NEW BIBLE COMPANION

New Bible Companion

Robert B. Hughes

AND

J. Carl Laney

Tyndale House Publishers, Inc.
Wheaton, Illinois

The authors wish to acknowledge all those who have had an influential or direct part in the production of this book. Numerous colleagues, especially Dr. Donald Launstein and Dr. Stanley Ellisen, and students through the years have greatly influenced the approach taken in this book. We also wish to acknowledge Mrs. Nancy Nasution, a Tyndale editor who worked many hours on this project. Although she did not live to see the completion of this book, her edits will be appreciated with each new page read. Our editor, Mr. Mark Norton, has skillfully led us through the entire editorial process. We are also happy to acknowledge his expertise, scholarship, and clarity of thought.

Library of Congress Catalog Card Number 90-70300

Printed in the United States of America.

ISBN 0-8423-4733-X

97 96 95
10 9 8 7 6 5 4 3

To DANIELLE ELLEN HUGHES

A daughter full of grace and beautiful moments

and

To JOHN, ELISABETH, LAURA, and DAVID LANEY

(2 Peter 3:18)

CONTENTS

INDEX OF BIBLE-WIDE THEMES

All of the following themes are Bible-wide in scope and could easily be traced through many, if not all, of the books of the Bible. This index connects these "Bible-wide" themes to the biblical books where they are discussed in the New Bible Companion. See the Bible-Wide Concepts sections in the books mentioned for more information on the listed themes.

Preface

INTRODUCTORY SECTIONS

The *New Bible Companion* presents each Biblical book by means of an introductory section followed by an outline and interpretive notes. The introduction to each Biblical book contains four subsections. First, the *BASIC FACTS* section discusses the book's historical setting, authorship, date, and essential purpose. Second, the *GUIDING CONCEPTS* section provides keys to understanding how the book's message unfolds and to identifying its major emphasis. Third, the *BIBLE-WIDE CONCEPTS* section explains how the book fits into the unified message of the Bible as a whole. Finally, a fourth section pinpoints the major *NEEDS MET BY* a particular book for its original hearers and for readers today. A fifth section discussing geographical concerns has been added to books in which geography plays a significant role. The idea of these introductory sections is to take the reader to the original time and setting of the book, to how the author developed his message, to the book's place in the entire scope of God's revelation, and, finally, to the major applications of its message—then and now.

OUTLINES AND NOTES

The introductory sections are followed by an overall outline of the book and then specific notes on each section of the book. The notes at the beginning of each major section of the book summarize the development of the author's thought over a major section. The interpretive notes that follow these *overviews* contain historical, geographical, and archaeological insights and help with major interpretive problems. We have tried to distill out the essential message of each book without adding extensive and overly technical data. While the notes are quite readable on their own, our hope is that you will read them in close conjunction with the Biblical text. We also hope that you will keep this volume close at hand to provide an initial orientation to particular books of the Bible before you begin reading them and to answer your questions as they arise along the way.

Introduction: The Big Picture

Every book from Genesis through Revelation has a special way of fitting into the Bible as a whole. Wonderful when studied one by one, the Biblical books form an even more enriching whole when viewed together. Like a diamond's facets, each book makes its own special contribution to God's unfolding revelation. It is beautiful to see how the smaller facets—verses, chapters, and books—contribute to and receive meaning from the whole of God's revelation. The benefit of studying passages in the full light of their immediate, bookwide, and Bible-wide contexts is great. And an investigation of Scripture with the narrow and wide contexts in mind is the best foundation for accurate interpretation and effective application. The following overview of the Bible's big picture will help the reader make applications that will be based on the truth revealed in the whole of God's word.

THE NEED FOR A BIG PICTURE

A BIBLE MAP

As tourists need maps to avoid getting lost in foreign cities, Bible readers need a map to keep from getting lost between the books of Genesis and Revelation. They need to see how the whole Bible is laid out—how Scripture's main freeways interconnect with its smaller streets and avenues. Although a child may recognize the houses where he and his grandparents live, he may not know how to get from one to the other. Likewise, Bible readers may know one Bible book here and another there, but have no real sense of how the one is connected to the other. How does Genesis lead to 1 and 2 Samuel? Or how are 1 and 2 Chronicles crucial for understanding Matthew? The books of Scripture are extremely diverse, yet in their diversity, they form a unified whole that reveals God's amazing work to save and redeem mankind. The New Bible Companion will provide a bird's eye view of the Bible, recognizing the diversity of its individual books and revealing how its diverse parts form a wonderful unity.

DIVERSITY WITHIN THE BIBLE
Different authors

The Bible was finished nearly two thousand years ago. Many different human authors wrote it over a period covering at least fifteen hundred years and including three different languages (Hebrew, Aramaic, and Greek). During that long period, history and culture changed radically—from the time of Moses, writing some fourteen hundred years before Christ, to the time of the apostle John, writing in the Roman Empire around A.D. 80. In addition to different cultures and languages, the Biblical writers had their own different personalities and abilities. Moses was a prince of ancient Egypt—Matthew was a Roman tax collector. Solomon lived securely in a palace—Ezekiel was a prisoner of war. Paul was highly educated— Peter was an unschooled fisherman.

Different purposes

Each Bible book was written with its own specific purpose in mind. Each author wrote to meet specific needs. He selected, under God's guidance, appropriate truths that matched the particular needs of God's people at that time. Therefore, many different needs and situations are represented from book to book: announcements of God's discipline, loving God for his redemption, the problem of family hatred and jealousy, wandering in the desert, wars with the Philistines, captivity in Babylon, church squabbles, and dealing with personal sin. Some books were written to individuals, others to large groups. Some were for singing, while others were poetry or narrative to be read aloud. Some were written to bring correction, while others were for information or historical record.

Different topics

Because the purposes differ from book to book, so does the subject matter. God did not present his word in long and organized lists of simple principles for living, detached from real people and their ancient historical situations. He wrapped his truths in greatly varied everyday history, language, and life. God gave us his truth in ancient books like Exodus, Joshua, Malachi, Romans, and 1 and 2 Peter. He did not give us books like *1 and 2 Thought Life* or *The Epistle To Parents*. God's principles and truth are embedded in the events of God's salvation history and the diverse experiences of God's people.

Neither life nor God's truth comes in a neat, self-contained package. Just as our daily experiences contain diverse situations and needs, the books from Genesis to Revelation contain a diverse presentation of truth; the Bible is not a systematized card file of questions and answers. Its diversity is important to consider when interpreting and applying the Bible. God presented his eternal truth in the context of communities and people with concerns and needs defined by distant places and cultures. Thus, Bible readers cannot ignore the various cultures and situations of the Biblical text. Part of the task of interpreting the Bible is to see how its ancient context actually sharpens and clarifies its message. Seeing how God's truth helped ancient people in the struggles of their varied lives shows how we can apply the same truths today. Understanding the diversity of the Bible's message and context is vital to properly interpreting and applying Scripture.

Different relevance

Becoming aware of the Bible's diversity may cause us to make a mistake. We may tend to ignore those parts of the Bible that seem strange or difficult to apply. When we read the New Testament, especially Paul's letters, God seems to be speaking directly to us. But in the Old Testament we may find it difficult to apply things like bloody battles, ancient rituals, and long genealogies. In the face of the Bible's strangeness, it is possible that we may read only the New Testament—and just parts of it, at that. But such a neglect of the difficult and culturally distant parts of Scripture is wrong. To correct this neglect that grows out of the Bible's cultural distance and diversity, we need to look to another truth—the Bible's essential unity.

THE UNITY OF THE BIBLE

But how do the various books of the Bible fit together? Although the Bible was written book by book over a period of around fifteen hundred years, the end result is a single work, each part of which contributes perfectly to the whole. Therefore, it is not enough to study only a book here or there. The Bible should be understood as a logically ordered whole, moving from Genesis through Revelation. Although there are many different historical contexts and human authors in the Bible, God is the unifying author behind it all. Behind each diverse passage of Scripture stands our unchanging God. Behind the Bible's many human authors stands the single divine Author. And he is the real solution to the needs of the people in the Bible and those living today. Since God intended for the diverse books of Scripture to fit together as a unified whole, the interrelationships of the various books are significant for understanding God's revelation as a whole.

It would be somewhat odd to begin reading a current best-seller in the middle of the fifth chapter, skip to the last chapter, and then go back and read the end of the third chapter. Although a reader could make some sense of what he had read, he would not have an accurate picture of what the book was all about. The reader would have to see why the chapters were arranged in their present order and how each chapter fit into the entire book. Likewise, Bible readers need to determine how each Bible book fits into Scripture as a whole. Then they will be able to understand how the Bible's development has resulted in a beautiful and cohesive whole, from Genesis through Revelation, that meets the practical needs of believers.

GETTING FROM THE BIBLE MAP TO LIFE

Questions concerning how the different books of the Bible are interrelated are not just academic questions. The question of how the Bible fits together is crucial for a believer's practical application of Scripture. In order to understand the relationships between the various books of Scripture it is important to emphasize God's single authorship and the literary unity of Scripture. An understanding of the unifying message of Scripture should serve as a Bible map, revealing the unity of God's revelation amidst its diversity. Without a sense of how each book relates to the others, historically and literarily, interpretations and applications are open to a number of potential problems.

First, verses or books might be taken out of their larger Biblical context. They might be read as if they can be properly interpreted without understanding their original God-given literary context. This approach sees the Bible as if it were just a long list of detached Christian principles. Scripture becomes like a stack of cards, each with a principle for living. This approach denies the true nature of the Biblical text and can be a cause for great misinterpretation.

One slightly humorous example of such misinterpretation would be to read Psalm 91:4, "He will cover you with his feathers, and under his wings you will find refuge," and conclude that God has feathers and wings. To convert these bare words into a meaningful interpretation demands placing the words in their original context. When that is done, it is clear that the key element of the context is poetry that involves figurative language. Thus the feathers and wings are not spoken of in a scientific sense but in a poetic sense describing God's love and care using the imagery of a mothering bird.

A less humorous example is found in Matthew 5:29: "If your right eye causes you to sin, gouge it out and throw it away." The gouging out of the eye might appear to solve the problem of sin, especially lust (see Matt. 5:27-28). But a look at the broader context of Jesus' entire Sermon on the Mount (Matt. 5:1-7:29) shows that God is against the notion that sin problems can be solved by external remedies. The context calls believers away from external actions (called hypocritical in Matthew 6:2, 5, 16) to making changes of the heart (Matt. 5:28; 6:21). Hands and eyes do not cause people to sin. They are just instruments, controlled not by themselves, but by man's inner desires and will. Removing them would not remove the inner bent of people toward sin. The context shows that the problem of lust is solved by correcting the warped vision of the spiritual eye ("eye" as symbolic of one's worldview, Matthew 6:22) not the gouging out of the physical eye.

If readers ignore the literary and historical context for the verses they study, they will inevitably pile up misunderstandings about God's original message. Each verse must be read in its immediate literary context (chapter and book) and then interpreted within the context of the entire Bible—a formidable but, never-theless, necessary and lifelong task.

Second, failing to study Scripture with its unity in mind creates a greater possibility of coming up with many conflicting interpretations. Without the control of the broader Biblical context, interpretations will be built on the interpreter's own experiences and ideas. The interpreter will tend to project his own needs and solutions into the text and, in doing so, miss what God originally intended. Interpretations may end up being as numerous and as creative as the interpreters themselves.

Third, fragmentary Scripture knowledge leaves the interpreter deficient when coping with the transition between Old and New Testaments. A great change came about at the coming of Christ, and that change is reflected in differences between the Testaments. But only a firm grip on the Bible-wide context can help interpreters move accurately from the Old to the New. How should Christians view the Old Testament laws and rituals? Why do some Christians still keep them while others do not? How are Christians supposed to use Genesis through Malachi?

Fourth, a Bible-wide picture is necessary for understanding how and why Christ, Paul, John, and the rest of the New Testament authors continually referred to the Old Testament in order to explain the fullness of God's redemption in Christ. What did the New Testament authors, who had known and experienced the person and work of Jesus Christ, find the same as they looked back to the Old Testament times of Moses? What had changed? How did they connect Christ with the Old Testament? How did they use the Old Testament to define Christian behav-ior? The identity of Christians rests on their appreciation of how the New Testa-ment grows out of the Old. Without that appreciation they may make the mistake in day-to-day practice of treating the content of Genesis through Malachi as somewhat inferior, if not excludable, information.

Discovering how the whole Bible fits together will help Bible readers avoid these four problems and others. It will become clear that in the New Testament the Bible developed progressively, both by adding new truth and by reinterpreting the old. After readers have become oriented to God's map from Genesis to Revelation, they will have accurate directions for avoiding interpretations rooted solely in their own situations or personalities, and they will find themselves nearer to God's intended truth.

FINDING PRESENT POWER IN ANCIENT SCRIPTURE

God made no mistakes when he chose the means for communicating his truth. He purposely used history, different kinds of literary form (poetry, prose, proverb, hymns), culture, the authors' personalities, and three languages (Hebrew, Aramaic, and Greek). These things are both antiquated and foreign to the world we live in today. Since God's word is conveyed in an ancient medium, what part should it play in contemporary interpretation and application of the Bible? Must we pay attention to the ancient forms used in Scripture to apply God's word today? How can God speak today through such a diverse and ancient document? Why did God not give his word in lists of timeless truth, rather than in truth wrapped up in time-bound language and culture?

Actually, we should be glad that God chose to communicate the way he did. He did not bring his message around the specifics of history. Rather, he brought his word right into the middle of the miracles and the messes of human life. So, rather than seeing the foreign people and cultures of Scripture as confusing, we need to see them and their occasional strangeness as part of the very message God intended for us to receive. The earthy quality of the Bible is a vital part of its divine message. It is not something to be ignored or peeled off in order to get at a supposed "real" and "timeless" Biblical message. Just as our Lord in his full humanity became the perfect medium for the message of God, so the written word of God, with all its ancient, diverse, and sometimes strange qualities, is the perfect expression of God's mind. God did not want to simply present truth. He wanted to present truth in the context of life's events. In that way God revealed truth in application, not in the abstract. And the applications of the Bible to its original readers should provide direction for our own applications. God wrapped his truth in the real world because he wants us to learn it and live it in the real world. And appreciating both the familiar and the foreign in the Bible is the best way to appreciating the fullness of God and his will for the world. If we fail to recognize Scripture's historical distance and diversity, we might interpret Scripture from the limited standpoint of modern culture—much like the artists of the Renaissance who painted all Biblical characters, whether Abraham or Paul, in the clothing and setting of contemporary Europe—thus distorting the true message of Scripture.

THE FOCUS OF GOD'S RULE

The entire Bible consistently develops God's three-part promise of his *presence,* his chosen *place,* and his redeemed *people.* God's presence, place, and people form the focus through which readers can discover and profit from the Bible's "big picture." Bible readers can use this threefold framework at each point in Scripture to discover how that section develops God's promises and speaks to believers today. Although many different and sometimes strange things happen in Scripture, they can all be unified around the three aspects of presence, place, and people.

PLACE

The first aspect, God's promised place, relates to the physical universe, and earth in particular. God's will and power stand behind the existence of the earth, sea, trees, birds, and animals. The physical creation perfectly manifests God's will and reveals much about his character and abilities, for example, his sheer power and incredible creativity. The earth also became the exciting arena in which God reveals his will and where humans respond to that will with either a yes or a no. God began with a perfect earth, cursed it with thorns and groanings (Rom. 8:22), gave a piece of it to Israel as a Promised Land, and promised to ultimately re-create an entirely new heaven and earth. The progressive revelation of what God wants to do with the physical earth is a unifying theme from Genesis through Revelation.

PEOPLE

The second aspect of the Bible's focus is God's desire for his people. He creates, rules over, and seeks intimacy with them. Under God's rule, his people experience a vast variety of situations, problems, and needs. His special beginnings with Adam, Noah, and Abraham are summed up and brought to completion in Christ. The progressive revealing of how God works through his people's needs is a unifying theme from Genesis through Revelation.

PRESENCE OF GOD

The third and most important aspect of the Bible's focus is God himself. The crown of the Bible is the proclamation of who God is. Believers know who God is both by what he does and by what he says. Although the physical universe reveals much about its Creator, reading the Creator's words shows in even more detail who he is. When God reveals what he wants, he reveals something about himself—God's will reveals his character.

And when believers look closely at what God wants, they are brought close to his character and heart. The presentation of God's character by means of his deeds and words is the comprehensive unifying theme from Genesis through Revelation. He is consistently characterized as a king ruling from his throne. And the Bible clearly explains what the rule of God looks like from Genesis through Revelation. It is a story of how the King became more intimately present with his estranged kingdom by following a consistent pattern through differing times and cultures. A series of interrelated agreements, or covenants, between God and his creation brought his promises concerning his *presence, place,* and *people* to ultimate fulfillment.

THE MAP OF GOD'S RULE

THE SIGNPOSTS OF GOD'S COVENANTS

From the time of the apostles, the sacred writings were collected under two names that greatly illuminate the big picture of Scripture: the Old Testament and the New Testament. The Bible is about two testaments, or covenants. The old covenant was given under Moses. The new covenant came through Christ. A covenant is an agreement to do something, like a contract or a promise. Some biblical covenants are like contracts where both parties, God and people, have responsibilities and conditions for the contract to be fulfilled. Other covenants place all the responsibility to carry out the conditions on God alone. Instead of being like contracts, these covenants are more like unconditional promises.

Although the two covenants of Moses and Christ receive the most attention in the Bible, several other covenants complete God's revelation. In fact, God's covenant promises form the basis for all of his redemptive actions throughout Scripture. The covenants inform and explain virtually all of the events and speeches in the Bible and frame the development of God's plans for his *presence,* chosen *place,* and *people.* A covenant is at the backbone of every book of the Bible and, taken together, the covenants form the blueprint of the entire Bible.

Covenants also pave the way to understanding how each book interrelates with the rest of the Bible. Each new covenant is a sign-post that shows the next major route opening up in Scripture and how to understand all the little side roads of biblical history. Because each book was written from the perspective of the covenant or covenants operating at that time, knowing the main promises of those covenants will help the reader understand a book's particular emphasis and point. It will also help him to avoid making major points out of minor details and keep him from missing the heart of God's message. From Genesis through Revelation the unfolding interrelationship between the covenants is the key to understanding and applying the Bible. This overview of how God expressed his rule of love and justice through his promises begins with the sad fact of a divinely blessed creation being broken under a divine curse.

Goodness

In Genesis 1 God evaluated his creative work as being very good. In Genesis 2 God sanctified the completion of his creative work with a great Sabbath rest. In Genesis 3 God cursed everything he had made and damned it to an eternity in hell. What caused the goodness of creation? And what caused the badness of the curse?

Creation was good because it was exactly the way God wanted it. The pattern in Genesis 1 is "God said, 'Let there be . . .' and there was. . . ." God got what he asked for. When he commanded that there be light, there was light, pure and simple. When he called for fish and birds, he got fish and birds. And when his word was perfectly obeyed, he recorded his response: "Very good." And this reveals the relationship between what God wants and who he is. What he wants springs from his essential goodness. When his will is accomplished it reflects the goodness of his divine character.

From its first lines, the Bible defines what makes something good. Things and people are not good because they are beautiful, smart, rich, productive, or fun. Goodness is that which matches up with what God wants and the standards he sets. To the extent that people and the earth are the way God wants them—to that extent, they are good. And what God wants reveals who he is—powerful, sovereign, and good.

Badness

In Genesis 3, God cursed the world because of Adam's sin. The pattern of "God said . . . and there was. . . ." was broken. God wanted obedience, but he did not get it. He said, "You must not eat from the tree of the knowledge of good and evil." But Adam and Eve said, "No." They did not shout it and they probably had, in their own views, very good reasons for saying no. But, while all creation had resounded up to that point with a very good yes to God, Adam quietly brought in the first no. God could not say "Very good" to that response. He could only say, "Cursed." Adam's sin infinitely offended God's infinitely holy character. God responded with an infinitely devastating curse.

From its first lines, the Bible defines what makes something bad. Things and people are not bad because they may be unattractive, ignorant, poor, unproductive, or no fun. Badness is that which does not match up with what God wants and the standards he alone sets. God's curse provides Scripture's constant background of brokenness and need for restoration. Behind each act of hate, lust, murder, or lying stand human sin and divine curse. Not only are the Bible's characters shot through with a sinful nature, they also have to labor in a world damned at every turn by God's own curse.

GOD'S PROMISE OF ULTIMATE VICTORY

Along with the curse, the Bible reader needs to keep God's promise continually in view. The curse was not the end of the human story; it became the reason for God's plan to offer worldwide salvation to a fallen creation. What could ever remedy the infinite offense of sin and remove the infinite curse? Only a correspondingly infinite sacrifice would be sufficient to do so. The entire scope of the Bible is about how God moves from the *very good* creation into the *very bad and cursed* creation and out again into a new and blessed second creation. It is a story of how God, at great cost, removed his offense at mankind's sin and restored a relationship of blessing with his creation. The Bible is first and foremost a story of God dealing with his problems with human sin. To put it another way, it is a simple story of two acts, one of offense, the other of forgiveness. It is about an intensely personal transaction between God and humanity.

Right in the middle of his curse regarding Adam, God gave a promise of ultimate victory (Gen. 3:15). He said that someday a son of Adam would crush the head of the serpent. Ultimately, the son of Adam was Christ and the serpent was Satan. Amazingly, God's curse and Satan's hatred would culminate in the crucifixion of Christ, an act that satisfied God's offense at sin and defeated Satan's power. But God did not move immediately to the fulfillment of his promised redemption in Christ. Thousands of years came between the promise to Adam and Christ's resurrection. And nearly two thousand years have passed since then.

THE COVENANTS AND GOD'S CHARACTER

How could Adam, Eve, and all people who have followed them know that there would be ultimate victory as the process of conflict with personal and world evil lengthened from days to thousands of years? As generations came and went through the cursed world, their faith had to be based on a God who would keep his word. To his original word of promise in Genesis 3:15, the Creator, who was by nature a sufficient object of trust, added many more words of promise.

Those words of redemptive promise blossom within the framework of the covenants recorded in Scripture. Behind each covenant stands the trustworthy character of God. God takes nearly all the responsibility in some covenants and shares it with his people in others. Biblical contracts form a blueprint that unifies the diverse Scriptural elements of *people, place,* and God's *presence* around God's faithful character. Also, those covenants clarify how believers may apply the truth of any passage.

THE COVENANTS AT A GLANCE

The grand Scriptural movement from infinite curse to eternal blessing is directed by a series of covenants between God and sinful mankind. Through these contracts, God brings promises of hope and blessing to a world that has been separated from its Creator by sin. See the accompanying chart.

As Bible readers discover what the Bible says about why God made contracts, three questions should continually be asked: (1) What can be learned about God in each covenant? (2) What does he want from the people he brings into those contract relationships? (3) In what way do God's conditions continue or change from covenant to covenant? These questions will provide a solid basis for applying the Bible to a reader's own situation. Each covenant contains the basic elements that provide sign-posts for tracking change and development from one covenant to another. These guidelines also show how the passages properly apply to a reader's own personal situation.

GOD'S COVENANT WITH NOAH

THE FOUNDATIONS OF LONGSUFFERING

God made a contract with Noah (Gen. 9:1-17) which, in part, echoed what he had originally said to Adam in Genesis 1:28. God restated his original commission to the human race. Though Noah, God was giving humankind a second start with a second "first family." The contract with Noah was necessary for all the others that would follow because in it God said he would never again destroy the entire earth by flood. Without that promise of restraint, humans could expect God to vent his global wrath at any moment. Every so often, God would have to destroy the world again. Why? Because the human problem of saying no to God still persisted. God would have had to punish sin.

By making a contract with Noah, God showed he could withhold his righteous retribution. And though God at times in Scripture judged some sins in order to warn and instruct, he let the vast majority of human sin go unpunished throughout the course of history. God refrained from immediate judgment by exhibiting the characteristic of longsuffering. From the time of Noah, Bible readers should

---

GOD'S COVENANTS WITH MANKIND

Promise of ultimate victory	Genesis 3:15
Noah	Genesis 9:8-17
Abraham	Genesis 12:1-3; 13:14-17; 15:1-21; 17:1-14
Moses	Exodus 20—Numbers 6; explained and elaborated throughout the Old Testament
David	2 Samuel 7:8-17
Christ	Jeremiah 31:31-34; Ezekiel 36:22-32; Hebrews 8:1–10:18; explained and elaborated throughout the New Testament

appreciate the concept of longsuffering in a new way. The holy God, whose attitude of loathing and grief toward sin had not changed, would now live with sin for a long time. Why?

THE COST OF LONGSUFFERING
The covenant with Noah reveals a God who is more concerned with the restoration of the human race than with its destruction; God is more concerned with humankind's salvation than he is with venting his own rightous anger. God's decision to be longsuffering toward sinful people was costly. It left his reputation open to human scoffing that he was powerless or indifferent regarding evil. It would cost him his own dear Son. Longsuffering would also become the only acceptable model for the life-styles of his followers.

Even after the flood, the earth was still under God's curse. And, as Noah's children show, people had not miraculously become any less sinful as a result of the flood. Above all, God had certainly not changed his mind about sin. He still hated it. But, in the contract with Noah, God determined to hold back the flood waters of his wrath in order to make room for his grace in the cross of Christ.

In Genesis 3:15 God had promised ultimate victory over the serpent. Through Noah, God promised to withold his global wrath on the road to ultimate victory. The next step toward that great victory was God's covenant with Abraham.

GOD'S COVENANT WITH ABRAHAM

THREE ELEMENTS
The basic elements of the covenant with Abraham are found in Genesis 12:1-3 (cf. also Gen. 13:14-17; 15:1-21; 17:1-14). Abraham was promised a *place,* the land of Israel; a *people,* the nation of Israel; and the blessings which come from the special *presence* of God. These three elements—place, people, and God's presence—were God's focus in the original creation and direct the way to his future final restoration of worldwide blessing. Although this promise begins with Abraham, eventually all the nations of the earth will find blessing (Gen. 12:3). The Abrahamic promise included every place and people of the entire earth. From this point on, each book of Scripture will be understood by finding out how it shows God's progress in fulfilling his promises to Abraham of place, people, and presence.

The Place
The initial place of Abrahamic promise, the Promised Land of Israel, was just a starting point. It began with Palestine, but it will eventually extend to the entire earth. In the beginning of history, God gave, as a starting point, a little patch of the earth to Adam and Eve. Although their ultimate goal was dominion over the entire earth, they had to start somewhere. The Garden of Eden was a small starting point. The finish line would be of global proportions. Likewise, the place of Abrahamic promise, beginning with the Promised Land of Israel, will also ultimately be global and will one day extend to the new heavens and earth. Each book of Scripture needs to be searched as to what it says about God's progress in giving the Promised Land to Israel and then about giving the new earth to all the saints.

The People

The starting point of the people aspect of the Abrahamic covenant was Abraham's children: from Isaac and Jacob to the twelve tribes of Israel. But it did not end there. It would eventually grow to include all the people of the earth. At creation, God gave his original commission for world dominion to just two people, Adam and Eve. But through them he addressed all the human race who would follow after them. In a similar way, God's promises were given to one man, Abraham. But through Abraham God addressed all peoples. The people of the Abrahamic promise are international. Each book needs to be searched as to what it says about how God extends his people from Abraham, to Israel, and finally into all nations.

The Presence of God

God promised Abraham great blessing. Blessing is not defined throughout Scripture as simply the material things God gives. The essence of blessing is having God present in a special way. Blessing is God's presence, not just his gifts. The blessings offered to Abraham were based on a new intimacy with God. God often told Abraham, "I am with you." Later, God would be with his people in greater intimacy as he moved from thundering Mount Sinai into the tabernacle at the center of Israel's camp. That initmate presence would later be extended to all lands and peoples in the new covenant in Christ. God would move from the tabernacle and temple into the center of believers' hearts. Finally, the joy of eternity will be the unhindered presence of God in the new earth. The divine presence of the Abrahamic promise is universal. Each book can yield rich truths about the conditions required for God's presence and how he became increasingly more intimate with his people on the basis of each new covenant.

ABRAHAM AND THE BIBLE

All the rest of the Bible is about how God fulfilled the three aspects of his great promise to Abraham. The next covenants, centered around Moses, David, and Christ, all flesh out and fulfill the great promises to Abraham. From Abraham on, the geographic starting places of Eden for Adam and the newly dried earth for Noah were replaced with the focus on the Promised Land of Israel. The human starting points, Adam and Noah, were replaced with Abraham. And the work of God to reverse his curse and restore his unhindered presence took a great leap forward in his deepened intimacy with Abraham. Long after Abraham, the apostle Paul would call him the father of all believers (Rom. 4:12).

THE PRESERVATION OF THE PROMISED NATION AND LAND
Nation

Once God had marked out his chosen man, Abraham, and his chosen line through Sarah's children, the history of Abraham's covenant revolves around how Abraham's descendants respond to God's grace and demands for obedience. Although God always remained faithful, more often than not his people were uncooperative and placed themselves at great risk. God had promised Adam ultimate victory. The covenant with Noah had shown that God was more interested in redemption than in destruction. But how would God preserve his continually rebellious people in order to bring in his promised blessings? That drama brings excitement to many portions of the stories of the Patriarchs and of Israel. Here are just a few examples of the drama of God's preserving his people despite their sins: Would Sarah be married off to the wrong man before she could bear the promised son (Gen. 12:10-20; 20:1-18)? Would Rebekah be married off to the wrong man in a similar way, putting a stop to God's chosen family (Gen. 26)?

In addition to individuals like Sarah and Rebekah, the drama of preserving Abraham's line also relates to the nation of Israel as a whole. God used Joseph's captivity in Egypt as the very thing needed to bring his family down out of Canaan and into Egypt to preserve the kernel nation of Israel from starvation during a great famine. God caused the tribe of Israel to increase miraculously while in Egypt. He preserved Israel from Pharaoh's army and from starvation in the wilderness after the exodus.

During the conquest of Canaan under Joshua, God preserved the nation and gave it great victory. God preserved Israel through the devastating Assyrian and Babylonian captivities. He once again saved the entire nation from being wiped out through the heroic efforts of Esther during the time of Persian rule.

Much can be learned about God and people from these events of preservation. God is faithful and is able to keep his words of promise no matter how many years and harrowing events pass. God preserved his chosen people, not because of their faithfulness, but because he remained faithful to his promise to Abraham.

Land

The drama of Israel's preservation also involves the second aspect of the Abrahamic covenant, the preservation of the land. Would God be strong enough and faithful enough to give Israel the land? Or would the constant failures of his people void the land promise?

The Old Testament gives great attention to the ups and downs involved in God's people and their land. Abraham received the promise, though he never owned any significant part of the land. The land was taken by Joshua, though it was never very secure until David's conquests and Israel's consolidation under Solomon.

But all of that security evaporated in the face of Assyrian and Babylonian devastation and captivity. Even when the people were allowed to return from the Babylonian captivity, the Promised Land was not their own. Until the time of Christ, Israel would be under a sequence of foreign domination by Persia, Greece, and Rome. God's promises of victory, peace, and international blessing seemed very far off.

GOD'S COVENANT WITH MOSES

THE DIVINE PRESENCE PROMISED TO ABRAHAM

Long after Abraham, God made another covenant, this time with Moses. Moses' covenant developed the promises and demands God had originally given to Abraham. The Mosaic covenant clarified two critical aspects of God's redemptive plans given through Abraham: human obedience and divine presence. God would be present only with a people obedient to his will.

Under Moses, the rituals surrounding the tabernacle defined the obedience required for remaining in God's blessed presence (Lev. 11:45; 15:31). The great feasts of the covenant clarified the major elements of God's promised blessing through Abraham. The Day of Atonement pictured a perfect forgiveness of sin (Lev. 16). The Jubilee, or Sabbath year, pictured the restored and perfect creation

Sabbath (Lev. 25). The blessings and curses spoke of the pleasure and pain arising from either keeping or breaking the covenant (Lev. 26:27-45). God would be with the nation for its blessing only if the people loved and obeyed him. God's law found its source in his love and was designed to lead to an improved relationship between God and his people.

HOLINESS

The tablets of the Ten Commandments, placed in the Most Holy Place of the tabernacle, summed up the grace and demands of the new relationship with God under Moses. Human obedience and God's presence rested on the demands arising from God's absolute holiness. Because God was holy, he would be redemptively present only with an obedient people. From Adam on, it was always clear that the believer's obedience was indispensible for enjoying the blessing of divine fellowship. The laws of the Mosaic covenant spelled out in black and white the holiness of God's character and how to have a redemptive relationship with him. The detailed laws of Exodus showed how far the people had fallen into lawlessness. The detailed sacrifices of Leviticus showed the gracious way back to obedience and holiness. All of these laws and sacrifices sprang from, and blazingly illustrated, God's holiness. His holiness demanded the believers' conformity to it. But that conformity of obedience was to spring from the heart (Deut. 6:4-9).

In the face of the Mosaic covenant's many laws and regulations, one point must not be lost. The Mosaic covenant grounded blessing squarely on a deep inner love for God which issued in doing what he wanted. While carrying out all the requirements of the Mosaic covenant, the believers' hearts were to match their external conformity to God's law. Only through heartfelt obedience would the curse on God's *people* and *land* be lifted. Sincere obedience alone could bring holiness and salvation from war, famine, and disease.

Adam was the source of humanity's fall. Noah's covenant opened up time for grace to overtake judgment. Abraham's promises outlined the route to international blessing. And Moses' covenant visualized the solutions to the two roadblocks to experiencing that blessing: forgiving human sin and perfecting human obedience. The covenant that God would make with David continued to clarify how God would remove those two roadblocks.

GOD'S COVENANT WITH DAVID

THE KING AS MEDIATOR FOR GOD'S PEOPLE

God's covenant with David was made during the most secure period of Israel's history. It was a special word of God's promise, not to the whole nation of Israel, but to the special kingly line of David. To Abraham, God had promised blessing on his offspring. To Moses, God had continued the blessing to Abraham's offspring, then known as the nation of Israel. But under David the personal blessing promised to Abraham and Moses focused on one man within the nation of Israel, the king. And that king functioned as the representative for the entire nation of Israel. As the king went, so went the people of Abrahamic promise. In the Davidic covenant a new drama arose in Scripture: the preservation of the kingly line. That drama is clearly seen throughout the books of Samuel, Kings, and Chronicles and reaches its height in the attempts on the life of the King of Israel, Jesus, during his life as a baby and as a man.

Under the Davidic covenant the king of Israel held a critical place of mediation between God and the nation. The king was responsible to ensure civil justice and the sanctity of the temple services. The preservation of the nation depended upon the king's obedience to God's commands. The whole story of how God enthroned his chosen king, David, is climaxed by the king's mediation for the entire nation of Israel. When the king did right in God's sight by keeping his commands, he answered prayers for the preservation of the people and the land (cf. 2 Sam. 21:14; 24:25). The king became the person through whom the nation experienced the rule of God. That rule finds its fulfillment in the sacrificial mediation and exalted rule of the ultimate seed of David, Jesus the Messiah.

THE KING AS GOD'S SON
In 2 Samuel 7:8-19, God promised that a royal line would extend from David onward forever. The critical emphasis was that each Davidic king of Israel would have a special Father-son relationship with God. Each king was a special son of God, blessed with a potentially close and powerful relationship with the Father. The kings of David's line realized that potential in degrees varying from better to worse. But the power of divine sonship found its fulfillment in the Son of God, Jesus, who had a perfect and unique form of sonship with God.

Through Christ, that sonship has been shared with his followers. The victory promised to Adam, the international blessing promised to Abraham, and the forgiveness and obedience required under Moses all zeroed in on one man. And that man was the second Adam, the single seed of Abraham, the prophet greater than Moses, and the perfect son of David. Where Adam, Abraham, Moses, and David failed, Christ succeeded. God's redemptive focus narrowed to one man, Christ, so that from his singular perfection it could expand outward into the international blessing promised to Adam and Abraham. Because of Christ's redemptive work, now all believers have the privilege of being called sons and daughters of God. See 2 Corinthians 6:18–7:1 where Paul applies the Davidic covenant to Christian believers (Paul quoted 2 Sam. 7:8, 14).

One man, Adam, brought sin and God's curse into the world. He received a promise that someday his son would crush the head of the serpent. To get to that ultimate victory, Noah was promised a period of patient and longsuffering grace. Abraham was given the promise of a special place, nation, and blessing that someday would extend around the world. Moses received the details of maintaining that blessing through forgiveness and obedience. And to David came the hope of one Israelite who would be the perfect king and mediator for the nation and the world. That one would bring in the fullness of the kingdom of God. But until he came, the nation went through traumatic times of failure, always warned, encouraged, or condemned by a long series of prophets.

GOD'S PROMISES AND THE PROPHETS

The Old Testament prophets primarily focused on the conditions for blessing found in the covenant with Moses. They inevitably spoke out because God's kings, priests, and people had broken their promise to love and obey God. Obedience to the commands in Moses' covenant was the key condition for God's people to be preserved in his land. The prophets are best arranged around the times during which they prophesied: *before, during,* and *after* the exile to Babylon.

BEFORE THE BABYLONIAN EXILE

Before the exile, the nation of Israel still had a chance to avoid destruction. The prophets who spoke before the Babylonian exile warned of impending judgment for unfaithfulness to the covenant with God (for example, see Isaiah, Jeremiah, and the minor prophets from Hosea through Zephaniah). Their message to Israel was to stop being like the nations that surrounded them. Their message to the nations was to repent and do justice to all men, especially Israel. The exhortations to the nations rested not on the Mosaic covenant, which was made only with Israel, but on God as the Creator who had rights to command and correct all of his creation. Also, God continually had more on his mind than just the well-being of the little nation of Israel. The Abrahamic covenant had shown God's ultimate intentions to bless all nations.

Another important prophetic message to Israel was that of the promise of exaltation after a period of chastisement and humiliation. Israel would have to undergo both deserved and undeserved suffering, after which God's people would be raised up and eternally blessed. That great truth is continually emphasized throughout Scripture, especially by the prophets, the Lord Jesus, and Paul: suffering before relief, humility before praise, perseverance before reward.

DURING THE EXILE

The prophets who spoke during the Babylonian exile told captive Israel to submit to and learn from God's chastisement (see Daniel, Ezekiel, and parts of Jeremiah; the books of 1 and 2 Kings were also written from the perspective of the exile). The prophets told Israel not to hope in the nations for deliverance. Israel was warned to make sure that idols were scrubbed out of their hearts (see Ezek. 14 with reference to the curses of Deut. 28). The captive Israelites in Babylon were not to hope in the temple still standing in Jerusalem. The temple was not a good luck charm against the consequences of Israel's rebellion. It was only a symbol of God's presence and would soon fall. The real issue of God's presence would hinge on their present obedience, no matter where in the world they might be. Wherever they were obedient to God's laws, God was with them.

Daniel brought a special message of the need to wait for the restoration to the Promised Land. After the seventy years of captivity another type of seventy would come, only this time it would be seven times seventy. Four hundred and ninety years of oppression under the nations would have to pass before the great king of Israel, the Messiah, would come.

AFTER THE EXILE

The prophets who spoke to Israel after she had returned from exile to the Promised Land called upon the nation to persevere (see Haggai, Zechariah, and Malachi; the books of 1 and 2 Chronicles were also written from the perspective of positive restoration after the exile). Daniel had told the nation about the years of oppression to come, but Israel had also been told to continue on in obedience to the requirements of the Mosaic covenant. So, lest Israel's courage fail, the prophets gave comfort and warning. The day of God would eventually come, bringing destruction to the rebellious but salvation and rest to the faithful remnant. That time of final restoration would be according to the Abrahamic covenant as it had been gradually elaborated in later revelation to Moses, David, and the prophets. In that final day: (1) God's *land* will be restored; (2) God's *people* will be saved; (3) God's *presence* will dwell with his people once again.

All of God's promises to Abraham would be fulfilled. But a final covenant, mentioned in Jeremiah and Ezekiel but not inaugurated until Jesus' life, addressed the major problem blocking the dawning of the kingdom of God: sin. All the sacrifices of the Mosaic covenant did not secure perfect and final forgiveness. Guilt persisted. All the laws of the Mosaic covenant could not ensure perfect obedience. Sin persisted. How could the infinite offense of past sin be removed? And how could people stop sinning in the future?

JESUS: THE NEW COVENANT

The new covenant was designed by God to remedy the long-standing problem of sin in Israel and the world. First, the new covenant brought a sacrifice that removed God's offense at human sin from Adam onward (Jer. 31:34). The basis of the new covenant is the better sacrifice of Christ (Heb. 8–9).

Second, through Christ, God created people who would no longer echo Adam's original no to God. God's people always had a bad habit of doing what he did not like. Adam ate the fruit. Abraham lied. Moses got angry. The nation of Israel grumbled and complained. David committed murder and adultery. Solomon supported idolatry. Peter denied his Lord. Church after church continued to fall prey to pride, bickering, and lapses in faith. Even in the face of God's great redemptive events from the exodus to the cross, his people persisted in falling down on their responsibility to respond in gratitude and obedience.

The new covenant in Christ aimed at correcting the weak link of disobedience. And that was begun by putting the law of God into the human heart by means of the interior regeneration of the human soul. The law was placed inside (Jer. 31:33-34). God had told Israel to put his will into their hearts (Deut. 6:4-6). But in the new covenant, God does the interior decorating himself. Humans receive a new heart, and the Spirit of God moves believers to obedience to his laws (Ezek. 36:26-27). Obedience becomes an instinctive response.

The Old Testament promised the fulfillment of the promises to Abraham: a restored earth and people enjoying God's unhindered presence and blessing. And the new covenant is the means for fulfilling those promises. The entire New Testament is an explanation and application of the new covenant for the people of God. Every New Testament book emphasizes the significance of Christ's sacrifice and its implications for past history, present salvation, and future hope.

In Revelation 21:1-7; 22:3 all the strands of covenant promise come together. The ruined creation, both people and earth, are re-created. Then God's place and people will experience the greatest blessing: unhindered divine presence. The curse will be lifted, disobedience will end, and all aspects of God's promises will be realized. God's kingdom will have come and his will will be done on earth just the way it is done in heaven—perfectly and from the heart.

THE PRESENT

But until that great day of heaven on earth, believers live in the challenge of a world still under God's curse and human sinfulness. Forgiven believers can experience the power of new hearts and the Holy Spirit. All sin is forgiven. The power for obedience is present. And a day will come when all who believe will cease to disobey. But for the present, as the apostle Paul explained in Romans 8:22-23, believers groan, awaiting the glorification of their all-too-mortal bodies. While much of God's promise has been completed, some critical areas await completion. Earth remains a maverick, prone to earthquakes, floods, droughts, and famines. And people continue to be their own worst enemies, prone to the jeopardy of their flesh and Satan's attacks.

But Scripture was written for people just like these, people caught in the weakness and pain of living on a cursed earth. They need Scripture's redemptive truth. The task in Bible study is to find out what redemptive help each section was designed to give. The map of the Bible outlined above will help Bible readers see how a text fits into the flow of God's redemptive plan. As they work to understand what has changed since the text was written and what remains the same, they will be able to link how it was designed to help its original readers to how it can relate to believers today.

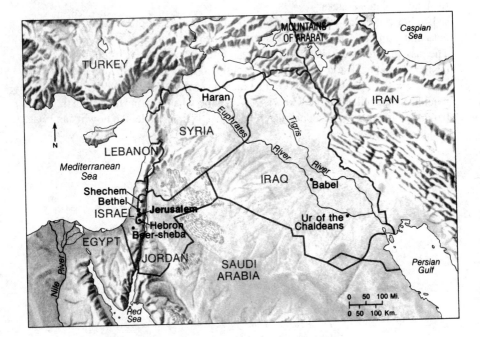

Genesis

BASIC FACTS

HISTORICAL SETTING
Genesis was written for the people of Israel, who had just been redeemed out of
Egypt under the leadership of Moses. They had been living on God's provisions in
the wilderness and had seen his awesome appearance on Mount Sinai. They were
being introduced to a new relationship with their God through his covenant and
through worship of him at the tabernacle.

AUTHOR
The authorship of Genesis through Deuteronomy
The authorship of Genesis is an integral part of the larger question of who wrote the
first five books of Scripture (called the Pentateuch by scholars). Scholars agree that
these five books have an overall thematic and literary unity and that Scripture and
tradition place these books under Moses' name. But scholars disagree as to the editorial process his material underwent to arrive at its present form. The question hinges
on the relationship between the material's present and original forms.

A more conservative view tends to see only minor differences between the forms
of the original and final compositions. According to the conservative view, the books
of Genesis through Deuteronomy contain, with the exception of later minor addi-
tions, essentially what God transmitted through Moses. A more liberal view sees a
long and complex history of editorial development and a vast difference between the
bits and pieces of the original materials and their final edited form. Scholars have
presented positions on the authorship of the Pentateuch ranging all the way from
direct dictation by God to Moses to seeing the books as a fragmented collection of
bits of tradition only brought into its present form after the Babylonian captivity.

Several key biblical passages, however, support Moses' significant part in the
original shaping of the Pentateuch. First of all, Moses was highly educated (Acts
7:22). Then, after the exodus from Egypt, God told Moses to write a specific
message concerning the destruction of the Amalekites (Exod. 17:14). Moses first

spoke and then recorded God's law given at Mount Sinai (Exod. 24:3-4; 34:27-28).
He recorded the stages of the wilderness journey (Num. 33:2). He wrote the "Book
of the Law" that probably refers to virtually all the Pentateuch except the last chapter
of Deuteronomy, which recounts the event of Moses' death (Deut. 31:24-26; see also
Neh. 13:1).

After Moses died, God referred Joshua to "all the law my servant Moses gave
you" and the "Book of the Law" (Josh. 1:7-8; see also 1 Kings 2:3; 1 Cor. 9:9).
Although it cannot be proven that the written material mentioned in these passages is
identical to the present Pentateuch, it is clear that Moses left for Joshua a comprehensive written record of the laws of God that would encompass the general material
now known as the Pentateuch.

Much later, when Jesus referred to the incident of Moses and the burning bush, he
revealed that Moses' name was also attached to the book of Genesis ("the book of
Moses, in the account of the bush," Mark 12:26). Luke reflects the common tradition
of putting the "law of the Lord" (in this case specifically referring to Exod. 13:2, 12
and Lev. 12:8) under the broad heading of "law of Moses" (Luke 2:23-24; see also
Acts 13:39). When Jesus said that Moses wrote of him, he again reflected the conventional view of Moses as the author of Genesis through Deuteronomy (John 5:46).

The first five books of the Bible were also commonly referred to simply as
"Moses" (Luke 16:29; 24:27, 44; Acts 26:22). Although biblical connections between the Pentateuch and Moses' name do not prove that Moses wrote every word
of these books, they do affirm him as both the chief figure in the books of the Pentateuch and as their primary human author. Any others who had a later part in editing
Moses' work remain unnamed. Moses was viewed as the human transmitter of the
laws of God and the chief literary figure behind the Pentateuch.

The authorship of Genesis

The book of Genesis itself does not name its author, who is therefore anonymous.
And although Moses was viewed as the figure behind Genesis, in the book, and
throughout the Pentateuch, he is always referred to in the third person "he," not in
the first person "I." The Pentateuch unfolds its message from a biographical, not an
autobiographical, perspective. But the central issue in authorship is the nature and
authority of the message.

The question of authorship is usually closely linked to the question of authority.
Although it cannot be proven, nor does it need to be proven exactly what Moses or
other possible editors wrote, believers can have absolute confidence that Genesis
comes with the full authority of God as transmitted through its original human
author, Moses. If, after Moses, others had a hand in editing his material, the crucial
issue of the book's divine authority through Moses is not altered. But that process of
editing, however it may be conceived, is never mentioned in the Bible. Moses and
Moses alone is viewed as the author and the mediator of God's authority inherent in
the Pentateuch.

DATE

Because the book of Genesis builds up to and ends with Israel's bondage in
Egypt and her hope of return to the Promised Land, it is clear that its purpose

was to lay out the background of Israel's election by God and her exodus from
Egypt. Therefore, the date of the book is from a time shortly after the exodus.
Because Moses had a significant hand in writing the material, it initially must
have been composed in the wilderness period prior to his death. The two most
commonly accepted dates for the wilderness wanderings of Israel, and therefore
for the composition of Genesis by Moses, are an early date of around 1446–1406
B.C. and a later date of around 1220–1180 B.C., depending on when one dates the
exodus. See the introduction to the book of Exodus for the issues involved in
dating Israel's exodus from Egypt.

PURPOSE

The general purpose of Genesis is to preserve an accurate record of the beginnings of the human race and the Hebrew nation. More specifically, it is designed
to record man's initial rebellion against God's rule and the beginnings of his
redemptive program through Israel. Genesis records the origins of the world,
plants, animals, humans, sin, death, and redemption. These origins were recorded
to provide the necessary background for Israel's appreciation of her election in
Abraham, her redemption from Egypt, and her obedience to the Mosaic Law. In
essence, the book of Genesis was designed to help God's redeemed people to
respond to their Redeemer in gratitude, love, and obedience.

GEOGRAPHY AND ITS IMPORTANCE

The Bible is a book about the entire world. Genesis begins with the creation of the
universe—the background against which all the little places in the Bible will be set.
Several places in Genesis cannot be identified today, like the Garden of Eden or
where Noah lived. But the major places where Abraham, Isaac, Jacob, and Joseph
lived have been found. Geographically the Genesis narrative moves from Adam and
Eve in the Garden, to Abraham in Ur and then in Israel, and to Joseph in Egypt.
Genesis makes the first important step in God's redemptive movement that spans
from Eden, to Israel's exodus from Egypt, to the Cross of Christ in Judea, and finally
to the new heavens and earth found in the book of Revelation. See the introductory
map.

GUIDING CONCEPTS

FROM EDEN TO EGYPT

Genesis is full of contrasts. It begins with the creation of the universe and ends with
Joseph's corpse in a coffin in Egypt. At the beginning of Genesis, Adam and Eve
were living in the purity and security of the Garden of Eden; at the end of the book,
the little family of Jacob was dwelling in the foreign land of Egypt. Adam and Eve
were offered the world and God's unhindered presence; the family of Abraham was
offered the promise of eventual deliverance out of Egypt. The earth was created and
cursed, destroyed and repopulated. Genesis tells the story of human failure and
divine help given to a special family on a journey from Eden to Egypt.

FAMILY ACCOUNTS IN GENESIS

2:4	The account of the heavens and earth
5:1	The account of Adam
6:9	The account of Noah
10:1	The account of Shem, Ham, and Japheth
11:10	The account of Shem
11:27	The account of Terah
25:12	The account of Ishmael
25:19	The account of Isaac
36:1	The account of Esau
37:2	The account of Jacob

PEOPLE: ADAM TO JOSEPH

The main interest in Genesis is the history of a single family. The repeated phrase, "this is the account of," helps divide the book around the family members (see chart above).

The Hebrew word that is translated "account" (this word is also commonly rendered "generations") is first used with reference to the heavens and earth (2:4) and represents more than just a list of descendants. It refers more generally to family origins and history. In Genesis such "accounts" are usually made up of two parts. The first part is a genealogy. (See the chart "Genealogies in Genesis.")

The second part of each "account" section is a record of important events in the family's history. Sometimes the family history comes before the genealogy, as in the following format: (1) family history (2:4–4:26); (2) the catchphrase "account of" (5:11); and (3) the family genealogy (5:2-32).

The phrase "account of" can refer both to what precedes and to what follows—to the family history and to the genealogy that follows from that history. The histories and lineages of God's chosen people form the backbone of the book of Genesis.

THE CENTRAL PERSON: ABRAHAM

The emphasis and main point of Genesis can be seen by the book's interest in certain people. The section 1:1–37:2 emphasizes Adam, Noah, Abraham, Isaac, and Jacob. The rest of the book (37:3–50:26) focuses on how God used Joseph, Jacob's son, to bring his family to Egypt and preserve them from starvation. So the major people on whom Genesis focuses are Abraham and his sons. Even the first eleven chapters form an introductory and crucial background to the story of Abraham and his children.

GENEALOGIES IN GENESIS

5:1–9:29	From Adam through Noah
10:1-32	Noah's three sons: Shem, Ham, and Japheth
11:10-26	From Shem through Abram and his brothers, Nahor and Haran.
11:27-32	From Terah through Abram in Haran
25:12-18	From Ishmael through his twelve tribes
36:1-19	From Esau through his sons, the chiefs of Edom

Individuals and family histories, however, take second place to the book's main thrust. Why is there such great emphasis on Abraham? Because of the covenant God made with him. God's covenant with Abraham and its importance for all of humanity is the book's main focus.

THE FOCUS OF GENESIS: ABRAHAM'S COVENANT

The space allowed for the various family histories, as well as the pace at which they are related, show what the original hearers needed. They needed to be informed about the events behind the history of the Abrahamic covenant and its implications for them. The way in which the narrative dwells on some people and moves quickly over others confirms this. For example, the first four chapters go from creation to Adam's first grandson, Enosh. Then a genealogy quickens the story's pace to bridge many hundreds of years from Adam through Noah's sons. Many interesting things probably happened to the various people mentioned in that genealogy. But those things were not included because they were not directly relevant to the book's purpose and main interest: God's special covenant work through Abraham's family.

After the story of the flood and the covenant with Noah, the pace quickens through hundreds of years of genealogy in order to move from Noah to Abraham. Thousands of years of history, with intervals for Noah and the Tower of Babel, are covered quickly in a short space. Genesis 1–11 covers thousands of years, but in Genesis 12–50 the narrative slows down and expands to tell about the lives of members of a single family, from the father, Abraham, through his great-grandchildren.

Even the space used for Abraham and his family clearly indicates where the emphasis lies. Abraham's story revolves around the covenant God made with him and how he came to have his promised son, Isaac. (1) From Genesis 12:1 through 25:11 the focus is on Abraham and his securing God's promise regarding his lineage and blessing. (2) The promised son, Isaac, is the focus for more than three chapters (25:18–28:9). (3) Then the focus moves to Isaac's son, Jacob, for the next eight chapters (28:10–35:29). (4) In the following fourteen chapters the focus shifts again from Jacob to Joseph and from Canaan to Egypt (36:1–50:26).

In summary, Genesis spends eleven chapters on the creation, the fall, the flood, and the Babel account and then thirty-nine chapters on Abraham's family history—fourteen of them for Abraham, three and a half for Isaac, eight for Jacob, and fourteen for Joseph. The most space is used for Abraham's life and

---

ABRAHAM'S FAMILY HISTORY

12:1–25:11	Life of Abraham
25:12–28:9	Lives of Abraham's sons: Isaac and Ishmael
28:10–49:33	Lives of Isaac's sons: Jacob and Esau
28:10–36:43	Jacob in Paddan Aram: birth of twelve sons
37:1–49:33	Jacob's son Joseph in Egypt: preservation of Jacob's family
50:1-26	The last years of Joseph in Egypt

Joseph's experiences in Egypt, both of which emphasize God's covenant with Abraham. Two chapters are spent on creation, nine on the curse of sin and its subsequent judgments, and thirty-nine on God's initial steps to remedy the curse through his covenant with Abraham.

BIBLE-WIDE CONCEPTS

ADAM, ABRAHAM, AND CHRIST

The book of Genesis introduces two men who have great significance throughout the Bible: Adam and Abraham. In the New Testament the apostle Paul drew a key parallel between Adam and Christ: "Consequently, just as the result of one trespass [Adams's sin] was condemnation for all men, so also the result of one act of righteousness [Christ's sacrifice] was justification that brings life for all men" (Rom. 5:18). Through Adam's sin, all of mankind are condemned. Only in Genesis can the details of Adam's transgression and its consequences be found.

Paul also linked Adam to Christ when he spoke of the believer's resurrection body. "So it is written: 'The first man Adam became a living being'; the last Adam [Jesus Christ], a life-giving spirit. The spiritual did not come first, but the natural, and after that the spiritual. The first man was of the dust of the earth, the second man from heaven" (1 Cor. 15:45-47). According to Paul's teaching, Adam is the first man, and Christ the second man. Humanity is divided between two poles: people are either in Adam and his sin or in Christ and his righteousness. Genesis provides the crucial first steps of mankind's movement out of Adam and into Christ.

Abraham is also a key figure throughout Scripture. He is the model for the true believer's faith: "Therefore, the promise comes by faith, so that it may be by grace and may be guaranteed to all Abraham's offspring—not only to those who are of the law but also to those who are of the faith of Abraham. He is the father of us all" (Rom. 4:16). Abraham became Paul's example, and an example for all believers, of one who had been justified by faith and not works.

Genesis provides all the basics of the promise of worldwide redemption through the Abrahamic covenant. In Christ believers can partake of the promise originally made to Abraham. His promise is the promise to all believers: "If you belong to Christ, then you are Abraham's seed, and heirs according to the promise" (Gal. 3:29). Genesis details the faith that Abraham had in God's promises—a faith that would become a Bible-wide model for the life of a righteous person.

THE CURSE

The fundamental problem throughout the Bible and at present is God's curse. All people labor under personal and world situations that are not fair and just. Therefore, the personal and corporate failings people experience are not only the result of their own disobedience; they are complicated by living in a world that is still under a divine curse.

Adam's sin was not just one little mistake. It infinitely offended the almighty God and set up a wall between the human race and its Creator. In response to Adam's sin, God plunged the original goodness of his creation into the horror of his divine curse.

That curse could only be reversed by an act that could remove the infinite offense of human sin against God. All of God's great acts of love toward Abraham, Moses, David, and others were steps that led to the only satisfactory means for removing sin's offense: the sacrifice of Jesus Christ.

Not until the events described in Revelation 22:3 take place, however, will the full weight of the curse be lifted in the re-created heavens and earth. All that takes place between the beginning in Eden and the end in the new heavens and earth illustrates the pain of the curse and the joy of redemption. The Bible is the story of how God reverses his curse upon sin. Although individuals and groups can experience aspects of God's blessing and presence now, the curse continually crouches behind the scenes as the awful spoiler that keeps believers from experiencing the fullness of a true relationship with him. Some humans perform beautiful acts of sacrifice and obedience, but God's full glory will remain hidden until he removes the curse at his own sovereignly appointed time. Even at the best of times the curse and its resultant human and cosmic brokenness are continual threats to the well-being of people and society.

CONFLICT BETWEEN GOD AND SATAN

The continual turbulence created by human sin and the divine curse clearly manifests itself in the conflicts found throughout Scripture. Those conflicts may be between individuals (Cain and Abel, Jesus and Satan), groups (Joseph and his brothers), nations (Israel and the Philistines), or within ourselves (flesh and spirit). Genesis 3:15 sketches the process of conflict that runs throughout the Bible. God put enmity between Satan's seed and Eve's seed. The chart, "victory through conflict," sketches out the basic direction that the conflict between the children of evil and the children of God takes throughout Scripture.

VICTORY THROUGH CONFLICT: Enmity between Satan's and Eve's Seed

Genesis 4	Cain with Abel (cf. 1 John 3:10-12)
Genesis 21:10	Ishmael with Isaac (cf. Gal. 4:28-29)
Genesis 3:15	Satan with Jesus (cf. Gal. 3:16)
Genesis 6:3-6	Flesh with spirit (cf. Rom. 16:20; Gal. 5:16-17)

Genesis explains the conflict between good and evil from two perspectives: (1) humans chose to say no to God; and (2) disobedience was an immense and infinite offense to God's love and holiness. Genesis provides the answer to why life is tragic and futile in so many ways. The curse and its ensuing conflict are behind all of the conflicts recounted in the Bible.

NEEDS MET BY GENESIS

Who were the original hearers of Genesis and what did they need? Genesis was written to people who needed to know about three things: creation, Abraham, and Egypt. The original hearers had a rich religious history preserved from Abraham onward. They were also face to face with God, who had redeemed them out of Egypt and now thundered in glory from Mount Sinai. God had redeemed Israel from Egyptian slavery and took them directly into another difficult situation in the wilderness. There, Israel had to rely solely upon God to guide and provide. The material in Genesis helped flesh out who God was and what the roots and purpose were for his people. The structure and content of Genesis show that it was written to give clear answers to questions like these.

- How did the Israelites get into Egypt in the first place?
- Who is the God who saved Israel out of Egypt?
- Who is the nation of Israel and why did God choose to come to them?
- What is the purpose for the earth?
- Why are there problems in the created world?
- What is the solution to the curse of sin?
- What is the basis of God's salvation for believers?

Believers ask many of these questions today, especially the last four. Although we were not redeemed out of Egypt in the first exodus, in a similar way we do stand before God, having been redeemed out of the bondage of sin and guilt in the second exodus in Christ. Like Israel, believers today need to understand how their future hope for the Promised Land of the new heavens and earth is directly rooted in the original purposes of the first creation. The rest of Scripture provides the answers to the questions of Genesis—questions that relate to the brokenness of God's creation and its eventual healing.

OUTLINE OF GENESIS

A. GOD'S PLAN FOR HIS CREATION (1:1–2:25)
    1. The Place: Eden As Earth's Place of Beginnings (1:1-25)
    2. The People: Adam and Eve As Parents of the World's Population (1:26–2:25)
B. GOD'S CURSE ON THE VIOLATION OF HIS CREATION (3:1–7:24)
    1. Primary Recipients: The Earth Cursed and Adam and Eve Cast Out of Eden (3:1-24)
    2. Secondary Recipients: The Creation Destroyed by Flood (4:1–7:24)
C. GOD'S COVENANT FOR A NEW CREATION (8:1–50:26)
    1. God's Covenant through a New People: Noah (8:1–11:32)
    2. God's Covenant through Abraham (12:1–21:34)
    3. God's Promises through Abraham's Son Isaac (22:1–26:35)
    4. God's Promises through Abraham's Grandson Jacob (27:1–36:43)
    5. God's Promises through Abraham's Great-grandson Joseph (37:1–50:26)

GENESIS NOTES

1:1–2:25 GOD'S PLAN FOR HIS CREATION

Overview: The first half of this section opens with a title, "In the beginning God created the heavens and the earth" (1:1), and closes by again identifying itself as a report of that creation: "This is the account of the heavens and the earth when they were created" (2:4). The words of 2:4 restate the title of 1:1 and end the opening section on creation.

Genesis 1:1–2:4 shows the original nature of creation in three ways. First, the creation revealed the character of its Creator. The nation of Israel and redeemed people of all ages need to know that God is the supreme Creator of the universe, the One who creates merely by speaking a word. Second, the original creation was very good. Believers need to know that everything God created was very good. God is not one who only approximates what is best in his creation, nor does he need help to finish a good job. All that he touches by his creative power is supremely good. Third, the original creation displayed its purpose. Believers need to know that creation was intended to continue being very good and that humanity's role in that process was one of working together with God to rule the earth and, in ruling, to obey God's guidelines.

1:1-25 The Place: Eden As Earth's Place of Beginnings

Overview: The heart of the creation account is revealed by the repetition of these three phrases: (1) "And God said. . . ." God's word was the potent force behind creation and it laid the foundation for the authority of his future words (see, for example, Heb. 11:1-3). (2) "And it was so." God speaks and it happens. The sure and potent force of the Creator is behind any other words he will speak, whether for judgment or for salvation. (3) "And God saw that it was good" (Gen. 1:4, 10, 12, 18, 21, 25, 31). Why is there a repetition of these words? What made creation good? It was the fact that it was exactly the way the Creator wanted it to be. It was a perfect manifestation of his will and purpose. The repeated declaration of creation's goodness forms one pole; the second pole is the re-creation of the new heavens and earth at the end of the age. The goodness of the first and last creations forms the framework for understanding both the horror of the evil and the hope for restoration that comes to believers today who stand between these two poles.

1:1 THE BEGINNING

Two major and differing translations of Genesis 1:1-2 are believed to be true today. The first reads: "When God began to create the heavens and the earth, the earth was formless and empty." This translation focuses on the state of the earth before God began the creative activity that is recorded in the Genesis account. Those who accept this translation believe that God's historical involvement with creation began after the earth already existed in a formless and empty state. That is, the earth was formless and empty, and then God began to create. According to this view, Genesis does not address how the earth originally came into existence in its formless and empty state, but what God did with a world already in existence.

The second translation reads: "In the beginning God created the heavens and the earth. Now the earth was formless and empty. . . ." This traditional translation teaches that God created everything out of nothing. Therefore, his first step was to create the earth, which prior to that time did not exist, and he created it without form and population (empty). God then proceeded to shape and populate the world he had made as witnessed by the Genesis account.

Although the validity of either translation cannot be proven by grammar and syntax alone, the second translation is preferred for several reasons. First of all, a literary comparison of "In the beginning God created the heavens and the earth" (1:1) and "This is the account of the heavens and the earth when they were created" (2:4*a*) supports the idea that Genesis 1:1 is the first part of a literary framework within which the creation account is presented. Genesis 2:4*a* stands as the closing phrase for this literary unit and it refers backward, not forward, ending the account of creation begun at 1:1.

This framework with its beginning and ending statements substantiates the argument for 1:1 ("In the beginning God created the heavens and the earth") being independent of 1:2 ("Now the earth was formless and empty") and standing alone as a comprehensive statement of God's creative work. Genesis 1:1 is a title that refers to the whole creative process described in Genesis 1:2–2:3. It is not a simple introduction that notes when God began to create. Literary form supports the conclusion that Genesis 1:1 is an independent and general statement of God's total creative activity from its start to its Sabbath wholeness.

Another argument supporting the second translation points out that the phrase "heaven and earth," in 1:1, functions much like the English idioms "A to Z" or "top to bottom." It is a phrase that covers not only the "heaven" and the "earth," but everything in between as well. This reveals that God created, that he created in the beginning, and that his creative work involved the heavens, the earth and everything in between.

1:2-25 SEVEN DAYS OF CREATION
Some see a time gap between 1:1 and 1:2 in which they place long geological ages and the chaos stemming from the fall of Satan to earth. If, however, God originally created the earth as formless and empty, there is no need for such a gap.

The term "now" that begins 1:2 introduces three environments for God's first step in creation: (1) a formless and empty earth, (2) darkness over the surface of the deep, and (3) the Spirit of God hovering over the waters.

The words "formless and empty" can be literally translated "unformed and unfilled." This phrase is the literary key to the creation account. In the first three days the earth was "formed," and in the second three it was "filled." The arrangement of those first six days shows a clear order in God's creation (see chart).

Days one, two, and three move creation from a formless to a formed state. Days four, five, and six move creation from an empty to a filled state. Order and population form the thrust of God's creative work.

1:26–2:25 The People: Adam and Eve As Parents of the World's Population

Overview: Some believe that 2:4-25 records a different account of creation than the account given in 1:1–2:3. This belief arises, in part, from viewing 2:4 as an introduction to what follows it rather than as a conclusion

to what preceded. Whichever view is taken, these verses actually presuppose and elaborate on events that happened on the sixth day of creation as mentioned in 1:24-31. Thus, Genesis 1 outlines God's creation of the world and everything in it, while Genesis 2 details the creation of man and woman.

1:26–2:17 HUMANITY'S PHYSICAL AND MORAL LIMITATIONS
It is important to notice that the end of Genesis 1 and the beginning of Genesis 2 take the creation account one step further by clarifying the following three roles which mankind was to fill: Mankind's first role was to populate the earth (1:28). This reveals some aspects of the nature and abilities of men and women: people were created to be members of families. Everyone was created to be a social creature. The image and likeness of God (1:26-27) is most immediately linked to humanity's power to rule over creation (1:26) and to reflect the nature and graces of male and female gender (1:27). Human rule over the earth reflects God's perfect and sovereign rule over the universe. Human gender reflects God's infinitely deep character as the potent Creator and the perfectly wise, loving, and nurturing Person. God's likeness passed on to Adam's son Seth (5:1, 3). Ultimately, every human shares in God's likeness (James 3:9), but the redeemed person undergoes a process of more perfect conformity to God's image (Col. 3:10). That image is more fully described as conformity to "true righteousness and holiness" (Eph. 4:24).

The second role for humanity was that of subduing the physical earth (1:26, 28). Subduing means taming the earth and caring for it so that it will continue to be of profitable use. Subduing is not destroying. The Hebrew word translated "subdue" is used in 2 Samuel 8:11 to describe the activity of overcoming nations, and in Jeremiah 34:16 the same word describes the activity of making people slaves. The idea carried here by "subdue" is to tame and train, not to destroy or consume.

Formation	*Population*
Day 1 Light	Day 4 Lights
Day 2 Waters/Expanse	Day 5 Fish/Birds
Day 3 Land	Day 6 Animals/People

The third role given to man was his rule over the animals, but not over other humans (1:26, 28). Eden was to be the starting place for a society of sinless development that would eventually encompass the entire world; what was just a small garden was to expand to worldwide proportions. The method of

This section also explains the moral context for humanity. God displayed his right to dictate: (1) where humans lived; (2) what they were to do; and even (3) what they were to eat. God alone is the sovereign King. The great expressions of his will in the laws of Moses and the teachings of Christ would

THE DAY-AGE THEORY

Many argue that the six creative days of Genesis 1 involved millions of years, not literal twenty-four-hour days. This view is essential to the evolutionary hypothesis that requires long time periods for mutation and natural selection. However, the terms "evening" and "morning" suggest days of a normal length. Throughout the Old Testament the word "day" is never used figuratively when accompanied by a number. But whether they are interpreted as literal or figurative days, God fashioned the literary portrayal of his creation of the universe around six literal days. If something other than literal days is in view, then the text uses the term "day" as a figure of speech. Although normal word usage upholds the argument for literal days, the creation narrative's literary form of elevated and poetic prose and the desire to correlate the days of creation with the long geological ages posited by science leave room for a figurative use of the word "day."

OTHER CREATION ACCOUNTS

Other creation accounts were written in the ancient Near East. The most well-known account outside of the Bible is called the Babylonian Genesis. Quite different from Genesis 1–2, the Babylonian account was designed to tell how the lesser gods were born. It says they were born from titanic clashes between the major gods, and that the universe is actually made up of parts of the destroyed bodies of several gods.

The Babylonian Genesis is based on sources dating back at least two thousand years before Christ. The similarities of that account with the Bible's are few and minor: they are: (1) the separation of earth and sky; and (2) the commissioning of humans to serve the gods. Both accounts have a similar order of events and a prevalence of the number seven. At best, the Babylonian Genesis presents a distorted account only distantly linked to the true record of God's original creation.

Another striking element of the Genesis account of creation can be seen in ancient Akkadian and Ugaritic literature, in which seven days equaled the period of perfection needed to develop an important work. The conclusion of any work of perfection always came on the seventh day. The Genesis record of a seven-day creation and its perfection is reflected in the literature of these ancient peoples.

The differences between the accounts are vast and involved. The Bible presents one God, not many, and he is totally above nature. He commissions mankind to serve him not out of necessity, as in the Babylonian accounts, but out of a desire for glory and fellowship with his creatures.

starting small but having a plan with worldwide intentions appears again in God's plans for the world, starting with the small family of Abraham, and once more in the smallness of the hidden kingdom of God that will someday grow into God's complete and righteous rule over the entire earth.

continue his right to determine how believers live, what they do, and even what they eat. God originally made all his creatures to be vegetarians (1:29-30). His command regarding this would change only after the flood (9:3).

God rested on the seventh day because all his work was completed (2:1-2). This completion of his incredible work of creation is the reason he set the seventh day apart as blessed. God's rest became the basis for human rest under the Mosaic covenant (Exod. 16:23; 20:11; 31:15-16); for redemptive rest in Christ's salvation (Matt. 11:28); and for eternal rest in the new heavens and earth (Heb. 4:8-9). God's rest on the seventh day meant that he stopped creating, not that he stopped doing everything. He continues to maintain his creation and works of redemption every day, including the Sabbath, as John 5:17 shows.

Adam was to till and take care of the garden (Gen. 2:15). The original earth presented sinless man not with thorns and frustrations, but with a real and healthy challenge to tame it and to bring it to its inherent potential. The meaning of the tree of knowledge of good and evil is understood by the consequences that Adam and Eve experienced by eating from it (2:16-17). God had said that eating from it would bring death. Thus, the knowledge regarding the tree was knowledge gained by committing a negative act; Adam and Eve gained firsthand knowledge of evil by doing evil. That kind of knowledge brought deadly enlightenment.

2:18-25 MALE AND FEMALE UNITY AS CORULERS OF THE EARTH

Adam had no human person-to-person relationships, so God made a "helper suitable for him" (2:18), one who was nearly a mirror image of him. The female was not inferior, she was, literally, "one corresponding to him"—like an image in a mirror. By saying, "she shall be called 'woman'" (2:23), Adam discerned her character. Of everything created, only woman was qualified to be called by a term related to the Hebrew word for man, *ish.* The word "woman" is formed simply by adding the feminine ending *ah,* thus making *ishah,* or "woman."

God instituted marriage for the human family (2:24). Marriage may be defined as a God-ordained, blessed, permanent, one-flesh, covenant relationship between a man and a woman. The permanence of the relationship is implied in the word "united" (2:24; cf. Mal. 2:14,16; Matt. 19:6-9; Mark 10:6-9; 1 Cor. 7:39). The phrase "for this" of 2:24 refers to the phrase "this is" in 2:23. The close unity between man and woman is demonstrated in the one-flesh relationship of 2:24. That was a unified physical, emotional, and spiritual relationship between male and female. Before sinning, they were not ashamed of their bodies. Their awareness of self was without guilt and shame. There were only two limitations on their relationship: physical (the universe in which they lived) and moral (the forbidden tree).

3:1–7:24 GOD'S CURSE ON THE VIOLATION OF HIS CREATION
3:1-24 Primary Recipients: The Earth Cursed and Adam and Eve Cast Out of Eden

3:1-7 SATAN'S STRATEGY

Satan denied God's word (3:4) and led Eve to doubt God's will (3:1) and his good intentions (3:5). Satan had argued that restrictions were not good and had told Eve that because God's plan contained restrictions, it was flawed. The serpent had brought into force a will other than God's by directly contradicting God's commandments and telling Eve that she would not die if she ate of the forbidden tree. The test of the serpent was an ethical one. It was a test that caused Adam and Eve to question the authority of God's perfect will, and thereby moved them to act against God's will and everything that they knew was right.

The created quality of Adam's and Eve's wills was indeed "very good." They had free wills that were in need of expression and maturity, and which were originally in line with God's command to subdue and rule the earth. Satan's subtle encouragement was for Eve to ask herself, "What do I think?" No doubt all that she observed was that the tree was beautiful and good for food. No created thing could be bad in itself, for God had created it. But she became the standard-maker. Sin, in this case, was the wrong use of good things—her own will and the beautiful, though forbidden, tree.

The desire for wisdom (3:6) is a theme that pervades all of Scripture and is the foundation for books like Proverbs and Ecclesiastes. This recurring theme of the "wise man," very prominent in the Old Testament, reaches its high point in the person and work of Jesus—the perfect wisdom of God (1 Cor. 1:24).

3:8-21 THE TWOFOLD CURSE

Each curse was twofold. The serpent was directly cursed; it received a physical curse and the promise that it would ultimately be crushed by the seed of the woman (3:15). God promised that he would execute his rule through the seed of the woman and Christ came as a fulfillment of that promise. The victory of Christ was a direct crushing of Satan in fulfillment of this curse, for Satan was behind the serpent in Eden (Rom. 16:20; Rev. 12:9; 20:2).

The woman received the consequences of her actions, though they were not called a curse. The conflict between the man and the woman, foretold in the words "desire" and "rule" in Genesis 3:16, is seen in the same Hebrew words used in 4:7 for "desires" and "master." The strain that would occur between man and woman was in regard to the man's ruling and supremacy over the woman. The world of man-woman relationships specifically and all relationships generally had fallen prey to the upside-down chaos that resulted from Adam's sin. The consequences for women also included suffering great pain in childbirth. Thus, the only means of fulfilling God's promise to crush the serpent's head with the heel of someone born of a woman was through the child-bearing sufferings of a woman.

Adam also was not directly cursed, but the earth was cursed on his account, as Paul later noted in Romans 8:20-22. The curse on the earth has caused toil and frustration for humanity. Work is not a result of the curse; toil and frustration are. Another result of Adam's sin was physical death (Gen. 3:19). Paul also noted that the root of death was in Adam's sin (Rom. 5:14-15).

Adam exercised faith and hope when he named the woman Eve (Gen. 3:20), for he looked to the life that the woman would bring forth. Adam and Eve could now only hope in the promise that someone born to Eve would undo the curses that they had caused through disobedience. The issue of Adam and Eve's shame at their nakedness confirmed the split between man and woman. They were no longer the original and pure "one flesh" that God had created them to be. God confirmed their instincts of shame by making clothing and covering them (3:21; cf. 3:7).

3:22-24 THE ISSUE OF ETERNAL LIFE

Another tree, the "tree of life," was then mentioned. But Adam and Eve were banished from the garden to keep them from it. That mysterious tree will not appear again until the dawn of the new heavens and earth spoken of in Revelation 2:7; 22:2, 14, 19.

4:1–7:24 Secondary Recipients: The Creation Destroyed by Flood

4:1-26 THE GENERATIONS OF CAIN

The genealogies of Genesis were designed to show both the multiplication of evil in the world and God's plan of redemption. In 4:16-24 the line from Cain through Lamech shows the spread of murderers. In 5:3-32 the narrative moves from Adam, through Seth, to Noah and his sons. Noah's father said about him, "He will comfort us in the labor and painful toil of our hands caused by the ground the Lord has cursed" (5:29). These family trees separate the world into two categories: the descendants of Adam through Cain and those through Seth.

The fighting between the godly and ungodly lines that were born of the woman was manifested when Cain murdered Abel. The apostle John later used Cain to typify those who murder and show hatred toward the righteous (1 John 3:12). The ground already had been cursed by God; then Cain was cursed from the ground that had soaked up Abel's blood (Gen. 4:9-15), revealing that God still held sovereign right and protection over life. Lamech's killing of a man (4:23) shows that moral advancement did not keep pace with cultural progress, for there was a growing presumption among mankind on God's protective grace.

5:1-32 FROM ADAM THROUGH NOAH

The purpose of the genealogy in 5:1-32 was to show the development of the human family from Adam through Noah and to illustrate the falsity of Satan's claim, "you will not surely die." Some have used the Bible's genealogies in an attempt to reconstruct a chronological record back to creation. On this basis, James Ussher (1581–1656) dated creation at 4004 B.C. However, the problem with such efforts is that biblical genealogies were not intended to present a full chronology, but to trace a family line back to a chief ancestor. Furthermore, there is evidence of some gaps in the genealogies of Scripture (e.g., compare Gen. 11:13 with Luke 3:36).

6:1-4 SONS OF GOD AND DAUGHTERS OF MEN

The "sons of God" mentioned in Genesis 6:2 have been identified in three different ways: (1) as Seth's apostate descendants who intermarried with the depraved descendants of Cain, (2) as fallen angels who took on physical bodies to cohabit with women of the human race, and (3) as despotic chieftains of Cainite descent who married a plurality of wives in order to expand their dominion.

Although each of the three views has its problems, those of the "angel" view can be most satisfactorily resolved. The expression "sons of God" is used exclusively in the Old Testament of angels (Job 1:6; 2:1; 38:7). According to this view, the Nephilim (from a Hebrew word meaning "to fall") were the monstrous offspring of these unnatural unions. (For more on the Nephilim, cf. Num. 13:33.) Although they were big, they were not stronger than God, who blotted them out (Gen. 6:7; 7:23) in the flood, along with the rest of the world.

In Genesis 6:3 a question arises. Evil mortals were striving with God, yet at the same time their lives were sustained by God alone. Why did God allow such enemies to continue existing? In answer, note that the meaning of the name *Israel* is "the one who strives with God." Even Israel (Jacob) and the Israelites, God's chosen people, often questioned God's will. If God destroyed all those who resisted his will, all people would soon be destroyed as they were in the flood. In contrast, Noah was one man who followed God's will totally.

6:5-12 NOAH IN THE CONTEXT OF AN EVIL SOCIETY

The Hebrew root for Noah is the same root behind the English words "comfort" and "grieved." Both God and humanity shared in the pain caused by sin. Both also shared in the pain of what their hands had labored over. And each in their own ways would share in the comfort brought by God's redemption. It is interesting to compare 6:6 with 5:29. Both verses use the same three Hebrew root words in a similar order. "Comfort" (5:29) and "grieved" (6:6) come from the same Hebrew root. "Labor" (5:29)

and "made" (6:6), as well as "toil" (5:29) and "filled with pain" (6:6), are related similarly.

Although God is perfect, he can still experience genuine sorrow over what he has created. He can grieve over his creation just as he can rejoice over it (cf. Gen. 1). In the same manner his perfect Son could also experience genuine sorrow over the lost condition of his world (Matt. 23:37). God's love and his hatred of sin form the indispensable foundation of his plans for redemption through the incarnation of Christ.

6:13-22 THE ARK

While God was grieved with mankind in general, there was one man, Noah, who pleased him. Therefore, God told him to make an ark to save him from the coming flood and destruction. Actually, the ark was more of a barge than a ship. It was 450 feet long, 75 feet broad, and 45 feet high, giving it a capacity of 1,400,000 cubic feet. As many as 522 modern railroad boxcars could have fit inside. But only 150 boxcars would have been sufficient to house two of every air-breathing creature, including animals now living and those that are now extinct. The covenant that God told Noah he would make with him (6:18) related to Noah's salvation (9:9-16) and contrasted with everything else on earth that would perish in the flood. God told Noah, "But I will establish my covenant with you."

7:1-24 THE FLOOD

Was the flood universal or local? Indications for a universal flood include the depth of the water (7:19), the death of all flesh (7:21-22), the duration of the flood (371 days), and the need for the ark. Had the flood been only a local one, God could have directed Noah, his family and the animals to migrate to a safe place. The ark's contents are emphasized in 7:13-16. The phrases "according to its kind" and "breath of life" refer back to the event of creation recorded in Genesis 1. There is repeated emphasis on the flood or waters and on the earth in 7:17-18; note also the mention of heavens. The water moved progessively higher; the ark was lifted up above the ground; the water greatly increased (7:18); all mountains under the heavens were covered (7:19); and finally the water was twenty feet ("15 cubits," KJV) higher than the mountaintops (7:20).

Every living thing was "wiped out" (7:23), just as God had said (6:7). All that had the breath of life—man, cattle, beasts, and swarming things—died. This portrays the unraveling of the act of creation recounted in Genesis 1. The rain (7:12) continued for 40 days; the ark rested on Ararat after 150 days (7:24; 8:4); and all the waters did not recede for a year and 10 days (7:11; 8:14).

8:1–50:26 GOD'S COVENANT FOR A NEW CREATION

Overview: The historical narrative moves quickly from Noah through Babel to Abraham. After Abraham received the great Abrahamic covenant, he went down to Egypt because a famine had occurred in Canaan. The relationship between the Promised Land and Egypt pervades Genesis 12–50 and makes preparation for understanding the book of Exodus. In Egypt Abraham saw God's power and miracles and was sent out of Egypt with great wealth from Pharaoh. At the end of Genesis a famine in Canaan would bring Abraham's children once again down into Egypt. Hundreds of years later their ancestors also would see the power of God and be sent out of Egypt by another pharaoh. Many years afterward a baby, Jesus, would make a trip with Mary and Joseph to Egypt in order to escape murder by Herod the Great.

Egypt functions not only as the place where Israel was placed into bondage but also as the place where God preserved his chosen line from famine and threat of death. For Abraham, Egypt served as a place of preservation. For Israel (Jacob), Egypt provided food in a time of famine and made possible the multiplication of his family into a great nation. For Jesus, Egypt provided a place of safety from Herod (cf. Hos. 11:1; Matt. 2:15). Egypt, therefore, often functions in the Bible as a place of preservation and salvation— preservation from the evils in the Promised Land (famine, death threats) until God's appointed time of salvation. A simple lesson for all eternity can be learned here: God does control and preserve the lives and destinies of all men according to his eternal plan.

But why did God choose not to sustain his people in the very land he had promised them? Why did they have to travel to the land of Egypt? The reason is that Egypt not only served as a place of preservation, but also functioned as a place of experiencing God's physical salvation. There are both physical and spiritual elements to salvation. In the history of God's people, they were often physically saved from human wrath and oppression. And through that history believers now can discern, along with the Israelites themselves, that the essential reality of God's spiritual salvation is release from divine wrath and satanic oppression. In addition, since Egypt was a land of "old" things and ways, it served for the Israelites as a place for learning things that they would later use while in the wilderness and the Promised Land.

8:1–11:32 God's Covenant through a New People

8:1–9:17 THE COVENANT WITH NOAH
After the earth had been flooded for 150 days, God remembered Noah. The word "remembered" (8:1) is one of the great words for expressing redemption and salvation in the Old Testament (cf. Exod. 2:24-25). Although the flood story ends with 8:22, there is a spiritual as well as physical watershed at 8:1 where the reader is reminded, "But God remembered Noah. . . ." In Scripture when something is said about God remembering, this signals a major act of redemption for the ones remembered (cf. 9:15-16; 19:29; 30:22; Exod. 2:24; 6:5). God's remembering of Noah explicitly begins his major design for bringing about worldwide redemption; the record of that design stretches from Genesis 8 through Genesis 50.

In some ways the flood returned the earth to a condition that was similar to its state at the beginning of God's creation. Although the earth still retained its basic form and probably had not changed drastically under the floodwaters, water covered the earth as it did in the beginning. Also, it was again empty of people and animal life, except for the handful of people and animals that were aboard the ark. After Genesis 8:13, time began to be reckoned by Noah's age. He was the head of a new race and father of a new beginning of history. He, like Adam, was commanded to be fruitful and multiply (8:17; cf. 1:28).

God's covenant with Noah was foundational for his grace seen later in the cross. (See the discussion of God's covenant with Noah in the introductory section, *The Bible's Big Picture.*) In the flood, God displayed his hatred and vengeance toward sin. In the rainbow he showed that man's deserved punishment for his acts of sin would not be immediately fulfilled. He also revealed that his hatred of sin would not be expressed until his plan of grace was completed. How then, could God stand to face mankind's continued sin? The answer lies in his character: though God is holy and just, he is also longsuffering. God is always more interested in salvation than in damnation.

9:18–10:1 NOAH'S DESCENDANTS
The story of Noah's offspring recounts a curse placed on Ham (Canaan). This curse would be very important for the Israelites, who were in the wilderness, about to enter the Promised Land where they would run up against the Canaanites. The sin of Ham was disrespect toward his father, Noah. The curse of Ham's son, Canaan, was actually a curse on all of Ham's descendants. Thus, the curse on Canaan was not specifically directed against the man Canaan himself, but against the Canaanite people in general. Ham's sin was his frivolous look upon his naked father, an act in which he abandoned God's moral code. Canaan's descendants acted as their ancestor had—with moral abandon (Lev. 18:24-30). The curse on Canaan was fulfilled in the destruction and the conquest of the land by the Israelites led by Joshua.

10:2-32 THE GENEALOGY THROUGH SHEM
Genesis 10 is a table of the ancient nations that reveals where the different peoples were scattered, and 11:1-9 tells why they were scattered. The sons of Japheth (10:2-5) are the Indo-Europeans; the sons of Ham (10:6-20) are the Africans and various peoples of Babylon, Assyria and Palestine; and the sons of Shem (10:21-32) are the Semitic peoples. "Eber," the son of Shem, is singled out in 10:24-25 and 11:16-17 and is probably the chief ancestor of the Hebrew people.

The genealogy in 10:2-32 serves two purposes: (1) It begins to focus on Abraham's line: the order is Japheth, Ham, and then Shem, the ancestor of Abraham. (2) It prepares for the story of the Tower of Babel, which explains how the "nations spread out over the earth after the flood" (10:32). This genealogy does not mention all the names or identify all the peoples (cf. 10:5, 20, 31-32). Shem is mentioned last in order to clear the way for Abraham. This shows that the story about Babel was included as part of the preparation for the story of Abraham. The unity of the human race was shattered and many nations were formed. This prepares the reader for the promise that all nations will be blessed in Abraham (Gen. 12:3). Babel is also traced to Ham (10:10; NASB, TLB), and thus stands as one of the results of the curse on Canaan. The people of Babel, along with Ham, failed to show respect toward their father, who was ultimately God.

11:1-9 THE TOWER OF BABEL
The "plain in Shinar" (11:2) is the fertile plain of Babylonia (modern Iraq) that lies between the Tigris and Euphrates rivers. The Tower of Babel may have been an early type of Babylonian ziggurat; these pyramid-like towers served as shrines for mountain-dwelling deities. The story of Babel shows how people banded together in an evil effort to block God's plan for mankind to fill the earth. (See "scattered over the face of the earth," 11:4, 9.)

11:10-32 FROM SHEM TO ABRAHAM
At this point, the Genesis narrative begins its focus on the family of Abraham (around 2166–1991 B.C.). The genealogies in Genesis 5 and 11 both move respectively toward the next key figures in God's redemptive history: Noah (5:29) and Abraham (11:26). Both of these men had a special part in God's plan to re-create his kingdom on earth. Ur, Abraham's hometown (11:31), was the ancient capital of the Sumerian kingdom, the earth's first great civilization (see introductory map). Situated on the bank of the Euphrates River, it was an important commercial center with two harbors. Nanna, the moon god, was the city's patron deity.

12:1–21:34 God's Covenant through Abraham
Overview: The section 12:1–21:34 emphasizes the personal and property aspects of the Abrahamic covenant. Abraham would gain the land promised to him and an heir to

inherit it. His blessing would extend to those closely associated with him, which at first included his nephew, Lot (13:10). Two potential conflicts are noted. First, even though Lot was not Abraham's own son, Abraham did not strive with him over how they would divide the land between them for the grazing of their flocks and herds. Instead, he relied on God, not quarreling with his relatives for the land he would receive. Readers may have wondered whether Abraham would fight with Lot over the land (13:5-8). Abraham allowed Lot to take the best land because he did not need to fight for the land that he believed God had given him. Later God would confirm his promise of giving the land to Abraham (13:14-17). The second potential conflict arose when Abraham was offered the spoils of war. Would Abraham take the spoils from the king of Sodom (14:21-24)? No, because it would show that he lacked faith in God. Afterward God confirmed his great reward to Abraham (15:1).

The major focus of 16:1–21:34 is the birth of the promised son of Abraham and Sarah. That son would become the first of many in the Abrahamic line that would stretch out until God would fulfill his promise to bless all the earth in Abraham through the greatest of all Abraham's descendants, Jesus Christ. The twists and turns leading to the birth and establishment of Isaac as Abraham's sole heir show God's sovereignty over human frailty. Then, during the bondage of Jacob, Isaac's son in Paddan Aram, God would increase the tribe of Abraham into the majority of the twelve tribes of Israel.

12:1-9 THE FOUNDATION OF THE ABRAHAMIC PROMISE

Abraham's initial call was at Ur in Chaldea (11:31; Acts 7:2-3), but the call was renewed at Haran (12:1) (see introductory map). God revealed his will for worldwide redemption, and all the nations would find their blessing in what he would do through his promises to Abraham. (For an overview of the covenant with Abraham, see the introductory section, *The Bible's Big Picture*.) God reinforced his promises to Abraham several times and in a number of different ways (see chart).

The promises would not come instantly or all at once, but they would gradually be realized over a period of thousands of years. Because that slow unfolding of God's promises could cause believers to weaken in their faith and desire an affirmation of God's faithfulness, God consistently and repeatedly affirmed his promises to Abraham and his offspring.

12:10-20 ABRAHAM'S EXODUS

Abraham and Sarah's departure from Egypt (12:10-20) is an event parallel to Israel's later national exodus from that land. Both events reveal something of God's might and plan. Since the bondage of God's people was not accidental, deliverance and preservation were sure. Abraham had gone to Egypt because of a famine (12:10). Famines were frequent in Palestine, a land with a marginal climate, where agriculture was dependent upon rainfall. Since the Nile River furnished a more certain supply of water for cattle and crops, it made Egypt a haven from hunger in times of famine. God inflicted Pharaoh and his household with diseases (12:17)

GOD'S PROMISES TO ABRAHAM

12:1-3	Blessings promised
12:7	Land identified
13:15-16	Land and seed emphasized
13:17-18	Land surveyed
15:5	Seed reemphasized
17:9-14	The sign of the covenant
17:15-21	Seed reemphasized
18:10	Seed reemphasized
21:1-7	Seed given
22:1-18	Certainty of the covenant reemphasized

and miraculously preserved Abraham and his family, especially Sarah, God's chosen bearer of the promised son. The great plagues on Egypt that occurred just before the exodus of Israel were not the first that God had sent upon an Egyptian pharaoh. This fact would have confirmed to the readers of Genesis, who had just witnessed another pharaoh's defeat at the exodus from Egypt, that nothing is accidental with God. Even great and powerful pharaohs could not keep him from doing his promised work.

13:1–15:21 ABRAHAM RESCUES LOT
Because their flocks and herds had become so large, Abraham and Lot divided the land (13:1-18). Lot chose to reside in the Jordan Valley. This valley, while barren and desolate today, was well watered before God destroyed Sodom and Gomorrah (13:10). A major environmental change appears to have taken place as a result of God's judgment.

Hebron, founded around 1700 B.C., did not exist as a city in Abraham's day (see introductory map). The site Abraham visited was called Mamre; the mention of Hebron (13:18) is a later scribal note indicating where Mamre was located.

Genesis 14 tells of an early invasion of Palestine by a coalition of four Mesopotamian kings who invaded the plain of the Jordan, subjugating the five cities there, including Sodom (14:1-3). Lot, Abraham's nephew, was among those taken captive. But God is sovereign over the nations, and Lot was saved because of his relationship to Abraham (cf. 12:3). In future generations when the nation of Israel was attacked and her people taken captive by Assyria and Babylon, nations also from Mesopotamia, she would find that her preservation as a nation was assured in much the same way— because of her relationship to Abraham.

When Abraham returned from defeating the four kings, he was met by Melchizedek, the king of "Salem" (14:18). "Salem" is believed to be an early name for Jerusalem (see introductory map). Melchizedek was not just a king; he was also a priest of the Most High God (cf. Ps. 110:4; Heb. 5:5-10; 7:1-10).

In Genesis 15 God confirmed his covenant with Abraham and foretold Israel's future enslavement in Egypt. This chapter's

importance in placing the Egyptian enslavement squarely in God's sovereign and predetermined plan for redemption can scarcely be overestimated. Abraham was told that a 400-year period of enslavement and oppression would come upon his family. The 400 years is a round figure that is given more exactly as 430 years in Exodus 12:40. After four generations (of 100 years each) Abraham's descendants would return to the land. At that time the oppressing nation (Egypt) would be judged (Gen. 15:14) and Israel would come out with many possessions.

After that prediction, the covenant between God and Abraham was finalized. This fact would be highly significant for the Israelites who, under Moses, had just been released from Egyptian bondage. Note that Israel's return to Canaan was linked to God's plan for the Amorites (Gen. 15:16), "Amorite" being a general term for the inhabitants of Canaan. Therefore, Israel's return and the end of the Amorite's iniquity were closely linked.

16:1-16 ABRAHAM'S MISGUIDED EFFORTS AT GAINING A SON
Ishmael was a son of Abraham but not of the promise (16:1-16). The Nuzi tablets, cuneiform documents dating from about 1500 B.C., shed light on why Sarah did what she did (16:1-4). Giving Hagar to Abraham was in keeping with an ancient custom that allowed a wife who was unable to bear children to give a concubine to her husband in order to gain an heir. What was missing, as noted in 16:2, was a request for the Lord's advice. Abraham's action was not rebellious, just hasty and unwise. Note the parallel between the statement, "Abram agreed to what Sarai said" (Gen. 16:2) and God's words to Adam, "you listened to your wife" (Gen. 3:17). Would a son by Hagar be the answer? No. But her son, Ishmael, was greatly blessed anyway.

Why was Ishmael blessed (16:10)? Because the Abrahamic covenant stated that any offspring of Abraham would be blessed, even if that offspring was not received according to the promise. The descendants of Ishmael are modern-day Arabs, blessed with incredible wealth that silently existed beneath their tents even at the time of Hagar: the wealth of oil.

17:1-27 THE COVENANT SIGN OF CIRCUMCISION

Abraham aligned himself with God's covenant sign of circumcision in an account that is sandwiched between two responses of his faithlessness: his attempt to gain a son through Hagar (16:1-4) and his reaction of falling down and laughing when God said he and Sarah would have a child (17:17-18). Circumcision, a sign pointing away from itself to something else, was the external mark or evidence of Abraham's covenant relationship to God. In view was God's intention to create a pure race of obedient people who would fill, rule, and subdue the earth—a race bearing a mark that showed they were followers of God's way.

18:1–19:38 SODOM AND GOMORRAH

Abraham still had to learn about God's wrath against sin and of his grace toward the righteous. God desired to share with Abraham how he would vent his wrath against Sodom and Gomorrah (18:16-33). God initiated the conversation (18:17), for he wanted Abraham to become aware of his grace toward the righteous. In talking with God, Abraham explored, but did not bargain with, God's mercy and justice. The direct relationship between the Abrahamic covenant and personal obedience is seen in 18:18-19. The blessings of that covenant would come by God's sovereign promise, but only for the particular people or groups that obeyed his commands.

Oriental etiquette has a strong emphasis on caring for the needs of strangers. Both Abraham and Lot proved that they were sensitive to these customs of hospitality, which were regarded as a sacred duty, since it was believed that guests were sent by God himself. The promises that God made to be fulfilled through Abraham included a blessing for all people, even those who were strangers to God's covenant (18:18). Because of this promise, Abraham's hospitality has reached out to strangers down through the centuries, even to believers today, through the work of his descendant, Jesus Christ.

According to oriental custom, a host was responsible for protecting his guests from harm, whatever the cost (19:4-8). Thus, Lot offered his daughters to the wicked men in order to protect his guests. The demands of hospitality explain, but do not justify, Lot's

actions. Why did God have compassion on Lot (19:16)? Because God "remembered Abraham, and he brought Lot out" (19:29), which was in accordance with his covenant with Abraham. God had told Abraham, "all peoples on earth will be blessed through you" (Gen. 12:3), and Lot was no exception. However, Lot's lineage, known later as the Moabites and Ammonites, would become enemies of Israel (19:30-38).

20:1-18 ABRAHAM AND THE PHILISTINES

Abraham moved into the land of the Philistines where he again told Sarah to say that she was his sister and not his wife (cf. Abraham's similar deception in Egypt in 12:11-19). As a result, Sarah was taken into the king's house. Would Sarah be lost to a Philistine king? No. This event, as was true of the one in Egypt, shows the importance of preserving Sarah's as well as Abraham's great claim to God's promises. God was greater than any human pharaoh or king. Notice God's power over the event of childbearing (20:18). All of this account needs to be read in the full light of the promise of Isaac's birth (17:21). Abraham should have waited for God's specific commands before following his own fleshly and logical options. As the people of Israel heard these stories, they would realize how secure they were as God's people. Nothing could stop his promised blessings of salvation and ultimate deliverance from taking place.

21:1-34 ISAAC IS BORN

God had said a son would be born to Abraham and Sarah (stressed three times in 21:1-2). Read this account in light of what Abraham had tried to do intentionally to achieve this promise through a son by Hagar, as well as what he had done unintentionally to block it by pawning Sarah off to Pharaoh and a Philistine king. According to custom, if a natural heir was born, the heir through the slave woman would lose the right of being chief inheritor (21:10-11). However, previous heirs were to be well treated. In the desert near Beersheba, God confirmed to Hagar that he would continue to care for Ishmael, the previous heir, and make of his descendants a great nation (21:17-18).

Abraham then settled near Beersheba, figuratively claiming the land God had promised him. The tree he planted (21:33) indicated to God his permanent residence there and his being at peace. Then Abraham worshiped God. The major migration of the Philistines (a group of "Sea Peoples") by boat from the Aegean Islands took place around 1168 B.C. The reference here to the Philistines (21:34), which is supported by archaeological discoveries, provides evidence of earlier movements of these people to Palestine.

22:1–26:35 God's Promises through Abraham's Son Isaac

22:1-24 GOD TESTS ABRAHAM'S FAITH
According to tradition, the mountain in the land of Moriah where God tested Abraham (22:1) is the hill upon which Solomon built the temple (2 Chron. 3:1). When Abraham had successfully passed the testing, God declared his promises to him (22:16-18). Was God's command that Abraham slay his son Isaac immoral? No, for God was testing Abraham's willingness to obey him completely, and he stopped him before he could actually kill Isaac. However, one day God would allow the sacrifice of his own Son for mankind's sins. God gave a special promise to Abraham (22:16-17) because of the combination of his obedience and faith (cf. 15:6).

23:1-20 ABRAHAM BURIES SARAH
After Sarah's death, Abraham just wanted to purchase a cave for her burial place (23:3-9), but Ephron would not sell his cave without the adjoining field. According to Hittite land laws, a land owner had to continue to pay taxes until he disposed of the entire property. It is very possible that Ephron insisted on selling the whole plot so he would not have to continue paying taxes. After bartering with Ephron over the price of the cave and field in a way typical of those in the Near East, Abraham gained a place to bury Sarah.

24:1–25:12 ABRAHAM FINDS
A BRIDE FOR ISAAC
When Abraham's servant was told to get a wife for Isaac, he placed his hand under Abraham's thigh. This gesture accompanied the servant's solemn oath to return with a wife for Isaac. The area beneath the thigh was regarded as the seat of procreative powers and the placing of the servant's hand there pointed to the nature of this oath. It would be the means for gaining a wife for

Isaac and making possible the birth of the next generation of Abraham's descendants; it also highlighted the importance of acquiring the proper wife, thus preserving the family line through which God's promises would be fulfilled.

The servant was sent to Mesopotamia (24:10), which refers to the land of Aram between the Tigris and Euphrates rivers. Isaac took a wife from among his relatives, not from among the Canaanites. There were to be no political marriage alliances in Abraham's family to secure the land God had promised (24:3). By arranging a marriage for his son that gained him nothing materially or politically, Abraham proved that he trusted God to give the land of Palestine to his descendants. Isaac then became Abraham's sole inheritor (25:1-12).

25:13-34 ISAAC AND ESAU
The life-style of Ishmael's descendants (25:12-18) is attested to by the words, "they lived in hostility toward all their brothers" (25:18).

Isaac's oldest son, Esau, had a birthright that included the right of a double inheritance, the privilege of becoming head of the family, and the right of a special parental blessing (25:19-34; cf. 27:19, 36; Deut. 21:17). Ancient clay tablets found at Nuzi indicate it was legitimate to exchange one's birthright for something else. Esau's problem was his casual and unconcerned attitude toward the birthright (25:31-34; Heb. 12:16-17). It was not simply the question of his despising his place as the firstborn. It was his indifference to the privilege of carrying on God's plan for world redemption through Abraham and his children. Esau did not care whether or not he was next in line for carrying on God's work of redemption to the world.

26:1-11 ISAAC AND ABIMELECH
When another famine occurred, God kept Isaac in the land rather than sending him to Egypt, in order to state his covenant to him. Isaac's being in Gerar set the atmosphere for his lie to the Philistines regarding Rebekah (26:7-11). He lied even though he had just been promised God's blessing and his heir had already been born. This section's close similarities to Abraham's lie to Pharaoh is designed to show how Abraham's and

Isaac's fears were equally groundless in light of God's promise. God would protect his chosen ones and fulfill his promises just as he had said. The fears of all God's people who follow after, as physical or spiritual descendants of Abraham, are equally groundless.

26:12-35 THE DISPUTES ABOUT WELLS
The disputes about the wells and their being stopped up amounted to an attempt by the Philistines to drive Isaac out of the land. This contributed to the whole drama of how God accomplished his promise for his people's possession of the land. Would Isaac, the promised heir, find no place to live in the Promised Land? God told him, "Do not be afraid" (26:24), and Isaac responded by calling upon the name of the Lord (26:25). The events surrounding the naming of Beersheba (26:26-33) are a confirmation of how God brings blessing from foreign peoples (Gen. 12:1-3). In contrast to all of Abraham's earlier efforts to make sure Isaac married a proper woman is a note concerning Isaac's concern about the wrong marriages of his son Esau (26:34-35).

27:1–36:43 God's Promises through Abraham's Grandson Jacob

Overview: The purpose of this section is to highlight the struggle between Jacob and Esau. It shows how the blessing would come to Jacob, and it also foreshadows the character of his descendants, the nation of Israel, whose name means, "one that struggles with God." Jacob (later named Israel) struggled at birth (25:22-26), for his birthright (25:27-34), in his deceptive grab for the blessing of the firstborn (27:1-46), and with God at the Jabbok River (32:1-32).

Who were the men who gained the birthright throughout the book of Genesis? Many times it was not the person expected to receive it. Much emphasis is placed on the reversal of birthrights from the older or oldest son to a younger one. Abraham, Isaac, Jacob and Joseph were all younger sons. Later on, two other younger sons would be chosen for God's blessings: David and Solomon.

Genesis 28–36 relates the births of each of Jacob's sons whose descendants would become the twelve tribes of Israel. The story would be of great interest to those who had recently come out of Egypt or to those who wanted the details of their heritage. But this story of origins is told with warts and all, because it ultimately is a story of how God brought redemption to his people. God is portrayed as perfect, but his agents are seen for what they really were—sinful, needy people trying to gain favor with God, even though at times it was for the wrong reasons.

Jacob's story tells of God's covenant that was given to him in the land, of God blessing him while he was working for Laban in Paddan Aram, and of his receiving a new name and new beginning as he reentered the Promised Land. Years earlier Jacob's grandfather, Abraham, had gone to Egypt, miracles had occurred there, and he had come out richer than he had gone in. Jacob was forced to go to Paddan Aram, he prospered during his stay there, and he left as a wealthy man who found God's favor upon his return to the Promised Land. For God's chosen people, even exile can be a time of preservation and renewed blessing.

27:1-45 GOD ALLOWS THE RIGHT MAN TO BE BLESSED: JACOB
In Isaac's plans to bless Esau, he was ignoring the plain word of God about which son should have supremacy (25:23). Isaac's blessing of Jacob, which was actually intended for Esau, pictured Jacob as master of his brothers (27:29; cf. 25:23). When Esau came in later and Isaac realized what had happened, he trembled because he saw the hand of God in what he had unknowingly done (27:33). The Nuzi tablets attest to the fact that an oral blessing was legally binding. Once given, the blessing could not be successfully contested (27:33). Afterward, Esau lamented loudly, hated Jacob, and made plans to kill him.

Jacob had highly valued the covenant blessing and had sought it eagerly, even though his methods were deceptive. God blessed him in spite of his sin, not because of it. The key actor in this story was God, not Jacob, Isaac or Esau. God was forging ahead with his redemptive plan. Since he was accomplishing his goals through real humans, his perfect plan was worked through sinful and error-ridden people. The long line of imperfect agents in God's redemptive plan forms a stark contrast to the single and perfect consummation of that plan—Jesus Christ.

27:46–36:43 JACOB SECURES THE PROMISE TO ABRAHAM

In the section 27:46–28:22, the covenant is reaffirmed to Abraham's grandson, Jacob. Isaac had given Jacob the blessing of Abraham's covenant (28:4), and then God confirmed that blessing to Jacob in a dream (28:10-17). The next morning Jacob made a vow to God (28:18-22) that anticipated his return to the Promised Land. Jacob could have been about seventy-seven years old as he served Laban for his daughter Rachel (29:1-20). He married both Leah and Rachel (29:21-30), and with them and their two maidservants he fathered his twelve children (29:31–30:24). Then Jacob used deception to gain provisions for his household (30:25-43). Why was he blessed by God in spite of his deceptive methods? Jacob did not receive God's blessing because he deserved it, but because he was a descendant of Abraham, and a recipient of God's promise to Abraham.

Although Jacob married two wives (29:27), bigamy was an exception to God's original plan for marriage (2:24; Mal. 2:13-15). It is never condoned or condemned in Scripture, but it also seems to result in unhappy situations (1 Sam. 1:2-7). The mandrakes that Leah's son found (30:14) were herbs similar in size and shape to a small apple. They were thought in ancient times to stimulate physical desire and aid in conception. Rachel's motive for wanting them was for increased fertility; but while she got the mandrakes, Leah got another son (30:17). God was in control, and later he gave Rachel her first child, Joseph, according to his own perfect timing (30:22-24).

In his breeding methods Jacob sought to influence the color of the animal's offspring by placing peeled, white striped branches before the animals as they bred (30:37-43). These strange actions were apparently based on a God-given dream (31:10-13). Whether or not God told Jacob to actually use such methods, it was he who sovereignly caused the birth of the animals that would prosper Jacob and give him success (31:9).

After the Lord commanded Jacob to return to the Promised Land, he began his journey with his wives, livestock and other possessions (31:13-20). Before leaving, Rachel stole her father's "household gods" (31:19). These were small figures of female deities that probably were important to Rachel for two reasons: they were thought to guarantee fertility, and they symbolized inheritance rights. No doubt Rachel wanted to guarantee that she would have more children and to maintain Jacob's right to a portion of Laban's wealth. Jacob later buried these images at Shechem (35:2-4).

When Jacob reached the entrance to the Promised Land, he prayed at the Jabbok River (32:9-12). Note the revelation of God's character in this section. Struggling with God will bring victory when such struggling is done by means of prayer, earnestly and humbly seeking his favor. The name "Israel" means "one who struggles with God." That explains the inclusion of the dialogue of 32:26-29. Jacob was struggling for a blessing. Hosea 12:1-5, which refers to Jacob, should be read in this connection. Ever since his birth, Jacob had struggled with men to receive the birthright that would give him the blessings of the Abrahamic covenant. Here he was shown that in all his previous human efforts to gain the blessing through deception, his real enemy had been God. In Hosea 12:6 the nation of Israel was told to do the same thing as Jacob did here—prevail by prayer to God, not by looking for help from human sources. Jacob's struggle was a physical picture of his need for God, and many years later the nation had the same need. Jacob learned that as heir of the covenant promises, he had nothing to fear from humans (32:11). Wrestling with God for his blessings should release all believers from their fear of lesser mortals.

Jacob's safe arrival in Shechem (33:1-20) fulfilled God's promise to him given in 28:15. Jacob's daughter was violated by Shechem, the son of Hamor, the area's ruler. Afterward Hamor advised Jacob and his sons of how to establish a union with the land's residents and achieve peace and prosperity there. Jacob demanded that the men of Shechem be circumcised, thus identifying themselves with God's covenant people, before allowing intermarriage. But instead of seeking a peaceful way, Simeon and Levi used deception and physical violence for survival in the land, killing all the men of Shechem in revenge for Shechem's violation of their sister. Jacob rebuked them for their excessive action (34:1-31), and years later he judged them for it (49:5-7). The incident at Shechem stood against intermarriage with the residents of Canaan—something that God opposed for Jacob and his family. This incident also resulted in great fear of Jacob's family among the resident Canaanites (35:5). That fear also was a result of the family members' purifying themselves before God at Bethel, for God was their real protection against anyone who might harm them.

At Bethel, where years earlier Jacob had vowed to make God his God (28:21), God reconfirmed his covenant with him (35:1-15). See introductory map for Bethel. As the family traveled on, Jacob's last son, Benjamin, was born and Rachel died in childbirth. Reuben wrongfully used his father's concubine, which resulted in the forfeiture of his birthright as the firstborn son (49:3-4; cf. 1 Chron. 5:1).

The generations of Isaac's son Esau are listed in 36:2-43. Note how many times it is mentioned that Esau was also called Edom (36:1, 8, 9, 43). Esau was the ancestor of the Edomites, perpetual enemies of Israel throughout the Old Testament period (cf. Obadiah, which is a book of prophecy against Edom). This genealogy told the Israelites, who had left Egypt in the exodus, where their enemies came from.

37:1–50:26 God's Promises through Abraham's Great-grandson Joseph

Overview: The section of 37:1–50:26 relates back to 15:13-16 and also prepares the reader for Israel's upcoming exodus from Egypt. It also emphasizes dreams, because when several of God's leaders were in bondage in foreign countries, God appeared to them by this means. See the parallels in the accounts of Abraham, Daniel, and the dreams of Joseph, Jesus' earthly stepfather. This section also shows how the seed of Israel was preserved (50:20) in spite of famine in the land. Although the ground was still cursed, God continued to protect his own people. Jacob was buried in the land, and Joseph would be also. Compare 49:26, where Jacob blessed Joseph, with 37:7-11, where Joseph told about his dreams and his family bowing down before him. Although this section ends with a coffin, that fact is not bad. Joseph's command to take his coffin to

the Promised Land represents the hope of God's future visit to the world (50:24) to make possible the salvation of mankind.

37:1-38 JOSEPH SOLD INTO SLAVERY

Joseph's special robe is variously interpreted as ornamented, varicolored, or long-sleeved. It designated Joseph as a favored son and was a garment that an overseer, not a worker, would wear. His exaltation by his father and the sharing of his dream of exaltation offended his family, but these facts were directly in line with what God had planned for him. Although the Ishmaelites and Midianites are interchangeable in this passage (cf. Judg. 8:22, 24), it is probable that Ishmael was their ancestor, whereas Midian was their land and place of origin.

38:1-30 JUDAH AND TAMAR

This story is designed to show the righteousness of Tamar and the negative attributes of Judah (compare 38:25-26 with 37:32-33). In 38:25-26, Tamar "sent a message" to Judah and Judah "recognized" the tokens she sent. In 37:32-33 Judah and his brothers "took" Joseph's bloodstained coat as a message to Jacob. Jacob "recognized" Joseph's coat and was thus deceived. This structure presents parallels involving the sight of personal items of clothing and the recognition of startling implications from them. Judah created a deception to trick Jacob into thinking Joseph was dead. Jacob's recognition of Joseph's bloody coat issued in his proclamation of the death of his son. Tamar created a deception to trick Judah. Judah was the cause of Jacob's deception in Genesis 37, and then he himself was the victim of deception in Genesis 38. Judah's recognition of his own seal, cord, and staff issued in his proclamation of the righteousness of Tamar and his own unrighteousness in not letting his son Shelah marry her. Meanwhile his great unrighteousness in selling Joseph into slavery awaited its exposure in Genesis 42:21-22 and 44:18-34.

Deuteronomy 25:5-6 commanded that a brother's offspring replace his dead brother, and that principle was in effect in Judah's day. Tamar may have been influenced by a Hittite law that held that when no brother-in-law existed to fulfill the levirite duty, the father-in-law was responsible. Note also the contrast of Judah's lusts with Joseph's purity in Egypt. Judah's son Onan sinned by refusing to perform his responsibility as a brother-in-law to father children by his brother's widow. He may have coveted the firstborn's property for himself (cf. Num. 27:8-11).

39:1–41:57 JOSEPH'S RISE, FALL AND RESTORATION

The Lord prospered Joseph and then allowed him to be thrown into prison, which was actually a light sentence for his alleged crime (39:1-23). The key phrase is "the Lord was with him" (39:21, 23). Again God worked through dreams—this time the dreams of Pharaoh's cupbearer and baker (40:1-22). The cupbearer did not remember Joseph (40:23), but God was always with him and did not forget.

Pharaoh's dreams (41:1-36) were interpreted by Joseph because God gave him the interpretations (41:16, 25; cf. 40:8). Joseph became prime minister of Egypt at age thirty (41:37-46). He received Pharaoh's signet ring by which he could transact affairs of the state in the name and with the authority of Pharaoh. Joseph was given a daughter of the priest of On for his wife. On (41:45, 50), which was located at the head of the Nile Delta, is the Hebrew name for Heliopolis, an early capital and principal center of sun worship in ancient Egypt. Joseph's rise to power saved Egypt from famine and allowed it to become a haven for famine relief, which was just what Jacob's family would need.

42:1–45:28 JOSEPH AND HIS BROTHERS

Joseph's dealings with his brothers were not motivated by his desire for vengeance. Rather, he was testing his brothers to determine if they had had a change of heart. His actions caused his brothers to reflect on their conduct of past years and to admit their guilt (42:21-22). Joseph's intentions are revealed in 42:9.

Divination by water, which Joseph told his steward to mention when finding his cup in Benjamin's sack (44:5), was a widespread practice in ancient times when precious gems or oil were put into the water and interpreted. It is highly unlikely that Joseph, to whom God had revealed so much regarding the interpretation of dreams, would practice divination, but the uniqueness of the cup

gave his scheme an air of authenticity. Note the role of Judah in confessing the brothers' guilt and pleading to replace Benjamin as Joseph's slave (44:18-34). Joseph knew that God had allowed all that had happened to him in order to preserve and bring Jacob's family into Egypt (45:5, 7; cf. 15:13-14). He also knew God's covenant promise to Abraham to preserve his descendants in the chosen line.

Jacob's family was allowed to settle in Goshen (45:10) in the western delta of the Nile, the best watered and fertile land in Egypt. During the next 430 years, until the exodus, the family of Jacob grew into the great nation of Israel.

46:1–47:31 JACOB'S FAMILY COMES TO EGYPT

At Joseph's request, Jacob and his family moved to Egypt, where they were kept alive during the drought and where they would live for the next four hundred years. Jacob's request for burial in the Promised Land of Canaan (47:27-31) was honored. He was trusting God's covenant promise as well as what God had told him before leaving the Promised Land about making his family into a great nation in Egypt and then bringing them back (46:3-4; 48:21; cf. Exod. 3:7 and Matt. 22:32).

48:1–49:33 JACOB'S FINAL BLESSINGS AND PREDICTIONS

Jacob adopted the two sons of Joseph, Ephraim and Manasseh (48:1-22), who took their father's place and became tribal heads. Some believe that this means that Joseph then took the leadership position of the firstborn since after Jacob's blessing of his sons, he had double representation among the tribes. The Scriptures explain that Reuben's "rights as firstborn were given to the sons of Joseph . . . and though Judah was the strongest of his brothers and a ruler came from him, the rights of the firstborn belonged to Joseph" (1 Chron. 5:1). Actually, the only "rights" that Joseph received were the "double portion" plus the blessings given to his sons. And although Joseph ruled over his brothers when they first went to Egypt because of his high position over the whole land, his descendants never assumed a leadership position over the later nation of Israel. God's covenant line of promise was continued through Judah, who was technically next in line for the birthright after it had been forfeited by Reuben, Simeon and Levi. And Judah was the royal line through which Christ, the promised One, came (49:8-10). After the book of Genesis ends, no tribe was singled out as that through which God's chosen line would continue until God told David, who was from the tribe of Judah, that he would establish the throne of his kingdom forever.

In Jacob's predictions regarding his twelve sons and their descendants (49:1-33), the exact meaning of the phrase "until Shiloh comes" (49:10, NASB and TLB) is uncertain. Traditional interpretation, both by Christian and Jewish scholars, is that it is a proper name for the coming Messiah. That view is in keeping with the context (cf. Rev. 5:5).

Jacob's charge to bury him in the Promised Land was an act of faith that one day God would allow his descendants to return and settle there (cf. 50:24-25; Heb. 11:22).

50:1-26 JOSEPH'S FINAL ACTS

After Joseph buried Jacob in the Promised Land (50:1-14), he subdued his brothers' fear that he might take revenge on them now that their father was dead (50:15-21) and exhorted them regarding God's faithfulness to Abraham and his descendants (50:22-24). He assured them that God would come to their family's aid and return them to the Promised Land. When that happened, they were to take Joseph's bones with them. No doubt Joseph had heard about and remembered what God had told Abraham regarding his descendants' spending four hundred years in a foreign country (cf. 15:13-14).

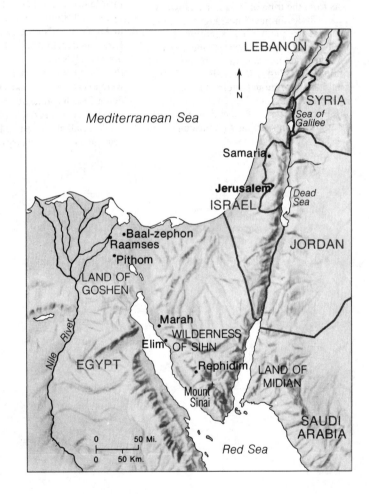

Exodus

BASIC FACTS

HISTORICAL SETTING

Discovering the date of Israel's exodus from Egypt is a difficult task. Dates which
have been put forth for the exodus fall into two major periods, one in the fifteenth
and the other in the thirteenth century B.C. (around 1446 B.C. and 1266 B.C. respectively). Scholars settle on one date or the other depending on how they evaluate
information from two major sources: biblical data and archaeological discoveries.

Biblical Data

The Bible has two primary references to the exodus that are accompanied by some
kind of time frame to help with dating. The interpretive issue in deciding for an
earlier or a later date for the exodus centers on whether the numbers in these two
passages should be taken literally or as symbolic and general time references. The
first passage is in 1 Kings 6:1, where the exodus is placed 480 years before the
dedication of the temple, an event which took place in 966 B.C. Taken at face value,
480 plus 966 yields a date for the exodus of 1446 B.C.

It appears, however, that the 480 years symbolically represent 12 generations.
Those who take a fifteenth-century B.C. date for the exodus calculate a generation at
forty years each ($12 \times 40 = 480$), so are able to maintain the date for the exodus
around 1446 B.C. For this view, the number 480 symbolizes 12 generations but also
closely approximates 480 real years.

Those who hold a thirteenth-century B.C. date calculate a generation at 25 years
each ($12 \times 25 = 300$) and place the exodus around 1266 B.C. They consider the 480
years a symbolic statement of time that differs from the actual historical record by
around 180 years.

The second biblical passage is Judges 11:26, in which Jephthah, who lived around
1100 B.C., said the conquest of Palestine happened 300 years earlier. Adding 40 years
for the wilderness wanderings puts the actual exodus about 340 years prior. Counting back from 1100 B.C. the 340 years place the exodus into the fifteenth century.

Those who take a thirteenth-century B.C. date conclude that Jephthah's figure of 300 years was only rough and general and not meant to be taken as a historically precise statement. The result is a date that is different from Jephthah's estimation by about 175 years, putting the exodus at around 1266 B.C.

Archaeological Discoveries

On the archaeological side, one important find is an ancient record called the Merneptah Stela, which notes that Pharaoh Merneptah encountered Israel in Palestine around 1220 B.C. Historically, then, the exodus must be dated before 1220 B.C. at the latest.

A second archaeological find concerns the Egyptian city of Rameses (see introductory map). The reference to the city of Rameses in Exodus 1:11 may substantiate that Rameses II (1304–1238 B.C.) was the pharaoh of the exodus. But those who hold to an earlier, fifteenth-century B.C. date believe that (1) the city may have been named for another Rameses or that (2) when Israel was in Egypt the city had a different name. After rebuilding the city, Rameses would then have renamed it in his own honor, and that new name found its way into the biblical text and replaced the older name current when Israel was in Egypt.

A third area of archaeology that is used to date the exodus concerns certain destruction levels in ancient city ruins found in Israel. The question centers on who did the destroying and when. For example, Deborah and Barak destroyed the city of Hazor during the period of the Judges. A destruction level that has been uncovered by archaeologists and attributed to Deborah and Barak's attack contains pieces of pottery that must be dated no later than the late thirteenth century. If that is indeed the destruction caused by Deborah and Barak, then the exodus had to have occurred much earlier than the date commonly given of around 1266 B.C.

Archaeological evidence from Jericho is also interpreted various ways, either to support an earlier or later date for the exodus. John Garstang's excavations at the site of Jericho resulted in the discovery of a violent destruction which he dated around 1400 B.C. This destruction level coincides with the biblical date of the conquest. But a later archaeologist, Kathleen Kenyon, concluded that the destruction level was from a significantly later date.

Other scholars conclude that certain destruction levels at other archaeological sites dated in the thirteenth century show that Israel did not begin the conquest until the thirteenth century B.C. Those who hold to a fifteenth-century date conclude that those destructions were caused by another nation, for example Egypt, after Israel had already been in the land since 1406 B.C. Again, the question of who caused the destruction levels is debated.

A fourth area of archaeology and the date of the exodus concerns the Amarna letters (around 1400–1366 B.C.). Those letters mention the Habiru, who invaded southern and central Palestine. Abdi-Hiba, governor of Jerusalem, wrote numerous letters to Pharaoh Akhnaton (1377–1358 B.C.) requesting Egyptian aid against the encroaching Habiru if the country was to be saved for Egypt. If the term "Habiru" either equates with or includes the Israelites, then that places the nation of Israel in Palestine and confirms a fifteenth-century date for the exodus. However, not all scholars agree that "Habiru" can even refer to, much less equate with, the Hebrews.

Theology and History

Amazingly, the Bible does not name the pharaoh of the exodus, and surviving
Egyptian records do not mention Joseph, Moses, the exodus or the pharaoh of that
time. God clearly had no desire to tell who the pharaoh was and thereby frame the
exodus in a specific time. In that light, the use of biblical and archaeological data to
date the exodus must remain tentative. Indeed, the foundational date for the beginning of this whole chronology, the date for Abraham, is still legitimately debated.
Also, the dates of the judges are far from certain, so a simple count backward from
the relatively certain dates of David and Solomon is tentative at best. Depending on
when Abraham and the judges are dated, the entire chronology for Israel's descent
into and exodus out of Egypt can slide hundreds of years either way.

But the important issue concerns how the biblical text is interpreted and applied.
No substantial difference in interpreting and applying the truths of Exodus results
from adopting either an earlier or a later date. Knowing the exact date of the exodus
does not add to or diminish experiencing the truth of the exodus, just as knowing the
exact date of the crucifixion of Christ neither adds to nor diminishes the believer's
experience of his exodus from the power of sin and death. Both the early and late
views of the date of the exodus give honor to the integrity of the biblical text. And
both allow for full appreciation of the great truth of God's power to redeem his
people from bondage.

Israel in Egypt

If Israel sojourned in Egypt 430 years (Exod. 12:40), and assuming an early date for
the exodus, Jacob's entrance into the land of Egypt would have taken place around
1876 B.C., during the reign of Sesostris III (1878–1841 B.C.). Joseph would have died
under the reign of Amenemhet III around 1805 B.C. For the next two hundred years
the Israelites lived in relative peace and prosperity in Egypt. They received favorable
treatment under the Hyksos (foreign rulers), who ruled Egypt from 1730 to 1580 B.C.,
because they too were largely Semitic.

Assuming an early date for the exodus, the setting of events in contemporary
Egyptian history can be reconstructed as follows: Ahmoses (1580–1548 B.C.), the
founder of the Eighteenth Dynasty who drove out the Hyksos from Egypt, was the
pharaoh who did not know Joseph (1:8). Amenhotep I (1548–1528 B.C.) carried out
oppressive measures against the Hebrews (1:22). Thutmoses I (1528–1508 B.C.) was
the father of Hatshepsut, perhaps the lady who was Pharaoh's daughter and who
rescued the baby Moses from the river. Moses was born around 1526 B.C. (2:2-5).
Thutmoses II (1508–1504 B.C.) was the brother and husband of Hatshepsut (1504–
1483 B.C.), who was also the daughter of Thutmoses I. Thutmoses III (1504–1448
B.C.) was the stepson of Hatshepsut and expanded the kingdom of Egypt. Amenhotep II
(1448–1423 B.C.) was possibly the pharaoh of the exodus (5:1-2). Thutmoses IV
(1423–1410 B.C.), the next pharaoh of Egypt, was not the eldest son of Amenhotep II.
In a dream it was revealed to him that he would be the next monarch of Egypt.

AUTHOR

For the question concerning the Pentateuch's authorship, see the *Author* section in
the introduction to Genesis. The book of Exodus itself does not name its author, who

is therefore anonymous. It is interesting to note that, though Moses was viewed as the figure behind the book of Exodus, in Exodus and throughout the Pentateuch, Moses is always referred to in the third person "he," not the first person "I." The Pentateuch unfolds its message through a biographical, not an autobiographical, perspective.

The traditional view concerning the authorship of Exodus is that it was written by Moses. This view is supported by the following considerations: (1) Joshua refers to the Mosaic authorship of the book of the law, which would have included much of Exodus (Josh. 8:34-35; cf. Exod. 24:3-4). (2) The book is closely connected with Genesis, which has traditionally been viewed as authored by Moses. (3) Moses names himself several times in connection with the Lord's command to write (Exod. 17:14; 24:4; 34:27), (4) Jesus ascribed texts from Exodus to Moses (see Mark 7:10, where Jesus quotes Exod. 20:12 and 21:17; and Mark 12:26, where he quotes Exod. 3:6). When Jesus said that Moses wrote of him, Jesus affirmed the conventional view of Moses being the author of Genesis through Deuteronomy (John 5:46). (5) The unity and literary construction of the work points to the Mosaic authorship of the whole book of Exodus.

Luke reflects the common tradition of putting the "law of the Lord" (in this case specifically referring to Exod. 13:2, 12 and Lev. 12:8) under the broad heading of "law of Moses" (Luke 2:23-24; see also Acts 13:39). Although referring to the Pentateuch by Moses' name does not mean that Moses wrote every word of these books, it does affirm him as the chief figure in the Pentateuch and as their primary human author. Any others who had a later part in editing Moses' work remain unnamed. Moses was viewed as the human transmitter of the laws of God and the chief literary figure behind the Pentateuch.

DATE

The book of Exodus contains a covenant given by God from Mount Sinai. The basic form of that covenant closely parallels secular covenants only current in the fifteenth to thirteenth centuries B.C., thereby dating the book's material to that time period. There is good reason to believe that the book itself was composed shortly after the events that it describes. Exodus was probably written shortly after the book of Genesis, during Israel's wilderness wanderings (1445–1406 B.C., assuming an early date for the exodus).

PURPOSE

The book of Exodus was designed to show how the Israelites got out of Egypt and how God came to dwell among them in the tabernacle. It formed the bridge from the story of Joseph in Egypt at the end of Genesis to the detailed laws of the Mosaic covenant in Leviticus.

Exodus was probably written during the forty years of Israel's wilderness wanderings. It therefore is not simply a bland historical record of the exodus and God's giving of the law. Rather, it is a book that was originally written to an extremely stubborn, sinful, and complaining group of people. They had seen God's miraculous salvation, and yet they complained against him and quickly turned to serve other gods. The book of Exodus was written to remind them how great their salvation was and how divine the origin of their law and tabernacle. It was given to them to deepen their love for their Redeemer and warn them against further disobedience.

GEOGRAPHY AND ITS IMPORTANCE

Exodus twice moves geographically between city and wilderness. It begins in Egypt in the area of Goshen and the cities of Pithom and Raamses and then moves with Moses out into the wilderness of Midian. The Exodus narrative then returns with Moses to the cities of Egypt and, as the entire nation leaves Egypt, moves back into the wilderness and to the foot of Mount Sinai. The cities of Egypt are the places of bondage. The areas of wilderness are where God intimately meets with his people. Therefore the most important geographical place in Exodus is a little tent at the foot of Mount Sinai called the tabernacle where God's glory came to dwell in awesome presence with his redeemed people.

Many places mentioned in the Exodus account have not been located with certainty. It is not known for sure where the sea was that God parted for Israel. Even the exact location of Mount Sinai and the wilderness Israel entered is debated. But the key geographical concept in the Exodus relates to Goshen being spared from the plagues while the rest of Egypt was not spared. This dividing line between God's plagues and his redemption became like a spiritual geographic line not limited to any one place. It moved out of Egypt with God's people, simultaneously separating them from and witnessing to the cursed world around them. See the introductory map.

GUIDING CONCEPTS

THE EXODUS, THE LAW, AND THE TABERNACLE
First, note the following points made concerning the exodus itself: (1) the unpreventable growth of Jacob's family until it became a large nation; (2) the preservation and growth of Israel's leader, Moses; (3) God's witness to and judgment of Egypt; and (4) Israel's miraculous deliverance from the Egyptians and her preservation in the wilderness.

Second, note these key events that took place during Israel's one-year stay at Mount Sinai: (1) the giving of the law; (2) Israel's doubts and disobedience right after seeing God's great salvation; and (3) the uncompromising balance between God's grace and judgment for his redeemed people. For example, read these passages to see how God's presence worked both to save and to judge: Exodus 2:24-25; 3:5-8; 4:22-23; 13:14-16; 19:19-22; 20:1-21; 24:1-11; 25:8; 29:45-46; 40:35.

Third, note the great detail surrounding the tabernacle's construction and the sacrificial aspects related to it. In the Bible, great detail means great importance. This was true in the description of the tabernacle, the place where humans would meet with God for forgiveness and worship. What might seem boring to the modern reader is, in reality, a painstakingly detailed literary effort to recreate the reality and importance of the earthly place where God would meet with humans.

For another example of lengthy description and great importance, see the passage describing Ezekiel's temple (Ezek. 40:1–44:31).

TWO PLACES AND ONE PERSON

Exodus is a book about two places and one person. The places are Egypt and Sinai, and the person is Moses, who led Israel from one place to the other. By way of a one-year stay at the foot of Mount Sinai, Israel was brought to the goal of the exodus: God coming to live among his people. Exodus should be viewed not only as a book about Israel's redemption from bondage but, in addition, as the nation's release so that they could experience a more intimate relationship with God.

A WILDERNESS TRAINING GROUND

In the book of Exodus, Israel was called out of a land with relative comforts to a barren wilderness. For the newly born nation, the wilderness was a severe and rough nursery. Although Israel was not born with the proverbial silver spoon in her mouth, she did come to life under the protection of a wise and gracious God. The One who called the world into being and hovered over the earth like a protective bird when it was formless and empty (Gen. 1) was also abiding over newborn Israel in her time of chaos and disobedience. God used the wilderness as a training ground for his chosen people.

BIBLE-WIDE CONCEPTS

FROM GENESIS TO EXODUS: THE LINK WITH ABRAHAM

In the book of Genesis God had revealed his greatness in creation, his holiness in response to sin, and his grace in re-creating a fallen world. The central focus of that grace lay in God's promise to Abraham to create a *people* of God who would live in the *land* God provided and experience the fullness of his divine presence and *blessing*. Those three elements—people, land, and blessing—form the link between Genesis and Exodus.

CURSE

In Genesis 3, Adam's sin brought both a great curse and a great promise from God. The curse caused human beings to experience broken relationships with one another, the earth, and God. Genesis 3 also records God's promise of a future son of Adam who would crush the head of the serpent. The roots of this promise's fulfillment deepen in the book of Exodus, where God sets apart a special group of people through whom the Messiah would come and bring ultimate victory over Satan and the curse of sin and death.

BLESSING

In Genesis 12:2-3, God promised that Abraham's descendants would become a large nation that would claim the land of Canaan as a homeland and be the source of inter-national blessing. At the close of Genesis, the family of Jacob in Egypt remained optimistic concerning the promise, though its fulfillment was still far off (see Gen. 15:13-14, where four hundred years of bondage were predicted).

At that time Abraham's descendants consisted of a family group of less than eighty, not a large nation by any means. Furthermore, they were living in Egypt, not

in the land God had promised. And finally, though Joseph had made a start at being a
local blessing to the Egyptians, the people of Jacob were nowhere near being the
international blessing God had promised. In the exodus, the people of Israel began a
journey that would not only take them from bondage in Egypt but would also make
them the source of great blessing for all mankind.

EXODUS

The events in Exodus narrow the gap in a stunning way between God's promise to
Abraham and his fulfillment of that promise. The small family of Jacob grew into a
large nation in Egypt, and was then redeemed out of that land. Israel was schooled
by God in the desert, pointed toward the Promised Land, and brought into a new and
more intimate relationship with God. At the end of the book of Exodus, Abraham's
descendants had become a nation that was being led toward the land promised by
God, and God's dwelling among them in the tabernacle set the scene for them to
become an international blessing.

THE INTERNATIONAL SCOPE OF BLESSING AND CURSING

In Genesis 12:2-3, God had told Abraham that his line would be both a blessing
and a curse to others. God's divine presence with Israel to bless and to curse other
people is seen throughout Exodus as he cursed those who did not treat Israel kindly and
blessed those who did. Israel indeed began to become the touchstone of God's
blessing and cursing in the world. That focus would eventually narrow to one person,
Jesus Christ, who would become the final watershed for God's blessings and curses.

The curse was carried out in judgments on the people of Egypt and Canaan. The
exodus from Egypt was the next major step in fulfilling what God had alluded to in
Genesis 15:16 regarding his plan for the Amorites, the inhabitants of the Promised
Land. At that time he had given them four hundred more years, but now their time
was up and judgment was about to fall upon them. God also had a purpose for the
Egyptians, a purpose foreshadowed in Genesis 12:14-20, where God had struck the
house of an earlier pharaoh with plagues in order for him to release Abraham's wife,
Sarah. God desired to reveal who he was to the Egyptians (Exod. 7:5) and to bring
some of them out of their country with Israel (12:38). These things were also a
foreshadowing of a final redemptive and successful move on God's part to win the
Egyptians (Isa. 19:19-25). In Exodus, God's great international promise of worldwide redemption took a giant step forward, which is seen in God's *people,* moving
toward God's *land* under the *blessing* of God's presence.

SALVATION AND LAW

The basic aspects of God's redemptive promises center on these two key concepts
that stretch from Genesis to Revelation: redemption and direction. God redeems his
people and then gives them direction as to how they should live. In the book of
Exodus, redemption is seen in the exodus from Egypt and the direction given Israel
in the Mosaic covenant.

Actually, the theme of redemption and direction had already been established in
Genesis. For example, see Genesis 18:19, where God's promise of blessing to
Abraham was intertwined with Abraham's duty to teach his children the way of

the Lord by doing righteousness and justice—the core descriptions of the law later to be given through Moses. In Exodus, the laws given at Mount Sinai are linked to God's eternal purpose for his re-creation: to create a perfectly obedient people.

The Passover lamb of Exodus 12 saved from death Israel's firstborn males, who were symbolic of the nation as a whole (see "Israel is my firstborn son," Exod. 4:22). The death plague broke the yoke of bondage, and the death of the Passover lamb saved Israel from death. From that point on, the Passover pictured the core of God's redemption: deliverance from death and bondage. In the New Testament, the shadows of the Passover lamb find their substance in Christ, the Passover (1 Cor. 5:7), who saved all believers from eternal death and bondage to sin. That great exodus from death and sin will be finalized in the next great exodus for believers, which will be from this age into the eternal Promised Land of the new heavens and earth.

God's self-revelation under Moses and the greater Moses, Jesus, is designed both to save and to aid obedience. God's pattern, whether it be to Abraham, to Israel, or to the church, is to follow redemption with direction, and forgiveness with instruction.

WHEN GOD TOUCHES EARTH TO SAVE AND JUDGE

One last link of Exodus to future biblical events was God's appearance on Mount Sinai. He appeared in fire, smoke, thunder, lightning, and earthquake. All of those fireworks were due to what happens when a piece of cursed and finite earth is touched by the almighty and holy God. The fire-and-smoke appearance of God was similar to when he made his covenant with Abraham (Gen. 15:17). But the most striking similarity to the fireworks on Mount Sinai appears in the book of Revelation, as God's holy presence appears not just on one mountaintop but over the entire world. When this is fulfilled the earth will quake, burn, and eventually disintegrate as God's presence causes thunder, lightning, and earthquakes (compare Exod. 19:16, 18 with Rev. 6:4; 8:5; 11:19; 15:8; 16:18). Mount Sinai in Exodus is a small picture of what is ahead for the entire world when God comes to finalize his covenant of redemption and require the full application of his law.

NEEDS MET BY EXODUS

The families of Israel were suffering physically and emotionally in slavery. But then God dazzled them with miracles, overcame their slavemasters and led them out into the barren and foreign wilderness. God's redemption had taken his people from one difficult situation to another. Although subservient to cruel slavemasters in Egypt, the Israelites were home in a relatively comfortable and known setting. They may have been oppressed, but at least they knew what to expect each day. In the wilderness, God's people had to learn to cope with the unexpected and the unknown.

Without the comfort zone of their past home they had to rely solely upon God. Where would their food come from? Where were they going? God fed and God led. The masters of Egypt were gone and replaced by the great master and Creator. But the unknowns were too great for most of the adult Israelites. In their view, God as master was not trustworthy, and his provisions of food and direction on the journey were not acceptable. The book of Exodus brings answers to the following questions and problems faced by God's people as they struggled to leave behind their place of bondage and faced the uncertainties of the journey to the Promised Land:

- What happened to God's promise to Abraham that his children would become great (Gen. 15:16) and return to the Promised Land?
- How did Moses become such a great leader?
- How did Israel get out of Egypt?
- Why did God come to dwell in the tabernacle in the midst of the people of Israel?
- What did God expect of the Israelites after they were redeemed?
- What were the conditions for their fellowship with God?
- What did God do when they rebelled or failed?
- What were the major areas about which God's redeemed people griped and disbelieved?
- How strong was God's commitment to his people?

These questions are similar to those that believers, the redeemed people of God in Christ, ask today as they struggle to leave their pasts behind, to know and trust their Redeemer more deeply, and to maintain faith in the uncertainties of their journey through life. Exodus affirms God's desire to dwell intimately with believers of all ages, to replace their past bondage with present worship and service for him, and, even though they fail in their commitment to him, to confirm his unbreakable commitment to them.

OUTLINE OF EXODUS

A. GOD'S PRESENCE FOR DELIVERANCE: SOCIAL, POLITICAL, AND SPIRITUAL (1:1–18:27)
  1. The Miracle of Preservation in Egypt (1:1–2:25)
  2. Moses and Aaron Commissioned as Mediators (3:1–4:26)
  3. The Miracle of Deliverance (4:27–13:16)
  4. Saved through the Red Sea (13:17–15:21)
  5. Preserved in the Wilderness (15:22–18:27)
B. GOD'S PRESENCE FOR HOLINESS: THE COVENANT IS GIVEN AND RECONFIRMED (19:1–34:35)
  1. Divine and Human Separation Highlighted (19:1-25)
  2. The Covenant Presented by God: Legal Paragraphs (20:1–23:33)
  3. The Covenant Ratified (24:1-11)
  4. Laws Given for Tabernacle and Priests (24:12–31:18)
  5. The Covenant Broken and Restored (32:1–34:35)
C. GOD'S PRESENCE FOR FELLOWSHIP: GOD DWELLS IN ISRAEL (35:1–40:38)
  1. The Dwelling Place Constructed (35:1–40:16)
  2. God Begins Dwelling in the Tabernacle (40:17-38)

EXODUS NOTES

1:1–18:27 GOD'S PRESENCE FOR DELIVERANCE: SOCIAL, POLITICAL, AND SPIRITUAL
1:1–2:25 The Miracle of Preservation in Egypt

Overview: Exodus 1 reemphasizes three keys first stated and developed in Genesis as to how God planned to bring his salvation to the world. First, Exodus 1 echoes the original creation mandate to God's people that they be fruitful and multiply. Note the use of the terms "fruitful," "multiply," and "numerous" throughout Exodus 1 (1:7, 9- 10, 12, 20). In the beginning of Genesis, God created the earth and commanded the human and animal population to be fruitful and increase (Gen. 1:22, 28). That command was restated to Noah after the flood (Gen. 9:1, 7). In the beginning of the book of Exodus, the Israelites obeyed that command and became fruitful and multiplied until the land of Egypt was filled with them (Exod. 1:7).

Second, Exodus 1 takes a major step in showing what God meant when he promised that Abraham's line would multiply and be mighty. Besides being a clear reference back to the creation account of Genesis, that fruitfulness was a fulfillment of God's promise to Abraham's line through Isaac (Gen. 12:2; 17:6; 22:17; 26:24; 35:11).

Third, this section shows how the fear of the Lord was used to fulfill God's promise of blessing. Note "feared God" in Exodus 1:17, 21. This chapter shows why and how the little family of Jacob was able to become a mighty nation that threatened the political stability of ancient Egypt. Not only does this chapter look back to the key themes of Genesis, it also acts as a prologue to the key themes of Exodus that begin in Exodus 2.

Exodus 1 shows how God preserved and multiplied the children of Abraham for hundreds of years and specifically how male children were preserved by women who feared God. Exodus 2 shows the specific story of the preservation of one male baby, Moses. The chapter scans Moses' birth, preservation as a baby, childhood, his act of murder, his flight to the Sinai Desert, his marriage, and the birth of his first son. Moses moved from being a stranger in Egypt to becoming an alien in Sinai (2:22), from being a baby in Egypt to fathering a baby in the desert. Exodus 2 ends with the death of Pharaoh and God's hearing the cries of his people.

The pharaohs who ruled over the Israelites fall into two groups: (1) those who were in power during Joseph's day and soon after, who allowed the children of Abraham to prosper in peace; and (2) those who ruled later and did not know who Joseph was (1:8). Two such pharaohs are noted, though not by name: (1) the one who began the initial persecution and ruled during Moses' early life; and (2) the ruler at the time of Moses' return and the exodus. It is during the reign of the latter that God began to take redemptive action in relieving his people's affliction and redeeming them out of bondage in Egypt and into his holy presence.

1:1-22 NATIONAL PRESERVATION

The Hebrews used the first words of the book of Exodus for its Hebrew title, which means, "the names of." The English Bible took the book's title from the Septuagint (Greek OT), which named the book according to its principal theme: the exodus. A strong allusion exists here (1:7) to the creation account in Genesis 1 and the blessing God promised in Genesis 35:11. God had promised to make Jacob a great nation; here he is fulfilling that promise.

The new king was probably Ahmoses (1:8; 1580–1548 B.C.), who drove out the Hyksos (the foreign rulers) and founded the Eighteenth Dynasty. Many scholars appeal to the reference to the city of Rameses (1:11) in arguing that Rameses II (1304–1238 B.C.) was the pharaoh of the exodus. That would place the exodus from Egypt at a later time than would be otherwise indicated by the biblical record. It may be that (1) the city was named for another Rameses; or (2) the name in the biblical text was updated from one of the site's earlier archaic names (Zoan, Tanis, Avaris). After rebuilding the city, Rameses renamed it in his own honor. For more on the use of the name of the city Rameses in dating the exodus, see the introductory section under *Historical Setting.*

The motivation behind the midwives' action (1:15-22) was that they feared God (1:17). The vigor of the Israelite women during the birth process is alluded to in 1:7. Evidently the midwives let the boys live (1:17), either by delaying their own arrival until after the births had taken place (1:19), or by lying to Pharaoh. At any rate, they were blessed because they feared the Lord and did not murder the male babies at birth. God showed his verdict on their actions by blessing them (1:20).

2:1-25 PERSONAL PRESERVATION: MOSES
Moses' parents, Amram and Jochebed (2:1-2; cf. 6:20), already had two children: Aaron, three years old (7:7), and Miriam, perhaps about seven years old. Pharaoh's daughter, who found Moses in the river (2:2-10), was probably Hatshepsut, who later ruled as the pharaoh (1504–1483 B.C.). Moses would have been raised in Thebes, the capital and center of Amun worship, where he was instructed in the wisdom of the Egyptians. The Exodus account does not dwell on Moses' childhood but moves directly from his being drawn out of the Nile to his act of murder at about the age of forty and his subsequent flight to the desert. The structure of this section shows how Moses was preserved twice from death—from drowning as an infant and then from death by execution near the age of forty.

Moses was almost forty when he fled from Pharaoh (2:15-25; cf. Acts 7:23). Midian was a desert land on the eastern fringe of the Sinai Peninsula. At that time Moses could not deliver Israel from Egypt, but he did deliver the daughters of Reuel, or Jethro, from some hostile shepherds (2:19). Later God would make Moses his chosen deliverer, but only at his own sovereignly appointed time. Moses married one of Jethro's daughters, and he named his first son Gershom, literally, "a stranger here" (2:22). His second son he named Eliezer, which means "God is my help" (18:3-4).

After spending forty years in the wilderness as a shepherd (2:23; cf. Acts 7:30), Moses was eighty years old when called by God to lead Israel. Four terms in 2:23-25 describe Israel's distress: "groaned," "cried out," "slavery," and "groaning." (The NASB uses the terms "sighed" for "groaned," and

"bondage" for "slavery.") Those terms of distress were matched by four terms describing God's personal activity on behalf of Israel that encapsulate the content of Exodus: "heard," "remembered," "looked on," and "was concerned about."

3:1–4:26 Moses and Aaron Commissioned as Mediators

Overview: In this section, God teaches Moses about his redemptive plans for Israel and commissions Moses and Aaron as his spokesmen before Pharaoh. Exodus 2 ended with God taking notice of Israel, and in Exodus 3 God begins to take action. Exodus 4 is structured around two questions from Moses concerning what to do if his hearers do not listen (4:1) and his inability to speak well (4:10, 13). The mountain where God spoke to Moses has two names: Horeb and Sinai (3:1; cf. 19:1; Deut. 4:10). Traditionally identified as Jebel Musa, it is 7,632 feet high and located in southern Sinai (see introductory map).

3:1-12 GOD ANNOUNCES HIS INTENTIONS TO SAVE ISRAEL
In 3:6 God implied that he remembered his covenant with Abraham. The four terms used in 2:23-25 for God's personal saving activity are restated or implied in 3:6-12, where God said Israel's cry had reached him and that he had seen, heard, and was concerned about his people. Those aspects of God's awareness of the Israelites' situation in slavery resulted in the great act found in 3:8—God had come down to rescue them.

3:13-22 GOD REVEALS HIS REDEMPTIVE NAME
Here God revealed the significance of his personal name, Yahweh (3:13-15). The name, probably derived from the verb "to be," speaks of God as the self-existent One. God had promised that his presence would be with Moses (3:12). "I will be" (in this case, "with you") forms the basis for his name in 3:14. God is the One who is known by what he is. Throughout history God proclaims: I Am—the Creator; I Am—the Judge; I Am—the Covenant-keeping One; I Am—the Faithful One. And in Exodus God was about to proclaim: I Am—the Redeemer.

God is who he is, known only by what he chooses to reveal about himself by his words or his actions. In Scripture God chose to reveal his character through his name and by what he said and did. That involved a progressive unfolding (cf. 20:1; Deut. 26:8-9; Judg. 2:12) as he was dynamic and active throughout biblical history. The name "Yahweh" is his memorial name to all generations (Exod. 3:14-15), and his name displays his character. God remembered his covenant, made long before with Abraham (2:24). There is nothing forgetful or arbitrary with regards to God's character. His consistency is the basis of all revelation and cements the continuity between the Old and New Testaments. That consistency also forms the basis of hope. The readers of Exodus from that time until the present can therefore wait for God to act again according to his promise.

Many Jewish people do not speak the divine name found in 3:14 but substitute instead the word "Lord." They often use Leviticus 24:16 and Exodus 20:7 as the background for God's name not being taken in vain. They believe they will avoid taking God's name in vain simply by never pronouncing it and by substituting another word, "Lord," for "Yahweh." Moses' request for only three days to offer sacrifices to the Lord (3:18) was not an attempt to trick Pharaoh, but probably reflects oriental bargaining. His first request was quite conservative in order to give Pharaoh every reason to respond positively.

4:1-17 GOD GIVES MOSES SIGNS OF AUTHORITY

The signs of authority given to Moses by God were designed to cause the Israelites to believe what he said (4:5) and show them that God was present (4:12; cf. 3:13-15).

4:18-26 THE AUTHORITY OF THE COVENANT SIGN

This section concerns Moses' departure from the desert. Here God also illustrates his high view of the firstborn by saying what he would do to Pharaoh for harming God's firstborn, Israel (4:22-23), and by what God almost did to Moses because he had not obeyed God regarding his own firstborn son (4:24-26). The hardening of Pharaoh's heart (4:21) was not only a divine judgment on one who had already hardened his own heart against the Lord (cf. 7:13; 8:15) but was also God's way to glorify himself (9:15-16).

The circumcision of Moses' son, a command decreed by God (4:24-26; cf. Gen. 17:9-14), had been neglected by Moses, perhaps to accommodate Zipporah. For that failure, God was about to take Moses' life. God was being consistent with his promise to and demands of Abraham and his descendants in the chosen line. Moses was not the beginning of God's redemption. Rather, he was God's man to bring about the next great step in the redemption promised to Abraham.

4:27-13:16 The Miracle of Deliverance

Overview: This section contains a series of actions and reactions between Moses and Pharaoh. The sequence is peppered with the repetition of two key thoughts that God had already given to Moses in the desert: (1) God would without doubt fulfill his promise of deliverance (Exod. 3:8, 16-17; 6:8; 7:4); and (2) Pharaoh would not let deliverance happen except under great compulsion (3:19; 6:1; 7:3-4; 9:35; 10:9-11). All the forces of Egyptian might were against Israel's release from bondage, but God's might was working to break that bondage.

What God could have done in an instant (9:15-16), he did by degrees in order to detail his great power and Pharaoh's great defiance. That detail produced a record of God's power and grace as a continual warning to those who would resist him, and as a display of his faithfulness and ability to save those to whom he promises redemption (that is nowhere better stated than in 10:1-2). Note the key phrase and variations: "That they may know that I am the Lord" (6:7; 7:5, 17; 8:22; 9:15-16, 27; 10:2). The plagues of Egypt were to display the knowledge of God for the Egyptians, Israelites, and their future generations.

4:27-6:27 OPPORTUNITY FOR VOLUNTARY OBEDIENCE

The essence of this section is Israel's response to Moses' message: they believed and worshiped when they saw the signs (4:29-31). But God had more to teach them about how to continue to believe and worship, even when experiencing unpleasant circumstances. Note their immediate hostility and doubt (5:21), which were indicative of their upcoming response to difficulties in the wilderness.

Pharaoh's question about God and negative response to Moses' first request would soon be answered (5:1-4). Both he and future generations of Egyptians and Israelites would be shown who God was. His question, "Who is the Lord, that I should obey him?" continues to be a question that troubles not only the unbeliever but, more pointedly, presents a continual challenge to the believer as well.

Moses' cry of dismay to God in 5:22-23 sums up the pain and frustration of people who on the one hand have the promise of God, but on the other hand have to suffer pain while waiting for its fulfillment (5:2-23). The person suffering unjustly is given a special challenge to hold onto God's promises in faith rather than to abandon hope because of difficulties and pain.

Previously the patriarchs had known God by the name "El Shaddai," which means, "God Almighty" (6:1-9), and the name "Yahweh" was also known (cf. Gen. 4:26), but its full significance was not known as it was now revealed to Moses (3:13-15). Here God clearly linked the approaching exodus to a fulfillment of his promise to Abraham to bless the descendants of his chosen line and return the Israelites to the Promised Land, eventually blessing all the nations of the earth through them. Thus, the exodus was a giant step toward fulfilling God's international mission for Israel. But, as 6:9 shows, personal pain and discouragement crowded out the Israelites' faith and hope in that great mission. Moses' protest that he could not speak well (6:10-13, 28-30) was mentioned both before and after the genealogies of his and Aaron's families. Thus, just prior to the formal inauguration of God's saving activity through Moses, his Levitical pedigree was given.

6:28–7:13 COUNTERFEIT MIRACLES

God gave Moses his full authority before Pharaoh, but he also hardened Pharaoh's heart (7:1-7). The reason for doing so is found in the latter part of 7:3—to multiply the signs and wonders of God in Egypt. The exodus was, first of all, a display of God's power (7:3) and judgment (7:4), and only secondarily an act of redemption. In other words, the exodus was essentially a statement concerning God, not humans. This event was to reveal God's glory first, and then secondarily

bring about human redemption. That vision of God's redeeming glory would serve as the focus of the redeemed community's motivation to serve him. Later, when they ceased to appreciate God's redeeming glory, they stopped appreciating their own redemption and wandered off to follow their own interests.

How Pharaoh's wisemen and sorcerers were able to counterfeit Moses' signs is not known (7:8-12). The text expresses no surprise at the magicians' abilities. But whatever the nature of their secret arts, the point of this event is the supremacy of the Lord's representative over the Egyptians. This was a small foreshadowing of God's devastating supremacy about to be shown in the final plagues.

7:14-25 THE DIVINE NILE

Because the Egyptians considered the Nile to be sacred, turning it into blood was an insult to their gods of the river—*Khnum* (guardian of the Nile sources) and *Hapi* (spirit of the Nile). This was also a judgment against another Nile river god, *Osiris* (god of the underworld), because the Egyptians believed that the Nile was his bloodstream.

8:1-15 SACRED FROGS

God had made Moses "like God" and Aaron as "Moses' prophet" to Pharaoh (7:1). At the Lord's command all that Moses told Aaron to do came to pass, and frogs appeared over the whole land of Egypt. In ancient Egypt, frogs were sacred and never intentionally killed, since they were regarded as deified representatives of the goddess *Heqt*. The Egyptians believed that *Heqt* assisted with fertility and was associated with childbirth. *Heqt's* popularity undoubtedly diminished as her devotees were tormented by the plague.

8:16-19 LICE

The dust becoming gnats (lice, TLB, KJV) was a judgment against the earth god, *Seth*. Pharaoh would not listen when his magicians acknowledged that this plague proved that God was at work (8:19). None of Pharaoh's magicians could duplicate this plague.

8:20-32 FLIES

Swarms of flies appeared in all the land of Egypt except Goshen, which God protected because the Israelites lived there. Besides being a great discomfort to the Egyptians, this and the next two plagues on livestock attacked Egypt's foremost goddess, *Hathor,* who was represented by the cow.

9:1-7 LIVESTOCK

The fifth plague destroyed the Egyptian livestock and was directed against *Ptah,* the god of Memphis, represented by the sacred Apis bull, and *Hathor,* the goddess of love, beauty, and joy who was represented by the cow.

9:8-12 BOILS

The sixth plague of boils caused great suffering for all Egyptians. It continued the assault upon the gods of Egypt (9:9; cf. 12:12), in particular the gods represented by animals. Since ashes were used by Egyptian priests to bless the people, this plague ironically used a mode of blessing as a means for a curse.

9:13-35 HAIL AND FIRE

The plague of hail and fire, destroying Egyptian herds and crops, was an insult to *Isis,* the goddess of life, and *Seth,* the protector of the crops. This judgment also would have humiliated *Nut,* the sky goddess who was looked to for blessing, and *Serapis,* the god of fire and water. The purpose of the plague is noted in 9:14, 16. Note that some Egyptians already feared the word of the Lord (9:20).

10:1-20 LOCUSTS

The devastation of all green living things by the plague of locusts demonstrated the impotence of *Isis,* the goddess of life, and *Seth,* the protector of the crops.

10:21-29 DARKNESS

The plague of darkness that covered all the land of Egypt except Goshen was an insult to *Re,* or *Amun,* the sun-god and chief deity of Thebes. When this plague struck, Pharaoh offered his third compromise to Moses (10:24).

11:1-10 DEATH

The last plague, the death of the firstborn, was announced (11:1-8), followed by a sum-

---

THE PLAGUES

Their Purpose. *The issue at stake throughout the plagues was that Pharaoh should recognize that God was supreme and therefore should be served, not ignored (see Pharaoh's response in 5:2). The issue in Pharaoh's mind hinged on the question of which was stronger, the Hebrew God or the gods of the Egyptians. Whenever his magicians duplicated a plague of God, Pharaoh's response was one of apathy and unconcern (7:23). He concluded that the God of the Hebrews was not so strong after all and could be ignored.*

The ten plagues of divine judgment upon Pharaoh and Egypt were supernatural events designed to: (1) authenticate God's messenger, Moses (4:21); (2) introduce Pharaoh to Israel's sovereign God (5:2; 7:17; 9:14); (3) demonstrate to the Egyptians the power of God (9:16; 14:4); (4) execute judgment on the gods of Egypt (12:12; Num. 33:4); and (5) witness to all the earth and to Israel's future generations the greatness of God (9:16; 10:2).

The plagues centered on the Nile as the focus of Egypt's religious idols. They covered a period from an unusually high flooding of the Nile river in July or August to the death of the firstborn around April of the next year. The recurring idea of all Egypt ("whole country," and "men and animals," 8:2, 17; 9:11, 19, 25; 10:22) builds to the climax of the death of the firstborn of both men and animals and the judgment of the gods of Egypt (12:12). Each plague was a progressively severe judgment not only on the gods of Egypt but on those who worshiped them as well.

Their Nature. *Anytime that God brings about changes in nature, he does it to remind mankind that he is the one and only Creator and that he does whatever he wants with his creation. These changes are usually negative in order to get the attention of people who are preoccupied with their lives of sin. Normally their attitude is the same as Pharaoh's: "Who is God that I should obey him?" Both the beginning and continuance of redemption are based on the believer's acknowledgment of God as the creator who is totally sovereign and powerful to save and to judge. Famines and droughts, plagues and fire, locusts and earthquakes from Genesis to Revelation all signaled the same problem: the Creator was trying to get the attention of some sinner.*

---

mary statement of all the plagues (11:9-10). The focus of Exodus 12 shifts to the people of Israel and their preparation for the Passover.

12:1-28 THE PASSOVER
In Exodus 12:1-28 God gave Moses instructions for the Passover and told him of its significance. It would be observed at the beginning of what God established as the first month of Israel's calendar year (12:2; Nisan, March–April). The essence of the Passover is found in 12:12. God would (1) strike down all the firstborn, both human and animal; (2) execute judgments against all the gods of Egypt; and (3) pass over the houses of the Israelites. Thus, the Passover was not only a divine judgment on humanity and the unseen demonic world but also served as a divine redemption for believers. The Passover, which was preceded by seven days of purification (12:15), was a sacrifice that spared the offerers from God's plague of death (12:13, 27).

12:29-51 THE PLAGUES' EFFECTS
This section recounts the effects of the plague upon Egypt as well as Israel's departure. Since the Egyptians considered every Pharaoh to be divine, this final plague would constitute a judgment on the divine heir to the throne. It would also insult the Egyptian gods' responsibility for protecting the royal family.

The number of adult men of Israel participating in the exodus was approximately 600,000 (12:37). Assuming that most were married and had children, a conservative estimate of Israel's total population at that time would be about 2,500,000. When Israel was later numbered before entering the Promised Land, the total number of men was approximately the same (Num. 26:51). Many liberal scholars reject these figures, arguing the impossibility of such a multitude surviving forty years in the wilderness of Sinai. But the exodus was a supernatural event, making the total number of people delivered from Egypt and their survival in the wilderness a testimony to God's great power.

The Israelites lived in Egypt 430 years, most of them in bondage, from the time of Jacob's entrance into the land (1876 B.C.) until the exodus (12:40-51). The four hundred years mentioned in Genesis 15:13 and Acts 7:6 is a round figure. Many people who

were not Israelites left Egypt with the nation of Israel (12:38); and since other foreigners would attach themselves to Israel in the future, rules were given regarding how a foreigner could eat the Passover and celebrate God's redemption with Israel (12:43-51). The emphasis here is not only on who was entitled to eat the Passover, but also on how a stranger could become qualified to eat it. That emphasis is elaborated in 13:1-16, where the focus shifts to celebrating the Passover feast after Israel entered the Promised Land.

13:1-16 REDEMPTION OF THE FIRSTBORN
God's provision through establishing a sacrificial offering for the redemption of Israel's firstborn males (13:13) released the Israelites from God's claim on them. God later took the Levites as his own in place of all the firstborn males (Num. 3:12). The firstborn functioned as a symbol for all Israel (cf. Exod. 4:22), for the firstborn became the Lord's (13:11-16) as a symbol of the nation's collective redemption. The continual sacrifice of firstborn animals and the redemption of the firstborn Israelite males was a graphic way to perpetuate the memory of Israel's deliverance from Egypt. The Passover also functioned as a reminder of God's redemption (13:8-10) in order to motivate the believers to keep the covenant of Moses (cf. 20:2). The Passover had diverted God's wrath (12:13, 27).

The Passover also pictured the sacrifice of Christ, who is our Passover. Christ, the firstborn of a new creation, represents all believers before God through sacrifice and makes it possible for God to "pass over" our sins. Believers today are to celebrate the Feast of Unleavened Bread by living lives of purity and sincerity, not for just one week a year, but every day through Christ's fulfillment of Israel's Passover (1 Cor. 5:7). See the *Historical Setting* section for a discussion of the date of Israel's exodus from Egypt.

13:17–15:21 Saved through the Red Sea
Exodus 13:17–15:21 records the first part of the three-month period from the exodus to Israel's arrival at Mount Sinai in the wilderness. This section is built around two acts of God: first, redemption from bondage—the Passover and the departure from Egypt; and second, God's provision in the wilderness—crossing through the Red Sea, manna, quails,

water, defeating Amalek, and Jethro's confession of faith in God and his advice to Moses on running the camp.

In this section God honored himself by means of Israel's salvation through the Red Sea (14:21-22) and the destruction of the Egyptian army (14:23-28). These events caused the Israelites to fear the Lord and to trust him and his servant Moses (14:31). The psalm of praise and instruction that resulted from the Red Sea incident (15:1-21) has a threefold emphasis: (1) God is a warrior for his people (15:3); (2) God leads his people in loving-kindness (15:13); and (3) he brings them to his holy habitation and mountain of his inheritance (15:17). The journey from bondage to the promised inheritance would be long and dangerous, but God would be there to protect and care for them. That period of danger and risk would become an example in both the Old and New Testaments. Redemption, whether achieved by means of the Passover or the Cross, involves a long and hard journey before the believer attains God's full promises.

Israel's first camping place had been at Succoth, a location just to the east of Pithom (12:37). They traveled next to Etham on the edge of the desert (13:20), a place somewhere to the southeast, not far from the northern tip of the Red Sea. The next camp at Pi Hahiroth (14:2) has not been identified. Most of these place names mentioned in the record of Israel's journey to Sinai have not been identified with certainty. (See the introductory map for a general idea of the route that Israel followed.) God led Israel by a circuitous route so that they would not have to face war immediately, which might cause them to lose their courage and return to Egypt (13:17). Later God would let his people experience war (13:17), but only after one year of teaching them his laws at Mount Sinai and coming into their midst in power and by fellowship through the tabernacle. The Red Sea (13:18) may be more literally translated Sea of Reeds, referring to a large body of water in the vicinity of the Bitter Lakes near the modern Suez Canal.

The key issues in the account of 14:1-31 are: (1) the Israelites' fear (14:10-12); (2) Pharaoh's desire to return Israel to his service (14:5); and (3) God's inexorable sovereignty in making himself known both to Egypt and

to Israel as he accomplished his great acts through his servant Moses (14:4, 17-18, 30-31). Naturalistic explanations of the crossing through the sea, such as calling it a shallow sea or saying it was at ebb tide, simply do not satisfy the text or explain the impact of this event on Israel's theology and literature.

These key elements in the psalm sung by Israel in 15:1-21 form the core of God's future redemptive revelation: (1) the Lord who is strong has become Israel's salvation (15:2); (2) the Lord is a warrior (15:3); (3) he is incomparable: "Who among the gods is like you, O Lord?" (15:11); (4) he would plant Israel in his inheritance (15:17); and (5) the Lord is an eternal king (15:18).

15:22–18:27 Preserved in the Wilderness

The Israelites' risky and dangerous journey to receive God's inheritance is emphasized as the focus shifts from their praise of God to their complaints about the lack of provisions and even about what God did supply when he gave them food. This period was designed to test the Israelites' opinions about God (15:25; 16:4). Their redemption from Egypt had been just the beginning. Heart-probing and faith-testing experiences were in God's design for them during their journey between Egypt and the Promised Land. The tests of their hearts would center on the bitter water at Marah (15:22-26); the manna and quail (15:27–16:36); water (17:1-7); the battle with the Amalekites (17:8-16); and Jethro's great confession of faith in God and his advice to Moses on how to solve Israel's judicial problems (18:1-27).

The sweetened water at Marah was a sign of God's healing power for those who would obey him (15:26). See the introductory map for the approximate locations of Marah and Israel's next camp, Elim (15:27). Equal manna provisions for each person (16:18) and the Sabbath commandment (16:28-29) tested Israel's willingness to trust in God to supply their needs and to obey his commands.

The name given to the bread from heaven, "manna," means, "What is it?" Consider its looks (Exod. 16:14; Num. 11:7), its taste (Exod. 16:31; Num. 11:8), its preparation (Exod. 16:23; Num. 11:8), its source (Exod. 16:4, 15; John 6:32), its purpose (Deut. 8:3), and its uniqueness (Deut. 8:3).

Manna is typical of Christ, the Bread of Life (John 6:33-35).

The people were not only thirsty, but they also doubted that God was even present with them (17:1-7). That is the heart of what it means to test the Lord. After all his great redemptive miracles, they still doubted that he was with them for their good. The key to Israel's victory over the Amalekites was God's power that was mediated through Moses, the sign of which was Moses' upraised hands (17:8-16).

The section 18:1-27 concerns two main events: (1) Jethro's great confession of faith in God (18:10-12); and (2) his advice to Moses on how to administrate Israel judicially (18:13-26).

19:1–34:35 GOD'S PRESENCE FOR HOLINESS: THE COVENANT IS GIVEN AND RECONFIRMED

Overview: This large section 19:1–34:35 is famous for two things: (1) the Ten Commandments and (2) Israel's idolatry with the golden calf. The following events are covered: God's descent upon Mount Sinai (19:1-25), God's giving the Ten Commandments (20:1-17), God's giving ordinances for worship and feasts (20:18–

23:33), Moses and Israel's leaders eating with God on the mountain (24:1-11), Moses going up onto the mountain for forty days to receive instructions for the tabernacle's priests and offerings (24:12–31:18), the Israelites worshiping the golden calf, their punishment and repentance, Moses receiving assurance of God's presence (32:1–34:9), and another forty days for Moses on the mountain for receiving instructions concerning Israel's behavior after entering the Promised Land (34:10-28). See chart below.

19:1-25 Divine and Human Separation Highlighted

God, who had called Israel his firstborn son (Exod. 4:22) and had just redeemed the nation out of Egypt, then told the people to stay away from him or die. Why would God redeem his people only to keep them away from himself? The great God of the exodus, who had been so lethal to the Egyptians, was just as much of a threat to Israel, for his holiness is nonpartisan. The only way God would be able to stop being so distant and dangerous to his people and come to dwell among them would be on the basis of the covenant he was about to make with them.

ISRAEL'S ONE-YEAR STAY AT SINAI

Approximate Dates	Biblical Dates and Events	References
FIRST YEAR:		
June 1?	Third month, first year at Sinai	Exod. 19:1
June 3	God appears	Exod. 19:11, 20
June 6?	Law and sacrifice	Exod. 20:1–24:11
June 7-12	Moses waits to ascend	Exod. 24:12-16
June 12–July 22	Moses receives the law	Exod. 24:18–31:18
July 23	Golden calf incident	Exod. 32:1-29
July 24	Moses intercedes for Israel	Exod. 32:30-35
? days	Moses outside the camp	Exod. 33:7-11
?	Moses spends forty days on Sinai	Exod. 34:4-29
?–March 30	Tabernacle built	Exod. 36–39
SECOND YEAR:		
April 1	Tabernacle erected	Exod. 40:2
April 1-30?	Laws and rules given	Lev. 1–27; cf. Num. 1:1
April 1-12	Gifts given for offerings	Num. 7
April 14	Second Passover observed	Num. 9:3
May 1	Census taken for God's army	Num. 1:1-4
May 20	Departure from Sinai	Num. 10:11-12

20:1–23:33 The Covenant Presented by God: Legal Paragraphs

20:1-26 ANCIENT CONTRACT FORMS

The Ten Commandments do not begin with hoops for God's people to jump through but with a reminder of his redemptive acts of love (20:1, 6). That saving grace forms the context of and motivation for keeping any specific commandment. God designed the immediate context of the thunder and lightning to give the people visible signs that would help them fear him and continue to keep his commandments (20:20).

During this biblical period in history, international treaties were used to outline the relationship between a king (suzerain) and his subject people (vassals). These treaties, copies of which have been discovered and translated, followed a regular pattern and included the following elements that also are found in God's treaty with Israel:

(1) Historical preparation. The date was identified (19:1), the geographical setting given (19:2), and the activity cited of both the suzerain (God, 19:4) and the mediator of the covenant (Moses, 19:7).

(2) Preamble. God was identified as the great Suzerain, the author of the covenant (20:1).

(3) Historical prologue. A record was given of previous relations between the two parties involved (20:2). Past benefits of the suzerain were set forth to inspire gratitude and obedience on the part of the vassal people.

(4) Stipulations or obligations. These were laid upon the vassal people by the suzerain. The basic stipulations gave a concise statement of the suzerain's will for his people (20:3-17). The detailed stipulations (20:18–23:33; 25:1–31:29) provided examples and applications.

(5) Provision for deposit and reading. A copy of the covenant would be placed in the sanctuary of the vassals and the suzerain (25:16, 21). From time to time there would be a public reading of the covenant terms to the people (Deut. 1–34; Josh. 24).

(6) Witnesses. Usually long lists of gods were called upon to witness the ratification of the covenant so that there would be legal witnesses to testify in case of default. Since there were no other gods for Israel, the witnesses invoked were the heavens and earth (Deut. 4:26; 32:1).

(7) Cursings. Curses were called down upon those who would break the covenant (Deut. 27:15-26; 28:15-68) and blessings on those who remain loyal to it (Deut. 28:1-14).

(8) Ratification. The covenant was ratified by its acceptance by the people, the sacrifice and sprinkling of blood, and the eating and drinking of the covenant meal (Exod. 24). The covenant was then officially in force.

In studying the Mosaic Law it becomes clear that God used a contemporary cultural institution, a contract form, to communicate his will to his people. This treaty form would have been especially meaningful to the Israelites since they had been bound to their Egyptian overlords under similar arrangements. By employing this form, Israel's freedom from worldly authority as well as the nation's submission to the Lord are given particular emphasis.

The point of any such contract was to show how the king would care for his new people and what the people had to do to stay in the king's favor. It is extremely important to understand that God used a covenant form that stressed the personal relationships involved. God did not use an impersonal list of laws. Instead, he presented himself as the King who had already done so much for his people that they, in return, should have been gratefully willing to return service and love to him.

The prohibition of Exodus 20:26 was a warning against ritual nakedness, which at the time was an integral part of fertility cult worship.

21:1-36 RESTITUTION

The principle of restitution was applied to the issues of the worth of a servant, or slave (21:1-11) and death penalties for various acts (21:12-36). The key principle (21:13-25) is that justice demands equality of restitution, no more (which would be revenge) and no less (which would trivialize the seriousness of the offense). In the case of mothers and children, special laws were given to protect the helpless and innocent (21:22-25). If a man caused a woman to give birth prematurely but the infant was not harmed, then a simple fine was to be levied. If the child or mother was harmed, then the law of retaliation was applied.

Punishment was restricted to that which was commensurate with the injury. In these verses God shows clear concern for protecting unborn children, a concern that people today would do well to heed. Surely the abortion of millions of unborn babies will fall under God's condemnation.

22:1-31 COMMUNITY LAWS
Restitution was required for both intentional and inadvertent breaches of trust (22:1-6). The section 22:18-31 covers various laws such as sorcery (22:18), afflicting the poor and foreigners (22:21-27) and offering of the firstborn son to God (22:29-31).

23:1-33 FEASTS
Some of the great feasts of Israel are presented here: the sabbatical year (23:10-13); and the three feasts of Unleavened Bread, Harvest, and Ingathering (23:14-17). The feasts were actually a time of humility and celebration before the Lord, not exclusively times to eat. The last sentence of 23:19 has been understood by Jewish people as a basis for separating meat and dairy products. But archaeological discoveries indicate that it was actually a warning against Canaanite cultic worship in which this ritual was practiced.

God promised that an angel would go before Israel and give the land of Canaan to them (23:20-33). The hornet (23:28) may be a figurative reference to the panic and terror that came upon the Canaanites as they anticipated the Israelite conquest (Josh. 2:9).

24:1-11 Covenant Ratified

Although Exodus 19 had presented a God who was virtually unapproachable on penalty of death, here several humans not only approached the mountain and saw a vision of God but also actually ate a communal meal in his presence. That meal celebrated the ratification of the Mosaic covenant. The people's response, which was a wise and sincere commitment to the covenant (24:3, 7), was pleasing in God's sight (Deut. 5:28-29).

24:12–31:18 Laws Given for Tabernacle and Priests

24:12-18 MOSES ON THE MOUNTAIN
The setting for the giving of the laws for the tabernacle and priests was the blazing mountaintop that enveloped Moses for forty days (24:17-18). For Israel that setting elevated the laws and gave them a visual portrayal of God's abiding glory. The laws of his glory were to be seen in that original light, not simply as good ideas from humans to follow.

The tabernacle served to remind Israel of God's presence among his people and prefigured the redemptive work of Christ who lived, or "tabernacled," among the human race (John 1:14). A type is an Old Testament illustration that, having its place and purpose in biblical history, is divinely appointed to foreshadow some New Testament truth. Many parts of the tabernacle are types of Christ (see chart below).

25:1-40 INTERIOR ARTICLES
Instructions were given for (1) collecting the peoples' contributions for the tabernacle (Exod. 25:1-9); (2) making the Ark of the Covenant (25:10-22), the place where God would meet with Moses (25:22); (3) making the table that would hold the bread of the presence (25:23-30); and (4) making the lampstand (25:31-40).

26:1-37 CURTAINS
Instructions were given for making (1) the tabernacle curtains and their supports (26:1-30); (2) the veil (26:31-35); and (3) the curtain, or screen, for the tabernacle doorway (26:36-37).

ILLUSTRATIONS OF CHRIST IN THE TABERNACLE

Table of Showbread	Christ, the Bread of Life (John 6:35, 48)
Golden Lampstand	Christ, the Light of the World (John 8:12; 9:5)
Inner Veil	Christ's broken body (Mark 15:38; Heb. 10:20)
Bronze Altar	Christ's perfect sacrifice (Heb. 9:14)
Incense Altar	Christ's intercessory prayer (Heb. 7:25)
Bronze Laver	Christ's blood that cleanses from sin (Rom. 5:9; 1 John 1:9)

27:1-21 EXTERIOR ARTICLES
Instructions were given for making (1) the
altar (27:1-8); and (2) the courtyard, or court,
of the tabernacle (27:9-19); as well as for
(3) the maintenance of the lamp (27:20-21).

28:1-43 PRIESTLY DRESS
Instructions for priestly garments included
the preparation of (1) Aaron's clothing
(28:1-5); (2) the ephod of gold (28:6-14)
that he would wear to represent Israel before
the Lord; (3) the breastpiece of judgment
(28:15-30), to which were attached the Urim
and Thummim (28:30), which would be used
to determine God's will (28:30-31; cf.
1 Sam. 23:9-12); (4) the gold plate to be
attached to his turban (28:36-38); and (5) the
robes, turbans, tunics, sashes and other items
for Aaron and his sons (28:31-43).

29:1-46 PRIESTLY DEDICATION
Instructions for dedicating and consecrating
the priests included: (1) dressing and anointing them (29:1-9); and (2) making the sin,
burnt and wave offerings that would purify
them before the Lord (29:10-35). Other offerings were to be offered on a daily basis to
consecrate the tabernacle (29:36-44). The
beautiful point of all this was that God would
dwell among Israel and that Israel would
know him (29:45-46).

30:1-38 INCENSE AND SUPPORT
Instructions were given for: (1) making the
altar of incense (30:1-10); (2) taking a census
of Israel's eligible fighting men, which
would bring financial support for the tabernacle services when each paid his half-shekel
offering (30:11-16); (3) making the bronze
basin, or laver (30:17-21); (4) preparing the
special oil for anointing the priests and tabernacle and its utensils (30:22-33); and
(5) making the special incense (30:34-38).

31:1-18 CRAFTSMEN
The men who made the tabernacle were
filled with the Spirit of God (31:3). The first
part of the law (Exod. 20–31) concludes with
the commanded sign of observing the
Sabbath (31:12-18).

32:1–34:35 The Covenant Broken and Restored

32:1-35 ISRAEL SPARED
The apparent reasons that God did not wipe
out the nation for its worship of the golden
calf were because of the negative witness

such action would give to the Egyptians
(32:12), as well as God's remembrance of his
covenant with Abraham (32:13). But God's
gracious act did not preclude his killing three
thousand people who had gone out of control
(32:25-29) or stopping Moses' continued
intercession on the nation's behalf (32:30-35).
The expression "blot me out" (32:32) was
borrowed from the register that was kept of
Israel's citizens. It means "Let me die an
untimely death and no longer be listed
among the living."

What made God angry with his enemies
was their stubborn opposition to him (4:21;
8:15; 14:17). What made him angry regarding Israel was her unfaithfulness (33:3).
That unfaithfulness would become the basis
in the future for the prophets' continual
remarks concerning Israel's having broken
the Mosaic covenant. See 15:26 and note
the close relationship between plagues and
sickness in 1 Kings 8:37.

God's anger has different effects. In
Exodus 19:4 God's judgments on Egypt
worked for Israel's salvation. In Exodus 32
his anger worked to purify and discipline
Israel. Thus, disaster for God's redeemed
people is not a time for the loss of hope and
faith, but rather, a time for growth through
discipline.

Although 32:14 reads "God relented" or
"changed His mind" (NASB), in actual fact
God does not change his mind or ways
(32:14; cf. Mal. 3:6; James 1:17). Rather, this
is a human expression that attributes human
emotions to God, emphasizing the pain,
sorrow and grief he experiences due to
mankind's sin.

33:1-23 MOSES' FAVOR
The intimate way in which God related to
Moses is seen in 33:7-11. This section
describes the favor with which God viewed
Moses, the critical issue of God's presence
with Israel, and Moses' desire to know God
even more intimately by seeing his glory
(33:12-23). The tent mentioned in 33:7 was
not the tabernacle, which was yet to be
completed, but a place where Moses could
meet with God privately.

34:1-35 MOSES' VISION OF GOD
Moses not only received the renewed
covenant (34:1, 27-28) but also glimpsed
God's person more closely. The words of

34:6-7, describing God's loving and uncompromisingly holy character, have become one of the most often quoted Bible passages. The description of the veil (34:29-35) rounds out the events that had led up to Moses' intimate meeting with God. Moses' new vision of God's glory was a source of awe and fright (34:30) and also a confirmation of God's glory surrounding the words Moses brought to Israel. Compare 34:26 with 23:19.

35:1–40:38 GOD'S PRESENCE FOR FELLOWSHIP: GOD DWELLS IN ISRAEL

Overview: This section (35:1–40:38) builds to the climax of Exodus 40, where God came to dwell with his people. Long, detailed instructions were given concerning how to build the tabernacle and worship there. Although many details are listed, the section really centers on one major thing—how God can once again dwell among humans. All the details of the tabernacle merely stress that it was to be a holy residence because of its holy Resident. These numerous details climax at the end of the book, when God, once deadly to approach on the mountain, was able to dwell in the center of Israel's camp.

35:1–40:16 The Dwelling Place Constructed

35:1-35 OFFERINGS FROM THE HEART
The key word in 35:1-35 concerning offerings for the tabernacle is "willing" (35:5, 21, 22, 26, 29). The people truly gave from a willing heart and a spirit stirred by God.

36:1-38 THE TABERNACLE IS CONSTRUCTED
The recounting of the people's heartfelt offerings overlaps with an account of the skill of the Spirit-filled workmen (36:4-6). The next section describes the construction of the inner tent curtains and outer covering (36:8-19); the boards, bases, and bars for

supporting the curtains (36:20-34); and the curtain, or veil, to go in front of the Holy of Holies, as well as the curtain, or screen, for the entrance to the tent (36:35-38).

37:1–38:31 THE ARTICLES ARE BUILT
The workmen constructed the Ark of the Covenant (37:1-9); the table and its utensils (37:10-16); the lampstand (37:17-24); and the altar of incense, as well as preparing the oil and incense (37:25-29). They made the altar of burnt offering (38:1-7); the bronze basin, or laver, and its stand (38:8); and the tabernacle courtyard, or court (38:9-20). An account is also given of the material used in the tabernacle's construction (38:21-31).

39:1–40:16 THE TABERNACLE IS COMPLETED
A description is given of the preparation of the priestly garments, with special emphasis on the breastpiece (39:8-21). The entire construction project was concluded and summarized, ending with Moses' inspection and blessing (31:32-42). The tabernacle was erected almost one year after the exodus from Egypt.

40:17-38 God Begins Dwelling in the Tabernacle

The instructions for setting up the tabernacle (40:1-16) were matched with Moses' obedience in carrying them out (40:17-33). Previously Moses had been able to enter his small tent of meeting outside the camp and observe God's partial glory (33:7-11). But not even Moses could enter this greater tent of meeting, a tent where God's full glory dwelt (40:35), for at that point God began to dwell with his people in a more intimate way. God was one step further away from the tragedy of man's fall into sin and one step closer to his future perfect dwelling among believers when his tabernacle will appear in the new heavens and earth (Rev. 21:3).

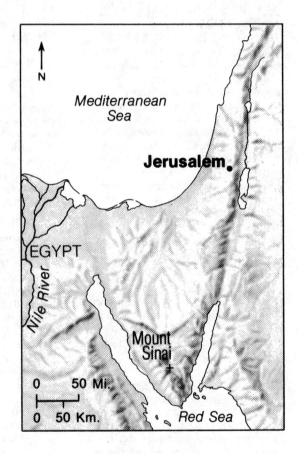

Leviticus

BASIC FACTS

HISTORICAL SETTING

The events recorded in the book took place at the foot of Mount Sinai. The time period goes from the setting up of the tabernacle to Israel's departure from Sinai about one month and twenty days later (cf. Exod. 40:17 with Num. 10:11). The people had been away from Egypt just one year when the events of this book took place. For a discussion of the date of Israel's exodus from Egypt, see the *Historical Setting* section to the book of Exodus.

AUTHOR

The author of Leviticus is not named. The Lord addressed Moses repeatedly throughout the book (1:1; 4:1; 6:1, 8, 19, 24; 7:22), making Moses the most likely person to have recorded these words. The Mosaic authorship of Leviticus is further supported by other evidence. The material in the book was revealed at Sinai, and it is highly probable that Moses would have recorded the revelations he received there from the Lord. The book follows and is closely linked with Exodus (Lev. 1:1), which was certainly authored by Moses. When Jesus called the laws concerning leprosy (Lev. 14:2-3) as those which Moses commanded (Matt. 8:4; Mark 1:44), he affirmed Moses as the one who first brought the words of Leviticus to Israel.

The third book of Moses is referred to in Jewish usage as "and he called," an English translation of the first Hebrew words in Leviticus 1:1. The Old Testament Greek translators gave it the name "The Levitical Book" because of its emphasis on priestly regulations for the tribe of Levi. The Latin Vulgate rendered the book's title "Leviticus," from which the English title is taken.

DATE

Modern criticism has questioned the antiquity of Leviticus, dating it in the period of 500–450 B.C. However, since the discovery of Ugaritic literature, some arguments against an early date are no longer valid. These arguments are based on a premise that the forms of ritual and sacrifice found in Leviticus were only developed late in

Israel's history. But the finds at Ugarit show these forms were in existence 1,500 years before Christ. The terminology used at Ugarit in the fifteenth century B.C. is remarkably parallel to that of Leviticus. Terms such as burnt offering, whole burnt offering, trespass offering, and peace offering are found in Ugaritic literature.

Leviticus was probably written shortly after the book of Exodus was written during the wilderness wanderings. It records the words God spoke to Moses out of the tabernacle (1:1) during Israel's last two months at Mount Sinai.

PURPOSE

Leviticus gives the details of how a believer could live in the presence of God and enjoy his blessings. It is designed to clarify both what is and what is not pleasing to God. The largest part of the book is used to describe how sinful man can attain forgiveness and restoration after breaking one of God's laws.

GEOGRAPHY AND ITS IMPORTANCE

The Israelites were camped at Mount Sinai at the time the events and revelations of Leviticus took place. Wherever the exact location of Mount Sinai may be, the book of Leviticus locates its readers right outside of the tabernacle's front curtains and lets them listen to the voice of God telling his people what they must do now that he has come to dwell with them. The stark and threatening aspects of Israel's journey through the wilderness, already seen in Exodus and about to be seen in Numbers, fade into the background. Leviticus focuses on a vision of God's holiness—a vision that is true no matter where the people are located. See the introductory map.

GUIDING CONCEPTS

FELLOWSHIP WITH GOD

God said, "I will put my dwelling place among you, and I will not abhor you. I will walk among you and be your God, and you will be my people" (Lev. 26:11-12). All the various rituals and laws in Leviticus have one main goal—to enable God and his children to have fellowship with each other. That fellowship would glorify God and graciously give blessing and joy to his people. Look for the following key concepts that made God's desires for fellowship with Israel possible: (1) holiness; (2) sacrifice; and (3) forgiveness. All the book's diverse aspects revolve around those three concepts.

BIBLE-WIDE CONCEPTS

BLESSING THROUGH OBEDIENCE

In Genesis 18:19 God had said that he had chosen Abraham "so that he will direct his children and his household after him to keep the way of the Lord by doing what is right and just, so that the Lord will bring about for Abraham what he has promised him." Notice the key words and phrases: "so that," "direct," "keep the way of the Lord," and "right and just." "So that" introduces the purpose for God having chosen

Abraham (this phrase appears twice in Genesis 18:19). God chose Abraham *so that* he could "direct his children," *so that* God would "bring about" his promises. Thus the purpose for God choosing Abraham was twofold: (1) to get Abraham and his descendants to pass on God's laws (2) in order to bring in God's promises. "Direct" reveals the task for Abraham and his children: to instruct and teach family members. "Keep the way of the Lord" and "right and just" are two technical terms for God's laws and describe what was to be taught and passed on from generation to generation. Abraham's election and salvation by faith were accompanied by the necessary call to obeying God's laws. The way to experiencing God's blessings was through obedience to the way of the Lord. No one who lived like the devil could expect to experience the blessing of Abraham.

The way of the Lord, that is, God's commands of righteousness and justice, were known to Abraham. In fact, all mankind was under obligation to honor the morality that God required (Rom. 1:18-20, 32). But in the covenant with Moses some of the laws of God were specifically noted as conditions for fellowship with God (for example, see the change that took place under the Mosaic covenant reflected in Rom. 5:13-14). Exodus 20–31 outlines the major laws of relationship within the community of the redeemed. The last part of Exodus outlines the construction of the the tabernacle which served as the central way of access to God. Leviticus continues the giving of the Mosaic covenant from the tabernacle, or the "Tent of Meeting" (1:1), rather than from smoke-covered Mount Sinai as was seen in Exodus.

LAW AS A BLESSING OR A CURSE

Leviticus 26 contains a list of blessings and curses that would result if a person kept or ignored God's commandments. The most important thing to note when reading this list is that keeping the law would bring the promised blessings. In other words, the law told the Israelites how to be blessed by God. That is why David could say that he loved the law, that it was a light on his path and that it was sweeter than honey. Paul also said that the law was holy, righteous, and good. The law is good because it reveals what God wants so that believers can please him.

The blessings and curses of the Mosaic covenant stem directly from the blessings and curses inherent in God's creation of the world. Adam and Eve were told that they would be blessed if they kept God's law concerning the tree of the knowledge of good and evil or cursed if they did not. Since they did not keep God's law they were cursed. All the smaller curses of the Mosaic Law are but pale reflections of the greater curse upon the world resulting from Adam's disobedience. All the smaller blessings of the Mosaic Law are but pale reflections of the greater blessing the world will ultimately experience based on Christ's obedience.

OBEDIENCE AS GRATITUDE FOR SALVATION

Abraham believed God, and it was reckoned to him as righteousness. From his initial and essential faith in God, Abraham was then required to keep the way of the Lord by doing righteousness and justice, no longer in order to be counted as righteous but to consistently confirm his original faith in and love for God. His obedience was the only appropriate response to God's gracious promise and acts on his behalf. The same was true for Israel before the tabernacle of God. As a nation,

Israel had placed its faith in God, believing and obeying his instructions for the exodus from Egypt. Only God knew those individuals who from the heart had truly believed in him and had been counted righteous. All were taken through the sea and were provided with manna from heaven and water from the rock. But many showed a deficiency in their relationship with God since they were destroyed in the wilderness. (Reflecting on this incident, Paul relates it to the Christian life in 1 Cor. 10:1-6.) Leviticus continues the theme of obedience of the redeemed by focusing on the place where God and humans met.

THE ISSUE OF THE HOLY SEED
From Genesis through Revelation the key issue concerning who will receive God's redemption centers on who will say yes to God, both in heart and in life. God wanted a people who would give him devotion and obedience. He was preparing a race of people who could be blessed instead of cursed. Leviticus shows the major step God took on the journey from Eden to the new earth to help people enjoy his blessings. Israel, as God's holy people, would become equipped to be a worldwide witness so that "in Abraham" all the nations of the earth could be blessed (Gen. 12:3).

THE ISSUE OF LAND PROMISES
The wickedness of the Canaanites would cause God to destroy and replace them with the Israelites (see Gen. 15:16). Leviticus first focuses on the implications of the presence of the tabernacle among the Israelites and then focuses on the implications of Israel's presence in the Promised Land. The holy God would enable Israel to purge the Promised Land of its enemies. The Israelites would only remain in the land as long as they remained faithful to their Redeemer.

THE LEVITICAL OFFERINGS AND CHRIST
The offerings were the shadows of which Christ's sacrifice would become the reality and substance. Each offering pictured his perfect atonement and forgiveness. Believers today must consider the significance of the sacrifices for the Old Testament worshiper, the illustrative significance of sacrifice for the Christian, and the principles that may be applied to all believers. The sacrifices were predictive, expressing a need that they could not perfectly satisfy (Heb. 10:4); but the promised Redeemer they prefigured would fulfill and complete these sacrifices (Eph. 5:2; 1 Cor. 10:11; Heb. 9:14; see accompanying chart).

THE OLD TESTAMENT SACRIFICES AND CHRIST

Burnt offering	Christ offered himself completely (Heb. 9:14) and without blemish (Heb.4:15) as a fragrant offering to God (Eph. 5:2).
Grain offering	Christ offered himself as spiritual food (John 6:33-58).
Peace offering	Christ proclaimed peace (Eph. 2:17), made peace (Col. 1:20), and is our peace (Eph. 2:14).
Sin offering	Christ took the believer's sin (John 1:29; 2 Cor. 5:21) and died in the sinner's place (Mark 10:45).
Guilt offering	Christ made compensation for the damage done by sin (2 Cor. 5:19).

NEEDS MET BY LEVITICUS

The book of Leviticus shows Israel during a very difficult time. They had been redeemed out of Egypt but now found themselves in the middle of the wilderness. They had already complained about God's provisions and fallen into idolatry during the golden calf incident. Any thoughts of a carefree life of freedom from Egyptian bondage had passed. God, who had redeemed them, now thundered and flashed over them from the top of Mount Sinai. God was so awesome and lethal that anyone who touched the mountain would die. For God's people, the grace of his redemption had been transformed into a vision of his terrifying holiness. And now that holy God dwelt among them in the tabernacle. The Israelites could only watch and wait to find out if their sinful nation could coexist with their holy God. The structure and content of Leviticus show that it was written to answer questions regarding the needs of the Israelite believers.

- What can be done about sins that are committed?
- How can God live so close and yet not destroy those who sin, even if it is inadvertently?
- How can the sinful people of Israel find forgiveness?
- How can the Israelites keep themselves clean before the Lord?
- Just how holy is the Lord and what does that mean for his people?

Believers ask these questions today. The redemption of believers from sin is wonderful, but, like Israel, they may find that God's uncompromising drive for holiness becomes overwhelming. The failures of sin can seem all too frequent and believers may wonder how God can exist with them without destroying them. But for God's redeemed people, then and now, Leviticus points the way to the balance between God's free redemption and uncompromising holiness. Sacrifice removes the guilt of sin. And only then, in the state of perfect forgiveness, can the believer have the grace and motivation to seek to be holy as God is holy.

OUTLINE OF LEVITICUS

A. REMAINING IN GOD'S PRESENCE (1:1–16:34)
1. Guidelines for the Offerings (1:1–7:38)
2. Mediator: Holiness of Priests (8:1–10:20)
3. The Holiness of the People (11:1–15:35)
4. Yearly Provision for National Holiness (16:1-34)

B. REMAINING IN GOD'S LAND (17:1–27:34)
1. Avoidance of Egyptian and Canaanite Perversions (17:1–20:27)
2. The Guardians of the Offerings (21:1–22:33)
3. Rests: Reminders of God's Creator-Owner Sovereignty (23:1–25:55)
4. Conditions for Remaining in Canaan (26:1-46)
5. Appendix: Vows (27:1-34)

LEVITICUS NOTES

1:1–16:34 REMAINING IN GOD'S PRESENCE

Overview: The section 1:1–16:34 focuses on the way Israel should relate to God in their midst. God moved from the awesome Mount Sinai, covered in lightning, thunder, and smoke, down into a tent in the very middle of the Israelites' camp. It moves from: (1) sacrifice (Lev. 1–7); to (2) priestly mediators (Lev. 8–10); to (3) removing all uncleanness that would defile the tabernacle (Lev. 11–16).

1:1–7:28 Guidelines for the Offerings

Overview: The first seven chapters of Leviticus introduce that which the Lord communicated to Moses from the doorway of the tabernacle. The subject matter immediately turns to offerings: "When any of you brings an offering to the Lord . . ." (1:2). The descriptions of the offerings presuppose a prior knowledge of their significance on the part of the Israelites. Terms such as burnt offering, whole burnt offering, trespass offering, and peace offering are found in extrabiblical writings contemporary with Leviticus. Therefore, the offerings themselves were not new for Israel. However, what was new was their incorporation into the religious life of God's covenant people. The offerings were

---

THE OFFERINGS

. . . As Gifts. The purpose of the offerings was summed up in the word "gift." First, as with the giving of any gift, the recipient was the key figure in view. The offerings were gifts to God, given to him because he is the sovereign Lord and everyone owes all to him. From Cain and Abel onward, God's people have known to give back to him part of what he, as sovereign Creator, has given to them.

Second, the one who gave to God became deprived of some necessities of life. But though the person lost the gift, he gained a bond of grace and forgiveness with God. The altar became the place of mediation between God and humans. Third, some of the offerings were totally burned up on the altar, but that burning was not seen as the gift's destruction. The burning symbolized, through the rising of the heat and smoke, the gift's transference into God's invisible realm. These offerings were literally called in Hebrew, "that which goes up," implying that the gift went up in the smoke into the realm of God. It also made the giving of the gift final—the offerer could not take it back. The burnt offering was, in that sense, the most perfect offering, for God received all of it.

. . . As Communion. Every offering signified an element of communion between God and the offerer that showed a certain degree of friendship and intimacy. The offerer ate a meal of renewed fellowship after he had been forgiven by God.

. . . As Forgiveness. Every offering was a means for receiving God's forgiveness. In one way or another the offerer had broken the covenant and stood unclean before the Lord. The offering was designed to reestablish a relationship with God by atoning for a particular sin. Sin put anyone in jeopardy with God, and the particular focus of offense throughout Leviticus was the defilement of the tabernacle, which was both God's dwelling place and the location of the covenant regulations (15:31; 20:3).

The offerings brought forgiveness for inadvertent sin (4:2, 13-14, 22, 27; 5:15) as well as conscious sin (5:1, 4; 6:1-7). No atonement was available for a defiant, high-handed sin (Num. 15:30-31), but see Numbers 16:46-48, where the offering of incense stopped the plague. For another example, David realized that no sacrifice was available for his sins of murder and adultery (2 Sam. 12:13); however, his true repentance did bring atonement for his sins. A resounding theme throughout the Old Testament was that the sacrifices were not mechanical. They could only bring forgiveness when accompanied by a sinner's contrite heart (cf. Pss. 4:4-5; 20:1-5; 40:6; 50:7-16; 51:14-19).

designed to bring forgiveness to an individual or to the nation as a whole when they had broken the covenant with God or had sinned against other people.

The theological key to these first seven chapters is the concept of bringing an offering "to the Lord" (1:2) in order to be "acceptable to the Lord" (1:3). The personal key is the repeated phrase of assured forgiveness (4:20, 26, 31, 35; 5:10, 13, 16, 18; 6:7). The Israelite who sacrificed for a particular sin would have the full assurance of being forgiven for that sin.

1:1-17 BURNT OFFERING

The burnt offering could be made with one of the following animals: a bull (1:1-9); a sheep or goat (1:10-13); or a bird (1:14-17). The literal meaning of the Hebrew word for burnt offering was "that which goes up," that is, what went up to God. The Hebrew word for "offering" (1:2; *qorban)* is derived from the Hebrew verb meaning "to draw near." Thus, an offering prepared the way for Israel to draw near to God. The laying of the offerer's hands on the sacrifice was a symbolic act of identification with the offering (1:4). It was just as if the worshiper was saying, "This animal represents me; its blood shall be shed in my behalf." The word "atonement" comes from the same Hebrew root as the noun meaning "ransom" or "ransom price." The verb form of this word means "to atone by offering a substitute." The image was of an aroma that was pleasing to God. Blood atonement was not the central feature of this offering. Rather, central were the cutting, washing, and arranging of the pieces of the offering on the altar and then the burning of them, by which was accomplished the actual sending of the gift up to God. This offering was often coupled with a sin, or peace, offering. The significance of this offering was that it called the offerer to complete surrender and dedication to God.

2:1-16 GRAIN OFFERING

The grain or cereal offering consisted either of portions of flour mixed with oil and incense (2:1-3), or baked or cooked offerings (2:4-10) prepared with no leaven but seasoned with salt (2:11-13), or roasted ripened heads of new grain (2:14-16). The salt signified the permanence and purity of

the worshiper's devotion to God (2:13; cf. Num. 18:19). The grain offering was usually made along with a burnt offering (Num. 28:5, 12-13) and was always made with a peace, or fellowship, offering (Lev. 7:12-14). The giver shared in, offered, and dedicated the fruits of his personal labors to the Lord.

3:1-17 PEACE, OR FELLOWSHIP, OFFERING

The peace, or fellowship, offering was either an animal from the herds (3:1-5), or a lamb (3:6-11), or a goat (3:12-17). This offering was brought on the basis of the offerer's voluntary desire. The name of the offering does not indicate that the offerer would gain peace with God, but that he was celebrating the fact of the peace and wholeness brought about by his faith in God's redemption and covenant.

4:1-35 SIN OFFERING

The law covered unintentional sins committed by either the priests (4:1-12), the whole congregation of Israel (4:13-21), a leader (4:22-26), or a lay person (4:27-35). The kind of offering was suited to the rank of the offerer. The ritual included the laying on of hands with its significance of identifying the sacrifice with the sinner whose sins it would atone for.

5:1-19 GUILT OFFERING

The guilt offering, a specialized type of sin offering, was either a lamb or goat (5:1-6), or two birds (5:7-10), or fine flour (5:11-13). It covered offenses against the Lord's holy things (5:14-16) or any unintentional sin (5:17-18). Three types of offense required a guilt offering: (1) an offense against God's holy things (5:15-16); (2) an offense against God's commands (5:17-19); and (3) an offense against one's neighbor (6:1-7).

6:1-7:30 RESTITUTION

The section 6:1–7:30 covers restitution, which comprised a guilt offering plus twenty percent of the damage incurred (6:1-7). The reiteration of the various offerings that were described earlier focuses on the priest's specific duties in performing those offerings (burnt offerings, 6:8-13; grain offerings, 6:14-18; grain offerings at priests' anointings, 6:19-23; sin offerings, 6:24-30; guilt offerings, 7:1-10; peace, or fellowship, offerings, 7:11-36; and a final summary, 7:37-38).

These principles were to be learned from the offerings: (1) God demands that sins be paid for and acquitted (sin and guilt offerings, Rom. 8:1); (2) God delivers assurance of forgiveness (peace, or fellowship, offering, John 14:27); (3) God desires adoration (grain offering, Heb. 13:15); (4) God delights in acknowledgment of his lordship (burnt offering, Rom. 12:1).

8:1–10:20 Mediator:
Holiness of Priests

Overview: Leviticus 1–7 focused on the offerings, whereas Leviticus 8–10 focused on the priests who mediated the offerings. Two points are stressed: (1) the priests were qualified to mediate on the basis of a complicated and completely obedient process of purification (Lev. 8–9); and (2) they could be fatally disqualified by one act of disobedient imperfection (Lev. 10).

8:1–9:24 OBEDIENCE TO GOD'S COMMANDS

Every major section of Leviticus 8 ends with the phrase, "as the Lord commanded Moses," or variations of it (8:5, 13, 17, 21, 29). That obedience was continued by Aaron and his sons (8:36), who were ordained and dedicated in this chapter. The consecration offering (8:22) when literally translated from the Hebrew meant "filling," since "to fill the hands" was a technical term for ordaining someone to an office (cf. Exod. 32:29, where this word is translated "set apart"). The blood (Lev. 8:23) was placed on the priest's "ear" (because he was to heed God's words), on the "thumb of his right hand" (because he was to perform God's work), and on the "big toe of his right foot" (because he was to follow God's ways). The theme of God's commandments being carried out continues in Leviticus 9 (9:7, 21) in reference to the nation's dedication and purification. The main point of all this was that the people be given an opportunity to see the Lord's glory (9:6, 23).

10:1-20 NADAB AND ABIHU

The phrase "contrary to his command" (10:1) bursts out in terrible contrast to the previously unbroken chain of "as the Lord commanded" seen throughout Leviticus 8–9. The nature of the sin of Aaron's sons is not fully explained. Possibly they were stirred by

the shouts of the people to present an offering of incense. Yet they did it at an improper time (not at God's direction) and in an improper way (not prepared from the altar fire). The fire was called "unauthorized" since it was contrary to what was prescribed (Exod. 30:9). Whatever the particular reason behind Nadab and Abihu's actions, the point was that they did not treat God as holy (10:3). A possibility is raised in 10:9 that the sons were intoxicated.

Eleazar and Ithamar disobeyed when they burned up the portion of the sin offering that they should have eaten (10:16-20). Aaron explained to Moses that, in light of the judgment on Nadab and Abihu, they did not consider themselves sufficiently free from sin to deserve to eat the designated portion of the sin offering. Moses was satisfied with the explanation. Although an ordinance had been broken, the violation had been motivated by a desire to treat God as holy.

11:1–15:35 The Holiness of the People

Overview: Leviticus 11–15 focused on the daily life and purity of the people. While these rules may seem strange to believers today, the underlying point is very much a part of the Christian life (15:31). The people were to stay pure as defined by these rules so that they would not defile either God who had redeemed them or the place of his dwelling. For the Israelite it was God's saving act in the exodus; for the Christian it is God's redemption in Christ.

11:1-23 CLEAN AND UNCLEAN CREATURES

The regulations of clean and unclean creatures (11:1-23) must be understood in light of the New Testament teaching in Acts 10:11-15; 11:9; 15:20, 29, and Mark 7:19. The criteria of clean and unclean were applied to animals, birds, water creatures, and insects. The principle of clean and unclean animals had been known since the flood, because Noah knew those distinctions (Gen. 7:2). The explicit purpose for clean and unclean distinctions is found in relating Leviticus 11:43-45 to 20:22-26. The food distinctions were to be a witness of Israel's holiness to her God. Ethical, health, and aesthetic reasons have also been given for the distinction between clean and unclean foods. However, the point is that God has always had a right as the Creator to tell the people he has created what they can and cannot eat. See, for example, Adam and Eve (Gen. 1:29-30; 2:16-17) and Noah (Gen. 9:3-4). Obedience to these dietary laws brought a person into conformity with God's own holiness (Lev. 11:44). Even touching the carcass of a dead animal would make a person unclean (11:24-40). Dead animal carcasses, just as dead human bodies, were defiling since death is the result of sin (Gen. 2:17; Rom. 3:23).

11:24–15:33 CLEAN AND UNCLEAN HUMAN BEINGS

The law for cleansing from birth impurity (12:1-8) was observed by Mary after the birth of the Lord Jesus (Luke 2:22-24). The reason for the uncleanness of childbirth may be traced to the Fall and the curse pronounced immediately afterward. Pain and suffering were to accompany childbirth (Gen. 3:15), and death would ultimately follow (Gen. 2:17; 3:19). Consequently, everything connected with procreation (childbirth, menstruation, seminal emission) was treated as unclean, rendering a person unfit for a specified period of time to perform religious duties.

The laws concerning infectious skin diseases, including leprosy, in people, or mildew in infected articles (13:1–14:57) were followed by a long section on the laws concerning what to do when a person or object was healed of such a disease (Lev. 14). Leprosy (Hansen's disease) was greatly feared by the Israelites, not only because of the physical damage done by the disease, but also because of the strict laws that isolated the leper from the rest of society. Leviticus 15 put forth the laws concerning male and female discharges and gave two examples for each. The point of this passage was to protect Israel from death (remember Nadab and Abihu) by teaching them how to avoid defiling the tabernacle (15:31), God's dwelling place among them.

16:1-34 Yearly Provision for National Holiness

Sitting squarely in the middle of the book is Leviticus 16, which describes how, once a year, all of Israel would stand in perfect forgiveness before the Lord. This chapter forms the climax to the sins, offerings and forgiveness described in Leviticus 1–15.

The Day of Atonement was a yearly provision for national holiness. (For the meaning of "atonement," see 1:4.) Even after all the sacrifices the people and priests would have made throughout the year, they still needed cleansing. There was always the possibility that some unnoticed sin would defile the people, priests, or tabernacle (16:33). This special day called attention to the basic nature of God's forgiveness provided in the Mosaic covenant: it was limited to specific sins and would only be complete when the leaders or priests were obedient to all the Mosaic stipulations. The inadequacy of the priesthood was shown (16:1, 6, 13) as was the priest's need to bathe and change clothing (16:4, 24). The consciousness of sin's guilt, whether known or unknown, real or potential, was always present (Heb. 9:6-10).

The ritual offering of the "scapegoat" (Lev. 16:10) is described (16:20-22). Although it is debated whether the Hebrew term *azazel,* translated as "scapegoat" in 16:26, means "complete destruction" or "the goat that has gone away," what the ritual symbolized is clear: sin had been removed from Israel. The scapegoat is typical of Christ "who takes away the sins of the world" (John 1:29). The expression "deny yourselves" (Lev. 16:31) is often associated with fasting, self-examination and prayer (cf. Ezra 8:21; Ps. 35:13; Isa. 58:3, 5) and speaks of true repentance. The Day of Atonement called attention to humanity's essential distance from God because of the curse's resultant impurities (Lev. 16:16). The nation was to humble itself (Exod. 10:3; Mic. 6:8). For one brief and holy day each year the entire nation would be cleansed from their sins (Lev. 16:30).

17:1–27:34 REMAINING IN GOD'S LAND

Overview: The section 17:1–27:34 emphasizes what Israel would have to do to remain in the Promised Land. They would remain there by avoiding the pagan practices in Egypt and Canaan (Lev. 17–20), by the priestly mediators of the sacrifices not committing any unclean acts (Lev. 21–22), and by the Israelites consistently honoring God's "Creator ownership" of the land by observing his ordained feasts and Sabbaths

(Lev. 23–26). The book concludes by including even free-will vows in the conditions for covenant blessing.

17:1–20:27 Avoidance of Egyptian and Canaanite Perversions

Overview: Leviticus 1–16 centered on the lives of the people in relation to God's holy presence in the tabernacle. Leviticus 17–20 centers on the people in relation to the sinful practices that surrounded them in Egypt and would surround them in Canaan. The land, symbolizing God, was going to vomit out the Canaanites because they had defiled it. The land also would do the same thing to the Israelites if they sinned in the same way.

17:1-16 THE ALTAR AND BLOOD
The altar in front of the tabernacle (17:1-9) was to be Israel's focus of true worship. God, the King, would brook no rival altars. The expression "cut off" (17:3-4) refers to the death penalty (Exod. 31:14). The "goat idols" (17:7) possibly were worshiped in an orgiastic ceremony (cf. 2 Chron. 11:15). The blood sacrifice (17:10-16) reveals the nature of the atonement: it was graciously given (17:11b), not the result of human perfection. Because of its sacrificial purpose, blood was not to be eaten. This law taught respect for human life, which the blood represented.

God provided various means for forgiving the Israelites' sins: (1) presenting the blood of a sacrifice and eating its flesh (10:17); (2) intercession (Exod. 32:30); (3) offering incense (Num. 16:47); and (4) laying one's hands on an animal sacrifice (Lev. 16:21-22). Ransom was central to the idea of atonement (cf. Exod. 21:30). The blood was effective because it represented life; if there is no blood, there is no life. The blood functioned as the symbol of life that ransomed the lives of God's people.

18:1-19:37 SEXUAL, CULTIC AND CIVIL SINS
Egyptian and Canaanite perversions were to be avoided (18:1-5). Specific examples involving sexual perversion involved blood relatives (18:6-23). Such sins were the reason why the land's inhabitants were about to be destroyed (18:24-30). This explains God's purpose for leaving Israel in Egypt for the four hundred years mentioned in Genesis 15:13. He had given these nations time to repent, but they had

not done so. The religious and civil laws given to Israel, with the repetition of the words "I am the Lord," revealed a close interrelationship between the worship of God (19:2, 4, 12, 16, 18, 28, 30-32, 36-37) and God's maintenance of the Promised Land (19:9-10, 23, 29, 33).

20:1-27 PUNISHMENT FOR SINS
The theme of avoiding sin in the Promised Land continues in Leviticus 20. God has revealed the future of man in his word, and seeking to know and control that future through mediums, spiritists or astrology is tantamount to unbelief and rebellion (20:6). "His blood will be on his own head" (20:9) meant that the law of blood revenge would not apply in this case. The offender would have to bear the guilt for his own death. This chapter rounds out the section on the Israelites avoiding pagan perversions so that the Promised Land would not vomit them out of it (20:22-23). It also stresses the reasons for dietary and religious separation (20:25-26).

21:1–22:33 The Guardians of the Offerings

Overview: Leviticus 21–22 describes the necessary wholeness and acceptability of the priests and offerings.

21:1-24 LONG-TERM QUALIFICATIONS
The long-term qualifications for the priests involved: (1) rules regarding touching the dead, shaving, cutting the hair and body, and marriage (21:1-9); (2) specific rules for the high priest (21:10-15); and (3) rules for those with physical defects (21:16-24). All this was so that God's sanctuary would not be profaned (21:23). Cutting the hair, beard, and body were pagan practices that both the people and priests were to avoid (21:5; cf. 19:27-28).

22:1-33 SHORT-TERM DISQUALIFICATIONS
The short-term disqualifications for the priests involved: (1) uncleanness (22:1-9); (2) eating holy things (22:10-16); (3) defects in the offerings (22:17-25); and (4) imperfection of sacrificial animals (22:26-33). The command of 22:28 was to guard against Israel's participation in Canaanite cultic worship (cf. Exod. 34:26).

23:1–25:55 Rests: Reminders of God's Creator-Owner Sovereignty

Overview: The section of 23:1–25:55 on Israel's feasts and sabbaths emphasizes God's creator ownership of all he gives to his redeemed. It looks back to the perfection of Eden and forward to the perfect justice and ecology of the new earth. Leviticus 17–22 focused on Israel's relationship to the Promised Land, and that relationship continues here. The Israelites had to realize that the land was on temporary lease to them from God and was not their own possession; it was theirs only as long as they satisfied the requirements of their covenant with God. They had been redeemed from Egypt to become God's servants, not their own masters (25:55).

God's sacred assemblies for the Israelites were designed to instruct them in holiness, remind them of their covenant relationship with God, and provide them with opportunities for worship. Each feast and convocation looked back to a specific historical event in Israel's past and forward to an end-time event in her future (see chart below).

23:1–24:23 WEEKLY WORSHIP AND SABBATH HOLINESS

The purpose for these Sabbath rests was to remind the Israelites of God who had created them and owned them. Feasts were actually holy convocations appointed for specific times (23:2) to be observed by all Israelites wherever they were living (23:3). These were in contrast to some unholy feasts that had occurred in Israel's history (Exod. 32:5; 1 Sam. 30:16). The holy observances are described as follows: (1) the weekly Sabbath (Lev. 23:3); (2) Passover and the Feast of Unleavened Bread (23:4-8); (3) Firstfruits (23:9-14); (4) the Feast of Harvest, or Weeks, or Pentecost (23:15-21); (5) the Feast of Trumpets or Ingathering (23:22-25); (6) the Day of Atonement (23:26-32); and (7) the Feast of Tabernacles, or Booths (23:33-44).

OLD TESTAMENT FEASTS AND THEIR SIGNIFICANCE

Sabbath	This looked back to the creation and the Mosaic covenant (Exod. 20:11; 31:12-17) and forward to the believer's rest in Christ's finished work (Heb. 4:1-11).
Passover	This looked back to Israel's redemption from bondage in Egypt (*Pesach,* Exod. 12:1-30) and forward to the redemption from sin through Christ (1 Cor. 5:7).
Unleavened Bread	This looked back to Israel's separation from Egypt (*Matsah,* Exod. 13:1-10) and forward to the fellowship possible because of Christ (1 Cor. 5:7-8; 1 John 1:1-4).
Firstfruits	This looked back to the first harvest God gave Israel in the Promised Land (Lev. 23:10) and forward to the first of the resurrection harvest (1 Cor. 15:20, 23; 1 Thess. 4:13-18).
Feast of Weeks	Later known as Pentecost, this celebration looked back to the firstfruits of the grain harvest (*Shevuoth,* Lev. 23:16) and forward to God's first harvest of the redeemed in Christ (Acts 2).
Trumpets	This looked back to the beginning of the civil year (*Rosh Hashana,* Lev. 23:23-25; 25:9) and forward to the regathering of God's people (Ezek. 37:12-14; 1 Cor. 15:52).
Day of Atonement	This looked back to the need for cleansing from national sin (*Yom Kippur,* Lev. 16) and forward to Christ's atonement (Heb. 9:28) and Israel's repentance (Zech. 12:10–13:1).
Tabernacles, or Booths	This looked back to the wilderness wanderings (*Succoth,* Lev. 23:43) and forward to Israel's joy in Christ's kingdom (Zech. 14:16).

The care of the lampstand (24:1-4) and the loaves of bread, or cakes (24:5-9), represented all of Israel in worship before the Lord. Blasphemy meant to demean and declare something cursed (24:10-23). Laying hands on the head of the offender represented the removal of the other Israelites from the blasphemy that they had heard (24:14). This is analogous to "washing one's hands" to remove guilt (Deut. 21:6). On the basis of Leviticus 24:16, Jews have traditionally refused to pronounce the name "Yahweh" and have substituted "Adonai" (Lord) to avoid the sin of blasphemy.

25:1-55 SPECIAL YEARS

The focus of the sabbatical year and the Year of Jubilee was on the Promised Land of Canaan (25:2). The purpose of the sabbatical year (25:1-7) was to concede that the basics of life are God's. Failure to keep this year resulted in the seventy years of captivity in Babylon (2 Chron. 36:21). The word "jubilee" is from the Hebrew word *yobel,* or "ram's horn," which was blown to announce the fiftieth year. The Year of Jubilee (Lev. 25:8-55) again affirmed that the land was God's (25:23) and that the people were his (25:55). Since everything belonged to him, the liberation and restoration of this year were under his sovereign ownership. The Israelite who had sold himself into bondage was to be treated more as a hired servant than a slave. Six years was the maximum period an Israelite could be required to serve (Exod. 21:2).

26:1-46 Conditions for Remaining in Canaan

The pattern of Israel's blessing for obedience, discipline for disobedience, and restoration for repentance was presented. It was a pattern that would be repeated many times throughout Israel's history from this point on. Blessings and provision for remaining in the Promised Land (26:1-13) were described conditionally: "If you follow my decrees and are careful to obey my commandments . . ." (Lev. 26:3). See the situation forty years later as Moses gave similar words (Deut. 27–28). Conditional curses followed (Lev. 26:14-39): "if you will not listen to me and carry out all these commands . . ." (26:14). The repeated use of "seven times" (26:18, 21, 24, 28) stressed the necessity of keeping the sabbaths (26:34). After necessary punishment, God promised the equally necessary restoration of his own people (26:40-46), as he remembered his covenant with Abraham (26:42, 45).

27:1-34 Appendix: Vows

The appendix of Leviticus 27 brought even the free-will vows under the morality of the Mosaic legislation. There was no requirement to ever make a vow (Deut. 23:21-22), but if someone did, then it had to be kept. A "devoted thing" (Lev. 27:28) was devoted to God, as were the spoils of Jericho (Josh. 6:17). For God's redeemed people, holiness involved the large and the small, the external and the internal.

Numbers

HISTORICAL SETTING
The historical events recorded in the book of Numbers began exactly one month after the completion of the tabernacle (Num. 1:1; Exod. 40:17). This book takes the reader through the nearly forty years of wilderness wanderings and ends its narrative on the plains of Moab near the Jordan River.

AUTHOR
Numbers 33:2 ascribes literary activity to Moses in relation to the material of the book, and it is stated repeatedly that God spoke these words to Moses (1:1; 2:1; 3:5, 14, 40). The Mosaic authorship of Numbers is supported by the following considerations: (1) The book is connected with the three previous books in which Mosaic authorship is confirmed. (2) Many references state the fact that God spoke these words to Moses (1:1; 2:1; 3:5), and it is most likely that Moses himself would have recorded this revelation. (3) The authorship of the record of Israel's journeys in the wilderness is ascribed to Moses (33:2), making it probable that the rest of Numbers was written by him as well. (4) The local color, authentic wilderness background, and antiquity of the material lend support to the Mosaic authorship of Numbers. A few editorial insertions, such as the enumeration of the Transjordan cities built by the offspring of Gad, Reuben, and Makir, son of Manasseh (32:33-35), were added subsequent to the time of Moses. For a fuller discussion of the authorship of the Pentateuch, see the introductory section for Genesis.

DATE
Numbers was written, or at least completed, after the death of Aaron (20:28), which took place on the first day of the fifth month of the fortieth year after the exodus (33:38-39). Aaron died at the age of 123 (33:39), just a few months before Moses, who was 120 years old when he died (Deut. 34:7).

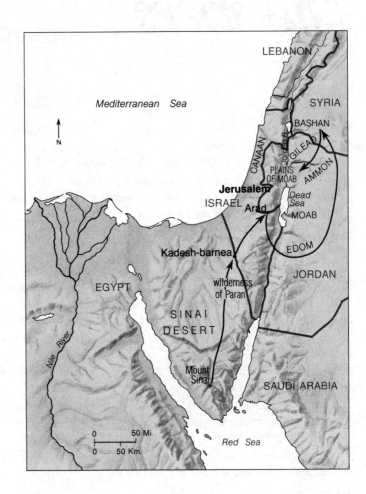

PURPOSE

The book of Numbers communicates that Israel was God's army and that God's people would take the Promised Land by the means of military force, as God's instrument of judgment upon the wicked people living in the land of Canaan. It also shows that God's children may sin and be disciplined, but that his promises for blessing are ultimately unstoppable. The wilderness wanderings brought about a denial of God's blessings for those who had sinned, but not for the faithful.

GEOGRAPHY AND ITS IMPORTANCE

The book of Numbers begins at Mount Sinai as Israel prepares to take the Promised Land by military force. The book then tells why Israel moved twice to Kadesh-barnea. The first time at Kadesh-barnea the nation disbelieved that God was a warrior strong enough to give them the land. As a result, God banished Israel to nearly forty years of waiting in the wilderness. The second time at Kadesh-barnea, after the completion of Israel's waiting period, the Israelites prepared to go around the east side of the Promised Land, heading north and arriving on the Plains of Moab, just across from Jericho. As that journey exposed Israel to the nations of Edom, Ammon, Bashan, and Moab, it also exposed Israel to her own weakness of faith and to God's great power and loyalty.

GUIDING CONCEPTS

A FORFEITED BLESSING

Numbers records how sin in a believer's life can prevent blessing. An entire generation sinned unto death and forfeited blessing as a result of the rebellion at Kadesh-barnea. The nation's full deliverance and inheritance of the land were delayed forty years because of their unbelief in God's provision and protection (Heb. 3:16-19). But because God was dealing with a redeemed people (Exod. 12; 1 Cor. 10:1-4), their unbelief resulted in their loss of blessing, not of salvation.

THE COMPLAINING OF THE REDEEMED

Israel's complaining is a major emphasis of Numbers. The people had only traveled three days' distance from Sinai when they began complaining (Num. 11:1-3; cf. 10:33). They complained about their diet of manna (11:4-6) and against the leadership provided by Moses and Aaron (12:1-2; 14:2, 36). Their complaining against God resulted in the judgment of death decreed on the first generation of Israelites in the wilderness (14:27-29). The people's constant grumbling was as bad as their refusal to enter the land (16:11, 41; 17:5, 10). By complaining against God they were breaking the covenant with their great King. The complaining about God's provision of food and drink must not overshadow for the reader of the book their more serious complaints against God's appointed leaders. Throughout Numbers, the people of Israel showed an attitude that was sometimes ambivalent, sometimes hostile, toward God's chosen leaders.

DIVINE JUDGMENT

The wrath of God, manifested in judgment against sin, is well illustrated in the book (11:1, 10, 33; 12:9-10). God's wrath is the natural expression of his holiness manifesting itself against the willful sin and rebellion of humans (1:53-54; 11:1, 10, 33; 12:9; 16:46; 18:5; 22:22-34; 25:3-4, 11; 32:10, 14). Numbers teaches that God's wrath may be stopped by an offering (16:46-48) or by intercession (14:11-20). While God's wrath is prominent in Numbers, it is revealed in the New Testament as well (Ananias and Sapphira, Acts 5:1-11; all mankind, Rom. 2:5-9; abusers of the Lord's table, 1 Cor. 11:28-30; unfaithful Christians, Heb. 10:30-31; 12:29; and the unbelieving world, Rev. 6:15-17; 16:19; 19:15). Only faith in God's Son, who has satisfied his wrath (Rom. 3:25; 1 John 2:2), can save the sinner from divine judgment.

THE ARMY OF GOD

Israel was forged into an army that was to carry out God's judgments upon the inhabitants of Canaan (Num. 1:3; 2:32). This judgment should always be read in the light of Genesis 15:16.

THE UNSTOPPABLE PROMISES OF GOD

Even in the light of Israel's continual failures, Numbers shows that God's promises to Abraham were absolutely certain (Num. 15:1-2; 23:8, 20). See the accompanying chart.

BIBLE-WIDE CONCEPTS

THREE MAJOR JOURNEYS

The first five books of the Bible present three major journeys undertaken by the people of Israel: (1) from Egypt to Mount Sinai (Exod. 12:37–19:2); (2) from Sinai to Kadesh-barnea (Num. 10–13); and (3) from Kadesh to the plains of Moab (Num. 15:1–21:35). Genesis presents a detailed prologue showing how humanity's hope for redemption narrowed down to one small family that was driven to Egypt by famine. Exodus details the first great journey of this family as it leaves Egypt and travels to Mount Sinai.

Numbers tells of the second and third fateful journeys of Israel. The second is the great journey of salvation from Sinai to Kadesh. The third is the re-grouping of Israel into God's holy army during the wilderness wanderings.

KEY EVENTS FROM THE EXODUS TO TRANSJORDAN

Exodus 12:41	Exodus from Egypt
Exodus 19:1	Arrival at Sinai
Exodus 40:17	Tabernacle erected
Numbers 1:2	Israel's first numbering
Numbers 13:23, 26	Arrival at Kadesh
Numbers 33:37-38	Departure from Kadesh (Aaron's death)
Deuteronomy 1:3	Moses' address to Israel
Joshua 4:19	Israel's crossing of the Jordan

Deuteronomy functions as a hinge between Genesis through Numbers and the historical books of Joshua through 2 Kings. It sums up Israel's history and salvation to that point and provides the perspective through which the rest of Israel's history is to be viewed.

NUMBERS IN THE NEW TESTAMENT

The apostle Paul in 1 Corinthians used Israel's wilderness experience as an example of how believers can be disqualified because of disobedience. The accompanying chart compares 1 Corinthians 10 with Israel's experience in the wilderness.

Note that both 1 Corinthians and Numbers are warnings for those in the covenant. The book of Hebrews also uses Israel's failures to encourage Christians not to make the same mistakes. But, above all, the book of Numbers takes its place in the Bible-wide concept of God's relentless commitment to keep his redemptive promises even in the light of his people's continual failures, whether under Moses or Christ.

NEEDS MET BY NUMBERS

God's people never learned. The book of Numbers shows both the old generation and the new one after it making the same mistakes. The book covers the time period in which hundreds of thousands of Israelites died after rebelling against the Lord. The Promised Land was so close, yet God kept the nation out for nearly forty years. The book spoke to the needs of those Israelites who had trouble holding on to their faith in God's great promises when they saw the tragedy of sin all around them. These questions probably bothered them:

- Why did an entire generation of God's people die in the wilderness?
- Had the sins of Israel voided God's great promises to Abraham and Moses?
- Why did God form the Israelite nation into an army on the march?
- What did God want believers to do as they experienced his discipline?

For the Christian, the book of Numbers is filled with bad examples which should be avoided. But it also presents a loud and clear message. It was written to show how prone God's people were to failure, how insistent God was that they be disciplined, and how equally persistent God was that his people get back up from the self-inflicted pain of their disobedience and move on toward God's promised blessings.

ISRAEL'S WILDERNESS EXPERIENCE IN THE NEW TESTAMENT

Exodus 32:4-6	1 Corinthians 10:7
Numbers 11:4	1 Corinthians 10:6
Numbers 16:41-49; 17:5, 10	1 Corinthians 10:10
Numbers 20:11	1 Corinthians 10:4
Numbers 21:5-6	1 Corinthians 10:9
Numbers 25:1-9	1 Corinthians 10:8
Numbers 26:65	1 Corinthians 10:5

OUTLINE OF NUMBERS

A. FROM SINAI TO KADESH (1:1–14:45)
  1. The Departure from Sinai (1:1–10:36)
  2. Complaint and Judgment: Blindness toward God's Provision (11:1-35)
  3. Complaint and Judgment: Blindness toward God's Prophet (12:1-16)
  4. Complaint and Judgment: Blindness toward God's Power (13:1–14:45)
B. ISRAEL'S WANDERINGS: DISINTEGRATION (15:1–19:22)
  1. Laws While in the Land (15:1-41)
  2. Complaint and Judgment: Blindness toward God's Priest (16:1–18:32)
  3. Cleansing after Touching Dead Bodies (19:1-22)
C. FROM KADESH TO MOAB: REGROUPING THE TROOPS (20:1–36:13)
  1. Complaint and Provision: Leaders Judged (20:1-29)
  2. Complaint and Judgment: Blindness toward God's Provision of Manna (21:1-35)
  3. God's Absolute and Sovereign Blessing of Israel Emphasized (22:1–24:25)
  4. Idolatry and Judgment: Blessing Lost through Human Irresponsibility (25:1-18)
  5. Second Census for War (26:1-65)
  6. Second Leader Commissioned (27:1-23)
  7. Continuity of Worship in the Land Emphasized (28:1–30:16)
  8. Transjordan Conquered (31:1–32:42)
  9. Review from Egypt to Canaan, with the Method for Dividing Canaan (33:1–36:13)

NUMBERS NOTES

1:1–14:45 FROM SINAI TO KADESH

Overview: Numbers 1–10 gives a series of dates that ranges from the day that the tabernacle was finished to the day that Israel broke camp (1:1; 7:1; 9:1, 15; 10:11). Throughout the book the stress is on doing everything exactly as God had commanded Moses (1:54; 2:34; 3:51; 4:49). The section 1:1–14:45 ends with the defeat of God's army by the Israelites' lack of faith in God's ability to beat their enemies. The nation lost the right to enter the Promised Land and had to wait for forty years to go in.

1:1–10:36 The Departure from Sinai

1:1 TITLE

The Hebrews called this book either "and he spoke" or "in the wilderness of," according to the words used in the first verse. The Septuagint translators gave it the title Numbers because of the prominence of the census figures in the book. This tradition was followed by the Latin Vulgate and English versions. Numbers begins with a chronological notice indicating that the numbering of the people took place just a year and one month after the exodus from Egypt. Just one month had passed since the completion of the tabernacle (Exod. 40:17).

1:2-54 THE CENSUS

The army of God was counted and positioned around the tabernacle for military purposes (1:1-4). Israel had 603,550 men over twenty years of age (1:46). Including women and children, the figure would rise to an estimated 2 million. Many have doubted that such a large multitude of people could survive in the wilderness for 40 years. Yet God had used a supernatural event to deliver them from Egypt, and in the same way he sustained them in the desert by his divine power.

The census was clearly designed to count those who were to go out to war (1:3, 20, 22, 24, 26, 28, 30, 32, 34, 36, 38, 40, 42, 45). While God would prove himself lethal to the inhabitants of Canaan, he also would be lethal to any Israelite who profaned his tabernacle. Thus the Levites formed a protective shield around the tabernacle that was set up in the center of the camp (1:51, 53).

2:1–3:51 THE ARMY CAMP

The Israelites' way of obedience would be to act as God's army against the inhabitants of Canaan. They were encamped according to their twelve tribal groups around the tabernacle (2:1-34), with three tribes on each side. In addition, the Levites, who were not counted among the twelve tribes, were numbered and organized to camp around all four sides of the tabernacle (3:1-51). Of all the Israelites, they encamped closest to the tabernacle. The main reason for doing so was to protect the lay person from death due to inadvertently profaning the tabernacle (3:10). The Hebrew word translated "ordained" (3:3) literally means "to fill one's hand." Aaron's sons were entrusted with the authority and responsibility to officiate at the sacrificial altar. The rest of the Levites, that is, all the remaining descendants of the tribe of Levi, were appointed to serve the priests (who were descendants of Aaron, a Levite). Thus, all priests were Levites, but not all Levites were priests.

Because all the firstborn males of Israel had been saved from the death angel in the Egyptian plagues (Exod. 12), the firstborn male of every family was to be set apart to God (3:12-13). The Levites were appointed to act as substitutes before God in their place. The total of 22,000 Levites given in 3:39 is correct if the Greek Old Testament (Septuagint text) is followed in 3:28, where the figure is 8,300 instead of the 8,600 in the Hebrew text. The discrepancy in the Hebrew text is due to a scribal omission of one letter that makes the difference between a "three" and a "six." The priests performed the sacrificial rites while the other Levites assisted by taking care of the outward elements of the tabernacle and its furnishings (1:50). The families were those of Gershon (3:21-26), Kohath (3:27-32), and Merari (3:33-37). The ransom of the firstborn (3:13, 41, 44-51) had been established at the Passover (Exod. 4:22-23). The Lord made a one-for-one substitution of the 22,000 Levites for each firstborn male of Israel, of whom there were 22,273. For the additional 273 firstborn Israelites, an equivalence of redemption money was paid to the priests (3:39-51).

4:1–6:21 THE HOLINESS OF THE TABERNACLE

The Levites' duties are described (4:1-49). The holiness of the tabernacle was emphasized, with special reference to protecting from death the sons of Kohath, whose

---

THE ARRANGEMENT OF THE TRIBES AROUND THE TABERNACLE

In the camp of Israel the twelve tribes were arranged symmetrically around the tabernacle. The physical location of the tabernacle in Israel's camp visualized two truths that the people needed to hold in tension. First, God was to be at the physical and spiritual center of the nation's life. Second, because God was too holy to dwell directly with his people, he ordained a protective barrier of priests and Levites between him and the nation. The Israelites needed to be close to God, making him the center of their lives, while also recognizing that they were unworthy of his holy presence among them.

The camp illustrates circles of holiness. The outside world was excluded from Israel's camp, and thus, from close fellowship with God. The vast majority of God's chosen people were within the camp, the first circle of holiness. Only the priests and Levites were allowed into the next circle of holiness. The most exclusive circle was limited to the high priest. Once a year, he alone could enter into the Most Holy Place—the inner room of the tabernacle. But even though these degrees of holiness and priestly barriers are done away with for believers in Christ, they still need to balance their desire for God's intimate fellowship with an awesome respect for his holiness.

responsibility was to care for the sanctuary (4:17-20). Whereas in Numbers the families of Gershon, Kohath, and Merari were numbered according to all males a month in age or older, in Numbers 4 those who were from thirty to fifty years of age were numbered. These men, who would serve in the work of the tabernacle, totaled 8,580 (4:46-48). Numbers 3 tells the work that each family was to do while the tabernacle was set up, whereas Numbers 4 details how they were to take care of the tabernacle and its parts when the camp would move to another place.

In Numbers 5, a new element to the laws of infectious skin disease, including leprosy (cf. Lev. 13–14), was introduced. The camp of God was to be pure from persons inflicted with these diseases, as well as those who were unclean due to contact with dead bodies (Num. 5:1-4). Any personal guilt of one Israelite against another was ultimately a direct offense to God (5:6). The test of a wife's adultery (5:11-31) was to help avoid the kind of family strife that could shake the camp to its roots. The mixture that a wife suspected of adultery was to drink was not a lethal poison; the terrible results for guilt came from a direct curse of God (5:27-28). The ritual test for adultery illustrated the seriousness of this issue in the Israelite community. God provided this means of exposing the guilty and vindicating the innocent. The underlying principle was that God knows and judges sin. See Leviticus 20:10 for a man's penalty for adultery and Hosea 4:14 for an amplification.

The Nazirite vow (6:1-21) gave the lay person an opportunity to come near to the status of priests (cf. 6:7 with Lev. 21:1-3, 11). The word *Nazirite* (Num. 6:2) is derived from a Hebrew verb meaning "to separate." The Nazirite vow provided opportunity for a voluntary dedication (or separation) of oneself to God (6:18). The idea was that of separation for a special ministry to God. Abstinence from wine signified giving up life's luxuries (cf. Jer. 35:6-8), and the uncut hair signified presenting oneself to God intact and whole (cf. Exod. 20:25 for uncut stones and Deut. 15:19 for unshorn animals). The vow could be temporary (e.g., Paul, Acts 18:18; four men, Acts 21:23-28) or for life (Samson, Samuel, and John the Baptist).

6:22-27 THE AARONIC BLESSING

The great Aaronic blessing (Num. 6:22-27) is placed here as a conclusion to the covenant God had given from the thundering top of Mount Sinai and from the glorious tabernacle. God would bless and keep (i.e., take care of) the nation (cf. "take care of" the garden in Gen. 2:15, which also can be translated "keep," NASB). He also would make his face shine on the Israelites and be gracious to them (cf. Exod. 34:6). The face of God's holiness that was to shine upon Israel could equal life or death, but God desired his blessings to fall upon those who were faithful so that they could experience peace (Num. 6:26) and wholeness in their relationship with their redeeming God.

7:1–8:26 THE DEDICATION OF THE TABERNACLE AND PRIESTS

The service of the tabernacle was completed in twelve days, during which the twelve tribes presented offerings (7:1-89) to be used for the dedication of the altar (7:84, 88), the special place where the Israelites could have their sins forgiven before God. These offerings were given after the tabernacle had been set up (7:1). The carts and oxen that were provided were used to transport the tabernacle and its fixtures when the Israelites were on the move. But the Ark of the Covenant was to be carried by the Kohathites on their shoulders (7:9).

The importance of the high priest was stressed (8:1-4), followed by a beautiful example of the Levites as "living sacrifices" (8:5-26). Regarding the Levites being presented as a wave offering to do the Lord's work (8:11), see 1 Chronicles 23–26 and 2 Chronicles 17:8-9; 19:8 for the varieties of priestly work assigned to them. The protection of Israel from violating God's holiness was again stressed (Num. 8:19). The age limits for Levitical service were twenty-five to fifty years (8:24-25). Numbers 4:3 gives a slightly different age period of thirty to fifty years. The five-year difference may have involved a training period before the official period of service began.

9:1-23 THE SECOND PASSOVER

The second Passover was observed fourteen days after the tabernacle was finished (9:1-14). A summary was given of the history of God's presence with the Israelites during their wanderings (9:15-23).

10:1-36 THE DEPARTURE FROM SINAI
After final instructions regarding trumpet blasts to be used for signals (10:1-10), the Israelites moved out of their camp for the first time since the tribes had been designated specific places to camp and the order in which they would travel (10:11-36). According to the Jewish Mishnah, the alarm for war was a succession of short blasts that made it distinct from a sustained blast that meant they should move from their camp (10:5). After eleven months at Mount Sinai (10:11; cf. Exod. 19:1), the cloud of God's glory lifted from the tabernacle and the people moved out. Moses' words were really a song that envisioned the Ark as God's warrior presence to fight against Israel's enemies (10:35-36). Israel was beginning a march that was to lead them into war against the inhabitants of the Promised Land.

11:1-35 Complaint and Judgment: Blindness toward God's Provision

Now the book moves into a series of complaints of the people and God's resultant judgments. Their first complaint was about their hardships, and they made it in God's hearing (11:1-3). This complaint was caused by their blindness toward God's provision. Moses called the place Taberah ("burning") because of the judgment God sent. Their second complaint (11:4-30) stemmed from their greed for food other than manna (11:4, 34; for more about manna cf. Exod. 16:31). The people wanted what was not provided by God's gracious presence (Num. 6:24-27). They fondly remembered the food of Egypt and wailed before God (11:4-10, 18-20). The seventy elders who helped Moses care for the people (Num. 11:16) were distinct from the rulers of thousands, hundreds, fifties, and tens who had been appointed earlier (Exod. 18:21-26). God met Moses' great emotional needs (11:10-15) by giving spiritual discernment to these leaders (11:16-30). Moses' prayer that the Lord would put his Spirit on all his people (11:29) would come true on the day of Pentecost. Perhaps the people's greedy craving indicated their unbelief in the adequacy of God's provision (11:33). The place was named Kibroth Hattaavah, meaning "the graves of greediness."

12:1-16 Complaint and Judgment: Blindness toward God's Prophet

The third complaint concerned Miriam and Aaron's blindness as to who was God's true prophet. In the Hebrew text the feminine ending on the verb "spoke" makes it clear that Miriam instigated the complaint and rebellion (12:1). Hence, she alone was judged with leprosy. To "spit in someone's face" (12:14) was a sign of shame imposed upon wrongdoers (Deut. 25:9; Isa. 50:6). Miriam and Aaron had confused Moses' function as God's spokesman (12:6) with his position as a believer before God. All Israel was equally favored before God in his saving grace. But God had different functions for different individuals. Humility in the Bible is one's appreciation of who he is in God's sight (12:3). Moses knew his place before God according to God's standards, and he did not cease to call on God's graciousness in his prayer (12:13).

13:1–14:45 Complaint and Judgment: Blindness toward God's Power

The fourth complaint and judgment concerned the people's blindness to God's power to give Israel the Promised Land. Deuteronomy 1:22 indicates that God had yielded to the people's request that the land be searched out (Num. 13:2). In listing the spies, note that Moses had added the name of God to the name of Hoshea (meaning "salvation"), making his name Joshua (meaning "Yahweh is salvation," 13:16). The spies brought back full and accurate knowledge concerning what Israel was up against (13:1-29), but they gave two conflicting reports. The spies who made the majority report only saw the giants (cf. Gen. 6:4), whereas Joshua and Caleb saw victory. The descendants of Anak, the giants, were noted for their great size and strength (13:28). They were described as being related to the Nephilim (13:33), who lived on the earth before and after the flood (Gen. 6:4). Using hyperbole (exaggeration for the sake of emphasis), the writer compares the Israelites to grasshoppers.

In the resulting rebellion the Israelites tried to appoint a new leader to take them back to Egypt (14:1-4) and to stone the old leaders (14:5-10). From God's point of view, the purpose for sending in the spies was not to determine if the conquest was possible, but to show Israel what God was going to give his people. All of the Israelites' actions were actually a rebellion against the Lord himself, not their leaders (14:9, 11). God's destruction of the people was stopped by Moses' intercession for them (14:11-19), but a forty-year period of wandering in the desert was God's verdict against them (14:20-38), along with a great failure in battle (14:39-45). Figuring that at least 1,200,000 people were to die in the next thirty-seven and a half years means that there were approximately eighty-five funerals a day, seven per waking hour. This would be a continuous reminder to Israel of God's wrath and judgment on sin (14:29). Of course, large numbers of them died during a few days' time in the rebellion of Korah and the following day's plague, as well as those who died by the snakes or in the plague following the worship of Baal of Peor.

15:1–19:22 ISRAEL'S WANDERINGS: DISINTEGRATION

Overview: This section introduces the forty-year period of Israel's wanderings, beginning with a surprising reaffirmation of God's land promise and ending with a massive sacrifice to cleanse the nation from the death that had pervaded the wanderings. The events of 15:1–19:22 happened in the early part of the wanderings because the sacrifice commanded in Numbers 19 was designed to cleanse the nation from the uncleanness caused by touching the many dead bodies of the first generation that was to die in the wilderness.

15:1-41 Laws While in the Land

Just after condemning the older Israelites to wander in the desert for forty years, God reaffirmed that the next generation of Israel would go into the land ("After you enter the land," 15:2, 18). That gave the nation a focus of hope in the wilderness. Their task was to remember God's great redemption (cf. 15:37-41 regarding tassels as a reminder). In spite of the Israelites' unbelief and unfaithfulness, God would eventually bring them into their inheritance (15:2). The word "defiantly" (15:30) literally reads, "with a high hand" (cf. Exod. 14:8, KJV), such as a fist

raised in defiance. There was no provision for atonement for such a sin. The offender would be put to death, "cut off from his people" (Exod. 31:14). The case of the wood gatherer showed that God regarded the intent to sin as being equivalent to the sin itself (15:32-36; cf. Matt. 5:21-28). The tassels, intended as a reminder to obey the law, came to be used hypocritically by the New Testament Pharisees (Num. 15:38-41; cf. Matt. 23:5).

16:1–18:32 Complaint and Judgment: Blindness toward God's Priest

16:1-50 THE BLINDNESS OF THE LEADERS AND PEOPLE

The fifth complaint concerned the people's blindness toward God's true priest, specifically the authority of the Aaronic line versus that of Korah (16:1-3, 6-7). The issue again was a confusion between the differing functions that God assigns to his leaders and the essential equality of every believer before God. While all were redeemed, not all could come into the holy places of God, at least not until Christ opened the way into God's Holy of Holies for all believers. The judgment that fell upon the rebels (16:28-35) caused the Israelites to make their sixth complaint the next day (16:41), and this again brought a plague. Throughout these complaints and judgments, Israel owed its continued existence to the gracious intercession of Moses (16:47-50).

17:1-13 GOD SIGNIFIES HIS PRIEST

God put to rest the matter of Aaron's authority as his chosen high priest by causing the sprouting of Aaron's rod (17:1-9). A rod symbolized a man's rule over his house, and the budding of the rod confirmed the divinely appointed spiritual leader, putting an end to the murmuring.

18:1-32 CLARIFICATION OF PRIESTLY AND LEVITICAL WORK

The people's response to Aaron's rod that budded (17:12-13) led to God's clarification of where the responsibility lay for the tabernacle service (18:1-32). Note the key phrase "I give you all" (18:12; cf. 18:19, 26). God provides for his own. The priests would guard the lay people, including the other Levites who were not priests, who would die if they offended against the sanctuary (18:3, 5, 7, 22, 32).

19:1-22 Cleansing after Touching Dead Bodies

Death pervades the book, and here God provided a relatively quick and easy way to cleanse a person from defiling the tabernacle as the nation wandered in the desert and witnessed the deaths of the members of the first generation (19:13, 20). Because of the mass defilement by so many deaths during the wilderness wanderings, God instituted the red heifer ritual to make cleansing readily acccessible from unavoidable contact with a dead body (cf. Lev. ll:24-47).

20:1–36:13 FROM KADESH TO MOAB: REGROUPING THE TROOPS

Overview: The events of section 20:l–36:13 take the reader to the fortieth year of Israel's wanderings. They were still complaining just like they had in the first year. There was no difference in the hearts of the people after the forty years of wandering, for they still were complaining as the old generation had done. But God relentlessly forged ahead to bring the nation to the border of the Promised Land.

20:1-29 Complaint and Provision: Leaders Judged

The seventh complaint concerned the need for water (cf. Exod. 15:22-26; 17:1-7). The account of Moses' disobedience when striking the rock at Meribah for water is similar to God's provision of water from a rock that is recorded in Exodus 17:1-7, but the settings, chronologies, and details distinguish the two incidents. Throughout Numbers there are recurring phrases regarding Moses' obedience according to the Lord's commands to him (1:54; 2:34; 3:51; 4:37, 49; 8:20; 9:5, 23; 10:13; 16:40; 20:9). They lead the reader to this one moment of Moses' disobedience. Moses was humble (12:3); that is, he did exactly what the Lord commanded him, except for this one instance.

Also, the long section of Numbers 15–18 had stressed the significance of God's authority behind the symbol of Aaron's rod, the very rod Moses used wrongly here to strike the rock. To disobey was to disbelieve

(20:12), and to disbelieve was to dishonor God among the believers.

The rivalry that had existed between Jacob and Esau (Gen. 25:20-34) now developed between their descendants, Israel and Edom (Num. 20:14-21). Edom became a continual enemy of Israel (Gen. 36:l, 8; Obad. 1-2l). The death of Aaron, the high priest, marked the end of an era and signified a new beginning for the second generation of Israelites (20:22-29).

21:1-35 Complaint and Judgment: Blindness toward God's Provision of Manna

The Israelites' eighth complaint again concerned their blindness toward God's provision of manna. God's deliverance of them in battle (21:1-3) had no connection in their minds with being grateful for his provision. Again Moses interceded for the people by providing them a focal point, the bronze snake, at which they could look for life despite their being bitten by poisonous snakes (21:8-9). Jesus compared this event to what would happen to himself (John 3:14-15). The bronze snake was later used as an idol and had to be destroyed (2 Kings 18:4).

The itinerary of places where Israel camped while traveling to Moab (Num. 21:10-20) is given in more detail in 33:41-49. "The Book of the Wars of the Lord" (21:14) was an ancient collection of war songs used by Moses and other scribes as a source of information.

22:1–24:25 God's Absolute and Sovereign Blessing of Israel Emphasized

Overview: Numbers 22–25 emphasize God's absolute and sovereign blessing of Israel. God had promised Abraham that the one who cursed him would be cursed and the one who blessed him would be blessed. In the account of Balaam (see also 2 Pet. 2:15; Jude 1:10-11), it is obvious that when he was speaking for God, it was impossible for him to curse Israel.

22:1-41 BALAAM COMMISSIONED

Balak realized that God's blessing was upon Israel (Num. 22:5-6) and soon Balaam would realize this also (22:12, 20; 23:8; 24:9-10), but that did not stop either of them from trying to curse her. God's lethal opposition (22:31-33) was against Balaam's intention to curse instead of bless Israel. God was clearly open to Balaam's going to Balak, but only if he intended to bless Israel (22:20, 35). Balak's fear of Israel was expressed in 22:2-4. God did indeed intend to completely destroy the inhabitants of Canaan, for he wanted the land of Canaan as well as the Israelites to be devoted to himself. This rationale is revealed in Deuteronomy 7:1-6.

Who and what was Balaam? His name in the biblical text literally means "he who destroys the people," possibly a distortion of his original name, meaning "a divine brings forth." Balaam was from Pethor, located in northern Mesopotamia about twelve miles south of Carchemish, four hundred miles from Moab. While his identity has been debated, it appears that Balaam was a *baru* prophet, that is, a kind of diviner who looks at animals, birds, ants and the livers of sacrificed animals to predict the future. He was hired by Balak, king of Moab, to curse Israel.

23:1–24:5 BALAAM'S ORACLES
OF BLESSING

Balaam's oracles are characterized by the repetition of the phrase "uttered his oracle" (23:7, 18; 24:3, 15, 20-21, 23). The movement from one hill to another (23:27) shows the then-prevalent pagan view regarding local gods. Balak thought that perhaps Balaam could move to a place where God, whom he considered to be a local god who was only powerful in a specific locality, would not have the power to stop him from cursing Israel. The oracles of Balaam, the pagan diviner, are masterpieces of Semitic poetry that reveal great truths concerning the relationship of God and Israel. Although Balaam was a wicked diviner, God spoke truth through him (22:35; 24:13). If God could speak through the mouth of a donkey, he also could speak through the mouth of Balaam. There were seven oracles: 23:7-12; 23:18-24; 24:3-9; 24:15-19; 24:20; 24:21-22; 24:23-24. Balaam's continued blessings upon Israel (24:1-9) turned into his cursings against Balak, Moab, Edom and other nations (24:10-25).

25:1-18 Idolatry and Judgment: Blessing Lost through Human Irresponsibility

Although Balaam could not bring a curse against Israel, the nation itself could bring a curse from within by its own disobedience. At this point Israel's sin consisted of idolatry with the Moabites. Balaam's counsel was behind this event (31:16). While camped in Moab, Israelites were enticed into sexual immorality with Moabite women, which resulted in their participating in the worship of Baal of Peor. Worship in the Baal cult involved dramatization of sexual acts intended to incite Baal to lust so that he would have sexual relations with Anath, the goddess of love and war, and thus fertilize the land.

The plague that followed the Israelites' sin killed 24,000 (25:9). When the apostle Paul mentioned this event in 1 Corinthians 10:18 he said that 23,000 had died. He did not include those who were executed by the judges (Num. 25:4-5). The Zadokites (25:10-13), who later replaced the priestly line because of the sin of Eli (1 Sam. 2:30-35), traced their descent through the priest Phinehas, who killed the Israelite man and the Midianite woman he had taken into his tent.

26:1-65 Second Census for War

The contrast is sharp between the terrible plague Israel had brought upon itself in Numbers 25 and the direct movement in Numbers 26 of renumbering the men of the nation who would fight to gain the Promised Land. Through all the Israelites' complaints and judgments, God's march toward fulfilling his promises to them was relentless and certain. Divine judgments, plagues, slayings, and hardships accounted for the lack of Israel's population growth during the forty years in the wilderness (26:51; cf. 2:32).

27:1-23 Second Leader Commissioned

Israel's anticipation of inheriting the land was given specific focus when God established a legal requirement regarding family lines without male heirs (27:1-11). When God told Moses of his impending death, he also instructed him to commission Joshua as his successor (27:12-23). The "mountain in the Abarim range" (27:12) is another name for Mount Nebo (Deut. 32:49). (See Deuteronomy's introductory map for Mount Nebo's location.) "God of the spirits of all mankind" (Num. 27:16) refers to God, who sustains the physical life of all creatures (cf. 16:22). "Urim" (27:21) is an abbreviated reference to the Urim and Thummim (Exod. 28:30).

28:1–30:16 Continuity of Worship in the Land Emphasized

Overview: The section 28:1–30:16 presents the instructions for feasts and vows from the perspective of Israel's being in the Promised Land. These three chapters, like Leviticus 23, record the annual events on the religious calendar. However, here the quantities of the offerings are given in anticipation of Israel's settlement in the land.

28:1–29:40 THE FEASTS OF ISRAEL
The focus here is on the daily offerings (28:1-8): those for the Sabbath (28:9-10); new months, or new year (28:11-15); the Passover (28:16-25); and the Feast of First-fruits, or Weeks (28:26-31). The seventh month (29:1) contained the Feast of Trumpets (29:1-6); the Day of Atonement (29:7-11); and the Feast of Tabernacles, or Booths (29:12-40). See Leviticus 16 and 23:23-44 for more details.

30:1-16 THE AUTHORITY OF MEN OVER THEIR WIVES AND DAUGHTERS
Numbers 30 describes the various levels of responsibility and authority between men and their wives as well as fathers and daughters in the matter of vows. The vow's essence was a humbling of the person (30:13) before the Lord for service and therefore was highly sacred. The question of vows by a woman under the authority of a man was bound to arise and was answered here. The regulations concerning the discharge of vows upheld the sanctity of the promise (cf. Eccles. 5:4-5) while also recognizing the principle of subjection to authority in the home (Num. 30:3-5).

31:1–32:42 Transjordan Conquered
31:1-54 THE MIDIANITES DESTROYED
The Midianites, on Balaam's counsel (31:16), had successfully tempted Israel to idolatry (25:1-3). Now, the destruction of the Midianites (31:1-24) brought an immense amount of wealth to Israel and to the taberna-

cle servants (31:25-54). Midian's destruction also secured the settlement of the Trans-jordan territories by the tribes of Reuben, Gad, and the half-tribe of Manasseh.

The war against Midian (31:3) was a holy war commanded by God to execute his vengeance (cf. 25:16-18). (See the introductory map in Exodus for Midian's location.) These executions (31:17-18) were designed to protect the Israelites from further defilement by involvement with the Midianites (cf. 25:1-3) and to prevent the propagation of the Midianite race. The young virgins were spared for marriage (Deut. 21:10-14) and slavery (Lev. 25:44-46). The gold accepted as a memorial (Num. 31:54) would serve as a reminder to Israel of the remarkable victory (31:49, 54).

32:1-42 THE SETTLEMENT
EAST OF THE JORDAN
The text does not indicate that there were any problems with some of the Israelites settling in the land east of the Jordan (Trans-jordan). Other Scriptures give the specific boundaries of the land promised to Abraham, and the Transjordan area is included in the general area described (Gen. 15:18; Exod. 23:31; Num. 34:1-15; Deut. 1:7-8). The only problem that concerned Moses was the potential loss of the Transjordanian tribes in helping the rest of Israel to take the land west of the Jordan, but this problem was peacefully solved (Num. 32:17). The Transjordan territories of Sihon, Bashan and Gilead (all in modern Jordan) were distributed among the tribes of Reuben, Gad, and the half-tribe of Manasseh (32:33-42). (See introductory map.)

33:1–36:13 Review from Egypt to Canaan, with the Method for Dividing Canaan

Overview: This final section of 33:1–36:13 gives a summary list of the wilderness wanderings (Num. 33), Canaan's boundaries and instructions for dividing the land (Num. 34), the locations of the Levitical cities and cities of refuge (Num. 35), and the maintenance of land portions allotted to each tribe (Num. 36). In spite of all the Israelites' failures recorded in this book, the people were now making detailed plans for entering the land as God had promised.

33:1-56 REVIEW OF THE JOURNEY

Numbers 33 begins by reviewing the Israelites' journey from Egypt to Moab (33:1-49) and ends with a pointed exhortation to them to carry out completely the destruction of the inhabitants of the land of Canaan (33:56). Listed are the encampments used during the thirty-seven and one-half years of wilderness wanderings (33:19-49). Few of these sites can be identified today. Instructions for the conquest were (1) to drive out the inhabitants, (2) to destroy everything connected with the false religions of Canaan, and (3) to divide the land among the tribes (33:52-54).

**34:1-29 MEN APPOINTED
TO DIVIDE CANAAN**

The land's boundaries were given, and men were appointed who would later distribute it among the tribes (cf. Gen. 15:18).

**35:1-34 PORTIONS FOR LEVITES AND
CITIES OF REFUGE**

Numbers 35 and 36 list God's commands given in the plains of Moab (35:1; 36:13) and provide specific instructions on how the land would be divided and maintained. Forty-eight cities were allocated for the Levites, who received no tribal territory. The Levitical cities were strategically located in order to allow their inhabitants an opportunity to provide a godly influence throughout the land. Six of the cities would serve as cities of refuge (35:9-34). Three of the six cities were located east of the Jordan River and the other three were located symmetrically on the west side. This made at least one of the six cities

of refuge easily accessible to all locations in Israel. The cities of refuge served as places of refuge for those who killed someone unintentionally. According to the law, a murderer was to be put to death (Exod. 21:12, 14), but the cities of refuge provided protection from the blood avenger (kinsman of the slain) if the bloodshed was unintentional (Num. 35:11-12). Moses regulated the custom of blood vengeance by (1) distinguishing between accidental and deliberate homicide, (2) providing a place of refuge for the offender, (3) interposing the judicial judgment of the elders, and (4) stipulating that no one could be put to death on the testimony of just one witness. The purpose of the regulation was to avoid bloodshed that would defile the land in which God would live among the people of Israel (35:33-34).

**36:1-13 MAINTENANCE OF PORTIONS
THROUGH INHERITANCE**

The book ends with a return to the question of keeping each tribe's land inheritance within that specific tribe (36:9). The concept of allotting portions of the land as special gifts of God to each tribe was very important, for it was one fruit of God's redemption from Egypt. Moses had ordered that daughters could inherit their father's property if there were no male heirs (27:1-11). Now, in order to preserve each tribe's inheritance, he decreed that such female heirs had to marry within their own tribes (36:8). If such female heirs chose to marry outside their own tribe, their inheritance would be forfeited.

Deuteronomy

BASIC FACTS

HISTORICAL SETTING

The journey from Egypt to Palestine, which might have taken less than two weeks, was lengthened to forty years because of Israel's disobedience. The restatement of the covenant, which included the law, for the new generation of Israel took place on the plains of Moab across the Jordan River from Jericho (Deut. 1:5; Num. 36:13). (See introductory map for Jericho's location.) This was followed by Moses' death and thirty days of mourning. The people, having received a new leader, a new high priest, and a new copy of the covenant, were ready to enter Canaan and conquer the Promised Land. Deuteronomy covers the period from the first of Shebat (a month corresponding to a time period in January and February; 1:3) to thirty days after Moses' death (34:8) and probably covered a time period of about sixty days (Josh. 4:19).

AUTHOR

The Mosaic authorship is rejected by liberal critics who date the book to the time of Josiah, making its publication the basis of his great reformation (2 Kings 22–23). However, the Mosaic authorship of the book is supported by several evidences.

Deuteronomy 31:9 states explicitly, "Moses wrote down this law." His authorship is also referred to in 31:24. The Jews of Jesus' day held to the Mosaic authorship (Matt. 22:24; Mark 10:3-4; 12:19). Jesus refers to Deuteronomy 24:1-4 as the commandment of Moses (Matt. 19:8).

Only Deuteronomy 34 is demonstrably post-Mosaic because it records the account of Moses' death. That account may well have been written by Joshua in keeping with early Jewish tradition. The book's unity and authenticity as a Mosaic product are also confirmed by the conformity of its structure to that of the covenant treaty form of the fifteenth to thirteenth centuries B.C. For a fuller discussion of the authorship of the Pentateuch see the introductory section to Genesis.

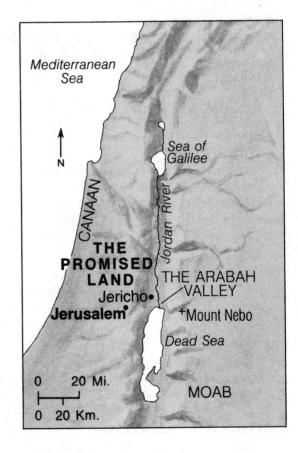

DATE

The three sermons of Moses, which make up the majority of the book of Deuteronomy, were given just before his death and before Israel crossed over into the Promised Land under the leadership of Joshua. The date for the original writing of
Deuteronomy would be nearly forty years after Israel's exodus from Egypt. The two
major positions concerning the dating of the exodus (around 1446 B.C. or 1266 B.C.)
would date Deuteronomy at around 1406 B.C. or 1226 B.C. respectively. See the introduction to Exodus for a discussion concerning the date of Israel's exodus from Egypt.

PURPOSE

The book of Deuteronomy was designed to present the link between the Israel of
Egypt and the Israel of the Promised Land, between the giving of the law at Sinai
and the application of that law in the Promised Land. It is a series of three sermons
by Moses designed to remind the nation of the past and prepare them for the problems of the future.

GEOGRAPHY AND ITS IMPORTANCE

The book of Deuteronomy takes place on the east side of the Jordan River across
from Jericho. With the sides of the Arabah Valley rising over one thousand feet on
either side and the great city of Jericho in the distance, Moses recounted the long
journey of Israel's Patriarchs from Ur to Egypt and related it to their present need for
obedience and faith. Moses' story of Israel's journey and his elaboration of God's
laws prepared the nation to cross the Jordan River, conquer Jericho and climb the
western side of the Arabah Valley to take the Promised Land.

GUIDING CONCEPTS

RELATIONSHIP TO THE NEW TESTAMENT

This is one of the most widely quoted books in the Bible. The New Testament
writers quote it over 80 times in 17 of the 27 New Testament books. Christ used it to
confirm his messiahship, to summarize the law, and to refute the devil (Matt. 4:4,
cf. Deut. 8:3; Matt. 4:7, cf. Deut. 6:16; Matt. 4:10, cf. Deut. 6:13). It is quoted 356
times in later Old Testament books as well, which points to the importance of its
contents and significance of its truths.

STRUCTURE

Deuteronomy 1:5 explains that the book is an exposition of the covenant of God.
The three addresses of Moses were designed not to give new laws but to deepen
Israel's appreciation of the law's significance. The first five verses (1:1-5) are an
editorial introduction to the whole book. The first address (1:6–4:43) retells the
great past saving acts of God for Israel. Deuteronomy 4:44-49 is an introduction
to the second address. The second address (5:1–28:68) explains the significance of
the law of God. The third address (29:1–30:20) is a final summary explanation
of the covenant's demands. The section 31:1–34:12 is the account of the last acts
of Moses and his death.

OBEDIENCE

Numbers brought the people to the border of the land, and Deuteronomy prepared them for entering it by emphasizing the necessity of their obedience to the law of God. The motive and goal for following God in obedience was the promise of God's blessing. The standard of obedience was God's Word. The incentive to obedience was God's faithfulness, whereas the alternative to obedience was God's judgment. Deuteronomy called on Israel to fear God, to walk in his ways, to love him, to serve him, and to keep his commandments (10:12-13).

RELATIONSHIP

The most important feature of the Mosaic covenant was the bond of relationship between God and humanity. God's original promises to Abraham provided a continual backdrop to the book's message. Abraham was mentioned directly or indirectly in 1:8, 11, 21, 35; 6:10; 9:5, 27; 26:5; 29:13; 31:20; 32:17; and 34:1-4. The benefits promised were direct effects of God's love (1:11; 7:13). That divine love was the primary source of the covenant bond (4:37; 7:7-13; 10:12-19; 11:1, 13, 22; 13:3; 19:9; 30:6, 16). Above all, God desired that Israel would return his love from the heart as a genuine expression of gratitude and obedience.

That concept of love pervades the book and should eliminate any thoughts that the Mosaic covenant was intended to be an external and heartless conformity to God's law (4:7-9, 29, 39; 5:29; 6:5-6; 8:2, 5, 10-14, 17-18; 10:15-21; 11:13-15, 18; 26:16; 30:6; 32:46-47). It had been love all along—all the way back to Abraham. The concept of God's love clarified the fact that his relationship with his people under the covenant was one of love rather than legalism. No stronger statement in this regard exists in the book than in 5:29. In light of that background, these words of Christ have an even more significant meaning for believers: "If you love me, you will obey what I command" (John 14:15).

THE NEED FOR RENEWING THE COVENANT

The Mosaic convenant needed renewal, not because God had changed but because humans change. Each new generation had to commit itself to God in love and obedience. This renewal was made in 26:16-19 and would later be repeated at Mount Ebal and Mount Gerizim (27:4-8; cf. Josh. 23–24).

BIBLE-WIDE CONCEPTS

Deuteronomy gives a basic perspective by which to view the rest of the Bible, especially from Joshua through 2 Kings. It takes the foundational Abrahamic promises of *land, people,* and *blessing,* puts them within the framework of the Mosaic covenant, and looks ahead to the day when the fulfillment of those promises would burst out of the old covenant into the glory of the new covenant in Christ. Here are the basic pillars of God's redemptive work laid out in Deuteronomy.

Israel's redemption from Egypt was completely bound up with her obedience to God's commands (29:25). God's blessing and judgment of Israel were completely dependent on the nation's obedience or disobedience to his commands (4:25-26; 6:3, 13-15). Just as 5:31 was the basis for Israel's gaining the land and staying in it (cf. Josh. 1:2-8), Deuteronomy 28:15 explains why Israel might be cast out of the land (cf. 2 Kings 17:13-18). And Deuteronomy 4:29-31 and 30:2-10 reveal the way in which the exiled nation could once again be restored into God's promised blessings (cf. 1 Kings 11:36; 2 Kings 25:27-30). The keeping of God's commands was completely related to Israel's worship at the place that God alone had chosen (Deut. 12:5, 11, 13-14; 14:23-25; 16:2, 5-7). Eventually that place would be the temple in Jerusalem.

Although the reign of David was still far off, verses 17:14-20 gave instructions as to how the kings of Israel were to act. Actually, long before this Abraham had been promised that there would be a line of kings among his descendants (Gen. 17:6, 17), and this promise had been repeated to Jacob (Gen. 35:11). The word of the Lord is potent; no matter how much time might pass, it will be accomplished (Deut. 32:46-47). Phrases about God fulfilling his word and keeping his promises, such as "according to the word of the Lord," occur repeatedly throughout 1 and 2 Kings (see, for example, 1 Kings 2:27; 6:11-12; 8:20; 2 Kings 1:16-17; 2:22; cf. 3:12).

NEEDS MET BY DEUTERONOMY

Since the exodus from Egypt, Israel had seen God save them through the Red Sea, supply food and safety for nearly forty years, come from the thundering top of Mount Sinai down into the relatively tiny tabernacle in the middle of the camp, and systematically destroy virtually all of the adult generation that had originally failed to enter the Promised Land. The redemption and vengeance of God stood in stark and possibly irreconcilable contrast. His holiness and grace could be seen by some as threats rather than as allies.

So, just before God's people entered the Promised Land, Deuteronomy taught that God's demands for holiness were driven by his character and that the essence of his character as expressed to his people was love. Did he redeem? It was because he loved. Did he discipline? It was because he loved. And through his redemption and discipline God showed himself to be absolutely holy. God wanted their hearts to stand in grateful remembrance of his past and present love. The book of Deuteronomy uncovers what had been implicit all along—the love of God—and meets some basic needs of God's people. The structure and content of Deuteronomy show that its author was answering questions like the following for the people of Israel:

- Why should Israel keep remembering things that God did so long ago?
- Why does God continue to love and care for the people of Israel?
- What is the appropriate response of God's people to his love?
- Can God's people expect the future to correct their past disobedience?
- Will the disobedience of Israel void God's promises to Abraham?
- What is the relationship between inner life and external behavior?

Christians ask similar questions today. All believers await entrance into the heavenly Promised Land. Meanwhile, Deuteronomy helps believers understand that dwelling with God now or in eternity involves holding together both his redemption and discipline. Deuteronomy encourages believers to remember how much they are loved by God and their original desperate need for that love. In this light, Deuteronomy asks that Christian service grow out of an honest love for God from the heart.

OUTLINE OF DEUTERONOMY

A. THE HISTORICAL BACKGROUND FOR THE COVENANT (1:1–4:43)
   1. From Sinai to Kadesh: The Old Generation (1:1-46)
   2. From Kadesh to the Plains of Moab: The New Generation (2:1–3:29)
   3. The Remembrance of God's Acts of Redemption (4:1-43)

B. BASIC STIPULATION OF THE COVENANT RELATIONSHIP: REMEMBER (4:44–11:32)
   1. The Ten Commandments Elaborated (4:44–5:33)
   2. Remember God in the Land: Redemption (6:1-25)
   3. Remember the Covenant with God: Avoiding Idolatry (7:1-26)
   4. Remember the Manna: Avoiding Self-Sufficiency (8:1-20)
   5. Remember Rebelliousness: Avoiding Self-Righteousness (9:1–10:22)
   6. Remember the Condition for Knowing God's Love: Obedience (11:1-32)

C. DETAILED STIPULATIONS OF THE COVENANT RELATIONSHIP (12:1–26:19)
   1. Fellowship and Diet (12:1–16:17)
   2. Persons in Leadership (16:18–18:22)
   3. Cities in the Land (19:1–20:20)
   4. Fresh Applications of the Moral Laws in the Land (21:1–26:19)

D. GOD'S SOVEREIGNTY AND HUMAN RESPONSIBILITY IN BLESSING (27:1–30:20)
   1. Blessings and Curses (27:1–28:68)
   2. Banishment and Restoration (29:1–30:20)

E. CORRECTIVE PICTURES (31:1–32:52)

F. THE FINAL BLESSING OF MOSES (33:1-29)

G. THE DEATH OF MOSES (34:1-12)

DEUTERONOMY NOTES

1:1–4:43 THE HISTORICAL BACKGROUND FOR THE COVENANT

Overview: The first address of Moses functioned as a reminder of Israel's failures. It was not intended to browbeat the nation, but to provide a context that magnified the great grace and love involved in God's continued commitment to her.

1:1-46 From Sinai to Kadesh: The Old Generation

1:1 TITLE

The Hebrew title for the book, which literally means "these are the words" or "words," was taken from the opening line of 1:1. Later, the translators of the Greek Septuagint descriptively entitled the book "second law," from 17:18, which says, "a copy of the law."

It was then rendered in the Latin Vulgate as *Deuteronomium* and in the English versions as Deuteronomy. The English title, which comes from the Latin title meaning, "second law," reflects an incorrect understanding of the words in 17:18. They are best translated "copy of the law," rather than "second law," which suggests that the book of Deuteronomy contains something new and distinct from the Mosaic covenant given at Sinai.

1:2-5 INTRODUCTION

A short introduction (1:2-5) sets the tone for the first subject, Israel's past history as they traveled from Sinai to Kadesh (1:2), as well as for that of the entire book, which is an exposition of God's covenant with Israel (1:5). Moses' explanation and application of the law to the second generation took place on the plains of Moab, in Transjordan, just east of Jericho and the Jordan River (1:5).

1:6-46 FROM SINAI TO KADESH

"Amorites" (1:7) was a general term for the inhabitants of Canaan (1:8). The promise to the patriarchs mentioned repeatedly in Deuteronomy (1:35; 4:31; 6:10, 18, 23, etc.) refers to the Abrahamic covenant (Gen. 12:1-3). The next step in fulfilling this promise was the occupation of the land. Some of Canaan's inhabitants were of extraordinary size. Og of Bashan was noted as having the first king-size bed, measuring more than thirteen feet long by six feet wide (Deut. 3:11).

The account of the trip from Sinai to the failure at Kadesh was punctuated with mentions of Israel's disputes (1:12) and the people's claim that God hated them (1:27). At that time Joshua was designated as the successor to Moses (1:37-38). The function of this four-chapter rehearsal of Israel's history was to heighten her anticipation of God's promises by taking to heart his past faithfulness. That faithfulness, coupled with his promise of future exaltation, was designed to bring about the present faithfulness of God's people.

2:1–3:29 From Kadesh to the Plains of Moab: The New Generation

In the journey from Kadesh to the plains of Moab, the Israelites saw the Lord's power as they defeated Sihon. The background to that and all their other victories was that the Lord had a pattern of dispossessing one nation of

its land by means of another nation (2:20-23). That cut both ways for Israel. God would have them dispossess and utterly destroy the inhabitants of Canaan, but he could, and would, also dispossess Israel of the Promised Land if she became unfaithful.

By Israel's defeat of Og (3:1-22), the way was cleared for the Transjordanian tribes to settle on the east side of the Jordan. The rest of the nation of Israel would soon cross the Jordan River and enter the Promised Land, but Moses would not enter it. He was only allowed to view the Promised Land from afar (3:23-29).

4:1-43 The Remembrance of God's Acts of Redemption

Moses urged the remembrance of God's acts of redemption (4:3, 9-10) and exhorted the nation to watch its behavior carefully (4:15, 23). Although Israel had been promised the title deed to the Promised Land (Gen. 13:15), only through obedience to the law would she actually possess the land and remain there (Deut. 4:1). Israel was warned by this reminder (4:3) of God's discipline of the disobedient in Numbers 25. The duty of remembering is stressed both positively and negatively throughout Deuteronomy (4:9; 5:15; 7:18; 8:2, 18; 9:7; 15:15). Forgetfulness opens the door to disobedience and failure. God is spirit, and true worship is after the pattern of his essential nature (4:15-19; cf. John 4:23-24). Exile from the Promised Land would be the ultimate discipline for breaking the covenant (Deut. 4:27; 28:41, 64; 29:22-28). God promised to be faithful to the covenant promises in spite of the disobedience of his people (4:31). Deuteronomy is comprised of the law (God's instruction), stipulations (exhortations or reminders), decrees (permanent rules of conduct), and laws (judgments, judicial decisions; 4:44-45). The core of the matter was God's absolutely unique love for Israel (4:32-40).

4:44–11:32 BASIC STIPULATION OF THE COVENANT RELATIONSHIP: REMEMBER

Overview: The basic theme of remembrance as the key to remaining faithful to God is continued throughout section 4:44–11:32. The emphasis was on a relationship from the heart that would breed allegiance to the God who loves, saves, and keeps.

4:44–5:33 The Ten Commandments Elaborated

The second address of Moses restated and explained the Ten Commandments. The basic stipulations of the covenant were reiterated (5:6-21; cf. Exod. 20:3-17). According to Mosaic Law each person was responsible for his or her own sins and they and their descendants after them would suffer consequences for those sins (Deut. 5:9). The innocent were not to be punished for the guilty (Deut. 24:16; Ezek. 18:4), yet the criminal acts of a father would affect the children. The parent would be judged for the sin, but the children would often suffer some of the consequences inadvertently. The people of Israel's motivation to keep the Sabbath came from the remembrance of their redemption from Egypt (5:15). In Exodus 20:11 the motivation had been a remembrance of the creation Sabbath.

Although legally binding, the law was intended not to restrict life, but to lead to fullness of life (Deut. 5:33). Blessing would accompany obedience. The exclamation of God in 5:29 displayed the depth of his desire to bless and have fellowship with Israel.

6:1-25 Remember God in the Land: Redemption

Deuteronomy 6 literally went to the heart of what God desired for Israel in the Mosaic covenant: love from the heart (6:5-6; cf. 11:18-19). Here God asked Israel to put the commands on her heart for her own good (6:4-6). In the new covenant in Christ, God did that work himself and placed the law within the believer (Heb. 8:10; Phil. 2:12-13). The section 6:4-9 is known in Jewish tradition as the *Shema* (literally, "hear" or "listen") which declares the uniqueness and unity of God. The words "the Lord is one" may be translated "God alone."

On the basis of 6:8, some pious Jews wear a phylactery, a small box containing portions of Scripture (cf. Matt. 23:5), on their forehead and forearm during prayer. Many Jewish homes have a *mezuzah*, a small scroll-shaped container, on the doorpost. The point is that the Israelite people were to learn the law and

not forget the Lord (Deut. 6:10-12). The home was to serve as the center for religious education (6:20-25). In response to a child's inquiry, the great truths about God were to be taught. Israel was to remember her redemption (6:12) and not repeat the mistakes of the past in the wilderness (6:16). Jesus quoted 6:16 during his time of temptation in the wilderness (Matt. 4:7).

7:1-26 Remember the Covenant with God: Avoiding Idolatry

The command not to intermarry with the Canaanites (7:1-5) was designed to keep Israel as God's special possession. God did not give Israel blessings because she was a great nation but because he loved her and was keeping his promise to Abraham (7:8).

Because the Israelites were to be a separated people, God reminded them of their election as his own special possession from among the people of the earth (7:1-6). Sacred stones, or pillars, were upright stones associated with male deities (7:5). Asherah (or Asherim) poles were wooden symbols of the female deity, Asherah. The reason for Israel's separation from the Canaanites lay in her election and holiness (7:6). Association with other nations would lead the Israelites into idolatry.

Lest the Israelites should become proud of being in such a select and favored position, God went on to remind them of the nature of his love (7:7-8) and of their responsibility to him (7:9-11). Israel did not merit the blessing through obedience, but rather, obedience was the means by which she was to maintain the covenant relationship that was God's established course and context for her blessing (7:12). God's love is an undeserved, selective affection by which he binds himself to his people and which results in the redemption of his people from bondage (7:17-26). Because God had demonstrated his love by the act of redemption, the redeemed were thus obligated to demonstrate their love for him in return. For comments on the "hornet" (7:20), see Exodus 23:28.

8:1-20 Remember the Manna: Avoiding Self-Sufficiency

The Israelites were to remember what happened to them in the wilderness (8:2, 11), specifically the reason why God gave them the manna: to humble them (8:3, 16) and find out what was in their hearts concerning obedience (8:2-3). The provision of manna was intended to teach Israel that God's word was more essential to their existence than food. The essence of forgetting God is the failure to keep his commands (8:11). Pride is the danger of success (8:14), for there is always the temptation to think that what has been achieved is the result of human effort rather than the gift of God. Proud self-sufficiency would be the Israelites' undoing (8:17-19), causing them to become like the nations that were destroyed before them (8:20).

9:1–10:22 Remember Rebelliousness: Avoiding Self-Righteousness

Lest Israel become self-righteous (9:4), she was to remember her continual rebelliousness in the wilderness (9:7, 13, 22, 24, 27). Israel was entering the Promised Land due to the wickedness of the people of Canaan (9:4-5; see "sin of the Amorites," Gen. 15:16). Those Israelites who might be foolish enough to claim that the gift of the land was a result of their righteousness would be suffering from a case of religious amnesia (Deut. 9:4). Against the background of the fulfillment of God's promise to Abraham to make him a great nation, God reemphasized that the conditions of the covenant (1) had come from God's love (10:15), (2) were for the people's good (10:13), and (3) were to be obeyed from the heart (10:16).

The covenant's basic requirements were summarized (10:12-13). Note that fear of the Lord and love for him were not mutually exclusive concepts, for God expected his people to do both at the same time. The command "circumcise your hearts" (10:16) was reminiscent of the Abrahamic covenant (Gen. 17:9-12), but it was used figuratively here for consecration to God (cf. Josh. 5:2-9). "Hold fast" (Deut. 10:20) is translated from the same Hebrew word as the word "united" in Genesis 2:24 and suggests an extremely close and intimate relationship with God.

11:1-32 Remember the Condition for Knowing God's Love: Obedience

Obedience (11:1, 13, 18, 22) to God's ways would bring the nation strength and victory (11:9). The Promised Land was under God's special care (11:12). The expression "flowing with milk and honey" (11:9) is a pastoral figure of abundance. The "early" or "autumn" rains in October, which fell before the beginning of the rainy season (November–April), softened the soil after the summer drought, enabling the farmer to plow and plant. The "late" or "spring" rains in May ensured a good harvest (11:14). If either of these failed, the crops would be sure to suffer.

12:1–26:19 DETAILED STIPULATIONS OF THE COVENANT RELATIONSHIP

Overview: In the section 12:1–26:19 detailed conditions for having a relationship with God are given—conditions that touch on all areas of human life. No area of life was left without a word, which revealed God's total concern for Israel. The purpose of the conditions was not that the people would center their attention on impersonal external rules for heartless

---

THE TEN COMMANDMENTS IN DEUTERONOMY

Commandment	Text	Description
1-2	12:1-31	Worship
3	13:1–14:27	Name of God
4	14:28–16:17	Sabbath
5	16:18–18:22	Authority
6	19:1–22:8	Homicide
7	22:9–23:19	Adultery
8	23:20–24:7	Theft
9	24:8–25:4	False Charges
10	25:6-16	Coveting

obedience, but on a holy and loving relationship with God. Those conditions were summarized and applied in 26:18-19.

The Ten Commandments (5:6-21) formed the basis for the laws expounded in Deuteronomy 12–25. See the accompanying chart.

12:1–16:17 Fellowship and Diet

12:1-32 FELLOWSHIP AT GOD'S PLACE

In contrast with the many places of pagan worship that had to be destroyed (12:1-4), Israel was to worship only at the place God would choose for her and where he would dwell; it would ultimately be Jerusalem (12:5, 11, 14). The place of sacrifice would indicate whether or not the true God was being served.

The command for the destruction of the Canaanite cultic centers (12:2-4) was designed both to punish the sinful inhabitants of Canaan (Lev. 18:25) and to protect the Israelites from false gods (Deut. 7:25-26). The centralization of Israel's worship was to prevent contaminating the worship of the Lord, Yahweh, with idolatrous practices (12:13-14).

13:1-18 IDOLATRY

Three possible means of seduction to idolatry were condemned: (1) a prophet (13:1-5); (2) a family member (13:6-11); and (3) wicked and worthless men (13:12-18). Note the repeated phrases "let us follow" or "let us go" (13:2, 6, 13). In Moses' day, treaties were made between kings and the subjects they had conquered (sometimes called suzerain-vassal treaties). In these ancient treaties, the king required his vassals (subject nations) to report any conspiracy, rebellion or disloyalty and to take active measures against offenders. This obligation finds its counterpart in Deuteronomy 13.

14:1-29 DIET

God as the Creator and Redeemer has a right to dictate even what his people can eat. Here the conditions of what to eat (14:3-21) and where to eat (14:22-29) were established along with Israel's responsibility to be separate and holy to God. Shaving the head and lacerating the body, activities forbidden to the Israelites, were pagan cultic practices performed to secure favor from false gods (1 Kings 18:28). Regulations were repeated for clean and unclean foods (cf. Lev. 11:1-45

with Deut. 14:3-20) and the pagan practice of boiling a young goat in its mother's milk was again forbidden (cf. 14:21 with Exodus 23:19).

Each year Israel was to bring its tithes to Jerusalem to share with the Levites and priests (Deut. 14:22-27). Every third year, the people were to store the tithes in their own towns to share with the Levites and the needy (14:28-29). That third-year offering appears to replace the regular yearly tithe that was to be taken to Jerusalem ("all the tithes of that year's produce," 14:28). Some scholars see the third-year tithe to be in addition to the regular yearly tithe. Both the local and the centralized locations for the tithes met the general command to share the yearly tithes with the Levites and the priests throughout the land (Lev. 27:30-33; Num. 18:21-32).

15:1-23 SABBATICAL YEARS

Sabbatical years and the period immediately prior to them were to be full of generous acts by the Israelites in light of their redemption by God. The motivation for that generosity was to be their remembrance of being redeemed out of Egyptian slavery. It is debated whether the debt of 15:1-6 was to be canceled permanently or simply suspended for the year. Servitude could be rendered for the repayment of a debt (15:12-18). But the limit was six years unless the slave requested to become a life-long servant.

16:1-17 FEASTS

Israel's three great feasts of the Passover ("Unleavened Bread," 16:1-8), the Feast of Weeks ("Pentecost," 16:9-12) and the Feast of Tabernacles ("Booths," 16:13-17) were designed to keep fresh in the Israelites' minds the remembrance of their redemption by God (16:3, 12).

16:18–18:22 Persons in Leadership

16:18–17:20 LEADERSHIP
DECISION MAKING

All of the conditions of the law called for accurate judgment. The section 16:18–17:20 gives instructions for judgment that moved from judges and officials (16:18-22), to the people (17:1-7), to the priests (17:8-13), and ultimately to the future king (17:14-20). Since the witnesses were to deliver the first lethal blows, this would tend to guard against possible perjury (17:7). The foundation for the establishment of the Israelite monarchy was laid (17:14-20; cf. Gen. 49:10; Num. 24:17; 1 Sam. 8–10). The survival of the kingly line (Deut. 17:18-20) would become a parallel theme to the survival of the nation as a whole. Kingly survival would become the backbone of the books of Kings and Chronicles and the foundation for Israel's messianic hope. Marriage into the royalty of foreign powers was used by pagan kings as a means of strengthening their treaties. But Israel's king was to depend on the Lord rather than on military strength, political alliances, or personal wealth, and he was not to take many wives, or his heart would be led astray from the Lord (17:16-20).

18:1-22 CARE FOR LEVITES

The Levites, who were to settle throughout the land, were to be cared for (18:1-8) by the other Israelites as they taught the people the conditions of the covenant. The occult flourished among the pagan inhabitants of Canaan, and the Israelites were warned against it (18:9-14).

Moses said that God would bring the nation a greater Prophet (18:15), that is, Jesus Christ (Acts 3:19-26). Every prophet that arose after Moses would share in an aspect of the hope for this greater Prophet. The word "prophet" (Deut. 18:15) means one who speaks for another (Exod. 7:1-2). The biblical prophet was one who spoke forth a message for God (Deut. 18:18; cf. Jer. 1:4-7).

19:1–20:20 Cities in the Land

Another aspect of God's judgment and mercy was found in the laws protecting those who unintentionally took a human life (19:1-21). The cities of refuge were given to allow a person time to gain a just trial.

Two factors stand out regarding the instructions for fighting against the cities of Canaan: (1) the God of the exodus would be with the Israelites and fight for them (20:1, 4); and (2) anyone or anything that breathed in the cities of Canaan had to be completely destroyed, in contrast with only the men having to be killed in cities taken outside the land (20:10-18). Because Israel's success did not depend upon military power but God's presence, allowance was made for exemption from military service (20:5-9). During a

military siege of a city it was customary in ancient times for an army to cut down the surrounding trees, both to destroy the enemy's land and to build siege equipment (20:19-20). This was prohibited in order to protect Israel's inheritance.

21:1–26:19 Fresh Applications of the Moral Laws in the Land

Overview: The section of 21:1–26:19 makes fresh applications of the moral laws given at Sinai to situations that would arise in the Promised Land. The themes of purging evil from the land and dealing with others in fairness and decency were based on the fact of God's holy presence with Israel (23:14).

21:1–22:11 CIVIL PURITY

These civil instructions were solely aimed at removing impurity and avoiding sin within the land: (1) atoning for the impurity of the guilt of innocent blood (21:1-9); (2) avoiding the mistreatment of captive women and maintaining the firstborn's rights (21:15-17); and (3) punishing rebellion and enforcing capital punishment (21:18-23). The public exposure of a corpse ("hang on a tree") was a means of adding disgrace to an executed criminal.

In 21:15-17 it is debatable whether Moses was legislating for a man who had two wives (polygamy) or had had two wives in succession. Since the text can be translated "has had two wives," it is questionable whether polygamy was involved. Deviant sexual behavior, not clothing styles, was the object of concern in 22:5.

22:12-30 MORAL PURITY

The social laws (22:1-12) were followed by moral laws (22:13-30), the theme of which was to purge evil from the congregation of Israel (22:21-22, 24). The legislation of 22:13-19 was designed to protect a virgin against false allegations of unchastity.

23:1-25 PURITY IN THE ASSEMBLY

Instructions for the holiness of the assembly (23:1-3, 7-8) and the camp (23:13) were dictated by the presence of God in Israel's midst (23:14). The "assembly of the Lord" refers to the people of God gathered in his presence for worship. The exclusion of Moabites and Ammonites (23:3) from the assembly continued the standard set forth to Abraham: "whoever curses you I will curse" (Gen. 12:3).

Self-emasculation was a heathen cultic practice performed to ingratiate a worshiper with the gods (23:1). "Male prostitute" is literally "dog" in Hebrew (23:18). Money from unclean sources could not be brought to the house of God (23:18).

24:1–26:19 PURITY AND JUSTICE MOTIVATED BY GRATITUDE

The various topics covered in 24:1–26:19 hinge on the purity of the land (24:4), the remembrance of events that had occurred in the wilderness (24:9), and the exodus (24:18, 22). The legislation of 24:1-4 neither instituted nor condoned divorce but simply prohibited a particular type of remarriage after divorce. The grammatical structure is "if" (24:1-3), "then" (24:4). A man could not remarry his divorced wife if, in the meantime, she had had an intervening marriage. The precise meaning of "something indecent" (24:1, literally, "a naked matter") is hotly debated by the Jewish rabbis, and is uncertain. Apparently the legislation was designed to discourage divorce and prevent the establishment of an illicit union.

While loans were permitted (24:10-13), charging a fellow Israelite interest was forbidden (23:19-20). The "pledge" functioned as collateral to secure repayment of the loan (24:10-12). However, the borrower was not to be deprived of his means of livelihood (24:6) or cloak (24:13).

Deuteronomy 25:6 continues the theme of human compassion, decency and fairness with laws regarding dignity in punishment (25:1-3); a proverb on wages for work (25:4); care for widows (25:5-10); indecency (25:11-12); accurate and honest weights and measures (25:13-16); and the command to destroy the Amalekites for their unfair war against Israel (25:17-19). The apostle Paul later appealed to 25:4 to support the principle that the worker was worthy of his hire (1 Cor. 9:9-11). The law of the levirate marriage (the word comes from the Latin *levir* which means "husband's brother") served as the essential background to Ruth's marriage (Deut. 25:5-10; cf. Ruth 3–4).

The offering of firstfruits was to be made in connection with a confession of God as the Redeemer (from Abraham to the exodus) and the Giver of the Promised Land (Deut.

26:4-11). The creedal confession of Hebrew history recalled God's mighty deeds in the exodus and conquest (26:5-10). The second speech of Moses ended with the formal commitment of Israel to keep God's instructions (26:16-19).

27:1–30:20 GOD'S SOVEREIGNTY AND HUMAN RESPONSIBILITY IN BLESSING

Overview: The blessings and curses (27:1–28:68) presented the two ways that were open to the children of God. The way of blessing was open to all (29:1-29), and in the end God would perform great acts of purification and inner perfection to bind his children to himself permanently (30:1-20).

27:1–28:68 Blessings and Curses

In the section 27:1–28:68 fourteen verses describe the blessings (28:1-14) and sixty-six verses the curses (27:15-26; 28:15-68). Clearly, the thrust was on warning the Israelites of what would happen when they disobeyed. Mount Ebal (3,083 feet high) and Mount Gerizim (2,890 feet high) are situated north and south, respectively, of Shechem (27:12-13). The slopes of these two mountains form a natural amphitheater suitable for the occasion. Israel's history of disobedience and divine discipline was anticipated (28:15-68). The cursing ended with the threat of a complete reversal of the exodus, with Israel once again in captivity in Egypt (28:68). This threat became a prophecy of Israel's doom because it was a model of human sinfulness. Given the opportunity to know God, humans inevitably fail.

29:1–30:20 Banishment and Restoration

The third speech of Moses began by including all the future believers in Israel in the covenant's demands (29:14-15) and by another reference to the curses (29:22-28). There could only be one reason why Israel would fall into destruction—her disobedience (29:24-25); it would not be a failure of God's love. The way of blessing, however, was plain and open to all (29:29).

God's discipline of Israel would end when she returned to him with all her heart (30:2). This promise enlarged and confirmed the provisions in the Abrahamic covenant regarding the land (Gen. 12:1, 7; 13:12; 17:7-8).

Although the people of Israel possessed the "title deed" to the Promised Land, their living in the land and enjoying its blessings would be dependent upon their obedience. Any future restoration to blessings in the land would be conditional on their repentance (Deut. 30:1-5). This concept was crucial in the messages of the prophets, including John the Baptist and Jesus (Matt. 3:2; 4:17). Obedience to the law was possible for a believing Israelite (Deut. 30:11-13). Love and loyalty to God would result in life and prosperity (30:15-20), whereas disobedience and desertion would result in death and adversity. God would perform an inner act of purification (30:6). Again, the accessibility of blessing was stressed (30:11-20).

31:1–32:52 CORRECTIVE PICTURES

The section 31:1–32:52 brings together two seemingly opposing concepts. On the one hand, Moses was told by God of Israel's certain failure (31:16-19) but ultimate restoration (32:36-43), and he composed a song about both events (32:1-44). On the other hand, he exhorted Israel to be faithful (32:44-47). Those concepts formed the backbone of all future prophetic addresses to the redeemed. Failure is bound to come, but believers are not to be the ones who live in failure. That Moses was the original author

of the material in Deuteronomy is made clear by 31:9 (see also 31:24). Moses' song presented the entire span—past, present and future—of Israel's history. Every time the Israelites sang it they would bear witness of their agreement to the terms and implications of their covenant relationship with God. "Jeshurun" (32:15), which means "the upright one," is an honorific title or "pet name" for Israel. Although used in a positive context in 33:5, it is also used reproachfully in 32:15 to express the thought that Israel failed to meet God's ideal.

33:1-29 THE FINAL BLESSING OF MOSES

Although failure would come, ultimate restoration was always the final note to be sounded when God's redemption was in view. Moses' final blessing stressed the love of God (33:3) and the incomparability both of God (33:26) and of his redeemed people (33:29).

34:1-12 THE DEATH OF MOSES

God linked Moses' view of the Promised Land to his covenant with Abraham, Isaac, and Jacob (34:4) and then took Moses to be with himself (34:5). The book ends with the passing of Moses' authority to Joshua (34:9) and a final exclamation of Moses' greatness (34:10-12), a greatness only to be surpassed by the greater Prophet, Jesus Christ (18:15).

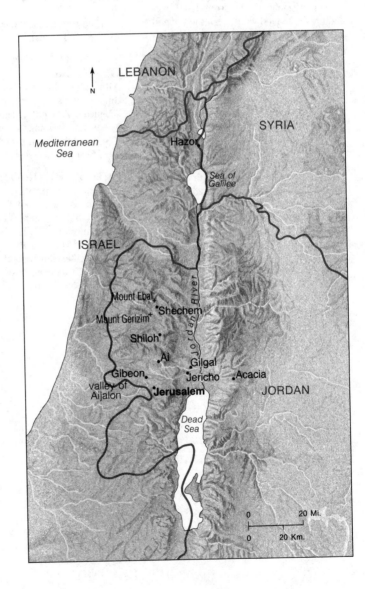

Joshua

BASIC FACTS

HISTORICAL SETTING

At the time of the conquest, Canaan was populated by a variety of people that
included Hittites, Amorites, Canaanites, Perizzites, Hivites and Jebusites (Josh. 9:1).
The Canaanites and Jebusites were native to the land. The Hittites were from Asia
Minor to the north, while the Amorites were from the Arabian Desert, and the
Hivites were from either the mountains of Seir (Gen. 36:20) or the mountains of
Lebanon (Gen. 10:17; Judg. 3:3). Little is known of the origin of the Perizzites. Most
of the inhabitants of Canaan lived in the lowlands rather than the hills, though there
were important cities in the hill country, including Kiriath Arba, Jebus, Luz and
Shechem. Canaan had been dominated earlier by Egypt, but from 1400 B.C. Egypt's
influence on the land of Canaan rapidly diminished.

The religions of Canaan were idolatrous and involved the worship of El, the
supreme god of the Canaanite pantheon, and Baal, his son and successor. Astarte,
Asherah, and Anath (who was a combination sister and spouse of Baal) were all
patronesses of sex and war. They were worshipped by the people of Canaan. Canaanite religion was so perverted that God actually drove the people out of the land in
judgment because of it (Gen. 15:16; Lev. 18:24-25; Deut. 9:4-5). Israel was
commanded to have nothing to do with the wicked ways of the people of Canaan
(Deut. 12:29-31).

AUTHOR

The central figure in the book is Joshua, who was appointed by God to bring the
people of Israel into the Promised Land (Deut. 31:14, 23). In his early life Joshua
distinguished himself in serving Moses (Exod. 17:9-13; 24:13). Moses had changed
his name from Hoshea to Joshua (Num. 13:16). Joshua and Caleb had brought back
the minority report after spying out the land (Num. 13:30; 14:6-9), and as a result
they were spared the judgment against the unbelieving Israelites.

Although the book is anonymous, it is reasonable to conclude from the following evidences that it was written from eyewitness and personal accounts by Joshua himself. Intimate biographical details, which only Joshua himself could have known, are given from the very first chapter (Josh. 1:2-9). Joshua wrote his own farewell address that is recorded in 24:1-25. In Joshua 5:1, 6 the first person plural is used, which points to the record of an eyewitness who had participated in the events.

Evidence of later editorial work is seen by the inclusion of events that occurred after Joshua's death (24:29-31; 15:13, 17; 19:47). Taken together, this evidence points to the substantial composition of Joshua by the man after whom the book is named. The supplementary material recording events after Joshua's death may have been added by Eleazar the high priest, or perhaps his son Phinehas.

DATE

The events of the book cover about thirty-one years from the beginning of the conquest (1406 B.C., taking an early date) to the death of Joshua around 1375 B.C. (24:29). While some hold to a late date for the book, there is evidence of an early date of composition. One argument in support of an early date for the book is that Canaanite cities are mentioned by their archaic names (15:9, 13, 49). The most direct evidence for an early date is that 13:4-6 and 19:28 indicate that Sidon was the most important city of Phoenicia. This indicates a date of writing before the twelfth century B.C. when Tyre began to grow in its power, taking supremacy from Sidon.

If Joshua was about the age of Caleb, who was 40 years old at the time of the mission into Canaan, then he would have died at about 1375 B.C. at 110 years of age (24:29). The book was written prior to the death of Joshua and most likely edited shortly thereafter.

PURPOSE

The purpose of Joshua was to show future readers that the Hebrews did ultimately conquer and occupy the Promised Land in accordance with God's divine purposes, demonstrating his faithfulness in keeping his covenant promises (Deut. 9:5).

GEOGRAPHY AND ITS IMPORTANCE

Israel's initial conquest of Palestine began with the taking of Jericho and the difficult climb up the west side of the Arabah Valley to conquer Ai. That first military campaign drove a wedge between the northern and southern regions of Palestine. Then, the campaign continued south to take Jerusalem and its surrounding regions. The last part of the initial conquest was to march north for a great victory at Hazor. Israel was able to take hold of the central mountain range of Palestine which gave them control over the east-west passages throughout the land. But Israel balked at fighting the Philistines who controlled the fertile coastal plains. The central, southern and northern campaigns provided rugged geographical and human opposition to display how God was the great warrior for his people and to test Israel's faith in his abilities.

GUIDING CONCEPTS

THE FORMER PROPHETS

The books of Joshua, Judges, 1 and 2 Samuel, and 1 and 2 Kings are known as the former prophets. (The latter prophets are Isaiah, Jeremiah, Ezekiel, Daniel, and Hosea through Malachi.) The former and latter prophets differ not only in the general time they were written but also in their style and content. The former prophets use historical narrative to communicate their goal, while the latter prophets in the main use prophetic speeches. The former prophets can be placed together to form a continuous historical story of Israel from Joshua's conquest to the Babylonian captivity, while the latter prophets present detailed prophetic speeches with very little historical narrative to help locate them in time. The essential difference between the two groups is their style and content. But both groups use their special contents to meet a common goal: the prophetic exhortation to the hearers to stop sinning and return to obeying God with grateful and awe-filled hearts.

The books of Joshua, Judges, Samuel and Kings are not just books of history; they have been received by God's people throughout the ages as books of prophecy. But they are not prophecy in the sense of telling the future. Rather, they are prophecy in the sense of proclaiming God's truth to instruct, challenge and encourage God's people. So, when these books are read they should not be viewed as dry history. They were purposely constructed from a pastoral perspective to provide messages of help to meet the needs of God's people.

GOD'S FAITHFULNESS

The book of Joshua is the culmination of God's promise to give the Israelites their own land (Gen. 12:1; 17:8). It is the record of the conquest of the land that God had promised to bring about (Deut. 7:1-2) and thus demonstrates God's faithfulness to his covenant with the patriarchs and the nation by settling the tribes in the Promised Land (Josh. 11:23; 21:43). Israel's victories were not attributed to her military skill and superiority, but to the power of God himself. While Joshua was Israel's leader and quite influential upon the spiritual lives of the people (24:31), the book makes it clear that the credit for the conquest belonged to God alone (3:10; 4:23-24; 5:13-14; 6:16; 21:44; 23:3, 9-10). The book emphasizes God's faithfulness in bringing about all that he had promised to do for the young nation of Israel.

God's covenant faithfulness also is seen in his provision of a leader to follow Moses. The man he selected had proven his faithfulness by encouraging Israel to be bold enough to enter the land in spite of its dangers (Num. 14:6-10, 29-30). Only Joshua and Caleb from the old generation were allowed to enter the land. God himself selected Joshua as the leader of his people (Num. 27:15-23; Deut. 31:23). Joshua's name in Hebrew means "God is salvation." That name in Greek was Jesus, the name given to the Lord because he would save his people (Matt. 1:21).

ISRAEL'S FAITHFULNESS

Central to the success of God's people was their obedience to the word of God, which, for them, was the law handed down by Moses. Both the leader, Joshua, and the people were to meditate on the law day and night in order for them to have success (Josh. 1:8; 8:32-35; 23:6-16; 24:26-27). Human effort alone was not able to bring victory. Only the blessing brought by obedience was the way to enter the fullness of God's promises.

GOD'S HOLINESS

God's holiness is seen in his command that Israel completely exterminate the inhabitants of Canaan (6:21; 8:26; Deut. 20:16). That judgment was the natural expression of God's holiness manifesting itself against sin and wickedness. God had long before promised that the inhabitants of Canaan were due for divine judg-ment—a prophesy fulfilled four hundred years later (Gen. 15:16; cf. Deut. 7:3-6). The moment of judg-ment had now come. As with all of God's promises, it never matters how much time elapses between his making of a promise and its fulfill-ment. His word of blessing or judgment will always be fulfilled. That aspect of God also relates to his own people. He shows no favorites and does not overlook the sins of his people. Israel was to have no other gods (Exod. 20:3; cf. Deut. 5:7, which restates Exod. 20:3). The holiness of God also is seen in his pronouncement of judgment upon the sin of Achan (Josh. 7:10-15).

BIBLE-WIDE CONCEPTS

PUTTING AN END TO SIN
Sin, Judgment, and Grace

The first Bible-wide contribution of Joshua concerns God's judgment on sin. Ever since the Garden of Eden, God had shown himself to be utterly against humanity's "no" to his desires. However, even in the face of his gracious long-suffering, human beings continued to deepen their commitment to do what they wanted instead of what he wanted. That unfortunate situation put God's reputation in jeopardy. Why did he not put an end to all the injustice and cruelty of humanity? If he really hated sin, why did he not stop it? Was he not strong enough? Or had he softened in his acceptance of sin? Did not the fact that he used sin to accom-plish his own ends betray some kind of sinister compromise of his holiness? Those questions have been asked or implied by both rebellious and pious people throughout Bible times to the present.

These questions, besides assuming that God has to justify his actions to mortals, miss one key point that pervades Scripture from Genesis to Joshua and is cemented in the Noahic covenant: God desires people's salvation more than their damnation. The Noahic covenant teaches that God will put up with people's sin in order to give them time to repent. The length of time he does so indicates the depth of his grace. So far, it has been thousands and thousands of years. However, his time of grace for repentance will come to an end, and that is what was seen happening to the people of Canaan in the book of Joshua. They had been given four hundred years to repent, but they did not respond (Gen. 15:13-16). The time for judgment had arrived. Much earlier, the world before the flood had been given 120 years to repent (Gen. 6:3) before its judgment came. Israel itself was given hundreds of years of opportunity in the Promised Land before the desolation of the land and the captivities of the people took place. Presently, the entire world has been given thousands of years, but its end will come at the Lord's return. And, individually, each person has been given a limited stretch of years on this earth to respond to God's ways.

Jericho and the Book of Revelation

In the nation's march around the city of Jericho, the imagery of the seven trumpets announcing God's presence enthroned above the Ark of the Covenant anticipated the seven cosmic trumpets of the book of Revelation that signal the mighty presence of God from the Ark of the Covenant in the heavenly temple (Rev. 8:2; 11:19). What was just one city in Joshua becomes the entire globe in the book of Revelation. The downfall of Jericho and the land of Canaan is simply one more picture of both God's grace and judgment. The time he gives for repentance shows his love. The flash of final judgment shows that he indeed has been in control. He does not overlook sin, and he is not too weak to judge. God's judgments are designed to show his inevitable evaluation of disobedience and evil, and in doing so he justifies both his holy character and his long-suffering compassion.

Judgment as Cleansing

God's judgment also paved the way for his people to receive their divine promises of redemption. The flood cleansed the earth for Noah's new, though unsuccessful, start. The death of the old generation of Israelites in the wilderness cleansed the nation for its new start in the land of Palestine. The destruction of the Canaanites cleansed the land for the holy tribes of Israel. And the destruction of the present heavens and earth will provide the final cleansing of the universe for the new and totally successful beginning for God's redeemed people.

A PROMISED LAND

What was so important about the particular plot of ground now called the Holy Land? We know that it was promised to Abraham. But there is something more important about it that stretches all the way back to the creation. God created the entire universe but began its human population on a small scale: two people in a small location called Eden. The people were told to multiply and spread over the whole earth and extend the perfection of the Garden of Eden worldwide. Likewise, the small band of Noah's family was to have another chance to provide worldwide blessing. In the same way, Israel was to start small and to extend God's blessings to the entire world. God has always had the entire world in view even though he has at various times started his plan for blessing the world with only a few people in a small location. Adam and Eve in Eden, Noah grounded on the mountains of Ararat, and the people of Israel in Palestine all represent new beginnings to God's plan for worldwide blessing.

So when God gave the land of Palestine to Israel, he simply gave another beginning with the goal of making possible a world right with God. The land was a down payment for a worldwide inheritance. That is what believers will see at the end of this age when there is a new start, this time in a new heavens and earth. The heavenly city of Revelation is described, in part, in terms taken from the Garden of Eden (Rev. 22:1-2). And God's rule and blessing will forever extend around the real Promised Land: heaven on earth. What is so important about the Holy Land? It foreshadows the perfect rest yet to come. It points toward the holy perfection of which Palestine is just a shadow.

GOD THE WARRIOR

Certainly the main thrust of the book of Joshua teaches that God was the warrior who fought for Israel in order to give all that he had promised to the nation of Israel. But why did the promise have to come through bloody battle? Back in Genesis 15:13, God had told Abraham that after a period of four hundred years of captivity in a foreign land, Abraham's children would return to Palestine. The reason for the four-hundred-year delay was then given: "for the sin of the Amorites has not yet reached its full measure" (Gen. 15:16). God had a plan, not made known to us, for the Amorites (Amorites is a general term used to describe all the inhabitants of Palestine). After that four-hundred-year period, Israel would return to take the land and, at that time, the sin of the inhabitants of Palestine would come to an end. Thus, Israel's return to the Promised Land was directly related to putting an end to the Canaanites' evil.

Israel's return would carry out God's judgment for iniquity (cf. Lev. 18:24-25). That explains why Israel's receipt of the land had to come through the divine warfare of judgment and also why Israel was not to take any of the spoils of the initial cities, which were holy to the Lord's judgment. The judgment was the Lord's; therefore, the battle was the Lord's (Josh. 1:2, 15; 10:14). Thus, the Lord described the giving of the land to Israel as a gift from him (1:2-3). The giving of the land was an accomplished fact from God's perspective of sovereignty and power even before the conquest began. Just as Abraham was instructed to rise up and walk through the Promised Land (Gen. 13:17), so Joshua could know that each step he took had been prepared for him by God (Josh. 1:3).

Because God was the warrior, Israel had hope for the future. God would give them rest (1:13-14; 22:4). That rest was, in part, anticipated in the days of Noah (Gen. 5:29). It was a rest that would give relief from the awful toils brought on by God's curse on Adam's sin. In this age, spiritual rest has been ushered in by Christ's death and resurrection which allowed the Holy Spirit to enter the lives of believers in a new and intimate way. Ultimately, the promised rest will come in its fullness in the new heavens and earth. God will never forsake or leave those who trust in him (Josh. 1:5; Matt. 28:20).

NEEDS MET BY JOSHUA

Israel needed to know several important facts that the book of Joshua supplied. The nation had been disciplined for her past failures to enter the land, but God's promise was not voided by disobedience. Israel was now poised to enter the Promised Land. Moses was dead but God would not leave the nation without a leader to bring them into God's promise. And once again God brought his chosen people from one difficult situation to another. He took them from Egypt into the wilderness to test their hearts (Deut. 8:1-5), and he was about to test his people again.

The taking of the Promised Land would not be easy. Although God's people had to do the physical fighting, their spiritual battle was to always affirm the invisible presence of the Lord at their side and to obey him. Past failures were forgotten, Joshua was God's leader and God himself was always present for victory. The following questions allude to the major needs met by the book of Joshua.

- How did God prove his commitment to give Israel the Promised Land?
- If God was powerful enough to give his people victory, what were the reasons they failed from time to time?
- What kind of leader did God provide after Moses?
- What was God's chosen leader like and what was the key to his success?
- Why did God not give his people immediate and complete victory?
- Why did God let his people go through an ongoing process of battles and challenges?
- Why was the Mosaic covenant crucial to the success of God's people in gaining the Promised Land?

The book of Joshua provides answers to these important questions. It is not made up of dry historical facts; it is alive with the author's purpose to help God's people face the challenges of ongoing battle, remain true to God's salvation, and enjoy the rewards of their victories. Israel seemed to always be in one fight or another. The Israelites no doubt wished they could just stop having to struggle all the time. Even after their military takeover of the land they would still have to struggle with the battles caused by personal and national sin. Christians may sometimes feel the same way. Will there never be a time to relax? Although Christians do not fight physical battles for the Promised Land, they fight the same spiritual fight as Israel of old. And, like Israel, the redemption of believers today has not lifted them out of the struggles of the world. If anything, their redemption has more sharply defined the nature of the enemy, the locations of the battlefields, and the only powerful way to victory.

OUTLINE OF JOSHUA

A. CONQUERING THE LAND (1:1–12:24)
1. The Central Campaign (1:1–10:28)
2. The Southern Campaign (10:29-43)
3. The Northern Campaign (11:1-23)
4. The Review of the Conquest (12:1-24)

B. DIVIDING THE LAND (13:1–22:34)
1. The Remaining Land (13:1-7)
2. The Transjordan (13:8-33)
3. Canaan (14:1–22:34)

C. EXHORTATION TO OBEDIENCE AND COVENANT REAFFIRMATION (23:1–24:33)

JOSHUA NOTES

1:1–12:24 CONQUERING THE LAND

Overview: Joshua 1–12 takes the reader from the crossing of the Jordan River to the destruction of Jericho; the failure at Ai; and the initial subduing of the north, south, and central portions of the Promised Land. The major themes are the saving power of God, the fierce opposition of the Canaanites, and the alternating fear and faith of the Israelites.

More specifically, Joshua 1–10 emphasizes: Joshua's God-given authority as the next leader in line after Moses (Josh. 1); the careful preparations for (Josh. 2) and actual taking of Jericho (Josh. 6), separated by a detailed section on the preparation of God's children to carry out his warfare by personal consecration and the crossing of the Jordan (Josh. 3–4), by their circumcision and the celebration of the Passover (Josh. 5). God would do the initial fighting, but his people were responsible to be pure before him. Joshua 7–8 details the people's first failure because of Achan's sin and the second victory as the nation purified itself and fought against Ai. Joshua 9 records Israel's mistake of making a covenant with the people of Gibeon who were Canaanites who should have been destroyed. That covenant obligated Israel to protect Gibeon from its enemies, an obligation that resulted in Israel's great victory in the valley of Aijalon where the sun and moon stood still (Josh. 10).

1:1–10:28 The Central Campaign

1:1-9 INTRODUCTION
Joshua 1:1-9 presents the following themes: (1) the giving of the land by God himself (cf. 1:11, 13, 15); (2) Joshua as the mediator of God's victory (1:5-6, 9); (3) the land as a promise to Abraham (1:6); and (4) the centrality of obedience to the conditions of Moses' covenant (1:7-8). Joshua's meditation on the word of God was to focus on obedience. From that obedience came the automatic presence of God to save.

God had promised this land to Abraham (1:3-4; cf. Gen. 15:18-21). It was a gift, but possession required Israel's corresponding military action. Divine sovereignty and human responsibility complement one another. Obedience (Josh. 1:7) enables a person to live according to God's divine order and thus enjoy God's best (cf. Deut. 30:15-20). The word "meditate" (Josh. 1:8) means to speak in an undertone, and it involves recitation as well as memorization.

1:10-18 THE LAND AS REST
Joshua 1:10-18 emphasizes that the giving of the land to Israel was equal to their receiving rest (1:13, 15), and that the strength and courage of Joshua, Israel's leader, was to be based on his full obedience to the word of God. Joshua's obedience was immediate and exemplary, which was especially significant because the Jordan River was at flood stage (3:15) and crossing it would be especially difficult. The Transjordanian tribes are the focus in 1:12-18 (cf. 12:1-6).

2:1-24 JOSHUA AND CALEB SPY OUT THE LAND
The spies were sent out secretly, perhaps because of what the public report by the spies sent out by Moses had brought about (Num. 13–14). Rahab's confession acknowledged that God had given Israel the land. She requested a blessing that reflected belief in what God had said in Genesis 12:3, that is, that he would bless those who blessed Abraham's line. The report that the hearts of the Canaanites had melted (Josh. 2:11, 24) continued the response to God's great works seen in kings Sihon and Og in Numbers 21:21-35. Attempts have been made since early times to represent Rahab as merely an innkeeper, but the Hebrew word confirms that she was a prostitute. Her house would have been a good place to spend the night unnoticed. Situated on the wall (Josh. 2:15), it allowed for the possibility, if necessary, of a secret escape by the spies.

But if God already had promised victory, why did Joshua choose to spy out the land? Joshua obviously discerned the need to exercise his human responsibility, understanding his part in accomplishing God's promised victory. But whatever was Joshua's specific reason, the point of the story lies in Rahab's confession of God's great power as well as his mercy. That confession earned Rahab a place in Scripture as one of the great people of faith (Matt. 1:5; Heb. 11:31). Rahab lied to protect the Israelite spies. Many have sought to justify her actions based on the situation, but that is unnecessary. What the New Testament commends here is her faith (Heb. 11:31), not the lie that she told. God could have protected the spies even if she had told the truth. Rahab's confession was much like that made earlier by Moses (Deut. 4:39).

3:1-17 THE CROSSING OF THE JORDAN
The Ark led the way into the Jordan River (Josh. 3:1-4), remained in the middle while the nation crossed (3:17), and was the sign of the presence of the God of heaven (3:11). A distance of a thousand yards (2,000 cubits) was to be kept between the people and the Ark (3:3). The people were consecrated (3:5), and the great crossing was God's way of exalting Joshua before the nation (3:7). The crossing of the Jordan River was as significant for these Israelites as the crossing of the Red Sea had been for their parents. The Jordan River was blocked by a landslide in A.D. 1267 for sixteen hours, and again in 1927 for twenty-one hours. However, the mention that the river was at flood stage at the time of Israel's crossing and that the people crossed on dry ground suggests a miraculous event (cf. 5:1). The crossing of the Jordan River took place in the spring of the year at the time of the barley harvest (3:15). That was a difficult time to ford the Jordan River due to the flooding that always resulted from the spring run of the melting snow on Mount Hermon. This miraculous event would fortify the Israelites' faith for the struggles that lay ahead of them (3:10). Joshua was exalted because God showed his presence with him.

4:1-24 MEMORIAL STONES FROM THE CROSSING
The stones that were set up both in the middle of the Jordan River and on the other side were to serve as future reminders that Israel had once been in the middle of the river and that God had taken them over to the other side (4:9, 20). The date (4:19) was probably Nisan (March–April) 10, 1406 B.C. Gilgal was the first Israelite camp in Canaan. While the exact location is uncertain, many have identified it with Khirbet el-Mefjer, two and one-half miles northeast of Jericho (see introductory map). The crossing of the

Jordan River is paralleled with the crossing of the Red Sea (4:23). It was a sign of God's might designed to help the people to remember and reverence God forever (4:24).

5:1-15 THE ABRAHAMIC COVENANT IS HONORED
The response of the Canaanites (5:1) to Israel's crossing of the Jordan River was linked to 4:24: "so that all the peoples of the earth might know." The circumcision of the male Israelites was their last link to "the reproach of Egypt," that is, of their ties to the journey out of Egypt to Canaan (5:9). The rite of circumcision, the sign of the Abrahamic covenant (Gen. 17:9-14), was not observed during the forty years of Israel's wilderness wanderings. Joshua renewed the rite, which was symbolic of the obedience promised by the second generation (Josh. 1:17). The Israelites' observance of the Passover in the land and their eating of food in the Promised Land broke their last tie with the exodus from Egypt. The manna ceased (5:12). As the Lord had appeared to Moses (Exod. 3), so he appeared to Joshua. Where the army of God was, in this case in front of Jericho, that place was holy (Josh. 5:13-15).

6:1-27 JERICHO IS DESTROYED
The message God gave to Joshua in 5:13-14 was elaborated (6:1-5). Jericho, one of the oldest fortified cities in the ancient Near East, was west of the Jordan River and six miles north of the Dead Sea. The key phrase is "I [the Lord] have delivered" (6:2), which was shouted in 6:16 as Israel actually took the city. The instructions for the conquest reveal that the city was to be overthrown by God's power, not military might. Rams' horns were generally used for religious, not military, festivals (cf. Exod. 19:16, 19; and Lev. 23:24; 25:9), while silver trumpets were used for announcing wars (Num. 10:2-10). Thus, the use of rams' horns shows that the taking of Jericho fell under the heading of a religous rather than a military activity.

The city was given by God through his judgment and was to be returned as an offering to him. Therefore, no human being was to receive any of the city's goods, for what was taken was to be God's exclusive property. Anything that could not be burned was to be placed in the sanctuary. The battle needed to be fought for two reasons: (1) sin needed to be punished; and (2) Israel's purity needed to be maintained (Deut. 9:5; Lev. 18:24-30). Israel was engaged in a holy war. It was no ordinary kind of battle, and it will occur only once again—at the second coming of the Lord.

The purpose of the seven rams' horns before the Ark was to announce the presence of the King of the universe. That announcement was made once each day for six days. The seventh day brought the perfection of God's judgment on Jericho and his promise of giving the city to Israel. To take anything from the city would bring a curse on the nation (Josh. 6:18). Achan would soon violate that command (7:1). The fall of Jericho is a capsule picture of God's judgment. Everything was destroyed, and any material objects that could not be burned were holy to the Lord.

The promise of redemption for Rahab and her family came about because she had hid the messengers of Israel (6:22-25). In the sovereignty of God, Rahab was spared (6:25) and became the great-grandmother of David (Ruth 4:21) and an ancestor of Christ (Matt. 1:5-6). Jericho was to remain ruined as a picture of God's attitude toward sin. The curse for rebuilding Jericho (Josh. 6:26) was fulfilled a long time later during the reign of Ahab (1 Kings 16:34).

7:1-26 THE SIN OF ACHAN

There is considerable debate regarding the location of Ai (see introductory map). The traditional identification, et-Tell, was not occupied at the time of the conquest. The defeat of Israel at Ai caused Joshua to question why God ever brought his people into the land only to let them be defeated. Joshua mistakenly thought the problem was with God. The sin of Achan illustrates how one person can influence the fate of the entire nation. The ban on taking anything from Jericho had been violated, and the entire nation suffered the consequences of defeat.

The Israelites began to wonder why God had let them down (Josh. 7:7). But the whole story of Achan's judgment was designed to show clearly to Israel that the problem was with them, not with God. Stones with markings indicating yes and no were cast like dice. God used this procedure to make his will known (Prov. 16:33). Achan's confes-

sion was to give glory to God by showing what the problem was (Josh. 7:19). In view of the prohibition against executing children for the sins of their parents (Deut. 24:16), it may be assumed that Achan's children were accomplices. However, the point of the story goes beyond who did and did not sin. Thirty-six innocent men suffered death in the first battle against Ai because of Achan's sin (Josh. 7:5).

This judgment on the house of Achan was a severe first-time lesson for the nation and takes its place in a line of similar actions by God throughout Scripture. There was the severe first-time lesson of the fall of Adam (Gen. 3); the flood (Gen. 6–8); the judgment on the worship of the golden calf (Exod. 32); the wilderness wanderings (Num. 14); and the deaths of Ananias and Sapphira (Acts 5). Surely someone else took things that were holy to God. Surely someone else worshiped an idol. Surely someone else lied to the church about his giving. But God makes his points in severe first-time lessons and then moves on in patience and grace. He desires that his people will learn their lessons without having to undergo catastrophic destruction every time they disobey.

8:1-35 AI IS DESTROYED

With purity restored and through clever military tactics, Israel was able to defeat Ai. God reconfirmed his promise of giving the land (Josh. 8:1) and the Israelites reconfirmed their commitment to him after their victory. They went to Mount Ebal and Mount Gerizim and reconfirmed the covenant God had made with them at Sinai (8:30-35). That fulfilled God's commands given in Deuteronomy 11:26-30 and 27:11-14. The covenant-renewal ceremony, begun on the plains of Moab (Deut. 12:26), was to be concluded in Canaan (Deut. 27:2-8). Shechem, situated between Mount Ebal and Mount Gerizim, was probably subjugated by Joshua at this time (cf. Josh. 11:19).

9:1-27 A COVENANT WITH THE CANAANITES

Gibeon is located at el-Jib, six miles northwest of Jerusalem (see introductory map). The Gibeonites deceived Israel into making a treaty with them. They must have known that Israel was permitted to make peace with the people who lived in far-off cities, but not with those from cities in the Promised Land. The Gibeonites' confession (9:24-25) showed that the nations rightly understood the great power of God on Israel's behalf. A covenant with the Canaanites flew in the face of God's command to destroy all of them. Israel's leaders failed to ask for the Lord's counsel (9:14) and relied instead upon their own ability to discern what was right. Thus, they violated God's commands in Exodus 23:32; 34:12 and Deuteronomy 7:2. Much later, this covenant with the Gibeonites was violated by King Saul, with devastating results (2 Sam. 21:1-6). The judgment mentioned in Joshua 9:27 may have had an evangelistic intent. It would expose the Gibeonites to God's continual revelation as displayed at the tabernacle.

10:1-28 GOD HONORS THE COVENANT WITH THE CANAANITES
Israel's alliance with Gibeon resulted in the nation having to fight to defend Gibeon against the coalition of five Canaanite kings. The march from Gilgal to Gibeon was twenty-four miles. God clearly promised Israel the victory (10:8, 19, 25) and even gave them a miraculous extension of daylight to finish the battle (10:12-14). The key to this section and to the conquest of the Promised Land as a whole is seen in 10:14: "the Lord was fighting for Israel!"

There are three basic interpretations of Joshua's long day: (1) Poetic interpretation: The story is poetry and not to be taken literally. The sun only seemed to stand still because of the weariness of the soldiers and the heat of the battle. (2) Total-eclipse view: On the basis of Babylonian astronomical texts, the words "stand still" (10:12) are rendered "became dark" or "eclipsed." (3) The prolongation-of-light view: The passage is taken literally to mean that Joshua was miraculously allowed to complete the battle before darkness set in. That may have taken place as a result of a passing comet (a theory of Velikovsky), the tilting of the earth's axis, or the refraction of the sun's rays on a local level. The Book of Jashar (10:13) may have been a history of Israel's wars in which some important events and great men were commemorated poetically (cf. 2 Sam. 1:18).

Joshua followed the custom of ancient conquerers to impress his army captains with

the significance of this victory (Josh. 10:24). Putting their feet on the necks of the kings symbolized the complete subjection of the enemy. (Cf. 10:27 with Deuteronomy 21:22-23.)

10:29-43 The Southern Campaign
This next section surveys the southern conquest. Israel had first driven a wedge between the north and south of Canaan, thus destroying the Canaanites' ability for unified opposition. Again, God fought for the nation (10:42). The purpose of Israel's initial campaigns through the middle of the land of Canaan and then the southern and northern parts was to make a preliminary conquest of the entire land. Not all of the land was taken, and some areas had to be retaken later (15:13-17). But these initial raids by the entire nation knocked out the key military centers and prepared the way for each tribe to go in and finish the conquest within its own apportioned area.

11:1-23 The Northern Campaign
A survey of the northern campaign is given in 11:1-15. Hazor was a very large and strategic Canaanite city located about ten miles north of the Sea of Galilee. North of Galilee, near Mount Merom, many kings assembled to make a last-ditch effort to stop Israel's conquest. Merom, noted for its large spring, was situated about seven miles southwest of Hazor. Again God made it clear that it was his battle and that victory was assured (11:6). Joshua was commanded to hamstring the horses, which disabled the animals for military activity by cutting the back sinews of the hind leg. They could still pull a plow but could not be used in battle. The remark to burn the cities (11:13) refers to the northern campaign. Both Jericho and Ai were also burned (6:24; 8:19).

The key phrase for defining the nature of this conquest is in 11:15 and 20. This all happened in complete obedience to the Lord's commands through Moses to Joshua. The entire campaign is summarized in 11:16-23, ending with the note that the Anakites (also spelled, Anakim, cf. KJV) were destroyed (11:21-22). The Anakites were the giants who brought so much fear to Israel earlier when the nation failed to have faith in God's ability to bring them into the land (cf. Num. 13:33, where they are called Nephilim, sons of Anak). The Nephilim were fearsome, but they always had to be viewed by Israel as being under God's power. Even though they were strong, there were Nephilim who had been destroyed in the flood (Gen.6:4), others who were killed in the conquest (Josh. 11:21-22), and Goliath who was killed later by David (1 Sam. 17:45-51). All of the people of Canaan, with the exception of the Gibeonites, were hardened by God, like Pharaoh, so that God might show his wrath against sin and his mercy to his chosen people.

The conquest of Canaan and the division of the land took about seven years to complete. Caleb was forty years old when Moses sent spies the first time into the land, and he was eighty-five at the time of Joshua's division of the land (Josh. 14:7-10). The final division of the land took place six or seven years after Israel entered the land. Joshua took the whole land, as God had promised (1:2-5), but that did not mean that the work was all done. While the military strength of the inhabitants of Canaan had been broken, much of the land was still not occupied (13:2-6). It would be the responsibility of the individual tribes to subjugate and occupy their designated territories.

12:1-24 The Review of the Conquest

The entire initial conquest was summarized by noting the Transjordan victories (12:1-6), then those of southern (12:8-16) and northern Canaan (12:17-24). The only information regarding how long these campaigns took is in 11:18. It was a period of about five years (cf. 14:10).

13:1–22:34 DIVIDING THE LAND

Overview: The section of 13:1–22:34 narrates the division of the land by highlighting Israel's failures and faith in finalizing the conquest (13:1–19:51). Even at the end of Joshua's life, not all of Canaan had been taken from the former inhabitants of that land (23:4-5). After the twelve tribes were alloted their lands, the cities for refuge and for the Levites were assigned (20:1–21:45). The building of an altar by the Transjordanian tribes in Canaan nearly brought about a civil war (22:1-34). The book concludes with the last addresses of Joshua,

which include a plea for faithfulness (23:1-16) and a witness to Israel's reaffirmation of the covenant (24:1-34).

13:1-7 The Remaining Land

Joshua 13 begins at the end of Joshua's life (13:1). The initial campaigns by the entire nation of Israel were in the past, and each tribe still had much work to do in trusting the Lord for complete victory. Much land remained to be captured. Joshua apportioned the Transjordan lands (13:2-33) and then the lands within Canaan (14:1–19:51). The detailed description of the tribal boundaries may seem very uninteresting to the contemporary reader, but these records served as the title deed for Israel's inheritance in the land. The tribes would have been extremely interested in these accurate and detailed boundary descriptions. Detailed descriptions of God's physical blessings of promise and redemption can be just as meaningful as descriptions of his spiritual blessings.

13:8-33 The Transjordan

The Transjordan lands, located east of the Jordan River, were apportioned to the two and a half tribes in the way that Moses had divided them (13:8, 15, 24, 29, 32; 14:5). The lands within Canaan were apportioned to the remaining tribes by the priest Eleazar, Joshua, and the heads of the households of the tribes (14:1).

14:1–22:34 Canaan

14:1–19:51 LAND FOR THE TWELVE TRIBES
The land was divided among the twelve tribes by lot (14:2; Num. 34:16-29) and according to need, which was determined by the size of each tribe (Num. 26:54-56). The general location was determined by the casting of lots, while the amount of territory given depended upon the tribe's size. Joshua 14:7-10 records information that makes it possible to calculate the conquest's duration. Caleb was forty years old at the time of the exodus and was eighty-five after forty years in the wilderness and the five years of the conquest. Caleb received as his personal inheritance the city of Hebron, known earlier as the city of Arba (15:13). Joseph's sons, Manasseh and Ephraim (16:4), took his place as tribal heads among the tribes of Israel (Gen. 48:5). Gezer (Josh. 16:10), a strategic fortress city on the coastal plain, did not

come under full Israelite control until the days of Solomon (1 Kings 9:16). Shiloh (Josh. 18:1), located in the hill country of Ephraim twenty miles north of Jerusalem, was to serve as Israel's political and religious center for the next three hundred years.

In fulfillment of Jacob's prophetic judgment (Gen. 49:5-7), the tribe of Simeon received no land inheritance of its own (Josh. 19:1-9). But Simeon did inherit seventeen cities within the large tribal territory of Judah. Some of the Simeonites later migrated north (2 Chron. 15:9; 34:6). Dan's allotment was very vulnerable to the Philistine menace (Josh. 19:40-48), and a remnant of the tribe later migrated north to Leshem (Laish), which they captured and renamed Dan (Judg. 18).

Throughout this long section describing the division of the land among the twelve tribes, notes of both faith and fear were sounded: Caleb's faith and resulting conquest (Josh. 14:11-15; 15:13-19); Judah's inability to drive out the Jebusites (15:63); Ephraim's inability to drive out the Canaanites in Gezer (16:10); Manasseh's inability to drive out the Canaanites (17:11-13); Ephraim and Manasseh's fear of the Canaanites (17:14-18); and the procrastination of seven tribes in taking their lands (18:2-3).

20:1-9 CITIES OF REFUGE
After the land was divided, cities of refuge were established, as Moses had instructed (20:1-9; Num. 35:9-34, Deut. 4:41-43; 19:1-3). Three were located east and three were west of the Jordan River. See the accompanying chart.

The cities of refuge were to give protection from revenge to someone who accidentally killed a person (cf. Deut. 19:1-13; 21:1-9; Num. 35:9-29). This concept went back to the Noahic covenant (Gen. 9) and the prohibition against murder. The person who had accidentally killed someone had to stay in the city where he had fled until the death of the current high priest (Num. 35:25-28).

21:1-45 CITIES FOR THE LEVITES
Yet another fulfillment of God's commands through Moses was the allotting of the cities for the Levites (Josh. 21:2-3). Those forty-eight cities were selected in locations that would make it possible for the Levites to provide a spiritual influence throughout all of the twelve tribes of Israel. The presence of those cities was also a reminder of the true inheritance of the Levites, and all of Israel as well: the Lord himself (13:33).

22:1-34 THE TRANSJORDAN ALTAR
Before returning across the Jordan River to their own lands, the Transjordanian tribes built a copy of the altar of sacrifice (22:10). The rest of the Israelites perceived their act to be one of idolatry (22:17) as well as a potential bringer of God's anger (22:18). The erection of the altar appeared to be a violation of the law of Deuteronomy 12:13-14 that required a central sanctuary. But the Transjordanian tribes explained that the altar was only a symbol to unify worship and was never to be used for sacrifices. The rest of the Israelites accepted that explanation (Josh. 22:26-29) and a civil war was avoided (22:33). Such a war would have been in accordance with Deuteronomy 13:12-18, which required the Israelites to destroy an apostate city.

23:1–24:33 EXHORTATION TO OBEDIENCE AND COVENANT REAFFIRMATION
An address was given by Joshua near the end of his life (Josh. 23). He commended Israel to have faith in God's ability to drive out the rest of the nations still remaining in the land (23:1-5) and to faithfulness in serving God alone (23:6-11). Like Moses, Joshua emphasized the curses of the covenant that would fall upon the disobedient (23:12-16; cf. Lev. 23:14-33; Deut. 28:15-68). He ended this message by noting God's unfailing

---

THE CITIES OF REFUGE

West	East
Kedesh in Galilee	Bezer in Reuben
Shechem in Ephraim	Ramoth in Gilead
Hebron in Judah	Golan in Bashan

consistency. God would bless obedience and punish disobedience.

Joshua's final address to Israel (Josh. 24) took place at Shechem. It was a formal renewal of the covenant that God had made with Israel through Moses. The preamble of his address rehearsed God's faithful election of Israel (24:1-2). The historical section told of God's redemption in detail (24:3-13). The next section called upon Israel to witness and reconfirm her allegiance to God's covenant (24:14-24). The final section tells about Joshua writing and storing the renewed covenant in the "Book of the Law of God" as a witness to the events of that day (24:25-28).

Some scholars have suggested that the hornet of 24:12 was the sacred symbol of the pharaohs and that the Egyptians had softened up the people of Canaan by fighting against them shortly before Israel's conquest. But God's sending of the hornet was still a future event on the eve of the conquest (Deut. 7:20). See the comments on Exodus 23:28 for another suggestion. The words "You are not able to serve the Lord" (Josh. 24:19) were intended to impress the Israelites with the weight of the responsibility before them. The statement "He will not forgive" was not a general rule (cf. 1 John 1:9), but it is to be understood in the context of certain divine judgment for denying God (Josh. 24:20; cf. Num. 15:30).

Joshua ordered the tribes to convene at Shechem (Josh. 24:1; cf. Deut. 27:4-8, 12-26) for a public reading of the covenant's terms and a renewal of the covenant relationship. Joshua 24:1-28 follows the outline of the ancient treaties between a king and his subjects (cf. Exod. 19–24). See the accompanying chart.

The conclusion of the book of Joshua rounded out the key themes of the books of Genesis through Deuteronomy. Joshua, Moses' successor, died. Joseph's bones found their final resting place in the Promised Land. And Eleazar, a son of Aaron, died. After many years, God had brought Abraham's descendants to the land that he had promised them. The years of wandering had come to a close and the era of the judges was about to begin.

JOSHUA 24 AS A VASSAL TREATY

24:1-2	The Preamble
24:2-13	The Historical Prologue
24:14-25	The Covenant Stipulations
24:26-27	The Deposit of the Covenant

Judges

BASIC FACTS

HISTORICAL SETTING

Most of Israel's oppressors of this period were local enemies near the borders of Canaan, for during this time in world history the large powers of the ancient Near East were not engaged in active domination of Palestine. Egypt's rulers after Amenhotep III were weaker and no longer interested in the control of Palestine. Mitanni, of northern Mesopotamia, was curtailed in strength due to the rise in power of the Hittites under Shuppiluliumas. Assyria and Babylon, farther to the east, did not play a significant role in Palestine at this time. The foreign oppressors that successively attacked Israel were the Mesopotamians, the Moabites, the Canaanites, the Midianites, the Ammonites and, most seriously of all, the Philistines.

AUTHOR

There is no clear indication in the book as to the identity of the author. According to tradition, Samuel was the author, although this tradition is difficult to substantiate. It is known that Samuel was a writer (1 Sam. 10:25), and he may have authored the book. The evidence concerning the date of writing (see below) would indicate that Judges was at least written by a contemporary of Samuel. The final editing of the book was completed during the monarchies of David and Solomon.

DATE

The following internal evidences point to an early origin of Judges, sometime during the monarchies of David and Solomon: (1) Judges 1:21 indicates that the Jebusites were still living in Jerusalem at the date of writing. This shows an ongoing Jebusite presence such as is noted in 2 Samuel 24:16, where David purchased the temple site from Araunah the Jebusite. (2) Judges 1:29 declares that the Canaanites were still living in Gezer, which indicates a date of composition prior to when the city was captured by Pharaoh and given as a dowry to his daughter, Solomon's wife (1 Kings 9:16). (3) Judges 3:3 indicates that Sidon, rather than Tyre, was the chief city of

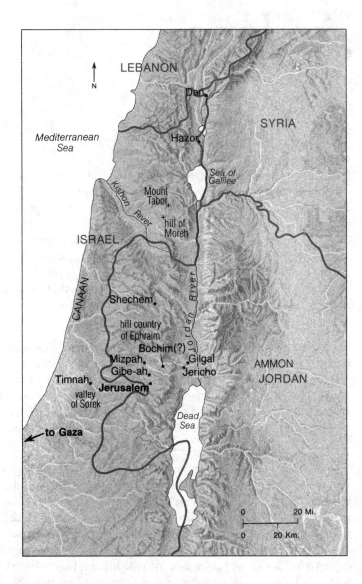

Phoenicia, which points to a date of writing around 1040 B.C., prior to Tyre's rise in influence. (4) The reference to the absence of a king in Israel (Judg. 17:6; 18:1; 21:25) implies composition in the early monarchy while the blessings and benefits of the monarchy were in the forefront of the people's minds.

The book of Judges presents a problem of chronology. If all of the terms of office of the judges are totaled, they equal 410 years. However, 1 Kings 6:1 states that only 480 years elapsed between the exodus and Solomon's fourth year when he began to build the temple. That leaves only 70 years for the wilderness wanderings, the conquest, the reign of Saul, the reign of David, and four years of Solomon's rule—all of which in reality total 145 years. The 410 year total for the events of Judges is, therefore, about 75 years too long.

The solution to this problem is that many of the careers of the judges overlapped. The judges ruled in their particular separated areas of Israel and could well have given leadership at the same time (Judg. 10:1-5). Judges 10:7ff. implies that Jephthah, who was occupied with the Ammonites to the east of the Jordan River, and Samson, who was concerned with the Philistines on the west, were contemporaries. The period of the judges, then, covers about 325 years from the death of Joshua (around 1375 B.C.) to the anointing of Saul as king of Israel (1050 B.C.).

PURPOSE
The book of Judges was designed to show the bridge between Joshua's conquest and David's monarchy. It shows God's protection of the faithful in Israel and how basic religious and governmental problems were solved by God's anointed king. The book corrects and encourages God's people by (1) showing how bad it was when there was no king to unite and deliver all of Israel; and (2) how good it was now that God had provided a single king bound to God by the Davidic covenant.

GEOGRAPHY AND ITS IMPORTANCE

The book of Judges shows how God allowed enemies from the surrounding regions to defeat the Israelites if they stopped obeying him. Moab to the southeast, Hazor to the north, Midian to the northeast, Ammon to the east and the Philistines to the west all captured parts of Israel. The nation was being militarily eaten away by the consequences of her sin. The defeats had driven Israel farther up into the central mountain range. The ability of the Israelites to expand down onto the fertile plains and defeat the enemy was directly related to their willingness to change from sin to obedience and to trust God for help.

GUIDING CONCEPTS

JUDGES AS ONE OF THE FORMER PROPHETS
Judges is one of the books of the former prophets (Joshua, Judges, 1 and 2 Samuel, 1 and 2 Kings). For a discussion of the differences between the former and latter prophets, see the introduction to Joshua under *Guiding Concepts*. The book might be

viewed as just a series of stories or a history of failures in Israel. But the book should be seen as prophecy—not prophecy that tells the future, but prophecy that exhorts God's people to live better lives and not to repeat the mistakes of the past. No book in the Bible is just history, for all history in the Bible is seen as illustrative of spiritual truth, especially of God's sovereignty over history to bring his salvation to the human race.

The Holy Spirit was given for specific tasks throughout the book (Judg. 3:10; 6:34; 11:29; 13:25; 14:6, 19; 15:14). This relation to the Spirit links back to Deuteronomy 34:9 and Numbers 11:17, 25, 29; 27:18-23. Victory was the mark of the presence of the Spirit. The anointing of the Spirit would eventually focus on the anointed king of Israel in the line of David (2 Sam. 7:12-16) and be fulfilled in the Anointed One, the Messiah Jesus (Matt. 3:16-17; Luke 4:17-21).

THE ILLUSTRATION OF THREE PROBLEMS

The book was designed to illustrate three problems: (1) incomplete conquest; (2) unfaithfulness to God's covenant; and (3) civil chaos.

Incomplete conquest

After the general conquest, there were still Canaanites in the Esdraelon and Aijalon valleys. Their foreign presence had driven wedges that divided Israel into northern, central, and southern sections, and almost totally destroyed Israel's ability to act as a unified whole. Full cooperation between the Israelites was not easily possible because Israel was not united. That situation was an almost identical reversal of Joshua's strategy during the initial conquest when he first drove a wedge into the center of Canaan and then took the north and south.

Unfaithfulness to God's covenant

The book mentions the sin of the people a number of times (2:11; 3:7-8, 12; 4:1; 6:1; 10:6; 13:1). After such disobedience, war was usually the test for faithfulness and God's means for reminding the people of their responsibilities under the covenant (cf. 2:20-23 and Deut. 8:2; 13:3).

Civil chaos

The problem of civil chaos is noted in the phrase "everyone did as he saw fit," linked to the phrase "in those days Israel had no king." These phrases sum up the situation in Israel (Judg. 17:6; 18:1; 19:1; 21:25), and expose two sides to a common problem—the problem of civil chaos. It was the king who would solve the problem of the people doing whatever they wanted. The king would bring an end to the civil and military defeats that came from the people's unfaithfulness to God's covenant.

The king would unite the nation civilly, politically, and religiously. The historical time for that perspective of kingship can only be placed within the reigns of David and Solomon and the framework of the Davidic covenant made in 2 Samuel 7. Although the book covers events that happened before a king arrived in Israel, it was clearly written after a king had begun to rule in Israel. The book looked back to the pre-king time to show how bad that period had been. This would encourage the readers not to make the same mistakes and it would encourage them to appreciate their present king and to look forward to the fullness of blessing that God would bring through his greater King to come.

TITLE

The Hebrew title of the book is translated as Judges. The name relates to the deliverers of the tribes of Israel following the conquest and until the time that a king ruled in Israel. The book's name makes one think of a law court with a presiding judge, but legal decision was only a part of what the judges in the book of Judges did. The judges were also military leaders, a fact supported by Judges 2:14; 4:5. The judges also had a special empowering by God to accomplish their civil and military tasks.

BIBLE-WIDE CONCEPTS

THE NEED FOR A LEADER

Judges shows that God's people desperately needed a spirit-anointed leader. Each time they fell into defeat, God provided a man of his choosing to bring about release. The people who were anointed by God as redeemers and judges throughout this book pointed forward to a time when God would choose his leaders from the single line of Davidic kings under the Davidic covenant's promises (cf. 2 Sam. 7). And that line of Davidic kings pointed to one single Redeemer, Jesus the Messiah. That great King would become the perfect Mediator and Deliverer for mankind; he would be the One who would fulfill the deepest of their needs.

The record of human failure stretches from Genesis to Revelation, but the contribution of Judges is that while repeating the cycle of sin, it also leaves hope for the faithful that God will provide leaders to deliver his people. Judges also emphasizes the power of repentance and the faithfulness of God. Each time God's people repented of their sin, God was faithful to forgive and restore.

PRESSURES FOR CULTURAL CONFORMITY

Judges also contributes to the understanding of how contemporary culture and other religions can bring immense pressure upon the people of God. The battle is with the world system that pressures believers, successfully at times, to reject God. The book of Judges emphasizes that a key problem for Israel was forgetting God's great acts of the past, especially the exodus from Egypt. The Passover and all of Israel's feasts were designed to keep the people remembering God's great redemptive acts. When they forgot what God had done in the past, they inevitably excluded God from their present. As the exodus was to the Jew, so the cross is to the Christian. The faith of believers continually calls them to remember God's great act on the cross. To forget that would be to loosen their moorings in forgiveness and to compromise their faith through legalistic or lawless living.

NEEDS MET BY JUDGES

The period of Israel's history from Joshua to King David was rough indeed. The Israelites forgot many truths about their past relationship to God through Moses and Joshua. The events of the great exodus from Egypt dimmed, and the religious, cultural, and military pressures of the surrounding countries burned brightly. By the time the book of Judges was written, Israel already had a king, probably David or Solomon, and needed to be reminded of what life was like without a God-anointed leader at the helm. The content and structure of Judges show that its author was answering questions like the following for the people of Israel:

- What are the reasons Israel is defeated so often?
- How can the Israelites end the severe discipline for their disobedience?
- How can the Israelites change their destructive patterns of behavior?
- Why is it good for Israel to have a king?
- What has happened to the covenant since Moses and Joshua have died?
- Is God still enforcing his covenant?
- Is God still rewarding and blessing obedience to his regulations and laws?

These questions are not unlike those that Christians are asking today. The "great exodus" provided for believers by Christ's death on the cross took place a long time ago. The pressures of life can be great, but this book reminds all believers, then and now, to appreciate how great it is to have the King of kings in charge of their lives. Cycles of destructive behavior can only be broken by submission to the gracious rule of our Lord and King.

OUTLINE OF JUDGES

A. TWO PROBLEMS NOTED (1:1–3:6)
   1. Incomplete Conquest (1:1-36)
   2. Covenant Unfaithfulness (2:1–3:6)

B. THE PROBLEMS ILLUSTRATED (3:7–16:31)
   1. Othniel (3:7-11)
   2. Ehud (3:12-30)
   3. Shamgar (3:31)
   4. Deborah and Barak (4:1–5:31)
   5. Gideon (6:1–8:32)
   6. Abimelech (8:33–9:57)
   7. Jephthah (10:6–12:7)
   8. Ibzan, Elon and Abdon (12:8-15)
   9. Samson (13:1–16:31)

C. A THIRD PROBLEM ILLUSTRATED: DOING RIGHT IN ONE'S OWN EYES (17:1–21:25)
   1. The Migration of the Tribe of Dan (17:1–18:31)
   2. The Events in the Tribe of Benjamin (19:1–21:25)

JUDGES NOTES

1:1–3:6 TWO PROBLEMS NOTED

Overview: The section of 1:1–3:6 takes the reader from the Israelites' partial victory to their pervasive failures in receiving the Promised Land and ends with their weeping before God (1:1–2:5). Judah and Simeon (1:1-7) had some major victories after the death of Joshua. There were links to Caleb, hero of the wanderings and conquest with Joshua (1:12-15), the family of Moses' father-in-law (1:16), and the sons of Joseph (1:22-29). But victory was only partial (1:27-35). The migration of the tribe of Dan into the hills (1:34) was a preparation for the Danites being mentioned later on in the book (17:1–18:31).

The Lord appeared to the Israelites (2:1-5) and explained why they had not driven out all the Canaanites. They had made covenants with the people of the land whose foreign gods would snare them (2:3). That set up the problems of the book of Judges and also pointed to their solutions: Israel would need a king to help the nation keep covenant faithfulness and provide military might that God would support. There is a flashback in 2:6-10 to the end of Joshua's life noting what happened after his death: Israel as a whole ceased to know God and his acts (2:10).

Judges 2:20-23 continues what was first stated in 2:1-5. Israel did not choose to follow in the ways of Joshua. In order to test Israel's desire to obey God, Joshua did not drive out their Canaanite enemies for them. This is similar to God's testing of Israel in the wilderness to see if they would obey him (Deut. 8:2-3) and to his testing of Jesus in the wilderness (Jesus quoted from Deut. 8:3 in Matt. 4:4). The rough times experienced by the Israelites were designed to expose where their hearts really were when it came to loving God. This is also true of difficulties experienced by believers today. A list of the nations God left in Canaan to test Israel is given in 3:1-6. Again, the purpose of testing was defined (3:4).

1:1-36 Incomplete Conquest

After the death of Joshua, Judah was singled out as having the Lord's presence for victory (1:2). The strength of the Canaanites had been shattered by Joshua during the conquest, but it was the responsibility of the tribes to complete the work and flush out remaining pockets of resistance. The law of retaliation (Lev. 24:17-21) was applied to Adoni-Bezek (Judg. 1:6-7). He was receiving the treatment he had given others.

The Israelites captured the heights but could not occupy the valleys, which were controlled by the Canaanites with their iron-reinforced chariots (1:19), or fully take Jerusalem (1:21). Two Canaanite worship centers, Beth Shemesh ("house of Sun") and Beth Anath ("house of Anath"), were allowed to remain (1:33). Anath, the sister and consort of Baal, was a goddess of fertility. That failure to completely drive out the Canaanites constituted disobedience to God's clear command (Exod. 23:33).

2:1–3:6 Covenant Unfaithfulness

In light of the military and religious compromises of Judges 1, the Lord appeared and condemned Israel for her disobedience (2:1-5). Israel's failure to obey God's instructions (Exod. 23:32; 34:12-13) encouraged idolatry and intermarriage with nonbelieving Canaanites (Judg. 2:11-13, 17, 19; 3:5-6; cf. Deut. 7:3; Exod.

ISRAEL'S CYCLE OF SIN AND RESTORATION

Relapse	Israel did evil in the sight of the Lord	3:7
Ruin	God sold them into foreign domination	3:8
Repentance	Israel cried out to the Lord	3:9
Restoration	Deliverance was given through a judge	3:9-10
Rest	The land had peace	3:11
Relapse	Israel returned to evil after the judge's death	3:12

34:15-16). When Israel lost a battle, the question that was inevitably asked was "Why?" God had promised Israel the land, but the blessing of full occupation was to be given only on the condition that Israel lived in obedience. Any failure was due to a problem with Israel, not God.

The name Bokim (Judg. 2:5) means "weepers." Subsequent history reveals that the Israelites lamented the consequences of their disobedience but did nothing about the cause of their judgment. The parents had not passed on the knowledge of the Lord to their children (2:10).

Baal (2:13) was the son and successor of El, the supreme god of the Canaanite pantheon. Baal, whose name meant "lord," was a fertility god whose domain was the sky. The worship of Baal involved sexual rituals thought to bring productivity to the people and the land. Astarte, or Ashtaroth, was the female counterpart to Baal. She served as a goddess of fertility and war.

The giving over of Israel into her enemies' hands (2:14) was in keeping with the curse of the covenant (Deut. 28:25), which was still in force even though Moses and Joshua were dead.

The judges functioned as Spirit-empowered deliverers (Judg. 2:16). During times of peace they arbitrated disputes and made decisions regarding judgments. During times of war they led the Israelite army in victory against its enemies.

Israel's cycles of apostasy (2:16-19) always began with a *relapse* into sin, followed by *ruin* and servitude to a foreign power. After crying out to God in *repentance,* the nation would be *restored* through a judge and enjoy a period of *rest.* This cycle, repeated throughout the book of Judges, formed the pattern for Israel's bondage and deliverance. The chart, *Israel's Cycle of Sin and Restoration,* furnishes an example of this often repeated sequence (Judges 3:7-12).

There was clearly a relationship between the living presence of the judge and the people's ability to remain faithful to God. It was as if the people were kept by the judge's spiritual power and leadership.

The presence of the enemy in the land (2:22–3:2) was to test the Israelites' faith in God and their obedience to his commands (2:22; 3:1, 4) as well as to teach them the art of warfare (3:2). God knew the hardness of their hearts. He wanted them to realize their errors and get back to living according to God's way.

3:7–16:31 THE PROBLEMS ILLUSTRATED

Overview: The chart, *Israel's Oppressors and Deliverers,* lists the leaders mentioned in this section of Judges. Although thirteen judges are mentioned, seven receive specific emphasis in illustrating the repeated cycle of sin, repentance, and deliverance. Those seven judges are related to seven episodes that are introduced with

ISRAEL'S OPPRESSORS AND DELIVERERS

Oppressor	Deliverer	Reference
Mesopotamian	Othniel	3:7-11
Moabite	Ehud	3:12-30
Philistine	Shamgar	3:31
Canaanite	Deborah	4:1–5:31
Midianite	Gideon	6:1–8:32
Civil war	Abimelech	8:33–9:57
Unknown	Tola	10:1-2
Unknown	Jair	10:3-5
Ammonite	Jephthah	10:6–12:7
Unknown	Ibzan	12:8-10
Unknown	Elon	12:11-12
Unknown	Abdon	12:13-15
Philistine	Samson	13:1–16:31

the concept of Israel doing evil in the sight of the Lord (3:7; 3:12; 4:1; 6:1; 8:33-34; 10:6; 13:1), and they should receive the most emphasis in studying the book. No specific enemy was mentioned in relation to the minor judges (Tola, Jair, Ibzan, Elon and Abdon). Instead, their prosperity before the Lord was established by noting their large families and many donkeys. For each judge, power for deliverance and prosperity marked them off as God's chosen leaders. Concepts like God raising up a judge, or deliverer (3:9, 15; 11:29), the deliverer saving Israel (3:31), and God being present with each judge in a special way (6:16, 34) show that these people point to the great Deliverer, Jesus Christ.

3:7-11 Othniel

Aram, or Mesopotamia (3:8), means "the land between the rivers" and refers to the region of the Tigris and Euphrates rivers. The Hebrew means "Aram of the rivers" and refers to the Aramean territory centered at Damascus. Othniel was Caleb's son-in-law (1:13; cf. Josh. 15:15-17).

The Holy Spirit came upon Othniel (Judg. 3:10), Gideon (6:34), Jephthah (11:29) and Samson (13:25). The Spirit served (1) to empower those judges for their appointed tasks of deliverance, (2) to show that victory came from God's power, and (3) to point toward the future anointed king of Israel and, through him, to the perfect King of kings, Jesus.

3:12-30 Ehud

The Moabites (3:12) were the incestuous offspring of Lot and his oldest daughter (Gen. 19:37). They occupied a territory in Transjordan east of the Dead Sea. Moab was behind the evil of Balak and Balaam (Num. 22–24) and the Midianite idolatry (Num. 25). The City of Palms (Judg. 3:13) was Jericho. This whole episode is a reminder of the initial conquest of Jericho by Joshua (3:28). Ehud (3:16) was the cloak-and-dagger judge. His message for King Eglon was fatal. The entire story was designed to delight the reader with its intrigue, misunderstandings, and perfect timing.

3:31 Shamgar

An oxgoad was a stout stick, often bronze-tipped, used to guide and impel oxen at work (3:31). Shamgar also saved Israel, though the enemy was not mentioned.

4:1–5:31 Deborah and Barak

Joshua had conquered Hazor (Josh. 11:1-15), but the Canaanites rebuilt the city. Jabin was apparently a dynastic title applied to each successive Canaanite king (Josh. 11:1), not a personal name. Deborah (Judg. 4:4) was a prophetess, wife and mother (4:4; 5:7). Before directing Barak in the defeat of the Canaanites, she served as a judge in settling civil disputes (4:5). The Kishon River (4:13) is a seasonal river that flows northwest through the Jezreel Valley (see introductory map). During the battle, a rainstorm filled the riverbed (5:4), immobilizing the Canaanites' chariots.

Jael's deception and treacherous murder of Sisera need not be justified (4:21). God clearly said the honor of victory would go to a woman (4:9). Israel's victory over Jabin and the Canaanites was commemorated poetically (5:1-31). The key to the meaning of this passage is found in 5:31.

6:1–8:32 Gideon

The story about Gideon shows that not all Israelites had forgotten what God had done for them in the past (2:10). Gideon knew the God of the exodus (6:13) and wondered why God had ceased doing miracles. Readers today can look back and realize that God's miracles were not happening in Israel at that time because of the sins of the people. But his miracles would appear through his anointed leaders, as Gideon was about to personally discover.

The Midianites (6:1) were descendants of Abraham through Keturah, his second wife (Gen. 25:2). They were a seminomadic desert people who lived south and southeast of Canaan. They had worked together with Moab in the days of Moses to bring Israel into idolatry (Num. 22–25). The Amalekites (Judg. 6:3) were descendants of Esau (Gen. 36:16). They were a nomadic desert tribe that moved about in the northern Sinai and the Negev.

Asherah (Judg. 6:25) was the chief consort of El in Canaanite mythology and served as a mother goddess. (For comments on Baal, cf. Judg. 2:13.) By his exploits,

Gideon acquired a new name, Jerub-Baal (6:32), meaning "let Baal contend."

Gideon's fleece (6:36-40) should not serve as a pattern to believers for determining the will of God. God's directive already had been given, and victory had been promised (6:14, 16, 36). Gideon had difficulty believing what God told him and was testing God to find out if he meant what he said (6:16-17). This account shows how God often patiently works through people like Gideon—people with little faith.

The troops were reduced (7:2) to prevent Israel from boasting in victory instead of giving God the glory he deserved. Gideon's victory was followed by tragic failure (8:27-30). He fashioned a golden ephod that became an object of worship (8:27), and he also acquired many wives who gave birth to his seventy sons (8:30). Gideon rightly understood that God alone was to be King over the nation (8:23). Surprisingly, Gideon named one of his sons Abimelech, which means "my father is king." That son, who was born of Gideon's concubine, would become ruler of the nation by murdering all but one of his brothers.

8:33–9:57 Abimelech

The judges demonstrated the great things that God could do for Israel through his anointed leaders. This story, by contrast, reveals the evils that could come to Israel through wicked leadership—in this case, the leadership of Abimelech. This story reveals the importance of following God's own Spirit-anointed leaders.

Baal-Berith (8:33) means "Baal of the covenant," whose shrine was at Shechem (9:1-4). The Israelites forgot that God was the only God of the covenant.

Jotham's fable proclaimed from Mount Gerizim (9:7-21) revealed the true character of Abimelech, Gideon's worthless son. The ignoble death of Abimelech (9:50-57) at Thebez, ten miles northeast of Shechem, illustrates the principle of divine retribution (9:56-57). An upper millstone (9:53) was the large upper stone that was moved back and forth on a larger stone when grinding corn. It was about ten inches long and easily gripped.

Tola in Ephraim, and Jair in Gilead (10:1-5) probably served contemporaneously. The Hebrew word translated "after" or "followed" can also be translated as "with" (10:3).

10:6–12:7 Jephthah

The story of Jephthah begins once again with Israel's sin and its resulting oppression causing the nation to cry out to God. God's mercy caused him to lift the nation out of its misery (10:16). He delivered the Israelites through his servant Jephthah, a man who, like Gideon, remembered God's great acts in the exodus and conquest (11:12-27). The thrust of Jephthah's message was "What God gives remains given!" And Jephthah acted on that belief.

The Israelites worshiped (10:6) the gods of Canaan (Baal and Ashtoroth), Aram (Hadad and Rimmon), Sidon (Baal Melqaret), Moab (Chemosh), Ammon (Molech), and Philistia (Baal-zebub and Dagon). The Ammonites (10:7) were the descendants of the incestuous relationship between Lot and his youngest daughter (Gen. 19:38). They occupied the Transjordan territory north of Moab. Jephthah attempted unsuccessfully to negotiate a settlement with the Ammonites (Judg. 11:12-28)

The three hundred years mentioned in 11:26 is an important figure in calculating the date of the exodus. Jephthah's judgeship began at about 1096 B.C. Three hundred years earlier would be the approximate date of Joshua's conquest (around 1406 B.C.). The forty years in the wilderness prior to the conquest would put the exodus at 1446 B.C.

Jephthah's rash vow (11:30-31) is the subject of considerable debate. Two common views on how Jephthah fulfilled his vow are: (1) he offered his daughter as a burnt sacrifice, or (2) he devoted his daughter to a life of service at the tabernacle. The most straightforward rendering of the Hebrew text suggests that his daughter died as a burnt sacrifice. But if this is so, why did the daughter bewail her virginity (11:37) rather than her impending death? Neither view is without problems, although the first view is preferred since it is supported by the most straightforward rendering of the text.

Because of certain dialectical changes in the Hebrew language, the Ephraimites could not pronounce "sh" but said "s" when forced to say Shibboleth (12:4-6).

12:8-15 Ibzan, Elon and Abdon

The mention of large families and many donkeys implies wealth and prosperity from the hand of God. The enemies and events relating to these three judges are not specifically mentioned.

13:1–16:31 Samson

Overview: The story of Samson is comprised of the announcement of his birth and call as a lifelong Nazirite (13:1-23), his ill-fated marriage (13:24–14:20), and his revenge (15:1-20). In addition to Samson's wife, the story ends with the mention of two more women, a prostitute (16:1-3) and Delilah (16:4-31). All three of the women in Samson's life were Philistines, the arch-enemies of Israel in the land of Canaan. Samson illustrates the uneasy and ultimately fatal alliance that the Israelites had with one of the nations that they should have destroyed when they entered the Promised Land. This Spirit-filled leader, a man with great potential, inspired great victory, but, paradoxically, he also suffered great defeat because of his own foolish-ness. The great, though limited, victory that Samson did attain was the goal toward which every king of Israel would strive, but a goal which Jesus alone would attain.

13:1-23 SAMSON'S BIRTH ANNOUNCED, THE NAZIRITE VOW EXPLAINED
Samson was to be a Nazirite to God from the womb (13:5). Accordingly, he was not to drink wine, cut his hair, or touch a dead body (cf. Num. 6:1-6). Manoah's response (Judg. 13:21) indicates that he viewed the angel of the Lord as actually an appearance of God himself.

Samson was set apart by God to begin the deliverance of the Israelites from the Philistines (13:1, 5). The Philistines were Indo-Europeans from the Aegean Islands who migrated eastward under the pressure of the Dorian Greeks. The main invasion took place around 1168 B.C. They were repulsed by the Egyptians and eventually settled on Israel's southern coastal plain. They controlled the coastal plain north to Mount Carmel and the Jezreel Valley to the Jordan River.

13:24–16:31 SAMSON'S STRUGGLES
Zorah and Eshtaol (13:25) are situated in the Sorek Valley that pierces the hill country about fifteen miles west of Jerusalem. Timnah (14:1) is about four miles west of Zorah, Samson's hometown. In helping himself to the tasty treat of honey (14:8-9), Samson violated his Nazirite vow that prohibited contact with a dead body. Samson carried the massive Gaza gate forty miles uphill to Hebron (16:3). (See the introductory map for the location of Samson's deeds.) He had so much potential, but it was wasted in his pursuit of pleasure.

Dagon (16:23) was the chief god of the Philistines. He was probably a fertility deity associated with grain production, the prominent agricultural pursuit in the Philistine territory.

The Philistine temple discovered at Tel Qasile illustrates the situation in which Samson found himself (16:26). The roof of the main hall was supported by two pillars close enough together for a large man to grasp both of them. Even though Samson judged Israel for twenty years and caused the Philistines a great deal of trouble and humiliation (16:30-31), he failed to remove the Philistine threat from the nation.

17:1–21:25 A THIRD PROBLEM ILLUSTRATED: DOING RIGHT IN ONE'S OWN EYES

Overview: Judges 1–16 illustrates the problems of an incomplete conquest and covenant unfaithfulness. Judges 17–21 illustrates the problem of civil chaos. That problem is highlighted by the repeated phrase "everyone did as he saw fit" (17:6; 21:25). But that problem is linked to another repeated phrase, "In those days Israel had no king" (17:6; 18:1; 19:1; 21:25). When there was a king in Israel, civil order and peace were enforced. The book of Judges showed its readers how bad it was before God ordained a king in order to help them realize how good conditions were under the king. Acceptance of the leadership of God's anointed king foreshadowed mankind's hope for a future ruler, the King of kings, Jesus.

17:1–18:31 The Migration of the Tribe of Dan

The idolatry of Micah and the migration of the tribe of Dan must be placed early in the period of the judges because Joshua 19:47 mentions this move and Joshua was written while Rahab was still alive (Josh. 6:25). Without a king, extensive religious apostasy like that of Micah took place in Israel (Judg. 17:6-13). The period of the judges was a time of loose morals, openness to many different gods and religions, and political chaos.

Bethlehem (17:7) was not one of the cities designated for the Levites (Josh. 21:9-42). The absurdity of Micah's situation (Judg. 17:13) is emphasized by the fact that he anticipated God's blessing because he had a genuine Levite to serve in his idolatrous shrine.

The powerful Philistines had not permitted the Danites to occupy the coastal plain (18:1), forcing them up into the mountains. Cramped between Judah and Philistia, the tribe of Dan searched for a new territory. Micah's gods (18:26) were not worth fighting over, for he could always make some more. Laish, far to the north, was captured and renamed Dan (18:29). (See introductory map for Dan's location.) From that time on, Dan was a center for idolatrous worship (1 Kings 12:29).

Some ancient versions read "Gershom, the son of Moses" (Judg. 18:30). Thus, the priests at Dan were descendants of Moses, not Aaron. The editorial note, "until the time of the captivity of the land" refers to the later conquest of Galilee by Tiglath Pileser III in 733 B.C. (2 Kings 15:29). This comment shows that editorial changes were made in the book of Judges after the time of the Assyrian conquest.

19:1–21:25 The Events in the Tribe of Benjamin

The section of 19:1–21:25 outlines a civil war among the sons of Israel. The perversions at Gibeah (19:1-30) led to civil war and the destruction of many of the males of the tribe of Benjamin (20:1-48). The section

ends with a strange scheme to allow the remaining males of Benjamin to find wives from among the Israelites (21:1-25).

A concubine (19:1) was a secondary wife, often acquired by purchase or as a war captive. In antiquity, when a marriage produced no heir, a barren wife would present a slave concubine to her husband to produce offspring. Although the practice was not condoned, the concubines were protected under the Mosaic law (Exod. 21:7-11). Since concubines were expensive to maintain, they were considered to be a sign of wealth and status.

Jebus (Judg. 19:10) is the Canaanite city that later became Jerusalem. Gibeah (19:12), located four miles north of Jerusalem, became Israel's capital in Saul's time. The moral intentions of the men of Gibeah (19:22) match those of the men of Sodom (Gen. 19:5). According to oriental custom (Judg. 19:23-24), a host had to protect his guests from harm, whatever the cost. The demands of hospitality and the low status of women in this period of apostasy help to explain this horrendous proposal.

The dismemberment and distribution of the concubine's body to the twelve tribes (19:29) constituted a warning concerning the nation's deep immorality as well as a challenge to make things right.

The two military defeats of Israel by Benjamin drove Israel to prayer and fasting in an earnest attempt to discern God's will (20:26). The rock of Rimmon was about four miles east of Bethel (20:45). The Israelites soon regretted their rash oath concerning Benjamin (21:1, 7, 18).

Jabesh Gilead (21:8), an Israelite city in Transjordan, was to be punished for failing to participate in the discipline of Benjamin. Years later, King Saul, a Benjamite, would rescue this city from the Ammonites (1 Sam. 11:8-11). As a result, the inhabitants of this city would show great bravery by coming to Beth Shan and removing the bodies of Saul and his sons from the city gate and burying them (1 Sam. 31:11-13).

Since the daughters of Shiloh were taken rather than given, the Israelites did not consider themselves in violation of their rash oath (21:19-23). Shiloh was situated in the hill country of Ephraim about twenty miles north of Jerusalem.

Moral decisions in the period of the judges were made on the basis of whatever seemed to suit the situation, not on God's unchanging character. The result was political, moral, and religious chaos. This situation was partially remedied through the Davidic kings and has been perfectly remedied through the Son of David, Jesus the Messiah.

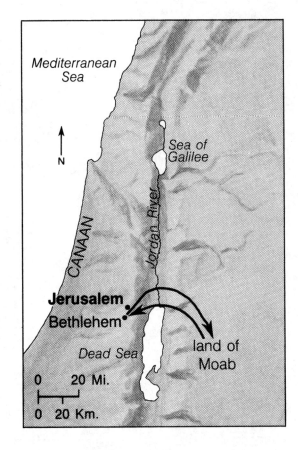

Ruth

BASIC FACTS

HISTORICAL SETTING
The events of the book happened sometime during the period of the judges (1375–1050 B.C.) as recorded in Ruth 1:1. Judges 21:25 is the key to the historical setting of the book: "In those days Israel had no king; everyone did as he saw fit."

The period of the judges was a time of political, religious, and moral chaos. The political chaos is seen in the cycles of apostasy that resulted in oppression by foreign powers. The religious chaos is seen in the person of Micah, who set up his own house priest instead of going to Shiloh to worship (Judg. 17). The moral chaos is illustrated in the perversions recorded in Judges 19. The book of Ruth must be seen in contrast with the book of Judges. The book of Ruth is an oasis of fidelity in a time of idolatry, sin, and infidelity.

AUTHOR
According to rabbinic tradition, Samuel was the author of the book of Ruth. While this is possible, it is unlikely since the concluding genealogy implies that David was well known at the time the book was written. The book is anonymous and the author is unknown.

DATE
The book of Ruth appears to have been written during David's reign (1010–970 B.C.). It could not have been written earlier than the time of King David since he is mentioned by name (Ruth 4:22), unless the genealogy was added later. Had the book been written later than the time of David, the name of his famous son Solomon probably would have been listed in the record of Ruth's descendants.

PURPOSE
The book's historical purpose was to relate an episode in David's ancestry that accounted for the introduction of non-Israelite blood into his family line. The theological purpose is to show the place of the spirit of the law over the letter of the law, illustrating that the exception to the law is based on faith and loyalty to God.

GEOGRAPHY AND ITS IMPORTANCE

The distance from the mountains of Moab to the city of Bethlehem is around forty miles as the crow flies. But on the ground the trip involved a descent and ascent of over four thousand feet. The journey of Naomi and her daughter-in-law Ruth first involved descending from Moab into the Arabah Valley, a descent of over four thousand feet from the valley's eastern rim to its floor, the lowest spot on the earth, 1,300 feet below sea level. Then the pair had to cross the thirteen miles of dry valley floor, ascend over four thousand feet up the valley's western side and make their way through the wilderness of Judea to the little village of Bethlehem. But the journey of that obscure pair of widows prepared the foundation of both a geographical and a spiritual bridge between the Gentile nation of Moab and God's nation of Israel. Ruth became a great-grandmother of King David and part of the family line leading to Jesus the Messiah. In David, and perfectly under Christ, Jews and Gentiles are unified, and when Christ's kingdom is completed, all nations will live at peace.

GUIDING CONCEPTS

THE SOVEREIGNTY OF GOD
God's sovereignty is so obvious in the book of Ruth that the author uses subtle irony when he writes that "as it turned out, she found herself working in a field belonging to Boaz" (2:3). It was within God's sovereign plan and purposes that Ruth would return to Bethlehem with Naomi, that Ruth would come to the field of Boaz, that Boaz was a near relative, that the nearest kinsman would be unwilling to redeem, and that Ruth would become the great-grandmother of David and be an important link in the genealogy of Jesus Christ (Matt. 1:1-17).

THE KINSMAN-REDEEMER
The qualifications and functions of the kinsman-redeemer are illustrated in the person of Boaz, who is typical of the Lord Jesus Christ. The kinsman-redeemer had to be a blood relative to have the right of redemption, even as Christ was a blood relative of man through the virgin birth (John 1:14; Phil. 2:5-8; Heb. 2:14-18). The kinsman-redeemer had to have the resources to purchase the forfeited inheritance, even as Christ had the resource of his own precious blood (1 Pet. 1:18-19). The kinsman-redeemer also had to have the resolve to redeem, even as Christ laid down his life of his own volition (Mark 10:45; John 10:15-18). The book of Ruth is one of the most instructive Old Testament books concerning the redemptive work of Christ.

PRAYER
The book records the prayers of Naomi (Ruth 1:9; 2:19-20), Boaz (2:4, 12; 3:10), and the people of Israel (2:4; 4:11-12, 14-15). God answered those prayers, giving Ruth rest and a fine son, and giving Boaz great blessing.

BIBLE-WIDE CONCEPTS

DAVIDIC COVENANT

The book of Ruth serves as an important background to the covenant God made with David in 2 Samuel 7. Some historical parallels are as follows: famine forced Elimelech to go to Moab, just as Israel had been forced to go to Egypt in the time of Joseph; Ruth aligned herself with Naomi and the true God and went to Canaan (1:15-16; 2:12), just as the mixed multitude had aligned itself with Israel when they left Egypt for Canaan. Rahab, the prostitute from Jericho, was married to Salmon and gave birth to Boaz. Boaz's mother was a Canaanite and his wife was a Moabite. What pervaded the international lineage of David and, ultimately, Jesus Christ, was the universal promise to Abraham: salvation by faith in God, no matter what one's race.

ABRAHAMIC COVENANT

The book contributes to the overall message of the Bible: the promise of worldwide redemption. The source of that redemption is God's promises to Abraham. He was promised a land, offspring, and blessing from God. Abraham also was promised to be a blessing to all the nations of the earth (Gen. 12:1-3). Although God started with an ethnic group from Abraham, he intended to include all ethnic groups in Abraham's blessings.

The book of Ruth contributes to the Abrahamic promise in two ways: (1) the background of David, to whom the kingdom was promised, is given and, more to the point, (2) the Gentile element in the great promises to David is noted. Ruth was from Moab, a nation of Gentiles, not Israel.

THE SPIRIT OF THE LAW

The book of Ruth shows the place of the spirit of the law over the letter of the law. The spirit of the law is seen in the action of Boaz, who went beyond the letter of the law, which said that the widows and foreigners could glean in the fields (Lev. 19:9-10). Boaz not only invited Ruth to glean among the sheaves, he even required his workers to drop grain for her (Ruth 2:15-16). The spirit of the law also is seen in the ancestry of David. The law said that no Moabite or any of his descendants, even to the tenth generation, could enter the assembly of God (Deut. 23:3). However, David was the third-generation descendant of Ruth, and yet he became king of Israel, built an altar, and sacrificed to God (2 Sam. 24:25). While God's moral law must never be violated, the book of Ruth illustrates a legitimate exception to the ceremonial law when it is based on faith and loyal love for God.

NEEDS MET BY RUTH

The Bible gives little detail of King David's birth or childhood. It picks up his life's story just before Samuel anointed him as king. But there was one part of David's background that held a special importance for God's people: his great-grandparents. The importance was in the Moabite background of Ruth, David's great-grandmother. Also important was the time in which she lived—the frequently corrupt period of the judges when there was no king and everyone did what was right in his own eyes, not God's. God wanted his people to know that his promises to Abraham concerning making a great nation were not ethnically limited.

The great nation God had in mind included both Jews and Gentiles. The entrance into that nation was by faith, not physical birth. Israelites could not claim a right to God's Abrahamic promises of blessing simply because they were Jewish. They needed faith and obedience to God. Likewise, even a Gentile from the despised Moabite nation could be honored by God on the basis of allegiance to God. When Israel was in the splendid period of King David's rule, God caused the book of Ruth to be written to remind the nation of how anyone stood before God: by faith and obedience alone. The structure and content of Ruth show that its author was answering questions like these for his readers.

- Is it true that King David had a Moabite among his ancestors?
- What is God's attitude toward receiving Gentiles, especially Moabites, into the nation of Israel?
- Were conditions all bad during the time of the judges?
- Which is more important, faith in God or a pure family lineage?

For the Christian, knowing that Ruth was of Moabite descent and that the way to God's blessings was equally accessible to all ethnic groups by faith is just as potent now as it was in King David's day. Throughout time, God's people have had a way of forgetting the simple truth that they stand before God in his grace alone, not in their own self-righteousness, ethnic background or social standing. Through its beauty and simplicity, the book of Ruth reminds believers again of that single and critical truth.

OUTLINE OF RUTH

A. NAOMI RETURNS TO BETHLEHEM WITH HER DAUGHTER-IN-LAW RUTH (1:1-22)
B. BOAZ CARES FOR RUTH DURING THE BARLEY HARVEST (2:1-23)
C. RUTH UPHOLDS THE LAW BY SEEKING BOAZ AS HER KINSMAN-REDEEMER (3:1-18)
D. BOAZ MARRIES RUTH: THEY BECOME GREAT-GRANDPARENTS OF DAVID (4:1-22)

RUTH NOTES

1:1-22 NAOMI RETURNS TO BETHLEHEM AS A WIDOW WITH HER DAUGHTER-IN-LAW RUTH

The book of Ruth is named after the principal character of the narrative, Ruth, a Moabitess, who after the death of her husband journeyed to Bethlehem with her widowed mother-in-law. The four major scenes in this dramatic story take place outdoors—on the road (Ruth 1:7-18), in the field (2:8-16), at the threshing floor (3:6-13) and at the gate (4:1-12). The lawless period of the judges (Judg. 21:25) provides the setting for the book of Ruth. Famine in a land of marginal rainfall is not uncommon, but for Israel it was a sign of God's judgment (Lev. 26:3-4, 19-20; Deut. 28:12, 23-24). The names of the children (Ruth 1:2), Mahlon, meaning "sickly," and Kilion, meaning "failing," reflect the circumstances in Judah resulting from famine.

Marriage to Moabite women (1:4) was a drastic step, for it banned ten generations of one's descendants from participation in Israel's worship (Deut. 23:3). Naomi referred (Ruth 1:11) to levirate marriage (cf. Deut. 25:5-10), which required a man to marry the childless widow of his deceased brother. The purpose of this institution was to preserve the family name and property. Naomi recognized God's chastening in her life (Ruth 1:20), and when she returned from Moab she asked to be no longer called Naomi, meaning "pleasant," but Mara, meaning "bitter." Barley (1:22) was harvested in the early spring (March–April).

2:1-23 BOAZ CARES FOR RUTH DURING THE BARLEY HARVEST

Ruth was qualified to glean (2:2) from the fields after the harvest because she was a widow and a stranger (Lev. 19:9-10; Deut. 24:19). "As it turned out" (Ruth 2:3) she came upon the field of Boaz. God's sovereign hand is clearly seen in leading Ruth to the field of this kinsman. Such God-honoring greetings (2:4) would have been very unusual during this period of the judges. The book of Ruth is an oasis of fidelity in a time of Israel's idolatry, sin and infidelity.

The poetic imagery "under whose wings" (2:12) depicts the shelter and protection that God provides (cf. Matt. 23:37). Ruth had found a place of refuge in Israel's God. The kindnesses of Boaz (Ruth 2:14-16) went far beyond what the law required. An ephah (2:17) was approximately the same amount as a bushel, which was an astounding amount for a day's gleaning.

Naomi disclosed that Boaz was a near kinsman or kinsman-redeemer (2:20). As such, he could be expected to function as a protector of family rights, protecting property (Lev. 25:25) and persons (Deut. 25:5-10).

3:1-18 RUTH UPHOLDS THE LAW BY SEEKING BOAZ AS HER KINSMAN-REDEEMER

The threshingfloor (Ruth 3:2) was a hard surface where the grain was trampled by animals in order to break the kernels from the stalks of grain. Winnowing involved separating the grain from the tiny broken pieces of the stalk (the chaff) after threshing. The mixture was tossed into the air, and the evening breeze would blow the lighter material away from the grain.

Boaz was going to sleep at the threshing floor to protect his grain (3:4). The uncovering of the feet of Boaz (3:7) was a symbol of Ruth's submission; it alerted her kinsman-redeemer to the fact that she sought his protection. In light of the culture and the high moral character of Ruth and Boaz, there was nothing improper about this procedure. The words "spread the corner of your garment" (3:9) functioned as a marriage proposal that Boaz was only too happy to consider. The word "garment" is the translation of the same Hebrew word that in 2:12 refers to the "wings" of God. Boaz took precaution against scandal (3:14), which showed that he already was functioning as Ruth's protector.

4:1-22 BOAZ MARRIES RUTH: THEY BECOME GREAT-GRANDPARENTS OF DAVID

The town gate (4:1) customarily served as a meeting place where legal transactions were authorized and judicial decisions were made. The offer of the opportunity to purchase Elimelech's land at first looked attractive to the nearest kinsman-redeemer (4:4). He assumed that this was the limit of his obligation. But then he refused to purchase it because he did not want to invest in property that would not ultimately be his (4:6). He also may have hoped to inherit this property and avoid paying for it (Num. 27:9).

By removing his sandal (Ruth 4:8), a symbol of land possession, the nearest kinsman permanently renounced his claim on the property. The marriage of Ruth to Boaz (4:10) was similar to a levirate marriage. But due to the fact that Boaz was the brother of Elimelech (4:3) rather than Mahlon, it differed slightly from the law of Deuteronomy 25:5-10. The reference to Judah and Tamar (Ruth 4:12) recalled a situation in which the levirate responsibility was not honored (Gen. 38). Obed (Ruth 4:17), Naomi's legal grandson, was the child of Mahlon according to Jewish law (4:10) and the child of Boaz by actual paternity (4:12). Boaz and Ruth became King David's great-grandparents (4:21-22).

1 & 2 Samuel

BASIC FACTS

HISTORICAL SETTING
The religious scene
The nation of Israel was at a religious low point. Even the priesthood was corrupt (1 Sam. 2:12-17). Samuel's sons, who served as judges, were dishonest and corrupt (8:1-3), and the people of Israel refused to listen to the voice of their prophet Samuel (8:19). Yet in the midst of that corruption, there was a remnant of righteous people who were faithfully worshiping and sacrificing to the Lord at Shiloh (1:3).

The Ark of the Covenant was at Shiloh (4:4), but it was taken from there to the battle of Ebenezer, where it was captured by the Philistines (4:11). The Ark was later returned to Beth Shemesh (6:19) and then to Kiriath Jearim (7:1). Eventually it was brought to Jerusalem by David twenty years later (2 Sam. 6). (See map.)

The political scene
Politically, the book begins with the last judge, Samuel. The people of Israel refused to listen to Samuel and insisted on having a king to rule over them (8:19). Samuel anointed Saul as Israel's first king (10:1), and he later anointed David (16:6-13). Gibeah was Saul's fortress and capital (10:26; 15:34). David reigned approximately seven years in Hebron before he moved his capital to Jerusalem after being appointed king over all of Israel (2 Sam. 5:3-5). At that time Israel began to move into its greatest religious, social, political, and miltary period.

The international setting during the united monarchy of David and Solomon was one of transition. The great empires of the ancient world were in a state of weakness that allowed Israel to develop nationally without external restraint. Assyria was in decline, and the Hittites of Asia Minor had passed into insignificance. Egypt was weak and involved in internal conflict.

The Philistines, having recently migrated from the Aegean Islands and Asia Minor under the pressure of the Dorian Greeks (around 1168 B.C.), constituted Israel's main threat. They had a monopoly on the manufacture and use of iron tools and weapons,

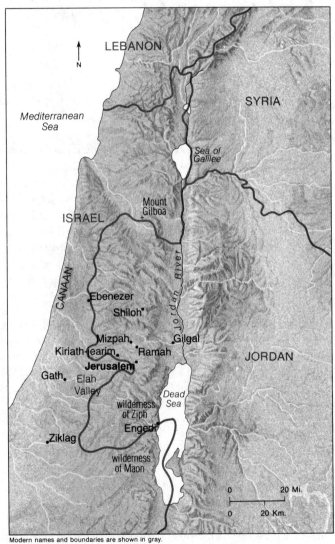

KEY PLACES IN 1 SAMUEL

which gave them a decided military and economic advantage and kept Israel on the defensive (1 Sam. 13:19-22).

The threat of the Philistines was an impetus to the nation to unite under the leadership of Samuel, Saul, and David. The weakness of the great international powers made possible the expansion of the kingdom under David until Israel reached its peak of military and political power.

AUTHOR

The author of 1 and 2 Samuel is not known. According to Jewish tradition, Samuel, Nathan, and Gad all had a part in the recording of the events of the book of Samuel. This theory is suggested by 1 Chronicles 29:29.

DATE

Parts of the book were written after Samuel died (1 Sam. 25:1; 28:13-20) and even after the division of Solomon's kingdom (see 1 Sam. 27:6, where the phrase "kings of Judah" implies the post-Solomonic division of the southern kingdom of Judah from the northern kingdom of Israel). The fall of Samaria in 722 B.C. is not mentioned, so it is reasonable to date the book somewhere between 931 and 722 B.C. The events cover the time from the ministry of Eli to the close of David's reign. Taking 931 B.C. as the date of the division of the kingdom after Solomon, the dates for Israel's first three kings are as follows: Saul reigned forty years (Acts 13:21) (1050–1010 B.C.); David reigned forty years (2 Sam. 5:4) (1010–970 B.C.); and Solomon reigned forty years (1 Kings 11:42) (970–931 B.C.).

Samuel's date of birth may be determined by the fact that he had sons old enough to be judges in Beersheba (1 Sam. 8:1-2) before Saul began to reign in 1050 B.C. That places Samuel's birth around 1100 B.C., just prior to the outbreak of Ammonite and Philistine oppression and the birth of Samson.

PURPOSE

The historical purpose of the book of Samuel was to provide an official account of Samuel's ministry as well as of the rise and development of the monarchy and the kingdom of Israel from the days of Saul through most of the reign of David. The theological purpose was to show God's sovereignty over the theocratic kingdom as he set up, deposed, and commanded the rulers of Israel. The heart of that sovereignty was God's commitment to his people through the covenant he made with King David (2 Sam. 7). That covenant is so crucial to understanding the message of 1 and 2 Samuel that its basic aspects are presented in the *Bible-Wide Concepts* section rather than being covered later in comments on 2 Samuel 7.

GEOGRAPHY AND ITS IMPORTANCE

The books of 1 and 2 Samuel were originally one unbroken book. Taken in its original unity, the book of Samuel begins with the Ark at Shiloh and ends with the purchase of the temple site in Jerusalem. The geographical movement from Shiloh to Jerusalem demonstrates the bookwide struggle to get two things into their proper place in Jerusalem—the Ark and the king. Both the Ark and the king were key

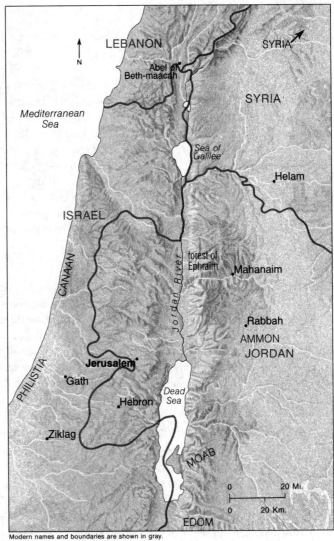

LEBANON

SYRIA

N

Abel of
Beth-maacah

Mediterranean
Sea

SYRIA

Sea of
Galilee

Helam

ISRAEL

CANAAN

forest of
Ephraim

Mahanaim

Jordan River

Rabbah

AMMON

JORDAN

Jerusalem

Gath

Dead
Sea

Hebron

Ziklag

PHILISTIA

MOAB

0   20 Mi.

0   20 Km.

EDOM

Modern names and boundaries are shown in gray.

KEY PLACES IN 2 SAMUEL

ingredients for establishing God's rule over the nation. The Ark represented the center of the temple and its priestly duties. The king had a special father-son relationship with God and became the director of the entire nation's prosperity or defeat. The enemies of Israel only had military victory when the people of Israel were experiencing spiritual defeat. In the book of Samuel, four surrounding nations were at war with Israel: the Philistines to the west, the Ammonites to the east, the Moabites and Edomites to the southeast, and the Amalekites to the south.

GUIDING CONCEPTS

THE ORIGINAL UNITY OF FIRST AND SECOND SAMUEL
The books of 1 and 2 Samuel are included in the former prophets. See the discussion of the significance of the former prophets in the introduction to Joshua. The main point is that the books are not dry ancient history. They are full of pointedly arranged stories designed to cause readers to think about making their lives more pleasing to God.

The two books of Samuel were originally inspired as one book. The same was true of the books of Kings. Later, the translators of the Greek Old Testament combined the books of Samuel and Kings into a complete history of the kings of Israel. The translators divided each book into two parts. The four parts were called Reigns A, B, C, and D.

Those who translated the Bible into Latin kept the four-part division of the Greek Old Testament but called the first two parts 1 and 2 Samuel and the third and fourth parts 1 and 2 Kings. These divisions have been used in the English translations as well. (See the chart below.)

Why is all this important? The original unity of Samuel is vital to maintain for understanding the original and God-given message of the book. The importance of this will become clear after looking at the book's structure. This *Bible Companion* will present all of these books in the light of their original unity. Thus, the books of 1 and 2 Samuel will be viewed as a single unit.

THE STRUCTURE OF SAMUEL
Although God's great covenant with David and its implications pervade 1 and 2 Samuel both in content and structure, the narrative of the book begins with the prophet Samuel. Samuel did not simply function as a transitional figure between the judges and the kings. He also functioned as the prophetic voice God used to

SAMUEL AND KINGS IN THE EARLY TRANSLATIONS

Original	*Greek Old Testament*	*Latin And English*
Samuel ————<	Reigns A ———>	1 Samuel
	Reigns B ———>	2 Samuel
Kings ————<	Reigns C ———>	1 Kings
	Reigns D ———>	2 Kings

announce his views regarding Israel's desires for a king. Then, after God had endorsed the monarchy, Samuel served as the wise spokesman from God who anointed the first two kings. The aborted reign of Saul, the first king anointed by Samuel, was not simply a mistake. The reign of Saul revealed what God demanded of Israel's kings and his attitude toward rebellion; it illustrated what it meant to have God's loving-kindness withdrawn. Because of the special covenant that God later made with David, the second king anointed by Samuel, God's loving-kindness would never depart from David's line.

The reign of David showed how God's demands for obedience were placed within a gracious commitment to continue with David's line even though it would fall into gross sin. Although the book of Samuel is superficially about the kings of Israel, at heart it is about a God who was more concerned about bringing in the rule of the Messiah-King than about taking away his loving-kindness from dynasty after failed dynasty. The end of the book of Samuel (2 Sam. 21–24; remember, it was originally one book) reveals the centrality of the Davidic covenant to the content and structure of the book. The author arranged the material to show the reality of human failure, while also recognizing the glory of God's promises to David:

National Judgment: Saul's Sin, David's Entreaty (2 Sam. 21:1-14)
> Military Victory through Mighty Men (2 Sam. 21:15-22)
>> Song of Praise for the Davidic Covenant: Past Victory (2 Sam. 22:1-51)
>> Song of Praise for the Davidic Covenant: Future Security (2 Sam. 23:1-7)
> Military Victory through Mighty Men (2 Sam. 23:8-39)
National Judgment: David's Sin, David's Entreaty (2 Sam. 24:1-25)

The above structure shows the perspective and basic themes of the book of Samuel: (1) When the king obeyed, God blessed the land. (2) God's covenant with David brought military peace and security. (3) The Davidic covenant brought to remembrance God's blessing in the past and provided hope for the future.

BIBLE-WIDE CONCEPTS

KINGSHIP IN ISRAEL

From Genesis on, God had promised to bring about a kingly rule in Israel. Kings would come from the line of Abraham (Gen. 17:6, 16; 35:11). Judah would have the scepter of rule (Gen. 49:10). The entire nation was to be a kingdom of priests (Exod. 19:6). A scepter would arise from Israel to defeat her enemies (Num. 24:7, 17). The king would be of God's choosing and subject to his rules (Deut. 17:14-20). Gideon argued that the Lord, not a king, should rule over Israel (Judg. 8:22-23). While a king would indeed arise in Israel, those quoted texts present an ambivalent attitude toward kingship. It was seen as something that would happen, but also as a thing that could cause some negative consequences for the nation.

THE DAVIDIC COVENANT
Abrahamic promise

Second Samuel 7:12-16 records the Davidic covenant, which amplifies and confirms the seed promises of the Abrahamic covenant (Gen. 12:1-3). Abraham was promised a land, a nation, a divine blessing and an international influence for good (Gen. 12:1-3). The Davidic covenant took up the nation and blessing aspects and focused them on one individual—the king of Israel. The Davidic covenant promised David an eternal house, an eternal throne and an eternal kingdom, guaranteeing that the right to rule over Israel would always belong to one of David's descendants (cf. Luke 1:31-33).

Mosaic Law and the temple
The king would become the catalyst for maintaining the temple worship, keeping the Mosaic covenant's laws, and guiding the nation into personal and international blessings. As the king went, so went the nation. Under a good king, there was good for the nation. But history shows that most of the kings were bad and ultimately led the nation away from God's blessings. Only Jesus, the Son of David, would be the One to bring God's people into a reign of perfect obedience and blessing.

The house of God
Just before God announced that he would make a covenant, David offered to build God a house. The tabernacle still housed the Ark of the Covenant, and David wanted to have a more splendid structure for Israel's worship (2 Sam. 7:1-3). God made a counteroffer to build a house for David, a royal house with a lineage that would go on forever (2 Sam. 7:4-17). The seed of Abraham now had a new focus: the royal line of David. The role of Israel among the nations also was refocused. The king would now be the mediator between Israel and the nations.

Permanent loving-kindness
Without a doubt the heart of the book's purpose is to illustrate the greatness of God's promises made to David in the Davidic covenant. That was accomplished by showing the difference between King Saul and King David. The covenant with David said that God would not take away his loving-kindness as he had taken it away from Saul (2 Sam. 7:15). God's loving-kindness in that case was equivalent to his gracious presence that enabled Saul or David to be king, God's anointed leader. God took his loving-kindness away from Saul, but he would not do so with David's royal line.

The most important section of the Davidic covenant is in 2 Samuel 7:14-15. David's son would be a son of God (7:14). God and the king would have a special relationship of Father-son intimacy. If the son committed sin, he would be disciplined by his heavenly father. But God's loving-kindness would never depart (2 Sam. 7:15).

This permanent loving-kindness is the seal of God's commitment to David's line and its ultimate victorious kingdom. Saul forms the contrast as one who lost God's loving-kindness regarding kingship. God withdrew his loving-kindness, the special anointing of his Spirit for kingship, from Saul because of his sin. That would not be the case with David's line. Even though David and his descendants would sin, God would still be committed to them on the basis of his promise (2 Sam. 7:14). In contrast to God's relationship with Saul, the book of Samuel shows how the relationship mediated by the Davidic covenant was powerful and enduring and continued even despite David's sins. Although David's descendants might sin, resulting in severe discipline, God's loving-kindness would never depart.

Why was David allowed to be king even though his sins far outstripped those of Saul? Because God was committed to bringing in a Ruler for Israel and the world through his promises to David, not on the basis that any son of David was sinless (2 Sam. 7:14). Only one Son of David would be sinless—Jesus the King, to whom all the Davidic promises pointed. All the others would, in one way or another, fall prey to human failure.

The hope for the Messiah

The book of Samuel illustrates the source of messianic hope for a King to rule the world. Saul was not all bad and David was not all good. The point of the book is that God alone is good and powerful enough to bring in the universal rule of Jesus, the King of his own choosing. David recognized that eternal and wonderful gift of promise as he praised God in 2 Samuel 7:18-29. The promise was for more than a line of kings. It was for a worldwide outpouring of blessing mediated by a future King of Israel. That great promise was fulfilled in Jesus the Messiah, the anointed King, not only of Israel, but of the whole world.

NEEDS MET BY SAMUEL

When the book of Samuel was written, God's anointed king had brought God's people great pleasure and great pain. The exhilarating first part of David's reign brought military victories and civil prosperity. The last part of David's reign brought defeat and civil war. The king had sinned greatly and everything seemed to be falling apart. What had happened to those great divine promises of a line of godly kings ruling forever in might and peace? The book of Samuel was written to explain the origins of God's chosen kings and also to show where the real potency lay in keeping those kings on the throne—in the sovereign covenant between God and David, not in the perfections or imperfections of the human kings. The book of Samuel answers a number of important questions for the children of Israel who were under the rule of David and Solomon.

- What was the history of God's work from the judges to the kings?
- Why did Israel need a king?
- Was it a bad thing for Israel to want a king in the first place?
- How committed was God to David and his lineage?
- What was God's ultimate goal in preserving the line of David?
- Would God someday reject David for his sin just as he had rejected Saul?
- In what way was the king a mediator for the entire nation?

The book of Samuel shows how deeply committed God was to the idea of kingship. God proved his commitment by maintaining a long series of earthly kings from Saul, eventually stretching to Jehoiachin. That mixed line of success and failure framed the goal of all earthly kingship—the ultimate coming of Jesus the King. The kings of Israel failed, but Jesus was perfect. The kings lost the link of mediation between their subjects and God, but Jesus brought the perfect mediation of king and priest combined. For Israel, as the king went, so went the people. The same is true now for all who are the people of the King of kings.

OUTLINE OF SAMUEL

A. GOD PROVIDES A SON TO LEAD ISRAEL (1 Samuel 1:1–2:11)
  1. Samuel Is Born and Dedicated (1:1-28)
  2. Hannah's Prayer (2:1-11)
B. GOD JUDGES RELIGIOUS GREED AND SUPERSTITION (2:12–7:17)
  1. Offerings Eaten in Greed (2:12-17)
  2. Judgment Predicted on Eli's Sons (2:18–3:12)
  3. Superstition Rejected (4:1–6:18)
  4. True Religion Restored (6:19–7:17)
C. GOD CHOOSES HIS KINGS (8:1–31:13)
  1. Saul (8:1–15:35)
  2. David (16:1–31:13)
D. DAVID GROWS STRONGER (2 Samuel 1:1–10:19)
  1. Lament for the House of Saul (1:1-27)
  2. Conflict with the House of Saul (2:1–4:12)
  3. Establishment of the House of David (5:1–10:19)
E. DAVID'S HOUSEHOLD EVIL (11:1–20:26)
  1. Adultery and Murder (11:1–12:31)
  2. Revenge (13:1-39)
  3. Insurrection in David's Kingdom (14:1–20:26)
F. DAVID AS A MEDIATOR AND PRESERVER (21:1–24:25)
  1. National Judgment: Saul's Sin, David's Entreaty (21:1-14)
  2. Military Victory through Mighty Men (21:15-22)
  3. Song of Praise for the Davidic Covenant: Past Victory (22:1-51)
  4. Song of Praise for the Davidic Covenant: Future Security (23:1-7)
  5. Military Victory (23:8-39)
  6. National Judgment: David's Sin, David's Entreaty (24:1-25)

FIRST SAMUEL NOTES

1:1–2:11 GOD PROVIDES A SON TO LEAD ISRAEL
Overview: The climax of the section 1 Samuel 1:1–2:11 is Hannah's prayer of exaltation in 2:1-11, where she praises God for his care for the lowly, his judgment on the proud, and his blessings on his king. The focus from the outset is on Samuel's relationship to God's future work through his kings. In Scripture, God often displayed his new works of redemption by choosing women to bear children in a miraculous way: Sarah (Gen. 21:1-2), Rachel (Gen. 30:22-23), Manoah's wife (Judg. 13:2-3), Hannah (1 Sam. 1:19-20; 2:21), Elizabeth (Luke 1:13), and Mary (Luke 1:26-31).

God showed that nothing stops his purposes, not even barren wombs, and that he is the source of these promised sons, seen most perfectly in the virgin conception of Jesus. In the birth of Samuel God provided a leader and intercessor for Israel.

1:1-28 Samuel is Born and Dedicated
Ramathaim Zuphim (meaning "the heights of the Zuphite," 1:1) is the longer name for "Ramah" (1:19), located about five miles north of Jerusalem. Elkanah lived in Ephraim, but he was a Levite by lineage (1 Chron. 6:26, 33). Although polygamy (1:2) was practiced in the biblical period, it was at variance with God's original plan for marriage (Gen. 2:24) and never resulted in

a happy homelife (1 Sam. 1:6). Shiloh (1:3) was the location of the tabernacle (Josh. 18:1). "Lord Almighty" (1 Sam. 1:11; 17:45) is a military designation referring to God as the One who commands the armies of Israel and the angelic armies of heaven (1 Kings. 22:19). The term emphasizes God's sovereignty and omnipotence.

Hannah promised (1 Sam. 1:11) that her son would be dedicated to lifelong Levitical service (Num. 4:3; 8:24-26) and would be a lifelong Nazirite (Num. 6:2-6). The son's name, Samuel (meaning "name of God" or perhaps "heard of God," 1 Sam. 1:20), served as a continual reminder of God's mercy toward those who call upon his name. Hebrew children were normally weaned at two to three years of age (1:23; 2 Macc. 7:27). The words "give him" (1 Sam. 1:28) literally mean "made him over to"; they speak of an irrevocable giving up of the child to the Lord.

2:1-11 Hannah's Prayer
Hannah's prayer was a psalm of praise about the incomparability of God. Based on his greatness, there should be no arrogance (2:3) but rather humility. Humility is submission to God's ways. Notice the upcoming bad example of Saul as he insists on his own way rather than listening to God. Humility is the essential quality for God's servants, seen most perfectly in the humble Son of Man, Jesus. The king would be the instrument of judgment against all evil.

The Hebrew word for "grave" (2:6) refers to the dark, shadowy, silent place of the dead. Both the righteous and the wicked will go there at death (Gen. 37:35; Ps. 9:17).

2:12–7:17 GOD JUDGES RELIGIOUS GREED AND SUPERSTITION
2:12-17 Offerings Eaten in Greed
Why were Eli's sons not immediately judged? Nadab and Abihu sinned at the tabernacle and were instantly judged (Lev. 10:1-11). God's delay of his judgment upon Eli's sons provides a longer example of God's sovereign plans to show himself holy whether by instant or delayed judgment (see 1 Sam. 2:25). To despise the offering was to make the wrong use

of it and actually to despise the Lord (cf. Deut. 31:20). They despised the link of sacrifice between God and the human race. They knew what the food was for, but they did with it as they pleased. Their immorality approached the immorality of the rituals of pagan cultic prostitution (1 Sam. 2:22).

Samuel's faithfulness contrasts with the unfaithfulness of Hophni and Phinehas. As priests, Eli's sons knew about God, but they did not know him in a personal way. Their disobedience was a process that would lead to their deaths (2:25).

2:18–3:12 Judgment Predicted on Eli's Sons
An ephod (2:18) was a close-fitting, sleeveless vest extending to the hips and worn almost exclusively by priests, especially when officiating before the altar (Exod. 28:6-14; 1 Sam. 2:28).

The prophecy of 2:35-36 indicates that God intended to transfer the high priesthood back to the line of Eleazar in the person of Zadok, the faithful priest of David during Absalom's revolt (1 Kings 2:26-27, 35).

The initial meeting between the Lord and Samuel was to give Samuel the prophecy of the death of Eli's sons (1 Sam. 3:1-18). A summary statement confirmed God's presence with Samuel and his renewed presence at Shiloh (3:19-21). "Dan to Beersheba" (3:20), a distance of about 150 miles, became an expression denoting the northern and southern extremities of the Israelite nation.

4:1–6:18 Superstition Rejected
4:1-22 THE ARK IS TAKEN AND ELI'S SONS ARE JUDGED
The Israelites treated the Ark of the Covenant like a good-luck charm. They did not pray to find out why they had been defeated, as Joshua had done at Ai (Josh. 7:6-11). They assumed the problem was with the Lord, not themselves (1 Sam. 4:3). The Philistines, on the other hand, simply plucked up their courage, entered the battle, and emerged victorious with the Ark. Aphek (4:1; NT "Antipatris") was a strategic Canaanite city on the coastal plain northeast of modern Tel-Aviv. It controlled the travel route that passed between the headwaters of the Yarkon River and the hill country of Ephraim.

The child born to Phinehas's wife was named Ichabod (4:21), meaning "no glory," for the loss of the Ark meant the absence of glory in Israel (4:22). Archaeological excavations at Shiloh indicate that the city was destroyed around 1050 B.C., perhaps by the Philistines after they captured the Ark (cf. Jer. 7:12-14). (See the introductory map for Shiloh's location.)

5:1-12 THE LORD GOD TREATED AS ONE GOD AMONG MANY

The Philistines treated the God of Israel as one god among many (1 Sam. 5:1–6:18). Ashdod (5:1) was a Philistine city located on the Mediterranean seacoast about twenty-two miles south of Joppa. There was a close relationship between Dagon (5:2) and Baal. In ancient literature, Baal is sometimes referred to as "the son of Dagon," Philistia's fertility deity. The Hebrew word translated "tumors" (5:6) is derived from the verb "to swell" and may refer to boils. In view of the rats that ravaged the land (6:5), these sores may have been symptomatic of bubonic plague.

Why did the Ark not help Israel when she had it? Why did it hurt the Philistines after they defeated Israel? Because God had two messages to deliver. To Israel, God was saying that he was to be treated as holy. Disobedience had resulted in the absence of his power to deliver. To the Philistines, God was proving his awesome character—a character unique and far above those of their imaginary gods. In both cases, the Ark proved to be the sign of God's presence, either to bless or to judge. Moving the Ark from city to city was the Philistines' attempt to see if they could find a place where God would not be powerful. It was similar to Balak's movement from mountain to mountain to try to move out of the area of God's power (Num. 23:13, 27). However, God was powerful everywhere and thus proved that he was not just one god among many.

Gath (1 Sam. 5:8), another of the five Philistine cities (6:17), was located twelve miles southeast of Ashdod. Ekron (5:10), probably located at Tell Miqne, was six miles north of Gath (see introductory map).

6:1-18 THE RETURN OF THE ARK

The fact that the Ark returned to Israel in the unattended ox cart showed the Philistines that the plagues they experienced were not by chance (6:9) but from the Lord. The Philistines believed in sympathetic magic, that is, the removal of evil or disaster via models of their sores (6:4-5). By sending away the golden models, they hoped to remove the disease from their land. These expensive articles also served as a sacrifice, intended to placate the angry God of Israel.

6:19–7:17 True Religion Restored

6:19-21 RESTORED THE HARD WAY

The return of the Ark began a restoration of true religion in Israel. The first step in this restoration was taken the hard way at Beth Shemesh (6:19-21). God showed the Israelites that he was still holy and powerful enough to judge those whose curiosity and irreverence caused them to peek into the Ark (6:19). Apparently this was a violation of Numbers 4:20. The number 50,070 (KJV; NASB) is doubted even by conservative scholars and is probably a scribal error in transmission. Three other Hebrew manuscripts read "seventy."

The question of 6:20 cuts both ways. God's holiness applies both to believers and unbelievers. God is consistent and therein lies the believer's security and way of blessing. There is never a context for irreverence.

The Ark was a spiritual work (Exod. 35:30-31; 31:3) and was built by a person gifted spiritually and artistically by God (37:1-9). It was the place where God met with his people (25:22). See 2 Samuel 6:6-11 for a reminder, twenty years later, of God's holiness.

7:1-17 RESTORED BY THE WAY OF OBEDIENCE

The second step in the restoration of true religion in Israel was taken by following the way of obedience. Guarding the Ark (1 Sam. 7:1) meant protecting it from theft and protecting the Israelites from potentially fatal curiosity. As a result of their obedience, the nation moved from repentance (7:6) to victorious battle. Samuel gathered Israel for a prayer meeting at Mizpah, seven miles north of Jerusalem (see introductory map). Having won the victory on their knees, they went out and won the battle. The image of victory is overlaid with the image of Samuel offering a burnt sacrifice during the actual battle (7:10). The stone (7:12) was named Ebenezer, meaning "stone of help," as a memorial of God's deliverance of his people (see introductory map for Ebenezer's location). Amorites (7:14) is a general term for the original inhabitants of Canaan (Gen. 15:16; Josh. 7:7).

8:1–31:13 GOD CHOOSES HIS KINGS
8:1–15:35 Saul

Overview: The background for this section is found in Deuteronomy 17:14-20. In 1 Samuel 8 the surface reason for wanting a king was the failure of Samuel's sons to judge rightly (8:5). God had always provided a leader for his people—from Moses, to tribal leaders and judges, to Samuel. The difference in having a king as a leader was one of style, in this case conformity to the nations around them (8:5). And therein lay the problem. The real reason was the people's rejection of the invisible God as their King (8:7). They wanted an earthly king to fight their battles for them, just as if God did not already do that.

First Samuel 8–15 focuses on Saul's reign as king. The people insisted on having a king even though Samuel told them a king would oppress them (8:17-19). The selection and anointing of Saul as king took place against the background of his journey to find his father's lost donkeys (9:3; 10:16). But the heart of this section can be seen in God's gracious choice of Saul as king, contrasted with Saul's less than satisfactory response to the honor God had bestowed upon him.

The Lord clearly chose Saul (9:15-17; 10:24). Saul had an initial victory over the Ammonites (11:1-13) that ended with a renewal of the kingdom celebration at Gilgal (11:14-15). Samuel spoke pointed remarks to the people concerning their wrong desire to have a king and, in spite of that desire, he also emphasized God's unceasing commitment to Israel (12:1-25). Saul disobeyed the Lord by not waiting for Samuel to offer the sacrifice (13:1-4). Then Saul acted foolishly concerning Jonathan and was contradicted by the people (14:1-52). Saul's second act of disobedience, concerning the spoils taken from the Amalekites, brought the final split with Samuel as well as God's regret for making Saul king (15:1-35).

But why did God allow this "false start" with Saul rather than going straight to David in the first place? This section on Saul prepares the reader for the reign of David in four significant ways: (1) The people's desire for a king was a mistake, but it was a mistake through which God would deliver his promised blessings. (2) Kingship would, on a human level, ultimately fail. (3) The choice of Israel's kings was up to God alone. (4) The nation's well-being was dependent on the obedience of the king. The failure of Saul's rule prepares the reader for the success of David's. However, David's success was based on God's covenant with him, not his obedience.

8:1-22 ISRAEL'S REQUEST FOR A KING

The people's request for a king showed that they thought their problem was an organizational one. They failed to recognize that their basic problem was one of sin. Samuel, like Eli, may have been too involved in his ministry to deal with his family, and God was dishonored as a result (8:3). Conformity to the ways of unbelievers (8:5, 20) was displeasing to the Lord and indicative of spiritual decline. God intended for Israel to ultimately have a king, but he was not pleased with their self-centered motivation. Nevertheless, he allowed the people to have their desire.

9:1–13:23 SAUL'S FIRST FAILURE AS KING

9:1–10:16 Saul is anointed and endued with the Spirit of God. The term "seer" (9:9, from "to see") points to the receptive aspect—a servant of God's ability to perceive God's will. The term "prophet" points to the seer's ability to communicate. A "high place" (9:12) was an elevated place of worship and sacrifice located on a hill or artificial platform. The custom of worshiping at high places was essentially Canaanite (Deut. 12:2-5), but Israel used such facilities to worship God before the construction of the temple. For example, Solomon worshiped at the high place at Gibeon (1 Kings 3:4).

Anointing involved a consecration or a setting apart for service (10:1). It was a religious act that established a special relationship between God and the king who served as his representative and ruler over the people. Before any engagement with the Philistines, Saul was to meet Samuel at

Gilgal, where Samuel would offer sacrifices of burnt offerings and fellowship offerings to God (10:8). Saul did not obey Samuel's orders (13:8-14). Casting lots to answer questions is also seen in Joshua 7:14 where the phrase "the clan that the Lord takes" refers to casting lots to select the clan of God's choice (cf. 1 Sam. 10:20-22; 28:16 where casting lots is also implied). The Bible describes, but does not command, the practice of casting lots. In the Old Testament casting lots seems to have been primarily connected with priestly ministry and the use of the Urim and Thummim. For a New Testament setting for drawing lots, see Acts 1:26. Saul's hometown of Gibeah, three miles north of Jerusalem, became the first capital of the Israelite monarchy (10:26).

10:17–11:15 Saul is publicly confirmed as king. Jabesh Gilead (11:1), east of the Jordan River in the territory of Manasseh, was under siege by Nahash, whose name means "snake." The morning watch (11:11) was the last of the night watches (Lam. 2:19; Judg. 7:19; Exod. 14:24-27; Mark 6:48). They attacked while the Ammonites were still asleep. Barak (12:11) is also known as Bedan (NASB; KJV) which may be a scribal error for the name Barak of Judges 4–5 or possibly Abdon (Judg. 12:13, 15).

12:1-25 Samuel's farewell address. Samuel focused on the essentials in his farewell speech. He got to the heart of the nation's problem in desiring to have a king. They had forgotten God, the One who had delivered them throughout all of their history (12:1-12). To emphasize the severity of asking for a king, God sent thunder and rain (12:18-19). In spite of the people's mistake, if they and the king would obey the conditions of the Mosaic covenant, then God would remain with them. The king himself would not be the solution to Israel's problems, because he would not be above the conditions of the Mosaic covenant. For both king and people the way to blessing remained the same: obedience to God (12:24-25). God's love and faithfulness had not changed.

13:1-23 The disobedience of Saul. Saul's disobedience is related in 13:1-23, which presents the first of three foolish acts of Saul. Here, he disobeyed God's orders for sacrifice. In 1 Samuel 15 he disobeyed

God's order for not keeping any spoils of war. Between those two failures, in 1 Samuel 14, he put the nation under a foolish oath. These three actions form a contrast with the great and wise first acts of David and Solomon, the kings to come.

There is an obvious textual difficulty in 13:1. Originally it probably read "Saul was one and [thirty or forty?] years old when he began to reign, and when he had reigned two years over Israel, . . ." The age of Saul in this passage is impossible to know for sure as the various ancient texts disagree. The figure of 3,000 chariots in 13:5 is given as 30,000 in some translations (cf. NASB and KJV), a number which is excessively large (13:5). Some versions of the Greek and Syriac Old Testament read 3,000.

The events of 10:8–13:8 cannot be compressed into seven days. The agreement had been made two years earlier that prior to any engagement with the Philistines, Saul would meet Samuel at Gilgal for sacrifice and worship. Samuel's delay was a test of Saul's faith and obedience. The Philistine monopoly on iron and metal-working craftsmen (13:19-23) continued until the time of David (1 Chron. 22:3).

14:1-52 SAUL'S FOOLISH ORDER
Instead of "the Ark of God" (1 Sam. 14:18), the Septuagint reads "ephod," perhaps in light of the statement in 1 Samuel 7:2. Beth Aven (14:23; meaning, "house of evil") is a purposeful corruption of the name Bethel (meaning, "house of God"; cf. 1 Kings 12:26-33). On eating meat with the blood (1 Sam. 14:33), compare Leviticus 17:10-14. Saul expanded his kingdom to the south (Edom), east (Moab and Ammon), north (Zobah), and west (Philistia).

15:1-35 SAUL'S DISQUALIFYING FAILURE
The Amalekites (15:2) fought against Israel at Rephidim (Exod. 17:8-13) and were placed under divine judgment by the Lord (Deut. 25:19). Note Saul's pious reasons for his disobedience in 1 Samuel 15:13, 20-21. God began to show how Saul, through his disobedience, was rejected from the kingship, preparing the way for David's anointing.

This sequence of Saul's rejection is the first feature of the "Dynastic Defense," which runs from 1 Samuel 15 through 2 Samuel 8, and outlines the reasons why the rule of David, the new king, was legitimate. Such a defense would be especially important in the case of a king like David, who founded a new dynasty and could have been charged with usurping the throne. The features of this defense included: (1) the disqualification of the preceding ruler (1 Sam. 15); (2) the ability of the successor to lead and rule as demonstrated by his military achievements (1 Sam. 17); (3) the new king's leniency on political foes (1 Sam. 24, 26); (4) the king's interest in religious matters (2 Sam. 6–7); and (5) the record of kingdom expansion as evidence of divine blessing (2 Sam. 8).

In 15:11 God does not change his mind (cf. 15:29; James 1:17). Rather, God's regret is an expression of sorrow over Saul's sinful rebellion (cf. Gen. 6:6). The "Glory of Israel" (1 Sam. 15:29) is a unique term for God, emphasizing his constancy and endurance. The word "see" (15:35) can be translated "look with regard or interest."

16:1–31:13 David

Overview: This long section was designed to show how God preserved David from attempts on his life by Saul and foreign leaders and how faithful David was in trusting God to vindicate and avenge the wrong that was done to him. That faith contrasts with Saul's self-assertive reliance on his own wisdom and military might. The essence of what God wanted from a king was a patient trust in God's own power and timing. David absolutely resisted taking the throne by his own scheming or according to his own schedule. He waited for the Lord even at the cost of exile, hardship, and personal loss. David is a fine example of the righteous sufferer who patiently waits for exaltation in God's own time. As such, he is a type of Jesus, the perfect righteous Sufferer. In this light, read Philippians 2:1-18.

16:1-23 ANOINTED AT BETHLEHEM, BROUGHT BEFORE SAUL
David was anointed by Samuel, and he played the harp to soothe Saul's torment. The Lord did not suggest deception (1 Sam. 16:2), but he gave Samuel official sacrificial business to do in Bethlehem. While there, Samuel would be able to anoint David. Saul's mental torment

(16:14) may refer to demonic attack or influence. Perhaps God appointed a demon to torment Saul in order to drive the king to repentance. David's appointment as Saul's armor-bearer (16:21) probably took place after he killed Goliath, but it is recorded here because it fits with the theme of his entrance into royal service. The physical anointing with oil was symbolic of the anointing with the Holy Spirit (16:3, 6-7, 12-13). This activity of the Spirit for leadership was seen in the events of Numbers 11:24-30 and throughout the book of Judges. Here the anointing is specifically for kingship and symbolizes God's special enablement of David to be king. The spiritual presence of God for the king was the essence of the love spoken of in 2 Samuel 7:15, the love that departed from Saul.

17:1–18:9 THE VICTORY OVER GOLIATH
Goliath's taunting was a new low for the nation of Israel. One man blocked the entire army of God, an army that had seen entire nations run before it in fear. The Israelites viewed the situation only in human terms, much like their forefathers had viewed with fear and faithlessness the giants in the land (Num. 13:26–14:10). Goliath was 9 feet, 9 inches tall and wore a coat of armor weighing 125 pounds; his bronze javelin weighed 17 pounds (1 Sam. 17:4-5). But the heart of this story is David's confession in 17:45-47. Outward physical appearances were nothing when compared with the power of the unseen God. David relied not on Saul's armor but on his own proven abilities (17:39-40). Above all, he remembered what was truly important (17:45). The victory would become a witness to the world of who God was. David's conquest over Goliath revealed the power that one faithful man could possess—the man with the kind of heart God looked for (13:14; 16:7). In 17:55-58 Saul knew David from his contact in the court (16:18-23), but he needed to know his father's name to reward the family for the victory (17:25).

When Saul became David's enemy and began his initial persecution of him, David escaped two attempts on his life. Saul is described in the terms of pure jealousy (18:1-9). Note the mentions of what Saul was thinking (18:11, 17, 21). His jealousy issued in his making two attempts to murder David: first by hurling his spear at him (18:11), and then by requesting David to kill one hundred Philistines (18:25). Note the gradual growth of Saul's hatred for David (18:9, 12, 15, 29).

19:1-24 FOUR LIFE-SAVING EVENTS FOR DAVID
Jonathan successfully interceded with Saul for David (19:1-7). But later David again escaped Saul's spear when it was thrown at him (19:8-10). Then Michal helped David in his escape from Saul's plan for his assassination (19:11-17). The Holy Spirit prevented four attempts by Saul and his men to kill David from taking place (19:18-24). The Spirit controlled the words and actions of Saul and his men, who spoke God's words instead of doing evil deeds. This section shows that the split between David and Saul was all caused by Saul, for David wanted peace within Israel.

20:1-42 SAUL'S HATRED SOLIDIFIES
Jonathan told David that he would find out Saul's feelings about him at the New Moon Festival (20:12-13). This was a sacrificial meal that had both religious and civil significance (Num. 10:10; 28:11-15). The peace between David and Jonathan contrasts with Saul's hostility. From this point on David was a fugitive and outcast with regard to the royal court.

21:1–22:23 THE TRAGEDY AT NOB
David went to Nob, a priestly community located just one mile north of Jerusalem. He planned to meet there with his band of men (cf. Matt. 12:3). David and his men ate the consecrated bread or showbread, which was reserved for the priests (Exod. 25:30). Psalms 34 and 56 have their background in this encounter.

The priests at Nob were slain because Saul thought they had conspired with David against him (1 Sam. 22:12-19). While their deaths (22:17-19) were a partial fulfillment of the prophesied judgment on Eli's house (2:27-36), Saul was nevertheless responsible for this condemnable act. The cave of Adullam (22:1) may have been the background of Psalms 57 and 142. The "stronghold" (Hebrew, *mesudah*) (1 Sam. 22:5) is probably a reference to Masada, the moun-

tain fortress that towers 1,320 feet above the Dead Sea. On 22:9, see Psalm 52:1.

23:1-29 TWO TOWNS BETRAY DAVID
The Lord delivered David from Saul at Keilah, and David fled to the wilderness where he was delivered again from Saul. Keilah (23:1) was situated near the border of Philistine territory, about three miles south of Adullam. The wilderness of Ziph (23:14) surrounds the city of Ziph, about four miles southeast of Jerusalem (see introductory map). Arabah (23:24) means "wasteland." Jeshimon means "desert" or "waste" and refers to the desolate wilderness southeast of Hebron.

24:1–26:25 THREE "SPARINGS"
The section of 24:1–26:25 focuses on three events in which people's lives were spared.

First, David spared Saul's life (24:1-22). Note David's care for the Lord's anointed (24:5, 10; cf. 26:9, 11, 23; 29:1-11). That was leading up to Saul's death in 31:1-13. When Saul died, his death was in no way connected to David. This section also contains two prophecies of David's kingdom by Saul (24:20; 26:25).

Second, David was spared from performing an act of rash vengeance against Nabal by the wisdom of Abigail (25:1-44). Abigail stopped David and thus protected him from possible retaliation by Nabal's relatives. The metaphor "bound securely in the bundle of the living" (25:29) is taken from the custom of binding valuables in a bundle to protect them from loss or injury. In a similar way, God cares for his own. David's growing number of wives (25:43-44) marked the beginning of his royal harem, which was in violation of Deuteronomy 17:17.

Third, David again spared Saul (1 Sam. 26:1-25; cf. 26:9, 11, 23). When David spared Saul's life in the camp, Saul again foretold David's future victory. En Gedi (24:1), a lovely fresh-water oasis surrounded by desert, was located on the western shore of the Dead Sea. David's experience in the cave (24:3) may have provided the background for Psalms 57 and 142. David trusted God to remove Saul from the kingship rather than taking matters into his own hands (1 Sam. 24:10). The expression "Go, serve other gods" (26:19) expressed David's concern that to be driven from the land of Israel would be the equivalent of abandoning the worship of the true God. Whether Saul was sincere or not in confessing that he had sinned (26:21), David recognized the king's mental instability and declined the invitation.

27:1–31:13 DAVID'S EXILE AMONG THE PHILISTINES

David pretended to be loyal to the Philistines (27:1-12), but he deceived them by destroying their cities. Gath (27:2), a Philistine city (6:17), was situated twelve miles east of Ashdod. Ziklag (27:6) was situated on the Philistine coastal plain about fifteen miles northwest of Beersheba (see introductory map). The sixteen months (27:7) David spent in enemy territory prepared him for later Philistine wars by acquainting him with the geography of Philistia. The term "Negev" (27:10) is Hebrew for "south" and refers to the dry country at the southern end of Israel.

Saul sought a word from God regarding his battle against the Philistines (28:1-25). In 1 Samuel 28–31 the focus of the narrative shifts back and forth between David and Saul. David is presented as the victorious and anointed one, and Saul, the failing and rejected one.

The results of Saul's visiting the medium at Endor were to affirm David as king and to confirm Saul's death (28:7-19). The removal of spiritists and mediums was in keeping with the law (28:3; cf. Exod. 22:18; Lev. 19:31; Deut. 18:9-13). The Philistines were camped in the Valley of Jezreel at Shunem, a city located at the foot of the Hill of Moreh, while the Israel-

ites were camped five miles to the south at Mount Gilboa (see introductory map). For Urim see the discussion on Exodus 28:30. The term "medium" (1 Sam. 28:7) literally means "a mistress of a ghost." Mediums consult the dead to determine the future. This medium practiced her forbidden profession at Endor, located between the Hill of Moreh and Mount Tabor.

Is the appearance of Samuel to be interpreted as a psychological experience, demonic impersonation, trickery, or genuine? The text says it was Samuel, and the message was clearly from God (28:16-19). Perhaps this event is akin to the appearance of Moses and Elijah on the Mount of Transfiguration (Matt. 17:3).

God delivered David from the dilemma of having to fight Israel or being slain by the Philistines for treason. David was spared from fighting God's anointed (1 Sam. 29:1-11). He defeated the Amalekites and showed justice to his troops. The Amalekite attack was a further consequence of Saul's failure to carry out God's command (15:2-3, 10-19). David's generosity (30:26-31) won him the support of the citizens of Judah who were later to name him king (2 Sam. 2:1-4).

Saul and his sons were killed in battle (1 Sam. 31:1-13). Their bodies were taken to Beth Shan, located at the junction of the Jezreel and Jordan valleys, and were hung on the wall by the city square (cf. 2 Sam. 21:12). The men of Jabesh Gilead had not forgotten Saul's kindness to them in the past (1 Sam. 11:1-11). They removed their bodies and gave them an honorable burial.

SECOND SAMUEL NOTES

1:1–10:19 DAVID GROWS STRONGER

Overview: The many events of this section make two central points: (1) David committed no deceit or treachery to gain his kingdom. He acted with compassion and justice. That forms a stark contrast with other people such as Joab, Rechab, and Baanah, who committed murder for revenge or favor with the king. (2) God blessed David with loyal subjects and military victory. All of that provided the context for the estab-

lishment of God's covenant with David in 2 Samuel 7. David dealt with attempts to overthrow his rule, defeated the Philistines, secured a place for the Ark, and finally was given an eternal covenant of blessing.

1:1-27 Lament for the House of Saul

1:1-16 THE AMALEKITE'S STORY

The Amalekite's story was a fabrication (see the true account in 1 Sam. 31:4-5). He must have come across Saul's body on the battlefield and taken his crown and bracelet to substantiate the lie. The event highlighted what has been proved throughout 1 Samuel—that David honored the Lord and in no way would harm Saul, the Lord's anointed.

1:17-27 DAVID'S LAMENT FOR SAUL AND JONATHAN

The book of Jashar (1:17) is also mentioned in Joshua 10:13 and appears to have contained poetry about Israel's military heroes. The book of Jashar itself has not been found. Presumably, the original readers of the book of Samuel had access to the book of Jashar, which was used to give support to the facts in Samuel. The facts of Samuel were well-supported by other contemporary documents. Although the contemporary support for Samuel, the book of Jashar, has disappeared, the book of God's choice and revelation remains.

How could David speak so well of Saul after all that Saul had done to him? David viewed Saul from the standpoint of all the good that Saul had accomplished in Israel and of his previously high position before the Lord. David left judgment up to God and gave honor where it was due. The "heights" (2 Sam. 1:19) refers to Mount Gilboa (cf. 1 Sam. 31:8). The key phrase "How the mighty have fallen" (2 Sam. 1:25, 27) expressed the burden of the lament.

2:1–4:12 Conflict with the House of Saul

2:1-32 ABNER AND JOAB'S FIRST CONFLICT

David settled in at Hebron, but Abner, Saul's commander of Israel's army, led a military attempt to make Saul's son Ish-Bosheth king of the northern part of Israel. That led to an initial defeat of Abner's forces by Joab, David's commander. Abner, with the tribe of Benjamin's support, retreated after killing Joab's brother. Benjamin was the tribe to which Saul belonged. This functions as an example of the resistance David encountered to his becoming king over all Israel; it is summarized in 3:1.

Hebron (2:1), located in the Judean hills nineteen miles south of Jerusalem (see introductory map), served as David's capital during the first seven and a half years of his reign (2:11). The name Ish-Bosheth (2:8) means "man of shame." This is a deliberate twisting of the original name Ish-baal

(meaning "Baal lives") in light of his demise. The contest between champions (2:12-17) on behalf of the opposing armies took place at Gibeon (el-Jib), six miles north of Jerusalem. The pool with its steps has been excavated and can be seen today.

3:1-39 JOAB MURDERS ABNER

David's marriage to the daughter of Talmai (3:3), king of Geshur, probably sealed an alliance between the two kings. Marriage alliances between royal houses as a means of concluding treaties and cementing relationships between nations were common in the ancient Near East. But David's multiple marriages violated Israelite law (Deut. 7:3; 17:17). The kings of Israel were to depend on God for help, not on alliances with foreign rulers.

Abner vowed to help make David king over all Israel (2 Sam. 3:9-10) and began by making unifying speeches before the Benjamites and David's subjects in Hebron (3:17-19). Abner was slain in Hebron, a city of refuge (Josh. 20:7), where not even a blood avenger could slay a murderer without a trial (2 Sam. 3:22-27; cf. Num. 35:22-25). The death of Abner is presented in such a way as to again confirm that David did not resort to murder to gain the kingdom (2 Sam. 3:28, 37).

4:1-12 DAVID JUSTLY ELIMINATES HIS OPPOSITION

The reference to Mephibosheth (4:4), a living descendant of Saul, lays the foundation for 2 Samuel 9. Ish-Bosheth was "innocent" (4:11) in that he was not guilty of any wicked deed or crime. He had merely assumed the throne upon Saul's death at the encouragement of Abner. Again, David was shown to be righteous and fair as he built his kingdom by justice, not treachery.

5:1–10:19 Establishing the House of David

5:1-25 DAVID WINS JERUSALEM AND DEFEATS THE PHILISTINES

The several references to the Lord's appointment of David confirm the central reason for his success (3:18; 5:2, 10, 12). David became king of the entire nation (5:1-5) and captured Jerusalem (5:6-10). Zion (5:7), the Jebusite fortress, became David's capital, the city of David. The city had steep cliffs on three sides, a good water supply, and was on the north-south travel route. The fortress (5:9), or Millo (NASB and KJV, from the Hebrew, "to fill"), was a mound or terrace that served as a foundation for a building. In 5:10 the secret of David's success is revealed: God's presence with him. The multiplication of David's wives (5:13) was a direct violation of Deuteronomy 17:17.

God gave David two initial victories over the Philistines. The valley of Rephaim (5:18) penetrated the hill country from the coastal plain to the west, giving strategic access to Jerusalem. Baal Perazim (5:20) is literally translated "the Lord of breaking forth." The image is that of floodwaters breaking through a dam just as David's troops broke through the Philistine assault.

6:1-23 DAVID RETURNS THE ARK TO JERUSALEM

The Ark was to be carried by the sons of Kohath (Num. 3:30-31), not to be placed on a cart or vehicle, and it was not to be touched (Num. 4:15). The violation cost Uzzah his life and again reminded Israel that no matter how long ago God had said something, he still meant it (2 Sam. 6:3-7). That was the basis both of their fear of God and of their confidence in his consistency.

The term "danced" (6:14) literally means "whirled around." It served as an exuberant expression of worship and praise (Ps. 149:3). For comments on "ephod," see 1 Samuel 2:18. The word "disrobing" (2 Sam. 6:20) is a derogatory reference to David's wearing an ephod. Normally, a longer robe was worn under the ephod (Exod. 28:31-35). Without the longer robe, more of David's body was exposed. However, the problem was with Michal's hard heart toward the Lord that resulted in her sarcastic and untrue criticism, not with any inappropriateness with David's dress.

7:1-29 A HOUSE FOR GOD AND A HOUSE FOR DAVID

Second Samuel 7 revolves around one main idea: the concept of "house." David wanted to build God a *house*—the temple. God made a covenant to build the *house* of royal lineage for David. The emphasis is on what God already had done and would do in the future for David (note the "I will" statements in 7:9, 10, 11, 12, 13, 14). The heart of the covenant was the promise of God's loving-kindness that would never depart. Saul's

experience had illustrated what it meant for God to remove his loving-kindness (7:15).

David was not allowed to build the temple (7:5) because he had waged wars and shed blood (1 Chron. 22:8; 28:3). David wanted to build God a house, but God told him that he would build a house or dynasty that would be a royal dynasty for him (2 Sam. 7:11-13). The promise God made to David, known as the Davidic covenant (Ps. 89:20-37), was built upon the promise God made to Abraham regarding a future nation (Gen. 12:2). God promised David an eternal house, throne and kingdom (2 Sam. 7:16). David's house or dynasty would always be the royal line and would continue forever. The right to rule on the throne would always belong to David's seed. Finally, the right to a literal kingdom or dominion would never be taken from David's posterity. The rule of David's dynasty was interrupted with the Babylonian exile, but the right to rule was never rescinded. The ultimate fulfillment of this promise will be realized in Jesus Christ (Luke 1:31-33; see the fuller discussion of the Davidic covenant in the introductory section).

David's response of praise to this great covenant revolved around three aspects of God's grace: (1) God's favor at the present time (2 Sam. 7:18-21); (2) God's work in the past (7:22-24); and (3) God's promise for the future (7:25-29).

8:1-18 DAVID SECURES PEACE FROM EXTERNAL ENEMIES

David's list of defeated enemies (the Philistines, 8:1; the Moabites, 8:2; Zobah, 8:3-4; the Arameans, or Syrians, 8:5-8) led to a summary statement of his rule: it was unified, just, and righteous (8:15). The chief city was Metheg Ammah, or Gath (8:1; 1 Chron. 18:1). (See the introductory map for Gath's location.) David either spared the young Moabites whose height was approximately one cord and executed the adults whose height was two cords, or he selected one of three rows of soldiers to be spared execution (2 Sam. 8:2). Zobah (8:3) was an Aramean kingdom north of Damascus. The figure 1,700 horsemen in some translations (8:4, NASB and KJV) is apparently a scribal error in transmission for 1,000 chariots and 7,000 horsemen or charioteers (NIV; see the Septuagint and 1 Chron. 18:4). The term "Syrians" for "Arameans" (8:5, KJV) is

not correct since Syria did not exist as a political entity until the Greek period. The Hebrew
reads "Aram" and the people were Arameans.
This territory was in the region of Damascus.
The reference in 8:13 to Edom rather than to
the Syrians (KJV) is probably correct (Ps. 60:1;
1 Chron. 18:12).

9:1-13 DAVID'S KINDNESS TO THE MEMORY OF JONATHAN

The expression "a dead dog" (2 Sam. 9:8)
refers to someone contemptible and useless.
David provided the necessities of life for
Mephibosheth (9:10), but he had to make
provision for the maintenance of his own
family and servants.

10:1-19 DAVID DEFEATS THE AMMONITES AND THE ARAMEANS

This is a mighty example of David's strength
in battle and forms the contrast to David's
upcoming great failure in 2 Samuel 11. The
shaving (10:4) was regarded as a form of
grave humiliation and indignity. The 700
charioteers (10:18) is probably a scribal error
in transmission for 7,000 (cf. 1 Chron.
19:18).

11:1–20:26 DAVID'S HOUSEHOLD EVIL

11:1–12:31 Adultery and Murder

11:1-27 THE SIN

The deadly result of David's actions regarding Bathsheba and Uriah is found in
2 Samuel 11:27, "The thing David had
done displeased the Lord" or "was evil in
the sight of the Lord" (NASB), the very
phrase found throughout the book of Judges
to describe the beginning of God's
judgments (Judg. 2:11; 3:7, 12; 4:1; 6:1).

Most oriental homes had an enclosed
courtyard that was regarded as part of the
house. But the interior of Bathsheba's courtyard could be seen from David's palace
roof (2 Sam. 11:2), which was at a higher
elevation on Mount Zion. David saw, he
inquired, and then he yielded to temptation
(11:2-5). This same progression of sin is
revealed in James 1:14-15. David's lust
gave birth to sin, which resulted in judgment. The words "purified herself" (2 Sam.
11:4) reflect the requirements of the Mosaic
Law (Lev. 15:18). The expression "wash
your feet" used by David in speaking to
Uriah (2 Sam. 11:8) is an idiom meaning
"spend some time at home." While David

had succeeded in concealing his sin from
the general public, the omniscient God
knew of the whole evil affair (11:27).

12:1-31 THE CONVICTION AND REPENTANCE

This event illustrates the power of the
Davidic covenant. God would indeed
punish David's disobedience, but his
loving-kindness would never be taken
away (7:14-15). The chapter describes the
indictment of David and the births of two
sons: one who died and the other who
was beloved by the Lord, Solomon
(12:24). Nathan brought the words of
God's condemnation of David's sin (12:1-4)
and his love for David's son (12:25).

These predictions of discipline (12:9-11)
were fulfilled in the violent deaths of Amnon
(13:28-29) and Absalom (18:15), and
Absalom's public appropriation of David's
royal concubines (16:22). David's confession
was immediate, as was God's gracious
forgiveness (12:13). The fuller expression of David's confession is found in
Psalm 51.

Many people use 12:23 to support the
view that infants and children who die are
taken to heaven. However, the verse is not
speaking to the question of afterlife, but of
the inevitability of death. The child could not
return to life and activity, but David would
someday join his son in death. David
expected to go to Sheol, the place of the
righteous and unrighteous dead (Ps. 16:10:
6:4-5). Although the Bible does not reveal
what happens to an infant that dies, the holy
and righteous God can be trusted to do what
is right. The name Jedidiah (2 Sam. 12:25,
meaning "beloved of the Lord") marked
Solomon as the successor to David's throne.

God's continued blessing on David's
military might was reconfirmed in 12:26-31.
Rabbah (12:29, modern Amman), located in
Transjordan at the border of the desert, was
the capital of Ammon. It was later rebuilt and
renamed Philadelphia. There are two views
regarding David's treatment of the Ammonites
(12:31). He either imposed hard labor (NIV)
or cruel death on the captives. The latter
view would be more in accordance with 1
Chronicles 20:3 (NASB; cf. KJV), which
says David "cut them with saws and with
sharp instruments and with axes." That punishment was in accordance with Ammonite

ways (1 Sam. 11:2; Amos 1:13) and was probably limited to those who resisted David.

13:1-39 Revenge

This story concerns Amnon's lust for and rape of Tamar (2 Sam. 13:1-14), Absalom's two-year-long grudge that resulted in revenge (13:15-29), and the initial exile of Absalom and David's longing for him. But why are these depressing stories recorded in Scripture? They are a direct fulfillment of God's punishment for David's sin with Bathsheba as spoken through Nathan the prophet (12:10-11). Like David, Amnon had a moment of sexual incontinence. Like David, Absalom resorted to murder. David was furious, but he took no action because he had been guilty of similar sins (13:21). In the same way Absalom was full of hatred but had no communication with Amnon (13:22).

Levitical law prohibited marriage to one's brother or sister (Lev. 18:11). Perhaps Tamar made the suggestion of marriage in the hope that there would be a chance for her to escape (2 Sam. 13:13). The Jewish Talmud assumes that Tamar was of illegitimate birth and therefore the two could have been married. Baal Hazor (13:23), located at the highest point in the mountains of Ephraim at 3,333 feet, is fifteen miles north of Jerusalem. The territory of Geshur (13:38) extends along the eastern shore of the Sea of Galilee and the northern bank of the Yarmuk River.

14:1–20:26 Insurrection in David's Kingdom

14:1-33 DAVID CALLS FOR ABSALOM'S RETURN
The woman from Tekoa (14:1-20) used the same technique as Nathan did in 2 Samuel 12 in order to convict David of his guilt. The technique was effective because it was easier for David to see sin in others than it was to see it in himself. The self-righteousness that covers personal sin in ourselves inevitably wants to see the same kind of sin punished in others. The unfolding of God's punishment for David's sin continued.

Three men were consumed by interpersonal conflicts and their uncontrolled personal lust: (1) Amnon wanted, got, and hated; (2) Absalom hated, murdered, wanted to see his father, David, deceived, and was murdered; and (3) David longed for his son

but would not see him. All of this created an awful state of family strife.

Tekoa (14:2), the hometown of the prophet Amos, was located five miles south of Bethlehem. David's unwillingness to completely forgive and restore Absalom (14:23-24) bore bitter fruit in the heart of his son (cf. 2 Sam. 15–18).

15:1-37 DAVID FLEES FROM ABSALOM
While in Hebron, Absalom accomplished a military coup, causing David to flee east out of Jerusalem. David saw himself as expendable and under the sovereign will of God (15:25-26; 16:12). David also was not without his own plans (15:34). Some translations (NASB; KJV) have the figure "forty" (15:7), which is probably a scribal error and should read "four" as do the Septuagint, Syriac, and Josephus (cf. NIV). David fled, fearing for his personal safety and seeking to avoid an attack on Jerusalem (15:14). The brook Kidron (15:23) separates the Mount of Olives from the temple mount.

16:1-23 ABSALOM SECURES JERUSALEM
Two remnants of Saul's old regime, Mephibosheth (16:1-4) and Shimei (16:5-14), begin the section of 16:1-23. Absalom's taking David's harem (16:20-23) fulfilled the judgments prophesied in 12:11-12. In ancient times the seizure of the royal harem demonstrated possession of the throne (16:21-22; cf. 3:7). This public spectacle was the greatest possible insult to David.

17:1-29 GOD PROTECTS DAVID
In case the reader wonders what God's attitude toward Absalom was at this point, 17:14 provides the answer. God had someone other than Absalom in mind for the next king after David. God gave David time to escape by thwarting the counsel of Ahithophel (17:14). En Rogel (17:17) is a spring situated a short distance south of the junction of the Kidron and Hinnom valleys, not far from Jerusalem. Ahithophel (17:23) committed suicide because (1) he was humiliated by Absalom's rejection of his advice, and (2) he could foresee Absalom's defeat and knew that he would then be accountable to David for his disloyalty. Mahanaim (17:24), situated in Transjordan, was Ish-Bosheth's former capital (2:8). (See the introductory map for the location of Mahanaim.)

18:1-33 DAVID DEFEATS ABSALOM

With the tragic words of 18:33, the prophecy that the sword would not depart from David's house took on terrible proportions. The forest of Ephraim (18:6) was north of the Jabbok River in Transjordan. Because of the rugged nature of the terrain, the pursuit through the forest resulted in more deaths than the battle (18:8). The tradition that Absalom was caught by his hair comes from Josephus, but it makes sense in light of 14:26. The coming of a band of men would signify a defeat to those waiting in the city, but the coming of one man signified a victory (18:26-27).

19:1-43 DAVID REESTABLISHES HIS RULE

Second Samuel 19 shows the return of David as he dealt with military unity by ending his mourning for Absalom (19:1-8) and by attaching Amasa to his army (19:9-15). The two remnants of Saul's regime that affected David as he left the city were dealt with again upon his return (19:16-30). Barzillai, the man who had supported David during his exile, was honored (19:31-43).

Joab warned that David's disposition was affecting the morale and loyalty of the people (19:7). David would be in deep trouble if he did not express appreciation for those who had fought for him. David replaced Joab with Amasa (19:13) to secure the allegiance of the rebel army (17:25) and to discipline Joab for slaying Absalom. The expression "house of Joseph" (19:20) refers to Ephraim (the offspring of Joseph's son), which, as a large tribe, was representative of the ten northern tribes. For 19:24-30, compare Mephibosheth's story with Ziba's (16:1-4). Did Mephibosheth or Ziba lie? Apparently David could not decide and gave both a share of the inheritance.

20:1-26 SHEBA

Again a split occurred between Israel and Judah under Sheba's rebellion. The slogan "Every man to his tent" (20:1) meant "Let's go home and from there we will offer resistance." A kiss on the cheek (20:9) was a customary oriental greeting. Joab committed another murder of David's ally Amasa (20:9-10). Abel Beth Maacah (20:14) was about twenty-five miles north of the Sea of Galilee in the Hula Valley. The expression "a mother in Israel" (20:19) refers to Abel Beth Maacah, which was a prominent city or capital of the region. The forced labor (20:24) was one of the evils of kingship promised by Samuel (1 Sam. 8:11-16).

The defeat of Sheba's civil war marked the end of the various attempts to overthrow or divide up David's kingdom listed in the book of Samuel. It continues the report of God's judgment on David's sins of adultery and murder, yet it also recounts God's grace, which is seen in the preservation of David's kingdom and in God not removing his loving-kindness as he had done with King Saul. Although David suffered discipline, he still ended up secure and victorious (2 Sam. 20:23-26).

21:1–24:25 DAVID AS A MEDIATOR AND PRESERVER

Second Samuel 21–24 forms one beautifully constructed literary unit. The accompanying chart outlines the arrangement of its content.

The Davidic covenant was at the heart and source of all of David's victories for the nation. Military victory only came about through God's covenanted support to establish David securely in the land (2 Sam. 7:9-10). The framework for this section begins and ends with two national judgments. The first (2 Sam. 21) was caused by Saul breaking the covenant with the Gibeonites,

---

OUTLINE OF 2 SAMUEL 21–24

National Judgment: Saul's Act (21:1-14)
   Military Victory through Mighty Men (21:15-22)
      Song of Praise for the Davidic Covenant: Past Victory (22:1-51)
      Song of Praise for the Davidic Covenant: Future Security (23:1-7)
   Military Victory through Mighty Men (23:8-39)
National Judgment: David's Act (24:1-25)

which was established under Joshua (Josh. 9:16-21). The last (2 Sam. 24) was caused by David's sin in counting the members of his armies. Both instances concluded with the phrase "God [the Lord] answered prayer in behalf of the land" (21:14; 24:25).

How was God moved and by whose entreaty? In 2 Samuel 21 it was on the basis of doing "everything the king commanded" (21:14). In 2 Samuel 24 God was moved through the king's priestly intercession. The message was clear: the king was the mediator between God and the nation. When he obeyed, God was moved to bless the people and the land. But the source and power of that blessing were in the covenant God had made with David.

Both books of Samuel need to be interpreted in the light of this concluding section. It reveals God's original intentions for the kingship in Israel: God alone was to be King. It explains the abortive reign of Saul: an example of what it means to have God take his loving-kindness away from the king. It also explains the ups and downs of David's rule: discipline with the rods of men (2 Sam. 7:14) but with love from God that never departs (7:15).

The great covenant with David points to the King of kings, God's Son. Every human king showed himself to be more or less imperfect. Originally, God alone was to be King. And he accomplished that through Jesus, who was both his incarnate Son and the Son of David. Through Jesus' mediation and obedience believers may all experience the nondeparting love of God (cf. 2 Sam. 7:15 with 2 Cor. 6:18).

21:1-14 National Judgment: Saul's Sin, David's Entreaty

Saul violated the treaty Joshua had made four hundred years earlier with the Gibeonites (Josh. 9:3-27). In light of Deuteronomy 24:16 and Ezekiel 18:1-4, 14-17, it is probable that the seven sons (2 Sam. 21:6) were directly implicated in the attack upon the Gibeonites. The word "hang" (21:6, NASB and KJV) refers to a solemn execution involving the exposure of the dead body. Since Michal died childless (6:23), it is likely that the reference (21:8) is to Merab, the wife of Adriel (1 Sam. 18:19). Rizpah (2 Samuel 21:10-11) remained by the dead

bodies from the time of the barley harvest in April to the early rains of October (cf. Deut. 21:23). When David was told what she had done, he took the bones of Saul and Jonathan from the citizens of Jabesh Gilead and buried them, as well as the bones of those who had been recently killed (2 Sam. 21:11-14).

21:15-22 Military Victory through Mighty Men

The spear of Ishbi-Benob (21:16) weighed about eight pounds. The "lamp of Israel" was David, whose life and actions served as a bright light for the nation (21:17). Here, the slaying of Goliath was attributed to Elhanan (21:19), in contradiction with 1 Samuel 17:50. The parallel account in 1 Chronicles 20:5 indicates that Elhanan killed "the brother of Goliath."

22:1-51 Song of Praise for the Davidic Covenant: Past Victory

This hymn of praise (2 Sam. 22:1-51) is almost identical to Psalm 18. The "horn" (2 Sam. 22:3) is a common symbol for strength in Hebrew poetry; animals often use their horns to defend themselves. The "word of the Lord" (22:31) is used in Scripture as an image of divine power.

23:1-7 Song of Praise for the Davidic Covenant: Future Security

The "last words of David" (23:1) were probably his last formal utterance. The basis of his hope was the everlasting covenant (23:5).

23:8-39 Military Victory

According to 1 Chronicles 11:10, these mighty men (2 Sam. 23:8-39) helped David to become king. The "thirty-seven" (23:39) included the three (23:8-12), Abishai and Benaiah (23:18-23), the thirty-one (23:24-39) and David's commander, Joab (23:37).

24:1-25 National Judgment: David's Sin, David's Entreaty

While Satan actually instigated the pride and rebellion that led to the numbering of the people (1 Chron. 21:1), God was using Satan to accomplish his plan (2 Sam. 24:1; cf. Gen. 50:20). Why was the numbering of the people wrong (2 Sam. 24:10)? Josephus speculated that David forgot to collect the half-shekel temple tax when he took the census (Exod. 30:12-13). Perhaps he had been commanded not to number the people but did so anyway. Perhaps the numbering was evidence of a lack of faith. David may have been trusting in his own resources rather than in the Lord. The exact reason is not important. The text simply asserts that it was wrong for him to do so.

David insisted on buying the threshing floor because he did not want to give the Lord something that had cost him nothing (2 Sam. 24:24). He believed in sacrificial giving (cf. 2 Cor. 8:1-3). The threshing floor that David purchased (2 Sam. 24:24) is identified in 2 Chronicles 3:1 as Mount Moriah. Traditionally this is understood to be the mountain in the land of Moriah where Abraham offered Isaac (Gen. 22:2), and it would soon be the site of Solomon's temple.

Religious, military, and civil unity was achieved under the king in Israel (2 Sam. 20:23-26). Those were the three continual problems that the Israelites had struggled with in the book of Judges. The book of Samuel shows that God's man on the throne could make significant intercession for the nation to bring about God's rule in Israel. All of this was a temporal and imperfect vision of the rule to be brought in by the perfect Son of David, Jesus the Messiah.

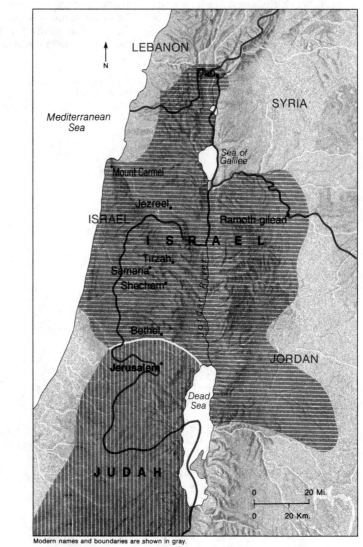

KEY PLACES IN 1 KINGS

1 & 2 Kings

BASIC FACTS

HISTORICAL SETTING
The books of Kings begin where the books of Samuel left off, with the death of David and the coronation of his son Solomon. The books then cover the histories of the united kingdom and the divided kingdoms, leading up to the fall of the northern kingdom, Israel, to Assyria in 722 B.C. and the later fall of Judah to Babylon in 586 B.C. Throughout the books, Syria, Assyria, and Babylon are the great political threats to God's people.

AUTHOR
The author of these books is unknown. Jeremiah has been named as author by some scholars because portions of his prophecy appear in 2 Kings 24–25 (cf. Jer. 39–42; 52 with 2 Kings 24–25). But the common consensus admits that the author(s) cannot be identified with any certainty.

DATE
The books cover the events during the time period between 970 and 586 B.C. They end with the elevation of King Jehoiachin in Babylon during the Babylonian captivity. Whatever the exact date of writing, the events recorded end in the middle of the Babylonian exile.

PURPOSE
The books are designed to explain why God's people fell into such great destruction and captivity. They show the people's consistent disobedience contrasted with God's consistent faithfulness to his words of blessing and discipline. God was faithful to his promises to David. But in light of the failures of David and Solomon, the great figures in the books of Kings are the prophets Elijah and Elisha. The prophets came in to rebuke sin and encourage a return to faithfulness.

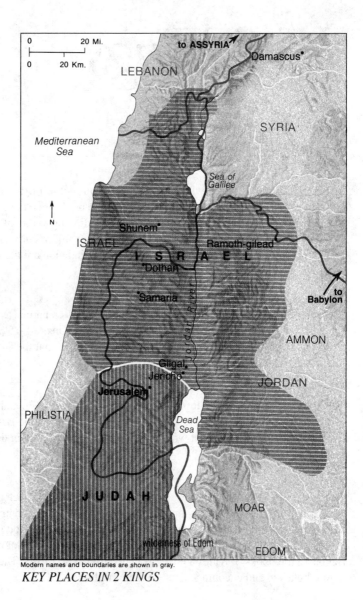

KEY PLACES IN 2 KINGS

GEOGRAPHY AND ITS IMPORTANCE

The books of 1 and 2 Kings were originally one unbroken book. The book was written while Israel was still in captivity, cut off from her homeland. Geographically, the single book of Kings begins in Jerusalem and ends in Babylon. This movement from Jerusalem to Babylon involves the split of God's people into two nations, north and south; the split of God's rule through kings into two lines, David's line and a series of dynasties in the north; and then the final destruction of first the northern and then the southern half of God's nation. The split of the kingdom into north and south resulted in several capital cities (Jerusalem in the south; Shechem, and later, Tirzah and Samaria in the north) and three centers of worship (Jerusalem in the south; Dan and Bethel in the north). By the end of the book of Kings, a small number of God's people had fled back to Egypt and most had been taken as captives to Babylon.

GUIDING CONCEPTS

THE FUNCTION OF THE PROPHETS
The book of Kings is part of the collection of books known as the former prophets (Joshua, Judges, Samuel, Kings). For a discussion concerning the former prophets see the *Guiding Concepts* section for Joshua. These books, when taken together with the book of Deuteronomy, form a beautiful history of God's relationship with his people. This means that the book of Kings is not merely a book of dry history. Rather, it is a book designed to bring a prophetic word of exhortation and encouragement to God's people in the midst of their failure and discipline for their sins. Throughout the book of Kings, great emphasis is placed on the certainty of the fulfillment of God's prophetic words of blessing and warning. No matter how long ago God had spoken a word, the certainty of its fulfillment remained in full force forever. That cut both ways to provide both security and warning to God's people, as God's words confirmed the potency of his covenants through Abraham, Moses, and David.

THE UNITY OF FIRST AND SECOND KINGS
The two books of Kings were inspired by God as one unified whole. Therefore, they can only be properly understood by studying them as a single unit. For example, the exaltation of King Jehoiachin by the king of Babylon in the last chapter of 2 Kings is the positive end toward which both 1 and 2 Kings are headed. Furthermore, 2 Kings 17:7-23 is the key to understanding the structure of 1 Kings and illustrates why Israel and Judah fell into captivity. Also, without the lesson taught in 2 Kings 17, Solomon's great speech at the dedication of the temple in 1 Kings 8 cannot be set into its proper context. This *Bible Companion* approaches 1 and 2 Kings as a single interpretive whole.

THE PERSPECTIVE OF THE BOOK
The end of 2 Kings gives a perspective for viewing the entire work. The last act described in the book of 2 Kings is the elevation of Jehoiachin out of prison

and into the king of Babylon's court. That event occurred a little past halfway through the seventy-year period of exile. The best that could be said when the book was written was that the king of Judah had been released from prison; it was a sign that God's favor through the Davidic covenant was still operative, even during Israel's exile. Therefore, the book of Kings was written from the perspective of being in the Babylonian exile, a time when failure still stung and release was still far off.

That exilic viewpoint was designed to make sure the exiles stopped blaming God for their defeats and instead confessed their own responsibility for failure. It also was geared to providing the only ray of hope possible in the middle of exile: God's unswerving faithfulness to David, even through the past reigns of faithless kings. Just as God's promise of discipline for sin was certain, so also was his promise of blessing. It was up to the people of God to decide if they would repent from their careless attitude toward God during the captivity and faithfully wait for his promised restoration of David's royal line.

KEY SPEECHES IN THE BOOK OF KINGS

Several key speeches enable readers to understand and apply the message of 1 and 2 Kings: (1) The temple as the location of both present and future hope (1 Kings 8:12-61). (2) Prophecy of the divided kingdom (1 Kings 11:31-39). (3) Reasons for the Assyrian captivity of Israel (2 Kings 17). Second Kings 17 is the key chapter for revealing the purpose and perspective of the book of Kings. (4) Reasons for the Babylonian captivity of Judah (2 Kings 21:10-15; cf. 24:1-4).

THE EVALUATIONS OF THE KINGS

Throughout 1 and 2 Kings, the description of each king's reign includes a moral evaluation. The northern kings were all given bad evaluations and are compared to Jeroboam I, who led the northern kingdom into idolatry (cf. 1 Kings 11:28-29; 14:16; 15:26, 30, 34; 16:2, 13, 26; 21:22; 2 Kings 3:3; 10:29, 31; 13:2, 6, 11; 14:24; 15:9, 18, 24, 28; 17:21; 21:10-16; there is a fulfillment of 1 Kings 13:1-3 in 2 Kings 23:15; note also 2 Kings 23:26-27). A phrase like the one in Judges occurs throughout the book of Kings: "did evil in the eyes of the Lord" (1 Kings 11:6; 14:22; 15:26, 34; 16:19, 25, 30; 21:20, 25; 22:52; 2 Kings 3:2; 8:18, 27; 13:2, 11; 14:24; 15:9, 18, 24, 28; 17:2, 17; 21:2, 6, 15-16, 20; 23:32; 24:9, 19). The evil done by the Israelites is described in 1 Kings 14:23-24 and 2 Kings 16:3; 17:7-12; 21:6 (cf. Deut. 12:2-3, 31). The central focus of obedience was true worship at the Jerusalem temple. The focus of disobedience involved other places of worship, even under the guise of worshiping the true God of Israel.

BIBLE-WIDE CONCEPTS

THE FOCUS ON THE DAVIDIC COVENANT

Another key concept is found in the phrases "David's sake" and "Lamp of David" (some selected verses are 1 Kings 2:33, 45; 8:66; 11:12-13, 32, 34, 36, 39; 15:4-5;

2 Kings 8:19; 19:34; 20:6). The rebellions of the various kings only served by contrast to highlight God's faithfulness to his covenant with David.

THE PERSPECTIVE OF THE EXODUS FROM EGYPT

The past acts of God's love were firmly rooted in the exodus from Egypt. The exodus was to Israel what the cross is to the Christian: the focus of God's love and power to break the bondage of evil. All of Israel's subsequent rebellions were viewed as sadly contradictory to the original salvation and purity brought about by the exodus. The book of Kings continually refers back to that great redemptive event. The temple's construction (1 Kings 6:1) and dedication (8:9, 16, 21, 51, 53; 9:9) were linked back to the exodus. Even the apostate Jeroboam I used the exodus to encourage the worship of his false gods (12:28). Israel's failure to love God from the exodus on is given as the primary reason for the Assyrian and Babylonian captivities (2 Kings 17:7, 36; 21:15). And the reason for those captivities already had been prophesied by God long before in Deuteronomy 29:24-25.

NEEDS MET BY FIRST AND SECOND KINGS

The book of Kings presents the history of Israel from David's final years to about halfway through the Babylonian captivity. The perspective given is one that recognized God's divine promise despite human failure. Israel had received the great promises of God to Abraham, Moses and David. Israel had also lost its temple and land and was now cast off into captivity. The book of Kings shows how the Babylonian captivity did not mean the end of God's promises to Abraham and David and that the reason for the sad state of God's people was not due to God's failure but to their own. The structure and content of Kings show that its author was answering questions like the following for his readers.

- Is God in control of Israel and the nations around them?
  (For the answer to that question see the following passages: 1 Kings 2:27; 6:11-12; 8:20, 56; 12:15; 13:1, 2, 5, 9, 16-18, 20-26, 32; 14:17-18; 15:29; 16:12, 34; 17:16, 24; 18:31, 36; 20:35-36; 2 Kings 2:22; 4:44; 7:1, 16; 9:36; 10:10, 17; 14:25; 15:12; 23:16-17; 24:2.)
- Why is Israel in such trouble if God is in control?
  (For the answer, see Deut. 28:9; Josh. 1:8; 2 Kings 17:13.)
- In light of Israel's past failures is there is any hope for a future with God?
  (See 1 Kings 8:28-30; 11:36; 2 Kings 23:25; 25:27-30.)

Christians today may find themselves in the middle of God's discipline, much like the Israelites found themselves in captivity. But that pain of discipline should not be taken as if God has voided all his promises. Believers first need to realize that the pain of discipline is due to their own failure, not God's. Then, the discipline should be seen as a clear confirmation that they are still his children, still under his disciplining care, and still participating in the hope of his promises. Discipline should result in a confession of failures, a reaffirmation of commitment to obedience, and hope for future restoration.

OUTLINE OF FIRST AND SECOND KINGS

A. OBEDIENCE: THE UNITED KINGDOM (1 Kings 1:1–11:43)
   1. The Kingdom Is Established (1:1–2:46)
   2. Kingdom Blessings from Obedience (3:1–10:29)
   3. Foundations of Chastisement (11:1-43)
B. CHASTISEMENT: THE DIVIDED KINGDOM (1 Kings 12:1—2 Kings 17:41)
   1. Jeroboam's Lost Opportunity (1 Kings 12:1–14:20)
   2. The Lamp of David in Jerusalem (1 Kings 14:21–15:24)
   3. The Prophetic Word Certified against Covenant Unfaithfulness (1 Kings 15:25—2 Kings 10:36)
   4. Covenant Blessing from Obedience (2 Kings 11:1–14:29)
   5. Chastisement Confirmed and Explained (2 Kings 15:1–17:41)
C. PRESERVATION: THE SOLITARY KINGDOM (2 Kings 18:1–25:30)
   1. Reform: Babylon Introduced (18:1–20:21)
   2. Irrevocable Chastisement: Manasseh and Amon (21:1-26)
   3. Reform in the Shadow of Judgment: Josiah (22:1–23:30)
   4. Chastisement Confirmed (23:31–25:26)
   5. Preservation of the Davidic Kingship: Jehoiachin Restored (25:27-30)

FIRST KINGS NOTES

1:1–11:43 OBEDIENCE: THE UNITED KINGDOM

Overview: First Kings 1–11 shows how Solomon overcame various threats to his reign, built the temple, and became the object of international respect. The key phrase is "his rule was firmly established" (1 Kings 2:12, 46), a fulfillment of the promise in 2 Samuel 7:12. The loving-kindness of the Davidic covenant was confirmed for Solomon (1 Kings 3:6) and illustrated in his great wisdom to rule with justice (3:28). First Kings 4 shows Israel at its greatest height and describes its greatness in the terms of the Abrahamic promise of land (cf. 4:21 with Gen. 15:18). First Kings 5–10 details the temple's completion and the kingdom's impact on the nations. First Kings 11 shows the split in the kingdom brought on by Solomon's sins. The great amount of detail used to describe the religious and international successes of Solomon's rule was to illustrate to the suffering exiles how great all of their lives could be when the king obeyed God, and why blessing could so quickly turn to destruction when the king rebelled. It also presents a picture of the hope for the future restored kingdom of David when God will once again establish the Son of David on the throne in Israel.

1:1–2:46 The Kingdom Is Established
1:1-53 LEADERSHIP IN CRISIS
First Kings 1–2 tells of struggles through which Solomon had to pass in order to be placed securely on the throne (2:46). Solomon ruled forty years (970–931 B.C.). The phrase "take care of" (1:2) refers to someone who is in an intimate relationship with another person. The fact that David did not have intimate sexual relations with Abishag (1:4) is recorded to demonstrate that she was not David's concubine and to explain how it could thus occur to Adonijah to ask that she become his wife (2:17; cf. Deut. 22:30).

Three statements about David (1 Kings 1:1; 2:1; 2:10) show the king's weakness and his openness to a military takeover. Adonijah's first rebellion took place because the king was ill. His second rebellion concerned taking David's virgin for his own wife (1:4). Adonijah (1:5), David's fourth but oldest surviving son (cf. 2 Sam. 3:2-4), regarded himself as next in line for the throne. Usually the king's oldest living son would reign, but Solomon had been promised the throne (1 Kings 1:13, 17, 30). Solomon had been singled out in 2 Samuel 12:24-25 as the one loved by the Lord (cf. 1 Chron. 22:6-10). Adonijah was either unaware of David's vow to make Solomon king, or he chose to ignore it. En Rogel (1 Kings 1:9), a spring marking the boundary between Judah and Benjamin (Josh. 18:16), is located near Jerusalem, just south of the junction of the Kidron and Hinnom valleys.

When his supporters dispersed (1 Kings 1:49-50), Adonijah took refuge at the tabernacle, which was at Gibeon (1 Chron. 16:39). Taking hold of the horns of the altar was a means of claiming refuge from an avenger (cf. Exod. 21:14). Adonijah was placed under severe conditions (1 Kings 1:52) and house arrest (1:53), forcing him to retire from public life.

2:1-12 THE CHARGE TO SOLOMON
David's charge to Solomon (2:1-4) echoed God's exhortation to Joshua (Josh. 1:6-7). Obedience was the key to success (1 Kings 2:4). The promise (2:4) referred to the covenant God had made with David (2 Sam. 7:12-16). "Rested with his fathers" (2:10) is a euphemism for death, like the English expression "passed away." "The City of David" refers to Zion, or Jerusalem, where David established his capital.

2:13-46 OLD BUSINESS CONCLUDED
Appropriating the royal harem of a deposed king was a recognized method of laying claim to the throne (2:22). This was Adonijah's second attempt to take the kingdom away from Solomon. Solomon understood Adonijah's request as an attempt to usurp his kingship (2:17), although Bathsheba naively believed the request to be merely motivated by love. She may not have regarded Abishag as a concubine since David had not known her intimately (1:4). Abiathar's dismissal from his position as priest (2:27) fulfilled the judgment on the house of Eli made in 1 Samuel 2:30-36. Abiathar, the last of Eli's descendants to serve as a priest, was replaced by Zadok (1 Kings 2:35), who had remained faithful to the house of David.

Shimei forfeited his life (2:46) by violating the conditions of his confinement (2:36-38). The judgments on Adonijah and Shimei cleared the way for the secure establishment of Solomon's reign (2:12, 46).

3:1–10:29 Kingdom Blessings from Obedience
3:1–4:34 WISDOM:
THE HEART OF BLESSING
3:1-28 Solomon asks for wisdom. The cornerstone of Solomon's foreign policy was his use of international marriage to conclude treaties and cement relationships (3:1). His treaty with Egypt was unique, for it is the only instance in history where the daughter of a pharaoh was given to a foreign ruler. Egypt was friendly toward Israel at that point, but it would not be later. Also, the potential for Solomon to fall into idolatry due to the influence of his non-Israelite wives was great (cf. 11:2). The high places (3:2) were elevated platforms, usually set on a hill, used by the Canaanites for worship. They were to be destroyed at the time of the conquest (Num. 33:52). The Israelites adapted the high place at Gibeon as a place to worship God after the destruction of the tabernacle at Shiloh (Jer. 7:12) and before the construction of the temple at Jerusalem (1 Chron. 16:39).

Solomon's "discerning heart" (1 Kings 3:9) was literally a hearing heart, that is, one that was quick to listen and obey. Such obedience was the central issue of kingship in God's kingdom—knowing the difference between good and evil and obeying God. Solomon's decision in the case of the two prostitutes (3:16-28) illustrates the wisdom that God gave him. Wisdom is the practical and successful application of God's truth to life's situations. See Proverbs 2:6-22 for a description of wisdom and its benefits. The result of Solomon's wisdom was national respect by the people of the king for his wisdom and justice (1 Kings 3:28).

4:1-28 National blessing. The national blessings of Solomon's rule clustered around Abrahamic themes: the numerous people of Israel (4:20; cf. Gen. 22:17); the boundaries of the land (1 Kings 4:21; cf. Gen. 15:18); the peace and prosperity

(1 Kings 4:22-25; cf. Gen. 22:17; Mic. 4:4). Seeking to mini-mize tribal rivalry, Solomon reorganized the kingdom into twelve admin-istrative districts that cut across old tribal boundaries (1 Kings 4:1-19). Although Solomon received tribute from lands as far north as the Euphrates (4:21), he did not possess these territories, nor did they fall under his permanent jurisdiction. "Under his own vine and fig tree" (4:25) is an image of security and contentment (cf. Mic. 4:4). The number of 4,000 stalls for chariot horses (1 Kings 4:26; cf. 2 Chron. 9:25) is given as 40,000 in some translations (NASB and KJV). That figure is exceptionally large and probably represents a scribal error in the transmission of the Hebrew text.

4:29-34 The fame of Solomon's wisdom.
Solomon was known internationally for his wisdom. Many of Solomon's proverbs (4:32) are recorded in the book of Proverbs. The best of his 1,005 songs is preserved as "The Song of Songs." Solomon's wisdom links back to Adam's insight into nature when he named the animals of God's origi-nal creation (4:34). God's original command for people to rule the earth came with their ability to understand how the earth works. The ability to name the plants and animals and to dis-cuss the world of nature shows an important element of dominion and wisdom at work.

5:1–7:51 THE TEMPLE IS CONSTRUCTED
The temple was the earthly focus of the kingdom and the symbol of God's presence in Israel. Solomon and Hiram, king of Tyre, entered into an economic alliance (5:11). Hiram provided materials and skilled craftsmen to build the temple in return for Israel's wheat and oil. The Phoeni-cians were great shipbuilders and merchants, but their land was lacking in agricul-tural productivity (cf. Acts 12:20). The slave status for the Israelites (1 Kings 5:13), although apparently only a tempo-rary measure (cf. 9:22), must have been a bitter pill for the freeborn Israelites to swallow.

The 1 Kings 6:1 text is important in determining the date of the exodus. The construction of the temple began 480 years after the exodus, in the fourth year of Solomon's reign. If the division of the

Israelite monarchy took place in 931 B.C., as is generally accepted, then the fourth year of Solomon's forty-year reign would have been in 966 B.C. The addition of 480 years to 966 B.C. makes the biblical date of the exodus 1446 B.C. Some scholars argue that 480 is symbolic in that it is representa-tive of twelve forty-year generations. But the historical nature of the text and specific chronological notes (fourth year, second month) support a literal, non-symbolic view of the *Kings* text.

However, the literary point of this look back to the exodus was to remind the readers, who were suffering in the exile, of the great redemptive reference point of the temple. Its source was in God's great prom-ises made so many years earlier in Egypt and at Mount Sinai. Solomon took seven years to build the temple (6:38), but thirteen years to build his own palace (7:1). The measurements of the temple were 90 by 30 by 45 feet, which made the temple twice the size of the tabernacle.

The Huram referred to in 7:13 ("Hiram," NASB and KJV) was not Hiram, the king of Tyre (5:1), but a skillful worker in bronze (7:14). Jakin ("Jachin," NASB and KJV) means "he shall establish," and Boaz means "in it is strength" (7:21). The dimen-sions of the bronze Sea, used for ritual cleansing (7:23), have raised questions about the accuracy of the original text of Scripture. According to the mathematical formula, a circle's circumference is equal to Pi multiplied by that circle's diameter. The difficulty is that, according to this formula, the diameter should have been 14.3 feet instead of 15 feet (10 cubits). Possible answers to this problem could be that the cast bronze Sea may have been several inches thick, or perhaps it had an outer lip that provided the extra inches necessary for the full 15-foot diameter.

8:1-66 THE DEDICATION OF THE TEMPLE
The dedication of the temple took place in the month of Ethanim (8:1-2, later known as "Tishri," which falls some-where in September–October). It was held eleven months after its completion (6:38), perhaps to coincide with the beginning of the new year. The feast of dedication held from the 8th through the 14th days of the

month was immediately followed by the
Feast of Tabernacles held from the 15th
through the 21st days. The veil of the tabernacle (2 Chron. 3:14) appears to have been
a slight distance inside the entrance of the
Most Holy Place so that the poles used to
carry the Ark were visible from the Holy
Place. The cloud (1 Kings 8:10), symbolizing God's presence, was not mentioned
again until Ezekiel's vision of its departure
(Ezek. 9:3; 10:4; 11:23). Repentance
(1 Kings 8:46-50) was set forth as the basis
for forgiveness and the restoration of blessing after the people's disobedience and
failure (cf. Deut. 30:1-10).

God had kept his covenant of loving-
kindness with David (1 Kings 8:22-26).
But that meant the nation was still responsible to obey him and his commandments.
The main part of the dedication stated the
conditions for restoration if the people
sinned. The temple was the place where
God would hear and forgive his repentant
people (8:27-53). Note the pattern of "if"
or "when" (8:31, 33, 35, 37, 42, 44, 46-48)
coupled with "hear" and "forgive" (8:32,
34, 36, 39, 43, 45, 49-50). Note especially 8:46-53 regarding captivity. Here
the purpose is given for all the details
surrounding the dedication of the temple.
The temple would be the only place where
God would hear and forgive.

Those in exile would read this section
and know what their duty was: to repent
and pray to God. The basis of their hope
was the two covenants that framed this
dedication: the Davidic (8:23-26) and
the Mosaic (8:56-61). At the heart of the
temple was the Most Holy Place, and at
the heart of that room was a copy of the
Mosaic covenant that formed the basis for
Israel's relationship with God.

9:1-9 THE DAVIDIC COVENANT PASSES TO SOLOMON

The Lord appeared to Solomon a second
time (9:2) and reconfirmed the Davidic
covenant. God's two appearances to
Solomon showed the grace of God that
Solomon ultimately abused (11:9). God
said that if the king obeyed, all would go
well; but if he did not, then adversity would
come upon the people and they would be
driven from the land (9:6-9). This would
be a clear reminder for the exiles in

Babylon, hearing the content of this book
for the first time, as to why they were there.
The key concepts of land, throne, temple,
and Egypt were repeated (9:4-9).

9:10-28 CIVIL AND MILITARY PROJECTS

Hiram, king of Tyre, had sent 120 talents of
gold to assist in financing Solomon's vast
building project (9:14). With his treasury
depleted, Solomon tried to pay his obligations by giving Hiram twenty towns in
Galilee (9:11), but Hiram called them "Cabul"
(9:13), meaning "as good as nothing." The
term "the supporting terraces" (9:15; or
"Millo," NASB and KJV), is derived from
a word that means "to fill," hence "a
mound," and refers to rock terraces used as
foundations for buildings in Jerusalem. The
exact location is uncertain. Other building
projects were noted (9:10-28). With the
completion of the temple, Solomon was able
to consolidate the worship of God in Jerusalem (9:25) and away from the pagan high
places (3:1-2).

10:1-13 INTERNATIONAL GLORY

First Kings 10 demonstrates the fulfillment
of God's promise that Solomon would be
extremely wealthy and uniquely honored
(3:10-14). The queen of Sheba's praise
(10:1-13) reflected a fulfillment of God's
promise to Abraham that all the nations
would be blessed through his descendants
(Gen. 12:3; 1 Kings 10:24). Sheba is identified with the southern part of the Arabian
Peninsula. Note the use of gold (1 Kings
10:14-22). A talent of gold (10:14) is the
equivalent of 66 pounds or 1,056 ounces.
To get an estimate of Solomon's yearly
revenue, multiply 703,296 ounces (666
talents) by the present price of gold. Acquiring large numbers of horses (10:26-28)
constituted a violation of the covenant
regulations for the king (Deut. 17:16).
Solomon was to trust in the Lord, not in
military might (cf. Isa. 31:1-3).

10:14-29 GLORIES AND BLESSINGS SUMMARIZED

The summary of Solomon's international
glory (1 Kings 10:23-29) describes the
highest point Israel had reached in experiencing the blessings promised to Abraham,
Moses, and David, and it forms a stark
contrast with the next chapter. The purpose
of the book of Kings was not to glory in the

past kingdom but to teach why Israel had lost it all in exile and what her hope was for the future.

11:1-43 Foundations of Chastisement
11:1-8 SOLOMON'S IDOLATRY
Solomon, who had a discerning or understanding heart (3:9), let his love for women (11:1-2) turn his heart away from God, a fact that is repeated three times in 11:2-4. By marrying foreign wives, he broke the Law of Moses. Solomon used marriage alliances to secure treaties with Egypt, Moab, Ammon, Edom, Sidon, and the Hittites. This multiplying of wives and alliances with foreign powers violated the covenant (Exod. 34:12; Deut. 17:16-17) and led to Solomon's ruin. No clear reason is given why he did this, but 1 Kings 11:4 links his idolatry with his old age.

Ashtoreth (11:5) was a fertility deity, the Canaanite counterpart of the Babylonian Ishtar; Molech (or Milcom, NASB and KJV) was a chief god of the Ammonites; and Chemosh (11:7) was a deity of the Moabites to whom children were sacrificed (cf. 2 Kings 3:26-27). Molech was an Ammonite deity whose worship also involved the ritual burning of children (Lev. 18:21). The "hill east of Jerusalem" (1 Kings 11:7) was what is now known as the Mount of Olives, from which the Lord ascended to heaven, and to which he will return. In Solomon's day it was dotted with pagan altars.

11:9-43 GOD OUTLINES HIS JUDGMENT
God brought disciplinary judgment on Solomon by dividing the kingdom (11:11-13) and raising up adversaries (11:14-28). Ten tribes were promised to Jeroboam (11:30-33), and one was promised to Rehoboam. That totaled eleven tribes, but the cloak was torn into twelve pieces. Technically, Rehoboam was promised the one tribe, Judah, but the tribe of Benjamin was allied with Judah (cf. 12:21). Jeroboam received the other ten tribes, including Simeon, a tribe that appears to have migrated north (2 Chron. 15:9; 34:6). Through all this discipline, God was faithful to his covenant with David. His loving-kindness would never depart, even in judgment (1 Kings 11:13, 32, 34, 36, 38-39; cf. also Gen. 22:16-18; 26:3-5 for the source of this love in Abraham's covenant).

Three men arose to carry out God's judgment: Hadad of Edom (from the south, 1 Kings 11:14); Rezon of Aram (or Syria, KJV, to the north, 11:23); and Jeroboam of Israel (in Israel's midst, 11:26).

1 KINGS 12:1—2 KINGS 17:41 CHASTISEMENT: THE DIVIDED KINGDOM
Overview: The divided monarchy (931–722 B.C.) can be divided into four major periods: (1) The Period of Conflict between Israel and Judah (1 Kings 12:1–16:28), 931–875 B.C. (2) The Period of Alliance between Israel and Judah (1 Kings 16:29—2 Kings 11:16), 874–835 B.C. (3) The Period of Independence for Israel and Judah (2 Kings 11:17–15:38), 835–740 B.C. (4) The Period of Assyrian Domination (2 Kings 16–17), 740–722 B.C.

The first period of the divided monarchy was characterized by military conflict between Israel and Judah until the border was finally established between Mizpah and Bethel (1 Kings 15:21-22). (See the introductory map.) This section extends from the original split between the north (Israel) and south (Judah) to the time when the north was taken captive to Assyria.

The stress throughout is on the fulfillment of God's words of warning concerning rebellion. No matter how long before he had spoken a word, what he had foretold would always happen. That fact was necessary to stress to the exiles in Babylon so that they would understand why they were there. God had not failed; on the contrary, Israel had. But just as God was true to his words of warning, so he would also be faithful to his words of promise and restoration.

12:1–14:20 Jeroboam's Lost Opportunity
12:1-24 JEROBOAM CONFIRMED AS KING
Jeroboam became king due to the foolishness of Rehoboam (12:12-14). But the point of this section is to show how the word of God was fulfilled through human events (12:15). Jeroboam was acting according to the will of God, and 1 Kings 12–14 shows how he lost his own opportunity to rule Israel. Discipline with scorpions

(12:11) refers to the use of whips with barbed hooks tied to the leather thongs.

12:25–13:34 GOD'S WORD AGAINST JEROBOAM CONFIRMED

Jeroboam (931–910 B.C.) established a substitute religion of golden calf worship (12:28), a substitute priesthood that was not of the tribe of Levi (12:31), and a substitute feast that was held just one month after the Feast of Tabernacles (12:32). By doing that, Jeroboam set out to stop the ten tribes of the nation of Israel from returning to the nation of Judah, the house of David (12:26-27). In other words, he purposely set out to defeat the clear-cut promise God had made to David (2 Sam. 7). Images of calves (1 Kings 12:28) were associated with Canaanite fertility rituals. Both El and Baal are frequently likened to bulls.

The test of the man of God illustrates the severe consequences of disobedience to divine revelation (13:1-34). The old (false) prophet deceived the man of God into being disobedient to God's original and clear direction. What prompted this deception is not revealed in the text. But the message for the reader is clear: not even the one who delivers the prophecy is above keeping its conditions. When God says something, he means it.

The word of God concerning Josiah was spoken in 13:2. The fatal judgment for the prophet's disobedience confirmed the potency and certainty of the prophecy (13:23-32). This prophecy would be fulfilled years later in 2 Kings 23:15-16. The pattern of the word of God being spoken and then confirmed occurs throughout the book of Kings. It was a pattern that needed to be repeated for those who had been taken into exile.

14:1-20 JUDGMENT ON JEROBOAM IS EXECUTED

As is true throughout the book of Kings, David was the model for a good king (1 Kings 14:8). David was set forth as the ideal servant to whom all other kings were compared (cf. 15:3). Just as David's heart for God secured blessing for Judah, so Jeroboam's disobedience secured destruction for the northern kingdom. The terrible disgrace of having their dead bodies eaten by wild animals (14:11) was one of the cursings of disobedience (Deut. 28:26). The ultimate disgrace for Jeroboam's disobedience was the Assyrian captivity (1 Kings 14:15). God's word of judgment (14:12) was confirmed in 14:17-18 by the recurring phrase "as the Lord had said." This is the first promise (14:15) of the Assyrian captivity (722 B.C.) resulting from the northern kingdom's disobedience to the covenant (cf. Deut. 28:63-64). The Jewish nation of Israel fell into captivity because of her disobedience, not because of God's lack of faithfulness.

14:21–15:24 The Lamp of David in Jerusalem

14:21-31 REHOBOAM

Rehoboam of Judah (931–913 B.C.) was just as apostate as Jeroboam. His idolatrous activities constituted a return to the Canaanite religion. According to his royal records, Shishak, king of Egypt (1 Kings 14:25), identified with Sheshonak I (945–924 B.C.), captured 150 cities in Palestine. This pharaoh may have been the father-in-law of Solomon (cf. 3:1).

15:1-8 ABIJAH

The reign of Abijah (or Abijam, NASB and KJV; 913–911 B.C.) functioned as an example of God's covenant-keeping acts in history. He was unfaithful, but God was faithful to his covenant with David (15:4-5). Abijah fashioned his life after the ungodly example of his father, Rehoboam. The lamp in Jerusalem (15:4) referred to the custom of keeping a lamp burning in the tent or house. Used here as a figure, no lamp meant no Davidic royal dynasty. God preserved the dynasty of Abijah for the sake of his promise to David (2 Sam. 7:12-16).

15:9-24 ASA

Asa's conformity to the heart of David (15:11) removed all idolatry in the land, even that of his own mother. Asa (911–870 B.C.) was the first great religious reformer in Judah. God blessed him with a reign of forty-one years. Ben-Hadad (15:18), king of Aram (Syria, KJV), was the first of three Aramean rulers to bear this name (2 Kings 6:24; 13:24). The name means "son of [the god] Hadad" and probably served as a dynastic title.

1 Kings 15:25—2 Kings 10:36
The Prophetic Word Certified
against Covenant Unfaithfulness

15:25–16:7 NADAB AND BAASHA

Nadab of Israel (910–909 B.C.; 1 Kings
15:25-28) succeeded his father Jeroboam
(15:26) to the throne and continued in his
evil ways. Baasha of Israel (909–886 B.C.;
15:28–16:7) killed Nadab and became king
in his place. That murder fulfilled the word
of God concerning the household of
Jeroboam (14:10). Again, the resounding
point made throughout the book is that when
God says something, it happens. His words
of judgment are as certain as his words of
blessing. The entire section from 1 Kings
15:25 through 2 Kings 10:36 shows how God's
prophetic words against covenant unfaithfulness were fulfilled. Baasha also was
like Jeroboam and suffered a similar fate
(1 Kings 16:2-7).

16:8-20 ELAH AND ZIMRI

Elah of Israel (886–885 B.C.; 16:8-14) had an
alcohol problem. He was overthrown by a
military leader, Zimri, in order to fulfill God's
word of judgment against Baasha (16:12).
Zimri of Israel (885 B.C.; 16:9-20) reigned
just one week. When the report of his conspiracy reached the army, Omri was declared
king; as a result Zimri burned the palace at
Tirzah over his own head.

16:21-34 THE DYNASTY OF OMRI
IS INTRODUCED

Omri of Israel (885–874 B.C.; 16:21-28)
disputed with Tibni for the throne and
became king after a four-year struggle. He
was best known for founding a new capital
at Samaria on a three hundred-foot-high
hill overlooking an important valley in the
heart of the northern kingdom. Omri's
conquest of Moab was recorded by Mesha
on the famous Moabite Stone.

The dynasty of Omri spans from 1 Kings
16:21 through 2 Kings 10:17. Its most famous
king was Ahab of Israel (874–853 B.C.;
1 Kings 16:29–22:40), who succeeded Omri
and became a powerful but very wicked king.
Ahab's wife, Jezebel (16:31), tried to make
Baal worship the official religion of the royal
court. Her name originally meant "my divine
father is a prince," a fitting name for the
daughter of a pagan king. But the biblical
writer has dropped one letter so that the name

means "unexalted," a mockery of the evil
queen. Like Baal, Asherah (16:33) was a
prominent fertility deity in the Canaanite
religion. She was the chief goddess of Tyre,
a city of Phoenicia, the homeland of Jezebel.

The reference in 16:34 is to child sacrifice
at the ground-breaking ceremony for the
rebuilding of Jericho (cf. Josh. 6:26). The
word of God, spoken long before in the days
of Joshua, was still potent in the days of
Ahab. No amount of time could diminish the
power of God's promises and warnings. The
power of the warnings explains the pain of
God's discipline. The power of God's promise gives hope and motivation for repentance.
That held true for Israel in captivity as it does
for people today in the bondage of their own
personal exiles.

17:1-24 ELIJAH IS PRESERVED
OUTSIDE OF THE LAND

Lack of rain (1 Kings 17:1) was one of the
curses of the covenant that would result from
disobedience (Deut. 28:23-24). Zarephath
(1 Kings 17:9) was situated between Tyre
and Sidon, the very center of the Baal cult.
There Elijah would demonstrate God's
power to provide flour, oil, and rain, blessings customarily attributed to Baal. Also, this
section emphasizes that God can protect the
faithful, in this case Elijah and the widow,
even when outside of the land of Israel. This
would be a powerful lesson to the Israelites
in captivity in Babylon that God can bless
his faithful people anywhere. The point of
the resurrection of the widow's son was
found in the widow's response to the miracle
(17:24). The prophet's word was truth, even
though the king and other Israelites did not
believe it.

18:1-46 GOD'S WORD THROUGH ELIJAH
IS CONFIRMED

The Obadiah of the Minor Prophets was not
the same man as this protector of the godly
(18:3). Ahab's comment that Elijah had
caused the famine (18:17) sums up the lessons of the book of Kings. The people had to
learn that it was not the prophets who had
troubled the land. Rather, it was their own sins
that had brought on the judgment of the exile.

Mount Carmel (18:20) a 1,742 foot-high
promontory jutting in a northwest direction
into the Mediterranean Sea, was thought by
the Canaanites to be a dwelling of the gods.

On this mountain, Elijah confronted the Baal cult. Elijah's mockery attributed basic bodily necessities to Baal (18:27). The word translated "busy" (NIV) or "occupied" (NASB) means to relieve oneself, and the word translated "traveling" means to have a bowel movement. Elijah was saying that Baal could not respond to his worshipers because he had gone to the toilet. The point of this display is summed up in 18:36, where Elijah acknowledged that the God of Abraham was behind all that he had done. God's people always had trouble believing that God was speaking through his prophets. The people gave the proper, though temporary, response in 18:39.

Elijah ran to Jezreel (18:46), Ahab's camp, to report the victory of God and encourage popular opinion against Jezebel. Note the confession in 18:39. God's control of the rain was a direct attack upon Baal's supposed power.

19:1-21 GOD'S FAITHFULNESS TO THE REMNANT

The section of 19:1–22:40 shows how the prophets' words against Ahab were confirmed. The "afraid" of 19:3 may be translated "and he saw." If Elijah had been afraid, he could have just fled to Judah and the safety Jehoshaphat could provide. What did he see and why did he flee to Sinai? It appears that Elijah realized that he would be no more successful at ending Israel's apostasy than the prophets who had preceded him had been (19:4). He mistakenly thought he was the last faithful person left (18:22, 36; 19:4, 10, 14). That observation led to his discouragement and deep despair.

He fled to Sinai, the source of Israel's covenant through Moses, to recapture the original vision for the nation. Horeb (19:8) was another name for the 7,363 foot Mount Sinai (Exod. 19:1-2; Deut. 4:10). There Elijah understood that the kingdom of God was hidden and easily missed, like God's still, small voice. However, the kingdom was potent and fully under God's sovereign plan. That idea of the hidden and powerful nature of the kingdom was taken up again in the parables of Jesus (Matt. 13) and in his role as the humiliated Son of Man. In 2 Kings, the Elisha narra-

tive will reveal more of the hidden and preserved faithful remnant.

The first two parts of Elijah's threefold commission (1 Kings 19:15-16) were carried out by Elijah's disciple Elisha. Elisha anointed Hazael and Jehu. So what did God mean by saying that Elijah would anoint those two (19:15-16)? Elijah passed his authority on to Elisha, and in that sense he anointed Jehu and Hazael. That is the beginning of the concept of Elijah as a type, as is seen later, for example, in John the Baptist (Matt. 17:10-12). Special prophets of God came as Elijah, that is, in Elijah's spirit and power.

The cloak (or mantle, NASB and KJV; 1 Kings 19:19) was an outer garment of distinction worn by prominent individuals, especially prophets. Putting the cloak on Elisha was a symbolic act indicating that Elijah's office and authority were to be inherited by Elisha.

20:1-34 A PROPHET'S WORD OF VICTORY IS CONFIRMED

Ben-Hadad stationed his army around Ahab's city, Samaria (20:1-21). *Aram* (20:1) is the correct Hebrew term. The people were the Arameans. The King James Version translates "Aram" as "Syria," but Syria did not exist as a political entity until the intertestamental period.

The next two battles provided lessons about God's character. The first battle (20:13-21) taught about God's greatness on Israel's behalf. The second (20:22-34) taught about God's greatness to Israel in contrast to the Arameans' limited concept of God's power (20:28). God gave Israel victory both at Samaria in the mountains and at Aphek in the plain to show that, unlike the localized gods of Canaan, God ruled all territories and regions. Ahab received two proofs of God's greatness.

20:35–22:40 THREE PROPHETS' WORDS OF JUDGMENT ARE CONFIRMED

The story of 20:35-36 again emphasized the necessity of honoring the word of God. At issue was honoring God who gave the message, not passing judgment on the message's seeming insignificance. The judgment prophesied in 20:42 was fulfilled in 22:29-38 (cf. also 21:19).

21:1-29 *Ahab's Murder of Naboth.* Ahab was sullen and angry (cf. 20:43 and 21:4). On the basis of the biblical laws of inheritance, Naboth had refused to give Ahab his land (cf. Lev. 25:23-28; Num. 36:7). Ahab's murder of Naboth led to an extremely negative evaluation of his reign (1 Kings 21:25-26). However, even Ahab was able to repent (21:27-29) and, because of his humility, he received God's kindness. That would have carried the clear message to the readers in exile that no one was beyond receiving God's favor if he would simply humble himself before God.

22:1-40 *Micaiah and the Death of Ahab.* Ahab's attitude was one of hatred toward the true prophets of God (22:8). Ahab called Elijah his enemy in 21:20. Far from being Ahab's enemies, the prophets of God were attempting to save the nation's life. That fact would be clear later to those who would read these words in exile and mourn over their repeated animosity toward God's spokesmen in the past.

Ramoth Gilead (22:3) was an important frontier town east of the Jordan River in the territory of Gad (see introductory map). Micaiah, the name of the true prophet, means "Who is like Yahweh?" (22:7-28). God is sovereign over the good and evil spirits, that is, angels and demons (22:20-23). He allowed the deceiving spirit of the false prophets to lead Ahab into battle and to his death. This is a clear example of why the nation went into exile—because God judged their idolatry and social sins by allowing them to believe false prophets. Essentially, the false prophets told sinners that they were really all right before God and that there was no need for repentance from sin. The people's belief in that contradiction of God's clearly revealed laws—the contradiction that had been made by the false prophets—would result in fitting judgment.

22:41-50 JEHOSHAPHAT INTRODUCED
Jehoshaphat (873–848 B.C.) was a spiritual reformer, but not without fault (22:43). His greatest failure was allowing his son, Jehoram, to marry Athaliah, the daughter of Ahab and Jezebel (cf. 2 Kings 8:16-18). The period of conflict between Israel and Judah ended when Jehoshaphat made peace with Ahab (1 Kings 22:44). The treaty was sealed by the marriage of Athaliah to Jehoram (2 Kings 8:16-18, 26-27).

1 KINGS 22:51—2 KINGS 1:18
AHAZIAH'S JUDGMENT IS CONFIRMED
Ahaziah, the son of Ahab, of Israel (853–852 B.C.), followed in the wicked ways of his father (1 Kings 22:51-53). The division between 1 and 2 Kings at 1 Kings 22:53, which splits the account of Ahaziah's reign in half, is the result of later editing.

SECOND KINGS NOTES

Second Kings 1 affirms that when God says something will happen, it does; in this case it was the death of Ahaziah (1:4, 17). The chapter also affirms the divine authority granted to the true prophet of God. Note the two "if" sentences (1:10, 12) followed by the proof: "Then fire fell from heaven" (1:10); "Then the fire of God fell" (1:12). Elijah called fire from heaven against the false prophets of Baal (1 Kings 18:36-38). But in this case it represented judgment against the Israelites.

Baal-Zebub (2 Kings 1:3) means "Baal of the fly," a mocking alteration of the god's true name, "Baal the prince." The leather belt (1:8; or girdle, NASB and KJV) was a belt used to bind garments about one's body. The soldiers (1:10) were participating in the king's rebellion against Elijah, God's representative, and thus were subjected to divine judgment. Joram (or Jehoram, NASB and KJV) of Israel (852–841 B.C.) was the son of Ahab of Israel. He succeeded his brother to the throne because Ahaziah had no son. He was wicked, but not to the extent of Ahab and Jezebel (3:2-3).

2:1-25 POWER IN ELISHA'S WORDS
The travel from Bethel (2:3) to Jericho (2:5) was punctuated with prophecies of Elijah's departure. The travel back from Jericho (2:18-21) to Bethel (2:23-24) proved Elisha's power. The central section was a reminder of God's parting of the waters at creation, at the Red Sea, and at the entrance into the land of

Israel. It showed how Elisha received the power. The double portion was the inheritance of the firstborn or heir (Deut. 21:17). Elisha was requesting that he might be the heir or successor of Elijah, which was indeed God's will (1 Kings 19:16). Like Enoch (Gen. 5:24), Elijah was translated to heaven without dying. He departed by a whirlwind or windstorm. Such a storm was often used as a visual symbol of God's presence (Job 38:1; 40:6; Ezek. 1:4; Zech. 9:14).

The youths (2 Kings 2:23-24) were not children but young men who could be held morally accountable for their actions (cf. 1 Sam. 16:11; 1 Kings 3:7; Jer. 1:6-7). Not only were their words disrespectful, but they also constituted a challenge to Elisha's divinely appointed ministry. Their judgment was in keeping with the curses pronounced in the Mosaic Law against those who were disobedient (Deut. 28:26).

3:1-27 WORDS OF VICTORY OVER MOAB

Second Kings 3 records how Israel campaigned with Judah and Edom against rebellious Moab (3:4-7). Kir Hareseth (3:25) is identified with Kerak on the Transjordan highlands, east of the Dead Sea. With his capital under siege, Mesha sacrificed his oldest son to Chemosh in a final desperate attempt to induce the god to give him victory (3:27). The "fury against Israel" may have been the Lord's fury because the siege resulted in human sacrifice, or the fury of the Moabites, who were challenged to rally against Israel. The three kings of Israel, Judah, and Edom were victorious.

4:1-6:7 THE POWER OF ELISHA

Second Kings 4:1–6:7 begins a long section in which the prophet's words against the house of Omri were confirmed (4:1–10:17). Second Kings 4 shows the blessings that came to those who aligned themselves with the true prophets of God. The wife of a deceased prophet received a miracle of oil (4:1-7). A woman who provided food and a room for Elisha received her dead son back by resurrection (4:8-37). The poisonous food of the sons of the prophets was transformed into good food (4:38-44).

The blessings that came from people aligning themselves with the true prophets of God continued. Naaman was blessed (5:1-27).

The lesson he learned, and that the reader should learn, is repeated in 5:8, 15, and 18. The healing of Naaman, the Aramean army captain, demonstrated God's lordship over the whole earth and showed his mercy on an obedient Gentile. Here the Abrahamic covenant (Gen. 12:1-3) was being fulfilled as Israel was bringing blessing to the Gentiles. Although expressing faith in God (2 Kings 5:17), Naaman still held to the view that no god could be worshiped properly except in his own land. Therefore, Naaman wanted two loads of earth from the land of Israel so he could worship the God of Israel on his own soil. "Rimmon," also known as Hadad Rimmon (5:18; Zech. 12:11), referred to the supreme deity of the Arameans.

Again, the blessings of the prophets continued. The sons of the prophets were given their lost ax head (6:1-7). The recovery of the ax head reveals that God is concerned even with small things and helps his faithful ones with such matters. Elisha's miraculous ministry in this section demonstrates that there is no need that God cannot meet when it comes to loving his faithful ones.

6:8–7:20 THE POWER OF GOD TO DELIVER FROM SYRIA

Dothan (6:13), where Joseph had found his brothers (Gen. 37:13-17), was located thirteen miles north of Samaria in a broad valley leading into the Jezreel Valley (see introductory map). Elisha taught love for one's enemies (2 Kings 6:22; cf. Matt. 5:43-45). This is the second Ben-Hadad mentioned in 1 and 2 Kings (2 Kings 6:24). A "cab" (6:25) was a unit of measurement that was the approximate equivalent to one pint. The horror of cannibalism (6:29) was one of the curses that would result from disobedience to the covenant (Deut. 28:53).

God gave Elisha power to deliver Israel from Syria once in 2 Kings 6:8-23 and again in 6:24–7:20. That kind of military victory could have been Israel's continually if she had just listened to God's warnings through his prophets.

The doubt of the officer in charge of guarding the gate of Samaria brought God's judgment upon him (7:2, 17-20), but Elisha's word was confirmed (7:16). The prediction of a return to reasonable prices and available commodities took place in the midst of a siege-induced famine (6:25). The point being made for the readers of this book who were in exile was that God would do the impossible, but only the faithful would experience those blessings.

8:1-6 THE WOMAN FROM SHUNEM IS PRESERVED

The story of the woman from Shunem (8:1-6) again stressed the blessings of God on his faithful people, not only while within the land, but also while outside of the land of Israel. (See the introductory map for Shunem's location.) This would be a message of encouragement to the faithful believers who were exiled to places far from their homeland.

8:7-15 HAZAEL BECOMES KING OF SYRIA

Hazael was a high officer in the court of Ben-Hadad II who killed his master and became one of the most powerful kings of Aram (or Syria). Why did Elisha command Hazael to lie to Ben-Hadad when the Lord had shown the prophet that the king would die (8:10)? Actually, Elisha predicted that Ben-Hadad's illness itself would not be fatal. However, Ben-Hadad would die, but at the hand of Hazael. The "he" of 8:11 was Hazael, who was gazing at the prophet, lost in his thoughts of how he might take the throne from the ailing Ben-Hadad.

8:16-24 PRESERVATION FOR JUDAH

Jehoram, the son of Jehoshaphat of Judah (853–841 B.C.), walked in the evil ways of the kings of Israel, for he had married Athaliah, Ahab's daughter (8:16-24). God disciplined him with the loss of territory, but God preserved the throne of Judah because of his promise to David (8:19; 2 Sam. 7:12-16).

8:25–10:17 THE HOUSE OF AHAB IS DESTROYED

Ahaziah, the son of Jehoram of Judah (841 B.C.), appears to have been strongly influenced by his mother, Athaliah, and thus followed the wicked example of the northern kings of Israel (2 Kings 8:25-29). Joram (8:28-29; whose name is sometimes spelled Jehoram) refers to the king of Israel, the son of Ahab (8:16). This king of Israel is to be distinguished from the king of Judah with the same name.

Jehu, the commander of Israel's army, brought the wicked dynasty of Omri to an end and became the next king of Israel (841–814 B.C.; 9:1-37). His rule was the most bloody of any king of Israel. The divine commission to destroy the house of Ahab (9:7-8) constituted God's retribution on Jezebel's sins and fulfilled the promised judgment on Ahab's son (1 Kings 21:19, 29). After Jehu was proclaimed king (2 Kings 9:13), he began his bloody purge that included the murder of Joram, king of Israel (9:14-26); Ahaziah, king of Judah (9:27-29); and Jezebel (9:30-37).

The power of God's word spoken through Elijah continued as Jehu judged Ahab's sons (10:1-11; note especially 10:10, 17). He extended his judgment to the supporters of Ahab (10:11), the relatives of Ahaziah (10:12-14) and of Ahab (10:17), and the prophets of Baal (10:18-28). But his zeal for the Lord was misguided (10:16). He overstepped the commission given him by the Lord (9:7-10). "The word of the Lord spoken to Elijah" (10:17) refers back to 1 Kings 21:19.

The pattern throughout the book of Kings was to show that every evil would be judged according to the word of God spoken through his prophets. The seventy-year Babylonian exile was simply the consistent culmination of God's righteous judgments upon Israel's disobedience.

10:18-36 JEHU IS CHASTENED

God chastened Jehu (2 Kings 10:29-36) through the Arameans, and the northern kingdom lost all of its Transjordan territories to Hazael. The records of Shalmaneser III also indicate that Jehu was forced to pay heavy tribute to the Assyrians.

11:1–14:29 Covenant Blessing from Obedience

11:1–12:21 THE RETURN OF THE PEOPLE TO THE COVENANT

11:1-20 Joash spared. The section of 11:1–14:29 shows the blessings that came to Judah when the king returned to keeping the Mosaic covenant. Athaliah of Judah (841–835 B.C.) usurped the throne when Ahaziah, her husband, was slain by Jehu. She immediately sought to revive the Baal cult in Judah (11:18) that her mother, Jezebel, had so successfully introduced in

Israel. Even though Athaliah tried to wipe out all of David's offspring, God preserved one royal son according to his covenant with David.

The period of alliance between Israel and Judah was brought to an end by the murder of Ahaziah by Jehu (9:27-29) and the killing of Athaliah by the captains of Judah (11:13-16). Then both of the two kingdoms entered a period of independence, power, and prosperity. The latter part of this period was considered the "Golden Age" for Israel and Judah.

12:1-21 Joash reigns. Joash, also known as Jehoash, the son of Ahaziah, reigned next in Judah (835–796 B.C.). He was brought to the throne as a lad of seven by Jehoiada the priest. The early years of the king's reign, when he ruled under the influence and guidance of Jehoiada, were marked by spiritual reform. But this did not continue after Jehoiada's death (2 Chron. 24:17-22). As soon as the temple was restored (12:4-16), its wealth was given to Hazael, the king of Aram (or Syria), to keep him from attacking Jerusalem (12:17-18).

13:1–14:29 GOD'S FAITHFULNESS TO THE ABRAHAMIC COVENANT
13:1-9 Jehoahaz. Second Kings 13–14 clearly shows all the weaknesses of the kings of Judah and Israel. Jehoahaz of Israel (814–798 B.C.) succeeded his father, Jehu, to the throne. His days were characterized by continual Aramean oppression (13:22). His glimmer of faith (13:4) was answered by victory. The unnamed deliverer (13:5) may refer to the Assyrian emperor Adad-nirari (810–783 B.C.) who attacked Damascus in 806 B.C., thus weakening the Arameans.

13:10-25 Joash. Jehoash (or Joash, NASB and KJV) of Israel (798–782 B.C.), another evil king, defeated Hazael and recovered Israel's territory that had been taken by the Arameans. Throughout the book of Kings, the reasons why God preserved the nation are clearly ascribed to his faithfulness to his covenant with David. In 13:23 the foundational reason for God's faithfulness is given: the covenant with Abraham.

The little story of 13:20-21 continues the theme of the power of God through his prophets. In this case, even the bones of

Elisha were powerful enough to raise the dead.

14:1-22 Amaziah. Amaziah of Judah (796–767 B.C.) improved on the record of his father, Joash, but failed to remove the tempting pagan high places from the land. Beth Shemesh (14:11), a city in the Judean foothills, is located at the head of the Sorek Valley, about fifteen miles southwest of Jerusalem.

14:23-29 Jeroboam II. Jeroboam II of Israel (793–753 B.C.), although an evil king, was noted for his great expansion of the northern kingdom. He recovered Damascus and Hamath (14:28) for Israel and extended Israel's border as far south as the Sea of the Arabah, that is, the Dead Sea (14:25). The prophet Jonah (14:25), who fled the Lord's commission to preach at Nineveh, lived at Gath Hepher in Galilee (cf. Josh. 19:13) during the reign of Jeroboam II.

15:1–17:61 Chastisement Confirmed
15:1-7 AZARIAH
The section of 15:1–17:41 confirms and explains the ultimate judgment upon Israel. Azariah (Uzziah) of Judah (791–739 B.C.) was known for his great building projects and strong military power. He expanded the southern kingdom east, west, and south. In the end, he succumbed to pride and had to live out his days under God's judgment as a leper.

15:8-12 ZECHARIAH
Zechariah of Israel (753 B.C.) was the fourth and last ruler of Jehu's dynasty. Again, the stress was on the fulfillment of God's word (15:12; cf. 10:30).

15:13-15 SHALLUM
During the Assyrian threat against Israel, Shallum of Israel (752 B.C.) ruled for just one month before being overthrown by Menahem. That was the beginning of the end for the northern kingdom. In just thirty years Israel would fall to the Assyrians.

15:16-22 MENAHEM
Menahem of Israel (752–742 B.C.) was a wicked king whose depravity can be illustrated by his dealings with the rebellious city of Tiphsah (15:16). Pul, the king of Assyria (15:19), is probably the original name of Tiglath Pileser III (754–727 B.C.), who

assumed the name of a great king of the past when he ascended to the throne of Assyria. Under the leadership of Pul, the kingdom of Assyria became a great empire that eventually swallowed up the petty kingdoms of Aram and Israel. At this time, both Judah and Israel began to enter a period of Assyrian domination (2 Kings 16–21). Menahem paid tribute to Assyria (15:19-20). In doing so he retained his throne but became an Assyrian vassal.

15:23-26 PEKAHIAH
Pekahiah of Israel (742–740 B.C.) ruled only two years before being overthrown by Pekah.

15:27-31 PEKAH
Pekah of Israel (740–732 B.C.) and Rezin of Damascus, the Aramean king, formed an alliance to resist Assyria. Ahaz, king of Judah, refused to join their anti-Assyrian alliance and was attacked by Pekah and Rezin (Isa. 7:1-7). Against the warnings of the prophet Isaiah, Ahaz called upon Assyria for help. Tiglath Pileser responded with three devastating campaigns against Israel and Damascus (734–732 B.C.). In 733 B.C. Assyria captured northern Israel (2 Kings 15:29) and exiled the population. The days of the northern kingdom were numbered.

15:32-38 JOTHAM
During the Assyrian threat against the southern kingdom, Jotham of Judah (750–731 B.C.) was a good king whose concern for the things of God was evidenced by his rebuilding of the upper gate of the temple (cf. 2 Chron. 27:3).

16:1-20 AHAZ
Ahaz of Judah (743–715 B.C.) was a wicked king who was faced with Assyrian domination. He chose to submit to Assyria rather than join the anti-Assyrian coalition of Rezin and Pekah (16:7). The phrase "sacrificed his son in the fire" (16:3) refers to the sacrifice of Ahaz's son to Molech, a Canaanite god of Ammonite origin. Damascus was captured by Assyria in 732 B.C. (16:9). Ahaz usurped the function of the priests by offering sacrifices himself upon an altar built to resemble the Assyrian altar at Damascus (16:11-13).

17:1-61 HOSHEA
Israel was taken into Assyrian captivity. Hoshea (732–722 B.C.), the last king of Israel, began his rule as an Assyrian vassal paying annual tribute to Tiglath Pileser III and his successor, Shalmaneser V (727–722 B.C.). Then, in league with Egypt, he revolted (17:4). After three years of siege, Samaria was captured. Sargon II (722–705 B.C.) succeeded Shalmaneser and claimed the victory. He then exiled Israel's inhabitants to distant regions of the Assyrian Empire.

17:7-41 Chastisement Explained
While 17:1-6 provides the political reason for Israel's captivity, 17:7-41 provides the religious explanation. Israel's sins against the God who had redeemed them from Egypt are described in 17:7-12. God had warned Israel through his prophets (17:13-18). First Kings 1–16 described that warning in detail. Why? In order to convince the exiled captives that their continual disobedience, not God's lack of interest, had caused their downfall. They had not departed from the sins instituted by Jerobam I (17:21). God's prophetic word of judgment was sure (17:23).

The Samaritans of the first century A.D. (John 4) had their origins in the mixture of ethnic backgrounds and worship institutions described here (2 Kings 17:24-41). Again, the exodus from Egypt and the Mosaic covenant were the focus of obedience and the measure for disobedience (17:36-38).

18:1–25:30 PRESERVATION: THE SOLITARY KINGDOM
Overview: The rest of 2 Kings describes the history of the solitary kingdom of Judah, which was subject to three foreign powers during this period: Assyria (2 Kings 18–21), Egypt (2 Kings 22–23), and Babylon (2 Kings 24–25). This section stresses that God is faithful to the slightest show of repentance and to his great covenant with David. Although this section appears to continue the judgment of Judah's sins on into the Babylonian captivity, it is actually an upbeat description of how God preserved the kingly line promised to David. When the northern kingdom, Israel, ended with the Assyrian captivity, the southern kingdom, Judah, continued to have a son of David as king. Even though the physical kingdom was destroyed and the people had no religious

or political independence, God was still faithful to keep a son of David alive to return and reign someday according to his promise.

18:1–20:21 Reform: Babylon Introduced

18:1-37 THE NORTHERN KINGDOM FALLS AND JERUSALEM IS ATTACKED

Hezekiah of Judah (728–686 B.C.) was one of the most godly descendants of David to sit on the throne of Judah. He began his reign with a revival of orthodox religion. The bronze serpent made by Moses in the wilderness (Num. 21:8-9) had become an object of worship (2 Kings 18:4). Its name "Nehushtan" means "a piece of bronze."

Hezekiah did not rebel against Assyria (18:7) until after the death of Sargon II (705 B.C.), who had captured Samaria. In 701 B.C. Sennacherib, king of Assyria (705–681 B.C.), invaded Judah; he captured forty-six cities and besieged Jerusalem. In his own annals he wrote of Hezekiah, "Himself I made a prisoner in Jerusalem, his royal residence, like a bird in a cage." Lachish (18:14), about seventeen miles west of Hebron, guards an important valley that gives access to the hill country of Judah. While Sennacherib was besieging the city, Hezekiah submitted to Assyria and met the demand for tribute (18:14-16). Sensing that Hezekiah could not stand up to him, Sennacherib decided to go ahead with the capture of Jerusalem. The meaning of the Hebrew word translated "field commander" (18:17; NIV) or transliterated as "Rab-shakeh" (NASB) is uncertain. The title implied a position of high-level leadership. This leader was an official emissary and spokesman for Sennacherib. The Rabshakeh (most likely a title, not a name) was sent to threaten Hezekiah so that he would surrender (18:17-25). For God's perspective on Judah's tendency to rely on Egypt for deliverance (18:21), see Isaiah 30:1-2 and 31:1-3.

Addressing the Judeans, the Assyrian Rabshakeh promised peace and prosperity in return for their submission to Assyria (2 Kings 18:27-36). He threatened the people of Israel with proud rhetorical questions (18:33-35).

19:1-37 GOD SPARES JERUSALEM FOR HIS NAME'S SAKE

The key to 2 Kings 19 is in verses 4 and 34. God repulsed Assyria from Jerusalem because Assyria had blasphemed against the Holy One of Israel and because God was faithful to his covenant with David. The tearing of one's clothes and putting on rough sackcloth (19:1) was a traditional sign of grief and mourning. Isaiah encouraged Hezekiah with a promise of deliverance from the Assyrian menace (19:7).

Some scholars believe that 2 Kings 18:17–19:37 refers to a later Assyrian campaign (around 688 B.C.), based on the reference to Tirhakah (19:9), who ascended the throne of Egypt in 690 or 689 B.C. However, Tirhakah was twenty years old at the time of this campaign and appears to have been summoned by his brother, the king, to lead the campaign into Judah. He assumed a responsible role in this endeavor, although he was only the crown prince at the time. But since he later became king, the application of the title of king in telling the story is appropriate.

Hoping to avoid fighting on two fronts at the same time, that is, against both Judah and Egypt, Sennacherib sent a letter to Hezekiah, demanding his submission (19:10). Hezekiah prayed that Judah's divine deliverance from Sennacherib would testify to Yahweh's uniqueness as the one true God (19:19). God said that he would preserve Judah and enable the people to prosper in their land (19:30). God accomplished the deliverance (19:34) for the sake of his own glory and his covenant faithfulness to David (cf. 2 Sam. 7:12-16). Esarhaddon (681–669 B.C.) succeeded his father to the throne of Assyria (19:36-37).

20:1-21 HEZEKIAH'S LIFE IS EXTENDED

It is generally held that Hezekiah's illness and recovery took place before Sennacherib's attack since the promise of deliverance from the Assyrians (20:6) would not have been necessary if Sennacherib's army had already been destroyed. The miraculous retreat of the shadow on the steps (20:10-11) was probably a local miracle accomplished by the refraction of light rather than a reversal of the earth's rotation. The foolish and unnecessary display of Jerusalem's wealth

(20:13) whetted the appetites of the Babylonians, who later brought their troops against Jerusalem. The pool and the tunnel, or water conduit (20:20), are further described in 2 Chronicles 32:30. Hezekiah built the tunnel to carry water from the Gihon spring, outside the city walls, to the pool of Siloam, which was within the protective defenses of Jerusalem. The Siloam inscription, discovered in the tunnel, indicates that the workers cut from opposite ends and met in the middle.

21:1-26 Irrevocable Chastisement: Manasseh and Amon

Second Kings 21 outlines the basis of the irrevocable chastisement that would fall on Judah. Manasseh of Judah (697–642 B.C.) was one of the most wicked kings to rule the southern kingdom. His apostasy actually exceeded the conditions of the Canaanites who had lived in the land of Israel before the conquest (21:9). Second Chronicles 33:10-13 records that he later repented of this evil, but he could not change the ways of the people. Like Ahaz (2 Kings 16:3), Manasseh practiced child sacrifice (21:6). Manasseh's son, Amon (642–640 B.C.; 21:19-26), followed the evil ways that his father had practiced before his change of heart. The end of God's patience and the extent of Judah's rebellion from the day the Israelites were taken out of Egypt are clearly shown (21:10-15).

22:1–23:30 Reform in the Shadow of Judgment: Josiah

Josiah (640–609 B.C.) brought reform in the very shadow of judgment. Because of his humility before God, he was spared from seeing Judah's downfall (22:11, 19-20). This reform was in the light of certain destruction (22:15-17). The exiles reading this would be encouraged that reform of any sort, even after discipline, would be received with favor by God. Josiah, Judah's greatest reformer, was compared with David (22:2) and noted for his unprecedented obedience (23:25). His first step in reform was to repair the Jerusalem temple, which had been neglected during the fifty-seven years of the reigns of Manasseh and Amon.

The eighteenth year of Josiah (22:3) would have been 622 B.C. Just four years earlier (626 B.C.), the city of Babylon had

rebelled and begun a destructive campaign against Assyria. In 612 B.C. the Babylonian and Median armies captured Nineveh, Assyria's capital. Assyria's last stronghold, Haran, fell to Babylon in 610 B.C. Both Egypt and Babylon were interested in ruling Judah. Egypt would have the first opportunity to do so.

Some scholars have suggested that the book of the law (22:8) was Deuteronomy, written by a pious scribe and planted in the temple area so that it might be discovered and accepted as Mosaic. The manuscript may well have been Deuteronomy, since it contained both the curses of disobedience as well as positive instruction, but there is no reason to suggest that it was a fabrication. Studies in form criticism have done much to confirm the authenticity of Deuteronomy and its Mosaic authorship.

Jeremiah was the son of Hilkiah the priest (22:14). Jeremiah, who had begun his prophetic ministry just five years earlier, in the thirteenth year of Josiah's reign (2 Kings 22:3; cf. Jer. 1:2), was not mentioned. This is not unusual, for he would not have gained a widespread reputation as a prophet by this time.

The first half of 2 Kings 23 describes Josiah's reformation. The act of 23:16 fulfilled the prophecy of 1 Kings 13:2. Although the prophecy had been spoken long before, God was in control to bring about his word of judgment and blessing.

The record of reform provides a stark commentary on the idolatry and apostasy that characterized the reigns of Manasseh and Amon. Topheth (2 Kings 23:10) literally means "place of burning" and refers to the altar hearth of Molech, a god to whom children were sacrificed by burning. With Assyria on the decline, Josiah was able to assert his influence even into Samaria (23:15-20).

Josiah lost his life at Megiddo when he went out to confront Pharaoh Neco of Egypt (23:29). Pharaoh Neco probably felt threatened by the rapid Assyrian demise in the face of aggressive Babylon. No doubt he sought to equalize the balance of power by rushing to the aid of Assyria's Asshuruballit, who was attempting to recapture Haran in 609 B.C. Assuming that any friend of Assyria was an enemy of Judah, Josiah tried to stop the Egyptian advance. He lost his life in the attempt, but he was spared the sadness of witnessing Judah's destruction.

23:31–25:26 Chastisement Confirmed

23:31-35 JEHOAHAZ

Jehoahaz of Judah (609 B.C.) was the first of Josiah's three sons to rule Judah. But his reign lasted only three months. When Pharaoh Neco returned from his campaign against Babylon, Jehoahaz was deposed and imprisoned. Judah fell under Egyptian domination.

23:36–24:7 JEHOIAKIM

Jehoiakim of Judah (609–597 B.C.) paid tribute to Egypt in order to keep his throne. The change of his name from Eliakim (23:34) was in keeping with a sovereign's privilege in dealing with a vassal ruler. In the fourth year of Jehoiakim's reign, 605 B.C., the Babylonians defeated the Egyptian army at Carchemish (Jer. 46:2) and became the new world power. Nebuchadnezzar (605–562 B.C.) moved quickly to secure his newly won territory of Judah. He proceeded to Jerusalem and took some of the royal family, along with many temple vessels, back to Babylon (Dan. 1:1). This is thought of as the first deportation to Babylon (605 B.C.).

24:8-17 JEHOIACHIN

Jehoiachin (597 B.C.), son of Jehoiakim, ruled only three months before Jerusalem was attacked by Nebuchadnezzar. This resulted in the second deportation of Judah to Babylon (2 Kings 24:14). Jehoiachin was also known as Coniah (Jer. 22:28, NASB and KJV) and Jeconiah (Matt. 1:12).

24:17–25:7 ZEDEKIAH

Zedekiah (597–586 B.C.), Josiah's third son, was installed as a puppet ruler by Nebuchad-

nezzar and reigned eleven years. After that period of submission to Babylon, Zedekiah decided to revolt (24:18-21; cf. 2 Chron. 36:13).

25:8-26 THE FINAL DEPORTATION TO BABYLON

Nebuchadnezzar began his final attack on Jerusalem in December of 588 B.C. After eighteen months of siege, the city walls were breached (July 586 B.C.). Then there was a third deportation of Judeans from their homeland. The three deportations of Judah are summarized in the chart below.

Riblah (2 Kings 25:20), located about sixty miles north of Damascus, was the staging grounds for Nebuchadnezzar's attack against Judah. Nebuchadnezzar appointed Gedaliah to govern Judah as a province of Babylon (25:22). Mizpah (25:23), usually identified with the site of Tell en-Nasbeh, located about eight miles north of Jerusalem, served as Gedaliah's residence and the administrative center for Judah. Jeremiah was kidnapped and taken to Egypt with the rebels (25:25-26; cf. Jer. 43:6-7).

25:27-30 Preservation of the Davidic Kingship: Jehoiachin Restored

The release of Jehoiachin in 560 B.C. by the king of Babylon (2 Kings 25:27) was evidence that the line of David was still under God's protective care (cf. 2 Sam. 7:12-16). The elevation of a king in captivity may not seem like much of an achievement, but to the captives it would be certain proof that God had not forgotten his people or his promises. That proof would encourage his people to get their lives squared away in order to honor God and prepare for his future acts of release and redemption.

THE THREE DEPORTATIONS OF JUDAH

First Deportation	Daniel 1:1	605 B.C.
Second Deportation	2 Kings 24:14-15	597 B.C.
Third Deportation	2 Kings 25:11	586 B.C.

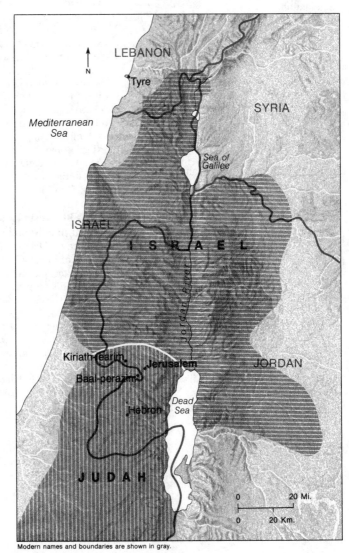

Modern names and boundaries are shown in gray.

KEY PLACES IN 1 CHRONICLES

1&2 Chronicles

BASIC FACTS

HISTORICAL SETTING
The books of 1 and 2 Chronicles cover the history from the first man, Adam, to the restoration of Israel from the Babylonian captivity (around 538 B.C.). Originally a single book, it was completed sometime after the Jews' return to Palestine during the difficult times when they tried to reestablish their nation and religion after the catastrophe of the Babylonian captivity. Babylon had fallen and Persia ruled that empire.

AUTHOR
The author of Chronicles is unknown. Since Ezra was a priest and scribe during the time it was probably written, he has often been accepted as the most likely candidate for the author. This is further substantiated by the fact that the book of Ezra begins exactly the way Chronicles ends.

DATE
If Ezra wrote Chronicles, it would put the date of writing around 457 B.C. The time period re-created in the book, no matter who the original author was, is the positive time of reconstruction after Israel had returned from captivity in Babylon.

PURPOSE
The book of Chronicles was designed to encourage the Jews who had returned to rebuild their nation and continue in faithfulness to God. Punishment for sins was in the past, and their future held the fulfillment of the bright promises God had made to Abraham and David.

GEOGRAPHY AND ITS IMPORTANCE

The book of Chronicles begins geographically at Hebron and ends with the Persian king Cyrus's decree for Israel to return from exile to her own land. Although the book begins at Hebron, it quickly moves to David capturing and

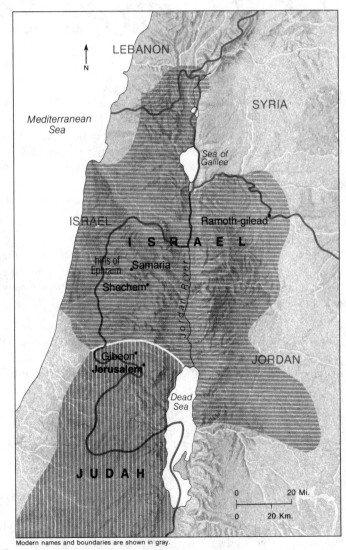

KEY PLACES IN 2 CHRONICLES

Modern names and boundaries are shown in gray.

settling Jerusalem. The focus from that point on is the temple. After the split of
Israel into northern and southern kingdoms, the focus is still on good kings like
Josiah and Hezekiah and their temple reforms. Even at the end of the book, when
Cyrus allowed Israel to return to her land, the central purpose was to restore the
temple (2 Chron. 36:23). The book of Chronicles has one geographic focus, the
temple at Jerusalem; and one corresponding thematic focus, encouraging faithfulness in the worship of God.

GUIDING CONCEPTS

THE ORIGINAL UNITY OF FIRST AND SECOND CHRONICLES

The books of 1 and 2 Chronicles were inspired as one book. The translators of the
Greek Old Testament (the Septuagint) split the book into two parts. They named
the books "The Things Left Out" because they thought Chronicles simply filled in
the gaps of events that had been left out of the books of Samuel and Kings. But
Chronicles is much more than material that fills in gaps. Although there is
some new material in Chronicles, large sections of the book are a nearly verbatim
repetition from Kings. In fact, nearly half of Chronicles is almost verbatim repetition from the books of Samuel and Kings. If the purpose of Chronicles was to fill
in gaps, why would there be the massive amounts of repetition? Obviously its
purpose was not to fill in gaps, and its repetition serves as the key to understanding its real purpose.

Actually, Chronicles was designed to build a foundation by repeating God's greatest past redemptive acts on Israel's behalf. Then, upon that foundation, the writer of
Chronicles gives a message of encouragement for Israel's future after the Babylonian captivity, a future which would be built upon the ruins of her past sins and upon
the power of God's unchanging promises.

THE END OF SECOND CHRONICLES

The end of the book of Chronicles takes the reader to the first year of Cyrus, king of
Persia (538 B.C.). Cyrus allowed the Israelites to return to their homeland, and that is
the note upon which the book ends. The last words are "go up" (2 Chron. 36:23), a
positive call to all Jews to return to the land of God's promises. The thrust was for
them to be optimistic about the future. God's disciplining punishment was past. It
was now the time for them to regroup and to rebuild what had been destroyed. God
had been faithful to his promises, and now the Jews were once more to receive their
part in his blessings of redemption.

The end of the book of Chronicles explains the thrust of the entire work. It was
designed to retell Israel's history by emphasizing the actions that brought God's
blessing. Those actions were to be models for Israel after she returned to the land.
The time for chastisement and dwelling on failure was past. The book of Kings
already had struck the notes of failure and its consequent judgment. Chronicles
emphasizes the positive past as a basis for a positive future. Israel was to learn from
the past and strive for a God-honoring future.

THE TEMPLE AS THE FOCUS OF A POSITIVE PERSPECTIVE

Chronicles has a clear focus on how the kings' righteous actions supported the pure worship of God at the temple. The temple was where the Mosaic covenant resided in the Most Holy Place. It was the place where God met with human beings to hear their prayers and forgive their sins. Chronicles emphasizes the proper treatment of the temple in order to encourage the same honor on the part of those who returned from the exile to rebuild the temple.

Once the story moves past David and Solomon, the bad points of the kings are mentioned, but nothing is written about the northern kingdom of Israel except as its kings came into contact with the kings of Judah. The focus is all on Judah—the good things that happened during the reigns of David and Solomon and the bad events that occurred after them. The emphasis is on the wonderful period of the unified kingdom when David and Solomon were obedient to God and maintained worship in the way that God desired. That was where the readers' minds were to dwell.

STRUCTURE

The emphasis of the book of Chronicles can be seen in the chart below.

Most of the content of Chronicles is about David and Solomon (28 out of 65 chapters), especially their work on the temple and Israel's worship there (21 out of 28 chapters). The focus is on the great work on the temple by the two great men of God, David and Solomon. That emphasis was needed to encourage the Israelites who had returned from the exile to work on rebuilding the temple and restoring the city of Jerusalem (see the books of Haggai and Zechariah).

THE STRUCTURE OF CHRONICLES

Genealogies	1 Chron. 1–9
Saul	1 Chron. 10
David (nineteen chapters)	1 Chron. 11–29
Military support unified	1 Chron. 11–12
Ark, temple, and Davidic covenant	1 Chron. 13–17
Military victories and support	1 Chron. 18–20
Plans and offerings for the temple	1 Chron. 21–29
Solomon (nine chapters)	2 Chron. 1–9
Building and dedication of the temple	2 Chron. 1–7
Activites, wealth, and power	2 Chron. 8–9
Rehoboam	2 Chron. 10–12
Abijah	2 Chron. 13
Asa	2 Chron. 14–16
Jehoshaphat	2 Chron. 17–20
Jehoram through Ahaz	2 Chron. 21–28
Hezekiah	2 Chron. 29–32
Manasseh	2 Chron. 33
Josiah	2 Chron. 34–35
Captivity and release	2 Chron. 36

BIBLE-WIDE CONCEPTS

THE COVENANT SUCCESSES OF DAVID AND SOLOMON

The book of Chronicles emphasizes the good deeds of David and Solomon. While the book of Kings showed how the sins of the kings brought about the captivity, the book of Chronicles shows how the kings' obedience brought blessing. The sins of David and Solomon are either not mentioned or are minimized. When the book of Chronicles covers the life of David, it does not mention the sad episodes of his adultery with Bathsheba and murder of Uriah, of Amnon's violation of Tamar, or of Absalom's rebellion. In telling of Solomon's life, no mention is made of Adonijah's problems, of Solomon's punishment of David's enemies, or of his polygamy and idolatry. The Jews had read of those problems in the book of Kings. The book of Chronicles leaves them out to emphasize a positive perspective for rebuilding the kingdom. The book recounts examples of God's commitment to the covenant blessings that he had promised to Abraham, Moses, and David.

NEEDS MET BY 1 & 2 CHRONICLES

Chronicles ends with the people of Israel being called to return to their homeland. But it leads up to that happy moment by rehearsing the successes and failures of Israel's past. At the moment of their release from God's discipline, God's people needed a reminder of what had made them successful and what had led to their disastrous failures. The emphasis is clearly on repeating in the future what had made them successful in the past. The book of Chronicles answered questions like the following for the Israelites who had returned from the Babylonian exile to rebuild the kingdom in Israel.

- How can the people of Israel go on with their lives after such a great destruction of their homeland and seventy years of exile?
- Can the future in any way be as great as the outstanding moments of Israel's past history?
- How can what happens "after" the captivity be anything like what happened "before" the captivity when the two periods are separated by a time of awful discipline?
- Has Israel's original hope for future redemption been completely destroyed by her terrible sin and long period of discipline?
- Can the Israelites still hope in the promises that God made to Abraham, Moses, and David?

The prophetic point of Chronicles is that God's people can count on God's promises even after a time of discipline for failure. He proved his commitment to Israel and the Davidic kingship by bringing Israel from exile back to the Promised Land. He has brought all believers into the age of the fulfillment of all his promises through Jesus Christ. The Christian must learn from the past what makes for success or for failure. Recovering from discipline involves leaving the negatives of the past behind and focusing on the positive actions that bring obedience and blessing.

OUTLINE OF 1 & 2 CHRONICLES

A. ESTABLISHING THE HOLY CITY (1 CHRONICLES 1:1—2 CHRONICLES 9:31)
  1. Legitimizing the Nation's Ancestry (1 Chron. 1:1–9:1)
  2. David: The Legitimate King (1 Chron. 9:2–29:30)
  3. Solomon: The Legitimate Heir (2 Chron. 1:1–9:31)
B. MAINTAINING THE HOLY CITY (2 CHRONICLES 10:1–36:23)
  1. Preservation of Lineage (10:1–23:21)
  2. Restoration to the Land (24:1–36:23)

1 CHRONICLES NOTES

1 CHRON. 1:1—2 CHRON. 9:31
ESTABLISHING THE HOLY CITY
1:1–9:1 Legitimizing the
Nation's Ancestry
Overview: First Chronicles 1–9 records genealogies that trace the development of the human race from Adam to David. The purpose was to define the place of God's chosen people in world history and to show the origins of the Davidic line through which the Messiah would come. While these genealogies are not very interesting to today's reader, they were of great value and importance to the returned exiles.

Genealogies trace one's lineage in order to legitimize one's background. These genealogies trace, in incomplete form, all the tribes of Israel back to Abraham and a line from Abraham all the way back to Adam. But only two family lines have unbroken genealogies extending through the Babylonian exile: those of David and Eleazar. That is, only the royal and priestly lines are emphasized. That emphasis shows the purpose of the genealogies: to legitimize the ancestry of the royal and priestly lines of the kingdom. The other lines are sketchy and do not form an unbroken line through the postexilic period.

The genealogies also have a set structure by which the reader can more fully understand their purpose: (1) the genealogy leading up to Israel (1 Chron. 1); (2) the genealogies of Judah, Levi and Benjamin (1 Chron. 2–8); and (3) the genealogy of postexilic Israel (1 Chron. 9).

The function of this structure is to show the continuity of the postexilic nation with respect to all of Israel's prior history. After the destruction of the nation and seventy years of captivity, the Israelites needed to regroup and reorient themselves to their nation's history and its purpose for existence. The genealogies rehearse both the history and the purpose of the line of Israel.

In 1 Chronicles 1 the important people are listed last, while in 2:1–8:40 the important tribes of Israel are listed first. The genealogy of 1:1-54 goes as far as the offspring of Israel (1:34; 2:1), and that of 2:1–8:40 works its way down from the most important offspring of Israel, the royal line of David (2:1–4:23), to the privileged but ill-fated tribe of Benjamin, of King Saul's family (8:29-40).

In 2:1 the tribes are introduced in this order: (1) Reuben, (2) Simeon, (3) Levi, (4) Judah, (5) Issachar, (6) Zebulun, (7) Dan, (8) Joseph, (9) Benjamin, (10) Naphtali, (11) Gad, (12) Asher. But the tribes' actual genealogies are listed in the order presented in the chart on the next page.

1:1-54 ADAM THROUGH ISAAC
In 1 Chronicles 1 the most important people are listed last. For example, the families of Shem, Ham, and Japheth (1:4) are listed in the order of Japheth (1:5-7), Ham (1:8-16), and then Shem (1:17-27), the line through which Abraham came. In the line of Abraham (1:28), Ishmael is listed first (1:29-33) and then Isaac (1:34). When the sons of Isaac are named (1:34), Esau is first (1:35-54) and then, as the most important, Israel (2:1–9:44).

First Chronicles 1:1-4 provides a condensed version of the genealogy of Genesis 5. Gaps in ancient genealogies were not regarded as inaccuracies because the purpose of a genealogy was not to provide a step by step historical chronology but to trace a family line to its chief ancestor. First Chronicles 1:5-27 reproduces, except for minor variations in spelling, the genealogy of Genesis 10. Abram's name (1 Chron. 1:27, meaning, "exalted father") was changed to Abraham (meaning, "father of a multitude"; cf. Gen. 17:5). Jacob (1 Chron. 1:34) is referred to here by his new name, Israel (meaning, "he who strives with God"), which he received after his night of wrestling with the Lord. The descendants of Esau, who was the ancestor of the Edomites, are given (1:35-54).

2:1–9:1 JACOB'S SONS

2:1–4:23 Judah. Shua (2:3) or Bath-shua (NASB), literally means "daughter of Shua," as in Genesis 38:2. Achar (1 Chron. 2:7) is a variation of the name for Achan (Josh. 7:1). According to 1 Samuel 16:10-11, Jesse had eight sons, David being the youngest. One apparently died in childhood and thus was omitted from the genealogy

---

THE LISTINGS OF TRIBAL GENEALOGIES IN CHRONICLES

Group One

- Judah (2:1–4:23): Judah was the house of the Davidic covenant, which was promised an unending royal reign. Clearly, the first major emphasis of Chronicles is on the past and future of the Davidic hope for the king.

- Simeon (4:24-43): Simeon was grouped with Judah off and on throughout its history (cf. Josh. 19:1; Judg. 1:3, 17). After the single kingdom split into the north (Israel) and the south (Judah), the tribe of Simeon apparently migrated into the northern kingdom (cf. 2 Chron. 15:9). However, the faithful of that tribe returned to Judah as the 2 Chronicles 15:9 passage shows.

Group Two

- Reuben (5:1-10): Reuben was Israel's firstborn. Gad and the half-tribe of Manasseh are grouped with Reuben because they all settled across the Jordan River to the east of the other ten tribes.

- Gad (5:11-22).

- The half-tribe of Manasseh (5:23-26).

Group Three

- Levi (6:1-81): Levi was the great tribe of priests and ministers for the temple worship. The second major emphasis of Chronicles is the establishment of the proper orders for worship at God's holy temple.

Group Four

- Issachar (7:1-5): The rest of the tribes north of Judah are listed, but Dan and Zebulun are not mentioned.

- Benjamin (7:6-12): Benjamin, King Saul's tribe, is mentioned twice, both at the beginning and the end of this section.

- Naphtali (7:13).

- The other half-tribe of Manasseh (7:14-19).

- Ephraim (7:20-29).

- Asher (7:30-40).

- Benjamin (8:1-40).

(1 Chron. 2:13). Bezalel (2:20) was the chief architect of the tabernacle (Exod. 31:2).

The content of 1 Chronicles 2:4–4:1 centers on the line of David, which came from Hezron (2:9) through Ram (2:10), and its structure is as follows:

Introduction: Sons of Judah (Jerahmeel, Ram, Caleb) (2:3-9)
    Line of Ram: David (2:10-17)
        Line of Caleb (2:18-24)
        Line of Jerahmeel (2:25-41)
        Supplement to Caleb (2:42-55)
        Supplement to David (3:1-24)
Conclusion: Sons of Judah (4:1)

The line of David is traced down to the grandsons of Zerubbabel after the return from Babylon.

First Chronicles 3 traces the line from David to the restoration from exile. Bathsheba (3:5) was another name for Bath-shua (NASB and KJV). Of those mentioned in 1 Chronicles 4, only Perez was a son of Judah. But the term "sons" is used loosely in the Hebrew language and can refer to grandsons or even more broadly to descendants. For the descendants of Simeon (4:24-43) and their territory, see Joshua 19:1-8.

5:1-26 The Transjordan tribes. Although Reuben (5:1) was the firstborn and had the right of double inheritance (Deut. 21:17), he lost this privileged position due to his uncontrolled passions (Gen. 35:22; 49:3-4). Tiglath Pileser (1 Chron. 5:6) is another spelling for Tilgath Pilneser (NASB and KJV), king of Assyria, who subjugated northern Israel in 733 B.C. (2 Kings 15:29). The descendants of Gad are listed (1 Chron. 5:11-17), as are the wars of the Transjordan tribes (5:18-22). The exile (5:22) refers to the Assyrian captivity of 722 B.C. The descendants of Manasseh are given in 5:23-24. Pul (5:26) is probably the original name of Tiglath Pileser (see the note on 2 Kings 15:19).

6:1-81 Levi. First Chronicles 6 revolves around the temple service inaugurated by David and Solomon. The three sons of Levi—Gershon, Kohath, and Merari—are mentioned (6:1). The structure of chapter 6 is outlined in the chart below, *The Sons of Levi.*

The emphasis is on the priestly line from Aaron on. That would legitimize the priestly line, which was beginning anew, and its mediatorial work at the postexilic temple in Jerusalem. This section would have been of special interest to Ezra, the probable author of Chronicles, who was himself a priest.

7:1–9:1 The remaining tribes. Listed in this section are the descendants of Issachar (7:1-5), Benjamin (7:6-12), Naphtali (7:13), Manasseh (7:14-19), Ephraim (7:20-29) and Asher (7:30-40). One key to the emphasis is the repetition of the phrase "fighting men" with reference to the first two and the last tribes mentioned in 1 Chronicles 7 (Issachar, 7:2, 5; Benjamin, 7:7, 9, 11; Asher, 7:40, "brave warriors"). Ephraim was the tribe of Joshua (7:27). Manasseh and Ephraim are listed together because they were the sons of Joseph (7:29).

First Chronicles 8 supplements the information provided in 7:6-12, tracing the ancestry of Saul (cf. 8:33), Israel's first king. Again the phrase "brave warriors" is repeated (8:40) with reference to the tribe of Benjamin. David would sin by wanting to number those mighty men of war rather than trusting in God to provide the victory no matter what the number of warriors (1 Chron. 21). The contents of 8:29-38 are repeated nearly verbatim in 9:35-44. "The book of the kings of Israel" (9:1) is not a reference to the canonical book of Kings, but to a royal court record that is now lost. The verse (9:1) functions as an end to the preexilic listing of families and prepares the reader for the list of postexilic returnees that is given next.

THE SONS OF LEVI

6:2-15	Kohath's line: Especially Aaron and Moses
6:16-30	Two Cycles of the Three Sons of Levi
6:31-48	David's Temple Musicians
6:49-53	Kohath's Line: Aaron's Sons
6:54-81	Kohath's Line: Settlements

9:2–29:30 David: The Legitimate King

Overview: First Chronicles 1–8 focused on the line of David, the ministers at the temple, and the surrounding tribes full of mighty men of valor to fight for the kingdom. In 1 Chronicles 9–29, which includes the rest of the book, the interest centers on David and his line of kings. More space is devoted to David than to any other ruler. He is set forth as the founder of the royal dynasty in Judah and as an example of a successful ruler for those who returned from exile to pick up the pieces of the earthly kingdom of God.

9:2-34 THE POPULATION OF JERUSALEM
The section of 9:2-34 gives the family names of those who returned to live in Jerusalem after the exile. First Chronicles 9 quotes extensively from Nehemiah 11, which lists the initial repopulation of Jerusalem. The purpose is to show the continuity with the original and God-ordained ministry of worship (1 Chron. 9:22). Just as it had been under David and Solomon, so it could be once again.

9:35-44 SAUL'S ANCESTRY
The members of the family of Saul (9:35-44) lived in Gibeon and Jerusalem. These verses, repeated from 8:29-38, serve to introduce Saul's fall in battle, which, in turn, prepared the way for David's ascent to the throne. Unlike the book of Kings, there is no interest here in the details of Saul's rise and fall as king.

10:1-14 SAUL'S REMOVAL
The story of Saul's death (1010 B.C.) is not told just to repeat the historical record (cf. 1 Sam. 31). Rather, the author has a definite moralistic emphasis. An important lesson is to be learned by the restored population of Israel (cf. 1 Chron. 10:13-14). Those verses assume a familiarity with the accounts in 1 Samuel and simply present a succinct summary of all that was wrong with Saul's rule as well as giving a warning to any future king.

This particular temple of Dagon (10:10), the chief god of the Philistines, was located in Beth Shan (1 Sam. 31:10). Archaeologists have uncovered a large temple at the site.

11:1-3 DAVID ANOINTED
The section of 1 Chronicles 11:1–12:40 shows how there was total support for God's legitimate king. David ruled over Judah from 1010 to 970 B.C. Key phrases used through-out the reigns of David and Solomon were "all Israel," "all the Israelites," "all the leaders of Israel" and "the entire assembly of Israel" (11:1, 4, 10; 12:38; 13:5; 15:3, 28; 19:17; 23:2; 29:23, 26; 2 Chron. 1:2; 5:6; 7:8). David's and Solomon's reigns had complete support from all of Israel, unlike the later times of the divided kingdom when the north and south fought against each other in civil war. David reigned for his first seven and a half years at Hebron, located in the hill country about twenty-five miles south of Jerusalem (see introductory map).

11:4-9 JERUSALEM CAPTURED
The capture of the Jebusite fortress (1 Chron. 11:4-7) gave David a strategic site for his capital. Its central location (actually in Benjamite territory) would help David secure the loyalties of the northern tribes. Jerusalem, also known as Jebus (11:4), became Zion, the city of David (11:5). The "supporting terraces" (11:8, or "the Millo," NASB and KJV), meaning "filling up," was a rock terrace probably used as a building's foundation. The exact location is uncertain. The author was very interested to point out the basis for David's success: the Lord was with him (11:9). Again, the spiritual aspect of the nation's history is highlighted.

11:10–12:40 MIGHTY MEN WHO SUPPORTED DAVID
David's mighty men and their feats (11:10-47) provided security and support for the kingdom. Mighty men figured largely in the events of 1 Chronicles 11:10-47 and also in 2 Samuel 21:15-22; 23:8-39. The cave of Adullam (1 Chron. 11:15) is located about seventeen miles southwest of Jerusalem in the vicinity of the city that bears the name. The Rephaim is a branch of the Sorek Valley which provides access to Jerusalem from the Philistine coastal plain. The Egyptian was seven and a half feet tall (11:23), or five cubits (NASB and KJV). A cubit is about eighteen inches in length.

The repeated phrase "warriors" or "brave warriors" (12:1, 8, 21) is connected with a list of warriors from the twelve tribes (12:23-38) to show the original and growing support for God's king, David. The entire nation was of one mind to make David king (12:38). Ziklag (12:1) was a Philistine city in the east Negev that David used as the base for various raids (1 Sam. 27:6-11). The warriors came to David at Hebron to help him establish his throne over all Israel. The total number of warriors was about 350,000. The mention of past joy (1 Chron. 12:40) was to kindle afresh a similar joy for restored Israel.

13:1-14 THE FIRST ATTEMPT TO RETURN THE ARK TO JERUSALEM

The author was very much interested in Israel's worship and religious institutions. He went to considerable length to show David's high regard for the Ark of the Covenant, as evidenced by his bringing it up to Jerusalem. The Ark (13:5) had remained at Kiriath Jearim (modern Abu-Ghosh), about ten miles east of Jerusalem, since it had been recovered from the Philistines in the days of Samuel (1 Sam. 7:1-2). The Shihor River of Egypt (1 Chron. 13:5) is identified with the Wadi el 'Arish and served as the southern boundary of the Israelite territory. Lebo Hamath, or the entrance of Hamath, was the northern border and probably was located between the Lebanon and Anti-Lebanon mountains at about the same latitude as the island of Cyprus.

The Ark was to be carried on poles, not transported on a cart, and it was not to be touched. The judgment on Uzzah (13:10) may seem severe, but God's holiness was at stake (cf. Num. 4:15). The author did not want any similar matters of ritual and procedure to be ignored by the returnees from Babylon for whom he was writing.

14:1-17 ENEMIES SUBDUED

First Chronicles 14 moves from David's kingdom being highly exalted (14:2) to the fame and fear of David spreading to all the nations, which was a sober reminder of what God would do again through his Davidic king to come. It was up to the fledgling nation to once again believe God's promises and work obediently to restore the kingdom. The king's marrying multiple wives (14:3) was a violation of Deuteronomy 17:17. David's example led the way for Solomon's excesses in this area. The Rephaim Valley (1 Chron. 14:9) gave the Philistines direct access to Jerusalem from the coastal plain. Baal Perazim (14:11) literally means "the lord of breaking forth." David's troops broke through

the Philistine offensive as raging waters might break through a dam. Gibeon (14:16) is in the hill country just north of Jerusalem, while Gezer is on the northwestern edge of the Shephelah, or foothills.

15:1-16:3 THE ARK IS SUCCESSFULLY BROUGHT TO JERUSALEM

The emphasis on the great joy in Israel (12:40) continued (15:16, 25; 16:4). Having learned from his previous bad experience (13:7-10), David instructed that the Ark be transported properly (15:2). David was the first Israelite to give significant recognition to the place of music in worship (15:16-24), the purpose of which was to "sing joyful songs, accompanied by musical instruments" (15:16). For a note on the ephod (15:27), see 1 Samuel 2:18.

16:4-43 REJOICING AND THE CARE OF THE ARK

The central thrust here is David's function in assigning Asaph to praise the Lord in poetry and song (16:7, 37). At the heart of 1 Chronicles 16 is an example of such praise (16:8-36), which is a compilation of Psalms 105:1-15 and 106:1, 47-48. For more on the burnt and fellowship (peace) offerings (1 Chron. 16:2), compare Leviticus 1-3. The expression "psalm of thanks" (1 Chron. 16:7), or "to give thanks" (NASB), literally means "to give public acknowledgment." That is the essence of biblical praise—a public declaration of God's greatness (his attributes) and his goodness (his actions). This psalm of thanksgiving rehearses the great elements of Israel's faith and hope: seeking the Lord (16:8-11), remembering his past deeds (16:12-14), remembering his covenant with Abraham (16:15-22), and praising him as Creator and coming Judge of all the nations (16:23-36). It would take the eyes of encouraged faith to believe in such a future for the small band of returned Jews. Zadok (16:39) was the priest who remained faithful to David in the time of Absalom's revolt. The Ark was now in Jerusalem, but the tabernacle stood at the worship center at Gibeon.

17:1-27 GOD'S HOUSE FOR DAVID

David was concerned because he had a lovely home in Jerusalem, while the Ark was in a mere tent. David wanted to build

God a house, but instead the Lord declared that he would build a house for David (17:10). Here the word "house" (17:10) is used in the sense of royal house, family, or dynasty. The Davidic covenant (17:11-14; cf. 2 Sam. 7:14-29) amplifies and confirms the promise God gave Abraham in Genesis 12:1-3 about his future long line of descendants.

One surprising aspect of God's promise to Abraham was the mention that kings would also be part of his line (Gen. 17:6, 16; 35:11). That promise of kings was made specific in the Davidic covenant. The royal line of Israel's kings was an original part of the wonderful promise that God made to Abraham. Here God promises David that he will have a son (the Messiah) who will sit on his throne and rule his kingdom forever (1 Chron. 17:11-14). This promise would serve as a tremendous encouragement to the struggling people of restored Israel.

18:1–20:8 WARS: ENEMIES SUBDUED
God promised David that his enemies would be subdued (1 Chron. 17:10). The subduing of various enemies of Israel is described (18:1). Further proof is given of God's loving-kindness upon David (18:13). David was the first to deal adequately with the Philistine menace. The record of David's conquests to the west, east, north, and south was designed to show the newly restored nation how God blesses those who love and serve him as David did.

Moab (18:2) was located in Transjordan, east of the Dead Sea. Zobah (18:3) was probably located somewhere northeast of Damascus. Modern Hama, located on the Orontes River, is identified with ancient Hamath (18:3). The Valley of Salt (18:12) is probably a reference to the Rift Valley, which is south of the Dead Sea. To the southeast of the sea lies the territory of Edom. Ahimelech (18:16; cf. 2 Sam. 8:17) is incorrectly given as Abimelech in some translations (NASB and KJV).

First Chronicles 19 gives a further illustration of how God, through his covenant with David, subdued all his enemies (cf. 17:10). The territory of the Ammonites (19:1) was located in Transjordan, northeast of the Dead Sea. Such treatment as that described in 19:4 would be regarded as a grave insult. The

1,000 talents of silver (19:6) would approximate 1,200,000 ounces. Medeba (19:7), located about twenty miles southwest of modern Amman, the capital of Jordan, is the location of the famous sixth-century Medeba Mosaic Map. "Arameans" (19:10) is incorrectly given as "Syrians" in the King James Version. The River mentioned in 19:16 is the Euphrates.

First Chronicles 20 covers the time of David's sins concerning Bathsheba and her husband, Uriah. However, 1 Chronicles does not mention them because its aim is to present the best of Israel's history in order to build the best kind of future. This rounds out the story of 1 Chronicles 19 concerning the Ammonites. Rabbah (20:1), the capital of the Ammonites, is identified with present-day Amman. For David's treatment of the Ammonites (20:3), see the note on 2 Samuel 12:31. Gezer (1 Chron. 20:4) is located on the northwestern edge of the Shephelah about twenty-two miles west of Jerusalem. The giants were members of a race of people who were very large in stature and among the original inhabitants of Canaan (cf. Gen. 15:18-21 and Num. 13:28, 33). Gath (1 Chron. 20:6), one of the five Philistine cities, was located on the coastal plain south of Ekron.

21:1-30 CENSUS AND PLAGUE
It is easy to miss the fact that this section of 1 Chronicles gives details about the significance of God's covenant with David (cf. 17:3-27). The essence of that covenant was that God would subdue Israel's enemies and build a royal house of kings for David. First Chronicles 18–20 illustrates God's promise to subdue David's enemies (17:10). But that was simply to provide the security for Israel to build and worship at God's house, which David desired to build (17:1-2; cf. 22:18-19).

First Chronicles 21 again takes up the theme of building a house for God and shows the surprising and tragic circumstances through which the temple's location was selected. Satan, as Israel's ultimate enemy, was behind the numbering of Israel's armies (21:1-8). David's prayer of intercession (21:8-17) was accepted, and he was commanded to provide an intercessory offering (21:18-27). The king's intercession for the nation was emphasized as a key element of the Davidic covenant (cf. 2 Sam. 21:14; 24:25).

When God responded to David's prayers by sending fire from heaven upon his altar, David realized that Jerusalem was where God's temple and altar should be (1 Chron. 21:28-30). Fire from heaven was a sign of God's presence; such affirmation had previously appeared at these several key junctures in God's redemptive history: at the altar before the tabernacle with Moses and Aaron (Lev. 9:24); with Gideon's offering (Judg. 6:21); with Elijah's offering on Mount Carmel (1 Kings 18:38); and with Solomon as God reaffirmed his choice of the temple site (2 Chron. 7:1).

For Satan's involvement (1 Chron. 21:1), see the note on 2 Samuel 24:1. But David took responsibility (1 Chron. 21:8, 17). He was taking a census to find out how many men he had for his army (cf. 27:1-23), which was an insult to God's already proven ability to deliver Israel from all her enemies and a misuse of the mighty men God had given to David. David (21:7) appears to have been trusting in his own resources rather than in God's (see the note on 2 Sam. 24:10).

"Beersheba to Dan" (1 Chron. 21:2) is a reference to the traditionally southern and northern extremities of the Israelite territory, respectively. The figures of 1,100,000 and 470,000 found in 21:5 are given as 800,000 and 500,000 for Israel and Judah, respectively in 2 Samuel 24:9. It may be that the figure for Israel in 1 Samuel does not include the nearly 300,000 men listed in 1 Chronicles 27. The figure for Judah in 1 Samuel 24:9 may not include the 30,000 of 2 Samuel 6:1. It is also possible that the figures in Chronicles have been rounded off.

The punishment options (1 Chron. 21:12) were of an increasing severity with a decreasing duration. Araunah (21:15) is also translated Ornan (NASB and KJV; cf. 2 Sam. 24:16). David adhered to the principle of sacrificial giving (1 Chron. 21:24). He knew that the value of a gift that he offered to God would be measured by his own degree of sacrifice (Luke 21:1-4). The total purchase price of 600 shekels of gold, about 300 ounces

(1 Chron. 21:25), covered the cost of the threshing floor and oxen and also included the surrounding area. This was where Solomon later built the temple. Although Solomon built the temple (cf. 17:11-12), it was David who had the vision for the project (22:5) and made arrangements for implementing its construction.

22:1-19 THE CHARGE TO SOLOMON

The theme of the temple's construction is here continued. David's wars and bloodshed disqualified him from the privilege of building God's temple (22:8-9), but they also were used by God to fulfill his promise of subduing Israel's enemies (cf. 22:18 with 17:10). The task of building the temple was reserved for Solomon, whose reign was characterized by peace. The resources set aside for the project included about 120 million ounces of gold and 1.2 billion ounces of silver.

23:1-24:31 TEMPLE ORDERS FOR PRIESTS

See 1 Kings 1 for more details about Solomon's turbulent ascent to the throne (1 Chron. 23:1). David's great administration and his organization of the temple ministry are described in 1 Chronicles 23–27. The army and civil administrators (1 Chron. 27) were supports for leading the nation in its mission to worship God and to be a living witness to his greatness. Assignments were given to the various priestly families, and the Levites were divided into twenty-four divisions, each of which would minister at the temple two weeks out of the year. David appears to have lowered the age requirement of those entering into Levitical service (23:3, 24; cf. Num. 4:3; 8:24). Zacharias, father of John the Baptist, was of the priesthood of Abijah (1 Chron. 24:10; cf. Luke 1:5) and was ministering in the temple when he received the angelic announcement that he was soon to be a father.

The organization of the temple personnel from Aaron's descendants and the rest of the sons of Levi was completed (1 Chron. 24:1-31). These lists are a reminder of the care that David took in organizing the temple worship. This probably encouraged the same care on the part of the returnees from the exile.

25:1-31 TEMPLE ORDERS FOR MUSICIANS

First Chronicles 25 reflects one of the great high points in the history of worship. Here David appointed temple musicians to lead the worship through music. The word "prophesying" (25:1) suggests some musical proclamations of divine revelation that came as expressions of praise and worship (cf. 1 Sam. 10:5; 2 Kings 3:15-16). Words and music that edified the hearers were the heart of biblical praise and worship.

26:1-32 TEMPLE ORDERS FOR GATEKEEPERS AND TREASURERS

The gatekeepers (1 Chron. 26:1-19) were appointed to guard the temple and prevent unauthorized persons from entering it. The court (26:18), also called the Parbar (NASB and KJV), probably refers to a colonnade or open chamber on the west side of the temple area. The Levites were responsible for the temple's treasures and dedicated offerings (26:20-28). Certain officers and judges were given responsibility for those matters relating to the temple that had to be dealt with outside Jerusalem (for example, hewing timber and quarrying stones; 26:29-32).

27:1-43 TEMPLE ORDERS FOR MILITARY HEADS

David organized his army into twelve divisions of 24,000 men, each of which served one month out of the year (27:1-15). David organized the tribes by placing certain leaders over them (27:16-24). It is not known why Gad and Asher were missing. David had a number of overseers and counselors to assist him in his administrative responsibilities (27:25-34).

28:1–29:30 COVENANT AFFIRMATION

In light of the selection of the temple site and the preparations for its building and use (1 Chron. 21–27), 1 Chronicles 28–29 contains a speech by David to his assembled nation. The speech centers on praise to God for his covenant with David (28:4-7), the passing on of the temple plans to Solomon (28:11-19), and the authority to command the builders (28:20-21). The phrase "for the footstool" (28:2) is better rendered "namely, for the footstool." The Ark of the Covenant is likened

to a footstool for God, who was enthroned above the cherubim (1 Chron. 13:6).

Although David was the appointed ruler, he recognized that God was the supreme King over Israel (28:5). A conditional aspect of God's covenant is reflected in 28:7-8. Such conditionality can only refer to individual and personal invalidation of covenant benefits. The promise, confirmed by God's oath, would be continued even though individual participation might be delayed or forfeited. In such cases, the promises would be passed on to the heirs. The cherubim (28:18) over the Ark of the Covenant were likened to God's chariot (cf. Ps. 18:10). The temple plans were not David's own but were the result of divine revelation (1 Chron. 28:19).

The key to understanding the significance of the offerings of David (29:1-5) and the people (29:6-9) can be found in the words, "over and above everything" (29:3), "willingly" and "willing" (29:6, 9, 17). The atmosphere was one of rejoicing (29:9) and joy (29:22). The message for the newly returned Jews was to adopt the same gladness and purity of heart in their work on the new temple. The offering of David (29:4) amounted to about 3.6 million ounces of gold and 8.4 million ounces of silver. The precious metals (29:7) amounted to over 6 million ounces of gold and 12 million ounces of silver.

The first coronation of Solomon (29:22; cf. 1 Kings 1:32-40; 1 Chron. 23:1) was in response to Adonijah's attempt to usurp the throne. Here Solomon's kingship was confirmed and publicly acknowledged. Zadok was confirmed as high priest as a result of Abiathar's disloyalty (1 Kings 1:5-8). Again, the phrase "all Israel" (1 Chron. 29:23, 26) was applied to both Solomon and David to show the original unity and support of both the northern and southern tribes of Israel. Special emphasis was given to the officials and the mighty men (29:24), the political and military powers. None of the writings mentioned in 29:29 have been preserved.

SECOND CHRONICLES NOTES

1:1–9:31 Solomon:
The Legitimate Heir

Overview: Second Chronicles 1–9 is devoted to Solomon's reign as king. Very little information is given here that is not found in 1 Kings. The writer's religious focus is evidenced by the attention given to the temple and the instructions for worship.

1:1-17 SOLOMON'S KINGDOM POWER

God established Solomon's kingdom (2 Chron. 1:1) as he had promised (cf. 1 Chron. 28:7). For "all Israel" (2 Chron. 1:2) see the usage throughout 1 Chronicles, for example, 29:23, 26. Solomon carried on the unified rule over all Israel. It was a unity that was maintained by those who returned from the exile. Solomon initiated a massive dedication of the king and nation to God (1:1-6). On that basis, the thrust of 1:7-17 is to show how Solomon's great wealth and international power came to him from God because he asked for wis-dom (1:7-12).

The tent of meeting (1:3) refers to the tabernacle situated at Gibeon, about six miles northwest of Jerusalem. For a description of the bronze altar (1:5), compare Exodus 27:1-8. In acquiring so many horses (2 Chron. 1:14-16), Solomon violated a specific prohibition given by God (Deut. 17:16). The king was to depend on the Lord, not his own military might. Kue (2 Chron. 1:16) was a region of southeast Asia Minor later known as Cilicia. Solomon paid about 240 ounces of silver for the chariots and about 60 ounces of silver for his horses (1:17). Presumably he made a good profit through his horse and chariot trade.

2:1-18 THE PLANS AND PURPOSE OF THE TEMPLE

Solomon decided to build a temple for God (2:1), and then he started to build (3:1). Plans were laid out for collecting the raw materials to be used in the building of the temple (2:1-18). The temple was to be a place for the name of the Lord (2:1) and a place to burn sacrifices to him (2:6); it was to be a place to worship and to remember the name of God (cf. 6:11, 22-24, 34-39, 41).

Hiram (2:3) sometimes appears as Huram and it is sometimes translated as such (NASB and KJV). Algum (2:8) is thought

by some to be red sandalwood. Huram-Abi (2:13) was a half-Israelite whose mother was of the tribe of Dan, but she appears to have lived in the territory of Naphtali (cf. 1 Kings 7:13-14). Joppa (2 Chron. 2:16), Jerusalem's closest Mediterranean seaport, was situated about thirty-five miles to the northwest.

3:1–5:1 THE TEMPLE IS COMPLETED

The golden walls of the temple's inner rooms, the sculptured cherubim overlaid with gold, the woven curtain, and the porch of the temple are described (3:1-17). Mount Moriah (3:1), where the temple was built, is believed to be the mountain in the land of Moriah where Abraham offered Isaac (Gen. 22:2). Solomon began to build the temple in the spring (April–May) in 966 B.C. The cubit (2 Chron. 3:3), a unit of measure, is approximately eighteen inches. The location of Parvaim (3:6) is uncertain, although some have suggested Arabia or Yemen. Six hundred talents of gold (3:8) is approximately 720,000 ounces. For the names of the pillars (3:17), see the note on 1 Kings 7:21.

The emphasis is on the altar (2 Chron. 4:1-6)—the place where Israel's sins were forgiven through sacrifice —and on the golden lampstands (4:7). The other items in the temple are only mentioned briefly. Three thousand baths (4:5) is equivalent to approximately 17,500 gallons. First Kings 7:26 mentions only 2,000 baths. Perhaps the 3,000 included the amount held by the smaller basins (4:6).

5:2-14 GOD'S GLORY FILLS THE TEMPLE

Upon the completion of the temple, the Ark was brought up from Jerusalem, the city of David, also known as Zion, to the temple mount, just to the north. Two key elements were present. First, the response of the people was summed up by the musicians: they praised and glorified God for his goodness and loving-kindness (5:13), the words that sum up all of God's character, kind covenants and acts of redemption. Second, the temple, like the tabernacle (Exod. 40:34-35), was filled with the glory of God (2 Chron. 5:14). That showed that God's presence and blessing were with the temple just as they had been with the tabernacle before it. The temple's size and ornamentation did not determine God's presence, but the Ark with its binding covenant did.

The feast of dedication (5:3), held in the seventh month (September–October), was followed by the Feast of Tabernacles (see the note on 1 Kings 8:2). Apparently Aaron's staff and the jar of manna (Heb. 9:4; cf. Exod. 16:33-34; Num. 17:10) had been lost by this time (2 Chron. 5:10).

6:1-42 SOLOMON'S PRAYER OF DEDICATION

The relationship between the Mosaic and Davidic covenants is clearly presented. The temple and Solomon were fulfillments of the promise that God had made to David in 2 Samuel 7 (2 Chron. 6:9-10). As God's chosen man, Solomon placed the Ark, which contained the Mosaic covenant (6:11), at Jerusalem, God's chosen place (6:6). On the basis of the Mosaic covenant, the king mediated between God and the people. That mediation found its ultimate fulfillment in the mediation of God's perfect Son of David, Jesus the Messiah.

The word "Name" appears throughout 2 Chronicles 6 and refers to God's reputation or attributes that were focused upon the temple and all that it signified (6:6-7, 10, 20, 24, 26, 33-34, 38). Solomon's prayer of dedication (6:12-42) acknowledged God's covenant commitment to David (6:14-17) and solicited forgiveness and restoration when the nation would fall into sin. The pattern throughout this section is "if/when . . . then" and covers various problem situations and their remedy of remembering God, praying to him in the temple, and hoping in his remembrance and covenant forgiveness. That same instruction and hope applied to the returned exiles.

7:1-22 THE DEDICATION FEAST AND WARNINGS FOR DISOBEDIENCE

After Solomon prayed, fire from heaven consumed the burnt offering and sacrifices (7:1). The three other times in the Old Testament when God showed his approval by sending fire from heaven were: when Gideon presented an offering (Judg. 6:20-21), the sacrifice of Elijah on Mount Carmel (1 Kings 18:38), and when David built the first altar on the threshing floor of Araunah, or Ornan (1 Chron. 21:26; on 2 Chron. 7:9, see the

note on 1 Kings 8:2). All Israel supported Solomon, observed the feast, and had great joy in God (2 Chron. 7:8).

God answered Solomon's dedicatory prayer by promising mercy and forgiveness on the basis of repentance (7:13-15), a new addition to what was given in 1 Kings 9:3-5, and the covenant with David (2 Chron. 7:17-22). This promise provided the theological foundation for the preaching of the Old Testament prophets in calling Israel to repentance and for the key role of the ruling son of David in preserving the nation from disaster. That role of preservation was perfected in the great Son of David, Jesus, whose perfect rule assures perfect peace and salvation.

8:1-18 SUMMARY OF SOLOMON'S PROJECTS

Solomon's great building projects were interspersed with the assurance that the temple was run exactly as the king commanded (8:15). Hamath Zobah (8:3) has not been specifically identified, but it was probably located somewhere northeast of Damascus. Tadmor (8:4), later known as Palmyra, is an oasis in the Syrian desert located halfway between Damascus and the Euphrates River. For Hamath (8:4), see 1 Chronicles 18:3. Upper Beth Horon and Lower Beth Horon (2 Chron. 8:5), situated on a strategic route into the hill country from the coastal plain, were located ten and twelve miles, respectively, northwest of Jerusalem. Baalath (8:6), of the tribe of Dan (Josh. 19:44), was situated at the edge of the coastal plain. Ezion Geber (2 Chron. 8:17), at the north end of the Gulf of Aqaba, was the port for Solomon's Red Sea fleet of ships (1 Kings 9:26). Elath (2 Chron. 8:17), sometimes spelled Eloth (NASB and KJV), was apparently located nearby, although some scholars have suggested that Elath and Ezion Geber were one and the same. Ophir (8:18) was situated along the Red Sea in southern Arabia, in the area of today's Yemen.

9:1-31 SOLOMON'S INTERNATIONAL WEALTH

There are two special aspects to the description of the greatness of Solomon in 9:1-31. First, the queen of Sheba rightly saw God's blessing behind all the impressive riches of the kingdom (9:8). Second, the longer descriptions of the greatness of the kingdom show the fulfillment of God's promises to both Solomon (regarding greater fame and riches than all kings, 9:22: cf. 1:11-12) and Abraham (regarding the boundaries of the land, 9:26; cf. Gen. 15:18). That was as close as Israel would come to the fulfillment of the Abrahamic and Davidic promises this side of the Millennium.

Sheba (2 Chron. 9:1) was located in southern Arabia, in the vicinity of today's Yemen. The 120 talents of gold (9:9) amount to about 144,000 ounces. The 666 talents (9:13) are about 799,200 ounces.

10:1–36:23 MAINTAINING THE HOLY CITY

Overview: The rest of 2 Chronicles (10–36) records the history of the kings of Judah, highlighting their spiritual successes and failures. The success of each king was measured by his faithfulness to God and the Mosaic covenant. This history was intended to instruct Israel's restoration community in the importance of obeying God so they might enjoy his blessings and avoid divine chastening.

10:1–23:21 Preservation of Lineage

10:1–12:16 REHOBOAM

The kingdom divided (10:1-19) under Rehoboam (931–913 B.C.). The division caused a tragic change in the meaning of the term "all Israel." Whereas all of Israel, that is, all the twelve tribes from both the northern and the southern parts of Israel, came to make Rehoboam king of the nation (10:1), the ten northern tribes, who from that time onward became known as Israel, departed in rebellion (10:16-19). "To your tents, O Israel" (10:16) was a call for the northern tribes to disassociate themselves from the dynasty of David, represented by Rehoboam, and thus declare independence from Judah. Adoniram (10:18) is also spelled Hadoram (NASB and KJB) or Adoram (1 Kings 12:18; NASB and KJV).

After his initial mistake of refusing to heed the advice of the elders (2 Chron. 10:3-16), Rehoboam began to rule wisely (11:1-23). Because the purpose of the book of Chronicles was to encourage the restored tribes toward unity and obedience, the unified aspects of the divided nation were emphasized. For example, the southern tribes of Judah and Benjamin drew the faithful from out of the north (11:3, 13–14). And in

12:1 "all Israel" refers just to the southern tribes under the Davidic king, Rehoboam.

A unique historical contribution of 2 Chronicles is the list of cities that Rehoboam fortified in anticipation of Shishak's invasion (11:5-12; cf. 12:1-4). Those cities were located at strategic points to the west, south, and east of the hill country of Judah. Jeroboam made goat idols (11:15, called "satyrs," in the NASB and "devils" in the KJV) that were fashioned after the idols of Canaan that bore the image of the goat. For more on the calf idols that he made (11:15), see the note on 1 Kings 12:28-29. Absalom's one daughter, called Maacah here (2 Chron. 11:20), was also named Tamar (2 Sam. 14:27). The Hebrew term for "daughter" may also mean "granddaughter" (cf. 1 Kings 15:2). (For the king's marriage regulations, 11:21; cf. Deut. 17:17.)

Rehoboam was humbled (2 Chron. 12:1-16) when Shishak, the king of Egypt (12:2), attacked Judah in 925 B.C. Inscriptions at Karnak list the cities that Shishak conquered. He was aided by Libyan (Lubim) and Cushite (Ethopian) forces. His other allies, the Sukkites (Sukkim), were another tribe of people apparently from Africa but not presently identified. The lesson of 12:8 would have special meaning for those who had just returned from seventy years of captivity in Babylon. Note the threefold use of the term "humbled" (12:7, 12) in connection with the conditions of 7:14. In or out of the land, a person's humble heart might not do away with all the negative consequences of his failure, but it would bring God's kindness and blessing.

13:1–16:14 ABIJAH TO ASA

13:1–14:1 Abijah. Abijah (913–911 B.C.) gave an address that was a reinforcement and reminder of the authority given to the ruling son of David on the basis of the Davidic covenant (13:5, 8). On that basis, God gave Abijah the victory over Jeroboam (13:15). That example (13:18) would be an encouragement for the citizens of Israel's restoration community. Mount Zemaraim (13:4) was located in southern Ephraim, about thirteen miles north of Jerusalem. The term "salt" (13:5) suggested that the covenant was one that would be preserved. Like David and Solomon, Abijah violated the marriage law for the king (13:21; cf. Deut. 17:17).

14:2-15 Asa. Asa (911–870 B.C.) cried to God for help in war (14:11-12) as his father, Abijah, had done (13:14-15), and was victorious. But later (16:1-14) he relied on help from Aram (or Syria), not God (16:7). Mareshah (14:10), situated halfway between Jerusalem and Gaza, was one of Rehoboam's fortresses (11:9). Gerar (14:13) was situated about nine miles northeast of Gaza.

15:1-19 Prophetic encouragement. Prophetic encouragement was given to Asa. A genuine response to the word of the Lord brought repentance, cleansing, and blessing. Again, the defections from the northern tribes to Judah were noted (15:9). Seeking God with all their heart brought rest (15:15; cf. also 14:6). Asherah (15:16) was a Canaanite fertility goddess. A problem of chronology appears in 15:19–16:1 because Baasha died before Asa's thirty-sixth year. The numbers thirty-fifth and thirty-sixth probably reflect a copyist's misreading of the numbers fifteenth and sixteenth.

16:1-14 Asa relies on Aram. Asa's spiritual life had gone sour. Instead of responding positively to the word of God, he became angry (16:10). The result was further divine discipline (16:12). The fire (16:14) refers to the burning of spices (cf. Jer. 34:5), not cremation.

17:1–21:3 JEHOSHAPHAT
17:1-19 Jehoshaphat's strength. Three key aspects of Jehoshaphat's rule (873–848 B.C.) were noted. First, he equipped the fortified cities (17:2, 12), as Solomon (8:5) and Rehoboam (11:5) had done. Second, the Lord established his kingdom (17:5) as he had done for David (1 Chron. 14:2) and Solomon (2 Chron. 1:1). And third, Jehoshaphat sent out officials to teach the ways of God to the Israelites (17:5-9; cf. 19:4). Baals (17:3) refer to the local varieties of idols used in Baal worship (cf. Num. 25:3; Josh. 11:17; Judg. 9:4; 2 Kings 1:2).

18:1-34 Jehoshaphat's alliance with Ahab. To seal the alliance (18:1), Ahab's daughter, Athaliah, was given in marriage to Jehoshaphat's son, Jehoram (cf. 2 Kings 8:16-18). Ramoth Gilead (2 Chron. 18:2) was located east of the Jordan River, about thirty miles southeast of the Sea of Galilee. God commissioned a demonic spirit (18:20-22) to induce the false prophets of Ahab to lie. While God

does not initiate evil, in the exercise of his sovereignty he can use even the actions of evil instruments to accomplish his purposes. The contrast is between the faithless King Ahab (18:6-7) and the faithful King Jehoshaphat (18:31).

19:1-11 Jehoshaphat's justice. Jehoshaphat's fourth great aspect is noted: his insistence on justice (19:8-9). Beersheba (19:4) is located at the center of the Negev, about twenty-six miles southwest of Hebron. The usual division between the administration of things of the Lord and of the king is noted (19:11; see, for example, 1 Chron. 10:11 and the lists of temple workers, things of the Lord, mighty men, and things of the king in 1 Chron. 11:10–12:40; 15:1–16:43).

20:1–21:3 Victory over Moab and Ammon. Again Jehoshaphat turned to the Lord in the time of war, but the emphasis was on God as the warrior for Israel (see especially the Spirit-inspired words of Jahaziel in 20:14-17). The great prayer of Jehoshaphat repeated the believer's confidence in the God of the initial conquest of Israel (20:7-8), the dedication of the temple (20:9; cf. 6:22-39) and the victories in the journey from Egypt to Canaan (20:10). The victory brought rest on all sides, a concept based on the Davidic covenant, and noted for David (1 Chron. 17:9-10; 18:1; 19:19; 22:8; 23:25), Solomon (1 Chron. 22:9; 2 Chron. 1:1) and Asa (14:7; 15:15).

Some Hebrew texts read "Aram," rather than "Edom" (20:2). But Edom harmonizes better with 20:22-23, which mentions Mount Seir (Edom). The invasion came from the east. En Gedi was situated along the western shore of the Dead Sea, about thirty miles south of Jericho. Undoubtedly the author included 20:4 to be an encouragement and a challenge to the restoration community. The Desert of Tekoa (20:20) was located east of Tekoa, about five miles southeast of Bethlehem. Beracah (20:26) means "blessing." The exact location of Tarshish, mentioned in 20:36 (NASB and KJV) is uncertain. It may have been situated in southern Spain or perhaps on the island of Sardinia. For Ezion Geber (20:36), see the note on 8:17.

21:4–23:21 JEHORAM AND ATHALIAH
21:4-20 Jehoram. The military security won by Jehoshaphat was lost by the disobedience of Jehoram (853–841 B.C.). God preserved

the nation because of his promise to David
(21:7), but he let Edom (21:8), the Philistines, and the Arabs (20:16) invade Israel.
The Davidic promise continued even though
the particular king was rejected (21:20), a
clear example of God's loving-kindness that
would never depart (cf. 1 Chron. 17:13).
Libnah (2 Chron. 21:10) was a Philistine city
located about twenty-five miles southwest of
Jerusalem. The expression "to prostitute
themselves" (21:11) has its background in
the Canaanite fertility cult in which sexual
immorality was practiced. It refers to the
spiritual unfaithfulness of the Israelites
toward God as they pursued other gods.
Elijah had ascended to heaven by this time
(21:12). The letter had been written by Elijah
but was delivered by another prophet. For
the significance of "no fire" (21:19), see the
note on 16:14.

22:1–23:21 Athaliah. The evil from the
house of Ahab, the king of the northern
tribes, continued. His grandson Ahaziah
(841 B.C.) was judged for his disobedience
(22:1-9). Then Ahab's daughter, Athaliah
(841–835 B.C.), killed all of the royal line of
David but one, Joash, who took the throne six
years later (22:10-12). The house of David
shriveled down to but one heir. Joash's
preservation illustrated once again God's
absolute faithfulness to his promises to
David that he would always have an heir to
the throne of the kingdom. Ramoth (22:6;
Ramah, NASB and KJV, Hebrew for "height")
is an abbreviation for Ramoth Gilead.

Joash (835–796 B.C.) was anointed king
through the political and military plans of
the high priest Jehoiada (23:1-21). The
basis for his action was the Davidic covenant
(23:3). Athaliah's death (23:12-15) cleared
the way for the reestablishment of the
Mosaic Law and the Davidic celebration of
God's redemption (23:18). The covenant
(23:11) refers to a copy of the Mosaic Law.

24:1–36:23 Restoration to the Land
24:1–28:27 JOASH TO AHAZ

24:1-27 Joash. Joash's chief triumph was
his effort to restore the temple under the high
priest Jehoiada's oversight (24:1-14). After
Jehoiada's death, Joash dropped God for
idols and killed Jehoiada's son, Zechariah
(24:15-22). (Jesus referred to the stoning of
Zechariah in Matthew 23:35.) Through it all,

God showed his kindness by sending prophets to warn the king and people to return to
loving God.

25:1-28 Amaziah. Again, the same pattern
occurred during the reign of a king, Amaziah
(796–767 B.C.): having the kingdom firmly
in hand (2 Chron. 25:3), gaining great victory
(25:11-12), worshiping idols (25:14-15), and
then losing his military security (25:22-24)
and, eventually, his life (25:27). God wanted
Amaziah to trust in him for the victory, not in
his own military might (cf. Deut. 17:16).

The Valley of Salt (2 Chron. 25:11) is that
section of the Rift Valley located at the south
end of the Dead Sea. Seir (25:14) is another
name for Edom. To the record of Kings,
Chronicles adds this account of Amaziah's
defection. He worshiped the gods of the
defeated enemy. Beth Shemesh (25:23) was
located about fifteen miles west of Jerusalem. Lachish (25:27) was about twenty-five
miles southwest of Jerusalem.

26:1-23 Uzziah. The key phrase for Uzziah
(791–739 B.C.), as well as for all the kings of
Judah and the returned exiles, is found in the
last part of 26:5. Uzziah's downfall was his
pride in his kingdom's military strength
(25:16; cf. Prov. 16:18), which led him to
want to function as a priest in addition to
being king (2 Chron. 26:18). That was Saul's
problem as well (1 Sam. 13:8-9; cf. Exod.
30:7-8). But only One could be both priest
and king, Jesus the Messiah and High Priest
of the Christian faith. Uzziah, like Jehoram
(2 Chron. 21:20), was not buried in the
tombs of the kings (26:23).

Elath (26:2, sometimes spelled Eloth,
NASB and KJV) was an important sea-
port located at the north end of the Gulf of
Aqaba. The Zechariah of 26:5 is not a refer-
ence to Zechariah the postexilic prophet.
Gur Baal (26:7) has not been identified.
The machines of war (26:15; also trans-
lated "engines") refer to catapults.

27:1-9 Jotham. As with many other good
kings, Jotham's positive contributions (750–
731 B.C.) included building fortresses and
temple renovation (27:3-4). The moral for his
life (27:6) was a direct message to the little
band of returned exiles. The silver (27:5)
amounted to about 120,000 ounces, and the
wheat and barley to about 62,500 bushels each.

28:1-27 Ahaz. Judah suffered terrible defeats by Aram (28:5; Syria, KJV), by the northern tribes of Israel (28:6-8), and by Assyria (28:20-21) because of the sins of Ahaz (743–715 B.C.). Yet Ahaz went on to do even worse (28:22-27). He showed a misconception common among God's people, that is, that defeat at the hands of another nation meant that the god of that nation was stronger than the God of Israel (28:23). Instead, the lesson of the book of Chronicles was that the defeat of God's people meant that there was a problem with their faithfulness, not with God's power. During Ahaz's reign the northern tribes were taken away into the Assyrian captivity, but Chronicles does not even mention that. Its focus is on Judah alone and her faith, faithlessness, and ultimate release from the Babylonian captivity.

For "sacrificed his sons in the fire" (28:3), see the note on 2 Kings 16:3. For more on Tiglath Pileser (2 Chron. 28:20; also spelled "Tilgath Pilneser"), see the note on 2 Kings 15:19.

29:1–35:27 HEZEKIAH TO JOSIAH
29:1–32:33 Hezekiah. Hezekiah (728–686 B.C.) repaired the temple and, unlike Ahaz before him, understood that the true reason for Israel's defeats was the king's unfaithfulness (29:1-11). He cleansed the temple (29:12-19), consecrated the people, and reestablished David's orders for the praise and worship of God in the temple service (29:20-36). Again there were joy and worship in the nation (29:30, 36) as a result of the restoration of the temple worship (29:35). The square on the east (29:4) refers to the open space east of the temple area.

A great Passover celebration was held (30:1-27). There were some Israelites (30:1) living in the north who had not been taken captive by the Assyrians in 722 B.C. with the rest of the northern tribes (cf. 30:10-11). Note the phrases "at the king's command" (30:6), "all Israel" (30:1), "throughout Israel" (30:5), "the Israelites" (31:1), and "unity of mind" (30:12). Those were reminders of the golden days of David and Solomon when the king's command was pleasing to God and coincided with his commands, and the unified nation supported the king with one heart.

Hezekiah's Passover prayer (30:18-20) illustrated the ultimate triumph of inner heart obedience over external legal details. In this exceptional case, Hezekiah's attitude was accepted by God even though external rituals were not followed. That great purity of heart extended the celebration another week (30:23) and marked a return to the greatness of Solomon's reign (30:26). The additional seven days of celebration coincided with the Feast of Unleavened Bread.

Hezekiah destroyed idolatry and increased the offerings (31:1-21). The people supported the king and destroyed idols in Judah, Benjamin, Ephraim, and Manasseh (31:1). Then Hezekiah established the divisions of the temple ministers and saw to their proper support through tithes. The summary of 30:20-21 rounds out the description begun in 29:2 of how Hezekiah did right in accordance with the ways of his father, David. The thrust of this entire section was to encourage the returned Jews to restore the temple and its wor-ship with all their hearts. The sacred stones, or pillars, and the Asherah poles, or Asherim (31:1), represented the Canaanite fertility deities (cf. the note on Deut. 7:5). The third month (2 Chron. 31:7) is Sivan (May–June), and the seventh month is Tishri (September–October).

The acts of faithfulness were directly linked to Assyria's attack on Judah (32:1-33). Usually such attacks were due to the king's disobedience, but this attack functioned as a vehicle to display the essence of Israel's faith in the presence of the God of heaven and earth (32:7; cf. 2 Kings 6:16). Sennacherib's speech asked the key questions that probed the heart of Israel's understanding of why she succeeded or failed: (1) "On what are you basing your confidence?" (32:10); and (2) Would a defeat in Israel be due to the fact that her God, Yahweh, was inferior? (32:13-14). Hezekiah's prayer brought about an indisputable answer from the true God (32:20-23). Hezekiah's prideful end was downplayed (32:24-26) in order to emphasize his God-given (32:29) wealth and devotion (32:32).

For "the supporting terraces" (32:5; the Millo, NASB and KJV), see the note on 1 Kings 9:15. For Sennacherib's attack (2 Chron. 32:9), see the notes on 2 Kings 18:1-37. For Hezekiah's water conduit (32:30), see the note on 2 Kings 20:20.

33:1-25 Manasseh and Amon. Manasseh (697–642 B.C.) brought Judah back to the spiritual darkness that existed in the land before Joshua conquered it (33:2). It was as if all the good done from the time of Joshua through the time of Hezekiah had been undone (33:9). Incredibly, the nation's worst king humbled himself in the Assyrian exile, was heard by God, and was returned to the land (33:10-13). Manasseh had the longest reign, was the worst king of Judah, and was the most brilliant example of restoration from the exile on the basis of his having a tender and humble heart before God. The key to restoration was a person's humility of heart when convicted of sin, no matter how great the sin. That was a lesson for the returned Jews and the people of God from then on. The Valley of Ben Hinnom (33:6; also known as the Hinnom, KJV) was the L-shaped valley that is situated west and south of Jerusalem. Amon (642–640 B.C.) functioned as an example of one who did not humble himself before God (33:23).

34:1–35:27 Josiah. The account of Josiah's reign (640–609 B.C.) can be divided into his eight years of rule (34:3) followed by his four years of seeking the Lord (34:3). Those years were followed by a nationwide six-year purging of idolatry (34:3-7) and a subsequent cleansing and rebuilding of the temple (34:8-13). Josiah's response to finding the Law of Moses (34:14; cf. 2 Kings 22:8-13) resulted in the prophetic speeches by Hilkiah the high priest and Huldah the prophetess that stated why the nation would fall (34:21, 25) and why Josiah's reign would be spared destruction (34:26-28). Even in the shadow of certain destruction, it was important to do right before God. The tension between undergoing consequences for past sins and at the same time maintaining obedience to God was something that the returned exiles had to endure and learn from.

Second Chronicles 35 ties together the key elements of Israel's faith: obedience according to David, Solomon (35:4) and Moses (35:6), all mediated according to the command of the present king, Josiah (35:16). Hezekiah's Passover celebration was linked to the time of Solomon (30:26), while Josiah's Passover looked back to the time of Samuel (35:18). The Ark, which apparently was removed from the temple during the apostasy

of Amon or Manasseh, was returned to the temple (35:3). For a discussion of Josiah's intentions in fighting the king of Egypt (35:20), see the note on 2 Kings 23:29. Megiddo (35:22) was a fortress city in the Jezreel Valley that guarded an important pass through Mount Carmel to the coastal plain.

36:1-21 JEHOAHAZ TO ZEDEKIAH
The four last kings of Judah were listed quickly; the last three all did evil in the sight of God: Jehoahaz (36:1-4; 609 B.C.); Jehoiakim (36:4-8; 609–597 B.C.); Jehoiachin (36:9-10; 597 B.C.); and Zedekiah (36:11-21; 597–586 B.C.). Nebuchadnezzar's first invasion of Jerusalem was in 605 B.C. when Jehoiakim was king. In his second invasion and deportation of the Israelites (36:10), the king and ten thousand Jews were taken into captivity. Even after all that horror, Zedekiah still did not soften his heart before God (36:13). God's compassion was seen in his continual warnings (36:15); his wrath was shown in the destruction of Jerusalem (36:16). For a note on Nebuchadnezzar's attack and siege (36:17-18), see the notes on 2 Kings 25:1. The third deportation to Babylon took place after the destruction of Jerusalem in 586 B.C. (2 Chron. 36:20).

The writer explains that the deportation was divine discipline for neglect of the sabbatical year (36:21; cf. Lev. 25:4; 26:34-35). That was another important lesson the writer wanted to emphasize for the newly returned Jews. They had just come out of that discipline and needed to be reminded of its cause and purpose.

36:22-23 THE DECREE OF CYRUS
Cyrus captured the city of Babylon in 539 B.C., and his first official year as king was 538 B.C. The reference to Jeremiah's prophecy (2 Chron. 36:21; cf. Jer. 25:12-13; 29:10) indicates that God was in control from the very beginning. After seventy years of discipline, God prepared the way for the Jews to return to their land. His promises to Abraham, Moses, and David were certain. The book ends with the upbeat words of release and restoration: "go up." The return of the exiles was, in effect, a second exodus—not from Egypt, but from Babylon. The nation reentered the land with a chance to start again.

Ezra

BASIC FACTS

HISTORICAL SETTING
Jewish exiles first returned from the Babylonian captivity under Zerubbabel in about 538 B.C. The date of Ezra's return to Jerusalem is a matter of some scholarly debate, but the biblical evidence points to 458 B.C., the seventh year of Artaxerxes (464–424 B.C.). Over sixty years separate the first part of the book (Ezra 1–6) and last part (Ezra 7–10). During Ezra's time Greece was in its golden age, Athens flourished, and Socrates was a young adult.

AUTHOR
Ezra, the priest and scribe, is the commonly accepted author of the book of Ezra. He probably had a part in editing the two books of Chronicles and Nehemiah as well.

DATE
The book of Ezra was written in the period after Israel's Babylonian captivity, sometime after Ezra returned to Jerusalem. The book mentions several specific dates that help the reader understand its structure and emphasis. For these dates, see the chart on page 192.

This overview of the dates and their events introduces the two main issues of the book: (1) the overcoming of attempts to stop the restoration of the temple, and (2) the overcoming of attempts to reintroduce foreign marriages of a kind that would introduce idolatry, the very reason for Israel's past downfall and her captivity in Babylon.

PURPOSE
The book of Ezra was designed to show how God supported those who returned from the captivity and to encourage faithfulness in regard to the hard task of rebuilding the nation.

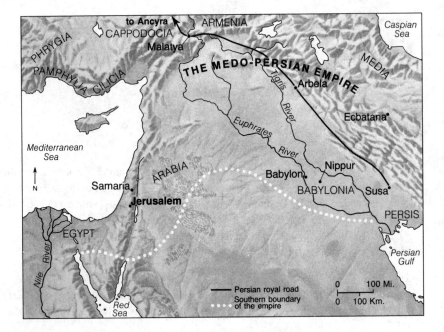

GEOGRAPHY AND ITS IMPORTANCE

The return of Israel to her land, followed by the special returns of Ezra and Nehemiah were made under the rule of the Medo-Persian Empire. God placed Israel under a long period of foreign rule by Assyria, Babylon, Persia, Greece, and Rome before he sent his Messiah to redeem the nation. Israel's exit from Babylon mirrored her exodus from Egypt and repeated the geographical and spiritual pattern of movement from bondage to release, from foreign captivity to captivity to God.

GUIDING CONCEPTS

FORM AND CONTENT
Three decrees
The book centers on three decrees that would result in the prosperity of Jerusalem and the Jewish people: (1) that of Cyrus (1:1), (2) that of Darius (6:8), and (3) that of Artaxerxes (7:11). In 6:14 the three decrees are seen in close unity, even though they relate to separate matters that occurred over a long period of time.

Two returns
The two returns of the Jews from the Babylonian captivity were made during the reign of Cyrus (539 B.C.), with Sheshbazzar as the leader, and during the reign of Artaxerxes (458 B.C.), with Ezra as the leader.

Two tasks
The two tasks of the people of Israel in the book were to rebuild the temple (6:15) and to obey the law concerning marriages and the purity of worship of God alone (7:10).

Form
The book focuses on the activities and leadership of two men: Sheshbazzar, the prince, and Ezra, the priest. (See the chart below.)

All of these events are seen through the light of Jeremiah's prophecy of restoration (1:1; cf. Jer. 29:1-14). According to Jeremiah, the nation was to settle down in Babylon and expect seventy years of captivity. After that, God promised that his plans to rebuild the nation and return his people to the land of Israel would come about. The book of Ezra focuses upon and describes that period of promised relocation and reconstruction as the period of a renewed building of the temple and teaching of the law for the nation of Israel.

THE WORK OF SHESHBAZZAR AND EZRA

Event	Sheshbazzar	Ezra
Release and Travel	1:1–2:70	7:1–8:34
Return and Worship	3:1-7	8:35-36
Task of Rebuilding	3:8–6:22	9:1–10:44
	Davidic Line	Aaronic Line
	Builder of the Temple	Teacher of the People

SPECIFIC DATES MENTIONED IN EZRA

1:1	The first year of Cyrus's reign (539–530 B.C.)	The time of Cyrus's decree to allow the Jews to return to Jerusalem.
4:5	Darius I (522–486 B.C.)	The temple's rebuilding was frustrated from the reign of Cyrus until the reign of Darius (Cambyses, 530–522 B.C., is not mentioned).
4:6	Xerxes I (486–464 B.C.)	He was the Ahasuerus of Esther's day and received an accusation against the returned Jews.
4:7	Artaxerxes I (464–423 B.C.)	This was Ezra's time. Artaxerxes I issued a decree to stop the work of rebuilding the city of Jerusalem.
6:15	Sixth year of Darius (516 B.C.)	The temple's rebuilding was completed. Note that this date goes back in time to the reign of Darius, mentioned in 4:5. It is out of chronological sequence to include the later work stoppages noted during the reigns of Xerxes (Ahasuerus) and Artaxerxes (4:6-7) and also to end the discussion of the stoppages happily with the completion of the second temple. Chronologically, the attacks on the efforts to rebuild Jerusalem continued long after the temple was restored. But the writer wanted to end the discussion of the frustrated rebuilding efforts and move on to the even more important point of the book: the purification of God's people.
7:7	The seventh year of Artaxerxes I (458 B.C.)	Ezra 7 has much to say about the seventh year. It was the year in which Ezra returned to Jerusalem and reformed the marriage practices of some of the Jewish returnees.
7:8	The fifth month, first day	Ezra arrived in Jerusalem under Artaxerxes' good decree.
8:31	The first month, twelfth day	This reflects back on the day that Ezra left to return to Jerusalem.
10:9	The ninth month, twentieth day	The people assembled to hear Ezra read the law.
10:16	The tenth month, first day	Ezra began to investigate the Israelite men who had married foreign wives.
10:17	First month, the first day of the next year (457 B.C.)	Ezra finished the investigation, and the Israelite men were separated from their foreign wives.

THE PROBLEM WITH FOREIGN WIVES

Why was it so bad for the Jews to marry foreign women? First of all, the law had prohibited marrying women of the Canaanite nations (cf. Exod. 23:31-33; 34:12-16; Deut. 7:1-4). Second, during Israel's history, foreign wives had always brought idolatry into the nation of Israel. Solomon's problems in this area are noted in 1 Kings 11:1-8. The postexilic community needed to avoid a relapse into the idolatry that brought about their downfall.

BIBLE-WIDE CONCEPTS

PROMISE OF RESTORATION

The geographic promise

God gave the newly created earth to Adam, the newly dried earth to Noah, and the land of Canaan to Abraham, Moses, and the nation of Israel. That land of Israel was an essential part of God's promise to the Jewish nation. But what happened to the promise of land when the nation of Israel was exiled during the Babylonian captivity? It remained firm and sure. Ezra showed his readers that the Israelites would be restored to the land that always had and would be theirs. And that promise looks forward ultimately to the new heavens and earth where the land promised will extend around the globe to all nations.

The Davidic promise

God had promised an eternal line of kingly rule through the Davidic covenant. What had exile done to that promise? Both Sheshbazzar and Zerubbabel were members of David's royal line (see the genealogy of 1 Chron. 3:18-19 where some scholars identify Shenazzar as Sheshbazzar). Other scholars believe Shenazzar to be an uncle of Sheshbazzar. The Davidic line was still in place and leading the return from exile. But how would that rule be fully reestablished? Under the domination of Persia, then Greece and Rome, Israel would wait for God's answer to that question. When Jesus, the King, finally came, he inaugurated a new kind of rule from heaven at the right hand of God. But he will come again and fully establish the Davidic rule promised so long ago.

The Mosaic promise

After the Babylonian exile, were the people of Israel still bound by the Mosaic covenant as they had been before it took place? From Ezra's viewpoint, the law was still as binding as ever. The keeping of it was still the way to receive divine blessing. The breaking of it, in the case of intermarriage, was still the way to destruction. The law's firmness and continuity stretched into the life of Jesus, the Prophet who was greater than Moses. In the Sermon on the Mount (Matt. 5–7), Jesus said he came to uphold and fulfill the Mosaic Law, and in his death he annulled Moses' covenant and replaced it with a deeper law and a more binding covenant that was sealed by his blood. But for those Israelites who were living in Ezra's time, the Mosaic covenant still held out its blessings and curses. People have always been and always will be responsible to obey God's desires, from the beginning of time in the Garden of Eden, to the coming glories of God's future kingdom.

NEEDS MET BY EZRA

The people of God returned to their land but they were still under the domination of Persia and under military threat from the surrounding peoples. Where was the great glory of the days of Solomon? Where was the powerful presence of God? The days of glory had to be patiently awaited and the power of God was present, but hidden, and had to be seen through the eyes of faith. God's promises and presence still remained. In that light, the returned exiles failed and succeeded in several ways. Their experiences were written down so that future readers would have a proper and realistic perspective on just what Israel's restoration from the captivity did and did not mean. These are some of the questions that the exiles probably asked and that the book of Ezra answers.

- What will God's promised restoration of Israel from the captivity be like?
- What are the problems that the people of Israel will face upon return?
- Has God's discipline through the exile made Israel immune to further sin and failure?
- Has God's restoration of the people of Israel to the Promised Land made them immune to external attacks?
- Are God's preexilic promises to Abraham, Moses, and David still in force?
- What good did the exile really do for Israel?

As the book of Ezra provided answers to these questions, it enabled God's people to move on under his guidance with their eyes wide open both to the greatness of his power to accomplish his promises and to the greatness of their own power to derail their blessings through their disobedience. The good news was that God had redeemed them from captivity and brought them back to their land. The bad news was that they were still the same old people; they were still weak and needed God's grace to keep them from sin. In Christ we share similar good and bad news and enjoy the same wonderful grace.

OUTLINE OF EZRA

A. RECONSTRUCTION OF THE PLACE OF THE COVENANT (1:1–6:22)
    1. Release: The Divine Stirring of Cyrus (1:1–2:70)
    2. Reconstruction of the Temple (3:1–6:22)
B. RESTORATION OF THE PRACTICE OF THE COVENANT (7:1–10:44)
    1. Release (7:1–8:34)
    2. Restoration of Covenant Purity (9:1–10:44)

EZRA NOTES

1:1–6:22 RECONSTRUCTION OF THE PLACE OF THE COVENANT
1:1–2:70 Release:
The Divine Stirring of Cyrus
Overview: The return of the Jews from the exile (1:1) was in accord with Jeremiah's prophecy (Jer. 29). The joy of return was to

be matched with human response, as seen throughout the book in key phrases like "go up" and "came up" (Ezra 1:3, 5, 11; 2:1), "assisted" and "extended his good favor" (1:6; 6:22; 7:28), God's gift of the law, and the "gracious hand of his God" (7:6, 9), and "gave their hands" (10:19). Ezra 2 lists the men of Israel (2:2-35), priests and Levites (2:36-42), servants (2:43-58), and unregistered people (2:59-63) who came back from the captivity.

1:1-4 THE DECREE OF CYRUS

Cyrus, the king of Anshan, a region in eastern Elam and part of the area populated by the Persian tribes, defeated the king of Media and welded the Median and Persian empires into a dual monarchy called Medo-Persia. In 539 B.C. he captured Babylon, bringing the Babylonian Empire to a close. Cyrus's proclamation (1:2-4) fulfilled Jeremiah's prophecy of restoration after seventy years of captivity in Babylon (Jer. 25:1-18; 29:10). As many as 160 years earlier, Isaiah had named Cyrus as God's chosen instrument to liberate the Jews (Isa. 44:28–45:7,13). Cyrus's accession year was 539 B.C., making 538 B.C. his first official year on the throne.

Although Cyrus acknowledged the Lord (Ezra 1:2), on the Cyrus Cylinder he ascribed his victories to Marduk, the god of Babylon. Scripture clearly states that Cyrus was an unbeliever (Isa. 45:4). The purpose of the Jews' return to Jerusalem from Babylon (Ezra 1:3) was to give them an opportunity to rebuild God's temple that Nebuchadnezzar had destroyed in 586 B.C.

1:5-11 ENCOURAGEMENT FOR THE RETURN

The Jewish historian Josephus (*Antiquities,* 11.8) reported that many of the Jews did not want to leave Babylon (1:5-6) because of their many possessions. Cyrus decreed that the Jews who were returning be given a portion of the treasure that Nebuchadnezzar had taken from the Jerusalem temple (1:7); Darius I apparently returned the rest (6:5).

There are three views regarding the identity of Sheshbazzar (1:8), whom Cyrus appointed as the governor (5:14). (1) Sheshbazzar was just another name for Zerubbabel. (2) Sheshbazzar was the officially appointed leader, and Zerubbabel was the popular but unofficial leader. (3) They were both leaders, but they led at different times, Sheshbazzar preceding Zerubbabel. Both men were called "governor of Judah" and were associated with laying the temple's foundation (Ezra 5:16; Zech. 4:9), but only Zerubbabel was associated with its completion (Hag. 1:12; Zech. 4:9). Possibly

Sheshbazzar died soon after the Jews' return to Jerusalem and was succeeded by Zerubbabel. Although 5,400 vessels were returned (1:11), only 2,499 of the more important ones are specifically listed (1:9-10).

2:1-67 THOSE WHO RETURNED

The list of the Jews who returned included men (2:2-35), priests (2:36-39), Levites (2:40-42), servants to the temple and to Solomon (2:43-58), unregistered families (2:59-63), and the totals (2:64-67). The same list with some variation (due to scribal errors or problems with the transmission of numbers) appears in Nehemiah 7:6-73. "Nehemiah" (Ezra 2:2) does not refer to Jerusalem's famous wall builder. While biblical genealogies (2:61-63) may seem boring and unimportant to readers today, these verses show why they were so essential for the Jews of ancient times. The actual number (2:64) by count was 42,360. They apparently arrived in Jerusalem at the ruined temple site in 537 B.C. (2:68).

2:68-70 THE FREEWILL OFFERING

Note the principle of giving (2:69; cf. 2 Cor. 8:3). The Israelites gave willingly and out of their ability, from hearts committed to God's revealed will.

3:1–6:22 Reconstruction of the Temple

Overview: There were two responses to the completion of the temple's foundation (Ezra 3:10). First, there was a mixed reaction among the Jews of joy for the present reconstruction and tears for the loss of past glory (3:11-13). Second, the enemies of Israel stopped the Jews from doing further work until the reign of Darius (6:14). That prepares the reader for the last part of the book, where another enemy appeared to threaten the fragile existence of the returned people of Israel: the Israelites were prone to marriages with foreigners which would only result in the acceptance of idolatrous practices. In 4:1-3 Israel's leaders excluded foreigners from working on the temple; yet, at the end of the book, some Jews had married foreigners.

3:1-7 SEVENTH-MONTH ACTIVITIES

The seventh month (3:1) was Tishri (September–October). It was noted for its three religious convocations: the Feast of

Trumpets (on the first of the month), the Day of Atonement (on the tenth of the month), and the Feast of Booths, or Tabernacles (during the fifteenth to the twentieth days of the month; cf. Lev. 23:1-36).

3:8-13 THE FOUNDATION IS LAID
The "second month" (Ezra 3:8) was Iyyar (April–May). The temple's foundation (3:10) was laid in 536 B.C. The great practice of praising God's loving-kindness, so prevalent in the Psalms before the exile, was begun once again (3:11).

4:1-24 FOREIGNERS ARE EXCLUDED
Ezra 4 records the opposition to the temple's construction that took place from 536 B.C. to the days of Artaxerxes (around 446 B.C.). Esar-haddon (4:2; 681–669 B.C.), son of Sennacherib, had brought foreigners to the land of Israel after expelling the Jews of the northern tribes to Assyria. They worshiped the God of Israel as well as many other gods (2 Kings 17:41). The opposition recorded here (4:4; 536 B.C.) was not unique. Ezra went on to cite two other examples of opposition in later history: (1) the opposition in the days of Xerxes I, also known as Ahasuerus (4:6), and (2) the opposition in the days of Artaxerxes (4:7-23). Xerxes I, or Ahasuerus (4:6; 486–464 B.C.), ruled Persia during the days of Esther (cf. Esther 1:1). Artaxerxes (Ezra 4:7; 464–424 B.C.) ruled Persia during the days of Nehemiah.

The enemies of the Jews wrote to Artaxerxes, asking that he not permit Jerusalem to be rebuilt (4:11-16). Ezra 4:8–6:18 was originally written in Aramaic, which served as the international language at the time of the Persian Empire. The word "until" (4:21) is crucial in the king's reply. In a few short years Artaxerxes would grant Nehemiah's request to rebuild Jerusalem (Neh. 2). With Ezra 4:24 the parenthesis of 4:6-23 is complete. Ezra 4:24 is a statement concerning the cessation of the temple's construction in 536 B.C. That cessation continued until 520 B.C., the second year of the reign of Darius (522–486 B.C.).

5:1-5 THE ROLE OF THE PROPHETS IN OPPOSITION
The ministry of the prophets Haggai and Zechariah (5:1) is further detailed in the books that bear their names. When once again challenged as to their right to build

the temple (5:3-5), the Jews continued their work while the matter was investigated by Tattenai.

5:6–6:12 THE LETTER TO AND DECREE FROM DARIUS I
In Ecbatana (6:2), a summer residence of the Persian kings located about two hundred miles south of the Caspian Sea, an official memorandum containing details of Cyrus's original decree was discovered (6:3-5). Darius must have stunned Tattenai by strengthening the original decree of Cyrus (6:8-11). This was no idle threat (6:11). Herodotus reports that Darius impaled three thousand Babylonians after he put down a rebellion in their capital city. He then destroyed the walls and gates of Babylon, something Cyrus had not done.

6:13-22 THE TEMPLE IS COMPLETED
Credit also was given to a later ruler, Artaxerxes (6:14; 464–424 B.C.), who helped in the maintenance of the temple (7:15-21). The work was completed in the month of Adar (February–March), 515 B.C., twenty-one years after the foundation had been laid (6:13-22). Again, the stress on the nation's purity (6:21) contrasts with the upcoming impurity of mixed marriages. The reference to the "king of Assyria" (6:22) is unexpected but not unusual. Obviously, Darius was meant. A similar expression is used in Nehemiah 9:32 to refer to Assyrian, Babylonian, and Persian kings. Since the Persians ruled former Assyrian territories, it could be said that Darius was king of Assyria, just as Cyrus claimed the title "king of Babylon."

7:1–10:44 RESTORATION OF THE PRACTICE OF THE COVENANT
Overview: Ezra's words in Ezra 7:10 echoed Deuteronomy 33:10. The hand of God was upon Ezra (Ezra 7:14, 23, 25) as he made preparations to return to Israel. As God had worked in Cyrus (1:1), he also worked in Artaxerxes (7:27). The problem of purity is met with Ezra's great confession (9:5-15) and careful correction (10:1-44).

7:1–8:34 Release
7:1-28 THE DECREE OF ARTAXERXES I
Almost sixty years separate the events recorded in Ezra 6 and Ezra 7. During this

period (515–458 B.C.), the events of the book of Esther took place in Susa (see introductory map). Ezra's family line (7:1-5) was traced back to Aaron, Israel's first high priest. At one time a "teacher" (7:6) was little more than a secretary, but later the office increased in importance. The teacher, or scribe, became a preserver and interpreter of the law. Ezra's desire to teach displayed the heart of a biblical philosophy of education (7:10). The order is significant. A person cannot practice what he has not thoroughly studied; and he should not teach principles he has not carefully applied. Perhaps Ezra was using some of the extra funds in an attempt to rebuild Jerusalem's walls (7:18; cf. 4:12). One talent of silver weighed about seventy-five pounds, one hundred kors of wheat were the equivalent of about four hundred to six hundred bushels, and one bath was about five and a half gallons (7:22). The term "Nethinim(s)" (7:24, NASB and KJV), also translated "temple servants" (NIV and RSV), literally means "those who are given" and refers to those dedicated to the temple service as assistants to the Levites.

8:1-20 THOSE WHO RETURNED
A shortage of Levites (8:15-19) would have greatly inhibited the program Ezra wanted to implement, so he sent out a last-minute appeal for reinforcements. As a result, 38 Levites and 220 temple servants responded to his appeal.

8:21-36 THE JOURNEY: SAFE DELIVERANCE OF THE OFFERING
Ezra took precautionary measures with regard to money matters (8:24-30), as did Paul with the money he collected and handled (cf. 2 Cor. 8:20-21). One talent (8:26) weighed about seventy-five pounds. God gave Ezra and the exiles traveling safety during the four months of their nine hundred-mile journey (8:31).

9:1–10:44 Restoration of Covenant Purity

9:1-15 EZRA'S CONFESSION
Ezra had been in Jerusalem about four and a half months when the officials brought to his attention the problem of mixed marriages. Deuteronomy 7:1-5 had forbidden the intermarriage of Israelites with unbelieving foreigners and warned of the idolatrous consequences of such a practice. If this continued, the Jews would soon lose their national identity and could end up in exile once again. Ezra displayed the customary signs of grief, evidence of his intense concern (Ezra 9:3-4). He did not stand apart from his people and condemn them, but he identified himself with them in their guilt and interceded on their behalf (9:5-15). The "remnant" (9:8; "peg," NASB, and "nail," KJV) probably refers to the Israelites who had returned from the exile. As a tent peg secures a tent, so the returned exiles secured Israel's national existence.

10:1-44 THE HOLY RACE IS PURIFIED
Shecaniah offered Ezra a suggestion as to how to deal with the matter of intermarriage: separation of the marriage partners (10:2-4). Since the normal Hebrew word for "divorce" is not used, it is uncertain whether remarriage was intended or allowed. The words "according to the Law" (10:3) probably referred to Deuteronomy 7:1-5, a text condemning mixed marriages with unbelievers. The people agreed to follow Shechaniah's suggestion. It took three months to complete the investigations and carry out the divorce proceedings. Seventeen priests, ten Levites, and eighty-four laymen (the NASB, KJV, and other versions list eighty-six due to a different textual reading of 10:38) were found guilty and put away their foreign wives (Ezra 10:18-43).

This sad incident (10:44) is not included in Ezra to provide a biblical basis for divorce. Rather, it illustrates the great tragedy of marital breakup. Any attempt to make application of this unusual situation by Christians seeking to divorce an unbelieving spouse would be prohibited by Paul's words in 1 Corinthians 7:12-13. It is a picture of the need for purity among God's people.

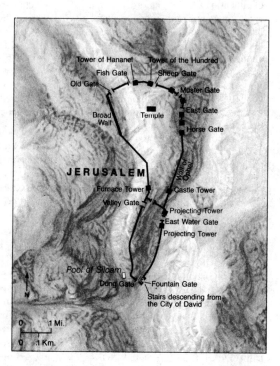

Nehemiah

HISTORICAL SETTING

In 539 B.C. Cyrus, king of Persia, destroyed the Babylonian Empire and released the Israelites from captivity. Nehemiah continues the story of Israel's reconstruction after the captivity. The book begins its record of events around thirteen years after the period of Ezra's temple reforms, and it shows how Jerusalem was finally rebuilt and repopulated. The events recorded in the book of Nehemiah span the reigns of five Persian kings: Cyrus, 559–530 B.C.; Cambyses, 530–522 B.C.; Darius I, 522–486 B.C.; Xerxes I, 486–465 B.C.; and Artaxerxes I, 464–423 B.C.

AUTHOR

Nehemiah was a Jewish servant to the king of Persia. Although it is difficult to know for certain who wrote the book in its final form, it is clearly based on Nehemiah's first-hand memoirs.

DATE

Nehemiah came to Jerusalem in 445 B.C. For the general conditions of those times, see the book of Ezra, Haggai 2:1-10, and Zechariah 2:6-13. The book of Nehemiah presents a chronology that clearly shows the emphasis and point of the book. (See chart on the following page.)

The dedication of the wall was done after Nehemiah returned from his trip to Babylon (13:4, 6). After his return, he purified the temple service and dedicated the wall. The exact date cannot be known.

The events of Nehemiah 13 happened before those of Nehemiah 12, while Nehemiah was away in Babylon. Nehemiah wrote about those events last because he wanted to emphasize the sins of the Jewish leaders and how he corrected them.

PURPOSE

The book of Nehemiah was designed to round out the story of the postexilic reconstruction of the nation of Israel. It shows God's support for the rebuilding through faithful men like Nehemiah who had to fight against hostile enemies and unfaithful Israelites.

GEOGRAPHY AND ITS IMPORTANCE

Jerusalem was a symbol either of God's blessing or of his curse. Because the time of his anger was past, Nehemiah wanted the city to reflect the new time of God's blessing. That would only happen when the walls and gates were repaired and the city repopulated. As the city's destruction had conformed to the people's sinfulness, the city's restoration would reflect the people's repentance and God's restored blessing.

GUIDING CONCEPTS

REPROACH

At the beginning of the book, Nehemiah was very concerned about the disgrace that Jerusalem was still under. The word "disgrace" (variously translated as "despised" and "reproach") is repeated several times (1:3; 2:17; 4:4; 5:9). That word reflects more than a tragic state of disrepair; it also reflects an attitude of God, which was why Nehemiah was so disturbed. The word was used by the Prophets to describe what God would do to Jerusalem because of its people's sins (cf. Jer. 23:40; 24:9; 29:18; 44:8, 12; Lam. 5:1; Ezek. 5:14-15). The reproach was grounded in God's judgment upon his sinful people.

It was terrible for the city of Jerusalem to look as if it still was under disgrace. The temple had been rebuilt for more than seventy-five years, and God had given his blessing, release, and restoration to the people of Israel. For the city to appear as if it was still under God's judgment was to insult God and to demean the dignity of his restored people. The reproach was not just a landscaping and construction problem. Rather, it involved the theological implications of judgment upon sinful people. Although the nation of Israel could not conquer the entire land again, it could make all the necessary efforts to show that the city of God's presence was rebuilt, inhabited, and prosperous.

PURIFICATION

Nehemiah was concerned that the Israelites should obey the Law of Moses so that the nation would be pure in God's sight (Neh. 1:5, 7-9; 5:7, 9; 7:2; 8:2, 9, 12, 17; 9:3; 10:28-29; 13:1-3). Passages like Leviticus 26:33 and Deuteronomy 23:3-5 lay

---

THE CHRONOLOGY OF NEHEMIAH

Reference	Text Marker	Date
1:1	Twentieth year of Artaxerxes	445–444 B.C.
2:1	Twentieth year of Artaxerxes	445–444 B.C.
5:14	Nehemiah governs twelve years	456–444 B.C.
6:15	Twenty-fifth day, sixth month	444 B.C.
7:73	Seventh month	444 B.C.
8:2	First day	444 B.C.
8:13-18	Second through the eighth days	444 B.C.
9:1	Twenty-fourth day	444 B.C.
12:27–13:3	The dedication of the wall	444 B.C.

behind Nehemiah's efforts. The specific areas in need of purification were the temple service, the observance of the Sabbath, and the observance of laws against usury (Neh. 5:7; 12:30, 45; 13:3, 9, 22, 30).

BIBLE-WIDE CONCEPTS

THE CITY AND TEMPLE OF GOD

Throughout the history recorded in Scripture, God designated special starting places in which his people could grow in their commission to rule the world and fellowship with him. Those places included the garden called Eden, the land of Palestine promised to Abraham's offspring, and at the heart of that land, the city of Jerusalem. At the center of the city, the temple was the place of fellowship between God and his people based on their obedience to the Mosaic covenant that rested in the Most Holy Place. For hundreds of years the peace or unrest of that city was the barometer of God's blessing or curse upon the entire land and people of God. But Jerusalem came to an abrupt end when destroyed by Babylon and lay in ruins for over seventy years. Those ruins were a sign of God's judgment on his people's sin. Even when Ezra and Nehemiah had done what they could to remove the reproach of the city's ruins, God's city and people awaited the full restoration of Jerusalem as the center of God's blessing.

The restored temple and city would only survive and be blessed when populated by people with restored obedience. Because God's blessing is always related to his personal presence, the restoration of Jerusalem by Nehemiah is a foreshadowing of the ultimate restoration of the city by God's own creative hand. The heavenly Jerusalem will descend from heaven and God will openly dwell among humanity. The temple, which was only a small building in the original city, will be replaced with the infinite presence of God himself (Rev. 21:3). The new Jerusalem will come from heaven prepared by God himself (Rev. 21:2). And the population of that city will live in perfect obedience and happiness (Rev. 21:3-27).

THE REMOVAL OF SIN'S REPROACH

Nehemiah saw the ruined city as a sign of God's reproach and disgrace (1:3; 2:17) for the nation's sins. He saw it as his responsibility to help remove that disgrace in light of the promises of the Mosaic covenant. Even after the Babylonian exile that covenant was still in force. Abraham's people were bound by God's covenant with Israel to love and obey God's commands from the heart. Nehemiah's task of exhorting people to remove the reproach of their sin is similar to the exhortations of Paul and others found throughout the New Testament to put away the patterns of the old ways of life that brought God's condemnation. The time for judgment was past, and it was time to put away the things of the past.

That human and divine cooperation in removing the signs of past judgment is also based on God's promises to Abraham. Two key elements of God's promises to Abraham were still in force in balancing human and divine responsibility. First, the world still had ill-will toward Israel ("whoever curses you, I will curse," Gen. 12:3; see also the hostility between the seed of the woman and the seed of the serpent in Gen. 3:15). The world was openly hostile to God's people succeeding in spiritual maturity and obedience. Second, God's people still had to obey and pass along the way of the Lord to following generations (see God's description of Abraham and his line's task in Gen. 18:19). That meant obeying the commands of the Mosaic covenant. Israel had to keep separate from the world in holiness and purity, the chief example in this book being when Nehemiah kept foreigners from working on Jerusalem and from marrying Israelites. The chief example in the New Testament is separation from sin and avoidance of being yoked together with unbelievers and thereby adopting their ungodly perspectives on life.

NEEDS MET BY NEHEMIAH

The book of Nehemiah gives a realistic picture of postexilic life. The nation's strengths and liabilities were still the same. Obedience would bring national and personal stability, while disobedience would put the nation in a state of jeopardy like that which existed before the exile. The task was to live in the light of God's presence and promises even though the earthly fulfillment of those promises was hidden in the future. The Israelites, who had recently returned from the exile, may have been asking questions like these.

- Does God still expect the people of Israel to keep the old Mosaic Law now that they have been released from exile?
- Why was it so bad that Jerusalem lay in relative ruins for nearly one hundred years after the return of the first Jews from the captivity?
- Has the captivity made the Jewish nation any less prone to social and civil evils?
- Is God still willing to stand behind Jewish resistance to the hostility of surrounding nations?

The people of Nehemiah's day and believers today need to have a realistic picture of where the nation of Israel stood in relation to other nations and God. As Israel recovered from the discipline for her sins she needed to be strong in two areas: faith and patience. Faith inspires believers to believe in God and in his ability to do what he promises. Faith keeps them working hard to recover and to avoid repeating the failures of the past. Patience keeps believers from losing heart during the time spent waiting for God to fulfill his promises.

OUTLINE OF NEHEMIAH

A. RELEASE (1:1–2:8)
    1. Reproach of the Remnant Noted (1:1-3)
    2. Petition for Remembering the Covenant (1:4-11)
    3. First Step in Remembrance Granted (2:1-8)
B. REMOVAL OF REPROACH IN THE FACE OF OPPOSITION (2:9–6:19)
    1. Opposition: Secret Survey (2:9-16)
    2. Work Commenced (2:17–3:32)
    3. Opposition: Work in Warfare (4:1-23)
    4. Opposition: Internal Reproach (5:1-19)
    5. Opposition: Wall Completed (6:1-19)

C. RESTORATION OF COVENANT PURITY (7:1–13:31)
   1. Population of Jerusalem: Protection and Increase (7:1-73)
   2. Care for the House of God: Seventh-Month Activities (8:1–10:39)
   3. Population of Jerusalem: Increase (11:1–12:26)
   4. Purity Restored: Dedication of the Wall (12:27–13:31)

NEHEMIAH NOTES

1:1–2:8 RELEASE
Overview: God is seen as being behind the scenes but powerfully causing Nehemiah's success in leaving Babylon (1:11) and getting the wall rebuilt (2:20; 4:9-10, 15). The great detail presented in Nehemiah 3 makes the rebuilding process graphic and also memorializes those brave individuals as models for later generations. The opponents of Israel's return were seen as enemies of God and under his judgment (4:4-5; 6:14).

1:1-3 Reproach of the Remnant Noted
The name "Nehemiah" means "comfort of Yahweh." The book contains Nehemiah's personal memoirs of the rebuilding of Jerusalem. The month of Chislev falls within the months of November–December, and the twentieth year (of the Persian king Artaxerxes) was 445 B.C. Susa, destroyed after the rise of Babylon, was later rebuilt and became the winter residence of Darius and his successors. The condition of Jerusalem mentioned in 1:3 reflects Artaxerxes' decision to stop the rebuilding of the city until an investigation could be completed. The work was stopped by force of arms (Ezra 4:21-23). Nehemiah prayed for his people and the situation in Jerusalem for four months (Neh. 1:1; 2:1).

1:4-11 Petition for Remembering the Covenant
Nehemiah's prayer (1:5-11) was a model of adoration (1:5), confession (1:6-7), and petition (1:8-11). He pleaded God's character. Note the place of Leviticus 26:33 in the prayer. As the king's "cupbearer" (Neh. 1:11), he held a position of great responsibility and influence in the Persian court. Not only did he drink first of the king's wine to guard against poisoning, but he also kept accounts and exercised other administrative responsibilities. Only a person of exceptional trustworthiness would be given such a post.

2:1-8 First Step in Remembrance Granted
The date was Nisan (March–April) of 445 B.C., Artaxerxes' twentieth year (464–424 B.C.). Although Nisan is the first month on the Jewish calendar, Artaxerxes' official year began in the month of Tishri (September–October). The date of the decree to rebuild Jerusalem is important prophetically, for it serves as the beginning point of the seventy weeks of Daniel 9:24-27. Nehemiah was fearful when the king noticed his sad face (Neh. 2:2), for he knew that sadness might suggest that he was dissatisfied with the king and was plotting against him. Nehemiah probably agreed to return to Susa soon after rebuilding Jerusalem's wall (2:6), but the time that he spent in Jerusalem eventually extended to twelve years (5:14). Nehemiah attributed his success to God's intervention and blessing (2:8).

2:9–6:19 REMOVAL OF REPROACH IN THE FACE OF OPPOSITION
2:9-16 Opposition: Secret Survey
Artaxerxes' decision (2:4-8) constituted a reversal of his own royal policy (Ezra 4:21). Sanballat was the governor of Samaria, north of Judah, and Tobiah was a Persian official having authority in Ammon, east of the Jordan River (Neh. 2:10). They probably learned of Nehemiah's mission through official correspondence and became opponents of the new governor. The distance from Susa to Jerusalem was approximately nine hundred miles, and travel between the two cities would have taken about four months (see the note on Ezra 8:31). Nehemiah surveyed Jerusalem at night in order to keep his plans secret until he could ascertain the magnitude

of the task (Neh. 2:12). Nehemiah left from the Valley Gate, on the east side of the city, and traveled south toward the Fountain Gate (2:13-15). It is not known if he completed the circuit around the walls or turned back because of the rubble. (See the introductory map for locations on the Jerusalem wall during Nehemiah's day.)

2:17–3:32 Work Commenced
Geshem (2:19), a powerful Arab chieftain, joined in opposing Nehemiah's work. But in the midst of opposition and persecution, Nehemiah remained confident in the God of the impossible (2:20; cf. Luke 1:37; Phil. 4:13).

Nehemiah described the repair of the walls with their ten gates and four defensive towers (Neh. 3). Beginning with the Sheep Gate at the northeast corner of the city, he moved in a counterclockwise direction, describing the work. All classes participated in the project, including priests (3:1), goldsmiths and perfumers (3:8), rulers and women (3:12), Levites (3:17), and merchants (3:32). In directing this project, Nehemiah demonstrated his administrative and organizational skills.

4:1-23 Opposition: Work in Warfare
Because the earlier efforts of Sanballat and his allies were insufficient to stop the work on the walls, they intensified their opposition. The rhetorical questions of 4:2 implied that the Jews could not expect to complete the project of rebuilding the walls. Nehemiah prayed for God to bring judgment on those enemies who were persecuting his people (4:4-5). The theological basis for this request was the Lord's promise to Abraham (Gen. 12:3), when God said, "Whoever curses you I will curse." Nehemiah was simply praying that the Lord would do as he had promised. Nehemiah prayed that their enemies' guilt would not go unpunished. Ridicule was overcome by the people's determination (4:6). Their enemies' conspiracy was overcome by their prayer and preparedness (4:9). Their despair was overcome by Nehemiah's encouragement (4:13-14) and their preparedness for attack (4:17). In summary, the opposition was overcome by faith, "Our God will fight for us" (4:20), and hard work, "guards by night and workmen by

day" (4:22). Even when washing or drinking, the workers were prepared to fight (4:23).

5:1-19 Opposition: Internal Reproach
According to the Jewish law, an Israelite was prohibited from charging interest on loans to poor fellow Israelites. An outcry arose among the oppressed people because this law was being neglected (Neh. 5:1-5). Usury was the loaning of money at excessive rates of interest (5:7; cf. Exod. 22:25 and Lev. 25:36). Nehemiah demanded that the practice of usury cease and that confiscated property be returned (Neh. 5:10-11). The "hundredth part" (5:11) probably referred to the interest being charged. If calculated on a monthly basis, it would have amounted to 12 percent per year. Nehemiah served his first term as governor of Judah from the twentieth to the thirty-second year of Artaxerxes, or 445–432 B.C. As a man of integrity, Nehemiah did not use his position of authority for self-enrichment (5:15). Instead, he provided hospitality for 150 Jews and officials who had no place to live in Jerusalem. Nehemiah's memoirs may have been a votive offering, presented to the Lord in the temple (5:19; cf. 13:14, 22, 31).

6:1-19 Opposition: Wall Completed
Continued opposition to the building of the wall consisted of three plots against Nehemiah: the first (6:1-4), the second (6:5-9), and the third (6:10-14). First, the enemy tried to lure Nehemiah away from Jerusalem where he could be kidnapped or put to death (6:2). Ono was a village situated about twenty miles northwest of Jerusalem. Second, Nehemiah was accused of rebelling against Persian rule (6:5-6). Third, they tried to lure Nehemiah into breaking the Jewish law by entering the temple, a privilege reserved only for priests (Num. 1:51; 18:7). Although Josephus records that the building program took two years and four months (*Antiquities* 11.179), the Hebrew text indicates clearly that the wall was completed by God's help in just fifty-two days on the twenty-fifth day of Elul (August–September), 444 B.C. (Neh. 6:15). Tobiah, Nehemiah's enemy, sought to infiltrate Jewish ranks by marrying into the family of a Jewish noble, Shecaniah

(6:17-18). His son also followed this pattern.

7:1–13:31 RESTORATION OF COVENANT PURITY

Overview: The heart of this book is the covenant renewal where the people recommitted themselves to keeping the law and maintaining the temple (Neh. 7–10). Nehemiah 11 narrates the repopulating of Jerusalem, the purpose of which was to remove the reproach from the city. The temple had been rebuilt, and Jerusalem's wall had been rebuilt. When the city's emptiness was filled, Nehemiah recorded the dedication of the city's wall, the symbol of the final removal of reproach and the commencement of religious and civil life on the preexilic order under David and Solomon (12:45-46). Finally, Nehemiah 13 shows the correction of impurities in the nation that were cleansed upon Nehemiah's return to Jerusalem and just before the dedication of the wall.

7:1-73 Population of Jerusalem: Protection and Increase

Although Jerusalem had been rebuilt, its inhabitants were few (7:4). For several generations the Jews had avoided making their home in the city that had no wall. The rest of Nehemiah 7 provides a register of the Jews who had returned to Jerusalem with Sheshbazzar and Zerubbabel in 537 B.C. The list is almost identical to that found in Ezra 2. Apparently Nehemiah wanted to make sure that those repopulating Jerusalem were of pure Jewish ancestry, and the record served to this end. Many attempts have been made to account for the numerical differences between this list and the one found in Ezra 2. Perhaps Ezra 2 was merely an estimate that was later revised and preserved here. The Nehemiah named in Nehemiah 7:7 was not Nehemiah the wall builder.

8:1–10:39 Care for the House of God: Seventh-Month Activities

8:1-12 LAW AND MOURNING
The seventh month (8:1) may provide a literary link between the events of Ezra 3:1-4 (the Feast of Tabernacles, or Booths) and the events of Nehemiah 8. Nehemiah appeared to be reminding the reader of

that great gathering with the hopes that a comparison would be made with the gathering spoken of in Nehemiah 8. The Water Gate (8:1) was in the east wall of the city and gave access to the Spring of Gihon. The first day of the seventh month was the day set aside to observe the Feast of Trumpets (8:2; Num. 29:1). That feast was a time to humble their souls and confess their sins of arrogance before God. Out of respect for the word of God, the people stood when it was being read (Neh. 8:5). Since many of the returned exiles had forgotten their Hebrew, the Levites translated the Scripture from Hebrew into Aramaic so that the Jews could understand the message (8:8).

8:13-18 THE FEAST OF TABERNACLES, OR BOOTHS
Reading the law (8:14), the Jews were reminded of the Lord's instructions to celebrate the Feast of Tabernacles by building "booths" (Lev. 23:39-43). The Feast of Tabernacles had not been kept with such enthusiasm since the entry of the Israelites into Canaan (Neh. 8:17).

9:1–10:39 CONFESSION AND DESIRE FOR RESTORATION
After the Feast of Tabernacles, the people gathered to hear the word of the Lord, confess their sins, and commit themselves to keeping the stipulations of the covenant. The prayer of 9:4-37 could well be used to trace Israel's religious history. It covers the covenants with Abraham and Moses, national rebellion, God's compassion, the period of the Judges, the exile and the captivity, and the present state of the returned nation. Wearing "sackcloth" (9:1) was a common expression of grief and sadness. The expression "for a quarter of the day" (9:3) was probably the same period as "from daybreak till noon" (8:3). God used the Holy Spirit to communicate his revelation to the prophets (9:30; cf. 2 Pet. 1:21).

Nehemiah recorded the names of the civic and religious leaders who signed the covenant renewal document (Neh. 10). Mosaic legislation required the payment of half a shekel (Exod. 30:11-16), but Nehemiah apparently reduced it in light of economic conditions (Neh. 10:32). The obligations agreed upon (10:29-39) may be summarized in their final words: "We will not neglect the house of our God" (10:39).

11:1–12:26 Population of Jerusalem: Increase

11:1-24 THE REGISTER OF CITY DWELLERS
Nehemiah used two procedures to encourage the resettlement of Jerusalem: he cast lots (11:1), and he asked for volunteers (11:2). Lot casting was a means of determining God's will prior to the permanent, indwelling ministry of the Spirit (cf. Prov. 16:33). Nehemiah listed the various heads of families living in Jerusalem (Neh. 11:4-24). A similar list with some differences appears in 1 Chronicles 9:2-34.

11:25-36 DWELLERS IN THE LAND
A very helpful list (Neh. 11:25-36) was given of postexilic Jewish communities in the areas formerly known as Judah and Benjamin.

12:1-26 PRIESTS
Nehemiah provided a list of the priests and Levites, the spiritual leaders who were living in Jerusalem (12:26).

12:27–13:31 Purity Restored: Dedication of the Wall

12:27–13:3 THE DAY OF DEDICATION
The historical narrative now continues in 12:27–13:3 from 11:2. Nehemiah described the dedication of the wall, which followed the covenant renewal of Nehemiah 10. Two great choirs (12:31-42), led by Ezra and Nehemiah, respectively, mounted the city wall at the Valley Gate and proceeded in opposite directions to a meeting point in the vicinity of the temple area. Like David, Nehemiah took great care in the administration of the Levitical temple ministry. He appointed personnel and saw to it that foreigners were excluded from the assembly (13:3; cf. Deut. 23:3-5).

13:4-29 EXAMPLES OF PURIFICATION
Nehemiah served as governor of Judah for twelve years before returning to Persia to report to Artaxerxes in 432 B.C. It is not known how long he stayed away from Jerusalem, but it was long enough for the people to begin to neglect tithing (Neh. 13:10-14) and the Sabbath laws (13:15-22), and to become involved once again in mixed marriages with unbelievers (13:23-29). In Nehemiah's absence, Malachi preached and rebuked the people for these failures. When Nehemiah returned to Jerusalem, he corrected these abuses. His reforms in Jerusalem during the early days of his second governorship are recorded in 13:30-31.

The thirty-second year of Artaxerxes (13:6) was 432 B.C. Artaxerxes was referred to as the king of Babylon just as Cyrus, who conquered and ruled the territory of Babylon, once claimed this title. Mixed marriages with unbelievers (13:23) had been a problem for Ezra about twenty-five years earlier (Ezra 9) and remained a thorny problem.

13:30-31 SUMMARY AND PETITION
Nehemiah concluded his memoirs with a summary of his contributions to the nation's spiritual welfare. He would be remembered as a gifted administrator and devoted servant of God. The book does not end with the happy dedication of the wall but with the prior and unhappy sins of the people that were corrected by God's faithful man, Nehemiah. The reader comes away recognizing the threat of personal sin, yet also having the hope that God will continue to provide faithful leaders such as Nehemiah.

Esther

BASIC FACTS

HISTORICAL SETTING

Esther's family was one of many Israelite families that chose to remain in Persia rather than return to Israel. The Jews first returned to Palestine in 536 B.C. Ezra and Nehemiah returned to Jerusalem in 475 B.C. and 444 B.C., respectively. Esther lived in the period of King Xerxes I, also identified as Ahasuerus (486–465 B.C.). Her story took place after Ezra's temple reforms and before Nehemiah's rebuilding of Jerusalem's wall. Just as Israel was striving to live once again in God's land, the political forces of Persia were about to try to destroy God's people.

AUTHOR

The author to the book of Esther remains unknown, although tradition has asserted that Mordecai wrote the book.

DATE

The story took place in 484 B.C., the third year of the reign of the Persian king Xerxes I, known elsewhere in Scripture as Ahasuerus. The temple had been built under Zerubbabel's leadership in 516 B.C. Ezra and Nehemiah would not arrive in Israel for another twenty-six to thirty-nine years. God's promise to return the nation to its land had been accomplished, but the Israelites' full restoration flickered like a candle in the wind. Enemies surrounded them.

PURPOSE

The purpose of the book of Esther was to give the origin of the feast of Purim, which was a time of both lamentation and celebration. The story was written to give a context for all the emotional elements of the feast.

GEOGRAPHY AND ITS IMPORTANCE

The key relationship of geography to theme in Esther concerns what happens to God's people who live outside the Promised Land. God shows that he blesses his people wherever they live. The power is not in the Promised Land itself. It is God

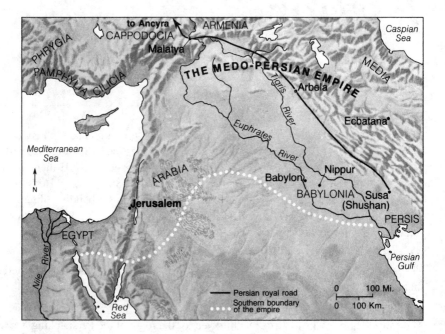

Mediterranean Sea

Caspian Sea

PHRYGIA
PAMPHYLIA CILICIA

to Ancyra
CAPPODOCIA
Malatya

ARMENIA

THE MEDO-PERSIAN EMPIRE

MEDIA

Arbela

Ecbatana

Tigris River

Euphrates River

ARABIA

Jerusalem

Babylon

Nippur

BABYLONIA

Susa
(Shushan)

PERSIS

EGYPT

Nile River

Red Sea

Persian Gulf

N

— Persian royal road
⋯ Southern boundary
     of the empire

0   100 Mi.
0   100 Km.

who controls all lands and spreads the power of his promises to Abraham and Moses around the earth. It was Esther, living far from Israel in Ahasuerus's palace at Susa, who was used to save all the Jews, in and out of the Promised Land.

GUIDING CONCEPTS

LITERARY STYLE
Esther was written in a style that is more interested in plot and action than in character and personality. The reader sees the characters' actions but rarely sees deeply into why they acted or how they felt. The book's emphasis is on decisions that issue action.

Esther also follows the classic form of comedy. It begins with the main characters in prosperity, moves them into potentially tragic events, and concludes with a quick rise to a happy ending. In addition, the book contains several elements of good dramatic writing such as suspense (5:2; 8:3-4), irony (6:1-6, 12; 7:10), passion (1:12; 2:1; 2:17; 3:6; 4:1), and plot conflict (6:1-10).

THE TWO LETTERS AT THE END OF THE BOOK
Two letters, one from Mordecai (9:20-28) and one from Esther (9:29-32), made the feast of Purim part of Israel's religious life. Mordecai wrote and told of all these events. The feast's celebration confirmed God's desire to keep Israel alive.

RELIGIOUS PERSPECTIVE
Is the book secular just because it does not mention God by name? No. Fasting would include prayer (4:16). Mordecai refused to worship Haman (3:5). Certainly those events show a religious perspective. But the broader Bible-wide concepts confirm the deep religious perspective of Israel's history and promise.

BIBLE-WIDE CONCEPTS

THE PRESERVATION OF ISRAEL
This book reminded the people of Israel of God's promises to preserve them. God had promised Abraham that his line would become a great nation and that he would be with Abraham to bless or curse the people of the world according to how they treated Abraham and his family (Gen. 12:1-3). Egypt had been a place of bondage and preservation for Israel. Like Egypt, Babylon served as a place of bondage for Israel, but it was also a place of preservation for the nation and a staging ground for Israel's return to the Promised Land.

The book was designed to be best appreciated by those who understood God's past revelation to Israel in Scripture. The king's edict would bring destruction to all the Jews who lived within the Persian provinces (3:14), which included the land of Israel. All the returned Jews could have been exterminated. Also, just as God's miraculous works before the Israelites' exodus from Egypt caused many non-Jews to join God's people, so what he accomplished through Esther caused many Persians to become Jewish, that is, believers in their religion (8:17; 9:27).

ISRAEL AND HER ENEMIES

Finally, the book reflects an old conflict between Israel and the Amalekites. Mordecai was a descendant of Kish, of the line of King Saul (2:5). Haman was a descendant of Agag (3:1), king of the ancient Amalekites. For the story of the conflict between these two family lines, read 1 Samuel 15:7-9, 32-33. For Israel's prior conflicts with the Amalekites, read Exodus 17:8-13 and Deuteronomy 25:17-19. Israel's enemies always tried to exterminate them, but God's promise to Abraham was always in force to preserve them. The book of Esther serves as another confirmation that God would always uphold his promise of preservation.

NEEDS MET BY ESTHER

With all of God's promises and power, he allowed his people to undergo some very harrowing experiences. His redeemed people were never immune to Satan's attempts to mar or destroy what was holy and good. In Esther, the nation of Israel came close to extermination. But the book does not explain why God allowed the nation to come to the brink of annihilation. It simply shows two Jews, Mordecai and Esther, being courageous and true to their heritage. And through them, the nation escaped yet another attempt on its life. The book answers some difficult questions that arise from the nation of Israel's troubled existence during captivity and exile. The structure and content of Esther show that its author was probably answering questions like these.

- Has God left Israel to the mercy of the nations who hate them and have power over them?
- God has restored Israel to the Promised Land, but does that mean the Jews have the fullness of God's promises to Abraham?
- Why do Jews celebrate a feast (Purim) related to their escape from extermination and how was God involved in their deliverance?
- Did Israel's failure cause God to annul his promises for their redemption?

Like Israel, Christians may at times feel like their recovery from past failures is being blocked by their present bad circumstances. Why does God not make things less difficult? Why do believers seem to move from one crisis to another? A book like Esther helps believers understand that, though they may not find out why things happen the way they do, they can know that their task is to affirm their heritage and God's presence and sovereignty. The believer's task is to be strong and do what is right no matter what situation he faces. The triune God has not left his people alone. The Father, his Son, who died at the hands of world hatred, and his Spirit, who grieves and groans over the broken creation, are all there to uphold believers. Amidst a world of hatred, God's hidden presence and promises stand firm.

OUTLINE OF ESTHER

A. ESTHER ATTAINS ROYALTY (1:1–2:23)
1. A Queen Lost (1:1-22)
2. A Queen Found (2:1-18)
3. A Favor Earned: Assassination Plot (2:19-23)

B. "SUCH A TIME AS THIS" (3:1–9:19)
   1. Problem: Jewish Insubordination (3:1-6)
   2. Edict: Jewish Annihilation (3:7–8:2)
   3. Edict: Jewish Preservation (8:3–9:19)
C. THE FORMULATION OF THE FEAST OF PURIM (9:20-22)
D. THE GREATNESS OF MORDECAI (10:1-3)

ESTHER NOTES

1:1–2:23 ESTHER ATTAINS ROYALTY

Overview: Esther 1 describes the problem created when Vashti disobeyed the king. All the men of the kingdom feared that their wives, following the example of Vashti, would also disobey them, so they advised a harsh and immediate punishment. That event made clear the great wrath that could result when the king was disobeyed. Esther would have to overcome her fear of the king's wrath when she boldly entered his presence without being summoned in order to save her people from sure destruction.

1:1-22 A Queen Lost

1:1-9 BANQUET: GLORY AND PLANNING
The story of Esther is set in the rule of Xerxes I, known in other sources as Ahasuerus (486–464 B.C.). The number of provinces varied as the empire's boundaries were extended or adjusted (cf. Dan. 6:1-2). For Susa (1:2), see the note on Nehemiah 1:1. The year was 483 B.C. According to the Greek historian Herodotus, the king laid plans for his unsuccessful campaign against Greece during these festivities. Customarily the king pledged his guests to drink a certain amount, but at this banquet they could drink as much or as little as they liked (Esther 1:8). Persian queens usually ate at the king's table, but on this occasion the men and women dined separately.

1:10-12 PROBLEM:
FEMALE INSUBORDINATION
The reason for Vashti's refusal is not given in the text. Herodotus notes that she feared for her dignity in the midst of such a drunken group. But the Jewish Talmud suggests that modesty was the issue, indicating that the king called Vashti to appear dressed "only with the royal crown."

1:13-22 EDICT: FEMALE SUBMISSION
The king's counselors were concerned that Vashti's refusal would set a pattern for other Persian wives (1:16-17). The king's decree required that the husband rule the home and that his native tongue be used by his family. The decree was sent throughout the Persian Empire, which boasted an efficient postal system (1:22). By using a relay system of riders on horseback, messages sent from Susa could reach Sardis, a distance of 1,200 miles, in less than a week!

2:1-18 A Queen Found

2:1-4 PROBLEM: NEED FOR A QUEEN
A three-year gap separates the events of Esther 1 and 2. During this period Xerxes I campaigned against Greece and was defeated at Salamis (480 B.C.). Upon his return he set out to find a replacement for Vashti.

2:5-18 EDICT: FINDING A QUEEN
Mordecai's great-grandfather, Kish (2:5), had been one of the exiles taken to Babylon with King Jehoiachin in 597 B.C. Hadassah (2:7) means "myrtle." Her Persian name, Esther, means "star." Esther "was taken" into the custody of Hegai (2:8). This was an involuntary decision. Why did Esther not reveal that she was a Jewess (2:10)? Perhaps she feared for her safety or did not want to prejudice the king against her. The women who entered the contest became members of the king's harem (2:8, 14). As concubines they were wives of secondary rank and regarded as the legal chattel of the king. Esther became queen of Persia in the month of Tebeth (December–January) of 479 B.C. (2:16-17).

2:19-23 A Favor Earned: Assassination Plot

Esther 2:19 refers to another occasion when Xerxes I added to his harem, after Esther had been made queen. Although not rewarded,

Mordecai's kindness was recorded in the royal chronicle (2:21-23). God's sovereignty is shown as the details of the narrative begin to fit together.

3:1–9:19 "SUCH A TIME AS THIS"

Overview: The section of 3:1–9:19 presents the plot to kill all Jews in the Persian Empire and the beginning of Esther's plan to avert the disaster. The irony of timing brought together the king's remembrance of Mordecai's favor and Haman's pride. The result was the reversal of Haman's intended evil. Haman was hanged and Mordecai was honored. The edict for the Jews' extermination was reversed.

3:1-6 Problem:
Jewish Insubordination

The events of Esther 3 occurred more than four years after Esther's coronation as queen. Haman, the "enemy of the Jews" (3:10), was descended from Agag, whom Saul had spared and Samuel had killed (1 Sam. 15:8, 33). This would make him an Amalekite, a traditional enemy of the Jews. To bow before a Persian ruler was regarded as paying homage to a divine being (Esther 3:2). Mordecai refused to bow before Haman or any human ruler. But killing Mordecai would not solve Haman's problem for all pious Jews would refuse to bow before a mere man (3:5-6); thus, he determined to destroy all the Jews throughout Persia.

3:7–8:2 Edict: Jewish Annihilation

3:7-15 EDICT ELLICITED

The date was Nisan (March–April), 474 B.C. Haman cast the lot (Hebrew, *pur*) to determine the most propitious time to carry out his plot against the Jews. The lot fell on the twelfth month, Adar (February–March). Financial incentives persuaded the king to accept Haman's proposal. Xerxes I entrusted the signet ring to Haman to validate the document. The king did not even bother to read the decree, which was signed on Nisan (March–April) 13. It would become effective on Adar (February–March) 13, 474 B.C. (3:12-13).

4:1–8:2 TWO REVELATIONS FOR XERXES

Shocked by the decree, Mordecai displayed the traditional signs of mourning (4:1). His message, revealed to Hathach (4:6-7), disclosed that Esther was a Jewess ("her people," 4:8). To protect the king's life, Persian law prohibited anyone from entering his inner court without invitation (4:11). As a Jewess, Esther the queen was subject to Haman's death edict (4:13). Mordecai was convinced that God would somehow intervene and save the Jewish people from extinction (4:14). Perhaps his conviction rested on God's promise in Jeremiah 31:36-37. Mordecai suggested the possibility that God may have brought Esther to her position as queen for the very purpose of intervening in behalf of her people. Esther's words, "If I perish, I perish," expressed her submission to do God's will no matter what the cost (4:16; cf. Luke 1:37).

In the context of the "three days" (Esther 4:16), the expression "on the third day" (5:1) reflects the Jewish view of time that regarded a part of any day as the whole. Following Oriental custom, Esther did not make her request known immediately (5:4). She either lost courage or sensed that the time was not right to bring her petition before the king (5:7-8). Providentially, that delay allowed for the king's sleepless night and began the sequence of events leading to Haman's humiliation. The gallows Haman had built was fifty cubits high, the equivalent of seventy-five feet (5:15).

In Esther 6 God's sovereign hand is seen working through seemingly insignificant events. Haman was a living illustration of Proverbs 16:18, "Pride goes before destruction, a haughty spirit before a fall." Haman's wife, Zeresh, and his advisers interpreted the turn of events in which Mordecai, a Jew, was honored as a bad omen (6:13). Perhaps they knew something of God's promise to judge those who would harm his Jewish people (Gen. 12:3; Zech. 2:8-9).

At last Esther identified herself as a Jewess (Esther 7:3). The word "sold" (7:4) reflected Haman's promise of silver for the king's treasury (3:9). Haman appeared to have been prostrating himself before the reclining queen, perhaps clasping her feet (cf. 2 Kings 4:27) as he begged for his life (Esther 7:8). Xerxes I interpreted this as a physical assault on Esther. As a condemned prisoner, Haman's face was "covered" (7:8) in preparation for his execution.

8:3–9:19 Edict: Jewish Preservation

8:3-17 ESTHER'S PETITION AND THE
KING'S RESPONSE

Esther petitioned the king to revoke Haman's
decree and prevent the impending calamity
on the Jewish people. Since according to
the law of the Medes and the Persians,
Haman's edict could not be repealed (cf.
1:19), Xerxes gave Mordecai authority to
enact a counteredict that would allow the
Jews to protect themselves against the
attack that already had been authorized
(8:7-8). Mordecai's decree was written on
Sivan (May–June) 23, about two months
after the first edict (8:9). That gave the
Jews eight months to prepare to defend
themselves against attack. The counteredict
was intended to discourage Persians from
taking advantage of Haman's decree (8:11).
The date set by Mordecai's decree was the
same as that of Haman's, Adar (February–
March) 13, 473 B.C. (8:12). This is the only
occurrence of the expression "became
Jews" (8:17) in the Old Testament.

9:1-19 THE JEWS DEFEND THEMSELVES

The killing of the sons of Haman would not
be justified unless they had shared in their
father's plot or were among those who had
attacked the Jews (9:12-14; cf. Deut. 24:16;
Ezek. 18:4). The repeated fact that the Jews
"did not lay their hands on the plunder"
(Esther 9:15-16) indicates that their actions
were in self-defense and not motivated
by the prospect of gain. The hanging of
Haman's sons involved the public exposure
of their bodies to shame the offenders and
deter further attacks (9:13). Esther apparently learned of a plot against the Jews in
Susa that was to be carried out on the
following day, so she asked the king for an
extension of the decree (9:12-16). Adar
(February–March) 13 and 14 were designated for the Jews' rejoicing over deliverance from enemy persecution (9:17).

9:20-22 THE FORMULATION OF THE FEAST OF PURIM

The salvation of the Jews involved a massive
and successful effort of self-protection. The
institution of the feast of Purim was made
by the means of two letters, and the book
concludes with its major thrust throughout:
the welfare of the whole nation of Israel. The
name of the feast of Purim is taken from the
word for "lot" (Hebrew, *pur*) (9:26); *purim*
is the plural form. The celebration of Purim
was designed to keep alive the memory of
this providential deliverance (9:28).

10:1-3 THE GREATNESS OF MORDECAI

It is not known how long Mordecai held
office, but historical records indicate that by
465 B.C. another ruler had taken his place.

Job

BASIC FACTS

HISTORICAL SETTING

The book of Job shows what life was like for people well before the coming of Moses and the Mosaic covenant. Job, rather than a priest, performed his own sacrifices (42:8) and lived in an age that was similar to that of the patriarchs (42:16). The location of the land of Uz (1:1), where Job lived, is difficult to know for sure. That it was situated somewhere southeast of Palestine is one prominent viewpoint. Although the precise date when Job lived and the location of his home are unknown, this is not important to unlocking the book's timeless message.

AUTHOR

The book of Job is without a named author. Jewish tradition has suggested that Moses either found or wrote the book. But again, knowing who wrote the book would do little to aid in understanding the significance of its message.

DATE

The events of the book are best set during the general time of Abraham, Isaac, and Jacob (around 2000 to 1800 B.C.). The date of writing is not known. Theories of authorship range from Job himself (date unknown), to Moses (around 1440 B.C.), to Solomon or someone of his time (around 950 B.C.), to an unknown writer who lived around 200 B.C.

PURPOSE

Is the purpose of the book to show that suffering is a sign of God's displeasure? No, for if it were, what could be said about the suffering of Abel, Uriah the Hittite, Naboth, the prophets, Christ, or the Christian martyrs? The book's beginning clearly answers no to the question of whether Job was sinful. There is a kind of human suffering that is not a result of God's displeasure over sin. The option of suffering for reasons other than personal sin remains open.

Is the purpose of the book to solve the problem of suffering? No solution is given for that problem in the book of Job, and to look for a solution to it will only warp a reader's interpretation. The answer to why God allows suffering in the world remains unanswered. The book teaches that during the times when believers suffer innocently, their relationship with God can still remain unbroken. God has neither forsaken them, nor is he angry with them. Job never lost his integrity (2:3, 9-10; 27:5; 31:6), and therefore he never lost his good relationship with God. After all, that was the very heart of the test in the first place—to see if Job would abandon God if God took away his material and physical blessings. Job's faith in God did not waver. He just needed to learn that some of his expectations of God, such as getting instant answers to his questions, would not be immediately or necessarily met.

The book of Job reveals the truth that believers should continue trusting in God even when undeserved suffering occurs in their lives. Believers often suffer like Job, without knowing why. They need to learn to admit that God has better control of their lives as the Creator than they do themselves. Also, there are some things about nature and suffering that believers are just not meant to know. Most important, if what believers know about the person of God is not motivation enough to keep them worshiping him, then they have forgotten that they are only finite mortals. The book of Job probes the hearts of believers, uncovering the reasons why they follow God. Do believers follow God because of the benefits he gives or out of a deep love and sacrificial reverence for God?

Satan was taught a lesson: the nature and person of God himself should be enough to motivate human devotion. Job's so-called comforters were taught a lesson: not all suffering is due to personal sin. Job was taught a lesson: if a person knows he is innocent but still suffers, then he must not accuse God of injustice but continue to believe in God's presence and trust in his ability to do the best for everyone concerned.

GUIDING CONCEPTS

THE PROSE INTRODUCTION AND CONCLUSION

The book's introduction (1:1–2:13) and conclusion (42:7-17) are written in prose. All of the contents between these verses, with the exception of the small prose section in 32:1-6, are written as poetry. So the book's beginning and end are set off from the majority of the book by their different literary form, creating brackets within which the poetry sections are to be understood.

The prose introduction clearly gives the reason for Job's suffering: it reveals that Job loved God for God's sake alone and not for the things that God could give him. Job's suffering was in no way due to his personal sin.

The book's prose conclusion clearly affirms that Job was right and that his friends were wrong. In fact, Job had to offer a sacrifice for his friends' sins. Also, Job received replacements for all the material things that he had lost. Job was totally affirmed for speaking what was right concerning God. That perspective of Job's innocent suffering presented at the beginning and end of the book is crucial for understanding the positions brought out in its central section.

THE CENTRAL POETIC SECTION

The ideas of God and five very fallible human beings dominate the book's central section. It is a poetic section designed to capture the reader's emotions as well as his intellect. The contents revolve around one question: Why is Job suffering? Job, his three friends, and Elihu all gave their best answers to this question. But the irony of the book is in the fact that the readers already know why, for they have already been given the reason in Job 1–2.

As readers study the intricate arguments regarding why Job was suffering, they should become increasingly aware that somehow all the speakers were missing the point. For Job was suffering because Satan incited God to ruin him without cause (2:3), and the human debaters all were on the wrong track.

Job felt wronged and wanted an answer for his unjust suffering. Job's three friends had made up their minds that he was suffering because of his sin. Moreover, Elihu asserted that Job not only had sinned, but if he did not get an answer right away, there was more that God wanted him to learn. All the human participants wrongly assumed that finding the cause of a person's suffering would provide the key to his coping with his suffering. Job's friends were sure that the cause was sin, and that is the cause usually sought by believers. Neither Job nor his friends would ever have guessed the real cause of his suffering (2:3). Nor would they have guessed that knowing the cause would have been of little help in successfully making it through the time of suffering.

The pursuit of the idea that sin is always the cause for suffering has continued into the present time. Some interpreters try to convict Job of committing a sin *during* his suffering because the first chapters of the book make it clear that Job had committed no blatant sin *before* his suffering. For example, some claim that Job's sin resulted from his having said that God had wronged him (19:6 and similar passages). But that position is based on the assumption that Job must have sinned in some way in order to justify his suffering as understandable punishment from God. But the book clearly does not allow the reader to assume that sin was the cause for Job's suffering. Its message comes from another, more surprising, direction.

THE MESSAGE OF THE BOOK

The way to cope with suffering is not in finding the cause of that suffering. Job never did find out why he had suffered; at least the book of Job does not say that he did. The way for believers to cope with suffering is not in finding out why they are suffering, but in finding out who God is. Job was eventually affirmed as blameless, but not until he had understood the point that simply knowing that he was innocent was not the way to cope with suffering. A profound knowlege of God as the Creator and Sustainer of the universe was all that God offered and all that Job needed.

Yes, Job was indeed innocent. Yes, God is righteous in his dealings with the world. But in Job's day, as well as today, personal innocence and divine justice are not what believers really need to stay true to God and to be assured of his presence during times of deep and undeserved suffering. Like Job, believers may not receive answers to their questions of innocence and justice. But what they need is a deeper, firsthand vision of who God is.

So the book of Job is not about why the righteous person suffers or about how suffering itself leads to a deeper view of God. It is ultimately about how believers can go on trusting God even when some of their most urgent questions are not answered. It is about how they can know the unseen God is with them and for them even when their lives are being crushed to pieces. It is about how they can continue trusting in God while living in a cursed world.

SOME ASSUMPTIONS ABOUT HOW LIFE WORKS
The characters in the book make several observations about life as well as several assumptions about why those observations are true.

Observations about life
(1) Some people are righteous and prosper. (2) Some people are unrighteous and suffer. (3) Some people are unrighteous and prosper. (4) Some people are righteous and suffer.

Assumptions about life
(1) Some people are righteous because they believe that will cause them to prosper (the view of Satan). (2) The unrighteous sufferer deserves to suffer because he has sinned (the common view of all the human characters in the book of Job). (3) The unrighteous person who prospers now will be judged in the afterlife (the argument of Job). (4) The idea of a righteous sufferer is an impossibility, for the righteous God would only bring suffering upon the sinner (the argument of Job's so-called comforters and Elihu). (5) Suffering does happen to the righteous, but if it does God owes the sufferer an immediate explanation (the argument of Job).

Conclusions about life
The book concludes by recognizing that Job had not been righteous just because he thought God would make him prosper, as Satan had accused. Job had been righteous for the proper motives. Job's assertion that he deserved a reason from God for his suffering was shown to be false, for he never received an explanation of why he was suffering. His assumption that he deserved an explanation was corrected to another conclusion: that he, like all people, was excluded from a certain area of God's knowledge. The crisis for Job was whether knowing much about God would suffice when he could not know everything about God.

The same is true for believers today. If they successfully weather the crisis they are undergoing by trusting in God, they will be able to continue on in life and in their faith in God. Without that trust in God their faith will not grow. They will live by the potentially devastating assumption that God owes them something that he has clearly stated no human being will receive in this life.

PRINCIPLES FOR APPLICATION
Do not generalize about the message of the book of Job. There is no concern in the book about the problem of evil. God sovereignly hid (Job 1–2) and upheld his righteous ethical and created order (Job 38–42). The book does not teach believers principles to follow for carefully choosing their mates or that God will double their blessings after a time of suffering.

It is especially true that the book does not teach that religious insight only comes after suffering. Job's insight about God did not come as the result of his suffering, for he was still as blind to the cause of his suffering after it had ended as he had been before and during it. Also, the book does not try to idealize suffering as a way to deeper spirituality. Job did not find God firsthand in his suffering because that would imply all believers need that type of awful experience in order to come to God. But the very point of wisdom literature is to help the reader not to have to experience that kind of pain in order to learn the insights given.

The book teaches that God must be appreciated by believers even in their suffering. Creation reveals God's power, not his righteousness. And that revelation shows that God is so much greater and wiser than anything created, including the human race, that no one has a legitimate excuse not to worship him.

The book encourages believers to be open to surprises in life and to avoid having closed minds about how life operates. The minds of Job's so-called comforters were closed to the possibility of the wicked prospering and the righteous suffering. Job's mind was closed to the reality of what his own function was within God's great scheme. The book asserts that God is upholding the moral order of life. In Job's case what God was doing was hidden, but Job was obligated to worship him nonetheless.

BIBLE-WIDE CONCEPTS

THE PROBLEM OF EVIL

Although the book itself does not answer why God has allowed evil, the question inevitably arises in the reader's mind. However, the book does provide insight: not into why there is evil, but into how a believer can cope with it. For Job, his way of coping was to accept his limitations. He did not know why he was suffering, nor could he do anything to find out. He might have wanted more knowledge and power. But if he was to find any peace, he had to accept the limitations God had placed on him. Such is man's limitation concerning evil. Job never knew why he was suffering at the hands of evil, but his way of going on in life was to accept his ignorance in the light of what he did know about God.

From the time of Genesis on, God and Satan have been in conflict. That conflict is pictured in the Bible as the conflict between the seed of the serpent and the seed of the woman (Gen. 3:15). Cain killed righteous Abel, righteous Lot suffered in Sodom, and King David suffered unjust persecution, as did many prophets of Israel. The Son of God suffered unjustly to bring redemption to the world.

The point is that the conflict between God and Satan has many dimensions, some known to believers and some known only to God in the hiddenness of heaven. The book of Job teaches that the righteous person will allow God to carry out his own purposes in the awful conflict with Satan. God does not have to share those purposes with the human race. Ultimately he will publicly expose, defeat, and condemn Satan to an eternity of damnation. But until then God must be trusted to have victory secure, even though believers cannot always know all the details of the process.

THE RIGHTEOUS SUFFERER

The book of Job reveals a biblical teaching concerning questions that the person who suffers without a sinful cause might have. The fact that people suffered innocently destroyed the serene philosophy that assumed that wrong was always punished and right always rewarded. What actually happens is that wrong is often rewarded while right is punished, at least in this age. A history deformed by sin slinks between the creation of the old heaven and earth and the future creation of the new heaven and earth. How will a person who seeks after God fare in such a world? Will he somehow escape the deformities of unfairness and injustice?

The book of Job takes its place in the Bible by answering no. Until God's new creation begins, the righteous person will be vulnerable to injustice and suffering. Like Abel, Lot, David, the prophets, and Jesus, today's follower of God suffers. But the book of Job teaches that such suffering in no way means that God has abandoned the sufferer or voided his future eternal blessings.

JOB AS WISDOM LITERATURE

The book of Job is a type of wisdom literature that asks the hard questions of life. Proverbs makes profound statements about how the world works and how people can enjoy prosperity and avoid foolishness. But books like Ecclesiastes and Job probe into the gray areas where answers are not easily found.

NEEDS MET BY JOB

Although the date of the book of Job is uncertain, it is clear that it was written for God's people who needed to understand how to cope with the injustices of life. The book attempts to correct the tendency among God's people to blame God for their pain whether by mild insinuation or by blatant attack. It also corrects the error of many to blame personal sin for all the sufferings that people experience. Pain brings hurt and hurt brings anger. But when the pain is undeserved, a believer may feel that he is suffering unjustly. It is easy to begin thinking that somehow God is not dealing fairly with his people. The book confronts head-on the issue of how believers should cope with unjust suffering. These are some of the difficult questions asked and answered in the book of Job:

- When a believer is hurting, does that always mean he is being punished for something he has done wrong?
- When a believer is hurting, does that mean he is suffering for someone else's sins?
- If a believer is innocent and still hurting, does that mean he is being wronged?
- How could God really be concerned about innocent people and yet allow them to suffer?
- If believers have to go on suffering in this broken world, can they really go on affirming God's goodness and trustworthiness?
- Will a believer hurt less if he can find out why he is suffering?

The book of Job meets the believer's need for a perspective on how to cope with undeserved suffering. Much of life's pain is not deserved. People do not deserve to hit their thumbs with a hammer or to break a leg while skiing. They do not deserve to be hit by careless drivers or to be laid off from their jobs. Many bad things happen to people because they live in a cursed world, not because God is out to get them. When he wants a person's attention, God does use fatherly discipline. But the book of Job makes it clear that there are additional reasons for human suffering other than just the narrow perspective of deserved discipline. Job opens up the more profound yet less black-and-white experience of unjust suffering—an experience chosen by the Lord Jesus and into which he beckons all believers to follow. The book of Job meets the believer's need to know how to face the challenge of unjust suffering with honest cries to God and absolute confidence in his sovereignty and goodness.

OUTLINE OF JOB

A. THE MOTIVE FOR ALLEGIANCE TO GOD (1:1–2:10)
    1. Character: Righteous and Blessed (1:1-5)
    2. Conflict: Righteous Because Blessed (1:6–2:10)
B. THE QUEST FOR THE CONDITIONS FOR DIVINE PRESENCE (2:11–42:17)
    1. Establishing the Reality of Job's Righteousness (2:11–14:22)
    2. Establishing the Reality of God's Justice (15:1–21:34)
    3. Establishing the Reality of Earthly Moral Government (22:1–25:6)
    4. Integrating God's Power and Wisdom with Innocent Suffering (26:1–31:40)
    5. The Teaching Ministry of Chastisement: Elihu (32:1–37:24)
    6. The Answer to Implied Injustice: God Speaks (38:1–42:6)
    7. The Answer to Implied Sin (42:7-17)

JOB NOTES

1:1–2:10 THE MOTIVE FOR ALLEGIANCE TO GOD

Overview: The book's two essential issues of character and conflict are exposed. Job's character was righteous, and he was blessed by God (1:1-5). But Satan caused conflict by contending that Job was being righteous because he knew he would be blessed as a result (1:6–2:10). The external and personal attacks of Satan confirmed Job's blameless integrity (1:22; 2:3, 10). The perfection of God's character alone was motive enough for Job's devotion to him.

1:1-5 Character: Righteous and Blessed

Job 1:1 is essential to an understanding of Job's suffering. Was it the result of sin? Not according to the clear statement found here and repeated by God in 1:8 and 2:3. Job was no mere formalist, for he recognized that sin was not only exhibited in wrong activities and deeds but could also be expressed as an attitude of the heart (1:5).

1:6–2:10 Conflict: Righteous Because Blessed

1:6-22 THE FIRST ATTACK

The Hebrew word translated "curse" in English (1:11; 2:9) is literally the word for "blessed." But the writer was unwilling to use the Hebrew word for "curse" with reference to God. So he wrote the word for "bless," knowing that the Hebrew reader would understand from the context that the opposite was intended. The word translated "angels" (1:6; cf. 38:7) is used elsewhere for "sons of God" (Gen. 6:2). Satan (Job 1:6), whose name means "adversary," was among the angels who appeared in heaven before God. Satan's access to heaven will be terminated during the tribulation (Rev. 12:9).

To begin the process of conflict between Satan and Job, God called attention to Job as an example of genuine faith and piety (Job 1:8). The "hedge" (1:9) refers to a protective hedge such as might be planted around a garden or vineyard (cf. Isa. 5:5). Satan suggested that Job was good because God had been good to him and that Job served

God only for the benefits he received. Satan argued that if God took away Job's possessions, his devotion would evaporate. It is encouraging to know that Satan is subject to God's sovereign control and brings trial to the lives of believers only by divine permission (1:12).

The Sabeans (1:15) were a powerful and wealthy people who lived in what is today southern Arabia. The fire of God was probably lightning (1:16). The Chaldeans mentioned in 1:17 were a regional group of nomadic marauders, not to be confused with the later Chaldeans who founded the Babylonian Empire.

Job exhibited the traditional signs of mourning (1:20; cf. Gen. 37:34; Jer. 7:29). He lost his possessions, but not his faith. Although tested through a most difficult trial, Job's piety was proven genuine (Job 1:22).

2:1-10 THE SECOND ATTACK
The words "to ruin him without any reason" (2:3) indicate that there was no sin in Job's life that God was judging. The expression "skin for skin" (2:4) suggests that a person will give some skin from his hands to save the skin on his nose. Satan was suggesting that Job was willing to lose all his possessions in order to escape with his life. The precise nature of Job's disease (2:7) has not been determined medically. The symptoms included enflamed eruptions of the skin (2:7), intense itching (2:8), magots in the open flesh (7:5), feverish nightmares (7:14), bad breath (19:17), pain in the bones (30:17), and fever and blackening of the skin (30:30).

Job did not call his wife a "foolish woman" (2:10), but he suggested that she was speaking like one. Job knew that she, too, was distraught after losing their children and possessions. He did not condemn her but, rather, encouraged and instructed her.

2:11–42:17 THE QUEST FOR THE CONDITIONS FOR DIVINE PRESENCE

Overview: The large section of 2:11–42:17 elaborates two basic assumptions: First, Job assumed that he deserved an answer from God as to why he was suffering for no cause. Second, Job's comforters assumed that Job was hiding his sins and was implying that the problem was with God and not with himself. If Job was righteous for God's sake alone,

would God alone be enough for him? Job's stalemate of faith was: "If I've not sinned, then the problem is with God." But Job would learn the other option: "I must take my finite place under God's infinite wisdom and sovereignty."

Readers of the book of Job already know why God let Job suffer—for no cause (2:3). So throughout this long exposition it is clear that Job was right and the others were wrong. Why does God want believers to listen to these long and mistaken arguments? To teach them that no matter how elaborate and flowery the argument, sin is not always the cause behind someone's suffering. A believer's first deep-seated and instinctive response to suffering is to wonder what he or others did wrong. That response is at times dead wrong. The long exposure in this section to impressive yet wrong assertions of sin is designed to hammer home their inadequacy.

As time passes, the reader also wonders if God will tell Job about what had happened earlier between him and Satan. Will God put an end to Job's pain and tell him that he indeed is righteous and that the situation started in heaven? The longer this section stretches out, the more pressing the need becomes for an answer from God. Surely God will affirm Job as blameless and Satan as the culprit.

But God's long-awaited reply goes in a completely unexpected and surprising direction. He says nothing about Job's righteousness or Satan's attacks. Instead, he asserts his power and sovereignty over creation. That authority provides the ultimate context for Job's assessment of what God owes him and what his next move should be. It also provides the key to a believer's next move when faced with undeserved suffering.

2:11–14:22 Establishing the Reality of Job's Righteousness

2:11–3:26 WHY THE RIGHTEOUS SUFFER
The locations of the homes of Job's friends (2:11) cannot be identified with any certainty. Teman, associated with Eliphaz, was a town or tribe in Edom (cf. Jer. 49:7). Seven days (Job 2:13) was the usual time for mourning the dead (cf. Gen. 50:10; 1 Sam. 31:13). Job lamented life and blessed death in Job 3. But he did not curse God as Satan

had anticipated, and he never did so later. The text moves from historical narrative (Job 1–2) to poetry (3:1–42:6), where imagery and figures of speech abound. Job viewed his conception as the beginning of his life (the Hebrew word for "conceived" is used in 3:3; cf. NASB and KJV, although NIV renders it "born"). Leviathan (3:8), also known as Rahab, was the name of a dragon monster that Baal is said to have killed in an ancient mythical story. Job wished that this monster had swallowed up the sun on the day of his birth so that his birthday had never dawned. Job, of course, knew that the stories of Leviathan were myths, but he referred to them in the same poetic way someone might refer to Santa Claus today in connection with Christmas giving. This is borrowed imagery, not borrowed theology.

Job lamented the fact that he had not been stillborn (3:16). The knees (3:12) refer to the knees of the father, on which the newborn child was placed (cf. Gen. 50:23). Job asserted that all of his life had been a big waste. Why had God let him get so far in life and then taken everything away?

4:1–5:27 ELIPHAZ'S CONCLUSION: JOB HAS SINNED
The cycles of talk between Job and his friends begin in Job 4:1–5:27. The first cycle in Job 4–14 forms a complete pattern of Job responding to each of the three friends. The next two cycles are not so complete, indicating a progressive breakdown of ideas and arguments.

Eliphaz (4:1), the first of Job's three friends to speak, argued on the basis of personal experience (4:8) and his mystical vision (4:12-21) that calamity was the lot of sinners, not saints. His thesis, and that of all his colleagues, was that suffering was always an immediate result of sin. However, though sin certainly brings trouble, not all trouble results from sin (cf. John 9:1-3). The truth that those who sow evil also reap it (Job 4:8) is reflected in Proverbs 22:8. But Eliphaz sought to make a universal dogma out of a general observation. He expected the negative answer, "No," to his questions (Job 4:17; cf. Rom. 3:23). The phrase "charges his angels with error" (Job 4:18) must be a reference to Satan and the fallen angels (cf. Rev. 12:4, 7-9).

Eliphaz suggested that Job's children had sinned (Job 5:4). He had a high view of God as being sovereign, righteous, and just (5:9-16). According to him, Job should have recognized God's discipline in his life and repented (5:17).

6:1–7:21 JOB'S RESPONSE: GIVE ME ONE EXAMPLE
In his reponse to Eliphaz (Job 6–7), Job argued that any sin he might have committed was far outweighed by the calamity he had suffered. He said there was no need for complaint when all was going well (6:5) and that food and salt go together (6:6) just as trouble and wailing do. Job wanted to be killed (6:9), the very thing that God would not allow Satan to do to him. Job told his friends to illustrate his sins concretely (6:14-30). An intermittent stream (6:15; wadi, NASB) is a river that flows in the winter when it rains but dries up in the summer heat. Job's friends were compared to such a stream.

"The grave" (7:9) is sometimes translated "Sheol" (NASB), a transliteration of the Hebrew word referring to the place of the dead. Some scholars believe that this may be the point where Job broke his good record of not sinning and did sin by complaining against God (7:11-21). He asked why, if he had sinned, God had not pardoned him (7:21), and he suggested that God had better do something before it was too late.

8:1-22 BILDAD
Bildad the Shuhite argued on the basis of tradition, presenting views that past generations had searched out and taught (8:8). Although he did not openly accuse Job of sin, he questioned his integrity because of his extensive suffering (8:6). In the end, he advised Job to seek God and be restored (8:5-7). Like Eliphaz (5:4), Bildad suggested that Job's children might have sinned (8:4). Bildad presented three illustrations of the godless man: he was like the papyrus plant that withered without water (8:11-13); his home and possessions were brushed aside like a spider's web (8:14); and like a quick-growing plant, he was uprooted (8:16-18).

But Bildad missed the key option in suffering, which is that the good person may be suffering for reasons known only to God. Notice the irony in 8:20. Despite all these accusations by his friends, Job never let go of his integrity (1:1, 8, 22; 2:3).

9:1–10:22 JOB

Job acknowledged that God was too powerful and great for any person to oppose or question (9:1-12). Underlying his comments was this unspoken question: Was God, perhaps, a cruel perfectionist? The Bear, Orion, and the Pleiades are constellations (9:9). Rahab (9:13) is another name for the mythical Leviathan (cf. 3:8). According to one myth, Rahab and her confederates made an assault on heaven, but they were thwarted. Job was actually saying, "If God overthrew the rebellious supernatural powers, what chance do I have before him?" One may think that here Job spoke wrongly about God (9:23), for is it true that God really "mocks the despair of the innocent"? But the meaning of the word "mock" must be understood in the context of 9:23-24, where Job was speaking of times of calamity or when wicked persons were in power. God destroys both the guiltless and the wicked in military or natural disasters (9:22), and in that sense he does mock the despair of the innocent. Innocence is no plea against suffering in this world. That sentiment is of one piece with the teaching of Ecclesiastes, which shows that being either good or bad is no guarantee of prosperity in this life because death mocks everyone.

Job sought a mediator to listen to both sides and arbitrate a fair decision (9:33). What a difference the incarnation of Jesus has made for believers (cf. 1 Tim. 2:5). In the absence of a mediator to represent him, Job made a direct appeal to God in an attempt to understand why God appeared to be against him (10:1-8). Job reflected on God's personal involvement in the formation of his body in the womb (10:9-12). He then repeated the theme of Job 3, lamenting his life (10:18-19).

11:1-20 ZOPHAR

Zophar, the rationalist, appealed to a commonsense application of an orthodox but impersonal theology in dealing with Job's suffering (11:7-12). He suggested that Job was guilty and should repent (11:11, 14-15), and he also implied that Job was getting only a portion of the punishment he deserved (11:6). The proverb he used in 11:12 was intended to stress Job's stupidity for not seeing things as clearly as he did. The implication was that if Job had God's wisdom, he would see how bad he really was.

12:1-14:22 JOB

Job concluded the first round of talks with a lengthy discourse in response to Zophar and his friends (12:1–14:22). He calculated that bringing his case before God might result in his death, but he was willing to risk it (13:14-15) because his hope in God was all that he had left. His words were a significant expression of his faith in the midst of trial. Job demanded to know the precise charges against him (13:23). He believed that a tree has more hope than man; for if a tree is cut down, it will sprout again (14:7). Job longed for a resurrection hope beyond the grave, or Sheol (14:13-14), for such hope would help him endure his present suffering. But rather than providing Job with hope, God had eroded what little hope he had (14:18-19).

In this first airing of the debaters' views, several mistakes were made and argued for on both sides. The friends mistakenly argued that Job had sinned, while Job mistakenly argued that he should be given a reason for his suffering.

15:1–21:34 Establishing the Reality of God's Justice

Overview: The section of 15:1–21:34 is the second cycle of exchanges between Job and his friends. It was a tug-of-war to establish the reality of God's justice. The friends argued that only evil people were punished. But Job proved that good people also suffered, so he asked where a person's hope was for being good (15:1–17:16). Again the friends argued that evil was punished and good was rewarded. But once more Job asserted that good people suffer, concluding that their only hope was related to life after death (18:1–19:29).

Then the friends changed their approach and admitted that evil people might prosper, but their prosperity would exist for only a brief time. But Job replied that some evil people prospered for a long time (20:1–21:34).

15:1–17:16 BOTH GOOD AND EVIL PEOPLE ARE PUNISHED: WHERE IS HOPE?

15:1-35 Eliphaz. Eliphaz suggested that Job's guilt caused his long defense (15:1-16);

a defense that would be unnecessary if Job was truly innocent. He continued to appeal to his own experience ("what I have seen") as the basis for his instruction to Job (15:17), declaring again that the wicked, not the righteous, suffer (15:20; cf. 15:25). He even described the destruction of the wicked in vivid detail (15:29-35).

16:1–17:16 Job. In 16:3 Job returned the remark made by Eliphaz in 15:2. Beginning to view God as an enemy, Job compared him to an animal that had hunted him down (16:9), a lion that had him by the neck (16:12), an archer shooting at him (16:13), and a warrior breaching a stronghold (16:14). Placing his hope in a heavenly advocate (16:19; cf. 19:25), with courtroom imagery Job appealed for God to pledge himself to appear in his behalf to prove his innocence (17:3-5). In despair, Job saw the grave as his only hope of relief from suffering (17:13-16).

18:1–19:29 BOTH GOOD AND EVIL PEOPLE ARE PUNISHED: HOPE IS AFTER DEATH
18:1-21 Bildad. Bildad, the traditionalist, expounds the fate of the wicked.

19:1-29 Job. Even if Job's suffering would turn out to be the result of some sin, the three friends had not yet identified his failure (19:4). They had spoken in generalities, not specifics. Here, for the sake of argument, Job overstepped the line of appropriate discussion regarding God (19:6). He presented the startling accusation of God doing wrong as the only possible conclusion in light of the contradiction between his friends' accusations and his own known innocence. He used a logical "if . . . then" conclusion about God, but it was an attack upon his accusers, not an article of faith from his own heart.

The writing of his words in a book was one of Job's desires that was realized (19:23). Earlier he had wished for a mediator (9:33), and later he expressed hope in a heavenly advocate (16:19-21). Here the idea was perfected (19:25). Although without hope in this life, he knew that God would vindicate him. The word "Redeemer" refers to a kinsman-redeemer (cf. Ruth 2:1), whose responsibility it was to redeem and restore a relative who had become a slave or had lost his property. Job's hope was ultimately realized in Christ (1 Tim. 2:5; Heb. 7:25). Job expressed his

belief in a bodily resurrection (Job 19:26-27). After death ("after my skin has been destroyed") he was certain that he would see God with his eyes.

20:1–21:34 EVIL PEOPLE PROSPER BRIEFLY; EVIL PEOPLE PROSPER FOR A LONG TIME!
20:1-29 Zophar. Zophar referred (20:3) to Job's sarcasm in 12:1-5. Responding to Job's earlier statement in 12:6 that the wicked do prosper, Zophar countered that their prosperity was brief (20:4-11; cf. 20:21). A fire unfanned (20:26) refers to one kindled by God rather than man, perhaps by lightning (cf. 1:16).

21:1-34 Job. Job continued to respond by pointing out the fallacy of his friends' analysis, for the wicked do indeed prosper (21:8-13). He highlighted the identical temporal destiny of the good and the wicked (21:23-26); both end up in the grave. The Hebrew word translated "body" (21:24; "sides," NASB; "breasts," KJV) may refer to the human body, milk pails, or some other kind of receptacle. Job meant that the wicked are spared or reserved in the day of calamity and delivered in safety from the day of wrath (21:30).

22:1–25:6 Establishing the Reality of Earthly Moral Government
22:1-30 ELIPHAZ
The section of 22:1-30 continues the debaters' intellectual struggle to establish the reality of earthly moral government. They all continued to have their own brands of problems with the idea that someone who had not sinned could suffer so badly. That idea seemed to go against their basic understanding of how God managed things in the world. Eliphaz argued that since God would not punish a man for his piety, Job must be guilty of great sin (22:4-5). Then he cataloged Job's supposed sins (22:6-9). But such wrongdoing was denied by Job (29:12-20), as well as by the author of the book (1:1), and by God himself (1:8). Eliphaz did not tell the truth about Job. Why? Because he was so hung up on suffering only being caused by sin. That narrow view made for his black-and-white approach to life, an approach that denied all the complexity and ambiguity of life brought about by the fall of Adam. In the end of the book God would

bring this view under divine judgment in need of sacrifice by the righteous Job.

Clothing (22:6), usually an outer garment, could be taken as a pledge of the repayment of a loan, but it was not to be kept overnight (Exod. 22:25-27). Although Eliphaz was sure Job was not innocent, he declared that God would pardon Job if he would repent and be cleansed of his wrong (Job 22:30).

23:1–24:25 JOB

Responding to Eliphaz, Job insisted on his innocence (23:1-17). He wondered why God did not at least appoint certain days to hear cases and pronounce judgment on those who practiced violence and oppression (24:2-17). In 24:18-20 Job seems to admit that evil men do suffer under God's judgment. Either Job had modified his previous analysis, now admitting that the wicked do sometimes come under judgment, or he was quoting the view of his friends. Translations that follow the second alternative insert the words: "You [Job's friends] say . . ." at the beginning of 24:18 (RSV). A third alternative is to assign 24:18-20 to Zophar as it seems to echo his earlier speeches.

25:1-6 BILDAD

Bildad avoided Job's challenge (24:25) to prove him wrong, but he tried to bring Job to his knees before God's power and holiness (25:1-6).

26:1–31:40 Integrating God's Power and Wisdom with Innocent Suffering

Overview: The section of 26:1–31:40 presents Job's best attempt at uniting the power and wisdom of God with his own experience of innocent suffering. It was a three-part effort (26:1-14; 27:1–28:28; 29:1–31:40). Job clearly asserted God's power (26:1-14). Then he asserted his own righteousness and God's great wisdom (27:1–28:28). Job ended this address by declaring that he was open to justified punishment for any sin of his that might be revealed to him (31:1-40).

26:1-14 ASSERTION OF GOD'S POWER

For Rahab (26:12; or Leviathan), see the note on 3:8. Job insisted that when a person had described God's wisdom and power to the best of his ability, he had just scratched the surface. There was infinitely more that could be said.

27:1–28:28 ASSERTION OF JOB'S RIGHTEOUSNESS AND GOD'S WISDOM

Some scholars suggest that Job 27 contains Zophar's speech. But the reference in 27:1 to Job being the speaker is clear. Zophar apparently dropped out of the dialogue after he last spoke in 20:1-29 and no more is heard from him.

In 27:13-23 Job appears to have modified his earlier position by admitting that the wicked would not enjoy their prosperity (27:14) and that it would not be their final destiny (27:19). But he held firm to his opinion that the wicked prosper for a season.

The heat of the debate was past, and Job reflected on the wisdom of God, where he was certain the answer to his dilemma had to be found. While man is able to mine the treasures hidden in the ground (28:1-11), wisdom cannot be found so easily. The major theme of the wisdom books (Job, Proverbs, Ecclesiastes, Song of Solomon) is introduced: "the fear of the Lord" (28:28). This concept is the beginning point and the fundamental lesson in one's search for wisdom (Prov. 1:7). The parallel phrase, "And to shun evil is understanding" (28:28), explains how the fear of the Lord may be practically applied.

29:1–31:40 JOB'S BEST SYNTHETIC EFFORT

Job listed God's past blessings to him (29:1-25). Producing evidence against the accusations of his friends, Job testified to his own kindness in helping the afflicted in the past (29:12-20).

Job lamented that while he used to be respected and appreciated for his kindnesses, he had become the object of taunts (30:1, 9). His garment (30:18) probably referred to his skin; his body had been disfigured as a result of his disease.

Job was open to justified punishment for any revealed sin that he might have committed (31:1-40). Job 31 is a high point in the ethical teaching of the Old Testament. Note the emphasis on a person's heart attitude, not just the outward observance of his good deeds. Job denied any private sins of his heart (31:1-8). In 31:10 he was really saying, "If I have sinned, may I die and my widow become another man's wife." He appealed for God to answer his claim of innocence (31:35), and he said he was willing to be punished if found guilty (31:38-40).

32:1–37:24 The Teaching Ministry of Chastisement: Elihu

Overview: The message of Elihu emphasizes two central points. First, God can teach, but he will not be forced into doing anything (32:1–35:16). And second, God will eventually inform mankind of its evil, but they must wait for him (36:1–37:24). Critical scholars believe that this is a later addition by a scribe who felt that Job's friends had overlooked some important points. However, the section fits well with the book's argument and provides a transition between the words of Job's friends and those of God. Elihu had a broader view of suffering and suggested that God might have intended to teach Job something (33:16; 35:11; 36:22).

32:1–35:16 GOD CAN TEACH BUT WILL NOT BE COERCED
Elihu was sure he could solve the problem that Job's friends had failed to solve (32:1-22). His words "they had found no way to refute Job" (32:3) appear to reflect the evaluation of the book's author on the comments made by Job's friends. Elihu said wisdom was not the exclusive possession of the aged (32:8-9), for the young could be wise if they knew that they should seek wisdom from the Lord.

Elihu maintained that God is able to keep people from sin and teach them about it (33:1-33). He told Job that he, too, was just a man, so Job should have nothing to fear from his words (33:6-7). He quoted Job's declarations of innocence, which also were indictments against God (33:9-11). He rightly declared that Job was out of line in making such statements about God (33:12). This is a key concept (33:13), especially in light of Job's experience, for God does not always reveal the reasons for his actions. In spite of man's perplexity, he must trust God to do what is right. Elihu recognized that God might use suffering and dying to turn people from their wicked ways and lead them to repentance (33:26).

In 34:1-37 Elihu argued that God is not unjust, for evil is ultimately punished. He summed up Job's complaint: God perverts justice (34:5-6), and righteousness does not pay (34:9). The first complaint was answered by Elihu in Job 34 and the second in Job 35. Elihu spoke for the wise who, having considered the evidence, would also condemn Job (34:34-37). Like Job's friends, he assumed that Job had sinned, but he was especially concerned about Job's rebellious attitude over the perplexity of his suffering (34:37).

In 35:1-16 Elihu dealt with the question of whether God was obligated to answer Job's request. He said human vice or virtue cannot bring any advantage to the transcendent God, so people cannot expect immediate recompense (35:6-7).

36:1–37:24 GOD WILL INFORM OF EVIL: WAIT FOR HIM
Elihu urged Job to let God teach him (36:1-33). He said that suffering was not inconsistent with divine justice, for God used it for constructive purposes—to teach people and lead them to repentance (36:10). Warning Job against turning aside to evil by developing a rebellious and critical attitude as a result of his affliction (36:21), Elihu exhorted him to transform his complaint into praise (36:24-33).

In 37:1-24 Elihu expounded on the power and justice of God. He described the greatness of God the Creator that is beyond full human comprehension (37:14-15). Since God is infinitely great, he must be infinitely just (37:23). The "breath of God" is a poetic expression for the wind (37:10). In ancient times, mirrors were made of molded, polished metal (37:18).

38:1–42:6 The Answer to Implied Injustice: God Speaks

Overview: God provided his own answer to Job's implication of divine injustice by proclaiming his knowledge of and ability in the creation and maintenance of the earth and heavens (38:1-38) and in his sovereignty over the animal kingdom (38:39–39:30). In conclusion, he measured the power required for any who would try to challenge him (40:1–41:34). The major point was that if God controls the intricate orders of creation, which Job could only dimly understand, surely Job could trust him to order his life even though God's doings were beyond his human comprehension. Amazingly, God never mentioned the problem of suffering. In response, Job declared his newly found insight and took the only logical next step: to stop challenging God and be quiet (42:1-6). Note the sarcasm in this section (38:3, 5, 21; 40:7).

38:1–39:30 CREATION KNOWLEDGE AND ABILITY

The "storm" (38:1; "whirlwind," NASB and KJV) represents a theophany, which is an appearance of God in visible form (cf. Ezek. 1:4, 28). In Job 38:4 and the following verses God is likened to a master builder or architect, and his creation is poetically described. Throughout this section God drew attention to his unsearchable wisdom, power, and sovereignty in order to impress Job with the immensity of Job's own ignorance and lack of power. The stars that are visible on the horizon in the early morning are Venus and Mercury (38:7). The angels, or the "sons of God," rejoiced as they witnessed creation (38:7; cf. 1:6). The constellations of Pleiades, Orion, and the Bear were mentioned again (38:31-32; cf. 9:9).

The point was that Job had to see God in relation to the world; this is also true of believers today. Job's problem was not sin; it was his inability to realize his own limited place in the world in relation to God. The way for Job to receive release from his mental turmoil was not by obtaining justice; it was by becoming aware of and accepting his proper place.

40:1–41:34 REQUIRED POWER TO CHALLENGE GOD

The illustrations of God's sovereignty and power had shown Job that he should not have found fault with God. Instead, he had to submit to God even though he did not completely understand his ways. This had been the major flaw in Job's response to suffering. The link between God's power over creation and his ability to make right judgments was made in 40:8. Job had called into question the righteousness of God's actions. Leviathan (41:1) referred to the dragon monster that was so prominent in ancient mythology and was known as an enemy of the created order. While he was untamable by man, for God he was a mere plaything (41:5). The behemoth (40:15) is the plural form of the Hebrew word for beast. The plural suggests that it was a beast of great size and strength. It is debated as to

what specific beast was meant—an elephant, hippopotamus, or rhinoceros. Such a beast was beyond man's control, but it was under God's power.

42:1-6 JOB'S INSIGHT INTO HIS PROPER POSITION

Job's suffering in and of itself brought him no new awareness of God. In fact, it brought him into a foolish position of challenging God's actions. Only God's self-revelation deepened Job's relationship with him. He had known about God, but the pain of his suffering and the folly of his challenge provided the context into which God brought a revelation that opened up for Job a deeper and more personal experience with God. Having seen God as he was, Job humbly repented before him, not because of a sin committed before his suffering, but due to his critical and judgmental attitude toward God that he had allowed to develop during his suffering. Job never deserted or cursed God. Actually, the very intensity and focus of his complaints toward God showed his insistence and faith that God alone was the source of his past, present, and future hope for life. His complaint was confirmation, not denial, of his faithfulness and integrity toward God. No greater passage than 13:15-16 can be found in the book to confirm that truth.

42:7-17 The Answer to Implied Sin

42:7-9 THE FRIENDS' ERROR

The end of the book provides a clear answer to the implication that Job's suffering was caused by sin. The friends, not Job, were condemned (42:7-9).

42:10-17 THE RESTORED FRUITS OF RIGHTEOUSNESS

After Job and his friends were evaluated by the Lord, Job's normal fruits of righteousness were restored (42:10-17). The view of Job's friends—that suffering is always a result of sin—had been proven wrong by God's spoken words. Job was not condemned because he had spoken rightly. He acquired twice as many animals as he had originally owned but the same number of children. Job fully recovered from his affliction and lived out his life in good health.

Psalms

BASIC FACTS

HISTORICAL SETTING
The general historical setting for the singing and reciting of psalms was the temple in Jerusalem, designed by David and built by Solomon. But though most of the psalms share this general focus of temple worship, the specific historical backgrounds and settings for each of the 150 psalms are quite diverse. The writing of the psalms grew out of specific concerns and events that spanned the time period from the exodus (Ps. 90) to the Babylonian captivity (Ps. 137).

AUTHOR
The majority of the authors represented in the book of Psalms were associated with the temple. David headed the group that included various temple musicians who contributed other psalms. A large number of the psalms are anonymous. (See the section regarding the book's structure.)

DATE
The earliest psalm (probably Ps. 90), was probably written by Moses shortly after the Israelites left their bondage in Egypt (around 1446 B.C.). The latest psalm (probably Ps. 137) was written some time during the Babylonian captivity (586–538 B.C.). All 150 psalms were collected into manuscripts sometime before the second century B.C. Manuscripts from this time period were recently discovered near the Dead Sea, showing that by then the collection of psalms was already complete in its present form.

PURPOSE
The book of Psalms was designed to aid in the worship of God by supplying poetic examples of life's ups and downs. Each event or struggle represented in the psalms is punctuated with the triumph and peace that can only be found through heartfelt praise to God. See *Background of the Use of the Psalms, Lament in the Psalms,* and *Praise in the Psalms* for more detail concerning the original and present purposes of the psalms.

GUIDING CONCEPTS

THE BACKGROUND OF THE USE OF PSALMS

The book of Psalms is the Bible's own hymnal. Its contents are psalms that were used to praise God for personal and national wonders of redemption. Sometimes psalms grew out of a psalmist's private experience of despair, and sometimes from Israel's national suffering as a result of military defeat. Some psalms were composed by temple priests and professional musicians and others were written by the kings of Israel. But in the collection of psalms as it now exists, the psalms center around the temple of God in Jerusalem, as a brief survey of the background of the psalms will show.

King David was the first to organize the musicians in the temple and to incorporate psalms into Israel's temple worship. The psalms were designed to be sung as joyful songs (1 Chron. 15:16), to praise the Lord (1 Chron. 23:5, 30), and actually to prophesy through the words and music (1 Chron. 25:1, 3). The psalms were not just songs of praise; they were also statements of prophecy, not only in the telling of the future, but especially in exhorting and comforting God's people to remain true to him through all the pressures of life that might cause them to fall away. David organized the temple's composers and musicians and became the catalyst for Israel's great tradition of psalms. See 1 Chronicles 16:7-36 (which quotes Ps. 105:1-15), where David first assigned and organized the singing of psalms at the temple.

Throughout the Old Testament, David and his musician Asaph are viewed as the originators of the temple's songs of praise. King Solomon used the psalms during the dedication of the temple (2 Chron. 5:7-14). Jehoshaphat encouraged his armies through an exhortation of psalms (2 Chron. 20:20-21). Hezekiah used the psalms of David and Asaph (2 Chron. 29:30). During the great Passover of Josiah, the psalms of David were used (2 Chron. 35:15). Even after the return of Israel from the Babylonian captivity, Zerubbabel celebrated the rebuilding of the foundation of the temple with psalms according to the directions of King David (Ezra 3:10-11). And when the rebuilt wall of Jerusalem was dedicated, Nehemiah had the priests sing psalms according to the command of David and his son Solomon (Neh. 12:27-29; 45-46).

HOW PSALMS COMMUNICATE THEIR MEANING

Although the psalms are poetry, they do not deliver their message through rhyming words. They get their point across by laying out a thought one way and then immediately following it with a parallel thought that takes the first thought a step further. It is this interplay between parallel thoughts that forms the individual bricks that add up to the meaning of each psalm. In order to understand the psalms, the reader must avoid seeing the sentences of each psalm as independent wholes and recognize the relationships between parallel lines and sentences.

Sometimes a parallel sentence does little more than say the same thing as the first sentence using slightly different words (e.g., Ps. 146:2). But be sure to grasp the contribution of those "slightly different words." For example, in the case of Psalm 146:2, the addition of the repeated word "my" deepens and personalizes the content of the first line.

Sometimes a parallel sentence repeats the same thought as the first, but does so by stating the opposite or the negative side of what was said in the first line. That opposite side drives home the truth of the first line by contrast and usually functions to provide the reader with an understanding of what could happen if the words of the first line are not taken seriously. For example, see Psalm 1:6.

Sometimes a parallel sentence simply illustrates the first line. Actually, each pair of parallel sentences in the psalms has its own unique relationship. It is up to the reader to seek out and enjoy the wonderful variety that God has woven into his book of poetry.

But, above all, the psalms communicate their meaning by speaking to the reader's emotions and feelings as well as his mind. And the reader who wants to know what a psalm means will have to open up his heart as well as his mind.

THE STRUCTURE OF THE BOOK OF PSALMS

The collection of 150 psalms in the book of Psalms contains five benedictions that mark off five sections (Pss. 41:13; 72:19-20; 89:52; 106:48; Ps. 150 is a doxology in its entirety). And each of the five collections is grouped around the psalms written by a specific author.

THE FIRST COLLECTION: PSALMS 1–41

David	37
Unknown author(s)	4

This first collection contains twenty-one psalms that lament life's problems and eleven that are purely praise psalms. Lament predominates, for nearly all of David's songs in this collection relate to his suffering at the hands of his enemies. Psalms 1 and 2, two of the four anonymous psalms in this section, serve as an introduction for all five collections in the book of Psalms.

THE SECOND COLLECTION: PSALMS 42–72

David	18
Sons of Korah	7
Asaph	1
Solomon	1
Unknown author(s)	4

This second collection centers around psalms written by David and the sons of Korah. Again, lament predominates in this section. All seven of the psalms written by the sons of Korah in this collection are included in the section of Psalms 42–49 (Ps. 43 is anonymous). Then, after a psalm of Asaph (Ps. 50), comes the Davidic group. David authored all the psalms in the section of Psalms 51–71 except for two anonymous psalms (Pss. 67; 71). The second collection ends with a final psalm from Solomon (Ps. 72).

The Davidic group is characterized by titles or superscriptions that note the wars and trials that inspired his writings (see Pss. 51; 52; 54; 56; 57; 59; 60; 63; and 70). In the first collection such superscriptions are found with Psalms 3; 18; 30; 34; and 38. The one remaining superscription of this type is not found until Psalm 142 in the fifth collection.

THE THIRD COLLECTION: PSALMS 73–89

Asaph	11
David	1
Sons of Korah	4
Heman	1
Ethan	1

Again lament predominates in the third collection. The Asaph group appears first (Pss. 73–83). The last section of this collection includes four psalms by the sons of Korah and one each by David, Heman, and Ethan.

THE FOURTH COLLECTION: PSALMS 90–106

Moses	1
David	2
Unknown author(s)	14

Among the psalms of the fourth collection, praise and the kingship of God are the predominant themes. This section, made up for the most part by anonymous psalms, is opened by what is thought to be the oldest of the psalms (Ps. 90), written by Moses soon after the Israelites made their exodus from Egyptian bondage.

THE FIFTH COLLECTION: PSALMS 107–150

David	15
Solomon	1
Unknown author(s)	28

The fifth collection of psalms exhibits a decided emphasis on wisdom psalms and the events of the postexilic period (for example, see Ps. 137). Psalms 120–134 help the reader visualize a pilgrim's ascent to the city of Jerusalem and the temple mountain. Psalms 146–150 are the hallelujah psalms, which form a resounding and essential conclusion to all five books.

It appears that David's psalms were originally collected into two separate groups, the collections perhaps being made at quite different times. These can be seen in collections one and two. Then a group of psalms, the third collection, that consists mostly of the psalms of Asaph, who was David's chief musician, was collected. The fourth and fifth collections contain mostly anonymous works. Possibly many of those psalms were thought to be by David and so were eventually collected together. Those collections emphasize special love for the city of Jerusalem and for praising God simply on the basis of who he is. In most of the psalms this praise is given to God, not by people in prosperity, but by those who suffered the difficulties of human pain.

LAMENT IN THE PSALMS

Why are so many of the psalms, especially those of David, full of the complaints and laments of God's people? Psalms of lament actually form the largest number of psalms. Why are not all of the songs focused on praising God for his great redemption? First of all, the psalms, like the rest of Scripture, express many of the realities of life, and those realities include pain and lament. Like the books of Job and Ecclesiastes, the book of Psalms shows God's people struggling, not only with the black-and-white issues of life, but also with the gray. These psalms show God's people doing right yet still suffering at the hands of powerful but lawless people. That is the context for all the encouragement given to believers to wait through the difficult times for God's deliverance. The idea is not to ignore evil; rather, it means that believers should do all they can and then wait for God to act.

Second, all psalms that begin by lamenting over the pain and injustice of life always end their lament with praise to God. So why does God take his people through all the pain? Because God wants his people to watch the psalmists time after time show trust *during* the trials of life. It is one thing to praise God when the pain has gone. But it is more profound to praise him when the pain is still present. The kind of complaint and lament found in the psalms is not faithless carping against God. On the contrary, it is actually an expression of ultimate faith in him to remedy the bad situation.

The lament psalms all follow a rather standard format. The following sections describe two basic patterns of lament. These patterns follow the work of Claus Westermann (*Praise and Lament in the Psalms,* John Knox Press, 1981).

An individual's lament: Psalms 6; 13; 22; 102; 142

This type of psalm is basically a petition or supplication based on the situation of someone in distress. Frequently the distress is described in detail and with pictur-esque vividness. The basic format of the lament involves:

1. An address and introductory cry for help and/or turning to God.

2. The actual lament, which summarizes the individual's problems, his external foes, and addresses God directly.

3. A confession of trust, which follows the lament and usually begins with "but." At this point the author has changed from complaining to confessing his ultimate trust in God's salvation.

4. A request for God to be favorable (with such words as "look" and "hear") and to intervene (with words like "help," "save," and "rescue").

5. A presentation of various reasons that should motivate God to intervene.

6. A statement by the writer of his assurance of being heard.

7. A conclusion that sometimes includes a double wish: blessing for those who love God, and cursing for those who do not.

8. A conclusion that sometimes features the author vowing to make a public confession of praise and promising to tell others what God has done if God should choose to intervene. This is not bargaining with God, with the psalmist saying, "If you save me, I'll praise you." Rather, the spirit of the vow is, "When you answer and save me, it will only be right that I answer you with public praise." The essence of truly biblical praise is the confession in public of who God is, what he has done, and how dependent his people are on him.

9. A conclusion that sometimes includes a word of praise to God after the petition has been answered.

In some psalms the "confession of trust" is so dominant that a distinctive subcate-gory appears—the song of trust (see Pss. 4; 11; 16; 23; 62; 63; and 131).

A national lament: Psalms 74; 79; 80

The psalm of national lament or lament of the people is very similar to the individ-ual's lament and can contain all or some of the same characteristics. The major difference between the two is that the national lament concerns the suffering and distress of the whole community rather than that of a single individual.

PRAISE IN THE PSALMS
Even in the psalms of lament, expressing praise to God for who he is and for what he has done is of major concern. But other psalms were designed to allow for even more emphasis on praise and less on the painful experiences of life.

Psalms of individual declarative praise: Psalms 18; 30; 40
Psalms of individual declarative praise are often more specific than the psalms that report how God has met the needs of the community. This praise is offered by an individual worshiper rather than a group. A psalm of individual declarative praise will usually feature:
1. A proclamation of praise.
2. An introductory summary.
3. A statement looking back to the time of need.
4. A report on God's deliverance.
5. A vow of praise to God (a promise to tell others what God has done).
6. Praise of God's mighty acts.

Psalms of national declarative praise: Psalms 124; 129
This kind of psalm reports that God has acted and met a specific need of the community. Three basic features of this kind of psalm are: (1) recognizing that God should be praised because he has acted on the nation's behalf, (2) praising God as a direct response to a specific act that has just occurred, and (3) praising God in a joyful manner. A psalm of national declarative praise usually includes:
1. An exhortation to praise God.
2. An introductory summary (God's deeds and praise declared).
3. A statement looking back to the time of need.
4. Praise to God.
5. A report on God's intervention.

Psalms of descriptive praise: Psalms 36; 105; 113; 117; 135; 136; 146
Descriptive praise is a public confession or acknowledgment of God's greatness or goodness. This praise does not necessarily arise out of a historical situation, but there remains at the core of such praise an experience in the history of the people with God. Declarative praise often passes into descriptive praise as the psalmist reflects on a unique occurrence in history and speaks of God's majesty and grace. These psalms feature the following characteristics:
1. An imperative call to praise God
2. Reasons for praise:
    a. God is great
        i. As the Creator
        ii. As the Lord of history
    b. God is good
        i. He saves
        ii. He preserves

Although many other categories of the psalms are set forth in various comment-aries, they generally are related to the content of the particular psalm rather than its structure.

SPECIAL VARIATIONS ON LAMENT AND PRAISE
Alphabetical psalms: Psalms 9; 25; 34; 37; 111; 112; 119; 145
In alphabetical psalms the initial letters of successive lines form the Hebrew alpha-bet or some part of it. This literary pattern was an aid for the Israelites in memoriz-ing these psalms.

Creation psalms: Psalms 8; 33; 104; 148
The creation of the physical universe is the central theme of the creation psalms. God's glory and power are demonstrated in these psalms by describing the unspeak-able wonders of his creation.

Exodus psalms: Psalms 44; 66; 68; 74; 77; 78; 80; 81; 95; 105; 106; 114; 135; 136
The theme of Israel's deliverance from Egyptian bondage is a central theme of the exodus psalms. God's greatness is demonstrated in these psalms by describing the numerous miracles performed to bring about freedom for the Israelites. The cross-ing of the Red Sea, perhaps one of the most spectacular miracles, is a prominent feature.

Imprecatory psalms: Psalms 7; 35; 58; 59; 69; 83; 109; 137; 139
Imprecatory psalms are psalms in which a prayer for judgment (an imprecation) on the psalmist's enemies is a leading feature of the psalm. These psalms have their theological basis in the Abrahamic covenant, which said that curses would come upon Israel's enemies.

Penitential psalms: Psalms 6; 32; 38; 51; 102; 130; 143
The key feature of the penitential psalms is the psalmist's penitence over his own sins and failures. He acknowledges his guilt before the Lord and recognizes his need for divine favor and forgiveness.

Pilgrim psalms: Psalms 120–134
The pilgrim psalms or "Songs of Ascent" were probably sung by the Jewish pilgrims going up to Jerusalem to celebrate the three major festivals of the year (Deut. 16:16). The psalms were sung as they ascended into the hill country to worship in Jerusalem. The pilgrim psalms praise God for his choice of Jerusalem as his holy city.

Royal psalms: Psalms 47; 93; 96–99
The royal or enthronement psalms extol God's choice of his king, David. These psalms ultimately emphasize the kingship of God and explain the establish-ment of God's rule through the Davidic covenant and its kings from David on to the promised Messiah, Jesus. God's universal rule is mediated through the earthly Davidic line, and the earthly and heavenly aspects of God's rule come together perfectly through the past, present, and future rule of Jesus the Messiah. The psalmist recognizes that God is reigning on the throne and repeatedly declares, "God is King!" These psalms are basically psalms of descriptive praise, which are expanded and modified by the theme of God's kingship.

Didactic psalms: Psalms 14; 15; 24; 50; 52; 53; 75; 78; 81; 95; 105
The didactic psalms form a category of psalms that has the common purpose of
teaching truth through a variety of forms. The wisdom psalms form a major
subgroup of the didactic psalms and express the thought patterns and themes of
the Wisdom Literature (Pss. 1, 37, 49, 73, 91, 112, 128, 133, 139).

Torah psalms: Psalms 19; 119
Torah psalms express the psalmist's praise for the Torah, the "instruction" of God.
In these psalms the Word of God is glorified and exalted. Torah psalms also can
be described as hymns to the law, mentioned under a series of synonyms: law,
statutes, words, testimonies, judgments, precepts, commandments, and promises.

Messianic psalms: Psalms 2; 8; 16; 22; 41; 45; 69; 72; 89; 102; 109-110; 118; 132
The messianic psalms are those that predict aspects of the person and work of
Jesus Christ. While skeptics have questioned the validity of such a category of
psalms, Christ explicitly declared in Luke 24:44 that the psalms speak of him.
Jesus quoted Psalm 22:1 as he hung on the cross (Matt. 27:46), thus demonstrat-
ing its messianic significance.

BIBLE-WIDE CONCEPTS

LAMENT OVER PERSONAL AND WORLD EVIL

Feelings of pain and grief over the horrible acts of human beings have been around
for nearly as long as people themselves. Shame and fear gripped Adam and Eve, and
Abel's blood cried out from the ground. Mankind's wickedness made God sorry that
he had made them (Gen. 6:6). From those early cries of people suffering from pain
and grief grew the tradition of the psalms. At the end of the Bible, in Revelation 6:10
the souls of the martyred saints cry out the lament concerning how long God had
waited to avenge their deaths. The psalmists put into words and music their experiences of the joys and sorrows of life.

The laments of life, which stretch from Genesis through Revelation, have two
aspects. First, biblical lament presupposes the ideal of good while a person is experiencing evil. The person laments because he knows and also desires God's ways in a
world that is shot through with evil. Second, biblical lament reinforces the absolute
truth of the world's cursed and bent nature that was brought about by the curse of
God in Genesis 3. Those two aspects form a continuous line from the blood of Abel,
through the blood of Christ, to the blood of the martyrs of the great tribulation. From
a biblical perspective, the cry of the faithful sufferer is the cry of one committed to
God's ways while living in a world under Satan's power. That lament will only cease
when God's curse is removed in the new heavens and earth.

HOPE FOR THE COMING OF THE MESSIAH

The great lament of the righteous sufferer in the book of Psalms usually gives rise to
the sufferer's burning desire for God's justice to be placed upon the one inflicting the
pain. Pain moves the person to hope for a deliverer. The psalms emphasize God's
absolute sovereignty over this world that has gone awry. God will come and set the
record straight. From the fear of Adam and Eve to the cry of the last martyr, mankind

has looked with hope for a redeemer. Throughout the psalms God confirms that a deliverer will come, and he will specifically come as a King after the line of David. The psalms forge the link of a divine Deliverer with the prior promise of the Davidic covenant and the future promise of redemption through the greater Son of David, Jesus the King.

THE TEMPLE AS THE CENTER FOR WORSHIP

The temple of Jerusalem and the psalms were closely related. In the temple was the Ark of the Covenant, which contained the covenant that God had made with Moses. That covenant was the means through which human beings reached upward in hope of redemption while God reached downward to fulfill that hope. It is no wonder that the 150 songs, which celebrate that wonderful redemptive relationship, have been collected in the book of Psalms in the Bible. Although the temple was destroyed, the songs of redemption continued to be remembered and sung by the Israelites. And today in the church, which is the temple of the living God, those same songs still continue to express the pain, joy, and hope of all believers. In the future new age, when the tabernacle of God will come to dwell fully among God's people, they will continue to sing these songs and, no doubt, even greater songs.

NEEDS MET BY THE PSALMS

There is one common link between the many diverse situations and needs of the people of God represented in the 150 psalms. Each psalm was written because something good had just happened—an act or insight that was directly the result of God's character or actions. The writer wanted the listeners to experience what had happened as a context for a mutual praise of God. Throughout their history, God's people needed reminders and experiences of his matchless character, redeeming actions, and just judgments. The psalms met that need for both reminder and experience. As reminders, the psalms present detailed teaching concerning God's laws and past history. As experience, the psalms stir the emotions as the pain of life is transformed by the grace of God's character and redemption. The 150 psalms have been used by God's people for thousands of years. Here are only a few of the questions that believers with needs ask as they read and recite the psalms:

- Can God ever forget believers when they are suffering?
- Do believers need to be reminded about God's control over everything?
- Is God ever going to make things right?
- What are some good things that could be said when God answers prayer?
- Have other believers ever felt the way I do about life and God?

The Christian stands in a long line of those who, though being a heavenly people, still experience the pain of living in a fallen world. In that pain a believer needs the same reminder and experience of God's love and redemption that was needed by Moses, David, Ezra, Matthew, or Paul—exactly what the psalms have offered God's people of all generations. The psalms provide concrete illustrations of how God turns the strain and pain of life into food for devotion and praise to God. And that praise was ultimately to be shared with others. Although many of the incidents represented in the book of Psalms originated in private experience, they had to find their way into open sharing with God's people. Praise, like God's redemption and glory, is not to remain private or hidden. The situations of believers today may differ from those experienced by the psalmists, but the needs are the same—to have sanity in stress, to know deliverance from evil, to be able to express gratitude for redemption, and to find profound delight in God's incomparable character.

OUTLINE OF PSALMS

A. COLLECTION ONE (Psalms 1–41)
B. COLLECTION TWO (Psalms 42–72)
C. COLLECTION THREE (Psalms 73–89)
D. COLLECTION FOUR (Psalms 90–106)
E. COLLECTION FIVE (Psalms 107–150)

PSALMS NOTES

PSALMS 1–41 COLLECTION ONE
Psalm 1 Two Ways of Life
A wisdom psalm

Psalm 1 gives a simple but comprehensive description of the state of the world's beginning from the time of God's curse upon Adam's sin. The godly seed of the woman is always confronted with the ways of the ungodly seed of Satan, the serpent, or snake. The entire world is on the way to the last judgment, but the righteous person will stand and be approved (1:6) by God. "Blessed" (1:1) can be literally rendered "happy." The verbs "walk," "stand," and "sit" (1:1) describe the successive steps of a person's involvement with evil. The Hebrew word translated "meditates" (1:2) can also be used for the growling of a lion over its prey. This suggests that meditation is a vocal, not just a mental, activity. The biblical concept of meditation involves a thoughtful and reflective recitation of the word of God. Wisdom psalms are noted for contrasting the ways of the righteous with the ways of the wicked. This psalm presents two contrasting ways of life and the two contrasting destinies that go along with them. This contrast sets the context for all the psalms that follow. What is "good" in a person's life is not relative to personal pain or pleasure. It is relative only to what God thinks about that life.

Psalm 2
The Messiah's Ultimate Victory
A messianic psalm of David (see Acts 4:25-26)

In Psalm 2 the "Anointed One" is the King in the Davidic line. He is the Son of God in the sense of 2 Samuel 7:14, "I will be his father, and he will be my son." This reference to the Son of God and Son of David found its fulfillment in the only begotten Son of God and greatest Son of David, Jesus, the anointed King of kings. Psalm 1 begins with a blessing (1:1), and Psalm 2 ends with a blessing (2:12). These first two psalms form the introduction to all the rest of the psalms and set the context of blessing and judgment, involving loving obedience (1:2), rebellion (1:4; 2:2), and devoted worship of God and his Son (2:11-12). The king of Israel was anointed with oil as part of a religious consecration (2:2), and he became known as "God's Anointed." The Hebrew word translated "anointed" literally means "Messiah." David's experience described in this psalm would be ultimately fulfilled in Christ. Jesus, the Messiah, will reign as King in Jerusalem during the millennium (2:6; Isa. 2:3). The New Testament links the words "Today I have become your father" (2:7; "begotten Thee," NASB and KJV) with Christ's resurrection (cf. Acts 13:33-34; Rom. 1:4; Heb. 1:5; 5:5). The Hebrew word for "kiss" (2:12), which is its literal meaning, is sometimes translated as "do homage" (NASB).

Psalm 3
A Morning Prayer of Trust in God
An individual's lament

As the chosen king of God, David waited for God to make right the wrong things that had been done against him. The king's patient waiting resulted in blessing for the people (3:8). Similarly, Christ's waiting for God's vindication has issued in his perfect blessing and salvation for all believers. Note the superscription to Psalm 3: "A Psalm of David. When he fled from his son Absalom." Thirteen psalms (3; 7; 18; 34; 51; 52; 54; 56; 57; 59; 60; 63; and 142) have similar superscriptions that provide the historical settings out of which these psalms were composed. It is hazardous to attempt to reconstruct the historical settings of the other psalms where no such indication is given as to the historical occasion for which they were written. The background of Psalm 3 is Absalom's revolt (cf. 2 Sam. 15). The word "Selah" (Ps. 3:2), which occurs seventy-one times in the book of Psalms, was probably a musical notation that signaled an interlude or a change of musical accompaniment.

Psalm 4
An Evening Prayer of Trust in God
A song of trust

Psalm 4 expresses the frustration of the godly king who is waiting, in the middle of criticism (4:2, 6), for God to reveal his righteousness. For all faithful believers, God alone brings peace and gladness in a world of contradictory evil (4:7). The words of the superscription, "For the director of music. With stringed instruments" (4:1), appear in fifty-five psalms and indi-cate that this psalm was to be set to music and sung in public worship in praise of God. "Right sacrifices" (4:5; "sacrifices of righteousness," NASB and KJV) refer to those sacrifices brought by a believer with a pure motive and sincere heart (cf. Mic. 6:6-8). "Let the light of your face shine upon us" (4:6; "Lift up the light of Thy countenance," NASB and KJV) is an expression from the priestly benediction (cf. Num. 6:25-26), that means "show favor."

Psalm 5
A Morning Prayer for Protection
An individual's lament

Requests for God to hear (Ps. 5:1), answer (4:1), or stop delaying (6:3) are found throughout the psalms. They are not disrespectful commands; rather, they are poignant cries of a suffering faithful believer going to his only possible source of hope. The first half of Psalm 5 speaks of prayer in the temple, while the latter half asks for judgment on enemies and blessings on the faithful. "Mercy" (5:7; "Loving-kindness," NASB) is one of God's attributes revealed in Exodus 34:6-7. The root meaning of the Hebrew word brings to mind the loyalty epitomized in the stork, a symbol of motherhood. It can be rendered "loyal love" or "covenant loyalty." That love is embodied in God's lovingkindness to David and his family line of descendants through the Davidic covenant (2 Sam. 7:15). In Psalm 5:10 the imprecation, or the prayer for God to judge (see "Imprecatory psalms" mentioned previously), David petitioned God to punish the wicked and thus vindicate his own righteousness. Such prayers were grounded on God's promise to "curse" those who persecuted Abraham's descendants (cf. Gen. 12:3).

Psalm 6
A Prayer for Physical Deliverance
An individual's lament, a penitential psalm

The king was being persecuted by his enemies (6:7), enemies who were fighting against God's anointed king. Assurance of relief (6:10) came only after the time of suffering. During that time, the assurance of being heard by God was sufficient for the king to remain faithful. In 6:5 David was simply saying that only the people who are living have an opportunity to give public praise to God on earth. The grave refers to the place of the dead. The phrase "Away from me, all you who do evil" in 6:8 was quoted by Jesus in condemnation of superficial religion (cf. Matt. 7:23). God had heard and answered David's prayer (6:8-9)!

Psalm 7 A Prayer for Justice
An individual's lament, an imprecatory psalm

David could take refuge in God because he was righteous. That was his defense and stabilizing foundation (7:8-10) when he was attacked by his enemies, which in this case was one of his Israelite brothers. "Shiggaion" in the superscription of Psalm 7 is a liturgical indicator, the actual meaning of which scholars have not discovered. The word translated "me" (7:2; "my soul," NASB and KJV) could also be rendered "my life." In 7:9-11 David prayed an imprecation (see "Imprecatory psalms" above), asking God to punish the wicked and preserve the righteous (cf. Gen. 12:3). The expression "give thanks" (7:17) could be better rendered "give public acknowledgment," referring to praise in which God's greatness and his goodness, his attributes, and his actions are declared publicly.

Psalm 8
God's Glory Revealed in Creation
A creation psalm, a messianic psalm

The majesty of God comes not only from his greatness displayed in creation but also in his crowning of lowly humanity with majesty. That bestowal of majesty was perfected in the perfect divine majesty of the incarnate Son of God. The "gittith" in the superscription of Psalm 8 is an obscure musical term, perhaps referring to an instrument or tune from Gath. The psalmist's lofty view of man reflects the fact that man was created in God's image (8:5; cf. Gen. 1:27). In Hebrews 2:6-8 the concept is applied to Christ in his incarnation.

Psalm 9 Praise for God's Judgment
A psalm of individual declarative praise

The present reign of evil against God will be resolved in God's last judgment. In the meantime, his faithful followers worship him in the present and trust in his victory that will occur in the future. The focus on the nations (Ps. 9:5, 8, 15, 17, 19-20) shows the original global intentions of God's rule through his chosen line of David. "Muth-labben" in the superscription of Psalm 9 (NASB) is a melody indicator of uncertain meaning. God, who is the avenger of blood, will not overlook deeds of violence (9:12). The words "Higgaion" and "Selah" (9:16) provide directions for a musical interlude. The grave (9:17) is the place of the dead.

Psalm 10
A Prayer against the Wicked
An individual's lament

In light of the predominance of world evil, the writer asked why God seemed far away (10:1). People were saying there was no God (10:4, NASB), that God had forgotten (10:11), and that God would not judge (10:13). However, God had heard the request and would act, but the righteous had to wait for him (10:16-18) to purify the world (10:15). In some Hebrew manu-scripts and ancient versions Psalms 9 and 10 are joined as one. In the Hebrew text, they form a partial alphabetic acrostic. This is an imprecation against the wicked (10:15; see "Imprecatory psalms" mentioned previously).

Psalm 11
God, the Refuge of the Righteous
A song of trust

The conflicts of this age are tests of character. The righteous will find rest and see the face of God (11:7), whereas the unrighteous will be judged in terms descriptive of the great tribulation and the lake of fire (11:6). The psalmist's friends advised him to "flee" while there was a chance (11:1). Like a building, society rests on "foundations" (11:3). If the foundation is undermined, the building will soon collapse. The image of "eyes" (11:4) is a powerful anthropomorphism (attributing human features to God) referring to God's careful scrutiny of mankind.

Psalm 12
The Prayer of a Faithful Believer
An individual's lament

As the godly people disappeared (12:1), David asserted his belief that God was in control and would protect the faithful believers for their ultimate safety and relief (12:5). The psalm was written by David to be set to music and sung in public worship (see the superscription of Ps. 12). The "faithful" person (12:1) is loyal to God and upright in character. The phrase "purified seven times" (12:6) indicates that the silver was completely pure.

Psalm 13 A Prayer for Help from God
An individual's lament

Aside from desiring survival for his own sake, David did not want his enemies to overcome him because he was God's chosen king. Again, God's love shown in the Davidic covenant was David's security (13:5). His four repetitions of the rhetorical question "How long?" reveal the depths of his despair (13:1-2).

Psalm 14 The Folly and Wickedness of Mankind
An individual's lament, a didactic psalm

The fool mentioned in Psalm 14 was David's fellow Israelite who in practice really was an agnostic. For although he knew that God existed, his words and his practical life denied that God was powerful enough to act. After quoting 14:1-3 in his letter to the Roman church in the New Testament (Rom. 3:10-12), the apostle Paul concluded that all mankind is corrupt, having fallen short of God's standard of righteousness (Rom. 3:23). Despite his despair over the wickedness of evildoers, David joyfully anticipated the blessings of the messianic kingdom, which would bring an end to the reign of evil (14:7; cf. Isa. 2:2-4; 4:2-6).

Psalm 15
The Character of a Faithful Believer
A didactic psalm

The essence of David's rhetorical question in Psalm 15:1 is, "What kind of person may enjoy fellowship with God?" The matter of lending money "without usury," or "interest," is related to the Old Testament prohibition of charging excessive rates of interest or charging interest on loans to the poor (15:5; cf. Lev. 25:35-46; Deut. 24:10-13). This prohibition does not relate to receiving modest interest on bank deposits today.

Psalm 16 The Joy of Trusting God
A song of trust, a messianic psalm

For the meaning of *miktam* (in the superscription) see Psalm 56. The "libations of blood" (16:4) referred either to sacrifices offered to idols or drink offerings made by those whose hands were bloodstained. The "boundary lines" (16:6) referred to measuring cords that were used to mark off a territory of land. In the New Testament Peter quoted 16:8-11 in Acts 2:25-28, commenting that David was speaking prophetically of the resurrection of Christ (Acts 2:31). Using the language of hyperbole to express his resurrection hope for faithful believers, David

predicted what would literally be fulfilled in the life of Christ (Ps. 16:10); for Jesus, God's "Holy One," underwent no bodily decay in the grave (cf. Acts 13:35).

Psalm 17 Prayer for the Vindication of the Righteous
An individual's lament

David was not making a claim for sinless perfection in Psalm 17:1 (cf. 51:3). Rather, he was presenting himself as a man of integrity, free from deceit (17:3). The "apple of your eye" (17:8) is a reference to the eye's precious and delicate pupil, which must be carefully protected. The wicked enjoy temporal prosperity or "reward" (17:14; "treasure," NASB and KJV), but the righteous who "awake" in the resurrection to life (cf. John 5:28-29) will enjoy the presence of God forever (Ps. 17:15).

Psalm 18
Praise for God's Deliverance
A psalm of individual declarative praise

Psalm 18, also found in 2 Samuel 22, celebrated the Lord's deliverance of David from Saul and the securing of David's kingdom. That victory was a brief and miniature picture of what the final victory of David's great Son, Jesus, will be at the end of the age. Until then, momentary victory, though soon swallowed up by conflicts and defeats, gives believers a basis for their hope in the future and final victory. The "horn" (Ps. 18:2), a symbol of great strength, was an illustration taken from the wild ox (Deut. 33:17). Psalm 18:7-15 contains the language of theophany, that is, the language describing an appearance of God. Here God is depicted as revealing himself through the upheavals of nature. In 18:20-24 David was not claiming to be sinless; he was simply recalling how he had obeyed God, particularly with regard to his dealings with Saul (cf. 1 Sam. 24:10-12). David viewed God's deliverance and blessing as rewards for his obedience in this area. God will act appropriately with every person whether he intentionally chooses evil or good (18:25-27). With God's help, David had completely overcome his enemies and made them his servants (18:43-45; cf. 2 Sam. 8). In the New Testament Paul quoted Psalm 18:49 (Rom. 15:9) with reference to Gentile worship of the

Messiah. The hope of the world centers on David's line of descendants and all those who align themselves with it (Ps. 18:49-50).

Psalm 19 Praise of God's Revelation
A Torah psalm

The great themes of creation (19:1-6), the law (19:7-11), and the fear of God (19:9) are linked together here as the motivation for man's verbal and heartfelt devotion to God (19:14). Without words or voices, the beauty and wonder of creation shouts, "God, the Creator, exists!" In 19:7-9 David provided a sixfold description of the law, God's special revelation. The various synonyms emphasize different aspects of God's word. The "law," in Hebrew, "Torah," is God's instruction to his people; the "statutes" are a witness to God's truth; the "precepts" are divine directions for man to follow; the "commands" are God's orders or imperatives; the "fear of the Lord" is the reverence that God's word fosters; and the "ordinances" are God's decisions. "Willful sins" (19:13; "presumptuous sins," NASB and KJV) are those sins done knowingly and deliberately (cf. Num. 15:30-31).

Psalm 20 A Prayer for Victory
A royal psalm

The repeated use of "may . . ." throughout Psalm 20 makes this psalm a confident wish for the reader or hearer to be helped by God. David promised to lead others in a song of praise when the help came from the Lord (20:5). For "Selah" (20:3), see the note for Psalm 3:2. In David's time there was often the temptation to trust in military might (20:7; "chariots" and "horses") rather than in God (cf. Isa. 31:1; Deut. 17:16). David, a mere earthly monarch, recognized that God is the true King and Deliverer.

Psalm 21 Thanksgiving for Victory
A royal psalm

The first half of Psalm 21 is a beautiful description of how God had blessed the king. The victories foretold in the second half were based on the loving-kindness of God found in the Davidic covenant (2 Sam. 7:14-15). The king was the mediator of God's victories over the enemies. This is most fully seen in the victory of Christ over sin, death, and the nations at his first and second comings. "Him" (Ps. 21:3) refers to David, the king

(cf. the superscription of Ps. 21). In 21:7-12 the nation expressed its wishes for the king.

Psalm 22 Triumph through Suffering
An individual's lament, a messianic psalm

Psalm 22 shows the tension David felt while knowing that God was totally powerful to help him at the same time that he was experiencing what appeared to be the absence of God's presence to help. The faithful person may cry out in great pain and yet affirm God's goodness and ultimate deliverance (22:3, 8, 10, 22). Jesus quoted the first part of 22:1 while he was dying on the cross (Matt. 27:46), acknowledging his sense of abandonment by the Father as he bore on his own person the sin of mankind. The imagery of Psalm 22:3 represents Israel's praise serving as a throne of glory for God. The "worm" (22:6) serves as an illustration of humiliation, one being trodden underfoot with contempt. For the fulfillment of 22:7 in Christ's suffering, see Matthew 27:39; and for Psalm 22:8, see Matthew 27:43. In Psalm 22:14-16 David prophetically described the crucifixion, for it was a means of execution that was not known until Roman times. The suffering that David described by using hyperboles was literally experienced by Christ. For the piercing of Christ's body foretold in 22:16, see John 20:25. For the fulfillment regarding his clothing in Psalm 22:18, see Matthew 27:35. David prayed for deliverance from death (Ps. 22:19-21), while Christ's deliverance was accomplished by his resurrection from the dead. For 22:22, see Hebrews 2:12. David predicted the universal worship of God during the millennial kingdom (Ps. 22:27-31; cf. Zech. 8:20-23; 14:6-11).

Psalm 23 The Divine Shepherd
A song of trust

Psalm 23 is a psalm of praise deeply rooted in God's covenant promise to David. See God's promise to build a house for David and provide him with permanent loving-kindness in 2 Samuel 7:11-16. In a pastoral community the "shepherd" would be recognized as an illustration of one who serves as a leader, companion, guide, and provider (Ps. 23:1). In the ancient Near East, the term was frequently applied to the king (cf. Ezek. 34:1-23). The shepherd used the "rod" as a weapon of defense to drive off beasts of prey, and the "staff" to lean upon as well as to guide straying sheep (Ps 23:4). The Hebrew words translated "valley of the shadow of death" (23:4) are better translated "valley of deep darkness."

Psalm 24 Greeting the King of Glory
A psalm of descriptive praise,
a messianic psalm

Psalm 24 moves from God as Creator, to the holy requirements for mortals to be in his presence, to a jubilant welcome for God to enter into his temple. For a question and answer similar to the one in 24:3, see Psalm 15. Jacob is an example of one who sought God (24:6; cf. Gen. 32:30). In Psalm 24:7-10 the gates were exhorted to look up and welcome God, the King of glory, as he entered the walled city of Jerusalem. The historical context may have been the transference of the Ark of the Covenant from the house of Obed-Edom to Jerusalem (2 Sam. 6:10-17).

Psalm 25
A Prayer for Help and Pardon
An individual's lament, an alphabetical psalm

The king of Israel prayed for his own forgiveness and ended with a prayer of mediation for the entire nation. The "name" (25:11) refers to God's reputation. David was actually praying, "In keeping with your reputation for grace and compassion, forgive my sin."

Psalm 26 A Prayer for Vindication and Protection
An individual's lament

The king of Israel sought personal vindication from God because of his purity and trust (26:1). "Examine" (26:2) literally means "judge" or "administer justice." Here David claimed to have conducted himself according to God's laws with sincerity of purpose, not sinless perfection. David did some bad things, but he was a good man, "a man after his [God's] own heart" (1 Sam. 13:14). "The house where you live" (Ps. 26:8) was the tabernacle where the Ark of the Covenant was kept (2 Sam. 6:17). David prayed that God would discriminate between him and the wicked so that he would not be taken into judgment with them (Ps. 26:9).

Psalm 27 A Song of Trust
An individual's lament

Light is a figure often used in Scripture to refer to God (27:1; cf. John 8:12; 9:5; 1 John 1:5), since it dispels darkness and brightens life. Again David's great desire surfaced to dwell in the "house of the LORD," that is, the tabernacle, which represented God's presence (27:4). David wanted to be with God and to do his will (27:11). His obedience assured him of God's presence, and that formed the basis of his requests for deliverance from his enemies and the stamina to wait for God (27:14). The tone of the psalm changes in 27:7 from that of explicit trust in God to a tone of lament for the hostile circumstances the psalmist was experiencing. David's comment, "Though my father and mother forsake me" (27:10), should be understood as conditional, not as something that actually had happened. He was pointing out that God's care is even more constant than that of parents. "Wait" (27:14) carries the sense of trust (cf. Isa. 40:31, where the same Hebrew word is translated "hope" in the NIV; "wait," NASB and KJV).

Psalm 28 An Answered Prayer
An individual's lament

In the face of evil, David prayed for his own deliverance and that of his people (28:1-2, 9). The king mediated for God's people, praying that God would not be unresponsive, that is, "turn a deaf ear" to his appeal, lest his life be endangered (28:1). The "pit" refers to the grave. The "Most Holy Place" (28:2) refers to the tabernacle (cf. 2 Sam. 6:17). The community of Israel was regarded as God's "inheritance" or "possession" (28:9; cf. Deut. 4:20).

Psalm 29
The Voice of God in the Storm
A psalm of descriptive praise

God, who is sovereign over nature's storms, is also the God of Israel's redemption (29:11). The link between God as Creator and as Savior is made strongly throughout the Old Testament. The "mighty ones" (29:1; "sons of the mighty," NASB) probably refers to angels (cf. 89:6-7). They were invoked to acknowledge God's majesty and sovereignty over nature. The priests who ministered in the tabernacle had to wear "holy garments" (29:2; "holy array," NASB; cf. Exod. 28:2).

David described an "epiphany," that is, an appearance of God, in the storm (Ps. 29:9). Seven times the "voice of the Lord" moved the elements of nature (29:3-9). Reflecting on the Lord's sovereignty over creation, David recalled the flood of Noah's day (29:10; cf. Gen. 6–8).

Psalm 30 Praise for Healing
A psalm of individual declarative praise

Psalm 30 speaks of a time of restoration for David (30:2) after a close brush with death (30:3) due to his prideful and self-sufficient attitude (30:6). It was a time of joy after suffering discipline. The superscription indicates that the psalm was composed for the "dedication of the temple," a reference to either David's palace (2 Sam. 5:11) or perhaps the house of Obed-Edom, where the Ark of the Covenant remained for three months before being brought up to Jerusalem (2 Sam. 6:10-11). Some scholars suggest that this refers to the dedication of the temple site after the outbreak of pestilence (2 Sam. 24:15-25). God delivered David from near death, for the pit was the grave, the place of the dead (Ps. 30:31). Some scholars hold that 30:6-7 refers to David's pride, which led him to number the people (2 Sam. 24:1-14). If David died, there would be no further opportunity for him to praise God on earth (Ps. 30:9; cf. Ps. 6:4-5).

Psalm 31 A Prayer for Deliverance
An individual's lament

David's hope for God's covenant love ("loving-kindness," NASB) forms the backbone of Psalm 31 (see 31:7, 16, 21). David committed his life to God (31:5). These words were quoted by Jesus on the cross (Luke 23:46) and by Stephen just before being stoned (Acts 7:59). In Psalm 31:9-13 David expressed his distress in exaggerated language for the sake of emphasis. Then in 31:17-18 he prayed for God's judgment on his persecutors in keeping with his promises in Genesis 12:3 and 2 Samuel 7.

Psalm 32 The Blessing of Forgiveness
A psalm of individual declarative praise

The covenant of God with Israel demanded a believer's careful attention to the confession of his sins. In Psalm 32, King David described his struggle with personal sin and his movement to confession and

forgiveness. So wonderful is that forgiveness that the psalm ends with instructions about how others may have the same blessing. The term *maskil* in the superscription labels thirteen psalms and probably meant that it was a contemplative or didactic poem. The word "blessed" (32:1) can be literally translated "happy." David described God's chastening prior to his confession (32:4). God responded with an admonition in light of David's experience (32:5). The reader is reminded that God will watch over the paths of those in danger of straying (32:8).

Psalm 33
Praise to the Creator and Sustainer
A psalm of descriptive praise,
a creation psalm

Creation (33:6-9) is an illustration of God's love (33:5), which forms the basis of hope (33:18, 22). Psalm 33:6-7 is a poetic reflection on Genesis 1–2. The "deep" (33:7) refers to the vast seas. The proper attitude to have in relationship to God the Creator is one of holy reverence and awe (33:9). God's sovereignty extends beyond creation to the rule of nations (33:10). For the "eyes of the LORD" (33:18), see Psalm 32:8.

Psalm 34 Praise and Instruction
A psalm of individual declarative praise,
an alphabetical psalm

Psalm 34:19 reveals a major theme of Psalm 34 and of all the psalms. Here the tension of suffering unjustly is balanced with the confidence of ultimate vindication. The superscription relates Psalm 34 to the incident of David's pretending to be insane in 1 Samuel 21:11-15. The Philistine king's name was "Achish," but he is referred to here by his dynastic title "Abimelech," meaning "my father is king." God's reputation is magnified by those who publicly acknowledge his goodness and greatness (Ps. 34:3). Psalm 34:5 is probably a generalization based on David's experience and could be rendered, "People look to him [God] and . . . their faces are never shamed." David was giving a general principle that people who look in faith to God for help will ultimately not suffer shame. David's bones not being broken (34:20) was ultimately realized by Jesus in his crucifixion (cf. John 19:36).

Psalm 35　A Plea for Vindication

An individual's lament, an imprecatory psalm

The key concepts of Psalm 35 are suffering without cause (35:7, 19) and praying for God to arise and provide salvation (35:2, 17, 22-23). The word "contend" (35:1) is a legal term that suggests a courtroom setting where David, the defendant, called on God, his Advocate, to defend him against accusers. "Say to my soul" (35:3) was his request for an encouraging message from God. In keeping with God's promises in Genesis 12:3 and 2 Samuel 7:9-11, David prayed that God would judge those who were persecuting him (35:4-8). David promised to give public acknowledgment, or praise, of God's goodness when the deliverance was accomplished (35:18).

Psalm 36　The Loyal Love of God

A psalm of descriptive praise

Sinfulness lurks in the heart of the wicked, inciting rebellion against God (36:1). The love of God refers to his loyal love or covenant loyalty (36:5). The attribute of God's love (36:5-12) is highlighted against the contrasting ways of the wicked (36:1-4). The "shadow of your wings" (36:7), picturing a hen with her chicks, is a beautiful figure of protection and refuge.

Psalm 37　The Problem of Evil

A wisdom psalm, an aphabetical psalm

David warned against being agitated or anxious about God's apparent inconsistency in letting evildoers triumph, for their prosperity is short-lived (37:1-2). Beginning with 37:1, every other verse begins with successive letters of the Hebrew alphabet. The word "delight" (37:4) speaks of "exquisite" joy. When believers delight in the Lord, his desires become their desires. Then their prayers are answered as they do his will. The statement of 37:19 regarding God's provision is characteristic of the Bible's Wisdom Literature; it is not a universal promise but a general statement that God will care for his own. In the present age believers may suffer the grief of poverty and starvation. But this passage looks to God's ideal for his people—an ideal that will only be realized in the new heavens and earth. The message of the psalm is summarized in 37:22. The psalmist's testimony in 37:25 is

not a promise or a doctrine and cannot be taken as a universal truth.

Psalm 38　A Prayer of the Penitent

An individual's lament, a penitential psalm

Psalm 38 clearly shows how righteous persons view their own sin within the broader context of their lives. David's sins were many (38:4), but he could say he followed what was good (38:20). The fact that David was a man after God's own heart illustrates that the righteous person is not sinless but is always eager to correct his errors. In contrast, the wicked person is content to stay in his sins. According to the superscription, this psalm of David was designed as "a petition" ("for a memorial," NASB). This indicates that it was to be recited in connection with the "memorial portion" of the grain offering (cf. Lev. 2:2, 9, 16; 5:12). David recognized God's hand of discipline on his life. The particular sin is not identified, but it was probably different from that of Psalm 51. Like one who could not hear or speak, David would make no defense or try to justify himself (38:13-14).

Psalm 39　A Prayer of the Afflicted

An individual's lament

In a time of discipline, David wanted to get a better perspective on the shortness and relative insignificance of his life. Only one thing mattered: hope in God. "Jeduthun" (in the superscription of Ps. 39) was one of the choir directors appointed by David to lead in public worship (cf. 1 Chron. 16:41). At first David suffered in silence (Ps. 39:1-2). Breaking his silence, he asked God to help him understand and accept the brevity of life (39:3-4). He asked God to turn away his gaze of wrath so that he might enjoy the time that was left him on earth (39:13).

Psalm 40　Praise and Prayer

A song of trust (40:1-11), an individual's lament (40:12-17), a messianic psalm

God always wanted his law to get into people's hearts so that it would become their instinctive response (40:8). In the new covenant, made through the death of Christ, he fulfills that desire (cf. Jer. 31:33 and Ezek. 36:26-27). For David, his own sins (Ps. 40:12) and the attacks from others simply thrust his hope more securely upon God's loving-kindness (40:11). Consistent with the prophets, David acknowledged that God was not pleased with sacrifice only but wanted a heart of faith and obedience (40:6; cf. Hos. 6:6; Mic. 6:6-8). Hebrews 10:5-7 quotes Psalm 40:6-8 with reference to Christ's obedience on the cross. Psalm 40:13-17 reappears separately as Psalm 70.

Psalm 41
Thanksgiving and Complaint
An individual's lament

David was suffering from a case of physical illness brought about because of sin (41:4). The king's enemies had taken advantage of the situation (41:5-6). But David's integrity and his essential willingness to correct his mistakes and seek after God would be honored by God (41:12). "He will bless him" (41:2) recalls the thought of Matthew 5:7. Jesus quoted Psalm 41:9 in connection with his betrayal by Judas (John 13:18). Psalm 41:13 was not a part of the psalm originally, but it was added as a concluding doxology to the first collection or book of Psalms (Pss. 1–41).

PSALMS 42–72
COLLECTION TWO
Psalm 42 Thirsting for God
An individual's lament

In Psalm 42 the psalmist's enemies had a twice-repeated response to his suffering, "Where is your God?" The psalmist's crisis of faith was only resolved by his realization of God's power and his own faith in eventual restoration. This *maskil,* or contemplative poem, was either written or sung by the sons of Korah, descendants of the noted rebel (cf. Num. 16–17; 26:11). These are words of introspection (Ps. 42:5). The "soul" refers to the psalmist himself. The 9,200-foot Mount Hermon (42:6) is situated about thirty-five miles northeast of the Sea of Galilee. The location of Mount Mizar (which means "littleness") has not been identified.

Psalm 43 A Prayer for Vindication and Restoration
An individual's lament

Several Hebrew manuscripts combine Psalms 43 and 42. This fact as well as the refrain (43:5), which is repeated from 42:11, suggest that the two psalms were originally one composition.

Psalm 44 A Prayer for National Deliverance
A national lament, an exodus psalm

Psalm 44 presents a case where the writer, like Job, was suffering, but not as a result of committing any sin. He did not know why he was suffering; he had not forgotten God (44:17). For no cause of sin within themselves, the people were as sheep about to be slaughtered (44:22). The psalm's superscription is similar to the one for Psalm 42. Psalm 44:3 contains the great truth of Israel's victorious conquest of Canaan (cf. Josh. 10:42). "Jacob" (Ps. 44:4) refers to the tribes of Israel, of which Jacob was the forefather. God, as it were, had sold his people into captivity, but he had derived no profit from the transaction (44:12). In 44:17-22 the people were lamenting that God's discipline had not been consistent with their own faithfulness to him. The apostle Paul quoted 44:22 in Romans 8:36 in describing the believers' experience in this unbelieving world.

Psalm 45 The Marriage of the King
A royal psalm, a messianic psalm

Psalm 45, a *maskil,* or contemplative poem, is a "song of love" or wedding song. The "king" (45:1) has been identified by scholars as either Solomon, Ahab, or the Messiah King. The latter view seems to be supported by 45:6-7. The historical king in view was probably Solomon, but Christ may be the ultimate fulfillment. In such a case, the people of God would be the bride (45:9). On the basis of 45:12, it has been suggested that the king was Ahab, bridegroom of Jezebel, the "Daughter of Tyre."

Psalm 46 God, a Mighty Fortress
A song of trust

Psalm 46 is an affirmation that God indeed will be exalted in the world. That fact forms the core of the believer's trust and ability to relax in the trials of this age (46:10). "Alamoth" (in the superscription) means "maidens" and was apparently a direction that the psalm was to be sung by soprano voices. The "city of God" refers to Zion (46:4; cf. 48:2). For "LORD Almighty" (46:11), see the note on 1 Samuel 1:3. God determines the destinies of the nations; therefore, believers are to depend on him rather than on political striving (46:10).

Psalm 47 God, the King of the Earth
A royal psalm

God is seen in Psalm 47 as a king ascending his throne on his coronation day. But his throne, unlike that of any earthly ruler, is above all the world. The "sons of Korah" (in the superscription) were descended from the man who rebelled against Moses (cf. Num. 16–17; 26:11). King David appointed them poets and musicians in the temple (cf. 1 Chron. 6:13-17). The theme of God's kingship is the major characteristic of the royal psalms, which look forward to God's reign on earth during Christ's millennial kingdom. God's kingship is absolute; he reigns over all creation.

Psalm 48 Zion, the City of the King
A psalm of descriptive praise

The "city of our God" (48:1) refers to Zion, site of the Jerusalem temple mount. In Canaanite legend, Zaphon, or "north," was where the gods reportedly dwelled (cf. Isa. 14:13). The implication is that Zion is where Yahweh, the true God, dwells. The ships of Tarshish (48:7; cf. Jonah 1:3) were noted for their size and voyaging capabilities.

Psalm 49
The Fate of the Wealthy Wicked
A wisdom psalm

Psalm 49 gives a believer's perspective for coping with enemies. The wicked will not gain eternal life (49:9). Although they may have power, it will only be during this life. This perspective demands a firm persuasion that this earthly life is extremely fleeting and will be replaced with eternal life or death (49:14-15). For the superscription, compare that of Psalm 42. The redemption and extension of a person's life cannot be bought from God (49:7). No amount of money can buy life when God has decreed one's death. Like the dumb beasts, even the wealthy must perish (49:12). While those wealthy persons who rely on their money will perish, those who trust in the Lord will be preserved from premature death ("the grave," 49:15; "the power of Sheol," NASB). There is no sin in being rich (49:16-20). But when one glories in material prosperity and forgets about God, then his life is little more than an animal's existence.

Psalm 50 The Nature of True Worship
A didactic psalm

Psalm 50 indicts the people who give superficial lip service to God while their hearts are actually opposing him (50:16-17). This is a psalm of Asaph, a famous and skilled musician David had appointed chief of the Levites who provided music at the ceremony held when the Ark of the Covenant was brought back to Jerusalem (1 Chron. 16:4-6). The expression "consecrated ones" (Ps. 50:5) refers to those with whom God was in a covenant relationship, that is, the believing Israelites. On 50:8-9, see Hosea 6:6; Micah 6:6-8; and Isaiah 1:11-15 for similar condemnations of empty ritual in worship. God's keeping "silent" (50:21) in response to the misdeeds of the wicked was wrongly interpreted by some as a reflection of God's own character, an indication of his approval.

Psalm 51
A Sinner's Prayer for Pardon
A penitential psalm

There was only one acceptable act to restore David after his adultery and murder—having a broken spirit and contrite heart (51:17). David's contrition was genuine; therefore he was accepted by God. The historical setting of Psalm 51 is found in 2 Samuel 11–12. David's confession of sin (2 Sam. 12:13) is expanded here. He made his appeal on the basis of God's "unfailing love" and "great compassion" (Ps. 51:1). David sinned against Bathsheba and Uriah, but all sin is ultimately an offense against God (51:4; cf. Gen. 39:9). In Psalm 51:5 David was not suggesting that his conception or birth involved acts of sin. Rather, he traced his own sin nature to his very beginning, that is, his conception. "Hyssop" (51:7) was used by the Israelites for cleansing from leprosy and purification from death (cf. Lev. 14:49; Num. 19:18-19). David prayed in accordance with the covenant that God had made with him (Ps. 51:11). God's lovingkindness would never depart, even in severe discipline (cf. 2 Sam. 7:14-15). The "Spirit" (Ps. 51:11) is here seen as the symbol of David's anointing as king, not in the sense of David's redemption. David's "bloodguilt" (51:14) was due to his murder of Uriah.

Psalm 52
The Judgment on the Wicked
An individual's lament, a didactic psalm

Psalm 52 is a *maskil*, or contemplative poem, that has its setting in 1 Samuel 21:1–22:19 where Doeg reported David's visit with Ahimelech the priest to Saul. The words "in the house of God" (Ps. 52:8) may begin a new sentence. The wicked is torn away from his own tent (52:5), but the righteous is always welcome in God's house.

Psalm 53
The Folly and Wickedness of Men
An individual's lament, a didactic psalm

Psalm 53, which is almost identical to Psalm 14, is a contemplative poem (a *maskil*) with an obscure melody indicator (*mahalath*). Paul quotes 53:1-3 in Romans 3:10-12 to show that all mankind is guilty of sin. Psalm 53:5 may refer to the occasion of deliverance that provided the impetus for the reworking of Psalm 14.

Psalm 54 A Prayer for Deliverance
An individual's lament

Psalm 54, a *maskil*, or contemplative poem, has its historical setting in 1 Samuel 23:19-29, where the Ziphites revealed David's hiding place to Saul. In 54:5 David trusted God to right the wrong done rather than taking matters into his own hands.

Psalm 55 Betrayal by a Friend
An individual's lament

While most psalms speak of life's problems, Psalm 55 highlights the betrayal by a most trusted and intimate friend (55:12-13) as the cause of pain. When David asked God to bring confusion to his enemies (55:9), he may have had the tower of Babel in mind (cf. Gen. 11). He prayed that God would judge his enemies, bringing an end to their lives as he had done with Korah and his followers (55:15; cf. Num. 16:30-32). The grave refers to the place of the dead. Psalm 55:22 contains the major lesson of the psalm.

Psalm 56 A Plea for Deliverance
An individual's lament

Although trampled by men, David trusted in God and would fulfill his vows to praise him for deliverance. The tune title in the psalm's superscription refers to the community of Israel ("A dove"; "The silent dove," NASB marg.) in a distant land. The meaning of *miktam* (in the superscription) is uncertain. The word is found introducing Psalms 16 and 56–60 and may refer to how the psalm should be performed. All *miktam* psalms are lamentations. The historical setting is 1 Samuel 21:10-15, which records David's feigned insanity at Gath (cf. the superscription of Ps. 34). God knew David's every hurt and was intimately concerned (56:8). For vows (56:12), see Ecclesiastes 5:4-5 and Numbers 30:2. For thank offerings, see Leviticus 7:11-18.

Psalm 57 A Prayer for Protection
An individual's lament

A key focus in Psalm 57 is the steadfastness of David's heart to praise God in the middle of his problems (57:7). The tune or melody indicator in the superscription, appears also in the superscriptions of Psalms 57–59 and 75. The word *miktam* (in the superscription), also appears elsewhere; see the note on Psalm 56 for an explanation. The historical setting for Psalm 57 is probably the cave of Adullam (1 Sam. 22:1) or possibly the cave at En Gedi (1 Sam. 24:1-7). Either David was actually fighting lions (57:4), or he was making free use of hyperbole, that is, exaggeration for the sake of emphasis.

Psalm 58 A Protest against Injustice
An individual's lament

The great tension for the righteous person is watching injustice go on and on without seeing God move in to right it. The heart of Psalm 58 is found in what the righteous do when God finally rewards and judges (58:10-11). For comments on the melody indicator and *miktam* in the superscription, see the note on Psalm 56. A biblical view of man's depravity from his earliest beginning is reflected in 58:3-5 (cf. 51:5). This fallen moral state shared by all humanity can be traced to Adam (Rom. 5:12).

Psalm 59 A Prayer for Rescue
An individual's lament

See the note on Psalm 56 for a discussion of *miktam* (in the superscription) and the note on Psalm 57 for an explanation of the melody indicator. The historical setting for

Psalm 59 is found in 1 Samuel 19:11-12. Like that of Psalm 58:6-9, the imprecation of 59:11-15 was motivated by a desire to teach people about God, specifically, "Then it will be known to the ends of the earth that God rules over Jacob" (59:13). God is sovereign, even over the wicked.

Psalm 60 A Prayer for National Crisis
A national lament

For the word *miktam* see the note on the superscription of Psalm 56. The historical setting is that of 2 Samuel 8 (also 1 Chron. 18) where David was fighting in the north with Aram Naharaim (Mesopotamia) and Aram Zobah (near Damascus) and was attacked in the south by Edom. Joab met the attack and achieved a great victory. God had given a "banner" (Ps. 60:4) as a rallying point for the people. God assured his people that he still was maintaining his sovereignty over the tribes of Israel (60:6-7). The other nations were regarded as mere servants of God (60:8). Moab and Edom were in the lands east of the Jordan River. Philistia was in Israel along the Mediterranean coast. Reliance upon God's strength is the key to success (60:12; cf. Phil. 4:13).

Psalm 61 A Prayer for Restoration
An individual's lament

The king sought refuge in his God. God's refuge and protection were illustrated by four figures: a high rock, a strong tower, a tent, and sheltering wings (61:2-4). In 61:6-7 David recalled God's promise given to him in 2 Samuel 7:16 of an everlasting lineage and kingdom.

Psalm 62
God, the Believer's Only Refuge
A song of trust

The heart of Psalm 62 is in its combination of God's power and loving-kindness (62:11-12) for judging human behavior. The meaning of "Jeduthun" in the superscription is disputed, but it may refer to one of the choir directors appointed by David (1 Chron. 16:41). David viewed God as his only real security and refuge (Ps. 62:2). Regardless of status or position, the wicked will be found wanting in the day of judgment (62:9).

Psalm 63
A Thirsting Soul Satisfied in God
A song of trust

David's faith pierced through life's problems to a deep enjoyment of God's loving-kindness (63:3). The superscription places the historical setting of the psalm at David's time in the wilderness of Judah, possibly during Absa-lom's revolt (2 Sam. 15:23, 28). The "sanctuary" (Ps. 63:2) refers not to the temple but the temporary tent for the Ark of the Covenant (2 Sam. 6:17). The Old Testament divided the night into three "watches" (Ps. 63:6): (1) the night watch for the night guard of soldiers and shepherds, from sunset to 10:00 P.M. (Lam. 2:19); (2) the middle watch from 10:00 P.M. to 2:00 A.M. (Judg. 7:19); and (3) the morning watch from 2:00 A.M. to sunrise (Exod. 14:24). The "king" (Ps. 63:11) is a reference to David.

Psalm 64 A Prayer for Deliverance
An individual's lament

What David's enemies intended to do to their victim, God would do to them (64:7; cf. Gal. 6:7). God's judgment on the wicked elicits, from both psalmist and reader alike, a healthy recognition of his holiness and high standards (Ps. 64:9; cf. Acts 5:11).

Psalm 65 A Hymn of Thanksgiving
A psalm of descriptive praise

After a brief mention of personal sin and forgiveness, David described God's righteousness in terms of nature and harvest. Zion (65:1) refers to Jerusalem. The "streams of God" (65:9) refer to God's provision of rain. The "bounty" (65:11) of the harvest was due to the abundance of rain along the paths where God had, as it were, walked.

Psalm 66 A Song of Deliverance
A psalm of national declarative praise (66:1-12), a psalm of individual declarative praise (66:13-20), an exodus psalm

God's saving of the nation Israel through the exodus became a pattern or type to remind the people of Israel of God's continual desire to save them. The psalmist recalled the great events of the exodus, crossing the Red Sea (Exod. 14–15) and the Jordan River (Josh. 4). For "burnt offerings" (Ps. 66:13), see Leviticus 1. This psalm

remindsthe reader that sinful attitudes
of the heart block effective prayer
(Ps. 66:18).

Psalm 67
A Call for Universal Praise to God
A psalm of national declarative praise

Psalm 67:1 is based on the priestly
blessing of Numbers 6:24-26. The psalmist
prayed for God's blessing for the purpose
of causing all peoples to know (Ps. 67:2)
and fear him (see 67:7).

Psalm 68 The Triumph of God
A psalm of national declarative praise,
an exodus psalm, a messianic psalm

God is described as ascending to his
throne in Jerusalem as King over all the
nations and receiving gifts of honor from
all (68:18, 29). This psalm contains a variety
of designations for God: *Elohim,* translated
"God" (68:1); *Yah,* an abbreviation for
Yahweh, translated "LORD" (68:4);
El-Shaddai, translated "Almighty" (68:14);
Yahweh, translated "LORD" (68:16); *Yah
Elohim,* translated "LORD God" (68:18);
Adonai, translated "Lord" (68:19); and
Yahweh Adonai, translated "God the LORD."
The reference in 68:7-14 is to the Israelite
exodus from Egypt to Canaan. The rebellious
were those who because of disobedience and
unbelief had died in the wilderness. "Zalmon"
(68:14) is a hill near Shechem. The "mountains of Bashan" (68:15) is probably a reference to the 9,200-foot Mount Hermon. In a
figurative sense, loftier peaks look with envy
at Mount Zion, the mountain chosen by God
as the place where he is to be worshiped
(68:16). Paul quotes 68:18 in Ephesians 4:8
with reference to Christ's person and work.
The "beast among the reeds" (Ps. 68:30)
refers to the hippopotamus, which represented Egypt, one of Israel's enemies.

Psalm 69 A Prayer for Retribution
An individual's lament, an imprecatory
psalm, a messianic psalm

Psalm 69 gives a clear explanation of why
so often good people are unjustly attacked.
The attackers are really reproaching God by
hating his faithful followers (69:9). David
experienced hatred (69:4), but Jesus endured
hatred in a more complete measure (see John
15:25; cf. Ps. 69:8 with John 7:3-5). The

disciples linked Psalm 69:9 with Jesus'
temple cleansing (see John 2:17). Matthew
linked Psalm 69:21 with Jesus' suffering at
Golgotha (Matt. 27:34). Jesus may have
been alluding to Psalm 69:25 in Matthew
23:38. Peter quoted it with reference to Judas
(Acts 1:20). The "book of life" (Ps. 69:28)
refers to the registry of the living. David
was praying for the premature death of the
wicked so that they might be distinguished
from the righteous.

Psalm 70 A Prayer for God's Help
An individual's lament

Nearly identical to Psalm 40:13-17,
Psalm 70 is designated in the superscription as "a petition," or "for a memorial"
(NASB) and was apparently used in connection with the memorial part of the grain
offering (cf. Lev. 2:2, 9, 16).

Psalm 71
The Prayer of an Experienced Saint
An individual's lament

Psalm 71 is an expression of trust based
on the psalmist's long walk of fellowship
with God. The expression "from my
mother's womb" (71:6) may be understood
to refer to God as a gracious benefactor.
Although it may seem that God is far away,
he has promised never to abandon or
forsake his own (71:12; cf. Heb. 13:5).
The psalmist, who viewed himself as good
as dead, expressed confidence in God's
power to restore him (Ps. 71:20).

Psalm 72 A Prayer for the King
A royal psalm, a messianic psalm

These key things, desired by God from
David and the line of kings descended from
him, are stressed in Psalm 72: justice in the
king's rule (72:2-4), the king's rule over the
entire kingdom (72:8), and peace in the land
and the fullness of harvest under the king's
rule (72:16). Solomon, who was the writer of
this psalm, also may have written Psalm 127.
The "king" (72:1) refers historically to
Solomon, but the expansive nature of the
prayer (72:8, 11, 17) suggests that the
prophetic reference looks to Christ in his
kingdom to come. Universal worship of
Christ by kings and nations will be characteristic of the messianic kingdom (72:11; cf.
Zech. 14:9). The editorial note of Psalm

72:20 indicates that at one time this psalm concluded a collection of Davidic prayers. Psalm 72 serves as a conclusion to the second collection of psalms.

PSALMS 73–89
COLLECTION THREE
Psalm 73
The Prosperity of the Wicked
A wisdom psalm

Psalm 73 is a frank confession by the writer of his being jealous of bad people who were prospering. But in the case of the wicked, their end explains the futility of their lives. They often prosper when alive, but death ends their prosperity. On the other hand, even when righteous people suffer trouble, their lives are full of God's goodness (73:1). Asaph (see the superscription and the note on Ps. 50) authored Psalms 73–83. Psalm 73 falls in the category of Wisdom Literature, which is noted for its use of generalization (73:3-5). Obviously there are exceptions to the psalmist's description of the wicked. But, from a temporal perspective, they often do prosper, or at least seem to do so. The wicked "lay claim to heaven" (73:9), that is, they blaspheme God. Their conduct tends to have a corrupting influence on God's people (73:10). Often believers turn to the wicked and drink deeply of their sayings, philosophies, and values. Who has not wondered if serving God is really worth the personal deprivation and discipline (73:13-14)? In 73:15-17 the psalmist provides a divine perspective on his thoughts expressed in 73:3-14.

Psalm 74
The Prayer of a Devastated Nation
A national lament, an exodus psalm

The term *maskil* in the superscription of Psalm 74 identifies this as a contemplative poem. The author, Asaph, probably does not refer to the contemporary of David but to one of his descendants. In lament psalms, the psalmist often expressed himself in terms of what he felt rather than what he actually believed theologically. The "ruins" (74:3) refer to the temple ("sanctuary," NASB and KJV), which was completely devastated by the Babylonian attack. For the burning of the sanctuary (74:7), see 2 Kings 25:8-9 and

2 Chronicles 36:18-19. "Every place where God was worshiped" (74:8) refers not to synagogues, which developed during the Babylonian captivity, but perhaps to places of prayer and private devotion. "Leviathan" (74:14) refers to a dragon monster that figures prominently as an enemy of the created order in ancient Babylonian mythology. The psalmist used this poetic image to emphasize God's power over his creation. "Your dove" (74:19) is a figure that likens Israel to a defenseless bird. In 74:20 the psalmist reminded God of the covenant promises made to Abraham (cf. Gen. 12:1-3).

Psalm 75 God Judges with Equity
A psalm of national declarative praise, a didactic psalm

Psalm 75 gives the key to how the righteous cope with seemingly unjudged evil in the world. God has set a time to judge (75:2). Although that time is known only to him and may be near or far, its fact is certain and forms the basis for hope and warning. The psalm's melody indicator "To the tune of 'Do Not Destroy'" in the superscription also is seen in Psalms 57–59. The "horns" (75:4), the powerful weapons of an ox or bull, were used as a poetic image of strength. God is absolutely sovereign. As the cup of wine may bring stumbling, so the cup of God's wrath will bring destruction (75:8; cf. Isa. 51:17).

Psalm 76 A Song of Victory
A psalm of descriptive praise

God's great deliverance of Jerusalem from its surrounding enemies is a sign that he saves the humble (76:9). "Salem" (76:2) is an abbreviation for the name Jerusalem, which was also called Zion. The defeat did not take place in Jerusalem, but the city served as God's headquarters. This psalm repeats the concept of fear (76:7-8, 11-12) as the context for praise and worship (76:11-12).

Psalm 77 Comfort through Remembering God's Works
An individual's lament (77:1-9), a psalm of national praise (77:13-20), an exodus psalm

Psalm 77 clearly shows one important aspect of comfort: believers remembering God's past acts of love when they are in the middle of difficult times. "Jeduthun" in the superscription is a disputed term appearing also in the superscriptions of Psalms 39 and 62. Thoughts about God disturbed the psalmist (77:3). How could he keep faith when God seemed to have rejected him (77:7-9)? But remembering God's great deeds in the past gave him faith and encouragement for his present struggles (77:11-15). In 77:16-20 the psalmist praised God for his deliverance of Israel at the time of the exodus. The "waters" (77:16, 19) refer to the waters of the Red Sea and the Jordan River, which parted at God's command.

Psalm 78
Israel's Failures and God's Grace
A didactic psalm, an exodus psalm,
a messianic psalm

The purpose of Psalm 78 was to pass along the old stories of God's judgment and redemption to future generations (78:3-4). It does that by recounting both the great redemptive acts of God in the exodus from Egypt and the forgetfulness and failures of Israel along the way. The story ends with God's grace prevailing in establishing his temple and his Davidic king in Jerusalem. The *maskil* in the superscription marks this as a contemplative poem. Matthew quoted 78:2 in Matthew 13:35 to show that Jesus' speaking in parables fulfilled prophecy. The reference in Psalm 78:9 is not to a specific battle but to a history of Israel's unfaithfulness in relationship to the things of God (cf. Judg. 1:29). Baal Shem Tov, founder of the Hassidic movement in eighteenth-century Poland, said, "Forgetfulness leads to exile, while remembrance is the secret of redemption." This man could very well have learned this lesson from 78:11. The "bread of angels" (78:25) refers to manna, the "grain of heaven" (78:24). The deaths of some Israelites led others to question how they had offended God (78:34). God's people were to learn from the mistakes of those who had gone before them.

Psalm 79 Lament over the Destruction of Jerusalem
A national lament, an imprecatory psalm

Psalm 79's prayer for judgment on the psalmist's enemies was based on God's promise in Genesis 12:1-3 to bring judgment on those who cursed Israel. The cry for

God's vengeance upon the enemies of his people was motivated in part by the desire to answer those who asked, "Where is their God?" (79:10). Another motivation for God to deliver his people came from their promise to praise him (79:13).

Psalm 80
A Prayer for Rescue from Calamity
A national lament, an exodus psalm

The "cherubim" (80:1) refers to the figures, representing spiritual beings, on the Ark of the Covenant (Exod. 25:22). The "vine" (Ps. 80:8) is Israel, the nation that sprouted in Egypt but was planted and took root in Canaan. The vine, Israel, expanded toward the Mediterranean "Sea" and the Euphrates "River" (80:11; cf. 80:12 with Isa. 5:5.) Psalm 80:17 is not a reference to Jesus the Messiah but to the people God's right hand planted (cf. 80:15), that is, Israel.

Psalm 81 God's Goodness and Israel's Waywardness
A didactic psalm, an exodus psalm

Psalm 81 presents a common pattern in the psalms, that is, the use of the exodus as a motivation for present faithfulness. For comments on "gittith," a disputed term used in the superscription, see the note on Psalm 8. The ram's horn was blown on the first day of the seventh month (80:3; cf. Num. 29:1). The "New Moon" refers to the fifteenth day of the seventh month when the celebration of the Feast of Tabernacles began. The incidents that took place at Meribah (Ps. 81:7) are recorded in Exodus 17:1-7 and Numbers 20:1-13. The psalmist's moving unexpectedly from the usage of the third to the second person (Ps. 81:8) was not uncommon in Hebrew writings.

Psalm 82
Judgment on the Unjust Judges
A national lament

Psalm 82 is a poetic presentation of the justice demanded in the law of God handed down at Mount Sinai. The term "gods" (82:6) was used in this context to describe those who were to "preside over" or "judge" others (82:1); these were men who had been given authority on earth to represent God's interests and enforce his law. Jesus used this verse in John 10:34 to defend his use of the title "Son of God" (John 10:35-36).

Psalm 83 A Prayer for Judgment on the Nations
An individual's lament, an imprecatory psalm, an exodus psalm

The harsh judgment of God that the psalmist demanded here (83:13-15) was ultimately for redemptive ends (83:16). In 83:6-8 the noteworthy enemies of Israel were identified. Two great victories, by Gideon over the Midianites (Judg. 7), and by Deborah and Barak over the Canaanites (Judg. 4–5) were recalled in Psalm 83:9. Oreb and Zeeb (Ps. 83:11) were Midianite princes (Judg. 7:25), and Zebah and Zalmunna were kings of Midian (Judg. 8:5-21). In Psalm 83:16, 18 the strong imprecation against Israel's enemies had an evangelistic purpose. God's judgment was, and still is today, designed to cause the wicked to "seek" him and recognize that he alone is the "Most High" over all the earth.

Psalm 84
The Delight of Fellowship with God
A psalm of descriptive praise

For the disputed term "gittith," used in the superscription of Psalm 84, see the note on Psalm 8; and for the "Sons of Korah," see the note on Psalm 42. How "blessed," or happy, are those who spend their lives in God's service! (84:4). "Baca" (84:6) is usually understood to mean "weeping." The idea here is that God turns weeping into blessing. To "be a doorkeeper" at God's house (84:10) expresses an attitude of worship and service.

Psalm 85 A Prayer for Restoration
A national lament

As usual, behind the desire for physical blessings is the more profound desire to experience the love, faithfulness, righteousness, and peace of a relationship with God (85:10-11). In 85:9-13 the psalmist described the millennial kingdom, during which God's "glory" will be exhibited in Israel in the person of Christ.

Psalm 86 A Prayer for Deliverance
An individual's lament

David trusted in the great revelation of God given so long ago to Moses in Exodus 34:6 (Ps. 86:5, 13). The Hebrew word translated as "devoted" (86:2) can also be translated "loyal" and refers to one who is faithful to his covenant relationship with God. In 86:11 David prayed that his heart would be totally focused on God's awesome reputation ("name"), not distracted by other interests or desires.

Psalm 87 A Song of Zion
A psalm of descriptive praise

Jerusalem has received the great blessing of God's presence. "Rahab" (87:4) is another name for Leviathan, the dragon monster mentioned frequently in ancient Babylonian mythology as an enemy of the created order. The psalmist was saying that the powerful enemies that once warred against Israel will one day bow the knee to God (Phil. 2:10-11). The future kingdom will be characterized as a time of great joy and celebration (Ps. 87:7).

Psalm 88
The Distress of Unanswered Prayer
An individual's lament

Psalm 88 is one of the bleakest psalms. No answer is given or hope specified. But, at least, the writer was still praying and clinging to God. The words *Mahalath leannoth* (in the superscription) are an obscure melody indicator literally meaning "sickness to afflict." The term *maskil* indicates that the psalm is a contemplative poem. "Heman the Ezrahite" was apparently one of the directors of the temple music. The "grave" (88:3-6) refers to the place of the dead. The point of 88:10 was that if God did not intervene, it would be too late; the psalmist would be dead.

Psalm 89 God's Covenant with David
A messianic psalm

The central fact of Psalm 89 is the permanent love that God gave to David in his covenant (89:28, 33). That permanence formed the foundation for the king's hope for restoration from personal sin and the ultimate preservation of the kingdom from its enemies (89:35-37). The psalm is a contemplative poem. The identity of Ethan is unknown. The theme of Psalm 89 is the Davidic covenant, the promise that God made to David in 2 Samuel 7:12-16. The "heavenly beings" (Ps. 89:6) refer here to angels (cf. 89:7). For "Rahab" (89:10), see the note on Psalm 87:4. "Tabor" and "Hermon" (89:12) are prominent mountains in Israel. The two men mentioned in 89:19 may refer to Gad and Nathan (1 Sam. 22:5; 2 Sam. 12:1), although some manuscripts are written in the singular, alluding to Nathan, the key figure in the historical context (2 Sam. 7). Psalm 89:25 is a reference to promised dominion, from the Mediterranean Sea to the Euphrates and Tigris rivers. The covenant promise to David and his dynasty is eternal (89:28-29), unconditional (89:30-34), and permanent (89:35-37). In 89:38-39 David lamented that his immediate experience did not seem to match what God had promised. Psalm 89:52 serves as the conclusion to the third book of the Psalter.

PSALMS 90–106
COLLECTION FOUR
Psalm 90
God's Eternity and Man's Brevity
A national lament

Psalm 90 is the oldest psalm and was authored by Moses. The return to "dust" (90:3) is part of the curse resulting from Adam's sin (Gen. 3:19). God's perspective is different than man's. A thousand years is but an instant in the context of eternity (Ps. 90:4). This verse is applied by Peter in 2 Peter 3:8. Realizing the brevity of life, the reader is reminded to make decisions that reflect wisdom (Ps. 90:12). The prayer is for God to return his expressions of grace instead of wrath and discipline (90:13). To confirm the works of one's hands (90:17) is to provide blessing that matches inward righteousness.

Psalm 91 Security in the Lord
A wisdom psalm

The deliverance of God is promised for the one who loves and knows him (91:14). The "shadow of the Almighty" suggests the image of a mother bird protecting her little ones under her wings (91:4). God will protect his own against danger and attack (91:5-7). Psalm 91:10 should not be taken as a personal promise for protection from every evil circumstance. It is a general principle, seen in the Wisdom Literature of the Bible, that the righteous will be spared

unnecessary and avoidable difficulties. Satan quoted Psalm 91:11-12 in the context of Christ's temptation (see Matt. 4:6; Luke 4:10-11).

Psalm 92 Praise for God's Goodness
A psalm of individual declarative praise

Meditation on the great works and deep thoughts of God is the way to avoid sin and deepen wisdom (92:5-6). Psalm 92 was designated for use on the Sabbath day (cf. Exod. 20:8; Deut. 5:12). The fool lacks spiritual perception (Ps. 92:6). For "horn" (92:10) see the note on Psalm 75:4.

Psalm 93 The Reign of God
A royal psalm

God reigns presently as sovereign Creator of the universe (Ps. 103:19), but his reign will one day be culminated when Christ takes his throne on earth. So Psalm 93 is prophetic as well as descriptive of present reality. The "seas" (93:3) refer figuratively to the enemy nations surrounding Israel.

Psalm 94 The Appeal to a Just Judge
A national lament

The Lord who has created the ear and the eye hears and sees all. In that light, the one who listens to him is blessed and will find support in God's love (94:18). Compare 94:14 with Hebrews 13:5. The "silence of death" (Ps. 94:17) refers to the grave. Like Habakkuk, the psalmist questioned how a righteous God can use an evil or wicked instrument to accomplish his purposes (94:20). The answer is found in the principle of divine retribution (94:23).

Psalm 95 A Call to Worship
A psalm of descriptive praise, an exodus psalm, a didactic psalm

God as Creator (Ps. 95:1-5) is the foundation for worship and softness of heart. The test of 95:7-11 is quoted in Hebrews 3:7-11 as a warning against unbelief. The wilderness wanderings were used to remind the readers of the importance of obedience (Ps. 95:8). For the historical situation, see Exodus 17:1-7. The unbelieving generation of Israelites forfeited the "rest" and blessing they could have enjoyed in Canaan (Ps. 95:11).

Psalm 96 A Call to Praise the Righteous Judge
A royal psalm

The major idea here is the coming of the Lord to judge the world. Psalm 96 is reproduced almost verbatim in 1 Chronicles 16:23-33, where it was said to have been composed when David brought the Ark of the Covenant to Jerusalem. While the Lord reigns in a sovereign sense today (Ps. 96:10), one day Christ's kingdom rule on earth will culminate the fulfillment of this prophecy (96:13). During the age of the kingdom, the curse on earth that resulted from man's sin will be removed (96:12). When peace and harmony return to the natural realm, even the the trees will "sing for joy."

Psalm 97 The Kingship of God
A royal psalm

For a note on "The Lord reigns" (97:1), see Psalm 96:10. In 97:2-6 language reminiscent of that used during God's self-revelation at Sinai is used to emphasize his awesome presence. The psalmist was not implying that the heathen idols were true gods (97:7). Rather, assuming the polytheistic viewpoint of the ancient world, he indicated that all so-called gods must bow before the one true God (cf. 97:9; 1 Cor. 8:4-6). Sharing God's attitude regarding evil is an essential characteristic of those who sincerely acknowledge his rule (97:10; cf. Prov. 8:13). The end notes of Psalm 97 are to hate evil and to be glad in the Lord (97:10, 12).

Psalm 98 Praise of God, the Judge
A royal psalm

Psalm 98 shows the two pillars, past and future, that enable hope and faithfulness in the present: God's past redemption and his future coming to judge. The psalmist's testimony (98:3) is similar to the promise of Isaiah 52:10. God has demonstrated his saving power in the great deliverances of the past. This mighty demonstration of his salvation was culminated at the cross. For Psalm 98:7-8, see the note on Psalm 96:12. God the Savior is also God the Judge (98:9). His second coming will be marked by his judgment of the nations (cf. Joel 3:13-17).

Psalm 99 Holy Is God
A royal psalm

The double-edged nature of God seen in his forgiving yet exacting ways (Ps. 99:8) forms the basis for worship. The truth that God reigns (99:1) means that the present, with its good and evil, is perfectly and fully under God's control and is being brought to its final end of judgment and reward (cf. 96:10). The word "holy" (99:3) basically means "separate." When used with reference to God, it means that God is separate from all that is contrary to his nature, from that which is common or unclean. Derived from the concept of "separation" is that of moral or ethical purity.

Psalm 100 An Exhortation to Worship
A psalm of descriptive praise

God's goodness, evidenced by his love and his faithfulness (100:5), is the theme of Psalm 100.

Psalm 101 Vows of a King
A royal psalm

David showed himself as the king after God's heart, eliminating evil and encouraging faithfulness. While David tried to apply these ethical standards to himself, they will be ultimately fulfilled by the Messiah in his kingdom (101:2-5). Each morning the king will administer justice, keeping Israel ("the land") and Jerusalem ("the city") morally clean (101:8).

Psalm 102 An Afflicted Man's Prayer for Himself and Zion
An individual's lament, a penitential psalm, a messianic psalm

The superscription of Psalm 102 reveals the life setting of the psalmist—a time of affliction and distress. The references to the condition of Zion suggest the time period of the captivity. In 102:3-5 the psalmist used exaggeration for the sake of emphasis to reveal the extent of his distress. He anticipated a time when God would extend his compassion to Zion (102:13). One such expression of divine compassion was when God raised up Cyrus to decree the return of the Jews (Ezra 1:1-4). Psalm 102:13 suggests that God's compassion on Zion will be ultimately realized in the messianic kingdom when the peoples and nations gather to serve him (102:22).

Psalm 103 The Great Benefits of a Gracious God

A psalm of descriptive praise

God's love (103:8, quoting Exod. 34:6) is demonstrated through his forgiveness (Ps. 103:8, 10, 12). David used the expression "O my soul!" (103:1-2) merely to address himself. For "holy" (103:1), see the note on Psalm 99:3. In the Hebrew parallelism of this verse, the term "diseases" (103:3) is a figurative reference to the sickness of sin. The "fear" of God (103:11) refers to reverential awe and respect that are exhibited in turning from evil and pursuing God's will (cf. Job 28:28; Ps. 111:10). Since east and west are at opposite points on the compass, they never meet (103:12). God's dominion extends to all of his creation (103:19).

Psalm 104
The Greatness of God the Creator

A creation psalm

Psalm 104 is a poetic reflection on Genesis 1–2. Here poetic imagery is used to describe God's heavenly abode. The "waters" (Ps. 104:6) refer to the moisture in the atmosphere (see Gen. 1:7, "the water above it"). Psalm 104:4 is quoted in Hebrews 1:7 with reference to the ministries of angels. Psalm 104:6 is not a reference to the world flood (Gen. 6), but to the separation of sea and dry land on the third day (Gen. 1:9-10). Leviathan (Ps. 104:26) is the dragon monster prominent in ancient Babylonian mythology as an enemy of the created order; see the note on it in Job 3:8.

Psalm 105 The Faithfulness of God in Israel's History

A psalm of descriptive praise, an exodus psalm, a didactic psalm

Psalm 105 sums up the immediate implication of God's prior covenant with Abraham and his great redemption of Israel from Egypt under Moses. God desired to have a people who would obey and praise him (105:45). For God's covenant with Abraham, see Genesis 12:1-3. The covenant was confirmed with Isaac (Gen. 26:2-4) and Jacob (Gen. 28:13-15; 35:11-12). The fact that God remembered his promise to Abraham (Ps. 105:42) provides the key to understanding all the blessings that God has bestowed on Israel. God was being faithful to the Abrahamic promise (Gen. 12:1-3; 15:18-21).

Psalm 106 Confession of National Sin

A national lament, an exodus psalm

The future glory of Israel (Ps. 106:5) is viewed through her past failures under Moses up into the Babylonian captivity. That view provides the basis for repentance and hope. The words "Praise the LORD" (106:1) are literally in Hebrew "hallelujah," which can be translated "Give a shout of praise for God." "Our inheritance" (106:5) refers to the inheritance of Israel (33:12). For the rebellious attitude of Israel by the Red Sea (106:7), see Exodus 14:11-12. For Psalm 106:17, see Numbers 16:1-35; for Psalm 106:19, see Exodus 32:1-4; for Psalm 106:28, see Numbers 25:1-9. The nation was not deserving of God's compassion, but he extended it anyway (Ps. 106:44). Psalm 106:48 serves as a doxology for the fourth section of the book of Psalms (Pss. 90–106).

PSALMS 107–150
COLLECTION FIVE
Psalm 107 God's Deliverance in a Time of Trouble

A psalm of individual declarative praise

The "love" (or, "loving-kindness," NASB) of God is Psalm 107's main theme (cf. 107:1-7, 8, 15, 21, 31, 43). The psalm illustrates God's gracious care and intervention for his own by several illustrations. Being lost in the desert, experiencing captivity, suffering from illness due to personal sin, sea storms, and agricultural drought are all opportunities for people to call on God and to see his loving-kindness in action. Similar imagery to 107:10 appears in Isaiah 42:7, describing the conditions of the exiles in Babylon.

Psalm 108
Praise and Prayer for Victory

An individual's lament

Psalm 108:1-5 corresponds with Psalm 57:7-11. The exact words of Psalm 108:7-12 also appear in Psalm 60:6-11.

Psalm 109 A Prayer for Retribution

An individual's lament, an imprecatory psalm

The root problem of David's enemies was that they did not reflect the loving-kindness of their God (109:16). In 109:6-20, David's prayer for retribution is based on God's promise in Genesis 12:1-3 to "curse" those who "curse" Abraham's descendants and also upon the Davidic covenant of 2 Samuel 7. Compare Psalm 109:25 with 22:7. The mockery of Christ (Matt. 27:39; Mark 15:29) was a fulfillment of these verses.

Psalm 110 The Messianic King-Priest
A messianic psalm

Psalm 110 pointed toward another King who would be above David; this King, Jesus the Messiah, would stand between David and God the Father. This psalm is an important Old Testament passage for the book of Hebrews (Heb. 1:3, 13; 5:6; 7:17, 21; 10:13). Psalm 110 was also a crucial Old Testament passage for Peter on the Day of Pentecost for showing that the greater Son of David, Jesus, had to ascend to the right hand of God (Acts 2:34-36). Jesus used Psalm 110:1 to prove his deity to the questioning Pharisees (Matt. 22:41-45). The "LORD" refers to God the Father, while "my Lord" refers to the second person of the Trinity, Jesus the Son (110:1). The rule of Christ will be culminated in the millennial kingdom (110:2). God's believing people will rally around the Messiah in recognition of his lordship and rule (110:3). The metaphor "the dew" (110:3) refers to the freshness and vitality of those who will serve God. Like Melchizedek (Gen. 14:18), Christ holds both offices of king and priest (Heb. 7:1-28). The battle scene described in Psalm 110:5-6 will take place at Christ's second coming (Zech. 14:1-15; Rev. 19:11-21).

Psalm 111
The Praise of God's Goodness
A psalm of descriptive praise,
an alphabetical psalm

The goodness of the Lord is here focused on his support of his people by providing food and redemptive covenant promises (Ps. 111:5-6). The "fear of the LORD" (111:10) is the major theme of the Bible's books of Wisdom Literature (cf. Job 28:28; Prov. 1:7; 9:10; Eccles. 12:13).

Psalm 112 The Happy Man
A wisdom psalm, an alphabetical psalm

Psalm 112 gives insight into the strength often seen in the suffering children of God. Because they know they are doing right before God, their hearts are steadfast and without fear

(112:7-8). The Hebrew parallelism likens the "fear of the LORD" with delighting in God's commands (112:1). The righteous will look with satisfaction upon the defeat of the wicked (112:8), who will see the triumph of the righteous and be dismayed (112:10).

Psalm 113
The Unique Greatness of God
A psalm of declarative praise

Psalms 113–118 are called the "Hallel" or "praise" psalms and are sung by Jewish families during their celebration of the Passover. Psalm 113:5 asks who is like God in order to give believers the perspective they need when, in their eyes, troubles get too big and God seems too small. "From the rising of the sun to the place where it sets" (113:3) means in all lands, from the east to the west. God is exalted (transcendent), but this does not preclude his concern for the welfare of his creatures (113:5-6). Hannah (1 Sam. 1:1–2:10) illustrates the truth of Psalm 113:9.

Psalm 114 The Wonder of the Exodus
A psalm of descriptive praise,
an exodus psalm

In Psalm 114 the exodus image is re-created with a few bold strokes to motivate holy fear and worship. Technically, the sanctuary (tabernacle or temple) was located in the land of Benjamin (Josh. 18:16), but in time it became associated with the tribe of Judah because the Judean kings ruled from Jerusalem (Ps. 114:2). Psalm 114:3 is a reference to the exodus events, crossing the Red Sea (Exod. 14) and the Jordan River (Josh. 3). Psalm 114:4 is a reference to the quaking of Mount Sinai (Exod. 19:18). And Psalm 114:8 is a reference to God's provision of water in the wilderness (Exod. 17:1-7).

Psalm 115
A Prayer for God to Honor His Name
A national lament

The nations mocked Israel concerning the perceived absence of her God. In that light the writer prayed for God to glorify his name (Ps 115:1). Compare 115:4-8 with Isaiah 44:9-20. Psalm 115:17 is not intended as a theological commentary on the afterlife. The point is simply that when God's people are dead they are not present to praise the Lord on earth.

Psalm 116 Thanksgiving for Deliverance from Death

A psalm of individual declarative praise

Compare Psalm 116:3-4 with 18:4-6. The second line of 116:11 could be rendered "the whole of man is deceptive." Thus, man is unreliable. The "cup of salvation" (116:13) alludes to the drink offering (Exod. 29:40-41; Num. 28:7). For "vows" (116:18), see Numbers 30 and Ecclesiastes 5:4-5.

Psalm 117 A Shout of Praise

A psalm of descriptive praise

God's love and faithfulness brings to remembrance his covenant loyalty and reflects the revelation of God's character to Moses in Exodus 34:6.

Psalm 118 Thanksgiving for Deliverance

A psalm of individual declarative praise, a messianic psalm

This is the last of the "Hallel" or "praise" psalms (Ps. 113–118), which were sung at the Passover. This was probably the hymn sung by Jesus and the disciples in the Upper Room before they departed for the Mount of Olives (see Matt. 26:30). He will "look in triumph" (Ps. 118:7) on God's judgment on the wicked. Jesus quoted 118:22-23 with reference to his being rejected by his own Jewish people (Matt. 21:42-44; Mark 12:10-11). They also were quoted by Peter (see Acts 4:11; 1 Peter 2:7). See also Isaiah 28:16. The people called out these words of praise (Ps. 118:25-26) at Christ's royal entry into Jerusalem (cf. Matt. 21:9; Mark 11:9-10; Luke 19:38). The "horns of the altar" (118:27) were projections at the four corners of the altar (cf. Lev. 4:7).

Psalm 119 The Law of the Lord

A Torah psalm, an alphabetical psalm

Psalm 119 consists of twenty-two stanzas corresponding successively to the letters in the Hebrew alphabet. The eight verses of each stanza all begin with the same letter. This pattern is maintained throughout the psalm until the alphabet is complete. The often-used term "law" has the idea of teaching, direction, or instruction. The law is the gracious revelation of what God wants in order for believers to have fellowship with him. It reveals who he is in holiness and justice. The wicked are insensitive to the ethical ideals set forth in the law (119:70). A "wineskin in the smoke" (119:83) is an image representing someone who has become dried, shriveled, and of little use. Man's knowledge of earthly matters is limited, but God's word is extensive and comprehensive in scope and application (119:96). The "willing praise" (119:108) of the psalmist's mouth is a true sacrifice of praise (Heb. 13:15). For "watches of the night" (Ps. 119:148) see the note on Psalm 63:6. In this context, the expression "seven times" (119:164) is used poetically to mean "many times" or "frequently." Praise should be part of a regular pattern for living.

Psalm 120 Prayer for Help against a Slanderer

An individual's lament, a pilgrim psalm

Psalm 120 shows the discomfort of a righteous person in the middle of people of ungodly speech. The superscription "song of ascents" is found attached to Psalms 120–134. The term "ascents" suggest that these psalms were sung as the Jews went up to Jerusalem for worship at the three annual pilgrim feasts (Deut. 16:16). God's judgment on the slanderer is likened to sharp arrows and burning coals (Ps. 120:4). Meshech (120:5; cf. Gen. 10:2) and Kedar (Gen. 25:13) were mountain and desert tribes, respectively, dwelling outside the land of Israel. The slander had made the psalmist feel as though he lived in hostile surroundings.

Psalm 121 God, the Keeper of Israel

A psalm of individual declarative praise, a pilgrim psalm

Psalm 121 asserts the absolute and ultimate safety of the child of God. The essence is found in 121:7, where God is praised as the one who protects his people from evil. For "song of ascents," see Psalm 120. The "hills" (121:1) may refer to those that surround Zion (cf. 125:2). The expression "your coming and going" (121:8) refers to all of one's affairs and undertakings.

Psalm 122 Prayer for the Prosperity of Jerusalem

A psalm of individual declarative praise, a pilgrim psalm

The blessings of the house of the Lord in Jerusalem begin and end this psalm (122:1, 9) and frame the central thrust of the psalm (122:2-8) which concerns the house of David (122:5). The key prayer for the peace of Jerusalem (repeated three times in 122:5-8) is for the benefit of those who love the city (122:6), that is, for those committed to the God of Israel and his statutes—the Law of Moses (122:4-5).

Psalm 123 Looking to the Lord

A national lament, a pilgrim psalm

Note the images of dependency used in 123:2 to help the reader visualize his dependency on God. The "hand" is that which supplies the need. The scorn and contempt by the proud were more than the psalmist could bear (123:4), and hence this prayer.

Psalm 124
Help in the Name of the Lord

A psalm of national declarative praise, a pilgrim psalm

Psalm 124:8 contains a major theme expressed by all the psalms. Help and deliverance are based on the reputation ("name") and power of God, the Creator.

Psalm 125
The Security of God's People

A national lament, a pilgrim psalm

Note the comparison of the righteous person to a mountain (125:1). Usually God is pictured that way. The mountains literally surround Jerusalem (125:2). To the north is Mount Moriah (2,425 feet high); to the east, the Mount of Olives (2,700 feet high); to the west, the Western Hill (2,550 feet high); and to the south, the so-called Mount of Evil Counsel where the .local United Nations Headquarters is presently located. The "scepter" (125:3) is an image of rule or domination.

Psalm 126
A Prayer for Full Restoration

A psalm of national declarative praise, a pilgrim psalm

The first group of exiled Jews returned to Jerusalem ("Zion") under the decree of Cyrus in 537 B.C. (Ezra 1:1-4). The psalmist prayed for a restoration blessing that was forfeited with captivity to the same degree that the dry riverbeds in the southern desert ("streams in the Negev," Ps. 126:4) are filled to overflowing with the winter rain. The metaphor of harvest in 126:5-6 is used to illustrate the results of the prayerful efforts of the exiles to reestablish themselves in the land.

Psalm 127
Prosperity Comes from the Lord

A wisdom psalm, a pilgrim psalm

This is the second of Solomon's two recorded psalms (cf. Ps. 72). Man's labor is in vain unless God is in it (127:2). The last line suggests that God will provide for his own, even during times of sleep. Hence, those who know God can be free from anxiety. Those with large families can have confidence in the face of personal threat or public criticism because of the support and encouragement of their offspring (127:5). The "gate" (127:5) was the place for settling legal disputes in ancient times (see Ruth 4:1ff.).

Psalm 128
The Blessing of Revering God

A wisdom psalm, a pilgrim psalm

The wife is likened to a "fruitful vine" (128:3) bringing the blessing of progeny. Because of the presence of the temple in "Zion," God was viewed as residing there (128:5). Thus the blessings from God come from Zion.

Psalm 129 God Delivers His People

A psalm of national declarative praise, a pilgrim psalm

Persecuted Israel is likened to a scourged man with welts on his back like the deep "furrows" made by a plow in a field (129:3). Grass often grows on the tops of flat roofed houses (129:6), but with little soil, it withers quickly under the hot sun.

Psalm 130
Hope in God's Forgiving Love

An individual's lament, a penitential psalm, a pilgrim psalm

God's pardon of sin is designed to turn man's heart toward him in reverence (130:4). The repetition of identical lines (130:6) is used here for emphasis, expressing urgency.

Psalm 131 The Virtue of Humility

A song of trust, a pilgrim psalm

The imagery "like a weaned child" (131:2) suggests one who is happy and secure, having gone through the difficult weaning process. Such is the psalmist's condition after being weaned from a desire for status.

Psalm 132 A Prayer for Blessing on the Sanctuary

A royal psalm, a messianic psalm, a pilgrim psalm

David's desire to build God a temple (Ps. 132:2-5) is reflected in 2 Samuel 7:1-7. "Ephrathah" (132:6), also known as Ephrath, is another name for Bethlehem (Gen. 35:19), but may be used here for the district in which Kiriath Jearim was located where the Ark of the Covenant was kept for twenty years (1 Sam. 7:1-2). The "anointed" (132:10) refers to the future kings of the Davidic dynasty. God's promise to David and his descendants (132:11-12; see 2 Sam. 7:12-16) was unconditional, yet participation in the benefits of this promise could be forfeited by disobedience ("if," Ps. 132:12). In such cases, the promise would be passed on to the next ruler. The promises of 132:15-17 will ultimately be fulfilled in Christ in the messianic kingdom.

Psalm 133 The Praise of Brotherly Unity

A wisdom psalm, a pilgrim psalm

Brotherly unity (133:1) is compared with three progressively powerful images: (1) oil on the head and beard; (2) dew on Mount Hermon; and (3) the bestowal of God's blessings on Mount Zion, that is, Jerusalem. Unity is a blessing that has its source in God himself. The oil on Aaron's head and beard refers to Leviticus 8:12 and Aaron's anointing with oil to begin the great ministry of atonement in the tabernacle. The blessing of God's people living in unity is like the oil of blessing being poured not only over the high priest Aaron but also over the entire city of Jerusalem. Moist, Mediterranean air blown inland to the foothills of Mount Hermon (9,200 feet high) results in a very heavy dew fall in the area mentioned (133:3). This represented the abundant blessing of unity that God would bring to Jerusalem.

Psalm 134 An Exhortation to Bless the Lord

A psalm of descriptive praise, a pilgrim psalm

Those who served at the temple throughout the night received a blessing. This psalm forms a benediction for the Songs of Ascent (Pss. 120–134). The biblical concept of "bless" (134:3) includes the good things God gives including his presence with his people.

Psalm 135 Praise of God's Greatness

A psalm of descriptive praise, an exodus psalm

God should be praised for his election of Israel (Ps. 135:4) and her redemption out of Egypt. Compare 135:7 with Jeremiah 10:13 and 51:16. For Israel's victories over Sihon and Og (135:11), see Numbers 21:21-35.

Psalm 136 Praise for God's Loyal Love

A psalm of descriptive praise, an exodus psalm

Psalm 136 exalts the Lord for the many expressions of his loving-kindness. That aspect of God's character is rooted in Exodus 34:6 and God's redemption of Israel out of Egypt. The psalm was probably used anti-phonally in temple worship, with the refrain being sung by the Levites or the congregation.

Psalm 137 The Song of the Exiles

A national lament, an imprecatory psalm

The "rivers of Babylon" were the irrigation canals that channeled water from the Tigris and Euphrates rivers (cf. Jer. 51:13; Ezek. 1:1). The Edomites were the descendants of Esau, Jacob's brother (137:7; cf. Gen. 36:8). Instead of showing kindness to their Israelite kinsmen, they called for Jerusalem's destruction. Some link Edom's crimes against Jerusalem with the judgment pronounced against them in Obadiah 1:11-14. The law of retaliation (Lev. 24:17-21) is applied in Psalm 137:8-9. Such crimes had been perpetrated against Israelite children (cf. 2 Kings 8:12; Hos. 10:14) and the Babylonians were guilty of them (cf. Jer. 51:24 with Isa. 13:16). This shocking imprecation is ultimately grounded on God's promise in Genesis 12:3.

Psalm 138 Great Is God's Glory
A psalm of individual declarative praise

The pagan "gods" or idols were mocked by the psalmist's praise of the true God. The "word" (138:2) refers to a specific answer to prayer. God's answer had surpassed all that David had previously understood his reputation ("name") to signify. Although God is glorious and greatly exalted, he is concerned for the "lowly," those who truly love and reverence him (138:5-6).

Psalm 139
A Devout Contemplation of God
An individual's lament, an imprecatory psalm, a wisdom psalm

David praised God for his knowledge (139:1-6), omnipresence (139:7-12), and his plan for all of his days (139:13-16). On that basis David praised God and asked for his judgment upon the wicked and upon himself as well (139:23-24). Psalm 139:13-15 makes a strong biblical statement concerning God's involvement in the development of life within the womb. The "depths of the earth" (139:15) refer to the mother's womb. Psalm 139:16 reveals God's prior knowledge of each individual life before birth (cf. Eph. 1:11). In Psalm 139:19-20, on the basis of God's promise to Abraham (Gen. 12:3), David prayed for God's judgment on the wicked and murderers ("bloodthirsty men").

Psalm 140 A Prayer for Protection
An individual's lament

As a protective helmet, God protects his own from the wicked enemy (140:7). David prayed that the mischief spoken by the "lips" of the wicked would recoil and entangle them (140:9). The "burning coals" (140:11) may allude to God's judgment of Sodom and Gomorrah (Gen. 19:24).

Psalm 141 A Prayer for Protection
An individual's lament

Before David prayed for protection from his enemies, he prayed for protection from his own evil potential (141:1-4). For the use of incense in the tabernacle (141:2),

see Exodus 30:8. For the evening offering, see Exodus 29:39-41. The "delicacies" (141:4) of the wicked are the fruits of their ungodly practices. Psalm 141:6-7 are variously interpreted. The wicked will be overthrown (141:6), but not without great cost to the righteous (141:7).

Psalm 142 A Prayer for Help
An individual's lament

The historical setting of this contemplative poem (*maskil*) was probably either the cave of Adullam (1 Sam. 22:1-5) or the cave at En Gedi (1 Sam. 24:1-7). The Lord told the Levites, who had no territorial inheritance, that he was their "portion" in the land of Israel (Ps. 142:5; cf. Num. 18:20). God was David's possession and provision. David's "prison" (142:7) was probably the cave where he was hiding from Saul.

Psalm 143 A Prayer for Deliverance
An individual's lament, a penitential psalm

David prayed for inner strength to do God's will (143:10) and outer protection from his enemies. The "level ground" (143:10) was used figuratively for conditions free from obstructions resulting in peace and prosperity. The imprecation of 143:12 was based on God's promise in Genesis 12:3.

Psalm 144
A Prayer for Rescue and Prosperity
A royal psalm

Compare Psalm 144:3 with 8:4. In 144:5-8 David prayed for God's divine intervention whereby the forces of nature were enlisted as allies with God's people (cf. Josh. 10:10-11; Judg. 5:20-21). Psalm 144:12-15 depicts the happy estate resulting from God's presence and protection.

Psalm 145 Glory to God
A psalm of declarative praise, an alphabetical psalm

Psalm 145 forms an alphabetical acrostic with each verse beginning with a successive letter of the Hebrew alphabet. The Hebrew letter *nun* is missing, but it appears in a Hebrew text from Qumran. The great revelation of Exodus 34:6 forms the core of and foundation for David's faith. The "saints" (145:10) refer to those who exercise covenant loyalty in their relationship with God and man.

Psalm 146 Praise of God's Power

A psalm of descriptive praise

The Lord was praised for his justice and provisions. He had shown himself to conform to his own laws. The five psalms that conclude the psalter all begin and end with the Hebrew imperative "Hallelujah" meaning "Praise the LORD." For 146:8, see Matthew 20:29-34 and John 9:1-7.

Psalm 147 Praise of God's Goodness

A psalm of descriptive praise

Psalm 147 moves its focus in three broad strokes from the stars to the afflicted, from all of nature to those persons who fear God, and from all the nations to Israel's special favor. Hundreds of billions of stars are known to exist in the Milky Way galaxy, which is regarded as but a speck in the star clusters of the known universe (147:4). Man depends upon physical strength for victory and accomplishment, but such things are not a factor in God's dealings (147:10). In ancient times, the "bars" of city gates would be strengthened against attack (147:13). God has done this for his people. He did something unique and special with Israel when he entrusted them with his special revelation ("his laws and decrees," 147:19-20).

Psalm 148 All Creation Invoked to Praise God

A psalm of descriptive praise,
a creation psalm

From nature to humanity, all are commanded to praise God. The term "heavenly hosts" (148:2) refers to numerous heavenly beings. The word "horn" (148:14) is used as an image of strength and is probably referring to a "strong one," or king.

Psalm 149 Praise for Victory

A psalm of descriptive praise

For "saints" (149:1, 5), see the note on Psalm 145:10. Psalm 149:6-9 anticipates the subjection of the nations under Christ's rule during the messianic kingdom (see Ps. 2:8).

Psalm 150 A Universal Call to Praise

A psalm of descriptive praise

The writers of the psalms recognized the importance of music as an instrument for praise. The listing of the various instruments (150:3-5) suggests that all resourses at one's disposal are to be called upon to exalt the great name of God. Praise is the essence of the redeemed person's life. It shows continual appreciation for the redemption God gives believers and continual appreciation of their frailty and need for God's strength. It shows continual appreciation of his desires to right the world.

Proverbs

BASIC FACTS

HISTORICAL SETTING
The courts of Solomon (Prov. 1:1) and Hezekiah (25:1), two of Israel's greatest kings, provide the historical setting for the book of Proverbs. The proverbs illustrate the wisdom that was desired by God for the kings of his Davidic line.

AUTHOR
The book of Proverbs includes material from several authors. Solomon, as God's chosen king of Israel, is the primary source for the wise sayings in this book. Other lesser authors are "the wise" (22:17), Agur (30:1), and Lemuel (31:1).

DATE
The book was originally composed in the days of Solomon (971–931 B.C.; see 1:1) and then completed in the days of Hezekiah (between 715 and 686 B.C.; see 25:1).

PURPOSE
The book of Proverbs was designed to help believers deepen their healthy fear of God and to apply that fear to the varied events of daily life. The proverbs graphically described these events as opportunities for making wise or foolish choices that could bring either blessing or disaster. But the book of Proverbs was not collected and compiled simply to give a long checklist of various items for successful living. Its purpose was to strengthen the confidence of believers in God's ultimate control over the world to help them take responsibility for their actions and accept the consequences of wrongdoing.

The book probes deeply into how people's thoughts affect their actions. The book divides thoughts and acts into two major categories, each one based on either true or false understandings of God's involvement in the world. The fool acts as if God does not exist. The wise conduct themselves in the full realization that God exists and that actions have unavoidable consequences, good or bad. Thus, the book's main purpose is to correct the worldviews of readers—to turn them away from foolish fantasies (see, for example, 12:11; 28:19) and back to the fear of God (1:7). Then the various wise actions described in the book will result from that inner awe and respect for God.

In summary, the purpose of the book of Proverbs is to save people from the realm of darkness and death caused by error and ignorance. It is also to save them in order that they might enter the realm of life as God originally intended.

GUIDING CONCEPTS

THE VIEWPOINT OF PROVERBS

The book of Proverbs uses pithy and vivid statements to equip the godly person for life (3:17-18). It strives to instill values as well as motivate behavior (1:3). It was very important for every Jewish son to learn a trade, usually one passed from father to son. Proverbs paints the picture of a son being groomed to take over after the father is gone, especially in the skills of daily life. It uses poetry in order to present truth to the heart as well as to the mind. Overall, there is no consistent grouping of the individual proverbs by topic. There is no need for a closely knit argument. Each day normal human experience brings many diverse topics to deal with. Proverbs matches life on the busy streets.

Proverbs speaks from the experience of age. It is as if wise and gentle people were sharing their years of experience with the younger generation. Proverbs probes the works of creation, seeing in it God's power to order the world he made. It is international in its scope because it recognizes that the entire world, not just a single nation, is under God, who created all things. The way in which he created the world to operate is beneficial for everyone. This universal perspective is different from that of the rest of the Old Testament, which emphasizes the relationship of Israel to God under the Mosaic covenant. The Old Testament generally has a national focus; Proverbs has a focus that is international.

THE COURT OF SOLOMON

Solomon had asked for and received great wisdom (1 Kings 3:9). He also was the one God spoke of in 2 Samuel 7:14, the one who, as king of Israel under the Davidic covenant, would have a special father-son relationship with God. The wisdom of Solomon, as described in 1 Kings 4:29-34, related to everything from trees to animals, birds, and fish. Solomon's wisdom did not pertain only to godly matters. The wisdom God gave him was insight into how the entire world operated, on the vegetable, animal, and mineral levels. And, as is true in his proverbs, that wisdom also related to how God intended the home, the body, the business, and the community to best operate. True wisdom looks at the world and finds out how things work the best. It is very practical.

BIBLE-WIDE CONCEPTS

PROVERBS AND CREATION

Wisdom is much more than a skill. It is actually God's underlying plan and thought for the universe. Proverbs 8:22-31 links wisdom with the very blueprint of creation.

Wisdom is God's detailed plan of how his creation was designed to operate. "The fear of the Lord" is the foundation of wisdom, for it connects people with God's original plan not only for creation but for their lives. A wise person follows that original plan as best he can so that his life will reflect order and not chaos.

God is sovereign over his creation and knows the heart of every man or woman (15:3, 11; 16:2). He rewards good and evil (12:2; 22:22-23). His control does away with an impersonal view of how life works. God is the personal sustainer of the universe. It is up to the wise person to ground his life not in high ethical or social norms but in the personal God who controls the world. From that relationship, which the Bible calls "the fear of the Lord," will then issue the particular ethics and behavior that match God's original intentions for creation. Only there will life be found (12:28; 13:9; 19:16).

But that wisdom does not come easily. It is a decision of faith to accept the revealed order and rule of God (1:23; 3:5-6; 4:7). Each person is responsible to search for it (2:2-5; 25:2; 28:12-28; 30:5-6). It is available to all people—from wise leaders to the farmer in his field (Isa. 28:23-29).

These words of wisdom often come in the form of commands (e.g., 1:8; 2:1; 3:1; 4:4; 6:23; 13:13; 28:4). They stand on the same level as Moses' commands and are to be bound on the tablet of the heart (3:3; cf. Deut. 6:8; 11:18). They are fulfilled and perfected in Jesus, the Son of God, the personified wisdom of God (Col. 2:1-3) and the upholder of creation (Col. 1:16).

NEEDS MET BY PROVERBS

The first readers of the book of Proverbs were not just people who enjoyed a special relationship with God. They were people called upon to reinvigorate God's original plan for humanity to have dominion over the earth and to make God an important part of every aspect of life. That original creation mandate for humanity allowed for no split between secular and sacred. From tilling the ground to fellowshiping with God, everything was of one noble and God-oriented whole. So, for the Israelite, religion stretched far beyond the tabernacle into the field, street, business, and home. All areas of life were to reflect God's designs for success. Proverbs extended the commands of the law into wise words to guide a person into godly living in all areas of his daily life. Questions like the following are answered in the book of Proverbs.

- What does God have to say about the parts of life that do not seem to be directly related to religion?
- How can a person become truly wise?
- Does God bring the consequences of a person's actions upon him immediately or do the consequences take awhile to appear?
- What makes a choice foolish or wise?
- How can a person avoid doing what so many of his friends are doing?
- If consequences of sin are not always immediate, where can a person find the stability to continue making wise choices?
- How long can a person get away with making foolish choices?
- What may motivate a person to keep trying to make wise choices?

The book of Proverbs portrays the situations of life as they really are, not the way people might wish them to be. Unfortunately, it is all too easy for people to live in a world of their own creation. The atheist creates a world that has no God. The disobedient believer creates a world in which God somehow winks at personal sins. The one who spends more than he earns creates an imaginary world in which bankruptcy somehow never finds him. The one who overeats and underexercises lives in a fantasy world in which heart attacks always happen to someone else.

But in the real world, the world of Proverbs, the norm is that bad actions have bad consequences—perhaps not immediately, but inevitably. In the real world overspending leads to financial problems, overeating leads to health problems, immorality leads to personal and family problems, and dishonesty leads to exposure and ruin. Such a world is not pretty. But most people would rather have reality over fantasy. Only through that reality can the book of Proverbs reveal the ultimate reality that is the ground of all wisdom: the fear of God.

OUTLINE OF PROVERBS

A. INTRODUCTION (1:1-7)
B. THE PARENTS' VIEW OF LIFE (1:8–9:18)
C. THE PROVERBS OF SOLOMON, PART ONE (10:1–22:16)
D. GENERAL COLLECTIONS OF PROVERBS (22:17–24:34)
E. THE PROVERBS OF SOLOMON, PART TWO (25:1–29:27)
F. THE WORDS OF AGUR (30:1-33)
G. THE WORDS OF LEMUEL (31:1-9)
H. POEM TO AN EXCELLENT WIFE (31:10-31)

PROVERBS NOTES*

1:1-7 INTRODUCTION
The reference to Solomon (1:1) does not mean that he wrote the whole book (24:23; 30:1; 31:1), but that he was the major and most illustrious contributor. The purpose of the book of Proverbs (1:2-4) is to bring to the reader an understanding of true "wisdom" and inspire him to allow it to guide his decisions and conduct (see Job 28:28). To exercise "wisdom" (1:2) means to order one's affairs according to God's righteous guidelines and thus avoid unnecessary difficulties in life. The word "instruction" is best translated "discipline" and contains the idea of training by word (24:32) or deed (23:13). In view are wise dealings (1:3) that lead to successful living; "right" is right behavior; "just" is the application of righteousness in making the right decision; and "fair" is moral

integrity. Wisdom will give prudence to the naive or simple minded, the person susceptible to being misled (1:4). The person without experience will learn how to avoid the pitfalls of life.

Proverbs will benefit both the wise and the simple (1:5-6). The wise will be able to navigate around life's hidden reefs with care. The "proverb" (in Hebrew, *mashal*) is simply a method of teaching by means of comparison. The theme of the proverbs is that the "fear of the LORD" (1:7) is the first lesson in the pursuit of wisdom. To "fear" God means acknowledging his standards and reverently submitting to his will. Numerous applications of the "fear of the LORD" are presented by the wisdom writers (see Job 28:28; Eccles. 12:13; Ps. 111:10; Prov. 2:5; 8:13; 9:10). Solomon wanted to emphasize that

---

* The substance of some of the notes for Proverbs was also published in the *Ryrie Study Bible*.

wisdom is not acquired by some mechanical formula but comes through a right relationship with God. The "fool" is the mentally naive and morally irresponsible person who has little regard for God's guidelines ("wisdom") and discipline ("instruction").

1:8–9:18 THE PARENTS' VIEW OF LIFE

Overview: The first nine chapters give the parents' view of life and prepare the reader for Solomon's words in 10:1–22:16. They form a foundation for wisdom that is world-wide in its application. It is not simply "religious wisdom," but it is applicable in all aspects of the world and people's personal lives. The mood in the book is like that seen in a loving father's hands on his son's shoulders. The mother also has a high position of honor as a teacher in the book of Proverbs (1:8; 4:3; 6:20; 10:1), a characteristic uncommon in literature of the ancient Near East.

These chapters were written by the overall editor of the book and were written in a royal setting in the court of the king. Although these chapters are anonymous, the rest of the book's contents have named authors. This editorial introduction sets the perspective and interpretive tone for the rest of the book. The first major and following section of Proverbs contains discourses on wisdom. Here Solomon taught by contrast, comparing the ways of the wise with those of the foolish.

1:8-33 The Father's Call to Wisdom

The individual proverbs had their original set-ting in the home where the wise parent ad-dressed his "son" concerning practical lessons in life (1:8-9). The word "listen" (1:8) means "to pay attention to and put into practice."

Sin is attractive (1:10-14) but deadly (1:15-19). The sinner may gain the world at the cost of his own soul (Mark 8:36). The grave (1:12) is the place of the dead, while wisdom is seen as a rejected street creature (1:20-33), who is not in the temple but out in life's everyday routine. Wisdom is personified as a godly woman inviting all to come and learn from her teaching, but the majority refuse to listen.

2:1-22 Wisdom's Benefits

The father spoke again as a wise master teacher, describing the benefits of pursuing wisdom. The concept that God is the ultimate source of wisdom makes Israel's Wisdom Literature unique (2:6). True wisdom is God-given, not merely the result of human effort or ability (cf. 1 Kings 3:9-12; James 1:5). Wisdom will deliver one from the ways of evil men (2:10-15) and adulteress women (2:16-19). The adulteress is referred to as a wayward woman in that she is outside the circle of a man's proper relationships (2:16).

3:1-35 Wisdom's Security

Wisdom not only protects one from evil, it also promises many earthly rewards (3:1-18). The word "acknowledge" (3:6) means to "know." In all of the activities and pursuits of life, God must be kept central. The words "make straight" mean to clear obstructions enabling one to reach the appointed goal. The "tree of life" (3:18; cf. Gen. 2:9; Rev. 2:7) is a metaphor for a "source of life." Wis-dom played a dynamic part in the creation of the universe (3:19-20), so it can have a significant part in ordering the affairs of each person's life.

4:1-27 Exhortation to Grasp Wisdom

Wisdom provides many benefits for any-one who will follow its direction (4:1-27). It is seen as the way or path (4:11) upon which people are to journey through life. The first step for a person in acquiring wisdom is to make up his mind that he really wants it and is willing to subject his own ideas and desires to God's revealed will (4:7). The two conflicting ways of the wicked and the righteous is a common theme of the wisdom writers (4:18-19). The "full light of day" (4:18) refers to noontime, when the sun is directly overhead. The "heart" (4:23) refers to one's inner being or mind. The expression "wellspring of life" is a reference to one's spiritual vitality.

5:1-23 Marital Fidelity

The exercise of wisdom will help guard a person against the temptations of adultery. The wisdom of marital fidelity is contrasted with its foolish and dishonoring alternative

(5:7-23). The figurative language in 5:15 refers to marital intercourse. The "springs" of 5:16 refer to one's offspring or children.

6:1-35 Debt and Adultery

To "put up security" (6:1) means to take responsibity for another person's loan; so if the borrower defaults, the cosigner has to pay the obligation. The wise teacher warned his son to avoid such financial folly. The proverbs are based on general observations about life. Job recognized that there are exceptions to this general prediction concerning the destiny of the wicked (Job 12:6). The proverbial expression "six . . . seven" (Prov. 6:16) means that the list, though specific, is not exhaustive (30:15, 18). The seventh commandment, "You shall not commit adultery" (Exod. 20:14), is the theme of Proverbs 6:20-35. With adultery there is no possible means of giving back to the rightful spouse what has been taken (6:35).

7:1-27 Description of a Son's Downfall

The "apple" of the eye (7:2) is the pupil. The imagery is used to emphasize how precious the teachings of God's word should be in the lives of his people. The theme of this section, the folly of yielding to the enticements of a harlot, is introduced in 7:5. Here the warnings against adultery were dramatized as the teacher described how a young fool succumbed to the temptations of an adulteress. Having offered sacrifices, she had a good supply of meat on hand to share with her guest (7:14; cf. Lev. 7:15).

8:1-36 Wisdom and Creation

Wisdom is personified and exalted by proclaiming her excellences. She is a guide offered to every person (Prov. 8:1-11) as the key to all success (8:12-21). The careful application of God's guidelines for living will generally result in a more favorable economic situation, but financial prosperity must always be kept in proper perspective (8:19).

Wisdom's eternal character is shown in 8:22-31 and ultimately points to Christ, in whom is found "all the treasures of wisdom" (Col. 2:3; cf. Phil. 2:3-11; 1 Cor. 1:24; Jer. 9:23-24). Christ, who is wisdom incarnate, is the ultimate wise man. Wisdom is pictured as a craftsman at God's side at creation (8:30). The sky, likened to a vaulted canopy over the earth, is described from the viewpoint of appearance. The "circle" refers to the horizon. The "deep" refers to the ocean. "Listen" (8:32) means to both hear and obey.

9:1-18 Wisdom and Foolishness Personified

The rival invitations of wisdom (9:1-6) and folly (9:13-18) serve to conclude this section. The "seven pillars" (9:1) signify an ideally constructed house. Mixed wine (9:2, 5) refers to wine flavored with spices (Song of Sol. 8:2). The theme of the book is repeated (1:7) in this concluding section (9:10). Like a harlot, folly promotes the attractiveness of what is forbidden (9:17). "Stolen water" and "food eaten in secret" (9:17) may be figures of illicit intercourse (see 5:15-20; 30:20).

10:1–22:16 THE PROVERBS OF SOLOMON, PART ONE

Overview: Here Solomon presents 375 of the over 3,000 proverbs he wrote (1 Kings 4:32). Proverbs are short sayings taken from everyday life that are intended to serve as practical guidelines for successful living. These proverbs are general principles that may have exceptions. They are not intended as personal promises or meant to apply in unusual or exceptional situations. This is not a problem with their inerrancy, but a matter of understanding the nature of proverbs and the contexts in which they do apply.

10:1-32 The Security of the Wise

Violent, vicious language flows from the mouth of the wicked (10:6). The "fountain of life" (10:11) is a source of spiritual vitality. The proverbs confirm the general principle that a person reaps what he sows (10:16). When one's prosperity comes as a blessing from the Lord, there is freedom from the usual anxieties and trouble accompanying the accumulation of wealth (10:22).

11:1-31 Wisdom's Blessing in Society

The term "guidance" (11:14) literally means "steering," or wise direction on the course of life. For "security" (11:15), see 6:1-5. The word "discretion" (11:22) can be literally translated "taste" and refers to moral perception. For "tree of life" (11:30), see 3:18. Spiritual salvation is not in view here but rather the winning of others to the ways of wisdom.

12:1-28 Security and Diligence in Work

"Discipline" (12:1) is training by word or deed. For an example of such a noble wife (12:4), see 31:10-31. The mouth of the upright will deliver the innocent from undeserved judgment (12:6). Better to be of humble circumstances and have something to eat than to have an honored position and be hungry (12:9). The wicked covets the possessions of others in order to stabilize his own position (12:12). But the righteous man works for what he has and enjoys the joy and security of earning one's due. "Annoyance" (12:16) means anger. A prudent man knows when to speak and when to remain quiet (12:23). The slothful man neglects essential responsibilities (12:27). An allusion to the immortality of the one who knows God is found in 12:28.

13:1-25 Wisdom's Gains and Life's Injustices

The "light" and "lamp" (13:9) serve here as symbols of joy and prosperity (cf. Esther 8:16). For "tree of life" (13:12), see the note on 3:18. The word "hard" (13:15) is better rendered "not lasting." Proverbs 13:21 is a general principle, but there are exceptions, as in the case of Job.

14:1-35 Wisdom and Earthly Power

There is always a price for growth and accomplishment (14:4). The prudent man does not walk blindly but carefully considers his steps and chooses his way (14:8). There is a way that seems to be ethically correct, but it leads to destruction (14:12). Wisdom generally does result in greater economic stability because financial entanglements (6:1-5) are avoided (14:24). For "fountain of life" (14:27), see 10:11. The righteous have an eternal hope in contrast to the wicked, who can expect only humiliation and judgment (14:32). The fool boasts of what little knowledge he has, while the wise man avoids making a display of himself (14:33).

15:1-33 Wisdom in Heart and Speech

"Death and destruction" (15:11; "Sheol and Abaddon," NASB; "Hell and destruction," KJV) both refer to the place of the dead, the grave. "Abaddon" is a Greek word from which "destruction" is rendered. "Sheol" is a Hebrew word meaning "place of the dead." "A cheerful look" (15:30) refers to the sparkle seen in the eyes of one who has received good news.

16:1-33 The Sovereignty of God over Life's Events

"Commit" (16:3) literally means "roll." It calls the reader to roll his burdens onto the Lord's shoulders; they are not too great for him. Atonement for man's sin is the result of God's love and faithfulness (16:6). A reverence for God and an appreciation of his power to judge motivate a person to turn from temptation. The expression "speak as an oracle" (16:10) points to the finality and authority of the king's words. The spring rain (16:15) falls just before harvest, assuring that there will be an abundant crop. A "fountain of life" (16:22) is a metaphor for a source of spiritual vitality. The expression "purses his lips" (16:30) refers to a nonverbal expression of malice; much evil can be communicated through body language. Lot casting was a means of determining the will of God (16:33). Although the casting of lots appears to be by chance, the decision is ultimately from the Lord.

17:1-28 Avoiding Injustice and Quarreling

A bribe can be used to secure a profitable business deal, but the practice is clearly condemned (17:8; cf. 17:23). Forgiveness preserves friendship unless someone takes advantage of such graciousness by repeating the offense (17:9). The fool thinks wisdom can be bought with a price (17:16). The term "pledge" (17:18, literally "strike hands") refers to confirming an agreement by a handshake. For "security," see Proverbs 6:1-5. The expression "builds a high gate" (17:19) refers to opening one's mouth with arrogant, boastful talk. Wisdom is readily accessible, but the foolish are preoccupied with other interests (17:24).

Hughes and Laney / 270

18:1-24 Consequences of Good and Bad Decisions

The expression "deep waters" (18:4) speaks of teaching that is dark and obscure. A "bubbling brook" refers to the teaching of the wise that is crystal clear, that is, easily understood. The "name of the LORD" (18:10) speaks of God's true character and reputation. The word "gift" (18:16) is a more neutral term than "bribe" and refers to an innocent courtesy (cf. 1 Sam. 17:18). The "barred gate" (18:19) refers to barriers in friendly relations. In the selection of friends, quality counts more than quantity (18:24).

19:1-29 Contrasts of Wealth and Wisdom

The fool blames the Lord for the disasters he brings upon himself (19:3). A comfortable living situation tends to reinforce the careless ways of a fool (19:10). Proverbs 19:16 speaks of temporal punishment, for example, premature death, not eternal judgment (cf. Deut. 30:15-20). The neglect of child discipline results in premature death for a disobedient or rebellious child (19:18; cf. Exod. 21:15). A simpleton needs to visualize or experience the consequences of folly ("strike a scoffer"), but a wise man will correct his conduct simply in response to a reproof (Prov. 19:25).

20:1-30 Discernment of Inner Motives

The words "in season" (20:4) reflect the custom in ancient Israel of planting the winter wheat in the fall. The intentions of a man's heart may be hidden ("like deep water"), but the wise person is able to penetrate below the surface and know the inner thoughts (20:5). Compare 20:7 with Exodus 20:5-6. The answer implied by the context is "nobody" (Prov. 20:9; cf. Rom. 3:10-18). For "security," see Proverbs 6:1-5. In ancient times a garment was often used as collateral against a loan (cf. Exod. 22:25-27). "Food gained by fraud" (Prov. 20:17) implies dishonest gain. The "lamp" (20:20) is a symbol for a person's life (cf. 13:9; 24:20; 2 Sam. 21:17). Compare Proverbs 20:25 with Ecclesiastes 5:4-5. Physical discipline may have very beneficial results in purging evil and correcting conduct (Prov. 20:30).

21:1-31 God's Sovereignty and Justice

The word "lamp" (21:4) is better translated "ground newly plowed" and refers to the schemings of the wicked. The "righteous one" is probably a reference to God, "the Righteous One" (21:12). Proverbs 21:14 reflects a fact of experience, but it does not promote bribery. The "bold front" (21:29) is an expression of defiance.

22:1–24:34 GENERAL COLLECTIONS OF PROVERBS

Overview: The next section contains the "sayings of the wise" (22:17). Here the pattern returns to that of chapters 1–9, using proverbial discourses.

22:1-29 Wealth and Poverty

A "good name" (22:1) speaks of a good reputation. The words "in the way he should go" (22:6) literally translate "according to his way," that is, the child's habits and interests. The proverb teaches the duty of reinforcing a child's interests and abilities during the early years of life. The "rod of his fury" (22:8) refers to the rod used in fury or anger. The last line of the verse appears to refer to bribery, which fails to accomplish its purpose (22:16). For 22:26 see the note on 17:18. The reference "you" is to the harsh creditor (22:27).

23:1-35 Self-Control and Discipline

The expression "put a knife to your throat" (23:2) refers to restraining one's appetite. A delicious meal may be provided with an ulterior motive. Like 23:1-3, the warning is against being deceived by an insincere host (23:4-8). For the "boundary" marker (23:10), see Deuteronomy 19:14. The "Defender" (Prov. 23:11) refers to the near kinsman, like Boaz who served as family protector for Ruth and Naomi (cf. Lev. 25:25-28 and Ruth 3:9). The term may also be used of God (Isa. 41:14). The words "he will not die" (23:13) infer that having learned obedience through parental discipline, the child will not die as an adult as a penalty for a crime. The expression "save his soul from death" (Prov. 23:14) means "prevent an untimely death." The "deep pit" and "narrow well" (23:27) have sexual associations, but they focus primarily on the inescapable doom of those who fall into the harlot's clutches. The image here is of a sailor who falls in a drunken stupor into the sea or goes to sleep in a precarious crow's nest at the top of a ship's mast (23:34).

24:1-34 Avoiding Envy of Successful but Evil People
The gate was the central meeting place for the city (24:7; cf. Ruth 4:1). Members of society have a responsibility to be informed concerning those whose lives are in danger (Prov. 24:11-12). Ignorance is no excuse for one's neglect of vital issues. The "lamp" (24:20) of the wicked refers to their short-lived joy and prosperity. The words "join with the rebellious" (24:21) refer in this context to a desire to alter or oppose recognized civil authority. The proverbs speak with high regard of the truth, an "honest answer" (24:26).

25:1–29:27 THE PROVERBS OF SOLOMON, PART TWO
Overview: In this section more of Solomon's proverbs are presented. They have been "copied" by an editorial committee of Hezekiah's men. The word means "to remove" and indicates that these proverbs were extracted from other Solomonic materials and incorporated into Proverbs during the reign of King Hezekiah (715–686 B.C.).

25:1-28 Self-Control in Speech
The proverbs highlight the difficulty of understanding the ways and decisions of a ruler (25:3). The proverb warns against striving after personal honor (25:6). It is acceptable to receive honor, but not to seek it. These proverbs speak of the caution necessary in bringing charges against someone (25:9). The reference in 25:11 appears to be to gold and silver sculptures. Although the illustration is obscure, the message is clear. The "coolness of snow" (25:13) refers to cold ice water from the mountain snow. Kindness extended to an enemy will incite him to shame and bring reward to the benefactor (25:21-22).

26:1-28 The Power of Words for Good or Evil
Observations about fools comprise the contents of 26:1-12. A curse without a cause will never be effective (26:2). While it is unwise to argue with a fool (26:4), there may be times when a sound reproof is appropriate (26:5). The rest of Proverbs 26 contains observations about sluggards (26:13-16) and scoundrels (26:17-28).

27:1-27 Friendship and Foresight
Compare 27:1 with James 4:13-16. "Hidden love" (27:5) does not demonstrate its existence by ministering a needed reproof. Love often demands reproof of the object of that love. Wealth and what wealth can buy never really satisfy, but such possessions look attractive to those who have so little (27:7). The value of a close friend in contrast to a relative who lacks interest in one's concerns is highlighted in 27:10. A good pupil will enhance the reputation of a teacher against his critics (27:11). For "security" (27:13), see the note on 6:1-5. For "Death and Destruction" (27:20), see the note on 15:11. A man's response to praise serves as a test of his true character (27:21). This treatise on pastoral life provides a balance between physical labor and trusting in God's sufficiency (27:23-27).

28:1-28 The Security of Obedience to the Law
A wise ruler can bring stability during a time of national upheaval. The poor oppressing the poor is as absurd as rain washing away crops instead of watering them (28:3). One's attitude toward the law reflects one's standing in relationship with the wicked (28:4). "Exorbitant interest" (28:8) refers to charging excessive rates of interest, a practice forbidden by Israelite law (Lev. 25:36). For Proverbs 28:9, see Psalm 66:18. The words "conceals his sins" (Prov. 28:13) mean "refuses to admit his guilt" (Ps. 32:5). In this context, "always fears" (Prov. 28:14) refers to sin and its consequences. Proverbs 28:17 refers to the pursuit of a murderer by the blood avenger (Num. 35:19). Some people will violate justice for the smallest bribe (Prov. 28:21).

29:1-27 Wisdom and Justice
Scorners delight in stirring people to controversy, but the wise seek to minimize nonessential differences (29:8). Some of God's blessings are enjoyed by both the oppressor

and the poor (29:13; cf. Matt. 5:45). Without prophetic revelation ("vision") from God, people are unrestrained and will fall under divine judgment (Prov. 29:18). The thought may be that a pampered slave will begin to act like an heir, conducting himself as though he were free from a servant's obligations (29:21).

30:1-33 THE WORDS OF AGUR
The author of Proverbs 30 is said to be Agur (meaning "gatherer"), son of Jakeh. Early rabbis and church fathers identified Solomon as the "gatherer" of wisdom. There is no certainty as to the author's identification. Although he had a high view of God, Agur did not pretend to have mastered wisdom and theology (30:3). Man is not able to fully comprehend the ways of an infinite God (30:4). Compare 30:6 with Revelation 22:18. In Proverbs 30:7-9 Agur prays for honesty and for circumstances that will not cause that character to deviate. In 30:11-14 four types of wicked men are highlighted: the disrespectful, the hypocrite, the proud, and the greedy. The proverbs that count (see "three . . . four" in 30:15, 18, 21, 29) illustrate the process of the wise person going through life making lists of observations about wise and foolish events. The first number "three" makes the basic emphasis. The additional number on the list "four" heightens the emphasis and suggests that more examples could be added. As in all proverbs, the readers are being probed to add their own observations to the list. One of the curses for violating the covenant was that the body would be left unburied for the birds to feed on (30:17; cf. Deut. 28:26). The exhortation is to self-restraint in light of the certain consequences of foolish behavior (30:32-33).

31:1-9 THE WORDS OF LEMUEL
This section and perhaps the verses that follow (31:10-31) are attributed to King Lemuel. Some have identified Lemuel (his name meaning "belonging to God") with Solomon, but that is simply speculation. Like Samuel (cf. 1 Sam. 1:11), Lemuel was born in response to his mother's vows (Prov. 31:2). Proverbs 31:6-7 does not advocate intoxication, but it simply reflects the medicinal use of wine in ancient times, much like a tranquilizer would be prescribed today. The phrase "those who cannot speak" (31:8) is used figuratively for the defenseless, those unable to plead their own cause.

31:10-31 POEM TO AN EXCELLENT WIFE
These verses describe an ideal woman who is both a challenge and an encouragement for women to strive in their own lives for such qualities as are exemplified here. The verses form an acrostic or alphabetical poem, with each verse beginning with successive letters of the Hebrew alphabet. The term translated "excellent" (31:10) refers elsewhere to strength, ability, efficiency, wealth, and valor. She works late into the night (31:18). For "gate" (31:23), see Proverbs 24:7. Earlier, the book noted that a wise wife is from the Lord (19:14). Here, that gift from God is described in detail. The key to the character of this worthy woman is found in the fact that she "fears the LORD" (31:30; cf. 1:7). The book begins and ends by focusing on this motivating concept.

Ecclesiastes

BASIC FACTS

HISTORICAL SETTING

The historical setting for the book of Ecclesiastes was the reign of Solomon (970–931 B.C.), the grandest in Israel's history. At its highest point it was the envy of all the surrounding kingdoms. Israel was also at the high point of its blessings under God's great Abrahamic, Davidic, and Mosaic promises.

AUTHOR

Solomon, king of Israel, was the author. Some scholars have argued on the basis of the unusual language in the book that another unknown author wrote the book at a much later date.

DATE

The book of Ecclesiastes was written somewhere during the last period of Solomon's reign of forty years (970–931 B.C.). Some have argued for a date as late as 400 B.C. on the basis of the unusual language in the work. But the linguistic arguments for a late date have been undermined by discoveries of fourteenth-century B.C. Ugaritic tablets that show linguistic similarities with Ecclesiastes.

PURPOSE

The book of Ecclesiastes was designed to make people wise and happy. It makes them wise by showing the futility of building their hopes on the material and social goods of this world. It makes them happy by showing how, within the context of fearing God, they can fully enjoy the goods of this world.

GUIDING CONCEPTS

THE PERSPECTIVE OF THE WRITER

Even during the wonderful and prosperous time of Solomon's reign there was still injustice. Did not innocent children die of disease? Did not some masters abuse their servants? Did not some wrongs go unpunished? Even during Solomon's great reign, the effects of the curse of God in Eden were still in ugly force. The effect of the curse on man and nature was not reversed. People still sinned.

Because people continued to sin, people continued to die. And death is at the heart of mankind's feelings of despair and futility (see Rom. 8; 1 Cor. 15). The writer of Ecclesiastes wanted his readers to see how seriously they should take living in a fallen world. For those who have lived since Christ's coming, death, and resurrection, this realistic perspective should help them to see the importance and necessity of Christ's death. What some might call pessimism and fatalism in the book, the writer calls realism. It is a realism bred from looking deeply into both the darkness of a cursed creation and into the sunlight of God's sovereignty.

Ecclesiastes is part of a wisdom tradition in Israel that took a long hard look at all sides of reality, not just at the sugar-plum fantasy life that believers can all too easily create for themselves. The writer looked at a world where wrongs went unpunished, children died, and cheaters won. Then he asked how someone could live in it. The writer's answer may not be easy to accept, but it is true to reality.

KEY PHRASES
Several key phrases are repeated throughout the book and give the reader insight into its primary truths.

"Everything is meaningless"
However the Hebrew word translated "meaningless" is rendered, its main idea is futility. Life is not ultimately meaningless, but it is futile because what people often start out to do escapes them in the end. People hope for long life, happiness, and health. But they cannot count on any of those. By repeating that life is meaningless (see, for example, 1:2, 14; 2:1, 11, 15, 17, 19, 21, 23, 26) the writer stressed the reality of this age—death puts an end to all earthly projects, noble or otherwise. A companion phrase is "chasing after the wind" (1:14; 2:11, 17, 26; 4:4, etc.). Life is not worthless or meaningless; it is just unpredictable, often unfair, and always ends in death. The book's wisdom seeks to show how to find meaning and worth in such a bent world.

"Under the sun"
The phrase "under the sun" sets the interpretive context of the book (1:3, 9, 14; 2:11, 17-20, 22, etc.). It deals with issues under the sun, that is, on the earth—the place of human work, frustration, and hope.

The writer also reveals the thought processes in coming to his conclusions in phrases like "I learned" or "I came to realize" (1:17; 2:14; 5:18), "thought in my heart" (see 2:1, 15; 3:17-18; 9:1; see also 1:13, 17; 2:3; 7:25; 8:9, 16; 9:1). Because of the book's depressing nature, the reader might think that the writer presents merely human reflection, apart from God's revelation. But that is not true. The author reflects upon life in full view of God's teaching concerning the human condition due to Adam's sin and concerning God's commands for human obedience.

"Enjoy"
The writer asks the reader eat, drink, and enjoy the good of life (for example, 2:24; 3:12-13, 22; 5:18-19; 8:15; 9:7, 9). That is not a fatalistic leap into decadence. Rather, it comes as God-given insight into how people are to work and live in a

cursed and fallen world. Difficult? Yes. Frustrating? Yes. But people are to rejoice in the good that comes their way. Note 3:22 and 8:15 in this regard. God's eternal work abides and that is the focus of the believer's hope. For now, in this life, people are not to put their hope or faith in human works, but they can and should enjoy them.

"Fear God"

The reader might think that the writer's admonition to "fear God" in 12:13 is the final conclusion of the book. But actually it is the perspective of the entire work (cf. 3:14; 5:7; 7:18; 8:12-13). It pervades the book and produces the insight into how to keep going on and finding joy in such a disappointing world. It creates a balance for enjoying the good and appreciating the bad without falling into either decadence or pessimism. Reverence for God (3:13; 5:1-7) and submission (12:13-14) grow out of fearing God. The fear of God keeps believers from giving up when evil strikes or diving into excess when they strike it rich. Faith is not found just at the end of the book; it is the book's whole perspective.

BIBLE-WIDE CONCEPTS

THE CURSE AND DEATH

The book of Ecclesiastes uses several themes that can be found from Genesis through Revelation. God's curse upon creation because of Adam's sin has bent the world against God's original Sabbath goodness and against humanity's hope for justice and satisfaction. Things do not work out the way they should. Death ends all the earthly joys of home, family, and business, and it is the same for people who are both good and bad. This does not seem fair. And, in the short run, it is not. Ecclesiastes describes in graphic and realistic detail what life has been like since Adam sinned. It portrays the devastation of the consequences of sin that stretch from Genesis through Revelation. Death takes everyone.

GOD'S SOVEREIGNTY AND JUSTICE

Also, Ecclesiastes speaks to the great issue of taking life as God deals it out, trusting in his wisdom and sovereignty. It asks the reader to trust that God will ultimately right all wrongs and reward all good. God has not revealed to mortal men all of his reasons for the way things are. People are kept in the dark about some very important issues. Ecclesiastes probes how God's people feel about those patches of darkness. Will they reject God and live for today? Or will they find in the darkness the clue to God's sovereignty and their humility? Throughout Scripture believers are told to take what God in his goodness gives to them. God keeps his secrets throughout the Bible. It is the wise person who accepts his limited knowledge and fears God, whether in the time of Adam, Abraham, Solomon, Isaiah, Christ, or the present.

NEEDS MET BY ECCLESIASTES

Ecclesiastes was written to people who needed to know that God's plans for his children included a full range of the world's experiences. Even under the great blessings of Solomon's early reign life was still hard. It was peppered with injustice; it was inexorably sliding downward into death. God did not innoculate his people against either life's pain and injustice or its pleasure and joy. Above all, God did not prevent his people from running into the inevitable wall of death—the dismantling of what they had sought to build and hang onto in this life. The book met the needs of God's people to be able both to accept the ultimate futility of life and, within that perspective, to have the presence of mind to please God and fully enjoy the good things of life. Ecclesiastes responds to difficult questions asked by people in Solomon's day and by people of today as well.

- Since all people are going to die anyway, what difference does it make in how they live?
- Why be good if the good and bad go down in death together?
- Why be good if it is no guarantee of being rich and successful in this life?
- How can people put their lives in the broader context of eternity rather than just living as if there were no tomorrow?
- How can people honestly face up to death and still have a positive outlook on life?
- How can people hold God's redemptive promises together while living in such a bent world?

One of the mysteries of the Christian faith is the unjust murder of God's Son on the cross. The perfect Son experienced suffering and pain along with joy and pleasure on this earth before he was taken up into heaven. The Christian is called to follow that pattern of suffering *now* and exaltation to heaven *later*. But being a child of God and yet suffering the wrongs of this world can create a great challenge to the Christian faith. But Ecclesiastes reveals a bigger picture: an understanding of life that sees beyond present moments of pain or pleasure. It points toward ultimate physical death and the subsequent evaluation of people by God. It reminds believers that even though their sins are forgiven and they have a place in the new heavens and earth, they must still cope with the daily problems of this age. They must make joyful and responsible choices that come, not from fleshly abandon, but from the fear of God.

OUTLINE OF ECCLESIASTES

A. PROPOSITION: LIFE IS FULL OF UNFULFILLED ASPIRATIONS (1:1-18)
   1. Statement: Life Is Futile (1:1-2)
   2. Summary Support: Nature Goes on, but People Come and Go (1:3-18)
B. ADVANTAGE SOUGHT (2:1–7:29)
   1. Attempts at Having Control over Life (2:1-26)
   2. Attempts at Understanding the Whole Plan of Life (3:1-22)
   3. Attempts to Find Advantages in Life (4:1–7:29)
C. WHERE ADVANTAGE CAN BE FOUND AND UNDERSTOOD (8:1–12:14)
   1. The Benefits of Wisdom and Fear of God (8:1–9:1)
   2. The Impact of Death (9:2-12)
   3. The Benefits of Wisdom (9:13–11:6)
   4. The Impact of Judgment (11:7–12:8)
   5. Conclusion: Fear the Lord (12:9-14)

E C C L E S I A S T E S   N O T E S *

1:1-18 PROPOSITION: LIFE IS FULL OF UNFULFILLED ASPIRATIONS

1:1-2 Statement: Life Is Futile

The word "Teacher" (1:1) is translated from the Hebrew term *Qohelet* and refers to one who convenes and speaks at an assembly. In the context of this book, the assembly is not a general congregation but a gathering of the wise (Jer. 18:18). The phrase "son of David, king in Jerusalem" (1:1) supports the Jewish tradition that Solomon wrote the book. The theme of futility is developed in 1:3-11 and continues throughout the book (1:2). It accords with Paul's words in Romans 8:20-22 that all creation is subject to futility because of sin (Gen. 3:17-18).

1:3-18 Summary Support: Nature Goes On, but People Come and Go

The word "gain" (1:3) is used ten times in Ecclesiastes, but nowhere else in the Bible. It is a commercial term meaning "surplus" on a balance sheet. The author asks, "Is there any guarantee of positive benefit or reward for a person's work?" The words "under the sun" are a figure of speech that means "upon the earth" where man dwells under the sun. The endless cycles of nature illustrate the monotonous futility of much of life on earth (1:4-11). The expression "chasing after the wind" speaks of futile activity (1:14-15). Solomon was convinced that the works of people on earth were permeated with futility and paradoxes that cannot be resolved. Solomon's great wisdom simply enabled him to see more clearly the frustrating futility of life (1:18).

2:1–7:29 ADVANTAGE SOUGHT

2:1-26 Attempts at Having Control over Life

2:1-11 EXPERIENCE OF PLEASURE
Solomon's unlimited resources enabled him to conduct a great experiment to search for meaning in life (2:1-11). He sought fulfillment in indulgence (2:1-3), achievements (2:4-6), possessions (2:7-8), and fame (2:9), but none of these brought meaning or satisfaction.

2:12-23 KNOWLEDGE OF INEVITABLE DEATH
Solomon was convinced that anyone trying his experiences would come up with the same conclusion (2:12). Death is the "same fate" that befalls both the wise and the fool (2:14). Solomon despaired over leaving the results of his labor to his heir (2:18-20) and over the lack of gratifying or lasting reward for his work.

2:24-26 CONCLUSION: ENJOY GOD'S GIFTS
Having contemplated the utter futility of life, Solomon presented his divinely inspired solution: Rather than chafe under frustration and futility, enjoy to the fullest the life God has given (2:24). This advice is repeated six times (3:12-13; 3:22; 5:18-19; 8:15; 9:7-9). Solomon's wise counsel was quite different from the Epicurean philosophy "Let us eat, drink, and be merry, for tomorrow we die." Solomon's solution to life's futility was balanced in the book's conclusion by the warning that one's life must be regulated by an awareness of coming judgment (12:14). Those who know God, the Creator, should enjoy life most (2:25). There is no real enjoyment of life apart from him.

3:1-22 Attempts at Understanding the Whole Plan of Life

3:1-8 THE OBSERVABLE PLAN
The words of 3:1 suggest a "divinely ordained" time, not just an appropriate time (Eph. 1:11). God has entrusted governmental authority with responsibility to carry out capital punishment in the case of murder (3:3; Gen. 9:6). The word "hate" (Eccles. 3:8) does not always suggest hostility or malice, for it can be an expression speaking of an appropriate attitude toward evil (Luke 14:26).

3:9-22 THE HIDDEN PLAN
There is beauty, yet mystery, to God's design (Eccles. 3:11). God gives people an eternal perspective ("set eternity in the hearts of men") to see beyond the futility of this life "under the sun." Yet he has not revealed all of life's mysteries. The words "nothing better" (3:12) emphasize by understatement.

* The substance of some of the notes for Ecclesiastes was also published in the *Ryrie Study Bible*.

The intended sense is "the best thing." As in 3:1, the reader is reminded that God ordained the continual cycles of life (3:15). Both human beings and animals face a common fate: death and the return to dust (3:19-22). But humans must also face judgment. Ecclesiastes 3:21, which should read as an affirmation rather than a question, reveals a distinction between human beings and animals (cf. 12:14).

4:1–7:29 Attempts to Find Advantages in Life

4:1-16 FIVE AREAS OF OBSERVATION

Oppression makes death look more attractive than life (4:1-3). Rest and work must be kept in proper balance (4:5-6). The futility of excessive work without need or purpose is highlighted in 4:8. There is strength in numbers (4:12). The instability and uncertainty of political support is emphasized in 4:14-16. Fickle crowds soon forget their favored rulers and replace them with others.

5:1–6:12 THE FEAR OF GOD AND RICHES

The words "Guard your steps" (5:1) mean "be careful." The "sacrifice of fools" refers to unworthy worship, mere religious externalism that exhibits no reverence for God. As preoccupation with one's work makes for many dreams, so excessive words are characteristic of the prayer of a fool (5:3). The "messenger" (5:6) refers to the Levitical priest who would receive what was vowed. The "much dreaming" (5:7) seems to reflect a preoccupation with one's work (cf. 5:3).

Often there is corruption at every level, with oppressors being subject to the same treatment by those higher up (5:8). For the fourth time Solomon presented his answer to the frustration and futility of life (5:18). A better translation of 5:18 is "Furthermore, as for every man to whom God has given riches and wealth and has empowered to eat from them and to receive his reward and rejoice in his labor—this is the gift of God." This verse indicates that a capacity to enjoy one's possessions is itself one of God's gifts to man (see 6:2). A long life without satisfaction and enjoyment is futile (6:6). The "same place" refers to the grave. Man is neither able to control his earthly destiny (6:10) nor able to know

his future (6:12). The context relates this truth to the futility of pursuing riches.

7:1-29 DEATH OBSERVED

Solomon offered a series of proverbial sayings concerning wisdom and folly (7:1-14). Visiting a home stricken by tragedy serves as a reminder of the brevity of life and the need for wisdom (7:2). Sorrow may have a beneficial effect, tempering mirth by life's realities (7:3). Wisdom is undoubtedly superior to wealth, but Solomon acknowledged that wealth with wisdom is better than wisdom alone (7:11). God is sovereign over all the circumstances of a person's life—both prosperity and adversity (7:13-14; cf. Eph. 1:11). In 7:15–8:15 Solomon reflected on the advantages and limitations of wisdom.

The polarity in Ecclesiastes, which reproduces the true character of this world, is reflected in 7:16. Exaggerated, superficial righteousness is to no avail. Solomon counsels that those who truly fear God should hold fast to wisdom and righteousness (7:18). Even Solomon's wisdom (1 Kings 3:12, 16-28) was insufficient to enable him to comprehend all the mysteries of life (7:23). A wise and upright man or woman is a rare find indeed (7:28-29).

8:1–12:14 WHERE ADVANTAGE CAN BE FOUND AND UNDERSTOOD

8:1–9:1 The Benefits of Wisdom and Fear of God

No one understands a situation or problem like a wise person (8:1). His wisdom "illuminates his mind" and is reflected on his countenance as he deals wisely with others. The "oath before God" (8:2) is the oath of allegiance made in God's name to a ruler at the time of coronation (2 Kings 11:17). Wisdom and authority have limits, even for a king like Solomon (Eccles. 8:6-8). Solomon observed that life did not always operate by the cause and effect, reward-for-good and punishment-for-bad principle of retribution (8:10-14). For the fifth time, Solomon commended the enjoyment of life as the only means of coping with life's perplexities (8:15). Although believers long to understand the intricate details of God's plan, even their most diligent efforts will not remove the mystery (8:17). Whether life's circumstances are happy ("love") or unhappy ("hatred"), there is consolation in knowing that God is in control (i.e., everything is "in God's hand," 9:1).

9:2-12 The Impact of Death

9:2-6 DEATH TREATS EVERYONE THE SAME
Death is no respecter of persons (9:2). One fate (death) awaits both the wicked and the righteous. Solomon conceded that the living have an advantage over the dead (9:4), for the dead have no further opportunities to secure reward for their life's labors (9:4-6).

9:7-12 ENJOY LIFE
Solomon once again (the sixth time) commended the enjoyment of life (9:7-10). White garments were customarily worn at a festival (9:8). Solomon was saying, "Don't wait for tomorrow's festival to find relief from today's frustrations. Enjoy life now; live each day as a celebration." Solomon added a new dimension to his advice—taking hold of a present opportunity (9:10). Life is not just a party; it is an opportunity to serve God and mankind. The fact that such opportunities are limited to life on earth makes it imperative that no day be wasted. There is no guarantee of reward for life's endeavors (9:11-12). A person's success and life span are not guaranteed by his ability or health.

9:13–11:6 The Benefits of Wisdom

9:13–10:4 WISDOM IMPRESSES OTHER PEOPLE
In 9:13–11:6 Solomon presented another series of proverbs on wisdom and folly (cf. 7:1-14). A confident and calm composure may dispel a king's anger (10:4).

10:5–11:6 BOLDNESS IN LIVING IN THE PRESENT
Successful living starts with the practical application of God's wisdom (10:10). Lacking discipline, the fool wastes his energies and is unable to accomplish even the most basic tasks (10:15). The attitude of the undisciplined princes mentioned in 10:16 is expressed in 10:19. In this context, "a bird of the air" (10:20) is a poetic expression referring to a disclosure by some unknown source.

The custom of shipping grain ("bread") from a seaport town is reflected in 11:1-2. Some active response to life's opportunities is necessary, even when success is not guaranteed (11:2). Many of life's circumstances are outside the sphere of man's influence or control (11:3). Uncertainty in life sometimes makes people overly cautious with the result that nothing gets done (11:4). The theme of God's mysterious ways is repeated once again (11:5; cf. 3:11; 7:14; 8:17).

11:7–12:8 The Impact of Judgment

11:7-10 ENJOY LIFE
God's gift of life ("light") should be fully enjoyed, especially in view of the fact that it will eventually terminate with death ("darkness"; 11:7-8). Once again, Solomon exhorted the reader to enjoy life (11:9-10). There is no suggestion of embracing sinful pleasures in his words, "follow the ways of your heart." The last line of 11:9 would curb any tendency toward excess.

12:1-8 LIVE CORRECTLY
Solomon exhorted his readers to remember God before they were overtaken by old age and poor health (12:1-7). Old age is described as a gathering storm (12:2), as an old house (12:3), and as an old man (12:5). The "keepers of the house" (12:3) are the arms and hands; "strong men stoop" means the legs become weak; "grinders" are the teeth; "those looking through the windows grow dim" equals failing eyesight. The "sound of the grinding fades" (12:4) signifies hearing loss; "rise up at the sound of the birds" describes one's inability to sleep; "songs grow faint" again describes hearing loss. Being "afraid of heights" (12:5) is difficulty in descending stairs; "dangers in the streets" describes the fear of stumbling when walking; "the almond tree blossoms" is white hair; "the grasshopper drags himself along" means crippled and bent limbs impair mobility. The phrase "the silver cord is severed" (12:6) means loss of life support; "golden bowl is broken" is the crash of death; "pitcher is shattered" is the loss of fragile life; "wheel broken" means that the apparatus for sustaining life is ruined.

The body returns to dust, but the spirit returns to God for judgment (12:7; cf. John 5:28-29). The original thesis is repeated (12:8; cf. 1:2).

12:9-14 Conclusion: Fear the Lord

Solomon affirmed that his writings were upright and true (12:10). The words of Ecclesiastes have a divine source (12:11). They come from "one Shepherd" (God). The parallel relationship between the words "fear God" and "keep his commandments" reveals that the fear of the Lord is observed and proved by obeying God's word (12:13). The words "whole duty of man" imply that wisdom is what the lives of human beings are really all about. The reminder regarding final accountability before God serves to curb any improper application of the counsel to enjoy life (12:14).

Song of Solomon

BASIC FACTS

HISTORICAL SETTING
This book gives the dialogue of a king, his wife, and her friends in the king's harem. The man and woman described their love for each other, while the friends praised the woman's beauty and favored place before the king. The reader hears about the beauty of love from several directions. The particular setting was the harem of King Solomon.

AUTHOR
The book itself names Solomon as the chief figure throughout (1:1, 5; 3:7, 9, 11; 8:11-12). Although Solomon's direct authorship has been debated, the text of the book affirms Solomon or someone in his immediate court as the writer. Some scholars believe that the song was written long after Solomon's days but attributed to his style as a writer of wisdom literature. They allege that certain words in the song come from later Persian and Greek times, making the possible composition or final editing of the work around the time of the Babylonian exile. In this case, the reference to Solomon in 1:1 is translated, "The Song of Songs Concerning Solomon." Although the final editing of the book may have been done around the time of the exile (around 587 B.C.), the book's wisdom and its description of the unity and luxury of the kingdom fit well with Solomon's reign and his own abilities as an author.

DATE
Solomonic authorship places the date during his reign (970–930 B.C.). It may have gone through a final editing process around the time of Judah's exile (around 587 B.C.).

PURPOSE
As in many of the psalms, the reader of the Song of Solomon is not directly addressed. He simply told what two lovers (Solomon and his bride) said and is thus drawn into their relationship. But what kind of application of this relationship are readers to make to their own lives? The purpose of the book was twofold. First, through its splendid poetry, God affirms the goodness of sexual love. Second, the

repeated passages of warning (2:7; 3:5; 8:4) command the listener to set love within its proper context of marriage. Like the Bible's other books that express the wisdom and poetry of Israel, the Song of Solomon instructs and inspires concerning the beauties and proper contexts of physical love.

GUIDING CONCEPTS

SOME APPROACHES TO INTERPRETING THE BOOK

Throughout history people have interpreted this book from various and quite different perspectives. Some interpreters view the book as a straightforward love song or collection of several love songs that speak of the beauties of human sexual love within the context of marriage. Other interpreters either exclude or diminish the erotic aspects in order to find a more symbolic purpose for the book. In this view, the man and woman are symbols of God and his people. The love of the man is compared to the love of God for Israel or to the love of Christ for his church.

Other interpreters have viewed the book as a collection of love or wedding songs, a dramatic script or a reflection of pagan fertility rites made over into acceptable Jewish theology. But the literal thrust of praising the love between a man and a woman, in this case, king Solomon and one of his wives, is the simplest and most straightforward way to interpret the book.

The symbolic approach to the book is deeply rooted in early Jewish and then Christian interpretations and essentially grows out of a discomfort with viewing a book of the Bible as so completely dedicated to the joys of the human sexual relationship. But the book in and of itself gives no clue that it is to be taken in a symbolic way. It presents itself as a literal poem extolling marital love. Thus, the book must first be seen as primarily instructive on the level of human sexual fulfillment. Another dimension to appreciate may then be explored when the book is placed into its Bible-wide context. Then the king and his love for his bride may secondarily take on a symbolic representation of God and his love for his people.

THE SHEPHERD

Some interpreters conclude that the figures of the shepherd and of Solomon are two different characters. Thus, Solomon becomes the villain who is trying to take the lady into his harem, away from her true love, the shepherd. Others view the shepherd and Solomon to be the same figure. Solomon was in casual dress when he visited his northern property, part of which was the vineyard of the Shulammite (6:13). That she first saw Solomon in shepherd's attire accounts for the kingly and shepherdly descriptions of him throughout the song.

DIALOGUE

One powerful feature of this song is the way the man and woman describe their love for each other in the second person: "I liken you, my darling" (1:9). That allows the reader to feel that he is being let into a very intimate relationship, much like reading someone else's love letter. Why this style? First, because it drives the sensualness and beauty of physical love deep into the reader's consciousness. Second, as the word of God, it provides a definition of love by which people can judge their own love relationships and it leads them to consider the vitality and sanctity of those relationships. Another powerful feature is the repeated command, issued to the other members of Solomon's harem, to keep love within its proper context (2:7; 3:5; 8:4).

BIBLE-WIDE CONCEPTS

HUMAN LOVE

Ever since Adam first saw Eve, human love at its best has been the driving force for populating the earth and bringing man and woman into a fulfilled relationship of marriage in light of God's original creation order. Although Scripture also describes numerous negative examples of human lust at its worst, the Song of Solomon takes its place in reinforcing what God really intended from the beginning. That this song concerns Solomon's wedding is especially significant. Here, the son of David, anointed over Israel as king according to the Davidic covenant, was about to take his bride. To have seen the king so passionately and appropriately in love with his bride would have been an encouragement to his people that he was strong, virile, and caring. But that leads the reader on to the divine dimension involved in the anointed king of Israel.

DIVINE LOVE

To see the greater Son of David, Jesus the anointed King, behind the figure of Solomon is inescapable. Whereas the Jewish interpretation viewed the Song of Solomon as an expression of God's love for Israel, the Christian interpretation put it within the frame of Christ's love for the church. But the symbolism is best established on the basis of the Davidic covenant, which always looked forward to the fullness of God's rule through his anointed King. Israel's king was always a visible representative for God in his love and sovereignty over his people. On human and divine levels, the Song of Solomon shows the beauties of physical and spiritual love—of a man for his wife and of God for his people.

NEEDS MET BY THE SONG OF SOLOMON

Throughout Scripture, poetry is part of God's word because it can draw a person's emotions, as well as his mind, into the subject at hand. With the Song of Solomon, the subject is erotic love. The point is to sanctify it and put it in its biblical context. In this case it is the context of the divinely anointed king of Israel. The following are some questions that were undoubtedly asked in Solomon's day. These same questions are often asked by people today as well.

• Are strong erotic feelings appropriate for godly people?
• What does God say about physical love?

God has created humanity with virtually insatiable sexual drives. But, as with the rest of the passions instilled at the original creation, sexual passion has been grossly perverted and distorted by Satan's schemes and the acts of sinful people. The Song of Solomon breaks into the sexual madness that so often surrounds believers today with a graphic description of God's blessing on erotic love. But that description also clearly sets the confines of such love within marriage. The Song of Solomon gives the person desiring to marry a beautiful goal to await. It gives the married person encouragement to seek similar mutual sexual fulfillment. It gives the immoral person a glimpse of the beauty God offers in place of degrading sexual counterfeits. It gives all believers a physical symbol of God's own spiritual love for them in Christ.

OUTLINE OF THE SONG OF SOLOMON

A. TITLE (1:1)

B. IN THE KING'S CHAMBERS: THE BRIDE DESCRIBES HERSELF AND HOW SHE FEELS ABOUT HER FIANCÉ (1:2–2:7)

C. THE KING INVITES HIS BRIDE FOR A SPRINGTIME TRIP; THE BRIDE DREAMS OF LOSING THE KING (2:8–3:5)

D. SOLOMON DESCRIBES HIS BRIDE (3:6–5:1)

E. THE BRIDE DESCRIBES HER HUSBAND (5:2–6:3)

F. THE KING DESCRIBES HIS WIFE (6:4–7:9)

G. THE DESIRES OF THE WOMAN (7:10–8:4)

H. THE POWER OF LOVE AND THE REWARDS OF PURITY (8:5-14)

SONG OF SOLOMON NOTES

1:1 TITLE

The words "song of songs" are a translation of the Hebrew superlative that could be rendered "most excellent of songs." Of the 1,005 songs Solomon wrote (1 Kings 4:32), this one was regarded as the very best.

1:2–2:7 IN THE KING'S CHAMBERS: THE BRIDE DESCRIBES HERSELF AND HOW SHE FEELS ABOUT HER FIANCÉ

The Shulammite spoke of Solomon (1:1-4). The word "Shulammite" means "a woman of Shulem" (or possibly "Shunem"). The Hebrew word for "love" (1:2) here refers to sexual love. The "maidens" (1:3) were the young ladies of the court, the "daughters of Jerusalem" (1:5). The Hebrew word for "love" in 1:3 refers to a love growing out of the will, similar to the Greek *agapé*. The word may sometimes include sexual love, but it is not limited to that. The daughters of Jerusalem spoke of Solomon (1:4).

The Shulammite spoke about herself (1:5-6) to Solomon (1:7). Her complexion had been darkened ("dark," 1:5) from working in the hot sun (1:6). The "tents of Kedar"

were made of black goat's hair. The family background of the Shulammite is revealed in the fact that she had two older brothers who forced her to work in their vineyard. As a result, she was unable to care for her own vineyard, a figurative reference to her own physical being. Solomon may have been on a hunting trip when he first encountered the Shulammite, who evidently mistook him for a shepherd (1:7). This verse is used by some interpreters in support of the "shepherd hypothesis," which posits that the cast of the book consists of three persons: (1) the shepherd; (2) the lady who loves the shepherd; and (3) Solomon, who tries to win her away from the shepherd.

The daughters of Jerusalem spoke to the Shulammite (1:8), and then Solomon spoke to her (1:9-10). The word "darling" (translated from the Hebrew, "to shepherd") refers to a beloved companion (1:9, 15; 2:2, 10, 13). The "mare" is an image of strength, form, and beauty (1:9; cf. 1 Kings 4:26). The daughters of Jerusalem spoke to the Shulammite (1:11), and she spoke about Solomon (1:12-14). The "henna blossoms" (1:14) refer to a fragrant yellow and white flower that grew at Engedi, an oasis on the west shore of the Dead Sea. Solomon spoke to the Shulammite (1:15), and she responded to his love (1:16-17).

She reflected on her appearance, expressing her own lack of self-esteem (2:1). The "rose" (lit., "crocus") was a humble meadow flower. Solomon talked to the Shulammite, elevating her sense of self-worth (2:2). She replied to Solomon telling of her contentment and delight in his love (2:3-6), and she also expressed her desire for sexual intimacies. The Hebrew word translated "embrace" is used in a sexual sense and may be rendered "fondle" (2:6; cf. Prov. 5:20).

The Shulammite addressed the young virgins of the royal court concerning the importance of remaining chaste prior to marriage (Song of Sol. 2:7). The words "awaken love" can better be rendered "arouse the sexual expression of love," while "until she pleases" can better be translated "until it pleases," that is, "until it is with the right person within the bounds of marriage." This warning against premarital sexual arousal appears three times (2:7; 3:5; 8:4).

2:8–3:5 THE KING INVITES HIS BRIDE FOR A SPRINGTIME TRIP; THE BRIDE DREAMS OF LOSING THE KING

The Shulammite talked about Solomon, recalling his marriage proposal (2:8-13). Then he spoke to her (2:14). The word "dove" (2:14) is a term of endearment. The Shulammite, in mentioning their relationship, resolved to prevent any distraction ("foxes") from spoiling it (2:15). She spoke again of her relationship with Solomon (2:16-17). The "rugged hills" or "hills of Bether" (2:17) can be translated from the Hebrew as "mountains of cleavage."

The Shulammite dreamed of seeking and then finding Solomon (3:1-5). She sensed a critical need for Solomon's companionship in the early days of their marriage. The warning against arousing sexual love prematurely was set against the background of the difficulties of marital adjustment (cf. 2:7).

3:6–5:1 SOLOMON DESCRIBES HIS BRIDE

The daughters of Jerusalem described the bridal procession to Jerusalem (3:6-11). Solomon's "traveling couch" or "sedan

chair" was a chair set on poles and enclosed by a small canopy. It would have been carried by the king's servants. Solomon's mother was Bathsheba (1 Kings 1:11).

Solomon described the beauty of his bride (Song of Sol. 4:1-5) in imaginative and highly poetic imagery. The Shulammite (cf. 2:17) interrupted the praise of Solomon anticipating the consummation of her marriage (4:6). In the meantime, she would spend time in Solomon's royal garden, where imported myrrh and frankincense grow. These fragrant trees were not native to any part of Israel. Solomon's marriage proposal and praise for his bride is given in 4:7–5:1. Solomon invited the Shulammite to leave her homeland, the mountains of Lebanon, and go with him to Jerusalem. The word "sister" (4:9) is used here as a term of endearment. The "garden" imagery is used to refer to the Shulammite's physical body, which she had saved exclusively ("locked") for her future husband, Solomon. The "spring enclosed" and "sealed fountain" (4:12) are poetic figures for virginity (cf. Prov. 5:15-18). The Shulammite invited Solomon to consummate their marriage (Song of Sol. 4:16). The imagery of eating and drinking was used as a euphemism for the sexual delights of marriage. After the marriage had been consummated (5:1), the lovers were instructed to enjoy their love fully.

5:2–6:3 THE BRIDE DESCRIBES HER HUSBAND

The Shulammite dreamed of refusing Solomon (5:2-7). After rejecting his late-night advances, she had sought help from the daughters of Jerusalem in finding him. After they ask her for a description of Solomon, she responded by describing her beloved in highly figurative poetic language (5:10-16). The daughters of Jerusalem then asked her where to look for Solomon (6:1). The Shulammite directed them to look in the king's garden (6:2-3).

6:4–7:9 THE KING DESCRIBES HIS WIFE

Solomon described the Shulammite as he and his bride were reunited (6:4-9). Tirzah was the capital of the northern kingdom until Omri built a new capital at Samaria

(1 Kings 14:17). Solomon eventually had seven hundred wives and three hundred concubines (1 Kings 11:3), but evidently he viewed the Shulammite as unique, possibly the only wife he truly loved. The daughters of Jerusalem praised the Shulammite's beauty (6:10). Verse 6:10 may reflect the praise of the Shulammite's beauty by the daughters of Jerusalem. Because of the response in 6:13, verses 6:11-12 may reflect the Shulammite's words rather than her lover's. Royalty came upon the Shulammite suddenly, before she had a chance to realize what was happening (6:12). The daughters asked to gaze upon the Shulammite's beauty (6:13). She questioned, "Why would you [the daughters of Jerusalem] want to gaze on the Shulammite as on the dance of Mahanaim [a festive dance]?" When Solomon spoke to the Shulammite, extolling her beauty (7:1-9), she responded to his expressions of love (7:9-10).

7:10–8:4 THE DESIRES OF THE WOMAN
The Shulammite asked Solomon to take her on a kind of marriage enrichment retreat in the country (7:10-13). In ancient times "mandrakes" (7:13), small apple-like herbs, were thought to stimulate sexual desire and aid in conception.

The Shulammite expressed her desire for a closer relationship with Solomon (8:1-4).

Once again (cf. 2:7; 3:5), the request for sexual intimacies was followed by a warning to avoid the premature arousal of sexual love.

8:5-14 THE POWER OF LOVE AND THE REWARDS OF PURITY
The villagers raised the question of 8:5 as they saw Solomon and the Shulammite approaching. Solomon recalled his courtship and spoke words of love to her (8:5-7). Genuine love can only be given, never bought. The last line of 8:7 is best translated "he would be utterly despised." The Shulammite spoke regarding the proper care of her young, immature sister (8:8). Her brothers responded, recognizing two possible situations (8:9). If she was virtuous ("a wall"), her chastity would be honored; but if she was yielding ("a door"), measures would be taken to protect her from the sexual advances of young men. The Shulammite reflected on her own virtue and submission to Solomon in marriage (8:10-12). She spoke of her physical body as, "my own vineyard" (8:12; cf. 1:6), which she had surrendered to Solomon in marriage. The "two hundred" shekels were for her brothers, who had a part in encouraging her own chastity (8:12). When Solomon requested that she sing him a song (8:13), she responded in song, inviting him to enjoy her as she had promised (8:14; cf. 7:12).

Isaiah

BASIC FACTS

HISTORICAL SETTING
Throughout Isaiah's life Assyria presented a great threat to God's people. In 853 B.C. Assyria came into direct conflict with Ahab of Israel. In 745 B.C. Menahem of Israel paid tribute money to Tiglath Pileser III. Two kings later, Hoshea rebelled against Assyria. That brought about the destruction and deportation of the northern kingdom of Israel (722 B.C.). Isaiah prophesied before and after the downfall of the northern kingdom of Israel and successfully warned the southern kingdom, Judah, to avoid the same fate by returning to God. Under Hezekiah, the nation repented and was saved from destruction by the Assyrians (701 B.C.). Although the threat of Assyria was diminished, the greater threat of the rising nation of Babylonia loomed in the future. Although Isaiah predicted the Babylonian captivity, he also proclaimed the future restoration of the nation to the glory of God.

The book of Isaiah is centered around three key historical events. The first is the coalition between Syria and Ephraim in the days of Ahaz (Isa. 7–12; cf. 2 Kings 16:5-9). The second is the fall of the northern kingdom of Samaria (722 B.C.; Isa. 28:1ff.). The third is the invasion of Judea by Sennacherib in 701 B.C. (Isa. 36–39).

AUTHOR
The book presents itself as the words of Isaiah the prophet, who ministered from around 740 to 700 B.C. Many scholars believe the book is divided between two authors—Isaiah, who wrote Isaiah 1–39 and another prophet who lived some two hundred years later (Isa. 40–66). To be sure, Isaiah 40–66 are quite different in content and mood from Isaiah 1–39. But that difference is due to Isaiah's looking beyond the eighth century B.C. to the time of the Babylonian captivity, and beyond, to the time of the new heavens and earth.

DATE
Isaiah's call came in the year of Uzziah's death (740 B.C.). Isaiah noted three kings under whom he ministered: Jotham of Judah (750–732 B.C.; who was co-regent with

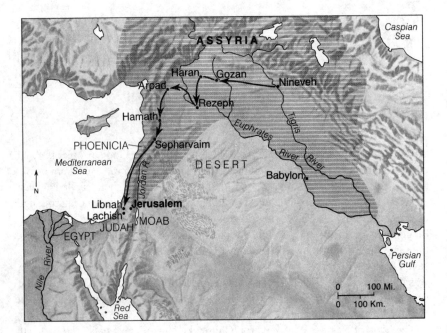

Uzziah), Ahaz of Israel (735–716 B.C.), and Hezekiah of Judah (716–687 B.C.).
The composition of Isaiah may be placed sometime after 701 B.C. and before the
prophet's death.

PURPOSE
Isaiah related prophecies predicting inescapable judgment for the world and highlighted the comfort offered to the righteous remnant. The anointed One of God
would be the leader of God's restored world. The catalysts for God's actions of
judgment and restoration were his holiness (Isa. 6) and his loving-kindness (Isa.
63:7). The message was that God's victory would come through a time of humiliation for his people and for his Servant. Exaltation would come after humiliation.
That message was designed to encourage repentance by looking to past and future
judgments and to the future blessings for service in times of suffering.

GEOGRAPHY AND ITS IMPORTANCE

The geographical scope of Isaiah moves from the land of Israel, to the nations of the
world, to the destruction and re-creation of the entire earth. The central focus moves
from the immediate threat of Assyria to the future conquests of Babylonia and
Persia. Israel is attacked, taken captive to foreign lands, and restored to her
homeland. These geographical cycles of captivity and restoration, and destruction
and creation ultimately reflect the great spiritual cycles of sin and forgiveness,
offense and reconciliation.

GUIDING CONCEPTS

THE STRUCTURE OF ISAIAH
Dates
Several dates are given in the book of Isaiah that mark off its structure and highlight its message. The book's first verse mentions several kings and also functions
as a summary title for the entire prophecy. The dates of those kings began in
792 B.C. (Uzziah) and ended in 687 B.C. (Hezekiah). Isaiah 1–5 is devoted to
Israel's condemnation and reflect no specific date. Isaiah 6 is dated around
740 B.C., the year Uzziah died. Isaiah 7–12 is dated in the days of Ahaz, around
735 B.C. (7:1). Isaiah 13–66 mentions the specific dates of the death of Ahaz
(14:28; 715 B.C.), the arrival of the commander under Sargon III at Ashdod (20:1;
711 B.C.), the fourteenth year of Hezekiah's reign (36:1; 701 B.C.), and the year
Sennacherib died (37:38; 681 B.C.). Isaiah 13–66 falls within the general time
period of King Hezekiah's reign (716–687 B.C.).

Judgment
The primary foci of the book are judgment (Isa. 1–39) and comfort (Isa. 40–66).
Isaiah 1–39 punctuates each specific judgment section with incredible announcements of God's worldwide judgment and the restoration of his people. See the
accompanying chart, *Judgment and Restoration.*

First, judgment was announced upon Israel (Isa. 1–12) for her broken covenant (1:1-31) and her pride (Isa. 2–6). But Israel would be exalted through chastisement because God would be with her (Isa. 7–12). The focus was on the faithless alliance of Ahaz with Assyria. Second, judgment was announced upon the nations (Isa. 13–27). Specific nations were named, but the section ends with God reigning supreme over all (27:13). Third, judgment was again announced upon Israel for her trust in foreign alliances with Egypt (Isa. 28–35) and Hezekiah's foolish boasting to the Babylonians (Isa. 36–39). In Isaiah 1–39 judgment fell upon the nations for their mistreatment of Israel and upon Israel for her inappropriate trust in them, especially in Assyria, Egypt, and Babylonia. The three centers of Israel's misplaced trust were the three centers of her most cruel captivities. Isaiah 36–39 forms a transition from Assyrian to Babylonian concerns.

Comfort

Isaiah 40–66 is divided into three sections each ending with similar phrases (48:22; 57:21; 66:24). The first section (40:1–48:22) emphasizes ultimate deliverance from Babylonia through the incomparable greatness of God. The second section (49:1–57:21) describes the servant of God, Israel, in her worldwide calling. Her leadership is rebuked (Isa. 56) and invitations to salvation are given (Isa. 51). The third section (58:1–66:24) provides the conditions for seeing the future glory of God. Israel is divided into the faithful and faithless. The faithful remnant cries out for deliverance (63:7–64:12), receives an answer from God (65:1-25), and learns about those who will be excluded from the new creation (66:1-24).

BIBLE-WIDE CONCEPTS

THE EXODUS AND ISAIAH
Exodus themes and the exiles

Isaiah frequently linked the Babylonian and Egyptian captivities together. The Egyptian bondage had both preserved and oppressed Israel. The same was true of Israel's captivity in Babylon. God had released Israel from Egypt in a mighty display of his love and power. The same applied to Israel's release from Babylon. Israel was released from Egypt to claim her Promised Land. Israel was released from Babylon to regather and reclaim her inheritance of land and redemptive promises. The tension between bondage and release would be repeated again as Christ released believers

---

JUDGMENT AND RESTORATION

	Specific Judgment	*Worldwide Judgment and Restoration*
On Israel	Isaiah 2–10	Isaiah 11–12
On the Nations	Isaiah 13–23	Isaiah 24–27
On Israel's Alliance with Egypt	Isaiah 28–33	Isaiah 34–35
On Israel's Boasting to Babylon	Isaiah 36–39	

---

from the bondage of personal sin, and it will occur for the final time as the new heavens and earth are released into the new creation. Jeremiah saw a future time when Israel would not refer to the exodus but to the restoration from the captivity as the most recent and great act of God's salvation (Jer. 16:14-15).

The exodus in Isaiah

The "exodus and release" theme pervades Isaiah's prophecy (10:24-27; 11:16; 19:24-25; 27:12-13; 30:1-3; 31:1; 36:6; 43:3; 45:14; 48:20-21; 52:4-6; 66:2, 22-23). For a nation entering captivity, the question of God's power over the gods of Assyria and Babylonia was a burning issue (21:9; 48:20-21), but God had already shown himself to be the victor over the gods of Egypt at the exodus.

The exodus and creation

Creation and redemption are closely intertwined in Scripture. Isaiah described Israel's past and future redemption in view of God being her Creator. Read carefully the following passages: Isaiah 43:1-7, 15-21; 51:12-16; 63:7-14 (cf. also 42:5-7; 44:21-28; 48:13; 45:18). Neither creation nor exodus were simply one-time events. They were continuous models of God's ability to bring freedom out of bondage and order out of chaos. Paul described Christianity in terms of the creation (2 Cor. 5:16-17), the exodus Passover (1 Cor. 5:7-8), and the wilderness wanderings (1 Cor. 10:1-4).

As Creator, God can judge evil by returning the earth to its pre-creation formlessness and void (Isa. 24:1-6; cf. Gen. 6–8). He is also always present and powerful to re-create both his people and a new universe (Isa. 51:16). That creative power became the basis for the redemption of his people and the commission of them to a worldwide mission of witness (45:18-25). The remnant was preserved through the destruction and recreation process, and the world was exhorted to join in that preservation and redemption.

THE HOPE FOR A DIVINE KING

Isaiah's prophecy deepened and broadened God's promise that a Davidic king would rule forever. The promises to David looked toward a Davidic Ruler who, contrary to worldly standards, would come to a throne of international proportions through suffering and humiliation. Isaiah called this Ruler the Branch, Servant, and Shoot (4:2; 7:14; 8:8, 10; 9:6-7; 11:1-5; 42:1-4; 52:13–53:12). That Davidic branch found its fulfillment in Jesus, the King of Israel. His humiliation brought the forgiveness of sins to all believers. His exaltation assured their eternal future in his presence. The combination of first the Servant's humiliation and second his exaltation also became the pattern for his followers. Jesus taught that a time of humble service and suffering comes before the time of the servant's exaltation and reward (Matt. 10:24-39; 24:9-13, 30-31; Mark 8:31-38; John 15:18-25).

THE FULFILLMENT OF ABRAHAMIC BLESSINGS

Isaiah described the fulfillment of God's promises to Abraham. The Abrahamic themes of *land, seed,* and *blessing* are found throughout the book (29:22; 41:8-11; 51:1-3; 63:16). All these promises look back to the original and perfect creation and ahead to the perfection of the new heavens and earth.

Israel's possession, or nonpossession, of the land promised to Abraham became a barometer for measuring their obedience. When discipline was needed, God used the hostility of and even captivity by other nations to bring about Israel's repentance, a punishment about which Moses and Solomon, among others, had repeatedly warned (Deut. 32:1-47; 1 Kings 8:33-34, 46-51; 9:6-9). Israel's disobedience resulted in God allowing hostile nations to succeed in their attacks and exile his people from the Promised Land. But God had also promised to protect Abraham and his descendants, blessing those who blessed them and cursing those who cursed them (Gen. 12:3). This promise of Israel's preservation pervades Isaiah (34:8; 35:4), while the enemies of Israel are cursed in judgment. In fact, the only way a curse could be brought upon God's people was for them to bring it upon themselves by their own rebellion against God.

God's judgment upon Israel's enemies is described in great detail (cf., for example, Isa. 12) and finds its completion in the gruesome judgments of the book of Revelation. Hostility against God's righteous people found its origin in Satan in Genesis 3. This hostility will find its end in Satan's judgment at the end of the age when Satan comes out in full force against God's people (Rev. 12:1-17). But God will defeat all of Satan's hostile nations, and then the promises to Abraham, which were always with a view to "all peoples" (Gen. 12:3), will be fulfilled when the Promised Land of God's blessing is fully realized in the new heavens and earth (Isa. 65:17, 25; 66:1-24; Rev. 21:1–22:6). Then the themes of creation and redemption will perfectly merge. The Promised Land will be global and perfect, populated by the redeemed who will be perfect in soul and in body.

NEEDS MET BY ISAIAH

The original readers of the book of Isaiah lived in an Israel that had recently lost its northern half to Assyrian captivity (722 B.C.) and whose southern half, including the holy city of Jerusalem, was escaping a similar fate only by God's grace and the rare obedience of a few of Judah's kings. Through Isaiah, God told his people of all the painful discipline and beautiful salvation he had in store. He exposed how his people tended to forget their call to be holy and blame God when being disciplined for their own sins. Because of their present and impending judgment, God showed his people how to maintain hope for salvation in the middle of painful judgment. Even though righteous people like Ezekiel and Daniel would have to undergo war and captivity, God's people were not to lose heart, become bitter, or give up seeking to fear God.

The book of Isaiah is of massive scope and proportions and therefore covers a multitude of topics and needs. At its heart is an announcement of judgment, a call to repentance, and a message of hope after suffering a time of humiliation. These central themes give answers to questions that God's people were asking in Isaiah's day.

- Why is the nation of Israel suffering military and economic trouble?
- Why is God angry at Israel—what did they do?
- Why is God allowing wicked foreign nations to attack Israel and get away with it?
- If God is punishing the people of Israel for their sins, is there any hope for the future?

- How can any good come out of Israel's personal and national humiliation?
- What can be done to escape God's terrible judgment?
- What do the people of Israel need to do to repent and turn from their sins?

Readers may find the long descriptions of Israel's and other nations' judgments repetitive and without any apparent Christian application. But the very length of the book of Isaiah is a large part of its point. Why did God tell in such detail that his people were forgetful and sinful, that their enemies would be destroyed, and that a glorious future lay ahead? God went to great lengths to remind his people of these things because they were so forgetful. He described at great length the ultimate defeat of Israel's enemies because his people tended to fear the forces of world evil and wondered if they would win out in the end. Because believers in Isaiah's day (like today) tended to forget what a bright future was in store for them, and especially how that future hope was to encourage and direct them into present joy and obedience, God described the future blessings in great detail. The long book of Isaiah meets three continuing needs of all believers: to be reminded of (1) God's past acts of redemption for them, (2) his present abilities to protect them from evil, and (3) his future plans for their complete blessing and his fully revealed glory.

OUTLINE OF ISAIAH

A. INESCAPABLE JUDGMENT AND HOPE FOR ISRAEL (1:1–12:6)
    1. God's Lawsuit against Judah (1:1-31)
    2. God's Exaltation over the Proud (2:1–6:13)
    3. Restoration through Chastisement: Judgment on Ahaz (7:1–12:6)

B. GLOBAL JUDGMENT: MOTIVATION FOR REPENTANCE (13:1–27:13)
    1. Babylon (13:1–14:27)
    2. Nations Surrounding Israel (14:28–17:14)
    3. Ethiopia and Egypt (18:1–20:6)
    4. Four Symbolic Titles of Judgment (21:1–22:25)
    5. Tyre (23:1–18)
    6. Global Response after Global Judgment (24:1–27:13)

C. BOOK OF WOES: FOREIGN ALLIANCES CONTINUED (28:1–35:10)
    1. Samaria and Jerusalem: Fall and Comfort (28:1-29)
    2. Ariel: Fall and Comfort (29:1-24)
    3. Results of Egyptian Alliance: Part One (30:1-33)
    4. Results of Egyptian Alliance: Part Two (31:1–32:30)
    5. Deliverance and Glory of Jerusalem (33:1-24)
    6. Finale of Judgment (34:1–35:10)

D. TWO SIGNS OF DELIVERANCE (36:1–39:8)
    1. Assyrian Threats: The Faith of Hezekiah (36:1–37:38)
    2. Babylonian Overtones (38:1–39:8)

E. CYCLES OF COMFORT AFTER CAPTIVITY (40:1–66:24)
    1. God Contrasted with Idols (40:1–48:22)
    2. The Servant's Humiliation and Exaltation (49:1–57:21)
    3. Israel: The Faithful and the Faithless (58:1–66:24)

ISAIAH NOTES

1:1–12:6 INESCAPABLE JUDGMENT AND HOPE FOR ISRAEL

1:1-31 God's Lawsuit against Judah

Overview: Isaiah 1 is an introductory message containing the themes of the entire book: the sinfulness of Israel, the tender appeals of God, certain judgment, and promised blessings of restoration. All the promises for Judah and Jerusalem can be found in summary form in the first chapter of Isaiah.

1:1 AUTHOR, DATE, ADDRESSEES
Isaiah prophesied during the reigns of four different kings, and he addressed the problems and people of those reigns. Uzziah (791–739 B.C.), also known as Azariah, was a good king. Jotham (750–731 B.C.) was also a good king. Ahaz (743–715 B.C.) was wicked and idolatrous. Hezekiah (728–686 B.C.) was a godly king and a religious reformer.

1:2-31 THE COMPLAINT IS DEVELOPED
Isaiah is first presented in his role as a prose-cuting attorney in behalf of God, indicting the sinful nation for breaking the law of the Mosaic covenant (1:2-3). The "heavens" and "earth" were called upon as "witnesses" against the covenant breakers (cf. Deut. 4:26; 30:19). Five terms are used for sin in 1:4 to describe the sinful condition of the people of Judah. "Sinful" means "to miss the mark"; "guilt" is "to bend or twist aside"; "evil-doers" are those who "do harm and injury"; "corruption" means "to ruin, to destroy"; and "spurned" means "to be estranged or to revolt." The title "the Holy One of Israel," which is almost unique to Isaiah, appears twenty-four times in the book.

The sickness described here is a metaphor for sin (1:5-6). God had disciplined the nation, but the people had not repented and been healed. During Isaiah's lifetime, the land of Judah was devastated by foreign armies that God used to discipline his people (1:7-9). The expression "Daughter of Zion" refers to the city of Jerusalem, which was being personified as a young woman (1:8).

In 1:11-15, God was not rejecting the Levitical blood sacrifices. He only rejected the religious hypocrisy that usually went along with them. Many brought sacrifices to God, but their worship was merely external and they lacked sincere love for God (cf. 1 Sam. 15:22; Jer. 7:21-23; Hos. 6:6; Amos 5:21-24). The "New Moon" (1:13) was a minor religious festival celebrating the appearance of a new moon (cf. 1 Chron. 23:31). Isaiah was not suggesting salvation by works (1:16). He simply emphasized the Lord's promise to cleanse those who come to him by faith and through the appointed way of sacrifice (Isa. 1:18; cf. Lev. 4:20).

The orphan and the widow were regarded as the defenseless in Israelite society (1:17; cf. Deut. 10:18; 24:19). There was a lament over the moral decline of God's people (Isa. 1:21-23). The "wine diluted with water" (1:22) is probably a reference to wheat beer. The "therefore" (1:24) refers to all that has preceded, principally the description of the nation's sinful condition. After disciplinary judgment (1:25) comes restoration (1:26). Isaiah carries the reader from history to eschatology, predicting kingdom blessing for the redeemed (1:27) and future judgment for the wicked (1:28-31).

2:1–6:13 God's Exaltation over the Proud

Overview: Isaiah 2:1 presents a clear break from Isaiah 1. Isaiah 2:1–6:13 forms the second subsection and shows the inevitable process leading up to God's international sovereignty (cf. the last phrase in 2:11 and 2:17). The link between Isaiah 1 and Isaiah 2–6 is God's exaltation over the proud (1:2, 4, 20, 31 and, for example, 2:11-17). The heart of 2:1–6:13 is God's specific criticism against his people (3:13–4:6). They were crushing the poor (3:13-15). The results of God's judgment upon his people would be final purification (4:2-6). Isaiah 2:1–4:6 presents a unified thought concerning what will happen in "that day" (2:2, 20; 3:7, 18; 4:2). Esteemed people will be humbled, and God's glory will be exalted.

Isaiah 5 presents the imagery of a vine-yard, Israel, that has worthless produce. That judgment and purification are compatible is confirmed in the following vision of God in the temple, purifying Isaiah's lips (6:1-13) in preparation for him to take his prophetic message to Israel. Isaiah's lips were burned unto purification (6:1-7), and the nation itself would endure a burning toward the same end (6:8-13). For God's people, judgment was not for destruction but for purification.

2:1–5:30 GOD'S INTERNATIONAL PROMINENCE IN THE LAST DAYS

2:1-22 A call to international repentance. These verses are nearly identical with Micah 4:1-5 and describe the blessings of the future Messianic, or kingdom, era. The "last days" (2:2) is a reference to the Messianic era when Jesus will return to rule his kingdom (cf. Hos. 3:5). Jerusalem will serve as the center for government, and both Gentiles and Jews will go there to worship Jesus the Messiah. The return to peace will involve a reversal of the prophecy of Joel 3:10. The "house of Jacob" (Isa. 2:5) refers to the nation Israel, which descended from Jacob. The "day in store" (2:12) is a reference to the day of the Lord, the major theme of Joel and Zephaniah. For "Tarshish" (2:16), see Jonah 1:3.

3:1-12 Judgment elaborated. Woe was pronounced for rebellion against God's presence. Judgments on Judah and Jerusalem included famine, drought (3:1), the removal of national leadership (3:4), and poverty (3:6).

3:13–4:6 God's contention. War would so greatly destroy Israel's male population that women would resort to polygamy or husband-sharing to avoid the reproach of childlessness (4:1). The glories of the Messianic kingdom were anticipated in 4:2-6. The "Branch" (4:2; lit., "sprout") is a reference to the Messiah (cf. Jer. 23:5), who would grow like a sprout from the fallen "tree" of David (6:13; cf. Luke 1:32-33). The "cloud of smoke by day" (4:5) and "flaming fire by night" recalled God's deliverance and protection at the time of the exodus.

5:1-30 Vineyard imagery. Woes were pronounced on worthless deeds. The nation of Israel was portrayed under the figure of a vineyard (5:7; cf. Jer. 12:10; Ps. 80:8-13). The destruction of the vineyard illustrated the judgment to come upon Israel for the nation's disobedience to the Mosaic covenant. Standing in judgment over his people, the Lord pronounced seven exclamatory woes. God condemned selfish greed (5:8-10), dissipation (5:11-17), skepticism (5:18-19), perverted standards (5:20),

proud self-sufficiency (5:21), alcoholic excess (5:22), and the perversion of justice (5:23). The "banner" (5:26) is a military banner that served as a gathering point for the nations (that is, Assyria and Babylonia).

6:1-13 JUDGMENT AND PRESERVATION AUTHENTICATE GOD'S MESSAGE

King Uzziah's death in 739 B.C. marked the end of a great period of expansion and prosperity for Judah. "Seraphs" (6:2), literally, "burning ones," are angelic creatures. Here their ministry focused on the worship of God. God was described as thrice holy, a superlative meaning that his holiness is beyond human expression. The theme of God's holiness pervaded Isaiah's prophetic ministry. Isaiah's lips were cleansed in preparation for the commencement of his prophetic ministry. Isaiah's ministry was divinely intended to harden the hearts of the people (6:9-10). This heartbreaking assignment rested on God's decision to judge the nation. Jesus quoted this text in Matthew 13:14-15, and Paul used it in Acts 28:26-27. The judgment would continue until Judah's removal from the land by the exile. The nation of Israel in exile was portrayed as a fallen and burned tree. But after seventy years in captivity, a "tenth" of the people would return. And there would be life in the roots of the stump from which the Messiah ("the holy seed") would "sprout" forth.

7:1–12:6 Restoration through Chastisement: Judgment on Ahaz

Overview: Isaiah 7–12 shows how God would bring about restoration through his chastisement of Israel. He used a series of signs that referred first to the contemporary nation and, second, to times beyond his own. Isaiah in 8:18 clearly referred to himself and his children as signs (see chart on following page).

Isaiah 7–12 was spoken in the context of the coalition by Ahaz against Judah. It stresses that a remnant of the nation will return (7:3). Immanuel ("God with us") is the sign of judgment and of salvation in "that day" (7:18, 20-21, 23; 10:5-34). That day of God is composed of at least two elements: (1) judgment on Israel on the basis of the Mosaic

covenant; (2) restoration of Israel around
the throne of David by judging Israel's
enemies and by restoring Israel's kings on
the basis of the Davidic covenant.

7:1-25 THE SIGN OF THE INFANT IMMANUEL

During the reign of Ahaz (743–715 B.C.)
Judah was attacked by Pekah (king of Israel)
and Rezin (king of Damascus) for refusing
to stand against Assyria's aggression under
Tiglath Pileser III (745–727 B.C.). The name
"Shear-Jashub" (7:3) means "a remnant shall
return" (that is, from captivity). Judgment on
the northern kingdom ("Ephraim") was to
come within sixty-five years. Actually, the
capital, Samaria, fell within eleven years in
722 B.C. The Lord commanded Ahaz to ask
for a supernatural sign that God would
accomplish the deliverance promised (7:11).
Ahaz had already made up his mind to
appeal to Assyria for help rather than trusting God.

The sign of the "virgin" (7:14) has been
variously interpreted. Some interpreters
suggest that the prophecy was completely
fulfilled in Isaiah's day. Others recognize a
fulfillment in the virgin-born Son of Mary
(Matt. 1:23). A third position recognizes
some kind of fulfillment in the time of Isaiah
with a final culmination in the virgin birth
of Jesus. Isaiah 8 suggests a fulfillment in
Isaiah's day through his wife (8:3, 8, 10, 18).
This was probably Isaiah's second wife, and
hence a virgin. Matthew recognized that the
prophecy had its most complete realization

in the birth of Christ. The name "Immanuel"
means "God with us" (8:8, 10).

The "curds and honey" (7:15) reflect a
diet of natural foods, the only foods available after the agricultural economy had been
destroyed (cf. 7:21-23). Before the virgin-
born child reached the age of moral perception, judgment would come upon the land
of Pekah and Rezin (7:16). That took place
during the campaigns of Tiglath Pileser III in
733 and 732 B.C., respectively. The "king of
Assyria" (7:17) refers to Tiglath Pileser III.
The devastation of Judah (7:20-23) took
place during Sennacherib's 701 B.C. campaign (cf. Isa. 36 –37).

8:1-4 THE SIGN OF THE TABLET AND SON

"Maher-Shalal-Hash-Baz," the name of
Isaiah's second son, means "swift is the
booty, speedy is the prey." This son was a
symbol of upcoming judgment by the troops
of Babylonia.

8:5–10:4 IMMINENT JUDGMENT IN IMMANUEL'S LAND

The "waters of Shiloah" (8:6) may be
identified with the "pool of Siloah" (Neh.
3:15) and was used figuratively here to
refer to God's help. While Assyria would
do its best to destory Judah, the nation
would be spared because of the promise of
God's presence (Isa. 8:10; for "Immanuel,"
see 7:14). Darkness and gloom characterized Galilee in Isaiah's day because of the
Assyrian crisis (9:1-2; cf. 2 Kings 15:29).
But this would be dispelled by the radiant
"light" of the Messiah who would one day

ISAIAH'S SIGNS AND THEIR SIGNIFICANCE

Sign	First reference	Second reference
Shear-Jashub "A remnant shall return" (7:3)	Return from the Babylonian exile	The regathering of Israel in the end times.
Immanuel "God with us" (7:14)	God's presence to judge and save in the time of Ahaz	Jesus at his first and second comings
Maher-Shalal-Hash-Baz "Swift is the booty; speedy is the prey" (8:3)	Fall of Israel to Babylon	Fall of the world at the Second Coming
Isaiah "God is salvation"	Salvation of the remnant through Babylonian captivity	The final salvation of the remnant (11:4, 11, 16; 12:2)

shine in Galilee (cf. quote in Matt. 4:15-16). The battle of Midian (Isa. 9:4) was fought by Gideon (Judg. 7–8). Four names were used to describe the coming Immanuel (Isa. 9:4). Each reflects the office of deity and humanity. "Wonderful Counselor" means an extraordinary (godlike) advisor; "Mighty God" means a heroic God; "Everlasting Father" means an everlasting overseer; and "Prince of Peace" means a captain who secures spiritual peace and tranquillity. His government will continue because it rests on the unconditional covenant God made with David (2 Sam. 7:12-16; cf. Luke 1:32-33). The section of Isaiah 9:8–10:4 reflects the doom about to befall the northern kingdom for its failure to respond to God's discipline. The key phrase "Yet for all this, his anger is not turned away, his hand is still upraised" (9:12, 17, 21; 10:4) was repeated four times.

10:5–12:6 RESTORATION IN THE LIGHT OF ASSYRIA'S DESTRUCTION
10:5-19 The time for Assyria's downfall. Assyria was simply the instrument that God used to judge his people (cf. 10:15). Assyria boasted of the cities north of Judah that it had conquered.

10:20–12:6 Further implications for Judah's restoration. The "remnant" referred to the small portion of Israel that would survive the captivity (6:13). They would return to the Lord (10:21) and to the land of Israel (10:22). Isaiah 10:28-32 graphically described the Assyrian advances through Judah toward Jerusalem in preparation for the 701 B.C. siege (cf. 36:1-2). The "shoot" (11:1) that would spring from Jesse (David's father) was the Messianic King (4:2; 6:13; 7:14; 8:8, 10; 9:6-7; 11:1-5; 42:1-4; 52:13–53:12; Jer. 23:5). The three pairs of gifts bestowed by the Spirit are intellectual, administrative, and spiritual. Isaiah proclaimed the harmony and peace that will characterize the kingdom as all creation is liberated from the curse resulting from man's fall (Isa. 11:6-9; cf. Gen. 3; Rom. 8:19-22; Rev. 22:3). The "second" (Isa. 11:11) time refers to a regathering of the Jewish people following the tribulation (Matt. 24:15-20, 31). This song of praise (Isa. 12:1) will be sung on that day when the Jews are regathered from among the nations as a believing people. "Isaiah" (meaning "God is

salvation") as a sign (8:18) is fulfilled when these events occur.

13:1–27:13 GLOBAL JUDGMENT: MOTIVATION FOR REPENTANCE
Overview: The section of 13:1–23:18, like 2:1, begins with a new heading (13:1). It is a further elaboration of Isaiah 1–12, especially of having God present with his people to judge and rule. The day of God's judgment and rule was elaborated (8:9-10; 13:6, 9-13). In Isaiah 13–23 Isaiah spoke prophecies of judgment on several foreign nations. The point was this: Since the other nations were held accountable for violations of social justice based on the law of conscience (Rom. 2:14), Israel certainly could not expect to escape God's judgment. The greater the light of revelation, the greater the responsibility. The basic topical structure of this section is laid out thus: Babylon (13:1–14:27); Israel's neighbors (14:28–17:14); Ethiopia and Egypt (18:1–20:6); four symbols of judgment (21:1–22:25); and Tyre (23:1-18). The section ends with the international response after God's international judgment (24:1–27:13). The God of Israel alone reigns supreme.

13:1–14:27 Babylon
13:1-22 BABYLON'S DESTRUCTION DESCRIBED
The first oracle concerned Babylon, which served as God's instrument of judgment against Judah in 701 and 586 B.C. In 13:4 the "army" refers to the Medo-Persian troops of Cyrus, who conquered Babylon in 539 B.C. The "day of the Lord" (13:6) is a term that can be used historically for God's judgment on a people or place, including Israel. The term is also used for that eschatological period when God will deal out wrath (the tribulation) and blessing (the Messianic kingdom). Sometimes when a historical day of the Lord was being described, the writer included some references to future end-time judgment and blessing. The events described in 13:10-13 go beyond the historical judgment on Babylon in 539 B.C. and suggest the end-time judgments of the tribulation. Strabo, the first century geographer, wrote of Babylon, "A great desert is the great city" (13:19-22).

14:1-27 ISRAEL'S TAUNT AGAINST BABYLON

When Israel returned to her land, enjoying peace and blessing (14:1-3), a taunt song would be sung against the tyrant, "the king of Babylon." The deceased tyrant's reception into Sheol, the place of the dead, was described (14:9-11). Instead of being honored as other great kings, this tyrant would receive only dishonor. The words "fallen from heaven" (14:12) figuratively describe the tyrant's loss of political prestige. The words "star of the dawn" can be literally translated "shining one." The Vulgate rendered it by the Latin term "lucifer," meaning "light-bringing." Eventually the Latin word "lucifer" came to be identified as a name for Satan. There is very little evidence to commend this view. Certainly the judgments described in 14:16-21 have not happened to Satan.

Like many proud kings of the ancient Near East, the "king of Babylon" sought divine position and privilege (14:13-15). But such would not be his. Instead, he would be subject to degradation and humiliation (14:16-21). The oracle against Assyria (14:24-27) was fulfilled in Assyria's destruction recorded in 37:21-38.

14:28–17:14
Nations Surrounding Israel

14:28-32 ORACLE AGAINST PHILISTIA

The prophetic oracle against Philistia was dated in the year of King Ahaz's death (715 B.C.). They sought to resist Assyria, but Isaiah predicted their demise (14:30).

15:1–16:14 ORACLE AGAINST MOAB

Moab's judgment, probably by Assyria, was described as swift and complete. Having arrived in Edom, the Moabite refugees appealed to Judah for political asylum. Moab's request was denied because of the nation's pride (16:6).

17:1-14 ORACLE AGAINST DAMASCUS

This oracle was not only against Damascus; it was also spoken against the northern kingdom of Israel. Damascus was the capital of Aram, which Tiglath Pileser III captured for Assyria in 732 B.C. "Asherah poles" (17:8) were wooden pillars representing the Canaanite fertility goddess.

18:1–20:6 Ethiopia and Egypt

18:1-7 ORACLE AGAINST ETHIOPIA

The phrase "whirring wings" describes the buzzing insects of "Cush," the land of Ethiopia, located south of Egypt. Ethiopia ruled Egypt from 715 to 663 B.C. and pursued an anti-Assyrian foreign policy like Judah's.

19:1–20:6 ORACLE AGAINST EGYPT

Egypt, involved in an anti-Assyrian conspiracy with Judah (cf. 2 Kings 18:21, 24), was conquered by Esarhaddon in 669 B.C. His son Ashurbanipal gained control of all of Egypt in 663 B.C. Egypt was regarded as a haven from famine in time of drought because its water came from the Nile, with its source in the mountain highlands of Africa (19:5-10). For the "waters" of Egypt to dry up would be regarded as a great natural calamity. The "year" (20:1) was 712 B.C., when Tartan, Sargon's general, captured Ashdod, which was situated east of Jerusalem on Israel's coastal plain. The word "stripped" (20:2) means without one's outer garment. Isaiah's scanty attire suggested the situation of a prisoner or a person in exile, which was the destiny of Egypt and Ethiopia.

21:1–22:25
Four Symbolic Titles of Judgment

21:1-10 ORACLE AGAINST BABYLON: WILDERNESS OF THE SEA

In cuneiform inscriptions, south Babylonia is called the "land of the sea" because of its proximity to the Persian Gulf. "Elam" and "Media" are the Persian territories to the north and east of Babylon. See Daniel 5 for the details of this feast. The city of Babylon fell to Cyrus in 539 B.C.

21:11-12 ORACLE AGAINST EDOM: SILENCE

"Dumah" (21:11) means "silence" or "stillness," a wordplay on a name for Edom that foretells its destruction. "Seir" (21:11) is a central mountain in the land of Edom that also served as a representative name for Edom.

21:13-17 ORACLE AGAINST ARABIA

Cuneiform inscriptions reveal that Arabian rulers paid tribute to Assyrian kings Tiglath Pileser III and Sargon II.

22:1-25 ORACLE AGAINST JERUSALEM: VALLEY OF VISION

The "Valley of Vision" referred to Jerusalem, the object of many prophetic visions, which is set in the valley between the western hill and the Mount of Olives. The oracle related to the 701 B.C. siege of Jerusalem by Sennacherib. The work of Hezekiah in securing Jerusalem's water supply in anticipation of the Assyrian siege was reflected in 22:11 (cf. 2 Chron. 32:3-4, 30). Shebna (22:15) was a powerful pro-Egyptian politician in the reign of Hezekiah (cf. 2 Kings 18:18). Eliakim became Shebna's replacement (cf. 2 Kings 18:18). The "key" (Isa. 22:22) served as symbol of authority that a steward had over a house (cf. Matt. 16:19).

23:1-18 Oracle against Tyre

Tyre was noted as one of the finest port cities of Phoenicia. For "Tarshish," see Jonah 1:3. The "Chaldeans" (23:13) was used synonymously with "Babylonians." A dynasty of Chaldeans ruled the land of Babylonia. For "seventy" years (23:15), from Nebuchadnezzar's conquest until the fall of Babylon, Tyre lapsed into poverty and insignificance.

24:1–27:13 Global Response after Global Judgment

Overview: The section of 24:1–27:13 forms the finale to Isaiah 13–23, as Isaiah 12 was to Isaiah 7–11. It is a great hymn to God's holiness. This is the essence of God's dealing with all of his enemies. Isaiah 27 revived the vineyard imagery (cf. Isa. 5), only this time the vineyard was under the eternal protection of God.

24:1-23 DESTRUCTION ENDS
IN GOD'S REIGN
The coming tribulation judgment will affect the whole earth and all classes of people. Sin is the basis of God's judgment. The "everlasting covenant" (24:5) must refer to the moral law of God revealed in his word and written in man's heart (cf. Rom. 2:14-15). This period of world devastation (Isa. 24:17-22) is also known as the "time of trouble for Jacob" (Jer. 30:7; "Jacob's distress," NASB). The sun and moon will darken in preparation for the full revelation of the Messiah's glorious kingdom (cf. Rev. 21:23).

25:1-12 SONG OF DELIVERANCE:
A GREAT BANQUET
The "city" (25:2) may be a reference to Babylon, which was representative of unbelieving opposition to God. The kingdom age (25:6) was likened to a great banquet (cf. Matt. 22:1-14). The "mountain" (25:6)

is Zion, that is, Jerusalem. Isaiah 25:8 is quoted in 1 Corinthians 15:54 and Revelation 21:4. There will be no physical death during the kingdom age.

26:1-21 ISRAEL BROUGHT BACK
FROM THE DEAD
The song of praise in Isaiah 26 will be sung by the redeemed as they enjoy the blessings of the Messianic kingdom. The dead tyrants of 26:13 could no longer trouble or threaten Israel. The comments on their destruction in 26:14 do not deny the doctrine of the universal resurrection (cf. 26:19; Rev. 20:11-15).

27:1-13 SONG OF THE PROTECTED
VINEYARD
"Leviathan" (27:1; cf. Job 3:8) is a figurative reference to the enemies or opposition of God. For "Asherah" (Isa. 27:9), see the comment on 17:8. The "Wadi of Egypt" (27:12) refers to the Wadi el-Arish, the main geographical barrier between Israel and Egypt.

28:1–35:10 BOOK OF WOES: FOREIGN ALLIANCES CONTINUED

Overview: The section of 28:1–35:10 contains five woes on Israel and the nations (28:1; 29:1, 15; 30:1; 31:1). God used Assyria (28:11 and 33:19 bracket this section) to judge Israel for her alliances with Egypt. The key verse is 35:4. Isaiah 28–33 contains prophecies to Samaria, and Isaiah 34–35 is the international finale to God's judgment.

28:1-29 Samaria and Jerusalem: Fall and Comfort

Ephraim was the chief tribe of the northern kingdom of Israel. As the people mocked Isaiah's prophecy as nonsense (28:9-10), so they would get their fill of the nonsensical language of the Assyrians (28:11). Paul used 28:11 in 1 Corinthians 14:21 to demonstrate the purpose of tongues as a sign of God's judgment on unbelieving Jews. Instead of trusting in shaking alliances (28:15), God's people were to rely on the firm Cornerstone, the Messiah (cf. Ps. 118:22; Rom. 9:33; 10:11; 1 Pet. 2:6). For the historical background of "Mount Perazim," see 2 Samuel 5:17-25. God works in many different ways to accomplish his purposes (Isa. 28:23-29).

29:1-24 Ariel: Fall and Comfort

Ariel (lit., "[altar] hearth of God") referred
to Jerusalem, the place of sacrifice. The
attack of Sennacherib in 701 B.C. was
prophesied. This condemnation of Israel's
empty formalism (29:13-14) is quoted by
Jesus in Mark 7:6-7. The secret negotiations with Egypt (cf. Isa. 31:1; 36:9) were
no secret to God. Paul used the illustration
of the potter in a lesson on the sovereignty
of God (Rom. 9:20-21). Isaiah portrayed
the blessings of the Messianic kingdom
(Isa. 29:17-24).

30:1-33 Results of Egyptian Alliance: Part One

30:1-17 DESTRUCTION FOR
RELIANCE ON EGYPT
This section reflects the existence of a pro-
Egyptian party in Hezekiah's court. God
warned that true deliverance was not to be
found in Egypt but in the security of his own
person. Zoan (better known today as Tanis)
is located in the northeast region of the Nile
Delta. Hanes (known today as Ahnas) is
located west of the Nile about fifty-five
miles south of Memphis.

30:18-33 COMFORT
To encourage the people, Isaiah described
the glories of the Messianic kingdom. The
destruction of Assyria (30:31) served to
foreshadow the eschatological day of the
Lord. Topheth (30:33; lit., "place of burning"), was where human sacrifices were
carried out in the Hinnom Valley located
southwest of Jerusalem (2 Kings 23:10).

31:1–32:30
Results of Egyptian Alliance: Part Two

31:1-9 DESTRUCTION
Isaiah contrasted the futility of human
resources with the security of divine protection. See 37:36 for the destruction of the
Assyrian army. The "stronghold" (31:9)
referred to the protective fortress of Assyria
(cf. 33:16), perhaps Nineveh.

32:1-8 COMFORT
Isaiah described the righteous rule of the
Messianic king (7:14; 9:6; 11:1).

32:9-20 APPENDIX: WOMEN OF JERUSALEM
The "complacent women" were the frivolous
women of Jerusalem who would soon
experience Assyria's wrath. In 32:15-20

Isaiah promised the blessings of the Spirit
during the righteous kingdom of the Messiah.

33:1-24 Deliverance and Glory of Jerusalem

The "destroyer," Sennacherib, king of
Assyria, was warned of coming divine
judgment (37:36-38). Isaiah described the
response of the sinners in Jerusalem to God's
judgment on Assyria (33:13-16). The glories
of the Messianic kingdom were previewed
(33:17-24). The Assyrian official who
counted out the captives, weighed out the
tribute, and considered the city towers in
preparation for siege was referred to in 33:18.

34:1–35:10 Finale of Judgment

34:1-17 THE CERTAINTY OF APOCALYPTIC
DESTRUCTION
The end-time judgments of the day of the
Lord were described in detail. "Edom"
(34:5), representative of the world powers
that have opposed Israel, would be utterly
destroyed. "Bozrah" (34:6) was the capital
of Edom. The "night creatures" (34:14; lit.,
"Lilith") were noted in ancient mythology as
night demons that frequented desolate
places. The imagery was used here to illustrate the total desolation of the heathen lands.
The "scroll of the Lord" (34:16) referred to
Isaiah's prophecies. All would be fulfilled.

35:1-10 THE JOY OF THE RANSOMED
The judgments of the tribulation (Isa. 34)
prepared the way for the blessings of the
Messianic kingdom. These prophecies will
be fulfilled at the Messiah's coming as God
lifts the curse from his creation.

36:1–39:8 TWO SIGNS OF DELIVERANCE

Overview: This section is arranged topically
rather than chronologically. Isaiah 36 and 37
showed the fulfillment of the prophecies
concerning the coming Assyrian attack on
Jerusalem. Isaiah 38 and 39 revealed Hezekiah's dealings with Babylon and prepared
the way for the chapters of consolation for
the exiles in the Babylonian captivity. Chronologically, the events were arranged as follows: (1) Hezekiah's illness, healing, and God's
promise of deliverance from Assyria (38:1-6);
(2) the visit by the Babylonian embassy
and Isaiah's rebuke of Hezekiah's foolish
conduct (39:1-8); and (3) the siege of Jerusalem by Sennacherib in 701 B.C. (Isa. 36–37).

This section on Hezekiah stands in contrast to the previous section on Ahaz (Isa. 7–35). God gave Ahaz a sign of deliverance from Assyria, but Ahaz rejected it. Hezekiah accepted God's ways and was accepted by him (37:3-4). In Isaiah 7–35 the threat of Assyria and prophecies of future judgment predominated. In Isaiah 40–66, Babylon loomed as a new threat, but even so, prophecies of future comfort were emphasized. Isaiah 36–39 functioned as a good example of faith that would lead to promises of ultimate restoration.

36:1–37:38 Assyrian Threats: The Faith of Hezekiah

36:1–37:7 THE FIRST THREAT

The "fourteenth" (36:1) year of Hezekiah corresponds with 701 B.C. Sennacherib reported in his royal annals that he had captured forty-six cities in his assault on Judah. The meaning of the Hebrew word translated "field commander" (36:2, NIV) or transliterated as "Rabshakeh" (NASB) is uncertain. The title implied a position of high-level leadership. This leader was an official emissary and spokesman for Sennacherib. Aramaic (36:11), a Semitic dialect similar to Hebrew, was the diplomatic and commercial language of the ancient Near East. Tearing one's clothes and wearing "sackcloth" was a sign of mourning and distress (37:1). The reference to newborn "children" (37:3) was a metaphor suggesting a critical moment when special help would be needed.

37:8-38 THE DEATH OF SENNACHERIB

Libnah (37:8) is situated in the Elah Valley about twenty miles west of Bethlehem. Lachish is located about ten miles south of Libnah. Tirhakah (37:9) was not the reigning king in 701 B.C. but later succeeded his brother to this office. The Rabshakeh (probably a title, not a name) cited historical evidence that the gods had been unable to protect the cities of Mesopotamia and Aram from Assyrian conquest (37:12-13).

God promised that Jerusalem would be spared (37:30-33). Although agricultural pursuits would be interrupted by the siege, normal conditions would return to the land within three years. Herodotus, a first-century Greek historian, recorded that a plague of field mice entered the camp and gnawed the weapons of the soldiers, making them defenseless (37:36). Ararat (37:38) is a mountainous region of eastern Turkey. Esarhaddon ruled Assyria from 680 to 669 B.C.

38:1–39:8 Babylonian Overtones

38:1-22 THE EXTENSION OF HEZEKIAH'S LIFE

The miracle was probably a local phenomenon rather than a total reversal of the earth's rotation. "Sheol" (38:18) refers to the grave, the place of the dead. In death, one is cut off from the public assembly, the historical context for "praise" (public acknowledgment of God's great works and deeds).

39:1-8 HEZEKIAH'S FOOLISHNESS BEFORE THE BABYLONIANS

The words "At that time" (39:1) link Hezekiah's foolishness with his illness and recovery, before Assyria's attack on Jerusalem. Merodach-Baladan (721–709 B.C.) reigned over the city of Babylon for periods during the reigns of Sargon II and Sennacherib. The prophecy of 39:6 would be realized in the days of the Babylonian king Nebuchadnezzar (cf. Dan. 1:2; 2 Kings 24–25).

40:1–66:24 CYCLES OF COMFORT AFTER CAPTIVITY

Overview: The section of 40:1–66:24 contains three cycles of comfort (Isa. 40–48; 49–57; 58–66). The first describes the incomparability of God and Israel as contrasted with idols and idolaters (40:1–48:22). The second shows how God's Servant, the promised Messiah, in his humiliation and exaltation, will bring Israel to its worldwide calling (49:1–57:21). The third divides Israel into two groups for eternal reward: the faithless and the faithful in a final invitation to repentance (58:1–66:24).

Many scholars believe that Isaiah 40–66 was written by a different author and refer to this section as "Deutero-Isaiah." Their main problem has to do with accepting the possibility of predictive prophecy. Isaiah lived during the Assyrian period, and the prophecies of Isaiah 40–66 assume a prophetic viewpoint. Isaiah wrote as if the Babylonian exile (586 B.C.) had already taken place. If the reader can accept the possibility that Isaiah could look into the future by divinely inspired prophecy, there is no real problem with him authoring both sections of the book.

40:1–48:22 God Contrasted with Idols

Overview: The words in 40:1–48:22 brought comfort by focusing on the greatness of God (40:1-31), the introduction of his Servant (42:1–43:13), and then a lengthy description of the destruction of Babylon (43:14–48:22).

40:1-31 GOD AS DELIVERER OF HIS PEOPLE

The prophets of Israel, Isaiah in particular, were exhorted to speak words of consolation to God's people in the Babylonian exile. A herald announced the coming of God among his people (40:3). The "voice" (40:3) was revealed by the New Testament to be that of John the Baptist (Matt. 3:3), the introducer of Jesus, the Messiah. The divine plan of the Messiah's coming depended on God, not man (40:6-8). This plan is as certain as his word, which stands forever.

Isaiah 40:12-26 demonstrated the awesome power of God. Nothing could hinder God's coming to the people of Judah. He is incomparably greater than any foe! The "breadth of his hand" or a "span" (40:12) is the distance between the thumb and little finger, about nine inches. The vault (40:22; lit., "circle") of the earth referred to the sky that appeared to be a canopy. Biblical cosmology describes the universe as it appears, not with detailed, scientific exactness. To the people of Judah, weary from exile, God promised that he had not lost sight of them in Babylon (40:27). God promised his unfailing strength to those who would "hope" patiently in him (40:31).

41:1-29 THE INCOMPARABLE POWER AND KNOWLEDGE OF GOD

The "islands" served as a figure referring to the people of the Mediterranean world. The one aroused "from the east" (41:2) referred to Cyrus, king of Anshan, who inherited the kingdom of the Medes (550 B.C.) and captured Babylon (539 B.C.) to found the Persian Empire. Although Cyrus was an unbeliever, he was called to do God's righteous will (cf. 45:1-5). In 41:8-9 the believers of Israel were addressed as God's "servant." The term also was used of Isaiah (20:3), Cyrus (41:2), and the Messiah (49:5). The context is the key to determining who was being referred to by the term "servant." The "mountains" (41:15) referred to mountain-like shrines (called "ziggurats") that were used for idolatrous worship. God

addressed the pagan idols, challenging them to prove their worth (41:21-24). They were asked to predict a near prophecy ("former things") or a distant prophecy ("things to come").

42:1–43:13 THE INTRODUCTION OF THE SERVANT

The first of four great Servant Songs was presented in 42:1-9. The "Servant" is identified by Matthew 12:18-20 as Jesus, the Messiah. The establishment of a just order ("justice") was a key theme in the song (42:1, 3-4). The Servant is the instrument by which a new "covenant" will be effected (cf. Jer. 31:31-34; Ezek. 36:25-28; Heb. 8:6-13). For the opening of blind eyes (42:7), see John 9:1-7. The song of praise in 42:10-17 glorified God for his future (tribulation) triumph over the wicked. "Kedar" (42:11), the second son of Ishmael (Gen. 25:13), occupied the desert east of Transjordan. The "servant" nation (Israel) was rebuked for its lethargic spiritual state (for being "blind" and "deaf"). In spite of Israel's unfaithfulness, God promised to restore the nation from exile (43:1-7). The return from Babylon may serve as a precursor of the Jews' return to Israel after the tribulation (Matt. 24:31).

43:14–44:5 BABYLON DESTROYED, ISRAEL RESTORED

Isaiah predicted that God was going to overthrow Babylon (43:14). The "first father" (43:27) probably referred to Jacob (cf. Hos. 12:3). The nation "servant" Israel was addressed (44:1). Jeshurun (44:2) literally means "upright one" and is a poetic term of honor for Israel (Deut. 32:15). The pouring out of God's Spirit speaks of Israel's spiritual revival as a believing people of God (44:3; cf. Joel 2:28; Ezek. 39:29).

44:6-23 GOD VERSUS THE GODS OF THE NATIONS

The foolishness of idolatry is illustrated by the man who used part of a log to make a "god" and the other part as fuel for his fire.

44:24–45:25 GOD USES CYRUS FOR ISRAEL'S RESTORATION

Cyrus, king of Persia, conquered Babylon and decreed the return of the Jews to their homeland (Ezra 1:1-4). Cyrus was called God's anointed (45:1-5; lit., "messiah"). As he freed the Jews from bondage to the Babylonians, so Jesus, the divine Messiah, delivers all who will believe in him from their penalty of sin. The words "you do not acknowledge me" (45:4) make it clear that Cyrus was an unbeliever. He spoke about God in political ways (Ezra 1:2-4), but he did not know him personally. The words "create disaster" (Isa. 45:7) were a strong statement concerning God's sovereignty over all events (Eph. 1:11). God raised up Cyrus ("him") to accomplish his purposes in restoring the Jews and rebuilding Jerusalem (cf. Phil. 2:10 with Isa. 45:23).

46:1-13 GOD DESTROYS BABEL'S GODS
Isaiah 46 illustrated the superiority of God over the gods of Babylon. "Bel" was the Babylonian equivalent to Baal. "Nebo," the son of Marduk, was the god of writing and education. The "bird of prey" (46:11) was a reference to Cyrus (41:2).

47:1-15 GOD DESTROYS BABYLON
The prophecy of 47:1-15 was of Babylon's destruction, which was fulfilled when Cyrus captured the city in 539 B.C. (Dan. 5). Babylon's failure was uncovered in 47:6. God had used the nation to discipline his people, but they went beyond reasonable punishment and showed no "mercy" (Zech. 1:15). The sorcerers of Babylon were challenged to do the impossible—to avert the disaster that would befall the city (47:12-15).

48:1-22 GOD DELIVERS ISRAEL FROM BABYLON
Isaiah 48 summarizes the message of Isaiah 40–47, reiterating Israel's promised deliverance through Cyrus (48:14-15). The best support in the Old Testament for the doctrine of the Trinity may be provided in 48:16. The Father ("Sovereign Lord") sent the Son ("me") and the Holy Spirit ("his Spirit"). Isaiah 40–66 closes with a solemn statement concerning the wicked (cf. 57:21; 66:24).

49:1–57:21 The Servant's Humiliation and Exaltation

Overview: The section of 49:1–57:21 shows how God uses his Servant's humiliation and exaltation to bring Israel to its worldwide calling. The historical perspective is from the time period after the return from Babylon. The Servant attested to the glory of God (Isa. 49) and his message (Isa. 50) and invited the righteous remnant in Israel to hear and receive God's blessings once his wrath had passed (51:1–52:12). The Servant himself would be exalted, but only after

undergoing intense, but redemptive, humiliation (52:13–53:12). After that profound insight into God's redemption plan follows a four-part invitation to accept such a costly salvation (54:1-17; 55:1-13; 56:1-8; 56:9–57:21).

49:1-26 THE SELF-ATTESTATION OF THE SERVANT
The second Servant Song was presented (cf. 42:1-9). Rejected by his own people (49:4), the Messiah would bring salvation to the Gentiles (49:5-6) and restore Israel to God (49:5). His mouth was likened to a "sharpened sword," a reference to the Messiah's speaking ministry (49:2; cf. Heb. 4:12). The name "Israel" was applied to the Messiah, the One who fulfilled God's expectation for his people (49:3). The Messiah appeared to have "labored to no purpose" to bring God's people to himself, but his work will eventually be rewarded (49:4). The Messiah was given literally "to be a covenant for the people," that is, Israel (49:8; cf. Gen. 12:1-3). The "region of Sinim" is of an uncertain location, perhaps Aswan in Egypt (49:12). One of the strongest statements in Scripture regarding God's faithfulness to his people is found in 49:15-16.

50:1-11 THE SERVANT'S FAITHFULNESS
Because of her sins, God divorced and sold Israel to her enemies (50:1). But those terms are descriptive of Israel's discipline only. God never broke his commitment to the relationship he had with Israel. The nation was temporarily rejected because of sin (cf. Jer. 31:35-37). The third Servant Song was presented (Isa. 50:4-9; cf. 42:1-9 and 49:1-13). Here it is revealed how the Servant learned through his own rejection to comfort the weary and discouraged. The phrase "Sovereign Lord" occurs four times and may be better translated "My Master God." It emphasized that the Servant had a Master (God) to whom he submitted and in whom he found help. The "instructed tongue" (50:4) was a reference to his speaking or prophetic ministry. The followers of the Servant were called upon to trust in God, who would bring judgment upon the disobedient (50:10-11).

51:1-23 INVITATION TO SALVATION AFTER WRATH
God encouraged the righteous remnant ("you who pursue righteousness") by promising deliverance from Babylon and future

blessings for his people. "Rahab" (51:9) is another name for the mythical dragon monster, Leviathan (27:1), that was at odds with God and his created order.

52:1-12 JERUSALEM RELEASED FROM CAPTIVITY

Zion (God's people) were called upon to throw off the stupor of God's judgment ("Awake") in preparation for the blessings of God's future kingdom reign (52:7). The "good news" for the exiles was that they could return to their homeland (52:7). Isaiah linked this historical message with a message about the end times: "Your God reigns!" (52:7). While Christ reigns presently at the right hand of God the Father through the work of the Spirit on the earth, he will one day return visibly to rule his kingdom on earth. Paul used this verse in Romans 10:15 of the messengers who herald the "good news" of salvation in Christ. The message was addressed to the Jews in Babylon, who would have to choose between economic security in Babylon and the hazards and hardships of returning to Judah (see note on Ezra 1:5).

52:13–53:12 THE EXALTATION OF THE SERVANT

Isaiah presented the fourth Servant Song, predicting that the Servant would die in the place of the guilty in order to satisfy God's judgment on sin. Early Jewish interpretation of this passage understood the "servant" (52:13) to refer to the Messiah. This also was the interpretation by the early church (cf. Acts 8:30-35). Not until the twelfth century was it suggested that the "servant" of Isaiah 53 was the nation of Israel. But the nation of Israel has not suffered innocently (53:9) or willingly (53:7). Nor did Israel's suffering provide substitutionary atonement (53:5).

The Messiah's resurrection, ascension, and exaltation were predicted in 52:13. For the disfigurement of Christ, see Matthew 27:28-31. The word "sprinkle" (Isa. 52:15) is the translation of the Hebrew word for "ceremonial cleansing." The Messiah's death would effect a spiritual cleansing potentially applicable even for the Gentiles ("nations").

Redeemed Israel spoke in retrospect and explained why they rejected the Messiah, Jesus (53:1-3). The Messiah bore the consequences of Israel's sin although they did not realize it at the time. Sin is pictured here in terms of its results or consequences in people's lives—sickness and pain. Matthew used this text with reference to Jesus' healing ministry (see note on Matt. 8:17). The emphasis in 53:5 is on substitution. What Christ suffered, he suffered for believers ("our transgressions," "our iniquities," "peace," and "healed"). The figure of straying sheep was used to describe the spiritual apostasy of Israel and all people (53:6; cf. Rom. 3:23). The Messiah Servant suffered willingly and silently (cf. Matt. 26:63; 27:11-14; Luke 23:9). The unjust judicial proceedings Christ was subjected to were reflected in 53:8. The Jewish Sanhedrin violated their own laws by (1) convening at the house of Caiaphas rather than the regular meeting place, (2) meeting at night rather than the day, (3) convening on the eve of a Sabbath and a festival, (4) pronouncing the judgment the same day as the trial, and (5) ignoring the formalities allowing for the possibility of acquittal in cases involving a capital sentence. Although condemned with wicked criminals (the two thieves), Christ was buried in the tomb of a rich man (cf. Matt. 27:57-60).

The Servant Song concluded with God's promise to exalt his Servant because he did the Father's will in dying as a guilt offering (53:10-12; cf. Phil. 2:9-11). The "offspring" was a reference to Christ's spiritual progeny who would trust in his redemptive work. Because of Christ's suffering, many would be justified (cf. Rom. 5:1,18).

54:1-17 JERUSALEM: RESTORED AS A WIFE

Israel was exhorted to "shout for joy" (54:1) for her punishment was past. Now the nation could anticipate blessing and prosperity. Israel's rejection was necessary because of sin, but it was temporary because of God's covenant promise. See Genesis 9:11 with reference to Isaiah 54:9. These verses await their complete fulfillment in the Messianic kingdom (Isa. 54:11-17).

55:1-13 INVITATION TO TASTE SALVATION

God offered salvation to all who would respond, whether Jew or Gentile. The word "thirsty" is used throughout Scripture as a metaphor for spiritual longing (cf. Ps. 42:1; John 4:14). The "everlasting covenant" (Isa. 55:3) or new covenant (Jer. 31:31) is associated with the Davidic covenant of 2 Samuel 7:12-16 ("my faithful love promised to

David," Isa. 55:3). Both are unconditional and are founded on God's promise to Abraham (Gen. 12:1-3). God's prophetic "word" will most certainly be fulfilled, for it rests on the character of his own person (55:11; 40:8).

56:1-8 COVENANT UNION FOR OUTCASTS
God emphasized that the Gentiles who believed (56:3) would not be excluded from his blessing (56:7). The inclusion of Gentiles in God's plan for world blessing is seen in Genesis 12:3; Amos 9:12; Acts 15:16-18; Romans 4:9-16; Galatians 3:7-9; and Ephesians 2:11-19; 3:4-6.

56:9–57:21 ISRAEL'S LEADERSHIP IS REBUKED
In contrast to the righteous, the wicked face certain condemnation and judgment. Isaiah used picturesque language to describe the prophets of Israel (Isa. 56:10). They were likened to blind "watchmen" and "dogs" that could not bark. Isaiah suggested a positive view of death in that it removed a righteous person (like Josiah in 2 Kings 23) from the evil of the day (Isa. 57:2-8). God is willing to provide deliverance from judgment for those who are truly humble and repentant (57:15; cf. 2 Pet. 3:9). The second section of Isaiah 40–66 concludes with a statement of God's judgment on the wicked (Isa. 57:21; cf. 48:22).

58:1–66:24 Israel:
The faithful and the faithless

Overview: In 58:1–66:24 Israel is divided into the faithful and the faithless to clarify the conditions for entering into God's future glory. It forms a final invitation and comfort. The heart of this section is the remnant's prayer for deliverance (63:7–64:12) and God's answer (65:1-25). The book ends by showing who will be excluded from the blessings of the new heavens and earth (66:1-24).

58:1-14 TRUE AND FALSE WORSHIP
Hand ritual (like fasting) without genuine heart righteousness (expressed by deeds of kindness) is unacceptable to God (cf. Matt. 23:13-36). The "Sabbath" was designed by God to be a day for turning aside from routine work to rest and be spiritually refreshed (Isa. 58:13). It was to be a day to "delight" in the Lord.

59:1-21 SIN'S PARTITION JUDGED
Isaiah 59 reveals the gospel in the Old Testament: "All have sinned" (Rom. 3:23; cf. Isa. 59:2). "The wages of sin" (Rom. 6:23; cf. Isa. 59:10). "While we were yet sinners, Christ died for us" (Rom. 5:8; cf. Isa. 59:16). The "one mediator" is Christ (1 Tim. 2:5). When Christ returns, he will judge the wicked and redeem his people, Israel, "those in Jacob who repent of their sins" (Isa. 59:20; "those who turn from transgression in Jacob," NASB).

60:1-22 LIGHT AND GLORY UPON JERUSALEM
Isaiah 60 reveals that Israel can anticipate a glorious future and significant ministry in the Messianic kingdom. The "darkness" that "covers the earth" (60:2) refers to the tribulation period that will precede Christ's return (cf. Matt. 24:29). In the Messianic kingdom Israel will fulfill its destiny as a "light" to the nations (cf. Zech. 8:20-23). The "riches of the nations" (Isa. 60:5) will come to Israel when the Gentiles (60:6-9) gather at Jerusalem to worship the Messianic King (cf. Zech. 8:20-22; Hag. 2:7-9). The "sanctuary" (Isa. 60:13) refers to the Messianic temple (cf. Ezek. 40–42). In contrast to Israel's national experience in history, Isaiah revealed the kingdom blessings the nation could anticipate (Isa. 60:15-22). The promise of land (Deut. 30:1-5) was once again affirmed.

61:1-11 THE SERVANT'S GLORY AND VENGEANCE
Isaiah 61 revealed that the Messiah, who ministered salvation at his first coming, will minister comfort for redeemed Israel at his second coming. Jesus read and applied 61:1-2 to his own ministry when he preached in the synagogue at Nazareth (Luke 4:16-21). Jesus did not quote 61:2-3 in the synagogue at Nazareth because they will be fulfilled at his second coming. In the kingdom, redeemed Israel will realize its destiny to be a priestly nation (Exod. 19:6).

62:1-12 JERUSALEM'S INTERNATIONAL GLORY
In the Messianic kingdom, redeemed Israel will be vindicated, honored, and protected. While Israel experienced separation from God because of her sin (Isa. 50:1), a day is coming when the believing nation will be fully restored as Yahweh's bride (cf. 54:4-10). "Married" (62:4) is a translation of the

familiar Hebrew term *Beulah.* What a contrast there is between Jerusalem's "watchmen" in the kingdom and those of Isaiah's day (62:6; cf. 56:10).

63:1-6 EDOM:
IMAGE OF INTERNATIONAL VENGEANCE
At the Messiah's coming, he will execute his wrathful judgment on the unbelieving enemies of his people. Edom, territory located southeast of Israel, was representative of Israel's enemies. Bozrah was the capital of Edom. The picture presented by the prophet was of a divine warrior returning from judgment. His garments were red from the blood of those he had judged. The imagery is precisely that of Revelation 14:18-20 and 19:3.

63:7–64:12 THE REMNANT'S PRAISE AND PLEA
Redeemed Israel acknowledged God's past mercies (Isa. 63:7-14) and prayed for him to deal kindly with his repentant people. The phrase "divided the waters" (63:12) is an allusion to one of the great miracles of the exodus, the parting of the Red Sea (Exod. 14:16). Even though "Abraham" and "Israel" might disown their descendants because of their sin, certainly God, "our Father," cannot deny his own children (Isa. 63:16; cf. 2 Tim. 2:13).

Paul quoted Isaiah 64:4 in 1 Corinthians 2:9 with reference to the heavenly glories awaiting the believer in Christ. Israel's unworthiness for God's mercy was highlighted. The appeal for forgiveness and restoration was based totally on God's grace (Isa. 64:5-12).

65:1-25 GOD'S ANSWER TO THE REMNANT'S PLEA
God declared that he would judge the wicked and preserve the righteous. Although Israel rejected God, he remained faithful in calling his people to repentance. The words "call on my name" (65:1) are an expression referring to public worship. Idolatry (65:3), eating forbidden food (65:4), and spiritual pride (65:5) were among the sins of the Israelites of Isaiah's day. The words "sit among the graves" (65:4) may refer to consulting with the dead (cf. 1 Sam. 28:3-25). The "descendants from Jacob" (Isa. 65:9) referred to the faithful remnant of God's people, Israel. The "Valley of Achor" (65:10) was where Achan was judged for his sin (Josh. 7:24). The point is, even places of past judgment will be blessed when God redeems his people. "Fortune . . . Destiny" (65:11) refer to Gad (the Aramaean god of luck) and Meni (the god of destiny). The future blessings anticipated by God's people were described in 65:17-25. The "new heavens" and "new earth" (66:22) are a unique contribution by Isaiah to biblical eschatology. This theme was picked up by Peter (2 Pet. 3:13) and John (Rev. 21:1). After the dissolution of the present heavens and earth, which have been cursed by sin and judgment, God will create new heavens and a new earth as the physical context for the eternal state for believers. The curse on the earth that came as a result of Adam's fall (Gen. 3:17-19) will be reversed in the eternal state (Rev. 22:3).

66:1-24 EXCLUSIONS FROM THE NEW HEAVENS AND EARTH
The future blessings of the redeemed were further described. Isaiah 66:2 revealed the kind of person that God truly delights in (cf. Mic. 6:8). Religious hypocrisy was strongly condemned (Isa. 66:3). God is never pleased with hand ritual apart from heart righteousness. Isaiah 66:7-9 anticipated the spiritual rebirth of the nation of Israel, an event to coincide with the second coming of the Messiah (cf. Zech. 12:10–13:1; Rom. 11:26). The blessings and prosperity of the Messianic kingdom (Isa. 66:10-14) were set in contrast with a vivid description of the judgment to be anticipated at the Lord's coming (66:15-17; cf. 2 Thess. 1:7-9). During the time of the Messianic kingdom, believers among the Gentile nations will gather in Jerusalem to worship the Messiah with believing Jews (Isa. 66:18-20). Isaiah's grand prophecy concluded with a description of the eternal state (66:22-23; cf. Rev. 21:1–22:5) and a final announcement of the certain divine judgment of the wicked (Isa. 66:24; cf. Rev. 20:15-20). The joy of the redeemed was contrasted with the pain of the damned, all of which glorifies the compassion and justice of God.

Jeremiah

BASIC FACTS

HISTORICAL SETTING

During Jeremiah's time, Egypt was involved in two decisive battles with Babylonia. The first was in 609 B.C. (cf. 2 Chron. 35:20-25). The second, in 605 B.C., saw Egypt broken in defeat (cf. 2 Chron. 36:1-6; Jer. 46:1-26). Assyria, in its attempt to block the rise of Babylonia, had unsuccessfully sided with Egypt. Babylonia was now strong and on the rise ultimately to defeat both Egypt and Assyria.

AUTHOR

The book of Jeremiah was written by the prophet Jeremiah. When his first volume of prophecies was destroyed by King Jehoiakim (Jer. 36:22-23), Jeremiah dictated the original prophecies as well as additional messages (36:32) to his secretary, Baruch.

DATE

The book begins by listing the kings under whom Jeremiah prophesied (1:2-3): Josiah (640–609 B.C.), Jehoiakim (609–597 B.C.), and Zedekiah (597–586 B.C.). Two other kings of this period, Jehoahaz (609 B.C.) and Jehoiachin (597 B.C.), are not mentioned in this first list of Jeremiah's kings. The thirteenth year of Josiah's reign (628 B.C.) was during a period when he had been aggressively seeking God since his eighth year (cf. 2 Chron. 34:3). In the eighteenth year of Josiah's reign he brought about one of Israel's greatest reforms. The fourth year of the reign of Jehoiakim (1:3; 606 B.C.) as king is mentioned in 36:32, in which he burned Jeremiah's scroll of prophecy. The fourth year of Zedekiah (27:1; 28:1; 51:59; 594 B.C.) was a year of great tragedy and upheaval as the nation drew closer to its final collapse.

PURPOSE

The book was designed to show the exiles the reasons for their captivity. They were not in Babylon because God had forgotten his promises to Israel but because Israel had been unfaithful to him. The book also taught the captives to wait patiently for the seventy years to elapse and not to seek a quick release through military or

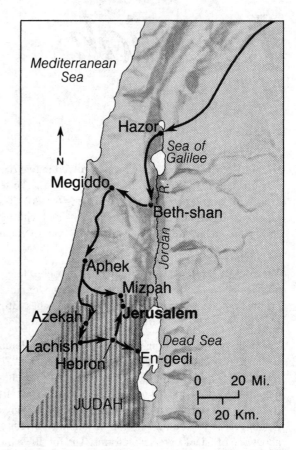

political means by trusting in other nations for deliverance. Finally, the book encouraged the captives that after their bondage there would come a time of restoration and renewal under the new covenant.

GEOGRAPHY AND ITS IMPORTANCE

Nebuchadnezzar's troops first destroyed the major cities to the north and south of Jerusalem. Then, without the support of her surrounding cities, Jerusalem also fell after a long siege. Jerusalem's destruction marked the end of the settlement of Palestine that began with Joshua's great defeat of Jericho. Early in Jeremiah's ministry, he predicted the coming exile of Judah in Babylon. And later during the Babylonian captivity, Jeremiah wrote that Israel would one day be restored to her land. The concept of getting back home was strong and deep for God's people. But Jeremiah placed geographical restoration squarely within a larger spiritual restoration. To "get home" physically demanded getting home in a spiritual sense, a sense described in the miracles of Jeremiah's new covenant. The physical captivity in Babylon reflected a spiritual bondage to sin and its consequences. The promise of geographical restoration to the Promised Land reflected an inner spiritual restoration. It was outward evidence of inner forgiveness and the indwelling of the Holy Spirit.

GUIDING CONCEPTS

JEREMIAH THE MAN

The book of Jeremiah provides numerous insights into the private and public life of Jeremiah the prophet. He originally came from the town of Anathoth, just north of Jerusalem (1:1; 11:21-23; 29:27; 32:7-9). Jeremiah revealed his feelings about his call (1:4-10). He gave up any hope of having a normal family life (16:1-13). His ministry was continually surrounded by hostility from his neighbors (11:21-23; 12:6) and his professional peers (5:31; 26:1-6). His life was threatened (26:24). He was publicly humiliated (20:1-6) and put in a hole in the ground (38:6-13). Throughout his trials, Jeremiah was honest and transparent. He freely shared his feelings and at the same time always maintained a vital trust in God (14:17-18; 15:15-23; 18:20; 20:7-18; 32:1-44; 38:1-13). Why did God give so much personal information about this prophet?

The descriptions of Jeremiah's personal feelings and troubles were not included just to make a good story but also to provide a personal context in which the prophetic message could be received. The inclusion of Jeremiah's feelings shows that God's prophets were not gloom-and-doom machines cranking out tirades against sinners. Rather, God's spokesmen were just as human as their audiences, and their sometimes harsh messages sprang from hearts broken by the rampant sin that surrounded them and from a desire to establish hope in God's wonderful promises of blessing.

But this picture of the prophet's heart being broken for God's people is a reflection of the pain in God's own heart. Thus, Jeremiah's pain and striving with the nation is a human reflection of God's divine and genuine pain as he strives to correct and bless his hard-hearted people. This genuine involvement of God with the pain of his sin-blasted creation is consummately seen in the agony of his Son on the cross. Jeremiah's personal life was revealed so that believers may be reminded to receive his harsh words of prophetic rebuke within the personal context of God's loving concern for their best.

THE ARRANGEMENT OF THE BOOK'S CONTENTS

The long book of Jeremiah, unlike the majority of the other prophets, is not arranged in chronological order. Stories and prophecies from various periods in Jeremiah's life are arranged together. Messages of hope or destruction, personal stories from Jeremiah's life, and historical events appear side by side. Some scholars account for this apparent lack of usual order in arrangement by noting the process leading up to the writing of the book.

Jeremiah had prophesied for twenty years before God told him to write his messages down. Thus the first compilation of Jeremiah contained some kind of listing ("all the words"; 36:2) or summary version of twenty years of warning and encouraging the nation. But when King Jehoiakim heard the prophecy, he burned the scroll section by section (36:22-23), showed no fear of God, and sought to arrest Jeremiah. Jeremiah then rewrote the original prophecy and added even more to it (36:32). Thus, some scholars believe the turbulent times surrounding the writing of Jeremiah account for the book's seeming lack of order.

The book does have an overall progression and order, however. It begins with the beginning of Jeremiah's ministry (1:1-19), then encourages God's people to repent (2:1–45:5), shows God's absolute rule over the nations (cf. this aspect of Jeremiah's call in 1:10), and concludes by describing not only the fall of Jerusalem but also the elevation of David's son, Jehoiachin, in captivity. This clearly shows that the book was purposely designed to contribute to the ongoing development of God's promises to Abraham's children. They had been told by Moses in Deuteronomy that disobedience would bring destruction. But they also had been told of God's promises to Abraham to bring in a large nation and universal blessing and of God's promises to David to always have one of his sons ruling on the throne of Israel. Jeremiah's structure shows how the prophecies of destruction were accomplished without destroying the promises of Davidic rule that would someday be perfectly fulfilled in the Messiah.

BLESSINGS LOST AND GAINED

Jeremiah 1–29 and 34–52 outline the loss of Israel's blessings under the Mosaic covenant. Israel lost her throne, her land, her temple, and a good number of her inhabitants because she had violated the conditions of the covenant. But at the heart of the book (Jer. 30–33) is a promised remedy for Israel's covenant violations: a new covenant. Israel, under that new covenant, would have the law placed in her heart so that she would never again lose God's blessings.

BIBLE-WIDE CONCEPTS

LINKS TO KINGS, CHRONICLES, AND EZRA

Jeremiah, like 1 and 2 Kings, presents a detailed description of the failures that led to the destruction of Jerusalem. See, for example, Jeremiah 52 and 2 Kings 24–25. Jeremiah has an even closer relationship to the book of Kings, for both end with the elevation of Jehoiachin in captivity (2 Kings 25:27-30; Jer. 52:31-34). Jeremiah presents a midexilic perspective, like 1 and 2 Kings. The most optimistic way the authors of these books could end their books was to show that the anointed son of David, Jehoiachin, was still under the Davidic promise of God, even while he was in captivity.

However, Jeremiah also contains a link to the even more positive ending of 1 and 2 Chronicles, where Cyrus, the Persian king, released Israel from captivity. The writer of Chronicles calls the words of Cyrus a fulfillment of Jeremiah's prophecy. Jeremiah 29:10-14 clearly prophesied a seventy-year captivity, after which God would release his people. Ezra 1:1 begins the account of the return of the Jews to the land with the words from Cyrus's decree (2 Chron. 36:22) and names that return as a fulfillment of Jeremiah's prophecy. Thus Jeremiah presents a clear link between Israel's chastisement and her restoration.

THE NEW COVENANT

A second exodus

In the first exodus God's people were led out from Egypt's captivity and into a relationship with God based on the covenant given to Moses. The captivity in Babylon also was followed by an exodus that led to a new relationship through a new covenant. Jeremiah spoke of the release from Babylon as a second exodus (Jer. 16:14-15; 23:7-8). That pattern of bondage, release, and relationship will be fulfilled at the end of this age when God brings complete release from the bondage of sin and death and allows the creation to enter into an unhindered relationship with him. That will be the third and final exodus from bondage to freedom. Jeremiah 31 speaks of Israel's inability to keep the Mosaic covenant (31:32), thus excluding her from the blessings of Abraham. But the new covenant would bring with it the ability to keep God's ways, thus opening up unhindered participation in the fullness of God's promises to Abraham concerning the land, the nation, and God's presence.

The time of Israel's restoration

Jeremiah described Israel's restoration as a time of release from captivity, victory over hostile nations' attacks, and the establishment of God's perfect rule through the fulfillment of Abrahamic and Davidic promises. Jeremiah described this time as if the release, victory, and rule would happen one right after the other and soon after the captivity took place. However, as Daniel found out, the release from Babylon and the full restoration of Israel's promises were separated by seventy weeks of years (Dan. 9:24-27). And as Jesus noted, the future time of full restoration is known only to God (Matt. 24:36).

Certainty, not chronological closeness, was the point of linking release, victory, and rule together. Although actually separated by thousands of years, the promised releases from oppression, victories over the nations, and the establishment of God's perfect rule will certainly happen. The actual time frame is secondary to God's people basing their present hope on a certain future. Knowing the certainty, not the date, is what provides a foundation for present repentance and hope. God's people tended to take God's threats or promises seriously only after it was too late. They put off making important decisions if they thought the deadline was far off. Jeremiah's point of present urgency would have been lost if he had told Israel that the events of victory and rule were thousands of years away. He presented future events as inevitable and certain, with present consequences for decisions of repentance and commitment, no matter how far in the future the fulfillment of the prophecies might be.

The place of the Gentiles

God's word to Abraham was that the nations would be blessed in him (Gen. 12:3). But how were the Gentiles related to Israel's blessing? Jeremiah spoke of a time when God's blessing would be international, for both Jew and Gentile. At that time all the nations would be obedient to the Lord (Jer. 3:16-18) and find their blessing in him (4:2). Jews and Gentiles are equal when it comes to God's evaluation of their hearts (9:25-26). All the nations of Jeremiah's day were subject to exile and, if they had responded in obedience to God, they would have been given his restoration (12:14-17; 25:29-31).

That accountability of the Gentiles before God went back to God's claim as Creator. The covenant with Abraham included all the people of the world. The covenant with Moses focused on the Jewish nation as an evangelistic witness to all the nations concerning God's salvation. The new covenant broke down all ethnic barriers between Jews and Gentiles, while maintaining the centrality of the seed of Abraham and of David through the promised Messiah (i.e., Jesus). The international blessing inherent in the promises to Abraham (Gen. 12:3) was no longer mediated by the priests in the Jerusalem temple but by the Son at the Father's right hand. Earthly ethnic and religious distinctions were done away with.

Covenant promises

God's promises were not frustrated by Israel's disobedience (31:35-37). His promises, though delayed from a human standpoint, would be fulfilled. God's words to Jacob (30:3, 7, 10) and David (30:9) were still in force, even in the light of Israel's disobedience and disastrous captivity. Paul (2 Cor. 3) and the writer to Hebrews (Heb. 8–10) explained what Jesus meant when he spoke of the new covenant in his blood (Luke 22:20). Indeed, the name "New Testament" shows that the entire New Testament is an exposition of the new covenant's meaning and implications. Jeremiah 31 begins an explanation of the new covenant that will be completed by the New Testament books.

NEEDS MET BY JEREMIAH

Jeremiah originally spoke to people who lived before and just after the downfall of Jerusalem to the Babylonians. But the book was finally composed after the middle of the seventy years of captivity, as its ending shows. Why would these people need to read about the past events of Israel's downfall? First, they needed to see God's heart of pain and compassion reflected through Jeremiah's own life and words. God cared about them, even in their rebellion and self-earned discipline. Second, God had not forgotten his promises to Abraham and David. The captivity in Babylon was a painful but temporary part of God's path to ultimate blessing. The hearers of the book of Jeremiah were challenged both to accept their discipline and to take hope in God's love and faithfulness to his promises. The book of Jeremiah answered some of the Israelites' hard, but necessary, questions.

- What hope remains for Israel after her destruction and captivity?
- Are God's covenant promises through Abraham and David still in force?
- Can God's people run away and escape God's judgment?
- How can a new covenant be any better than the covenants God has already made with Abraham, Moses, and David?

The Christian reader of Jeremiah must hold together two interesting concepts. First, the new covenant about which Jeremiah spoke has been inaugurated in Christ. The New Testament is devoted to explaining the implications of the new covenant for the believer. That covenant brings a more effective and intimate relationship with God than the one offered through Moses. Second, Christian readers must try to understand how they are to relate to the words of warning and potential disaster facing the nation of Israel. Do words of potential judgment for disobedience relate to believers who are participants in the new covenant? Are Jeremiah's words without present application, or is Israel to be viewed as a type of the church and her judgments somehow spiritualized into personal disciplines for the Christian?

The answer lies in realizing that the historical specifics unique to Israel at the time of her captivity are secondary to God's continuing attitude toward sin in his people. He hates any sin in his people's lives. The chronological dates of the captivity and of future restoration are also secondary to God's desire that his people take seriously their call to love him and pass his desires on to others, no matter how far in the future judgment or blessing may be. Jeremiah meets the needs of believers today by warning that God will bring discipline for their rebellion just as he did for Israel's. But believers can be assured that during the times of discipline, God's heart hurts for them and remains committed to their ultimate restoration in his promised blessings. To participate in his new covenant in Christ is to remain subject both to his discipline and to his inevitable blessing.

OUTLINE OF JEREMIAH

A. INTRODUCTION: END-TIME WORDS OF WARNING (1:1-19)
   1. The Times (1:1-3)
   2. The Commission (1:4-19)

B. ACCUSATION: COVENANT UNFAITHFULNESS (2:1–6:30)
1. The Initial Confrontation (2:1-37)
2. God's Desire for Repentance and Reason for Discipline (3:1–6:30)
C. COVENANT RENEWAL AND CHASTISEMENTS (7:1–19:13)
1. Understanding in Chastisement (7:1–10:25)
2. Covenant Recall (11:1–19:13)
D. GOING OVER THE LEADERS' HEADS TO THE PEOPLE (19:14–29:32)
1. Priestly Opposition (19:14–20:18)
2. Kingly Reproach (21:1–22:30)
3. Prophetic Hostility (23:1–29:32)
E. NEW COVENANT RESTORATION (30:1–33:26)
1. Promise of Discernment in the End (30:1–31:40)
2. A Picture of Restoration (32:1-44)
3. Certainty of Restoration (33:1-26)
F. COVENANT CHASTISEMENT CONFIRMED: SUBMIT OR DIE! (34:1–45:5)
1. Siege: Submit to Babylon (34:1-22)
2. Kingly Lack of Submission (35:1–36:32)
3. Zedekiah's End (37:1–39:10)
4. Gedaliah's End (39:11–44:30)
5. Summary (45:1-5)
G. GOD'S RULE OVER THE NATIONS (46:1–51:64)
1. Egypt (46:1-28)
2. Philistia (47:1-7)
3. Moab (48:1-47)
4. Ammon (49:1-6)
5. Edom (49:7-22)
6. Damascus (49:23-27)
7. Hazor (49:28-33)
8. Elam (49:34-39)
9. Babylon's Scroll of Destruction (50:1–51:64)
H. FROM JERUSALEM'S FALL TO THE ELEVATION OF JEHOIACHIN (52:1-34)

JEREMIAH NOTES

1:1-19 INTRODUCTION: END-TIME WORDS OF WARNING
Overview: After a short historical prologue (1:1-3), Jeremiah's commission sets forth the thrust of the book (1:4-19). He was known personally by God from before his birth, and God's word through him was to be certain. His appointment for building up and destroying nations (1:10) is related to the various themes used throughout the book. The book of Jeremiah describes Israel's downfall and restoration and concludes with a long section that shows God's ultimate rule over all the nations (46:1–51:64). The very end of the book reaffirms God's promises to build up Israel by the elevation of King Jehoiachin, the son of David, while still in exile.

1:1-3 The Times
Jeremiah, whose name means "Yahweh establishes," was of the priestly family residing at Anathoth (modern Anata), located about three miles north of Jerusalem. Although Jeremiah was the author, the "words" were recorded by Baruch, the prophet's amanuensis (36:4, 32). The

thirteenth year of Josiah (640–609 B.C.) was 627 B.C. Jeremiah continued his ministry in Jerusalem through the reigns of the last kings of Judah and until the exile to Babylon had begun in 586 B.C.

1:4-19 The Commission

In 1:4-10 two key thoughts dominated Jeremiah's commissioning as a prophet: (1) his divine appointment (1:5), and (2) the provision of God's word (1:7, 9). The word "child" (1:6) was used to denote a young person from the age of infancy to early manhood. The words "I knew you" (1:5) speak of God's intimate awareness and purposeful affection. While yet in his mother's womb, Jeremiah was set apart by God for his prophetic ministry. Jeremiah's mission was described in terms of judgment and edification (1:10). The four synonyms used for destruction, in comparison to the two used for building up, indicate that the prophet's message was to be predominately one of warning about Judah's coming judgment.

In Israel, the almond tree is the first tree to blossom, and thus it announces the coming of spring (1:11-12). As spring always follows the blossoming of the almond, so prophetic fulfillment would follow Jeremiah's predictions. The boiling pot (1:13-16) was tilted from the north, the direction from which Babylon's invasion would come (3:18). Soon the scalding contents, the Babylonian invaders, would flow south over Israel.

The girding of the loins involved tucking the end of a man's long outer robe into his belt in preparation for walking or working (1:17). The command signified a readiness for work, and for Jeremiah it meant the work of preaching. The prophet had to expect opposition (cf. John 15:18-25), but he would not be overcome by it (1:18-19; cf. Rom. 8:31-39).

2:1–6:30 ACCUSATION: COVENANT UNFAITHFULNESS

Overview: The section of Jeremiah 2:1–6:30 was God's initial confrontation with the nation. It progressed on the basis of the following themes: The Israelites loved God at the first, but they soon stopped loving him (2:2-3); God asked what wrong he had done to them (2:5). He then asked why they were

on the roads to Assyria and Egypt (2:18). The implied answer was that, even though he had disciplined them in the past, they had not responded (2:30). The nations' leaders, pictured here as shepherds, were corrupt but would be replaced with others who would be men after God's own heart (3:15). And all Israelites needed a heart cleansing (4:4). Because of Israel's sin, God's future judgment was pictured as the earth returning to formlessness and void (4:23-26). But that would not be a complete destruction (5:18). Finally, the prophets and priests gave the people false words of peace and were condemned for their deceit (6:13-14; cf. 14:13-16). These condemnations and promises in the first chapters form a foundation for all the themes introduced and developed throughout the book.

2:1-37 The Initial Confrontation

God's love for Israel (2:1-37) contrasts with the apostasy of the nation. The figures of bride and bridegroom (2:2-3) depict the relationship between God and Israel during the nation's early life after the exodus ("through the desert"). Although God had been faithful to Israel, the people were unfaithful to him (2:5-8). They forsook the Lord (2:5-6) and defiled the land (2:7). The leaders (priests, teachers, rulers, and prophets) led the way to apostasy. The result was that the Lord had a case against Israel for violating the Mosaic covenant (2:9). The words "bring charges" denoted the activity of making an accusation or a complaint. "Kittim" (2:10) referred to Cyprus, and "Kedar" to Arabia.

There are two kinds of water sources in Israel—springs with "living" or fresh water, and cisterns (small reservoirs) with stale or stagnant water. The metaphor of water sources (2:13) graphically illustrated Israel's apostasy. Jeremiah 2:15 apparently referred to the destruction of the northern kingdom in 722 B.C. by Assyria. Jeremiah 2:16 probably referred to the killing of Josiah by the Egyptians (cf. 2 Kings 23:29). Memphis (near modern Cairo) was the ancient capital of Lower Egypt. Tahpanhes was on the eastern border of the Nile Delta commanding the road to Israel.

For 2:21, see the vineyard imagery in Isaiah 5:1-7 and Psalm 80:8-13. The apostate nation was likened to a wild donkey in heat whose desire was so great that any mate that wanted her could have her without effort (2:24). Judah should not have expected to find help through an alliance with Egypt (2:36). The reference to "Assyria" recalled Ahaz's attempt to secure help from Assyria when the nation was threatened by Pekah (2 Kings 16:5-18).

3:1–6:30 God's Desire for Repentance and Reason for Discipline

3:1-5 RETURNING ADULTERESS
Deuteronomy 24:1-4 provides the legal background for 3:1. The law prohibited a man from remarrying his former wife if in the meantime she had been married to another man. This law was referred to in order to illustrate defiled Israel's condition resulting from apostasy (3:2-3).

3:6–6:30 REPENTANCE AND DESTRUCTION
Israel's punishment should have caused Judah to repent, but she didn't (3:10). The comment in 3:10 sheds light on the Lord's view of Josiah's reform (3:6), which appears to have been superficial. In 3:12–4:4 God addressed the northern kingdom ("toward the north," 3:12) in exile in order to set forth a warning for Judah, the southern kingdom, to repent. Jeremiah spoke of a future day when both kingdoms would be regathered to the land by the Shepherd after God's own heart (3:15-18). In that future kingdom, the believing nation would not miss the Ark of the Covenant because her attention would be focused on the throne of the Lamb (3:17). Israel's repentance and confession of sin were an example for Judah (3:22-25). But God demanded that the repentance had to be sincere (4:1-2). He looked for evidence of repentance, which can be found in the fruit of true faith. The application was made for Judah and Jerusalem (4:3-4). Only genuine repentance could avert judgment. The sign of circumcision was an outward witness of an inward, spiritual reality. The command "Circumcise yourselves" (4:4) spoke figuratively of the need to separate oneself from sin and reconsecrate oneself to God.

Jeremiah announced coming destruction from the north (4:5-31). Babylon was likened to a "lion" seeking prey (4:7), a "scorching wind" (4:11), and threatening "clouds" (4:13). The words "formless and empty" (4:23) were used in Genesis 1:2 to describe the earth before the six days of God's creative work. The strong metaphor suggested that the earth would be reduced to its state before the creation (4:24-26).

Jeremiah 5 gives the reason for God's judgment on Judah. The essence of the answer is found in 5:18-19. The people had forsaken God and had served other gods. Jeremiah was instructed to search the streets of Jerusalem for one righteous man because God promised to pardon Judah if just one such person could be found (5:1; cf. Gen. 18:22-23). However, a complete destruction of Judah was decreed (Jer. 5:10). For the imagery of the vine (5:10), see Isaiah 5:1-7 and John 15:1-11. In spite of Israel's apostasy, God promised not to destroy the nation completely (Jer. 5:18). The basis of this encouragement was God's unconditional commitment to keeping his promise (Gen. 12:1-3; 2 Sam. 7:12-16). Both "Jacob" (the northern kingdom) and "Judah" (the southern kingdom) were exceedingly wicked and deserving of divine discipline (5:20-31).

In Jeremiah 6 the prophet predicted the inevitable and imminent destruction of unrepentant Jerusalem (6:6), a prophecy fulfilled in the 586 B.C. destruction of the city by the Babylonians. The people of "Benjamin" (6:1) were exhorted to flee from Jerusalem because of its impending judgment. Tekoa (6:1) was situated on the edge of the Judean wilderness, twelve miles south of Jerusalem. Beth Hakkerem (6:1) has been identified with Ramat Rahel, located two miles south of Jerusalem.

The phrase "shepherds with their flocks" (6:3) was used figuratively to refer to the enemy kings and flocks of invaders (cf. 12:10) coming to feed on Judah. The "watchmen" were the prophets (6:17; cf. Ezek. 3:17), who were supposed to rebuke the nation's sins and warn the people of coming disaster. Costly but superficial sacrifices could not please God (6:20). Ancient "Sheba" (6:20) was located in the southern Arabian Peninsula in the vicinity of modern Yemen. To arouse the nation from its apathy, the approaching Babylonian enemy was described in terrifying terms (6:22-26). A "tester" (6:27) tested the quality of a metal to determine its value.

7:1–19:13 COVENANT RENEWAL AND CHASTISEMENTS

Overview: The people were to understand why they were going to be disciplined so severely (7:1–10:25). From the temple's gates (7:2) Jeremiah criticized Israel's false hope in the temple building (7:4). He urged them to remember what had happened at Shiloh and why it had happened (7:8-15). He drove them to search for true heart-level service to God rather than depend on the false security of an external and legalistic religion (9:23-24). He is God the Creator, not a false god of human imagination (Jer. 10). The command for heart-level obedience would be fulfilled in the new covenant mentioned in Jeremiah 31. The punishment of the nation was done in full light of the future promises of blessing and restoration.

The nation's sins were so great that God told Jeremiah not to pray for the people's deliverance (7:16; 11:14; 14:11). The potential still remained for international blessing for the nations who learned the ways of God through the ways of his people (12:14-17). The prophecy foretelling the Babylonian captivity (Jer. 13) was followed by a list of sins and judgments (14:1–19:13), including drought (14:1–15:21), military judgment, and Sabbath breaking (17:1-27). This section ended with the mention of the potter's rights (18:1-23) over the pot's destruction (19:1-13).

7:1–10:25 Understanding in Chastisement

7:1-34 UNDERSTAND SHILOH'S JUDGMENT
In Jeremiah's "temple sermon," which he delivered at the gate of the temple, he warned that the people could not expect to be delivered from attack simply because of the presence of the temple in Jerusalem (7:4). They were reminded of God's past judgment on Shiloh (7:12), where the tabernacle had been set up. What had happened at Shiloh could also happen to Jerusalem. The theme of Jeremiah's temple sermon was presented in 7:3. Jesus quoted 7:11 in Mark 11:17; cf. Luke 19:46. Shiloh (7:12), located about twenty miles north of Jerusalem, was the location of the tabernacle in the time of the judges (Josh. 18:1). The city was destroyed by the Philistines around 1050 B.C. The

"queen of heaven" (Jer. 7:18) referred to the heathen fertility goddess Astarte, known in Babylon as Ishtar (cf. 44:17).

With stinging sarcasm, God rebuked the people whose sacrifices meant nothing as expressions of genuine worship (7:21-22). Obedience, not ritual, had been God's overriding concern when he instituted the sacrifices at Sinai (1 Sam. 15:22; Hos. 6:6). "Topheth" (Jer. 7:31) probably meant "fireplace." "Hinnom" (6:31) referred to the L-shaped valley situated west and south of Jerusalem where the heathen custom of child sacrifice was practiced (cf. 2 Kings 16:3; 21:6).

8:1–10:25 UNDERSTAND WISDOM VERSUS FOOLISHNESS
The desecration of graves was practiced as a supreme insult to the dead (Jer. 8:1-2; cf. Deut. 21:22-23). The Lord warned that Judah's stubborn apostasy was the sure way to national ruin (Jer. 8:4-17). Jeremiah lamented the iniquity of Zion (8:18–9:22). The "balm" (8:22) referred to a resin used for healing purposes. Gilead (8:22), a region east of the Jordan River, was famous for its balm from early times (cf. Gen. 37:25). Jeremiah 9:16 was the prophet's first mention of Judah's dispersion from the land. It was the ultimate judgment on the nation for violating the stipulations of the covenant (cf. Lev. 26:33; Deut. 28:64). The "mourning women" (Jer. 9:17) were professional and hired mourners (cf. Matt. 9:23). Those who "clip the hair by their temples" (Jer. 9:26, NASB and NIV footnote) referred to an idolatrous religious practice that violated Leviticus 19:27. For the significance of circumcision, see the note on 4:3-4.

Jeremiah 10 set forth the greatness of God, the Creator and Sustainer of the universe, contrasted with impotent idols. For "Tarshish" (10:9), see the note on Jonah 1:3. The location of "Uphaz" (10:9) is unknown. Jeremiah 10:11 was written in Aramaic, a Semitic language similar to Hebrew and the common language of the people in exile. The Lord instructed the people, "gather up your belongings" for the trip into exile (10:17). The land was likened to a tent that had been pulled down and destroyed (10:20). The "shepherds" (10:21) is a figurative reference to the leaders of the nation.

11:1–19:13 Covenant Recall

11:1–13:27 THE CALL TO OBEDIENCE

11:1-23 Impending curses. In 11:1-5 the
prophet called the people into remembrance
of the Mosaic covenant, which God had instituted with his people at Sinai. The covenant
promised blessings for obedience and curses
for disobedience (Deut. 28–30). Because
the Israelites had violated the covenant,
they would receive the judgments that God
had promised (11:10-11). A plot against
Jeremiah's life by the men of his hometown,
Anathoth, was reflected in 11:18-23. They
wanted to kill him and thus silence his
message (11:19).

12:1-17 Times of judgment and compassion.
Reflecting on his own sufferings, Jeremiah
wrestled with the age-old question of why
the wicked prosper (12:6). God responded,
"The worst is yet to come!" The Lord
described the judgment coming on Judah
with such certainty that he spoke as if it had
already occurred (12:7-13). The "wicked"
(12:14) were nations neighboring Judah
(Aram, Moab, and Ammon) that would share
her fate of exile from the land.

13:1-27 Waistband: obedience. The "linen
belt" was used in ancient times to brace a
man's hip joints for prolonged periods of
exertion and to hold up his robe for greater
freedom in walking and work. The Euphrates
River is 350 to 400 miles northeast of the
land of Judah (13:4). Some scholars suggest
that the text refers not to the Euphrates but to
the village of Parah, located about three
miles from Jeremiah's hometown. The two
names are almost identical in the Hebrew.
Just as the waistband was ruined by the
waters of the Euphrates, in the same way
the Lord would also destroy Jerusalem and
Judah because of their sin (13:7).

The filled wine jugs symbolized the fact
that God would fill the people with confusion, as when men are drunk (13:12-14).
Their drunkenness would lead to their
destruction. The prophet was instructed to
address King Jehoiachin and the queen
mother, Nehushta (13:18; cf. 2 Kings 24:8).
"Those coming from the north" were the
Babylonians (13:20). The stark metaphor of
13:26 was taken from the public shaming of
a harlot. The "adulteries" (13:27) referred to
the peoples' idolatrous worship that
frequently involved cultic prostitution.

14:1–19:13 THE LIST OF CURSES

14:1–15:21 Drought. The drought that came
upon Judah was one of the curses of disobedience spoken of in the Mosaic covenant
(14:1-6; cf. Deut. 28:24; Lev. 26:19).
Jeremiah prayed twice (Jer. 14:7-9, 19-22)
that the Lord would spare Judah the
promised judgment, but twice he was told
that the prayers for the nation were futile
(14:10-12; 15:1-9). Nothing could alter the
judgment for which the nation was destined.
Jeremiah also appealed to God's covenant
promise (Gen. 12:1-3) as a theological basis
for his sparing the nation (Jer. 14:21).

Moses (15:1; cf. Exod. 32:11-14) and
Samuel (1 Sam. 7:5-9; 12:19-25) were noted
as great prayer warriors who had prayed in
behalf of the nation. For Manasseh's sin (Jer.
15:4), see 2 Kings 23:26; 24:3. The
"winnowing" process was a means of
separating wheat from chaff (Jer. 15:7).
Grain was tossed into the air, and the wind
blew the lighter chaff away while the grain's
kernels fell at the feet of the winnower.

Jeremiah experienced both despair and
strengthening by the Lord (15:10-21). In
Jeremiah's day the hardest iron came from
regions in the north (15:12). Certainly
Judah's "iron" had no chance to break the
stronger "iron" of Babylonia. In the depths
of his despair, Jeremiah charged God with
deception (15:18). Like a brook that dries up
in the summer when it is most needed, so
God had seemingly failed him.

16:1-21 Military judgment and restoration.
The life of Jeremiah was to illustrate his
message to Judah of her coming judgment.
He was prohibited from marrying (16:1-4),
mourning (16:5-7), and feasting (16:8-9).
The expression "offer food" (16:7) referred
to the custom of providing a meal for mourners after the funeral (2 Sam. 3:35). The
"drink to console" may have referred to a
similar custom. Although God would exile
the people, he promised to restore them later
to their homeland (16:13-15; cf. Deut. 30:1-
10). The thought of 16:13 regarding the
captivity was continued in 16:16. Like
"fishermen" and "hunters," the Babylonians
would capture and destroy the Judeans.

17:1-27 Sabbath breaking. The sin of the nation and the consequent judgment were once again highlighted. Indelible sin meant inevitable judgment. The "Asherah" (17:2) referred to the Canaanite fertility goddess whose image was set up on hills and in sacred groves of trees. The words "My mountain" (17:3) probably referred to Jerusalem. Compare Psalm 1 with Jeremiah 17:7-8. Jeremiah saw the Sabbath as a test case for obedience (17:19-27). The observance of the Sabbath was the prerequisite for the return of national glory and prosperity. The "Negev" (17:26) is the dry region located just south of Judah, centering around Beersheba.

18:1–19:13 The land as a reproach. Just as the potter had control over the clay on his wheel, the Lord was sovereign over the nations of the earth—to build them up or to destroy them. The potter's "wheel" (18:3) consisted of two flat, circular stones connected by a vertical axis. The potter turned the lower stone with his feet, which caused the upper "wheel" to revolve. The rhetorical questions in 18:14 sought a negative answer. The point was that while nature pursues its God-directed course unchanged, the nation had unnaturally changed its course by turning from God. In response to his enemies' plot against his life, Jeremiah prayed that God would bring upon them the curses of the covenant (18:18-23; cf. Deut. 28:15-68). The theological basis for this prayer is found in God's promise in Genesis 12:3.

In Jeremiah 19 the breaking of the potter's jar illustrated the calamity that was soon to come upon Judah and Jerusalem (19:3). The "Valley of Ben Hinnom" is identical with the valley of the sons ("ben") of Hinnom. See the note on 7:31. The "blood of the innocent" (19:4) referred to the children who were sacrificed in heathen ceremonies in the Hinnom Valley. The "drink offerings" (19:13) were sacrifices or offerings of wine (cf. Num. 15:4-5).

19:14–29:32 GOING OVER THE LEADERS' HEADS TO THE PEOPLE

Overview: Jeremiah was beaten and imprisoned by the priests (Jer. 19:14–20:18). He then reproached King Zedekiah for his sinful leadership (21:1–24:10). The shepherd theme (12:10; 23:1) reappeared. At this point

in the book, the time shifts backward to the fourth year of Jehoiakim and his twenty-three-year rebellion against God (25:1-38; cf. 25:3-4, 12-14). Moving back farther to events during the first year of Jehoiakim's reign (26:1-24), the author records Jeremiah's escape from the king's death sentence. The next scene moves ahead to the fourth year of Zedekiah (28:1). There, Zedekiah was warned to submit to Nebuchadnezzar (27:1-22), and Hananiah received a death sentence from Jeremiah for his false prophecy (28:1-17). But prophets also were lying to the Israelite exiles in Babylon, promising a quick release. In response, Jeremiah wrote his famous letter to the exiles in which he clearly told them to settle in for a seventy-year stay (29:1-32).

19:14–20:18 Priestly Opposition

Jeremiah 20 records the response of the religious establishment to Jeremiah's message of coming judgment on Judah and Jerusalem. "Pashhur" (20:1) ranked next to the high priest in authority and had charge of the temple area. His position may have been identical with the "captain of the temple guard" (Acts 4:1). Jeremiah gave Pashhur a new name, Magor-Missabib, meaning "terror on every side," symbolic of the coming judgment on Jerusalem by the Babylonians. In 20:7-18 is found one of Jeremiah's most revealing confessions. His prayer illustrates the personal cost of faithfully declaring God's word (20:8).

21:1–22:30 Kingly Reproach

The prophecy recorded in Jeremiah 21 took place in the reign of Zedekiah (597–586 B.C.), the last king of Judah. He was urged to submit to Nebuchadnezzar in light of the certainty of Jerusalem's fall (21:10). The words "you who live above this valley" (21:13) were a reference to Jerusalem's inhabitants.

There are two possible interpretations of Jeremiah 22: (1) It is a prophecy concerning judgment on Shallum, Jehoiakim, and Coniah (or Jehoiachin); or (2) it is a prophecy of judgment on Zedekiah (21:1, 3; 22:1, 6, 10, 30), illustrated by the divine judgment that fell on his three predecessors. According to the second view, there was no curse on the line of Coniah (22:24-30) because Jeremiah was referring to Zedekiah. The fact that

Matthew did not recognize a curse on Jehoia-chin (Matt. 1:11) lends support to this inter-pretation.

In Jeremiah 22:1-9 the prophet addressed Zedekiah, the reigning "king of Judah" (22:1). Shallum (or Jehoahaz) took the throne after Josiah's death but reigned only three months (2 Kings 23:31-34). In 22:13-23 Jehoiakim (609–597 B.C.) succeeded Shallum. This wicked king received a donkey's burial, which actually was no burial at all (Jer. 22:18-19; 2 Kings 24:6). Coniah (Jer. 22:24-28), also called Jehoia-chin and Jeconiah, reigned only three months before Nebuchadezzer captured Jerusalem in 597 B.C. and exiled ten thousand Judeans (2 Kings 24:8-16). Coniah was imprisoned in Babylon but later released (2 Kings 25:27-30). The book of Jeremiah ends by recount-ing the event of Coniah's release (52:28-34).

In 22:29-30 Jeremiah concluded his oracle with an application that went back to Zedekiah ("This man," 22:30), the addressee of Jeremiah 21–22. The word "childless" referred to the fact that Zedekiah's sons were slain by Nebuchadnezzar before he was exiled to Babylon. None of his children sat on the throne of David.

23:1–29:32 Prophetic Hostility

23:1-40 THE RESULTANT REPROACH
Jeremiah describes the coming of the Messiah, the righteous King. The "shepherds" referred to the wicked rulers of Judah (10:21). The term "Branch" (23:5) is a Messianic title (cf. Isa. 11:1; Zech. 3:8; 6:12) and indicated that the Messiah would be a fresh sprout from the stump of a felled tree, that is, the seemingly dead line of David. The religious leaders, that is, the false proph-ets and apostate priests, were condemned (Jer. 23:9-40). The Hebrew term translated "oracle" (23:33) was a standard term for a message received by divine revelation. The misuse of this term by the false prophets and apostate priests brought it into disrepute (23:36).

24:1-10 THE REPROACH OF ZEDEKIAH
AND HIS OFFICIALS
Jeremiah's vision of 24:1-10 took place after the captivity of Jehoiachin in 597 B.C. The "good figs" were Judeans removed from the land, whereas the "bad figs" were those, like Zedekiah, who remained.

25:1-38 THE FOURTH YEAR OF JEHOIAKIM
The duration of the Babylonian captivity was revealed. The "fourth year of Jehoiakim" was 605 B.C. The "seventy" years (25:12) can be calculated from either 605 B.C. or 586 B.C. It is probably best to figure the period from 605 B.C., since that was the date of the proph-ecy. The conclusion of the period was 536 B.C. (including both 605 and 586 B.C. in the seventy years), when the returned Jewish exiles began rebuilding the Jerusalem temple (Ezra 3:1-6). Judgments would come on apostate Israel and the nations that had oppressed God's people (Jer. 25:15-38). The universal extent of that judgment (25:30-31) suggests that the verses referred all the way ahead to the future end-time tribulation events.

26:1-24 THE FIRST YEAR OF JEHOIAKIM
Jeremiah 26 records the circumstances surrounding Jeremiah's preaching of the temple sermon (7:1–8:3). For "Shiloh" (26:6), see the note on 7:12. Micah's proph-ecy of judgment against Jerusalem and the temple (Mic. 3:12) was recalled as evidence against putting Jeremiah to death (Jer. 26:8, 18). But the ultimate reason that Jeremiah was spared death was because of God's promise (26:24; cf. 1:18-19).

27:1–28:17 THE FOURTH YEAR
OF ZEDEKIAH
27:1-22 Submission to Nebuchadnezzar.
Zedekiah (597–586 B.C.) was placed on the throne by Nebuchadnezzar and was the last king of Judah. Although at first Zedekiah submitted to Babylonian rule, he later conspired with neighboring kings to over-throw Babylon. Jeremiah sought to correct the notion that such an overthrow was possi-ble (27:12), urging submission rather than rebellion. The "yoke and crossbars" (27:2) were symbolic of Judah's certain subjection by Babylon. The "articles from the Lord's house" (27:16) had been taken by Nebuchad-nezzar when he sacked Jerusalem in 597 B.C. (2 Kings 24:13). Usually a conqueror took a defeated nation's idols as a symbolic gesture of victory. But since the Jewish faith toler-ated no idols, the temple vessels were taken instead. The promise of Jeremiah 27:22 was fulfilled in 537 B.C. when Sheshbazzar led the first group of exiles back to Jerusalem (Ezra 1:7-11).

28:1-17 False Hananiah. Hananiah, a false prophet, broke Jeremiah's "yoke" (Jer. 27:2) and predicted that Babylon would fall and the exiles would return within two years (cf. 25:11). In 28:1 it seems unusual to call the fourth year of Zedekiah the "early" part of his reign. But according to Jewish practice, the reign was divided into halves—the beginning and the end. The beginning was simply the first half of his reign. The word "Amen!" (28:6) means "may it be confirmed." Jeremiah wished such a prophecy could be true. About two months elapsed between Hananiah's false prophecy and his death (cf. 28:1).

29:1-32 FALSE PROPHETS IN BABYLON
Jeremiah 29 records Jeremiah's letter written to the Judean exiles who had been taken to Babylon in 597 B.C. (2 Kings 24:10-17). Once again (29:10; cf. 25:11), a seventy-year captivity was anticipated. But a return to the land of Israel was also promised (cf. Deut. 30:1-5). The punishment of Zedekiah and Ahab was like that experienced by Daniel's three friends (Dan. 3:20). Only, for these two false prophets, there was no deliverance. Instead, they became an object lesson of the Lord's wrath (Jer. 29:23). Jeremiah's letter (29:24-28) provoked opposition from Shemaiah, a Judean leader in Babylon who called for the Jerusalem temple's authorities ("Zephaniah" the priest, and "all the priests") to rebuke Jeremiah for his prophecies.

30:1-33:22 NEW COVENANT RESTORATION
Overview: The section of 30:1-33:22 is the central section on the restoration of God's people (30:3). It begins with the certainty of God's promise to David (30:9) and ends with an explosion of covenant promises that will be as certain as the covenant for day and night (33:25): the covenants with David (33:15-17, 26), Moses (33:18), and Abraham (33:26). God explained that Israel would understand his discipline and his lovingkindness in the latter days (30:24). Jeremiah 31 elaborates on the time of restoration and understanding. The shepherd theme reappears (31:10), but unlike the hostile shepherds of the past, this Shepherd will be the Lord himself. Note the appearance of the section divider, "Behold the days are coming" (31:27, 31, 38; 33:14). Jeremiah 32,

in the tenth year of Zedekiah, describes not only the downfall of Jerusalem but also the promise of restoration.

30:1-31:40 Promise of Discernment in the End
30:1-31:26 RESTORED FORTUNES: LAND
If Jeremiah 30-31 was written at the same time as Jeremiah 32-33, then the year was 587 B.C., and Jerusalem was under Nebuchadnezzar's siege (32:1). Jeremiah was in prison while famine and pestilence raged in Jerusalem and the Babylonians were at the city's gates. This was Judah's darkest hour, and the people were in need of hope and comfort. Jeremiah announced that the nation of Israel would be preserved, restored, and given a new covenant. The "time of trouble for Jacob" (30:7) refers to the coming tribulation during which the people of Israel will suffer intense persecution (Matt. 24:9-22). "That day" (Jer. 30:8) is the day of the Messiah's return to judge his enemies and deliver the believing remnant of Israel from the antichrist's persecution (cf. Zech. 14:1-4).

After the tribulation (30:12-17), God will bring healing to the seemingly incurable wounds received by Israel as the result of her sin and God's divine judgment. The healing will be both physical (restoration to prosperity) and spiritual (restoration of blessing). In the Messiah's kingdom, Jerusalem will be reestablished as the center of rightful rule and true worship. The "leader" (30:21) is the Messiah. The often-repeated phrase of 30:22 (cf. Exod. 6:7; Jer. 32:38; Ezek. 36:28; Hos. 2:23; Zech. 13:9) expresses God's covenantal intention for his people.

During a time of future blessing the faithful of both Israel (Jer. 31:1-22) and Judah (31:23-26) will be gathered from their dispersion into the Land of Promise. Ramah (31:15), the home of Samuel (1 Sam. 7:17), was located about five miles north of Jerusalem. It was there that the captives were gathered before being taken to Babylon (40:1). In this poetic figure, Rachel, the mother of Joseph and Benjamin, is portrayed as weeping for her descendants going into exile. Matthew saw fulfillment of this verse in Herod's slaughter of the children in Bethlehem (Matt. 2:17-18). The meaning of the prophecy "a woman will surround a man" (31:22) is debated. Among the views are:

(1) the virgin birth of Christ; (2) the strength of Israel ("a woman"); she will become strong enough to protect others; (3) the return to God; Israel will encompass or cling to the Lord. The context lends support to the third view.

31:27-30 BUILD AND PLANT: INDIVIDUAL ACCOUNTABILITY

The words of Jeremiah 31:28 are based on the commission given to Jeremiah in 1:10.

31:31-37 THE NEW COVENANT

The section of 31:31-37 is the central Old Testament passage on the new covenant (quoted in Heb. 8:6-13). Because Israel had failed to keep the old covenant (the contractual obligation begun at Mount Sinai), God promised that he would institute a new and better one. This promise amplified and confirmed the blessing promise of the Abrahamic covenant (Gen. 12:3). It was unconditional ("I will"), everlasting (Ezek. 37:6) and promised regeneration and the forgiveness of sin (31:33-34) through faith in Christ, based on his sacrificial death for sins (1 Cor. 11:25; Heb. 7:22; 8:6-13).

The repeated words "declares the Lord" (31:31-34) divide the promise into its major sections. The first section "At that time" (31:31; "Behold, days are coming," NASB) makes the promise certain for a future time. The second section (31:31-32) stresses that the new covenant will not be like the old covenant that people broke. The implication is that something will happen to keep people from breaking the new covenant. The third section (31:33) announces the new covenant. The fourth section (31:33-34) shows in what way the covenant is new. It puts the law of God in a new place—the heart (cf. 24:7; 29:13; 32:40). That results in a universal relationship with and knowledge of God. The fifth section (31:34) gives the reason ("for") why the new covenant can happen. The iniquity and sin of God's people will be forgiven and forgotten.

The new covenant was a renewed covenant that replaced the shadow of the Mosaic covenant with the substance of Christ's sacrifice and heavenly mediation. It was made with the same people of God, the children of Abraham by faith. It contained the same law of God (cf. Deut. 6:6-7; 10:12; 30:6) but placed it in the heart. It promised a saving relationship with the same God (cf. Exod. 34:6-7 and 2 Cor. 6:16). And it offered complete forgiveness (cf. Exod. 34:6-7; Lev. 4:20; Num. 14:18; Deut. 5:9-10). The new covenant took up the elements of the Mosaic covenant but expanded and deepened them into fulfillment. The permanence of the cycles of nature (31:35-36) illustrated the certainty of God's preservation of the Hebrew people.

31:38-40 THE CITY IS REBUILT

The "Tower of Hananel" was located along the north wall of ancient Jerusalem. The "Corner Gate" was probably situated at the northwest corner of the wall. The locations of "Gareb" and "Goah" are unknown. The "valley where dead bodies are thrown" referred to the Hinnom (7:31). The brook "Kidron" separated the temple mount from the Mount of Olives. The "Horse Gate" was in the east wall of the city.

32:1-44 A Picture of Restoration

Jeremiah's purchase of a field near Jerusalem demonstrated the prophet's faith in God's promise of restoration. The "tenth" year of Zedekiah (32:1) was 587 B.C. Jerusalem was under siege and Jeremiah was in prison, having been incarcerated by Zedekiah for prophesying the fall of Jerusalem. The transaction in 32:7 was based on the law of redemption (cf. Lev. 25:25, 32-34).

Jeremiah's purchase of the field (32:10) took on greater significance when it was realized that it had already fallen to the Babylonians. The purchase was Jeremiah's expression of faith that God would one day restore Israel to the land as he had promised (32:15). Baruch was Jeremiah's scribe, or secretary, who wrote much of the book under the prophet's direction (cf. 36:27-28). The "siege ramps" (32:24) were earthen ramps built against the city walls by the invaders. The ramps provided access to the weaker, upper sections of the walls. The L-shaped Ben Hinnom Valley lies west and south of Jerusalem. Molech was the god of the Ammonites whose worship included child sacrifice.

33:1-26 Certainty of Restoration

Jeremiah 33 continues the theme of restoration that was introduced in Jeremiah 30. Here Jeremiah predicted restoration to the land (33:1-9), restoration to prosperity (33:10-13), and restoration of the Davidic throne (33:14-26). These prophecies related to Israel's future. The "Branch of David" is a Messianic title (23:5-6; cf. Isa. 4:2; 11:1-5; Zech. 3:8; 6:12). Jesus, the Messiah, will sit on David's throne and rule his kingdom (cf. 2 Sam. 7:12-16; Luke 1:32-33). "My covenant with David" (Jer. 33:21) referred to God's promise in 2 Samuel 7:12-16. It was as certain as the ordinances of heaven.

34:1–45:5 COVENANT CHASTISEMENT CONFIRMED: SUBMIT OR DIE!

Overview: The section of Jeremiah 34:1–45:5 is a section of contrasts. The Babylonian captivity mirrored the nation's captivity of its own people in slavery (34:1-22). The Rechabites' obedience to their ancestral father stood in stark contrast to Israel's disobedience to her heavenly Father (35:1-19). God commanded that a scroll be written so that its hearers might repent and release God's forgiveness (36:3). But the king's officials feared the king, and the king did not fear God. Instead, he burned the scroll that was designed to avert destruction and bring about God's blessing (36:1-32).

The section of 37:1–45:5 revolved around Israel's hope in Egypt versus her hope in God. Zedekiah received no help from Egypt (38:1-28) or from trying to escape from Jerusalem (39:1-18). The Jews who remained after the downfall of Jerusalem were commanded to stay in Israel (40:1-16) and definitely not go down to Egypt (42:1-22). But they murdered Gedeliah (41:1-18) and chose flight into Egypt (42:1-22). From Egypt, Jeremiah predicted destruction by Babylon (43:1-13) due to the Jews' idolatry (44:1-30). There was painful irony to see Israel returning to Egypt, the place of her original bondage and redemption. A short prophecy of Jeremiah 45 serves as a summary of Jeremiah's prophecies and concludes the broad section of Jeremiah 1–45.

34:1-22 Siege: Submit to Babylon

The events of Jeremiah 34 illustrate the depths to which the king and people of Jeremiah's day had plunged. While Jerusa-

lem was under attack (34:6-7), Jeremiah delivered a message from God to King Zedekiah (34:1-2) and the people (34:8-22). The fate of Zedekiah (34:4) was recorded in 2 Kings 25:5-7. Lachish (34:7) was a fortress city located twenty-three miles southwest of Jerusalem. Azekah (34:7) was located eleven miles north of Lachish (see introductory map). Both cities are well known from the "Lachish Letters," which were written in Hebrew at the time of Nebuchadnezzar's invasion of Judah and discovered in 1935. Letter IV reads, "We are watching for the signals of Lachish . . . for we no longer can see the signals of Azekah."

Perhaps to gain God's favor, Zedekiah induced the people to promise to emancipate their Hebrew slaves, who according to the law were supposed to be given their freedom after six years (34:8-10; cf. Exod. 21:1-6; Deut. 15:12-18). When the Babylonian siege lifted temporarily due to the approach of the Egyptian army (Jer. 37:6-11), the pledge was broken and the slaves were returned to servitude. When ancient covenants were ratified, an animal was sacrificed, and those participating in the agreement walked between the parts (34:18). By this they were saying, "So may I be [that is, dead] if I break this covenant" (cf. Gen. 15:9-17).

35:1–36:32 Kingly Lack of Submission

35:1-19 RECHABITE OBEDIENCE

The Rechabites were descendants of a nomadic tribe of Kenites who had joined with the Israelites when the Babylonians invaded the land (Jer. 35:11). They were followers of Jehonadab, the son of Rechab (2 Kings 10:15-16, 23), who sought to maintain the desert ideal by avoiding the "corruptions" of city life, such as farming, wine, and houses. The Rechabites were obedient to their dead ancestor in contrast to the Judeans who had disobeyed their living God.

36:1-32 DISOBEDIENCE IN THE DAVIDIC LINE

Jeremiah 36 recorded the contempt of Jehoiakim for the word of God. The "scroll" (36:2), which was made of papyrus or vellum, would be used to record Jeremiah's prophecies from 627 B.C. until the "fourth year of Jehoiakim" (36:1) or 605 B.C. For "Baruch"

(36:4), see the note on 32:12. The date was December 604 B.C. The probable reason for the "fasting" (36:9) was the increased threat of a Babylonian invasion of Judah. The "winter apartment" (36:22) may have referred to a warmer, more sheltered room of the palace. No historical record was provided about the details of Jehoiakim's death (36:30; cf. 2 Kings 24:6). This judgment was one of the curses of disobedience specified in the covenant (Deut. 28:26).

37:1–39:10 Zedekiah's End

37:1-21 NO HELP FROM PHARAOH
During a brief lifting of the Babylonian siege due to the advance of the Egyptians (Jer. 37:5), Jeremiah sought to leave Jerusalem to attend to some family property (37:12). Apparently he was charged with desertion (37:13) and imprisoned underground (37:15-16). The "vaulted cell in a dungeon" (37:16) was probably an empty cistern, an underground water reservoir. Pharaoh Hophra (44:30), ruler of Egypt (589–570 B.C.), may have encouraged Zedekiah to revolt and then came to his aid.

38:1–39:10 NO HELP IN FLIGHT
The term "official" (38:7) or "eunuch" (NASB and KJV) originally referred to one who cared for the king's harem (cf. "the women," 38:22). Later the term was used of a trusted officer or palace official. The fall and destruction of Jerusalem are described in greater detail in Jeremiah 52. After eighteen months of siege, the walls of Jerusalem were breached on the ninth of Tammuz (our June–July) in 586 B.C. (39:1-2). One month later the city was burned (cf. 52:12-13). Some have equated "Nergal-Sharezer" (39:3) with Neriglissar, who succeeded Nebuchadnezzar's son (560–556 B.C.). For 39:10, see Jeremiah 24:8-10.

39:11–44:30 Gedeliah's End

39:11–43:7 MURDER AND FLIGHT TO EGYPT
At Ramah (40:1), situated five miles north of Jerusalem, the Judeans were gathered in preparation for deportation. In the absence of a Judean king, Gedaliah was appointed governor of Judah (40:5; cf. 2 Kings 25:22-24). Mizpah (now Tell en-Nasbeh) was located eight miles north of Jerusalem. It became the administrative center during Gedaliah's short governorship (Jer. 40:6).

Why was Gedaliah assassinated (41:1-2)? It may have been that Ishmael, a member of the royal family, was jealous for the throne. Or perhaps Gedaliah was viewed as a traitor for assuming a post under the appointment of the Babylonians. The men demonstrated extreme signs of mourning at his death (41:5). "Geruth Kimham" meant the lodging place of Kimham, the son of Barzillai, who exhibited such kindness to David (41:17; cf. 2 Sam. 17:27-29; 19:31-39).

Afraid to stay in Judah after the murder of Gedaliah (Jer. 42:1–43:7), the people who were on the way to Egypt (41:17) stopped to ask Jeremiah to ask God what they should do (42:1-3). The answer came from God that they should stay in the land and not go to Egypt (42:19), but they decided to go to Egypt anyway, forcing Jeremiah to go with them (43:1-7). For Tahpanhes (43:7), see the note on 2:16.

43:8–44:30 NO HELP IN EGYPT
Jeremiah's prediction of the Babylonian conquest of Egypt was fulfilled in 568 B.C. by Nebuchadnezzar during the reign of Pharaoh Ahmosis II (43:8-13). Heliopolis ("city of the sun"), located near modern Cairo, was a worship center for the sun-god Re. The "sacred pillars" (43:13) were tall, tapered granite shafts used by the Egyptians as monuments.

Jeremiah warned the Jews in Egypt of the consequences of idolatry (44:1-10). For Tahpanhes, see the note on 2:16. Migdol (44:1) was located near the northeast boundary of Egypt. Memphis (44:1), still in existence today, is located about fifteen miles south of modern Cairo. In Upper Egypt (44:1) some Jews established a military colony at Yeb (Elephantine). Rejecting the words of Jeremiah, the Jews declared their allegiance to the "Queen of Heaven" (44:17), a reference to the heathen fertility deity known in Canaan as Astarte (the Babylonian Ishtar). The downfall of Pharaoh Hophra (588–569 B.C.) would serve to confirm God's word through Jeremiah (44:29-30). He was assassinated by a former government official Amasis, also known as Ahmoses II (569–526 B.C.).

45:1-5 Summary

The brief message of Jeremiah in 45:1-5 to his scribe, Baruch, was dictated in the fourth year of Jehoiakim, or 605 B.C. Baruch's reward was his physical preservation. He would suffer with the Judeans, but his life would be spared.

46:1–51:64 GOD'S RULE OVER THE NATIONS

Overview: In the middle of all the gloom of Jeremiah 1–45, Jeremiah 30–33 stood out as a bright light of God's ultimate restoration of Israel to be over the nations. In Jeremiah 46–51 are collected several prophecies against foreign nations that reinforced that ultimate restoration. The nations' hostile attitudes toward Israel are summed up in 50:7, 11 and 51:24, 49. The judgment was a direct reflection of God's promise to Abraham to curse those who cursed Israel (Gen. 12:3). Jeremiah was ordained "a prophet to the nations" (Jer. 1:5, 10). The nations prophesied against were Egypt (46:1-28), Philistia (47:1-7), Moab (48:1-47), Ammon (49:1-6), Edom (49:7-22), Damascus (49:23-27), Hazor (49:28-33), Elam (49:34-39), and Babylonia (50:1–51:64). Egypt and Babylonia begin and end the list as the two nations that had held Israel in bondage. Babylonia received the most space concerning judgment. The relation of this list to Israel's hope was found in 46:28; 50:33-34; 51:5. God also had gracious plans for many of the hostile nations (48:47; 49:6, 39).

46:1-28 Egypt

The defeat of Egypt at the battle of Carchemish in 605 B.C. gave Babylonia dominion over the land of Israel. "Cush" (46:9), "Ethiopia" (NASB), or "Ethiopians" (KJV) referred to the region south of Egypt (the Upper Nile region). "Put" referred to the northern coast of Africa. The Lydians were inhabitants of Asia Minor, and the Egyptians employed them as mercenaries. For the "balm" of Gilead (46:11), see the note on Jeremiah 8:22. For locations of cities in 46:14, see the note on 44:1. Mount Tabor (46:18) is located in the Jezreel Valley. Mount Carmel reaches its peak on the Mediterranean coast near modern Haifa. Thebes (46:25) is located about four hundred miles up the Nile from Cairo. Amon was the chief deity worshiped there.

47:1-7 Philistia

The Philistines migrated from the Aegean Islands under pressure from the Dorian Greeks around 1168 B.C. They were repulsed from the Delta of Egypt and settled on the southern coastal plain of Israel. The name Palestine is derived from Philistine. The reference in 47:1 was to Pharaoh Neco's campaign in 609 B.C. when he went to the aid of Assyria against Babylonia (2 Kings 23:29). The "waters . . . in the north" (47:2) referred to the invasion by Babylonia. Tyre and Sidon were Phoenician cities. Caphtor referred to Crete, one of the Mediterranean islands from which the Philistines came (Amos 9:7). Gaza and Ashkelon were two of Philistia's five principal cities located on the Mediterranean coast of Philistia to the southwest of Israel.

48:1-47 Moab

The Moabites were the descendants of the incestuous union of Lot and his eldest daughter (Gen. 19:30-38). They occupied the region east of the Dead Sea between the Arnon and Zered rivers. The background of the prophetic judgments may have been the attack mentioned in 2 Kings 24:2. Chemosh (48:7) was the chief deity of the Moabites (Num. 21:29; 2 Kings 23:13). The "dregs" (48:11; "lees," NASB, KJV) referred to the sludge at the bottom of a flask of wine. Like the undisturbed lees, Moab had not yet gone into exile. Dibon (48:18), famous for the discovery of the Moabite Stone, was located north of the Arnon, thirteen miles east of the Dead Sea. The land of Moab (48:42) was inhabited by the Nabateans in the first century B.C. and later by the Arabs.

49:1-6 Ammon

The Ammonites were the descendants of the incestuous union of Lot and his youngest daughter (Gen. 19:30-38). They occupied the desert region north of Moab. Malcam (also spelled Milcom) was the chief deity of Ammon (1 Kings 11:5). Rabbah, the capital of Ammon, was located at the site of modern Amman, the capital of Jordan.

49:7-22 Edom

The Edomites were the descendants of Esau, Jacob's twin brother (Gen. 25:21-25; 36:8).

They lived in the desert region south of the Dead Sea. Teman was a city in Edom thought to be located about three miles east of Petra. Dedan was a tribe of traders descended from Abraham and Keturah (Gen. 25:3) dwelling southeast of Edom. Bozrah was a fortified city in Edom located about thirty miles north of Petra.

49:23-27 Damascus

Damascus, the capital of the Aramaeans (Syria), survives as a major city today and is located about 130 miles north of Jerusalem. Hamath was located on the Orontes River about 110 miles north of Damascus. Arpad was situated about 20 miles northwest of Aleppo.

49:28-33 Hazor

Jeremiah 49:28-33 is related to Nebuchadnezzar's attempt to bring certain regions of the Syrian desert under Babylonian control (599 B.C.). Kedar was the son of Ishmael (Gen. 25:13). The Hazor mentioned here was a desert area, not the city in northern Israel.

49:34-39 Elam

Elam was a region of Mesopotamia located just north of the Persian Gulf. Elam was overrun by Nebuchadnezzar in the winter of 596 B.C. This nation, as a part of the Medo-Persian Empire, later overthrew Babylonian rule (cf. Isa. 21:2; Dan. 8:2).

50:1–51:64
Babylon's Scroll of Destruction

Babylon, located in central Mesopotamia on the Euphrates, was the capital of the Babylonian Empire. The term "Chaldean" referred to the ruling dynasty of Babylon but was used synonymously with the term "Babylonian." Bel (50:2) was the Babylonian equivalent of the Canaanite Baal. Marduk was the chief god of Babylon. The nation (50:3) that rose against Babylon was Persia under the leadership of Cyrus. He came from Media, "north" of Babylon, and captured the city in 539 B.C. (cf. Dan. 5). In 514 B.C. Darius Hystaspes put down a revolt in Babylon and partially destroyed the city walls (50:13). In 478 B.C. Xerxes destroyed Babylon's walls and temples. The names Merathaim (50:21; "double rebellion") and Pekod ("visitation") were a play on the names of actual places in southern Babylonia. The Jerusalem temple

was destroyed and burned by the Babylonians (50:28; cf. 2 Kings 25:9). The reference in 50:44 is to Cyrus, God's instrument of judgment against Babylon (cf. Isa. 45:1-5).

Leb Kamai (51:1) means in Hebrew "the heart of those who rise against me." It is a cryptic reference to Babylon. The fall of Babylon was seen to be so certain in the mind of the prophet that it was described in the past tense (51:8). The Medes lived east of the Tigris River and south of the Caspian Sea (51:11). Cyrus, who overthrew Babylon, was of Median descent. He succeeded in uniting the Medes and the Persians into one empire. Jeremiah 51:20-23 referred to Cyrus (cf. 50:44). The "kingdoms of Ararat, Minni, and Ashkenaz" (51:27) referred to regions north of Babylon that were conquered by the Medes and became a part of Cyrus's empire. The "sea" (51:36) may refer to the moat that surrounded the city of Babylon or possibly a reservoir. Sheshach (51:41) was apparently another cryptic name for Babylon (cf. 51:1). Seraiah was the brother of Baruch (51:59; cf. 32:12). As quartermaster he was responsible for the king's accommodations during travel.

52:1-34 FROM JERUSALEM'S FALL TO THE ELEVATION OF JEHOIACHIN

The book of Jeremiah's prophecies ends with a summary from Jerusalem's fall to the elevation of Jehoiachin (52:1-34). That gave further encouragement that God had not abandoned his promises to King David. God's loving-kindness still remained. In the closing chapter (Jer. 52), Jeremiah presented the fate of Jerusalem, Zedekiah, and Jehoiachin. The material here is nearly identical to that of 2 Kings 24:18–25:30. This historical appendix was added to show how Jeremiah's message of judgment was fulfilled and to remind the reader of the continuing power of the Davidic covenant. The siege of Jerusalem began in the winter of 587 B.C. and continued until midsummer of the next year (586 B.C.) when the conquest was completed. Riblah (52:9), located thirty-five miles northeast of Baalbek, was the site of the Babylonian military headquarters (2 Kings 25:6, 20-21).

The first deportation to Babylon occurred in 605 B.C., during which choice young men were taken to be servants in the Babylonian court (2 Kings 24:1; Dan. 1:1). A second deportation took place in 597 B.C. and involved around 10,000 Judeans (2 Kings 24:12-16). The count of 3,023 exiles (Jer. 52:28) was probably the number of adult males. A third deportation (2 Kings 25:8-21) took place in 586 B.C. in connection with the destruction of Jerusalem and the burning of the temple (Jer. 52:29). After the assassina-tion of Gedaliah, the governor appointed by Babylon (52:30; cf. 40:7–41:18), the people feared further retaliation from the Babyloni-ans and fled to Egypt. The release of Jehoia-chin from prison in 560 B.C. suggested to the exiled Jews that God had not forgotten his people. He was preserving the Davidic line even in exile, and his promises for the future were certain.

Lamentations

BASIC FACTS

HISTORICAL SETTING
The setting of Lamentations was the destruction of Jerusalem by the armies of Babylon under Nebuchadnezzar.

AUTHOR
The author has traditionally been named as Jeremiah, but the work itself does not name the author. However, it gives all the appearance of an eyewitness report.

DATE
The eyewitness quality and charged emotionalism of the work suggest a date of writing shortly after Jerusalem's destruction in 586 B.C.

PURPOSE
The book clearly shows why Jerusalem was destroyed: Judah's prophets, priests, and people had sinned (1:8; 2:14; 4:13-14) and had broken God's commandments given in the Mosaic covenant long before (1:18; 2:6-17). But at the heart of the book is a confession of trust in God's "great love" (3:22; "lovingkindnesses," NASB; "mercies," KJV) and compassion. Although the terrible destruction of Jerusalem was due to Israel's sin (1:8), God's love still provided a glimmer of future hope. The purpose of the book was to express lament for the destruction of Jerusalem and to provide a platform for moving on in life. That platform was repentance (3:39-40) based on trust in God's unceasing love (3:22-23). Lamentations 5, the last chapter, sums up the thrust of the book. God would remember Israel's reproach (5:1) and restore the nation (5:21-22).

GUIDING CONCEPTS

Lamentations is a collection of five poems, each comprising a chapter in the English versions. The major concepts developed are the destruction of Jerusalem and the temple (1:1, 10; 2:1, 6-7), famine (1:11), cries for judgment on Israel's destroyers (1:21-22; 3:64-66; 4:21-22), and the tragic irresponsibility of her prophets and priests (2:13-14; 4:13-14).

BIBLE-WIDE CONCEPTS

The book related back to the promises of God to Abraham and Moses. In the Mosaic covenant, exile from the land was a promised consequence of sin. Lamentations showed that nearly one thousand years after the covenant had been made, it was still in force. Also, God's promise of unceasing love (3:22-23) reached back to the revelation of God to Moses at Sinai (Exod. 34:6) and the covenant with David (2 Sam. 7:14-15). It was that long-standing promise of permanent love that gave the writer of Lamentations hope. Finally, the desires for the judgment of Israel's enemies had their source in the promise to Abraham that all who cursed Israel would be cursed by God (Gen. 12:3).

NEEDS MET BY LAMENTATIONS

Lamentations takes the particular event of Jerusalem's downfall and shapes it into a timeless cry of anyone of God's children who suffers—for his own or for others' sins. The core confession of trust in God's love, even in the most tragic of situations (3:32-33), forms the center of the book's answers to these questions regarding the Israelites' life needs.
  • Why has the nation of Israel's life fallen apart (1:8)?
  • Why was God not on the side of Israel, his chosen people (4:12)?
  • What should be Israel's next step (3:39-40)?
  • What could possibly provide the security for any hope for the future (3:32-33)?
  Jeremiah's agony over Jerusalem's destruction mirrors God's own pain over disciplining his children (3:31-33). The reason for discipline is the sin of God's children. The application of discipline comes from God's love and holiness. The purpose of reading about the past act of God's judgment on Jerusalem is hopefully to avert the need for God disciplining believers today in a similar way (3:40). In the flurry of present activities it is easy to forget that God exists and still demands holy living. Reading about the great judgment on God's holy city of Jerusalem should remind believers that as temples of God's Holy Spirit they also are not immune to God's severe discipline should they fall into sin. The book also serves as an example of how to mourn for sins and cry to God. Grief and pain are to be expressed, not denied or kept within. Lamentations gives believers something to identify with when they experience discipline. God's anger toward sin is real. But it is the anger of a loving father who will deal out pain if it is necessary to mature his children. And believers can always say, with Jeremiah, the "punishment will end" (4:22).

OUTLINE OF LAMENTATIONS

A. MOURNING AND CRYING FOR VENGEANCE (1:1-22)

B. THE NEGLIGENCE OF THE PROPHETS (2:1-22)

C. CALL FOR REPENTANCE (3:1-66)

D. THE NEGLIGENCE OF THE PRIESTS AND PROPHETS (4:1-22)

E. THE REMNANT PRAYS FOR RESTORATION (5:1-22)

LAMENTATIONS NOTES

1:1-22 MOURNING AND CRYING FOR VENGEANCE

The author used poetry packed with strong and vivid imagery to lament the condition of Jerusalem, the city of Zion. The nation's "lovers" (1:2) were the neighboring countries with whom Judah tried to form alliances against Babylon—Egypt, Edom, Moab, Ammon, Tyre, and Sidon. The roads, once full of worshipers traveling to Jerusalem, were deserted (1:4). Like Zedekiah, Israel's leadership "fled" from Jerusalem (1:6; cf. Jer. 39:4-7). The siege conditions in Jerusalem were reflected in 1:11, when people exchanged their precious treasures for food. The figures of "fire" (meaning "total destruction") and a "net" (that is, "captivity") describe the calamities that befell Jerusalem (1:13). "Allies" (1:19) comes from the same Hebrew word that was translated "lovers" in 1:2. The author prayed that God would bring about "the day" of Babylon's judgment (1:22; cf. Jer. 50–51).

2:1-22 THE NEGLIGENCE OF THE PROPHETS

The author reflected on the fact that Zion's sorrows had come as a judgment from the Lord. "His footstool" (Lam. 2:1) was a reference to the Jerusalem temple (cf. Ps. 132:7). The conditions described in Lamentations 2:11-12 reflect the famine, which was one of the accompaniments of siege warfare. The false prophets had predicted a return to peace and prosperity (2:14; cf. Jer. 14:13). Clapping one's hands and hissing were ancient gestures of malicious joy and contempt (Lam. 2:15). In ancient times the night was divided into three four-hour

periods (2:19). The writer suggested that the people awaken at the beginning of each of these periods ("the night watches") so they could continue weeping. Cannibalism was one of the horrors experienced by the starving Judeans in Jerusalem during the Babylonian siege (2:20). This was one of the judgments God promised for disobedience (Deut. 28:53).

3:1-66 CALL FOR REPENTANCE

The author reflected on his personal experiences of affliction during his prophetic ministry (Lam. 3:1-18). He then received encouragement and consolation by reflecting on God's faithfulness (3:21-29). He used the imagery of hyperbole, that is, exaggeration for the sake of emphasis. The words "great love" (3:22) are translated from a Hebrew term related to the Hebrew word for "stork," suggesting a mother's love and faithfulness. It can be translated "loyal love" or "covenant loyalty." Burying "his face in the dust" (3:29) was an Oriental expression of submission. In 3:37-38 is a strong statement of God's sovereignty over all circumstances (cf. Eccles. 7:14; Rom. 8:28; Eph. 1:11). The writer referred to his own imprisonment in the "pit" (Lam. 3:53; cf. Jer. 38:6). The expression "I was about to be cut off" (3:54) means "I was as good as dead." In 3:64-66 the author did not take personal vengeance on his persecutors, but left retribution to the Lord (cf. Rom. 12:19).

4:1-22 THE NEGLIGENCE OF THE PRIESTS AND PROPHETS

Jeremiah reflected on the horrors of Jerusalem's suffering during the Babylonian siege.

Those "nurtured in purple" (Lam. 4:5) were the wealthy. No one helped Sodom (4:6). For cannibalism (4:10), see the note on 2:20. After their true character was recognized, the false prophets and wicked priests were condemned as "unclean" like lepers (4:15; cf. Lev. 13:45-46). The "nation that could not save us" (Lam. 4:17) refers to Egypt, with whom Zedekiah attempted to form an alliance against Babylon (cf. Jer. 37:7). Edom (Lam. 4:21), whose people were descendants of Esau, Judah's neighbor to the southeast, was warned of God's judgment for her part in the sufferings of the Judeans, the descendants of Jacob. "Uz" (4:21), situated in the territory of Edom, was the home of Job (cf. Job. 1:1).

5:1-22 THE REMNANT PRAYS FOR RESTORATION

Jeremiah confessed the sins of the nation, recounting the calamities, and then petitioned God for restoration. The reference to Assyria (5:6) is a bit confusing unless one understands that Babylonia was meant. The Babylonian Empire had inherited the territory that had once been Assyria. For a similar usage, see Ezra 6:22. In 5:13 is a reference to the forced labor imposed upon the Judeans by their conquerors. According to Jewish custom, the request of 5:21 is repeated at the conclusion of the book in order to avoid ending on an unpleasant note. But history has shown that God had certainly not rejected his people (Rom. 11:1-5).

Ezekiel

BASIC FACTS

HISTORICAL SETTING
The book of Ezekiel records prophecies and events that took place during the early part of the Babylonian captivity. Ezekiel was probably taken captive to Babylon in 597 B.C. From Babylon he wrote of Jerusalem's final downfall in 586 B.C. and prophesied the future glories that God had in store for his people.

AUTHOR
The author was the priest (1:3) and prophet Ezekiel. He lived in Jerusalem at the same time as Jeremiah. Ezekiel was probably taken captive to Babylon in 597 B.C. and may have personally known Daniel, who had been taken to Babylon during the earlier deportation of 605 B.C. The book shows a uniform style throughout, indicating the work of a single author.

DATE
Ezekiel began to prophesy in 593 B.C., the fifth year of Jehoiachin's captivity (1:2). The last dated message is from 573 B.C. (29:17). The compilation of the complete book may be dated shortly after 573 B.C.

PURPOSE
At this point in history, the people of the northern kingdom had been in exile for over a century (since 722 B.C.), and the people of the southern kingdom (Judah) had already suffered two of their three exiles to Babylon (in 605 and 597 B.C.). Jerusalem had not yet been destroyed, and the exiled Jews would naturally have had great hopes that Jerusalem might somehow survive. But God had clearly spoken otherwise. Their false hopes kept God's people from facing the truth: their own sins would soon bring about the destruction of their city and nation (586 B.C.). Ezekiel's prophecy was designed to place the responsibility for Jerusalem's downfall squarely on the shoulders of the Jews. But the prophecy's message also provided comfort for the Jews after the destruction of Jerusalem by graphically presenting the prediction of a restored Jerusalem, temple, and land.

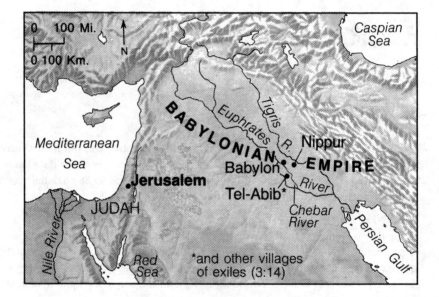

GEOGRAPHY AND ITS IMPORTANCE

Two geographical images control the themes of Ezekiel: the mobile presence of God and the new temple. First, God was described as being mobile, moving about on beautiful wheels. The temple remained in Jerusalem, but God was not restricted to the temple. His presence moved all over the earth, and thus moved freely between Jerusalem and the captives in Babylon. Second, though the temple was destroyed, God would rebuild it, and Ezekiel described that new temple in graphic terms. Ezekiel called the captives to purify themselves and develop their relationship with God while exiled in Babylon. Then they would be ready to return to Jerusalem and worship in his purified and rebuilt temple. The idea is similar to the woman at the Samaritan well in Jesus' day who debated about worshiping God at Samaria or at Jerusalem (John 4). Jesus replied that the issue was spirit and truth, not the geographical location of worship. Believers will all worship at the new temple in the heavenly Jerusalem, but first they must be ready to worship and obey God wherever they are in this present world. The geography of Ezekiel follows the presence of God as it departs from the old temple, exhorts the exiles in Babylon, and then returns to dwell forever in the new temple.

GUIDING CONCEPTS

CHRONOLOGY AND CONTENT
Ezekiel consistently gave precise dates for each of his major prophecies. Those dates were in chronological order, with minor exceptions.

This overview covers the major sections and messages of Ezekiel: the commission of Ezekiel; the events surrounding the departure of the glory of God from the temple; the failure of Israel's leadership; and the destruction of Israel and her enemies. Then after thirteen years came the prophecy of the return of God's glory and the restoration of the temple. The book takes the readers from the time when the glory departed to when the glory returned.

LINKS TO KING JEHOIACHIN
Ezekiel's prophecy can be linked to the years of King Jehoiachin's exile. The date in 1:2, the fifth year of the king's exile, becomes the book's chronological starting point. Zedekiah, the king ruling in Jerusalem while Ezekiel prophesied in Babylon, was not seen as the legitimate ruler because he was set in place by Nebuchadnezzar as a "puppet" ruler. Jeremiah had already made it clear that the nation was destined for seventy years of captivity (cf. Jer. 25). No one in Jerusalem could change that fact. Jehoiachin, living in Babylonian exile, was the focus of Israel's national hope. Second Kings 25:27-30 records that about halfway through the captivity, Jehoiachin was released from prison and elevated to a high position under the Babylonian king. Thus, in Jehoiachin's elevation in exile, Israel's hopes for the temple and Davidic throne were kept alive.

BIBLE-WIDE CONCEPTS

THE PURPOSE OF DISCIPLINE
Although part of Judah's people had been taken captive to Babylon, many of the Jews were still in Jerusalem, causing some to falsely believe that complete destruction of the nation would not take place. The captives' minds were still in Jerusalem and not on God's purpose for them in captivity. They wanted to escape God's discipline, but God wanted them to stay and learn vital lessons from it. The recurring phrase that the Jews heard from God in Babylon, "You will know that I am the LORD" (7:4, 27; 11:10; 34:27; 36:11, 38; 37:6, 13, 28; 38:23; 39:22, 28), had also been spoken to Israel when God took her out of Egypt. The exodus itself and the judgments on Egypt revealed to Israel (Exod. 6:7) and to the Egyptians (Exod. 7:5, 17; 9:14) who God is and provided graphic instruction and encouragement for Israel (Exod. 10:1-2). In Ezekiel the phrase functions in a similar way. Israel would know that God is the Lord first by means of judgment, and later, by restoration.

THE DWELLING PLACES OF GOD'S GLORY
The book of Ezekiel begins with the departure of God's glory from the temple and ends with the return of God's glory. The prophet wanted to tell his readers the reasons for and implications of God's presence and absence. In the beginning, God's

---

THE CHRONOLOGY OF EZEKIEL

Passage	Ezekiel's Date Year / Month / Day			Julian Date B.C.	Content
1:2	5	4	5	July 31, 593	Commission and message of Ezekiel
8:1	6	6	5	Sept. 17, 592	God's glory departs from the temple; don't trust in a brief exile
20:1	7	5	10	Aug. 9, 591	False trust in leadership
24:1	9	10	10	Jan. 15, 588	Jerusalem and her enemies will be destroyed
26:1	11	(10)	1	Feb. 12, 586	Tyre destroyed
29:1	10	10	12	Jan. 7, 587	Egypt cannot save
29:17	27	1	1	Apr. 26, 571	Egypt cannot save
30:20	11	1	7	Apr. 29, 587	Egypt cannot save
31:1	11	3	1	June 21, 587	Egypt destroyed
32:1	12	12	1	Mar. 3, 585	Egypt destroyed
32:17	12	(12)	15	Mar. 17, 585	Egypt destroyed
33:21	12	10	5	Jan. 19, 586	Jerusalem destroyed
40:1	25	1	10	Apr. 20, 573	Prophecy of the new temple and God's returned glory

presence rested upon the perfectly created earth. At Sinai he filled the tabernacle with his glory (Exod. 40:34-38); and later, Solomon's temple also was filled with God's presence (1 Kings 8:10-11). In the future, the entire new earth will be God's temple, filled with his unhindered presence (Rev. 21:3). God has always come to dwell with humans on the basis of his saving grace. But man's sin and stubborn refusal to repent caused the removal of God's holy presence. Ezekiel spoke of a future time when God would make believers perfect in obedience so that his presence could abide with them forever (11:19-20; 36:25-35). Place those passages together with Jeremiah 31:31-34 to gain a fuller understanding of God's promised new covenant. That covenant was also referred to as a covenant of peace (34:25-31; 37:26).

THE LEADERSHIP OF KING AND PRIEST

God would again establish the rule of David's throne. In the section on leadership (Ezek. 20–23), God said he would put a rightful heir on the throne (21:27). The Davidic covenant was still in force. Also, in the section on restoration (Ezek. 34), God promised the return of good shepherds (34:11-31) for the nation. At their head would be one shepherd, David (34:23-24; 37:24). That figure of David looked to an earthly son of David on the throne and also to the greater Son of David, Jesus the Messiah.

THE SEED OF ABRAHAM

Although, from a human standpoint, Israel would be lost in captivity, God promised that the seed of Abraham would always survive and would someday be restored. The vision of the dry bones (Ezek. 37) affirmed that God would keep his promise to Abraham.

NEEDS MET BY EZEKIEL

The original hearers of Ezekiel's message needed to understand that the temple, Jerusalem, and the land of Palestine (the "Promised Land") were not good luck charms against the consequences of personal sin. The buildings and land only gained worth and power from God's presence. When Israel lost her temple, holy city, and land, she blamed God and thought that he had abandoned her forever. Ezekiel met the people's need both to accept responsibility for their own sins and not to give up hope in God's ultimate restoration and forgiveness. They needed to place their faith in God, not in things, and let that personal relationship turn them from sin to obedience. Some special needs are met by the book of Ezekiel, needs that are only felt when believers are under the heavy hand of God's discipline. The content and structure of Ezekiel show that the exiled Jews were probably asking questions like these.

- Should Israel worry more about their suffering under God's discipline than about hearing what God had to teach them through it?
- Is the temple so sacred that God would never destroy it, no matter how bad his people might be?
- Is the temple a kind of national security blanket for Israel?
- If God actually does destroy the temple, does that mean he has also destroyed all his other promises to his people?
- What does the future hold for Israel's hopes of a good king, a temple, and the presence of God?

The point of the vision of God's glory in Ezekiel 1 and 8–10 was to show the exiled Israelites that God's presence was not restricted to the temple or to the land of Israel. God was in Israel, Babylon, and everywhere. All that counted was obedience to his laws, not a superstitious clinging to his temple or land. In fact, he had even more incredible plans for a new temple in a renewed land (Ezek. 36–48). But, in the present or future, in the Promised Land or in temporary exile in a foreign land, believers were to enjoy the presence of God available through obedience, and trust in God for a better future.

The book of Ezekiel encourages believers to avoid putting anything in the place of a vital relationship with the living God. They are to repent, turn from idols, and renounce their detestable practices (14:6). Ezekiel presents a vision to lift the heads of believers from the present works of God through his people, beautiful though they may be, to see an incredibly glorious future. Ezekiel encourages believers to live with the vision of a new earth in their minds, with God alone reigning in their hearts, and with a commitment to responsible obedience in the present world.

OUTLINE OF EZEKIEL

A. JUDGMENT: GOD'S GLORY AND MAN'S REBELLION (1:1–7:27)
   1. Ezekiel's Commission: Bound and Loosed for Judgment (1:1–3:27)
   2. Object Lessons of Jerusalem's Destruction (4:1–7:27)
B. THE VACANT TEMPLE: DEPARTED GLORY (8:1–39:29)
   1. Do Not Trust in the Temple Being Preserved (8:1–11:25)
   2. Do Not Trust in a Brief Exile (12:1–19:14)
   3. Do Not Trust the Leaders for Deliverance (20:1–23:49)
   4. Do Not Trust Other Nations for Deliverance (24:1–33:20)
   5. Jerusalem Falls: Now Is the Time for Hope and Rest (33:21–39:29)
C. THE OCCUPIED TEMPLE: RETURNED GLORY (40:1–48:35)
   1. The Setting: A City and a Guide (40:1-4)
   2. The Temple Described (40:5–42:20)
   3. The Temple Occupied: God's Holiness (43:1-9)
   4. Temple Obligations: Humans' Holiness (43:10–46:24)
   5. The New Land (47:1–48:35)

EZEKIEL NOTES

1:1–7:27 JUDGMENT: GOD'S GLORY AND MAN'S REBELLION
1:1–3:27 Ezekiel's Commission: Bound and Loosed for Judgment
Overview: God was pictured in 1:26-28 as riding a throne on a platform with wheels, showing that his presence was not limited to the temple in Jerusalem. His presence is mobile, able to go anywhere for blessing or for judgment. He could be with the remnant left in Jerusalem or with those in Babylonian exile. The splendor of God in judgment and restoration was a vision that was continually behind all the words of this book. The watchman theme (3:17) would appear again in 33:7-9. Note the theme of a "rebellious house " (2:5-6, 8; 3:9, 26-27). Ezekiel's eating of the scroll (3:3) was in contrast with Israel's refusal to hear and apply the words of God (3:7-8).

1:1-28 GOD APPEARS IN HIS GLORY
1:1-3 The setting. The "thirtieth year" (1:1) referred to Ezekiel's age, the age at which Old Testament priests began their ministries (cf. Num. 4:3, 23-30). The "fourth month" (1:1) was Tammuz (our June–July). The "Kebar River" (1:1) was one of the navigable canals branching from the Euphrates, which flowed southeast from Babylon. The "fifth year" (1:2) from King Jehoiachin's exile (597 B.C.) would have been 593 B.C. The name "Ezekiel" means "God strengthens."

1:4-28 The vision is described. Interpreters often become so engrossed in guessing the meaning of the details of this vision that they overlook its major significance. It was a vision of the glory of the Lord (1:1, 28). The vision left Ezekiel with an abiding sense of God's glory, which was often reflected in his prophetic ministry (3:23; 8:4; 10:4; 11:22). Whatever Ezekiel saw, he was limited in his ability to describe it. He used the Hebrew words translated "like" and "appearance" to describe what was completely beyond his earthly experience.

The "four living creatures" (1:5) were later identified by Ezekiel as "cherubim" (10:20), an order of angels sometimes associated with the worship of God (cf. Gen. 3:24; Exod. 25:18-22). The singular was *cherub* and perhaps related to the Akkadian root meaning "to bless, praise, adore." The spirit (1:12) was identified in 1:20 as the "spirit of the living creatures," not the Holy Spirit. The chrysolite (1:16; "beryl," NASB and KJV), literally, "tarshish," is a stone perhaps like topaz. Over the heads of the living creatures was an "expanse" that served as a platform for the "throne" (1:26). Comparison of 1:26-27 with Revelation 1:13-18 suggests that the one sitting on the throne was Christ.

2:1–3:27 GOD COMMISSIONS EZEKIEL
2:1-7 The target group is described. Ezekiel recorded his call and commissioning. The expression "son of man" (2:1, 3, 6, 8; 3:1, 3-4, 10, 17, 25; etc.) is used ninety-three times in this book and simply meant "mortal man," in contrast with the majestic God. See the note on Daniel 7:13 for a contrasting usage of the term. The "briers" (2:6; "thistles," NASB), "thorns," and "scorpions" suggested the difficulty of Ezekiel's ministry.

2:8–3:3 Ezekiel eats the scroll. Contrary to usual practice, this scroll was written on both sides, front and back (2:10). Another scroll written on both sides is found in the seven-sealed judgment scroll of Revelation 5:1. The writing on both sides suggested an extensive and detailed message. The eating of the scroll (3:1-3) suggested the assimilation of the message (cf. Rev. 10:8-11). In spite of the message of judgment, the scroll was "sweet as honey" (3:3) because it was the word of God (cf. Ps. 19:10).

3:4-15 Ezekiel is sent to the exiles. To meet the challenge of a difficult ministry, God made Ezekiel as hardened as Israel's heart (3:8). The phrase "the Spirit lifted me up" (3:12) should not be understood as physical removal, but as an expression for prophetic vision (cf. 8:3; 11:1, 24). Tel Abib (3:15), whose location is uncertain, was the major settlement of the exiles in Babylon. The words "bitterness" and "anger" (3:14) suggested Ezekiel's awareness of impending judgment.

3:16-27 Ezekiel's watchman ministry. The work of the "watchman" (3:17) was depicted in 2 Samuel 18:24-27 and 2 Kings 9:17-20. Ezekiel's job was to warn the nation, both the wicked and the righteous (3:18-21), of impending divine judgment. While each group was responsible for its own actions, Ezekiel was accountable to present the warning. Some have found support in 3:20 for the view that the believer ("righteous") can turn from God and die an eternal death, that is, lose his or her salvation. However, the context is that of the Mosaic covenant where physical (not spiritual) life and death were in view (Deut. 30:15-20). The "ropes" (3:25) suggested some physical restraint and possibly the rejection of Ezekiel's ministry. Ezekiel remained unable to speak except when the Lord opened his mouth to proclaim his word. This situation continued for seven and a half years until the fall of Jerusalem (cf. 33:22).

4:1–7:27 Object Lessons of Jerusalem's Destruction

Overview: Throughout Ezekiel's declarations of judgment on Judah and Jerusalem, he used a number of symbolic actions or revelatory signs that caused the people to ask what he meant (12:9; 24:19; 37:18) and gave him an opportunity to explain their significance and drive home the application. The process of judgment described in Ezekiel 4 and throughout the book was linked by the forty years of 4:6 and the explicit statement of 20:34-36. The refining process of the wilderness wanderings was to purify the nation before the conquest of the Promised Land under Joshua. Similarly, God's punishment of Israel in war and captivity was designed to achieve the same end.

The cause of the Babylonian captivity was Israel's defilement of God's sanctuary (5:11). After God's wrath the nation would know that he had spoken (5:13; cf. also 6:7, 13-14; 7:4, 9, 27). That would confirm God's ability to enforce his covenant laws (6:9-10) and complete his covenant promises. For example, God hid his face from Israel in 7:22 and uncovered his face in 39:29.

4:1-17 JERUSALEM BESIEGED: THE CLAY TABLET

The sign of the "clay tablet" (4:1; "brick," NASB; "tile," KJV) depicted Jerusalem's coming siege and fall. The "iron pan" (4:3) is thought to represent (1) the severity of the siege, (2) the barrier of sin between God and the people, or (3) God's protection of Ezekiel as he pronounced judgment. The sign of the prophet's posture depicted the duration of Jerusalem's punishment (4:4-8). The total of 430 days was based upon the past years of Israel's iniquity and corresponded to the years of coming judgment. Because all numbering in the book is dated from the captivity of Jehoiachin (597 B.C.), the 430 could be subtracted from 597 to give 167 B.C. (the year of the Maccabean revolt) as the end of the period of judgment. The sign of the famine portrayed the suffering and deprivation of siege conditions (4:9-17). This procedure was not only repulsive but polluting (cf. Deut. 23:12-14). The point was that Israel would soon be eating the unclean food of the foreign nations in exile.

5:1-17 JERUSALEM'S INHABITANTS: THE HAIR AND REPROACH

The signs of the "sword," "razor" (5:1; "knife" and "razor," KJV), and dividing of the shaved hair portrayed the coming destruction of the people by fire, sword, and scattering in exile. The preservation of a few hairs in the edge of Ezekiel's robe suggested that a remnant would be spared. This is stated more explicitly in 6:8-9; 7:16-18. The "laws and decrees" referred to the stipulations of the covenant (5:6). Disobedience resulted in the curses of the covenant rather than its blessings (cf. Deut. 28:15-68). The horror of cannibalism became a historical fact as recorded by Jeremiah (see the note on Lam. 2:20).

6:1-14 MOUNTAINS OF ISRAEL: HIGH PLACES DESTROYED

The "mountains" (6:2) referred to the hilltop shrines where Canaanite cultic worship was practiced (6:3-4; cf. Jer. 3:6). Certain "valleys" were also used for the worship of Molech (cf. Jer. 7:31-32). The phrase "you will know that I am the LORD" (6:7) was repeated sixty-eight times in the book of Ezekiel. God's judgment had an evangelistic purpose: God would prove to his own people and all the nations of the world that he is truly God. God seasoned judgment with grace by the promise to preserve a remnant (6:8; cf. Isa. 6:13). Clapping (6:11) was sometimes an expression of joyous praise (cf. Ps. 47:1), but here it referred to remorse and derision over Judah's sin and judgment.

7:1-27 THE NATION'S END

Ezekiel described the imminent and complete destruction of Judah (7:5, 9). The "rod" (7:10) may have referred to Babylon or possibly the Israelite kings who had "budded" with violence and wickedness. Neither the buyer nor the seller should have rejoiced over a good transaction because of the coming disaster. The coming captivity would make it impossible for the seller to regain his property in the Year of Jubilee (Lev. 25:10-12) because he would not be in the land. God's "treasured place" (7:22; "secret place," NASB and KJV) referred to the Jerusalem temple. The sign of the "chain" (7:23) portrayed the coming captivity in Babylon. The calamity of the captivity would leave the Judeans without spiritual leadership, instruction, and counsel (7:26).

8:1–39:29 THE VACANT TEMPLE: DEPARTED GLORY
8:1–11:25 Do Not Trust in the Temple Being Preserved

Overview: The section of 8:1–11:25 showed what God would do to Jerusalem and why. This was preparation for his message to the exiles. Ezekiel 1–7 describes the judgment in general. Ezekiel 8–39 goes into the specifics. Ezekiel's vision of Jerusalem was designed to cut through any sentimental or romanticizing thoughts about why God should spare the holy city. In reality, it was a place of rank paganism. Because of that, the exiles were not to think that the temple would, at all costs, be preserved. Note the repetition of "even more detestable" (8:6, 13, 15; "still greater," NASB; "greater," KJV) with reference to Jerusalem's idolatry. The faithful of the city were to be marked (9:4, 6) for salvation, but none was found. All were candidates for death (9:8).

As God's glory departed (Ezek. 9–10), God answered Ezekiel's twice-repeated question concerning the survival of the remnant (9:8; 11:13). The temple might fall and Jerusalem might be razed, but God himself would be the captives' sanctuary (11:16). That is exactly how the book ends (48:35). The new hearts of flesh and spirit would enable the redeemed to follow God and keep his laws (11:19-20). That promise would be a tremendous comfort to the captives. The true temple had always been God himself. And his people could dwell in that temple anywhere on earth.

8:1-4 EZEKIEL IS TAKEN IN A VISION TO JERUSALEM

The date was Elul (August–September) 5, 592 B.C., fourteen months after Ezekiel's first vision (1:1-2). Although Ezekiel was in Babylon, he was transported to Jerusalem by prophetic vision so that he might report to the exiles why God had to bring such severe judgment on the city. The "idol" (8:3) was an idolatrous image, perhaps the Canaanite goddess Asherah (cf. 2 Chron. 33:7, 15), which provoked God to jealous anger.

8:5-9:11 THE GLORY MOVES TO THE THRESHOLD

The seventy elders had become involved in idolatry because they believed that God had abandoned the nation. Tammuz (8:14) was the ancient Babylonian god of vegetation and lover of Ishtar, whose death at the time of the summer heat was mourned annually and whose resurrection was celebrated in the spring. In the inner court of the temple, an area restricted to the priests, Ezekiel observed the worship of Shamash, the sun-god of the Babylonians (8:16). The expression "putting the branch to their nose" (8:17) referred to some obscure or obscene practice, perhaps connected with the worship of the sun. The "six men" were probably angels (9:2). A "writing kit" (9:2) would contain pens, ink, and a knife for cutting the parchment of papyrus. This marked the beginning of the departure of the glory of the Lord from Jerusalem (9:3). It first left the Most Holy Place, where it had dwelt over the cherubim (see the note on 1:5) mounted on top of the Ark of the Covenant. It then proceeded to the threshold of the temple, to the east gate (10:19), and finally to the Mount of Olives, east of the city (11:23). The "mark" on the righteous was intended for their protection throughout the forthcoming judgment (9:4; cf. Gen. 4:15; Rev. 7:3).

10:1-11:21 EAST GATE EVENTS

The central truth of Ezekiel 10 is that the judgment to fall on Jerusalem was from the hand of God (10:2, 6-8). The "wheels" (10:2) were described in 1:15-21. The "city" (10:2) referred to Jerusalem. The "burning coals" (10:2) suggested the manner of Jerusalem's destruction in 586 B.C., that is, by burning. For "chrysolite" (10:9), see the note on 1:16. One of the four faces was described as that of a "cherub" (10:14), but in 1:10, one was that of an "ox." Since cherubs were angelic beings with a basic animal form and wings, the ox could be regarded as the form of a cherub. Ezekiel linked the "cherub" with the "living creatures" he saw in 1:5 at the Kebar River (10:22).

The leaders of Jerusalem argued that as the pot protects the meat from the fire, so the walls of Jerusalem would protect the people from judgment (11:3). Ezekiel denied that they would find such protection in the doomed city (11:11). The death of Pelatiah, one of the leaders of the people, was a striking confirmation of Ezekiel's message of judgment (11:13). This led the prophet to intercede for the remnant. God reaffirmed his promise of Deuteronomy 30:1-4 to regather his people to their land after their exile (11:14-17). The promise of a new heart and a new spirit described by Ezekiel were part of what Jeremiah called the new covenant (11:19-20; cf. Jer. 31:31-40).

11:22-25 THE GLORY DEPARTS TO THE EAST MOUNTAIN

After his vision of Jerusalem had ended, Ezekiel reported what he had seen to the community of exiles in Babylonia (11:24; "Chaldea," NASB).

12:1–19:14 Do Not Trust in a Brief Exile

Overview: The false prophets were mentioned in 12:24-25 and elaborated upon in Ezekiel 13–14. In Ezekiel 13 the false prophets were condemned for predicting Jerusalem's survival. In Ezekiel 14, those who fell prey to the false prophets were described. They had set up idols in their hearts (14:3-7). As the false prophet was, so would be the one who listened to him (14:10). All of God's judgment in this regard sought to recapture his people's hearts (14:5), to bring them into a more intimate relationship with him (14:11, 23). But only personal repentance could allow this to occur; great people of the past could not help (14:12-20), and distant relatives (14:18) could not be blamed for Israel's downfall.

The purpose of Ezekiel 15–16 was to contrast the people's great sinfulness and rebellion with God's great forgiveness (16:63). And the purpose of that great forgiveness was to make his people ashamed and humbled before him, and lead them to repentance. The last part of this book, Ezekiel 40–48, greatly detailed God's forgiveness and covenant of peace. Therefore, the function of the entire book was to impact the reader with the glory of God's forgiveness so that he would become humble now and not risk the dangers of God's judgment.

Ezekiel 17 describes Zedekiah's attempt to use Egypt's help to defend Israel against Babylon. That prepared the reader for the lengthy section concerning Egypt's destruction (Ezek. 29–32). Rather than blaming their fathers, the Israelites were to change their lives (18:21, 24-25, 30-31). This section ends with a formal lament for the leaders of Israel.

12:1-28 IMMINENT DESTRUCTION

12:1-16 Exile of the prince of Jerusalem. The sign of the baggage ("pack your belongings," 12:3) portrayed the coming siege of Jerusalem and exile of the inhabitants

(12:11). The "wall" (12:5) was probably the wall of Ezekiel's house. The message of 12:10 concerned both the people of Jerusalem ("house of Israel") and the "prince," a reference to Zedekiah, Judah's last king. Although taken captive, Zedekiah never saw the land of Babylon (12:13), for he was blinded by his captors (2 Kings 25:1-7).

12:17-28 Picture of fear: eating and trembling. The sign of trembling (12:18) portrayed the distressing conditions of Jerusalem during the Babylonian invasion, siege, and resulting captivity. Encouraged by the false prophets, the people thought the prophecies of judgment would never be fulfilled, or that they would be fulfilled in the distant future (12:22, 27).

13:1–14:11 TRUE AND FALSE PROPHETS

13:1-23 False prophecies of peace. The false prophets who promised peace when there was no peace were denounced (13:2-16). "Jackals" (13:4; "foxes," NASB and KJV) were noted for being mischievous, deceptive, and destructive. The false prophets merely whitewashed the insecure walls of the nation instead of strengthening them (13:10-16). Such walls could never withstand the storms of God's judgment. The false prophetesses spoke their own messages, instead of God's, and practiced sorcery (13:17-23; cf. Lev. 19:26). The exact nature and purpose of the "charms" and "veils" (13:18; "bands" and "veils," NASB; "pillows" and "kerchiefs," KJV) are unknown.

14:1-11 True prophecy: idols in their hearts. The "elders" (14:1) were supposed to be the spiritual leaders of the nation, but they had "set up idols in their hearts" (14:3).

14:12-18:32 ESCAPE FROM JUDGMENT BY REPENTANCE

14:12-23 The coming judgment is inescapable. The exiles implied that they could rely on their forefathers: Noah, Daniel, and Job. God declared that judgment on the wicked was not going to be averted by the righteousness of a few. Some scholars have identified "Daniel" with "Dani'el" of the Ugaritic legend discovered in the Ras Shamra Tablets (around 1400 B.C.). But the immoral character of the legendary Dani'el (a participant in drunkenness, cursing, and murder) makes such a view very unlikely. The "survivors" (14:22), a wicked remnant, would be sent to

Babylon to show the righteous in exile that God's judgment on Jerusalem was neither excessive nor arbitrary.

15:1-8 Once burned, but not twice. The parable of the unproductive vine showed that Jerusalem, God's vine (Ps. 80:8-12; Isa. 5:1-7), was no longer good for anything but burning.

16:1-63 The abominations of Israel are made known. The allegory of the adulterous wife forcefully depicted the history of God's dealings with Israel and her response to him. The place of Jerusalem's origin—in Canaan, the land of the Amorites and Hittites—was emphasized (16:3; cf. Gen. 10:15-19; 15:16; Num. 13:29; Josh. 5:1). The rubbing with salt (16:4) was intended to cleanse the skin and strengthen the body. The spreading of the "garment" (16:8; "skirt," NASB and KJV) over Jerusalem symbolized God's marriage with his people (cf. Ruth 3:9). The "covenant" (16:8) may have referred to the Mosaic covenant or possibly the marriage contract between God and Jerusalem. Jerusalem "rose to be a queen" (16:13; "advanced to royalty," NASB; "didst prosper into a kingdom," KJV) serving as capital of the united kingdom under David and Solomon.

The image of the "prostitute" (16:15) was often used by the prophets to depict the unfaithfulness of God's people. Since Canaanite worship often included acts of cultic prostitution, the figure of speech was most appropriate. Child sacrifice was one of the horrors of pagan worship (16:20-21; cf. Jer. 7:30-32). Unlike other prostitutes who were paid for their favors, Jerusalem paid others to engage in her illicit activities (16:33-34).

The tribute money was the price of consorting with foreign powers. Jerusalem's corruption was highlighted by comparing her with two wicked "sisters," the cities of Samaria and Sodom (16:46). Jerusalem's wickedness exceeded both (16:48). God promised restoration on the basis of Deuteronomy 30:1-10 (cf. 16:53). If God could restore devastated Sodom, then he would have no trouble restoring Jerusalem. God would remember his "covenant" (the Abrahamic covenant of Gen. 12:1-3) and establish an "everlasting covenant" (16:60; cf. the "new covenant" of Jer. 31:31-34).

17:1-24 Can Israel rely on Egypt? Ezekiel 17 is both a riddle and an allegory. As a riddle, it needs to be explained; and as an allegory, it makes several points of comparison. The "great eagle" (17:3) is identified in 17:12 as the king of Babylon, Nebuchadnezzar (605–562 B.C.), who exiled Jehoiachin and other nobles in 597 B.C. (cf. 2 Kings 24:10-12). The second "great eagle" (17:7) is identified in 17:15-17 as the king of Egypt, Pharaoh Hophra (589–570 B.C.), to whom Zedekiah looked for help in his rebellion against Nebuchadnezzar.

The features of the allegory are explained in 17:11-21. After the exile of Jehoiachin to Babylon (17:12), Zedekiah was placed on the throne as a vassal of Nebuchadnezzar (17:13). He was obedient at first, but then he rebelled, looking to Egypt for help to overthrow the Babylonian yoke (17:15). Zedekiah was exiled to Babylon (17:20) and his troops slain (17:21). The parable of the "cedar" (17:22-24), representative of the house of David, is a Messianic prophecy regarding the preservation of David's dynasty (2 Sam. 7:12-16) in spite of the judgment on Jehoiachin and Zedekiah. The "shoot" (Ezek. 17:22) referred to the Messiah (cf. Isa. 11:1; Jer. 23:5), and the "high and lofty mountain" (Ezek. 17:22) was Zion (cf. 20:40).

18:1-18 Individual responsibility for repentance. The exiles were accepting the view reflected in the popular proverb that they were suffering the consequences of the sins of their forefathers. Ezekiel declared the principle of individual responsibility for sin ("The soul who sins is the one who will die," 18:4) and expounded it through the chapter. For an understanding of the "pledge" (18:7), see Exodus 22:26. Loans to fellow Israelites were to be without interest (Ezek. 18:8; cf. Exod. 22:25). Eternal life is always secured by grace through faith (Ezek. 18:9; cf. Gen. 15:6; Eph. 2:8). The promise "will surely live" (Ezek. 18:9) referred to physical salvation—deliverance from the curses of the covenant (cf. Deut. 28:15-68).

18:19-32 The principle is summarized. Each person was responsible for his or her own actions. The Israelites were not accountable for the sins of the previous generation. God's ways are just because he deals with people according to their present condition rather than their family history (Ezek. 18:25-29).

19:1-14 LAMENTATION FOR THE PRINCES
The "lioness" (19:2) represented Judah (cf. Gen. 49:9), and the "cubs" (Ezek. 19:3) represented two of her kings. The first of the "cubs" was Jehoahaz, who was taken captive to Egypt by Pharaoh Neco in 609 B.C. (cf. 2 Kings 23:30-34). Judah's next ruler, Jehoiakim, was passed by, and the second of the "cubs" may be identified with Jehoiachin, who was taken to Babylon in 597 B.C. (cf. 2 Kings 24:8-16). The destruction of Judah was likened to the removal of a "vine" (Ezek. 19:10-12). Judah's removal took place in 586 B.C. The "branches" referred to the office of king.

20:1–23:49 Do Not Trust the Leaders for Deliverance

Overview: Behind God's past restraint (20:9, 14, 22) and present judgment (20:44) was the witness of his name to the nations. The section of 20:1–23:49 condemned the sins of the prophets, priests, princes, and people. The Babylonian captivity was compared with Israel's past wilderness wanderings (20:36). The purpose of both was to judge and purify the children of God.

20:1-44 THE IDOLATROUS LEADERS
The oracles of Ezekiel 20 were given just before the fall of Jerusalem. Here Ezekiel described in literal terms the history of Israel's rebellion, which was figuratively portrayed in Ezekiel 16. The leaders ("elders") had continually rebelled against God; therefore, he refused to answer them when they came to "inquire" of him (20:3). What had been true in the past (20:5-29) was true in the present (20:30-32). The people persisted in idolatry and false worship. God's dealings with the nation described in these verses appear to be referring to the future tribulation period (20:33-44; cf. Zech. 13:8-9). Then, as a purged and purified people, they will be united with their Messiah and restored to his land (Ezek. 20:40-42).

20:45–21:32 CERTAIN JUDGMENT ON LEADERS
The passage of 20:45–21:32 concerned the southern region of Judah. The sign of the sharpened sword (21:3), a symbol of divine judgment, indicated that Judah's destruction was imminent (21:1-17). The sanctuary (21:2) denoted the various buildings that together comprised the Jerusalem temple. Compare Ezekiel's mourning (21:12) to Jeremiah 31:19. The intensity of the judgment was indicated by the words "Let the sword strike . . . three times" (21:14; "the third time," NASB and KJV), which was perhaps a reference to the three deportations of people to Babylon in 605, 597, and 586 B.C. The sign of Nebuchadnezzar's sword identified the king of Babylon as God's agent of judgment (21:18-27). Rabbah (21:20) was the capital of Ammon, the country east of Israel across the Jordan River.

Divination (21:21) was the art of knowing or foretelling the unknown apart from God's way of prophetic revelation. Among the ways this was done in ancient times included shaking "arrows" from a quiver, consulting "idols," and examining the "liver" of a sacrificed animal. The "prince of Israel" (21:25) referred to King Zedekiah. Israel would have no king until the Messiah came (21:27; cf. Gen. 49:10). The restoration of Jehoiachin to the throne (cf. 2 Kings 25:27-30) was only a temporary measure. Nebuchadnezzar postponed but did not give up his plans to attack Ammon (Ezek. 21:28-32).

22:1–23:49 IDOLATRIES REHEARSED
22:1-31 Cause the city to know its abominations. The purpose of Ezekiel 22 was to make sure that Jerusalem understood "why" judgment was coming. The essence of her sin is found in 22:12, "You have forgotten me, declares the Sovereign LORD." "Disperse you among the nations" (22:15) was the ultimate curse of the covenant (cf. Deut. 28:41, 63-64). The sign of the smelting furnace was designed to show the intent of God's judgment (22:17-22). He did not want to destroy his people but desired rather to remove her impurities (her sin) as raw ore must be smelted to remove the dross.

23:1-49 Political and religious prostitution. As he had done in Ezekiel 16, the prophet used an allegory in Ezekiel 23 to depict the adulterous character of God's people. However, in Ezekiel 16 the emphasis was upon Israel's spiritual adultery (idolatry), while in Ezekiel 23 the emphasis was upon the nation's political adultery (alliances with Egypt, Assyria, and Babylon). The nation's unfaithfulness began in her youth, even while Israel was still in Egypt. The name "Oholah" (23:4) means "tent woman" and referred to Samaria, representing the northern kingdom. The name "Oholibah" means "My tent is in her" (a reference to the "tabernacle" or temple in Judah) and referred to Jerusalem, representing the southern kingdom. Jerusalem was condemned for alliances with Assyria (by Ahaz, 2 Kings 16:7), Babylon (by Hezekiah, 2 Kings 20:12-15), and Egypt (by Zedekiah, Jer. 2:18; 37:7). "Pekod and Shoa and Koa" (Ezek. 23:23) were tribal groups east of the Tigris River within the Babylonian Empire.

A punishment causing physical deformity was often practiced on a convicted adulteress in Egypt and Babylon (23:25). Jerusalem would experience the same judgment as Samaria (23:32; "You will drink your sister's cup")—the judgment of death that was due the adulteress (23:47; cf. Deut. 22:21-22).

24:1–33:20 Do Not Trust Other Nations for Deliverance

Overview: God is the Judge of all the nations, not just Jerusalem. In Ezekiel 24:1–33:20 the foreign nations were accountable to God on the basis of general revelation and the law of conscience. If they were accountable, how much more accountable were the Judeans, who had been entrusted with the very word of God? This section describes the beginning of the siege of Jerusalem (Ezek. 24) and then shows how happy Israel's surrounding nations were about Israel's imminent destruction. In that light, much is written concerning the judgment on those nations. God's judgment on these nations reflects the background of the Abrahamic covenant (28:26; cf. Gen. 12:3).

As a mighty political and trade center, Tyre received much attention (Ezek. 26:1–28:26). Egypt received much prophecy because of its own pride and Israel's mistaken notion that Egypt could defeat Babylon and save Israel (29:1–33:20). However, like Assyria, Egypt too would fall to Babylon (31:1–32:32).

24:1–25:17 JERUSALEM AND NEAR NATIONS DESTROYED
24:1-27 No mourning over the destruction of Jerusalem. The long prophesied attack and siege of Jerusalem began in December of 588 B.C. ("the ninth year, in the tenth month,"

24:1) and culminated with the destruction of the city in June and July of 586 B.C. The parable of the cooking pot depicted God's judgment on Jerusalem (24:3-14). The cooking pot (Jerusalem) would boil its contents (the people), and then the empty pot would itself be burned up.

The death of Ezekiel's wife was a sign designed to portray the loss of God's blessing for Jerusalem (24:15-24). The "delight of your eyes" (24:16) referred to Ezekiel's wife. The same expression was used in 24:21 to refer to the Jerusalem temple. As Ezekiel was forbidden the customary mourning practices with regard to his wife's death, the people were not to mourn God's judgment on Jerusalem, for it was just (24:22-23). On the day the fall of Jerusalem was reported to Ezekiel, his tongue would no longer be dumb (cf. 3:25-27), and he would be free to speak messages of hope and consolation (24:27).

25:1-17 Judgment on Jerusalem's neighbors. The Ammonites (25:2) were descendants of the incestuous relationship between Lot and his younger daughter (Gen. 19:36-38). Rabbah (25:5), later known as Philadelphia, was the chief city of Ammon. The Moabites were the descendants of the incestuous relationship between Lot and his eldest daughter (25:8-11; cf. Gen. 19:36-38). Seir is another name for Edom (cf. Gen. 36:8), the land of the descendants of Esau. Josephus recorded that Nebuchadnezzar attacked and subjugated the regions of Ammon and Moab five years after the destruction of Jerusalem (*Antiquities,* 10.9.7). Edom, the region of the descendants of Esau (25:12-14; cf. Gen. 36:8), was overrun first by the Nabateans and later by the Maccabeans during the intertestamental period. For Edom's sins, see Jeremiah 49:7-22 and Obadiah 1:10-14. Most of the Philistines migrated from the Aegean Islands to the southern coast of Israel around the twelfth century B.C. (25:15-17). They were a powerful and aggressive people and were Israel's greatest threat at the beginning of the monarchy. For more on the judgment of the Philistines (25:16), see Isaiah 14:29-32 and Zephaniah 2:5.

26:1–28:26 TYRE DESTROYED
26:1-21 The oracle of judgment. Ezekiel 26–28 contains judgments against Tyre. Tyre was a Phoenician seaport which had been

allied with Israel during the reigns of David and Solomon, but the allies later drifted apart (cf. Joel 3:4-8; Amos 1:9-10). The city was well known for its merchant fleet and commerce. Much of the imagery describing its fall was related to its commercial importance. The "eleventh year" (26:1) was 586 B.C. Nebuchadnezzar besieged Tyre for thirteen years and destroyed the city on the coast, but not the island fortress. Alexander the Great took the fortress in 332 B.C. by building a causeway from the rubble of the city out to the island. Although rebuilt during the Roman period, Tyre was once again destroyed during the Crusades.

27:1-36 Lamentation for Tyre: mighty ship. Senir (27:5) was another name for Mount Hermon. Lebanon is the mountain range north of Galilee. Bashan (27:6) referred to the Transjordan hills northeast of Galilee. Elishah (27:7) probably referred to the island of Cyprus. Sidon (27:8) is another Phoenician seaport north of Tyre. Arvad was the most northerly Phoenician town. It was situated on a rocky island directly opposite the island of Cyprus. Gebal (27:9), later known as Byblos, was a Phoenician city just north of modern Beirut. Tyre was depicted as a great merchant vessel that was completely destroyed by an "east wind" (27:26), apparently a reference to Nebuchadnezzar. The ruined Tyre was described and lamented (27:26-36) under the image of a sailing ship.

28:1-26 The ruler of Tyre is condemned. While Ezekiel 27 focused on the destruction of the city of Tyre, Ezekiel 28 emphasized the fall and destruction of the leader of Tyre, King Ithobaal II. Following the church fathers, many have suggested that this text describes the person and work of Satan. But some of these verses could not be applied to Satan (cf. 28:18-19). The most natural way to understand this poetical passage is as a satirical attack on the pagan king of Tyre. Many of the images used in the passage were taken from the religious background of Tyre. The patron deity of the city was Baal Melqart ("Baal, king of the city"). Apparently Ithobaal appropriated divine honors ("I am a god," 28:2). To call a king a god was common at that time.

Ezekiel predicted the king's humiliation and demise with poetic language and terms that could be understood by the people of his day who would have been familiar with the religion of Tyre. For "Daniel" (28:3), see the note on 14:14. Like many rulers of his day, this king claimed deity ("I am a god," 28:2), but he was only a man. The prophet lamented the destruction of the king of Tyre (28:11-19). The phrase "perfect in beauty" (28:12) was taken from the city's proud boast in 27:3. The name Eden (28:13; cf. Gen. 2:8) was again used in 36:35 to describe a place that was like Eden in vegetation and beauty.

The king viewed himself as the "[anointed] guardian cherub" (28:14) of the sacred sanctuary of Baal Melqart. The king was "blameless" (28:15) until he became guilty of pride and commercial transgressions. His sin took place in the commercial "trade" area (28:16, 18), something that could not be said of Satan. Sidon, located twenty miles north of Tyre, was subjugated by Nebuchadnezzar when Tyre was defeated (28:20-26; cf. Jer. 27:3, 6). See the note on 26:3-14 for Nebuchadnezzar's siege of Tyre.

29:1–33:20 EGYPT DESTROYED
29:1-16 Initial condemnation: pride. The prophecies against Egypt were delivered in January of 586 B.C., about seven months before the fall of Jerusalem. The "king of Egypt" (29:3) at this time was Pharaoh Hophra (588–569 B.C.). Judgment fell on Egypt around 570 B.C., when the country was conquered by Nebuchadnezzar (29:8). Migdol (29:10) was located on the northeast border of Egypt. Egypt was restored to independence around 530 B.C. after the conquest of Babylon by Cyrus (539 B.C.).

29:17–30:19 Two oracles: Egypt's destruction. This was Ezekiel's last dated prophecy (570 B.C.). The "horn" (29:21), a symbol of power, suggested Israel's future restoration. The prophecy of Egypt's fall was fulfilled in Nebuchadnezzar's campaign against Egypt (30:1-19), around 570 B.C. Here the term "day of the LORD" (30:3) was used of the time of Egypt's fall and destruction. The expression may also refer to the future eschatological "day of the LORD." "Put" (30:5) is usually identified with either Somolia or

Libya. "Lydia" (30:5; "Lud," NASB) is thought to refer to the Ludites (Gen. 10:13; "Ludim," NASB and KJV). The Ludim were probably an otherwise unknown African nation. Some have identified the Ludim with the Lydians of Asia Minor. "Libya" is literally "Chub," a people that has not been identified. For "Migdol to Aswan" (30:6; "Migdol to Syene," NASB and KJV), see 29:10. Ezekiel named the principal cities of Egypt existing in the sixth century B.C. that were destined for destruction (30:13-18).

30:20-26 A sign of complete defeat. The date was 586 B.C., about three months before the fall of Jerusalem. The reference was to Pharaoh Hophra (cf. 29:3).

31:1-18 Egypt compared with Assyria. The allegory of the cedar of Lebanon in Ezekiel 31 depicted the pride and fall of Assyria as a warning to Egypt. The date was 586 B.C., just one month before Jerusalem's fall. Assyria, the great Mesopotamian power to the north, ruled the ancient Near East from 860 to 612 B.C. The figurative descent into the "grave," the place of the dead, was used to depict the humiliation of Babylon (31:15-17; cf. Isa. 14:15), Tyre (Ezek. 26:20), and Egypt (32:18).

32:1-16 Lamentation for Pharaoh. Ezekiel lamented the destruction of Pharaoh Hophra and Egypt (cf. 29:8). The date was February–March 585 B.C., one year and seven months after the fall of Jerusalem (32:1).

32:17-32 Lamentation for the multitude of Egypt. This prophecy was given just two weeks after that of 32:1. "Elam" (32:24) referred to a region of southeast Mesopotamia just north of the Persian Gulf. "Meshech and Tubal" were descendants of Japheth (32:26; cf. Gen. 10:2), who occupied a mountainous area of Asia south of the Black Sea. "Edom," the descendants of Esau (32:29; cf. Gen. 36:8), occupied a region southeast of the Dead Sea.

33:1-20 The watchman theme is repeated. Ezekiel 33 is a transitional chapter. The message, delivered in February–March of 585 B.C., echoed Ezekiel's commissioning as a watchman. The exiles recognized their own sin and iniquity and questioned what they should do next. God's ways had not changed, and he commanded them to repent (33:11; cf. Deut. 30:15-20).

33:21–39:29 Jerusalem Falls: Now Is the Time for Hope and Rest

Overview: This section examined the accusation that God was not doing right (33:17, 20). This accusation was made by people with hearts that were committed to doing their own evil, no matter what God said (33:31-32). They laid a false claim on the promise to Abraham (33:24). Once Jerusalem had fallen (33:21), God moved on to tell of restoration and peace. The central concepts of Ezekiel 35–39 are found in 34:25-31. The evil shepherds (34:2, 7) would be replaced by the one good shepherd (34:23, 25, 27).

A central concern throughout this section was the vindication of God's holy name (36:21). Ezekiel 37 functions as an illustration of the restoration spoken of in 36:16-38. The covenant of peace was tested for the last time (Ezek. 38–39). While Israel had been regathered, she would undergo one last attempt to displace her from the land.

33:21-33 A FINAL CLAIM
FOR DELIVERANCE
The report of Jerusalem's fall was received by the Jews in Babylon in December–January 585 B.C., about a year and a half after the event. Some manuscripts, however, read the "eleventh" month which allowed for six months rather than eighteen for the news to travel to Babylon. With the fall of Jerusalem, Ezekiel's tongue was loosed to begin a ministry of comfort and encouragement (24:25-27). Enjoyment of the land was conditioned on obedience to the covenant.

34:1-31 CASE ANSWERED:
DESTROYED BUT FINALLY RESTORED
Ezekiel 34 is an indictment against the wicked leaders of Israel under the figure of "shepherds" (34:2), a common metaphor for kings and rulers. God was Israel's true Shepherd in contrast to the false ones Israel had previously followed (cf. Ps. 23:1; John 10:1-18). God himself would shepherd his people ("sheep"), restoring them to their land after a period of persecution and scattering (34:13). The image changed, and the designations "sheep," "rams," and "goats" were used to refer to the leaders of the people, who took advantage of their privileged positions to enrich themselves at the expense of the people (34:17). "My servant David" referred

to David's greater Son, the Messiah (34:23-24; cf. Isa. 9:6-7; Jer. 23:5-6). David's name was being used typically as the one who realized the promises given to David in 2 Samuel 7:12-16. The "covenant of peace" (34:25) was associated with but not identical to the new covenant (34:25-31; cf. Jer. 31:31-34). The provisions included the physical blessings of the Messianic kingdom.

35:1–36:15 TWO MOUNTAINS: ONE FALLEN, ONE RESTORED
This prophecy against Edom or "Mount Seir" (cf. Gen. 36:8-9) elaborated the judgment pronounced in 25:12-14. The "two nations" (35:10) referred to Israel and Judah. Ezekiel 36 contains the most comprehensive description of God's plan of redemption found in this book. The "mountains of Israel" (36:1) were representative of all of Israel's land. Restored Israel would be productive (36:8-9), populated (36:10-11), and peaceful (36:13-15).

36:16–37:28 GOD'S HOLY NAME AND ISRAEL'S RENEWAL
36:16–37:14 The holy name vindicated. The restoration promised was the second (36:24; cf. Isa. 11:11), or final, return to the land by the Jews after the tribulation's scattering. This return is based on the provisions of Deuteronomy 30:1-10. Ezekiel did not use the expression "new covenant" in this passage (36:25-28), but the provisions are identical with those of the new covenant described in Jeremiah 31:31-34. The remnant of Israel will be gathered back to their land as a believing, redeemed people (Ezek. 36:28; cf. Matt. 24:31).

The vision of the dry bones illustrated how the restoration of the nation (Ezek. 36:24) will be accomplished. There were two stages in the resurrection of the dry bones (37:7-10). As Ezekiel prophesied over the bones, they came together and formed human beings, but without the breath of life. Ezekiel prophesied again and "breath" came into them and they came to life (37:9-10). In the interpretation of the vision it was revealed that Israel would first be brought to national life and restored to the land (37:12), and then the Lord would give the nation spiritual life (37:14). The first stage may have taken place on May 14, 1948, when Israel once again became a nation after a 2,000-year eclipse. The "graves" (37:12)

may have been a reference to the foreign countries of Israel's captivities or were simply a reference to Israel's lost hope (similar to the "dry bones").

37:15-17 Unification under one king: the hand of God. The union of the two sticks, "Israel" and "Judah," represented the reuniting of the northern and southern kingdoms into one nation (37:22). "My servant David" (37:24) was a reference to the Messianic king, Jesus (cf. 34:23-24). For the "covenant of peace" (37:26), see 34:25-31.

38:1–39:29 THE LAST TEST OF THE COVENANT OF PEACE
38:1-23 Gog defeated: God magnified. Ezekiel 38–39 described the invasion and the destruction of a great northern power, "Gog." One of the major interpretive problems of the book, especially this section, is where in history to put the invasion spoken of here. There are four main views: (1) during the church age, probably at its close; (2) during the tribulation, after the Rapture; (3) after the second coming, just before the beginning of the Millennium; (4) after the millennial reign of Christ. Another possibility is a dual fulfillment during the tribulation (Rev. 19:17-19) and after the millennium (Rev. 20:7-10).

There has been considerable discussion over the five names mentioned in these verses (38:2-6). "Gog" is the leader of the land of Magog, a name not found outside the Bible. This land is north of Israel (38:15; 39:2). "Meshech" and "Tubal" have been identified as Phrygia and Cappadocia. "Put" (38:5) was a reference to Libya of North Africa. "Gomer" (38:6) referred to the Cimmerians, tribes settled along the Danube and Rhine that later formed the Germanic peoples. "Beth Togarmah" referred to the Armenians.

The invasion was scheduled for the "future years" (38:8), an eschatological designation, when Israel is restored to the land and living in security. "Sheba and Dedan" (38:13) refer to Arab peoples. "Tarshish" is also mentioned in Jonah 1:3. God is sovereign over all events (Ezek. 38:16; cf. Eph. 1:11), including the invasion of Gog. He will use this wicked nation to discipline his own people (cf. Zech. 13:8-9). The instrument of judgment ("Gog") will then be judged by God (38:17-23). Ezekiel then provided a more detailed and vivid account of the disaster that will befall Gog's armies (39:1-16).

39:1-29 Gog defeated: results elaborated.
The birds and beasts eating of the bodies of the slain was one of the curses of God's covenant with Israel (cf. Deut. 28:26), and here it is visited upon Israel's enemies. The burning of the weapons of war for "seven" years (Ezek. 39:9) is problematic if interpreted literally. The number "seven" may be used symbolically to represent the complete destruction of military weapons. "Hamon Gog" (39:11) literally means "the multitude of Gog." Cleansing will be required because bloodshed defiles the land (39:14; cf. Num. 35:33-34). "Hamonah" (39:16) literally means "multitude." The bird supper may correspond with the events recorded in Revelation 19:17-19 or those of Revelation 20:8-9, or perhaps both. The full and final restoration of Israel, both physically and spiritually, will take place after the tribulation and second coming (Ezek. 39:25-29; Zech. 12:10–13:1; Matt. 24:31).

40:1–48:35 THE OCCUPIED TEMPLE: RETURNED GLORY

Overview: There are differences of opinion among scholars regarding the interpretation of the description of Ezekiel's temple. Some interpreters believe it to be the postexilic temple built during the time of Zerubbabel. But there are too many differences between this glorious temple and the temple built after the exile. Others believe that it describes the kingdom of God in its heavenly state. This equates Ezekiel 40–48 with Revelation 21–22. Others see a figurative description of the present church age. Another view is to see a future temple during a period called the Millennium. Other prophets confirm that there will be a literal, physical temple in the Messianic age (Isa. 60:13; Jer. 33:17-18; Joel 3:18; Hag. 2:7; Zech. 6:12; 14:20).

The exact time and nature implied by the vision, however, is secondary to its main point. It is a graphic portrayal that underscores the absolute certainty of the future restoration of Israel and her friends. Ezekiel did not have the benefits of television or motion pictures by which he could visualize the certain message of restoration. His finely detailed and elaborate brick-by-brick description of the new city and temple achieves a similar end: affirmation of future hope. That future hope was to form the basis for present repentance (43:10-11) and obedience to God.

God waited fourteen years after the fall of Jerusalem before he gave this vision (40:1). He started by giving the setting and a guide (40:1-4). Then he described the temple (40:5–42:20). The phrase "I saw" (40:5; 43:2) marks the two sections of the vision so far: the two descriptions of the temple and God's returning glory. The movement is from the outside to the inside of the temple.

The temple is occupied by God (43:1-9). The east gate events are a direct link to the earlier vision of the sins of Jerusalem and the departure of God's glory (10:18-19). The human obligations of order and faithfulness are still the same (43:10–44:31). The new land is ruled by a prince who provides for the temple worship and feasts (45:1-24). As in the original conquest of the land under Joshua, the land is described and then divided for the twelve tribes (47:1–48:35). The book even ends like the book of Joshua, with the land allotments and a farewell address.

40:1-4 The Setting: A City and a Guide

The vision of Ezekiel's temple was received in the fifteenth year of Jehoiachin's exile, or 573 B.C. It was the tenth of Nisan (March–April), the day when Jewish families began to prepare for the Passover. The "man" (40:3) was apparently an angel who showed Ezekiel the temple. The "linen cord" was for longer measurements, and the "rod" for shorter measurements.

40:5–42:20 The Temple Described
40:5-47 THE WALL, GATES, AND INNER COURT
Measurements are given in terms of Ezekiel's rod that measured "six long cubits" (40:5), each of which was a "cubit and a handbreadth." A cubit was eighteen inches. One handbreadth was about three inches. So these "long" cubits were about twenty-one inches. Thus the measuring rod was ten and a half feet long. This "wall" surrounding the temple court was not to be confused with the wall that surrounded the entire temple region

(42:15-20). The "sons of Zadok" (40:46) were descendants of the priest who had been faithful to David and Solomon at the time of Adonijah's attempt on the throne (cf. 1 Kings 1:8; 2:35). The "court" (40:47) refers to the inner courtyard of the temple. The "altar" refers to the altar for sacrifice (43:13-17).

40:48–41:26 THE TEMPLE
Unlike the tabernacle or the Jerusalem temple, there is no Ark or any furniture found in its Most Holy Place. The purpose of this separate building (41:12) is unknown. It has been suggested that it was to be used for the disposal of refuse from the sacrifices. This "wooden altar" (41:22) was not the altar for sacrifice, but it corresponds to the altar of incense in the tabernacle.

42:1-20 PRIESTS' CHAMBERS AND OVERALL MEASUREMENTS
The Hebrew word translated "rod" (42:16; "reed," NASB and KJV) is the same word as in 40:5 also translated "rod," hence a ten and a half foot unit of measure. The large "wall" (42:20) was different from that in 40:5; it enclosed the whole temple complex, separating it from the rest of the land.

43:1-9 The Temple Occupied: God's Holiness

The same "glory of the God of Israel" (43:2) that Ezekiel had seen departing from Jerusalem (11:22-23) now returns to fill the temple (43:4-5).

43:10–46:24 Temple Obligations: Humans' Holiness

43:10–44:3 THE PROCLAMATION OF HOLINESS
The altar of burnt offerings was designed for use in worship in the Messiah's kingdom (43:13-27). The existence of this altar is the major objection to a literal view of the millennial temple. How can sacrifices be offered if Christ's redemptive work is finished (cf. Heb. 10:3-14)? But it should be noted that Ezekiel was not alone in mentioning animal sacrifice during the time of Israel's restoration (cf. Jer. 33:15-18). The Old Testament sacrifices did not have redemptive power in and of themselves (Heb. 10:4), and neither will these sacrifices. Yet the Old Testament sacrifices did point to Christ, the One

who would fully and finally deal with sin. And so the millennial sacrifices will point back to the death of Christ in commemoration or remembrance of the perfect sacrifice and salvation that he accomplished at Calvary.

The closure of the East Gate is often linked to the present closure of the East Gate in modern-day Jerusalem (44:1-3). But the closure spoken of here is yet future and will take place during the restored kingdom. Who is the "prince" (44:3)? He has been identified as the Messiah. However, this prince must offer a sin offering (46:12) and will have sons (46:16). Others have identified him with David. But the texts used (34:23-24; 37:24) speak of the Messiah, not the historical David. Thus, the prince is probably a future individual who will serve as a ruler or Messianic representative in the kingdom.

44:4–45:8 CARE IN WORSHIP AND LAND PORTIONS
The Levites who were unfaithful during the periods of Israel's history (cf. 1 Kings 2:26-35) will not be able to offer sacrifices (44:13), but they will perform duties in the outer court of the temple (44:14). For the "descendants of Zadok" (44:15; "sons of Zadok," NASB and KJV), see 40:46.

The temple was situated in the middle of a sacred territory measuring about eight square miles, surrounded by the priests' houses (45:1-8).

45:9–46:24 THE WORSHIP OFFERED BY THE PRINCE
An "ephah" (45:10) was a dry measure equal to two-thirds of a bushel. A "bath" was a liquid measure equal to about six gallons. In 45:25 Ezekiel was referring to the Feast of Tabernacles (cf. Deut. 16:13-15; Zech. 14:16-19). For the "day of the New Moon" (46:1), note 2 Kings 4:23; Isaiah 66:23; Amos 8:5.

47:1–48:35 The New Land

47:1-12 THE RIVER
The main point in 47:1-12 is that the land will be restored and blessed with prosperity as the curse of sin is lifted (cf. Rev. 22:3). The river flowing from the temple eastward toward the Dead Sea will bring healing to the parched desert land. This river is similar to but not identical with that found in

Revelation 22:1-2. It is symbolic of the blessings that will flow from God's presence in the sanctuary to the land.

47:13–48:35 DIVISIONS FOR THE TRIBES
The northern boundary will run from the "Great Sea" (47:15, the Mediterranean) north of Tyre to a point near Damascus. The eastern boundary will run along the Jordan River Valley to the "eastern sea" (47:18, the Dead Sea). The southern boundary will run from a point south of the Dead Sea to the "Wadi [of Egypt]" (47:19, the Wadi el-'Arish). The western boundary will run along the coast of the "Great Sea" (the Mediterranean). The "aliens" (47:22-23) is a reference to Gentile believers who will live in the land and share in the blessings of the Messiah's kingdom.

Ezekiel provided another description of the land and its divisions (48:8-22; cf. 45:1-8). "Joseph" (48:32) was representative of Ephraim and Manasseh, Joseph's two sons. Jerusalem shall be known as "The Lord Is There," a promise of God's abiding presence among his people (48:35). The book ends like the book of Joshua. The Promised Land is given to the cleansed and faithful people of God.

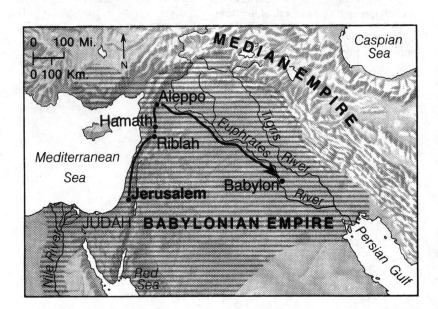

Daniel

HISTORICAL SETTING
The three deportations of Judah to Babylon
The first deportation of Judah, the southern kingdom, to Babylon was in 605 B.C., during which Daniel was taken as a young man to Babylon (Dan. 1:1). In 597 B.C., after Daniel had been in Babylon for eight years, a second deportation occurred (cf. 2 Kings 24:11-16). In 586 B.C. the third deportation occurred (cf. 2 Kings 25:1-21), and the city of Jerusalem was destroyed. By that time, Daniel had been in captivity for seventeen years.

The return of the Jews to Jerusalem
In 538 B.C. the Persian king, Cyrus, allowed the Jews to return to Israel (cf. Ezra 1:1-4). Daniel's last dated prophecy was made in the third year of Cyrus (Dan. 10:1), around two years after Zerubbabel's return to Palestine. Throughout the entire span of Israel's captivity, Daniel spoke to Israel and influenced her for good. Some captives thought that God had cast Israel aside (Jer. 33:24), but God's work through Daniel in exile showed that he was still present, powerful, and willing to forgive his people.

AUTHOR
The book itself makes the claim to have been written by Daniel, who prophesied for nearly seventy years throughout the Babylonian captivity (Dan. 7:1). He was taken into captivity in the deportation of 605 B.C., maintained a brilliant testimony before his captors, and was blessed with divine revelations of the immediate and far future. Because of the predictive element in the book, some scholars date the book about four hundred years after the captivity, during the persecution by Antiochus Epiphanes (176–164 B.C.). But the practice of using an ancient hero's name for a book written by someone else does not have enough support here or with any other book in Scripture.

DATE

The writing of the book probably took place soon after the latest date mentioned in the book (10:1), that is, around 536 B.C. The explicit dates in the book cover a time period of approximately sixty-eight years. They were purposely listed to link up with the great kings and movements in Israel's captivity and Babylon's fall under Persia. The issue of international sovereignty was central. The book of Daniel showed that the rise and fall of kingdoms, even secular kingdoms, was in God's hands. See the accompanying chart for a list of dates and events mentioned in Daniel.

PURPOSE

The book of Daniel was designed to encourage the Israelites to live holy lives before God in order to maintain a good witness to those who held them captive in Babylonia. It did this by three means: First, it showed the examples of Daniel and his friends risking their lives to remain faithful to God. Second, it showed how God was totally in control of their present circumstances to care for and preserve his faithful people. Third, it showed the extent of that control through visions of the future, building present faithfulness upon future hope for restoration and fulfillment of God's promises.

GEOGRAPHY AND ITS IMPORTANCE

Daniel had been taken captive from Jerusalem to Babylon. Many years later, while he was still cut off from his homeland, Daniel received visions of Israel going through a long period of domination by the foreign nations of Babylon, Persia, Greece, and the Roman Empire. But Daniel also saw that those geographical and national shifts of power were under the sovereign control of God who would ultimately unify the world under his rule.

GUIDING CONCEPTS

DREAMS AND VISIONS

When one looks at the order of the dreams and visions in the book of Daniel and puts them together with their dates, an even clearer picture of the book's purpose emerges.

THE CHRONOLOGY OF DANIEL

Reference	Date	Event
1:1	605 B.C.	Third year of Jehoiakim
1:21	539 B.C.	First year of Cyrus
2:1	604 B.C.	Second year of Nebuchadnezzar
5:1	539 B.C.	Last year of Belshazzar
5:31	539 B.C.	Darius the Mede
7:1	553 B.C.	First year of Belshazzar
8:1	551 B.C.	Third year of Belshazzar
9:1	539 B.C.	First year of Darius
10:1	537 B.C.	Third year of Cyrus

Three of the visions found in the book of Daniel were dated at the beginning of the reigns of each of the three kings mentioned in the book: (1) Nebuchadnezzar (Dan. 2:1-49); (2) Belshazzar (7:1-28); and (3) Darius (9:1-27). But a look at the section that was originally set off in the Aramaic language (Dan. 2–7) reveals the heart of the book's message. See the accompanying chart, *Dreams and Visions in Daniel*.

The Aramaic section consists of six dreams and the events surrounding those dreams. The beginning and ending dreams in this section (2:4–7:28) consist of two four-part visions that visualize events spanning the course of history. The second and second to last dreams relate two acts of deliverance: from the fiery furnace and the lions' den. The middle two dreams recount God's humbling of two great rulers of Babylon: Nebuchadnezzar, the one who destroyed Jerusalem; and Belshazzar, the last king to rule Babylon before being conquered by the Persian king, Cyrus.

This is how the arrangement looks when grouped by the content of each vision:

The Four-Part Statue (2:1-49).

The Golden Image: Deliverance from the Furnace (3:1-30).

The Tree: Nebuchadnezzar Humbled (4:1-37).

The Wall: Belshazzar Humbled (5:1-31).

Edict against Prayer: Deliverance from Lions (6:1-28).

The Four Beasts (7:1-28).

The section of Daniel 2–7 was written in a language understood internationally at that time, Aramaic. This was important as it contained truth concerning the Gentile nations. Its content was framed at the beginning and the end with a description of international rule from the present on into the dark future (the two four-part visions). Then, the next level told of two great acts of God's power and mercy to the Jews in captivity (deliverance from the furnace and the lions). But at the heart of the book, two great rulers were humbled and dethroned by God, proving that God alone was sovereign over the international scene. That was the message needed by the captives and the newly returned Jews.

The sequence of visions in this section answered the question of what life would be like for the Jewish nation. It would be under continual domination by the Gentile powers. But an end would come and God would reign. Until then, the book assured

---

DREAMS AND VISIONS IN DANIEL

Section One (originally written in Aramaic, not Hebrew)

2:1-49	Four-part statue	Nebuchadnezzar's dream (604 B.C.)
3:1-30	Golden Image	Deliverance of the three Hebrews
4:1-37	Tree	Dream of Nebuchadnezzar's humbling
5:1-31	Writing on Wall	Prediction of Belshazzar's end (539 B.C.)
6:1-28	Edict against Prayer	Deliverance of Daniel (539 B.C.)
7:1-28	Four Beasts	Dream: General (553 B.C.)

Section Two (the Aramaic section ends, the Hebrew section begins)

8:1-27	Ram and Goat	Dream: Specific (551 B.C.)
9:1-27	Seventy Weeks	Dream: General (539 B.C.)
10:1–12:13	End-Time Conflicts	Dream: Specific (537 B.C.)

the readers, God was in total control of any and all international powers. The book gave a balanced perspective to the present and hope for the future by showing that God was sovereign.

The rest of the book (Dan. 8–12) was written in the Hebrew language to the Jewish people and was a sequence of general and specific visions that elaborated on the visions of the four-part statue (Dan. 2) and the four beasts (Dan. 7).

THE ENDINGS OF THREE VISIONS
The four-part statue vision (2:1-49) ends with the eternal kingdom being established. The vision of the four beasts (7:1-28) ends with the eternal kingdom being established for the saints of the highest One (7:14, 18, 22, 27). The vision of the seventy weeks (9:1-27) ends with complete destruction of the enemy and complete victory, purification, and honor for God's people (9:24). Throughout, God shows his power to rule over hostile forces and bring in his kingdom. That is why the specific events in Daniel 9–12 were so necessary for God's people to hear as they faced that awful time of chastisement and the prospect of an indefinite period of Gentile domination stretching into the future.

BIBLE-WIDE CONCEPTS

THE RELATIONSHIP TO JEREMIAH
Jeremiah 25:11-12 and 29:10 first announced that the Babylonian captivity would last seventy years. Jeremiah 34:13-14 linked the captivity to Israel's lack of observing the seventh-year Sabbaths (cf. 2 Chron. 36:21). The number seventy symbolized the seventy seventh-year Sabbath rests that Israel had not kept. That added up to a 490-year period stretching back into Israel's disobedient history. So, when Daniel was meditating over the seventy years of captivity, he was also meditating over a 490-year period of disobedience. And that seventy-times-seven framework was exactly what God used in the vision of the seventy weeks in Daniel 9. He presented a series of seventy weeks, but of years, not days. The number 490 was already on Daniel's mind. Thus the six aspects (9:24) of purifying at the end of the seventieth week were similar to the function of the seventy years of Israel's captivity.

MIRACLES AND WORLD RULERS
Israel would be dominated by a number of international rulers before the end of Daniel's seventieth week. Israel, the northern kingdom, had earlier suffered under Assyrian domination; Babylon was the present power; and Persia, Greece, and Rome would soon follow, one after the other. Daniel's message was that God would allow those nations a time of international dominance. But eventually he would destroy all national attempts at world rule and replace them with his own worldwide reign.

God had allowed periods of increased miracles at great junctures in history. Those periods stand out clearly: Moses and the exodus from Egypt; Elijah and Elisha; Daniel and the exile; and the time of Christ and the apostles. At times of great new developments God also supplied the faithful with visible proof of his omnipotence. But the faithful also needed proof of his control of the future. The dreams and visions of the future were given to show that God not only had power over the present but he also had knowledge and control of the future. The Lord used Daniel to confirm the end of the age and the certain fact of his future return (cf. Matt. 24:15).

NEEDS MET BY DANIEL

Daniel wrote during Israel's captivity in Babylon, a time of great physical and spiritual loss for the nation. To those who cared, it seemed as if all of God's promises had been permanently broken. There was no temple or land, and no son of David was ruling over God's people. Perhaps the gods of Babylon were stonger than the God of Israel. Perhaps the Israelites should just forget their past and go along with Babylon and its cultural and religious ways. But the book of Daniel affirmed that it was Israel's sin, not God's weakness or lack of care, that brought about captivity. Israel's call to do God's will and prepare for his wonderful future was still in force. Far from conforming to the religion of Babylon, Israel was to conform to God's holiness. His people might be in or out of the Promised Land or in present or future times of trouble, but neither the place nor the problem was to affect the commitment of the people of Israel to their all-powerful and ever-present God. They were probably struggling with thoughts and questions much like these.

- Many of the Israelites thought the kingdom would come after the seventy years of captivity, but Daniel said they had 490 more years to wait. How could God be in control of that?
- If Israel is going to have to wait for deliverance, what is their task in the meantime?
- What possible purposes could God have in letting things go on and on, rather than bringing this age to an end quickly?
- Since Israel is under the godless domination of world rulers, is God still powerful and present to help?

The book of Daniel meets some needs that believers face today—needs born from having to wait for God's victory and not having all the answers. First, modern believers, like Israel, have the great challenge of waiting for God's promises for a better future without losing their hope and desire to please God in the present. Daniel's seventy years of captivity stretched into 490 years until the Messiah would come. And for believers today, the years of waiting for the Messiah's return now approach two thousand. For some believers, their desire to be faithful is inversely proportional to how long it will be before Christ returns. Because the date of his return seems so far in the future, they feel no need to work on the project of personal holiness day by day. But Daniel's words about the distant future were to encourage and sober believers to recognize the powerful hope they actually have. Although Daniel does not diminish the pain and depression of living so long in a sinful world, neither does he allow believers to give up walking with God. On the contrary, the evil of the world that stretches into the future is to be a showcase for the purity and goodness of the faithful.

Second, like Israel in captivity, believers today have the problem of living with and learning from the consequences of their own or others' sins. Daniel's greatest pain is expressed not over the sins of unbelievers, but of believers. Daniel speaks to believers of all ages as those who, like Israel, have suffered discipline for their disobedience yet still are prone to be faithless. But far from browbeating, he shows them how lovingly God preserves them through world evil to the end when they will be fully restored and unbelievers will be judged. The vision of God's present sovereignty and creation's ultimate rest is the fire God sought to light in hearts needing stability and purity. The world and its evil will run its course. But the task of all believers, like Daniel's, is to shine as pure witnesses to the world of God's call to redemption.

OUTLINE OF DANIEL

A. DANIEL BECOMES ESTABLISHED IN THE COURT OF NEBUCHADNEZ-
ZAR (1:1-21)
 1. Taken to Babylon (1:1-7)
 2. Daniel Refuses to Be Defiled (1:8-16)
 3. God Grants Knowledge and Understanding (1:17-21)
B. THE TIMES OF THE NATIONS (Aramaic section 2:1–7:28)
 1. The Four-Part Statue (2:1-49)
 2. The Golden Image: Deliverance from the Furnace (3:1-30)
 3. The Tree: Nebuchadnezzar Humbled (4:1-37)
 4. The Writing on the Wall: Belshazzar Humbled (5:1-30)
 5. The Edict against Prayer: Deliverance from the Lions (5:31–6:28)
 6. The Four Beasts (7:1-28)
C. THE NATIONS' IMPACT ON ISRAEL (8:1–12:13)
 1. Ram and Goat: Holiness Defiled and Restored (8:1-27)
 2. Seventy Weeks: Holiness Defiled and Restored (9:1-27)
 3. End-Time Conflicts: From Cyrus to the End of the Age (10:1–12:13)

DANIEL NOTES

1:1-21 DANIEL BECOMES ESTABLISHED IN THE COURT OF NEBUCHADNEZZAR

Overview: Daniel 1 shows the pure character of Daniel and his friends. They understood that the Babylonian captivity was for the purification, not the destruction, of God's people. The chapter also emphasizes what God, in his sovereignty, gave to his people. God gave Jehoiakim into the hands of the Babylonians (Dan. 1:2), showing how Daniel came into captivity. God gave Daniel favor and sympathy from the Babylonians (1:9), showing a fulfillment of Solomon's prayer for captives in 1 Kings 8:50. God gave Daniel and his friends knowledge and under-

standing (Dan. 1:17), setting the foundation for the revelations to come. These men proved the purity of their character. All the visions and interpretations that are seen throughout this book should be viewed as the gifts of God as he had compassion on his people in bondage.

1:1-7 Taken to Babylon

In 626 B.C. Nabopolassar (626–605 B.C.) became the king of the city of Babylon and began a campaign to overthrow the Assyrian yoke. In 612 B.C. Nineveh was captured, and in 610 B.C. Haran, the last Assyrian stronghold, was conquered. Concerned by Babylon's rapid rise to power, Egypt intervened and gained control of Israel for a brief period. But Egyptian sovereignty was lost when Babylon defeated Egypt at Carchemish in 605 B.C. Babylon became the new world power, and Nebuchadnezzar (605–562 B.C.) moved quickly to secure his newly won territory.

The "third" year of Jehoiakim (605 B.C.) reflects the Babylonian custom of designating the first year of rule as the accession year. Thus, the "third" year (Dan. 1:1) coincides with the "fourth" year of Jehoiakim as reflected in the more common method of reckoning (cf. Jer. 46:2). Jehoiakim (609–597 B.C.) submitted to Babylon and became a vassal king. The appropriation of the temple's vessels reflects the practice of a conqueror placing the gods of the vanquished enemy in his own sanctuary. This gesture claimed victory for the Babylonian gods. Babylonia (1:2) is also called Shinar (NASB) (see NIV footnote; cf. Gen. 10:10; 11:2).

The siege against Jerusalem in 605 B.C. resulted in the deportation of some of the royal family and nobles, including Daniel and his three friends. Ashpenaz was the chief of the "court officials" (Dan. 1:3), literally, "eunuchs." While the term was originally used of those who tended to the king's harem, it came to have a general usage for a trusted advisor of the king.

Nabopolassar, the first king of Babylon, was of Chaldean (Kaldu) descent. The term was later applied to the land of Babylonia (i.e., Chaldea) and its inhabitants. Daniel and his friends were given names that honored the Babylonian deities: Bel (Babylonian for the Semitic Baal), Aku (the moon god), and Nebo (son of Bel). Their Hebrew and Babylonian names had these meanings: Daniel ("God is my judge") was changed to Belteshazzar ("May Bel protect his life"); Hananiah ("Yahweh is gracious") was changed to Shadrach ("command of Aku"); Mishael ("Who is what God is?") was changed to Meshach ("Who is what Aku is?"); Azariah ("Yahweh helps") was changed to Abednego ("servant of Nebo").

1:8-16 Daniel Refuses to Be Defiled

The problem with the palace food was that it would not have been prepared according to the Mosaic Law (cf. Lev. 17:10); it may have included unclean meat (cf. Lev. 11); and it

may have been dedicated to Babylonian deities (cf. Exod. 34:15). Actually, all food in Babylon was considered unclean by the Hebrews (cf. Ezek. 4:13; Hos. 9:3-4). But the point is that the men were submissive to their captors in everything except those things that would lead to disobedience to God. They would not be defiled.

1:17-21 God Grants Knowledge and Understanding

The words "ten times better" (Dan. 1:20) are probably hyperbole (i.e., exaggeration for emphasis). Daniel 1:21 does not indicate that Daniel's ministry concluded in the first year of Cyrus (10:1; 538 B.C.). Rather, his ministry continued through the Babylonian and into the Persian period.

2:1-7:28 THE TIMES OF THE NATIONS (ARAMAIC SECTION)

Overview: The section of Daniel 2:1–7:28 was written in Aramaic, the language used by the Jews in Babylon, instead of Hebrew (cf. Ezra 4:7). Daniel 2, 3, and 4 all start with Nebuchadnezzar and end with his praise to God. Getting the identification and interpretation of the dream was a matter of life and death (Dan. 2:17-18). The prayer was for God's compassion (cf. 1 Kings 8:50). Daniel's praise (Dan. 2:19-23) forms the background to all of the actions in the book. God is totally sovereign over times and kings (2:21), and he is the only true source of revelations (2:22). The dreams and visions throughout the book are reflections of God's sovereign control. The three confessions of Nebuchadnezzar (2:46-49; 3:28-30; 4:34-37) confirm God's sovereignty and trustworthiness. God is above all gods and kings (2:47), is able to deliver (3:29), and humbles the proud (4:37).

Nebuchadnezzar, the greatest Babylonian king, had his pride humbled in Daniel 4. Belshazzar, Babylonia's last king, was humbled in Daniel 5. Daniel 6 is about Daniel's deliverance from the lions; it matches up with Daniel 3 and the deliverance of Shadrach, Meshach, and Abednego from the fiery furnace. Darius's praise of God (6:26-27) matches the three praises of Nebuchadnezzar (2:46-49; 3:28-30; 4:34-37). Again, God shows compassion to his captive people through the deeds of their Babylonian captors (6:28;

cf. 3:30). The purpose of this section is to detail God's plans to give the kingdom to the people of God through a long process of international ups and downs (7:27).

2:1-49 The Four-Part Statue

2:1-13 MAGICIANS UNABLE TO INTERPRET THE DREAM

The "second" year of Nebuchadnezzar (2:1; 603 B.C.) was actually the third year of Daniel's training. The first year (605 B.C.) would have been Nebuchadnezzar's accession year. Four classes of wise men were identified (2:2): "magicians" were sacred writers or scholars; "enchanters" were sacred priests; "sorcerers" were those who practiced sorcery or incantations; "astrologers" or "Chaldeans" referred to a priestly class in the Babylonian religion.

It is clear that Nebuchadnezzar did not forget the dream (2:5) but required that the dream be revealed in order to validate the interpretation (cf. 2:9). How else could he have known that the interpretation was valid and that his wise men were not deceiving him?

2:14-49 DANIEL RECEIVES AND INTERPRETS THE VISION

The petition led to God's answer and Daniel's praise. Prophetically, Israel has two ages: (1) the present age—the age of promise, and (2) the age to come—the Messianic age when the covenant promises will be fulfilled (2:28). Daniel's vision concerned the "days to come" (2:28), the time from Daniel's day to the establishment of God's kingdom.

From the head downward, the image was made of materials that were of decreasing value but of increasing strength, until the feet (2:31-35), where weakness and deterioration set in. Interpreters vary in identifying the parts of the figure with ancient kingdoms (2:36-45). The commonly accepted view that fits best with the context of the book (cf. Dan. 7–8) is presented in the accompanying chart.

The "rock" (2:45; "stone," NASB and KJV) image is used often in the Old Testament to refer to the Messiah (cf. Ps. 118:22; Isa. 28:16; Zech. 3:9). It becomes one of the most important figures used for Christ throughout the New Testament (cf. Matt. 21:42; Acts 4:11; Rom. 9:33; 1 Pet. 2:6-8).

3:1-30 The Golden Image: Deliverance from the Furnace

3:1-7 THE SETTING

A "cubit" is a unit of measure equivalent to eighteen inches (this ancient unit of measure is retained in NASB and KJV). The image was ninety feet high and nine feet wide (Dan. 3:1). Dura was a city six miles south of Babylon. Archaeologists have discovered a large platform forty-five feet square and twenty feet high that may have served as the pedestal for Nebuchadnezzar's image. The "satraps" (3:2-3) were chief ruling officials over the provinces in Babylon. The furnace (3:6) may have been a brick kiln used for firing bricks. Several such furnaces have been excavated outside the site of ancient Babylon.

3:8-27 THE DELIVERANCE

The three Jews believed that God was able to deliver them, but they did not presume to know his will (3:17-18). Even in the face of possible martyrdom, they refused to participate in idolatry (3:18). Their confidence may have been based on Isaiah 43:1-2. The "seven times" (Dan. 3:19) was a proverbial expression (cf. Prov. 24:16). The point was to exclude the possibility of supernatural intervention. The Talmud identifies the one "like a son of the gods" (Dan. 3:25) as the angel Gabriel. Christians usually identify the figure as the preincarnate Christ.

NEBUCHADNEZZAR'S IMAGE AND ITS SIGNIFICANCE

2:36-38	Golden head	Nebuchadnezzar—Babylon
2:39	Silver chest and arms	Persia
2:39	Bronze abdomen and thighs	Greece
2:40	Iron legs	Rome
2:41-43	Iron and clay feet	Divided Roman Empire
2:44-45	The rock cut out of a mountain	The Messiah's kingdom

3:28-30 NEBUCHADNEZZAR'S RESPONSE
Nebuchadnezzar's decree served as the
climax of this story. It provided for the recognition of Judaism and protection for its
followers.

4:1-37 The Tree:
Nebuchadnezzar Humbled
4:1-18 THE DREAM
Chronologically, Daniel 4:1-3 belongs at the
end of Daniel 4 because the words grew out
of Nebuchadnezzar's experiences. This story
has an introduction (4:1-3) and conclusion
(4:34-37). Nebuchadnezzar must have
realized that the dream had special significance for him because he was alarmed by it
(4:5). See the note on 2:2 regarding the
various wise men (4:6). Daniel's late arrival
allowed for the incompetence of the king's
wise men to be clearly demonstrated and
gave Daniel's interpretation greater impact
(4:8). Daniel's Babylonian name, "Belteshazzar" means "may Bel protect his life." The
expression "the spirit of the holy gods" (4:8)
suggests that Nebuchadnezzar was coming to
a realization that Daniel's God was different,
and more powerful, than his own.
  The expression "messenger" (4:13)
referred to an observing angel. The purpose
of the "iron and bronze" (4:15) is unclear. It
may suggest that the stump was to be
preserved in order that it might grow again.
The pronoun "him" (4:15) indicates that the
tree represented a person. The "seven times"
(4:16) are time periods of uncertain duration.
Following the Septuagint, most scholars
interpret them to be "years." Daniel 4:17
reveals the major theme of the book—the
sovereignty of God.

4:19-27 EVANGELISTIC INTERPRETATION
Through his experience, Nebuchadnezzar
(4:20-22) was to learn that the Lord is the
ultimate Sovereign and that he delegates
dominion so that man cannot take the glory
or credit. Daniel counseled the king to repent
in order to avoid God's judgment (4:27).

4:28-37 THE KING IS RESTORED
Nebuchadnezzar had every reason to take
pride in Babylon. The building of this
famous city, with its hanging gardens,
massive walls, and many temples, was one
of his greatest accomplishments. However he
failed to acknowledge that none of this
would have been possible apart from God's

sovereign will. Nebuchadnezzar suffered
from a known form of mental illness called
"zoanthropy," which is the delusion that one
has become an animal. Nebuchadnezzar
learned his lesson concerning God's
judgment on pride. Many believe that he was
genuinely converted and became a believer
in God.

5:1-30 The Writing on the Wall:
Belshazzar Humbled
5:1-12 THE WRITING:
THE DEMAND FOR DANIEL
Daniel 5 records the downfall of Babylonia
and the rise of Persia in fulfillment of the
second part of Nebuchadnezzar's vision
(2:39). This forms an abrupt shift to the end
of Nebuchadnezzar's kingdom. Note the link
of 5:2 to 1:2. The year was 539 B.C., and
Babylon was surrounded by the armies of
Cyrus. Daniel was probably eighty years old
at this time, having been taken captive from
Jerusalem in 605 B.C. Until recently, the
existence of "Belshazzar" as king of Babylon
was in question, and thus, the historical credibility of the book of Daniel was also in
question. But the discovery of the Nabonidus
Chronicle has confirmed that Belshazzar was
the eldest son and coregent of Nabonidus,
reigning with his father from 553 to 539 B.C.
Nabonidus was in charge of the military, and
Belshazzar was in charge of the administration of the empire. The sacred vessels (5:2)
were part of the temple's treasure taken from
Jerusalem by Nebuchadnezzar in 605 B.C.
(cf. 1:2).
  The Hebrew word translated "father"
(5:2) can be used of ancestors, which was
true in this case. In 5:4 Belshazzar was
saying in effect, "What god is great enough
to do us any harm? We even conquered the
people of Israel, and their God." The "third
highest ruler" (5:7) was the ruler after
Nabonidus and Belshazzar. The "queen"
(5:10) was Nitocris, the wife of Nabonidus
and mother of Belshazzar.

5:13-30 INTERPRETATION
AND FULFILLMENT
The Aramaic words have been transliterated
into English: *Mene, Mene, Tekel*, and
Upharsin (5:25). God gave Daniel the ability
to declare the meaning of this cryptic message: *Mene* meant "numbered": God had
numbered the days of the kingdom; the

repetition of *Mene* was for emphasis. *Tekel* meant "weighed": God had weighed the king in the balances and found him deficient. *Peres* meant "divided": God had divided the kingdom and given it to the Medes and the Persians. *Upharsin* meant "divided": the plural noun form of *Peres,* the plural being used for emphasis.

Daniel became the "third" ruler, along with Nabonidus and Belshazzar (5:29). Ancient historians Herodotus and Zenophon reported that Cyrus had his soldiers divert the Euphrates River, which ran under the walls and through the city. The army then used the river channel to enter and capture Babylon without a fight (5:30; 539 B.C.).

5:31–6:28 The Edict against Prayer: Deliverance from the Lions
5:31–6:9 THE EDICT SIGNED
There are differences of opinion among scholars as to the identity of "Darius the Mede" (5:31). The two major views identify him with (1) Gubaru, whom Cyrus appointed governor over Babylon immediately after taking the city, or (2) Cyrus the Persian (cf. 6:28). Daniel 6 contains one of the most familiar stories in the Old Testament, that of Daniel in the lions' den. "Darius" (6:1) may have been Cyrus or Gubaru (cf. 5:31). For "satraps" (6:1), see the note on 3:2-3. The laws of the Medes and Persians were irrevocable (6:8; cf. Esther 1:19; 8:8).

6:10-28 DANIEL DELIVERED FROM THE LIONS
Daniel 6:10 reflects Hebrew prayer habits in the biblical period. The faithful Hebrews faced Jerusalem (cf. 1 Kings 8:41-43; Tobit 3:11), got on their knees (cf. 1 Kings 8:54; Ezra 9:5; Ps. 95:6), and prayed three times a day (Ps. 55:17). The words of Darius may have indicated true faith or mere hope (cf. Dan. 6:16, with 3:15-17; and cf. 6:26-27 with 2:20-23; 3:28-29; 4:33-35; and cf. 6:28 with 3:30). The "angel" (6:22) may be the same person who was with the three young men in the furnace (cf. 3:25), possibly the preincarnate Christ. Persian law (6:24), in contrast to the Mosaic code (cf. Deut. 24:16; Jer. 31:29), required the punishment of the criminals' families along with the offenders. Some scholars translate Daniel 6:28 as "Daniel prospered during the reign of Darius, that is, the reign of Cyrus the Persian,"

identifying Darius and Cyrus as the same person (see NIV footnote). Cyrus ruled Persia from 539 to 530 B.C.

7:1-28 The Four Beasts
7:1-14 THE DREAM
Chronologically, Daniel 7 follows Daniel 4. It deals with the Babylonian rather than the Persian period. Thematically, however, it builds on the revelation of Nebuchadnezzar's vision in Daniel 2 and forms the ending bracket to the section of Daniel 2–7.

The "first year of Belshazzar" (7:1) was 553 B.C., when he began to serve as coregent with his father, Nabonidus (556–539 B.C.). The "four great beasts" (7:3) compare with the "four" major parts of Nebuchadnezzar's image (cf. 7:17, 2:31-45). The gate of Babylon was decorated with images of winged lions (7:4). The "lion" and "eagle" were both used in Jeremiah 49:19-22 to refer to Nebuchadnezzar, king of Babylon.

Medo-Persia, which succeeded Babylon, was a lopsided coalition like the lopsided bear (Dan. 7:5). Greece, under the leadership of Alexander the Great, conquered Persia in 331 B.C. The "four wings" on the swift leopard (7:6) suggested the speed of Alexander's conquest, and the "four heads," the division of the empire among his generals after his death: (1) Egypt and Palestine were given to Ptolemy; (2) the area of Phrygia to the Indus River was given to Seleucus; (3) Thrace and Bithynia were put under Lysimachus; and (4) Macedonia was given to Cassander. Rome (7:7-8) succeeded Greece with the coming of Pompey to Palestine in 63 B.C.

The little horn (7:8) is the subject of further revelation in 7:24-25. The "Ancient of Days" (7:9) is a reference to God the Father (cf. 7:13). The "one like a son of man" (7:13) was distinguished from the "Ancient of Days" (God the Father) and received a "kingdom" (7:14). This would suggest that he was identified with the coming Messiah and would someday be revealed as the preincarnate Christ (cf. 2 Sam. 7:12-16; Luke 1:32-33).

7:15-28 THE DREAM INTERPRETED
The interpretation of Daniel's vision is first given in summary form (Dan. 7:17-18) and then in further detail (7:19-27). Daniel was particularly interested in the fourth beast and

the boastful little horn (7:8). The fourth beast was actually a "kingdom" that would be powerful enough to dominate the whole earth (7:23). The "ten horns" (7:24) of the beast (7:7) were identified as ten kings who were contemporaneous with the fourth kingdom. Out of this group would arise the little horn (7:8) who would gain control of the fourth kingdom. His character and activities identify him with the antichrist of the tribulation period (cf. Rev. 13:1-10). If the word "time" (Dan. 7:25) may be translated "year," the period, "time, times and half a time," would then refer to three and a half years.

8:1–12:13 THE NATIONS' IMPACT ON ISRAEL

Overview: Daniel 8–12 details the future for God's people. Daniel 2–7 detailed the future for the Gentile powers. God was sovereign over the Gentile kingdoms. Daniel 8–12 shows that he is also sovereign to bring ultimate victory to his people. The pattern in this section is to move from the oppression of God's people to their final victory. The explanation of the vision of the ram, goat, and horns in Daniel 8 ended with God's total victory for his people (8:25). Daniel's prayer in Daniel 9 reflected Solomon's prayer long before at the dedication of the temple. It was a prayer that confessed the reason for the captivity in Babylon (9:12-13), petitioned for the end of God's anger toward Jerusalem (9:16), and requested God's compassion, hearing, and forgiveness (cf. 1 Kings 8:30, 34, 36, 39, 43, 45; and especially 8:49-50). God's response to that prayer was the decree of seventy weeks. A period of oppression would end with the complete destruction of the anti-God forces (Dan. 9:27). Jerusalem, once defiled, would have her holiness restored. The great suffering involved here was to instruct the captives that not all suffering under God's sovereignty was due to divine punishment, as was the captivity in Babylon. Much conflict would come from human sources.

Daniel 10 revealed that another and related conflict was in the angelic realm. The subject was what would happen to the people of God in the latter days (10:14). But more space was given to the subject of the struggle to bring the message. Angelic conflict and angelic strength for Israel were stressed. The

details of the content of the prophecy of the future were meant to be obscure (12:9). But the overall point was crystal clear: God is absolutely for his people's complete victory and would bring it about.

Daniel 11 continues the speech of the angel and specific details about the kingdoms to come. It concludes with the end of the "contemptible person" (11:21, 45). In the various descriptions of the future, note the difference between human attempts to bring in the end (11:14, 27, 35) and the real end of the age and the establishment of the kingdom of God (12:1-3). God's people would suffer, but ultimate victory was certain.

8:1-27 Ram and Goat: Holiness Defiled and Restored

8:1-14 THE DREAM
In Daniel 8, Daniel returned to the Hebrew language (cf. 2:4) because these chapters relate to the history and destiny of Israel. Daniel 8 provides the details concerning the second and third kingdoms, Medo-Persia and Greece. The "third year" (8:1) would be around 551 B.C., when Cyrus established a joint state of Medes and Persians. Elam (8:2) was a province located about 230 miles east of Babylon. Susa was the ancient capital of the Elamite Empire and later became one of the capitals of Persia.

The "ram" (8:3) is identified in 8:20 with Medo-Persia (the lopsided bear of 7:5). The "goat" (8:5) is identified in 8:21 with Greece, and the "prominent horn" (8:5) symbolizes the empire's first king, Alexander the Great. The destruction of the "large horn" (8:8) was realized with Alexander's death in Babylon (323 B.C.) at the age of thirty-three. The small horn (8:9) is not to be identified with the little horn of 7:8, for this horn arose out of the Greek Empire, while the previous one arose out of the Roman Empire. The little horn should be identified with Antiochus IV Epiphanes (175–164 B.C.), who sought to unify Greek rule through the Hellenization of the empire. He sought to extend his rule south toward Palestine, and he persecuted the Jewish people there.

Antiochus went to Jerusalem and converted the temple into a shrine dedicated to Zeus (8:10-12). On December 16, 167 B.C., he had a sow (an unclean animal according to God's law) sacrificed on the sacred altar, and "daily sacrifice" at the temple (8:11) by the Jews ceased. This defilement interrupted sacrifice for 2,300 evenings and mornings, a reference to the evening and morning offering (8:14). The period, then, was just a little over three years, from 167 to 164 B.C., when the temple sacrifices were reinstated by the Maccabeans.

8:15-27 THE INTERPRETATION
"Gabriel" (8:16) is one of the two angels mentioned by name in the Bible. He has often served God by relaying important messages (cf. Luke 1:19, 26). Daniel 8:23-26 provides further detail regarding the person and work of Antiochus IV Ephipanes (cf. 1 Maccabees 1–6).

9:1-27 Seventy Sevens: Holiness Defiled and Restored

9:1-19 THE PRAYER OF DANIEL
As Daniel 2 and 7 outlined God's prophetic program for the Gentile nations, so Daniel 9 revealed God's prophetic program for Israel. The "first year of Darius" (9:1) was 538 B.C. He actually took the throne in 539 B.C. Daniel had been studying Jeremiah 25:11 and 29:10 regarding God's promise to restore the Judeans to their homeland after seventy years of captivity (Dan. 9:2). Daniel realized that the period was almost complete (605–539 B.C., sixty-six years of seventy had passed). He wondered how God would bring about the restoration and what would follow.

Daniel is an example of a man of prayer (9:3-19; 2:19-23; 6:10). The "time of the evening sacrifice" would be about 3:00 P.M. (9:21; cf. Exod. 29:39). The "seventy 'sevens'" (Dan. 9:24) may be weeks of "years." The prophecy would then concern seventy seven-year periods, or 490 years. Daniel 9:24 outlines and summarizes the program for this period.

9:20-27 SEVENTY WEEKS FOR RESTORATION
The seventy weeks begin with the "decree to restore and rebuild Jerusalem" (9:25), which was issued by Artaxerxes for Nehemiah (cf. Neh. 2:1-8). The date was March 5, 444 B.C. The seventy weeks are divided into three periods: During the first (7 weeks, or 49 years), Jerusalem was rebuilt. The second (62 weeks, or 434 years) concludes with the coming of the Messiah at his royal entry, March 30, A.D. 33. The third (one week, or

seven years) is still in the future and is possibly to be identified with the tribulation period.

After the sixty-nine weeks (the 62 + 7), the Messiah would be "cut off" (Dan. 9:26), an apparent reference to his crucifixion, and "the city and the sanctuary" of Jerusalem would be destroyed. The "people of the ruler who will come" (9:26; "the prince who is to come," NASB) were the Roman people, who destroyed Jerusalem and the temple in A.D. 70. There is evidence of a gap between the 69th and 70th week, for what is predicted in 9:27 has not yet taken place. The "ruler who will come" (9:26) is the antichrist, who will rise out of what may possibly be a revived type of the Roman Empire (7:8, 24-26). In the middle of the "week" he will take control of the Jewish temple and put a stop to worship, demanding that *he* be worshiped (cf. Matt. 24:15; 2 Thess. 2:4). But he will be destroyed at Christ's second coming (cf. Rev. 19:11, 20-21).

10:1–12:13 End-Time Conflicts: From Cyrus to the End of the Age

10:1–11:1 THE GLORIOUS DELIVERER OF THE VISION
In Daniel 9, the prophet was praying as a result of reading Jeremiah. In Daniel 10, he was praying during the season of the Passover (the fourteenth day of the first month) and the Feast of Unleavened Bread (the fifteenth to the twenty-first days of the first month). The "third year of Cyrus" (10:1) was 536 B.C. Daniel had been in Babylon approximately seventy years. The "first month" (10:4) was Nisan (March–April). The "man dressed in linen" (10:5) has been identified as either the preincarnate Christ (cf. Rev. 1:12-20) or an angelic messenger (Dan. 10:11). The messenger mentioned here had a human appearance (10:18) and was an associate of Michael (10:13). He may have been Gabriel (cf. 8:16; 9:21). The "prince of the Persian kingdom" (10:13) was apparently a supernatural figure who tried to oppose God's plan. Michael (the name means "Who is like God?") is one of two angels specifically named in Scripture. He is designated "archangel" in Jude 1:9. These verses (10:13, 20–11:1) provide some insight into the believers' spiritual warfare (cf. Eph.

6:12). The revelation concerns "the future" (Dan. 10:14; cf. 2:28), from the period of Daniel's day until the inauguration of Christ's kingdom.

11:2–12:4 THE VISION OF THE END

The four kings to follow Cyrus included: Cambyses (530–522 B.C.), Pseudo-Smerdis (an imposter), Darius I (522–486 B.C.), and Xerxes I (486–464 B.C.). The "mighty king" (11:3) referred to Alexander the Great (334–323 B.C), who conquered the Persian Empire. The section of 11:5-20 reveals the warfare that would take place between two of the four generals that inherited Alexander's empire—Seleucus, who ruled Syria, and Ptolemy, who ruled Egypt. These generals fought against one another and used Palestine as their battlefield. The primary purpose of this section was to provide background for Antiochus IV Epiphanes.

Antiochus IV Epiphanes (175–163 B.C.) encouraged the worship of himself in the form of the Olympian Zeus (11:21-35). His name Epiphanes meant "the manifest god," but his enemies perverted it to "Epimanes" ("madman"). This section further elaborates what was revealed about him in 8:9-14. In 170 B.C. Antiochus invaded Egypt and besieged Alexandria (11:25). An insurrection in Jerusalem forced Antiochus to withdraw (11:28). He went to Jerusalem and plundered the temple (1 Macc. 1:20-29). Returning to Egypt in 168 B.C., he was confronted by a Roman commander who forced him to withdraw (Dan. 11:29-30). Bitter about this turn of events, he took out his hostilities on Jerusalem (1 Macc. 1:29-67).

The "western coastlands" (Dan. 11:30) referred to Cyprus. On December 16, 167 B.C., Antiochus desecrated the Jerusalem temple by dedicating it to the worship of Zeus (11:31). The Maccabees resisted Antiochus and eventually cleansed the temple (December 14, 164 B.C.), but many Jews lost their lives during this awful period (11:32-35). In 11:36–12:3 the focus shifts to the prophetic future, from the Antiochus of history to the antichrist of the end time (7:8). The king of 11:36 was distinguished from "the king of the North" (11:40) and therefore could not have been Antiochus. The "gods of his fathers" (11:37) may have referred to religion in general or his personal religious heritage (11:37-38). His "god" (11:38) would be military might and power. The "one desired by women" (11:37) has been variously interpreted to refer to human love, a desire for peace, or the Messianic hope. Daniel 11:40-45 revealed the end-time campaign of Armageddon (cf. Rev. 16:16). The ultimate conclusion will be the antichrist's destruction at Christ's second coming (Dan. 11:45; cf. Rev. 19:11-21). The "Beautiful Land" (Dan. 11:41) referred to Palestine. The "holy mountain" (11:45) referred to Jerusalem.

For "Michael" (12:1), see the note on 10:13. The "time of distress" (12:1) is the tribulation (cf. Matt. 24:9-26). Those "delivered" (Dan. 12:1) are the faithful believers who will respond to Christ at his second coming (cf. Zech. 12:10–13:1) and be spared judgment. Two kinds of resurrection were recognized—one to life and one to judgment (cf. John 5:28-29). The "scroll" (Dan. 12:4) of Daniel's prophecies was to be sealed up or preserved intact until the period to which they applied came about.

12:5-13 FINAL WORDS TO DANIEL

In answer to the question in 12:6, it was revealed that the period of oppression under the antichrist's dominion would be "time, times and half a time" (12:7), or three and a half years (cf. 7:25). This period coincides with the last three and a half years of the tribulation. The "abomination that causes desolation" (12:11) referred to the antichrist (cf. Matt. 24:15), who will abolish Jewish sacrifice and take a position in the temple, demanding the worship due only to God (2 Thess. 2:3-8). The 1,290 days is three and a half years plus thirty days. That period will bring some aspect of the tribulation judgments to a complete conclusion. The 1,335 days (Dan. 12:12) is three and a half years plus seventy-five days. Some unspecified blessing will be realized for believers who endure to that time, perhaps the beginning of Christ's kingdom reign. Daniel's death ("rest") will culminate in resurrection ("rise") so he can share in the glory of Christ's kingdom (12:13). The book encourages purity while believers wait for the end of this age and the beginning of the next.

Hosea

BASIC FACTS

HISTORICAL SETTING
Hosea began his ministry in Israel during the prosperous reign of Jeroboam II (cf.
2 Kings 14:25, 28). After Jeroboam's death, anarchy and confusion ensued. Four of
the last six kings of Israel were assassinated. Internationally, Assyria was in the
ascendency and moving west toward Palestine. The kingdom of Israel was at a spiritual low point during Hosea's ministry. The priests were leading the people into sin
(Hos. 4:6-9; 6:9); idolatry and temple prostitution were rampant (4:11-14); and
drunkenness and adultery were characteristic of the kings (7:3-5). Amos and possibly Jonah were Hosea's contemporaries in Israel while Isaiah and Micah were his
contemporaries in Judah. Hosea and Amos prophesied during the closing years of
the northern kingdom of Israel, even as Jeremiah prophesied during the last years
of the southern kingdom of Judah.

AUTHOR
The book begins by attributing the prophecies to Hosea, the son of Beeri (1:1). Even
liberal critics have attributed most of this prophecy to the historical prophet Hosea.
The author is not mentioned outside this book, and little is known about him. He was
probably a citizen of the northern kingdom and exercised his prophetic office there.
He wrote with familiarity of the circumstances and the topography of the north (5:1;
6:8-9; 12:12; 14:6) and spoke of Israel's king as "our king" (7:5).

DATE
Hosea began his prophetic work in the reign of Israel's king Jeroboam II (793–753
B.C.). Because the fall of Samaria was not mentioned by Hosea, it is probable that he
completed his ministry before 722 B.C. His book may be regarded as containing
messages delivered over a period of about thirty years, from 755 to 725 B.C. The
prophecy was probably committed to writing around 725 B.C.

PURPOSE

The book of Hosea was designed to convince the Israelites that they needed to repent and to turn to their long-suffering God so that judgment might be averted. They needed to know that God loved them in spite of their unfaithfulness.

GUIDING CONCEPTS

TITLE

The prophecy was named after its author, Hosea, whose name means "salvation" or "deliverance." The name of the prophet was the same as that of the last king of the northern kingdom, Hoshea. In order to keep the two names separate, the English Bible always spells the name of the prophet without the second "h," that is, Hosea.

GOD'S COMPASSION AND CONTENTION

God's loving-kindness was expressed in the terms of the relationships between father and child (11:1) or husband and wife (2:19). But God's compassion also made room for the chastisement of his disobedient people. Those who disobeyed had to be judged (as in a court of law) and God's complaint against them took the form of a lawsuit (4:1; 6:7; 8:1; 12:2). They would be punished according to their fulfillment of God's covenant requirements.

But the chastisement of God's people took place within the context of God's unchanging commitment. His goal through discipline was his people's perfection, never his people's eternal destruction. Through his unfailing love, God desired to inspire a similar love in his people. Hosea emphasized that the essence of God's kingdom was a relationship of response to God's love.

STRUCTURE

The book of Hosea is structured around a movement between passages declaring punishment and passages declaring healing for God's people. Hosea 14:4 lays out the program for the entire book: "I will heal their waywardness and love them freely, for my anger has turned away from them." To compare passages of apostasy and healing in Hosea, see the accompanying chart.

Although God's discipline for sin may have gotten the attention of his children, it was his love and healing that caused them to repent and return to him. In Hosea, God's lawsuit was completely surrounded by his loyal love.

BIBLE-WIDE CONCEPTS

The priority of God's love over his judgment in the book of Hosea can be seen in how the New Testament writers quoted from the book. Hosea was perfect for expressing how God loved his people even while they were still sinners. The following passages

---

APOSTASY AND HEALING IN HOSEA

Apostasy	1:1-9; 3:1-3; 4:1–5:15; 6:4-11; 7:1–11:7; 11:12–13:13; 13:15-16
Healing	1:10–2:23; 3:4-5; 6:1-3; 6:11; 11:8-11; 13:14; 14:1-9

from Hosea are quoted in the New Testament: Hosea 1:10 in Romans 9:26; Hosea 2:23 in Romans 9:25; Hosea 6:6 in Matthew 9:13 and 12:7; Hosea 11:1 in Matthew 2:15; and Hosea 13:14 in 1 Corinthians 15:55.

God's compassion for his people had its source in his character. The classic and often-quoted passages on his compassion are Exodus 33:19 and 34:5-16. God's sovereign goodness would restore Israel under Davidic leadership (Hos. 1:11; 3:5) and as a whole nation (2:23). The promises to Abraham would be fulfilled. Compare Genesis 22:17 with Hosea 1:10; 2:23; and Genesis 18:19 with Hosea 2:19.

The future Assyrian captivity (8:9; 9:3; 10:6; 11:5, 11; 12:1; 14:3) that God had planned for his people of the northern kingdom was compared and contrasted with the past bondage of Israel in Egypt (2:15; 8:13; 9:3, 6; 11:1, 11; 12:1, 9, 13; 13:4). God's restoration of Israel from Assyrian (and Babylonian) captivity was seen as another saving event, similar to the great exodus from Egypt under Moses.

NEEDS MET BY HOSEA

When God's people suffered, they instinctively asked God why. Hosea wanted to know how Israel's pain, caused by pagan nations, squared with what he knew about God's holiness and love for his people. Why would God allow them to suffer so much? Hosea's audience needed to know that their problems were caused by their own spiritual adultery. The pain of discipline through military defeat had long before been promised in the Law of Moses should the covenant be broken. But the readers' deepest need was to know that the pain was just a step along the way of God's efforts, not to destroy, but to get his people to respond to his love. God stood as the faithful and loving husband. His people stood condemned as unfaithful. But they needed to know that the combination of God's discipline and love was his call to return to him. This book clearly revealed to the people of Israel the goal of and motivation behind God's punishment. The content and structure of Hosea's prophecy show that the Israelites were probably asking questions like the following. Hosea gave them very clear answers.

- Why is the nation of Israel being punished? (Because they have broken God's covenant relationship.)
- Does God now hate his chosen people? (No. He is punishing them because he loves them.)
- Have God's people lost the promises God made to them? (No. He was punishing them so that he could gain their repentance and restore them in the future.)

God's people continually have to struggle with living in a cursed world. In addition, believers have to struggle with their own tendencies to disobey God. And, like Israel, Christians may experience God's painful discipline. During the times of discipline, they need to hear Hosea's message that God's love should be motivation enough to keep them faithful. It was the believers, not God, who broke the bond of faithfulness to such a degree that only the pain of discipline would be sufficient to bring them back. To the question of why, believers receive a twofold answer. The pain was caused by their sin but was motivated by God's loving desire to restore their original relationship of love and obedience. The pain is designed not to make believers run away from God but back to him.

OUTLINE OF HOSEA

A. INTRODUCTION: AUTHOR AND DATE (1:1)
B. HUMAN UNFAITHFULNESS AND GOD'S LOYAL LOVE (1:2–3:5)
   1. God's First Address: Take a Wife (1:2–2:23)
   2. God's Second Address: Love an Adulteress (3:1-5)
C. ISRAEL'S PROSECUTION OVER HER BROKEN VOWS (4:1–13:16)
   1. The Threefold Complaint of God (4:1-3)
   2. The Complaint Elaborated (4:4–13:16)
D. GOD'S APPEAL OF LOYAL LOVE (14:1-9)

HOSEA NOTES

1:1 INTRODUCTION: AUTHOR AND DATE

"Hosea" means "salvation." Hosea ministered under the reigns of the following kings: Uzziah, or Azariah (791–739 B.C.), Jotham (750–731 B.C.), Ahaz (743–715 B.C.), Hezekiah (728–686 B.C.), and Jeroboam II (793–753 B.C.).

1:2–3:5 HUMAN UNFAITHFULNESS AND GOD'S LOYAL LOVE
1:2–2:23 God's First Address: Take a Wife

1:2-9 THREE CHILDREN
AS PICTURES OF JUDGMENT
The prophet's marriage and children were symbolic of the deteriorating relationship between God and his people due to Israel's waywardness. The expression "adulterous wife" (1:2; "wife of harlotry," NASB) is interpreted to mean that Gomer had an inclination toward harlotry that developed after her marriage, or that she was a harlot when she married Hosea. The latter view is probably more in keeping with Israel's history of idolatry from the beginning (cf. Josh. 24:14; Ezek. 23:8; Amos 5:25-26).

The name "Jezreel" (Hos. 1:4) means "God sows," and in this context it referred to the sowing of God's judgment. Jezreel was also a geographical place name used for the broad valley of Esdraelon that separated the hills of Samaria from Galilee. The sins committed by Jehu, king of Israel (841–814 B.C.), in the Valley of Jezreel (cf. 2 Kings 9:11–10:36) would be punished. Jehu's dynasty came to an end in 753 B.C. with

the slaying of King Zechariah (cf. 2 Kings 15:8-12). The "end" of the northern kingdom of Israel came in the Assyrian conquest of Samaria in 722 B.C. The expression "break Israel's bow" (Hos. 1:5) referred to utter defeat (cf. Ps. 46:9).

The name "Lo-Ruhamah" (Hos. 1:6) means "not pitied," signifying that the northern kingdom of Israel could not expect mercy or compassion from the Lord. The Lord's compassion on Judah, in contrast to Israel, was demonstrated in Judah's miraculous deliverance from the Assyrian siege in 701 B.C. (Hos. 1:7; cf. 2 Kings 19:34-37). The name "Lo-Ammi" (Hos. 1:9) means "not my people." This name represented a reversal of the terms of the covenant that God had made with his people (cf. Lev. 26:9-12). This rejection would not be permanent, in light of the unconditional promise of the Abrahamic covenant (cf. Gen. 12:1-3).

1:10–2:23 THREE CHILDREN
AS PICTURES OF RESTORATION
Immediately following his words of judgment, Hosea proclaimed a message of hope. He summarized the restoration in the terms of the Abrahamic promise (Hos. 1:10-11), then he gave the details of restoration in 2:1-23. Here God promised physical and spiritual blessing for Israel. The names of Hosea's children, which were previously symbolic of judgment, were changed to symbols of hope. "Ammi" means "my people," and "Ruhamah" means "pitied."

The metaphor of marital separation was used to depict the relationship between God and Israel due to the nation's apostasy. As harlotry undermined marriage, so sin and apostasy separated the people of Israel from their God. The Nuzi Tablets attest to the fact that public exposure of an adulterous wife was common in the culture of the ancient Near East (Hos. 2:3; cf. Ezek. 16:37-38). The "lovers" (Hos. 2:5) of the people were the Canaanite gods, Baal and Asherah, whom they credited with providing the necessities of life.

Hosea described the coming judgment on Israel's unfaithfulness (2:6-13). For "expose her lewdness" (2:10), see the note on 2:3. Once again Hosea turned from prophecies of judgment to promises of blessing (2:14-23). The logic ("therefore," 2:14) was found only in the unceasing love of God for his people. The "Valley of Achor" (2:15), where Achan died (Josh. 7:26), would become a "door of hope." Judgment would lead the way to blessing. Affection was implied in "my husband," while rule was implied in "my master" (Hos. 2:16). The "covenant" (2:18) was simply a divine ordinance that brought harmony to all creation. The words of 2:19-20 are traditionally recited by Jews when they put on their phylacteries (cf. Deut. 6:8). The word "love" (Hos. 2:19; "loving-kindness," NASB and KJV), or loyal love, reflects a central theme in Hosea of God's unceasing love (covenant loyalty) for his people.

The blessings of God's unhindered reign were described (2:21-23). The land that was once made desolate by God's judgment would bring forth grain, wine, and oil. The names once associated with judgment were now associated with blessing: "My people," "sow," and "compassion" (NASB).

3:1-5 God's Second Address: Love an Adulteress

Hosea 3 records one of the greatest expressions of God's unceasing love found anywhere in the Bible. It reveals the apostasy of God's people, Israel, and their future repentance and restoration. Although Gomer had been unfaithful, God commanded Hosea to take her back as a wife and love her again. Hosea modeled the alternative to divorce for marital unfaithfulness. The "raisin-cakes" (3:1) were a reference to idol sacrifices. The price of a slave during the Old Testament period was thirty shekels, but Gomer was worth only half that (3:2; cf. Exod. 21:32).

Hosea paid part of the price in grain. A "homer" was a dry unit of measure estimated at four to six bushels.

Hosea 3:4 depicted the present condition of Israel—neither idolatrous nor enjoying fellowship with God. The "ephod" was part of the high priest's attire (cf. Exod. 28:6-14). The Messianic era, the "last days," when God will be reunited with his repentant and believing people ,was described in Hosea 3:5. "David their king" referred to the Messiah (cf. Ezek. 34:23-24).

4:1–13:16 ISRAEL'S PROSECUTION OVER HER BROKEN VOWS
4:1-3 The Threefold Complaint of God

In Hosea 4–13 the prophet gave the details of what was set forth through the illustration of his marriage to Gomer in Hosea 1–3. In 4:1-3 Hosea represented the Lord as a prosecuting attorney bringing an indictment ("a charge" [NIV] or "a case" [NASB]) against the people for their violation of the covenant's stipulations.

4:4–13:16 The Complaint Elaborated
4:4–6:3 NO KNOWLEDGE OF GOD
4:4-19 The sins of Israel. The term "mother" (4:5) was used with reference to the nation. Prostitution (4:11-15) was used as an image of spiritual unfaithfulness. The people were unfaithful to God by turning from him to worship idols. The content of 4:14 is an enigma. Why wouldn't God punish the adulterous daughters? Perhaps because the men were the worse offenders. "Gilgal" and "Beth Aven" (4:15) were centers of false worship. "Beth Aven" ("house of iniquity") was Hosea's name for Bethel ("house of God"). "Ephraim" (4:17), used here as a synonym for Israel, was bent on idolatry and in a hopeless condition.

5:1-15 Priests and kings condemned. The priests and kings were condemned for ensnaring the people with false worship. "Mizpah" (5:1) was located in Gilead, east of the Jordan River (cf. Gen. 31:49). Several biblical cities bore the name "Tabor" (Hos. 5:1). The "New Moon festivals will devour them" (5:7) meant that in a very short time (a month) they would be judged. "Gibeah" and "Ramah" (5:8) were cities located on hills in the central territory of Benjamin. They would serve as good places from which to sound an alarm. Moving a "boundary" mark was forbidden by law (5:10; cf. Deut. 19:14).

The "great king" (Hos. 5:13) was probably a reference to Tiglath Pileser III, to whom Ahab appealed for help against the attacks of Rezin and Pekah (cf. 2 Kings 16:7-9). The Lord's withdrawal from Israel's presence (Hos. 5:15) may have referred to the Babylonian exile or possibly the future tribulation.

6:1-3 Exhortation to return to the Lord. The words "after two days . . . on the third day" (6:2) were a Hebrew idiom for "a short time."

6:4–10:15 NO LOYAL LOVE FOR GOD
6:4-11 The covenant transgressed. The "love" (6:4) referred to the covenant loyalty. Hosea did not deny the validity of sacrifice offered in the right spirit, but he declared that mere sacrificial ritual meant nothing apart from a person's heart righteousness (6:6; cf. 1 Sam. 15:22). "Adam" (Hos. 6:7), literally, "man," may have referred to Adam's disobedience to God's command in the garden, or mankind's disobedience in general. "Shechem" (6:9), located about thirty-two miles north of Jerusalem, was the site of the covenant renewal ceremony when the Israelites entered Canaan (cf. Deut. 27:11-14; Josh. 8:30-35).

7:1-16 False trust in the nations. "Samaria" (Hos. 7:1), the capital of the northern kingdom (also called "Ephraim"), was used here to refer to the whole country. Only eight of the seventeen kings of Israel died natural deaths (7:7). The other nine were murdered by their successors. Ephraim had joined in alliances with other nations (7:11), and she came out like a "cake not turned" (7:8), that is, half-baked.

8:1–9:17 Ultimate captivity among the nations. Israel's enemy, Assyria, was likened to an eagle swooping down upon its prey to attack (8:1). The reasons for God's judgment were recorded (8:1-14). The "calf-idol" (8:5) referred to the golden calf worship established by Jeroboam (cf. 1 Kings 12:28-29). The worship of idols would result not in feast but in famine, which was God's judgment on disobedience (Hos. 8:7). The "oppression of the mighty king" (8:10) referred to the tribute imposed upon Israel

by the king of Assyria. The "return to Egypt" (8:13) is a figurative reference to Israel being carried into Assyria. God would reverse the exodus and send Israel back into captivity.

Because of their spiritual harlotry (9:1-3), the Israelites would be rejected from God's land. They would return to bondage, or "Egypt" (9:3). Unable to offer the firstfruits of harvest in the Jerusalem temple (Exod. 22:29; 23:19; Lev. 23:10-12), their food would be considered "unclean" (Hos. 9:3). The reference to "Egypt" as a gathering place (9:6) may have alluded to the migration of the Judeans after the assassination of Gedaliah (2 Kings 25:26). "Memphis," situated on the Nile just south of Cairo, was regarded as an important burial center.

The "corruption" (9:9) of Gibeah was an allusion to the atrocity recorded in Judges 19:22-30. Israel's past apostasy was illustrated from the incident at Baal Peor (Hos. 9:10-14; cf. Num. 25). Israel's present apostasy was illustrated by what was going on at Gilgal, an important site in Israel's history (cf. 1 Sam. 11:15) that had become a center for idolatrous worship (Hos. 4:15; 12:11).

10:1-15 Sinful independence from God as King. "We have no king" (10:3) meant that there was no king worthy of the title. "Beth Aven" (10:5) referred to Bethel (see the note on 4:15). The Hebrew for "wickedness" (10:8) is possibly better rendered as a place name "Aven" (NASB), a shortened form for Beth Aven. The words of the last part of 10:8 appear in Revelation 6:16. From the days of the abuse of the Levite's concubine at Gibeah (Hos. 10:9; cf. Judg. 19:22-30), Israel had had a history of sin and immorality. Hosea issued a last-minute call to repentance (Hos. 10:12). "Shalman" (10:14) was probably a reference to Shalmaneser V (cf. 2 Kings 17:3). "Beth Arbel" (Hos. 10:14) was a town located east of the Jordan River in Gilead.

11:1-11 THE TRIUMPH OF LOYAL LOVE:
THE SON ISRAEL
Israel's waywardness and God's unceasing love for the nation were emphasized (11:1). The deliverance of Israel from Egypt was likened to God's care for a son. The calling "out of Egypt" (11:1) was a reference to Israel's exodus. This text was used by Matthew (Matt. 2:15) with reference to

Jesus' return to Israel after being taken to Egypt by Joseph and Mary. On the basis of the solidarity of the Jewish people, what was vital in the nation's corporate experience found its ultimate fulfillment in the Messiah, Jesus.

The more "I" (Hos. 11:2; that is, God through the prophets) called "Israel" (the people), the more persistent was their idolatry. "Admah" and "Zeboiim" (11:8) were towns destroyed with Sodom and Gomorrah (cf. Deut. 29:23). Hosea looked to a day of restoration when the "lion" (Hos. 11:10; cf. Rev. 5:5) would roar and his dispersed people would return from the east and west to resettle in Israel (cf. Matt. 24:31; Deut. 30:1-10).

11:12–13:16 NO TRUTH: THE SON'S HISTORY IS RECALLED
11:12–12:14 Return to the God of the exodus. Israel played one nation against another, to her own destruction (Hos. 12:1). "Jacob" (12:2) was used here with reference to his descendants, the tribes of Israel. For these incidents in the life of Jacob (12:3-4), see Genesis 25:26 and 32:24-28. Hosea reflected on the past deliverance of Jacob from Esau when he fled to Aram (12:12; cf. Gen. 29) and Israel's deliverance from Egypt by "a prophet," that is, Moses (cf. Exod. 1–14). Failing to respond to God's grace, "Ephraim" (Israel) would have to bear the consequences of sin ("guilt," Hos. 12:14).

13:1-16 Destruction and restoration. Because Israel had forgotten God their Savior (13:6), the Lord would be to them like a devouring beast (13:7-8). "Kiss the calf-idols" (13:2) referred to Israel's worship of the golden calves. The allusion (13:10) was to the Israelites' earlier demand for a king so that they might be like other nations and protected from their enemies (1 Sam. 8:20). Israel unwisely delayed responding to "pains as of a woman in childbirth" (Hos. 13:13), a reference to God's discipline.

In spite of Israel's disobedience, God made a gracious promise (13:14). Paul quoted part of this verse in 1 Corinthians 15:55. The Assyrians were noted for terrible atrocities (Hos. 13:16). For example, Ashurnasirpal (883–859 B.C.) boasted of burning men and maidens alive, cutting off the hands and feet of his captives, and putting out their eyes.

14:1-9 GOD'S APPEAL OF LOYAL LOVE
The prophet issued a final call to repentance and promised pardon and gracious restoration (14:1-2). The people promised that they would no longer turn to Assyria (14:3; cf. 2 Kings 16:7-9), Egyptian war-horses (Hos. 14:3; cf. 1 Kings 10:28), or idols (cf. Jer. 10:1-10) for help. God's promise of pardon and blessing (Hos. 14:5-7) will be realized in the Messianic kingdom. Believing Israel will enjoy such blessing then that those associated with them will also greatly benefit (cf. Gen. 12:3). God looked with favor upon Ephraim's renunciation of idolatry (Hos. 14:8). God's final words were an exhortation to see the heart of true wisdom and the justice of God (14:9).

Joel

BASIC FACTS

HISTORICAL SETTING
The exact historical setting for Joel's prophecy is not known. One possibility is that
he prophesied to the southern kingdom of Judah while Joash served as king. Joash
began his reign (835–796 B.C.) when he was a boy, after having been hidden in the
temple by Jehosheba to protect him from the murder of the royal offspring instigated
by Athaliah as she usurped the throne (cf. 2 Kings 11:1-3). Joash was crowned king
at the age of seven by his high priest and advisor, Jehoiada (cf. 2 Kings 11:21–12:2).
A devastating locust swarm invaded Judah sometime early in the reign of the young
king. That great catastrophe sounded the alarm for a call to repentance in view of a
greater judgment to come, the day of the Lord. If Joel prophesied during the reign of
Joash, the ministry of the prophet Elisha was going on at the same time in Israel to
the north.

AUTHOR
The author of the book was Joel, the son of Pethuel. Nothing is known about the
author's circumstances in life except that he lived and prophesied in Judah and
Jerusalem (Joel 1:9; 2:15-17, 23, 32; 3:1).

DATE
Scholars suggest possible dates for Joel's ministry ranging from the reign of Joash
(835–796 B.C.) to after the Babylonian captivity sometime in the sixth century B.C.
Joel, whose name means "Yahweh is God," lived and prophesied in Judah and
Jerusalem (1:9; 2:15-17, 23, 32; 3:1). The book does not mention any reigning king
or otherwise datable event. It appears that Amos borrowed from Joel (cf. Joel 3:16
with Amos 1:2; Joel 3:18 with Amos 9:13). This would put Joel before 760 B.C. Also,
the position of the book between Hosea and Amos in the Hebrew canon suggests a
preexilic date.

PURPOSE
The book of Joel was designed to call the nation to repentance on the basis of the calamity of the locust plague, a token of the more devastating judgment of the coming day of the Lord. The prophecy was also intended to comfort the nation with promises of future salvation and prosperity in the day of the Lord, a day of deliverance for Israel and destruction for her foes.

GUIDING CONCEPTS

JUDGMENT AND BLESSING
This book was to be told and retold throughout generations (Joel 1:3) in order to keep its message before the people of God. In view were two locust plagues: one in Israel's past, the other in the future. The locust attack had destroyed the crops of the land and linked back to the promised punishment for disobeying God (1 Kings 8:37-40). The future plague was equated with the day of the Lord and pictured the army of God coming to destroy his foes (Joel 2:1). The link between the past and future plagues was that both were gracious calls from God for human repentance (2:32).

Some Israelites only saw the redemptive aspect of the day of the Lord, when God would come to save his people. But they missed its other aspect in which the people of God would experience judgment (cf. Amos 5:18-20). They cheered judgment on their enemies but denied judgment would ever be leveled against themselves.

But even in discipline God would be faithful to preserve the nation (2:32; 3:1, 16). He would also judge the nations for their past acts of injustice toward Israel (3:2). Joel asked his readers to think about the future in light of the past. The future would only escalate and perfect the partial judgment seen in the past attack of locusts. Therefore, the readers were to call upon God so that they would be spared from his wrath.

BIBLE-WIDE CONCEPTS

LOCUSTS AS CURSES FOR COVENANT DISOBEDIENCE
God chose Jerusalem to be the earthly location of his presence (3:16, 21). His people were to keep the laws of the Mosaic covenant and enjoy the blessing of his presence. If they obeyed, God promised his care and provision. If they disobeyed, they could expect his curses. When Solomon dedicated the temple, he mentioned locusts as an example of one such curse (cf. 1 Kings 8:37). Before that, the Mosaic covenant had also spoken of locusts as a curse on covenant disobedience (cf. Deut. 28:38). The locust curse was one of many signs and wonders from God (Joel 2:30; cf. Deut. 28:46).

THE DAY OF THE LORD
The day of the Lord was first a time of judgment for Israel, and then for the nations. It was a time when God would rule. It would be a terrible day, and Joel asked who could endure it (Joel 2:11). His answer is found in 2:12, 32. The function of the locusts and other signs and wonders was to cause the people to repent. They were acts of a gracious God reaching out to his people.

Joel spoke of a time when the Spirit would be poured out on all humanity for prophecy (2:28), and great cosmic signs and wonders would come about (2:30-31). The prophecies and signs were intended to motivate people to call on the Lord's name (2:32). Peter, in Acts 2, showed how today's believers are participating in that time of the Spirit, even though they still await the completion of all the listed signs and wonders. Paul also used Joel 2:32 to confirm how God saves those who call upon him (cf. Rom. 10:12-14).

NEEDS MET BY JOEL

Joel's audience needed to be reminded of several things. First, they needed to learn that for God's chosen people, painful judgment was yet one more gracious call of God for repentance and restoration. Second, they needed to be reminded of their sin, which had become a way of life. As a first step toward that end, they needed to picture their disobedience not in the context of their limited setting in time but within the grand panorama of God's past and future judgments on sin. In that context they were to ask themselves if their sins were worth their shunning God's love and risking his judgment.

Getting this broad past and future perspective did not come easily. Israel needed to be reminded that the past locust plague, devastating though it was, was only a small taste of the greater future judgment of God. Past judgments were previews of even greater future judgment. It was too easy for the people simply to think that when the locust plague was past, there was no more judgment to worry about. They forgot that God's judgments are not like the days on a calendar to be torn off and forgotten. God's past judgment defines his future judgment, and both are brought into the present by the prophet to show God's never-changing attitude toward sin.

The issue was not, Is judgment here right now? The issue was, Is God here and what is his attitude toward sin? The people who wanted a relationship with God would repent in response to this last question. The one who would rather sin and gamble with God's judgment would not repent. The structure and content of Joel show that the Israelites were asking questions like the following.

- The locust plague was bad enough; what will the day of the Lord be like?
- If Israel must participate in the day of the Lord, how can they know that they will survive it?
- Why is it necessary to suffer under all this judgment before God can come to dwell with his people forever?

Like Israel in Joel's day, believers today also need a broad perspective to show them that the past judgment of God against sin was evidenced in the cross and that future judgment will come at the end of the age. Until then, believers are to live in full remembrance of God's hatred toward sin, which cost his Son great suffering and will cost unbelievers an eternity of anguish. How much does God hate sin and want people to return to him? Enough to take the life of his dear Son, to bring judgment upon the world at the end of the age, and to proclaim eternal rewards for the faithful or suffering for the faithless. The judgments on the cross and in eternity are not to be seen only as far in the past and far into the future without present implications. They are to be seen as God's present call to people to repent and live with him in holy fellowship. The book of Joel teaches its readers to be mindful of both the past and future judgments now, and encourages them to fill the present with God's presence and live to please him.

OUTLINE OF JOEL

A. SUMMONS TO HEAR AND TRANSMIT (1:1-3)

B. LOCUSTS AS GOD'S JUDGMENT AND CALL TO REPENTANCE (1:4–2:17)
    1. The Certainty of Destruction (1:4)
    2. Commands for Mourning (1:5-20)
    3. The Day of the Lord: Who Can Endure It? (2:1-11)
    4. Command to Repent (2:12-17)

C. FUTURE REMOVAL OF THE SAINTS' REPROACH (2:18-27)
    1. Removal of the Northerners (2:18-20)
    2. Restoration of the Locust Years (2:21-27)

D. FUTURE RESTORATION OF ISRAEL (2:28–3:21)
    1. The Spirit Poured Out (2:28-29)
    2. Wonders Displayed (2:30-31)
    3. Survivors Called (2:32–3:21)

JOEL NOTES

1:1-3 SUMMONS TO HEAR AND TRANSMIT

In Joel 1 the prophet described the devastating effect of the locust plague on the country of Judah. Here Joel reminded the people of the serious nature of the unprecedented calamity and made it the basis for an appeal for national mourning and repentance. The name "Joel" means "Yahweh is God." The rhetorical question (1:2-3) suggests a negative answer.

1:4–2:17 LOCUSTS AS GOD'S JUDGMENT AND CALL TO REPENTANCE

1:4 The Certainty of Destruction

Joel described dramatically and poetically how swarm after swarm of locusts had diminished the potential harvest to nothing. The four different terms used for locusts were probably poetic synonyms rather than four distinct kinds of locusts or stages of locust development. Locust plagues were one of the curses of the covenant for disobedience (cf. Deut. 28:38, 42).

1:5-20 Commands for Mourning

1:5-7 WINE DRINKERS: LOCUSTS

The "nation" (Joel 1:6) referred to the locusts. With serrated jaws rasping from side to side, adult locusts consume daily their body weight in food. It is estimated that a single swarm can eat in one day what forty thousand people eat in one year. They are able to live four days without feeding, surviving on stored fat. Locust swarms have been known to blanket two thousand square miles, stripping vegetation, fouling the air with their excrement, and triggering epidemics as they die and rot. Branches (1:7) stripped of bark by the rasping teeth of the locusts were left splintered and ghostly white. The "grain offerings and drink offerings" (1:9; "The grain offering and the libation," NASB) could not be offered because the locusts had destroyed the crops.

1:8-12 SONS OF MEN: DROUGHT

The nation, priests, and people were called to mourn the desolation of the land. The nation was likened to a young woman who was widowed on her wedding day. The Judeans had anticipated the joy of harvest (cf. Isa. 9:3; Ps. 4:7), but now because of the disaster, "the joy . . . is withered away" (Joel 1:12; "rejoicing dries up," NASB).

1:13-20 NATIONAL ASSEMBLY
AT THE HOUSE OF GOD
Joel reminded the leaders that repentance was the prerequisite to restoration of God's provision (1:13-14; cf. Deut. 30:1-5; 2 Chron. 7:14) and called the nation to repentance. The "day of the Lord" (Joel 1:15) referred to a time of judgment and deliverance either in the past or in the future. Joel viewed the locust plague as a historical day of judgment that served as a premonition of an even greater future day of the Lord. Apparently drought followed the locust plague and contributed to the desolation of the land (1:17). Even the animals suffered from the drought and "pant" (1:20) for a renewal of God's provision (cf. Rom. 8:22).

2:1-11 The Day of the Lord: Who Can Endure It?
Joel returned to the words of 1:15, "the day of the Lord." Here he used the illustration of the locust plague to turn the minds of the Judeans to a far worse judgment yet ahead. The "trumpet" (2:1, lit., "shophar"), or ram's horn, was used in ancient times to signal a military alarm (cf. Jer. 6:17; Amos 3:6). The darkness caused by the locust swarms was used as imagery for the judgment of the day of the Lord (Joel 2:2). Darkness in Scripture is often a figure for misery, distress, and judgment (cf. Isa. 8:22; 60:2; Jer. 13:16). The "forces" that invaded Judah were clearly the locusts (cf. Joel 2:11). They were mentioned as a warning of even greater future judgment. Joel described the locusts and their destruction of the land in vivid, poetic terms (2:3-11). Hyperbole (that is, exaggeration for emphasis) was used to elicit images of greater judgment in the minds of the people (2:10).

2:12-17 Command to Repent
Having warned of the nearness of the approaching day of the Lord (2:1), Joel called the nation to repentance. The character of God, revealed to Moses in Exodus 34:6, was repeated here (Joel 2:13) as a basis for an appeal for repentance. According to the Jewish Mishnah, newlyweds were excused

from reciting daily prayers on their wedding day, but not in such a time of spiritual emergency (2:16).

2:18-27 FUTURE REMOVAL OF THE SAINTS' REPROACH
2:18-20 Removal of the Northerners
Joel 2:18 is also translated, "Then the Lord was zealous . . . and had pity. . . ." In response to the people's repentance, God promised restoration (2:19). The "never again" (2:19) may have been a promise of deliverance from another wave of locusts, or perhaps it looked forward to a time when Israel would enjoy the blessings of God's future kingdom. The "northern army" (2:20) probably referred to the army of locusts that served as the illustration of judgment in 2:1-11. The "eastern sea" (2:20) referred to the Dead Sea. The "western sea" (2:20) referred to the Mediterranean.

2:21-27 Restoration of the Locust Years
The "autumn" and "spring" rains (2:23) fall in the early autumn and early spring, respectively. The autumn rains serve to soften the soil for planting winter wheat. The spring rains cause the ripe grain to swell and ensure a good harvest.

2:28–3:21 FUTURE RESTORATION OF ISRAEL
2:28-29 The Spirit Poured Out
Joel described spiritual blessings that God promised to bestow on his people at a future time (2:28-29). The passage was quoted by Peter in Acts 2:17-21 on the day of Pentecost to explain the outpouring of the Holy Spirit. The "afterward" (Joel 2:28) indicated that the spiritual blessings of 2:28-32 would follow sometime after the physical blessings of 2:21-27. The expression "pour out" (2:28) is a metaphor for abundance (cf. Prov. 1:23) and was mentioned twice for emphasis. The ministries of the Spirit promised here were fulfilled at Pentecost (cf. Acts 11:28; 21:9; 2 Cor. 12:1-4; Rev. 1:1-3).

2:30-31 Wonders Displayed
The heavenly signs promised (Joel 2:30) will take place before the "great and dreadful" day of the Lord (2:31), apparently the period of the most severe judgment (cf. Rev. 16). The kinds of judgments mentioned here also

appear in the context of end-time judgment (cf. Rev. 6:12; 8:7-8, 12; 9:18).

2:32–3:21 Survivors Called

2:32 THE PROMISE OF DELIVERANCE
Joel promised that those who repented ("everyone who calls on the name of the LORD") would be delivered. Zechariah 14:1-5 describes this end-time situation as involving a remnant of Jews who repent and believe in the Messiah at his second coming.

3:1-16 THE PLACE OF DELIVERANCE
Just as the Lord had brought judgment on Judah through the locust plague, he promised judgment on the foreign nations for their mistreatment of Judah (Joel 3:2). The time of this judgment is the second coming of Christ (cf. Zech. 14:1-3; Matt. 25:31-46) and God's restoration of Israel will take place at the same time (cf. Matt. 24:31). "Jehoshaphat" (Joel 3:2) literally means "Yahweh judges" and the location of the valley of that name has not been identified with certainty. The basis of God's judgment was the Gentile nations' treatment of the Israelite people (3:2-8). From his experience with Gentile oppression in his own day, Joel listed the kinds of things that the Gentiles will be accountable for—crimes against the land (3:2), the people (3:3, 6), and the temple (3:5).

Some scholars have argued that the mention of the "Greeks" (3:6) supports a postexilic date for Joel. However, Greek people were known to be in Assyria by the time of Sargon II (722–705 B.C.). They also were known to be in Egypt before 1300 B.C.

With a touch of sarcasm, God called the nations to prepare for the judgment that is to take place at the Messiah's second advent (3:9-12; cf. Rev. 19:11-15). The nations' weapons will be insufficient to stand against God (Joel 3:10); thus, their "plowshares" should be fashioned into "swords," and their "pruning hooks" into "spears" (3:10). This exhortation is later reversed in Isaiah 2:4 and Micah 4:3. The "warriors" referred to angels (Joel 3:11; cf. Mark 8:38; Rev. 19:14).

The "valley of decision" (Joel 3:14) was another name for the "Valley of Jehoshaphat" (3:2). The nations will not be making their decision, but God will be making his, which will be a verdict of "guilty."

3:17-21 THE RESULTS OF DELIVERANCE
After the judgment on the nations, Judah will enjoy the fulfillment of God's promises to them. Joel concluded the prophecy with a description of the conditions that will exist in the Messianic age. An abundance of "wine" (3:18) is representative of the joy that will overflow during the Messianic age. Jesus was giving an insight into his person and work when he produced an abundance of wine at the wedding at Cana (John 2:1-11). The "valley of acacias" (Joel 3:18), literally, "Valley of Shittim," was the location of the last Israelite encampment before they entered Canaan (cf. Num. 25:1; Josh. 3:1). "Egypt" and "Edom" (Joel 3:19) were representative of the Gentile nations that have been judged by the Lord. They were set in contrast with Judah, which will be blessed by the presence of the Lord (3:21).

Amos

HISTORICAL SETTING

Amos prophesied at a time when the southern kingdom of Judah under Uzziah and the northern kingdom of Israel under Jeroboam II were at the height of their prosperity. The northern kingdom's expansion caused it to become the largest and most influential country along the eastern Mediterranean seacoast. Uzziah had expanded the southern kingdom west to the Philistine territory (cf. 2 Chron. 26:6), south into the Negev (cf. 2 Chron. 26:10), and into the territory of the Arabians and Meunites (cf. 2 Chron. 26:7). During this period the relationship between Judah and Israel was peaceful, and both kingdoms enjoyed peace and prosperity that had not been equaled since the reign of Solomon. Assyria was no present threat to Israel, but Amos as well as Isaiah saw that that nation would be the instrument of God's impending judgment on his rebellious people (Amos 5:27; 7:11, 16-17; cf. Isa. 10:5).

AUTHOR

The prophet Amos, whose name means "burden," lived in Tekoa (Amos 1:1), a village five miles southeast of Bethlehem in the hill country of Judah. His occupation was that of a shepherd (1:1) and gardener (taking care of sycamore fig trees) (7:14). Thus he lived in the southern kingdom of Judah but prophesied in the northern kingdom of Israel.

DATE

The prophecy can be dated by the reference in 1:1 to kings Uzziah (791–739 B.C.) and Jeroboam II (793–753 B.C.). A probable date of composition would be around 760 B.C.

PURPOSE

The book of Amos was designed to pronounce judgment against the northern kingdom's social injustices, moral degeneracy, and spiritual apostasy. Amos intended to show the nation's accountability to comply with the covenant's obligations, both in letter and spirit. The prophet insisted that the external practice of religious rituals, divorced from right ethical conduct in society, was unacceptable to God.

GUIDING CONCEPTS

REPEATED PHRASES

An earthquake figured largely in the book (cf. 1:1; 8:8; 9:1, 5). The phrase "This is what the Lord says" ("Thus says the Lord"; NASB) signals the start of each new section (1:3, 6, 9, 11, 13; 2:1, 4, 6) in Amos 1–2. Also note the "for, because, so" pattern (1:3-4, etc.). There are three short hymns in 4:13; 5:8-9; and 9:5-6. There is a threefold repetition of "Hear this word" (3:1; 4:1; 5:1).

The repeated phrase "yet you have not returned to me" shows the intended result of God's discipline (4:6, 8-11). Any pain God caused was designed to bring the people back to himself. There is a cause and effect relationship repeated throughout Amos 5–6 by the use of "therefore" (5:13, 16, 27; 6:7). Evidently God's people would only admit to the "light" aspect of the day of the Lord, that is, his redemption (5:18). However, they needed to understand the corrective aspects of the day of the Lord: judgment first for all, and only then redemption for those who repent.

BIBLE-WIDE CONCEPTS

In 9:8-15, reference was made to the restoration of the fallen tent of David and the blessings to come for all the Gentiles. The goal of reaching the Gentiles explains the list of offending nations at the beginning of the book. They were listed not only as recipients of God's judgment but also because, like Israel, their faithful remnants would receive God's salvation. The Davidic hope of Israel was also the hope of the nations. The implications of this truth were not fully realized until after Christ's resurrection. The apostles and early Christians struggled with how the Gentiles fit into God's plan of salvation (cf. Acts 15).

The original Christian community, primarily composed of Jews, had to accept that the line of David, always so centrally a Jewish hope, was in reality a blessing and hope for the entire world. To substantiate that fact, James quoted Amos 9:8-15 in the Jerusalem council (Acts 15:16-18) that debated whether Gentiles had to follow the rituals of the Mosaic Law, or if they could be saved on the basis of faith in the Messiah (Jesus) alone. Like the promises to Abraham (Gen. 12:1-3), the promises of God to David begin with Israel but inevitably extend to all races because these promises are based on faithfulness to God. In fact, at times God had to bypass blessing the vast majority of the Jewish nation.

At the beginning of the Christian witness in Jerusalem, Stephen quoted Amos 5:25-27 when referring to the Jews' own long history of rebelling against God, who graciously came to dwell with them in the tabernacle. Israel constantly rejected God's prophets. Throughout Scripture God's people, whether under Moses or Christ, could never get away with replacing obedience with claims of religious status based on race, history, or land. See also Acts 7:42-43 regarding Amos 5:25-27.

NEEDS MET BY AMOS

Amos's audience had two problems needing correction: arrogance and despair.
First, some of Amos's hearers were arrogant because they thought their religious
heritage exempted them from God's judgment. Because they were Jewish, lived
in the holy land, and had the temple, they concluded that God would indeed
judge the world but certainly never punish them. In their view, the day of the
Lord was light for them and darkness for the world. They were condemning sin
in unbelievers but were blind to their own gross offenses against God.

Second, others of Amos's hearers were in despair. They felt that Jewish disobedience had completely wrecked any hope for the fulfillment of God's promises
to Abraham and David. If the arrogant were blind to God's comprehensive judgment, the despairing group was blind to God's unbreakable loyalty. His loyalty
to his promises could never be broken by human disloyalty. Thus, the book of
Amos met basic needs for two quite different groups of people: those who thought
their sins would not be judged by God, and those who thought their failures had
destroyed all hope for the fulfillment of God's promises. The content and structure
of Amos show that the Israelites were struggling with questions like these.

- Are the people of Israel somehow exempt from God's judgment because they
  are God's people?
- Will the day of the Lord be a day of judgment for everyone except God's people?
- Have all of Israel's failures voided God's promises to Abraham and David?

Arrogance and despair are also found within the Christian community. Christians
may think that because they are in Christ, they are immune to God's disciplining
judgment. Or they may think that their failures have cut them off from God's love.
Amos asserts that neither one of these positions is true because neither one is true to
God's character. He remains holy, and his forgiveness of sins in Christ does not do
away with his absolute demand that believers live holy lives. But at the same time
God remains loyal to his people, and acts of disobedience can never void his promises
in Christ. Amos meets the needs of believers, for rebuke when they snobbishly presume on God's grace, and for encouragement when they foolishly forget God's loyalty.

OUTLINE OF AMOS

A. INTRODUCTION: AUTHOR, DATE, ADDRESSES (1:1-2)
B. INTERNATIONAL CONDEMNATION: VIOLATION OF BROTHERHOOD
   (1:3–2:16)
   1. The Nations Surrounding Israel Condemned (1:3–2:3)
   2. Israel Condemned (2:4-16)
C. THE ULTIMATE SOURCE OF CONDEMNATION: GOD'S CHARACTER
   (3:1–6:14)
   1. Certainty of Destruction (3:1-15)
   2. Correction Disregarded (4:1-13)
   3. The Dirge Resulting from Sinful Violations (5:1–6:14)

AMOS NOTES

1:1-2 INTRODUCTION: AUTHOR, DATE, ADDRESSES

Tekoa was located in Judah about twelve miles south of Jerusalem. Amos prophesied around 760 B.C. in the days of Uzziah (791–739 B.C.) and Jeroboam II (793–753 B.C.). The earthquake, referred to two centuries later by Zechariah (Zech. 14:4-5), is said by Josephus to have occurred in connection with Uzziah's sin (cf. 2 Chron. 26:16). Zion is a synonym for Jerusalem. Carmel, the mountain range separating Samaria from the Jezreel Valley, was noted for luxuriant vegetation (Song of Sol. 7:5; Isa. 35:2). If Carmel "withers" under God's judgment, how great will be the desolation elsewhere where conditions are normally less favorable?

1:3–2:16 INTERNATIONAL CONDEMNATION: VIOLATION OF BROTHERHOOD

Overview: Although the book of Amos is full of flashes of God's judgment, it, like all the books of the prophets, was also a call to repentance (Amos 5:4). Amos 1–2 records the prophecies against the foreign nations. Since the other nations were to be punished for breaches of the law of social justice (1:3, 6, 11; cf. Rom. 2:14), so Israel could not escape. As the list of foreign nations about to be punished grew, so would the glee of the Israelite readers. But Amos went on to expose Israel's mistake, that is, their conception that the day of the Lord would not touch them. Amos told the readers that the coming day of the Lord would not be a day of light but one of darkness, both for the Gentile nations and for the people of God (Amos 5:18). The list moved directly from the nations to Judah (2:4) and Israel (2:6).

1:3–2:3 The Nations Surrounding Israel Condemned

1:3-10 DAMASCUS, GAZA, AND TYRE
The numeric sequence "for three . . . even for four" (1:3) indicated that the list, though specific, was not exhaustive. The threshing of "Gilead" (1:3) in Transjordan involved driving heavy threshing sledges with iron spikes over their fallen enemies. "Hazael" (1:4; cf. 2 Kings 8:7-15) ruled Aram at the time of Amos. "Ben-Hadad" (2 Kings 13:3, 25) was his son and successor.

The prophecy was fulfilled when Tiglath Pileser III captured Damascus in 732 B.C. and exiled its inhabitants (Amos 1:5; cf. 2 Kings 16:9). The "Valley of Aven" (Amos 1:5) referred to the Beka Valley in Lebanon. Kir was a province of Mesopotamia from which the Arameans came (cf. 9:7). Gaza (1:6) was one of the major Philistine cities on the southern coastal plain of Judah (cf. 1 Sam. 6:17). It fell to Tiglath Pileser III of Assyria in 734 B.C. Ashdod, Ashkelon, and Ekron (Amos 1:8) were major cities of Philistia (cf. 1 Sam. 6:17). Tyre (Amos 1:9) was a great trade center and port in Phoenicia. The merchants of Tyre were guilty of Israelite slave trade with Edom. The "treaty of brotherhood" (1:9) was between Hiram, king of Tyre, and David and Solomon (cf. 1 Kings 5:1-12). Tyre was besieged by Nebuchadnezzar (Amos 1:10) for thirteen years (585–573 B.C.) and was eventually destroyed by Alexander the Great in 332 B.C.

1:11–2:3 EDOM, AMMON, AND MOAB
Enmity between Edom and Israel can be traced back to the strife between Esau and Jacob, from whom the two nations descended (1:11). Teman (1:12) was a district of Edom, and Bozrah was the chief city. Judgment fell on Edom when the Hasmonean priest John Hyrcanus (135–104 B.C.)

conquered the region around 120 B.C., compelling all its inhabitants to adopt Judaism.

The Ammonites descended from Lot's incestuous relationship with his youngest daughter (1:13; cf. Gen. 19:36-38). They occupied Transjordan territory north of Moab. The atrocities mentioned here were perpetuated for the purpose of territorial expansion (cf. 2 Kings 8:12). Rabbah (Amos 1:14), later known as Philadelphia, was the capital of Ammon. The Ammonites were subjugated by Tiglath Pileser III (745–727 B.C.) and by Sennacherib (705–681 B.C.).

The Moabites descended from Lot's incestuous relationship with his eldest daughter (2:1; cf. Gen. 19:36-37). They occupied the land east of the Dead Sea, south of Ammon. Kerioth (Amos 2:2) was one of Moab's prominent cities (cf. Jer. 48:24). Judgment fell on Moab when Nebuchadnezzar completely subjugated the region (cf. Jer. 48:46-47; Josephus, *Antiquities* 10.9.7).

2:4-16 Israel Condemned

While the other nations were punished for sins against the laws of nature and conscience, Judah was judged for sinning against the revealed will ("the law") of God (Amos 2:4). Land-hungry creditors begrudged the poor even the "dust" that they cast on their heads as mourners (2:7). The statement "Father and son use the same girl" (2:7) referred to father and son having sexual relations with the same temple prostitute. Garments taken as security for loans were to be returned before sunset, not kept overnight (2:8; cf. Exod. 22:26-27). The "Amorite" (Amos 2:9) was a name often used to designate the people of Canaan generally (cf. Deut. 1:20). They forced the Nazirites to drink wine in violation of their vow (Amos 2:12; cf. Num. 6:1-21).

3:1–6:14 THE ULTIMATE SOURCE OF CONDEMNATION: GOD'S CHARACTER

Overview: Each of Amos's three sermons began with the call "Hear this word" (3:1; 4:1; 5:1). Amos 4 recounted how all the judgments that God had sent to Israel had not caused them to repent (4:6, 8-11) and ended with a "therefore" of final judgment (4:12). God desired to give them life (5:4, 14-15),

but their sins would eventually carry them into exile (5:27). Amos 6 brought criticism on Israel's arrogance and lack of grief (6:6) over their spiritual ruin.

3:1-15 Certainty of Destruction

Because God had taken the Israelites into a special relationship with himself, he would hold them accountable for the unique privilege of having him as their loving and disciplining Father (3:1-2). Amos made an appeal to the law of cause and effect to prove that no calamity came upon Jerusalem except by God's sovereign determination (3:6). Ashdod and Egypt (3:9) were representative of heathen nations that had witnessed Israel's iniquity, and they would witness against Israel before God.

The judgment on the northern kingdom (3:11-15) was fulfilled in 722 B.C. after a three-year siege and capture of Samaria by the Assyrians (cf. 2 Kings 17:1-6). Bethel (Amos 3:14), an idolatrous worship center, would be desecrated (1 Kings 12:32). The "horns of the altar" were a place of refuge (Amos 3:14; cf. Exod. 21:14; 1 Kings 1:50), but even this refuge would be denied Israel in her day of judgment. The "houses adorned with ivory" (Amos 3:15; "houses of ivory," NASB) referred to houses with ivory inlays in wooden panels and revealed the vast wealth and waste in Israel. Many of these ivory inlays have been found in the excavation of Samaria.

4:1-13 Correction Disregarded

Amos began his second sermon by addressing the women of Samaria who were likened to the well-fed cows of "Bashan," a territory noted for its luxuriant pastures and fat cattle (cf. Deut. 32:14). Assyrian reliefs sometimes depict captives being pulled along with a rope fastened to a ring in the lip (cf. 2 Chron. 33:11). With biting sarcasm, Amos rebuked the false worship of the Israelites (Amos 4:4-5). Bethel and Gilgal (4:4) were singled out because they had once been such sacred places (cf. Gen. 35:1-16; Josh. 5:1-9) but had been perverted. God brought disciplinary judgment (the curses of the Mosaic covenant) on the people, but they were unresponsive to his chastening (Amos 4:6-11). The phrase "yet you have not returned to me" (4:6; etc.) was repeated five times.

5:1–6:14 The Dirge Resulting from Sinful Violations

5:1-27 A CALL TO SEEK THE LORD
Amos's closing sermon called the nation to repentance and restated the outcome of the nation's moral and religious apostasy. The emphasis was a call to seek the Lord (5:4, 6, 14). The past tense ("Fallen," 5:2) indicates that the fall of Israel was so certain that it could be viewed as already having taken place. In 5:4-17 Amos called the people to repentance with the words "seek God and live" (5:4, 6, 14). "Bitterness" (5:7; "wormwood," NASB and KJV) is a reference to a bitter, poisonous herb (cf. Deut. 29:18; Jer. 9:15). Those who were responsible to administer justice produced bitter injustice. "Pleiades and Orion" (Amos 5:8) were constellations (cf. Job 9:9; 38:31). Speaking out against injustice may not have been in his best interests, but Amos considered it necessary (Amos 5:13). The "remnant of Joseph" (5:15) referred to the faithful of Israel with whom the Old Testament prophecies would be fulfilled (cf. Isa. 6:13; 11:11; Mic. 2:12; 4:7).

In Amos 5:18-20 the prophet noted that some people were looking forward to the coming day of the Lord, believing that God would deliver and vindicate Israel. Amos corrected that view, showing that the judgment of the day of the Lord was inescapable. Although the Israelites worshiped God during their forty years in the wilderness, they also served idols (5:26). "Shrine" is a translation of "Sikkuth" (see NASB and NIV footnote), the Assyrian god of war. "Pedestal" is a translation of "Kiyyun," also spelled "kaiwan" (see NASB and NIV footnote), and may have been the Babylonian name of this same war deity. The prophecy of 5:27 was fulfilled in 722 B.C. (cf. 2 Kings 17:1-6).

6:1-14 THE WOE OF ISRAEL'S SINS
The great cities of Mesopotamia, Calneh, and Hamath (Amos 6:2) declined, lost their independence, and were annexed to Assyria. Certainly Israel could not expect to escape judgment. In 6:8-11 Amos predicted the siege and destruction of Samaria ("the city," 6:8). In the midst of such divine judgment, the name of God was not to be used, for to call upon him after such apostasy would be sheer hypocrisy and would invite further

judgment. Israel's perversion of justice was contrary to the natural order of things (6:12)—like expecting horses to run on rocks or oxen to plow on rocks.

Lo Debar and Karnaim (6:13) were cities in Transjordan (cf. Gen. 14:5; 2 Sam. 9:4) which Jeroboam II may have captured when he restored the boundaries of Israel (cf. 2 Kings 14:25). Hamath (Amos 6:14) was located in the extreme north of Israel, and the Arabah is located in the south. The enemy would overrun the whole land.

7:1–8:3 THE END OF OPPORTUNITY: VISIONS OF FINAL JUDGMENT

Overview: God showed that he could graciously avert further disaster on the land (7:3, 6). But his offer of grace met with no repentance, so the last three visions revealed certain destruction. Amos 8–9 presented a discussion of God's rights as Creator to judge Israel (cf. especially 8:7-9; 9:5-6). The formula "This is what the Sovereign LORD showed me" ("Thus the Lord GOD showed me," NASB) introduced the first four of the five visions (7:1, 4, 7; 8:1).

7:1-6 Times of Opportunity

The first judgment envisioned was a locust plague (7:1; cf. Deut. 28:38). The words "the LORD relented" (Amos 7:3; "changed His mind," NASB) referred to God changing his method of dealing with sinful creatures. While his attitude toward sin remained the same (7:4; cf. 1 Sam. 15:29; James 1:17), he could change his method of dealing with it, showing mercy in response to his people's repentance. The second vision (Amos 7:4-6) was of a consuming fire about to destroy both the land and the sea ("the great deep," 7:4).

7:7–8:3 The End of Opportunity

The third vision was of a plumb line (7:7-9), an instrument designed to measure whether or not a wall was vertical. Just as a tilted wall would have to be removed, so the nation of Israel would have to be judged. The judgment on Jeroboam II's dynasty was fulfilled with his son Zechariah's assassination by Shallum (2 Kings 15:8-10).

Amaziah (Amos 7:10-17), the priest of the apostate worship center at Bethel, accused Amos of being a conspirator against Jeroboam II and ordered him to return to Judah (7:12). The expression "earn your bread" (7:12) means "earn your living." Amos was a farmer until God called him to a prophetic ministry (7:14). A small incision in the "sycamore figs" was necessary to make them ripen properly. The fourth vision (8:1-3) was of a basket of summer fruit. As the gathering of summer fruit marked the end of the harvest, so Israel had come to the end of her national existence.

8:4–9:15 WHEN GOD SWEARS NOT TO FORGET
8:4–9:8 Destruction Detailed

The section of 8:4–9:8 stressed God's sovereignty as the Creator. He has intimate knowledge and power to judge and to restore. The people of Israel were glad when the Sabbaths and religious festivals concluded so that they could get on with their crooked business practices. The practice of swearing in the name of the gods was referred to in 8:14 (cf. Deut. 6:13; Josh. 23:7). Such deities would be powerless to help in the coming calamity.

The fifth vision depicted the Lord at the altar of an idolatrous shrine, possibly at Bethel (Amos 9:1), about to execute judgment (9:1-8). No matter where the people fled, they would not escape God's wrath (9:2-4). "Grave" (9:2; "Sheol," NASB; "hell," KJV) referred to the place of the dead. "Carmel" (9:3) referred to the mountain range separating Samaria from the valley of Jezreel. Since God is sovereign over the migrations of nations, Israel could not appeal to her deliverance from Egypt as evidence of divine privilege and exemption from the consequences of sin (9:7). Caphtor (9:7) referred to Crete. The fifth vision (9:1) began with "I saw" (cf. also 7:1, 4, 7; 8:1).

9:9-15 Restoration of the Faithful Kernel

The end of the book turned to restoration of the faithful remnant, the "kernel" (9:9; "pebble," NASB), of God's faithful people. A promise of restoration and blessing concluded the prophecy. "David's fallen tent" (9:11) referred to the Davidic dynasty, which God promised to restore (cf. 2 Sam. 7:12-16; Luke 1:32-33; and especially Acts 15:16-18). Edom (Amos 9:12) was representative of the Gentile nations that will have a part in the Messiah's kingdom. James appealed to Amos 9:11-12 in Acts 15:16-18 to argue for including believing Gentiles in the church. The kingdom of the Messiah will be characterized by prosperity and security for the people of God (Amos 9:13-15).

Obadiah

BASIC FACTS

HISTORICAL SETTING
Accepting an early date of 845 B.C. for Obadiah places its writing during the reign of
Jehoram (853–841 B.C.). During this time the Edomites expressed their hatred for
Israel (cf. 2 Kings 8:20-22; 2 Chron. 21:8-10), and Israel also experienced some
major invasions by the Philistines and Arabs (cf. 2 Chron. 21:16-17; Joel 3:3-6).

AUTHOR
Obadiah means "servant of Yahweh." Beyond his name, nothing is known of the life
of this prophet.

DATE
The book of Obadiah describes judgment on Edom for its hostilities against Israel.
The two most commonly accepted dates for the Edomite hostility described in
Obadiah are 845 B.C., during the reign of Jehoram (2 Chron. 21:8-10, 16-17), and
586 B.C., after the destruction of Jerusalem in which the Edomites rejoiced (Ps.
137:7; Lam. 4:21; Ezek. 25:12). Obadiah seemed to be describing a situation that
stopped short of the severe Edomite activities of 586 B.C. Thus, the more probable
date of composition is during the reign of Jehoram (853–841 B.C.) after Edom
revolted against Judah (cf. 2 Kings 8:20-22; 2 Chron. 21:8-17).

Support for the early date of Obadiah is also found in observing that both Amos
(760 B.C.) and Jeremiah (627 B.C.) showed an acquaintance with the book. Compare
Obadiah 1:4 with Amos 9:2; Obadiah 1:14 with Amos 1:6; Obadiah 1:19 with Amos
9:12; and Obadiah 1:1-6 with Jeremiah 49:7-16. Thus, a very probable date for
Obadiah is around 845 B.C., near the end of Jehoram's reign.

PURPOSE
The book of Obadiah was designed to show God's covenant faithfulness to Israel,
not to gloat in Israel's ultimate victory over her arch rival, Edom. God showed that
he held sovereign rule over all the nations. The book brought comfort to Israel
during a low time, and the Lord promised restoration after deep humiliation. Edom

was shown as a representative entity of the ungodly powers of this world that threatened the people of God. God would judge Edom's pride and humiliation of Israel (Obad. 1:10-14).

GUIDING CONCEPTS

KEY THEMES

Some of the key themes in this short book are the sovereignty of God (1:2, 8, 15, 21), the causes of Edom's self-deception (1:3, 7-9), and the reason for Edom's approaching downfall (1:10). The day of the Lord was in view in various passages (1:11-15, 16-18). The book encouraged the remnant of believers (1:17, 19-21) by making firm the promise of restoration to the land. Obadiah taught that judgment and the day of the Lord were the necessary means to establishing the kingdom. There was constant interplay between the images of two mountains, "Mount Zion" representing the nation of Israel, and "the mountains of Esau" representing the nation of Edom (1:3, 8-9, 16-17, 19, 21).

BIBLE-WIDE CONCEPTS

JACOB AND ESAU

Throughout the Old Testament there had been conflict between the family lines of Jacob and Esau. Those brothers each fathered a nation; Jacob fathered the nation of Israel, and Esau's descendants became the nation of Edom (cf. Gen. 27:29, 39-40; 36:8; Num. 20:14-21). Edom was ultimately destroyed in A.D. 70 by the Romans. The problem addressed in Obadiah was how the kingdom (Obad. 1:21) of the Lord could be regained. God would repay the evil done against Israel by Edom. That was a fulfillment of the covenant of Genesis 12:3—God would curse those who cursed Israel. The promise to Abraham is still in effect (Obad. 1:10, 15; cf. Gen. 27:29). Abraham's land will be restored (Obad. 1:17, 19-20), and all the nations will be judged (1:15).

THE EDOMITES AND CHRIST

Even in the New Testament times strife between the Hebrews and Edomites continued in the Jews' hatred for King Herod who was of Idumean (Edomite) descent. Herod tried to kill the ultimate Representative of Israel, Christ (Matt. 2:1-18). The judgment that would come upon the Edomites because of their cruelty and lack of compassion toward the descendants of Jacob was described in many Old Testament prophecies (cf. Isa. 34:5-15; Jer. 49:7-22; Lam. 4:21-22; Ezek. 25:12-14; Amos 1:11-12).

NEEDS MET BY OBADIAH

The military and cultural wars between Israel and Edom had stretched on for centuries and, at the time of Obadiah's prophecy, Israel seemed to be on the losing side. God's people needed to know two things: victory was certain and it was for God's glory alone. The book ends with its main point: the kingdom will be the Lord's. The people of God needed to see their present unfortunate circumstances in the light of their future victory. This perspective would not lessen the pain of the present, but it would provide hope and faith: two things necessary for keeping God's people faithful to him. The book of Obadiah met many long-standing needs of the people of God. During this time of difficulty, the people of Israel were probably asking questions like these.

- Will God let Israel's enemies go on harming them forever?
- When will God put an end to Israel's age-old rivalry with Edom?
- Is Israel still being protected by God's promise to Abraham?

The problems between Israel and Edom were not simply minor ancient skirmishes between two little nations. Edom represents all nations (1:15) in two ways: pride against God and hostility against God's people. This pride and hostility took its most ugly form in Christ's crucifixion and received its most destructive blow in Christ's resurrection. From this point on, believers may read the book of Obadiah as a confirmation of God's ultimate rule over the nations. The present aggravation of believers over the pain and injustice of the world needs to be viewed through God's promises. Obadiah should give believers hope during times of suffering and revive their faith in God's certain future. At the same time it calls them to avoid acting with the same arrogance and hostility as God's enemies.

OUTLINE OF OBADIAH

A. GOD'S PROCESS OF CUTTING DOWN EDOM (1:1-9)
   1. Judgment by the Nations (1:1)
   2. Inner Deception: Not Knowing God (1:2-6)
   3. Outer Deception: The Removal of Insight (1:7-9)
B. THE CAUSE AND EFFECT IN EDOM'S DESTRUCTION (1:10-14)
   1. Reason for Judgment (1:10-11)
   2. Warning Not to Repeat Disobedience (1:12-14)
C. THE PURPOSE OF EDOM'S JUDGMENT: RESTORATION OF THE KINGDOM (1:15-21)
   1. International Recompense for Past Deeds (1:15-16)
   2. Jacob's Place in the Recompense of Edom (1:17-18)
   3. The Possession of the Kingdom (1:19-21)

OBADIAH NOTES

1:1-9 GOD'S PROCESS OF CUTTING DOWN EDOM
1:1 Judgment by the Nations
The prophet's name, "Obadiah," meaning "servant of the Lord," was quite a common name in the Old Testament. Nothing is known about this particular Obadiah except that he appears to have lived in the southern kingdom of Judah. "Edom" (1:1), meaning "red," was the name given to Esau when he sold his birthright to his brother Jacob for some reddish soup (cf. Gen. 25:30). The land of Edom was located in a mountainous area southeast of the Dead Sea.

1:2-6 Inner Deception: Not Knowing God

Edom deceived herself (repeated twice in 1:3) by means of her arrogance. She dreamed up an unreal world in which she could never be brought down (1:3). The word "rocks" (lit., "sela") probably referred to Petra, an important commercial center of Edom. The city was surrounded by high mountains and could be entered only by a narrow ravine. Although seemingly inaccessible in her secure mountain fortress, Edom was not outside the range of God's judgment. The completeness of Edom's approaching destruction was illustrated by referring to the pattern of thieves and harvesters who had to leave something behind (1:5). By contrast, the plunderers of Edom would leave nothing. Trade routes passing through Edom enabled the people to acquire great wealth. But such "treasures" would be plundered (1:6).

1:7-9 Outer Deception: The Removal of Insight

Edom's prideful inner deception results in her being deceived by the surrounding nations (1:7). Her self-deception made her blind and foolishly susceptible to being deceived by others. Historically, Edom was renowned for her wisdom. Access to international trade routes enabled the Edomites to acquire wisdom from abroad. Thus, Obadiah's statement that they would be deceived contained a tone of sarcasm. Teman (1:9; cf. Job. 2:11), an important city of Edom, was located about five miles northeast of Petra.

1:10-14 THE CAUSE AND EFFECT IN EDOM'S DESTRUCTION

1:10-11 Reason for Judgment

Obadiah explained the reason for Edom's coming destruction. The major scholarly debate over this section relates to the historical circumstances of Edom's sin against Judah. Many scholars would place it in connection with the 586 B.C. destruction of Jerusalem. However, Obadiah made no mention of the Babylonians, Nebuchadnezzar, the deportation, or the burning of the Jerusalem temple. The more probable historical situation was the attack on Jerusalem during the reign of Jehoram (2 Chron. 21:8-10, 16-17), which the Edomites applauded. "Jacob"

(Obad. 1:10) referred here to the Israelites and reminded the people of the brotherly relationship between Esau and his brother Jacob. The Hasmonean leader John Hyrcanus (135–104 B.C.) forced the people of Edom to adopt Judaism or be killed. Edom, known later as Idumea, was attacked and devastated by Simon ben Gioras during the Jewish War (A.D. 66–70). Josephus reported that the land was totally destroyed.

1:12-14 Warning Not to Repeat Disobedience

Obadiah described the actions of the Edomites as if he were viewing an instant playback. The eight imperatives (1:12-14) described what the Edomites actually did while Jerusalem was being destroyed. The "gates" (1:13) referred to the gates of Jerusalem. The Edomites took up positions around the city where they could prevent the escape of the Jewish fugitives and turn them over to the enemy (1:14).

1:15-21 THE PURPOSE OF EDOM'S JUDGMENT: RESTORATION OF THE KINGDOM

1:15-16 International Recompense for Past Deeds

Obadiah described the "day of the LORD" (1:15) as drawing near. This expression was used to describe both the judgment and blessing that Edom would experience historically and the future judgment and blessing that will be experienced in the final day of the Lord. Obadiah appeared to blend both elements to show that what Edom would experience historically would be the fate of all godless nations in the future. The words "all nations" (not just Edom) indicate that the prophet had a future judgment in view.

1:17-18 Jacob's Place in the Recompense of Edom

Whereas nations like Edom could expect only judgment, the righteous, like the faithful of Israel, awaited restoration and blessing. The "house of Esau" (1:18), representative of the wicked nations that persecuted God's people, would be totally destroyed, in keeping with the promise of Genesis 12:3.

1:19-21 The Possession of the Kingdom

Obadiah described the full extent of Israel's restoration to the land. The "Negev" (Obad. 1:19) referred to the southern, dry region centering around Beer-sheba. The "foothills" ("Shephelah," NASB) referred to the low hills between the Philistine coastal plain and the hill country of Judea. Ephraim and Samaria (1:19) referred to the territories of the northern kingdom. Benjamin was located just north of Judah. Gilead was in Transjordan, southeast of the Sea of Galilee.

Zarephath (1:20) was located in Phoenicia. Sepharad is of uncertain location. Recent scholarship suggests that it was identical with Sardis of Asia Minor. The "deliverers" (1:21) who ascended Mount Zion (Jerusalem) probably referred to returned exiles (1:17). They may have been appointed to help in the Lord Messiah's kingdom rule. At that time the kingdom was not the Lord's (1:21); it was in the hands of sinful leaders and followers. But someday it would be fully under the Lord's rule (1:21).

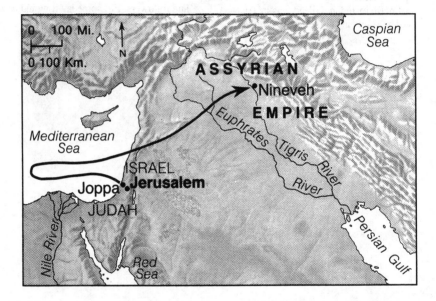

Jonah

BASIC FACTS

HISTORICAL SETTING
Jonah ministered under Jeroboam II (793–753 B.C.). Nineveh, the greatest city of the Assyrian Empire, had already begun to take tribute from Israel as early as 841 B.C.,; thus Jonah was called to go to the dominant city of Israel's enemy nation. Assyria would continue to have supremacy until its destruction by Babylonia in 612 B.C.

AUTHOR
Jonah was only mentioned once elsewhere in Old Testament Scripture (2 Kings 14:25). No other facts about Jonah are known, except the name of his father (Jon. 1:1) and his birthplace (2 Kings 14:25).

DATE
Jonah ministered during the reign of Jeroboam II, who ruled from 793 to 753 B.C. If the Jonah mentioned in 2 Kings 14:25 was the author of this book, then the date of writing was around 760 B.C.

PURPOSE
The book of Jonah was designed to convict the readers of their selfishness and bigotry concerning the spread of God's message of salvation to all ethnic groups. It contrasted the great unbiased compassion of God with the miserly and inbred self-interest of Jonah and his provincial religion.

GEOGRAPHY AND ITS IMPORTANCE

Jonah wanted to flee to Tarshish because it was in the opposite direction from Nineveh. The great geographical distance between Tarshish and Nineveh matched Jonah's emotional distance from the spiritually needy people in Nineveh. God loved and wanted to save Nineveh, but Jonah did not want God to have mercy on Israel's great enemy. In the middle of the great fish Jonah received God's mercy and praised God for his salvation. But when Jonah arrived in the middle of Nineveh, his heart was far away from the people and God's love for them.

GUIDING CONCEPTS

STRUCTURE

The book of Jonah is not a typical prophetic address. It is a very personal story about the prophet's disgust at thinking that God might forgive a group of non-Israelite pagans. The book was structured around two commands for Jonah to go to Nineveh (1:2; 3:2). Those two commands support two interpretive points. First, God confirmed the calling of Jonah, and the nation of Israel along with him, to be evangelistic lights to the nations. Jonah had to wrestle with his own choice of confessing or denying God's love for the nations. Second, God confirmed his own unchanging desire for the redemption of the world outside of Israel. At the structural center of the book is Jonah's psalm of praise (2:1-9). This psalm provides the book with a basic theological viewpoint ("salvation comes from the Lord," 2:9). That viewpoint resulted in conflict for Jonah but redemption for the sailors on Jonah's "get-away" ship and for the people of Nineveh.

The content of the book was organized in a layered manner.
1:1-3 Jonah's Unexplained Disobedience
1:4-16 God Saves the Sailors
1:17–2:10 God Saves Jonah
3:1-10 God Saves Nineveh
4:1-11 Jonah's Disobedience Explained and Challenged
Note the relationships between the first and last parts, and the second and fourth parts of the outline above. Part three (1:17–2:10) was at the very heart of the book and was framed between the layers of God's salvation of the sailors on the "get-away" boat and the people of Nineveh. The outer layers formed a book-wide frame of Jonah's disobedience. The questions of 4:4 and 4:9 pointed the way to the book's message and application. If God was so willing to save sailors, Jonah, and Nineveh, why was Jonah so angry?

MESSAGE

Why did Jonah not delight in telling Nineveh of its possible destruction (1:2)? Jonah's disobedience was not explained until 4:2, where he quoted Exodus 34:6. He knew that if the people of Nineveh repented, God would forgive them. And that galled him. God's final questions to Jonah were questions for the readers as well (Jon. 4:9). The message of impending judgment had one major purpose: to get people to repent and avoid judgment. Only a sour person like Jonah would get angry because God had forgiven someone else.

BIBLE-WIDE CONCEPTS

God's universal rule and offer of redemption were mentioned throughout the Old Testament (cf. Gen. 9:27; 12:3; Lev. 19:33-34; 1 Sam. 2:10; Isa. 2:2; Joel 2:28-32). God greatly desired for all the people in Nineveh to come to know him. Jonah's quote of Exodus 34:6 in 4:2 showed that God's compassion extended worldwide, not just to the Jews under the Mosaic covenant. But Jonah did not want to accept the worldwide perspective of the Abrahamic covenant, in which all nations would be blessed. Compassion (Exod. 34:6) is of the very character of God; therefore, it is universal, not bound by ethnic and geographic limits.

The Lord used the book of Jonah as a prophetic sign of the future redemption in Christ for both Jew and Gentile (cf. Matt. 12:39-41; Luke 11:29-32). It looked forward to Christ's redemptive work that would offer peace and salvation to all people.

NEEDS MET BY JONAH

Israel needed to know that God did not play favorites. His grace extended equally to all who asked for it and his judgment fell on all who disobeyed—and that included Israel. Simply being born into Israel played no part in receiving God's grace or avoiding his judgment. The deciding factor was faith and obedience, not ethnic or religious background. That leveling of everyone before God cleared the way for Israel to understand that her world mission was redemption, not condemnation.

Jonah and his hearers needed to stop giving their racial and cultural hatred a religious stamp of approval. Their personal hatred for cruel and ungodly nations like Assyria did not give them the right to withhold the message of God's grace and rejoice when God's judgment fell. On the contrary, a pagan nation's impending doom should have filled their hearts with compassion, causing them to rush to share God's grace and possibly avert the judgment. Israel needed to replace her judgmental heart with one full of compassion for the lost world. The book of Jonah pointed the way to a less narrow and ethnic view of religion. The structure and content of Jonah show that the Israelites were probably asking questions like these.

- Why should anyone go to tell foreign enemies about how to avoid God's judgment?
- What is the relationship between Israel's salvation and the world's possible damnation?
- What is the relationship between the desire of Israel to receive compassion and her desire for the world to receive it?

When one person causes another person pain, not only pain is felt, but anger as well. Continued hurt only increases both the pain and anger. Jonah (and his nation) lived with the constant cruel oppression of Assyria, and it was easy for his anger to grow right along with his nation's pain. When people are hurt and angry they tend to fight back with the best weapons they have at their disposal. In Jonah's case it was his supposed ability to affect the eternal destiny of his enemies. What better weapon than to be able to let someone go to hell? But the Bible calls believers to take their hurts before God and to replace their hate with compassion. Christ is the supreme example of one exhibiting compassion in a situation where most people would show hate. He had all the best reasons to hate the human race in all their selfishness, sin, and offensive ways. He had the power to let them just slide off into a deserved hell. But his anger against sin was replaced with compassion for the lost and he suffered the sins and insults of mankind in order to bring them the message of redemption. The book of Jonah makes it clear that though there are indeed things in life to hate, a believer's anger is never to eclipse his compassion and call to share God's grace.

OUTLINE OF JONAH

A. THE FIRST COMMISSIONING: GOD'S LONG-SUFFERING TOWARD
   JONAH (1:1–2:10)
   1. Jonah's Unexplained Disobedience (1:1-3)
   2. God Saves the Sailors (1:4-16)
   3. God Saves Jonah (1:17–2:10)
B. THE SECOND COMMISSIONING: GOD'S LONG-SUFFERING TOWARD
   NINEVEH (3:1–4:11)
   1. God Saves Nineveh (3:1-10)
   2. Jonah's Disobedience Explained and Challenged (4:1-11)

JONAH NOTES

1:1–2:10 THE FIRST COMMISSIONING: GOD'S LONG-SUFFERING TOWARD JONAH
1:1-3 Jonah's Unexplained Disobedience

The name "Jonah" (1:1) means "dove." Second Kings 14:25 records that he lived and ministered during the reign of Israel's King Jeroboam II (793–753 B.C.). The historicity of the prophet was confirmed by Jesus (Matt. 12:39-41; Luke 11:29-32). Nineveh was located just east of the Tigris River in northern Mesopotamia (see introductory map). Although Nineveh was the largest Assyrian city in the time of Jonah, it was not the capital. At the time of Jonah's visit, the capital was at Calah, about twenty-five miles to the southeast. Nineveh, the last capital of the Assyrian Empire, was destroyed by the Babylonian and Median armies in 612 B.C.

The city was surrounded by a wall seven and three quarters miles in length. The "great city" had an area sufficient to house a population of 120,000 (1:2; 4:11). It is probable that the whole district administered by Nineveh encompassed a very wide area, including the surrounding lesser cities and villages. Thus "three days" would be

necessary to reach the city center from the outlying suburbs (3:4). The Hebrew language does not distinguish between the metropolis itself and the general region. Tarshish (1:3), according to the Greek historian Herodotus, was a mining and smelting center in southern Spain. An inscription found in A.D. 1773 suggests that Tarshish might have been located on the island of Sardinia.

1:4-16 God Saves the Sailors

1:4-9 JONAH'S CONFESSION
The sovereignty of God was evidenced throughout the book of Jonah. God "sent a great wind" (1:4) and "provided a great fish" (1:17), a "vine" (4:6), and a scorching "east wind" (4:8). Lot casting (1:7) was a means of determining the will of God (cf. Josh. 7:16; 1 Sam. 10:20-24; Prov. 16:33; Acts 1:23-26).

1:10-16 THE SAILORS' CONFESSION
Jonah's response can be interpreted in at least two ways: (1) he would rather die than obey God, or (2) he recognized his worthiness of death and was willing to endure this punishment. The sailors prayed that in throwing Jonah overboard, they would not be held guilty for his death ("innocent man," 1:14).

1:17–2:10 God Saves Jonah

Jesus compared his own impending death and resurrection with Jonah's "three days and three nights" in the fish (1:17; cf. Matt. 12:39-40; 16:4; Luke 11:29-30). The time periods were essentially the same, and both ended with a surprise—Jonah delivered and Jesus resurrected. Jonah was probably near drowning (2:3, 5-6) as he sank to the bottom of the sea. He viewed the fish as salvation from death and a sign that God would bring him safely back to Jerusalem.

Jonah prayed "from inside the fish" (Jon. 2:1) and recorded his prayer and recollections subsequent to his release and his ministry at Nineveh. The "depths of the grave" (2:2) literally reads, "the belly of Sheol," referring to the grave as a devouring monster that had swallowed Jonah. Jonah thought of himself as good as dead. There is no evidence to suggest that he actually died and was resurrected like Christ. The primary point of similarity between the experience of Jonah and Jesus was the time element—"three days and three nights" (1:17) and being in a "grave" (2:2).

Although he had sinned, Jonah knew that God would forgive him, and he looked with anticipation to worshiping in Jerusalem ("your holy temple") again (2:4). Jonah promised to praise God for the deliverance he anticipated by faith (2:9). The fish obeyed God more readily than Jonah had (2:10)!

3:1–4:11 THE SECOND COMMISSIONING: GOD'S LONG-SUFFERING TOWARD NINEVEH

3:1-10 God Saves Nineveh

3:1-4 JONAH'S WITNESS
God gave Jonah a second chance, as he did John Mark (Acts 13:13; 2 Tim. 4:11). The city of Nineveh was large but smaller than the language may seem to imply. The "great city" (Jon. 3:2) probably referred to "greater Nineveh," including the lesser cities and villages situated nearby. The "three days" (3:3) would have been necessary to completely traverse the metropolis, including its outlying suburbs.

The moral corruption and wickedness of the city and people were attested to by the prophet Nahum. Jonah came to Nineveh

either during the reign of Adad-mirari III (810–783 B.C.), Shalmaneser IV (782–773 B.C.), Ashur-dan III (772–755 B.C.), or Ashur-nirari V (754–745 B.C.). If his appearance is put within the reign of Ashur-dan III, then the plagues recorded in Assyrian annals in 765 and 759 B.C., and the total eclipse of 763 B.C., may have been regarded as portents of divine wrath that prepared the city for Jonah's message. During this period Assyria was experiencing weakness and degeneration caused by the rising menace of the Urartu peoples, internal dissension within Assyria itself, and a succession of weak rulers. This turn of events for the empire also may have prepared the city of Nineveh to respond to Jonah's call to repentance. The Hebrew word for "destruction" (3:10) expresses the idea of complete devastation (cf. Gen. 19:25).

3:5-10 NINEVEH'S CONFESSION
An eclipse on June 15, 763 B.C., may have been taken as a warning of impending disaster and helped to kindle a repentant spirit among the people of Nineveh (Jon. 3:5). The "king of Nineveh" (3:6) was probably Ashur-dan III (772–755 B.C.). Sitting in "dust" or ashes was a sign of mourning (3:6; cf. Job 2:8; Mic. 1:10). While God's character does not change (cf. 1 Sam. 15:29; James 1:17), he may show mercy instead of wrath in response to man's genuine repentance.

4:1-11 Jonah's Disobedience Explained and Challenged

4:1-4 JONAH'S ANGER OVER GOD'S SAVING CHARACTER
Jonah explained why he fled his commission (Jon. 4:2). He had proper doctrine (cf. Exod. 34:6), but he did not share God's love for the lost. While he had been forgiven, he did not want to accept the fact that non-Israelites would be forgiven too.

4:5-11 JONAH'S ANGER COMPARED WITH GOD' COMPASSION
Jonah apparently thought the Ninevites might fall back into sin and that God might judge Nineveh after all, so he went outside the city to watch what would happen (Jon. 4:5). It has been suggested that the "vine" or plant (4:6) was the quick-growing castor oil plant that can grow to about eight feet in height during its growing season.

The "east wind" (4:8) is known for its excessive heat and dryness (cf. Ps. 103:16; Isa. 27:8; Jer. 4:11).

In Jonah 4:9-11 God explained his compassion on Nineveh by making an analogy with Jonah's concern for the plant. If Jonah was concerned about a mere plant that grew up on its own without the care of a gardener, how much more compassion might God extend to the people of Nineveh whom he had loved and labored to bring to repentance? The 120,000 persons who "cannot tell their right hand from their left" (4:11) may have referred to literal children or mature people who were like children in terms of their spiritual perception.

Micah

BASIC FACTS

HISTORICAL SETTING

Micah ministered in the period surrounding the destruction of the northern kingdom of Israel (722 B.C.) by Assyria. That destruction also terrorized the inhabitants of the southern kingdom of Judah. Micah warned the people of both the north and the south to change their ways. The quotation of Micah 3:12 in Jeremiah 26:18-19 indicates that Micah's warnings were taken seriously and made a contribution to the reform that took place under Hezekiah. Micah prophesied contemporaneously with Hosea and Amos in the northern kingdom and Isaiah in Jerusalem in the southern kingdom.

AUTHOR

Micah was the only prophet whose writing ministry was directed to both the northern and southern kingdoms (Mic. 1:1). Although his father's name was not given, Micah's name (meaning, "Who is like the Lord?") indicates that his parents were pious and faithful worshipers of God. Although Micah 1–3 is accepted by most scholars as written by Micah the prophet, Micah 4–5 is believed by some to have been added during the exile and Micah 6:1–7:6 is viewed as a later anonymous prophecy from the period of King Manasseh. However, the repeated expressions "hear" and "listen" (1:2; 3:1; 6:1) and the book-wide pattern of alternating sections of judgment and salvation (see the section below on structure) support the unity of the book and in no way undermine Micah as the single author.

DATE

Micah's prophecies began at least a decade before the fall of Samaria in 722 B.C. (cf. 1:6). He prophesied during the reigns of Jotham (750–731 B.C.), Ahaz (743–715 B.C.), and Hezekiah (728–686 B.C.). Micah's prophetic ministry in writing can be dated between 735 and 700 B.C.

PURPOSE

The book of Micah was designed to encourage repentance by threats of judgment
and promises of the ultimate triumph of God's promises to Abraham and to King
David.

GUIDING CONCEPTS

STRUCTURE

Note the repetition of "hear" and "listen" (1:2; 3:1; 6:1). The book is structured in layers of judgment (1:2–2:11; 3:1-12; 6:1–7:6) and salvation (2:12-13; 4:1–5:15; 7:7-20).
In his prophecies, Micah balanced God's judgment with the reality of his love.

BIBLE-WIDE CONCEPTS

Jesus used Micah 7:6 to support how he came not to bring peace, but a sword (cf.
Matt. 10:34-39). The central problem in both Micah's and Jesus' times was the same:
a lack of commitment to God (cf. Mic. 6:7-8 with Matt. 10:31-33). The coming of
the Messianic kingdom involved judgment first, then peace. And that judgment and
turbulence involved a potential crisis of family allegiance versus trust in God (Mic.
7:6).

The priests and scribes quoted Micah 5:2 to show Herod where the promised King
of Israel would be born (Matt. 2:6). The coming of the promised King includes all
the concepts of land, blessing, and rule promised from Abraham, through Moses, to
David. The last verse of Micah grounds all of his hopes and fears in God's loving-
kindness to Abraham (Mic. 7:20). That great promise describes the essence of God's
character: God "will be true" and "will show mercy" (7:20; cf. John 1:17 for the
equivalent "grace and truth").

NEEDS MET BY MICAH

Micah's hearers faced certain destruction and captivity because they had stubbornly
refused to stop their private and public sins. Because of that, the Assyrians would
soon come and destroy the northern half of God's nation. To the rebellious, Micah
offered the way to repent and return to God. But a small group had remained faithful
to God. And to that group Micah brought special words of encouragement. He told
them that the nation's sin had not voided God's promises to Abraham and that there
was a way for them to get through the time of discipline and pain.

It was hard for the faithful to have to suffer the punishment brought on by the
unfaithful. Good and bad alike lost their land, homes, and lives. Micah explained
that the nation as a whole would suffer discipline, but only temporarily. Beyond lay
a future of restoration and peace. Micah's task was to strengthen that future hope in
the face of a present that threatened to dismantle all hope. His intention was not to
make the present pain of sin's consequences go away. It was to get the people to the
point where, when the discipline ended, they could receive future blessings either by
the repentance of the unfaithful or by strengthening the hope and endurance of the

faithful. The book of Micah called God's people to stop sinning and encouraged them to persevere during the period of God's discipline. The content and structure of Micah show that the Israelites were probably asking questions like these.

- How long will God let the injustice of Israel's leaders go on?
- What future hope will there be when the entire nation of Israel is torn apart by exile?
- What are God's people supposed to do in the light of certain judgment?
- Have the great promises to Abraham been voided by the sins of Israel?

The problems faced by God's people in Micah's day continue today. Christians face living in a society where leaders are corrupt and do not do right by those they are supposed to serve. Many of God's people face the potential economic or military collapse of their nations and wonder how they can live through an uncertain future. Other believers face hard times of discipline for their ventures into disobedience. But Micah speaks now as he did long ago. Although people today indeed will have to live with the consequences of their sins and the sins of others, God's promises of future blessing are still secure. The task for the present is to increase obedience and readiness to glorify God now and to receive his blessings in the future.

OUTLINE OF MICAH

A. INTRODUCTION (1:1)

B. REBELLION PUNISHED (1:2–2:13)
  1. God's Witness (1:2)
  2. Destruction upon the Nation (1:3-7)
  3. Captivity Promised (1:8-16)
  4. Woe Speech: Injustice to the Family of God (2:1-11)
  5. Divine Headship Restored (2:12-13)

C. LEADERSHIP CORRECTED (3:1–5:15)
  1. Leadership Condemned (3:1-12)
  2. The Kingdom Restored (4:1-8)
  3. Babylon and the Day of God (4:9-13)
  4. The Rule of One Who Is Peace (5:1-15)

D. REBELLION PUNISHED (6:1–7:20)
  1. God's Lawsuit (6:1-16)
  2. Woe Speech: Injustice to the Family (7:1-6)
  3. God's Rule Restored: Abrahamic Promise (7:7-20)

MICAH NOTES

1:1 INTRODUCTION

Micah 1–2 formed Micah's first message. The name "Micah" means "Who is like Yahweh?" The city of "Moresheth" was located in the vicinity of "Gath" (cf. 1:14) about six miles northeast of Lachish. Micah carried out his ministry during the reigns of Jotham (750–731 B.C.), Ahaz (743–715 B.C.), and Hezekiah (728–686 B.C.). His message concerned both the northern ("Samaria") and southern ("Jerusalem") kingdoms.

1:2–2:13 REBELLION PUNISHED
1:2 God's Witness

Using the imagery of a law court with the divine Judge, witnesses, and the accused, Micah announced God's judgment.

1:3-7 Destruction upon the Nation

The "high places" referred to the centers of idolatrous worship in Samaria and Jerusalem (1:3). Samaria was ravaged by the Assyrians in 722 B.C. (cf. 2 Kings 17:1-6). The "wages of prostitutes" (Mic. 1:7) referred to payment given to a temple prostitute. The treasures of Samaria would be used by the Assyrians in worshiping their gods.

1:8-16 Captivity Promised

Going barefoot (1:8; cf. 2 Sam. 15:30) and without one's outer cloak ("naked," 1:8; cf. Isa. 20:2-4) were traditional signs of mourning. Micah singled out for mourning a number of towns situated in the Shephelah, a ridge of hills located between the hill country of Judea and the lowlands descending to the Mediterranean Sea (Mic. 1:10-15). Although it is difficult to detect in the English text, Micah employed a play on words suggesting a symbolic significance in many of the names. Knowing the meaning of the Hebrew names helps in appreciating the puns employed by Micah. Beth-Ophrah (1:10) means "house of dust." Shaphir (1:11) means "beauty-town." Zaanan (1:11) means "going out." Maroth (1:12) means "bitterness." Aczib (1:14) means "deception." Mareshah (1:15) means "possession." Adullam (1:15) means "retreat" or "refuge." The shaving of the head (1:16, "baldness") was apparently also a mourning custom (cf. Isa. 3:24; Amos 8:10; see also Deut. 14:1).

2:1-11 Woe Speech:
Injustice to the Family of God

Micah revealed the reason for the coming judgment. To "divide the land by lot" (Mic. 2:5) is a reference to doing a survey with a view to distributing land. No survey would be necessary because the people would be exiled. The words "Do not prophesy" (2:6) were apparently spoken by those who opposed Micah's ministry. Micah quoted the wicked who doubted that God would allow a calamity such as exile. But the prophet pointed out that God cares for those who

obey him. The "defiled" place (2:10) was reminiscent of Leviticus 18:25-28. With biting sarcasm, Micah declared that the people would rather listen to a lying windbag than a true prophet of God (Mic. 2:11).

2:12-13 Divine Headship Restored

Having announced severe judgment, Micah provided a word of encouragement regarding the regathering of dispersed Israel to their land (cf. Deut. 30:1-10). The "one who breaks open" (2:13), who clears the obstacles for this return, is probably the Messianic King.

3:1–5:15 LEADERSHIP CORRECTED
3:1-12 Leadership Condemned

Micah 3–5 formed Micah's second message. The Lord as supreme head (2:13) addressed the heads of Israel (3:1). The image of the holy mountain linked Micah 3 and Micah 4 (cf. 3:12 and 4:1). "Justice" is the key word in Micah 3. While the corrupt national leaders abhorred justice, God delighted in it. Using the figure of a defenseless flock, Micah portrayed the violence carried out against the people (3:2-3). The false prophets predicted "peace" to make the people happy and to make sure that the people would pay them generously (3:5).

Micah's qualifications to speak for God included the presence of the Holy Spirit, a sense of justice, and courage to denounce and expose sin (3:8). Micah was the first of the prophets to threaten Judah with the annihilation of its capital and the destruction of the temple (3:12). This prophecy made such an impression that it was quoted by the elders in defense of Jeremiah a century later (cf. Jer. 26:18).

4:1-8 The Kingdom Restored

There were great contrasts between nations that desired to worship God (Mic. 4:2) and those that desired to destroy Israel (4:11). The fall of Jerusalem in 586 B.C. merged with the image of the final day of the Lord (4:12-13).

The prophecy of 4:1-3, concerning the Messianic era, is nearly identical to that found in Isaiah 2:2-4. The same revelation may have been granted to both prophets about the same time. This prophecy constituted a reversal of the prophecy given by Joel in the context of anticipated judgment (cf. Joel 3:10). Micah's day was contrasted with the Messianic era in Micah 4:5. Israel's future recognition of God was to prompt true worship now. The "watchtower of the flock" (4:8) was a poetic synonym for Jerusalem, likening the city to a tower from which a shepherd watched his sheep.

4:9-13 Babylon and the Day of God

Dispersion and captivity in Babylon (4:10) were two of the sufferings that had to precede Israel's restoration and blessing. Both the exile and the return from captivity were predicted (4:10; cf. Ezra 1:1-4). In Micah 4:11-13 the prophet moved to the distant future, describing the gathering of the nations around Jerusalem for judgment (cf. Joel 3:1-16). At that time, God will give Israel victory over all her enemies (Mic. 4:13).

5:1-15 The Rule of One Who Is Peace

A promised ruler would come to Israel and have international dominion (5:4, 6, 15). Israel would be purged first, then the nations (5:12-15). In 5:1 Micah referred back to the thought of 4:9. At the time of Babylon's invasion, Zedekiah ("Israel's ruler") was smitten and humiliated (cf. 2 Kings 25:6-7). In contrast to the smitten king (Mic. 5:1), a great ruler (5:2) would come for God's people. Ephrathah (5:2, meaning "fruitful") was an ancient name for Bethlehem (cf. Gen. 35:19; Ruth 4:11). This additional name served to distinguish Bethlehem of Judah from Bethlehem of Zebulun (cf. Josh. 19:15). The last sentence of 5:2 affirmed the existence of this Messianic Ruler before his birth (cf. John 1:1). Micah 5:2 provided the answer to the Magi's question in Matthew 2:1-6. The solution to the leadership problem will be a perfect Ruler of the Davidic line.

The "she" (Mic. 5:3) referred to the Virgin Mary (cf. Isa. 7:14). As the good shepherd, Christ will care for the needs of his flock (Mic. 5:4; cf. John 10:1-18). "Peace" (Mic. 5:5-6) summed up what the Messiah would mean for Israel and the world. The Assyrian foe of Micah's day was representative of the enemies of Israel that God would enable his people to overcome. Nimrod, the son of Cush, founded a kingdom in Babylonia that later extended to Assyria (cf. Gen. 10:8-12). Micah revealed God's dealings with Israel's remnant, which will be purged, purified, and converted (Mic. 5:7-15). Military weapons will be unnecessary in the Messianic age (5:10-11; cf. Isa. 2:4).

6:1–7:20 REBELLION PUNISHED
6:1-16 God's Lawsuit

Micah 6–7 formed Micah's third message. Just as the mountains, hills, and earth were invoked as witnesses to the ratification of Israel's covenant (cf. Deut. 4:26; 32:1), so they were called upon as witnesses of the covenant violations (Mic. 6:1-2). The Lord led Israel from Egypt, provided national leadership, and delivered the people from their enemies (6:4-5). God's gracious dealings with his people in the past should have resulted in their love and obedience. For "Balak" and "Balaam" (6:5), see Numbers 22–24. The rhetorical questions (Mic. 6:6, 7) imply a negative answer. What does the Lord desire of his people? No matter how great the sacrifice made, the sacrifice alone is insufficient to satisfy God's requirements for justice. God's demand (6:8) links ethics with piety, duty toward people with duty toward God. He wants believers' hearts to be pure and requires that they prove their purity through their actions (cf. Deut. 6:5-6; 10:12).

In Micah 6:9-16 the prophet set forth the sinfulness of Jerusalem (6:9-12) and described her coming judgment (6:13-16). The "statutes of Omri" and "the practices of Ahab's house" (6:16) referred to the unbridled wickedness, oppression, and idolatry that characterized the reigns of these two kings (cf. 1 Kings 16:25-26, 29-33; 18:4; 21:25).

7:1-6 Woe Speech:
Injustice to the Family

In 7:1-6 Micah lamented the iniquity of the nation. Like an orchard or vineyard devoid of fruit after harvest, there were no godly or righteous people left in Judah.

7:7-20 God's Rule Restored: Abrahamic Promise

The "enemy" (7:8) that threatened Judah was either Assyria or Babylon. In 7:11-17 the Lord promised the restoration of his people. Micah predicted a reversal of all exiles, allowing the Jewish people to return to their land (cf. Matt. 24:31). Bashan and Gilead (7:14) were northern Transjordan territories.

In Micah 7:18-20, encouraged by the revelation of God's ultimate deliverance of his people, the prophet broke forth in praise of God's mercy and forgiveness. Note how 7:18-20 relates to Jeremiah 31:34 and the forgiving of iniquities. The Jews joined these verses to the book of Jonah for reading in the synagogue on the afternoon of the Day of Atonement. All that God did for his people by way of forgiveness, compassion, and loyal love was based on his promise to Abraham (7:20; cf. Gen. 12:1-3). Micah affirmed that godly leadership would be restored.

Nahum

BASIC FACTS

HISTORICAL SETTING

The events surrounding the book of Nahum took place before 612 B.C., when Nineveh was destroyed by the Babylonian and Median armies. Assyria was still dominant in the west (1:12-13; 2:12-13; 3:1-4). Nahum probably prophesied during the long reign of wicked Manasseh (697–642 B.C.). Ashurbanipal, king of Assyria, placed Manasseh on the throne of Judah as one of his vassals who assisted in his campaign against Egypt. Manasseh introduced into Judah the official Assyrian religious cult and many other pagan practices (cf. 2 Kings 21:1-18; 2 Chron. 33:1-9). Assyria had extended its dominion into Palestine and Egypt and dominated the international scene of the ancient Near East. Ashurbanipal was especially noted for the ruthless cruelty and atrocities that he brought upon the victims of his campaigns. Through Nahum, the Lord judged and condemned Nineveh's power and oppression (1:1-15), despite its seeming invulnerability.

AUTHOR

The book is titled as "the book of the vision of Nahum" (1:1). Nothing is known about Nahum except that he was a native of Elkosh, the location of which has not been determined with certainty. The prophet's name means "comfort" or "consolation," which probably related to his message of comfort to Judah from the threats of Assyrian oppression.

DATE

The reference to the capture of "Thebes" (3:8; "No-Amon," NASB; "No," KJV) by the Assyrians in 663 B.C. reveals the earliest possible date for the writing of the book. As Egypt was plundered by Assyria (3:8-9; cf. Isa. 20:1-6), so Assyria would be plundered by the Babylonians. The destruction of Nineveh by the Babylonian and Median armies took place in 612 B.C. Nahum 1:12-13; 2:12-13; and 3:1-4 suggest that Assyria, whose power began to decline rapidly after the death of Ashurbanipal (660–633 B.C.), was still dominant in the west. Therefore, the probable date of Nahum's prophetic ministry and the composition of the book was around 650 B.C. while Nineveh was still in its glory.

PURPOSE
The book of Nahum was designed to console Judah by its announcement of coming judgment on her enemy, Nineveh. Nahum warned concerning God's wrath toward persistent wickedness and vindicated God's holiness in the eyes of the heathen empire of Assyria. The book demonstrated that the God of Israel, the nation that the Assyrians had despised, was in fact the sovereign Controller of the destiny of all nations. Even the greatest of world powers had to submit to his sovereign will and justice.

GUIDING CONCEPTS

The main themes of the book of Nahum can be found in its revelation of God as the Avenger (1:2) and the Restorer (2:2). Nineveh's military campaigns were viewed as direct assaults upon God (1:9, 11) and as the vehicles of God's punishment of Israel (1:12). Therefore, God would judge Nineveh for its assaults and would put an end to his discipline of Israel. Note the emphasis on "great in power" (1:3). Nahum is primarily a book of judgment, but it also reveals the consistency of God's loving-kindness.

BIBLE-WIDE CONCEPTS

GOD'S JEALOUSY AND PATIENCE
Exodus 34:6-7 provided the background for God's jealousy, wrath, and slowness to anger (Nah. 1:2-3). The Hebrew word translated "jealous" (1:2) is used throughout the Old Testament and is sometimes translated zealous (cf. Exod. 20:5; Isa. 9:7; 59:16-21; Joel 2:18). The words of Exodus 34:6-7 were spoken to Moses at Sinai and became a two-edged sword of protection and punishment for Israel and the nations.

CITIES AND THE RULE OF GOD
Several cities were singled out for destruction by God in the Bible: Babel (Gen. 11:1-9), Sodom and Gomorrah (Gen. 19), Jericho (Josh. 6), Nineveh (Nahum), and Babylon (Babel), which will be destroyed in the end times (Rev. 18:21). These cities were destroyed because they epitomized all that was against the rule of God. Even Jerusalem was destroyed when it rebelled against God. But a city could also express God's reign and, like the new Jerusalem, be full of his glory and blessing. And even Nineveh had been spared judgment at one time when its people repented (cf. Jonah).

NEEDS MET BY NAHUM

The Assyrian atrocities against the Jewish nation put God's people in a complex psychological bind. Assyria had cut off the northern tribes from Israel and was known for her fierce and merciless destruction. Although the people of Israel's own sin had brought judgment upon them, God had used a gross pagan nation as his instrument of discipline. What did that mean for Assyria? Was that nation ever going to be punished for what it did to Israel? And how could God's people endure such difficult times where God's judgment on Israel's enemies seemed not to exist? Nahum showed that Nineveh was indeed God's enemy and would eventually be judged. The more difficult question of how to endure the times of pain and discipline was also answered by Nahum. God was good, was a refuge, and never lost track of those who sought him for protection (1:7). The structure and content of Nahum show that the Israelites under Nineveh's sword were asking questions like the following.

- Does God care that Nineveh has done such damage to Israel and the rest of the world?
- Is God for or against Nineveh (2:13; 3:5)?
- Will God ever stop Israel's oppression and restore it to its former glory (1:15)?

Nineveh is not just an ancient city, long-since destroyed for equally ancient reasons. It stands as an illustration of God's enemies throughout the ages (1:3-5). With this is mind, the book of Nahum provides a very sensitive balance for God's people in tough times. The book helps believers walk a balance between rejoicing when God's enemies get what they deserve, avoiding a self-righteous arrogance that brings the same judgment, and finding encouragement in bad times to hope in the future. Nahum's message of certain judgment at the end of a period of grace has been fully amplified in this time between the cross of Christ and his return to judge and reward. Believers need to know not only that God will indeed punish the guilty (1:3) but also that his wrath is slow in coming in order to allow time for many to find their refuge in him (1:7).

OUTLINE OF NAHUM

A. PATIENCE AND POWER: GOD'S CHARACTER FOCUSED ON NINEVEH (1:1-15)
1. Introduction (1:1)
2. The Power of God in Wrath toward His Enemies (1:2-8)
3. The Destruction of Nineveh's Evil Plots against God (1:9-14)
4. What Nineveh's Cutting off Means for Judah (1:15)

B. GOD'S ATTACK ON NINEVEH DESCRIBED (2:1-13)
1. Jacob Restored by God's Attack (2:1-2)
2. The Attack Described: Horror and Completeness (2:3-12)
3. The Destroyer Delivers the Sentence (2:13)

C. THE CAUSE AND CERTAINTY OF NINEVEH'S CAPTIVITY (3:1-19)
1. Woe Speech: International Corruption (3:1-7)
2. Certain Captivity: God Shows No Partiality (3:8-19)

NAHUM NOTES

1:1-15 PATIENCE AND POWER: GOD'S CHARACTER FOCUSED ON NINEVEH

1:1 Introduction

Nineveh was the last capital of the Assyrian Empire. The prophet's name, "Nahum," means "comfort" or "consolation," probably reinforcing his message of comfort to Judah from the threats of Assyria. The location of "Elkosh" (1:1) has not been determined with certainty.

1:2-8 The Power of God in Wrath toward His Enemies

In Hebrew, Nahum 1:2-8 forms an alphabetic acrostic. The theme of this poem was the certainty and severity of God's judgment on the enemies of his people. Bashan, Carmel, and Lebanon (1:4) were places known for their lush fertility (cf. Amos 1:2; 4:1; Ezek. 31:16). The rhetorical questions in Nahum 1:6 imply the answer "No one." Divine wrath is not indiscriminate (1:7). The Lord is inherently good and a stronghold for the righteous who seek refuge in his person. God promised to make "an end" of Nineveh (1:8). The Greek historian Ctesias recounted that the overthrow of Nineveh took place at a time of great flooding that swept away the city's gates and the foundations of the king's palace.

1:9-14 The Destruction of Nineveh's Evil Plots against God

God would not have to raise up a nation against Nineveh "a second time" (1:9) for the city would never rise to power again. The words "plot against the LORD" (1:9) have been taken to refer to either Assyria's Sennacherib (705–681 B.C.) or the reigning king, Sinsharrishkun (623–612 B.C.). The extinction of the king's dynasty was fulfilled in the suicide of Sennacherib's great-grandson, Saracus, in the last days of the Assyrian Empire (1:14). Sennacherib's death took place in the "temple" (2 Kings 19:37; "house," NASB and KJV) of his god, Nisroch.

1:15 What Nineveh's Cutting Off Means for Judah

The "good news" (Nah. 1:15) in this context was Judah's deliverance from the threat of Assyria, which coincided with the fall of

Nineveh in 612 B.C. The Judeans were called upon to celebrate their "festivals" (1:15; "feasts," NASB and KJV), which were interrupted by the Assyrian invasion (cf. Deut. 16:16), and pay their "vows" (1:15; cf. Eccles. 5:4, 5) made during times of distress. This text is almost identical with Isaiah 52:7, which speaks of deliverance from Babylon.

2:1-13 GOD'S ATTACK ON NINEVEH DESCRIBED

2:1-2 Jacob Restored by God's Attack

Nahum 2 described the destruction of Nineveh. The "attacker" (2:1) was a reference to the combined armies of the Medes and Babylonians, who would conquer Nineveh in 612 B.C. "Jacob" (Nah. 2:2) denotes the kingdom of Judah, and "Israel," the northern kingdom.

2:3-12 The Attack Described: Horror and Completeness

"Red" (2:3) was the favorite color of the fighting men of Media. Both their shields and cloaks were dyed crimson. The "metal on the chariots" (2:3) may have referred to metal plating or to sharp scythes projecting from the axle hubs. The "protective shield" (2:5; lit., "covering") was a framework of wood covered with leather. It provided protection for the soldiers who worked the battering ram against the city walls.

Unusually high flooding at the time of Nineveh's fall resulted in the destruction of the king's palace (2:6). The city of Nineveh was captured and sacked for her treasures (2:7-10). Nineveh had been like a "pool" of water (2:8), a trade center where people would gather. The taunt song of 2:11-12 depicted the overthrow of the once-proud city of Nineveh. Nineveh was pictured as a den of "lions" (2:11), symbolizing the city's power, pride, and fearlessness.

2:13 The Destroyer Delivers the Sentence

With the fall of Nineveh, the Assyrian "messengers," or royal emissaries like Rabshakeh (cf. 2 Kings 19:23), would no longer be heard demanding tribute from subject kingdoms.

3:1-19 THE CAUSE AND CERTAINTY OF NINEVEH'S CAPTIVITY

3:1-7 Woe Speech: International Corruption

Nahum concluded with a statement on the reason for Nineveh's destruction. Nineveh was called a "city of blood" (Nah. 3:1), alluding to the bloody and ruthless Assyrian military activities. Shalmaneser III boasted that he used the bodies of the slain to span the Orontes River before there was a bridge. One of the most vivid battle scenes in all of Hebrew literature is described in 3:1-7. Nineveh was likened to a harlot, a favorite metaphor of the biblical prophets. Nineveh's "shame" (3:5) consisted of treachery against other peoples and nations. The exposure of one's nakedness (3:5) was a great humiliation and often served as the punishment for adultery (cf. Ezek. 16:37-41).

3:8-19 Certain Captivity: God Shows No Partiality

In Nahum 3:8-15 the prophet provided Nineveh with a historical illustration of No Amon (lit., "the city of Amon"), later known as Thebes. The city was the capital of Upper Egypt during the time of the new kingdom (1580–1085 B.C.). It was situated on the Nile and was noted for its fine temples, royal palaces, and great strength. In many ways it was much like Nineveh. Yet it fell to the Assyrians in 663 B.C., and Nineveh too would fall. Thebes had powerful alliances with the neighboring nations of the Ethiopians to the south, "Put "(3:9), identified with Somalia, and "Libya" (3:11; "Lubim," NASB), probably a reference to Libya in North Africa. The cruelties mentioned in 3:10 were customary in ancient warfare (cf. 2 Kings 8:12; Ps. 137:7-9).

A similar fate ("You too") was to overtake Nineveh (Nah. 3:11-19). The people of Nineveh would be like "women" (3:13), that is, unprepared militarily to defend the city. With a note of satire, Nahum invited the city to prepare for siege (3:14). The "shepherds" (3:18) were the leaders of the Assyrian Empire who were dead ("lie still," Ps. 76:6; "sleeping," NASB). Nineveh was destroyed in 612 B.C. and disappeared from history until the rediscovery of the site by British excavators in A.D. 1846.

Habakkuk

BASIC FACTS

HISTORICAL SETTING
The people of Israel had persisted in telling God no even though for hundreds of years he had been asking them to obey. Now God was using two giant world powers to discipline his people. The great nation of Assyria had already lopped off the northern half of the nation in 722 B.C., and God was bringing the greater nation of Babylon down to finish the job by destroying the southern half. In 605 B.C. Babylonia had just destroyed the Egyptian armies that had marched north of Israel to try to stop the southward advance of the Babylonians. Although the exact setting of Habakkuk's ministry is uncertain, he probably ministered in the times of kings Josiah, Jehoahaz, and Jehoiakim (640–597 B.C.).

AUTHOR
The name "Habakkuk" means "embrace" or "embracer." Little is known about the author except that he lived and ministered during the last days of the southern kingdom of Judah just before the first Babylonian attack on Jerusalem in 605 B.C.

DATE
The book of Habakkuk has been dated by conservative scholars in the reigns of Manasseh (697–642 B.C.), Josiah (640–609 B.C.), and Jehoiakim (609–597 B.C.). The only clear historical reference in the book is in Habakkuk 1:6, probably referring to the Chaldeans as an actual threat to Judah in 605 B.C. The ministry of Habakkuk and the composition of the book both took place early in the reign of Jehoiakim, probably around 607–606 B.C.

PURPOSE
The book of Habakkuk provided comfort and hope during one of the darkest periods of Israel's history, a time during which she suffered the deserved punishment for her sins.

GUIDING CONCEPTS

QUESTION-AND-ANSWER STYLE

The book of Habakkuk was written in the form of a question and answer session between Habakkuk and God. The questions of Habakkuk were similar to those asked by most honest seekers of God who see evil that has gone unpunished. These questions reveal to the reader much of the book's content and the direction of its application. The book begins like a lament psalm: "How long?" "I cry out," "Why?" (1:2-3). Then Habakkuk asked another set of questions concerning God's silence in the face of evil (1:13-14). Although God would eventually judge evil, the answer to the questions of "How long?" and "Does he care?" was given in 2:4. The righteous were called to wait and be faithful, even when some questions could not be answered immediately.

BIBLE-WIDE CONCEPTS

This book has been quoted by several New Testament authors. Habakkuk 2:4 was quoted in Romans 1:17, Galatians 3:11, and Hebrews 10:38. Habakkuk 1:5 was quoted in Acts 13:40-41, where the judgment of God on Israel by using the Babylonians was used to illustrate the judgment that God would bring on the world in the day of the Lord.

Habakkuk saw violence among his people (1:2; cf. Gen. 6:11; Job 19:7; Jer. 20:8; Ezek. 45:9) that resulted in neglect of the law (Hab. 1:4). The prophet longed for judgment (1:12) in order to find restoration. The process of judgment followed by restoration found in the book of Habakkuk is central to the entire Bible's teaching of the purpose of judgment on this side of the grave. God judges his people to cause them to repent so that he can restore them.

NEEDS MET BY HABAKKUK

Habakkuk wanted God to end the rampant sin in the nation of Israel. But he faced another crisis when he found out that God was going to use the godless nation of Babylonia to put an end to that sin. Habakkuk spoke to people who desired purity and who also were experiencing God's judgment. The content and structure of Habakkuk's prophecy show that he was answering questions like the following for the people of Israel.

- How long will it be before God will judge sin?
- How can God use a pagan nation to judge and purify his people?
- What are God's people supposed to do during the time of judgment?

Two elements of Habakkuk continue to puzzle and encourage believers today. The first concerns their desire for God to put an end to evil. Believers may think that God is not doing anything about the evil that surrounds them. The second area concerns the conflict that believers have with the means God chooses to punish sin. They may think he is waiting too long or not using the proper methods.

Modern Christians may wonder exactly why Habakkuk had a problem with Babylon being God's instrument of discipline for Israel. From Moses on, God had spoken about military defeat and captivity in a foreign land as the way he would bring discipline to his disobedient people. By what other means could Habakkuk have expected God to bring discipline? Perhaps he expected either plague or drought as more acceptable ways for God to bring discipline. At any rate, Habakkuk could not conceive of a holy God using unholy people to destroy Jerusalem and bring Israel into captivity.

God's holiness is not diminished by his working his will through good and evil alike. On the one hand, it may appear that God is not doing anything about evil. On the other hand, Habakkuk encourages his readers to believe that God, in his own way and time, is doing something about evil and that they must persist in hope and faithful obedience. Habakkuk teaches that even in discipline God is a faithful friend who will enable those who trust in him to bear the pain and come out purified.

OUTLINE OF HABAKKUK

A. LAMENT OF HABAKKUK: WAITING FOR GOD TO SAVE (1:1-4)

B. GOD'S INSTRUMENT OF SALVATION: EXTERNAL FORCE (1:5-11)
    1. God's Answer (1:5-6)
    2. The Chaldeans Described (1:7-11)

C. HABAKKUK'S QUESTION: HOW LONG WILL EVIL BE ALLOWED TO CONTINUE? (1:12–2:1)
    1. Habakkuk's Perplexity (1:12-13)
    2. The Enemy Described (1:14–2:1)

D. GOD'S RESPONSE: SALVATION OF THE RIGHTEOUS AND CERTAINTY OF JUDGMENT (2:2-20)
    1. Certainty of Judgment (2:2-3)
    2. The Destruction of the Proud "Home Builder" (2:4-20)

E. HABAKKUK'S RESPONSE (3:1-19)
    1. Introduction (3:1)
    2. Twofold Response to the Revelation in Habakkuk 1–2 (3:2-19)

HABAKKUK NOTES

1:1-4 LAMENT OF HABAKKUK: WAITING FOR GOD TO SAVE

Habakkuk was perplexed over Judah's unpunished wickedness. He asked, "Why does evil triumph?" "Why doesn't God intervene?" Habakkuk reflected on Judah's wickedness. "How," Habakkuk wondered, "can a holy God look upon such sin with complacency?" The Hebrew word trans- lated "paralyzed" (1:4; "ignored," NASB) literally means "chilled," or "numbed."

1:5-11 GOD'S INSTRUMENT OF SALVATION: EXTERNAL FORCE
1:5-6 God's Answer

The Lord answered Habakkuk's question (cf. 1:2-4) by informing him that Judah would be judged by God through the Babylonians. The

Babylonians ("Kaldu" in the Assyrian annals) were a Semitic people of southern Babylonia. When Nabopolassar, a native Chaldean governor, took the Babylonian throne in 626 B.C., he inaugurated a dynasty that made the "Chaldean" name famous. The word is used in the Bible as a virtual synonym for "Babylonian."

1:7-11 The Chaldeans Described

The Chaldeans or Babylonians were described as a fierce and terrifying people. They were a law unto themselves and were known for taking conquered peoples into captivity. The words "build earthen ramps" (1:10) refer to the practice of placing earth against a city's wall so that the siege equipment could batter down the weaker upper sections. Although the Chaldeans were God's instrument to punish the Judeans, they were held accountable for their excessive violence against Judah (1:11; cf. Zech. 1:15). Divine sovereignty does not annul human responsibility.

1:12–2:1 HABAKKUK'S QUESTION: HOW LONG WILL EVIL BE ALLOWED TO CONTINUE?

1:12-13 Habakkuk's Perplexity

Habakkuk expressed his perplexity that God could use such a wicked instrument as the Chaldeans to punish a people more righteous than they. How could this be consistent with God's holy character? The words "we will not die" (Hab. 1:12) must be grounded on Habakkuk's confidence in God's unchangable purposes (cf. Gen. 12:1-3; 2 Sam. 7:12-16). Because God is too pure to regard iniquity, how could he look with apparent favor on the treacherous Chaldeans?

1:14–2:1 The Enemy Described

In Habakkuk 1:14-17 the prophet described the Chaldeans as fishermen who used every means ("hook" and "net") to capture the helpless Hebrews ("fish in the sea," 1:14). The "sacrifices to his net" (1:16) may have referred to sacrifices to their weapons of war as was practiced by the Scythians, who offered a yearly sacrifice to a curved sword, the symbol of the war god Ares. Like a watchman on a city wall, Habakkuk waited patiently for God's reply or correction (2:1).

2:2-20 GOD'S RESPONSE: SALVATION OF THE RIGHTEOUS AND CERTAINTY OF JUDGMENT

2:2-3 Certainty of Judgment

In response to Habakkuk's perplexity, the Lord set forth the principle of divine recompense. Habakkuk 2:2 may have referred to announcing the message or to living obediently in response to the divine revelation. Three assurances were given that the promise of God would certainly come to pass (2:3).

2:4-20 The Destruction of the Proud "Home Builder"

2:4-5 THE BASIC INSIGHT

"Puffed up" (2:4) referred to the Chaldeans whose arrogance had already been alluded to (1:10-11). Such were destined for destruction. The "righteous" (2:4) referred to the godly of Judah in contrast to the proud and wicked Chaldeans. The "righteous" shall "live," that is, "prosper and be blessed." The words "by his faith" referred to the godly person's deep reliance upon God.

The New Testament quoted this reference (2:4) three times (cf. Rom. 1:17; Gal. 3:11; Heb. 10:38). Habakkuk emphasized that the righteous man would live. Paul emphasized that the righteous man ("the just," KJV) would live by faith. Habakkuk 2:5 was a transitional verse in which the Chaldeans were further described. The "grave" (2:5; "Sheol," NASB; "Hell," KJV) was a reference to the grave, the place of the dead.

2:6-8 THE OPPRESSORS BECOME THE OPPRESSED

Habakkuk concluded this section of the book with a taunt song against the Chaldean oppressor. Five woes were pronounced. In the first woe, the victims of injustice ("all of them," 2:6) were to take up a taunt song against the wicked Chaldeans.

2:9-11 THE HOUSE CRIES FOR VENGEANCE

In the second woe, destruction is predicted for all those who gained power and wealth unjustly. To "set his nest on high" (2:9) was to build a seemingly secure and invulnerable home (cf. Obad. 1:4).

2:12-14 DESTRUCTION DISPLAYS GOD'S GLORY

In the third woe, punishment is promised for the unjust and God's glory is foreseen. The "glory of the Lord" spoken of in Habakkuk 2:14 was prophetic and looked to the Messianic kingdom for fulfillment. This prophecy is found five times in the Old Testament (cf. Num. 14:21; Ps. 72:19; Isa. 6:3; 11:9).

2:15-17 DRINKING FROM GOD'S CUP OF WRATH

In the fourth woe, disaster was predicted for those who did shameless deeds. The "violence you have done to Lebanon" (Hab. 2:17) referred to the destruction of trees and cattle in the mountainous region north of Galilee (cf. Isa. 14:7-8).

2:18-20 POWERLESS NATIONAL GODS

In the fifth woe, the makers of idols were called to account. In contrast with the impotent idols, the Lord of heaven was about to execute judgment. The earth was to keep silent—a hushed expectancy of imminent judgment (cf. Zeph. 1:7; Zech. 2:13; Rev. 8:1).

3:1-19 HABAKKUK'S RESPONSE
3:1 Introduction

The response of 3:1 was a model for the proper view of the nation's downfall. Habakkuk concluded with a prayer that would be set to music and was to be used in worship (cf. 3:19). The term "shigionoth" (3:1) was a musical signal that indicated its usage as a song and may have indicated more specifically that it was "an irregular or wandering song."

3:2-19 Twofold Response to the Revelation in Habakkuk 1–2

3:2 REQUEST FOR WRATH AND MERCY

Habakkuk prayed that God would put into effect his program of judgment on Judah and then on Babylon. But he asked that in executing judgment, God would temper his wrath with mercy. The word "mercy" (3:2; lit., "womb") refers to a motherly sense of compassion and pity.

3:3-15 GOD'S WAR FOR HIS PEOPLE'S SALVATION

Habakkuk 3:3-15 described an appearance of God to the prophet. God approached from "Paran" (northwest of Mount Sinai) and "Teman" (a city of importance in Edom). Even in the greatest of God's displays in nature, his full power is hidden (3:4, "his power was hidden"). Cushan (3:7) was a neighbor of Midian in the Sinai Peninsula.

The rhetorical questions of 3:8 ask whether or not God was angry at his creation. The implied answer is "No, this is the exercise of his wrath against the wicked nations." As the prophet prayed (3:2), the Lord remembered mercy (3:13). He went forth as a divine warrior to deliver his people. This forms an answer to Habakkuk's opening question in 1:2.

3:16-19 DESCRIPTION OF THE FRUIT OF FAITH

The "nation invading us" (3:16) referred to the Chaldeans who invaded Judah in 605 B.C. after Nebuchadnezzar defeated Egypt at the battle of Carchemish. In 3:17-19 Habakkuk expressed his quiet trust in the Lord's sovereign purposes. Although judgment would come to Judah (3:17), Habakkuk determined to rejoice in the Lord (3:18), for the One who led his people into trial would enable them to bear it (3:19).

Zephaniah

BASIC FACTS

HISTORICAL SETTING
The spiritual condition of the kingdom of Judah progressively worsened from the death of Hezekiah (728–686 B.C.) until the reign of Josiah (612 B.C.). Josiah was the greatest of the reformers of Judah. In 627 B.C. he began religious reform in Judah and Jerusalem (cf. 2 Chron. 34:3). This great era of reform was influenced by the ministries of the prophets Zephaniah, Jeremiah, and Nahum. During this period Judah was free from foreign intervention but was facing a rapid Babylonian expansion. The prophecy of Zephaniah was an announcement of judgment on Judah in particular and the world in general. It is most probable that the threat of the Babylonian invasion provided the political background for the prophecy.

AUTHOR
Zephaniah's ancestry was traced back four generations to show the prophet's relationship with Hezekiah, who was inferred to be King Hezekiah of Judah (Zeph. 1:1). Therefore, Zephaniah was a prophet of royal blood and a distant relative of Josiah, the king under whose reign he prophesied. Zephaniah apparently lived in Jerusalem (1:4, 10-11) and may have been influential in stirring Josiah to his reforms (cf. 2 Chron. 34:1-7). The prophet's contemporaries included Nahum and Jeremiah.

DATE
Zephaniah ministered in the days of Josiah (640–609 B.C.). The moral and religious conditions described by Zephaniah (1:3-6, 8-9, 12; 3:1-7) indicate that the prophecy was given before Josiah's reforms while the spiritual condition of Judah was still low as a result of the evil reigns of Manasseh and Amon. The book should be dated between 640 and 621 B.C.

PURPOSE
The book of Zephaniah was designed to warn of the impending universal judgment of the day of the Lord and to call the remnant of God's people to repent (2:3) and be protected.

GUIDING CONCEPTS

THE DAY OF THE LORD
Zephaniah has much to say about the day of the Lord (1:7-8, 10, 12, 14, 18; 2:2; 3:8, 11, 16, 20). The message elaborated on the judgment that would take place as well as the purifying and redeeming effect the day of the Lord would have on the righteous remnant (1:4; 2:7, 9; 3:9, 12-13, 19-20). Until that time of restoration, Zephaniah gave several explicit commands to the remnant (1:7; 2:1, 3; 3:8, 14).

BIBLE-WIDE CONCEPTS

The message began with images that reached back to the flood of Noah's day (1:2-3). Compare the same terms in 1:2-3 with Genesis 6:7. The focus was on Judah, but the message related to a global judgment (Zeph. 1:2).

The words "humble" (2:3; 3:12), "humility" (2:3), and "meek" (3:12) described those who would survive the coming judgment (cf. Hab. 3:2; Matt. 3:7). Those descriptions were taken up by Jesus as he described those who are blessed (Matt. 5:3, 5). Another phrase concerning the lame and the outcast (Zeph. 3:19) had its significance expanded as Jesus healed those who were both physically and spiritually lame or outcast. That humble remnant is a group that suffers, either justly or unjustly, but comes out at the end as faithful and committed to God's ways.

The nations (2:4) were again drawn within God's plans for Israel. God told Abraham that he would bless those who blessed Israel and curse those who cursed Israel. In 2:8, 10, God carried out that promise. All nations would bring homage to the God of Israel as a result of his acts of judgment (2:11; cf. Phil. 2:9-11). Jesus expanded the teachings of the day of the Lord in his Olivet discourse (Matt. 24:1–25:46; Luke 21:10-36). The nations functioned as a witness of God's wrath and restoration (Zeph. 3:9).

NEEDS MET BY ZEPHANIAH

Zephaniah's audience was about to experience the most severe judgment in Israel's history. It was too late to avert it and there was no way out. At this point, even repentance could not stop national destruction. But when God's holiness finally caused his long-suffering to end and his judgment to begin, his people always seemed to misunderstand what was going on. The judgment came as a shock, even though the prophets had warned of it for years. So, before judgment fell, Zephaniah's hearers needed to understand the cause of and purpose for their judgment. Zephaniah helped the people of Israel to understand why they were about to be judged (for their own personal sin), what the purpose was (personal purity), and what it implied about the character of God (that he was holy and loving). The fears of the righteous people of God were addressed in full view of the coming day of the Lord. The content and structure of Zephaniah's prophecy show that he answered questions like the following for the people of Israel.

- If the day of the Lord is coming soon can the judgment still be avoided?
- What will happen to the people who are righteous?
- What will happen to God's enemies?

Unlike the people of Zephaniah's day, believers today have no certain word that their nation is going to be destroyed by God's judgment. But they do know that his condemnation of Israel's sins falls equally on any present nation's sins. Believers also know that the day of the Lord still lies ahead for the just and unjust alike. And for God's people, Zephaniah's calls to repentance and assertion of the purifying effect of the day of the Lord are as pointed today as they were in his own time. Believers need to respond to the pictures of God's jealousy, vengeance, and holiness with humility and consistent commitment.

OUTLINE OF ZEPHANIAH

A. SENTENCE AND ACCUSATION: TOTAL DESTRUCTION (1:1-6)
B. THE DAY OF GOD: IMMINENT (1:7-18)
    1. Focus on Jerusalem's Inhabitants (1:7-13)
    2. Focus on International Destruction (1:14-18)
C. GATHER AND SEEK: ALL THE HUMBLE OF THE LAND (2:1-15)
    1. Plea for Repentance (2:1-3)
    2. Repent in the Light of International Devastation (2:4-15)
D. WOE SPEECH: WAIT THROUGH DESTRUCTION FOR RESTORATION
    (3:1-20)
    1. Unheeded Admonitions (3:1-7)
    2. Words for the Faithful Remnant (3:8-20)

ZEPHANIAH NOTES

1:1-6 SENTENCE AND ACCUSATION: TOTAL DESTRUCTION

The name "Zephaniah" means "Yahweh hides" or "hidden of Yahweh," and suggests that God hides or protects those who belong to him. The prophecy began with a declaration of universal judgment (Zeph. 1:2-3). This judgment was virtually a reversal of God's work at the creation of the world. The word "rubble" (1:3) is used elsewhere to describe idols (cf. Ezek. 14:3). Zephaniah set forth the reason for God's judgment on Judah (Zeph. 1:4-6). Baal was the Canaanite god of fertility whose worship involved sexual rites. The worship of heavenly bodies (forbidden by Deut. 4:19; 17:3) was practiced by the Assyrians and Babylonians and became common among the idolaters of Judah (Jer. 19:13; Ezek. 8:16). "Molech" (1:5; "Milcom" NASB; "Malcham," KJV) was the chief deity of the Ammonites (see 1 Kings 11:5).

1:7-18 THE DAY OF GOD: IMMINENT
1:7-13 Focus on Jerusalem's Inhabitants

The "day of the LORD" is that period during which God will deal with his people through judgment or deliverance. The "day of the LORD" can refer to an event in past history or future prophecy. Here Zephaniah used it to refer to the coming "sacrifice" (Zeph. 1:7) of Judah to the army of Babylon. Those who clothed themselves in "foreign clothes" (1:8) were the wealthy rulers who had taken on pagan customs and values. To step "on the threshold" (1:9) was a practice of the Philistine priests (cf. 1 Sam. 5:5). Zephaniah 1:10 pictured the Babylonian enemy coming into the city from the north and occupying the prominent positions of the city ("the hills"). The "Fish Gate" was in the northern wall (cf. Neh. 3:3; 12:39), which gave access to the "New Quarter" (2 Kings 22:14; "Second Quarter," NASB). The "market district" (Zeph. 1:11) is thought to have been a section of Jerusalem possibly located in the Tyropoean Valley. The expression "complacent" people (1:12) referred to those who were self-satisfied and apathetic in regard to their character or circumstances.

1:14-18 Focus on International Destruction

The Babylonian attack on Jerusalem was a portent of the universal judgment ("the whole world," 1:18) that the eschatological day of the Lord will bring. Compare this description of judgment with the description in 2 Peter 3:10.

2:1-15 GATHER AND SEEK: ALL THE HUMBLE OF THE LAND
2:1-3 Plea for Repentance

Judah, the "shameful nation," was called to repent and thus escape God's wrath. The "appointed time" referred to the divinely determined judgment on Judah by the Babylonians (Zeph. 1:8-13). The Hebrew word used in the expression "Perhaps you will be sheltered" (2:3) is a close synonym to the Hebrew word that forms the prophet's name, Zephaniah, "Hidden of Yahweh."

2:4-15 Repent in the Light of International Devastation

2:4-7 PHILISTINE DESTRUCTION BRINGS JUDAH'S RESTORATION

Zephaniah focused on the historical day of the Lord that was experienced by the Gentile nations that had persecuted God's people. Philistia was one of the Gentile nations in line for God's judgment. The Philistines migrated from the Aegean Islands and Asia Minor under the pressure of the Dorian Greeks. Repulsed by Egypt, these people settled on the coastal plains of Israel and became a formidable enemy.

Gaza, Ashkelon, Ashdod, and Ekron were all major Philistine cities (cf. 1 Sam. 6:17). They were subdued by Nebuchadnezzar in

586 B.C. The Kerethites (Zeph. 2:5) were a subgroup of the Philistines that came from Crete (cf. Amos 9:7). A remnant of Judah would inherit the Philistine coastal plain after the return from exile (Zeph. 2:7). Ultimate fulfillment of these prophecies would be realized in the Messianic kingdom.

2:8-10 MOAB AND AMMON DESTROYED BY THE REMNANT

The nations of Moab and Ammon had long been enemies of the Israelites and they too would suffer judgment. Moab and Ammon were treated together because they were both located east of Judah and shared a common ancestor, Lot (cf. Gen. 19:36-38). The "salt pits" (Zeph. 2:9) referred to evaporation pits into which Dead Sea water was channeled for the purpose of extracting salt.

2:11 TRANSITION VERSE: GOD DOES ALL THIS

To destroy "all the gods" referred to the pagan idols being deprived of sacrifices by which they were thought to be fed.

2:12-15 ETHIOPIA AND ASSYRIA DESTROYED

2:12 Judgment on Ethiopia. Since Ethiopia (Cush) ruled Egypt from about 720 to 654 B.C. and its fortunes were bound up with those of Egypt, it is probable that the reference to to the "Cushites" ("Ethiopians," NASB and KJV) was a general reference to Egypt and its allies. The prophecy may have been fulfilled with Nebuchadnezzar's punitive invasion of Egypt in 568 B.C.

2:13-15 Judgment on Assyria. The destruction of Assyria and its capital, Nineveh (2:13), was given fuller treatment in the prophecy of Nahum. Nineveh fell to the combined forces of the Babylonians and the Medes in 612 B.C.

3:1-20 WOE SPEECH: WAIT THROUGH DESTRUCTION FOR RESTORATION
3:1-7 Unheeded Admonitions

Despite the fact that Jerusalem was special in God's plan for man's redemption, her people would suffer judgment because they would not repent of their sin. Although the city was not mentioned by name, it is quite apparent from the context that Jerusalem, the capital of the southern kingdom, was meant. Four classes of national leaders were singled out for condemnation (3:3-4).

3:8-20 Words for the Faithful Remnant

3:8-13 CLEANSED OF REBELLION WITHIN Zephaniah announced the universal judgment on the nations in the eschatological day of the Lord. Contextually, it seems that this judgment will be realized during the future tribulation and Christ's second advent. The destruction of "the whole world" by "fire" may suggest the purging of the heavens and earth (cf. 2 Pet. 3:10-13). The phrase "purify the lips" (Zeph. 3:9) does not mean that they will worship God with the Hebrew language, but with lips uncontaminated by the mention of idols. God's people Israel will become this spiritual people when they see their Messiah and repent (cf. Zech. 12:10–13:1).

3:14-20 CLEANSED FROM ALL ENEMIES In Zephaniah 3:15-17 the Lord is pictured with his people as a present King (3:15), a protective warrior (3:16-17), and a rejoicing bridegroom (3:17).

Haggai

BASIC FACTS

HISTORICAL SETTING

In 539 B.C. Babylon fell to the armies of Persia, and soon afterward (538 B.C.) Cyrus gave permission to the Jews to return to their homeland and renew their worship of God in Jerusalem (Ezra 1:1-4). In 537 B.C. a group of Jews returned under the leadership of the prince of Judah, Sheshbazzar (Ezra 1:8). The foundation of the temple was laid during the second year of their return (Ezra 3:8-13; 536 B.C.), but the builders soon met with opposition. The Samaritans to the north requested to participate in the temple's construction, but they were refused by Zerubbabel and the leaders of the people (Ezra 4:1-3). The Samaritans then discouraged the builders through false counselors (Ezra 4:4-5) and the temple's construction was halted (Ezra 4:24).

It was not until the second year of Darius I that Haggai and Zechariah appeared and encouraged the people to rise up and rebuild the temple (Ezra 5:1-2; 520 B.C.). The work again met with opposition (Ezra 5:3), but the opposition was overcome by the decree of Darius (Ezra 6:8-12) and the temple was completed in 515 B.C. (Ezra 6:13-22).

Haggai ministered during a period characterized by spiritual indifference. The people of Judah were procrastinating concerning their religious duties (Hag. 1:2) and were occupied with their personal interests (1:4, 9). Because of this sinful attitude the people were not experiencing God's blessing (1:6, 10-11). Although they were engaging in some degree of worship, their sacrifices were regarded as unclean because of their sinful attitude (2:14). Haggai exhorted the Jews of that day to observe their spiritual priorities if they were to enjoy material prosperity and divine blessing.

AUTHOR

Haggai was the first of the three postexilic prophets. His ministry to the Jews of Jerusalem is referred to in Ezra 5:1-2 and 6:14. Both Haggai and his contemporary, Zechariah, had great influence in encouraging the Jews to rebuild the temple. Haggai was probably born in Babylon and returned to Judah with the first contingent of Jews under Sheshbazzar (Ezra 5:14) in 537 B.C.

DATE

The book of Haggai may be dated in the reign of Darius, who ruled Persia from 522 to 486 B.C. Haggai's first message was delivered on the first of Elul (August–September) in the second year of Darius (520 B.C.). The last of the four messages came on the twenty-fourth of Kislev (November–December) in the same year. All four messages were given within a period of about four months during the year 520 B.C.

PURPOSE

The book of Haggai was designed to stimulate the lethargic leaders and people of Judah to recognize their spiritual responsibilities and rebuild the temple. Renewed devotion to God would overcome the problems of drought and economic depression.

GUIDING CONCEPTS

STRUCTURE

Several dates given in the book of Haggai (1:1, 15; 2:1, 10, 20) keep the reader's attention focused on the contemporary historical context and the rebuilding of the temple. The prophetic message called the people to consider their ways (1:5, 7). God also made several statements about himself: "I am with you" (1:13; 2:4-5), "I will shake" (2:6-7), "I will grant peace" (2:9), and "I will make you [Zerubbabel] like my signet ring" (2:23). The means of moving from judgment to blessing was by showing obedience to the king, priest, and people. And that call to obedience (1:12) is placed between the sections on judgment (1:1-11) and blessing (2:1-23).

Portions of the book also parallel each other (cf. 1:1-15 with 2:10-19, concerning poor crops; God shaking the nations to bring wealth for the temple (2:1-9); and glory for the ruler (2:20-23). Note the repetition of "Zerubbabel," "Joshua," and "remnant" or "people of the land" (1:12, 14; 2:2, 4). Haggai tried to encourage the postexilic people with promises for the present and future.

BIBLE-WIDE CONCEPTS

THE REMNANT

Haggai spoke to the remnant that had returned from exile. It was a living fulfillment of Isaiah's son Shear-Jashub, whose name meant "a remnant shall return" (cf. Isa. 6:11-13; 7:3; 10:21; 11:11). Although God had fulfilled his promise of return, the nation was still obligated to obey him. The true nature of the release from captivity was a return to God, not simply to a land (Hag. 2:17; cf. Amos 4:9). Restoration did not do away with the need for obedience or for a relationship with God.

PRESENCE AND SPIRIT

God's phrase "I am with you" finds its greater fulfillment in Matthew 28:20 and Revelation 21:3. The powers of the heavens will be shaken in the day of the Lord (Hag. 2:6; cf. Matt. 24:29; Luke 21:26; Heb. 12:26).

The thrice-repeated "stirred up the spirit of" (Hag. 1:14) takes its place in the Bible-wide presentation of God stirring up people's spirits to do his will (cf. Exod. 36:1-2; 1 Chron 5:26; 2 Chron. 21:16; 36:22; Ezra 1:5).

ENRICHING GOD'S PEOPLE

The first part of Haggai 2 took place during the seventh month (Hag. 2:1-9). For Israel that month contained the Feast of Trumpets on the first day, the Day of Atonement on the tenth day, and the Feast of Tabernacles from the fifteenth to the twenty-third day. The Feast of Tabernacles celebrated Israel's exodus from Egypt and God's tender care for them in the wilderness. During the Feast of Tabernacles (the twenty-first day, 2:1) the Lord paralleled Israel's present postexilic state with Israel when she first came out of Egypt (2:5-6). As God had shaken Egypt and given wealth to his people (cf. Exod. 12:35-36), so he would also shake the world to restore Israel and her king to great prosperity.

THE HOPE FOR A KING FROM DAVID'S LINE

Clearly, the hope for a king in David's line ends the book (Hag. 2:20-23). The king will sit with international authority (cf. Jer. 22:24, for the king as God's signet ring). The shaking of the heavens and earth spoken of here was the foundation for later theological developments such as the role of the Spirit in stirring up his people to action (Hag. 1:12-15); the greater glory for the temple (2:1-9); a great blessing because of the renewed temple (2:10-19); and a greater king on the throne (2:20-23).

NEEDS MET BY HAGGAI

Haggai's hearers needed to understand the cause and effect relationship between their sin and their problems like drought, national economic depression, and personal lack of money. They had problems because they put their own interests before God's. They needed to understand the high priority of commitment to rebuilding God's temple. And all of that was in the face of not having learned God's intended lessons from the discipline of seventy years of captivity in Babylon. True, they no longer had a problem with worshiping pagan idols. But they simply moved on to another form of idolatry—putting personal comfort over advancing the kingdom of God. Once again, the slow coming of God's promises became a potential trap for discouragement and diversion of their commitment to God. They needed to understand that no matter how long God took to fulfill all his promises, they had to remain sharp in their obedience. The structure and content of Haggai's prophecy show that the people of Israel were probably struggling with questions like these.

- Why do those of God's people who returned from exile not have enough food and money?
- Is rebuilding a temple, which will be much less beautiful than Solomon's temple, really that important now that God's people are back from exile?
- Is the small rebuilt temple all that Israel has to show for the great promises that God made to Abraham, Moses, and David?
- Why doesn't Israel's restoration look as great as the prophets made it out to be?
- Will there be another, greater restoration sometime in the future?

Christians today are not faced with rebuilding God's temple after a period of seventy years of captivity. The lands and economies of modern believers are not experiencing drought and depression because they have not rebuilt God's city and temple. But in Haggai the hearers were encouraged to rebuild the temple, small though it was compared to Solomon's temple, as a sign of their commitment to the law of God and to his greater future temple. The people's present commitment to God was a token of their faith in and hope for the future final and glorious presence of God on earth. God's presence with his people was typified by the temple but realized in the real presence of God in Christ and in his Spirit. For the Christian, Haggai's mention of agricultural or financial troubles being remedied by commitment to God's temple do not need to be spiritualized into modern economic principles of success. The issue for God's people then and now is commitment to God's manner of presence—in the temple back then and in the Holy Spirit now.

OUTLINE OF HAGGAI

A. THE FIRST MESSAGE: AN EXHORTATION TO REBUILD (1:1-15)
    1. A Call to Consider: Rationale for Rebuilding (1:1-11)
    2. Building Commenced: Stirred up by the Spirit (1:12-15)

B. ASSURANCE IN REBUILDING (2:1-23)
    1. The Second Message: Wealth for the New Temple (2:1-9)
    2. The Third Message: Prosperity for the Land (2:10-19)
    3. The Fourth Message: Prominence for the Ruler (2:20-23)

HAGGAI NOTES

1:1-15 THE FIRST MESSAGE: AN EXHORTATION TO REBUILD
1:1-11 A Call to Consider: Rationale for Rebuilding

1:1-2 THE FACT OF PROCRASTINATION
The "second year" (1:1) of Darius (522–486 B.C) corresponds with 520 B.C. The "sixth" (1:1) month was Elul (August–September). The name "Haggai" means "festal" or "my feast," suggesting that he may have been born on some festal occasion. "Zerubbabel" apparently succeeded Sheshbazzar as governor of Judah (see the note on Ezra 1:8). Joshua, known by the name "Jeshua" in Ezra and Nehemiah, was the son of Jehozadak, who was high priest at the time of the Babylonian invasion (cf. 1 Chron. 6:15). The foundation of the temple was laid in 536 B.C. (cf. Ezra 3:1-10), but for fifteen years

the people procrastinated, being content with just a foundation and altar.

1:3-4 QUESTIONS OF MOTIVATION
The first message was an exhortation to rebuild. Instead of focusing on the priority of the temple, the people were busy building their own luxury ("paneled") homes (Hag. 1:3). Good things had crowded out the best. They had allowed concern for their own comfort to get in the way of doing the work God had for them to do.

1:5-6 CONSIDER:
YOU DO NOT HAVE ENOUGH
The exhortation "Give careful thought to your ways" (1:5; "Consider your ways," NASB) suggests that the people were to reflect on their activities and the results that would come about because of those activities. The fruitless expenditures and disappointed

expectations seen in Haggai 1:6 reflected the chastening of the Lord.

1:7-11 CONSIDER:
THE REASON FOR YOUR LACK
The meager harvest was traced to the neglect of the temple (1:9). Drought and famine were instruments of God's wrath that were intended to turn his people back to himself (1:10-11; cf. Lev. 26:19-20).

1:12-15 Building Commenced: Stirred up by the Spirit
The people responded wholeheartedly to Haggai's exhortation. The "remnant of the people" (1:12) was a reference to those who had returned to Judah from the Babylonian captivity (cf. Isa. 6:11-13; 7:3; 10:21; 11:11). Twenty-three days had passed since the message (Hag. 1:2-11) was declared by Haggai. Note the repetition of the words "Zerubbabel," "Joshua," and "remnant" or "people of the land" (1:12, 14; 2:2, 4). The future was great for the obedient prince, priest, and purified people. The Lord stirred up the spirits of Zerubbabel, Joshua, and the remnant (1:14). This stirring up of Israel's leaders ends a section that began with 1:1, when Haggai first brought them the "word of the Lord" (cf. also Exod. 36:1-2; 1 Chron. 5:26; 2 Chron. 21:16; 36:22; Ezra 1:5).

2:1-23 ASSURANCE IN REBUILDING
2:1-9 The Second Message: Wealth for the New Temple
The second message (2:1-9) was a word of encouragement to the remnant of Israel. The date of the second message was the twenty-first of "the seventh month," known as "Tishri" (September–October). This was a busy day in a busy month on the Jewish religious calendar. The Feast of Trumpets was observed on the first day, the Day of Atonement on the tenth day, and the Feast of Tabernacles on the fifteenth through twenty-first days.

There were those among the community of the returned exiles who had seen the Jerusalem temple before its destruction by the Babylonians (Hag. 2:3). They compared the past glories of Solomon's temple with the present realities of the restoration temple and became quite discouraged. According to Jewish tradition, missing

from the second temple were: the Ark of the Covenant, the Urim and Thummim, the holy fire, the Shekinah, and the Holy Spirit (Babylonian Talmud, Yoma 21b).

The people were reflecting on what was missing, not on what they had. Haggai encouraged the people with a promise of God's personal presence. The shaking of the "heavens" and the "nations" (Hag. 2:6-7) probably referred to God's future intervention into the affairs of men whereby he would overthrow earthly kingdoms in preparation for the establishment of the Messianic kingdom. These words were quoted by the writer of Hebrews (Heb. 12:26-27) in connection with Christ's second advent.

The rabbis and church fathers have taken the well-known translation "the desired of all nations" to refer to the Messiah (Hag. 2:7). The "glory of this present house" (2:9) may refer to the second temple refurbished by Herod the Great, or to the Messianic temple (cf. Ezek. 40–43). The promise of "peace" (2:9; cf. Isa. 9:6-7) would suggest the Messianic interpretation.

2:10-19 The Third Message: Prosperity for the Land
The third message (2:10-19), a promise of blessing and restoration, was given in the "ninth" month, Kislev (November–December). Haggai used an illustration to explain the absence of God's blessing in past years (Hag. 2:11-14). Holiness could not be transmitted by mere contact with holy things. However, defilement could be transmitted by personal contact (cf. Num. 19:11-13). The application is in Haggai 2:14. Judah's disobedience brought defilement and rendered even sacrificial worship unacceptable. The words "this people" (2:14) referred to the Judeans and contain a note of censure.

In 2:15-19 Haggai compared the past problems with the future possibilities. The Hebrew term for the words "this day on" (2:15) is better translated "backward." Haggai wanted the people to look back to past chastening (2:16-17) before they began to obey and rebuild the temple ("one stone was laid on another," 2:15). In 2:19 Haggai looked to God's future blessing of the repentant people.

2:20-23 The Fourth Message: Prominence for the Ruler

The fourth message, a Messianic prophecy, looked forward to a righteous ruler who would bring peace and prosperity to Israel. This message was given on the same day as the third message. The Persian Empire was quite unstable at this time. What was the future of Israel in this insecure situation? God promised to overthrow and destroy the Gentile world powers and preserve Israel.

The "signet ring" (2:23) was used to make the mark of its owner on a document or clay tablet. It reflected authority and was to be guarded and preserved. God promised that Zerubbabel would be his signet, or representative authority to the people. The promise related primarily to Zerubbabel's dynasty. His family line would be honored and preserved and through Zerubbabel's lineage would come Jesus the Messiah (cf. Matt. 1:12; Luke 3:27).

Zechariah

HISTORICAL SETTING

The Jews had returned from captivity in Babylon to their homeland in 537 B.C. The temple's foundations had been laid in 536 B.C. (Ezra 3:10), but the construction had ceased because of opposition from the Samaritans (cf. Ezra 4:1-5). For sixteen years the temple building was neglected by the selfish returned exiles who did not recognize their spiritual priorities (cf. Hag. 1:4). Throughout the ministries of Haggai and Zechariah the people were encouraged to rise up and rebuild the temple (cf. Ezra 5:1-2).

The prophet saw Greece as a menace to the Persian Empire, and the prophecy fits well into Zechariah's day. From 520 B.C. onward the Greeks of Asia Minor were a continual source of trouble for Darius, and in 500 B.C. the great Ionian revolt occurred. By 490 B.C. Darius had stamped out the Ionian uprising, but the Persians were later defeated at Marathon (490 B.C.) and Salamis (480 B.C.). This was a time of insecurity in the Persian Empire.

AUTHOR

Zechariah was the grandson of Iddo, who was one of the heads of the priestly families that returned to Judah after the exile (cf. Neh. 12:4). A contemporary with Haggai, he was influential in encouraging the people of Judah to rise up and rebuild the temple (cf. Ezra 5:1-2; 6:14). Zechariah seemed to have succeeded his grandfather, Iddo, as head of the priestly family (Neh. 12:12-16), from which it may be inferred that his father, Berekiah (Zech. 1:1), died before he was able to succeed to the priesthood. Zechariah is generally considered to have been a young man when he received the visions of Zechariah 1–7 (cf. 2:4). He entered his prophetic ministry two months after Haggai concluded his first oracle.

Some believe that Zechariah 9–14 was not original to Zechariah and contains anonymous prophecies from a later period. These arguments are based on what some see as different styles and vocabularies. However, the prophetic end-time thrust of this section, and a time period of about twenty years between the giving of the two main sections of the book, may well account for such differences. It was accepted early as part of Zechariah's prophecy, since no Hebrew manuscripts have been discovered with this section of Zechariah missing.

DATE

Zechariah began his ministry in the second year of Darius (522–486 B.C.) in 520 B.C. His last dated prophecy (7:1) was two years later on the fourth day of Kislev (November–December) in 518 B.C. The latter chapters of the prophecy (Zech. 9–14) appear to have been composed sometime later, possibly around 500 B.C., in view of the reference to Greece (9:13). The book of Zechariah was thus composed between 520 and 500 B.C.

PURPOSE

The book of Zechariah was designed to provide a detailed picture of God's future dealings with his chosen people. Zechariah 1–8 demanded the ethical responsibility of the people, while Zechariah 9–14 moved on to revive the hopes of the obedient. The believers needed to turn from their sins. The book comforted and encouraged the remnant by revealing future glories, the overthrow of Israel's enemies, and the universal reign of the Messiah. They had undergone an immense amount of suffering, but if they expected future blessings from God they would have to reform their civil and religious practices.

GUIDING CONCEPTS

The two major concepts that controlled the book were the necessity of a functioning temple and the return of the people's hearts and actions to the conditions of the Mosaic covenant. All the various visions of hope and judgment were centered on those two concepts. Zechariah 1–8 contains a series of visions designed to encourage personal repentance and reconstruction of the temple. Zechariah 9–14 moved away from the specifics of Zechariah's day and looked to the furious struggles of the end times. Evil did its worst but, in the end, God remained the victorious King.

BIBLE-WIDE CONCEPTS

Zechariah taught a great deal concerning the first and second comings of the Messiah. He referred to the Messiah as God's servant (3:8), the Branch, the stone (3:9), and the shepherd (13:7). Concerning the first coming of Christ, Zechariah prophesied his entrance into Jerusalem on a colt (9:9), his rejection by Israel (11:1-17), his betrayal for thirty pieces of silver (11:12-13), the piercing of his hands and feet (12:10), and his work on the cross (13:1).

Concerning the Messiah's second coming, Zechariah prophesied the conversion of Israel (13:1-9), the destruction of Israel's enemies by the Messiah (14:3, 12-15), the restoration of Jerusalem (14:8-11, 16-21), and the reign of the promised Messiah from Zion (14:9). The prophecy of Zechariah contains one of the most outstanding passages in the Old Testament concerning the removal of sin and imputation of righteousness (3:1-5).

NEEDS MET BY ZECHARIAH

In Zechariah's day, even though the Jews had been restored from captivity they were still under foreign domination. The promises of God's unhindered worldwide reign seemed as far off as ever. Added to that, God's people were still entrenched in sin as if the lessons of captivity had never been learned. Zechariah encouraged his hearers to return to the Lord by giving graphic descriptions of God's future end-time judgments. God's people had lost their will to consistently obey because they had lost sight of God's absolute control and presence. Just because they could not see stupendous evidences of God's presence did not mean he was absent or was not running history exactly as he wanted. As Zechariah affirmed God's complete present control, he also affirmed God's ability to judge or reward those in the present. God's control over history meant moral accountability. The returned nation of Israel had a long list of promises for great prosperity. But those promises seemed very far off, if still in effect at all. Zechariah presented a rather full picture of what lay ahead for Israel in order to confirm the promises and to comfort God's people. The content and structure of Zechariah show that the people of Israel were probably struggling with questions like these.

- What will happen to the priesthood and the line of David?
- Will Israel ever be able to overcome her enemies?
- Because God has returned his people to their land, are they now immune to God's judgment?
- Will the people of Israel ever be the kind of people God wants them to be?

Two of the greatest strains on faith are tough present circumstances and the long time it takes before God's promises are fulfilled. When it seems that God is not actively present in history, it is easy to think he will neither hold his people accountable for their sins nor reward them for their faithfulness. In such a situation their faithfulness tends to collapse and sin tends to increase. Zechariah works to combine the great past acts of God and graphic descriptions of his future judgments and rewards into a package that fills the present with a sense of God's complete control. With this perspective believers can move through this time of waiting, no matter how long ahead it stretches, with a firm sense of God's control and presence to judge and reward.

OUTLINE OF ZECHARIAH

A. CALL TO REPENTANCE: DO NOT BE LIKE YOUR FATHERS (1:1-6)
B. EIGHT VISIONS: GOD'S PROTECTION OF HIS HOUSE (1:7–6:15)
    1. The Temple Built and Enemies Punished (1:7-21)
    2. The Temple Built: Enemies Punished and Leaders Accepted (2:1–4:14)
    3. A Rival Temple Built and Enemies Punished (5:1–6:8)
    4. Returnees Encouraged: The Branch Builds the Temple (6:9-15)
C. THE POSTEXILIC MIND-SET: SADNESS TURNED TO JOY (7:1–8:23)
    1. The Setting: The Question about Fasting (7:1-3)
    2. Motivation and Rebellion Exposed (7:4-14)
    3. Words of Assurance (8:1-17)
    4. Questions Answered and Illustrated (8:18-23)

D. TWO BURDENS (9:1–14:21)
  1. Against Nations and Leadership: The Victorious Flock (9:1–11:17)
  2. Israel's Victory through Mourning (12:1–14:21)

ZECHARIAH NOTES

1:1-6 CALL TO REPENTANCE: DO NOT BE LIKE YOUR FATHERS

The date was Marchesvan, "the eighth month" (which falls in October–November), 520 B.C., "the second year of Darius" (1:1). The name "Zechariah" means "Yahweh remembers." The words "your forefathers" (1:2) referred to the forefathers of the present generation. Their sins resulted in the Babylonian exile. The words "Return to me" (1:3) speak of repentance, that is, a change of attitude resulting in a change of conduct. And Zechariah said, "Repentance is the prerequisite for enjoying God's blessing." The "earlier prophets" (1:4) were those who lived before the exile and warned of coming judgment. Zechariah warned that life is short, and it is perilous to pass up the opportunity to repent when it is available.

1:7–6:15 EIGHT VISIONS: GOD'S PROTECTION OF HIS HOUSE
1:7-21 The Temple Built and Enemies Punished

1:7-17 THE WORLDWIDE PATROL: NATIONS AT EASE

Note the following pattern in Zechariah's visions: (1) "I saw"; (2) "What does this mean?" (3) An explanation given by the interpreting angel.

In the vision of the red horse's rider among the myrtle trees (1:7-17) God promised to bless Israel by showing compassion and rebuilding Jerusalem. The date of this vision was the "eleventh month" (1:7), Shebat (which falls in January–February), 519 B.C., three months after the call to repentance (1:1-6). In 1:8-12 there were four participants in the vision: Zechariah, the rider on the red horse, the interpreting angel, and the angel of the Lord (1:11). Myrtle is an evergreen tree, once very common in the vicinity of Jerusalem (Neh. 8:15). Early in his rule, Darius had trouble with rebellion in

parts of his empire. Now all was quiet and peaceful.

The "seventy years" (Zech. 1:12) referred to the period the temple had lain in ruins (586–516 B.C.). The question was, How much longer would Israel be under Gentile domination? The "measuring line" (1:16) was used to survey a site for construction. God promised to rebuild Jerusalem and the temple ("my house," 1:16). Jerusalem's election ("again . . . choose Jerusalem") was emphasized prominently in Zechariah (1:17; cf. 2:12; 3:2).

1:18-21 FOUR HORNS AND FOUR CRAFTSMEN

Zechariah was given a vision of four horns and four craftsmen (1:18-21) in which God promised to destroy Israel's enemies. The horn was an image of invincible strength (cf. Dan. 8:5-8). The "horns" (Zech. 1:18) that persecuted Israel and Judah were Assyria, Babylon, Medo-Persia, and Greece. The "craftsmen" (1:20), or smiths, would destroy the "horns" (1:21). Babylon destroyed Assyria, Medo-Persia destroyed Babylon, Greece destroyed Medo-Persia, and Greece was succeeded by the Roman Empire.

2:1–4:14 The Temple Built: Enemies Punished and Leaders Accepted

2:1-13 PROTECTION: NO WALLS NEEDED

The vision of a surveyor with a measuring line (2:1-13) gave the remnant hope that Jerusalem would be restored and rebuilt. The "measuring line" (2:1) was a surveyor's tool. The measuring of Jerusalem was with a view to rebuilding the city. God promised his protection, a "wall of fire" (2:5; cf. Exod. 13:22). Those who had not yet returned to Judah from Babylon were urged to do so. The "north" (Zech. 2:6) was the direction of travel routes between Israel and Babylon, although Babylon was located directly east of Israel. In 2:9 God promised to protect his people (cf. Gen. 12:3). The "apple of his eye" (Zech. 2:8) referred to the eye's pupil. The word "touches" spoke of a touch with the intent to harm. Zechariah 2:10-12 appears to have its fulfillment in the Messianic kingdom ("I will live among you," 2:11).

3:1-10 PRIEST ACCEPTED
Zechariah's vision of the cleansing of Joshua the high priest (3:1-10) led the way to the cleansing of the whole nation. The nation was to be cleansed spiritually by the promised Messiah. The scene of this vision was a heavenly courtroom where Joshua, the representative of the people of Judah, was standing before the "angel of the Lord" while being accused by Satan. The "stick snatched from the fire" (3:2) referred to Judah, delivered from the "fire" of the Babylonian captivity. The "filthy clothes" (3:3) symbolized the pollution of sin that needed to be removed (cf. Isa. 4:4).

The cleansing of Joshua (Zech. 3:4-5) symbolized the removal of the guilt of sin ("I have taken away your sin," 3:4) and the imputation of God's righteousness ("rich garments," 3:4). Joshua was recommissioned and promised God's blessing for obedience (3:7). In 3:8-9 the Messiah was depicted as a servant (cf. Isa. 53:11), a Branch (cf. Isa. 4:2), and a stone (cf. Ps. 118:22; Isa. 28:16). The Hebrew word translated "eyes" (Zech. 3:9) may also be translated "springs" or "fountains," which symbolized the spiritual cleansing of the people by the Messiah (cf. 3:4). The image of sitting under a person's vine and fig tree (3:10) was an image of peace and tranquility and spoke of the Messianic kingdom (cf. Micah 4:4).

4:1-14 TEMPLE COMPLETED
The vision of the gold lampstand and two olive trees (4:1-14) pointed to the rebuilding of the temple. This rebuilding would take place by God's enablement. In Zechariah 4:2-3 the prophet saw a lampstand with seven lights, each having seven channels (or "spouts"). The "olive trees" provided the supply of oil for the lamps through "gold pipes" (4:11-12). The key message of the vision is contained in 4:6. The rebuilding of the temple would be accomplished by the ministry of God's Spirit. The "mountain" (4:7) referred to mountainous opposition or obstacles. The "seven" (4:10), identified as

"the eyes of the LORD," should probably be understood with reference to the "seven lights" (4:2). The "two olive branches" (4:12) were identified as "two who are anointed" (4:14), representative of the political and religious offices in Israel: king and priest. Many identify the "two" with Joshua, the high priest, and Zerubbabel, the governor.

5:1–6:8 A Rival Temple Built and Enemies Punished

5:1-4 SCROLL: UNIVERSAL JUDGMENT
Zechariah's vision of the flying scroll (5:1-4) indicated that there would be severe judgment on those who neglected the law. The "scroll" was the size of a billboard, thirty by fifteen feet (5:2; 20 by 10 cubits, NASB and KJV; a "cubit" was a unit of measure equivalent to eighteen inches). The scroll, containing the curses of disobedience (cf. Deut. 28:15-68), signified that lawbreakers would be judged. God's judgment was sure, penetrating, and severe.

5:5-11 EPHAH: THE RIVAL IDOL IN SHINAR
The vision of the woman in a measuring basket (5:5-11) was a prophecy of hope that sin and wickedness would be removed from Israel. The "measuring basket" (5:6; "ephah," NASB and KJV) was a unit of dry measure estimated at around two-thirds of a bushel, or almost four and a half gallons. This ephah basket may have been larger since it contained a woman (5:7). The woman in the basket ("wickedness") was a personification of sin (5:8).

6:1-8 WORLDWIDE PATROL: UNIVERSAL JUDGMENT
The vision of the four chariots (6:1-8) foretold the divine judgment that would fall upon the Gentile nations. The chariot and teams represented four divine agents of judgment. The "four spirits of heaven" (6:5) referred to heavenly messengers or agents. As a result of their activity, God's wrath was appeased (6:8). Victory in the turbulent "north" (6:8) suggested that there was victory over every foe.

6:9-15 Returnees Encouraged: The Branch Builds the Temple
The Messiah will be crowned as High Priest and King. The "exiles" (6:10) referred to the new arrivals from Babylon, who brought gifts of silver and gold (6:11) to help the

restoration community. The Hebrew word translated "crown" (6:11) is literally "crowns" and could refer to an ornate or double crown. The "Branch" (6:12) was a reference to the Messiah (cf. 3:8-9) who would build "the temple of the Lord," the millennial temple (cf. Hag. 2:6-9; Ezek. 40–43). In the Messiah the two offices of king and priest will be united in one Person (Zech. 6:13; cf. John 1:49; Heb. 3:1). The expression "those who are far away" referred to Gentiles (Zech. 6:15; cf. Eph. 2:13).

7:1–8:23 THE POSTEXILIC MIND-SET: SADNESS TURNED TO JOY
7:1-3 The Setting: The Question about Fasting
The date was the "ninth month," or Kislev (November–December), the "fourth year" (7:1), or 518 B.C. Bethel (7:2) was located about twelve miles north of Jerusalem. The people of Bethel sent a delegation to inquire of the priests in Jerusalem. The question was (7:3), "Is it necessary to fast in the fifth month, the month of Ab (July–August), as we did during the Babylonian exile to commemorate the 586 B.C. destruction of Jerusalem?"

7:4-14 Motivation and Rebellion Exposed
Zechariah exposed the selfish motives of the people in their self-righteous fasting. The fast during the "seventh" month lamented the slaying of Gedaliah (cf. 2 Kings 25:25). Zechariah's prophecies were in continuity with those prophets who preceded him (7:7). The "Negev," meaning "south," referred to the desert area in southern Judah centering around Beersheba. The "western foothills" referred to the Shephelah, a low ridge of hills between the hill country of Judah and the coastal plain. The "they" (7:11) referred to the disobedient Judeans living in the land before the Babylonian exile (cf. 7:14).

8:1-17 Words of Assurance
In 8:1-8 the prophet turned from the subject of Judah's desolation to speak of her future restoration. God's return to "Zion" (8:3; Jerusalem) provided the theological basis for the blessings that would follow. This regathering of the God's people (8:7) corresponds with the idea of regathering in

Matthew 24:31. The foundation of the temple was laid in 536 B.C. (Ezra 3:7-13).

8:18-23 Questions Answered and Illustrated
The former fasts would become feasts as a result of God's blessing on his obedient people. The fast of the "fourth" (Zech. 8:19) month commemorated the breach of Jerusalem's walls (cf. Jer. 39:2); the "fifth" (Zech. 8:19) commemorated the temple's destruction (cf. 2 Kings 25:8-9); the "seventh" commemorated the slaying of Gedaliah (cf. 2 Kings 25:25); and the "tenth" commemorated the beginning of Nebuchadnezzar's siege (2 Kings 25:1). The expression "to entreat the Lord" (8:21) meant to sacrifice to God and worship him. In 8:22-23 Zechariah anticipated a time when Gentiles would seek to worship God in Jerusalem. Gentiles would be included among the people of God by faith (cf. Eph. 2:13-19).

9:1–14:21 TWO BURDENS
9:1–11:17 Against Nations and Leadership: the Victorious Flock
9:1-10 THE COMING KING: DOMINION AND PEACE
Zechariah's oracle concerning the Gentile nations and Israel (Zech. 9:1-8) looks forward to God's judgment of Israel's enemies. There has been much scholarly debate regarding the text of 9:1-8. Scholars disagree about which historical circumstances were the subject of the prophecy's predictions. Most identify the contents of this section with Alexander the Great's campaign through Palestine (332–331 B.C.). Others have argued that it refers to a military campaign during the time of Josiah, Tiglath Pileser III, Sargon, or the Maccabees. The difficulty is that no one historical setting really answers to all the details of the situation described in these verses. More recently, it has been suggested that the section was set in the literary form of a "divine warrior hymn," a poem that describes a warrior-god's battle and the establishment of peace. In this view, no specific historical situation lies at the background. Rather, the poem presents God's intervention among the nations with a view to the establishment of the ideal that Yahweh had promised Israel.

Hadrach (9:1) was situated north of Hamath on the Orontes River southwest of Aleppo. Damascus, located sixty miles northeast of the Sea of Galilee, was the capital of Aram. Hamath (9:2) was named in some texts to represent the northern limits of the Promised Land (cf. Num. 13:21; Josh. 13:5). Tyre and Sidon were important port cities located in Phoenicia on the Mediterranean coast. Ashkelon, Gaza, Ekron, and Ashdod (9:5-6) were Philistine cities located on the coastal plain south of Joppa (cf. 1 Sam. 6:17). Having subjugated the nations, Yahweh returned as a victorious warrior to his temple (Zech. 9:8, "my house").

In 9:9-10 the first coming of Christ was set against the background of God's victory march (9:1-8). This prophecy was fulfilled when Jesus rode into Jerusalem on the colt of a donkey (cf. Matt. 21:2-7; John 12:12-15). A donkey was not regarded as a lowly creature in the ancient Near East, but rather as a king's mount. The inauguration of the Messiah's reign at his second coming was described in 9:10. During his future reign, instruments of warfare will be destroyed and universal peace established. "Ephraim" (9:10) was a reference to the northern tribes of Israel. The "River" (9:10) referred to the Euphrates.

9:11-17 VICTORY AND RESTORATION
Zechariah 9:11-17 spoke of the release of captives ("prisoners") in exile. They were exhorted to return to Jerusalem ("your fortress," 9:12). God was depicted as fashioning Judah and Ephraim into a bow and arrow, which would be used against Greece. The appearance of Greece (9:13; lit., "Javan") has led many scholars to date this section of Zechariah at a much later time. However, the term is used elsewhere for nations on the edge of civilization (cf. Gen. 20:2, 4; Isa. 66:19), which appears to be the usage here. The appearance of God (Zech. 9:14) was patterned after Israel's experience with God at Sinai, revealing God's sovereignty and power to protect his own.

The victory banquet of God's people in celebration of his victory over the nations and securing Zion was recorded in 9:15. The people would be filled with drink like a sacrificial basin and filled with meat like

the corners of a sacrificial altar. God would shepherd and provide for his restored and repentant people.

10:1–11:3 LEADERSHIP CONDEMNED: RETURN FROM EXILE
The prophet described how God would restore his people to their land. The unifying theme of the section of 10:1–11:3 is the restoration of the Jewish people by divine power. The "idols" (10:2) were household idols (cf. Gen. 31:19), which led the people to their own destruction. The term "shepherd" (Zech. 10:2) is a figure for a leader or king. The metaphors in Zechariah 10:4-5 reflected the strength, stability, and victory that God would impart to his people, Judah (10:6). God's scattered people would be regathered to the land from worldwide dispersion (10:8-12). Assyria (10:10) referred to the region of northern Mesopotamia. Gilead was the Transjordan territory southeast of the Sea of Galilee. Lebanon referred to the region north of Galilee. God would overcome any obstacles or impediments, like "the sea" or "the Nile" (10:11), to Israel's return.

Zechariah 11 prophesied the rejection of the good shepherd of God's flock and his replacement by a worthless shepherd who would bring them ruin. Zechariah 11:1-3 depicted the devastation of the land of Israel due to the people's rejection of the Messiah, the good shepherd (11:4-17; cf. Matt. 23:37-39). The judgment was probably fulfilled in the A.D. 70 destruction of Jerusalem by the Romans. The dominant image of this passage was the wailing that would express the horror of Israel's devastation.

11:4-17 LEADERSHIP REJECTED
Zechariah revealed the destiny of the shepherd and the flock. The flock was said to be "marked for slaughter" (Zech. 11:7), destined for judgment. As shepherds carried implements to guide and protect the sheep (Ps. 23:4), so Zechariah carried two staffs. Their names suggest that he wanted the flock to enjoy God's "Favor" and experience national unity ("Union"). At least forty different conjectures have been offered as to the identity of the three shepherds whom Zechariah deposed (Zech. 11:8). Such speculation is unnecessary. These shepherds, whoever they were, did not share the true shepherd's vision and were removed from leadership.

The breaking of the staff "Favor" was symbolic of the termination of God's gracious dealings with his people (11:10). Then judgment was inevitable. The "covenant" referred not to the Abrahamic (Gen. 12:1-3) or Davidic covenants (2 Sam. 7:12-16), but to one made with the Gentile nations ("all the peoples") on Israel's behalf. Zechariah, taking the role of the Messianic shepherd, requested his wages for service rendered (Zech. 11:12-13). The "thirty pieces of silver" (11:12; "thirty shekels," NASB) was the price of an injured slave (cf. Exod. 21:32) and was the price paid to Judas for the betrayal of Jesus (cf. Matt. 26:14-15).

The rejection of the good shepherd meant that the national unity Zechariah had hoped for would not be achieved at this time (Zech. 11:14). In 11:15-17 the rejection of the good shepherd resulted in a leadership vacuum that would be filled by a wicked shepherd who would actually destroy the flock. A comparison of this shepherd with the sinister figure of Daniel 7:25 and 11:36-39 indicates that he represented the antichrist (2 Thess. 2:1-12; Rev. 13:1-10).

12:1–14:21 Israel's Victory through Mourning

12:1-9 NATIONS DESTROYED

Zechariah looked to the future day of Israel's deliverance from her enemies when the Gentile nations would be destroyed. The end-time setting is the campaign of Armageddon (Rev. 16:16) when the nations will come against Jerusalem (cf. Zech. 14:2). When the nations are gathered against Jerusalem, the Messiah will return and execute judgment on the Gentile powers so that he may rule the nations himself (12:4-9). Judah is likened to a "firepot" (12:6), a clay vessel used to carry hot coals for the purpose of building a fire. The "sheaves" referred to the grain that was cut, bound, and left standing in the field to dry. The Lord, the Messiah, would be the agent of judgment on the enemy and the agent of deliverance (12:8) for his people.

12:10–13:1 GRACE POURED OUT: ISRAEL MOURNS

In 12:10–13:6 Zechariah described Israel's spiritual deliverance. At the time of Christ's second coming, the remnant of Israel, which will have survived the tribulation judgments, will repent and believe in Jesus, the Messiah whom they "pierced" (12:10). The expression "a spirit of grace" (12:10) referred to the work of the Spirit in Israel's conversion. The "weeping of Hadad Rimmon" (12:11; "mourning," NASB) may have referred to a place noted for some intense lamentation, or to the combined names of the vegetation gods "Hadad" and "Rimmon." The "plain of Megiddo" (12:11) referred to the plain that Megiddo controlled, the Jezreel Valley.

Zechariah 12:12-14 emphasizes the universal aspect of mourning for the Messiah, the royal family ("house of David," 12:12), the priestly family ("house of Levi," 12:13), and all citizens ("all the rest," 12:14). Shimei was Levi's grandson (cf. Num. 3:18, 21).

The "fountain . . . to cleanse" (Zech. 13:1) speaks of the cleansing from the impurity of sin that Christ made available at the cross. At the time of Christ's second coming, the remnant of Israel ("house of David") will appropriate that provision and be saved (Rom. 11:26).

13:2-6 FALSE PROPHETS EXPOSED

Zechariah announced that a day was coming when false prophets would be purged from the land along with idolatry and demonic influence. The execution of the false prophet was based on the Mosaic Law (Zech. 13:3; cf. Deut. 13:5; 18:20). The "garment of hair" (Zech. 13:4; "hairy robe," NASB), that the false prophets would want to avoid, had been worn by Elijah (2 Kings 1:8) and seems to have been the distinctive attire of the prophets. The "wounds" (Zech. 13:6) appeared to betray the profession of an ecstatic prophet who had slashed himself on the back and breast to gain the attention and blessing of his god (cf. 1 Kings 18:28).

13:7-9 SHEPHERD STRUCK: REMNANT PRESERVED

In 13:7-9, Zechariah resumed the shepherd motif and returned to the theme of the Messiah's rejection. The Lord commanded the sword to strike the Messiah shepherd. This indicates that the death of Christ was no mere accident but had been divinely determined (cf. Acts 2:23). The shepherd's death resulted in the scattering of his flock (cf. Matt. 26:31; Mark 14:27). The scattered flock would face great judgment (the tribulation), which only one-third of the people would survive (cf. Matt. 24:15-22). The remnant that survived would be purged, purified, and reestablished in a covenant relationship with God (cf. Hos. 2:23; Rom. 11:26-27).

14:1-21 JERUSALEM DIVIDES THE SPOIL: FEAST OF BOOTHS KEPT
In Zechariah 14:1-5 the prophet described the events associated with the second coming of the Messiah at the end of the campaign of Armageddon (Rev. 16:16). Just before the Messiah's return, the unbelieving Gentile nations will gather at Jerusalem to besiege and destroy the city (Zech. 12:2). Christ's return to Jerusalem will turn what seems an unavoidable defeat into victory (14:4-9). Christ will return to the Mount of Olives, the very mountain from which he ascended (Acts 1:10-11). The splitting of the Mount of Olives will provide a way of escape for the besieged and defeated people in Jerusalem. The site of "Azel" (Zech. 14:5) has not been identified but must be somewhere in the desert east of Jerusalem. According to Josephus, the "earthquake" (14:5) occurred when Uzziah went into the temple to offer incense (cf. 2 Chron. 26:16-21).

Cosmic upheaval is associated with the second coming (Zech. 14:6-7). The glory of the Messiah's kingdom will be preceded by the darkness of the tribulation (Joel 2:30-32). In Zechariah 14:8-11 the prophet described the culmination of the prophetic promise of a kingdom in which Israel's Messiah will rule on David's throne (cf. 2 Sam. 7:12-16; Luke 1:31-33). "Living water" (Zech. 14:8) was a reference to flowing water as opposed to stagnant water. The "eastern sea" referred to the Dead Sea. The "western sea" was a reference to the Mediterranean. Certain topographical changes will take place in the environs of Jerusalem to accomodate the Messianic temple (14:10). "Geba" was situated six miles northeast of Jerusalem. "Rimmon" was about thirty-five miles southwest of Jerusalem.

While the surrounding terrain will be leveled, Jerusalem itself will be elevated so that the city will dominate the land (14:10; cf. Isa. 2:2; Mic. 4:1). "The Benjamin Gate" (Zech. 14:10) probably referred to a gate in the northern wall of the city. The "First Gate" has not been identified. The "Corner Gate" probably marked the northwest limit of Jerusalem. The "Tower of Hananel" was a defensive fortification on the northern wall.

Zechariah 14:12-15 elaborates on the content of 12:4-9 and 14:3, providing further details of how God will fight against and destroy those nations that attack Jerusalem. In 14:16-21 Zechariah concluded with a description of worship in the Messiah's kingdom. The "Feast of Tabernacles" (14:16) referred to the fall feast of ingathering that commemorated the wilderness experience of Israel (cf. Lev. 23:33-43). In the Messianic kingdom, the people of Judah and Jerusalem will be holy, as a priestly nation. The words "HOLY TO THE LORD" (Zech. 14:20) were inscribed on the gold headband of the high priest (cf. Exod. 28:36). The "Canaanite" (Zech. 14:21) referred to the merchants who frequented the courts with their wares (cf. Neh. 13:19-22; Matt. 21:12; John 2:14). In the kingdom, there will be no distinction between the sacred and the secular. The bells, pots, and people all will be "HOLY TO THE LORD."

Malachi

BASIC FACTS

HISTORICAL SETTING

In the thirty-second year of Artaxerxes (432 B.C.), Nehemiah left Jerusalem to visit the king in Babylon (Neh. 13:6). Some time after the visit he returned to Jerusalem and initiated the temple, Sabbath, and marriage reforms (Neh. 13:4-31). A Persian governor was apparently in authority during Nehemiah's absence (Mal. 1:8). Such a ruler would not have been in office during Nehemiah's governorship of 444–432 B.C. or his governorship following his visit to Babylon.

There is close agreement between the sins that Malachi denounced and those that Nehemiah sought to correct. Both books refer to the problems of priestly laxity (Mal. 1:6–2:9; Neh. 13:4-9, 29), the neglect of tithes (Mal. 3:7-12; Neh. 13:10-13), and intermarriage with foreign women (Mal. 2:10-16; Neh. 13:23-28).

Malachi prophesied about seventy-five years after the temple had been completed in 515 B.C.. The Jews had been home from exile for around one hundred years. Although they were cured of idolatry, they had lost the enthusiasm over the return and reestablishment of proper worship. Nehemiah had brought reform and revival (Neh. 10:28-39), but the people had again succumbed to religious indifference and moral laxity.

Having suffered plague and famine (Mal. 3:11), the people had begun to doubt God's love (1:2). They questioned his justice (2:17) and the benefit of obeying his commandments (3:14-15). The priesthood was corrupt (1:6; 2:1-9) and the Levitical offerings were unacceptable for sacrifice (1:8-10). The people were neglecting their responsibility of tithing (3:7-9) and were wearying God with their hypocrisy (2:17). They were even involved in the scandal of mixed marriage and divorce (2:10-16), activities condemned by the Mosaic Law. It was such a wayward people that the Lord through the prophet Malachi called to repentance and obedience and warned of future judgment.

AUTHOR

The name Malachi means "my messenger." Because of this, some scholars have taken the name Malachi to simply be a generic name and regard the prophecy as anonymous. However, the writings of the prophets were never anonymous works. Nothing is recorded concerning the prophet's background or circumstances, but Talmudic tradition includes him as a member of the "Great Synagogue" with Haggai and Zechariah. This shows that he was considered an individual prophet at an early date, making it likely that "Malachi" was a personal name and not a generic one.

DATE

While the book of Malachi is not dated, scholars are in agreement that internal evidence indicates it is postexilic. The book must be dated after the ministry of Haggai and Zechariah, for the temple had been built and Levitical worship was in effect (Mal. 1:6-10; 2:1-3; 3:1, 10). While some have dated the prophecy just before the reform that was instigated by Ezra following his return in 458 B.C., a date of around 432 B.C. has much to commend it. It was probably during Nehemiah's absence between his first and second governorships that the corruption and abuses developed. It is reasonable to assume that Malachi protested those abuses prior to Nehemiah's return and reform, and hence a very probable date for the composition of the book is around 432–431 B.C.

PURPOSE

The book of Malachi was designed to restore the Jewish people to a right relationship with God by exposing the causes of their spiritual deterioration and setting forth the steps through which the community could be renewed. Malachi presented God's case against Israel as well as his promises for blessing.

GUIDING CONCEPTS

The argument of the people with the Lord pervades the entire book: "says the LORD"; "But you ask" (1:2, 6, 11-12, 13-14; 2:14, 17; 3:7, 13). The last chapter of Malachi resounds with the key themes of the Old Testament: the fear of the Lord (4:1); the remembrance of the law (4:4); blessings and curses (2:2; 4:6); Moses, Elijah, and the Lord (4:4-5).

The general failure of God's people dominates until the messenger of God comes to chastise and the Lord himself comes to judge and preserve the remnant. Worship of God will then be a global event (1:11, 14).

BIBLE-WIDE CONCEPTS

Malachi made an important contribution to Old Testament theology in his statements regarding the Lord's love for Israel as demonstrated by his choice of Jacob over Esau (1:2-5). The book is also instructive concerning the day of the Lord (3:2, 17; 4:1, 3, 5). In announcing that day's approach, he pointed to the fact that it will be both a day of judgment (3:2; 4:1) and of deliverance (3:3, 4, 6, 16-18; 4:2-3). Malachi concluded his prophecy with a promise of the coming of the Messiah's forerunner, Elijah (John the Baptist), before the "great and dreadful day of the LORD" (Mal. 4:5; cf. Matt. 17:10-13; Mark 9:11-13). See also Matthew 3:1-3; 11:10, 14; and Luke 1:17.

NEEDS MET BY MALACHI

The last book of the Old Testament portrays God's people still struggling to understand God and what he desires from them. They still did not understand the reasons for their problems. Throughout the book of Malachi the people ask why they are having problems even though God had been telling them why for centuries. Continually, God's people showed an amazing stamina and ability to deny their own sin and seek other reasons for their problems—blaming either God or others. Malachi sought to break through their denial of personal responsibility for their problems and called them to return to God. They also needed to be encouraged to work hard at building the focal point of God's presence, the temple. More than just a building for ritual, it was a gauge of the quality of their fellowship with the living God. The questions posed by God's people throughout the book provide the clearest indication of the needs the book was intended to meet.

- How has God shown love to his people (1:2)?
- How have the people of Israel defiled God (1:7)?
- Why is the Lord not answering the prayers of his people (2:13-14)?
- Why is God not doing something about injustice (2:17)?
- How have God's people robbed God (3:8)?
- What have the people said that has been against God (3:13-14)?
- God also asked a crucial question: Who can endure the day of the Lord's coming (3:2)? (This question was answered in 4:1-2.)

When, like Israel, believers suffer the consequences of their disobedience, it is easy for them to doubt God's love. The self-centered definition of God's love held by many believers coupled with their denial of their own evil makes them prime candidates for the exhortations of Malachi. Believers need to lift their heads above their own limited problems and see the great love of God in Christ. And they need to find the answers to why they are being disciplined and how they have offended God through a clear acceptance of their own part in disobedience. Malachi shows believers how denial of their sins furthers their discomfort, but admittance of their offenses opens the way for forgiveness and renewed fellowship with God. This will prepare believers for that eventual meeting with God face-to-face.

OUTLINE OF MALACHI

A. GOD'S LOVE QUESTIONED (1:1-5)
    1. Title (1:1)
    2. The Question of Past and Future Acts of Love Answered (1:2-5)
B. CORRUPT PRIESTHOOD: GOD'S NAME DEFILED (1:6–2:16)
    1. Defiled Offerings: What King Would Receive Them? (1:6-14)
    2. Defiled Covenant (2:1-16)

C. THE SONS OF LEVI PURIFIED (2:17–4:3)
   1. The Calls for Divine Accountability (2:17)
   2. The Divine Response (3:1–4:3)
D. COVENANT OBEDIENCE RESTORED TO THE RIGHTEOUS REMNANT
   (4:4-6)

MALACHI NOTES

1:1-5 GOD'S LOVE QUESTIONED
1:1 Title

The name "Malachi" means "my messenger," an appropriate designation for a prophet of God.

1:2-5 The Question of Past and Future Acts of Love Answered

Malachi used questions and answers as a literary device to develop the message. The pattern is as follows: (1) an assertion or charge was made by God (a statement); (2) an objection in the form of a question was asked from the perspective of the people (a challenge); (3) a refutation of the objection was made by God (defense). In each section, the prophet dealt with a problem. This section dealt with the problem of the people doubting or denying God's love for them. The Lord's love for Israel was demonstrated by his choice of Jacob over Esau (Gen. 25:23) and by his severe dealings with Edom, the descendants of Esau (cf. Obadiah). During the intertestamental period, John Hyrcanus (135–104 B.C.) forced the people of Edom to adopt Judaism or be killed (Mal. 1:4). Edom, later known as Idumea, was attacked and devastated by Simon ben Gioras during the Jewish War (A.D. 66–70). Josephus reported that the land was totally destroyed. Malachi anticipated that God's people would one day acknowledge his greatness and his love (1:5).

1:6–2:16
CORRUPT PRIESTHOOD: GOD'S NAME DEFILED
1:6-14 Defiled Offerings: What King Would Receive Them?

1:6-12 QUALITY:
BLIND, CRIPPLED, AND DISEASED
The problem in 1:6-12 was the failure of the priests to truly honor God. God's "name" (1:6) represents his character or reputation.

The meat placed on God's altar was defiled by the disobedience of the people (1:8; cf. Hag. 2:12-14). They vowed to give God their best (cf. Eccles. 5:4-5), but when it came time to pay, they gave unworthy offerings—crippled and diseased animals. "From the rising to the setting of the sun" (Mal. 1:11) was a reference to the entire world, from east to west, over which God would rule. The offerings that God anticipated would be given in the true worship of the future kingdom (cf. Ezek. 40–44).

1:13-14 INNER ATTITUDE: TIRESOME
The curses were based on the provisions in the Mosaic covenant for curses and blessings—curses for disobedience (Mal. 1:14; cf. Deut. 28:15-68) and blessings for obedience (Deut. 28:1-14).

2:1-16 Defiled Covenant

2:1-3 ADDRESS AND CURSE
Malachi spoke regarding the priests who had the responsibility to instruct God's people (Mal. 2:7; cf. Lev. 10:8-11; Deut. 33:10). They had failed in that sacred trust. For the curses of the covenant, see Deuteronomy 27:15-26 and 28:15-68.

2:4-16 COVENANT CONTINUED: TRUE AND FALSE MESSENGERS CONTRASTED
2:4-9 True messenger: Levi. The "covenant with Levi" referred to God's provision for the priesthood in Levi and his descendants (Num. 1:50). In Malachi 2:5-7 the prophet contrasted the ideal priest, represented by the name "Levi," the chief ancestor of the priests, with the ungodly priests of his day.

2:10-16 False messengers. The intermarriage of the Judeans with unbelieving heathen women was a continual problem in the restoration community (Ezra 9–10; cf. Neh. 13:23-29). The rhetorical question "Have we not all one Father?" (Mal. 2:10) was intended to be answered yes. In one sense, God is the Father of all, since he is the Creator. The "daughter of a foreign god" (Mal. 2:11) referred to "an idolatrous woman." Throughout 2:13-16 the Lord identified "divorce" as a breaking of faith. In order to marry the idolatrous pagan women, the Judean men were divorcing their wives. In light of their treacherous dealings with their spouses (Mal. 2:14), God had no regard for their offerings.

Note that God is a "witness" of the marriage union, and that such a union is a "covenant" relationship, not something liable to be broken with God's approval (2:14). The emphasis is clear: "Remain true to the wife of your youth." Garments (2:16) were often used to symbolize the moral coverings of a person's actions (see, e.g., Zech. 3:3-4).

2:17–4:3 THE SONS OF LEVI PURIFIED
2:17 The Calls for Divine Accountability
The problem in Malachi 2:17–3:5 was the cynical unbelief that "wearied" God, that is, nearly exhausted his patience. The Judeans doubted God's justice.

3:1–4:3 The Divine Response
3:1-6 JUDGMENT:
THE MESSENGER PURIFIES
The "messenger" (3:1) was identified by Jesus as John the Baptist (Matt. 11:10, 14), who served as Christ's forerunner, inviting people to repent and believe in him. The "Lord" and the "messenger of the [new] covenant" (3:1; cf. Matt. 26:28) referred to Jesus. Malachi focused on the second coming of Christ, which will purge and purify both the priests and the people in preparation for the Messianic kingdom. The "refiner's fire" (3:2) referred to a smelters fire, used to purify ore. The "launderer's soap" was for cleaning. Since God is unchanging in his covenant relationship with Israel (Gen. 12:1-3), he will not completely destroy them (Mal. 3:6).

3:7-15 EXHORTATION:
THE WAY OF REPENTANCE
The problem in 3:7-12 was the people's departure from God as reflected by their neglect of tithes and offerings. Two annual tithes were required according to Israelite law—one for the Levites (Lev. 27:30; Num. 18:21), and one to be used in worship at the annual feasts in Jerusalem (Deut. 14:22). A tithe was required every three years to provide for the needs of the poor (Deut. 14:28-29). There is debate as to whether this tithe for the poor was in addition to or served as a substitute for the tithe used in worship.

The New Testament pattern for tithing is proportionate giving—a person is to give "in keeping with his income" (1 Cor. 16:2). Certainly a tithe should be given proportionate to one's wealth, but not all proportionate giving is a tithe.

The anticipation of blessing for obedience to God's command to tithe was based on the Mosaic covenant, which promised blessings for obedience and curses for disobedience (Mal. 3:10; cf. Deut. 28:15-68). Generally, God will meet the needs of his own people (Ps. 34:9-10; Phil. 4:19), but that is not an unconditional guarantee. There certainly were and are exceptions. Yet, where God chooses not to provide physically, he gives sufficient grace to go without (2 Cor. 12:9). The "devouring" (Mal. 3:11) probably referred to drought and general infertility.

The problem in 3:14-15 was that the people were guilty of arrogant words against God. They were saying, "There is no prophet who is serving God," and "God is not concerned about justice." God responded by showing that he did distinguish between the wicked and the righteous. The righteous would be blessed, and the wicked would be judged.

3:16–4:3 PRESERVATION:
GOD-FEARERS SPARED
This section emphasizes the blessings that come to those who fear God, a concept repeated several times (3:16; 4:2; cf. also in 1:14; 2:2; and 3:5). The "scroll of remembrance" (3:16) was a figure derived from the custom of recording names of public benefactors (cf. Esther 6:1-2) so that they might be rewarded. God referred to the righteous remnant of his people as his "treasured possession" (Mal. 3:17). Malachi anticipated a day of the Lord (4:1; cf. 4:5) as a day of judgment on the wicked. The "sun of righteousness" (4:2) was a strong poetic image for a righteousness on the scale of the sun's brightness.

4:4-6 COVENANT OBEDIENCE RESTORED TO THE RIGHTEOUS REMNANT

The Old Testament concludes with an exhortation to remember the "law," God's instruction, and to anticipate the coming of "Elijah." Horeb (4:4) was another name for Mount Sinai (Deut. 5:2). The "great and dreadful day of the LORD" (Mal. 4:5) referred to the most severe period of God's judgment that will come just before the second coming of Christ. Before that time, Elijah would come to call people to repentance and reunite disintegrating families, turning people's hearts to God. For the fulfillment of the promise concerning the coming of Elijah, see Matthew 3:1-3; 11:10, 14; 17:10-12; Luke 1:17; and John 1:21.

Matthew

BASIC FACTS

HISTORICAL SETTING
The historical setting for the book of Matthew was the life of Jesus and the period of his resurrection ministry that continued for forty days after his resurrection (Acts 1:3). Like the other synoptic Gospels (Mark and Luke), Matthew focused on the Galilean ministry of Jesus.

AUTHOR
The Gospel of Matthew is anonymous, but from a very early period the author has been identified as Matthew (Levi), the Galilean tax collector who became one of Jesus' disciples. The tradition of Matthean authorship can be found in the writings of Papias, Eusebius, and Origen. Matthew, originally named Levi, was the son of Alphaeus (cf. Mark 2:14). He worked at a tax collection station in Capernaum (Matt. 9:9), a city in the territory of Herod Antipas. Matthew promptly responded to Jesus' call and became one of only three writing apostles.

DATE
Scholars are divided as to whether Matthew or Mark was written first. Early tradition suggested that Matthew's Gospel account was the first written. Eusebius quoted Clement of Alexandria (A.D. 144–200) as saying that the Gospels with the genealogies (Matthew and Luke) were written first (*Historia Ecclesiastica*, 6.14). Recent scholarship has tended to place Mark first, with Matthew quoting 601 of Mark's 678 verses. But whether Matthew wrote his Gospel before Mark or not, the date of Matthew's account must have been prior to the destruction of Jerusalem in A.D. 70 because there was no hint in Matthew's record that Jerusalem was in ruins. The prophecies concerning Jerusalem's destruction clearly indicated that the event would still take place in the future (23:37-38; 24:1-2).

The expression "to this day" (27:8; 28:15) indicated a period of years from the time of the events referred to and the writing of the Gospel account, but a period of

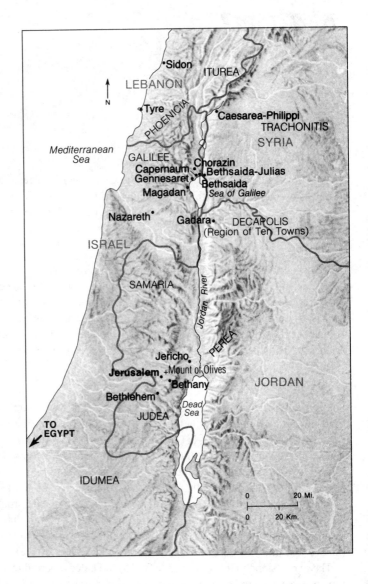

twenty years would certainly satisfy the time lapse indicated in these passages. The account would probably not have been written before the first dispersion of the Jewish Christians under the persecution of Herod Agrippa I in A.D. 44 (Acts 12:1-7). Before that time the apostles would have been present with the Christians in Jerusalem and would have been able to impart authoritative teaching. The Gospel of Matthew was probably written around A.D. 50 to meet the needs of the Jewish Christians in Judea and those dispersed around the Roman Empire.

PURPOSE

Matthew desired his readers to understand that Jesus was the fulfillment of God's promises to Abraham, Israel's greatest patriarch, and to David, Israel's greatest king (1:1). The Gospel of Matthew was designed to convince its readers that Jesus of Nazareth was the promised Messiah of Old Testament prophecy. The book was also intended to reveal that the Messianic kingdom was not fully realized in Jesus' day, but its fulfillment awaits his glorious return. Until then, Jesus the Messiah reigns in full authority over the earth as he seeks to make disciples around the world.

GEOGRAPHY AND ITS IMPORTANCE

Matthew used the geography of Israel's past to show how Jesus alone could be Israel's and the world's hope for the future. Matthew used the image of a sunrise dawning upon the Gentiles and foreigners in Galilee to introduce Jesus' ministry. Galilee is called Galilee of the foreigners (Matt. 4:16) because it had often been overtaken by hostile foreign enemies and in Christ's day was a mix of Jewish and Gentile inhabitants. The book focuses on Jesus' ministry in Galilee and ends with his resurrection appearance there and his promise to be forever present with those who believe in him. Galilee of the Gentiles is where Jew and Greek met with Jesus, the greater son of David who will bring kingly rule and the greater son of Abraham who will bring universal blessing to all nations of the world.

In addition to the Gentile thrust of Jesus' ministry in Galilee, Matthew saw many correspondences between the places in Jesus' life and Israel's past history. The geography involved in Jesus' birth in Bethlehem overlays Israel's past history of King David's birth. The killing of the babies in the Bethlehem area revived the horrors of Israel's captivity in Babylon. Jesus' trip to Egypt and return to Israel retraced Israel's ancient descent into and exodus from Egyptian bondage. Jesus' wandering in the Judean wilderness for forty days followed the pattern of Israel's forty-year wilderness wanderings. Jesus' sermon from the mountain (Matt. 5–7) and his glorious appearance on the mountain (Matt. 17) linked back to Moses' declaration of God's laws and the radiance of his face. But the correspondence between where Jesus and Israel went was designed to show what kind of man Jesus was. In all the places where Israel failed, Jesus was perfectly obedient and powerful. Circumstances and geography combine to reveal Jesus' perfect authority.

GUIDING CONCEPTS

OLD TESTAMENT QUOTATIONS

Jesus used Old Testament Scripture to emphasize key Old Testament concepts as he proclaimed the gospel and instructed his disciples. Matthew quoted Old Testament Scripture to show how it was fulfilled by the life of Jesus (1:22-23; 2:15, 17-18, 23; 4:13-16; 8:17; 12:17-21; 13:35; 21:4-5; 27:9-10). Matthew's purpose was to illustrate the sure fulfillment and power of God's covenant word and to identify Jesus as God's Messiah. What God had begun with Abraham, Moses, and David, he fulfilled in Jesus. The pattern of quoting Old Testament Scripture was set down by Jesus himself in 26:54-56. The Old Testament truths that were brought to their fulfillment in the life of Jesus revealed the redemptive heart of a loving God manifested through his Son.

COMPASSION

Compassion (sometimes translated "loyalty" or "loving-kindness") was an important concept taken up by Jesus from the Old Testament Scriptures. The central passage on the Lord's compassion in the Old Testament is Exodus 34:6-7 (cf. Deut. 30:1-6, 19-20). Jesus revealed God's compassion through everything he did while also calling his followers to do the same. He required mercy and compassion from his followers and pointed to the key Old Testament passage of Hosea 6:6, "For I desire mercy, not sacrifice" (cf. Matt. 5:7; 9:13, 27, 36; 12:7; 14:14; 15:22, 32; 17:15; 18:27, 33; 20:30-31, 34; 23:23). The kind of compassion taught by Jesus was not just a feeling. It was an act (9:13) that reflected the bringing of God's salvation to the world. The righteous remnant was to show compassion while they waited for God to judge and restore the world.

STUMBLING

"Stumbling" or "falling away" or "taking offense" was the opposite of having faith in Jesus. Matthew presented the majority of the "stumbling" sayings that appear in the New Testament. He was concerned to show his readers how to avoid falling away from, or stumbling over, the claims and person of Jesus Christ (5:29-30; 11:6; 13:21, 41, 57; 15:12; 16:23; 17:27; 18:6-9; 24:10; 26:31-33). Matthew desired to convince people of Jesus' Messianic identity so they would not reject him and his message of the kingdom. The essence of stumbling (16:23) was part of a satanic trap to block the spread of God's redemption in Jesus the Messiah. Satan first sought to cause Jesus to stumble (cf. 4:1-11) and after failing to do this, set out to cause people to reject Jesus' claims to Messiahship by any means possible.

AUTHORITY

The authority about which Matthew spoke was not just Jesus' physical power to do miracles. Jesus' authority was also shown in his power to command and expect obedience (7:28-29; 8:8-9; 9:6-8; 10:1; 21:23-24, 27; 28:18). The book of Matthew ends with the words of Jesus the Messiah's eternal claim to authority ringing loud and clear (28:18-20).

IDENTITY

The people mentioned in the book of Matthew had various opinions about who Jesus was (8:27; 9:14; 11:3; 14:1-2, 33; 16:13-16). That difference of opinion concerning his identity was used to make several points in the book. Outsiders never seemed to fully realize that Jesus was the Messiah. His disciples may have realized the truth about Jesus' Messiahship, but they still struggled with understanding the deeper truths of his identity, such as the predictions of his death on the cross. The question of Jesus' identity demanded that the honest disciple come to understand the heart of God's plan for world redemption through the suffering and sacrifice of his own Son. The closer Jesus' followers came to knowing who Jesus was, the closer they were to understanding the depth of God's compassionate and redemptive heart.

PRESENCE

Matthew began and ended his book by teaching about the presence of God in Jesus Christ. At the beginning of the book, the baby Jesus was named "Immanuel" (1:23), which means "God with us." At the end, he was the crucified and risen Lord of heaven and earth, present with his people "to the very end of the age" (28:18-20). All that Jesus did and said between these accounts expanded and deepened the readers' understanding of their own responsibilities to obey the God who was eternally present with them. In this way, the concepts of God's authority and eternal presence were brought together.

BIBLE-WIDE CONCEPTS

Matthew is the first book in the New Testament canon. As such, it provides a bridge between the Old and New Testaments. This bridge was built on deep prophetic and theological foundations. Matthew showed continuity with the Old Testament in several ways. In his book, Matthew showed how Jesus fulfilled the promises that God had made to Abraham, Moses, and David to restore the divine presence with Israel. He developed profound links between the life of Jesus and the history of Israel (1:1–4:16). He showed how Jesus fulfilled the demands of the law and how he founded the Messianic community of the faithful (4:17–16:20). Jesus was the greater Joshua who would save his people from their sins. He was Immanuel, the God who was present with his people to judge and to save. These themes, that can be seen in both Old and New Testaments, will be expanded in the following notes.

NEEDS MET BY MATTHEW

The original readers of Matthew's Gospel had a great need for assurance that God was still with them. In the past, God's people had clung to that assurance throughout centuries of captivity and persecution. But believers in Jesus as the Messiah faced harsh criticism from the Jewish religious establishment that asserted that God could not possibly be with what they called a new and heretical sect. Matthew's reply was that God had indeed made himself present in the man from Nazareth called Jesus. For those who disbelieved, Matthew's Gospel provided extensive Old Testament proof that the man Jesus was also the Son of God, the Messiah. For those who believed, Matthew affirmed that, though absent physically, Jesus was spiritually and powerfully present until the end of the age. God had not abandoned his people. The suffering his people experienced was a sign, not of being abandoned by God, but of faithfully following in the steps of their suffering Savior.

Jesus' presence met a second need for the original readers. Along with comfort, Jesus presented a challenge to faith. As the prophet greater than Moses and the king greater than David, Jesus elaborated God's law and demanded self-sacrificing obedience. Like Israel of old, the new Israel of the church was prone to stumbling and lapses of faith and obedience. The presence of Jesus cut two ways for his church. It was both a comfort in hard times and a challenge to more consistent faithfulness. Matthew wrote to a community that needed help with its own faith and with its mission to witness to others. The structure and content of Matthew's Gospel reveal that he was answering questions like the following for his readers.

- Is Jesus the Messiah?
- If he is, how does he fit into Old Testament prophecy?
- What has happened to God's promises to Abraham, Moses, and David?
- Why did Jesus act in an unexpectedly quiet and humble way? (I thought the Messiah would come and break the power that Rome held over Israel.)
- If believers are really children of God, why are they being treated so badly? (I thought that when the Messiah came all would be well for those who believed in him.)
- Exactly where is this kingdom he came to bring about?
- How much longer will believers have to wait before the kingdom finally comes?
- What are believers in Jesus the Messiah supposed to be doing while they wait?

If the original readers of Matthew needed to be assured that God was with them, believers today need that assurance even more. When Matthew wrote his Gospel, Jesus had only been physically gone a few decades, whereas now he has been gone nearly two hundred decades. Matthew helps today's readers understand what Jesus' spiritual presence means for them today.

First, Matthew meets the need of believers to know how Jesus fits into the Old Testament promises. Many in Jesus' day and today believe that Jesus had no right to claim Old Testament roots and that he was just a religious zealot or imposter without God's prophetic authority. By showing that Jesus was indeed the one prophesied by the Old Testament, Matthew assures believers that God did not change his mind between the Old and the New Testaments. He did not abandon all he had promised before the appearance of Jesus. God's great promises to Abraham, Moses, and David have not been replaced with a new set of promises in Christ. In Jesus these great promises and laws were elaborated and deepened, not abrogated. Because Jesus came to fulfill, not destroy, God's Old Testament promises and laws, Matthew records many of Jesus' speeches that elaborate and apply God's Old Testament laws for Christ's disciples. Thus the religion of Jesus was not new and rootless. It was the perfection of God's will for obedience and redemption that reached from the first day of creation, to Moses on Mount Sinai, to David in Jerusalem, to Jesus resurrected and glorified in Galilee.

Second, Matthew explains Jesus' quiet and humble ways. Early in his ministry, people wondered why, if Jesus really was the promised Messiah, he lived life in such a quiet and humble way. Matthew shows how Jesus' humble life was the very vehicle for bringing world redemption. The time of Christ was the time for redemption, not judgment and destruction. Throughout his Gospel Matthew explains how Jesus' sufferings and sacrifices set a pattern for the cross-bearing ministry of all who follow him. Although believers do not know when Jesus will return, they do know what he wants them to do while they wait. The time of waiting is the time for selfless ministry to the world, not for a selfish attempt to reign and be served. The Gospel of Matthew helps to show how, like Jesus, the believers' time of glory and reigning must come only after a time of humble redemptive service to the world. Jesus' life brought salvation for the world. The humble works of believers today will serve to witness to that great redemption in Christ.

OUTLINE OF MATTHEW

A. CREDENTIALS AND CONTINUITY: JESUS FULFILLS OLD TESTAMENT PROPHECIES REGARDING THE MESSIAH (1:1–4:16)
1. The Background and Birth of Jesus (1:1-25)
2. Jesus in Egypt: Bondage and Exodus (2:1-23)
3. John the Baptist Is Presented (3:1-12)
4. Jesus Is Baptized (3:13-17)
5. Jesus Is Tempted: Identity with Israel's Testing (4:1-11)
6. The Location of Jesus' Ministry: Light Dawns on the Gentiles (4:12-16)
B. MESSIANIC IDENTITY: FULL AUTHORITY AS SERVANT AND SON OF GOD TO INAUGURATE HIS NEW COMMUNITY (4:17–16:20)
1. The Community Is Called (4:17-25)
2. Authority of Words: The Fulfilled Law (5:1–7:29)
3. Authority and True Cleanness (8:1–11:1)
4. The Question of Faith and Further Revelation about the Kingdom (11:2–13:58)
5. Faith and True Cleanness: Controversies concerning Eating Bread with Unwashed Hands (14:1–16:12)
6. Identity to the Community Supernaturally Revealed: Authority to Bind and Loose (16:13-20)
C. MESSIANIC DESTINY: FULL AUTHORITY TO COMMISSION AND PRESIDE OVER HIS NEW COMMUNITY (16:21–28:20)
1. The Son and the Cross: The Stumbling Block of Self-Preservation (16:21–17:23)
2. Sonship and Privilege in the New Community (17:24–18:35)
3. Obedience and Privilege in the Kingdom (19:1–20:16)
4. The Purpose of the Son's Coming: a Ransom (20:17-34)
5. The Servant and Son Is Praised: Triumphal Entry (21:1-11)
6. Jesus Redefines Temple Functions (21:12-17)
7. The Fig Tree Cursed: a Faith Lesson in the Context of Rejection (21:18-22)
8. The Past Disobedience to God's Messengers (21:23–23:39)

9. The Final Evaluation of Obedience (24:1–25:46)
10. A Passion Prediction and Plot (26:1-5)
11. Betrayal and Arrest (26:6-56)
12. The Passion Narrative: Guilt and Identity (26:57–27:56)
13. Burial and Resurrection (27:57–28:15)
14. Commission to the Community: Identity, Authority, and Presence (28:16-20)

MATTHEW NOTES

1:1–4:16 CREDENTIALS AND CONTINUITY: JESUS FULFILLS OLD TESTAMENT PROPHECIES REGARDING THE MESSIAH

Overview: The record of the background and birth of Jesus in the book of Matthew revealed Jesus' links to the promises and prophecies of the Old Testament (1:1-25). The cornerstone of this section was the genealogy of Jesus, which included both Abraham and David. Although Jesus was a son of David, the most prominent of Jewish kings, his links to Abraham were also stressed. Abraham was named to lay the foundation for Jesus' being the one who would bring salvation to all the nations (cf. Gen. 12:3). This emphasis on international salvation also explains the presence of Gentile women in Jesus' genealogy, and the book's thrust to include all nations in the Messianic kingdom. Drawing an ethnic circle around God's salvation, whether done by the disciples or the Jewish religious leaders, is soundly condemned by the power of God's universal promises to Abraham.

The reader cannot claim that the Davidic aspects of the genealogy were stressed simply because David was mentioned first (1:1). If Jesus was a son of David, he was also a son of Abraham. The element of Jesus' genealogy that was stressed was the Abrahamic element. The genealogy established Jesus' role as a son of David and highlighted the inclusion of the Gentiles in salvation history stemming from God's promises to Abraham. Note the Gentile elements in the genealogy (Tamar, 1:3; Rahab, 1:5; Ruth, 1:5; Uriah's wife, Bathsheba, 1:6). The genealogy showed that God sovereignly brought his salvation into the world through a long and complicated history. Jesus, the son of Abraham and David, brought together the Abrahamic (Gen. 12:1-3) and

Davidic (2 Sam. 7:16-19) covenants. That union had international (Abrahamic) and royal (Davidic) implications for God's saving work through Israel.

The most important point of the birth story was the establishment of Jesus' divine sonship (1:18-25). Joseph's negative response to the news of Mary's pregnancy was corrected by divine revelation. Joseph became the first model of a faithful disciple who listened to and obeyed God's heavenly messages (1:18-21). From that point on, Matthew showed that Jesus' life paralleled Israel's history. Just as the nation of Israel had done many centuries earlier, Jesus was taken into and out of Egypt (1:15). His absence from Palestine was compared to the time of Israel's captivity in Babylon (2:18). He suffered temptations in the wilderness like Israel (4:4, 7, 10). He was the light promised both to Israel and the Gentiles (4:15-16). But whereas Israel often failed in her role as witness to God's redemption, Jesus proved himself to be all that Israel was not. He perfectly fulfilled the destiny that God had planned for Israel by mediating God's work of redemption for the whole world.

1:1-25 The Background and Birth of Jesus

Matthew began his Gospel with Jesus' genealogy, centering on two ancestors with whom God enacted major covenants: (1) Abraham (Gen. 12:1-3) and (2) David (2 Sam. 7:12-16). The genealogy demonstrated Jesus' legal right to the throne of David. Matthew apparently did not consider Jeconiah (Jehoiachin) as cursed (1:11; cf. Jer. 22:28-30). The prophet Jeremiah had questioned whether Jehoiachin was "a despised and broken pot" (Jer. 22:28). The two verses that followed this description (Jer. 22:29-30) cursed

Israel's king and stated that "none of his offspring . . . will sit on the throne of David." If the curse in these two verses referred to Jehoiachin, one of Jesus' ancestors, the curse against Jehoiachin's descendants and Jesus' Messiahship would be contradictory. But this is not a problem, for Jeremiah 22:28 referred to Jehoiachin, while Jeremiah 22:29-30 referred back to Zedekiah, the one to whom Jeremiah was addressing his words. The curse was on Zedekiah, not Jeconiah (Jehoiachin). With the words "O land, land, land" (Jer. 22:29), Jeremiah started a new section and renewed his words to Zedekiah.

Although Jesus was the legal son of Joseph, the words "of whom" (1:16) indicated that he was the physical son of Mary (cf. 1:18). The number "fourteen" (1:17) was used as a memory device. There are gaps in this genealogy (cf. 1 Chron. 3:10-16), but its purpose was to show the relationship between Jesus and his important ancestors, not to record a complete family history.

A betrothal (1:18) was enacted by the payment of a bride's price and coming to a binding agreement regarding a future marriage. During the six to twelve month betrothal, the future husband would prepare a home for his bride. Betrothal was much more binding than modern engagements. A formal "divorce" (1:19) was necessary to break such a contract. The application of the term "husband" (1:19) to Joseph illustrates the binding nature of the betrothal relationship.

The name "Jesus" (1:21), a Greek form of the Hebrew name "Joshua," means "Salvation is of God." His name revealed the redemptive nature of his ministry. Matthew saw the fulfillment of Isaiah's prophecy (Isa. 7:14) in the birth of Jesus to the virgin Mary (1:23). The virgin birth of Jesus testified to his uniqueness and sinlessness. Without a human father he inherited no sin nature from Adam. The baby was given two names: "Jesus" (1:21) and "Immanuel" (1:23). The first, "Jesus," revealed his mission, to "save his people from their sins." The second, "Immanuel," revealed who he was in that redemptive mission, "God with us" to save and also to judge. Matthew confirmed the presence of God at the beginning (1:23) and at the end (28:20) of his Gospel.

Since King Herod the Great (2:1) died in the spring of 4 B.C., the birth of Jesus took place sometime before that date, perhaps during the winter of 5 or 4 B.C. (1:25). The present Christian Era, beginning in A.D. 1, should have had its beginning four or five years earlier. The dating followed today was based on the somewhat inaccurate calculations of Dionysius Exiguus (c. A.D. 496–540).

2:1-23 Jesus in Egypt: Bondage and Exodus

Overview: Matthew showed how Jesus was the Messiah by his identification with the experiences of the people of Israel in the Old Testament record. Jesus was presented as the one who fulfilled the role that God had intended the rebellious nation of Israel to play. Jesus' sojourn in Egypt was compared to the bondage that had been experienced by the people of Israel in that same land. Jesus was presented as the perfect Israelite in bondage (2:13-14) and in exodus (2:15). During the birth narrative (1:18-25), the historical setting of the events recorded was unclear. But at the coming of the Magi and the subsequent escape to Egypt (2:1-18), the surrounding world of Herod's evil reign came sharply into focus.

2:1-12 THE MAGI VISIT

"King Herod" (2:1) was a descendant of the Edomites, who were commonly called Idumeans in Jesus' day (cf. Gen. 36:8; Obad.). Herod had ruled as governor of Galilee from 47–37 B.C. He was then promoted to rule as king over all Palestine from 37 to 4 B.C. He became famous for building cities, fortresses, and temples throughout the land but was generally opposed by the people because of his Edomite ancestry. The "Magi" (2:1) were originally a priestly tribe in the Persian Empire. As astronomers, they may have learned of the Jewish Messianic expectation and understood the significance of the appearance of the star (cf. Num. 24:17). The Magi often held positions of considerable political influence in Persia. In 40 B.C. Jewish rebels and the Persians had joined together to push the Romans and Herod, their puppet king, out of Palestine. But in 37 B.C. Herod came back with the Romans and again took control of Jerusalem. Ever since, the Jews had shown a continual desire to overthrow Herod. In this historical context it was not surprising that Herod was disturbed and reacted with great violence when the Magi came in pomp from Persia, supported with cavalry for safety, looking for the new "king of the Jews."

The past and current high priests made up the council of "chief priests" (2:4). According to Old Testament custom the high priest officiated until he died, but the Roman authorities did not follow this system and appointed new high priests at their own discretion. The "teachers of the law" (2:4; "scribes," NASB and KJV), originally copiers of the Scriptures, were regarded as experts in Jewish law. The one "born king of the Jews" (2:2) was assumed also to be the Messiah.

The "prophet" (2:5) who foresaw the birth of the Messiah in Bethlehem was Micah (cf. Mic. 5:2). Bethlehem (2:8), the birthplace of King David, was located just five miles south of Jerusalem. By the time the Magi had arrived, Joseph had moved his family from the stable to a "house" (2:11; cf. Luke 2:39). According to the Luke account, the family of Joseph had returned to Nazareth, then back to Bethlehem before leaving for Egypt. God spoke through dreams (2:12) as he actively protected his Son from the deadly designs of Herod. The Magi's gifts of gold, incense, and myrrh were worthy of a king.

2:13-15 BONDAGE IN EGYPT:
THE SON IS CALLED OUT
Note the importance of dreams (2:13) in the early life of Jesus and in the Old Testament for Joseph in Egypt (Gen. 40–41) and Daniel in Babylon (Dan. 2–12). Matthew saw Joseph and his family's departure for Egypt as prophetically significant in the life of Jesus (2:15; cf. Hos. 11:1). The prophecy of Hosea 11:1 originally made reference to Israel's exodus from Egypt. Matthew saw a parallel relationship between the experiences of Jesus and Israel, and he understood by the Holy Spirit's inspiration that Hosea's prophecy applied to both.

Israel's great exodus from Egypt, so vital for the nation's corporate and redemptive experience, found its ultimate fulfillment in Jesus the Messiah. Israel was loved by God as a youth and was released from Egypt. Jesus was loved by God as a youth and released from Egypt. Matthew linked Jesus' experience in Egypt with the bondage, exodus, and preservation experienced by Israel during the Egyptian and Babylonian captivities. Jesus brought a fullness and completion to these earlier events in Israel's history.

2:16-18 PRESERVATION IN BABYLONIAN
EXILE: RACHEL WEEPING
Quoting from Jeremiah 31:15, Matthew viewed the Babylonian exile and Herod's murder of the baby boys as part of the same broad picture of persecution and suffering experienced by God's people. In the original historical context, Jeremiah spoke of the "weeping and great mourning" by Israelite mothers whose children had been taken in the Babylonian exile. But that exile was a prelude to a brighter future through divine preservation in a foreign land and later restoration to Israel. Rachel (2:18) was the favorite wife of Jacob and was representative of the mothers of Israel who were weeping for their lost children. In Jeremiah 31 all the children of Israel are pictured under the image of Ephraim, who is called God's "firstborn son" (Jer. 31:9; see also Jer. 31:6, 18, 20; Exod. 4:22). This figurative son was taken into captivity amidst great pain and death. The figure of Ephraim's sonship is fulfilled in God's unique son, Jesus, who was taken down into Egypt amidst the suffering of his people. But despite the suffering of his descendants, Ephraim was Joseph's favored son who was favored and blessed by his grandfather Jacob (cf. Gen. 48:14-20).

2:19-23 HUMBLE REMNANT:
THE SON CALLED A NAZARENE
Archelaus (2:22; 4 B.C.–A.D. 6) was a cruel and oppressive ruler. Complaints against him by both Jews and Samaritans resulted in his banishment by Augustus Caesar. Matthew viewed Jesus' residence in Nazareth as prophetically significant (2:23). Nazareth was a despised town because of its association with Sepphoris, the Roman capital of Galilee, situated just four miles to the north. Matthew related the name "Nazareth" to the Messianic title in Isaiah 11:1 (Heb. *netzer*, meaning "Branch," "sprout," or "shoot"). Matthew's mention of the city of Nazareth combined the concepts of lowliness and the wordplay on a Messianic title.

3:1-12 John the Baptist Is Presented

The "Desert of Judea" (3:1) was a barren desert region west of the Dead Sea. John's message was "Repent, for the kingdom of heaven is near" (3:1-2). For years, people had been saying the kingdom of heaven was coming. John announced that it was at hand. John was identified as the one who would "Prepare the way for the Lord" (3:3; cf. Isa. 40:3). See the context of Matthew's quote in the book of Isaiah (Isa. 40:1-11). John the Baptist came as a prelude to the Messianic age. John's appearance (3:4) was similar to that of Elijah (2 Kings 1:8) and this was the only explicit connection made between John the Baptist and Elijah in the Matthew account. John was in the wilderness "to prepare the way for the Lord." He had to be sought out (3:5) because his ministry was to a separated people who were willing to come away from society to confess their sins.

John's message had a twofold thrust (3:2). First, he wanted people to repent and be saved. This directed listeners to acknowledge their guilt (3:6) and change the attitudes of their hearts. Second, his end-time message, "the kingdom of heaven is near," had to do with the fulfillment of God's promise to David of a Messianic kingdom (2 Sam. 7:12-16). Through his ministry, John the Baptist became the "voice . . . calling in the desert" (3:3) foreseen in Isaiah 40:3. He came as the Messianic forerunner, the one sent ahead to announce the Messiah's coming.

The "coming wrath" (3:7) was related to the coming of the Messianic kingdom. According to Josephus, the "Pharisees" (3:7) were "a body of Jews with the reputation of excelling the rest of their nation in the observances of religion, and as exact exponents of the laws." They were middle class Jews, primarily associated with the synagogue. The "Sadducees" (3:7) were the priestly aristocracy associated with the Jewish temple. Unlike the Pharisees, they did not believe in the bodily resurrection, since they did not believe this doctrine was taught in the Mosaic Scriptures. They did not accept anything except the Mosaic Scriptures (Genesis, Exodus, Leviticus, Numbers, and Deuteronomy) as authoritative.

The expression "brood of vipers" (23:3) characterized the religious leaders as evil and deceitful. These leaders had misunderstood the significance of the original international scope of the Abrahamic covenant. John the Baptist anticipated judgment on the unrepentant and corrupt Jewish religious establish-

ment (3:10; cf. 23:37-38; John 15:1-2, 6). John the Baptist's mission was to call Israel to repent and be changed at the level of the heart and character, not on the level of outward religious ritual.

The word "baptize" (3:11) was a transliteration of the Greek word *baptizo,* meaning "to dip" or "to immerse." The Greek root *bapto* was used by those in the dye trade to describe the "dipping" of cloth. As a result of this "dipping," the cloth would be identified with a new color. The word was used here of a religious act of baptism that would result in one becoming identified as a follower of John and his movement. The baptism "with the Holy Spirit and with fire" (3:11) foreseen by John suggested the work of Christ at Pentecost (Acts 2) and the final judgment (3:12; 13:40-42). The "winnowing fork" (3:12) was an instrument used for tossing threshed grain into the air to separate the wheat from the broken bits of straw (chaff). In the judgment, God would separate the repentant (grain) from the unrepentant (chaff) (cf. 25:31-46).

3:13-17 Jesus Is Baptized

John misunderstood Jesus' intentions at his baptism. John understood baptism to represent an act of repentance, and thus, protested Jesus' baptism. But Jesus did not come to repent of sin. He came to identify with his people in righteous alignment with God's purposes. He came to "fulfill all righteousness" (3:15) by identifying himself with the righteous remnant of God's chosen people— the people he had come to represent and save (cf. 12:18-21). The righteousness Jesus sought to fulfill included God's plans and demands for his people and John the Baptist. It also included Jesus' identification with the righteous remnant in Israel.

God's announcement (3:17) was the first of three times when God spoke from heaven regarding his Son (cf. 17:5; John 12:28). There were two titles given here: (1) "Son" (cf. Exod. 4:22, where God spoke of the nation of Israel as his son) and (2) "beloved" (cf. Gen. 22:2, where Abraham called his only son, Isaac, "beloved"). Jesus was both the Messiah and the representative of the covenant people before God. That representation would become the basis for the mediating role he would take in God's ongoing work of redemption.

4:1-11 Jesus Is Tempted: Identity with Israel's Testing

Satan's intent in the temptations was to cause Jesus to sin by taking shortcuts to the accomplishment of his kingdom purposes. God's purpose was to demonstrate Jesus' sinlessness (cf. 2 Cor. 5:21; Heb. 4:15) through his obedience to the Father's will. Jesus responded to the temptations by quoting Scripture (Matt. 4:4, cf. Deut. 8:3; Matt. 4:7, cf. Deut. 6:16; and Matt. 4:10, cf. Deut. 6:13) and refusing to fall into sin.

During Jesus' temptations in the wilderness, he quoted from the Old Testament Scriptures connected with Israel's own wilderness experience. But where Israel had failed to obey God during its wilderness experience, Jesus succeeded in perfect obedience during his. God was well pleased (Matt. 3:17) with Jesus' righteousness (3:15). His baptism and subsequent temptation in the wilderness was compared to Israel's passing through the Red Sea into the wilderness. Israel was tested for forty years and Jesus for forty days.

The first temptation (4:3-4) was with regard to food. It was a test of Jesus' dependence on and trust in the Father to provide for everyday needs. In his defense against Satan Jesus quoted from Deuteronomy 8:1-3, where Moses was reminding the people of Israel of God's provision of manna in the wilderness. Satan was tempting Jesus to make his own manna and not trust in God's provision. In Deuteronomy 8, the people were reminded that the purpose of manna was to test the heart's devotion to God. The Israelites had to depend on God's provision since there was no other food supply available. This first temptation was intended to thwart Jesus' dependence upon his Father by causing him to use his own resources to meet his need. The words of Satan, "the tempter" (Matt. 4:3), could be translated, "Since you are the Son of God . . ."

The second temptation (4:5-7) was with regard to safety. Satan hoped to tempt Jesus into trying or testing the power and ability of God. This would have been a rash self-assertion to prove a point that did not need proving. Such an act would have shown a lack of faith in the power of the Father. Compare the commandment "Do not put the Lord your God to the test" (4:7; Deut. 6:16) with the time Israel put the Lord to the test in the wilderness because they were angry and lacked faith (Exod. 17:1-7). This test would prove whether or not God was with the nation of Israel in the Sinai wilderness or with Jesus in the Judean wilderness. But the people of Israel and Jesus needed no such proof. To test God again would only prove a lack of faith. Thus, this second temptation tested Jesus' faith in God's presence and control over life's events. The "pinnacle" (4:5) referred to the southeast corner of the temple that overlooked the deep Kidron Valley. The second temptation was intended to cause Jesus to put God to the test by placing himself in a precarious situation that would require divine intervention (4:6).

The third temptation (4:8-9) was with regard to power and wealth. It was a temptation to short-circuit God's plan for salvation that required the redemptive suffering of Jesus. Satan offered Jesus immediate glory and riches, while God's plan would take Jesus down a road of suffering and death. Jesus quoted Deuteronomy 6:13 in his defense against Satan. In Deuteronomy 6:10-15, Moses had warned the people of Israel as they entered the Promised Land to avoid the temptation to fall into idolatry. He warned Israel not to forget that God had given them all that they owned in the Promised Land. Similarly, Jesus had to avoid the temptation to embrace riches and forget God. Jesus was offered all of this world's kingdoms under Satan's authority (cf. John 12:30-32; Eph. 2:1-2) for just one little act of worship. But such sin would have disqualified Jesus as God's means of redemption to the world.

During his own wilderness experience, Jesus, the perfect Israelite, was identified with his people in the wilderness of Sinai. All his quotations of Old Testament Scripture reflected similar temptations experienced by the nation of Israel in the wilderness. But where Israel had failed, Jesus succeeded. Jesus' use of the Old Testament pointed to his temptations being the fulfillment and summation of Israel's wilderness temptations. Jesus, who would represent the people as a perfect sacrifice, had proved worthy of the task by conquering the temptations that had overcome Israel centuries before. Jesus banished Satan and as a result enjoyed God's provision (4:10-11).

4:12-16 The Location of Jesus' Ministry: Light Dawns on the Gentiles

Jesus identified with the nation of Israel through his ancestry and birth, as well as through his parallel experiences. The events of Jesus' youth summed up the major events of Israel's history. His temptations paralleled Israel's failures in the wilderness. He further identified with Israel by the locale of his ministry. But his work of salvation would not be for Israel alone. He also came to bring light to the Gentiles (4:12-16). Leaving Nazareth, he moved directly into the territory of Herod Antipas, the one who had imprisoned John the Baptist (4:12-13). For more on John the Baptist's arrest and execution (4:12), see Matthew 14:1-12.

"Zebulun and Naphtali" (4:13) were Israelite tribes that occupied the region of Galilee. Luke recorded that after his rejection, Jesus left Nazareth and settled in Capernaum, a fishing village and tax collection station along the northwest shore of the Sea of Galilee. Matthew did not mention Jesus' one-year Judean ministry noted in John 1–3.

The location of Zebulun and Naphtali related to the Old Testament prophecy of Isaiah (4:14-16; cf. Isa. 9:1-7). Although Galilee was occupied by the descendants of these tribes, a variety of Gentile people groups lived in the area as well. Jesus was beginning a major new movement; he was bringing a new light to the Gentiles. Matthew saw in Jesus' arrival in Galilee a fulfillment of Isaiah 9:1-2. A new era had dawned for a region that once lay in spiritual darkness. Jesus' ministry had started with Israel but would extend to all the nations.

4:17–16:20 MESSIANIC IDENTITY: FULL AUTHORITY AS SERVANT AND SON OF GOD TO INAUGURATE HIS NEW COMMUNITY

Overview: This section of the book of Matthew (4:17–16:20) is introduced by the phrase "from that time on" (4:17). The events of this section elaborate the meaning of the simple message: "Repent, for the kingdom of heaven is near" (4:17). The phrase "from that time on" also introduces the final major section of the book (cf. 16:21). In that section, the passion or suffering of Jesus will be the primary focus.

The kingdom proclaimed by Jesus would come at God's own time and in God's own way. In section 4:17–16:20, that "time" and "way" were greatly illuminated and defined by the Lord's words and actions. The problem of man's sin was especially significant for the coming of the kingdom (cf. Isa. 51:1-8; 62:1-2; Dan. 9:24). Jesus' new covenant was based on a complete forgiveness of sins (cf. Jer. 31:33). The very name "Jesus" meant that he would save his people from their sins (Matt. 1:21). Therefore, whether people rejected or accepted Jesus, his death as the substitute for mankind's punishment was indispensable. The resolution of the sin problem was the only way to open the "gates" to the kingdom of God. The cross and the kingdom were inseparably linked.

This section presents four major events in the life of Jesus: (1) the calling of his new community of disciples (4:18-22); (2) the authority of his words in fulfillment of the law (5:1–7:29); (3) the authority of his deeds as his identity is questioned (8:1–16:12); and (4) the revelation of his identity, supernaturally revealed to his community of disciples, along with his gift of authority to "bind" and "loose" (16:13-20).

4:17-25 The Community Is Called

Jesus' message was precisely the same as John the Baptist's (4:17; cf. 3:2). Jesus started where John left off, but he would soon go far beyond all that John had said and done (cf., for example, 4:23-25; 5:1–7:29). The call of the first disciples in 4:18-22 chronologically follows the events of John 1:35-51. This was not the first contact that these men had had with Jesus. They had heard John the Baptist identify him as the Lamb of God and had traveled with Jesus to Cana where they had seen his first miracle (John 2:1-11). But now at Jesus' invitation, they left their fishing to become fishers of men by proclaiming the gospel. The gospel was the "good news" of forgiveness for those who would repent and align themselves with the righteous remnant (cf. Isa. 1:19-20; 25:6-9; 51:1-8; Mal. 4:1-2).

Jesus was teaching in the synagogues (Matt. 4:23; cf. Luke 4:16-22), announcing the kingdom (cf. Matt. 4:17), and authenticating his message by miracles (12:28;

cf. John 20:30-31). The stress on healing was leading up to the Matthew 8:17 quote of Isaiah 53:4. Healing was a picture or outward sign of a greater restoration based on the forgiveness of sins (Matt. 9:6). Many interesting things happened during this part of Jesus' ministry, but Matthew rushed through the events to give the reader a sense of the general impact and growing ministry of Jesus.

"Decapolis" (4:25) was a Gentile district east of the Jordan River known for its splendid Greek cities. This section (4:17-25) gave a quick summary of Jesus' teaching, preaching, and healing ministries as a contextual background for Jesus' well-known Sermon on the Mount in the following chapters (Matt. 5–7).

5:1–7:29 Authority of Words: the Fulfilled Law

Overview: Matthew 5–7 is commonly called the Sermon on the Mount. In it Jesus gave his definition of true righteousness. These chapters reveal the nature of true righteousness (Matt. 5), the question of rewards and which master should be served to receive those rewards (Matt. 6), and repentance as an individual responsibility and choice (Matt. 7). Some of the key elements reflected problems with the religious leaders (6:2, 5, 7, 16), questions about the nature and application of the Mosaic Law (5:17, 20, 48), and questions about the means of entering the kingdom of heaven (7:20-23).

The Sermon on the Mount served as an extended example of Jesus' preaching of repentance and the kingdom of God (cf. 4:17). He proclaimed the kingdom in order to inspire repentance in his listeners. He desired that his listeners might turn away from sinful attitudes and deeds in order to bring about a change in their standing before God. He wanted to lead people away from their fallible human wills so that they might follow the infallible will of God. The Sermon gave descriptions of and demands for potential and aspiring kingdom dwellers.

The Sermon was spoken to a curious multitude who had responded with interest to Jesus' message and miracles. They knew that righteousness was required for entrance into God's kingdom (cf. Ps. 24:3-6). But they wondered if the righteousness of their Pharisaic practices was sufficient for entrance into the kingdom. Jesus delivered the theme of his message in Matthew 5:20 where he said, "Unless your righteousness surpasses that of the Pharisees and the teachers of the law, you will certainly not enter the kingdom of heaven." The righteousness necessary for entering the kingdom was to be found through faith in Christ (6:33). The "blessed" people (5:1-12) were those that were closely related to the kingdom of God. When the kingdom came, it would be theirs.

5:1-12 EIGHT CHARACTERISTICS OF KINGDOM DWELLERS

The Beatitudes (5:1-12) revealed eight characteristics that should be true of the righteous remnant in the promised kingdom. The truths implied in these characteristics all reflect pervasive themes in the Old Testament. They revealed to the listeners what the lives of people in the process of repentance should be like and caused them to reflect upon their own character in relation to the character of God. The Beatitudes were built upon an *if/then* logic and hidden in each Beatitude was an *if/then* relationship. For example, the first Beatitude says in essence, "*If* you are poor in spirit, *then* you will receive the kingdom of God" (5:3). The Beatitudes both describe and demand. They *demand* good character as they *describe* the "blessed" results of following the demands of kingdom living.

The attitudes of "poor in spirit," "mourning," and "meekness" all draw upon Old Testament themes and underscore the need for human responsibility and the work of divine grace. The basic element demanded by all the Beatitudes was a right relationship with God. The Beatitudes were intended to inspire Matthew's readers to think about the character of the repentant person so that they also could follow the path of repentance.

Matthew 5:3-16 should be seen as one single unit of thought. The word "blessed" (5:3; etc.) literally means "happy." For "poor in spirit" (5:3) see Psalms 40:17; 69:29-30, 33-34; and Isaiah 57:15; 61:1; 66:2, 5. This characteristic describes the inner attitude of a person when confronted with the holy God and his demands. Being "poor in spirit" means admitting that no one can have spiritual wealth in and of themselves—that all are dependent on God alone for spiritual salvation and daily grace. Such a person aligns with God's will, even against the desires of his own.

For the attitude of "mourning" (Matt. 5:4), see Isaiah 1:17, 23; 2:11, 17; 61:2. The afflicted were often seen as God's favorites in contrast with the powerful. This "mourning" was a reaction to seeing all that God had demanded for the kingdom and then seeing how far all of mankind had fallen short.

For the attitude of "meekness" (Matt. 5:5) read Psalm 37:7-11 and Isaiah 57:15. Having the quality of "meekness" would result in possession of the new heavens and new earth (cf. Isa. 66; Rev. 21–22). The Beatitudes and the Sermon on the Mount as a whole continually looked forward to the time of judgment and reward in the end times.

To "hunger and thirst for righteousness" (Matt. 5:6) was to seek to live life as God intended for it to be lived. Concepts drawn from Old Testament Wisdom Literature were being applied here (cf. Prov. 8:22-36). For "pure in heart" (Matt. 5:8), see what it meant under the old covenant (Deut. 6) as well as under the new covenant (Jer. 31; Ezek. 36).

The "peacemakers" (Matt. 5:9) will be called "sons of God." They will be heirs to God's kingdom of which "peace" will be an important characteristic (cf. Isa. 9:6-7; 66:12-13; Mic. 4:3). Note the emphasis in 5:3, 4, 9, 10. In each of these verses, an implied contrast was being made between those who would be blessed in the age to come and the religious leaders of Jesus' day.

Those "persecuted because of righteousness" (5:10) would also be heirs to the kingdom. This relates back to 5:3 regarding the kingdom and to 5:6 regarding righteousness. The idea of this verse carried a bit of irony. These people were being persecuted because they were hungry and thirsty for righteousness. But their persecutors would be the religious leaders of Israel, the ones who claimed to strictly follow the way of righteousness.

Jesus made a personal elaboration (5:11-12) of the comments in 5:10. He would become the cause for the persecution of the righteous ("because of me," 5:11). The people who desired to be among the "blessed" of the kingdom would not find their time on earth easy. Matthew wrote for people who faced a time of persecution prior to the establishment of the kingdom. There

was a parallel drawn in 5:12 with the prophets of the past who had suffered for the sake of righteousness.

5:13-16 TWO FUNCTIONS OF BLESSED PEOPLE

Those who had repented and suffered for righteousness were linked to the prophets of old (Matt. 5:12). The message that God called them to proclaim was the message of the gospel to all the world (28:19-20). The fact that believers were to be like "salt" (5:13) communicated the prophetic function of living righteous lives and calling others to repentance. It meant having an impact for God and not being ineffectual. Salt, by its very nature, flavors and preserves everything that it comes in contact with. If it did not do these things, then it would not be salt. Salt, a valuable commodity in the dry Middle East, was used in the biblical period for barter. In fact the word "salary" comes from the Latin *salarius* ("salt"). A person lacking integrity might have mixed white sand with the salt and then had more for trade. But salt mixed with sand lost some of its salty quality and became useless.

The fact that believers were to be like "light" (5:14-16) emphasized the aspect of visibility. As light attracts people and dispels darkness, so believers were to illumine the way to Jesus the Messiah, the true source of light. The doing of good works was a form of that light. Good works would inspire others to believe in and glorify God. The giving of "light to everyone in the house" (5:15) looked ahead to the final commission to go into all the world (28:19).

5:17-48 THE FULFILLED LAW: DIVINE PERFECTION

Jesus gave five examples of the fulfillment of the law. He corrected a possible misunderstanding concerning the purpose of his coming (5:17-20). He did not come to abolish the law (5:17). But he did come to demand perfection (cf. 5:48). Jesus had just spoken of good works (5:16), and he, like the prophets of old, demanded the same holy character and acts of obedience. He brought no new way of living in God's kingdom. He simply expanded and deepened God's long-standing desire for his creation's obedience and holiness. He started with the Pharisees' standard of righteousness: obedience to the law. But he applied that law not only to the external deeds that a person might do, but also to the attitudes and thoughts in the depths of a person's heart. Fulfilled law is no longer the law imposed upon a person from the outside, but that which is written on the heart and becomes an integral part of that person (cf. 5:22, 28, 32, 34, 39, 44). If the law becomes internalized, obedience becomes instinctive and pleasant, not something a person is forced to do. Throughout the Sermon on the Mount, Jesus called his hearers to move from external obedience to an obedience motivated by the law written upon the heart (5:22, 28, 32, 34, 39, 44; 6:19-24).

The word "fulfill" (5:17) meant "to clarify" the true meaning of the law as a way to walk or a way of life. It also meant "to complete," the opposite of "to abolish" (5:17). The "smallest letter" (5:18) of the Hebrew alphabet is the *yod*, about the size of an apostrophe. The "least stroke of a pen" is a very small mark that distinguishes the Hebrew letter *dalet* from the letter *resh*. Notice the consequences if a person "breaks one of the least of these commandments" (5:19) or "teaches others to do the same." Jesus was teaching full and complete obedience to all the law.

True believers were to exhibit a righteousness surpassing that of the Pharisees (5:20). Righteousness equals the tally sheet of kept commands. The religious leaders of the day served as the foil in Jesus' sermon. What righteousness could they possibly have lacked? Five examples of how the Pharisees failed to fulfill the law were given in 5:21-28: (1) murder and anger 5:21-26; (2) adultery and lust 5:27-32; (3) vows and simplicity (5:33-37; cf. Lev. 19:12; Num. 30:2); (4) revenge and nonresistance (Matt. 5:38-42); and (5) loving enemies (5:43-48).

The words "You have heard" (5:21) referred not to the teaching of Moses but to the imbalanced Pharisaic interpretation of the law. "Raca" (5:22) is an Aramaic word that means "empty-headed." The word translated "hell" (Gehenna) referred literally to the L-shaped Hinnom Valley, south and west of Jerusalem. Child sacrifices had once been offered there (cf. Jer. 7:31), but it had become in Jesus' time an

unclean rubbish heap noted for its continual burning. It became a metaphor for the place of eternal punishment.

Jesus' words specifically condemned lust as a form of adultery (Matt. 5:28). In 5:29-30 Jesus used hyperbole (exaggeration for the sake of emphasis) which was a common biblical means of making a strong point. While Jesus did not intend physical maiming, he did emphasize the seriousness of the sin and its consequences.

Jesus referred to the faulty Pharisaic interpretation of Moses' teaching on divorce (5:31; cf. Deut. 24:1-4). Jesus condemned divorce for any reason except for "marital unfaithfulness" (Matt. 5:32). This has been interpreted to refer to adultery, unfaithfulness during betrothal (cf. 1:19), or incestuous marriage (cf. Lev. 18:6-18). This exception to the permanence of marriage appears only in Matthew (cf. Mark 10:2-12; Luke 16:18). Jesus said that one who divorces a spouse contributes to the adultery that may result in the following remarriage. He added that in many cases marriage to a divorced person constitutes adultery since divorce did not dissolve the "one-flesh" covenant relationship of the original marriage.

The Old Testament strongly condemned false oaths (cf. Exod. 20:7; Lev. 19:12), but the rabbis made hair-splitting distinctions between oaths that had to be fulfilled and those that did not (Matt. 5:33). The "law of retaliation" (Exod. 21:24) was not designed to encourage retaliation but to limit it with a view to justice (Matt. 5:38). The Pharisees mistook this as an encouragement for revenge. The Old Testament had taught love for one's neighbor (Lev. 19:18), and the principle of hatred for one's enemies was a Pharisaic perversion (Matt. 5:43). Passages like Deuteronomy 23:3-4 were not excuses to hate one's enemies but needed to be interpreted in context. Deuteronomy 23:7-8 goes on to require the acceptance of Edomites and Egyptians. The issue was holiness in God's assembly, not a generic excuse to hate anyone who was offensive. The essential teaching for dealing with the problem of enemies was reliance upon God's, not man's, justice. For Matthew 5:40, compare 1 Corinthians 6:7. These acts of nonresistance motivated by unselfish love would clearly represent the shining good works that were to character-ize the kingdom of heaven (Matt. 5:16).

God was the model for the characteristics of righteousness spoken of in the Sermon on the Mount. Believers were being asked to do what was humanly impossible. They were to do what God did: love their enemies—the very thing God did for mankind through the incarnation of his Son. This passage was not talking about ethical perfection (5:4). Rather, it was commanding believers to be as con-sistent and generous toward people as God is (causing rain and sun). The law of Christ freed believers from having a provincial attitude toward other people, toward the extent of God's love, and toward the intent of the law. In 5:21-48 Jesus rejected the Pharisaic interpretation of the law as superfi-cial. He emphasized inner conformity to the spirit of the law rather than mere out-ward conformity to the letter of the law. The true requirements of the law were high-lighted to convict listeners of their need to turn to Jesus, the one true source of righ-teousness.

6:1-34 REWARDS: SINGULAR MASTERY Matthew 5 dealt with righteousness and God's demands. The subject in Matthew 6 turns to that which motivates most people to performance: rewards. The subjects covered were prayer, fasting, and the giving of alms. Because none of these three practices were demanded by the law, there was a greater tendency to boast about doing them. Jesus rejected the common practice among the Pharisees of parading their piety to be noticed by men, and he condemned doing good works for personal glory.

6:2-4 Alms. Jesus struck at the heart of Pharisaic hypocrisy when he condemned the Pharisees for the way they performed their acts of prayer, fasting, and the giving of alms—the pillars of Jewish piety (cf. Tobit 12:8). To "announce it with trumpets" (6:2) was possibly a reference to the noisy manner in which offerings were tossed into the thir-teen trumpet-shaped chests in the temple. The alms given in secret (6:4) may have been a reference to the "Chamber of Secrets" in the temple where, according to the Mish-nah, the devout gave their gifts in secret.

6:5-15 Prayer. The "room" (6:6; "inner room," NASB; "closet," KJV) probably referred to the storeroom. In most first-century Jewish homes, it was the only room that had a door. The "pagans" (6:7; "Gen-tiles," NASB; "heathen," KJV) were men-tioned as people who prayed endlessly for fear that their gods might not hear them. But God does not need to be informed when prayers are being said. He already knows. Prayer should consist of a humble, yet confi-dent, conversation with God.

The "Lord's Prayer" (Matt. 6:9-13) was clearly a model for the disciples to follow, not an exact formula to recite in each prayer. In the parallel passage in Luke 11:2-4, the words vary, but the pattern remains the same. The Bible teaches that God does not tempt man to sin (Matt. 6:13; cf. James 1:13-14). The words of Matthew 6:13 meant "Do not allow us to succumb to temptation." Prayer should align the will of the person praying with God's will ("your will be done," 6:10). It calls the believer to realize that God is the source of all blessing and that his creation is in need of his sustaining hand.

6:16-18 Fasting. Only one fast was required by the Mosaic Law, the Day of Atonement (Lev. 16:29-34), but many other fast days developed in Jewish tradition (cf. Zech. 8:19). Jesus advised his followers to go about their business on a fast day as they would on any other, so that only God would know of their sacrificial deed.

6:19-24 Treasures evidence heart attach-ment. In Matthew 6:1-8 the focus was on the choice between receiving rewards from men or from God. In 6:19-34 the focus is on the choice between the treasures of earth or the treasures of heaven. Notice the reason for God being concerned about where believers hoard their treasures (6:21). God wants the hearts of his followers to be permanently with him, not captured by the things of earth that will soon disappear.

Impaired vision affects a person's whole body (6:22-23), and similar damaging conse-quences result from an obsession with money (6:24). The eye illuminates the body and gives it the ability to see the world around it. Without the aid of sight, it is easy to get lost or be deceived. Similarly, when a person lives for money, he is blinded to the truth about life and can be easily led astray. For such a person, dark and light are difficult to distinguish. True vision can only be found by serving God alone, the true master.

6:25-34 The avoidance of anxiety. Along with the Pharisees' concern for material gain came the problem of anxiety (6:25). The command "Do not worry" was repeated three times (6:25, 31, 34) for emphasis. When God is the master of a person's life, that person has no need to be anxious about his physical needs. This does not mean that believers should refuse to work and expect God to provide for them. The fulfillment of human responsibility is necessary (like the bird that is fed only by seeking the food that has been provided). God will meet the needs of those who responsibly seek to obey him. With the problem of daily provision solved, believers are free to seek more important things in life, such as the kingdom of heaven (6:33).

In Matthew 5 the Father was presented as the model for perfect righteousness (5:21-48). Therefore, God the Father was the one to please with obedience and to seek after, not the hypocritical Jewish leaders (Matt. 6). In Matthew 7 a starting place for curing hypocrisy (for effecting true repentance) was presented; it called believers and any person who might judge other people to purify their own lives first before trying to change others (7:1-27; especially 7:5).

7:1-29 REPENTANCE: RESPONSIBLE INDIVIDUAL CHOICE

For the godly leader, personal inner reform must always precede the teaching of others. Jesus condemned the hypocritical judgments commonly made by the Pharisees. He called leaders to judge with humble discernment, not prideful criticism (7:1-5). See 2 Samuel 12:1-7 for an example of how King David found it easy to judge someone else while he had a giant log in his own eye. The tendency for most people working for reform is to start by condemning others. Jesus reminded people to judge themselves before criticizing others because missing their own faults would leave them condemned. Jesus was not against people correcting and evaluating each other. On the contrary, he supported criticism that was done with humility and

love (cf. Matt. 7:5). It is important to distinguish between judging self-righteously and discerning sin with proper humility (cf. Matt. 18:15; Gal. 6:1).

Jesus ended this section on avoiding self-righteous criticism with a warning to beware of false disciples (Matt. 7:6, "dogs," "pigs"). The section on throwing pearls (7:6) immediately followed Jesus' command to see clearly and without hypocrisy. Such clear sight was necessary for those who followed Jesus. He wanted them to be able to discriminate between the holy and unholy in order to give what was appropriate to where it was needed. The two illustrations of dogs and pigs were not designed to insult the very people God came to save. Figuratively, were not all people unholy like dogs and pigs? Jesus taught here that when someone seeks to take the speck out of another's eye (7:5), he needs to have the wisdom to discern the specific situation and to bring the appropriate remedy. It is not appropriate, for example, to feed dogs the holy food used in the temple. Nor is it appropriate to trick pigs by giving them pearls instead of real food. The link between the two illustrations is the inappropriateness of the remedy for the need. The holy food was for the priests, not dogs, and pearls are for jewelry, not for angering hungry pigs. It is doubtful that Jesus was calling any particular religious or secular group of people dogs or swine. He and his disciples shared God's holy truth with Jews, Gentiles, men and women alike. Some received his word and some responded to it with murderous anger. Jesus was not teaching to withhold God's truth from unworthy people. He was teaching his followers to be as wise and effective as possible while ministering the gospel.

Jesus concluded the Sermon on the Mount by offering entrance to the kingdom to those who would act on his words (7:7-27). The present imperatives could be translated in a continuous sense, "keep on asking," "keep on seeking," "keep on knocking" (7:7). This section also served as a warning ("Watch out," 7:15) against false doctrines and ungodly living. To show how crucial this warning was, Jesus placed it in the context of the end times; it was important to act immediately, for the end was near ("destruction," 7:13; "life," 7:14; "fire," 7:19; "on that day," 7:22; "Away from me," 7:23; "it fell with a great crash," 7:27). Jesus compared life's way, that could lead either into the kingdom or into destruction, to two roads (7:13-14), two trees (7:15-23), and two houses (7:24-27).

In his sermon, Jesus stressed the importance of doing God's will, that is, keeping his commandments within the covenant bond. Jesus illustrated the doing of God's will or the doing of its opposite by such concepts as good and bad "fruits" (7:16-20), or phrases like, "does the will of my Father" (7:21); "you evildoers," (7:23; "you who practice lawlessness," NASB; "ye that work iniquity," KJV); and "puts them [the words of Jesus] into practice" (7:24, 26). This was the application section of the Sermon on the Mount. The "narrow gate" (7:13) was the way of faith in Jesus Christ (inward righteousness). The wide gate was the way of Pharisaism (outward righteousness). The words of Jesus in this section reflected the blessings and curses given in Deuteronomy 11:26-29.

The false prophets (professing disciples) would be identified by their fruits—their deeds as well as their doctrines (Matt. 7:15-23). It would be practice, not mere profession, that would reflect a genuine relationship with God. This was an expansion of John the Baptist's message. Jesus was warning against false or hypocritical obedience (7:21).

The story of the two houses (7:24-27) illustrated the importance of practicing the wise words of Jesus. The common biblical motif of comparing the practices of wisdom and foolishness was employed in these verses. See Deuteronomy 30:19-20 on the blessings or curses that result from either listening to or ignoring the wise counsel of God.

After Jesus had completed the Sermon on the Mount, the audience was amazed at his authority (Matt. 7:28-29). In contrast with the scribes who simply quoted the rabbinic interpretations of the law, Jesus spoke in a manner that reflected his intrinsic authority as the Son of God. Their response of awe and amazement should be the response of people today. Jesus spoke many other times in Matthew, but this was the only address with an audience response noted (11:1; 13:53; 19:1-2; 26:1-2).

8:1–11:1 Authority and True Cleanness

Overview: There are three guiding concepts found in this section: (1) the source of authority; (2) the source of cleanness; and (3) the source of revelation. In this section Jesus illustrated with his own life the principles given in the Sermon on the Mount.

8:1-34 AUTHORITY OVER ILLNESS AND DEMONS

The significant points to note in the section of 8:1-34 are the authority of Jesus over sin and suffering and the Gentile aspects of his ministry.

8:1-4 The healing of a leper. Lepers were regarded as unclean on the basis of Old Testament Levitical law (8:3; cf. Lev. 13:45-46). The removal of sickness was one of the great blessings anticipated in the kingdom (Matt. 8:4; cf. Isa. 33:24). The purpose of this miracle was not only to cure the leper but to alert the Jewish religious establishment in Jerusalem that there was someone in Galilee exhibiting Messianic credentials. The religious leaders in Jerusalem were notified and began an investigation of Jesus (cf. Matt. 9:1-8).

8:5-13 A centurion's faith. The "centurion" (8:5) was an officer in the Roman army who was in charge of one hundred men (a "century"), though by Jesus' time the actual number of men had dropped to eighty. They were responsible for training their men, leading them into battle, keeping track of military equipment, posting guards, and making inspections.

Why were only Abraham, Isaac, and Jacob mentioned as those who would be in the kingdom and not Moses and David (8:11-12)? Because the Gentile, not the Jewish, inclusion into God's salvation was being stressed. Indeed, the sons of the kingdom had to be obedient, and their very sonship was a privilege, not a guarantee. Any obedient person would ultimately be included in the kingdom promised by Jesus without respect to his ethnic background.

Those who "come from the east and the west" (8:11) was a reference to the Gentiles. The teachings of Jesus reflected the universal aspect of the Abrahamic covenant (Gen. 12:1-3). The "subjects of the kingdom" (Matt. 8:12) was a reference to Jews who thought they would gain access to God's kingdom simply because they were descendants of Abraham. It is personal faith that enables one to appropriate the Messiah's promised benefits and blessings (8:13).

8:14-17 The healing of Peter's mother-in-law. In Matthew 8:17, Matthew quoted from Isaiah 53:4. Diseases, griefs, and iniquities were seen as interrelated in the Old Testament. The root cause of all sickness and suffering was sin. By removing the effects of sin, that is, sickness, Jesus was demonstrating his ability to deal with the ultimate cause—sin itself.

The healings pointed forward to the work of Jesus on the cross by beginning the conquest of sin's effects (cf. Matt. 27:27-31 with Isa. 53:4-5). Matthew quoted from Isaiah 53 to show that in Jesus' works of physical healing and bringing forgiveness for sin, he was fulfilling the visible signs that the prophets attributed to the promised Messiah. The event recorded in Matthew 9:6 carried the concept of Jesus' forgiving sin further, though Matthew did not elaborate or theologize upon Jesus' substitutionary death. The work of theology was left for the apostle Paul.

8:18-22 The focus and priority of discipleship. This is a departure saying and includes the first occurrence in Matthew of the phrase, "Son of Man." Jesus' use of the term went against the common Messianic concepts of the day, including the Messianic concept of militant Judaism. Jesus did not first come to reign victorious or destroy the military might of Rome. Where would Jesus take his followers in the political, military, or religious terms of the world (8:20)? Nowhere. Jesus cautioned the disciples to evaluate their reason for following him. He wanted to make sure that they knew that glory and conquest would only come after they had suffered humiliation in the eyes of the world.

The term "Son of Man" (8:20) was used thirty-two times in Matthew by Jesus to refer to himself. As used by Jesus, the term drew on the implications of its use in Daniel 7:13 (for more on the "Son of Man," see the guiding concepts for the Gospel of Mark). In Matthew 8:22 Jesus was saying, "let the spiritually dead bury the physically dead." There was no greater priority than following the Author of Life.

8:23-27 The obedient storm: What kind of man is this? The "lake" (8:24) was a reference to the fresh water Sea of Galilee, situated about 680 feet below sea level. The Mediterranean winds often rush through the valleys of Galilee and swoop down into the basin of the Sea of Galilee causing strong tempests. The audience's response was noted in 8:27. Jesus's authority was demonstrated by his power over nature, and his calming of the storm also gave support to his claim to authority over sin and death (cf. 9:4-7).

8:28-34 Jesus rejected in Gentile territory. The "region of the Gadarenes" (8:28) was the region of Gadara, a city located six miles southeast of the Sea of Galilee (see introductory map). Mark and Luke located the miracle in connection with the better known, but more distant, city of Gerasa (cf. Mark 5:1; Luke 8:26). In destroying the swine, the demons may have wanted to discredit Jesus by causing people to associate him with the loss of material possessions (Matt. 8:32-34).

9:1-13 AUTHORITY OVER SIN

Jesus' "own town" (9:1) was Capernaum (cf. 4:13) (see introductory map). The background for this incident was in the previous chapter (8:4). The Pharisees and teachers of the law (9:3; cf. Luke 5:17, 21) had come from Jerusalem to investigate Jesus' ministry. The miracle was intended to validate Jesus' divine and Messianic authority before the officials of Israel (Matt. 9:6).

Matthew was a tax collector who collaborated with the Roman government to raise taxes from the Jewish people (9:9). They were classed with harlots and thieves by their fellow Jews and were excluded from Jewish religious activities. In 9:13 Jesus quoted from Hosea 6:6, contrasting his own attitude toward ministry with that of the Pharisees.

Jesus' authority over sin related directly to the condition and needs of humanity. It would not have been enough if he had just had authority over nature and demons. Authority over sin was the significant aspect of Jesus' miracles. Miracles were signs (Matt. 9:6) that pointed to something even greater. An important key to understanding the significance of Jesus' miracles is that they were signs of salvation. They verified the claims of Jesus: "that you may know" (9:6). They were linked to the Son of Man and his authority on earth. Matthew's quote of Hosea 6:6 in Matthew 9:13 brought judgment against the false religious ritual of the Pharisees and teachers of the law. It required that they match, as God does, their character with their deeds. God's desire to save the lost was the controlling force in Jesus' ministry to sinners.

9:14-17 WINESKINS: JESUS' IDENTITY IS CLARIFIED FOR JOHN THE BAPTIST
In the light of Jesus' rejection by the Gentiles of Gadara (8:28-34), the hostility of the religious leaders, the meekness shown by Jesus (9:1-8), and his eating with those who were ritually unclean, John began to wonder whether Jesus was the Messiah. Why was he away in Galilee rather than in Jerusalem? Using the illustration of wineskins, Jesus told John's disciples not to try to make the new conform to old preconceptions and traditions.

John's disciples were fasting because John had been imprisoned by Herod Antipas (9:14; cf. 4:12; 14:1-3). The Pharisees fasted in accordance with Levitical commandment and Jewish tradition (cf. Lev. 16:29-34; Zech. 8:19). Jesus explained that it would be inappropriate to fast while the Messiah ("the bridegroom") was present with his disciples (Matt. 9:15). Jesus did not intend to patch up Pharisaic Judaism but to initiate a vital new way of life through faith in his own person (9:16-17).

9:18-34 TWO CONCLUSIONS CONCERNING JESUS' AUTHORITY: PRAISE AND BLASPHEMY
This collection of miracles was, in part, preparatory for the section of 9:35–11:6 and in particular would serve to allay John the Baptist's doubts about the identity of Jesus (11:2-6). The four miracles mentioned in this section made Jesus famous throughout the land (9:26, 31). Two daughters were healed in this passage (9:18, 22). The "edge" (9:20) that the sick woman touched may have been a reference to the tassels worn at the edge of Jewish garments to remind them to follow God's laws (cf. Num. 15:37-40). The healing of the ruler's daughter (9:23-26) was the first of three resurrection miracles that demonstrated Jesus' authority to give life and resurrect the dead (cf. John 5:25-29).

The blind men appealed to Jesus as the Messiah, the "Son of David" (Matt. 9:27).

Jesus' instruction "see that no one knows" (9:30) was intended to prevent increased opposition and a premature crisis in his ministry. The accusation made by the Pharisees that Jesus was empowered by demons (9:34) was repeated in 12:24.

10:1-4 THE RECIPIENTS OF THE AUTHORITY
Jesus shared his identity and authority with the community as they witnessed in a hostile world (9:35–11:1). The question of who Jesus was pervades this section (10:18, 22, 25, 32, 40). Persecution had already been predicted in 5:10-12. Note the contextual link of Matthew 10:25 with 9:34. The term "apostle" means one who is a special representative, in this case of Jesus the Messiah. The concept of "apostle" may have developed from the authorized representatives who were sent out in behalf of the Jewish religious establishment to render decisions and make pronouncements in the synagogues of the dispersion. So too, the twelve disciples were sent with Jesus' message and authority. The Zealots (10:4) were members of an extremist political party that sought the overthrow of Rome by force.

10:5-33 PERSEVERANCE IN PERSECUTION: WITNESS
The disciples were to go only to the "lost sheep of Israel" (Matt. 10:5-6). Israel was to be the key to world evangelism. Jesus began his work of evangelism with the Jews, the children of Abraham. Then, after his resurrection, he commanded them to make disciples around the world.

Jesus' comments on the persecution of his followers moved from the sufferings of his contemporaries to the persecution that would take place in the end times. The words of 10:9-10 suggest that the disciples anticipated that the mission was going to be short. The disciples were not to waste time raising support for this ministry. Their work would be limited to a time of crisis and extremity. The underlying principle, however, is timeless: God cares for those who seek to serve him.

The Lord's message in 10:16-39 was given in the form of an Old Testament prophetic discourse. It blended together prophecies of times that were both near and distant. Jesus offered hope for the persecuted disciple

(10:22-23). The sermon was built on the principle of 10:24. Just as Jesus, their master, would suffer, his followers were to expect suffering—lest any be tempted to stumble over the cross and persecution. "Beelzebub" (10:25) literally means "lord of flies," an Israelite term of mockery for the Philistine deity (cf. 2 Kings 1:2). Later the term became an epithet for Satan (cf. Matt. 9:34; 12:24). Confidence in confession was linked to confidence in God's sovereign care and intimate knowledge of his people (10:29-31).

10:34-39 PERSEVERANCE IN PERSECUTION: CROSS-BEARING
The "sword" (10:34) was a symbol of division and separation. Commitment to the Lord would bring about a division between Jesus' followers and the world. Jesus showed his disciples that acceptance of their own personal crosses was the way to finding life (10:39). "Take up your cross" was also a battle cry for certain of the zealots as they sacrificed themselves in the battle to overcome Rome. The "cross" (10:38) was an instrument of execution perfected by the Romans. Here it was used as a symbol of one's willingness to identify with Jesus and endure the pain of rejection and persecution.

10:40-42 REWARDS FOR RECEIVING CHRIST'S PROPHETS
The persecuted disciples needed to know that God was behind them (10:40). They were of the same status as the Old Testament prophets (10:41); the rewards of the people who would receive them can be compared to the rewards received by the widow of Zarephath who served Elijah (1 Kings 17:7-24). Eternal rewards would be given to all who served those of God's family, including the poor and needy, as if Jesus himself had been served (cf. Matt. 25:34-46). A summary statement in 11:1 links the preceding discourse to the narrative that follows.

11:2–13:58 The Question of Faith and Further Revelation about the Kingdom

11:2-6 JOHN THE BAPTIST QUESTIONS JESUS' MESSIAHSHIP
John had been imprisoned by Herod Antipas at Machaerus, a fortress east of the Dead Sea (11:2). The phrase "the one who was to come" (11:3; lit., "coming one") was a Messianic designation (cf. Ps. 118:26). Jesus

intended that John's disciples would report to John (Matt. 11:5) that he was fulfilling the Messianic expectations revealed by Isaiah 35:5-6 and 61:1.

John the Baptist's questions and doubts were promoted by Jesus' works that apparently did not fit John's preconceptions of what the Messiah would be like (Matt. 11:2). Jesus gave his answer to John's question in 11:4-6, affirming his Messianic identity. In his answer, Jesus showed how his actions fulfilled Isaiah's Old Testament prophecies concerning the Messiah (cf. 11:5 with Isa. 35:5-6 and 61:1 regarding the poor). Jesus pointed to his works as evidence of his Messianic identity. If this was so, what works did Jesus perform that caused John to question his identity as the Messiah? John probably questioned Jesus' identity because he failed to connect Jesus' works with the prophecies of the Old Testament. Even though John had been confronted with Messianic acts, he was still asking if Jesus was the Messiah. He also had probably been influenced by the popular notion of the day that expected the Messiah to come as a victorious and mighty king, not as a carpenter's son who spent his time serving the poor and needy. John was about to "fall away" (11:6), or stumble, because of his presuppositions about how the Messiah was supposed to behave or speak. Although Jesus had not measured up to John's expectations, Jesus' actions did not need to change; John's perceptions did.

11:7-24 JESUS QUESTIONS AND WARNS THE MULTITUDES CONCERNING THEIR EXPECTATIONS OF JOHN AND HIMSELF
The rhetorical questions of 11:7-8 anticipated negative answers. Jesus indicated (11:10) that the ministry of John the Baptist was the prophetic fulfillment of Malachi 3:1 and 4:5. John the Baptist fulfilled Malachi's expectation of the coming of "Elijah" (11:14; cf. Mal. 4:5) by coming in "the spirit and power of Elijah" (cf. Luke 1:17). The truth of Matthew 11:12 was illustrated by the imprisonment of John the Baptist and the hostility and rejection aimed at Jesus.

The woes (Matt. 11:20-24) showed the great responsibility that would fall on those who heard the gospel and rejected it. Chorazin (11:21) was located about two miles north of the Sea of Galilee. Bethsaida (Bethsaida-Julias) was located just east of where the Jordan River enters the Dead Sea. Tyre and Sidon were located in Phoenicia, on the Mediterranean coast north of Galilee. Capernaum (11:23) was located on the northwest shore of the Sea of Galilee. Sodom was probably located in the Rift Valley in the vicinity of the south end of the Dead Sea. (For the above locations, see introductory map.)

11:25-30 JESUS INVITES REPENTANCE AND UNVEILS HIS CHARACTER

Jesus revealed his relationship with God the Father, thus showing how the character of the Father was revealed in him and how he, as the Son, represented the Father's sovereign authority (11:27). This revelation provided a foundation for Jesus' authoritative teaching ministry represented in the parables of Matthew 13. There are Old Testament allusions throughout this section. The "little children" (11:25) were the humble and repentant listeners. To such listeners Jesus revealed the Father and taught the lessons of discipleship. Matthew 11:27 revealed the sovereignty of the Son of God, both in his relationship with the Father and his revealing the Father to mankind. But the gentle and humble way in which Jesus the Messiah chose to come would cause many to stumble or "fall away" (cf. 11:6). The "yoke" (11:29) of the Jewish people was heavy under the laws and traditions of the Pharisees. Jesus offered an easy yoke because he would carry the load (cf. Jer. 6:16). The concept of "rest" (11:29) points forward to the discussion of the Sabbath rest in Matthew 12.

12:1-14 THE CONTROVERSY OVER THE SABBATH

The Sabbath had been designated the sign of the Mosaic covenant (Exod. 31:13-17). That the Sabbath observance had become superficial and external was evidenced by the Pharisees' condemnation of Jesus' disciples.

In the section of Matthew 12:1-14, Jesus applied the principle of Hosea 6:6 to the Sabbath laws (Matt. 12:7). Jesus showed the Pharisees that the Sabbath was a day for mercy and rest, not for adding extra burdens to the lives of the people. Eating grain while passing through fields was permitted by Old Testament law (12:1; cf. Deut. 23:25). The fourth commandment (Exod. 20:8-11) set the Sabbath (seventh day) apart as a day to

reflect on God's work of creation and delight in the Lord (Isa. 58:13-14). This was an example of what Jesus meant in saying that his yoke was easy (Matt. 11:29). This passage compared the heavy burdens imposed by the Pharisees with the light burdens given by the Lord.

In 12:3-5 Jesus cited two examples where greater priorities took precedence over the Levitical law: (1) David's eating of the "consecrated bread" (1 Sam. 21:1-6) and (2) the priest's labor on the Sabbath (Lev. 24:8). As in Matthew 9:13, Jesus (12:7) once again cited Hosea 6:6. A heart of mercy and compassion would recognize that meeting a person's needs was more important than following every ritual element of Sabbath observance.

Jesus further illustrated the importance of doing acts of mercy before practicing religious ritual by healing a man with a shriveled hand on the Sabbath (Matt. 12:9-14). The Jewish religious leaders reacted by meeting to plan Jesus' death (12:14). This was the first indication that the religious leaders would plan to kill their Messiah.

12:15-21 THE REASON FOR SECRECY: VICTORY AND GENTILE HOPE

The withdrawal of Jesus from the mainstream of Jewish society in section 12:15-21 came as a result of the death plots against him (cf. 12:14). Jesus' secrecy fulfilled the prophecy about him (12:17-21) recorded in Isaiah 42:1-4. The purpose was to extend salvation to the Gentiles (Matt. 12:18, 21). This Gentile extension showed that the Jewish mission of Matthew 10 was only a first step in bringing the message of the kingdom to the world. The narrower Jewish mission of Matthew 10 was, in Matthew 12, expanded to include all nations. Jesus' love and care for the poor and sick (12:15) also illustrated the broadly inclusive nature of the kingdom.

12:22-45 THE KEY TO OBTAINING FURTHER REVELATION: OBEDIENCE TO THE WILL OF GOD

The section of 12:22-45 centered on the agent of revelation: the Holy Spirit. The Pharisees attempted to destroy the people's growing belief in Jesus as they debated his identity (12:22-37). Jesus was accused by the religious leaders of doing his miracles by the power of Satan (12:24, "Beelzebub").

They were attributing the works of the Holy Spirit to Satan rather than to God. Jesus identified that as speaking "against the Spirit" (12:31), a sin that would not be forgiven.

There were Jewish exorcists who claimed to have the authority to cast out demons (12:27; cf. Acts 19:13-20). Whether they actually had this power is uncertain. But since they were regarded as having this authority from God, it would be inconsistent to attribute Jesus' miracles of exorcism to Satan. The unforgivable sin may be defined as knowingly attributing the works of the Holy Spirit to Satan (Matt. 12:31). This was tantamount to final rejection of the Holy Spirit's testimony concerning the person of Jesus Christ.

In the section of 12:38-45, two examples of Gentile faith (12:41-42) were contrasted with the Jewish leaders' unbelief and desire for a sign (12:38). Jesus referred to the prophet Jonah's mission to the Gentiles of Nineveh to reveal the breadth of the salvation he offered and the unbelief of his chosen people, the Jews. See the notes concerning the purpose of the book of Jonah and on Jonah 4:10-11 regarding compassion. No further attesting miracles were promised the Jews except the "sign of Jonah" (12:39-40; cf. 16:4), which would be represented by the resurrection of Jesus from the grave. Jonah's three-day experience in the great fish was typical of Jesus' experience in the grave. Both Jonah and Jesus suffered what appeared to be tragic and final deaths, but instead, they both experienced miraculous deliverances. The point of comparison, the "three days and three nights," does not actually require that Jesus spend seventy-two hours in the grave. According to Jewish reckoning, any part of a day was regarded as the whole. Jesus spent parts of three days in the grave (Friday, Saturday, and Sunday), which met the requirement from the viewpoint of first century Jewish culture. The "evil spirit" (Matt. 12:43) was a reference to a demon.

12:46-50 FURTHER REVELATION TO THE FAITHFUL

In 12:46-50 Jesus revealed that those who obeyed his Father were the people truly related to him. Obedience to the faith was what established a spiritual relationship with Jesus the Messiah. Note the link of 12:50

with 13:55-56. The religious leaders saw and understood only Jesus' earthly relations and failed completely to understand his relationship to God the Father.

13:1-52 THE OBEDIENT RECEIVE MORE REVELATION: THE PARABLES

Matthew 13 contains a series of parables, true-to-life stories that teach spiritual truth. The Greek word "parable" (13:3) suggests the idea of comparison. Parables often place two concepts, one known, the other unknown, side by side for comparison. They use the known concept, like the work of a farmer planting seed (13:3-9), to explain a central truth about the less familiar concept, like the way people receive the word of God concerning the kingdom of heaven (13:18-23). Although parables are fictitious stories, they present content and situations that are true-to-life. Parables contain wisdom elements, making them, in some ways, much like the Old Testament proverbs. They show how the truth being taught relates to the hearer, who, but for keen and obedient hearing, might well miss the parable's personal implications (13:9, 43: cf. 2 Samuel 12:1-7).

Here are some basic principles for interpreting the parables: (1) Knowing the original setting in which the parable was given is important for understanding its intended meaning. The known must be understood to make the transference to the realm of the unknown. (2) The central problem of the parable must be discovered. The parables were designed to deal with a particular problem or question. This can usually be discovered from the immediate context or related verses. (3) The central truth of the parable must be determined. Most of the parables focus on one central truth. Even those that have multiple points of comparison are usually designed to answer one question.

Why did Jesus teach in parables (Matt. 13:10-23)? There were two major purposes: (1) to reveal truth to the receptive (13:11-12) and (2) to conceal truth from the unresponsive—those who rejected Jesus (13:13-15). Jesus quoted Isaiah 6:9-10, originally written to describe the hard-hearted Jews of preexilic Israel, to describe the unbelieving Jews of his own day. In addition, Jesus' use of parables fulfilled prophecy, for Psalm 78:2

predicted that the Messiah would teach by this means (Matt. 13:34-35).

Jesus used parables to explain to his hearers what would happen in the kingdom as a result of the leaders' blasphemy and rejection of him (cf. 12:22-45). They also explained why some rejected God's Messiah. The parable of the soils (13:1-8) explained much in this regard. This parable made it clear that the people's rejection of Jesus was not because his preaching was unsuccessful. The problem was with the unresponsive minds and hearts of his hearers, not with the truth or power of the speaker. The hearts of many who listened to the parables of Jesus were like the hardened path (13:4), the rocky soil (13:5-6), or the thorny ground (13:7). But others would be like the good soil, and through them the kingdom of God would grow (13:8).

The "secrets of the kingdom" (13:11; "mysteries," NASB and KJV) revealed by the parables were those things that had not previously been known but were then being revealed. The kingdom of God had certainly been previously known and had been anticipated throughout the Old Testament. The "secrets of the kingdom" were that it was revealed but rejected, that it was present but small and hidden like the mustard seed or the leaven, and that its members were the humble and poor, not the powerful and wealthy.

The key to receiving more revelation was revealed in 13:12. But what is it believers can have or not have? The concepts of "having" and "not having" are defined in 13:13-17 as closely related to seeing, hearing, understanding, and turning from sin. The audience of the parables ("the people," 13:10; "them," 13:11, 13-14) saw and heard but did not understand or perceive (13:14) or turn from their sins (13:15). The disciples had open hearts toward God and a basic understanding of Christ to which Jesus would add more and more understanding. The others had "calloused" (13:15) hearts and would lose the value of whatever meager knowledge of God they already had. Self-righteous people think they have something before God, but in God's eyes they have nothing. Matthew used the prophet Isaiah's words describing the willful rebellion of Israel (Isa. 6:9-10) to explain Jesus' use of parables to hide truth

from the ungodly (Matt. 13:14-15). This would become a form of judgment upon the unrepentant. The call to "understand" (Matt. 13:19, 51) was a theme that Matthew used throughout his Gospel.

Note Isaiah 6:12-13 and the prophecy of the holy seed in the stump. Matthew 13:14-16 is a quotation of Isaiah 6:9-10 that scolds God's people for their hardness of heart and speaks of the time of their punishment. In the same Isaiah context, Isaiah 6:11-12 goes on to answer the question of how long the punishment would continue. Isaiah 6:13 then shows how the restoration of God's people comes about. The image of the shattered stump that sends forth a new shoot and springs back to life represents the spiritual process that unfolds in Matthew. Amidst the shattered stump of hard hearts and spiritual blindness, the "holy seed" begins to bring forth spiritual life and vitality.

The "weeds" (13:24-30; "tares," NASB and KJV) were weeds that appeared quite similar to wheat when immature, but were of an inferior quality. When full-grown, they could be distinguished from the wheat and removed before harvest. These weeds or tares were sometimes used for chicken feed. Later Jesus explained that the parable of the weeds or tares was a revelation of what would happen at the last judgment (Matt. 13:36-43).

The "mustard seed" (13:31-32) was the smallest of the garden seeds used by first century Jewish farmers. The mustard seed was often referred to in the Jewish Mishnah as an illustration of something quite small. Like the mustard seed, the kingdom would begin very small, but would grow to become a resting place for the godly. The "yeast" (13:33; "leaven," NASB and KJV) functioned in a manner similar to the yeast used in modern times, causing dough to rise. It revealed the kingdom's hidden power to pervade and reshape the world. Like yeast, the kingdom, though hidden to the eye, would work its way through the whole world (the lump of dough) powerfully and completely. In 13:34-35 Matthew showed how Jesus' use of parables fulfilled the prophecy of Psalm 78:2. Jesus was seen as one of the Old Testament prophets speaking to a dull and rebellious people.

In the next set of parables, Jesus described the value of the kingdom in terms of treasure and pearls (13:44-46) and how opposition to the kingdom would be judged (13:47 50). The kingdom was seen as so valuable that it was worth all that the seeker owned.

The parable of the fishing net (13:47-50), like that of the weeds, revealed events of judgment and reward that would take place in the future. Jesus used the well-known activity of fishing to show that God would separate the worthy and unworthy in his kingdom (cf. Matt. 25:31-46). The following two verses (13:51-52) revealed what a disciple of the kingdom was called to do. The disciple was to be perceptive and listen to God's words. Then he was to relate the old to the new, that is, the work of Jesus to the revelation already given in the Old Testament.

Jesus' rejection at Nazareth (13:53-58) by his relatives and neighbors was a clear example of those who would "fall away" and reject Jesus (cf. 11:6). They were unable to accept Jesus' offer of the new treasures along with the old (13:52). Note the link of 13:55-56 with 12:50. Those who had been closest to Jesus when he was a child rejected him. It was not the closeness of human relationship that proved one's relationship to Jesus, it was obedience to the will of his Father.

14:1–16:12 Faith and True Cleanness: Controversies concerning Eating Bread with Unwashed Hands

Overview: The entire section of 14:1–16:12 is concerned with eating. Two guiding concepts found in this section are: (1) the juxtaposition of the physical with the spiritual,

and (2) Jesus' elaboration of Deuteronomy 8:3. This important section has been summarized in the accompanying chart.

Jesus taught that when it concerned such items as food, shelter, and safety, the faith of his people should be automatic. He showed that his followers needed to be tuned into the more important concerns of his kingdom. The disciples were hung up on the mundane concern for bread. Though they had two well-known opinions concerning the meaning of leaven (bread and teaching), they chose to understand his teaching on the mundane level of bread and missed what he was really trying to tell them. They failed to receive Jesus' words from a faith perspective and almost missed his warning about the unclean teachings of the Pharisees.

14:1-12 IDENTITY: IS JESUS JOHN THE BAPTIST?

When Herod Antipas heard of Jesus, he feared that he was John the Baptist come back from the dead. At an earlier time, Herod had ordered that John be beheaded. Herod's confusion about the identity of Jesus showed the people's confusion about what God was doing through his great men. This set the background for the discussion regarding the identity of Jesus in Matthew 16. When his father (King Herod the Great) died, Herod Antipas received the title, "tetrarch" ("ruler of a fourth part") and the authority to rule over Galilee and Perea (4 B.C.–A.D. 39). Herod Antipas, who was married to the daughter of a Nabatean king, fell in love with his brother Philip's wife, Herodias, who was also his niece (14:4). Herod Antipas divorced his wife and married Herodias in violation of the Mosaic Laws concerning incestuous marriages (Lev. 18:6-18). John condemned

---

SUMMARY OF MATTHEW 14:1–16:12

Jesus' identity: not a resurrected John the Baptist	14:1-12
Feeding number one: 5,000 satisfied	14:13-21
Jesus' walk on water: worship and confession	4:22-33
Recognition of Christ: healed at a touch	14:34-36
Teaching about what is clean or unclean	15:1-20
A clean Gentile woman	15:21-28
Coming to Christ: healing and worship	15:29-31
Feeding number two: 4,000 satisfied	15:32-39
Feedings explained: a warning of unclean teachings	16:1-12

this marriage as "unlawful," and as a result was killed in A.D. 31 or 32 (Matt. 14:10).

14:13–15:39 THE WILDERNESS LESSON OF FAITH IS ELABORATED
14:13-21 Five thousand are fed. The feeding of the five thousand took place at a lonely or deserted place on the northeast shore of the Sea of Galilee near Bethsaida (cf. Luke 9:10). This miracle was the only one of Jesus' thirty-six recorded miracles that appears in all four Gospels. Jesus' withdrawal from the crowds was probably due to Herod's interest in him (cf. Matt. 14:2). The news of his deeds had spread to the king's palace (14:13). Although Jesus had sought solitude, he looked with compassion on the multitude that had followed him. His miracles of healing and feeding would serve as illustrations to teach his disciples (16:5-12), and at that point, comments on the significance of the feeding would be given. Note the progression of events in 14:14, 16, 18, 21.

14:22-33 Walking on water: God's Son worshiped. The disciples responded to this sign of Jesus' power by worshiping him (14:33; cf. 28:17). The night was divided into four periods: 6:00 to 9:00 P.M., 9:00 to 12:00 P.M., 12:00 to 3:00 A.M., and 3:00 to 6:00 A.M. The "fourth watch" (14:25) was between 3:00 and 6:00 A.M. If the disciples had started out around sunset (14:22-23), they had been rowing for about nine hours.

14:34-36 Healings from the cloak: the Messiah recognized. Gennesaret (14:34) was a fertile plain on the northwest shore of the Sea of Galilee. The Sea of Galilee was sometimes referred to as the Lake of Gennesaret (cf. Luke 5:1) (see introductory map). The people brought their sick to Jesus, showing their recognition of the promised Messiah.

15:1-20 Confusion about the clean and unclean. Jesus sought to make clear to his disciples that true purity and faith began with the heart, not with external rituals. The "tradition of the elders" (Matt. 15:2) was a reference to the *Halachah* or the "law of custom." This tradition was regarded by the Pharisees as equally binding as the written law. The "law of custom" called for ritual hand cleansing before eating. Neglect of this custom brought defilement. The Mishnah states, "Bread eaten with unwashed hands

was as if it had been filth." This law is an example of the heavy burdens imposed by the Pharisees. The Pharisees' criticism of Jesus and his disciples was ironic in that the feeding of the multitude came from the absolutely pure hands of God's Son.

The professed commitment of the Pharisees to God and his law was used by them to avoid the parental obligations demanded by the law (15:4-5; cf. Exod. 20:12). Jesus used the sixth commandment (Exod. 20:12), which was the first one that applied to man's relationships with his fellowmen, because it exposed one of the Pharisees' sins.

In Matthew 15:7-9 Jesus identified the Pharisees with the hypocrites of Isaiah 29:13. Isaiah himself had contrasted a false religion of the lips with a true religion of the heart. Even in Isaiah's day, most of the Jews had worshiped vainly on the basis of human traditions. The Pharisees vividly exemplified the "out of the mouth" (Matt. 15:11) type of impurity. Jesus taught that people were not defiled by ceremonial uncleanness but by moral impurity that issued from the heart (15:11). He sought to drive home the importance of honoring God in heartfelt sincerity. See 15:10, 16 regarding Jesus' desire to bring about true understanding among his hearers (cf. 13:51; 16:6, 9, 12).

In the section of 15:12-20 Jesus made clear the source of true impurity—the heart. The distinction between ethical impurity (purity of heart) and ritual impurity (purity in terms of law and tradition) was also further clarified (15:15-20). Jesus showed that a lack of understanding could indicate a problem with the purity of one's heart (15:19).

15:21-28 The Canaanite woman: an impure person. Tyre and Sidon (15:21) were located in Phoenicia, a Mediterranean coastal region north of Galilee (see introductory map). Why did Jesus make this woman beg? Was she asking for a Messianic blessing ("Son of David," 15:22)? Jesus' silence raised a response from his disciples: "Send her away" (15:23). They responded with the assumption that the benefits brought by Jesus were exclusively for the Jews and thus failed to respond with compassion. Jesus' statement "I was sent only to the lost sheep of Israel" (15:24) seems to support the disciples' request to send her away. Yet Jesus intended to meet her need. In 15:24 he was simply clarifying the scope of his commission; he had been sent only to Israel. Jesus clarified the priorities that exist in any household (15:25-26). Children were always fed as a priority before the pets of the household. Jesus did not intend to insult the woman by calling her a dog; rather, he used a form of the word dog that meant "pet."

After clearly enunciating the priority that the Israelites took in his ministry, Jesus went on to teach the disciples and the woman that the Gentiles would also see benefits from his presence. Her claim to blessing was through the Abrahamic covenant which promised that all nations would be blessed through Israel (cf. Gen. 12:3). After making his point about priority in the Messianic ministry, Jesus healed her. The location, Tyre and Sidon, might have influenced Jesus' actions. Jesus waited until it was crystal clear that the woman would participate by faith in the blessing he would give her. For other examples of Jesus healing Gentiles, see Matthew 4:24; 8:5-13, 28-34.

15:29-39 Healings glorify God and four thousand are fed. Matthew was painting a picture of the Lord's compassion by recounting his works of healing and the second feeding of a multitude (15:32; cf. 14:14). Magadan (15:39) was located on the southern end of the plain of Gennesaret (see introductory map). It was probably identical with Magdala (modern Migdol). See the comment on Dalmanutha in the notes on Mark 8:10.

16:1-12 CONCLUSION: BEWARE OF UNCLEAN TEACHING

16:1-4 Magadan: leaders seek a sign. The power of a sign is not in its display, but in that to which it points. Jesus presented an analogy based on the ability of the Pharisees and Sadducees to forecast the weather (Matt. 16:3). They could predict the weather but could not "interpret the signs of the times." The signs of the times were his miracles of healing that authenticated him as the Messiah. The "sign of Jonah" (16:4) referred to the resurrection of Jesus (cf. 12:39-40).

16:5-12 Leaven: watch out for false teaching. Until this point Matthew had not revealed to the reader the significance of the feedings. In these verses Matthew presented the key to understanding the life setting of the feedings and applications that could be

made concerning them. The feedings revealed the sustaining power of God for his people in the wilderness of life. They were signs to encourage the people's faith in Jesus as the physical and spiritual sustainer of mankind. In his discussion of the feedings, Jesus warned his disciples to beware of a kind of leaven other than that used in bread. Jesus warned his disciples concerning the teachings of the Pharisees and Sadducees that, like leaven, had permeated and distorted the belief system of the whole nation (16:12).

16:13-20 Identity to the Community Supernaturally Revealed: Authority to Bind and Loose

The previous section (14:1–16:12) was started and immediately followed by accounts in which people sought to understand who Jesus really was. In 14:1-12 Herod believed Jesus to be John the Baptist returned from the dead (14:2). In 16:13-20 Jesus was confessed by Peter to be the Christ (Messiah), the true Son of God. Peter's confession stands at the heart of Matthew's Gospel. Did the disciples know who Jesus was? The range of opinions given (16:13-14) shows that though all viewed him as special, many did not view Jesus as a truly unique individual, the Son of God. But Peter's confession revealed that Jesus was a unique individual (16:15-17). And Jesus affirmed that confession as a supernatural revelation from the Father (16:17). Furthermore, the confession of Jesus as the Messiah intimated that Jesus had a direct revelatory link with the Father as the "Son of God" (cf. 11:25; 13:11). The word "man" (16:17; "flesh and blood," NASB and KJV) should probably be taken in this context to refer to natural reason. The knowledge reflected in Peter's confession was based on special revelation.

This was not the first time Peter realized who Jesus was (cf. 14:33). The disciples had been convinced that Jesus was the Messiah at least since the events recorded in Matthew 10 took place. But until this point the disciples had thought of the Messiah as a powerful and victorious king who would deliver them from Roman oppression. This was Jesus' time to redefine his identity as the Messiah. As the Messiah, Jesus would not free his people from Roman oppression. Rather he would follow his destiny of building his church and going through death to resurrection. Understanding his identity as the Messiah had been the disciples' first step. The idea of the Messiah's destiny to suffer on the cross and be raised from the dead would be much more difficult for them to grasp.

Caesarea Philippi (16:13) was in northern Galilee near the foot of Mount Hermon (see introductory map). Philip, Herod's son who ruled this district (4 B.C.–A.D. 34), rebuilt the ancient pagan worship center of Paneion and named it after Caesar Augustus. It was called Caesarea Philippi to distinguish it from Caesarea on the Mediterranean seacoast. Some thought Jesus was John the Baptist risen from the dead (16:14; cf. 14:2), Elijah (cf. Mal. 4:5), Jeremiah (cf. 2 Macc. 2:4-8), or simply one of God's many prophets.

In Matthew 16:18-19 Jesus commissioned Peter to be the foundation of a new community. It was inconceivable to have a Messiah without his special community. The word "church" (16:18) simply means "the assembly of those called out." The "gates of Hades" (16:18) was a figure of speech that referred to death. Even death would not prevail against this special community. What would the Messianic community be like? The community that Jesus revealed would be different from anything his disciples had ever imagined.

The name "Peter" (16:18) is simply the masculine form of the Greek word for "rock." Peter's name revealed his function in the Messiah's new community; he was to be a foundation. Jesus made a word play on Peter's name. Peter (*Petros* in Greek) means "a movable rock or stone." The word translated "rock" (*petra* in Greek) means "an immovable rock formation or rock mass." Scholars have debated whether the "rock" was a reference to Peter himself, Jesus, Peter's confession, or the truth of Peter's confession—that Jesus was the divine Messiah.

The "keys" (16:19) were a symbol of authority to open or close doors (cf. Isa. 22:22). "Binding" and "loosing" (Matt. 16:19) were terms used by the rabbis to describe what they permitted or prohibited, that is, declared lawful or unlawful. By judicial pronouncement they would bind or loose someone with respect to a particular law. The authority given Peter was later given the other apostles (18:18). They

pronounced people loosed from the consequences of sin on the basis of repentance, and bound to sin's consequences (judgment) without repentance. What was the point of binding and loosing? It was related to allowing entrance into the kingdom of God and was given in contrast to the Pharisees' rules for kingdom entry.

16:21–28:20 MESSIANIC DESTINY: FULL AUTHORITY TO COMMISSION AND PRESIDE OVER HIS NEW COMMUNITY
16:21–17:23 The Son and the Cross: the Stumbling Block of Self-Preservation
16:21-28 TWO CROSSES: JESUS' AND THE DISCIPLES'

Jesus made the first specific prediction of his death and resurrection in 16:21-28. The key elements of the passion predictions were that Jesus would go to Jerusalem, suffer, die, and be raised from the dead. That plan was not immediately acceptable to the disciples. The essence of the "stumbling block" (16:23) was the placing of human interests and plans over God's plans for world redemption. Peter was expressing the desire of Satan, to keep Jesus from his work of redemptive suffering on the cross. But Peter was really trying to preserve himself when he said, "Never Lord" (16:22). Peter, along with the other disciples, was looking for glory in the new kingdom and had no desire to participate in suffering and self-denial (16:24-25). The opposite option to following the natural human inclination of self-preservation was to follow Jesus and carry his cross (16:24). The self-denial demanded of those who would follow Jesus went against the disciples' natural inclinations. And what was natural to them as human beings, as is true so often, was also contrary to God's purposes. Peter, like the other disciples, would have to learn that "he must deny himself" (16:24) in order to "save his life" (16:25). For to deny self would be to follow Jesus' pattern (the way to life) rather than Satan's (the way to death).

Jesus revealed the perils of following the path of self-preservation (16:25-27). Note the twofold use of "For" (16:25, 27). Jesus exposed the selfish and materialistic attitudes (16:26) that motivated Peter to rebuke him.

Peter probably dreamed of a place of glory in the Messianic kingdom, and the death of the Messiah did not fit into his vision of glory. This desire for power and material wealth was at the heart of his desire for self-preservation. But Jesus revealed that the final evaluation by the sovereign Evaluator would bring all deeds and motivations to light (16:27). The motivation of rewards and punishment was given to provide an eternal perspective to the self-denial demanded in 16:24-26. The divine call to carry the cross and the natural human revulsion to that call was the basis for the community instructions that followed. People tend naturally to avoid the self-denial demanded by the cross. The following instructions were designed to solve the problem. Jesus spoke of the two major aspects of his second coming: glory and judgment (16:27; cf. Ps. 62:12).

Jesus promised his followers that the kingdom would soon come (Matt. 16:28). After revealing to his followers the agonies they would face, Jesus, having just spoken of recompense and final judgment, offered a vision of his coming in the kingdom. Matthew 16 laid down the two foundations of the Christian faith: the cross and the second coming.

17:1-13 THE TRANSFIGURATION
The greater the impact made by the discussion of Jesus' taking up his cross (16:21), the greater the readers' appreciation of what the transfiguration (17:1-8) had to do with their taking up the cross and following him. The words of 16:28 suggested that the transfiguration (17:1-8) would provide a foretaste of the Messiah's kingdom glory. That foretaste would greatly encourage those who would soon suffer persecution for their faith. Its purpose was to reveal the breadth of God's kingdom and Jesus' position within it. Jesus "shone like the sun" (17:2; cf. Exod. 24:1, 16; 34:29-35). Moses and Elijah were the surrounding figures who functioned to show how much superior Jesus the Messiah was (Matt. 17:5). Jesus was the fulfillment of the law (represented by Moses) and the prophets (represented by Elijah), especially with regards to his work as the suffering Messiah.

This event became a confirmation of Jesus Christ's divinity and a commission for the disciples. It made it clear to the disciples

that Jesus' words were God's words. God's statement "Listen to him!" (17:5) implied "Because this Son is mine and beloved, you had better listen to him." Therefore, if the Son spoke of a cross for himself and his disciples (16:21-24), his disciples would have to accept that. But the disciples continued to struggle with Jesus' command to take up the cross, as can be seen throughout the rest of the book of Matthew. The glory seen in the transfiguration was to help the disciples dispel doubts about Jesus' call to self-denial.

The "high mountain" (17:1) probably was a reference to Mount Hermon (9,200 feet high), although the traditional site was Mount Tabor (1,843 feet high). Peter and John both mentioned this experience in their later writings (2 Pet. 1:16-18; John 1:14). According to Luke 9:31, Moses and Elijah were talking with Jesus about his departure, that is, his death and ascension to the right hand of God (Matt. 17:3). Peter wanted to build the three tabernacles (temporary shelters) to celebrate the Feast of Tabernacles (cf. Lev. 23:33-44), which would be observed in the kingdom (cf. Zech. 14:16). He had the right idea but was off on his timing. Relate Zechariah 14:16-19 to Peter's desire to set up booths for Jesus, Moses, and Elijah. This was the second time God spoke from heaven about his Son (Matt. 17:5; cf. 3:17; John 12:28).

The disciples discussed with Jesus the teaching that Elijah would appear before the coming of the Messiah (Matt. 17:9-13). In answer to the disciples' question about the coming of Elijah, Jesus affirmed the temporal sequence of Malachi 4:5-6 that Elijah would come first (Matt. 17:11). He also revealed that the prophecy of Elijah's coming had already been fulfilled (17:12). The disciples understood Jesus to be referring to John the Baptist (17:13) who fulfilled the prophecy in an unexpected way. John the Baptist had come in the spirit and power of Elijah (cf. Luke 1:17; John 1:19-27), and his coming was set against the background of Malachi 4:5-6. The suffering of Jesus and John were linked together (cf. Matt. 14:1-12; 17:9, 12).

The vision of the transfiguration looked forward to the time after Jesus' resurrection (17:9). But Jesus the Messiah's lifetime on earth would be spent in suffering and humility (16:21; 17:12), not glory. The prelude to the kingdom's coming was the suffering of Jesus and John the Baptist. After their suffering was complete, the time of restoration would begin (17:11).

17:14-21 THE EPILEPTIC BOY: LITTLE FAITH DURING JESUS' ABSENCE
This little story moves powerfully to its climax in 17:20, "Nothing will be impossible for you." The immediate problem was the inability of the disciples to heal in Jesus' absence. Jesus had been up on the mountain, like Moses had been away from his people on Mount Sinai. When the disciples failed to heal the boy, Jesus pointed to their lack of faith as the problem. But Jesus did not demand an extraordinarily large amount of faith; he described the amount of faith he had in mind. It was the size of a mustard seed—very small and quite attainable by all his disciples. But faith is not a physical quantity, so the essence of Jesus' response is that success comes not from the amount of a believer's faith but from the fact that he has even the smallest amount of true faith and wholly relies upon the power of God. The words of 17:21 are not found in many important Greek manuscripts.

17:22-23 A SECOND PASSION PREDICTION
Even with a second mention of his resurrection, the disciples were still grieved. Their grief masked their inability to accept and understand Jesus' mission as a suffering Savior and their own mission to follow in his footsteps. Peter could not accept Jesus' death in Matthew 16:21-23. In Matthew 20:17-19, the only recorded response to Jesus' third passion prediction was the disciples' quarrel about who would be the greatest in the kingdom (Matt. 20:20-27). They had replaced acceptance of Jesus' death with a self-centered striving for status.

17:24–18:35 Sonship and Privilege in the New Community
17:24-27 THE PRIORITY OF MINISTRY: THE TEMPLE TAX
In his conflict with the collectors of the temple tax, Jesus avoided causing even these religious leaders to be angry with him (17:27). His decisions were always ministry oriented. Here Jesus taught by his example that though sonship has privileges, those

privileges should be given up in order to offer redemption to others. Capernaum (17:24; cf. 4:13) was located on the northwest shore of the Sea of Galilee. The question asked by the tax collectors (17:24) dealt with the payment of the annual half-shekel temple tax (cf. Exod. 30:11-15). Two drachmas were the Greek equivalent to the Jewish half-shekel. The "four-drachma coin" (Matt. 17:27; "stater," NASB; "piece of money," KJV) was the equivalent of two half-shekels and provided sufficient payment for both Jesus and Peter.

18:1-6 GREATNESS AND GOD'S INTENTIONS
If the sons of the kingdom had to give up their rights to minister to others (17:27), Peter asked, "Who is the greatest?" (18:1). Why should the sons give up rights for strangers? The disciples could not accept the fact that sonship and servanthood were compatible. Jesus revealed the heart of the matter in 18:3-4. The disciples needed to become like little children, humble and dependent on the power of God. Humility, a proper and biblical evaluation of self, would be the mark of true greatness in God's kingdom. The "millstone" (18:6) was a heavy disc-shaped stone used for grinding grain. The "little ones" (18:10) was probably a figurative reference to believers, young or old (cf. 18:6). Matthew was continuing the use of the "child" metaphor used earlier (18:2, 5).

18:7-14 CAUSES OF STUMBLING AND THE PARABLE OF THE LOST SHEEP
Jesus made it clear (18:7-9) that impediments to following him in righteous humility had to be overcome and destroyed. This included the punishment of any person that might cause another to stumble (18:7; cf. 18:15-20). But the point being made by these words of admonition was not that Jesus desired to exclude people from the kingdom. In the following section (18:10-14) Jesus told the parable of the lost sheep. In this story Jesus showed that his goal was to bring salvation, even to the sheep that ran away (8:14), at the price of great personal sacrifice. The point behind avoiding all stumbling blocks that might deter a person from humbly following Jesus, and the point of this parable, was that Jesus desired that all might be saved.

18:15-20 DEALING WITH A SINFUL BROTHER

In 18:15-17 Jesus outlined four steps for dealing with a believing brother who is embroiled in sin: (1) Personal confrontation of the sinner (18:15), (2) Private conference with witnesses in order to verify both sides of the argument (18:16), (3) Public announcement to the church (18:17), and (4) Exclusion from fellowship (18:17). At each step, even after step four, opportunity was provided for repentance and restoration. This section on judgment and discipline is followed by one of the great passages on forgiveness (18:21-35). The ultimate purpose of church discipline was restoration and forgiveness.

The "two or three witnesses" (18:16; cf. Deut. 19:15) would serve to confirm the evidence and either strengthen the reproof or invalidate the accusation. A "pagan or a tax collector" (Matt. 18:17) served as a metaphor for unbelievers. For "binding" and "loosing" (18:18), see the notes on 16:19. The "two" (18:19-20) do not constitute a "church." In this context "two or three" referred to those who were gathered for prayer regarding a matter of church discipline.

The power to "bind" and "loose" (18:18) was granted by Jesus in connection with decisions concerning community purity and discipline. Notice that the power to "bind" and "loose" in the similar verse of Matthew 16:19 was given with respect to entrance into the community of Christ.

18:21-35 THE PARABLE OF THE UNFORGIVING SERVANT

Note how in 18:21, Peter still seemed to be thinking of the discussion in 18:15. He wondered how many times he should forgive someone who was offending him. The rabbis believed that they were required to forgive another person only three times (18:21-22). Peter doubled it and added one more for good measure. But Jesus demanded that his followers give unlimited forgiveness (18:22). A "talent" (18:24) was a unit of weight equal to sixty-six pounds, usually used for measuring precious metals. A "hundred denarii" (18:28) was the equivalent of one hundred days wages. Compassion or "pity" (18:27) lies at the root of forgiveness (cf. 18:33). The Lord's compassionate desire to feed (14:14; 15:32) and to heal (20:34) was a manifestation of his even deeper compassionate desire

to forgive (18:27). In 18:33 Jesus pointed his disciples to the divine pattern: be perfect in forgiveness as the Father is perfect (cf. Matt. 5:43-48).

19:1–20:16 Obedience and Privilege in the Kingdom

19:1-12 GOD MUST RULE OVER MAN'S WANDERING DESIRES: DIVORCE

"The other side of the Jordan" (19:1) referred to the district east of the Jordan known as Perea, ruled by Herod Antipas (see introductory map). In the first century A.D., there were two prominent views on the subject of divorce and remarriage among the Jews (19:3). Rabbi Shammai taught that divorce was allowed only on the grounds of adultery. Rabbi Hillel taught that divorce for any reason was permitted. Both viewed remarriage as permitted after legitimate divorce.

The Pharisees used the problem of divorce to test Jesus. They pitted God's prohibition of divorce against Moses' allowance of it, as if the latter superseded the former. Jesus pointed out that the Mosaic permission for divorce was also of divine origin and served only to highlight the hardness of human hearts, then and now, in not being able to live according to God's will for marriage.

In 19:4-6 Jesus demonstrated from Genesis 1:27 and 2:24 that divorce was alien to God's original plan for marriage. He concluded by rejecting both the liberal and conservative views of his day with the words of Matthew 19:6. The question of Moses' teaching on divorce (Deut. 24:1-4) was answered by pointing to the hard-hearted attitude that necessitated it, and that the Mosaic permission was not in keeping with God's plan "from the beginning" (Matt. 19:7-8). For "marital unfaithfulness" (19:9; "immorality," NASB; "fornication," KJV), compare the note on Matthew 5:32.

The words of 19:10-12 related to those who had been divorced or had divorced in the case of immorality. Jesus' rather strict teaching led the disciples to conclude that it was "better not to marry" in the first place (19:10). The term "eunuch" (19:12) was used metaphorically here of those who were not married. Some never married because of physical limitations, others because they were never asked. Then there were those who "renounced marriage" or "made

themselves eunuchs" for the sake of the
Messiah's kingdom. The disciples thought
the option to the strict rules of marriage was
a life of singleness. But Jesus' point was that
remaining single for any reason, whether
because of physical defects, personal choice,
or by divorce, needed the gracious help of
God (19:11). People were not to use a return
to single life as a way to get out of a marriage. God wanted people who were married
to submit to his rules for love and purity
within the marriage bond.

19:13-15 GOD CALLS THE LITTLE CHILDREN

Immediately following his discussion of
marriage, divorce, and the single life, which
revealed that people often try to get out of
certain commandments, Jesus returned to the
subject of children and their important place
in the kingdom of heaven. Jesus taught that
the humble submission found in innocent
children was required both in marriage (19:3-
12) and in obtaining eternal life (19:16-22).
The problem of people failing to follow
Jesus and the law with humble obedience
links back to the discussion in 17:22–18:35.

19:16-22 RICHES AND PRIVILEGE

A rich young man asked Jesus how he
might gain eternal life (19:16). Jesus' reply
demanded that the man focus on God and his
word (19:17). All he needed to know was
already there. But Jesus demanded that the
man not only follow external laws but also
work for inner change and submission to
himself as God's Messiah (19:20-22). External conformity alone has never been pleasing
to God; a contrite heart has always pleased
him. The point of 19:21-22 was to probe into
and identify the objects of the young man's
inner commitment. He failed the test of true
commitment to God because he was mater-
ialistically minded (19:22; cf. 6:24). Jesus
demanded that the man give away his riches,
which stood as a stumbling block between
him and true righteousness (cf. 18:7-9). God
must be the object of a person's ultimate
commitment; riches must take the backseat
(19:16-29).

19:23-29 REWARDS FOR OBEDIENCE: TRUE RICHES

Salvation cannot be bought (9:23-26). For a
camel to pass through the eye of a sewing
needle is impossible, just as it is impossible

for someone who is unwilling to make
material sacrifice to follow Jesus and enter
his kingdom (19:24; cf. Luke 18:25). Jesus
showed that in the kingdom of heaven there
was no room for misplaced priorities or
disobedience. Humble submission to the
Father's will was a necessity. He wanted
his disciples to demonstrate the surpassing
righteousness he spoke of in the Sermon on
the Mount (Matt. 5–7). Peter wondered if
those who denied themselves for the sake of
Jesus would ever receive a reward (19:27).
Jesus made it clear that riches would only
be given to his followers after the kingdom
was fully realized (19:28-30). The "renewal"
(19:28) referred to the future renewal of
Israel's kingdom (cf. Acts 3:19-21). The
parable of the workers in the vineyard (Matt.
20:1-16) would more fully develop Jesus'
answer to Peter's question in 19:27.

19:30–20:16 NO SPECIAL PRIVILEGE: THE FIRST MAY BE LAST

The assertion that "many who are first will
be last, and many who are last will be first"
(19:30) was illustrated by Jesus' parable of
the workers in the vineyard (20:1-16). The
context for this parable was a discussion of
the rewards that would be given in the future
day of "renewal" (19:28). In the parable,
people grumbled over equal pay for less
work (20:11). Jesus was revealing the leveling character of God's justice. The eternal
life promised to Jesus' followers would be
a reward given equally to those who had
followed him a long time and to those
who had known him only a short time (cf.
20:14-15). This would quell the tendency
of man to seek preeminence. The parable
of 20:1-16 served to illustrate the point of
19:30—that the first would be last, and the
last first (cf. 20:16). A "denarius" (20:2) was
one day's wage.

20:17-34 The Purpose of the Son's Coming: a Ransom

20:17-19 ANOTHER PASSION PREDICTION: GENTILES

This prediction added the new element of
Jesus being delivered to the Gentiles (20:19).
It also made the first specific mention of his
mode of death by crucifixion, a Roman
means of execution. Jesus' prediction of
humble suffering contrasted with the attitude
of the disciples who desired positions of

authority in the new kingdom (20:25). Their desire for power and position became clear as they neared Jerusalem, and their hope for the establishment of Jesus' kingdom over all the Gentiles was at its height.

20:20-28 THE MODEL OF THE SON OF MAN: TRUE GREATNESS IS REDEMPTIVE SERVICE
The rest of the disciples were indignant at the request of James and John's mother (20:24) because they also wanted the best positions in the kingdom. The disciples had completely misunderstood the nature of the kingdom that Jesus would bring. It would not be like the Gentile kingdoms in which rulers "lord it over" the people they rule (20:25). The disciples were not to be like the Gentiles, but like Jesus Christ. Jesus, in predicting his passion, desired to teach submission and humility to his disciples. The "cup" (20:22) referred to Jesus' impending suffering and death. James later drank the "cup" (cf. Acts 12:2). Jesus gave his life a ransom "for" (Matt. 20:28, "in the place of") many. These words by Jesus clearly taught the doctrine of the substitutionary atonement.

20:29-34 THE SON SERVES: JERICHO BLIND MEN HEALED
Matthew's account mentioned two blind men, while Mark 10:46-52 and Luke 18:35-43 mention only Bartimaeus, the more prominent of the two. Luke said that the miracle took place as they entered Jericho (Luke 18:35), while Matthew indicated that the miracle took place as they left (Matt. 20:29). Apparently the miracle took place as they left the old city of Jericho (Old Testament) and were nearing the newer city of Jericho (New Testament); the sites of these two towns lie about a half a mile apart. The expression "Son of David" (20:30) was a Messianic title (cf. 2 Sam. 7:11-16; Isa. 9:7).

21:1-11 The Servant and Son Is Praised: Triumphal Entry
Bethphage (Matt. 21:1) was a village in the vicinity of the Mount of Olives about a half a mile east of Jerusalem. The donkey was the mount of royalty in the biblical period (21:2). The Zechariah passage (21:5; cf. Zech. 9:9) concerned God's great offer of salvation and restoration for Israel. Jesus rode the young colt of a donkey in fulfillment of Zechariah's prophecy. Jesus came in a gentle manner, not

as a warrior on a war horse. Palm "branches" (Matt. 21:8; cf. John 12:13) were associated with rejoicing (cf. Lev. 23:40), and later with expressions of triumph or victory (1 Macc. 13:51). The passage surrounding Psalm 118:26, quoted by the crowds in Matthew 21:9, also concerned God's restoration of Israel through his chosen messenger (cf. Ps. 118:22-29). "Hosanna" (21:9), a Hebrew imperative, means "save now." The crowd identified Jesus as "the prophet from Nazareth in Galilee" (Matt. 21:10-11).

21:12-17 Jesus Redefines Temple Functions
These debates between Jesus and the religious leaders achieved several ends. They revealed the false arguments being made against Jesus for what they were and his true identity was recognized. He was the Messiah, "the Son of David" (21:15). Jesus' words and deeds in the temple also served to teach his followers about true religion. The book of Matthew, as a whole, built to this confrontation between Jesus and the Jewish leaders with their distorted form of religion. The conclusion of this confrontation recognized the authority of Jesus, the Messiah. These debates also provided an inspirational model of boldness in opposition to false religion.

In the context of Jesus driving the money changers from the temple (21:12-13), read Isaiah 56:6-8 and Jeremiah 7:8-11. Jesus redirected the minds and hearts of the people to God in prayer (Matt. 21:12-13) and praise (21:14-17). Read the entire verse of Psalm 8:2 to understand what Jesus intended in Matthew 21:16. The words of the psalm speak of praise and strength to confound his enemies. Also, the "child" image is found throughout Matthew's Gospel (cf. Matt. 11:25-30; 18:1-6; 19:13-15).

21:18-22 The Fig Tree Cursed: a Faith Lesson in the Context of Rejection
The cursing of the fig tree was a lesson in the relationship between faith and prayer (21:21). Jesus demonstrated to his disciples the power that was available to them through prayer. The foliage on the fig tree indicated that there should have been some early, small figs, but there were none. Jesus judged the

tree for its false profession and its unfruitfulness (cf. John 15:6). This was Jesus' only destructive miracle.

21:23–23:39 The Past Disobedience to God's Messengers

21:23-27 JESUS AND JOHN THE BAPTIST: THE WAY OF RIGHTEOUSNESS
The debate concerning Jesus' authority was just a smoke screen used by the Jewish religious leaders to avoid obedience (21:23-27). The three parables that follow this debate (21:28–22:14) were designed to deal with this challenge to his authority (cf. 21:23).

21:28-32 THE PARABLE OF TWO SONS
In this parable Jesus showed the difference between professions of faith and the practice of faith. Jesus required that his followers do, not just agree with, the will of the Father. The "tax collectors" and "prostitutes" (21:31) functioned as examples of those who had truly repented, and Jesus sought to motivate the Jewish leaders to repentance by citing their example. Deeds, not words alone, were necessary to make a person acceptable to God.

21:33-46 THE PARABLE OF THE REJECTED SON
The kingdom was not cancelled, rather it was taken away from the proud Jewish leaders and would be given to a repentant people (21:43) who would produce the fruit of righteousness (cf. Zech. 12:10–13:1; Rom. 11:26-27). The present generation was under judgment based on their rejection of Jesus the Messiah (cf. Matt. 23:38). Psalm 118, quoted in Matthew 21:42 (Ps. 118:22-23), was also quoted in 21:9. Matthew 21 was built around Jesus' fulfillment of the prophetic words of Psalm 118 (cf. Matt. 21:9, 13, 16, 42; 23:39). The people who would lose the kingdom were those who thought they had it (21:43). The nation that would bear fruit would be composed of anyone who did the will of God (cf. 21:31). The response of hatred by the Jewish leaders toward Jesus was restrained by fear of the crowds (21:45-46).

22:1-14 THE PARABLE OF THE MARRIAGE FEAST
This parable elaborated on the idea that few are chosen to be a part of the kingdom (22:14; cf. 21:43). The historical context reflected in the parable was the rejection of

God's messengers throughout Israel's history (cf. 21:33-39). It revealed qualifications necessary for a person to be called to the feast of God's kingdom. Many Jews had been invited to the banquet but showed themselves to be unworthy (22:8). Others (Gentiles) were then invited, but even among this group was found a fool who was not prepared to accept the invitation and enter the feast. The second invitation, like the first, required that the person invited be worthy of the invitation.

Following these parables, a number of debates occurred with the scheming Jewish leaders. The leaders had already been shown to be deficient regarding their understanding of the Scriptures (21:16, 42) and to be excluded from the kingdom due to their lack of faith (22:15, 23, 31-32). Now, exposed as people without faith, they debate with Jesus.

22:15-46 JESUS DEALS WITH HIS OPPOSITION AND ANSWERS POLITICAL, DOCTRINAL, AND RELIGIOUS QUESTIONS
22:15-22 Paying taxes to Caesar. The Pharisees marveled at Jesus' response to their question concerning payment of the Roman poll tax (Matt. 22:15-22). Instead of becoming flustered, Jesus called them to reevaluate their own priorities. The "Herodians" (22:16) are usually identified as political supporters of the Herodian dynasty, but the dynasty of Herod had not been ruling in Judah since the expulsion of Archelaus in A.D. 6. When Herod became king in 37 B.C., he adopted the policy of selecting his own high priest. The "Herodians" mentioned here were probably descendants of the family of Boethus, whom Herod had selected as his high priest. The question involved the legitimacy of the Roman government in Palestine (22:17). Everyone would agree that a legitimate government has a right to tax its citizens. But the issue behind the question was: "Is the Roman government legitimate?" This was an attempt by the Jewish leaders to make Jesus say something against the Roman government that would result in his arrest. But the Jewish leaders also knew that if Jesus defended the Roman poll tax, he would alienate his Jewish followers. Jesus avoided the two-way trap by acknowledging two legitimate spheres of authority—governmental and religious—both of which needed to be recognized (22:21).

22:23-33 Marriage and the resurrection.
Jesus' response to the question of the Sadducees about marriage in the resurrection astonished his listeners (22:23-24). Jesus saw
through the falsity of their question, realizing
that the Sadducees did not even believe in
the resurrection of the dead as the Pharisees
did. For more on the Sadducees (22:23),
see the note on 3:7. The question of 22:24
was based on the law of levirate marriage
(cf. Deut. 25:5-10). The Sadducees referred
to this provision to demonstrate the absurdity
of belief in the resurrection. Jesus produced
evidence for the resurrection from the
Pentateuch (Exod. 3:6), which the Sadducees recognized as their sole source for
authoritative teaching (Matt. 22:32).

22:34-40 The greatest commandment.
The Pharisees questioned Jesus concerning the greatest of the commandments
(22:34-40). They had reduced the law to
365 negative and 248 positive commandments (22:36). Because it was difficult to
know them all, a priority list was needed.
The Pharisees' question related to the
debates common among them over which
commandments were "heavy" (most important) and which ones were "light" (less
important). What commandment was at
the top of Jesus' list? Jesus quoted Deuteronomy 6:5 and Leviticus 19:18 in answer
to their question. What was startling was
Jesus' connection of the command to love
one's neighbor (Lev. 19:18) with the
command to love God (Deut. 6:5). He
made the command to love one's neighbor
equally heavy with the command to love
God, showing that the two were closely
connected.

22:41-46 The identity of the Messiah.
After Jesus asked the question concerning
whose son the Messiah was, no one else
dared question him (Matt. 22:41-46). The
Messiah would in their thinking be a human
son, the "son of David" (22:42; cf. Ps.
110:1). But Jesus revealed that the Messiah
would be not only David's son; he would
also be David's Lord (Matt. 22:45). Jesus
quoted Psalm 110:1 in Matthew 22:44. The
only way David would call his descendant
"Lord" (22:45) would be if his descendant,
the Messiah, was divine.

**23:1-36 WOES ON THE LEADERS:
UNCLEAN AND WITHOUT THE LAW**
This scathing denunciation of the scribes and
Pharisees arose out of the incidents described
in the preceding chapters. The religious
leaders of Israel were presented as professional hypocrites. "Moses' seat" (23:2) was
a special chair in the synagogue assigned to
the most honored scribe of the community.
Jesus was implying that the Pharisees were
assuming Mosaic authority for their petty
laws and traditions. "Phylacteries" (23:5)
were small boxes containing portions of
Scripture (cf. Exod. 13:2-10; Deut. 6:4-9)
that were strapped on the forehead and forearm during prayer (cf. Exod. 13:9, 16; Deut.
11:18). The "tassels" (Matt. 23:5; cf. Deut.
22:12) served as reminders to keep the law.

The term "Rabbi" (Matt. 23:7), from the
Hebrew *rab* (meaning "great"), was a reverential form of address and title of respect.
Note the threefold use of "for" in 23:8-10.
Jesus called the Pharisees to give up their
religion of human deeds and short-lived
glory (23:5-7) and to seek God in humble
repentance. Humility (23:12) was the key
concept in Matthew 21–23.

Jesus gave seven woes (23:13-36). For
tithing (23:23), see Deuteronomy 14:22-29.
The leaders did not understand the true
meaning of the law. They debated the outer
and inner cleanness of utensils while the
law really was concerned with people and
their moral purity (Matt. 23:25-26). "Whitewashed tombs" (23:27) were clean on the
outside but were full of hidden death and
decay. Inner purity (23:27-28) was demanded in order to escape destruction
(23:29-36).

The identity of the Zechariah who was
murdered (23:5) cannot be known with certainty. In Old Testament Scripture, "Zechariah son of Berekiah" refers to the prophet
Zechariah (Zech. 1:1). But nowhere else in
Scripture is there an indication that he was
killed. The prophet Zechariah was also called
"descendant of Iddo" (Ezra 6:14) after his
grandfather's name. In 2 Chronicles 24:20-
22 a Zechariah, son of Jehoiada, was murdered in the way described by Jesus. If this
Zechariah is the one Jesus had in mind, then
the use of father's and grandfather's names,
seen in the references to the Old Testament
prophet Zechariah, may also be reflected in

Matthew 23:35. If this were true, then Jesus would have referred to Zechariah through his grandfather's name, Berekiah, while 2 Chronicles refers to him through his father's name, Jehoiada. Second Chronicles was the last book in the canon of Hebrew Scripture. The murder of "righteous Abel" (23:35) recorded in Genesis, and Zechariah's death recorded in 2 Chronicles, the last book of the Hebrew Bible, show how God's faithful followers have been persecuted throughout biblical history (cf. 23:37).

23:37-39 SUMMARY: CRY OF LONGING AND JUDGMENT
Jesus longed to be reconciled with his people, the Jews. Jesus had longed to restore the blessings on his people, but the key to unlocking those blessings was their own desire to ask. Jesus had asked two blind men what they wanted him to do for them (Matt. 20:32). Jesus was willing to restore the nation, but the nation did not want it from him ("you were not willing"; 23:37). Notice how Psalm 118 was used throughout Matthew 21–23; see Matthew 21:9 (cf. Ps. 118:25), Matthew 21:42-43 (cf. Ps. 118:22-23), and Matthew 23:37-39 (cf. Ps. 118:26). The "house" (Matt. 23:38) referred to the Jerusalem temple. Jesus concluded his comments by looking forward to his second coming when the Jewish people would welcome him and call him blessed (23:39; cf. Zech. 12:10–13:1).

24:1–25:46 The Final Evaluation of Obedience

Overview: With all Jesus had said about the errors of the Jewish leaders, one might wonder if he had any concern for the Jewish nation. This was answered in Matthew 24–25. The end-time perspective of this passage followed from the "comes" in 23:39 and the hypocrites' resistance to God's ways. Matthew 24:1–25:26 functioned in a number of different ways. It gave: (1) warnings against being misled (24:4-5, 11, 24); (2) encouragement to be diligent and faithful (24:6, 10, 12-13, 23, 26); and (3) insight into the essence of obedience exemplified by love (24:12, 14; 25:40, 45). These chapters revealed the loving heart of Jesus arming his followers for the potential problems to be faced in his absence. The Olivet Discourse was a loving, warm-hearted prophetic

departure saying and took its place with the other departure sayings of the Bible (cf. Moses, Deut. 31–32; Joshua, Josh. 23–24; and Paul, Acts 16:13-36). The background of the Olivet Discourse was Jesus' announcement recorded in Matthew 23:37-39. Jesus had hinted of his second coming and the judgment that would come against Jerusalem. The disciples needed some clarification on these two matters.

24:1-31 THE DESTRUCTION OF JERUSALEM PREDICTED: SIGNS OF THE END TIMES
24:1-3 Questions concerning the future. The "Mount of Olives" (24:3) is a long north-south ridge that lies just east of Jerusalem. The disciples had two basic questions on their minds (24:3): (1) When would the temple be destroyed? (2) What would be the sign of Jesus' second coming that would coincide with the end of this age? The first question had to do with the destruction of Jerusalem in A.D. 70 and was answered in Luke 21:20-24. The second question concerned the end of the age as it related to Israel's prophetic history.

Jesus' prediction of the destruction of Jerusalem (24:1-2) brought to mind their question "When shall these things be?" (24:3). The content of the Olivet Discourse illustrated and reflected the content of Matthew's Gospel as a whole. It revealed how those with the character traits of the Beatitudes, especially salt and light in persecution, would live in relationship with others and the end to which they would come. Jesus expected his followers to live out the command "Love your neighbor as yourself" (Matt. 22:39) as the observable, tangible proof of love for God (24:45-51). The sermon gave to the disciples comfort and assurance for a ministry in a time of great conflict (25:40, 45).

The disciples' question concerning Jesus' return (24:3) showed that they had not yet come to grips with his departure, suffering, and resurrection. Jesus had mentioned his coming in 23:39. As a result the disciples then ask when that will be and what it will look like.

24:4-14 The correction to potential misleading. Note the "time" words used in Matthew 24–25 (cf. 24:15, 23, 29, 33). Jesus warned his disciples to beware of the false teachers that would come (24:4). Why did Jesus not directly answer their questions concerning the future? Because he had another purpose. He wanted to help them avoid falling away from doing his will while he was gone (24:45-46). The "beginning of birth pains" (24:8) was a technical phrase for the end times. The events described in 24:4-14 did not paint a picture of the very end (cf. 24:6, 8). Jesus encouraged endurance through a long time of persecution to continue preaching the gospel (24:9-14). Persecution of Jesus' followers links back to 5:11. Jesus' response in 24:14 more directly related to the disciples' question about the end times (24:3). The disciples were looking for the end. Jesus wanted them to look at what they were to do until the end arrived: witness for him (cf. Acts 1:6-8). That was the reason for this age of trial and persecution. Jesus defined "love" as the opposite of "wickedness" (24:12; "lawlessness," NASB; "iniquity," KJV). In this sermon, Jesus was dealing with the disciples' motive for asking when the end would come (24:3). They were looking forward to the coming of the kingdom, in which they hoped to receive great glory as the disciples of the Messiah. Jesus continually redirected their thoughts to their present responsibilities to witness for him in a world that was hostile to their message.

24:15-22 The signs of the end. The events described in 24:1-14 were not the end. The greatest tribulation would come later (24:15-22). The "So" of 24:15 was a conclusion based on the warning against being misled (24:4). The "abomination that causes desolation" (24:15) referred to the antichrist (cf. Dan. 9:27; 2 Thess. 2:4). If the tribulation continued indefinitely, all living things would be exterminated (Matt. 24:22). To prevent such extermination, the period would be "shortened."

24:23-28 The unmistakable return. During times of great tribulation, one would naturally look for relief. This would be the attraction of the false messiahs. The content of 24:27 was Jesus' first specific answer to the question concerning the signs of his return (24:3). The middle part of this section (24:24-26) showed Jesus' concern that his disciples not be deceived.

24:29-31 The Son comes. Jesus quoted Isaiah 13:10 and 34:4 in Matthew 24:29. Note the context of these verses in the book of Isaiah. Jesus continued the answer to his disciples' question concerning the end times (Matt. 24:3) in 24:29-31 (cf. 24:36). Matthew 24:29-31 stressed the point made in 24:27 and emphasized Jesus' concern for those who would suffer. Jesus feared that their suffering would open them up to possible deception by false messiahs. Thus, he made it clear that his coming would be unmistakable, accompanied by great glory, angels, and a loud trumpet call (24:30-31). The desire for relief by the elect would be great, but Jesus left them with a message of comfort (24:31, "gather the elect"; cf. 24:4, 22, 24).

24:32–25:46 EXHORTATIONS TO FAITHFULNESS IN ABSENCE: PARABLES OF READINESS
24:32-36 The fig tree: certainty, but in ignorance of the exact time. The parable of the fig tree related to the cursing of the fig tree in 21:18-22. The word "generation" (24:34) probably referred to the generation that would experience the period of tribulation (24:4-28). The encouragement implicit in the passage was that they would not be totally destroyed before Jesus returned. Compare Matthew 24:30 with Daniel 7:13, and Matthew 24:31 with Isaiah 27:13. Matthew 24:36 gave the complete answer to 24:3 (cf. also 24:37; 25:46). Jesus' words "No one knows about that day or hour" (24:36) answered the disciples' question in 24:3 and set the stage for the need of endurance (24:13) during Jesus' absence (24:36–25:46).

24:37-44 Noah: remain alert and ready. Just as the people of Noah's day were not ready for the impending judgment, the people in the end times would be blind and unprepared. Note that "took" (24:39) and "taken" (24:40-41) referred to being taken in judgment, not to being taken to be with God in heaven. People did not understand (24:39) the signs of the times and the coming judgment. They continued on eating, drinking, marrying (24:38), working, and grinding (24:40-41) without insight into their impending doom.

24:45-51 Evil and faithful slaves. This parable examined the perils of "long-time" responsibility. All followers of Jesus have been put "in charge" as faithful slaves. The words "long time" (24:48; cf. 25:5, 19) gave the key to understanding the message Jesus was trying to get across in this section. Jesus was preparing his disciples for what would turn out to be a long absence. Jesus expected his followers to live according to the law of love (cf. 22:37-39; 25:31-46) and always be ready no matter how long he might wait to return.

25:1-13 The parable of the ten virgins. The parable of the ten virgins taught about the proper preparation necessary to enter the kingdom. Only those who were prepared to serve the Messiah (25:1, "the bridegroom") would enter in. The groom's delay in coming caused some to be unready (25:5). Again, the length of the wait for the Messiah's return and the need to be ready no matter how long he might take was emphasized.

25:14-30 Talents: laziness with the Master's entrusted possessions. In this parable the concept of reward was central (25:21, 23; cf. 24:47). The parable of the talents spoke of the rewards that would be given to those entering the kingdom on the basis of their faithfulness to God-given opportunity for service. Those who failed to use their gifts and opportunities for service would suffer judgment (25:28-30).

25:31-46 True obedience defined: love for the King's brothers. This passage elaborated the concept in 25:26 that not only blatant acts of evil would reap judgment. The failure to do the will of the Father and to use his gifts for the sake of others would also bring judgment. It also described the gathering and evaluation of the elect (25:32; cf. 24:31). The subjects of judgment would be people from all the nations. The separation of the sheep and goats depicted the judgment on the Gentile nations that would precede the inauguration of the kingdom and determine who would enter. The basis for entrance was faith, evidenced by works of kindness (25:35-39). No unbelievers ("goats") would be permitted to enter.

The two commands in 25:34, 41 brought some surprises (cf. 25:37, 44) for both the saved and the unsaved. For each group Jesus stressed the way they treated their fellow brothers and sisters (cf. 22:39). He had already defined who they were in 12:48-50. He placed great emphasis on community life in the gospel ministry. Jesus taught that the rewards of the kingdom were based on the good deeds performed for others. Showing love toward others would prove love for God (cf. 22:37-40; 1 John 4:7-8). Love for Jesus' family rounded out the concept of "theirs is the kingdom of heaven" of the Beatitudes (Matt. 5) and summed up all the character traits desired by Jesus for his followers: gentleness, humility, compassion, and obedience.

26:1-5 A Passion Prediction and Plot
Jesus' resurrection was not mentioned as it was in the other predictions of his death (cf. 16:21; 20:17-19). In this passage, Jesus focused on his impending death. Passover was a Jewish feast that commemorated God's deliverance of his people from Egypt (Exod. 12:1-30). It was observed annually on the fourteenth day of Nisan (Lev. 23:5), March–April, and was followed by the seven-day Feast of Unleavened Bread (Lev. 23:6-8) and the celebration of First Fruits (Lev. 23:10-14). Caiaphas (26:3) was installed as high priest from A.D. 18 to 36, when his father-in-law, Annas (cf. John 18:13), was removed from the office.

26:6-56 Betrayal and Arrest
26:6-13 BURIAL PREPARATIONS: ONE PERSON LISTENED TO HIS PREDICTIONS
The apostle John identified the "woman" (Matt. 26:7) as Mary, the sister of Martha and Lazarus (cf. John 12:3). Jesus said that she had done a good deed toward him (26:10; cf. 25:40, 45). The merit of what this woman did for Jesus (Matt. 26:12-13) had to do with the fact that she knew what she was doing. The disciples were slow to believe that Jesus was going to die. Mary believed the words of Jesus and proved her belief by making preparations for his burial (26:12) at great personal sacrifice.

26:14-16 JUDAS'S PLOTTING
Judas's decision was influenced by Satan (cf. Luke 22:3) and motivated by a desire for financial gain (Matt. 26:15). Apparently Judas did not believe that Jesus was fulfilling the Messianic role.

26:17-29 PASSOVER KEPT: COVENANT SYMBOLIZED

The "Feast of Unleavened Bread" (27:17) was so closely associated with the Passover that the term was used to designate the Passover season. Preparations for the Passover included: selection of a lamb (the tenth day of Nisan); burning all leaven (noon, the fourteenth day of Nisan); sacrifice of the lamb (1:30–2:30 P.M., the fourteenth day of Nisan); roasting of the lamb on a spit in preparation for the Passover supper. It was common in ancient Israel to recline propped up on one's elbow on cushions around a table (26:20). The "bowl" (26:23) may have been a bowl of salt water into which the bitter herbs were dipped as part of the Passover ritual.

The forgiveness of sins was linked to the breaking of Jesus' body and the shedding of his blood (26:26-29). The sacrifice of Jesus, memorialized in this Passover supper, would be the means of man's forgiveness in the new covenant. Jesus used the elements of the Passover meal to provide a memorial of his body and blood (26:26-29). The "covenant" (26:28) referred to the new covenant (cf. Jer. 31:31-34; Ezek. 36:25-28) that was inaugurated by Jesus' death (Heb. 8:6). Jesus implied that he would soon be absent (26:29; cf. the absence in 24:48; 25:5, 19).

26:30-56 ARREST IN GETHSEMANE

26:30-35 Jesus predicts the disciples' falling away. The "hymn" (26:30) was probably Psalm 118, the last of the Hallel psalms (Ps. 113–118) that were sung at Passover. Compare Jesus' prediction of the disciples' "falling away" (26:31) with the concept of endurance that he taught in Matthew 24–25. Jesus used Zechariah's prophecy of God's shepherd being struck and his sheep scattered (Zech. 13:7) to describe what would happen to himself and the disciples, his sheep (Matt. 26:31). The words "fall away" (26:31, 33; "be offended," KJV) are nearly synonymous with "disown" (26:34; "deny," NASB and KJV). Galilee (26:32) will again become significant (cf. 28:7, 10, 16; see also 4:15-16).

26:36-46 Jesus' prayer for deliverance: strengthening the flesh. Jesus' prayer in Gethsemane and the agony he experienced

as he submitted to the will of his Father became a model for his disciples. Jesus prayed to aid his weak flesh in doing what his Father and his own spirit so willingly desired. Submission to God's will (Matt. 26:39, 44) was central to Jesus' prayer and should be the heart of prayer for all of his followers. Although Jesus always submitted to his Father's will, he kept asking for deliverance just as he had taught his followers to do (cf. 7:7). The name "Gethsemane" (26:36) means "oil press." This olive grove was located, according to tradition, at the foot of the eastern slope of the Mount of Olives.

26:47-56 Jesus is arrested: flesh strengthened to obey God's word. One of the disciples tried to stop Jesus' arrest, and they all were confused about why Jesus would allow such a thing to happen. John identified Peter as the one responsible for this defensive action (26:51; cf. John 18:10). They still did not understand Jesus' role as the suffering Messiah. Jesus' disciples were not willing to face up to God's plan that had been revealed through his prophets (Matt. 26:54, 56). These verses reveal the nature of true discipleship and the problem of "falling away" or "stumbling" because of Jesus' mission of suffering on the cross. A Roman "legion" (26:53) had about 5,300 men.

26:57–27:56 The Passion Narrative: Guilt and Identity

26:57–27:26 THE TRIALS: TWO CONTRADICTORY VERDICTS

Jesus was brought before the religious court of the Jews and then the civil court of Rome. The civil trial was necessary because the Jewish leaders did not have authority to execute the death penalty (John 18:31). His religious trial was before Annas (John 18:12-14), Caiaphas (Matt. 26:57), and then before the Sanhedrin (Mark 15:1). His civil trial was before Pilate, the Roman governor (Matt. 27:2), Herod Antipas (Luke 23:6-12), and once again before Pilate (Matt. 27:15-26).

The leaders brought false testimony against Jesus (26:57-68). Jesus' silence (26:63) was in fulfillment of Isaiah 53:7. Jesus combined Daniel 7:13 and Psalm 110:1 in his defense (Matt. 26:64). Tearing one's garments (26:65) was a traditional sign of grief or mourning. Peter denied Jesus, just as had been predicted (26:69-75; cf. 26:31-35). Peter's Galilean accent suggested that he may have been one of Jesus' disciples (26:73).

The witnesses to Jesus' innocence came from surprising sources, Judas (27:3-10) and Pilate (27:11-26). Following the expulsion of Herod's son Archelaus from Judea in A.D. 6, Judea became a Roman Imperial Province governed by a Roman prefect (27:2). Pontius Pilate served as prefect from A.D. 26 to 36. He normally lived in Caesarea but stayed in Jerusalem during Jewish festivals to keep order. Pilate was staying in the "Palace" (John 18:28; "Praetorium," NASB; "judgment hall," KJV), probably the Antonia Fortress, located just north of the temple area. The Jews did not have the authority to execute captial punishment, though they took it anyway several times (for example, cf. Acts 7:58). The message sent to Pilate from his wife while he was judging Jesus further attested his innocence (Matt. 27:19).

Judas's death fulfilled the prophecy of Zechariah 11:12-13. The "potter's field" (Matt. 27:7) was a section of property apparently used by the potters of Jerusalem to dig for clay. It was known in Acts 1:19 as "Akeldama," meaning "field of blood." In Matthew 27:9-10 Matthew quoted Zechariah 11:12-13 and alluded to Jeremiah 19:1-4 and 32:6-9. Composite quotations were often assigned to the more prominent author, in this case Jeremiah.

The Roman scourge, or whip, consisted of a short wooden handle to which several leather thongs were attached (Matt. 27:26). To the ends of the thongs were attached bits of lead, brass, or sharp bones. Josephus told of a man whose ribs were laid bare by scourging.

27:27-56 THE CRUCIFIXION
27:27-44 The mockers of Jesus. Matthew connected those who insulted Jesus while he was on the cross with the fulfillment of Old Testament Scripture (cf. Isa. 53:3, 7). All the mocking was thematically similar. The mockers expected that if Jesus was the Messiah, he would be able to get off the cross. They were questioning his ability to fulfill the Messianic role that he claimed to be fulfilling. But the problem was not with

Jesus' ability. It was with the people's conception of what the Messiah's role was. What looked to the unenlightened like a humiliating disaster was really the powerful work of God fulfilling his promise of redemption.

For more on the "Praetorium" (27:27), see the note on 27:2. Simon (27:32) was from Cyrene, the capital of Cyrenaica, a Roman province located in North Africa. The name "Golgotha" (27:33) is Aramaic for "the place of the skull." The "gall" (27:34) was a bitter, and perhaps poisonous, herb. It has been suggested that this drink was given to the condemned to lessen the pain of crucifixion. The dividing of Jesus' clothes (27:35) was in fulfillment of Psalm 22:18.

27:45-56 The believers in Jesus, the Son of God. The "sixth . . . until the ninth hour" (Matt. 27:45) was from noon until 3:00 P.M. The words *"Eloi, Eloi, lama sabachthani"* (27:46) are Aramaic for "My God, My God, why have you forsaken me?" They were quoted from Psalm 22:1. Some in the crowd mistook *"Eloi"* for "Elijah" (27:47). The "curtain" (27:51) separated the Holy Place from the Most Holy Place. According to Josephus it was ninety feet high. The tearing of the veil had great significance, for after the work of Jesus Christ the mediator was complete, the veil was no longer necessary to separate man from the holiness of God (cf. Heb. 10:19-20). Some people were raised through Christ's death and resurrection (Matt. 27:52; cf. 1 Cor. 15:20-23). Like Lazarus, they died again, but their resurrection marked off the dynamic witness of God's approval for his Son at this moment.

27:57–28:15 Burial and Resurrection
27:57-66 BURIAL AND SECURITY
Joseph was from Arimathea, a town of uncertain location (Matt. 27:57). He secured permission to bury Jesus in his own tomb. Jesus' burial in the tomb of a rich man took place in accordance with Messianic prophecy (27:60; cf. Isa. 53:9). The securing of the grave with a sealed entrance and guards was an attempt to thwart the fulfillment of Jesus' prediction of his resurrection (Matt. 27:62-66). This was yet one more attempt to thwart God's work through Jesus. Such attempts to block the will of God

had been seen earlier in Herod's murder of the babies in Bethlehem (2:13-18), the temptation of Jesus in the wilderness (4:1-11), and Peter's denial that Jesus should die (16:21-23). But nothing would stop the fulfillment of God's plan.

28:1-15 RESURRECTION AND BRIBERY

The "Sabbath" (28:1) was a Saturday. The "first day of the week" was Sunday. The resurrection of Jesus was the sign of Jonah (cf. 12:39-40), the last public sign to the Jews that Jesus was who he claimed to be (28:6). The disciples were commanded to return to Galilee (28:7, 10). That command was delivered by an angel and by Jesus himself. Jesus appeared five times on resurrection day: (1) to Mary Magdalene (Matt. 28:1; Mark 16:9-11; John 20:11-18), (2) to the other women (Matt. 28:8-10), (3) to Simon Peter (Luke 24:33-35; 1 Cor. 15:5), (4) to the two disciples (Mark 16:12-13; Luke 24:13-32), and (5) to the eleven apostles (Matt. 28:16-20; Mark 16:14; Luke 24:36-49; John 20:19-25).

28:16-20 Commission to the Community: Identity, Authority, and Presence

As was true throughout Matthew's Gospel, even at the end some doubted Jesus' identity (Matt. 28:17). They doubted whether he was one whom they should worship. But to their doubts Jesus gave the proclamation of his authority and his presence (28:18-20). Matthew 28:19 could be translated, "As you are going, make disciples. . . ." The imperative was "make disciples." The "going" was assumed. This ministry extended to "all nations," which was in keeping with the universal prospect of blessing in the Abrahamic covenant (cf. Gen. 12:2-3). The ministries to accompany making disciples included "baptizing" (identifying believers with a local assembly) and "teaching" (laying the foundation for application). Jesus would fulfill his name "Immanuel," meaning "God with us," by being present with his people through the work of the Holy Spirit even "to the very end of the age" (28:20; cf. Acts 1:1-8; 2:1-4).

Mark

BASIC FACTS

HISTORICAL SETTING

The Gospel of Mark makes no reference to the birth of Jesus or his early ministry in Judea (cf. John 2:13–4:3). The record begins with the commencement of Jesus' public ministry at his baptism, which most likely took place in the summer or autumn of A.D. 29. Mark records the ministry of Jesus in Galilee (Mark 1:14–9:50), Perea (10:1-52), and Judea (11:1–13:37). The Gospel continues the record of Jesus' life to include his death and resurrection.

AUTHOR

Mark's Gospel is anonymous, but the testimony of the early church fathers, including Irenaeus, Clement of Alexandria, Origen, and Jerome, indicates that John Mark was the author of the work. John Mark was the son of a certain Mary in Jerusalem (Acts 12:12) and the cousin of Barnabas (Col. 4:10). His home was Jerusalem, and he may have witnessed some of the events of the life of Jesus. He may possibly have been the young man referred to in Mark 14:51.

Mark accompanied Paul and Barnabas from Jerusalem to Antioch and set out with them on their first missionary journey (Acts 12:25; 13:5). Upon reaching Perga, Mark returned home to Jerusalem (Acts 13:13). He later accompanied Barnabas on a missionary journey to Cyprus (Acts 15:37-39). Mark was probably in Rome with Peter before Peter's death (1 Pet. 5:13). Later he was with Paul at Rome (Col. 4:10; Philem. 23-24). While Mark had experienced an initial failure in his early ministry, he later proved himself a valuable servant of Jesus. Paul desired his presence in Rome during the final days of his second imprisonment (2 Tim. 4:11).

According to tradition, Mark was in Rome serving as Peter's interpreter before his death. Tradition also records that Mark ministered in Alexandria, founded a church there, and became its first bishop.

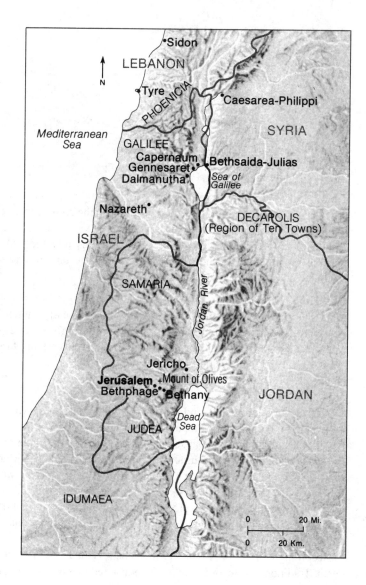

- Sidon
- LEBANON
- N
- Tyre
- PHOENICIA
- Caesarea-Philippi
- Mediterranean Sea
- SYRIA
- GALILEE
- Capernaum
- Bethsaida-Julias
- Gennesaret
- Sea of Galilee
- Dalmanutha
- Nazareth
- DECAPOLIS (Region of Ten Towns)
- ISRAEL
- SAMARIA
- Jordan River
- Jericho
- Mount of Olives
- Jerusalem
- Bethphage
- Bethany
- JORDAN
- Dead Sea
- JUDEA
- IDUMAEA
- 0   20 Mi.
- 0   20 Km.

DATE
There is no explicit statement in the book of Mark as to its date or origin. Mark was undoubtedly written before A.D. 70 because there is no reference to the destruction of Jerusalem. Clement of Alexandria mentions that the Gospels with the genealogies were written first, so Mark would have been written after Matthew and Luke, sometime after A.D. 60.

Many scholars believe that Mark was written around A.D. 50 and was used by Matthew and Luke in writing their Gospels. The thesis of the priority of Mark is based in large part on the theory that the Gospel writers were dependent on each other.

PURPOSE
The book of Mark was designed to present the person and works of Jesus as God's servant and Son attested by his mighty works. The abundance of miracles in the book is a key to discerning its purpose. While Mark records no more miracles than the other Gospel writers, he does have a greater concentration of miracles. Those mighty works authenticate the person of Jesus as a servant (10:45) and as the Son of God. This would create the kind of holy fear in the early believers that would cause them to obey his will and share his Good News.

GEOGRAPHY AND ITS IMPORTANCE

Mark begins geographically in the wilderness and ends at the empty tomb. At the center of the book is the revelation at Caesarea Philippi (Mark 8:27-38) of the deity of Jesus and his destiny to die on the cross. Isolated places like the wilderness, the stormy Sea of Galilee, open country, or a quiet early morning graveyard become the contexts for Jesus' followers to come to grips with how Jesus' destiny is intricately bound up with their own.

GUIDING CONCEPTS

WILDERNESS
Mark mentions the wilderness many times in the early chapters of his Gospel (1:3, 4, 12-13, 45; 6:31, 35). The wilderness was a place that was in many ways opposite to the city; it was a place where one would go out to meet God's prophet (1:5; cf. 1:38). It was the place of beasts (1:13) and loneliness (1:35; 6:31; cf. Matt. 14:13; Luke 4:42). The wilderness was the place of Jesus' testing and the stage for his initial victory over Satan. Mark, unlike Matthew, does not recall Israel's earlier experiences in the wilderness and thus compare and identify the Hebrew nation with Jesus. For Mark, the wilderness was a place set apart from the rebellious society of Israel, where the true seeker could hear the voice of God and seek to follow him. It was the place where the gospel had its beginnings (see his use of Isa. 40:3 in Mark 1:3) and the place to seek God in repentance (1:2; cf. Mal. 3:1).

IMMEDIATELY
Mark used the Greek word for "immediately," translated variously as "at once," "without delay," "just then," "just as," "quickly," "immediately," or "as soon as" far more than the other Gospel writers (Matthew, six times; Luke, one time; John, three times;

Mark, forty-two times; for example, see Mark 1:12, 18, 20, 23, 28, 42-43; 2:8; 4:5, 15-17, 29; 5:29-30, 42; 6:25, 45, 50, 54; 7:25; 9:15, 24; 10:52; 11:2; 14:43, 45, 72). Mark used the word in the contexts of miracles, narrative, and the words of Jesus to show the reader that the time to repent and follow Jesus was right then. Jesus moved with immediacy, not because he was in a rush, but because the time to act was "now," and not a moment was to be lost in indecision and delay. The repetition of the word "immediately" drives the urgency of repentance home to the readers of Mark's Gospel.

FEAR
Mark used the concept of fear throughout his Gospel to teach the believers the proper response to the gospel of Jesus the Messiah (cf. 4:41; 5:15, 33, 36; 6:20, 50; 9:32; 10:32; 11:18, 32; 12:12; 16:8). Many hold that originally Mark's Gospel ended at 16:8 and that the present verses after that were added at a later time. If Mark ended his work at 16:8, then he purposely wanted to end with the concept of fear. While he certainly knew the rest of the gospel story, he wanted to stop there in order to drive home the absolute astonishment and fear that comprehension of Jesus' resurrection should cause. As disciples, believers are to reflect on that astonishment and fear to see if they have truly comprehended the meaning of the resurrection. The disciple fears, not because of possible punishment, but because of astonishment, awe, and respect in the presence of God's great redemptive act in Jesus Christ.

INCOMPREHENSION
Mark also wanted to show what the disciples did and did not understand about Jesus. That would help the believers see their own blind spots when it came to believing and following Jesus (4:12-13, 41; cf. Matt. 13:13-15, 19, 23, 51). Matthew focused on the end of the disciples' process of enlightenment. But Mark showed the disciples in the middle of the process, before the light of understanding had dawned on them (Mark 6:52; cf. Matt. 14:22-32). With the problems of physical and spiritual blindness in mind, compare Mark 8:17, 21 with Matthew 16:12. Note how both Matthew (Matt. 13:14-15) and Mark (Mark 4:12) use Isaiah 6:9.

Mark highlighted three of the disciples' misunderstandings about Jesus' nature and mission that became obvious after each of Jesus' three predictions of his death and resurrection (Mark 8:27-31; 9:30-32; 10:32-34). Mark's recording of the blindness of the disciples followed immediately after each prediction (8:32-33; 9:33-34; 10:35-37). Each time Jesus predicted his death, the disciples became concerned with other things, such as their desires for personal greatness or fear for their own lives. They could not seem to comprehend the significance of Jesus' death and resurrection. That was why, at the end of the book, Mark left his readers with the event of Jesus' resurrection; an event that demanded a reaction of utter astonishment, fear, and silence. The readers of Mark's Gospel, like the disciples, were called to pause and let this amazing revelation sink in.

THE REASON FOR JESUS' SECRECY
Mark 8:27-33 is the pivotal section of the book. The disciples had little trouble comprehending that Jesus was the Messiah, the Son of God (8:27-30). His identity was relatively easily grasped. But the challenge for the disciples, then and now, was to come

to grips with the role that the Messiah would play during his time on earth. Jesus' role included death on a cross and a subsequent resurrection from the dead (8:31-33).

Jesus often moved about in secrecy or asked his followers not to talk about him (4:10-11; 5:43; 7:24; 8:30; 9:9, 30). Jesus proclaimed the gospel openly, but when he met with hard-hearted resistance, he often revealed truth in parables that were difficult to understand. He shared fuller explanations and insights into the kingdom only with those who believed in him (4:11, 34). He unsuccessfully tried to keep his presence a secret (7:24, 36). He told several people not to tell anyone about him (5:43; 8:30; 9:9). Jesus' secrecy was an attempt on his part to clear the way for special teaching to his disciples (9:30-31). Jesus' amazing acts of raising the dead, healings, and feeding of thousands were certainly not geared to keeping a low profile. But Jesus had a twofold mission: to build a solid group of disciples and to move on to his goal of Jerusalem and the cross. He had no desire to build his own kingdom among the people of Galilee. Perhaps Matthew 12:18-21, quoting Isaiah 42:1-4, is the best explanation of Jesus' secrecy. His gentle teaching marked the men and women who would be his disciples, and his quiet ways allowed him to bring justice to victory through his death and resurrection. He was moving toward the cross and avoided the kind of public presence that would be more suitable to building an earthly kingdom then and there.

In part, Jesus' secrecy was explained in 8:27-33. His identity was being hidden from unbelievers who refused to hear him. His destiny was also partially hidden from the believing disciples, but his destiny to die was revealed to them that they might seek to understand its significance. The unveiling of the secret of Jesus' identity as the Messiah paved the way for the unveiling of the mystery of his destiny to die on the cross. The death of Jesus, which Peter so adamantly rejected (8:32-33), the church was called on to embrace. The church needed to comprehend the mystery of Jesus' destiny on the cross and in his resurrection. The cross became the model for earthly Christian experience; the resurrection became the basis for Christian hope.

BIBLE-WIDE CONCEPTS

THE SON OF MAN

The disciples quickly recognized Jesus' identity as the Messiah (8:27-30) but found it hard to understand the implications of his suffering (8:31-33). They needed to understand what Jesus meant when he called himself the "Son of Man." In Jesus' day the phrase was not commonly used as a title, and in Mark, only Jesus used the phrase with reference to himself. Therefore, Jesus' use of the phrase was unusual and worthy of close attention. It was Jesus' own unique way of naming himself.

Jesus referred to himself as the Son of Man in each of his passion predictions. The Old Testament background for the phrase can be found in Psalms 8:4; 80:17; Ezekiel 4:1; and Daniel 7:13. Jesus used the term in three different contexts. First, he used it in connection with his claim to authority in the forgiveness of sins (Mark 2:10) and his authority over the Sabbath (2:28). These were the only times Jesus used the title "Son of Man" before he used it in Mark 8 in connection with the revelation of his destiny of suffering.

Second, the title "Son of Man" was used by Jesus to reveal the fact of his incarnational limitation and humbling. Jesus the Messiah would not seek personal greatness, and he thus chose a title that would not bring him exaltation. "Son of Man" revealed the nature of God as savior and the bringer of atonement for sin through suffering and self-sacrifice (Mark 10:45). He called himself the "Son of Man" in each of his passion predictions (8:31; 9:31; 10:33). In addition, the phrase was used when Jesus further discussed his betrayal (14:21, 41), suffering (9:31), and resurrection (9:9). The suffering of the "Son of Man" would come in submission to God's will. He let God make the claim for his Messiahship. That was done first through humiliation as the "Son of Man," and then through exaltation as the "Son of God" (Phil. 2). God in his voice from heaven approved Jesus at his baptism and transfiguration. The practical application of the entire book rests on one word: "even" (10:45, "For *even* the Son of Man . . ."). *Even* Jesus did not come to be served, but to serve. Should not believers follow in the same role of humble, and if necessary, suffering service?

Third, Jesus also used the phrase "Son of Man" with reference to his exaltation and return (8:38; 13:26; 14:62). He would reign exalted and would return, but only after the time of his suffering and humiliation. Mark laid out this same pattern of suffering before exaltation as the model for Jesus' followers. They would first have to humble themselves to be servants in bringing God's redemption to the world. That would involve varying degrees of suffering. Only then could they expect to share in Jesus' resurrection and exaltation. Jesus' first coming is the model for the present age of ministry. The glory of his second coming will belong to believers forever in the next age.

The phrase "Son of Man" was what Jesus used to explain his ministry. Because there were many ideas of how God would send his Messiah, Jesus used a phrase to describe himself that no one would recognize. Therefore, no one could read their presuppositions about how Jesus should act into the title. "Messiah" and "Son of God" brought up images of a conquering and reigning king. "Lord" as a title also only contained ideas of power, victory, and divinity. But "Son of Man" carried no clear content. Although some people in Jesus' day knew of Daniel's prophecy of a "Son of Man" who would be given the kingdom (Dan. 7:13), they were also used to hearing the phrase "son of man" used simply as a way of referring to someone as being human (as in Ezekiel 2:1; 3:1; 4:1; 31:1; 33:1; 34:1). In addition, Jesus brought new content to what the people were expecting from God's chosen Messiah. This is why the crowds were not clear as to what Jesus meant by applying the phrase to himself (see, for example, John 12:34). Jesus poured into this phrase the concepts of servanthood, suffering, and ultimate resurrection.

Jesus was indeed Lord, Messiah, and God, but the power and model of his mission as ransom payment for the world was summed up in the title "Son of Man." The church is to follow that model and not try to be great before the time when God will exalt all who are faithful.

NEEDS MET BY MARK

Mark wanted to help his readers come to grips with the difficult issues of belief in Jesus. Belief brought persecution, and that persecution would give rise to many hard questions about the purpose and benefits of believing in Jesus. Mark showed how the pain of persecution was closely linked to the cross of Christ. Faith in the cross of Jesus Christ also demanded the believer's own daily experience of the cross. Mark outlined major reasons why the disciples had difficulty in comprehending how their own lives were to conform to the humiliation and pain of Christ's cross. The days during which Mark wrote were very dangerous, and he helped his readers understand the seriousness of their faith in Jesus and the holy fear it demanded. Finally, Mark envisioned sharing in Christ's future exaltation and freedom from pain and suffering. But Mark always wanted his readers to keep the order straight: humble service in this age, glorious exaltation in the next. Mark met some basic needs for those who believed and yet struggled with embracing the full message of the gospel. The structure and content of Mark's Gospel show that he was answering questions like the following for his readers.

- What is required of believers beyond their initial belief in Jesus as Savior and God's Son?
- What encouragement can believers find in suffering for the sake of Christ?
- Why is it so hard for believers to accept their destiny of bearing the cross?
- What kind of life are believers called to in Jesus the Messiah's resurrection?

There are many things believers are afraid of today, but Mark speaks most effectively about a fear believers actually need. Mark wanted to replace the tendency of believers to live selfishly with a holy fear of God that would cause them to act and speak under the influence of Christ's astounding resurrection. Mark wrote to a Christian community that needed to understand that following Christ was a difficult and challenging task. It brought a great salvation but also stood against the natural desire of people to live selfishly. Status seeking and luxury building were to be weeded out of their lives and replaced with an aggressive commitment to bringing God's redemption to the world. Mark revealed the struggle the disciples had with giving up their desire for mortal greatness, a struggle shared by believers today. They were not immune to fear, misunderstanding, and status seeking. Like believers today, the disciples had trouble understanding and accepting the suffering that resulted from following their great Savior.

OUTLINE OF MARK

A. THE PROPHETIC FOUNDATION: JOHN THE BAPTIST (1:1-15)
  1. Title: The Beginning of the Gospel about Jesus Christ (1:1)
  2. The Prophetic Foundation: John the Baptist (1:2-15)
B. THE FOUNDATION OF POWER: ITS IMPLICATION FOR THE IDENTITY OF JESUS (1:16–8:30)
  1. The First Impact of Power (1:16-39)
  2. Jesus Explains the Significance of His Acts of Power (1:40–3:6)

3. The Obedient Are Initiated into Power and Mystery (3:7–4:34)
4. Extreme Power for Extreme Cases (4:35–6:6)
5. Progressive Enlightenment: From Physical to Spiritual Reality (6:6–8:30)
C. THE FOUNDATION OF SUFFERING: ITS IMPLICATION FOR THE
DISCIPLES' SUBMISSION (8:31–16:20)
1. The Way to Jerusalem: The Struggles of Self-Denial (8:31–10:52)
2. Victory over Anti-Christian Delusion (11:1–13:37)
3. Betrayal and Arrest: The Disciples' Defeat by Flesh Unprepared by Prayer
(14:1-52)
4. The Trial (14:53–15:15)
5. The Crucifixion and Burial (15:16-47)
6. Resurrection Events (16:1-20)

MARK NOTES

1:1-15 THE PROPHETIC FOUNDATION
1:1 Title: The Beginning of the Gospel about Jesus Christ
The "gospel" is the "good news" concerning Jesus Christ. The title gives shape and direction to the book by setting forth the beginning components of the timeless Christian message. Mark began his book by giving believers in every generation the first principles of the gospel. He used the words "gospel" or "good news" more than any other Gospel writer (cf. 1:1, 14-15; 8:35; 10:29; 14:9; 16:15). Matthew used it in 4:23; 9:35; 24:14; 26:13. The Greek noun translated "gospel" was not used in either Luke or John. Luke used the verb form "preach the gospel" twenty-five times, but Matthew used it only once; Mark and John did not use the verb form at all.

1:2-15 The Prophetic Foundation: John the Baptist
1:2-11 JOHN THE BAPTIST IS INTRODUCED
The coming of John the Baptist (1:2-3) was in fulfillment of Isaiah 40:3 and Malachi 3:1. John was contrasted with the "one more powerful" (Mark 1:7) who would follow after him. John's baptism (1:4) signified repentance from sin on the part of the one baptized. This was done with a view to the redemption that would come through God's Messiah and his shed blood. The traditional site of John's ministry was on the Jordan River about eight miles southeast of Jericho. Locusts (1:6) were clean insects and could

be eaten (cf. Lev. 11:22). Wild honey (1:6) was plentiful in Israel (Judg. 14:8; 1 Sam. 14:25). The baptism with the Holy Spirit (Mark 1:8) took place at Pentecost (Acts 1:5; 2:33). This was the first of three times that God spoke words in affirmation of his Son from heaven (Mark 1:11; cf. 9:7; John 12:28).

1:12-15 THE TEMPTATION OF JESUS
Jesus was severely tempted (Mark 1:13), yet he did not yield to sin (Heb. 4:15). John's arrest and imprisonment (Mark 1:14) is recorded in Matthew 14:1-12 and Mark 6:17-29. The events recorded in John 1:19–4:54 took place before John the Baptist's arrest. For Mark 1:15, see the comments on the kingdom of God in the notes on Matthew 3:2. The word "repent" (1:15) means "to change one's mind" and assumes a consequent change in one's behavior. The word "believe" (1:15) means to "trust" or "rely upon."

1:16–8:30 THE FOUNDATION OF POWER: ITS IMPLICATION FOR THE IDENTITY OF JESUS
1:16-39 The First Impact of Power
This section traces Jesus' work from his first impact in calling fishermen to follow him and healing needy people, demon possessed, and sick, to his expanded ministry to all Galilee (1:38). This was not the first encounter Simon and Andrew had had with Jesus (1:16; cf. John 1:35-42). Capernaum (Mark 1:21), situated on the northwest shore of the Sea of

Galilee, was an important tax collection station on the caravan route to Damascus. This was the home of Peter, Andrew, James, and John. Jesus relocated in Capernaum after his rejection from Nazareth (Matt. 9:1; Mark 2:1). The "teachers of the law" (1:22) debated the opinions and interpretations of leading rabbis, depending on second-hand tradition. Jesus did not need to refer to such authorities to authenticate his words.

1:40–3:6 Jesus Explains the Significance of His Acts of Power

This section stresses the importance of healings (leper and paralytic) for revealing the purpose of Jesus' coming (for sinners and humanity). For the laws regarding leprosy (1:40), see Leviticus 13–14. The miracle (1:40-42) was intended by Jesus to alert the Jewish establishment of his miraculous ministry in Galilee. For this reason, Jesus instructed the healed man to go straight to Jerusalem (1:44) rather than taking time to tell his story locally. The term "Son of Man" (2:10) is used fourteen times in Mark by Jesus to refer to himself. This strongly Messianic term appears to be derived from Daniel 7:13 (see comments in the introductory notes). Levi (Mark 2:14), another name for "Matthew," was a tax collector in Capernaum, an important city for the collection of customs from caravans traveling north and south. The Baptist's disciples were fasting because John had been imprisoned by Herod Antipas (2:18). The Pharisees fasted according to Levitical commandment and Jewish tradition (cf. Lev. 16:29-34; Zech. 8:19). For a discussion of the Sabbath (Mark 2:23), see the notes on Matthew 12:2. For David's actions (Mark 2:25), see 1 Samuel 21:1-6. Jesus' point in Mark 3:4 was that refusing to do good was itself evil. For a note on the Pharisees (3:6), see Matthew 3:7. For a note on the Herodians, see Matthew 22:16.

3:7–4:34 The Obedient Are Initiated into Power and Mystery

3:7-35 POWER AND PARABLES OF OBEDIENCE

The secret of the kingdom was explained to the intimate group of obedient followers (Mark 3:7-35). The author put stress on how obedient people receive the mysteries of God. Idumea (3:8; from the Hebrew "Edom") refers to the region south of Judea,

in the vicinity of the Negev and extending as far north as Hebron (see introductory map). For other lists of the apostles (3:16-19), see Matthew 10:1-4; Luke 6:13-16; and Acts 1:13. For an explanation of the term "Zealot," see the note on Matthew 10:4. For Beelzebul (Mark 3:22), see the note on Matthew 10:25.

4:1-34 THE SECRET OF KINGDOM GROWTH: FERTILE SOIL

The secret of the kingdom of God (Mark 4:11) was how the Messiah could come and be rejected and how the kingdom could be present but hidden in seed form (4:26, 31). The Greek word translated as "parable" (4:2) suggests the idea of comparison. The parables are true to life stories that teach spiritual truth by comparison. The realm of the known is used to teach something in the realm of the unknown. For a further discussion on parables, see the notes on Matthew 13:3, 10-17. The pagan mystery religions had teachings that only the initiated insiders were taught. So too, the secrets of the kingdom of God were revealed only to Jesus' followers, but non-disciples heard only the parables without the explanations (Mark 4:11). For the mustard seed (4:31), see the note on Matthew 13:31-32.

4:35–6:6 Extreme Power for Extreme Cases

4:35-41 POWER OVER NATURE AND DEMONS

This event was designed to show the disciples more about Jesus' identity. The disciples' fear revealed their lack of faith and understanding as to Jesus' true identity (4:40). At the time of this event, the disciples were not yet ready to be taught. They were still astounded that Jesus could stop a storm. Their question, "Who is this?" carries its own answer. They were in the presence of God and understanding this fact would be the key to solving their problems of fear and faithlessness. He was to be the only object of their faith and he was sufficient to deliver them from fear. The "other side" (4:35) referred to the opposite side of the Sea of Galilee, a fresh water lake situated in Galilee about 680 feet below sea level. The valleys to the west allow the Mediterranean winds to funnel down on the sea, raising great tempests on the otherwise calm sea.

5:1-20 POWER OVER NUMEROUS DEMONS: DECAPOLIS PROCLAMATION

The "region of the Gerasenes" (5:1) referred to the district of the well-known Greek city of Geresa, located about thirty miles southeast of the Sea of Galilee. The city apparently shared water and commerce rights on the Sea of Galilee with other cities of the Decapolis. Matthew 8:28 referred to the lesser known city of Gadara which, having a sizable Jewish population, would be more familiar to his Jewish readers. A "Legion" (Mark 5:9) in the Roman army consisted of about 5,300 men. The man was possessed by a host of demons. "Decapolis" (5:20) was a reference to a Gentile district east of the Jordan River known for its splendid Greek cities (see introductory map). The cities may have originally been ten (*deca*) in number, although their number varied from time to time. One of these cities, Scythopolis, lay west of the Jordan.

5:21-43 THE POWER OF FAITH

Jesus clarified the relation between his power and the woman's faith. She was not healed impersonally, but upon the meeting of her personal faith with Jesus' personal power. This stands in great contrast to the pagan concepts of impersonal divine power. The continual hemorrhage (5:25) would have rendered the woman perpetually unclean (cf. Lev. 15:25-27), unable to participate in temple worship. The language Jesus spoke (Mark 5:41) was Aramaic, a Semitic language like Hebrew, which was the common tongue of the Jewish people in the first century A.D.

6:1-6 THE POWER OF UNBELIEF

Although he had been born in Bethlehem, Jesus' "hometown" was Nazareth, the city in which he was raised (6:1) (see introductory map). Mark 6:3 tells of other children that were born to Joseph and Mary. Jesus had four half brothers and two half sisters. James became a leader in the Jerusalem church and authored the epistle of James. Judas or Jude wrote the epistle that bears his name.

6:6–8:30 Progressive Enlightenment: from Physical to Spiritual Reality

6:6-29 MISSION TO THE MULTITUDES: THE HOSTILE CONTEXT

After traveling through Gentile territory, Jews would shake the dust from their sandals and garments lest they contaminate the land of Israel. Here the act was to be done in protest against those who rejected Jesus the Messiah's messengers (6:11). King Herod (6:14) was a reference to Herod Antipas who ruled over Galilee and Perea (4 B.C.–A.D. 39). Herod Antipas divorced his wife and married his brother Philip's wife who was also Antipas's niece (6:17-18). John condemned this incestuous marriage as unlawful (cf. Lev. 18:6-18). According to Josephus (*Antiquities,* 18.5.4), the dancing daughter of Herodias was named "Salome" (Mark 6:22). To save face with his guests, Herod Antipas kept his oath even though it was rash and wicked (6:26).

6:30-56 MISSION TO THE MULTITUDES: THE HIDDEN SOURCE OF SUSTENANCE

6:30-44 The symbol of bread. The feeding of the five thousand was not immediately explained by Mark. It was simply narrated. It was not until 7:52 that Mark revealed that the feeding was a symbol of Jesus' great power and divine nature. To stop with amazement at the feeding without taking to heart its implications for the one who did the feeding would be to make the same mistake as the disciples. The "shepherd" (6:34) was a common metaphor in the ancient Near East for a leader (cf. Ezek. 34:1-23) and has Messianic implications (cf. John 10:11-16). The denarius (6:37; plural, denarii) was a silver coin that amounted to approximately one day's wage in the New Testament period. The number "five thousand" (6:44) did not include the large number of women and children who were also present.

6:45-52 The implications of the symbol of bread. Bethsaida (6:45), also known as Bethsaida-Julias, was a double site with a fishing village on the shore of the Sea of Galilee about one and a half miles south of the fortified city. It was located just east of the Jordan near the northeast shore of the Sea of Galilee (see introductory map). The "fourth watch of the night" (6:48) referred to the time between 3:00 and 6:00 A.M. The words "He was about to pass by them" (6:48) suggest that Jesus intended to "pass by" to give the disciples an opportunity to confess their need.

The disciples should have received insight from the feeding of the five thousand (6:44; cf. 6:52) that Jesus had full power over nature. Jesus was powerful, just as God was powerful. He was not just a miracle worker. Mark was dealing with the problem of fear and how believers should cope with it. The disciples understood the details of the feeding but only saw it as a marvel with no significance regarding who Jesus was. This reveals the parabolic nature of some of Jesus' acts. The apostle John called these miracles "signs." Jesus' miracles were signs that pointed away from the dazzle of the act to its significance: God was present to save those who would believe. The disciples' problem of hard-heartedness was also shared by those who did not understand the parables (4:11-12).

6:53-56 The recognition of power. In contrast with the disciples' hard hearts and lack of understanding about Jesus' power (6:52), these people recognized Jesus and his power (6:54) and sought his healing. They even understood that his power was so great that just touching his clothing would bring healing (6:56). Gennesaret (6:53) was the plain located on the northwest shore of the Sea of Galilee southwest of Capernaum (see introductory map).

7:1-23 THE HIDDEN SOURCE OF UNCLEANNESS: THE HEART
For a note on the Pharisees (7:1), see Matthew 3:7. The "teachers of the law" (7:1; "scribes," NASB and KJV) were originally copiers of the Scriptures who became regarded as experts in Jewish law. The "tradition of the elders" (7:3) was a reference to the oral tradition of the Pharisees which amplified and applied the biblical law. Included were detailed specifications for such procedures as ritual cleansing before meals. The issue was Jewish ceremony, not personal hygiene. The Pharisees regarded bread eaten with unwashed hands as if it were filth (7:5). In 7:6-7 Jesus quotes from Isaiah 29:13. "Corban" (Mark 7:11) is the transliteration of a Hebrew word that means "offering." The word was used to refer to that which had been dedicated to God and withdrawn from secular use. The custom was used by the Pharisees as a means of avoiding parental obligations. Legal loopholes allowed for

these funds required of children to support ageing parents to be returned for personal use. Mark 7:16 is absent in several important Greek manuscripts.

7:24-8:30 THE SYMBOL OF BREAD: THE HIDDEN SOURCE OF SALVATION
7:24-30 Bread crumbs as salvation for a Gentile. Tyre (7:24) was located in Phoenicia, about twenty-five miles north of Ptolemais (Old Testament Acco) (see introductory map). The designation "Syrian Phoenicia" (7:26) indicates that the woman was of Phoenician stock and resided in the Roman province of Syria. Matthew referred to her as Canaanite, based on the name of the people that once occupied Israel and Phoenicia. For "dogs" (7:27), see the note on Matthew 15:26. Once she understood that her relationship to Jesus could be only received by faith, Jesus granted her request.

7:31-37 Hearing and speaking restored. For why Jesus commanded the crowds to be quiet (7:36) see the discussion concerning "The Reason for Jesus' Secrecy" in the Guiding Concepts section. However, the real emphasis in 7:36-37 was not on Jesus' desire for silence, but on the crowd's overwhelming excitement over Jesus' power to heal. The pattern of an awesome miracle followed by a command for silence and a rapid spreading of the word about Jesus stands in stark contrast with the situation at the end of the book where after Jesus' greatest miracle, his resurrection, the women were so awestricken they could, for a time, say nothing. It is easy to spread the word about Jesus' great miracles. It is much more difficult for believers to take to heart who they should be in light of who Jesus is. Such a recognition of personal responsibility takes a period of silent awestricken meditation. Sidon (7:31) was located in Phoenicia, about twenty-five miles north of Tyre (see introductory map). For "Decapolis" (7:31), see the note on 5:20.

8:1-9 The source of sustenance questioned. The disciples had still not gained insight from the time Jesus fed five thousand people. Their question in 8:4 shows the same blindness toward Jesus' power as they had in 6:51-52. They still did not consistently realize who Jesus was and what he was able to do for them. Jesus was the answer to all their spiritual and physical needs, but they blindly lamented the absence of a local bakery.

8:10-21 Hard hearts hide spiritual insight. Crossing from the eastern shore of the Sea of Galilee, Jesus came to the district of "Dalmanutha," a Syriac word that literally means "of the harbor" (see introductory map). Jesus' encounter with the Pharisees (8:11-13) took place at Magadan (Matt. 15:39) in the vicinity of the harbor. The leaders sought a sign from Jesus that would prove he was the Messiah (Mark 8:11). "Yeast" (8:15; "leaven," NASB and KJV) was noted for its characteristic of permeating and influencing the dough in contact with it. The "yeast of the Pharisees and that of Herod" referred to their false understanding of who Jesus was—a false understanding that was permeating the nation and leading many astray. The "yeast of the Pharisees and Herod" brought doubt to those listening to Jesus' claims to be the Son of Man. Herod thought Jesus was John the Baptist risen from the dead (6:14-16). The religious leaders only wanted to test him and argue with him. Jesus took the time to warn against the "yeast of Herod and the Pharisees" (8:14-21). Note the significance of Jesus' statement regarding unseeing eyes and unhearing ears. The disciples were capable of being just as blind as Herod or the Pharisees.

In 8:17-21 the fuller significance of the two miraculous feedings and why the leftover baskets of bread were counted is explained. Jesus requested that the leftover baskets of bread be counted to show the disciples his more-than-adequate ability to provide for physical needs. They would later learn that spiritual things, not bread, should be their focus. But this section ends with an unanswered question (8:21). The disciples were to understand that when it came to physical things, Jesus could do whatever he wished. He could feed thousands, walk on water, and bring instant health. But the disciples continued to be stuck on the physical level. Jesus wanted them to think on a spiritual level. Their thoughts dwelt on the problem of having no bread (8:16). They should have known Jesus could make all the bread he wanted and that his real concern was with providing for their spiritual needs.

The question of 8:21 becomes a direct question to Mark's readers. Will they continue to misunderstand Jesus' absolute power to provide them with daily bread? Will they continue to worry about physical needs and be blind to the deeper life of spirit and insight into God's ways?

8:22-26 Progressive healing: sight restored. Jesus healed this man in two stages because he wanted to illustrate, through this physical healing, the progressive way in which his disciples' spiritual blindness could be healed. Spiritual insight did not come instantly, as illustrated by the disciples' problems in comprehending who Jesus was and what role he would play. For Bethsaida (8:22), see the note on 6:45. Caesarea Philippi (8:27), built by Herod Philip in honor of Caesar Augustus, was located near the foot of Mount Hermon about twenty-five miles north of the Sea of Galilee (see introductory map).

8:27-30 The first step in seeing clearly: Jesus is the Messiah. The conversation recorded in Mark 8:27-30 clearly reveals Jesus' identity as God's Messiah.

8:31–16:20 THE FOUNDATION OF SUFFERING: ITS IMPLICATION FOR THE DISCIPLES' SUBMISSION
8:31–10:52 The Way to Jerusalem: the Struggles of Self-Denial
8:31–9:13 THE PASSION AND SELF-PRESERVATION: NEGATION OF SUFFERING

8:31-38 Two rebukes. In this section, contrary to the plans and hopes of the disciples, Jesus makes it clear that he, as God's Son, will go to the cross. The conversation recorded in Mark 8:27-30 clearly revealed his identity. The events recorded in Mark 8:31-38 showed the disciples the mystery of Jesus' impending suffering and death. The disciples had expected the Messiah to come as a conquering king, not a sacrificial lamb, and as a result could not comprehend Jesus' predictions. The unveiling of the secret of Jesus' identity paved the way for the unveiling of the mystery of his destiny. The destiny of suffering that Peter rejected in his rebuke of Jesus, the church would be called upon to embrace. The church needs to comprehend and participate in the mystery of Jesus' destiny of suffering. The law of the cross prevails. The task is to realize that God's ultimate good does not necessarily guarantee comfort and easy living for all believers. Jesus' death on the cross was painful for him, but good for the world. That model of the cross bringing personal pain but corporate good is also the model of Christian experience (8:34). Peter could handle Jesus being the Messiah. But he rejected the Messiah's destiny of going to the cross. Why? Because Peter was worried that he might have to follow Jesus to the cross. That was why Jesus spoke also of the cross his disciples would have to bear (8:34). In not accepting all of Jesus' gospel, his followers were in danger of keeping him at a distance and not listening to or understanding him.

9:1-8 The transfiguration: his coming certified. The words recorded in 9:1 suggested that the transfiguration of Jesus (9:2-9) was a foretaste of the kingdom glory promised in the future. Luke 9:28 says "about eight days." Mark's "six days" (Mark 9:2) include the last part of the first day and the beginning of the eighth. According to Jewish chronological reckoning, any part of the day would be regarded as the whole. The "high mountain" was probably 9,200 foot-high Mount Hermon. Peter's "shelters" (9:5) were probably intended for celebrating the Feast of Tabernacles—the feast that would be celebrated in God's kingdom (Zech. 14:16).

9:9-13 The transfiguration's lesson: suffering must precede resurrection. Jesus wanted the vision of his glory to be kept until after his resurrection. Before then, the focus was on his suffering. For comments on the promise of Elijah's coming, see Matthew 17:10-13.

9:14-29 PRAYERLESS EXERCISE OF POWER
The disciples learn that Jesus' works were done by prayerful connection with the Father, not by some kind of magic or force of will.

9:30-50 THE PASSION AND
SELF-EXALTATION: NO EXCLUSIVISM
This was the second time that Jesus predicted his death (Mark 9:31; cf. 8:31). The "millstone" (9:42) was a large disc-shaped stone used for grinding corn. Some background on "salt" (9:49-50) is helpful in the interpretation of this trilogy. Salt was used in ancient times as a preservative for

meats and as a means of payment. The soldier who was "not worth his salt" had not earned his "salary" (a word derived from the Latin word for "salt"). Salt was sometimes diluted by the addition of white sand, which made it "unsalty." Such salt was cast on the roadbeds to inhibit the growth of weeds.

10:1-31 SUBMISSION TO THE DIVINE
POWER IN SALVATION
10:1-12 Submission to God's joining: hard hearts condemned. The phrase "across the Jordan" (10:1) referred to Perea, a territory ruled by Herod Antipas. For the first century views on divorce, see the note on Matthew 19:3. For the "command" (Mark 10:3) of Moses, see the note on Deuteronomy 24:1-4. Jesus said in this passage that divorce and remarriage constituted adultery (Mark 10:11-12). See the note on Matthew 19:10-12 for a further discussion on this topic.

10:13-16 Submission to God's requirements for the kingdom. The disciples tried to keep the young children away from Jesus, but Jesus condemned their rebuking of the children who desired to come to him. The little children formed a contrast with the religious leaders who resisted God's plan for marriage (10:1-10) and with the rich man who would not trade earthly wealth for heavenly treasure (10:17-23). The little children came to Jesus and willingly received his embrace, touch, and blessing (10:16). Receiving the kingdom like little children (10:15) involves believers allowing themselves to have this kind of intimate and warm relationship with Jesus. The willing and trusting relationships exhibited by children are key ingredients in receiving the kingdom. The children also represented humble and servant-oriented lives (9:35-37). Prior to the obedience involved in keeping God's marriage laws or giving wealth to the poor must come the initial child-like trust and relationship with Jesus.

10:17-31 The impossibility of saving one's self. In Mark 10:18 Jesus was asking, "Why do you call me 'good' when you don't recognize my deity?" For a camel to pass through the "eye of a needle" (10:25), that is, a sewing needle, is impossible, just as it is impossible for one who is unwilling to make material sacrifices to follow Jesus and enter his kingdom.

10:32-52 THE PASSION AND
SELF-EXALTATION: THE CORRECTIVE
OF SERVANTHOOD
Jerusalem was about 2,500 feet above
sea level, so the phrase "on their way up"
(10:32) was topographically correct. Jesus'
third and final death announcement was the
most precise (10:33-34). The prediction indicated that Jesus was sovereign over circumstances, not the victim of chance. The words
"in your glory" (10:37) referred to the
Messiah's future kingdom. The "cup" and
"baptism" (10:39) were figures of speech
referring to Jesus' sorrow and suffering,
which James and John would share. James
was executed by Herod Agrippa (Acts 12:2)
and John exiled on the island of Patmos
(Rev. 1:9). For the apparent discrepancy in
this account (Mark 10:46-52) with Matthew
and Luke, see the note on Matthew 20:29-34.

11:1–13:37
Victory over Anti-Christian Delusion
11:1-11 THE PUBLIC ENTRANCE
INTO JERUSALEM
"Bethphage" and "Bethany" (Mark 11:1)
were villages in the vicinity of the Mount of
Olives about a half-mile east of Jerusalem
(see introductory map). The word "Hosanna"
(11:9) is a transliteration of a Hebrew word
which means "save now."

11:12-26 THE CONSTANT OBJECT OF FAITH
The "kingdom of our father David" (11:10)
was a reference to the kingdom that God had
promised David's descendant would inherit
(2 Sam. 7:12-16; Luke 1:32-33). This "buying and selling" (Mark 11:15) was going on
in the outer court (Court of the Gentiles) of
the temple. In 11:17 Jesus quoted Isaiah
56:7 and Jeremiah 7:11. Mark 11:26 is
absent from many early manuscripts but
does appear in Matthew 6:15. Many scholars
believe it was added to Mark's Gospel at a
later time from the Matthew account.

11:27–12:44 DEBATES WITH
DISOBEDIENT LEADERS
In Mark 12:1 Jesus quoted from Isaiah 5:2.
Jesus was the "capstone" (Mark 12:10) that
the "builders," the leaders of the nation,
rejected (Ps. 118:22-23). For the Pharisees
(Mark 12:13), see the note on Matthew 3:7.
For the Herodians, see the comments on
Matthew 22:16. The two sects were at
opposite ends of the theological spectrum but

had teamed up to trap Jesus with a political
question. Everyone acknowledged that a legitimate government had the right to tax its subjects (Mark 12:14). The ultimate question
was, "Is the Roman government legitimate?"
For "denarius" (12:15), see the note on 6:37.
For more on the Sadducees (12:18), see the
notes on Matthew 3:7. The question of Mark
12:23 was based on the law of levirate marriage (cf. Deut. 25:5-10). The Sadducees
referred to this provision to demonstrate the
absurdity of belief in the resurrection. In
Mark 12:26 Jesus produced evidence for the
resurrection from the Pentateuch (Exod. 3:6),
which the Sadducees recognized as their sole
source for authoritative teaching. In Mark
12:36 Jesus quoted from David's Psalm
110:1.
   The only possible answer to Jesus'
question in Mark 12:37 was that David's
descendant ("son") was a divine ("Lord")
Messiah. The "treasury" (12:41) was in the
temple in the Court of the Women. Located
there were thirteen large brass receptacles
with trumpet shaped mouths. Nine were for
sacrifice-tribute money, and four were for
free-will offerings. The "copper coins"
(12:42) were worth very little but represented all the woman owned.

13:1-37 VICTORY IN JESUS' ABSENCE:
PERSEVERANCE
The purpose of this sermon was to encourage and protect the disciples during Jesus'
absence. It was a sermon designed to
promote faith and obedience during a
time of distress. It was the longest
discourse in Mark, and it was the only
extended speech of Jesus or anyone else
recorded in Mark's Gospel. It functioned as
a bridge between the public ministry of
Jesus and the events of his passion. It was
also a farewell discourse following the
biblical pattern (cf. Gen. 49; Deut. 33;
Josh. 23; and Acts 20:17-35).
   The "Mount of Olives" (Mark 13:3) is
a long north-south ridge that lies just east
of Jerusalem. The two basic questions in
13:4 were: (1) "When will the temple be
destroyed?" and (2) "When will these 'end
of the age' events be fulfilled?" The discourse focused on answering the second
question. The message covered the events
leading up to the time of the end (13:5-13),

the preservation of the faithful through the time of the judgments (13:14-27), and the concluding encouragements to perseverance (13:28-37).

There were nineteen commands given in 13:5-37. Note phrases like "watch out" and "be on your guard" (13:5, 9, 23, 33). Note that the things Jesus described always related back to 13:4 (13:5-8, 9-12, 14, 23, 24-27). The purpose was to show that believers were not to be disturbed by preliminary signs or to confuse them with the end of the age. Jesus' comments in Mark 13:32-37 were the real answer to the disciples' questions, not a mere afterthought. Jesus makes it clear that no one knows the time of his return and calls all his followers to stay faithful while awaiting this glorious event.

The time references used by Jesus speak of those who will be alive whenever the predicted events should happen (see the idea of "when" or "whenever" in 13:7, 11, 14, 29). These were words of concern, love, and compassion that had been sparked by the disciples' desire for a sign. Jesus first gave an exhortation and then followed it with the reasons for the warning (see "because," "for," and "therefore" in 13:19, 22, 35).

The reference to the "synagogues" (13:9), Jewish meeting places for prayer and Scripture reading, reflected the Jewish setting of this discourse. The "abomination that causes desolation" (13:14) was a reference to the antichrist (Dan. 9:27; 2 Thess. 2:4).

14:1-52 Betrayal and Arrest: the Disciples' Defeat by Flesh Unprepared by Prayer

14:1-11 MURDER PLOTS

The "Passover" (Mark 14:1) was one of the three annual festivals that the Jews attended in Jerusalem (Deut. 16:16). It commemorated the deliverance of Israel from Egypt (Exod. 12) and how God "passed over" the Israelite houses where the blood of the lamb had been applied. This feast on the fourteenth day of Nisan was followed by the Feast of Unleavened Bread (Nisan, days fifteen through twenty-one). The woman (Mark 14:3) was Mary of Bethany (cf. John 12:3). The costly ointment (Mark 14:5) was worth the equivalent of three hundred days' wages.

14:12-25 THE PASSOVER

This "upper room" (14:15) was apparently in the home of Mary, the mother of John Mark (cf. Luke 22:12; Acts 1:13-15; 12:12). The "covenant" (Mark 14:24) was a reference to the new covenant mentioned in Jeremiah 31:31-34, which Jesus brought into fruition by shedding his blood on the cross (Heb. 8:6-13).

14:26-52 THE ARREST

The name "Gethsemane" (Mark 14:32) means "oil press." This olive grove was traditionally thought to be located across the Kidron from the Eastern Gate of Jerusalem at the foot of the Mount of Olives. The "betrayer" (14:42) was a reference to Judas (14:43). All had promised loyalty, but all left him and fled (14:50). One wonders why such an insignificant incident would be included in the Gospel unless the young man was Mark, the writer (14:51-52). The incident may have been included to authenticate him as an eyewitness. The word "naked" (14:51) may simply mean "without an outer garment."

14:53-15:15 The Trial

14:53-65 CONDEMNED BY THE JEWS AS THE MESSIAH

The accusation made against Jesus in Mark 14:58 used a perversion of Jesus' teaching concerning his bodily resurrection as evidence against him (cf. John 2:19-21).

14:66-72 DENIED BY PETER

The Galileans spoke Aramaic with a noticable accent which is how Peter's association with Jesus and his disciples was revealed (14:70). Jesus had predicted Peter's denial in 14:27-31. He had also spoken of his ongoing relationship with the disciples afterward in Galilee (14:28). Peter's denial was tragic, but not fatal to his relationship with Christ. Throughout their time with Jesus, the disciples misunderstood the nature of his mission. They struggled most with Jesus' humility and suffering and with his demand that they follow him down the path toward a cross. Peter had earlier denied the place of the cross in Jesus' life (8:31-38), and at this point he denied his own part in taking on the sufferings of Jesus. The striving of the disciples for greatness (9:33-37) resulted in their rejection of the lowliness associated with Jesus as he turned his way toward the cross.

15:1-15 CONDEMNED BY PILATE AS KING
In the early morning hours (possibly April 3,
A.D. 33), the Sanhedrin ("Council") met
again to give their night verdict some
semblance of officiality (15:1). Jesus was
then delivered up to the Roman authorities
because the Jews had no authority to execute
capital punishment. Pilate was the Roman
prefect, or governor, of Judea who ruled
from A.D. 26 to 36. He normally resided in
Caesarea but was in Jerusalem to maintain
control over the Jewish crowds at Passover.

Jesus admitted his claim to kingship, but
he clarified what kind of king he claimed to
be (15:2; cf. John 18:36-37). Jesus was silent
before his accusers in fulfillment of prophecy (Mark 15:5; Isa. 53:7).

Pilate's response to the Jews (Mark 15:15)
in contrast to his previous hostile dealings
(cf. Luke 13:1) can be better understood in
light of the A.D. 32 execution of Sejanus,
Pilate's protector and supporter in Rome.
Pilate's position as prefect was now insecure,
and he did not want the Jews to raise trouble
for him that might reach the ears of the
emperor, Tiberias. For this reason, he reluctantly submitted to the demand of the Jews
that Jesus be crucified.

15:16-47 The Crucifixion and Burial

15:16-21 LED TO THE CROSS
The term "Praetorium" (15:16) was derived
from praetor, originally the name for Rome's
highest magistrate, later called "consul." The
Praetorium was the praetor's tent or military
headquarters. The term was used here to
refer either to Herod's palace or, more likely,
to the Antonia fortress, located just north of
the temple area. This fortress quartered the
Roman "cohort," a battalion of six hundred
soldiers. Simon was from Cyrene, the chief
city of Cyrenaica in North Africa (15:21).

15:22-32 INSULTS AT THE CROSS
The "wine mixed with myrrh" (15:23) was
intended as a sedative to ease the pain of
crucifixion. The "third hour" (15:25) was
9:00 A.M. All the details of the suffering
borne by Jesus on the cross were recounted.
Jesus was crucified with robbers; he bore
insults regarding the temple; he chose not to

vindicate himself by saving himself; and he
did not show a miraculous sign to the sneering crowd.

15:33-41 RESPONSES TO JESUS' DEATH
The "ninth hour" (15:33) corresponds with
3:00 P.M. Jesus quoted Psalm 22:1 in the
Aramaic language (Mark 15:34). Apparently
"Eloi" was misunderstood to be a reference
to "Elijah," whose return the Jews expected
(Mal. 3:1; 4:5). Josephus reported that the
temple "veil" was thirty feet wide and ninety
feet high (*Jewish War,* 5.5.5). The "curtain"
(Mark 15:38) is typical of the body of Christ
(Heb. 10:19-20). "Salome" (Mark 15:40)
was the wife of Zebedee and mother of
James and John (Matt. 27:56).

15:42-47 BURIAL
Joseph was from "Arimathea" (Mark 15:43),
a town of uncertain location. He was a
member of the Sanhedrin ("Council") which
had condemned Jesus. Victims of crucifixion
sometimes hung on their crosses a day or
more (15:44). Jesus' death came after six
hours. The burial of Jesus in the tomb of
Joseph (15:46-47) was done in fulfillment
of Isaiah 53:9.

16:1-20 Resurrection Events
Some Greek manuscripts of Mark end with
16:8. Others add two or as many as twelve
verses to the text. The vast majority of Greek
scholars today would say that the last twelve
verses are not authentic since they are not
supported by the two oldest and complete
manuscripts of the New Testament. Not
everyone agrees, however. In fact the vast
majority of the surviving Greek manuscripts
have the traditional ending, and the evidence
supporting the inclusion of the traditional
ending is older than the manuscripts that
omit it. Until scholars settle this debated
issue, it would be wise to retain the text but
not develop any peculiar doctrines from it.

Mark 16:16 has been used by some to
prove that baptism is necessary for salvation.
But more careful observation reveals that the
only basis for condemnation is a refusal to
believe. Therefore, the only basis for salvation is faith (cf. Eph. 2:8-9).

Luke

BASIC FACTS

HISTORICAL SETTING

Luke was written for a certain prominent individual named Theophilus (Luke 1:3). The Greek meaning of the name "Theophilus" is "lover of God." Some interpreters theorize that the name may be symbolic for all Christians rather than referring to an actual person. But without clear proof for symbolism, "Theophilus" should probably be understood to be a real person to whom Luke addressed his two-volume work of the Gospel and Acts. The reference to this individual, however, was really a dedication characteristic of Greek and Roman literature. The work was clearly written for the benefit of Gentiles in general and Greeks in particular. As a result of Paul's missionary journeys the gospel spread through the Greek world, and there developed a need for a gospel record that would speak to the Greek mind.

The Greek nature of the book can be seen in the fact that the genealogy was traced to Adam, the father of the human race, rather than Abraham, the father of the Hebrew nation. Luke avoided the use of Jewish terminology like "rabbi" and instead used "master" or "teacher." Luke placed less emphasis on the fulfillment of prophecy, and he substituted Greek names for Hebrew names (cf. Luke 6:16; 23:33 with Mark 3:18). Abundant evidence indicates that Luke addressed his Gospel to Greek Gentiles.

AUTHOR

Although the Gospel of Luke is anonymous, both internal and external evidence point to Luke, the Gentile physician and companion of Paul, as the author. Internal confirmation of Luke's authorship is assumed by the close relationship between Luke and Acts. Acts was clearly authored by Luke, for only he could have written the "we" section of Acts, having joined Paul at Troas (Acts 16:10-17; 20:5–21:18; 27:1–28:16). Both Luke and Acts were addressed to the same man, Theophilus (Luke 1:3; Acts 1:1), and both use medical terminology. That strongly suggests that Luke, the author of Acts, also authored the Gospel of Luke. The writings of the early church fathers also attest to Luke's authorship.

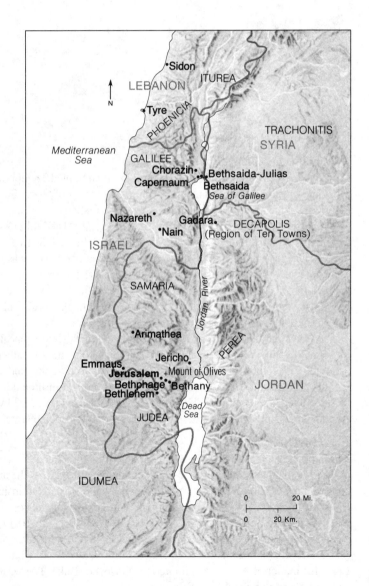

Luke was a Gentile convert (Col. 4:10-14), possibly of the church at Antioch, as stated by Jerome and Eusebius. Luke joined Paul at Troas (Acts 16:10) during his second missionary journey and accompanied him to Philippi. Luke later accompanied Paul to Jerusalem (Acts 20:5–21:15) and finally to Rome (Acts 27:1–28:15). He was referred to by Paul as "our dear friend Luke, the doctor" (Col. 4:14; Philem. 24), and was his last friend to remain with him during Paul's second imprisonment (2 Tim. 4:11). Luke was an able historian, physician, missionary, and author.

DATE
The Gospel of Luke was written before Acts (Acts 1:1) and after the development of Christianity to the point where it would attract the attention of a Gentile inquirer like Theophilus. The abrupt ending of Acts indicates that Luke concluded his writing at the end of Paul's imprisonment in Rome in A.D. 62. The Gospel was composed prior to that, probably about A.D. 60. Paul's two year imprisonment at Caesarea would have afforded Luke an opportunity to research and write the Gospel.

PURPOSE
The book of Luke was designed to promote certainty concerning the historical events and facts that form a foundation for the Christian faith (Luke 1:1-4). It did that by presenting Jesus' life in its historical context and by the great amount of detail gained by Luke's research. The heart of the book's teaching can be seen in how Jesus' life prepared believers for the power of the Spirit, who came at Pentecost after Jesus had been exalted to God's right hand.

GEOGRAPHY AND ITS IMPORTANCE

The book of Luke begins and ends in the Jerusalem temple. In between, Luke emphasized a long journey section that moves from Galilee down to Jerusalem—a journey that focuses on Jesus' victorious ascension from Jerusalem up to his Father's right hand. The progression from the spiritual state of God's people in the temple at the beginning of the book to the happy disciples praising God in the temple at the end of the book involves a journey that reveals the greatness of Jesus, outlines the costs of following him, and teaches the central place of the Holy Spirit in the lives of Jesus and the believers.

GUIDING CONCEPTS

THE UNITY OF LUKE WITH ACTS
Luke and Acts are parts of a two-volume set. Therefore, they need to be interpreted recognizing the connections between the two. The first volume, the Gospel of Luke, was a record of all that Jesus had done during his life—from his birth to his ascension (Luke 1:1-4). The second volume, the book of Acts, continued the record of the acts of the risen Lord through the work of his apostles (Acts 1:1-2). The Gospel of Luke began with the announcement in the temple of the coming of the Lord and his forerunner (Luke 1:13-17). The book of Acts ended with Paul in Rome preaching the gospel unhindered (Acts 28:30-31). Throughout the two

books, whether Luke or Acts, the author presented one undivided message about the person and work of Jesus. Therefore, this study on Luke's Gospel will often recognize the connection between Luke and Acts.

THE FOCUS ON THE ASCENSION OF JESUS

Luke made the ascension of Jesus into heaven the central focus in both Luke and Acts. Luke made special reference to Jesus' ascension at his transfiguration (Luke 9:31) and put the major part of his account of Jesus' ministry (9:51–19:28) into a journey to Jerusalem, a journey that would find its completion in the ascension (9:51). So important was the ascension that Luke described it twice, once at the end of Luke and again at the begining of Acts.

Only in Acts 2 did Luke clarify why he found the ascension so important (Luke 2:34-36). At that event, God the Father exalted Jesus to his right hand in heaven. But more important, the ascension was where Jesus promised the community of believers that the Spirit would soon be poured out upon them (Acts 2:33). Peter quoted Psalm 110:1 (Acts 2:34-35; quoted first by Jesus in Luke 20:41-44). From the beginning of his Gospel, Luke built toward the event of Jesus' enthronement and the subsequent "pouring out" of the Spirit upon God's people. The goal of Jesus in Luke was not simply to die on the cross but also to be exalted to the right hand of God, to send his Spirit, and to powerfully enable his people to continue proclaiming the gospel. The Gospel of Luke builds toward the event of the ascension and the gift of the Spirit. The book of Acts illustrates the unhindered witness to Jesus Christ through the power of the Spirit. The Gospel looks ahead to the ascension; the book of Acts looks back to it. The ascension and its resultant power for witness is at the very heart of the Luke-Acts account.

BRINGING GOOD NEWS

Luke used the concept of bringing good news or proclaiming the gospel twenty-five times in the Luke-Acts account. Mark and John did not use it at all, and Matthew used it only once. Old Testament background for that phrase can be found in 1 Kings 1:42; Isaiah 52:7; Jeremiah 20:15. The phrase is used in contexts of joy, the expectation of the end times, and the inclusion of Gentiles in salvation. The book of Luke gives a special focus on how the Good News came to the world in the person of Jesus. Acts shows how the Good News spread through the power of the Holy Spirit. In Luke the gospel was proclaimed by the perfect Man of the Spirit, Jesus. In Acts it was proclaimed by believers empowered by the Spirit.

POWER AND SPIRIT

Power and Spirit are nearly synonymous in Luke-Acts (see especially Luke 1:35 and 24:49). Both found their source in God the Father and were given to Jesus or to his followers through the Spirit. Luke used the word for Spirit 109 times in Luke-Acts (Matt., 19 times; Mark, 22 times; John, 22 times). Luke introduced Jesus as a person conceived by the Spirit (Luke 1:35), as the Man of the Spirit (3:22; 4:18; Acts 10:38), and after his resurrection, as the Lord of the Spirit (Luke 24:49; Acts 2:33). Therefore, on earth the Spirit was not the instrument of Jesus' power. Jesus was the instrument of the Spirit's power. And from that model believers can discover the nature of true discipleship. True disciples do not use the Spirit; the Spirit uses them.

PRAYER

Luke used the words for prayer thirty-four times in Luke-Acts (Matt., 15 times; Mark, 4 times; John, zero times). Luke recounted a number of special contexts for Jesus' prayers (Luke 3:21; 6:12; 9:18, 28; 11:1). Luke alone told his readers that at Jesus' baptism Jesus was praying when the Spirit descended upon him (3:21), that Jesus spent the night in prayer before he chose his disciples (6:12-13), that Jesus was praying before he told his disciples of his impending death (9:18), and that Jesus was praying as he became transfigured (9:28-29). Luke wanted his readers to know that at the critical new movements of Jesus' ministry he was in prayer and God answered. The same pattern would become evident for the disciples in the book of Acts. When they prayed, God's Spirit moved in powerful ways.

BIBLE-WIDE CONCEPTS

JESUS' USE OF THE OLD TESTAMENT

Jesus' own method of interpreting the Old Testament was taken up by Luke and the rest of the New Testament writers. Luke 24:27, 45 and Acts 1:3 show how Jesus' interpretations were impressed upon the minds of his followers and provided a foundation for their approach to the message of Old Testament Scripture. Through-out the New Testament, the Holy Spirit continued to guide the writers to show how Jesus the Messiah fulfilled the prophecies of Old Testament Scripture. Such fulfill-ment ratified the claims of Jesus and his followers and became the heart of the gospel proclamation.

THE LINKS WITH ADAM

Luke's genealogy tied Jesus all the way back to Adam's sonship from God (Luke 3:38). As such, it set up two poles upon which the human race was strung: Adam and Jesus. From Luke's perspective, only those two men were critical to the history of the world. Paul also saw a similar relationship between Adam and Jesus (cf. Rom. 5:17; 1 Cor. 15:45). For Luke, Jesus was the Man who could stretch across the uncounted centuries of human sin and restore humanity's sonship with God.

THE KINGDOM OF GOD

In Luke-Acts, Luke laid the foundation for answering how Jesus could come and go and the kingdom of God still not be fully established on earth. The disci-ples had expected the Messiah to come and establish the visible kingdom of God. Luke explained that the Messiah came first to redeem humanity by his death on the cross. Later he would return in power and glory to reign forever (2:35; 5:35; 9:22; 9:31; 9:44, 51; 17:25; 20:17; 22:19-20; 24:25-26, 46; Acts 5:31; 10:38-43). The surprise was that in between his first and second comings would come the age of the Spirit—an age marked by a fellowship of humble suffering and spiritual power modeled after Jesus' life on earth. Jesus reigned at the right hand of God and ministered his rule through the outpoured Spirit on earth. Such was the present form of the kingdom that Luke sought to explain.

NEEDS MET BY LUKE

Luke's audience needed truth that would make their commitment to Christ more solid and complete. They needed a stronger faith because believing in Jesus during Luke's day often brought persecution. Luke began his task by answering questions his readers had about Jesus' life on earth, knowing that by doing this he would strengthen their faith in Jesus. Next, Luke helped to deepen his readers' confidence in Jesus by showing how Jesus fulfilled Old Testament truths and prophecies. Finally, Luke built all of his two-volume work around the great day of Pentecost when Jesus sent the Holy Spirit to earth. Luke knew that faith and confidence in Jesus was dependent on the indwelling power of the Spirit among his readers. Jesus had come and gone. How could people maintain a solid commitment to an invisible Savior, especially during times of persecution and hardship? Only through the fact of the fulfilled Old Testament, the experience of the invisible but potent Holy Spirit, and the reminder and instruction brought by a book like Luke. Luke let his readers know what needs he wanted to meet (1:4). He wanted to give the reader the exact truth—that which was needed for assurance. Luke laid down the foundation for certainty (1:4) and provided facts that would inspire his readers to confidence and faith in Jesus the Messiah. The following questions reflect some of the thoughts of those who sought certainty in their relationship with Jesus.

- How did John the Baptist's parents respond to John's birth?
- How did God confirm that he was behind John's birth?
- How did John the Baptist and Jesus fit in with Old Testament prophecy?
- What were some of the events surrounding the birth and early life of Jesus?
- How do the events of Jesus' birth and life relate to Old Testament prophetic hope?
- How did Jesus relate to the Holy Spirit?
- What was Jesus' prayer life like?
- What did Jesus teach regarding discipleship?
- What happened to the kingdom Jesus proclaimed?
- How could Jesus come and go and the kingdom still not be fully established?

Luke's goal that his readers might know the certainty of the things they had been taught (1:4) meets more than a need to know simple facts. Certainty is a condition of the heart as well as of the mind. It is an inner confidence that grows out of the facts of Jesus' life and becomes a foundation for a believer's consistent Christian living and witness. Without confidence, Christian obedience will not survive the pressures of daily life and the potential problems Jesus' absence creates. Luke helps believers cope with a redemption gained but a kingdom still awaiting its perfection. He shows that Jesus' life was a journey through real time and history and that he made that journey successfully only by complete dependence on the Holy Spirit. The Holy Spirit is the key to having the needs of believers met as well. It is only through the Spirit's power that believers can realize the full potential in their own lives.

OUTLINE OF LUKE

A. PROLOGUE: PRAYER AND ANNOINTING (1:1–3:38)
 1. The Purpose of the Book (1:1-4)
 2. Two Pregnancies Predicted (1:5-56)
 3. Two Sons Are Born (1:57–2:52)
 4. John's Ministry of Preparation (3:1-20)
 5. Jesus' Ministry: The Anointed One (3:21-38)
B. SPIRIT AND POWER IN GALILEE (4:1–9:50)
 1. The Testing of Jesus (4:1-13)
 2. Proclamation and Power (4:14-44)
 3. Power Interpreted and Focused (5:1–6:11)
 4. Power and God's Purposes: Rejection and Acceptance (6:12–7:50)
 5. Power and the Soils (8:1-56)
 6. Ministry in a Hostile World (9:1-9)
 7. The Crucial Interpretation of Jesus' Ministry: Passion (9:10-50)
C. TOWARD THE GOAL: DEBATES AND INSTRUCTION (9:51–19:27)
 1. Preparation for Departure (9:51–13:21)
 2. On the Journey: Faith during Conflict (13:22–17:10)
 3. On the Journey: Perseverance (17:11–19:27)
D. THE GOAL ATTAINED: JERUSALEM (19:28–24:53)
 1. The Entrance into Jerusalem (19:28-48)
 2. The Religious Opposition to Jesus (20:1–21:38)
 3. The Passover (22:1-38)
 4. Arrest and Trial (22:39–23:25)
 5. Crucifixion and Burial (23:26-56)
 6. The Resurrection (24:1-53)

LUKE NOTES

1:1–3:38 PROLOGUE: PRAYER AND ANOINTING
Overview: In Luke 1–3, the author shifted between the stories of John the Baptist and Jesus. Two pregnancies were announced: John the Baptist (1:5-25); Jesus (1:26-38). Two births were recounted: John the Baptist (1:57-80); Jesus (2:1-52). Two ministries were followed: John the Baptist's ministry of preparation (3:1-20); Jesus' ministry as the Anointed One (3:21-38). Throughout, the Spirit was behind the acts and speeches of those involved: pregnancy of Elizabeth (1:15, 41-42); pregnancy of Mary (1:35); Zechariah at the birth of John (1:67); Simeon at his recognition of Jesus (2:25). Luke gave

insight to his readers concerning the people who awaited the Messiah and the Spirit's work that was accomplished through them.

1:1-4 The Purpose of the Book
The prologue of Luke is similar to the prefaces used by such classical historians as Herodotus and medical writers like Hippocrates. This reveals something of the method Luke used in composing his Gospel and what he intended to accomplish with it. The purpose of his Gospel was assurance (1:4, "certainty"). Reading this Gospel should bring assurance of the truth of Jesus the Messiah's life, death, and resurrection. And that assurance is only strengthened by the

meticulous process of writing and research that Luke described. Assurance is built upon the events seen by eyewitnesses, handed down to Luke and others, and finally carefully researched and written by Luke. Luke wrote for the confirmation of the faith. He wrote to correct problem areas with regards to the facts and implications of Christianity.

The words "from the first" (1:2) referred to the beginning of Jesus' ministry at his baptism by John (Acts 1:22). Luke was not an eyewitness but a historian who researched the facts carefully and composed a point by point ("orderly," Luke 1:3) account of the information. The book was dedicated to "Theophilus," apparently a person of rank or nobility. Theophilus may have assisted in financing Luke's research and writing.

1:5-56 Two Pregnancies Predicted

1:5-25 THE CONCEPTION OF
JOHN THE BAPTIST
"Herod" (1:5) was a king of Idumean descent who ruled Palestine from 37 to 4 B.C. under Roman auspices (see note on Matt. 2:1). The "division of Abijah" (1:5) was one of the twenty-four orders into which David divided the Levites (cf. 1 Chron. 24:10). Both Zechariah and Elizabeth were of priestly descent. Their characters (Luke 1:6) were noted to show that they were part of the righteous remnant awaiting the coming of the Messiah.

An angel appeared to Zechariah (1:8-23). The temple location is significant. This was a once-in-a-lifetime opportunity for Zechariah to be in the temple. Lots (1:9) were cast (cf. Prov. 16:33) to determine which priest would have the privilege of burning incense in the Holy Place during the hour of prayer (Exod. 30:7-8). According to the Jewish Mishnah, this was a once-in-a-lifetime privilege. The angel referred to Zechariah's petition (Luke 1:13), probably for a child. Zechariah's response was the same as Abraham's (1:18; cf. Gen. 15:8). The angel was Gabriel (1:11; cf. 1:19). Gabriel had made earlier appearances in Daniel 8:16 and 9:21. He is the angel of mercy. John the Baptist would function as the Messiah's forerunner (Luke 1:17). Ministering in the "spirit and power" of Elijah (1:17), he fulfilled the prophecies of Malachi 3:1 and 4:5. The name "Gabriel" (Luke 1:19) means "man of God." He is

one of two angels mentioned by name in Scripture. The other is Michael, the archangel. Gabriel is associated with the bearing of messages (1:26; cf. Dan. 8:16; 9:21). According to custom, the priest who had offered the incense was to pronounce a concluding benediction (Luke 1:22). But Zechariah was mute. As the angel promised, Elizabeth became pregnant (1:24-25).

1:26-38 GABRIEL ANNOUNCES
MARY'S PREGNANCY
Mary was troubled at Gabriel's greeting (1:26-29). The announcement to Mary was made in the insignificant little village of Nazareth six months after John the Baptist's conception (1:36). Mary was engaged, or betrothed, to Joseph (1:27). Betrothal was a formal relationship that existed for six months to a year before the marriage was consummated. There was no sexual union during that period (cf. Matt. 1:18). In Luke 1:27, 32-33 the author emphasized that the child was a descendant of David and thus the heir through whom the Davidic covenant would be fulfilled (2 Sam. 7:12-16). Mary submitted herself as God's servant, completely obedient to the will of her Master (Luke 1:38). The angel's message was full of Messianic promises and predictions (1:30-33). The name "Jesus" is a Greek translation of Joshua, the one who led Israel across the Jordan into great military victories during the initial conquest of Israel. The references to sonship, throne, and David (1:32) and to reign and kingdom (1:33) all refer to the fulfillment of the Davidic covenant for a perfect king to rule over Israel in an eternal kingdom (2 Sam. 7:12-16). Note the coupling of "Holy Spirit" and "power" (1:35) and compare this with Acts 1:8 where the same coupling was made. Unlike that of Zechariah, Mary's response (1:34-38) carried no request for a sign.

1:39-56 MARY'S VISIT TO ELIZABETH
The city in Judah (1:39) was not specifically identified, although tradition associates this event with En Karem, a town located several miles west of Jerusalem. Various Christian denominations have built churches and monasteries there to commemorate the birth of John the Baptist. Mary's "Magnificat" (1:46-56) drew upon a series of Old Testament quotations to magnify the Lord. It

resembles Hannah's prayer in 1 Samuel 2:1-10. This section brought both confirmation and exultation to the promise of Jesus. It was a prophetic confirmation of the events that had been given in Old Testament covenantal contexts. Elizabeth's song (Luke 1:41-45) spoke of being "filled with the Holy Spirit." That concept occurred in the Old Testament (cf. Num. 11:24-30; Deut. 34:9; Mic. 3:8) as well as in Luke's writings in the New Testament (Luke 1:15, 41; Acts 2:4; 4:8, 31; 9:17; 13:9). The filling with the Spirit was closely associated with the act of speaking. It took the sense of prophetic utterance involving the sovereign work of the Spirit of God. For Elizabeth, this filling was for a particular task, to praise the work of God in Jesus the Messiah.

The words of Mary's song (Luke 1:46-55) recognized that God's work through Jesus fulfilled the promise God made to Abraham (1:55). Mary praised God's acts of exalting the humble and bringing humiliation upon the proud and rich. In Jesus, God had reversed the means of attaining greatness in the world.

1:57–2:52 Two Sons Are Born

1:57-80 THE COMING OF JOHN THE BAPTIST

1:57-66 Controversy over the name of the son. It was common to call a son by his father's name. But Zechariah's willingness to name the baby John confirmed the work of God in his birth. According to the law, a male child was to be circumcised on the eighth day after his birth (1:59). It was a common Jewish custom to name the firstborn son after his father, but Elizabeth emphatically rejected that idea and followed Gabriel's instructions (1:60; cf. 1:13). The name "John" means "God is gracious."

1:67-80 The Song of Zechariah. Note the background of Malachi 4:1-6 (Luke 1:76) and Isaiah 9:1-2 (Luke 1:79). Mercy, remembrance, and oath are key Old Testament concepts. This prophetic hymn of Zechariah is known as the "Benedictus" from its opening word in the Latin translation. Zechariah's use of Isaiah 9:1-2 (Luke 1:79) was used by Matthew to introduce the impact that Jesus would have upon the Gentiles (Matt. 4:16). John grew up in the desert, outside of the Levitical system and established Judaism

(Luke 1:80). He would be calling a people out of that system to come to the Messiah and the promised kingdom.

2:1-52 THE COMING OF JESUS

2:1-7 The time and place. Caesar Augustus (27 B.C.–A.D. 14), who brought great reform to the Roman Empire, commanded the registration of his subject population for the purpose of assessing the value of property and levying taxes. Quirinius (2:2) was governor of Syria twice (3–2 B.C. and A.D. 6–7), but neither of his governorships fit with what is known to have been the date of Jesus' birth (around 5/4 B.C.). Many solutions have been offered for this problem. It is possible to translate 2:2, "This census took place before Quirinius was governor of Syria." This would place the census around 6/5 B.C., a year or two before Herod's death. It is likely that Augustus would have wanted to have an estimate of the condition of the state before Herod's death.

The journey to Bethlehem was necessary to fulfill Messianic prophecy (2:4; Micah 5:2). Jesus was born in either an enclosed courtyard or as tradition says, a cave, because there was no room in the inn (Luke 2:7). The point is that he was born in obscurity and poverty as a son of David.

2:8-20 The worship of the shepherds. The Mishnah indicates that some flocks around Bethlehem were out all year, and those to be used at Passover were in the fields thirty days before the feast, as early as February (2:8). Shepherds were of low social status and were a people shunned by the rich and famous. The Lord was announced to the shepherds ("to you," 2:11), illustrating his importance for "all" (2:10) the people. What makes one exalted in God's sight is faith and obedience, not worldly might. See, for example, Mary's song (1:52-53). Notice the importance of divine signs in Luke's Gospel so far. Signs have been given to Zechariah (1:18-20), Mary (1:34-35), and to the shepherds (2:12). Those signs further Luke's purpose to establish certainty and assurance concerning the coming of Jesus the Messiah. God's message of peace was directed to people "on whom God's favor rests" (2:14).

2:21-40 Purification and presentation. See Numbers 18:15-16 and Leviticus 12:8 for the Old Testament background to purification.

For "circumcision" (Luke 2:21), see 1:59. The "time of their purification" (2:22) was a reference to the uncleanness of childbirth (cf. Lev. 12:1-8), which required that a sacrifice be offered for cleansing forty days after the birth of a male child. The offering of birds reflects the poverty of Joseph and Mary (Luke 2:24). They could not afford a sacrificial lamb.

Simeon's recognition and adoration of Jesus (2:25-35) further confirmed to Luke's readers that Jesus was the promised Messiah. Simeon had been looking for the coming of Messiah, "the consolation of Israel" (2:25). He invoked a blessing on the holy family and predicted the world's response to God's provision of salvation (2:35). His message confirmed Jesus' identity as God's Messiah. It showed that he would be salvation, light to the Gentiles, and that he was appointed to fulfill the promises of Isaiah 8:14 and 42:6. Simeon was another block in Luke's presentation of assurance and certainty.

Luke continued his presentation with the adoration of Anna (Luke 2:36-38). Simeon and Anna illustrate the godly character of the righteous remnant. They were faithful to God's promises and were looking for God's redemption. Anna was a descendant of one of the northern tribes, Asher, which had gone into captivity in 722 B.C.

2:41-52 Jesus' youth. It was at the age of thirteen that Jewish boys became "sons of the law" and assumed adult responsibilities. Jesus became a son of the law and was eligible to keep feasts, fasts, and so forth. These first recorded words of the Messiah (2:49) served as the capstone to the infancy narratives. They set the tone for his coming ministry and for the believers' responsibilities as his disciples. He asserted the authority of his divine sonship.

Mary asked why Jesus had treated them that way, saying that they both had been anxious (2:48). She expressed all the normal emotions of parents who have lost their children. This is the interpretive key to this section. Mary and Joseph were acting like they had a normal parent-child relationship with Jesus. They were not living in the light of the great miracles and prophecies they had experienced concerning their son. He was the Son of God, not just an average teenager. In 1:49 Jesus

answered Mary's why with another why question. Jesus' response implies that they should not have been looking all over Jerusalem for Jesus but should have known where he would be because of who he was. The Son would be found in the Father's house. Mary and Joseph had to learn to think of Jesus as the Son of God who had come to do his Father's redemptive will, not as an average person.

Although his parents misunderstood his mission, Jesus clarified the relationship between himself and his parents. All his concerns were Father-centered. Such a misunderstanding of his person and mission is possible for all believers. Joseph and Mary returned to Nazareth, in Lower Galilee, where Jesus grew to adulthood (2:51). Nothing more was recorded about Jesus' youth. The record of Jesus' life was not resumed until he was baptized by John.

3:1-20 John's Ministry of Preparation

3:1-18 JOHN'S MESSAGE

Luke the historian places the beginning of John the Baptist's ministry in the context of the political and religious leadership of the day (3:1-2). The fifteenth year of Tiberius Caesar (A.D. 14–37) would be between August 19, A.D. 28, and December 31, A.D. 29 (reckoned from the Julian calendar or Tiberius' regnal year). Assuming Jesus had a three-year ministry and an A.D. 33 crucifixion, John's ministry would have begun in A.D. 29, and Jesus' ministry shortly thereafter. Pontius Pilate served as governor of Judea (A.D. 26 to 36). Herod Antipas (a son of Herod the Great) ruled Galilee and Perea (4 B.C.–A.D. 39). Philip, another son of Herod, ruled territories northeast of Galilee (4 B.C.–A.D. 34). Annas was high priest (A.D. 6–15) before being deposed by the Romans. His son-in-law, Caiaphas, was later appointed to the position (A.D. 18–36). John warned the Jews against trusting merely in their religious ancestry to secure a good relationship with God (3:8). John called the people to repentance. Repentance reveals itself by producing fruit—deeds for God. Note the thrice-repeated question asked by the hearers of John the Baptist's message concerning what they should do to show repentance (3:10-14; cf. Acts 2:37).

John the Baptist used the imagery of harvest to describe events of the second coming—deliverance of the righteous into God's kingdom and punishment of the wicked in the fires of hell (Luke 3:17; cf. Matt. 25:46; Isa. 30:24). John had been preaching the gospel of the coming kingdom (3:18) and called the people to repent of all sin.

3:19-20 JOHN'S REMOVAL
Because of his criticism of Herod Antipas's marriage to Herodias, John the Baptist was put in prison (Luke 3:18-20). Herodias had been the wife (and niece) of Herod's brother Philip (3:19). Herod Antipas divorced his wife and married Herodias in violation of the Mosaic laws against incestuous marriage (Lev. 18:6-18).

3:21-38 Jesus' Ministry: The Anointed One

3:21-22 JESUS' BAPTISM
John's role was played down in order to focus on Jesus. This was the only Gospel account to mention the heavens being opened and that Jesus was praying when the Spirit descended upon him.

3:23-38 JESUS' GENEALOGY
The genealogy that Luke chose to include in his account must have had a special purpose because every human being can be traced back to Adam. But perhaps that was just the point. The genealogy allowed Jesus to take his place in and identify with the human race. Also, Adam provided a universal link with Jesus and God for the Gentiles as well as the Jews. As Adam was a son of God, Jesus was the Son of God. As the sin of Adam destroyed the human race, Jesus would open up the way for its redemption. The genealogy was inserted at this point because Jewish literature often placed the genealogy before the start of a man's ministry (see for example, Exod. 6:14-27).

How could Joseph be called the "son of Jacob" in Matthew 1:16 and the "son of Heli" in Luke 3:23? It has been suggested that this genealogy was really that of Mary who was the daugher of Heli. Joseph would have been the "son of Heli" by marriage (as son-in-law). One ancient explanation is that Heli died childless, and Jacob, his half

brother, in accordance with the law of levirate marriages (Deut. 25:5-6), took his widow as wife and became the father of Joseph. While Matthew's genealogy descends from Abraham to Jesus, Luke's genealogy ascends from Jesus to God, linking Jesus not only with Israel but the whole human race. Both genealogies demonstrate Jesus' right to the throne as an heir of David (Luke 3:31; cf. Matt. 1:1, 6).

4:1–9:50 SPIRIT AND POWER IN GALILEE

Overview: The section of 4:1–9:50 emphasizes several key points. Jesus was anointed by the Spirit (Luke 4:18-21) in accordance with Isaiah 61:1. He came to build a community of witnesses (Luke 5:9-11). The power of his words was set in the context of the power of his acts (cf. 6:19; 20-49). Love for Jesus was related to the forgiveness of sins (7:47). And finally, a series of miracles and the sending out of the disciples led up to the confession of Peter (9:20) and the transfiguration (9:28-36). The climax was in God's own proclamation, "This is my Son, whom I have chosen; listen to him" (9:35).

4:1-13 The Testing of Jesus

Jesus was "full of the Holy Spirit" (4:1). That means he was in full submission to the Spirit. The "desert" (4:1; "wilderness," NASB and KJV) was a reference to the twelve-mile wide desert region southeast of Jerusalem paralleling the Dead Sea. The "highest point" (4:9) of the temple referred to the southeast corner overlooking the Kidron Valley. Luke left the testing of Jesus open-ended (4:13). Satan would return at a later time of opportunity.

4:14-44 Proclamation and Power

4:14-30 THE FIRST REJECTION AT NAZARETH
A linking phrase moves the reader from an account of the people's praise (4:14-15) to an account of those who did not praise him (4:16-30). Matthew moved from the temptation, to selecting the disciples, and then on to the first major discourse in Matthew 5–7. In contrast, Luke moved from the temptation of the Spirit-filled Jesus to his Nazareth sermon on the anointing by the Spirit spoken of in Isaiah 61:1. For Matthew, Nazareth was the

fulfillment of prophecy (Matt. 2:23). For
Luke, the Spirit's presence upon Jesus was
the fulfillment of prophecy. In Luke 4:18-19
Jesus said the purpose of his anointing was
the proclamation of the gospel to the poor
and handicapped. Jesus offered physical
and spiritual healings (4:18). God's mercy
was given to those who saw themselves in
need.

Nazareth was located in lower Galilee
just north of the Valley of Jezreel and four
miles south of Sepphoris, the capital of
Galilee until A.D. 18 (see introductory map).
The synagogue was an institution that arose
during the Babylonian exile and was a place
where Jews gathered for worship, study, and
prayer. Jesus stopped reading from Isaiah
61:1-2 in the middle of 61:2 indicating that
"the day of vengeance of our God" (Isa.
61:2) would be an event associated with his
second coming and not his present ministry
(Luke 4:18). Two specific elements of the
prophecy were fulfilled (4:21). Jesus, the one
who was "anointed," had come and Jesus'
audience was about to prove itself blind to
the gospel. Only the first line of Jesus' message was recorded by Luke. Luke jumped
ahead to show how the hearers responded
to Jesus' message.

The rejection of Jesus by the people of
Nazareth (4:25-30) was preceded by a statement of the basic problem (4:23-24). How
could Jesus say he was not accepted (4:24)
when 4:22 seems to say that he was well
received? Jesus defined "accepted" as his
hearers receiving the gospel in faith from the
heart. All other responses or praises were
worthless and not accepted. Jesus illustrated
the hardness of the people's hearts by recalling events of Elijah's day (4:25-27).
Elements of "hardheartedness" from ancient
Israel remained in the Israel of Jesus' day.
The nation of Israel was like the people of
the "hometown." With Elijah and Elisha,
God went to the Gentiles before going to the
faithless in Israel. Similarly, Jesus would not
be accepted by people of his own hometown. That was a slap in the face to the Jews
of Jesus' day. The people initially responded
with wonder at Jesus' preaching, but were
not willing to take it to heart (4:28-30). They
would not admit to having hard and faithless
hearts and thus failed to cry out to God in
repentance.

4:31-44 HEALINGS AT CAPERNAUM
Capernaum (4:31), a tax collection station on
the Via Maris, was located on the northwest
shore of the Sea of Galilee (see introductory
map). Contrast what the demons knew about
Jesus (4:34) and the ignorance of the men of
Nazareth (4:22).

5:1–6:11 Power Interpreted and Focused

5:1-16 POWER OVER HUMANITY
Jesus demonstrated his power to catch
people by showing his power to catch fish.
The "Lake of Gennesaret" (5:1) was another
name for the Sea of Galilee (see introductory map). The name "Gennesaret" was
taken from the name of the large plain that
lies along the northwest shore of the lake.
This time, instead of demons (4:34), a disciple acknowledged Jesus as Lord (5:8). It
was God's power that enabled Jesus to catch
people for his kingdom—a power that would
be more fully revealed in Acts 2.

Jesus also used his power as a testimony
to the leaders of Israel by healing a leper
(Luke 5:12-16). Leprosy is a skin disease,
certain forms of which are described in
Leviticus 13. Lepers were regarded as
"unclean" on the basis of Levitical law (Lev.
13:45-46). The words "as a testimony to
them" (Luke 5:14) are important. This
miracle of cleansing was designed to alert
the religious establishment in Jerusalem that
there was someone up in Galilee exhibiting
Messianic credentials.

5:17-26 POWER OVER SIN
Jesus used his healing of a paralytic to illustrate and demonstrate his power to forgive
sins (5:17-26). In doing this, Jesus identified
his miracles of physical healing as signs that
pointed to his power to work the greater
miracle of forgiving sins (5:24).

5:27-39 POWER OVER TRADITIONS
"Levi" (5:27) was another name for
Matthew. Jesus demonstrated his power
over the traditions of Judaism (5:27-39). He
showed that spending time with tax collectors and sinners was not sinning, but a means
of bringing salvation to those in need. He
showed that following the traditions of
fasting did not make one spiritually acceptable to God. In the following section, Jesus
will show that it is more important to serve
others than to fulfill the requirements of

Sabbath observance. The problems of "sin" (5:17-32) and the keeping of the "Sabbath" (6:1-11) were rooted in the old Mosaic system—a system that would soon be replaced. The parable of new and old clothes and wineskins means that people should adjust their behavior to what fits a new situation, not try to continue on with old and inappropriate ways. The new situation here is the presence of Jesus the bridegroom (5:34-35). While he was on the earth, fasting was inappropriate. When he left, fasting would resume (5:35). Jesus required flexibility as he began his new work on earth. Those who held to the old ways ended up rejecting the very God whom they thought they were honoring. They were the ones in the parable who would rather continue using the old wineskins (5:39).

6:1-11 POWER OVER THE SABBATH
For "what David did" (6:3), see 1 Samuel 21:1-6. Jesus was demonstrating that it was more important to fulfill the higher commands to bring love and justice by serving people's needs than to follow the traditions of men. To claim to be Lord over the Sabbath (6:5) was the same as claiming to be equal with the Creator of the Sabbath (Gen. 2:1-3).

6:12–7:50 Power and God's Purposes: Rejection and Acceptance
6:12-49 MINISTRY OF THE DISCIPLES IN LIGHT OF REJECTION
6:12-19 Prayer before choosing the disciples. The link to the historical context is in 6:11-12. In direct response to his trouble with the Jewish leaders resulting from the Sabbath conflict (6:1-11), Jesus began to build his community of apostles (6:13). Luke emphasized the importance of prayer in all that Jesus did, and choosing the twelve apostles was no exception (6:12).

6:20-49 Preparation for kingdom entrance. Jesus' sermon has the following structure: blessings and curses (6:20-26); the obligation to love (6:27-36); refraining from criticism (6:27-45); the importance of obedience (6:46-49). Luke's "Sermon on the Plain" is quite similar to the "Sermon on the Mount" recorded by Matthew (Matt. 5–7). However, they are located at different times in Jesus' life chronologically, and Matthew's account was considerably longer than Luke's (107

verses in contrast to 30). It is probable that Jesus repeated the essential message of the Sermon on the Mount several times during his ministry. Luke recorded a similar sermon but with more brevity and slightly different language and phraseology. Luke's use of the phrase "kingdom of God" (Luke 6:20) and Matthew's "kingdom of heaven" are virtually equivalent. "Heaven" was a respectful, Jewish form of reference to God.

7:1-50 PITFALLS IN INTERPRETING JESUS' POWER
7:1-10 The centurion's faith. In 7:1-17 the context is given for John's questions in 7:18-23. This miracle shows Jesus' ability to heal even though he was far away. This long-distance power for good would be especially important after Jesus ascended into heaven. Although far away, his power for good would still be available everywhere. A "centurion" (7:2) was an officer in the Roman army who was in charge of approximately one hundred men (a century). They were responsible for training their men, leading them into battle, keeping track of military equipment, posting guards, and making inspections. Jesus said the centurion's faith was greater than any Israelite's he had found. This contrast between a Gentile centurion and the Jewish nation continues the theme of Jesus' special inclusion of Gentiles in his ministry and the pronounced rejection of Jesus by his own people (see 4:14-30).

7:11-17 A widow's son. "Nain" was located in the Valley of Jezreel at the foot of the Hill of Moreh, about six miles south of Nazareth (see introductory map). The widow was an example of the troubled and needy kind of person to whom Jesus came to minister (4:18). Luke 7:15 describes one of three resurrection miracles of Jesus (cf. Mark 5:41; John 11:44). It was this kind of miracle, contrasted by Jesus' own humility, that would give John the Baptist doubts about who Jesus was (Luke 7:18-19).

7:18-35 Expectations of the Messiah. John the Baptist doubted Jesus' identity (7:18-19). For "these things" (7:18) that caused John to doubt if Jesus was the Messiah, see 4:14, 37, 44; 5:14-15; 6:17; 7:1-17. The Old Testament had predicted that the Messiah would bring relief from physical suffering even as

Jesus was doing (7:22; cf. Isa. 35:5-6). Old Testament prophecy also looked forward to the poor having the Good News preached to them (Isa. 61:1). Jesus' answer to John's disciples essentially quoted Isaiah 66:1 (cf. Luke 4:18). Even the disciples needed to watch their preconceptions of what Jesus the Messiah would do, otherwise they might stumble or "fall away" (7:23).

In his discussion of John the Baptist (7:24-35), Jesus showed how the Jewish leaders had rejected John and would reject Jesus himself because John and Jesus did not fit with their preconceived ideas of what they should be like. Jesus clearly linked John the Baptist to the prophecy of Malachi 3:1 (Luke 7:27; cf. Matt. 17:10-13). That was how his baptisms were to be understood. However, for both Jesus and John, their association with sinners brought rejection.

7:36-50 Two examples of forgiveness. This event and its subsequent parable show how those who receive forgiveness for great sins will be likely to return great love to the person who forgave them. Jesus was talking about the relationship between loving him and appreciating his forgiveness. Those who see the awfulness of their sin along with the greatness of God's forgiveness will have the greatest love for Jesus. This incident must not be confused with the similar one involving Mary, sister to Martha and Lazarus, which took place during the last week of Jesus' life (cf. Matt. 26:6-31). A denarius (Luke 7:41; the plural form is *denarii*) was a Roman coin worth one day's wage.

8:1-56 Power and the Soils

8:1-3 LINKING PHRASE: SUPPORT OF JESUS' MINISTRY

Note the linking phrases in the progression of his ministry (4:14-15, 44; 8:1-3). These women were ministering to Jesus and the disciples. Mary "Magdalene" (8:2) was from the village of Magdala located in the Plain of Gennesaret north of Tiberias. Joanna's husband, "Cuza" (8:3), was identified as "the manager of Herod's household." The reference was to Herod Antipas. Cuza had some position of rank as an administrator in Herod's government.

8:4-21 THE REASONS FOR PITFALLS IN INTERPRETING JESUS' POWER

For a note on parables, see Matthew 13:3. The parable of the sower and the soils dealt with the reception of God's word. Luke added some clarifying details in 8:15 concerning a good heart. Jesus was interested in how people listened to the word of God.

8:22-56 MIRACLES

The function of these miracles was to show faith and its opposition. The audience's response was given at the end of each of the miracles.

8:22-25 Calming the storm. The "lake" (8:22) was the Sea of Galilee, a body of water situated 680 feet below sea level and noted for its sudden storms that occur when the Mediterranean winds rush through the narrow valleys of Galilee onto the lakeshore. This miracle revealed Jesus' unbelievable power to his disciples. Their reaction was one of fear and amazement (8:25).

8:26-39 Healing a demoniac. The disciples' question about Jesus, "Who is this?" (8:25), was answered by the demon in 8:28. A "legion" (8:30) in the Roman army consisted of 5,300 men. The "abyss" (8:31) was apparently a reference to a place of imprisonment for wicked spirits destined for the lake of fire (cf. Matt. 25:41; Jude 1:6; Rev. 20:3). The people who saw this miracle reacted with great fear (Luke 8:35).

8:40-56 Healing a sick woman and Jairus's daughter raised. In section 8:40-56, Luke looked at faith in two different ways. First, the faith of a woman was hidden because of her fear (8:50). Second, the faith of a man, shown by his inviting Jesus to come heal his daughter, was openly laughed at (8:53). Faith and fear are in opposition to each other. For in the person of faith, there is no reason for fear. The "edge" (8:44) of Jesus' cloak was probably a reference to one of the four blue tassels that were worn by strict Jews according to Levitical law (Num. 15:38-40). Jesus said that Jairus's daughter was "asleep" (Luke 8:52), knowing that she would be raised from death. "Asleep" is a common euphemism for death. This term carries with it the assumption that people can look forward to being resurrected after they die (1 Thess. 4:13).

9:1-9 Ministry in a Hostile World

Jesus shared his power with his twelve disciples. He shared that authority even more broadly when he sent the Spirit to all his disciples (Acts 2). "Herod the tetrarch" (9:7) referred to Herod Antipas, ruler of Galilee and Perea (4 B.C.–A.D. 39). The term "tetrarch" means "ruler of a fourth part."

9:10-50 The Crucial Interpretation of Jesus' Ministry: Passion

9:10-17 FIVE THOUSAND FED
"Bethsaida" (9:10) was located on the northeast shore of the Sea of Galilee, just east of the Jordan River's entrance (see introductory map). See the note on Mark 6:45 for more on this miracle.

9:18-27 CONFESSION
AT CAESAREA PHILIPPI
The feeding at Bethsaida was linked to the question, "Who do the crowds say I am?" (9:18) by the use of "people" and "crowds" in 9:16 and 9:18. The central issue was not bread, but understanding the identity of Jesus as the Son of God. Again, only Luke recorded that Jesus prayed just before he revealed his destiny to die on the cross (9:18). Luke 9:21-22 clearly reveals why his Messianic identity had to be kept secret. Jesus had the goal of the cross and ascension before him, not great public recognition. He would leave the worldwide spread of his reputation up to his Spirit-empowered followers.

9:28-36 TRANSFIGURATION
Images from Israel's exodus from Egypt are prominent in the events surrounding the transfiguration. Moses and Elijah were talking with Jesus about his own exodus (departure) from Jerusalem. That happened at his ascension (24:51; Acts 1:9). The "mountain" (9:28) probably referred to 9,200 foot-high Mount Hermon (see note on Matt. 17:1). The "three shelters" (9:33) apparently were intended by Peter for the observance of the Feast of Tabernacles. This feast was to be observed in the Messianic kingdom (cf. Zech. 14:16), which Peter anticipated would come soon.

9:37-43 A DEMON-POSSESSED BOY HEALED
For the reason the disciples were unable to drive out this demon (9:40), see Mark 9:29.

9:43-45 PASSION PREDICTION
Although the crowds marvelled at his miracles, Jesus wanted his disciples to grasp the fact of his upcoming death. The disciples, expecting Jesus to usher in his kingdom immediately with power and glory, had difficulty accepting Jesus' passion predictions. Jesus' time for bearing the cross was fast approaching; this was not a time to receive permanent praise. There was only one thing on Jesus' mind regarding his purpose on earth: the cross and the empty place waiting at the Father's right hand.

9:46-50 SECULAR PRIDE
The disciples argued within their ranks and denied acceptance to other followers of Jesus. Their pride revealed that they still did not understand the nature of the kingdom Jesus promised. They were still seeking power and riches. This attitude was obvious in their inability to understand Jesus' predictions of his upcoming suffering and death. They still had to learn to accept Jesus' and later, their own, bearing of the cross. They still had to learn that "he who is least among you all—he is the greatest" (9:48).

9:51–19:27 TOWARD THE GOAL: DEBATES AND INSTRUCTION

Overview: This section of the Gospel has long been a problem for biblical scholars. Luke specifically indicated that Jesus was traveling to Jerusalem (Luke 9:51, 53; 13:22, 33; 17:11; 18:31; 19:11, 28). The difficulty is in trying to trace the course of this journey. The vast majority of scholars see no literal journey in Luke's account, believing that the author arranged miscellaneous material into a "journey motif" to provide a place to record researched material Luke wanted to preserve but did not know its original historical or geographical context.

Another possibility, however, is to suggest that Luke's three main geographical notices (9:51; 13:22; 17:11) correspond with Jesus' three journeys to Jerusalem (recorded by John) that took place in the last months of Jesus' ministry (John 7:2, 10; 10:22; 12:1). Several passages show Jesus on the move (Luke 9:57; 10:1, 17, 38; 11:1; 13:10; 14:1, 25). Other passages focus on Jesus' destination (9:51; 13:22, 33; 17:11; 18:35; 19:1, 11). In light of the debate on the issue, it should be pointed out that it is not essential to the interpretation of this material to know the precise geographical setting in which it was originally given.

The ascension was Jesus' goal in going to Jerusalem (9:51). His death and resurrection were subordinate to the primary goal: Jesus' exaltation to the right hand of the Father and the subsequent pouring out of the Holy Spirit to empower the ongoing proclamation of his gospel. The focus of this long section was not on suffering and rejection at Jerusalem, but on discipleship in the shadow of the cross. Suffering is presented as an opportunity for full consecration and for following Jesus at all points of life. This section is in the form of a travel narrative to show the conflicts and lessons to be learned while the disciples walked with Jesus in this life. It recounts instruction in and opposition to the gospel proclamation.

The section divides into three cycles: (1) resolution to depart (9:51–13:21); (2) lessons on faith, conflict in the kingdom (13:22–17:10); and (3) lessons on perseverance (17:11–19:27). The key subjects covered are faithfulness, courage, service, the cost of discipleship, humility, riches, and stewardship. There is also a stress on how the "self" and the world's goods can be hindrances to devoted discipleship (9:23; 10:4; 12:15; 14:27; 16:14, 19; 17:27; 18:23; 19:2). This section emphasizes discipleship in the shadow of the cross.

9:51–13:21 Preparation for Departure
9:51-56 REBUFF AND REBUKE
Jesus focused on his ascension. He did not speak here of his death or resurrection. The Samaritans (9:52) were descendants from the idolatrous foreigners brought into the northern kingdom after the fall of Samaria in 722 B.C. and some of the Jews who had remained there (cf. 2 Kings 17). Although claiming adherence to the *Torah*, they were regarded by the Jews as religiously and ethnically impure. This section shows the character and attitude of a witness and how one should respond to rejection. One should continue to offer salvation and leave judgment for later (cf. Luke 6:35). Pride and exclusivism were behind the disciples' question in 9:54. The disciples were looking for a repeat of the miraculous judgment recorded in 2 Kings 1:10-12.

9:57–10:24 THE SEVENTY ARE INSTRUCTED: WITNESS AND REJECTION
Halfhearted discipleship is condemned (Luke 9:57-62). For a discussion of the term "Son of Man" (9:58), see note on Matthew 8:20 and the Guiding Concepts for Mark. The meaning of Luke 9:60 is: "Allow the spiritually dead to bury those who are physically dead." Jesus was emphasizing the demands, priorities, and importance of God's kingdom program.

In 10:1-24 Jesus extended his ministry through seventy men (10:4, 16). Only Luke recorded this mission of the seventy. It was similar to the mission of the twelve recorded in Matthew 10:1–11:1. Note the definition of true joy (Luke 10:20). That joy is elaborated in 10:21-24. A "fall . . . from heaven" (10:18) was a phrase that reflected a loss of power and authority (cf. Isa. 14:12-15). Satan's counterfeit kingdom was subject to a major setback as a result of the disciples' ministry.

10:25-37 THE GOOD SAMARITAN
The parable of the Good Samaritan illustrated the depth of God's love, while also calling everyone to show compassion in the same way. The "expert in the law" (10:25) was one of the scribes, who spent their time studying and copying the Jewish law. It was a dishonest disciple who asked, "Who is my neighbor?" (10:29). New Testament or Herodian Jericho (10:30) was located in the Jordan Valley just north of the Dead Sea about 1,300 feet below sea level. Jerusalem is situated about 2,500 feet above sea level. Hence the expression "down from Jerusalem to Jericho" (10:30). The route through the Wadi Qilt is rocky and rugged with many places for robbers to hide in wait of travelers. For "Samaritan" (10:33), see the note on 9:52. The Samaritan was the least expected traveler to assist the injured Jew. The coins (10:35) were Roman and worth about a day's wage. Jesus showed that a neighbor is anyone who is in need (10:37). The point of the parable of the Good Samaritan (Luke 10:25-36) was made in 10:37. All are called to show compassion to those in need.

10:38-42 LISTENING TO THE WORD
In this account about Mary and Martha, the disciples' and Martha's priorities were examined and corrected. Martha questions Jesus' care for her in 10:40 and commands

him to tell Mary to help with the chores. But Jesus cut through the "many things" (10:41) pressing in on Martha and focused on one thing. Jesus showed his care for Martha by helping her see what was truly important and of eternal value. Rather than commanding Mary to get busy, Jesus instead emphasized the better choice Mary had made. Seeking to be with Jesus and listening to him was of the highest priority. The "village" (10:38) was Bethany, located about half a mile from Jerusalem on the east side of the Mount of Olives (see introductory map).

11:1-13 ON PRAYER: PERSISTENCE
Luke placed this discourse on prayer directly after his account of Mary insisting on staying at the feet of Jesus (10:39-42). Thematically these two events are related. Jesus was making it clear that it was important to be persistent in prayer. In the contrast made between earthly and heavenly fathers (11:13), the gift promised by God was the Holy Spirit. The Holy Spirit is the only crucial gift needed by believers in this age.

11:14–13:21 DEBATES WITH LEADERS: HYPOCRITES
11:14-28 Obedience to the stronger Man. The section of 11:14-28 encourages obedience to the "stronger Man" (11:21-22), Jesus the Messiah. For "Beelzebub" (11:15), see the note on Matthew 10:25. Notice the people who are truly blessed: "those who hear the word of God and obey it" (Luke 11:27-28).

11:29-36 The sign of Jonah. For a discussion of the sign of Jonah, see comments on Matthew 12:22-45. Without faith, many simply sought signs and miracles with unclear eyes (11:29-36).

11:37-54 Six woes for the Jewish leaders. The unclean leaders were condemned for their hypocrisy (11:37-54). It was customary in the biblical period to recline on cushions around a low table when eating (Luke 11:37). Contact with a dead body would bring ceremonial defilement upon a Jew (11:44; cf. Num. 19:16). To avoid this, tombs were usually marked with whitewash (cf. Matt. 23:27). Unmarked tombs would result in contamination. For the death of Zechariah (11:51), see the discussion on Matthew 23:35. Jesus' strong words against the Jewish leaders led them to plot his death

(11:53-54). As he turned to address the crowd (Luke 12), they waited for him to say something they could use against him.

12:1-12 Courage during attack. The word "meanwhile" (Luke 12:1) showed that while Jesus was speaking to the Jewish leaders (Luke 11), a crowd had gathered. Jesus then turned and addressed the crowd. The setting was similar to that of the sermon on the plain (6:19). "Yeast" (12:1; "leaven," NASB and KJV) is known for its ability to permeate bread dough and work great changes in it. Just as yeast permeates bread dough, the disciples were urged to beware of the hypocrisy of the Pharisees, which was having a similar influence on the nation of Israel. The Pharisees were teaching falsehoods about Jesus to maintain their own security in Jewish society. For "blasphemes against the Holy Spirit" (12:10), see Matthew 12:31.

12:13–13:9 Serving with an end-time life perspective. Jesus encouraged his followers to get their hearts in the correct place (Luke 12:13-34) in view of the fast approaching end times. He called his listeners to center their energy and service on God. When a man asked Jesus to tell his brother to share an inheritance (12:13-15), Jesus refused to arbitrate the matter. Jesus apparently recognized the man's selfishness and lack of concern for the things of God (cf. 12:16-21). To impress upon this man the importance of reorienting his values, Jesus told the parable of the rich fool (12:16-20). For treasures to last, they had to be eternal treasures gained in service of God, not self (12:21-34).

Jesus called his followers to serve in readiness (12:35-48). He emphasized the importance of being prepared—watchful and ready—for his second coming (12:40). Peter questioned Jesus (12:41) as to whether the thoughts of 12:40 applied to the disciples or to everyone. The stringent demands were for all who desired to follow Jesus. Jesus was setting the tone for all who await his return in the present age. The temptations of the long-term absence (12:45) of Jesus could cause some to forget their master's return and thus result in their destruction. Jesus emphasized that his followers were not only to be watchful, but also caring for the Master's own (12:42, 45).

Serving the Messiah in this age would include undergoing hostility (12:49-53). The "fire" (12:49) referred to the judgment on Satan and his domain that would commence at the cross (John 12:31). Jesus' "baptism" (Luke 12:50) referred to his sacrificial death on the cross (cf. Mark 10:38-39).

Despite all the harsh warnings of judgment, Jesus would allow time for repentance (Luke 12:54–13:9). The theme of this section is the necessity for repentance in a limited time. The incident involving Pilate (13:1) is not known from any other source, but it fits well with what is known of Pilate's character. This brutal act against the Galileans undoubtedly contributed to the enmity between Pilate and Herod Antipas (cf. 23:12). In 13:2-3 Jesus pointed out that this incident did not fall on the Galileans because they were exceptionally sinful. God's judgment would fall upon all who failed to repent, not just the exceedingly sinful. The "tower in Siloam" (13:4) must have been located in the vicinity of the pool of "Siloam" (cf. John 9:11) just south of Jerusalem near the junction of the Kidron and Tyropoean valleys.

13:10-21 Establishment of and entrance into the kingdom. On the Sabbath, Jesus healed a daughter of Abraham (a Jewess) who had been crippled by a spirit for many years (Luke 13:16). The Abrahamic promises found fulfillment in this woman's life, not in spite of, but especially, on the Sabbath. Therefore, 13:18-21 should be read in that light. What better day than the Sabbath to give rest to this woman who had probably not enjoyed a truly restful day for eighteen years. The "mustard seed" (13:19) was the smallest of the garden seeds. This image was used frequently in Jewish rabbinic literature to represent something small. The function of "yeast" (13:21; "leaven," NASB and KJV) was to cause dough to rise. A little yeast is known to permeate and transform a whole lump of bread dough.

13:22–17:10 On the Journey: Faith during Conflict

13:22-35 INVITATION AND
LAMENT OVER JERUSALEM
Jesus stressed the need for obedience (13:27) and not just acquaintance (13:26) when it came to salvation (13:23). Jesus called his followers to travel a narrow and difficult road. After receiving death threats from Herod, Jesus lamented over Jerusalem and again predicted his passion (13:31-35). This "Herod" (13:31) was Herod Antipas who had murdered John the Baptist (cf. Matt. 14:1-12). Herod was likened to a "fox" (Luke 13:32), a creature that lacks real power and dignity but accomplishes evil by cunning schemes. The lament of 13:34-35 was also recorded by Matthew after Jesus' royal entry into Jerusalem (Matt. 23:37-39). Jesus' prediction in Luke 13:35 anticipated the A.D. 70 destruction of Jerusalem by the Romans. It also looks forward to the Jews' recognition of Jesus' Messiahship at his second coming (cf. Zech. 12:10–13:1).

14:1-35 THE NATURE AND COST
OF DISCIPLESHIP
14:1-11 Humility. "Dropsy" (14:2) is a disease symptom involving swelling due to the retention of excessive fluids in body tissues. Jesus noticed how the Jewish leaders lived in contrast to the way of humility that he exemplified (14:7) and told a parable to illustrate their folly (14:8-10). The truth that the exalted will be humbled and the humble will be exalted (14:11) was exemplified by Jesus' own humiliation and then exaltation to the right hand of God. Jesus' healing of the man with dropsy was his seventh and last Sabbath healing. Jesus made it clear that humility (14:11), not self-exaltation, was the passport to promotion in the kingdom of God.

14:12-14 Generosity. Jesus called his followers to give without any hope of return. This continued the theme of selfless discipleship already touched upon in his call to humility. The "resurrection of the righteous" (14:14) promised to the generous was distinguished from the resurrection of the wicked (cf. John 5:29; Rev. 20:11-15).

14:15-35 Qualified discipleship. Jesus continued his comments on the selflessness of the true disciple with a parable about a great wedding banquet (14:15-24). Many refused to come because of their worldly concerns. What was the purpose of Jesus' statement in 14:24? He desired to make it clear that only those willing to give up everything to enter the kingdom would find a place at God's table. Relate the discussion of the banquet to Isaiah 61:1. After the parable, Jesus continued his call to count the cost of following him (Luke 14:25-35). Following Jesus had to have priority over all other relationships (14:26). The word "hate" (14:26) expressed a disciple's turning from others in preference for God's kingdom when called to choose between family loyalty and discipleship.

15:1-32 THREE PARABLES OF THINGS LOST BUT FOUND AGAIN

The three parables of Luke 15 must be understood in the context or life setting given in 15:1-2. Jesus was showing the "sinners" that salvation was available to even them (15:7, 10, 32), while also answering the complaints of the Pharisees about Jesus spending time with sinners (15:2). Note the ending statements for each of the parables (15:7, 10, 32). Jesus was giving hope to the "sinners," while also calling the "righteous" Pharisees to rejoice with the hosts of heaven over the fact that someone who had been lost was found.

The three parables of Luke 15 (the lost sheep, the lost coin, and the lost son) were directed to the Pharisees who did not share God's loving attitude toward sinners. True to their name, Pharisee (meaning, "separate one"), they believed in separation from sinners because God obviously hated such people. The parables were designed to correct the error of the Pharisees, showing how God loves sinners and takes delight when a lost sinner is restored. Readers of Luke's Gospel are forced to ask, "Where do we line up in our attitude toward sinners? Do we condemn them as did the Pharisees, or do we love them as God does?"

The "coins" (15:8) that had been lost were probably part of the woman's dowry and had sentimental value in addition to monetary worth. Luke 15:11-32 is often called the parable of the Prodigal Son. "Prodigal" means "addicted to wasteful expenditure." The story reveals the heart of the father, representative of God, watching, loving, and rejoicing at the return of his lost son. The angry son who had remained at home (15:28-32) was representative of the "righteous" Pharisees.

16:1–17:10 DISCIPLESHIP: FAITH AND STEWARDSHIP

16:1-13 Men's love for the Father is contrasted with riches. Jesus used the parable of the shrewd steward (16:1-8) to make a

comparison between the handling of earthly and spiritual affairs. These verses are closely linked with the three parables in Luke 15. Luke 15 concerned Jesus' response to the Pharisees' criticism of his welcoming sinners (15:1). God's love for sinners caused him to seek them out as the three parables in Luke 15 demonstrate. In Luke 16 Jesus brings his lesson home to the Pharisees. The parable concerns a servant who does everything he can to smooth his way with potential masters. Jesus encouraged his listeners to work just as hard to keep the way smooth with their heavenly Master. But because of the Pharisees' love for money (16:13-14), they were, in reality, the same as the sinners they condemned in 15:2. But the Pharisees, like everyone else, were sought after by the loving Father and would also have to conform to all of God's unchangeable law (16:16). The master commended the steward, not for his dishonesty, but for his wise foresight in preparing for the future (16:8). Similarly, the believer is to make wise use of material resources so that they will bring eternal benefit and reward. Jesus also warned his listeners that they needed to recognize the danger of money becoming the master and God taking second place (16:13). The transition from 16:13 to 16:14 shows that the following section also concerns the use of money.

16:14-18 Jesus rebukes the Pharisees as manipulators of God's law. The Pharisees' love of money caused further animosity between them and Jesus (note the link between 16:13 and 16:14). The "least stroke of a pen" (16:17) was a reference to the very small mark that distinguishes the Hebrew letter *dalet* from the letter *resh*. Jesus was saying that he did not come to take away the law; he came to give the law new life. Jesus' teaching on divorce was presented in Matthew 5:32; 19:1-12; and Mark 10:1-12 (see the notes there). Since marriage can be terminated only by death (1 Cor. 7:39), Jesus taught that remarriage after divorce constitutes adultery (16:18).

16:19-31 The rich man and Lazarus. What was the point of the story about Lazarus and the rich man? Abraham appeared a number of times in this story (16:22, 23, 24, 25, 27, 29, 30, 31). There is debate about whether this was a parable or an actual historical incident. It was probably a parable intended to correct the Pharisees (16:14) who were lovers of money. Being rich was not necessarily a sign of God's blessing—it could signal a faithless heart bound for hell. "Abraham's side" (16:22; "Abraham's bosom," NASB and KJV) was a figurative reference to "paradise" or the presence of God (cf. Luke 23:43; 2 Cor. 12:4). Like the Hebrew *Sheol* in the Old Testament, "hell" (or "Hades," Luke 16:23) refers to the abode of the departed dead. "Hades" was never used in the New Testament as the place of the righteous. Rather, it was used like the Greek term *Gehenna* for a place of flames and conscious torment (16:24, 28). Care should be taken to avoid building a detailed theology of the afterlife based solely on this parable.

17:1-10 Learning to serve and avoiding the leaders' hardness. A "millstone" (17:2) was a circular stone used for grinding grain into flour. The disciples realized that in order to receive powerful forgiveness (17:4), they needed a powerful faith (17:5). Unlimited forgiveness was the standard for those who had been forgiven much. The disciple's proper self-image was to be a servant (17:10)—one who is there to serve, not be served (17:5-10). The obligation of a slave was never discharged, neither was he to expect any commendation. Similarly, even the Christian's best and most selfless service would not place God under any obligation.

17:11–19:27 On the Journey: Perseverance

17:11-19 THE PROPER FOCUS OF GLORY TO RETURN TO GIVE PRAISE

The words "between Samaria and Galilee" (17:11) apparently referred to the Valley of Jezreel in which the official border between the regions was situated. It was necessary to present themselves before the priests to demonstrate that they had been healed and to offer the sacrifice of purification (17:14; cf. Lev. 14:1-32).

17:20-37 THE SON OF MAN'S COMING

At the request of his followers, Jesus described the coming of God's kingdom. Jesus confirmed that his return would be like that of a thief in the night (Luke 17:20-21, 30-31; cf. 12:39). He desired to make it clear that the kingdom would catch everyone off

guard, warning his followers to be continually faithful. Jesus, the King, was offering his kingdom to those who would respond and believe (17:21). In a real sense the kingdom was present in the person of Jesus Christ ("within you"). In the "days of Noah" (17:26-27) people were going about their everyday tasks and not heeding God's warning. They were unprepared for judgment and were destroyed. So shall it be before the second coming of Jesus. The background for the terse warning given in 17:32 is found in Genesis 19:26. Many manuscripts omit Luke 17:36 although it appears with certainty in Matthew 24:40. The "vultures" (Luke 17:37) will feed on the bodies of the slain at the second coming (Rev. 19:17-18).

18:1-8 THE DISCIPLES' PREPARATION

In Jesus' parable of the persistent widow, the judge had the responsibility of settling disputes and avenging wrongs, but he cared little for those who made appeals before him (Luke 18:2). The term "quickly" (18:8) does not necessarily mean "immediately," but "in due time," according to God's economy and timing. Notice the question in 18:8. The Son of Man will come looking for faith and wonders whether or not he will find any. He will judge the faithless (17:37) and reward the faithful.

18:9-14 HUMILITY IN PRAYER AND IN THE KINGDOM

The context for the parable of the Pharisee and the tax collector is set up in 18:9 and rounded out in 18:14. Jesus was speaking to some Jews who thought themselves beyond reproach. The ancient Israelites fasted on the Day of Atonement (18:12; cf. Lev. 16:29-34). Other fasts were added by Jewish tradition (cf. Zech. 8:19). The Pharisees had advanced this practice to excess (cf. Matt. 6:16-18). Regarding their "tithes," see Deuteronomy 14:22-23 and comments there. The tax collector requested that God's wrath against his sin be satisfied and that he be extended mercy. Jesus Christ, "the atoning sacrifice for our sins" (1 John 2:2), would soon become the answer to his prayer.

18:15-17 JESUS AND THE LITTLE CHILDREN

Receiving the kingdom like a little child contrasts with the arrogance and pride in the surrounding acts of the indignant disciples

(18:15), the Pharisee (18:11-12), and the rich ruler (18:22-23). Jesus' call to be like children was not a call to be ignorant or naive. It was a call to believers to be humble, that is, willing to see themselves as God sees them and accepting that perspective (like the tax collector in 18:13) and then moving on in obedience to do what he wants (like the disciples in 18:28).

18:18-30 FALSE AND TRUE RICHES WITH REGARD TO ENTERING THE KINGDOM
A rich young man came seeking eternal life. Jesus pointed out the significance of his use of the word "good" (18:19). In essence Jesus was saying, "Why do you call me 'good' if you do not recognize my deity?" The rich man's problem was that he would not obey Jesus' final command (18:22). His riches were only the surface problem; the real problem lay in the love he had for his wealth. For the word "needle" (18:25) Luke the physician used the Greek term for "surgeon's needle."

18:31-43 THE BLIND MAN HEALED
In recounting the healing of the blind man, Luke also emphasized the spiritual blindness of Jesus' disciples (18:31-34). They continually failed to accept Jesus' predictions of his upcoming death (18:34) and other teachings as well. Many of Jesus' teachings were understood only after he sent the Holy Spirit (18:34; cf. John 16:12-15). Matthew 20:29-34 indicates that the miracle took place as they were leaving Jericho. The account in Luke says it took place as they approached the town (Luke 18:35). Apparently the miracle took place as they were leaving Old Testament Jericho and were nearing New Testament or Herodian Jericho. The sites are about one-half mile apart. "Son of David" (18:39) was a Messianic term (2 Sam. 7:12-16; Isa. 9:7) showing a general awareness of Jesus' Messianic identity.

19:1-27 A TAX COLLECTOR CONVERTED: ZACCHAEUS
As a tax collector, Zacchaeus had enriched himself at the expense of his fellow Jews by charging excessive taxes (Luke 19:2). Collaborating with the Romans, he had worked himself up to a prominent position as "chief tax collector" (19:2). Zacchaeus proved the sincerity of his repentance by making restitu-

tion far beyond that which was required by the law (19:8; cf. Num. 5:6-7).

Note the relationship of the story of Zacchaeus (Luke 19:1-10) and the parables that begin in 19:11. They grow out of Zacchaeus's confession and proclamation that he would return what he had wrongly taken (19:8). For the significance of Zacchaeus's relationship to Abraham (19:9), compare 3:8 and 13:16. The parables of 19:11-27 clearly corrected the misconception that the kingdom was going to come immediately (19:11). Jesus asked that his followers continue in faithful service no matter how long it might take before Jesus returned. Jesus taught regarding the rejection of the king (representing himself) and announced judgment on the rejecting generation (19:11-27). A "mina" (19:13) was a measure of money worth one hundred drachmas or denarii. It amounted to about three months' wages.

19:28–24:53 THE GOAL ATTAINED: JERUSALEM
Overview: Luke's travel narrative (9:51–19:27) ends in 19:28 (see comments introducing this section). Next, Luke follows the sequence of events of the last week of Jesus' ministry recorded also by Matthew and Mark. This section was designed to show the innocence of Jesus before his judges. In line with Luke's purpose of presenting the exact truth so that the readers would find certainty in the faith, the book ends with proofs of Jesus' resurrection. Luke concludes his Gospel with the disciples in the temple praising God, waiting for the Spirit and power from on high.

19:28-48 The Entrance into Jerusalem
19:28-40 APPROACH IN PRAISE
Although Bethphage (Luke 19:29) has not been precisely located, Bethany was situated just east of the Mount of Olives about half a mile from Jerusalem. Bethphage was probably located in the immediate vicinity (see introductory map). The quotation in 19:38 was from Psalm 118:26, one of the Hallel psalms (Pss. 115–118) sung at Passover. The cry of the crowds (Luke 19:38) echoed the cry of the angels at Jesus' birth (2:14).

An inspiring encouragement for witnessing in the face of rejection is found in 19:39-40.

19:41-44 JESUS' LAMENT OVER JERUSALEM
The "day" (19:42) of Jesus' royal entry into Jerusalem had been predicted by Daniel 9:25-27. The Messiah would be "cut off" sixty-nine weeks (of years) after the issuing of the decree to rebuild Jerusalem. The "sixty-nine" weeks calculates to be 173,880 days (69 x 7 x 360). Jesus' royal entry took place on March 30, A.D. 33, exactly 173,880 days after the issuing of Artaxerxes' decree to rebuild Jersalem, March 5, 444 B.C. (cf. Neh. 2:1-8). The "embankment" (Luke 19:43) was a siege wall designed to prevent citizens from fleeing and to keep supplies from being smuggled in. The Romans built such a siege wall around Jerusalem when the city was attacked by Titus in A.D. 70.

19:45-48 THE FIRST CRISIS AND ITS RESULT
Upon entering the temple and seeing its courts being used as a market place, Jesus accused the traders of making the temple "a den of robbers" (19:45-46). The temple area (the Court of the Gentiles) had become a place for selling animals for sacrifice and changing Roman coin into the Jewish half-shekel (19:45). In demonstration of his Messianic authority, Jesus "cast out" those who were misusing the worship center. He quoted Isaiah 56:7 and Jeremiah 7:11 to support his actions (Luke 19:46). Luke took note of the multitude's acceptance of Jesus and how that had a restraining effect on the Jewish leaders who were bent on destroying him (19:47-48; cf. 20:19).

20:1–21:38 The Religious Opposition to Jesus

20:1-19 OPPOSITION REGARDING AUTHORITY
Jesus linked his authority to John's baptism (20:2-8) and to the "stone" predicted in Psalm 118:22 (Luke 20:17). Jesus told a parable about vineyard tenants to show how he would be rejected by the religious leaders just as they had rejected the prophets before him. The "vineyard" (20:9) imagery was familiar to first century Judeans. The same imagery was used by the prophet Isaiah to describe God's dealings with his people (Isa. 5:1-7). Jesus was to be the "capstone"

(Luke 20:17; cf. Ps. 118:22) bringing unity and completion to God's redemptive program. Yet he was rejected by the Jewish religious leaders ("the builders").

20:20-26 OPPOSITION REGARDING POLITICAL RESPONSIBILITY
Behind the leaders' questions concerning the payment of taxes to Rome was a plot to accuse Jesus (Luke 20:20). Everyone would agree that a legitimate government has the right to tax its citizens (20:22). The question really concerned the legitimacy of the Roman government in Palestine. This was an attempt by the Jewish leaders to make Jesus say something against Rome and thus come into conflict with the authorities. On the other hand, if Jesus defended the legitimacy of Rome's authority, he would be taking a position unpopular with the Jewish people and would likely lose popular support. Jesus' answer amazingly avoided both pitfalls.

20:27-40 OPPOSITION REGARDING RESURRECTION
The question the Sadducees asked Jesus concerning levirate marriage and the resurrection of the dead was ironic because this Jewish sect rejected the idea of resurrection. Thus, they did not seek an honest answer but only desired to test Jesus. There is a note on levirate marriage (20:28) in Deuteronomy 25:5-10. The point Jesus made in Luke 20:35-36 was that marriage is an institution limited to life on this earth. There will be no marriage or procreation in heaven. The Sadducees rejected the idea of resurrection because they could not find the idea in Mosaic Law, the only Scriptures they accepted as authoritative. But Jesus pointed out evidence for the resurrection in Mosaic Law (20:37; cf. Exod. 3:6), leaving them speechless. He showed that the resurrection of the dead was implied by the fact that God continued to be the God of the patriarchs long after they had died.

20:41-44 OPPOSITION RESULTING FROM MISUNDERSTANDING THE MESSIAH
In Luke 20:42-43 Jesus quoted Psalm 110:1 to clarify his identity as the divine Son of God. He pointed out that the only way David could call his son (or descendant) "Lord" was if his son (that is, Jesus) was divine (Luke 20:44). Thus, David's state-

ment prophetically looked forward to a
descendant who would be divine, that is,
Jesus. Psalm 110:1 was later used by Peter
in Acts 2:34-35 to validate Jesus' deity and
exaltation to the right hand of God.

20:45–21:4 PRIDE AND GENEROSITY
Luke set in contrast the deeds of the proud
Pharisees (20:45-47) and the deed of a poor
and humble widow (21:1-4) and showed the
widow to be the one who was truly righteous. The value of giving was based on the
amount of sacrifice and the attitude of heart,
not on the amount given or the ostentation.

21:5-38 THE END OF THE TEMPLE
AND THE AGE
Luke's version of the Olivet Discourse
begins with some mention of the eschatological signs of the final tribulation (Luke
21:8-11) but then provides a parenthesis on
Jerusalem's more immediate future—the
Roman attack and destruction of the city in
A.D. 70 (21:12-24). The sermon from 21:25
and following parallels Matthew's account
describing the events of the second advent
(21:25-28) and giving exhortations to
watchfulness (21:29-38). The discourse is a
straightforward encouragement to perseverance (21:19) and strength (21:36). The key
elements are perseverance of witness in
persecution (21:10-19) and exhortations to
enable recognition of the returning Messiah
(21:29-33) and readiness for that return
(21:34-36). Apparently Jesus and the disciples were used to sleeping in the open air on
the Mount of Olives (21:37).

22:1-38 The Passover

22:1-6 THE PLOTTERS UNIFY
According to Jewish law, Passover was
observed on Nisan 14 and the Feast of
Unleavened Bread followed, being observed
on Nisan 15-21 (cf. Exod. 12:1-28; Lev. 23:5-
6). The two feasts emphasized the removal
of leaven or yeast, and the term "Unleavened
Bread" was often applied to the whole
season including Passover and Unleavened
Bread (cf. Luke 22:7). The Jewish leaders,
looking for a way of getting rid of Jesus,
found Judas Iscariot willing to participate.
The role of Satan was mentioned (22:3),
reminding the reader that though Satan had
failed to stop Jesus earlier (cf. 4:1-13), he
had not stopped trying (cf. 4:13).

22:7-23 THE PASSOVER MEAL
A man carrying water would have been an
unusual sight in the ancient world since this
was normally a woman's job (22:10). The
man may have been John Mark. It was probably in his mother's house that the disciples
observed the Last Supper with Jesus (Acts
12:12). In the first century meals were taken
around a low table where the guests reclined
on cushions (Luke 22:14). The "bread"
(22:19) was to serve as a memorial ("remembrance") of Jesus' sacrificial death on the
cross. The "cup" (22:20) was to serve as a
memorial to the shed blood of Jesus, the
sacrifice that made the new covenant possible (cf. Jer. 31:31-34). The death of Jesus on
the cross was scandalous and surprising. He
clearly emphasized that his death was in
accord with what God had previously determined in the Old Testament Scriptures (Luke
22:22; cf. 24:44-47; and Acts 2:23; 4:28;
10:42; 17:31).

22:24-38 SERVANTS IN A NEW SERVICE
The section of Luke 22:24-38 can be sub-
divided further: greatness through service
(22:24-30); preservation through failure (22:31-
34); preparation for persecution (22:35-38).
The term "Benefactors" (22:25) was often
inscribed on coins along with the name of
the ruling official. For most, it was a hollow
and worthless title. The word "sift" (22:31)
was an agricultural term that referred to the
process of separating the kernels of grain
from the chaff. The reference to the "sword"
(22:36) was a bit confusing since Jesus apparently did not intend for his disciples to use
force to deliver him (22:49-51; cf. Matt.
26:52). Perhaps Jesus used the term figuratively to speak of the perilous and difficult
days ahead. The disciples apparently took
him literally and produced two swords
(Luke 22:38). Jesus' words "That is enough"
(22:38) may simply mean "Enough of this
talk" (see in that regard, 22:51).

22:39–23:25 Arrest and Trial

22:39-53 PRAYER AND ARREST
IN THE GARDEN
Luke 22:43-44 are omitted in certain important manuscripts. However, their presence in
many manuscripts as well as their citation by
many church Fathers proves their antiquity.
The text does not say that Jesus sweated
blood (22:44). Rather, Luke the physician

observed that Jesus' perspiration was so profuse that it was "like" blood dripping from an open wound. The name of the servant of the high priest was Malchus (22:50; cf. John 18:10). At his arrest, Jesus noted with irony that the Jews had arrested him when no one could see them, though they had had numerous opportunities at the temple in broad daylight (22:53). This was because the religious leaders feared the general population who revered him (cf. 19:47-48), but Jesus also noted that coming in the darkness reflected on the religious leaders' character.

22:54-65 DENIALS AND BEATINGS
Matthew began his passion account with the beating of Jesus by the soldiers (Matt. 26:67). Luke's passion account started out with the denials of Peter and was followed by the beatings. Luke's account tells the reader that Peter denied Jesus to his face (Luke 22:61). The place was the house of Caiaphas (22:54; cf. Matt. 26:57). The crowing of the rooster or cock (Luke 22:61) signified the end of the third night watch, 12:00 to 3:00 A.M.

22:66–23:25 BEFORE PRIESTS AND KINGS
The "council" (22:66) was a reference to the Sanhedrin, the highest court of the Jews. Jesus made an undeniable affirmation of his deity (22:70). The listeners understood his claim and wanted to put him to death. Since the Sanhedrin had no authority to execute the death penalty, the case had to be brought before the Roman authorities (23:1). Pilate was the Roman prefect, or governor, of Judea (A.D. 26–36). The case the Jews made against Jesus concerning Jesus' opposition to Roman taxes (23:2) was a distortion of the truth (cf. 20:20-26). The "Herod" (23:7) mentioned was Herod Antipas, ruler of Galilee and Perea (4 B.C.– A.D. 39) who had murdered John the Baptist. Herod Antipas had no authority to decide the case against Jesus. The gesture was politically motivated and resulted in better relations between Pilate and Herod Antipas (23:12). The robe (23:11) signified for Pilate that Herod thought Jesus' claim to be king was a joke and not to be taken as a serious threat to the rule of Rome (23:13-15). Many manuscripts omitted 23:17. It may have been inserted to explain

the basis for the release of Barabbas (23:18, 25). Luke made it plain that Jesus was innocent of any crime (23:14, 20, 22).

23:26-56 Crucifixion and Burial
Simon (23:26) was from Cyrene, the chief city of Cyrenaica in North Africa. The women were weeping for the wrong reason. The suffering of the Righteous One was only a foreshadowing of the awful persecution of the saints and the judgments of God that would happen in the future. Compare 23:30 with Hosea 10:8 and Revelation 6:16. The cryptic words of Luke 23:31 may mean: "If they act so shamefully when the nation ('tree') is prospering ('green'), how will they act during times of difficulty ('dry')?" For the same imagery, see Ezekiel 20:47.

"The Skull" (Luke 23:33) is a translation of the Aramaic term "Golgotha" (cf. Matt. 27:33). "Wine vinegar" (Luke 23:36; "sour wine," NASB; "vinegar," KJV) was a common drink often used by laborers and soldiers. "Paradise" (23:43) was derived from the Persian word for a "king's garden." It was used here by Jesus to refer to heaven, the dwelling place of God. The "sixth" (23:44) hour referred to noon. Again, Jesus' righteousness was stressed (23:41, 47). Jesus also framed his last words in the words of Psalm 31:5. All had happened according to the Scriptures. The "curtain" (Luke 23:45; "veil," NASB and KJV) separated the Holy Place from the Most Holy Place. According to Josephus it was ninety feet high. Its tearing symbolized the opening up of the Most Holy Place, which symbolized God's very presence, to the saints of Jesus Christ (Heb. 10:19-20).

Joseph (Luke 23:50-51), a member of the Sanhedrin, was from Arimathea, a town of uncertain location. The term "Preparation Day" (23:54) referred to Friday, the day of preparation for the Sabbath rest that began Friday at sunset. The commandment not to work on the Sabbath (23:56) is found in Exodus 20:10.

24:1-53 The Resurrection
24:1-12 AT THE TOMB
The reports of Jesus' resurrection were first met with disbelief (Luke 24:11). In 24:6-8 Luke reveals the reason for Jesus' passion

predictions. They were to give assurance that his death was according to God's plan. That was the assurance Luke set out to give to his readers (1:4). The "first day of the week" referred to Sunday. It was customary in ancient Palestine to use a circular stone about one foot thick as the door for a tomb (24:2). It was rolled along a groove in the rock to seal the tomb.

24:13-35 ON THE ROAD
These verses are unique to Luke. One of the "two" (24:13) disciples was identified as Cleopas (24:18). The other, perhaps his wife, was not identified. If this Cleopas was the same person as mentioned in John 19:25, his wife was named Mary. "Emmaus" (24:13) was said to be "seven miles" (lit., "sixty stadia") from Jerusalem. The traditional site of 'Amwas is approximately twenty miles from Jerusalem. Perhaps a better location is el-Qubeibeh situated just sixty-three stadia or seven miles north of Jerusalem (see introductory map). The site is marked by the ruins of a Crusader basilica and perhaps a Byzantine church. Jesus' appearance to Simon Peter (Luke 24:34) was also mentioned in 1 Corinthians 15:5. The point of this story was to show why people might not believe that Jesus had been raised from the dead—fool-ishness and slowness to believe the word of God (Luke 24:25).

24:36-53 IN JERUSALEM
Again, Jesus' appearance was designed to dispel all doubt that he had risen from the dead (24:38-39). The certainty Luke desired to build in his readers was rooted in understanding how the Old Testament spoke of the Messiah (24:44-47). Many Greek manuscripts do not contain 24:40. Jesus alluded to the common Jewish divisions of the Old Testament: the Law of Moses, the Prophets, and the Psalms which were representative of the Writings. Luke ended his book where he began it—in the temple. This time the disciples were in the temple praising God and waiting for the power of the Spirit to come. "What my Father has promised" (24:49) was a reference to the promise of the Holy Spirit, an event that was realized at Pentecost (cf. Acts 1:1-4; 2:33). "Bethany" (Luke 24:50) was located about half a mile from Jerusalem, just east of the Mount of Olives. Luke recorded the details of Jesus' ascension (24:50-53) in Acts 1:6-11 and the coming of the Holy Spirit in Acts 2:1-42.

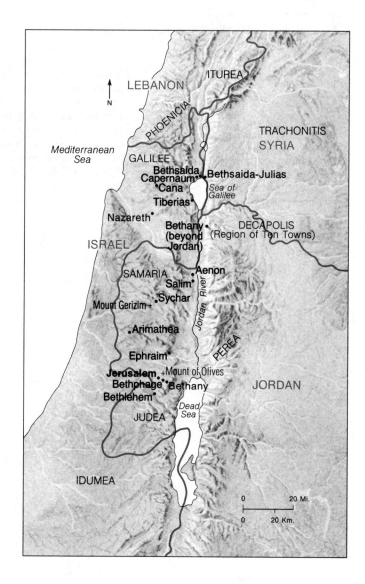

John

BASIC FACTS

HISTORICAL SETTING

The uncertainties in dating the book (see below) make a discussion of the precise historical setting difficult. The book's contents placed the earthly life of Jesus the Messiah into the context of his eternal preexistence. He was with the Father; he came to earth; and then he returned to the Father. Historically, this revelation spoke against criticisms that Jesus was just a mortal man or that he was just a man who was, for a time, empowered by God. John's desire to convince his readers to "believe" in Jesus' divine Messiahship was not only appropriate in John's day but is appropriate in any historical setting. He desired both believers and unbelievers to allow the signs that Jesus performed to reveal his eternal glory and create initial or deeper faith.

AUTHOR

Although the Gospel of John is anonymous, both internal and external evidence point to John the apostle, the son of Zebedee, as the author of the work. From internal evidence it is clear that the author was a Palestinian Jew, for he quoted the Old Testament (John 6:45; 13:18; 19:37), and had first hand knowledge of Palestine's geography (1:44; 2:1; 5:2; 9:7; 11:18). The author was an eyewitness of the events he recorded (1:29, 35, 43; 2:6; 4:40, 43; 5:5; 12:1, 6, 12). John 21:20, 24 indicates that the author was the "disciple whom Jesus loved," the one who leaned on Jesus' breast at the Passover supper (cf. 13:23; 19:26; 20:2; 21:7). The author was one of the inner circle Jesus' disciples. This group was comprised of Peter and the brothers James and John, the sons of Zebedee (13:23, 24; 20:2-10; 21:2, 7, 20). Since James was martyred not long after Jesus' ascension (Acts 12:1-5), and Peter appears as a different person from the beloved disciple (John 21:7), only John is left to be the beloved disciple and author of the Gospel.

External evidence from the time of the church fathers has confirmed the authorship by the apostle John. Irenaeus (A.D. 120–202) wrote, "Afterwards, John, the disciple of the Lord, who also had leaned upon his breast, did himself publish a gospel during his residence at Ephesus in Asia" (*Against Heresies,* 3.1.1). As for the reliability of Irenaeus, Eusebius said that his authority was Polycarp (A.D. 70–155/160) who had personally known John the apostle (*Historia Ecclesiastica,* 4.14). Theophilus of Antioch (A.D. 115–188), Clement of Alexandria (A.D. 190), Origen (c. A.D. 220), and Hippolytus (A.D. 170) all agree that John wrote this Gospel.

DATE

The discovery of the Rylands fragment of John's Gospel in Egypt (dated c. A.D. 135) requires that the date of John be sometime in the first century. Some scholars suggest that the Gospel was written around A.D. 85–90. They would argue that John's Gospel was written after the other Gospels as a supplement to them. But John's lack of reference to the fall of Jerusalem in A.D. 70 may indicate a date of writing some time before that event.

Some scholars conclude that the Gospel should be dated before A.D. 70. They feel that John wrote as if he had not seen Matthew, Mark, or Luke's Gospels. They also note that John referred to the followers of Jesus as "disciples" rather than "apostles" ("apostles" being a later designation). Perhaps the strongest argument for a date before A.D. 70 is in 5:2 where John wrote "there *is* . . . a pool," not "there *was* a pool." This may indicate a composition before the fall of Jerusalem (A.D. 70). Later in 18:1 he wrote, "there was a garden," probably referring to the King's Garden that was located just outside the city. These verb tenses would allow John's writing before or even during the time Jerusalem was under siege by the Romans, but before the city had actually been destroyed (c. A.D. 68–69). However, precise dating of the book is not necessary to appreciate its many contributions to the Christian's life of faith.

PURPOSE

The Gospel of John was designed to convince those who had not seen Jesus to believe in him (John 20:29-31). Believers were to read John's Gospel to bring about a deepening of their faith. Unbelievers were to read it so that they might come to believe in Jesus Christ. Both groups were addressed through John's arrangement of Jesus' signs, which progressively ascended in importance to the resurrection of Lazarus and then to Jesus' own resurrection. The reader was to receive the spiritual bread, drink, light, and life that Jesus offered.

GEOGRAPHY AND ITS IMPORTANCE

Although Jesus moved in the surrounding areas, John's major geographical focus was on Jerusalem. Jesus always returned to Jerusalem, specifically, to participate in various temple feasts. He returned from the Jordan and Cana of Galilee to the Feast of the Passover (John 2). His trip to the Jordan, Samaria, and Cana of Galilee ended with his return to another, unknown feast in Jerusalem (John 5). John even linked Jesus' feeding of the five thousand in the wilderness to the Feast of the Passover in Jerusalem (John 6:4-5). Jesus returned to Jerusalem for the feasts of Tabernacles (John 7) and Dedication (John 10). After raising Lazarus in Bethany (John 11), which was just over the Mount of Olives from Jerusalem, Jesus returned to Jerusalem for his final Passover (John 12). The geographical focus on Jerusalem and its feasts undergirds

John's purpose to reveal that Jesus was the fulfillment of all the feasts and, especially, represented the perfect Passover Lamb of God. Around him alone, not the temple with its festivals, are believers to worship, celebrate, and find their redemption.

GUIDING CONCEPTS

JOHN'S COMMENTARY ON GENESIS 1

In his Gospel, John stressed the creative and powerful Word of God. Jesus himself was the Word (1:1). And when he spoke, his word was powerful to create and redeem. That pattern of creation by God's Word relates back to Genesis 1 and the creation of the world. John 1:1-13 takes up the themes of Genesis 1 and applies them to Jesus the Messiah. As the Word, Christ existed before the creation in close relationship to God and was himself God (John 1:1). He was the agent of creation (1:3). He was light in the darkness (1:4-5), and that light was symbolic of life itself (1:4). Jesus, the Life, was connected to God's Word, the Creator (1:4), and was given as the Mediator by which all men could have true life as children of God (1:12). As the Word created the world in the beginning, Jesus the Word came to re-create what had been broken by sin.

Throughout Scripture there is a relationship between wisdom and creation (1:3; cf. Prov. 8:22). Proverbs makes it clear that wisdom was at God's side at creation as a master workman (Prov. 8:22; cf. also Col. 1:16; 2:2-3). The first creation saw light separated from the darkness and brought both physical and spiritual life. The new creation account portrayed by John shows the light in the midst of darkness—a light not from the sun or stars, but from the presence of eternal life itself.

The "world" is presented in John 1:1-18 as all that is opposed to the "Word," Jesus the Messiah (1:10). In 3:16, the world that opposed Jesus is shown to be the very thing he came to save. For the Greek Gentiles, the Word represented the rational principle of the universe and the link between God and man. In Jewish usage, the Word was understood as the effective word of God and was sometimes used as a reverential substitute for his holy name. John 1 serves as a commentary on Genesis 1, but it also points toward a second creation by the Word by which the first creation would be redeemed. Creation themes of "Word," "light," and "life" all find their fulfillment in the life of Jesus the Messiah.

SIGNS AND BELIEF

John began and ended his Gospel by presenting events within the context of one-week periods. John counted out some of the days that represent the first one-week period (1:28, day one; 1:29, day two; 1:35, day three; 1:43, day four; 2:1, the seventh day, three days after the day mentioned in 1:43). The seventh day contains the first of Jesus' seven pre-resurrection signs or miracles—the creation of wine out of water. It is as if John wanted his readers to recognize in the life and works of Jesus a reenacted seven-day creation account (cf. Gen. 1); this time the new creation would be worked by Jesus the Messiah as he made possible his Father's offer of eternal life. At the end of the Gospel John detailed another week (12:1); one that would end with the resurrection of the Light of Life (20:1).

Only John called Jesus' miracles "signs." He recounted seven signs that were performed before Jesus' death and resurrection: (1) the turning of water into wine at Cana (2:1-11); (2) the healing of the official's son (4:46-54); (3) the healing at the Bethesda pool (5:1-15); (4) the feeding of the multitude (6:5-14); (5) the walk on water (6:16-21); (6) the healing of the blind man (9:1-12); and (7) the raising of Lazarus (11:1-44). These signs formed the backbone of John's presentation of the person of Jesus. They revealed Jesus' character as the Son of God and were designed to cause the reader to believe in his glory (2:11, 23; 4:48; 11:47-48; 12:37; 20:30-31). A sign points away from itself to something else. In the case of Jesus, the signs he performed pointed to his glory, a glory that would be transferred from himself to those who believed in him (17:20-22).

MISUNDERSTANDINGS IN JOHN

Throughout the book, John showed his readers how people misunderstood the words and actions of Jesus. Jesus taught his audience by using illustrations from things they understood in order to reveal things they did not understand. He used the ordinary physical things of life to teach them about God and the eternal kingdom he promised. He came as a man so that he might truly and clearly reveal the nature of God. The misunderstandings of Jesus' listeners concerned: (1) the identification of Jesus' body with the temple of God (2:18-22); (2) the possibility of a second and spiritual birth (3:3); (3) the nature of spiritual, living water (4:10); (4) the nature of a spiritual bread of obedience to God (4:32); (5) the authority of Jesus (5:44-47); (6) the nature of the true bread of life (6:30-36); and (7) the true origin of Jesus (7:25-29).

In all these misunderstandings there was movement from the physical to the spiritual. The misunderstandings took place when the people failed to move beyond a merely physical understanding of Jesus' words to a spiritual understanding; from seeing the outer meaning to discovering the inner one; from knowing Jesus, the man, to knowing Jesus, the Son of God. The purpose of the signs and witness of Jesus was to help those who saw and heard him to see beyond the physical miracles, like the turning of water into wine, to see that to which those signs pointed—the presence of the creative Word of God to bring eternal life. These "misunderstandings" are related to the theme of "incomprehension" examined in Mark (see the Guiding Concepts section for the book of Mark).

BIBLE-WIDE CONCEPTS

THE WILDERNESS

John showed how Jesus reenacted and fulfilled several Old Testament events and concepts. Most of these came from the exodus and wilderness period of Israel's history. Jesus was presented as the true tabernacle (1:14); the true bronze serpent (3:14); the true manna of God (6:49-50); the true rock of water (7:37-38); the true light of the cloud of glory (8:12); and the true Passover Lamb (1:29; 19:14). These links of Jesus to Israel's wilderness experience showed that the promises that had been made to Israel were fulfilled in him. On the one hand, the subtlety and pervasiveness of these themes from Israel's past mark John's gospel as deeply Jewish in origin. On the other hand, his roots in the creation of the world (cf. John 1 and Gen. 1) mark John out as vastly universal in scope. And that is as it should be. From the beginning, God promised that all nations would be blessed, but that that blessing would come through the Jewish line of Abraham (Gen. 12:3).

BELIEF

Ever since the Garden of Eden humans have been responsible to believe what God tells them. Abraham believed God and acted upon his word (Gen. 15:6). Israel in the wilderness was given several tests of belief (cf. Deut. 8:1-3). Throughout the history of the Bible, belief was defined as trust that leads to obedience (Ps. 78:21-31). Behind the Hebrew verb for "believe" stood the ideas of stability, reliability, and faithfulness. Believers can believe in God because he is stable and faithful, but God also calls believers to be faithful and worthy of trust as well. The book of John was designed to enable belief (John 20:30-31). It was not just a tool for evangelism; it was also designed to strengthen the belief of those who already believed. For the one who already had eternal life, the Gospel of John would serve to increase the power and experience of life in Jesus Christ. The signs he presented were to convince his readers to believe and rely upon Jesus as the Son of God—the provider of eternal life.

NEEDS MET BY JOHN

John wrote to believers who were suffering persecution and conflict. Different groups within the early Christian church held faulty ideas about who Jesus was, and unbelievers from outside the church also persecuted the Christians. John provided comfort and faith-strengthening answers to questions about where Jesus came from, why he was rejected by most people while he was on earth, how he was with believers in Spirit though bodily absent, and where he would take believers in the future. The structure and content of John's Gospel show that his readers were asking the following questions.

- How is Jesus related to the beginnings of the world?
- What does Jesus have to say about the present sufferings of believers?
- Why does the world reject Jesus if he really is the Son of God?
- How is God's glory revealed on earth today?
- What does it really mean to have eternal life?
- What is the believer's relationship to Jesus and to God?
- What is Jesus' relationship to his Father in heaven?
- Where is Jesus going to finally take those who believe in him?

Jesus' physical absence after his resurrection and the perceived delay of his kingdom is always a potential crisis for his followers. Where is God? How can those who seek him see his glory in the midst of day-to-day life? Continually, the New Testament writers try to increase the faith of Jesus' followers by making God's presence more vivid and real. But the visions of faith are easily overcome by the all too real visions of the world. With this problem in mind, John's Gospel reveals a Jesus who first existed in glory before the world's creation, then in a humble life on earth, and finally in resurrected glory forever at God's right hand. To the question of how believers can see Christ's invisible glory today, John's Gospel replies that the glory is seen in the lives of Jesus' followers—in their love for each other and their witness to the world. The Spirit is with them and is making God's glory known to the world.

But John's Gospel speaks to another more pressing question. If Jesus was God's glory and believers now share in that glory, why does the world hate Jesus and his followers? John helped his readers to understand world hatred and to cope with rejection and suffering. The heart of this understanding centers on defining what is the best kind of life. John showed that the best life is eternal and related to the life of God that flows out through Christ. The stark contrast of eternal life with the world's limited life should help believers cope with worldly problems. They can view all short-lived human problems from the perspective of eternity. Jesus is not physically present, but believers are not alone. As they let the Gospel of John increase their belief, their faith will find deep roots and steadfastness in the vision of Christ's glory at God's right hand and in his believing church on earth.

OUTLINE OF JOHN

JOHN NOTES

1:1-18 THE POSSIBILITY OF WITNESS IS EXPLAINED

Overview: The function of the prologue was to show how the hidden Word of God was able to be known; how the Word moved from hiddenness into openness; how the Word was able to be observed and spoken about. Three sets of key words progressively show how the knowledge of God came through Jesus. The first set of words concerns Christ's existence before the world and his life-giving power (1:1-4: "was," "with," "through," "life"). The second set shows Christ's reception in the world and the results of rejecting or accepting him (1:5-13: "has not understood," "light," "witness," "receive," "believe," "children of God"). The third set of words shows how the message about Christ was transmitted from the original eyewitnesses to the ever larger circle of believers (1:14-18: "we have seen his glory," "testifies," "received," "grace and truth," "made him known"). Each of the three sections of the prologue was designed to show how the coming of Jesus enables believers to know the Father. The knowledge of the Father through the Son was the foundation of the book's evangelistic purpose (20:30-31).

1:1-5 From Unknown to Known

The term "Word" was an established philosophical concept that John used, added to, and enriched, to communicate the nature of Jesus Christ. John's presentation of the "Word" incorporates both Greek and Jewish ideas.

Philo, the Alexandrian Jew who sought to bring about a synthesis of Greek philosophy with Old Testament thought, used the concept of the "word" to denote how God created and communicated with the material world. In keeping with Greek thought, Philo conceived of the philosophical "word" as a bridge between the transcendent holy God and the material evil universe. To the Greek of the first century, the word was a mediating principle between God and the world of created matter.

But John's usage of the term was also centrally located in the Old Testament Scripture's account concerning God and creation. Using the concept of the "Word," points

were made in 1:1 concerning Christ's eternal existence, relationship to the Father, and character as God. Jesus the Messiah was the "Word," the Creator, come to bring about the redemption of the fallen creation—to re-create what had been broken by sin. John used the concept of the powerful and creative Word, a concept familiar to both Jews and Greeks, and gave it greater meaning, identifying the Word as the divine Person, Jesus, who came to reveal God to man. He was God's creative presence, present to redeem what had fallen into the bondage of sin and to mediate between the Creator and creation.

In the Old Testament the "word of God" is often personified as an instrument for doing God's will (Pss. 33:6; 107:20; 119:89; 147:15). Jesus, the Word, came to earth expressly to do God's will by bringing about God's plan for redemption. John repeats the statement that Christ was with God in order to show his close relationship with God (1:2). Jesus, the Word, was the creative and effective extension of God, given to show God's love to lost mankind.

In Genesis 1 God spoke (his word) and the entire universe came into being. In the Bible generally, the "Word" is the personification of God's revelation. Throughout Scripture *creation* and *salvation* are closely linked as forms of God's self-revelation (1:3). God revealed himself first as Creator (Gen. 1) and then as Redeemer or Re-creator in the person of Jesus Christ. John presents Christ's work as the beginning of a new creation. Similarly, Paul calls the Christian a "new creation" in Christ (2 Cor. 5:17).

The themes of light and life, both describing God's work in the creation, are related to the person of Christ (1:4-5). Light shines in the darkness of creation. Light was the first element (cf. Gen. 1). All that will follow in John's account of Christ's life is done with a comparison of the creation account of Genesis in mind. For example, the first miracle, the sign of water changed into wine, receives the evaluation of "very good" by the master of the banquet (2:10). That parallels God's evaluation of his creation in Genesis 1 where he calls all "very good" (Gen. 1:31). In addition, this miracle comes as the culmination of a week of creative activity by Jesus the "Word," further paralleling the Genesis account (see "Signs and Belief" in the Guiding Concepts section).

"Light" and "darkness" (1:5) are frequently used metaphors in John's Gospel. Jesus was the source of spiritual light (cf. 8:12; 9:5). "Darkness" referred to the realm of spiritual evil—the satanic world system set against God (1:5; 3:19; 8:12). John tells his readers right at the beginning of his Gospel that the darkness could not extinguish the light of Christ.

1:6-13 John the Baptist: Witness and Belief

The function of John 1:6-13 is to explain how the "world" did not comprehend Jesus the Messiah. The "man" (1:6) was John the Baptist (cf. Luke 1:5-17). John the Baptist's purpose was to be a witness to the world (1:29, 36; note the repetition of witness in 1:7-8). John 1:7 has the first of ninety-eight occurrences of the word "believe" in the Gospel of John. The word essentially means "trust" and suggests not just an intellectual agreement with facts, but a committed reliance upon the truth concerning Jesus. "Light" (1:9) is here used differently than in Matthew 4:16, where Isaiah 9:2 is quoted. Matthew and John both suggest a close relationship between light and life as the remedy for darkness and death. But while Matthew portrays light as the dawning of the Messiah's presence near the end of the age, John presents light as the dawn of the original creation light and the first burst of mankind's life upon the earth.

Three connected statements (1:10) centered on the "world" reveal the good news of God's presence in the "world" (the incarnation) and the tragedy of the "world's" rejection of that presence. The only birth narrative about which John was concerned is in 1:12-13. He was concerned with the Christian's spiritual birth, not Jesus' physical birth. To "receive" (1:13) is to believe—a belief that results in a new birth into God's family.

1:14-18 The Object of Witness Enters the World

The section 1:14-18 makes the point that God took on human flesh in the person of Jesus. Jesus came to reveal and explain the nature of God (1:18), and everything he said

and did revealed something of the nature of God the Father. John 1:14-18 serves as a bridge from the prologue to the narrative of Jesus' life. It shows that Jesus was a reliable representative of God the Father and that because of his presence among men, the record of which is to follow in the rest of the book, the believer can also bear witness to God's work on mankind's behalf. It also reveals that the circle of witnesses to the powerful work of God is exclusive. Not everyone is able to bear witness, but only those who have seen and believed God's glory and witness through Jesus.

The incarnation of the Word is observed (1:14). This is a reference to the tabernacle in the wilderness and its link to glory. The Greek word translated "lived for a while" pictures living in a tent. Jesus, in becoming a man, tented on earth with the rest of mankind. John systematically shows how Jesus fulfilled many of the events of God's glory to Israel in the wilderness of Sinai (see "The Wilderness" in the Bible-Wide Concepts section for John). This suggests that this little reference to Jesus' glory being seen while he "tented among us" is a reference to how Jesus was the fullness of what was begun when God's glory tented with Israel in the tabernacle in the wilderness. Some examples of how John speaks of glory are: 1:14; 2:11; 5:41, 44; 7:18, 39; 8:50, 54; 9:24; 11:4, 40; 12:16, 23, 28, 41, 43; 13:31; 14:13; 16:14; 17:1, 4-5, 10, 22, 24; 21:19. The most frequent occurrence of the word is in John 17. The term "one and only" (1:14, 18; "only begotten," NASB and KJV) is best understood as implying "unique" or "one-of-a-kind" (cf. Heb. 11:17 where the same word is used of Isaac, not Abraham's only son, but his unique, special son of promise).

The mention of Moses, the law, and grace is a supporting witness to the greatness of Jesus Christ (1:16-17). This is the introduction to the wilderness concept in John (see Bible-Wide Concepts). In the Old Testament God sometimes displayed his glory by a vision (Isa. 6:1) or in some physical way (Exod. 34:5-8; Judg. 13:22). But through the person of Jesus Christ, God would make himself known in a new and personal way (1:18). Compare the revelation of God in Jesus Christ with his revelation in Exodus 33:7-8, 10-11, 20, 23.

But God is spirit (cf. John 4:24) and has no physical body. Jesus, in his incarnation, is the most complete revelation of the Father. This is the climax of John's introduction (1:18). Moses never really saw God, but Jesus did. And Jesus, as God's incarnate Son, revealed to mankind the very person of God. He is the bridge between God and man. This is the foundation of Christian faith—God revealed and explained in the person of the Messiah, Jesus.

1:19–2:11 A WEEK OF WITNESS: THE SIGNS BEGIN
1:19-42 John's Witness
1:19-28 THE WITNESS TO THOSE IN DARKNESS
1:19-23 John functions as a witness to the Light. The "Jews" (1:19) were the religious leaders in Jerusalem who had heard about his preaching and baptism of repentance. They wanted to know how John saw himself in relationship to God's prophetic program. John denied being "Elijah" (1:21), yet the angel Gabriel (Luke 1:17) and Jesus (Matt. 11:10, 14; 17:10-13) clearly view John as fulfilling the Malachi 3:1 and 4:5 prophecies of Elijah's return. If Jesus confirmed John's identification with Elijah, why did John himself deny it? Since the Jews of the first century believed that Elijah would actually return in the flesh, John denied being the physically reincarnated Elijah that they anticipated. Although he did fulfill the prophecy of Malachi 3:1 and 4:5, he did so in an unexpected way. He came and ministered in "the spirit and power of Elijah" (Luke 1:17). In 1:23 John quotes Isaiah 40:3 with reference to the place and purpose of his ministry.

1:24-28 The identity of the coming One. There is here no explicit reference to Jesus' "Holy Spirit and fire" baptism mentioned, for example, in Matthew 3:11. John simply notes the surpassing worth of the One to come, a worth that forms the basis for John's witness in John 1:33. This Bethany (1:28), the place where John baptized, is distinguished from the Bethany near Jerusalem (cf. Mark 11:1). The Bethany where John baptized was a village east of the Jordan about five miles north of the Dead Sea. The changing course and flooding of the Jordan over the years has completely

obliterated the site so that no ruins exist today (see 3:22, 26; 4:1-2; 10:40).

1:29-34 THE WITNESS TO THE LIGHT
The actual event of Jesus' baptism was not mentioned by John. The writer's focus was on the witness to Jesus' identity as Son and Lamb of God. The phrase "Lamb of God" (1:29) contains much Old Testament imagery, taking the Jewish mind back to Genesis 22:8 when Abraham said, "God himself will provide the lamb." A ram was provided as a substitute for Isaac, but God's Lamb was yet to come.

The Passover lamb (Exod. 12:3) pointed the way to the full and final provision of God's sacrificial Lamb, Jesus (1 Cor. 5:7). John did not emphasize the repentance element of John the Baptist's preaching. Instead, he emphasized Jesus as the one on whom the Holy Spirit would remain—the very Son of God, who would baptize in the Spirit.

1:35-42 THE WITNESS TO THE DISCIPLES
Compare this event with Matthew 16:13-20. From the first meeting, Jesus was identified as the Messiah and had identified Simon as Peter (1:41-42). The "tenth hour" (1:39) would refer to 4:00 P.M. by Jewish reckoning. The Hebrew term "Messiah" (1:41) means "Anointed One" and was translated into the Greek as "Christ." "Cephas" (1:42) was an Aramaic name; "Peter" was the same name in Greek. Both words mean "stone."

1:43–2:11 Jesus' Initial Witness
1:43-51 HIS CAPACITY AS REVEALER OF HEAVEN'S GLORY
This section shows the growth of the results of Jesus' witness. Bethsaida (1:44), also known as Bethsaida-Julias, was a double site with a fishing village on the shore of the Sea of Galilee about one and a half miles south of the fortified city. It was located just east of the Jordan near the northeast shore of the Sea of Galilee. Nazareth (1:46) was not highly regarded because it was not even mentioned in the Old Testament and because it was in the immediate proximity of Sepphoris, the old Roman capital of Galilee. Nathanael, not Peter, was the first to identify Jesus as the divine "Son of God" and "King of Israel" (1:49). He was the first to recognize what John the apostle was trying to communicate in his Gospel (cf. 20:30-31).

The focus in this section was on Jesus' origin, not on his exact links to the law and prophets. His hometown origin, Nazareth, became insignificant in the light of his supernatural origin, recognized by Nathanael. Exactly what happened between Philip and Nathanael under the fig tree is not important The point was that Jesus had been supernaturally there and already knew Nathanael (1:48-49).

Jesus described the "greater things" (1:50) in terms of Jacob's ladder at Bethel (1:50-51; cf. Gen. 28:11-17). Jesus was making the point that he was the revealer of heavenly things and the medium through whom heaven and earth would meet. Jesus was the one who would fulfill Jacob's dream, providing access and communication between God and man. The words "I tell you the truth" occur twenty-five times in John and nowhere else. They serve to introduce a truth of special solemnity or importance.

2:1-11 HIS CAPACITY DEMONSTRATED IN THE FIRST SIGN

In the dialogue between Jesus and Mary (2:1-5), no disrespect was intended in Jesus' use of the term "woman." The word simply meant "madam." The phrase "Why do you involve me?" (see a similar phrase used in Matt. 8:29; Mark 1:24; 5:7; and Luke 8:28) indicates a new relationship between Jesus and his mother. Cana (John 2:1) was located in Galilee, a three day's walk (about seventy-five miles) from Bethany (see introductory map). The exact site is debated. Kefr Kenna is popularly regarded by tourists as the place of Jesus' miracle, but there is little substantial evidence for this recent tradition. The better choice is Khirbet Kana, about nine miles north of Nazareth. This identification is supported by geographical references in Josephus, archaeological evidence, and early pilgrim itineraries.

The concept of Jesus' "time" (2:4) relates to the time for a display of his Messianic powers and glory either by miracle or by death and resurrection (cf. 7:6, 8, 30; 8:20; 12:23, 27; 13:1; 17:1). The water had been brought for the "ceremonial washing" (2:6), the ritual cleansing of hands before eating (cf. Mark 7:1-4). The word "wine" (2:9) refers to an alcoholic beverage. There is some doubt that Jesus would have made an intoxicating drink. But that is a cultural,

not a moral, problem. Wine was the most frequently used beverage in the first century. Also, wine was commonly diluted, one part wine to three parts water. It was considered barbaric to drink undiluted wine.

Jesus' miracle should be understood in light of kingdom expectations. According to Joel 3:18, the mountains of Judah will "drip new wine" in the Messianic kingdom. Jesus' miracle was a sign of his Messiahship and a foretaste of kingdom blessings. The master of the banquet was quoted (2:10) to show how good the wine was. That qualitative evaluation was the key to this miracle. It was "very good," like God's creation in Genesis 1. That creative act displayed Jesus' glory. This revealed glory would result in belief for those who witnessed it. His glory was manifested to show people what the Father is like (cf. John 1:18).

In the Bible, creation is linked to salvation and God's communication of blessing. In his Gospel, John bore witness to the Creator at work; light in the darkness was forming a "new creation" through the work of his glorious Son (cf. 1 Cor. 5:17). The good wine was the first example of the Creator's presence and the goodness of his second creation. This was the first sign (2:11), that is, there were more to come. The signs of bread, healings, and resurrection life were still ahead.

2:12–4:54 JERUSALEM, SAMARIA, AND BACK TO CAPERNAUM: A SECOND SIGN
2:12–3:21 To Jerusalem
2:12-25 PASSOVER

2:12 The stay in Capernaum. Capernaum, a fishing village and tax collection station, was located along the northwest shore of the Sea of Galilee.

2:13-22 The cleansing of the Jerusalem temple. The temple businessmen were selling animals and changing money so that the worshipers would have supposedly "pure" offerings. Some of the money was used for the offerings and some for the temple tax. Note the two things remembered (2:17, 22): (1) the Scriptures (Ps. 69:9 quoted in John 2:17) and (2) Jesus' words. This event clearly shows the transfer of significance from the temple to the body of Christ.

This "Passover" (2:13) has been dated April 7, A.D. 30. The Passover Feast commemorated the deliverance of Israel from Egypt (cf. Exod. 12) and foreshadowed Jesus' sacrificial death on the cross (1 Cor. 5:7). This is the first of two temple cleansings—one at the beginning and the other at the end of Jesus' ministry (cf. Matt. 21:12-17).

Herod began to refurbish the Jerusalem temple in 20/19 B.C. (2:20), and while the sanctuary was completed after one and a half years of work, the project was not finished until around A.D. 63. The "forty-six years" (2:20) was the period during which the sanctuary had stood. The question would probably be better translated, "How can you destroy and rebuild in a mere three days such a structure which has stood for forty-six years?"

2:23-25 Summary of his ministry: aspects of trust. John showed that the basis of trust was in knowing the trustworthiness of the object of that trust. Jesus revealed his distrust of the crowds that had begun to follow him. Jesus came to reveal the Father, not to rely on humans. Although humans might believe, Jesus did not trust in them because of the witness he had regarding humans. Jesus saw this belief, based only on miracles, as superficial (2:24). He did not trust himself to these people and accept them as his disciples. The only fame he sought was in doing the will of his Father (4:34).

3:1-21 JESUS IS THE UNIQUE SON, NOT ANOTHER TEACHER
Jesus' encounter with Nicodemus (3:1-21) is related to the preceding verses concerning Jesus' trust of those who followed him (2:23-25). The encounter with Nicodemus was an example of Jesus not entrusting himself to humans. He knew people and knew their need for a new birth. He did not need Nicodemus's authority as a religious leader. He needed to tell him about being born again. John 3:1-21 describes a Jew's questions about Jesus. The section comprises the dialogue of Jesus and Nicodemus (3:1-15) and John's commentary on Jesus' words (3:16-21). John sought to show how entrance into the kingdom came by regeneration (3:1-8). The content of the entire book concerns the offer of a second birth

from God (1:12-13) and the things in this world that try to block that new birth. John 3 is yet another example of the offer and its conflicts. The word "Now" (3:1) ties John 2 and 3 together. The historical context for this conversation is given in 2:23-25, the feasts of Passover and Unleavened Bread.

The Pharisees were a sect of Judaism that came into existence during the intertestamental period. They were middle-class separatists, associated with the synagogue and characterized by legalistic interpretations of the law. Nicodemus was a member of the Sanhedrin, an aristocratic supreme court possessing jurisdiction over the Jews in both civil and religious matters. The signs that Jesus had performed were seen as pointing to God and establishing Jesus as a great teacher but not as the Son of God. But would Nicodemus, or anyone, take the next logical step and learn from this Teacher? That is the question of John's Gospel.

John 3:6 expresses a central theme of the book. The labor of Jesus was to teach the spiritual dimension of life so that, with the difference between flesh and spirit clearly drawn, people might believe in his offer of eternal life. Water and Spirit (3:5) define the "second time" of 3:4 and the "again" of 3:3, 7. The Greek word for "again" is also found in Galatians 4:9 (see "from above" in John 3:31; 19:11).

The concept of being "born again" must also relate to the physical versus spiritual birth from God discussed in 1:12-13. Although the kingdom of God is mentioned (3:3, 5), the concept of eternal life is the most emphasized truth in John's Gospel. Note the emphasis that is made with the statement "I tell you the truth."

The one "born of the Spirit" (3:8) is like the wind to the unregenerate person. The unbeliever does not know the origin of the life that is in him nor his final destiny. God's working in regeneration is not explainable by natural laws. Like the wind, the effects can be seen, but not explained.

Nicodemus struggled with the parables of the new birth (3:9-15). He was locked into thinking on the level of the flesh. But only a new spiritual creation could bring salvation. Jesus had been teaching some of the basic truths about the new covenant (Jer. 31:31-34; Ezek. 36:26-27; Joel 2:28-32), concepts that Nicodemus, "Israel's teacher," should have understood (3:10).

John included in his account an explanation of the relationship between the first and second births (3:11-15). Jesus was qualified to speak of heavenly things because he had been in heaven and was there to share the heavenly glory with humans (3:11). John again brought up the wilderness theme from Israel's history. Jesus' glory would be seen through the humiliation of being lifted up on the cross. What to people was a disgrace, to God would be the manifestation of his glory. The "snake in the desert" (3:14) referred back to Numbers 21 where Moses prepared a bronze serpent to deliver the people from death by poisonous snake bites. The bronze serpent was an Old Testament illustration of the Messiah, Jesus. As the serpent was "lifted up," so would Jesus be lifted up on the cross, that people might look upon him with faith and receive spiritual healing.

In Jesus' elaboration on new birth, belief, and judgment there was a heavy emphasis on personal choice (3:16-21). John 3:20-21 implies the element of free choice and personal responsibility with reference to human actions after the initial confrontation with the light.

3:22-36 To Judea

3:22-30 AUTHORITY TO PURIFY: JOHN'S PARTICIPATION
The section of 3:22-30 describes the dialogue of John the Baptist and a Jew, and 3:31-36 is the apostle John's commentary on John the Baptist's words. The question of 3:25 concerns whose baptism, Jesus' or John's, is approved by God. "Aenon near Salim" (3:23) was a site located near the junction of the Jordan and Jezreel valleys. The site of Salim was located about eight miles south of Scythopolis and Aenon, although the location is uncertain. John the Baptist was later imprisoned by Herod Antipas at Machaerus, a fortress east of the Dead Sea (cf. Matt. 14:1-12). John the Baptist recognized that his place was that of a servant who would of necessity decrease, for it was his place to exalt the Master (John 3:30). John had introduced Jesus and thus had fulfilled his

mission. These are the last words by John the Baptist recorded in this Gospel.

3:31-36 AUTHORITY TO MAKE ALIVE: JESUS' PREEMINENCE
These verses probably come from the mind of the author of this Gospel and again stress the thoughts of 3:6. Jesus was from heaven, stood above all earthly authority, and opened the doors of spiritual understanding and rebirth into eternal life.

4:1-42 To Samaria

Overview: This section links back to the question concerning Jesus' authority and his Jewish opposition (3:25-26). Jesus left Judea and began traveling north to Galilee (4:3-4). While it was common for more scrupulous Jews, like the Pharisees, to travel through Perea (east of the Jordan), Josephus says that some Jewish travelers went through Samaria because it was the most direct route. The necessity ("had to," 4:4) is not directly explained in the text. The results of Jesus' passing through Samaria (4:39-42) indicate that the necessity was related to bringing the word of redemption to the Samaritans. As the "light of the world," it was necessary for Jesus to take his message to Samaria also.

4:1-4 THE TRIP TO SAMARIA
The background of the Samaritans can be found in 2 Kings 17 where it is recorded that after the fall of the northern kingdom in 722 B.C. , the Assyrians exiled the Israelites and brought in foreigners to occupy their land. These foreigners brought their own gods, and a syncretistic religion developed in which the God of Israel was worshiped along with other gods. The Samaritans developed their own Pentateuch in which scribes emended the text to legitimize their place of worship on Mount Gerizim, rather than Jerusalem. The leading Israelites were taken by Sargon. The remaining Jews continued to worship God and maintained close relationships with Judah (see 2 Kings 23:19-20; 2 Chron. 30:1-5; Jer. 41:4-13).

Under the Persian influence in 537 B.C. the returning Jews clashed with the Samaritans concerning the rebuilding of the temple. The drives of Ezra and Nehemiah for the purity of the Israelite race heightened tensions. This may have been the period in which the Samaritans, rejected from Jerusalem, built their own temple on Mount Gerizim.

Around 128 B.C. Jewish forces zealous for the purity of the Jerusalem temple captured Shechem and destroyed the Gerizim temple. In A.D. 6–9 the Samaritans defiled the Jerusalem temple on Passover by scattering bones in the temple precincts. This strife between Jews and Samaritans was not significant to the Romans. Under Roman rule both Jews and Samaritans together suffered Roman oppression.

As far as doctrine and practice were concerned, the Jews viewed the Samaritans as schismatics, not Gentiles. Their main problem was with the Gerizim temple. Here are some New Testament references to the Samaritans: Matthew 10:5-6; Luke 9:52-56; 10:33; 17:16; John 4:7-42; 8:48; Acts 1:8; 9:31; 15:3. In the first century A.D., the relations between the Jews and Samaritans continued to be quite strained. Jews regarded Samaritans as unclean religious apostates.

4:5-30 ANOTHER MISINTERPRETATION: JESUS AS JUST A PROPHET
4:5-9 Jesus is misunderstood as only an ethnic Jew. Sychar (4:5) was located at the modern village of Askar, about half a mile north of Jacob's well. The Old Testament site of Shechem that lies nearby was in ruins at this time. The water of "Jacob's well" (4:6) is noted for its fine quality—cold, pure, and refreshing. It produces a softer water than other springs in the area. The site can be visited today in the crypt of an unfinished church. The "sixth" hour was noon, not the usual time to carry water. Note the irony of the Samaritan woman's statement (4:9) as she mistakes the Creator of the universe for a simple Jewish man.

4:10-12 The source of spiritual "water." The woman, like Nicodemus, must move from thinking on the physical level to the spiritual level. The woman must move from the figure of physical water to its spiritual counterpart, eternal life. The gift of living water relates to the gift of life-giving bread from heaven (6:30-35) and the ongoing theme of Israel in the wilderness. Spiritual thirst and hunger are satisfied by the living water and bread from heaven. The term "living water" (4:10) was a common

reference to spring water in contrast to that which was found in a cistern (cf. Jer. 2:13). Jesus took this common term and filled it with new meaning—spiritual cleansing and refreshment through Christ. The well is 120 to 200 feet deep (John 4:11).

4:13-26 The woman's life is exposed. Jesus exposed the woman's life in order to bring her to the point of receiving the living water (4:13-18). Due to Jesus' insight into her private life the woman thought that he had the divinely given insight characteristic of a prophet (4:19-20). But Jesus raised the issue, not of his identity, but of the location and nature of true worship. Jesus only identified himself as the Messiah (4:26) after the woman herself raised the issue of the coming Messiah (4:25). The Samaritans believed God had designated Mount Gerizim ("this mountain," 4:20) as the proper place for worship. They had built a temple there to rival the worship center in Jerusalem. The Samaritans believed in a coming Messiah who was to be primarily a teacher, a priest, and a restorer of true worship on Mount Gerizim. Jesus articulated the difference between worship that was expressed in external rituals alone and true worship in spirit (4:23). The term "spirit" refers to the sphere of worship. True worship happens when a believer's spirit is connected with God's Spirit, not when a believer is in any particular physical place like Jerusalem or Samaria. God's Spirit is everywhere, therefore worship can happen anywhere. The term "truth" implies that the human worshiper is open and conforming to God's revealed ways of worship and life, specifically Jesus' call to repentance and honest, spiritual worship.

4:27-30 Light exposes darkness. The disciples were surprised that Jesus had been speaking with the woman since it was not the custom for rabbis to converse with women in public (4:27). The woman was tentative as to Jesus being the Messiah (4:29). He had great knowledge—a point that had also impressed Nathanael with Jesus' deity (1:48-49; cf. also 4:39).

4:31-38 MISUNDERSTANDINGS CONCERNING "FOOD" AND "HARVEST"
Jesus used the symbol of food to represent doing God's will (4:34) and used the acts of eating and drinking as symbols of eternal versus earthly life. Jesus made statements

that confused his disciples in order to go on to make his contrasting spiritual points. That same contrast was presented concerning the earthly versus spiritual harvests (4:35). The date may be calculated as January/February, A.D. 31. The grain harvest in April/May would have been four months away.

4:39-42 FIRSTHAND FAITH
The Samaritans believed because they had heard for themselves (see Thomas in 20:29). Their confession is the high point of this story. Jesus is Savior of the world (4:42), not just of a small ethnic handful of Israelites or Samaritans. The universal scope of Jesus' redemption is rooted in his role as Creator and Son of God (cf. 1:1-18).

4:43-54 To Capernaum
4:43-48 SIGNS AND SINCERITY
Jesus again examined the relationship between seeing and believing. Receiving Jesus because of his miracles (4:45) was not the kind of faith Jesus saw as honoring him (4:44). Jesus desired belief based on faith, not just in miracles, but in his word alone (20:29). This explains why the nobleman's request for his son's healing was criticized by Jesus (4:48). The royal official was an officer in the court of Herod Antipas (4 B.C.–A.D. 39), ruler of Galilee. Was it not natural to want his son to live? Certainly. But Jesus used a plural "you" in 4:48. He moved beyond the father and spoke to all his hearers. He knew human hearts and their desire for flashy externals like miracles rather than sincerely taking Jesus at his word. At that moment, heart belief in Jesus was more important than a dying son. For Cana of Galilee (4:46), see note on 2:11.

4:49-54 FAITH IN WORD
AND FAITH IN DEED
The nobleman believed in Jesus' word alone, without proof (4:49-50). When the hour of healing was discovered, the man again believed, having seen the proof of Jesus' word (4:53). The movement was from believing the words of Jesus to seeing and believing the deeds of Jesus. The man first believed in Jesus' word. Then he believed in the deed and character of Jesus. That was a second sign (4:54). This event showed that Jesus' signs were not presented simply for evangelism. They were also for

those who had already believed, yet needed to believe in Jesus on a more deep and sincere level.

5:1–11:57 FROM JERUSALEM TO JERUSALEM: THE FATHER'S WITNESS TO HIS SON
Overview: The section of 5:1–11:57 develops around Jesus' words in 5:21, 24-26, 28-29. In John 5 Jesus moved from the healing of the man by the Bethesda pool to proclaiming a future time when he would call all to a resurrection of life or of judgment (5:28-29). In John 11 Jesus called one man, Lazarus, to a resurrection from the dead. In between, Jesus used several figures to illustrate his ability to give eternal life. Jesus described himself as bread from heaven (6:32, 35, 51); the living water of life (7:38-39); the light of life (8:12; 9:5); the gate and good shepherd 10:9-11; and the resurrection life (11:25-26).

Jesus stressed throughout that his words and actions reflected the nature and will of the Father (5:19-20; 6:46; 7:15-18; 8:26; 9:3-4; 10:18, 37-38) and were the basis for receiving the life he offered. This illustrates the point made in 1:18, that Jesus explained what the Father was like.

5:1-47 The Witness Patterns of the Father in Jesus
Overview: In John 5, the author shows how Jesus redefined the Sabbath day as a time for saving people. He went on to reveal how all that Jesus said and did was a reflection of the Father's will (5:17, 19); every word and deed of Jesus on earth found its source in his Father (5:19, 30). Jesus' glory also found its source in the Father. These verses prepare the reader for Jesus' words in John 17.

5:1-18 A CRISIS: CAN GOD WORK
ON THE SABBATH?
5:1-9 The work is done: a third sign. This feast (5:1) is not identified. It was probably in the fall because the next feast mentioned is the Passover the following spring (6:4). The pool of Bethesda (5:2) was located just north of the temple area near the Sheep Gate (Neh. 3:32) and may have been used for washing sheep before Passover sacrifices.

John 5:4, omitted in many manuscripts, clarifies why there were so many ill people gathered around the pool and the reason behind the sick man's words in 5:7. The questionable material of 5:3-4 may have come to be deleted by a copyist concerned about what seemed to him to be a pagan or superstitious influence. Thus, it can be argued that all of 5:3-4 may have been included in the original manuscripts.

The question "Do you want to get well?" (5:6) was geared to encourage an expression of the man's desire, not his faith. That would come later. Jesus asked the man to get up and walk in order to provide a highly visible sign on the Sabbath (5:9). Jesus wanted to provoke the dialogue with the Jewish leaders concerning what should be allowed on the Sabbath day (5:10-47).

5:10-18 The proposition is stated: God is working. Oral traditions advanced by the Pharisees forbade carrying certain things on the Sabbath (5:10). While Jesus associated the man's sickness with sin, the story of Job illustrates that this is not always the case (5:14). Jesus was criticized by the Jews on two counts: (1) healing on the Sabbath and (2) claiming equality with God (5:18). Had he not intended this, Jesus could have easily corrected their notion. Jesus' startling revelation was that his Father worked on the Sabbath and so Jesus would work as well (5:17). This brings out the true meaning of Sabbath—not inactivity but activity to restore and redeem. Jesus identified himself with the divine worker, and through his work he revealed the nature of God (1:18). Sabbath activity is the same as the saving work of God (cf. Matt. 12:1-8; Mark 2:23-28; Luke 6:5).

5:19-47 THE PATTERN OF JESUS' SONSHIP
5:19-23 Patterned after the Father. Requirements for Sabbath observance were patterned after the example of God the Father who works even on the Sabbath. Jesus quickly moved from his deed of healing on the Sabbath to the hope of resurrection and life (5:21). Greater things (5:20) are life and judgment with a view to honoring the Son's authority. Jesus only did what he saw his Father do. To look at Jesus was to see God the Father in action (1:18). The fact that Jesus did the will of his Father without question established the reason for the glory of his ministry and the stumbling block for those who would not receive him.

5:24-29 Functioning as a judge. In 5:24-29 the "life" and "judgment" offered by Jesus are elaborated. His hearers were not to marvel at his earthly acts like healings or knowledge (5:28) because they simply pointed to the ultimate and eternal resurrections to either life or death (5:29). His hearers already knew about the last judgment. But they would also find out that Jesus would be the one in charge.

5:30-37a The authenticating witness to Jesus. Note the link of 5:30 with 5:19. According to Jewish tradition, self-testimony without supporting witnesses was not regarded as legally valid (5:31). Jesus' witness was not "true" in the sense that it was not legally acceptable in a court of law. But Jesus never intended to be his own authority (5:30). Nor was John the Baptist Jesus' authority (5:33-35). His authority found its source in the Father (5:36-37). It was the Father who gave the works and words to his divine Son, Jesus. Jesus did not receive the witness of people (5:34, 41; cf. 2:24-25). Jesus presented five witnesses to the truth of his divine Person and authority: himself (5:30-31), John the Baptist (5:33-35), his own works or miracles (5:36), the Father (5:37-38), and the Old Testament Scriptures (5:39-47). The greatest witness of the five was the Father's authority (5:36). All of those focus on Jesus as the source of eternal life.

5:37b-47 The people's history of rejecting God's witness. The people had rejected God's witness in history (5:37-38), in word (5:39-40), in true devotion (5:41-42), in self-glory (5:43-44), and in Moses' words (5:45-47). Scriptures that bore witness to the truth of Jesus include Genesis 3:15; 12:1-3; 49:10; Numbers 24:17; and Deuteronomy 18:15-18. The rejection was based on preferring human over divine glory (John 5:43-44), an example of loving darkness instead of light (1:10-11).

6:1-71 The Implications of Bread Developed: The Old Testament and Manna

Overview: The heart of this chapter is Jesus' comparison of his feeding miracle with the manna God gave to Israel in the wilderness after the exodus from Egypt (6:31-32). During the temptations of Jesus (Matt. 4:4), he quoted Deuteronomy 8:3 with reference to making bread in the wilderness. The broader context of Deuteronomy 8:1-3 is crucial for understanding the ongoing significance of manna. The purpose of manna was to test the hearts of the people for faith and obedience to God's ways. The same was true in John 6. Note the use of "humble" in Deuteronomy 8:3; Exodus 10:3; Leviticus 16:29-31; 23:27, 32 (see also Mark 9:20; Exod. 16:4, 8, 12, 15, 22, 32; Ps. 78:24-25).

John 6 focuses on Jesus as the only way to life by election (6:65) and by faith (6:35). Jesus stressed the spiritual over the physical ("I tell you the truth," 6:26, 32, 47, 53), but only those chosen by the Father believed him. The others misunderstood the sign of feeding (6:26) and the Old Testament sign of manna (6:32). Jesus defined true bread as himself and true eating as faith in him (6:35, 47).

6:1-15 THE POPULAR INTERPRETATION OF THE BREAD SIGN

6:1-6 Bread and testing. The miracle of feeding the five thousand took place near the time of Passover, mid-April, A.D. 32. Because the Passover celebration was at hand (6:4), this incident should also be related to the idea of Jesus as the true Passover Lamb (1:29, 36; cf. 1 Cor. 5:7). The feeding of the five thousand took place on the east side of the Sea of Galilee near Bethsaida (Luke 9:10) in a remote place (Mark 6:35). The word "test" in 6:6 was the same word used to describe what Satan did to Jesus in Matthew 4:1. That word was also used in Genesis 22:1 in the Septuagint (the Greek Old Testament) for the testing of Abraham. Jesus intended to test his disciples' insight and faith and to show them that he was the true bread of life.

6:7-9 Two failures of the test: Philip and Andrew. Philip and Andrew did not pass Jesus' test. The people of Israel failed a similar test given to them by Moses in the wilderness (Num. 11:13-15, 20-23). A denarius (John 6:7) was a coin that represented about one day's wage.

6:10-15 The miracle of bread from heaven: a fourth sign. The people associated Jesus (6:14) with the prophet of Deuteronomy 18:15. But they assumed that prophet would break Roman rule over Israel as Moses had

broken Egypt's (1:21; cf. Deut. 18:15; Acts 3:22; 7:37). Jesus withdrew because they had missed the point and not accepted him on his terms. The crowd intended to force him to become king. He knew that this offer of kingship was superficial, motivated by a desire for bread rather than as a result of true recognition of his person. They wanted bread for physical life and independence for political life. But Jesus offered himself as the foundation for a new spiritual and eternal life.

6:16-21 THE SIGN OF WALKING ON WATER: A FIFTH SIGN

John placed this sign in the middle of his discussion of Jesus as the bread of life. It strengthened the disciples' faith. Jesus had just rejected earthly kingship, but he was still full of divine power and greatness. The disciples were crossing from the northeast side of the sea toward Bethsaida (Mark 6:45) with Capernaum on the northwest side of the sea as their destination. Their fears were changed to receptivity when they understood that it was Jesus (John 6:20-21). As God had power over the waters of the Red Sea and the Jordan River in the Old Testament, so his Son had power over the Sea of Galilee.

6:22-71 THE CAPERNAUM SYNAGOGUE: THE FULL INTENTION OF THE BREAD SIGN

6:22-40 Jesus gave a clear invitation to believe and receive. Tiberias (6:23) was the Roman capital of Galilee built between A.D. 18 and 22 by Herod Antipas in honor of the Roman emperor Tiberius. The city was located on the west side of the sea and was famous in ancient times for its hot springs. Jesus' response (6:26) to the people's question (6:25) relates to their mistaken notion that Jesus came to meet all their physical needs. The problem Jesus sought to correct concerned the people's inability to see that the signs he performed pointed not to material prosperity but to spiritual wholeness and eternal life.

The people wanted Jesus to do what Moses did—give them manna (6:30-31). But Jesus helped the people realize that the ultimate source of manna was not Moses, but the Father (6:32). Then he identified himself as the Father's true bread (6:35). For more on the manna in the wilderness, see Exodus 16:15 and Numbers 11:8. Jesus contrasts Moses' manna, which was life sustaining but not life giving. He is the true bread which is life giving and permanently satisfying. Note the phrase "raise them up at the last day" (John 6:39, 40, 44, 54). Throughout, the option of resurrection to eternal life or resurrection to eternal judgment lies behind Jesus' words.

6:41-59 Jewish grumblings over Jesus' origins. The people could not believe Jesus was from heaven because they could only see his earthly parentage. They were grumbling because they were caught up in the "how" of his descent from heaven rather than in his sufficiency (6:42). John 6:45 refers to the time of the new covenant mentioned in Jeremiah 31:34 and also to the universal extension of God's redemption mentioned in the Abrahamic covenant (Gen. 12:3). Jesus' claim that he was the "living bread" (6:51) raised the objection of cannibalism (6:52). Again the people were unable to see beyond the literal, physical meaning of Jesus' words.

The words "eat" and "drink" (John 6:53-54) are figures of speech that denote the operation of the mind or spirit in receiving, understanding, and applying teaching or instruction. People today also think in terms of "digesting" ideas. This does not refer to the Last Supper, which had not yet taken place (cf. Matt. 26:20-29).

6:60-71 The disciples grumble or confess. Those who were not drawn to Jesus withdrew (John 6:60-65), but those who were chosen remained (6:66-71). The characteristic that separated those who left and those who stayed was a God-given ability to discern between the things of the flesh and the things of the Spirit (6:63). Jesus did not give these people a second taste of his miraculous physical bread. He had made his point about the bread of life, of which, by faith, people could have as many tastes as they desired. The lesson was to linger, because the true bread of life remained.

7:1–11:57 Jerusalem

Overview: Jesus was either rejected or received as he presented himself in the images of water (John 7), light (John 8–9), the shepherd (John 10), and the resurrection (John 11). As light, Jesus illuminated and exposed. As the shepherd, Jesus guided and sacrificed. Those images were preparing the readers of John's Gospel for the intimate

words of the shepherd to the sheep in John 13–17. As the resurrection, Jesus was the very life of God; a new life over which death had no power.

7:1-53 THE FEAST OF TABERNACLES
7:1-9 Pressures in Judea and Galilee. Opposition sets the tone for John 7–8. The date was September 10-17, A.D. 32, about one-half a year before Jesus' crucifixion. The "Feast of Booths" or "Tabernacles" (7:2) was one of the three pilgrim festivals (Deut. 16:16) that the Jews attended in Jerusalem. The feast originally involved thanksgiving for God's preservation of Israel in the wilderness (manna and water, for example). As a fall harvest festival it commemorated the first harvest in the land after the wilderness wanderings. Jesus' relatives felt he was staying too long in the shadows. They wanted him to act in a grand public way. That manipulation of Jesus may sound pious, but John calls it unbelief (John 7:5). Jesus' brothers did not believe at this point, but later they would (1 Cor. 9:5; 15:7). Jesus explained why the world hated him (John 7:7). It was becoming clear that the rejection of Jesus noted in 1:11 would lead to murderous hate. The seeming confusion about Jesus not going (7:8) and then going (7:10) up to the feast was avoided by understanding Jesus' "time" (7:6, 8). Jesus followed the pattern that God had laid out for him (5:19); he rejected going when his brothers wanted him to, and then went later.

7:10-13 Secret speculation about the Messiah. The "fear of the Jews" (7:13) was a reference to the people fearing the Jewish religious leaders (7:26, "authorities").

7:14-24 Public exhortation to judge rightly. This relates to the Sabbath controversy of the healing at the Bethesda pool (5:2-9, 16). Jesus used this opportunity to authenticate his origin and authority (7:14-18). Jesus had never attended the leading rabbinical schools, yet all had to admit that he was an eloquent and knowledgeable teacher (7:15). He defined a teachable spirit as one with willingness to do his will (7:17). He attacks narrow vision and defines righteousness (7:19-24). The "one miracle" (7:21) was the healing of the lame man on the Sabbath (5:1-16). Jesus desired to clarify the intent and emphasize the application of the law of

Moses (7:23-24). Jesus pointed out that since circumcision was allowed on the Sabbath (Lev. 12:3), then certainly it should be permissible to do a deed of mercy on the Sabbath (7:23).

7:25-36 Response to signs. Jesus claims God as his Father (7:25-30). Some of the people held to the unscriptural tradition that the Messiah's origin would be unknown and that he would be an unknown individual until anointed by Elijah (7:27). Because the people of Jerusalem knew all about Jesus they were sure that he could not be the Messiah. Those people that did believe, believed because of the signs Jesus had performed (7:31-36). The paragraph ends (7:35-36) with an unanswered question, showing a misunderstanding regarding Jesus' arrival and future absence. The disciples would soon have similar questions (John 13–14).

7:37-52 The last and great day of the feast. Jesus gave the promise of the Spirit (7:37-39). It became the custom each day during the Feast of Tabernacles for the priests to bring a vessel of water from the Pool of Siloam and pour it out at the base of the altar in Jerusalem. The ceremony was a symbolic confession of physical thirst and looked forward to the end of the dry season and the coming of the winter rains. For seven days the libations were made. The eighth day ("last day") was observed as a Sabbath and no water was poured. It was on this day that Jesus invited the people to have their spiritual thirst satisfied in him (7:37). Jesus had already used the image of springs of water with the woman from Samaria (4:13-14). The Old Testament mentions springs of water in significant ways (Exod. 17:6; Num. 20:11; Ps. 78:15; Isa. 48:21; 35:6-7; 41:17-18; 44:3; Jer. 2:13; Ezek. 36:25; cf. also Rev. 21:6; 22:1, 17). Note in John 7:39 "since" and its implication that the Spirit could not be given until he had been glorified. The glorification of Jesus was directly related to the giving of the Spirit. Peter would clarify the link between Jesus' ascension and the outpouring of the Spirit in Acts 2:33 (see also Peter's use of Ps. 110:1 and Joel 2:28 in Acts 2:16-21, 34-36).

There was division over Jesus' geographical origin (John 7:40-43). Ironically, they did not know Jesus was indeed born in Bethlehem (7:42; cf. Mic. 5:2; Matt. 2:5-6). They were blind even to the facts because they were blind to God and not willing to do his will (John 7:17).

7:53–8:11 THE FUNCTION OF LIGHT

This story is omitted in many manuscripts, yet there seems to be substantial evidence that this was part of John's original text. The stylistic trait of short explanatory phrases that appear elsewhere in John (6:6; 6:71; 11:31; 11:51; 13:11, 28) also appear here (8:6). The same type of legal language that appears in John 1–12 also appears here ("questioning," "accusing"). And the evidence for inclusion of the story is very early (Jerome and Augustine), mid-fifth century A.D. About 450 Greek texts include the story.

If Jesus had advocated stoning the woman he would have gone against the official policy of Rome that prohibited the Jews from executing the death penalty for adultery (8:6). If he advocated her release, then Jesus would be accused of contradicting Mosaic Law (Lev. 20:10; Deut. 22:23-24). By his response (8:6-11), Jesus escaped the trap set for him. They could not accuse him of showing disrespect for either Roman authority or Mosaic Law. Jesus' response in 8:11 did not condone the woman's sin and cannot be used as an argument for the validity of situation ethics. Jesus named sin for what it was. He granted forgiveness, not permission to sin (note the relation to 8:15-16). This relates to a constant theme of Jesus: the necessity of inner, rather than merely outer, purity. His point was that stoning was only a part of God's government, and if one was guilty of sin, all were guilty.

8:12-20 THE LIGHT OF THE WORLD

This teaching was probably presented at the Feast of Tabernacles (7:2). In the Court of the Women in the temple were four golden candelabras that burned brightly throughout the festival (8:12). The light symbolized the pillar of fire in the wilderness and the glory that had once filled the temple. At the close of the feast, after the lights had been darkened, Jesus made the impressive claim, "I am the light of the world" (8:12).

Light in Jewish literature is often a reference to the Messiah (cf. Isa. 9:2). The Jews could not have mistaken the meaning of his words. Self-testimony (8:13) was not regarded as acceptable in a Jewish court of law.

8:21-30 THE LIGHT'S REMOVAL

Jesus had much to say about his glory and departure (2:19-22; 7:36; 13:33-37; 14:1-4, 18-19, 28-29; 17:24). The hearers believed Jesus' words (8:30), but, as 8:31-59 will show, they were not willing to abide in his words (8:31).

8:31-59 JESUS' FOLLOW-UP FOR NEW BELIEVERS: TRUE FATHERHOOD

Even while under Rome's subjection, the Jews claimed that they were servants of God, not of Rome (8:33; see Josephus, *Jewish War*, 7.323). The Jews were Abraham's physical offspring, but were not his spiritual children because they did not share the justifying faith of Abraham (8:39). It is ironic that they claimed never to have been enslaved, especially since they had been under the thumbs of Egypt, Assyria, Babylon, Greece, and finally, Rome. The characters of the two fathers, God and Satan, were being manifested by the actions and words of their followers (8:43-47).

Jesus' accusers misunderstood what Jesus meant by death, and thus were unable to understand or believe in Jesus (8:48-53). The foundation of life is the keeping of Jesus' word. Jesus had already spoken about death in sins (8:24). The way to life was to hold to his teachings (8:31) and keep (8:51) his words. He spoke of eternal life; the hearers could only think of physical life and death. Physical death may come for the believer, but it won't be the final victor (8:51; cf. 1 Cor. 15:54-57).

Jesus clarified what life meant (8:54-58). His eternality was the only basis for the believers not seeing death. Again, their claim to be children of Abraham was exposed for the sham it was (8:53). With the words "I am" (8:58), Jesus laid claim to the great Old Testament revelation of God's personal name, the One who eternally exists (cf. Exod. 3:14). Jesus claimed to be the Old Testament God. There was no doubt in the mind of the Jews that this was a claim for deity (8:59). When Jesus explained his true nature, they responded in hate. But true

believers, from John the Baptist on (1:31), believed in Jesus' eternal existence (1:2).

9:1-41 THE LIGHT AND TRUE BLINDNESS

9:1-3 The reason for the blindness. John 9 continues the theme of light and darkness, sight and blindness. It was held, though not widely, that the soul of a man could sin in a preexistent state (9:2). Others held that the offspring would be punished by God for the sins of the parents. But the reason for this man's suffering was not that anyone had sinned; this man's blindness was allowed so that through his life God's glorious light might be displayed.

9:4-12 The Light enlightens. Jesus, the Light, came to relieve both physical (9:11) and spiritual (9:39-41) blindness. This was a clear example of the Light coming to his own people and either being received or rejected (1:11-12). The blind man had spiritual sight, but the Pharisees were spiritually blind, and thus rejected Jesus. The Pool of Siloam (9:7) was located at the south end of Mount Zion, the City of David in the Tyropoeon Valley. The pool was fed by the Gihon Spring through Hezekiah's tunnel. The miracle of giving sight to the blind should have brought to the minds of the observers Isaiah's prophecies that in the kingdom, the blind would see (Isa. 29:18; 35:5; 42:7, 16). The miracle was a foretaste of kingdom blessings, both physical and spiritual.

9:13-34 The Healer's nature is debated. To be "put out of the synagogue" (John 9:22; that is, excommunicated) was a most serious punishment because it involved forfeiting one's social relations and religious privileges as a Jew. The words "give glory to God" (9:24) imply "give glory to God by telling the truth." Again, the question of Jesus' origin (9:29) arises. The Jewish leaders looked to his earthly origin. The healed man worked backwards from his healing to recognize the divine origin of his Healer.

9:35-41 The Light is worshiped and rejected. Jesus did not come into the world for the purpose of condemnatory judgment (cf. 3:17), but his coming represented a judgment since the people who met him had to decide how to respond to his person (9:39). The Pharisees rejected the light Jesus offered and thus cast a dark shadow over their nation. Jesus not only sought to bring healing to the physically blind; he also desired to bring healing light to the spiritually blind.

10:1-39 THE SHEPHERD AND TRUE GUIDANCE

10:1-18 Intimate sheep and shepherd relationship. The good shepherd presented in John 10 stands in contrast to the blind leaders of 9:41 who were in reality Satan's children (8:44). The author intended this chapter as part of the preceding discourse (10:21; reference to the blind man). Jesus' discourse on the good shepherd needs to be understood in light of the Old Testament references to the good and bad human shepherds (cf. Ps. 23:1; Isa. 40:11; 56:9-12; Jer. 23:1-4; Ezek. 34:23; Zech. 11:1-17). Jesus used this familiar image to communicate important truths regarding himself.

The sheep "pen" (10:1) was usually a rock enclosure designed to protect and shelter the sheep. The shepherd would actually lie down across the entrance of the sheepfold and become the "gate" (10:7). Note the editorial comment in John 10:6. It again reminds the reader that not seeing the spiritual truth behind Jesus' earthly words and acts was the main block to understanding him. In contrast to the Jewish leaders, Jesus leads his followers sacrificially (10:11, 15). On "one flock" (10:16) see 11:52 and 17:20-23. The "other sheep" (10:16) are the Gentiles who would be brought into God's family as heirs of the promise by faith (Eph. 2:16). The implications for the hearers are: Jesus is the good shepherd (10:11); God gave authority regarding the sheep and the sacrifice of Jesus (10:18); and obedience to Jesus' voice is necessary for those who desire to be one of his flock (10:27).

10:19-21 The debate over the source of Jesus' power. The people debated the source of Jesus' power as they struggled to understand the implications of the healing of the blind man.

10:22-39 Feast of Dedication: plain statement of identity. The Feast of Dedication commemorated the cleansing and rededication of the temple by Judas Maccabeus in 164 B.C. after the defilement by Antiochus Epiphanes (1 Macc. 4:52-59; 2 Macc. 10:5). It was also called the Feast of Lights because when the temple was cleansed, the lamps in the temple burned miraculously for eight days when the oil was sufficient for only one. The date was December 18, A.D. 32. "Solomon's Colonnade" (10:23) was the column-lined, covered porch along the east wall of the Court of the Gentiles. Belonging to and believing in Jesus is directly related to being given to Jesus by God (10:29). Jesus clearly stated his "oneness" with the Father (10:30). The security and comfort for his sheep lies in the essential link between Jesus and the Father. Jesus still tried to help the people even when they were about to stone him. He attempted to help them reason from the signs he had performed to their real significance (10:37-38). In 10:34 Jesus cites Psalm 82:6 to support his claim to deity.

10:40-42 BELIEF BEYOND THE JORDAN: CONFIRMED WORDS

This section, in which Jesus goes out into the wilderness (10:40), sets the stage for John 11:1-57. The hostility in Judea became so great that Jesus withdrew across the Jordan to Bethany, the place where John the Baptist had baptized (cf. 1:28). This Bethany must be distinguished from the Bethany near Jerusalem, where Mary, Martha, and Lazarus lived. The truth of John the Baptist's words, confirmed by Jesus' acts, brought about belief in the hearts of those who followed Jesus there.

11:1-57 THE SIGN OF LIFE

11:1-16 Background: death and threats. This sign of Lazarus's return to life is a fitting climax for the seven signs recorded by the apostle John. They all relate to the central truth of Jesus: that he is eternal life (1:4; 20:30-31). Note the relationship of love (11:3, 5, 11, 36) and glory (11:4, 15, 26, 40) in these verses. The ultimate way for Jesus to show love in this situation was not by rushing back to heal Lazarus before he died. It was to reveal the greater love and glory of resurrection.

The word "yet" in 11:6 is important. The delay was for God's glory and in the best love for Martha, Mary, and Lazarus. Compare 11:15 with 11:21, 32 regarding Jesus being there or not. Jesus' actions were designed to encourage belief (11:15). This "Bethany" (11:1), identified as the village of Mary and Martha, was located just east of the Mount of Olives, about half a mile from Jerusalem.

The disciples feared returning to Judea because of the opposition to Jesus that was growing there (11:7-16). But Jesus taught his disciples to see circumstances from the perspective of divine light (11:9-10), not from the perspective of the dark (11:8). Again the disciples felt and thought on the physical, rather than spiritual, level and therefore misunderstood Jesus' words (11:11-13). Jesus referred to death (cf. 11:14) as "sleep" since a resurrection to life was anticipated for those who believed in him. The benefit of Jesus' absence (11:14-15) was resurrection for Lazarus and a great sign of the eternal life that was promised in Jesus the Messiah.

11:17-37 Two interviews. Both Martha and Mary thought that Jesus could have kept Lazarus alive if he had been there (11:21, 32). But the implication of their statements is that now that Lazarus was dead, Jesus' being there could do no good. The "four days" (11:17) were significant, since it was held by some Jews that the spirit left the body only after the third day. In her talk with Jesus (11:17-29), Martha learned that he is a present power for life whether a person is in need of life for healing or resurrection life. She had faith in spite of her partial understanding of what Jesus said (11:23-27). The point is that Jesus is the resurrection to eternal life. Lazarus's physical resurrection, like the other physical healings by Jesus, points to a spiritual and eternal resurrection to life.

The Jews with Mary (11:30-37) also took up the sisters' questions concerning why Jesus had not arrived when Lazarus was still alive (11:37). The implication is that if Jesus really loved Lazarus, he could have kept him alive. Jesus would make a much greater point. Notice how the crowd took Jesus' ability to heal the blind man as proof that he would have been able to heal Lazarus too. See Luke 19:41-42 for another time Jesus cried (11:35).

11:38-44 At the tomb. The "glory of God" (11:40) was seen in the life given by God. Jesus prayed out of concern for the believer (11:42). He was giving an object lesson in prayer that emphasized that God had sent

him. This miracle of resurrection (11:44) exhibited the kingdom condition excluding death (cf. Isa. 25:8) and vindicated Jesus' claim to be the bringer of life (John 11:25; cf. 5:21). Lazarus eventually died again. But this sign of physical resurrection was to point to the greater truth of resurrection to eternal life. This same point was made in the feeding of the five thousand. The people got physically hungry again, but the greater promise was the spiritual bread of eternal life.

11:45-57 The sign's impact. Two responses to Jesus can be found here: the response of belief (11:45) and the response of rejection (11:46). The Jewish leaders feared that Jesus would spark political upheaval that would result in further subjugation by Rome (11:47-48). Caiaphas (11:49) served as high priest from A.D. 18 to 36. Caiaphas thought that it would be better for one man (that is, Jesus) to die than for the nation to be subject to a heavier Roman yoke (11:50). Note 11:52 with reference to 10:16. The "village called Ephraim" (11:54) has been identified as et-Taiyibeh, fourteen miles north of Jerusalem. The Passover of A.D. 33 was fast approaching, and many Galileans were going up to Jerusalem to participate in the festival (11:55).

12:1–20:31 THE SIGN OF THE RESURRECTION

Overview: Jesus returned to Jerusalem (12:1), despite knowlege that the Jewish leaders had given orders to seize him (11:55-57). The entire passion account is introduced with Jesus' willful movement to Jerusalem (cf. 2:19; 10:18). He was the Lamb of God willfully giving up his life for his sheep.

12:1-50 Focus on Death and Rejection

12:1-11 MARY ANOINTS JESUS
This may have been a thanksgiving party for Lazarus's resurrection. John puts this event into its historical time frame—the night before (12:12) Jesus' entry into Jerusalem. For "Bethany" (12:1), see note on 11:1. Judas was the treasurer and regularly stole funds (12:6). The result of Jesus' resurrection of Lazarus was belief for those who had seen the miracle (12:9-11).

12:12-19 INSIGHTS INTO THE JERUSALEM ENTRANCE

The royal entry took place on Monday, rather than Sunday. It was March 30 (Nisan 10), A.D. 33. John's use of Zechariah 9:9 (12:14-15) resulted from his looking back on Jesus' life from a time after Jesus' resurrection (12:16). There were mysteries about parts of Jesus' earthly life that were solved only after he was glorified and had sent the Holy Spirit to teach and remind his followers (14:26, 29).

12:20-26 FRUIT FOR THE GENTILES: FALLEN SEED

Note the link of 12:19 to 12:20. The "whole world" (12:19) was represented by the "Greeks" (12:20). "The hour has come" (12:23). The "hour" was that long-awaited time (2:4; 7:6, 30; 13:1; 17:1) in which Jesus would be glorified through his crucifixion and resurrection. Jesus was about to begin the culmination of his ministry as the Lamb of God. Jesus used the illustration of the fallen seed (12:24) to predict his death and its results; his death would bring salvation to the world. Jesus' death could easily have been seen as defeat. But the gospel message claims that his death was necessary and of eternal benefit to the world (12:24). The gospel calls believers to give up their lives to God that his kingdom of light and life might take root in a dark and dying world. Love of life in this world can be a block to eternal life (12:25).

12:27-36 MISUNDERSTANDINGS CONCERNING JESUS' DEATH

God's authenticating witness to Jesus' person and authority (12:27-30) was for the crowd's benefit to help them believe (cf. 11:42). The crowd misunderstood the most important role of the Messiah—his responsibility to be lifted up as a sacrifice for sin. They only understood his permanence (12:31-36). Jesus used the phrase "Son of Man" to help educate them about his crucifixion. That is why they wondered who the Son of Man was (12:34). A crucified Messiah was a new and difficult concept for them to grasp (cf. 12:25-26).

12:37-50 PASSIONATE PLEA FOR BELIEF

This section serves to expand and explain the words of John's prologue (1:1-18) concerning light, life, and belief. The crowds listening to Jesus were still confused about who he was (12:34, 37, 42, 43).

The words of 12:39-41 were quoted from Isaiah 6:10. In Jesus' last appeal to the crowds (12:44), he gave reasons for belief and emphasized the people's responsibility to believe. The divine person whom Isaiah saw (Isa. 6:1-4) was none other than the preincarnate Christ. The words concerning God's commands to Jesus (12:49-50) formed the foundation for Jesus' call to obedience and abiding in John 13–17.

13:1–16:33 Focus on Departure and Disciples

Overview: The four gospels contain three great discourses of Jesus. In the Sermon on the Mount (Matt. 5–7) Jesus detailed the demands of righteousness and repentance. That sermon was given to those who wanted to know how to enter the kingdom. The stress was on fulfilling the law and Jesus interpreted the law for the present.

The second major discourse, the Olivet Discourse (Matt. 24–25; Mark 13; Luke 21), described the end times and the endurance that would be required of the faithful. That discourse was given to the disciples and centered on personal stability during a time of great temptation to depart from the faith. It was future oriented.

The third discourse, the Upper Room Discourse, defined the love of God. It was instruction concerning the new relationship between God and humanity brought about by the start of the new covenant founded in Jesus' blood. This discourse forms the key link to the "in Christ" emphasis of the epistles, especially Paul's writings. This instruction was Jesus' response to those few who believed and were insecure about living life after he had gone away.

The purpose of the Upper Room Discourse was to prepare the disciples for Jesus' death, resurrection, and absence (John 13:14; 14:2-3, 18, 21, 23; 15:18-27; 16:5, 16-22, 28-33). Jesus instructed his disciples about their future. Unlike the Olivet Discourse's emphasis on the end-time events of tribulation and apostasy, the Upper Room Discourse viewed the future from the perspective of how God would be present with them even though Jesus had gone away. It focused on the elements of abiding and love, so important for the life of faith during his absence.

The promise of the Holy Spirit was one of Jesus' central concerns (14:16-18, 26; 15:26-27; 16:7-15). The Holy Spirit would be the one who would help believers cooperate with God. The return of Jesus was discussed (14:1-3), but the coming of the Holy Spirit was viewed as the bridge of God's presence until Jesus returned. Jesus made it clear that there would be conflict with the world (15:18-27). But the believer's response to the world was to be controlled by love. Similarly, conduct between believers was to be governed by love (13:3-35; 15:1-17). Love contrasts with how the unbeliever responds to the light—with hate and hostility.

Finally, Jesus prayed for the preservation, sanctification, and unification of his disciples (17:1-26). Jesus' followers were to be assured that if anyone's prayers would be answered, Jesus' would. Every word in his prayer in John 17 will be answered for those who believe in him.

The accompanying chart shows the basic content of the discourse. It contains three sections that divide into two subsections each.

The key concepts are: (1) finding comfort through Jesus' peace and the coming of the Holy Spirit; (2) the importance of remaining faithful to (abiding in) Jesus' commands; and (3) showing love for one another by following Jesus' example. These three concepts spoke to the disciples on the levels of emotion, the will, and behavior.

13:1-30 THE PREPARATION
FOR THE INSTRUCTION
13:1-20 Illustration of humiliation. Before Jesus could go on to speak of the disciples' glory, he first clearly illustrated the humble service that would lead to glory. The lines of rejection (Judas) and acceptance (the disciples) were drawn. Jesus' departure would be

the start of his disciples' continuance of expressing his love. Just before the Feast of Passover Jesus purposed to give his disciples a very practical demonstration of his love. The "full extent" of Jesus' love (13:1) referred to both the time and quality of his love. Feet were usually washed before the meal. But Jesus waited until during the supper (13:2) to make the act stand out as noteworthy. Jesus knew that he could take a servant's role without losing anything (13:3). The purpose of this action was to fix in their minds the nature of true greatness.

The background of this event can be found in Luke 22:24-30. The disciples were in the midst of a dispute over who was going to be the greatest in the kingdom. Jesus had taught them that greatness in the kingdom comes through serving others (Matt. 20:26-27), but they had not learned the lesson. Thus, he gave them this unforgettable illustration.

At first Peter rejected Jesus' humble service of foot washing (13:6-11), which pointed toward Jesus' humble, cleansing work on the cross. But when Peter saw that this foot washing was symbolic of cleansing from sin, he wanted to be washed from head to foot. Peter had discovered the spiritual aspect of the foot-washing ceremony but would need to think about the more literal aspects of service. He misunderstood Jesus the Messiah's servant role and therefore his own role as disciple. In 13:10 Jesus came back to the literal point. The spiritual point had already been understood. They were already clean. Jesus was also showing his disciples what it meant to serve—what it meant to be great in the kingdom of God.

As teacher, Jesus should be believed (13:12-15); as Lord, he should be obeyed. The teacher is the one from whom truth is

THE UPPER ROOM DISCOURSE

I.   A. Jesus' Example of Humility (13:1-20)
     B. The Prediction of Jesus' Betrayal (13:21-30)
II. A. The Command to Love (13:31-35)
     B. Comfort in Absence (13:36–14:31)
III. A. The Command to Love in the Face of World Hatred (15:1-27)
     B. Comfort in Absence (16:1-33)

learned; and the Lord is the one to be obeyed (13:13). Jesus explained his act of foot washing as a symbol and linked it to 13:34 and his new command to love. He linked being a servant of God to salvation and to the perfecting of discipleship. Jesus explained the significance of the foot washing in terms of a pattern of humble service that the disciples needed to follow.

Many view this act as an illustration of the "washing of rebirth" (Titus 3:5) and the "purifying" of 1 John 1:9. Others prefer a more literal reading of humble service pictured by foot washing (13:15). John 13:17 is the classic passage on the relationship between knowing and the blessing of doing. In 13:18 Jesus quoted Psalm 41:9 as finding its ultimate fulfillment in Judas. That was a sign of Jesus' knowledge to encourage belief in him and a relationship with God the Father (13:9-20).

13:21-30 The separation of the son of perdition. The separation was to get the unbelief (Judas) out in order to make room for instruction to the immature (disciples). The disciples ate while lying on their sides. John was "reclining next to Jesus" (13:23; cf. 21:20, 24). The words "next to" literally mean "in the sphere of." As the disciples reclined around a low table, they turned on their sides, propping themselves up with an elbow. The "piece of bread" (13:26) was like a small sandwich with a bit of lamb with bitter herbs folded in a small piece of what is known today as Middle Eastern pocket bread.

13:31–16:33 THE PARTICULARS OF THE INSTRUCTION
Jesus made it clear that he was the exclusive means of salvation. The comfort he left behind was founded on his promises: he will return (14:3); he prepares a place for us (14:2); he answers prayer (14:13-14); he sends the Comforter (14:16); our obedience manifests the Father's love (14:21); the Spirit will instruct (14:26); and Jesus leaves peace with believers (14:27).

13:31–14:31 Instruction regarding God's presence. The prologue to this section is in 13:31-35. Jesus addressed the problem of his absence (13:33). Behavior during his absence is to be governed by love (13:34).

The problems centered on comfort in Jesus' coming absence (13:36–14:24). Jesus' statement in 13:33 about his absence provoked insecurities and questions from the disciples. Peter asked the first questions: where? (13:36) and why? (13:37). Peter's claim that he would lay down his life for Jesus was serious (13:37). Later that night he attempted to defend Jesus against those who arrested him in the garden (cf. 18:10). Peter wondered why he could not follow Jesus (13:36-38). Jesus' reply (14:1-4) shows what was behind Peter's question—a troubled and insecure heart. Jesus taught Peter and the others about the importance of love during Jesus' coming absence. Another aspect of comfort can be found in Jesus' foreknowledge (14:29).

Note especially 14:2, 23. Jesus will prepare a dwelling place for those who believe, and he and the Father will dwell with the obedient believer on this earth (14:23). The preparation of the place is certainly not heavenly carpentry but relates to Jesus' ascension and sending forth of the Spirit to take up his dwelling place with believers, whether now on earth, or later in heaven.

The cross was a stage in the glorification of Jesus. That symbol of shame was also a symbol of glory (see 1 Cor. 1:17). Jesus' departure (13:33) was the central issue of his ministry here. He emphasized the children's immaturity and the Father's care.

Thomas wondered how they would know how to find the Father if Jesus was not there to show them the way (14:5-7). Behind Thomas's questions was a burning desire to be where Jesus was and not to be left behind and alone. Philip (14:8-21) asked specifically for a demonstration of who the Father was (14:8). Jesus taught that he was the link between man and God. To see Jesus was to see the Father. John 14:11 presents the central idea of John's entire Gospel—belief (cf. 20:30-31).

The context would indicate that the "greater things" (14:12) are those things accomplished by Jesus' disciples through prayer in his name (cf. 14:13-14). In the biblical period, one's name represented the person; it was a summary statement of someone's character or reputation (14:14). The name of Jesus pointed to his attributes, his person, and all that he had accomplished. It was no mere magical formula, but a confession of dependence, trust, and confidence in the person and work of Jesus the Messiah. Again the obedient saint would be the one who experiences God in this earthly life (14:21). Jesus' answer to Judas' questions (14:22-24) brings the discussion around full-circle back to 13:34 (cf. 14:23).

In the epilogue (14:25-31), Jesus continued to show concern for the believers' comfort in his absence. He gave the promise of the Comforter (14:25-26). Jesus' promise of the Holy Spirit's power for remembrance meets the disciples' needs for insight and strength of faith after Jesus had gone (especially 2:22; see also 2:17; 7:39; 13:19; 14:20, "you will realize"; 15:20; 16:4; 17:13; 19:35-37; 20:8-10).

The promise of peace (14:27) was a positive blessing (cf. Isa. 54:10; Ezek 34:25; 37:26). The promise of parting was in John 14:28-31. Jesus could have banished the "prince of this world" (14:30). But he did not because he wanted to show God's love and his own obedience to the world (14:31). See 14:31 for the relationship between love and keeping commandments.

The words "let us leave" may mean that Jesus and the disciples were departing from the Upper Room and that the discourse was finished along the way to the garden. Others suggest that Jesus made the statement at this time but did not leave until after his words in John 17. John included this statement in order to mark off a major division in the discourse.

15:1–16:4 Instruction regarding the harvest. In the section of 15:1–16:4, Jesus elaborated on keeping the Father's word (14:23), especially the commandment to love (13:34; 14:31). The cause of the disciple's fruit-bearing was explained by using the metaphor of the vine (15:1-11). This metaphor was common in the Old Testament (cf. Ps. 80:8; Isa. 5:1-7; Jer. 2:21; Ezek. 15:1-8; Hos. 10:1). Israel was the vine in the Old Testament passages. In John's Gospel Jesus was depicted as the true vine. Two types of branches were described: fruit-bearing and fruitless (John 15:2). The fruit-bearing branches were "trimmed" (lit., "cleansed") while the fruitless branches were cut off and destroyed.

What would happen to these fruitless branches was revealed in 15:6. Fruit was what the vinedresser intended for his vines—in this context, the keeping of God's commands. Trimming, in this context, would increase the disciple's obedience to the word of Jesus for a greater harvest. The harvest, in this context, would be acts of obedience that follow Jesus' acts of obedience and love. For a similar illustration, see Jeremiah 15:1-8. It appears that the fruitless branch was in fact a lifeless branch that had no life-giving connection with Jesus, the vine.

The vineyard image was simply another way of expressing the teaching of John 1:1-8. Jesus the Messiah is the light of the world. Some will accept him and gain eternal life. Others will reject him and gain death. Jesus is the vine to whom some will respond and bear fruit. Others will not respond to him and will gain death. The "in me" (15:2) is not the same as Paul's "in Christ." It is the place where the light of Christ shines on everyone (cf. 1:4, 9). The benefits of "remaining" or "abiding" (NASB and KJV) are obedience and joy (cf. 15:10, 12).

Jesus exemplified the totally honest friend who would be willing to lay down his life for his friends (15:13-16). The term "friends" (15:14) was used both in a general sense and a technical sense in the Roman period. In the technical sense, to be a "friend of Caesar" meant that you held the highest position possible in relationship to the emperor and the Roman government. Such "friends" of Caesar knew the emperor so well they actually opened his mail and carried out his correspondence. In addition, they were willing to go wherever the emperor commanded to conduct his affairs. Who is a "friend" of Jesus? Those who know him intimately and obey him willingly.

Jesus also taught his disciples how to relate to their enemies (15:18–16:4). This section taught them to show love in the face of hatred. The disciple would be equal to Jesus in showing love and in bearing the world's hate (15:20; 13:16). In Greek grammar, the "if" describes a condition that is assumed as true (15:18). The phrase "*If* the world hates you . . ." could also be translated, "*Since* the world hates you. . . ."

The witness of the Holy Spirit and the disciples (15:26-27) was behind the writing

of the Gospel of John in the first place
(20:30-31). That witness in Jesus' name
would produce the same hatred as John
and Jesus experienced. Jesus warned of
these negative things to keep his followers
from stumbling after experiencing this
hatred from the world.

Excommunication from the synagogue
involved being cut off from all normal
dealings with the Jewish community (16:2;
cf. 9:22). The term "service" (16:2) referred
to "religious service." Like Paul, they would
persecute the Christians, thinking they were
serving God in doing so (Phil. 3:6).

16:5-33 Revelation regarding comfort.
The Holy Spirit would work during Jesus'
absence. Jesus' departure was necessary for
the sending of the Holy Spirit (cf. Luke
24:49; Acts 1:4-5; 2:1-40). The Holy Spirit
would work in the world as prosecutor and
as comforter (John 16:8-11). The word
"convict" (16:8) was a legal term meaning to
cross-examine for the purpose of convincing
or refuting an opponent. It involved the
setting forth in a clear and convincing manner the true character of a person or thing.
The disciples would also be the recipients of
the guiding and revealing work of the Father
by means of the Spirit (16:12-15). The outcome of the resurrection would be Jesus'
absence, but he would someday return
(16:16-24).

Jesus promised to give peace during the
times of tribulation. The section of 16:25-33
is foundational for 17:7-8. Jesus' stay on
earth was just one half of a circle that began
and ended with the Father. The way down,
through obedience and the cross, was the
way back to glory. In John 17 Jesus would
include his followers in that journey back to
the glory of God. Up to this time in Jesus'
ministry he had spoken enigmatically—
through parables, allegories, and figures
with implications not easy to understand.
From this point on, things would be different
(16:25; cf. 16:29).

17:1-26 Prayer following the Instruction

Overview: This prayer was, in part, the basis
for John's meditation which was presented
in the prologue (1:1-18). Compare 1:1 with
17:5, 11, 24; 1:3 with 17:2; 1:4 with 17:2;
1:9-10 with 17:14; 1:12 with 17:3; 1:14 with

17:4, 24; and 1:18 with 17:3, 6, 26. Jesus
used many purpose statements that added up
to a powerful world mission (note the use of
"that"; 17:1-3, 11, 13, 19, 21-23, 26). Along
with the purpose statements, Jesus used
comparison statements between himself and
his followers (17:11, 14, 16, 18, 21-23). The
purpose of unity is world witness. This was
communicated by comparing the disciples
and Jesus and by the transference of Jesus'
glory to the disciples (17:22-23).

17:1-5 THE LORD AND THE FATHER
John 17 is the longest of Jesus' recorded
prayers and was spoken in the presence of
the disciples in the Upper Room or somewhere along the way to the Garden of Gethsemane. Jesus prayed for himself (17:1-5),
his disciples (17:6-19), and for future believers
(17:20-24).

17:6-19 THE LORD AND THE DISCIPLES
The essence of what Jesus did for his followers was to convince them that he was a
true reflection of the Father (17:7). This
explained his words in the prologue (1:18).
Jesus gave the reason for his petition for the
disciples (17:6-8) and then requested their
preservation (17:9-16). The "one doomed"
(17:12) was Judas, whose betrayal was anticipated in Psalm 41:9 (cf. John 13:18). The
way to sanctification is through God's Word
becoming reality in a believer's life (17:17;
cf. 13:17). The "evil one" (17:15) referred
to Satan. "Sanctify" (17:17) meant to "set
apart." Jesus prayed that the disciples would
be "set apart" for God and his purposes by
the truth. Jesus' commission of the disciples
was an extension of God's commission of
Jesus (17:18). The disciples would be Jesus'
representatives.

17:20-26 THE LORD AND THE FAMILY
Jesus prayed for the unification of future
believers (17:20-23; see also 20:29). The
purpose of the glory spoken of in 17:22 was
for worldwide evangelization. This prayer
for unity had an evangelistic purpose—"so
that the world may believe" that God the
Father sent his divine Son. The glory of
believers is the unity shared between the
Son, the Father, and themselves (17:22).
Jesus wanted the disciples to behold his
glory as proof of his eternal oneness with
the Father (17:24). On this earth Jesus
promised to continue to make the Father's

name known (17:26). Sharing God's love (17:26) was the purpose of both his prayer and the entire section of John 13–17.

18:1–19:42 The Passion of the Passover Lamb of God

Overview: The passion was the last aspect of the wilderness theme in John (Jesus as the tabernacle, John 1; the bronze serpent, John 3; manna, John 6; rock of water, John 7; light, John 8; and Jesus as the Passover lamb, 18:28; 19:14; 1:29). Notice what Jesus knew during the passion events. He was seen as in full control of the situation. He knew his hour had come (13:1), what was about to happen (18:4), and that all was completed or accomplished (19:28). His hour of glory was related to the Greeks (12:23) and to Judas' exit (13:31).

18:1-11 THE ARREST

Darkness and light meet in these verses. Jesus' actions revealed the character and will of the Father (1:18; 17:6-7). His movement to the cross was the climax of explaining the loving heart of God. The "Kidron" (18:1) is a small north-south valley with a stream that flows during the rainy season. The valley is situated between the Temple Mount and the Mount of Olives. The "grove" referred to Gethsemane (cf. Matt. 26:36). A Roman "detachment" (18:3) consisted of a company of six hundred soldiers. The text does not indicate that the whole company came to arrest Jesus. Like the modern expression "the police came," so representatives of the Roman military forces went to the garden. John 18:8-9 shows the fulfillment of 17:12. On 18:10 see Luke 22:51 for the healing of Malchus's ear.

18:12–19:16 THE TRIALS

18:12-27 The Jewish trial. John contrasted the denials of Peter with the strong witness of Jesus. This gave the reader a good example to follow and completed Jesus' mission of explaining the Father through faithful witness. The examination by Annas (18:13), the high priest (A.D. 6–15) was unique to John's Gospel. Although he had been removed from office by the Romans, he was still regarded as a person of authority by the Jews since the high priest was to hold office for life. Caiaphas (John 18:14, 24), the son-in-law of Annas, was officially serving

as high priest at that time (A.D. 18–36). Details of the trial before Caiaphas were recorded by Matthew. After questioning Jesus, Annas gave permission to proceed with the trial before Caiaphas (John 18:24).

Peter provided a negative example for the believer's witness in the world (18:15-18). Jesus provided a just question for all who would be unjustly persecuted in his name (18:23). John, known to the high priest, secured Peter's entrance (18:15). Since his mother, Salome, may have been the sister of Mary (John 19:25; Mark 15:40), and Mary was related to Elizabeth, a daughter of Aaron (Luke 1:5), John was of priestly descent. This is confirmed by Polycrates as recorded by Eusebius (*Historia Ecclesiastica,* 3.31).

18:28–19:16 The Roman trial. More of the Roman trial is seen here than in Matthew, Mark, and Luke. The emphases are: (1) the innocence of Jesus; (2) the attempted release by Pilate; and (3) the hardened unbelief of the religious leaders. The "palace" (John 18:28) was the governor's residence, perhaps Herod's Palace, but more likely the Antonia Fortress located just north of the temple area. The Jews did not want to enter the fortress, the dwelling of Gentiles, lest they be defiled and rendered unfit to eat the Passover meal.

How was it that Jesus and the disciples ate the Passover (the "Last Supper") on the day before his crucifixion (Matt. 26:20; Mark 14:17; Luke 22:14; John 13:2) and the Jews yet expected to eat the Passover on the evening of Jesus' crucifixion? Many solutions have been offered to solve this problem. It may be that there were actually two Passovers observed on the basis of two different methods of reckoning a day. The Galileans and Pharisees may have begun counting their day at sunrise whereas the Judeans and Sadducees may have begun their days at sunset. Thus the disciples from Galilee would have begun their Passover in the morning, but the religious leaders in Jerusalem would have not begun their official Passover until that evening, with their major preparations not starting until the following morning, the morning of Jesus' trial and crucifixion.

With the Galileans, Jesus and his disciples observed Passover on Thursday, Nisan 14. The Judeans sacrificed their Passover lambs

Friday afternoon, Nisan 14 according to their reckoning, and observed the feast that evening. There is no explicit statement of Scripture to support the theory of two Passovers except for the evidence for two Jewish ways of reckoning a day. This view does explain John 18:28, allowing Jesus to be the Passover Lamb in fulfillment of Old Testament typology (John 19:36; 1 Cor. 5:7), and harmonizing the data found in the Synoptics and the Gospel of John.

Following the expulsion of Herod's son Archelaus in A.D. 6, Judea became a Roman Imperial Province governed by a prefect (John 18:29). Pontius Pilate served as prefect from A.D. 26 to 36. He normally lived in Caesarea but stayed in Jerusalem during Jewish festivals to help maintain order. The Jews, under Roman rule, were denied the authority to execute capital punishment except in situations that violated the sanctity of the Jerusalem temple (18:31).

In 18:34-35 Jesus inquired whether Pilate had been prompted by the Jews and was therefore thinking of a king as a Messianic person, or whether his question was strictly political. Pilate's response (18:35) reflects the fact that he was only interested in finding out if Jesus had done anything to warrant prosecution by Rome. Jesus admitted to having a kingdom, but not one that was a threat to Rome (18:36).

Pilate made the first of several attempts to free Jesus (18:38-40). Josephus wrote of a man whose ribs were laid bare by scourging (19:1). Pilate was unable to save Jesus. Note the three "not guilty" remarks (18:38; 19:4, 12). Pilate was obviously using sarcasm with his words, "You take him and crucify him" (19:6). In fact, the right to execute capital punishment was the most jealously guarded privilege of the Roman government. The Jews had no such authority (18:31). The fear of losing his status as "friend of Caesar" (19:12; see the note on John 15:14) convinced Pilate that it was necessary, for his own sake, to allow the Jews to put Jesus to death. Pilate had been sent to Palestine to keep the peace at all cost.

Pilate had been a ruthless ruler (Luke 13:1), but in A.D. 32 his friend and protector (Sejanus) in Rome who had been covering up his abuses had been executed. Pilate was no longer secure and comfortable in his

relationship with Caesar. He had to guard against any negative reports coming to the emperor's ears. The Jews knew that he was vulnerable at this point and forced Pilate's decision to crucify Jesus.

The "Pavement" (John 19:13) was located in the Antonia Fortress. The "sixth" hour was 6:00 A.M. The crucifixion took place at 9:00 A.M. (Mark 15:25). In John 19:14-15 there may be yet a fourth attempt by Pilate to set Jesus free.

19:17-42 THE CRUCIFIXION

19:17-22 The inscription. Golgotha was probably located at the site of the Church of the Holy Sepulcher, situated about one quarter mile southwest of the Antonia Fortress. The site was identified by Helena, the emperor Constantine's mother, when she visited the Holy Land in A.D. 326. A church was built over the site. This structure was later destroyed and rebuilt several times. The present church was completed in A.D. 1149 by the Crusaders.

19:23-27 Gambling and adoption. Crucifixion, a horrible and prolonged means of execution, was perfected by the Romans. Having been hung with arms stretched wide above the head on an upright wooden post, the victim eventually succumbed to asphyxiation as his diaphragm became distended and lost its ability to fill the lungs with air. "The disciple whom Jesus loved" (13:23; 19:26; 20:2; 21:7, 20) was John, the author of this Gospel. Jesus assigned to him the responsibility of caring for his mother.

19:28-42 The death of Jesus. "Wine vinegar" (19:29) was a common drink, often used by soldiers and laborers. "Hyssop" is a plant with stems two to three feet in length. Even Jesus' thirst was related to the fulfillment of God's word through the Old Testament Scriptures (19:28).

The "day of Preparation" (19:31) meant that Friday was the day of preparation for the Sabbath. The Sabbath was to be a "special Sabbath" in that it would coincide with Passover. Breaking the legs (19:32) was intended to bring death by preventing the victim from using the legs to raise himself up in order to breath. Victims often surged and plunged on the cross for amazingly long periods before dying of respiratory failure. However, Jesus had died early. Even the time of his death honored God and fulfilled his word (19:36). Joseph was from Arimathea, a town of uncertain location (19:38). Nicodemus's (19:39) visit with Jesus was recorded in 3:1-15. Matthew also recorded that the tomb belonged to Joseph of Arimathea (Matt. 27:57-60).

20:1-29 The Resurrection

20:1-10 THE EMPTY GRAVE
The "other disciple" (20:2) referred to the apostle John, the author of this Gospel. The orderly state of the tomb implied that a super-natural exit of Jesus from his burial wrappings had taken place (20:6-7). The effect was the same for the next group of eyewitnesses (20:8-10). What did John believe? Apparently he believed in the resur-rection of Jesus. John 20:9 indicates that this belief preceded an understanding that the resurrection was foretold in Scripture (cf. Pss. 2:7; 16:10; Isa. 52:12-13). The disciples were convinced of the resurrection first and then later came to an understanding of the Old Testament prophetic Scriptures. This suggests that they did not manufacture a resurrection story to agree with their inter-pretation of prophecy.

20:11-18 THE LORD APPEARS TO MARY
This was the first of five appearances of Jesus on resurrection day: to Mary Magda-lene (Mark 16:9-11; John 20:11-18); to the other women (Matt. 28:9-10); to Simon Peter (Luke 24:33-35; 1 Cor. 15:5); to the two disciples on the road to Emmaus (Mark 16:12-13; Luke 24:13-32); and to the eleven apostles (Mark 16:14; Luke 24:36-43; John 20:19-25). The words "Do not hold on to me" (20:17) indicate that Mary needed to realize that Jesus' presence was not permanent. He explained that he had not yet ascended to the Father. That ascent was on the surface a sad departure of Jesus from those who loved him. On a deeper level, Jesus' ascent to the Father opened up the new presence of Jesus and the Father with the believer through the Holy Spirit.

20:19-23 THE LORD APPEARS
TO THE DISCIPLES
In his first resurrection appearance Jesus reconfirmed his words of comfort, his promise of the Holy Spirit (20:19-20), and his commission to them (20:21-23). The

disciples were commanded to receive the Holy Spirit (20:22). Jesus breathed on his disciples as he commanded them to receive the Spirit. (When the day of Pentecost came, the disciples would complete their obedience to this command to receive the Spirit and would see the Spirit as the very breath of the risen and ascended Lord.) As they had received Jesus, so they would receive the Spirit. The next verse (20:23) unpacks the full implication of receiving the Spirit: it was the reception of God's authority to announce forgiveness and judgment in the name of Jesus.

20:24-29 THE SECOND APPEARANCE: FROM DOUBT TO BELIEF
The climax of the Gospel has two aspects. First, Thomas's confession of Jesus as Lord and God (20:28-29) was the perfect expression of faith and worship by a disci-ple of Jesus. Second, Jesus clarified the relation between faith and sight. Faith was not dependent on actually seeing the risen Lord. The next section made this very clear.

20:30-31 THE CALL TO DECISION
Here John disclosed the purpose of his Gospel—to encourage belief in the truth that Jesus was Israel's divine Messiah. The signs presented by John were to stand as the basis for belief. Unlike Thomas, the reader would not have access to seeing and touching the risen Lord before belief could take place. See 2:21-22 for how the signs operated for even the faith of the eyewitnesses.

21:1-25 ASSURANCE AND COMMISSION
21:1-23 The Galilean Appearance
21:1-14 THE CATCH OF FISH
AND BREAKFAST
This was the third appearance of the risen Lord. In this narrative, Jesus told his dis-ciples how they were to function as apostles. The catch of fish and the breakfast were certainly miracles and related to encourag-ing the disciples in their lives of faith. But this appearance had special significance for Peter and John. The "Sea of Tiberias" (21:1) was another name for the Sea of Galilee. This name was derived from the name of the prominent town built by Herod Antipas and named for Tiberius Caesar. For "Cana in Galilee" (21:2), see note on 2:1.

21:15-23 PETER'S INSTRUCTIONS

In this section Jesus spoke with his disciples concerning love and service (21:15-19). Jesus had already met with Peter privately and probably dealt with his denial at that time (Luke 24:34; 1 Cor. 15:5). Here Jesus instructed Peter concerning his ministry and motives as a church leader. There is debate as to whether John intended a distinction between the two Greek words for "love," *agapao* (Jesus' word) and *phileo* (Peter's word), or whether John used the variation without intending any distinction. Those holding that a distinction is being made suggest that *agapao* is a volitional love that can be commanded. It seeks the good of the object loved even to the point of personal sacrifice. The other word, *phileo,* was understood to refer to an emotional love based on personal affection. Jesus was asking Peter about the depth of his commitment, and the apostle was responding by expressing affection. In his third question (21:17), Jesus used Peter's word (*phileo*), asking if his professed affection was real and sincere. Peter assured Jesus that it was. But 21:17 recounts Jesus asking three similar questions "the third time." In that light neither Jesus, Peter, nor John saw any significant difference between the two words for love in this context. The crucial point of this passage was that Jesus was highlighting Peter's responsibility of feeding and caring for Jesus' sheep, the believers. Peter's love for Jesus would be essential to being faithful to the task.

In 21:18-19 Jesus revealed that Peter would die a martyr's death, a death that would glorify God. Eusebius reported that Peter was crucified head down in Rome under the persecution of Nero in A.D. 64. John's future (21:20-23) was in God's hands. Peter's task was to follow Jesus.

21:24-25 Postscript

The conclusion concerns the true witness (21:24). That witness was claimed by the author ("I," 21:25) and by his circle of friends ("we," 21:24). Those other acts of Jesus were lost to history, but the signs included in John's Gospel would be sufficient to bring its readers to believe in Jesus, the Son of God.

Acts

BASIC FACTS

HISTORICAL SETTING

The book of Acts covers the period from the ascension of Jesus (around A.D. 33) to Paul's first imprisonment in Rome (from around A.D. 60 to 62). Some of the events recorded in the book of Acts were also recorded in secular history, making it possible to build a basic chronology: the death of Herod Agrippa in A.D. 44 (12:20-23); the expulsion of the Jews from Rome by Claudius in A.D. 49 (18:2); the proconsulship of Gallio in A.D. 51 or 52 (18:12); and the procuratorship of Festus in A.D. 59 (24:27).

AUTHOR

Although the author of Acts is not named, the evidence points to Luke. The Muratorian Canon indicates that as early as the middle of the second century A.D., the church believed Acts to be written by Luke the physician, the friend and fellow traveler of Paul. The church fathers, Irenaeus, Clement of Alexandria, Tertullian, and Origen, support the view of Lukan authorship. No evidence in the other New Testament books conflicts with the view that Luke was the author.

The book indicates that the author is also the author of the Gospel of Luke (Luke 1:3-4; Acts 1:1). The dedication to Theophilus links the two works. The medical vocabulary used in Acts supports the tradition that Acts was authored by Luke. Luke is the apparent writer of the "we" sections of Acts (16:10-17; 20:5–21:18; 27:1–28:16), having joined Paul, Silas, and Timothy at Troas (16:11).

Luke was a Gentile convert (Col. 4:14), possibly of the church at Antioch (claimed by Jerome and Eusebius). Luke joined Paul at Troas (Acts 16:10-11) during his second missionary journey and accompanied him to Philippi. He later accompanied Paul to Jerusalem (20:5–21:15) and finally to Rome (27:1–28:15). He was called by Paul "our dear friend, the doctor" and "fellow worker" (Col. 4:14; Philem. 1:24) and was his last friend to remain with him during his second imprisonment (2 Tim. 4:11). Luke was an able historian, doctor, missionary, and theologian.

Modern names and boundaries are shown in gray.

DATE

The book of Acts was probably written in Rome during or following Paul's first imprisonment there (A.D. 60–62). That the work was published around A.D. 63 is indicated by the lack of reference to the fall of Jerusalem (A.D. 70) or the persecution of the Christians by Nero following the fire of Rome in A.D. 64. There is no hint in Acts that Nero's anti-Christian policy had yet manifested itself. The fact that Paul's imprisonment and death (A.D. 67 or 68) were not recorded is also evidence that Acts was written around A.D. 63.

PURPOSE

The book was designed to be the second half of a two-volume work by Luke, completing the story begun in Luke's Gospel. Acts shows how the coming of the Holy Spirit was the initial goal of Jesus' ascension; he was the continued presence of Jesus on earth to proclaim his kingdom. Acts solidly demonstrated how the Spirit would preserve and empower the gospel message through people who followed the sometimes hard road of worldwide evangelization.

GEOGRAPHY AND ITS IMPORTANCE

The book of Acts follows the geographical pattern mandated by the risen Lord (Acts 1:8). Beginning in Jerusalem, the geography expands to Judea, Samaria, and to the remote parts of the earth—in this case, to Rome, the book's geographical and thematic goal. The expansion of Christianity from Jerusalem to Rome exposed Christians to different cultures, but the responses to the gospel followed along two consistent lines. People either embraced the faith, or, for political and religious reasons, rejected the faith. Some of the rejections were extremely hostile, even fatal. But nothing stopped the geographical and spiritual spread of Christianity—not human hostility, political intrigue, storms, or illness. The power behind the spread of the gospel across the miles of mountains and seas was the Holy Spirit, who came at the beginning of the book and never ceased to empower the proclamation.

GUIDING CONCEPTS

STRUCTURE
The unhindered gospel

The events in the book of Acts move in a straight line from Jerusalem to Paul's unhindered preaching of the gospel in Rome. The entire book can be summed up in the words "without hindrance" (Acts 28:31). Although the believers sometimes suffered in chains, shipwreck, or martyrdom, the power of the gospel was not hindered. From Jerusalem in Acts 1 to the triumphal proclamation of the gospel in Rome in Acts 28, the book is about the power of the Lord through his Spirit to spread the message of redemption worldwide.

Key places

The spread of the gospel in Acts follows the geographic plan laid out by Jesus in 1:8. The book begins in Jerusalem (1:1–8:3), moves to Judea and Samaria (8:4-40), and concludes in the remote (from the viewpoint of Jerusalem) regions of the world (9:1–28:31).

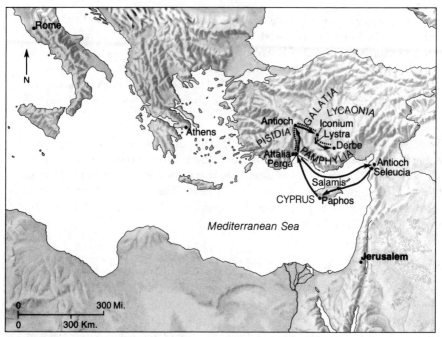

PAUL'S FIRST MISSIONARY JOURNEY

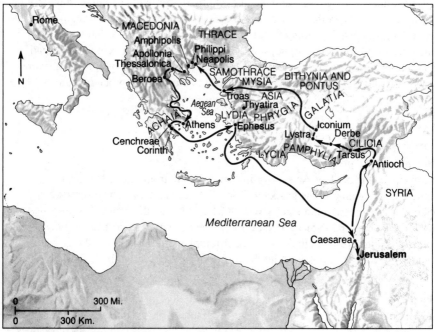

PAUL'S SECOND MISSIONARY JOURNEY

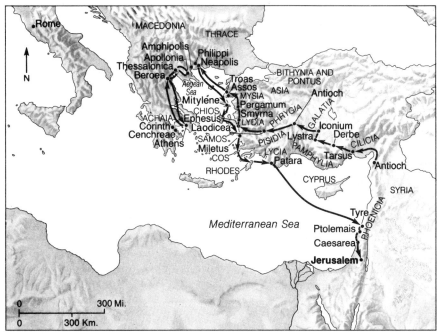

PAUL'S THIRD MISSIONARY JOURNEY

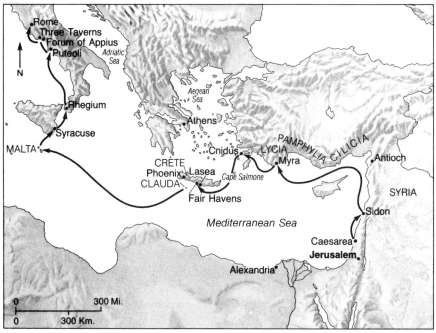

PAUL'S VOYAGE TO ROME

Key people

The book also presents the lives of two famous missionaries, Peter and Paul. Peter receives the first focus (1:1–8:40). Then the book introduces Paul and moves back and forth between the ministries of these two great men (9:1–12:24). The book's largest and final part focuses on Paul's ministry (12:25–28:31).

THREE MAJOR PROBLEMS

The book of Acts focuses first on the spread of Christianity and its resultant problems within the Jewish community (1:1–8:25). Then the book shows the problems inside and outside Christianity when the gospel spread to the Gentiles (8:26–12:24). The last part of the book focuses more on the impact of the gospel on Gentile communities. In this section opposition comes from the Jewish and the civil realms (12:25–28:31). Overall, the book of Acts deals with the following three problems:

The problem of Jesus of Nazareth as the exalted Messiah

The Jews of the first century viewed Christianity as a new religion. The first part of Acts focuses on the problems within the Jewish community concerning the Christians' claim that Jesus was the Messiah and exalted Lord (1:1–8:40). It was difficult for the Jewish establishment to believe that a humble man from Nazareth could be the promised Messiah, much less God in the flesh. As Lord, he brought a new perspective on obedience to God's commands.

The problem of new perspectives on law and covenant

The new way in which the Christians understood the Mosaic Law aroused anger and persecution from the religious authorities. The new changes in the conditions for how humans had fellowship with God were hard for the Jewish religious leaders to accept. The book of Hebrews gives the most complete explanation of the movement from Moses to the Messiah. God had replaced Moses' covenant with Christ's. But he had not thrown away his demands for obedience and personal purity. The Christians believed that though the old covenant in Moses had been replaced with the new covenant in Christ, the perfect law of God still remained and had to be obeyed.

The covenant structure was certainly different between Moses and Christ. To be sure, instead of ritual sacrifices at the temple, the new covenant had but one perfect and eternally effective sacrifice, the Lord. But the new covenant also had its laws. While Christians did not have to follow the dietary and cleansing laws of Moses, they were duty bound to obey the original and deeper intentions of those laws, calling believers to separation and personal purity.

Even in Moses' day it was never good enough just to cleanse the hands and allow an unclean heart—to eat kosher foods but feed the mind with unclean thoughts. The covenant had changed and some external rituals had found their spiritual fulfillment, but God's laws for morality and purity were, as always, still binding on the believer in Christ. The covenant structure around the law was subject to change—for example, from Adam to Noah, or from Abraham to Moses—but the essence of godly behavior remained. The religious leaders argued, however, that the Christians had thrown away both the covenant of Moses and his law and were therefore dangerously lawless.

The problem was that Christianity's critics had wrongly interpreted the Old Testament as teaching that salvation was gained by keeping the law of Moses. They believed that God was gracious, but salvation by grace without the merits of law-keeping was an impossibility for them to accept. But for the Christians, grace was God's gift of redemption that provided the only powerful motivation for obeying God's commands. Christianity did not do away with God's laws, it simply reestablished grace as motivation for obedience. Christians obeyed God's laws because they had already received God's grace—not in order to gain grace.

The problem of Gentile and Jewish equality

The misunderstanding concerning how law related to grace led to a third problem addressed in Acts and most other New Testament books as well. If the Mosaic Law was done away with as a standard for gaining salvation, then a non-Jewish Gentile person could be saved without going through the process of conforming to the Mosaic commands such as circumcision, temple rituals, cleansings, and dietary restrictions.

That freedom from Mosaic Laws was profoundly disturbing to the Jewish religious establishment and brought about much persecution. It also was a bitter pill for some Christians from Jewish backgrounds, who also caused bitter disputes within the fold of Christianity. These people were known as Judaizers, Christians who tried to make other Christians conform to the Mosaic Law (15:1).

THE USE OF THE OLD TESTAMENT IN THE SPEECHES

When Jesus instructed his disciples to be witnesses to the the "remotest part of the earth" (Acts 1:8), he was quoting from Isaiah 49:6. He used the Old Testament to describe the spread of Christianity around the world. Indeed, Jesus' entire life fulfilled God's will as laid down in the Old Testament Scriptures. Luke recorded in his Gospel that Jesus explained how his life related to the Old Testament Scriptures (Luke 24:27) and opened the disciples' minds to understand his explanation (Luke 24:44-45).

Jesus passed down that method of using the Old Testament to his disciples. He taught them about the kingdom of God during the period of forty days following his resurrection (Acts 1:3). Paul himself was so taught and quoted the same Isaiah 49:6 passage in Acts 13:47 to describe the Scriptural basis for his ministry. Paul thus showed that he had also been taught by the risen Lord (26:22-23).

Throughout Acts the speeches that were made by Jesus' followers show that they were taught how to relate the Old Testament Scriptures to Jesus' life and the Christian mission by the Holy Spirit. Even after the ascension, Jesus continued to teach them through his Spirit how to use the Old Testament.

BIBLE-WIDE CONCEPTS

JESUS RELATED TO DAVID, MOSES, AND ABRAHAM
Jesus and David: resurrection

In Acts 2:25-35 Luke gave the two most important links between Jesus and David. The first was in the quotation of Psalm 16:8-11 (2:25-28), which speaks of Jesus' resurrection. Because many Jews thought that passage related in some way to David, Peter had to explain its true meaning in 2:29-32.

Jesus' resurrection was directly related to Jesus being seated on the throne of David according to God's promise to David (2:30). That was the promise of the Davidic covenant made in 2 Samuel 7:1-29. And though Acts 2:25-28 spoke of Jesus' resurrection, it also spoke of the humiliation and pain of the death he had to suffer. But through that humiliation of death came the exaltation to the throne of God's promise.

Jesus and David: exaltation

The second major link between Jesus and David was in the quotation of Psalm 110:1 in Acts 2:34-35. That passage spoke of Jesus' exaltation to the right hand of God. After resurrection came exaltation. That was how the disciples understood Jesus' departure up into the cloud (1:9)—as a coronation procession. Now Jesus was at God's right hand, ruling according to the promise of David. Jesus now functioned as the administrator of the great promises of God to Abraham and Moses.

But that promise involved a certain time period noted in the phrase "until I make your enemies a footstool for your feet" (2:35). Jesus was and is reigning in the "until" period of conflict and of subduing his enemies. That sets the scene for the conflicts throughout Acts, the New Testament, and the history of Christianity as a whole. The present is a time for conflict as God's enemies are subdued. The final conflict and establishment of God's perfect kingdom is still future.

The startling revelation was that the Messiah had come, died, had been raised and exalted to the right hand of God, yet still the kingdom had not come in its historical fullness. Evil could still have temporal victories; flesh could still aggravate spirit. As Jesus, and David before him, had to undergo attacks from their enemies, so Christians would have to follow in the same path of humble obedience, but always knowing they would also follow in resurrection and exaltation.

Jesus and Moses

Jesus was the greater prophet whom Moses foretold. Peter quoted Deuteronomy 18:15, 19 in Acts 3:22-23. That meant that Jesus had now replaced Moses as the one to listen to (3:23, 26). Throughout Israel's history the Mosaic Law had been broken and ignored time after time. In Jeremiah's day God had spoken about making a new covenant sometime in the future (Jer. 31:31-34). It was Jesus who had inaugurated that new covenant (Luke 22:20).

Now Jesus was the greater prophet and lawgiver. God had spoken about the new covenant as including putting his Spirit within the hearts of the people (Ezek. 36:26). Jesus as the exalted prophet would send that Spirit forth to baptize his followers (Acts 1:4-5; 2:3-4). From that time on, the believer in Jesus would have to hear *his* voice for the final decision on matters of God's law, not Moses'.

Jesus and Abraham

One of the most difficult problems faced by Christians as well as their critics in Acts was the inclusion of Gentiles in salvation and worship. Most zealous Jews allowed for Gentiles to be included in Judaism, but with clear discrimination against them. Never would the Gentile be viewed as an equal participant in salvation with a Jew. Even after a Gentile had undergone the rituals such as circumcision, cleansings, and dietary laws, he would still not be viewed as equal with one born of Abraham's line.

And that mentality was naturally brought into Christianity by the first Jewish believers. But God would not let those cultural biases last for long.

God made both the Jews who did not believe in Jesus the Messiah as well as the Jewish Christians rethink their bias against Gentiles. God gave his Spirit to Gentiles on the basis of faith alone (Acts 15:8-9). Unlike the Jews, God did not show partiality (10:34-35). That meant that the Lord who reigned at God's right hand was sending his Holy Spirit upon Jew and Gentile alike. There was no distinction between them when it came to salvation. All were equal in need and were accepted on the same terms. That truth of equality would become Paul's central theme as he spoke against a return to the old standards of law and racial discrimination within the church.

That act of giving the Holy Spirit to the Gentiles clarified what God had intended all along when he first gave a covenant to Abraham (Gen. 12:1-3). All the world would someday be blessed in Abraham (Gen. 12:3). Peter quoted that promise in Acts 3:25-26. When God raised Jesus up and exalted him to his throne, that was the moment when the blessing to all families of the earth took a giant and final step forward.

No longer would there be Jews and Gentiles. All were equal candidates for direct blessing, not through the Mosaic conditions, but through the conditions of the greater prophet, greater son of David, and final fulfiller of the promise to Abraham, Jesus the Lord. Acts upholds the ethnic equality of all races in the new covenant of Christ. This realization provided the foundation for the necessary geographic spread of the message from Jerusalem to the ends of the earth (1:8).

RELATIONSHIP TO THE GOSPEL OF LUKE

As was said in the introduction to Luke's Gospel, Luke and Acts form a two-volume set. Each needs to be read with an awareness of the relationship between the two books. Acts builds on the truths of Luke's Gospel and continues the ministry of Jesus through the work of his Spirit and his body, represented by the church.

The place of the genealogy

Luke placed Jesus' genealogy right before the account of Jesus' ministry (Luke 3:23-28). Placing a person's genealogy before the recorded events of his life was an Old Testament pattern (cf. Exod. 6:14-27 regarding Aaron and Moses). Luke developed Jesus' ministry from this Old Testament pattern, thereby placing Jesus' works clearly within God's acts of salvation in history. Jesus was the Anointed One of God who had come to proclaim God's salvation (Luke 4:18-19). Jesus followed the pattern of the great ancestors in his genealogy by devoting himself to prayer at the great turning points of his life (Luke 3:21; 9:18, 28).

Jesus was the Man of the Spirit

Luke's Gospel highlighted how God gave his Spirit for prophecy to Elizabeth (Luke 1:41-42), Zechariah (Luke 1:67), Simeon (Luke 2:25-28), and Jesus (Luke 4:17-18). Acts shows God's next great advance in the gospel through the Spirit. He gave his Spirit to believers in Jesus the Messiah to enable them to proclaim the gospel. The Spirit is viewed as coming from the exalted Lord who sits at the right hand of God (Acts 2:33-36). The Spirit is the person through whom God touches and rules the world.

THE PRESENT AND FUTURE KINGDOM

The early believers struggled with how the Messiah could have come without ushering in the kingdom. Jesus explained how the kingdom was present in a hidden but powerful way (Matt. 13:1-52). The Messiah had come and so had the kingdom, but not in the way people had expected. It was a matter of misunderstanding how the kingdom was present, not of its postponement or delay.

In the book of Acts Jesus reigns over his kingdom from God's right hand. The kingdom was present, but not in the way it would be in its full historical manifestation at the end of the age. It was a time of sowing both wheat and tares, of leaven hidden in a lump of dough, of a mustard seed slowly growing to maturity.

The kingdom had not been delayed. Its present hidden but powerful presence was the way the kingdom would come to fullness. The visible physical kingdom, though now absent, was the hope of the Christian. The challenge was to see its glorious presence in the Spirit by faith and faithfully obey the King who reigned from God's throne until he came again. The present and the future manifestations of the kingdom are linked by a common bond: doing the will of God, on *earth* or in *heaven* (Matt. 6:10). The spread of the gospel was the only acceptable occupation for those who awaited the coming kingdom.

The gospel of the kingdom was the essence of the gospel message throughout Acts (3:19-21; 28:23, 31). The universalism of the Abrahamic blessing was becoming a reality. The shift from Moses to Jesus was debated and described (13:39; 15:9). The Spirit was poured out to provide strength for witness, comfort, and obedience (1:8; Ezek. 36:26-27; John 14:25-26; 15:26-27).

THE RELATIONSHIP OF ACTS
TO THE OTHER NEW TESTAMENT BOOKS

As the books of the New Testament were written, they were first collected into two groups: the Gospels and the Epistles. The book of Acts filled the gap between what was recorded about the earthly life of Jesus (the Gospels) and the work of the risen Lord recorded through the Epistles. Acts gives both historical and theological links. It is at once a sequel to the Gospels and the background to the Epistles. Therefore, it is a crucial book for understanding the continuity between the earthly and resurrected life of Christ.

NEEDS MET BY ACTS

Times were not easy for the original readers of Acts. Many faced religious persecution from Jewish or civil organizations. Many lost their jobs and social standing and others were beaten or even killed for their faith. Luke wanted his readers to gain a deeper certainty about their faith in Christ—a certainty that would keep them faithful to God during hard times. The heart of that certainty was a need to understand where Christ went after his resurrection and how he could still be present with his followers. Christ had been exalted to the right hand of God, but his Spirit was poured out among his believers on earth. The certain presence of God's Spirit brought believers power for certainty in their faith and for witness.

Other needs addressed by Luke relate to how the followers of Christ were supposed to relate their new faith to the ancient ways of Israel. Throughout the book, Luke shows the deep Old Testament roots of faith in Jesus. The kingdom of God would come and be ruled by the Messiah as promised. Until then, the Messiah's people, both Jews and Gentiles, were to witness in the power of the Spirit. The structure and content of Luke's Gospel show that he was answering questions like these for his readers.

- How can Jews give up the Mosaic Law to follow Jesus?
- If Mosaic Law and Jewish tradition are unimportant for salvation, what good are they?
- How do Jesus and his teachings relate to God's promises to Abraham, Moses, and David?
- Does Jesus annul the Old Testament promises or does he somehow enlarge or modify them?
- How can it be possible that Gentiles do not have to follow the Laws of Moses in order to be saved?
- How is the kingdom of God operating now that Jesus is no longer on earth?
- What does it mean for the Holy Spirit to be here?
- How does the presence of the Holy Spirit relate to Christian life and witness?
- What is the connection between the Spirit and the rule of the risen Lord?
- Has the coming of God's kingdom somehow been put off or delayed?
- Is the Christian faith a threat to the Roman Empire?
- Should Christianity be a legal religion?
- What should believers be doing while they wait for Jesus to come back?
- Can hostility from religious and civil authorities hinder or even stop the spread of the gospel?

Luke's long narrative of Christ's acts after his resurrection helps meet three key needs for believers today. First, and most important, Acts explains how God is present with believers in his Spirit. That divine presence is the foundation for joy in life, awe in worship, and power in witness.

Second, Acts provides great insight into how Christians are to relate to the Laws of Moses. When Luke wrote, there was much controversy about how Christians were to relate to Old Testament laws. Luke described how the early church handled some of these difficult questions. And these point the way to how believers today are to relate to the laws of the Old Testament and contemporary pressures to false legalism.

Third, Luke helps believers understand why the kingdom did not come immediately after Christ's resurrection. God's plans for the kingdom were not somehow derailed. Luke showed that the present is fully part of God's plan and is pervaded with essential kingdom blessings because Christ is ruling from his place at God's right hand and his Spirit is present to work his wonders of power and blessing. Persecution then or now does not diminish the truth that the proclamation of the kingdom continues on "without hindrance" (Acts 28:31). God's work may experience opposition and hostility, but it will not be stopped. And until faith is replaced by sight, Acts helps meet the needs of believers for a pattern of prayer, witness, and worship.

OUTLINE OF ACTS

A. WITNESS POWER: MESSIANIC EXALTATION (1:1–2:47)
   1. The Final Departure (1:1-11)
   2. The Community of Prayer (1:12-26)
   3. The First Witness in Power (2:1-47)

B. THE JERUSALEM CAMPAIGN: HOSTILITY AND DIVINE PROTECTION (3:1–8:1)
   1. Events at the Beautiful Gate (3:1–4:4)
   2. The Interrogation of Peter and John (4:5-22)
   3. The Empowered Community (4:23–5:16)
   4. The Imprisoned Apostles (5:17-42)
   5. Ethnic and Administrative Squabbles (6:1-7)
   6. Stephen Is Arrested and Murdered (6:8–8:1)

C. THE SCATTERED WITNESS: THE DIRECTION AND DIRECTOR (8:2–9:31)
   1. Rise of Persecution (8:2-3)
   2. Philip in Samaria (8:4-25).
   3. Philip Preaches to an Ethiopian (8:26-40)
   4. The Conversion of Saul (9:1-31)

D. THE GENTILES: INCLUDED BY GOD (9:32–11:26)
   1. Two Miracles in Neighboring Towns (9:32-43)
   2. Confirmation of Gentile Salvation (10:1–11:26)

E. JERUSALEM PERSECUTION: THE KING VERSUS A KING (11:27–12:24)
   1. Famine Relief (11:27-30)
   2. Herod's Final Atrocities (12:1-24)

F. PAUL'S LONG-RANGE MISSION: JEW AND GENTILE CONFLICT (12:25–14:28)
   1. Commission and Preparation (12:25–13:3)
   2. Cyprus (13:4-12)
   3. Asia Minor (13:13–14:25)
   4. Return and Report to the Antioch Community (14:26-28)

G. TOWARD A JEW AND GENTILE RESOLUTION (15:1-35)
   1. The Problem Arises (15:1-5)
   2. The Problem Debated and Solved (15:6-21)
   3. The Answer Is Formulated (15:22-29)
   4. The Response to the Answer (15:30-35)

H. THE SECOND MISSION: GENTILE EXTENSION INTO EUROPE (15:36–18:21)
   1. The Personnel Selected (15:36-41)
   2. The Journey to the Edge of Europe (16:1-10)
   3. In Philippi (16:11-40)
   4. Thessalonica and Persecution (17:1-9)
   5. Berea and Persecution (17:10-15)
   6. Athens (17:16-34)

A C T S   N O T E S

1:1–2:47 WITNESS POWER: MESSIANIC EXALTATION

1:1-11 The Final Departure

1:1-5 THE COMMAND TO WAIT FOR THE SPIRIT

This introduction to the book emphasizes two aspects: (1) Christ's ministry from its beginning to his ascension and (2) his task of giving instructions by the Holy Spirit to his apostles after his resurrection. The rest of the book is the result of the apostles carrying out these instructions given by the risen Lord. These instructions (Acts 1:2; see "command," 1:4) and the Holy Spirit stand behind all the great acts of witness throughout the book.

Note the central place of the Spirit. Even the orders of the risen Lord were "through the Holy Spirit" (1:2). Although the author of Acts is not named, all the evidence points to Luke. The dedication to "Theophilus," the mention of the "former book" (the Gospel of Luke), and the medical vocabulary support the tradition cited by Irenaeus, Clement of Alexandria, Tertullian, and Origen that Luke authored the book. The reference to Theophilus, some prominent individual who may have assisted in the publication of Luke's research, is a dedication characteristic of Greco-Roman literature.

Jesus had promised that the coming of the Holy Spirit would be indicative of the kingdom's presence (1:3-5). This post-resurrection teaching about the kingdom of God is foundational for the book. Jesus appeared and ministered to his disciples for a period of forty days between Jesus' resurrection and ascension. The "kingdom of God" was the major subject of his teaching. The book of Acts begins and concludes with this subject (28:31).

The speeches of Peter (Acts 2–3) and Stephen (Acts 7) reflected their schooling during this forty-day period sitting under the teaching of the risen Lord as he told them the details about the kingdom (1:3). Acts 1:3 follows and guards the "taken up" (1:2) by showing that Jesus was alive, well, and seen by his apostles for a long time before he disappeared. What the "Father promised" (1:4) was the indwelling ministry of the Holy Spirit to be given as divine enablement (cf. Luke 24:49; John 14:16-17; Acts 2:33; Ezek. 36:27; Joel 2:28). The baptism performed by John the Baptist was about to find a new fulfillment in the coming of the Holy Spirit (Acts 1:5).

1:6-11 THE PROMISE OF CHRIST'S RETURN
1:6-8 The commission of the disciples. The disciples linked the coming of the Spirit (1:5) to the coming of the kingdom (1:6). They would find out that though the Holy Spirit would soon come, the fullness of the kingdom would not. They had to learn a balance between rejoicing in the power of the Spirit and humbly waiting through the conflicts of this age for the kingdom to come. In spite of Christ's rejection, the disciples still anticipated a literal Messianic kingdom (1:6). The word "restore" (1:6) implied a pattern that had existed before—the rule by kings in the Old Testament.

Acts 1:8 provides the outline for the entire book: (1) witness in Jerusalem (2:5–8:3), (2) witness in Judea and Samaria (8:4–12:25), and (3) witness in the Mediterranean world

(13:1–28:31). The Spirit's function was to provide power for witness worldwide. The redeemed believers were being told what their primary function would be while they waited for Jesus to return. This is similar to the Olivet Discourse in Matthew 24–25. There the believers were told to be faithful and spread the gospel to the whole world (Matt. 24:14).

The phrase "the ends of the earth" is a quotation of Isaiah 49:6. This showed that the mission of Israel, of Jesus, and the church was to spread the news of God's redemption. Paul applied the same passage to his ministry to the Gentiles in Acts 13:47.

1:9-11 Christ's glorious departure. The ascension (1:9), an event prophesied in Isaiah 52:13, took place on the Mount of Olives and demonstrated that Jesus was the perfect pattern of righteousness acceptable to the Father (John 16:10). A cloud (1:9) had also enveloped Jesus and the disciples during his transfiguration (Luke 9:34) and was an image mentioned in relation to his second coming (Luke 21:27; Mark 14:62).

Jesus' visible departure upward was different from his other disappearances during the forty days following his resurrection (John 20:19-29; Luke 24:31, 36). It made a clear point as to where he went—up, in simple human terms, to the right hand of God (Ps. 110:1). Peter used Psalm 110:1 to describe this event (Acts 2:33-35).

The point behind the conversation with the angel (1:10-11) was to assert that Jesus could go and would someday come again, but the task of witness still remained. The unknown time of his return had nothing to do with a lessening of the command to witness. For his second coming, see Matthew 24:26-31; Revelation 19:11-16; Zechariah 12:10–13:1; 14:1-4.

1:12-26 The Community of Prayer

1:12-14 RETURN TO JERUSALEM
FOR PRAYERFUL WAITING
A "Sabbath day's walk" (Acts 1:12) was about three-quarters of a mile. This limit had been calculated by the rabbis on the basis of Exodus 16:29 as interpreted by Numbers 35:5. The disciples were told to wait for the promise of the Spirit (Acts 1:4). The disciples waited prayerfully (1:14), presumably for the Spirit's coming. The disciples may have been following Jesus' prayer (Matt. 6:10) that the kingdom would come. The book of Acts shows how the believers' desire for God's power from the Holy Spirit impacted their obedience and witness.

1:15-19 JUDAS'S DESTRUCTION
Within the context of expectant prayer, Peter's thoughts were led to Scriptures instructing how to complete the original number of the Lord's twelve apostles. This book tells about the apostolic spread of the gospel, and the first step was to complete the original apostolic body. Matthew 27:6-7 notes that the temple priests bought Judas's field. For "Scripture" (1:16), see 1:20 and the use of Psalms 69:25 and 109:8. The word "hanged" in Matthew 27:5 may be literally translated "strangled" and is used of Ahithophel in the Septuagint version (the Greek Old Testament) of 2 Samuel 17:23.

1:20-26 JUDAS'S REPLACEMENT
The fulfilled Scripture (Acts 1:20) came from two of David's psalms (Acts 1:16). It affirmed two principles that were applied to Judas: the judgment on rejectors (Ps. 69:25) and the replacement of defectors (Ps. 109:8). Psalm 69 is thoroughly Messianic. Other portions of it are used elsewhere in the New Testament (see Ps. 69:9 in John 2:17 and Rom. 15:3; and Ps. 69:21 in Luke 23:36). Psalm 109:22 is quoted in Matthew 27:39 ("shaking their heads," also see Ps. 22:7-8). The name of the field, "Blood," implied that no one was to live there. The "place of leadership" (Acts 1:20) was not just a position. It demanded the experience of the full period of Jesus' earthly ministry (1:21-22).

To be qualified (1:21-22), this new leader was to have witnessed the resurrection (1:22) and experienced Jesus' life from his baptism to the ascension (1:22). Simply having seen the risen Lord, as for example, the five hundred of 1 Corinthians 15:6, was not sufficient for qualification as an apostolic witness. That witness demanded the experience that would enable him to put the risen Lord's appearance into the context of his whole life and teaching concerning the kingdom.

The apostles used a method of both rational and supernatural selection (Acts 1:23-26). Lot casting (1:26) was a means of determining the will of God (Prov. 16:33).

It does not appear again in the Bible after Pentecost (cf. Rom. 8:14). Some have argued that the apostles were wrong in recognizing Matthias and should have waited until God filled the vacancy with Paul. However, Paul would not have been qualified on the basis of Acts 1:21-22, and the choice made was God's, not man's (1:24).

2:1-47 The First Witness in Power

2:1-4 THE FILLING OF THE SPIRIT FOR PROPHECY

The Holy Spirit's coming was accompanied by a sound (2:2) and a symbol (2:3). The day of Pentecost ("Feast of Weeks," Exod. 34:22; Deut. 16:10) was celebrated on the fiftieth day after the Feast of First Fruits (Lev. 23:15; Exod. 34:22). This spring celebration commemorated the first of the grain harvest. The Spirit's coming at Pentecost signaled the presence of God predicted by the Old Testament prophets, John the Baptist, and Jesus (Acts 1:5). The fire appeared on the believers (2:3), much like the flames of God's holy presence appeared on the burning bush for Moses (Exod. 3:2).

With the coming of the Holy Spirit came also enablement to communicate God's message supernaturally (Acts 2:4). The believers were filled with the Spirit for the specific function of proclaiming the gospel (2:11). The disciples were all filled with the Spirit, baptized into the body of Christ, and indwelt by the Holy Spirit (1 Cor. 12:13; cf. Ezek. 36:27; John 14:17). Luke's Gospel presented people being filled with the Spirit to speak (Luke 1:41-42, 67). But the difference in Acts from the early chapters of Luke is the speaking in foreign languages—"in other tongues."

2:5-12 AMAZEMENT

There were Jews from every nation in Jerusalem for the feast (Acts 2:5). They became the first illustration of the Lord's intentions to bring the gospel to the ends of the earth (1:8). They were amazed at hearing the message in their own language. The tongues were known languages (2:6, 8) used to communicate the gospel. The hearers could speak Greek or Aramaic so they did not need to hear the message in their own language. But God provided a special sign to communicate his gospel.

Peter's explanation of the phenomenon of tongues (2:14-42) appears to have been in a single language, probably Aramaic or Greek. The sign came in many tongues—an unusual act of God to highlight and define the scope of his message. But the explanation and invitation to believe came in one language.

The countries mentioned in 2:9-11 are the lands of the Jewish dispersion in the eastern Mediterranean. The message was about "the wonders of God" (2:11), a first definition of the content of the gospel. "Converts to Judaism" (2:10; "proselytes," NASB and KJV) were Gentiles who kept the Jewish law and were admitted into full fellowship with the people of Israel. Three steps were required: (1) circumcision, (2) purification through self-baptism, and (3) the offering of a sacrifice. Many Gentiles were content with a more informal attachment to the Jewish religion and were called God-fearers (cf. 10:2).

2:13 MOCKING

Some people made fun of the miracle of tongues (2:13; cf. 1 Cor. 14:23). The communication of the great acts of God was clear (Acts 2:11). What needed explanation was how the believers could speak in other languages. That sign and its mocking by some of the listeners formed the transition to Peter's speech of interpretation. His speech explained the sign through teaching and evangelism.

2:14-36 PETER'S EXPLANATION OF THE SIGN OF TONGUES

The introduction (2:14) set the tone by being formal and impressive. Then Peter explained the languages (2:15-21). The "third hour" (2:15; NASB and KJV) was 9:00 A.M. Jews engaged in worship on feast days and customarily abstained from eating or drinking until 10:00 A.M.

2:14-21 Peter's use of Joel 2:28-32. In 2:16-21 Peter quoted Joel 2:28-32 in order to explain the miracle of tongues. There are three basic views regarding how Peter viewed the fulfillment of Joel 2:28-32. (1) The nonfulfillment view holds that Peter used the prophecy only as an illustration of what was transpiring in his day, not as a fulfillment. The only fulfillment would come later at the second coming of Christ. (2) The partial fulfillment view regards the part of

Joel's prophecy that concerns the Holy Spirit as fulfilled (Acts 2:28-29), but the signs in the sky (2:30-32) as still to be fulfilled in the tribulation. (3) The full fulfillment view regards the essence of the prophecy as being fulfilled with additional fulfillments in the future (cf. Isa. 32:15; 44:3; Zech. 12:10–13:1).

Whatever the overall view taken, the essence of Peter's use of Joel can be better understood by examining the quotation in its original context. Joel presented a message about how God calls people to himself. He called upon the people to return with all their hearts, before the terrible day of the Lord came (Joel 2:11-12). Salvation would come to any who called upon the name of the Lord (Joel 2:32). But actually, God himself was calling the people to himself through the great signs and wonders (Joel 2:32). So the context was God calling people to himself by means of signs and wonders.

Peter's purpose in his sermon was similar to that of the prophet Joel. That is, Joel shared the same overall context with Peter's speech in Acts 2. Peter wanted his listeners to call upon the name of the Lord (Acts 2:21), but he ended with acknowledging that God was ultimately calling people to himself. The people's faith in God was a response to God's call through the signs and wonders in Jesus' life and the miracle of tongues. Seeing signs was to issue in faith and repentance.

Joel predicted that God would pour out his Spirit (Joel 2:28) and present signs and wonders (Joel 2:30) in order to cause people to call upon him for salvation (Joel 2:32). That was precisely Peter's point. Tongues showed that God had poured out his Spirit (Acts 2:15-17). God had presented signs and wonders through the life and resurrection of Christ (Acts 3:19, 22, 43). Therefore, the people should repent and respond in faith to God's call (2:38-39).

Peter linked the speaking in tongues to the Holy Spirit by adding "they shall prophesy" (2:18) to his quotation of Joel 2:29. He linked the signs and wonders predicted in Joel 2 to the work of God in Jesus' life on earth (Acts 2:19, 22). Prophecy was the pouring forth of the Spirit. Signs and wonders were seen in the life of Christ and would continue through the work of the

apostles (2:43). Peter linked his present time to the time of threat and urgency that will surround the end of the age (2:20-21). The tongues were a sign confirming the predicted advance in God's redemptive and prophetic program.

The speaking in tongues was directly linked to the outpouring of the Spirit (2:16-17). The pouring forth of the Spirit was directly linked to the exaltation of Jesus to the right hand of God (2:33). Thus, the signs of the apostles, whether healings or tongues, were confirmations that God had exalted his Son to his right hand and now summoned people to respond in faith to his redemptive call. This sign was not simply a miracle; it was a sign pointing to the power and call of the risen and reigning Lord.

2:22-36 New elements in proclaiming the Christian gospel. A radical shift was being presented. Now, for the Jew and the Gentile, the only acceptable response to God was to believe in his Son. That response of faith would then unlock forgiveness and the gift of the Spirit. Peter went on to show how Jesus was approved by God (2:22-23). "Wonders and signs" (2:22) link back to 2:19. Although approved by God, the people nailed him to the cross, but God was behind it all (2:23).

Appealing to Old Testament quotations, Peter presented three proofs that Jesus was the Messiah: (1) his miracles (Acts 2:22-23; cf. Joel 2:28-32), (2) his resurrection (Acts 2:24-32; cf. Ps. 16:8-11) and (3) his exaltation (Acts 2:33-35; cf. Ps. 110:1). Christ's resurrection and exaltation were presented as fulfillments of God's promise to David.

As a prophet, David spoke of the resurrection and reign of a future son according to the Davidic covenant (Acts 2:30; cf. Ps. 16:8-11). As that future son, Jesus experienced what was predicted for David's son, exaltation to the right hand of God (Acts 2:33-36; cf. Ps. 110:1). Peter viewed the raising up and exaltation of Jesus as one and the same event. See Matthew 22:43-45 and 26:64 for Jesus' use of Psalm 110:1. The conclusion (Acts 2:33) clearly links the pouring forth of the Spirit with Joel's prediction (2:17).

This first proclamation by a Christian prophet contains some basic elements of early Christian preaching. (1) The age of fulfillment has arrived as initially described by the Joel 2 context. (2) The message is universal but always comes to the Jew first. The speech focuses on devout "God-fearing" (2:5) Jews and Gentile converts (2:10). (3) The life, death, and resurrection of Jesus is recounted. Its essence is to show that the man Jesus was the promised Messiah (2:36). (4) The Old Testament is used as proof for Jesus' Messiahship. The next speeches expand the message to include the impending kingdom (Acts 3), the Messiah as Savior (Acts 4–5), and the long-standing Jewish resistance to God's affirmation of his prophets (Acts 7).

2:37-47 THE RESPONSE.
2:37-40 Direction is sought and given.
Direction is sought by the listeners (2:37) and given by Peter (2:38-40). Repentance and baptism enabled the believer to receive forgiveness and the Holy Spirit (2:38). Forgiveness of sins always came through faith in Jesus (Eph. 2:8-9). Baptism was a rite of identification by which new believers became associated with Jesus and his followers. The benefits of repentance were called a promise for Jews and Gentiles alike (near and "far off," Acts 2:39; cf. Eph. 2:11-13). Luke only recorded the gist of Peter's message; his many other words (Acts 2:40) were not recorded.

2:41-42 Community growth in numbers and maturity. The rapid growth mentioned here was related to the repentance and belief of new members (2:41-42). Community teaching and fellowship was the only acceptable result of belief in Jesus as Messiah. The "breaking of bread" (2:42) referred to the celebration of the Lord's Supper (cf. 1 Cor. 11:20-34; Jude 1:12).

2:43-47 Growth and maturity is elaborated. The wonders and signs (2:43) link back to Joel's prediction (2:19-20) and the life of Jesus (2:22). Certain aspects of Joel's prediction of signs and wonders were still future, like the prediction of a radical change in the sun and moon. But enough signs and wonders were performed by Jesus and his disciples after him to demonstrate that the time of Joel's prediction had begun—the time of special awe (2:43).

The communal sharing was voluntary and met the needs of believers who lingered in Jerusalem after Pentecost or lost jobs due to persecution. It was the natural expression of spiritual unity. The spontaneous sharing of personal property was consistent with other principles of Scripture. The intentions behind God's distribution of manna would be taken up by Paul with reference to supplying the needs of the Christians (Exod. 16:18; 2 Cor. 8:14-15). The Mosaic Law had much to say about supporting the poor, needy, and widows (Deut. 10:18; 14:29; 16:11, 14; 24:17, 19-21; 26:12-13; 27:19).

3:1–8:1 THE JERUSALEM CAMPAIGN: HOSTILITY AND DIVINE PROTECTION
3:1–4:4 Events at the Beautiful Gate
3:1-10 THE LAME BEGGAR HEALED
Peter and John continued to follow the customs of temple worship (Acts 3:1). The events that took place there form the second major witness to Christ. The "ninth hour" (NASB and KJV) was 3:00 P.M., the time for the prayer service that accompanied the evening sacrifice (cf. Exod. 29:39-46).

SOME IMPLICATIONS OF THE NEW RELIGION
The linking of Jesus and the Spirit to the Old Testament and the end of the age was a giant step forward in God's plan of redemption. Christianity claimed that the Messiah had been identified: Jesus. As a result, to the extent that the existing Jewish religion rejected Jesus as Messiah, it was now insufficient with respect to salvation. Therefore God's approach to the sin problem had been radically advanced. Forgiveness was now to be found exclusively in Jesus.

A mind change was needed regarding Jesus in order to avoid rejecting the authority of Judaism. Mainline Judaism was apostate from God's perspective, to the extent of its resistance to the new proclamation. That resistance would grow stronger over time. Passages like Matthew 13 and Romans 9–11 explain why the Jews as a whole did not receive Jesus as God's Son. But their rejection of Jesus would be used to bring light to the Gentiles (Matt. 4:15-16).

Peter healed the lame beggar with power granted by the Holy Spirit through the *name* of Jesus (Acts 3:2-8). Alms giving in the New Testament period was regarded as a meritorious act with sacrificial and atoning value. It was regarded above prayer and fasting as a means of attaining rightousness. The Beautiful Gate was located east of the sanctuary and gave access to the Court of Women from the Court of Gentiles.

The people who saw the healed beggar responded in amazement (3:9-10). The man had been lame from birth and known by many. The miracle became an occasion for preaching the gospel and for the first arrest of Christians.

3:11-26 PETER INTERPRETS THE SIGN
The controling image of this sermon is Jesus as servant. The "servant" image begins and ends this sermon (3:13, 26) and cements not only Jesus' role in God's plan for world redemption but the believers' as well. They must be servants of God's salvation blessings. The book of Acts describes the glories and the costs of that servanthood. The Old Testament supports the idea that the Messiah was to be a servant and a blessing for all nations in Abraham (see Gen. 22:18 in Acts 3:25-26) and in the raising up of the prophet greater than Moses (see Deut. 18:15, 19 in Acts 3:22-23).

The source of the healing was Jesus (3:11-16). The power for healing came through faith in his name. Scholars are divided as to whether the faith for healing was granted on the part of Peter or the lame man. "Solomon's Colonnade" (3:11; "portico of Solomon," NASB; "porch that is called Solomon's," KJV) was a covered, colonnaded porch that ran the length of the Court of the Gentiles on the east. As servant, Jesus had been glorified (3:13) by the exaltation to the right hand of God as described in Acts 1–2 (cf. Isa. 42:1; 52:13–53:12; Luke 1:54-55). The servant theme will be taken up again in Acts 4:25, 27, 30.

Peter proclaimed the coming kingdom (3:17-26). His logic was that the predicted suffering of Jesus was in the past. Therefore the people needed to repent and receive the coming time of restoration (3:18-19). The words "repent . . . and turn" mean "change your mind about Jesus and return to God."

The time of restoration (3:21) was a reference to the future blessings of the Messianic kingdom.

Acts 3:20-26 contains four key themes: (1) Jesus' return is for the Jews in a special way ("for you," 3:20; and "first to you," 3:26). (2) The prophets predicted that time ("prophets" repeated three times 3:21, 24, 25). (3) God has raised up a prophet greater than Moses ("raise up," 3:22; and "raised up," 3:26). (4) Jesus' raising up begins the special blessing promised to all the nations through Abraham ("blessed," 3:25; "bless," 3:26). The people are to return to God (3:19), so that Jesus might return and restore (3:20-21). In the present, God had already sent the risen Jesus to the people (3:26) through the proclamation of the gospel and the presence of his Spirit.

The key Old Testament passages in this speech are Deuteronomy 18:15, 19 and Genesis 22:18. The "until" of Acts 3:21 reflects Psalm 110:1 which was also used in Acts 2:35 ("until I make your enemies a footstool for your feet").

4:1-4 THE FIRST PERSECUTION BEGINS
Peter and John were arrested (4:1-4), ushering in the first persecution. The "captain of the temple guard" (4:1) was responsible for maintaining order in the temple and was second only to the high priest. The Sadducees were theological conservatives associated with the temple and priesthood. They objected to Jesus being called the Messiah and the concept of resurrection (Matt. 22:23-33). The ruling Sadducees may have presented a pious front, but they were motivated by jealousy. Luke links their jealousy (Acts 5:17) with a long-standing jealousy within Israel of God's chosen leaders (7:9). The initial persecution did not stop the effectiveness of the gospel message (4:4). That is one key point of Acts—prison could not imprison the power of the gospel.

4:5-22 The Interrogation of Peter and John
4:5-7 THE QUESTION OF AUTHORITY
This is the third major act of witness in the book. It took place before all the major religious rulers in Jerusalem (4:5-6). This was a meeting of the Sanhedrin (4:5, 15),

the highest religious court of Judaism. Annas (4:6) was high priest (A.D. 6–15) before being deposed by the Romans. His son-in-law, Caiaphas (A.D. 18–36), was later appointed to the position. Nothing is known of John and Alexander (4:6) except that they were members of the high priest's family.

4:8-12 PETER'S REPLY
Peter's bold reply to the accusations of the Sanhedrin exemplified the prophetic enabling of the Spirit to proclaim God's message with boldness (cf. Luke 1:15, 67; Acts 4:31; 13:9). The core of the message concerned the resurrection (4:10) based on the Scripture of Psalm 118:22. The resurrection was seen as God's affirmation of Jesus the Messiah. Humans rejected the stone; God put it back in place permanently. The key themes were Jesus' humiliation at human hands and exaltation by God's hands (Ps. 118:22). See the themes of humiliation and exaltation in Psalm 118:22. Jesus quoted the same passage in Matthew 21:42-44, possibly before the very same people. Peter inserted "you" (Acts 4:11) before "builders" to make the passage more pointed. Peter explained the nature of the sign miracles. They were to move the onlookers from the physical healing of the lame man to the spiritual healing offered by Jesus the Messiah. Salvation was to be found in Jesus alone (4:21).

4:13-22 THREAT AND RELEASE: NO GUILT
The religious leaders ordered Peter and John not to witness (4:13-18). The leaders could not deny the miracle, but they did deny that Jesus did it. The word "unschooled" (4:13) simply means that Peter and John had not been formally trained in the rabbinic schools (note 4:13). The disciples had been with Jesus and now sounded like him, especially after his forty-day resurrection teaching ministry and the sending of the Holy Spirit. Their motivation to witness was the demand of truth from eyewitness authority and doing right in God's sight (4:19-22).

4:23–5:16 The Empowered Community
4:23-31 EMPOWERED IN PRAYER
This section builds to the disciples' again being filled with the Holy Spirit to speak the word boldly (4:31). The power behind that filling was prayer based on Scripture. They confessed God as Creator of all (4:24). They also confessed that their persecution had been predicted, that is, that their pain was not a surprise to God. He was in total control. Hostility against Jesus the Messiah and Christians was part and parcel of God's intentions for the spread of the gospel in Acts and beyond (note Ps. 2:7; Acts 13:33). The believers related the Scripture (Ps. 2:1-2) to their own circumstances (see "peoples" and "nations" in Acts 4:25, 27). Psalm 2:7 will be quoted in Acts 13:33 to refer to Jesus' resurrection. "Herod" (4:27) refers to Herod Antipas (Luke 23:7-12). For "Pontius Pilate" (4:27), see note on Matthew 27:2. Their next step for the Christians was to ask for "enabling to speak" (Acts 4:29) and miracles (4:30). That request was right in line with Jesus' commands to witness (1:8). The result was that the believers were again filled for bold sharing of the gospel (4:31). But more, it was a confirmation from God of his continued control and presence with this little band of believers, even though it was cursed by the religious leaders.

4:32–5:11 EMPOWERED IN GIVING
4:32-35 The believers share their possessions. The acts of giving in 4:32-35 were the result of the believers' prayer and the powerful work of the Holy Spirit (4:23-31). The great power of the Spirit led to great acts of grace. The same Greek word translates "great" with reference to the apostles' power and "much" with reference to the grace upon them all (4:33).

4:36-37 The positive example of Joseph (Barnabas). Acts 4:36–5:11 gives two specific examples of giving, one negative and one positive. Joseph's nickname was "Barnabas," Aramaic for "son of refreshment" or "son of a prophet." The word "son" (4:36) was used in the Semitic sense, as a reference to the man's character. The word "encouragement" (4:36) may mean "consolation" or "exhortation." He was a Jew and a Levite, from Cyprus (4:36). Joseph freely gave the purchase price of the land to be distributed by the apostles to meet the needs of the community (4:37).

5:1-11 The negative example of Ananias and Sapphira. This couple lied to God (5:3-4), specifically the Holy Spirit (5:3, 9). Their sin was not in withholding some of the proceeds of the sale, but in pretending to give all they had received. Satan desired this kind of prideful deception among the Christian community. They pretended greater devotion than was real in their lives. In the biblical period, burial normally took place on the day of death in view of the rapid deterioration of the body in the hot Middle Eastern climate (5:6).

Their testing of the Spirit (5:9) became another of the first-time lessons provided by God in Scripture (see the fall, Gen. 3; the flood, Gen. 6–8; and the sin of Achan, Josh. 7). In 1 Corinthians 10:9 Paul also spoke of Israel testing the Lord. The essence of testing God was to push God to prove his presence, either to judge or to bless (cf. Matt. 4:7; see also Deut. 6:16; Exod. 17:7). Ananias and Sapphira "test the Spirit of the Lord" (Acts 5:9) by presuming his unwillingness to judge sin. In this case God indeed was with the Christian community both to bless and to judge.

Others have doubtless lied in a similar manner since then. But God had made his lesson at the first occurrence and continued to move on in grace. Here the emphasis was on giving rather than witnessing. The character of the witnesses had to be pure. In this flash of judgment it became clear that God was the audience for ministry, not men. To pervert the great grace (4:33) was to pervert the witness concerning Jesus Christ. The result of this judgment was "great fear" (5:5, 11).

5:12-16 EMPOWERED IN GEOGRAPHICAL EXTENT

God produced great awe through his miracles (2:43), great grace (4:33) and great fear (5:5, 11). These led to a purity of lifestyle among the believers that brought high esteem from unbelievers (5:13) and an increased spread of the gospel. For "Solomon's Colonnade" (5:12), see note on Acts 3:11.

5:17-42 The Imprisoned Apostles

5:17-25 THE MIRACULOUS RELEASE

All twelve of the apostles were arrested by the Jewish leaders. The source of the hatred shown was the jealousy of the religious leaders—jealousy based on the high esteem in which the Christians were held (5:13). The "high priest" (5:17) was Caiaphas

(A.D. 18–36). For the "Sadducees," see note on 4:1. The miracle of release (5:19-20) was another confirmation of God's blessing and presence with the believers. Humans locked the door on the gospel's progress, but God opened it. This continues the tone set in 4:23-30.

5:26-32 SECOND ARREST AND DEFENSE

The continued threat of imprisonment was restated (5:26-28). At the heart of Peter's response to the Jewish leaders was the exaltation of Jesus to God's right hand, justifying their belief and witness (5:29-32; cf. 2:33-35). The end of Peter's response implied that the religious leaders were not obeying God because they did not believe in Jesus as Messiah (5:32).

5:33-40 GAMALIEL'S PROPOSITION

The response of the leaders was to kill all twelve of the apostles (5:33). "Gamaliel" (5:34), a respected Jewish rabbi often quoted in the Mishnah, was the grandson of Hillel and Paul's teacher (Acts 22:3). He gave a "wait-and-see" proposition (5:34-40). A certain Theudas (5:36) was mentioned by Josephus with reference to later historical events around A.D. 44 (Josephus, *Antiquities,* 20.5.1). It is possible that Josephus was wrong in the dating of Theudas or that there were two men with the same name. Judas the Galilean (Acts 5:37) inaugurated a religious and nationalist revolt in A.D. 6, but the rebellion was crushed by Rome.

Note Gamaliel's skepticism, which reveals an attitude toward Christianity common among Jews of that day. Gamaliel had seen many false religious leaders come and go, and he placed Jesus among them. But his skepticism was tempered with a healthy understanding of God's sovereignty. He had an attitude, not of faith in Jesus, but of waiting to see if the small group of Jesus' followers would survive and grow. But Gamaliel ignored the best proof he would ever get—the resurrection of Christ. The proof of Jesus' claims is in his resurrection, not in the relative prosperity or growth of his followers. Flogging (5:40) was the same punishment that Jesus had received (John 19:1). Pilate also attempted to follow a punish-and-release pattern with Jesus (Acts 5:40; cf. Luke 23:16). The end of this second crisis with

Jewish leadership was the result of them having no basis for convicting the apostles (Acts 4:21) and the impossibility of fighting against God (5:39).

5:41-42 TEACHING CONTINUED
The disciples continued to witness, and the split between Christianity and Judaism continued to widen. The command to stop sharing the gospel did not invalidate God's commission to witness (1:8; 5:20).

6:1-7 Ethnic and Administrative Squabbles
6:1 THE MATERIAL AND ETHNIC PROBLEM
The heart of the problem was racial tension over the daily ration of food for widows. This was a breakdown of the kindhearted sharing of goods seen in 2:44-45 and 4:34-37. It was a violation of a prime biblical command to care for widows while also being an ethnic slur against the Greek Christians. The common good had to be maintained. Compare with 2 Corinthians 8:14-15 and Exodus 16:18 regarding the equality in the distribution of manna.

But the overall thrust of this story was in surmounting this hindrance to prayer and the ministry of the word. This section moves from the possible neglect of the word of God (Acts 6:2) to the continued spreading of that word (6:7). The problem may have been material or racial, but the real problem was how this squabble could have kept the apostles from praying, preaching, and spreading the gospel. The book of Acts reveals that neither persecution from unbelievers nor squabbles with believers could hinder the spread of the gospel. The Hellenistic Jews were those of a Greek background; they spoke Greek rather than Aramaic.

6:2-6 THE NEED IS MET
The expression "wait on tables" (6:2) was a figure of speech referring to the ministry of providing food for the widows. The word "deacon" was derived from the Greek word for "serve." The phrase "full of the Spirit and wisdom" (6:3) meant that the person's life was characterized by the virtues and power of the Holy Spirit, in this case the quality of wisdom was emphasized.

This movement to care for the Gentile Greek Christians was just a small taste of the massive Gentile movement to come. The

laying on of hands (6:6) identified this already spiritual man with the blessing and authority of the apostles. In the biblical period, the laying on of hands was a rite of identification that signified the link or association between the parties involved (cf. Lev. 3:2). It is interesting to note that the names of the men chosen to mediate this racial problem (6:5) indicate that these men were of Greek or Hellenistic backgrounds. The deacons were chosen from among the Hellenistic Christians to balance the representation of the two groups (Hellenistic and Judaistic) in leadership.

6:7 THE INCREASE OF DISCIPLES IN JERUSALEM
This verse functions not only to show how the word was unhindered by human problems and that the number of believers had grown; but it contributes to the building of tension between the believers and the religious leaders who were already hostile and jealous (Acts 5:17-18, 33). This relates most closely with the following section concerning one of the Hellenistic deacons, Stephen. Note some other linking phrases in Acts (9:31; 12:24; 16:5; 19:20; 28:30-31).

6:8–8:1 Stephen Is Arrested and Murdered
6:8–7:1 BROUGHT BEFORE THE HIGH PRIEST
Stephen, one of the deacons, had been gifted with the signs and wonders shared by Jesus (2:22) and the apostles (2:43). The "Freedmen" (6:9) were Jews who had once been slaves of Rome but had been set free and settled in Jerusalem. They built their own synagogue in Jerusalem. Stephen, like Jesus, suffered a farce of a trial built on false accusations. Those accusations centered on the temple building, the temple customs, and the Mosaic Law (6:13-14).

7:2-53 STEPHEN EVALUATES HIS JUDGES
Stephen's message was designed to show that God's presence was not limited to the temple nor its customs. He pointed out that the leaders' rejection of the Holy Spirit was just like that of their ancestors, which had resulted in exile and punishment. Stephen's discussion of God's presence and redemptive purpose was based on God's promises to Abraham. His discussion of the temple and the laws was based on the Mosaic covenant.

Finally, his second discussion of the temple and law was based on the Davidic covenant. The whole speech was a brief but complete interpretation of Israel's history based on Jesus' teachings about the Old Testament. Stephen argued that God was not restricted to one nation or one building. He also showed the religious leaders that rejection of God's ways had been a pattern with Israel throughout history.

7:2-16 Abraham to the Exodus. Stephen's sermon has been criticized for supposed historical inaccuracies. While it does contain some difficult interpretive problems, they are not beyond solution. Stephen's point in 7:2-8 was that Abraham had God's presence even without the Promised Land or the temple. The thrust was that Abraham had the word of promise that said God would give the land but only after a time of oppression in and deliverance from a foreign land (7:5-6).

The problem in Acts 7:2 is that Genesis 11:31-32 records no divine call of Abraham at Ur in Mesopotamia. Genesis 11:31–12:4 reveals a call from Haran. However, Genesis 15:7 and Nehemiah 9:7 record that Abraham was first called at Ur. Apparently he was first called to leave Ur (Gen. 15:7; Neh. 9:7; Heb. 11:8) and then from Haran was called to go to Canaan (Gen. 11:31–12:4). Stephen referred only to Abraham's first call at Ur.

Many have accused Stephen of an inaccuracy in Acts 7:6 when he referred to the period of Egyptian bondage as being "four hundred years" in length. Exodus 12:40 and Galatians 3:17 speak of the period as 430 years. Was Stephen in error? No. Genesis 15:13 refers to four hundred years of Egyptian bondage. Evidence from Genesis 15:16 suggests this was a rounded number. Stephen was probably thinking of the Genesis 15:13 text with the rounded number, or else he may have been calculating the period from a different starting point.

In Acts 7:9-16, Stephen used the jealousy shown against Joseph as an example of the kind of jealousy shown against God's leaders, especially Jesus, that was present in Stephen's day (cf. 5:17). Like Jesus, Joseph was rejected as a brother, rescued by God, exalted, and eventually received by his people. In 7:14, Stephen said that seventy-five of Joseph's relatives went with him to Egypt. Exodus 1:5, however, records the

number "seventy." Was Stephen wrong? No. The Septuagint and the Dead Sea Scrolls support the reading "seventy-five." Stephen was probably following these texts, which apparently included Joseph's five grandsons in the final sum (cf. Num. 26:29, 35).

In Acts 7:16 Stephen appeared to confuse Jacob's purchase of property at Shechem (Gen. 33:18-19; Josh. 24:32) with Abraham's purchase of the cave of Machpelah at Hebron (Gen. 23:16-18). The problem was that Stephen named Abraham when the transaction at Shechem involved Jacob. One approach views the two purchases of land as telescoped in the same way the two separate calls of Abraham were telescoped in Acts 7:2. Another position points out that Abraham was in Shechem long before Jacob (Gen. 12:6) and perhaps made a first purchase of property there. Later it was reoccupied and purchased again by Jacob (Gen. 33:19). This is a reasonable hypothesis and would adequately explain Stephen's statement in Acts 7:16. The historical data presently available is insufficient to make a final judgment on this matter.

7:17-44 Moses and the law. With Moses, as with Joseph before him, his brothers failed to understand his role as their deliverer. This would be mentioned again in 7:35. God's rejected ruler and deliverer was rescued and exalted at God's own time (7:35). The people of Israel rejected God's chosen one. Note Stephen's use of Deuteronomy 18:15 in Acts 7:37 (cf. 3:22). The people were neither obedient to Moses (7:39) nor to the prophet raised up after him, Jesus the Messiah.

The nation indeed had the tabernacle, but they did not worship God (7:42-44). Amos 5:25-27 was quoted to support the continued idolatry among the people in the wilderness. "Molech" (Acts 7:43) was the name of a Canaanite god whose worship included child sacrifice (Lev. 18:21). "Rephan" (Acts 7:43) was the name of an astral deity associated with the planet Saturn.

7:45-50 Dwellings as symbols of God's presence. Stephen used Isaiah 66:1-2 to show that the tabernacle and temple were only symbols of God's presence, not the substance or actual residence of God. Throughout Israel's history, the people had thought the temple or its equipment had a special ability in and of itself to save or bless. But that was just a pagan attitude toward the temple as a good luck charm. Even though they had the tabernacle and after that the temple, they were exiled from the temple and the land to Babylon (Acts 7:43). Jesus had reminded his people of what the real temple was (John 2:20-22; 4:21-24; cf. also 1 Kings 8:26-27). It is important to remember that Stephen was speaking to the accusation that he was destroying respect for the temple and it customs.

7:51-53 Application to the hearers. Remember the charges against Stephen? They accused him of blaspheming Moses and God (6:11) and of destroying respect for the temple (6:14). But Stephen said that the leaders, his very accusers, had blasphemed and ignored God's true intentions for the Mosaic covenant and the temple regulations.

7:54–8:1 STEPHEN IS MURDERED
Filled with the Spirit, Stephen related a startling vision (7:55-56). The disciples had seen Jesus ascend up into a cloud (1:9), and Peter had preached that Jesus had ascended to sit at the right hand of God (2:33-35). But this was the first time Jesus' presence there was actually revealed. And it came from the final vision of the first martyr for Jesus Christ. Jesus stood to receive Stephen. Stephen's prophecy echoed the words of Jesus spoken before the same group (cf. Mark 14:62; and Jesus' use of Ps. 110:1 and Dan. 7:13). The presence of the Messiah at God's right hand provided a more universal and satisfying way of access to God and comfort during persecution.

Capital punishment was a carefully guarded privilege in Roman government (Acts 7:57-58; cf. John 18:31). This was not a punishment the Jews had the authority to inflict, with one exception—when the case involved the sanctity of the temple. In the temple a barrier wall separated the Court of the Gentiles from the area restricted only for Jews. Accordingly, Gentiles who crossed the barrier could be stoned—even if it were a Roman (Josephus, *Jewish War,* 6.126). The Jews may have justified their actions against Stephen because of what he said about the temple (6:13) or this may have simply been a case of mob violence. The reference to "witnesses" (7:58) suggests that they sought

conformity to the requirements of a legal execution (Deut. 19:15). Saul (7:58), who would soon figure prominently in the record of Christian history, was introduced as an enemy of the faith. Stephen's last words echoed those of Jesus (Acts 7:60; cf. Luke 23:34). It was as if Jesus was suffering all over again through his first martyr.

8:2–9:31 THE SCATTERED WITNESS: THE DIRECTION AND DIRECTOR
8:2-3 Rise of Persecution
The primary result of the growing persecution of believers in Jerusalem was not death to the new faith, but the spreading of the church to Judea and Samaria in obedience to the Lord's command in Acts 1:8. It appears that Saul was the chief mover behind the persecution (8:3) because when he stopped, the church enjoyed a measure of peace (9:30-31).

8:4-25 Philip in Samaria
8:4-8 INITIAL SUCCESS
Although there was no indication that the church was complacent, God used the pain of persecution to scatter the witness from Jerusalem. Samaria was the first example of the preaching ministry of those scattered. The elements confirming God's work abroad were "attention" (8:6), "miraculous signs" (8:6) and "great joy" (8:8). This prepares the way for Simon the sorcerer's problem with materialism and the Samaritans' receiving of the Holy Spirit. Samaria had traditionally been a rival center of worship to Jerusalem and was hated by the religious Jews (see John 4 for Jesus' witness to the Samaritans). From Jerusalem, Philip "went down" (8:5; cf. 6:5) in elevation from Jerusalem to the city of Samaria. This city, about thirty-five miles north of Jerusalem, had been rebuilt by Herod the Great and named "Sebaste" in honor of Augustus Caesar. It was in the heart of the region occupied by the Samaritans, a people of low regard in the sight of the Jews (see note on John 4:3-4).

8:9-13 SIMON THE SORCERER
IS INTRODUCED
Simon's belief (8:13) was later seen to be superficial (8:20-23). It apparently was based on miracles alone and did not issue in faith unto salvation (James 2:20-24). His

title (8:10) was a direct affront to the real power of God in Jesus, poured out through his Spirit. The Samaritans received the Good News about the kingdom of God and the name of Jesus.

8:14-25 SAMARITAN MINISTRY CONFIRMED
The interest in this section is in Simon's materialistic attitude toward the gift of the Holy Spirit. It compares with the story of Ananias and Sapphira's materialistic lies concerning their property (5:1-11). The simple authority given to Peter and John (8:17) was contrasted with Simon's desire to buy the same authority as if it were another magic spell (8:9, 18-19). But the divine cost and the glory that led to the simple act of laying on of the apostles' hands had already been paid for. Behind that act lay the death and exaltation of Jesus, something that could not be bought with mere money.

The Spirit coming upon the Samaritans confirmed God's presence and blessing on this next crucial advance in the unhindered spread of the gospel (1:8). As at Pentecost, this new outpouring of the Spirit was preceded by prayer (8:15; cf. 1:14).

Simon was reprimanded for his commercial attitude toward the gift of the Holy Spirit (8:20-23). Throughout 8:9-24 Simon's praise by the people around him was stressed ("boasted," 8:9; "attention," 8:10; "amazed," 8:11). When he lost that praise to the apostles, Simon became jealous, not for God's glory, but for his own (8:23). This continues the theme of how those within the community responded to the Holy Spirit. Simon desired the status of authority without the required knowledge and purity. Normally the Spirit was given at the moment of faith (cf. 10:44; Eph. 1:13), but this situation was unique (8:17).

The Jews had no dealings with the Samaritans. Had the Spirit been given while Philip was preaching, the Jews might have regarded Samaritan Christianity as distinct from the Judean brand; thus there would have been two churches. The laying on of hands by Peter and John associated the Samaritan believers with the Jerusalem church. That preserved the unity of the body of Christ and clearly marked out the next extension from Jerusalem to Judea and

Samaria. The linking phrase (Acts 8:25) supplied the purpose of Peter and John's trip: to proclaim the word of the Lord.

8:26-40 Philip Preaches to an Ethiopian

8:26-28 PREPARATION
The Ethiopian was reading and wondering. Gaza (8:26) was located on the coastal plain about thirty-five miles west of Hebron (see introductory map). The Ethiopian eunuch (8:27) was a court official of the queen who ruled the northern region of modern Sudan. Candace (8:27) was a dynastic title. Eunuchs were in a position to secure the trust of royalty. They could have no children to begin a new usurping dynasty and were thus commonly promoted into positions as court officials.

8:29-35 PRESENTATION
The Ethiopian was baffled by the Scriptures (8:34). He was reading Isaiah 53:7-8, about the suffering servant of God. Philip followed Jesus' own interpretation of the Old Testament (8:35; cf. Luke 24:27, 44, 48).

8:36-40 BAPTISM
In a startling way, God gave a sign to the Ethiopian by snatching Philip away. Most Greek manuscripts do not contain Acts 8:37. Azotus (8:40), known as Ashdod in the Old Testament, was about twenty miles north of Gaza. Caesarea was located on the Mediterranean coast about fifty miles north of Azotus (see introductory map).

9:1-31 The Conversion of Saul

9:1-19 SAUL'S SALVATION
9:1-9 Saul's confrontation with Jesus. Saul had authority to arrest Christians as far north as Damascus (9:1-2). Note the great change between rage (9:1) and peace (9:31) that resulted for the Christians because of Saul's conversion. The "Way" (9:2) was an expression used in the first century to refer to the Christian faith, that is, "the way of salvation" (cf. John 14:6; Acts 19:9, 23; 22:4; 24:14, 22). Damascus was an important oasis and caravan stopover east of the Anti-Lebanon mountains, about sixty miles north of the Sea of Galilee (see introductory map).

As he approached Damascus, Saul had a vision in which Jesus validated the claims of his gospel (9:3-6). The key question Jesus asked was, "Why?" Saul responded, "Who are you?" The divine response (9:5) linked Jesus and the Lord as one and the same. This confrontation with the risen Lord brought radical change to Saul's life. Saul had discovered that the man Jesus from Nazareth was in fact the promised and exalted Lord. Saul's conversion continues the theme of how God overcame all hindrances to the gospel message. Under God's power, the worst persecutor of the church was changed into its most influential evangelist.

Saul spent three days fasting (9:9). It is not known what Saul was thinking during this time, but when he again opened his mouth it was to proclaim Jesus as the Son of God (9:20, 22). This time was spent making the basic connections between Old Testament Scriptures predicting the coming of the Davidic Son of God, Jesus of Nazareth. Saul's conversion was also recorded in Acts 22:4-21 and 26:12-23 (cf. also 1 Cor. 9:1; 15:8; Gal. 1:15; Phil. 3:12; 1 Tim. 1:13). The conversion of Saul took place in the summer of A.D. 35.

9:10-19 Saul's commission. In the dialogue between Ananias and God, Saul's mission to the Gentiles was foreseen (9:15). Saul was chosen to witness and suffer. The laying of Ananias's hands on Saul was a means of identifying him with the Christians whom he had been persecuting (19:17). Saul's baptism identified him further with the movement. His filling with the Holy Spirit was his commission as God's prophet.

9:19-22 SAUL'S PERSUASIVENESS
Saul amazed all groups (9:19-21), the Christians and Jews alike. Proving that Jesus was the Messiah (9:22) was at the core of Saul's early thought and preaching.

9:23-30 INITIAL PERSECUTION AGAINST SAUL
9:23-25 Persecution in Damascus. Saul's escape from Jewish persecution in Damascus took place somewhere between A.D. 37-40. Galatians 1:17 reveals that immediately after his conversion Saul had spent three years in Arabia. This may be alluded to in the words "after many days had gone by" (Acts 9:23). Saul's return to Damascus after a three-year absence was greeted by this death plot. He used this incident in 2 Corinthians 11:32 as his final example of weakness and humiliation.

9:26-31 Persecution in Jerusalem. After Saul arrived in Jerusalem, he faced initial opposition from the Christian community. Barnabas befriended Saul because all the other Christians remembered Saul's past hatred toward the church and were slow to accept him (9:26-27). For more on Barnabas, see 4:36. Hellenistic or Grecian Jews (9:29) were those who spoke Greek and were at home with Greek culture and customs. The Hellenistic Jewish Christians were referred to in an earlier conflict within the church (cf. 6:1). Here the Hellenistic Jews tried to kill Saul (9:29) as they had done to Stephen (6:9). Saul was sent to Tarsus (see introductory map) by the Christian community to avoid the death plots against him (9:30). His aggressive style seems to have stirred up stronger opposition to the Christian community; after Saul left, the church enjoyed a measure of peace (9:31; cf. 9:1). Caesarea (9:30) was located on the Mediterranean coast about sixty miles northwest of Jerusalem. Tarsus (9:30) was Saul's hometown and was situated on the Cilician plain (cf. Gal. 1:21) about ten miles inland from the Mediterranean (see introductory map).

9:32–11:26 THE GENTILES: INCLUDED BY GOD
Overview: The section of 9:32–11:26 relates to the preceding section (8:2–9:31) in two ways. It resumes the account of the work of the original apostles, Peter in particular. And it introduces the expansion of the church among the Gentiles—a necessary precedent to Saul's later work among them.

9:32-43 Two Miracles in Neighboring Towns
Overview: These two miracles show how the message spread in two more areas of Jewish population (9:35, 42). The miracles of healing and resurrection mirror the signs and wonders of Jesus (2:19, 22, 43). Peter was traveling only to the Jewish people. With Dorcas's death, her friends came and called for Peter to come. He came willingly and Dorcas, who was already a believer, was raised. Peter's willingness to bring salvation to the Jews stands in contrast to his unwillingness to bring the message of spiritual life to the Gentiles. Peter's unwillingness was corrected by the great lesson of 10:9-16, 28.

9:32-35 AENEAS HEALED: LYDDA

Lydda (9:32), Old Testament Lod, was located about eleven miles southeast of Joppa (see introductory map). Sharon (9:35) was a reference to the fertile plain that extends for about fifty miles along the Mediterranean coast from Joppa to the Crocodile River (just north of Caesarea).

9:36-43 TABITHA RAISED: JOPPA

"Tabitha" (9:36) means "gazelle." "Dorcas" is the Greek rendering of the name. Joppa (9:38) was an important port city on the Mediterranean coast located about thirty miles northwest of Jerusalem (see introductory map). The ancient city, now called Jaffa, has been completely surrounded by modern Tel-Aviv. Peter was staying in the home of a "tanner" (9:43)—one who preserved the skins of dead animals. This was considered an unclean profession by the Jews in view of the tanner's regular contact with dead bodies. This may reflect Peter's increasing emancipation from Jewish ceremonial traditions; an emancipation that will be completed when he brings the gospel to the "unclean" Gentiles (Acts 10).

10:1–11:26 Confirmation of Gentile Salvation

10:1-8 THE GENTILE IS INTRODUCED

Cornelius is introduced by his character (10:1-2), prayerfulness and compassion (10:3-6), and obedience (10:7-8). Caesarea (10:1), located twenty-seven miles north of Joppa, was a major seaport and the seat of the Roman procurators of Judea. Cornelius was a centurion who commanded around one hundred (a "century") soldiers. A cohort was a military unit of six hundred men. Five cohorts were stationed in Caesarea and one in Jerusalem. Cornelius was not a Jewish proselyte but accepted the Jewish religion and revered their God (10:2). The "ninth hour" (10:3; NASB and KJV) was 3:00 P.M.

10:9-16 PETER'S VISION

The point of this vision was that God is not partial to any one ethnic or racial group (10:15). To eat all foods was symbolic for fellowshiping without discrimination with people of all races and people groups (10:28, 34). This was a direct fulfillment of 3:25-26 and all families being blessed in Abraham (cf. Gen. 12:3). The cleanness problem came from the commands of the Mosaic

Law (Lev. 11). But Jesus had replaced the Mosaic covenant with the new covenant. The old was now fulfilled, but Peter was still learning what was old and what was new. This explains how Peter could disobey God's thrice repeated command to eat, while still thinking he was obeying the Mosaic Law (cf. Acts 11:8).

It seemed to Peter that God was contradicting his own law (but see Mark 7:19). But the dietary laws of the Mosaic covenant served, in part, to visualize the separation of Israel from the unclean nations. Now that Jesus had broken down that dividing wall, the old food restrictions were no longer needed. God had changed the covenant and ended the food distinctions. In Christ, no person was unholy or unclean (Acts 10:28; cf. Eph. 2:11-22).

10:17-33 PETER GOES TO CAESAREA

The message arrived from Cornelius (Acts 10:17-23), and Peter began to understand (10:23-33). The vision was about "food," yet it really concerned "race" (10:28). He understood that God's cleansing of the "impure" foods (10:15) related to his cleansing of the Gentiles. There were six brethren who went with Peter to Caesarea (10:23; cf. 11:12). Peter had grasped the meaning of the vision (10:28). The primary point was not that Peter should change his diet, but that God had dissolved the traditional distinction between Jew and Gentile. This concept would become foundational for the unity of the church, proclamation of the gospel, and mission outreach.

10:34-43 PETER'S ADDRESS

Peter's words at this primarily Gentile gathering revealed a new understanding of how God relates to humans through the gospel. Peter summarized the life of Jesus (10:37-41). The emphasis was on Jesus' anointing with the Holy Spirit and power (10:38), the exact terms used for Christians' anointing (1:5, 8; Luke 24:49). Note the carefully selected witnesses (Acts 10:41). The resurrection ministry of Jesus before his ascension was to prepare witnesses. The orders to preach (10:42) had been given in 1:2. The forgiveness of sins (10:43) was given through the work of Jesus, the author of the new covenant.

10:44-48 THE SPIRIT EMPOWERS
NEW WITNESSES
The key words are "astonished" and "even on" (10:45). There was no difference in the way God confirmed faith in Christ, whether to the Jew or Gentile. Therefore, ethnicity was no longer of any consequence. They were cleansed by faith in Jesus' name. Baptism identified this group of Gentiles with the community of the redeemed (10:47-48). The outpouring of the Holy Spirit and speaking in tongues served to authenticate that these Gentiles had truly believed and were to be regarded no differently than Jewish believers.

11:1-18 THE LARGER COMMUNITY'S
RESPONSE AT JERUSALEM
But the issue of Jewish and Gentile distinctions had to be further resolved (11:1-3). Those "circumcised" (11:2) referred to Jewish believers who were unhappy at the report that Gentiles were being saved without becoming Jews (that is, circumcised) first. Peter explained the changes that were coming about (11:4-17). The "beginning" (11:15) referred to the day of Pentecost (Acts 2) when the church began. The essential issue was human versus divine, water versus Spirit (11:16). Spirit baptism was God's final word of acceptability (11:17). The church was satisfied with Peter's explanation (11:18), but the issue later came to a climax in Acts 15. This was a direct granting of repentance to Gentiles without the practices of Judaism and the Mosaic covenant as a middleman. Not all would stay quiet over this issue.

The door was now open to carry the gospel from Jerusalem to the ends of the earth (1:8). From this point on the book provides examples of how the gospel was not hindered and clarifications about how Christianity related to Mosaic Law and Gentile ways.

11:19-26 GENTILE RESPONSE AT ANTIOCH
Some Christians continued only witnessing to Jews (11:19). Phoenicia is the coastal plain region stretching about 120 miles north from Mount Carmel. Cyprus (11:19) is the large island (140 x 60 miles) located in the northeast corner of the Mediterranean Sea. Antioch (11:19) was the capital of the Roman province of Syria and the third largest city in the empire. It was located on the Orontes River about fifteen miles from the Mediterranean Sea. Cyrene (11:20) was the chief city of a district of North Africa called Cyrenaica. (For the locations of these cities, see introductory map.)

Other Christians ventured out to the Gentiles and God encouraged them with large numbers of believers (11:20-26). The Gentile community was strengthened by Barnabas (11:22-24) and by Saul (11:25-26). This was Saul's first appearance in about six years (9:30) and can be dated around A.D. 43–44. Saul came to Antioch in A.D. 43 to begin a teaching ministry in the city (11:26). It was in Antioch that the disciples were first called "Christians," or "Christ-people."

11:27–12:24
JERUSALEM PERSECUTION:
THE KING VERSUS A KING
11:27-30 Famine Relief
The function of the famine relief was to forge a link of fellowship between Gentile Antioch and the predominantly Jewish church of Jerusalem. The link with Jerusalem was important for establishing apostolic foundations and connections to Jesus' earthly life. The Gentile church was not a mere "off-shoot" of Christianity, but was an integral extension of Christ's international body. Luke linked Agabus's prophecy of the famine (11:28) to the reign of the emperor Claudius (A.D. 41–54). Josephus reported that the great famine did, in fact, occur during Claudius's reign, about A.D. 46.

12:1-24 Herod's Final Atrocities
12:1-2 JAMES IS PUT TO DEATH
"King Herod" (12:1) is a reference to Agrippa I (A.D. 37–44) who was the grandson of Herod the Great. In A.D. 37 Caligula endowed him with Philip's tetrarchy, and in A.D. 39 he received Galilee and Perea as well. In A.D. 41, Claudius added Samaria and Judea to his charge. Thus he ruled practically the same territory as his grandfather, Herod the Great. The apostle James was the first of the twelve to be martyred (12:2). Jesus had predicted James's harsh death in Mark 10:35-39. Herod's desire to please the Jews (12:3) by persecuting the believers was later repeated by the governors Felix (24:27) and Festus (25:9).

12:3-19 PETER IS DELIVERED

Peter was imprisoned (Acts 12:3-5) and released through God's power (12:6-11). The significance of this and the other releases from prison was to show God's power to overcome physical hindrances and God's verdict of "not guilty" on the activities of his witnesses. For Passover (12:4), see the note on Matthew 26:17.

After his release, Peter reported to the local gathering of Christians and then left Jerusalem for a safer place (12:12-17). James (12:17) is the brother of Jesus and the author of the book of James. The apostle James, the brother of John, had recently been murdered (12:2; cf. Mark 10:35-39). The "house of Mary" (12:12) was probably the location of the upper room where the Last Supper was observed (Mark 14:13-16) and where the early church met for prayer (Acts 1:13-14). John Mark (12:12) was the cousin of Barnabas and participated in Paul's first missionary journey (cf. 12:25). John Mark is probably best known for writing the Gospel of Mark. "His angel" (12:15) might have been a reference to Peter's guardian angel (cf. Matt. 18:10) or his helping angel (cf. Heb. 1:14). At any rate, the believers could not believe that their prayers for Peter's release had actually been answered (Acts 12:15).

Herod killed the guards who had allowed Peter's escape (12:18-19). According to Roman law, a guard who allowed a prisoner to escape became liable to the same penalty the prisoner would have suffered.

12:20-24 HEROD IS JUDGED

This section graphically demonstrates how the gospel could not be hindered even by a great and powerful king (note the contrast of 12:24). He died after Passover in A.D. 44. Tyre and Sidon (12:20) were the major port cities of Phoenicia (see introductory map). While the Phoenicians were noted for their shipping and trade, they depended on the grain of Galilee for their food supply.

12:25–14:28 PAUL'S LONG-RANGE MISSION: JEW AND GENTILE CONFLICT

Overview: The expeditions of Paul share several characteristics: First, Paul went to the Jews first. That was not a reversal of God's

mission to the Gentiles. It was a continued pattern that dated back to Abraham. It was not just to the Jews or just to the Gentiles. It was to the Jews first, but certainly also then to the Gentiles (cf. 13:46-47). The new covenant opened up the no-distinction ministry to Jews and Gentiles. Second, persecution of Christians came first from the Jews and then from the Gentiles. The Jewish persecution reflected the ancient conflict within God's chosen community (Esau and Jacob). Gentile persecution related to questions of the Roman government and reflected the concept of the nations rising up against God's people (4:25-26). Third, Paul returned to strengthen the communities he had already planted (cf. Matt. 28:20). Fourth, Paul returned to his home base.

The geographical spheres of Paul's expeditions reflected the progressive nature of Jesus' commission in Acts 1:8. Paul moved through Asia Minor, to the Aegean regions, and finally to Rome.

12:25–13:3 Commission and Preparation

Paul and Barnabas escaped the trials experienced by Peter while in Jerusalem (12:1-19). John Mark, who returned to Antioch with Paul and Barnabas, had been introduced in the context of the Jerusalem persecutions (12:12). The church in Antioch sought God's direction (13:1-2) and prayed for his blessing (13:3). The Holy Spirit represented God's sending power (13:4) and was behind all Paul's expeditions. The Latin name "Niger" (13:1) probably indicates that Simeon was a black man. For "Cyrene" (13:1), see the note on 11:20. Apparently Manaen (13:1) was the foster-brother of "Herod the tetrarch," that is, Herod Antipas, ruler of Galilee and Perea (4 B.C.–A.D. 39). The laying on of hands (13:3) symbolized the relationship between the church at Antioch and the missionaries sent out as their representatives. Essentially, it was a rite of identification.

13:4-12 Cyprus

13:4-5 TO THE JEW FIRST

Sent out by the Spirit, the apostles mirrored Christ's ministry (cf. 13:47; Matt. 4:15-16; Luke 4:18). Cyprus (Acts 13:4; see the note on 11:19) is located in the Mediterranean Sea about eighty miles southwest of Seleucia, the port of Antioch (see map of *Paul's First Missionary Journey* on page 566). The island was about a twenty-four hour journey from Seleucia by boat. Salamis (13:5) was a major port and commercial center on eastern Cyprus. It boasted the largest marketplace in the Roman colonial Empire. "John" (13:5) refers to John Mark (cf. 12:25).

13:6-12 SERGIUS PAULUS

Bar-Jesus, or Elymas, an attendant of the proconsul Sergius Paulus, tried to oppose the ministry of Paul and Barnabas (13:6-8). Paphos (13:6) was the capital of Cyprus in Roman times and a worship center for Aphrodite, the Greek goddess of love. Procounsul (13:7) was the title given to the official chosen to rule a senatorial province such as Cyprus.

Elymas, an enemy of the gospel, was miraculously blinded. This miracle served as a sign for Sergius Paulus pointing to the truth of the gospel (13:9-12). God had used blindness in Paul's own life. "Saul" (13:9) was a Jewish name and "Paul" a Roman name. Both were probably given at birth, but Paul apparently began going by his Roman name as he began ministering in a Roman environment.

13:13–14:25 Asia Minor

13:13-52 PISIDIAN ANTIOCH

No reason was given for John Mark's return (13:13). In 13:16-41, Luke recounted the longest of Paul's recorded sermons. It was quite similar to Stephen's defense (Acts 7). Paul recounted Israel's history (13:14-22). He started with the Abrahamic covenant (13:17), moved to the Davidic covenant (13:22), and concluded by presenting Jesus as the Messiah promised by the Davidic covenant (13:23-25).

Paul addressed Jews and God-fearing Gentiles (13:16, 26). Perga (13:13), located in Pamphylia, a coastal district of Asia Minor, was about twelve miles from Attalia, the probable port of entry for the missionary team. Entering the region of Galatia, the missionaries came to Pisidian Antioch, an important commercial and religious center (13:14). The city served as a major stop on the trade route from Ephesus to the Euphrates River. Antioch was near the district of Pisidia, but actually in the lesser known district of Phrygia. "Pisidian" distinguishes

this city from "Syrian" Antioch, the city Paul had come from. The 450 years (13:19) was apparently a rounded figure that included the years of bondage (400 years, cf. Acts 7:6), wandering (40 years) and conquest (7 years).

Paul concluded his sermon with an application and warning (13:38-51). Note the use of the Old Testament in Acts 13:33-35, 41, 47 (Ps. 2:7; Isa. 55:3; Ps. 16:10; Hab. 1:5; Isa. 49:6). Compare the use of Psalm 2 here with its use in Acts 4:25-26. Compare the use of Habakkuk 1:5 (Acts 13:41) with Habakkuk 2:4 in Romans 1. Paul received the typical twofold response (Acts 13:42-43). For "devout converts" (13:43), see the note on 2:10. The split from the synagogue (13:44-52) was caused by jealousy (13:45; cf. 5:17; 7:9).

In Acts 13:47 the fuller significance of the phrase "to the remotest part of the earth" (1:8) is revealed. It was a quotation of Isaiah 49:6 that Jesus had applied to the mission of the church. Previously, Simeon had applied the passage to Jesus when he was brought into the temple (Luke 2:32). Here, Paul applied the same passage as a command of God to his own mission (Acts 13:47; see also Matt. 4:15-16 and its use of Isa. 9:1-2). It was a commission in terms of the universal Abrahamic blessing.

Despite strong persecution from the Jews, disciples multiplied quickly (13:50-52). A Jew returning from travel in Gentile lands would shake off his garments to prevent carrying any "unclean" dust back into Israel. This action was commanded by Jesus (cf. Matt. 10:14) and symbolized the rejection of those who had rejected Christ. It was an acknowledgment that those who refused the gospel were like unbelieving heathen.

14:1-7 ICONIUM

After arriving in Iconium, persecution again arose from Jewish leaders who stirred up the leading citizens (14:2). This opposition came because so many of the Jews believed the gospel message (14:1). In order to protect their interests, the Jewish leaders had to get rid of the upstart missionaries. As in 8:1-4, persecution grew out of the generally favorable response to the gospel, not because the overwhelming majority opposed it (14:5-7). Despite the persecution, the gospel was spread.

Iconium (14:1; modern Konia) was located about eighty miles southeast of Pisidian Antioch. Iconium was a prosperous Greek city and was situated on a well-watered plain in the Galatian heartland of Asia Minor. Lycaonia (14:6) was a region of southern Asia Minor north of Cilicia. Its major cities were Lystra and Derbe.

14:8-20 LYSTRA
After seeing a miracle performed by Paul and Barnabus, the people of Lystra began to worship them as gods (14:8-13). Paul was forced to reinterpret this miracle for them (14:14-18). He began with their understanding of gods and from there taught them of the real God. He did this by using illustrations from creation, God's control of history, and nature. He stressed the unity and singularity of God.

Lystra, once a military outpost of Rome, was located about twenty miles southwest of Iconium. After the area was subdued by Rome, the city declined in population. It was so far off the main road that most of its inhabitants did not even speak Greek (14:11). It was probably at Lystra that Timothy was converted (cf. Acts 15:41–16:3).

Zeus (14:12) was the chief god of the Greek pantheon. Hermes was the patron god of orators. It may have been as a result of this stoning that Paul bore the "marks of Jesus" (14:19; Gal. 6:17; cf. also 2 Cor. 11:25). Derbe was located seventy miles southeast of Lystra. Only recently has the city been identified with certainty, and little is known about it.

14:20-25 DERBE TO ATTALIA
After moving on to Derbe (14:20), Paul returned to establish the churches he had already planted (14:21-23). Paul's message to the churches established during the first missionary journey was summarized in 14:22. Persecution was not a hindrance to the kingdom of God. Paul called persecution the very gateway for entrance into God's kingdom (14:22). This statement contributes to the book's purpose of bringing encouragement to those suffering persecution. Elders (14:23) were appointed early on in Paul's ministry. For the appointment of elders, see the qualifications given by Paul in 1 Timothy 3:1-7. Pisidia (14:24) was a mountainous district of Asia Minor south of Phrygia.

Pamphylia was the coastal district south of Pisidia. Perga, located about eight miles inland from the coast, was the chief city of Pamphylia. Attalia was an important seaport in Pamphylia.

14:26-28 Return and Report to the Antioch Community
Paul's first journey took about one and a half years (A.D. 48–49) and involved about 1,250 miles of travel. In this journey Paul and Barnabas widened the open door for including the Gentiles in the Christian church. Thus, Paul's first missionary journey continued the work already begun by Peter's first opening of the door to Gentile faith at the home of Cornelius (Acts 10).

15:1-35 TOWARD A JEW AND GENTILE RESOLUTION
15:1-5 The Problem Arises
The Christians who had once been Pharisees (15:5) asserted that Gentile Christians had to obey the Laws of Moses. They believed in the resurrection and Messiahship of Jesus, but placed that faith within the Mosaic covenant rather than the new covenant. The dispute centered upon the question of how salvation is received (15:1, 5). Jesus had anticipated this conflict between old and new in Matthew 13:51-52. The book of Hebrews presents a more elaborate discussion of this conflict.

Judea (15:1) was the central district of Palestine. These Jewish believers came to Antioch insisting that circumcision according to Mosaic Law (Gen. 17:11; Exod. 12:48; Lev. 12:3) was necessary for salvation. The church was faced with the question, Is a Gentile acceptable to God without becoming a Jew? For Phoenicia (15:3), see note on Acts 11:19. Samaria (15:3) was the district north of Judea. For more on the Pharisees (15:5), see note on Matthew 3:7.

15:6-21 The Problem Debated and Solved
15:6-11 PETER CLAIMS GRACE ALONE
The Holy Spirit was God's affirming witness of approval for Gentile inclusion in the fold of Christianity (15:8). Those of Jewish background were demanding external signs, like circumcision, to prove inclusion, but Peter pointed out that God proved his accep-

tance of the Gentiles through the witness of the Spirit (15:8). Peter recounted how God's Spirit had been given as completely to uncircumcised Gentile converts (cf. Acts 10) as to the circumcised Jews. This divine witness confirmed that salvation came by faith, not by keeping the Mosaic Laws (15:9). Salvation by anything else tested God (15:10) and his salvation through grace (15:11).

15:12-21 JAMES ADDS
OLD TESTAMENT SUPPORT
Again, God's signs and wonders were used to show his approval of the believing Gentiles (15:12; cf. 2:19, 22, 43; 14:3). Amos 9:11-12 was used (15:15-18) to show that the inclusion of Gentiles was a long-standing part of God's promised restoration of Israel according to his promise to David. The prophecy concerned God's future blessing on disobedient Israel. The Davidic dynasty ("David's fallen tent," 15:16) would be restored in the kingdom, and then even the Gentile nations would know and worship the Lord. James was saying, "What God is doing today in blessing Gentiles is in harmony with his program for the future."

The suggested prohibitions of 15:20 were common sense items—the reason being given in 15:21, "For." There was no need to wave red flags in front of those Jews who were culturally steeped in the Laws of Moses. However, those prohibitions were not at all connected to the issue of salvation. They were to increase community between Jews and Gentiles. The prohibitions come from Leviticus 17 and 18 and include idol sacrifices (Lev. 17:8-9), eating blood (Lev. 17:10-12), eating animals that had not been properly butchered and the blood drained, that is, "things strangled" (Lev. 17:13-14), and "sexual immorality."

15:22-29 The Answer Is Formulated
The letter written here (15:23-29) became the official word from the apostles concerning the place of the Mosaic system in relation to salvation for Gentiles. By implication, it also became the official word on the sufficiency of faith in Jesus alone to bring salvation. Judas and Silas were chosen by the church in Jerusalem to return to Antioch with Paul and Barnabas to announce the decision of the Jerusalem church. Silas joined Paul on his second missionary journey (cf. Acts 15:40).

15:30-35 The Response to the Answer
The people of the Antioch church rejoiced in the decisions made at the Jerusalem council (15:30-31). The nature and work of the New Testament prophets was revealed in the work of Judas and Silas (15:32-33). Their work was primarily that of encouragement and strengthening. The party from Jerusalem returned, but Paul and Barnabas remained to minister in the Antioch church (15:34-35).

15:36–18:21 THE SECOND MISSION: GENTILE EXTENSION INTO EUROPE
15:36-41 The Personnel Selected
15:36-39 THE CYPRUS MISSION
The argument between Paul and Barnabas about whether John Mark should accompany them on the second journey carried no judgment as to who was right or wrong. It simply described how Silas came to be Paul's companion rather than Barnabas. The account of Mark's desertion during the first journey (15:38) is found in 13:13. Despite Paul's negative feelings toward Mark at this point, Paul later found him to be useful for the ministry (cf. 2 Tim. 4:11). Cyprus (15:39; see note on Acts 13:4) was the native homeland of Barnabas (4:36).

15:40-41 PAUL AND SILAS
GO TO ASIA MINOR
Paul and Silas traveled north from Antioch through the provinces of Syria and Cilicia into Asia Minor (15:41). (See map of *Paul's Second Missionary Journey*, page 566.) Silas's Roman citizenship turned out to be very helpful (16:37). Perhaps the dispute that resulted in Silas's selection was allowed by God for just this reason.

16:1-10 The Journey to the Edge of Europe
16:1-3 TIMOTHY CHOSEN
AND CIRCUMCISED
It was probably at Lystra that Paul asked Timothy, apparently converted through Paul's ministry on the first journey (1 Tim. 1:2), to join the missionary team. Timothy was circumcised in the spirit of Acts 15:21, i.e., to avoid offending the sensibilities of the Jews (16:3, "because of the Jews"), not as a means of gaining saving grace. The act would help regularize Timothy's status as a Jew and enlarge his usefulness

in ministry. Compare Paul's dealings with Titus (Gal. 2:3). For the cities of Lystra, Derbe, and Iconium, see notes on Acts 14:1, 6, 19.

16:4-5 THE DECREE IS DELIVERED

The important "decisions reached by the apostles and elders in Jerusalem" (16:4) were those reached at the Jerusalem council and recorded in their official statement (15:23-29). Paul and Silas were spreading the news that salvation came through faith alone and not by following the Laws of Moses. The result of this message was that the churches were strengthened and the believers grew in number (16:5).

16:6-10 THE DECISION TO GO TO MACEDONIA

The Holy Spirit led Paul to Troas by denying him entrance to other areas (16:6-7). The "go ahead" for God's choice came through a night vision (16:9). The Phrygian and Galatian regions (16:6) were located in central Asia Minor and would include within them the cities Paul ministered to on his first journey. Asia (16:6) referred to the Roman province located in western Asia Minor. Mysia (16:7) was the district of northwestern Asia Minor. Bithynia (16:7) was the district of northern Asia Minor bordering the Black Sea. Troas (16:8) was the major port on the Aegean coast of western Asia Minor. Macedonia (16:9) was a Roman province that encompassed much of northern Greece.

16:11-40 In Philippi

16:11-15 LYDIA: HOME BASE CHURCH

Samothrace (16:11) was a small island about halfway between the two ports of Troas and Neapolis. Neapolis, located on the northern shore of the Aegean, was the major port of Philippi. Philippi (16:12), ten miles inland from Neapolis, was a Roman colony. It was a leading city of Macedonia both politically and economically. The city commanded a fertile plain and was strategically located on the Egnatian Way, the major east-west travel route through Macedonia. Lydia (16:14) was from Thyatira, a city in Asia Minor noted as a textile center (see note on Rev. 2:18). In the ancient world the color purple was a mark of high rank and nobility. A special purple dye was extracted from the murex shellfish found in the east Mediterranean region.

16:16-18 A DEMON IS CAST OUT

The slave girl's prophecies were an annoyance to Paul because they blurred the fact that salvation came through Jesus alone. The girl was possessed by a spirit, literally a "spirit of Pythia." Pythia was the priestess of Apollo at Delphi who was believed to be inspired by the god to speak oracles when sitting over a sacred rock in his temple. The young girl at Philippi was apparently demon possessed.

16:19-34 SALVATION IN PRISON

Here a new element of resistance to the gospel is experienced by the missionaries— arrest by the civil authorities, not the religious Jews. It was important that Christianity not be seen by Rome as an illegal religion. The false accusations (16:19-21) sought to brand Paul and Silas as Jewish subverters of Roman law and order (16:20-21). The initial punishment (16:22-24) was reversed by the power of God (16:25-26). Again, not even prison could hinder the movement of God's message in this new region. In fact, God used this difficulty as an opportunity to bring the jailer to salvation in Christ (16:27-34).

16:35-40 RELEASE AND ENCOURAGEMENT FOR THE CHURCH

In order to avert Roman retaliation, Paul clearly emphasized his Roman status (16:37). This secured a footing for the church within the Roman Empire. A similar judgment was made by Gallio in Corinth (18:14-15). Roman law exempted Roman citizens from degrading forms of punishment. A Roman citizen could claim his legal rights by declaring "I am a Roman citizen." Acts 16 should also be read as background for Paul's letter to the Philippians.

17:1-9 Thessalonica and Persecution

17:1-4 IN THE SYNAGOGUE

Amphipolis and Apollonia (17:1) were cities located on the Egnatian Way west of Philippi. Thessalonica, about one hundred miles from Philippi, was the capital of Macedonia. It was a large city (about 200,000). Situated on the Thermaic Gulf and the Egnatian Way, the city was very important commercially. The "three Sabbaths" (17:2) does not seem to have been the duration, but only the beginning of Paul's ministry in Thessalonica (Phil. 4:16; 1 Thess. 2:9; 2 Thess. 3:8).

17:5-9 JEWISH JEALOUSY BRINGS PERSECUTION

Again in Thessalonica, Jewish jealousy created problems for the church (Acts 17:5; cf. 5:17; 7:9). The charges were treason against Rome (17:7). Jesus was also accused of being a king to challenge Caesar (cf. John 19:12). The "bond" (17:9; "pledge," NASB; "security," KJV) was probably a sum of money that would be forfeited should there be further trouble. The account clarifies that Christianity did not cause the problems that followed it wherever it went. The problems were caused by unfounded religious, social, or civil hostility.

17:10-15 Berea and Persecution

17:10-12 INITIAL SUCCESS

The noble-mindedness of the Bereans came from comparing human thoughts with God's word. They compared the human words of the gospel with Old Testament Scripture and found it to be true. Berea (17:10) was a small city about forty miles west of Thessalonica. Located a considerable distance from the Egnatian Way, it was a place of no particular political or historical importance.

17:13-15 THE FOCUS OF PERSECUTION

Most of the persecution in Berea was focused on Paul. Silas and Timothy were able to remain for further ministry after Paul left the city. Paul left for Athens by sea, leaving Silas and Timothy to complete the work in Berea. They later joined him in Athens (17:16; 1 Thess. 3:1-2). This section is helpful background for understanding Paul's letters to the Thessalonians (see also comments on 18:5-11).

17:16-34 Athens

17:16-17 ACTIVITY AROUND THE SYNAGOGUE

The personal context for this section was Paul's spiritual distress over the idolatry of Athens (Acts 17:16). Athens was located about two hundred miles south of Berea, just five miles from the Aegean Sea. Athens, the birth place of democracy, was a cultural and intellectual community and was the worship center for Athena, the Greek goddess of wisdom. The road from the port at Piraeus, where Paul arrived, was lined with idols devoted to the many Greek deities.

17:18-21 PAUL GAINS A HEARING

The initial opinions of his hearers were negative (17:18). The "Epicurean" philosophers believed that the avoidance of pain was the chief end of life. The "Stoics" were those who embraced a philosophy of stern self-denial. The Areopagus (17:19) was a council of men entrusted with the oversight of matters pertaining to religion, culture, and education in Athens. They met on the Hill of Ares (Mars, the god of war), a rock knoll northwest of the Acropolis.

17:22-31 PAUL'S ADDRESS

In his sermon, Paul promised to identify the "unknown God" (17:22-23). Paul's calling the Athenians "very religious" was not a compliment, just a statement of fact. The emphasis of the message was actually on their ignorance (17:23, 30). Around 600 B.C. a terrible plague hit Athens (17:23). It was believed that one of the many gods of Athens had been offended and thus brought the plague. Sacrifices were offered, but the plague continued. Then Epimenides suggested that the Athenians had possibly offended an "unknown" god. It was ordered that a number of sheep be released in Athens, and that wherever they lay down, a sacrifice would be offered. The sheep were sacrificed to the "unknown" god and the plague lifted. Paul had observed one of the altars to this "unknown god" and used it as a cultural analogy in presenting the gospel to the Athenians.

After establishing a starting point, Paul went on to present the true and exalted God (17:24-28). Paul presented God exalted as Creator (17:24), exalted in sufficiency (17:25, no service needed), exalted in life-giving (17:25), and exalted in ordering the creation toward himself (17:26-28); and although God is partially hidden (17:27), he has also partially revealed himself (17:27-28). The poet (17:28) quoted by Paul was Aratus of Cilicia.

Paul gave a reasoned conclusion to his sermon (17:29-31). Because mankind is related to God, they should not think he is like silver or stone (17:29). The image of God is seen in human beings. Paul taught that in trying to find out about the real God, people should start by looking at themselves rather than creating nonhuman images of stone. Paul made it clear that the time for repentance was then (17:30-31; cf.

2 Cor. 6:1-2). Paul ended as he had begun, by offering a solution to their ignorance (Acts 17:23, 30). The mention of the resurrection was decisive and brought either radical rejection or acceptance of the gospel (17:31).

17:32-34 THE RESPONSE

The response to Paul's message in Athens appears to have been small. There is no record of a church being established in Athens as a result of Paul's ministry, but according to Eusebius, Dionysius became the first bishop of the city.

18:1-17 Corinth

18:1-4 PAUL FOUND HIS TRADE

Corinth was located about sixty miles west of Athens and was situated beside the isthmus that links the Peloponnesus with mainland Greece. Corinth was an important trade center with two fine ports: Cenchrea on the Aegean to the east and Lechaeum on the Adriatic to the west. The city was also the worship center of Aphrodite, goddess of love. A temple dedicated to Aphrodite was situated on the 1,886 foot high Acro-Corinth. Paul ministered for one and a half years in Corinth (18:11).

For other references to Aquila and Priscilla (18:2), see Acts 18:18, 26; Romans 16:3; 1 Corinthians 16:19; and 2 Timothy 4:19. The imperial edict of Claudius (A.D. 41–54) commanding the Jews to leave Rome was issued around A.D. 50. The ancient historian Seutonius indicated that it was because "the Jews were indulging in constant riots at the instigation of Chrestus." He apparently wrongly imagined that Chrestus was the leader of these riots when in fact they were riots about Chrestus, a reference to Christ. Paul continued his pattern of starting his ministry in the Jewish synagogue and then speaking to the Greek Gentiles (18:4).

18:5-11 EIGHTEEN-MONTH GENTILE MINISTRY

Notice how separate the Jews and Greeks were as Paul left the synagogue and went next door to the Gentiles (18:6-7). Because of the great hostility in Corinth, God gave Paul special encouragement to minister there (18:7-11). This ministry in Corinth was the time during which Paul wrote the letters of 1 and 2 Thessalonians. When Silas and Timothy joined Paul in Corinth, they brought an encouraging report concerning the church

at Thessalonica (1 Thess. 3:6-7). Having received this report, Paul sat down and wrote 1 Thessalonians (A.D. 51). He probably wrote 2 Thessalonians several months later.

18:12-17 GALLIO LEGITIMIZES THE NEW RELIGION

Christianity was a new religion in Rome's eyes and therefore shared the protection of Roman law. Gallio (A.D. 51–65) was a well-loved proconsul in Achaia. He apparently viewed Christianity as a branch of Judaism and therefore refused to become involved in the sectarian dispute. He later became involved in a conspiracy to overthrow Nero and was either forced to suicide or put to death. Sosthenes (18:17), who had succeeded Crispus as ruler of the synagogue (18:8), was beaten. If this is the same Sosthenes of 1 Corinthians 1:1, he eventually became a Christian.

18:18-21 From Corinth to Ephesus

Paul left Corinth from Cenchrea, Corinth's seaport on the Aegean, after one and a half year's of ministry. The cutting of his hair apparently concluded a Nazirite vow (Num. 6:1-21) voluntarily undertaken during his ministry in Corinth. The exact reason for this vow (Acts 18:18) is not known. The vow may have been for Paul's prosperous ministry at Corinth. At any rate, the vow shows that aspects of Old Testament worship were acceptable within the Christian faith. Paul would also conform to temple procedures in 21:24. Paul made a brief stopover at Ephesus, a place he had been denied entrance to earlier (16:6-7). He would come back to Ephesus on his next journey for a long and successful ministry.

18:22–21:16 THE THIRD MISSION: STRENGTHENING

18:22-23 Rest and Strengthening: Summary

Paul's second missionary journey had lasted two and a half years (A.D. 50–52) and included two thousand miles of travel. In the spring of A.D. 53, Paul set out from Antioch for Asia Minor (18:23) by the same land route he and Silas had followed on the second journey. (See map of *Paul's Third Missionary Journey,* page 567.) Having passed through Galatia and Phrygia, he headed for Ephesus (19:1).

18:24-28 Apollos Strengthened

The pre-Pentecost teaching of Apollos was corrected by Priscilla and Aquila (18:25-26). Apollos was from Alexandria, an important seaport and educational center on the western edge of Egypt's Nile delta. The city had a large Jewish population that had been strongly influenced by Greek culture and philosophy. The power of Apollos's witness was based on his use of the Old Testament Scriptures to prove that Jesus was the Messiah (cf. Luke 24:27, 44-47).

19:1-41 Paul in Ephesus

19:1-7 DISCIPLES STRENGTHENED

Paul advanced this little group's knowledge of salvation from John's baptism to the baptism of the Holy Spirit based on the resurrection and exaltation of Jesus. Ephesus became a new center of Gentile ministry. The speaking in tongues indicated a new advance in the spreading of the gospel. The link was to the Samaritan mission of Acts 8:15-17. As usual, the tongues served as a sign to the Jewish community that God was working at Ephesus (cf. 1 Cor. 14:22; Isa. 28:11-12). Ephesus, a port city located near the Aegean Sea on the Cayster River, was the foremost city of Asia Minor. It was at the west end of the caravan route that linked Mesopotamia with Asia. Ephesus was also the worship center of Artemis, the many-breasted mother goddess of Asia (Acts 19:35). "Diana" (KJV) is a Romanization of Artemis. The temple of Artemis was one of the Seven Wonders of the ancient world. It was 425 feet long, 220 feet wide, and 60 feet high.

19:8-20 WONDERS IN EPHESUS AND ASIA

19:8-9 The school of Tyrannus. After being rejected by the Jews in the synagogue, Paul rented the lecture hall of Tyrannus as a place to instruct the growing body of believers. One Greek text indicates that he instructed them from the fifth to the tenth hour of the day (from 11:00 A.M. to 4:00 P.M.).

19:10-20 Evil overcome by God's power. From this lecture hall all of Asia Minor heard the gospel over a two-year period. Apparently Paul taught for two of the three years he minstered at Ephesus (20:31). It was during Paul's ministry at Ephesus, around the spring of A.D. 56, that he wrote the letter now known as 1 Corinthians. The exorcists

professed to have the power to exorcise demons (19:13; cf. Matt. 12:43-45). The "scrolls" (Acts 19:19) had magic spells written on them. Again, the section ends with the book's major theme, the prevailing of the gospel—in this case over the powers of black magic.

19:21-22 THE END OF THE AEGEAN MINISTRY

Two major aspects of Paul's ministry arise— the desire to see Rome and the plan to take an offering to the Jerusalem church. The desire to see Rome caused Paul to write the Epistle to the Romans from Corinth. The plan to collect an offering for the Jerusalem church figured largely in the problems Paul faced as he wrote 1 and 2 Corinthians.

19:23-41 RIOT OVER THE CITY PATRON DEITY

Christianity started to threaten the business and reputation of Ephesian idolatry (19:23-27). The small silver shrines housed minature figures of Artemis that worshipers would purchase and dedicate in the temple. Gaius (19:29) was from Derbe (20:4) and Aristarchus from Thessalonica (27:2).

The two-hour shouting match in the stadium (19:28-34) ended with the town clerk persuading the crowd to disperse (19:35-41). The clerk was the most important man in Ephesus. His argument that truth should order their action (19:35-36, 40) provides a most eloquent sermon from an idolator. Again, Christianity was shown to be innocent of causing riots or spreading sedition.

20:1–21:14 The Return to Jerusalem

20:1-6 EPHESUS TO TROAS

Paul left Ephesus in the spring of A.D. 56 and headed for Macedonia. It was there in the fall of A.D. 56 that he wrote 2 Corinthians, preparing them for his next visit. Paul spent the winter of A.D. 56/57 in Greece, probably mostly at Corinth (20:3). There he wrote the great doctrinal treatise, the Epistle to the Romans. In the spring, Paul returned to Asia by way of Macedonia (20:6). The week of Unleavened Bread (20:6) refers to the seven-day festival following Passover (early April, A.D. 57). Troas was the Aegean port city from which Paul received his Macedonian call (cf. Acts 16:8-10).

20:7-12 THE SERMON AT TROAS
The "first day of the week" (20:7, Sunday)
became the regular day of worship for the
Christians. This day commemorated the day
of Christ's resurrection from the tomb. The
incident of Eutychus's healing served as yet
another sign that confirmed God's presence
and blessing on his gospel ministry.

20:13-38 MILETUS
Paul hurried to make it to Jerusalem by
Pentecost, the anniversary of the day when
God poured forth his Spirit upon the church
(20:13-16). Pentecost was due to be
observed in Jerusalem on May 27, A.D. 57.
Leaving Troas (20:13), Paul decided to walk
the twenty miles to Assos, a strategic port
city in Mysia, while Luke and the other
travelers went by ship. Mitylene (20:14)
was the chief city on the Aegean island of
Lesbos. Kios and Samos (20:15) are small
Aegean islands just off the coast of Asia.
Miletus, a port city located at the mouth of
the Meander River, was situated about thirty
miles south of Ephesus.

At Miletus Paul made his final farewell
address to the Ephesian elders (20:17-35).
This farewell message was similar to those
given in Deuteronomy 29–31, Joshua
24:2-27, and Matthew 24–25. It contains
the elements of farewell, blessing, and warning against falling away from the faith. Paul
discussed past faithfulness (Acts 20:17-21),
the uncertainty of the future (20:22-24), and
the potential of the present (20:25-31). The
"elders" were the leaders of the church at
Ephesus. The term "elder" suggests the
maturity of those who hold that office. These
leaders were also known as "overseers"
(20:28), a term that emphasized the responsibility of spiritual oversight. The elders and
overseers were responsible to shepherd (that
is, pastor) God's flock, the church (20:28).

Paul ended his farewell sermon with a
commendation (20:32-35). The words of
Jesus quoted by Paul (20:35) are not found
in the Gospels, although the substance is
there (cf. Luke 6:38). The gospel of grace
(Acts 20:24) is the same as the preaching of
the kingdom (20:25). God's kingdom is the
framework within which Paul preached the
gospel. Acts 2:33-35 established that Jesus
was already reigning at God's side in this
period of subduing his enemies. Even though
it created hostility from both Jews and

Greeks, Paul did not shrink from telling the
whole gospel (20:26-27). He never gave in
to temptations to water down the message in
order to escape conflict. This farewell causes
those who read it to feel the sadness and
emotions along with Paul and the Ephesian
leaders (20:36-38).

21:1-6 MILETUS TO TYRE
From Miletus Paul and his associates sailed
to the island of Cos, and then to the island
of Rhodes. From Rhodes they sailed east
along the southern coast of Lycia, putting in
at Patara. From there they arranged a cross-
sea voyage to the Phoenician port of Tyre.

Some regard Paul's decision to continue
on to Jerusalem (21:4) an act of disobedience, and that his imprisonment in Caesarea
was God's discipline for this disobedience.
Yet the Holy Spirit only warned of suffering
and never said, "Do not go." And Paul never
referred to his imprisonment as suffering
for disobedience. The warnings (21:4, 11-12)
may have been designed to test Paul's commitment. He proved himself willing to go in
spite of the cost (cf. 20:22-24). The prophecies surrounding his original calling also
included great suffering in the name of the
Lord (9:16).

21:7-14 CAESAREA WARNINGS
The warnings here continue the warning
theme of 21:1-6. Ptolemais (21:7, Old Testament "Acco," Crusader "Acre") was a port
city on the north side of the Bay of Haifa.
Caesarea (21:8), located about fifty-five
miles northwest of Jerusalem, was a major
port in New Testament times and the center
for the Roman government in Judea. Philip
the evangelist (6:5; 8:5) had come to minister
there. Agabus (21:10) may have been the
same prophet who foretold of the famine in
Palestine (11:28). Paul's comment in 21:14
summed up the thrust of his life as well as
that of the book of Acts. In all that he did,
Paul sought to do the Lord's will.

21:15–28:31 THE FOURTH
MISSION: TOWARD THE GOAL
21:15–26:32 Arrest and Defense
to Kings
21:15-26 THE VOW PROBLEM
Paul completed his final lap to Jerusalem.
Paul's arrival in Jerusalem marked the end of
his third missionary journey, a trip that had

taken four years (A.D. 53–57) and had involved 2,700 miles of travel. Paul recounted to the believers in Jerusalem his successful witness among the Gentiles (21:17-19). The Jerusalem Christians, in turn, related Jewish successes (21:20-21). Thousands had believed and many tenaciously held on to the Mosaic Law. Acts 21:21 provided an excellent description of the Judaiser mentality that believed that all Christians should keep the Mosaic Law. Reports of Paul's ministry among the Gentiles were interpreted by Jewish believers in Jerusalem to imply that Paul was against the Mosaic Law! Of course this was untrue (cf. Rom. 7:12), but how could Paul prove it?

Paul demonstrated his relation to the old Mosaic system (Acts 21:22-26). Paul was asked to join four Jewish believers in a purification rite and pay the expenses of their temple offering (not necessarily a blood sacrifice, see Lev. 2). This was intended to prove that Paul was not against the Mosaic Law. Paul's motive in making this vow is reflected in 1 Corinthians 9:20. He saw no problem in observing a Jewish ritual as long as it was viewed in the light of Jesus Christ and was not seen as a means of salvation.

21:27–22:30 ARREST AND ADDRESS
21:27-36 The arrest of Paul. Paul received the same accusations from the Jewish leaders as Stephen had earlier (cf. 21:28 with 6:14). And only rescue by the Roman troops saved Paul from the same fate. Paul was falsely accused by the Jews of bringing "Greeks" (that is, Gentiles) into the temple area. There were strict prohibitions against Gentiles entering beyond the barrier that separated the Court of the Gentiles from the courts that only Jews could enter. Notices around the barrier read, "No foreigner may enter within the barricade that surrounds the temple and enclosure. Anyone who is caught doing so will have himself to blame for his ensuing death." The cohort (21:31) was a unit of six hundred Roman soldiers. One cohort was stationed at Antonia Fortress, just north of the temple area, at all times.

21:37–22:21 Paul's address. Paul spoke to the Roman commander and gained a hearing (21:37-40). The commander had thought Paul was the Egyptian rebel leader who had

led Jewish rebels out to the Mount of Olives. Felix, the Roman procurator, had put down that revolt. The Jewish historian Josephus recorded the incident about the Egyptian (Josephus, *Jewish War,* 2.261-263). Paul's knowledge of the Greek language (21:37) proved to the Roman commander that Paul could not have been that Egyptian rebel (21:38). The "terrorists" (21:38) was a reference to the "sicarri," from *sica,* Latin for a "curved dagger." This radical group of Jews mingled with crowds at festivals and stabbed their pro-Roman opponents with hidden daggers.

Aramaic (21:40) was the common spoken language of first century Jews. When Paul spoke in this language, the Jews became silent and listened. Paul began his defense before the Jews by recounting his testimony (22:1-21). He recalled his persecutions (22:1-5), salvation (22:6-11), commission (22:12-16), and vision (22:17-21). Acts 22:16 does not teach baptismal regeneration. As the arising precedes the baptism, so calling on the name of the Lord precedes the forgiveness. The vision of 22:17-21 probably took place during Paul's first visit to Jerusalem after his conversion (9:26-30). It amplified and confirmed the commission he had received on the Damascus road (26:17). The command to go to the Gentiles (22:21) related to previous warnings that Paul would have no success in Jerusalem (22:18-19; cf. 13:46).

22:22-29 Paul is arrested as a Roman. A Roman citizen was entitled to certain rights, including a public hearing before the application of any punishment. Somehow Paul's parents in Tarsus had earned this right before his birth. Even the Roman commander was afraid of what would happen to him if it was found out that he had treated a Roman citizen the way he had treated Paul (22:29).

22:30–23:10 PAUL'S ADDRESS
BEFORE THE JEWISH COUNCIL
The Sanhedrin was the same Jewish court that had tried Jesus. The court attempted to find the basis of Paul's crime. Paul showed his accord with the Old Testament law of respect for rulers (23:1-5). The high priest (23:2) was Ananias (A.D. 47–66) who was very pro-Roman and was executed by insurgents at the beginning of the Jewish revolt. Paul's failing eyesight (Gal. 4:15; 6:11) may have accounted for his failure to recognize

the high priest (Acts 23:5). Or perhaps he was simply saying, "I didn't believe the high priest would speak like that."

Paul caused a split between the religious parties, finding support with his past group, the Pharisees (23:6-10). While the Pharisees affirmed the doctrine of resurrection, the Sadducees denied it (23:7; see the note on Matt. 3:7). Paul used this difference of opinion to his advantage before the Sanhedrin.

23:11-22 THE PLOT TO KILL PAUL

God gave Paul a special word of comfort assuring him of the opportunity to witness in the city of Rome (23:11). This vision explains why there was so much detail given in Acts 21–22 concerning Paul's escape from harm and his innocence before the religious and civil leaders. Paul was taking his place alongside Peter and Stephen. This was the Lord's fourth appearance to Paul (cf. Acts 9:5; 18:9-10; 22:17-18). From this point on, Luke focused on how God sovereignly worked the circumstances to move Paul to Rome.

Paul's journey to Rome (23:12-30) began with his escape from forty murderers in ambush. The large number was needed to overcome Paul and the Roman soldiers guarding him. Through God's providence Paul was saved. This event again showed how the gospel was unhindered, in this case by forty radical murderers. Acts 23:16 is the only reference in Scripture to Paul's immediate relatives.

23:23–26:32 PAUL IN CAESAREA

23:23-33 Paul is transferred to Caesarea.
Arrangements were made to transfer Paul to Caesarea, the center of Roman government in Judea (23:23). Antonius Felix served as procurator, or governor (A.D. 52–58), of Judea and resided in Caesarea (23:24). The ancient historian Tacitus reported that "He exercised the power of a king with the mind of a slave." Lysias (23:26) was the military tribune over the Roman forces in Jerusalem. The letter to Felix (23:26-30) continued to support the book's theme of the innocence of the Christians from plots to overthrow the Roman government. This element of innocence gained greater detail as Paul got closer to Rome. This may indicate that Acts was written for a Roman audience. Antipatris

(23:31) was located on the coastal plain about thirty-five miles from Jerusalem.

23:34–24:21 The initial interview with Felix. Paul's home province of Cilicia (23:34) was located in southeastern Asia Minor. Herod's "palace" (23:35) was the palace built by Herod the Great, which at this time served as the official residence of the Roman provincial governor.

Paul was forced to defend himself under Felix against accusations made by the Jews (24:1-21). The Jewish accusation was made (24:1-9). For Ananias (24:1), see the note on 23:2. Tertullus was a lawyer hired by the Jews to prosecute Paul. The "Nazarene sect" (24:5) was a reference to the those who followed Jesus of Nazareth. Acts 24:6-8 is absent in many manuscripts.

Paul's rebuttal (24:10-21) emphasized his obedience to God's word (24:14) and his innocence of any civil crime (24:12-13). The "Way" (24:14, 22) was a reference to the "Way of Christ," that is, Christianity. Paul protested the absence of appropriate witnesses at his hearing (24:19).

24:22-27 Felix's procrastination. It is not known how Felix obtained this special information about Christianity. It may have been through his present wife, Drusilla, a member of the Herodian family. Drusilla (24:24), the third wife of Felix, was the youngest daughter of Herod Agrippa I (A.D. 37–44). She had been wooed by Felix from her first husband, king of Emesa. When Felix was recalled by Nero in A.D. 58, he left Paul in prison as a favor to the Jews (24:27). Porcius Festus succeeded Felix and served as procurator until his death in A.D. 61. Paul's imprisonment was used by God to afford two years of witness in Caesarea (24:24-27).

25:1-12 Paul's defense under Festus. The preparation was made for Paul's trial (25:1-5). Festus (25:1) became procurator at a time of considerable unrest including a breakdown in law and order. His visit to Jerusalem, the religious capital of Judea, was intended to placate the Jews. While in Jerusalem, the Jewish leaders sought to re-open Paul's case.

At the Jews' request, Festus prepared to try Paul (25:6). Festus did not want to alienate the Jewish population of Judea and sought to make concessions to those who accused Paul (25:9). The "appeal to Caesar" (25:11) was one of the most ancient and cherished rights of a Roman citizen. The right applied only to extraordinary cases, that is, those not specifically defined by statute laws. It was usually used to appeal the verdict of a lower court but could be exercised at any stage in the proceedings. The case would then be transferred to Rome and a verdict rendered by the emperor. This allowed Paul to realize his ambition to witness in Rome. At this time, the ruling Caesar was Nero.

25:13–26:32 Agrippa joins Festus. Festus sought Agrippa's advice on Paul's case, and as a result, Agrippa asked to see Paul (25:13-22). Herod Agrippa II (25:13; A.D. 50–100) was the son of Herod Agrippa of Acts 12:1. When his father died, Claudius decided to rule Judea by procurators. Herod Agrippa II received the tetrarchy of Philip and was later given authority to rule virtually all the territory that had been in Herod the Great's domain. Bernice was Herod Agrippa's sister with whom he was living incestuously. Herod Agrippa, a Jewish king, was interested in Paul's case, and Festus was happy to gain his insight into the charges against Paul in order to write a proper statement regarding the appeal to Caesar (25:22).

Paul addressed Agrippa (25:23–26:23) and asserted that there was no basis for the accusations made by the Jews (25:23-27). This is the fullest address by Paul recorded in Acts (26:1-23). The length of the address was implied in Paul's opening statements (26:3). The address was delivered to one who knew a great deal about the Jewish religion. Paul described his previous early life (26:4-5), God's promise (26:6-8), his persecution (26:9-11), and his conversion on the Damascus road (26:12-18). His conclusion (26:19-23) again asserted his conformity to God's word, to the Law of Moses, and to the prophets.

It is debated whether the words "cast my vote against them" (26:10) indicate that Paul was a member of the Sanhedrin, or simply that he was in agreement with their decision. The "goads" (26:14) were pointed implements used to prod oxen in the proper direction. The expression "kick against the goads" was used metaphorically of Paul's resistance against God's prodding in his life.

Paul sought the conversion of the king (26:24-29). Agrippa's words can be paraphrased, "In short, you are trying to persuade me to become a Christian" (26:28). By appealing to Caesar, Paul had put himself into a new relationship with the Roman government (26:32). In order for the law of appeal to proceed, Paul was required to go to Rome. The final verdict confirmed Paul's innocence (26:30-32), but since he had appealed to Caesar, he was required to go to Rome for a further hearing.

27:1–28:31 The Expedition to Rome

27:1-44 FROM SAFETY TO A SHIPWRECK

27:1-8 The voyage to Fair Havens. The detail in this account of Paul's journey to Rome was not given simply for excitement. It was to give a graphic example of the power of the book's last word: "without hindrance." When God wanted a proclamation to be made, he enabled it to be made by removing all hindrances.

The centurion (27:1) was a commander of around one hundred soldiers (a "century") in the Roman army. A cohort was a battallion of six hundred men. This particular cohort was named for the Roman emperor Augustus (27 B.C.–A.D. 14). The "we" (27:2) indicated that Luke sailed with Paul. The ship (27:2) was from the city of Adramyttium, on the west coast of Asia Minor, southeast of Troas. Note the sites along Paul's sea route on the map, *Paul's Voayage to Rome* (page 567).

Sidon (27:3) was an ancient Phoenician harbor located seventy miles north of Caesarea. The ship sailed along the east coast of Cyprus to get shelter from the winds blowing from the west. The ship sailed along the coast of the Asian provinces of Cilicia, Pamphylia, and Lycia, landing at Myra, one of the chief ports of the grain fleet that brought wheat from Egypt to Rome (27:4-5).

At Myra (27:6), Paul transferred to a ship that had Alexandria, Egypt, as its home port. From Myra to Cnidus (27:7) sailing was slow because of the strong wind blowing out of the northwest. There they made the decision to sail south to Crete and then along the lee side of the island where they could be sheltered from the northwest wind. Fair Havens (27:8) was located on the island of Crete. Unfortunately its harbor faced west and would not provide suitable protection against the easterly winter winds. Because it was inadequate as a winter harbor, the sailors decided to move on to a better winter port.

27:9-26 Paul's advice goes unheeded. It was fast appproaching the end of the winter sailing season on the Mediterranean (April–August). Mid-September through mid-November, and February to March were regarded as dangerous times for sea travel (27:9). Mid-November to January was the off season when there was no safe sailing on the Mediterranean.

It was already October, for the Day of Atonement ("the Fast," 27:9; cf. Lev. 16:29-34) had past. Paul's warning was based on plenty of experience (cf. 2 Cor. 11:25). The harbor at Phoenix (Acts 27:12) promised greater protection against the winter winds. The "northeaster" (27:14; "Euraquilo," NASB; "Euroclydon," KJV) referred to the strong winter wind that blows onto the Mediterranean from the northeast. Blown southwest of Crete (26:16), the ship found shelter off the island of Clauda, about twenty-three miles to the south. The ship was undergirded with cables to prevent the hull from breaking apart in the rough water (27:17). The "sandbars of Syrtis" (27:17) were located off the coast of North Africa.

27:27-44 The shipwreck. The ship's "lifeboat" (27:30) was a small dinghy that was normally towed, but in bad weather it was taken aboard in case it was needed. The "Adriatic Sea" (27:27) was the ancient name applied to the Mediterranean Sea east of Sicily. Do Paul's words in 27:31 contradict his encouragement in 27:24? No, for God's will would be accomplished, but this never annuls the fact of human responsibility. Paul was insisting that all the ship's hands be available to help get the passengers safely ashore. They lightened the ship so that it would draw as little water as possible and run aground well up on the beach (27:38).

28:1-6 SNAKEBITE DOES PAUL NO HARM
Even a bite from a poisonous snake could not hinder God's proclamation. The small island of Malta (28:1) is located just south of Sicily. Paul'surviving the snake bite led the islanders to conclude that he was a god, a misidentification he had experienced previously (28:6; cf. 14:11).

28:7-10 MALTA MIRACLES
The Christians found honor and respect (28:10) on Malta. That is, they did nothing to support the accusations that they were criminals.

28:11-16 ARRIVAL AT ROMAN SUBURBS
After three months on Malta, Paul set sail around the first of February for Rome (28:11). The "Twin Brothers" on the ships figurehead were Castor and Pollux, sons of Zeus, who were regarded as the patrons of navigation. Sailing from Malta, Paul traveled north to Sicily and landed at Syracuse on the east coast of the island (28:12-13). After three days, they made their way to Rhegium on the toe of Italy.

When a favorable wind came up, they sailed along the coast of Italy and landed at Puteoli, the principle port of southern Italy, in the Bay of Naples. Hearing of Paul's approach, some Christians came from Rome to escort him to the city (28:15). Some met him at the Market of Appius, forty-three miles south of Rome. Others met him at Three Inns, thirty-three miles south of Rome. Paul was under the watch of the Praetorian guard (Phil. 1:13), the elite soldiers of the Roman military whose primary function was to guard the imperial palace (28:16).

28:17-28 PAUL INTRODUCES HIMSELF AND THE "SECT"
28:17-22 Paul is given a cool reception. Paul centered his remarks around facts proving that he had done no wrong against Israel (28:17) and that he had no grievance against his people (28:19). The "hope of Israel" (28:20) was an eschatological expectation focusing on the resurrection, the Messiah, or the kingdom. Paul was received as an unknown stranger representing a sect with a bad reputation (28:21-22).

28:23-28 Paul speaks of the Way. Paul used the Old Testament to link Jesus to the kingdom of God, the law, and the Prophets, a technique taught by the risen Lord (Luke 24:27, 44-45; Acts 1:3). The book ends with one parting word (28:25) that was an application of Isaiah 6:9-10 to the Jews in Rome (Acts 28:26-27). Jesus had used Isaiah 6 in Matthew 13:14-15. The unbelief of the Jews moved the focus of the Christian witness to the Gentiles (Acts 28:28). Many manuscripts omit 28:29.

28:30-31 SUMMARY OF PAUL'S
TWO-YEAR ROMAN MINISTRY

The book concludes with two verses that
cover the two full years of Paul's Roman
ministry. During those two years Paul
preached, unhindered, the kingdom of God
(28:31) and sought to persuade visitors that
Jesus was the Messiah of Old Testament
prophecy.

Luke recounted nothing of Paul's trial
or hearing before Caesar. There does not
appear to be any first-century evidence for
a procedure permitting a case to lapse automatically by default. It may have been that
his accusers never appeared or it may have
taken two years for his case to clear the
courts. Whatever the precise circumstances,
Paul was released after two years and then
had an opportunity to continue his ministry
in the Mediterranean world until his death
in the spring of A.D. 68. The exalted Lord
had poured forth the Holy Spirit and enabled
a witness to Jesus Christ that neither death,
persecution, corruption, shipwreck, lies, nor
hostility could hinder.

Throughout the book, the clashes between
Christianity and Rome clearly revealed to
Jew and Gentile alike that Paul's religion
did not subvert Roman law. The problems
of social unrest stemmed from trumped up
charges by Jews against Christians. Because
of its ending (28:26-28), Acts stands as a
final appeal to the Jews to convince them
that God was behind the movement that
claimed Jesus to be the Messiah.

Acts is a foundational record of Christian
experience during the time spoken of in
Jesus' parables (Matt. 13). These were the
times when the believer was hurt by hostility
and persecution. It was the time when the
very power of God through the Holy Spirit
seemed to be hidden in the shadows of world
hatred. It was the time when the Spirit was
accomplishing an unhindered witness that
would one day issue in the coming of God's
kingdom. The book of Acts revealed that
God's salvation did not discriminate on the
basis of race or politics. All had been brought
near by the reigning Christ, and all could be
saved through faith in his name.

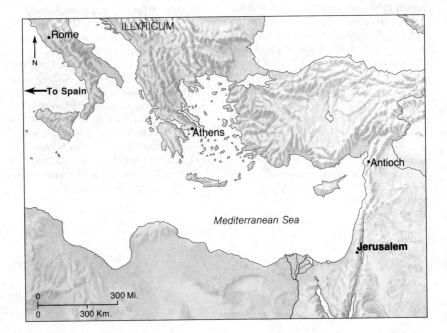

Romans

BASIC FACTS

HISTORICAL SETTING

The letter to the Romans was written in Corinth toward the end of Paul's third missionary journey. Paul had collected and was about to deliver an offering for the Jerusalem church (Rom. 15:25-27; 1 Cor. 16:3-5; 2 Cor. 8). Paul had never visited Rome. After his visit there, he desired to move on to Spain (15:22-33). Paul had recently worked through severe problems with the Corinthian church (cf. 1 and 2 Corinthians). And it was from Corinth that he wrote his letter to the Romans—a letter which described the power of the gospel and the problems of human pride and the weakness of the flesh.

The city of Rome was founded in 753 B.C. on the Tiber River at a ford that was indispensable for traveling between northern and southern Italy. The ridges surrounding the Tiber River valley provided hilltop fortifications for times of attack. In Paul's day, Rome had a population of approximately one million (the largest city in the world) and was the political hub of the vast Roman Empire.

The church at Rome was not founded by Paul. Perhaps some Jews and proselytes from Rome who were in Jerusalem on the day of Pentecost (Acts 2:10) became believers and carried the gospel back to their city. The church was predominately Gentile (Rom. 1:5-6, 13; 11:13; 15:15-16), yet Paul's frequent quotations from the Old Testament and other references indicate that believing Jews would also read his letter (2:17).

AUTHOR

The Pauline authorship of Romans is almost universally accepted. Internal evidence of authorship abounds (1:1; 15:25; 16:3). The external testimony of the church fathers who quote Romans, among whom are Clement, Ignatius, Polycarp, and Justin, confirms the view that Paul was the author. The actual writing of the letter was done by Tertius, the secretary to whom Paul dictated the letter (16:22).

Paul as tentmaker and Pharisee

Paul was a strict Pharisee of the tribe of Benjamin (Phil. 3:5). Although he was born in Tarsus, he was educated in Jerusalem under Gamaliel (Acts 22:3). He was born in Tarsus with the privilege of Roman citizenship (Acts 22:28). Paul was a tentmaker by trade and used that craft to support himself while ministering in Corinth on his second missionary journey (Acts 18:1-3).

Paul may have been a member of the Sanhedrin (Acts 26:10) and was so zealous for his Jewish faith that he persecuted the church (Acts 26:9-11; Phil 3:6). Paul was first mentioned as Saul at the stoning of Stephen (Acts 8:1), an execution with which he was in hearty agreement (Acts 26:10).

Paul's conversion

Paul's conversion took place on the road from Jerusalem to Damascus (Acts 9:1-7), probably in A.D. 35. He remained in Damascus witnessing to the deity of Jesus in the Jewish synagogues (Acts 9:20). When it was learned that the Jews were plotting to kill Paul, he escaped from the city (Acts 9:25) and lived in Arabia for several years (Gal. 1:17).

Paul's early ministry

After revisiting Damascus, Paul went to Jerusalem where he visited with Peter and preached to the Hellenistic, or Grecian, Jews (Acts 9:26-29; Gal. 1:18-20). Threatened in Jerusalem, Paul went to Tarsus (Acts 9:30) and visited the regions of Syria and Cilicia (Gal. 1:21). Later while Barnabas was ministering in Antioch, he invited Paul to join him (Acts 11:25). The two ministered together for an entire year at Antioch (Acts 11:26). During the famine predicted by Agabus (Acts 11:28), Paul and Barnabas took relief aid from Antioch to the believers in Jerusalem (Acts 11:30). Paul and Barnabas then returned to Antioch, taking John Mark with them (Acts 12:25).

Paul's missionary journeys

Paul's three missionary journeys all began at Antioch. His first journey (Acts 13–14), from A.D. 48 to 49, was followed by another visit to Jerusalem (Acts 15). The second journey lasted from A.D. 50 to 52, and the third from A.D. 53 to 57. It was following Paul's third expedition that he was arrested in Jerusalem (Acts 21:27-36) and then imprisoned in Caesarea for two years (Acts 23:23–26:32) from A.D. 57 to 59. Having appealed to Caesar (Acts 25:11), Paul was transferred to Rome where he was confined for approximately two years (Acts 28:30-31).

After two years in Rome, Paul was released, apparently because no Jews had appeared to bring a charge against him (cf. Phil. 1:19, 25; 2:24). Paul then went east through Ephesus, where he left Timothy (1 Tim. 1:3), and then to Colosse (Philem. 1:22). From there he proceeded to Macedonia where he wrote his first letter to Timothy (1 Tim. 1:3). Paul may have at that time realized his desire to journey to Spain (Rom. 15:28; 1 Clement 5:7).

Paul again journeyed east and visited Crete (Titus 1:5), where he left Titus to set the church in order and appoint elders in A.D. 66. Paul wrote Titus concerning his responsibilities just before he journeyed from Asia Minor (2 Tim. 4:13, 20) to Nicopolis, where he spent the winter of A.D. 66/67 (Titus 3:12). Having spent spring and autumn in Macedonia and Greece (1 Tim. 1:4; 2 Tim. 4:20), Paul was arrested a second time and brought to Rome, where he was martyred in the spring of A.D. 68 (see the *Date* section below).

DATE

Early church fathers such as Clement of Rome, Eusebius, and Dionysius of Corinth generally support the second arrest of Paul and his martyrdom sometime near the end of Nero's persecutions. The date for Paul's death is based on early church tradition and is not certain. The letter was probably written from Corinth around A.D. 57.

PURPOSE

The letter to the Romans was designed to pave the way for Paul's visit to Rome by giving a straightforward presentation of the gospel. But the goal was not the conversion of the readers. They were already Christians. The goal was to show the implications of the gospel for Christians who mixed ethnic bigotry, fleshly works, and stubborn pride with the pure word of redemption in Christ alone. Paul desired to wean his readers away from self-sufficiency with its source in human achievement and pride, whether religious or secular. The goal was to bring the readers to the point of being living and acceptable sacrifices to God (Rom. 12:1-2).

GEOGRAPHY AND ITS IMPORTANCE

From Corinth to Rome

At the time Paul wrote this letter to Rome from Corinth, he planned to return to Jerusalem, with an offering for the Christians there. After his journey to Jerusalem he planned to set out for Rome and possibly Spain. The letter to the Romans outlined Paul's beliefs about Jesus Christ so that the readers would be informed about him when he finally arrived.

GUIDING CONCEPTS

CORINTH AND THE LETTER TO THE ROMANS

Paul's letter to the Romans is often viewed as a formal presentation of Christian doctrine, as if in it Paul organized his beliefs in a timeless way, untouched by the usual problems and debates with his readers found in all the rest of his writings. On the contrary, Romans throbs with real-life needs and carries the still glowing heat of Paul's most recent problems with the Corinthian church.

Paul had spent three years of his third missionary journey (A.D. 53 to 57) ministering in Ephesus. After the riot in Ephesus (Acts 19:23-41), Paul departed for Greece and spent three months there (Acts 20:2-3) before his departure for Jerusalem with the contribution for the saints (Rom. 15:25-26). Paul spent a good part of that three months in Corinth and wrote his letter to the Romans from that city. This is clear from his reference to Gaius in 16:23 and 1 Corinthians 1:14. Paul's recommendation of Phoebe from Cenchrea, the eastern seaport of Corinth, is another indication that Corinth was the place of writing (Rom. 16:1). Perhaps Phoebe carried the letter to Rome.

Paul's letters to the Corinthians provide the best immediate background to the problems and the passion behind his letter to the Romans. The Corinthians had problems with pride and arrogance (1 Cor. 4:5-6; 2 Cor. 3:5-6, 15-16; 11:21-22). And they were not sure they needed to believe in a physical resurrection (see 1 Cor. 15; 2 Cor. 5 concerning the resurrection and the nature of flesh). Compare that with the problems of arrogance spoken of in Romans 11:18, 20, 25; 12:3, 16. Romans also dealt with the problem of causing other Christians to stumble (cf. Rom. 14 with 1 Cor. 8).

Romans is not an abstract formal presentation of doctrine. It is a throbbing presentation of the impact of Jesus Christ on the most cherished but fatal presuppositions of Jew and Gentile alike.

BIBLE-WIDE CONCEPTS

THE FOUNDATIONS OF REDEMPTION
The nature of God
Paul recounts a number of God's characteristics and brings God's character directly to bear on the Romans' needs.

God is the Creator. As Creator he is free to act upon and within his creation. He makes the rules for his creatures, not the other way around (Rom. 1:20, 25; 4:17; 8:18-23; 9:19-21).

God is also just. This characteristic of God is crucial at several points in the letter (for example, see 2:11; 3:3-4, 25-26; 9:6, 14, 19; 11:1-2) and is supported by numerous Old Testament quotations.

God is completely righteous. Paul used the Old Testament to show how God has always been righteous (for example, see Rom. 3:21; also, 3:4 and its quotation of Ps. 51:4). Paul stressed that the possibility of human righteousness is based only on the fact that God is righteous. Human righteousness is a participation in God's righteousness. That is the foundation of righteousness in Jesus Christ. Any righteousness must be linked to a relationship with him. Paul's point throughout Romans was that righteousness is a relationship with God himself, not simply external obedience to a set of rules.

The nature of human beings
Paul laid down several truths about the nature of human beings. Humanity is suffering under the effects of Adam's sin (5:12-21). People come to God by faith and receive salvation through the promises to Abraham (4:1-15). They are under the rule of the King of the line of David (1:3; cf. 1 Kings 11:36; 2 Kings 8:19). The human race is stretched out between two men, Adam and Christ. People live either in the first man, Adam, or in the last man, Christ (Rom. 5:15). And the movement from Adam to Christ is through the doorway of faith in the redeeming work of Christ, not by means of law, ethnic background, religious tradition, or worldly tokens of status. Paul's letter to the Romans directly assaults human aversion, whether Jewish or Gentile (1:16), to salvation by faith alone.

THE CONCEPT OF RIGHTEOUSNESS
The big picture
Righteousness is the central concept in Romans; and the key element of being right with God is being like God. Righteousness involves obedience to God's commands (power for life) and a remedy for disobedience (forgiveness for sin). But Paul wrote to people who either wanted to do away completely with any standards or laws for living righteously (the Gentiles) or wanted to put every Christian back under all the laws of the Mosaic covenant (the Jews). So Paul presented a full-orbed view of how righteousness is achieved and how it relates to righteous living.

Righteousness has its beginning in the power of God to declare a believer righteous on the basis of faith in Christ (1:16-17). Everyone is equal in being declared unrighteous so that they all may be equally exalted in the righteousness of Christ (3:9, 21-24).

The middle phase of righteousness involves God's gift of strength and endurance to live righteously. That power comes not from self-effort but from the powerful work of the Holy Spirit (8:1-4, 12-13).

The final phase of righteousness is the realized power of resurrection and judgment in the life of the believer (2:5-6, 14-16; 8:23; 16:20). In Judaism, justification would only be known in the future judgment. For the Christian, justification is a fact based on the past act of God in Christ, the present power of the Holy Spirit, and the future hope for resurrection and reward.

Covenantal appearances
Righteousness stems from the character of God. God has always given specific commands that let believers know what a truly righteous life is. Those commands do not create righteousness; they define it. For example, Noah's righteous acts showed that he was righteous in his character (Gen. 6:9). The commands given to Abraham gave him a description of how he, as a righteous person, should behave (Gen. 12:1-3; 15:6; 18:19). The letter to the Romans gave extensive explanations about how the Christian receives the fulfillment of God's promises to Abraham. The commands given in the Mosaic covenant put God's laws into clear statements that give a clear gauge of one's righteousness.

Even people who did not have God's commands in the Mosaic Law could behave righteously (Rom. 2:14-16). Righteousness is an inner transformation brought about by the Holy Spirit. In Romans 5:21 righteousness is that which acquits mankind of sin and is the living power given to break sin's bondage.

The new covenant in Jesus Christ solves two problems that have been present since the fall of Adam and Eve in Eden—forgiveness for sin and ability for righteous living. Isaiah 53:11 spoke of God's act of justifying man on the basis of the Servant's suffering. The new covenant passages of Jeremiah 31:31-34 and Ezekiel 36:26 spoke of God putting the law and the Spirit inside believers to instruct and enable their obedience. The Old Testament and New Testament order was always forgiveness first, instruction in obedience second. The entire question of law-keeping concerns not what people have to do to be saved, but what they are compelled by gratitude to do because they have been saved. Such was the answer Paul set out to give in Romans.

NEEDS MET BY ROMANS

Paul wrote to meet several key needs of his readers. First, he addressed some of their political questions by affirming that Christianity supported Roman laws and was not out to overthrow Roman rule. An early way to bring persecution upon Christianity was to claim that the religion was against the laws of Rome and sought to depose Caesar.

Second, Paul addressed the question of possible ethnic superiority. The Romans were experiencing some conflict between the Gentile and Jewish elements of the church. But neither being Jewish nor Gentile put someone in a better standing before God. Paul wanted the jealousy and fighting between Jewish and Gentile Christians to stop. He stressed that no ethnic group had special salvation standing before God. Jews and Gentiles all equally needed Christ's redemption. In that connection, Romans addressed the new role of the Old Testament Laws of Moses since the coming of Christ. Were Christians bound to keep the Laws of Moses? If not, then how was Christianity connected to all of God's Old Testament promises of redemption? Jews were pressuring the Gentile Christians to keep all of Moses' laws. Paul had to carefully explain the role of Old Testament law within Christ's redemption.

Third, Paul showed how two invisible things, faith and the Holy Spirit, were needed for gaining a secure salvation. Paul stressed that the entire witness of the Old Testament confirmed faith and the Spirit as the only means to salvation. Although Paul may not have known his readers in Rome, he knew from experience the kinds of problems they were having. These problems ranged from religious to civil matters. The structure and content of Romans show that Paul was answering questions like the following for his Roman readers.

- Does Christianity respect the laws of Roman government or does it promote rebellion?
- How can something as intangible as faith be a more secure a way of salvation than the more tangible obedience to Mosaic Law?
- How can Jesus do away with the Mosaic Law and yet require his followers to obey the laws of God?
- How does complete forgiveness in Christ relate to his demands that people live righteously?
- What is the role of the Holy Spirit?
- Why are Jewish people not better off with God than Gentiles?
- Does not the heritage of Jews automatically give them special standing before God?
- How is the Christian supposed to relate to the civil authorities?
- How are Jews and Gentiles supposed to relate to each other within the church?

Throughout Romans Paul worked to break through the kind of human pride that insists on gaining salvation through human works rather than accepting the perfect righteousness God offers in Christ. The book seeks to do away with any thoughts of superiority believers might harbor based on their race or religious obedience, no matter how well-intentioned. Paul wanted all ethnic groups to take an equal place on the level ground around the cross of Christ and live in peace.

Believers may face frequent pressures to obey religious laws and be judged by their external conformity to religious norms—some biblical, others not. If believers just focus on these external rules, it is easy for them to become satisfied with giving good impressions to the people around them, when in reality God may not be so pleased with their inner spiritual life. To this situation Romans opens up the world of God's perfect righteousness revealed in his character and his laws, impossible for believers to achieve on their own, but freely given in Christ. Paul proclaimed that in Christ believers are free to obey God, not as a means of becoming righteous, but because they have already been made righteous.

Often what believers can see seems more substantial than what they can hear. Romans shows how the seemingly uncertain facts of faith and the Spirit, heard but not seen, are eternally secure grounds for their redemption. Visible obedience to God's laws may seem to be a more substantial way to certify merit before God. But Paul argued that the presently invisible rewards of faith and the Spirit are the only true grounds for eternal redemption. In Christ, God had brought to perfection all the Old Testament ways and promises of salvation.

OUTLINE OF ROMANS

A. RIGHTEOUSNESS FOR ACCEPTANCE BY FAITH (1:1–8:39)
1. The Introduction of Paul and His Message (1:1-17)
2. Righteousness Rejected by All Men (1:18–3:20)
3. Righteousness Accepted by Faith (3:21–5:21)
4. Righteousness and Personal Sin (6:1–8:39)
B. RIGHTEOUSNESS IN GOD'S ACTS WITH ISRAEL (9:1–11:36)
1. God's Righteous Election of Israel (9:1-29)
2. God's Righteous Witness to Israel (9:30–10:21)
3. God's Righteous Restoration of Israel (11:1-36)
C. RIGHTEOUSNESS IN HUMAN OBEDIENCE UNDER GOD (12:1–16:27)
1. The Renewed Mind: Proper Perspectives on Self, Church, and Society (12:1–13:14)
2. The Renewed Mind: Acceptance and Edification of the Weak (14:1–15:13)
3. The Trip to Rome: Reasons (15:14-33)
4. Final Remarks: Friends and Enemies (16:1-24)
5. Ascription of Glory (16:25-27)

ROMANS NOTES

1:1–8:39 RIGHTEOUSNESS FOR ACCEPTANCE BY FAITH

Overview: This entire section of 1:1–8:39 explores the relationship between faith and redemption linked to Abraham versus the merits of obedience to the Mosaic Law. Faith was always the way of salvation before and during the time of Moses. As seen in Acts, Christ's new covenant opened up salvation by faith in new ways to both Jews and Gentiles alike.

With or without the Mosaic Law, Jews and Gentiles are under God's condemnation (Rom. 1–3). Because both Jews and Gentiles were used to thinking of salvation in terms of religious merit through works, Romans 4 demonstrates how secure redemption through faith can be, especially when it is a faith like Abraham's. Romans 5 continues the theme of the security of faith by showing how faith alone removes believers from death in Adam to life in Christ. Believers are "much more" (5:9-10, 15, 20) secure in Christ than they would be in Adam. In light of the security in Christ by faith, Romans 6–8 addresses how the demands of the law and the flesh relate to the power of Christ and the Holy Spirit.

1:1-17 The Introduction of Paul and His Message

1:1 PAUL'S CHARACTER AND CALLING
This introduction clarifies Paul's identity and the nature of his message. He called himself an apostle of Christ to the Gentiles to bring the gospel of righteousness by faith in Christ. His personal role was that of being a servant of Christ (see Phil 1:1; Titus 1:1).

1:2 THE GOSPEL'S FOUNDATION: PROMISE
This greeting was designed to elaborate how the gospel in Christ was related to Old Testament promises (Rom. 1:2). Note the connecting first words in each verse (1:2-6). They build an elaborate description of how Jesus relates to Old Testament promises. This will also serve as a foundation to the arguments concerning promises in Romans 4 and 9–11. The promises of God, from Abraham to Christ, form the foundation and definition of present experience and future hope.

1:3-6 THE GOSPEL'S SUBJECT
The subject of the gospel is Jesus from two perspectives. He was the human seed of David (1:3) and the divine Son of God (1:4). As such, he is the ultimate King according to Davidic promise (2 Sam. 7)—eternal, divine, and exalted at God's right hand (Ps. 110:1; Acts 2:33-35). But he is also the Son of God in the flesh. Christ's identity as a human being will be foundational for the comparison between Adam and Christ in Romans 5 and the role of the Spirit in the Christian's life (Rom. 6–8).

Although consistent with Old Testament promise, Christ's kingly and divine nature combined with his humiliation and crucifixion broke all the Jewish presuppositions and expectations about how the Messiah would come. It also cut against their presup-

positions about how the Messiah's followers should conduct themselves.

Jesus the Messiah's resurrection (1:4) was God's declaration of his sonship in power. That power was the Spirit of holiness—the foundation for all this letter's comments concerning the Christian's war with sin and victory in resurrection. Paul's ministry found its potency in the power of Christ's resurrection. The same power that raised Christ from death operates in the Christian's righteousness, Christ's lordship, Israel's hope, and the world's release from bondage. The entire book's perspective on power for salvation and Christian victory is based on the person and work of the Holy Spirit.

The instrument ("through him") of Paul's calling (1:5-6) is the risen Lord who commissioned him. That idea of mediation ("through") is foundational to all of the letter. Every forgiven sin, every gift of the Spirit, every act of power in ministry comes mediated from God the Father, through the risen Lord, and by the enabling power of the Spirit. Notice, for example, the great stress on mediation ("through") in Romans 5:1-2, 5, 9-12, 16-19, 21.

In Romans 1:5, Paul's solid base of identity and authority is presented. The "we" here focuses generally on the Gentiles (1:5-6). The readers have an equality with Paul; both are considered "called" ones (1:1, 6).

1:7 THE ADDRESSEES ARE FURTHER IDENTIFIED AND BLESSED
In expressing their calling and nature (1:7), Paul broadened his address to include the Jews as well. On saints (1:7; "holy ones"), see 1:4; 12:1-2. The content of Romans 12–15 was founded on the fact that Christians are to behave in accordance with their nature as "holy ones."

1:8-17 PAUL'S DESIRE TO VISIT ROME AND REASONS FOR DELAY
The purpose of this section was to clear the air for his visit. Paul was positive and gracious; he had a message of encouragement that they needed, but he never talked down to them.

Paul's thanksgiving for the faith of the Romans (1:8) blends with the main body of the introduction. Compare what Paul wrote to the believers in Rome with Acts 28:15. Paul emphasized his interest in the Romans both in prayer and in his desire to visit them

(1:9-15). He had long desired to travel to Rome (Acts 18:21; Rom. 1:13; 15:32), but his desire was ministry-oriented (1:11-12). He wanted to do them some spiritual good. Community sharing and encouragement is the vehicle of growth and stability.

As Paul affirmed his travel plans (1:13) he was not simply sharing a travelog. He was assuring them that he had not purposely been staying away from Rome. He was not embarrassed to come to the great city of Rome but had wanted to come for a long time. His visit was part of his Gentile calling and was an obligation from God (1:14-15). Paul was aware of the obligation that God had committed to him (cf. 1 Cor. 9:16-17; Acts 9:15).

The "Greeks" (1:14) were those who spoke Greek in contrast to the "non-Greeks" (1:14; "barbarians," NASB and KJV) who did not. Note that Paul wanted to preach the gospel to the Christians (1:15) in Rome. But the "good news" (Isa. 52:7; 61:1-2) was a message for the saved as well as the unsaved.

Paul gave another reason for his desire to see them (1:16-17). The possible accusation that Paul was ashamed (1:16) to come to Rome was contrasted with his eagerness (1:15). Paul had not stayed out in the provinces because he was weak. On the contrary, he had the very power of God—the gospel (1:16). Although Paul was commissioned to witness to the Gentiles (Acts 9:15), he recognized an obligation to carry the gospel to the Jews first. That was in line with the great covenant with Abraham that promised redemption for the world through Abraham first (Gen. 12:3).

The "righteousness from God" (1:17) is the righteousness that God approves and provides. The words "by faith from first to last" (1:17; "from faith to faith," NASB and KJV) mean that God's provision of salvation is by faith from start to finish. This illustrates Paul's desire in 1:15. He will pass the gospel on from his faith to the faith of others. "For" (1:17) explains why the Gentiles ("Greeks") are included. Paul used Habakkuk 2:4 to support his point (cf. also Gal. 3:11; Heb. 10:38). This use of the Old Testament speaks to possible Jewish resistance to this message. This relationship between faith and righteousness is leading up to the conclusion of Romans 3:28.

1:18–3:20 Righteousness Rejected by All Men

Overview: This section, which reveals man's sinfulness, lays the foundation for the line of thought that moves through 3:31 and leads finally to God's promise of mercy (11:32). In the section 1:18–11:32 an explanation is given of how all people, Jew and Gentile, are included in and impacted by sin. It calls all ethnic groups to recognize their sinfulness and to understand God's promise that in Abraham all the nations of the world would be blessed. This obligated the readers of the Roman letter to receive all peoples as equal candidates for God's redemption.

This section functions in two ways. First, it shows how all are equally needy of God's remedy for sin. Second, it shows the great need that people have of the Holy Spirit's power in order to live righteously. Paul will present remedies to these problems in order. Here, Paul was speaking of the present exhibition of God's wrath, not the final wrath to come.

1:18-32 WRATH REVEALED AGAINST GENTILES

Romans 1:18 presents God's wrath, the opposite of God's revealed righteousness (1:16-17), and begins the long section that shows why faith is the only way to righteousness. Wrath is God's attitude toward sin. Note the links to Habakkuk's context (Hab. 2:4). Wrath is revealed by the "giving over" of man to his sin; it is the twisting of God's image into its opposite.

1:18-23 Mankind's willful rejection of God. God made his truth evident (1:18-20), but humans suppressed and rejected it (1:18-19). Romans 1:18 is added to begin Paul's thoughts on how all humanity is responsible for their sins. The core of the law is summed up in 1:19: "What may be known about God is plain" (cf. 1:32). That basic knowledge about God is available by simply viewing God's creation (1:20). People are without excuse. This statement implicates Paul's audience—people who made excuses for why they were exempt from God's wrath (cf. 9:19-20)—in mankind's universal guilt. Mankind rejected the true God (1:21-23) for its own image (see Acts 14:11-13, Lystra; Acts 17, Athens; Acts 19, Ephesus). The source of this data was the Old Testament and Paul's own experience.

1:24-32 God's willful rejection of humanity.
Because man rejected God's truth, he "gave
them over to the sinful desires of their
hearts" (1:24-27). The "therefore" (1:24)
links the punishment that follows with the
just-mentioned sins. The words "gave them
over" speak of God's judicial abandonment
of sinners to their wicked ways. This was
the divine penalty for rejecting God. Their
life was based on a lie—the opposite of
God's character and ways (1:24-25). The
due penalty (1:27) was to suffer the consequences of the perversion itself.

Because man forgot his knowledge about
God, God "gave them over to a depraved
mind" (1:28-32). This is a severe marring
of the image of God. It involves being controlled by the fleshly mind (1:28-31). This is
a list of vices that lead to the willful disobedience to the ordinances of God (1:32). Note
the split between knowing and practicing.

2:1–3:8 WRATH REVEALED AGAINST "MORALITY"
Paul had the Jews in mind primarily, though
not exclusively, in this section. Paul had this
section in mind when he wrote 1:18—"all"
are under God's wrath. To convince the Jews
of their need for redemption, much less a
redemption through faith in Jesus, was a
difficult task. Paul began by attempting to
wean them, and any others, away from the
self-righteousness of law-keeping. The issue
was not in knowing the laws of God (1:32)
but in keeping them (2:1). It is in keeping
God's law that all fail. In Romans 2, Paul
showed, first subtly (2:1-16) and then openly
(2:17-29), that the Jews, like the Gentiles, are
without excuse (1:20; 2:1) and stand under
God's condemnation.

*2:1-16 God judges according to deeds, not
words.* Deeds, not words, are the object of
God's judgment. The concept of "practice"
links Romans 1 and Romans 2 (1:32; 2:1-2,
"do"; 2:25, "observe"; 2:26-27, "keep").
Some give hearty approval to sin (1:32),
and some condemn it (2:1). But they both
do it—and that is the fatal flaw that brings
humanity under the wrath of God. Neither
the wallowing in nor the judging of sin can
overcome the universal and fatal flaw—the
practice of sin.

Therefore, the "wallowers" and the
"judges" receive the same condemnation

(2:2-10). Paul is building to 2:29. The externals of race or the hurling of pious judgments cannot bring the internal cleanness
granted by the Spirit; it is only the cleanness
given by the Spirit that merits God's praise
(2:29). Romans 2:7-8 defines the concept of
rewards based on deeds (2:6). God's judgment of deeds is not partial (2:11) to Jew or
Gentile. His judgment is ethically, not ethnically, defined. Paul was quite clear that good
works do not save (Eph. 2:8-9) but are the
product of regeneration. The Jews were first
in privilege, but also first in guilt and responsibility (2:9).

God will give impartial judgment to all
(2:11-16). Paul was revealing that obedience
was a criterion used in God's judgment of
mankind, not because he supported salvation
by works, but in order to establish that mankind, Jew or Gentile, does not have what
God requires—a life of perfect righteousness.

Paul was being general here in regarding
the principles of "practice" or "obedience" as
being essential before God. James 2:10 says
that just one sin breaks all the law. Those
"apart from the law" (2:12) are the Gentiles
who had not been entrusted with the Mosaic
Law. Romans 2:13 is key to Paul's argument
showing that it is not in hearing the law that
righteousness is achieved but in the doing of
it. This shows that the Jews who have heard
the law are no better off than the Gentiles
who have not heard it, for both have failed
to do it. The Gentiles, nevertheless, do have
a "law" of conscience that commends or
corrects their actions (2:14).

*2:17-29 The externals of Judaism are
negated.* Paul asked those who had the
Mosaic Law where their confidence was—
in words or in lives conforming to the law
(2:17-25). He addressed those who relied
on law (2:17, 23) and boasted in God but
did not obey either the law or God. And this
was precisely what the Jews and Gentiles
had in common—rejection of the truth and
light God had given them. Note Isaiah 52:5
quoted in Romans 2:24.

Circumcision (2:25, lit., "a cutting
around") is a reference to the removal of
the foreskin of the male penis. This was
common practice among Semitic peoples,
including the Hebrews. In the Old Testament, God introduced the custom as the sign
of the Abrahamic covenant (Gen. 17:10-14;

cf. Exod. 12:48; Lev. 12:3). The rite was a sign that one had entered the covenant community of Israel. All too frequently, the real meaning of the rite was lost and it became an external practice without any spiritual content.

Because of that, externals such as circumcision were of no value (Rom. 2:26-29). Spiritual circumcision (Ezek. 36:26) of the heart (see Deut. 10:16 and context; Deut. 30:6; Jer. 4:4; 9:25-26) was an Old Testament concept. Paul's thoughts echoed Jeremiah's words regarding a circumcision of the heart (Jer. 4:4; 9:25-26). It was the inward reality, not the outward sign, that counted most with God. The Spirit and letter contrast (Rom. 2:29) was central in Paul's most recent letter (2 Corinthians) preceding his writing of Romans (2 Cor. 3:6). Note the link of Romans 2:29 with 3:1.

3:1-8 Promises for Judaism are upheld. Paul will elaborate further on God's faithfulness to Israel in Romans 9–11. At this point, Paul provided a correction to a possible misunderstanding that he was implying that it was no longer of any worth being Jewish—that somehow, with the coming of Christ, God emptied the nation Israel of all worth and promise. However, the issue was not the failures of Israel, but the faithfulness of God (3:3). Paul responded to the question, "What is the benefit of being Jewish if it doesn't save me from sin and presents no advantage over heathenism?" He made it clear that God's promises would be upheld in spite of human unfaithfulness (3:3). Paul stressed Jewish disobedience to God's Messiah, though he began the stress on what the Jewish future would be. Paul met two objections (3:5-8). The first concerned the justice of God (3:5). The second concerned the false accusation of lawlessness hurled at Christians (3:8).

3:9-20 GOD'S WRATH REVEALED AGAINST ALL HUMANITY
In light of 3:1-8, is the Jew better off when it comes to escaping God's wrath (3:9)? Paul answers no, because sin has brought everyone to the same level. The "we" (3:9) referred to the believers, with a possible Gentile emphasis. Paul had "already made the charge" that all have sinned (Rom. 1–2).

The organizing image for the string of Old Testament quotations (3:10-18) was the parts of the human body. This revealed the numerical (none) and particular (parts of each one) pervasiveness of unrighteousness. The basic cause of this state of sin was a lack of fear of God (3:18). Paul appealed to the testimony of Old Testament Scripture (Pss. 14:1-3; 53:1-3; 5:9; 140:3; 10:7; Isa. 59:7-8; Ps. 36:1) to confirm that both Jew and Gentile were under sin and guilty.

Paul had already revealed how the law could not bring salvation, and next he revealed the purpose of the law (3:19-20). On 3:20, see Psalm 143:2. No one could in reality keep the law. Everyone knew that. What they missed, and what Paul was trying to teach, was that knowledge of sin did not equal a knowledge of damnation. The problem was serious. While everyone might have admitted they were not perfect, Paul had to convince them that their imperfections, minor as they might be, were fatal.

In 1:18–3:20, Paul established the universal guilt of both Jews and Gentiles by stacking their deeds up against God's revealed law. But Paul also did this to show that the law was inadequate. Mankind would need more than the law to achieve righteousness before God. They would need the grace of God.

Paul showed that all people had sinned in order to speak to the necessity of justification by faith. The problem was not so much that people were hell-bound, but that they were arguing that they were not. Their self-righteousness had blinded them to their sin. This blind self-righteousness was shared by the non-Christian as well as by the Christian. Because of this, Paul would bring the message of the gospel to both groups (1:8, 15).

3:21–5:21 Righteousness Accepted by Faith

3:21-26 RIGHTEOUSNESS MANIFESTED
Paul answered the question, If it is impossible to keep the law perfectly, where can righteousness be found? The manifestation of righteousness returns to the topic of 1:17. Righteousness is manifested apart from the keeping of the Mosaic Law (3:21). The words "apart from the law" (3:21) are key to Paul's theology of justification. Righteousness is attained through faith (3:22) and witnessed to by the law and the Prophets (as Paul's Old Testament quotations

throughout the letter confirm). Justification is free to people but cost God an infinite price (3:23-26). Redemption (3:24) is a price paid as a ransom. Jesus Christ was the price; God was the one who paid. All people were in bondage. The word "redemption" means "to purchase and set free." The word contemplates mankind's bondage to sin and God's provision of grace to release them from that bondage. The word "justified" (3:24) means "to be declared righteous" as by a judge. This righteousness is not something earned, but something given as a gift on the basis of faith. For an Old Testament illustration of imputed righteousness, see Zechariah 3:1-5.

"A sacrifice of atonement" (3:25; "propitiation," NASB and KJV) is a satisfactory sacrifice (1 John 2:2; 4:10). Such a sacrifice has God's wrath in full view. The need for the sacrifice and the cause of God's wrath were painfully explained in Romans 1:18–3:20. God sent Christ to satisfy that need of a sacrifice. The atoning sacrifice or propitiation contemplates mankind's liability to God's wrath against sin and is God's gracious provision to deliver them from that wrath. Christ is the believer's atoning sacrifice, satisfying with his blood God's holy demand that sin be judged.

God has demonstrated and satisfied his righteousness through the sacrifice of his Son (3:25-26). Some ask what God is doing about sin. Why doesn't he fully deal with it? Does his passing over sins mean the sinner is justified? Paul answers no. Ever since the Noahic covenant God has pledged himself to long-suffering and patience (Gen. 8:21–9:17). Humans had not become more holy, but God would not immediately judge each and every sin. He waited for Christ to do that (see Acts 17:30). God suspended judgment on sins during the Old Testament period in anticipation of Christ's full and final sacrifice for sins (Rom. 3:25; cf. Hebrews 10:1-18).

Yes, God judged sin in the Old Testament, but sin's offense against God was infinite and his Old Testament judgments were merely finite. It was only in Christ that God showed his justice in matching the infinite crime with an infinite punishment. Sin's infinite offense has now been satisfied—

justly and perfectly. That satisfaction is the foundation for God's justice in declaring all forgiven. Since Christ's death, God could be just in judging sin perfectly, but could also be the justifier of those for whom Christ died (Rom. 3:26).

The section of 3:21-26 emphasizes faith as the only way to justification. It clarifies the relationship of God's forgiveness of sin to his inherent justice. Paul could have ended his letter right here. But at this point another critical issue was addressed—boasting (3:27-31). Relate this to 2:17; 3:1, 9, and Paul's recent experience with the Corinthians' boastings (1 Cor. 4:18; 5:2; 8:1; 13:4).

3:27-31 BOASTING EXCLUDED

Salvation by faith excludes boasting (3:27-28). Where there is no room for self-effort, there is no room for boasting (cf. 1 Cor. 4:7). Take note of Romans 3:28. Because God is sovereign over Jews and Gentiles, there is a unity in his chosen means of redemption by faith (3:29-30).

Paul had to defend and describe his claims about what had happened to the law (3:31). This problem was hinted at in 3:1, 5-8. The law had been both done away with and established in a new way (3:31). This showed that Paul did not advocate a lawless life. On the contrary, he established the importance of the law. Two views of the law surface in Paul's discussion. The wrong view thought that keeping the law could bring salvation. The correct view saw the law as a set of directions for those who had already been brought into a saving relationship with God through faith.

Paul's references to the law (3:20, 28) could lead his readers to conclude that it was useless. On the contrary, it fulfills a vital role in confronting people with their sin and accountability before God. The law is vital and currently operative as a means for conviction (3:31; cf. 1 Tim. 1:8) but not as a means of salvation.

Romans 5–8 will further relate to establishing the law. See Matthew 5:17. Surprisingly, to maintain the law is to maintain faith. The law continually reveals mankind's need for Christ and reminds them of their forgiveness and perfection in him. Paul's work of establishing the law was to help his readers see the law, not as a way of attaining righteousness, but as a means of discovering their sinfulness and need for God's gracious forgiveness.

4:1-25 JUSTIFICATION THROUGH FAITH AS AN OLD TESTAMENT PRINCIPLE

4:1-8 For Abraham in faith. Paul demonstrated in Romans 4 that justification by faith was nothing new. This section is a powerful exposition of Genesis 15:6 (quoted in Rom. 4:3, 9, 22) and how God has always forgiven his people on the basis of faith—whether Abraham before the law (4:3) or David within the time of the law (4:6-8). Both Abraham (4:3-5) and David (4:6-8) were justified in this manner. The entrance of the law in Moses' day did not interrupt this way of righteousness by faith. The two pillars of Genesis 15:6 are "faith" (Rom. 4:3, 5, 9, 11-13, 16, 18-20, 24) and "credited" (4:3, 5, 9-11, 22-23).

This explanation of faith and its righteousness explains what Paul meant in 3:20 and 3:31. The law was never designed to save, just to instruct and condemn (3:20). And to see faith's priority over the law was to set the law into its proper perspective, thus establishing it properly (3:31).

4:9-12 For Abraham in uncircumcision. This section clarifies what Paul meant in 2:29. Circumcision was a sign (4:11), that is, its real meaning pointed away from the physical act to something else, in this case a heart of faith. See, for example, Acts 15:9. The point here (4:9) is that Abraham was declared righteous before (Gen. 15:6), not after, his circumcision (Gen. 17:9-14). The fact that Abraham was justified apart from circumcision opens the doorway of faith to Gentiles—"all who believe but have not been circumcised" (Rom. 4:11).

4:13-25 For Abraham and his worldwide seed. Abraham was promised the world as his inheritance, not through the law, but through faith (4:13; see "heirs" in 4:14). Paul shows that the law of circumcision came after Abraham's justification by faith. Again, this established the proper framework for the law. It came to those who were already righteous by faith; therefore it must have a purpose other than justification. Its purpose was to correct and condemn where needed, thus driving its followers to God's grace

through the offerings of the tabernacle, then the temple, and finally, Christ.

Law was not the vehicle of promise (4:13). Paul's use of Genesis 17:5 and 15:5 (Rom. 4:17-18) was Old Testament proof that Abraham was "the father" (4:16) through God's promise to him and through his own faith. The resurrection and creation themes of 4:17 are the foundation for Paul's faith that God would do something with his "as good as dead" body (4:19) and for the faith of all believers that God raised up the dead body of Jesus (4:24).

5:1-21 THE PEACEFUL SECURITY OF RIGHTEOUSNESS

For Paul, justification through faith was not just a matter of sound doctrine. It was also a source of great blessing (5:1-11). In Romans 1–4 Paul explained the correct way to God's righteousness through faith. This was an explanation of 1:17. But Paul established law, not as a way to gain salvation, but as a means to find condemnation.

For many, faith did not seem to be a very secure mark of salvation. How could something so intangible bring security? Paul answers that question here. He offsets insecurity by showing how "much more" (5:9-10, 15, 17, 20) they have in Christ. Other key words are "through" and "by" (5:1-2, 5, 9-12, 17, 19, 21). Salvation through faith is as secure as the work of God through Christ.

5:1-11 Security is based on God's demonstration of love. The "therefore" of 5:1 indicates that a logical inference is being drawn from the preceding discussion (3:21–4:25). The text of 5:1 may be paraphrased, "Let us keep and enjoy peace with God." Justification brings peace, not wrath, and is mediated by the Lord (5:1-2). It brings a future hope of glory (5:2). The Greek word translated "rejoice" in 5:2-3, 11 is translated "brag" in Romans 2:17, 23, where the element of self-centered boasting is present. In 5:2-3, 11 the element of self-confidence is removed. The substitute is accepting the mediation achieved "through" God's sacrifice.

Even difficulties and hardships exhibit the love of God (5:3-11). Paul made it clear that there was great benefit in trials (5:3-4). Note the relationship of weakness in tribulation and God's manifested glory through earthen vessels. This removes the validity of any boasting in law-keeping. Another proof of security is the presence of the love and Spirit of God (5:5).

The term "reconcile" means "to change" (5:10-11). Reconciliation by the death of Christ means that man's state of alienation from God is changed so that he is now able to be saved (2 Cor. 5:19).

5:12-21 The security is based on God's free gift. Paul concluded his consideration of justification by faith with an analogy demonstrating that while all men are in fact sinners (in Adam), all are potential beneficiaries of Christ's death and justification. The links are drawn between Adam and Christ. Paul's point was that security in Christ is even more secure than damnation in Adam.

Paul showed that even before the law, people died because of Adam's sin. Adam infected humanity with death. In a greater way Christ injected humanity with life. The human race is directly related to Adam and his sin. The theology of this verse is based on the concept of the corporate solidarity of the human race (cf. Heb. 7:9-10). With or without the law people sinned and died (Rom. 5:12; cf. 3:23). Adam's disobedience caused humanity to be "made sinners" (5:19; cf. 1 Cor. 15:21). Sin could not be charged as a violation of a specific command where there was no law. But sin existed, nevertheless, before the law was given at Sinai, as was evidenced by universal death from Adam to Moses.

Paul used Adam as a "pattern" (5:14), indicating that while he had a place and purpose historically, he was also divinely intended to teach by means of analogy something about Christ. Paul took Genesis 3 and the curse of God on Adam's sin very seriously. Humanity's death was rooted in Adam's sin. Paul used that certain root to compare and contrast with the certain rooting of life in Christ. See the accompanying chart.

The key to seeing "because all sinned" (5:12) as meaning "in Adam" is the "for" of 5:13. What is it explaining? All are reckoned as sinners by Adam's one sin. Again, Romans 5:20-21 continues to establish the law (3:31) in its proper perspective.

6:1–8:39 Righteousness and Personal Sin

Overview: In Romans 6–8 Paul deals with how righteousness is imparted to people through sanctification. The word "sanctify" means to "set apart" for God's possession and use. There are three aspects: (1) positional—all believers are set apart for God at redemption (1 Cor. 1:2, 30); (2) experiential—conforming the believers' experience of righteousness to their position of being righteous in Christ (John 17:17; Rom. 8:3-4); and (3) final—when the believers see the Lord and are made holy like him (1 Cor. 15:54; 1 John 3:2). Romans 6–8 focuses on the second, experiential aspect of sanctification.

6:1-14 DOES SIN ENLARGE GRACE?
The link between Romans 5 and 6 can be found in how the heightened awareness of sin due to the law's condemnation (5:13, 20; 6:1) is met with abounding grace (5:20).

6:1-2 Sin is a moral contradiction to salvation. Paul was forced to answer the criticism already mentioned (3:8) that Christians did not bother keeping rules (6:1). This criticism came primarily from Jewish Christians who wondered what would happen to people who claimed freedom from the law. But Paul moved the issue away from law-keeping to the Christian's new nature, in this case, his death to sin (6:2-3). The words "died to sin" (6:2) indicate that those who have believed in Christ have been separated from the ruling power of sin. Sin is no longer the master of one who has given his allegiance to Christ. Thus, the answer to the question in 6:1 is "By no means!"

ADAM AND CHRIST

Death in Adam	*Life in Christ*
Sin	Righteousness
Condemnation	Justification
Death	Life

6:3-4 Identification with Christ through baptism. Paul used the imagery of baptism to illustrate the vital union that the believer has with Christ. The Greek word for "baptize" was used in the dyeing trade for dipping cloth into dye. This dipping process brought about a change in the cloth's color and identity. Christian baptism also brings a change in identity—an identification with a new community.

Paul used baptism as a picture of the believer's change in identity—separated from the old life in Adam and united with Christ. The words "baptized into Christ" mean "identified and united with Christ." This begins to explain more fully the believer's solid link with Christ as opposed to Adam. It was man's link to Adam, not to the Law of Moses, that was fatal. Therefore, it was man's link to Christ, not to the Law of Moses, that would bring redemption. This is all based on the implications of chapter 5 for those who are in Christ rather than in Adam. Two "reigns" (5:14, 17, 21), the reign of death in Adam and the reign of grace in Christ, are in view.

Paul returned to the question regarding law for the justified (6:4; "live"). The Christian's walk is not defined by any particular set of laws but by conformity to the resurrected life of Christ. Conformity to a law code has been replaced with conformity to Christ's death and resurrection.

6:5-11 Identification with Christ's life. The function of this section is to clarify 6:3-4 by the example of Christ. This also relates back to Romans 5 and the believer's links to Adam and Christ. Paul continues to deal with the criticism that Christians can continue in sin in order to enjoy more and more grace (6:1). The issue here is conformity to Christ, not only in his resurrection power, but in the purpose of his death—to do away with servitude to sin (6:5-6). The believer's union with Christ in his death is designed to free him from sin's mastery. The term "old self" (6:6) refers to the unregenerate person, the condition of the human race in Adam before having faith in Christ.

The "body of sin" (6:6) refers to the physical body as conditioned and controlled by sin. Paul concludes his first words on sin and the believer by reinforcing the model of Christ (6:10)—dead to sin, alive to God

(6:10-11). The word "count" (6:11) is a mathematician's term and means "to add up" or "calculate." Paul is saying, "Add up the facts and live accordingly."

6:12-14 Willful presentation of the body. Paul's use of "reign" (6:12) continues the topic's discussion from 5:17, 21. Two reigns are in view—the reigns of sin and grace. Although sin can plague all believers, they are to consider themselves dead to sin and choose to walk in the reign of resurrection grace rather than the reign of Adamic death. Reign equals obedience to the call of either sin or grace. It is the presentation of oneself (cf. 12:1 for the same word) in response to one or the other.

The entire Christian life is a response to one reign or the other. Paul implies that sin has been reigning over the physical bodies of believers. Now he says, "Stop! Don't place your physical body at the disposal of sin. Rather, present yourselves to God for his service."

Compare 6:14 with 5:21. Romans 6:14 shows that the believer has already been judged a perfect person in Christ; therefore, questions of law-keeping are not relevant. Paul is trying to keep a careful balance between affirming the Christian's completed righteousness by faith in Christ and the expectation that a believer will live a holy life, not in order to get righteous before God, but because he is already righteous.

"Not under law" (6:14) means believers are not alone and faced with the insurmountable mountain of keeping God's law. Paul puts it another way in 8:15. There is no fear of condemnation. Being "under law" in this sense is to be liable to God's retribution in a final sense of eternal wrath.

6:15–7:6 THE IMPLICATIONS OF BEING A BONDSLAVE

6:15-23 Should believers sidestep the law? Triggered by his statement that believers are not under law (6:14), Paul continued to assert both the righteousness of believers and their absolute mandate to live holy lives. Paul's critics assumed that those who were under grace alone would have no standard for behavior. They claimed it was the law that was the motivation to obedience. But Paul showed that those justified by faith were motivated to love and obey God by grace, not the law. Paul came to the conclusion that believers do not need the law to love righteousness. The lives of believers in Christ are not determined by the limited provisions and resources of the "law," but rather by the redeeming and renewing resources of "grace."

The believer, not under the threat of condemnation for failure, is enabled to obey God from the inside ("heart," 6:17). It is in that internal sense that the believer becomes a slave to righteousness (6:18). Paul appealed to a familiar principle: you are a slave to the one you serve. People are either slaves to sin resulting in death, or slaves to righteousness resulting in life.

Paul continues by showing the consequences of being enslaved by either sin or righteousness (6:19-23). Paul showed that true believers are not lawless. Actually, their slavery to Christ results in sanctification. Paul's illustration of the two types of presentation ("offer," 6:19) needs to be taken seriously. Little more than this (6:23) can be said once salvation by faith has been elaborated. Verse 6:23 contains a fundamental law of God's moral universe. Sin ends in death, and grace ends in eternal life. Death is earned as a consequence of sin; eternal life is received as free and unmerited favor.

7:1-6 The death of believers to the demands of the law. Paul continues to establish the law (3:31) by showing that through Christ believers have died to the law's condemnation so that they might live lives of righteousness. Apart from Christ, the demands of the law are upon the flesh. This continues the thrust from Romans 4. First, faith precedes and makes possible the way to righteousness (Rom. 4). Second, faith is secure (Rom. 5). Third, through the death of Christ believers are free to present themselves to God (Rom. 6). There is a standard for behavior under grace (6:1, 15-17).

Paul shows one exception to his observation in 7:1; one can live and still be free from the law's demands. In 6:14 Paul made the statement "you are not under law," and now he returns to develop that subject. The major point that he makes is that death dissolves the dominion of the law. Paul used marriage to illustrate the concept (7:2-3) and then applied the teaching (7:4-6). Believers have died to the law and have been joined to a new master, Christ. Paul consistently taught that death brings an end to a marriage (7:2; cf. 1 Cor. 7:39). Used in this context, the word "bound" (7:2) means married. What is the parallel being drawn here? Just as a woman and man become one flesh in marriage (Gen. 2:24), people are bound to the law while living as sons of Adam. Just as the woman is free from her husband when he dies, believers are free from the law when they have died to the law and sin. The death to sin and the law experienced by believers opens them up to a new state of freedom from the law. They are free to live out the death and resurrection of Christ through the Holy Spirit's power.

To match the Christian experience of dying to sin and living to God, Paul used an illustration in which someone is set free by death, but still lives. Jesus Christ acted both as the husband in the believer's bondage to the law and as the new and living husband in righteousness. The human illustration requires two husbands to make its point. But the great truth of Romans 7 is that Christ is at the same time the one husband who dies to the state of bondage and the one who brings his bride, the church, into a new state of freedom. Romans 6 shows that believers are dead to sin; Romans 7 shows they are dead to their old relationship to law.

7:7-25 THE LAW'S TRUE FUNCTION

7:7 The law reveals sin. These are Paul's final words on the law, completing the thought begun in Romans 6. The key question of 7:7 continues the line of thought from 6:1-2, 15 concerning how law is to be viewed from the standpoint of grace. Paul's point here is that the law reveals what sin is and must be distinguished from the sin itself. The law is not sin (5:20; 7:4-6), just as light is not that which it illuminates. Paul attacked legalism, not the law (7:14). Paul kept the situation in Romans 5 behind his discussions of law and righteousness. The believer could never escape his death-link to Adam by keeping the law.

7:8-12 Sin uses the law. Paul's focus in these verses was not on whether the person is regenerate or unregenerate. The power of sin is present in any person who tries to keep the law on his own. Note Galatians 5:17-26 as a summary of Romans 7–8.

7:13-20 Sin, not the law, causes death. Does the law cause death? Sin is based on the reality of being in Adam (Rom. 5). The presence of sin is what creates the inherent tension within people. This paves the way for the explanation in Romans 8 regarding this time of groaning (8:22-23, 26).

Who is this person who struggles so much with sin? Among the most prominent views, it is held that these verses describe: (1) Paul's life either before or after he became a Christian, (2) the experience of all people in Adam, (3) the experience of any person who relies on the law and his own efforts for sanctification, or (4) the experience of someone whose "true self" is struggling with the flesh (physical desires of the human body). It is likely that Paul was using himself as a picture of every human's struggle with good and evil.

7:21-25 The power of sin. How does this relate to the Christian? Romans 7 is talking about a walking-in-the-flesh approach to being righteous. After describing the believer's struggle with the flesh, Paul affirms that believers are not without hope for deliverance (7:25). The answer comes generally in 7:25 and more specifically in Romans 8.

8:1-39 THE SPIRIT ILLUMINATES THE NEW BONDAGE
In Romans 3–5 Paul presented how the powerful union of faith in Christ makes all who believe righteous. In Romans 6–8 Paul tells how to live righteously through the power of the Spirit. To sat it another way, faith, not law, brings about righteousness (Rom. 3–5) and the Spirit, not self-effort, brings about righteous living (Rom. 6–8).

Paul was still speaking to the issue of continuing in sin (6:1) versus living obediently to God's commands. See Paul's use of "offer" (6:13, 19), "live" (8:4), "minds set" (8:5-7), and "led" (8:14). The underlying structure is the process and path to holiness and glorification. Paul noted that believers still have unglorified bodies (8:23). But the Spirit gives them comfort in suffering, freedom from a condemned conscience, and freedom from the inability to do right.

8:1-11 God meets the law's requirements in Christ. Christ met the law's requirements and thus set all believers free (8:1-11). Believers do not need to work to gain standing before God. Romans 8:2 sums up the thrust of Romans 5–7. The directing power of the believer drawing on new covenant resources is not the flesh, but the Holy Spirit. The principle of a Spirit-produced life ("law of the Spirit of life") brings release from the sin principle ("law of sin") that produces separation from God ("death"). The law is established (cf. 3:31) in its proper way in the Christian's life (8:4).

The mind (8:5-11; cf. 7:22-23; 8:5-7) is allowed to have its way in the Spirit. There is an absolute separation between being in the flesh and in the Spirit. In this section the potency of life in the Spirit is stressed, not the details of how such a life comes about. These verses expand and elucidate the contrast between the mind conditioned on and patterned after the flesh and the mind conditioned on and patterned after the Spirit. The provision of the Spirit is universal for all believers (8:9). No one who belongs to Christ lacks the Holy Spirit (cf. 1 Cor. 12:13). Believers can experience Christ's resurrection life now (8:9-11).

8:12-17 Sons of God through the Spirit. The cause of release from the law and sin is that believers have become sons of God (8:13-14). Putting to death (8:13) is what was described in 6:19. The "fear" (8:15) is a fear of penalty in terms of God's final wrath at the end of the age. Note especially 8:11, 17. "Sonship" (8:15; "adoption," NASB and KJV) was a very significant matter in Roman law and culture. The adoptee was taken out of his previous state and placed in a new relationship as son to a new father. As such, all his former debts were cancelled and he was able to start a new life. As adoptees of God the Father, believers are freed from their debt of sin and receive the rights, privileges, and responsibilities of God's own children.

8:18-30 A focus on future hope. Paul addressed the potential discouragement faced by all Christians in suffering and in waiting for complete redemption from pain in the world. The Christian has great promises for the future (5:2). Romans 6–8 address how believers are to live until then. Paul deals with the question and problem of the "not yet" aspects of Christian experience (8:17).

Creation groans (8:19-22). In the Old Testament the Spirit hovered over the creation (Gen. 1:2). God cursed the world (Gen. 3) and opened it up to futility (Eccles. 3:20-22). Creation was subjected to futility as a part of God's curse on sin (cf. Gen. 3:17-18). Here, creation is personified as longing for deliverance from the consequences of the fall. One day this longing will be realized (cf. Rev. 22:3).

Christians groan (8:23-25). Why? Because they want glorified bodies. The believers' present bodies cause the groaning. The expression "firstfruits of the Spirit" (8:23) draws on the Old Testament custom of presenting the first of the harvest as an offering to the Lord in confident expectation of the complete harvest yet to come (cf. Exod. 23:16; 34:22; Deut. 18:4). So, the Holy Spirit is God's pledge of the ultimate completion of the salvation process—the bodily resurrection.

The Spirit groans (8:26-30). Why? He groans for the needs of all believers and groans to lead them to redemption glory. The Spirit helps in the believers' prayers (8:26-27) by going beyond their conscious words to express their needs. See the same word for "our weakness" (8:26) in 6:19. While divine foreknowledge (8:29) emphasizes God's love and points to the initiating cause, predestination (8:29) emphasizes God's choice and points to ultimate destiny (8:29-30). Those who are summoned to God for salvation ("called") are declared righteous ("justified") and will be "glorified" at the rapture or resurrection (1 Cor. 15:43, 49; Phil. 3:21; 1 John 3:2).

8:31-39 The ultimate statement of security. In light of religious and civil persecution ("bring any charge," 8:33; "condemns," 8:34; "separate," 8:35), Paul summed up God's security in Christ. Nothing can separate the believer from God. Note that 8:32 sums up Romans 1-5, and 8:33-34 sums up Romans 6-8. Paul proclaimed the believer's ultimate and eternal victory: justification by God (8:31-33), security in Christ (8:34), and conquest in all things (8:35-39). In 8:36 Paul quotes Psalm 44:22.

In Romans 1-8 Paul has presented the gospel (1:15). He has clarified the relationship between faith and law as a means of righteousness. He has shown how faith is secure

and the Spirit accomplishes God's desires for the believer's obedience and prayers.

9:1–11:36 RIGHTEOUSNESS IN GOD'S ACTS WITH ISRAEL

Overview: In Romans 9–11 the emphasis is on the question of a future for Israel. All that God promises is in line with his righteousness. Paul is clearly speaking to a Jewish criticism that Christianity evaporates the wonderful promises of God specifically for the nation of Israel. This discussion of the potential failure of God's promises to Israel (9:6) directly relates to God's promises of love and security for Christians generally (8:31-39). If it could be shown that God dropped his promises to Israel, then he might do the same to the church. Paul deals with the criticisms and supposed insecurities of God's failure (9:6), injustice (9:14), bullying (9:19), and rejection of his people (11:1).

In light of the seemingly radical shift of God's blessing from Israel to the church, Paul labors to show that the blessing of God on his church in no way violates his previous blessing or promise for Israel. Romans 9–11 forms the link between Paul's statements of the believer's great security in Christ through faith (Rom. 1–8) and his specific responsibilities of righteous sacrifice in everyday life (Rom. 12–15).

Romans 9–11 justifies God's righteousness regarding Israel, and 9:6 gives the thesis. Salvation indeed moves from the Jew first and then to the Gentile (1:16). But Paul clarifies who exactly is the Jew (9:27, quoting Isa. 10:22). He clarifies the distinction between the Israel of flesh and the Israel of promise. Paul expounds on the unbelief of Israel. He makes liberal use of Old Testament quotations to answer such questions as the following: Why are the Jews refusing the gospel? Has the purpose of God been frustrated? What does the future hold for Israel? How do the Gentiles fit into God's plan of salvation?

In this section Paul also speaks to a possible Gentile arrogance and pride in being selected for God's blessings (Rom. 11:17-18, 25). He had seen such arrogance and its sad social consequences in the Corinthian church, the setting from which he wrote this letter to the Romans. This section builds up to the exhortation to believers in 12:1-3 to renew their mind and not to think more highly of themselves than they should. This kind of arrogance regarding believers' standing before God could spill over into and damage relations with the Jews (Rom. 9–11), the body of Christ (Rom. 12), the government (Rom. 13), and the weaker Christians (Rom. 14–15). For the Gentile Christians to think that God's plans began and ended with them was a grave and short-sighted error.

9:1-29 God's Righteous Election of Israel

9:1-5 PAUL WOULD SEPARATE FROM CHRIST FOR HIS BROTHERS
For more on "the adoption as sons" (9:4), see Romans 8:15. Paul declared that if it were possible (which it is not, 8:39), he would gladly have traded his own salvation for Israel's (9:3; cf. Exod. 32:32). Romans 9:4-5 gives more details regarding the benefits of being a Jew.

9:6-13 ONE QUALIFICATION: ISRAEL OF PROMISE
Being recipients of the promise involves God's selective will. The "true" Israel had received all God's promises so far. See 9:13 regarding the continual conflict between the true and false people of God. Romans 9:6 gives the thesis of Romans 9–11. The promise of 9:8 relates to the Abrahamic covenant (cf. 4:13). The Israel spoken of in the Old Testament promises is not identical with the natural and physical descendants of Jacob. In Romans 9:7 Paul quoted Genesis 21:12 to prove the point of 9:6 that physical descent does not in and of itself make one a child of God and a recipient of the promise. Both Isaac and Ishmael were physical sons of Abraham, but Isaac was designated Abraham's heir. In Romans 9:9 Paul quoted Genesis 18:10, a prophecy of Isaac's birth. In Romans 9:12-13 Paul quoted from Genesis 25:23 and Malachi 1:2-3 to illustrate that God's elective purposes are often contrary to human expectation.

9:14-18 DOES GOD'S SELECTION FOR SALVATION IMPLY DIVINE INJUSTICE?
The concept of promise (9:8) by divine selection (9:11) leads to the question of 9:14. The source of the selection is God's mercy (9:15; cf. 12:1). This reveals how good God is to show any mercy at all. What part do humans play? See Exodus 7:3, 14, 22 regarding God

and Pharaoh. Romans 9:16 is given in the context of all humans being in Adam (cf. Rom. 5). There is nothing believers could have done to attain their salvation. It would be a cruel trick if God made believers jump through hoops of righteousness in order to gain redemption. In 9:15 Paul quoted from Exodus 33:19 to illustrate God's sovereignty in the bestowal of his mercy and compassion. The hardening of Pharaoh's heart (Rom. 9:17; Exod. 9:16) was part of God's sovereign purpose.

9:19-29 DOES DIVINE SELECTION MAKE DIVINE JUDGMENT UNJUST?
The Creator has full rights over his creation (9:20). We have no basis to question the acts of God; he is beyond human evaluation. He is not accountable to his creatures. In 9:22-24 the point is that God's judgments and decisions are ultimately a display of and context for the riches of his mercy.

The Old Testament quotations support the idea of God choosing some for mercy. Hosea 2:23 and 1:10 in Romans 9:25-26 illustrate God's call to the Gentiles for salvation. Paul quoted Isaiah 10:22-23 and 1:9 to show that it was prophesied that only a remnant would be saved. Paul quoted Isaiah 1:9 in Romans 9:29. The point is that unbelief, not a failure on God's part, is what kept Israel from salvation blessings. How this personal unbelief fits together with God's sovereignty is one of the difficult questions in Christian theology.

9:30–10:21 God's Righteous Witness to Israel

9:30-33 THE ELECT WILL RESPOND IN FAITH
This section pits the "stumbling stone" (9:33) of salvation through faith against salvation sought through works of the law. This is based on the Old Testament quotation of Isaiah 28:16 ("trusts in him," Rom. 9:33; 10:11). Paul quoted Isaiah 28:16 to specify Israel's problem—unbelief in Jesus the Messiah. To summarize: God's promises relate to his elect (Rom. 9:6-29), and the elect will respond in faith (9:30-33). Therefore God has not been unjust with Israel. Israel has simply not responded in faith to God.

10:1-15 THE ACCESSABILITY OF RIGHTEOUSNESS BY FAITH
In Romans 10 Paul develops the concept of righteousness that comes by faith, not by

works, and shows Israel's failure in that area. Jewish unbelief is not due to God withholding his grace, but to Israel's own failure to appropriate God's provision of righteousness by faith. Romans 10:3 is the key verse (cf. with 1:17). This elaborates 9:31-33. For "law of righteousness" (10:4), see 9:31.

The word "end" (10:4) combines the idea of aim (goal) and termination (see the use in 1 Pet. 1:9; 1 Tim. 1:5). The law points to Christ (Luke 24:44; Gal. 3:24) and is fulfilled in Christ (Matt. 5:17-18). The new covenant in Christ has ended the law as a contractual obligation. Yet the law as a reflection of God's values and standard has abiding significance for the new covenant believer. Note the bracket of Isaiah 28:16 in Romans 9:33 and 10:11. This section emphasizes the importance of faith over law-keeping.

In Romans 10:6-8 Paul quoted from Deuteronomy 30:12-14 to reflect his own thoughts concerning the fact that faith-righteousness simply accepts what God has provided. In Romans 10:11 Paul quoted from Isaiah 28:16 as further proof that salvation is by faith. The ideas tied to "confess," "heart," and "mouth" (10:7-8) are drawn from the quotation of Deuteronomy 30:14. This continues the concept of Romans 9 regarding personal unbelief as the cause for condemnation. In 10:11-12 Paul linked "believes" to "call upon," which leads into the Joel 2:32 quotation of 10:13 (cf. Acts 2:21, 39). Paul quoted from Joel 2:32 to emphasize the universal application of salvation by faith. The text quoted in Romans 10:15 (Isa. 52:7) refers to those messengers announcing deliverance from Babylonian captivity. The idea is that the swiftness of the messenger's pace revealed the character of the message being delivered.

10:16-21 THE INCLUSION OF THE GENTILES
Quoted in Romans 10:16, Isaiah 53:1 anticipated Israel's rejection of the Good News of salvation. In Romans 10:18 Paul applied Psalm 19:4 to the proclamation of the gospel, which was just as effective and far reaching as the proclamation of nature. In Romans 10:19-20 Paul quoted Deuteronomy 23:21 and Isaiah 65:1, which predicted Gentile acceptance of the provision

of faith-righteousness. In Romans 10:21 Paul quoted Isaiah 65:2 to show that God never ceases to plead with his people to repent and believe. But his immediate concern is to reinforce that the Gentiles have God's blessing because of Israel's unfaithfulness.

11:1-36 God's Righteous Restoration of Israel

Overview: The section of 11:1-36 shows the consequences for Gentiles as a result of Jewish disobedience and the promise of Israel's future restoration. The discussion in Romans 10 may lead some to conclude that God is through with Israel. Paul responded to this idea with an emphatic no. Salvation issued from Israel's rejection (11:11-24). But that is quite different from saying God had rejected his people (11:1). God's inclusion of the Gentiles should not result in their pride (11:18, 25; 12:3, 16). And Paul goes on to show that Israel's rejection is only partial (11:1-10) and temporary (11:25-32).

11:1-10 IN THE PRESENT REMNANT
Note the key questions in 11:1, 11. Foreknowledge (11:2) equals certain salvation. The present remnant of believing Israel (11:5) confirms God's faithfulness to his promises. Note the quotation of 1 Kings 19:18 in Romans 11:4. God had a remnant even in the dark days of Elijah (1 Kings 19:10, 18). In Romans 11:8-10 Paul quoted from Isaiah 29:10 and Psalm 69:22-23 to show that Israel's rejection and spiritual blindness was predicted by Scripture.

11:11-32 IN THE FUTURE REVIVAL
In Romans 11:11-24 Paul revealed the good that came as a result of Israel's rejection— the provision of salvation for the Gentiles. The first piece of dough (11:16; cf. Num. 15:17-21) and the root (cf. Rom. 9:5; 11:28) refer to Abraham and the patriarchs. The holiness attributed to the part is applied to the whole. Israel was consecrated by virtue of its patriarchal heritage; thus, its rejection was not final. The branches (11:17) represent Israel; the wild olive shoot, the Gentiles; and the root of fatness, the Abrahamic covenant—the source of blessing for Israel and all nations.

The promise of future restoration shows God's equal mercy to Israel (11:25-32; also note 11:25-26, 29). Note 11:32 as the end of the presentation of the gospel. A divine "mystery" is something hidden in the counsels of God, not accessible except as God is pleased to make it known. In Romans 11:26-27 Paul quoted from Isaiah 59:20-21 and perhaps Isaiah 27:9 to show that Israel would one day be saved and enjoy the benefits of the new covenant. Romans 11:32 is a restatement of all Paul tried to assert in Romans 1–3.

11:33-36 IN PAUL'S ESTIMATION OF PRAISE
Paul quoted from Isaiah 40:13 and Job 35:7; 41:11. This serves as the climax and benediction for the first half of the book (Rom. 1–11).

12:1–16:27 RIGHTEOUSNESS IN HUMAN OBEDIENCE UNDER GOD
Overview: The key concept in Romans 12–16 is the renewal of the believer's mind. See 11:34 for the mind of the Lord. Note what 1:21-22, 28 have to do with the need for a renewed mind (cf. Eph. 4:23).

12:1–13:14 The Renewed Mind: Proper Perspectives on Self, Church, and Society
12:1-2 EXHORTATION TO A TESTED PRESENTATION AND TRANSFORMATION
The mercies of God are those of which Paul spoke throughout Romans 1–11. The "therefore" of 12:1 is a conclusion based on the entirety of the first eleven chapters. The word "offer" (12:1) is the same as in 6:13, 16, 19. True worship is seen as a presentation of the self to God. The body is the vehicle of presentation. Remember what was said about the body in Romans 6–8.

The specifics of mind renewal (12:1) involve the proving of God's will (law) in everyday experience (12:2). Rather than being conformed to the world's mold, the believers are to be transformed (lit., "metamorphosis") from the inside out.

12:3–13:14 COMMANDS TO HUMILITY AND LOVE
12:3-8 Humility. Humility is the key to remaining in the root of Abraham (cf. 11:17-24). This call to humility links back to Jewish (Rom. 2–3) and Gentile (11:18, 25)

tendencies toward arrogance. Paul desired that believers find their proper place in the body of Christ, using the gifts of God's salvation (cf. 1 Cor. 12–13). They are to be interdependent. Their exercise of gifts is limited (12:6-8). The exercise of gifts needs to be done without envy or pride; believers should not seek to get gifts in order to stay within God's measure of grace. God gives the different gifts according to his will.

12:9–13:14 Love. Love in this context is recognizing one's proper place in society and the Christian community—humility before God and people. Love must be honestly applied (12:9-16), not like that of Ananias and Sapphira (Acts 5:1-11). Romans 12:9-21 gives extensive illustrations of what unhypocritical love looks like. In 12:19-21 Paul quoted Deuteronomy 32:35 and Proverbs 25:21-22 to demonstrate that vengeance is God's prerogative. Kindness, like the penetrating intensity of burning coals, is the Christian's means of conquering evil.

Love calls believers to be subject to the civil authorities (13:1-7). The words "must submit" (13:1) mean "to place oneself under" and refer to support as well as submission (cf. Titus 3:1; 1 Pet. 2:13). Paul says nothing about certain forms of government being ordained by God. It is significant that these instructions were given during the reign of the emperor Nero, a particularly evil ruler in his later years. Paul's words concerning government are important in light of accusations that Christianity was rebellious and anti-Roman. Taxes (13:7) are tribute paid by subjects of a ruling state; customs are levied on goods being transported for sale.

Love stands as a bridge between the Testaments (13:8-10). This section shows that Paul is still describing the nature of true love (begun in 12:9). Love fulfills the law (13:8). Paul's words on Christ being the "end of the law" (10:4) do not mean that the law has no application for the believer (13:9). Paul says that the law (cf. Exod. 20:13-17) can be summed up in the commandment of love (Lev. 19:18; cf. John 13:34). Paul continued his exhortations on love by pointing out the end-time motivation (13:11-14). Knowing that the time is near is a foundational motivation to show love.

14:1–15:13 The Renewed Mind: Acceptance and Edification of the Weak

14:1-12 THE LORD, NOT MAN, WILL JUDGE BOTH THE WEAK AND THE STRONG

Rome was a cosmopolitan city, and the believers there came from differing backgrounds and cultures. Some practices of the Jews and the Gentiles were mutually unacceptable. Here Paul provided guidelines for believers' actions where there had been no specific revelation. He called these believers from different backgrounds to mutual acceptance (14:1-12) and brotherly obligation (14:13-23). The issues are different for modern believers, but the principles are still applicable.

The "weak" (14:1) is the believer whose faith is not strong enough to enable him to perceive the full liberty he has in Christ to partake of all things. The "strong" (15:1) is the believer whose faith is mature enough to appreciate and apply his full liberty in Christ, while at the same time not demanding the exercise of this right. In Romans 14:11 Paul appealed to Isaiah 45:23 to support the fact that God would judge all men (cf. 1 Cor. 3:10-15; 2 Cor. 5:10). In Romans 14:13 Paul appealed for believers to do nothing that would cause a brother to fall spiritually or become ensnared by a temptation to sin. The kingdom of God (14:17) is focused not on outward but on inward realities.

Note the link between 14:3 and 14:10 concerning looking down on or showing contempt toward "weaker" Christians (cf. also 15:1, "please ourselves"). The focus is on the end (service to God), not the means. The "weak" here were for the most part Jews who still held to strict obedience to the Mosaic Law without understanding how it was fulfilled in Christ. The stronger believers should always seek to live with and encourage those who are weak in faith.

14:13–15:13 THE RESPONSIBLE SUPPORT OF THE STRONG FOR THE WEAK

One way of supporting the weaker Christian is to remove activities or objects that might cause him to sin (14:13-23). Paul moved to a consideration of stumbling as in Romans 12. Another way of support is by living out the Christ-like perspective of pleasing others

before self (15:1-13). Believers are exhorted to follow Christ's example of self-denial in order to edify others (15:1-3). In 15:3 Paul appealed to Psalm 69:9 to support his exhortation. Throughout, the Old Testament is used to support Paul's words. Having "a spirit of unity" (15:5; "the same mind," NASB; "likeminded," KJV) does not mean total uniformity. It means unity regarding the object of the believer's love and glory (15:6).

The conclusion of this section on acceptance (15:7-13) clearly shows how Jew and Gentile Christians must be unified. Christ was a servant to both Jew and Gentile (15:8-9). Paul used a series of quotations from the Old Testament to demonstrate God's plan to include Gentiles in his plan for world blessing (cf. Ps. 18:49; Deut. 32:43; Ps. 117:1; Isa. 11:10). Romans 15:13 serves as the conclusion for section 12:1–15:13.

15:14-33 The Trip to Rome: Reasons

15:14-21 REASON FOR WRITING

Paul knew of their ability to instruct one another (15:14), but he desired to extend his own ministry (15:15-21). Illyricum (15:19) was located in present-day Yugoslavia, along the eastern shore of the Adriatic. The visit may have taken place toward the end of Paul's third missionary journey when he visited Macedonia (Acts 20:1-2). In Romans 15:21 Paul appealed to Isaiah 52:15 in support of his desire to preach the gospel where Christ was unknown.

15:22-29 REASON FOR DELAYING

Paul was completing his ministry in Asia (15:22) and was tending to the Jerusalem offering (15:23-29). This discussion of what hindered Paul from coming to Rome returns to the thought of Romans 1, where Paul asserted that he had not stayed away because of fear or shame of the gospel. One purpose for writing was to enlist Roman support for Paul's projected visit to Spain (15:24). According to 1 Clement 5:7 and the Muratorian Canon, Paul eventually made the trip. The offering for the Jerusalem Christians (15:26) was the subject of Paul's lengthy exhortation in 2 Corinthians 8–9. The believers in Macedonia and Achaia responded positively to Paul's instruction.

15:30-33 REQUEST FOR DELIVERANCE
Paul knew of potential trouble in Jerusalem.
He desired to come to Rome and find rest.
This is the end of the body of his letter
(15:33).

16:1-24 Final Remarks: Friends and Enemies

16:1-2 COMMENDATION OF PHOEBE
Phoebe (16:1), a member of the church at
Cenchrea (the eastern port of Corinth), is
believed to have carried the letter to Rome.
The term "servant" (16:1) is often transliterated "deacon," leading some to conclude
that Phoebe was a deaconess (cf. Eph. 6:21;
1 Tim. 3:11).

16:3-16 GREETINGS TO FRIENDS IN ROME
Just how Priscilla (Prisca, NASB) and
Aquila (16:3; cf. Acts 18:2, 26; 1 Cor.
16:19; 2 Tim. 4:19) had risked their lives
for Paul (16:4) is not disclosed. It is
debated whether "Junias" (16:7) was a
male or female. Rather than being included
as apostles, Andronicus and Junias may
have been "well known to the apostles."

The "holy kiss" (16:16; cf. 1 Cor. 16:20;
2 Cor. 13:12; 1 Thess. 5:26) was a culturally
accepted Christian greeting that corresponds in Western culture to the handshake.

16:17-20 AVOIDANCE OF ENEMIES
IN THE CHURCH
In 16:20 Paul saw the second coming of
Christ as the final end to the conflict be-
tween the seed of the woman and the seed
of the serpent prophesied in Genesis 3:15.

16:21-23 GREETINGS FROM FRIENDS
IN CORINTH
Tertius (16:22) was Paul's amanuensis, or
stenographer, who did the actual writing of
the letter (cf. 1 Cor. 16:21; Gal. 6:11; Col.
4:18). Romans 16:24 is not found in many
ancient manuscripts and is most likely not
original.

16:25-27 Ascription of Glory

The book ends with a final confession of the
power of God through the gospel—a gospel
in full accord with God's word and universally the standard for faith.

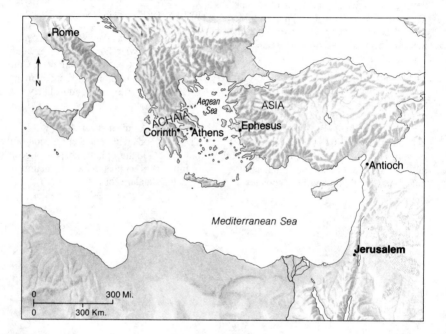

1 Corinthians

HISTORICAL SETTING

The recipients of 1 Corinthians were the believers at Corinth (1:2). Corinth was strategically situated on the isthmus that links the Peloponnesus with mainland Greece, about sixty miles west of Athens (see introductory map). The city lay at the foot of the 1,886 foot high Acro-Corinth and thus could be easily defended. In ancient times the city controlled the land route between the Peloponnesus and the mainland. Because of its control over that land route, Corinth was considered one of the most strategically located cities in the ancient world. Corinth was also a great trade center that could boast of two very fine ports: Cenchrea on the Aegean to the east, and Lechaeum on the Adriatic to the west. Mariners avoided the treacherous two hundred-mile trip around the Peloponnesus by moving their ships on rollers across the narrow isthmus. Corinth was a commercial center known for its wealth, indulgence, and immorality. In addition to being an important commercial center, Corinth was the worship center of Aphrodite, the goddess of love.

Paul first visited Corinth in March of A.D. 51 during his second missionary journey after his visit to Athens (Acts 18:1). There he met Aquila and Priscilla and joined them in their trade of tentmaking while he ministered in the synagogue on the Sabbath. He was later joined in this Corinthian ministry by Silas and Timothy (Acts 18:5). Paul had a very successful ministry for a year and a half at Corinth (Acts 18:8, 11). It was during this time that Paul wrote 1 and 2 Thessalonians.

Paul left Corinth in A.D. 52 for Jerusalem (Acts 18:18-19). Apollos (Acts 18:26) was invited by the Corinthian believers to minister in Corinth, and he helped the church there in a significant way (Acts 18:27–19:1). Apollos later joined Paul in Ephesus (1 Cor. 16:12) and reported to him about the situation at the church in Corinth.

The occasion for 1 Corinthians was that Paul had received a letter asking about certain problems (7:1, 25; 8:1; 12:1; 16:1). Paul replied in writing before he could come and deal with the problems in greater detail (16:3-7).

AUTHOR

The Pauline authorship of the epistle is clear from 1:1 and 16:21 and is practically uncontested. Paul made at least three visits and wrote at least three letters to Corinth. Scholars debate exactly how the letters and visits of Paul to Corinth are to be arranged. For example, did Paul's second visit to Corinth (mentioned in 2 Cor. 13:2) occur before or after he wrote 1 Corinthians?

The following order of events appears most likely. Approximately three years after his first visit to Corinth, Paul heard of some new Corinthian problems when he arrived in Ephesus on his third missionary journey (Acts 19:1–20:1). Paul then made a second visit to Corinth (not recorded in Acts but mentioned in 2 Cor. 2:1; 12:14; 13:2), where he did what he could to gain a hearing and solve the problems. But Paul's attempt failed, and he left with an ultimatum: if he returned, he would "not spare those who sinned earlier or any of the others" (2 Cor. 13:2). Then soon after his departure, he sent a letter telling the Corinthians to avoid immoral Christians (the letter mentioned in 1 Cor. 5:9), most likely speaking to the primary problem encountered on his recently completed second visit. Soon after, Paul wrote 1 Corinthians to clear up some new and some persistent problems. Second Corinthians was written later, within six months of 1 Corinthians.

This order of events is based on several conclusions. (1) First Corinthians 16:5-7 presents Paul's "Plan B" itinerary, a change from his original travel plans. (2) Second Corinthians 1:15-16 explains why Paul changed his travel plans. On or before his second visit, Paul had spoken of a final double visit, passing through Corinth both going to and coming back from Macedonia (2 Cor. 1:15-16). But the pain of his second visit caused him to change his original plans and to stay away as long as possible, returning only after he had passed through Macedonia. The change is announced in 1 Corinthians 16:5-7 and explained in 2 Corinthians 1:15-16. (3) If 1 Corinthians 16:5-7 is a change from Paul's original double-visit plan, then his statement in 2 Corinthians 1:23, "I did not return to Corinth," meant that he had not been to Corinth since he wrote 1 Corinthians. A visit between the writing of 1 and 2 Corinthians is thus excluded. The letter mentioned in 2 Corinthians 2:3-9 and 7:8-12 is therefore best explained as being 1 Corinthians, and the visit mentioned in 2 Corinthians 2:1, 12:14, and 13:1 is Paul's second visit, made prior to writing 1 Corinthians.

This view of 1 Corinthians 16:5-7 and 2 Corinthinans 1:23 produces the following order of events: Paul makes his first and second visits to Corinth; Paul writes the letter mentioned in 1 Corinthians 5:9; Paul writes 1 Corinthians, and then 2 Corinthians; and finally, Paul makes his third visit.

DATE

Paul wrote his letter to the Corinthian believers from Ephesus (16:8) toward the end of his three-year ministry there, during his third missionary journey (spring A.D. 53 to May A.D. 57). It is probable that the letter was written in the winter of A.D. 55 or spring of 56.

PURPOSE

This letter to the Corinthians was designed to give Paul's corrections to a number of concerns that had arisen in the Corinthian church. These concerns were based on two singular problems: human arrogance and denial of the importance and power of the cross of Christ. Paul's reply called the church to unity and selfless love motivated by God's love in Christ.

GEOGRAPHY AND ITS IMPORTANCE

From Ephesus to Corinth
Paul had spent two years in Ephesus, right across the Aegean Sea from Corinth. During that time he had made a second visit to Corinth that ended badly, and Paul left Corinth under unfair criticism and humiliation. He planned to pay a third visit to Corinth, but until the problems there were resolved, he wanted to stay away and try to solve the problems by letter and a visit from one of his coworkers, possibly Titus.

GUIDING CONCEPTS

PROBLEMS ADDRESSED
The Corinthian church had many problems. The believers there divided up into parties following different religious leaders (1 Cor. 1:12). They still participated in immoral practices (5:1). Some were involved in lawsuits (6:1). They abused the Lord's Supper and squabbled over spiritual gifts (1 Cor. 12–14). Some denied the resurrection (15:12). Earlier, Paul had written a letter (5:9) and sent Timothy to minister to the needs of the church (4:17; 16:10).

The problems may be summarized as follows. The Corinthians had fallen into serious errors based on arrogance developed from worldly wisdom that focused on riches, social standing, and personality traits. Paul was judged as an inferior apostle, one who could be left behind (4:6, 8) as the Corinthians marched on in their kingdom living. Paul's simple speech and life-style were criticized by the ostentatious Corinthians.

Paul mentioned his upcoming visit twice—at the beginning and end of the letter (4:18-21; 16:3-9). Paul placed his pending arrival before his readers in the hope that they would solve their problems before he arrived. Therefore, the discussions of purity (5:1–7:40), idols and sacrifices (8:1–11:1), traditions (11:2-33), spiritual gifts (12:1–14:40), the resurrection (15:1-58), and the offering for Jerusalem (16:1-4) were framed with the fact that Paul would soon be coming to visit the Corinthians— either in love or in discipline.

BIBLE-WIDE CONCEPTS

WISDOM
Throughout the Old Testament, wisdom was considered insight into the mind of God for physical and spiritual matters. Proverbs portrays wisdom as the very blueprint for how creation operates (Prov. 8). Thus, wisdom is knowledge of reality as God intended it, whether physical or spiritual. Also, humans have consistently tried to replace God's wisdom with a wisdom constructed of their own making. But God calls that human wisdom foolishness.

Paul mentioned wisdom and foolishness over thirty times in 1 Corinthians. The words "wisdom" or "wise" are used twenty-three times in chapters 1–3 and three more times in the remaining thirteen chapters. The first chapters of the letter contrast the Old Testament concepts of wisdom and foolishness. Paul drew from Isaiah and Jeremiah for the backbone of his assault on the false wisdom of the Corinthian believers (1:19, 31; see also 3:19-20 for his use of Job and Psalms). He contrasted their foolishness with the true wisdom and mysteries of God (2:7; 4:1)—mysteries that were hinted at in the Old Testament but only fully revealed by Jesus Christ through the Spirit.

THE KINGDOM OF GOD

The kingdom of God was a central Old Testament way of describing God's rule. It was a partial reality in the earthly kingdom of Israel and was also a future hope. The day of the Lord would usher in the kingdom in its fullness. Jesus also presented the kingdom as both here now in part (Matt. 13:11, 19, 24, 31, 33, 38, 44-45, 47; 28:20) and yet future in its final fulfillment (Matt. 6:10). Peter proclaimed that Christ was presently reigning over the world from the right hand of God (Acts 2:33-36). Paul also preached the gospel of the kingdom of God (Acts 14:22; 28:23, 31).

In 1 Corinthians Paul continued to proclaim how the great Old Testament truths of the kingdom had to be hoped for in the future and worked out in the present. Paul addressed the Corinthians' infatuation with pride and schisms within the framework of the kingdom of God (4:20). Although the kingdom was not realized among the Corinthian Christians perfectly, it was there spiritually in the power of the Holy Spirit sent from the risen and exalted Christ (Acts 2:33).

Looking toward the future aspect of the kingdom, Paul said behavior in the present could exclude entrance later on (1 Cor. 6:9-10; cf. Matt. 5:1-10). In the future, Jesus will deliver up the kingdom to God (1 Cor. 15:24). For now, the church enjoys the privileges and liabilities of Israel of old. Believers now have the greater blessing of the Spirit dwelling within them, not just in the tabernacle or temple (3:16-17). Israel's Passover and exodus have been fulfilled in Christ, the present believer's Passover (5:5-8). Like Israel, the church has been baptized into Christ and now enjoys the spiritual food and drink of Christ (10:1-4). Also like Israel, the church is subject to God's discipline (10:5-13; 11:28-31).

NEEDS MET BY FIRST CORINTHIANS

The Corinthians had problems with arrogance and pride. They tended to see themselves as the beginning and end of God's concerns (4:7; 14:36-38). That self-infatuation warped several of God's good gifts. It turned seeking the best for others into selfish status seeking. It turned the spiritual gifts of God into prizes to be gloated over or envied. It turned forgiveness into revenge and replaced the cross of Christ with partisan pride in flashy human ministers. Paul tried first to solve the problem of their arrogance and then to deal with each of the specific problems that had been mentioned to him. The structure and content of 1 Corinthians show that Paul was answering questions like these.

- What is wrong with having a favorite Christian leader?
- Should believers not have a high and lofty view of their leaders?
- Do their followers not have a share in the leaders' status?
- How can believers know who are the truly spiritual among them?
- Should Christians take other Christians to court?
- Do sexual relations with an unsaved spouse defile a believing spouse?
- Is marriage good or bad?
- Do strong Christians have to alter their behavior just to keep weaker Christians from copying them?
- How can believers live in unity with the great diversity of spiritual gifts in the community?
- Is it necessary for Christians to believe in a physical resurrection?

Although Paul addressed many different topics ranging from eating idol-sacrificed meat to partaking of the Lord's Supper, from immorality to marital relationships, from spiritual gifts to his travel plans, just one central truth informed each of his solutions—the cross of Christ. Believers today can, along with the Corinthians, discover how the cross of Christ is the answer to their problems. In regard to the problems of jealousy, pride, and division, the cross puts all believers on the same level and teaches them to forgive each other and wait for Christ's perfect evaluation of them all at the end of the age. In regard to the tendencies of believers toward immorality, the cross teaches them to purify their lives and celebrate Christ's sacrifice in holiness. The cross shows believers the way to resolve their conflicts out of court and to appreciate the work of the Holy Spirit for edification. The specific situations have changed from first-century Corinth to the lives of believers today, but the issues addressed by Paul of pride, immorality, care, and generosity are still the same.

OUTLINE OF FIRST CORINTHIANS

A. SPIRITUAL ENRICHMENT WHILE WAITING FOR CHRIST (1:1-9)
  1. The Greeting: Unity with All the Churches (1:1-3)
  2. The Thanksgiving: Enrichment in All the Gifts (1:4-9)

B. THE PROBLEM OF DIVISION: ARROGANCE IN THE COMMUNITY (1:10–6:20)
  1. The Exhortation to Unity in the Light of Partisan Quarrels (1:10–4:21)
  2. Community Purity versus Arrogant Liberty (5:1–6:20)

C. FALSE AND TRUE SEXUAL PURITY (7:1-40)
  1. Marriage and Purity (7:1-16)
  2. The Guiding Principle (7:17-24)
  3. Marriage and Virgins (7:25-38)
  4. Marriage and Widows (7:39-40)

D. LIMITATION AND EDIFICATION: IDOL MEATS (8:1–11:1)
  1. Limitation Described (8:1-13)
  2. Limitation Defended (9:1–10:13)
  3. Limitation Encouraged (10:14–11:1)

E. ORDER IN WORSHIP AND SERVICE (11:2–14:40)
1. The Order of Authority for Women (11:2-16)
2. The Order of the Lord's Supper (11:17-34)
3. The Order of Spiritual Gifts (12:1–14:40)

F. THE IMPLICATIONS OF UNITY WITH CHRIST'S RESURRECTION (15:1-58)
1. The Fact of the Resurrection of Christ (15:1-11)
2. The Fact of Bodily Resurrection (15:12-34)
3. The Nature of Bodily Resurrection (15:35-49)
4. Transformation in Place of Resurrection (15:50-53)
5. Final Triumph in Immortality (15:54-58)

G. THE JERUSALEM OFFERING (16:1-9)
1. The Order for the Collection (16:1-4)
2. The New Order for Paul's Itinerary (16:5-9)

H. EXAMPLES OF EXCELLENT LEADERS (16:10-24)
1. The Itineraries of Timothy and Apollos (16:10-12)
2. Exhortations regarding Traveling Leaders (16:13-18)
3. Final Greetings (16:19-24)

FIRST CORINTHIANS NOTES

1:1-9 SPIRITUAL ENRICHMENT WHILE WAITING FOR CHRIST
1:1-3 The Greeting:
Unity with All the Churches

Sosthenes (1:1) was Paul's associate and may have once been the ruler of the synagogue at Corinth (Acts 18:17). In spite of their many problems, the Corinthians were "sanctified" (1:2), that is, set apart for God's possession and use. There are three aspects of the believer's sanctification—positional (made right before God at the moment of salvation, Acts 20:32; 1 Cor. 6:11), progressive (being conformed to Christ in word and deed, John 17:17), and final (transformation at the return of Christ, 1 John 3:2).

Paul's greeting was extended to "all those everywhere" (1:2), in order to begin correcting the Corinthians' narrow preoccupation with themselves (1 Cor. 4:7; 14:36). This hinted at the problem Paul sought to correct throughout the epistle. Paul placed the Corinthian church in the much larger context of all the churches of God (7:17; 11:16; 14:33; cf. also 2 Cor. 2:14; 1 Thess. 1:8; 1 Tim. 2:8). By using the word "grace" (1:3), Paul was recognizing that everything of worth that the Corinthians had was given by God (cf. 4:7) and was thus no ground for boasting.

1:4-9 The Thanksgiving:
Enrichment in All the Gifts
1:4-7 ENRICHED EXPECTATION

The Corinthians' gifts were given (1:4), not earned. The people were enriched by God (1:5), not self-made. Paul was already seeking to correct the tendency of the Corinthians to boast in the gifts they were given by God. The gifts were given for the edification of the church during the time of waiting for Christ's return (1:7; cf. 13:8-13). Paul was emphasizing that the ultimate goal and hope of the believer was the return of Christ, not the spiritual gifts given during the time awaiting that return. The Corinthians had forgotten the ultimate goal of Christ's return (cf. 4:5).

1:8-9 DIVINE SECURITY

Until that day of Christ's return, God would do the confirming of character. God would keep his people "strong to the end" (1:8). Again, the fact that God did the work was emphasized. This began a corrective to the Corinthians' judgmental and prideful tendencies. Paul emphasized that "calling" and "fellowship" (1:9) were not exclusive experiences for just one part of Christ's church. These blessings belonged to all believers in the church of Jesus Christ. Paul made it clear that the security found in Christ related to him keeping believers blameless till the end. The fact that salvation is a work of God, the faithful one, is the true ground for security.

1:10–6:20 THE PROBLEM OF DIVISION: ARROGANCE IN THE COMMUNITY
1:10–4:21 The Exhortation to Unity in the Light of Partisan Quarrels

Overview: The first four chapters move between (1) Paul's statement of facts concerning the Corinthians' problems and his actions when he was with them, and (2) God's view of the implications of those problems.

Facts (1:10-17) The problem of religious cliques—Paul's original preaching of the cross.

Implications (1:18-31) God's method: wisdom only found in the cross.

Facts (2:1-5) Paul's original preaching of Christ crucified.

Implications (2:6-16) God's medium: wisdom through the Spirit.

Facts (3:1-4) Paul's inability to speak to them as spiritual people.

Implications (3:5-17) God's evaluation of final work: what conforms to the foundation, Jesus Christ.

Summary exhortations (3:18–4:21)

1:10-17 THE ISSUE:
MAKING THE CROSS OF CHRIST VOID
In this section, Paul was concerned with the growing disunity in the Corinthian church. The people were forming religious cliques and making them the objects of their faith rather than finding unity in the cross of Christ. The cross was to be the focus of the Christian life and an illustration of what it meant to follow Christ. The Corinthians were enjoying spiritual exaltation to the point that they were ignoring the implications of sacrifice and service found in the cross of Jesus Christ.

The word "divisions" (1 Cor. 1:10) referred to internal dissensions over the leadership of the church. Paul appealed to the people to make adjustments that there might be unity in the church. The believers were giving spiritual allegiance to different leaders (1:12). Paul expected that each of the questions in 1:13 would be answered with a resounding no! Paul was careful not to distort the truth of the gospel by embellishing

it with clever rhetoric because he desired to avoid diminishing the cross of Christ (1:17). Paul's concern focused on "the cross." This focus emphasized that God alone had worked man's salvation, not the various leaders who preached the word of God. It also called the Corinthians to identify with the cross, through service and self-sacrifice. The Corinthians' problems needed the corrective emphasis of the cross; the cross needed to be the focus of their ways because it exemplified God's way. The next section develops this principle. Voiding the cross was the mistake that led the Corinthians to exalt themselves and various leaders. Paul returned their minds to the crucified Christ, through whose suffering they were saved, and in whose steps they needed to follow.

Although Paul dealt with many subjects in this long letter, the underlying concepts that guided him were few. In evaluating ideas that stretched from idol-sacrificed meat to the Lord's Supper, from immorality to marital relationships, from spiritual gifts to travel plans, only one thought directed his conclusions—the cross of Christ (1:17). Each solution Paul presented came from his discernment of a problem's relationship to that great truth.

1:18-25 THE CROSS:
FOOLISH AND POWERFUL
The central thesis statement for this letter was given in 1:18. The two groups, the "perishing" and the "saved," were mentioned in order to cause the readers to identify with one or the other group when it came to the strife between the religious parties (1:12). Paul used Isaiah 29:14 to support his claim (1:19) that preaching a crucified Christ was considered foolishness in the eyes of the lost world. The worldly views of the Corinthian church also fell under Paul's condemnation. History supports this view (1:20-25). The wise of this world are made foolish by God bringing salvation to those who believe. This is paralleled in 1:22-24.

Paul used paradoxical language (1:25) because of the Corinthians' involvement with wisdom that was really foolishness. True wisdom is found in the salvation power of the cross. Any other means of salvation or supposed wisdom makes void the cross of Jesus Christ and in God's eyes is actually "foolishness."

1:26-31 THEIR CALLING: FOOLISH AND WISE

This relates to 1:18-25 as another example of Isaiah 29:14 in action. Their calling was considered foolish according to the flesh (1:26-31). Note the broader context of Jeremiah 9:12-24. To boast in the Lord is to boast in the cross of Christ. Paul emphasized God's choice three times (1:27-29, cf. 1:9, "called"). Contrary to the world's approach, God chose to use, not the wise, but the foolish and the weak to convey the Good News (1:26-29). Paul emphasized this fact to deny the Corinthians any occasion of boasting about their salvation.

Boasting (1:30-31) was a problem among the Corinthian Christians. They boasted of their salvation and spiritual gifts. Paul wanted them to realize that because their salvation was a gift from God, all their boasting should center in him. Their pride in their spiritual gifts was being cloaked in a guise of wisdom. Christ and his work on the cross had lost its hold on their thoughts and actions. In 1:31 Paul quoted Jeremiah 9:24 in support of his point.

2:1-16 PAUL'S COMING: WEAKNESS AND WISDOM

2:1-5 Wisdom and power in evangelism. Paul admitted his lack of human wisdom (2:2, "know nothing"), not because he was unlearned and foolish in the world's terms, but to bring to focus the mystery of God's work on the cross and to reestablish faith in the power of God. Why did Paul come to Corinth in "weakness and fear" (2:3)? He had recently been run out of Thessalonica (Acts 17:1-10) and had not had a very encouraging experience in Athens (Acts 17:15-34). But Paul came to every city in "weakness and fear" (cf. 2 Cor. 7:15; Eph. 6:5; Phil. 2:12). Paul's attitude of "weakness and fear" was the way he ordered his ways in humility and awe before God, rather than in the self-reliant and cocky manner of worldly wisdom. Paul came to them humbly to show them that wisdom was not in him but in the power of God through Christ's work on the cross.

2:6-9 Wisdom and the mature. In these verses, Paul explained how he could be rejected or misunderstood, even if his way was God's way. He revealed that the hidden mind of Christ is above human understanding and evaluation. The "rulers of this age" were contrasted with God and his wisdom (2:6-8). These "rulers" had failed to understand God's mysterious wisdom and would be excluded from his kingdom. Those with the "wisdom of this age" even crucified the Messiah, Jesus. "God's secret wisdom" (2:7), the truth of the gospel, was a divine secret— a truth undiscoverable apart from divine revelation. Paul's quotations of the Old Testament (2:9; Isa. 64:4; 65:17; Jer. 3:16) were used to defend the nature of the gospel, not simply to describe future glory in heaven (see Isa. 6:9-10 in Matt. 13:14-15).

2:10-16 The communication of this wisdom. Paul revealed that the things long hidden are now revealed by the illuminating work of the Holy Spirit, not by human wisdom. Only spiritual people could receive this revelation. The spiritual person is one who thinks like Christ.

The meaning of the last phrase, "expressing spiritual truths with spiritual words," (2:13) is uncertain. Among the possible interpretations are: (1) giving spiritual truth a spiritual form, (2) comparing spiritual truths with spiritual truths, (3) interpreting spiritual truths to spiritual men, (4) explaining spiritual truths with spiritual words (that is, filled with spiritual meaning).

In 2:14–3:3 Paul described people in four ways: (1) the "man without the Spirit" (unsaved) (2:14; "natural man," NASB and KJV); (2) the "spiritual man" (mature Christian) (2:15-16); (3) "worldly" or "infant" person (having characteristics of the flesh; spiritually weak or immature Christian) (3:1-2; "carnal," KJV); (4) the "worldly" person (composed of a fleshly nature; characterized by a willful refusal to grow) (3:3; "fleshly," NASB; "carnal," KJV). The Greek words for "worldly" (3:1; "flesh," NASB) and "worldly" (3:3; "fleshly," NASB) seem to be interchangeable and simply describe a person under the control of the flesh.

3:1-23 PAUL'S PERSPECTIVE OF LEADERSHIP

Note the concept of "puffed up" (cf. 4:6, 18-19; 5:2; 8:1; 13:4; cf. also Col. 2:18; Rom. 11–12, "mind"). In the Corinthian church was a growing puffed-up attitude that, if not immediately stopped, would ruin much of God's work in the church.

3:1-4 Paul's inability. The problem for the Corinthians was not doctrine but lack of spirituality. The people only thought they were spiritual. Paul was not able (3:1) to talk to them as mature believers because they were not able (3:2) to relate to such a mature address. The mode of ministry had to be as to babes, not as to mature Christians. Their inability was related to their worldly or fleshly nature. They had been fleshly to begin with, and they were "still" (3:3) in that state. They had not grown since they had come to Christ.

Paul continued his analogy of "infants" versus "spiritual" Christians with the illustration of feeding with "milk" or "solid food" (3:2-4). Paul sought to respond appropriately (3:1, "as" two times) to the needs of the Corinthians. He did not want to teach them truths they could not handle or understand. He had already spoken of the "secret" (2:7) to them and of the "superior wisdom" of God (2:1). Paul had not held back deep spiritual truths from the Corinthians. But he had limited his manner of speaking to them for their good. He gave them only milk.

3:5-9 The corrective: God's perspective. God's view of servants (3:5) was that they were channels "through whom" God worked. Their work was limited to Christ's gifts through the Holy Spirit within them. Any success they had was a gift from God. While Paul planted the church at Corinth, Apollos came to Corinth after Paul's visit and helped the ministry to grow (3:6; cf. Acts 18:27–19:1). But God, not the workers, caused the growth.

The unity of the workers was a result of their "one purpose" (3:8) and the fact that they all belonged to God. God was mentioned three times (3:9). The phrase "God's fellow workers" may mean either "fellow workers with God" or "fellow

workers who belong to God." The context favors the latter.

3:10-17 Responsible to God for the work. In this section, the builders were being warned about the quality of their work. The foundation of the church is a Person, not a doctrine (3:11). True building of the church involves a person's participation in the very life of Christ. This cuts against the "I am of Paul" mentality. For the final evaluation (3:12-15), see Amos 4:11 and Zechariah 3:2 regarding being saved through fire.

Paul shifted from God's building (the church) to his dwelling (the individual Christian) (3:16-17). Paul reminded the Corinthians that their work would be evaluated at the judgment seat of Christ (2 Cor. 5:10; Rom. 14:10). Paul did not explain the nature of the reward (1 Cor. 3:14) but elsewhere referred to "crowns" as representative of the believers' reward (1 Thess. 2:19; 2 Tim. 4:8; cf. also James 1:12; 1 Pet. 5:4).

3:18-23 Do not boast in men. The people of Corinth had deceived themselves concerning the nature of the building (the church) and its builders (the church leaders). In 3:19-20 Paul quoted from Job 5:13 and Psalm 94:11 as a warning to those who thought themselves to be wise. This was the high point of Paul's discussion of the problem of division in the church. He ended the discussion with the focus on God, not God's servants. If they had had the choice, the "proud" in Corinth would probably have ignored 1 Corinthians 3:23 because for them to be "of Christ" would put them under his authority, and they wanted to be under no one's authority. To add "and Christ is of God" was to put the Corinthians even one more level down from the top of the authority chain. They would want to stop with the statement "all things are yours" (3:21). They would have agreed with 3:21 but would not have seen its fuller implications until this point in the letter. All things

SUMMARY OF FIRST CORINTHIANS 1–3

Chapter 1	God did not send his wisdom through great men in order to level all men. The Corinthians were not great.
Chapter 2	God sent his message to men by the Spirit.
Chapter 3	The Corinthians were not spiritual.

were theirs but only in the context of taking their place of submission under Christ and under God. Some of the Corinthians mistakenly conceived all things as being theirs in a selfish sense—an attitude that Paul sarcastically criticized in 1 Corinthians 4:8. To claim to have great spiritual riches as a Christian also includes the obligation to take a humble and submissive place under Christ and God.

4:1-21 EXHORTATIONS FROM PAUL'S PERSPECTIVE ON LEADERSHIP

4:1-5 Paul and personal criticism. These verses are concerned with the evaluation of humans by humans. Although the term "servants" (4:1) denotes subordination, "given a trust" (4:2) emphasizes privilege and responsibility. The call to leadership was a call to a pure and trustworthy character (4:2). The Corinthians acted as if they were the judges at the last day, but they had judged much too early (4:5, "before the appointed time"). Their judgments of Christians were not for edification, but to put a final tag of good or bad, in or out, on the ones they judged. It was a nonministry judgment that had its source in pride.

4:6-13 Paul applies his message. Paul spoke of himself and other leaders to illustrate to the people their problems in the area of arrogance (4:6). Paul's concern for the problem of pride is reflected throughout the book (cf. 4:18-19; 5:2; 8:1). He used himself and Apollos as illustrations of leaders in the Corinthian situation and probably omitted the names of the real culprits to avoid their resentment.

Paul used the tool of sarcasm to reveal the pride of the Corinthians (4:7-13). The readers were acting as if the coming of the Lord and his judgment were already behind them. It is easy to see how this wrong perspective could grow out of the doctrine of the judgment of sin at the cross. If they were forgiven, how could there be any future evaluation? But this was a misunderstanding. Who regarded them as superior (4:7)? Only themselves. The answer to the second question of 4:7 is, "nothing." The answer to the third question reveals the self-centered pride of the readers.

Paul, during much persecution, had left Thessalonica, passed through Berea (Acts 17:10) and entered Athens. He sarcastically

used his persecuted life-style to show how far he had been left behind by the exalted and reigning Corinthians (4:8-14).

4:14-21 Paul clarifies his attitudes. As a loving father (4:14-17) Paul admonished the Corinthians; he did not seek to shame them. Tutors (4:15) were slaves and guardians responsible for the general supervision of children until they reached adulthood (cf. Gal. 3:24). Timothy (4:17), who was ministering with Paul in Ephesus (Acts 19:22), was sent to Corinth to remind the believers of Paul's teachings.

5:1–6:20 Community Purity versus Arrogant Liberty

Overview: First Corinthians 5–6 is part of a larger section that also includes 1 Corinthians 7. All three chapters are concerned with how individual purity affects the community. The emphasis moves from sexual purity (1 Cor. 5) to social purity (6:1-11), then back to sexual purity (6:12–7:40). The subject of immoral actions, sexual or otherwise, is traced from 5:1 through 6:8-10 to 7:2, 28, 36.

5:1-8 CLEANSING COMMUNITY IMPURITY

The problem in 1 Corinthians 5 was immoral sexual union. The words "father's wife" (5:1) was an Old Testament and rabbinical phrase for stepmother (Gen. 35:22; 49:4; 2 Sam. 16:22; 20:3; 1 Chron. 5:1). Marriage to a stepson was forbidden by Jewish and Roman law.

5:1-2 The response: puffed up boasting. Removal from the assembly was the final step of church discipline outlined by Jesus in Matthew 18:15-18.

5:3-5 Paul's response. The concept of "judgment" may be traced from 5:3 to 5:12-13. See 1 Corinthians 5:11 for a fuller description of handing someone "over to Satan" (5:5). Deliverance over to Satan is equivalent to being removed from the assembly, that is, excommunicated. Delivered into Satan's domain, the offender would no longer enjoy the protective fellowship of the church. The "destroyed" sinful nature (5:5) may refer (1) to the ruin of one's physical body through sickness, even death, or (2) the destruction of the fleshly hold over the person. The context (cf. 3:1-3) gives credence to the latter view. This view is more consistent with the ultimate purpose of church discipline, which is to restore the offender to fellowship with God and his people.

5:6-8 Paul's critique of the Corinthians' response. Paul used the leaven proverb to illustrate how "boasting" can soon permeate and destroy the church (5:6). For more on Old Testament Passover concepts (5:7-8), see Exodus 12:15, 19; 13:7; and Deuteronomy 16:3-4. Leaven was cleaned out of all Israelite homes before the Passover sacrifice could be made. Paul characterized the whole Christian life as a celebration in the purity of Passover.

The Jewish feasts of Passover and Unleavened Bread (Exod. 12:1-28) served as the background for Paul's remarks. Just as leaven was removed from Jewish homes to celebrate these religious festivals, so the Corinthians should remove the leaven of unholiness from their assembly. This was especially appropriate since Christ, who fulfilled the typical significance of Passover, had been sacrificed. The Christian life was likened to a continual observance of the Feast of Unleavened Bread (1 Cor. 5:8). The leaven of unholiness had to constantly be removed.

5:9-13 CLARIFYING COMMUNITY PURITY
Paul mentioned here (5:9) a lost letter. The earlier epistle that Paul wrote to the Corinthians has not been preserved. While daily contact with the unbelieving people of the world is unavoidable, Christians should not have familiar fellowship with professing Christians who are involved in sin and refuse to respond to church discipline (5:11). Paul appealed to the Old Testament principle of the removal of the wicked (5:13; cf. Deut. 13:5; 17:7, 12; 21:21).

6:1-11 CRITICIZING FALSE RIGHTS
First Corinthians 6 continues the theme of judging others (5:3, 12-13; 6:2-3, 5). Paul had earlier emphasized judging the sinful among them (5:1-8). At this point he examines the need for church members to work out disputes among themselves within the church (5:9-13). He did not want them seeking judges from outside the church. If needed, they were to go before Christian arbiters (6:1-6). In 6:2-4 Paul pointed out the incongruity of believers appealing to civil courts when the saints would someday judge

the world (6:2) and angels (6:3; cf. Isa. 24:21; 2 Pet. 2:4; Jude 1:6; Rev. 20:10). The phrase "appoint as judges even men of little account in the church!" (6:4) might be better translated "do you appoint as judges men of little account in the church?" (NASB and KJV). The saints should not be judged by those "of little account" (NASB) or "least esteemed" (KJV), that is, by unbelievers.

Paul wondered why judgment should even be needed among Christians living holy lives (6:7-11). It was a sign of defeat to get even that far (6:7). The questions Paul asked pierce to the heart of how worldliness can void the work of Christ on the cross (1:17). In 6:5-8 Paul presented two alternatives to appealing to civil courts: (1) have a believer judge the case (6:5-6) or (2) be wronged rather than wronging others and destroying one's testimony in the community (6:7-8).

Paul gave a list of vices that were apparently evident in the Corinthian church (6:8-11). These vices are in sharp contrast to the life of true believers. The term "washed" (6:11) was a reference to the "washing of rebirth" (Titus 3:5).

6:12-20 FOCUSING ON PHYSICAL PURITY
This section elaborates the principle behind 1 Corinthians 5:1–6:11 and reveals the root problem. The Corinthian Christians were willing to live with someone else's sin (5:1) because they were living with sin in their own lives (6:12-20). Apparently, some Corinthian believers were trying to use Christian freedom to justify their sins. Paul insisted that Christian liberty was limited by expedience and self-control. Their formal right to freedom did not equal the right to do anything they desired. Paul would not, however, substitute a new or old legalism. The way out of this problem was in a different direction.

Paul put forth a principle that applied to belly and body (6:13-20). Freedom in eating food does not equal freedom for immorality. The body is an eternal aspect of the person. It cannot be treated as separate from the real person.

The questions of 6:15-16 are not about physical possibility but ethical incompatibility. In 1 Corinthians 6:16 Paul used Genesis 2:24, a foundational text on marriage, to show that even in an adulterous relationship a union is established. A sexual union in and of itself does not make a marriage (cf. Gen. 2:24), but sexual intercourse does result in a one-flesh relationship and undermines the uniqueness of the one-flesh relationship of marriage.

Paul gave the Corinthians a strong warning to run from sexual immorality (6:18-20). Such sin is a sin against one's own body, which is the temple of the Holy Spirit (6:19), bought with the price of Jesus' suffering on the cross (6:20). It is sin against a body that will some-day be resurrected from the dead through God's gracious gift of grace. Paul has moved his readers away from an attitude of fleshly arrogance and has prepared them for answers to the various questions they had sent to him.

7:1-40 FALSE AND TRUE SEXUAL PURITY
Overview: Note the word "now" in 7:1, 25; 8:1; 12:1; 16:1, 12. It introduces the various questions the Corinthians had sent to Paul. The general questions at issue in 1 Corinthians 7 are, Is it bad to be married? and, Are sexual relations with unsaved or even saved spouses unholy?

7:1-16 Marriage and Purity
1:1-7 THE GENERAL PRINCIPLE
The general principle is stated in 7:1. The phrase "it is good . . ." probably reflects a Corinthian slogan Paul wanted to modify. Then Paul applied the principle to marriage (7:2-7). Monogamy, not celibacy, is the norm for Christians (7:3). Marriage, just as much as celibacy, is a gift of God (7:7). Paul was in agreement with the principle of celibacy, but not because he advocated sexual asceticism in marriage. Marriage is good but not required. And temporary sexual abstinence is not commanded.

"As I am" (7:7) means Paul was sexually controlled—not just unmarried, but having the character to stay both unmarried and pure. While most Orthodox Jews were opposed to celibacy and regarded marriage as a duty, there were apparently some ascet-ics at Corinth who advocated celibacy and wanted Paul to approve it as a duty for all.

7:8-16 TRUE AND FALSE PURITY IN MARRIAGE
To the unmarried men and widows, Paul approved, but did not command, the single

life (7:9). In 7:10-11 Paul addressed the issue of marriage and commanded, on the authority of Jesus, that married believers ought to maintain their marriage relation-ship. In the case of separation, Paul pre-sented the believer with two options: (1) remain unmarried or (2) be reconciled to one's partner. Paul's teaching summarized previous revelation that married people are not to be divorced (Matt. 5:32; 19:3-12; Mark 10:1-12; Luke 16:18).

Unbelievers cannot defile a believing spouse (7:12-14). Here Paul dealt with the possibility of one partner becoming a believer after marriage. While Christ did not give any teaching concerning spiritually mixed marriages, Paul did ("I, not the Lord"), and his teaching is authoritative. Four times he instructed Christians to continue to live with their unbelieving partners. The "sancti-fied" and "holy" (7:14) influence is limited to the one who does the sanctifying—in this case the believing spouse. Therefore, the issue in 7:14 is not God's saving and sancti-fying work through Christ, but the blessed efforts of the believing spouse to provide an atmosphere of holy words and deeds.

Is the believer required by the command of Jesus and teaching of Paul to preserve the marriage at the cost of becoming a slave to the unbelieving spouse (7:15)? No. Paul says that if the unbeliever demands separation, the believer may accept it and be at peace with the situation. In such a case the believer is left with the two options mentioned in 7:11.

7:17-24 The Guiding Principle
7:17-19 STATED ONCE: WALK AS CALLED
No religious changes were needed to make a believer better off before God. Is a change of marriage status advisable for the believer? Paul repeated the principle three times: remain in your present condition; lead the life that God has assigned you. How could someone become "uncircumcised" (7:18)? The author of 1 Maccabees 1:15-16 recorded that under Hellenistic influence, certain Jews in the time of the Seleucid ruler Antiochus Epiphanes (175–164 B.C.) disguised their circumcision.

7:20-23 STATED TWICE: REMAIN
No social alterations should be made simply on the basis of worry about religious status. Apparently some of the Christians in Corinth

were taking on various ascetic activities, even putting away their wives, so that they would have greater "spiritual" status among the people of the church there.

7:24 STATED THRICE: REMAIN
Paul reemphasized that there was no need to maneuver out of marriage, circumcision, or social position. God's call and salvation were not based on physical or social status but on Christ alone.

7:25-38 Marriage and Virgins
7:25-26 HISTORICAL CONCERNS
The next question Paul responded to concerned "virgins"—young, unmarried women. The point Paul made was that celibacy is desirable but not demanded. It is not a sin for a virgin to marry (7:28). The word "crisis" (7:26) should read "constraint" or "compulsion." The same Greek word is translated "compulsion" in 7:37 and "compelled" in 9:16. Paul defined the nature of the "present constraint" in 7:28-31 (cf. also 2 Cor. 9:7; Philem. 1:14). Paul's mind was on constraints that came to the married, not on political or social upheavals. The main constraint Paul had in mind here was that being married cut into one's all-too-little time to serve the Lord (7:32-35). Because of the present shortness of time before the return of the Lord, men and women need to maximize their service to God.

7:27-34 CORRECTIVE FOR BALANCE
Paul again advised, "stay as you are" (7:27-28). He emphasized that the issue he was addressing was not one of sin. Paul recognized that with marriage come additional cares and concerns (7:28). First Corinthians 7:28 could be paraphrased, "But if you, a man, should marry, don't think you have done anything sinful. And the same applies to a woman." The nature of the times (7:29-31) called for unhindered service to the Lord (cf. Matt. 6:25, 27-28, 31, 34).

7:35 THE REASON FOR THIS ENTIRE SECTION
Paul desired that all Christians live with "undivided devotion to the Lord" (7:35). This idea was behind all his statements concerning marriage and celibacy in this section. Distracted versus undistracted devotion has a parallel in the lives of Mary and Martha in Luke 10:39-42.

7:36-38 ON FATHERS AND THEIR VIRGINS
Apparently the Corinthians had asked Paul about the duty of a father to a daughter of marriageable age (7:38). Paul advised that if there is no evidence of the gift of celibacy, the father should let his daughter marry.

7:39-40 Marriage and Widows
Bound in life and freed in death. The last issue Paul dealt with here is the question of widows. Paul recognized that since death ended a marriage, the widow was free to remarry. Yet, in his opinion, it would be better to remain single.

8:1–11:1 LIMITATION AND EDIFICATION: IDOL MEATS
Overview: This section concerns food that had been sacrificed to idols. Could a Christian eat that food? The focus of 1 Corinthians 8–11 is on the use of Christian liberty (8:9; 9:4-6, 12, 18; 10:23). Christian liberty had to be balanced with concern that other Christians not be led into sin. Paul used the specific example of idol meats to show the Corinthians how their freedom was being misused and was ruining fellow Christians (8:11). In 1 Corinthians 9 Paul cited his own refusal to accept pay for his ministry as an example of how Christian liberty should be curbed by concern for other Christians and a desire to spread the gospel. Finally, in 1 Corinthians 10 he used the illustration of ancient Israel to show that membership in God's redeemed community was no automatic guard against avoiding his displeasure. First Corinthians 10 uncovers the real and potentially disqualifying truth behind the exercise of the Corinthians' freedom: they were participating with demons.

8:1-13 Limitation Described
8:1-3 ORIENTATION TO THE BASIC ISSUE
Read 10:23-33 for the overall perspective. Paul's immediate concern was the use and limitations of knowledge (8:1-4, 7, 10, 11). Paul admitted that knowledge alone was not the solution to the problem. Just setting a brother or sister straight about the facts would not achieve the edification and love God desired. Paul's thesis that "knowledge puffs up, but love builds up" (8:1) was

supported by two examples (8:2-3). Paul showed that the problem was how knowledge was used, not how much was known.

Paul introduced a new subject—meat sacrificed to idols. In Paul's day when portions of an animal were offered to heathen gods, part of the meat was eaten. If offered as a private sacrifice, the meat might be used for a banquet to which the offerer invited friends. If the offering was a public sacrifice, the meat could be sold in the markets to the people of the city. Should Christians buy and eat meat that has been offered to heathen gods? When invited to the home of a friend, should Christians eat meat that has been offered to idols?

In answering these questions, Paul developed important principles that enable believers to make the right decisions on questionable or debated matters: (1) Is it profitable? (6:12); (2) Is it enslaving? (6:12); (3) Will it hinder the spiritual growth of a brother or sister? (8:13); (4) Does it edify? (10:23); (5) Does it glorify God? (10:31).

8:4-6 THE "WE KNOWS" ARE LISTED
Paul began his solution to the problem of meat and idols by recognizing that idols are not true gods (8:4). All "gods" are excluded from the realm of power. Although Paul granted that there were "so-called gods," such as those recognized in Greek and Roman mythology, there was only one true God with divine and sovereign power.

8:7-13 THE "DON'T KNOWS"
ARE DEFENDED
But some still believed that eating meat sacrificed to idols was wrong (8:7). On the northern slopes of the Acro-Corinth was a temple dedicated to Demeter, the Greek goddess of agriculture, marriage, and fertility. Located within the temple were a number of dining rooms where worshipers could eat their sacrifices. Some of the Corinthian believers had once dined there in honor of this goddess and thus they associated the eating of this meat with idol worship. Because of this association, eating the sacrificed meat probably defiled the consciences of many of the Christians there. Paul illustrated the power of example (8:10-11), which could cause others to sin against Christ and their consciences (8:12-13). Those who flaunted their Christian freedom would not have seen that their

actions, though not wrong in God's sight, might cause a weaker brother or sister to sin. First Corinthians 8:13 provides the principle that should regulate Christian conduct in morally neutral matters. The believers' use of liberty must be regulated by love for God and other Christians and governed by self-restraint.

9:1–10:13 Limitation Defended

Overview: Paul had thought through one area of possible criticism, his work and financial support, long before he went to Corinth. In the Thessalonian correspondence he argued that Christians ought to work for their food (1 Thess. 2:7-10), and he used himself as a model of self-support (2 Thess. 3:6-15). Paul addressed this issue at length in 1 Corinthians 9.

Paul had worked with Priscilla and Aquila in making tents (Acts. 18:3) in Corinth, an endeavor that had been thrown back in his face as an indication that he was neither strong nor using his full apostolic rights (1 Cor. 9:6, 15; 2 Cor. 11:7-9; 12:13).

9:1-2 THE NEED FOR THE DEFENSE:
TO THOSE TO WHOM PAUL
HAD NOT MINISTERED
Note the four questions. They all expect a yes answer. Paul established his absolute right to receive full financial support for his work. But he had set aside his right to receive support to avoid the criticism that he was preaching for money, not for God. Paul used this setting aside of his freedom to illustrate the truth that at times Christian freedom had to be set aside for higher service. Paul refused to be paid so that people could not be offended by it, and thus more people could be saved through his ministry (9:19-22).

9:3-12 THE DEFENSE: "I HAVE ALL THE
RIGHTS ANY APOSTLE HAS"
Paul addressed the problem of other people making incorrect evaluations of his person and authority (2:14-15; 4:3; 9:3; 10:29-30). Paul asked eleven questions about his rights (9:4-12). The central issue was liberty (cf. 8:9; 9:4-6, 12, 18). Paul argued his right to receive financial support for his ministry. First Corinthians 9:5 reveals a little about the family life of the apostles. Peter and the rest of the apostles, including the half brothers of Jesus, were

married. In 9:9-10 Paul quoted Deuteronomy 25:4 in support of the right to receive remuneration for one's ministry.

9:12-27 THE DEFENSE:
"I DO NOT USE ALL RIGHTS
IN ORDER TO WIN MORE TO CHRIST"
Paul presents two views of ministry. The issue was one of entrustment, not salary. For Jesus' teaching that the laborer is worthy of his hire (9:14), see Luke 10:7 and Matthew 10:10. Paul clarified his reason for giving up his various apostolic rights: "to win as many as possible" (9:19-23). Note the use of "win" (9:19-22). In 9:19-23 Paul revealed the whole scope of his ministry, of which the Corinthians had seen but a part. They had accused him of being limited because they concluded he was less than qualified to be an apostle. But Paul showed that his limitations were self-imposed and ministry-oriented. The Corinthians had made a value judgment without seeing the context of Paul's whole life. Paul's reward (9:18) was the privilege of presenting the gospel without accusations that he was doing it for personal gain.

Paul explains his regimen in the terms of running a race (9:24-27). Paul drew upon the cultural background of Corinth. Seven miles to the east was Isthmia, home of the Isthmian games held every other year in honor of the sea-god Neptune (Gk., *Poseidon*). In light of this background, Paul knew that the athletic imagery of running and boxing would be very familiar to the readers. The disqualification Paul feared (9:27) was that of being rejected with regard to his reward, not with regard to his salvation.

10:1-13 THE AVOIDANCE OF
DISQUALIFICATION
Paul moved on from the challenge to avoid disqualification (9:27) to address the avoidance of disqualification with respect to their specific problem of idolatry (10:20). His drive to "win as many as possible," no matter what freedoms had to be given up, should have been their drive as well. Any lapse in this drive might subject them to the displeasure of God. First Corinthians 9–10 shows how to avoid standing in the way of the ongoing thrust of the cross of Christ.

10:1-4 Privileges of the forefathers. Here Paul set forth the example of the Israelites who, although greatly privileged (10:1-4), through lack of self-restraint (10:6-10) died

in the wilderness, being disqualified (cf. 9:27) from entrance into the Promised Land. Paul used Israel's experiences as an example that the Corinthians would be wise to heed. Paul was making it clear that being a member of God's community did not insure against disqualification.

The word "for" (10:1) connects 1 Corinthians 9 and 10. Paul singled out the key factors of baptism (10:2) and the Lord's Table (10:3-4) as signs of membership in God's community. The Israelites were identified and united with Moses ("baptized into Moses," 10:2) by the crossing of the Red Sea. The rock that provided water (10:4) for the people in the wilderness was really a manifestation of Christ's presence. Paul did not believe the rabbinical legend that a material rock rolled along after the tribes, sending forth springs of water whenever the march stopped. Rather, Christ, the supplier of the water, was with them all along the way.

10:6-10 Israel's experience in the wilderness. Israel's experience in the wilderness provided an example for the Corinthians. Drawing upon the Old Testament illustration, Paul warned the Corinthians to beware of lust (10:6; Num. 11:4), idolatry (10:7; Num. 25), immorality (10:8; Num. 25), testing God (10:9; Num. 21:4-6), and grumbling (10:10; Num. 16:41-50). First Corinthians 10:7 gets Old Testament support due to the special Corinthian problems with temples, idols, meat, and the Lord's Supper of 1 Corinthians 11. The list of problems drawn from Israel's history was a perfect match to the problems at Corinth.

10:11-13 The escape from failure. After outlining the sins problematic to both Old Testament Israel and the Corinthian church, Paul assured the Corinthians of God's faithfulness to give initial endurance and a path of escape from falling into sin (10:13). God in his faithfulness always arranges a way of escape from temptation (lit., "a way out") and before that, gives strength to endure it.

10:14–11:1 Limitation Encouraged

10:14-22 LIMITATION IN IDOL FEASTS
Paul linked the Corinthian idolatry problem to the other temptations of 10:13. He set forth specific applications of Christian liberty to the issues facing the Corinthians. Partaking in a religious feast meant fellowshiping

with the one worshiped at that feast (10:14-22). Since fellowship with God and with demons is incompatible (10:20), believers must not participate at pagan feasts. Pagan religious feasts are regarded as "the table of demons" (10:21).

10:23–11:1 LIMITATION IN IDOL FEASTS: SEEKING TRUE EDIFICATION

Paul put forth his central thesis in 10:23. He advised that believers may eat meat sold in the marketplace without asking questions that might perplex one's conscience. He appealed to Psalms 24:1 and 50:12 for support. As for eating meat in the home of an unbeliever, Paul advised that the believer not ask questions and just enjoy the meal (10:27-30). But if a fellow guest should inform the believer that the meat has been offered to idols, then he should abstain for the sake of the other man's conscience. Liberty to eat the meat was not in question—edifying other Christians was. Christian liberty must always be subordinate to God's glory and the spread of his gospel (10:31).

11:2–14:40 ORDER IN WORSHIP AND SERVICE
11:2-16 The Order of Authority for Women

11:2-3 BASED ON A DIVINE ORDER

All creation has levels of honor and authority. Within the Trinity, the Father is supreme (cf. 15:23-28). Although the Father, Son, and Spirit are equal in essence and worth, the Son and Spirit carry out different subordinate functions. The Son is under the authority of the Father, and the Spirit is under the authority of the Father and Son. Likewise, God has made male and female of equal worth but has given them different functions. The man has authority over the woman, not because he is better, but because God has given him that function.

According to Jewish custom, a bride went bareheaded until her marriage, but when she married, she wore a veil as a sign that she was under the authority of her husband. It is quite probable that both Jewish women and respectable Greek women wore head coverings in public. There were those at Corinth who were not wearing the traditional veil (11:5, 10). Paul, who was otherwise quite careful not to subject new converts to old traditions (Gal. 2:11-14), here ruled that the tradition needed to be followed.

The term "head" (11:3) was used figuratively to denote superior rank or authority (cf. Eph. 4:15; 5:23). Superior rank and authority does not imply inequality (11:11), for Christ is subordinate to the Father, yet they are equal (John 10:30; 14:9; 5:18).

11:4-6 APPLIED TO A PRACTICAL EXAMPLE OF ORDER

It is uncertain if Paul was acknowledging the praying and prophesying of women as appropriate and indicating his approval (11:5; cf. 14:34-35; 1 Tim. 2:12). Scholars differ in how they compare this section with 11:33-36. Some see it as addressing the question of female prophesying outside (11:3) or inside (14:33-36) the formal church assembly. Others conclude that the issue of female prophesying, whether in or out of the church, (11:3) and the problem of female silence in the assembly, relates only to one specific type of speaking—to thoughtless chatter and needless interruptions. But whichever view is taken, this section on head coverings must be seen as an answer to a minor problem; one that could be finally concluded with an appeal to common sense (11:13), the natural order (11:14-15), and church tradition (11:16). Also, this discussion is within the context of "praise" (11:2) rather than "no praise" (11:17). The overall point of his argument, however, was that women need to show proper respect for headship as do men. Although the woman was under the headship of the man, that was a subordination of function only and, therefore, maintained the essential equality of male and female. This equality is similar to the way Jesus, though subordinate in his function as servant to his Father, was nevertheless still fully equal to God in essence.

11:7-12 WOMEN NEED A VEIL: CREATION ORDER

The "angels" (11:10) must refer to the elect angels who know of no insubordination (Col. 1:16; Eph. 1:21). Male and female share essential equality in their origin from God (11:12).

11:13-16 BASED ON AN INTUITIVE SENSE OF ORDER

Paul's appeal to "nature" (11:14) reflected the general principle that throughout the world men wear short hair and women wear their hair long. He appealed to an intuitive general sense that male hair is shorter than female. He was not appealing to nature in the sense of zoology or botany. There are, of course, exceptions, just as the Spartans wore long hair, but tied it up for battle. Paul did not mean that the woman's hair was provided in place of a head covering and that she needed no veil (11:15). This would render most of the preceding discussion nonsensical. The long hair answers to the need for a covering.

11:17-34 The Order of the Lord's Supper

11:17-22 SPLIT BY THE MANIFESTATION OF PRIDE

The rest of 1 Corinthians 11 is devoted to the Corinthians' participation in the Lord's Supper (cf. Matt. 26:26-29; Luke 22:19). The believers would meet together for a "love feast" (Jude 1:12), or fellowship meal, following which they would pass the bread and cup, observing the Lord's Supper (11:20). Unfortunately, many of the Corinthians were intent on getting filled up, overindulging in food and drink, rather than sharing in spiritual fellowship.

11:23-26 FOCUSED ON THE HISTORICAL EVENT

Paul emphasized the importance of remembrance (11:25-26), the essence of which is personal conformity to the body and blood of Christ. This relates to the problem in Corinth. They tended to misuse the body and avoid conformity to Christ and the shedding of his blood on the cross. The new covenant (11:25; Jer. 31:31-34; Ezek. 36:25-28; Heb. 8:6-13) amplifies and confirms the blessing promises of the Abrahamic covenant (Gen. 12:3). It also promises regeneration and the forgiveness of sin through faith in Christ and his sacrificial death for sins. The Lord's Supper is a dramatic sermon that looks back

to Christ's death and forward to his return. In addition to remembrance, it calls all believers to actually participate in Christ's death and resurrection (11:26; cf. Matt. 26:29).

11:27-34 ACHIEVED BY PASSING THE TEST

Paul warned the Corinthians against profaning Christ's person and work by partaking in the Lord's Supper in an unworthy manner— with unconfessed sin (11:27). Christ was potently present to judge the snobbish and hasty eaters of the Lord's Table. For other references to the Christian's death under the image of "sleep" (11:30), see John 11:11 and Acts 7:60. Paul had other items to address, but he would wait to handle them in person (11:34; 4:18-21). But the next item could not wait; the issue of spiritual gifts was doing too much damage to the church and its witness to unbelievers.

12:1–14:40 The Order of Spiritual Gifts

Overview: First Corinthians 12 helped the Corinthians realize that different gifts did not mean a different spiritual source or a position of lesser worth (12:14, 19-20, 29-31). Diversity in function did not annul spiritual worth and unity. First Corinthians 12 teaches that all spiritual gifts are worthy of equal honor. Therefore, the Corinthians should not exalt one gift over another. First Corinthians 13 collects the majority of the Corinthians' problems under the solution of love. It shows the necessity of love operating behind each gift. First Corinthians 14 teaches that the application of love in the specific gift of tongues should always bring about edification.

To look at 1 Corinthians 12–14 another way, see the accompanying chart.

12:1-3 THE FOUNDATION

Paul asserted that there was a standard in ecstasy—the glory of God. The word Paul used for spiritual gifts in 12:1 is literally

---

SUMMARY OF FIRST CORINTHIANS 12–14

Chapter 12	Diversity does not imply inferiority. Unity does not demand uniformity.
Chapter 13	Love is preeminent, to be practiced, and permanent.
Chapter 14	Therefore, gifts are to be used for other-oriented, not self-oriented, purposes.

"spirituals," that is, "spiritual things or matters." In 12:4 he used the word "gifts," a term that is sometimes translated "grace." Spiritual gifts are God-given abilities for service. Every believer possesses a spiritual gift, but not all possess the same gift. Lists of spiritual gifts are found in Romans 12:6-8 and 1 Corinthians 12:8-10. These gifts are to be used in serving others (1 Pet. 4:10). The problem at Corinth was that certain spectacular gifts were emphasized and people were seeking the spectacular gifts for the sake of personal glory.

12:4-31 THE CONTROL AND VALUE OF THE GIFTS

Believers are not to exalt one gift and despise another. The divine source of all the gifts determines their equal worth. All gifts are from God and therefore may have differing functions, but all are of equal worth. There is a unity of origin behind the variety of effects. The purpose, not the source, of the gifts is emphasized: the common good (12:7). Note the use of this concept in 6:12; 7:35; 10:23; 10:33. A spiritual gift is the manifestation of the Spirit for the common good. Spiritual gifts are bestowed, not on the basis of merit, but according to God's sovereign purposes (12:11).

Paul used the human body to illustrate how the church was to function—with a unified diversity of gifts (12:12-26). This takes up the themes of 12:7 (common good) and 12:11 (as he wills). Paul wanted the Corinthians to accept the diversity of gifts given by God. The Corinthian problem was living with this diversity. They sought a false unity that was based on everyone seeking the same gift. Such a quest was not the basis for true unity.

Using the illustration of the human body, Paul described the relation of the gifted believers to one another and to Christ and explained how each was necessary and important. By the baptizing work of the Holy Spirit (12:13), believers were united with the universal body of Christ. The word "baptized" was used metaphorically here and carries the sense of "identification with." The Spirit is the criterion for identifying God's gifted people and for evaluating the worth of the gift. The worth is dictated by source, not function (12:15-26). Membership in God's community is not based on the type of gift he has given.

All members are equal (12:19-26). The nature of the church demands a variety that leads to interdependence and appreciation, not schism (cf. 12:14, 20). Some in Corinth had a foot-and-ear complex. They said or were told that they were not important. Others had an eye-and-hand complex. They boasted that they did not need anyone else. But Paul sought to show them that they all needed each other and were given diverse gifts so that they could care for each other (12:25).

Paul applied the illustration of the body to the Corinthian church (12:27-31). In 12:29-30 Paul used a series of rhetorical questions to emphasize the point that God never intended to give the same gifts to all believers. The word "way" (12:31) has the sense of road rather than manner. Paul was showing that the function of the spiritual gifts was to express and be driven by the all-encompassing nature of love (12:31). In 1 Corinthians 13 Paul would present a way of life superior to a life spent in seeking and displaying spiritual gifts.

13:1-13 THE PRIORITY AND CONTROL OF LOVE

13:1-3 The superiority of love. Paul made it clear in these verses that the spiritual gifts were a means, not an end. The gifts were merely the means by which love was shown and edification brought about. Paul revealed the inadequacy of the gifts and knowledge without love, an idea already noted in 8:1. When angels speak in the Bible, they speak in the languages understood by their human hearers. Paul's distinction between tongues of humans and angels implied that the angels spoke another language among themselves. In Paul's day there was speculation about what languages the angels spoke among themselves and in God's presence. Paul covered the entire range of language, from the languages spoken in heaven to the languages of men, in order to stress that the form of any language without the content of edifying love is worthless.

13:4-7 Then Paul shows the way of love in the world. This is a practical definition of love in the daily routine of life. Note how these descriptions relate to the Corinthians' problems: jealousy (3:3); bragging (4:7); arrogance (4:6); seeking their own (10:24);

taking wrong into account (6:7); rejoicing in unrighteousness (5:2).

In the exercise of spiritual gifts, it is necessary to understand their place in relationship to God's priorities. Christ's new commandment (John 13:34-35) is to love one another. Christian love is preeminent, permanent, and most noble. The spiritual gifts are subordinate to love.

13:8-12 The eternality of love. In 13:10 Paul explained that the temporal gifts would pass away when the "perfect" came. There are three main views on the identity of the "perfection": (1) the complete canon of Scripture, (2) the second advent of Christ, (3) the maturity of the body of Christ. The third approach is broad enough to embrace the relative maturity implied in the illustration of 13:11 as well as the absolute maturity that is depicted in 13:12. The church would be mature at the return of Christ (13:12) or at the point where continuing revelation would no longer be necessary (13:11). The spiritual gifts are for the present period of immaturity; the period before believers see God face to face.

14:1-19 THE VIRTUES OF PROPHECY
Paul cautioned the Corinthian believers not to exercise any gifts without love. He zeroed in on a specific gift, tongues.

14:1-2 The exhortation. Paul discussed the regulation of the speaking gifts and set forth guidelines for the use of tongues. Tongues were given as a genuine spiritual gift on the day of Pentecost (Acts 2:4) as a sign to the unbelieving Jews (14:22) and for the purpose of building up the body of Christ (12:7). Tongues were known languages, understood by men on earth (Acts 2:4, 6, 8, 11). Not everyone in the early church had this gift (12:30).

14:3-5 Two contrasts showing the superiority of prophecy. "Greater" (14:5) is determined by the ability of the gift to bring edification (14:3; cf. 12:31; 13:13; 14:39). Gifts (1 Cor. 12) plus love (1 Cor. 13) equal edification (1 Cor. 14).

14:6-8 Three examples of sounds that profit. Edification determines the use and priority of the gift of tongues. Words spoken in public worship should always be clear so people will understand.

14:9-19 The application. Paul desired that everyone listening understand what was spoken (14:9). This takes the thought back to 12:1-3. Knowing the content allows hearers to know if the utterance proclaims Jesus as Lord (12:3). Paul urged that zeal for gifts equal zeal for edification (14:12). The mind is the controlling factor (14:13). The context for Paul's remarks was the assembled church (14:19).

14:20-25 THE PURPOSE OF TONGUES
In 14:20-21 Paul called for mature thinking with regard to tongues and gave the criterion. Paul quoted the Old Testament (Isa. 28:11) to show the result of hearing tongues spoken in a disorderly manner—unbelief. The sign was not the result of loving edification and would bar their access to the kingdom. Paul provided here the only direct statement regarding the specific purpose of the gift of tongues. Paul used the quote from Isaiah 28:11-12 to show that tongues are a sign of God's judgment. The tongues of Isaiah's day were the tongues of the Assyrians, which the people would hear if they rejected Isaiah's message. The Assyrian tongue was a sign of judgment to a generation of Israelites rejecting the word of God. So, Paul explained, tongues are a sign of coming judgment for rejecting Jesus the Messiah and the gospel of grace (cf. Matt. 23:37-38).

Paul recounted the results of mature thinking (14:22-25). The gift of tongues should be valued in proportion to the edification it brings to the church. Tongues spoken without interpretation are forbidden since they have a negative effect on the body of Christ and bring division and confusion without bringing edification.

14:26-40 THE ORDER FOR TONGUES AND PROPHECY
All that is done in worship is to be for edification (14:26). This is the theme of Paul's letter. There is an order given for speaking in tongues (14:27-28), for prophesying (14:29-33), and for women in the church (14:34-36). Compare 1 Corinthians 11:2-16 and 1 Timothy 2:11-15 with 1 Corinthians 14:34-35. Paul's reference to "the Law" (14:34) probably reflects Numbers 30 (on vows), which sets forth the principle of subjection of wives and daughters.

15:1-58 THE IMPLICATIONS OF UNITY WITH CHRIST'S RESURRECTION

Overview: The structure of 1 Corinthians 15 surrounds a lively question and answer format. See the accompanying chart, *Questions and Answers about the Resurrection.* The ultimate problem in this passage centers on the question of whether believers need to be changed to enter the kingdom.

15:1-11 The Fact of the Resurrection of Christ

15:1-2 THEIR COMMITMENT TO THE MESSAGE OF THE GOSPEL

One of the problems the Corinthian church faced was that some were saying, "There is no resurrection of the dead" (15:12). It has been suggested that these were Sadducees (Matt. 22:23-33), but this is unlikely since the Sadducees were associated with the Jerusalem temple, which was far from Corinth. They were probably Gentiles influenced by Greek philosophy. To the Greeks, immortality was a spiritual concept, and they had no place for the resurrection of the physical body. Since matter was considered essentially evil, release from a physical body was regarded as liberation, and a physical resurrection would amount to a return to bondage. Paul addressed these views through implications drawn from Christ's resurrection.

15:3-4 THE GOSPEL PRIORITIES

Paul put forward two foundations of the Christian faith (15:3-4). Each foundation was accompanied by two proofs—Scripture and a verifying historical fact. Paul set forth the two essential elements of the gospel: (1) the death of Christ for sins, authenticated by his burial, and (2) the resurrection of Christ on the third day, authenticated by his appearances.

15:4-11 THE REASON FOR EMPHASIZING THE RESURRECTION OF CHRIST

The resurrection of Christ was not an isolated event but the opening of the door to the resurrection of the dead in general. The appearance to James, Christ's half brother and a leader in the Jerusalem church (Acts 15:13), and to Paul, is recorded only here (15:7). James apparently did not come to faith until after the resurrection of Christ (cf. John 7:5; Acts 1:14). Paul viewed himself as one untimely born, prematurely converted in relationship to unbelieving Israel (1 Cor. 15:8; cf. Rom. 11:26). In 1 Corinthians 15:9-10 Paul corrected a possible attack on his past by providing the balancing view of God's grace.

15:12-34 The Fact of Bodily Resurrection

15:12-19 THE PROBLEM REVEALED BY A QUESTION

In this section Paul revealed the necessity of belief in the historical event of Jesus' resurrection. Paul's question implied that there was a close link between the resurrection of Christ and the salvation and resurrection of the believer. The resurrection of Christ was linked to the very fiber of faith (15:13-19). The false teaching of no resurrection could give hope only in this life (15:19).

15:20-28 THE RESURRECTION OF CHRIST INITIATES THE BELIEVER'S RESURRECTION

Paul explained the connection of Jesus' resurrection to the resurrection of believers by looking at Jesus' resurrection as the first-fruits of what was to come (15:20; cf. 16:15; Rom. 16:5). Paul drew upon a metaphor from Jewish worship, "the firstfruits" (Lev. 23:10-11). According to the law, the firstfruits of the harvest were to be brought to the temple and offered to the Lord. The firstfruits

---

QUESTIONS AND ANSWERS ABOUT THE RESURRECTION

15:1-11	Christian facts about the resurrection.
15:12-34	Resurrection of the dead is established.
	The problem is raised by a question (15:12).
15:35-49	The nature of the resurrected dead is defined.
	The problem is raised by a question (15:35).
15:50-58	The necessity of all being changed.

implied that more of like kind was to follow. Because Christ is the firstfruits, his resurrection implies that the resurrection of believers will follow. Christ has initiated a new order. Now resurrection is as certain as death.

Paul put forward a certain order of exaltation (15:23-28). This explained the various stages experienced before final glorification. A problem was present as to how one could be saved but not yet glorified. Paul referred in 15:24 to the termination of the Messianic kingdom when Christ will deliver his earthly rule up to God the Father who will rule for all eternity (see Ps. 110:1). It shows that the subjection of death is a process of time ("reign until," 15:25). When Christ rose to God's right hand, he began a period of time in which God would put "all his enemies under his feet" (15:25, 27, quoting Psalm 8:6). The revelation of that reign is rooted in Psalm 110:1, which notes that the reign lasts "until" Christ's enemies are subdued. Because the church is now in that period and is waiting until Christ finishes the battle with his enemies, believers are not to be surprised when they experience that intense warfare's conflicts and pain.

15:29-34 RESURRECTION AS A MOTIVE FOR SUFFERING
To deny the resurrection was to give a false power to death. Dying and rising again are inseparable concepts. What did Paul mean when he referred to those "who are baptized for the dead" (15:29)? Some have taken Paul to refer to baptism "in behalf of" dead believers. That vicarious baptism did not necessarily have Paul's approval, but he referred to it to argue the logic of the resurrection. However, Christian baptism was normally administered without delay (cf. Acts 2:38; 16:31-33), and it is unlikely that Paul would have referred to such a practice without condemning it. It is probable that Paul was referring to believers who were being baptized "in place of" the dead—to fill up the ranks of those dying or being martyred. Baptism is being used figuratively to refer to what it signified—people coming to faith in Christ and being identified with his church on earth. The point is, the progress of such faith and church growth is to no avail if the dead be not raised.

In 1 Corinthians 15:32 Paul quoted Isaiah 23:13, a parody of the message of Solomon in Ecclesiastes 2:24. With no hope for the resurrection, life offers little more than eating and drinking.

15:35-49 The Nature of Bodily Resurrection

Paul continued to emphasize the believer's certain link to a glorified body. A question reveals a problem (15:35). There was a basic problem with the concept of raising a dead body (cf. Acts 17:32) or the possibility of flesh being glorified (15:36-49). Paul's distinctions between flesh and glory show that distinctions apply also to the next life as well as this one. The resurrection body is up to God, as are the gifts. Paul illustrated from nature that there are various kinds of bodies, each uniquely suited to the existence of the particular living thing. A body suited for life in the eternal kingdom must be different from a body of this present age. That follows the pattern of Adam and Christ (15:45). Adam, the first man, was a source of physical life for all men (Gen. 2:7). Christ, the last Adam, is a source of spiritual life for all who would believe.

15:50-53 Transformation in Place of Resurrection

Although not all will go through the process of death, all need to be changed. The parallel thoughts that stress the concept (15:50) answer more fully the question of 15:35, especially concerning what kind of body. If there were no resurrection, then the Corinthians were ready as they were to enter the kingdom.

A question also arose about believers who would be living at the last trumpet (15:52). The "last trumpet" does not correlate with the "seventh trumpet" of Revelation 11:15. Paul was drawing upon the practice of the Roman army to illustrate the removal of the church from the earth. The "first trumpet" signaled the troops to break camp. The "last trumpet" was the signal to begin to march (Josephus, *Jewish War*, 3.89-92). The "last trumpet" will signal the removal of the church to heaven.

15:54-58 Final Triumph in Immortality

Note the use of the Old Testament in 15:54-55. "Sting" means the potency of death. On

15:57, see Romans 7:24-25. Paul used Isaiah 25:8 and Hosea 13:14 to expound the believers' ultimate triumph over death.

Summary of 1 Corinthians 15: The resurrection of Jesus Christ is essential to the gospel (15:1-11). Take away Jesus' resurrection and you take away salvation (15:12-19). Add Jesus' resurrection and you add the believers' resurrection (15:20-28). Take away the resurrection and you take away the motivation to keep on in godly living (15:29-34). Add the resurrection and you add the believers' resurrection in glory (15:35-49). The new body is a necessity—all believers need to be changed (15:50-58).

16:1-9 THE JERUSALEM OFFERING
16:1-4 The Order for the Collection
The collection to which Paul referred (16:1) was for the believers in Jerusalem (Acts 24:17) who had endured famine and extensive persecution. Paul had instructed the churches of Galatia similarly on his first journey through that region (Gal. 2:10).

16:5-9 The New Order for Paul's Itinerary
The groundwork for some of the problems in 2 Corinthians resulted from this change of travel plans (2 Cor. 1:15-24). Paul's new plan was to travel from Ephesus across the Aegean to Macedonia, and then travel on to Corinth, where he planned to spend the winter. Paul planned to remain at Ephesus until Pentecost, when travel on the Mediterranean would once again be safe (see note on Acts 27:9).

16:10-24 EXAMPLES OF EXCELLENT LEADERS
16:10-12 The Itineraries of Timothy and Apollos
Although Paul encouraged Apollos (cf. Acts 18:24–19:1) to go to Corinth, the eloquent Alexandrian Jewish believer did not desire to do so at the time. Apollos's decision may have been based on the leadership problems in Corinth (1 Cor. 1:12).

16:13-18 Exhortations regarding Traveling Leaders
Paul touched on the key elements mentioned here elsewhere in his letter: be alert (16:13), love (16:14), and be in subjection (16:15-18). Stephanas, Fortunatus, and Achaicus (16:17) may have brought Paul the letter from Corinth to which he was making this reply (7:1).

16:19-24 Final Greetings
The "holy kiss" (16:20) was an expression of Christian love and fellowship, corresponding to today's handshake (cf. Rom. 16:16; 1 Pet. 5:14). The Aramaic phrase *Marana tha* is behind the words of 1 Corinthians 16:22, "Come, O Lord" (cf. Rev. 22:20). The personal hand-written note from Paul (16:21-24) again returns to the overall theme of the letter and Paul's life—love for the Lord.

2 Corinthians

BASIC FACTS

HISTORICAL SETTING

See the Historical Setting for 1 Corinthians. Second Corinthians was written about six months after 1 Corinthians. Paul had made two previous visits to Corinth—his first visit and a second follow-up visit to try to solve some painful problems. Paul's second visit is only briefly mentioned in 2 Corinthians 13:2-3, but that brief mention has great importance for understanding Paul's relationship with the Corinthians. The passage in 2 Corinthians 13:2-3 uncovers several problems Paul addressed. First, the problems were so bad that during Paul's second visit he had to threaten severe discipline. Second, Paul made that threat with his return in view, not as something he would do during that visit. With the problems still uncorrected by his second visit, Paul chose to leave and try to solve the problems from a distance. Third, the central problem related to Paul proving that Christ spoke through him (13:3). Some argued that Paul did not have divine approval and authority.

But Paul did not plan on staying away from Corinth forever. He sent Timothy and Erastus to Macedonia (Acts 19:22) and endured hard times in Asia (2 Cor. 1:8) before he left for Greece to hear the news from Corinth (Acts 20:1). Not finding Titus at Troas, Paul went to Macedonia (2 Cor. 2:12-13), finally finding Titus somewhere there (2 Cor. 7:6). Paul spent much time there exhorting (Acts 20:2), collecting the Macedonians' offering (2 Cor. 8:1), and writing 2 Corinthians.

During this time, Paul heard some good and bad news from Corinth through Titus and others (2 Cor. 10:2, 10; 11:4). Outsiders had come and worsened the problems (2:17–3:1; 11:4). They were promoting excessive punishment (2 Cor. 2:11) and were false apostles (2 Cor. 11:13-15, 18, 23) challenging Paul's adequacy (2 Cor. 12:14-18). They also used Paul's change of itinerary for another barrage of criticism, which took Paul seven chapters of 2 Corinthians to answer. Paul's motive in staying absent was to spare the Corinthians (2 Cor. 1:23), but his change of plans became fuel for his critics.

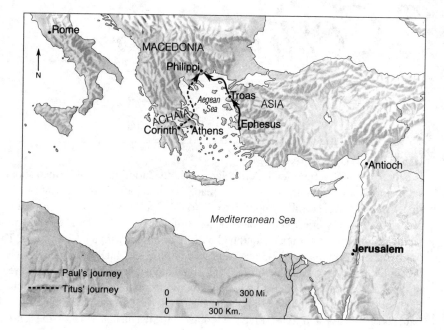

AUTHOR

The Pauline authorship of 2 Corinthians is clearly seen in the salutation (1:1) and throughout the epistle. The Pauline authorship of the letter is practically uncontested. See the Author section in 1 Corinthians for a discussion of the order of Paul's letters and visits to Corinth.

DATE

Second Corinthians was written during Paul's third missionary journey (A.D. 53–57) after his departure from Ephesus (Acts 20:1; 2 Cor. 2:13) for Troas and Macedonia. Paul spent some time in Macedonia (Acts 20:1-2) where he wrote 2 Corinthians, probably in the fall of A.D. 56. The letter was written a few months before Paul returned to Corinth (2 Cor. 12:14; 13:1) in the winter of A.D. 56/57.

PURPOSE

The letter of 2 Corinthians was designed to cement Paul's bond of love with the Corinthians after they had repented of their hard attitudes toward him and God. This was accomplished primarily by Paul's sharing of his pastoral calling under the new covenant and his pastoral love for God's people. But the letter also presented Paul's last words of warning to those who still persisted in doubting his authority. Even his warning, however, was couched in his strong desire to avoid fighting and return to Corinth in love and peace.

GEOGRAPHY AND ITS IMPORTANCE

The background for Paul's encouragement and warnings in 2 Corinthians was his past journey from Ephesus and his impending journey to Corinth. After Paul was asked to leave Ephesus, he went to Troas to find Titus and receive word about the situation in Corinth. Not finding Titus in Troas, Paul pushed on into Macedonia, where he finally found Titus, heard the good news about the Corinthian church, and wrote 2 Corinthians. The physical strains of the journey were used to support Paul's claims of deep concern and affection for the Corinthians. Paul let the Corinthians know that physical distance was acting as a buffer between them and his discipline. That distance was also proof that Paul wanted peace and was not rushing across the miles to fight and to bring harsh discipline.

GUIDING CONCEPTS

PAST VICTORIES AND FUTURE VISIT

Two events cast their shadows over this letter: one past, one future. In both areas Paul presented a picture of true apostolic adequacy and pleaded for full reconciliation. Adequacy and reconciliation are the foundations of the letter.

Past victories

Paul used his travels with all their ups and downs to provide the framework for his correctives to the Corinthians' disdain for weakness and preoccupation with externals. Paul wrote 1 Corinthians from Ephesus, and it announced his intended visit to Macedonia and Corinth (1 Cor. 16:5-6). The Corinthians had caused Paul much pain and sorrow. He had written and visited the church there but still had made no major breakthrough.

Although Paul planned to stay in Ephesus until Pentecost (1 Cor. 16:8), he was forced to flee the city on account of the riot caused by the silversmiths (Acts 19:23-31). He proceeded north to Troas (2 Cor. 2:12-13) where he hoped to meet Titus (2:13), whom he had recently sent to Corinth to solve some serious problems (12:18).

Paul went on to Macedonia where his afflictions and troubles increased (7:5). While helping the Macedonian churches with their offering for the Jerusalem church, Paul was greatly encouraged by the arrival of Titus and his favorable report concerning the church at Corinth (7:6-7, 13-15). With this encouragement, Paul wrote 2 Corinthians.

Second Corinthians 1–7 focuses on the present implications of past problems and successes. Paul stayed away from Corinth for one reason. He wanted to spare them from his authority to severely discipline (1:23). In fact, he remained absent and wrote 2 Corinthians for the same reason—they were still not ready for him to come in peace. The theme of sparing concludes in 13:2, where Paul reasserted that when he came again, he would spare no one. Until then, he wanted the Corinthians to focus on the things of the heart, not of outward appearance (5:12). Paul used his journeys, with all their hopes, fears, and failures, to correct lingering problems in Corinth; problems that inhibited the Corinthians from giving him the full commendation he deserved and the full blessing available to them as believers.

Future visit

Second Corinthians 8–13 focuses on the problems relating to Paul's upcoming visit. Overall, 2 Corinthians is preparatory for Paul's visit. He was close to returning and wanted to prepare his way from one specific perspective; the perspective given in 12:19-21. Paul knew that the readers would think he was being defensive and self-protective (2 Cor. 12:19), but he was actually speaking for the sake of their "strengthening." What may appear to be Paul protecting or defending himself is in reality his effort to build up his readers in order to avoid the conflicts and humiliation he experienced during his second visit (2 Cor. 12:20-21). Paul's point was that everything in the letter was for the readers' good, not for his own justification or defense. Paul rejected a defense rooted in self-exaltation and external accomplishments. Nevertheless, Paul spoke quite a bit about his personal adequacy, a touchy matter that could easily be misinterpreted as self-serving. Perhaps for that reason, he always carefully noted that he was not qualified in and of himself, but only as a result of receiving God's gifts (3:5; 4:7; 10:18; 12:9; 13:7). He spoke only to build up his readers and to glorify God, not himself (2:14; 4:5). This should be kept in mind throughout the letter.

The expectation of Paul's approaching (future) visit to Corinth—his third visit— pervades the entire letter. Second Corinthians 1–7 shows how Paul had to change his original plans (1:15, 23; 2:12-13; 7:5). Second Corinthians 8–9 speaks of Titus's work with the Corinthians to complete their offering for Jerusalem. Paul wanted the matter to be settled before he arrived (8:6; 9:4). Second Corinthians 10–13 focuses on Paul's upcoming arrival. He hoped for a solution to their problems, but he would not spare discipline for anyone who persisted in rebellion (10:2; 12:14, 20; 13:1-2, 10).

PROBLEMS
The major problem of the letter is summed up in 6:12—interpersonal friction bred by the Corinthians' hard hearts. The solution was to replace arrogance with weakness and see God's grace alone as the source of adequacy and sufficiency (12:9).

AUTHORITY
Some were not convinced that Paul was a qualified apostle (1 Cor. 9:1). He did not use his right to be paid for his services (1 Cor. 9:1, 6, 11-12, 18). And that opened him up to slander. Second Corinthians 10:8 and 13:10 begin and end with Paul's reply to slanders against his status as an apostle and his honesty in money matters. His authority was based on God's grace, not his own personal talents and status (2 Cor. 12:9).

TEST
The Corinthians tested Paul's divine authority. By questioning Paul's God-given authority, the Corinthians opened themselves up to false apostles (11:12-15). They wanted proof that Christ was speaking through Paul (13:3). One Corinthian test of proper life-style involved accepting their financial support (11:7). They expected formal letters of commendation (3:1). They wrongly assumed that God's apostles would have smooth, trouble-free lives (4:7-10). None of this was true for Paul.

   Some accused him of walking according to the flesh (1:17; 10:2) and of being full of crafty schemes to get their money (4:2; 12:16). Paul offered proof for these tests of authority, but not the kind his readers expected. The true test was graded by the Lord, not the people (10:18). In the end, Paul commanded them to test themselves (13:5).

COMMENDATION
Second Corinthians almost has a monopoly on Paul's use of the word "commendation." The perspective on commendation that pervades the book is in 12:11. But the readers were not mature enough to recognize God's blessing on Paul (cf. 3:1; 4:2; 10:12, 18). The Corinthians boasted in appearance rather than in the issues of the heart (5:12). Paul had tried to correct this wrong boasting (2 Cor. 1:14, 21; 7:4, 14; 5:12; 8:24; 9:2; cf. also 1 Cor. 1:29, 31; 3:21; 4:7; 5:6). Paul boasted only in relation to the work God was doing through him (2 Cor. 10:1, 13, 15-17; 11:10, 12).

WEAKNESS
Above all, Paul's greatest commendation came through boasting in his weakness (cf. 11:16-18, 30 with 12:1, 5-6, 9). The Corinthians were infatuated with a superficial and worldly outlook (5:12; 6:14–7:1). But weakness was the way to true adequacy. Weakness was a topic in 1 Corinthians 8:7, 9-12; 9:22. The weakness of

fear and trembling before God was commendable (2 Cor. 7:15; Eph. 6:5; Phil. 2:12). In 2 Corinthians weakness was also a means of glorifying God (10:1; 11:21, 30; 12:5, 9-10).

COMFORT
Second Corinthians 1 and 7 focus on how the Corinthians' repentance gave Paul great comfort. Comfort comes from the Corinthians' earnestness for Paul and forms the basis for the continued ministry of the offering (2 Cor. 8–9) and the last-minute discipline for those who still needed it (2 Cor. 10–13).

BIBLE-WIDE CONCEPTS

DIVINE PRESENCE, PURITY, AND SONSHIP
Paul believed that all the promises of God throughout the Old Testament were fulfilled in Christ. In him all the promises of God are answered with a yes (1:20). These Old Testament promises involved the presence of God for salvation and the indwelling Spirit. Paul specifically mentioned three Old Testament promises that would be central to solving the Corinthians' problems (6:14–7:1). They were (1) God's presence (6:16, quoting Lev. 26:12), (2) the exodus from the Babylonian captivity (6:17, quoting Isa. 52:11), and (3) becoming sons and daughters of God (6:18, quoting 2 Sam. 7:14). Paul understood that the great Old Testament events of God's dwelling among Israel in the tabernacle, redeeming them out of captivity, and adopting the line of David as his special sons were fulfilled in Christ and extremely relevant to the needs of Christ's church.

Paul continued to apply the Old Testament patterns of how God dealt with his redeemed community when he applied the equality God showed in providing manna in the wilderness to the equality to be shown through the Jerusalem offering (8:15, quoting Exod. 16:18).

PAUL AS SERVANT OF THE NEW COVENANT
Paul saw himself as a servant of the new covenant in Christ (2 Cor. 3:6, 14). Jeremiah had predicted a coming new covenant, and Jesus had proclaimed its inauguration (Jer. 33:31-33; Luke 22:20). Paul showed the implications of that new covenant for understanding true, but hidden, glory and how people could reject such a glorious covenant. The Old Testament background of the new covenant was crucial for accepting the genuine version of Christianity in the face of false apostles.

THE RIGHTEOUS SUFFERER
Throughout Scripture, people such as Abel, Joseph, David, and Job have suffered unjustly—usually because of the fact that they were righteous. Jesus the righteous sufferer was the one through whomGod expressed his favor and accomplished redemption. The pattern that Jesus set for suffering unjustly was uncompromisingly followed by Paul and urged upon his readers (1:5; 4:6-10). It was that very pattern of humiliation and righteous suffering that was the mark of Christ and the Christian—a mark totally avoided and shunned by the false apostles who attacked the reputation and authority of Paul.

NEEDS MET BY SECOND CORINTHIANS

Fleshly desires for money and status were the continual problems Paul faced at Corinth. The Corinthians cloaked their status-seeking in the guise of wisdom and maturity but actually opened themselves to immoral relations, a disregard for God's words through Paul, and ultimately a rejection of the reconciling power of the cross of Christ. Some of the Corinthians unfairly attacked Paul's free ministry as a cover for second-rate qualifications and a sneaky way to get money by means of his associates. Second Corinthians presents a moving example of a spiritual response to difficulties by means of a fusion of praise and correction. This letter to the Corinthians attacks the attitude that takes pride in appearances rather than in purity of heart. Paul sought to overcome the attitude that looks only on the outside for commendation and criticism (5:12). This attack answers a number of questions and meets many needs.

- How can suffering and low status reflect the glory of God?
- Is Christianity not supposed to bring exaltation and superiority?
- How can believers judge what makes a minister adequate?
- How can believers learn to view people in Christ rather than according to their external demeanor and abilities?
- What are the best motivations for giving money to Christian needs?
- What is the place and purpose of boasting in personal blessings given by God?
- How do personal weaknesses relate to God's great power and adequacy?

Christians face a great paradox. On the one hand, they are greatly gifted and exalted in Christ. On the other hand, they are not to exalt themselves over others, and, in comparison to God's holy adequacy, they soon sense their own great weaknesses. The desire of believers to boast pridefully directly conflicts with the Spirit's desire that they be humble and admit their weaknesses. Second Corinthians should help believers avoid either covering their weaknesses with prideful boasting or becoming so depressed by their weaknesses that they cannot enjoy their great blessings in Christ. Second Corinthians provides the balance between pride and depression by answering the questions above—questions that have been asked by Christians for two thousand years.

OUTLINE OF SECOND CORINTHIANS

A. A TEST PASSED: CONFIDENCE FOR CONTINUED OBEDIENCE (1:1–7:16)
  1. Mutual Trust Reaffirmed: A First Defense (1:1–2:17)
  2. Adequacy in Ministry Commended: A Second Defense (3:1–5:19)
  3. Exhortations to Reconciliation (5:20–7:16)

B. A TEST FOR THE SINCERITY OF LOVE: GIVING FROM THE HEART (8:1–9:15)
  1. Motivation by Example (8:1-7)
  2. Exhortation to Sincere Love (8:8-15)
  3. Commendation of the Administrators (8:16–9:5)
  4. Motivation by Principle (9:6-15)

C. TRUE VERSUS FOOLISH COMMENDATION: THE REAL SOURCE OF
STRENGTH (10:1–13:14)
1. Warning to Recognize Paul's Authority (10:1-18)
2. A Demonstration of Paul's Authority (11:1–12:13)
3. A Plea to Avoid Pending Judgment (12:14–13:14)

SECOND CORINTHIANS NOTES

1:1–7:16 A TEST PASSED: CONFIDENCE FOR CONTINUED OBEDIENCE

Overview: This section contains three mentions of Paul's travels from Ephesus to Macedonia with two corrective sections layered in between. See the accompanying chart for the structure of 2 Corinthians 1–7.

The central problem in the first seven chapters is the Corinthians' restraint in their own affections (6:12). Paul offered the solution in 5:17, 6:13, and 7:1-2. The overall perspective is given in 5:12. The root of the problem was in their worldly affections, which had closed their hearts toward God and Paul. Paul's solution encouraged the readers to make room for him in their hearts (6:13; 7:2). Although Paul claimed great glory for his ministry (2 Cor. 3), the treasure was in earthen vessels (2 Cor. 4). Therefore, true glory could easily be missed if one focused on the container rather than its contents. This is why Paul only related to realities of people's hearts in Christ (5:12, 16).

As Paul drove his point home, he exposed the core of the problem. It was a problem of the heart (6:12) and could only be remedied by perfecting holiness in the fear of God (7:1). The entire discussion concerning Paul's ministry in weakness and glory must not be seen as a defensive reaction but as a loving correction (12:19).

1:1–2:17 Mutual Trust Reaffirmed: A First Defense

1:1-2 GREETING

Achaia (1:1) was the Roman province south of Macedonia comprising most of central and southern Greece. Timothy (1:1) was Paul's associate during his ministry in Corinth (Acts 18:5) and was with him when he wrote this letter.

1:3-11 MUTUALITY IN SUFFERING AND COMFORT

1:3-5 Individual enablement. The Lord Jesus Christ (1:3) is the medium for comfort and compassion. Paul also became an expression of God's words of comfort. His comfort had the purpose of being shared with others (1:4). Second Corinthians 1:5 restates and emphasizes the balance between sufferings and comfort. Paul reflected on his recent difficulties in Ephesus (cf. Acts 19:23-41) and on how God had been his comfort. He recognized that God had given him a ministry of giving comfort just as he had received comfort from God.

1:6-7 Mutual fellowship. Paul stressed that even his sufferings were designed to give benefit to the Corinthians. He was building to 2 Corinthians 7 and the full expression of fellowship. His sufferings did not point to weakness and lack of qualification or love— just the opposite. On "patient endurance" (1:6), see 1 Corinthians 10:13. The point is that comfort works simultaneously with suffering.

SUMMARY OF SECOND CORINTHIANS 1–7

1:8-11	Itinerary: Affliction in Asia
1:9–2:11	A corrected perspective on Paul's change of itinerary
2:12-13	Itinerary: Troas to Macedonia
2:14–7:4	A corrected perspective on Paul's adequacy
7:5-16	Itinerary: Arrival in Macedonia and Titus's Good News

1:8-11 Sharing the sufferings. Here Paul is sharing his experiences of suffering to give a lesson in encouragement. The sharing of Paul's weaknesses was not idle storytelling. It was the vehicle for sharing comfort. Ignorance is the block to sharing comfort. To hide his weaknesses from the Corinthians would only pander to those who thought weakness equaled disqualification. Part of the affliction Paul had experienced in Asia is recounted in Acts 19:23-41. The focus is on God's purpose of comfort, not the trouble itself. This was a lesson needed by the readers. Another description of God follows (1:10). Paul's appreciation for the effectiveness of intercessory prayer (1:11) is evidenced also in Romans 15:30-31; Philippians 1:9; and Colossians 4:12.

1:12-22 PAUL'S GOOD INTENTIONS FOR HIS FIRST TRAVEL PLANS
From this point on the purpose expressed in 2 Corinthians 5:12 controlled Paul's thoughts as he corrected the Corinthians' attitude of pride in appearances rather than purity of heart. He supplied internal standards of commendation and adequacy rather than the externals in which his opponents boasted.

1:12-14 Paul's confidence: clear conscience. Paul's letters were as honest as his life. Paul desired a mutual appreciation with the Corinthians in the Lord (1:14). He wanted them to join him in boasting in the works accomplished by the Lord, rather than quibbling about the external accomplishments of various people.

1:15-16 Paul's change in travel plans is described. While Paul was still in Ephesus he had written to Corinth and said that he would come soon "if the Lord wills" (1 Cor. 4:19). Paul's original travel plans are noted in 2 Corinthians 1:15-16. His plan was to visit Corinth, travel north to Macedonia to gather the collection for the Jerusalem church, and then return to Corinth again to get help for his travel back to Jerusalem. But his plans had changed.

His change from those plans is recorded in 1 Corinthians 16:5-7. Instead of traveling first to Corinth, Paul had gone directly to Macedonia (2 Cor. 2:12-13; Acts 20:1). Now Paul had to defend himself against accusations of insincerity and vacillation.

1:17-22 The charge and its implications are described. Paul responded to criticisms about his change in itinerary, not defensively, but theologically. His defense was God's consistency—which Paul followed rigorously—based on God's faithfulness in the gospel and on the foundation of the character of Christ. Essential to the thrust of the letter are the establishment of the believers by God and the internal pledge of the Spirit in the heart (1:21-22).

Paul asserted that he followed a consistent God, and therefore his own actions, done only at the Holy Spirit's leading, were consistent. It is clear that Paul saw a potential link between the charge that his actions were fickle with the more devastating charge that the gospel he preached was not consistent. One so-called charge of fickleness had great implications from Paul's perspective. Why would this one change in plans tend to void his credibility? Because some people were just waiting for an excuse to discredit Paul (cf. 2 Cor. 10–13). "Silas" (1:19) was a variant for the name "Silvanus" (cf. Acts 17:1-9; 1 Thess. 1:1; 2 Thess. 1:1).

1:23–2:11 THE REASON FOR HIS CHANGE OF PLANS
1:23-24 Paul's desire to spare the Corinthians. The link to the previous section is mutual pride and joy (1:24) in the day of the Lord (cf. 1:14). If joy is to be the future's aim, it must also be the present's reality. This explains Paul's change of plans. He would remain absent as long as possible to ensure mutual joy when present. Because of the highly sensitive situation in Corinth, Paul had to be defensive and careful.

Paul stayed away to spare them grief (1:23) and to share joy later (1:24). This is key to Paul's ministry. He saw his readers as objects of joy (cf. John 17:13; 1 John 1:4). Paul had made a second visit to Corinth (2 Cor. 13:2), and it had been a sorrowful experience. Now Paul wanted to spare the Corinthians and himself another such sorrowful experience (cf. 2:1-2).

2:1-4 The reversed situation. Instead of another visit, Paul had written a stern letter to correct the believers. This letter may have been lost. Some hold that these verses refer to 1 Corinthians, which certainly contains subject matter that caused Paul grief and sorrow. Paul desired to show love, not judgment (1 Cor. 4:21; 12:20–13:1).

2:5-7 The goal of discipline is restoration.
Paul's last words to the Corinthians, probably in 1 Corinthians, were words of sorrow and correction. One problem that may have given rise to Paul's severe letter was the failure of the church to deal with the gross immorality Paul had rebuked in 1 Corinthians 5:1-13. Now they had responded, and the sinner had been disciplined. Yet they had failed to forgive and restore the repentant offender. They were to avoid sorrow that overwhelmed the benefits of the discipline (2 Cor. 2:5-7; cf. 5:4 and 1 Cor. 15:54 for the Greek word translated "overwhelmed" or "swallowed up").

2:8-11 Avoid deception by Satan. Excessive discipline is one of Satan's schemes. Paul exhorted the Corinthians to restore the brother to fellowship and thus prevent Satan from using the situation to his advantage.

2:12-17 THE CONTINUED CONCERN OF PAUL

2:12-13 Resumption of itinerary. Paul mentioned his lack of rest in spirit to reinforce his genuine concern for the Corinthians. After leaving Ephesus, Paul traveled north to Troas, a port city on the Aegean (2:12). There he waited for Titus whom he had sent to Corinth (7:6-7). When Titus failed to arrive, Paul departed for Macedonia where the two were reunited (7:5-7).

2:14-17 A digression to 7:4. From 2:14 to 7:4 Paul launched out into a discussion that contrasts true Christian adequacy of the heart and the superficial adequacy of appearances (5:12). Paul used a number of concepts to illustrate this contrast: heart versus appearance, spirit versus stone, new covenant versus old covenant. Paul's point in 2:14-17 is that victory in his ministry did not equal news of success from Corinth. In earthly victory or defeat, Paul's success was gauged by his manifestation of Christ, not human response or acceptance.

The concepts of 2:15-16 lead to the broader concept of adequacy. Paul showed his sincere love toward the Corinthians even in his seemingly erratic itinerary. In 2 Corinthians 2:17 Paul both defended himself and attacked the "many" false apostles in Corinth (11:12-15). Second Corinthians 3:1–7:4 reveals the genuine quality of Paul's ministry. As Paul corrected the misunderstandings

created by his change in itinerary, he provided tremendous insight into his own life, ministry, and motivation.

3:1–5:19 Adequacy in Ministry Commended: A Second Defense

Overview: The section of 3:1–5:19 presents the heart of Paul's answer to the question, "Who is equal to such a task?" (2:16). Note the threefold mention of adequacy in 3:5-6. The contrasts of 2 Corinthians 3 are rooted in the life-or-death reactions to his ministry (2:16). Paul used such responses to reach his goal in 5:12, to assure the Corinthians of his love, and to expose true glory through the Spirit. Second Corinthians 3–4 show the surpassing greatness of Paul's ministry, though it operated in "jars of clay" (4:7).

3:1-11 NEW COVENANT ADEQUACY
The truths of this section are built upon a number of different concepts: (1) letters of commendation, (2) tablets of law, (3) old and new covenants, and (4) worthiness. The questioning of Paul's credentials always led him back to fundamentals in his own defense. Three interconnected lines demonstrate the superiority of the new covenant over the old: (1) the superior nature of the new covenant, (2) the resultant superior new covenant ministry, and (3) the superior benefit for those who receive that ministry.

In view are two kinds of ministry, not just the contents of the two covenants. Paul did not call the Mosaic covenant itself "condemnation" and "death" (3:7-9; cf. also Rom. 7:12, 14, 16). He kept the content of the covenant distinct from the concept of "letter" (3:6). Here his focus is on how God's word was communicated—in the old covenant by the "letter" written on stone, in the new covenant by the Spirit's writing on the heart. The new covenant's ministry far surpasses the great, though fading, ministry of the old covenant. It produces a change of heart as well as changes in external behavior.

Some itinerant teachers were circulating among the churches, bearing letters of commendation from other congregations (3:1-3). Paul wrote that his life and ministry spoke for themselves. He needed no such commendations. The Corinthian converts were his "credentials."

Note the contrasts of stone/flesh, ink/Spirit, old covenant/new covenant. Paul's ministry was one of the Spirit and the greater glory of the new covenant (Jer. 31:34; Heb. 8:6-13). The radiance of the old was fading (3:12-18).

3:12–4:6 NEW COVENANT INTIMACY

3:12-18 The removal of the old covenant veil. Paul did not not need letters of commendation because of his firsthand intimacy and its ensuing boldness (3:12) and stability (4:1). Paul's boldness in speech is elaborated in 3:12-18.

Paul compared his own speaking with the speaking of Moses (3:12-13). But the comparison is really between two ministries, not just two ways of speaking. Skip from 3:13 to 3:18 in order to see that 3:14-17 is an explanatory digression. The "but" of 3:14 is then put in perspective. The continual use of the veil blinds, deafens, and dulls the minds of the people to God's glory in Christ (see 2:11; 4:4; Rom. 11:7, 25). The Corinthians should have realized the temporary nature of the old covenant's glory.

In 3:13 Paul explained the purpose of Moses' veil—to conceal the reality that the glory was fading (cf. Exod. 34:33-35). The "veil" (3:13-18) also had been used to interrupt the people's vision of God's glory. Moses put his veil on after he had spoken to the people of Israel (see Exod. 34:29-35). But in the new covenant, the veil is no longer needed (3:16). The glory is given through the Spirit, hidden but powerful (2 Cor. 3:3, 6, 8, 16-18; cf. 1 Cor. 15:45). The Spirit is the new means of covenant ministry. Moses beheld God's glory and his face was changed temporarily (2 Cor. 3:18; cf. 3:13). New covenant believers behold the glory of the Lord, though imperfectly, and are supernaturally transformed into the same image of glory. The idea of reflection (3:18) best fits the context of Moses' reflection of glory and Paul's reflection of the glory in clay jars (cf. 4:7).

4:1-6 Stability in heart. Take note of 4:1, 7, 16. The subject of stability was Paul's launching pad for the mention of despair and restlessness in spirit (2:13). Since Paul was adequate in Christ, rejection and persecution did not cause him to lose heart. Surpassing glory (3:1-11) and veiled hearts (3:12-18) explain the context and problems surrounding new covenant glory. In 4:6 Paul was loosely quoting from Genesis 1:3. The God who created physical light can illumine the minds of his spiritually blinded creatures. What then could be the reason that not all acknowledged and understood Paul's great adequacy?

4:7-15 NEW COVENANT SUFFERING

The answer to the final question in the previous section is: because the great glory of new covenant adequacy is within the earthen vessels of human frailty. This contrast between glory and weakness finds its source in a lesson Paul previously learned from God, which he waited until the end of the letter to recount (12:7-9). Weakness allows the glory of God to be revealed. To point to difficult physical circumstances was not to point to spiritual inner despair or inferiority (4:8-12). Both the psalmist and Paul spoke of their trials in order to glorify God (4:13, quoting Ps. 116:10). Paul poured out his heart with reference to his suffering for the sake of Christ. He shared a divine perspective on suffering that has been an encouragement to many in the straits of affliction.

4:16–5:10 NEW COVENANT IMMORTALITY

4:16-18 The promise of renewal and eternal glory. Why did Paul not lose heart? First, he knew the difference between the problems of an earthen vessel and the strength found through the glory within (4:1-15). Second, he looked forward to an eternal state in which a body of glory would replace the mortal body of weakness (4:16–5:10). This is building to his point in 5:12 that commendation must be made on heart realities, not external abilities or personality. Paul found strength of heart because of the promise of his future eternal state (4:16-18).

5:1-5 Physical death is not a reason to lose heart. Second Corinthians 5:1-10 shows that one's attitude toward the future life is fundamental to one's ethical conduct on earth. "Now" (5:1) is a link back to 4:18 (cf. 4:1, 16 and the use of "therefore"). Paul provided one example of the eternal things that are not seen (5:1-5). Again, Paul confirmed that his groanings were not because he was weak or unqualified but because he longed for the eternal and perfect body (5:4, 6; see the same groaning in Rom. 8:23).

Because of the burdens of life lived in a physical body, the believer longs, not to be bodiless ("naked" or "unclothed"), but to live in a resurrected, glorified body. The "deposit" (5:5; "pledge," NASB; "earnest," KJV) is a down payment that renders further or final payments obligatory. The Holy Spirit is God's deposit or pledge of the believer's future and complete redemption. Paul explained that even the threat of physical death is no reason to lose heart.

5:6-10 Continued good courage. Excavations in ancient Corinth have uncovered a raised platform known as the *bema* ("judgment") seat (5:10). It was there that Paul was accused before Gallio (A.D. 51–65), proconsul of Achaia (Acts 18:12). Paul used this terminology and imagery to describe the future judgment of the works of believers (cf. 1 Cor. 3:13-15).

5:11-19 ADEQUACY AS AN OPPORTUNITY FOR GENUINE PRIDE
The purpose of 2 Corinthians 1–7, if not of the entire letter, is revealed in 5:12. At this point Paul gave an answer to pride in appearances (5:11-15). The struggle was to communicate the hidden message, the veiled glory (3:14-15), the treasure in earthen vessels (4:6-7). Although not manifest to humans, Paul's adequacy and approval were manifest to the only one who counted—God. The fear of the Lord is a major theme of Old Testament Wisdom Literature (5:11; cf. Prov. 1:7). The fear of the Lord is expressed, not so much in trembling knees, but in obeying God (Eccles. 12:13) and departing from evil (Job 28:28). The contrasts in 2 Corinthians 5:13 will take full expression in 2 Corinthians 10–12, where Paul will play the fool to teach true wisdom.

Paul continued his discourse on adequacy in Christ by putting forth his means of regarding people (5:16-19). The key "heart" versus "appearance" distinction (5:12) was used to regard people in light of God's grace in Christ, not according to the flesh (5:16-17). Paul no longer judged from a perspective that limited itself to what the eyes could see and the mind deduce. Paul saw all men according to their potential as "new creations" in Christ. To reconcile (5:18) implies "to change." Reconciliation by the

death of Christ means that humanity's state of alienation from God is changed by the death of Christ (Rom. 5:11) so that all are now able to be saved.

5:20–7:16 Exhortations to Reconciliation
5:20–6:10 GODWARD RECONCILIATION
5:20-21 A return to 5:14-15. From the world's perspective, the paradox of Christian glory is that Christ's sin-bearing suffering accomplished righteousness for the believer. Second Corinthians 5:21 declares the essence of Christ's work. The sinless Savior has taken mankind's sins in order that believers might share in God's righteousness.

6:1-10 Specific application to the Corinthians. To receive grace in vain (6:1) is similar to the concept of emptying the cross of its power (1 Cor. 1:17). It would thwart the full intended purpose of God's redemption in Christ—in this case, renouncing God's ways of true glory through weakness and suffering. In 2 Corinthians 6:2 Paul quoted the Septuagint translation of Isaiah 49:8 to provide Scriptural support for the exhortation of 6:1. Isaiah promised that God would hear and help his people. Paul interpreted and applied the promise to his own day. Isaiah's words to Israel become God's words to the church. Note the context of Isaiah's frustration in ministering to Israel (Isa. 49:4).

The descriptions of Paul's life ("putting no stumbling block," 6:3; "commending," 6:4; "dying," 6:9; "making many rich," 6:10; "possessing everything," 6:10) all hinge on the "we urge" of 6:1 and show the manner of the exhortation. Paul provided very personal insight into his own experiences in his service for Christ. All that Paul said and did took into account the readers' best interests.

6:11–7:16 MANWARD RECONCILIATION
6:11-13 Paul's yearning for reconciliation with the Corinthians. Paul's reconciliation with the Corinthians was based on purity from sin (6:11–7:4). Paul provided an example of restraint in affection (cf. 6:12). He made a plea for full fellowship (6:11-13) based on his character of good faith (6:1-10). The real problem in Paul's relationship with the Corinthians lay, not with Paul's attitude

or qualifications, but with the Corinthians' own affections—their inner attitudes toward Paul (6:12).

6:14–7:1 Avoiding being yoked with unbelievers. The unbelievers in view (6:14) were the false apostles who were trying to take over the affections of the Corinthian believers (11:3-4, 12-15, 18-21). Much of the trouble at Corinth stemmed from the believers' association with impure believers and unbelievers. The five questions of 6:14-16 all expected a negative answer and were intended to stress the incompatibility of Christianity with heathenism. Belial (6:15) is a transliterated Hebrew term that means "worthlessness." In later Jewish writings the term became a proper name for Satan.

In 6:16 Paul quoted Leviticus 26:11-12 which gave God's promise to move into a new stage of intimacy with his people as he came to dwell in his tabernacle. See Leviticus 26:1 for the need to separate from idolatry and Leviticus 26:13 for the concept of yoke (cf. also Deut. 22:10; Lev. 19:19 for unequal yokes).

In 6:17 Paul quoted Isaiah 52:11, which was a call to Israel to come out from the impurity of the Babylonian captivity and reenter the holiness of life in the Promised Land. It was a second exodus from bondage into life centered around the presence of God in the temple.

Paul's third quotation (6:18) was from 2 Samuel 7:14 which originally was God's promise to take the sons of David and give them a special Father-son relationship with God as they served as kings of Israel. Paul broadened out the thought by the addition of "and daughters" to show that what was originally a promise to the male Davidic line of kings had, in Christ, become a reality of divine relationship for male and female believers.

Paul claimed that the above Old Testament quotations were promises for the Christian as well (7:1). In Christ, God's presence in the tabernacle (6:16), his call for purity after release from bondage (6:17), and his relationship as Father to his children (6:18) are all realities (cf. 1:20). As God was present with Israel in the Old Testament tabernacle, so the presence of God through the Spirit is seen in the church. As God brought Israel out from bondage in Babylon, God would also bring about the greater exodus from sin and death into purity through Christ's sacrificial death. As God had chosen to bless the royal line of David, God would also view believers as royal sons and daughters. This grand understanding of the Old Testament promises as they relate to New Testament believers illustrates the truth that in Christ every believer is a "new creation" (5:12, 16-17). God had taken what was old and made it new in Christ.

7:2-16 Joy over repentance and fellowship. Paul's primary focus in 2 Corinthians 1–7 was the need to correct the Corinthians' alignment with the worldly ways taught by the false apostles. But these chapters were written with Paul's full knowledge of the readers' repentance. Next, he spoke specifically of that good news. He made a confident plea for reconciliation (7:2-4) based on the Corinthians' proper repentance from sin (7:5-16).

Paul recounted his separation from and search for Titus (7:5-12; cf. 2:12) and resumed the discussion regarding his travel and ministry itinerary (cf. 2:13). Having left Ephesus, Paul traveled north to Troas, crossed the Aegean to Macedonia, and looked for Titus whom he had earlier sent to Corinth (7:5-7). From Titus Paul received the encouraging report about the Corinthians. Proper sorrow brought repentance without regret (7:8-10) that was centered on God, not self.

The letter that caused the Corinthians sorrow (7:8) is believed by most scholars to be a letter written after 1 Corinthians and delivered by Titus. Others believe it refers to 1 Corinthians. Although the letter brought sorrow, there was genuine repentance on the part of the Corinthians (7:9-10) and other beneficial results (7:11-12).

Paul revealed the results of proper sorrow (7:11-13). Why was Paul comforted? Because the Corinthians' sorrow at his rebuke had brought about repentance and obedience to God. The "one who did the wrong" (7:12) referred to the immoral man who was disciplined by the church (cf. 1 Cor. 5:1; 2 Cor. 2:6). Because of the Corinthians' repentance, Paul had full confidence in them (7:13-16). Titus had a very positive ministry with the Corinthians, and they grew in mutual affection for one another.

8:1–9:15 A TEST FOR THE SINCERITY OF LOVE: GIVING FROM THE HEART

Overview: Paul waited until this point to mention the offering because he could not speak about money when he knew some of his readers, though obedient in one area, were still yoked with unbelievers in their hearts. Not only was he being condemned by the false apostles for having a supposedly erratic and uncaring ministry, he was also being criticized for being dishonest. In 2 Corinthians 1–7 Paul addressed these and other issues in a caring and reconciling way. He tried to do the near impossible: to combine his personal defense and correctives for their worldliness with praise for their innocence in the matter of immorality (7:11).

The Corinthian problems with the Jerusalem offering concerned equality in giving. They asked why they should have to give up their money for others. What if they should need that money later on? Paul answered their question by discussing God's long-standing emphasis on equality dating back to how manna was divided up for the Israelites in the wilderness (8:10-15).

The second problem concerned covetousness (9:6-14). Paul's readers needed to learn how to give freely from the heart, trusting God to provide for their own needs. The third problem dealt with the trustworthiness of the bearers of the offering (8:16-24). This section represents part of the entire epistle's concern for financial matters (cf. 2:17; 4:2; 11:7-12; 12:13-18).

Paul clearly presented the problem (8:11), the solution (8:15; 9:9), and the purpose of his discussion (8:8). In 2 Corinthians 8–9 Paul commended those who would deliver the collection for the poor in Jerusalem. Charges of greed and thievery against Paul had blocked the progress of the collection (1:17; 2:17; 4:2; 10:2; 11:7; 12:13-18). Paul tried to correct two problems: (1) the question of equality (8:13-15) and (2) the question of giving freely from the heart (9:7-9). He wanted the offering to issue from sincere love (8:8), not from guilt or pride.

8:1-7 Motivation by Example

Second Corinthians 8:1-6 was written as one sentence in the original Greek. Paul spoke of the offering here, just after his warm-hearted commendation of their repentance and just before he made a final attack on the false apostles (2 Cor. 10-13). The offering was a duty (Rom. 15:25-27; cf. Gal. 2:10, "poor in Jerusalem"). Paul had instructed the Corinthians concerning giving to the needs of the saints (1 Cor. 16:1-4; cf. Acts 11:29; Gal. 2:10). Now he encouraged them to complete the preparations for their gift to the Jerusalem church. Their positive response to this exhortation is evidenced in Romans 15:25-26.

The churches of Macedonia (2 Cor. 8:1), the province of northern Greece, included Philippi, Thessalonica, and Berea. These churches were cited as examples in sacrificial giving (cf. Phil. 4:15-18). Paul's concern was that the work on the collection for the Jerusalem church (2 Cor. 8:6), a project begun a year earlier (8:10), be brought to completion.

8:8-15 Exhortation to Sincere Love

This exhortation to sincere love was based on a divine example (8:8-11). For an application of Christ's selfless example in 8:9, see Paul's experience in 6:10. The Corinthians were to continue that line of enriching and sacrificial giving.

Sincere love was also based on human equality (8:12-15). Paul's quotation of Exodus 16:18 showed that God always intended for needs to be met on the basis of relative need. The one who needs much should receive much (cf. 1 Cor. 16:2). When God gave the Israelites manna in the wilderness, those who gathered more than others were not able to save it, and those who gathered less had a sufficient amount. Equality was a sign of divine intention and provision. Paul's use of the term "equality" (8:13) did not mean that everyone had to have the same amount. Rather, everyone's basic needs were to be met; those in need were to be helped by those with plenty.

8:16–9:5 Commendation of the Administrators

The motivation of Titus, 8:16-23, came from God putting earnestness within him. The Macedonians' motivation to give their offering also came from God (8:3). Paul continued to support his views with Old Testament Scripture (8:21, quoting Prov. 3:4). The "brother" (8:18) is not identified, although it has been suggested that he was perhaps Luke or Trophimus.

Paul's purpose for sending the Christian brothers (9:1-5) was that he desired the churches to see his reason for boasting (8:24). Macedonia (9:2) was the Roman province of northern Greece, and Achaia was the province of southern Greece. Paul encouraged giving that was unaffected by covetousness (9:5), that is, given with a view to helping others, not motivated by the thanks or recognition one might receive.

9:6-15 Motivation by Principle

Overview: Paul set forth four principles of Christian giving: the principles of harvest (9:6), willingness (9:7), divine grace (9:8-10), and thanksgiving (9:11-15).

9:6 GIVING IS SOWING
In giving, the harvest is always in view. The farmer does not plant seed and then walk away, saying, "Well, I'll never see that again." Although it is out of sight and given away to the ground, he knows he will someday see the harvest.

9:7 GIVING IS FROM THE HEART, NOT THE PURSE
Note the quotation (9:7) from Proverbs 22:9. The first place to look when giving is how much honest willingness is in the heart, not how much money is in the wallet.

9:8-15 GIVING ENRICHES FOR FURTHER GIVING
Paul used Psalm 112:9 (9:9) and the quotation and broader context of Isaiah 55:10 (9:10) to show that the giver shall be provided a means of giving. Paul also connected the thoughts of Hosea 10:12. The farming images of sowing and harvesting illustrate the fact that if righteousness is sown, a great harvest of righteousness will be given in return. Thus, it conveys the realities of moral living after repentance.

10:1–13:14 TRUE VERSUS FOOLISH COMMENDATION: THE REAL SOURCE OF STRENGTH

Overview: Second Corinthians 10–13 successfully holds two seemingly contradictory attitudes: edification and sarcasm. Paul's sarcastic attack on his opponents is clear throughout (10:1; 11:4, 8, 11, 19-21; 12:13, 16). But

that strong offense is set within a context of the meekness and gentleness of Christ (10:1). The harsh and critical content must be read within the intentions of humble and temperate emotion. If Paul's goal had been to put down the Corinthians and justify himself, his sarcasm could not have been called meek and gentle. But because his motives were for the upbuilding of the Corinthians (12:19), his words, though strong, were intended to nurture, not destroy.

The content of 12:19 is behind all of these words. Although some of Paul's words could be mistaken as defensive backlashes, the clear framework of "gentleness" (10:1) and "strengthening" (12:19; "upbuilding," NASB; "edifying," KJV) alerts the reader to the true heart and point of this section: edification.

Paul put forward the problem (10:2), the solution (12:9), and the purpose of his discussion (12:19). In this section he commended himself as an eminent apostle. However, his boasting in weakness was quite different from that of his opponents. He corrected their assertion that he lived by the standards of this world (10:2).

Also, he pointed out that his free service of ministry should not have branded him as inferior or as a person cunningly trying to cheat them. The Corinthians needed their appearance-oriented evaluation of Paul turned around (12:11). They would only be able to follow the correct pattern of godliness after they understood what made a person commendable before God (11:3).

Second Corinthians 12:19-21 is the core of this section. Paul defended himself against attacks by certain opponents and false apostles (11:3). The Corinthians had been taken in by these criticisms. As a result, their evaluation of the apostle was appearance-oriented (10:7). They were focused on external matters rather than internal issues. Paul had to defend himself against these criticisms to prevent his ministry and teaching from being undermined (13:3).

10:1-18 Warning to Recognize Paul's Authority

10:1-6 REQUEST FOR COMPLETE OBEDIENCE
Paul desired no punishment for the readers (10:1-2), but he would punish those who needed it (10:3-6). On 10:5, see

1 Corinthians 1:17 concerning the opposition to the knowledge of God. This shows how the spiritual person wages war.

10:7-11 REMINDER OF HIS SUFFICIENT AUTHORITY

Apparently the false apostles had spread doubt about whether Paul belonged to Christ (2 Cor. 10:7, 11; 13:5). Again, Paul corrected the outward-oriented judgments (10:7; cf. 5:12). Paul boasted (10:8) because of the extravagant boasting of his opponents. He did not like to boast (cf. 10:13, 15; 12:1) but was forced to do so because of the criticism he had received. His boasts were not about what he had done, but what God had done. In the Apocryphal "Acts of Paul and Thecla," Paul was described as, "baldheaded, bow-legged, strongly built, a man small in size, with meeting eyebrows, with a rather large nose, full of grace, for at times he looked like a man and at times he had the face of an angel." It is believed by some scholars that this plain and unflattering account embodies a very early tradition.

10:12-18 REMINDER OF THE PROPER SPHERE OF COMMENDATION

All of Paul's boasting and commendation were based on what the Lord gave him. His opponents commended themselves (10:12-18). Paul quoted Jeremiah 9:24 to reinforce this idea (10:17; cf. 1 Cor. 1:31). The words of 2 Corinthians 10:17-18 should have been enough, but the situation in Corinth was out of hand. Paul had to continue. The subject returns to that of 3:1 and 5:12.

11:1–12:13 A Demonstration of Paul's Authority

11:1-6 THE PROBLEM PRECIPITATING PAUL'S FOOLISHNESS

Paul's "little foolishness" (11:1) grows out of 10:12; to commend oneself is to be without understanding, a fool. Because Paul was going to commend himself, he called this foolishness. When compared with 10:8, this forms a startling conclusion. Paul would not be put to shame if he boasted because he would speak the truth. But even though he would speak truth, it would still be foolishness. Paul was saying that what makes boasting foolish is not the truth or falsity of the boast but the self-serving attitude motivating it. The goal of Paul's "foolishness" was to bring about edification (12:19).

Paul began by expressing his wish that his readers would put up with his foolishness (11:1). He asked that they bear with him (11:1, 4, 19-20) and made it crystal clear that he was acting the fool. The foolishness to which Paul referred was that of boasting. Self-commendation is foolish, but Paul engaged in it briefly to make a point.

Paul continued his argument by exposing and illustrating the problem (11:2-4). In 2 Corinthians 11–12 Paul was waging spiritual warfare according to his definition in 10:5. Paul was seeking to demolish the falsehoods that had taken root in the Corinthian congregation (cf. 2:11; 3:14; 4:4; 10:5; 11:3). For the deception of Eve (11:3), see Genesis 3:4, 13 and 1 Timothy 2:14. Paul gave a reasoned evaluation of himself in 11:5-6. In this case, the message was more important than the medium.

11:7-15 THE ISSUE OF "FREE" MINISTRY

Note the reason why Paul had to be "foolish": accusations by false apostles and the acceptance of false apostles by the Corinthians. He raised a question relative to his being unskilled in speech (11:7). Paul's critics rudely implied that the Corinthians got what they paid for. But Paul did not work for free—it had cost someone besides the Corinthians. Paul "robbed" (11:8) other churches in the sense that he received gifts from them in order that he might not be a financial burden on the church at Corinth. Macedonia (11:9) is the northern province of Greece. Paul served the Corinthians freely out of love (11:10-11) in order to cut off opportunity from his enemies (11:12-15). They wanted to be regarded like Paul, but Satan was behind their deception.

11:16-29 FOOLISHNESS DISPLAYED

11:16-21 Sarcastic opening. Paul continued his attack on his enemies by using sharp sarcasm (11:16-21). He spoke to the wise and unwise (11:16) and recounted his experiences of personal suffering as evidence of his apostolic authority (cf. John 15:18-25). He disassociated his boasting from anything God might do (11:17). He was making it clear that he was acting the fool (cf. 11:16-18, 21, 23, 30, "must"; 12:1, 6, 11). Boasting according to flesh was well received in Corinth (11:18-21).

11:22-29 Foolish boasting. Paul's pedigree (11:22) made it likely that his opponents were Judaizers, probably with a Jewish ethnic background. Paul continued by recounting his past performance (11:23-29). The thirty-nine lashes (11:24) referred to beatings Paul had received at the hands of the Jewish religious leaders. The law called for forty lashes (Deut. 25:1-3), but only thirty-nine were administered to avoid the possibility of exceeding the limit by miscounting. Paul had been shipwrecked (11:25) three times before his shipwreck on the island of Malta enroute to Rome (Acts 27:40-44).

11:30-33 THE FOCUS OF PAUL'S BOASTING
Paul's boasting was in his very weakness (11:30-31). His glory was in earthen vessels (4:7, "jars of clay") in order to glorify God. He gave another example of his weakness in the account of his escape from Damascus (11:32-33). Paul's experience in Damascus is recorded in Acts 9:24-25. The term "governor" (11:32), meaning "ruler of a people," was the title of a leader of a town or country. This ruler was a subordinate of the Arabian king Aretas IV (9 B.C.–A.D. 40), the father-in-law of Herod Antipas. During the years A.D. 37–40 Aretas was given power to appoint an ethnarch by the emperors Caligula and Claudius.

12:1-10 FURTHER FOOLISHNESS
DISPLAYED
12:1-6 Paul's visions and revelations. Paul continued his "foolish" boasting by recounting the visions and revelations he had received (12:1). These revelations did not illustrate Paul's weakness (11:30), but they set the context for the weakness of his "thorn in the flesh" (12:7). The point was that even though Paul had extremely privileged knowledge, he did not flaunt it. His visions had occurred fourteen years earlier, and yet Paul had kept them secret. The visions (12:2) Paul recalled took place around A.D. 42 (A.D. 56 minus 14 years) while Paul was still in Tarsus before Barnabas brought him to Antioch (Acts 11:25-26). The "third heaven" (12:2) and "paradise" (12:4; Luke 23:43; Rev. 2:7) refer to the place where God dwells. Paul's credentials were based on firsthand witness, not past glories (12:6).

12:7-10 Under God's direction. Paul's sphere of boasting was in his weakness (12:5-10; cf. 5:12; 11:16-33). No one knows

for sure what Paul's "thorn in the flesh" (12:7) was, but it has been speculated that it was some kind of eye disease (cf. Gal. 4:13-15; 6:11).

The focus in these verses is on Paul's weakness. He had asked God for deliverance from a specific weakness three times. Finally, a direct word from God showed Paul that he was, in reality, trying to throw away God's gift that kept his fleshly nature from boasting of his privileged position. Paul may have been caught up to heaven, but during his time of struggle with his "thorn," God had kept him in the dark. His affliction had to meet grace in order to bring about its God-intended result.

Paul thought God's grace would include the removal of the suffering. But God's grace was related to his sufficiency at all times, not to the presence or absence of suffering. Paul wanted to increase his power by the removal of the "thorn." God showed him where his true sufficiency was. Power came through seeing weakness as the very vehicle for manifesting the power of Christ, not through gradually eliminating mortal weaknesses. Weaknesses show the inadequacy of the vessel and affirm the ever-present grace and power of the Spirit within. This had been Paul's argument throughout the letter (1:9; 4:7, 11, 16-18).

12:11-13 THE NEEDLESSNESS
OF THE DISPLAY
The Corinthians should have commended Paul, but instead they condemned him and forced him to defend himself. Miracles (12:12) had the specific purpose, in biblical times, of authenticating messengers and their message. Paul's miracles authenticated his apostleship. Paul had given patient exhortations throughout 2 Corinthians 1–7. In 11:1–12:10 he gave a most intimate look into his private reasons for boasting in weakness. Here, his sarcasm (12:13) is still set in the context of patient and careful exhortation.

12:14–13:14 A Plea to Avoid Pending Judgment
12:14-18 PAUL'S CONTINUED DESIRE
FOR TRUE MINISTRY
In 12:15-18 two elements introduce the conclusion of the letter: (1) Paul was about to make his third visit, and (2) he sought the Corinthians, not their money. Titus had gone

to Corinth in Paul's behalf (12:18; cf. 2 Cor. 7:6, 13; 8:6). The slander against Paul in this section was that he used his friends to take people's money while he himself came off as self-sacrificing and innocent.

12:19-21 THE PURPOSE OF THE LETTER: EDIFICATION, NOT DEFENSE
Paul's purpose was edification in God's sight, not self-seeking defense (cf. 2:17). The Corinthians thought Paul was on the defensive, trying to vindicate himself from a wrong that he had committed. But he had done no wrong.

The concepts of defense and commendation (3:1; 4:2; 5:12; 6:4; 7:11; 10:11-12) are closely related. In 12:19 Paul clarified the difference between how the letter might be perceived (defensive) and how it was actually designed (for edification). The letter's many defensive and sarcastic sounding passages just show how extreme the situation was. Paul had to go to extreme lengths to get through to the Corinthians.

13:1-10 THIRD-TIME WARNINGS
13:1-3 Warning. All the sarcasm and foolish boasting of 2 Corinthians 10–12 comes to an end here. Paul's third visit would bring talking to an end. In 2 Corinthians 1–12 Paul hoped that he would be able to come and find obedience. In 2 Corinthians 13 he vowed he would come and punish disobedience. Paul said he could come in love or with a whip (1 Cor. 4:21). Now was the time to see which one he would use. In 2 Corinthians 13:1 Paul quoted from Deuteronomy

19:15, which requires two or three witnesses to secure a conviction against a defendant (cf. Matt. 18:16; 1 Tim. 5:19). The issue to be proved was not the Corinthians' sins but Paul's authority in Christ (2 Cor. 13:3). His third visit would bring proof that he was God's appointed apostle.

13:4 Explanations. Paul presents a perfect model of ministry in 13:4. This verse gives a perfect outline of the letter's major themes of God's power becoming evident and active despite the weakness of its vessels.

13:5-10 Warning and explanation. Paul turned the tables on his critics (cf. 10:7, 11). He instructed the Corinthians to examine their character and conduct to see if they were truly Christian (cf. Titus 1:16). Paul again asserted his desire for the Corinthians' approval even if he could not win it (2 Cor. 13:7-10).

13:11-14 FINAL GOOD WISHES
The "holy kiss" (13:12; cf. 1 Cor. 16:20; Rom. 16:16; 1 Thess. 5:26) was a culturally accepted Christian greeting and corresponds in Western culture to the handshake. In this particular case it symbolized the reconciliation and peace needed in the Corinthian situation. Paul concluded the epistle with a great trinitarian benediction (13:14), emphasizing the grace that finds its source in the Son, the love manifested by the Father, and the fellowship established and sustained by the Holy Spirit. This letter contains Paul's longest benediction.

Galatians

BASIC FACTS

HISTORICAL SETTING
The term "Galatia" (1:2) can be understood in two different ways. One refers to the area inhabited by the Galatian ethnic group in northern Asia Minor—a place visited, if at all by Paul, on his second or third expeditions. A second usage refers to a political division of central and southern Asia Minor that became part of the Roman Empire in 25 B.C. Most scholars favor the view that this letter was addressed to the churches in the southern cities of this region—cities visited by Paul on his first and second missionary expeditions.

AUTHOR
The Pauline authorship of Galatians is confirmed by internal and external evidence. The author is named in 1:1 and 5:2. The early church fathers, from Clement of Rome on, affirm the Pauline authorship and authenticity of Galatians.

DATE
Scholars are divided as to the date and location of the original recipients of this letter. Some believe that Paul addressed the epistle to Galatia proper, which he did not personally visit until his second journey on his way to Troas. If this was the case, the letter would have been written after his second missionary journey any time from A.D. 53 to 56. Others hold that Paul addressed the letter to the churches of southern Galatia, which he had established on his first missionary journey. Identifying the recipients thus would put the writing of the letter at an earlier date, around A.D. 49.

The key issue in dating Galatians has to do with how Paul used the term "Galatia," whether he referred to Galatia as the official Roman province or as the more general pre-Roman territory founded by the Gauls. The provincial use of the term "Galatia" would direct the letter to the churches Paul founded on his first missionary journey. The territorial use of the name would date the letter later, with its addressees being the churches Paul founded during his second and third missionary journeys. Paul's writings show the use of both regional (Rom. 15:31; 2 Cor.1:16; Gal. 1:17, 21;

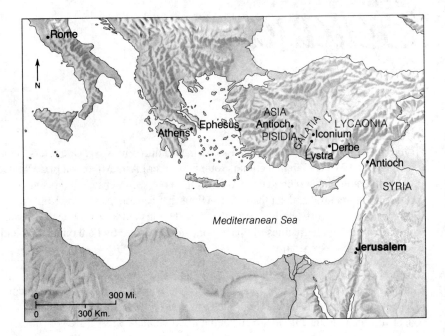

1 Thess. 2:14) and provincial names (1 Cor. 16:1, 5, 15, 19). No completely conclusive argument for Paul's use of Galatia as the provincial or territorial name has been made, though more recent scholarship has favored the southern Galatian view, and thus the earlier date. The decision to adopt either view does not materially alter the interpretation or application of the letter to the Galatians.

PURPOSE
The letter to the Galatians was designed to correct legalistic approaches to Christianity by demonstrating the priority of righteousness by faith over the works of the law. Paul made his argument by showing the priority of the promises to Abraham over the covenant with Moses. The goal of both the Abrahamic promise and Mosaic obedience was fulfilled in the righteousness brought through faith in Jesus Christ.

GEOGRAPHY AND ITS IMPORTANCE

Cities in Galatia
Paul passed through Galatia on all three of his missionary journeys. The four cities of Antioch, Iconium, Lystra, and Derbe received several visits from Paul during these journeys. Although it is not known exactly which of these churches were being addressed in Paul's letter to the Galatians, the letter makes it clear that the readers shared a common problem of falling to the pressures of legalism.

GUIDING CONCEPTS

The major problem presented in the letter to the Galatians was the challenge to Paul's gospel that believers are justified by faith in Christ alone, apart from the works of the law. Among the Galatian believers were false teachers who insisted on a Judaistic model for Christianity (Gal. 1:7; 4:17; 5:10).

The practical result of these doctrinal debates was an atmosphere of critical fighting (5:25), snobbish dismissal rather than restoration of sinning believers (6:1, 3), and a general tendency to give up and lose heart (6:9). The Galatian squabbles were not simply doctrinal niceties. They were damaging the fibre of the believers' compassion and perseverance.

BIBLE-WIDE CONCEPTS

Paul viewed Christians as the true Israel of God (6:16). This concept sums up all the Old Testament connections made in the letter. Paul contrasted the work of the Holy Spirit in the church with the work of the law under Moses (3:3, 5, 14; 4:6, 29, 5:16-18, 22-25). The Spirit is the Christian's link to the family of God (4:6). The sonship found in the Spirit was the link to Paul's discussion of the relationship between Abraham and the law (3:14-29).

The historical conflict between Isaac and Ishmael foreshadowed the conflict between the children of Spirit and promise (Christians) and the children of flesh (the hostile Jews, cf. 4:29). But that conflict also had a personal counterpart within each Christian in the form of hostility between flesh and Spirit (5:15-17).

Thus Paul's words reflect the line of conflict and hostility predicted by God in Genesis 3:15, where enmity between the seed of the woman and the seed of the serpent would wind through history. That enmity first took form with the murder of Abel by Cain and will take its final form when Jesus returns and casts Satan into the lake of fire. In between, all the conflicts between good and evil, flesh and Spirit, whether on the national or personal level, reflect the ongoing conflict between Satan and Jesus.

NEEDS MET BY GALATIANS

The question concerning who had true authority from God pressed hard against the Galatians. They admired both Paul and the Jewish leaders who were also Paul's critics. To complicate matters, both Paul and his critics claimed the authority of God and the Scriptures. But the issue for the Galatians was much deeper than a theological squabble between Christian leaders. Paul's critics claimed that the Law of Moses could save people from hell. But to imply that the law brought salvation denied the power of what God had done through Christ's death and resurrection. The legalistic stance of Paul's opponents also missed the point of God's work through Abraham. More personally, legalism left the Galatians in bondage to the fear of failure. It bound them to trying to save themselves through obedience rather than allowing them to relax and enjoy the freedom of fully won forgiveness in Christ. The central issue in this letter had to do with how much obedience was needed to merit salvation. The structure and content of Galatians show that Paul intended to answer questions like the following for his readers.

- How could God throw out the Mosaic Law and replace it with a gospel of grace?
- If God's grace through Christ was sufficient for salvation, what was the purpose of the law?
- Does a Christian not have to obey the Laws of Moses in order to be saved?
- How do faith in Christ and law-keeping go together?

Christians must struggle on two fronts. They must admit their tendencies to sin and thankfully acknowledge God's complete and rich forgiveness by faith in Christ alone. But they also need to evidence their saving faith with good actions and deeds. While doing this, it is very easy to fall into replacing honest acts of faith with works of law that are subtly motivated by the desire to gain favor with God. There is a conscious effort at times for believers to earn at least a piece of their own salvation by doing good and piling up merit. The struggle between humbly receiving and legalistically meriting God's grace can be complicated by God continually asking his people throughout Scripture to obey him. What are believers to make of God's continual commands to keep his laws. What does he have in mind? Must believers keep laws to gain his favor? Or do they keep his commands because they already have the full measure of his favor?

Galatians opens the way to understanding how faith and law-keeping go together. It shows believers how faith alone realizes the complete riches of God's grace in their lives. And, once believers are inside of God's grace, they fulfill the law's demands by reliance on the Spirit and through love (5:13-14). Galatians shows that obedience is given to God, not in order to merit his grace, but because by faith it has already been obtained. Galatians provides an important balance. It emphasizes the proper place of faith for salvation and the necessity of loving obedience to God as a response to that grace.

OUTLINE OF GALATIANS

A. INTRODUCTION: AUTHOR AND AUTHORITY (1:1-9)
   1. Greeting (1:1-5)
   2. The Problem of Another Gospel (1:6-9)
B. AUTHOR AND HIS AUTHORITATIVE MESSAGE (1:10–6:10)
   1. The Authority from a Revelation-Gospel (1:10–2:21)
   2. The Faith of Abraham: Primacy and Permanence (3:1–4:7)
   3. Personal Application and Exhortation (4:8-20)
   4. Freedom from the Yoke of Slavery (4:21–6:10)
C. THE FINAL EXPOSURE OF THE JUDAIZERS (6:11-18)
   1. Insights into Enemies (6:11-16)
   2. Final Warning and Benediction (6:17-18)

GALATIANS NOTES

1:1-9 INTRODUCTION: AUTHOR AND AUTHORITY
1:1-5 Greeting
1:1-2 COMMON IDENTIFICATION
Paul began this letter with an unusual description of himself. He described how he was commissioned as an apostle—not through men, but through Jesus and God. This immediately addressed one of the problems at hand. The Galatians apparently wondered if Paul was a divinely authorized apostle, or if he preached a merely human message. The term "apostle" (1:1) means "special representative." An apostle was commissioned and sent with authority to carry on a task. Paul emphasized that his apostleship did not originate from man, but from God. Along with these words defending his authority, Paul also stressed God's great resurrection power through Christ that was available for the believer's benefit (1:1). The "brothers" with Paul (1:2) would have included Barnabas, Paul's fellow missionary to Galatia, and other believers at Antioch (Acts 13:1).

1:3-5 BENEDICTION
Jesus Christ was characterized as the one who gave himself for all believers. He brought deliverance from this present evil age, and all that he did was done according to the will of God his Father. This set the foundation for Paul's arguments in this letter: (1) Paul was divinely authorized; (2) his message embodied the pure will of God; and (3) he spoke his message in an age of evil conflict.

1:6-9 The Problem of Another Gospel
Overview: This letter does not have the usual section of thanksgiving for the readers' spiritual growth. Instead, it plunges directly into the problem.

1:6-7 DESERTION FROM GOD
Paul used the word "astonished" (1:6) in an ironic way. The "quickly" (1:6) could be paraphrased "easily." Paul was not referring to the time since their conversion. He was amazed that they could slip so quickly and easily into the lies of another gospel. They had deserted a person, not a doctrine ("the

one," 1:6). The issue was personal. They had left the one who called them. Paul had described the context of their calling in 1:3-5. The Corinthians faced a similar temptation to follow another Jesus and a different gospel (1:6; cf. 2 Cor. 11:4). The word "deserting" is used elsewhere to describe a military revolt. This desertion was in process; it was not yet an accomplished fact. The two results of the problem among the Galatians were: (1) the believers were being troubled and (2) the true gospel was being distorted. These are two areas that Paul developed throughout the letter.

1:8-9 CURSING THE PREACHER OF ANOTHER GOSPEL
The source of the other gospel does not matter (1:8). Paul presented a hypothetical situation. The phrase "eternally condemned" (lit., "anathema") means "devoted to destruction" (cf. Josh. 6:17; 7:12). Paul was praying divine judgment on those who would pervert the truth. The repetition (1:9) was for emphasis. Paul had already given a previous warning about some who would present a different gospel. Paul's strong language shows the severity of the problem.

1:10–6:10 AUTHOR AND HIS AUTHORITATIVE MESSAGE
Overview: In this section Paul discussed why the gospel of Christ did not need the addition of the Mosaic Law for salvation. Paul built his argument on (1) his own firsthand revelation from God (1:1–2:21); (2) the priority of the promises to Abraham by faith over those to Moses through law (3:1-29); (3) the priority of Abrahamic sonship over the law (4:1–5:15); and (4) the priority of the way of the Spirit over the way of the law (5:16–6:10). Clearly, Paul's opponents in Galatia were urging Christians to conform to the Mosaic Law; a situation seen also in Acts 15:1.

1:10–2:21 The Authority from a Revelation-Gospel
1:10 NOT FOR PLEASING PEOPLE
Paul's critics accused him of being out to gain human approval at any cost. But Paul was out to please God, not other people.

1:11-17 NOT FOR SUPPLEMENT BY HUMANS
The gospel Paul preached came by revelation from God (1:11-12), not from men. That rev-

elation began with the vision of Christ near Damascus. Paul asserted that he received his gospel, not by fallible man, but as direct revelation from the risen Christ (Acts 9:1-9; 2 Cor. 12:1-11). Jesus Christ was both the source and subject of the revelation.

Paul's mention that he stayed away from Jerusalem reinforced his lack of need to supplement his revelation with insight from the leaders in Jerusalem (1:13-17). His gospel needed no human confirmation. The "traditions" (1:14) mentioned by Paul referred to the *Halachah,* the Jewish oral law that applied the written law to new circumstances. These laws were collected and now appear in the Jewish Talmud. God had set Paul apart for his ministry from birth (1:15). See Isaiah 49:1 and Jeremiah 1:5 for the same sense of calling.

After his conversion on the Damascus road (Acts 9:1-7), Paul did not immediately return to Jerusalem but traveled first to Arabia and then back to Damascus (Gal. 1:17). The visit to Arabia was not mentioned in Acts but probably took place between Acts 9:21 and 9:22. The term "Arabia" (1:17) probably refers to the kingdom of the Nabateans, a territory of Transjordan extending south from Damascus to the northwestern part of Arabia. During his time alone in Arabia, Paul was able to reorient his theology and understanding of the Old Testament Scriptures in light of his encounter with the risen Christ.

1:18–2:10 NEEDS NO ALTERATION BY HUMANS
1:18-24 A first short and polite meeting in Jerusalem. This account of Paul's travels reinforced the fact that he had authority independent of the Jerusalem leaders. This is in contrast with Paul's usual claim to close ties with Jerusalem (Rom. 15:25-27). He stayed away from Jerusalem for three years following his conversion (1:18). After his three-year absence, he returned once again to Jerusalem and had a brief visit with Peter and James, the half brother of Jesus. This visit to Jerusalem is dated around A.D. 37.

After this brief visit, he was still basically unknown in the Judean churches. But he brought glory to God anyway (1:24). The point was that Paul had virtually no contact with the Jerusalem leaders concerning the content or authority of his gospel message.

After his brief visit in Jerusalem, Paul traveled north through Syria and Cilicia to Tarsus, his hometown, where he remained until his call to Antioch (Acts 11:25-26).

2:1-10 A second visit to Jerusalem: no change required. Paul was in no rush to return to Jerusalem. He waited fourteen years and then returned to Jerusalem to "set before them the gospel" he had been preaching for so long (2:1-2).

This section of Galatians contains one of the historical puzzles of Paul's life. Was Paul recounting his famine relief visit to Jerusalem (Acts 11:29-30) or his experience at the Jerusalem Council (Acts 15)? Those who believe that Paul was writing believers in northern Galatia understand this as a reference to the Jerusalem Council. Those who believe that Paul was writing to believers in southern Galatia view this as a reference to the earlier famine relief visit.

There are at least two convincing evidences for the latter view: (1) Paul mentioned that it was "because of a revelation" that he went up to Jerusalem. This appears to refer to Agabus's vision of the forthcoming famine (Acts 11:28-30). (2) Had the Jerusalem Council already met, Paul would cer-tainly have appealed to their decision as a strong argument against those Judaizers who were advocating circumcision and the keep-ing of Jewish traditions. The point of Gala-tians 2:1-10 is that Paul had contact with the Jerusalem church, but they added nothing to his message. The Jerusalem church simply recognized and approved Paul's ministry to the Gentiles.

The "fourteen years" (2:1) dates from Paul's conversion (A.D. 35) until the autumn of A.D. 47. Actually, there are twelve complete years and a fraction of a year at the beginning and end of this period. The Jews regarded any portion of a time period as equivalent with the whole (see note on Matt. 12:39-40). The "revelation" (2:2) referred to Agabus's prophecy of a coming world famine (cf. Acts 11:27-29).

Paul recalled the case of Titus as a test case for Gentile salvation apart from circum-cision (2:3). He was building evidence for his claim that salvation was gained through faith in Christ alone, not by following the law. He showed how this true gospel was also upheld by the leaders in Jerusalem.

Paul also reported how the gospel had been distorted by false brothers (2:4-5). The implication was that the criticisms Paul faced in Jerusalem should not be entertained as possibly coming from God. The same false thoughts were apparently being pawned off as gospel in Galatian churches.

The gospel was not supplemented by the authorities or "pillars" of the church (2:6-10). The same God effectually worked in both Paul and Peter (2:8). Peter, James, and John recognized the God-given ministry of Paul and Barnabas (2:9). James was not the apostle (cf. Acts 12:2), but the half brother of the Lord and one of the leaders in the Jerusalem church (1:19).

2:11-21 PETER IS OPPOSED BY PAUL IN ANTIOCH

Having established that he was independent of Peter and the rest of the Jerusalem leaders, Paul showed his equality to them in God's power and authority. At this point, he recalled a time in which Peter failed to uphold the true gospel. First, Paul continued to demonstrate that he was not out to please men, not even the great Peter. Second, Peter was claimed as the great champion of Jewish Christianity (2:8). Paul showed that even Peter did not maintain strict orthodox separation from the Gentiles. When Peter did separate from the Gentiles, Paul corrected his hypocrisy (2:13-14). Paul viewed Peter's actions as inconsistent. Paul opposed Peter (2:11) because Peter twisted the implications of the gospel (2:14, "not acting in line"). The men from James were Jewish Christians from Jerusalem. Peter's hypocrisy had public consequences, and therefore the issue needed public clarification. Although Peter had not been teaching that Gentiles should adopt Jewish customs, his actions had implied that they should.

There was no other mention in the New Testament of Peter's visit to Antioch and his clash there with Paul. This probably took place after the famine relief visit (Acts 11:29-30; Gal. 2:1-10) and either before or just after Paul's first missionary journey (Acts 13:1; 14:26-28).

How were the Jews saved (2:15-16)? Paul referred to the Gentiles (from a Jewish perspective) as sinners, that is, unbelievers. Galatians 2:16 contains the key thought of this letter. Notice how many times Paul asserts here that a man is not justified (that is, declared righteous) by the works of the law. But Paul did not totally reject the law (2:17-19). He stated strongly that freedom from the law does not promote sin—"Absolutely not!" (2:17). Verse 2:18 explains 2:17. Those who had died to the law were not to try to live again to the law (cf. Rom. 6:1, 15).

Paul then made a transition to his debate in Galatians 3 (2:20-21). This debate concerned the relationship between faith and the law. The phrase "crucified with Christ" (2:20) means identified with Christ in his death (Rom. 6:3-8) and thus freed from the authority and penalty of the law. The fact of the resurrection implies a new life—a life in perfect righteousness. Since this is the case, Paul could not see why one would return to trying to keep the law to gain righteousness that is already achieved in Christ. Paul was alert to anything that might void the necessity that Christ die on the cross. To nullify the grace of God was to assert that Christ died needlessly (see Gal. 5:11; 6:12-14).

3:1–4:7 The Faith of Abraham: Primacy and Permanence

3:1-5 FAITH AS THE SOURCE OF SALVATION
Paul cried out to his addressees by name (3:1). Paul suggested that the Galatians had been "bewitched"—put under a spell. He forced the image of Christ on the cross into their minds to bring them back to their senses. Paul asked a series of pointed questions in 3:2-5 as he relied on the Spirit to convict them as they thought about their answers. It was foolish to begin the Christian life by faith and then revert to slavery to the law's demands (3:3).

3:6-9 ABRAHAM AND LAW:
SONSHIP BY FAITH
Paul built his arguments on the foundation of Old Testament Scripture, which when applied to the life of Christ, provided a sure support for faith. Note the key concept of promise in 3:14, 16, 21, 29. Notice that the gospel had been preached even to Abraham—the promise of God's redemption by faith. Paul appealed to Genesis 15:6 to show that even Abraham, the chief patriarch of the Jews, was reckoned righteous on the basis of faith (3:6). Those who share Abraham's faith are his spiritual descendants (3:7). Gentile justification by faith was not Paul's

innovation (3:8) but was anticipated long ago in Genesis 12:3. Gentiles may receive the blessing of justification by faith just as Abraham did.

3:10-14 SALVATION FROM THE
CURSE OF LAW
Having expounded the doctrine of justification by faith positively (3:6-9), Paul next presented the negative counterpart: the impossibility of justification by the law. In this section Paul compared lives lived by faith and lives lived by the law. Law is work-oriented, demands perfect obedience, and issues in a curse if even one commandment is broken (3:12-13). Faith is belief-oriented and conforms to the means of Abraham's blessing (3:14), bringing justification by grace (3:11).

Paul appealed to Deuteronomy 27:26 to show that those living under the principle of the law were also under the law's curse (3:10). Paul quoted Habakkuk 2:4 to show that the Old Testament itself taught that men are justified by faith (3:11). Paul appealed to Leviticus 18:5 to show that the law is antithetical to faith for it demands "doing," while faith involves receiving what Christ has done (3:12). Paul quoted Deuteronomy 21:23 as proof that Christ became a curse for believers (3:13). The hanging of a criminal indicates his accursed state.

3:15-18 THE PERMANENCE
OF RATIFIED FAITH
God's promise to Abraham is viewed from one perspective only—from the perspective of its fulfillment in Christ. No other person in the line (seed) of Abraham qualified as the bringer of promise. The promise stretches in an unbroken line from Abraham to its fulfillment in Christ. The next section develops how the law, which came in between Abraham and Christ, is to be understood. Israel was in bondage (3:17) for 430 years (cf. Exod. 12:40): from the time of Jacob's entrance into Egypt (c. 1876 B.C.) until the exodus (c. 1446 B.C.). The covenant was ratified to Jacob just before his departure for Egypt (Gen. 46:1-4).

3:19–4:7 REASONS FOR THE LAW
3:19-22 The law reveals mankind's sin. The curse of the law came because the principle of the law demanded perfection, something no human could attain. One sin brought a

curse on a person's life. The law trapped all people in sin (3:19-22). The law as an ethical standard existed before its codification at Sinai (cf. Gen. 18:19). But at Sinai the law was "added" as a contractual obligation with blessings promised for obedience and discipline promised for disobedience. The angelic involvement in the giving of the law is not fully explained in Scripture but is referred to elsewhere (Ps. 68:17; Acts 7:53; Heb. 2:2). Deuteronomy 33:2 mentions thousands of holy ones, probably angels, at the giving of the law at Mount Sinai.

If people cannot be justified before God by the law, then why did God institute it in the first place? Paul pointed out that the purpose of the law was to reveal sin (3:19) and lead people to Christ (3:22-25). A mediator, Moses, was needed because two parties were involved, the people of Israel and God. This made the Mosaic covenant conditional on human obedience—something that had failed up to that point in Scripture. But with the Abrahamic covenant there was no mediator bringing God and people into a conditional relationship. God alone was the one on whom the fulfillment of the conditions and promises rested (cf. Rom. 1:21-22).

3:23-29 The law leads to sonship in Christ. Paul used "before faith" (3:23) to refer to "faith in Jesus Christ" (3:22). Faith itself existed before Christ, as Paul's discussion of Abraham's faith emphasized. The image of the law "put in charge" (3:24) is of a slave in charge of his master's children. His job was to ensure the safe arrival of the children at school. So, the law is a child-minder to lead people to Christ, the Savior and Teacher.

Galatians 3:28 has been used by some to deny the biblical concept of role-relationships within ethnic, social, and gender groups. However, the focus here is on spiritual equality in Christ. Equality of spiritual position and privilege does not necessitate that there be identical secular or spiritual activity (cf. Eph. 5:22, 27; 6:1, 5). Even Gentiles could be Abraham's spiritual offspring and heirs of God's promise by faith in the person of Christ (3:29).

4:1-7 The law leads to sonship. In Galatians 3 Paul showed that faith was the only way of salvation from Abraham to Christ. In Galatians 4 he continued this thought by showing

that faith brings mature sonship and law brings slavery. It considers heirs (3:29; 4:1) as children and as adults to explain the progression of time from Moses (the child period) to Christ (the adult period, 4:7). The term *"Abba"* (4:7) is an Aramaic word for father. The term suggests both intimacy and reverence.

Paul answered the question of why the law was not binding as a contractual obligation as it had been on the Old Testament saints. The law's guardianship ended with Christ's coming. Believers in Christ enjoy the full status of sonship and are free from the legal limitations of slavery. Christ's redemption releases believers from the law's claim and confers on them the rights of sonship. In the first century, adoption meant that all old debts were cancelled and the adoptee started a new life as part of a new family (cf. note on Rom. 8:15).

4:8-20 Personal Application and Exhortation

4:8-11 CONCERNED APPLICATION
The Galatians were turning back to old ways (Gal. 4:8-9; cf. 4:3 with 4:9), and Paul feared his work among them had been in vain (4:10-11). What made it vain was the lack of the formation of Christ in their lives (4:19). The days, months, seasons, and years (4:10) refer to such Jewish celebrations as Sabbaths, new moon festivals, other religious festivals, and the year of Jubilee.

4:12-20 EXHORTATION TO MUTUALITY
4:12-15 Paul pleads for mutuality. Paul made it clear that he was not taking these ministry problems personally (4:12). The Galatians had not wronged him. Quite to the contrary, they had given much to him. Acts does not recount what Paul's bodily ailment was. Some have speculated that Paul contracted malaria in the lowlands around Perga and was compelled to go to the higher elevations of Pisidian Antioch in order to recover.

The reference to the Galatians' willingness to have "torn out" their eyes (4:15) has been interpreted by some to suggest that Paul had poor eyesight. Eyes are a priceless possession (Deut. 32:10; Ps. 17:8; Zech. 2:8). The expression suggests the Galatians' willingness to give up anything for Paul. But that original warmth toward Paul had now turned to hostility (4:16).

4:16-20 Desire for face-to-face ministry.
Does the truth make enemies? Yes (4:16).
A key statement about the false teachers in
Galatia is in 4:17. The false teachers desired
to alienate the Galatians from Paul and the
other true apostles. These teachers desired
to force the Galatians to rely on their false
instruction and help.

Paul called the Galatians to return to the
basic truths of the Christian faith (4:19-20).
The "tone" Paul desired to change (4:20)
pervades the entire book. It was a tone of
amazement and fatherly distress over children who were throwing away life itself.

4:21–6:10 Freedom from the Yoke of Slavery

4:21-31 FREEDOM BY SONSHIP

4:21-23 Past children of flesh and promise.
Here Paul vindicated his gospel by using an
Old Testament incident to contrast the
principle of law with the principle of grace.
Abra-ham had two sons—Isaac and
Ishmael—but only one (Isaac) inherited
God's promises to Abraham. Paul wanted the
believers to real-ize that they were spiritual
heirs of Abraham by faith and thus needed to
repudiate their bondage to the law.

*4:24-28 Present children of flesh and
promise.* Paul continued his image of two
covenants, the Abrahamic and the Mosaic
(4:24). He showed how the Mosaic Law was
for the immature and how faith in Christ
according to Abrahamic faith would set
believers free from sin and law. Galatians 3
reveals who Abraham's true sons are and the
temporal nature of law. Galatians 4 explains
the slave nature of the Ishmael line and its
conflict with Isaac's line. This can all be seen
under the concept of the "slave" and the
"heir" (3:29; 4:1, 7).

What did Paul mean by taking things
"figuratively" (4:24)? He was certainly not
suggesting that Genesis contains allegory,
not history. Nor was he interpreting the Old
Testament allegorically as did the Jewish
rabbis. Rather, he was appealing to a historical situation (Gen. 16–17; 21) that had application to the Galatian crisis. The value of
Paul's use of allegory was twofold: (1) Paul
defended the principle of grace from the Old
Testament, the chief authority of the Judaizers. (2) If the Judaizers were employing

allegorical methods of interpretation, Paul
answered them with their own method.

The two covenants represented by Ishmael
and Isaac were characterized as being "born
in the ordinary way" (according to flesh) and
being "born as the result of a promise" (4:23),
or by "the power of the Spirit" (4:29). The
mother of Ishmael, Hagar, represented
Mount Sinai, the Mosaic Law; and
Jerusalem, Judaism of Paul's day (4:24-25).
False teachers in Galatia were claiming the
necessity of obeying the law as was being
done in Jerusalem by the Orthodox Jews.
The other mother in the passage is the
"Jerusalem that is above" (4:26), a reference
to God's abode in the heavenly city that will
one day appear on earth (Rev. 21:2). In
Galatians 4:27 Paul cited Isaiah 54:1, which
describes the restoration of God's people.

4:29-31 Conflict between flesh and promise.
The conflict between flesh and promise
existed among the believers in Galatia (4:29-
31). Paul appealed to Genesis 21:10, 12 as
the basis for his command that the believers
abandon legalism (4:30). This directly condemned the false teachers as being according
to the flesh and persecuting the work of the
Spirit. But this was not only an attack on
false teachers. This also explained that persecution was not the Galatian believers' fault
and did not imply something was wrong with
them and their original faith in Christ. They
were not to change beliefs and start following the law in order to avoid persecution.
Their very beliefs showed that they were
right in the middle of God's truth. In fact,
Paul would show that this desire to avoid
persecution was the very reason why the
false teachers acted the way they did (6:12).

5:1 DIRECTION AND MAINTENANCE OF CHRIST'S WORK

Paul exhorted the Galatians to stand firm
in the liberty that Christ has provided. The
present imperative, "Stand firm" (5:1) could
be translated, "Keep on standing firm."

5:2-12 FREEDOM FROM LEGAL OBLIGATION

This section relates back to the two sections
on Abraham in Galatians 3–4. The discussion continues along the two lines, flesh and
Spirit, law and promise. Paul argued that
freedom was not found under the law. Paul
was not talking about losing one's salvation.

He was simply saying that turning to law was falling away from grace (5:4). This would amount to alienation from Christ. Falling into legalism was falling from grace. Paul used other terms to describe the fall from grace: "deserting" (1:6); "bewitched" (3:1); "attain . . . by human effort" (3:3); "burdened again by a yoke of slavery" (5:1).

The source of the wrong persuasion was not from God (5:7-11). Source determines authority, and Paul had already belabored the truth that the source of his authority was from God (1:1–2:10). The source of the Galatians' problems was human, not divine (5:8). God was calling them (5:8). On "yeast" (5:9; "leaven," NASB and KJV), see 1 Corinthians 5:6. The "offense" of the cross (5:11; "stumbling block," NASB) was exactly what the legalists wanted to avoid (6:12). Paul made a strong statement against the Judaizers. The verb "emasculate" (5:12) refers to castration or similar mutilation (cf. Deut. 23:1). Such physical mutilation for religious purposes was commonly practiced in the worship of Cybele, the Phrygian goddess of nature. Paul expressed his wish that those who advocated circumcision should go all the way.

5:13-15 A WIDENING OF SCOPE TO LOVE

The false teachers pressured the Christians to keep all of the law. Paul argued that this should be done through love, not by wrangling over legalistic applications of the law (5:13-15). Galatians 5:13 is central to the exhortations in 5:26 and 6:1-10 because it describes the problem that led to 5:26 and the exhortations in 6:1-10. These hostilities and interpersonal problems were linked to the debates over the false teachings.

5:16-26 FREEDOM FROM FLESH

The illustration of the two lines of Abraham—one flesh, the other Spirit—became an image that revealed the internal state of the believer. The same hostility between the flesh and Spirit takes place inside each believer. The false teachers said, "Obey the law." But Paul argued that this command always finds an impossible barrier in the flesh. Only the Spirit could overcome it, and the Spirit only comes through faith in Christ, not legalism. Paul urged his readers to have a faith/Spirit approach to life, not a law/flesh attitude.

The present imperative "live" (5:16) could be translated, "keep on living." By continually depending upon and yielding to God, the believer can live under the control of the Holy Spirit and does not need to carry out the desires that seek to hold sway over his physical body (the "flesh"). Paul recognized that there was a continual war going on between the physical flesh and the Holy Spirit to control the life of a believer (5:17). In light of the Galatian conflict over keeping the law, Paul was saying that walking by the Spirit is living by grace, not by law-keeping. It is living because of God's grace, not in order to gain it. Paul contrasted the acts of the sinful nature (5:19-21) with the fruit of the Spirit (5:22-23) in order to show that the way of the Spirit actually accomplishes the goals of the law.

6:1-5 MUTUAL FORGIVENESS

The conflicts over law had led to "conceit" and "envy" (5:26). The law did not inspire gentleness and the bearing of each other's burdens (6:1-2). Paul had to instruct them how to restore the power of the Spirit in their lives. The legalistic perspectives of the false teachers had no room for gentleness or restoration (4:17). They compared themselves to others (6:4; cf. 6:13) and were hindered by pride (6:3). This is the outcome of legalism—false pride and lack of compassion.

Paul dealt with the subject of church discipline (cf. Matt. 18:15-18). When a believer falls into sin, those who are spiritually mature should deal with the matter in a spirit of gentleness. The words "caught in a sin" (6:1) could mean (1) overtaken and surprised by the transgression; (2) surprised in the transgression, that is, caught "red-handed"; or (3) simply caught up in sin, with no refernce to being seen or caught by others. The word "restore" (6:1) was used for mending nets, setting bones, re-outfitting a ship for a voyage. It means "to restore to its former condition." While every Christian should bear his own part of the common load (6:5), believers should assist those excessively burdened.

6:6-10 FOCUSING ON THE GOOD THINGS IN LIFE

This section directly relates to the problems of the letter. False teachers were taking the support that was due true teachers. They caused the Galatians to distrust and not support the true representatives of God. The obligation of believers to support their teachers financially and materially was a frequent Pauline theme (cf. 1 Cor. 9:3-14; 2 Cor. 11:7-9; Phil. 4:10-19; 2 Thess. 3:7-9; 1 Tim. 5:17-18). While believers should be willing to help all those in need, there is a priority (6:10). Their first responsibility is to those of the Christian family of faith.

6:11-18 THE FINAL EXPOSURE OF THE JUDAIZERS
6:11-16 Insights into Enemies
6:11-13 ENEMY MOTIVES

The false teachers demanded that Christians be circumcised in order to avoid persecution from Jews; they argued that Paul's way was the way of needless persecution (6:12). Paul openly exposed the real motives of the opponents. They were full of pride in their adherence to the law, but were failures at their own game (6:13; cf. 6:4). Paul took the pen from the scribe and wrote the closing words of the epistle himself. The large letters mentioned by Paul served to authenticate to the believers that this letter was genuinely Pauline.

6:14-16 MOTIVE OF THE TRUE TEACHERS

Paul moved from the crucified Christ to the "new creation" (5:6; cf. 1 Cor. 7:19; 2 Cor. 5:17). For Paul to call Christians the "Israel of God" is his final blow against the Judaizers. Some believe that Paul was distinguishing two groups of believers in Galatians 6:16—believing Gentiles and Christian Jews ("the Israel of God"). Others hold that the translation "even" identifies the Gentile believers with the true (spiritual) Israel. It seems unlikely that Paul would distinguish two branches of Christianity in light of his remarks about the Gentiles being heirs of the promise by faith (cf. 3:7, 14, 29; 5:6; 6:15).

6:17-18 Final Warning and Benediction

Paul would stand for Christ to the point of suffering. The brand marks on Paul's body were the scars he had suffered as a result of persecution for the sake of Christ (6:17; cf. Acts 14:19). These were more impressive than the mark of circumcision that the Judaizers sought to impose. Paul ended his letter with its central theme: the grace of Christ.

Ephesians

BASIC FACTS

HISTORICAL SETTING

The words "in Ephesus" (1:1) are absent from the oldest Greek manuscripts. This may be accounted for in two ways: (1) The epistle may have been addressed to a single church but was later adapted to a general reading by the omission of the name, or (2) the epistle was originally written for general publication or for many churches, and one particular copy was addressed to the church at Ephesus.

Because Marcion knew this letter in the second century as *The Epistle to the Laodiceans,* copies of the letter may have been possessed originally by both Laodicea and Ephesus. The letter may have been intended to be read by a larger circle of Christian communities. Without the words "in Ephesus," the address reads "to the saints who are also faithful in Christ Jesus."

Paul first visited Ephesus on his second missionary journey (Acts 18:19). He also spent between two and three years of his third journey in Ephesus (Acts 19:8-10; 20:31). He left the city during a riot caused by silver craftsmen who felt their religion and trade were being threatened (Acts 19:24-28; 20:1). Paul later visited with the Ephesian elders at Miletus on his journey to Jerusalem (Acts 20:17-38).

The city ranked with Alexandria and Antioch of Syria as one of the most important cities of the eastern Mediterranean Roman world. It was a port city located on the Cayster River, three miles from the Aegean. It was an important city commercially as the starting place of a great overland trade route to the east.

Ephesus was the worship center of the Greek goddess Artemis (Diana in Latin). The temple of Artemis was 340 feet long, 160 feet wide, and richly decorated with 100 columns more than 55 feet high. The city was the guardian of the sacred image of Artemis, which was believed to have fallen from heaven (Acts 19:35).

AUTHOR

The Pauline authorship of Ephesians is attested both by internal and external evidence. Paul names himself twice in the letter (Eph. 1:1; 3:1). Pauline authorship was also attested by the early church fathers. Only in recent times have liberal critics

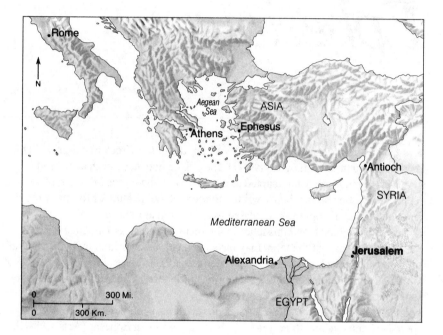

questioned Paul's authorship of the letter to the Ephesians. They conclude that someone other than Paul was the author because the letter addressed the Ephesians as if they did not know Paul (3:2), and it did not mention anyone by name except the person who delivered it (6:21). But the letter may have been written by Paul to be read in several cities in the area of Ephesus. The oldest manuscripts of the letter do not have the phrase "in Ephesus" (1:1) but do contain Paul as the named author. This would explain the general nature of the letter and still maintain Pauline authorship.

DATE
Ephesians is the first of Paul's Prison Epistles, the others being Philippians, Colossians, and Philemon (3:1; 4:1). Paul was in prison several times: Philippi (Acts 16:23); Jerusalem (Acts 23:18); Caesarea (Acts 23:33; 24:27; 25:14); and Rome (Acts 28:16, 20, 30). The imprisonments in Rome and Caesarea gave enough time for considerable correspondence. Since Paul anticipates in Philippians 1:19 and Philemon 1:22 his forthcoming release, and no such release was anticipated at Caesarea, it is most probable that Paul wrote the Prison Epistles, including Ephesians, during his first imprisonment at Rome, which lasted from A.D. 60 to 62.

PURPOSE
Paul's letter to the Ephesians was designed to deepen the walk of Christians who had no major spiritual problems. Paul sought to enlighten them by recounting the greatness of their past sins, God's great redemption, and the present power of the Spirit for waging victorious spiritual warfare.

GEOGRAPHY AND ITS IMPORTANCE

The City of Ephesus
Paul spent over two years in this strategic city. Ephesus was the largest city in the province of Asia, with a population of around 300,000 people. The city had the best seaport in Asia and was an important trade center. It also boasted a refined culture and a well-known religion that worshiped in a massive temple built to honor the goddess Artemis, a daughter of Zeus.

GUIDING CONCEPTS

PROBLEMS
Ephesians does not present the severe problems found in books like Romans or 1 Corinthians. But it does deal with critical problems for the Christian life. It is a book designed for those with a need for a deeper and more consistent fellowship with God and his people. Paul's desires for the Christians at Ephesus, that they might have wisdom and intimate knowledge of God (Eph. 1:17-19), reveal the weaknesses he was seeking to correct by this letter.

The readers needed to learn more of the racial unity brought through Christ (2:11-18; 3:4-10). They needed to provide a more settled place for Christ in their hearts (3:16-17). They needed to learn how to cope with suffering (3:13) without losing heart. They needed to discern truth from error concerning a walk that would please God (5:6, 15). And they needed to understand where strength for the struggle with the flesh is found (6:10). All these problems are summed up in Paul's first great prayer that their hearts would become more enlightened about God's salvation (1:18). They needed their inner darkness changed to light. The light will only come as the believers wake up and let Christ shine on them (5:14-15). Throughout the letter Paul sought to bring to fruition his prayer for the enlightenment of the Ephesians and all believers generally.

THE HEAVENLY REALMS

Paul mentioned the concept of the heavenly places throughout the letter. The concept involves the place of Christ's reign (1:20-21) at God's right hand, the place of the believers' exaltation with Christ (1:3; 2:6), and the place of the believers' conflict on earth (6:12). Therefore, believers should not think of themselves as being here and the heavenly places as being far distant. The heavenly places are a reality on earth, and believers find themselves in a spiritual realm where both God's exalted Son and spiritual forces of wickedness exist. The idea is not that wickedness and Christ exist in the same place, but that they exist in the realm of the spirit, not of flesh and blood. Christ can only be enjoyed and wickedness overcome in the realm of the spirit through the Holy Spirit (6:12).

BIBLE-WIDE CONCEPTS

THE BLESSINGS OF ONE SHARED WITH THE MANY

Throughout the Old Testament, human leaders like Moses, Joshua, the judges, David, or Solomon functioned as God's saviors of his people. But all along there was the expectation that one day God would send the perfect and final Savior, in whom his people would find victory and rest. Each individual human leader only expressed in part what the promised Messiah would achieve in full. The promise of victory through conflict (Gen. 3:15) would then find its fulfillment (Rom. 16:20). But the critical need at each point in God's history of salvation was that God be "in" his appointed leader, that is, that the leader be under the blessing of God working through him, whether he be Abraham, Moses, or David. God's victory only came to the individual believers through the blessings bestowed on their leaders.

In Ephesians Paul helped readers to understand that their victory could only come through being in Christ (see, for example, "in him" and "with him," 1:4, 7, 13; 2:6). The victory of believers over the flesh is also "in the Lord" (6:10), not in their own power. Christian victory is described in Old Testament terms. The notes will show that the Christian's victory is defined in Old Testament passages describing the Messiah.

THE BREAKDOWN OF RACIAL DISCRIMINATION

Paul labored to show that in Christ there were no walls between the Jew and non-Jew. He built his case around the Old Testament concept of peace taken from Isaiah 57:19, quoted in 2:17. Those who were historically distant from (the Gentiles) or near to (the Jews) God's covenants of promise (2:12) now had peace with God and each other—a peace forged by the single sacrifice of Christ (2:13) and the single

Spirit of God (2:18). Peace means a restoration of the original unity and wholeness God intended for all people in creation—a restoration now in the process of being fulfilled in Christ.

NEEDS MET BY EPHESIANS

The readers of this Ephesian letter were addressed as Gentile believers (2:11; 3:1). They had a number of needs that Paul sought to meet. They needed to have their hearts enlightened as to the greatness of their salvation (1:18). They needed to feel full participation in the redemption given through Christ and overcome the feeling that they were outsiders or second class compared to the Jewish believers. Finally, they needed to know more about living in the power of the Holy Spirit and fighting evil with the weapons of Christ. The letter to the Ephesians sought to shed God's light on spiritual darkness within the Christian. Paul wrote this letter to answer questions the Ephesians may have been asking.

- What steps should be taken by believers to deepen their appreciation of their salvation in Christ?
- What more do the Ephesian believers need to learn about Jesus Christ?
- How can Jews and non-Jews live together as brothers in Christ?
- What are some concrete signs that prove a believer is filled with the Spirit?
- How can believers learn how to have more victory in their Christian experience?

The letter to the Ephesians did not expose any particularly severe problems among its readers. They appeared to be doing very well in their Christian faith. But that was not good enough for Paul. He exhorted his readers to a deeper appreciation of Christ, an exhortation of great value in the lives of believers today. Paul announced that no matter what the level of a believer's Christian maturity, there was always more room for him to grow in Christ. Believers always need a deeper appreciation of the depths of God's love, more consistent application of God's universal salvation to all ethnic groups, and more experience of the wisdom and power of the Holy Spirit in inner spirituality and external warfare with evil.

OUTLINE OF EPHESIANS

A. GREETING (1:1-2)

B. THANKSGIVING (1:3-23)
1. Thanksgiving to God: Praise (1:3-14)
2. Thanksgiving for Humans: Petition (1:15-23)

C. REMEMBERING: PAST AND PRESENT (2:1-22)
1. Separation: Restoration (2:1-10)
2. Separation: Unification (2:11-22)

D. STRENGTHENING: PRESENT TRIBULATION (3:1-21)
1. Prison: Strengthening the Heart (3:1-13)
2. Prayer: Strengthening the Inner Person (3:14-19)
3. Praise: For Unrequested Power (3:20-21)

E. WALKING WORTHILY (4:1–6:9)
1. Gifted for Maturity (4:1-16)
2. Putting on the New Self (4:17-24)
3. Laying Aside Sins (4:25–5:14)
4. Wise Submission (5:15–6:9)
F. STANDING FIRMLY (6:10-20)
1. The Focus of Strength and Attack (6:10-12)
2. Alert and in Armor (6:13-20)
G. PAUL'S MESSENGER OF COMFORT: TYCHICUS (6:21-22)
H. BENEDICTION (6:23-24)

EPHESIANS NOTES

1:1-2 GREETING

Paul addressed his letter to the "faithful."
Thus the purpose of his letter was not to
correct flagrant disobedience. Paul desired
to teach the believers in Asia Minor about
seeking the deeper spiritual life. The words
"in Ephesus" are absent from the oldest
Greek manuscripts (see the Historical Setting
section).

1:3-23 THANKSGIVING

Overview: This section (1:3-23) is made up
of two sentences in Greek: the first in 1:3-14
and the second in 1:15-23. The first section
of the letter (1:1–3:21) has around sixteen
Greek sentences, while the second section of
the letter (4:1–6:24) is made up of around
forty-two Greek sentences. Paul's thoughts
in the first three chapters are expressed in
broader and grander scope than the short and
to-the-point statements of Ephesians 4–6.

1:3-14 Thanksgiving to God: Praise

Overview: This grand expression is made
up of three sections(1:3-6, 7-12, 13-14). The
first proclaims the believers' being chosen
by God for "sonship" (1:3-6). The second
describes the believers' redemption (1:7-12).
The third affirms the believers' present
pledge of the Spirit for future hope (1:13-14).
Each section ends with "to the praise of his
glory." Christ, the Son, is the central link in
the praise to the Father, Son, and Holy Spirit.
The spiritual blessings (1:3) stem from the
believers' Father/child relationship with God
(1:5) and their resultant inheritance (1:11, 14).

1:3-6 SPIRITUAL BLESSINGS: CHOSEN ONES

Paul brought praise to God for the blessings
he gives to believers in Christ (1:3). For
the "heavenly realms," see 1:20; 2:6; 3:10;
4:8; 6:12 (see also the Guiding Concepts
section). The riches promised to believers
in the heavenly realms throughout this letter
prepare them for a successful battle with
the forces of evil who are also part of the
"heavenly realms" (6:12).

Paul next introduced the foundation of
God's blessing: the fact that believers are
chosen by God (1:4-6). The spiritual blessings are described. God's choosing of believers is directly related to their holiness in
behavior (1:4). The doctrine of election ("he
chose us") must be balanced with man's
responsibility (cf. John 3:36) and undergirded
with the teaching that God is loving, sovereign, and just. "Predestined" (1:5) means to
mark out by boundaries beforehand. For
"adopted" (1:5), see note on Romans 8:15.
The words "to the praise of his glorious
grace" or "his glory" (1:6, 12, 14) reflect
the most important consideration in the
universe—the glory of God (cf. Isa. 43:7;
1 Cor. 10:31). The "One he loves" (1:6) is a
reference to Christ.

1:7-12 SPIRITUAL BLESSINGS: FORGIVEN BY GOD

Part of the spiritual blessing believers receive
is redemption through Christ's blood (1:7).
The focus here shifts from God the Father to
Christ and the present fact of redemption
through his work. The word "redemption"
(1:7) denotes release from a state of bondage

and servitude effected by the payment of a ransom. The word was used in the first century A.D. for purchasing a slave out of the marketplace and setting him free.

God not only paid the price for man's redemption, he also graciously made it known (1:8-9). The "mystery" (1:9) is the full gospel of Christ. This introduction prepares the reader for a further discussion in 3:1-12. A divine mystery is something not previously revealed and therefore unknown apart from divine revelation. Paul referred to the "mystery" in 3:6 as the union of believing Jews and Gentiles in one body in Christ.

The content of the mystery is the unity that can come through Christ and his gospel (1:10). Christ is the sum of all; he defines all thought, action, and rule. The corresponding result of the mystery is the redemption of all those who believe (1:11-12).

1:13-14 SPIRITUAL BLESSINGS: SEALED BY GOD
God seals believers with the mark of the Holy Spirit (1:13). The phrase "the promised Holy Spirit" sums up the Old Testament hope that God would send his Spirit for power and wisdom (see, for example, Num. 11:29; Ezek. 36:26-27; Joel 2:28-29; Acts 2:33; 1 Cor. 12:13). The sealing is elaborated in Ephesians 1:14. In ancient times the term "sealed" was used of an identifying mark, like a brand on a donkey, suggesting both possession and security. "Marked in him with a seal," believers are possessed by Christ and secure in him.

1:15-23 Thanksgiving for Humans: Petition

1:15-16 UNCEASING PRAYER
What's left after the great truths of Ephesians 1:3-14? Unceasing prayer (1:15-16). The words "For this reason" (1:15) refer back to the promises of 1:3-14. Paul's prayer (1:15-23) is based on what God has accomplished for the believer through Christ.

1:17-23 ENLIGHTENED HEART
Paul prays for the Ephesians' full knowledge of God (1:17). The knowledge comes by the enlightening of the heart as to God's hope, glory, and power (1:18-23). These truths are empowered by the resurrection and exaltation power of God (1:20-23). The resurrection and exaltation of Christ to God's right hand (cf. Acts. 2:33-35) have great

implications for the believer. They are the very center of the Christian's life and are foundational for all Paul says throughout the letter concerning Jew and Gentile relations and power for waging spiritual warfare. The church is Christ's body. In ancient times, being seated at someone's "right hand" (1:20) was regarded as being in a position of honor and influence (cf. Ps. 110:1).

2:1-22 REMEMBERING: PAST AND PRESENT
Overview: Ephesians 2 begins with Paul's answer to his prayer of 1:15-23 for the enlightenment of believers. His petition to God was complete, but Paul's advice continued and would serve as a part of God's answer to that prayer. Paul contrasted the believers' past lives of sin (2:1-3) with their new lives, raised up with Christ in the heavenly realms (2:4-10). Appreciation of God's grace always demands that believers begin with an awareness of their past sin. People most aware of their sin appreciate most their need for grace.

2:1-10 Separation: Restoration
Overview: Ephesians 2:1-10 is one long sentence in Greek.

2:1-3 OBJECTS OF GOD'S WRATH
Two kinds of "walk" are compared throughout the letter: (1) the dead person's walk in sin (2:1-3) and (2) the living person's walk in love (2:4-7; 5:1-2). Prior to regeneration, the Ephesians were spiritually dead (Rom. 5:12). The "ruler of the kingdom of the air" (2:2) refers to Satan (6:12; cf. John 12:31). The "disobedient" (2:2) are unbelievers who are characterized by disobedience.

2:4-7 EXALTED TO LIFE
Paul dredged up the dirt from the past only to show the grace of the present. The passage moves from "you were dead" (2:1) to "But . . . God" (2:4) to "Therefore, remember" (2:11) to "But now in Christ" (2:13). The past provides the context for the appreciation of the grace given by God in the present. When God's mercy meets mankind's deadness, his grace brings exalted life. Only that context of past sins can enlighten people's hearts to the wonderful power of God's present grace.

Salvation is based on God's attitude of mercy and motivated by his *agape* love

(2:4; cf. John 3:16). Ephesians 2:5 contains the solution to the state of spiritual death set forth in 2:1. The parenthesis "by grace you have been saved" is expanded in 2:8. The key word "seated" (2:6) indicates the believers' position in Christ as partakers of a finished, accomplished redemption. By virtue of the union of believers in Christ, they are positionally already in heaven. Christ's exaltation was their exaltation (2:6). The believers' deep need for grace will form the context for their eternal praise of God in the ages to come (2:7). They will remember their former need so that they can, with perfectly enlightened hearts, praise God.

2:8-10 SALVATION IS GOD'S GIFT
The "gift of God" (2:8) refers to the salvation promised to all who believe. To get the over-all thrust of this section, read 2:11 directly after 2:1-2. Salvation is provided through God's grace and received on the basis of faith in God's promise of forgiveness because of Christ's shed blood. Good works are also a gift (2:10) from the God who made all creation. While good works cannot save (2:9), they always accompany salvation and are the result and evidence of a genuine faith.

2:11-22 Separation: Unification
2:11-18 PEACE BETWEEN JEW AND GENTILE
In the rest of chapter 2, Paul expounded on the unity of mankind in Christ. He wrote first of the alienation of Jew and Gentile (2:11-12) and then of their reconciliation by the blood of Christ (2:13-16). He showed how believing Gentiles had entered into the family of believing Israel by faith, so that there was, as a result, one people of God united in the one body of Christ.

Paul used Isaiah 57:19 (quoted in 2:17) and Psalm 118:22 or Isaiah 28:16 (alluded to in 2:20) to show how Christ, as the corner-stone, brought those who were near and far together into one holy temple in the Spirit. The words "But now" (2:13) introduce a contrast with the Gentile's previous position (2:11-12). Christ brought peace (2:14) by joining the two groups into one. The "barrier" (2:14) is an allusion to the wall on the temple grounds that separated the court of the Gentiles from the court that only Jews

could enter. The death penalty would be inflicted if a Gentile passed that barrier. That wall of hostility had been broken down in Christ.

2:19-22 THE RESULTANT EFFECT
Both Gentiles and Jews are now members of God's household (2:19). On the contrast with "fellow citizens" (2:19), see 2:12. A "cornerstone" (2:20) provided the proper angles and perspective for a building's construction. It can refer to a stone in the foundation, the key-stone of an arch, or the capstone of a pyramid. It is the stone that brings unity and completion.

3:1-21 STRENGTHENING: PRESENT TRIBULATION
3:1-13 Prison: Strengthening the Heart
3:1-7 THE GIFT OF A MYSTERY
Paul was a prisoner on the readers' behalf (3:1). The thought is interrupted from 3:2-13 and resumes in 3:14. Paul wrote this epistle while he was a prisoner in Rome (Acts 28:16). Paul's "administration" (3:2) was the message of God's grace given to him as the apostle to the Gentiles (Gal. 2:7). Paul next began to develop the con-cept of "mystery" that he introduced in 1:9. Paul made no claim to be the sole recipient of this revelation (3:5). His digression on the place of the Gentiles in Christ stressed their equality in the mystery of Christ. The "mystery" (3:4) was not that Gentiles would someday be included in salvation. That had been known since Genesis 12:3 ("all nations"). The mystery centered on Gentile status as fellow "heirs" (3:6) to God's promises to the Jews. Note the three-fold repetition of "together" in 3:6 to drive the point of equality home. The mystery was not that Gentiles would receive spiri-tual blessing (cf. Joel 2:28; Amos 9:12), but that Jew and Gentile would be united on an equal basis in one body, sharing a spiritual inheritance in the promises of God.

3:8-13 A WORD ABOUT PAUL'S PURPOSE
Paul went on to point out that sufferings are a glory, not something to be avoided. In light of all that God had done for the believing Gentiles (3:2-12), Paul asked that they not let his problems cause them to lose heart. Instead he enlightened their

hearts to the glory hidden in tribulation. Paul also spoke of not losing heart in 2 Corinthians 4:1, 16.

3:14-19 Prayer:
Strengthening the Inner Person
The first section of the epistle (Eph. 1–3) concludes with the apostle's second prayer for the spiritual lives of the believers. He returned to the themes of power (3:18; cf. 1:19) and the importance of a Christ-indwelling heart (3:19; cf. 1:18). It takes the power of the Spirit to allow the unhindered dwelling of Christ in the heart. Sin is unsettling. To "grasp" (3:18) and "know" (3:19) the love of Christ could only come from the settled presence of Christ in the believers' lives. That fullness is the purpose of this letter regarding "enlightened hearts" (1:18).

3:20-21 Praise:
For Unrequested Power
Paul's praise of God and his power pushed the perspective of his readers beyond what they could ask and conceive—to the infinite capabilities of God's power. God can do far more with and through those who believe in him than those people can ask for or even think about.

4:1–6:9 WALKING WORTHILY
Overview: In Ephesians 1–3 Paul revealed the wonderful benefits of believing in Christ: the unity found in the Spirit, the heavenly dimension of the Christian walk, and edifying speech and behavior among believers. All of these characteristics were modeled by Paul, and at this point (4:1–6:9) Paul urged the readers to live out the benefits of salvation. Paul desired that the lives and "walk" of the believers would be worthy of their calling as Christians.

4:1-16 Gifted for Maturity
4:1-6 CALLED IN THE UNITY OF THE SPIRIT
This section is built around Christ's ascension (4:8), an event that marked the believers' ascension as well (2:6). Ephesians 4:1 introduces the exhortations that build on the doctrines set forth in chapters 1–3. The key word is "live" (4:1), a term used frequently by Paul to describe the believers' manner of life. Paul's main point was

that believers should conduct themselves in a manner worthy of their high calling in Christ.

The believers' high calling in Christ called for unity in the body of Christ (4:2-6). Believers were in fact united positionally through their spiritual bond in Christ. They needed to be diligent to maintain this unity (John 17:21), allowing its implications to be lived out in their lives. The unity demanded of Christians comes from the "Spirit through the bond of peace" (4:3). This builds on earlier words about the "Spirit," the divine seal of redemption (1:13-14), and "peace," that wholeness with humans and God bought by Christ's blood (2:13-14). The unity of believers is grounded on what they share in common through Christ. The "baptism" (4:5) referred to here is the baptism by the Holy Spirit into the body of Christ (1 Cor. 12:13).

4:7-8 VARIOUS GIFTS FOR THE UNITY OF THE FAITH
Paul used Psalm 68:18 to describe the resultant gift-giving of Christ's ascension. Here Paul discussed spiritual gifts—the abilities given by God for service in the Christian community (cf. 1 Cor. 12–14). Although there is unity in the body (4:1-6), there is a diversity of gifts given by Christ for the edification of the body (4:7, 11). Paul quoted and somewhat adapted Psalm 68:18 to show the biblical basis for the giving of spiritual gifts. There are two possible backgrounds for this quote: (1) A victorious warrior is elevated when he returns with a group of prisoners. Having received gifts from the conquered people, he distributes them to his followers. (2) The Levites were taken from among the Israelites as captives for God's service and given as gifts to Aaron to serve the priesthood (cf. Num. 8:6, 19). At Christ's exaltation (Acts 2:33) his gifts were spiritual. The point is that the believers needed to be enlightened concerning their experience of the Spirit. The grace they all experienced was a direct evidence of the gifts given by Christ.

4:9-10 CHRIST'S DESCENT AND ASCENT
Paul again presented Christ's humble life on earth, by which readers would better appreciate Christ's exaltation (John 3:13; 6:38; 16:28).

Christ's exaltation came after his time of humiliation, and the same will be true for his followers. This is the meaning of Paul's statement in 3:13.

The parenthetical comment in 4:9-10 on "he ascended" (4:8) was written to show that only Christ fits the description. Some interpret 4:9 as evidence of a descent into hell by Christ between his death and resurrection (cf. 1 Pet. 3:19-20). More likely, 4:9 simply refers to Christ's coming down from heaven to earth. He descended to the "lower" regions of the universe, that is, "the earth." The phrase is used in Isaiah 44:24 for the earth; Psalm 139:15 for the womb; Ezekiel 32:24 for the netherworld; and Psalm 63:9 for the grave. The point is, however, that Christ alone fits the description of one who both "descended" and "ascended." Thus, he is able to give gifts to men.

4:11-16 GIFTS THAT BRING MATURITY FOR STABLE GROWTH
These are the gifts of Christ (4:7, 8, 11, "gave"). The purpose of mentioning the gifts was to enlighten the readers to the value of the people mentioned in 4:11. They were literally Christ's gift to the church. Some hold that the terms "pastors" and "teachers" represent one gifted person, not two. Elsewhere, however, the ministries are separated (Rom. 12:7; 1 Pet. 5:2). Certainly a pastor should be able to teach (1 Tim. 3:2; 5:17), but there may be teachers in the church who do not function in the office or role of pastor. The purpose of these gifts is to equip the saints for ministry. The phrase "builds itself up" (4:16) is used in ancient medical literature of setting a bone. It has the idea of "making fit." The Ephesians were being told that the way out of cunning, craftiness, and deceitful scheming (4:14) is to benefit from Christ's gifts to the church.

4:17-24 Putting on the New Self
4:17-19 THE NEGATIVE ASPECT
Paul had prayed for the enlightenment of their hearts in 1:18. The related concepts here are "thinking" (4:17, 23, "minds"), "darkened understanding" and "hardness of heart" (4:18). One of Satan's goals is to so conform believers to the ways of the world that no one will know they are Christians. Paul described the believers' walk as

a different walk. He contrasted the conduct of Christians with that of unbelieving Gentiles (cf. also Matt. 6:7).

4:20-24 BEING RENEWED IN MIND
Paul made the contrasts between the old and new self and darkened and renewed minds. "Put off" (4:22, 25) means changing the "former manner of life" to a manner conforming to God's "righteousness and holiness" (4:24). That is only possible based on the prayers of 1:18-19 and 3:14-21.

4:25–5:14 Laying Aside Sins
4:25–5:2 SEPARATE FROM SINFUL DEEDS
Paul presented a contrast between the old and new manners of life. The new manner is directed in each case toward giving grace (4:29; cf. 4:7) to another person (4:25, "members"; 4:28, "need"; 4:29, "needs"; 4:32, "forgiving"). This is based on God's grace toward believers (4:32). They were to be appropriately angry over sin (4:26) like Paul was in 1 Corinthians 5:3-5, 12-13. But they were not to sin by not seeking to bring about forgiveness and restoration like the Corinthians did in 2 Corinthians 2:5-11. There is a place for a proper anger, that is, a righteous indignation, but one must be careful to avoid giving the devil opportunity. One of the ten commandments prohibited stealing (4:28; Exod. 20:15).

Paul warned against causing the Holy Spirit pain and sorrow through sin and a refusal to follow his leading (4:30). Christians grieve the Spirit when they do not "benefit" (4:29) themselves or others. Although the Spirit can be grieved by believers' sins, he will never abandon those who belong to him (Rom. 8:9).

As children imitate their earthly fathers, so believers are to imitate their heavenly Father (5:1), and 5:2 tells how. The exhortation of 5:2 could be translated, "Keep on walking in love." The words "fragrant offering" (5:2) look back to the sweet savor offerings of Leviticus 1–3, which prefigured Christ's voluntary sacrifice of himself.

5:3-14 SEPARATE FROM SINFUL PEOPLE
The "disobedient" (5:6) are unbelievers who are characterized by disobedience to God. Paul admonished the believers to walk in the light, a metaphor for a life of holiness. While spiritual darkness is the

realm of unbelievers, light is the realm of Christians (Col. 1:12-13; John 8:12; 12:35). Believers "expose" the things of darkness (5:11) by living differently (4:17-24), walking with God (1 John 1:7), being a light (Matt. 5:14-16), and rebuking sin (2 Tim. 3:16). Paul's quotes in Ephesians 5:14 were probably taken from Isaiah 26:19 and 60:1. This verse contains a sample of how one might reprove a sinner.

5:15–6:9 Wise Submission

Overview: The essential elements of a renewed walk as Paul presented them were: (1) unity in love, (2) gifts in proper use, (3) a renewed mind, (4) separation from sin, and (5) submission. It was the last one, submission, that Paul focused on in Ephesians 5:15–6:9.

5:15-17 IN LIGHT OF EVIL DAYS

Since the time is short and the days are evil, a Christian's use of time needs redeeming or he will use it as most do—for evil. "Making the most of every opportunity" (5:16; "Redeeming the time," KJV) means to "buy it back"—to use wisely the short time that believers do have (cf. John 9:4). This demands an understanding of what evil is in the first place and an understanding of God's will. From this knowledge should follow action; Christians should use their time pursuing that which avoids evil and works to fulfill God's will.

5:18-21 AS A RESULT OF FULLNESS

Paul had already shown that the Spirit's power was behind the Christians' victories (1:13-14; 1:19-21; 2:18; 3:16; 4:4, 30). Ephesus was a center for the cult of Dionysus (Greek, "Bacchus"), the god of wine. Celebrations in honor of Dionysus emphasized fertility, sex, and intoxication. Intoxication would allow Dionysus to control the body of the worshiper. Thus the worshiper would do the will of the deity. Paul was saying in 5:18, "Don't be filled with the spirit of Dionysus through wine, but be filled with the true and living God by his Spirit." Paul's key illustration of being wise was to be filled with the Spirit for all the behaviors he described in 5:19–6:9. Paul described that fullness in several ways: speaking and singing (5:19), thankfulness (5:20), and submission (5:21).

The last point, submission, receives detailed development (submission in marriage, 5:22-33; submission of children to parents, 6:1-4; submission of slaves to masters, 6:5-9). In each area of submission Paul was careful to exhort those commanding the submission to show love to those under them, not to abuse them (husbands, 5:25-33; fathers, 6:4; masters, 6:9).

This passage further explains what Paul meant by laying aside the old self and putting on the new self (4:22-25). The acts of speaking, thankfulness, and submission show what believers should "put on" in the fullness of the Spirit's power and intention for their "walk" with God in Christ. They are visible manifestations of the grace and power that belong to believers in the "heavenly realms." Paul desired that the believers wake up and, with enlightened hearts, realize the power for life that God has given (3:14-21). All Christians possess God's fullness through Christ (1:23).

In 5:21 many have thought that Paul was teaching the principle of mutual submission of all believers to each other. Rather, Paul enjoined believers to submit themselves to and obey rightful authorities. He then proceeded to give some specific examples of proper submission—wives to husbands, children to parents, slaves to masters (5:22–6:9)—examples that ought not be reversed.

5:22-24 FOCUSED ON WIVES AND HUSBANDS

The submission of the wife to her husband does not suggest inequality, for Christ was in submission to the Father but was also his equal (John 14:9; 17:22; 1 Cor. 11:3; Phil. 2:6-8). The relationship between the husband and wife is one governed by unselfish love, where both meet the needs of each other.

5:25-33 FOCUSED ON HUSBANDS AND WIVES

Husbands are to have a Christ-like passion to bring their wives into deeper purity and holiness before God. Christ's sacrificial love for the church is set forth as the pattern for the husband's love for his wife. Husbands ought to consider whether they are loving their wives according to this pattern. Paul quoted Genesis 2:24, the scriptural basis for marriage (5:31). There is a symbolic purpose in marriage (5:32). The union is designed to be a reflection of the relationship between Christ and his church.

6:1-4 FOCUSED ON CHILDREN AND PARENTS

Obedience to parents can amount to obedience to God (Exod. 20:12; cf. also Deut. 5:16). A child's obedience led to a long life. This was especially true in the Old Testament where disobedience leads to death (Exod. 21:15, 17). Paul also described the father's proper relationship to his children (6:4). Fathers are to be gentle and patient like the Lord and are to avoid provoking their children.

6:5-9 FOCUSED ON SLAVES AND MASTERS

The Bible does not advocate slavery but rather assumes it as part of the cultural setting. Slavery was not instituted by God but by sinful and fallen man. What God does through his word is to regulate this evil until such a time as it is recognized as morally wrong and is changed. What Paul emphasized is one's perspective on slavery (cf. Gal. 3:28; 1 Cor. 7:20-23). Paul's word of admonition to the masters is like his word to fathers in Ephesians 6:4. Paul added a command for seeing the position of master in perspective. Paul reminded them that slave and slave owner alike are servants to the Master in heaven.

6:10-20 STANDING FIRMLY
6:10-12 The Focus of Strength and Attack

What kind of armor is available to protect believers from the evil in this world? (cf. 6:14-20). The armor comes from the Lord and "his mighty power" (6:10). Paul called believers to arms so that they would be able to stand firm against the attacks of the devil. The God who calls believers to receive blessings in the "heavenly realms" (cf. 1:3) also provides armor for the struggle with evil in that same realm (see note on 1:3).

6:13-20 Alert and in Armor

Note the pervasive use of the Old Testament throughout this section: Isaiah 11:5 and 59:17 in 6:14; Isaiah 52:7 in 6:15; Psalm 7:10, 13 in 6:16; Isaiah 59:17 in 6:17; and Isaiah 49:2 in 6:17. These passages speak of God's great and promised redemption through his Messiah. The armor of God is not something the believers put on to fight on their own. The armor is Christ himself. Putting on the armor is equivalent to putting on Christ. The power of Christ is sufficient to stand against all evil and temptation that a believer will encounter.

Paul wrote this letter from Rome where he was under the custody of Roman soldiers (cf. Acts 28:16). Knowing that his readers would be familiar with the dress and armor of Roman soldiers, Paul used this imagery to communicate a spiritual message. Roman soldiers used a broad belt (6:14) to fasten their sword to their body. A soldier girded in such a manner would be recognized as being on active duty. Paul wanted believers to gird themselves with "truth," the foundation for all spiritual activity.

The soldier's breastplate (6:14), made of bronze scales or plates sewn on leather, protected his front and sometimes his back. Paul exhorted believers to find their protection in righteousness.

Roman soldiers prepared for battle by putting on sandals that had short nails in their soles (6:15). These enabled them to stand firm and avoid slipping on the ground. Paul wanted believers to prepare themselves for spiritual battle with the gospel of peace. The Old Testament allusion is to Isaiah 52:7.

Two types of shields were used by Roman soldiers: a large shield that protected the whole body and was carried by the infantry, and a smaller shield, made of wood overlaid with leather, which was carried by the archers (6:16). Paul wanted the believers to take up the shield that consists of faith. The "evil one" (6:16) is a reference to Satan himself.

In 6:17 Paul quoted Isaiah 59:17. The soldier's helmet, made of metal or leather, was designed to protect his head, the most vital part of the body. The "helmet of salvation" is the helmet that consists of salvation and protects the believer's spiritual destiny. The sword, a two-foot, double-edged blade, was the soldier's most important weapon. He was trained to stab instead of swing and cut. The "sword of the Spirit" is the only offensive weapon mentioned. It is supplied by the Holy Spirit and is identified as the utterance or spoken word of God (cf. Heb. 4:12). Although Paul was under house arrest during his Roman imprisonment (Acts 28:16), he was probably chained to a Roman soldier and had these images before him as he wrote this letter (Acts 28:20).

6:21-22 PAUL'S MESSENGER OF COMFORT: TYCHICUS

Tychicus apparently carried the letter to the readers in Ephesus and Asia Minor for Paul (6:21; Col. 4:7). Paul's report as to how he was doing was linked to his situation as an "ambassador in chains" (3:1; 4:1; 6:20). Paul, who was in a situation that most would consider difficult, was sending a letter and messenger to bring encouragement and comfort to the Ephesian Christians.

6:23-24 BENEDICTION

Paul wished that the Ephesians would have "love with faith" (6:23). The readers had faith, but they needed love with it. Paul's final benediction (6:24) summarized all the important elements of life in Christ.

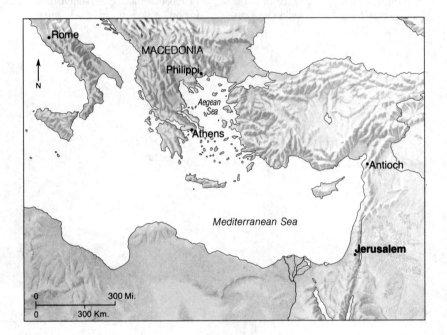

Philippians

BASIC FACTS

HISTORICAL SETTING

The readers of the letter are named in 1:1. Paul referred to them as "brothers" (3:13, 17; 4:1, 8). The Philippian church may have been largely a Gentile church because there was apparently no synagogue at Philippi when Paul first arrived there (Acts 16:13, 16).

The city of Philippi, named after Philip of Macedonia (the father of Alexander the Great), was strategically located on a fertile plain ten miles north of Neapolis, the city's nearest port. Through the plain passed the Egnatian Way, an important ancient highway that ran through Macedonia linking the Aegean and Adriatic Seas. Travelers to Rome would cross the Adriatic and continue up the boot of Italy on the Appian Way. The city was famous in antiquity for its gold deposits and became a Roman colony in 42 B.C. The city had a famous school of medicine and may have been the home of Luke or perhaps the place where he studied as a medical student.

Paul established the church in Philippi during his second missionary journey in A.D. 50 (Acts 16:11-40). Philippi was the first European city in which Paul preached, and Lydia was the first convert. Paul and Silas were imprisoned there and miraculously released. Some believe that Luke, previously a resident of Philippi, remained at Philippi to work among the churches of Macedonia while Paul went on to Thessalonica (Acts 17:1; 20:5). The Philippian church became a significant source of financial support for Paul (4:15-16; 2 Cor. 11:9).

The church at Philippi was around twelve years old when Paul wrote this letter. Epaphroditus had recently arrived to bring Paul some aid (2:25; 4:18). The immediate occasion of the letter was the return of Epaphroditus following his illness (2:25-30). This gave Paul an opportunity to commend his fellow worker and encourage the readers.

AUTHOR

The Pauline authorship is attested by internal and external evidence. Paul is named as the author (1:1). Although Timothy was also mentioned in the greeting, the use of the first person throughout the letter indicates that Paul alone was addressing the believers. The biographical references are distinctly Pauline (3:4-11; 4:10-16), and the entire letter bears the stamp of Pauline thought. Early church fathers such as Polycarp and Irenaeus support Paul's authorship of the Philippian letter.

DATE

Philippians is one of Paul's prison letters (1:7, 13, 17; cf. Ephesians, Colossians, and Philemon). For the possible location of Paul's imprisonment, see the Date section for Ephesians. A Roman imprisonment explains the references to the praetorian guard (1:13, "palace guard") and to Caesar's household (4:22). Because Paul anticipated his release (1:19; 2:24), the letter was probably written late in his first imprisonment, possibly during the spring of A.D. 62.

PURPOSE

The letter to the Philippians was designed to encourage joy and unity among the Christians there. It achieved this by exhibiting Paul's example of joy in Christ even during his imprisonment and by giving the supreme example of Christ's own humiliation and exaltation.

GEOGRAPHY AND ITS IMPORTANCE

The City of Philippi

Philippi was named by the father of Alexander the Great, Philip II, after he enlarged and renovated the city. In 42 B.C. Philippi was made into a Roman colony. The city was on the Egnatian Way, the major overland route to the west.

GUIDING CONCEPTS

STRUCTURE

The letter was designed to dispel any depression and discouragement surrounding Paul's imprisonment. It was no easy matter for Christians to accept persecution and imprisonment. Such treatment seemed to stand in stark contrast with the gospel of blessing and exaltation promised in Christ. It may have been a source of doubt among believers. They may have wondered if they had made the right choice in following Jesus into such persecution. Paul urged a divine perspective on suffering that leads from discouragement to rejoicing.

In this light, Paul showed how his prison sentence was really a cause for rejoicing (1:12-26), how the Philippians should live in the encouragement of Christ's model (1:27–2:18), how they should resist the pressures to conform to false doctrine (3:2-21), and how they should receive Paul's gratitude for their support in a balanced manner (4:10-20).

BIBLE-WIDE CONCEPTS

THE DAY OF CHRIST

Paul's desire was that the Philippian believers would be blameless in the day of Christ (1:6, 10; 2:16). That day was the broad time period of resurrection, evaluation, and reward for God's people (cf. also 1 Cor. 1:8; 5:5; 2 Cor. 1:14; 5:10;

1 Thess. 5:2; 2 Thess. 2:2). Jesus linked this day to his coming as the Son of Man. This involved the entire period of his second coming, a period of judgment and restoration mentioned throughout the Old Testament. The essence of this period is the process in which the faithful are rewarded, the rebellious are judged, and the eternal kingdom of God is established (broadly described in 1 Cor. 15:23-28). Only at that time would believers move from their period of groaning into resurrection glory (Rom. 8:23).

"GOD WITH US"

Paul's great joy and hope for victory was to have God with his people. Paul desired to have the joy of being with Christ in heaven (1:23; 3:20-21) and, before that, on earth (3:10-11). He desired for believers to have the God of peace with them (4:9) so that they could live lives of peace and joy no matter what the circumstances.

Ever since Adam and Eve were sent from God's presence in the Garden of Eden, humans had been longing for God to be with them once again. God's repeated promise to Abraham, "I am with you," hinted at a time of restored and unhindered divine presence. God dwelt with Israel in the tabernacle and temple, and through the Spirit, now dwells within Christian believers in a more intimate and complete way. The entire structure of Matthew's Gospel begins and ends with the fact of God being with the believers (Matt. 1:23; 28:20).

Paul's desire for God to be with the Philippians (4:9) echoed a theme prominent in the entire Old Testament by implying more than simple redemption. Yes, God had redeemed the Philippians, and his Spirit was indeed with them. But Paul was speaking of the experience of God's presence that comes from the "practice" (4:9) of truth, a firsthand experience of the sufferings and power of Christ (3:10; 4:13). God has always desired to be with his people firsthand in the difficulties of life.

HUMILIATION AND EXALTATION

Paul urged his readers to follow Christ's pattern of humility in order to attain a subsequent exaltation (2:8-9; 3:10-11). The order was always humiliation first, exaltation second. But some Christians lived as if they could skip the humiliation and go directly to the exaltation (1 Cor. 4:5-7). As a result of their faulty attitude, their suffering was a potential cause for alarm (1:28) and disunity (2:1-4; 3:17–4:3). But the pattern of the righteous sufferer who humbly waits in humiliation for God's timing of exaltation pervades the Old Testament and is perfected in Christ (cf. for example Mark 8:31; 9:31; 10:33-34; 1 Pet. 2:21-23; 4:12-19). The believers in Philippi were to follow this model.

NEEDS MET BY PHILIPPIANS

When Paul first came to Philippi, he was thrown into jail for casting a demon out of a slave girl who then could no longer tell people's fortunes and make money for her masters (Acts 16:11-40). Paul, with his companion Silas, then sang praises to God in the jail. As he wrote this letter to the Philippians, Paul was again suffering imprisonment, but this time in Rome. He called the Philippians to rejoice even as he suffered imprisonment. Persecution against Paul was a potential cause of discouragement for the Philippians. But Paul presented them with a new way of looking at suffering. He showed them that it could be the grounds, not for discouragement, but for rejoicing. The structure and content of Philippians reveal that Paul intended to answer the following questions for his readers.

- Has Paul's arrest stopped the progress of the gospel?
- How is Paul feeling during his imprisonment in Rome?
- Is he discouraged and depressed because he cannot be out preaching?
- How does he feel about those preaching the gospel from envy and strife?
- How does he maintain a positive attitude about Christ?
- How does Christ's humble earthly life and final heavenly exaltation relate to peace and unity among Christians?

The readers needed to understand the significance of Christ's experience of suffering for their own experiences of persecution. Only then would they be able to experience the significance of Christ's exaltation in their own eventual reward. The Philippians needed to understand that their blessed position before God did not make them immune to pain and suffering. To think that suffering was a sign of some defect with themselves or God would open them up to the very discouragement and bickering Paul was trying to get them to avoid. In that light, the Philippians needed to be reminded that the pleasure of knowing Christ was not diminished by circumstances—a difficult truth to accept during times of persecution. Paul showed the Philippians how to live in joy and in peace with each other no matter what the circumstances.

OUTLINE OF PHILIPPIANS

A. GREETING (1:1-2)

B. THANKSGIVING: PARTICIPATION IN THE GOSPEL (1:3-11)
1. Mutual Participation (1:3-8)
2. Prayer for Fullness in the Day of Christ (1:9-11)

C. FROM PRISON: OBEY AND REJOICE (1:12–2:30)
1. Release: For Joy and Progress (1:12-26)
2. Exhortations to Joy and Progress: Unity (1:27–2:18)
3. Mutual Joy by Messenger (2:19-30)

D. EXHORTATIONS TO FOLLOW GODLY PATTERNS (3:1–4:1)
1. Beware of Fleshly Boasting (3:1-16)
2. Focus on Good Patterns (3:17–4:1)

E. FROM PHILIPPI: REPORTS FROM EPAPHRODITUS (4:2-20)
1. Helps for Standing Firm (4:2-9)
2. Rejoicing for the Offering (4:10-20)

F. FINAL GREETINGS AND BENEDICTION (4:21-23)

PHILIPPIANS NOTES

1:1-2 GREETING

The greeting is friendly and casual. Paul does not call himself an apostle but links himself equally with Timothy. Paul had no need to defend his apostolic authority as he did when writing to some of the other churches (cf. Rom. 1:1; 1 Cor. 1:1; 2 Cor. 1:1; Gal. 1:1). While Paul is clearly the author of the epistle (3:4-11; 4:10-16), Timothy was Paul's amanuensis and cofounder of the church at Philippi (Acts 16:1-4). For the terms "overseers" and "deacons," see the notes on 1 Timothy 3:1, 8. Paul singled out the leadership to emphasize the responsibilities they had in being good examples to those who followed them (2:29; 3:17).

1:3-11 THANKSGIVING: PARTICIPATION IN THE GOSPEL

1:3-8 Mutual Participation

The focus of Paul's thanksgiving was mutual fellowship in the gospel ("partnership," 1:5; "partakers," 1:7). Paul thanked God for the Philippians' partnership in the progress of the gospel. The word "partnership" (koinonia) refers to what is shared in common, in this case, a joint ministry in the gospel of grace.

Paul's confidence was in God's continual work (1:6). The words "chains," "defending," and "confirming" were courtroom terms that reflected Paul's circumstances in Rome (1:7; cf. Acts 28:16, 20).

Paul longed for fellowship with the Philippians in Christ (1:8). Prison did not depress Paul into a "me-centered" wallowing. His longings still conformed to his Lord's desires for the Philippians' perfection (1:9-11). The longings of Paul's heart (1:7) matched those of Christ. Prison did not deflect Paul's desire to know Christ or to make him known (3:8).

1:9-11 Prayer for Fullness in the Day of Christ

Paul prayed that the Philippians would abound with love (1:9). But that love needed to be channeled "in knowledge and depth of insight." They needed to find discerning ways to exercise love and righteousness. The elements of real knowledge brought out in the letter are knowledge of Paul's own circumstances as causes of rejoicing rather

than being depressed (1:12); standing firm rather than alarmed by opponents (1:27-28); being of one mind in the face of selfishness and conceit (2:1-4); putting confidence in Christ when pressured to put confidence in the flesh (3:2-4); standing firm in the face of disharmony (4:1); and knowing how to face circumstances of prosperity as well as need (4:10-13)—a return to the first perspective on Paul's prison circumstances. Throughout the letter Paul taught knowledge and discernment for choices and action that would produce love. On the "day of Christ" (1:10), see the Bible-Wide Concepts for this book.

1:12–2:30 FROM PRISON: OBEY AND REJOICE

1:12-26 Release: For Joy and Progress

1:12-14 CIRCUMSTANCES SPREAD THE GOSPEL

Paul's joy and success were not based on where he was but on how effectively Christ was being proclaimed, again the emphasis of 3:10. Paul related how his circumstances had turned out for the greater progress of the gospel. Rather than thwarting the proclamation of the gospel, his imprisonment actually advanced the cause of Christ. The word "advance" (1:12) was used in ancient times of a pioneer cutting his way through the brush. The "palace guard" (1:13; "praetorian guard," NASB) was an elite corp of Roman soldiers that functioned as the imperial palace guard. They were responsible for prisoners who had appealed to the emperor. They heard the gospel when they were on duty guarding Paul.

1:15-26 DELIVERANCE FOR EXALTING CHRIST

1:15-17 Two attitudes regarding the gospel. Even in the face of bad motives for preaching Christ, Paul found good in the situation (1:18). To the discerning, the success of ministry transcended personality. While some were preaching Christ out of love, others were motivated by selfishness. They apparently wanted to outdo Paul's evangelistic ministry while his activity was limited by his imprisonment. Paul disagreed with their motives as believers today sometimes disagree with different methods of spreading the gospel. But Paul's one concern was: Is Christ being proclaimed?

1:18-26 Confidence in future release. Paul did not imply that his "deliverance" (1:19) would be from prison. He was ready to die (1:20). He meant continued deliverance from distress (1:17) and any hindrance to the proclamation of Christ (1:18). He was confident that he would be able to continue to exalt Christ (1:20). Release from prison would be desired only for the benefit of ministry (1:25-26). Paul allowed that he might remain absent (1:27), possibly permanently (2:17). For Paul, Christ was the one who gave meaning and significance to his existence. His life was wrapped up in Christ—witnessing, fellowshiping, and serving. Christ was the focal point and culmination of Paul's life experience.

Paul was confident that he would be delivered for the profit of the Philippians (1:22-26). Life for Christ (1:21) was a life given over to others (1:24). This reference (1:26) provides a clue as to Paul's travel plans. He anticipated a visit with the Philippians after his release from Roman imprisonment.

1:27–2:18 Exhortations to Joy and Progress: Unity

1:27-30 UNITY OF SPIRIT AND MIND
The Philippians' unity of spirit and firm standing in the face of their opponents was a sign of God's blessing on them and his displeasure of their opponents. Opposition to the gospel would result in ultimate divine judgment, while being persecuted was an indication of being among the redeemed (John 15:18-25). The believers were to resist the idea that questioned God's care and control. This potential idea and lapse of faith was the major problem Paul sought to avert in his letter.

Philippi was a Roman colony, and the people there were recognized as Roman citizens with the same legal position and privileges as those living in Rome itself. But they also had certain obligations and responsibilities—loyalty to the emperor and obedience to the law. Likewise, believers are citizens of heaven (3:20), and with that citizenship they also have obligations. Paul explained that believers were responsible as citizens of

heaven to conduct themselves in a manner worthy of the gospel that they represented.

2:1-11 UNITY: MAINTAINED BY HUMILITY
2:1-4 Paul's exhortation. Paul presented the one who exemplified perfect love and who exercised it with true knowledge and discernment: Christ. Paul focused on the mind (2:1-2) and on the mind's tendencies during times of need and trouble. Paul's exhortation in this passage is in keeping with Christ's prayer for unity among believers (John 17:21-23). The four "if"s of Philipians 2:1 represent conditions that are assumed as true and could be translated "since." The first verse sets forth the grounds for the believers' unity in Christ (2:2).

Apparently some believers at Philippi were characterized by vain conceit and selfish ambition (2:3-4). They thought more highly of themselves than they ought to have and neglected their responsibility to serve others (cf. John 13:1-17). Humility ("lowliness of mind") might be defined as a proper evaluation of oneself in the sight of God and others (2:3; cf. Rom. 12:3; 1 Pet. 3:8; 5:6).

2:5-11 The example of Christ. The best example Paul could use to exemplify the qualities demanded by his exhortation (2:1-4) was the person of Jesus Christ (2:5-11). Christ emptied himself in order to be filled up with obedience. The emphasis was on the two modes of Christ's existence: the first in divine glory and splendor, the second as humble servant. Paul presented the supreme illustration of humility: Christ's example of sacrificing himself for others. Although in his preincarnate state Jesus possessed the essential qualities of God, he did not regard his status of divine equality a prize to be selfishly hoarded (2:6). The word "nature" (2:6) refers to "appearance backed up by reality." Christ is of the same nature and essence as God.

There are various interpretations regarding what Christ actually did in becoming a man (2:7): (1) he emptied himself of some aspect of his deity (cf. James 1:17; Mal. 3:6); (2) he veiled his glory (cf. John 17:5; Matt. 17:1-2); (3) he laid aside the independent exercise of some of his attributes (Acts 10:38; Matt. 24:36); (4) he received the form of a servant and became a man. The last view is most commended by the context.

Christ lost nothing in his incarnation. He simply received the essential nature of a man and became a servant.

The result ("Therefore," 2:9) of Christ's humiliation was exaltation (2:9-11). Paul made free use of Isaiah 45:23 (cf. Isa. 45:21-25), making it a universal and Christ-centered statement. The purpose of Christ's exaltation was to secure for him universal worship. All will someday acknowledge his lordship (cf. Rev. 5:13). The words "Jesus Christ is Lord" (2:11) probably reflect an early creed of the Christians. But Jesus' exaltation is mentioned not as a hope for the believer's own future glorification. Rather, it is mentioned to cause the believer in the present to bow and confess Christ's authority in times of prosperity or opposition. In this context, Paul was recognizing Christ's authority to command humility and unity of mind among believers.

2:12-18 UNITY: THE FRUIT OF OBEDIENCE
2:12-13 Obedience and salvation. Paul's "presence" or "absence" (2:12) is linked to Philippians 1:27. Paul's emphasis in these verses was on "fear and trembling," not "work out your salvation." This fact is evidenced in Paul's emphasis on the awesome glory of the exalted Lord and the presence of the Creator in the following verse (2:13). Paul was not advocating salvation by works in contradiction to Ephesians 2:8. There are three aspects of the believer's salvation: (1) past (justification), (2) present (sanctification), and (3) future (glorification). Paul was speaking of the present aspect of salvation: deliverance from the troubles the believer faces, such as complaining and arguing mentioned in the very next verse (2:14). God works in the believer, supplying the will to obey and then helping him do the things that please God.

2:14-18 Exhortations. Paul gave these commands only after he mentioned that believers are given the ability to do them. Each act of disobedience to Christ's lordship makes ministry in his name vain and meaningless (2:16). Paul employed the language of Jewish offerings to illustrate his sacrificial service and ministry to the Philippians (2:17). Paul viewed his life as a drink offering, or wine libation. Such an offering normally accompanied the burnt and peace

offerings (Num. 15:1-10; 28:7) and was mentioned with the daily offering (Exod. 29:40-41). Verses 2:17-18 link Paul's exhortations (2:14-18) to his words about Timothy and Epaphroditus (2:19-30). Even if Paul might not be able to come to them, he would try to send Timothy as a middleman to minister to them.

2:19-30 Mutual Joy by Messenger
2:19-24 TIMOTHY
Timothy would function as a reporter to Paul (2:19) and as a helper to the Philippians (2:20-21; cf. 1:17). He was a tested worker (2:22-24). Paul planned to send Timothy to Philippi immediately and hoped that he would be able to visit the believers himself. This reference provides an indication of Paul's travel itinerary after his departure from Rome.

2:25-30 EPAPHRODITUS
Epaphroditus had been sent from Philippi with a gift for the apostle Paul (2:25; cf. 4:18). After delivering the gift, he had remained to minister to Paul. While in Rome, Epaphroditus became very ill and was delayed from returning to Philippi. His illness was not described, but it caused both Paul and the Philippians much concern. Paul regarded Epaphroditus highly because he followed Christ's pattern of humble service to the truth. Epaphroditus had done for Paul what the Philippians had not been able do for him because of their distance.

3:1–4:1 EXHORTATIONS TO FOLLOW GODLY PATTERNS
3:1-16 Beware of Fleshly Boasting
3:1-6 CONFIDENCE IN HUMAN ACHIEVEMENT GAINED
3:1 Rejoice in the Lord! The Lord alone is the focus of rejoicing (3:1). This rejoicing is inseparably linked to the avoidance of evil (3:2). The focus is on the Lord, not self-interest. The word "finally" (3:1) is an indication of an impending conclusion. Paul did not hesitate to repeat himself.

3:2-3 True worship. A continual temptation for believers is to work for the advancement of self, not the Lord (cf. 1:17). Paul was referring here to the Judaizers and described them from three points of view. As to their character, they were "dogs" (3:2), a term used by Jews for Gentiles. As to their conduct, they did "evil." As to their creed, they advocated "circumcision" as a vital part of Christianity and necessary for salvation. Paul contrasted true circumcision and the false circumcision advocated by the Judaizers (3:3). Paul made it clear that true circumcision was not of the flesh, but of the heart (cf. Rom. 2:25-29). The true Jews are Abraham's descendants by faith, not by the flesh.

3:4-6 Confidence in the flesh. To illustrate the sufficiency of faith-righteousness apart from legalistic Judaism, Paul set forth his previous grounds for confidence—his Hebrew heritage and Pharisaic practices. Paul had been a Pharisee of great status. He brought up this fact to show that status and self-motivated achievement can indeed be gained. But Paul gave up these achievements that seemed great in the world's eyes and in return gained real knowledge and discernment. Everything he once thought worthwhile he now considered "loss for the sake of Christ" (3:7).

3:7-16 CONFIDENCE IN HUMAN
ACHIEVEMENT REPLACED BY CHRIST
3:7-11 Knowing Christ. Paul "considered" all that was to his "profit" (2:7), the righteousness he could claim as a Pharisee, to be worthless (3:7-8). See the same concept in 2:6, where Christ "did not consider" his nature as God "something to be grasped." Paul wanted to know Christ (3:8, 10; cf. 1:9, "knowledge and depth of insight"; 2:13, "works . . . according to his good pleasure"; and 1:11 "the fruit of righteousness"). While it would be natural to be proud of his Jewish heritage and attainments, Paul counted it all loss (worse than useless) for the greater gain of knowing Christ. Paul gave up Judaism to gain a righteousness based on faith (3:9), a knowledge of Christ and his resurrection (3:10), a sharing with Christ in his sufferings (3:10), a likeness to his death (3:10), and a participation in the resurrection (3:11).

3:12-14 Pressing on. In this section Paul was referring to the moral and spiritual perfection spoken of in 3:8-10, not the resurrection of 3:11. Paul forgot the past, Christian and non-Christian, because his goal was continual present-tense obedience that yields the knowledge of Christ. Each new moment is fresh and powerful for gaining the fruit of righteousness. Paul used the image of a runner with hopes of winning the prize stretching for the finish line to describe his Christian walk.

3:15-16 The mature attitude. The mature person is able to understand Paul's perspective on humility, rejoicing in difficult circumstances and desiring to know Christ afresh each day. Paul suggested that if the Philippians did not agree with him, God would assuredly correct their views.

3:17–4:1 Focus on Good Patterns
3:17-19 THE BAD PATTERNS
Paul and the leaders (1:1), Timothy and Epaphroditus, were good models contrasted with their opponents. Paul exhorted the Philippians to join with one another in imitating him.

3:20–4:1 THE PATTERN OF CHRIST
The end of the enemies of the cross (3:19) is contrasted with the end of the Christian (3:20-21). All believers share in Christ's past humble state (3:21; 2:7-8) but will also share in his exalted state (3:21; 2:9). Although they lived on earth, the Philippian believers were also citizens of heaven. The Philippians would immediately grasp Paul's point. As Roman citizens living in the outpost of Philippi, a Roman colony, they were entitled to the same rights and privileges as those living in Rome. In the same way, Christians, who were citizens of heaven, lived on earth with all the rights and responsibilities of heaven's citizens.

The word "therefore" (4:1) looks back across the previous verses and sums up the entire letter. In view of their heavenly citizenship and future transformation, believers are to be steadfast and are not to defect from their faith (cf. 3:2-3).

4:2-20 FROM PHILIPPI: REPORTS FROM EPAPHRODITUS
4:2-9 Helps for Standing Firm
4:2-3 RESTORE HARMONY
Disharmony in the church is often a by-product of personal conflicts, so Paul directed the readers to the matter of inner joy and peace. The comrade Paul addressed here, although possibly Epaphroditus, was not identified. The book of life records

the names of the redeemed (cf. Exod. 32:32-33; Rev. 3:5; 13:8; 20:12).

4:4-7 REQUEST FROM GOD: PEACE
Rejoicing is linked to "gentleness" (4:4-5; "forbearing spirit," NASB). Gentleness and forbearance issue from knowing the truth regarding this world and the next; this is real knowledge and discernment (1:9-10). The imperative could be translated, "Keep on rejoicing" (4:4). The return of the Lord serves as a motivation for gentleness and forbearance.

Paul called believers to have peace in all circumstances (4:6-7). On anxiety or worry (4:6), see Matthew 6:25, 27-28, 31, 33-34. Worry implies that God is not present. To pray with thanksgiving shows a spirit of humble submissiveness. God does not promise to answer all the prayers of believers. But he does promise peace. The word "guard" (4:7) is a military term meaning "to keep under guard as with a garrison."

4:8-9 DWELL AND DO: PEACE
Right thinking is the first step toward righteous living (4:8). But thinking, learning, receiving, and hearing demand practice (4:9) if one desires to experience the God of peace.

4:10-20 Rejoicing for the Offering

4:10-14 THANKSGIVING FOR THE GIFT
This can sound like a thankless thanksgiving for their gift. Paul essentially said that he was quite content without their gift; he did not need it. But Paul was not being thankless. He was making a crucial point. His thanks arose, not because the gift had moved him from discontent to contentment, but because the

Philippians had done a compassionate and good deed (4:14) that brought them profit before God (4:17-18). Paul did not want them to think he was emotionally or spiritually deprived without their gift. Lack of freedom or lack of goods was not critical for Paul's contentment or joy. His contentment came from inward self-sufficiency in Christ (1:21; 4:13), not from outward circumstances. Paul was saying, "I can do all things through the one who continually empowers me" (see 2:13 for the power of God working within the believer). While this verse is applied to many situations, the immediate context indicates that Paul was acknowledging God's enablement to find contentment in all circumstances, in plenty or in poverty.

4:15-20 THE VALUE OF THE GIFT: FRUIT
The Philippians sent more than one gift while Paul was ministering in Thessalonica (Acts 17:1-10). This suggests that he stayed there longer than just three weeks (cf. Acts 17:2; 2 Thess. 3:8). God promises to meet all the "needs" of believers, not necessarily all their "wants" (4:19; Ps. 34:10; Prov. 10:3; Matt. 6:25-34; Rom. 8:32). Paul gave the perspective of discernment. Their gift to Paul was in reality a gift to God.

4:21-23 FINAL GREETINGS AND BENEDICTION

"Caesar's household" (4:22) probably referred to slaves or employees in the emperor's palace rather than members of the imperial family. There is no evidence of Christians within the family of Nero (A.D. 54–68) who ruled at this time.

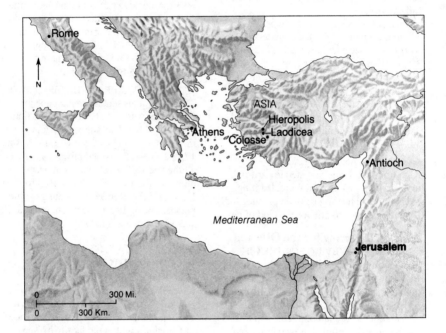

Colossians

BASIC FACTS

HISTORICAL SETTING

The Christians at Colosse were mostly Gentiles. Paul seemed to equate "among the Gentiles" and "in you" in 1:27. Later, he classed them among the uncircumcised, (2:13) indicating a Gentile origin. Paul also intended that the Laodiceans read this letter (4:16).

Colosse was located in the Lycus Valley about 120 miles east of Ephesus. The Lycus Valley, branching off from the Neander River, served as the natural gateway to Lydia and Phrygia, placing Colosse on an important trade route. Colosse's sister cities, Laodicea and Hierapolis, were located about ten miles northwest of Colosse.

The Greek historian Herodotus mentioned Colosse as a place of strategic importance. The city may have found its origin as a military base. The chief article of commerce, for which the city was well known, was *colossinus,* a peculiar wool that was somewhat purple in color.

There was a distinctive Jewish element at Colosse, but the majority of the citizens were Gentiles. The gospel was introduced to Colosse as a result of Paul's long and influential ministry at Ephesus (Acts 19:10, 26; 4:12-13). Epaphras, who brought the news of the church to Paul in Rome, may have been influential in bringing the gospel to Colosse (Col. 1:7-8). Archippus was also actively ministering there (Col. 4:17; Philem. 1:2). From all indications, it appears that Paul had not visited Colosse before he wrote to the believers there, and many in Colosse had not met Paul (2:1).

The occasion of the letter was the arrival of Epaphras from Colosse (1:7-9; 4:12) with the information about the growth of the church in witness and love (1:3-8). But opponents had come into the area as Paul had predicted (Acts 20:29) and were presenting false doctrine.

That false doctrine combined two main elements. The first was drawn from Old Testament ordinances of the Mosaic covenant (Col. 2:8, 11, 16), human traditions (2:8) and the worship of angels (2:18). The second was drawn from a philosophy that claimed special privileged knowledge and insight into the nature of the universe (2:4, 8, 18). The result of that doctrine was to demean the completeness and sufficiency of the nature and work of Christ.

Paul's response stressed Christ as Creator and head over the church (1:16-18); the source of all wisdom and knowledge (2:3-4); the fullness of the Deity and head over all authority (2:9-10); and the only source of hope for future resurrection glory (3:1-4). All believers, who are Christ's body, are connected to Christ, their head (2:19). They are to seek after heavenly things (3:1-2), put on the new self (3:9-10), and let the word of Christ dwell in them richly (3:16).

AUTHOR

Pauline authorship is clearly indicated by 1:1 and 4:18. The use of the first person throughout (1:24; 2:1, 4; 4:4) and the personal tone of the letter (1:7, 9; 3:18-21; 4:7-18) support Pauline authorship. The autobiographical material intertwined with the argument of the book (1:24-25, 29; 2:1; 4:18) and the similarity of Colossians with Paul's other letters bring additional support to his authorship.

DATE

Colossians is one of Paul's Prision Epistles. For a discussion of the possible location of his imprisonment, see the Date section for Ephesians. The Roman location has the strongest support. Also, Luke's use of "we" in Acts 28:16 indicates that he was in Rome with Paul, a fact mentioned in Colossians 4:14 as well. The letter was probably written in A.D. 62.

PURPOSE

The letter to the Colossians was designed to help the readers understand that there was no power greater than Christ. Paul did this by showing how Christ is responsible for maintaining the entire universe, redeeming the world, and overseeing his church. Thoughts and activities based on anything less than Christ's supremacy were to be corrected and conformed to his truth.

GEOGRAPHY AND ITS IMPORTANCE

The City of Colosse

Originally on a main road running eastward from Ephesus, Colosse diminished in importance when the road was moved westward through Laodicea. Paul had not been to this city when he wrote Colossians, but his influence probably reached the city during his long stay in Ephesus.

GUIDING CONCEPTS

Throughout the letter Paul confronts two problems that had arisen in the Colossian church. The first was a combining of legalism with Christianity. The second was an incorporation of mystical philosophies with Christianity. Both issues are compared and contrasted with the character and works of Christ.

Now that Christ had been exalted to the right hand of God (3:1; Acts 2:33-35), all things were reconciled to Christ and had to be evaluated according to his wisdom. Paul stressed that Christ alone was now the measurement of knowledge and wisdom (Col. 2:3). The believer was raised with Christ (2:12; 3:1) and shared in his exalted wisdom. The believer was moved from hostility to peace. And that peace through reconciliation (1:20; 3:15) was the source of wisdom for the Christian in speaking (1:28; 3:16) and witnessing to unbelievers (4:5).

BIBLE-WIDE CONCEPTS

CREATION AND KINGDOM

Paul presented a black and white contrast between the kingdoms of light and darkness (1:13). From Genesis 3 onward God's history of redemption involved moving people from the darkness of Satan's kingdom to the light of Christ's. In Christ, believers could live and work for the kingdom of God (Col. 4:11).

But Christ was not one source of power and wisdom among many. Paul identified the exalted Christ as the Creator of the universe (1:16-17). Throughout the Old Testament creation and wisdom were closely related. God's creation was very good (Gen. 1:31). So to follow the natural laws set up in God's creation was to follow the way of wisdom (Prov. 8:22-36). The wisdom and knowledge found in Christ were not simply one mortal's ideas but expressions of the very imagination and knowledge that conceived and created the universe.

THE NEW COVENANT AND THE HIDDEN KINGDOM

One problem with living in Christ's present kingdom was the fact that it is hidden. The treasures of wisdom and knowledge were hidden in Christ (2:2-3). Christ was in the believer (1:25-27) and the believer's life and Christ himself were hidden in God (3:3). The mighty power at work in the believer (1:29) came from this hidden spiritual source.

But the hidden nature of the kingdom and God's covenant had long been predicted. Jeremiah had spoken of a new covenant by which God's commands would be placed in the heart (Jer. 31:33; quoted in Heb. 8:10). Ezekiel further revealed that the power to keep those commands would come from the Spirit placed within the believer (Ezek. 36:27).

To be sure, the kingdom of God would someday be visible for all to see (Col. 3:4). But Jesus inaugurated a time period where the kingdom would be present but hidden. In his parables he compared the kingdom to a small seed or yeast hidden in a loaf of bread (Matt. 13:31-33). That hidden but potent existence of Christ's kingdom tempted some to look for more obvious outward manifestations of religion and wisdom (Col. 2:23). For others the hidden nature of the kingdom was a cause of groaning and eager expectation (Rom. 8:23). But Paul drove his readers back to the long-standing descriptions of the hidden kingdom of God in the Old Testament as fulfilled by Christ. Paul reminded his readers that though God's kingdom was hidden, it was still present, providing a basis for stability and hope.

NEEDS MET BY COLOSSIANS

The Colossians needed to be convinced that Christ was the supreme and final Mediator between God and mankind. No other heavenly or earthly being was to control the lives of believers. Therefore, worrying about right days or right foods to appease unseen angels was actually an insult to Christ's supremacy. Life was not to be seen as an intricate maze of angelic powers through which only those initiated in secret wisdom could navigate. Life was simple, a negotiation of daily events with Christ alone. But the Colossians were faced with a conflict of authority between Christ and the non-Christians. The Colossians were tempted to treat Christ's teachings as debatable and subject to being compared and modified with other positions. Paul argued the absolute superiority and completeness of Christ and his wisdom. The structure and content of Colossians show that Paul intended to answer the following questions for his readers.

- Can believers draw from both Christ and other sources for spiritual wisdom and knowledge?
- How does Christ compare with other voices of religious authority?
- How can believers tell if a suggested religious behavior is good or not?
- How can believers know which authority figures should be listened to?

The Colossians faced problems quite like those faced by believers today. People are seeking answers to questions about how the spiritual world works. What spirit beings live in heaven? How do they move between earth and heaven? Do they ever communicate with people? How might they influence the lives of people? Continual interest in fortune-telling, seances, and astrology confirms the world's desire to see more clearly into the unseen spirit world. People want to feel more in control of their lives and destinies, to have more insight and direction in winding their way through the seen and unseen elements of life. But to that need Colossians clearly presents two facts. First, believers are not to concern themselves with understanding or submitting to whatever angelic orders of rank and authority that may exist. Second, believers are better off submitting to Christ's control of their lives rather than seeking to control their own lives. Christ alone is perfectly capable of guiding believers safely through life, a life that he sovereignly designed and will sovereignly accomplish.

OUTLINE OF COLOSSIANS

A. INTRODUCTION: CHRIST AS SOVEREIGN AND PEACE (1:1-23)
  1. Greeting (1:1-2)
  2. Thanksgiving (1:3-8)
  3. Petition (1:9-23)

B. CORRECTIONS AGAINST DIMINISHING CHRIST (1:24–4:6)
  1. The Purpose of Apostolic Concern (1:24–2:5)
  2. The Fact of Continual Completeness (2:6–3:4)
  3. The Acts of Reckoned Completeness (3:5–4:6)

C. CONCLUSION: NEWS ABOUT THE MINISTERS (4:7-18)
1. Sharers of the News (4:7-9)
2. Closing Greetings (4:10-17)
3. Benediction (4:18)

COLOSSIANS NOTES

1:1-23 INTRODUCTION: CHRIST AS SOVEREIGN AND PEACE
1:1-2 Greeting
This is a standard Pauline greeting (cf. Rom. 1:1; 1 Cor. 1:1; Gal. 1:1; Eph. 1:1). Timothy, Paul's faithful associate, was with the apostle when he penned this letter.

1:3-8 Thanksgiving
Colossians 1:3-8 is one sentence in the Greek. Paul's gratitude to God for the Colossian believers is expressed in the three graces that he bestowed upon them: their faith, love, and hope (1:4-5). Paul's global perspective (1:6, 23) reveals the global power and scope of God's work in the gospel. The Christian faith was not just a localized religious cult. Paul needed to establish this to combat the Colossians' tendency to see Christianity as just another religion.

The gospel had been communicated to the Colossians by a faithful minister (1:7-8). The gospel message reached Colosse through Paul's coworker Epaphras, who apparently planted and organized the church. Epaphras is the only coworker of Paul designated a fellow bond-servant. While Epaphras had undoubtedly reported to Paul in Rome concerning the errors threatening the believers, he also told of the love fostered in their hearts by the Holy Spirit.

1:9-23 Petition
1:9-12 WALK WORTHILY OF GOD
This petition comprises two long thoughts (1:9-20 and 1:21-23). Paul desired that their walk match the worth of the Lord (1:9-12). They had understood the gospel (1:6). Now they needed to deepen their knowledge of his wise will, a will that is spiritual and unseen. Paul's unceasing prayer for the believers was that they might attain a full knowledge of God's will. He made a subtle contrast between the partial knowledge advocated by the false teachers and full

knowledge that is available in Christ. The result of being filled with knowledge is practical, a worthy life (1:10; cf. Eph. 4:1) accomplished in the power of God (Col. 1:11).

The thanksgiving of 1:12 is for complete and present qualification to share in salvation. This was foundational for arguing against the opponents who implied that such qualification had to be earned by progressively gaining knowledge. Light and dark symbolize the kingdoms of God and Satan. Believers have moved from darkness to light under the same God who moved the original creation from dark chaos to enlightened goodness.

1:13-17 WALK IN A MIGHTY REDEEMER
The Father's deliverance and the Son's reign are central for the Colossians' understanding and wisdom regarding their walk. Believers have been delivered from Satan's domain of darkness (Eph. 2:2) and brought into the kingdom of God's beloved Son (1:13). As those who have submitted to Christ the King, believers are in Christ's kingdom now, though the full realization of this fact is yet future (Rev. 20). The Son is the means of redemption (1:14). Redemption speaks of a release from slavery based on the payment of the purchase price or ransom.

Paul continued the letter by emphasizing the priority of the Son's creation (1:15-17). Christ is the Creator and Sustainer of all creation. The primary characteristic of the Colossian error was a deficient view of Christ and his work. Rather than attacking the Colossian error outright, Paul wisely began by setting forth the person and work of Christ and the believers' completeness in him. The word "image" (1:15) means "archetype," like the stamp that makes the impression on a coin. Christ is the one on whom the Father has set his mark. The word "firstborn" (1:15) may have a temporal (first of many to come) or a positional (chief heir) emphasis.

Here the emphasis is on primacy of position. The Colossians thought that angels had similar authority to Christ. But Paul showed that even the levels of angelic authority were under Christ's sovereign power. Paul's use of "thrones or powers or rulers or authorities" (1:16) may appear to refer to human authorities. But in this context these words refer to unseen angelic powers, as other Pauline passages confirm (e.g., 2:15; Eph. 1:21; 3:10; 6:12).

1:18-23 LIVE UNDER CHRIST'S RECONCILING HEADSHIP
The progression of thought is from Christ as the image of God (1:15), to his rank in creation (1:16-17), to his rank in the church (1:18). His rank in the church comes from his fullness of deity (1:19). Paul declared that all the "fullness" of God (1:19) dwells in Christ. The word "fullness" was apparently used by the false teachers at Colosse (and in later Gnosticism) to denote the divine nature distributed among numerous intermediaries between God and the world. Paul insisted that Christ alone embodies the full measure of deity. Reconciliation and peace can come only through him (1:20; 3:15).

Paul applied the fact of God's reconciliation with man to the lives of all believers and declared himself a servant of that truth (1:21-23). The "if" (1:23) does not cast doubt on the security of truly saved people (John 10:28) but stresses the fact that the proof of the genuineness of the believers' salvation is their continuance in faith and hope.

1:24–4:6 CORRECTIONS AGAINST DIMINISHING CHRIST
1:24–2:5 The Purpose of Apostolic Concern
1:24-29 INTRODUCTION OF PAUL'S MINISTRY
Paul's goal was the completion of the Colossian believers in Christ (1:28). This goal led him into sufferings which, rightly seen, were the completion of Christ's sufferings. But Paul was not completing the vicarious suffering of Christ for sin (Heb. 9:28). Because of the unity between Christ and the church, Paul's sufferings for the sake of the church could be called Christ's sufferings as well.

Paul was the servant of a mystery that had been disclosed through the person and work

of Christ (1:25-29). The exalted Creator (1:16-17) and head of the church (1:18) had revealed himself and lived within all the believers (1:27). That truth was an assault on those who implied that Christians needed knowledge and rituals to supplement the revelation of truth through Christ (2:4). Paul labored for their maturity (1:28-29).

2:1-5 APPLICATION OF PAUL'S MINISTRY
The city of Laodicea (2:1; see note on Rev. 3:14) was located in the Lycus Valley about ten miles northwest of Colosse. Paul was concerned that the Colossians would be deceived by the persuasive arguments of the false teachers. He admonished them to continue to live focused on Christ rather than pursuing less stable and speculative theories. Since in Christ the believer has the treasures of wisdom and knowledge, there is no reason to pursue philosophical speculation (Col. 2:3). The "persuasive argument" (2:4) is elaborated in 2:16-23.

2:6–3:4 The Fact of Continual Completeness
2:6-15 INITIAL COMPLETENESS
The Christians needed nothing else but to continue on in faith. The second step was the same as the first ("just as" they had received, so they should live). There was not a switch from the first step of faith to some supposed second step of legalistic or mystical ritual (2:23). Paul used two metaphors to describe the relationship of believers with Christ. Like a firmly rooted tree (2:7), they were grounded in the truth of Christ. Like a house with a solid foundation (2:7), they were founded on their faith in Christ and were continually being built up in him.

To avoid being led astray by "deceptive philosophy," Paul emphasized the need to be deeply rooted in Christ (2:8-15). Two ways of living are identified: according to the world or according to Christ (2:8). Paul warned the believers against getting sidetracked by persuasive arguments and speculative theories. He emphasized that Christ alone is sufficient for salvation and spiritual growth. "Philosophy" (2:8) means "love of wisdom" and refers here to any system of thought that does not recognize the centrality of Christ. The problem with philosophy is that it has no basis of authority other than man's reason. Paul used the vocabulary of the false teachers to show how Christ epitomizes all they hoped to find in philosophy.

Paul continued by giving reasons for living according to Christ (2:9-15). Christ has the fullness of deity (2:9) and believers can find fullness or completeness in him (2:10) and live above all lesser rule and authority. The results are freedom from human judges and hollow rituals (2:16, 20). Spiritual circumcision (2:11) takes place when a believer is identified with Christ through personal faith.

Paul reminded the believers that they once stood as debtors, condemned because of the law (Eph. 2:15; Gal. 3:10). But Christ fulfilled the requirements of the law (Matt. 5:17) and by his death liberated believers from its condemnation (Col. 2:14). He erased the legal ordinances that condemned, nailing the document that was against believers to the cross. Not only was the debt of sins cancelled, but Satan's forces were conquered and humiliated through the cross (2:15). Paul drew on the imagery of a triumphant Roman procession where the victorious general and his troops led captives and captured booty in public display through the city streets. Similarly, Christ defeated Satan and led him in triumph through his resurrection.

2:16-19 CONTINUED COMPLETENESS
Believers are not subject to any authority and judgment except Christ's. "Eat and drink" referred to the ceremonial food laws observed by the Jews (Lev. 11); "festival" referred to the Jewish holy convocations (Lev. 16); "New Moon" referred to a minor festival that was observed monthly (1 Sam. 20:5; Isa. 1:13); and "Sabbath" referred to the law of Sabbath keeping (Exod. 20:8). These ceremonies were to be regarded by Christians as shadows of the realities now available in Christ. Their observance could not add to or subtract from the believers' completeness in Christ (2:17). The opponents were motivated by selfish pride (2:18-19).

2:20–3:4 CONTINUAL FOCUS ON CHRIST
Paul was describing man-made religion in any form. It could not overcome fleshly or sensual indulgence (2:23). Paul warned against asceticism, self-denial as a means of gaining acceptance by God. All human decrees and prohibitions have the appearance of wisdom but are of no eternal significance apart from the knowledge of God.

The man-made facade of glory (2:23) is not to blind believers as to where their true glory resides, hidden in God (3:4). This glory will be revealed when Christ is revealed. Paul instructed the believers to set their affections on things above, things consistent with one's position in Christ, not the things that were earthly and had no eternal significance. Believers are to become in experience what they already are in Christ positionally.

3:5–4:6 The Acts of Reckoned Completeness

3:5-17 PUTTING ON THE NEW SELF
Paul revealed the absolute deity and authority of Christ and affirmed that Christ resides in the believers, making them complete and above man-made religious efforts. Next he gave specific examples of conduct worthy of the Christians' salvation.

Paul showed that believers should be dead to old ways and alive to the new (3:5-14). With the "therefore" (3:5) Paul made a transition from doctrine (1:1–3:4) to practice (3:5–4:6). (Paul made such a transition in most of his other letters as well.) The doctrine of Christ and the believers' completeness in him provides the basis for a discussion of proper Christian conduct. In the face of temptations that might lead to sin, Paul used a striking image of viewing the body as dead to sin. How the believers' death with Christ works out in practice is explained by more images in the following verses: "rid yourselves" (3:8; "put . . . aside," NASB; "put off," KJV); "taken off" (3:9; "laid aside," NASB; "put off," KJV); "clothe yourselves" (3:12; "put on," NASB and KJV); "let . . . peace . . . rule" (3:15); and "let . . . Christ . . . dwell" (3:15-16).

The "old self" (3:9) refers, not to the unregenerate nature, but to the flesh's disposition to follow physical desires and leave God out of the picture. The "new self" (3:10) refers to the disposition created in the believer by the Holy Spirit to obey God and live consistently with his spiritual inheritance. Paul exhorted the believers to put on new virtues that were more consistent with their new nature in Christ.

Christ's rule of peace (3:15) pulls believers together in unity (cf. 1:15-18). When differences threaten the unity of the body, the peace of Christ must be accepted as arbitrator. This peace was defined by Christ's words (3:16-17). This section has close parallels with Ephesians 5:18 where submission in marriage, family, and work flowed from the fullness of the Spirit. Here, the same groups were addressed from the perspective of the rich indwelling of Christ's word (3:16). Christ's teachings are to "dwell" in the believer. The context suggests that this may be accomplished through teaching, admonition, and singing. One's reputation is usually associated with one's "name" (3:17). Paul was saying that believers' activities ought to be consistent with the reputation of Christ. Could they participate in this activity in association with Jesus' reputation (cf. 1 Cor. 10:31)?

3:18–4:1 SPECIFIC RELATIONSHIPS
Note the motivations for keeping these commands (3:18, 20-25). This section is closely parallel to Ephesians 5:21–6:9. Here Paul illustrated how the principles of Christian living may be expressed in everyday affairs. For submission (3:18), see note on Ephesians 5:22. For slavery (3:22), see note on Ephesians 6:5-9.

4:2-6 SPEECH PATTERNS
On the subject of prayer (4:2-4), see Ephesians 6:18-20. Paul recognized the power and potential available through prayer (Phil. 4:6-7; 1 Thess. 5:17). Here he exhorted the believers to continue steadfastly in prayer. For Paul's imprisonment in Rome (4:3), see Acts 28:16, 23, 30-31.

Wisdom to outsiders (4:5) is the context for seasoned speech (4:6). The believer's speech is to be gracious and "seasoned with salt" (4:6). In the context of speech, "salt" was referred to as a metaphor for "wit." Here Paul was probably referring to speech that is "appetizing," a witness to unbelievers that is well prepared and focused on the individual needs of each person.

4:7-18 CONCLUSION: NEWS ABOUT THE MINISTERS
4:7-9 Sharers of the News
Tychicus (4:7; cf. Acts 20:4; Eph. 6:21; 2 Tim. 4:12; Titus 3:12) apparently carried this epistle to the church at Colosse. Onesimus (4:9), Philemon's runaway slave, accompanied Tychicus back to Colosse (cf. Philem. 1:10).

4:10-17 Closing Greetings
Many of the names mentioned in Paul's greetings are also mentioned elsewhere. Aristarchus (4:10; cf. Acts 19:29; 20:1-4; 27:2; Philem. 1:23-24) may have shared Paul's imprisonment on a voluntary basis, perhaps passing as his servant. John Mark (Acts 13:13; 15:36-40; 2 Tim. 4:11; Philem. 1:24), author of the second Gospel, having been restored to Paul's favor, was to be welcomed at Colosse should he travel there. Jesus, also called Justus (4:11), is not mentioned elsewhere. Epaphras (4:12-13; 1:7-8; Philem. 1:23) was influential in bringing the gospel to Colosse. Laodicea and Hierapolis were located in the Lycus Valley about ten miles northwest of Colosse. Luke (4:14; cf. 2 Tim. 4:11; Philem. 1:24), the author of Acts and the third Gospel, is referred to by Paul as "our dear friend." Demas (2 Tim. 4:10; Philem. 1:24) was a helper who defected.

With his greetings Paul included circulation instructions (4:15-16). Paul not only greeted the Laodicean believers (cf. Rev. 3:14) but asked that this letter be shared with them and that his letter to Laodicea be read to the Colossians. Some take it that the letter from Laodicea was the encyclical letter now known as Ephesians (see note on Eph. 1:1). The church met at Nympha's (or Nymphas; masculine) house (cf. Acts 12:12; Rom. 16:5, 23). It wasn't until the third century that separate buildings were used for church worship.

Archippus (4:17), Paul's fellow worker (Philem. 1:2), was actively ministering in Colosse. Paul encouraged him to give this letter his full attention.

4:18 Benediction
Paul's greeting with his own hand confirms the genuineness of the epistle. For Paul's Roman imprisonment, see Acts 28:16, 20, 23, 30-31. The remembrance of Paul's bonds was not for sympathy. It was a reminder to see trials from the proper perspective (1:24-25) and, in that light, stand firm no matter what the situation (4:3-5).

1 Thessalonians

BASIC FACTS

HISTORICAL SETTING

Thessalonica, named in 315 B.C. by Cassander for his wife, the half sister of Alexander the Great, is strategically located on the Egnatian Way, which stretched across Macedonia to the west. Located on an excellent harbor at the northeastern corner of the Thermaic Gulf, Thessalonica was commercially very important. Due to its location, the city has been called "the key to the whole of Macedonia."

In Paul's day Thessalonica was a large city with as many as two hundred thousand people, the largest city of Macedonia. It had a sizable Jewish population, and Paul recognized it as a strategic place to begin a ministry (1 Thess. 1:8).

Luke gave a detailed account of Paul's ministry in Thessalonica (Acts 17:1-10). Paul taught in the synagogue for three Sabbaths. He worked to bring in support (1 Thess. 2:9; 2 Thess. 3:8) and also received offerings from the Philippian church (Phil. 4:16).

Paul was forced out of the city and went to Berea (Acts 17:11-12). Jews from Thessalonica disrupted the ministry in Berea, forcing Paul to depart (Acts 17:13-15). Paul moved on to Athens and left Silas and Timothy in Berea to continue the work. Silas and Timothy eventually joined Paul in Athens (1 Thess. 3:1-2). From there Paul sent Timothy to Thessalonica. Paul had gone on to Corinth where Timothy again caught up with him and brought news from Thessalonica (Acts 18:1-5). Paul wrote 1 Thessalonians from Corinth.

AUTHOR

Pauline authorship of this letter is attested both by internal and external evidence. The letter presents itself as being from Paul (1:1). His named companions were known to have been with him on his second journey (1:1; 3:2, 6; Acts 15:40; 16:1-3, 19; 17:4, 10, 14; 18:5). The form, vocabulary, and theological thought are clearly Pauline. Finally, the major early church fathers (Origen, Clement of Alexandria, Tertullian, and Irenaeus) testify to the authenticity of the letter.

DATE

Paul first visited Thessalonica on his second missionary journey (A.D. 50–52). The letter was written in A.D. 51, about six months after Paul left Thessalonica.

PURPOSE

Paul's first letter to the Thessalonians was designed to give comfort and encourage steadfastness in their commitment to Christ. This was done by reminding the believers of the past powerful realities of Christ in their lives and by clarifying some of the future events of Christ's return. Whether discussing the past or the future, Paul's purpose was to increase their present faithfulness and joy in Christ.

GEOGRAPHY AND ITS IMPORTANCE

The City of Thessalonica

Paul was in Corinth when he wrote to the Thessalonians. Thessalonica was the major port for Macedonia. Cassander founded the city around 315 B.C. and named it for his wife, Thessalonica, who was also the half sister of Alexander the Great. During Paul's time Thessalonica was the capital and largest city of Macedonia.

GUIDING CONCEPTS

DISTINGUISHING BETWEEN HUMAN AND DIVINE WRATH

Paul clarified the difference between human and divine wrath. The Thessalonians were undergoing great afflictions from Jewish opposition (3:3). Paul said they were destined for this human type of tribulation (3:3; see Acts 14:22). But they were not destined to undergo God's wrath in the future (1:10; 5:9). The suffering believers confused human and divine wrath. This error opened them up to misunderstandings in their conception of Christ's second coming, which would be their ultimate relief from suffering, and a potential lapse of steadfastness.

EXCELLENCE AND SANCTIFICATION

Paul wanted his friends to excel in their Christian lives (4:1, 10). He also wanted them to live sanctified lives (3:13; 4:3-4, 7; 5:23). All the instructions concerning persecution, morality, and the second coming were geared toward enabling excellence and sanctification. Even the section where Paul defended the integrity of his ministry among them (1:2–2:20) was designed to strengthen the foundation of the believers' faith and obedience.

BIBLE-WIDE CONCEPTS

THE DAY OF THE LORD

The day of Christ's return forms a constant background for Paul's thoughts in this letter (1:10; 2:19; 3:13; 4:13–5:11; 5:23). A correct understanding of that day was essential for accomplishing the sanctification of the believers. In the Old Testament, the day of the Lord was presented as having a number of distinct characteristics.

"Thy will be done"

First of all, because it is the day of the Lord, it implies that all the other days of history are not the Lord's in the way this one will be. History's days are permeated with the ungodly acts of rebellious humanity. The day of the Lord will be a day that begins a new eternal era in which the perfect will of God will find exact fulfillment.

Supernatural and worldwide

Second, the day of the Lord will bring supernatural interventions. The righting of wrongs in that day will not be dependent on human effort. Throughout the Bible, the day of the Lord is revealed as a day that cannot be accomplished by people, only by God. Third, the day of the Lord will be worldwide. It looks back to creation and to the fullness of the Abrahamic promises to all nations (Isa. 51:1-8).

The day of the Lord stretches on into the promised golden age for Israel and the earth. Isaiah moves through a whole series of end-time events as if through a single grand day. Daniel includes both judgment and the establishment of the Messiah's kingdom in that day (Dan. 7:10-14). Note Jesus' use of that Daniel passage as recorded in Matthew 26:64 and Mark 14:62. The day of the Lord will bring international judgment and an eternal kingdom for the saints. There is a close interrelationship between the kingdom to come, the Son of Man, and the saints of Christ's church.

A process of redemption and judgment

Fourth, the day of the Lord will involve both redemption and judgment (Isa. 24:20-23; 25:6-9). It will be a day when the faithful are received into the fullness of their redemption. It will be a day when unbelievers are rejected into the fullness of their damnation. Thus, the day of the Lord will actually be a broad period of time that stretches from the time of antichrist and tribulation through the Millennium and final judgments. The Old Testament views the day of the Lord as the final conquest over evil; it will be a day when faithfulness is rewarded and the heavens and earth re-created.

The day of the Lord is not simply a future historical fact. It will bring a moral evaluation of people's lives by Christ. And that future evaluation impinges on the present. The promise of future judgment should encourage believers to live properly now (Amos 5:18). God has given many days that prefigure the final day of the Lord (for example, Zeph. 1:11-18; the downfall of Judah to Babylon; the locust plague of Joel 2:1-11).

Nearness

Fifth, the day of the Lord is near. It is near because the Judge is near. Christ reigns at God's right hand and is present with power. All he needs to do is to start his judgments and restoration. He is not far away. He can begin in an instant. That is what makes the day near, that sense of instant possibility.

The concept of nearness is not built on nearness in the sense of time, a short or long time. The day of the Lord has been near for close to two thousand years because it is like death. All people know they are going to die. They do not know when they will die, but they do know it could happen at any minute. In that sense, death and the day of the Lord are always near.

Summary

The day of the Lord is God's future visible entrance into history and retribution for people who have rebelled from his way. That history has stretched from the fall of Adam to the present. At present, the kingdom of God is like a tiny mustard seed. And the conflict is between the people of God and those who hate them. When Christ returns, the conflict will be directly between himself and his opponents will result in a visible kingdom. The seed will have become a mature tree spreading around the world in the fulfillment of God's promises to Abraham (Isa. 51:1-8).

THE RULE OF THE LORD

The Lord to whom the day belongs is both the suffering Servant (Isa. 53:1-12) and the exalted Son of Man (Isa. 9:1-7; Jer. 33:14-18; note Daniel 7:13 and Ps. 110:1 combined in Matt. 26:64). The hope for the day of the Lord is hope for redemption based on the suffering of the Lord. There could be no kingdom without the cross (Matt. 16:21; Mark 10:45). The doctrines of future things and salvation must always go together (2 Sam. 7:14-15; Isa. 11:1-9; Zech. 6:12-13). Those who believe must always look back to the cross and ahead to the second coming.

NEEDS MET BY FIRST THESSALONIANS

The Thessalonians' blessings in Christ had come up against the realities of life. They were being persecuted by religious and civil groups and some Christians had already died. They wondered why they should be so blessed by God and at the same time be so cursed by the world. The doctrinal truth of the line between relief for the saints and divine wrath on God's enemies had blurred. The pain of their hard circumstances could have blinded them to the broader realities of God's plan for history. By clearly distinguishing between human and divine wrath, Paul enabled the Thessalonian readers to go on in faith and steadfastness. The content of the letter indicates that the Thessalonians were probably asking questions like these.

- Have believers made the right and secure choice in accepting a Savior who has led them into persecution?
- With all the religious and civil leaders criticizing Paul, can believers be secure in accepting his authority?
- How can believers know that the persecution and tribulation they are suffering is not a result of God's wrath?
- How can believers feel secure about what has and will happen to deceased Christians?
- How can believers see this troubled life as designed to deepen their sanctification?

As with the Thessalonians, life's pain can cause today's believers to doubt that God is in control and wants the best for his people. Present conflicts can make believers insecure about the future and dull their perception and enjoyment of God's present goodness. When friends or relatives doubt the faith of believers and criticize their trust in the authority of the Bible, this letter encourages them to see beyond the problems to God's ultimate control of history. God's ordination of a process of time that involves some pain and injustice should not diminish the absolute certainty that the process will inevitably lead to righting all wrongs and rewarding the faithful. Believers need to hold fast to the future while living in the present. This combination will give them the perspective to maintain their personal purity, joy, and witness in an often joyless and hostile world.

OUTLINE OF FIRST THESSALONIANS

A. INFORMAL GREETING (1:1)
B. THANKSGIVING FOR AN EFFECTIVE INITIAL WITNESS (1:2-10)
    1. For Manifested Character (1:2-3)
    2. For Assurance of Election and Witness in Affliction (1:4-10)
C. DEFENSE OF PAST WITNESS (2:1–3:13)
    1. A Witness of Integrity (2:1-12)
    2. Paul's Thanksgiving for a Receptive Hearing (2:13-16)
    3. Paul's Thanksgiving for Timothy's Good Report (2:17–3:13)
D. REQUEST FOR INCREASED EXCELLENCE (4:1–5:24)
    1. Exhortations to Excellence (4:1-12)
    2. Concerning Those Who Died (4:13-18)
    3. Concerning the Day of God (5:1-11)
    4. Specific Community Relationships (5:12-24)
E. CLOSING REQUESTS (5:25-28)

FIRST THESSALONIANS NOTES

1:1 INFORMAL GREETING

The focus in Paul's greeting was on the three who ministered in Thessalonica, not on Paul and his apostleship (see 2:6). "Silas" is the shorter form of the name "Silvanus" (Acts 15:40). In 315 B.C. Cassander reconstructed Therma, a harbor city located on the Thermaic Gulf, and named it "Thessalonica" after his wife, the daughter of Philip of Macedon. Paul, Silas, and Timothy visited the city on Paul's second missionary journey (Acts 17:1-9) in A.D. 50. His ministry for "three Sabbath days" (Acts 17:2) was probably only the beginning of his ministry there rather than the full extent of it (cf. 1 Thess. 2:9; 2 Thess. 3:8; Phil. 4:16).

Because of the persecutions they were suffering, Paul identified this church closely with God and his Son who had also suffered. The believers were not alone in a hostile world. And despite the hostility of the world, they had peace with God. Although the people around the Christians may have been offended or threatened, God was not.

1:2-10 THANKSGIVING FOR AN EFFECTIVE INITIAL WITNESS

Overview: The section of 1:2–3:13 moves between Paul's ministry and its reception by the Thessalonians (reception, 1:2-3; ministry, 1:4-5; reception, 1:6-10; ministry, 2:1-12; reception, 2:13-16; ministry, 2:17–3:13). Clearly Paul was trying to reaffirm his godly ministry and the readers' godly responses in the light of critical hostility (cf. 2:3; 3:4-5; Acts 17:9; Phil. 4:16). It was customary for ancient letters to open with a word of gratitude, but Paul's thanksgiving is no mere formality. He is thankful for the believers virtues (1:2-3), conversion (1:4-7), and testimony (1:8-10).

1:2-3 For Manifested Character

Paul answered his critics point for point (cf. 1 Thess. 3:4-5; 2:3; Acts 17:6-9; Phil. 4:16-17): greed, 2:8-9; cowardice, 2:1-2; not caring, 2:7-8; mistaken message, 2:13-16; persecution, 3:1-4. "Endurance" (1:3; "steadfastness," NASB; "patience," KJV) literally means "to abide under," that is, to hold up under trial with a positive and optimistic outlook. This outlook is inspired by hope.

1:4-10 For Assurance of Election and Witness in Affliction

The "deep conviction" (1:5) relates to Paul's own affirmation of his sincerity (1:5). His sincerity was matched by the Thessalonians' commitment (1:6). The Greek word translated "imitators" (1:6) is related to the English word "mimic." Paul's integrity and their commitment cemented Paul's knowledge of their election (1:4). They reflected Paul and the Lord (1:6). Macedonia (1:7) was the province of northern Greece where Philippi was located. Achaia was the province to the south where Corinth was situated.

Paul noticed how the Thessalonians' witness confirmed what a positive and godly influence he had had. The hostility some of the Thessalonians felt toward him could not overshadow what God had done through him (1:9-10). The strategic location of Thessalonica on the Egnatian Way and at the head of the Thermaic Gulf undoubtedly did much to further the rapid spread of the gospel. Repentance (1:9) refers to a "change of mind" and involves a turning from sin and self to God. It is a synonym for believing, not a condition for salvation (Acts 26:20; Rom. 2:4; 2 Pet. 3:9).

The process of waiting (1:10) involves hope (1:3). "From" is used three times (1:10) and outlines the past, present, and future hopes of believers ("Son from heaven," "raised from the dead," "rescued from wrath").

"The coming" (1:10) is added to "wrath" in order to delineate between present tribulation and future wrath. For "rescues from," see Matthew 6:13; 27:43; Romans 7:24; 2 Corinthians 1:10; Colossians 1:13; 2 Thessalonians 3:2; 2 Timothy 3:11; 4:17-18; 2 Peter 2:7, 9. The return of Christ is a very prominent theme in 1 Thessalonians. Paul concluded every chapter in this letter with some reference to the coming of Christ (1:10; 2:19; 3:13; 4:17; 5:23).

2:1–3:13 DEFENSE OF PAST WITNESS

2:1-12 A Witness of Integrity

2:1-6 NOT A VAIN ENTRANCE

The words "visit" (2:1) and "reception" (1:9) are from the same Greek word. Paul recalled his first work among them. The

gospel had been spoken after and amidst persecution (2:1-2). This showed the sincerity of Paul's work among them. A false minister would not have persevered in the persecution Paul had experienced. Paul defended the missionary team against criticism from some who believed that Paul and his associates were motivated by selfish desires (2:3; 5:6).

In refuting the accusations, Paul used the method of letting the record of his ministry speak for itself. When evaluated in the light of truth, the malicious charges being made against the missionaries could not survive. For Paul's experience in Philippi, see Acts 16:12-40. Paul, a Roman citizen, had been beaten and imprisoned without a trial. The apostle had also experienced opposition in Thessalonica (Acts 17:5-9).

Paul spoke to please God, not people. His message was true, pure, and without deceit (1 Thess. 2:3). This verse reflects three charges that had been made against the missionaries: (1) their preaching was based on "error," (2) they gained followers by "impure motives," and (3) they tried to "trick" them. The word "trick" means "to catch with bait" and suggests deception. "Flattery" and "greed" were given as examples of methods used by those seeking "praise from men" (2:5-6). First negatively (2:5-6) and then positively (2:7-8), Paul recounted the missionaries' previous conduct among the Thessalonians.

2:7-12 A SACRIFICIAL ENTRANCE

Paul was full of affection for the Thessalonian Christians (2:7). He was not selfish or disinterested. His professional expertise was combined with the love of a mother for her children. He shared his life, not just words (2:8). The image of a caring mother points to the word "gentle." The phrase "like a mother caring" is a technical term for a professional wet nurse. But in this case the professional wet nurse is nursing her own children—the combination of professional expertise with personal love.

Paul continued to remind the Thessalonians of his irreproachable behavior (2:9-12). Paul early on had sized up the situation in Thessalonica and realized it was best not to receive money or gifts from the believers there. Because of this, Paul and his associates worked hard not to become a burden to them. They also received gifts from Philippi to support themselves financially (Phil. 4:16). This strategy is further explained in 2 Corinthians 11:7-11. Paul had the right to receive remuneration for his ministry (1 Cor. 9:3-14) but gave up that right so that no one would charge him with greed.

Paul mentioned three aspects of his preaching ministry: encouraging, comforting, and urging (2:11). Once again (cf. Eph. 4:1), Paul used the word "live" to describe the believers' conduct or manner of life (2:12).

2:13-16 Paul's Thanksgiving for a Receptive Hearing

Paul wanted the Thessalonians to look toward God, not men, as the end of true ministry (2:13). The preachers would come and go, but God would always remain. Ministers must eventually hand their work over, but God energizes. The work accomplished by the word of God (2:13) was a church that remained faithful in persecution (2:14-16). For a glimpse of how the Thessalonians suffered at the hands of their own countrymen, see Acts 17:5-9. The main offense of Paul's opponents was that they hindered the gospel (2:15-16). For "wrath" (2:16), see Romans 1:18.

2:17–3:13 Paul's Thanksgiving for Timothy's Good Report

2:17-20 PAUL'S DESIRE TO SEE THE THESSALONIANS

Paul had been kept away from this church because of Satan (2:17-18), not because he had a careless attitude (2:3-4, 7). After Paul left Thessalonica, the believers there were out of sight, but not out of mind. Several times Paul planned to return to Thessalonica, but his efforts were thwarted by Satan. Happily for believers today that satanic thwarting resulted in Paul having to write this very letter.

Paul answered the accusation that he did not care about them by telling of his desire to see them and that one day they would be together with the Lord forever (2:19; cf. Matt. 24:3, 27, 37, 39; 1 Cor. 15:23). Paul emphasized Jesus' bodily presence at the "coming" of the Lord.

3:1-10 PAUL'S SUBSTITUTE MINISTER

Timothy was sent to strengthen and encourage the Thessalonians (3:1-5). Paul had left Silas and Timothy at Berea to complete the work there (Acts 17:13-15) and had traveled on to Athens (Acts 17:16) by sea where he was later rejoined by his associates. After several attempts to return to Thessalonica, he decided to go on alone to Athens and sent Timothy (and probably Silas, Acts 18:5) to strengthen and encourage the believers. The Thessalonian believers were destined to suffer (3:3-4). But suffering at the hands of hostile people is radically different from suffering the wrath of God (5:9). They were destined for affliction but not destined for wrath. "Useless efforts" (3:5; "vain labor," NASB and KJV) would be the silencing of the Thessalonians' witness due to satanic temptations in persecution. The "tempter" (3:5) refers to Satan by his characteristic activity.

Timothy brought good news back to Paul (3:6-10). After Paul had traveled on to Corinth (Acts 18:1), he was joined by Silas and Timothy who brought an encouraging report from Thessalonica (Acts 18:5). Paul was so thankful for their continued progress in the faith that words could barely express his joy (3:9). The expression "supply what is lacking" (3:10) was used of repairing a fishing net (Matt. 4:21). Paul wanted to build up the believers' faith so that they would not be deficient in any way.

3:11-13 PAUL'S DESIRE FOR THEIR ESTABLISHED HOLINESS

Paul prayed that God would remove the obstacles that Satan had put in his way (3:10) so that their fellowship could be renewed (3:11).

4:1–5:24 REQUEST FOR INCREASED EXCELLENCE

Overview: The key words are "blameless" and "holy" (3:13; 4:3-4, 7; 5:23) and "more and more" (4:1, 10; "excel," NASB). This entire section from 4:13 to 5:23 reveals important elements in the process of sanctification. The Thessalonians needed encouragement; their faith lacked strength. Paul would at this point seek to begin correcting them in the areas in which they were deficient. He would talk about personal purity (4:3-8) and comfort (4:9–5:11); he would continue talking about living with leaders who probed them about what they lacked (5:12-14). The main thought in all of this section is holiness (3:13; 5:23) and the means by which it is attained.

4:1-12 Exhortations to Excellence

4:1-8 EXHORTATION TO EXCEL IN PURITY
The word "finally" (4:1) does not indicate the close of the letter but serves to introduce a new subject (Phil. 3:1). Paul passed from matters of personal history to practical application. "Instructions" (4:2) is a military term used for a "word of command" received from a superior officer to be passed down to others. The sanctification referred to here is the believer's present sanctification—being set apart to God from the controlling influence of sin (4:3; see note on 1 Cor. 1:2).

The idea of men confining sexual intercourse to marriage was foreign to Greek morality of the first century A.D. Men were said to have mistresses for pleasure, harlots for casual sex, and wives for marriage and children. Although pagan religions knew nothing of sexual purity, and some even encouraged cultic prostitution as part of their fertility rites, God's will for Christians is sexual purity (1 Cor. 6:12-20).

Paul emphasized the importance of self-control (4:4-6). Some interpret "body" (4:4) as referring to one's own body (cf. 2 Tim. 2:21) or to one's own wife (1 Pet. 3:7). Since "to control" may also be rendered "acquire," Paul could be referring to premarital chastity during courtship and the contracting of marriage. The word translated "body" normally meant "body" in Greek usage and "wife" in Jewish usage. Either way, believers were to be the masters of their desires, not controlled by them.

4:9-12 EXHORTATION TO EXCEL IN LOVE
On brotherly love, see John 13:34. Paul encouraged the believers to work to supply their own needs while doing ministry so that their witness might not be suspect. This followed Paul's own model for ministry (2:9).

4:13-18 Concerning Those Who Died

Overview: This passage revealed the fact that deceased and living believers would meet again at the Lord's return. This focus

uncovered a confusion among the Thessalonians. They wondered what would happen to already dead believers when it came time for Christ to return. Comfort and encouragement (4:18; 5:11) were Paul's aim in these verses. The dead may have been lost to their relatives, but they were not lost to God (4:13-14). They would be seen again when Christ is revealed. Perhaps some thought that the dead would not be raised to resurrection bodies (4:14, 16). But the main issue concerned how they would all come together again at Christ's coming. Note the concepts of "bring with" (4:14), "precede" (4:15), "first" (4:16), and "with them" (4:17). Sanctification would be greatly hindered by people depressed over lost loved ones whom they were not sure they would ever see again. Paul wrote to give hope to the grieving believers.

4:13-14 THE PATTERN OF CHRIST'S DEATH AND RESURRECTION
The believers at Thessalonica were apparently upset because they mistakenly thought that those who died before the Lord's coming would miss out on it completely. Paul wrote to clarify the relationship between the living and the dead at the time of Christ's return. His point was that the living would not precede the dead (4:15). The Lord's coming will begin with the dead believers but will also include the living saints, for they are all part of the one body of Christ. "Fall asleep" (4:13) is a metaphor for death (cf. John 11:11) emphasizing the idea of resurrection, just as one awakens from sleep. The certainty of the believers' resurrection is based on the fact of Christ's resurrection (4:14; 1 Cor. 15:20-22). "We believe" (4:14) reveals that the Thessalonian Christians did believe that the resurrection of Christ was true.

4:15-18 THE SEQUENCE OF APPEARANCE AT HIS COMING
The "dead in Christ" (4:16), the believers who had died and are present with Christ (2 Cor. 5:8) will be physically resurrected and receive their glorified bodies at the time of Christ's return (1 John 3:2). The word translated "caught up" (4:17) literally means "to seize" or "to snatch." It is from the Latin translation of this word that the term "rapture" is derived. The words "to meet" (4:17) were used of meeting a

dignitary paying an official visit to one's city. The leading citizens would go out to meet the honored guest. Paul's instruction concerning the Lord's coming and believers' resurrection was to be a source of comfort and hope to the Thessalonians (4:18).

5:1-11 Concerning the Day of God

5:1-3 CERTAIN DESTRUCTION
See Matthew 24:36-44. The day of the Lord is one of the major themes of the Old Testament prophets (cf. Isa. 13:6, 9; Joel 1:15; Zeph. 1:14-18). The day of the Lord is that period of time during which God will deal with Israel and the nations through judgment and deliverance. According to Peter, that day will conclude with the purging of the heavens and earth in preparation for the creation of the new heavens and earth (2 Pet. 3:10-13; cf. Isa. 65:17; 66:22). The expression "like a thief in the night" (5:2) emphasizes the unexpectedness of the event and the unpreparedness of those to whom he comes. The expression "as labor pains" (5:3) is a common figure for increasingly intense pain and sorrow (Matt. 24:8).

5:4-11 CERTAIN SALVATION
Paul encouraged the Thessalonians to conform to God's light, not the darkness that leads to destruction in the day of the Lord. Since the day of the Lord will result in judgment for the wicked and deliverance for the righteous, self-examination was important. Believers are associated with "light" (spiritually enlightened because of the new birth) rather than "darkness" (the realm of sin and spiritual emptiness). The coming of the Lord should motivate believers to be mentally alert and morally vigilant. Paul used an illustration of a Roman soldier on duty (5:8). The believer must be on guard against a hostile world, putting on spiritual armor as protection against Satan's attacks (cf. Eph. 6:13-17). God has not appointed believers to be the subjects of divine wrath, but rather to be delivered from the day-of-the-Lord judgments by the coming of Christ (5:9). Whatever pain the Thessalonians would experience, they were not to think they had been abandoned to God's wrath (see the problem worsen in 2 Thess. 2:1-2).

First Thessalonians 5:10 shows that 4:13-18 has not been far from Paul's mind. The issues of discouragement (5:11) and sorrow (4:18) were definite threats to sobriety, faith, love, and hope (5:8). The point of speaking about the future coming of Christ was to give them hope and strengthen their present witness and sanctification.

5:12-24 Specific Community Relationships

Overview: Paul taught about living with people when the going gets rough. He had just encouraged them to build each other up (5:11). Next he asked that they honor those whose primary task is to do the building up— the church leaders (5:12).

5:12-14 APPRECIATION OF LEADERS
Paul explained that leaders are there to push believers to maturity. But their legitimate criticisms, no matter how difficult to accept, should result in peace and appreciation. Paul provided a helpful summary of the responsibilities of spiritual leaders (5:12). They are to "work hard" ("diligently labor," NASB), rule or govern ("over you"), and "admonish" ("give instruction," NASB). They are to match their ministry to the particular needs of the people. "Admonishing" is appropriate for the unruly, "encouragment" for the fainthearted, and "help" for the weak. The ministries match the needs. "Idle" (5:14) is a military term signifying the marching soldier who does not keep in proper step. Thus, it refers to those who are out of line.

5:15-22 PRAYER AND DISCERNMENT
This section provides the framework for seeking after being "kind" (5:15) and "good" (5:21). In the original Greek, 1 Thessalonians 5:16 is the shortest verse in the Bible. The Christian who prays "continually" is living in constant communion with God and is always ready to pray. "Putting out" or quenching the Spirit (1:19) is illustrated in the next verses: "treating with contempt" (1:20) rather than "testing" (1:21) spiritual truths. This was probably going on in Thessalonica and is reminiscent of what went on in Corinth (1 Cor. 14:23, 27, 29, 33, 39). To "treat with contempt" means to despise and count as nothing. Paul did not advocate

an uncritical acceptance of every person that claims to be of the Spirit. Teaching must be carefully examined to determine what is true and what is not. Sound doctrine must be retained and unsound doctrine rejected (5:22).

5:23-24 PRAYER FOR COMPLETE SANCTIFICATON

Paul's closing prayer covered all the areas addressed in 1 Thessalonians 4–5, especially regarding sanctification (3:13; 4:3-4, 7; 5:23). Paul prayed for complete sanctification among the believers. He elaborated further by praying that the immaterial (soul and spirit) and material (body) parts of the believers might be presented blameless at the coming of Christ.

5:25-28 CLOSING REQUESTS

In Paul's closing words he made requests for prayer, sent greetings, and gave instructions for sharing the letter. The "holy kiss" (5:26) was a common oriental greeting in ancient times and corresponds to the practice in Western culture of shaking hands (cf. Rom. 16:16).

2 Thessalonians

BASIC FACTS

HISTORICAL SETTING
For the founding of the church at Thessalonica, read Acts 17:1-10 and the Historical Setting section for 1 Thessalonians. The immediate occasion of 2 Thessalonians was a report that Paul received concerning the positive faith and love of the Thessalonian Christians (1:3-4) and their misunderstandings concerning the day of the Lord which were caused by false teachers (2:2). Some believers thought they were in the day of the Lord and had given up working to live in idleness (3:6-12), apparently waiting for the Lord's return.

AUTHOR
Paul is identified as the author in 1:1 and 3:17. The authenticity of the letter was recognized by Irenaeus (c. A.D. 170). The objections to Pauline authorship by some scholars are based on criticisms that have little substance compared to the certainty that the early Christians showed as to the letter's genuineness.

DATE
Because Paul, Silvanus (Silas), and Timothy were still together when the letter was written, it is probable that the second letter was written from Corinth not long after the writing of 1 Thessalonians. The close connection between the two letters makes it unlikely that a long interval separated them. It is generally held that two or three months passed between the writing of the two letters. In harmony with the date of 1 Thessalonians (early summer of A.D. 51), 2 Thessalonians may be dated in the summer of A.D. 51.

PURPOSE
Paul's second letter to the Thessalonians was designed to encourage believers that all their persecution and suffering would ultimately be worth it all. Throughout the letter, the question of how all their pain could be a good and righteous part of God's plan is addressed.

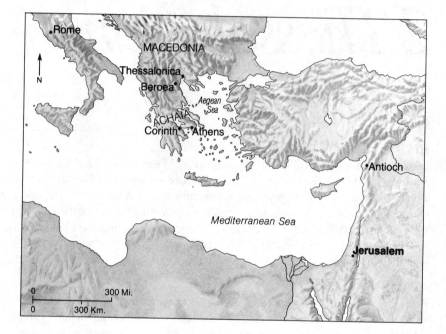

GUIDING CONCEPTS

This letter deals with three basic concepts, one in each chapter. The first concerns whether or not it was right for believers to be undergoing such persecution as they were experiencing (1:1-12). The second concerns whether or not the readers had fallen under the wrath of the day of the Lord (2:1-17). The third relates to whether following Christ under such persecutions was really worth all the pain and effort (3:1-18).

BIBLE-WIDE CONCEPTS

THE RIGHTEOUS SUFFERER
One problem addressed in 2 Thessalonians was the question of God's justice in the suffering of the righteous believer (1:5-8). Job could not understand why he suffered unjustly. Hebrews 11 is full of examples of those who suffered unjustly because they were righteous. Jesus became the supreme example of the righteous sufferer (1 Pet. 2:22-24). The question for the righteous sufferer throughout Scripture was how to keep going on with God and believing in his goodness (1 Pet. 2:20-21). Unjust suffering can easily cause a believer to lose steadfastness (2 Thess. 3:5) and become weary of doing good (3:13).

CONFLICT BETWEEN GOD AND SATAN
The letter also explains the conflict between the children of God and Satan that began at the fall of Adam (Gen. 3:15). The description of the antichrist (2 Thess. 2:3-12) contributes to the revelations in Scripture concerning the end times (see, for example, Dan. 7:23-27; Matt. 24–25; Rev. 12:9-17). Throughout the Bible, the reason for discussing the day of the Lord was to show that the Lord of that day is present now, whether that day is near or far. It also serves to remind believers that their future evaluation is built on their actions in the present.

NEEDS MET BY SECOND THESSALONIANS

The Thessalonians went through much criticism and hostility because they had believed Paul's message about Christ. The message of great blessing in Christ seemed a bit contradictory to their experience of persecution. Not only did they have questions and worries about what God was doing, they also needed confirmation that Paul, the one who first brought the gospel to them, was trustworthy. Paul's brief second letter to the Thessalonians met three crucial needs. These needs are reflected in the following questions that were probably being asked by the Thessalonians.
- Is God doing the right thing by allowing believers to suffer so much?
- What is God doing about the evil people who are persecuting believers?
- Have the terrible days of the antichrist already arrived?
- Is it really worth being godly when it brings so much pain?

The joy the Thessalonians experienced at the beginning of their Christian walk soon met with the painful and unjust realities of life. And when this happens, believers today, like them, have some pressing needs to be met. This letter should help believers to become honestly and deeply convinced that what God is allowing to happen is part of his process of justice. The temptation is to quietly think that God is not being fair. But the proper balance will come when believers learn to be content with present suffering without blaming God. They must anticipate the future judgment of their enemies while still witnessing to them and seeking their salvation. Another need the letter addresses is how to keep going during the tough times. The goal is not a tight-fisted teeth-clenched resignation to life's problems, but rather a joyful, optimistic, and very wise assessment of the good and the bad in life with a view to maximizing all the good for Christ. This letter should help believers learn to keep their eyes both on the realities of this age and the rewards of the next.

OUTLINE OF SECOND THESSALONIANS

A. INFORMAL GREETING (1:1-2)
B. THANKSGIVING FOR THEIR BEHAVIOR IN TRIBULATION (1:3-12)
    1. Faith and Love in Affliction (1:3-10)
    2. Prayer for Fulfilled Desires (1:11-12)
C. A CORRECTED CHRONOLOGY FOR THE DAY OF THE LORD (2:1-17)
    1. Its Futurity and Components (2:1-12)
    2. Exhortation to Hold to the Traditions (2:13-17)
D. CLOSING REQUESTS FOR PRAYER AND DISCIPLINE (3:1-15)
    1. Request for Prayer (3:1-5)
    2. Command for Discipline in Work (3:6-15)
E. BENEDICTION AND CLOSING (3:16-18)

SECOND THESSALONIANS NOTES

1:1-2 INFORMAL GREETING

In his greeting, Paul recognized a personal relationship (1:1) based on a divine source (1:2). Timothy and Silvanus were Paul's associates during his ministry in Thessalonica (Acts 17:10, 14). "Silvanus" is the longer name for "Silas" (see note on 1 Thess. 1:1). For matters concerning the city of Thessalonica, see note on 1 Thessalonians 1:1. Second Thessalonians was sent by Paul from Corinth in the summer of A.D. 51, not long after the writing of 1 Thessalonians.

1:3-12 THANKSGIVING FOR THEIR BEHAVIOR IN TRIBULATION

1:3-10 Faith and Love in Affliction

1:3-5 WHAT GOD THINKS OF THEIR SUFFERINGS

There is a cause and effect relationship between their love (1:3) and their perseverance in afflictions—a key theme of the letter (1:4). The idea behind perseverance is putting up with negatives in order to achieve another more constructive end. Because of the steadfastness of the Thessalonians under trial, Paul seized every opportunity to praise them.

God's verdict concerning the Thessalonians was: "You will be counted worthy" (1:5). Their worthiness was the verdict built on their perseverance and faith under suffering (1:3-4). Their perseverance rendered them worthy. God would be right in judging them worthy to enter his kingdom. The church at Thessalonica was born in persecution (Acts 17:1-9) and grew in spite of continued persecution (1 Thess. 1:6; 2:14; 3:1-3). Some believers were beginning to question the righteousness of God in all this. Paul declared that their response in suffering was proof that God was working in them and that their faith was genuine.

1:6-10 WHAT GOD WILL DO ABOUT THEIR SUFFERINGS

The question of how God could be doing right regarding those who suffer or cause suffering had to be related to the question of when God would act. The question of God's justice in the Thessalonians' suffering would not be completely answered until Christ was finally revealed (1:7). Paul declared that at Christ's coming there would be a reversal of present circumstances. God would bring judgment on the wicked who were persecuting the Thessalonians and would provide rest for those who had endured such hostility. The word translated "rest" or "relief" (1:7) was used to describe relief from tension, like that which comes from relaxing a taut bowstring. Old Testament appearances of God were frequently marked by the presence of fire (1:7; cf. Exod. 3:2; 19:18; 24:17; Ps. 18:12). A fiery manifestation of God's presence would be displayed at Christ's return. The words "everlasting destruction" (1:9) do not suggest the annihilation of the wicked but rather their everlasting ruin by reason of their eternal separation from the presence of God.

1:11-12 Prayer for Fulfilled Desires

Knowledge of Christ's future return was to encourage powerful works of faith. The believers were to glorify Christ in the present (1:12), and he would be glorified in the believers at his return (1:10). For now, the believers are to glorify Christ by proclaiming his great love and holy purposes. At his return, Christ will glorify the believers by proclaiming their exalted, vindicated, and holy nature as children of God. The combination of those two glories, Christ in Christians now and Christians in Christ then, was vital for maintaining hope for the future and a vigorous witness in the present.

2:1-17 A CORRECTED CHRONOLOGY FOR THE DAY OF THE LORD

2:1-12 Its Futurity and Components

2:1-2 ASSERTION: IT IS IN THE FUTURE

Paul referred to the subject of Christ's second coming throughout the first chapter of this letter. His coming would mean rest for the saints (1:7). During Paul's stay in Thessalonica he had explained many of the details

of prophecy to the believers (2:5; cf. 1 Thess. 4:13-18; 5:1-11). Paul had taught that the believers would have no part in the day of God's wrath (1 Thess. 5:9). Now, due to intense persecution and some misinformation (2 Thess. 2:2), some of the Thessalonians had come to believe they were in the midst of the day-of-the-Lord judgments. Paul wrote this letter to clarify that Christ's coming was still in the future.

Paul sought to clarify the fact that Christ's return and the day of the Lord were future events. He wanted to further explain that particular aspect of Christ's return that involved the believers' gathering together to meet their returning Lord. The potential problem (2:2) was that some claimed the day of the Lord was present. Had Paul changed his teaching regarding when that day would come? The Thessalonians were confusing present tribulation from men with the promised future judgments from God. They thought the day of the Lord had come and they were suffering under God's judgment. They also wondered why Jesus had not returned to redeem them out of the tribulation. They were disturbed due to a seeming change in the inaugural events of the day of the Lord. Paul explained that the day of the Lord had not yet arrived and that their suffering was not judgment from God but persecution from evil men. He turned the focus to how they should deal with the persecution they were experiencing. Paul explained that suffering severe tribulation should not be a cause of distress for them (cf. 1 Thess. 3:3).

2:3-12 INSTRUCTION: HOW THE DAY OF THE LORD WOULD COME

The Greek word translated "rebellion" (2:3) is only used again in Acts 21:21 to describe a political or religious "turning away." Here the context relates the word to the general events of the revelation of the antichrist (2:4-12) and the gathering of the church to the Lord (2:1). The antichrist's works parallel the works of Christ. He will have a "coming" (2:9; cf. 2:1); a revelation (2:3; cf. 1:7-8); and a gospel, "a powerful delusion" (2:11; cf. 2:10). Paul wrote that two events needed to take place before the day of the Lord's judgments began: (1) the apostasy and (2) the revelation of the man of lawlessness (cf. Dan. 7:25; 8:25; 11:36). The term "rebellion" literally means "departure" and may refer to a departure from doctrine or the departure of the believers to meet Christ at his return. The "man of lawlessness" (2:3, 8-9) refers to the "little horn" of Daniel 7:8, the antichrist of the end times (cf. Rev. 11:7; 13:1-10).

After the restraint's removal, the lawless one will seek to deceive and destroy (2:5-7). While the identity of this restrainer may be debated, its function is to show that this is the time of restraint, of grace for belief. The evil of this age has the stamp of the antichrist's lawlessness (2:7). Yet the antichrist cannot be revealed until "what is holding him back" (2:6) has been removed. The restrainer has been identified by some to be the Roman government, but there was no appearance of the antichrist after the decline of the Roman Empire. The restrainer must be more powerful than Satan who empowers the lawless (Rev. 13:4). It may be that Paul was referring to the restraining ministry of the Holy Spirit.

After the restraint of the lawless one is removed, the Lord will move to destroy the antichrist (2:8-12). This is the actual day of the Lord. Paul provided a description of the character and activity of the antichrist. The antichrist's career will be terminated at the second coming of Christ (2:8; Rev. 19:20; 20:10). The antichrist, empowered by Satan (Rev. 13:4), will demonstrate signs and false wonders in order to deceive people into following him (2:9).

2:13-17 Exhortation to Hold to the Traditions

2:13-15 PRAYER IS BASED ON BEING CHOSEN FOR SALVATION
Paul turned from the punishment of the antichrist and his followers to the bright prospects of the Thessalonians. Here he thanked God for the believers and for what God had done in their hearts (2:13-14). Compare 2:13 with 1:3. A proper understanding of the day of the Lord would help the believers to stand firm (2:15). The purpose of the believers' election was their ultimate salvation (glorification), and that would be achieved by the sanctifying work of the Holy Spirit.

2:16-17 PRAYER FOR THOSE CHOSEN
Paul desired that the Thessalonians would let truth push its way into their daily lives. The promise of the truth of future deliverance would give them steadfastness and faith in the present. God might let them suffer under persecution and tribulation, but that would serve to prove their perseverance and the evil of their persecutors.

3:1-15 CLOSING REQUESTS FOR PRAYER AND DISCIPLINE

Overview: Second Thessalonians 1 showed that God had just and blessed reasons for allowing the believers to be persecuted. Second Thessalonians 2 explained that the Thessalonians were not to be shaken from good works by thinking they had been misled and had fallen under God's judgments in the day of the Lord. In 2 Thessalonians 3 Paul encouraged them to be steadfast and not grow weary of doing good.

3:1-5 Request for Prayer
Paul requested that the believers pray for deliverance (3:2) and strength (3:3) so that Paul and the believers might continue in Christ's "love" and "perseverance" (3:5; "steadfastness," NASB). Paul desired that the gospel "spread rapidly" (3:1), a metaphor taken from the athletic arena (cf. 1 Cor. 9:24). Paul undoubtedly had in mind his Jewish opponents in Corinth (3:2; Acts 18:1-18). This chapter presents the commands of Paul (3:4, 6, 12) for perseverance (3:5) and discipline (3:6, 7, 11, 14).

3:6-15 Command for Discipline in Work
Doctrinal error often leads to practical misconduct. The misunderstanding concerning the day of the Lord led some to think that since the Lord was coming soon, there was no need to continue working. Some had quit their jobs and were leading undisciplined lives.

There was a connection between lack of discipline and the problem of perseverance (3:6, 7, 11; see "idle" in 1 Thess. 5:14). The strain of persecution and the misguided pressures of thinking they were in the day of the Lord led to weariness in doing good (3:13). That weariness resulted in unruly and undisciplined living. Paul used the future events of the day of the Lord to drive his readers into a clearer present world-mission. The function of Paul's command was to drive them to a world redemptive ministry (cf. 1 Thess. 4:11-12).

Paul set himself forth as an example for others to follow (3:7-9). He reminded the Thessalonians that while he had a right to receive support for his ministry (3:9; cf. 1 Cor. 9:1-18), he had worked night and day to avoid being a financial burden on them.

Paul clarified his original command concerning the necessity of work (3:10). While Christians have a responsibility to help those in need, Paul corrected misguided charity that only encourages idleness. The problem and the cure (3:11-15) were similar to those in 1 Thessalonians 4:11; 5:14. Life's strains caused some to tire of trying to do good (3:13). In Ephesians 3:13 the Greek word for "tire" is translated "discouraged." Note the common factor in Luke 18:1-8; 2 Corinthians 4:1, 16; Galatians 6:9; and Ephesians 3:13. People lost heart because they somehow misunderstood the future blessed results of life's trials.

Paul ordered the church to keep away from and not have social contact (3:14; lit., "mix themselves up") with the disobedient and disorderly. This coincides with the final step of dicipline described by Jesus—excommunication (cf. Matt. 18:15-17). The discipline was designed to cause them to "turn inwardly" ("feel ashamed," 3:14), reflect on their conduct, and repent of it. Second Thessalonians 3:15 emphasizes that the whole procedure is with a view to reformation and restoration to usefulness in the church.

3:16-18 BENEDICTION AND CLOSING

Although Paul dictated the letter, the final greeting was written in his own hand (cf. 1 Cor. 16:21; Gal. 6:11; Col. 4:18). This was an indication that the letter was genuine and was particularly important since some forged letters had been circulated in Paul's name (cf. 2:2). "Peace at all times" (3:16) is the theme of this letter, and Paul gave several clear examples of how such peace could be found.

1 Timothy

HISTORICAL SETTING

This letter was addressed to Timothy (1:2) but speaks to a broader audience (6:21 has the plural form of "you"). Timothy was first met by Paul on Paul's second missionary journey (Acts 16:1-3). Lystra was apparently Timothy's home. His father was a Greek, and his mother, Eunice, and grandmother Lois were devout Jews (Acts 16:1; 2 Tim. 1:5). Timothy had been trained in the Old Testament Scriptures (2 Tim. 3:14-15) and may have been converted by Paul on his first visit to Lystra (Acts 14:6-7; 1 Cor. 4:17; 1 Tim. 1:2). The words "my true son in the faith" suggest that Timothy was converted under Paul's ministry. Timothy worked with Paul on his missionary journeys (Acts 16:3; 17:14-15; 19:22; 1 Cor. 4:17; 16:10; 1 Thess. 3:1-2). He joined Paul and Silas when they traveled through the region of Lystra and Derbe on the second missionary journey (Acts 16:1-3) and faithfully served Paul during his second and third missionary journeys as well. He was with Paul during his first Roman imprisonment (Phil. 1:1; 2:19-24; Col. 1:1; Philem. 1:1). Timothy was his close companion and is associated with him in writing Philippians, Colossians, and Philemon. After Paul's release from Roman imprisonment, Timothy was appointed to lead the church at Ephesus (1 Tim. 1:3; 2 Tim. 1:16-18; 4:19). Timothy was also imprisoned (Heb. 13:23). Timothy was a prime example of a servant of God (Phil. 2:20-22). At the time Paul wrote 1 Timothy he expected to return to Ephesus, but he wrote this letter to give Timothy some directions for his ministry in case he should be delayed (cf. 1 Tim. 3:14-15).

AUTHOR

The letter names Paul as the author (1:1), and the autobiographical remarks fit his life (1:12, 13). The early church fathers accepted the letter as genuine. A possible reconstruction of Paul's travels after his first Roman imprisonment can provide the background for the Pastoral Epistles (1 Timothy, 2 Timothy, and Titus). The accompanying chart, *Paul's Travels after His Roman Imprisonment*, attempts to reconstruct a likely itinerary based on the biblical data.

Since Paul had announced his coming to the Colossians, he probably left for the east upon his release from Rome (spring of A.D. 62). He apparently went to Colosse (Philem. 1:22) and then to Ephesus where he left Timothy (1 Tim. 1:3). From there he proceeded to Macedonia where he wrote to Timothy (1 Tim. 1:3) and visited Philippi (Phil. 1:25; 2:24). Paul may have then returned to Ephesus as he had hoped would be possible (1 Tim. 3:14). Paul may have then realized his desire in the spring of A.D. 64 to journey to Spain (Rom. 15:24).

After a possible stay of two years in Spain (A.D. 64–66), Paul again journeyed east and visited Crete (Titus 1:5), where he left Titus to set the church in order and appoint elders (A.D. 66). Paul may have then journeyed to Asia Minor to visit Miletus (2 Tim. 4:20) and Troas (2 Tim. 4:13). He probably wrote Titus concerning his reponsibilities before traveling to Nicopolis, where he spent the winter (Titus 3:12). Paul may then have spent the spring and autumn of A.D. 67 in Macedonia and Greece, perhaps visiting Corinth (2 Tim. 4:20). Paul was then arrested a second time and brought to Rome. There he wrote 2 Timothy, requesting that Timothy join him in Rome before the winter of A.D. 67/68. Paul's martyrdom is placed by Eusebius in the thirteenth year of Nero. Paul's death probably occurred in the spring of A.D. 68.

The occasion for writing 1 Timothy was the possibility of Paul's visit to Timothy at Ephesus being delayed (3:14-15). Timothy needed the instructions concerning specific matters of church policy and practice that only Paul could give.

DATE

The letter was written after Paul's release from his first Roman imprisonment (A.D. 62) and before his death in the spring of A.D. 68. First Timothy appears to have been written soon after his release and after his visits to Ephesus (1:3) and Colosse (Philem. 1:22) and his journey to Macedonia (1 Tim. 1:3). The letter was probably written in the autumn of A.D. 62.

PAUL'S TRAVELS AFTER HIS ROMAN IMPRISONMENT

Place	*References*	*Key Phrases*
To Asia Minor	Philem. 1:22	"prepare a guest room" in Colosse
To Ephesus	1 Tim. 1:3	"stay there in Ephesus"
To Macedonia	1 Tim. 1:3	"went into Macedonia"
To Philippi	Phil. 1:25; 2:24	"come soon"
To Ephesus	1 Tim. 3:15	"if I am delayed"
To Spain	Rom. 15:24	"when I go to Spain"
	1 Clement 5:7	"the extreme limit of the west"
	Muratorian Canon	"the journey of Saint Paul to Spain"
To Crete	Titus 1:5	"I left you in Crete"
To Asia Minor	2 Tim. 4:13	"the cloak I left at Troas"
	2 Tim. 4:20	"I left Trophimus sick at Miletus"
To Greece	Titus 3:12	"come to me at Nicopolis"
	2 Tim. 4:20	"Erastus stayed in Corinth"
To Rome	2 Tim. 1:16-17	"in Rome, he searched hard for me"

PURPOSE

Paul's first letter to Timothy was designed to give the church clear directions for establishing the kind of leadership and decorum that would most effectively establish and support the truth of God in the gospel. This was done by focusing on love rather than speculation, salvation rather than squabbling, and true rather than false leadership. Throughout the letter Paul sought to encourage family love and respect among the believers.

GUIDING CONCEPTS

SUPPORTING THE TRUTH OF CHRIST

The key section for this letter is 3:14-16. It shows that the entire enterprise of the church is to be a pillar and support for the truth. That truth is embodied in the incarnation of Christ and lived out in the various practical issues dealt with in the letter. Everything Paul said about church life and leadership comes from the need for leaders to teach the wonderful truth about godliness in Christ.

BIBLE-WIDE CONCEPTS

PAST CORRESPONDENCE WITH EPHESUS

The Ephesian Christians tended to withhold their prayers for Gentile Christians in preference for Jews (2:1-7). But Paul had already shown the Ephesians that because the old covenant had been done away with (Eph. 2:15), the Gentiles were now fully included in the promise of salvation (Eph. 2:15). On that basis Paul continually pleaded for unity within the body of Christ (Eph. 4:16). Unity needed to be shown in an aggressive desire to match God's desire for the spread of salvation (1 Tim. 2:3-4). Paul had commanded that all anger and bitterness be put away (cf. Eph. 4:31 with 1 Tim. 2:8). And he had also warned that false teachers would come bringing deception and conflict (Eph. 5:6; Acts 20:29-31). The section of 1 Timothy 5:1–6:2 deals at length with the problems of submission and order within the family of God.

ISSUES FROM THE OLD COVENANT

The errant teachers of the law in Ephesus misunderstood and were abusing several Old Testament concepts. Paul dealt with these misunderstandings in his first letter to Timothy.

Law and faith

There was a conflict between law and faith. The foundational Old Testament passage on faith is Genesis 15:6. But the false teachers did not emphasize faith (1 Tim. 1:3-5) and thereby missed the original point of the law (1:7-10).

Riches

The Old Testament has much to say about the Ephesians' problem with riches (6:3-10, 17-19). Some key Old Testament passages are Deuteronomy 8:1-18; Jeremiah 9:23-24; 17:11; and Micah 6:12. Other important New Testament references are 1 Corinthians 1:26-31; 2 Corinthians 10:17; Mark 10:23-24, and James 5:1-6.

Widows
Paul dealt with the important Old Testament subject of widows in 1 Timothy 5:3-16. The Old Testament viewed the treatment of widows as a prime indication of a believer's devotion to God (cf. Exod. 22:22-24; Deut. 10:12-22; 14:29; 24:17-18; 26:13; 27:19; Isa. 1:17, 23; Jer. 7:6; Prov. 15:25; Zech. 7:8-10; Mal. 3:5). The New Testament also addresses this problem in James 1:27.

Truth
The false teachers misunderstood the nature of truth. For Paul truth was the very person of Christ (1 Tim. 3:16). All laws and conduct were to mirror God's ways as revealed in Christ. Anything that did not reflect Christ was not truth (cf. 2:4, 7; 3:15; 4:3; 6:5). For key Old Testament passages on truth (sometimes translated "faithfulness"), see Exodus 34:6; Nehemiah 9:13; and Psalm 31:5. In the New Testament see John 1:17; 14:6; 17:17; 18:37; and 1 Corinthians 5:8.

NEEDS MET BY FIRST TIMOTHY

Timothy had his work cut out for him when Paul left him to minister at Ephesus. Some Christians were trying to get rich by assuming roles of leadership in the church. Various social groups such as widows, elders, masters, and slaves were at odds with each other. And worst of all, status-seeking men were trying to become church leaders while teaching false doctrine and being completely inept at interpreting God's word. The Ephesian Christians needed to understand some basic distinctions between the proper and improper use of Scripture within the Christian community. The structure and content of 1 Timothy show that Paul intended to answer the following questions for his readers.

- When Scripture is quoted to support someone's position, how can believers know if the right interpretation is being made?
- Are believers supposed to pray for even the most ungodly national leaders?
- What else, besides a strong desire for leadership, is required for someone who wants to have authority in the church?
- How are believers supposed to relate to the various age and social groups in the church?
- What is the godly perspective on being wealthy?

For the Christians in first-century Ephesus and for believers today the issues concerning how Christians should live together are the same. This letter to Timothy helps believers to know how to test a person's claim to being a Christian leader. Desire for leadership must be matched by depth of character and skill in interpreting the Bible. The letter also gives advice as to how various social and age groups are to live together in harmony. The heart of church life is revealed to be the person of Christ. All church activity should further Christ's purposes and reflect his character. The letter also gives great insight into developing a balanced Christian perspective on spiritual and financial wealth.

OUTLINE OF FIRST TIMOTHY

A. FORMAL GREETING (1:1-2)

B. THE INSTRUCTION TO KEEP SOUND DOCTRINE (1:3-20)
1. The Instruction to End Fruitless Teaching (1:3-11)
2. The Gospel Entrusted to Paul (1:12-17)
3. The Command Entrusted to Timothy (1:18-20)

C. THE INSTRUCTION APPLIED: COMMUNITY TRADITIONS (2:1–6:19)
1. Prayer: Adopt God's Desires (2:1-15)
2. Leadership: Serve God's Truth (3:1–4:16)
3. Honor for Household Members (5:1–6:2)
4. Correctives to Materialism (6:3-19)

D. CLOSING CHARGE (6:20-21)

FIRST TIMOTHY NOTES

1:1-2 FORMAL GREETING

Although Paul addressed the letter to Timothy as an individual, it was clearly meant for the edification and instruction of the whole church. Paul stressed his divine authority for the church leaders in Ephesus as well as for Timothy. They were not to take Paul's call by God lightly.

God is portrayed as Savior (1:1). Paul was stressing to Timothy the fact that his call to the ministry should remain fresh. Timothy was said to be Paul's "true" son in faith (1:2), probably reflecting his conversion under Paul's ministry. The greeting in this letter adds "mercy" to Paul's standard "grace and peace." On God as Father (1:2), see Deuteronomy 32:6, 19; 2 Samuel 7:14 compared with 2 Corinthians 6:18.

1:3-20 THE INSTRUCTION TO KEEP SOUND DOCTRINE
1:3-11 The Instruction to End Fruitless Teaching

Overview: After his release from his first Roman imprisonment in the spring of A.D. 62, Paul traveled to Asia (cf. Philem. 1:22) and then to Macedonia (cf. Phil. 2:24). When he departed for Macedonia, Paul left Timothy in Ephesus for the specific purpose of correcting certain false teachers. For a description of Ephesus, see the note on Ephesians 1:1.

1:3-7 THE GOAL OF PAUL'S INSTRUCTION
Paul desired to turn fruitless teachings into acts of love (1:3-7). Some in Ephesus were addicted to strange myths. Paul may be referring here to Jewish myths and legends that are found in the noncanonical books of the Apocrypha (hidden writings), Pseudepigrapha (false writings), and Talmud. Books such as the *Assumption of Moses,* the *Life of Adam and Eve,* the *Secrets of Enoch,* and the *Book of Jubilees* relate speculative events, conversations, and prophecies.

The false teachers were focusing on these useless speculations rather than sound doctrine. Myths gave rise to speculation. The false teachers' hearts were not searching for godliness. They were just exchanging words. Speculation provided no foundation for acts of faith. The Greek word translated "speculation" indicates an exchange of words rather than a true search (see also Titus 3:9). God's administration (lit., "house rules") operated on the basis of faith, not speculation. That is, God wants believers to have clear and solid facts to believe in and act upon, not just words to debate over.

The context of being pure in heart (1:5) contrasts with what speculation could not accomplish. It did not accomplish purity in heart, a clear conscience, or faith. A good conscience is related to being pure in heart. True faith emphasizes how God feels toward believers, not how believers feel they are doing in relation to others. A sincere faith shows outwardly what is true in the inner life before God.

First Timothy 1:6-7 shows the results of neglecting character growth. The men desired to be teachers of the law (cf. Acts 5:34 regarding Gamaliel) but did not have the character to back up their desire. Paul dealt more fully with the relationship between desire and character in 1 Timothy 3.

1:8-11 THE VALUE OF THE MOSAIC LAW FOR THE LAWLESS

Paul's words stood in contrast to the useless words of the false teachers (1:9). The law was not for the righteous. It was a corrective for the lawless (2 Tim. 3:16; Rom. 3:19-20; Gal. 3:24). Paul pointed out that the law was good if used correctly because some in Ephesus had been using it ignorantly. The law was not being used according to its intended function, that is, to correct error. It was not for playing around with (1:3-4) or for teaching error (4:1-5). The proper use of the law was application in light of its purpose (1:9).

The list of sinful deeds elaborates upon those subject to the law (1:9-10). If they had been righteous, they would not need the law. The law's function was now defined by the gospel of grace in Christ (1:10-11). Paul used the expression "sound doctrine" frequently (1:10; 6:3; 2 Tim. 1:13; 4:3). It refers to teaching that is healthy and wholesome in contrast to that which is false. The gospel, not the law, is what now fully and clearly reveals the will of God to redeemed people.

1:12-17 The Gospel Entrusted to Paul

Paul brought up his past life to show one example of the proper use of the law—to bring sinners to salvation in Christ. But he also showed how the gospel came to bring redemption after the law had brought condemnation. He showed that law had to be combined with patience and grace. Paul had been a blasphemer as a persecutor of Christians. The law brought condemnation upon him as a blasphemer. But God came to Paul, not by the corrective of the law, but in mercy (see Acts 3:17; 17:30). In that light, Paul told his readers to stop playing with the law, unless it was needed (1:8-11). And even if it was needed, the correction

that the law demanded was to be tempered by the gospel of grace (1:12-17). The essence of salvation was to be found in understanding grace in Christ.

The Old Testament made a distinction between sins of ignorance and sins of defiance (1:13; Lev. 4:2; Num. 15:27-31). Atonement was available for the former, but not for the latter. Paul's sins against Christ and the church were in ignorance but still needed God's atoning mercy. The expression "trustworthy saying" (1:15) is literally, "faithful is the word." This was a formula used by Paul in 1 and 2 Timothy and Titus to introduce important truths (3:1; 4:9; 2 Tim. 2:11; Titus 3:8).

1:18-20 The Command Entrusted to Timothy

The command to stop teaching false doctrines had been stated in 1:3. The goal of that command was godly character (1:5). This command had been entrusted to Timothy and was a major purpose for his going to Ephesus. The "good fight" (1:18) had to do with moving others to love and disciplining the rebellious. The means of fighting are stressed: keeping faith and a good conscience. Fighting the good fight is moving people on to a pure heart, good conscience, and sincere faith.

The false teachers were excommunicated, but the purpose was corrective, not final, judgment. This was a proper use of the law according to the gospel. Paul dealt with the false teachers by delivering them over to Satan. This remedial discipline, also known as excommunication (cf. Matt. 18:17), was designed to destroy their fleshly attitudes and drive them back to Christ (see note on 1 Cor. 5:5).

2:1–6:19 THE INSTRUCTION APPLIED: COMMUNITY TRADITIONS

Overview: The central thought behind this instruction is found in 3:14-15—proper conduct in the house of God. Notice the support of the truth and proper use of the law. The discussion of prayer (2:1-15) was designed to help the readers adopt God's desires for world salvation. The section on leadership (3:1-16) urges men and women to adequately serve God's truth.

The condemnation of the lying teachers (4:1-16) comes because they have denied God's truth.

2:1-15 Prayer: Adopt God's Desires

2:1-2 EXCLUSIONS IN PRAYER
"Then" connects this section with the previous verses. First Timothy 2:2 elaborates the "everyone" of 2:1. Paul was revealing possible areas being excluded in prayer. Paul's instruction to pray for kings was especially significant in light of the fact that Nero (A.D. 54–68) was in office at this time. Love that comes out of a pure heart, good conscience, and a sincere faith reaches out beyond the community. Paul used four terms to describe the ministry of prayer: "requests"—specific petition or supplication; "prayers"—a general word for prayer emphasizing worship and reverence; "intercession"—a technical term for approaching a king, suggesting intercession on behalf of others; and "thanksgiving"—an attitude of thankfulness and gratitude that should always accompany prayer.

2:3-4 GOD HAS A UNIVERSAL DESIRE TO REDEEM HUMANITY
Paul's desire for universal prayer was based on the universal desire of God—the salvation of all the human race. God's desire defines and shapes the nature of this age and should also shape the behavior of believers. Paul desired that the Ephesian believers would pray sincerely for the salvation of all people. This would provide the link between praying and having a quiet life. Prayer for the world's salvation would also bring peace and righteousness. Salvation is characterized as "good" and pleasing to God (2:3). Sadly, in their disputes the believers were excluding some from their prayers who needed salvation. God is not partisan (cf. 1:16; 4:10). This fact is the reason why it is good to pray for the salvation of all people (cf. 1:13).

2:5-7 THE UNIVERSAL RANSOM
The "for" of 2:5 explains why it is good to pray for the salvation of others (2:3) and why God desires all to be saved (2:4). A "mediator" (2:5) is one who stands between two parties to remove a disagreement or reach a common goal. The mediator must perfectly represent both parties. Christ, the God-man, is the perfect mediator, representing both God's interests and man's without prejudice

or compromise. This verse supports the doctrine of *hypostatic union*—that the deity and humanity of Jesus Christ were united in one person forever without the mingling of attributes.

Paul indicated that their prayer life did not reflect the character of God who desires all to be saved. Adopting God's attitude toward the world issued in truth, redemption, and prayer. Blocking God's desire by refusing to pray for unbelievers would issue in God's wrath and dissension in the church.

Paul had already given three reasons to pray for all people: all people have one God, one mediator, and one ransom. But he returned to his own experience (2:7) to provide the fourth reason of why prayers should be made for all: God had assigned Paul to work with the Gentiles, the group disregarded by most Jewish Christians.

2:8-15 PROPER CHARACTER IN PRAYER
2:8-10 Effective prayer and holy living.
Believers are to live holy lives (2:8). To "lift up holy hands" was a common posture for prayer in the biblical period (cf. 1 Kings 8:22; Pss. 28:2; 63:4; 134:2). The "holy hands" symbolized a pure and holy life. Prayers of believers should reflect what has been said about God, Christ, and Paul's worldwide ministry. Truth is now applied to the community. God wants all people to know the truth. Prayer is related to the pure heart and should reflect God's desire for universal salvation.

Women should also live holy lives. The "clothing" of a godly woman is to be respectable and they are expected to behave with self-restraint. Their good works spring from inner goodness (2:10). Regardless of popular fashion, discreet and modest apparel is the standard for Christian women. The expression "braided hair or gold" refers to "gold-braided hair." In Paul's day it was the custom of dancing girls to braid their hair with golden bangles that shimmered as they moved. Hands are viewed as symbols of life; clothing is viewed as a symbol of character. People mirroring God's desire for universal salvation cannot come to prayer in an unholy way.

2:11-15 Leadership and proper order in the church. Paul moves from strife between people regardless of gender (2:8) to strife between men and women (2:11-15). Paul encouraged women to receive doctrine and instruction with a teachable and submissive attitude. In Paul's day, Jewish men and boys were required to learn the law, but there was no such requirement for women. Paul did not want Christian women to be ignorant of the Scriptures and encouraged them to learn. The words "full submission" (2:11) literally mean "under orders." As they learned, women were to listen to and respect those whom God had placed in positions of church leadership.

Paul's words in 2:12 do not mean that women should never teach. They are encouraged to teach in certain contexts (cf. Titus 2:3). Although debated, this appears to prohibit women from holding permanent positions of authoritative teaching in the church. "To have authority" (2:12) is to act as one's own authority, to have mastery over, or to exercise dominion. Teaching in the meeting of the church is apparently viewed by Paul as an exercise of authority (cf. also 1 Cor. 14:34-35). Women are to maintain their proper relationships with their husbands. To "learn in quietness" refers to an outer expression of an inward state.

The focus of 2:13-14 is on Genesis 1–3. Eve overstepped the bounds set by Adam and God (cf. Gen. 3:17, "because you listened to [obeyed] your wife"). See also Genesis 3:13; 16:2; and 2 Corinthians 11:3. In this context the woman was deceived into usurping the authority placed over her. Paul sought to show that if she had listened to Adam she would not have sinned. Eve and women generally, by accepting their God-given functions, can be saved the trouble that results from overstepping their bounds. Although equal in spiritual privilege (1 Pet. 3:7), men and women have different roles in terms of ministry. God's created order establishes these role relationships for men and women which, if bypassed, lead to disaster as illustrated by the fall.

"Through childbirth" (2:15) is Paul's way of summarizing the role of the woman (cf. 5:14). It refers to the whole process and related activities of bearing and raising children. Many evangelicals believe Paul is referring to salvation through the incarnation of Christ. But this seems like an obscure way to refer to this doctrine. Contextually, Paul seems to be referring to physical salvation or deliverance from the temptation to usurp authority (the problem of 2:12). Such deliverance is possible for the woman who gives herself to the ministry of home and family life.

3:1–4:16 Leadership: Serve God's Truth

3:1-16 THE QUALITIES OF TRUE AND FALSE LEADERS

3:1 Choosing appropriate leadership. True and effective leadership supports and serves God's truth. The point of this section is to make sure that a person with a great desire for leadership (3:1) has the appropriate character. The problem was not with desiring to be a leader. It was with being qualified to be a leader. Leadership is not something a person gets just because he wants it. "Overseer" (3:1) emphasizes the responsibility of giving oversight. The parallel term "elder" (Titus 1:5, 7) emphasizes the dignity and maturity required for the office. The stress on these qualifications was the moral and spiritual qualities necessary to give leadership to God's people. The first and last qualifications are foundational (3:1, 7). The others are more specific.

3:2-7 The man: overseer. "Above reproach" (3:2) summarizes all the qualifying characteristics that follow. "Must be" (3:2) controls all the traits that follow. "Husband of but one wife" refers to a character trait: a faithful husband or a sexually controlled single person. The expression literally reads "one wife's husband." The grammar also suggests that character, not just a head count of wives is in view. To be qualified for the office of elder, a married man must be faithful to his one wife. With reference to women, see 1 Timothy 5:9, 14-15. The temperate man knows his functions and limitations and is able to exercise his abilities accordingly. "Hospitable" (3:2) is related to Exodus 22:21-22. The overseer must have a household that can be run similarly to the household of God. The home always reflects the character and ability of its leader.

3:8-10 The man: deacon. The deacon is just as important as an overseer. The word "deacon" literally means "servant." The term can be used of an officer in the church or in an unofficial sense of anyone who serves (cf. Eph. 6:21). The origin of the office of deacon can be traced to Acts 6:1-6. The qualifications are similar to those of the elder. Dignity is related to that which produces worship. A deacon is dignified if signs of a higher order can be detected in him (cf. also 1 Tim. 2:2; 3:4). Three negatives follow which further define and explain dignity. Conscience (3:9) is the source of love (cf. 1:5, 19). The deacon also is worthy of being tested to ascertain that he is blameless. The "likewise" (3:8) presumes the testing of elders. Lest some should think that the "lesser" office of deacon does not require this, Paul adds this emphatic command.

3:11 The woman: deaconess. The women mentioned in 3:11 are logically related to deacons. But the Greek word for women does not necessarily mean wives. It is debated whether the women mentioned here refer to the wives of deacons or to deaconesses. If they were deaconesses, one would expect that they would be mentioned after the discussion of deacons. The placement of the verse in the middle of the paragraph about deacons seems to suggest that they were the wives of deacons. Yet one wonders why this qualification would be mentioned for deacons and not for elders (cf. 3:1-7). It has been suggested that deacons could be men or women and that verse 11 just adds qualifications relevant to those deacons who are female. It is oriented to an office of deacon relative to women. Phoebe is called a deaconess (Rom. 16:1), but this may reflect the unofficial use of the word ("service") as in 1 Corinthians 16:15.

3:12-13 The man: deacon. Paul returns to the office of deacon to stress further qualifications (3:12) and rewards (3:13).

3:14-16 The reason for writing: conduct in God's household. Paul revealed at this point the purpose of his letter to Timothy: it was to inform his associate and the church at Ephesus concerning the proper conduct of members in the local church. The "mystery of godliness" (3:16) is the bringing together of the spheres of heaven and earth in the incarnation of Christ. It focuses on Christ, who is able to produce a life of godliness in those who trust him. This verse may have been an early creed or perhaps a Christian hymn. This verse details the "truth" that is upheld by the church. That definition functions to underscore the importance of qualified church leadership. Leaders support the truth of Christ by their lives.

4:1-16 FALSE AND TRUE LEADERSHIP MANIFESTED

4:1-5 False: fallen from the faith. Paul set forth instructions for dealing with false teachers. God has a certain intention for those who believe and know the truth: the enjoyment of creation. But false leaders have rejected what God called good, his creation (Gen. 1–3 is still on Paul's mind). These teachers are liars and hypocrites. The "later times" (4:1) is a term virtually equivalent to "the last days" (2 Tim. 3:1; Heb. 1:2; James 5:3; 2 Pet. 3:3) and refers to the latter days of the present age, the age of promise, which anticipates the age to come, the age of fulfillment. The false teachers' consciences were "seared" so that they had lost sensitivity to moral issues (4:2). The practices of celibacy and fasting are not meritorious in themselves; in fact, their practice may imply unbelief in the complete and free salvation God does provide (4:3). Paul's words, along with Acts 10:15 and Mark 7:19, demonstrate that the Jewish distinctions in food (Lev. 11) are no longer valid (4:4).

4:6-16 True: discipline in the faith. Paul explained the nature of beneficial discipline. Timothy was to feed on the word of God. He was to be constantly nourished in and trained by its teachings (4:6). "Godless myths and old wives' tales" (4:7) refer to the Jewish myths mentioned in 1:4. Satan loves to get believers sidetracked to speculations on religious trivia. The phrase "train yourself" (4:7) comes from the Greek verb from which the English word "gymnasium" is derived. Like the disciplined athlete, the Christian is to pursue the development of his spiritual life. This is a continued corrective to the asceticism of 4:3. Profitable teaching, not fables, is needed.

First Timothy 4:9-10 refers back to 2:3-4. Timothy was to strive for the maturity that counts (4:11-16). The verbs in 4:11 encourage Timothy to keep on prescribing and teaching these things. Paul kept going back to the basics. Modeling is an essential component to education (4:12). Paul listed five areas in which Timothy should serve as an example. Note the "work" words, 1:3, 18; 4:6-7, 10. Timothy's young age was not of ultimate importance. Paul used the Greek verb translated "devote," "keep hold" and "agree" several times (1:4; 3:9; 4:13; 6:3). All three terms of 4:13 describe an area of public ministry: "reading" Scripture in worship services, "preaching"—encouraging people to respond, and "teaching"—formal instruction based on the word of God.

In 4:14 it is debated whether Paul was referring to Timothy's spiritual gift or his spiritual office. Spiritual gifts are divine enablements for service in the body of Christ (see notes on 1 Cor. 12:1–14:20). The laying on of the elders' hands, an act of identification (Acts 13:3), accompanied Timothy's prophetic training. The result of Timothy's training and "gift" was a transparent character (4:15-16). "Save" (4:16) refers to deliverance from the reigning power and influence of sin, the present aspect of salvation (also referred to as sanctification).

5:1–6:2 Honor for Household Members

5:1-16 HONOR AND CARE BY AGE GROUPS
5:1-2 The family perspective. This section teaches how to view members of the congregation while trying to move them on to maturity. The family perspective is based on God's desire to save all people. Dealing with people in the body of Christ is a practical extension of what it means to be thinking like God. The section covers honor for widows (5:3-16), leaders (5:17-25), and masters (6:1-2). The key word throughout is "honor," and Paul encouraged Timothy to show honor appropriately to each group of people in the church (5:3, 17; 6:1). Timothy is to continue appealing to the older men rather than issuing sharp rebukes (lit., "to strike with blows"—in this case referring to words rather than fists).

5:3-16 Widows. Believers have an obligation to care for widows in the church. This is first a family responsibility (5:4, 8, 16) but becomes a church responsibility when there is no family available (5:16). Not all widows were qualified to receive financial support from the church. Those who did qualify took a "pledge" (5:12) and were placed on a "list" (5:9). These widows were apparently prayer warriors who committed themselves to

serving the church. The age qualification would mean that there would be no chance for remarriage (5:9; cf. 5:14). The phrase "washing the feet of the saints" (5:10) is a figurative reference for sacrificial service to others (cf. John 13:1-17). On the phrase "faithful to her husband," see the male counterpart in 3:2. Some young widows had already allowed Satan to lead them into sin (5:15). The final case (5:16) is a woman, probably a widow herself, with dependent widows.

5:17-25 HONOR FOR FAMILY LEADERS
5:17-21 Showing honor to elders. The use of the words "recognition" (5:3) and "respect" (6:1) show that "double honor" (5:17) refers to high esteem, not money (Matt. 10:10; 1 Cor. 9:1-14). "Elders" (5:17; cf. 3:1) have the responsibility of superintending the affairs of the church. The quotations of 5:18 are taken from Deuteronomy 25:4 and the words of Christ in Luke 10:7 and Matthew 10:10.

Honor must also relate to a leader's reputation (5:19-21). Although high standards had been set for elders (3:1-7), Paul knew that their office would not make them immune to sin. Here Paul applied the principles of church discipline (Matt. 18:15-18) to the case of a sinning elder. Discipline of leadership must be founded on fact, not rumor. The requirement for several witnesses was a Mosaic command (Deut. 17:6; cf. Matt. 18:16; 2 Cor. 13:1). The purpose of the public rebuke was to give a warning (5:20). It is debated whether the public rebuke (a reproof that brings conviction) applied only to the elder who continued in sin or to any elder who sinned on a particular occasion. The purpose "that the others [of the elders] may take warning" may favor the latter viewpoint.

No partiality was to be shown to certain elders of the church (5:21). This relates to allowing accusations to be received for some and not others, publicly rebuking some and not others, laying hands on some and not others.

5:22-25 The importance of purity in church leaders. The section of 5:22-25 concerns freedom from sin and care in ordination. Timothy was careful to avoid any appearance of evil and totally abstained from alcoholic beverages at the expense of his personal health (5:23). Paul explained that keeping himself free from sin (5:22) did not necessitate his abstaining from a medicinal use of wine (cf. Prov. 31:6-7; Luke 10:34).

Paul warned against the hasty appointment of an elder to office (5:24-25). While many have understood Paul to be forbidding a hasty ordination, the context seems to suggest that the concern was over a hasty restoration of a leader to his former position after discipline. The principle of caution would apply in both situations. The key idea here was that an elder is known by his fruits. While some men's character immediately disqualifies them from the office, the character of others will be revealed only with the passing of time. Both the good (5:24) and the bad (5:25) will ultimately be apparent. The "judgment" of 5:24 concerns the evaluation of a person's qualifications for leadership, not the final judgment of God.

6:1-2 HONOR IN WORKING ROLES
Slaves were to show respect to their masters for the sake of Christ's name. Slaves with Christian masters were to show respect for their masters even though they were also brothers in Christ. Slavery was an accepted social and economic institution during the biblical period. Rather than seeking to abolish the institution, Paul sought to improve the situation by giving directives to servants and masters (cf. 1 Cor. 7:21; Eph. 6:5-9; Col. 3:22–4:1; Titus 2:9-10).

6:3-19 Correctives to Materialism
6:3-10 THOSE WHO WANT:
FALSE TEACHERS
Materialism was the motivation for the false teachers' ministries (6:3-5). "False doctrines" (6:3) are those not in agreement with the teachings of Jesus and that do not lead to godliness (Gal. 1:6-7). The results of refusing the path of contentment are given in 6:9-10. In contrast to the materialistic motives of the false teachers, Paul pointed out that godly Christian living does result in gain, both material and spiritual (Ps. 34:10; Phil. 4:19). The key is the development of "contentment"—an inner satisfaction no

matter what the situation God has ordained (Phil. 4:11-12). The focus of contentment is on God's gifts. People are born and die with nothing, except the life God has given. Anything else a person might add is temporary or optional and should not affect contentment with God's gifts. The "love of money," not money itself, is the root of all sorts of evil (6:10).

6:11-16 THE CHARGE TO
FLEE MATERIALISM
The flight from materialism is achieved by pursuing godly character traits. The person consumed with seeking righteousness will not have time to be consumed by materialism. Paul's words in 6:12 are taken from the athletic arena. Timothy was challenged to fight on in the arena entered by all who become Christians. He was to grasp life as opposed to wandering from it (6:10). See also 1:6, 19 for a similar concept. For Jesus' confession before Pontius Pilate (6:13), see Matthew 27:11; Mark 15:2; Luke 23:2-3; and John 18:36-37. Paul linked a good life to the good confession of Christ. The unseen God (6:16) was the center of Paul's life. God alone possesses immortality by his divine nature, and believers inherit it by their new birth. This grasp of eternal life is the foundation for purity in leadership and community life.

6:17-19 THOSE WHO HAVE: THE RICH
The wealthy have special challenges in the area of pride and contentment. They are to see their wealth as given by God, not by their own abilities. The purpose for their wealth is to enjoy by giving, not to covet or hoard. If the rich are free to give (6:18), they will be able to take hold of true riches (6:19). The material goods of this life are a mere shadow of the eternal reality to come.

6:20-21 CLOSING CHARGE
Paul repeated his charge to guard the truth in true knowledge. Paul's final admonition to "turn away from godless chatter" (6:20) reminded the readers of the central problem of the letter (cf. 1:3-4; 4:1-3, 7; 6:3-5).

2 Timothy

BASIC FACTS

HISTORICAL SETTING

The primary recipient of this letter was Timothy (1:2). For information on Timothy, see the Historical Setting section for 1 Timothy. Since his first letter to Timothy, Paul may have visited Ephesus (1 Tim. 3:14) and ministered in Asia Minor, Macedonia, Spain, and on the island of Crete. The persecution of Christians in Rome began shortly after Rome burned in July of A.D. 64. Nero blamed the Christians for that catastrophe, and Christianity was made an illegal religion. It was probably in the summer of A.D. 64 under the persecution of Nero that Peter was martyred.

Paul knew that his death was imminent and that his work on earth was done (4:6-8). He was alone in Rome except for Luke (4:11). Apparently some had deserted him at his first defense before the Roman authorities (4:16). Paul desired Timothy and John Mark to join him before winter (4:9-13).

The immediate occasion for writting this letter was the need to encourage Timothy to stand fast in the face of opposition and apostasy. Paul could not be sure Timothy would arrive in Rome before his death, and he wanted to present some final instructions to his most intimate disciple.

AUTHOR

The letter identifies Paul as the author (1:1), and the letter contains autobiographical material that fits the life of Paul as recorded elsewhere (2 Tim. 3:10-11; 4:10-11, 19-20).

DATE

The letter was probably written while Paul was a prisoner in Rome (1:8, 16-17) for the second time. Paul was martyred in the spring of A.D. 68, so the letter may be dated around autumn of A.D. 67.

PURPOSE

Paul's second letter to Timothy was designed to encourage the readers by showing how Paul was able to cope with his impending death by his security in God's commitment to the spread of the gospel. Paul desired the readers to be more concerned with the ongoing success of the gospel than with their own personal status and comfort.

GUIDING CONCEPTS

GOOD WORKS
In this letter, Paul stressed good works (2:21; 3:17; cf. also 4:5, 7, 17). Good works are designed for the profit of the individual, but their end is the furtherance of redemption. Good works are based on the truth of God's word (3:16-17), which is profitable (3:16) and offers eternal life (1:1, 10; 2:10). Paul gave Timothy insight into wisdom in a crisis situation and helped him find stability in God's control over all of life's crises.

OPPOSITION
Opposition is seen in relationship to shame and suffering. The concept of shame occurs frequently (1:8, 12, 16; 2:15; 4:16). The opposition mentioned in 2 Timothy stems primarily from within the Christian community. The purpose of suffering is seen throughout the letter (1:8; 1:12; 2:3, 7, 10; 3:11; 4:5, 14, 18). Opposition is to be met with solid preaching of God's word (4:2) and consistent purity of character (2:21-22).

USEFULNESS
Three parables are used to describe a faithful person (2:2-6). The focus is on service that pleases the master, in this case God. The useful person is described as one who can use the word of God accurately, that is, apply God's word as he intended. Usefulness is grounded in following the will of God through his word (2:14-15, 21, 26; 4:11).

BIBLE-WIDE CONCEPTS

THE KINGDOM PROMISED TO DAVID
In a section on endurance in suffering hardship, Paul asked Timothy to remember two things about Jesus: that he was risen from the dead and that he was descended from David (2:8). The link between Christ's death and resurrection and David reveals the Old Testament perspective through which Paul viewed his sufferings. Jesus was the risen and exalted King who now reigned in the kingdom promised to a son of David. The pattern of death, resurrection, and reigning can be followed by Christ's faithful followers (2:11-12). If Christ's disciples die with him, they will reign with him. This Davidic link belongs to all believers through Christ. Finally, Paul looked forward to entering the kingdom of the greater Son of David (4:18). The reality of the Davidic kingdom, predicted from 2 Samuel 7 onward, was an essential part of Paul's encouragement and commands to Timothy (2 Tim. 4:1).

CONFLICT IN THE LAST DAYS
Throughout this letter Paul spoke of events in the last days (specifically mentioned in 3:1). The opposition and hypocrisy of the last days is a pervasive theme in the New Testament (Matt. 24:24; John 2:17; 15:18-25; 16:33; Acts 14:22; 20:29; 1 Thess. 3:3; 1 Pet. 2:21; 4:19), and it was also foreseen in the Old Testament (Ps. 69:1-12).

NEEDS MET BY SECOND TIMOTHY

This very personal letter, written toward the end of Paul's life, was directly aimed at meeting specific needs for Timothy. Paul wrote to strengthen the church in Ephesus, to encourage Timothy's own perseverance, and to remind Timothy of the central place of Scripture in his ministry. Paul assured Timothy that Christianity would survive in the face of Roman persecution because God, not just people, was ultimately guarding his gospel and preserving those who responded in faith. Paul reinforced God's unwavering personal commitment to Timothy to strengthen his desire to maintain a vital relationship with God. Finally, Timothy's focus was to be on the Scriptures—the document that had been for generations the authoritative guide to salvation and proper living. Paul's words of advice met a number of needs felt by Timothy in particular and the church in general. The content and structure of 2 Timothy show that Paul intended to answer the following questions for his readers.

- What truths will help believers resist the pressures of opposition to the truth of the gospel in Christ?
- How can believers avoid being ashamed of the gospel?
- How central should the Scriptures be for guidance and instruction in godliness?

As Paul met the personal needs of Timothy, he also met the needs of Christians throughout the ages. As in so many other Biblical books, the central issue concerns believing in God when life is difficult and unfair. Second Timothy gives two vital reasons for remaining faithful to God during hard times. First, Paul shows steps to affirming that God has not abandoned his people. Not only is God perfectly guarding the continuance of his worldwide spread of the gospel, he is also noting every individual good deed believers do and will justly reward them. Second, hard times must not distract believers from rigorous attention to God's word. They must counter fuzzy thinking about God and misinterpretations of the Bible by accurate teaching. They must resist feeling ashamed of their position in Christ and letting fear of hostility silence their witness to the world.

OUTLINE OF SECOND TIMOTHY

A. GREETING (1:1-2)

B. THANKSGIVING FOR A SINCERE FAITH (1:3-5)

C. REKINDLED CONVICTION AND DISCIPLINE (1:6–2:26)
    1. On the Basis of Attitude: Controlled Boldness (1:6-7)
    2. On the Basis of Attitude: Commitment to Suffer (1:8-11)
    3. On the Basis of Attitude: Suffering and Shame (1:12-14)
    4. Guarding the Trust: Discipline and Purity in Suffering (1:15–2:26)

D. FAITHFULNESS AMIDST OPPOSITION TO THE TRUTH (3:1–4:8)
    1. Biblical Commitment in Difficult Times (3:1-17)
    2. Paul's Solemn Charge: Preach the Word (4:1-8)

E. PAUL'S CONTINUED NEED FOR FAITHFUL MINISTERS (4:9-18)

1. Need for Friends (4:9-13)
2. A Warning about an Enemy (4:14-15)
3. The Lord's Faithfulness (4:16-18)

F. CLOSING GREETINGS (4:19-21)

G. BENEDICTION (4:22)

SECOND TIMOTHY NOTES

1:1-2 GREETING

Timothy was Paul's "son" in the sense that Paul had led him to the Lord and nourished him in the faith (cf. 1 Tim. 1:2). For more on Timothy, see note on 1 Timothy 1:2. The author (1:1) is an apostle; he is not to be taken lightly, even by his dear friend Timothy. The promise of eternal life is an important theme of this letter (1:1, 10; 2:11; 4:8, 18; cf. with John 6:31-33). The concept of "promise" (1:1) takes the reader back through the ages to God the Father who has been consistently working to bring about man's redemption.

1:3-5 THANKSGIVING FOR A SINCERE FAITH

Paul longed to see Timothy (1:3-4). Note the clarity of Paul's conscience despite the fact that he was facing criminal charges in a Roman prison. Paul's forefathers had served God with clear consciences. Paul displayed a strong sense of continuity with the Old Testament remnant through his piety and reverence for God. "Tears" (1:4) had been shed at Paul's last parting from Timothy, as in Acts 20:37. Paul's remembrance of Timothy's tears colors this letter.

Timothy had a sincere faith (1:5). Paul made a link back to the God of Timothy's mother and grandmother. He wanted to remind Timothy of all the people throughout history who had served God properly. Timothy was "sincere" (cf. 1 Tim. 1:5) in continuity with his ancestors. Timothy's faith had been cultivated by his godly grandmother, Lois, and mother, Eunice, who had trained him in the Old Testament Scriptures (cf. 3:14-15). The faith of his mother and grandmother represented the long line of those who had truly believed in the God of Israel (cf. 3:15).

1:6–2:26 REKINDLED CONVICTION AND DISCIPLINE

1:6-7 On the Basis of Attitude: Controlled Boldness

1:6 FAN THE FIRE INTO FLAME
The historical context for Paul's words in this verse was persecution. Paul saw Timothy as one who was going to have to carry on in this situation (cf. 1:3-5). As the coals of a fire need to be stirred to keep it from dying out, so Timothy needed to constantly exercise the spiritual gifts that God had bestowed upon him. The phrase "fan into flame" (1:6) is better translated "keep it hot." Timothy had not let his fire go out. The laying on of Paul's hands did not procure the gift but was the accompanying circumstance associated with the announcement of Timothy's gift (cf. 1 Tim. 4:14).

At the time he wrote 2 Timothy, Paul was a prisoner in Rome. He was chained as a criminal (2:9) in the Mamertine prison adjacent to the Roman forum. He knew that his death was imminent and that his work on earth was done (4:6-8). Paul recognized that though individuals will die, Christianity will live on.

1:7 THE NATURE OF THE GIFT IS DESCRIBED
The effect of God's gift should not result in cowardice but power. Of the three characteristics of God's gift, "power" is the ability to accomplish what God wants, "love" is the focus of and end result of power, and "self-discipline" is sound judgment to know how to combine power with love in a time of crisis. Paul urged Timothy to think about who was with him (1:6-7) and then urged him to think about what he was doing in the world (1:8-11).

1:8-11 On the Basis of Attitude: Commitment to Suffer

Paul warned Timothy never to be ashamed of the gospel (1:8; cf. 1:12, 16). The "power of God" (1:8) is power to endure suffering and 1:9-11 defines that power: it is the power of God's gospel of grace.

1:12-14 On the Basis of Attitude: Suffering and Shame

The words "what I have entrusted" (1:12) literally read "my entrustment." This may refer to what Paul had entrusted to Christ, that is, his faith or commitment. But it most likely refers to what Christ had entrusted to Paul, that is, the gospel. The context on the concept of entrustment relates also to what had been entrusted to Timothy (1:14) and what he would entrust to others (2:2; cf. also 1 Tim. 6:20). God will guard the entrustment of the gospel until the day of Christ's return when all dangers for the believer have past. Paul knew that God had every intention of preserving and maintaining the gospel ministry on the earth. Security is not founded upon human effort but upon God and his work of grace through Christ.

1:15–2:26 Guarding the Trust: Discipline and Purity in Suffering

1:15-18 AN EXAMPLE OF ONE WHO REMAINED FAITHFUL
These verses give positive and negative examples of those who had been entrusted with the gospel. Christianity had become an illegal religion. Paul referred to those now in Asia, a Roman province in Asia Minor (western Turkey), who refused to speak on his behalf in Rome. Onesiphorus stands in stark contrast to the defectors. He had ministered to Paul in Ephesus and had sought him out in Rome despite the persecution he might suffer as a result.

2:1-2 TIMOTHY'S TASK: TEACH THE FAITHFUL
Paul's circumstances during his second Roman imprisonment (2:9) were quite different from his first imprisonment as described in Acts 28:16, 23, 30-31. Paul's conclusion "then" (2:1) was based on the preceding examples. Timothy must have

strength (Eph. 6:10; Phil. 4:13; 2 Tim. 4:17) for passing on the truth. Paul used six illustrations in chapter 2 to emphasize the need for diligence and sacrifice in serving Christ: a son (2:1), a soldier (2:3), an athlete (2:5), a farmer (2:6), a workman (2:15), a vessel (2:21), and a bondservant (2:24). Paul's concern was for the faithful proclamation of his teaching without addition or subtraction. The key was to find those who were faithful (trustworthy, reliable) and capable (competent, qualified).

2:3-7 TIMOTHY'S TASK: SUFFER HARDSHIP
In 2:2 Paul presented two important concepts: faithfulness and the necessity of transmitting the gospel message. Paul used three parables to describe a faithful person. Male images were used because he was discussing the pastoral role. The Christian life involves warfare (2:3; cf. Eph. 6:10-17), and the Christian soldier must regard hardship as inevitable in a world that is hostile to Christ (John 15:18-25). Paul emphasized that hardship, struggle, discipline, and labor precede the enjoyment of reward. For any working person the master's pleasure is most important. The soldier always seeks to please his commander (2:3-4). The athlete abides by the rules for his event to win the prize (2:5). Only after the farmer has worked his fields long and hard may he accept his privilege to feed himself first (2:6). Paul made it clear that the prize to be won in the Christian life would only come after hardship and sacrifice.

2:8-13 TIMOTHY'S FOCUS: REMEMBER
God's promises to David as fulfilled in Christ were the foundation of Paul's hope for deliverance after suffering. The present suffering and opposition could not deter God from keeping his promises (2:9). The word Paul used for "criminal" (2:9) was a strong word used to describe the two criminals who hung beside Christ at his crucifixion (cf. Luke 23:32-33, 39). Paul's chains did not hinder his proclamation of the gospel (2:10).

Paul appealed to a familiar Christian poem or hymn to emphasize that present suffering was necessary for future glory (2:11-13). The four lines are built around an "if-then" logic. It is a powerful and uncompromising statement of the commitment of God to furthering his gospel message. Even if many (like the examples in 2:17-18; 3:1-5) should end up denying Christ, Christ will be faithful to continue to proclaim his gospel through someone else. The fact that some "disown" Christ (2:12) may indicate that their initial faith was not genuine. Such a denial would be the evidence of unbelief. It is also possible that Paul was referring to a temporary denial of Christ such as Peter's (Matt. 26:69-75). The character of God is the foundation for faithfulness and strength. He is faithful (Rom. 3:3) to his mission of world redemption and judgment. Believers may disown him, but he will not disown those who believe in him. The faithful person is the one who acts like Jesus to bring redemption to the elect. The believer's strength is found in Christ Jesus and his strength and commitment to the task.

2:14-19 CORRECTING THE UNFAITHFUL: SPEAKING GOD'S WORD ACCURATELY
God's laborers were to handle his word accurately, proclaiming and applying it to life (2:15). The expression "correctly handles" (2:15) literally means "to cut straight" and may have it's background in Paul's tent-making business. At any rate, it is the opposite of the condition described in 2:16-18. These two false teachers taught that the resurrection was already past, apparently suggesting that the resurrection was a spiritual rather than a physical reality. "God's solid foundation" (2:19) refers to the foundation of the church (Matt. 16:18; 1 Tim. 3:15; Eph. 2:19-22). This foundation is based on God's faithfulness in fulfilling his promises.

2:20-26 CORRECTING THE UNFAITHFUL: PURITY IN GOD'S HOUSE
Honored vessels are cleansed vessels (2:20-21). Paul gave three descriptions of how to find cleansing: flee lusts (2:22); refuse arguments or speculations (2:23); and be patient and gentle (2:24-26). These attributes describe a useful vessel (2:21) and one that will keep the gospel, not self-interest, in mind (2:10). The command of 2:22 is a present imperative, "keep on fleeing." "His" (2:26) could refer to God or Satan. It may be that the capturing is parenthetical: those having been held captive by Satan will come to their senses and do God's will.

3:1-4:8 FAITHFULNESS AMIDST OPPOSITION TO THE TRUTH
3:1-17 Biblical Commitment in Difficult Times
3:1-9 EVIL HEARERS BRING DIFFICULTY FOR GOD'S MINISTER
Paul reminded Timothy that men will love themselves (3:1-5). The "last days" refers to the last part of this present age (the age of promise), which anticipates the age to come (the age of fulfillment). The New Testament writers regarded Christians as living in the "last days" (1 John 2:18; Acts 2:16-17). The apostates referred to in 3:2-5 were the unsaved who met with the church.

Paul continued by showing that these opponents to truth would come to a bad end (3:6-9). Jannes and Jambres (3:8) are not named elsewhere in Scripture, although they are named in the Targum of Jonathan on Exodus 7:11, 22. The Jewish Targums are free renderings of the Hebrew text into Aramaic. These men were Egyptian magicians who performed counterfeit miracles in opposition to Moses. Their names were preserved by Jewish tradition and thus known to Paul.

3:10-17 ABIDING IN WISDOM BRINGS SALVATION
Timothy was to follow Paul's example (3:10-13). But he also had the greater example of the Scriptures (3:14-17). Timothy had a lifetime acquaintance with the Scriptures due to the faithful teaching of his mother and grandmother (3:15; 1:5).

Second Timothy 3:16 is a very important verse for the doctrine of Scripture. Paul declared that "all" (not some) of Scripture is God-breathed. This term refers to the source of Scripture. It came from God (as if it were his breath) to the men who wrote it (cf. 2 Pet. 1:21). This means that God so directed the human authors of Scripture that, using their individual interests and literary styles, his complete thought for man was recorded without error. As a result, the Bible is inerrant (an accurate record) and infallible (a reliable guide).

In theory the doctrine of inspiration relates only to the original manuscripts. But Paul was not being theoretical here. He was saying that even the Greek translation of the Old Testament, the Septuagint, which he consistently used in his quotations, was God-breathed. His point was not a technical discussion of original versus present copies of

Scripture. His point was to emphasize the God-breathed profitability that comes from opening up the Scriptures and humbly applying them to life. Because it finds its source in God, it is profitable. And it was that profitability that was being eroded by the careless attitudes fostered in the last days (3:1-13). But the Bible has the wisdom that leads to salvation (3:15) and profitability in godly living (3:16-17). No element of doubt exists. When believers go to Scripture, they will be met with divine profit.

4:1-8 Paul's Solemn Charge: Preach the Word

4:1-2 PREPARED TO PREACH
Paul reminded Timothy that the certainty of Christ's appearing and his coming kingdom were incentives to faithfulness. The preaching of God's word was to be powerful (reprove, rebuke, exhort), but the preacher was to be patient. Content must be delivered through pure character. Whether the time was opportune or not, Timothy was to preach the truth of God recorded in Scripture.

4:3-8 PAUL'S EXAMPLE OF FAITHFULNESS
Paul took opportunities to speak without worrying about the interest of the listeners. His eloquent and confident testimony (4:6-8) touched on his present readiness for death, his past faithfulness in service, and his future reward in glory. Paul used a metaphor taken from the custom of offering a wine libation as the concluding act in the sacrificial rite (4:6; cf. Num. 15:1-10). Paul's "departure" refers to his death. The word is used of loosing a vessel from its moorings or of a soldier striking his tent. Paul drew upon athletic imagery to refer to his past faithful service to Christ (2 Tim. 4:7). Like a wrestler, he had agonized through the fight. Like a runner, he had finished the foot race. Paul kept the faith by defending it from attacks and by observing its obligations. At the end of the race course there awaited a laurel wreath that would be placed on the head of the victor (4:8). It was a perishable wreath (1 Cor. 9:25), but Paul's reward was an imperishable crown. For other crowns, see 1 Thessalonians 2:19; James 1:12; and 1 Peter 5:4. Paul emphasized the appearing of Christ at both the beginning and end of this section (4:1, 8).

4:9-18 PAUL'S CONTINUED NEED FOR FAITHFUL MINISTERS

4:9-13 Need for Friends
For Thessalonica, see the note on 1 Thessalonians 1:1. For Galatia, see the note on Galatians 1:2. Dalmatia was located in the southern part of Illyricum (Rom. 15:19), modern Yugoslavia. Mark's earlier failure in his Christian life (Acts 13:13; 15:37-40) did not destroy his usefulness for Christ (4:11). For Ephesus, see the note on Ephesians 1:1. Troas (4:13) was a port on the Aegean coast of western Asia Minor (cf. Acts 16:11). Paul's "scrolls" (4:13) were papyrus rolls; his "parchments" were skins of vellum, perhaps portions of the Old Testament.

4:14-15 A Warning about an Enemy
The description of Alexander as "the metalworker" (4:14) may be intended to distinguish him from the Alexander mentioned in 1 Timothy 1:20 (cf. Acts 19:33).

4:16-18 The Lord's Faithfulness
At Paul's first defense, or preliminary hearing, before the Roman court, no one came to vouch for him. Luke may have not have arrived yet. Others may have feared for their own lives. The "lion's mouth" (4:17; cf. Ps. 22:21) may be a figure of extreme and immediate danger from which Paul was spared. But Paul knew his Lord (1:12). And he would keep Paul from every "evil attack" (4:18; "evil deed," NASB; "evil work," KJV), that is, the temptations to sin arising from Paul's difficult circumstances—temptations to compromise his life and message in order to avoid persecution. Others have taken this to refer to deliverance from all the attacks of various people against Paul.

4:19-21 CLOSING GREETINGS
Prisca (or Priscilla) and Aquila (4:19) were Paul's fellow workers (Acts 18:2; Rom. 16:3; 1 Cor. 16:19). For Onesiphorus, see the note on 1:16-18. For Erastus (4:20), see Acts 19:22. He is probably not to be identified with the city treasurer of Corinth (Rom. 16:23). Trophimus was from Ephesus (Acts 20:4; 21:29), one of two Asians to carry the collection with Paul to Jerusalem (Acts 20:4-6; 21:29). Since Paul did not leave Trophimus in Miletus on their visit

recorded in Acts 20:15, this incident must have happened after Paul's release from his first Roman imprisonment. Nothing is known of the four faithful persons (4:21) named here who had not deserted the apostle Paul.

4:22 BENEDICTION

Paul's words of benediction in 2 Timothy were his last recorded words. According to Eusebius, Paul's martyrdom took place in the thirteenth year of Nero, which commenced in October, A.D. 67. Jerome places Paul's death in A.D. 68. Paul probably died in the spring of A.D. 68, for he was hoping that Timothy would join him for the winter. According to tradition, Paul was beheaded with a sword, a method of execution used for Roman citizens, on the Ostian Way, a road leading south from Rome. According to tradition, he was buried in the catacombs south of the city.

Titus

BASIC FACTS

HISTORICAL SETTING

The recipient of this letter was Titus (1:4), one of Paul's partners in ministry (1:5; cf. 2 Cor. 7:6; 8:16-18, 23; 12:18; Gal. 2:1, 3). Titus, a Greek Gentile, accompanied Paul and Barnabas to Jerusalem during the famine relief visit (Acts 11:29-30; Gal. 2:1). Evidently, Paul took him along as a test case for Gentile salvation apart from circumcision. The fact that Titus was not compelled to be circumcised confirmed the believer's liberty and freedom from the law (Gal. 2:3).

Paul's first visit to Crete was on his voyage to Rome (Acts 27:7-8). About four years after Paul's release from his first Roman imprisonment Titus accompanied Paul to the island of Crete, where he was left to set the church in order and to appoint elders in every city (1:5). Titus later joined Paul in Rome for awhile. Second Timothy 4:10 speaks also of Titus having left Paul in Rome for a journey to Dalmatia. Eusebius (A.D. 339) indicated that Titus returned to Crete where he was made bishop and remained there until his old age. Paul apparently took the opportunity to visit Crete on his return voyage from Spain (A.D. 66). The immediate occasion for writing was that Titus was facing a difficult assignment (1:5) and Paul wanted to encourage him.

AUTHOR

Titus is one of the three Pastoral Epistles of Paul (cf. 1 and 2 Timothy). The letter itself identifies Paul as its author (1:1). The personal tone of the letter (1:4; 3:12-13, 15) also points to the genuineness of Pauline authorship. In addition to this internal evidence, the church fathers added their support to Pauline authorship.

DATE

The letter was probably written in the summer of A.D. 66, after Paul's return from Spain in the spring of that year. He probably wrote Titus before traveling to Nicopolis, where he spent the winter (3:12).

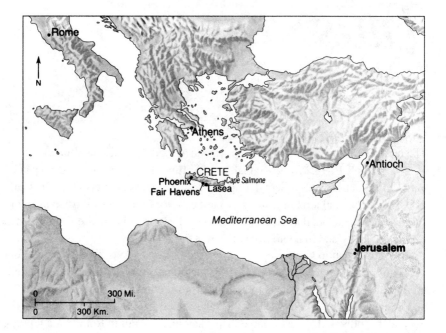

PURPOSE

Paul's letter to Titus was designed to establish the basic elements of church order and witness. It achieves this by emphasizing the need for purity in leadership and soundness in doctrine.

GEOGRAPHY AND ITS IMPORTANCE

The Island of Crete

It appears that after Paul's imprisonment in Rome, mentioned at the end of Acts, he was released and continued his missionary travels. Traveling to the island of Crete with Titus appears to have been one such mission. The mountainous island is around 156 miles long and from 7 to 35 miles wide.

GUIDING CONCEPTS

SOUND DOCTRINE

Throughout the letter Paul stressed the importance of sound doctrine (1:1, 3, 9, 13; 2:1, 7).

THE APPEARANCE OF GOD'S GRACE

The letter is structured around three different appearances of God's grace: (1) God's grace manifested in his word (1:3); (2) God's grace manifested in Christ who will appear yet again at the end of the age (2:11-13); (3) God's grace shown in his kindness and love (3:4). Each one of these appearances functions as the basis for instruction and behavior. God's word was promised and revealed and now forms the basis of the Christian's entrustment (1:3). The appearance of God's grace (2:11) instructs believers to live sensibly (2:12). Finally, the kindness of God (3:4) is foundational to the behavior of believers commended in 3:1-2.

GOOD DEEDS

Considering the smallness of the book, Paul mentioned "good deeds" many times (1:16; 2:7, 14; 3:1, 8, 14). There is a close link between sound doctrine and good deeds (2:7). Doing good works springs from the very heart of why Christ gave himself for mankind's redemption (2:14). The movement in 2:14 is from lawless deeds to good deeds.

BIBLE-WIDE CONCEPTS

Three topics show the deep connections of this letter with the Old Testament. First, there is a heavy emphasis on correcting false teaching from the law (1:10-11, 14, 16; 3:9) bred from misunderstandings concerning the role of the law in the Christian's life. Paul called the believers to do good deeds but insisted that those deeds be directed by faith, not by a legalistic attitude toward the law. Second, the threefold mention of Christ's redemptive appearance is placed within the age-old promise of God from the Old Testament (1:2-3). The promise of redemption in Christ had priority over the manifestation of the law. Third, the relationship of sound doctrine and good deeds was Paul's understanding of how Christ's appearance both freed believers from the law and yet bound them to a life of obedience. God's desire to make Israel his special possession (Exod. 19:5; Deut. 14:2) was fulfilled in the people of Christ (2:14).

NEEDS MET BY TITUS

The Christians on the island of Crete experienced the same problems with doctrine as did the major cities of Asia Minor and Greece. False teaching, spread by those not qualified to minister God's word, tended to move believers away from a clear and secure focus on the hope, discipline, and power stemming from the imminent return of Christ. Paul's letter to Titus met some basic needs of the church for security and direction in the face of opposition. The structure and content of Titus show that Paul intended to answer the following questions for the Christians on Crete.

- What kind of people do church leaders need to be?
- How should believers answer those who argue about the law and want them to keep it?
- How should the appearance of God's grace in Christ affect the behavior of believers?

The question of what and who believers should believe is always difficult to answer. Christian leaders may or may not be trustworthy. At times they may even ask believers to do things that contradict what others are teaching. Paul, in his letter to Titus, set out to give guidelines for evaluating leaders and their teaching. He also called believers to scrutinize themselves under the same tough evaluation. First, believers need to have an honest and accurate assessment of the leader's character. Are his motives good or based on desires for material gain? Second, they need to observe the results of the leader's teaching. Does it issue in Christian growth in grace or does it end up in pointless debates? Third, believers themselves are to have a deep understanding of what the appearance of Christ's grace means for the everyday events of life. These three guidelines are not easily followed, but Paul placed the challenge before the believers on Crete to continually probe character, evaluate results, and compare all things against the yardstick of grace alone.

OUTLINE OF TITUS

TITUS NOTES

1:1-4 GREETING: THE RELATIONSHIPS IN PAUL'S COMMAND

1:1 Paul's Relationship to the Father and to Christ

In chapter 1 Paul informed Titus of the administrative matters that would serve as the solid foundation for sound doctrine in the church. He encouraged Titus to set things in order in the church and appoint qualified elders (1:5). This was especially important in Crete because of the false teachers that were there.

Paul's introduction shows the scope, function, and nature of his apostleship and message. Paul used the term "servant of God" (1:1; "bond-servant of God," NASB) only in this letter. This term emphasized Paul's function of doing God's bidding. Paul presented the major concern of this letter here: he desired to teach the "knowledge of the truth that leads to godliness." Paul insisted that the truth of the gospel should result in personal godliness in the lives of believers.

1:2-4 Paul's Relationships with People

"Truth" (1:1) and "hope" (1:2) are founded on God's eternal promise (1:2; cf. Eph. 1:4; 2 Tim. 1:9) and God's revelation in history (1:3; cf. Rom. 5:6; Gal. 4:4; Eph. 1:10). The designations "God our Savior" (1:3) and "Christ Jesus our Savior" (1:4) cluster around the three mentions of the appearance of God's grace (1:3-4; 2:11, 13; 3:4, 6). The designation "true son" (1:4) would indicate that Titus was one of Paul's converts. Titus was a Greek Christian (Gal. 2:3) and one of Paul's travel companions and fellow workers (1:5; cf. 2 Cor. 8:23; 12:18; Gal. 2:1; 2 Tim. 4:10).

1:5–3:15 THE SEARCH FOR COMMUNITY ORDER

Overview: In Titus 1:5-16 good works are related to usefulness in faith and truth. In 2:2-15 they are related to works stemming from instructive grace. In 3:1-11 good deeds grow out of compassionate grace. The emphases are different, but the basic foundation is the same in all three sections.

1:5-16 A Basic for Order: Irreproachable Leaders

1:5-9 THE BASIC QUALIFICATIONS

The island of Crete (156 miles long and between 7 and 35 miles wide) forms the southern boundary of the Aegean Sea. The center of the island is formed by a mountain chain rising to the height of 8,193 feet (Mount Ida, birthplace of Zeus) which is fringed by lower valleys along the coast. Jews from Crete were present at Pentecost (Acts 2:11) and may have carried the gospel message back to the island. The culture of these island people was strongly influenced by Cretan myth and legend.

Paul's first visit to the island took place on his voyage to Rome (Acts 27:7-8). He had suggested to the captain of the ship that they spend the winter there. Since he probably had not had the opportunity to evangelize the island during his first visit, he took the opportunity to return to Crete sometime after being released from his first Roman imprisonment. This letter indicates that Paul and Titus had a successful ministry there.

Paul's directive was twofold: set things in order and appoint irreproachable elders (1:6). Paul then set forth the qualifications for irreproachable elders (cf. 1 Tim. 3:1-7). Note that "elders" (1:5-6) and "overseer" (1:7) are used synonymously. The term "elder" emphasizes the dignity and maturity required for the office; the term "overseer" emphasizes function, giving oversight. The determining factor for qualification stems from being God's steward (1:7). The church leader had to be one who held fast to the word of God, promoting truth and refuting error. Pure character was a necessity for the people with the roles of teaching and correcting. Good character plus sound doctrine were necessary to enable a ministry of exhortation and correction.

1:10-16 THE CORRECTIVE TO DISORDER

1:10-12 The source of the disorder: greed.
The character traits described in 1:10-12 are opposite to the traits of a qualified leader. Here Paul gave the reason for Titus's assignment and revealed the need to appoint qualified elders. There were false teachers among the Cretans. Paul used a strong

expression, saying that these false teachers must be "silenced" (1:11). Paul cited the testimony of a Cretan poet and self-styled prophet, Epimenides (1:12; c. 600 B.C.). According to tradition, Epimenides slept for fifty years and then became a prophet. He possessed great knowledge of medicine and natural history. His statement concerning the Cretans was apparently very accurate.

1:13-16 The corrective: establish soundness in the faith. The command "rebuke them sharply" (1:13) is a present imperative and could be rendered: "*keep on* rebuking them sharply." This severe rebuke matches a correspondingly severe problem. Such a rebuke was designed to bring conviction. It had to be sharp but was designed to be restorative, not vindictive. For "Jewish myths" (1:14), see the note on 1 Timothy 1:4. The concept of purity (1:15) was brought up to contrast the false way of purity that was represented in the "commands" of 1:14. True purity in Christ does not come from obedience to the law or Jewish myths.

Titus 1:16 expresses the major theme of Titus: "A believer's character and conduct must be consistent with his confession." This is the basic message of the epistle of James: faith without works is a fallacy.

2:1-10 A Basic for Order: Family Love and Honor

2:1-2 OLDER MEN

This section details the elements that are necessary to sound teaching (2:1). Character and behavior are the object of the teaching (cf. 1 Tim. 1:5). In contrast with the conduct of the false teachers, Paul insisted that the gospel must be graced with a godly life. The command "You must teach" (2:1) is continuous and could be rendered, "Keep on teaching." The virtues of 2:2 are appropriate for all Christians but are especially imporant for older men who are naturally looked to as leaders in the church whether or not they hold office.

2:3-5 WOMEN

The older women are to be teachers of younger women, a task that mature Christian women are admirably suited for (2:3-5). The general character of godly women is stated first, then is followed by specific illustrations. Paul not only gave the mature Chris-

tian women the responsibility to teach, he also assigned a specific curriculum (2:4-5). In 2:5 the wife and mother has her primary sphere of responsibility in the home. Yet Proverbs 31:10-31 indicates that the home is not necessarily the limit of her sphere of activity.

2:6-8 YOUNG MEN

Paul's request that the conduct of the young men be exemplary was intended to quiet any criticism or attacks from outside the church (2:6-8). Paul emphasized the need, in the face of false teachers and others who desired to give Christianity a bad name, to be self-controlled (2:2, 5-6, 12).

2:9-10 SERVANTS

For a note on slavery, see Ephesians 6:5-9. Paul insisted that even the lowest slave of the Roman social order could adorn God's truth by manifesting Christian character in keeping with his confession. The servant was to make God as Savior look good in the real and present world.

2:11-15 The Model for Community Order: Grace and Obedience

The grace that saves believers (Titus 2:11) and instructs them (2:12) also gives them hope for the future (2:13). Grace as an instructor is seen throughout Scripture (Deut. 8:5; Prov. 1:2; 3:11-12 quoted in Heb. 12:4-7; Eph. 6:4; 2 Tim. 2:25; 3:16). The provision of salvation has been presented to all and is effective for all who believe. This is a universal provision (John 3:16; 2 Cor. 5:19), not a universal salvation. The "blessed hope" and the "appearing" are one event (2:13)—the coming of the Lord Jesus for his church.

Paul's combination of Old Testament truths in 2:14 relates Christ to cleansing (Ezek. 37:23) and redemption (Ps. 130:8; cf. Mark 10:45 and Exod. 19:5-6). The imperatives of Titus 2:15 are in the present tense, "encourage and rebuke." Titus's authority was in accord with God's purpose in sending Christ.

3:1-11 A Basic for Order: Wise Subordination

3:1-2 "OTHER-CENTERED" CONSIDERATIONS

Paul considered the practical implications of sound doctrine and commanded Titus to keep on reminding the believers of the importance of good deeds. Paul's remarks were especially appropriate for the Cretans. The Greek historian Polybius remarks that they tended to be a seditious and rebellious people (cf. also Rom. 13:1; 1 Pet. 2:13). Paul, knowing the Cretans to be this way, made the godly qualifications in 3:1-2 a call to civil obedience. The purpose of this inward focus of godliness was also evangelistic. Through their godliness, the believers would exhibit God's grace to the people around them.

3:3-8 GOOD DEEDS FROM JUSTIFICATION BY GRACE

Paul reminded the believers on Crete of their sinful past (3:3) to inspire them to show kindness and consideration toward others. Paul cautioned them not to become spiritual snobs who were insensitive to their continuing need for God's grace. This was foundational for Paul's discussion of God's act of kindness toward the world (3:5-7). Paul set forth a capsule summary of the doctrine of salvation and expounded on several of the provisions of the new covenant (Ezek. 36:25-28). Salvation is not merited by any righteous works, but wholly determined by God's mercy. The "washing of rebirth" (3:5) speaks of the spiritual cleansing experienced in the new birth (cf. Ezek. 36:25; Acts 22:16). "Rebirth" (3:5; "regeneration," NASB and KJV) is the supernatural imparting of spiritual life to believers in Christ (John 3:7). The "renewal by the Holy Spirit" (3:5) refers to the Spirit's regenerating and indwelling ministry (cf. Ezek. 36:27). God's rich outpouring is to be mirrored in the believers' rich outpouring of kindness to others. To be justified (3:7) means to be declared righteous (Rom. 5:1).

3:9-11 THE ORDER FOR INSUBORDINATION

A "divisive person" (3:10; "factious man," NASB; "heretic," KJV) is one who argues foolishly without accurate Scriptural support. See Acts 24:14 where Paul explained that Christianity was not a sect (a factious group) because it was in complete harmony with the Old Testament Scriptures. Paul's instructions for dealing with divisive people (3:10) reflect the teachings of Jesus concerning discipline in the church (Matt. 18:15-17).

3:12-15 A Basic for Order: Meeting Pressing Needs

In this section Paul brought up his need for companionship (3:12) and emphasized the importance of helping Christian travelers (3:13-14). Tychicus was a close friend and fellow worker of Paul (cf. Acts 20:4; Eph. 6:21; Col. 4:7; 2 Tim. 4:12). Nicopolis was located in the province of Achaia on the Adriatic coast. Zenas the lawyer and Apollos the well-known preacher (3:13; cf. Acts 18:24) were on their way to Crete. They may have been carrying this letter to Titus. Even in his final words, Paul once again emphasized the important theme of good works (3:14). The Cretans were to take the lead in good deeds; they were to be fruitful, not fruitless.

Philemon

BASIC FACTS

HISTORICAL SETTING

This letter is the only source of information about Philemon. He was a slaveholder who had been converted, possibly as a result of Paul's ministry (Philem. 1:19). At least, Philemon was indebted to Paul in some way. Because the church met at his house, he must have been a person of wealth and influence. Apphia is not specifically identified. Paul calls her a sister (1:2), and this is evidence that she was a believer. Archippus was a believer at Colosse and a fellow soldier with Paul and Timothy (1:2; cf. Phil. 2:25 for the only other use of "fellow soldier"). Although the letter contains personal matters, it is also addressed to the church (1:2). Paul wanted to make this a public matter, perhaps to encourage other slaveholders to follow Philemon's example, or to apply social pressure on Philemon so that he might heed Paul's request.

Paul wrote this letter to Philemon on behalf of Philemon's slave, Onesimus of Colosse (Col. 4:9), who had run away to Rome. There he had evidently been converted under Paul's ministry. Onesimus had become a useful servant of the apostle in his imprisonment (Col. 4:9), and Paul desired to keep Onesimus with him to continue his ministry. But Paul recognized that Onesimus was the property of Philemon and must be subject to his master (cf. Eph. 6:5). Paul sent Onesimus back to Philemon with Tychicus (Col. 4:7-9) with a letter requesting Philemon to demonstrate grace and receive Onesimus as a brother in the Lord.

AUTHOR

Paul's letter to Philemon indicates that Paul was the author (1:1, 9, 19). The historical setting of the letter fits that of Colossians (1:23-24; cf. Col. 4:10-14).

DATE

The close connection of Philemon with Colossians makes it virtually certain that the two letters belong to the same period. Tychicus, accompanied by Onesimus, probably carried both letters to Colosse at the same time, probably in A.D. 62 (Col. 4:7-9).

PURPOSE

The letter to Philemon was designed to encourage a simple yet profound personal transaction—the substitution of forgiveness and acceptance for the legal rights of ownership. The letter encouraged seeing relationships in light of the deep bonds created in Christ, rather than the earthly social structures of status and self-achievement.

GUIDING CONCEPTS

SLAVERY IN THE ROMAN WORLD

Slavery was universally taken for granted in the first century A.D. It was practiced in Jewish, Roman, and Greek cultures, although the institution varied in some degree from culture to culture. Jewish slaves had certain privileges and were under legal protection. The Jews prided themselves in the fact that they never treated their slaves with cruelty. Slaves among non-Jewish peoples did not receive such protection. The Greek civilization was built on the institution of slavery. Greek slaves were used for industrial purposes and worked in the mines under terrible conditions. Roman slaves, although considered the legal property of their master, could obtain freedom and become legal persons. They were generally used in houses or on farms. A slave could not be legally married or own property. Any children born to a female slave would become the property of her master.

The main sources of slavery were: (1) birth, being borne by a woman who was a slave; (2) the practice of exposing unwanted children whom anyone could claim; (3) the sale of one's own children into slavery; (4) voluntary slavery as a means of paying a debt; (5) penal slavery as punishment for a crime; (6) kidnapping and piracy; (7) military conquest and capture of peoples. Slave dealers often followed military campaigns, buying captured prisoners and shipping them off to the slave markets to be sold at a nice profit.

Cruel punishments were inflicted upon slaves for mistakes and disobedience. Slaves were often beaten with sticks or whipped. Runaway slaves and thieves were branded on the forehead with a mark. Others were imprisoned. Although many died as a result of mistreatment, it was illegal to take the life of a slave without a court order.

The rights of a master over a slave were in no way affected by a slave's running away. It was the duty of civil authorities to aid in the recovery of slaves. Some citizens made it their business to capture and return runaway slaves for a profit. It was a serious criminal offense to harbor a runaway slave.

The chief way a slave might become free was by a legal act of the owner called manumission—the act of setting a slave free. This was accomplished by either the payment of a ransom, or by an act of the state. In Rome, manumission was often granted in a slave owner's will. At times legal limits had to be placed on the release of slaves to prevent too rapid an integration of Rome with persons of foreign extraction. In Greek states emancipated slaves became

resident aliens, but in Rome they could be granted citizenship. This resulted in
a great flow of slaves to Italy, especially in the last two centuries before Christ.
This could account for Onesimus's traveling to Rome. He was undoubtedly
aware that there were many freed slaves in the city who might be willing to
offer him some assistance.

Rather than trying to overthrow the cultural institution of slavery, Paul
sought to work within the system, requiring that slaves obey their masters
(Eph. 6:5-8; Col. 3:22-24) and that masters not mistreat their slaves (Col. 4:1;
1 Pet. 2:18-20). Although Paul seems to have been supportive of emancipation
(cf. 1 Cor. 7:21), he was definitely more concerned with spiritual freedom than
with the release of slaves. He remarked in 1 Corinthians 7:22 that a believing
slave is "the Lord's freedman" and that a free believer is "Christ's slave."

BIBLE-WIDE CONCEPTS

Paul's letter to Philemon is a powerful cameo illustration of God's grace
exhibited in the Bible-wide movement from the offense of human sin to repentance and reconciliation. This movement is based on God's willingness to
receive sinful people as his brothers (cf. Heb. 2:11) by charging their debts
of sin to Christ's account (2 Cor. 5:19). Paul commended this pattern to Philemon, and through him to believers today. All believers should be willing to
receive past offenders as brothers and sisters in Christ (1:16) and forgive them
(1:18-19).

NEEDS MET BY PHILEMON

Paul's letter to Philemon meets some basic needs that apply to situations beyond
the specific needs of Philemon and Onesimus. The Colossian believers probably
wondered how Christianity should affect the relationships between Christians of
different social classes. The structure and content of Philemon show that Paul was
answering questions like the following.
   • How can Christian leaders encourage people to reconcile relationships without
     commanding them harshly?
   • How should Christ affect the way believers view their relationships with people
     of differing social and vocational status?
Behind the issue of how Christians are to relate to others of various ethnic and
social backgrounds lies their need to give up certain rights in order to display
forgiving grace. God has every right to punish people for their sins. He has every
right to put an end to a world that does not care about him. But he has given up
his rights in order to display his grace in forgiveness and an intimate relationship
of love. Likewise, the letter to Philemon encourages believers to choose grace
and deeper relationships rather than insisting on formal rights and relationships of
social status.

OUTLINE OF PHILEMON

A. GREETING (1:1-3)

B. THANKSGIVING (1:4-7)

C. PAUL'S RETURN OF ONESIMUS (1:8-16)

D. PHILEMON'S RECEPTION OF ONESIMUS (1:17-22)

E. CLOSING GREETINGS (1:23-25)

PHILEMON NOTES

1:1-3 GREETING
Paul wrote to Philemon during his first Roman imprisonment (cf. Acts 28:16-31). Timothy (see note on 1 Tim. 1:2) is associated with him in writing the epistle, but Paul is clearly the sole author (cf. 1:9, 19). Philemon was a slaveholder (1:15-16) who had been converted, possibly as a result of Paul's ministry (1:19). He was fondly regarded by the apostle and had worked with Paul or helped him in the ministry (1:1). A careful comparison of the letter of Philemon with Colossians indicates that they were written at the same time to people of the same city. Philemon resided in the Lycus valley in the city of Colosse.

Apphia (1:2), some have speculated, may have been the wife of Philemon, although this is not specifically stated in the text. Archippus (1:2), a believer at Colosse, is regarded as a "fellow soldier" of Paul and Timothy. (For a note on the city of Colosse, see Col. 1:2.) The term "fellow soldier" is used figuratively as an expression of honor and appreciation for some sacrificial or risky service (cf. Phil. 2:25). Archippus resided at Colosse and was involved in the ministry there (Col. 4:17). The letter, while being personal in content, is also addressed to the church at Philemon's house. Perhaps Paul wanted to encourage other slaveholders to follow Philemon's example, or to apply pressure to Philemon that he might heed his request to forgive Onesimus.

1:4-7 THANKSGIVING
These verses begin with Paul's encouragement of Philemon to be gracious toward Onesimus. Paul reminded Philemon first to consider all the good things Christ had given him so that he would have an effective sharing (fellowship) of his faith, in this case good-will toward Onesimus.

1:8-16 PAUL'S RETURN OF ONESIMUS
Paul could have used his apostolic authority to command Philemon to do what was right, but instead he appealed to the principle of "love" to encourage Philemon to show kindness to Onesimus. The name "Onesimus" means "useful." As a runaway, Onesimus was useless, but now, returning as a believer, he had become "useful," both to Paul and to Philemon. Onesimus left as a mere slave but would return as a beloved brother in Christ. Paul's request on Onesimus's behalf was the practical outworking of his prayer in Philemon 1:6.

1:17-22 PHILEMON'S RECEPTION OF ONESIMUS
Paul asked that any debts or damages charged to Onesimus be placed on his own account. Paul promised to pay them in full. The word "charge" (1:18) means to "impute" or "reckon" (cf. Rom. 5:13). This well illustrates Christ's work for the Christian. The debt of the believer's sin has been charged to Christ's account. Now God the Father receives all who believe in him as he would his own dear Son. Philemon 1:21 may indicate that Paul was hoping that Philemon would release Onesimus from slavery. Philemon 1:22 provides an important clue regarding Paul's travel plans after being released from his first Roman imprisonment. His first destination appears to have been Colosse.

1:23-25 CLOSING GREETINGS

Epaphras (1:23) was a native of Colosse and was apparently the founder of the church (Col. 1:7). The term "fellow prisoner" suggests that he voluntarily remained with Paul during his house arrest in Rome (Acts 28:16, 23). Mark (1:24) refers to John Mark, author of the second Gospel (cf. Acts 13:5, 13; 15:37, 39). Aristarchus was a Thessalonian and traveling companion with Paul (Acts 19:29; 20:4; 27:2; Col. 4:10). Demas was a companion of Paul's (cf. Col. 4:14) who deserted him during his last imprisonment (2 Tim. 4:10). Luke was the Gentile physician, companion of Paul, and author of the third Gospel and Acts (Acts 16:10; Col. 4:14; 2 Tim. 4:11).

Hebrews

BASIC FACTS

HISTORICAL SETTING
The ancient title of this letter designates the readers as Hebrews, but the letter does not mention the readers as either Jews or Gentiles. Most conservative scholars agree on the basis of internal evidence that the readers were Hebrew Christians. Some believe the readers resided in Jerusalem because of the references to the temple and temple institutions. Closer observation, however, reveals that the author writes of the tabernacle (Heb. 9:2), not the temple. Furthermore, the Jerusalem Christians were known for receiving charity, not giving it (6:10; 10:34). It has also been suggested that Alexandria was the place of residence of the readers due to a temple located nearby at Leontopolis. The letter also reflects an Alexandrian influence as seen in the quotations of the Septuagint.

Others have suggested on the basis of 13:24 that the readers resided in Rome. The salutation could be that of Christians originally from Italy sending back greetings to their friends. On the other hand, the phrase could merely refer to the present location of the writer and greeters. Because the letter was first known in Rome where there appears to have been an influential group of Hebrew Christians (Rom. 9–11; cf. Acts 28:17-31), it was either addressed to Hebrew Christians at Rome, or possibly somewhere else in the Roman world.

AUTHOR
The author is not identified in the letter. Tradition has variously ascribed the letter to Paul, Barnabas, Apollos, Luke, Silas, Philip, Priscilla, or John Mark. Because of the dispute regarding the authorship of Hebrews, the letter was not regarded as fully canonical by the Western church until the fourth century A.D.

DATE
Because Hebrews was quoted by Clement of Rome in his *Epistle to the Corinthians,* it had to have been written prior to A.D. 96. Hebrews would have been written at a time when Timothy was still alive (Heb. 13:23), but some of the original leaders of

the Hebrew Christian assembly had died (13:7). The readers were apparently second generation Christians (2:3). The indications are that the Jewish sacrificial system was still in operation (7:8; 8:4; 10:1-2, 8, 11). This would demand a date prior to A.D. 70 when the Jerusalem temple was destroyed.

If the letter was written from Rome, and Timothy was able to come to Rome as Paul requested (2 Tim. 4:11-13) and was also imprisoned at that time (Heb. 13:23), then the date of writing would have followed his release, about A.D. 68 to 69. But the reference in 12:4, if interpreted literally, would indicate that the letter was written before the persecution of Christians under Nero, which began in July of A.D. 64. Thus, a date of origin in the sixties accords well with the available data.

PURPOSE

The letter was designed to correct the readers' desires to substitute old religious ways for the greatness of the new revelation of God in Christ. Although the geographical setting and date of the letter is uncertain, the spiritual condition of its readers is clear. The believers had demonstrated Christian love (6:10) and had endured persecution (10:32-34). In spite of these favorable traits, there were some areas of weakness.

The letter encourages the readers to make spiritual progress (5:11-12). Their failure to grow in the Lord was reflected in their Christian conduct (10:25; 13:2-17). The Hebrew Christians were looking back to their Jewish ways instead of ahead to Christ, the author and perfecter of faith (12:2). Facing the hardships of the Christian faith, they were in danger of drifting away (2:1) from the substance, Christ, to the shadow of the Old Testament sacrificial system (8:5; 10:1). It was to deal with such spiritual stagnation that the author wrote his letter to the Hebrew Christians.

GUIDING CONCEPTS

The first ten chapters of the book are built around five groups of Old Testament quotations. This amounts to a sermon about Christ based on Old Testament passages. Clearly the writer wanted to show how Christ related to well-known Old Testament themes and promises. The Old Testament passages are listed in the accompanying chart.

CHRIST IN THE OLD TESTAMENT

Hebrews Passage	*Quoted Old Testament Passages*
Hebrews 1:2-14	Psalms 2:7; 104:4; 45:6-7; 102:25-27; 110:1; 2 Samuel 7:14; Deuteronomy 32:43 from the Greek Old Testament (the Septuagint).
Hebrews 2:5-18	Psalms 8:4-6; 22:22; Isaiah 8:17-18.
Hebrews 3:1–4:13	Psalm 95:7-11.
Hebrews 4:14–7:28	Psalms 2:7; 110:4.
Hebrews 8:1–10:39	Jeremiah 31:31-34; Psalms 40:6-8; 110:1; 26:11; Habakkuk 2:3-11. (The Jeremiah passage is the longest Old Testament quotation in the New Testament.)

The key Old Testament passage in the book of Hebrews is Psalm 110:1, 4 (cf. 1:3, "sat down at the right hand"; and 1:13). It is also used in 5:5-6; 7:17, 21 and 10:11-14 where it is combined with the new covenant. Psalm 110 speaks of the eternal order of Melchizedek and the sitting down of the Son at God's right hand, the two key themes of the book. The entire book of Hebrews shows the implications of the answers to two questions: Why is Jesus sitting at God's right hand? And what does it mean for him to be a priest like Melchizedek?

BIBLE-WIDE CONCEPTS

The first ten chapters of the book reach back into the Old Testament to show how Moses, the law, and the priesthood have been completed in the new covenant inaugurated by Jesus. The rest of the book, Hebrews 11–13, is a series of exhortations built upon the message of Hebrews 1–10. The entire book is an exposition of how the Old Testament is fulfilled in Christ. But several Bible-wide concepts deserve special mention here.

First, Hebrews 1:2-14 clearly shows in its interpretations of Psalm 2:7, 2 Samuel 7:14, and Psalm 110:1 that Jesus was the long-awaited promised son of David, the King who would rule God's people and mediate between them and God. Adam was the first man, and he represented all humanity as he chose to sin rather than obey God. The chosen man Abraham was the recipient of a promise that mediated the blessing of all nations through him. The great leader Moses was also the mediator for God's people and several times saved them from destruction. God promised King David that a son of his would be the eternal Mediator between humanity and God. That greater son of David would be an eternal King ruling under God's unceasing loving-kindness. Hebrews shows how Jesus fulfilled that ancient promise of kingship and blessing.

Second, the interpretation of Psalm 95:7-11 in Hebrews 3:1–4:13 links those who profess faith in Christ to ancient Israel as they wandered in the wilderness from Egypt toward the Promised Land. And the Promised Land functions throughout the Bible as the middle ground between the Garden of Eden and the new heavens and earth. Like Eden, the Promised Land was a place of new beginnings and potential blessings. It represented a return to what had been lost when Adam and Eve were thrown out of Eden. But the path to the new Eden of the Promised Land had many pitfalls and barriers for the faith and steadfastness of God's pilgrims. All the weaknesses and forces that resulted in Adam and Eve's original loss of Eden's blessings still plagued those who journeyed across Sinai to the anticipated beauties of the Promised Land. Some pilgrims made it. Others fell by the wayside. Eden and the Promised Land were but preludes to the permanent place of God's blessing, the new and eternal heaven and earth. Hebrews links the journey through the desert of Sinai to the journey of believers through this age into the next. Some will make it into the new heavens and earth. Others will fall by the way.

Third, the letter to the Hebrews shows how Christ is the fulfillment of God's new covenant promised in Jeremiah 31:31-34 and other Old Testament passages. All the various promises and covenants God had previously used to restore his relationship with his creation pointed to and were fulfilled by his new covenant in Christ. The promise of victory over the seed of the serpent (Gen. 3:15), the perfection of God's promise to Noah to withhold his global wrath, the blessings promised through Moses' covenant, the inauguration of worldwide blessings through Abraham, and the perfect rule promised through David's greater son all come to fulfillment and perfection in Christ's new covenant. The new covenant remedied the problem of guilt now. The covenant's provision of inner change and power through God's Spirit would also help diminish disobedience now and would finally end all disobedience in the future. The details of how Hebrews elaborates these Bible-wide concepts will be seen in the following Notes section.

NEEDS MET BY HEBREWS

The original readers of the letter to the Hebrews faced a crisis of authority. The Jewish leaders they had trusted before believing in Jesus as the Messiah had seemed so wise and so true to God's revelations. Then Christian prophets had presented a convincing message that God had brought a new revelation of his will through Jesus of Nazareth. But now the new believers were having second thoughts. Their old Jewish leaders put pressure on them to return to the fold of Judaism. Some of the pressure was severe persecution, some was simple social shunning. But the real issue lay in the question of how an unknown man like Jesus from an obscure town called Nazareth could be accepted as being greater than famous leaders and prophets like Abraham and Moses.

To any who needed to be convinced of Jesus' absolute supremacy over Moses and Abraham, this letter demonstrated that the Bible itself predicted and identified that such a One would come. But the need to believe that Jesus' covenant was better than Moses' was just the foundation for the author's goals. He also sought to establish his readers' love and stability before God and their holy living and witness before the world. The issue began with doctrine but ended with an increased effectiveness in spreading the wonderful message of God's redemption in Christ. The book of Hebrews speaks to crucial needs felt by those under religious and cultural pressure to return to pre-conversion commitments. The structure and content of Hebrews show that the author was answering questions like the following.

- In what way is Jesus better than all the great heroes of the Old Testament?
- How does Jesus' new covenant improve upon Moses' old covenant?
- How can believers reconcile the hostility that comes their way because they are Christians with God's promises of security in his kingdom?
- What are some of the consequences of believers softening their commitment to Christ?
- What are some concrete ways of understanding the sometimes intangible reality of faith?

Many Christians face pressures to return to their old beliefs and life-styles. Family, friends, or just the flesh may pull them back toward living as they did before they met Christ. To correct this downward pull the writer of Hebrews presented a simple comparison between better and best. Christ is better than any of the old beliefs believers used to hold. His redemption is not only better, it is the only real salvation in the world. His forgiveness is perfect and eternal. Taken alone, who would not follow the best and choose Christ over what the world has to offer? The issue of who is the best is fairly easily settled. But that is only the first step to dealing with the more difficult issues met by Hebrews.

The writer was also aware that when a Christian chooses Christ as the only Redeemer, he also chooses to participate in Christ's sufferings. And when a Christian is suffering for Christ, it is tempting to end the pain by ending what caused it—the witness for Christ. The writer's argument for the supremacy of Christ on the basis of the Scriptures is but one support for persevering. His other argument is a more personal and less tangible matter. And that is how to make faith, that hard-to-grasp action, more solid and visible. Arguments for the supremacy of Christ are not going to produce steadfast Christian character without an accompanying faith that is strong and honest. The writer meets the needs of believers for stronger faith by providing a long list of people who believed that what God said, he would do. God's word promised many things, most of which, like God himself, are presently invisible. The writer of Hebrews used believers from the past to illustrate how God's invisible word had the power to move ordinary people to live obedient and even sacrificial lives. Only real things can affect the lives of believers, and only faith can make God a real force in their lives. The letter meets the need for a doctrinal presentation upholding Christ as the only supreme Redeemer. At the same time it seeks to deepen inner convictions so that believers will move from an intellectual assent that the doctrine is true to a committed life-style that can weather even persecution and hostility.

OUTLINE OF HEBREWS

A. THE EXALTED SON: BETTER THAN ANGELS (1:1–2:18)
   1. Better by Nature (1:1–2:4)
   2. Better by Empathy (2:5-18)

B. THE FAITHFUL SON: MORE GLORY THAN MOSES (3:1–4:16)
   1. Greater Glory (3:1-6)
   2. Conclusion: The Requirement of Consistent Belief (3:7–4:13)
   3. Transition from Apostle to High Priest (4:14-16)

C. THE PERFECT PRIEST: ETERNAL AND EFFECTIVE (5:1–12:13)
   1. Eternal: Melchizedek (5:1–7:28)
   2. Effective: Better Covenant Administered (8:1–10:18)
   3. Exhortations to Effective Faith (10:19–12:13)

D. PATTERNS FOR MATURE PEOPLE (12:14–13:17)
   1. Peace (12:14-29)
   2. Love (13:1-6)
   3. Obedience (13:7-17)

E. CLOSING REQUESTS (13:18-25)

HEBREWS NOTES

1:1–2:18 THE EXALTED SON: BETTER THAN ANGELS

Overview: In addition to being divinely inspired Scripture, the book of Hebrews is great literature. The first sentences are illustrative of the writer's lofty style, full of noble expressions and fine rhetoric. The book was clearly written by someone who was able and eloquent. Hebrews 1:3 sets out the two major themes of the book: (1) the purification of humanity's sin, which led to (2) Jesus taking his place at God's right hand.

Three points are made in Hebrews 1–2: Jesus is the Creator; angels are servants of the redeemed; and Jesus is the brother of all those who believe. While the topics initially were of concern to Jewish believers, the truths of Christ's inherent greatness over creation and the world of spirit beings is important for all Christians. The excellence of Jesus is critical for those who might consider withdrawing from Jesus to return to their pre-Christian commitments.

Tradition viewed angels as being the mediators who gave the law to Moses (cf. Deut. 33:2; Gal. 3:19; Acts 7:38, 53). Christ is better than any other mediatorial agent God had used in his revelation. By using numerous quotations from the Old Testament Scriptures, the writer demonstrates the superiority of Christ over angels. Angels were also highly regarded by the Jews as administrators of the nations (Dan. 10:20-21; 12:1). The writer does not disparage angels but simply shows how Christ is "better," a term used thirteen times in Hebrews to contrast Christ with the old order. Seven truths are stated about the Son that emphasize his greatness and show why the revelation given through him is full and final: (1) Heir of all things, (2) Creator of the world, (3) the radiance of God's glory, (4) the exact representation of God's divine nature, (5) the sustainer of creation, (6) the Redeemer of mankind, and (7) intercessor for believers.

1:1–2:4 Better by Nature

1:1-4 THE INHERITED NAME

1:1-2 Contexts of divine speaking. The author clearly recognized that God spoke both through his prophets (Old Testament) and his Son (New Testament). He viewed God's self-revelation through two eras (then and now) and two sources (the prophets and the Son). God was the source of the revelation that came to the forefathers of the nation Israel. But that revelation came bit by bit and by various methods: dreams, visions, signs, laws, institutions, and ceremonies. In contrast to the former revelation, the full and final revelation in these "last days" is in God's Son (John 1:18). Old Testament saints could say, "God speaks." Believers today say, "God has spoken."

1:2-4 The new way described. Jesus' supremacy is based on two facts: (1) he was appointed heir of all things and (2) before that he was the vehicle of creation (1:2). Here the writer emphasized the incomparable greatness, power, and majesty of the Son. Jesus has a better nature than angels. Christ is characterized as the Creator himself. His word sustains creation, and he has the very character of God.

1:5-14 BIBLICAL PROOF FOR THE SON'S NAME

1:5-6 Sonship. Jesus' excellence is confirmed by quoting Psalm 2:7 (cf. Acts 13:33) along with 2 Samuel 7:14. These are passages that speak of the coronation of God's chosen King according to God's promise to David. In view was Christ's exaltation to the right hand of God in resurrection power (cf. Acts 2:33-35). Christ is Son in terms of the kingship promised in 2 Samuel 7:14.

1:7-14 Vocation. This section shows that angels are ministers (see the beginning and end bracket in 1:7, 14) whereas Christ is the exalted Son (1:13 again quoting Ps. 110:1). The angels are servants (1:7 quoting Ps. 104:4) for the Christians (1:14). Therefore, Christians are not to worship angels. They are to be served by them.

Christ is better because of the worship he receives (1:6 quoting Deut. 32:43). Christ is better because of his eternal sovereignty (1:8-13 quoting Ps. 45:6-7; 102:25-27; and 110:1). Christ is better because of the work he accomplished at creation (1:10-12 quoting Ps. 102:25-27). And Christ is better because of the triumph he achieved (1:13 quoting Ps. 110:1). To sit at the right hand of royalty was regarded as a great honor and proved that someone was worthy of great respect. Treating one's conquered enemies as a footstool is a metaphor taken from the ancient practice of a conquering king placing his foot on the neck of a defeated king as a symbolic gesture of triumph. Why is Jesus sitting, rather than standing, at God's right hand? The book of Hebrews proceeds to answer this question. He has done his priestly work of purification for sin and now waits until the final judgment (Ps. 110:1). Jesus used Psalm 110:1 with reference to himself in Mark 14:62. Even the Jews of the first century A.D. understood Psalm 110 to refer to the Messiah.

The "salvation" mentioned in 1:14 looks to the final consummation of salvation where believers will be changed to full conformity with Christ (Rom. 8:29; 1 John 3:2). The writer has spoken about Christ as Creator and Sovereign over the angels. He next moves on to speak of something more personal than Christ as Creator; he reveals Christ's identity as brother to humanity.

2:1-4 STATEMENT OF NEED: PAY MUCH CLOSER ATTENTION

Here the writer presents the first of five warning passages (cf. Heb. 2:1-4; 3:7–4:13; 5:11–6:20; 10:26-31; 12:25-29). In this first warning, the writer shows that the Son's superiority to angels should not be neglected. Since the revelation through Christ is superior to that mediated by angels, and earlier disregard for God's revelation was duly punished, disobedience to the Christian message of salvation would not go unpunished.

Hebrews 2:1 reflects the major difficulty with the readers. They were drifting from the substance, Christ, back to the shadows of the old covenant system. They were failing to appropriate the blessings of their salvation (2:3). They would not be saved from the power of sin by drifting from grace back to the law and Judaism. The message of salvation was confirmed to the Hebrew readers by the apostles who heard firsthand; their message was certified to the Jewish hearers by apostolic miracles (2:4).

2:5-18 Better by Empathy

2:5-8 ALL IS SUBJECT TO HIM

The writer presents another example of the superiority of the Son over angels. The administration of the present world has been entrusted to angels (cf. Deut. 32:8; Dan. 10:20-21; 12:1; Eph. 6:12), but administration in the world to come is reserved for the Son (Heb. 2:5; 6:5). The writer refers to Psalm 8:4-6 (Heb. 2:6-8) in which the psalmist reflects on the original state of man and his dominion over creation (Gen. 1:26). The original psalm spoke of God putting all creation under the rule of humans (Gen. 1:28). That state of perfect rule will be a future reality. For now, believers have the vision of the Son of Man through his work of redemption to live by.

2:9-18 FAMILY RELATIONSHIPS

2:9 Jesus made lower than the angels. In this verse the author goes from *son of man* (mankind) in Psalm 8 to the *Son of Man.* Jesus will give humanity the ability to completely subject the world in the future. The purpose of Christ being made a little lower than the angels was that he might taste death for all believers. The exposition interweaves with Old Testament text, especially Hebrews 2:9. The expression "taste" is a metaphor for experience. The atonement is sufficient for all and effective for all who believe (John 10:15; 2 Cor. 5:18-19; Eph. 5:25; 1 John 2:2).

2:10 A mutual partaker in humanity. Hebrews 2:10 presents the writer's thesis. It was fitting for Jesus to experience humility and death because it was in accord with God's plan to perfect him. The sufferings of Christ were necessary to complete his identification with humanity. Christ's sufferings made him truly qualified to be the perfect high priest. The word "author" means "originator, leader, or pioneer."

2:11-13 Scriptural proof. Both he who sanctifies and those who are sanctified are from one Father. That unity of source was a driving force in Christ's empathy for sinful mankind. The author used Psalm 22 to support his statement. All who believe are Christ's brothers and sisters; therefore, he is not ashamed to call believers family. But more pointedly, Psalm 22:22 (Heb. 2:12), along with the quotations of Isaiah 8:17-18 (Heb. 2:13) shows that as Mediator, Christ is God's King speaking to his royal family. The Isaiah 8:18 passage (quoted in 2:13) refers to children as signs of God's judgment and salvation ("Isaiah" means "salvation is of God"; the name of his son "Shear-Jashub" means "a remnant will return," Isa. 7:3; and "Maher-Shalal-Hash-Baz" means "quick to the plunder, swift to the spoil" in judgment, Isa. 8:3). As signs, Isaiah and his sons were pictures of Christ and his children. These quotations demonstrate the unity of Christ and the believers.

2:14-18 Conclusion. This conclusion takes up the "children" concept of Hebrews 2:13. The incarnation makes a difference in the believer's approach to the one who is the Creator. Again the contrast is between what is done for angels and for believers (Heb. 2:16). The delivery from fear of death (2:14-15) is elaborated with reference to Abraham's offspring (cf. Isa. 41:8-10). The purpose of the incarnation of Christ was to defeat the prince of death (Heb. 2:14), deliver believers from the fear of death (2:15-16), and qualify him as a merciful high priest (2:17). The topic of the high priest is introduced (2:17; cf. Heb. 5–7). The term "atonement" (2:17; "propitiation," NASB; "reconciliation," KJV) speaks of the satisfaction of God's wrath. The death of Christ satisfied God's wrath toward sin, enabling him to receive those who place their faith in Jesus (cf. Rom. 3:25).

Since Christ was tempted through his human suffering, he is able to sympathetically assist those who are spiritually distressed (Heb. 2:18). He understands the temptations of believers and is able to help them remain faithful. These exhortation passages help believers understand why the letter was written. They explained the new word from God, not from Sinai, but from the promised Messiah. These passages do not differ significantly from Paul's. They emphasize a worthy walk. The point the author wanted to make is this: if what God said through Sinai was impressive, think about what he has said through Jesus. The author is speaking about the world to come (2:5). That new world will end the present period of Christ's reign at God's right hand (1:13; Ps. 110:1, "until"). The world is moving toward the end of that period. The author was speaking of the coming age in Hebrews 1:2 and 2:3.

3:1–4:16 THE FAITHFUL SON: MORE GLORY THAN MOSES

Overview: Jesus is contrasted with Moses by using the metaphors Son versus servant and builder versus house. The exodus theme of Moses changes to the conquest theme under Joshua as the rest in the Promised Land is contrasted with the eternal Sabbath rest to come.

3:1-6 Greater Glory

3:1-2 THESIS STATEMENT: BOTH MOSES AND JESUS ARE FAITHFUL
Consider Jesus who was faithful like Moses. Moses was a great servant (Num. 12:7), but Jesus is the Son. Note the whole context of Numbers 12. In Judaism, Moses was regarded as the great prophet and leader of Israel, delivering the people from bondage in Egypt and leading them up to the Promised Land (Deut. 34:10-12). While careful to avoid deprecating Moses, the writer sets forth the superior person and position of Christ. The author addressed his readers as "holy brothers" (3:1), indicating that they were fellow Christians. The expression "share in the heavenly calling" (3:1) indicates that they have received an effective call of God to salvation.

3:3-4 JESUS' FAITHFULNESS AS BUILDER
Christ is Son and builder of the house of which Moses was just a part. As the real credit for a building belongs to the architect and builder, so Jesus as the builder of God's house is entitled to more glory than Moses, who was merely an important part of the building.

3:5-6 JESUS' FAITHFULNESS AS SON
Christ's faithfulness is based on the relationship of being a Son, rather than a servant, in the house. The words "if we hold on" (3:6) suggest that an abandonment of grace in favor of Judaism would demonstrate that the readers had never become genuine believers. True believers are those who persevere in the faith.

3:7–4:13 Conclusion: The Requirement of Consistent Belief

3:7-19 SCRIPTURAL COMMAND: DO NOT HARDEN YOUR HEART
3:7-11 The principle. The writer warned that as the Israelites failed to enter into Canaan because of their sinful disobedience, an

expression of unbelief (3:19), the believers also would miss out on a similar blessing if they did not continue steadfastly in their faith (3:12; 4:1). The reason for bringing up Moses was to talk about the wilderness and rest. The key elements are "today" (3:7) and "desert" (3:8). Having a great man like Moses did not stop the Israelites from great failure of faith and loss of rest in the Promised Land. Psalm 95 speaks of the rest in the Promised Land of Israel. Hardness of heart raised God's anger and blocked entrance into his rest. For the illustration of unbelief, the author quoted Psalm 95:7-11 (cf. Exod. 17:1-7; Num. 20:1-13) in which David warned his own generation against the rebellion and unbelief that had characterized God's people in the wilderness. A whole generation of the nation of Israel forfeited the privilege of entering the Promised Land (cf. Num. 14:22-23).

3:12-19 The exposition. The basic problem for the original readers of this book was unbelief (3:12 and 3:19 frame this section). The writer warned the believers that as rebellion in the wilderness resulted in a forfeiture of God's rest in Canaan, so a retreat from Christ back to Judaism would also result in a forfeiture of God's blessing. Since they "share in Christ" (3:14), they should not be tricked into such apostasy. Professed Christians who, through a lack of trust in Christ, reverted to Judaism would be exhibiting the same unfaithfulness to God's revelation as their forefathers had in the wilderness. And the consequences could be equally disastrous.

4:1-13 APPLICATION:
BE DILIGENT TO ENTER TRUE REST
4:1-10 The need for hearing plus faith. The Promised Land of rest was just a picture of a future entrance into God's rest that began on the first Sabbath, the seventh day of creation. It is a rest in the perfection and wholeness of a restored creation. God's creation Sabbath rest confirmed that everything was very good, just the way he wanted it. Psalm 95 is used to show the hard-heartedness of the people. The writer was answering the question of how there could be a rest other than that of the Promised Land. The writer demonstrated that "rest" was part of God's plan from the very beginning and that his plan for providing rest is

still in effect. Hebrews 4:9 summarizes the conclusion of the arguments presented in 4:3-8.

God intends for believers to find rest (4:10). As God rested on the seventh day in light of the completion of creation, so his people may rest in the satisfaction that Christ's work of redemption is completed. The word translated "rest" may be translated "a Sabbath-kind of rest." The believer who rests completely in the finished work of Christ has ceased from self-efforts, human merit, and legalism as means of commending himself to God (4:10).

4:11-13 Exhortation to diligence. Everyday is today in the believer's experience before God. The author was talking about the way believers think about God and respond to him. The exodus under Moses and the conquest under Joshua were not once-for-all events. They were pictures of an ongoing process of redemption and conquest that will lead ultimately into the eternal Promised Land of the new heavens and earth. Until then, there is no time to coast or retreat in Christian commitment. Believers either go forward or backward.

The discussion of the sharpness of the word (4:12) cements the certainty of a fall (4:11) for those who doubt God's interest or ability to keep track of his peoples' maturity. People cannot hide from God (cf. 1:1-2). The word of God is living and active, filled with God's vitality and energy. It is able to probe the deepest recesses of the human heart and leave nothing hidden. Confronted by God's word, people are confronted with God before whom they must give an account and from whom nothing can be concealed.

4:14-16 Transition from Apostle to High Priest

Jesus being a priest has always been in the writer's mind, but now in Hebrews 5–10 he will discuss it more clearly. Israel's high priest held the highest official religious office in the nation (4:14). The writer of Hebrews sought to show that Christianity also had a high priest, but one who was in every way superior to the priests of Judaism. The proof of Christ's ability to understand human weakness sympathetically is found in his own experience of temptation (4:15). Christ was tempted in all areas in which man is tempted (Matt. 4:1-11; 1 John 2:16), and with particular temptations suited for him. He experienced temptation to the full degree and yet did not sin.

5:1–12:13 THE PERFECT PRIEST: ETERNAL AND EFFECTIVE
5:1–7:28 Eternal: Melchizedek
Overview: The writer demonstrated Christ's superiority to prophets, angels, and Moses. Next he explained that Christ is superior to Israel's high priest, Aaron. The basis of his greatness is his exaltation by God (5:5) and his appointment as a priest according to the order of Melchizedek (5:6). The oath of God mentioned in Psalm 110:4 is linked to the oath he made to Abraham. In Christ the perfect priesthood of Melchizedek and the promises for Abraham are certain.

5:1-10 CHOSEN AND PERFECTED
5:1-6 Designated to be empathetic. Here the author set forth two general qualifications that any high priest needed to satisfy. He had to be taken from among humanity so he could sympathize with those he represented, and he had to be divinely appointed to the office. The author showed how Jesus met both of these qualifications. On the gentle (5:2) work of Christ, see Matthew 12:18-21, quoting Isaiah 42:1-4, and Luke 4:18, quoting Isaiah 61:1-2. Two Old Testament texts (Pss. 2:7 and 110:4) are cited as proofs of Christ's divine appointment to the priestly office. Aaron, Israel's first high priest, and his successors occupied their office by divine appointment (Exod. 28:1; Num. 20:23-29). The issue was the call of God and his public declaration of his designated priest (Heb. 5:4). Again Psalm 110:4 is quoted (5:6) in conjunction with Psalm 2 (5:5; cf. 1:5). The public declaration of Christ's lordship and priestly calling was his resurrection (cf. Acts 13:33). Jesus is a high priest after the order of Melchizedek.

5:7-10 Perfected for eternal priesthood by suffering. The real suffering of the Son cannot be downplayed (5:7-8). Jesus' incarnation enabled him to meet the second qualification for serving as high priest: he was taken from among men (5:1). Christ met the qualifications for the high priesthood, but he would not have qualified as a priest of the Aaronic order because he was not of the tribe of Levi. Thus, Jesus fills the priestly office of

the order of Melchizedek (cf. Gen. 14:18-20; Ps. 110:4). The writer develops the significance of this priestly order in Hebrews 7.

5:11–6:20 EXHORTATION TO DILIGENCE
In the third warning passage of Hebrews, the writer rebuked the believers for their lack of spiritual progress and encouraged them to press on to maturity.

5:11-14 The problem exposed: dull hearing. Lack of movement toward maturity was what made these people dull of hearing. Their hearing was not matched by character growth and maturity. The "this" (5:11) referred to Melchizedek (5:10). Melchizedek is mentioned in Genesis 14 and is prominent in the Dead Sea Scrolls. Sufficient time had passed since their conversion for them to have been well grounded in the faith so as to teach others, yet they were still in need of learning some of the basic principles of Christian growth. The readers had become sluggish in responding to God's word. They should have been able to communicate what was well-known about the person of Christ. The concepts of milk and solid food (5:13-14) match up with those of trained or untrained senses in discerning good and evil (5:14). Lack of a consistent desire to apply doctrine, not complexity of doctrine, was the issue.

6:1-8 The singular solution: move on to maturity. Because of their spiritual immaturity, the writer encouraged his readers to move on to maturity. "Leave" (6:1) does not mean "repudiate" but merely "advance beyond the first step." The author mentioned six things (three pairs) that he regards as the fundamentals of Christianity. They relate to conversion, ordinances, and the doctrine of future events. As important as these matters are, they are foundational. After the foundation is laid, the house is built. One does not keep going back and re-laying the foundation.

The author addressed true believers (cf. 3:1) and emphasized their deep experience in the things of Christ: they had been enlightened by the gospel, had experienced Christ, and had shared in the Spirit's indwelling ministry. He told them that it was impossible, when renewing their lagging commitment to Christ, to start all over again with a spiritual rebirth. They could not be born again—

again. The offering of Christ was once-for-all. A falling away could not be remedied with a second regeneration. Even the worst-case example (6:8) could only be remedied by a pressing on to maturity. They were to get back on the road from where they fell off, not go back to the very beginning and start all over again.

Hebrews 6:6 has been understood to refer to saved persons who are subsequently lost (but see John 10:28-30), professing believers who have never really been saved (but see Heb. 3:1; 6:4-5), or saved persons who fail to go on to maturity. The context commends the third viewpoint. The sin involved a departure from grace back to Judaism. The writer pointed out that it was impossible to retreat to the cross for repentance by recrucifying Christ. By seeking to return to the cross to get saved again, the Hebrew Christians were bringing public shame to Christ by slighting his person and work. Since beginning the Christian life again is impossible, the only option for the readers was to press on to maturity.

However, some were not interested in getting back on the way of Christ but were insisting on staying immature. This put them in grave jeopardy before God (6:8). The author drew an illustration from the natural world to show God's blessing on fruitfulness, progressing to maturity (6:7); he continued the illustration to show God's judgment on fruitlessness, regressing back to Judaism (6:8). The judgment on fruitlessness is the loss of reward at the judgment seat of Christ (cf. 1 Cor. 3:13-15).

6:9-20 Encouragement to diligence. The writer commended the justice of God (6:10) in remembering the diligence of believers (6:10-12). The subject of becoming "lazy" (6:12) shows the continuation of the same thoughts and problems of being slow to learn (5:11), not paying careful attention (2:1-4), and hardening of the heart (3:7–4:13). Then follows an example of faith, patience, and divine justice (6:13-20). The writer quoted God's promise to Abraham (6:14; cf. Gen. 22:16-18), which is a promise for all who believe. In view of the faithfulness of God to Abraham, believers in Christ may have confidence that God will fulfill all he has promised.

But God wanted to prove his promise to believers "even more" than he did to Abraham (6:17). So he gave Christians both a promise and an oath (6:17-18). "Promise" (6:15) and "oath" (6:16) are the keys to this section. By God's granting both the oath and the promise, believers have the strongest encouragement for trusting God's promises (6:18).

The writer alluded to Israel's cities of refuge (6:18; cf. Num. 35:6, 9-32) that provided protection for Israelites who had slain someone accidently. So, too, the Christians have a place of refuge in Christ. An anchor (6:19) in a secure spot would keep a ship from drifting. Christ, the believer's anchor, is in the safest place possible. The anchor, a symbol for Christ, has been found engraved in early Christian tombs.

7:1-28 THE NEED FOR A NEW PRIESTHOOD
7:1-3 Melchizedek's order: perpetual.
Melchizedek is mentioned in only two Old Testament passages (Gen. 14:18-20; Ps. 110:4). The writer of Hebrews was not interested in anything that might be known about Melchizedek outside of the biblical narrative. What he appealed to was true about Melchizedek in a limited, literary sense. The lack of biblical details about Melchizedek is used at several points to show the analogy between Christ and Melchizedek. Melchizedek prefigures Christ in that he was both a king and a priest, and his priesthood abides forever. Some have interpreted 7:3 to mean that Melchizedek had no parents and thus was a divine figure, an appearance of God. But all the writer was saying is that there is no genealogy for Melchizedek in Genesis and no record of his death. The absence of this material is used by way of analogy with Christ's eternality. Hebrews 7:2 clarifies this by explaining Melchizedek's name in a symbolic manner. Hebrews 7:3 continues that symbolic explanation.

7:4-10 Melchizedek's greatness. Abraham and Levi paid tithes. A new priestly order was needed because the first one was imperfect (cf. 5:10; 6:20). Melchizedek and Jesus after him were not dependent upon the qualifications for Levitical priests. The greatness of Melchizedek over Aaron is evidenced by (1) the fact that Abraham, the father of the Hebrew nation, paid tithes to Melchizedek, thus acknowledging the priest's superiority; (2) Melchizedek blessed Abraham; (3) there is no record of Melchizedek's death, whereas the Aaronic priests died and the office was passed to their heirs; (4) Levi, yet unborn in the loins of Abraham, paid tithes to Melchizedek.

7:11-17 The imperfect priesthood and Melchizedek's new order. This section builds to another quotation of Psalm 110, this time 110:4. The emphasis was on a priesthood that will last forever. The first order was imperfect because it could not create a perfect people in God's sight (note the question of 7:11). This makes sense of 7:12. If the priesthood could be changed, so could the law because the priest administered the law. This brings in a new covenant. The Levitical priesthood was unable to make people acceptable before God, therefore a new order was necessary. The Levitical priesthood required the Mosaic Law to support it. Any basic change in the priesthood required a corresponding change in the law. The writer was building to the transition from the old to the new covenant (cf. 8:13). What is "even more clear" (7:15) refers back to the need for a change in law along with a change of priesthood. Christ's priesthood is better than that of the Aaronic priests since it is not based on the law but according to the power of his resurrection life.

7:18-25 A better hope and covenant. Again, Psalm 110:4 was quoted, this time with the emphasis on "sworn." The concept of oath stems from the discussion of God's oath to Abraham in 6:13, 16-17. The "former regulation" (7:18) was the law (7:19). Since Christ's priesthood had been established by an oath, he guarantees a better covenant (7:22). His priesthood is eternal and perfect (7:23-25).

7:26-28 Perfection described. The death of the high priests prevented them from continuing their ministry. Eighty-three high priests officiated from Aaron until the destruction of Jerusalem in A.D. 70. But Christ's resurrection means that he can hold his priesthood permanently. His perfection "meets our need" (7:26) in light of the oath that appointed him (7:28, referring to Ps. 110:4). The concept of meeting needs relates to Christ's work being fitting or proper, a

concept that occurs elsewhere in 2:10; Matthew 3:15 at the baptism of Christ; 1 Corinthians 11:13 with reference to hair; Ephesians 5:3 regarding saints; 1 Timothy 2:10 regarding women; and Titus 2:1 regarding doctrine. Because of the obvious weaknesses of the Aaronic priests, the Old Testament itself anticipated a contrasting perfect and eternal order that would come "after the law" (7:28).

8:1–10:18 Effective: Better Covenant Administered

Overview: Levi administered an old law. It was a copy. The old covenant was administered to hearts of stone. This section sets out to answer the question of why Christ is sitting at God's right hand. See 8:1-3 and the "and so" of 8:3. The concept of offerings and where they were offered are also keys to understanding Hebrews 8–10. In this section contrasts were made between the offerings of the priests and the offering of Jesus and between the places of the tabernacle and the heavenly temple. Moses' tabernacle was a copy or a pattern (Exod. 25:40). The Levitical priests ministered only a copy (Heb. 8:4-5; 9:9-11).

Another question being answered in 8:1–10:18 concerns what creates a bad conscience. Note the division of earth (seen) and heaven (unseen) throughout. The subject of Christ's shed blood becomes the climax of the doctrinal section of Hebrews. Christ's sacrifice is superior because of its price (9:15-22), its finality (9:23-28), and its efficacy (10:1-18).

8:1-13 THE NEED FOR A CHANGE: IMPERFECT PATTERN OF MINISTRY
8:1-6 The place of ministry: a copy. Christ is at the right hand of God in the heavens and in the true tabernacle. The crowning point of the discussion is that the believers do have a high priest at the right hand of God who discharged his ministry, not in an earthly shrine, but in the heavenly dwelling place of God. In contrast to the Aaronic high priests, Christ ministers in a heavenly sanctuary, the real tabernacle, as opposed to the earthly copy. The earthly tabernacle seems to have been a mere copy of the authentic tabernacle in heaven. This is evidenced by the fact that at Mount Sinai Moses was instructed by God to erect the earthly tabernacle after the

pattern shown to him (cf. Exod.25:40). Moses saw something for which the verbal directions (Exod. 25–30) served as commentary. A "mediator" (8:6) is one who stands in between two parties as an umpire or arbitrator and negotiates a settlement. Christ's mediatorial activity was his atoning death that provided a basis for reconciling man to God. For the "better promises" (8:6), see 6:17-18; 7:21.

8:7-13 Basis of ministry: imperfect. The copy administered by the Aaronic priesthood was imperfect; the covenant around which the priests ministered was imperfect. The essential problem was that the old covenant made demands that it could not help its followers to achieve (8:7). But the Old Testament spoke of a change in covenants (8:8-13). The writer contrasts the old covenant instituted at Mount Sinai with the new covenant enacted on the basis of Christ's atonement. The old covenant promised blessings for obedience and curses for disobedience. The new covenant secures unconditional blessings for believers on the basis of the finished redemptive work of Christ (cf. Jer. 31:31-34; Ezek. 36:25-28).

The writer quoted Jeremiah 31:31-34. The problem with the old covenant was that its followers continually broke it. Its laws stood outside of its subjects and they had little desire to follow them. The new covenant puts the law inside the hearts of its followers, leading ultimately to perfect, spontaneous, and heart-felt obedience. The old covenant could not accomplish that. The new covenant brings a new ability in relationship with God, not full of apostasy like the old covenant.

Christ is a high priest after the order of Melchizedek. He ministers the new covenant that gives new hearts. God's will is now internalized so that his people may instinctively do what he wants. He gives a new and intimate knowledge of himself. It is personal and individual rather than working through levels of priests and earthly leaders (8:11). The promise of a new covenant made the old covenant obsolete (8:13). From the writer's perspective, it was ready to "disappear." This took place in A.D. 70 when the Jewish temple in Jerusalem was destroyed by the Romans, thus ending the Old Testament sacrificial system.

9:1-10 THE FIRST MINISTRY: THE HIDDEN HOLY PLACE
This section points out the need for the Most Holy Place to be hidden away. Verse 1 introduces this section on the general features of the tabernacle. The author presented a general description of the tabernacle (cf. Exod. 25–27, 35–40). He associated the incense altar with the Most Holy Place. The altar of incense actually stood in the Holy Place before the veil (Exod. 40:26-27), though its ritual use was connected with the Most Holy Place, especially on the Day of Atonement (Lev. 16:12-13).

The divine lesson (Heb. 9:6-10) is that these articles had no ability to cleanse the conscience. Why did the high priest have to enter the Most Holy Place once a year when sacrifices were made all year long outside the Most Holy Place (9:7)? Because of sins done in ignorance. No matter how careful the nation was in offering sacrifices for their sins, they were always aware that some unconfessed and unsacrificed sin was probably out there putting the entire nation in jeopardy. This was the reason for the Day of Atonement (Lev. 16:16-17). While individual sins could be forgiven through the sacrifices, there always remained a consciousness of other unforgiven and unknown sins.

The fact that the priests daily entered the Holy Place to burn incense (cf. Exod. 30:1-8) and that the high priest yearly entered behind the veil to make atonement (Lev. 16) indicated that there was no final offering for sin under the Mosaic system. The old covenant provided only limited access to God (9:8) and limited cleansing from sin (9:9-10).

9:11-14 THE SECOND MINISTRY: A CLEANSED CONSCIENCE
Believers in Christ have access to the genuine Holy Place where God dwells. The sacrifice made for human sin was once for all and eternal. Christ fulfilled the ministry that was typified by the ministry of the high priests when he entered once for all into the Holy Place in the heavenly tabernacle, offering his own blood to obtain for believers' eternal (not to be repeated) redemption. Christ's sacrifice made a cleansed conscience possible, something animal sacrifices could never do.

9:15-22 THE SECOND MINISTRY: A CONFIRMED HOPE OF INHERITANCE

The inauguration of the new covenant came with the shedding of blood. The reason for the stress on blood was to show that it was not a negative in considering Christ as Redeemer. It was an established and crucial Old Testament truth. Almost everything needing ceremonial cleansing under the Old Testament law required blood. There were exceptions (Exod. 19:10; Num. 31:21-24). Apart from the shedding of blood (death) there is no remission (forgiveness) of sin. Believers have not been redeemed with perishable things like silver and gold but with the precious blood of Christ (1 Pet. 1:18-20). No animal sacrifice could have accomplished the perfect and final redemption effected by Christ's blood. As a last will and testament is valid only when the testator dies, so the new covenant was validated by Christ's death.

9:23-28 THE SECOND MINISTRY: APPLICATION OF THE TYPE AND ANTITYPE

The necessity of a better cleansing hinged on the better realities of the heavenly tabernacle (9:23). At the focal point of redemptive history ("the end of the ages," 9:26), Christ put away sin for all time ("once"). There is no need for further sacrifice. This explains why Christ is sitting at God's right hand (10:12; cf. Ps. 110:1). He has no further sacrificial priestly work to do. Christ's second coming will not be for the purpose of offering another sacrifice, but to take redeemed believers to himself in the consummation of their salvation.

10:1-10 THE NEED FOR A SINGULAR OFFERING

The writer emphasized that Christ's sacrifice was completely efficacious and final (10:10, 12, 18). It needs no repetition or supplement. The atoning value of the Old Testament sacrifices was temporary and typical. They expressed a need that in themselves they could not ultimately fulfill. Their efficacy depended upon Christ whose sacrifice they anticipated (John 1:29). In Hebrews 10:5-7 the author quoted Psalm 40:6-8 and interpreted it as being fulfilled in Christ. The inadequacy of the Old Testament sacrificial system is seen by the fact that Christ replaced it. He took away the "first" (10:9, the Old Testament system) to

establish the "second" (Christ's atonement and new covenant). Jesus fulfilled the Old Testament types and provided the actual forgiveness that the animal sacrifices could only symbolize.

The fact that multiple offerings were needed in the Old Testament implied the inadequacy of those offerings. Psalm 40 was used to emphasize the singularity of Christ's offering. The first part of this psalm is an acknowledgment psalm with a transitional phrase in the middle followed by a lament psalm. It is this middle section that the writer of Hebrews uses with reference to the Lord.

Elsewhere Scripture emphasizes that God does not desire Levitical sacrifices when one's inner life is not right before him (cf. 1 Sam. 15:22; Ps. 51:16-17; Isa. 1:11-15; Jer. 7:2-23; Hos. 6:6; Mic. 6:6-8; Mark 12:33). God does want offerings because he has commanded them. However, those offerings are always seen in light of the offerer's purity of heart. The point of Psalm 40 is that God wants the person, not sacrifices. And what he especially desired was the body (10:5, 10) of his Son. The reference to "ears" (Ps. 40:6) is to the human body. The Greek Old Testament translated "ears" of Psalm 40:6 as "body," and this is what the writer of Hebrews quoted to refer to the offering of Jesus' body once for the atonement of all.

10:11-18 FORGIVENESS FROM THE SINGULAR OFFERING IS CONFIRMED

Christ's singular offering (Ps. 40:5-8) resulted in his "sitting down" (Ps. 110:1, again quoted in Heb. 10:13) and the inauguration of the new covenant (Jer. 31:31-34). The fact that Christ "sat down" indicates that his work is completed. The writer confirms the finality of Christ's sacrifice (Heb. 10:15-17) by the witness of Jeremiah 31:33-34. Hebrews 10:18 provides the grand conclusion to the doctrinal section of the epistle to the Hebrews. From this point on the writer would give exhortations to appropriate the benefits secured for the believers by Christ. Sins are no longer remembered (10:17; contrast with 10:3) so there is no longer any need for sacrifice. The mention of "laws in their hearts" (10:16; Jer. 31:33) shows the extent of the perfection gained by Christ (10:14).

10:19–12:13 Exhortations to Effective Faith

Overview: The writer pleads for endurance. The heart of endurance is a faith that believes that what God says regarding unseen and unfulfilled promises will indeed happen. Hebrews 11 provides a long list of people who believed in the unseen promises of God.

10:19-25 THREE FUNDAMENTAL PROBLEMS
The new and living way in Hebrews 10:20 is through the perfect and complete forgiveness found in Christ and having God's law written upon ones' heart. The writer now moves into a long section on exhortations. Three fundamental problems are dealt with: a clear conscience, a strong witness, and supporting the assembly. He first exhorted the believers to draw near to God by having a sincere heart, full assurance of faith and purity (10:19-22). The temple veil was typical of Christ, the only access into the presence of God. It is significant that at the crucifixion, the veil in the temple was torn (Mark 15:38), illustrating the inauguration of a new way of access to God through Christ. Second, believers were advised to hold fast to their confession based on God's faithfulness (10:23). Third, the believers were reminded that stimulation to love and do good deeds should occur when Christians continue to meet together and share their faith with others (10:24-25). The "Day approaching" (10:25) refers to the imminent return of Christ (1 Cor. 3:13; Phil. 1:10), which serves as a motivation to faithfulness.

10:26-31 THE PENALTY FOR WILLFUL SIN
In the fourth warning passage the readers are exhorted to beware of God's judgment upon deliberate disobedience to the truth. There is considerable debate regarding the identity of those who would "deliberately keep on sinning" (10:26). Some have suggested that they were not Christians at all but were those who, though having made a profession, were not genuinely saved. But this view is not consistent with the view that Hebrews was written to believers (cf. 3:1). And note the references in Hebrews 10:29-30 to "sanctified" and "his people." More likely, these are true believers who will be disciplined by God

for sinning against a knowledge of the truth (cf. Heb. 12:5-11). Having made profession of faith, these believers were reverting to Jewish ritualism.

If Christ's sacrifice is viewed as inadequate, what sacrifice is there? Only judgment remains (10:27). For those who doubted God's judgment (10:30-31), the writer appealed to Deuteronomy 32:35 and Psalm 135:4. God's own people had not been exempt from accountability to act on what they knew. Willful sin is equivalent to not drawing near, not confessing, and not assembling. In this startling warning, even the penalties of the old and new covenants are compared. The writer compared the penalties from the lesser to the greater; if there was judgment for breaking the Mosaic covenant, would there not be even greater penalties for breaking the greater covenant in Christ?

10:32-39 THE PROMISE FOR ENDURANCE
The writer encouraged the readers to remember their sufferings and victories of the past. He appealed to Habakkuk 2:3-4 to support the principle that those who are made righteous by God "shall live," that is, "survive the ordeals of life" by the faith principle (10:37-38). The perseverance of 10:36 is defined by the Habakkuk quotation as living by faith (10:38; cf. also 6:9-20). See also Paul's use of Habakkuk 2:3-4 in Romans 1:17 and Galatians 3:11. The author reminded the believers that he knew they would endure as he elaborated what "hold unswervingly" (10:23) meant in light of God's faithfulness.

11:1-2 FAITH AS THE WAY TO APPROVAL
This chapter expands the thought of Hebrews 6:12. The time period covered by the first part of this list of faithful people is from the creation of the universe to Israel's entrance into Canaan (11:1-31). Having discussed the importance of maintaining faith and not turning back (10:32-39), the author illustrated from a number of Old Testament heroes the principle of enduring faith. The author began with a description of true faith. It is the "being sure" (the expression is used of a title deed that guarantees a future possession) that what is anticipated will be realized (11:1). Faith treats unseen things as realities, not mere

wishes or hopes. Throughout this chapter the issue of faith hinges on believing in what is not seen or what is future (11:1, 3, 7-8, 11, 13, 19-22, 27, 39; cf. Rom. 8:24-25).

11:3-12 APPROVED EXAMPLES

Faith's bedrock foundation is belief that when God speaks, it will happen. And the consummate example of the power of God's word was when God's word created the universe out of nothing. Faith believes that God's word can make the invisible visible. This world was created out of nothing, without the use of preexisting materials. Each example that follows illustrates that belief in the unseen is based upon a promise of God. Hebrews 11:6 presents two unseen truths for faith: God's existence (that he is there) and nature (that he is consistent and good). Faith is the key to knowing God. As people respond by faith to the general revelation of God in nature (Rom. 1:19-21), God directs them to the special revelation of himself found in his Son through his word.

For the Old Testament references to these heroes of faith, see the accompanying chart.

11:13-16 EXPLANATORY ELABORATION

These people died in faith without receiving God's great promises for the future. But they were not bound to this earth (11:13). More than this physical life, they desired a better country and a city of promise (11:16).

11:17-31 FURTHER APPROVED EXAMPLES

Abraham (11:17-19) is the central figure of the list as the beginning of the nation of Israel, but especially because he believed in God's unseen power of resurrection. His belief was a signal of the actual resurrection of Christ and, through him, all those of faith (cf. 11:35). After making note of the patriarchs from Isaac through Joseph (11:20-22), Moses' exodus (11:23-29) forms the next high point (note 11:27). The section ends with the conquest of the Promised Land starting with Jericho (11:30) and faithful Rahab (11:31; for Rahab in the line of Christ, cf. Matt. 1:5; Josh. 2:1-24; 6:22-25).

11:32-40 APPROVAL BUT NO RECEPTION OF THE PROMISES

These last examples cement the critical truth of faith: they believed in the unseen realities of promise as defined by God's word. These believers suffered in pain, but they held fast to his word (cf. Heb. 1:1). One reason that

HEROS OF FAITH IN HEBREWS

Heroes	*Old Testament References*
Abel	Genesis 4:2-5 (Hebrews 11:4 provides a clue as to why Abel's sacrifice was accepted and Cain's was not. Abel's sacrifice was an expression of faith.)
Enoch	Genesis 5:22-24
Noah	Genesis 6:13-22
Abraham	Genesis 12:1-4; 22:1-19
Sarah	Genesis 21:1-7
Isaac	Genesis 27:26-40
Jacob	Genesis 48:1-22
Joseph	Genesis 50:24-25
Moses	Exodus 2:1-15; 12:1-28; 14:13-31
Joshua	Joshua 6
Rahab	Joshua 2:1-21; 6:22-25
Gideon	Judges 6:11; 8:32
Barak	Judges 4:6–5:31
Samson	Judges 13:24–16:31
Jephthah	Judges 11:1–12:7
David	1 Samuel 16–17
Samuel	1 Samuel 7–10
Daniel	Daniel 6

these Old Testament saints did not realize the fulfillment of all God had promised was that the atonement of Christ had not yet taken place. The readers of this letter had something far better—the blessings of the new covenant (8:6-13). But believers still live with the unseen promise of Christ's return as a challenge to their worldly and faithless tendencies.

12:1-13 CONCLUSION: THEREFORE, ENDURE GOD'S DISCIPLINE THROUGH THE LONG RUN
The "cloud of witnesses" (12:1) refers to the heroes of the faith mentioned in chapter 11. Like a dedicated runner, Christians are to free themselves from entanglements and encumbrances so that there is nothing to hinder their life of faith. The expression "fix our eyes on" (12:2) means to turn away from all distractions and to focus on just one thing. Christ endured through suffering. Again Psalm 110:1 is used, this time to describe Christ's reward after his suffering (12:2). His endurance is set forth as an incentive and encouragement for the believers also to endure.

This section shows that the original readers were under some form of persecution. Their only way to endure would be to heed all that had been said in Hebrews 1–11, especially maintaining faith in the unseen but powerful promises of God. Apparently none associated with these Hebrew Christians had yet suffered martyrdom (12:4). The writer appealed to Proverbs 3:11-12 to introduce the subject of divine discipline (12:5-6). As a father disciplines his children, so God disciplines believers. While God's discipline is sorrowful in its experience, it produces spiritual results—holiness (12:10) and righteousness (12:11). God's discipline is not intended to destroy believers but to produce endurance (12:2, 3, 7) and healing (12:12-13). The pain of discipline is only understood in a positive way when the connection is made between the all too visible discipline and the unseen love of the heavenly Father.

12:14–13:17 PATTERNS FOR MATURE PEOPLE
12:14-29 Peace
Peace is linked to sanctification and the concept of avoiding sin (12:1). The bitterness arises in the context of persecution. The

persecuted person is likely to become bitter toward God, his people, and those who persecute. The result is a backing away from Christian commitment like Esau backed away from his birthright. The Esau illustration sums up the problem that arises throughout the letter—falling away from aggressive faith in Christ. The warning passages throughout have cautioned against facing a time when, like Esau, it would be too late to regain the blessing (cf. 2:1-4; 3:7–4:13; 5:11–6:20; 10:26-31; 12:25-29). Because of Esau's selfish, materialistic desires, he was rejected with respect to the blessing (Gen. 27:30-40).

Hebrews 12:18-29 uses the event of God's giving the law on Mount Sinai as an illustration of the even greater experience of coming to the real dwelling of God, the heavenly Jerusalem. Hebrews 12:18-24 is one long sentence in the Greek. Hebrews 12:18 looks back to 12:15-17 and applies the lesson of Esau to the readers.

In contrasting the old and new covenants, Mount Sinai serves as a symbol of law under the old covenant (12:18-21), and Mount Zion serves as a symbol of grace under the new covenant (12:22-24). The implicit question is, Do you want to return to the old? The "church of the firstborn" (12:23) referred to believers who belonged to the body of Christ. They were on earth, but their names were registered in heaven. The "spirits of righteous men made perfect" was a reference to Old Testament saints who were yet to be raised (Dan. 12:2). The "blood of Abel" (12:24) referred to Abel's blood sacrifice (Gen. 4:3-5). Abel's sacrifice was good, but Christ's is better.

The writer pictured the history of God's grace from his speaking at Mount Sinai through Moses to his speaking from the heavenly mountain of Zion through his Son (cf. Heb. 1:1-2). Israel had only come as far as Sinai. To stay at Sinai was to fall short of God's revealed grace in Christ (cf. 12:15).

The fifth and final warning urged the readers to think seriously about heeding what God had spoken (12:25-29). A reminder of the awesome scene at Sinai was used to emphasize the importance of absolute compliance with God's word. The earth/heaven image of 12:26 was based upon the earth/heaven images in the quotation from Haggai

2:6 in 12:26. As God shook the earth in the past (Exod. 19:18), he will shake heaven and earth in the future at the second coming of Christ.

13:1-6 Love

The previous section (12:14-29) was an exhortation to pursue peace and sanctification (12:14). This paragraph exhorts God's people to love each other (13:1). For examples of entertaining angels without knowing it, see Genesis 18:1-3; 19:1-2; and Judges 6:11-24. The avoidance of love of money and what it brings is placed within the context of having possessions taken away during persecution (cf. Heb. 10:34). The writer appeals to either Deuteronomy 31:6 or Joshua 1:5 and Psalm 118:6-7 to encourage Christian contentment (cf. Matt. 6:24-34). Contentment is based on "what we have." The scriptural quotations of Hebrews 13:5-6 show that what believers have is God himself. God has promised a permanent commitment to be with and help those who believe in him.

13:7-17 Obedience

This section begins and ends with a response to the teaching of Christian leaders (13:7, 17). In between, the content of that teaching is explained. While Christ's one sacrifice for sin stands for all time (cf. 10:12, 18), other kinds of sacrifices continue—praise, good works, and obedience (13:15-17). The "altar" (13:10) of Christians refers either to the cross or Christ's sacrifice made outside of the temple. As the bodies of certain sacrificial animals were burned outside the camp (Lev. 4:21; 16:27), so Christ suffered outside the gate of Jerusalem (John 19:17-20). The "enduring city" (13:14) is the heavenly Jerusalem (cf. 12:22).

13:18-25 CLOSING REQUESTS

The author concluded his letter focusing on Christ as the Shepherd and his eternal covenant, the new covenant (13:18-21). Timothy had apparently been imprisoned but had recently been released (13:23). It was hoped that the author and Timothy would make a joint visit to the readers. The implication is that the author was not a prisoner at this time since his visit hinged on Timothy's coming. "Those from Italy" (13:24) could refer to those presently with the author who were from Italy (perhaps Rome), or those with the author who was presently in Italy.

James

HISTORICAL SETTING

The twelve tribes scattered among the nations (James 1:1) were believing Hebrew Christians (1:2, 16; 2:1; 5:7). They were scattered as a result of the persecution in Jerusalem after the stoning of Stephen in A.D. 35 (Acts 8:1; cf. Acts 12:1-23). The letter indicates that the readers were suffering persecution and trials (James 1:2-4, 12; 2:6; 5:4). They were also lacking in fervor for good works and the practical application of truth to Christian living (1:26-27; 2:14-26).

AUTHOR

The author designated himself as the "servant of God and of the Lord Jesus Christ" (1:1). Little more is revealed about the author by the letter itself. Of the several men named James mentioned in the New Testament (Matt. 4:21; 10:3; Luke 6:16), James the half brother of the Lord (Matt. 13:55; Gal. 1:19) is the probable author. Eusebius and many others after him identify the author as the half brother of the Lord Jesus.

James grew up in Nazareth. He and his brothers remained unbelievers during the time of Christ's ministry on earth (John 7:5), but he had a significant role in the leadership of the Jerusalem church after Pentecost (Acts 12:17; 15:13-21; 21:18; Gal. 1:19; 2:9). The risen Lord appeared to James (1 Cor. 15:7), and shortly after that James appeared on the scene of the early church as a believer (cf. Acts. 1:14). Eusebius records that James lived as a perpetual Nazirite (Num. 6:1-21) and spent so much time in prayer that his knees became as hard as a camel's. The scribes and Pharisees of Jerusalem tried to persuade James to restrain the people who were following Jesus. He was taken to the pinnacle of the temple and told to speak against Christ. Instead, he took the opportunity to give testimony to Jesus. The enraged priests and Pharisees had James thrown from the temple. As the fall did not kill him, James was then stoned. Before his death, he prayed for his murderers, "Father, forgive them, for they know not what they do" (Eusebius, *Historia Ecclesiastica*, 2.23).

DATE

Josephus places the martyrdom of James in A.D. 62, so the letter must have been written earlier. An early date for the writing would be indicated by the use of the word "meeting" (lit., "synagogue," 2:2) for the place of the assembly of the believers and by the simplicity of ecclesiastical organization, which mentions elders alone (5:14). While difficult to date precisely, James was probably written between A.D. 45 and 49. This would make this letter the earliest book in the New Testament.

PURPOSE

The letter by James was designed to produce a vision for wisdom, good works, and the power of prayer. It did this by showing practical ways to live out the ethical implications of Christianity. Behind each of James's corrections are the unwavering holiness, goodness, and power of God.

GUIDING CONCEPTS

Three major themes shape the vigorous message of the book. (1) James insisted uncompromisingly on human equality in Christ. Watch for this in his discussions of wisdom (1:9-11), status (2:5), and wealth (5:1-6). (2) He was also a relentless activist. Words without actions to back them up are no better than what the devils say about God (2:19). (3) Finally, James was driven by a commitment to expose pride in all its awful and piously covered manifestations (cf. 4:1-3).

BIBLE-WIDE CONCEPTS

WISDOM LITERATURE

The book of James is a New Testament example of wisdom literature. Proverbs, Ecclesiastes, and Job are Old Testament examples. One characteristic of wisdom literature is its diversity. Life is diverse, and so wisdom instruction covers the whole range of life's situations. Another characteristic of wisdom literature is its unifying foundation: the fear of God. This is what allows the diversity of life to make sense. It is focused on God's character, not thousands of individual insights into life. The wise person is one who knows who God is. Knowledge of the character of God enables believers to act in a wise way in all of life's situations. Jesus' Sermon on the Mount (Matt. 5–7) and his parables (Matt. 13) are examples of New Testament wisdom literature. James has close affinities with the content of Jesus' Sermon on the Mount.

FAITH AND WORKS

James's argument that faith without works is useless (1:22-27; 2:14-26; 4:17; 5:19-20) is part of a pattern found throughout Scripture. God's people are to trust him and him alone for salvation and always affirm their trust by works of obedience. But James's letter is not an abstract theoretical discussion of salvation by works or by faith. He discusses faith and works as necessary and complimentary realities for any believer's life-style.

Faith reflects a person's valuation of God

From the very beginning of creation, the link between goodness and obedience
was defined by doing what God wanted. God said something and it was done.
Light, dry land, animals, and humans were all created when God commanded it to
happen. That link between God's command and creation's follow-through was to
be the same in human behavior. When God said to do or not do something, people
were supposed to carry out God's will. Adam and Eve did not question whether or
not God existed. The question was what value they placed on God's character and
ability to run the world. If they valued God highly, they would obey him. If they
did not value God, then they would disobey him. So, from the very beginning the
issue of obedience revolved around the issue of how highly people would esteem
God. And that is the essence of biblical faith—not the intellectual assent that God
exists, but the heartfelt assent to the high value of the joys and regulations of
being in a personal relationship with God.

Adam and Eve were to see God as the highest and last word on what they
should think, do, or say. God noted Adam's lack of priority in that he listened to
his wife (Gen. 3:17), implying that Adam should have listened instead to God. At
the moment Adam took his wife's word over God's, he showed whom he valued
the most. Faith is therefore a gauge of how much people value God and their
relationship with him. But the only way people can exhibit their faith is through
external and visible actions.

A person's claim of love for God has to be proven by appropriate visible actions.
This is why throughout Scripture God showed disgust for people who claimed to love
him but whose actions demonstrated nothing but hate. God criticized people who
said good things about him but whose hearts were far from him (Isa. 29:13; Matt.
15:8; Mark 7:6). He even condemned the hypocrites who had what looked like godly
devotion but in reality were motivated by selfishness (Matt. 6:1-2, 5, 16, 19-21). This
adds another dimension to the relationship between faith (what people believe or
claim to believe) and works (what people actually do); this is the dimension of underlying motives.

Actions should be motivated by a heart that loves and honors God. Love and
honor for God are the essence of faith. Any works that look like they spring from
hearts that love God but in reality spring from hearts that seek status and human
praise are counterfeit and bring no pleasure to or reward from God. Throughout the
Bible God desired his people to love him. He did not want them to obey him just
because of promised punishments or rewards. Moses (Deut. 6:5; 11:13), Joshua
(Josh. 24:23), Solomon (1 Kings 8:58), David (Pss. 37:31; 51:10, 17), Jehoshaphat
(2 Chron. 20:33), Isaiah (Isa. 29:13; 51:7), Jeremiah (Jer. 31:33), Ezekiel (Ezek.
14:3; 36:26), and others all called for an obedience to God's laws that was motivated
by a heart full of genuine love for God. People value what they love, and the more
they value something, the higher will be their commitment to it during times of
adversity. Behavior reveals people's values, and behavior is what the Bible calls
"works." Aside from the hypocrite who masks his evil heart with religious works,
works gauge where people are with God; they measure the love or lack of love
people have for God (e.g. 1 John 2:4-6; 3:21-24; 4:7-11, 20-21; 5:2-3).

The link of faith and works to salvation

The Bible puts forth a very interesting paradox. No one who acts like the devil can be saved, and no one can save himself by acting like a saint. Both the proverbial saint and sinner are equally doomed under God's curse on Adam. But people are delivered from this doom by God's action in two different ways.

First, God pushes people to obedience. His laws of life are absolutes. God never allows believers to pick and choose among his laws. He demands moral conformity to himself and cannot live with people who sin. Abraham (Gen. 19:18), Moses (Deut. 30:11-16), and Jesus (Matt. 5:17-20) all insisted that believers must keep God's commandments. Adam's sin infinitely offended God. Because God's curse on the world sprang from that infinite offense, only an equally infinite sacrifice could reconcile God's offense. This makes any hope that works of obedience can bring salvation impossible. Yet God never stops demanding complete obedience to his laws from people who are hopelessly flawed. Clearly, obedience to God's commands is a seperate issue from earning forgiveness or remedying the sin problem. Obedience is owed to God simply because of who he is. Salvation is God's business alone.

Second, God pushes people toward forgiveness. Throughout Scripture, God's push for obedience to his laws is kept clearly separate from his drive to bring believers into forgiveness. He shows that people cannot save themselves or make themselves acceptable to him by their works. God alone has brought the ultimate sacrifice for their sins, and they must accept that gift as complete, without a thought of bettering it by adding works of their own. Having received salvation by faith, believers keep God's laws, not in order to achieve forgiveness, but in order to show the value and honor felt for the one who already graciously saved them. Believers work to validate their claim of faith in God. That validation of their claim of faith is what James means when he speaks of works justifying or saving a person (James 2:14, 17, 21-22, 24-26). Without faith, works are hypocritical. Without works, a believer's faith is like the faith of demons, only intellectual (James 2:19). James's point is simple: just as fire gives off heat or the sun gives light, so faith will produce works.

NEEDS MET BY JAMES

James wrote to Christians who were suffering under the trials of family conflict and social ostracism. These difficulties pushed their belief in God's goodness to the limit. They found it tempting to respond to their problems with anger. They were tempted to hurt those who caused them pain. This anger even found its way into the Christian community where believers fought among themselves. Despite all the persecution the Christians were suffering, they still found it impossible to avoid acting like those who were oppressing them. They, like the worldly people around them, showed favor to the rich and ignored the poor; they sought the status of leadership without first being qualified; they had a soft attitude toward sin and exhibited little faith in prayer. The structure and content of James's letter shows that he intended to answer the following questions for his readers.

• What possible good can come from trials and suffering?
• How can believers continue to believe God is good when they are hurting so badly?
• Should believers look to worldly status and wealth as a protection against world problems?
• What is the relationship between a believer's beliefs and what he actually does?
• When believers are suffering, how can they resist striking back either verbally or physically?
• Is it possible that a believer's suffering is a result of personal sin?

The trials and sufferings experienced by believers today need the solutions James offered his readers. It is easy for believers to blame God when suffering is experienced. They may begin to think that God does not have their best interests in mind. Counter to this, James reminded his readers that God does only good. He is the Father of all good and never tries to cause his people to sin. To overcome the tendency of believers to base their joys on what the world has to offer, James taught that true joy comes from knowing God better and from growing in Christian character and witness. Instead of focusing on the material welfare of believers, James urged them to focus on how they could help others live purer lives. He helped them see the often wide gap between what they said and what they did. His advice for narrowing that gap relates to helping others live purer lives and living according to the law of love.

OUTLINE OF JAMES

A. GREETING (1:1)
B. EXHORTATION: BE JOYFUL IN TRIALS (1:2-27)
   1. The Purpose: Maturity (1:2-4)
   2. Desire for Insight: Asking in Faith (1:5-11)
   3. The Essential Insight: The Character of God (1:12-18)
   4. The Practice of Maturity (1:19-27)
C. EXHORTATION: BE IMPARTIAL (2:1–26)
   1. Implications of Partiality (2:1-13)
   2. The Practice of Impartiality (2:14-26)
D. EXHORTATION: BE MATURE IN SPEECH (3:1–4:12)
   1. The Tongue as a Revealer of Maturity or Immaturity (3:1-12)
   2. The Practice of Maturity (3:13-18)
   3. The Source of Immaturity (4:1-12)
E. CONDEMNATION: ATTITUDES AND END OF THE RICH (4:13–5:6)
   1. Arrogance of the Will (4:13-17)
   2. Judgment on the Rich (5:1-6)
F. EXHORTATIONS: MATURE ENDURANCE (5:7-20)
   1. Patient Endurance (5:7-11)
   2. Arrogant Oaths (5:12)
   3. Sharing in Prayer (5:13-18)
   4. The Essence of the Letter (5:19-20)

JAMES NOTES

1:1 GREETING

One of the key themes in James is the call to sinners to put their lives in order. The concepts of perfection and purity begin and end the letter (1:2; 5:19-20). James had a significant role in the leadership of the Jerusalem church (Acts 12:17; 15:13-21; 21:8; Gal. 1:19; 2:9). The "twelve tribes scattered among the nations" (1:1) was a reference to the believing Hebrew Christians who, because of persecution (Acts 8:1-4), were scattered throughout the Roman Empire.

1:2-27 EXHORTATION: BE JOYFUL IN TRIALS

1:2-4 The Purpose: Maturity

A "trial" (1:2) is a testing sent by God to prove the genuineness of the believer's faith (cf. with 1 Pet. 1:6). An attitude of joy is the proper perspective for such tests of faith. The command of James 1:2 is issued because joy in trials is easily missed. James spoke of trials and temptations in general. The letter specifically addressed the temptations arising from the flesh and from persecution. The way to finding joy while suffering trials is to see the direct result of perseverance developed in one's life (1:3; "endurance," NASB; "patience," KJV). Perseverance means to bear up under any given situation, not to escape it. The author's exhortation was to stay in the testing so that it would result in perseverance rather than sin. The result of perseverance is maturity (1:4); the purpose of the testing is to produce maturity. A process is in view: enduring just one trial is not enough. James encouraged his readers to let the process of trials keep working to bring complete maturity; for this reason trials had to come in all areas of life.

1:5-11 Desire for Insight: Asking in Faith

1:5 GAINING INSIGHT THROUGH ASKING
Prayer makes available the needed wisdom to endure and profit from testing. The purpose of prayer is to gain the wisdom needed to see suffering as a gift, not to gain wisdom for making decisions. The focus is on viewing sufferings as a source of joy, not on general requests for what believers should do, where they should go, or what they should buy. Believers are to ask, Is suffering really joy in my life? In prayer they need to ask for the wisdom to see their suffering in this way. God is characterized as the one who gives generously to all men without reproach. God's generosity is the foundation upon which James builds his discussion about doubt (1:6-8) and the rich and poor (1:9-11). There are no hidden strings in God's dealings with his people. He does not reproach believers for asking or needing to ask.

1:6-8 DOUBTING GOD'S CHARACTER
The doubt of James 1:6 is not about whether or not God will give believers what they want. The asking of 1:5 was specifically for wisdom to see trials as joy. The doubting of 1:6 concerns whether or not God is generous and willing to hear his people without reproach (see the description of God in 1:5). James likened the doubter, the one who thinks God is stingy and reproachful, to the wind-tossed surf, blown here and there. This image describes a believer who is influenced by many different ideas about what God is up to: (1) whether God is of such a character as 1:5 asserts; (2) whether one really wants what God freely offers; and (3) whether God is giving the best to his people.

1:9-11 ASKING IN AN ETERNAL CONTEXT, NOT FROM EARTHLY STATUS
The poor are exalted and the rich are humbled. The point is that all people, whether rich or poor, are equal before God. No one receives special treatment on the basis of his earthly status, a point central to the readers' problems (cf. 2:1, 15-16; 4:1-2, 12). Since the readers of James's letter had trouble with "asking" and "doubting," James needed to explain what it meant to be a doubter or a double-minded person. Both rich and poor needed a proper view of the essential elements of life. The poor may have thought their earthly circumstances determined their spiritual status before God. Thus, they may have "doubted" God's goodness and failed to "ask" for his

gifts. The rich may have thought themselves above reproach spiritually because of their material wealth. But both rich and poor are equal in God's sight. All have equal access before God to ask and receive. James exhorted his readers to focus on the eternal rather than the earthly. God is not partial. The illustration concerning the transience of earthly wealth (1:10-11) is taken from Isaiah 40:6-7.

1:12-18 The Essential Insight: The Character of God

1:12 REWARD FOR PERSEVERANCE

The key ideas concerning trials and developing perseverance (1:2-3) are again discussed. Being "approved" (1:12) can be compared to persevering during times of testing (1:3). James's thoughts concerning joy amidst trials (1:2) and asking for help if lacking wisdom (1:5) are elaborated. Seeking heavenly reward (crown of life), not earthly riches, is the way of the wise. The "crown of life" may refer to abundant life in its fullness and completeness or eternal life as the consummation of the believer's salvation.

1:13-15 FOUNDATION OF PERSEVERANCE: THE CHARACTER OF GOD

Asserting that God tempts believers to do evil (1:13) makes God responsible for their failures. After all, if God wants believers to fall, how can they resist? This wrong perspective is another example of doubting God's true character and therefore being double-minded. James returned to the crucial issue of how believers should view God when they are hurting (1:5). A proper view of God is the starting point for perseverance during times of trial. James 1:14-15 shows how temptation cannot have its source in God. Temptation has its source in mankind's own evil desires. It leads to sin and sin leads to death. James 1:14 shows more specifically what the various trials implied in 1:2 entailed. Evidently some of the believers thought that since God allowed trials in their lives, he was also the source of temptation. The fact that the same Greek word can be translated "trial" or "temptation," depending on the context, may have contributed to their misunderstanding. They thus excused their sin by declaring that

God had brought the temptation. James corrected his readers by declaring that God was not the source evil.

1:16-18 THE CONSISTENT PURPOSE FOR HUMANS

This section continues the thoughts concerning sin and its resulting in death (1:15). "Father of the heavenly lights" (1:17) visualizes God as the sovereign and perfect Creator of the sun, moon, and stars in Genesis 1. God wishes people well, not entrapment in sin and its resulting death. James told his readers that this God was also their Father (1:18). By his will believers are firstfruits of a new and sinless creation, not sinners. Sin comes from a will other than God's. This is a key insight into trials suffered by believers: God wills the best for his people. Again, see the description of God in 1:5. God, the source of all good things, does not change. He will not be different tomorrow, bringing evil instead of good. As Jewish believers, the readers were a "guarantee" to others that a fuller harvest of believers was yet to come (cf. 1 Cor. 15:20).

1:19-27 The Practice of Maturity

1:19-21 BUILT ON A TEACHABLE SPIRIT

The key ingredient in a teachable spirit is the willingness to listen. The person who listens is the person who is humble before God. The goal of humility is the righteousness of God, not the self-gratification gained by venting anger. A response of self-righteous anger during times of trial may feel good momentarily, but it will not accomplish the righteousness of God. This was a major problem addressed in the letter. God was blamed by believers for their temptations (1:13). Arrogance and anger were criticized by James throughout the book (2:1; 3:9; 4:2, 16; 5:6). The entire discussion concerning the tongue (1:26; 3:1-12) and fighting (4:1-12) arose because of human arrogance and anger. In putting aside all wickedness, believers are to respond to the word of God "planted" in the hearts of believers by the Spirit (Heb. 8:10). This resource is able to deliver (1:21; "save") all believers from the reigning influence and dominion of sin (Phil. 2:12).

1:22-27 BUILT ON THINKING RIGHTLY ABOUT RELIGION

These verses show what the results of receiving the implanted word will be. Receiving God's word is doing what he asks, not just hearing what he says (1:22). The hearer who deludes himself is like a person who sees himself in a mirror, walks away, forgets what he saw, and then reconstructs a good image of himself (1:26). This person has forgotten his true self, then made up a false self to his own liking and pronounced himself pure and religious. But the essence of religion is humility. James mentioned orphans and widows as classic examples of how true religion makes room for the lowly. Throughout the Old Testament the widows and orphans were always test cases for Israel's humility, compassion, and obedience before God. But the readers were having trouble making room for the poor, as the discussions of the rich and poor show (see 1:9-11; 2:1-6; 5:1-6). The "perfect law" (1:25; "law of liberty," NASB and KJV) may refer to (1) the word of God which sets believers free in Christ (John 8:32); (2) the law of the new covenant written on the hearts of believers (Jer. 31:33); or (3) the Old Testament ethic as explained and developed by Jesus (Matt. 5–7). This "perfect law" is a way of describing the application of God's love to life's circumstances. James was not thinking of "religion without God" but rather the outward expression of a genuine, inner faith. True religion involves ethical responsibilities.

2:1-26 EXHORTATION: BE IMPARTIAL
2:1-13 Implications of Partiality
2:1-7 THE IMPLICATIONS OF GOD'S MOTIVES IN SALVATION

James admonished his readers against playing favorites. They were to avoid showing special regard for people of position, wealth, or influence. Partiality, vividly pictured in James 2:2-4, is shown to be inconsistent with the Christian faith. Some in the church did not care for the lowly and made false distinctions between people. These distinctions came from evil motives (2:4). These motives were evil because they cut against God's motives in salvation

(2:5). God gives generously to all (cf. 1:5, 9). To view people as less than God views them is to dishonor them (2:6). It is important that believers ask themselves if they are reflecting a ministry that gives generously to all men without reproach.

2:8-13 IMPLICATIONS OF THE ROYAL LAW

James placed the concept of law within the total context of God's salvation in Christ (cf. Matt. 22:40). The readers were some-how able to show partiality to the rich and snub the poor and still think they were religious (2:1-4; 2:9). They were deluded into thinking that some wrong things were not violations of God's will. They had not made the connection between showing partiality and God's demand that they love their neighbors. James helped them to see the full damage of sin; he refused to minimize it. The "law that gives freedom" (2:12) is the love of God applied to each particular circumstance in life (see the progression of thought in 1:12, 18, 21, 25). By contrast, God shows no mercy to those who are merciless (Matt. 18:21-35).

2:14-26 The Practice of Impartiality

Overview: At first glance it appears that James was directly opposed to Paul on the doctrine of justification. Paul insisted that "a man is not justified by observing the law, but by faith in Jesus Christ" (Gal. 2:16; cf. Rom. 3:20; Eph. 2:8-9). James, however, argued that "a person is justified by what he does and not by faith alone" (James 2:24). But it is possible to reconcile these apparently contradictory viewpoints. James and Paul were confronting different issues. Paul was refuting those who advocated works, circumcision, and the observance of Jewish ceremonial law as necessary for justification. James, on the other hand, was challenging those who presumed that mere intellectual assent to doctrine was sufficient for salvation. Paul was confronting Judaizers who wanted to add works to grace; James was confronting dead orthodoxy, which denied that a genuine faith was evidenced by works. Both agree that while faith alone saves, the faith that saves is not alone. It comes with good works (see Paul's comments in Eph. 2:9-10).

2:14-17 USEFUL FAITH

James gives a practical illustration of the person who is a hearer and not a doer of the word. This is the person who forgets what he has seen in the mirror of God's word (1:23-24). "What good" (2:14) refers to the obedience mentioned in 1:25. The claim of having faith (2:14) implies that the person is quite satisfactory in God's sight and does not need to worry about doing acts of obedience. Such people think they are religious but act like the person in 1:26 or 2:1. The implied answer to the last question of 2:14 is no. James allowed no special pleading. He was also not concerned with a theological discussion of faith. Rather, he was concerned with its practical aspects. Faith without works has no use for others, illustrated in 2:15-16 ("useless," 2:20; "worthless," 1:26). The passive verbs "keep warm and well fed" (2:16) imply that someone else will do the warming and filling. Their snobbery led them to shirk their works of faith and love. At the heart of the question is the issue: "Is an inactive, non-working faith a genuine, saving faith?" James's implied answer is no! Such an "unworking" profession of faith is not a biblical faith! Faith without works is a fallacy (2:17).

2:18-26 EXAMPLES OF USEFUL
AND USELESS FAITH

Good deeds are objective proof that faith is alive and useful. Without works, faith is useless (2:20; cf. 2:14) and dead (2:26). James's point is to have belief issue in helpful actions for others. Faith without works may expose an inner character that matches the character of demons (2:19). James was talking about the person who believes in everything that is good but does nothing that is good. The question hinges on a person's willingness (2:20), unlike the demons, to add good behavior to sound doctrine.

The concepts of "complete" (2:22) and "fulfilled" (2:23) show how believers are to understand James's use of "righteous" (2:21; "justified," NASB and KJV). Paul used the term "justified" in a legal way, "to be declared righteous." James, however, used the term more in keeping with its use in the Greek translation of the Old Testament (the Septuagint), "shown to be righteous." Works fulfill and make

visible one's claim to have believed in God. For Abraham to disobey God's command to offer Isaac and yet claim to be justified before God on the basis of Genesis 15:6 (quoted in 2:23) would prove that he had not truly believed in the first place. This all relates back to the issue of believers hearing the truth but then forgetting to do it (1:22). Such people deceive their own hearts (1:26). Abraham heard and obeyed God's word. His faith was fulfilled, brought to its goal, thirty years later as Abraham obeyed God's command regarding Isaac. His works showed that he was indeed a friend of God (cf. Isa. 41:8). By the testing of Abraham's faith in Genesis 22, the patriarch was proven to be righteous. In like manner, the various testings of James's readers (1:2-3) were to have the same effect.

The comparison of Rahab with Abraham is another illustration of James's contrasts between the rich and the poor (cf. Josh. 2:4; 6:17; Matt. 1:5; Heb. 11:31), believers of high and low status. Read Rahab's great confession of the character of God in Joshua 2:8-13. James' examples of useful versus useless faith have ranged from demons to Abraham, a Jew, and Rahab, a Gentile. Again, James restated his thesis (2:26). Faith demonstrates its living and vital nature by what it enables believers to do for others.

3:1–4:12 EXHORTATION: BE MATURE IN SPEECH

Overview: James returns to the thoughts of 1:19-21 and emphasizes the importance of controlling one's tongue. The status-conscious readers would easily have desired the status position of teacher (see "envy and selfish ambition," 3:14, 16). But James also included all acts of speaking, public and private, in this section. As works reveal the depth of people's faith, so words show the depth of their maturity. As belief without works is demonic (2:19), so also are words without heavenly wisdom (3:15; cf. also 4:7).

3:1-12 The Tongue as a Revealer of Maturity or Immaturity

Since the teacher's work is performed primarily through the use of his tongue, control of this instrument is of utmost importance. The greater the privilege in terms of knowledge and education, the greater the accountability for the use of that information (Luke 12:48). The word "perfect" (3:2) may best be translated "mature."

The tongue is a symbol for the overall discipline and maturity of the whole person (3:2). The images of bridle, rudder, fire, untamed animal, poison, fountain, and fig tree all illustrate the cause and effect relationship between maturity and words. James has clearly shown the relationship between inner lust and outward expression (1:14-15). The images applied to the tongue illustrate the outward effects of inner lusts (cf. 4:2-4). The questions of 3:11-12 uncover the real issue: external behavior in sharp contrast with claims to purity and righteousness before God.

3:13-18 The Practice of Maturity

James gave two suggestions for handling the tongue. For the wise, he gave examples that revealed inner wisdom (3:13, 17). For the jealous and ambitious, he simply asked that they admit their arrogance and not try to cover up their evil with pious claims (3:14; and "sincere," 3:17). He directed both groups to pursue righteousness through making peace (3:18).

True wisdom is the practical and successful application of knowledge. Such wisdom comes from God and bears good fruit. The fruit, which consists of righteousness produces peace, the very opposite of the sin and disorder of 3:14, 16 and 4:1-3.

4:1-12 The Source of Immaturity

4:1-6 GOD'S OPPOSITION TO PRIDE
James held up the mirror of God's word (1:23-25) to show his readers their true faces. The contrast with seeking peace (3:17-18) is seeking pleasure (4:1-2). James uncovered the heart of the readers' false claims to faith and righteousness: friendship with the world (4:4). They either forgot to go to God to meet their needs (4:2) or they tried to use God as a celestial shopping center for worldly goods (4:3). They either forgot the source or tried to manipulate the source. Either way, they were manifesting the ambivalent view of God that James had already addressed (1:5-18). Worldliness is an attitude that places self and the things of this world at the center of the

believers' aspirations and activities. This attitude caused disputes among the saints.

James used the word "adulterous" (4:4) metaphorically, as did the Old Testament prophets who spoke of disobedient Israel as God's unfaithful wife (cf. Isa. 54:5; Jer. 3:20; Ezek. 16:15-17; Hos. 9:1). No specific Old Testament passage contains the words of James 4:5, but many passages express a similar sentiment—God is a jealous God (Exod. 20:5; 34:14; Deut. 32:16; Zech. 8:2). He will tolerate no rivals. He jealously desires the Spirit to dwell in believers.

But the heart of James's letter is found in the quotation of Proverbs 3:34 in James 4:6. The rest of the letter gives specific examples of what "humble" in Proverbs 3:34 means (see "submit," 4:7; "come near" 4:8; "humble," 4:10; "grieve," 4:9; "weep," 5:1; "be patient," 5:7; "confess your sins," 5:16). The purpose is that God's grace, not his opposition, may be experienced.

4:7-12 GOD'S GRACE FOR THE HUMBLE
The way to exaltation is through mourning and humility (4:9-10), not through fighting and arrogance. The double-minded attitude has been in view from 1:8 throughout. A string of commands (4:7-10) is built around the Old Testament quotation of Proverbs 3:34 as James sets forth the remedy for worldliness. Resistance to the devil (4:7) is done by coming near to God (4:8). Submission to God and his will results in a heart purged from worldliness. James 4:9 issues a call to repentance in the face of the seriousness of sin. The cries of mourning and weeping reflect an attitude of sobriety in contrast with deluded and arrogant attitudes. The Beatitudes of Christ are behind this description of the one who truly sees the need for God (cf. Matt. 5:4). It is then up to God to deliver and exalt (4:10).

James 4:11-12 relates to the tongue analogy but more specifically to taking over authority that belongs to God alone. James exhorted believers to avoid slandering their brothers. He condemned a censorious, hypocritical judgment (cf. Matt. 7:1-5). He was not rejecting the appropriateness of judging others in proper contexts (cf. Matt. 18:15-18). His very letter is an example of proper, humble, and loving evaluations.

4:13–5:6 CONDEMNATION: ATTITUDES AND END OF THE RICH

4:13-17 Arrogance of the Will

The examples James presented in these verses reveal the opposite of a humble and teachable spirit under God. The key here is the inability of people to know what their lives will be like in the future (4:14). This prideful assumption of a prosperous future echoes the prideful arrogance against the poor, and the selfish ambitions of life seen earlier. James was not condemning intelligent planning but rebuking presumptuous planning that disregards God. When making plans, the Christian should acknowledge his dependence upon God and submission to his will. For Paul's example in this, see Acts 18:21, 1 Corinthians 4:19, and 16:7. Although some of James's readers disregarded God's sovereign and mostly unknown plans and were deluded as to their self-knowledge, they really knew better (4:17).

5:1-6 Judgment on the Rich

The "rich" (5:1) who were condemned by James were probably not Christians. At least their conduct would make their profession of faith suspect. They were laying up destruction for themselves in the last days (5:3). The corrosion of gold and silver reveals its worth for buying a safe standing before God in the judgment. The term "Lord Almighty" (5:4) is an Old Testament description of God. In this section James was probably referring to judicial murder—taking the poor to court to rob them of possessions that sustain and support their lives (5:6).

5:7-20 EXHORTATIONS: MATURE ENDURANCE

5:7-11 Patient Endurance

The two concepts of patient endurance (5:7-8, 10-11) and the Lord's coming (5:7-9, 11) are built upon the outcome of the Lord's dealings: compassion and mercy (5:11). James has returned again to perseverance during life's various trials (1:3-4). And again, the corrective to complaining and lack of perseverance is a firm grasp on the character of God. Patience is the inner quality that produces the outer manifestation of perseverance. The phrase "fall and spring rains" (5:7) refers to the two brief

rainy periods that precede and follow the main season of rain in Palestine, November through April (cf. Deut. 11:14). The Lord's coming is a practical doctrine. James used it to encourage believers to exercise patience. Complaining against a Christian is taking over the prerogatives of the Judge (5:9). Job is set forth as an example of one who "persevered" (5:11). In spite of his sufferings, he refused to renounce God (Job 1:21; 2:10; 13:15; 16:19; 19:25). The outcome of the Lord's dealings with him was Job's complete vindication (Job 42:7-17).

5:12 Arrogant Oaths

James is here concerned with oaths that are given in arrogance. He warned Christians not to make oaths merely to appear spiritual before others. He was also concerned that making such oaths was evidence of an even deeper spiritual disease—the belief that man could be holy without the grace of God. God swore (Heb. 6:17) and Jesus spoke under oath (Matt. 26:63-64). But James has in view the oaths arising from the prideful and mistaken notion of human sovereignty (cf. Matt. 5:34-37). James stressed dependence on God, not on self. Among the Jews, oaths were often made for reasons of spiritual pride, but then they were undone on the basis of technicalities in Mosaic Law. But James called for constant honesty that could be depended on and could not be conveniently "recalled."

5:13-18 Sharing in Prayer

Rather than swearing when in trouble, James urged believers to pray and give praise. Rather than complaining to each other or praising themselves, James commended believers for lifting their pain and praise to God. In sickness, the patient is to call for the elders. Anointing with oil was a common practice (Mark 6:13). Here it is done in the name of the Lord. It is debated whether this passage commends a healing ministry for the physically sick or a spiritual ministry to those who are emotionally distressed or spiritually exhausted. The word "sick" (5:14) is used both of spiritual weakness and physical weakness. The word "well" (5:15) can refer to a healing of the heart. The connection of 5:16-18 is to do the praying and sin-bearing before one gets sick as well as in times of crisis. The reference to the incident in the life of Elijah (5:17; cf. 1 Kings 17:1; 18:1, 42, 45) confirms the power of prayer. In addition, while it is not always God's will for the sick to be healed (2 Cor. 12:8), it is always his will for the spiritually weak to be encouraged in their struggles against sin (5:15).

5:19-20 The Essence of the Letter

The essence of James's letter is a call to action (works) that allows truth to triumph over sin and error. This is the essence of everything he wrote. The individual under consideration (5:19, "one of you") is a Christian who has strayed from the truth. By turning that one back to God, the ultimate discipline of death (1 Cor. 11:30; 1 John 5:16) would be avoided. The multitude of sins covered were those that had been committed and those that would never happen because of a person's repentance. Through genuine repentance, forgiveness is appropriated and sins are hidden from the sight of God (cf. Ps. 32:1; 1 Pet. 4:8).

1 Peter

BASIC FACTS

HISTORICAL SETTING

The letter is addressed to believers scattered throughout several Roman provinces
(1 Pet. 1:1). Most were of Gentile background (2:10; 4:3), though some were
Hebrew Christians (2:12; 4:3). They lived in a region north of the Taurus mountains
where the apostle Paul had not preached (Acts 16:6, 7).

The suffering of persecution was a major background to the letter (1 Pet. 1:6-7;
2:11-12, 18-20; 3:13-17; 4:3-5, 12-19; 5:8-10). Such sufferings were common to
most first-century Christians. The suffering was referred to as "all kinds of trials"
(1:6) and appears to be of a more personal nature (2:15). Persecution arose from the
believers' refusal to participate in their former life-styles of sin (4:1-4). The place
of the writing was referred to as "Babylon" (5:13). Most scholars favor taking
Babylon as symbolic for Rome (cf. Rev. 17:5, 9; 18:2, 10, 21). This view finds
support in that Mark, who was with Peter (5:13), was also in Rome with Paul during
his imprisonment (Col. 4:10).

AUTHOR

The apostle Peter was the author. Both internal evidence and the testimony of the
early church confirms the statement in 1:1 that the apostle Peter authored this letter.
He shows an intimate knowledge of the life and teachings of Jesus (cf. 1 Pet. 5:5
with John 13:3-5, and 5:2 with John 21:15-17). The author was an eyewitness of the
sufferings of Christ (2:19-24; 3:18; 4:1; 5:1).

Simon Peter, originally from Bethsaida (John 1:44), was the son of Jonah (Matt.
16:17) and brother of Andrew, with whom he was a partner in a fishing business at
Capernaum. Peter first met Jesus near Bethany beyond the Jordan when he was led
to the Lord by Andrew and received his name "Cephas" (Aramaic), or "Peter" (Greek),
meaning "rock" (John 1:42). Peter was chosen by Jesus as an apostle (Mark 3:16).
Peter was a natural leader and often served as a spokesman for the Twelve (Matt.
16:15-16). With James and John he belonged to the innermost circle of the Twelve
and was present at the raising of Jairus's daughter (Mark 5:37), the transfiguration

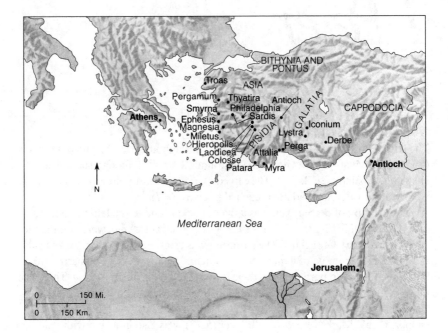

(Matt. 17:1-2), Gethsemane (Matt. 26:36-37), and the empty tomb (John 20:6). He took a position of leadership among the disciples after Christ's ascension (Acts 1:15-22; 3:11-26; 5:1-11; 8:14-25, 10:1–11:18) and was the key preacher on the day of Pentecost (Acts 2). Peter was God's instrument to open the way of salvation to the Samaritans (Acts 8:14-15) and the Gentiles (Acts 10–11). In later years Peter traveled in an itinerant ministry with his wife (1 Cor. 1:12; 9:5).

According to tradition, Peter went to Rome around A.D. 62 and there was crucified during Nero's persecution, which began in A.D. 64. Peter's martyrdom is hinted at by Christ in John 21:18-19. According to early tradition, Peter insisted on being cruci-fied head downward.

DATE

The letter reflected impending persecution, suggesting that it was written not long before Peter's death. But Peter's teaching that the government could be expected to administer justice (1 Pet. 2:13-14) and that a man who did what was right would be unmolested (3:13) indicate that this may have been written before the severe persecu-tions of Nero began in A.D. 64. Peter arrived in Rome in A.D. 62 and probably wrote this letter in A.D. 63 or 64.

PURPOSE

This letter by Peter was designed to exhort its readers to conduct themselves in accordance with the living hope they possessed as redeemed believers. The letter confirmed the believers' knowledge of salvation and encouraged them in their sub-mission to authority and joyful response to suffering for Christ's sake.

GEOGRAPHY AND ITS IMPORTANCE

The Churches of Peter's Letter

Peter wrote to Jewish Christians who had been exiled from their homeland, Israel, because of their faith in Jesus (see Acts 8:1-4). Forced to spread out into strange lands, they no doubt also spread their faith. Paul extensively evangelized many of the areas mentioned by Peter.

GUIDING CONCEPTS

HOPE AND SUFFERING

The two major concepts to look for in 1 Peter are suffering and hope. Throughout, the short letter speaks of suffering. But it does not simply discuss the pain of suf-fering. It places the fact of suffering within three contexts of hope. First, suffering takes place under the ultimate power of God to bring believers into full redemp-tion (1:5-7; 5:6-7, 10). Second, those causing unjust suffering will someday face the judgment of God who judges all evil (1:17; 2:23; 4:5, 17). Third, as Christians suffer, they do so in the presence of the Christ whose example has gone before them (2:21; 3:17-18; 4:12-14). In addition to suffering, Peter continually raised the issue of godly conduct (1:6-7, 13-17, 22; 2:1-2; 2:12–3:17; 4:1-19; 5:1-10). All of his words about suffering and hope point toward one result: godly behavior in the present. But that behavior is not demanded in order to get into heaven. It is done because of the secure redemption of believers in Christ. Any hope they have for the future is secured, not by their actions, but by the resurrection of Christ (1:3).

GODLY CONDUCT IN THE MIDST OF SUFFERING
Peter called his readers to godly conduct (1:15, 17-18; 2:12; 3:1-2, 16). The problem Peter addressed was the real or potential complaining and disobedience brought on by unjust suffering. His readers were in danger of misunderstanding the source and reason for their trials (cf. 4:12-13). This misunderstanding could cause the believers to drift from their intimate relation with Christ. It would be easier for them to follow their hate and lusts (2:23; 4:1-3) than to follow the perfect example of Christ.

Peter met these problems by reminding his readers of the history of their redemption (1:3–2:3). Without being rooted in history, they could become rootless in holiness. He founded their witness upon the Rock of Christ's witness (2:4–3:7). He revealed the problem of unjust suffering (3:8-22) to be resolved in God's final evaluation (1:17).

BIBLE-WIDE CONCEPTS

STONE TESTIMONIES
Peter's use of "stone"
Peter linked together three Old Testament texts that spoke of the nature of Christ as "stone" (2:6-8; quoting Isa. 28:16; Ps. 118:22; Isa. 8:14). All three Old Testament passages are from contexts of judgment and restoration. All speak of God being a source of rest and safety. Isaiah 8 and 28 were already connected in the book of Isaiah itself. Both passages are built around similar events. Compare Isaiah 8:8 with 28:15-16; 8:15 with 28:13; and Isaiah 8:10, 14 with 28:15, 18. Both passages deal with judgment and with false and true refuge. The "stone" conveys the dual image of stability and judgment. That dual image is also seen in 1 Peter 3:10-12 where Peter quoted Psalm 34:12-16. Peter also made a passing reference to Isaiah 8:12-13 in 1 Peter 3:14-15. Peter's readers evidently needed some powerful words concerning Jesus as both a security to the believers and a liability to the opponents of God.

Broader Christian use of "stone" testimonies
Other New Testament writers also saw an important place for the three Old Testament "stone" passages that Peter used. Isaiah 8:14 is quoted in Romans 9:32; Isaiah 8:14-15 in Luke 2:34-35; Isaiah 8:17-18 in Hebrews 2:13; Isaiah 28:16 in Romans 9:33; 10:11. The parable of the vineyard is an example of how Christ used the "stone" testimonies. Mark 12:10 quotes Psalm 118:22. Christ, the rejected "stone," was connected to the rejected and then exalted Son. Matthew 21:42 quotes Psalm 118:22. Luke 20:17, 18 uses Isaiah 8:14-15 with Psalm 118:22.

Relation of "stone" to Psalm 34 (1 Peter 3:10-12)
Peter also quoted another Old Testament passage that rounds out the "stone" imagery. Peter used the "stone" to picture a divine anchor and example. He used Psalm 34 to portray the human response of obedience. The "stone" testimony draws on Israel's hope as completed in Jesus. Also the image gives the comfort of security and exhortation. Psalm 34 applies the truths portrayed in the "stone" image to believers.

THE FLOOD

Peter compared the flood of Noah's day with Christian baptism (1 Pet. 3:18-22). Noah went through the waters of the flood and was saved by being in the ark. The Christian goes through the waters of baptism and is saved by the power of Christ's own resurrection (3:21). The redemptive images of ark and cross point toward God's redemption in Christ.

NEEDS MET BY FIRST PETER

This letter from Peter met the needs of believers who were hurting and were tempted to lash out in pain and revenge. In contrast with their blessed salvation in Christ, believers faced unjust persecution and loss of their material goods in the world. God called them to lives obedient to his word. But it was that very obedience that brought on world hatred and persecution. The Christians faced a fork in the road. They could continue to obey and continue receiving the world's hostility or they could weaken their obedience to live more comfortable and persecution-free lives. The structure and content of 1 Peter show that Peter intended to answer questions like the following for his readers.

- In what way are believers protected by God's power (1:5)?
- What is the reason and purpose for pain in this life?
- What kind of perspective can help believers not respond with anger and hate to life's hurts at home and on the job?
- Why are believers experiencing so much distress if they are really God's children?

Peter tried to help his readers experience the reality of two events. The first was the past example of Christ during his life on earth. When Christ was unjustly treated, he was able to behave graciously and did not fall into the trap of seeking revenge. The second event was the resurrection of the saints that is yet to take place. During times of suffering, pain, and injustice, Peter encouraged believers to think about what their certain, though future, resurrection means for the present. Peter urged them not to let present sufferings blind them to these past and future truths.

OUTLINE OF FIRST PETER

A. GREETING (1:1-2)

B. THE FOUNDATION OF OBEDIENCE: THE LIVING WORD (1:3–2:12)
   1. Doxology: The Word's Focus (1:3-12)
   2. The Focus of the Believer's Calling: God's Holiness (1:13-21)
   3. Redemption's Foundation: Imperishable Word (1:22–2:12)

C. THE TESTIMONY FROM OBEDIENCE (2:13–4:11)
   1. In Life Relationships (2:13–3:7)
   2. Summary and Elaboration: Blessing though Maligned (3:8–4:6)
   3. Conclusion: The End Impinges on the Present (4:7-11)

D. THE FOCUS IN OBEDIENCE: FAITHFUL CREATOR (4:12–5:11)
   1. The Suffering of Christ: God's Presence (4:12-19)
   2. Trusting His Appointed Leaders (5:1-5)
   3. Trusting His Powerful Grace (5:6-11)
E. CLOSING REMARKS AND BENEDICTION (5:12-14)

FIRST PETER NOTES

1:1-2 GREETING

This letter from Peter was addressed to the believers scattered throughout the provinces of Pontus, Galatia, Cappadocia, Asia, and Bithynia. For those who were suffering under persecution, the truth of God's foreknowledge was of great encouragement and gave them strength to persevere. Peter stressed the believers' election, obedience, and sanctification (1:2). While 1:1 refers to the addressees as "elect," 1:2 mentions that this election is according to divine "foreknowledge." While "election" points to God's selective choice, "foreknowledge" emphasizes the loving, personal aspect of that choice.

1:3–2:12 THE FOUNDATION OF OBEDIENCE: THE LIVING WORD
1:3-12 Doxology: The Word's Focus

1:3-5 PAST: SECURE SALVATION
The elements in this doxology move from God's past saving events to their present results and future perfection. God has caused believers to be born again to a living hope. Their faith rests on the resurrection of Christ. Peter contemplated the nature of salvation and poured out thanksgiving to God for this divine work accomplished through Christ's death and resurrection. He gave praise to God for the regeneration of the believers. He used the term "new birth" (1:3), which may have been suggested by Jesus' phrase "born again" (John 3:3). This new birth leads to a "living" hope and an eternal inheritance. The word "shielded" (1:5) is a military term (see "guarded" in Phil. 4:7) that means "garrisoned about." Throughout their earthly pilgrimage, God's divine power will protect believers.

1:6-9 PRESENT: PROVEN FAITH
God allows trials (cf. with James 1:2) in order to prove by testing the eternal quality

of the believer's faith. As fire distinguishes true gold from the counterfeit, so trials distinguish genuine faith from superficial profession. The focus is on the present as well as the future outcome of a believer's faith (1 Pet. 1:7, 9).

1:10-12 PRESENT: FOCUS OF HISTORY
The focus is on the Messiah. The future element is mentioned once more. There are great glories to follow (1:11). Peter reflected on the revelation of mankind's salvation through the Old Testament prophets who, by the Spirit, predicted the coming of Jesus the Messiah (Luke 24:44). Although they sought the precise details regarding the coming Messiah ("time and circumstances"), these matters were not revealed. The prophets did, however, predict the sufferings (Isa. 53) and glories of Christ (Isa. 11), without distinguishing his two comings.

1:13-21 The Focus of the Believer's Calling: God's Holiness

A practical conclusion ("therefore," 1:13) arises from the discussion of Christ's redemption in 1:10-12. History is the foundation of hope. The future revelation of Christ's grace should result in present godly behavior. Peter reflected on the implications of the great cost of the believer's salvation for present obedience. The expression translated "prepare" (1:13; "gird up," NASB and KJV) was used in the Old Testament for tucking one's robes into one's belt to prevent stumbling while engaged in rigorous activity. Here the activity is mental and spiritual.

Holiness is based on God's character (1:14-16). The quotation in 1:16 is from Leviticus 11:44-45. Peter used the word "also" throughout the letter to make critical comparisons between God and the believer (1 Pet. 1:15; 2:5, 21; 3:18; 4:1, 13). The character of God, the one calling the believers, is the standard for their behavior. The primary meaning of "holy" (1:15) is "separation." Moral purity is an outgrowth of the concept of holiness, for that which is separated unto the Lord must be in conformity to his righteous standards.

"Reverent fear" is the result of addressing God as an impartial judge (1:17). The future hope of believers is based on a redemption that God had in mind from eternity past. The relationship believers have with God does not diminish his demand for their holiness. It is the means whereby they have the ability to seek holiness. First Peter 1:18 deepens the motivation for obeying God. The concept of "foreknowledge" (1:20) links back to 1:2. The broad sweep of God's redemptive history is the viewpoint for the security of believers while suffering unjustly. The word "redeemed" (1:18) means to secure release by the payment of a ransom. Silver and gold are perishable in the sense that they can lose their value in a deflationary economy. They suggest temporary wealth, not eternal resources. As the Old Testament sacrifices had to be without flaw (Lev. 22:19-25), so Christ was unblemished and spotless, without sin (1:19; cf. Heb. 4:15).

1:22–2:12 Redemption's Foundation: The Imperishable Word
The great worth of salvation in Christ is the basis for sincere love (1:22-25). The "imperishable" concept (1:23) is key to Peter's desire to encourage steadfastness in the face of potentially fatal human persecutions. It gives the future hope spoken of in 1:5, 7, 9. "Sincere love" (1:22) is the opposite of conformity to "evil desires" (1:14). It sums up all the exhortations to obedience throughout the letter. The means by which salvation was brought to believers was the word of God—the preaching of the gospel (Rom. 10:14). While to some the word of God may appear to be frail, Peter quoted Isaiah 40:6-8 in 1:24-25 to show that it will outlast all natural phenomena. Isaiah contrasts the transitory natural creation with the unfailing and abiding nature of God's word.

Peter pointed out that Christ's followers should expect rejection just as Christ was rejected. The issue is one of value, whether value is defined by people or God. Believers are to seek what God sees as valuable—his rejected Son. The "therefore" of 2:1 looks

back to 1 Peter 1 regarding the word of God. The word is not only the basis for spiritual birth but also for spiritual growth. A taste of God's goodness should produce an appetite for more (2:3).

In 2:4-10 Peter contemplated the privileges that accompany the believers' gift of salvation. As "living stones" believers are to worship God (2:4-8), and as priests they are to witness to the world (2:9-10). As Christ is the living Stone (2:4), believers are living stones (2:5) joined together to form one building. The metaphor shifts in the second half of 2:5. Here believers are consecrated "priests" who offer up spiritual sacrifices to God through Christ (cf. Rom. 12:1; Heb. 13:15-16). In 2:6 Peter appealed to Isaiah 28:16 to show that Christ is the primary foundation stone. In 2:7-8 Peter appealed to Psalm 118:22 and Isaiah 8:14 to show that Christ is a stumbling stone to those who refuse faith in him. In 2:9 Peter used several Old Testament terms (cf. Deut. 10:15; Exod. 19:6; Isa. 61:6) to declare what believers have become in Christ. The spiritual sacrifices (2:5) are summed up as proclaiming God's character and acts (2:9). In 2:10 Peter quoted Hosea 2:23. Paul used Hosea 2:23 linked to Isaiah 8:14 in Romans 9:25-26, 33. The Old Testament as fulfilled in Christ is the solid foundation for faith and hope.

In 2:11–3:12 Peter developed the doctrine of the believers' submission to appropriate authorities—kings, masters, husbands. Even in the light of severe persecution they must submit, as Christ did before them. Unjust suffering in Christ's name is a sign of God's Spirit resting on them and blessing (3:14; 4:14). And good works will glorify God (2:12). Even if unbelievers reject Christians now, they will glorify God later when he comes again. The most important relationship for Christians to be concerned about is the one between themselves and God.

2:13–4:11 THE TESTIMONY FROM OBEDIENCE
Overview: This section on submission comes out of the discussion of what it means to minister God's redemption to the world (2:9). The practical implications of being "living stones" and "priests" are developed. The focus is on the task of 2:12.

2:13–3:7 In Life Relationships

2:13-17 HUMAN INSTITUTIONS

The word "submit" (2:13) means to "place oneself under" and implies support as well as submission. Note that Peter said nothing about certain forms of government. He approved no special kind of government, but supported law and order in general. Peter referred to God in each verse ("Lord's sake," "sent by him," "God's will," "servants of God," "fear God"). Submission to civil authority was not only the will of God, it was also designed to "silence" (2:15) ignorant talk against Christians.

2:18-25 SERVANTS: UNJUST SUFFERING

What example did Christ give (see Isa. 53:4-9 quotation)? In 1 Peter 2:25 the apostle borrowed a sheep allusion from Isaiah 53:6. The principle of submission, even through unjust suffering, is supremely illustrated by Peter as he directed his readers to the death of Christ. First Peter 2:22-25 contains Peter's exposition of Isaiah 53. In 2:22 Peter quoted Isaiah 53:9. It was tempting to strike back while suffering unjustly, but Christ did just the opposite (cf. also 1 Pet. 3:9). This theology of Christ's sufferings was very relevant in this section on submission to authority because the authorities over the readers of this letter were often unjust. Here Peter reveals what it means for believers to be living stones (2:4-5). Christ as the stone (2:6-7) was an appropriate image for Peter to use because it was a perfect illustration of the prophetic certainty stressed in 1:10-12. For some, the stone is a problem and brings judgment. For believers, the stone is precious in God's sight.

3:1-6 WIVES: A WORDLESS WITNESS

This section continues the topic of submission ("in the same way," 3:1, 7). The submission of the wife to her husband does not suggest inequality, for Christ was submissive to and yet equal with the Father. In 3:3 Peter does not forbid jewelry or nice clothes. Rather he is pointing out by way of contrast what makes a really beautiful woman—the inner character qualities. Again, the contrast between what does and does not perish is made (1:4). Only the one who sees the difference will have the insight to build on the imperishable. Sarah called Abraham

"master" (3:6; cf. Gen. 18:12), acknowledging him with the respect due a husband.

3:7 HUSBANDS: UNHINDERED PRAYERS

The husbands follow the pattern of submission ("in the same way"), though the word itself is not used. The issue is understanding and submitting to the requirements of any relationship, in this case between husband and wife. The husband submits to the requirements by meeting the wife's needs. How is the woman a "weaker" partner? Conclusions range from physical, spiritual, or emotional weakness. Although this is debated, the point of equality before God ("heirs with you") that results in receiving honor is central. Note that the husband who fails to undertand and honor his wife will have a hindered prayer life. What it means to have hindered prayers is explained in 3:12. A righteous person in relationship with his wife has the full attention of God in his prayers. God is against those who do evil to their wives, and their prayers will not be heard.

3:8–4:6 Summary and Elaboration: Blessing though Maligned

3:8-12 SUMMARY: HARMONY WITH GOD

Peter desired that believers give an honest blessing, not one muttered through clenched teeth, to those who persecuted them. The honest blessing should flow out of sincere love (1:22–2:12). There is a close relationship between giving and inheriting a blessing (3:9). Peter supported this point (3:10-12) with Psalm 34:12-16. Love of life and seeing good days (3:10) is the miraculous possibility of faith and obedience in the midst of life's problems.

3:13-16 SANCTIFY CHRIST AS LORD

The unswerving commitment to doing God's will at any cost (4:2) is the driving theme of this section. Christ is sanctified as Lord by doing the will of the Father (3:13-16). Peter continued the discussion in 2:20 concerning suffering for the sake of righteousness. He pointed out that believers who maintain a clear conscience while suffering unjustly will put their critics to shame.

3:17-22 REMAIN IN CHRIST'S ARK OF REDEMPTION

In 3:18-22 Peter presented the supreme example of undeserved suffering: the crucifixion of Christ. Jesus suffered death on the cross for the sins others had committed. In similar fashion, the suffering of the innocent could be God's will.

In 3:18 Peter reminded the believers of the suffering of Christ and what it accomplished. Christ's death for sins constituted a substitutionary judgment on behalf of sinners. His death prepared the way for the reconciliation of sinners with God ("to bring you to God," cf. 2 Cor. 5:18). But Christ's death was not a defeat. Having been "put to death in the body," he was "made alive by the Spirit." The two participles ("put to death" and "made alive") define the main verb "died." There is a balance and correlation between the two terms "body" and "Spirit." Both terms emphasize quality and denote two contrasting modes of Christ's existence—his earthly sphere of existence as a man ("body") and his heavenly sphere of existence as divine Spirit ("Spirit"). The point of 3:18 is that Christ's death was not a defeat but a triumph. While Christ died to his earthly sphere of existence, by resurrection ("made alive") he entered into a fuller life and was liberated for greater ministry (Matt. 28:20; John 14:12).

One interpretive problem in 1 Peter concerns the identity of the "spirits in prison" (3:19), the location of this prison, and when Christ preached to them. There are several different viewpoints with regard to "the spirits in prison" and when Christ "preached" to them:

(1) The earliest view identifies the "spirits in prison" with the fallen angels ("sons of God") in Genesis 6 (cf. 2 Pet. 2:4; Jude 1:6). But it is difficult to scripturally support the idea of the gospel being brought to demons.

(2) Some understand the "spirits in prison" to be unbelievers to whom the gospel was preached by Christ through the apostles after Pentecost. But this view fails to explain the reference to Noah.

(3) Others understand the "spirits in prison" to refer to those of Noah's day who are now dead and awaiting the final judgment. According to this viewpoint, Christ descended to hell between his death and resurrection. His preaching is viewed as being either condemnatory, no hope, or conciliatory, offering the antediluvians a second chance for salvation. However, there is no evidence in Scripture that anyone is offered

a "second chance" after death (cf. Heb. 9:27). And why would Peter exclusively single out the people who lived before the flood to be the recipients of this pre-resurrection ministry of Jesus? The viewpoint is quite complex and requires a great deal of hypothesis and speculation.

(4) A view that can be traced as far back as Augustine holds that 3:19-20 refers to the preincarnate preaching of Christ through Noah (cf. 1:11 for the Spirit of Christ working within the Old Testament prophets). The preaching was accomplished by ("through which") Christ's divine Spirit, the immaterial aspect of his person. The "spirits in prison" were the souls of those who heard the message, rejected it, and now find themselves in judgment. This view eliminates references to the obscure "doctrine" of Christ's descent into hell and the question of what his "preaching" might have accomplished there. It also has the advantage of clarity and simplicity.

But the point of the illustration in 3:19-20 is that Christ's past spiritual ministry in the Old Testament was resumed at his death. Christ's death was a victory, not a defeat. While death ended the physical, earthly dimension of his life and ministry, it inaugurated once again, and in a new and better way, his ministry as divine Spirit.

The ark built by Noah (3:20) is a symbol of the resurrection. It is the means of bringing people to God (3:18). The people in the ark were brought safely through the water (3:20). In a similar way, believers are brought safely to God through the cross. Water baptism and all it symbolizes is the picture of the believer coming to God through Christ. Like Noah, the people Peter was addressing had responded to God's message and were trusting Christ to bring them to God. The implication is that believers are not to jump out but wait patiently in their ark of Christ's cross through the storms of life. Believers are not to jump out of the ark to fight or retreat back into the world's ways.

4:1-6 OBEDIENCE TO THE JUDGE OF ALL
Obedience brings about a good conscience (3:16) and a good account in the last judgment (4:2, 5-6). Peter brought up the subject of death and people being judged in the flesh

in order to bring encouragement. His readers were suffering in the flesh, but they needed to know that even the threat of physical death was not a valid reason for losing sobriety and self-control (4:7-8). They might physically die, but they would have held on to true spiritual life (4:6). The approach is similar to that of 3:19-20. Peter looked back to Noah ("those who are now dead," 4:6) and probably included those believers after Noah's day up to the present. They had physically died, whether through martyrdom or other causes ("judged," 4:6). Peter was saying that the death and resurrection of Christ served to arm believers with the appropriate attitude for their daily battle against sin. The one who has identified with Christ's redemptive suffering is no longer responding to the lusts of the flesh, but to the will of God. The main point is that there is life, not condemnatory judgment, for believers who have died in Christ.

4:7-11 Conclusion:
The End Impinges on the Present

The conclusion ("therefore," 4:7) calls for a total focus of life on glorifying God. Peter set forth the proper conduct of those experiencing suffering. Even during suffering believers were to meet the practical demands of Christian discipleship. Love, being ready to forgive again and again, covers the sins of others. Peter encouraged believers to use their spiritual gifts in serving one another (cf. 1 Cor. 12) and glorifying God.

4:12–5:11 THE FOCUS IN OBEDIENCE: FAITHFUL CREATOR
4:12-19 The Suffering of Christ: God's Presence

The thrust of this section was to explain the judgment of God. The Old Testament Scripture quoted here (4:18) is Proverbs 11:31. Some thought that judgment could only mean punishment for sin. To them, the "painful trial" of persecution seemed strange and out of keeping with God's salvation. This had once been Peter's view of suffering when he told Jesus not to go to the cross (Matt. 16:21-23). This was a satanic view of life for believers. Others understood that judgment can be both punishment for

unbelievers and purifying for believers. This perspective on judgment enables believers to submit in peace to God's ways of judgment, starting with the church first and then the world (cf. also 1 Pet. 5:10). Peter wanted his readers to understand that there was judgment for the family of God that follows the pattern of Christ's own sufferings. In that light, continued rejoicing is the proper response to suffering as a Christian (4:13). In 4:17 Peter alluded to Ezekiel 9:5-6. Persecution is divinely permitted to purge believers and serves as a warning of judgment on the ungodly. The implication of the use of Proverbs 11:31 is that the ungodly face terrifying final judgment. Those who suffer according to God's will must place their confidence in God who is faithful and can be counted on to do what is right.

5:1-5 Trusting His Appointed Leaders

The concept of a faithful Creator (4:19) is pivotal to 1 Peter 5. As the Creator, God ordained the sufferings of Christ and his future glory (5:1). Leadership is to be carried out in conformity to that plan. In 5:1-4 Peter explained the way leaders were to shepherd their congregations. He exhorted the elders to shepherd (that is, feed and care for) the flock of God among them. The imagery of the shepherd and the flock was used by Jesus when instructing Peter (John 21:15-17). Faithful church leaders are promised a reward that they will receive from Christ, the Chief Shepherd (5:4). In 5:5 Peter quoted Proverbs 3:34 to show the reason for humility. It reaches to the very character of God.

5:6-11 Trusting His Powerful Grace

The thrust of this letter concerning humility and subsequent exaltation is clearly stated in 5:6. The "due time" is when Christ returns (cf. 4:13). Until then, believers must cast their anxiety upon him only if they truly believe the great truths in this letter. The next contrast is suffering for a little time to gain perfection for eternity (5:10). But whether now or then, the dominion is always his (5:11).

5:12-14 CLOSING REMARKS AND BENEDICTION

Apparently Paul's companion Silvanus, or Silas (Acts 15:22; 18:5), is the scribe who wrote as Peter dictated the letter (1 Pet. 5:12). The earliest understanding of "Babylon" (5:13) interprets it as referring to Rome. Other interpretations that were held later are the ancient city of Babylon, a city in Egypt named Babylon, or a cryptogram for a place of exile. The majority of scholars favor Rome as the place of writing and take "Babylon" as a symbolic designation for the city, as in Revelation 17:5, 9 and 18:2, 10, 21. The "kiss of love" (1 Pet. 5:14) corresponds to Paul's "holy kiss" (see note on Rom. 16:16), a culturally acceptable Christian greeting.

2 Peter

HISTORICAL SETTING
The readers of this letter were believers (1:1) and apparently the same group as addressed in 1 Peter (2 Pet. 3:1). See the Guiding Concepts section for 1 Peter. The problem facing the readers in 1 Peter was persecution. The problem facing the readers of 2 Peter was false teaching (2:1, 21). It was a teaching that advocated loose moral standards (2:10) resulting in enslavement to lusts (2:19). The false teachers denied the second coming of Christ (3:4). In contrast with the opponents' claims to knowledge, Peter emphasized the true knowledge of Christ (1:2, 3, 8; 2:20; 3:18).

AUTHOR
Although the authorship of Peter has been questioned, the letter itself names Peter as its author (1:1). The author referred to his approaching death (1:13-14). He witnessed the transfiguration of Jesus (1:16-18) as Peter had done (Matt. 17:1-4). A previous letter sent to the same readers is mentioned (3:1). The author had knowledge of Paul and his writings (3:15-16) as Peter must have had (Gal. 1:18; 2:9, 11, 14; Acts 15:1-29). There is nothing in the letter that might have motivated a forgery; it contains no heresy or new historical data about the life of Peter. The differences in form and style between 1 and 2 Peter may be due to his using a different scribe to actually put the words on paper. It is possible that he wrote this second letter himself but dictated the first one to a scribe.

DATE
Written after 1 Peter (2 Pet. 3:1), this letter was written shortly before Peter's death, which he believed to be imminent (1:14-15). The letter was probably written from Rome in the summer of A.D. 64.

PURPOSE
This letter from Peter was designed to warn its readers against false teachers in the church (2:1-2; 3:17). Peter intended for the letter to stir the readers to

remembrance of the true teachings of their prophets and Savior (3:1-2) and encourage growth in knowledge of the Lord Jesus (3:18).

GUIDING CONCEPTS

DIVINE PROVIDENCE

Peter dealt with the concept of divine providence in 2:3-9; 3:7, 9-13. He was involved in an argument that was common in his day and one whose roots can be traced back to Epicurean philosophy. The Epicureans (from 300 B.C. on) were interested in having a trouble-free life. Because their god had to be the supreme model of being trouble-free, the concept of a god trying to keep the world together made no sense. He could not be trouble-free if he had to be concerned with the world. Therefore, there could be no divine providence.

Man's ideal also was to be trouble-free. He was to have the promise of freedom. In order to achieve this trouble-free state, the Epicureans denied the existence of a god who evaluated people after this life. Thus both the concept of an afterlife and that of judgment were done away with. The Epicurean argument was based on two premises. First, the wicked are not judged. Second, the righteous very often seem to be punished. From this, the philosophers reasoned there could be no sovereign god who was in control. The foremost enemy to the untroubled state of humanity was the concept of a sovereign and judging deity.

Some Jewish writings bring forth this same argument against Providence. In a Targum of Genesis 4:8, Cain and Abel debate about the justice of God. Cain claimed that God did not accept Cain's offering because he was partial toward Abel. Cain then went on to conclude that "there is no judgment, there is no judge, there is no other world, there is no gift of good reward for the just and punishment for the wicked." Scholars believe that this Targum reflects the thinking of the Sadducees, the Jewish sect that denied the concepts of resurrection, afterlife, and free will. This Jewish sect was in existence during New Testament times.

AFTERLIFE

Peter spoke of the afterlife in 2 Peter 3:7, 10-13. The statement in 3:4 that all things would continue as they always had implies that history would continue on in the same way. Thus, talk of divine intervention into history with a second coming and judgment did not fit the philosophers' theories. In talking about the afterlife and judgment, Peter desired to illustrate God's ability to keep and preserve his people. Passages that relate to this are 2:4, 9, 17; and 3:7. Deuteronomy 32:34-35 reveals that there are treasuries of judgment, but they are sealed. They are sealed for a future opening in order to give time for repentance now (3:9, 15).

JUDGMENT AFTER THIS LIFE

Peter spoke of judgment after death in 2:4, 9, 17; 3:7, 10. The false teachers in 2:1 were denying the return of the Lord. They were practical atheists. Practical atheists, seen also in Psalm 10:4, 6, 11, do not deny God's existence. They just live their day-to-day lives as if God does not exist. Psalms 14:1; 73:11; and Jeremiah 5:12 also relate to this idea. These people have no fear of God. They believe that they will not be punished because they think that God is not concerned.

BIBLE-WIDE CONCEPTS

This letter from Peter was an incredible collection of biblical references ranging from the beginning to the end of time. Peter's encouragement to purity and steadfastness was rooted in a deep appreciation of God's words and deeds throughout history. Peter brought to his readers' attention the hope of God's promises (2 Pet. 1:4; 3:9, 13). He viewed all as under God's sovereign kingdom (1:11). He revealed the present implications of the transfiguration of Christ (1:16-18). He pointed his readers to the words spoken by the Old and New Testament prophets and apostles (1:19-21; 3:2). He related present false prophets to the line of false prophets throughout the history of God's people (2:1). He graphically illustrated the present implications of ancient judgments upon angels (2:4), the world by flood (2:5; 3:6), Sodom and Gomorrah (2:6), and Balaam (2:15-16). Peter showed that obedience to God was demanded by his power as Creator and Sustainer of the heavens and earth. Finally, Peter reflected the words of Jesus (3:10) and Paul (3:15-16). Far from a casual collection of biblical concepts, this letter reveals a mind steeped in Old and New Testament truths and a heart of wisdom that knew precisely how to bring the right truths to bear on the particular problems at hand.

NEEDS MET BY SECOND PETER

This letter from Peter was designed to meet some continual and basic needs of God's people, especially as they were surrounded by conflicting and, without doubt, false teachings. Those conflicting doctrines bred insecurity and doubt, especially about the promise of Christ's return to establish justice and reward the faithful for their sufferings and witness. The structure and content of 2 Peter show that Peter was answering questions like the following for his readers.

- With so many contradictory views, how can sincere people know what to believe?
- What are believers to make of the fact that it has been many years since Jesus said he would come back and make things right?
- What does the long wait for Christ's return say about God?
- How can believers be sure that they are really called and chosen by God for redemption?

Peter wrote to people who needed to be certain about their salvation in the face of many conflicting doctrines. But he showed that security is obtained, not by theoretical teachings of doctrine, but by one's own personal growth in Christian graces and by conformity to God's nature. To have the "perfect doctrine" is no substitute for exhibiting godly qualities (2 Pet. 1:5-8). In today's society, which is so bent on gathering information, Peter urges believers to develop godly qualities. He also helps today's believers to cope with the long wait for Christ's return. Christ said he would be returning soon, but it has now been almost two thousand years. Peter revealed what this long wait says about humanity and, most important, what it says about God. Peter also sought to convince his readers that Christianity was not something that someone made up. He showed how to appropriate the apostolic witness of Christ's life (God's word) in one's personal experience to build a firm foundation for security and witness.

OUTLINE OF SECOND PETER

A. GREETING (1:1-2)
B. REMINDER: DILIGENCE TO PARTAKE OF THE PROMISES (1:3-21)
    1. Diligence in Growth (1:3-11)
    2. Attention to God's Word (1:12-21)
C. WARNING: FALSE TEACHERS (2:1-22)
    1. Consider Their End: Divine Destruction (2:1-16)
    2. Consider Their State: Slavery to Sin (2:17-22)
D. REMINDER: DILIGENCE IN THE MIDST OF SKEPTICISM (3:1-18)
    1. Skepticism over Historical Continuity (3:1-7)
    2. Correction from Divine Chronology: Certainty (3:8-13)
    3. Concluding Exhortation from Divine Purpose: Salvation (3:14-18)

SECOND PETER NOTES

1:1-2 GREETING

Peter's greeting was based on a shared faith (1:1) within the sphere of growth in God's grace (1:2). Although the readers were apparently the same group of believers addressed in 1 Peter (cf. 2 Pet. 3:1), the more general address is used here because of the general applicability of the message to all Christians. The faith of the readers was the same kind of faith as was exhibited by the apostles; it was a true and genuine faith. The theme of the epistle (3:18) is introduced by the word "knowledge." The word Peter used means "full or true knowledge." His strong emphasis on true knowledge indicated that the false teachers also were claiming special access to divine truth.

1:3-21 REMINDER: DILIGENCE TO PARTAKE OF THE PROMISES
1:3-11 Diligence in Growth

1:3-4 A STATEMENT OF FACT: PARTAKING OF THE DIVINE NATURE
In these verses Peter considered the process of the believer's growth. Endowed with divine power, divine promises, and a divine nature, God enables the believer to grow in

Christian virtue (1:5-7). Peter used philosophical terms and religious catch words that would grab the attention of the Greeks (1:3-4). The words "participate in the divine nature" (1:4) refer to the believers as present sharers in the life of God through Christ (1:3) and future recipients of a glorified body (1:11). Peter's emphasis was not on the doctrine of salvation or on the doctrine of Christ. His letter was about God the Father. This gives further insight into the life-setting of the letter. Peter dealt with the readers' questions about how it seemed that God was not doing much to bring his kingdom into the world.

1:5-9 ENLIGHTENMENT AND PURIFICATION
Because of the spiritual endowment believers had received, Peter urged the believers to cooperate with God's plan for producing certain virtues (1:5-7). Ultimately these virtues are produced by Christ (Phil. 2:13), but believers must be yielded to God's will and word for the growth to take place. In 1:8-11 Peter pointed out the positive benefits of having developed the virtues listed in 1:5-7. Believers who do not manifest these virtues are spiritually nearsighted (1:9). They have forgotten that their sins have been forgiven.

These people have not really forgotten about their salvation, but they have forgotten the implications of past forgiveness on present behavior. They have been living as if their past forgiveness had no relationship to present holy living.

1:10-11 CERTAINTY FROM PRACTICE
The virtues listed in 1:5-8 provide true knowledge about God (1:8) and build a basis of certainty for believers about their salvation (1:10). Peter wanted his readers to be certain of their salvation so that they would stay true to the faith. But only their own firsthand experience of seeing God produce his character in their lives could create that certainty. Experiencing the divine nature of God now (1:4) will provide a rich reward later (1:11).

1:12-21 Attention to God's Word
1:12-15 AN ENDURING REMINDER
Peter and Paul both described their bodies as tents (1:13; cf. 2 Cor. 5:1). Peter wanted to leave a written record of reminder after he died (2 Pet. 1:15). The Lord had spoken about Peter's death in general terms (John 13:16; 21:19). At the time of writing this letter Peter had been made aware by the Lord that his death was imminent.

1:16-18 EYEWITNESSES OF GLORY
Peter showed that true knowledge had its basis, not in cleverly devised tales, but in the testimony of the apostles (2 Pet. 1:16-18) and the prophetic word (1:19-21). In 1:16-18 Peter joined hands with the apostles James and John in his claim that they were "eyewitnesses" of Christ's majesty at his transfiguration (Matt. 17:1-8). The term "eyewitnesses" was used by others as a technical term in various pagan religions of a person who had been fully initiated and allowed to watch a sacred ritual.

1:19-21 FIRM PROPHECY
The goal of this letter, protecting Christians from false teachings, depended on presenting the true authority to whom all believers would listen. Here, Jesus was the only one who had the Father's full approval, as seen in God's words quoted by Peter (1:17). It is debated whether Peter was saying that prophetic word (Scripture) confirms apostolic witness, or that apostolic witness confirms Scripture. Peter seemed to be saying that the truth of God's revelation is more certain,

having been confirmed by two witnesses (Scripture and apostolic testimony) rather than just one. The phrase "until the day dawns" (1:19) probably refers to the coming of Christ to establish his kingdom. The "morning star" (1:19) is a clear reference to Christ (Rev. 22:16). In 1:20-21 the apostle explained that no prophecy of Scripture was a matter of private origination. No true prophet thinks up a prophecy himself. The prophetic revelation comes from God through human instrumentality under the impulse of the Holy Spirit. This was why Peter spoke of the transfiguration and God's witness to Jesus as his approved Son. Only that which conforms to Jesus' words is acceptable teaching. Only God speaking through his Spirit, not ideas peculiar to a person's wishes, results in true divine prophecy. This prepares the reader for Peter's words about false prophets in 2:1-22. The chapter break would be more logical between 1:19 and 1:20 than it is at the end of 1:21.

2:1-22 WARNING:
FALSE TEACHERS
2:1-16 Consider Their End:
Divine Destruction
2:1-3 THEIR MESSAGE, JUDGMENT, AND AUDIENCE
Peter warned that false teachers would come among the believers, denying Christ and influencing others toward evil (2:1; cf. Acts 20:29-30). Peter emphasized the sure destruction of the false teachers (noted twice, 2:1, 3). The rest of the chapter outlines their judgment in graphic detail. By contrast, Peter also encouraged his readers by pointing to the ultimate preservation of the faithful (2:9). Peter asserted that the judgment of the false teachers had been clouded by delay. Some thought that the lack of immediate judgment on these heretics showed an idleness on the part of God (2:3). But the issue with God's prophecies is never how long it takes them to be fulfilled, but how certain they are. Although these false teachers are seen to be unbelievers (2:12), salvation was available if they would but repent. The penalty for their sins was paid in full by Christ. The "way of truth" (2:2) refers to God's full salvation (cf. Acts 9:2; 16:17; 18:25-26; 19:9, 23; 22:4; 24:14, 22).

2:4-16 PAST EXAMPLE

Having pointed out the certain destruction of the false teachers (2 Pet. 2:3), Peter went on to give some examples of God's impartial judgment on the wicked. This is a long "if-then" idea that can be quickly seen by reading 2:4 and 2:9 together. Until the last judgment, God is able to keep good and evil sorted out, one for preservation, the other for destruction. The concepts of "hold" (2:9), "rescue" (2:7, 9) and "spare" (2:4-5) are emphasized. The righteous are preserved through, not out of, times of evil (2:5, 7-9, "godly"). If God can really punish people and keep them for that purpose, he can also preserve the righteous. The implied logic is as follows: If God punished the wicked in the past, would he spare the false teachers now? Although debated, it is most likely that Peter was referring in 2:4 to the sin of the fallen angels of Genesis 6:1-4, who intermarried with mortal women and thus corrupted the human race.

The second example of God's judgment is the flood in Noah's day (2:5; cf. Gen. 6:5–8:22). The third example of judgment is God's wrath on Sodom and Gomorrah (2:6-8; cf. Gen. 19). The Genesis account gives the impression that Lot was not as righteous as Peter states (3:7). But Peter evaluated Lot's faith and belief. Lot did believe and obey God and did not condone the sexual perversion of the men of Sodom (Gen. 19:7). Peter's application (2:9) for the readers was that God would rescue the godly from temptation and bring judgment on the wicked. The "day of judgment" (2:9) referred to the great white throne judgment (Rev. 20:11-15). The basic elements of the judgment are elaborated in 2 Peter 2:10-16. The "way of Balaam" (2:15) referred to Balaam's materialistic motivation (Num. 22:5, 7; Deut. 23:4).

2:17-22 Consider Their State: Slavery to Sin

In 2:10-19 Peter proceeded to describe the character of the false teachers. He looked for the fruit of genuine faith and discovered that there was none. It is debated whether 2:20 refers to the false teachers or the new converts ("who are just escaping," 2:18). According to the first view, the false teachers knew of the truth of Christ and apparently made some profession of this truth, but then strayed from it. They professed faith but never

possessed it. In 2:21 Peter explained why their last state was worse than their first. Having been exposed to the truth, they had incurred a greater accountability (cf. Luke 12:47-48). According to the new convert view, Peter was pointing out the inconsistency of being delivered from sin's defilement and then returning to such slavery. Although applied in this case to believers, the impact of 2:21 remains the same. To return to previous sin after becoming cleansed by Christ is, in that context, worse than the preconversion state. Second Peter 2:22 shows in what way it is worse. It is worse because it is a great offense before God for believers to return to their old ways after receiving his cleansing. The two illustrations (2:22), one biblical (Prov. 26:11) and the other secular, show the inconsistency of being delivered from sin and then wallowing in it.

3:1-18 REMINDER: DILIGENCE IN THE MIDST OF SKEPTICISM
3:1-7 Skepticism over Historical Continuity

Peter referred to this as the "second" letter, 1 Peter being the first. Peter stressed two truths: (1) remember who brought the word of God (3:1-2); and (2) remember the potency of God's word to create and to destroy (3:3-7). From the viewpoint of prophecy (3:3), history divides into two periods: the present age (the age of promise) and the age to come (the time of fulfillment). The "last days" (3:3) refer to the end of the present age. One of the major doctrinal deviations of the false teachers was their denial of the second coming of Christ (3:4). They mocked the doctrine because so many years had passed since the promise had been given. But those who wondered whether God's promise would ever take place were forgetting God's creation of the world by his word and his act of judgment in the flood. Instead, they argued that God's seemingly present failure to judge world evil voided his promise that he would judge the world in the future. They were not the first to ask, "What happened to your promises, God?" (cf. Deut. 32:37; Judg. 6:13). But they were asking in sarcasm, not faith.

Peter claimed that those who said the world would continue as it always had, had forgotten to ask how the world came to be in the first place. Drawing upon biblical history (the creation and the flood), Peter pointed out that God was active in this world's affairs. He went on to appeal to biblical prophecy, the purging of the world by fire (3:7; cf. Isa. 66:15) and the judgment on the wicked (3:7; cf. Dan. 12:2), as further evidences of God's divine intervention into the affairs of this world. Peter showed that the future is built consistently upon the past. Faith is built upon certainty based on the previous acts of God. Imposing a human time frame within which God is supposed to act leads to error.

3:8-13 Correction from Divine Chronology: Certainty

3:8-10 GOD IS NOT BOUND TO A HUMAN SCHEDULE

God's plan and timing are divine (3:8). Sovereignty, not slowness, is the issue. Appealing to the teaching of Psalm 90:4, Peter pointed out that what was regarded as a long time to people was like a mere day in God's reckoning. God is not bound by earthly time. The phrase "as some understand slowness" (3:9) is intended as a slur against the opponents who say that delay functions as a prime argument against providential judgment. But, understood correctly, the present lack of God's full judgment is actually a proof for God's providence. God's so-called slowness is actually providing time to repent based on God's benevolent character. He is patient, not slow. That patience is clearly seen in God's covenant with Noah. Humans would continue to be as sinful as ever (Gen. 8:21), but God bound himself to withholding his full judgment so that he could show grace in Christ. A Jewish paraphrase of Genesis 6:3 notes that the 120 years God gave to Noah before the flood was for the people so "that they may work repentance and not perish." The Judaism of Peter's day understood the delay of God to be for repentance. This beautiful insight into the long-suffering nature of God is most clearly expressed in Exodus 34:6-7. Peter stressed this in 3:15. Peter's opponents had forgotten what should have shaped the God-centered person's

worldview: God is compassionate and gracious and abounding in loving-kindness. They were not to have a black-and-white worldview that bound God to either instant retribution or no retribution. Both Christians and unbelievers receive the kindness of God leading them away from destruction (3:9).

Peter explained that the apparent delay of God's judgment was not an evidence of God's indifference regarding sin. The delay of Christ's return is redemptive in purpose; it is to allow more people to believe before judgment comes. The future day of the Lord is that period during which God will deal with his people through judgment and deliverance (3:10). It will include the tribulation, Christ's second advent, the millennial kingdom, and the purging of the heavens and earth (see note on 1 Thess. 5:2). Peter focused on the cataclysmic consummation of the day of the Lord, the purging of the earth by fire in preparation for the new heavens and earth (Isa. 65:17; 66:22; Rev. 21:1). This event will take place at the final revolt of Satan (Rev. 20:7–21:1).

3:11-13 EXHORTATION: BEHAVIOR AND HOPE

Peter set forth the coming judgments of the day of the Lord as an incentive to godly living. The "day of God" (3:12) probably refers to that time when Christ hands over the reins of millennial government to God the Father, and the eternal state begins (cf. 1 Cor. 15:24-28; Rev. 21:1). For "promise" (3:13), see 1:4; 2:19; 3:4, 9, 13. The new heavens and earth were prophesied by Isaiah (Isa. 65:17; 66:22; cf. Rev. 21:1).

3:14-18 Concluding Exhortation from Divine Purpose: Salvation

The long wait for Christ's return displays the greatness of God's patience (3:14-15). Although Peter recognized that some of Paul's writings were hard to understand, he did regard them as Scripture (3:16). Peter hung the key to understanding his letter at the very end (3:18). There he put forth his central goal and theme: "Growing in the grace and knowledge of Christ."

1 John

BASIC FACTS

HISTORICAL SETTING

The readers are believers (3:1-2) of Gentile background (5:21). Because John spent his later years at Ephesus, it is likely that the letter was written from that city to a nearby group of Asian churches with which John was personally acquainted. The supposition of Augustine that the churches of Parthia are in mind has no foundation and probably arose from a corruption of the text.

False teachers appeared in the church (4:1) who drew some professing Christians from fellowship with true believers (2:19). The false teachers claimed a special illumination by the Spirit (2:27) that imparted a deeper spiritual knowledge. John combats this error by emphasizing the source and nature of true knowledge (2:3, 5; 3:16, 19, 24; 4:2, 6, 13; 5:2). The opponents also claimed to have reached a state of moral perfection (1:8-10). This ethical error brought pride and haughtiness, and John combats such attitudes by placing a strong emphasis on love for the brethren (4:7-21).

The major error among the readers was a denial of the incarnation of Christ (2:22; 4:2-3). This reflects an early form of Gnosticism known as Docetism, which claimed that Christ only "seemed" to take on an earthly human form. Many went farther to deny the reality of Christ's sufferings. In refuting the heresy, John did not attack the false teachers but carefully expounded the truth, encouraging his readers to continue in the faith and live consistent Christian lives with an awareness and concern for the errors that surrounded them.

AUTHOR

The author is not named in the letter. He claims to have been an eyewitness of the life and ministry of Christ (1:1). He expects not only to be heard but obeyed (4:6). Most scholars recognize the similarity in thought, vocabulary, and style between the Gospel of John and 1 John. Both works contain expressions such as "light," "love," "eternal life," "truth," "witness," "abide," "comforter," "new commandment," "begotten of God," and "Savior of the world." Early church fathers such as Irenaeus, Clement of Alexandria, and later, Tertullian support John's authorship. See the Guiding Concepts section for the Gospel of John.

DATE

The date is related to the date assigned to John's Gospel (A.D. 85–90). First John was probably written after John's Gospel because the author seems to assume an acquaintance on the part of the readers with the facts of his Gospel. The absence of any reference to persecution may indicate that the letter was written before the persecution of Domitian (A.D. 81–96) against the church (ca. A.D. 95). The letter should probably be dated after John's Gospel, around A.D. 90.

PURPOSE

This first letter by John was designed to combat false teaching by a clear presentation of the truth. The primary purpose was to promote Christian fellowship (1:3) and knowledge in Christian truth and experience (5:13). John sought to promote fellowship in the family of God through instruction in true knowledge and by encouraging the believers in their love for one another.

GUIDING CONCEPTS

John corrects several problems that contrast with the heart of his desires for his readers. Some claimed to be able to have fellowship with God without practicing the truth (1:6; 2:3-4). But the heart of truth in practice was showing love to fellow Christians, something their opponents were not doing (2:9, 11; 3:23; 4:20). These false teachers also claimed that they had no personal sin (1:8, 10). Because of the confusion about who was and was not in fellowship with God, the believers' confidence in their own salvation was shaken (2:28; 3:21; 4:17; 5:14).

The problems and solutions of the letter may be summed up under three areas of question. First was the question of sin. Is it possible for believers to sin, and does sin destroy their relationship with God? Can or should believers pray for fellow believers who are in sin? Second was the question of incarnation. Did Jesus really come in the flesh or was it just an appearance? Do believers have to believe in a real flesh and blood experience of Christ on the cross? Third was the question of power. If believers are so hated by the world, where is the security and power to confirm them fully and ultimately as the children of God? The letter is to help believers know that they have eternal life (5:13).

The concept of "remaining" or "abiding" in God is the major theme of the letter. It is John's central desire for the believers and it penetrates all of John's arguments against his opponents. The Gospel of John uses "remain" ("abide," NASB and KJV) forty times, once for every twenty-two verses. First John speaks of "remaining" twenty-four times, once for every four or five verses (see for example, 2:24, 27-28). John shows how believers can know they "remain" or "abide" in God. Such assurance will encourage them to continue in their love and prayer for other Christians.

BIBLE-WIDE CONCEPTS

WAITING FOR CHRIST'S RETURN

The letter examines how life can best be lived in this time of waiting for God's promise to be fulfilled (2:25; 3:2). This is the time of experiencing world hatred and inner conflict (3:13). This is the period when Christ reigns at the right hand of God (Ps. 110:1; Acts 2:34-35) and his people have times of groaning (Rom. 8:19-25). In 1 Corinthians 15:23-28 Paul made the clear link between the time of Jesus' reign and the time of the present in which believers have to cope with death and other problems that remain. All the promises of God are yes in Christ (2 Cor. 1:20), but believers must wait for some of them to be fully realized at the return of Christ.

THE NEW COVENANT

John shows the implications of being in the new covenant (1 John 2:18-29; 3:6; 4:12-16; 5:1-12). The new covenant promised a great and perfect sacrifice for sin (Jer. 31:34; cf. 1 John 2:2; 4:10). The new covenant promised the indwelling of the Holy Spirit (Ezek. 36:26-27; cf. 1 John 2:20, 27; 4:13). But it also provided a new way of obeying God, by placing the law in the hearts of all believers (cf. Jer. 31:33). It is that inner prompting of the Spirit that is behind all of John's discussion of keeping God's commands and knowing about him (1 John 2:4-6; 3:6-12; 4:13; 5:3).

CONFLICT BETWEEN THE CHILDREN OF GOD AND OF THE DEVIL

In Genesis 3:15 God predicted a continual struggle between the seed of Eve and the seed of the serpent. That conflict still existed in John's day (1 John 3:11-12). The world's hatred for God's people was not new. It reached all the way back into the Garden of Eden. Cain is the only mortal mentioned by name in the letter and is used as a model of the child of the devil. By implication, Abel is a model of the child of God who experiences hatred by the world. Also, like the serpent tempted Eve with divine knowledge apart from God's explicit commands, so those present-day antichrists sought to build a religion that claimed fellowship with God apart from his crucified and risen Son.

RELATION TO THE GOSPEL OF JOHN

In his Gospel John reported three appearances of Christ after his resurrection (John 20:11-18; 19-23; 24-29). By mentioning the fact of Christ's physical post-resurrection appearances, John was validating his claim of Christ's bodily resurrection. He could be seen, heard, and felt. He was really there. This made the link between the earthly and the resurrected life of Christ concrete. In his first letter John argued against some who had broken that link and had done away with the real body, death, and resurrection for Christ. The issue in the Gospel of John was that the man Jesus was also truly God (John 20:31). The issue in 1 John is that the divine heavenly Jesus is also truly man and lived on earth (1 John 4:2).

NEEDS MET BY FIRST JOHN

John wrote this letter to meet the needs of Christians who were wondering if they believed the right things about God and were really secure in his salvation. They were being told that if they were truly related to God they would not have any sin. They were also being told that it was foolish to believe that the Son of God would come in a literal physical body and that somehow his physical death could atone for sins. The content and structure of John's first letter show that he was answering questions like the following.

- How can believers have fellowship with God?
- What does sin do to the fellowship of believers with God?
- Is it important to believe that Jesus had a real human body and literally died on a cross?
- What is the mark of a true child of God?
- What is the mark of a true child of the devil?
- How can believers possibly cope with God's commands for righteousness?
- Should believers pray for other believers who are in sin?

Throughout Scripture people have tried to create religions that have all the trappings but do away with obedience to God's commands. Such an attempt is the target of John's words in 1 John. In the modern environment of competing religions, John meets the need of believers today to find security in their Christian faith (1 John 5:13). Today, as in John's day, believers face heresies that say salvation and a relationship with God can be had without worrying about keeping his commands. John makes it clear that the only way to salvation and a relationship with God is through the sacrifice of Christ and obeying God's commands.

Believers may find God's commands impossible to follow and almost oppressive in their demands. First, John encourages believers by confirming that their sins are already forgiven through Christ's sacrifice. He then points out that the commandments of God are not burdensome (1 John 5:3) because they are kept, not in order to gain salvation, but out of gratitude to God the Savior. In addition, the Holy Spirit instructs and enables believers to obey.

OUTLINE OF FIRST JOHN

A. THE LETTER'S PURPOSE: TO ANNOUNCE THE SOURCE OF FELLOW-
SHIP (1:1-4)
B. THE INCOMPATIBILITY OF FELLOWSHIP AND PRACTICED SIN (1:5–2:2)
1. God Is Light (1:5)
2. Fellowship and Sin (1:6–2:2)
C. VICTORY IN COMMANDMENT KEEPING (2:3-17)
1. Specific Ethical Demand: Commandment Keeping (2:3-11)
2. Victory by Present Knowledge of Christ (2:12-17)
D. CONFORMITY TO THE MODEL OF CHRIST (2:18–3:24)
1. Doctrinal: Jesus Is the Messiah (2:18-27)
2. Living amidst World Hatred (2:28–3:24)

E. THE INCARNATION AND LOVE FOR EACH OTHER (4:1-20)
   1. The Doctrinal Battle: Jesus the Messiah Has Come in the Flesh (4:1-6)
   2. The Practical Battle: Loving One's Brother (4:7-20)
F. ENABLEMENT FOR COMMANDMENT KEEPING (4:21–5:12)
   1. Ability through Faith (4:21–5:4)
   2. The Validation of Faith (5:5-12)
G. THE INDISPENSABLE ADVOCACY OF CHRIST (5:13-21)
   1. The Resumption of Intercession for Sin (5:13-17)
   2. A Summary of the Work of God in Christ (5:18-21)

FIRST JOHN NOTES

1:1-4 THE LETTER'S PURPOSE: TO ANNOUNCE THE SOURCE OF FELLOWSHIP

Like his Gospel, John's first epistle begins with a prologue in which he sets forth some of the major ideas he will develop as the message unfolds. "From the beginning" (1:1) may refer to either the eternality (cf. John 1:1) or incarnation (2:7, 24) of Christ. The letter concerns the "Word of life" (1:1; 5:11-13). But "Word" and "life" are intangible and often wrongly defined. False teachers had come in and were redefining "Word" and "life" in heretical ways. To counter the problem, John began by noting that he and other eyewitnesses had heard, seen, and touched the very real and physical Word. John referred especially to the senses ("heard," "seen," "touched") in order to refute the denial of the incarnation of God in Christ (4:2). On this physical and bodily reality John based the rest of his truth regarding Christ's real death, resurrection, and ability to offer life. But only the group of apostolic eyewitnesses could validate the testimony concerning the "Word of life." Any other ideas about Christ not approved by the eyewitnesses of Christ's life were not to be received. John drew the line of truth around the testimony of the apostles.

John presented a process that moves from the abstract spiritual presence of the "Word of life" in heaven to the earthly experience of Christ's life. The "eternal life" (1:2, "Christ") was manifested to the world in the incarnation of God in Jesus. Christ was proclaimed by the apostles (1:3). The link between the Father and his people is the apostolic proclamation now recorded in Scripture. This section describes how the Word was manifested and the resultant unique authority of the eyewitnesses.

Fellowship is the thrust of the letter. There is no true fellowship with God apart from fellowship with the eyewitness community (1:3). Their fellowship was with God and with Christ. Christ was noted second because the opponents claimed to have fellowship with God and yet totally disagreed with John's testimony about Christ. Fellowship is sharing or participating in the life of God and the family of believers. Joy (1:4) was John's pastoral intent in writing the letter. Joy will come when the contents of this letter result in fellowship.

1:5–2:2 THE INCOMPATIBILITY OF FELLOWSHIP AND PRACTICED SIN
1:5 God Is Light

"Light" (1:7) is used by John to describe ethical character and spiritual illumination (2:9). God's character is light with no darkness. This sets the context for discussing which doctrines or practices are suitable for a Christian. John began his message using the abstracts of light and darkness. But as long as light and dark remained abstract, it could not be proven that a person did or did not have fellowship with God. Therefore John immediately moved from the abstract to the specific by relating light to God's commands. John used love for Christians as the standard to prove whether a person conformed to God's light or not. John's admonition to walk in the light by showing love to fellow Christians was the cornerstone of his intention to bring about the joy of fellowship (1:3).

Because light and darkness could refer to either knowledge or ethics (cf. John 3:19-21), John took up both topics in the letter. He shed God's light on both false doctrine (knowledge) and false practices (ethics). The false doctrines about Christ had led to ungodly behavior toward fellow Christians. The rest of the letter explains the implications of God being light in the lives of believers.

1:6–2:2 Fellowship and Sin

1:6-7 WALKING IN THE LIGHT

This section makes the general ethical demand that fellowship not be accompanied by practiced sin. It begins by giving the conditions of fellowship: one's walk must match God's character (1:6). John contrasted saying with doing. To claim fellowship with God and yet persist in sin is to deny the reality of one's profession (1:6; cf. Titus 1:16). Some of John's opponents denied that evil could harm their enlightened spirits. They claimed to be righteous and did not acknowledge any sin in their lives (cf. 1:8). This first "if" test (1:6) formed John's foundational criticism of his opponents. The rest of the tests are elaborations on this one (cf. 1:8, 10).

John also reminded his readers of the positive results for those who walk in the light (1:7). Two things happen when believers walk in the light. They have fellowship with each other, and they are cleansed of sin. At this point, John was still focusing on the Christian "walk" in terms of commandment keeping. God's light shines forth his divine nature, which issues in his divine character. Because God's children partake of his nature, they should also display his character in godly behavior (note 4:17). John stressed fellowship with the eyewitness community of the apostles because they gave observable proof of true faith. The problem was that John's opponents claimed fellowship with God without having any fellowship with the community of believers (cf. 2:19).

John stressed behavior (walk) by looking to the ultimate model of divine behavior, God in Jesus Christ (2:6). Christians can talk about righteous living because they have a model. To walk in the light is to live in active obedience to God's command to love as illustrated by Christ. When believers are in the habit of walking in the light (i.e., participating in the life of God), they will naturally confess their sins, and their consciences will be cleansed.

John brought up the problem of sin (1:7) because his opponents were against keeping God's clearly stated commandments (see "burdensome," 5:3). They also did not believe in sin (1:8, 10). To speak of commandments was to speak of possible failure to keep them. But his opponents believed that their mystical brand of fellowship with God did away with the fact of any ongoing sin. Therefore, John commenced the attack by reminding his readers of God's commandments and the sins committed by failing to keep them.

John desired both to encourage the keeping of God's commands and to assure that occasional failure to keep the commandments was not fatal to the one cleansed by Christ's blood. He showed that such sin was done while walking in the light (1:7). Therefore, in John's mind, being in the light does not mean perfection. And it also means that sin does not take a believer out of the light and into the darkness. For John, being in the light was a way to describe the believer's standing in Christ. It was not a way of describing any single act of obedience or disobedience for the believer. John placed all true believers in the light and all opponents in the dark. For John, being in the light and being in fellowship were one and the same. In John's terms, it is impossible for a true Christian not to be in fellowship. This is the basis of John's wonderful encouragement. His opponents were saying that people who sinned could not have fellowship. John taught that occasional sin does not take believers out of their saving relationship of light and fellowship with God. In fact, the sins of believers are forgiven and cleansed by Christ's blood.

The blood of Jesus was a literal sacrifice. But John's opponents did not believe in a literal flesh and blood body for Christ nor in literal commandments that were valid. So with no standard for sin and no literal body for sacrifice, the idea of a literal blood sacrifice was totally out of the question. Such was the heresy of the antichrists. Their false teachings took the life and merit out of Christ's death and blood.

1:8-10 FELLOWSHIP AND OCCASIONAL SIN "Sin" in the singular (1:7, 8) means "guilt" (cf. John 9:41; 15:22, 24; 19:11). The claim here is to have done nothing that needed the blood of Christ's sacrifice. But believers are to admit that they do occasionally sin (1:9). Their sins and the sins of the world have been forgiven. For believers to confess sin is to admit the continual need of Christ's cleansing blood. While occasional sin will not place them in darkness, they must always affirm and confess their need for Christ's sacrifice. Also, believers must always affirm their fellowship with the "light" by actions of righteousness that include practice of truth and dependence upon ongoing forgiveness. First John 1:8 is the opposite of 1:9; it speaks of those who deny sins rather than confessing them. Confession of sin is simply agreeing with God that the sin is wrong and inconsistent with one's participation in the life of God.

By saying "and purify us from all unrighteousness" (1:9), John drove home the point that sin is not to be denied in Christian lives but that its effects have been and will be completely dealt with by the blood of Christ. This is both a past and present experience of cleansing. God is faithful to his covenant promise. He is "righteous" because he indeed has perfectly dealt with sin. "Confess" (1:9) refers to public, not private, admission of having a continual need for the forgiveness and cleansing of Christ's blood. In this particular context it does not refer to the public listing of particular sins. The opponents said they no longer sinned or needed the blood of Christ. The believers were to publicly admit their need for Christ. On the public nature of confession, see Ezra 10:11; Leviticus 26:40-42; and Psalm 32:5. The idea is confession within the secure conditions of the covenant. In 4:2-3 "confess" has the idea of admitting or proclaiming or acknowledging that something is true. In 4:15 "confess" has the idea of profession (cf. Matt. 10:32-33; Rev. 3:5). Throughout the Old Testament confession is related to thanksgiving for forgiveness.

The response that one has never done specific acts of sin that need confessing (1:10) again reflects the error of John's opponents. John had just mentioned the importance of confessing sins (1:9). The assertion of 1:10 is nearly the same as the assertion of 1:8 but more emphatic and cutting. First John 1:8 speeks of self-deception and 1:10 shows that such claims make all that God said and did in Christ a lie.

2:1-2 A REALISTIC BALANCE
On the one side, the purpose of John's writing was to encourage his readers to avoid sin. His opponents left the door wide open to excessive sin, especially denying Christ and hating Christians. The "my dear children" draws the readers close to him. The opponents had chosen to escape the problem of sin (breaking commandments) by doing away with commandments. John's way was not only to affirm commandments and the rigorous avoidance of sin, but also to affirm the depths of forgiveness available when believers sin by breaking God's commandments. This is a present reality ("have") in the presence ("to the Father") of God. Jesus is the advocate of all believers, like a legal counsel for the defense, someone called upon to speak in defense of another. When Satan accuses (Rev. 12:10), Christ defends.

First John 2:2 supports John's line of reasoning. Jesus also serves as the "atoning sacrifice" (cf. Rom. 3:25), or satisfaction, for God's wrath on sin. While Christ's sacrifice was sufficient for the sins of the whole world, only those who believe may enjoy the benefits of his atoning work. The pronoun "He" takes the primary empasis here. The sacrifice is not external to Christ. John's point is that not only is sin to be an admitted reality, there is no limit to the potency of Christ's advocacy because of the effectiveness of his propitiation. John clearly says this, not to encourage sin, but to discourage fear and insecurity in admitting it.

2:3-17 VICTORY IN COMMANDMENT KEEPING
2:3-11 Specific Ethical Demand: Commandment Keeping
2:3-6 COMMANDMENTS MUST BE KEPT
John declared that true fellowship with God should be evidenced in the life of a believer by his obedience to God's word (2:3-6) and

love for the brothers (2:7-11). First John 2:3-6 refers back to the assertion in 1:6 of having fellowship. What is new is the specific command to keep the commandments. Commandments are objective and verifiable statements passed on by apostolic tradition. The opponents' response is in 2:22 and 3:7. John discussed the sin aspect first (1:7–2:2) and then the subject of commandments because the commandments imply a failure from time to time. This idea of failure needed to be dealt with first. Believers have complete sufficiency in Christ.

Conformity to God as light is done by conformity to his nature as expressed in his commands. The perfection or completion of the love of God (2:5) takes place as a believer appreciates God's act of love and is thereby led to walk as Christ walked. One's profession is proved true by obedience and proved false by disobedience. Behavior provides an observable model for knowing if a person is in or out of God's light. In 2:6 John used the word "live in" ("to remain," or "continue in") as the equivalent to confessing Jesus to be the Son of God (4:15) and believing in him (2:24; 3:23-24).

2:7-11 A SPECIFIC OF CHRIST'S WALK: LOVE OF THE BROTHER

John gave new teaching for the new era ushered in at Christ's first coming (2:7-8). The teaching was not new regarding its source: the teachings of Christ. It was new regarding the quality of the age. The new age of grace was dawning, and the future age was already moving into the present. People may know whether they are in a right relationship with God by their love for the Christian brethren (cf. John 13:34-35). This is in line with John's whole approach to the problem: a focus on observable behavior. Fear and insecurity in one's relationship with God vanish as his behavior reflects God's love in Christ (1:3; 1:7; 2:3). Thus in 2:10-11 John has come full circle back to the heretics' claim of fellowship (1:6). Fellowship with God is confirmed, not by sinless perfection, but by an orthodox confession of the deity and sacrifice of Christ, an open admission of a continual need for the blood of Christ, and a consistent walk that reflects the example of Christ. The term "darkness" (2:11) is used metaphorically to refer to the

spiritual and moral condition of the unbelieving world. Unbelievers love darkness because it covers their evil deeds, but believers have no part in it (cf. John 8:12).

2:12-17 Victory by Present Knowledge of Christ

Continuous victory over the world is based on present knowledge and doing God's will (2:12-17). John used the term "children" to refer to all the believers (cf. 2:1, 28). Then John referred to both the old and young believers. The term "fathers" refers to those who are older or more spiritually mature. The term "young men" refers to younger members of the congregation. He repeated himself in 2:14 to emphasize why he wrote. He wrote, not because the readers were ignorant and weak, but because they were already strong and victorious. It was the opponents who viewed the believers as ignorant and weak. The sins of believers have been forgiven and continue to stand forgiven. The "world" (2:15) refers to the ungodly world and its wicked system, which is apart from and in opposition to God. Believers are not to love the world (2:15). Love of God the Father (2:15) is doing his will (2:17; cf. John 14:15). John's description of the world is also his description of the motives and attachments of his opponents.

2:18–3:24 CONFORMITY TO THE MODEL OF CHRIST
2:18-27 Doctrinal: Jesus Is the Messiah

John's opponents revealed their character by their action of leaving the church's fellowship. They also denied that Jesus was the Messiah and could not believe that the Messiah came in human form (2:22). In 2:18 John announced the coming of the antichrist (cf. Rev. 13:1-10) and the presence of many antichrists. The term "anti" means that they opposed Christ and substituted themselves for Christ. The "last hour" (2:18) refers to the final period of the present age, the age of promise (cf. Dan. 2:28). John has prepared his readers for the exposure of his opponents as antichrists by clarifying the issues of sin and forgiveness (1:5–2:6) and by confirming the believers' victory in keeping the commandment to love (2:7-17). Next he reminded them of the time (the "last hour,"

2:18), the character of his opponents ("antichrists," 2:22), and the abilities of believers ("anointed" and "discerning," 2:27). First John 2:27 indicates that the Holy Spirit is completely adequate for teaching believers, and they have no need to depend upon false teachers. The Spirit may use gifted teachers to expound God's word (cf. Eph. 4:11; 1 Cor. 12:28). What they all "know" (2:20) concerned the false claims of fellowship with God (cf. 1:8, 10; 2:4, 20, 24, 27). The anointing by the Holy Spirit (Rom. 8:9) would enable the believers to discern between truth and error (cf. John 16:13-15). John concluded chapter 2 by setting forth a threefold defense against doctrinal defection: adhere to the truth (1 John 2:24-26), rely upon the Holy Spirit (2:27), and anticipate Christ's return (2:28-29).

2:28–3:24 Living amidst World Hatred

2:28-29 RIGHTEOUSNESS AND CHRIST'S SECOND COMING

In 2:28 John encouraged believers to have confidence in Christ's coming despite criticism by the antichrists. John summed up his point in 4:17. A knowledge is spoken of in 2:28-29 in relation to and in the context of Christ's return. Christ is not just righteous in an abstract way. He is righteous and will come to seek those who are also righteous. This should motivate believers to lead godly lives so that they might have joy in anticipating his return. The practice of righteousness, not the knowledge of righteousness, is the assuring mark of one born of God.

3:1-3 THE MORAL IMPLICATIONS OF SONSHIP AND THE RETURN OF CHRIST

Being called children of God is a sign of God's love. With wonder in his heart, John marveled that believers should be called "children of God," an expression that emphasizes their relationship with God. Those who believe are his children now (3:2). This relationship to God results in the world not knowing them (cf. John 1:9-13); but it also gives believers confidence (cf. 2:28). John asserted that there was no progressive process by which believers gradually become God's children. Although the future does bring changes in believers' bodies, the future will in no way make them more God's children than they are today. In Christ believers are as related to God as they will ever be. When Christ appears to take his church to heaven, believers "shall be like him," possessing glorified, resurrected bodies (Rom. 8:17, 29-30; 1 Cor. 15:51-53). The anticipation of Christ's return for the church is an incentive to purity. The word "purifies" (1:3), given in the present tense, indicates that a continual, personal effort is involved. Purity is linked to the second coming. The present unglorified body should not block the expression of one's true relationship to God. Now is the time for purification. The coming of Christ will only be a change in the mode of the believer's existence, not a change in his position before God. But John's opponents had raised questions about a believer's present standing with God.

3:4-12 THE PURPOSE OF CHRIST'S FIRST APPEARING: TO TAKE AWAY SINS

In 3:1-3 John stressed that believers are children of God in the present. Next he emphasized that Christ came to take away the sins of all who believe (3:5). When John noted that true believers do not continue in sin (3:6, 9), he was describing the purifying efforts of 3:3. Christians will see Christ "as he is" (3:2), so they are to purify themselves "just as he is" (3:3; cf. 3:7). The false teachers believed that knowledge was all important and conduct did not matter. John showed that conduct not only counts but is the essential ingredient in proving true knowledge and spiritual rebirth. John emphasized the concept of "practice" (four times in 3:7-10). The term "righteous" (3:7) was used by his opponents who were supposedly righteous irrespective of their behavior. John pointed out that righteous deeds spring from righteous character and are the proof of regeneration.

The believer should not practice sin. The expression "does what is sinful" (3:8) is in the present tense and suggests a continual practice, that is, "habitually sins." The "seed" (3:9) may refer to the divine nature of those born of God (1 Pet. 1:3-4) or perhaps to the divine resources inherited through new birth (Jer. 31:31-34). But the specific sin that John warned believers not to practice is described at length in 3:10–4:21. The true believer should consistently practice love for God and his children. The children of the devil will consistently practice hate toward God and his children. In 3:9-12 John clarified what he meant by the antichrists (2:18, 22). They are children of the devil. John picked up the theme of brotherly love (3:10) and developed it. Cain (cf. Gen. 4:8) was set forth as a negative illustration of the concept of brotherly love.

3:13-24 SPECIFIC RIGHTEOUSNESS: LOVE THAT FOLLOWS CHRIST'S MODEL

John warned believers to "not be surprised" if the world's hate is experienced (3:13). One who has an attitude of hatred toward Christ and Christians is potentially capable of murdering Christians (cf. Matt. 5:21-22). Such a person demonstrates that he is not a possessor of eternal life. The readers had a problem with being hated. It made them wonder if they were really recipients of God's redemption. This explained why love of Christian brothers was so important to John. In a world controlled by the evil one's power, anti-Christian teachings and acts are to be expected. Only the children of God can bring comfort and instruct in truth. John showed that the teachings of both God and the devil centered on the truth of God's incarnation in Christ. See the accompanying chart for a comparison of true and false teachings.

In order to discern the source of the teaching, the believers were to examine the works that followed out of a set of teachings. This was John's approach. Assurance of salvation is based on conformity to the character of Christ who perfectly illustrated what it means to live by the law of love. And by discerning the validity of a teaching by examining its fruit, believers could avoid falling into error.

In 1 John 3:16-24 perfect love is related to the absence of fear. Christ's sacrificial death is a beautiful example of the love for others that should characterize believers. Assurance of salvation comes through loving in deed and truth (3:19-24). The false teachers sounded as if they knew God, but their deeds

of hatred toward Christians betrayed them. Believers may be too strict or too lenient in their self-evaluations, but since God is omniscient, his evaluation will be just and fair (3:20).

Obedience confirms that believers are abiding in God (3:24). The witness of the Holy Spirit also serves to assure believers that they are God's own (cf. Rom. 8:9; 1 Cor. 12:13).

4:1-20 THE INCARNATION AND LOVE FOR EACH OTHER

4:1-6 The Doctrinal Battle: Jesus the Messiah Has Come in the Flesh

John moved from the importance of tangible obedience (3:24) to the experience of God's presence by his Spirit (4:1). He showed that the one who listens to God's truth is also of God's truth. Note the use of "believe" in 3:23; 4:1, 16; 5:1, 10, 13. The emphasis throughout these verses is on how believers can be assured that they and others have truly believed in God. The reference to the Spirit (3:24) raises the question of how to distinguish between true believers and false teachers who claim that the Spirit abides in them. Here John presented tests for truth and error. The first test is confession (4:2-3): What do they say about the deity and incarnation of Christ? The second test is their crowd (4:4-5): Who are they associated with and who listens to them? The third test is their consistency (4:6): Do they hear and obey the teaching of John and the other apostles (that is, apostolic doctrine)?

4:7-20 The Practical Battle: Loving One's Brother

4:7-10 THE SACRIFICE OF LOVE
John rounded out his test of truth regarding knowledge of God (3:14, 16, 19, 21, 24; 4:13, 17-18). He had already made the point that one must walk in the light, confess sin, keep God's commands, and love like Christ. At this point he added one more aspect: the

TRUE AND FALSE TEACHINGS

Two sources:	*Evil One*	*God*
Two teachings:	Anti-Christian	Christ/Apostolic Witness
Two acts:	Hate	Love

true definition and motivation for love. The false teachers had redefined love according to the lusts of the world (2:15-16; 3:12). First John 4:7-21 contains John's classic exposition on the nature of love. Since God is love, the believer who is begotten by God should be characterized by the same kind of sacrificial love (4:7). The supreme manifestation of God's love was the giving of his unique Son that believers might enjoy life, both abundant and eternal, in him (4:9). For "atoning sacrifice" (4:10; "propitiation," NASB and KJV), see the note on 2:2.

4:11-16 GOD'S PRESENCE IN LOVE
God has never been seen by humans, but when certain individuals show divine love, people come as close to seeing him as they can (4:12-13). Believers can know that they live in God and he in them because he has given them his Spirit. The love John was talking about was something concrete—something that follows the pattern of Christ. "Living" (4:15; "abiding," NASB and KJV) in God is the equivalent of confessing Jesus to be the Son of God; this includes keeping his commandments (3:24).

4:17-18 THE CONFIDENCE FROM LOVE
Confidence grows in believers as they match their acts of love in the world with God's loving nature. Believers should have confidence because they are like God. Perfect love is shown in acts that reveal God's character. See the concept of "as he is" in 3:2-3. When God comes to judge the world, only that which conforms to his will and nature will remain. God will selectively destroy all that does not conform to his will. In 4:17 the relationship between God's will, his commands, and his character is clarified ("as he is"). He will spare those from destruction who conform to himself. The believer who has practiced love during his earthly life will be able to approach the judgment seat of Christ without fear of punishment.

4:19-20 THE OBLIGATORY CIRCLE OF LOVE: GOD AND HUMANS
These verses link back to 4:10. People never love God directly from an original starting point within themselves. Whatever love they bring to God is but a response to his infinite and original love in Christ. This means that the love of believers must be like the love shown by God. Therefore, those who say they love God but hate the people God loves show themselves in error.

4:21–5:12 ENABLEMENT FOR COMMANDMENT KEEPING
4:21–5:4 Ability through Faith
The test of true love for God is whether or not a person keeps God's commandments (4:21–5:4). John set forth three tests for true faith: (1) belief in Jesus, God's Son and the divine Messiah (5:1), (2) love for the brethren and for God (5:1-2), and (3) obedience to God's commandments (5:3). The commandment is to love the one born of God. And that commandment is not burdensome (5:3). John returned to the concept of "commandment" (cf. 2:4) because it was the only standard by which believers could judge their security as God's children and confirm the anti-Christian nature of those outside. Commandments are burdensome to those who cannot or will not keep them. Commandments are burdensome to the one who denies the possibility of sin and failure. But, for the person of faith, commandments are the way to victory. Failures are forgiven and the model of God's love in Christ stands, not as a frustratingly impossible hurdle to surmount, but as an encouraging model to follow. Commandments are burdensome only to those not born of God. God has both required and enabled believers to keep his commands. Love for God is not mystical, as the false teachers argued, but behavioral—the keeping of God's commands. The present tense of "overcomes" (5:5) implies a continuous battle, while the past tense of "has overcome" (5:4) indicates an assured victory.

5:5-12 The Validation of Faith
5:5 OVERCOMING AND FAITH
The ideas of commandments not being burdensome (5:3) and overcoming the world (5:4-5) are closely linked. The pressures of the world are against obedience to God. Only the power and grace unlocked by the faith of believers can lift the burdens weighted against God's commands. The "overcomer" is identified as the one who is a believer in Jesus Christ, God's divine Son.

5:6-9 VALIDATION

John spent much time at the end of his letter proving that Jesus came in the flesh. This was because without a Christ who came fully in the flesh, believers do not have God's true witness. And without God's witness they do not have his Son. And without his Son they do not have eternal life. The assertion, therefore, of Christ's flesh is no mere academic trifle. It makes a literal life or death difference for humanity. The three witnesses that are unified in their testimony concerning Jesus are the Holy Spirit (cf. Acts 10:38; Matt. 12:31-32), the water (that is, Jesus' baptism; Mark 1:9-11), and the blood (Jesus' death; Heb. 9:12). These three witnesses attest to the same truth about Christ and are therefore wholly reliable (cf. Deut. 19:15). The Holy Spirit is the divine and active force of witness in the community. The three witnesses are a single unit (1 John 5:9). Believers cannot reject a part of God's witness without rejecting the whole.

5:10-12 THE RESULTS

The security of believers comes back to the character of God. He is truthful and always faithful. Believers must follow Christ and exhibit his presence in their lives to prove the validity of their faith. Verse 5:12 summarizes all the testable aspects of salvation that John has elaborated on throughout the letter.

5:13-21 THE INDISPENSABLE ADVOCACY OF CHRIST
5:13-17 The Resumption of Intercession for Sin

There are two problems addressed in this section. The first is an insecurity concerning whether or not God hears prayer. The second is whether or not believers should pray for sinning Christians. What were in view were wrong judgments of sin that cause intercessory prayer to cease.

Here John linked the confidence of believers in God to their requests to him in prayer (3:21-22). Praying for sinning Christians is not an incidental concern used to illustrate praying with confidence. It was a very practical thrust of the letter. One purpose of John's letter was to give believers assurance of their eternal life (cf. John

5:24; 17:3). Now he showed them what to do with their confidence in God. False teachers, by claiming that a believer in true fellowship with God never sins, had created a problem. When Christians saw sin in another's life, they were not certain if they should pray for that person. So John had to clarify, in a way similar to 1 John 1:6–2:3, that the sins of Christians were to be confessed and prayed for.

John taught that there are two categories of sin—one leads to death, the other does not. He stressed that there was sin that did not lead to deat possibly because his readers thought all sin led to death (5:17). For "all wrongdoing," see the similar phrase in 1:9 ("all unrighteousness"). If all unrighteousness is sin, then John had an exception in mind that led to death. It was perhaps a sin that was not to be prayed for (5:16), for John was non-committal about praying for it (5:16).

There is considerable debate regarding the sin leading "to death." The basic views are: (1) A specific sin punishable by death (cf. Lev. 20:1-27); (2) renunciation of the faith and denial of Christ; (3) blasphemy against the Holy Spirit (Matt. 12:31-32); and (4) a state of persistent sin judged with physical death (1 Cor. 11:30). It is possible that John is contrasting spiritual life (5:13) with spiritual death (5:16). And he may be using the term "brother" in a broad sense, like "neighbor" (2:9, 11; 3:16-17). These considerations, along with the context, suggest that John is referring to the persistent rejection of the gospel by the "antichrists," or false teachers. John does not explicitly forbid praying for such people, but he does not advise it.

Being an antichrist is the one class of sin in this letter that is clearly outside the usual bounds of human unrighteousness brought under the cleansing blood of Christ (2:18-22). Nowhere did John say that believers should pray for the antichrist's conversion or the salvation of his followers. Normal world hatred and denial of Christ was not in John's view here. In view were a group that claimed fellowship with God on the basis of Christ, used all the Christian terminology, and yet adamantly denied the truth of Christ's literal atoning death (cf. 2:26).

5:18-21 A Summary of the Work of God in Christ

The section of 5:18-19 gives the final context for the sin unto death. In view was the habitual sin of the antichrists, those who had been touched by the "evil one" and were children of the devil (3:10). It is apparent that John was not writing an evangelistic tract. He had clearly laid the lines of siege separating God and Satan (5:19). His concern here was not saving the lost but affirming and assuring the saved.

"The true God and eternal life" (5:20) is often replaced with false replicas. This explains John's mention of idols in 5:21. It also reveals the essential error of the antichrists against which John argued throughout the letter. Antichrists are not those who deny Christ and substitute a deity of another name. The essence of anti-Christian heresy is to keep the name and acts of Christ but remove all reference to the atoning work of the reality of Christ's blood. The antichrists' idol looks like Christ on the outside but has the life of Satan coursing through its veins. The warning against idols is a most appropriate warning for readers in the ancient society of pagan Rome or for modern-society believers today. An "idol" is any substitute for God.

2 John

HISTORICAL SETTING

This letter from John the apostle was addressed to the "chosen lady and her children" (1:1). This may refer to a church or an individual. Taking this as a metaphor carrying the idea of "church" seems out of harmony with the simplicity of the message (cf. 1:13). It is most likely that the addressee of this letter was an individual Christian woman and her family. She apparently had a sister whose children were in Ephesus and had contact with John's ministry there.

In Ephesus John had apparently become acquainted with the children of the "chosen lady" and was pleased to find them walking in the truth. From them John learned of the false teachers who were denying the humanity of Jesus (1:7). Second John is simpler than 1 John and makes a good introduction to it. The common elements between the letters form a needed repetition. The false teachers in both letters seem to be of the same heretical nature.

AUTHOR

The author's name is not mentioned in the letter. He is simply identified as "the elder," which has caused some to conclude that the letter was authored by someone other than John the apostle. The simple title, however, implies that the author had unique preeminence. A lesser author would have needed to begin his letter with authoritative titles. The letter bears a close resemblance in language and thought to 1 John (cf. 2 John 1:9 with 1 John 2:23; 4:20; 3:6). The references to "truth" (1:1-4), "love" (1:5-6), "obedience" (1:6), "antichrist" (1:7), and "abiding" (1:8) are certainly typical of the apostle John.

DATE

The false teaching mentioned in the letter links it closely with the circumstances of 1 John. The references to the "new commandment" (1:5) and "the antichrist" (1:7) depend upon the fuller development of these concepts in 1 John. Quite probably it was written soon after 1 John had been sent, around A.D. 90.

PURPOSE

The letter of 2 John was designed to warn believers of the dangerous error infiltrating the church. John did this by exposing the nature of the false teachers and their doctrine. John also intended for the letter to challenge his readers to brotherly love and self-examination.

GUIDING CONCEPTS

This short letter vigorously hammers away at a single concept: participate only with those who love God and keep his commandments. Note the uses of "commandment" in 1:4, 5-6; "walking in truth" in 1:4; "teaching" three times in 1:9-10; "work" in 1:11; and notice the repetition of "truth," mentioned five times in 1:1-4.

BIBLE-WIDE CONCEPTS

The brief letter contains references to Christ's new covenant teaching on love and commandment keeping ("abides in us"). John revealed details of the kingdom struggle on a personal level, the struggle between antichrists and Christians, a struggle that goes all the way back to the struggle in Genesis 3:15.

NEEDS MET BY SECOND JOHN

This letter from John answered some basic questions about how Christians should draw the lines of fellowship with religious opponents. The original readers were faced with many traveling ministers who came in the name of Christ but were really imposters who taught lies about Christ, specifically that he never really came in the flesh. The denial that Christ had a human body led to the denial of Christ's physical death on the cross. Salvation became a matter of spiritual illumination rather than acceptance of Christ's death in payment for sin. The structure and content of 2 John show that John was answering questions like the following for his readers.

- What is the basic requirement for Christian belief and practice?
- What is lost if believers abandon the belief that Jesus came in the flesh?
- How can believers know Christian love when they see it?

While believers today often think that they are very sophisticated and able to tell whether someone is telling the truth about God or not, John warns that anyone is capable of being deceived (1:8). In the search for love (1:5-6) it is easy to miss the truth that love has a very specific sign: conformity to the commandments of God. John clearly revealed what lies at the heart of God's commandments: belief that Jesus came in the flesh. Without the link of Jesus to human flesh, it is easy to lose the link between believing Christian truth and living ("fleshing") that belief out in one's daily life. John's great desire was for believers to exhibit God's love, in true Christian behavior and not be religious counterfeits.

OUTLINE OF SECOND JOHN

A. GREETING IN LOVE AND TRUTH (1:1-3)
B. THANKSGIVING AND CONSEQUENT EXHORTATIONS (1:4-11)
    1. Thanksgiving (1:4)
    2. The First Exhortation: Love One Another (1:5-7)
    3. The Second Exhortation: Watch Yourselves (1:8-9)
    4. The Third Exhortation: Do Not Receive Them (1:10-11)
C. CONCLUSION: PREFERENCE FOR A PASTORAL VISIT (1:12-13)

SECOND JOHN NOTES

1:1-3 GREETING IN LOVE AND TRUTH

The term "elder" (1:1), rather than "apostle," has caused some to conclude that the letter was authored by someone other than the apostle John. However, the title would be especially fitting for the apostle John who was advanced in years at the time of writing. John addressed the letter to the "chosen lady" (1:1). On "chosen," see John 15:16. This has been understood by some interpreters as a personification of the church as the bride of Christ (cf. Eph. 5:29-32). But the reference to her "children" seems to suggest an individual rather than the church. John appears to have been writing a Christian woman and her family. Perhaps a church met in her home and would have benefited from the letter.

John began his letter by laying out the framework for understanding "love in the truth" (1:1). He was concerned that truth have an impact on the deeds of those who claimed to believe it. They were not to love because they felt like it but because their love was true. The future (1:2, "will be with us forever") gives believers an eternal model for present behavior. The truth "lives in us" now. The "truth" (1:2), a term used five times in the first four verses, is central to the message of this letter.

1:4-11 THANKSGIVING AND CONSEQUENT EXHORTATIONS

1:4 Thanksgiving

Walking in truth is the key thought in the letter. It came as a command directly from God the Father (cf. 1:3, 9). John rejoiced to find some of the lady's children "walking in truth," a metaphor for godly living, ordering one's life by the truth of God's word.

1:5-7 The First Exhortation: Love One Another

Second John 1:5 gives a reminder and 1:6 defines it. The framework is the commands of God (1:4-6). The concept of walking in truth begins and ends in 1:4-6. The "new commandment" was taught by Jesus in John 13:34-35. Love is defined in terms of obeying Christ's commandments (cf. John 14:15). Second John 1:7 supplies a reason for the exhortation in 1:5 and specifies one aspect of the truth. The basic error of the false teachers was a denial of the incarnation of Christ (cf. John 1:14).

1:8-9 The Second Exhortation: Watch Yourselves

To deny that Christ came in the flesh would result in losing heavenly reward. Second John 1:9 critiques the wrong theology of the antichrists. They went beyond the limits of Christ's own teaching, as if he had only given insufficient teachings while on earth. The indispensible link between people and God is the truth of Christ. The presence of error calls for self-examination on the part of believers lest the false teachers hinder the work of the ministry, resulting in a loss of reward at the judgment seat of Christ (cf. 1 Cor. 3:10-15; 2 Cor. 5:10). Obedience, not mere profession, is the mark of true faith (John 3:36; Titus 1:16).

1:10-11 The Third Exhortation: Do Not Receive Them

Second John 1:10 describes a point-by-point examination of doctrine. John does not advocate fellowship with heretics, those who substitute the teaching of Satan under the guise of Christ's. He is not speaking of a need to agree on every minor point of doctrine. To fellowship with antichrists is to fellowship with their destructive actions. Apparently, false teachers were being entertained in the homes of the believers in the name of hospitality. The command "do not take him into your house" (1:10) relates to the heretic who seeks entrance among Christian communities in order to do his proselytizing among them. The apostle was referring to false teachers, not simply those who have been led astray and deluded by false doctrine. While hospitality is forbidden, mildness, politeness, and respectfulness to all mankind ought to be characteristic of those who know Christ. Verse 1:11 describes

true guilt by association. To be on friendly terms with the evil, unbelieving, hostile world is to be God's enemy (cf. James 4:4).

1:12-13 CONCLUSION: PREFERENCE FOR A PASTORAL VISIT

The concept of joy looks back to 1 John 1:4 and before that to Christ's words in John 15:10-11. In his closing words, John anticipated a personal visit to complete his words of instruction. He would rather talk than write. Paper in ancient times was made from papyrus reeds that were cut into strips and pressed together at right angles. The procedure produced a stiff, durable writing paper. The word "ink" simply means "black," since in ancient times most ink was made from charcoal.

3 John

BASIC FACTS

HISTORICAL SETTING
The addressee of this letter was the beloved Gaius. Three other men in the New
Testament are known by this rather common name (cf. Acts 19:29; 20:4; Rom.
16:23; 1 Cor. 1:14). It is not likely that this Gaius is to be identified with any other
in the New Testament. He was a "dear friend" of the apostle John. John had received
a report from some of his itinerant representatives who had visited the district where
Gaius lived (1:3). The apostle enlisted the help of Gaius to assure acceptance of
and support for the ministering brethren who had been attacked by a man named
Diotrephes (1:5-10).

AUTHOR
The author of this letter is not named. He is identified as "the elder." The style and
thought of the letter unites it with 2 John and points to the authorship of the apostle
John. Both letters stress "truth" (2 John 1:1-4; 3 John 1:1, 2-4, 8) and refer to hospitality (2 John 1:10-11; 3 John 1:5, 8). The author of both letters rejoices over those
who are "walking in truth." In both letters the author expresses in almost identical
language his intention to visit the readers (2 John 1:12; 3 John 1:14).

DATE
The letter was probably written about the same time as 2 John. It is unlikely that
3 John 1:9 refers to either 1 or 2 John. The letter referred to in 1:9 would have been
intended for a small circle of readers and has probably been lost. It must be assumed
that the second and third letters were written about the same time, around A.D. 90.

PURPOSE
This letter by John was designed to encourage the believers under the shadow of
Roman persecution by reminding them of the ultimate victory of Christ over his
enemies. He also warned the churches of the dangers of spiritual lethargy and
apostasy. Another purpose was to bring the Old Testament prophecy and promises

to full consummation, showing how God would deal with the nations, judge sin on the earth, establish his kingdom, and bring in everlasting righteousness. The final purpose is to present a picture of the glory of Christ in directing the churches, judging the world, and ruling his kingdom.

GUIDING CONCEPTS

As in 2 John, the apostle spoke of "walking in truth" (3 John 1:1, 3-4) and then illustrated the particular aspect of truth the readers needed to hear (1:8, 12). Here the need was for welcoming the true ministers of Christ. In 1 John the apostle warned not to welcome false teachers. In 2 John to welcome false teachers was to participate in their deeds (2 John 1:11). In 3 John to welcome true ministers was to participate in the truth (3 John 1:8).

BIBLE-WIDE CONCEPTS

Both 2 and 3 John give historical clues to understanding the situation of 1 John concerning the need to assert the truth of God's full incarnation in Christ. The commandment of Christ was that believers love one another (John 13:34). Third John gives a specific example of that love relating to traveling ministers of Christ.

NEEDS MET BY THIRD JOHN

This letter from John answered questions concerning church authority and traveling teachers. The readers faced a conflict between the apostle John and one of their church leaders. In that light, John showed them how to apply God's truth to the situation, thus avoiding a personal confrontation. The structure and content of 3 John show that John was answering questions like the following for his readers.
- Why should Christians be hospitable to traveling ministers of Christ?
- What is the basis for church discipline and authority?

John gives two good examples of how to apply God's truth to life's situations. The first was a simple application of truth to helping ministers traveling for Christ. The second illustrates the use of truth in church conflicts. The truth realistically states the problems involved but also drives the hearers to a deeper experience of God's love.

OUTLINE OF THIRD JOHN

A. INTRODUCTION: APOSTOLIC JOY (1:1-4)
B. APOSTOLIC CORRECTION: HOSPITALITY TO MISSIONARIES (1:5-12)
    1. Gaius's Faithfulness (1:5-8)
    2. Diotrephes' Challenge (1:9-10)
    3. Demetrius as a Model and an Ally (1:11-12)
C. CONCLUSION AND GREETING (1:13-14)

THIRD JOHN NOTES

1:1-4 INTRODUCTION: APOSTOLIC JOY

John hoped that the external prosperity of Gaius and the believers matched the prosperity of their souls (1:2). John referred to himself as the "elder," a less authoritative designation than "apostle" (cf. 2 John 1:1). The letter was addressed to Gaius, possibly the Gaius of Derbe (Acts 20:4), the Gaius of Corinth (Rom. 16:23), the Gaius of Macedonia (Acts 19:29), or Gaius the bishop of Pergamos (*Apostolic Constitutions,* 7.40). Perhaps Gaius had been recently ill. John began the letter with a prayer for Gaius's health and prosperity. For the phrase "walk in truth" (1:3), see the note on 2 John 1:4. John used the term "children" to refer to his spiritual children, those who had been converted or discipled under his ministry.

1:5-12 APOSTOLIC CORRECTION: HOSPITALITY TO MISSIONARIES
1:5-8 Gaius's Faithfulness

John assured his readers of the correctness of Gaius's actions in caring for traveling ministers (1:5). The basis of their hospitality was the name of Christ (1:7). They were to participate with truth, not personalities. Hospitality is not only an opportunity but an obligation (Rom. 12:13) and a qualification for elders (1 Tim. 3:2). The missionaries went out to minister for the sake of Jesus' name (1:7). They accepted no support from unbelieving "pagans" lest it should appear that they had compromised the gospel or were selling salvation. Paul's strategy was the same (cf. 1 Cor. 9; 2 Cor. 11:7-15). The work of the ministry is to be supported by believers, not unbelievers.

In 1:8 John presented the believers with an obligation and an opportunity; he asked them to share in the support of those proclaiming the name of Christ. Those who share financially in such a ministry "work together" (1:8) for the truth. Giving allows them to have a ministry in other lands as co-laborers with dedicated missionaries.

1:9-10 Diotrephes' Challenge

Diotrephes was characterized as being one who loved to be first. The particular problem revolved around interchurch relations with regard to receiving traveling ministers. He had apparently accused John with wicked words. The arrogance of Diotrephes was demonstrated by his ambition to be pre-eminent in the church and his rejection of apostolic authority. He had usurped authority by excommunicating (1:10, "puts them out of the church") believers who were exercising hospitality.

1:11-12 Demetrius as a Model and an Ally

Third John 1:11 calls Diotrephes' salvation into question. The evil deeds of Diotrephes evidenced that he did not really know God (cf. James 2:16-26). The contrast was Demetrius (1:12). He was probably the bearer of the letter and an ally with John. Demetrius received a good testimony from other believers and "by the truth itself" (1:12), that is, his life squared with the truth.

1:13-14 CONCLUSION AND GREETING

John had more to say but would have preferred to say it in person rather than by letter. In some ancient texts, the phrase "Peace to you" (1:14) begins a new verse.

Jude

BASIC FACTS

HISTORICAL SETTING
The specific locality of the readers of this letter is unknown. They had heard of the words of the apostles and were acquainted with the teachings of Paul (1:18-19). The letter dealt with an outbreak of false teaching. The problem is similar to that mentioned in 2 Peter 2:1-2, 10. The false teachers who had crept into the church were denying Christ and perverting the doctrine of grace, considering immoral indulgence perfectly legitimate (1:4). They were guilty of rejecting authority and preferred their own dreamings to God's revelation (1:8). These people were critical of the orthodox doctrine of angels and used language against good angels that even Michael the archangel did not dare use against evil angels (1:8-10). They were ruled by their passions (1:4, 16) and scoffed at the accepted Christian ways (1:17). The character and activity of the false teachers was certain evidence that they were devoid of God's Spirit (1:16, 19).

AUTHOR
Jude, the brother of James (1:1), was one of Jesus' half brothers (cf. Matt. 13:55; Mark 6:3). The author would not have been Judas the apostle, the son (or brother) of James (Luke 6:16) because the author seems to distinguish himself from the apostles (Jude 1:17). Little is known about him. Although he was not a believer until after the resurrection (John 7:5; Acts 1:14), he no doubt was influenced by his devout parents and the personal contact he had with Jesus. Jude and some of the other believing brothers of the Lord later engaged in some itinerant preaching (1 Cor. 9:5).

DATE
Jude 1:17-18 relates closely to 2 Peter 3:2-3. The lack of mentioning the downfall of Jerusalem may indicate a date before A.D. 70, possibly around A.D. 65–68.

PURPOSE

This letter from Jude was designed to encourage its readers to contend for the orthodox faith (1:3), to remind them of the certain divine judgment upon the ungodly
(1:5), and to instruct the believers how to offset the evil effects of the false teachers
(1:17-23). Jude did not refute the heretical doctrine of the false teachers, nor did
he outline the specifics of orthodox belief. His purposes were simply to denounce
heretical doctrine and to warn readers of the certain judgment that would come upon
those who pursued such wicked ways.

GUIDING CONCEPTS

The basic elements of Jude center on contending (1:3) for the faith. But the letter
immediately moves on to a long description of the opponents of the faith (1:4-16)
with no specifics as to how to contend against them. This section is followed by a
reminder of how these opponents were predicted by the apostles (1:17-19). But,
again, Jude gave no specific information on contending with them. Next the readers
are encouraged to be built up and kept in the love of God (1:20-21). Finally, Jude
urged the believers to be merciful to those who doubted and who were sinning
(1:22-23). All the while, they were to maintain a holy hatred for coruption (1:23).

Putting all of this together, believers can understand what Jude meant by "contend
for the faith" (1:3). Jude did not advise believers to argue hotly with the false teachers. Instead he told them to seek to understand the evil nature of their opponents and
to remember their part in God's prophetic plan. He urged them to build themselves
up in the love of God and mercifully try to correct and save those who would listen.
In a word, contending is not winning a doctrinal argument. It is striving to win a
brother or sister to Christ.

BIBLE-WIDE CONCEPTS

Jude pulled information from several Old Testament events such as the exodus
(1:5), the destruction of Sodom and Gomorrah (1:7), and the wicked deeds of
Cain, Balaam, and Korah (1:11). He also drew from the New Testament teachings
of the apostles (1:17). This short letter shows that the events it describes are
completely in line with God's perfect plan from the beginning of God's word.
Jude's harsh condemnation of sinners coupled with his command to mercifully
seek their redemption has affinities with James 5:19-20.

NEEDS MET BY JUDE

The letter from Jude provides helpful answers for those in the middle of debates
about true belief and proper Christian behavior. The readers needed to know why
the opponents could look so good and yet be so condemned by God. They also
needed to know how to contend with the false teachers without falling into error
and stumbling. The structure and content of Jude's letter show that he was answering questions like the following for his readers.

• Why are there so many false teachers in the church?

• The false teachers appear to be so good, but what are they really like?

• What priorities should believers maintain when they debate with false teachers?

Jude tells believers how to cope with the fighting and false teaching often found in the church. The first reaction of sincere believers may be to wonder how so many contentious people got into the church and why God let this happen. Second, they might want to respond with equally destructive hostility. But Jude reminded the believers to purify the church by avoiding the false teachers, and, if possible, by extending God's grace and offer of salvation to them.

OUTLINE OF JUDE

A. GREETING (1:1-2)

B. DESCRIPTION OF THE FALSE TEACHERS (1:3-16)

  1. The Problem and Past Examples (1:3-7)

  2. The False Teachers Described (1:8-16)

C. EXHORTATIONS TO HOLINESS AND MERCY (1:17-23)

D. BENEDICTION (1:24-25)

JUDE NOTES

1:1-2 GREETING

The author identified himself as the brother of James. While there may have been another Jude with a brother named James, there was only one eminent, well-known James—the half brother of the Lord Jesus (James 1:1; Gal. 1:19; 2:9; 1 Cor. 15:7). Early church tradition confirms the view that this letter was authored by Jude, the half brother of Jesus. The readers were those who have been "called," "loved," and "kept." The rare greeting "mercy" (1:2) may be understood in light of the background of false teaching (2 John 1:3; 1 Tim. 1:2; 2 Tim. 1:2).

1:3-16 DESCRIPTION OF THE FALSE TEACHERS

1:3-7 The Problem and Past Examples

Jude had intended to write a doctrinal treatise, but upon hearing of the false teachers in the church, he decided it was more necessary to encourage and exhort the believers to contend for the faith. The word "contend" (1:3) suggests a striving as in an athletic contest. The false teachers had actually crept into the fellowship of the church and were using God's grace as a license to sin (1:4). In 1:5-7 Jude cited three

examples of past divine judgment to demonstrate to the false teachers the principle that God does judge the wicked. The first example (1:5) was from the period of the exodus. The second example (1:6) related to the sin of Genesis 6:1-4 (see note on Gen. 6:1-4). The third example is the judgment on Sodom and Gomorrah (Gen. 19). All three examples illustrate the fact that God judges unbelief and disobedience.

1:8-16 The False Teachers Described

In 1:8-16 Jude turned from the examples of the past to the false teachers of the present. These apostates were following the same pattern of unbelief and disobedience and were destined for a similar judgment. The basic charges against these false teachers were: immorality, insubordination, and presumption (1:8). In 1:9-10 Jude contrasted the restraint of Michael the archangel with the presumption of the apostates. When Michael contended with the devil about the body of Moses, he did not presume to use insulting words or appeal to his own authority. If an angel was careful in what he said, how much more should mortals be careful. This incident is described more fully in the

noncanonical, or apocryphal, book called
the Assumption of Moses. Jude's reference
indicates that he affirmed the truth of this
incident. Both Jude and the writer of the
Assumption of Moses may have drawn
upon a common tradition. In 1:11 three
examples of God's judgment on the wicked
are presented: Cain (Gen. 4:4-9; Heb. 11:4;
1 John 3:12), Balaam (Num. 22–24; 2 Pet.
2:15; Rev. 2:14), and Korah (Num. 16).

In 1:12-13 Jude described the character
of the false teachers. As Jesus said, "By their
fruit you will recognize them" (Matt. 7:16).
The "love-feasts" (1:12) were fellowship
meals eaten in connection with the observance of the Lord's Supper (cf. 1 Cor. 11:20).
In 1:14-16 Jude interpreted the prophecy
of the noncanonical book of Enoch to be a
prediction of the judgment that will fall
upon such apostates and false teachers at
the second coming of Christ. It is likely that
the original prophecy was uttered by Enoch
(Gen. 5:19-24; Heb. 11:5-6), and it was later
incorporated into the book of Enoch. Jude
knew of the prophecy and recorded it by
divine inspiration.

1:17-23 EXHORTATIONS TO HOLINESS AND MERCY

In 1:17-19 Jude warned the believers to
guard themselves from doctrinal error by
remembering the apostolic teaching. The
"last times" (1:18) are equivalent to the
"last days" (cf. 2 Tim. 3:1). In 1:22-23 Jude
reflected on three kinds of defectors and
directed his readers in dealing appropriately

with each situation. First, they were to "be
merciful" to the doubters (1:22). The primary
need was to convince the doubters of the
truth. Second, they were to "save" those who
could be saved (1:23). The "others" seems
to refer to those who have already become
involved in the false teaching but are not
beyond help. No effort should be spared to
snatch them from the error. Third, they were
to separate from apostates those who were
confirmed in their error. One can only pity
them and take care not to become defiled by
their false teaching. The "clothing stained
by corrupted flesh" (1:23) may allude to
the requirement of Leviticus 13:47-52 that
a garment contaminated with leprosy was
to be burnt.

1:24-25 BENEDICTION

In the benediction Jude praised God for his
power to preserve and perfect the believers
that they might one day stand faultless before
the glorious person of Christ. This benediction takes its place with some other outstanding benedictions throughout Scripture.
Aaron blessed the nation of Israel by invoking the character of God upon it (Num.
6:24-26). Paul emphasized the access of
believers to God through Christ (Rom.
16:25-27) and the total power and control
of God (Rom. 11:36). Jude's benediction
contrasts stumbling with arriving safely
"before his glorious presence" and places the
lives and great hopes of believers squarely
in the middle of God's past, present, and
future glory and sovereignty.

Revelation

BASIC FACTS

HISTORICAL SETTING

The original readers were seven churches of Asia (Rev. 1:4) identified as the churches in Ephesus (2:1), Smyrna (2:8), Pergamum (1:12), Thyatira (2:18), Sardis (3:1), Philadelphia (3:7), and Laodicea (3:14). These were the leading cities of the province of Asia and were connected by a road on which one could make a complete circuit from Ephesus to Laodicea, passing through all seven cities.

Revelation was received by John while he was in exile. Patmos was a small rocky island in the Aegean Sea off the coast of Asia Minor, about thirty-five miles southwest of Miletus. The island served as a place of banishment during the time of Roman rule. The small mountainous island measures only six by ten miles. John had been exiled to the island as part of Domitian's persecution against the Christians.

During the period of Roman rulers from Nero to Domitian, emperor worship became the official policy of Rome. Not all the emperors took their divine honors seriously, but Domitian did and took steps to enforce them. He took the title of "Lord and God" and proclaimed his infant son a god and his mother, Domitia, a goddess. The Christians refused to worship Domitian and as a result were severely persecuted under his reign. It was probably the refusal of John to submit to the imperial decree of emperor worship that led to his exile on Patmos. The persecution of the believers during the reign of Domitian is reflected in the message of Revelation (1:9; 2:10, 13; 6:9). Eusebius recorded that the apostle John returned to Ephesus upon being released from exile after the accession of Nerva in A.D. 96.

AUTHOR

Tradition ascribes the authorship of Revelation to John the apostle. The author calls himself John (1:1, 4, 9; 22:8). The author received his revelation while on the island of Patmos where the apostle John remained until after the death of Domitian in A.D. 96. There are also many resemblances between Revelation and John's Gospel. Only in Revelation 19:13, John 1:1, 14, and 1 John 1:1 is "Word" used for the person of Christ.

THE SEVEN CHURCHES

The seven churches were located on a major Roman road. A letter carrier would leave the island of Patmos (where John was exiled), arriving first at Ephesus. He would travel north to Smyrna and Pergamum (Pergamos), turn southeast to Thyatira, and continue on to Sardis, Philadelphia, and Laodicea—in the exact order in which the letters were dictated.

Jesus is referred to as the Lamb in John 1:29, 36 and twenty-eight times in Revelation (and implied as the Passover lamb by the constant mention of the Passover in John 11:55; 12:1, 20; 13:1; 18:28, 39; 19:14, 31, 42). The expression "springs of living water" or its equivalent is found only in Revelation 7:17; 21:6; and John 4:14; 7:38.

DATE
The weight of historical evidence points to a date toward the end of the reign of Domitian in A.D. 95 or 96. This later date allows for the growth and decline of the churches in Asia. The book reflects considerable persecution (Rev. 1:9; 2:10, 13; 6:9), and this certainly would have been the case during Domitian's rule. He initiated persecution against Christians who refused to worship him. Revelation is best dated toward the end of the reign of Domitian, around A.D. 96.

PURPOSE
The book of Revelation was designed to encourage believers under the shadow of Roman persecution by showing them the ultimate victory of Christ over his enemies and to warn churches of the dangers of spiritual disobedience. The book achieves this by bringing the Old Testament prophecy and promises to completion, showing how God will deal with the nations, judge sin on the earth, establish his kingdom, and bring in everlasting righteousness. Christ's glory in directing the churches, judging the world, and ruling his kingdom is the central feature of this book.

GEOGRAPHY AND ITS IMPORTANCE

THE SEVEN CHURCHES
The book of Revelation is a letter addressed to seven churches. The order in which those seven churches are addressed in the letter matches one possible route for its delivery. The seven churches were on a roughly circular road that connected the cities of the western part of the province of Asia. The letter may have left John's home on the island of Patmos, arrived in Ephesus, moved on to Smyrna and Pergamum, and then circled southeast to Thyatira, Sardis, Philadelphia, and Laodicea.

GUIDING CONCEPTS

THE NATURE OF THE BOOK
One aspect of interpreting and applying Revelation concerns the exotic images it uses. Modern readers can easily identify with the control of God over history, his long conflict with Satan, and his coming judgment. But Revelation presents these events in a type of literature that makes little sense to today's readers. Trumpets, bowls of wrath, fire from heaven, mountains falling into the sea, beasts emerging from the smoke that issues up from the core of the earth, dragons, and many-headed beasts stand outside the usual ideas about God and his present work on earth. Such imagery sounds like science fiction and myth. Not only that, but understanding such imagery seems to lie beyond any interpretive scheme. What do these images mean today? The interpretation believers come to will be greatly enhanced if they first understand that the book represents three different literary forms.

THREE LITERARY FORMS IN REVELATION

First of all, the book is a letter (1:4), as seen by its form and style. This letter was written to meet a particular need or set of needs in the first-century church. It contains a greeting (1:4-7). It ends with a benediction (22:21). The fact that it was written as a letter sets Revelation apart from other prophetic and apocalyptic litera-ture. John intended the book to meet the immediate needs of the first-century churches (cf. 2:10, 13).

Second, the book is a prophecy (1:3). As with all prophetic literature, this proph-ecy refers to the future's impact on the present comfort and obedience of its readers, in this case, believers in the first century A.D. (cf. 22:7, 10, 18-19). This revelation of the future was designed to meet the needs of honest curiosity and hunger for God. The future becomes the motivation to fulfill God's will in the present. In common with all prophecy, Revelation sets the call for present obedience within the context of the history of mankind's resistance to God's will. As prophecy, Revelation was given for the same reason prophecy was given throughout Scripture: because God's people were unfaithful.

Third, the book is filled with a literary form called apocalyptic. Apocalyptic contains the presentation, in highly figurative language, of a radical shift from this age into the next (1:1). The word "apocalyptic" means "that which is revealed." The subject of apocalyptic literature is always the day of the Lord.

The period between the Old and New Testaments was a time of silence. Although the people living during that silence had great faith in God, they were not seeing the promises for Israel fulfilled. The promises seemed far away, and the people were asking why there was so much evil in the world. This was the situation the writers of extra-biblical apocalyptic literature were addressing as well. They asserted that God was still at work among his people, and through their writings they called for a response of faith in adverse times. The righteous remnant of the Jews preserved these writings, and as Christianity arose, Christians identified with and preserved these writings.

CHARACTERISTICS OF APOCALYPTIC WRITINGS

The following are some characteristics of apocalyptic literature: (1) Apocalyptic literature found outside the Bible usually does not give the author's name. Biblical apocalyptic literature does. For example, see Daniel and Revelation. (2) Historical events are described figuratively. The content concerns the end times. Beasts are used for people, and the use of numbers is also important, for example, 3, 4, 7, 10, 12. (3) In apocalyptic writings a great person from the past leads the author on a heavenly journey (e.g., Moses, Elijah, Adam, Enoch, Noah). In John's revelation, Jesus is the one who leads the author. (4) Extra-biblical apocalyptic literature presents a pessimistic worldview. Apocalyptic usually addressed a small group of the faithful, exhorting them to persevere despite the evil and suffering in the world. It brought comfort rather than castigation. In John's Revelation, the present world is shown to be hopeless. But the hopeless present is offset by a promise of future victory for those who stand firm and "do not shrink from death" (12:11). The Lamb gives present history meaning. Apocalyptic writings outside of the Bible answered the question, Why are we being persecuted? By contrast, the prophetic element in John's Revelation asks believers why they are sinning and commands them to stop it.

In summary, because Revelation contains the traditional imagery of apocalyptic, it is not concerned with detailing each event that will usher in God's future kingdom. Its concern is to impact its readers with a summary picture of future blessings and judgments. God used this medium because he wanted believers to be more impressed with the impact of the coming kingdom than with the identification of specific events that would come in the future. And though these events are described in figurative apocalyptic imagery, they also carry the message of all the Bible's prophets: the call to repentance and perseverance. The explosive images of prophetic apocalyptic emphasize the only logical remedy for sin: re-creation on both a personal and cosmic level. See Amos 8:8-9; 9:5-6 (760 B.C.) and the book of Joel (835 B.C.) for early examples of prophetic apocalyptic in the Bible. The re-creation of the world will not come through the normal flow of historical events but only by God's direct replacement of the old universe with the new.

Apocalyptic literature is just one of many background areas of study that are helpful for Bible students in understanding John's Revelation. A study of the book also requires a sound knowledge of both the Old and New Testaments. But an appreciation of the aspects that Revelation and apocalyptic literature have in common clarifies the literary reasons for the complex imagery it contains. Such an appreciation also points the way to a proper interpretation of the book, helping readers apply its prophetic call to live lives of obedience in the present age.

INTERPRETING THE BOOK OF REVELATION
Figurative imagery is only meaningful to the one who knows the future and the reality behind the figures used. Throughout history believers have matched God's prophetic promises with current events seeking to identify specific fulfillments of prophecy. But only God can identify the meaning behind the images used in Revelation. But modern readers can, at least, appreciate the effect of specific symbols even if they cannot be certain of the reality behind the figures used. A number of different approaches to interpreting Revelation have been used throughout the church's history.

Contemporary-Historical
This approach takes the view that everything symbolized in the book of Revelation found its fulfillment in the downfall of Jerusalem (A.D. 70) or of Rome (A.D. 476). This position views the events symbolized in the book as having been fulfilled by events contemporary to its original readers in the first century A.D. The events were symbolic of the destruction of either Jerusalem or Rome and have all long been fulfilled.

Historicist
According to this approach, the events symbolized in Revelation began at the time John wrote the book, but they continue into the present. This was the view of people like Wycliffe and Luther. This approach interprets the book recognizing that the events recorded in Revelation reflect events throughout the ongoing history of the church as believers await the coming kingdom.

Futurist

The futurist view generally sees the majority of events in Revelation as happening in the future. Those who hold this view may find foreshadowings of the future judgments in present events, but they believe that Revelation 4–19 represents future events only.

There are three variations of this view. The first variation sees Revelation 1–3 as relating to the first century church. The seven seals of Revelation 4–19 refer to a future period of tribulation climaxed by the return of Christ.

The second variation also sees Revelation 4–19 as referring to future tribulation and judgment but views the seven churches in 1–3 as symbols of churches throughout the ages and as possible stages in church history.

The third variation views the churches in the first three chapters as real historical churches but with lessons from which churches of all ages can profit. This view's main distinction concerns when the seven seals are opened. It holds that the opening of the seven seals began in the first century A.D., continues into the present, and will end at the future return of Christ. It does not see the seven churches of Revelation 1–3 as symbolic, and it places the severe tribulations and judgments of Revelation 4–19 in the future.

Timeless and Symbolic

In this view the churches and seals refer to the ageless conflict between God and Satan. The book is not to be interpreted with reference to any one set of historical events. The book presents the ageless struggle of the kingdom of God with the kingdom of Satan, concluding with God's final and complete triumph.

BIBLE-WIDE CONCEPTS

USE OF OLD AND NEW TESTAMENT THEMES

Revelation completes all the promises and predictions made throughout the Bible. It fulfills the promises for a new creation and a fully redeemed people who are able to dwell in the returned and unhindered presence of God. It also fulfills the promises for full judgment of sin and the vindication of God's holiness and justice. The themes of the temple and God's presence are fulfilled in the new earth. The central theme of God's redemption through the Lamb provides the power for both salvation and judgment.

EARTHQUAKES AND THE APPEARING OF GOD

The appearance of God is the foundation of the warnings and promises throughout Revelation. Throughout the Bible when God appears, the earth goes into convulsions at his holy presence. This relates to God's appearance in battles (Judg. 5:4-5; Mic. 1:4), in his reign over the nations (Pss. 97:5; 99:1), in activities prior to world judgment (Isa. 13:13; Ezek. 38:19-20), at the giving of the Mosaic covenant at Mount Sinai (Exod. 19:18; Ps. 68:8), and at the day of the Lord (Isa. 64:1-7; Joel 2:10). In Revelation, the future appearance of God is modeled on his past appearances to save or to judge.

Earthquakes are part of the signs involved in making way for the new heavens and earth (Matt. 24:7; Mark 13:8; Luke 21:11; Heb. 12:27). In the book of Revelation earthquakes occur at the seventh seal (Rev. 8:1), trumpet (11:15), and bowl (16:17;

cf. 8:5; 11:19; 16:18). The earthquakes are presented in words descriptive of the appearance of God at Mount Sinai (cf. 4:5; 6:12-17). Only one mountain shook in the desert of Sinai. But in Revelation God's appearance shakes the whole earth. Also, the divine appearance in Revelation is an appearance of Christ (1:7; 19:11-12).

NEEDS MET BY REVELATION

The book of Revelation speaks to the needs of the faithful believers and the unfaithful who are succumbing to the pressures of sin and persecution. Jesus had been away for what seemed like a very long time. The pain of persecution tempted some to wonder how God could be with them and how long it would be before he came back to set things right. The pleasures of wealth tempted some to abandon their zeal for Christ. They wondered why they should witness for Christ and risk losing everything they had worked so hard for and enjoyed so much. Faithful Christians wondered how much pain they would have to endure and needed to understand how their pain could be reconciled with God's love and justice. The structure and content of Revelation show that John was answering questions like the following for his readers.

- What does Jesus think about the present successes and failures of the church?
- What can believers expect in the period of time before Jesus returns?
- How will God ultimately be victorious over all of his powerful enemies?
- In what ways will believers be or not be protected from Satan's hostility?

The problems of the seven churches of Revelation 1–3 are identical with many of the problems of today's church. Believers today struggle with witnessing to unbelievers, keeping themselves morally pure, remaining steadfast through life's problems, and maintaining a vibrant love for God. All the overt and subtle forces of hell seem to stand against their attempts to give their best for God. Daily they find themselves attacked by evil forces, causing them to wonder if seeking God is really worth it. It becomes natural to lapse into moving mechanically through the motions of worship and Christian living.

Believers know the future holds an eternity of either reward and bliss or horrible suffering. But at times that future seems far off and unrelated to keeping people on track with God in the present. But John's Revelation breaks into the apathy and brings the future into crystal sharp focus. Revelation takes the vague and potentially non-motivating future and brings it alive in all its splendor and horror. It splashes a cold dose of reality over the church's apathetic attitudes. It wakes believers up to their materialism; it wakes them to their fears and apathy toward God and toward a world in need of the gospel. It also breeds a holy fear concerning how long people can continue in sin and apathy and how far they think they can push God's grace.

Revelation combines the need of believers to be evaluated by Jesus with their need to know about the trials of the future. Were it not for salvation in Christ, believers would suffer the judgments described in the book. That mixed sense of relief and fear should motivate those who are not truly committed to God to stop wasting time and despising God's grace. The book also meets the need of more faithful Christians by balancing the question, How long until Christ returns? with the concern about how a just God could allow world evil to go on for so long. The book clearly shows that Christians may experience unjust and evil deeds. But it also reveals the terror of God's judgment that is reserved for those who have rejected Christ.

OUTLINE OF REVELATION

A. THE SOURCE AND SETTING OF THE MESSAGE (1:1-20)
    1. Prologue (1:1-3)
    2. Greeting (1:4-8)
    3. Prophetic Commissioning (1:9-20)
B. PRESENT EXHORTATIONS TO THE CHURCHES (2:1–3:22)
    1. Ephesus (2:1-7)
    2. Smyrna (2:8-11)
    3. Pergamum (2:12-17)
    4. Thyatira (2:18-29)
    5. Sardis (3:1-6)
    6. Philadelphia (3:7-13)
    7. Laodicea (3:14-22)
C. FUTURE EXPECTATIONS FOR THE WORLD (4:1–22:5)
    1. The Perfect Source of Glory and of Judgment (4:1–5:14)
    2. Seven Seals Broken (6:1–8:1)
    3. The First Four Trumpets (8:2-12)
    4. The First Two Woes (8:13–9:21)
    5. The Little Book and the Two Prophets (10:1–11:14)
    6. Seventh Angel Sounds (11:15-19)
    7. The Dragon, the Beasts, and the Lamb (12:1–14:20)
    8. The First Bowl Emptied (15:1–16:2)
    9. The Second through Seventh Bowls (16:3-21)
    10. The Woman and the Beast (17:1-18)
    11. Babylon's Downfall Described (18:1-24)
    12. The Marriage of the Lamb (19:1-21)
    13. A Final Rebellion Is Put Down (20:1-15)
    14. The Perfection of Creation's Glory (21:1–22:5)
D. BLESSINGS AND CURSES (22:6-21)

REVELATION NOTES

1:1-20 THE SOURCE AND SETTING OF THE MESSAGE

Overview: Revelation 1 sets the context for the book. The prologue (1:1-3) shows that Revelation came from God through Christ, an angel, and John. It also presents the purpose of the book: blessing from hearing and heeding the book's message. Throughout the book the hidden message of God is centered on the contents of a scroll with seven seals (5:5, 7; 6:1, 3, 5, 7, 9, 12; 8:1). It is the vision of Christ in 1:9-20 and the contents of the scroll that contain the revelation. The vision of Christ for the churches shows that he is at present the awesome and potentially lethal God who will in the future come to judge the world.

1:1-3 Prologue

The prologue was composed by John after he experienced the visions recorded in the book. He used this prologue to introduce his readers to what the book was about and how they were to respond to it. The book is first of all a revelation concerning Jesus Christ. "Revelation" means "disclosure" or "unveiling." Jesus is both the source and the subject of the revelation. The message is for his "servants." The book begins and ends by stressing Christ's return for his servants (1:1, 3; 22:3, 6-7, 10, 12, 20). For the concept of "shortly" (or "suddenly," or "certainly"), see Luke 18:8 and Romans 16:20. Also, consider 2 Peter 3:8-13. This is a letter to slaves encouraging them to obey their Master's commands in light of his expected return.

"To show" (1:1) indicates that the message was presented largely in signs and symbols. Signs and symbols teach truth by transference. What is known about the sign in a known realm reveals something about the unknown realm toward which the sign points. Most of the symbols or signs in Revelation are explained in the context or in some other place in Scripture. A blessing is promised for those who read and heed the words of the prophecy.

What is there to "take to heart" (1:3) in the book of Revelation? Revelation 1:3 is a beatitude promising blessing for those who heed what is in the book. Revelation reveals other blessings in 14:13; 16:15; 19:9; 20:6; 22:7, 14 (cf. Luke 11:28). These blessings form a stark contrast with the curses at the end of the book (22:18-19). The essence of taking the message of the book into one's life is maintaining love for Christ and one's family. This will result in "overcoming" (cf. 2:7, 11, 17, 26; 3:5, 12, 21; 5:5; 11:7; 13:7; 17:14; 21:7; Matt. 24:13). For seeing the letter as "prophecy" (1:3), see 22:7, 10, 18-19.

1:4-8 Greeting

As with the prologue in 1:1-3, the greeting was written after John had experienced the visions of the book. It presents the major themes of the book: seven churches, the eternality of God, Jesus the faithful witness, and God's eternal glory and dominion. These themes will be illustrated throughout the book. John gave a standard blessing: "grace to you and peace." Revelation is addressed to the seven churches of Asia. The churches were in cities Paul had visited on his second and third missionary journeys. As elder, or bishop, of Ephesus, the apostle John was responsible for these churches. Note the structure of 1:4-8. It starts and ends with the eternality of God (cf. Exod. 3:14-15). The middle part describes the person and work of Jesus, which results in believers being "priests" (1:6). The servants of God do their priestly ministry in Christ surrounded by the eternal power and nature of the Father.

The "seven spirits" (1:4) are variously interpreted as referring to: (1) the seven angels (1:16, 20); (2) the fullness of the Holy Spirit in all his ministries (2:7, 11, 17, 29; cf. Isa. 11:2-5; 1 Cor. 12:4, 13); or (3) a heavenly entourage of spirits that have a special ministry in connection with the Lamb. It is always best to see if the book itself can shed light on an issue. In this case 3:1; 4:5; and 5:6 refer to the seven spirits. These verses show that the main emphasis is on the power and presence ("horns and eyes," 5:6) of God on the earth (cf. Zech. 4:2, 10). The number "seven" appears fifty-four times in Revelation. Throughout the Bible the number seven is associated with the idea of completion and perfection (cf. Gen. 2:2; Exod. 20:10).

Jesus Christ is described as "the faithful witness" (1:5; cf. 2:13; 11:3; 17:6) in order to encourage the same from the readers. This relates to the book-wide theme of "overcoming" (2:7, 11, 17, 26; 3:5, 12, 21; 5:5; 11:7; 13:7; 17:14; 21:7; cf. Matt. 24:13), enduring to the end faithfully. The "first-born from the dead" (1:5) refers to Christ (cf. Col. 1:15). He was the first to receive an immortal, resurrection body (cf. 1 Cor. 15:20). As such, he is able to resurrect those who die for their faith (cf. 20:6). The term "kingdom" (1:6) reflects the present unity of believers under their King ("the glory and dominion"). The term "priests" (1:6) reflects the service to God by believers (cf. 5:10; Exod. 19:5-6; Isa. 61:6; 1 Pet. 2:5, 9). This service will continue throughout eternity (cf. 22:3).

Revelation 1:7 breaks the flow of the narrative. It is an outburst that clearly presents the theme of the book. Daniel 7:13 and Zechariah 12:10 are combined. Their predictions will be fulfilled at Christ's return (cf. also Matt. 16:27; 24:30; and John 19:37). Note the two "amens" (1:6-7). This glorious picture was needed by those who looked forward to a future filled with uncertainty and tribulation.

God confirmed his eternal sovereignty in 1:8. For Alpha and Omega, see 21:6; 22:13; and Isaiah 41:4. While some take "the Alpha and the Omega" (1:8) to refer to Christ (21:6), in this context it refers to God who is verifying the contents of the prophecy. He is the "A" to "Z," that is, the complete God. "Almighty" is used only ten times in the New Testament and nine of its appearances are in this book (1:8; 4:8; 11:17; 15:3; 16:7, 14; 19:6, 15; 21:22; cf. 2 Cor. 6:18). Triumph in tribulation is based on trusting in God to be the most powerful of all.

1:9-20 Prophetic Commissioning

1:9-11 THE FIRST COMMAND TO WRITE
The first Roman persecution of Christians was under Nero in A.D. 64-67. He ordered the burning and mutilation of Christians and brought about the deaths of Peter and Paul. The second persecution was under Domitian, around A.D. 95. This persecution brought John to Patmos. At the time of writing Revelation, John was in exile on the island of Patmos, a six by ten mile island in the Aegean Sea about thirty-five miles southwest of Miletus. This island served as a place of banishment during Roman times.

Revelation 1:9 recounts the major themes of the book: suffering, the kingdom, and patient endurance in Jesus (cf. 3:10; 2 Thess. 3:5). The "Lord's Day" (1:10) may refer to Sunday, the first day of the week (cf. Acts 20:7; 1 Cor. 16:2). If this was the case, John had his vision on the day the seven churches he would address were meeting to worship. It is also possible that the "Lord's Day" may not refer to Sunday but may to the kind of day (that is, a day totally given over to the Lord's words and acts) on which John received this revelation. For the phrase "in the Spirit" (1:10), see Acts 10:10; 11:5; 22:17; and 2 Corinthians 12:2-4. The loud voice was like a trumpet (1:10; cf. Exod. 19:16, 19; cf. Heb. 12:19; Matt. 24:31; 1 Cor. 15:52; 1 Thess. 4:16). The book was originally written as a prophetic exhortation to seven churches (1:11).

1:12-16 DESCRIPTION OF THE SPEAKER
John's vision was of the majestic person of Christ, the risen and glorified Lord, standing among the churches. The vision is similar to that recorded in Daniel 7:9-14. But this picture of the risen Lord is radically different from the picture presented in the Gospels, where the risen Lord was mistaken for a gardener and made breakfast for his disciples by the Sea of Galilee. In Revelation the risen Lord is revealed as the fearsome Judge, first of the churches and then of the world. The Lord is presented in this startling way in order to motivate the readers to pay attention. The "seven golden lampstands" (1:12) are identified in 1:20 as the seven churches. The picture of seven lamps occurs in Exodus 25:37; 37:23; and Zechariah 4:2. The "seven stars" (1:16) are identified in 1:20 as "seven angels."

There are a variety of opinions regarding the identity of the seven "angels." Some have understood John to be referring to the human leader or pastor of each local church. Others have viewed them as guardian angels of the churches (1 Cor. 11:10). And others believe the term "angel" should be understood literally as "messenger," referring to the human messengers sent by the churches to visit John and receive Christ's letter to their churches (cf. 2:1; for other human messengers in Scripture see Hag. 1:13; Mal. 2:7; Matt. 11:10; Luke 9:52; James 2:25). The order in which the churches are addressed is strictly according to geographical arrangement.

1:17-20 THE SECOND COMMAND TO WRITE
John revealed his personal response to what he saw (1:17), and by doing this, called believers to share his feelings of awe at the vision of Christ among the churches. Jesus comforts John with his right hand (1:17). His charge of the "keys" (1:18) reveals his full power over death. The risen Lord exhibits his full authority to command (1:19; cf. Dan. 8:18; 10:10, 12). The commission in Revelation 1:19 is often seen as the key to understanding the structure of the entire book: "the things you have seen" (referring to Rev. 1), "the things which are" (referring to Rev. 2–3), and "the things which shall take place" (referring to Rev. 4–22). John was being instructed to write down the entirety of what he saw and to leave nothing out.

2:1–3:22 PRESENT EXHORTATIONS TO THE CHURCHES

Overview: Each message follows a standard format: (1) the charge to write to the angel of the church; (2) identification of Christ in terms of his appearance in Revelation 1; (3) the church's positive qualities; (4) words of exhortation; (5) a closing with an exhortation to hear and a promise to those who "overcome." The closing to each message broadens the scope to all the churches. All seven messages are to all churches in every age. The impact of this format for the overall message and purpose of the book is that there is a critical need for Christians to endure a future period of terrible persecution. The churches are told to "overcome" by returning to their original commitment and guarding against cultural conformity.

Each of the churches' letters begins with a vision or characterization of Christ similar to the vision of 1:9-20. The selection of each reference to the vision of Christ matches the special needs of each of the seven churches. See the accompanying chart on the seven churches.

Each message was intended to deal with the specific internal conditions of each individual church. The churches were commended for their good traits and condemned for their failings.

2:1-7 Ephesus

Ephesus, the foremost city of Asia Minor, was located near the Aegean Sea on the Cayster River and had a population of around 250,000 (see introductory map). The city was the guardian of the temple of Artemis (Diana) and of her image. According to legend, the image fell from heaven (Acts 19:35). The emperor cult flourished at Ephesus, and temples were built there to Claudius, Hadrian, and Severus. The magic arts and mystery cults also flourished there (Acts 19:13-19). Ephesus had a fine harbor, which served as an export center at the west end of the Asiatic caravan route. The city had a fine theater that seated 25,000 people. The church at Ephesus was founded by Aquila, Priscilla, and Paul (Acts 18:18-19). By the time of John's Revelation, the church had persevered through the trouble of false teachers but had lost its first love.

2:1 VISION OF CHRIST: HOLDS AND WALKS
The vision of Christ holding and walking (2:1) reinforces his intimate knowledge of their hearts and actions. The picture of Christ with a letter to each church relates to his intimate knowledge of the problems each church faces (cf. 1:12, 16; 2:4).

2:2-3 PRAISE
The Lord praised the Ephesian Christians for their deeds, perseverance, and endurance. Toil and patience characterized their overall life-style. They were doctrinally sound and had exposed false teachers (cf. Matt. 7:15; Acts 20:29). They had persevered and endured many trials and hardships.

2:4-5 PROBLEM
Although endurance is a key theme throughout the book, it is not the only or final criterion for pleasing Christ. The Lord told these believers that they had left their first love and exhorted them to repent. See Matthew 24:12 for Jesus' warning that the "love of most will grow cold." The idea of "first love" (2:4) is purposely left general to let the readers specify what their own first love for God was (cf. Jer. 2:2; John 13:35; 2 John 1:5). The remedy is to "remember," "repent," and "do" (2:5). Doctrinal purity

THE SEVEN CHURCHES OF ASIA

Ephesus (2:1)	See 1:12, 16.
Smyrna (2:8)	See 1:17-18.
Pergamum (2:12)	See 1:16.
Thyatira (2:18)	See 1:14-15.
Sardis (3:1)	See 1:16.
Philadelphia (3:7)	See 1:18.
Laodicea (3:14)	See 1:5.

and endurance did not guarantee vital inner love for God. The remembrance by believers of their first state of love for Christ is potent for bringing about repentance and action. Christ's coming to judge (2:5) would be realized by his extinguishing the life of that particular church. There is a close relationship between Christ's coming to judge the churches (Rev. 2–3) and his coming to judge the world in the day of the Lord (Rev. 4–22).

2:6-7 EXHORTATION
According to the early church fathers, the Nicolaitans were the followers of Nicolas (cf. Acts 6:5). Others understand the name etymologically to refer to those who "conquer the people," that is, those who usurped authority and dominated the people. In context, their problem is linked to the teaching of Balaam (2:14-15) and may also be related to the works of 2:20-21 concerning food and idols. This also relates to the Jerusalem council's decrees in Acts 15:29. These exhortations to the churches of Asia Minor (2:7, 11, 17, 29; 3:6, 13, 22) are applicable to all churches and to individual believers as well (cf. Matt. 11:5). "Overcoming" (2:7) is a combination of doctrinal purity, faithful witness, and vital love for Christ. Those who "overcome" are not a special group of Christians but true believers who persevere faithfully to the end (21:7; 2:7, 11, 17, 26; 3:5, 12, 21; cf. 1 John 5:4-5). For the "tree of life," see Revelation 22:2 and Genesis 2:9; 3:22-24. "Paradise" signifies the place of Edenic fellowship with God.

2:8-11 Smyrna
Smyrna (modern Ismir) is located about thirty-five miles north of Ephesus (see introductory map). It was an important port city and trade center that also boasted of schools of science and medicine. Smyrna was also a center for the imperial cult of emperor worship. Temples at Smyrna were dedicated to the emperor Tiberius, Zeus, and Cybele. The gospel probably reached Smyrna at an early date, presumably from Ephesus (Acts 19:10). The church at Smyrna suffered from poverty and persecution by the Jews. Polycarp, one of the apostle John's disciples, served as bishop of Smyrna and was martyred there around A.D. 156 when he refused to recant his faith. He was burned alive on a wooden pyre.

2:8 VISION OF CHRIST
The vision of Christ's experience of suffering (2:8) matches the suffering and death that would be faced by the church in Smyrna (2:10; cf. the picture of Christ in 1:17-18).

2:9 PRAISE
The church at Smyrna experienced great affliction and poverty. Christ's words, "I know" (2:9), reveal the heart of the Christians' comfort. It is far from trite to say that God knows about the needs of his people. The spiritual riches of the believers in Smyrna contrasted with their material poverty. This stands in contrast with the state of the believers in the Laodicean church (3:17). For the concept of real versus false Jews, see Romans 2:28-29 and John 8:31-47. The "synagogue of Satan"

THE SEVEN CHURCHES: REAL OR SYMBOLIC?
Some have viewed these churches as picturing seven successive periods of church history. But this view involves considerable speculation and subjectivity. As with any of the letters in the New Testament addressed to particular churches, the churches in Revelation should be understood as real first-century churches, but modern interpreters must also realize that the message is to all of Christ's churches throughout time. To defend the timelessness of the message is not to withold the original historical reality of the seven churches. The churches are like those addressed in Romans, Ephesians, Philippians, and so forth.

In addition, emphasis needs to be placed on the prophetic nature of the messages to the churches in Revelation. They are more like oracles than letters, and the command to write (repeated in 2:1, 8, 12, 18; 3:1, 7, 14) is used in the Greek Old Testament to announce prophetic messages. Thus, the letters are prophetic messages written to real churches with timeless messages to Christ's church throughout the centuries.

referred to those who were Jews by birth but did not share Abraham's faith (cf. Rom. 2:28-29).

2:10-11 EXHORTATION

The "ten days" (2:10) refers to a brief period of suffering (Gen. 24:55; Neh. 5:18; Jer. 42:7; Acts 25:6). Satan was behind the suffering and tribulations of the saints throughout the book. Satan's work serves as a testing (2:10) for the saints (cf. 3:10). Faithfulness results in getting the crown of life, but only after death. The "second death" (2:11) is described in 20:6, 14 and 21:8. The "second death" refers to eternal separation from God in the lake of fire.

2:12-17 Pergamum

Pergamum was located about fifty miles north of Smyrna and about fifteen miles from the sea (see introductory map). To reach the city from the coast, one could travel up the Caicus River, which was navigable by small craft. Pergamum had a fine library and was the place where parchment was first used. The city was chiefly noted as the religious center of the province of Asia. It was the center of four of the great pagan cults honoring Zeus, Athena, Dionysus, and Asclerius. Each of these deities had a beautiful temple. The first temple dedicated to the imperial cult (in honor of Augustus) was built at Pergamum in 29 B.C. The pagan temples and idolatry undoubtedly led John to refer to the city as the place "where Satan has his throne" (2:13).

2:12 VISION OF CHRIST

The Lord is pictured as having a two-edged sword (cf. 1:16). This sword is seen in terrible use later (19:15, 21; cf. also Isa. 49:2; Heb. 4:12). The sword is related to the Lord's impending visit to the church (2:16).

2:13 PRAISE

The Lord praised the believers in Pergamum for having kept the faith. Antipas (2:13) is described as being a "faithful witness," an attribute he shared with Christ (1:5). Satan's work and throne are seen throughout Revelation 2 (2:9, 10, 13, 24; and also 3:9) and are connected to the Old Testament characters of Balaam (2:14) and Jezebel (2:20). Satan's work to destroy the church will extend into his terrible deeds recorded in Revelation 4–20.

2:14-16 PROBLEM

The Lord pointed out to them that they had allowed immoral teachings to come into their lives. The teachings were not a body of doctrine but a manner of behavior as described by the last part of 2:14. Their problem had two aspects: (1) They were eating food before idols in the temples; and (2) they were engaged in sexual immorality as pagan worship. For Balaam leading the Israelites into immoral activity, see Numbers 25:1-5 in connection with Numbers 31:16. They were involved in worship of false gods, which involved immoral sexual practices. Revelation 2:15 links the above sin to the teachings of the Nicolaitans and sheds light on the teachings of this basically unknown group. The center of their problem was that they were conforming to the ungodly activities of the surrounding society. "Come" (2:16) refers to Christ's second coming (cf. 3:11; 22:7, 12, 20).

2:17 EXHORTATION

The "overcomer" is promised three things. The "hidden manna" probably refers to the sufficiency of the person of Christ, the bread of life (cf. John 6:31-35). The theme of manna has its roots in the Old Testament. It is also seen in John 6 where Jesus indicated that he was the bread of life. The "hidden" concept may refer to the manna that was placed in the Ark for a memorial (Exod. 16:32-34; cf. Heb. 9:4). Tradition says that it was taken by Jeremiah at the time of captivity and hidden in the ground at Mount Nebo (2 Macc. 2:4-7). It was to remain there until the coming of the Messiah when the Ark would be brought to the new temple. Or it might refer to the "bread of the angels" (Ps. 78:25) that would descend from heaven during the Millennium to feed the blessed (2 Baruch 29:8; *Sibylline Oracles*, 7.149). A "white stone" was used in antiquity for voting and signified acquittal or acceptance. A white stone also was used as an admission ticket to a banquet, in this case the Messianic banquet. According to the rabbis, precious stones fell from heaven with manna. Christ received a "new name" after his resurrection (cf. Phil. 2:8-11), and believers will also. The essential contrast in this verse is between God's "hidden manna" and the unclean food and immorality offered by the false teachers at Pergamum.

2:18-29 Thyatira

This longest letter to the churches is addressed to the least known church. Thyatira was an important manufacturing center located approximately forty miles southeast of Pergamum (see introductory map). The city was situated in a valley on the road from Pergamum to Laodicea. Thyatira was especially noted for its trade guilds, which were more organized than in any other ancient city. Their meetings were bound up with acts of pagan worship and immorality. Dye manufacturing was an important industry in Thyatira. The purple dye was made from a root instead of from shellfish. Garment weaving, pottery making, and brass working were also trades known to have existed in Thyatira. In its early days, Thyatira had a temple dedicated to Tyrimnos, an ancient sun god. The gospel may have been brought to the city by Lydia of Thyatira who was converted under Paul's ministry in Philippi (Acts 16:14). The city is commended in Revelation for its deeds, love, faith, service, and perseverance, but it is rebuked for tolerating the false prophetess "Jezebel" (2:20).

2:18 VISION OF CHRIST

The eyes and feet of the Lord are stressed (cf. 1:14-15; 2:23; Dan. 10:6). The image of eyes like "blazing fire" indicates Christ's ability to search the minds and hearts of believers.

2:19 PRAISE

This church is praised for its works, love, faith, and perseverance. They had continued growing and were doing more for God than they had done during the the first days of their faith.

2:20-25 PROBLEM

Although this church was given high praise, it also had a problem with immorality. It tolerated immoral teachings. The reference to "Jezebel" (2:20) indicates sins of fornication and eating idol food, sins parallel to those practiced by the Israelites in their worship of Baal (1 Kings 16:29-33; 2 Kings 9:30-37). Again, the church was falling prey to cultural pressure to accommodate the pagan custom of idolatry. This pressure may have had its source in the commitment of trade guilds of that day to

their patron deities. "Bed of suffering" (2:22) is a punishment for sin (cf. 1 Cor. 11:27-30). They will be cast into great tribulation so that the churches will know God as the one who tries hearts (17:2; 18:19; cf. Jer. 17:10; Matt. 16:27; Rom. 2:6).

"Satan's so-called deep secrets" (2:24) may either be a sarcastic reversal of the claim to know the deep things of God, or a claim to have mystical power over Satan by entering into his realm and showing him powerless. "Until I come" (2:25) refers to Christ's second coming.

2:26-29 EXHORTATION

The Lord's exhortation to this church relates to rule in the Millennium. In 2:26-27 John quoted Psalm 2:9 indicating that the "overcomer" will be associated with Christ in his kingdom reign (5:10; 12:5; 19:15; 2 Tim. 2:12; 1 Cor. 6:3). The context of Psalm 2 is very important, especially Psalm 2:7. True believers will share in Christ's rule. The "morning star" (2:28) refers to Christ himself (cf. 22:16). In the Old Testament the concept functions as an allusion to an evil being (Isa. 14:12) and to the immortality of the righteous (Dan. 12:3). Again, "hearing" and "doing" mark the end of this and all the letters to the churches. This is also how Jesus ended his Sermon on the Mount (Matt. 5–7).

3:1-6 Sardis

Sardis was situated in the western part of the Roman province of Asia about thirty miles southeast of Thyatira (see introductory map). The city stood on the northern slope of a mountain with a river flowing at its base. This setting rendered the city almost impregnable. Sardis was once the capital of the kingdom of Lydia. In A.D. 17 the city was destroyed by a great earthquake. Although rebuilt by Tiberius, Sardis never recovered its former glory and importance. The ancient city was noted for its fruits and wool. The making and dyeing of woolen garments was the chief industry of Sardis (cf. Rev. 3:4-5). Worship at Sardis had a sexual emphasis and focused on Sybele, a goddess similar to Diana in Ephesus. The church was probably founded during the time of Paul's ministry at Ephesus (Acts 19:10).

3:1 VISION OF CHRIST
The Lord is pictured as having the seven spirits and the seven stars (cf. 1:16).

3:1 PRAISE
The Lord praised the Christians at Sardis for their good deeds (see also 3:4).

3:1-3 PROBLEM
The Lord did not find the deeds of this church complete in God's sight. Although the church had a reputation of being alive, it was dead on the inside. This is similar to the loss of first love for Christ (cf. 2:4). Again, as in 2:5, the remedy was to "remember" and "return" to original behavior and teaching. Throughout the Old Testament, Israel was also called to "remember" and "return" to God's redemption and commands. This is the most severe denunciation given to the churches. But this church had no named heresy or outside opposition, only incomplete acts of obedience to Christ (3:2).

3:4-6 EXHORTATION
The Lord talked about future rewards to be given to those who "overcome." The righteousness of those who "overcome" will be acknowledged by Christ before the Father (cf. Matt. 10:32). The "book of life" (3:5) refers to the book of the redeemed (cf. 20:15; 21:27). The concept of the "book of life" is seen in Exodus 32:32-33, Psalm 69:28, and Daniel 12:1. For "dressed in white" (3:5), see 3:18; 4:4; 6:11; 7:9, 13; and 19:14.

3:7-13 Philadelphia

Philadelphia, located twenty-eight miles southeast of Sardis, was a wealthy trade center in the wine producing district of Asia (see introductory map). The city was situated on a 650 foot terrace above the banks of the Cogamus River at the threshold of a fertile plateau from which its agricultural prosperity was derived. Philadelphia was called "little Athens" because of the magnificence of its temples and public buildings. Dionysus, the god of wine, was the chief deity of the city. The believers at Philadelphia were commended for their deeds, their obedience to God's word, and their loyalty to Christ (3:8). It is the only one of the seven churches of Revelation not subject to some measure of condemnation or criticism.

3:7 VISION OF CHRIST
The Lord is pictured as holy and true and as having the "key of David" (3:7; cf. Isa. 22:15-25). This is a change from the usual reference back to the vision of Christ in Revelation 1:18. The "key of David" refers to Christ's control over the Messianic kingdom. The content of this letter is similar to the one to Smyrna. The readers were assured that Christ could bring them safely through persecution and into God's kingdom.

3:8-10 PRAISE
The Lord praised the believers at Philadelphia for their deeds. They had an open ministry (3:8) and experienced victory (3:9). They were promised to be kept from the "hour of trial" (3:10) in contrast with "those who live on the earth," referring to the people who continue to reject the salvation of God (6:10; 8:13; 11:10; 13:8, 14; 17:8).

3:11-13 EXHORTATION
The believers are reminded to hold fast until Christ returns (3:11; cf. 6:9-11; John 16:33; 17:15; Rev. 7:1-8; 12:6). Satan is the chief accuser and persecutor of Christ's children (12:10; 2:9; John 8:44; 17:15; 2 Cor. 11:14-15). Those who "overcome" will gain a place in the new city (cf. 21:1-2). The "pillar" (3:12) may allude to the custom of honoring a magistrate by setting up a pillar in one of the temples of Philadelphia in his name. The writing of the name of God on the "overcomer" identifies the believer as God's own possession.

3:14-22 Laodicea

Laodicea was located in the Lycus Valley on an important crossroads forty-five miles southeast of Philadelphia and about ninety miles east of Ephesus (see introductory map). The city prospered in banking, commerce, and the manufacturing of clothing made from the glossy black wool of the sheep raised nearby. It had a medical school and was noted for its production of a salve used to cure eye diseases (cf. 3:18). The church at Laodicea, with the other Lycus Valley churches of Hierapolis and Colosse, was probably established during Paul's ministry at Ephesus (Acts 19:10), perhaps through the work of Epaphras (Col. 4:12-13).

3:14 VISION OF CHRIST

The picture of the Lord in 3:14 looks back to that of Revelation 1:5. Christ's work is certain ("Amen") and his witness is faithful.

3:15-18 PROBLEM

Laodicea (3:16) had no local water supply, so water was brought in by conduit from hot springs some distance away. The water no doubt arrived lukewarm, like the spiritual condition of the Laodiceans. The point is that the cold and pure waters of Colosse and the hot and medicinal waters of Hierapolis both could be put to good use. But lukewarm water was good for nothing.

3:19-22 EXHORTATION

The Lord invites them to repent (3:20). Christ was depicted as outside the church, inviting the Christians within to receive him. In view is the final invitation to Christ's Messianic banquet (3:21). The believer is promised the privilege of sitting with Christ on his throne and reigning with him throughout eternity (22:5; cf. 2 Tim. 2:12).

4:1–22:5 FUTURE EXPECTATIONS FOR THE WORLD

Overview: The third section of Revelation looks ahead to the future (cf. 1:19). Revelation 4–5 forms a prologue to this major prophetic section by providing a heavenly perspective for the earthly events to come. These chapters move from earth to heaven to provide a glorious vision of God that will pervade all the following chapters. The source of glory and judgment comes from a God who deserves ceaseless worship. Against the background of the adoration of God in heaven, the awesome events of the last days are revealed.

This section shows the specific challenges involved in following Christ's call to "overcome" (2:7, 11, 17, 26; 3:5, 12, 21). It provides consolation and courage in the coming tribulation (2:10; 3:10; 7:14). It also gives insight into how history is run—not by human political power but by a God who is active and enthroned. In light of human and satanic persecution, the church appears unable to overcome earthly powers. But the scroll is the key to the end of such injustice and the beginning of God's unhindered reign.

4:1–5:14 The Perfect Source of Glory and of Judgment

4:1-11 THE SOURCE OF GLORY AND THE RESPONSE OF CEASELESS PRAISE

"After this" (4:1) is a recurring phrase referring to a movement from one vision to another (cf. 7:9; 9:12; 15:5; 18:1; 19:1). John was invited to go to heaven for a preview of coming events. He did this by means of a spiritual vision. John was on Patmos but saw the glories of heaven. The "door standing open in heaven" (4:1) was used to show that John was going into a hidden realm to reveal what was unseen. These events are to be viewed from the perspective of heaven, not earth. John was "in the Spirit" (4:2), that is, caught up in a continued ecstatic state.

The vision of God closely resembles the vision of God in Ezekiel 1:22-28. It also has links to Isaiah 6:1-5; Psalms 47:8; 104:2; and 1 Timothy 6:16. All the terrible suffering of the saints is to be viewed through the perspective of this vision of God's glory and worthiness for worship. The stones (4:3) signify the first and last tribes of Israel in Exodus 28:17-21. In Ezekiel 28:13 these stones are counted among the treasures of the king of Tyre.

The ones "surrounding the throne" (4:4) were the elders. There is considerable debate as to the identity of the twenty-four elders. Some interpreters regard them as a special order of angels. Others believe they represent the redeemed of all ages; twelve representing Israel and twelve representing the church. Since there were "twenty-four" orders in the Levitical priesthood (1 Chron. 24:4; 25:9-31), some have taken the number to be representative of believer priests. But in 5:9-10 the elders seem to be set off from those redeemed by Christ. In 7:13 one elder equals one being. It is probably best to regard them as human or celestial beings who have some responsibility for leading in heavenly worship (4:9-11; 5:8-12). Whatever their actual identity, their function in the book is clear. They were to reveal to the readers of John's revelation the proper response to God—ceaseless praise and worship.

For the "seven spirits of God" (4:5), see the note on 1:4. The thunder and lightning were reminders of how God appeared to his people at Mount Sinai (Exod. 19:16-18; cf. Pss. 18:7-14; 77:18). In Revelation the presence of thunder and lightning marks off important events and is always connected with the temple scene in heaven (8:5; 11:19; 16:18). The four creatures also function as leaders in unceasing praise for God as a background for the unfolding of his seven-sealed scroll of judgment (see also 5:9-10, 14; 11:16-18; 19:4). They are related to the cherubim of Ezekiel 1 and Isaiah 6:2-3. In Ezekiel's vision of the glory of God, he saw four "living creatures" (1:5) who were later identified as cherubim (Ezek. 10:15), an order of angelic creatures. These creatures are additional to the traditional orders of heavenly beings. Each of the four creatures had a unique face. One had the face of a lion, another the face of a calf, another the face of an eagle, and the last had a human face. Whether these are to be taken as four actual creatures or as symbols, their function is clear. They were involved in ceaseless praise. The specific focus of praise was needed by the readers of this letter, especially those undergoing difficult times.

The creatures praise God for his holiness (4:8) and the elders praise God for his worthiness as Creator of all things (4:11). Seeing God in his holiness and Creator-sovereignty is indispensable for appreciating the upcoming judgment of the contrasting evil on the earth. The praise of a holy God results in seeing how bad it is on earth and how glorious it is in heaven.

5:1-14 THE SOURCE OF JUDGMENT
Revelation 5 is a continuation of the heavenly scene. John focuses his attention on a sealed book in the right hand of the one sitting on the throne. The question of worthiness for judgment (5:2) is answered. The fact that the scroll is written on the inside and on the back indicates that there was a lot to say (cf. Ezek. 2:10). The drama of seeking a worthy opener heightens the importance of the sealed scroll. To break the seals was to open the scroll. The function of seals in the ancient world was to protect important documents for private and select viewing. This scroll is so confidential that it has not one, but seven seals. Only when all seven are broken will the contents of the book be revealed. The "mighty angel" (5:2) will appear again in 10:1 and 18:21. The one worthy to open the seals would have to

match the worthiness of the Father (4:11). The revealing of God's judgment involves worthiness (5:2), not power. The challenge goes out to heaven above, earth beneath, and underneath the earth (5:3; cf. Exod. 20:4; Phil. 2:10). When the seven seals are broken, the judgments of God are poured out on the earth (cf. 6:1).

The question "Who is worthy to break the seals and open the scroll?" (5:2) is answered in 5:4-7. Christ overcame (5:5), and his triumph serves as the model for the believers' "overcoming." Christ's overcoming is explained in 5:9-10. Jesus the Messiah is the one who overcame death and thus demonstrates his right to open the book. The terms "Lion of the tribe of Judah" (5:5; Gen. 49:8-10) and "Root of David" (Isa. 11:1, 10; Rom. 15:12) are Messianic. Christ is the royal figure coming from the tribe of Judah and the descendant of King David. His victory, and that of his followers, is victory through righteous suffering, sacrifice, and conflict. The "seven horns" (5:6) are an image of strength (Zech. 1:18). For the "seven spirits of God" (5:6), see note on 1:4. Lamb (5:6) is used of Jesus in Revelation twenty-eight times (cf. Isa. 53:7; "our Passover lamb," 1 Cor. 5:7).

The worthy one is worshiped (5:8-14). "The prayers of the saints" (5:8) relate to the prayers for the end of evil and the beginning of God's kingdom. This is especially true of the prayers noted in the fifth seal (6:9-11). Both Father and Son are praised. For "new song" (5:9), see Psalm 98:1 and Isaiah 42:10. For being made "a kingdom and priests" (5:10) see 1:6 and 20:6. The new song is sung by all heavenly and earthly creation (5:13). The universality of Christ's work calls for this universal praise.

6:1–8:1 Seven Seals Broken

Overview: Revelation 6:1–8:1 records the breaking of the seven seals of the scroll (5:2). It is important to realize that breaking only some of the seals does not open the book. The contents of the scroll are not revealed until after the seventh seal is broken. The events associated with the opening of the seals are simply an overture to the dreaded and final judgments of the scroll itself. The first four seals are the beginning of sufferings that lead up to the final great sufferings of the tribulation and second coming of Christ. The first four seals relate to the events alluded to in Daniel 9, Matthew 24:4-31, Mark 13:4-37, and Luke 21:7-36.

6:1-2 A WHITE HORSE

The breaking of the first seal marks the coming of the antichrist, the "little horn" of Daniel 7:8, the "man of lawlessness" of 2 Thessalonians 2:3. The "bow" (6:2) may refer to a rainbow as in Genesis 9:12-17 and symbolize a conquest by peaceful means and diplomacy. There are similarities with Zechariah 1:8-17; 6:1-8. The figures of riders and horses form a stark contrast with Christ on a white horse in Revelation 19:11-16.

6:3-4 A RED HORSE

This is the horse of war. The breaking of the second seal marks the removal of peace from the earth. The red color of the horse suggests bloodshed, and the "large sword" (6:4) confirms it.

6:5-6 A BLACK HORSE

This is the horse of famine. There is a cause and effect relationship between the taking of peace at the breaking of the second seal and the increase of famine and inflation after the third seal is broken. The "pair of scales" (6:5) symbolize the coming inflation and famine. A "day's wages" (6:6; "denarius," NASB; "penny," KJV) is literally "a denarius," which was a Roman monetary unit worth approximately one day's wage.

6:7-8 A PALE HORSE

Death results from war and famine. Ezekiel 14:21 is quoted in 6:8. These four seals are separated from the last three. They are preliminary to the opening of the scroll's contents. The fourth seal reveals an ashen or yellowish-green horse that carries the horseman "death," resulting in the destruction of one-fourth of the earth's population. Being eaten by wild beasts was one of the curses of the Mosaic covenant (Deut. 28:26).

6:9-11 SOULS UNDER THE ALTAR

The fifth seal is now opened. The location is the temple in heaven (cf. Hab. 2:20). At the opening of this fifth seal the souls of martyred saints are revealed. They represent those who were slain for their faith. Their location under the altar shows that they are seen as a sacrifice. The answer to their question "how long?" (6:10) is that

they must wait "until" (6:11) the final number of martyrs have died. At present, they are praying for judgment that has not yet come but will justify God's reputation (cf. Pss. 79:10; 94:3; Hab. 1:2). The phrase "inhabitants of the earth" refers to those who are against God (6:10; cf. 11:10; 13:8, 12; 17:2, 8; 3:10; 8:13). After the devastation accompanied by the first four horsemen (seals 1-4), the martyrs are revealed praying for God's vengeance (seal 5). The sixth seal begins the vengeance requested by the martyred saints. The seventh seal reveals the scroll's contents and the heart of God's judgments. This relates to the purpose of the book by being a word of comfort for the redeemed during this and prior periods. The fifth seal is important because it implies that the first four seals were not divine wrath upon the unrighteous. This wrath would come, however, in the great tribulation seen in the sixth and seventh seals.

6:12-7:17 HEAVENLY CATACLYSM

The breaking of the sixth seal unleashes universal havoc in the heavens and on earth (6:12-7:17). These cosmic disturbances characterize the day of the Lord and are predicted in Isaiah 34:4, Joel 2:30-31, and Matthew 24:29. The imagery used in these verses is from Joel 2:28-32. For the earthquake, see 8:10; 9:1; and Matthew 24:29. For the moon and sun, see Acts 2:20, Joel 2:28-32, Isaiah 34:4, and Mark 13:25-26. For the mountains moving, see Nahum 1:5 and Jeremiah 4:24. Those trying to hide from all this know that the day of God's wrath has finally come (6:16-17). The term "wrath" (6:16-17) expresses a major characteristic of the day of the Lord (cf. 1 Thess. 1:10; 5:9).

Before the final devastation is unleashed, God sets apart 144,000 sealed ones (7:1-8). Revelation 7 records a parenthesis between the sixth and seventh seals. From the severity of the judgments it would appear that not a single person could be delivered (6:17). The question was "Who can stand?" (6:17). But the God of wrath is also the God of mercy. Revelation 7 records the manifestation of God's grace in the face of his wrath by giving two visions of the sealed and the slain. This vision is between the breaking of the sixth and seventh seals, a pattern repeated between the sixth and seventh trumpets (10:1–11:13). For the "four winds" (7:1), see Daniel 7:2 and Jeremiah 49:36. There is a direct relationship between the sealing of these "servants" (7:3) and their safety. They are sealed for faithfulness and safety (cf. 9:4). The "seal" is a mark of ownership. It does not have to be visible to be real (Eph. 4:30). The 144,000 (7:4) are identified as coming from the twelve tribes of Israel. The tribe of Dan is missing, and Joseph is included instead of Ephraim. The important thing is that they are drawn from twelve groups. Since John did not reveal the function of the 144,000, any view concerning their role is conjectural. The point is that they and a great multitude will be kept through the tribulation and will make it safely into the eternal kingdom (7:15-17). This may relate to the prophecy of Joel 2:3 (cf. 14:1, 3-4).

John also sees a great company of Gentiles who were martyred (7:9-17) during the tribulation (7:14). This is the group referred to in 6:11. In 7:15-17 John records the blessings to be enjoyed by the redeemed during the kingdom and the eternal state. For the great tribulation, see 3:10; 6:11; Daniel 12:1; and Mark 13:9. The concept of eternal service (7:15) is completed in 22:3. The tabernacle represents the new heavens and earth. For Jesus as the Lamb and shepherd, see Ezekiel 34:23 and Revelation 2:27; 12:5; 19:15.

8:1 THE SEVENTH SEAL IS OPENED

After the interlude of Revelation 7, the seventh seal is broken. The scroll's contents are now revealed, framed within the seven trumpet judgments of God's wrath (8:2–11:19).

8:2-12 The First Four Trumpets

8:2-7 HAIL, FIRE, AND BLOOD

Casting the incense burner to the earth initiates the next series of judgments. The first trumpet is a judgment of fire. A third of the trees and all of the grass of the earth is destroyed.

8:8-9 FIRE MOUNTAIN

The second judgment is upon the sea. A huge object is thrown into the sea that destroys one third of the sea life and one third of the ships. The mountain (8:8-9) and star (8:10-11; cf. Exod. 7:20) are from the coals of the altar (cf. Exod. 9:18-26).

8:10-11 FIRE STAR

The third judgment is on the fresh water. Wormwood is a plant with a strong, bitter taste and is used as a symbol of bitterness and calamity.

8:12 DARKNESS

God used darkness at several key points in his history of redemption (Exod. 10:21-23; Joel 2:2; Mark 13:24). The first four trumpets systematically unravel God's work of creation in Genesis 1. The fourth judgment affects the sun and stars. Not only will the light diminish, but it appears that the day and night cycle will be shortened. In Joel 2:10 a plague of locusts darkened the sun and the moon.

THE RELATIONSHIP BETWEEN THE SEALS, TRUMPETS, AND BOWLS

The seven seals build up to the revelation of the scroll's contents. The seven trumpets reveal God's judgments. The fifth, sixth, and seventh trumpets are called the "woe" judgments (8:13; 9:12; 11:14). The seven bowls are the terrible exposition of the seventh trumpet (note 10:6-7; 11:15-19; 15:1; 16:17-21). The imagery of seven trumpets relates to the seven trumpets that sounded before Jericho (Josh. 6:4-5). But here when the trumpets blast, the world, not just a city, falls apart. Like the first seven-day creation, another series of seven will precede the new heavens and earth. Like the exodus, bowls of God's judgment will bring release for God's people. Like at Mount Sinai, God's thunder, earthquake, and smoke (8:5) will signal his presence on earth. In the Old Testament, trumpets announced important events (cf. Zeph. 1:14-16). At Jericho, they announced the presence of God (Josh. 6:3). For the altar of incense (8:3), see Exodus 30:1-10; 1 Kings 6:22; and Hebrews 9:4. In Revelation 5:8 incense represents the prayers of the martyred saints for God's vengeance. There is a direct link with the beginning of the trumpets and the prayers of the saints in Revelation 5. The contents of the scroll are presented as the answer to the martyrs' prayers.

8:13–9:21 The First Two Woes

8:13 THREE WOES ANNOUNCED

The final three trumpets are trumpets of even greater woe than the first four. These signal the period of the great tribulation (Matt. 24:21-29).

9:1-12 TORMENTING LOCUSTS

The "Abyss" (9:1) is seen again in 9:11; 11:7; 17:8; 20:1-3 (cf. Luke 8:31; Rom. 10:7). The fifth trumpet, identified as the first of three woes, is a judgment of locusts. The locusts are not ordinary locusts, for they attack people, not just plants, and their "king" (9:11) is Satan, the ruler of the demons (Matt. 12:24). See Exodus 10:1-20 for the locust plague at the time of the exodus. The prophet Joel drew a close comparison between the locust plague and the day of the Lord (Joel 1:2-2:11). Locusts were referred to as symbols of judgment throughout the Old Testament. Here the locusts torment like scorpions, that is, they are like scorpions in their power, not their appearance. As in the first four seals, the image of horses in battle is used again (9:7; cf. Joel 2:4-5). The locusts are seen as a terrible combination of man and beast. They only hurt those who have not been sealed (9:4). The trumpets are God's wrath, which falls on none of God's redeemed community. See Israel's protection (Exod. 8:22; 9:4, 26; 10:23; 11:7). The locusts have power limited to five months (9:3-6). The point of this limited time is to still offer time for repentance (cf. Luke 21:25-26). Using the known reality of locusts, God has revealed the nature of the torment that is to come. "Abaddon" (9:11; cf. Job 31:12; 28:22) means destroyer. The Greek form of this name is Apollyon. Caligula and Nero claimed identification with Apollo; and Domitian, the persecutor of John, claimed to be his incarnation.

9:13-21 MURDERING HORSES

The sixth trumpet, and second woe, brings death and destruction to a third of mankind (9:18). The second woe is introduced by the sixth trumpet. It comes as a voice from the altar, the place of the prayers of the martyred souls (6:9-11). The horsemen are described in 9:13-21. They are called plagues in 9:18. The Euphrates functioned as a source of battle and destruction for Israel (Isa. 8:5-8).

It was the northern boundary of the Promised Land (Gen. 15:18). Note the lack of repentance in 9:20-21. Believers are spared (cf. 9:4). Under the fourth seal one quarter of the earth's population had been slain, and here an additional third are to be destroyed. Though one-third of humanity is destroyed, the remainder still does not repent. The point for the readers in the seven churches of Revelation 2–3 is clear. Will Christ's sacrifice and words of warning be enough to cause them to repent of their sins?

10:1–11:14 The Little Book and the Two Prophets

Overview: Again, there is an interruption between the sixth and seventh elements in a sequence. Sandwiched between the sixth and seventh trumpets, Revelation 10:1–11:14 shows God's answer to the lack of repentance mentioned in 9:21. He will no longer delay the end (10:6), and he will force his enemies to give him glory through the resurrection of his two witnesses and the accompanying signs (11:12-13). People may not repent, but they will give God the glory. This section answers two questions. The first concerns how much longer it would be before the judgments were finished (10:6). The second concerns the elaboration of further prophetic details concerning the events of the tribulation and the kingdom to come (10:11). Although the seventh trumpet marks the end of the tribulation (cf. 11:15), the book does not conclude there. John is told to prophesy again, focusing this time on the major characters and movements of the tribulation (cf. Rev. 13–19).

10:1-7 DELAY NO LONGER

The "mighty angel" shows his signs of conquest (10:2-3, 5, 7). The mystery of the seven thunders (10:4) shows that there are still things to come that have not yet been revealed (see also 15:1; 16:17). The angel announces that there will be no further delay in the completion of God's wrath and the inauguration of God's kingdom on earth.

10:8-11 THE PROPHECY PASSED TO JOHN

Eating the little scroll (10:9) was an allusion to Ezekiel 2:8–3:3. The New Testament speaks of other mysteries of God (10:7; Rom. 11:25; 1 Cor. 15:51; Col. 2:2; 2 Thess. 2:7). Here, the mystery has to do with all that is unknown concerning God's prophecies of how he will triumph over evil and usher in his kingdom. The mystery of God refers to the program of God declared by the prophets that brings about the consummation of human history, specifically, the kingdom (cf. 11:15). Again, this is a message of exhortation to the present churches and an encouragement to those going through the tribulation.

11:1-14 THE TWO PROPHETS
This vision is given in anticipation of a major construction project during the tribulation—the building of the Jewish temple in Jerusalem (cf. 2 Thess. 2:4). Reference is made to the Gentile domination (cf. Dan. 8:9-14; Luke 21:24). To measure the temple and its worshipers (11:1) is to claim sovereign ownership and protection of them. Similar measurements take place in Ezekiel 40:5–43:17; Zechariah 2:1-13; and Revelation 21:15-17. Revelation 11:6 describes the power of these witnesses. Links are drawn to Moses ("blood," Exod. 7:20, and "plague," Exod. 8:12), Elijah (no rain, 1 Kings 17:1; 18:41-45; 2 Kings 1:10-12) and the witnesses in Zechariah 4:3, 11, 14 (olive trees and lampstands). The actual persons of Moses and Elijah were seen with Christ at his transfiguration (Matt. 17:2-3) and were mentioned in Malachi 4:4-5. The witnesses are protected by God's power. They are presented as real people, though some interpreters view them as symbolic of the witnessing believers who are martyred during the tribulation. The point is that God still continues to graciously offer salvation through men who genuinely mourn the evil state of the earth. The months and days mentioned in 11:2-3 may refer to the last three and a half years of the tribulation. It is during the last half of the tribulation that the antichrist will overthrow Jewish worship and establish his own (cf. Dan. 9:27; 2 Thess. 2:4). The "beast" (11:7) refers to the antichrist (cf. 13:1). The identity of the "great city" (11:8) appears to be Jerusalem, but also see 16:19; 17:18; 18:10, 16, 18-19, 21. The names "Sodom and Egypt" are used to refer to Jerusalem and suggest the spiritual condition of that city. God's overall sovereignty is designed to encourage the readers as they go through their own tribulations.

11:15-19 Seventh Angel Sounds
This trumpet introduces the third woe. With this trumpet, the kingdom of the world becomes the kingdom of the Lord. The content of the seventh trumpet is not immediately described. First, comes the great outburst of praise that summarizes the results of God's final judgments. The covenant (11:19) appears to be the archetype of all God's earthly covenants; it is the eternal covenant that asserts his right as Creator to be obeyed, to judge, and to redeem. Revelation 11:18 records different aspects of judgment based upon Christ taking his dominion over the nations. The wicked dead will be judged (cf. 20:11-15); the prophets and Old Testament saints will be rewarded (cf. 20:4-6); and the destroyers of the earth will be destroyed (cf. 19:19-21).

12:1–14:20 The Dragon, the Beasts, and the Lamb
Overview: This section is placed between the seventh trumpet and the execution of the seven bowl judgments. The narrative flow of the book breaks between the sixth and seventh seals (7:1-17), the sixth and seventh trumpets (10:1–11:14), and between the seventh trumpet and the seven bowls (12:1–14:20). The breaks increase in length as the narrative moves closer to the climax of God's seven bowl judgments. Each break elaborates the nature of the times and how God is punishing evil and preserving his saints even through death (13:10; 14:13).

Revelation 12–14 contains explanatory prophecies and deals with the principle characters and major movements of the tribulation period. These chapters elaborate the implications of the rage of the nations (11:18) for believers throughout history and especially during the tribulation. Revelation 12 presents the persecution of Christians (12:17) by Satan. Its point is to stress the ultimate defeat of the devil and the triumph ("overcoming") of faithful Christians (12:10-12). Revelation 13 details the persecution of Christians by Satan through his two beasts. Thus, in Revelation 12–13 the focus is on Satan's war with the saints (12:17; 13:7; cf. 11:7). Revelation 14 proclaims and then illustrates the terrible fate of those who follow the beasts and the triumph of those who follow Jesus.

12:1-17 THE DRAGON AND THE WOMAN

In Revelation 12 two signs are given. The first is a woman clothed with the sun, with the moon at her feet and a crown of twelve stars on her head (12:1; cf. Isa. 66:7-8). The second sign, an enormous red dragon, is given in 12:3. This imagery relates to an age-old desire for salvation. The slain Lamb (12:10-11) has a special place in Revelation 12. The victory is due to Christ alone, who is seen as the fulfillment of all pagan hopes. The conflict in heaven continues on earth. It unveils the activities of Satan and his angels in their attempt to destroy the Messiah and Israel. The woman with child represents Israel who gave Christ to the world (12:5) and will be severely persecuted during the tribulation (12:13). Satan's ultimate objective is to destroy the woman's child, Christ (12:4). The son of the woman (12:5) is Christ, as is seen by the fact that he is the ultimate ruler of the nations. Israel's flight to the wilderness is designed to avoid the persecution of the antichrist during the last three and a half years (1,260 days) of the tribulation period (Matt. 24:15-21). In Revelation 12:7-12 the scene shifts from earth to heaven. Satan and Michael, the archangel, are involved in a conflict. Satan and his angels are thrown out of heaven and are confined to the earth (12:9) for the rest of the tribulation period. He will now vent his wrath on earth. In 12:13-17, having been cast out of heaven, Satan will center his hostilities on the "woman," Israel (12:5). His goal is to destroy Israel so that Christ will not have a people over whom to rule.

13:1-18 THE TWO BEASTS

The beast, or antichrist, is Satan's counterpart to what God offers the world in Christ. The beast is a political figure who arises from the Gentile nations ("the sea," 13:1; cf. Dan. 7:3) and receives his power and authority from Satan himself (13:2). The miraculous healing of the beast's death wound results in amazement and worship (13:3-4). The whole earth worships the dragon and follows the beast to whom he had given authority (13:3-4). The beast is given authority to engage in his evil exploits for forty-two months, the last three and a half years of the tribulation period. The "endurance" (13:10) is submission to

the sufferings of the tribulation without submission to Satan and his representatives.

The second beast (13:11-18) functions to witness to the antichrist (2 Thess. 2:4). He is referred to as the "false prophet" (19:20). This would serve as a warning against false prophets to the original readers of John's revelation, just as it is for believers today. When God's purposes are finished through the beast, he will be judged (20:10). The assurance that God will punish evildoers sustains the faith of the persecuted. The number representing the beast is identified as "666" (13:18). Many have sought to identify the antichrist on the basis of this number, but such attempts will be futile until the tribulation begins.

14:1-20 THE TRIUMPH OF THE LAMB

These people, by way of contrast with those in 13:16, have the name of the Lamb and his Father stamped on their foreheads (cf. Joel 2:32). Revelation 14 continues detailing the age-old conflict between Satan and God. Although in Revelation 13 it may look like the corruption of the earth by the antichrist is out of control, 14:1-5 tells the other side of the story. John tells of the 144,000 who have not defiled themselves with the beast's religious system. The words "did not defile themselves with women" (14:4) are probably a reference to the beast's religious system: the "prostitute" of Revelation 17. They are separated to God as women are separated to their husbands (cf. 2 Cor. 11:2).

The three angels (14:6-12) continue to extend God's grace for repentance (note Matt. 24:14). John recorded three angelic announcements intended to warn those on earth of God's impending judgment. The first angel announced the "eternal gospel" (14:6-7); the second angel announced the doom of Babylon (14:8; cf. Rev. 17–18); and the third angel announced the judgment on those who worship the beast (14:9-13). The fall of Babylon (14:8) is initially described in terms drawn from Isaiah 21:9 and Jeremiah 51:7. Babylon is mentioned throughout the book (Rev. 16:19; 17:5; 18:2, 10, 21; cf. 1 Pet. 5:13) and seems to stand for the world system that is totally against God and his people.

John next recounts his vision of two judgments by God's sickles (14:13-20). In the middle of the devastation of the tribulation period, God gives his verdict concerning the martyrs: they are blessed (14:13). Using the imagery of harvest, the judgment on the earth is detailed. These verses are a preview of the judgment at the second coming described in 19:17-21. These two reapings may relate to the two reapings mentioned by Christ in Matthew 13:24-30, 36-43. The "city" (14:20) most likely refers to Jerusalem (Dan. 11:45; Zech. 14:1-5).

15:1–16:2 The First Bowl Emptied

Another sign is now given. The wrath of God is completed in the seven plagues mentioned in 15:1. They are called seven bowls of wrath in Revelation 16. But before the final wrath, God provides a picture of final bliss for those who have "overcome" (15:2-4). Those earthly saints are now connected with the place of God's glory mentioned in Revelation 4. Being in the very presence of God is the goal for the exhortations to "overcoming" throughout the book. The "tabernacle of the Testimony" in heaven (15:5) is the true tabernacle after which the earthly one was patterned (Heb. 8:5; 9:23-24). In Revelation 15:5-8 the temple is opened, the four living creatures again appear (cf. 4:6), and the temple becomes unapproachable in God's judgment glory (cf. Isa. 66:6). Judgment is an expression of God's righteous character (15:4; 16:7; 19:2). This chapter evokes images from the exodus: the plagues, the sea, the song of Moses, the tabernacle of testimony, and smoke.

16:3-21 The Second through Seventh Bowls

16:3 SEAS OF BLOOD
The second bowl, like the second trumpet (8:8-9), is poured out upon the sea but is more severe. As a result of the judgment, the sea is turned to blood.

16:4-7 RIVERS OF BLOOD
The martyrs' prayer of 5:8 is now being answered (16:6-7; cf. 2 Thess. 1:5-6). The third bowl, like the third trumpet (8:10-11) is poured out upon the fresh water so that it becomes blood.

16:8-9 SCORCHING SUN
The fourth bowl, like the fourth trumpet (8:12), affects the sun. The increased intensity of the sun scorches the inhabitants of earth.

16:10-11 DARKNESS
Even at this terrible point, people still resist God (cf. 13:1, 5-6; 10:10-11; 17:3). The fifth plague falls upon the throne of the beast and brings darkness to his empire.

16:12-16 EUPHRATES DRIED
The sixth bowl judgment will dry up the Euphrates River to facilitate the crossing of the armies of the kings of the east (cf. Dan. 11:44) as they rush to involve themselves in the campaign of Armageddon. "Armageddon" is literally "the hill of Megiddo," referring to the hill upon which the ancient city of Megiddo was located. Megiddo was strategically situated at the foot of Mount Carmel to con-trol travel through the Jezreel Valley.

16:17-21 EARTHQUAKE
The wrath of God is completed (16:17). The great earthquake (4:5; 8:5; 11:19) destroys the city of Babylon. The city's downfall is elaborated in Revelation 17–18.

THE RELATIONSHIP OF THE SEAL, TRUMPET, AND BOWL JUDGMENTS
The seal and trumpet judgments brought partial destruction and afforded opportunity for repentance. But the seven bowl judgments dispense 100 percent judgment and zero percent opportunity for repentance. All is at an end; the evil are evil and the righteous are righteous (cf. 22:11). There are no pauses for elaboration. The bowls empty in rapid fire. This third series is explicitly called the "wrath of God" (15:7).

The first four bowls are similar to the first four trumpet judgments, but they are more intense and complete the wrath of God. These judgments are poured out during a brief period at the end of the tribulation just prior to Christ's second coming. The first bowl (16:1-2), like the first trumpet (8:7), is poured out upon the earth. This judgment of malignant sores falls upon the followers of the beast.

17:1-18 The Woman and the Beast

Revelation 17 describes the downfall of Babylon (14:8; 16:19) in greater detail. Babylon probably refers to the religious, political, and commercial aspects of the antichrist's empire. Revelation 17 focuses on the "prostitute," the false religious system controlled by the beast of 13:1. Revelation 18 will describe the judgment on the beast and his empire.

The same angel will show the bride of Christ (17:1; 21:9). The beast (17:3) appears to represent satanic influence throughout history. Its various heads are its attempts at world rule throughout history. The eighth head is the antichrist of 13:1-10 (cf. Dan. 7:19-21).

The "prostitute" imagery is seen also in Nahum 3:4 and Isaiah 23:16-17. This woman is to be contrasted with the woman of 12:1-6 and the bride of Christ (21:9). The prostitute is given a name that reveals she is the representative of the false religious system that began in ancient Babylon (cf. Gen. 11:1-9). The name is a "mystery" (17:5), that is, the city of Babylon on the Euphrates is not meant. This is a secret, or symbolic, use of the name, the exact understanding of which remains to be revealed (cf. 14:8; 16:19; 17:6, 18; 18:24). Names on foreheads (17:5) appear throughout the book for evil (13:16; 14:9; 20:4) and for good (7:3; 9:4; 14:1; 22:4). This vision answers a question asked by saints throughout the ages: Why do the enemies of God often seem so victorious instead of being judged? The vision shows that she will indeed be destroyed at God's chosen time. The beast and harlot's descriptions function as guides to interpreting their destruction in 18:1–19:5.

The seven heads, horns, and hills have been variously interpreted as Rome, other countries and kings, or simply as a symbol for all the kingdoms of history. More specifically, the seven heads are seven mountains or kings; five have fallen, one exists, and the other is yet to come. The first five kingdoms would include Assyria, Babylon, Persia, Greece, and Egypt. The kingdom in existence while John wrote was the Roman Empire (sixth). The kingdom yet to come will be the final form of world government. It is identified in 17:11 with the beast's

own empire. The idea of "was and was not" arises from past and future expressions of Satan through rulers. "Ten kings" (17:12) may mean ten actual nations or may be symbolic for all the nations of the world.

For "waters" (17:15) ,see Jeremiah 51:13. The destruction of the prostitute is described in images drawn from Ezekiel 23:11-35. Once in power, the beast and his associates will reject the authority of the prostitute's system and throw off her rule. With that system destroyed, the beast will then be introduced by the false prophet as the true god (13:12; cf. 2 Thess. 2:4).

18:1-24 Babylon's Downfall Described

18:1-3 THE ANNOUNCEMENT OF BABYLON'S DESTRUCTION
Revelation 18 describes the judgment on the final form of Babylon, the beast and his empire. The imagery of Babylon falling is taken from Isaiah 21:9, where the ancient city of Babylon was destroyed.

18:4-20 LAMENT OF THE WORLD OVER BABYLON
Revelation 18:4-20 is a message from "another voice from heaven" (18:4). The message begins with a call to separate from the city (18:4) and ends with a call to rejoice (18:20). The heavenly rejoicing forms a stark contrast with the world's mourning (18:9-19). The prayer of the martyrs (6:10) is answered. The call to separate is to believers living in the tribulation period who might be tempted to compromise their convictions and become associated with the beast. The world's leaders give three laments over fallen Babylon (18:9-10, 11-17a, 17b-19). Compare this with Ezekiel's lamentation over Tyre (Ezek. 27). Half the commodities mentioned in 18:11-13 are mentioned also in Ezekiel. Mariners, kings, and merchants are also mentioned in the Ezekiel lamentation. The merchants mourn over the long list of commodities rather than their long list of sins. The judgment against Babylon is on behalf of heaven and the saints (18:20).

18:21-24 BABYLON DESTROYED
The reason for the destruction is Babylon's deception (18:23) and murder of the saints (18:24).

CHIEF EXECUTIVE OFFICER

The dark brown whiskey splashed sullenly over the ice in the bottom of Cliff Morris's glass. He raised the cold rim to his parched lips. The sharp musty odor of the single-malt Scotch flung him back, back in time like a plane trapped in jet stream winds, an airborne Flying Dutchman spiraling down out of tomorrow into yesterday. So many memories thickened, clotted in his big throbbing body, coalescing with that old companion, fear, for a moment he thought of death as simplicity, a cleansing.

No. He let the living liquid slide down his hollow throat to burn beneath his breastbone. It was a foul taste, harsh, almost brackish, like water sucked from a crankcase. Was that why he liked it? Was this whiskey borne out of memory and misery telling him something about himself? Life still beat stubbornly in his middle-aged body, mocking the withered crybaby who clawed at the soft inner flesh of his belly like a pilot in a doomed plane. Maybe his bravery was not a fake.

Why? shrilled the crybaby. Why? Give me one reason why you deserve anything but oblivion? Cliff drowned the wail in another gulp of Scotch. The ice slid against his teeth. He sucked a cube into his mouth and crunched it slowly, bitterly, on the right side of his John Wayne jaw.

Clunk went the glass on the teak desk. Cliff loosened his 150-dollar Gucci tie and struggled for altitude: a deep relaxing breath. He was sitting in the tenth-floor boardroom of the Buchanan Aircraft Corporation. The floor-to-ceiling windows looked out on Los Angeles International Airport, known to the air traveling world as LAX. The runways were dark and silent; it was close to midnight. Beyond the airport tens of thousands of car headlights streamed along the city's freeways and boulevards. Millions of house windows glowed against the night all the way to the guardian mountains. Cliff liked to contemplate Los Angeles. He liked everything about it—its immensity, its variety, its incomprehensibility.

Cliff Morris had helped create this opulent planetary metropolis with its endless eccentric moons of towns and subcities and villages sprawling from the sea to the desert. It was no longer the city of his birth, a laughingstock full of loony cults and glitzy movie moguls and their sycophants and stars, with endless miles of orange groves on its borders. He and his fellow plane makers had made it a megacity, a megaregion that rivaled Pittsburgh and Chicago as an industrial giant, New York as a financial powerhouse.

For thirteen years Cliff had enjoyed being one of the leaders of this phenomenal place. Heads turned, smiles of recognition blossomed when he entered the Polo Lounge or the California Club. From surf-swept Malibu to sunbaked Palm Springs, from the jutting headlands of Palos Verdes to the teetering mansions of Holmby Hills, Cliff Morris was recognized, flattered, favored, sought.

Now there was an undercurrent of mockery, disdain, even contempt in that recognition. If a career can be imagined as a plane and the man inside the career as the pilot, Cliff's aircraft had recently taken a terrific beating in the all-or-nothing war American executives fought in their heads and hearts and boardrooms. He was struggling to stay in the air in spite of shredded ailerons and ravaged tail surfaces and wings that were starting to flap like feathers. Cliff was in danger of vanishing into the realm of the crashed, the cremated, the forgotten. The thought filled him with sullen rage—and that old companion, the secret crybaby in his belly—anxiety.

The boardroom was splendidly decorated in California style. The walls were white. A series of abstract paintings in red, white, and blue added color and a hint of patriotism. The gleaming oval table, the high-backed, gull-winged armchairs, were teak, adding a Hawaiian or South Seas effect. At the far end of the room a solid silver shield emblazoned with the Buchanan Corporation's seal, a plane soaring above a rainbow, glistened in the subdued lighting.

Dick Stone was sitting a few feet away from Cliff Morris, who was in the CEO's chair at the head of the table. Burly, short-armed, thick-necked, Dick was Buchanan's executive vice president for finance. His hunched aggressive posture emanated a tense urgent energy, part physical, part mental. If an audience were watching them, Cliff was sure his six-foot-four physique and laidback California style would win most of the applause.

But there was no audience at this movie. For the previous hour, on a screen that had just returned to its recess in the ceiling, Dick Stone had displayed an array of flow charts and summaries, depicting the current and future profits of the company's divisions. The bottom line was a shortfall of 240 million dollars for fiscal 1979. Unless they got a government bailout or persuaded several banks to loan them serious money, they were broke.

"Our corporate budget this year is six billion dollars. How in Christ can you go bankrupt on six billion dollars?"

"You know the answer to that, Cliff. Almost every cent is locked into total-performance contracts with the Pentagon that don't give us room to breathe," Dick Stone said.

First the right cross, then the left hook, Cliff Morris thought. He tried to weave, duck, clinch.

"What does Shannon say about our chances of getting more money on the Article?"

"Zero minus, unless Reagan wins next year."

"And then?"

"Five, maybe seven on a scale of ten."

The Article—a secret plane that was costing them millions of dollars—drew Cliff's eyes to the two paintings on the boardroom wall facing the windows. Cliff Morris had supplied old photographs that helped the artist capture their founder and chief designer, Frank Buchanan, in his prime. His bear-like physique, his shock of uncombed red hair, the lined hawk-nosed face vivid with visionary force all but leaped from the wall. From one angle he seemed to be glaring at the nearby portrait of the man who considered himself Buchanan's real founder—Adrian Van Ness. Adrian's response was an enigmatic smile. His domed forehead, his hooded eyes, seemed to deepen the enigma, stirring new anxiety deep in Cliff Morris's body and mind.

"What about Adrian's trip to England? If he can get a hundred million from their banks it could loosen things up over here."

Adrian Van Ness had gone to England with the head of the Armed Services Committee of the House of Representatives and the chairman of the Senate Finance Committee to bolster his plea for a major loan. He was probably over the Atlantic at this moment in his Argusair business jet, bringing home the good—or bad—news.

"I don't think he's going to get a damn thing out of them," Dick Stone said. "Unless we do something dramatic."

Cliff Morris had begun to suspect Dick Stone knew exactly what *something dramatic* meant. Sitting on Cliff's desk in his house on the Palos Verdes peninsula was a letter that told him in Adrian Van Ness's oblique, soothing way that he should consider resigning as president. It was the only way they could persuade bankers and congressmen that the Buchanan Corporation deserved to be forgiven for its recent financial and political sins.

Cliff lit a cigarette and put his voice, his face, into his chief executive officer mode. "How much did we make in the last quarter playing the exchange rates, Shylock?"

It was dirty, using the Jewish thing. He knew it disrupted Dick Stone's concentration. But Dick's invitation to this midnight movie was pretty dirty too. His old friend had not spent thirty years in the plane business without learning how to fight dirty. Especially in the last ten years, when Adrian Van Ness had coldly, consciously pitted them against each other, like two gladiators competing for Caesar's approval.

"About fifty million," Dick Stone said.

"That's more than the goddamn aircraft division made last year. Maybe we ought to sell everything and turn the joint into a bank."

"What fun would that be?" Dick Stone said. He looked up at the portraits on the wall, his eyes lingering wistfully on Frank Buchanan's visionary face. "They'd both come back and lead a stockholder revolt. It would be the first time they agreed on anything."

Cliff Morris nodded. "It's always meant more than money. That's been the best part of it. Imagine coming to work every day and figuring out how to sell refrigerators or aspirin? How do those guys stand it?"

Suddenly they were together, not in the boardroom but in a B-17 called the *Rainbow Express*. They were hurtling above burning German cities, with Captain Cliff Morris telling his skeptical navigator they were flying into a future as conquerors of the sky. For reasons only Cliff Morris understood, Dick Stone's intensity faltered. Cliff had time to breathe, to think.

The telephone rang. Both Cliff Morris and Dick Stone froze. The big clock on the wall, showing the time zones of the world, told them it was 10 A.M. in Tel Aviv and 8 A.M. in London and 2 A.M. the next day in Tokyo. Cliff thought of the other times the phone had rung in the middle of the night.

Whenever a Buchanan plane went down anywhere in the world, the tentacles of the long distance lines reached out on undersea cables or on whirling satellites to clutch the maker by the throat with the gruesome statistics—and the threat of ruinous lawsuits.

"Christ," Cliff Morris said, and picked up the white receiver.

The hollow voice belonged to Mike Shannon, head of Buchanan's Washington office, former tailgunner of the *Rainbow Express*. "The Charlottesville police—Adrian—dead." Cliff could not tell whether Shannon was gasping for breath or the stunning impact of the news disconnected the sentences in his own mind.

"Are you still in Washington?"

"Yes."

"Get the hell down to Charlottesville. Make sure no one but you gets into his safe. Bring someone from the National Security Agency with you to handle the local cops. There's stuff in that safe that could put us out of business!"

Cliff Morris dropped the white earpiece into its cradle and stared numbly at Dick Stone. "Adrian's dead."

Dick shook his head, like a boxer who had just been hit with a Sunday punch. He could not believe it either. "A crash?" he said.

"A heart attack. In Charlottesville. The housekeeper called the police. They contacted Shannon."

Dick shook his head again. His incredulity summed up both their relationships to Adrian Van Ness. Neither could imagine life without this man. The absurdity—and the reality—of that thought momentarily appalled Cliff. Fifty-six years old and he could not imagine life without the son of a bitch?

Cliff took a deep slow breath. He could imagine it. He could handle it. Sudden death was part of the plane business. For thirty-five years Cliff had trained himself not to think about death as anything more than a fact.

Except for certain deaths. One was a death Cliff still found unbearable to contemplate, a death that had left him falling free for a long time, like a jumper whose parachute had failed to open. Another was a death he and Adrian had shared, as mourners, accomplices, betrayers. A death that stirred his buried hatred of the man who had made him chief executive officer of this six-billion dollar corporation.

Nothing could heal the free-fall death. Part of him would spin through space into eternity regretting it. But Cliff was suddenly able to believe Adrian's death was connected by a shadowy cosmic justice to the betrayal death. Maybe that made Adrian's death a large, breathtaking fact that led to an even larger possibility. For the first time Cliff Morris might become the real chief executive officer of the Buchanan Corporation.

Cliff pondered Dick Stone's stunned face. He sensed a state of mind or soul radically different from his own. Dick was bereft. He was almost—perhaps actually—mourning Adrian Van Ness. Cliff did not understand why. He did not even try.

Other possibilities churned through Cliff's mind. Perhaps it was not too late to reach an understanding with a woman in a Malibu mansion where he had once been welcomed with extravagant love. For a moment she was naked in his arms, teasing, laughing, resisting, finally surrendering with a rueful cry. For another moment their son was in his arms, almost repealing the eternal gravity of the free-fall death.

Where did that leave another woman who was living in the desert near Palm Springs—his wife of thirty-six years? Cliff's response to that question was a mixture of animosity and regret almost as complex as the one Adrian's death had evoked. He had reasons—good reasons—for hating Sarah Chapman Morris and she had equally good reasons for hating him. Maybe they should leave it that way.

Fleeing that cruel thought, Cliff lurched to his feet. The important thing now was to concentrate on a return from the limbo of defeat and humiliation. "Where are you going?" Dick Stone asked.

"Never mind. I'll see you in the morning. We'll talk. We've got a lot to talk about," Cliff said.

The misgiving in Stone's eyes was almost an accusation. Did he know about Adrian's letter? That made it all the more important for Cliff to see Frank Buchanan as soon as possible. But the woman in the house on the beach at Malibu was almost as crucial in Cliff's new scheme of things.

He groped for his original exultance and regained it. Love, power, happiness—all the meanings of a California life were still possible. Cliff Morris strode out of the boardroom, his big confident body alive with hope.

NIGHT FLIGHT

For another ten minutes Dick Stone sat in the empty boardroom staring at the portraits of Adrian Van Ness and Frank Buchanan. For thirty years his feelings, his ideas, his life had been interwoven with these opposites. He had alternated between admiration and dislike from decade to decade.

For a while Dick had given his allegiance to Frank Buchanan, to his vision of the plane as a spiritual symbol, carrying man's hope toward a better world. But the vision had not been enough to enable the Buchanan Corporation to survive. That had required Adrian Van Ness's guile. He was proof that guile transcended vision in the second half of the American century.

Or did it? Dick Stone wondered. Did the man of guile need vision to justify playing the game by survival rules? Was that why Dick Stone was telling Cliff Morris it was time to pay the price guile finally exacts? What's your answer, Adrian? Dick asked the man who had won his grudging allegiance.

Back in his office, Stone regained his executive instincts. He had been running the day-to-day operations of the Buchanan Corporation for almost a decade while Cliff sold their planes around the world. He decided Mike Shannon was not the man to put in charge of safeguarding Adrian's papers. Grabbing the telephone, he told the night operator to get him Daniel Hanrahan.

In sixty seconds, the sleep-heavy voice of Buchanan's security chief was on the line. Dick told him what had happened. "Mrs. Van Ness. Is she all right?" Hanrahan asked, instantly wide-awake.

"As far as we know," Dick said.

"Can you spare me a plane to get to Virginia?" Hanrahan said.

"I'll spare you a SkyDemon. You'll be there before you've started."

The SkyDemon was a jet fighter-bomber that could hit 1,600 miles an hour. "Roll it out," Hanrahan said. "I'll be there in a half hour."

Dick punched the phone again and told the operator to get medical director Kirk Willoughby. In a moment, Buchanan's chief physician was on the line. Stone told him what had happened. Willoughby groaned. "I knew that goddamn anticoagulant wasn't working. I wanted him to have open heart surgery."

"Why the hell didn't you insist on it?" Dick snarled.

"You know Adrian. He always had the final say. He decided the unknowns were about the same in both routes."

"You should have decided that for him!"

"Calm down, Dick. Adrian wasn't your father."

The words froze the telephone in Dick Stone's hand. Willoughby had nailed him. He was feeling *filial*, he was grieving for Adrian Van Ness. While his real

16

father babbled passages from the Torah in a nursing home in New York.

Was it a reaction to Cliff Morris's barely disguised delight? Stone knew Cliff had several reasons to hate Adrian Van Ness. Cliff had almost as many reasons to mourn him. But hatred was a more powerful emotion. That was why Cliff had to be stopped.

"He wasn't your father either," Dick said. "But we all owe him enough loyalty not to bad-mouth him. It won't do the company any good, for one thing. That's what we have to worry about now. The company."

"Has Cliff heard the news?"

"That's why I'm calling you. I'm the new CEO. Cliff's resigning. But he may not go quietly. Get your ass out of bed and into a helicopter. I want you to talk to Frank Buchanan before dawn. Make sure he's on my side."

Dick Stone punched the phone again to rouse the night operator. "Get me a Hydra and a pilot. I'll be leaving in five minutes."

"Mr. Morris just asked for one too. There's only one pilot on duty."

"I'll fly my own."

Dick slammed down the phone and sat there, appalled by his recklessness. He had a pilot's license but that did not mean he was qualified to handle a Hydra. He had received a thorough checkout from Buchanan's chief pilot only a week ago. But going solo was still close to insanity.

The plane was out on the runway. Buchanan's chief mechanic, an ex–Navy aviation machinist named Kline, was giving it a final checkoff with another mechanic. "Where you headed, Mr. Stone?" Kline asked. "I got to file a flight plan."

"Dreamland. Notify the usual characters so they don't blow me away."

"I got you, Mr. Stone."

Dick buckled himself into the pilot's seat and studied the controls for a moment. Okay. Ready to go on a wing and a prayer, even if no one was interested in prayers from Dick Stone. No one named God, anyway.

He applied the power to the rotors and rose vertically into the night sky. In two minutes he was roaring north above the coast highway at 1,500 feet. Flight! It always aroused fierce exultance in Stone's throat.

Behind him he left a half dozen Dick Stones. The fugitive from Jewish New York enjoying a different shiksa each night at the Villa Hermosa with the Pacific's surf rumbling in the distance. The lover prowling the lobby of the Bel Air Hotel in search of a woman who did not exist beyond her ability to torment him. The husband whose embittered wife drunkenly accused him of loving planes more than people.

Past, gone, obliterated, Stone told himself. The future was the only thing that mattered. The past was a junkyard of false hopes and naive dreams. He was flying above it, beyond it into a new dimension.

It almost worked. He almost stopped hearing Amalie Borne whispering his name.

A dozen miles further up the coast Dick shoved the Hydra's throttle to full and in less than five minutes he was whizzing over the San Gabriel Mountains into the empty immensity of the Mojave Desert. He roared over Edwards Air Force Base where Billy McCall and Buchanan's other test pilots had risked their necks in new planes. For a moment all of them—the planes—flew in Dick Stone's mind. He marveled at the way they made men delirious with pride and pleasure and snuffed out their lives as inexplicably and as unpredictably as a woman broke a man's heart.

In an hour Dick was far up the Mojave, where the California desert met Nevada. Ahead of him was Dreamland, a base whose exact location was known only to a few hundred Air Force officers and aircraft executives. From the air it was an innocuous setup, a scattering of hangars with no planes visible. It looked like an abandoned airport, a place old pilots and plane lovers visited in their nightmares. Dreamland was where the Black Programs, the planes that would protect America in the twenty-first century, were tested.

The desert was turning from gloomy night to graying dawn. In a few minutes the first glow of the rising sun crept over the Sierras. Runway lights clicked on and an air controller in an invisible tower said: "Good morning, Mr. Stone. You are cleared for landing on runway two. Wind from the east at twelve knots."

The sensible thing to do was switch to the tilt rotors and make a helicopter descent. But Dick Stone had found out a long time ago that in the aircraft business the sensible thing was often the wrong thing. There were people watching him land and most of them—99 percent of them—would not land the Hydra that way when there was 4,000 feet of runway waiting for it. Unlike its competitor, the Osprey, the Hydra's propellers were not too big for a conventional landing. Why not show off—and demonstrate the aircraft's flexibility? It was an unbeatable argument.

Dick could hear Billy McCall telling him thirty-seven years ago: *Any asshole can get a plane in the air. Getting it back on the ground is the real trick.* Sweat oozed down Stone's chest as he cut his airspeed and lined up the Hydra for a propeller landing. Down, down, flaps lowered, altimeter reading—the tilt rotors on the wings made it a very unforgiving plane to handle. *Whump.* It was a heavy-footed performance. But he was on the ground, taxiing toward the nearest hangar.

Major General Anthony Sirocca, the burly commander of Dreamland, was waiting in front of the operations building. They were old friends. "We got a flash from Washington about Adrian," Sirocca said, as they shook hands. "Is it true?"

"I'm afraid it is."

"Anything suspicious about it?" asked Tom Guilford, the gaunt six-foot-six Buchanan vice president who had spent most of the last three years at Dreamland. His wife had divorced him a month ago, adding two more emotional casualties to the history of the aircraft business.

"We don't know yet," Dick Stone said. "We don't know a goddamn thing except he's dead."

They walked to the operations building, where Dick gratefully accepted a cup of coffee. Sleeplessness was beginning to suck life out of his brain. "We'll be having a special board meeting soon. I thought it might be a good idea to give the bankers a firsthand report on how things are going up here."

Tony Sirocca's bushy brows rose a fraction of an inch. He knew that was not the real reason Dick Stone was here. Tony heard things over the military grapevine. He knew a lot about Buchanan's financial problems. "Things couldn't be better," Sirocca said. "We've got ourselves a hell of a plane."

"You're just in time for a demonstration," Guilford said. "She's coming in from the Canadian border in about fifteen minutes."

In the checklist on Buchanan's executives Dick Stone carried in his head, Tom Guilford acquired a bundle of white points. He had understood the purpose of the visit the moment he heard about it.

They walked down the concrete walled corridor, freshly painted Air Force blue, to the communications center. At least thirty men and women sat before consoles. The officer in command of the room, a brisk blond major named Wallis Thompson, gave Stone a cheerful hello.

"How's it going?" he said.

"We've got every kind of radar in the book out there looking for him, including a whole fighter wing. Not a trace," she said in a throaty voice that made Dick consider inquiring about her next leave. But the business at hand swiftly sidetracked this erotic impulse.

Roaring toward them across the desert was an immense black plane made not of steel or aluminum but of carbon fiber and epoxy, materials created in the laboratory. Her radical design and the complex counter-radar devices in her belly made the latest version of the BX bomber invisible to the most sophisticated air defenses the minds of men in Moscow or Beijing or Washington could devise.

Tony Sirocca looked at his watch. "She'll be overhead in about two minutes."

They strolled out a side door and walked to the runway. The rising sun was almost visible over the peaks of the Sierras. The upper horizon was fringed with red. But everyone's eyes were on the empty desert that stretched for a hundred miles between them and the mountains. Suddenly it was there, a black blur against the brown slopes of the Sierras.

On she came, a bare fifty feet off the ground, traveling just below the speed of sound. Over their heads she whizzed in a roar that was almost instantly consumed by distance. An incredible sight as she banked far out on the desert and began a landing approach. The minuscule tail, the fusion of wing and fuselage, the beaked nose made her look like a creature from a science fiction movie. A true denizen of dreamland.

For a moment Dick Stone could only think of the heartbreak this plane had caused so many people in Buchanan Aircraft over the last twenty years. Denounced, junked, revived, reviled. Yet here she was, Frank Buchanan's last and perhaps greatest gift to the country he no longer loved. Adrian Van Ness's final triumph. And Dick Stone? Was it his consolation? Or his nemesis?

The plane lived. But she threatened the life of the company that had created her. Dick Stone was here to see if he had the courage—or the cowardice—to kill her. Take your pick of motives and alternatives. The world into which this plane was flying had become so complex, words lost their meanings, motives wavered and shimmered like air in the desert at high noon.

Down, down came the black bomber, exhaust pouring from her four turbofan engines. Without a trace of a bump, her tires kissed the runway and she rolled past them. In the cockpit window, the pilot gave them a thumbs up. General Sirocca and Tom Guilford raised their thumbs in response. Dick Stone found his hand high in an involuntary wave.

Dick took a deep slow breath. He was part of it again, the brotherhood he had joined when he climbed aboard the *Rainbow Express* in 1942. He had come out here hoping to find a reason to kill this plane. To tell Tony Sirocca and Tom Guilford that the numbers no longer made sense. A company that was running out of money could not keep spending a hundred million dollars a year on a plane that the U.S. government might not buy.

"There's only one thing wrong, Tony," Dick said. "You could paint two hundred of the goddamn things with the red ink she's generating."

"We'll get some real money for you next year. I guarantee it."

"You've been guaranteeing that for a long time, Tony."

"I'll get it or I'm out of this uniform," Tony said.

"The things we're learning will change the history of aviation, I swear it," Tom Guilford said.

For a moment exhaustion and the emotional side of Dick Stone's Jewish-American nature overwhelmed him. Guilford was frowning at him like a son who could not believe his father would betray him. He was a sort of son. Dick had picked him for this difficult job. He knew what it had already cost him.

"It'll guarantee the survival of the fucking country. That's what I care about," Tony Sirocca said.

Stone sighed. He had heard similar things said about other planes. But this one, with its freight of history and heartbreak, might be the one that deserved the rhetoric.

"You know me. I like to take a look at things close up," Dick said.

"Sure. Sure," Sirocca said. "I wish you came out more often."

"Tom keeps me up on everything. He writes a good report."

They walked toward the Hydra that Stone had flown to their impromptu demonstration as the sun slanted tentative red rays across the desert. "Don't you think it'd be a good idea to let a pilot fly you back?" Guilford said.

Again, the pain of fatherhood stirred in Dick Stone's chest. He could not get used to it. He had played a son's part to Adrian Van Ness and Frank Buchanan for so long. A difficult, combative son. Once—a memory that still filled him with twisting regret—a treacherous son.

"What do you mean 'good idea'?" Tony Sirocca said. "It's an absolute necessity. It's a miracle this asshole got here without killing himself in that screwy machine."

"Go to hell," Dick said. "I survived three and a half years in the U.S. Army Air Force with generals like you trying to kill me every day."

"After seeing you land tonight, I'm ready to believe you're indestructible. But why ruin a perfectly good aircraft, even if it's more or less useless?" Sirocca said.

General Sirocca was letting Stone know that the Air Force was not happy with the way the Marines, the Coast Guard, and the Navy were salivating over the Hydra. Tony wanted Buchanan to work exclusively for the boys in blue. Dick Stone had no intention of going broke to keep Sirocca happy. He could hear Adrian Van Ness telling him that governments and their departments and branches did not know the existence—much less the meaning—of the word *gratitude.*

Did that mean second thoughts about the BX bomber? Maybe.

Another cup of coffee and ten minutes with the ebullient young major who had flown the BX and Dick Stone was on his way. He dozed in his seat beside the baby-faced twenty-six-year-old Air Force captain who was flying the Hydra after a ten-minute conference with Tom Guilford. The captain was ecstatic at the chance to get his hands on the controls of such a top-secret item. It was making his day, his week, his month, his year.

Stone nodded and in his mind walked across miles of desert to a woman waiting in the silence. For years now he had found a strange monkish satisfaction in thinking of her there in the arid wastes. She was a kind of sentry, guarding a border that he some day hoped to cross. Now he began to think—to fear—it was going to become another failed dream, another hope that would never fly. Mournfully, while the boyish captain chortled, Dick talked to Sarah Morris.

If Cliff refuses to leave quietly I can deal with it one of two ways. I can cancel the BX, and stand tall as Buchanan's rescuer, the man who can make the hard decisions. If I keep the plane, that exposes me to Cliff coming forward as the BX's executioner, the man with the titanium backbone. He'll never convince a majority of the board but he may confuse enough people to make us a setup for a corporate raider, someone who'll carve us up and sell off the pieces. To stop Cliff I'll need your help. That means I can never ask you for anything else.

Could he do it? Could he dismiss happiness so finally, so irretrievably? Was this Adrian Van Ness's last demand, the final requirement of sonship? As he drifted down into sleep, Dick wondered if it was the only way he could reach out to Adrian now, the only way he could say: *I'm sorry.*

THE MEDICINE MAN

In his shack on the slopes of the San Jacinto Mountains, eighty-three-year-old Frank Buchanan lay awake. In his head he was soaring through the desert's blue sky, while in the front seat of his gull-winged fiberglass sailplane Sarah Chapman Morris uttered cries that could only be described as erotic. He had begun flying these engineless creatures about a year ago, at her suggestion. It was a uniquely spiritual sensation, riding the winds blowing off the mountains for an hour or two before gravity made its ultimate claim on the body and the airship. Frank always came home feeling renewed, able to endure his creaking physique and the nauseating American world of the 1970s for a while longer.

What an interesting woman Sarah had become. Frank realized he had rated her much too low because she was Cliff Morris's wife. He was amused by her insatiable curiosity about Buchanan Aircraft. She wanted to know everything, back to the dawn of time. She said she hoped understanding would lead to forgiveness, a lovely idea. It had not worked for him. Frank thought he understood almost everything about Adrian Van Ness but he still hated him.

Dozing off, Frank dreamt he was flying a Bleriot Experimental Model 2 biplane over southwestern England. The cranky sixty-horsepower engine pulled him along in the stiff headwind at a satisfying forty miles an hour. Below him in the darkening sky was another BE2 piloted by a man whom he had begun to regard as an older brother. Edward "Teddy" Busk was an ebullient Cambridge University mathematician who had devoted his first-class mind to the new science of aerodynamics. His insights had prompted Geoffrey de Havilland to reposition the wing, redesign the lateral tail and create the first truly stable plane. Not only had Busk shared his ideas with Frank Buchanan and other eager pupils—he had learned to fly as an act of faith in his computations.

As Frank looked down on Busk's plane, he saw a twenty-foot ribbon of flame streaming behind him. In sixty seconds, the fabric-covered wings and fuselage were engulfed by livid tongues of fire. As Frank watched, horrified, Busk made a perfect landing on a wide swath of downs called Laffan Plain. It was an ironic tribute to the stability of the BE2—but it did nothing to extinguish the flames.

Awake, his body twisting in anguish, Frank remembered the rest of the story. He had landed at nearby Farnborough, the home of the Royal Flying Corps, and raced back to Laffan Plain in a fire truck. They were much too late. Teddy Busk's blackened corpse sat in the charred skeleton of the plane, his grimaced teeth gleaming in the truck's headlights. They took the body and the remnants of the plane back to Farnborough and found that the fire had been caused by the motor's vibration breaking a pipe joint. The motor had run out of fuel and backfired, igniting the gasoline tank. Mournfully, they redesigned the fuel system to make sure it did not happen again.

Tears streamed down Frank Buchanan's face. The sacrifices men had made to create planes! His mind leaped from this lost brother to other brothers and sons. One above all, whose name he still could not pronounce without tears. Part of the reason he was living in this shack was a desperate wish to reach Billy McCall, wherever he was, beyond the sky.

Frank lay on his back on the boards that served for his bed, hearing his mother hiss: *death machine.* Slowly, carefully, he sat up and waited for the blood to circulate in his numbed feet and hands. Seizing his cane, he hoisted himself erect and waited again to make sure he had located his center of gravity. His body had become as fragile, as unpredictable as the planes of 1910, with their translucent fabric wings and fuselages, their jungle of guy wires and primitive controls.

Carefully, creakily, Frank heaved himself from his narrow bed and hobbled to a table. Switching on a battery-powered lamp, he sat before a blank sheet of white paper in a loose-leaf folder, pen in hand. For an hour, the paper remained pristine. The gnarled hand, with the blotchy skin where it had been burned off in the crash of a long vanished plane, remained motionless.

Finally, the hand began to move. *Father. Father,* it wrote. It was Billy, still calling for help. Frank had heard from him a dozen times since he retreated here. Once more Frank struggled to send a message to his mother. *Find him and rescue him. Even if you never loved him. Even if you hated him in my name.*

As usual, Althea Buchanan replied: *I can't find him in the spirit world. He has no soul. It often happens when a child is born of fierce opposites.* She had told him this when Billy was eleven. Frank had struggled to prove she was wrong. But history, another word for mystery, had been like a gigantic windshear, undercutting his hopes and prayers.

Frank stumbled out on the porch and sat down in a cane-bottomed rocking chair. The wind rushed up the mountain to tear at his loose shirt and pants. He looked down on the darkened desert and beyond it, a glare against the overcast, the lights of the city of Los Angeles behind her barrier mountains.

Two hundred years ago, the great Indian medicine man, Tahquitz, had withdrawn to this mountain to brood in lonely despair about the decline of his people. Frank Buchanan had followed him here, also a man in mourning for his people. The Americans of the seventies seemed to have lost their way. Sexual, political, religious extremists hurled insults and slogans. A president betrayed his office and senators and congressmen revealed themselves as hypocrites worshipping the newest goddess, Publicity. Night after night, Buchanan sat at his desk opening his mind to the guardian spirits, hoping for wisdom—an old man's consolation for his losses. But Tahquitz remained silent.

Frank could almost hear Adrian Van Ness laughing. For a moment he had to struggle against a demoralizing surge of hatred.

Thinking again of Edward Busk in his burning plane, Frank wondered if there was another meaning in the memory. Somewhere a compatriot had died in the long upward struggle men called flight. He was still linked to the great enterprise, so crucial in the conflict between darkness and light, above all to the company he had founded, now an immense family of machinists and designers and analysts and salesmen and executives, working beneath his name. Scarcely a day passed without a letter or a postcard from one of them, recalling the rollout of a famous plane, the triumph of a controversial design, the pathos of an old failure.

They were all linked, the living and the dead, in the cosmic sea of the worldsoul. Frank Buchanan still retained that primary faith, imparted to him by his mother. Within that cosmic soul, each individual soul was part of an eternal struggle between good and evil, between the guardians and the destroyers.

Adrian Van Ness had mocked that childhood faith. Adrian had mocked many things. His soul was an abyss of hatred or loss that Frank Buchanan had never been able to penetrate. That was another reason for his sojourn in the desert— he wanted to eradicate the last vestige of hatred for Adrian from his spirit. All he had to show for it was another failure.

A clattering, poppering roar in the sky above him. Searchlights blazing, a Buchanan helicopter was descending to the small landing strip a few hundred yards from the shack. In a few minutes Bruce Simons, Buchanan's tall flashy director of public relations, and a young stranger approached the porch. Behind them came Kirk Willoughby, the company's pink-cheeked, balding chief physician.

"Frank, how the hell are you?" Bruce said in his breeziest style, pumping his hand. "I hope you don't mind us dropping in this way at five A.M. We tried to call you but your phone doesn't seem to be working."

"I disconnected it a month ago."

"This is Mark Casey of the *L.A. Times*. Their aviation reporter."

"I told you I was through giving interviews, Bruce."

"This isn't just another interview, Frank. Adrian Van Ness died last night. Mark would like to talk to you about your memories of him—the early days of the company—where you see it going now that his influence—"

"Adrian! You're sure? How—what was the cause?"

"A heart attack, apparently. The doc here was treating him for heart disease—"

"Amanda—Mrs. Van Ness—how is she—where is she?"

"She's still in Virginia. But I presume she'll return to California. We're going to have a memorial service for Adrian at the company next week," Simons said.

Suddenly Frank Buchanan's world was no longer a gray meaningless place. He no longer belonged in the desert. But he could not possibly explain that to Simons or to this earnest young reporter, who looked as if he was born the day before yesterday.

Kirk Willoughby understood, of course. He knew more about Adrian and Frank and Amanda than anyone in the company, except inquisitive Sarah Chapman Morris. He was here to make sure the news did not abort Frank's laboring heart. A superfluous worry.

They sat down on the porch and Mark Casey began asking him the standard questions. What was the secret of his long, successful collaboration with Adrian Van Ness? What was their most important plane? What was Adrian Van Ness's contribution to Buchanan's success? Was he involved in the company's recent difficulties with the government? How did Frank see Buchanan's future now?

Frank's answers were not lies. He said the secret of his collaboration with Adrian was mutual respect. Of course they argued now and then, ho ho ho. But they realized each had a part to play. As for their most important plane— each one was important while they were building it. Frequently important enough to be the margin between bankruptcy and solvency, ho ho ho.

Adrian's greatest contribution was forethought. He was always thinking ahead to the next generation airliner or fighter plane. Of course he wasn't always right but neither were Douglas or Lockheed or Boeing right all the time, ho ho ho. As for Adrian's involvement with the company in recent years—he had retired to the cheering section, like him. The company's future? It was bright. The Buchanan rainbow—Adrian's idea, by the way—still reached over the horizon—and the plane soaring above it might soon be flying at hypersonic speed.

Almost all of it was true. But it was only one percent of the truth. Watching the boyish reporter take it down, Frank remembered so many things he could never tell him, so many things a thirty-five-year-old would find it hard—perhaps impossible—to understand.

Mark Casey said he was delighted with the interview. Bruce Simons said they had to get back to Los Angeles as soon as possible. "I think I'll stay with this old curmudgeon for a while. Check out a few things like his blood pressure and his heartbeat," Kirk Willoughby said. "You can send the chopper back for me in an hour or two."

The helicopter clattered into the sky. Frank Buchanan gazed at Willoughby. "It's impossible to explain," he said.

"I know," Willoughby said.

"You'd have to go back to the beginning."

"I know," Willoughby said.

He pulled a flask of Scotch out of his pocket and poured a drink for himself and Frank. "Dick Stone's going to be the new CEO. Cliff's out. Does that bother you?"

"It's a pretty raw deal in some ways. Cliff isn't really responsible for our sins. Adrian's the culprit."

Frank sipped the Scotch. Bitter memories flowed into his mind with the taste. "The culprit—in so many ways."

"I think you've got Adrian wrong. You've always had him wrong."

"You're saying you never know the whole truth about a man—even when you work with him for forty-seven years?"

"I'm afraid not."

Maybe he was right. Maybe none of them, including himself, were as innocent as they wished they were—or as guilty as they feared they were. "Amanda—do you think it's possible—?"

"I don't know. I hope so."

"If I can hold her in my arms for a year—or even a month—I'll forgive the universe."

The two men sipped their Scotch in silence, while from the empty desert welled the faces and the voices, the illusions and the heartbreak of the living and the dead. Above them flew the planes—from the wobbling fabric creatures of the first decade to the titanium projectiles of today. Seventy-six years of flight through Frank Buchanan's life and Adrian Van Ness's life and so many other lives.

This was their journey, Frank thought. Only someone who flew the route across memory and time and history could decide who should be forgiven, who should be condemned. For himself, he relied on two lines from his favorite poet.

> *Let the gods forgive what I*
> *have made.*
> *Let those I love try to forgive*
> *what I have made.*

EXILE

As usual, Sarah Chapman Morris awoke an hour before dawn. She lay in bed, watching the windowpane grow gray. Around the house stretched the southern California desert, arid mile after mile to the Salton Sea and Death Valley. It was a landscape as different from the green flowering England of her youth as nature—or the imagination—could devise. The aridity, the emptiness corresponded exactly with her state of mind and soul.

Thirty-six years. Thirty-six years since Sarah Chapman walked down the aisle of the country church outside Rackreath Air Base arm in arm with Captain Clifford Morris, the handsome American bomber pilot, whose indifference to religion dismayed her devout Catholic mother. Her brother Derek, flying fighters for the RAF, had asked in his brutal way how she could marry anyone from the "Bloody 103rd" bombardment group. Did she have some peculiar desire to become a widow?

Sarah put on a dressing gown and padded through the silent house to the room that had been her husband's study. She pressed a button on the desk. Along the wall to the right of the terrace doors, concealed lights illuminated an immense painting of a B-17 plowing through flak-infested skies, spewing bullets from its turret and tail and waist guns at German fighters. Beneath the cockpit window was a crescent rainbow with a plane soaring above it. At least once a day, Sarah stared at the painting as if she needed to convince herself that her life was not a dream.

On the empty desk was a letter from Adrian Van Ness.

Dear Cliff:

We have weathered the worst of the scandal without losing a single contract. This is a tribute to your reputation within the aircraft industry and in Congress. Alas, the same thing cannot be said for the Buchanan Corporation. Over the years we have acquired enemies in the press and in Washington, D.C. who are still pursuing us. The other day I heard from one of our closest Pentagon friends that our chief tormentor in the Senate was threatening to start a new round of hearings to explore our "continuing culpability" because we have, he claims, displayed not a single sign of repentance for our sins. I am sure you realize more negative publicity would make it impossible for us to obtain the financing we so badly need.

For thirty years you have demonstrated a readiness to work, to serve, to sacrifice for Buchanan. Can I ask you to consider an ultimate sacrifice, your resignation?

I have told Dick Stone you might want to discuss the terms of your retirement. He has orders from me to be even more generous than he would be under ordinary circumstances.

Regretfully,
Adrian

The bastard, Sarah Chapman Morris thought. The corrupt ruthless brilliant bastard. She should have known it was coming. She should have known Adrian Van Ness would send her a copy of this letter. It was exactly what a master of forethought would do. He was trying to stir pity in her forlorn heart.

A crash. The wind was blowing a shutter or a door somewhere in the house. Sarah padded through the rooms full of sleek chrome-and-glass furniture. The noise was coming from one of the patio doors. She stepped outside and let the cold desert wind cut into her flesh for a long minute. A plane was coming over the Funeral Mountains, beginning its descent to Los Angeles. The way she and Cliff had arrived thirty-four years ago.

The passengers would soon be looking down on the awesome sea of lights, the forty-six square miles of a city that was not a city, a vast collection of canyons and arroyos and flats and seacoast in search of an identity, with Hollywood in the center of it, infecting everything with its amoral hedonism.

No. That was the old Sarah talking, the once proper English girl with her devotion to spiritual ideals. That woman was dead. As obliterated as the test pilots who smashed their experimental jets into the desert floor at 2,500 miles an hour. Miss Sarah Chapman was gone into some region where souls occasionally communicated with the living. Now she was a semi-divorced American wife named Ms. Sarah Morris shivering in the desert wind beneath a starry California sky with the blank black bulk of the mountains looming in the night a few dozen miles away.

They had all come so far.

Was the distance the human equivalent of losing your soul—or finding it? Sarah pondered that question for another thirty seconds as the jetliner descended, wingtip lights blinking. In a few more minutes the landing headlights would come on and it would resemble a prehistoric creature, a pterodactyl or some other monster plunging out of time into man's exhausted mind.

She hated planes.

Was that true? She had always loved the idea of planes. Maybe she just hated what men did to make and sell them. That thought led to eighty-three year-old Frank Buchanan in his shack above Tahquitz Canyon. To memories of yesterday's soaring session in his sailplane, *Rainbow's End*. My God, how she loved those motorless hours in the sky with him! Almost as much as she loved the hours of reminiscence she had mined from his shy, reclusive soul.

Sleep was out of the question now. In the bathroom, Sarah washed her face and studied herself in the mirror by the dim glow of the night light. She looked ghostly as well as ghastly. Maybe she had become Miss Sarah Chapman again. Maybe she had died and was starting to relive her life, backwards. But Adrian's letter to Cliff mocked that silly idea. The letter was like a gaff in her flesh, flinging her forward into time again.

Sarah padded into the sunken living room and pulled a video at random from a rack beside the television set. She shoved it into the VCR and sat down. A stubby-winged, thick-bodied plane hurtled toward her on the television screen. She almost cried out.

"The Wild Aces," growled a gravel-voiced narrator. "They take the fight to the enemy. They hit him where it hurts."

It was a video of a film Buchanan had made to help sell their ground-support plane, the Thunderer. The narrator told why it was the best plane the U.S. Marines had ever bought for the money, his voice rasping against the rising beat of a frenzied orchestra. The Thunderer could carry more bombs, more hardware than anything the enemy could put in the sky. It could carry two-hundred-and-fifty-, five-hundred-, thousand-pound bombs. It had a twenty-millimeter cannon that fired 600 rounds a minute. It had Shrike missiles that could demolish the enemy's surface-to-air missile sites. That was the Thunderer's job. To come in low and get those SAM sites to make things safe for the bombers following them.

Sarah sat and watched the pilots getting into their G suits. She prayed she would not see her son. She no longer thought God was listening but she prayed anyway. It did no good. They all looked like Charlie. They were all young and cheerful and had short hair and strong jaws and firm, proud American mouths.

Sarah watched them climb into their cockpits and put on their shiny plastic helmets and clamp the oxygen masks on their faces. She watched them taxi down the runway, shove the throttles forward and vault into the sky, flame spewing from their afterburners.

"Taking it to the enemy," roared the narrator. Sarah watched the bombs explode on bridges, rail yards, factories, on what the narrator called troop concentrations but looked like trees and farms. The bombs burst and burst, sometimes leaping up in great orange gushes of flame, usually mushrooming into serrated puffs of earth and exploding dust.

Click. The screen went dark. Susan Hardy stood beside it, a blur against the gray desert dawn. "Are you crazy?" she said. "Are you trying to drive yourself crazy?"

"Maybe," Sarah said.

Her fellow pilgrim, with the burning passion for peace in her eyes. Sarah had traded her life as the wife of the chief executive officer of the Buchanan Corporation for exile with this woman. Susan was her oldest American friend. She had divorced her unfaithful husband years ago. She had led Sarah into the exhilarating bewildering worlds of the women's movement and the peace movement.

Without turning on a light, Susan sat down on the couch beside Sarah and kissed her on the cheek. "You're trying to accept it, aren't you? The whole thing. But that's the wrong way to go. Acceptance is just another word for surrendering to the bastards."

"Yes," Sarah said automatically. She no longer agreed with Susan but it was too exhausting to argue with her.

"Once and for all you have to ask yourself—what, who do you love," Susan said.

"I'll do that," Sarah said.

"The right answer is you love yourself. You are the most important person in your world."

Susan retreated to her bed. Sarah sat on the couch and watched the sun tip the Sierra's peaks with fire. Was I ever in love with anyone? she wondered. Was I really in love with a dream of glory, a destiny in the sky? Was I as drunk with the beauty, the terror, the mystery of planes as all the rest of them?

The telephone rang. Who in the world could be calling at this time of day? She walked into the hall to answer it. "Sarah?" Dick Stone said. "Adrian Van Ness died of a heart attack about four hours ago. I think it's time you came home. Cliff needs you."

Trailing the extension cord, Sarah stumbled back into the living room and sat down on the couch again with the phone in her numb hand. The fiery light was spilling over the Funeral Mountains. In the nearer distance, it created an aureole around a Joshua tree. The giant cactus seemed to be thrusting its prickly stumps into the glowing air in a silent hallelujah. Or was it a desperate plea?

And you don't? You don't need me? cried the ghost of Miss Sarah Chapman somewhere in her married mind. The ghost wanted to shout those words into the phone's white mouthpiece. But Sarah only sat there staring at the Joshua tree, deciding to let the ghost write the whole story. She would tell it objectively, with the crystalline clarity of the stratosphere, tell it without so much as a whimper of an I, an echo of an ego. She would tell everything she had learned in England and America, in Los Angeles and in the Mojave and on the ridge above Tahquitz Canyon.

29

"Sarah?" Dick Stone said. "Sarah?"

She would begin with Adrian Van Ness and Frank Buchanan, the original spinners of the web of profit and loss, betrayal and commitment, exaltation and compulsion that became the years of their lives. She would go back to the moment when men first discovered the omnipotence, the wonder, of the sky and began to explore the meaning, the power, of wings. Only by regaining the illusion of innocence could she hope to explain the stunning inevitability of it all.

She would *control* her *rage* at the *obscenities* they *committed* in the *name* of their *planes*. She would not *lament* the *women* they *mutilated*, the *lives* they *twisted* and *tormented* like the metal they *bent* and *hammered* into *shapes* they *loved* more than their *children*. She would *write* of *love* and *hate* and *despair* with the debonair *courtesy* of the *dammed*, the irony of the *unforgiven*, the blank-eyed *calm* of the angel of *death*.

The ghost would live in all the tormented hearts and anguished heads with a phantasm's duplicity, telling the truth the truth the truth about everyone, even about that riven ruin of reproach and regret known as Sarah Chapman Morris.

"Sarah?" Dick Stone said. "Sarah?"

BOOK TWO

BOOK TWO

BROTHERLY LOVE

In 1912 Americans were dancing the Crab Step, the Kangaroo Dip, the Chicken Scratch, and the Bunny Hug. The slang expressions of the year were *flossy, beat it!, peeved,* and *it's a cinch.* Movies were attracting five million people a day. An eastern Democrat named Woodrow Wilson was running for president. The U.S. Marines landed in Cuba to restore order. Frank Buchanan did not pay much attention to any of these things. He was too busy being the happiest sixteen-year-old in California, working as mechanic and factotum for his brother Craig, the pilot of a bright green biplane called *Rag Time.*

Craig had thundered up to Frank's door in his Harley-Davidson motorcar two years before to take his younger brother to the Dominguez Hills air meet outside Los Angeles. His mother had begged Frank not to go. She did not want him to have anything to do with her swarthy swaggering older son, who had defied her exhortations and admonitions practically from birth. In 1905, at the age of eighteen, Craig had gone off to race motor cars, becoming as famous as Cal Rodgers and Eddie Rickenbacker in that daredevil sport.

Frank had found the invitation to Dominguez Hills irresistible. Craig had said it would be the first air show in the United States. Airmen from France and America were going to fly balloons, dirigibles, and planes. It was going to make California famous for something besides orange groves and sunshine.

On the green mesa between Compton and Long Beach, a crowd of 20,000 swarmed off the big red Pacific Electric Railway cars to see the most miraculous sight in history—men flying through the air. The planes were the main attraction. Balloons were old stuff and dirigibles had been wobbling through the California sky for several years. One had raced an automobile from Los Angeles to Pasadena in 1905 and won.

Frank watched easterner Glenn Curtiss begin the festivities with a flight in his gleaming yellow biplane, the *Golden Flyer*, which had won the world's first air meet in Rheims, France in 1909 with a top speed of 46.5 miles an hour. The *Flyer* had a tricycle landing gear and a sixty-horsepower "pusher" motor that purred away behind the pilot's back. The crowd roared with excitement as Curtiss circled the field at a height of fifty feet, flying over a half mile and making a smooth landing in front of the grandstand.

Other pilots took to the air in similar machines. They soon demonstrated that flying was not only marvelous—it was dangerous. For reasons no one seemed to understand, planes suddenly slipped sideways out of the air or plunged to the ground nose first. The organizers of the meet did not let these accidents stop the show. Ambulances rushed to haul the fliers from the wreckage of their planes, the mangled struts and wires and fabric were towed out of sight into a nearby ravine—and another plane was in the air, dazzling the spectators again. Only the next day did they learn in the newspapers that the crashed flier was badly injured—or dead.

The star of the meet turned out to be a Frenchman, Louis Paulhan. He performed sharp banks and dives that made Curtiss and other fliers look timid. In eleven days of flying before crowds that totalled 176,000, Paulhan won 14,000 dollars in prize money.

"That does it, kid," Craig said. "From now on we're in the plane business." With his usual magnificent self-confidence, Craig introduced himself to Paulhan and soon learned the secret of his acrobatic skills. "It's those hinged sections on the wings. He calls them ailerons," Craig said. "They keep the ship steady in a turn."

Craig paid Paulhan five hundred dollars for a week's flying lessons. This gave him a chance to inspect Paulhan's plane and discreetly sketch the design. At night Craig gave lessons of another kind to the Baroness von Sonnenschein, a statuesque blond Viennese who had traveled to America with Paulhan's party. She liked Craig's lessons so much, she rented a cottage in the Malibu Hills and let Paulhan go back to France without her.

Craig and Frank went to work on building an imitation of Paulhan's plane. Frank took a course at the Los Angeles YMCA to improve his woodworking skills and did so well he personally carved the laminated walnut propeller the day before they rolled the plane out of Craig's Santa Monica garage. *Rag Time* had a wingspan of thirty-three feet. The hickory and ash struts were covered with green pegamoid, a fabric made of calico treated with celluloid. Craig had improved the rudder controls and widened the ailerons to give the ship added stability. They put a sixty-horsepower motor developed by a San Francisco automaker behind the pilot's seat and *Rag Time* was ready to fly.

The Baroness was naturally the first passenger. She cried out in French and German as Craig zoomed over the ocean and dipped and banked and dove to within inches of the whitecaps. Later Craig told Frank the exclamations were identical to those he heard at midnight in the cottage in Malibu.

Frank found Craig's attitude toward women confusing. He often came back from a visit to the Baroness and described in vivid detail what they had done, while Frank worked on *Rag Time*. Then Craig would drink a cup of coffee to sober up, take off his coat and say: "That's all they're good for, kid. The rest is yak-yak."

Craig completed *Rag Time*'s maiden flight with a perfect three-point landing. Frank helped the ecstatic Baroness descend from the passenger seat. Craig winked and said: "Get aboard, kid."

Down the grassy meadow they raced to soar above the horizon as Craig pulled back on the control stick. Up up they mounted against a strong headwind until the entire coast—the great headlands of Palos Verdes, the flat undulating shore of Long Beach and San Pedro, the wooded crests of the Santa Monica Mountains and the scattering of houses and business buildings called Los Angeles were visible in one magnificent sweep.

It was not simply the vista, it was the sensation of riding the wind that made Frank Buchanan an instant convert to the air age. Flight created a lightness, a happiness in his body and mind that seemed exactly like his mother's description of the soul's journey to the realm of peace and light after death. It was heaven on earth, divinity within the grasp of living men!

Craig was soon flying *Rag Time* all over California, winning prizes at other air meets, including a second show at Dominquez Hills in 1911, where he picked up 450 dollars as the best novice flyer. At that show, the organizers had added something new to the excitement. They staged a mock bombing raid. A detachment of national guardsman hunkered down behind some earthworks and Craig and another pilot dropped smoke bombs on them. The soldiers ran out and surrendered.

The extra seat they had added to the plane was a moneymaker. After William Randolph Hearst took a ride with Louis Paulhan and reported it in his newspapers like the Angel Gabriel announcing the second coming, hundreds of people were eager to fly at five dollars a head. Few pilots were more popular than Craig. With his racing car driver's peaked hat perched sideways on his head, a big cigar clamped in his mouth, he was the essence of heroism on the ground and in the air.

So here it was, 1912. They were on the way to an air show in San Diego. As they climbed aboard *Rag Time*, Frank said: "Can we stop in Santa Ana and see Mother?"

"How many times do I have to tell you to put that crazy woman out of your mind once and for all?" Craig said.

That was not easy for Frank to do. He had spent his boyhood defending Althea Buchanan from the ridicule of her neighbors and his friends. She never sought the messages that came to her in the night, voices of guardian spirits who told her of forgotten wars and evil conspiracies in the blank centuries before history began in books. The English-born pastor of the Church of the Questing Spirit said she was one of the rare few who could communicate directly with the world beyond the grave. But outside the tiny circle of true believers in the church, her gift had brought Althea Buchanan little but scorn and heartbreak.

Craig flew *Rag Time* above the coast highway, telling Frank to get over his "momma's boyitis." They were going straight to San Diego. But Frank knew they had to land for gas somewhere. When the village of Santa Ana appeared on the left, he grabbed Craig's sleeve and pointed to it. Cursing, Craig banked over the town and circled the Buchanan ceramics factory, with its beds of blooming flowers between the office and kiln. He landed in a grassy field just beyond it.

Althea Buchanan manufactured plates and pitchers and platters portraying Spanish days in old California. She had no training as a painter. Her designs were primitive but the colors were vivid and the expressions on the faces of her Mexicans and Indians emanated an innocence that Anglos found irresistible. There was scarcely a house in the Southwest that did not have at least one of her creations.

She had come to the sleepy town in Orange County just after Frank was born in freezing Kansas. One of her guardian spirits had told her to seek warmth and sunshine for the infant or he was doomed. Her husband, delighted (according to Craig) to find an excuse to split up, declined to accompany her. She had taken ten thousand dollars from him and headed for California with her two sons, confident that her guardian spirits would guide her when she arrived. They had told her to found the ceramics factory and she had done so with astonishing success.

Althea hurtled toward Frank and Craig, her cheeks streaked with dirt, her red hair cascading in all directions beneath an immense sun hat. Behind her trooped the twenty Mexicans who did the hard labor at the furnaces. Althea was only four feet eleven and at fifty still had the complexion of a sixteen-year-old. Her perpetual youth sharpened the aura of unreality that always surrounded her.

"What is it? Where did you get it?" she cried.

"It's a plane, Madam," Craig said. He always treated her with mocking courtesy, no matter how much she abused him.

"It's beautiful," she said, making a wide circle around *Rag Time*. "Does it have a soul?"

"It's a machine, Madam. Machines don't have souls."

"I've seen a creature like it in a dream," she said. "Galdur, the tyrant who ruled Palestine a thousand years before the Jews came there, used it to conquer Atlantis." She glared at Craig. "You were born under the same dark sign. You'll turn this into a death machine!"

She whirled on Frank. "Have you given up your great ambition—to worship this evil thing?"

Frank blanched. She was talking about the project to which he had vowed to dedicate his life until Craig took him to the Dominguez Hills air meet—to prove scientifically the survival of the soul after death.

"I'll never give it up entirely, Mother. But flying is so marvelous. You can't believe how wonderful it is until you try it. Why don't you let Craig take you for a ride?"

"If we crash, you can nag me for all eternity," Craig said.

"Your pride will be your undoing, Craig. You'll meet the same fate as your ur-soul, Gath."

According to the Church of the Questing Spirit, every person in the world was an emanation of a handful of primary ur-souls, some of them evil, others good. The world was in perpetual conflict between these agents of light and darkness. If, as in Craig's case, his ur-soul was evil, it required extra effort to achieve the light. Effort he of course declined to make.

"In the meantime, Madam, I hope to enjoy myself," Craig said. "You should see how excited this death machine makes the girls in Long Beach. Frank is finding that out too, right?"

"Just—by observation," Frank said, blushing the color of his mother's hair.

"Abominable!" Althea cried. "He's a child of light, an emanation of Mana, the noblest of the ur-souls. That's why I brought him to California. So he would thrive in sunlight. If you corrupt him, you'll wander among the galaxies for ten thousand years, I warn you. Not even Gath will consider you worthy of rebirth."

Craig laughed. He picked up Althea and announced he was going to give her one of his "Long Beach kisses." Althea punched at him furiously. "I won't accept your affection. I no longer consider you my son."

Craig kissed her anyway and set her down with a jolt. Frank saw he was angry. "I knew this was going to be a waste of time," he said. He climbed back aboard *Rag Time*. "Let's get on to San Diego, kid."

"Frank, I beg you. Don't let him seduce you with this evil creature," Althea said. "The spirit should soar without man-made wings! This will only swell men's pride and folly."

Craig was in the pilot's seat, adjusting his goggles. Frank hesitated, in torment. On one side was adventure, heroism, on the other side, the life of the spirit, the exploration of its mysteries.

"Let's *go*, kid," Craig said.

Suddenly Frank was almost as angry at his mother as Craig was. Couldn't she see he was a *man*? Craig was right. She was trying to make him a momma's boy for the rest of his life. Women were dangerous.

He spun the prop and leaped into the passenger seat. In a moment they were in the air, climbing to five hundred feet. Frank watched his mother dwindle to a speck in the green field where for a moment she had seemed so formidable.

The air meet in San Diego was a big success. Craig won four thousand dollars in prizes. His bombing routine was the hit of the show. He used giant firecrackers that went off with a big bang. That night Craig urged Frank to join him and Muriel Halsey, an actress who followed him everywhere in her white Dusenberg touring car, for a night on the town. (The Baroness had returned to Vienna "haxausted," according to Craig.) Muriel said she would find him a girl.

Frank shook his head. He was feeling guilty about making his mother unhappy. She had warned him against drinking liquor. She said it was dangerous for a child of light. She also warned him against women who did not match his emanations. They could destroy his spiritual gifts.

Craig returned to the hotel room around 1 A.M. with two Mexicans. Half asleep, Frank heard only snatches of the conversation. It had something to do with bombing and revolution and a town named Los Banyos. There was laughter, the clinking of glasses.

Craig shook Frank awake at dawn. This was unusual. The day after a meet, they usually slept until noon. At the air field, they gassed up *Rag Time* and took off into a splendid sunrise. "We're heading south!" Frank shouted, pointing to the Pacific, which was on their right.

Craig nodded. "Mexico!" he shouted. "We're going to war!"

A civil war had been raging in Mexico for several years. In a half hour they were over the border, flying across a barren, rocky landscape. In another hour they landed in a field not far from a camp with a half-dozen tents and hundreds of horses tethered in rows on wires stretched between posts. Soldiers rushed up to them firing rifles and pistols in the air. The two Mexicans who had visited the hotel room appeared, smiling broadly. With them was a big-nosed sweaty man wearing a white sun helmet.

"I have six bombs for you," he said in a thick German accent. "The fuses are set to explode on contact. Do you understand?"

"*Jawohl,*" Craig said.

The German examined *Rag Time* with great interest. "We have better in Germany," he said.

"Yeah, but we're in Mexico," Craig said. "Where's the money?"

The Mexicans gave him a thick roll of bills. They loaded the six bombs, snub-nosed artillery shells, into the bomb basket along with one or two smoke bombs. Someone blew a bugle and the soldiers rushed to their horses. Craig studied a map supplied by the German, Frank spun the prop and they took off.

At least, they tried to take off. *Rag Time* bounced down the field and Craig hauled back on the stick. They wobbled into the air and came back down with a shuddering crash. Cursing, Craig gave her full power and this time they got off the ground. But they were not climbing. They were heading straight for the face of a nearby ridge.

"Throw out two of those goddamn bombs!" Craig shouted.

The bombs created awesome explosions. Lighter by a hundred pounds, *Rag Time* cleared the ridge and zoomed down a road that wound behind it. The Mexican army galloped after them, shouting and firing their rifles in the air. Beyond another ridge lay a small valley with a town full of white-walled buildings at the end of it. Craig flew back and forth until the horsemen caught up to them. They formed up in a long line under the directions of the German. He waved a red flag and they charged. *Rag Time* roared ahead of them until they reached the outskirts of the town.

"Smoke bombs!" Craig yelled.

Frank hurled two bombs over the side, creating a billow of white smoke that drifted across the fronts of the houses. Below them, on the roofs of the houses, dozens of men were lying down aiming rifles at the charging horsemen. In one place three men crouched around a machine gun.

Craig roared over the rooftops at two hundred feet. Some of the riflemen rolled onto their backs and began shooting at *Rag Time*. A bullet whined by Frank's head. Another one snapped a wing strut. "Give 'em the first one, kid!" Craig bellowed.

Frank hauled one of the shells out of the basket and held it over the edge of his seat. It had small fins wired to the side to guide it down. He let it go and it hit only a few feet from the men on one of the roofs. It exploded with a tremendous crash and the roof, the men, vanished. Through a swirl of smoke Frank saw nothing but a dark hole between shattered walls. A man crawled out of the house into the street. Frank realized he was crawling because one of his legs had been blown off below the knee. After a few feet he stopped and lay facedown while a stream of blood trickled from the stump into the gutter.

"Nice going, kid!" Craig shouted. "Get ready for another run."

Frank looked over his shoulder and saw the Mexican army was charging through the smoke, firing their rifles from horseback. The machine gun chattered, emptying a dozen saddles. Craig came in even lower this time. "Get the machine gun," he shouted, pointing below them.

Frank shook his head. All he could hear was his mother hissing *death machine*. He clutched the bomb to his chest. "We're killing them!" he screamed.

"That's the idea!" Craig yelled. "They're paying us a thousand bucks to do it."

"Why are we killing them? What have they done to us?"

"It's a goddamn war!" Craig bellowed.

"I won't do it. It's wrong!" Frank cried.

"Jesus Christ, you're still a momma's boy!" Craig snarled.

He grabbed the bomb out of Frank's hands, banked and came in even lower, no more than fifty feet above the roofs. More enemy soldiers were shooting at them. But others were jumping off the roofs into the streets in panic. Craig planted the bomb about twenty feet from the machine gun. It blew the men firing the gun off the roof into the field in front of the town. The gun lay on its side like a dead insect.

The charging horsemen hurtled into the town. Some of the defenders tried to make a stand in the streets but the horsemen rode into them, swinging sabers, firing pistols. Those who were still alive fled out the other end of the town. Craig followed them and demanded another bomb.

"They're beaten! Let them go!" Frank said. He grabbed the last two bombs and threw them over the side. They blew big holes in the ground and probably made the fleeing defenders run a little faster. Craig banked back over the town. The victors were dragging people out of houses and shooting them in the streets.

"Jesus," Craig said. "Let's go home."

Back in California, Frank made Craig promise he would not fly *Rag Time* as a bomber again. Frank even wanted Craig to give up the bombing part of the act at air shows but Craig refused. "We've got to keep eating, kid," he said.

A month later, on August 23, 1912, Craig was flying low over the ocean before a huge crowd at Long Beach. The concessionaires along the Long Beach Pike, a big amusement park, had hired him to attract customers. On the beach beside Frank, in a swimsuit that displayed a lot of her knockout figure, Muriel Halsey wiggled her bottom excitedly in the sand and said: "He promised to show me something special."

A moment later, Craig took his hands off the stick and spread his arms wide. *"That's how safe flying is, ladies and gentlemen,"* boomed the Pike's master of ceremonies through a big megaphone.

"Gosh, he's got nerve," cried Muriel. She had just finished a movie in Hollywood and was sure she could get Craig a part in one. They were shooting five and six pictures a week and were desperate for brawny leading men. She had already urged a director to write a script about a pilot who rescued a blond American girl from Mexican bandits.

Suddenly *Rag Time* yawed to the right, her nose dipped and she dove straight down. *A trick. He'll pull it out,* Frank thought. This was the stunt Craig was going to show Muriel. He must have learned it in secret so not even Frank knew about it.

But *Rag Time* did not pull out. The plane plunged into a flock of gulls riding just beyond the surf. It happened so fast, no one in the crowd made a sound for a full minute. Then a kind of wail swept the beach. The fuselage and the right wing crumpled around Craig, trapping him in the wreckage.

Frank rowed frantically out with some lifeguards to pull Craig from the hulk minutes before *Rag Time* sank. But there was nothing more they could for Craig. His neck was broken. He died in the hospital about an hour later, trying to say something to Frank.

"Care—care—"

Take care of Mother? Be careful? It did not matter. As he closed Craig's eyes, Frank Buchanan vowed to build a better, safer plane, one that was not a death machine. He would learn the science of flight, instead of merely tinkering with ailerons and controls like a clever mechanic, which was all Craig had been. He would care about planes in Craig's memory. He would abandon his mother's dream of proving the survival of the soul after death. That was a job for a momma's boy. Building planes was a job for a man.

Craig's spirit entered Frank with that word, care. He did not know whether it partook of darkness or of light. It did not matter. Part of Frank became the swaggering older brother who loved and left women as casually as he risked death in the air. Part of shy, studious Frank Buchanan was abandoned that day in 1912 so life could triumph over death.

Muriel Halsey had sobbed beside the hospital bed as Craig died. She took Frank home to her villa in the Hollywood hills overlooking Los Angeles and fixed him something powerful to drink. Frank gulped it in Craig's memory, as part of his determination to keep him alive in his mind and body.

They had several drinks in Craig's memory. Pretty soon Muriel was telling him how much he looked like Craig. His hair was redder but he had the same build. The same big heart. Muriel joined him on the couch and began kissing him. She said she wanted to give him something to remember Craig by, something Craig liked even more than flying. Frank did not object. He did not worry about Muriel's emanations. It was another way of becoming Craig.

In the bedroom, Frank marveled at the design of a woman's body. All those fascinating curves and cunning concavities and fragile bones. It made him wonder if his mother was right when she contended that Eve, the Creator's second attempt, was an improvement on the first clumsy model, Adam. As Muriel slithered up his chest to slide her tongue into his mouth, Frank decided the answer was yes yes yes. Women and planes—two aspects of beauty in space and time—two ascents to bliss.

THE FUTURE IN THE SKY

"Here he comes!"

"We're in the perfect spot!"

Nine-year-old Adrian Van Ness stood beside his mother and her English friends on Shakespeare Cliff at Dover, where King Lear once raved against malignant fate. They were watching an incredible sight—a man flying an airplane from France to England. Hundreds of people had flocked to the white chalk bluffs to witness this sensation of the new century.

"By jove, it makes my blood boil to think a frog's doing it first," said a husky English voice above Adrian's head. Geoffrey Tillotson had broad shoulders and hooded eyes. His black bowler seemed to blot out the sky.

"It's glorious nonetheless, Geoffrey."

That silken American voice belonged to Adrian's mother, Clarissa Ames Van Ness. She was almost as tall as Geoffrey Tillotson. She wore a wide-brimmed black straw hat with a spume of white aigrettes. The hat was tilted on her beautiful head like a Jules Verne spaceship.

"You're right about that. Keep your eye on him, young fellows. You're seeing the future overhead. Everyone's future!" Geoffrey Tillotson said.

The white monoplane sailed over their heads, its motor clattering. At first it looked more like an insect than a bird, with the whirring propeller in its snout. But the outspread wings, the wheels jutting below the fuselage, recaptured a resemblance to the gulls that glided overhead, shrilling excitedly at this intruder in their sky.

"What keeps him up?" Adrian's mother asked.

"Aerodynamics," Geoffrey said.

The plane was so low you could see the pilot at the controls, wearing a helmet and goggles. "I say, Father, I'm going to learn to fly one of those things straightaway," said Peter Tillotson, Geoffrey's fourteen-year-old son. He was thick-bodied and muscular like his father.

Adrian did not like Peter very much. At the Tillotson house in Kent, not far from Dover, he had insisted on teaching Adrian how to play rugby, knocking him down repeatedly in the process. Adrian hated sports. Books were what he loved. He was reading Edward Gibbon's *Decline and Fall of the Roman Empire*. He had found it in the Tillotson library. He was enthralled by the descriptions of Rome's armies and emperors.

Peter had called *Decline and Fall* "eighteenth-century rubbish." Geoffrey Tillotson had defended Adrian's fascination with it. He said it was a great book. Then he told a funny story about it. When the author completed the second volume, he presented it to his patron, the Duke of Gloucester, who said, "Another damn thick square book. Always scribble scribble scribble. Eh, Gibbon?"

Everyone laughed and Adrian felt his face, his whole body grow hot. He thought they were laughing at him. He did not know exactly why he was often afraid people were laughing at him. It had something to do with his father. At St. Edmund's School in New York several boys had told him his father should be in jail. When Adrian asked his mother about it, she had gotten very angry. "That's a filthy lie!" she said.

Adrian thought she was angry at him and began to cry. His mother had cried too. Then she wrote the headmaster a letter. He had preached a sermon in chapel about the sin of slander. The next day at lunch, one of the boys had said, "My father still says your father belongs in jail, Van Ness." Everyone at the table had laughed.

The airplane tilted to the left after it passed over their heads and soared over Dover Castle. It tilted again and dropped lower and lower. He was going to land! They rushed to a big open touring car that Geoffrey Tillotson owned. The chauffeur cranked the motor and they beeped through the crowd pouring down the narrow street into town.

The plane was sitting in the center of the North Fall Meadow behind the eastern cliffs. The pilot, a stocky Frenchman named Louis Bleriot, was standing beside it, pleading with the hundreds of people swirling around him. "*Non, non, s'il vous plaît*, do not touch," he begged as they pressed closer. "It is easily damaged."

The thing looked very fragile. You could almost see through the fabric on the body and wings. Above them loomed Dover Castle, with its scarred octagonal Pharos, a relic of an original Roman fort. It was the oldest standing building in England. Geoffrey Tillotson pointed to it and said: "Forts, armies, ships, this thing will make them obsolete, mark my words."

Back in New York, Adrian's mother transferred him to the Trinity School. No one taunted or laughed at him there but Adrian often thought he saw hints of it in some boys' eyes. He made no friends. He spent most of his free time reading or talking to his mother or the maids. The following summer when they returned to England, Adrian's mother enrolled him in the Anson School. She told him he would be happier there than he was at Trinity or St. Edmund's in New York. She was wrong.

The school was in a gloomy set of buildings on a hill in Sussex. Adrian did not like any of the boys in his form any more than he liked Peter Tillotson. They all seemed to take special pleasure in flattening him in the compulsory rugby games. Night after night Adrian lay in bed, his body an aching bruise.

He spent most of his free time in the library, reading history books like *Decline and Fall*, which seemed to infuriate the boys in his form. They called him the American wog and massacred him relentlessly on the rugby field. He became a prime target of sixth formers who selected lower formers to be initiated into a tradition of the Anson School known as The Deflowering.

Adrian declined to cooperate. This soon led to a midnight summons. A rough hand shook him awake in his darkened dormitory. "Get up, wog. The council is meeting," hissed a commanding voice. In his bare feet, Adrian hurried along the icy floor and up the equally icy stone stairs to the top floor of the three-hundred-year-old dormitory.

Candles flickered in teacups. The council sat in an awesome row, their faces obscured by silk stockings they had stolen from their mothers. "Who's this?" asked the chairman.

"The American wog."

"What's the charge?"

"For the fifth consecutive night, he was told to get a pound of butter from dinner for the usual purpose and he refused. He also failed to save the correct portion of his dessert. We suspect he's trying to start a bloody revolution."

"We've been checking on you, wog. We think your real name's Von Ness. We think you're a bloody German," the chairman said.

"I'm not. Van Ness is a Dutch name. My father is descended from some of the first settlers in America."

"What does your father do for a living, wog?"

"Nothing."

Laughter. "Why doesn't he do anything, wog?"

"None of your business."

"We're making it our business, wog. Explain."

"My mother has money. He doesn't have to work."

"Very suspicious. He's either a spy or a layabout. Tell us more about your mother."

"Her maiden name was Ames. She's from Boston."

"Why is she living in England while your father stays in New York?"

"I don't know."

"Is she a spy, wog?"

"No. She hates the Germans like everyone else."

Adrian did not pretend to understand the antagonism for Germany seething through England in 1911. Even schoolboys talked confidently, eagerly, of fighting a war to teach the Kaiser and his generals a lesson in humility.

"You know what the butter is used for, wog?"

"It's for the Rammer," Adrian said.

"What does the Rammer do, wog?"

"He—he breaks in virgins."

"Why didn't you bring the butter, wog?"

"I don't want to be broken in."

"Wog, how many times do you have to be told what you want doesn't matter? We're the rulers, you're the slave. Tomorrow night you will visit the Rammer with the pound of butter or your life will cease. You will become one of the living dead. Do you understand that, wog?"

"Yes."

No one spoke to the living dead. They were treated as if they were invisible. Everyone walked straight at them in the corridors. They stepped on their feet in class. They refused to pass them food in the dining hall.

"For the present you are sentenced to double the usual punishment. Bend over."

Adrian pulled down his pants and bent double, his hands gripping the back of a chair.

"My god, that's a fat one. I can practically hear the Rammer salivating," one of the council said.

"Apply the punishment."

Again and again the paddle smashed against Adrian's buttocks. Waves of pain flooded his body. He thought for a while he was going to suffocate. Tears poured down his face. The council counted each stroke in chorus. "Twenty-one, twenty-two, twenty-three." They stopped at twenty-five.

Curled into a sobbing fetal ball in his icy bed, Adrian vowed not to tell anyone why his father lived in such a peculiar way. Last spring, before they left for England, Adrian had found the courage to ask his mother to explain it. His mother had taken him into her bedroom, which smelled of lilacs. They sat in two barrel chairs by the bay window overlooking Central Park. She told him how his father had been ruined in 1893, seven years before he was born.

The word *ruined* had tolled on her lips like a funeral bell. The stock market on Wall Street had crashed and some people who had given his father money to invest blamed him for losing it. She said the crash had not been his fault and no one really thought he should go to jail. When people lost money they said mean things.

His mother had seized Adrian by his shoulders and said: "Your father is a good man. We live on my money. You must never mention any of this to your father or anyone else."

It was enormously confusing. *Ruined* meant your wife seldom used your first name. In England his mother called many people by their first names. In New York his mother called his father *you*. Will you be home for dinner tonight? Do you plan to go to Bar Harbor this summer? Are you going to Long Island this weekend?

Ruined acquired spiritual as well as financial reverberations for Adrian Van Ness. As far as he could see, his father had almost ceased to exist. He was an adult version of a living dead man, haunting the house, the city. At dinner he seldom spoke about anything important. He talked about the weather—he could discourse on a late frost or an early snowfall for a full half hour—on who was marrying whom, or on who had just been admitted to the Union League

Club or the Century. He seldom talked to Adrian; he seemed to think there was no hope of winning his respect or friendship.

Ruined became another reason why Adrian liked to read history books. The past made the dismal present easier to accept, if not to understand. History often made people unhappy. He imagined himself as the son of a baron who had supported King Richard II, or of a general who had fought for Napoleon. They too had been ruined by different kinds of catastrophes. What happened to their sons? The history books never mentioned the sons.

His mother pretended she was staying in England for his sake but Adrian suspected she was enjoying herself. She was much more cheerful in London than she was in New York. There she was always solemn. Her eyes had a dull, pained expression. It had to have something to do with his father. She was glad to stay away from him. Why?

Adrian lay in his icy bed thinking about these mysteries until the pain in his buttocks subsided. Should he get the butter and let the Rammer have him tomorrow? The boy in the bed next to him, Carlo Pontecorvo, whom everyone called Ponty, had obeyed the summons last week. He was the son of an Italian nobleman who was a passionate admirer of England. Ponty had cried all night and told Adrian there was blood in the toilet bowl when he shit. Maybe it was better to be one of the living dead. He would be like his father. *Ruined*.

The next night, Adrian came back from the dining hall without the butter. He was consigned to the living dead. On the way to dinner the following day, Ponty whispered he had done the right thing. Someone ratted and Ponty got fifty strokes of the paddle for speaking to a living dead man.

Day after day, Adrian went to class and ate in the dining hall and studied in study hall and went to bed without speaking to anyone. At first he did not mind. He felt close to his father. It was almost as good as getting a letter from him. His father never wrote to him. His mother wrote almost every day, telling him about the war between Turkey and Bulgaria and the wild protests of the suffragettes, women who wanted the right to vote and threatened to blow up Parliament if they did not get it. She kept him up to date on what their friends were doing. Peter Tillotson had graduated from Sandhurst, the British West Point and joined the newly formed Royal Flying Corps to become a pilot.

One day in the spring of 1912 Adrian was walking across the school's inner quadrangle. Ponty strode toward him. Suddenly Adrian wanted to say hello to him. He wanted Ponty to answer him. Both lonely outsiders, they had naturally gravitated to each other. Ponty used to make Adrian laugh. He did funny imitations of their fat headmaster, Mr. Deakwell. When Ponty passed him without even letting his eyes flicker toward Adrian, it hurt in a new way deep inside. It was a pain worse than the paddle.

Even stranger things began happening inside Adrian as he continued walking across the quadrangle. Something almost as big as Louis Bleriot's monoplane began doing loops inside him. He felt hot and cold at the same time. His heart pounded and he thought he was going to faint. When it did not stop he thought he was going to die.

When the looping finally stopped Adrian felt so tired he went to bed. He did not go to supper and he did not get up for class the next day. He lay in bed and listened to the rain falling outside. *Ruined ruined ruined* it said with every drop. It was so sad. He wept for himself and his father. *Ruined* filled the whole world with fog and drizzle and mist.

After a while Adrian lost track of time. He vaguely remembered being hot and thirsty and hungry and being carried from the dormitory through the rain to another part of the school. The next comprehensible thing he heard was a man's hoarse voice.

"A living dead man? I don't understand. Is it some sort of American expression?"

Adrian was in the infirmary. The headmaster, Augustine Deakwell, was standing on the right side of his bed. He was very fat and wore sideburns, big white puffs of hair on both cheeks.

"It's a form of coventry, Mr. Deakwell. The senior boys invoke it for various reasons."

That was Mr. Goggins, the young master who was in charge of the third form. He was on the left side of Adrian's bed. He had big teeth and a stiff brush mustache. He had brought Adrian to the infirmary when he found him lying in his dormitory bed, sobbing.

"Hah? What's he done? Ratted on someone?" the headmaster asked.

"I think it's a good deal more malicious, Mr. Deakwell."

"If what Goggins tells me is true, Deakwell, you've got a first-class scandal on your hands."

It was his mother's friend, Geoffrey Tillotson. He loomed at the foot of Adrian's bed, scowling at the headmaster. His cheeks seemed pinker than usual, his jowls more formidable. He was wearing a black suit and a gray vest and gray tie with a large pearl stickpin in the center of it. His black derby was perfectly straight on his large head.

"If my son Peter wasn't a graduate, I'd have your head on a platter by next Monday, Deakwell. I leave it to you to straighten things swiftly—and mercilessly. In the meantime, I'll take this lad to his mother."

On the train, Tillotson bought Adrian a roast beef sandwich and a mug of cocoa. He told him he was proud of him for defying the sixth formers and becoming a living dead man. He said he was very sorry for what had happened and he hoped it would not make him dislike England. It was the fault of a few boys who misused their power as sixth formers. They forgot it was their responsibility to teach second and third formers the traditions of Anson, to make them proud of the famous men who had graduated from it.

"Every so often in all sorts of places, from schools to Parliament, rotters get into power," Tillotson said. "Eventually some brave fellows stand up to them and put things right."

"Like the Reform Acts," Adrian said. He had read about this great struggle for democracy in Macaulay's *History of England*.

"Exactly."

For the rest of the trip Tillotson talked about airplanes. He said his son Peter was becoming a very good pilot. An Englishman named de Havilland was building planes that were better than the ones the French made. Even better than the ones made by the Wrights, the Americans who had invented the machine. He gave Adrian a book full of photographs of planes at an air show outside Paris.

After a week with his mother, Adrian returned to Anson with Geoffrey Tillotson. On the train Tillotson assured him matters had been "put right." Remembering St. Edmund's, Adrian was not so sure. He still felt very sad.

In the quadrangle, Adrian encountered Ponty, who gave him a broad smile and said: " 'Allo, Van Ness. Glad you've come back."

That night Mr. Goggins had Adrian and Ponty and a half-dozen other third formers to dinner in his rooms. He talked about things having "gone wrong" but would be "ripping" now, he was sure of it. He said he hoped they would all try to be more friendly to their American guest, who had proved himself a "brave fellow."

"*Bravissimo!*" Ponty said. The other boys rapped their tea mugs on the table and said, "Hear, hear."

The next day, something even more remarkable happened. A biplane zoomed low over the school and climbed high into the sky to do a series of spectacular dives and banks. The pilot landed on the north playing field and the entire student body rushed there for a close look at the machine. The pilot climbed out and everyone gasped. It was Peter Tillotson, who had graduated two years ago.

"Where's my friend Van Ness?" Peter asked.

Adrian was shoved forward by wide-eyed third formers. "Get in," Peter said in his rough way.

Adrian climbed into the front seat and Peter buckled a thick belt around his waist. He asked Mr. Goggins to spin the propeller. In a moment they were bouncing down the playing field toward a line of trees in the distance. "Hang on!" Peter shouted, and they cleared the trees by a foot.

Aloft, Adrian looked down on the school and marveled at the way it was dwindling, exactly the way Shakespeare had described the men and boats below the cliffs at Dover in the scene where Lear went mad. Everyone was mouse-size and the buildings looked more and more like toys. The sadness started to fall away from him. He began to feel proud and free and happy.

"How do you like it?" Peter shouted above the roaring motor.

"Ripping!" Adrian shouted.

"This is only the third time I've been up alone. Soloing, they call it. You can get killed with no warning but it's worth it. Hang on, we'll try a loop."

He pointed the nose of the plane toward the sky and climbed straight up. Instead of flipping over, they hung there for a second, then fell off to the right in a screaming dive. "Afraid I've got to practice that," Peter said, after they pulled out.

They made a rather bumpy landing. The entire student body swarmed

47

around them again. "I've only got time for one more ride. Who will it be, Adrian?"

"Ponty," Adrian said.

Peter took him up and this time completed a loop. Ponty said it was the most remarkable sensation of his life. He vowed to learn to fly as soon as possible.

From living dead man, Adrian soared to leader of the third form. No more was heard of Von Ness, son of the German spy. The next two months were the happiest of his life.

One afternoon in mid-May, as Adrian sat in the library reading about the Battle of Waterloo, Ponty tapped him on the shoulder. "The head wants you, Van." He puffed his cheeks and stuck out his stomach and waddled away in a perfect imitation of Mr. Deakwell.

In the headmaster's office, his mother sat alone. She looked unusually beautiful in a jet-black suit. Adrian often thought she resembled one of those tall, proud Gibson girls in magazine illustrations. "Oh, darling," she said. "I've got some bad news. We have to go home."

"Why?"

"Your father's dead. He was killed in an accident. Foxhunting. He ran into a low-hanging limb and broke his neck."

Adrian waited for her to weep, to let him weep. But she did nothing of the sort. She told him to go to his room and pack. They were catching the fastest ship home, the SS *Lusitania*. It was sailing from Southampton the next day.

Adrian trudged across the quadrangle, suddenly remembering everything. Von Ness the spy, the months as a living dead man, the sadness. He felt angry at his mother for having exposed him to these ordeals. Beneath that anger was a deeper, colder enmity for her refusal to weep for his ruined father. He found himself wishing he could get in a plane and fly thousands of miles away from his mother and never see her again.

HISTORY'S LASH

"You—you there, young fellow—is that an American accent I hear?"

Frank Buchanan paused in his effort to tune the motor of a de Havilland Scout, wiped grease from his hands and nodded. The man had the lean face, the spaded beard, the fiery eyes of Mephistopheles in his youth, when his hair was bright red. A flowing gray coat enveloped him almost to his shoetops. He gestured at Frank with an ebony cane. He was surrounded by a half dozen of the most elegant women Frank had ever seen.

"It sounds like I'm hearing one too," Frank shouted as his helper got the motor to stop choking and sputtering and emit a racketing roar.

"Hailey, Idaho," the man shouted, holding out his hand. "The name's Pound. Ezra Pound."

"The author of *Canzoni*?" Frank said.

"A mechanic who reads poetry!" Pound cried. "You see what I've been saying? Americans aren't a lost cause. There's hope—if we can get more of them to Europe."

They were standing on the grassy airfield at Hendon, a suburb of London, on a sunny Saturday afternoon in May 1914. Every week some two hundred thousand people came out to see the latest planes race around the pyloned course. Britons of all classes had become fascinated by flight. A pilgrimage to Hendon was a must to those who hoped to have any claim to sophistication.

"Do you understand how these things work?" Pound said, leading Frank away from the snarling Rhone rotary engine. "Why one crashes, another stays in the air? The principle behind it?"

"I've learned a few things from Geoffrey de Havilland," Frank said modestly. He could have said much more. He had spent a year in France working for Louis Paulhan, the pilot he had met at the Dominquez Hills air show. Paulhan and other designers were churning out planes in a dozen factories around Paris. He had even accompanied Paulhan to the wind tunnel constructed by Louis Eiffel, builder of the famous tower. In the tunnel French designers studied the effect of airflow on models of the planes they were building.

In England, a photograph of *Rag Time* had won him a job in de Havilland's design department. The big blond Englishman had built one of Britain's first flyable planes in 1910. He was now working for the Aircraft Manufacturing Company, which operated from an old bus garage in Hendon. Frank had come to England to learn more about the changes the British were making in the airplane's basic design. De Havilland was working with scientists who had been studying aerodynamic problems in their laboratories. They recommended moving the wings of a plane back to the middle of the fuselage, closer to the center of gravity, enlarging the tail and the ailerons—all aimed at giving the aircraft as much stability in the air as a boat on the water.

A few minutes' conversation convinced Pound that his American discovery was the perfect man to introduce his circle of poets and poetry lovers to the mysteries of flight. Pound saw the plane as a prime example of his artistic theories. Since he arrived in England in 1908, he had become a one-man cultural crusade, churning out poetry and critical essays proclaiming that the new century required an entirely new art. He called his theory Vorticism and he publicized it in the pages of a magazine called *Blast*.

Vorticists believed art could and should represent reality with the same precision as an equation in fluid dynamics or solid geometry. They wanted to make a poem or story work as precisely as a machine. At the heart of every work of art there was a vortex, a pulsing fist of forces that gave it energy and meaning. It was the critic or the editor's task to find that vortex and help the writer exploit it to the utmost.

Within a week, Frank Buchanan found himself the center of attention in

Pound's small dark apartment in Kensington. A dozen guests, most of them women, listened wide-eyed as he proposed to demonstrate the central idea of flight. He took a piece of paper and curled one end of it over a pencil. Raising it to the level of his lips, he blew on it. The paper rose. "I have just produced lift," he said. "You are now in the world of aerodynamics."

Why does air traveling over a wing create lift? "The air on top of the wing moves faster than the air under the bottom. In the eighteenth century, a Swiss mathematician named Bernoulli experimented with water flowing through a pipe. He proved that the faster it flowed, the lower the pressure in the pipe. Later, an Italian scientist named Venturi proved the same thing was true for air. That's why the higher pressure of the slower air under the wing creates lift."

"Exactly how emotion works in a poem or story!" Pound cried.

"The other components of a plane are weight, drag, and thrust," Frank continued. "These are easier to understand. Drag is created by the resistance the surface of the plane meets as it moves through the air. Weight is the force of gravity and thrust is the forward motion we get from the engine."

"In a poem or story," Pound said, "Drag corresponds to the writer's ability, weight to the reader's stupidity, and thrust to the publisher's greed."

So it went for the length of the lecture, Pound finding literary analogies for all Frank's aeronautical terms. Pound was particularly fascinated by the way air flowing over the wings and down the fuselage of a plane formed negative vortexes that created a phenomenon known as *flutter*, which could tear a wing or a tail apart.

"Precisely the way the wrong metaphor can wreck a stanza, the wrong rhythm can ruin a poem, the wrong character can mangle a story!" Pound said.

A blond young woman in the center of the semicircle asked: "What is the future of this marvelous machine?" She had the face of a Pre-Raphaelite angel—the pale cheeks, the wide blue eyes, seemingly vacant, waiting to be charged with emotion.

"Its future is as unlimited as the sky above our heads," Frank said. "The plane can abolish distance, annihilate frontiers, unite peoples in Tennyson's wonderful vision of a Parliament of Man!"

"Tennyson!" Pound exclaimed. "My dear fellow—that's a name we don't allow in this house. He's a has-been."

"He never will be, to me," Frank said. His mother had read the great English poet aloud to him almost every night in his boyhood. *"The Idylls of the King"* was his favorite poem.

"The danger of teaching mechanics to read has now become visible," Pound said. "They form their own opinions."

"But Ezra," said the blond young woman. "He also likes your *Canzoni*."

"That only demonstrates, to use an aeronautical term, his instability," Pound said.

The highlight of the evening was a midnight supper cooked by Pound, a delicious oyster stew, complemented by an Italian white wine that he served with an inimitable toast. "Come let us pity those who are better off than we are. Remember that the rich have butlers and no friends and we have friends and no butlers."

The conversation swirled over art and politics, with the blond girl quizzically probing Frank's opinions. Her name was Penelope Foster and she was unquestionably attracted to him. "Do you think we shall have peace or war, Mr. Buchanan?" she said in a liquid voice that sent shimmers of desire through Frank's flesh.

"Oh, peace," Frank said. "War would be a ridiculous waste of time and energy."

"The British upper class can hardly wait to go to war with Germany. Proving, among other things, their imbecility," Pound said.

"You're quite wrong, Ezra. The Huns need to be taught a lesson," Penelope Foster said.

The rising power of Germany obsessed almost everyone in England. Their fleet and army were challenging Britain's supremacy everywhere, in Africa, China, the south Pacific. Their corporations were invading markets such as America, where English goods had once been supreme.

"If we have a war, do you think your planes will be in it?" Penelope asked.

"As scouts," Frank said. "They'll be the eyes of the army. In fact, their mere presence may make war impossible. How can a general maneuver a great army when a plane can swoop down and discover it miles before he can reach his objective? Planes can produce a stalemate, where neither side can gain an advantage."

"I think you badly underestimate the brutality of generals," Pound said. "What about planes as bombers? In the *Arabian Nights*, Sinbad the Sailor describes how two ships were destroyed by Rocs, giant birds carrying huge stones."

"We don't have motors powerful enough to lift a serious amount of bombs," Frank said, guiltily omitting his experience bombing Mexicans from *Rag Time*. He did not want to believe that anyone who experienced the exaltation of flight could use it to rain death on human beings. Even Craig had been dismayed by the effect of their bombs on Los Banyos.

Frank escorted Penelope Foster home to a nearby flat. The daughter of a colonial office civil servant, she was a poet who tried to create small, exact word portraits of nature and humanity in a style Pound had dubbed *imagism*. Pound told her she had talent and the samples she showed Frank in her rooms proved it. She called them *London Lives*. In ten lines or less, each depicted a London type, a burly bus driver, a screeching fishmonger, a banker flourishing his umbrella "like a scepter," a scrawny messenger on his bike, risking his life in the traffic "like a sparrow in a gale."

"All lift, no drag," Frank said. "I hope I can create planes like these some day."

"You will. I can sense it in you. A pulsing thing Ezra calls the gold thread in the pattern. Some people possess it instinctively."

"How does it work?" Frank asked.

"I'm not sure. It's part spirit, part technical mastery. A desire to grasp the essence of things—in art, in machines."

A plaintive sadness throbbed in Penelope's voice. Her lovely head drooped in a kind of mourning. "I sense the gift has passed to you Americans. You're the guardians of it now. We English nurtured it for a century—"

"Can I—may I—kiss you?" Frank said.

He wanted to possess this Sibyl, to explore her body as well as her soul. "No," she said. "It's much too soon."

"I want to make you part of my golden thread, my essence," Frank whispered. "In California, we believe it's never too soon."

The first part of that plea was Frank Buchanan, the second part was Craig. Frank was still an unstable blend of the two personalities. But Penelope proved she was worthy of her classic name when it came to evading suitors.

"This isn't California," she said.

In love for the first time, Frank became a regular visitor to Pound's Kensington circle. He listened to the poet read his magical translations from the Provençal and the Chinese and discourse with casual brilliance on Dante, Shakespeare, Homer. Frank took Penelope Foster up for a ride in a de Havilland Scout, the sturdy two-seat reconnaissance plane they were building for the Royal Flying Corps. She adored it but unlike the Baroness Sonnenschein and Muriel Halsey, she still declined Frank's offer of a similar ascent in her bedroom. Instead, she gave him a poem.

> *Crouched on the grass*
> *The plane is a clumsy cicada*
> *Who could believe*
> *It devours clouds*
> *Consumes cities and rivers*
> *Challenges the sun*
> *With its growling shadow?*

Frank called Penelope his priestess and accepted the celibacy she imposed on him. Although they saw themselves as citizens of the new century it was a very Victorian love. Pound was their high priest, weaving a spell of beauty, a promise of triumphant art, around their lives. For three months Frank Buchanan, soaring in planes and poetry, was a happy young man.

But history was rumbling toward them on the continent. The Great Powers, as the newspapers called them, had devoted millions to building huge armies while their frantic diplomats devoted hundreds of hours to weaving intricate alliances to maintain a balance of power that was supposed to make war impossible. When a Serbian anarchist assassinated the crown prince of Austria, the illusion of peace evaporated. Austria threatened Serbia, Russia warned Austria, Germany threatened Russia. France warned Germany.

On August 4, 1914, Frank Buchanan awoke in his Hendon rooming house.

Guy Chapman, his fellow junior designer, was pounding on his door. "Frank, Frank!" he was shouting. "It's the bloody war. It's started!"

Frank stumbled out of bed and found Chapman clutching a copy of the *London Times*. GERMANS INVADE BELGIUM roared the headline. England had warned Germany that if they violated Belgium's neutrality to attack France, Britain would declare war. At the Aircraft Manufacturing Company, chaos reigned. Geoffrey de Havilland and several other key people had been drafted by the Royal Flying Corps. Frank and Guy Chapman were the only designers still on the job.

Over the next year, Frank watched the airplane turn into a weapon of war. From the scout the generals had envisioned it became a fighter plane, when a Dutch designer named Anthony Fokker taught the Germans how to synchronize a machine gun to fire through the propeller. Then it became a bomber as more and more powerful motors created larger and larger planes capable of carrying as much as a thousand pounds of high explosives.

Penelope Foster's first reaction to the war was exultation. She was sure Germany would be smashed in a matter of weeks. As dozens of her friends and relatives, including her older brother, were killed by German machine guns and artillery in France, rage became her dominant emotion. She changed from a cool, detached imagist poet to a ranting, chanting writer of patriotic verse in the Kipling tradition. She shouted her poems from platforms to intimidate men into enlisting in the British army.

At night, in her Kensington flat, Penelope wrote more bad poetry to the heroic dead, and abused Frank Buchanan. She still refused to let him touch her. "Where are your heroic countrymen?" she hissed. "Why aren't they here, fighting for civilization? The barbarians are at the gates!"

Frank tried to defend President Woodrow Wilson's neutrality. He portrayed America as the one nation that could negotiate a just peace between the warring powers before they destroyed each other. Penelope called him a coward and a fool.

One terrible night at Pound's flat, after one of the best imagist poets, T. H. Hulme, was killed in Flanders, Penelope reviled Pound for not fighting beside him. Her diatribe was a paradigm of the way the war annihilated Pound's dream of a civilization redeemed by art. He began to sneer at the idea of patriotism, to see literature and art, not as a vortex transforming the world, but as a refuge from a world gone mad.

When German zeppelins and Gotha bombers appeared over London, smashing churches and homes, killing hundreds of people, Pound mocked Frank's vision of the plane annihilating frontiers. Its new goal was the annihilation of the countries behind the frontiers.

"I can hardly wait for them to bomb you American cowards," Penelope raged. She glared at Frank, her Pre-Raphaelite face livid with loathing.

The dreamer-designer Frank Buchanan shuddered under these blows. He wandered the streets of London consoling himself with streetwalkers while Craig whispered in his soul. *They're only good for one thing, kid. When you listen to their yak-yak they drive you nuts.*

One night, after a particularly unsatisfying encounter with a prostitute, Frank found himself on Brompton Road, standing before a building with a small sign crudely lettered over the doorway: *Church of the Questing Spirit.* Inside about two dozen people listened to a gray-haired minister talk about a world beyond their tormented visible one. The rectangular room, with a dome of stars painted on the ceiling, was the London headquarters of the sect Althea Buchanan had joined in California.

At the end of the sermon, the minister gestured to Frank, in the first row, and said: "Young man, are you as troubled as you look?"

Frank poured out his growing despair and confusion over the war. The woman he loved called him a coward for defending his own and his country's refusal to fight. What should he do?

The minister stepped into an anteroom and emerged with a shirt that had somehow been ripped almost to shreds. "Put this on," he said.

Frank shrugged off his jacket and thrust his arms into the shirt. Instantly he felt an incredible lash of pain across his back. Again again again, a fiery agony unlike anything he had ever experienced seared his flesh. He ripped off the shirt and flung it at the minister.

"What is it? What are you trying to do?" Frank gasped.

"That shirt belonged to a seaman in Nelson's navy who was lashed to death," the minister said. "You're one of us. Everyone in this room has felt that pain when they wore this shirt. Most people feel nothing."

"What does it mean?"

"Each of us has to find his own interpretation of that pain."

Outside the church, Frank found the night sky full of searchlights and flares. The Gothas were raiding London again. Huge explosions made the sidewalk tremble. The bombs were falling only a few blocks away, around Marble Arch. A man grabbed his arm. "Where's the nearest subway station, pal?" he asked. His accent was as American as his vocabulary. People were using London's underground for air-raid shelters.

"I don't know this neighborhood."

"Ah, what the hell. Let's have a drink."

They pounded on the door of a nearby pub. Behind the blacked-out windows a dozen fatalists were savoring what could be their last pints. The American ordered double Scotches for himself and Frank and held out his hand.

"Buzz McCall's the name, flying's my game."

"Likewise," Frank said.

Buzz was a chunk of a man, with black hair and a complexion as swarthy as an Italian's. He had a square fighter's jaw and a swagger to his walk and talk. Except for his stockier physique, the resemblance to Craig was uncanny.

Buzz began telling Frank he was on his way to France. A group of Americans had volunteered to form a squadron in the French air force. They were going to call it the Lafayette Escadrille. "We're gonna teach these German fuckers a couple of lessons for bombin' women and children," he said.

"Have you got room for another pilot?" Frank said.

Death machine, his mother whispered. But Frank dismissed her once and for all. Buzz and Craig and this war-maddened world were suddenly connected to the fiery shirt he had just torn from his back in the Church of the Questing Spirit. If he hoped to live as a man and not a momma's boy, he would have to wear that ancient shirt, no matter how much pain it cost him. He would have to endure history's lash.

THE GIRL FROM THE GLORIOUS WEST

"America stands for peace and nothing but peace!"

Auburn hair streaming to her waist, Amanda Cadwallader trembled in the icy January wind cutting through Harvard Square. The barbaric weather was not the only reason for her tremors. It was her first public speech, her first attempt to bring California's message of peace to war-infatuated eastern America.

As a crowd gathered, two of her fellow sophomores at Wellesley handed out leaflets quoting poets and philosophers, including Harvard's own William James, on the folly of war as the solution to settling quarrels between nations. A big bulky young man in a well-tailored dark suit snatched one of the leaflets, glanced at it and crumpled it into a contemptuous ball. He planted himself directly in front of Amanda and shouted: "Are you German?"

"I'm from California," Amanda said.

"That explains the nonsense you're preaching. You've got an orange for a brain!" the young man bellowed. His thick-lipped wide-boned face had an adult cast. He looked like a faculty member.

"Yeah, yeah," jeered a half-dozen grinning young men in the crowd. "An orange for a brain."

"I've got a perfectly good brain," Amanda said. "I had a straight-A average at Stanford. I'm getting the same grades at Wellesley. Why can't you discuss the subject like—like gentlemen?"

"Because there's nothing gentle about a German. A German is a Hun," her chief antagonist said. "If we had any guts, we'd be over there fighting them now."

"Right. Absolutely right," rumbled from the crowd.

"We don't agree with you in California," Amanda said. "America should be a voice of peace in the councils of the nations."

"Tell it to the Kaiser," sneered her antagonist.

Amanda glanced at her two followers, one of whom was her Wellesley roommate. Both easterners, they had been dubious about this venture. She had persuaded them to try it with the sheer force of her western enthusiasm.

"My friends told me this would happen. I had to see for myself. You're nothing but—barbarians."

She began to weep. Abominable! Amanda hated the way she wept whenever she was extremely angry—or extremely happy. Her mother had opposed the idea of letting Amanda go east. Her half-brother had been almost gleeful, he was so sure she would make a fool of herself. Her father had encouraged her. He said it would be a good way for her to find out just how confused and spiritually sick America was on the Atlantic seaboard.

The crowd began to disperse. But Amanda's chief antagonist remained behind—and was strangely contrite. "We're not barbarians," he said. "We're perfect gentlemen on every topic but the one you've chosen. To prove it—let me buy you all lunch."

Amanda turned to her two followers. The idea unquestionably appealed to them. The young man was remarkably self-possessed. His tailoring was expensive and foreign. There was something mysterious, intriguing, about his tufted brows and hooded eyes.

Twenty minutes later, Amanda and her friends were gorging on lobster salad, caramel cake, and ice cream sodas in the Crimson Cafe off Harvard Square. Adrian Van Ness talked to them earnestly and honestly about the war in Europe as he saw it in January 1916.

"I spent a year at the Anson School in England," he said. "Ten of my friends from the upper forms have died in Flanders, at Ypres, on the Somme. I've had letters from some of them. There was no doubt in their minds—or in mine—that they were fighting civilization's battle against the German hordes. Almost every faculty member and every student at Harvard believes this by now. We're all in favor of American intervention. There are over two hundred graduates already serving with the French and British armies as volunteers. Over a dozen have been killed—"

"Doesn't all this prove the madness, the stupidity of war?" Amanda said.

"It proves the courage, the heroism of ordinary men," Adrian said. "The war is a great testament to our civilization's capacity for self-sacrifice—and courage. Especially in the air. I have a number of friends in the Royal Flying Corps. One of them, Peter Tillotson, is the leading British ace at the moment with forty victories. Another friend, Carlo Pontecorvo, is flying for Italy. He thinks single combat in the plane is reviving some of the ancient ideals of chivalry. It may create a whole new race of men, with a code of honor like the knights of the Crusades."

Amanda was fascinated by the glow of idealism on Adrian's face as he talked about planes. Her followers, both from the east, began to change their minds about the war. Adrian was a remarkably persuasive young man. Amanda was losing the argument, but to her surprise she did not care. She sensed Adrian was genuinely distressed that he had hurt her feelings. Almost everything he said was for her. He barely glanced at her followers.

Outwardly, Amanda remained unconverted. She quoted Stanford's pacifist president, David Starr Jordan, at length. He had inspired her and a half-dozen other "peace missionaries" to transfer to Wellesley and Smith and Mount Holyoke to convert the warmongering easterners. She could hardly surrender to a spokesman for the evil East in her first encounter. But she secretly hoped she would see Adrian Van Ness again.

Within the week Adrian telephoned Amanda and invited her to another lunch at the Crimson Cafe—alone. Over more lobster salad he apologized for his slurs on California. "Actually, I know nothing about the place. What's it like?" he said.

A delighted Amanda talked about southern California—she dismissed the northern half of the state as a foggy, chilly wasteland—with an eloquence even she found surprising. She described the lush beauty of the mountain-ringed San Fernando Valley, the majesty of the coast above Los Angeles, the vistas of the desert.

"Southern California is the last paradise in the Western world," Amanda said. "A place where art and poetry and philosophy will flower in a new renaissance."

"Who said that?" Adrian asked.

Amanda blushed and cast her eyes down: "My father."

"What does he do for a living?"

"He grows oranges. Cadwallader Groves is the largest producer in Orange County. He serves in the state legislature too. In 1910 he was one of the leaders in the fight to reform the constitution. He helped break the power of the railroad barons and other vested interests."

Amanda sipped the last of her ice cream soda. "What does your father do?" she asked.

"Nothing. He's dead."

Adrian's voice was so cold and curt, Amanda wondered if she had somehow offended him. "I—was never close to him. He was an—introvert," Adrian said.

Even in 1916, psychology had become an instant explanation for everything. Amanda murmured sympathetically. "My father hates crowds, cities," she said.

"Maybe I'll pay you a visit," Adrian said. "See if southern California improves my poetry."

Amanda asked to see some of this poetry. Surprise, surprise, Adrian had a half-dozen poems in his pocket. She made him read them to her. Many were about the nobility, the glory of flight.

"They're very good," Amanda said.

Adrian glowed. "When I showed them to my mother, she said 'most poets die poor.'"

"What's wrong with being poor? All the Mexican pickers at our grove are poor. But they're happy."

As Adrian opened the door of the taxi that would take Amanda back to Wellesley, she kissed him on the lips. "I like you," she said.

When Amanda told her roommate about the kiss, she was horrified. "You can't be that *forward*. It just isn't *done* in this part of the country. He'll never call you again."

Adrian called the next night to arrange another Saturday lunch at the Crimson Cafe—and a trip to the movies after it. That soon became a Saturday routine. At lunch Adrian read her other poems full of sadness and anger at life's cruelty. Amanda sensed some wound deep in his soul and longed to heal it. She also discerned how lonely he was at Harvard. He seemed to have made almost no friends.

Adrian said he did not get along with New Yorkers even though he had been born there. They were only interested in making money. He disdained Bostonians—although he had numerous cousins there—because they thought making money was vulgar. At other times he claimed most of his fellow students were childish. "They haven't found out what life is all about," he said. "You have to read history—and experience it—to do that."

As Amanda puzzled over his melancholy, Adrian invited her for dinner with his mother at her Beacon Hill town house on a rainy night in late March 1916. Amanda wore a loose blue lace dress and a soft blue velvet hat she had rushed into Boston to buy the previous day. Clarissa was regal in black silk and a pearl choker. She sat with her back as straight as a West Point cadet's, barely smiling as Amanda said hello.

She was awed by Clarissa's hauteur. Amanda was sure there were no women like her in California. Her own mother, so indifferent to clothes and style, so moody and impulsive, gave her no preparation for dealing with such glacial self-control. Clarissa was a block of dark New England ice. Trembling, Amanda understood Adrian's melancholy. This woman did not know how to love anyone—even a son.

"Adrian tells me you're from California," Clarissa said. She made it sound as if it were a communicable disease.

"Yes," Amanda said. She talked nervously, defensively, about her birthplace. "I had a letter from my mother yesterday. The temperature hasn't gone below seventy since January. I told her here it hasn't gone above twenty-five."

"No question, the entire state is a gigantic playground," Clarissa said. "But doesn't that get rather boring? You can't play all the time."

Floundering, Amanda pictured herself as the heroine of her favorite novel, *Ramona*. She too had been despised by arrogant easterners. But she had found pride and love in her California heritage. "We don't play all the time," she said. "We've produced some important literature."

"Oh?"

"Frank Norris's *The Octopus*, Mary Austin's *The Land of Little Rain*."

By this time they had sat down to dinner. Clarissa carefully carved another small slice from her lamb chop. "Personally, I prefer Richard Henry Dana's view of California."

Amanda replied with equal care: "He was one of those New Englanders who hated California."

"He loved it on his first visit. It was his second visit that disillusioned him. It had changed so utterly—for the worse."

"He hated it," Amanda said. "The second visit was his way of satisfying his puritan conscience for falling in love with it the first time."

"You think poorly of a puritan conscience?"

"My father says California makes puritanism superfluous."

Amanda glanced at Adrian. He was watching them with disbelieving eyes. He apparently never imagined anyone could challenge his formidable mother this way. In spite of his adult physique, he looked like a bewildered boy.

Love, the emotion that Amanda's father had taught her was life's noblest experience, stirred in her soul. With it came a wish to share with Adrian the richest memory of her childhood, the gift her father had told her she could only offer to the Precious One.

In the silence at dawn her mother and father and Amanda and her brother Gordon drank cool orange juice on the porch of their turreted white mansion, which her father had named Casa Felicidad, the house of happiness. They stepped out of their night clothes and walked naked among the blossoming trees. "There is no shame," her father said. "California is a new beginning. We can stop believing in ridiculous things like God. We're free to be noble and good without God."

He let Amanda touch the dangling part of his body. She put her hand into the russet hair beneath her mother's belly and felt her cleft. Her brother Gordon did the same things. Then in the dawn stillness on the dewy grass with orange blossoms drifting around them her father and mother showed Amanda and Gordon how men and women loved each other.

Amanda gazed at Adrian and spoke the meaning of this memory carefully, softly, intending the words only for him, indifferent to what Clarissa thought. "For those who believe in it, California is Eden," she said.

WAR HERO

A week after he brought Amanda Cadwallader to dinner, Adrian Van Ness visited his mother's Beacon Hill town house for tea. She was wearing the pearl choker that Geoffrey Tillotson had given her for her fortieth birthday. The Tiffany lamp beside the tea table cast a golden glow on the silvery jewels.

"Your little girl from the golden West is charming," Clarissa said. "So unspoiled. It's hard to believe they even have schools out there."

"I think I'm in love with her," Adrian said.

"Darling, never confuse love and sympathy. You feel sorry for someone who's such a lost lamb. Can you imagine her as hostess at a New York dinner party?"

"She's very intelligent. She has excellent taste in poetry."

"You mean she likes yours."

Clarissa Ames Van Ness smiled mockingly at Adrian. She was so sure of her social and intellectual superiority, so certain of her ability to control her son. It was exactly what Adrian needed to convince him he was in love with Amanda Cadwallader.

Physically, Amanda was the total opposite of Adrian's dark, elegant mother. Amanda's face was long and angular, more sensitive than beautiful. Her slim body was almost boyish. Her streaming auburn hair proclaimed both her femininity and her western innocence. All of which made her attractive to Adrian.

Beneath his hyperactive intellect, Adrian was searching for a woman who would help him escape his mother's looming presence. He was emotionally exhausted by their alternating bouts of affection and anger. He did not, he could not, stop loving Clarissa Van Ness. But he could not resolve her apparent indifference to his father's fate.

Defying and irritating his mother—and enjoying every minute of it—Adrian continued to see Amanda. He struggled to change her mind about the war in Europe. But her California naivete was impenetrable. She simply insisted America had everything to lose and nothing to gain by entering the war. Her knowledge of European history was zero, her interest in it zero minus. She did not really argue. She believed. Adrian told himself it was part of her innocence. He even began to doubt his own arguments in favor of intervention.

They did not spend all their time arguing about peace and war. At the movies, Adrian teased Amanda about her resemblance to Mary Pickford, whose beatific smile and cascades of auburn ringlets had made her America's sweetheart. Amanda disarmed him by taking his hand and whispering. "I only want to be your sweetheart."

As spring advanced, they went for walks in the country and rows on the Charles River. Amanda was a fervent believer in exercise in the open air. On one of these excursions on the water, Amanda revealed more than an enthusiasm for California's scenery behind her smile. Adrian grew weary at the oars and suggested they tie up at a grassy spot on the river above Watertown. They ate sandwiches Amanda had packed and washed them down with iced tea. The rich May sunshine inspired Amanda to rhapsodies on California. In a month they would separate for the summer.

"Will you miss me?" Amanda asked.

"Yes," Adrian said.

"A part of you likes me—and a part doesn't."

"That's not so," Adrian said, vehemently trying to conceal the truth from her—and from himself. His mother's critique of Amanda often troubled him.

Amanda flung herself into his arms. Her kiss was wilder, more intense, than anything Adrian had ever imagined. He was still a virgin. In his head women were divided into good and bad. Some of his fellow freshmen were already sampling what the bad ones had to offer in Boston's Scollay Square brothels. But Adrian had remained aloof from this ritual as well as the other forms of college friendship.

"There's nothing to be ashamed of," Amanda whispered. "Come to California and I'll show you there's nothing to be ashamed of."

Dimly aware that he was being invited to play Adam to Amanda's Eve, Adrian spent the summer in Maine resisting a procession of young women Clarissa considered more suitable than his California temptress. To his mother's almost visible distress, the romance resumed when school reopened in the fall of 1916. Not even Amanda's enthusiastic support of Woodrow Wilson's campaign for a second term on the slogan "He kept us out of war" diminished Adrian's ardor. There were more kisses on the Charles and more dinners on Beacon Hill at which Amanda jousted with Clarissa with growing skill.

Amanda reiterated her invitation to California, which acquired orgiastic overtones in Adrian's mind. For a while he almost lost interest in the war in Europe. Then the Germans began proving all the nasty things interventionists like Adrian said about them, sinking American ships and trying to turn Mexico into a hostile foe on America's flank. Woodrow Wilson's balancing act on the neutrality tightrope ended with a crash and America declared war. Adrian wondered if this spelled finis to his romance with Amanda.

He was surprised—and pleased—to discover a warrior maiden on their next date. Like many other pacifists, she had been swept away by the president's soaring call for America to wage a war without hatred or greed, to make the world safe for democracy. Her father had volunteered for the army the day he read Wilson's speech in the *Los Angeles Times*.

On a Saturday night two months later, Adrian was lounging in his room, enjoying the prospect of taking Amanda to dinner in Boston. One of his floor mates said: "Van Ness. There's a red-haired creature outside weeping and wailing to see you."

Behind Amanda in Harvard Yard a battalion of seniors was practicing the manual of arms with wooden rifles. Like most of America, the school was feverishly committed to the war. Tears streamed down Amanda's face. She clutched a telegram in her hand. FATHER KILLED TRAINING ACCIDENT STOP. RETURN HOME AT ONCE STOP. MOTHER VERY ILL.

Her tears stirred the guilt Adrian had felt the day they met, when he had mocked her pacifism. He was swept with a masculine desire to comfort this fragile, wounded creature. "Darling, it's terrible. My heart breaks for you. But you have me. You have me to take care of you. I love you," he said.

Adrian took Amanda back to Wellesley where sobbing friends helped her pack. He hired a taxi that took them to Boston where Amanda boarded a train in North Station for her return to California. He wiped away her tears and kissed her. "I'll see you in a month. Two at the most."

Adrian rushed to his mother's house on Beacon Hill and announced his plan to move to California, marry Amanda Cadwallader and complete his education in some local college at night. "That is an absolutely absurd idea," Clarissa said.

Before Adrian could begin to think of an answer, Clarissa outlined her plan for Adrian's life. "I want you to become a man of substance, Adrian. You can't do that growing oranges in southern California. You also can't do it with a woman like Amanda for your wife. A man of substance needs a wife who glories in his success as her success, who understands his ambition and defers to it."

Defer? Adrian raged behind his impassive expression. Is that what you did to my father? Is that what you call it?

"Your little California friend will never defer because she doesn't understand. She doesn't have a worldly mind, Adrian. I daresay no one in southern California does. One acquires worldliness painfully, through disappointment, yes, through pain. Through an awareness that there are winters as well as summers in every life, cold and snow and icy rain as well as sunshine."

"She knows pain now," Adrian said. "We both know it. We know what it means to lose a father."

Adrian's reply suggested more than the loss inflicted by death. It evoked the several ways he had lost Robert Van Ness. The implied accusation aroused his mother to fury. "Go to California if you want to. But you'll go without a cent of my money."

Adrian was stunned. For some reason—perhaps the unstinting way his mother had always given him money—it never occurred to him that she would invoke this ultimate weapon. He stalked out of the house and spent the next month in an agony of indecision. A letter from Amanda reported nothing but chaos and despair at Casa Felicidad. Her mother was having a nervous breakdown. Her overbearing older brother had taken charge of the orange groves and the household. She begged Adrian to join her as soon as possible.

Adrian spent a week composing a reply.

Dearest One:
   Your letter tore at my heart. I wish I could rush to your side. But my mother is absolutely opposed to our marriage and has vowed to disinherit me if we go through with it. This leaves me in an impossible position. I can only see one solution: to submit and get my degree so that I can make my way in the world—which will, I hope, lead me with all possible speed to your side. Until that day, you have my undying love. Tell me I have yours.

Adrian showed the letter to his mother before he mailed it. It was a gesture of defiance but Clarissa chose to ignore it. She put her hands on Adrian's shoulders. "That is a manly letter. And a wise one," she said. "But I hope you don't mean that last sentence about undying love."

"I do."

With a stifled cry she threw her arms around him. Adrian remained rigid, his arms at his side, refusing to return the embrace.

Clarissa kissed him on the forehead and let him go. Adrian retreated to the bathroom and wiped off the kiss with a cold washcloth. He knew it was an infantile gesture. But it had symbolic power.

Idealism thundered in Adrian's soul. He was too young to fight to make the world safe for democracy. But he could and would make love and honor his guiding principles. He would marry Amanda Cadwallader and teach her to be the wife of a man of substance. He would acquire enough of that substance to defy Clarissa Ames Van Ness forever.

THE LAST PATROL

From ten thousand feet in the cloudless blue sky of November 1918, the Argonne battlefield was a crazy quilt of green fields and toy farmhouses and the dun gouged earth of no-man's-land. Beside Lieutenant Frank Buchanan flew his wingmate and best friend, Captain Buzz McCall, who had painted death's heads inside the red, white, and blue circles on his wings. They had transferred from the Lafayette Escadrille to the American Air Service when the United States entered the war in 1917.

Around them droned a half-dozen other planes in loose formation. They were finally flying swift stubby-winged French Spads, a plane that could out-speed and outdive the German Fokkers. For months they had been forced to fly Nieuport 28s, a tricky unforgiving plane that had killed more American pilots in training than the Germans had killed in combat. It stalled without warning and the wings had a tendency to fail in a roll or dive.

There were no American-designed planes on the western front. The inventors of the twentieth century's miracle machine had barely advanced beyond the clumsy craft the Wright Brothers flew at Kitty Hawk, while the British, the French, the Germans, the Italians, all had fighter planes that could fly over a hundred miles an hour.

A burst of machine-gun fire on his left broke through Frank's gloomy meditation. It was Buzz McCall, telling him to wake him up. Buzz was squinting above and behind them. At first Frank could see nothing. The trick was not to focus your eyes but to let them roam the empty sky. It was one of the first things a pilot learned on the western front. A cluster of specks rapidly grew and acquired color: at least a dozen Fokker Dr 1 triplanes with black crosses on their green wings.

Down they came out of the sun, hoping for surprise. In their eagerness they forgot that their three winged planes, having very little weight and a lot of drag, dove slowly. They were violating one of the modern world's fundamental laws, the machine must be obeyed before it will obey. The Americans had time to react.

Frank pulled back on the stick and shoved his right foot down on the rudder pedal. Up, up he soared into a loop. Just over the vertical he cut his engine and pulled the stick back sharply. There he was, slightly dazed by the gravity pounding his chest, behind the lead Fokker as the German came out of his dive. Frank's Vickers .303 machine guns hammered and two streams of tracers tore into the German's cockpit. The Fokker went into a writhing spin, an unmistakable death throe.

His fifth kill. He was an ace. He could hardly compare himself to Buzz McCall or Eddie Rickenbacker, who had five times that many victories. Moreover, he might soon be a dead ace if he did not do something about another Fokker on his tail. Red tracer bullets whizzed between his wings, snapping struts as Frank took violent evasive action, essing left and right, his brain turning to terrified mush.

Behind him the German abruptly spun out of control, smoke gushing from his engine. Buzz McCall hung on his tail, pouring extra bullets into him to make sure he was not faking. It was the tenth or eleventh time Buzz had saved Frank's life.

Around them the sky was crisscrossed by diving, rolling, spinning Fokkers and Spads. Buzz pointed below them, where two Fokkers were about to give a floundering American the coup de grace. Down they roared to pull out on the Germans' tails. Frank had a perfect shot at the Fokker on the right. He pressed the trigger. Nothing. Cursing, he grabbed a small hammer he wore around his wrist and whacked at one of the Vickers' outside levers, just in front of his windshield. The guns stayed jammed.

Buzz's first burst, short and deadly as always, set the other German on fire. He spun away, gushing smoke and flames. But Frank's German methodically blasted a stream of lead into the American's cockpit. Frank saw the pilot, a boyish Iowan named Waller on his first mission, shudder in agony. He shoved his Spad into a dive. The German, smelling blood, followed him. A thousand feet down Waller pulled out and tried to roll to the right. The German anticipated the move and caught him with another burst, riddling the cockpit. Waller spun in, exploded and burned.

A second later the Fokker pulled up into a twisting loop called an immelman, after the German pilot who invented it. He came down on Frank's tail. It was a maneuver the lightweight triplane was designed to perform. But Buzz McCall was waiting for him down below. He rolled over and fired a burst into the Fokker's belly while flying upside down. The German, probably wounded, banked away and fled for home.

Frank flew in a daze, not quite sure he was alive. Six American planes were still in the sky. They had lost two of their green pilots. At least half the replacements failed to survive their first mission. Hardly surprising, when the average life of all the pilots on the western front was six weeks. Below them were four, five, burning wrecks. His stomach churning, Frank dove with the survivors to waggle his wings above the fallen. In his head he heard his mother's voice hissing: *death machine.*

On the ground, Buzz threw his arm around him. "Good shootin' up there, Wingman," he said. "Too bad your lousy limey guns jammed and we couldn't save Waller."

"We're sending those kids up without enough training. It's murder, Buzz!"

"What's this, what happened?"

It was their squadron commander, a lean West Pointer named Kinkaid. With him was a handsome soldier in gleaming black riding boots and a broad-brimmed campaign hat tipped at a cocky angle. He had a brigadier general's star on his collar. Behind him trailed a photographer and several reporters.

"We ran into the flying circus and whipped their asses, Colonel," Buzz said. "I got two of them, Frank here got one. We lost two of the new guys—Waller and Kane."

"Two more kills," said the brigadier. "That means you're only three behind Rickenbacker. I'm Billy Mitchell. I came down to pin a medal on you, Captain."

Buzz remembered he was in the army and saluted the most popular general in the American Air Service. "Pleased to meet you, sir. This is Lieutenant Frank Buchanan. He got his fifth today. A real beauty."

Buzz described the way they had attacked the Germans as they came out of their dive. "That's the kind of aggressive tactics I want up there. That's the American style," Mitchell said.

They adjourned to the officers' mess, where champagne bottles popped and glasses were raised in a silent toast to the dead, then flung into the fireplace. Outside, the ground crews and pilots lined up in a semblance of military formation and Mitchell pinned a Distinguished Service Cross on Buzz McCall.

He added to the commendation a speech full of fiery prophecy. Fliers like Buzz McCall were demonstrating what Americans could do in the air against German veterans. "If this war lasts another six months, we'll wipe the Germans out of the sky. Then we'll show General Pershing and that circle of dunderheads he's got around him what air power can do for their infantry."

Flashbulbs popped, the reporters took notes. General Mitchell was already semi-famous for his running battle with Pershing's staff, who scoffed at the importance of air power. Mitchell told them he was assembling a force of de Havilland bombers that would demolish enemy airfields and supply dumps and arms factories if the Germans rejected the Allies' armistice terms and kept fighting.

Two hours later, led by General Mitchell driving a black sedan at ninety miles an hour, the squadron headed for the nearby city of Toul to celebrate Buzz's medal. They started with dinner at the Three Hussars, the best restaurant in town. Fueled by more champagne, Mitchell talked about air power in future wars with visionary fervor. The plane would soon make the infantry and the warship superfluous.

"The bombers of tomorrow will make this war's attacks on London and Paris look like acts of tender mercy," roared the general. "They'll be no need to send millions of men to die in the trenches. The war will be over the moment one side achieves air superiority."

"Let's drink to that!" Buzz shouted. "Air superiority!"

Frank Buchanan lurched to his feet with the rest of his by now ossified squadron mates. "General," he said. "I hope you're not saying Americans— would bomb cities—kill women and children—the way the Germans—"

"The British are doing it right now in the Rhineland," Mitchell roared. "They dropped some bombs in a fucking schoolyard last week and killed about sixty *kinder*. Those things'll happen till we get better bombsights. Then—*plunk*—we'll be able to put a thousand-pounder down a goddamn factory chimney!"

After dinner, the squadron and General Mitchell adjourned next door to Madame Undine's, the best brothel in the city. It was stocked with enough champagne to drown an infantry division and enough mademoiselles from Armentieres and elsewhere to make Valhalla look like a Methodist camp meeting.

At midnight Frank found himself in bed with two dimpled whores named Cheri and Marguerite. They were sisters. Marguerite was going around the world, licking him from the back of his neck to the soles of his feet, while Cheri was rolling her tongue around and around his aching joystick. He was Craig again, happy, proud, indifferent to death. He passed out as he came in Cheri's mouth.

The party raged around him and in the blank darkness Frank dreamt of a plane with a fuselage as round and smooth as a gun barrel, a plane that swallowed its wheels after takeoff and had only one wing, unsupported by struts. He leaped out of bed and stumbled over male and female bodies in various stages of undress to find a pen and paper and sketch it.

His mother hissed *death machine* but he defied her. This was a creature of speed and beauty, as vibrant with life as the Elgin marbles he had seen in the British Museum. It would make American pilots supreme in the air. That meant peace, not war.

"What the hell is that?"

It was Buzz McCall, glowering over his shoulder at the sketch.

"A plane we ought to build."

"You'd never get me to fly a fucking monoplane."

Louis Bleriot had flown the English Channel in a monoplane. But he soon gave the design a bad name because his wings frequently fell off. Frank began explaining that the problem was not the single wing but its shape and its position on Bleriot's monoplanes.

"Let's go," Buzz said. "We've got the dawn patrol."

In a flash, as if the champagne fumes in his head had exploded, Frank was back in the dogfight. The motors roared, the machine guns chattered, the planes blazed and spun down to doom.

He could not go up again. He was not Craig, he was Frank, the younger brother with these beautiful creatures of the sky in his head. He had no confidence in either his luck or his skill as a pursuit pilot.

"I can't do it, Buzz. I don't want to die until I see this plane—other planes—in the air—"

"What the fuck is this?"

Buzz stepped back as if he wanted to get a better look at his contemptible wingman. "Why should I die?" he mocked. "Do you think you're better than the rest of us, because you can draw pretty paper airplanes?"

Yes, Frank wanted to shout. He wanted to denounce everything, the war, the drunken parties at Madame Undine's, the dying. The endless dying. Before he could speak, Buzz hit him with a right cross that sent him hurtling across the room to crash into the opposite wall.

The next thing Frank knew he was on the floor and Buzz was shoving a foot his chest. "Are you comin'?"

Frank lurched to his feet. He was a head taller than Buzz but there was no thought of hitting him back. Buzz was Craig, curing another outbreak of momma's boyitis. "I'm sorry," he said.

"Nobody's gonna shoot you down as long as I'm up there with you," Buzz said. "We went into this fuckin' war together and we're comin' out together."

Buzz rounded up the rest of the patrol and they wobbled into the semi-dark street. Toward them panted Madame Undine, the fat blond-ringleted mistress of their revels. Her eyes bulged, tears streaked the layer of powder on her dumpling face. *"C'est fini!"* she cried. *"La guerre, c'est fini!"*

Frank threw his arms around Madame Undine and gave her a kiss. He was going to live. He was going to build the beautiful planes that flew in his head.

"Son of a bitch!" Buzz said. Peace meant he would never pass Eddie Rickenbacker and become the top American ace.

Behind him, General Mitchell looked even more disappointed. "What the hell am I going to do with all those beautiful bombers?" he said.

LOVE IN A COLD CLIMATE

The Negro jazz band in the SS *Berengaria*'s main salon was playing "There'll Be a Hot Time in the Old Town Tonight." In his mind's eye twenty-year-old Adrian Van Ness could see the dancers gyrating across the polished teak dance floor, the men in bright sports coats, the women in beaded dresses, their bobbed hair bouncing, their skirts revealing legs all the way to the knees and occasionally a silk-stockinged thigh.

Adrian wanted to be out there with the dancers. Instead he was standing on the main deck, holding his wife Amanda's hand while she fretted over the future health of a child they had yet to conceive. For a moment Adrian felt bewildered by the way life had catapulted him from carefree youth to husband and prospective father.

"Darling, I assure you England isn't an unhealthy country."

"Adrian, I can bear it for your sake. But what if the baby has weak lungs? All that dreadful fog and rain—"

"If the slightest problem develops, I'll quit my job in an instant and we'll take the first ship to California."

"I dread the thought of asking you that. I love you, Adrian. I'm terrified I'll make you unhappy."

The jazz band fell silent. It was past midnight. "Why don't you say good night to your mother?" Amanda said.

Adrian threaded his way through the tables to a corner of the salon, where Clarissa Van Ness was chatting with a sleek, gray-haired Italian nobleman. She wore a single strand of pearls around her swan-like neck, long white gloves, and a low-cut beaded black dress by Paul Poiret, the latest rage among Paris couturiers.

"Where's Amanda?" Clarissa said in her silkiest voice. "I was hoping you'd both join me for a nightcap."

"She's not feeling very well."

"Poor dear. I hope she gets her sea legs soon."

Everyone was being marvelously polite. Adrian's excuse avoided saying Amanda wanted to have as little to do with Clarissa Van Ness as possible, a sentiment that Adrian endorsed—and Clarissa ignored. She had blithely insisted on sailing with them to help Adrian launch his career as a merchant banker in London.

Her presence made Adrian uneasy. He wondered if she thought he carried his father's failure with him, like a virus. Did she plan to supervise his office conduct, his business decisions, to make sure he did not repeat Robert Van Ness's blunder?

Adrian had married Amanda in spite of Clarissa's desperate attempts to dissuade him. In fact, he had used her disapproval to wangle this opportunity to make himself a man of substance as rapidly as possible. He let Clarissa lure him to England last summer to renew their ties with Geoffrey Tillotson and other friends.

Tillotson's son Peter had been shot down and killed on the last day of the war. He seemed especially touched by Adrian's sympathy. Before long he was urging him to consider the possibility of coming to work for his family's merchant banking firm, Tillotson Brothers, Ltd., after his graduation from Harvard.

In the next year, Clarissa had mustered all her finesse to make this invitation as attractive as possible. She talked about the power and prestige of London's merchant bankers. She bombarded Adrian with stories from their glory days, when Byron celebrated them as men whose "every loan . . . seats a Nation or upsets a throne."

After a deliciously sadistic show of reluctance, Adrian accepted Tillotson's offer—and announced his plans to marry Amanda within a week of his graduation. A stunned Clarissa could only accept it with muted murmurs of regret. The wedding took place in Boston. Amanda's mother's mental condition had worsened, making Casa Felicidad, the family's Orange County home, unsuitable.

The newlyweds honeymooned for a week in Bar Harbor. It did not take Adrian long to realize Amanda had changed. Her father's death, her mother's nervous collapse, had damaged her ebullient trust in the future, which had been one of the most appealing aspects of her innocence. She felt guilty about leaving her mother to the not very tender care of her half-brother. She had no enthusiasm for further clashes with Clarissa.

A northeast storm engulfed the Maine coast with freezing rain and wind for their entire honeymoon. Although a shivering Amanda offered herself wholeheartedly, even frantically, to Adrian, she kept apologizing for her failure to "let go," to make him truly happy. She blamed the awful weather and herself for not overruling her penny-pinching brother and insisting on a California wedding. Adrian, for whom self-control was basic, saw no virtue in letting go and could not understand her distress.

Amanda's dislike of Maine in June soon extended to worries about England's fog and rain. Adrian gradually realized she saw this sojourn in London as little more than an extended honeymoon before they moved to California. Adrian soothed her with vague promises and hoped she would like England in spite of her doubts.

Geoffrey Tillotson met the *Berengaria* at Southampton and they drove to London in his yellow Hispano-Suiza Cabriolet. Listening to him talk, Adrian had the heady sense of being at the vital center of the civilized world. Having just won the most stupendous war in history, England was the most powerful nation on the globe. India, South Africa, Iraq, Palestine, Persia, Bulgaria, Turkey, Greece—their condition, their fate, rested on decisions made in Parliament and 10 Downing Street—and in the banks where the financial resources of the empire were mustered.

There were some parts of the world that were not under English control. Adrian was surprised by a note of uneasiness in Tillotson's voice as he discussed Russia, where the Bolsheviks were on their way to winning a civil war and taking charge of the country. He was almost as disturbed by the emergence of an Italian socialist, Benito Mussolini, as a power in Italy.

"Communism—socialism—they're both demagogic rot—," Tillotson growled.

"I'm not sure that's true," Amanda said as the chauffeur eased the Hispano-Suiza to a stop in front of the Ritz Hotel. "In California we've seen the evil results of unrestrained capitalism. My father was one of the leaders in the fight against the railroad barons."

Clarissa's eyes asked Adrian what he thought of his California bride. In their room, Adrian told Amanda to keep her opinions to herself from now on. They went to bed angry, not the best beginning for an extended honeymoon.

The next day Adrian reported for work at Tillotson Brothers, Ltd. His American eyes were dismayed by the company's offices. The redbrick Queen Anne building was two hundred years old and looked it. A barely legible rusty sign next to the entrance was the only evidence of ownership. Inside there was a rabbit warren of extra floors and rooms and cubicles where aging clerks clipped stock coupons or entered mysterious figures in thick red ledgers. Cage-like elevators creaked and clattered.

In the oak-paneled partners' room, cravatted Tillotsons of earlier generations stared with aplomb from the walls. A half-dozen partners sat at polished mahogany tables, conferring with clients in low tones or reading the *London Times*. The stationery had the firm's address, 16 Old Jewry Lane, and the telephone number on it but not its name. Unobtrusive was the watchword of British merchant banking.

Geoffrey Tillotson helped the newlyweds find a comfortable flat in Mayfair on a tiny street called Islington Mews and proposed Adrian for the Garrick and the Athenaeum clubs. He arranged invitations to weekend parties at a half-dozen country houses. Usually Tillotson and Clarissa came to the same party and Geoffrey introduced Adrian to prospective clients. It was all so low-keyed, so casual, Adrian had no sense of being under examination.

His fear that Clarissa would breathe down his neck soon vanished. But his hope that Amanda would like England evaporated almost as fast. Deprived of her native sunshine, she got one cold after another. She sat around their flat shivering in two sweaters, gulping cough medicine, inserting nose drops. This did not do much for their sex life. The ardor Amanda had promised him in his Harvard days vanished in tearful laments for California.

At work, Adrian filed routine letters from the African loans department. Occasionally, familiar names from Anson days relieved the tedium. Many of his former schoolmates were in the army or the civil service in Nigeria, East Africa, and other outposts. A letter from Kenya was especially welcome—it was from his Italian friend Ponty, who was running a vast coffee plantation purchased by his family with some help from Tillotson Brothers. He was still in love with flying. He had a French-made Caudron R11 three-seater that he flew all over East Africa.

Adrian lunched with Tillotson several times a month in the partners' top-floor dining room and was told he was doing splendidly. Tillotson talked off-handedly about the firm's recent investments in Chilean copper mines, South African railroads, Canadian lumbering, explaining why each one seemed a good idea. Invariably it came down to knowing that up the road certain events or changes in government policy would make the investment very profitable.

"A merchant banker has to be a bit of a crystal-ball gazer," Tillotson said. "Forethought. It's the key to success. Of course it helps to know a bit more than the next fellow."

To acquire this inside information, Tillotson partners crisscrossed the globe, hobnobbing with politicians and business leaders on every continent, sojourning for a year at a time in Hong Kong, Melbourne, Singapore, New York. The firm no longer invested much of its own money. It acted as a middleman, bringing together potential lenders and borrowers. Lately, the emergence of an aggressive Labour Party preaching socialism in England inclined a great many people to look abroad for safe places to put their money. Tillotson thought a bright young American like Adrian Van Ness might be just the man to encourage the worriers to make their investments through Tillotson Brothers, who had a long tradition of successful investing in the United States.

"We put two hundred million pounds into your country during and after the Civil War," Tillotson said. "We did especially well on the Union Pacific."

"The railroad?" Adrian said.

"We built the bloody thing," Tillotson said. "Sent you the Irishmen to do the digging and the money for the rails and locomotives. Your great-grandfather did wonders with the money."

"My great-grandfather?"

"You Americans are unbelievable. You only remember what happened yesterday. My grandfather, Geoffrey Tillotson the third, advanced most of the money from here. Your great-grandfather, Congressman Oakes Ames, was the man who organized Credit Mobilier. Surely you've heard of that?"

Adrian could only shake his head. He had majored in European history at Harvard. "Hmm," Tillotson said. "Maybe I'm talking out of turn. Don't mention it to your mother."

Obviously trying to change the subject, Tillotson said: "What do you know about the airplane business in America?"

"There isn't any, as far as I know."

"There's bound to be one. Everybody in Europe's building planes and starting airlines. Even the bloody Germans. We've got four airlines flying the Channel and the French have two. We've put money into all of the British lines. Eventually they'll consolidate and we might well control the whole kit. The plane is the machine of the future, my boy. That's been the root of my interest in it from the day I saw one fly."

For the moment, Tillotson's remarks about Oakes Ames had more impact than his prophecies about the airplane. The historian in Adrian was chagrinned by his ignorance of his mother's family. On the way home from work, he stopped at the London Library and got out a book on Credit Mobilier. He read it with mounting astonishment until midnight.

Credit Mobilier was a holding company that had built the Union Pacific, a railroad that had a decisive impact on the outcome of the Civil War. Mobilier was also a conduit for massive bribes that Adrian's maternal great-grandfather, Congressman Oakes Ames, paid to dozens of congressmen and senators to get the railroad government subsidies and a clear title to its right of way. When one of the promoters, feeling he had not gotten a fair share of the profits, sent a batch of Ames's letters to the *New York Sun,* a stupendous scandal erupted, which ended in 1869 with the House of Representatives voting 182 to 36 to "absolutely condemn the conduct of Oakes Ames."

In his astonishment, Adrian read quite a lot of this aloud to Amanda. At midnight, he decided he had to discuss it with his mother and rushed from his flat into a classic London fog. As his cab chugged though shrouded Mayfair, he began anticipating the first frank conversation he had ever had with Clarissa Ames Van Ness. Perhaps it would lead to an explanation of his father's ruin. Had he been persecuted because he was Oakes Ames's grandson-in-law?

Adrian bolted across the Ritz's long marbled lobby and rode to the fifth floor in the elephantine lift. As he charged down the red-carpeted upper hall, a door opened at the far end and a voice, which he recognized as his mother's, said: "Good night, my dearest."

A man's voice said: "I look forward to the weekend."

A few doors away was a room-service pantry. Adrian bounded into it and watched from its dark recess as Geoffrey Tillotson walked to the elevator, pressed the button, and departed.

Adrian did not confront his mother with this new, infinitely more stunning revelation. He was her son, with the same instinct for secrecy and evasion. He walked back through the fog to his flat, where he ignored Amanda's pleas to tell him what was wrong. He sent her to bed and sat in the small study composing a list of adjectives to describe his mother.

lascivious	profligate	lubricious
loose	amoral	hedonistic
adulterous	lecherous	disreputable

He decided he preferred *lubricious*. It best described the cold, concealed lust with which Clarissa and Geoffrey satisfied their appetites. Adrian stared out at the fog, seeing life for the first time with adult eyes. Tugboats hooted derisively on the Thames. Occasionally a larger vessel emitted a long, mocking moan.

In the bedroom slept his California wife whom he had married in his adolescent American idealism, never realizing that a different way of life awaited men of substance. If his mother had only had the courage to tell him. But she clung to her shameful secret, knowing he would condemn her in his ruined father's name.

Now Adrian saw the hidden purpose of the weekend house parties. They were all assignations between lovers like Geoffrey and Clarissa. Men of substance, men with forethought, parked their wives elsewhere and rendezvoused with lubricious women, while the middle and lower classes plodded through torturous moral lives.

The sheer duration of Clarissa's deception staggered Adrian almost as much as the fact. Geoffrey had been her lover when they watched Bleriot fly the Channel. For years before that, probably. All the years she had left her ruined husband behind her in New York to enjoy the company of a man of substance.

Substance? Money! That night the word was scorched into Adrian's brain. The word and its synonyms. Power, pleasure, freedom, lust, desire, fulfillment. And its antonyms: weakness, pain, humiliation, bondage, frustration, deception, loss.

In the morning, a snuffling Amanda begged him to tell her why he had not come to bed until dawn. Was he disturbed to discover he had an ancestor like Oakes Ames, a man as crooked and corrupt as the worst of the California railroad barons?

Adrian's arm froze in the act of raising his coffee cup to his mouth. His historian's brain shifted into gear. Crooked, corrupt? Oakes Ames, the bluff, blunt shovel maker from Massachusetts who had built the railroad that rescued the United States from dissolution?

Condemned by the hypocrites and thieves in Congress who took his money, Oakes Ames scorned them all and went home refusing to admit an iota of guilt. Here was a man who looked ruin in the eye and defied it. Who did not give a damn if the world considered him corrupt or disgraced. He was a hero who had saved his country.

In a flash Adrian saw an ancestor he could respect, even love. An ancestor who ignored—no, transcended—the approval of women. The fact that both Clarissa and Amanda condemned Oakes Ames, the one in her Boston silence, the other in her California naivete, was the best possible argument in his favor. Oakes Ames combined substance and heroism, money and patriotism, power and indifference to the vacuous morality of the herd.

"I don't think he was corrupt," Adrian said. "I think you need a different word for him. Effective?"

"He debauched Congress!"

"I suspect that was a contradiction in terms then—and probably still is one."

"Adrian—that's the crudest sort of cynicism. Is that what merchant banking does to you?"

"No. It's what history does to you," Adrian said.

DOWN BY THE RIVERSIDE

A few feet away, the Yellowstone River was a silent silver ribbon in the twilight. The snow-tipped peaks of the Bitterroot Range towered in the distance, cold, silent, serene. The frowning curly-haired young pilot sat with his back against a tree, his face toward the mountains. "The war was a disgrace," Charles Lindbergh said. "A national disgrace."

"In more ways than one, Lindy," Frank Buchanan said.

Fellow members of the Reynolds Air Circus, Frank and Lindbergh had spent the summer of 1922 barnstorming across Montana and Wyoming, risking their planes and their necks at county fairs and rodeos. Frank admired Lindbergh's skill as a pilot. There was nothing he could not make his Lincoln Standard biplane do in the air. Inside loops, stall spins, rolling pullouts. Only Buzz McCall could match him. Two members of the circus had been killed trying to imitate them. Frank, flying a Curtiss Jenny, a leftover wartime trainer that he had picked up for fifty dollars and rebuilt himself, did not even try.

Lindbergh had been too young to get into the war. But he would have refused to fight, even if he had been drafted. He had inherited a violent opposition to it from his congressman father, who had written a book accusing the British and Wall Street of sucking America into the carnage. His father had been called a traitor and his political career had been destroyed, leaving Lindy with a deep contempt for popular opinion. Already detesting the war for his own reasons, Frank was delighted to add Lindy's populist litany to his creed.

When they were not denouncing the war, Frank and Lindy bemoaned the current state of American aviation. The public only seemed interested in the daring and spectacular side of flying. When two army lieutenants piloted a Dutch Fokker T-2 coast-to-coast in just under twenty-seven hours, Frank had been in San Diego when they landed. The city had gone crazy, honking car horns and blowing factory whistles. But no one seemed interested in using airplanes in any practical or constructive way.

Not even in the military could the advocates of air power make any headway. General Billy Mitchell was still predicting that the plane could make fleets and armies obsolete. No one paid the slightest attention to him, even when he proved it by sinking two obsolete battleships with two-thousand-pound bombs off the Virginia coast. The United States was manufacturing automobiles and vacuum cleaners and radio sets by the millions. Planes? A handful of stubborn believers in isolated hangars in upstate New York, central Kansas, and southern California were making a few hundred.

None of the plane makers was interested in the ideas Frank Buchanan had brought back from the three years he had spent studying aerodynamics and aircraft design with French and British manufacturers. So here he was, barnstorming.

"What are you going to do for the winter, Lindy?" Frank asked. "Head for California?"

Lindbergh shook his head. "I'm going home to make enough money to buy a better plane. First, though, I'm going to float down the Yellowstone to the mouth of the Missouri in that." He pointed to a big wide-bottomed rowboat tied to a stake on the riverbank.

"Not a bad idea. You want to improve it?" Frank pointed across the green grass of their camp to the main tent. In front of it, a tiny girl with streaming blond hair was grilling steaks on a bed of coals. "Take Sammy with you," he said. "Two weeks on the Yellowstone with her will blow the gloom out of your head."

Lindbergh pulled a fistful of grass out of the ground and studied the wet roots. "No. I need some time alone."

Lindbergh stalked down to the riverbank to inspect his boat. Frank Buchanan contemplated Samantha Soames against the backdrop of the Rockies. She was as beautiful—and as wild—as an eagle or a mountain lion on those looming slopes. She appealed simultaneously to Craig, the buccaneering pilot whose spirit Frank was sustaining, and Frank, the artist-designer who found beautiful women irresistible.

Sammy was a Wyoming rancher's daughter. Her father had kicked her into a snowdrift when he caught her in the bunkhouse with one of the hired hands. She soon decided aviators were more interesting than cowboys and wound up with Raynald Reynolds. He had made her America's first female wing walker—and his mistress.

Frank strolled over to the chuckfire. "I was just talking to the Silent Swede. Lindy. He says he's going to float down the Yellowstone in that boat and he wants you to come with him. But he doesn't have the nerve to ask you."

Samantha Soames flipped a three-inch-thick steak. "Ain't there a poem about a guy who goes to a girl to ask her favor for some third party?"

" 'The Courtship of Miles Standish' by Henry Wadsworth Longfellow."

"Yeah. Longfellow. I always liked his name. Do you think he was?" She grinned and flipped another steak. "Guess only Mrs. Longfellow knew for sure. Anyway, there's this punch line in the poem. What was it?"

" 'Speak for yourself, John.' "

"Are you gettin' the message? Or do I have to hit you on the head with a sledgehammer? Daddy used to say that was the only way to get a steer's attention. Some pilots'r dumber than steers, I swear."

"I promised Buzz McCall I'd go to California with him."

"So? I like him too. If you go along with that sort of effrontery." Samantha grinned and flipped another steak. "Did I use that word right? I heard you use it the other night around the campfire. Somethin' about Reynolds havin' it."

"The effrontery to keep ninety percent of the money and only do ten percent of the flying."

Samantha held out a small, grimy hand. "Tell Lindy he's out of luck. I'm lookin' for some education. That's what I like about flyin' out with you and Buzz. You got lots of poetry and big words in your head. I figure Buzz'll take care of the other side of my ruined character."

Frank plucked a steak off the fire and strolled over to the tent he shared with Buzz McCall. He raised the flap and there was Buzz on his back, smiling at him upside down, not an unusual way of looking at things for a pilot. Buzz had both hands on the oversize breasts of a lady rancher who owned forty thousand acres near Fort Peck. She had been following them from show to show for weeks. Her husband had been killed in France.

"Come back in a half hour, sport," Buzz said.

From the darkening distance rose the incongruous sound of voices singing: "What a Friend We Have in Jesus." Booming above the mostly off-key chorus were the basso tones of the Rev. Abel Flutterman. Abel had been following the Reynolds Circus around all summer, preaching "the winged gospel" to the thousands of patrons the air shows attracted. According to Abel, who was five-five and weighed about three hundred pounds, the plane was proof that mankind had entered a new spiritual phase, in which they would surmount the evils of the flesh and achieve unparalleled purity of spirit.

Frank sat down under a tree and listened to the sacred music mingling with the lady rancher's cries of ecstasy while he consumed the steak. Sweet music of the sort he soon hoped to be making with Samantha Soames. Buzz eventually emerged from the tent while the lady rancher used the more discreet rear entrance.

"She wants me to marry her," Buzz said, combing his jet-black hair. "She'll buy me any kind of plane I want."

Buchanan offered Buzz a chunk of steak. It was not the first nor would it be the last proposition of this sort Buzz received. His compact body emanated animal magnetism. Recklessness of an ultimate variety glinted in his gray eyes, flashed in his slanting grin. Why any woman thought she could domesticate him was a mystery.

"Sammy's coming to California with us. She says she can keep us both happy."

Buzz squinted though the deepening twilight toward the chuckfire. "Is that okay with you?"

"Sure."

"Reynolds won't like it."

"Doesn't that make it even more appealing?"

"What about next summer when we need the work?"

"Who knows where we'll be next summer? You could be back in the army. I could be running my own aircraft company."

"Yeah. Or we could both be on some bread line in Dubuque behind Billy Mitchell and the rest of the Army Air Corps."

Buzz was bitter about the way America had abandoned her fliers. General Billy Mitchell had recruited Buzz for the provisional air brigade that had dropped the bombs on the battleships to demonstrate the potency of air power. The brigade had been disbanded a week later. The Navy and Army brass had combined forces to smear Mitchell as a liar and a publicity hound.

A short figure in a black flight jacket, white scarf, and tan jodhpurs strutted up to them. Raynald Reynolds had flown for the British during the war and had acquired pretensions to being a gentleman. "Where are you lads winging it for the winter?" he said.

"Florida," Frank said. "Or Texas."

"I'm thinking of Mexico," Reynolds said. "They'd love Sammy down there. Mexicans adore blond hair. But she doesn't want to go."

"Maybe she's bored with the way you fly your crate like an old lady with rheumatism," Buzz said.

"I don't believe in taking unnecessary chances," Reynolds huffed. "I don't ask my pilots to take any either. You and Lindbergh take chances up there that aren't necessary to please the public. I've made that veddy clear."

"Veddy clear," Buzz said.

"I don't think I want you back next year, McCall. You're a disruptive influence. The same goes for you, Buchanan."

"Who knows where we'll all be next year?" Buzz said, winking at Frank.

At dawn the next morning Buzz and Frank bumped down the pasture that passed for an airfield. Sammy was in the front seat of Frank's Jenny; her suitcase was stashed in the backseat of Buzz's Spad. Reynolds came running out of his tent, pulling on his jodhpurs and gesticulating wildly. The combination resulted in loss of control of the jodhpurs, which collapsed to knee level, pitching him into a nose-first landing.

At five hundred feet, Buzz did one of his more spectacular loops, pulling out so low Lindbergh and other pilots who were emerging from their tents threw themselves flat to escape decapitation. As Buzz whizzed over the prone Reynolds, something pink fluttered from his cockpit: a pair of Sammy's panties.

Reynolds raced to his Sopwith Camel and took off in pursuit. The Camel's superior airspeed soon overtook Frank and Buzz. Reynolds pulled alongside Frank's Jenny, shouting *"I love you."* The words were drowned by the roar of the motors. But Frank had no trouble reading the Englishman's lips. Sammy paid no attention to him.

Buzz McCall did a double barrel roll that put him directly above Reynolds's Camel. *Whump*—his wheels crunched into Reynolds's top wing. *Whump*—he did it again. Spars and fabric flew off. The appalled Reynolds dove for safety. Buzz followed him down, firing the machine guns mounted on his cowling. He was shooting blanks, of course. All the planes were equipped with guns to simulate dogfights at the air shows. Buzz was only adding to Reynolds's humiliation.

Reynolds pulled out of his dive at about 1,000 feet with Buzz still on his tail. As the Englishman rolled to the left, the top wing on that side crumpled like a piece of wet cardboard. The Camel slid into a spin, whirling down, down toward the green earth. Frank heard Sammy cry: "Oh, my God!"

Reynolds never even came close to pulling out. He hit nose first and the plane exploded into a geyser of flame. "He murdered him," Sammy cried.

They landed outside a town in northern Idaho and telephoned the Montana state police to report the "accident." Sammy was so furious with Buzz, she would not go near him that first night. In Frank Buchanan's tent, she was almost as reluctant to let him touch her, especially when he tried to tell her Buzz had not intended to kill Reynolds.

Sammy wiped away tears. "It's just awful thinkin' of someone dyin' like that for no reason."

Having seen so many pilots die for no apparent reason in France, Frank was unable to share her grief. But he respected it. "You don't have to do anything for me tonight," he said. "I'll read you a poem instead."

He pulled out a thin volume with the word *Lustra* in large letters on the ocher cover.

"What's that word mean?" Sammy asked.

"It's Latin. *Lustra* are offerings to the gods to atone for the sins of the people."

He opened the book at random and began reading "Dance Figure."

> *Dark eyed, O woman of my dreams*
> *Thine arms are as a young sapling under the bark;*
> *Thy face as a river with lights.*

"Shhhhh-it" Sammy said. "Who wrote that?"

"Ezra Pound. A poet I met in England."

"Do you think my face is a river with lights?"

"There's light in it. Beautiful shimmering light sometimes."

"Effrontery." Sammy giggled. She rolled off her cot onto Frank's. "There's nothin' we can do for Renny, is there?"

She kissed him on the mouth. "Read me another poem by this guy Pound." Frank flipped the pages of *Lustra*.

> *Woman? O Woman is a consummate rage,*
> *But dead, or asleep, she pleases.*
> *Take her. She has two excellent seasons.*

Sammy kissed him harder. "I like that."

For the first time Frank allowed himself to admit how much he wanted this woman. Trembling with a summer's desire that a dozen other women had not satisfied, he lifted Sammy's blouse over her head and kissed the nipples of her small snub breasts. Her neck was wreathed in her golden hair. She kicked off her denim skirt and more golden hair gleamed in the moonlit darkness.

"You don't have to," he whispered, suddenly afraid he would disappoint her.

"It's my lustra," she murmured. She took his hand and placed it on the mound of yellow hair below her waist. "Can you find the right place down there?"

He found the place with no difficulty. "Hey," Sammy gasped. "We're gainin' altitude." She wrapped her small hand around his ecstatic penis. "Damn," she said. "Whyn't you tell me you had a stick this big? I would've been flyin' with you in July."

"I wanted to surprise you."

"Ready for some stunts, pilot?"

Her fragile body was so light, so limber, yet so taut with desire, so vivid with movement, Frank Buchanan almost spoke. He almost shoved aside Craig and said the unthinkable words, *I love you*. Did Sammy sense love there beneath his pulsing skin? Frank hoped so.

It was long past midnight when they subsided into sleep. At dawn they were awakened by the roar of Buzz's engine. "Let's go, lovebirds," he shouted outside the tent flap. "We got a day's flyin' to do. The weather don't look so great to me."

Sullen cirrostratus clouds were covering most of the sky. That usually meant rain within twenty-four hours. They flew south across Wyoming and Colorado into Arizona. It was spectacular open country, with the Sierras towering on the right and endless miles of prairie and desert beneath them. A headwind blew the bad weather north into Canada, and they landed that night outside Flagstaff.

"Am I still on the blacklist?" Buzz asked, after dinner.

"Oh, I guess not," Sammy said. "A deal's a deal."

Frank was amazed by the pain he felt when Sammy disappeared into Buzz's tent. He ordered himself to grow up. He reminded himself of how often Buzz had saved his life on the western front. He tried to tell himself there was nothing special about Samantha Soames except that spectacular blond hair. She was like a hundred, a thousand other women who were crazy about pilots.

An hour later, Sammy was still inside Buzz's tent and Frank was pacing up and down in the desert beyond the glow of the campfire, barely able to restrain his rage. He finally went to bed and lay rigid on his cot, trying to think of other things. He did not know what time it was when Sammy lay down in the cot beside him.

In the morning Frank recoiled from Buzz's casual cheer. Sammy seemed almost as morose. Frank could not decide whether that was a good or bad sign. They flew across Arizona into California. Soon they were in the high desert, with its miles of scrub grass and lonely Joshua trees. They landed on a dry lake bed outside the tiny town of Muroc. Los Angeles was just over the San Gabriel Mountains, less than an hour's flying away.

A half-dozen people came out to inspect the planes but no one seemed interested in paying five dollars for a half hour in the air. Buzz could not resist taking two younger women up free. Around the campfire they discussed their prospects for making a living in California. The care and feeding of gasoline engines was expensive. Buzz thought Sammy would draw crowds as a wing walker. He had ideas for a series of hair-raising stunts, including a barrel roll with her on the wing and a midair transfer from his Spad to Frank's Jenny.

"Are you willing, Sammy?" Frank said. "We're asking you to take most of the chances."

"Sure," Sammy said.

That night Sammy came to Frank's tent and asked him to read her more poetry. He chose his favorite among Pound's translations from the Provençal, in which the troubadour tells his unfaithful beloved he will never find another woman like her, so he is going to select traits from a dozen women and "make me a borrowed lady."

"Why did you read that one?"

"I have a feeling I've lost you."

"Buzz is in his tent right now with one of the girls he took up today. Yet I'll come to him if he wants me. I wanted him the first time I saw him. It just grew and grew all summer. Why is that, Frank?"

"I don't know."

"I'll be good to you too. I really do want to learn some more poems and big words. Teach me another one now."

"Hedonist."

"What's it mean?"

"Someone who lives only for pleasure."

"That's Buzz, isn't it. Or is it me?"

"It's all of us."

Throughout the winter of 1921, Frank and Buzz and Sammy worked the great central valley of California, where people seldom saw planes. They fitted

Buzz's plane with the foot grips and the wire that would enable Sammy to stand on his wing, only a few feet from the whirling propeller. The first time Buzz did a barrel roll with her in that position, her right hand holding the wire, the left held defiantly aloft, Frank almost lost control of his Jenny. But Sammy came out of the roll unfazed, smiling, her blond hair streaming behind her in the airflow.

The midair transfer was a tricky business in even a moderate wind. Sammy walked out on Buzz's lower wing and held up one finger. They both started counting to thirteen. Precisely at that number, chosen by Sammy as a defiance of fate, she stepped gracefully, casually from Buzz's wing onto Frank's, and strolled to his front cockpit.

Thousands of California's farmers paid five dollars a head to see a beautiful woman risk death in an airplane. A man could never have attracted the crowds they drew that winter from towns like Grenada, Weed, Yreka, Tulare. At night there was love in the separate tents. Love that soon became as complex and dangerous as the stunts they were doing in the air.

Sammy wanted to respond to Frank's poetic vision of her. But she could not escape her dark compulsion for Buzz. That made her more and more contemptuous of her own character. Not a good frame of mind for a woman who was defying death in the air two or three times a week.

At first Buzz continued to take other women into his tent. He was trying to deny Sammy's growing power over him. Buzz began drinking harder. He was always a drinker, like most pilots. Drinking was part of the code, part of the way you controlled your fear and defied the groundlings. But this was a different kind of drinking. Buzz was using liquor to escape Sammy.

One night, outside Coachello, Buzz stumbled into the camp as drunk as Frank had ever seen him. "Sammy's not goin' near your goddamn tent tonight," he said.

"Did she say that?"

"No. I did."

"Why don't we ask her?"

"I won't ask her. I'll tell her. Just like I'm tellin' you."

Sammy strolled into the firelight with the groceries for dinner. "You're not fuckin' him any more. I just told him," Buzz said.

"I don't fuck him. I love him."

"No, you don't. You're saying that because you don't want to hurt me," Frank said.

"Shut up!" Sammy cried. "You're a pair of bastards. Why did I ever go near you?"

Long after midnight, Sammy slipped into Frank's tent and pressed her lips on his mouth. "I do love you," she said. "I'm so sorry. I love the poems, the words. Teach me one more."

"Euphoria."

"What does it mean?"

"A feeling of great happiness. What we feel when we fly. What I felt the first night with you."

They made love one last time. Behind his closed eyes Frank saw Sammy on the wing, the blond hair streaming almost to the tail of the stubby Spad, a miraculous figure against the blue dome of the sky. Tomorrow or the next day or some day in the next week or month, one of them, perhaps all of them, would die if he tried to fight Buzz for her.

The next day they flew to Ukiah to participate in the town's annual rodeo. They went up to do their usual assortment of death-defying dives and spins and barrel rolls. As always the climax of the stunts was Sammy's wing walk. Frank thought she looked unsteady when she got up on the wing. With her feet in the grips and the wire wound around her right wrist, Buzz went into his barrel roll. Halfway around Sammy flew into the air and stopped only when the wire ran out.

She dangled there with Buzz flying upside down. If he rolled rightside up the wire might cut through the spars and fabric and amputate his wing. Frank went to full throttle and pulled under the swaying figure. Inch by inch, he moved closer, praying he would not slash her with the propeller. It required exquisite judgment to place the plane just far enough ahead of her to get Sammy's feet into the front cockpit.

"Now!" Frank roared.

She dropped into the cockpit. Below them, the crowd went wild. They thought it was part of the show. On the ground, Sammy could not explain it. When Buzz rolled, she had blacked out. The next thing she knew she was dangling by the wire. While the cowboys rode their bucking broncos, Sammy went in search of a doctor in Ukiah. She came back with astonishing news. She was pregnant.

"How could you let that happen?" Buzz shouted.

"I don't know. I guess maybe the diaphragm wore out. Or God wants us to have a kid."

"There are ways to get rid of it," Buzz said.

"Not in my book there ain't," Sammy said.

Frank could not believe Sammy's transformation over the next several months. She stopped wing walking and started going to church services and prayer meetings. She began urging Buzz to figure out some other way to make a living in aviation. She did not want their son growing up in a barnstormer's world. Buzz defiantly insisted he could make enough money to support them.

To prove it, Buzz developed a new repertoire of stunts that were so dangerous he did not even ask Frank Buchanan to try them. Buzz flew under highway bridges and through walls of fire, he did barrel rolls at twenty-five feet and landed the Spad on the roof of a speeding car. When they reenacted aerial combat and Frank shot him down, Buzz did not pull out of the spin until he was close to treetop level. Every show, Frank was braced for a crash that did not happen.

The baby was born while they were performing in Turlock. Who should be there to baptize him but the Rev. Abel Flutterman? He had bought himself a Jenny and was flying it around California spreading his winged gospel with spectacular success. Sammy brought the infant to a prayer meeting and Flutterman dunked him in a tin tub and pronounced him "a son of the sky." William Craig McCall (his middle name chosen by Frank) responded with a spluttering squawk.

A month later, Sammy said she was ready to start wing walking again. Buzz objected. His stunts were drawing big crowds all over the state. They did not need her help. Sammy insisted and as usual got her way—and then some. She announced they would do the stunt they had improvised on her last outing— a fall from Buzz's wing and a rescue by Frank.

They flew to Petaluma to help celebrate its claim to being the chicken capital of the world. Crowds had driven down from San Francisco and Sacramento to feast on the hundreds of pounds of broiling birds and enjoy the Buzz McCall Air Show. Up they climbed into an azure June sky, without a sign of a cloud. Onto the wing sprang Sammy to clutch the wire and wave exultantly to the sun, the crowd below, perhaps to God. Over Buzz went for the climactic barrel roll. Sammy flew into space.

The wire snapped. They had left it coiled in the rear cockpit of Buzz's plane for eight months. It had never occurred to them to replace it. They knew nothing about the tensile capacity of one-inch wound steel cable, its shelf life, its eventual fatigue. Down tumbled Sammy, her blond hair streaming. After her dove Buzz. Did he really think he could snatch her from oblivion?

A farewell word leaped into Frank's mind: *expiate*. Sammy walked on wings because deep in her woman's soul she could not forgive herself for the dark compulsion at the center of her wildness. She had hoped a child would atone for it. But she had found it necessary to go back to challenging death again.

Expiate. What would he and Buzz have to do to atone for their stupidity and arrogance and lust? In a frenzy Frank pounded his fists against his windscreen and cursed at the uncaring sky.

They were at a thousand feet when the wire parted. At two hundred feet Buzz overtook Sammy but there was no possibility of maneuvering the plane into position to stop her fall. Above them, Frank saw Buzz's outstretched arm reaching for that ribbon of yellow hair. He closed his eyes, unable to bear the sight of the woman and the plane going into the ground together.

When Frank looked down again, Sammy's body was on the grass, arms flung out in a final plea. Buzz was circling above her. Somehow he had pulled out of the dive.

Only as Frank landed did he realize that he and Buzz were the bereaved parents of William Craig McCall, already known as Billy—the son of the uncaring sky.

REALIST IN LOVE

It took Adrian Van Ness several months to absorb the discovery that his mother and Geoffrey Tillotson were lovers. Already adept at masking his feelings, Adrian was able to deal coolly, affably with both of them at business and on social occasions. But the revelation inevitably affected his feelings for his wife. From a figure of pity and sympathy, Amanda became a burden, a walking, talking mistake.

Amanda also changed her mind about him. Their disagreement over Oakes Ames meant a great deal to her. She brought it up again and again until Adrian finally told her he was sick of arguing about it. Having jettisoned idealism, he found it hard to grasp how much it still meant to Amanda. She blamed his fall from grace on Geoffrey Tillotson, whom she saw changing her sensitive poet into a hard-hearted banker—the sort of grasping amoral capitalist her father had fought in California.

Adrian also grew irked by Amanda's inability—he saw it as unwillingness—to adapt to their social life. When she accompanied him to house parties, she was intimidated by the upper class. She thought they were snubbing her. Adrian tried to explain the difference between English and American manners. "Just because they don't use your first name doesn't mean they're unfriendly," he said.

"I know when I'm being snubbed, Adrian," Amanda insisted. "You're so eager to kowtow to them, you barely notice it."

"There's no need for you to come. I'm perfectly happy to kowtow on my own," Adrian said.

A few weeks after that nasty exchange, Adrian was invited to a house party in Sussex. Amanda, wheezing and sneezing with her worst cold yet, stayed in London. The house was Ravenswood, country home of Lord Elgin, chairman of the Cunard Line. It had a hundred rooms and at least that many servants. Around it were miles of woods and fields where guests shot grouse and hunted foxes.

The weather was cold and rainy. After unpacking, Adrian descended to the great hall and drank mulled wine before a blazing fire. A small dark-eyed brunette joined him, introducing herself as Beryl Suydam. She ordered sherry, remarking she was half frozen.

"What brings you here? Are you a member of the family?" Adrian asked.

"I was engaged to Lord Elgin's son, William. He was killed on the Somme."

"Oh. I'm—sorry."

"Don't be. It wasn't your fault. It wasn't anyone's fault. At least, that's what they want us to think."

"Are you inclined to blame someone?"

"Yes. But I don't know who."

Her bitterness coincided with Adrian's inchoate sense of betrayal and his deeper melancholy about history's pain. He felt an extraordinarily powerful attraction to dark, mournful Beryl Suydam. This was a woman who was grappling with more than a personal loss. She was trying to think about her pain historically, as Adrian had struggled to do since boyhood.

"What was he like—your fiancé?" Adrian asked.

"He was quite homely. A great lumbering bear of a man. But with the kindest heart, the most sympathetic nature I've ever seen. He was deeply interested in the social question. If he lived I think he might well have led a bloodless revolution in this country. He was not your ordinary aristocrat."

"A tragedy for you—and England," Adrian said.

"Beryl darling." Lady Elgin, a tall elegant blonde, clutched Beryl's hands and kissed her on the cheek.

Beryl introduced her to Adrian. "Are you married?" Lady Elgin asked.

Adrian reluctantly admitted he was. Lady Elgin sighed. "I drag Beryl to these parties because I want her to meet some eligible men. They're few and far between to her discriminating taste."

Beryl smiled gravely. "I'd like to pay a visit tomorrow. Will you come?"

Lady Elgin's good cheer disintegrated. "Oh, my darling girl. I don't think so. There's such a thing as too much sorrow. Edward's forbidden me to go there. I think he's right."

More guests arrived in the great hall. Lady Elgin regained her social smile and began greeting them. Among them were Clarissa Van Ness and Geoffrey Tillotson. Adrian enjoyed his mother's inquisitive glance at Beryl.

"What—where—are you going to visit?" Adrian asked.

"William's grave. It's about a mile away. On a lovely hill."

"I hate to think of you going there alone. May I come with you?"

"You're very kind."

"I lost some friends of my own on the Somme. From the Anson School. I'd much rather join you than make a fool of myself on horseback or shooting."

Adrian was a terrible shot and his enthusiasm for fox hunting was sharply curtailed by the memory of Robert Van Ness's fatal accident.

"Do you object to killing birds and beasts on principle?"

"If you think I should, I'll become a fanatic on the subject."

"I object to killing anything," Beryl Suydam said with sudden vehemence.

The next day, rain poured down but the shooters, the beaters, the whole party, struggled into macs and wellies and vanished into the drizzle. Adrian and Beryl enjoyed a second coffee before the fire and donned similar raingear for the walk to Viscount William Elgin's grave.

The rain stopped as they labored up the modest hill. An ancient cast-iron fence surrounded the two dozen graves, each guarded by a simple headstone. From the crest the rolling Sussex countryside, with its thick woods and pastures, was visible for several miles. Beryl opened the gate with a key and walked to William's grave.

"I used to bring flowers," she said. "I don't anymore. Maybe that's a good sign."

She did not kneel or say any sort of prayer that Adrian could detect. This was sorrow untouched by religious faith. Sympathy in its root meaning—the same feeling—stirred Adrian. He wanted to love or at least console this dark-haired wounded woman although history may have destroyed the very possibility of her loving him in return. For some reason he liked that idea.

The rain came down again. They walked back to Ravenswood while hunting guns thundered in the distance. William, the large-hearted nobleman with a social conscience, walked beside them, an invisible, formidable third. Adrian resolved to challenge him.

"Five years is a long time to mourn someone."

"It isn't just William's death. My father was a surgeon in France. What he saw there has left him a wreck. He can barely practice. I worked as a nurse, here. I saw some of the same things. I'll never forget what one man told me—the soldiers in the trenches hated everyone back here, enjoying the English way of life. We were their executioners."

"No you weren't. You were all—all of us—were—are—history's victims. Once you realize that, once you realize history's essential barbarism, you can begin to accept it—"

Beryl's face was almost invisible in the recesses of her hooded green mackintosh. "I like that idea," she said.

"It helps if you share the experience with another person."

"Where shall I find this historical hero?"

"He doesn't have to be heroic. We're talking about spiritual courage. That may occur in the most unlikely people—even in those who detest killing birds and beasts—and human beings."

Adrian yearned to tell her about his ruined father, his faithless mother, his naive California wife. But it was too soon. Beryl seemed to retreat deeper inside her green hood. They trudged silently through the rain, which had turned to a fine cold mist. Adrian sensed the third's looming presence.

"Have I made a fool of myself?" Adrian said.

"No," Beryl said.

That night after dinner Adrian sat down next to his mother and told her about the remarkable young woman he had met today. "She's very knowing," he said. "She tells me these house parties are really nothing but discreet assignations. Half the guests here are seeing each other illicitly, as the tabloids say."

"I'm sure that's an exaggeration," Clarissa said.

"Ah, here he is," Geoffrey Tillotson said, handing Clarissa a demitasse. "I've got a man over there who's ready to put a million pounds into an airline somewhere—Australia, America. Convince him of the glorious possibilities in your native land."

He nodded toward a rotund Liverpool shipping executive named Edward Jenkins. He had sideburns that reminded Adrian of his Anson headmaster, Mr. Deakwell.

"I wish I could stay in London a bit longer," Clarissa said. "But I must get home. There are so many things to do."

"I'm—I'm sorry to hear that," Tillotson said, sitting down on the couch opposite her like a man who has suddenly had a heavy sack dumped in his lap. Adrian strolled over to sell a paper airline to the man from Liverpool.

When a young man is angry at someone, it comes out in cruel ways. But retaliation never solves the deeper more dangerous anger at fate. That required a father's mediation—and a son's acceptance. For the time being Adrian had no father—and he was no man's son. He was at war with his world. As in most wars, the first victim was an innocent—Amanda.

LOOP THE LOOP

The Waco 10 biplane came in low and fast, just missing a line of eucalyptus trees. Frank Buchanan slammed the plane down for a rough three-point landing and bounced ten feet into the air. A crouching man scuttled beneath him. The Waco came down for another tremendous bounce and headed toward a second line of eucalyptus trees on the other side of the field.

In a perfect imitation of a pilot who had lost control of his plane, Frank tore between two of the trees. He sheared off the right wings within two feet of the fuselage. The left wings lost only their tips. Still going fifty miles an hour, the Waco flipped on her side and Frank dove into the bottom of the cockpit to keep his head from being mashed into the dirt. The plane hurtled to a cracking, crunching stop, the propeller spewing up sod until it splintered.

Silence except for the *plop* of leaking gasoline. Frank struggled to unfasten his safety belt. Pounding feet. Hands reached to help him. They dragged him away from the plane, yelling "Are you okay?" He nodded. As far as he could tell, he still had the use of his arms and legs.

"That was great," cried the excited unit director. He was standing in an open truck with the cameras. "I can hardly wait to see the rushes."

Buzz McCall was waiting on the other side of the field, his arm around the picture's second lead, a sultry Theda Bara–type named Tama Moreno. "Nice going, sport," Buzz said. "Now we can have a party instead of a funeral."

It was the last stunt on their list for this movie, a comedy called *Loop the Loop*, about a rich idiot learning to fly. Tomorrow they would collect two thousand dollars for two weeks of risking their necks. They had wrecked four planes and come close to smashing a half-dozen more, flying them upside down under bridges and around telephone poles. As usual, Buzz had done the really dangerous stunts, leaving the obvious ones like crash landings to Frank.

They had gone into the movie stunt business after trying several other ways to make a living in aviation after Sammy's death. Frank had been adamant about

86

getting out of the barnstorming game. He told Buzz it was Sammy's last wish and they had to fulfill it. That did not solve the problem of what to do with one-month-old Billy McCall. At first they tried boarding him with Frank's mother but her hostility to the boy disturbed Frank. She told him Billy was not a child of light or of darkness. She did not know what he was. They moved Buzz's widowed mother from Detroit and set her up in a house in Laguna Beach with the infant. It took six hundred dollars a month to pay the mortgage and support them—more money than most people were making from planes in the twenties.

At first they tried flying the mail. Their old barnstorming buddy, Charles Lindbergh, recommended it. The pay was eight hundred dollars a month, which left enough to do some carousing—a must with Buzz. But the risks were so hair-raising, even he started to wonder if they were out of their minds. The planes had no instruments and a lot of the flying was at night. As a pilot came in for a landing, he had to listen to the sound of the wind whistling through the struts to estimate his airspeed.

Flying through clouds, pilots became completely disoriented and flipped upside down and spun to their dooms. There were no official weather reports. A pilot had to land and ask local farmers their opinion of what tomorrow might bring. Worst of all was the cold. Even with bulky bearskin suits, the below-zero wind whipping through holes in the base of the windshields was agonizing. Soon a pilot was so numb he no longer cared whether he lived or died. Many died. Planes crashed by the dozen. Twice Lindbergh escaped death by bailing out at the last second.

Buzz got a better idea. On a mail flight to Houston, he met the state's richest bootlegger. The gangster offered ten thousand dollars to build a plane big enough to carry two hundred cases of Scotch per flight from Mexico. Frank spent three months designing and constructing a gullwinged monoplane with this awesome load capacity. To his disgust the bootlegger refused to pay another thousand dollars for a decent engine. They had to settle for a motor from a Curtiss-Wright Jenny. The plane needed about a mile to take off and could barely maintain a survivable airspeed.

They wobbled back and forth from Mexico in this flying disgrace for several months, making money for their employer and a fair amount for themselves. One day they heard a strange sound, a sort of angry thud in the fuselage. "I'd swear that was a bullet," Buzz said.

Frank saw numerous white clusters of smoke on the ground. A lot of people were down there shooting at them. The bootlegger's friends apparently disliked airborne competition. After a few more trips the plane looked like a flying sieve. This did not improve its handling characteristics. Buzz decided it was time to try to get back into the Army Air Service, where dodging bullets would be an honorable profession if a war started.

Old friends such as Jimmy Doolittle and George Kenney, still flying World War I–vintage crates, told him to forget it. The Air Corps was the Army's unloved, unwanted stepchild. General Billy Mitchell was in imminent danger of being court-martialed for complaining about it. They flew back to California with about ten thousand dollars from their Scotch running and tried to find someone who would back Frank's monoplane with a real engine in it.

They built another version of the plane. But no one could see beyond the struts and wire biplanes being used by the army and the airmail service. Broke again, Buzz took charge and did the only thing that occurred to him—use his skills as a pilot to get a cut of the tidal wave of cash pouring into Hollywood. By this time Sammy had been dead almost three years—and he was also ready to enjoy the other commodity that Hollywood had in abundance: beautiful women.

Enjoyment was the watchword of the party to celebrate the completion of *Loop the Loop*. The festivities got going around 8:00. The movie company had rented all the bungalows around a small lake near Modesto. The star, a baby-faced blonde named Mabel Durand, had the biggest bungalow, of course. Everyone called it the Villa Modesto—not a bad joke, if you knew Mabel. Modesty was not among her virtues. The villa was party headquarters but they had the whole lake to themselves, which fueled an exorbitant excitement in everyone.

In Mabel's bathroom was a tub full of iced champagne. For those with cruder palates, there was Scotch, bourbon, and gin, all guaranteed to have genuine labels, direct from Canada. Mabel's favorite bootlegger, a bullnecked Italian from San Francisco, had brought it in by plane earlier in the day. There was also plenty of cocaine on the side, delivered by a cheerful Mexican who was kicked out for daring to think he could snort with the Anglos.

Before everyone got too drunk, they had to see a rough cut of the film, which they spiced with exuberantly obscene comments. As usual, Tama Moreno had lined up one of the extras for Frank. She was a blonde from Texas named Gloria, a good ole cowgirl. She drawled about her heart bein' half out of her mouth when he crashed the Waco. After that gush of praise, conversation became a desperate struggle.

Buzz could never figure out why Frank wanted to talk to them in the first place. "Let them talk to each other," he said, a piece of wisdom that virtually echoed Craig.

By ten o'clock the party was taking off. Everyone was drunk and the grips were starting to snort cocaine. A black band was floating around the lake on a raft, playing New Orleans jazz. Buzz decided it would be fun to throw them into the water and see how well they played wet. Their British director organized a rowboat flotilla and commanded it Lord Nelson–style, screaming at every man to do his duty. They threw the terrified musicians into the lake, ignoring their pleas that they could not swim. Frank and a few others sensitive to race relations rescued them. They were left to shiver in their sodden clothes on Mabel's porch while the director staged a scene from *Anthony and Cleopatra*, the way he claimed it was played in ancient Egypt.

On a barge christened the HMS *Pussy*, Mabel and her ladies in waiting wore nothing at all. Floodlights were used to guarantee no one missed a detail. Mabel did a shimmy while her ladies Charlestoned around her. It was memorable. All that female pulchritude gyrating and jiggling in the white intensity of the ten-thousand-candlepower lights. "Hieronymus Bosch, Rabelais, Breughel—it beats them all!" the director shrilled.

Buzz commandeered a crew of stripped galley slaves in one of the larger rowboats who towed the HMS *Pussy* around the lake to massed applause from the drinkers and sniffers on shore. From another boat the director filmed the whole thing and shrieked he was sending it to *Ripley's Believe or Not* to claim the record for the most pubic hair in a single frame.

By midnight the orgy was in the stratosphere. The jazzmen had gotten into the champagne and cocaine and were playing very strange music, a dissonant assortment of howls and groans and wails. Buzz reeled past with his hand in Tama's black pussy. "Ain't this livin', Sport?" he roared. "I just fucked Mabel. Put in a good word for my ole wingman. Go for it, kiddo. She liked the way you crashed that plane."

Whether he took Buzz's advice, Frank was unsure. He dimly recalled swimming to the raft but the next thing he clearly remembered was a bungalow room with Gloria. She had shed her clothes and was telling him she liked to get on top. She liked almost everything, including Tama, who was in the room too, giving them instructions. Gloria and Tama went down on each other while half the crew, including Mabel and the director with his ubiquitous camera, screamed encouragement.

Suddenly a voice boomed in Frank's head. *Ain't this living?* It was Buzz's words but the voice seemed to belong to his brother Craig. Instead of the swaggering satisfaction in Buzz's question, the voice seemed mocking, almost contemptuous. Dazed, Frank slowly backed away from the two groaning, panting women on the bed. He shoved through the drunken crowd and stumbled to the shore of the lake in the darkness. *Ain't this living?* boomed the voice.

Pulling on a discarded shirt and pants, Frank wandered forlornly around the lake wishing he had hit the left-hand tree head-on in the Waco. Wishing, wondering, weeping in the darkness, while the jazzmen howled despair on the wind. Maybe the best thing to do was walk into the lake and abandon the mess he was making of his life.

He was sick of risking his neck for two hundred dollars a stunt, sick of crashing planes instead of building them. He knew why he could not find a backer to build the planes flying in his head. Most people found it hard to believe that Frank Buchanan, with his sloppy clothes, his rambling swooping conversation, which could leap from planes to poetry to mystical religion in a single sentence, was businessman enough to run a company, pay his bills and produce a given number of planes according to a contract.

For the past six months he had been begging Buzz to join him in another try at manufacturing. Buzz had the toughness, the leadership qualities, to get things done on schedule. But Buzz had fallen in love with the movies. He had already played a daring pilot in two films and Tama Moreno, among others, thought he had a future as an actor. Frank knew what he was really doing—using broads and booze to drown his dreams of warrior glory—and forget Sammy and her son, Billy.

Frank refused to forget Sammy—and to Tama Moreno's barely concealed chagrin, he made sure Buzz did not forget Billy. He insisted on a ritual weekly visit. He frequently reminded Buzz that Sammy did not want their son to become a barnstorming bum like his two fathers. She would have had the same opinion of stunt-flying bums. They made more money than barnstorming bums but they were still moral and spiritual disasters.

"Excuse me, mister. Have you seen my mother? The lady was supposed to stay with me but she left me all alone and there was all kinds of noises and I'm scared."

The voice belonged to a small figure a half-dozen cautious feet away in the darkness. It was Cliff, Tama Moreno's six-year-old son by a vanished husband. She took the boy on location with her, claiming she had no relatives or friends to mind him. He was one of the reasons she liked Buzz. She thought he was the kind of father Cliff needed—a man's man.

The little boy reminded Frank of Billy, the only person in the world Frank loved at this forlorn point in his life. "There's nothing to be afraid of," he said, putting his arm around him. "You know me. I'm Frank. Buzz's friend. We'll sit here together for a while and talk about planes. Do you like them?"

"Sure."

"Would you want to learn to fly them some day?"

"I guess so."

"You're not sure?"

"If they crash you can get hurt—even killed—can't you?"

"Not if you're a good pilot."

Frank described the new planes that were appearing in the American sky—the Ford trimotor, the Sikorsky seaplane, lumbering creatures that were lucky to go 115 miles an hour. He told Cliff someday they would have planes that could whiz across the continent in a single day. Even fly the Atlantic and Pacific.

"Hey, Sport, where the hell have you been? We were gettin' ready to drag the lake."

It was Buzz, followed by Tama. The night sky was turning gray. It was almost dawn. Tama exploded when she saw Cliff. Why wasn't he in bed? He tried to explain as she dragged him back to their cottage on the other side of the lake.

"What's wrong, Sport?" Buzz asked.

Frank shook his head. He was not about to do a momma's-boy act and cry on Buzz's shoulder. He let the jazzmen wail their woes into the dawn.

Buzz sat down beside him. He understood what was wrong. Beneath his tough-guy act, he felt as lost and betrayed by the aviation world as Frank. "We'll figure something out, Sport. I promise you. I want to build those goddamn planes of yours as much as you do. Meantime we gotta keep eatin'."

Frank heard another voice saying: *we got to eat, kid.* It was Craig, speaking through Buzz, telling him he still cared.

A trumpet howled sardonically. Frank struggled for faith that he was being guided by a presence that would somehow help him survive these wasted years.

SON AND LOVER

"Now put your feet on the rudder controls," Adrian Van Ness said. "To keep level, the nose should cut the horizon just above the top of the engine cylinders. Press the stick and it goes above them. Pull and it drops below. You try."

"Marvelous!" Beryl Suydam cried. Adrian understood what she was feeling. Discovering you could control this strange creature in the sky was an extraordinary thrill.

Adrian and Beryl were two thousand feet above the green Wiltshire countryside in a de Havilland Moth, everyone's favorite sport plane. At Geoffrey Tillotson's urging, Adrian had learned to fly to impress potential investors in the aircraft business.

"For level flying we keep the wings parallel with the horizon. Move the stick to the left and the port wing will drop. Move it to the right and we'll come back again. Try."

Beryl dipped the left wing and they got a glimpse of the landscape Thomas Hardy had made famous in his novels about fate-haunted lovers. She moved the stick to the right and they were level again.

"Last we have the rudder. It's like a boat. We steer for a fixed point on the horizon. A gentle push with the left foot and the nose slides left. Reverse, and we recover. Try."

Beryl tried and the Moth veered dramatically left. Adrian straightened the plane and explained that the rudder was much more sensitive than the other controls. It did not have to contend with as much air pressure. He let Beryl handle the rudder again and she did much better.

"Easy, isn't it?" Adrian said. "Try a turn."

Beryl tried it and almost panicked. The nose wavered up and down, the plane skidded and sideslipped. Adrian took charge as they wallowed around. "Feel for the angle of the bank," he said, "Try again. Use your toes on the rudder. Nothing else."

Beryl obeyed and made a remarkably smooth right turn. She was catching on fast. "Adrian, I adore it!" she cried.

They cruised over the west country, Adrian pointing out places of interest below them. "Those are the Berkshire Downs to the north. That smudge is

Reading. Now you can see the channel and the Isle of Wight. There's Southampton Water."

A liner was standing out to sea from Southampton. Adrian thought of his mother and her friends, plodding along on their boats and trains, and felt a gratifying surge of superiority. Geoffrey Tillotson was right. This was the machine of his generation. They were flying over the dull dismal past into the future.

In fact, they were flying to Ravenswood. The plane had become the smart way to arrive for a country weekend. In a half hour Adrian made a bumpy but adequate landing on the great lawn. A half-dozen other planes, most of them de Havilland Moths, were already parked in front of the house. As they taxied toward this impromptu flight line, Clarissa Van Ness and Geoffrey Tillotson stepped out of his Hispano-Suiza.

"What a marvelous surprise," Geoffrey said. Clarissa looked less pleased. A month ago, Amanda had returned to California. Seeing Adrian with Beryl confirmed a long-running rumor she had undoubtedly heard many times. But what could Clarissa say, when she was enjoying the amiable charms of her man of substance again? Adrian found his mother's dilemma deliciously satisfying.

For almost two years, Adrian had watched his marriage deteriorate, telling himself it was not his fault, it was a historical process in which he was unhappily participating. Amanda grew more and more melancholy at the prospect of a second winter in England. Her colds accumulated into the grippe and then into a bout of pneumonia—a very serious illness in the 1920s. In a flurry of guilt Adrian had asked Clarissa to return and nurse her back to health. She and Amanda spent the summer at the Tillotson house in Kent—giving Adrian time to pursue Beryl Suydam in London.

She proved elusive. The ghostly third was a formidable antagonist. But Adrian, convinced he was a man of the future and time was his ally, was tenacious. Slowly, inevitably, Beryl's melancholy receded. Soon Adrian was her lover, visiting her flat in London at night, lying to Amanda about his long hours at the bank.

Finally came news from California that Amanda converted into an ultimatum. Her mother's mental condition had deteriorated so badly, Amanda's half-brother had placed her in a sanitarium a few miles from Cadwallader Groves. Violently distressed, Amanda reminded Adrian of his promise to quit his job and return to California with her if circumstances warranted it. Here, surely, were the circumstances. Her doctor had told her not to spend another winter in England. Her mother was being hounded into insanity by her monstrous brother.

Adrian calmly, coldly, declined to go. He said his career as a merchant banker was just beginning to prosper. It took years to accumulate clients. But he urged Amanda to go. In fact, he insisted on it. She had wept and asked him if he were going to divorce her. It was a painful moment. Adrian gave her the only possible reply. "No." It was a lie, of course. But men of substance regularly lied to their wives.

That night at Ravenswood, Adrian, Beryl and the other fliers came to dinner in their jodhpurs and flying jackets. Planes were the main topic of conversation at the table, upstaging the establishment of the Irish Free State and the jailing of the German agitator, Adolf Hitler, for attempting a coup d'état in Munich. Later, sipping brandy before the fire while his mother glared in the middle distance, Adrian turned to Beryl and murmured, "Can I come to your room tonight?"

Beryl understood the significance of accepting Adrian in her arms in this house. It would be a decisive break with her sorrow, with the ghostly third. "I can't make you happy. I have no happiness in me," she whispered.

Adrian was not listening. "I want to make *you* happy," he said.

That night for Adrian flight was a new gospel, an escape from his empty marriage, a transcendence of the wounded naive adolescent who had sailed on the *Berengaria*. Flight fused with his desire for Beryl Suydam, his wish to heal her grief with his American faith in the future. Doubtful yet suffused with a wish to make an escape of her own, Beryl opened her arms to him. For a while that night in her room on Ravenswood's second floor, the ghostly third who walked beside her vanished.

The next day, while most of the guests shot grouse, Geoffrey Tillotson suggested a stroll through the woods. "A shame about Amanda going home like that," he said. "But our bloody climate is hard on Americans. She may well be better off in California."

He cleared his throat. "Your mother's a bit disturbed—as am I—about Beryl Suydam."

"Why?" Adrian said.

"The whole bloody family is full of socialist rot, dear boy. Socialist rot of the worst sort. Which makes her a bit inconsistent with your profession."

"We don't talk politics."

"You will, I assure you."

"I can handle politics quite nicely," Adrian said. "I'm not a fanatic on the subject."

"Not politics with a woman, old fellow," Tillotson said. "They add a dimension that can be quite devastating."

Adrian strode along, his eyes on the leafy path. "You and Clarissa don't talk politics? Is that the secret of your success?"

Now it was Tillotson's turn to walk a dozen paces in silence. He put his arm around Adrian's shoulder. "We must have a good talk one of these days."

Two weeks later, after a leisurely lunch, Tillotson led Adrian to a secluded corner of the Athenaeum Club's long lofty library. He ordered a turn of the century Sandeman's port and told Adrian how he had fallen in love with Clarissa Van Ness. His older brother's death in a climbing accident in Switzerland had brought him back from India, where he had been supervising Tillotson's numerous investments. He had married the daughter of a British civil servant out there and found her incapable of making the transition to social London. He was thrown on his own in society and seldom saw his wife, who preferred to remain "buried in Yorkshire."

When he met Clarissa Van Ness in 1898, Geoffrey Tillotson was a lonely man. She was a lonely woman. "Your father—her husband's—failure made him—how shall I say it?—less than adequate. Do you understand me?"

He finished his port in a nervous gulp and ordered another glass.

"Wrong as it was, her love has been the solace of my life, Adrian," Tillotson said. "And you, dear boy. I won't attempt to tell you what you mean to me now. Though I realize I don't have the slightest claim on you. I wanted to tell you immediately after your—your—mother's husband—your unfortunate father—I suppose you will always think of him that way—died. But your mother couldn't bring herself to do it. Of course you understand you must never tell her of this talk."

"Of course," Adrian said. He was too astonished to think or feel anything. He had just discovered Robert Van Ness was not his father. He was not the legitimate son of a failure, but the bastard son of a man of substance.

On a shelf behind Geoffrey Tillotson's head, illuminated mostly by the glow from the nearby fireplace, was a leatherbound book with a title in faded gold: *The Essays of Sir Francis Bacon*. The first man to write frankly about the pursuit of wealth and power. Thackeray had sat in this room writing *Vanity Fair*, another book that told how the world worked.

Something indefinable, an acceptance of the world's ways, filtered into Adrian's soul. It did not change his anger into milky benevolence. The wariness, the suspicion that life was a maze of secrets, would always be there. Along with a stubborn loyalty to the ruined speculator who had given him his name. But now this vortex of feelings belonged to a different man.

A man who saw himself telling Beryl Suydam he was half-English, ready to love her not as a visiting American but as a part of her own country, prepared to share its destiny with her at his side. For a little while, suffused with love and sonship, Adrian was no longer American.

A week later, Tillotson summoned Adrian to his office. "The chancellor of the exchequer—Winston Churchill—has asked me to form a commission to investigate our airline problems. We need a clever fellow who can find out how much money these confounded Europeans are losing whilst they pretend to prosperity. I'm quite sure the bloody beggars are all getting money from their governments. While our fellows are wobbling along on the edge of bankruptcy."

"I know someone who might be rather good at that," Adrian said.

Adrian was talking about his old schoolmate, Carlo Pontecorvo. He had returned from Africa when his father died in 1922 and assumed the family's ancient papal title. He was now Prince Carlo. But Italian politics had made his position precarious. His father, a believer in democracy, had opposed Mussolini and the Fascists had expropriated the family's estates in Calabria. They had been forced to sell their African lands at a catastrophic loss. In spite of his comparative poverty, Ponty was still passionately interested in flying. His letters to Adrian were full of descriptions of the latest airliners being developed by designers such as Antony Fokker and Gianni Caproni. He seemed to be in touch with all aspects of the European air world.

Tillotson approved the choice. "It's a job for a young fellow. Everyone in the business is young. Tell him we'll see that he's well treated for his time and trouble."

Ponty accepted Adrian's proposal by return mail. He planned to pose as the spokesman of a syndicate of investors who were considering the purchase of one or several existing airlines. He would refer doubters to Tillotson Brothers, who would confirm his authenticity. "I would also suggest setting up an account in the name of a third party in a Swiss bank," he wrote. "There may be a need for a certain amount of *douceurs*. Or as you Americans say, sweeteners."

Oakes Ames's great-grandson had no hesitation about suggesting all this, including the douceur account, to Geoffrey Tillotson, who approved it with a nod of his head.

Two months later, Ponty flew into Croydon Airport aboard a French Loire et Olivier Air Union biplane with reams of information on how much money all the European airlines were losing and how much their governments were paying to subsidize them. He also included some startling information on how Lufthansa, the German airline, was secretly training pilots for their military air force.

"Good job," Geoffrey Tillotson said after reading Adrian's digest of Ponty's espionage. "But we won't send this stuff to anyone in the government just yet. Let's take some of that Liverpool fellow's money and put two hundred thousand into Air France, two hundred thousand into Lufthansa and the rest into Alitalia."

"What about Lufthansa training military pilots?" Adrian asked.

"Forget that. It would raise hob with the stock," Tillotson said. "They're just playing the great game. As we'd be playing it if we lost the war."

Within a month, the British government announced a plan to consolidate the four faltering British airlines into Imperial Airways, with a government subsidy to keep it flying. Tillotson Brothers had, of course, bought into the company at bargain prices weeks before the announcement. Forethought at work again, Tillotson said, with his insider's smile. To reward their secret agent, a nice block of stock was signed over to Prince Carlo Pontecorvo.

Meanwhile, Adrian enjoyed Ponty's companionship. He combined aristocratic Italian good looks with a nonchalance that put men at ease—and if Beryl Suydam was a sample—women found enchanting. His stories of flying in Africa—crash-landing in the Nile, daring the downdrafts of Mt. Kilimanjaro—soon had him on everyone's list for dinner parties and country weekends.

On one of these outings, Beryl asked Ponty if he would give her flying lessons. Adrian's sporadic instruction had taught her the basics of flight but she had yet to solo. Ponty was evasive about his "commitments" in Rome. That night he took Adrian aside and asked him if he approved the idea.

"Why not?" he said.

"Learning to fly disturbs the equilibrium of many men," Ponty said. "I would be uneasy, if I were you, about its effect on a woman."

Adrian dismissed this warning as offhandedly as he had ignored Geoffrey Tillotson's concern about Beryl's politics. She had moved into his Islington Mews flat. True, she was working for a left-wing publishing house that seemed to specialize in books praising the Soviet Union. She was violently critical of the Conservative government that was ruling England. But Adrian saw this as a continuation of his contest with the ghostly third and avoided arguments by claiming an American should be neutral in British politics.

Within the week, Adrian and Beryl were airborne with Ponty in a biplane called the Lucifer 3 Seater. To Adrian's chagrin, Ponty was soon pronouncing Beryl a born pilot. She had the indefinable instinct that blended human and machine in the air. Adrian on the other hand was constantly trying to think his way through the process. The result was safe but clumsy flying.

Adrian simply did not understand Ponty when he urged him to "let the plane tell you what to do." The plane was an unthinking collection of struts and wood and metal that would kill him if it got a chance. Beryl had no such apprehension. She borrowed money from her father to buy a de Havilland Moth and was soon flying all over England, ferrying her authors to speaking engagements and participating in air shows, where she rapidly acquired a collection of prizes.

Adrian was not particularly troubled by Beryl's superiority in the air—until he began hearing more and more about a writer named Guy Petersham, who had been her late fiancé's roommate at Cambridge. He had just published a book about his visit to Russia. She invited him to dinner one night, along with Ponty and one of the half-dozen young Englishwomen who had fallen in love with the prince. Petersham arrived wearing baggy unpressed trousers and a dirty Shetland sweater. Tall, languid, he was totally convinced of his own intellectual brilliance.

For an hour he lectured them on Vladimir Lenin and Joseph Stalin as the prophets of the new age. "I begin to think the entire raison d'être of the slaughter of the Great War has been the creation of the Soviet Union. The war was the birth pangs of a new world."

"I've been led to believe America was the new world," Adrian said.

"Dear fellow," Petersham said. "You primitive capitalists are positively quaint."

You are positively asinine, Adrian thought. But he repressed the words. He did not like the excitement in Beryl's eyes.

"Communism looks to me like another name for fascism," Ponty said. "Both are disguises for the oldest form of government in the world—rule by the sword. I thought it was impossible for an Englishman to admire such a system."

"My dear prince," Petersham said. "You're a charming anachronism. If you stay around England long enough we may shoot and stuff you for some museum."

"Guy wants me to go with him to the Soviet Union on his next trip," Beryl said. "He thinks we can get permission to fly all over the country bringing a message of friendship from the British people. Do you think I'm up to it, Ponty?"

"If you fly in the summer, and they provide you with decent maps, yes," Ponty said.

His grave eyes met Adrian's. Were they saying *I told you so*? After the guests departed, Beryl cleared the table while Adrian poured the last of the wine into a decanter. "You're not really serious about that trip, are you?" he said.

"It's a once-in-a-lifetime opportunity, Adrian. A chance to see a part of the world I care about deeply. And perhaps set some records for overland flight."

"It's not a part of the world I care about," Adrian said.

"Perhaps you should. Perhaps you should at least let me explore it and find out if Guy is right about the Soviet Union being the only way to justify the war."

The third, the large-hearted noble ghost was back. Now his voice was more threatening, more formidable. Beryl Suydam was no longer the wounded woman he had met at Ravenswood. She had acquired a sense of mastery in the air and was prepared to demonstrate it on the ground. But Adrian was no longer the fatherless son, confused by his devious powerful mother. He spoke with a man's voice.

"I'm afraid I take a dim view of your spending three months in a foreign country with another man to explore an idea that I consider absolute trash."

"Maybe the trash is in your mind, Adrian. You talk about the plane as the symbol of our bright future. But what have you done with it here in England, with the help of your noble friend, Prince Carlo? Captured it for the ruling classes. Imperial Airways. Are you proud of helping to create that? The very name cries out exploitation."

"The ruling classes have the money. Planes cost a great deal of money. For the time being the rich will be their chief users. But America will change that. Look at the motorcar. Only a few hundred thousand people own one in Europe. In America there are millions of them on the road. The plane will go the same way."

"Bosh. You're lying to yourself. And to me."

"I love you. I've never lied to you. I try not to lie to myself."

Beryl began to weep. "I wish you'd taken me to America. Maybe this wouldn't be happening."

"I wish you hadn't met Guy Petersham. He's stirred up all the socialist rot in the bottom of your mind."

"Who told you that?"

"Never mind."

"It was your beastly boss, Geoffrey Tillotson. That man's a perfect example of what's wrong with this country. My father knew him in school. He was a snob then. The epitome of the ruling class."

"I disagree, totally," Adrian said.

"I know what I'm talking about. You don't," Beryl said.

Adrian felt like a man who had put his plane into a spin and failed to pull out. Instead of telling Beryl that Geoffrey Tillotson was his father, revealing himself as half-English and asking her to marry him, he was finding Tillotson's name the instrument of separation, desolation, loss. He was an outsider again, the American wog.

"You're talking about a man I—I admire. Admire deeply. Can you appreciate that?" Adrian said.

"I'm afraid I can't appreciate any such thing," Beryl said. "I'm afraid I can no longer appreciate anything you might have to say to me."

She packed her suitcases and departed. Adrian was certain she would be living with Guy Petersham within a fortnight. For a while he thought of taking a de Havilland Moth up to two thousand feet and pointing its nose toward the earth for a final dive. Ponty tried to soothe his turmoil with worldly advice. "She was charming, beautiful, sensual. But she was not a suitable wife, Adrian. She doesn't have a penny."

Ponty calmly explained the European view of the sexes. Next year he was going to marry Constance di Burgos, who would soon inherit huge swaths of southern France and Tuscany. She was a mousy woman with stringy hair and a will of iron. But her dowry made her an excellent wife. "The man who looks for love in marriage is naive," Ponty said. "Love is impermanent. Wealth—especially wealth in land—is what endures."

Ponty urged Adrian to investigate land values in California and reconsider his marriage with Amanda Cadwallader. Two thousand acres of orange groves might be the foundation of a comfortable fortune. "But don't teach her to fly," Ponty added with a grave smile.

One afternoon in the office a week later, Geoffrey Tillotson put his hand on Adrian's shoulder. "You're in the most awful funk, aren't you? Let's have a drink."

This time they went to the Garrick, smaller, more intimate than the Athenaeum in its Greek cathedral on Pall Mall. "Thought you'd be interested in this," he said and handed him a publicity release from de Havilland Aircraft. Beryl Suydam had just announced her plan to fly to Moscow in a DH Moth with Eric Petersham as her navigator.

"I knew her father at Cambridge," Tillotson said. "We were deadly enemies from the first days. Primal antagonism seems to be the only answer. It may go back to the Wars of the Roses. Or the Roundheads and the Cavaliers. The Tillotsons were royalists to a man. At any rate, it's not your fault."

Adrian said nothing. Tillotson sipped his sherry. "It's a blow, of course. But life is full of blows. Men carry on. Old Samuel Johnson probably put it best—'It does a man no good to whine.'"

Tillotson ordered another sherry. "It's time you thought about going back to America. You have a wife there. You ought to decide what to do about her."

Inwardly, Adrian bristled. Was Tillotson speaking as Clarissa's agent here? Or was he telling him it was time to accept another part of a man's task? Adrian's wound was too raw to think clearly about it. But he sensed pain, he saw sympathy in Geoffrey Tillotson's hooded eyes. He felt a father's love.

Tillotson began talking about their favorite topic, planes. With the formation of Imperial Airways, British commercial aviation was at a dead end. Imperial would buy only a few planes in the next decade. The other European airlines, secure in their state subsidies, would do no better. The sport-plane market was limited to the rich. The military market was hopeless. Grappling with massive unemployment, the British government had no money for weaponry of any sort. Parliament had actually forbidden the RAF to buy warplanes. There was only one place where the plane could multiply: America. He wanted Adrian to be there from the very beginning.

"You have an expression for it, from one of the generals in your Civil War. Get there first with the most?"

"I think it was firstest with the mostest. He was from Tennessee."

"Ah, yes. At any rate—I'll send you the mostest. I'm sure you'll put it to good use—for both of us."

"I'll try."

"Good-o." He slapped Adrian's knee. "There'll be other women. No reason for more than the normal regrets."

Adrian wanted to agree. But in his mind Beryl Suydam flew into a vast icy steppe of bitterness. Never again would Adrian think of the plane as a mystical machine that blended love and optimism into a future aglow with happiness. But he retained a wary faith in its ability to make him a man of substance.

ONCE IN GOLCONDA

In the cockpit of his World War I Jenny, Frank Buchanan climbed into an overcast California sky that was a mirror of his mood. The year 1926 was drawing to a dismal close. He was still a movie stunt flyer, part of Buzz McCall's circus, crashing planes instead of building them. Admiral Richard Byrd had just flown over the North Pole. Americans applauded but they remained more interested in cars, bathtub gin, and the ever-rising stock market.

Frank was on his way to San Diego to see an Arizona rancher who might be interested in backing an aircraft company. Buzz was to join him if the man talked real money. Five thousand feet above Orange County the Jenny's motor sputtered and quit. Once, twice, three times, he tried to restart the ancient engine, while the crate began losing altitude. Below him he could see nothing but miles of orange groves and the winding Santa Ana River. He chose the river as preferable to a collision with an orange tree at forty miles an hour.

Keeping his nose up, he pancaked in the center of the river. Unfortunately, the Santa Ana was one of those California rivers Mark Twain said he fell into and came out dusty. The Jenny's wheels dug into the mud and the plane flipped. The impact simultaneously snapped Frank's safety belt and his forehead smashed against the windshield, knocking him cold.

The next thing he heard was a voice saying: "Put him down here."

Two solemn Mexicans deposited him on the grass. He was drenched in muddy water. Otherwise his situation was totally unreal. The air was thick with the scent of orange blossoms. A young woman with the kindest, saddest eyes he had ever seen was bending over him. Her auburn hair fell in thick ringlets down both sides of her rather long, narrow face. She was wearing a dark green riding outfit with a derby and a slit skirt.

"Are you badly hurt?" she asked.

"I may be dead. I can't think of any other reason for this heavenly vision."

She blushed. "I was riding along the riverbank and saw you crash. I'm Amanda Van Ness."

"Frank Buchanan."

When he tried to stand up, Frank discovered he had also bashed his knee against the instrument panel. The Mexicans helped him to Amanda's horse and she led him like a wounded knight down a broad green swath through the orange groves to Casa Felicidad, a turreted Victorian house made of white sandstone. A blond, impatient young man, who turned out to be Amanda's older brother, Gordon Cadwallader, called a doctor with a German accent who diagnosed a slight concussion and a badly bruised but not otherwise damaged knee.

For a week Frank recuperated between clean sheets, on a mattress stuffed with feathers. When he was not sketching planes, he talked with Amanda Van Ness. He soon learned she was separated from her husband, who lived in New York. Gradually, Frank picked up other details that explained the sadness in her eyes—her father's death in the war, her mother's breakdown. Her mother was confined to a sanatorium run by the German doctor. Her brother ran the family's orange groves—and Amanda. She intimated that she hated him and was often lonely.

She was different from Sammy, from the other women Frank had met and occasionally bedded. Her willowy body was not immediately erotic. She seemed barely conscious of her sexual identity. But beneath her sadness was an idealism Frank had never encountered before.

Brooding on her father's death, Amanda had become profoundly interested in world peace. She corresponded with peace advocates around the United States and the world. She was surprised and pleased to discover that Frank shared her detestation of war. "My brother says that proves I'm a fool," she said.

"When it comes to war, most people are fools," Frank said.

She wanted to found a peace colony at Casa Felicidad and import famous philosophers and religious thinkers to hold seminars on the folly of war. She read the numerous books that were appearing, ridiculing the idea that the World War was a crusade for democracy. She could recite statistics proving the arms and munitions makers had gotten rich on the blood of the soldiers on both sides.

Frank Buchanan agreed with everything she said. "We have a lot in common. Everyone thinks I'm a fool too. I design planes that will never fly."

"Show me some of them."

He took out some of his sketches. Amanda instantly grasped the thrust of Frank's vision—toward simplicity, clean lines, a stark modern beauty. Although she knew nothing about aerodynamics, her enthusiasm stirred Frank enormously.

"These planes are going to fly," Amanda said. "I can see them flying now in my mind."

"I'm afraid that's the only place they'll fly," Frank said. "I have no money."

"I'll get you money," Amanda said. "My brother is always looking for businesses to invest in. He hates growing oranges."

Alas, Gordon Cadwallader declined to entrust his money to a wandering movie stunt flier with no track record in the business side of the aircraft world. At the end of the week, Amanda had to confess she had failed to persuade her brother to risk a cent on Frank's planes.

They were sitting on Casa Felicidad's side porch, breathing air fragrant with orange blossoms. The flowering trees sighed in the warm wind. "I can't tell you how much I appreciate your—your concern," Frank said.

For a thunderous moment, Frank realized he could have said "love." He sensed Amanda Van Ness loved him in a lost despairing way that she could not admit. "Can I see you again?" Frank said.

"There's no point to it," Amanda said. "I—I can only wish you well—"

Her brother Gordon stamped up the steps to announce the Mexican orange pickers had hauled Frank's plane out of the river and deposited the sodden wreck on the back lawn. Frank had apparently recovered from his injuries. Would he come upstairs for a final examination by the doctor?

In the bedroom, the examination consisted of flexing his knee. "My bill is five hundred dollars. Can you pay me before you go?" the doctor said in his heavy German accent.

"No," Frank said.

"We may have to confiscate the plane and sell it for junk," Gordon Cadwallader said. "Unless you can repair it and fly yourself out of here in the next two days. In that case, I'll take care of the doctor's bill."

"You can't get rid of me that easily. I'm in love with Amanda. I think she's in love with me."

"I know she is. But I advise you—I urge you—to forget it."

Gordon let the doctor explain it. "Amanda has to lead a quiet life. Nervous disorders are rampant in her mother's family. Bad genes. She came very close to breaking down when she returned from England."

"I don't see what harm an occasional visit can do."

"If you had a steady job, there might be some point to it," Gordon said.

Frank put his Jenny back together with some help from the orange pickers, one of whom drove the Cadwallader truck and was a pretty good mechanic. While Amanda watched mournfully, the truck towed the Jenny to an open field and Frank took off. He swooped low over the house and released a stream of fluttering paper—watercolors of some of his planes, which he had stayed up half the night completing.

Frank flew to Clover Field in Santa Monica and telephoned Buzz McCall to tell him he was through with stunt flying. He hitched a ride to an abandoned film studio where a man named Donald Douglas was building planes. He showed the bluff, florid-faced Scotsman his sketchbook. Douglas snorted and shoved it aside. "Not a damn one of them will ever fly," he said. "But we could use some fresh ideas. We're building float planes for the Navy and having a hell of a time with the wings. If we make them too thick, the plane has too much drag. If we go for thinness, we can't put bombs on them."

Frank came back in a day with a wing that was a foot longer and half the weight of the one Douglas had been using. By redistributing the center of gravity, it could handle 250-pound bombs with no problems. Douglas put him on the payroll at twenty dollars a week. He himself was only taking home twenty-two dollars.

Frank's ability to design wings spread through California's small aviation community. In San Diego, a man named Claude Ryan was putting together a monoplane rugged enough to carry the U.S. mail. He borrowed Frank to solve another weight problem. Ryan was easier to work for than the gruff, dictatorial Douglas, but Ryan's idea of a plane made Frank recoil. It was all squares and rectangles, like a packing case with wings. Nevertheless, a Buchanan-redesigned wing won Ryan a contract to build mail planes.

A few months later, in the spring of 1927, Frank got another call from Ryan Aircraft. The company had been taken over by a young man named Mahoney and they needed help on another wing. Frank cranked up his Jenny and flew to San Diego, where the plane maker introduced him to an ex–mail pilot named Charles A. Lindbergh. He was as slim and boyish as the night they parted on the Yellowstone five years ago. "Lindy's going for the New York to Paris prize. He wants to use one of our planes but he's got some load problems," Mahoney said.

When they were alone, Lindbergh told Frank he was far from happy with the Ryan plane but it was the best he could get for the ten thousand dollars his backers in St. Louis were ready to risk. Anyway, Lindbergh pointed out in his practical Swedish way, the prize was only 25,000 dollars and it made no sense to spend it all on the plane. When Lindbergh revealed he planned to carry an extra 300 gallons of gas in special cockpit tanks, raising his total weight to 5,200 pounds, Frank urged him to forget the whole idea. Four men had already died trying to cross the Atlantic.

Lindbergh calmly convinced Frank he knew what he was doing. He was betting on the reliability of the air-cooled radial motors that had replaced the water-cooled engines of the World War. The rest was fuel management and navigation, which he planned to handle himself, saving the weight of a navigator.

Frank went to work and in a week of concentrated effort redesigned the wing for the N-X-211, as it was called in the Ryan factory before Lindy christened it the *Spirit of St. Louis*. He created a series of interior metal angles, easily formed on ordinary shop tools, that solved Lindbergh's lift problem with several hundred pounds to spare. Lindbergh was at his elbow constantly, asking questions, making suggestions, checking Frank's computation of the plane's ratio of lift to drag, the crucial factor in every design. Lindy had obviously learned a lot about planes since his stunt-flying days.

At the end of April 1927, they rolled the completed plane out of the hangar and Lindbergh took it up for her first flight. She performed well in spite of her ugly shape, bounding from the runway in 165 feet. Frank stayed for the more important load tests at San Diego's Dutch Flats airport. Lindbergh cautiously added fifty gallons of fuel for each test, until they reached the maximum load of 300 gallons. This time it took the *Spirit of St. Louis* 1,026 feet to get off the ground, but the wing did the job. Frank wished Lindy luck and headed back to Los Angeles to resume his toils for Donald Douglas.

The next day he landed in the grassy field behind the Cadwallader orange groves. He had become a regular weekend visitor, ignoring scowls from brother Gordon. Amanda welcomed him eagerly. "You look tired," she said as they drank iced tea on the porch.

"I didn't get much sleep this week," Frank said. "I had to design a new wing for a fellow named Lindbergh who's going to fly the Atlantic."

"Can he do it?" Amanda asked.

"I wouldn't be surprised," Frank said. "He's got it figured out to the last ounce of gas and pound of lift."

"If he succeeds, maybe you could take some of the credit and raise enough money to start your own company."

This had never occurred to Frank. Neither he nor anyone else in California considered Lindbergh's projected flight a significant event. Pilots were setting long-distance records all the time. Lieutenant Jimmy Doolittle had flown across the country in a single day in 1922. Two army planes had flown around the world in 1924. Two other army fliers were planning a flight from Oakland to Honolulu sometime in June.

"Look at this." Gordon Cadwallader strode onto the porch and threw a copy of the *Los Angeles Times* on the tea table. A streamer headline announced Lindbergh was halfway across the Atlantic and had an excellent chance of reaching Paris. Amanda read the story and gasped: "He's flying alone?"

Reading over her shoulder, Frank nodded: "All he has to do is keep himself awake."

"Now I know you can raise the money," Amanda said.

She told her brother that Frank had designed the *Spirit of St. Louis*'s wing. Gordon Cadwallader sat down and struggled to put a friendly expression on his usually sour face. "I've been studying the stocks of plane companies," Gordon said. "Compared to the rest of the market, they're all incredibly low. If someone like Lindbergh changed the way people think about planes, they could become the hottest investment in sight. If you agree to share the management with good businessmen, maybe we could start a company."

Beneath the table, Amanda took Frank's hand. She was telling him she was ready to start something more serious than a company. The gesture annihilated Frank's first inclination to explore Cadwallader's offer with Buzz McCall and a lawyer at his side. Frank held out his hand. "I can put us in business in a month."

For the moment Frank was ready to believe love conquered everything— even greed.

GOOD-BYE TO EVERYTHING

Martini in hand, Adrian Van Ness sat beside John Hay Whitney on a leather banquette in the elegant cabin of Whitney's Sikorsky Amphibian, one of the first business planes in America. Opposite the banquette, in a stylish wicker pullup chair, sat Jock's cousin, strapping Richard Whitfield, vice president of the New York Stock Exchange. They were all listening to Winston Churchill, the volatile British politician who had been England's chancellor of the exchequer for the past five years, tell how he had accidentally made a fortune in the stock market.

"My old friend Tillotson asked me just before I sailed if I had any money to invest and I told him I could always find two or three thousand pounds. I meant this was the limit for me and let it go at that. I had no intention of speculating. He went out and bought shares on margin in your aircraft stocks through this young rascal—"

He beamed at Adrian Van Ness and took a hefty swallow of his brandy and soda.

"I get off the boat and find out I'm a bloody millionaire. I'm tempted to call him Santa Claus but he's too young."

"There's no question, the market Adrian's made in aircraft stocks is one of the accomplishments of the decade," Richard Whitfield said in his clipped Locust Valley lockjaw way.

"I think the real credit belongs to one Charles E. Lindbergh," Adrian said.

There was more than a little truth to Adrian's modesty. Since the Lone Eagle flew the Atlantic, Americans had invested an astonishing four hundred million dollars in aircraft stocks. Airlines had sprung into operation in all parts of the continent. Manufacturers were eagerly building planes to meet their growing schedules.

"Nonsense," Richard Whitfield said. "You were the only man on Wall Street ready to do something about it."

The praise was equally true. Adrian, backed by Tillotson's money, had already bought into many of these airlines and aircraft companies at bargain rates—and was in an ideal position to become Wall Street's leader in financing new ventures through stock offerings.

It was hardly surprising that Adrian had become Richard Whitfield's favorite young comer. He was escorting Whitfield's older daughter, Cynthia, around New York. Adrian's yellow Hispano-Suiza roadster was parked outside the Whitfield Seventy-third Street town house two or three nights a week. He had put off indefinitely a reconciliation with his wife Amanda. He soothed his conscience by sending her a hefty check each month—and advising her brother Gordon on his investments. Recently he had helped Gordon make a million dollars selling a small aircraft company he had founded with a designer named Buchanan to United American Aircraft, a Detroit company that proposed to become the General Motors of the plane makers.

Very little of the airplane investments had yet to return a nickel but the paper profits were marvelous. That was the way things worked in America in the year 1929. You could buy town houses and diamond necklaces and Hispano-Suizas simply by displaying your stock portfolio to your banker. Stocks had been going up for eight years and there seemed to be no reason why they would not go up indefinitely. In the White House, President Herbert Hoover was confidently predicting the end of poverty. A jingle in the *Saturday Evening Post* summed up the national attitude, in which Adrian heartily, even defiantly, concurred.

O hush thee, my babe, granny's bought some more shares,
Daddy's gone out to play with the bulls and the bears,
Mother's buying on tips and she simply can't lose,
And baby shall have some expensive new shoes.

Down came the New Haven Amphibian for a gossamer landing a few hundred yards from John Hay Whitney's dock. The plane taxied to the pier and the copilot helped them debark. Cynthia Whitfield strolled toward them in gray slacks and a monogrammed white Bergdorf blouse, pouting. "Why didn't you wake me? I adore that plane."

Adrian smiled tolerantly. Vassar had taught Cynthia that most men were lunkheads. But Adrian did not particularly care what she thought of him. Cynthia was an appurtenance he needed to be a man of substance as successful as Richard Whitfield and possibly, in the not-too-distant future, as rich as John Hay Whitney, with his strings of polo ponies and racehorses and mansions in Cannes and Long Island and North Carolina and Florida.

"If you spent less time imitating Scott and Zelda you wouldn't have to sleep until ten-thirty every morning," Adrian said.

"What's all that about?" Churchill asked.

"A writer named Fitzgerald and his wife. Wrote a book about a gangster. Typical Irish moonshine," Whitfield said.

Churchill chuckled and they all trooped into the house for lunch. Adrian entertained them with tales of new air records. Two Australians had flown the Pacific, British flyers had winged nonstop from London to India. You could fly all over the Caribbean now thanks to enterprising Juan Trippe, who had launched an international airline named Pan American. Adrian basked in the glow of admiration these stories evoked.

Cynthia announced a determination to take flying lessons. Adrian coolly declared he was opposed to it. He said there was some evidence that frequent flying disordered a woman's body chemistry. They were studying the problem in Germany. It was a lie but Cynthia promptly lost interest in flight. As she left with the other females for tea on the terrace, Adrian lit a cigar and smiled at Mr. Churchill. Women were as easy to manipulate as the stock market.

The pain of losing Beryl Suydam had receded to a bittersweet memory. In fact, Beryl's fame as a long-distance pilot was worldwide since she flew from Moscow to Vladivostok. It added to Adrian's aviation persona when he casually remarked that he had given Beryl her first flying lessons.

The next day, Adrian sat in his mother's Fifth Avenue dining room, eating this sense of male superiority—and little else. Clarissa had come back from England only a week ago—and become an instant critic of the bull market. The burden of her speech was a grave warning to get most of his money into cash as soon as possible. She saw portents of the crash of 1893 everywhere.

"What does Geoffrey think?" Adrian said.

"He's as bad as you. Totally infatuated with the airplane. Irrational on the subject. He feels he's creating a monument to Peter, I think."

That remark made Adrian even less inclined to take her advice. With icy élan, he explained Wall Street to his mother. "They simply won't let the market go down," he said. "There's too much money at stake."

"They" were the big operators, the bankers and brokers who had loaned six billion dollars to speculators who had bought stocks on margin. Then there were the investment trusts, worth eight billion dollars. With such titans involved, the idea of a crash was ludicrous.

Clarissa Ames Van Ness raised her wineglass to her lips. Her hand trembled. "Adrian, for God's sake. I heard your—your father say the same thing thirty-six years ago."

Icy fury replaced icy élan. She was still mouthing the lie. For a moment Adrian almost told her he knew everything. He knew his real father. But forethought rescued him. He recoiled from the ensuing scene. What would he do if she wept and begged his forgiveness?

"You're talking about another century, Mother. You're hopelessly out of your depth. Do you know how much I'm worth, personally?"

"No," Clarissa Ames Van Ness said, her head bowed. She was still beautiful, even with age's wrinkles making their first inroads around her eyes and mouth.

"Ten million dollars."

Clarissa rang for the maid to take away their unfinished dinner. That done, she gazed at Adrian with something very close to loathing in her eyes. "I won't give you a cent if you fail. I won't go destitute into my old age to support your

New York arrogance. I told your father the same thing in 1893."

"Your compassion is overwhelming. It makes me think he was glad he ran into that tree limb. He may even have done it on purpose."

His mother struggled to her feet, knocking over her wineglass. She was as white as the tablecloth. "I think we've said more than enough for one evening."

A month later, on October 24, 1929, Adrian stood in the visitors gallery of the New York Stock Exchange beside Winston Churchill, watching traders scream orders on the jammed floor. Huge blocks of stock in companies such as General Motors and Kennecott Copper were being thrown on the market. There were no buyers. Prices were in a vertical dive and "they"—the big operators and investment trusts—seemed powerless to pull them out.

With class A stocks dropping ten points an hour, it was almost a waste of time to ask the latest quotation on anything as speculative as airline and plane maker stocks such as United American Aircraft. They were already in the dust, mangled bits of wreckage.

"My boy," Churchill said. "We're both learning a lesson here today. There's no such thing as Santa Claus."

Adrian could not even muster a smile. All he could hear amid the frenzy on the exchange floor was his mother's voice tolling *ruined*. Was it his turn now to dwindle beneath her scorn? To live as her humble servant until fate or his own decision arranged an accident to remove him permanently from the scene?

Alone in his office, Adrian struggled to still the winged thing that looped in his chest. He was back in Anson, the American wog again. He was watching Beryl Suydam walk out the door, her radical shoulders squared. There was only one hope—his British father. The fountain pen slithered and slipped in Adrian's sweaty fingers as he composed the cable. CAN FIRM EXTEND FIVE HUNDRED THOUSAND POUNDS CREDIT? SITUATION GRAVE BUT GREAT OPPORTUNITIES FOR THOSE WHO STAY CALM.

He sat in his office for another two hours, watching the stock ticker fall farther and farther behind. Richard Whitfield called asking Adrian if he could spare any cash. "I've had to sell out my Harvard roommate," he said. "He's threatening to kill himself."

Adrian's male secretary came in with the brown cable from London. "What should I do, Mr. Van Ness?" he asked. "I'm getting creamed."

"Sell," Adrian said, ripping open the cable.

DEEPLY REGRET MR. GEOFFREY TILLOTSON HAS RESIGNED AS MANAGING PARTNER EFFECTIVE IMMEDIATELY.

Ruined. He had hoped a reply that was even faintly encouraging would open his mother's checkbook too. Once and for all he abandoned that alternative. What was the other alternative? As he returned from the visitors' gallery, his secretary told him that eleven men had already committed suicide.

Adrian stared at the brown cable. Faintly, as if it were coming from a great distance, he heard Geoffrey Tillotson say: *Men carry on. It does a man no good to whine.* Adrian Van Ness was not the son of that ruined speculator of 1893, no matter how much sympathy he would always feel for him. He was the son of that hearty chunk of England, who stood with feet planted wide and told life to deal what blows it might, he would take them standing. He was the great-grandson of Oakes Ames, the flinty Yankee who had defied a world that pronounced him ruined.

Adrian summoned Bleriot's plane soaring over Dover Castle in 1909. He remembered Peter Tillotson in the Bristol Scout banking over Anson in 1912. He recalled the transcendence of flight above England, the sense of soaring above history into the future. He still believed tomorrow belonged to these miraculous machines.

The future. Forethought. He could hear Geoffrey Tillotson pronouncing them. The words would always have an English echo in his ear.

Father, Adrian whispered. *O Father.*

Although a winged creature looped in his chest, Adrian Van Ness would carry on.

Where, how? In the chaos of a collapsing economy, mere determination seemed futile. As he sat in his Wall Street office, his mother's presence uptown loomed above the skyline. It was only a matter of time before he succumbed to that invincible checkbook.

Unless he got out of New York. Unless he went someplace where planes were being made, some place Clarissa Van Ness would never follow him.

That was when Adrian remembered Amanda and Prince Carlo Pontecorvo's advice about those two thousand acres of orange trees in California.

GREED: THE SECOND ACT

While a half-dozen reporters watched, the gleaming white monoplane emerged from Buchanan Aircraft's dim main hangar into the brilliant California sunshine. The plane emanated modernity. Her sleek fuselage had a shark-like shape. Her streamlined engine cowling, her art deco wheel pants, added speed as well as beauty. The twin tail fins doubled her stability and maneuverability. Her 400-horsepower radial engine would enable her to fly twice as fast as the lumbering Ford Trimotors which most airlines were currently using. The multicellular wing, each cell a complex of metal angles, was so strong a steamroller could be driven across it repeatedly without damaging it.

"What's her name?" asked one of the reporters who had not bothered to read the publicity release.

"Lustra Two," Frank Buchanan said and explained the poetic allusion. He did not have to explain Lustra I. That plane was already well known to aviation writers. It had challenged the Lockheed Vega for the supremacy of the skies, setting records for speed at air races and on distance flights. Lustra II was an attempt to take the basic design and convert it into a ten-passenger airliner.

"I'm in favor of changing it to Hot Pants," Buzz McCall said. "In a minute, you guys'll see why."

Buzz climbed into the cockpit and the engine rumbled. Minutes later, the Lustra leaped off the runway and whirled around Buchanan Field at 500 feet. At this dangerous height, Buzz did stalls and spins and banks that demonstrated the plane's amazing responsiveness. He opened her up to full throttle and whizzed across the airport again, a white blur, then all but turned her on her axis to slide in for a perfect landing.

"You're looking at the next generation airliner," Tama Morris (aka Moreno) said.

They were all working for Buchanan Aircraft—Buzz, Tama and her friend Gloria Packer, and several former mechanics from the Buzz McCall Flying Circus. Frank had hired them when Buzz agreed to take over as chief of production. Buzz and Tama had gotten married in 1929, shortly before the stock market crashed.

Frank had not had much difficulty persuading Buzz to take the job. His movie career had popped like a soap bubble in the sun as talking pictures arrived in 1927. Airplane movies went into eclipse around the same time when several stunt pilots died trying to fulfill impossible demands by directors who knew nothing about flying. The talkies had been fatal to Tama too. Her acting skills were rudimentary.

The reporters drank champagne in the hangar and peered at exhibits of the Lustra's wing structure and ultra-safe fuel system. Standing on the sidelines watching the party, a glum look on his foxy face, was their original backer, Gordon Cadwallader. Beside Cadwallader was Buchanan's chief financial officer, a small desiccated accountant named Arnold Appleby, from United American Aircraft, the Detroit company that had bought Buchanan, Lockheed and a dozen other aircraft companies in the bull market frenzy of the late 1920s. He was probably computing the cost of the champagne and the gasoline to fly the Lustra II for five minutes and adding it to his list of complaints in his daily memorandum on cutting costs.

It was March of 1930 and Wall Street showed no sign of reviving. United American stock, which had once sold as high as 70—close to what people had been paying for General Motors—was now valued at one and a half.

Beside the accountant stood Amanda Cadwallader in a flowery print dress, her shining eyes on Frank as he explained Lustra II's virtues to the reporters. Working under terrific pressure to produce planes that would make a profit in spite of the country's economic collapse, Frank had twice postponed their marriage. She had finally convinced him that she did not care whether he was rich or poor. They were to be married as soon as Lustra II was certified as airworthy by the federal government and she obtained her divorce from Adrian Van Ness.

Frank was determined to marry Amanda without a trace of Craig's misogynism in his soul. He had acquired a small library of books on the female body and applied his original mind to the problem of producing perfect bliss between husband and wife with the same passion for perfection he brought to the creation of a new plane. Their love would be as superior to the casual sex of the aircraft world as the Lustra II was to *Rag Time*.

"Tonight at our house—a real celebration," Buzz said, as the reporters departed.

"You're all invited," Tama cooed after the newsmen.

"I think we better have a talk," Appleby said to Frank and Buzz.

Gordon Cadwallader joined them in Appleby's office. Amanda was left to explore the cabin and cockpit of Lustra II. Appleby wasted no time. "We're broke," he said. "We can't even meet this week's payroll."

"The hell you say," Buzz roared. "We've sold twenty Lustra Ones in the last twelve months and we've got orders for another six."

"Whatever we've made on those transactions—which is damn little, with the salaries you're paying yourselves, has been requisitioned as an extraordinary expense to meet corporate financial problems," Appleby said.

"You son of a bitch!" Frank roared, seizing Appleby by the shirt. "You're robbing us to keep your Detroit friends driving around in their lousy Packards."

"Robbing is hardly the correct term," Appleby said, disengaging his shirt. "We own you, Mr. Buchanan. You are a division of United American Aircraft and we can do what we please with your cash."

"What about my stock?" Buzz cried. In the heyday of the bull market, with Lustras selling at the rate of three a month, he had put every cent he had into UAA.

"You're a very minor stockholder," Appleby said.

"We're all minor," Gordon Cadwallader growled. "UAA has twenty million shares outstanding."

"We're declaring bankruptcy and selling off our assets to satisfy class A stockholders and creditors," Appleby said.

"What the hell's a class A stockholder?" Frank said.

"You're looking at one," Gordon Cadwallader snarled. "I'll only get about ten cents on the dollar. You drew a salary while I got nothing. Not even a dividend."

"It was your idea to put us into that Detroit deal!" Frank shouted.

"You didn't complain when your stock was worth a half million dollars," Cadwallader said.

"You're robbing my company—my name," Frank said. "I'm going to sue hell out of you."

"I don't think you have a case," Cadwallader said. "If you threaten me, I'll make sure you don't have a case."

"Consider yourself threatened," Frank said.

"You're not welcome in my house any longer."

"It's not your house. Amanda owns it just as much as you do," Frank shouted. "The same thing goes for those two thousand acres of orange trees. The day after we're married, I plan to have a lawyer go over the books of Cadwallader Groves and find exactly where the profits are going. Your days of intimidating her into being a silent partner will be over."

"You can hire all the lawyers in California," Appleby said, in his infuriating drone. "This company is out of business, as of tomorrow morning. Notices will be posted, informing the employees before they leave tonight. Its assets and liabilities will be in the hands of the bankruptcy court of Los Angeles County within twenty-four hours."

"Why did you torment us—let us fly Lustra Two?" Frank cried.

Appleby grimaced. It was as close as he ever came to a smile. "Someone may want to buy the plane—and the design. Make sure when you leave tonight that all aspects of your design work will be available to prospective purchasers."

"The design of that plane is not for sale," Frank roared. "That came out of my head."

"Your head—as well as your hands—were working for United American Aircraft," Appleby said.

The enormous fact of his impotence, of all their impotences, descended on Frank. Gordon Cadwallader completed his humiliation. "Stay away from Amanda. Consider that a warning."

Gordon Cadwallader took a bewildered Amanda home. Frank retreated to the McCalls' house in Long Beach, where a funeral for Buchanan Aircraft lasted far into the night. Bootleg liquor flowed and everyone got very drunk. Frank awoke at noon the following day to find himself in a bed with Gloria Packer. "You looked so sad, Frank. I just wanted you to know I still cared," Gloria said.

Frank had tried to stay celibate for the last three years. It had not been easy, with Buzz for a partner. Ten-year-old Billy McCall appeared in the doorway with a pitcher of orange juice, intensifying Frank's guilt. Buzz had taken Billy into his household when he married Tama. "Any chance of a ride in Lustra Two, Pops?" he said, using the nickname he had given Frank years ago.

"No one's ever going to ride in Lustra Two if I can help it," Frank said.

Before he could execute his revenge, Frank had to extricate Amanda from her brother's custody. He drove to Long Beach Airport, where he kept his Lustra I. In a half hour he was circling over the white turreted Cadwallader mansion in Fullerton. Amanda stood on the lawn, waving to him. But it was Gordon Cadwallader who greeted him as he got out of the plane.

"I think we better have a talk," Gordon said.

"I'm through talking to you. I'm here to take Amanda away with me."

"If you really love Amanda, you'll do what I tell you. Get in the car."

They climbed into his Hupmobile Six and drove to the nearby mental hospital where Amanda's mother was an apparently perpetual patient. There were a half-dozen people on the lawn talking to themselves, wandering dazedly with glazed eyes. "It costs me five thousand dollars a year to keep her here," Gordon Cadwallader said. "If it weren't for Amanda's feelings, I'd have sent her to a state hospital years ago. She's my father's second wife. She never liked me."

Inside, they were greeted by Carl Farber, the German doctor who ran the place. He led Frank to the second floor and stopped before a door marked 13. He opened a small window and invited Frank to look inside. A woman with

Amanda's russet hair and angular face paced up and down the tiny room. She sensed Frank's eyes on her and flung herself at the door. "Stop these men from tormenting me!" she screamed. "Tell my warriors where I am! Tell them Queen Califia is calling on them to rise again!"

"Mrs. Cadwallader thinks she's Califia, the mythical Amazon queen of California," Dr. Farber said. "An interesting schizophrenic delusion. It enables her to despise the entire male sex."

Back at Casa Felicidad, Gordon led Frank into his office, locked the door and set up a small motion picture projector and screen. He pulled down the shade and they sat in semi-darkness. At first Frank was bewildered by the flickering images. A dark lake, sodden Negro musicians stumbling ashore clutching their instruments, naked women on a barge. He realized it was the British director's outtake of the party at Modesto, after finishing *Loop the Loop*. There was Mabel Durand doing a show-it-all shimmy while her ladies in waiting Charlestoned around her in the buff.

In the next frames Mabel was alone on the raft, stretched on her chaise longue while various members of the cast and crew rose dripping from the black waters of the lake to enjoy her. One was unmistakably Buzz McCall. With his clothes off, he looked part ape. Then another man, bigger than Buzz, with pale skin and reddish hair that looked almost white in the kleig lights. Frank watched himself, sick with shame.

Gordon Cadwallader stopped the camera. "I had a private detective investigate you last year when it began to look like you might actually marry Amanda. He picked this up on the blackmail market. Do you think I should show it to Amanda?"

"What do you want me to do?"

"Write her a letter, telling her you're bankrupt and you think it best to stop seeing her."

Frank sat down at Cadwallader's desk and wrote the letter. He stalked to his Lustra I and flew to Santa Monica, where he found the Buchanan Aircraft Company hangar padlocked and a notice of bankruptcy pasted on the doors. He borrowed a sledgehammer from one of the other hangars, smashed the lock and got into the cockpit of Lustra II.

Airborne, he roared above Los Angeles and its curving boulevards. Gordon Cadwallader and United American Aircraft had stolen his happiness, his future. But they would not steal Lustra II. Without this plane, Buchanan Aircraft was worth nothing.

Pulling a parachute from beneath the copilot's seat, Frank turned Lustra II's sleek nose east, toward the Mojave. Over the desert, he shoved the controls forward, kicked open the cockpit door and flung himself into space. By a miracle he evaded the tail and his parachute soon opened. Beneath his feet, the beautiful white plane exploded in a blossom of orange flame on the desert floor.

The sight made him feel guilty of a crime almost as brutal as the one Gordon Cadwallader had committed against him and Amanda. How could he ever explain it to Buzz and the men who had worked on the plane, who loved it as their creation as much as his? There was only one thing to do—obliterate all trace of Frank Buchanan, the plane designer. Hitching a ride back to Santa Monica, he began methodically destroying the thousands of drawings and blueprints that had gone into the creation of Lustra II and Lustra I.

He was interrupted by a woman's voice crying "Frank" at the far end of the hangar. It echoed around him like a spirit from the other world. He walked through the dimness to confront Amanda.

"What does this letter mean?"

"It means I—can't marry you."

"Why?"

"I'm bankrupt. I haven't a cent. Surely your brother's told you."

"He told me a great many things. I want to hear them from you."

"What did he tell you?"

"He said this letter proved what he'd suspected all along. You never wanted anything from us but money and now that the money is gone—we're almost as poor as you these days—you're no longer interested. You came out there today to ask him for money and when he told you how little we had you wrote this—this abominable letter."

She was weeping now. What could he say? Gordon Cadwallader was perfectly capable of showing her that film. She might end up in Farber's sanitarium raving like her mother. "That's something of an exaggeration. I still care for you—"

"What else matters? I don't give a damn whether you're rich or poor. I never have. I'd give myself to you right now if I thought—"

She struggled to control the tears that were flooding her voice.

"If I thought you were telling the truth."

She turned and walked slowly toward the open doors at the front of the hangar. Sunlight blazed outside. A yellow Lockheed Vega was racing down the runway to zoom into the sky. The plane evoked his dream of soaring in this woman's arms to new altitudes.

"Tell your brother I crashed Lustra Two. Tell him there's nothing here for him to sell."

It was better to play the madman. Better to be nothing but the stunt-flying bum who had plummeted into her life three years ago. Any humiliation, the worst possible disguise, was better than her seeing that film. His performance was a last twisted gesture of love. Weeping, cursing, Frank Buchanan went back to destroying his paper airplanes.

LOVE AMONG THE ORANGES

Six months later, Adrian Van Ness sat on the porch of Casa Felicidad, holding his wife Amanda's hand. California sunshine streamed down on them. The air was thick with the perfume of orange blossoms. For Adrian it was the scent of the promised land.

The situation was unreal but Adrian had grown used to unreality since Wall Street crashed. Clinging to his fragments of fatherhood from Geoffrey Tillotson, he had driven west through a landscape of pain. The Great Depression was twisting America on a continental rack. On the outskirts of city after city, homeless men lived in hobo jungles, clusters of tin shacks and empty packing cases. They crowded around fires in trash cans on street corners and glared at him as he drove past in his yellow Hispano-Suiza. He was frequently tempted to tell them the car was his last remaining asset.

Adrian went to California with only the dimmest idea of what he was going to do when he got there. Amanda and her orange groves were a faint hope, no more. When he wrote to explain why he was unable to continue the support money he had sent her since their separation, there had been no answer.

In Orange County, he discovered Amanda was, if anything, more forlorn than the woman he had sent home from England. Her brother hinted there had been a romance that had recently expired. He urged Adrian to consider a reconciliation. He also filled Adrian in on the chaos in the California aircraft industry. Companies were going bankrupt and being sold at knockdown prices every third day. He added his personal tale of woe—the paper million he had lost in United American Aircraft. Adrian, who had lost ten times that amount in the same and similar companies, pretended to be sympathetic.

For a month Adrian had concealed his desperation and waited for a sign of forgiveness from Amanda. She had maintained a melancholy distance. With his money running low, he had decided to gamble on a frontal assault. "After the way I treated you in London, I have absolutely no claim on your affections," he said. "I see now I was completely under my mother's influence."

"I understood, Adrian. I was afraid it would happen."

"In the past month I've come to feel we never really separated. I feel as if we we've been sharing similar experiences. The pain of loneliness—and heartbreak. Will you take me back, Amanda?"

"Adrian I—I'm afraid the same thing would happen. I'm sure your mother still hates me."

"My mother's approval or disapproval no longer interests me. I doubt if we'll ever see her in California. The only thing that matters is the way I've regained my old feeling for you."

"I'm not sure what I feel—"

"Darling, I know you still love me. I admit—why should I deny it?—I've been trying to reawaken that love for the past month. Say yes."

Amanda wept and told him about her chaste romance with Frank Buchanan and his abominable behavior at its close. In her heart she felt she had been unfaithful to Adrian. Could he forgive her? Adrian considered matching the story with his far less platonic heartbreak with Beryl Suydam and decided against it.

"There's nothing to forgive," he assured her. "I hope someday soon I can give that bastard Buchanan what he deserves."

"Oh Adrian. Yes. Yes. Yes."

They kissed across the tea table.

That night, while Amanda waited upstairs, Adrian and Gordon Cadwallader met in the study and executed a legal document. For fifty thousand dollars, Adrian sold Amanda's rights to 50 percent of Cadwallader Groves. Adrian also agreed to take over the expense of maintaining Amanda's mother in Dr. Farber's sanitarium.

Upstairs, Adrian discovered that fifty thousand dollars was erotic, even if his trembling wife was almost its opposite. Amanda returned to his arms with a stifled, possibly regretful cry that only made him feel more powerful, more confident in the future, in spite of the comatose stock market and the doom-crying newspapers.

In the morning Amanda began packing for a second honeymoon on Catalina Island. Adrian told her they would have to delay their idyl for a day. He was due in bankruptcy court at 10 A.M., where he expected to buy the Buchanan Aircraft Company. "Then I'm going down to the factory, where I gather your former friend Mr. Buchanan is still lurking, and throw him out on his head."

Amanda kissed him fiercely. "Let me come. I want to see it!"

"No. Gordon tells me he may get violent."

"I *want* to come," Amanda said, displaying a willfulness Adrian thought life's disappointments had demolished.

Trained from birth to please women whenever possible, Adrian shrugged. "All right. But it may be unpleasant."

They drove to the Los Angeles County Courthouse with Gordon Cadwallader's lawyer, who was handling the legal details. The lawyer had told Adrian the business would not take five minutes and he was right. There were no other bidders. The balding judge obviously regarded Adrian as slightly insane as he banged his gavel and informed him that he was the sole owner of Buchanan Aircraft, including its debts and liabilities, for thirty thousand dollars.

Adrian shook hands with the lawyer and whizzed to the Buchanan plant in Santa Monica with Amanda beside him in the Hispano-Suiza. In the design and engineering offices at the rear of the main hangar, they found a swarthy man in a flying jacket and overalls cleaning out his desk. He looked at Adrian in his dark blue Savile Row suit as if he was a somewhat comic figure and introduced himself as Buzz McCall, the former chief of production.

Adrian informed McCall that he was the new owner and asked if Frank

Buchanan was in the building. "He's been drunk for the last three months," Buzz said. "Ever since he crashed Lustra Two."

Adrian sat down slowly. Gordon Cadwallader had shown him the press clippings of Lustra Two's debut. They had convinced him that Buchanan Aircraft had a plane he could sell to the airlines.

"How long will it take to build another one?"

"That depends on when Buchanan sobers up."

"What do you mean?"

"He tore up all the designs. Ditto the blueprints. He did the same thing to the Lustra One files."

"I thought you had a half dozen orders for Lustra Ones." Again, Adrian was relying on Gordon Cadwallader's information.

"We did. Frank wrote letters, cancelling them."

"I'll sue him. I'll put him in jail," Adrian said.

Buzz shrugged. "You can probably do both. But it won't get you any closer to building some planes."

"There are other designers."

"Look at this before you start hiring someone else," Buzz said. "I found it in the mailbox when I came in."

It was a letter on the stationery of TWA, the new airline recently put together from the wreckage of Trans Western and several other lines that had collapsed since the stock market crashed. Adrian read it and handed it to Amanda.

Dear Frank: I have just taken on the job of consultant to TWA. They have financing from Howard Hughes, the Texas multimillionaire and are planning to buy quite a number of planes. I told them if it was at all possible, they should get a model with a Buchanan wing. Can your company produce a transport capable of carrying 25 or 30 people within the next six months?

Sincerely,
Charles Lindbergh

"You know Mr. Buchanan well, Mr. McCall?"

"Pretty well."

"Do you want to keep working here?"

Buzz shrugged. "I gotta work somewhere. I got a wife and two kids."

"Tell him if he wants to save your job—everyone's job—he should consider coming back to work as soon as possible. Assure him I will let him have complete autonomy as chief designer. I have no intention of changing the company's name. Everyone knows Buchanan means quality planes. Tell him I can sell planes better than anyone else in the country. I know almost every airline executive in the business personally."

"I'll tell him," Buzz said. "I don't know whether it will do any good."

"Tell the office people to report for work tomorrow," Adrian said.

Buzz nodded and swaggered out. Adrian sighed and turned to Amanda. "I'm terribly afraid we'll have to postpone our second honeymoon."

Amanda did not speak until she was back in the Hispano-Suiza. As Adrian drove out of the Buchanan Aircraft parking lot, she hissed a single word: "Liar."

116

REVELATIONS

For a long time that word *liar* encompassed all of them—Adrian, Frank, her brother. Amanda did not know the exact content of the lie. But she sensed its presence the moment Adrian rehired Frank. She saw the cold-eyed banker she had disliked in England. She was equally sure the contrite husband she had seen on Casa Felicidad's porch was a fraud.

She decided to leave them all. She was going to flee to New York, walk the streets, sell herself to men if necessary. She was going to escape California and its lies. Everything about it had become a lie, even the beauty of the land itself, its perpetual sunshine that denied the evil festering in the souls of men like her brother Gordon.

As she planned her escape, hoarding small amounts from the money that Adrian gave her to run their house in Westwood, only a few miles from the Buchanan plant, she had to struggle to retain her intuition of deceit. Adrian did everything in his power to annihilate it. He wielded arguments like a master duelist, portraying the golden future they would share, vowing that he had done nothing that any rational man would not have done when he discovered the truth about Buchanan Aircraft.

"The money!" Amanda raged. "Where did you get the money?"

"From your brother."

Adrian did not tell her how or why Gordon had produced the cash. He described it as a loan. She was even more confused by his repeated protestations of love. Still she refused to let him touch her. Adrian was not exactly importunate on this point. He was working fifteen hours a day, organizing a sales force, pleading with bankers for loans, trying to accommodate Frank Buchanan's erratic work habits.

Early in 1932, Amanda felt a presence in her body. She recognized it immediately as a child and knew in the next instant it was a girl. A few days later she met one of the Mexican pickers from Cadwallader Groves working in a grocery store in Westwood. Impulsively, she told him about the baby, then realized how strange the encounter was. Miguel had worked at Cadwallader Groves for over twenty years. "What are you doing here?" she asked.

"No more orange work," he said. "They cut down the trees."

She drove to Casa Felicidad in a wild rage. Sure enough, men were sawing down tree after tree. The landscape lay bare all the way to the river. Tractors were ripping up the stumps, leaving raw wounds in the green grass. The earth was being raped in front of her eyes.

"I won't let you do this!" she raged at her brother.

"It's none of your business," he said.

"I own half of it. I should have been consulted!"

"Adrian sold your half to me months ago."

A saw emitted an especially piercing shriek. For a moment Gordon almost lost his business aplomb. "Something like this had to be done soon," he snarled. "I mortgaged the place to the last tree to play the stock market. It's either drill for oil or let the goddamn banks grab it."

Amanda knew why there was a snarl in Gordon's voice. She knew why he had been secretly glad to risk Cadwallader Groves to make millions on Wall Street. She knew why he did not care about what he was desecrating here with his tractors and saws.

Gordon was destroying Eden. He was destroying the memory of their father and her mother walking naked among the trees, making love on the cool grass. Five-year-old Amanda had adored the lovemaking. She had clapped her hands and begged them to do it again. Seven-year-old Gordon had screamed *no* and had run frantically around the grove, clutching his dangling thing. Eden had made him afraid. It required courage to live in Eden.

Gordon was destroying Eden because there was evil in his soul. Adrian was his collaborator. He did not care if Gordon erected grimy rigs that spewed black stinking oil over the green grass where love had flowered in the sunlight. That meant there was evil in Adrian's soul too.

The wish to flee them all swelled in Amanda's throat with new desperation. But what could she do, where could she go with a child? The whole country was bankrupt. People were standing on endless lines to get a bowl of soup in New York and Chicago. Motherhood, motherness, consumed her.

She went home to Westwood and lay in bed remembering the loneliness of Casa Felicidad after her father died in the army and her mother retreated to her room and began to imagine she was Queen Califia, betrayed by her subjects.

For the first time Amanda thought about her mother's delusion. She had chanted songs about the cruel fate of Califia, abandoned as a prisoner, a victim, to the power of men. The words had a meaning for her. Now Amanda was in the middle of the same meaning.

Did her mother include her husband, Amanda's father, in her denunciations of male cruelty and lust? No, he was the exception, one of the rare ones who had no evil in his soul. Amanda had dreamt of finding Eden again with Frank Buchanan. Not at Casa Felicidad with Gordon watching. They would fly to it in one of Frank's planes.

She had been sure they could find another Eden in some remote canyon in the Cascades or the Sierras. They would swoop into it and strip off their clothes, strip off shame and civilization and discover the redeeming power of love.

What had gone wrong? Was Frank really no different from Adrian? Amanda could not believe it. All her instincts denied it. A hundred times, she got out the letter Frank had written, breaking his promise to marry her. She relived the conversation in the hangar. She wept. When Adrian came home at midnight, he found her in the kitchen staring at nothing, weeping.

He was profoundly, genuinely alarmed. When she told him Gordon had revealed his sale of her share of Cadwallader Groves, Adrian swore her brother had given her the most venal, the most atrocious version of the story. He had planned to raise the money from a bank, offering her share of Cadwallader Groves as equity, guaranteeing her continued half ownership of the property. He said he never would have taken such a step without her approval. But the bankruptcy court had moved the date of the Buchanan sale forward with no warning. He had been afraid to tell her before their reconciliation and there had been no time to tell her afterward.

It was almost convincing. Amanda discerned in Adrian's vehemence a kind of caring. She stopped crying. The child swelled in her belly, independent, indifferent to memory, regret, hatred. Amanda lived with Adrian Van Ness and the daily drama of Buchanan Aircraft's struggle to survive. It was impossible to remain indifferent to it. Adrian talked about nothing else. Her own happiness, the happiness of her child, was at stake.

With help from Buzz McCall, they had persuaded Frank Buchanan to come back to work and begin building another Lustra II for TWA. Adrian made an important contribution to the new design. Waiting at the Los Angeles airport one day, he watched a single-engined Varney Speed Line Vega take off, followed by a lumbering Ford Trimotor flying for Braniff. He suddenly remembered a story Carlo Pontecorvo had told him about how nervous single-engine planes made passengers on European airlines. He cancelled his flight and rushed back to the plant to persuade Frank to put two engines on the new Lustra II.

A day later, Adrian had sold the idea to Jack Frye, the president of TWA, and changed the plane's name to the SkyRanger. He disliked Frank's fondness for classical names, which few customers would ever understand.

The child grew. It leaped in Amanda's belly now, especially when Adrian put his hand there. Amanda permitted this much touching. She could not remove the word *liar* from Adrian's forehead. But she found it difficult to remain in a state of rage at him. He was so polite, so urbane, so determined to make her like him again. Amanda began to wonder if she could ever leave him.

A rhythm developed between the baby and the new plane at the factory. Both seemed to be growing on the same schedule. Adrian told Amanda he had promised a bonus to the workforce if the SkyRanger flew on or before the day his daughter was born. When Adrian invited Amanda to visit the factory in the middle of her eighth month, she could not resist the idea.

Inside the cavernous hangar, four dozen workmen swarmed around the ribbed fuselage, which rested on jigs, erector set–like metal platforms about six feet above the floor. It looked like the stripped skeleton of a whale on the deck of the *Pequod* in Melville's *Moby-Dick*. But this creature was coming to life. An obsequious smile on his tough guy's face, production chief Buzz McCall introduced her to foremen and riveters and machinists and explained that tomorrow they were going to give the SkyRanger her skin. Twin shells of lightweight steel would be glued together around the ribs.

"How many more weeks, Mrs. Van Ness?" one of the workmen yelled, as they departed. Amanda held up three fingers.

"We're way ahead. We're gonna finish this baby in two!"

In Adrian's office, she met Buzz McCall's dark-haired wife, Tama, who was, she cheerfully explained, Buchanan's publicity director.

"And office manager and payroll clerk and bookkeeper," Adrian added.

"This'll make a terrific story," Tama said.

A grinning little man with a flash camera materialized and began taking pictures of Amanda and Adrian, smiling, their arms around each other. Tama posed Amanda in the window of the office, so her bulging stomach was profiled against the light. "Terrific," she cried as the flashbulb popped again.

Amanda felt violated by the whole process. But she did not know how to protest it. Tama led her back to the assembly line, where Amanda posed with a half-dozen grinning workmen while the photographer blazed away.

The SkyRanger was completed in two weeks and rolled out for her first tests. It was a time of terrific tension for Adrian and everyone else. Would she live up to the promise of her design?

Precisely on the day her obstetrician predicted, Amanda went into labor. As she struggled to cope with the pains, she found herself hoping fiercely for a girl. She did not want a son. Adrian would corrupt him. She could protect a daughter from him. Confirming her intuition, the child was a girl.

"Do you have a name for her?" the formidable floor nurse demanded, as she filled out the tag for the tiny wrist.

"No," Amanda said, dismayed that she had never discussed it with Adrian. Would he name her Clarissa after his mother? She hated the name. She was afraid to use her own mother's name. She half-believed that names had power, that they carried meaning, fate, into a life.

"Where's my husband?" she asked.

"I have no idea," the nurse said, her opinion of Adrian's absence all too clear.

"He's here at last," Adrian said from the doorway of her room.

He kissed her limp hand. "I kept in touch by telephone. We were putting the plane through the final tests. She passed them all. The TWA people were there. They signed a contract for twenty planes on the spot."

"Marvelous. They want—a name."

Adrian took the tiny bundle out of the nurse's arms. She had been fussing and whining. She stopped and seemed to gaze up at him. "Do babies this young smile?" Adrian asked. "I could swear she's smiling."

"You are," Amanda said. The expression on Adrian's face was miraculous. It evoked the memory of her father's smile. The reality of unqualified love. She could never leave him now, Amanda thought. She might even learn to love him.

"Mr. Van Ness," said the impatient nurse. "Does the child have a name?"

"Victoria. Her name is Victoria."

The next day, Tama Morris arrived with a huge spray of roses—and her friend the photographer. Once more Amanda experienced the violated feeling, this time on her own and Victoria's behalf. Again she found it impossible to protest. Tama was so agreeable, so enthusiastic about the baby and the wonderful story and the wonderful news at the plant. Dark eyes aglow, she recited the dazzling figures. TWA was going to pay two and a half million dollars for the twenty planes.

A final blinding flash made Victoria whimper. "That's it, Roscoe, scram," Tama said.

The photographer fled as if he was afraid Tama might do him bodily harm. She lit a cigarette and sat down on the edge of the bed. "You're really glad it's a girl?"

"Yes," Amanda said.

"Why? Men get all the breaks in this world."

Propped on her white pillows, lying beneath the white hospital blanket in the white-walled room with thick white sunshine pouring through the window, Amanda contemplated Tama's darkness. It was in her hair, her eyes, her olive skin—and those bitter words. Suddenly Amanda saw this beautiful woman's entire life. Her willfulness, her pride, her despair. She felt a kinship with her beyond the power of words, something she had never felt for another woman.

"Do you have any children?" she asked.

"A son by my first husband and a stepson by Buzz's first wife. They make me almost wish for a daughter. It'd be nice not to have to play drill sergeant all the time."

"Adrian seems pleased to have a daughter."

"Adrian's different. He's not your average flyboy. They think a woman's only good for one thing."

Amanda saw new darkness, new perils in Tama's soul. Tama inhaled her cigarette. "You're lucky."

Amanda's heart almost broke. Tama was explaining her fate to herself. Amanda wanted to offer her some consolation. "But you've got an important job."

"Nah," Tama said. "They just hired a man to be my boss. Some yo-yo from the *LA Times*. Adrian was nice enough to try to explain it to me, at least. It's a man's business. As if I didn't know that. It's a man's world. Even if you're Norma Shearer. You've still got some SOB studio executive telling you what to do."

Amanda saw how hopeless it really was. "Thank you for the roses," she said.

"Hey, it's the least we could do. You've gotten us more publicity this week then we've had in a year."

The next day, a totally unexpected figure filled the doorway: Frank Buchanan. He carried a gigantic white rabbit and a huge bouquet. "What a wonderful surprise," she said.

He kissed her hand. "Are you happy?" he said.

"Yes," she said. "Are you?"

He shrugged.

"I thought the good news about the plane would make you happy."

"That's my consolation. Not the same as happiness. I designed it for you—and this little creature—as much as for myself."

Suddenly she wanted to scream, rage at him. "I don't know what you mean," she said, her voice empty and cold, her eyes averted.

"I would never have come back for any other reason. Adrian said he'd spent every cent he borrowed from your brother to buy the company. Everything you owned was at stake. I'm glad I came now. Consolation is better than nothing."

"I still don't know what you're saying!" she cried. She meant of course that he was not explaining the most important thing.

"What happened was entirely my fault," Frank said. "A—lamentable swinishness on my part. I deserve everything I've suffered for it. I only wish you hadn't suffered."

Suddenly nothing mattered, the child, Adrian's adoration of his daughter, the possibility of a happy marriage. Nothing mattered but the memory of that morning when Lindbergh was flying the Atlantic and she had taken Frank Buchanan's hand.

"I'm through with suffering!" she raged. "We're going to be very rich. I'm going to enjoy myself."

"I hope so," Frank said.

For the rest of the day, Amanda waited for Adrian. She wanted him to smile at Victoria again, to tell her more good news. But Adrian never appeared. She tried to feed Victoria but the baby could not get enough milk from her small breasts. "I knew she'd have to go on a bottle," the Valkyrian floor nurse said and carried the baby triumphantly away to the nursery.

Amanda lay alone in the white-walled room, watching darkness fall. She thought of Tama's despair, Frank's defeat, Adrian's smiling lies. She thought of her helplessness, her mother's madness, her brother's greed. When, how, could it change?

Darkness crept into the room. She did not bother to put on her bed lamp. She lay there, listening to wails and whimpers and random voices in the hall. When, how, could it change?

Califia could change it. Her mother sat beside her, wreathed in the golden light of Eden, telling her about Califia, when Amanda was five. What if Califia came by night to challenge the vile rule of men? She could enlist a million women like Tama, women who had been used for only one thing. A new army of Amazons would arise to reconquer California and restore the kingdom of women.

"Mrs. Van Ness. What in the world are you doing, lying here in the dark?" asked the floor nurse.

"I was thinking," Amanda said.

"There's only one thing you should think about," the nurse said. "Getting some milk in those breasts. I've brought you an extra glass for supper. Drink it all. If you can't nurse your baby, you don't feel like a woman. After all, it's what nature intended us to do. I've never seen a bottle baby who's been happy. They cry all the time."

Obediently Amanda gulped two huge glasses of foaming milk, while her keeper nodded approvingly. Califia was gone. But not forgotten.

BOOK THREE

MEN AND BOYS

Birdsong and sunlight. A beautiful spring morning. Half awake, Frank Buchanan imagined himself wandering through the green ravines of Topanga Canyon with his golden labrador, Winston. He wondered how long this unspoiled wilderness so close to Los Angeles would last if half the unemployed in America persisted in moving to California.

Wham wham wham. A fist was pounding on the front door. Winston was barking thunderously. Frank pushed himself up on one elbow. Jesus. There was a woman in his bed. What the hell was her name? Gladys? Gloria? She was a blonde. They were always blondes, in memory of Sammy. Never russets or even redheads. His pathetic way of honoring his chaste love for Amanda.

Where had this woman come from? Oh, yes. He had spent the weekend in Palm Springs, a little town in the Mojave desert, at a meeting of the Conquistadores del Cielo, the club Adrian Van Ness and other company presidents had organized to try to mold the airframe and engine makers and airlines into a group that could have some impact on the American psyche. Adrian had suggested the title to emphasize the airframe makers' largely California origins—and the grandeur of their ambitions. The conquistadores Frank had met in Palm Springs struck him as the biggest bunch of drunks he had ever seen. They had spent the weekend consuming immense amounts of booze and lamenting their imminent bankruptcy.

Frank's only pleasant moments had come when he watched Adrian trying to compete in the macho games the Conquistadores played—skeet shooting and archery from horseback, lancing targets à la the knights of the round table, running races with one leg strapped to a partner (Frank and Adrian had been matched and—predictably—came in last). But the gloom pervading the aircraft business far outweighed the droll moments.

After growing at an astonishing rate in the first half of the 1930s, defying the otherwise depressed national economy, the airlines were now in a fearful slide. Buchanan had boomed along for a while on a flood of orders for SkyRanger I and recently celebrated the rollout of SkyRanger II, bigger, faster, with a pressurized cabin. But Boeing and Douglas had both came out with competing models and Lockheed's Electra was also in the brawl. The future of SkyRanger II was uncertain at best. All they had so far was an order for ten copies from TWA.

If the rumors swirling around the company were true, SkyRanger II might be the last plane Buchanan would produce. Frank remembered Amanda's defiant prophecy about getting rich, five years ago. He wondered what she felt now, on the edge of bankruptcy. Most of the time he tried not to think about Amanda. It was too painful.

To console themselves, the floundering Conquistadores had flown in a covey of girls for the last night of their desert conclave. Each was a beauty, selected by their companies for their willingness to brighten the proceedings for an hour or two. The blonde in Frank's bed had obviously been one of them. *Wham wham wham.* The fist pounding on his door was not going away. Frank pulled on a pair of pants, telling himself he had to stop this drinking and random screwing. He flung water in his face and stumbled to the front door, as the fist continued to pound. Who could it be? A bill collector? They usually pursued Adrian Van Ness and good luck to them.

Wham wham wham. Had he made his monthly payment on his car? He depended on his secretary for those details. Was that her in bed? Marian? She was blond too.

He flung open the door and found himself face to face with sixteen-year-old Billy McCall. Literally face to face. Billy was no longer the cheerful chubby boy Frank had visited in Laguna Beach. He was almost six feet tall with solid shoulders and a craggy face that blended innocence and disillusion in a way that troubled Frank every time he saw him.

"I just had another go-round with Tama," Billy said. "I've had it with that bitch. I want to move in with you."

"Why sure. But—"

"I won't cramp your style. I just need a place to sleep. I got friends with wheels. I don't need an allowance. I got a job at the Long Beach airport."

"What about school?"

"The hell with school."

Billy was going to the public school in Westwood, one of Los Angeles's best. He studied just enough to stay one step ahead of expulsion. He was currently on his spring vacation.

"No deal," Frank said. "If that's why you're fighting with Tama you're going to have the same fight with me."

"I'm not fighting with Tama about school. I've had it with her lousy remarks. She never stops trying to make me look like a bum. While her big handsome momma's boy Cliff is always *wonderful*."

Frank waved him into the house. "You had any breakfast?"

Billy shook his head. Frank led him into the kitchen and began cooking bacon and eggs. As he was about to serve them, the blonde wandered in wearing his old army bathrobe. "Hi," she said. "Who's this?"

"My nephew, sort of," Frank said, winking at Billy. "I hate to admit it but I've forgotten your name."

"Sylvia. Sylvia Sydenham. My real name's Jones. You got some coffee? What the hell were they putting in those drinks?"

"I think it was gin."

The telephone rang. Tama Morris McCall's angry voice bored into Frank's throbbing skull. "Is Billy there?"

"Yes."

"You tell him to get the hell home here and simonize our cars. It's his turn. Cliff did it last month. If he doesn't have them both finished before sundown I'm going to tell his father what he called me."

"What did he say?"

"Never mind. It's too disgusting to repeat."

Tama had grown more and more proper as her movie career receded over the horizon. She could sound as straitlaced as a Midwest Methodist these days. Although her sex life was apparently still steamy. When Buzz married her, he had made it clear that he reserved the right to enjoy other women. Tama soon demonstrated two could play the reservations game. She had personally escorted Buchanan's contingent of beauties to the Conquistadores party.

"Give him until tomorrow on the simonizing," Frank said. "I'll take him for a ride in SkyRanger Two and calm things down."

"That's no way to teach him discipline," Tama said. "You're going to ruin that boy, Frank."

"He doesn't look that bad to me."

"Put Sylvia on the line."

Sylvia came alive when she heard Tama's name. "Hi," she said in her brightest actress voice.

Her kewpie-doll face darkened. "Gee, Tama, I don't feel so hot. Does it have to be tonight?"

Sylvia sighed. "Okay. I'll be there. The Biltmore at six."

She slammed down the phone. "One of your goddamn airline big shots wants some more entertainment after he sees your wonderful new plane."

Billy shoveled down his ham and eggs. Frank avoided his eyes. Sixteen-year-olds should not be hearing the unlovely details of the way planes were sold.

"That SkyRanger Two sounds like some plane, Pops," Billy said. "Where we going in her?"

Billy thought, ate, slept, drank, dreamt planes. He never read a book or magazine about anything else. He never stopped badgering Frank and Buzz to teach him to fly.

"No place in particular. Our savior and leader, Adrian Van Ness, wants to

127

know how much money it will cost to fix some problems. We're going to run a few tests."

Frank regarded Adrian Van Ness with an unstable mixture of hostility and respect. He had rescued Buchanan Aircraft from oblivion. Adrian had also reclaimed the only woman Frank Buchanan had loved since Sammy. He struggled not to blame Adrian for that fact. But every time Frank saw Amanda at a company party or rollout of a new plane, she looked unhappy. That made Adrian harder to like.

Frank gave Sylvia twenty dollars for a taxi and drove to the factory in his Ford. Billy fiddled with the radio and soon they were listening to an announcer describing an air raid on Madrid. "What about this civil war in Spain?" Billy asked. "Do you think the Russian planes can handle those German and Italian jobs? That Messerschmitt One-oh-nine sounds like quite a plane."

"The Polikaparpovs are pretty good fighter planes. The Russians have some first-class designers. I think they'll do okay."

"Who's gonna win the war?"

"The Loyalists, I hope."

"You mean you're for the Communists? Buzz says anyone who's for the Reds is a traitor."

"The loyalists aren't all Communists."

"Do you think we're gonna get into a war with the Germans or the Russians, Pops?"

"I hope not. People get killed in wars. I lost a lot of friends in the last one."

"You don't get killed if you're good enough. That's what Buzz says."

"I don't agree with him. We were lucky."

Billy looked disappointed. Buzz's bravado was much more appealing to a sixteen-year-old. "Buzz says if we don't start building some decent planes fast, we're gonna get wiped out. He gave me that book by Billy Mitchell. What do you think of it, Pops?"

"I'm afraid Buzz and the general could be right."

Last month Frank and Buzz and Adrian Van Ness had flown to Milwaukee for Billy Mitchell's funeral. He had died of heart disease but believers in air power like Buzz preferred to call it heartbreak. Frank had always felt uneasy about Mitchell's vision of the plane as the supreme weapon of war. But he knew too much about aerodynamics to ignore the progress the Germans and the Russians had made in designing fast, powerful fighters and bombers.

At the airport, Frank ordered the chief mechanic on duty to gas up a SkyRanger II. While they were waiting for the tanks to fill, Frank got a motion-picture camera from the hangar. On the SkyRanger's wings were one of Frank's newest ideas, flexible flaps that could be extended to add lift in short takeoff airports. They were going up to shoot some film of how the flaps behaved in flight. They had developed a flutter problem during recent tests.

As they talked, Buzz McCall pulled up in his white Chrysler convertible with seventeen-year-old Cliff Morris beside him. Buzz parked the car beside the hangar and walked out to the plane with Cliff. The contrast between Cliff and Billy was remarkable. Billy was so blond and fair-skinned he sometimes looked bleached. Cliff had his mother's olive skin and black hair. He too was over six feet, with a Latin profile that had half the girls in Santa Monica palpitating, his mother claimed.

Frank liked both boys. Their personalities were as different as their looks. Outwardly nonchalant and easygoing, Cliff wanted badly to be liked. Billy seemed indifferent to everyone's opinion but his own and occasionally Frank's.

Buzz strolled up to Billy and without saying a word drove his left fist into his stomach. Billy gasped and bent double. Buzz clipped him with a right-hand uppercut that knocked him under the fuselage of SkyRanger II.

"What the hell was that for?" Frank said.

"Stay out of this," Buzz said. He dragged Billy out from under the plane by his shirt front. "Don't ever call your stepmother a name like that again, get me?"

"I get you," Billy said, blood trickling from a split lip. He glared at Cliff. "Did you tell him, you fucking momma's boy freako?"

"No," Cliff said. He was clearly baffled by Billy's dislike, which began the day they met.

"Tama told me. She was shaking and crying when I came home," Buzz said.

Frank sighed. It never seemed to dawn on Buzz that even a mediocre actress like Tama could make a man believe almost anything with a carefully calculated performance. Frank could practically hear Tama declaiming: *that kid is going up in your new plane after insulting me while my son sits home? What kind of a father are you?*

"Let's get going." Frank said.

He beckoned Billy into the copilot's seat and taxied out for takeoff. The big plane leaped from the runway in thirty-two seconds while Buzz took pictures of the flaps extended. "The goddamn things are vibrating a foot and a half minimum," Buzz said.

Frank circled the field, touched down and took off again three more times, while Buzz took more pictures. "We may have to reposition the damn things," Frank said.

"Adrian'll shit a brick," Buzz said. "It'll cost at least fifty grand."

"That's cheaper than a new plane, if the wings come off," Frank said.

"Worse things could happen," Buzz said. "Maybe Adrian'd finally wise up and get into the right end of the business."

For at least a year Buzz had been urging Adrian to start building military planes. He had persuaded their designated leader to attend Billy Mitchell's funeral to introduce him to Army Air Corps brass.

"Could the wings come off now?" Cliff asked.

"No. We're putting the flaps up," Frank said, throwing a switch that raised the flaps level with the wing's trailing edge.

They soared over Los Angeles and up the coast toward Santa Barbara. Frank shoved the throttles forward and the Ranger was soon hitting her top speed, 320 miles an hour. "Wow," Billy said.

He was used to flying. Frank had been taking him up in his single-engine Lustra I since he was five or six. "She's all yours, copilot," Frank said, relinquishing the yoke.

"Aye, aye, Captain," Billy said, his sore stomach and aching jaw forgotten. Frank looked over his shoulder at Buzz, sitting in the flight engineer's seat behind them. Cliff Morris was a few feet behind him in the observer's seat. Buzz was watching Billy with unrelenting eyes. Was there fatherhood in the tough-guy stare? Frank hoped so.

Billy swung the plane into a steep bank, then into a shallow dive. Frank had been letting him take the controls of his Lustra I for three years. "Beautiful!" he yelled as he leveled off.

"Can I try it?" Cliff Morris said.

"Sure. Let him take over," Buzz said.

Billy reluctantly surrendered his seat. Cliff obviously had no feel for how a plane handled. He put the Ranger into a clumsy bank and Frank had to rescue them before they slipped into a spin.

"What'd I tell you about keepin' the nose up?" Buzz said. He had been teaching Cliff in his Lustra I, a flyspeck compared to this muscular airliner.

"This is a lot more plane," Frank said, trying to comfort Cliff.

"Get outta the way," Buzz said to Frank. He planted himself in the pilot's seat and made Cliff follow him, hands on his copilot's yoke, as Buzz spun the plane into a banking turn that only a veteran pilot could handle.

"Now let's see you get us out of some real trouble," Buzz said.

He pulled back sharply on his yoke as the Ranger came out of the turn and the airspeed fell away. In ten seconds they tilted left into a spin. Buzz sat there, arms folded. "Pull it out," he said.

The airstream whined over the wing surfaces. The big plane began hurtling toward the blue Pacific. Sky and water blended in a whirling blur.

"Wow!" Billy yelled. "Great!"

He had the born pilot's certainty that he was indestructible. Cliff Morris sat there, his hands frozen on the yoke.

"Pull it out!" Buzz roared.

"I don't know how!" Cliff screamed.

"Then we're goin' in! I'm tired of buildin' planes nobody buys. Uncle Frank ain't good enough to get us out and neither is your wiseguy brother. You save your own ass in a plane. Nobody else's gonna do it."

For the first time Frank realized Buzz hated his stepson—and really loved Billy. But Tama would not tolerate a sign of it. Maybe he even loved Tama but he was afraid to let her know it because it might force him to disown Billy and favor Cliff.

Down they spun, close to being in serious trouble as the centrifugal force of the spin locked them in its grip. "I *caaaan't*," Cliff screamed, his hands over his ears as if he could not bear the sound of his own terror.

This was going much too far. Frank lunged over Buzz's shoulder and pushed forward on the yoke. "Stamp on that right rudder," he roared. Everyone rose a foot out of his seat and Frank's head almost hit the roof as the Ranger came out of the spin with two thousand feet to spare and roared toward the Pacific horizon.

"Whattya know," Buzz said. "The fuckin' wings stayed on."

Frank flew back to Santa Monica with Cliff Morris slumped in the copilot's seat. "You'll do a lot better when you get some lessons from an instructor who's not your father," Frank said. "Fathers shouldn't teach their kids to fly or drive."

"You wanta teach him, he's all yours," Buzz said.

"I'll teach both of them."

"I don't know whether I want to fly," Cliff said. "I'm not sure I'm good enough."

"I know I'm good enough," Billy said.

"You don't know a fucking thing," Buzz snarled. "You never open a book, you're flunkin' every subject in the curriculum and you think you're good enough to fly? How, why?"

"I just know it," Billy said.

"Flyin' takes brains. So far you haven't convinced me you've got any." Buzz glowered at Cliff. "It takes guts too. So far momma's boy here hasn't convinced me he's got much of that item."

Frank patted Cliff's shoulder. "You don't have to be as tough as he is. Adrian Van Ness thinks millions of people will learn to fly in the next twenty years. It'll be as common as knowing how to drive."

"I don't buy that idea," Buzz said. "Planes are gettin' faster, hotter all the time."

Frank hoped Buzz was wrong. He shared Adrian's belief that the plane would help create jobs and prosperity, like the automobile. So far it was a faith with few followers.

"You'll be surprised how fast you learn to fly," Frank said to Cliff. "Pretty soon you feel like you're part of the plane."

"I feel that way already," Billy said.

"Shut the fuck up," Buzz said.

Billy's face remained expressionless. But there were tears in his eyes.

THE GREAT GAME

Adrian Van Ness sat in his shabby office on the first floor of Buchanan Aircraft's main building watching their latest plane, a sleek stylish trainer for the Army Air Force, come in for a smooth landing. On his desk was an invitation to the spring meeting of the Conquistadores del Cielo. Beside it was a letter from Jim Redwood, Buchanan's sales manager, dolefully reporting he had failed to sell a single copy of SkyRanger II on his latest foray to New York.

Ruined whispered in Adrian's soul. He had begun to hate the bravura name the historian in him had selected for their trade association in 1935—the very year the bottom had started to fall out of the plane business. He watched Frank Buchanan climb out of the trainer and stroll across the tarmac, his arm around Billy McCall's slim shoulders. A few minutes later Frank took off with Cliff Morris in the second seat. The chief designer was giving teenagers flying lessons on company time. Why not, when the company had nothing to sell?

Buzz McCall stood in the doorway, a sketch in his hand. "Here's Frank's idea for the next-generation fighter," he said. "It'll make that crummy P-Thirty-nine look like a Curtiss Jenny."

The P-39 was the current fighter plane of the Army Air Force. The bulky creature was inferior in speed and maneuverability to the fighters of every major power. Adrian pondered Buchanan's replacement—an angular craft with gull wings. "Who's going to pay for it?"

"I've practically got a guarantee—"

"Practically a guarantee doesn't pay the rent or the salaries or the taxes," Adrian said.

"Adrian—you gotta gamble to win in this business," Buzz said. "You gotta bet the goddamn company."

"It's easy to be a high roller with someone else's money," Adrian said. "Put this in a drawer until a war starts."

Buzz's recklessness was as unnerving to Adrian as Frank Buchanan's indifference to profit and loss. Both clashed with Adrian's belief in forethought. For the moment the dolorous facts were on Adrian's side. So far their plunge into the military plane business had been a financial disaster. They had sold only 150 trainers. Mockups of dive bombers, reconnaissance planes, fighters, cluttered the hangars. The Army and Navy procurement officers were delighted to encourage bold experiments. But other companies were competing for the same extremely limited appropriations. Don Douglas, an Annapolis dropout, had the inside track with the Navy. Boeing up in Seattle had a similar whammy on the Army.

Adrian's office intercom beeped. "Prince Carlo Ponte—something is here to see you."

Ponty was as handsome and urbane as ever. He was in California with his mistress, a Hungarian film star who was making a movie directed by the most lecherous mogul in Hollywood. "I am here to protect my investment," he said. He added a hilarious imitation of the mogul's assaults on the English language.

Ponty's sex life stirred envy in Adrian. He was usually too tired to do more than kiss Amanda when he stumbled home from Buchanan Aircraft at midnight. Amanda never even hinted she was interested in anything more amorous. They made love only when Adrian suggested it. Even in the bedroom he sensed an element of mockery in Amanda's manner. Again and again her eyes seemed to ask him why they were not rich. What had happened to his promises of a golden future as her compensation for turning Cadwallader Groves into a smelly, oozing oil field?

Yet Adrian struggled to keep his wife happy. He bought her expensive jewelry he could not afford. He swallowed her awful cooking. She had the power to make him miserable if she chose. She had daily access to the mind and heart of the one female in this world Adrian loved without reservations, his six-year-old daughter Victoria.

Ponty had married his French heiress. She seemed content to share him with other women—and with planes. He was known as the Italian Lindbergh for his record-breaking distance flights across Asia and Africa—and the elegant books he wrote to celebrate them. Like Lindbergh's books, his narratives combined high adventure with philosophy—in Ponty's case an uncompromising disdain for Europe's drift toward totalitarianism. He roamed the world to escape "the pygmies of the right and left."

Adrian had kept Ponty in close touch with the fortunes of Buchanan Aircraft. He was an admirer of Frank Buchanan's clean designs. "So, my old friend—how goes the profits and losses?" Ponty asked.

"Unless a miracle occurs, we'll be bankrupt in six months."

"I've suggested before, Adrian—and suggest again—you should see the whole world as your market."

Adrian sighed. "We're not a merchant bank. We don't have partners all over the globe, telling us where the deals are."

"That is something I would be happy to undertake. For old time's sake—and whatever douceurs you might be inclined to add. Breaking long-distance records is expensive. My wife's enthusiasm for financing me has distinct limits."

"I'm ready to add enough sweeteners to give you dyspepsia. Do you know anything we could go after right now?"

Ponty pointed to a copy of the *Los Angeles Times* on Adrian's desk. A black headline announced Adolf Hitler's agreement with British Prime Minister Neville Chamberlain at Munich, giving Germany the right to dismember Czechoslovakia. "Although the world sees it as a shameful surrender, the British are buying time. They've begun to rearm. But their aircraft industry has been starved for so long, they haven't the capacity to meet half their needs."

"Can you arrange something? My—my mentor, Geoffrey Tillotson, died two years ago."

His reputation ruined by the catastrophic losses Tillotson Brothers had suffered in the collapse of airline stocks in 1929, Adrian's English father had never returned to the business world. He had remained a stubborn believer in the airplane, writing Adrian letters full of praise for Buchanan's modest early success.

"It would be better for you to go yourself—and work through Winston Churchill. He's out of power but he's been calling for rearmament and has numerous friends in the military. I'd bring Frank Buchanan with you to deal with their design people. I would also contact your mother. She has many friends in English society. In these matters, every kind of influence helps."

Two weeks later, Adrian and Frank Buchanan were drinking tea with Clarissa Van Ness in her Mayfair flat. She had stayed in England almost continuously since Tillotson's death, saying she felt more at home there. They talked about Victoria, who had charmed her grandmother when Clarissa visited California last year.

On her home ground, Amanda had been an unruffled hostess. Clarissa even conceded a mild admiration for the scenery. But the visit had been marred by Adrian's desperate attempts to conceal the parlous state of Buchanan Aircraft. He had even rented a sleek black Packard for a week, ignoring the disapproval in Amanda's eyes. They had taken Clarissa to the best restaurants. But when they visited the factory, the charade had exploded. Outside Adrian's office, a small angry man in a derby declared he was not leaving until his client received three thousand dollars for a half dozen rivet guns purchased six months ago.

Clarissa had said nothing, of course. But *ruined* clanged in Adrian's head like a fire alarm. He had slept barely two hours a night for a month after his mother went back to London.

Frank Buchanan was telling Clarissa about the radical designs they had experimented with when he worked at de Havilland before the last war. His favorite was a flying wing. It had the best lift-to-drag ratio of any plane he had ever seen. Clarissa beamed. "I remember my dear friend Geoffrey Tillotson talking about that. He put up a great deal of the money for de Havilland in those days."

"We're hoping to sell the Royal Air Force some planes," Adrian said. "We're seeing Winston Churchill at the Athenaeum tomorrow at five o'clock. Can you put in a good word for us with him or anyone else?"

"I sat next to Winston at a dinner last night," Clarissa said. "I'll be happy to mention your plight if I see him again. But I doubt if it will do much good. He could not be gloomier about his political situation. He blames a great deal on the Oxford Oath. That woman you used to escort, Beryl Suydam, was one of the leaders."

Beryl's name had an extraordinary effect on Adrian. Her radical politics had not prevented her from becoming one of the best known women in English aviation. Except for those euphoric days when he had been a Wall Street wonder, he had never been able to read about her record-setting flights without pain. Now, in the center of London, he was filled with old longing.

Adrian was familiar with the Oxford Oath, promoted by British left-wing intellectuals in the mid-1930s. Tens of thousands of students and professors and union members vowed not to serve England in another war. "No wonder Herr Hitler decided he could forget about the British and concentrate on intimidating the French and the rest of Europe," his mother said, glaring at Adrian as if it were all his fault.

"I hope the British and French don't expect the Americans to fight this time," Frank Buchanan said. "All we did was make the world safe for their revenge on the Germans."

"Keep your isolationism to yourself when we see Churchill tomorrow," Adrian said.

Back at their hotel, although he was exhausted by the two-day flight from

Los Angeles, Adrian put through an overseas telephone call. It took an hour to complete the connection. Finally, Amanda's voice was on the line. "I suppose you want to talk to the birthday girl?"

In a moment, Victoria was on the line. "Hello, Daddy," she said.

An enormous tenderness swelled in Adrian's chest. "Hello, Gorgeous," he said. "Happy birthday. I'm so sorry I can't be there to give you a kiss."

Victoria said she loved her present, a paint set. She promised to paint him a whole fleet of planes. She asked him about England and hoped she could go there with him someday. Adrian told her they would visit all sorts of wonderful places—New York, Paris, London—when she was older.

"Mommy says we won't have enough money," Victoria said.

A flush of anger and anxiety swept Adrian. "Yes we will, Sweetness. I promise you we will."

Amanda came on the line. "At forty dollars a minute, I think someone should stop you two."

"Any news I should hear?"

"Douglas got a new Navy contract for some dive bombers. It's on the front page of the *Times*."

Adrian hung up and composed a cable to Buzz McCall, urging him to contact his fellow veteran of the air war in France, Colonel George C. Kenney, chief of Army production, and fan his envy of the Navy's decision to buy dive bombers. Frank Buchanan had a plane in his files that was superior to the Douglas plane in bomb load and speed.

Adrian realized he was hoping for the impossible, even as he wrote the cable. The Army had a new bombsight that was supposedly so accurate, it made dive bombers obsolete. That was why they were in bed with Boeing and their lumbering B-17 Flying Fortress, which was supposed to be able to shoot its way to distant targets without fighter escorts. That meant the Army was not particularly interested in fighters either.

Adrian went to bed and stared into the darkness, thinking of the future of Buchanan Aircraft. Amanda was right. After seven years of struggle, they had no money. This foray to England was their last gasp. It would be ironic if his attempt to become a man of substance ended where it had begun.

The following afternoon, Adrian and Frank Buchanan drank brandy in the lofty library of the Athenaeum Club with Winston Churchill and Major George Knightly, a trim mustached man in a blue RAF uniform. Adrian proposed their trainer, touting the Army Air Force's enthusiasm for it.

"I rather think we have all the trainers we need for the moment," Knightly said. "What we don't have is a light bomber. Do you have any ideas?"

"We've got a plane we call the SkyRanger Two," Frank Buchanan said. "I could turn that into a bomber for you in ten minutes."

Knightly pretended to set his watch. "Give it a try."

Frank seized pen and paper from a nearby writing desk and swiftly sketched the SkyRanger. Hurling technical terms that only Knightly understood, he redesigned the wings for extra strength and larger fuel tanks and reworked the interior to carry a 2,000-pound bomb load and a crew of five, with machine guns in the nose, tail, and a revolving top turret.

"How much?" Knightly asked.

"Two hundred and fifty thousand a plane," Frank said, looking warily at Adrian.

"Three hundred thousand," Adrian said.

"Umm," Knightly said. "I like it. If things go the way Winston thinks they will—you may hear from us."

"Any idea how many you'd want?" Adrian asked.

"Two hundred for starters."

Adrian barely managed to conceal his astonishment. Knightly was talking about six million dollars. "Surely you can spare a few thousand for the design work," Adrian said.

"Afraid not. We're counting every shilling at the moment."

"We'll manage it," Adrian said.

"Then we have an understanding."

Knightly went off to a staff meeting and Churchill ordered another brandy. "Is this man reliable?" he asked, eyeing Frank Buchanan.

"Oh, absolutely," Adrian lied, hoping Frank would keep his mouth shut.

"Your old friend Geoffrey Tillotson, whose loss I still regret, spoke to me of you now and then in matters more important than stocks and bonds. If war comes as I'm sure it will, you may be contacted from time to time by a small cadre we're sending over to offset German propaganda. I hope you'll be helpful."

"I'll try."

"Prince Carlo Pontecorvo will be handling matters in California."

Adrian, a student of the great game, wondered if Ponty's casual advice to sell planes in England and Churchill's prompt response were as accidental as they seemed.

On the ride back to the hotel Frank Buchanan was his usual erratic self. "Do you realize what he just asked you to do? The same goddamm stuff they pulled in the last war. Lindbergh's father wrote a book about it. They're going to drag us into it to save their imperialistic asses. Are you going to help them?"

"Yes," Adrian said. "So are you. The day we get home, I want you to go to work on designing that bomber. Hire twenty extra people if you have to. We'll finance it out of the trainer sale."

"Whose side are we on, anyway?" Frank said.

"Our side."

"Where is it?" Frank said. "Give me a moral or spiritual location."

"Beyond the rainbow," Adrian said. "Where the pots of gold are waiting."

"Why don't we make that our insignia?" Frank sneered.

"Not a bad idea. Give me a sketch."

In the lobby of the hotel, Frank grabbed a piece of stationery and drew a plane flying above a crescent rainbow. Adrian thanked him and put it in his pocket, deciding it was pointless to try to explain to his chief designer how

136

little morality had to do with playing the great game, the hidden struggle for power that nations waged. Like Ponty, he felt a sentimental loyalty to England, a belief that despite her flaws she stood for something valuable. But the thrill of the game was a far more powerful motive.

At the hotel desk, the clerk handed Adrian a phone message. *Miss Beryl Suydam 05-03-421.*

"Not *the* Beryl Suydam," Frank Buchanan said, reading it over his shoulder.

"I met her years ago," Adrian said.

Upstairs, his hand trembled slightly as he picked up the telephone and gave the operator the number. "Adrian," Beryl said in that silky voice, unchanged by a decade. "A friend saw you in your hotel lobby. I couldn't resist calling you."

"How nice," he said.

"For one thing, you've got a plane that interests me. That SkyRanger? I think I could beat Howard Hughes's around-the-world record in it, with some help from the brilliant designer fellow you've got on your staff. What's his name?"

"Frank Buchanan."

"Yes. Could we meet in the next day or two?"

Adrian decided they would meet without Frank Buchanan. He was anxious to visit de Havilland and a few other companies where he had old friends. While Frank rode a train out of London, Adrian met Beryl at the Savoy Grill. She arrived in a flight jacket and slacks and the headwaiter refused to seat them. She led him to a small Greek restaurant in Soho, a place full of shadowy corners. Someone played a zither in another room.

Beryl had changed little physically. The face was still the same lovely oval, the dark hair still framing it in a twentyish bob. "You don't look a day older," Adrian said.

"You do," she said. "Your hair."

Adrian brushed self-consciously at his receding hair line. "They say bald men are sexier."

"You'll never be sexy, Adrian. But you'll always be attractive to women."

"Why?"

"Every woman likes to explore an enigma."

"I don't think of myself as enigmatic."

"You are. I didn't feel I could devote my life to solving you. Are you still married?"

"More or less. How about you?"

"You know I'm not married."

"Not even in love?"

"Not at the moment."

"You still think the Soviet Union is the hope of the world?"

"I've grown a bit more sophisticated. I think socialism is the hope of the world. Hasn't it arrived in Washington, D.C., under the flag of the New Deal?"

"Roosevelt isn't a socialist. He isn't anything. That's his problem."

"Perhaps it's your problem too, Adrian. Not being anything eventually becomes distressing."

"I'm not sure you're right about that. I know exactly what I want to be at the moment."

"What?"

"Your lover again."

Beryl did not display the slightest surprise or shock—which only made her more desirable. "Does that make any sense?" she said.

"We have quite a lot in common. Planes—memories."

Beryl raised her wineglass. "Let's rely on memories for the time being."

In Adrian's middle-class hotel off Picadilly, memory created a bittersweet aura. Beryl's skin was still wet, glistening from the shower as they embraced. He licked drops of water from her small rounded breasts. His hand moved easily, knowingly, up her firm thighs.

"I've had other women. But I've never loved anyone else," Adrian said.

"It's been the same with me," Beryl said.

Over a nightcap they talked about her flight around the world. She had a backer lined up, the publisher of the *Daily Mail*. Adrian assured her the plane would be provided free of charge. He would put Frank Buchanan in touch with her the moment they got back to California.

"You're such a dear," Beryl said, with a contented sigh.

"Tomorrow—dinner again?"

"Why not," she said.

It was the old Beryl without her radical animosity, her war wounds healed by time or the progress of socialism. Politics were not important, Adrian told himself. Love transcended politics as it transcended time and space.

The next morning, Adrian was awakened by a call from George Knightly, the RAF officer who had come to the Athenaeum Club with Winston Churchill. "Could you spare a few minutes for another talk about that bomber?"

"My designer's off in the country visiting friends."

"We can chat just as well without him."

Adrian was sure Knightly was going to beat his price down to nothing to help save dear old England's ass. He was not going to let sentimentality bankrupt him. He arrived at the Air Ministry determined to bargain hard for every shilling.

Knightly shoved a chair beside his desk and tugged at his mustache. "This is a bit awkward but it has to be done. I take it you're an old friend of Beryl Suydam? That explains the—er—reunion last night in your room?"

"Why is that any of your goddamn business?"

"It shouldn't be. I gather she's quite a piece in bed, if half the hangar talk I've heard is true. But the fact is, old boy, she's a Soviet spy."

"Absolutely ridiculous!"

"I wish it was. She's a marvelous flier. Quite a personage, you might say. But the evidence is rather overwhelming. Since you're going to be building a bomber for us, if things develop with Herr Hitler, I thought you should know."

"Can you prove this—this—slander?"

"This may be a bit painful. But you've asked for it."

Knightly took a folder out of his desk and handed it to Adrian. In it were a number of photocopied letters from Beryl to someone named Sergei. "You'd be most interested in the one on the bottom. She wrote it last night in the lobby of your hotel," Knightly said.

The letter was on hotel stationery.

Dear Sergei:

The fish bit the moment I dangled the hook. I'm sure I can get you all you want on the light bomber in a week's time. He wants to marry me! That can be dealt with, of course. I'm inclined to go ahead with the round-the-world flight and see what else I can get from Frank Buchanan's files. I'll probe Adrian about that fighter plane tomorrow night.

Beryl.

"Sergei is her Soviet control. He's been working for us for several years."

Adrian was too dazed and humiliated to do anything but nod.

"We've no objections if you want to go on seeing her for a bit. You might pass on some rather useful misinformation to her. Multiply the number of planes we're buying by the order of five, say."

"Why?"

"We've reason to think it'll get to Herr Hitler via Moscow. The Germans have a covey of agents there. Trying to play the intimidation game a bit on our side. You might throw in some bull about orders with other plane makers. Heavy stuff."

"I see."

"She'll be doing her damndest to please you, old chap. Don't see how you can lose."

Knightly's smile sickened Adrian. The man of course had no idea what Beryl Suydam meant to him. For a moment, Adrian contemplated something much more vicious than repaying deception with deception. He imagined murder. He saw his fingers around Beryl Suydam's fragile throat, his thumb pressing hard on the hollow he loved to kiss. *Bitch*, howled a voice that did not belong to him. It wailed down from the stratosphere, where Beryl had found the strength, the guile, to make him a fool.

Forethought rescued Adrian. Outside the air ministry, he stared at the traffic on the Thames and told himself this was simply another phase of the great game. He had been given a license to enjoy himself. He would use it to the full.

For the next two nights, Beryl played Delilah to Adrian's cunning Samson. When she whispered *I love you* at the climax, his mask almost slipped, he almost reached for her lying throat. When she did it again the next night, Adrian almost believed it. He wondered if Knightly knew everything. Was this woman secretly pleading with him to rescue her from deception?

139

How could he speak? Knightly had warned him it was vital to keep Sergei's double agentry concealed. He would not live twelve hours if Beryl discovered it.

Beryl lit a cigarette while Adrian poured her a brandy. She curled up on the bed, oozing charm. "I've heard wonderful things about the planes you're making."

" 'Want to make' would be better. We've had a hell of a time selling most of them. The competition is tough and the airlines are going broke. The Army and the Navy have no money. That's why this order for a thousand bombers from the British is a godsend."

"A thousand?" Beryl said. "I wonder where they're getting the money."

"I don't know and I don't care."

"What other planes do you have?"

"A pursuit plane. It can outfly anything in the air."

"I smell a speed record. Can you send me the plans?"

Adrian shook his head. "We're keeping that one in a locked file."

"Adrian. You can trust me. I might even help you sell it to someone else."

The lovely lips curled into a Cheshire-cat smile. She was devouring him in her lying mind. Adrian no longer had any doubt that Knightly was right. Still he could not let go of those whispered words. *I love you.* Was she, even in the slimy gutter of deceit, asking him to forgive her?

Adrian finished his brandy and told himself he was a fool. Take what you can get and forget the rest. Forget the soaring and adoring. From now on, Adrian Van Ness would enjoy his women without the emotional window dressing of love.

"I've got bad news," he said. "I have to go home tomorrow. A labor crisis."

He teased her left nipple until it came erect. "Once more for auld lang syne?" he said.

For a moment he was sure she knew. He wanted her to know. He let the coldness in his mind fill his voice, his eyes. But he said nothing. It would be much more satisfying to let her dangle on the hook of doubt for the next year as he made excuses about the round-the-world flight and fed her more misinformation about the light bomber and other planes. Revenge could be sweetened by time—and more nostalgic encounters in hotel rooms.

But there was still a corner of Adrian's soul where *I love you* whispered, where memory wept and hope mourned.

WHEN DREAMS COME TRUE

Adrian returned from his trip to England deeply depressed. Amanda assumed it was because he had failed to sell a single plane. When Victoria asked him if they could go to Hawaii over the Christmas holidays, he snapped "no" so harshly she burst into tears. He rushed out and bought her a seventy-five-dollar Shirley Temple doll, then excoriated Amanda in private for letting her daughter have delusions of wealth.

"We're not going to be rich, ever," he said. "Get that through your head. The aircraft business is a penny-ante game and it's going to stay that way."

"You're the one who talked about going to Hawaii," Amanda said. "You buy her the most expensive doll in the store. Then you tell me her delusions are my fault?"

"She's your responsibility. I don't have time to educate her. I wish I did."

"Gordon is forming his own oil company," Amanda said. "He called to ask if we wanted to buy any of the stock."

"We'll be lucky to pay the mortgage on this house," Adrian snarled.

"He's brought in another dozen wells. He's going to be a millionaire," Amanda said.

"Are you going to hate me for the rest of your life?"

"I don't hate you," Amanda said. "But you obviously have no intention of giving me a chance to love you, either."

"What do I have to do to merit that," Adrian said. "Grovel?"

"Give me some evidence that you want me to love you."

"I do!" Adrian said.

"For whose sake? Mine or Victoria's?"

She saw fear flicker in Adrian's eyes. She had read him correctly. Instead of admitting she was right, he retreated into sullen isolation again.

"Do I have to fill out a goddamn questionnaire?"

They went back to being antagonists in small things and large things. One of the large things was the drift toward war in Europe. Hitler swallowed Austria and Czechoslovakia, making the British politicians who favored appeasing him look more and more foolish. The British and French began rearming to meet the German threat. Adrian frankly, unabashedly welcomed the prospect of an explosion.

"How can you say such a thing?" Amanda gasped. For her it was a grisly replay of the First World War. All she could think of was her father's death, the destruction of Eden.

"Because it will be good for the airplane business," Adrian said.

"It will mean death, suffering for thousands, millions of people," Amanda said.

"I don't know any of them," Adrian said. "I can only sympathize with people I know."

"I'm not sure you can even do that," Amanda said.

Amanda of course had no idea that the Adrian who said those heartless words was the man whom Beryl Suydam had wounded. For the first time in years, she felt repelled by her husband. His good manners, his dislike of argument, had held such feelings at a distance. She was even more dismayed a few weeks later, when the newspaper informed her that the British had placed an unprecedented order for two hundred light bombers with Buchanan Aircraft. That day, Adrian came home brimming with good cheer. He had a huge teddy bear for Victoria and a string of pearls for her.

"I'm beginning to change my mind about the aircraft business. It may not be penny-ante after all."

"I don't want them," Amanda said, giving him back the pearls.

"Why, for God's sake?"

"I don't want to wear anything that comes from planes built to kill people."

"I always knew your intelligence was limited. This proves it," Adrian snarled. "These planes will defend decent people against barbarians. Do you want Hitler and his friends to conquer the world?"

It was too late to advance this rational argument. Amanda could only remember Adrian's declared indifference to slaughtering people. "I don't care who wins as long as we stay out of it," Amanda said. "This sort of thing—making planes for one side—will drag us into it."

Amanda was speaking out of the depths of her California self, in a voice that millions of Americans shared. To her, Europe was a land of literature and monuments, the dead past that could be explored from a distance but was not worth the death of a single American. Adrian, with his deep ties to England, could only respond with outrage. Seven-year-old Victoria watched, bewildered and tearful, as her mother and father insulted and reviled each other.

Amanda joined America First, an organization committed to keeping the United States out of any future war. Henry Ford, former governor Alfred E. Smith of New York, Senator Burton K. Wheeler of Montana were among its leaders. Its chief spokesman was aviation's hero, Charles Lindbergh. Adrian was infuriated but how could he object to a policy that Lindbergh was advocating? Polls showed 80 percent of the voters backed America First's call for strict neutrality. Earlier in the decade, Congress had passed a neutrality act which forbade the United States to sell arms to any country at war.

On September 1, 1939, huge headlines blossomed in all the Los Angeles newspapers, announcing that the Germans had invaded Poland. Two days later, Britain and France declared war on Adolf Hitler's Third Reich. For Amanda that only made America First's task even more important. Adrian had other things on his mind. He rushed to Washington, D.C., to wangle a change in the neutrality act, which forbade him to ship his bombers to England.

Adrian came back to California with a self-satisfied smile on his face. At his suggestion, Roosevelt had persuaded Congress to amend the neutrality act to permit the bombers to be delivered, as long as they did not leave the country under their own power. Adrian had found an airfield in North Dakota on the Canadian border. Buchanan pilots would fly the planes there and Canadians would tow them across the border, where British pilots would be waiting to fly them to England.

When Adrian described this coup at dinner on the night of his return, Amanda denounced it as a criminal evasion of the law. "Who did you bribe?" she asked.

"Do you realize where we'd be if we can't deliver those planes?" Adrian shouted. "Bankrupt. Ruined."

"In a good cause, that wouldn't bother me in the least," Amanda said.

"It would bother the hell out of me," Adrian said. "Especially when the cause is brainlessness masquerading as idealism."

"Please stop, please!" Victoria cried, putting her hands over her ears.

For Victoria's sake, Adrian and Amanda negotiated a private neutrality act. She would say no more about his bombers and he would let her continue to support America First. A few weeks later, Lindbergh came to Los Angeles to speak at a rally. Amanda announced she was going and Adrian sullenly assented.

In the flag-decorated auditorium on Wilshire Boulevard, Amanda was stunned to see Frank Buchanan in the front row. "What are you doing here?" she said, sitting down beside him.

"I could ask you the same question," he said.

"I'm sure Adrian is considering divorce. But I feel this so strongly."

"So do I."

"But you're still designing those bombers. How can you live with that?"

"I'm here to prevent American boys from flying in them."

"I thought making them at all was reprehensible. Don't you think it puts us squarely on one side—against the Germans?"

"I hope not."

The pain in Frank's eyes made it clear that his conscience had asked the same question. She saw the anguish of his position and dropped the argument. She no longer despised this man. He seemed sad and lonely in his shabby flight jacket and tieless shirt.

Lindbergh gave a stirring speech, denouncing Franklin Roosevelt's attempts to evade the neutrality act and edge the United States into the war on England's side. He grimly declared Germany was going to win the war and there was nothing the United States could do about it but adjust to a world of new political realities. Amanda applauded fiercely, agreeing with every word of it. She noticed that Frank did not applaud. He sat with his arms folded on his chest, looking troubled.

Amanda drove Frank home to his house in Topanga Canyon, listening to him argue with himself. He was not sure Lindbergh was right about the Germans winning the war. He was unsure about Germany. Did Hitler's rampant anti-Semitism justify building planes for the British? Didn't every country have its anti-Semites? Could they possibly be right? His friend Ezra Pound, the greatest poet of the era, thought so.

Amanda said she disliked anti-Semitism as much as Frank—but she hated war. When they reached Frank's Topanga house, he urged her to stay for coffee. She sensed his loneliness. His anguish over the bombers was only a small part of his need for her companionship.

Inside the crude three-room house, she was appalled by the dirty clothes flung in corners, dishes piled in the sink. "Forgive my bachelor's style," Frank said. "I should have a woman come in once a week at least. But I can't afford it."

The words gouged her nerves. The chief designer at Buchanan Aircraft could not afford a cleaning woman? Frank saw the question in her eyes and began telling her what he did with his money. Some of it went to causes like America First. More went to Ezra Pound, whom he had been helping to support for years. More went to help Billy McCall, Buzz McCall's son, who was in college at UCLA. Buzz and the boy did not get along. Or, more precisely, Billy did not get along with Buzz's wife, Tama.

There was a mystery here, Amanda thought, as Frank Buchanan poured her coffee. This man was not the money-hungry manipulator her brother had portrayed. But how could she begin to search for the truth without telling him about her own unhappiness with Adrian? She knew what that might suggest to this lonely man. Anyway, how could she trust these intuitions? She was a naive woman, cut off from the politics of Buchanan Aircraft, the constant jockeying for power and money. She talked for an hour behind a shield of noncommittal politeness and went home troubled, full of inchoate wishes she could not even express to herself.

A month later, Hitler's armies swept into France and defeated the French and British in a few stunning weeks. Adrian went almost berserk with anxiety. He prowled the house from midnight to dawn, listening to the latest radio bulletins. He was terrified for England—and for Buchanan Aircraft. If the Germans bludgeoned the English into surrender, the 200 bombers already in production would never be paid for and Buchanan would be bankrupt.

In the middle of this turmoil, the first bomber came off the production line and was rolled out for a maiden flight. The desperate British decided to make it a symbol of their determination to fight on. They arranged for national publicity. Adrian was of course delighted but he still could not sleep and Amanda deduced that publicity was all the British were putting up. Nevertheless, to the press and public, Adrian was a picture of confidence and pride.

Amanda refused to go to the rollout celebration. Adrian almost exploded. "The British ambassador will be there with his wife! Harry Hopkins, Roosevelt's right-hand man, is flying out from Washington! The governor, both senators will be there. I insist on you coming."

"I can be sick. Make excuses. You're very good at that."

"*I* want you there."

Amanda shook her head.

"I'll take Victoria instead."

"I can't stop you. But I think you shouldn't. She's too young to understand any of this. All she knows is we seem to hate each other."

"I'm taking her. I want her to see what her father is doing to defend democracy. Let her figure out why her mother sides with the barbarians."

On rollout day Amanda stayed home, working in the garden. It was a beautifully sunny June morning, without a cloud in the sky. She listened on NBC radio, which was devoting an hour to the ceremony. The British ambassador, Adrian, California's governor, made brief speeches. Then the announcer described the preparations for the test flight. The test pilot and chief designer Frank Buchanan were introduced. Frank discussed some of the features of the bomber, such as two counter-rotating variable pitch propellers on each engine, which would add to the plane's stability.

"Are you going along, Mr. Buchanan?" the announcer asked.

"I always go along on test flights of planes I design," Frank said. "I believe the designer ought to risk his own neck to demonstrate his faith in his ideas."

The announcer described the two men boarding the plane, settling into the cockpit. He let the audience hear the roar of the two Wright Cyclone engines as they warmed up. In a moment he was describing the takeoff, the climb. Suddenly his voice changed tone. "Something seems wrong! The plane is pitching and yawing up there. The pilot doesn't seem to have complete control! He's trying to turn back to the field but he can't do it. He's losing altitude fast!"

A roaring filled the sky. The plane was coming toward her. Suddenly Amanda was in the cockpit with Frank and the test pilot, as they fought to control the berserk machine. Her body remained in the sunny garden but she was in the careening plane, the thunder of the motors tearing her brain apart, hearing Frank shout to the test pilot. "Bail out! Bail out!"

The pilot leaped and his chute billowed like an immense question mark. Frank was alone in the cockpit. Amanda could see what he was trying to do, turn in a wide wobbly circle to head back to the Buchanan airfield, five miles away. But he could not do it. The plane roared over Amanda in her garden and tore through the top of a house on the next street, smashed through a half-dozen trees and cars and disintegrated. The wings ripped through two other houses and the fuselage hurtled down the street for another block.

Amanda saw the terrible things that happened to Frank in the cockpit. His seat ripped loose and he was catapulted into the windshield, then flung against both sides of the fuselage as fearsome forces smashed the plane back and forth in its passage down the street.

Amanda raced for her car. The swath of destruction on the next street made her brain reel. Two houses, three cars were on fire. Women and children ran toward her, screaming hysterically. Amanda roared through the burning debris to the plane. Flames were swirling inside the fuselage. A fire truck came clanging around the other corner. "The cockpit. Get him out of the cockpit!" she cried, as firemen spilled from the truck.

The fire was in the cockpit now. The firemen hesitated, afraid the plane would blow up. "Look!" Amanda cried.

Frank was on his feet, clawing at the cockpit window. Two firemen raced forward with a hose spraying foam. Another one hacked at the window and the metal around it with an ax. In two frantic minutes they had Frank out of the plane. His face and hands were seared black. Blood drooled from his nose. An ambulance arrived, siren whooping. Amanda climbed in beside Frank and they raced for the nearest hospital while an intern gave him oxygen and monitored his vital signs.

"He's not going to die!" Amanda said.

"If he makes it, I'm going to hire you as my full-time fortune teller," the intern said.

Frank was conscious. He stared dazedly at her. "What are you doing here?"

"You almost crashed in my garden," Amanda said.

"Tell Buzz it was the propeller. I knew those counter-rotating propellers were a bad idea—"

"Damn the propellers. Concentrate on staying alive," Amanda said.

Frank feebly shook his head. "My mother was right. Death machine. That's what she called it the first time she saw a plane."

"Damn your mother too," Amanda said. "You're not going to die!"

Frank managed a feeble smile. "There's something—I want to tell you. I—never stopped loving you. Your brother forced me to—write that letter. He had a film of me—Buzz—we were all naked—a drunken party. I was ashamed—afraid it would hurt you—"

"I don't care," Amanda said, barely listening. "It's ancient history. You're not going to die."

She sensed, she knew, death was loose in Frank's soul, a huge black spider clutching him with multiple legs. She had to slay the creature.

At the hospital, they rushed Frank to the operating room. Buzz McCall and Adrian and others from the company soon joined Amanda. Gradually, she absorbed what Frank had told her in the ambulance. She looked at Adrian with a new, almost visible loathing. He must have been in the conspiracy. He must have known about Gordon's scheme.

Late in the afternoon, a grim-faced doctor in an operating-room gown gave them a gloomy prognosis. "His skull is fractured, his chest is crushed, both legs are broken, his pelvis is smashed. I'll be amazed if he lives until morning."

"He's not going to die," Amanda said.

The look Adrian gave her was loaded with suspicion and dislike. Buzz McCall and others were obviously curious about her passionate concern. She did not try to explain it away. "I want to see him," she said.

"I don't think that would be wise," the doctor said. "He's hanging on by a thread. Any disturbance—"

"I'm not a disturbance. I'm a friend. I will only stay ten seconds. I want to tell him something—that could save him."

"Is this some religious thing?" the doctor said.

"Yes."

"All right. Ten seconds," the doctor said, while Adrian glared.

Amanda stood beside the bed, trembling. Frank was a virtual mummy, his burned face, including his eyes, swathed in bandages, his chest encased in a cast. Instinctively she seized his hand. He groaned with pain. "Morphine," he said. "Please give me some more. I won't bother you much longer. The pain—"

"Frank," she said. "It's Amanda. I promise you, somewhere, somehow, we'll love each other again."

"Amanda," he said, half-sob, half-sigh.

Come war or Adrian's hatred or even the loss of Victoria, Amanda vowed she would create Eden with this man. They would find it somewhere in their California.

THE GREAT GAME II

Beryl Suydam stood beside Adrian in his office overlooking Buchanan's airfield as a green two-engined light bomber emerged from the factory. Adrian had christened it the *Nelson* in honor of the famous admiral who presided over Picadilly Square on his soot-blackened pillar. "Such a beautiful plane, Adrian," she said. "I can't wait to fly the Atlantic in it."

"I can't wait either," he said. "I have reservations at the most beautiful hotel in California."

"That other plane—the pursuit plane Frank Buchanan is working on—that's the one I'd *really* like to fly."

"We should have a test model ready in about six months."

"Marvelous," Beryl said. "Another excuse to come back. I've changed my mind about America. It makes me almost ashamed of the way we broke up."

"We were both young."

Was the contrition in her silky voice genuine? For the last year Adrian had tried to enjoy a different kind of satisfaction in his meetings with Beryl—the pleasure of deceiving a woman, of accepting her open arms, her inviting thighs, while inwardly a secret sharer laughed coldly. But it had not worked as well as he expected. Instead of a new dimension of power and pleasure, he was constantly listening, looking, for signs of genuine affection.

"I begin to think you Americans may be the hope of the world. With all your vulgarity, your materialism, there's an underlying honesty I find moving. Compared to the cynicism of certain other countries."

She was talking about her great disillusionment. In August 1939, just as the impending war canceled Beryl's plans for her around-the-world flight, Joseph Stalin signed a nonaggression pact with Adolf Hitler, enabling the German dictator to invade Poland and start his war with France and Britain with impunity.

The shock had left fellow travelers and worshipers of the future Soviet style numb. In an outburst of patriotism, many like Beryl joined the war effort. She was in California to ferry one of the new bombers to Britain.

"Americans can be cynical too," he said.

"Are you telling me to stop trying to save the world?"

"Perhaps. Just concentrate on saving me."

"Where is this wonderful hotel?"

"You'll see. I'll pick you up at the Beverly Wilshire at four o'clock."

Beryl departed and within five minutes she was replaced by a twitchy, suspicious Colonel George Knightly, Adrian's original RAF contact, who was at the plant supervising the delivery of the Nelson bombers. With him was the man in charge of British propaganda in California, Adrian's old friend, Prince Carlo Pontecorvo.

"I think she's changed sides," Adrian said.

"She's got some doubts, no question of that. But she's still sending dear Sergei anything she can lay her hands on," Knightly said.

"Are you sure?"

"I only know what the intelligence boys tell me, old chap. I urge you—indeed beg you—not to lose your head."

"Don't worry," Adrian snapped.

"We have two RAF pilots in town who flew against the Germans in Norway," Ponty said. "Good copy. Can you line up some press coverage for them?"

"I'll talk to our publicity director. Tell them to call his assistant, Tama Morris."

"These blokes will do more than call her, if they get a look at her. Whew!" Knightly said. "Is she as free with that stuff as I hear?"

"I wouldn't know. I don't ask that sort of question," Adrian said. The memory of his humiliation at the air ministry made it hard for him to be polite to Knightly.

"Of course," Knightly said, dropping his pilot's persona for his British officer's decorum. "I just thought she could prove useful in certain situations, depending on her—er—willingness."

"I'm inclined to reserve that willingness for the greater glory of Buchanan Aircraft, thank you."

"Perhaps we should ask the lady herself?" Ponty said, with a smile. "Or have you staked out a personal claim there too, Adrian?"

"Not at the moment," Adrian said, struggling to regain his savoir faire.

Knightly departed. Ponty stayed to discuss a dinner he had persuaded Adrian to sponsor at which speakers were to call for repeal of the neutrality act so the United States could directly assist England. These legislative fits of pacifist hysteria had been signed into law by President Roosevelt before war exploded across the globe. Adrian found FDR badly lacking in forethought—a crucial requirement for presidential leadership.

There were times when Ponty acted as if Buchanan Aircraft was a department of his British propaganda machine. In spite of the finesse with which his old schoolmate handled such matters, Adrian was American enough to dislike the assumption that they were at His Majesty's service every time Ponty crooked a finger. His affair with Beryl inevitably sharpened this conflict.

Adrian was a tangle of emotions when he picked up Beryl at the Beverly Wilshire Hotel. With the Pacific rumbling and splashing almost beneath their wheels, they drove down Route 101A to the pink stucco La Valencia Hotel in La Jolla. The inner courtyard was full of fresh flowers in February. Their room looked down on La Jolla cove, one of the loveliest seascapes in California. The Pacific rushed against jagged rocks and cliffs. Beyond the cove, white beaches stretched north and south. La V, as everyone called the hotel, was where Hollywood's stars and directors and producers took their illicit loves.

They ate in the dining room overlooking the ocean. A full moon bathed the sea in golden light. Later, as they made love, Adrian found himself loathing the secret sharer who mocked their passionate charade. "I love you," he whispered, and meant it for the first time since their reunion night in London.

"I love you too, dearest dearest Adrian."

She meant it. As a man who had spent a great deal of time reading nuances of tone and emotion in women's voices, Adrian was sure he had just heard the real thing. "Let's put aside the masks," he said.

"Masks? What mask? Are you wearing one?"

Beryl's elbows were against his chest. She was suddenly a sharp object, even a dangerous one. "Has someone been telling you vicious lies about me? Your friend Mr. Churchill for instance? He's never forgiven me for my part in the Oxford Oath."

"Nothing of the sort," Adrian said. "I meant—you as a famous flier, me as an aircraft tycoon. I wish we could reach—some new depth. Something that blends the past and the present."

He was babbling but it had an unexpected impact on Beryl. She trembled, her elbows withdrew. She pressed herself against him. "Oh Adrian. I wish—I wish that were possible."

"Why isn't it?" he said.

"Dear dear Adrian." She spread herself on top him. "I love your awful American need for sincerity."

"Why is it awful?"

"Because the world has gotten on without it for centuries."

"I'll accept your insufferable condescension—in the name of love."

"Oh do, do. Wait for me. Be patient. I'll come. Someday, somehow, I'll come to you the way I was that night at Ravenswood. Hoping, wanting to believe in your indestructible American optimism."

For one of the few times in his life, Adrian lost his self-control. "You don't love Sergei?"

The silence was thunderous. He lay there watching her make the connections. She began to weep. "How long have you known?" she said.

"Knightly told me yesterday," Adrian lied. He cradled her in his arms and offered her more sincerity to mock. "I'll wait and wait and wait."

They drove back the next morning in the sunrise. Adrian was ready to believe the spectacular red-and-gold sky was being displayed only for them, old-new lovers on the brink of profound happiness. He felt triumphant, a conqueror of both women and politics, a master of the great game on his own terms. He was stealing a spy from the Russians, rescuing a patriot for the British-American alliance.

He dropped Beryl at the Beverly Wilshire and drove to the factory. Tama Morris was in his office, smiling slyly. "Where the hell was Beryl Suydam last night?" she said. "I had three reporters desperate to interview her."

"I have no idea."

"The doorman at the Wilshire said she was picked up by a balding guy driving a Cadillac."

"She'll be here soon. She's taking off at noon."

"That's what I told them," Tama said. "I just wanted to make sure the takeoff might not be delayed for a week or two."

"Patriotism before passion, that's my motto. But don't quote me," Adrian said, smiling. He found himself liking the idea of Tama knowing he had a secret sex life.

Beryl had already checked out the Nelson and flown it a half-dozen times. She stood beside the huge three-bladed propeller on the left motor and talked to the reporters about a woman's desire to help her country in a time of crisis. She had changed her mind about the war, she said. "I'm changing my mind about a lot of things. I attribute some of it to my seeing America, seeing democracy and freedom in the flesh, here."

Adrian smiled and kissed her on the cheek. He posed for a picture with his arm around her. Beryl waved good-bye and climbed into the plane. The big propellers turned, she taxied out and took off for the thousand-mile flight to the airfield in North Dakota, where the plane would be towed across the Canadian border. The field was a dangerous destination in February and Adrian found himself suddenly anxious for Beryl.

Sleep was impossible for him that night. He called the airport in North Dakota and was told it was snowing heavily and Beryl Suydam had not yet arrived. Two hours later, she still had not arrived. Premonition swelled to dread. Four hours later, Beryl still had not arrived and was now considered overdue.

The next afternoon, a TWA pilot flying a SkyRanger II reported seeing the wreckage of a green bomber on the slopes of one of the Sierras. It took a rescue team two days to reach the plane and radio back that Beryl Suydam, the queen of British airwomen, was dead. The cause? A faulty altimeter. The instrument had told her she was flying at twenty thousand feet when she was actually at twelve thousand—and the mountain was eighteen thousand feet.

Adrian had every altimeter in Buchanan Aircraft tested. All worked perfectly.

Why had this one failed? He summoned production chief Buzz McCall to his office and asked him. "How the hell do I know?" Buzz said.

Buzz could have done it. He had killed twenty-three pilots on the western front in World War I. Adrian had heard him boast about strafing German trenches. If a British agent came to Buzz and said it was time to dispose of Beryl, Buzz would have simply nodded and agreed to maladjust the altimeter.

A sleepless night later, Ponty visited Adrian's office to ask Buchanan Aircraft to stage a memorial service for Beryl. "Go to hell," Adrian said. "Hold it at the British consulate in San Francisco."

Ponty sighed. "This is the last favor I will ask, Adrian. I'm flying back to England next week to help organize underground resistance in France and Italy."

"Did you have anything to do with fixing that altimeter?" Adrian said.

"My old friend," Ponty said. "I am not, strictly speaking, a member of British intelligence. But I understand certain things. Walls have ears. For those who play the great game, they have always had that peculiar quality—but now electronics makes the most private moments audible."

"It wasn't necessary! She was ready to change sides!"

Ponty lit a cigarette and looked out the window at a half-dozen new bombers waiting to be flown to North Dakota. "Adrian—surely you must know this arrangement between us and the Russians is a marriage of convenience that won't survive the war, presuming we win it. They are enemies of all the things we value. You and I can't really estimate what Sergei might mean to us in twenty years. You were wrong to sacrifice him. Wrong to place your personal desire ahead of history's imperatives."

Ponty put his hand on Adrian's shoulder. "Yet I understand, old friend. I understand why you did it. She was very beautiful."

Adrian wept. For Beryl and the self he had chosen to become, the boy, the man who vowed to learn history's lessons, to play by rules that only the powerful understood. "We'll stage—we'll hold the memorial service," he said.

To Adrian's surprise, Amanda offered to go to the service with him. As the British consul and a half-dozen British film stars praised Beryl's courage and patriotism, Adrian sat in a cockpit of private sorrow. Through the window he peered at his wife. Should he try to persuade her to love him again?

To his amazement, Amanda seemed to be thinking similar thoughts. That night as they were going to bed, she put her arms around him. "Adrian," she said. "I can see how much she meant to you. She was a woman you loved in England, I'm sure of it. She talked you into building those bombers. I know you're not religious and neither am I in the ordinary sense. But I do believe in the great precepts. The wages of sin is death. Doesn't this prove it?"

"I don't think it proves anything of the sort," Adrian said.

"Perhaps not. But I thought we might try to love each other again. All you have to do is tell me you won't build another warplane."

"I'm afraid I can't do that," Adrian said.

In a world already half engulfed by war, this naive woman was telling him to abandon the great game. Adrian vowed to go on playing it, to accumulate enough power and wealth to bar *ruined* from his soul, no matter what it cost him.

"I knew that would be your answer," Amanda said. "I had to ask the question."

For a moment Adrian sensed he was losing something precious—a chance to regain that youthful mixture of idealism and pity and desire that had drawn him to Amanda. So be it, he told himself. He was too absorbed by his grief and his determination to stay in the great game to wonder why his wife felt compelled to give him one last chance to love her.

AT WAR IN EDEN

On the third day of the year 1941, Amanda Van Ness put her nine-year-old daughter Victoria on the school bus and drove to Santa Monica Hospital to take Frank Buchanan home to his house in Topanga Canyon. He had made an amazing recovery from his injuries. Within a week of the crash, he was sitting up in bed reworking the Nelson bomber's design to give it the speed the British wanted without the extra propellers that had almost killed him.

The doctors warned him not to go to work for at least six months. Buzz McCall arranged for the work to come to Frank. Buchanan Aircraft was competing for dozens of contracts from the U.S. Army and Navy for every imaginable kind of plane. Congress, prodded by Franklin Roosevelt, had begun rearming the United States to deal with a world in which German power might be awesomely dominant.

For Amanda this only meant a renewed commitment to America First. Frank remained equally committed to keeping America neutral. He told Amanda that the planes he was designing would prevent a war because no one would dare to attack a strong United States. Amanda listened without argument, waiting for a sign that Frank was ready to respond to her declaration of love.

Frank was sitting on his hospital bed, dressed and smiling. Skin grafts had repaired most of the burn damage to his face and hands. His only disability was a limp. His right leg, which had been badly shattered, was still weak. He leaned on Amanda's arm as they walked to the parking lot. The temperature was in the seventies. The sun poured down and Amanda felt something—a voice or a single string of an instrument—begin to vibrate within her.

Frank was so quiet. He barely spoke as they drove through a changing landscape. People were surging into California by the tens of thousands. Clusters of houses were springing up on every other hillside. "From what I hear, half of them are probably working for you," Amanda said.

"Buzz told me they hired another thousand men last week," Frank said. "They're buying up all the houses on about four square blocks to expand the factory. Adrian predicts we'll go over ten thousand by the end of the year."

"He adores it," Amanda said. "I've never seen him so happy."

In a half hour they were winding through the green stillness in Topanga Canyon. There were no crowds of newcomers here; only a scattered handful of "settlers," as they liked to call themselves. In Topanga, Amanda could still imagine early California. That was another reason for the singing in her soul. Topanga was a place where Eden could be recaptured.

Up the steep road to Frank's house she climbed in second gear. "I've gotten experienced," she said. "A few more times and I'll apply for my pilot's license."

Frank nodded, smiling in an inward way that deepened the singing voice within her. Sunlight poured through the leaves of the sycamores surrounding the house. Inside, Frank stared in bewilderment. The place was immaculate. Books had been put on shelves, the bed was made, the closets were full of clean sheets and pillowcases. The floor had acquired flowery rugs. A painting, a Matisse-like view of sailboats off Santa Monica, hung on the bedroom wall.

"You did this?" Frank said.

Amanda nodded. "You're going to keep it this way. There's no reason in the world why a man without a woman has to live like an ape. What would you like to eat?"

"Waffles," Frank said. "Waffles and ice cream. I've been dreaming of waffles and ice cream ever since I woke up in that hospital room."

"Is that all you dreamt about?"

"No. I had a very strange dream, the first day. A beautiful woman stood beside the bed and promised to love me."

"That was unquestionably delirium," Amanda said. "There were no beautiful women in your room that day."

"Yes there was."

They stood there in the sunny stillness. The living room window was long and wide. They had left the door open. More sunlight, full of birdsong, wreathed them. "Oh my darling," Frank said. "Did you mean it? Or were you just trying to keep a wreck alive for pity's sake?"

"Would I be here if I didn't mean it?"

They were standing a dozen feet apart, speaking through the shafts of sunlight.

"What about Adrian? Victoria?" Frank said.

"Damn Adrian. He's a greedy swine who doesn't know the meaning of the word love. Victoria will be a woman someday. She'll understand."

The telephone rang. They stood there while the clang shattered the sunlight, the birdsong, the singing in Amanda's soul. Frank picked it up. "Velly solly," he said, "Missa Boocannon no here. This Chinee man who clean up slop. Missa Boocannon come in from hospital and go out again. I tell him to call you. Missa Van Ness? I write down chop chop."

He hung up and stood there, smiling. Amanda walked through the sunlight into his arms. A wind swept through the sycamores. The world shimmered. Amanda saw sunlight breaking, exploding into great globules of vanilla light.

She swam up a milky river of hope and wish to Frank Buchanan's arms.

She wept when she saw the purple patches of grafted skin on his chest. "I don't want you to fly again. Ever," she said.

He promised her no such thing, of course. He presumed it was wish, not reality, she was invoking. "Only with you beside me," he said.

They lay on the sunny bed for a long time, savoring the moment, touching only hands at first, then hair, then tongues, lips. Then kisses, deeper and deeper and longer and longer, kisses and caresses drawing her out of her self into a new dimension. It was totally different from Adrian, the only other man she had known. Adrian could not escape his knowing self, his awareness of his performance. "Do you like that?" he would ask. He wanted applause!

Frank wanted nothing but Amanda. He wanted what Amanda gave him and gave Amanda what she wanted from him without words, without hesitations and questions and egotism. There were no selves, no divisions in the pool of light in which they swam, only a blinding oneness that annihilated thought and fear and responsibility. Adrian and Victoria and her mother and father and even her dream of world peace vanished. She was Frank and Frank was Amanda and simultaneously they had ceased to exist. They had become memories, rumors, beings beyond time.

Still her body spoke and acted and his body responded. Hands and tongues and lips and hair and legs and thighs touched and white fire leaped within the pool of light like voices singing against a full orchestra. Amanda prayed for a child. It would be a savior, a saint. She was losing faith in Victoria, who reminded her of Adrian in too many ways, especially her willfulness.

The rational mind can explain this ecstasy, of course. Two people with a grudge against a third, two believers in love, two souls who had challenged death and won, two rebels against respectability and convention and habit. A lonely bachelor and a repressed, neglected wife. Tristan and Isolde reunited in spite of treachery and betrayal. Eden regained by an act of will, a surge of faith.

The analytic mind is a wonderful thing. But its logic cannot—in fact, must not—explain away what happened to Frank and Amanda in Topanga Canyon on January 3, 1941. Nor can the mind, if it feeds data into its brain cells for a million years, reproduce that wonder.

Finally there was consummation. A light richer and milkier than sunlight engulfed them. A golden light, shot through with shards of diamonds. As Frank's life, his self, his being leaped in her, Amanda broke the silence with his name. *Frank*. The word named everything in the known world. Happiness and unhappiness, victory and defeat, hope and despair. It embodied light and dark and warmth and cold and wealth and poverty. *Frank*. Everything was possible within the compass of those five ordinary letters.

They lay there, folded in the golden light, in each other's arms, for hours. They only spoke in fragments. Love. Life. Forever. Then Frank began to laugh. At first Amanda was shocked, almost frightened by the violence pouring out of his big chest until she realized what it meant. He was laughing at everything.

At death, at Adrian, at Buzz McCall, at Adolf Hitler and Franklin D. Roosevelt. At the newcomers in their ugly houses on the hillsides.

He was Eden, California, laughing in its golden light at the rest of the world. She joined him, laughing, touching, kissing, laughing, weeping finally, both of them, weeping and licking away the salt tears. That was how the wonder ended, salty.

"Believe it or not," Frank whispered. "There's an earthbound part of me that has somehow survived annihilation and still wants those waffles and ice cream."

"With champagne?"

"Is there any in the house?"

"The refrigerator is full of it."

Frank opened a bottle while Amanda cooked the waffles. As they sat down and clinked glasses, the telephone rang again. Frank answered it and went into his Chinese routine. "No Missa Ran Ness. Missa Boocannon not here. But he come in and I tell him you called. He go out again and say he come to factory chop chop."

"You're not really going," Amanda said as Frank hung up.

"They're having all sorts of problems with the pursuit plane we're building for the army. It killed one of our best test pilots yesterday."

They ate the waffles and drank the champagne in silence. Light drained from the room. A colder wind sighed through the trees. Amanda saw she had loved without conditions and now could not impose them. This man designed planes for a living. Could she expect him to stop doing it because they had lived in Eden for a day? The best she could ask was a future of visits to Eden. She tried not to think of that as a diminution, a pollution of the golden light. But it was hard. Suddenly all she could remember was the salt taste of tears on her lips.

Eden remained Eden for the next few months. But other realities revealed a dismaying persistence, an indifference to the way the world had been transformed. Franklin Roosevelt continued to nudge America toward war. Adrian was his ally. He talked, thought, ate, breathed war and warplanes. That made Amanda redouble her struggle against the war. Scarcely a day passed without a rally, a seminar, a letter-writing campaign to congressmen. All diminishments of Eden.

Intensifying her anguish was the awareness that it was a losing struggle. Radio broadcasts and news films dramatized the merciless German bombing of London and Coventry and Liverpool, arousing sympathy for the British. Their local propaganda, often generated from the offices of Buchanan Aircraft, was relentless.

Frank began to drift away from his commitment to peace. The pressure of work was enormous. They had built a new wind tunnel at the factory, the largest in America, and it was teaching him all sorts of fascinating things about airflow's effect on a plane's speed and stability. Another enemy to Eden.

Occasionally Frank deserted his wind tunnel and his designs to go to America

First rallies, ignoring a directive from Adrian that forbade anyone in the company to support what he now called a subversive organization. But Amanda could see Frank's mind was dividing on the subject of peace or war. Germany's brutal use of airpower had aroused his male blood. He wanted to build planes that would enable America to strike back with the same savagery if Germany attacked us.

Another enemy to Eden, where division, disagreement, was intolerable, where a single string untuned could turn the singing into wails of regret. Still they met there on sunlit mornings and afternoons. Never at night. Amanda had acquired a dislike of making love at night. She blamed it on Adrian, who would never dream of taking the time to do anything during daylight hours but make money.

Adrian, unaware of Eden, remained maddeningly unpredictable. He was growing richer and more powerful each day and he wanted to share it with her and Victoria. They moved to a fifteen-room Tudor house in Bel Air, one of the most expensive sections of Los Angeles. They began going to dinner parties with wealthy descendants of the scoundrels who had looted California until her father and other honest men broke their political power in 1910.

More enemies of Eden. Amanda was barely polite to them. She tried to maintain a similar surface politeness with Adrian. But that was not easy. After a party, Adrian was sometimes amorous. She could not always refuse him. He was playing the patient, generous husband.

Almost instantly she saw it was a mistake. She had not realized how central her body was to the experience of Eden. She had attributed the ecstasy to California's sunlight, to Topanga's stillness, to Frank's lovemaking skill. She had to complete the performance with Adrian although her flesh shriveled at every touch.

"Is this the way it's going to be for the rest of our lives?" Adrian said when it was over. "Are you ever going to stop sitting in judgment on me?"

Amanda almost confessed Frank, Eden. But she realized Adrian would never tolerate it. She saw how dangerously she was living. She was trapped between Adrian and Frank. She was at war with herself in Eden.

The big war spread across another quarter of the globe when Germany attacked Russia. The newspapers, the radio, grew frenzied with it. Roosevelt flourished a map before Congress, reputedly proof that Germany planned to invade South America next. Amanda felt war rising like a scummy, frothy flood, its sickening surface lapping at the gates of Eden. America First announced another poll still showed 80 percent of Americans wanted to stay out of it. Buchanan Aircraft's Nelson bombers flew in droves to North Dakota to be towed across the border into Canada. Adrian came home to report that he had just signed a contract to produce Boeing's B-17 Flying Fortresses, a program that would virtually double Buchanan's workforce.

So they came to a sunny Sunday in December. Adrian was in Washington, D.C. to work out the final details of the B-17 contract. Victoria was at home with the housekeeper and a half-dozen friends, giving a pool party. Eden had never been milkier, more full of golden light. For a while Amanda forgot the carnage swirling around them.

Afterward, as they consumed their ritual waffles and champagne, Frank said: "I'm beginning to think we may stay out of this war after all. Even if the Germans eventually beat the Russians, they won't have the strength or inclination to attack anyone for a decade. By that time we'll be strong enough to maul them if they come our way."

"Last week Adrian predicted we'd be at war with the Germans and the Japanese before Christmas."

"The Japanese?" Frank said. "We're negotiating with them. I don't think they want a war with us. They're using themselves up in China, like the Germans in Russia."

Hope, love, his yearning for peace, were so visible on Frank's face, Amanda reached out to touch it. Never had she felt more whole, more certain that her life was complete.

The telephone rang. Was it Adrian? No, he was in Washington. But it probably was someone else from Buchanan, invading Eden with a problem in the design or engineering departments. Amanda brooded. She considered demanding the removal of that telephone.

Frank was on the phone. But he was not doing his Chinese houseboy routine. He was not doing anything. He was standing with the telephone clutched against his ear as if he had been turned into stone.

"Fly as many planes as possible to smaller airports!" he shouted. "Get all our design and engineering papers underground, as deep as possible. Bury them in a ditch if necessary. Stop the production line and send everyone home for twenty-four hours. We have to assume we're a primary target."

He put down the telephone and blinked into the sunlight. "Adrian was right," he said. "The Japanese bombed Pearl Harbor this morning. They sank most of our battleships. Maybe now our dimwit admirals and generals will start believing in air power."

War was in Frank's voice. Rage and revenge and death was in his name. The five letters no longer named everything beautiful in the world. Frank was part of the ugly flood that was swirling through Eden with all war's flotsam, gouged bodies and smashed homes and shattered planes.

Now Amanda knew what her mother had felt twenty-five years ago. She understood the undertow that had dragged her down into madness. It was not weak genes, as her vile brother Gordon claimed. It was the destruction of Eden. It made a woman welcome the obliteration of her mind, her memory.

"Don't," Frank said, trying to brush the tears from her cheeks. "I know how much this means to you—"

"It's the end of this. The end of us."

"Hitler, Tojo, Mussolini—all of them together can't do that."

Amanda shook her head. "The war will change everything. It won't be the same country. It won't be the same California."

"But we'll be the same."

"No. You've already changed. I'll change too."

"Maybe we won't see each other so often. But why should we stop loving each other?"

"The love won't stop. It will always be there. But we'll stop living in it the way we have this year."

"If I have anything to say about it, that won't happen."

Amanda watched him fling on clothes for the trip to the factory. "It's happening already," she said.

BOOK FOUR

THE YANK AND THE SKYLARK

"Geoffrey!" Sarah Chapman said, as the tall airman in his bomber jacket strode past her.

Geoffrey Archer squinted into the spring sunlight, simultaneously managing to look past Sarah—or through her—across the runways of RAF Bedlington. Geoffrey was what Sarah and her friends at St. Agatha's School called a Profile. Deep-socketed eyes that suggested haunted thoughts of lost love or suppressed sexual desires, a resolute mouth that intimated a readiness to face death with dauntless courage. (Romantic mush, but that was the way seventeen-year-olds thought in 1943.) At a dance at the Grantham Country Club for the pilots of the nearby air-base where he was training, Geoffrey had been Sarah's constant partner. Only when the band cut loose with a boogie-woogie beat did he abandon her—explaining that he detested American dancing. Sarah liked to jitterbug but she meekly agreed with his condemnation and sat out the jive, watching her friend Felicity Kingswood swirling her skirts to mid-thigh on the floor with a peppery Welshman.

At the end of the night, as they stood on the terrace drinking punch, Sarah had told Geoffrey a secret she had withheld even from her parents. She was planning to join the Woman's Auxiliary Air Force when she graduated from St. Agatha's next month. "The WAAFs are an absolutely rotten idea," Geoffrey said. "My brother says they do nothing but muck up procedures wherever they go."

Stunned and angry, Sarah had said good night to Geoffrey without a kiss and conferred with her friend Felicity, who downgraded Geoffrey from a Profile to a Poltroon. Now here they were, face to face again nine months later.

"Oh—hello," Geoffrey said.

"I didn't take your advice about the WAAFs, as you can see," she said, gesturing to her crinkly new uniform.

161

"Too bad," Geoffrey said. "Everything I've seen so far here at Bedlington has only convinced me my brother was right. You'd be doing much more for the war effort working in a factory or nursing in an army hospital."

Off he went into the sunshine, leaving Sarah in a stew of embarrassment and fury. She had been at Bedlington exactly one week and so far she had found very little that pleased her. Most of the pilots, those beings she had hero-worshiped since girlhood, seemed to share Geoffrey's opinion of WAAFs. Their aircrews and the ground officers at Bedlington were not much better.

Things had started going wrong the first day, when Sarah made the mistake of strolling in the front door of the former guardhouse that had been converted into the Waafery—their headquarters building where the CO and officers lived. The CO, who looked like the Queen Mum having a permanent tantrum, had excoriated her for such a breach of etiquette. Mere privates used the back door, as befitted servants. Imbued with a healthy detestation of England's class system thanks to her father and one or two radical teachers at St. Agatha's, Sarah had almost strangled with rage.

Worse, the so-called officers of the WAAF administrative staff were so foggy, they did not even know what an RTO—radio telephone operator—was. One suggested they go to the orderly room and learn to read timetables and absorb other information necessary to train railway transport officers.

Sarah and Felicity and three others were the first RTOs to reach Bedlington, and everyone, male and female, seemed baffled by their appearance. Someone finally sent them out to the Watch Office, a square box-like building on the edge of the airfield's perimeter where male RTOs talked to incoming planes over upright microphones. An officer wearing the rings of a squadron leader on his sleeve hemmed and hawed and confessed no one had warned him of their arrival. He suggested they take a weekend pass while he figured out what to do with them.

On fourteen shillings every two weeks, none of them had the train or bus fare to go home—if they had the desire. Like Sarah, most of them had spent exhausting months convincing their parents to sign the waiver that permitted them to join up and they did not want to face inevitable interrogation and admit even a moment's disillusion.

Now Geoffrey Archer's epitome of male condescension! Steam all but flowing from her ears, Sarah stormed back to their brick hut filled with facing rows of iron beds and told Felicity about the latest insult. "Let's show the bastards we know where the grass is greener," Felicity said. "The Yanks are having a dance at Rackreath. They're sending over a bus to the village at seventeen hundred hours. Get on your war paint."

"Wizzo!" Sarah said, displaying her RAF slang in an ironic mode.

Best blues were pressed and buttons polished with Silvo (rather than Brasso) until they looked like the genuine expensive article. Shoes gleamed; freshly laundered shirts and collars were sacrificed without a murmur. Jane Newhouse was the only one with silk stockings. The rest of them had to tolerate the government's lisle. They all washed and set their hair and combed it just a little longer than the regulation length, so that it curled on their collars and below their ears. Sarah enjoyed the sensation of shaking her head and feeling her dark brown curls swing softly, loose from the ribbon she usually wore.

Finally came the makeup. Beneath her mother's puritanical eye, Sarah had never worn any. Felicity had introduced her to buying theatrical greasepaint for lipstick and eye shadow. It was much cheaper than commercial makeup and looked perfectly natural, if it was used with care. At Jane's suggestion—she was in her twenties and talked a lot about attracting men—Sarah blended a spot of greasepaint along her cheekbone to give her pale skin a bit more color.

A dash of Evening in Paris here and there and they were ready. They gamboled down Green Lane, an old Roman road that ran across the airbase and continued between low hedges and budding trees to the thatched roofs of Woodbastwick village. A tan U.S. Army Air Forces bus was purring on the narrow main street. They joined a dozen women from the village and rode across the wide Norfolk plain, as level and green as the top of a billiard table, past more villages like Woodbastwick full of the timeless tranquillity that inspired visitors to murmur "There'll always be an England." It was hard to believe that across the North Sea were ninety million Germans and their fanatic führer, determined to make that remark an anachronism.

War. Sarah could not quite grasp the horror with which her parents said the word. She knew her mother had lost two brothers in France during the Great War, as the textbooks called it—and her father had been shot down and badly injured in the Royal Flying Corps. But to her this second Great War was still an adventure, a marvelous opportunity to escape her mother's dominating grasp. Besides, they were going to win this time without so much slaughter. The Americans had come into the war early—instead of waiting until the last possible minute, as they had done in 1917. Her mother was quite bitter about the Americans for waiting so long the last time.

Sarah had no such prejudices. Individually, Americans were creatures she had only seen in the movies. Craggy-jawed cowboys in ten-gallon hats who said "howdy" instead of "hello"—or squat gangsters who said "troo" instead of "through"—or wiseguys who called women "Babe." She shared her father's admiration for their industrial and military might. As senior designer for de Havilland Aircraft company, he was awed by the statistics that emanated from Washington, D.C.. "Last month the Americans turned out three thousand planes," he said one night at supper, shortly before she left for the WAAFs. "Three thousand planes!"

That was twice what England could produce in a month. It meant victory was guaranteed. It entitled Sarah to regard her plunge into WAAFdom as an adventure, with no darker overtones. Mother could brood on England's losses, on another generation of broken hearts. She was eighteen and the world was enormously exciting. It teemed with brave men in hurtling planes, defying death and a vicious enemy. She loved them all—at least, she did until she met Geoffrey Archer and the assembled male supremacists and attendant female dodos of RAF Bedlington.

The American dance was in the Rackreath officers' club, in a big darkened room with a bar on one side and a band jammed against the opposite wall. The band was playing Glenn Miller's "In the Mood" with a wild intensity that made Sarah's flesh tingle. The whole room reverberated with the music and a cacophony of voices from the crowd of airmen around the bar. There was a frantic undercurrent to the voices and the jitterbugging couples on the floor. Everyone seemed to be flinging themselves into the party with something very close to frenzy.

There were no introductions, no formalities. The women trickled along the wall and stood shyly waiting for something to happen. It did not take long. The womanless drinkers around the bar stormed toward them in a cheerful, chortling mob. The village girls were snatched onto the floor like slaves off an auction block. It took a little longer to reconnoiter the WAAFs.

"Did anyone ever tell you you've got beautiful eyes?" said a deep confident voice. Sarah gazed up at one of the handsomest man she had ever seen. He was well over six feet with a profile that capitalized the entire word, a tough mouth and thick dark hair combed straight back à la Robert Taylor. "I think my nanny used to whisper that to me in my cradle," Sarah said. "After her, you're the very first."

It was such an obvious come-on, she felt her irony was justified. It was also a way of warding off the impact of his overwhelming maleness. He led her out on the floor before he bothered to introduce himself. "Cliff Morris, California."

She realized he was slightly drunk. That did not disturb her. Hard drinking and planes more or less went together. Her father often came home "snookered," as her mother called it. Her mother did not approve, of course. But her mother approved of very little.

"Sarah Chapman, Sussex," she said. "Are you a pilot?"

"Captain of the *Rainbow Express*," he said. "What are you doing in that uniform?"

"Not much of anything for the moment. But I expect to be talking to pilots like you in a week or so—in the RAF. I'm a radio telephone operator, stationed at Bedlington."

"You may be talking to us too," he said. "A half dozen of our flying wrecks went into Bedlington after the last raid. You're fourteen miles closer to the North Sea. That can make a lot of difference when you're operating on one motor."

Totally unaware of what the Eighth Air Force was experiencing over Germany, Sarah expressed surprise. "The communiques are all so upbeat," she said. "Have your losses been heavy?"

Cliff Morris seemed to hold her a little closer, as if he needed warmth or comfort. "We lost a hundred and sixty-eight planes over Schweinfurt last week. In our bomb group the losses were fifty percent."

"My God. How many missions have you flown?" Sarah asked.

"Sixteen," Cliff said. "We were one of the first to get here. We've had the privilege of learning the hard way."

Sarah felt an enormous surge of sympathy. This man had come six thousand miles—from that state with the exotic name, California—to help fight England's battle. He was talking about the deaths of his friends—his own death—with the calm steady voice of courage.

"My father's a tremendous admirer of your bomber, the B-Seventeen," she said.

"Oh? You should see the list of things I just sent to my father—stepfather, actually—telling him what's wrong with the damn thing."

"Your father's in the aircraft business?"

"He's head of production for Buchanan Aircraft."

"Oh, I say. This is a coincidence. My father's with de Havilland. He often talks of the man who founded Buchanan—was his name Frank?"

"Frank Buchanan's practically my uncle. I've known him since I was six years old. My stepfather started the company with him."

"My father and he worked together before the first war, designing planes for de Havilland."

In the shadowy room, her eyes burning from the cigarette smoke, the brassy music exploding in her ears, surrounded by the swirling swaying bodies of the other dancers, Sarah felt an aura envelop them, a compound of sympathy and fatality and attraction. Cliff Morris's arms crushed her against his broad chest as he talked excitedly about Buchanan Aircraft and its future. Planes were going to change the world after they won the war and Buchanan was going to be among the leaders in designing and making them. Frank Buchanan was a genius who would keep them perpetually ahead of the competition.

Into Sarah's mind flashed a vision of a dynastic marriage in the grand tradition. Her brother Derek would rise to power and fame in de Havilland while Cliff Morris rose to similar heights at Buchanan. She would be the link between them, urging each to greater and greater achievements, to better and better planes to defend the Anglo-American empire and preserve a peaceful world.

Cliff led her across the floor to a table where a half-dozen men were sitting with glasses of liquor in front of them. Five had English girls in their laps, two of them behaving amorously. "Hey, you bums," he said. "I found us a lucky charmer. This girl knows Frank Buchanan. Knows what a great designer he is. Wait'll you see the job he does on our flying coffins after he gets my letter."

He introduced Sarah to the crew of the *Rainbow Express*. They were a blur of names and titles—bombardier, waist gunners, belly gunners—except for two. One was the tail gunner, Mike Shannon. He was distinguished by his diminutive size—and the presence of her friend Felicity in his lap. The other man was the navigator, Dick Stone, who did not have a girl in his lap. Cliff drunkenly insisted Sarah should talk to Stone. "He doesn't think we should be bombing the goddamn Nazis," Cliff said. "Tell him what the bastards did to London."

Sarah did not know much more about what the Germans had done to London than anyone else who read the papers and listened to the radio. "Why don't you think we should be bombing the Huns?" she asked Stone, trying to make a semi-joke of it.

"I don't think anything of the sort," Stone said. He was a swarthy, square-jawed young man with horn-rimmed glasses that gave him a rather scholarly air. "I think we should be bombing them more accurately. To make sure we aren't killing women and children—or destroying irreplaceable cultural treasures. I'm all for bombing military targets."

"Isn't that what everyone bombs?" Sarah said.

"Miss Chapman—I don't want to upset you—but the British in my opinion are becoming mass murderers on a scale infinitely beyond Hitler's Luftwaffe. Your night raids on German cities don't have even a pretense of attacking military targets. They're terror bombing, pure and simple—or should I say impure and simply horrifying?"

Sarah was simultaneously angry and bewildered. It was the first time she had ever heard anyone connect morality and airplanes. Heretofore planes existed in a world beyond morality, the transcendent universe of the sky. They were an escape from the trivial groundling world of shoulds and shouldn'ts that her mother was perpetually invoking. She knew planes could be as maddening as an inconstant lover, as dangerous as a loaded gun. But she never thought of them as vessels of morality.

"See what I mean?" Cliff Morris said. "How would you like to have a navigator like this guy? To make it even worse, he's Jewish—you'd think he'd be cheering every bomb we dropped."

"Hitler and his crowd are anti-Semites. But I think the German people's anti-Semitism has been exaggerated," Dick Stone said.

"I'm not qualified to comment on their anti-Semitism," Sarah said. "But I think your opinion of the RAF should be reconsidered, Mr. Stone. I might even say the same about your comments on the Eighth Air Force. Captain Morris has told me about your terrible losses."

"Trying to bomb the lousy military targets he says we're missing half the time," Cliff said. "I say so what."

"Okay, okay," Dick Stone said. "I'll reconsider. I may even change my mind if Cliff reads Goethe's *Faust* and tells me how people who can produce that kind of literature should be bombed into extinction."

"I've read Goethe's *Faust*," Sarah said. "It's wonderful poetry, but I don't think the Germans have learned much from it. Wouldn't you say it's a warning against the danger of gaining the whole world and losing your soul?"

"I'd say Faust is a warning against loving a woman too much. A woman who seems to embody the whole world."

Dick Stone said this so softly, so calmly, in a voice that was such a contrast to the shouts and laughs and wisecracks flying around them, for a moment Sarah was ashamed of her reckless attack on him on Cliff Morris's behalf. The man was a *thinker*. At eighteen, she had never contemplated the possibility of a man who shared his thoughts with a woman. Men were like her father, creatures with short tempers, rough jokes, long obscure silences.

They sat down and Cliff poured Sarah a drink from a bottle on the table. It was her first taste of bourbon whiskey. Its sweetness made her think it was an

American version of sherry—which her mother allowed her to sip at her graduation party. Anyway, Mother was a hundred miles away. She was on her own, an adult woman with a grudge against the RAF and an exultant sense of exploring a new world.

There were more dances, more drinks. More discussions with Dick Stone, who still lacked a girl for his lap. Someone explained that Stone had made the idiotic mistake of getting engaged before he left home and he was being faithful to his fiancée. "He's a veritable tower of rectitude," Sarah said, still feeling some of Cliff's hostility to the scholarly navigator.

"A tower of Stone," Cliff said. "Full of bullshit. Come on, Stone, take a drink, at least. I don't like it when I get drunk and you stay sober."

"I have too much respect for my stomach to put that rotgut into it," Stone said.

"The guy's a snob. That's his problem," Cliff said. "He thinks he's better than everybody else. He even thinks he's got a better stomach."

"Maybe it is," Sarah said. "It's made of stone."

"I've got stone feet too," the navigator said. "Want to risk a dance?"

Out on the floor, they swayed to a raucous version of "Don't Get Around Much Anymore." "Are you Jewish?" he said.

"Catholic," Sarah said.

"Ah. That explains your innocent look. You remind me of several very protected Jewish girls I knew in New York."

"Are you engaged to one of them?"

"As a matter of fact, I am. If she was here, I'd give her some advice. Instead I'll give it to you. Go home while the going's good. This party is bound to get wild."

"Leftenant Stone," Sarah said. "You are one of the most—most presumptuous men I've ever met. Why is it bound to get wild?"

"Because we're going back to Schweinfurt the day after tomorrow. A good half the people you see dancing around you won't be here next week."

"That only makes me want to stay! What kind of a shirker do you think I am?"

"I think you're a sweet beautiful girl who should have stayed home with her mother."

"If you knew my mother you wouldn't say that! For your information, Leftenant Stone, women are not going to accept condescension in any form after this war is won. We're helping to win it and we're going to demand respect as our reward!"

They returned to the table and Sarah declared her independence from Lieutenant Stone and his obnoxious advice by demanding another drink of bourbon. The room careened and she was on the dance floor doing a lindy with Cliff Morris. Her skirt was up her around her waist and she was laughing boldly into his handsome face. She felt as if she were in midair, performing a preternatural stunt. In the middle of her laughter she remembered what Dick Stone had told her about Schweinfurt and almost wept. Was it possible? Would half of these laughing young men die in burning planes the day after tomorrow?

Unthinkable. She wanted to be powerful enough to prevent it. Another drink of bourbon and she was sure she possessed some sort of supernatural power. She would bestow it on Cliff, on the *Rainbow Express*, at least. If she could not protect them all she would protect him with her sheltering arms, her bursting heart.

They were outside in the cool spring night. A million stars crowded the incomprehensible sky. Dozens of couples were wandering across Rackreath Air Base, disappearing into the woods and fields that surrounded it. Air bases in England were inserted into the countryside with a view to doing as little damage as possible to existing farmland and orchards. The trees and grass were only a few yards beyond the runways.

"Dick Stone told me you're going back to Schweinfurt the day after to-morrow," Sarah said.

"I don't want to think about it."

"I want you to know I'll be thinking about it. Thinking about you. Praying for you."

"Praying?" Cliff said. "You'll be the only one. My mother stopped going to church when she was six. My old man—my stepfather—never went. How do you pray? I've never even tried."

"You—open your heart to God. You talk to Him."

"If He's there."

"He's there."

"You're the one I want to open my heart to. Can you open yours? I loved you the second I saw you coming in the door. I know that's a crazy thing to say. I know we've only been together a few hours. But when I look at you something like a prayer forms on my lips."

They were on a country lane between more low hedges. A sweet scent of new-mown grass rose from the fields. Nearby was the babble of a Wordsworthian brook. Cliff Morris took Sarah Chapman in his arms and kissed her for a long time. His hands moved slowly up and down her body, along her outer thighs, down her arms, over her breasts. "Say yes, Sarah, please. Say yes so I can get that plane off the ground the day after tomorrow. You can help me do it. With that prayer in your heart."

"Yes, oh yes, Cliff. Yes yes yes."

Off the lane the ground was soft, moist with night dew. Cliff spread his coat on the grass and slowly undressed her, whispering over and over: "You're so beautiful. You're so beautiful."

It was innocent, Sarah told herself. Her heart was overflowing with compassion and pity. This gift of herself, this prayer of herself was the least she could offer this man who was facing violent death on England's behalf. Juliet would have offered herself to Mercutio, Ophelia to Hamlet if the plots had given them the opportunity. It was a Wordsworthian parable for the twentieth century, love among the daffodils beside a babbling brook.

Except for certain things that Wordsworth forgot to mention. The brook at ground level had anything but a sylvan breath. It was probably the sewer for one or several nearby villages. Nor did sweet William or sister Dorothy ever encounter this mass of maleness on top of her blotting out the stars, this tongue plunging into her mouth, until her lungs, her whole body was bursting.

Lawrencian. That forbidden genius whose books were smuggled into St. Agatha's with the risk of expulsion by certain girls who read them between the covers of other books in study hall, their eyes wide with astonishment and glee. Sarah had yearned to be one of the smugglers but all she had done was skim selected passages copied out and passed from hand to trembling hand. Were men that way? Was any woman that way? She simply could not believe it.

Now it was happening here in the Wordsworthian countryside, abandon in the daffodils. In a swift sure thrust Cliff entered her. With a flicker of pain came the flash of awareness that he had done this before; he knew exactly how to lay her down, open her thighs, lunge. Did it mean Dick Stone was right, she should have stayed home with Mother?

Like a daregale skylark scanted in a cage. Poetry was answering that obnoxious question. Her spirit, her heart was the skylark in the cage of home, of Mother's perpetual prohibitions, in the larger cage of St. Agatha's with its frowning nuns and old-maid lay teachers. It was her heart in the cage of her body, her timid heart, partaking now of male courage, from an explorer of the skylark's home, the sky. She was bursting out of the cage of girlhood into womanhood, adulthood, into the word that gave meaning to a woman's life—into love.

Marvelous thoughts but the reality somehow failed to live up to them. The brook's odors assailed her nostrils; Cliff was stroking her with drunken, careless ardor, his weight crushing her into the grass, his mouth against her throat. She tried to let go, to give herself to him, the night, the vanished sky. They were one thing, a kind of plane, soaring into faith and hope and trust—and prayer.

Yes, her prayer for him was on her lips, it flowed into his body. But she did not feel a similar flow from him. She wanted to soar with him, to hurtle beyond earth, beyond Lawrencian orgies into the happiness that belonged exclusively to those who conquered the sky. Nothing else could justify the sin they were committing, the implicit awful condemnation that was always in Mother's eyes when she argued against joining the WAAFs.

Before she could begin to soar Cliff gave a shuddering groan and came—a tremendous gush that lifted her at least to treetop level with a surge of inexplicable sweetness. She cried out with a wild mixture of pleasure and regret. The sky, the stars, remained blank behind his massive shoulders and head.

They spiraled down to the waiting earth. On the other side of the brook there were similar cries and groans of pleasure. Sarah found it somehow disillusioning to realize they were not the only ones in England performing this ancient rite. Earthbound ideas crowded her dazed mind. She had given herself to this man. She had surrendered what she had vowed she would never yield, without the certainty of deep and abiding love.

"What do we do now?" she blurted.

"We do it again," Cliff said. "Again and again and again. Whenever we get a chance."

For a moment Sarah almost wept. There was too much male delectation in those words. They revealed things she did not want to confront. "You do love me?" she said. It was almost a wail.

"Of course I love you. Get dressed. I'll drive you back to Bedlington. We've got a long day tomorrow getting ready for Schweinfurt. And a longer one the day after that."

"You'll be all right. I know you will. I know it!"

"Sure," he said. "Just remember. Be there to pray me down."

"I know you'll be all right!"

She was omnipotent again. Love's goddess, ruling the sky.

RAINBOW EXPRESS

"Grab your cocks and pull up your socks, here we go!" Cliff Morris shouted over the intercom.

Down the rain-slick runway at Rackreath Air Base raced the B–17E with a red, white, and blue rainbow painted below the left cockpit window. She was fighting for airspeed with two tons of bombs in her belly and a ton of high octane gasoline in her fuel tanks. In the pilot's seat, Cliff poured on the power. The four Wright R1820 Cyclone engines responded with a deepening roar. When the airspeed indicator read 110, he gently pulled back on the control column and *Rainbow Express*, all thirty-three tons of her, lumbered into the air for her seventeenth mission over Germany.

"Ain't she beautiful?" Cliff shouted over the intercom.

"She's got my vote," Mike Shannon whooped. He was hunched in his tail gunner's seat, watching the rest of the 103rd Bombardment Group take off behind them. No one else aboard the *Rainbow Express* said a thing. Their morale was as low as the rest of the 103rd, which was as low as the rest of the Eighth Air Force in the spring of 1943.

Below the cockpit, in the Plexiglas nose, navigator Dick Stone hunched over his charts and remembered what Colonel Darwin H. Atwood had said when the 103rd Bombardment Group reported for training at Kearney Air Force Base in Nebraska in mid-1942. "Don't get the notion that your job is going to be glorious or glamorous. You've got dirty work to do and you might as well face the facts. You're going to be baby killers and women killers."

Tall and balding, Colonel Atwood had been a professor of modern history at Stanford before his elevation to rank and power. He seemed to carry history like a burden on his slumped shoulders. An unspoken pain lurked in his squinting eyes. If he did not know better, Stone would have sworn he was Jewish. Atwood knew all about the strategic bombing campaigns of World War I, which had killed hundreds of civilians in Paris, London, and German cities in the Ruhr.

Dick Stone was vulnerable to doubts about bombing German civilians. His paternal grandfather had been a professor of German literature at the City College of New York. Born in Germany, he was one of those Jews who were forever torn between admiration for its culture and dismay at its virulent anti-Semitism. He loved Goethe, Heine, Schiller and insisted on Stone learning German as a boy so he could read them in the original.

The pilots in the 103rd despised Colonel Atwood. For that reason alone Dick Stone was inclined to defend him—or at least take him seriously. Atwood had given some thought to what they were going to do over Germany. As far as Stone could see, none of the pilots had ever had a thought beyond their arrogant affirmation of their flyboy status and the inevitable superiority of the B-17.

Cliff Morris personified the goggles-and-scarf tradition Colonel Atwood struggled in vain to eradicate from the 103rd Bombardment Group. On their first flight Cliff had buzzed the field at fifty feet, missing the tower by inches, according to the terrified traffic controllers. Colonel Atwood threatened Cliff with a court-martial. "I was trying to give my crew some positive leadership," Cliff replied. "It's in short supply around here." When the outraged Atwood reported Morris to the commanding general, nothing happened. Morris's stepfather, a World War I ace, knew bigger generals.

Everyone in the *Rainbow Express*'s ten-man crew except Stone soon worshiped Cliff Morris. He made them feel like fliers. They joined his campaign to outdrink and outscrew every other airman in the Eighth Air Force. Stone went along on their "reconnaissances" in Nebraska and in England but he remained aloofly sober and disdainful of the girls they picked up. He was a rabbi's son and he felt he owed his father moral allegiance, even if he no longer agreed with his theology. Rather than try to explain anything so complicated, he cooked up the fiction of being engaged to silence Cliff Morris and other needlers in the crew.

"Hey, Stone," Cliff said as they reached their prescribed height of 20,000 feet and plowed through the icy sky toward Schweinfurt. "You got Little Miss England so upset with your criticism of the RAF, she couldn't wait to show me how true blue she was."

"What was blue? Once you got rid of her uniform," said Beck, the bombardier, who preferred London prostitutes to nice girls.

"Her eyes, you miserable whoremaster. I didn't have to pay for it either. The old record is still intact."

Cliff was inordinately proud of his ability to seduce women. They all listened while he gave them a condensed version of his line with Sarah Chapman. He always talked about a seduction as if he were a movie director setting up a scene. Dick sighed and wondered what Sarah Chapman thought of it now, two days after she sobered up.

"You should have heard the stuff she babbled on the way back to Bedlington," Cliff said. "Something about a skylark in a gale trapped in a cage. She got so excited we stopped in a lane just outside the base and did it once more for good measure."

"Like a daregale skylark scanted in a cage," Dick Stone said.

"That's it, Shylock. What the hell does it mean?"

"It's from a poem by someone who feels spiritually trapped and discouraged," Dick said.

A groan filled the earphones. "Don't knock it, you fucking atheists. She's gonna pray us back," Cliff said. "We could use some prayers flying this miserable crate."

Back in the States during their training, when Cliff was not talking about girls, he talked about the B-17. Again and again he proclaimed it the best plane ever built. Family pride was partly involved. Buchanan Aircraft was turning out hundreds of the big bombers under a contract from the original maker, Boeing. Cliff had named their bomber after the Buchanan company symbol, a plane soaring over a rainbow.

Now no one, including Cliff Morris, was sure of the B-17's superiority, though he usually tried to disguise his doubts with bravado. On the first few raids over Germany their losses had been light. Everyone assumed the Germans were afraid to attack the Flying Fortresses, with their bristling array of machine guns. Alas, the Luftwaffe was only reorganizing its defenses, which had been devoted to defending the fatherland against British bombers by night. The American decision to bomb in daylight and prove the precision of the Norden bombsight and the invulnerability of the B-17 took the Germans by surprise. But not for long.

Soon the sky above their targets was thick with ugly black bursts of .88 millimeter shells. An .88 could knock out a Sherman tank. When it struck something as fragile as a plane, the results were horrendous. B-17s exploded into fragments, broke in half, spun down with wings or tails gone. Out of the sun hurtled swarms of Focke-Wulf and Messerschmitt fighters firing 20- and 30-millimeter cannons. Formations dissolved. B-17s began burning all over the sky or spinning down with dead pilots and copilots in shattered cockpits. Instead of the eight or ten planes that they had expected to lose on each mission, they started to lose sixty or seventy. Whole squadrons were wiped out.

People with mathematical ability soon estimated that only 34 percent of them would make it through the required tour of twenty-five missions. Colonel Atwood addressed this chilling computation with his usual candor. "I'll give you a little clue on how to fight this war. Make believe you're dead already. The rest will come easy."

On the B-17s plowed in two huge box formations. Below them, Europe was invisible as usual beneath its semi-permanent clouds. The weathermen said the skies would be clear but they had been wrong so often, no one even bothered to curse them anymore.

Dick Stone found himself thinking about Sarah Chapman again. Amazing how poetry could connect people. He still felt linked to his grandfather by certain poems by Goethe and other German writers that the old man had read to him. He identified with that poem by Gerard Manley Hopkins because he too felt trapped in a spiritual cage. In an odd way he also identified with the word *Catholic*, spelled with a small *c*. He could hear his grandfather saying: *catholic, that's what we all must become. That's what America is about, catholicity, diversity yet brotherhood.*

"Any fucking cultural monuments you don't want to hit on this run, Stone?" Cliff asked.

On a recent raid the primary target, Dusseldorf, had been invisible under heavy clouds and they had scattered to bomb secondary targets. Breaking through the overcast to get some idea where they were, the *Rainbow Express* saw a city full of church spires and eighteenth-century houses, with some factories on the outskirts. Dick Stone flipped his maps, did some rapid calculations of their airspeed and course and concluded it was Weimar, where Goethe spent most of his life. He urged Cliff not to bomb it. The place was a living museum. Cliff had bombed it anyway and was still needling him about it.

"Nothing to worry about but women and children," Dick said.

They droned on in subzero boredom for another two hours. Finally, navigator Stone informed Captain Morris they were less than fifteen minutes from Schweinfurt. Below them was a growing number of fleecy cumulus clouds. In ten minutes they began to darken into a gray cumulonimbus blanket. The weathermen were wrong again.

"Bandits at two o'clock!" screamed the top turret gunner, Smithfield. He was coming apart. He started firing his guns when the Germans were at least a mile away, hysterically holding the triggers down, instead of squeezing off three-second bursts. The planes were thick-bodied Focke-Wulfs. They did a barrel roll and came down ready to work on the outer edge of the American formation where the *Rainbow Express* was flying. It was known as the Purple Heart corner.

Smithfield was not the only member of the crew Dick Stone worried about. Cliff Morris was also showing signs of strain. He was getting drunk much too often at the Rackreath officers' club. Already a licensed pilot when the Japs bombed Pearl Harbor, Cliff had a personal motive for seeing action. His stepfather had told him a good war record guaranteed him a job at Buchanan Aircraft. Cliff had converted this promise into guaranteed jobs for all of them. But Cliff had never imagined that winning this pot of gold involved sitting behind a half inch of glass watching Focke-Wulfs closing on him at a combined airspeed of five hundred miles an hour, their wings aflame with machine guns and cannon.

Cliff shoved the *Rainbow Express*'s nose down, putting her into a shallow dive to give top turret gunner Smithfield a better shot at the oncoming Focke-Wulfs. The Germans' wings flickered fire. A slamming tearing sound, then a scream of anguish over the intercom. "Smitty's hit!" shouted the radioman.

"Get up there and man his gun," Cliff said.

The Focke-Wulfs rolled into a dive that brought them beneath the formation for another blast of cannon fire. A new cry of anguish. Dick Stone turned to find bombardier Beck slumped over his bombsight, blood gushing from his mouth. Dick dragged him aside and told Cliff he was going to bomb.

Cliff held the *Rainbow Express* on course while Dick flicked on the rack switches and the intervalvometer switch that controlled the spacing between bomb drops. He peered through the sight at the target area. The clouds were now shrouding Schweinfurt. But the bombers were all too visible on German radar. Up through the clouds hurtled a firestorm of .88 millimeter shells. The blue sky looked as if a madman was flicking gobs of intensely black indigo paint on it.

"*Marvelous Mabel*'s hit," shouted Mike Shannon from the tail. She had been flying directly behind them. A shell had blown off *Mabel*'s wing. As she spun down the leggy blonde on the fuselage below the name seemed to smile up at them. "Not one goddamn parachute," Mike said.

Baby killers and women killers, Dick Stone thought, waiting for a break in the clouds to give him at least a glimpse of their target, ballbearing factories on the outskirts of Schweinfurt.

"Open bomb bay doors," Cliff said. A blast of freezing air swept through the plane. Dick could feel the motors straining against the extra drag.

A tremendous crash. Stone saw flames gushing from the number-two engine. "We're in trouble," Cliff shouted as the *Rainbow Express* lost airspeed. "Get rid of those goddamn bombs. Now."

"I can't see a thing," Dick said.

"I said *bomb!*" Cliff said, pulling the CO_2 switch to douse the fire in the burning engine.

Dick Stone's grandfather—or was it Colonel Atwood—began reciting a poem in Stone's head. It was by the great German Jewish poet, Heinrich Heine, asking his mistress to listen to his breaking heart. He said the hammering sound was a carpenter fashioning a coffin for him. Now the coffin maker was in the sky and Stone's heart was hammering not from love but a berserk mixture of fear and revulsion. What if he refused to press the bomb release?

"Stone, I said *bomb!*" Cliff Morris roared.

Dick pressed the button and the four five-hundred-pound bombs fell from their racks. He pressed a second button that fired a white flare, a signal for the rest of the group to bomb at the same time. God only knew what they were hitting in Schweinfurt.

The B-17 soared up at least a hundred feet without the bomb load. "Let's go home," Cliff said, banking the *Rainbow Express* like a pursuit plane to make the tightest possible turn.

"Bandits at two-three-four-five-six o'clock," screamed the radioman. There were at least two hundred of them and they all seemed to be heading toward the Purple Heart corner. A wave of bullets and shells hurtled into the 103rd Bombardment Group. Tail gunner Mike Shannon shouted reports of B-17s burning and exploding all around them. The *Rainbow Express* shuddered and groaned as she took her share of the bullets and shells.

Shouts from the waist. The radioman was dead, the second top turret gunner to go down. "Shannon, take over those guns," Cliff said. "You're having a goddamn vacation back there."

"Fire in the radio room," shouted one of the waist gunners.

"Number three engine's on fire," cried the copilot who was on his first mission. The regular copilot had been decapitated by a twenty-millimeter shell on their previous outing.

Smoke swirled through the plane. Dick Stone and the waist gunners used handheld extinguishers to snuff out the radio room flames, standing back as far as they could, praying they did not inhale any of the fumes, which were a deadly poison gas, phosgene.

Cliff used the automatic CO^2 in the wing to douse the number-three engine. That left them with only two engines. Their airspeed dropped below two hundred miles an hour. The surviving members of the formation soon passed them. They were alone in the sky with at least a dozen Focke-Wulfs barreling around them.

There were more slamming, tearing, clanking sounds as shells and bullets struck the plane. On the intercom Stone could hear Mike Shannon whooping: "I got one. I got one of the bastards."

A scream of pain erupted from one of the waist gunners. Stone realized it was only a matter of minutes before they went down. The rest of the bombardment group was on the way back to England, leaving the crippled *Rainbow Express* behind. The other planes were only obeying orders. There was no way to help a cripple. It was survival of the fittest up here in the enemy skies. Stone felt the detachment he had struggled to achieve under Colonel Atwood's tutelage slipping from his mind's grasp. Bombardier Beck's blood oozed from his dead body in a half dozen dark rivulets.

Death. He was going to die like Beck. He was going to turn into inert flotsam in history's stream. Garbage. Dust. Nothingness. Before he understood what life, history, America, Jewishness really meant. A terrible cry of rage, of pain, almost burst from his lips.

Did Cliff Morris, in the cockpit of the *Rainbow Express,* know this? Or was it only Cliff's hand that knew what Stone was thinking and feeling, what everyone was thinking and feeling in the belly of the *Rainbow Express*? Was the hand protesting that mutual terror, that common dread as it reached for the switch that released the landing gear? Then and for years to come Dick preferred to think of it as an involuntary thing, as impersonal as one of the motor's throbbing pistons. Somehow that made it easier to accept.

Thunk. The wheels came down and the *Rainbow Express* almost fell out of the sky as her airspeed faltered with the sudden increase in drag. Did Cliff know what his hand was doing? Dick wondered. Lowering your wheels in enemy skies meant you were surrendering. You were agreeing to fly your plane to the nearest German airfield.

No one in the 103rd Bombardment Group had done this. But planes in other groups had done it. The Germans had captured enough B-17s to fly some into formations and cause chaos by opening fire just as the Americans were starting to bomb.

"What the hell's happening?" the copilot said.

"Shut up," Cliff Morris said.

"Like hell I'll shut up," the copilot said. "We've still got two engines and plenty of ammunition. Why the hell are we surrendering?"

"Yeah, Cliff. Why?" Mike Shannon said over the intercom.

Dick Stone did not say a word. He was paralyzed there in the navigator's compartment face to face with death and the realization that Colonel Atwood's solution was balderdash.

The Focke-Wulfs had stopped shooting at them. One of them pulled alongside the *Rainbow Express*'s right wing tip. A second one appeared off to the left. The first pilot hand-signaled Cliff to head northeast. He banked in that direction and Cliff followed him. The other Focke-Wulf stayed on their left wing-tip.

"Listen to me," Cliff said. "I'm trying to save our goddamn asses. When I say *go*, I want you to blast these two bastards out of the sky. Shannon, you take the guy on the right. Byrd, the guy on the left." Byrd was the ball turret gunner, curled in his glass sphere underneath the belly of the plane.

The other Focke-Wulfs were specks in the distance, pursuing the rest of the B-17s. Did fighting Germans justify this dirty double-cross? Dick Stone wondered. Were these two pilots who had accepted their surrender Jew-baiters and Nazis, out to rule the world? Or had they been in their second year of college like Dick Stone, more interested in literature than politics when the war exploded in their faces?

Still, Dick did not protest. No one protested. No one wanted to sit out the war in a German prison camp. Dick did not want to put his fate in the hands of something as murky as the Geneva Convention, which supposedly protected everyone, even a Jew, as a prisoner of the Nazis. Dick waited in silence, barely breathing.

"Now!" Cliff shouted.

The Browning machine guns clattered above and below the navigator's compartment. Dick saw the Focke-Wulf pilot on the right clutch his throat. The plane dropped into a spin, gushing smoke. Dick whirled in time to see the plane on the left spin in the opposite direction, afire. The pilot bailed out and hung there in his harness as Cliff retracted the *Rainbow Express*'s landing gear and dove for the cloud cover. The German shook his fist in rage as they roared past him.

The clouds remained thick all the way to the North Sea, a remarkable piece of luck. But when they emerged over the water, they found a half-dozen Messerschmitt 109s waiting for them. Cliff ordered the engineer to man the tail guns and they fought off a furious ten-minute attack, living up to their flying fortress nickname for once. Mike Shannon shot down another plane and Dick Stone, manning the nose gun in his compartment, amazed everyone, including himself, by getting a second as he pulled up after a head-on attack.

Cliff dove to less than 100 feet and let the Germans decide whether another attack was worth the possible cost. They tried one more pass and Mike Shannon got his third plane of the day. The 109s cut for home, probably reporting the *Rainbow Express* would never make it to England.

The plane was practically scrap metal. Mike Shannon counted over 200 holes in the fuselage. The horizontal stabilizer was hanging in shreds, giving them no elevator control. The ailerons were equally shredded. When Cliff tried to climb to a safer altitude, they almost stalled out. "Get rid of everything you can tear loose," he ordered.

They jettisoned the ammunition, the machine guns, their bulky flying gear, their boots, the fire extinguishers. Finally, at Dick Stone's suggestion, they dumped the dead bodies of Bombardier Beck, the radio man, and the top turret gunner out the bomb-bay doors. Coaxing maximum rpm's out of their two engines, one of which was making ominous noises, Cliff reached the Norfolk coast at treetop level.

There, almost under their wings, was RAF Bedlington. "Let's hope Sarah's saying her prayers," Cliff said. There was another, more realistic reason for landing at Bedlington. If that gasping engine quit now, it would not be a water landing, it would be on top of apple orchards, thatched roof cottages, it would be fire and explosions frying and rending their flesh.

"Hello Bedlington, this is *Rainbow*, do you read me? We've got a Mayday here. Request permission to land. Over," Cliff said.

"Hello *Rainbow*, this is Bedlington," said a liquid feminine voice. "Receiving you poorly. Strength two, over."

"Need wind direction. Airspeed down to one hundred and ten," Cliff shouted into the microphone. "Designate runway immediately!"

"Wind from the west at ten. All runways open. Fire trucks spraying foam. Good luck!"

"We're going to make it, guys. We're going to make it!" Cliff shouted over the intercom.

In ten minutes they were over the field. The fire trucks had just finished spreading foam on the runway that ran southwest. The wings wobbled. Cliff fought them back to horizontal as they turned into the approach. Dick Stone saw a slim WAAF standing outside the Watch Office, her hands clasped together before her lips.

It was Sarah Chapman, praying them in. For a fleeting moment he felt a strange, wild gratitude—and a regret for his unbelief, which prevented him from sharing her plea to the faceless baffling God who held them in the palm of his omnipotent hand.

The runway rushed up at them. "Full flaps!" Cliff yelled and they pancaked in, skidding down the foam-covered runway to a shuddering, smoking stop.

Fire trucks clanged toward them. The smell of scorched metal filled the plane. "Didn't I tell you guys this was one hell of a plane?" Cliff said.

As Cliff and Dick helped the vomiting copilot off the plane, Sarah ran toward them. "Oh, oh, oh!" she cried. Tears were streaming down her face. She flung her arms around Cliff and kissed him wildly. Standing to one side, watching the romantic spectacle, Dick Stone felt an odd, painful regret. Did he simply want those no-longer-innocent lips on his mouth? Or was he deploring the probability that she and Cliff would be inseparable now?

The surviving members of the crew were pounding Cliff on the back. Only the copilot, still green, and Dick Stone declined to join the celebration. Cliff's eyes explored the circle of faces with an almost preternatural wariness. For the first time Dick sensed something or someone trapped inside Cliff that he was trying to conceal.

For the moment they had a more immediate problem to conceal. What they had done over Schweinfurt was a violation of the rules of war, not to mention morality. In the circle of faces Dick Stone saw mutual guilt, heightened, somehow, by the adulation in Sarah Chapman's innocent blue eyes.

AMERICAN KAMIKAZES

Bless 'em all! Bless 'em all!
Bless the needle, the airspeed, the ball;
Bless all those instructors who taught me to fly—
Sent me up solo and left me to die.
If ever your plane starts to stall,
You're in for one hell of a fall.
No lilies or violets for dead strafer pilots,
So cheer up, my lads, bless 'em all!

The young American voices were bellowing these words off-key when Frank Buchanan emerged from Major General George C. Kenney's tent into the humid twilight of the New Guinea jungle a few miles from Port Moresby. "Thanks for dragging your ass out here to the end of the earth on such short notice, Frank. I wish I could give you something more concrete, like money. Or at least a medal," Kenney said.

"There's one thing you could do, George," Frank Buchanan said. They were old friends from World War I days. "Let me fly with the kids tomorrow. I always like to see how my planes perform under stress."

"You know as well as I do those bombers can't handle passengers. They've got enough weight problems."

"My nephew's copilot is down with malaria. They're going to give him some green kid who flew in yesterday."

"My ass will be in a sling with Richard K. Sutherland stamped on it if you get shot down."

Sutherland was General Douglas MacArthur's overbearing chief of staff. When he tried to browbeat Kenney the way he had intimidated other generals, Kenney had taken a blank piece of paper and drawn a tiny black dot in the corner. "The blank area represents what I know about airplanes. The dot represents what you know," Kenney said. Sutherland had not bothered him since that exchange.

Tomorrow the whole world would find out if Kenney knew as much as he claimed. He had taken over the Fifth Air Force with its reputation at zero and its morale at zero minus. Bombing from twenty thousand feet, their planes had hit almost nothing. Occasionally they attacked American ships by mistake. Kenney had fired five generals and a dozen colonels and totally revamped their strategy.

He had summoned Frank Buchanan to the Pacific to redesign the Samson light bomber, another plane Frank had created from the SkyRanger II configuration. It had more armor and more powerful motors than the Nelson version they had shipped to the British. Buchanan Aircraft was building hundreds of them at a new plant they had opened in the Mojave Desert.

Working with the crudest tools, but with dedicated mechanics, Frank had put eight fifty-caliber machine guns in the nose and bolted four more on the outside of the fuselage. All were fired from a button on the pilot's control wheel. Nose-heavy and loaded to the limit of their weight ratio, the Samsons required maximum skill from their pilots to keep them in the air.

Kenney added another requirement for his pilots: fearlessness. He announced the days of high-level bombing were over. They were going to come in at 150 feet or lower. For three months they had been practicing on a sunken ship in shallow water off Port Moresby.

Last night coast watchers and reconnaissance planes had reported a Japanese fleet carrying a full division of reinforcements heading for New Guinea, the key to the South Pacific. There was not a single U.S. Navy ship close enough to stop them. Kenney's strafers were the only available weapons.

"Come on, George," Frank said. "I want to see if Billy Mitchell was right when he said planes could sink a fleet."

Kenney could not resist this appeal to the hero of every U.S. Army airman. "Okay. Just don't tell anyone about it when you get back to the States."

Frank limped off to the tents of the 345th Bomb Group's 499th Squadron, better known as Bats Outa Hell. His right leg had still not entirely recovered from the crash of the Nelson bomber three years ago. He had wanted to die that day. The pain had been unbearable. Now he was volunteering to fly in what was basically the same plane at a near-suicidal altitude. But the pain had led to the miracle of regaining Amanda's love. Perhaps this flight, even if it ended in another crash, would reestablish a link with another person he loved.

He and Amanda seldom met in his house in Topanga Canyon now. He was away so often on overseas assignments such as this one. When he was in California, the pressure of work was all-consuming. Buchanan Aircraft had expanded a hundred, a thousand times. Proposals for patrol planes, heavy bombers, transports, poured in from Washington D.C.

But there was always the future, that almost mythical world of tomorrow, when the war was over and a victorious America was at peace again. What would he and Amanda do? Even before the war exploded, Frank had started to hate the furtive element in their love. He found it harder and harder to confer with Adrian Van Ness, to eat lunch and dinner with him—and on that very day, perhaps, make love to his wife.

Amanda belonged to him, not Adrian. Frank was absolutely certain of that on the spiritual plane. But in the everyday world of legality and custom she belonged to Adrian. Frank could not adjust his mind to a future of endless liaisons, perpetual deception. But he recognized Amanda's dilemma. Although she had talked bravely about risking Victoria's affection, she flinched from demanding a divorce from Adrian. Frank also had a dilemma—a deep reluctance to leave the company he had founded, to abandon the designers and engineers who had him helped create his planes—and would, he hoped, help him build even better ones after the war.

In front of the Bats Outa Hell tents, Frank listened to a short, slim hatchet-faced Texan describe his week's R&R in Sydney, Australia. "You go back and forth between satchel fever and sweet ass."

"What the hell are you talkin' about, Patch?" asked his younger more naive copilot.

"Satchel fever's like you and me gettin' us a couple of gals in Sydney and goin' to Mansion's Bar or some other pub and drinkin' and just sayin' anythin' in front of 'em. Then hustlin' the women back to our apartment for some more drinkin' and fuckin' and maybe in the middle of the night we switch women.

"But sweet ass. That's somethin' else entirely. That's when you think you've found the virgin, the one and only woman who hasn't been touched by any other male member of the human race. Then you take her to Bondi Beach the next day for a swim, and she sees McCall stretched out on the sand with two or three dames just as virginal breathin' perfume on him and you find out from the expression on your sweet ass's face that this California son of a bitch was there first!"

Captain Billy McCall had propped himself against a palm tree. His canteen—and all the other canteens—were full of Scotch from a case Frank Buchanan had brought with him. Billy smiled at Patch's complaint and Frank thought his heart would stop. He was remembering the four-year-old, the eleven-year-old, he had visited at Buzz McCall's mother's house in Laguna Beach.

Now Billy was wearing a hat with a fifty-mission crush and Frank could easily imagine the swath he cut through the women of Sydney. He had been cutting quite a swath through the girls of Santa Monica until he joined the air force. Women fell into his arms the way men had gone crazy over his mother.

"What's the word from the big brass, Pops?" Billy said.

"I'm flying with you. But it's a military secret."

"How come I don't get a copilot with five thousand hours' experience?" Patch groused.

A siren awoke them at 4:30 A.M. Frank sat in the operations tent looking at the sleepy young faces, remembering the haphazard briefings of World War I. This briefing was far more complex. They were going to fly almost five hundred miles down the coast to hit the Japanese fleet as it turned into a strait between New Guinea and New Britain.

Billy's bomber, named *Surfing Sue* after one of his Santa Monica girlfriends, awaited them inside the dirt revetment. She was black from nose to tail, with an evil-looking bat's head on the fin. Frank joined Billy in the walk-around to make sure nothing obvious was wrong with the plane. "Oh-oh," Frank said and pulled a screwdriver from the nacelle of the left engine.

"Jesus," Billy said. "Braun!"

His scrawny crew chief came running. "You forgot this," Billy said, handing him the tool. "Tomorrow Braun, I want you to get drunk and stay that way for twenty-four hours."

They climbed into the plane. "Braun got a Dear John letter yesterday. He hasn't slept for two nights," Billy said. "Imagine letting a chick bug you that much?"

"Sure. I felt that way about your mother."

He had given Billy a sanitized version of his love for Sammy.

"There's one thing I can't figure out in that story, Pops. Why she preferred my old man. It doesn't say much for her judgment."

The navigator, a chunky Tennessean named Forrest, informed Billy that he and the three gunners were ready to take off. The 1,700-horsepower motors split their eardrums as they burst into life. Many people swore they were the loudest engines in the world. "Any instructions for the copilot?" Frank shouted.

"Remember to flip the toggle switch that turns on the camera as we go over the target," Billy bellowed.

As squadron leader Billy led the other five planes to the runway. Ahead of them another squadron was taking off at thirty-second intervals. Billy's planes paused, roaring, belching, backfiring, as each pilot tested his engines one last time. "Kit Bag Leader to squadron," Billy said. "I'll circle a half turn to the left at two thousand feet. Follow me."

Thirty seconds after the other squadron's last plane took off, the green light in the ramshackle control tower flashed and Billy pushed the throttles to the wall. They hurtled down the runway toward a green mass of jungle five thousand feet away, bouncing wildly through chuckholes and dips in the dirt strip. Frank, who had his hands on the copilot's controls, could feel the elevators and rudder coming to life. At the halfway mark they reached the point of no return and it was up to Billy to get this seventeen tons of plane and bombs off the ground.

As the airspeed hit 120, he pulled smoothly back on the yoke and they cleared the trees by twenty feet. But they were by no means safe. The prop wash of the planes ahead of them had stirred the air like a giant eggbeater. Frank could feel the plane trying to fall off on her left wing, a common reaction to such turbulence. A novice pilot would try to right the plane with his aileron— an instinctive reaction, but one that would be fatal in this situation. The prop wash was momentary and when it vanished, the down aileron would throw the plane onto its side at virtually zero altitude. Good pilots like Billy repressed instinct and kicked the laggard wing up with the opposite rudder.

Frank was tempted to say nice going. Billy grinned at him, making it clear that he knew exactly what he had done right. They were both pros now. This was no boy sitting beside him.

They climbed laboriously to 2,000 feet to await the rest of the squadron. Forming up in a tight *V* formation they headed down the coast. Other squadrons of Samsons, Australian Beaufighters, and A-20s, designed by Douglas Aircraft's resident genius, Ed Heinemann, joined them. In an hour there were over a hundred planes around them, with the Bats Outa Hell in the lead. In another hour the navigator told Billy they were within fifty miles of the strait where they hoped to find the Japanese fleet.

"Let's ride some waves," Billy said. He switched on the intership radio. "This is Kit Bag Leader. We're going down to attack altitude."

Down, down Billy slanted *Surfing Sue*'s black nose until she was only 150 feet above the water. The other planes joined them, forming a wide arc, each squadron flying in a tight *V* behind its leader.

"There they are!" Billy shouted.

Ahead Frank saw at least two dozen ships, a mix of troop transports and destroyers, spread across several miles of sea. "This is Kit Bag Leader," Billy said over the radio. "We'll take the ones at the end of the line. Good hunting."

Billy increased the propeller pitch to 2,100 rpms and moved the fuel mixture control from cruising lean to rich to give them maximum power. "Kosloski, watch for bandits out of the sun," Billy told the top turret gunner, as they headed for the transport that was bringing up the rear of the convoy.

They achieved almost total surprise. The guardian destroyers fired only a few rounds at them as they came in. Far above them, the Japanese air cover waited for the usual high-level attack. *Surfin' Sue* roared toward a black-hulled transport. Its decks were crowded with men. "Hang on!" Billy howled and pressed the button on the twelve fifty-caliber machine guns.

A stream of fire spewed from *Surfin' Sue*'s nose. Each of the twelve guns was firing 750 rounds a minute. That added up to the firepower of a battalion of infantry. The plane shook so violently, Frank would not have been surprised to see one of the engines fall off.

The blast of bullets from Billy's guns and the guns of the other planes in the squadron literally melted the superstructure of the transport before Frank's eyes. Most of the men on the deck never knew what hit them.

"Good shooting," Billy said. Ten seconds later he hit the bomb release and two of their one-hundred-pound bombs and twenty of their fragmentation bombs tore chunks out of the deck. Flame and smoke spewed from the transport and it went dead in the water

"Patch, Wilson, this is Kit Bag Leader. Follow me onto that destroyer," Billy said. "The rest of you finish the transport."

Billy banked to port, his wingtip all but touching the waves, and roared toward the long low-slung warship. Flames winkled from the muzzles of a dozen guns along the deck. This ship could fight back. A five-inch gun belched and Patch's plane exploded into a thousand fragments.

"You son of a bitch!" Billy roared. He was pure warrior now. The expression on his face was one Frank had never seen before, jaw rigid, eyes bulging, mouth a slit. Billy pressed the button and the machine guns spewed fire again. Terrified Japanese flung themselves behind their gun shields. Parts of the destroyer's superstructure sagged and all but disintegrated under the firestorm of steel.

"Now," Billy said and pressed the bomb release. Two one-hundred-pound-bombs added to the chaos on the destroyer's deck.

Wheeling, Billy and his surviving wingmate came back for another run. This time, the gunners on the other side of the ship blew the wingmate out of the sky. Billy called on the rest of the squadron to join him. In five minutes there was no one alive on the destroyer's deck. She was drifting aimlessly, gushing flames and smoke. Billy planted the last of his hundred-pound bombs on her bridge.

"Skip bombers, this is Kit Bag Leader. Finish this guy off."

A trio of Samsons wheeled along the horizon and roared toward the destroyer. While their nose machine guns poured in the same blast of death, from their bays leaped five-hundred-pound bombs that bounded off the water into the hull. Three tremendous explosions blew half the ruined superstructure into the sea.

Carnage. Along the ten-mile length of the convoy, other destroyers and transports were sinking and burning. Japanese sailors and soldiers leaped from them into the sea, where they clung to rafts and drifted in open boats. "Take the swimmers. Even the score for Bataan," Billy said.

"No!" Frank cried.

"Orders, Pops," Billy said. "These guys don't surrender. If they get ashore we'll have to kill 'em all over again."

They dropped to less than fifty feet and the machine guns churned the water white around the hapless survivors. "This isn't war!" Frank cried.

"Yes it is, Pops," Billy said. "These guys shoot pilots when they bail out. They behead pilots who bomb their sacred homeland. What the hell's wrong with you?"

"Bandits at six o'clock!" yelled the turret gunner.

The Japanese air cover was roaring down from their high-altitude patrol to protect the convoy. They were much too late. Not a single troop transport was still afloat. Four destroyers had survived by fleeing over the horizon, leaving the soldiers to their fate. Billy Mitchell was right. A fleet could be destroyed by air power alone.

The Japanese wanted to prove that enemy air power could at least exact revenge. Samsons and Beaufighters plunged burning into the sea as the marvelously maneuverable Japanese Zero fighters zoomed around them. "Long-range fighters," Billy shouted, weaving across the water at no more than twenty feet. "Build us some long-range fighters, Pops."

"Zeke at eleven o'clock. He's trying to ram us!" the top turret gunner shouted.

Billy swung the plane violently to the right and the Zero crashed into the sea.

"I'm out of ammo," the turret gunner reported. He had used most of his bullets on the ships and swimmers.

"I only got enough for two or three bursts," the tail gunner said.

"Here come three more Zeros," the navigator said. He was in charge of guns in the waist but like most navigators had little gunnery training and was a lousy shot.

Billy raced for the shore of New Guinea and zoomed along the beach, still at twenty feet. The Zeros could not dive on him and pull out without plowing into the jungle. Ahead, Billy saw the mouth of a river. He banked into it and roared along its snaking surface, the Zeros still buzzing angrily overhead. The river made several turns around various mountains and the Japanese, low on fuel, gave up the chase.

Billy swung south toward their home base. They too were low on gas and he did not want to waste an ounce of it. Suddenly they were flying down a box canyon at minimum altitude. About a mile ahead was the ugly stone face of a mountain at least 2,500 feet high. "We better get the hell out of here," Billy said.

He pushed the props to 2,300 rpm, shoved the throttles to full power and started climbing. *Surfin' Sue* failed to respond. Instead of going faster, the plane slowed to near stalling speed as it struggled to ascend.

"What the hell's happening, Pops?" Billy said.

"A downdraft," Frank said. "In the worst possible place."

"This thing stalls at one-thirty. I bet we're below that now. What's holding us up?" Billy said.

"I don't know. Maybe the spirit of Billy Mitchell," Frank said.

They were climbing but the mountain still blotted out the horizon. Frank began preparing to die in the jungle beside Billy. He could think of worse ways to go. At least he was with someone he loved. Maybe Sammy would be there to greet them on the other side. It would solve the dilemma of his future with Amanda.

"Jesus Christ!" Billy said. He was still pushing the engines to their limits. Instruments showed cylinder head temperatures creeping over the red line. Billy had the yoke jammed against his chest, trying to haul the plane over the top of the mountain by sheer physical effort. Frank could see the flat peak of the mountain now. They were going to hit about fifty feet below it.

"Full flaps!" Billy roared. "Give me full flaps. Fast."

Frank slammed down the lever and the flaps fell. *Surfin' Sue* ballooned straight up like a helicopter and they cleared the top of the mountain by ten feet. Billy had realized that by changing the shape of the surface of the wing, he could gain fifty feet of lift.

On the back side of the mountain, Billy quickly regained airspeed and roared back to the base at treetop level. "Do you think I'll always be able to get out of a tight spot that way, Pops?" Billy said.

"I hope so," Frank said. "But remember the saying, 'there are old pilots and bold pilots but no old bold pilots.' "

"Who wants to get old?" Billy said.

Over the base, Billy decided to celebrate their victory. He roared up to two thousand feet and rolled into a steep turn, which put the wings vertical to the ground. He cut the throttles, dropped the wheels and let down thirty degrees of flaps as *Surfin' Sue* started falling toward the jungle. Billy yanked the plane out of the turn, leveled the wings and was on the runway before Frank could get his breath.

General Kenney was waiting for them, his hands on his hips, as they taxied into their revetment. "If you weren't Frank Buchanan's nephew I'd have you court-martialed, Captain!" he roared. "You were never trained to do that in a bomber. I don't know many fighter pilots who'd land that way."

"It's a great way to build morale, General," Billy said. "I'll be glad to teach it to the whole bomb group."

"There's not a hell of a lot left of the group," Kenney said.

Three of the six planes Billy had led into the air that morning were at the bottom of the sea. Losses in other squadrons were equally heavy. Low-level bombing was murderously effective—Kenney had proved that. But it was also murderously dangerous.

"I hate to ask these kids to keep doing it," Kenney said that night in his tent. "But Bupp Halsey's got it right. He said you can't win a war without losing ships and you can't do it without losing planes either."

Frank said nothing. He knew Kenney was talking more to himself than to him, agonizing over a decision he could not retract.

"You lost a lot of your planes to Zeros, George," Frank said. "What you need is a good long-range fighter. I've got some ideas for one. They could use it in Europe to protect the B-Seventeens too."

He began sketching a plane with a pointed snout and thin square-tipped wings. "Those wings will make her hot to handle on takeoffs and landings," he said. "But they'll let a pilot do wild things in the sky." Next came a long lean fuselage that would have room for twice as much fuel as the average fighter. The cruciform tail rode high above the body. "We've learned a lot in our wind tunnel," he said. "Putting the tail up there solves the flutter problem with this size fuselage."

"If I knew you had that plane in your head I would have court-martialed myself for letting you go up in that bomber!" Kenney said. "Go home and get to work on it."

Later that night Frank sat on the beach with Billy, getting drunk beneath the starry Pacific sky, with the Southern Cross blazing in the center of the constellations. "Tell me the truth man to man, Pops," Billy said. "What happened to my mother? How did she die? I asked Buzz a hundred times and all he'd say was 'Don't worry about it.'"

Frank told him, leaving out his own anguish, though it was probably audible in his voice. "Buzz loved her, Billy. That's why he can't talk about it. He blames himself for it."

Billy was not interested in Frank's defense of Buzz. "It doesn't make any sense, does it? No more sense than poor old Patch gettin' creamed by that five-inch shell this afternoon while I make it back in one piece. What'd he do to deserve that, Pops? Why'd I make it back?"

"I don't know, Billy. War makes you realize how mysterious life is. How each of us is working out a destiny—how little we control it."

"I don't like it. Whoever's running the show is doing a lousy job."

Billy sprang to his feet and raised his fist at the dark glowing sky. *"Do you hear me up there? Are you listening, you fucking assholes? Tell the head asshole he's doing a lousy job!"*

Frank staggered to his feet, appalled by Billy's blasphemy. This was Sammy's son, the boy she had insisted on baptizing as a symbol of her repentance, her yearning to escape from her dark driven wildness to a life of caring love. With his dual nature, Frank understood it was not simply God Billy was cursing, it was all his failed fathers.

Frank saw he had to give Billy something more than the comradeship of terror and danger they had shared in the cockpit. That was Craig's love, older brother's love, a substitute at best for fathering love. In his desperation Frank offered his deepest and purest gift, his talent.

"Billy," he said. "You're a great pilot. After the war you'll fly planes that will go ten times faster and higher and farther than these crates. They're flying in my head now. I'll build them for you. I promise you."

With that pledge Frank knew he was abandoning Amanda, Eden, love in Topanga's green silence. He was accepting the warriors' dark code, their love of danger, their fascination with war and death. He was offering them his talent in Billy's name, for Sammy's sake.

"I won't forget that, Pops," Billy said.

They clung to each other there in the New Guinea darkness, fabricating fatherhood and sonship, their only shield against the misshapen world men and their gods had created.

MAN OF SUBSTANCE

Down the half-mile long assembly line Adrian Van Ness strolled, smiling at his workers. He stopped to talk to a woman riveter in slacks, her hair tied back by a bandana. "How's it going, Muriel?" he asked.

"Pretty good, Mr. Van Ness. But we're gettin' kinda tired. The overtime pay is great but after six months of twelve-hour days—"

"I know. It's even tougher on the night shift. But we're winning the war."

Muriel gave him a V for victory sign. "Anything that gets my husband home faster is okay with me."

The Fox Movietone news announcer took over the narration. "The human touch," he said. "That's how Adrian Van Ness and his company, Buchanan Aircraft, are setting records in airplane production. Van Ness knows an amazing number of his workers by their first names. When he isn't on a plane to Washington, D.C. to confer with generals or admirals or at an air base where his latest planes are being tested, he walks these assembly lines, keeping in touch with his people and their problems. This year Buchanan will turn out an astonishing six thousand fighters and bombers, planes that have proven they can outfly anything the Nazis and the Nips can put in the air."

Tama Morris flipped off the projector and pulled up the blinds on the big window overlooking the airfield. "Not bad?" she said, virtually uncoiling as she strolled across Adrian Van Ness's office. Her face, her figure were still remarkably youthful. A tight blouse accentuated the full breasts. Her legs deserved the black-market nylons Adrian bought for her in the east.

"You're a wonder," Adrian said, as she sat down beside his desk.

She was a wonder, in her own way. Not only did she get Buchanan reams of good publicity like the Movietone News feature, she also helped them sell planes in a less visible, more direct way. When generals, admirals, civilian bureaucrats, and congressmen began visiting Buchanan Aircraft with millions of dollars to spend, Tama reorganized the casual prewar dating service she had created to entertain visiting airline executives. She compiled a master list of women employees who were willing to keep these new VIPs happy in California. She also made sure her volunteers were rewarded with nylons, dresses, extra gas and ration coupons, if the visitor turned out to be too cheap or insensitive to leave a gift behind. Buzz McCall liked to say Frank Buchanan might design the best planes in the world, but Tama's volunteers sold them.

"We've got a problem with General Slade," Tama said.

Newton Slade was in charge of procurement for the Army Air Force's tactical branch. He had ordered a thousand copies of the long-range fighter Frank Buchanan had designed after visiting Billy McCall in the South Pacific. It was winning the air war in the skies over Hitler's collapsing Third Reich. Slade was about to order another five hundred, modified as fighter bombers.

"He needs a hundred thousand dollars to invest in some real estate in Santa Monica."

"Really?"

"Yeah. He says North American has a fighter bomber almost as good as ours."

"Why did he tell you all this? Is he afraid to come to me?"

Tama's eyes glowed with dark light. "We've gotten very friendly."

"What does Buzz think about that?"

"He couldn't care less. He's too busy screwing the whole assembly line."

"Oh? I didn't realize he was that ambitious."

"I'm not complaining. He doesn't care what I do, I don't care what he does. That was the deal I bought when we got married." She frowned and lit a cigarette. "One of these days I'm going to tell him to forget it."

"Why don't you?"

"Buzz doesn't let any woman walk away from him. I'm afraid he'd get me fired."

"That's a superfluous worry, as long as I'm around."

Adrian was certain Tama was not really worried about getting fired. She knew a man was stirred by having a woman ask for his protection. Adrian, a lifetime student of the feminine psyche, enjoyed the mating dance he and Tama were conducting.

For a year Adrian had mourned Beryl Suydam's death by working twelve- and eighteen-hour days. Gradually the pain had ebbed into regret. He began to see women as desirable again. But the pressures of his job and the fear of another wound made it a game he played mostly in his mind. In recent months he had begun to see Tama as the solution.

Her sultry reputation attracted him. But she was Buzz McCall's wife. What if Buzz suddenly played outraged husband? Even he stayed away from the wives of his fellow executives. On the other hand it would be a small step toward evening the score for Beryl. It might also deflate Buzz's ego, which had swelled to enormous proportions since the war began. He took credit for the avalanche of contracts from the U.S. Army Air Forces.

"How's Cliff?" Adrian asked.

"Still flying. I almost had a heart attack when he volunteered for another twenty-five missions."

"It was a remarkable thing to do. We're all proud of him."

"Do you think his English wife put him up to it? Could any woman be that crazy?"

"He might have done it for her. Love and idealism are easily connected when you're young."

Adrian understood Tama's relationship with her son. It was a crude version of his own involvement with his mother. It made him feel confident that he could deal with this woman. At the very least Tama would be a change from the tepid sex he got at home, when he got anything at all.

"Adrian—could you get Cliff transferred to this country? I can't ask Buzz. He'd have a tantrum. I'd be so damn grateful."

"I'll make a call or two. I can't promise anything."

"Thanks. What do you want to do about Slade?"

"Tell him to give me a ring tomorrow." He pulled an expense chit out of his desk and filled it out for five hundred dollars. "Buy yourself a new dress."

Tama strolled out the door, smiling. Adrian telephoned the president of the Los Angeles National Bank. He got through to him in ten seconds. These days Buchanan Aircraft kept a running account at the bank that seldom dropped below twenty million dollars.

"Joe," he said. "I've got an old army friend, Newton Slade. He's got a chance to make some money in Santa Monica real estate and needs a hundred thousand dollars. Can you get it to him fast, if he comes to see you tomorrow? Of course I'll cosign it."

Adrian buzzed his secretary. "Get me Hanrahan."

In a moment the rough voice of his new security chief was on the phone. Before the war, Daniel Hanrahan had been a career detective in the Los Angeles Police Department. Adrian had hired him at four times his detective's salary. With the company awash in money, Adrian used it to buy loyalty whenever possible. "Have we got a file on Buzz McCall?"

"You told me to run a file on everybody, Mr. Van Ness."

"Let me see it."

The government had ordered Buchanan Aircraft to hire a security chief. Adrian soon realized security was a good excuse to find out all sorts of useful things about his employees. Hanrahan arrived with the file in his left hand and handed it to Adrian. A remarkable feat if you knew the left arm, the stiff hand were plastic. A shell had blown off Hanrahan's real arm in a sea battle off Guadalcanal. It had been replaced by a prosthetic device designed by Frank Buchanan. Tama had gotten Buchanan reams of good publicity for this invention, which was being used to rehabilitate amputees all over the country.

Adrian opened Buzz's file. Hanrahan did not depart. He stood there, all two hundred pounds of him, feet spread wide. "What's wrong?" Adrian said.

"I don't intend to let one of those files out of my sight, Mr. Van Ness. Not even for you. You want to look at it, go ahead. But I'm staying here while you finish it."

Adrian read a sample page. *On August 18, 1944, at 8:31 P.M., Mr. McCall left the plant with two women, a riveter named Dora Kinkaid and his secretary, Helene Quinn. They drove to the Kit Kat Club in Long Beach where they met several friends, including Albert (Moon) Davis, Buchanan's chief test pilot. They had dinner and drinks and danced until 1:36 A.M. Leaving the club Mr. McCall was too drunk to drive and Miss Kinkaid took the wheel. They drove to her house in east Los Angeles, where a party was in progress. A glance in the window revealed a remarkable amount of nudity and orgiastic sex in every room. The party continued until 4 A.M.*

There was nothing to worry about from Buzz McCall.

"One other thing, Mr. Van Ness," Hanrahan said as Adrian gave him back the file. "The purpose of these files is to make sure there are no lapses of *military* security, no government secrets leaked. Is that correct?"

"Absolutely."

"Then I'm not obligated to inform you or anyone else about what you might call personal matters?"

"Definitely not."

"I'm glad we understand each other on that point."

Something—was it the intensity in Hanrahan's voice?—made Adrian uneasy. Did he mean matters relating to Adrian Van Ness's personal life? Adrian could not imagine what these might be. His personal life was humdrum to the point of boredom. He had a wife who spent far more time in hospitals working with amputees than she did with him. (Amanda had discovered Hanrahan in the hospital and recommended him to Adrian.) He had a thirteen-year-old daughter who adored him almost as much as she worshipped Frank Sinatra and was in all other respects a typical American teenager.

Adrian decided Hanrahan, a devout Catholic, was probably in a state of shock from discovering the sexual liberation of the aircraft world. Two days later, Adrian flew to Washington, D.C., to confer with Army Air Force planners at the Pentagon about a new military transport they were considering to carry supplies and wounded across the Pacific. The Japanese kamikazes had proven fearfully effective, blowing up hospital ships as well as warships. With B-17 production winding town, Buchanan had the capacity to build this plane.

As usual, Adrian took Frank Buchanan with him to discuss the design. He turned out to be the worst imaginable company. He was in a funk about the way the air war was being conducted over Germany and Japan. He said he did not object to the airplane as a weapon. He had resigned himself to that a long time ago. But the thousand-bomber raids on Berlin and Dresden were barbarism. Ditto for the firebomb raids on Tokyo and other Japanese cities. "If I'd known planes were going to be used to kill innocent civilians, I never would have designed one," he said.

"The terror raids were approved at the highest levels," Adrian said. "The Americans and the British fought over it for months. It finally went all the way to the White House. Roosevelt ordered us to go along with the British. You can't really blame them. The Germans did it to them first."

"Is that our morality? An eye for an eye? Surely we've advanced beyond the Old Testament. Even there, the prophets reminded Israel that the Lord said, 'Vengeance is mine.' "

"I don't see how it's any of our business. We're not running the war. Do you really want me to start lecturing the air force for killing civilians?"

"Someone should. I will, if I get a chance."

"Jesus Christ, you're as bad as Amanda. She carries on like this all the time. It's gotten to the point where I'm afraid to introduce her to a general or an admiral."

Buchanan buried his nose in a book for the rest of the flight. Adrian decided

Frank was mortified to find himself being compared to a woman as feather-brained as Amanda.

Adrian skimmed the war news in the *Los Angeles Times*. In Europe, the end was in sight. The Americans were across the Rhine, battering their way into Germany. The Russians were rampaging in from the east. The Japanese were another matter. Although they were being pounded nightly by Boeing's B-29 superfortresses, they showed no sign of giving up.

In the taxi on the way to the hotel, Adrian tried to thaw Frank Buchanan by telling him about Tama's plea to bring Cliff home. Adrian thought Frank would applaud getting a friend's son out of the air war he was denouncing. Instead, the chief designer became enraged again.

"Let him take his chances like the rest of them," he roared. "She didn't ask to bring Billy home, did she? He's still bombing at fifty feet out there in the Pacific. Their casualties have been ninety percent. But they don't bomb civilians. Those Eighth Air Force crybabies have nothing to worry about. They've got fighter cover all around them now."

Adrian was undeterred by this explosion. He knew nothing about Frank's complex relationship with Billy McCall. He thought it was one more proof of his chief designer's eccentricity.

At the Pentagon, the five-sided fortress the government had erected on the Virginia side of the Potomac to house the War Department's brass, they conferred with the head of the Army's Air Forces transportation command, a tall cigar-smoking southerner named Mellow. He was enthusiastic about Clay's sleek, whale-shaped transport. He even liked the name Adrian had selected, the *Skylord*. But there were problems about going into production immediately. To explain them required a visit to General Hap Arnold's deputy chief of staff, Major General George Crockett.

They marched down the hall for what seemed a mile and a half to General Crockett's office. A short intense Texan, Crockett wore the crispest uniform Adrian had ever seen. He pumped Frank Buchanan's hand and praised the magnificent work his long-range fighter was doing over Europe and in the Pacific.

"We think we can end the war with Japan by strategic bombing alone," Crockett said. "To do it we need four hundred more B-Twenty-nines. Can you go into production on them immediately? Boeing will give you everything they've learned. They've gotten the man-hours down to seventeen thousand a copy. A year ago it was a hundred and fifty-seven thousand."

"What about the transport? We can't do both," Adrian said.

"We'll sign the contracts for it and you can go to work on it the day after you deliver the four hundredth B-Twenty-nine."

"I thought you needed the transports for the invasion of Japan," Frank Buchanan said.

"There won't have to be an invasion if we can deliver the kind of stuff we laid on Tokyo a couple of nights ago," Crockett said. "We put three hundred and twenty-five Supers over the city, each with six tons of incendiaries. We burned out the whole goddamn joint. Take a look at these pictures."

He pulled some reconnaissance photos from his desk. Tokyo was a moonscape, with a random steel-and-concrete building such as the Imperial Hotel isolated by endless blocks of charred ruins.

"How many civilians did you kill?" Frank Buchanan asked.

"Hell, I don't know," the general said, missing the hostility in Frank's voice. "The Nips claimed eighty-four thousand but the Russian embassy estimated it at twice that. The temperature on the ground hit twelve hundred degrees fahrenheit. The last planes to bomb said there were whole streets that'd turned to red hot sludge."

The general smiled fondly at the photos. "We're gonna make these bastards cry uncle without sendin' a single Navy ship anywhere near the coast. The GIs and Marines can just play volleyball all day on Saipan or wherever and leave the war to us."

Air power, Adrian thought. They were all part of the mystique. The planes they built were put into the hands of men who were using them to settle an argument that had started twenty years ago.

"Do you call incinerating a hundred and sixty thousand civilians war?" Frank Buchanan roared.

"Jesus Christ, Frank," the general said. "Who's side are you on? Didn't these bastards bomb Pearl Harbor?"

"I don't believe there were any women or children aboard those battleships!" Frank shouted.

General Crockett's lip curled. "This here's war, Frank. It sort of separates the men from the boys and girls."

Adrian seized Frank Buchanan's arm in a decisive grip before he could bellow a reply. "I don't believe this is the time or place for us to debate these difficult questions," he said. "None of us here are responsible for the decision to bomb Japan. As far as I'm concerned, speaking as the president of Buchanan Aircraft, we're ready to go to work on those B-Twenty-nines the moment you get us the blueprints."

Crockett glanced at the reconnaissance photos of Tokyo for another moment, then banged the drawer shut. "Okay," he said. "We'll get 'em to you."

Back in General Mellow's office, Adrian braced himself for a lecture on diplomacy. Instead, Mellow whacked Frank Buchanan on the back. "I'm glad somebody told off those bomber maniacs," he said. "There's a lot of us in the Air Corps who don't agree with what they're doing. When you try to discuss it, they pull that men against the boys and girls crap."

Adrian decided this was a good time to ask the general's advice about getting Cliff Morris rotated home from Europe. Frank glowered but said nothing. "Hell, that shouldn't be hard," Mellow drawled. "Damn fool shouldn'ta been allowed to go over twenty-five missions in the first place. Most pilots're so strung out by that time they start takin' off with the flaps down and landin' with the wheels up."

Frank continued to glower while the general made a call to a friend in operations. "They'll check his file," he said. "Now—about my transports—I want a hundred of them by June and I don't care how you do it. Those bomber blowhards aren't goin' to make the Japs surrender. Down in War Plans they're talkin' about invadin' Kyushu in September and the casualties are estimated to be five hundred thousand men."

"We'll see what we can do," Adrian said. "Buzz McCall has pulled off a lot of miracles for us. I think he can handle this one."

"How is that son of a gun?" the general beamed. "Still got a cock as long as a windsock?"

Adrian nodded. "Unanimous testimony of the entire female work force. Cliff Morris is his stepson, by the way."

On the way to the airport, Frank reopened the argument against bringing Cliff home. "Buzz will go wild when he hears about it," he said.

"I did it as a personal favor to Tama," Adrian said.

He was daring Frank to tell that to Buzz. Frank seemed impressed by the revelation, which suggested Adrian and Tama were seeing a lot of each other. That was exactly what he planned to do, Adrian decided. See a lot of Tama. In fact, every luscious inch of her.

Frank, Buzz, and the rest of the company plunged into a frenzied effort to get the B-29s and the SkyLord into production, on top of the five hundred fighter bombers that General Newton Slade, happy with his Santa Monica real estate, had ordered on the same manic schedule. Adrian approved hiring another ten thousand workers if they could find them. That would give Buchanan a payroll of 101,000, making it the largest aircraft company in the world.

A week later, Adrian and Tama drove south across the San Gabriel River past the rambling white Pio Pico mansion, home of California's last Spanish governor. They followed Route 101 through the thick forest of oil derricks in Santa Fe Springs, Fullerton and Brea to the village of San Juan Capistrano. Tama had chosen it without explaining why. They rented a suite in a white-walled inn overlooking the ruined mission.

"I was born here," she said. "I used to walk with my mother in the mission grounds. My mother was Mexican. Does that bother you?"

"No," Adrian said.

Adrian began undressing her. He was full of triumphant desire. He thought of Beryl, of old sorrow, and dismissed it. He was beyond sorrow and regret now, the ultimate man of substance, with this beautiful woman eager to give herself to him.

Would she betray him too in some way? He could not imagine how. Tama let him lead her to a sunken tub where he bathed her as if she were an expensive toy. She was as beautiful as Beryl Suydam in a more ample American style. The dark triangle of hair below her belly was incredibly smooth and fine. Her olive skin gleamed when water flowed across it.

On the bed, after he had patted her dry, she responded to his kisses with sighs and cries that filled him with dark music. She was like an instrument he was playing, a kind of cello that emanated desire and a thousand deeper more intricate wishes. His hand found the little tip of love. She closed her eyes and trembled, her lips parted, the red edge of her tongue beckoned him.

"Are you really—or is it just—to even the score?" she whispered.

"What score? What are you talking about?" Adrian said.

"Amanda—and Frank."

Every imaginable kind of music vanished. A dozen memories coalesced. Hanrahan asking Adrian if he had to report personal misconduct. Hanrahan's amputated arm and Frank Buchanan's extraordinary interest in amputees and Amanda's devotion to them. Frank's abrupt silence when Adrian compared his tirade against bombing civilians to Amanda's monologues.

"Adrian," Tama said. "I thought you knew."

Of course she thought he knew. Everyone in Buchanan Aircraft knew. Why not the president? The presumption was completely logical, especially for Buzz McCall's wife. Why would she think his marriage was any different from hers?

No, that was too crude, the question had been asked out of that sea of secret sorrow that flowed through every woman, that invisible web of yearning for ideal love they wove around every man, even when their own minds mocked the idea.

"Adrian," Tama sobbed. "I didn't think anything could hurt you. You're always so calm, so aloof."

Women. Women. Adrian stumbled to his feet and stared out at the ruins of San Juan Capistrano. The crumbled walls were an image of his self. Behind him there was a thud of footsteps and Tama had her arms around him. "Adrian, Adrian," she whispered. "You don't know how much it means. You cared. You really cared. I've never met a man who cared that way. Not a man like you."

He shook his head. It was hopeless. He was fated to be tortured by women. Tortured and mocked and humiliated like ruined Robert Van Ness. Not even success protected him.

"Now we can really begin," Tama whispered.

She turned him, faithless, passive, to meet her kiss. Nothing happened, of course, as she revolved her gleaming black pussy against his inert stump. He was an amputee. Why couldn't she see that? Why didn't she leave him alone with his misery?

Tama did not seem in the least surprised or disappointed or offended by his plight. She led him back to the bed, step by step, her tongue deep in his mouth and drew him down on top of her. Then the slithering began, the coiling and uncoiling of that sinuous body, that electric tongue as she traveled up and down the moonscape of Adrian's flesh and finally took the still indifferent stump in her mouth. Around and around the doleful little snout her tongue revolved.

Amazing things began happening inside the burnt shell of Adrian's desire. He found himself imagining a thousand positions from some primeval Kama Sutra—he had never read the famous book itself. He saw himself taking Tama with inexhaustible desire in every imaginable way. He saw his tongue probing the pink flesh beneath the black frond of silky hair between her thighs.

He could never love this woman. She had no education, no taste, no refinement. But in some profound and triumphant way she was a woman and he would love that womanness, he would mingle his regret and humiliation and success and achieve an approximation of love and an acme of desire. He would be a man of substance with a woman every other man desired.

Yes, yes, he whispered, as his penis, a stump no more, plunged deep into Tama's darkness. Yes Yes Yes. A man in spite of all of them. A man with the power to betray and humiliate in turn.

"Oh, Adrian, love me, really love me." Tama whispered. "Tell me you do—now."

"I do, I do," Adrian lied.

The room filled with a triumphant roaring. The 400 B-29 Superfortresses that would soon roll off the assembly line in the Mojave thundered across the Pacific to sow flaming death over Tokyo and Yokohama. Adrian accepted that too. He accepted the life he was living in the middle of the twentieth century. A player of the great game. A conqueror of women and nations.

LOVE AMONG THE RUINS

Horns hooted, whistles blew, sirens howled, guns boomed, planes zoomed overhead doing loops. The war in Europe was over. Germany had surrendered. Amanda Van Ness heard the news in the amputee ward of Wainright Army Hospital in Long Beach. Around her, young men without arms or legs, some without arms and legs, expressed little emotion. Europe was not California's war. In the Pacific, men were still dying aboard ships and on islands where the Japanese continued to resist in spite of two years of defeats. In the skies above Japan hundreds of planes, many of them made by Buchanan Aircraft, dumped tons of bombs on city after city.

Amanda tried to banish the bombers from her mind as she left the hospital and drove through California's sunshine to Topanga Canyon. Although gasoline was supposedly rationed, the boulevards were clogged with cars full of whooping celebrators. But Topanga was still immersed in green silence. In five minutes, she was driving up the steep hill to Eden.

The word had a sad hollow ring now, like the sound of a temple bell in the abandoned monastery of a forgotten god. Amanda prowled the empty rooms, remembering happiness, how palpable it had been for a while. In Frank's study, she pondered a sketch of the immense transport plane he had designed, with room for two decks of beds for wounded men.

Frank was somewhere in the Mojave Desert testing a new kind of plane, a bullet-shaped creature that spewed flame from its tail. It had a new engine and a new fuel that might revolutionize flying. He was always somewhere else, even when he was here, lying beside her. His planes flew in his head, sowing death and devastation over half the world. They flew in her head too, sowing devastation on Eden. On their love.

She tried not to think of the last time they had talked about it, when he came back from New Guinea. He had turned into a different being before her eyes. Darkness oozed from his pores, his skin had seemed to grow swarthy as he roared his memories of the first war at her. How Americans had died flying bad planes and he was not going to let that happen again. Young men like Billy McCall and Cliff Morris deserved a chance to live and if she wanted to think of him as a murderer so be it. He thought of himself as a savior. It was blasphemous and sad.

She picked up the telephone and dialed her own number. "Victoria? I just wanted to make sure you got home from school in one piece. The city is going slightly crazy over the German surrender.

"No. You can't go downtown. It'll be full of drunken sailors and soldiers."

Victoria was fourteen. A very precocious fourteen. The war had vulgarized everything. Crooner Frank Sinatra sold sexual hysteria to every teenage girl in the country. They necked with sailors and soldiers on buses and had sex in the city parks.

A distant rustle of the temple bell. Go, it said. Go in peace if possible. Eden was over. Treasure its memory. It was never more than a dream, a hope. Now you have to find your way back to Adrian. You've abandoned him for almost four years.

If abandoned was the right word. Adrian was so self-contained Amanda never felt he needed her. Even when he was mourning his English mistress, Beryl Suydam. But Amanda had been indifferent to him for a long time and he knew it. He was uneasy at her independence from him. Recently he had begun making sarcastic remarks about the time she gave to her amputees.

It was time to try to return to his territory, to live within his domain again. It would be difficult at first. Her indifference to Adrian could so quickly turn to hatred. She would risk it for Victoria's sake. She was another reason for Eden's decline and fall. Motherhood and Eden did not mix.

What would happen to Frank? She would go on loving him, of course. Perhaps they could resurrect Eden for a few precarious hours some place, some time. But it could never be here. This place throbbed with the thunder of Wright Cyclone engines, with the crunch of exploding bombs, with the screams of dying women and children.

On Frank's design table was a letter from Billy McCall. It described a daring flight across a thousand miles of the Pacific to bomb Japanese ships in Saigon. The letter exulted in the destruction they had wreaked. Billy said he hoped they had a chance to do a similar job in Tokyo harbor soon. He talked about how many Japanese he had killed to even the score for all the men in his bomb group who had died in their wave-top attacks.

Amanda recoiled from the hatred in Billy's soul. War had entered his bloodstream. He would bring it home with him. She dreaded what it would do to

Frank. Amanda knew why Frank loved Billy. There were no secrets in Eden. He knew about Amanda's first Eden, the orange blossoms in the dawn. He even knew her temptation to a dream life with Califia, a confession that had disturbed him almost as much as her revulsion at the bombing. She knew about Craig, Frank's long struggle with his dark spirit.

Sad how absolute honesty between lovers made love more imperiled. But so perfect, so unstained, for a little while. No matter what happened to her for the rest of her life, she had lived in Eden. She had tasted the forbidden fruit of innocence and hope and now she was ready to be an American wife and mother again.

Farewell, whispered the temple bell as Amanda closed the door.

She drove down more boulevards clogged with cars, past sidewalks jammed with cavorting soldiers and sailors. At home, Victoria was on the telephone, telling her best friend, Susan, daughter of a Warner Brothers mogul, what a freak her mother was. "She's prehistoric. I mean your mother's living in the nineteenth century but mine's prehistoric."

A pound of lipstick and rouge on her face, Victoria announced she was going downtown no matter what Amanda said. "I'm not going to *do* anything. I promise you absolutely I'll be a virgin on my wedding day."

"You're not going anywhere. Invite Susan over here."

"She's going downtown. Her mother's getting one of the studio security guards to escort us."

Amanda shook her head.

"Mother, it's a great historic moment! I want to see it."

"It's a lot of vulgar people doing vulgar things."

"They're not vulgar, they're happy. Something you couldn't be if you lived a thousand years."

"I'm not that morose, am I?"

"Yes, you are. I'm going going gone!"

She left, all but smashing the windows with the slam of the front door. Amanda stood in the silence, helpless. What was going to happen to Victoria if she insisted on making her voracious will her dominant trait? No man would tolerate it.

Adrian came home for dinner, an event in itself. He was somewhat drunk, even more unusual. "We've been celebrating," he said. "Victory through air power. Planes beat Hitler."

"Hurrah," Amanda said.

"You don't agree?"

"I have no opinion."

"Where's Victoria?"

"Helping sailors celebrate downtown."

"You let her go?" Adrian shouted.

"I tried to stop her. I'm not a policeman. Perhaps you should hire one for her."

"I couldn't afford it. I'm spending too much money hiring them to watch you."

They were in the sunken living room of their Hancock Park house. Adrian had hired a decorator who had chosen California mission furniture. Huge slatted chairs and couches made of dark woods, with red upholstery. Amanda had wanted blue but Adrian ruled in favor of the decorator. It was not a restful room. Not a *living* room, in Amanda's opinion. Now it was a trap. The red pillows oozed blood.

Adrian knew.

She had wondered more than once what he would do if he found out. Frank had told her there were rumors floating through the company. People were watched and followed all the time to make sure no military secrets were being leaked. Which led, of course, to all sorts of other secrets being discovered.

"How long have you known?"

"Years. I let it go on because it kept you quiet and Frank Buchanan happy. Lockheed, North American, have offered him tons of money to switch jobs. He's a genius."

The glee on Adrian's face was horrendous. Her husband had sold her, sold his wife for profits, money. Unspeakable. But how could she protest? She had betrayed him. He was entitled to this or any other kind of revenge.

"Do you want a divorce?"

"Of course not. I loathe the very idea of divorce. That's the coward's solution to unhappiness."

"I wasn't going to see him again."

"Why not?"

Amanda shrugged. "Why did you decide to tell me now?"

"The war is as good as over. We're going to reduce Japan to rubble in a few months. They'll surrender and decorum will return to our lives. I will no longer be able to tolerate my wife being screwed by my chief designer."

Amanda sensed this was a lie. The exultance in Adrian's eyes suggested that he had been aching to speak and liquor and events had combined to make this moment irresistible.

"I have a dossier on you two a foot thick. It's crammed with details. Even a few pictures. If you ever see him again, I'll show it to Victoria."

She saw what Adrian was doing. Sentencing her to a life with him as his spiritual and moral prisoner. She heard the clang of a cell door, she breathed the rank odor of the dungeon. In the distance, the temple bell of Eden tolled one last time.

Adrian made a dinner reservation at the Ambassador Hotel for twenty people. Buchanan's executives were celebrating victory through air power. "Get dressed," Adrian said. "You're coming with me. I need you for ceremonial occasions. Otherwise, you're superfluous. I've got a woman who's ten thousand times more satisfying in bed than you."

It was Tama. Amanda was sure of it. She remembered the bitterness at the core of her spirit and wondered how Adrian had subjected her. Simply for money? Or revenge against her loathsome husband, Buzz McCall?

Amanda breathed the overpowering sweetness of Califia's perfume.

Madness, warned her mother's voice. But it was also freedom.

Smiling, Amanda went upstairs to dress for the celebration.

POWER PLAYS

His head still aching from the champagne he had drunk to celebrate the victory over Germany, Adrian Van Ness flew to Muroc Air Force Base in the Mojave Desert, where Frank Buchanan was testing a rocket engine using liquid hydrogen fuel in a silver bullet of a plane, nicknamed White Lightning. No one was sure what the next-generation plane-engine configuration would be. A half-dozen aircraft companies had experimental models flying out of Muroc, some using hydrogen, others kerosene in a jet engine developed by the British.

Frank Buchanan was exultant about their progress. He thought hydrogen was an ideal fuel for a plane engine. It was odorless, powerful. Unfortunately it was ten times more expensive than kerosene but Frank was sure they could solve that problem. Adrian was not so sure. He watched White Lightning fly at a speed close to six hundred miles an hour after it was launched from a pod beneath a B-29 bomber.

The amount of money being spent was breathtaking. But it was all on that wonderful World War II invention, the cost-plus contract, so there was no reason to wring his hands. Uncle Sam paid for everything designated as costs and Buchanan still got the plus—the fixed fee. Anyway, he was not here to fret about money or even to check out White Lightning.

He brought a case of California champagne with him to help the Buchanan team celebrate the end of the war in Europe. After a liquid lunch, he strolled to the small office at one end of the hangar where Frank Buchanan was designing planes that might utilize what they were learning from White Lightning's high-speed flights. Frank began discussing compressibility—the phenomenon that buffeted a plane almost to pieces as it approached the speed of sound.

"Interesting," Adrian said. "By the way, will you please stop screwing my wife?"

The desert glare filled the end of the hangar. In the center of it stood the white plane with its stubby wings and burnt black tail section. It would be hard to conceive a more perfect setting. Here was the resident genius, being permitted to spend a hundred thousand dollars a day to indulge his fantasies of future flight by his admiring boss. Now, with pain and sadness in his heart, the boss reveals the awful truth he has accidentally discovered.

"Who told you that?" Frank said, perhaps trying to gauge the value of a denial.

"She did," Adrian said. "It finally got to her conscience. Sounds old fashioned, I know. But she's been worried about Victoria's—proclivities, shall we say? It gradually dawned on her that she couldn't very well preach to her daughter while she was committing adultery herself."

"I love Amanda," Frank said. "You have to understand that. I was afraid she'd begin to feel this way. Are you going to divorce her?"

Adrian shook his head. "I don't intend to ruin my daughter's life by exposing her to such an ugly truth at the age of fourteen."

"I suppose you want me out of the company as soon as possible."

"There's no need for you to leave if you promise me you'll never touch Amanda again."

"Of course," Frank said. He was utterly, totally crushed.

It was all so convincing, for a moment Adrian almost believed his own invention. It was true, he did not want to expose Victoria to a messy divorce. But the rest was a carefully calculated performance, infinitely superior to sputtering outrage and angry dismissal. He now had Frank Buchanan in his grasp forever. No one else would ever make a plane designed by this strange combination of genius and fool.

Back at the plant in Santa Monica, Adrian conferred with Buzz McCall and the treasurer, a big bulky man named Thompson, whom he had hired away from Lockheed. The B-29s were in full production and Buzz had somehow found enough workers to produce Newton Slade's five hundred fighter-bombers at the same time. The last of these were rolling off the assembly lines and work would soon begin on the Skylord transport.

Buzz was all business, urging Adrian to put more money into jet engines as well as the rocket engine Frank was testing, telling him to use his influence with General Slade to get their hands on one of the jet fighters the Nazis had deployed in the skies over Germany in the final months of the war.

Buzz unquestionably knew Tama had become Adrian's mistress. If it had any impact, he concealed it behind his usual swagger. Probably a better index of his feelings was his reaction to Adrian's attempt to have Cliff Morris brought home. The moment Buzz heard it, he had gotten on the phone to Mellow and other generals and bullied them into forgetting it.

Thompson was telling them how much money they would have to pay in excess profits taxes when the door burst open. Tama stood there, tears streaming down her face. "Cliff's gone!" she cried. "He went down over Berlin three nights ago!"

When she saw Buzz, Tama went berserk. "Are you happy now?" she screamed. "Are you glad you killed him, you rotten bastard?"

"When I get home tonight, I want you out of the house," Buzz said.

Treasurer Thompson fled and Adrian telephoned General Slade at the Pentagon. The general got through to Rackreath Air Base and talked to someone who told him other pilots had seen parachutes from the *Rainbow Express* as it spun down into burning Berlin.

Adrian spent the next two days consoling, calming, a frantic Tama. On the third day, Newton Slade's oily voice crooned over the wires from the Pentagon. "Adrian. Cliff's okay. He and two other guys got out. They came down behind the Russian lines."

A month later, Cliff flew into Los Angeles aboard a TWA SkyRanger II with his British wife, Sarah. Adrian found her shy but charming. He gave Cliff high marks for marrying the daughter of the chief designer of de Havilland Aircraft, the best plane maker in England. Cliff was undoubtedly coming to work at Buchanan after the war and the connection could be useful.

Tama outdid herself with a publicity extravaganza that got Cliff and Sarah on the pages of every major newspaper in California. It was climaxed by Cliff taking delivery of the 200th B-29, which they named the *Rainbow Express II*. He and Sarah, in her WAAF's uniform, took off on a savings bond tour, along with a half-dozen other air heroes. Offhandedly, Adrian checked with Newton Slade and made sure Cliff would not be assigned to bombing Japan. With the end of the war in Europe, there was no shortage of pilots.

Tama filed for divorce from Buzz and she and Adrian resumed their weekly visits to San Juan Capistrano. Adrian's ardor mounted with Tama's ingenuity. He had never met a woman for whom sex was both love and a game. Her sense of humor, which was almost nonexistent verbally, seemed to emerge in bed. He also discovered something less entertaining. For Tama, sex meant not only pleasure but power.

She announced she wanted to be Adrian's executive secretary. She said it would give her more authority over her volunteer escorts. Adrian saw it would also give her power over a lot of other people. Soon no one would get to see Adrian Van Ness without consulting her. He finessed this move by doubling Tama's salary and insisting no one could replace her in the publicity department.

Adrian was more amenable to Tama's penchant for sharing gossip about the shortcomings of Buchanan's executives, suggesting promotions and demotions. It did not take him long to notice most of these stories were directed against Buzz McCall.

Buchanan's production chief maintained a stable known as Buzz's beauties, who did very little work on the assembly line when they showed up at all. Others in his department were imitating his example. Tama shuddered at what might happen if the story got into the newspapers.

Buzz was not the sort of man who sat quietly, letting any woman, above all his ex-wife, ruin him. He marched into Adrian's office one day with Frank Buchanan beside him. "I hear someone's tellin' you my guys are exploitin' the ravishin' beauties we got on the line," he said. "I checked into it and found a couple of bozos were guilty. I fired them yesterday. I got an idea to make sure it doesn't happen again."

Adrian was forced to admire his effrontery. "I'm listening," he said.

"Frank here's movin' out of his house in Topanga Canyon. He's ready to sell it to us for practically nothin'. I think we should convert it into a club for our top guys—where they can relax without anyone tellin' stories about them. A club where guys call the shots and the women don't have nothin' to do with Buchanan. We'll pay everyone's dues, just the way we pay your dues and mine at the Conquistadores del Ciclo and other clubs."

"What do you think, Frank?" Adrian asked their chief designer.

Frank was drunk. Tama had told Adrian that Frank was drunk alarmingly often lately. He was not taking Amanda's loss well. "You haven't heard the best part of it," he mumbled.

"The women ain't gonna wear a goddamn thing. It's gonna be the ultimate in realistic advertising," Buzz said.

"Can you find enough of them to do that?" Adrian said, momentarily staggered.

"Sure. They had a speakeasy like it in Kansas City I used to drink at when I flew the mail for a while in the twenties. This is Los Angeles. The canyons are full of dames who'll take it off in ten seconds to get a part in a picture. We'll pay them plenty to take it off permanently. I guarantee you they'll like it. We'll have twice as many applications as we can handle."

"Let's understand a few things," Adrian said. "First of all, we never had this conversation. Frank here doesn't know a thing about what you're planning to do with the property. This was your idea and we approved it without asking any questions."

"Sure," Buzz said, defiance flashing in his gray eyes. "You can do me the same kind of favor."

"What?" Adrian said.

"Tell Tama all about it."

The Honeycomb Club—a name suggested by Frank Buchanan—enraged Tama and simultaneously demoralized her. Adrian realized time was the enemy here as well as Buzz. Like many Californians, Tama found the approach of middle age terrifying. Buzz's ability to defy it, to continue his unlimited access to young women, was more than an affront, it was a judgment on Tama's fading youth. She clung to Adrian with almost frantic ardor, not quite able to believe his assurances that he found her much more desirable than some naive twenty-year-old.

In the Pacific, the B-29s pounded Japan. The war surged toward a climax. Something similar surged in Adrian's blood—a new sense of dimension and pathos and pride. There seemed to be nothing that the conquerors of the sky could not have for the asking. Buzz McCall's descriptions of the Honeycomb Club turned the executive dining room into a passion pit. Adrian, determined to avoid any hint of approval, declined to visit it. He sought his climaxes with Tama in San Juan Capistrano.

"Your choice," she would whisper. "Tell me what you want to do."

At first Adrian's ideas were mundane. But as the summer of 1945 wrapped southern California in a haze of heat and humidity, he became more ambitious. One night in August he said: "Tie you up."

He was amazed by the words. They came out of an unknown part of his mind. Tama liked it. Giggling, she let him spread-eagle her on the bed and tie her wrists and ankles to the walnut bedposts. Adrian knelt beside her and Tama added touches out of her silent movie repertoire. She whimpered and begged for mercy, she writhed in mock fear.

The barrier Adrian maintained between his ego and his desires crumbled. A fist began to pound inside his chest. A red film filled the room with sunset light. His penis was a sword of revenge and celebration. It was more than Buzz McCall's ex-wife on the bed. It was woman in all her maddening ambivalence and ambiguity. His hands clutched Tama's breasts until she cried out with pain and pleasure.

Tama enjoyed it as much as he did. She loved and hated men in almost the same proportion that Adrian loved and hated women. They were a fusion of hatred and love emitting the energy of a hundred suns. "More, more," she begged. "Hurt me a little more."

Grunting, growling, Adrian seized fistfuls of her ample rump. His penis was spewing fire like the White Lightning rocket plane. He was a hydrogen engine annihilating himself and this woman. He and Tama had become a machine driving pleasure, pleasure, great thundering waves of it, thick and foaming as Pacific surf, through Adrian's soul. He could not stop, it would never stop, it was eternal, they were reaching some shore wreathed in red light.

Of course it was not eternal. Adrian was not a machine. An hour later, he lay on top of a whimpering, laughing, writhing Tama, his penis a dry aching stalk.

"Adrian, Adrian, make me the happiest woman in the world."

"Yes, yes, anything."

"Fire Buzz. Fire him even if Frank Buchanan goes with him."

Overreach, overload. The Adrian of desire was gone. The Adrian of intellect and forethought reappeared. He had lost control. He was in danger of losing another kind of control. He did not like it.

"Did I spoil it?" Tama asked, clinging to him. "I couldn't help it. It just came out."

"No, no," Adrian lied. "You couldn't spoil anything that beautiful."

"I'm afraid of what Buzz will do to Cliff. He's always hated him."

"I'll take good care of Cliff. Don't worry."

That night Adrian lay awake for hours brooding about women, the maddening way in which money, history, politics, entangled and so often strangled their love. Would he ever find one who loved him without a secret agenda in her head? Was part of it his fault? He remembered Amanda in freezing Maine yearning to let go. Was that what they wanted? He had let go tonight and where had it gotten him? Back to his first trauma, mother love.

The next morning a sleepless Adrian felt depressed, distant from a still-amorous Tama. As they drove back to Santa Monica he turned on the car radio to avoid conversation. A newsman's voice said: "The White House announced that sixteen hours ago an American airplane dropped an atomic bomb on the Japanese city of Hiroshima. President Harry S. Truman described it as a device that harnessed the power of the sun. The president said the United States had spent two billion dollars to produce it."

"My God," Tama said. "Did you know about this, Adrian?"

Adrian's first reaction was outrage. How could he not have known this secret, after spending so many hours in wartime Washington? Why, how, had the generals ordered an extra four hundred B-29s when a single plane was about to drop more explosive power than all four hundred combined? He raced to the factory at suicide speed and called General Crockett in Washington. The general ruefully admitted that he had known no more about it than Adrian.

"But it don't really matter whether it was one plane or four hundred," he said. "We did the job, Adrian."

Victory through air power, Adrian thought. But there was something wrong with this victory. At lunch in the corporate dining room, Frank Buchanan voiced the thought Adrian had deflected. "It's a disgrace."

He was drunk again. That should have made him easier to dismiss, but Adrian discovered the contrary. The drunkenness reiterated that Frank was speaking not only for himself but Amanda.

"It's a victory that couldn't have been achieved without an airplane," Adrian said. "Anyone who criticizes it shouldn't be working in this industry. I find it rather sickening to see a self-appointed moralist ready to lecture the rest of us. May I ask what your qualifications are when it comes to morality, Mr. Buchanan?"

Frank slumped in his chair, reduced to silence. "Adrian's right," Buzz McCall said. "It's what we've said from the start. We could win the war without the goddamn Army and Navy and we've done it."

"By incinerating women and children," Frank said.

"I don't like that part of it any more than you do," Buzz said. "But what were we supposed to do when the bastards wouldn't surrender?"

"You would have dropped that bomb?"

"If I got an order, yes."

"That's where you and I part company."

For a moment Adrian wondered if he could fire McCall and keep Buchanan. At some deep level, did Frank loathe Buzz as much as he did?

Frank lurched to his feet and pointed a trembling finger at Adrian. "I predict we're making a horrendous mistake, getting in bed with the generals. We didn't start out to build planes for them. We built them because we loved flying. Because we wanted to create a better world, not blow it up. People aren't going to forget a plane dropped this bomb. We're going to be haunted by it for the rest of our lives."

He's right, whispered the historian in Adrian as Frank reeled out of the dining room. But the words could not be spoken. Adrian Van Ness was the president of the world's largest aircraft company. He could not let this bizarre eccentric, whom he had reduced to his obedient servant in perpetuity, tell him what to think, much less force him to eat his words in public.

Adrian's eyes traveled past the faces of the two dozen executives at other tables. Among the designers, all Frank Buchanan disciples, he saw anxiety on almost every face. Around Buzz McCall and his production engineers he saw only contempt. On the other faces the dominant emotion was consternation.

"I don't believe a talent for designing planes includes an ability to predict the future," Adrian said. He raised his wineglass. "To air power," he said.

"Second the motion," Buzz McCall said, hoisting his Scotch.

There were no objections to the toast. Everyone drank to air power. "Incidentally," Buzz said. "I've been on the phone to the Pentagon. They're cancelin' everything on the books but fifty B-Twenty-nines. Unless someone starts another war real quick we're gonna have to fire fifty thousand people next week."

Ruined clanged in Adrian's soul. "Peace, it's wonderful," he said.

MOONLIGHT

An immense moon dangled above Los Angeles, bathing the city and the beaches and the boulevards in its pale yellow light. Amanda Van Ness paced the rooms of her empty house. For three months the world had been at peace. She was sure Adrian spent his nights in Tama's arms, although he claimed to be grappling with the horrendous problems of converting Buchanan Aircraft to a builder of commercial planes. Victoria was always out with her fellow teenagers. Amanda was alone most of the time.

Alone but not lonely because in the darkest corner of her soul, Califia lay in an ivory casket, her golden sword in her pale hands. Amanda vowed she would not utter the fateful word that would awaken her. Memory would warm her heart. Those years in Eden would be her refuge.

For centuries, the moon had summoned lovers to rendezvous. Amanda thought of it gleaming on the forest of grimy oil derricks that Cadwallader Groves had become. She thought of it shining through the sycamores in Topanga Canyon. When Frank was away during the war, she often drove there and sat on the porch, bathing in the glow, relishing the silent affirmation of Eden.

Why not go again? Why not touch the memory? It would help keep Califia in the tomb. Adrian had told her Frank had sold the house and moved to another canyon. If someone else was living there, she would explain that she had spent four happy years in the house and was simply returning for a look at it. She would be content to sit in her car for a few minutes in the moonlight.

The most nervous householder could hardly object to a forty-five-year-old housewife sitting in his driveway for five minutes.

Amanda drove out Santa Monica Boulevard to the coast highway and swung north beside the ocean. Santa Monica was full of young people with ebullient eyes, laughing mouths. They were Americans, winners of the greatest war in history. The future belonged to them. She wondered if among them there were a few like her, for whom the victory was a wound.

Oh, Father, with your dream of a world reborn as Eden. Maybe to wish for too much happiness was the worst sin. Perhaps your daughter has learned the lesson of survival. Happiness preserved in the memory, like the beautiful butterflies you used to catch and mount in glass cases on Casa Felicidad's walls.

On the coast road the moonlight was incredibly bright. People were driving without headlights. The ocean undulated like an immense shimmering carpet. The narrow entrance to Topanga appeared on the right. In five minutes she was approaching the road to Frank's house. She shifted into second gear for the steep climb.

Up the slope labored her 1940 Ford to burst into a clearing twice the size of the one Amanda had known. Half of it was a parking lot filled with at least two dozen cars. Frank's house was gone. It had been replaced by a hangar-shaped building, the front painted gold and illuminated by concealed searchlights. There were a half-dozen oval windows cut in the side walls. Amanda walked to one of them and looked inside.

A beautiful dark-haired woman was bending low, serving food to a bald, grinning fat man. The woman was naked. Amanda recognized the man. It was Moon Davis, Buchanan's chief test pilot. Next to him, an equally obscene grin on his face, was Buzz McCall, Buchanan's production chief. Beside him, leering drunkenly, sat Frank Buchanan. In the distance were a half-dozen other beautiful naked women serving food to other members of the Buchanan hierarchy.

Amanda did not know how long she stood there in the moonlight watching them swill their liquor and chomp on their steaks and ogle the naked women. She looked for Adrian but could not find him. That was hardly a consolation. He was unquestionably a steady customer. But Frank! His presence meant he not only approved, he had collaborated in this desecration of Eden.

Amanda drove home through the moonlight, blinded by tears. It was a miracle that she reached her Hancock Park driveway alive. In the house, the moonlight continued to flood her mind. Everything in her life was revealed with scarifying clarity. All the truths she had suspected and tried to banish, the truths that she had hoped love would keep at bay.

Women were men's victims from the dawn of time. From the days when they oiled their bodies with frankincense and myrrh to please a pharaoh to the gift of their fidelity to lying medieval troubadours to their public prostitution in the celluloid world of Hollywood, they were always victims, exploited, used, abused. Only once, in a dim past before male historians began to write their lies, was there a country where women reigned.

The land of Califia. California before time began.

In the theater of her mind, this land would be reborn. Slowly, solemnly, Amanda descended to the ivory casket and spoke the word. *Awake*, she whispered. *Awake, my queen.*

The casket opened. There lay Califia in her silver robes, clutching her golden sword. Her dark-blue eyelids fluttered. The wide sensual mouth trembled. She opened her eyes and spoke. *Did someone call my name?*

Almost blinded by the moonlight streaming from Califia's eyes, Amanda fell to her knees. *Your servant, summoning you to restore the reign of women, my queen.*

Will you obey my commands?

Yes! Yes!

The ecstasy of surrender flooded Amanda's soul with the radiance of a thousand moons.

Then I will arise and ride the winds of night with you. All our deeds will be done in darkness. In the dawn you will resume your disguise of the faithful wife and I will retire to my tomb.

Yes! Yes!

With a smile, Califia stepped from the casket and held out her hand to the kneeling Amanda.

Arise. Let us seek out the worst of the oppressors and design fitting punishments for them.

Dazedly, Amanda imitated Califia and stripped naked. Together they walked through the silent house to the lawn, where a gleaming silver plane awaited them in the moonlight. At the controls, also naked, was Tama! She too was a servant of Califia! She too had the knowledge of oppression that opened the secret door in the female soul. She smiled a welcome to Amanda and they soared into the moonlit sky.

Amanda chose their first target, the club on Topanga's ridge where women were groveling naked before the conquerors of the sky. Down, down they swooped to let Califia and Tama see the obscenity with their own eyes. The rage it ignited there! It was a flame in Amanda's heart. *What will their punishment be, my Queen?* Amanda asked as they circled above the building.

I will lay my most terrible curse on them, Califia said in a voice that had the thunder of surf in Pacific caves. *They will labor and labor but they will never profit, they will never know happiness with a woman again. They will emanate a stench that drives women mad, a foulness that inspires revenge and retaliation in sunlight and moonlight.*

They swooped down again and Califia aimed her golden sword at the building. A terrifying yellow flame leaped from the tip and surged in the window, enveloping everyone in the room. Amanda could see the skulls and the bones beneath the revelers' flesh. The yellow flame sank into all of them, a divine electrocution that left them looking like putrefying corpses.

Amanda rejoiced until her eyes found Frank Buchanan. Frank! The five letters that had once encompassed a world. That too was being destroyed by Califia's vengeance. For a moment grief tore at Amanda's heart. Was Frank truly among the guilty? Was he too a victim of Buzz McCall, Adrian? It was too late to ask Califia for mercy. She could only weep as he too joined the ranks of the living dead.

Amanda awoke with sunlight streaming in the window. It was almost noon. Adrian was in the doorway frowning at her. "I'm going to work, even though it's Saturday," he said. "Since when have you taken to sleeping in the raw?"

She said nothing. She was terrified that she might betray Califia.

"You can sleep any way you please—but you ought to get under the covers—or shut the door. It's not a habit I want Victoria to acquire."

She knew what he was thinking. That was the way she had slept with Frank. He was right, of course. Just in time she remembered her promise to be a dutiful wife by daylight. "I won't do it again," she said.

Adrian walked over to the bed and kissed her. With a terrific effort she managed to accept the touch of his loathsome lips. "You could also get pneumonia. It got quite chilly last night."

"Thank you for taking such good care of me."

From the darkness Califia whispered: *Well done, my good and faithful servant.*

For a moment Amanda wondered if this was freedom or a new more terrible bondage.

It was too late to do anything but obey. *Thank you, my queen.*

As Adrian regarded her with his usual condescension, Amanda slowly regained her joy. All the atomic bombs and flying superfortresses in the world would not protect this man from Califia's vengeance.

BOOK FIVE

WELCOME TO CALIFORNIA

Sarah Chapman Morris sat on the patio of her south Los Angeles tract house in the February sunshine, reading a letter from her mother. It was one long lament about everything that was wrong with England. The country was bankrupt, freezing, starving. The winter of 1946 was the coldest in memory and the winter of 1947 was no better.

Sarah's two-year-old, Elizabeth, tugged at her sleeve. "Want a cookie, Mommy. Cookie—and ice cream."

Why not? Sarah could not get over living in this land of abundance. She scooped some creamy dark chocolate chip ice cream into a dish and put a chocolate chip cookie beside it. She fixed another dish for herself—with two scoops. They sat out on the patio eating this delicious mid-afternoon treat.

"Can I have a bite?" called her neighbor, Susan Hardy, from her patio. She also had a two-year-old—a boy—staggering around.

"Come on over, we'll have a party," Sarah said. Susan's husband worked at Buchanan Aircraft as a designer. That in itself was a bond. Cliff was already working there two days a week, making calls with the head of the sales department. When he graduated from UCLA next term, he would go to work full time.

Sarah liked Susan because she was so American. She was utterly totally disrespectful about everything. She called President Harry S. Truman "the haberdasher." She was equally contemptuous of the governor of California and its two senators. "Pointy-heads," she called them. She called her husband "the Hardy Boy," a reference to a series of books for adolescents. She never stopped complaining about the long hours he worked—and frequently hinted that instead of designing planes at midnight he was seeing other women—which did not seem to bother her.

A Vassar graduate, class of 1942, Susan was just that much older than Sarah

211

to give her a voice of authority. She was a chunky woman, with a strong sensual mouth, overgenerous breasts, and a heavy bottom. She smoked continuously, dropping ashes into everything. Some probably fell into her ice cream but she slurped it down nonstop. Susan leaned back, lit another cigarette and sighed. "California! It's so goddamn boring!"

She was off on one of her favorite topics, comparing Los Angeles and New York, where she grew up. There was no comparison, in Susan's opinion. Los Angeles had no Broadway theater, no decent restaurants, no art museums, no department stores worth patronizing—nothing. "I've been much too busy to be bored," Sarah said.

"What are you going to do when you finally get Cliff through college?"

"Oh—I don't know. Have another baby, probably."

"You're the one who should be going to college."

There was some truth to that. Cliff had absolutely no interest in the required history and English and French courses he was taking. Sarah had written all his term papers. She had even written a paper for one of his economics courses. He was getting a B.S. in that weighty subject. "But I don't have a job waiting for me at Buchanan," she said.

"He may not have one either, from what I hear," Susan said. "They're in a lot of trouble."

Sarah simply could not believe it. The biggest plane maker of the country that had built a thousand planes a month—with Buchanan frequently accounting for half of them—could not possibly go bankrupt. The English aircraft business was in the doldrums, like the rest of England. But that was understandable, if regrettable. Flying to California had given Sarah a sense of the immensity of America. Gazing down from the plane at the endless miles of prairies, the snowcapped mountains rimming them, she had felt awed, even privileged to find herself part of this tremendous nation.

"How's your mother-in-law treating you these days?"

"She still hasn't called me Sarah."

"Be nice to her anyway. She reminds me of my mother. The kind of woman you shouldn't cross. Because she'll never forget it."

Susan did not have much respect for her ultra-dignified mother. She made upper-class New York sound as stuffy and proper as England. From that viewpoint, she was glad to be in California, where there was no proper way of doing anything. Susan's father, who had died in World War I a few months before she was born, was the only person she respected. Sarah sometimes wondered if his loss was the real reason for Susan's anger at the United States of America. In the name of her dead father she seemed to be determined to take a man's jaundiced viewpoint on everything. That made her a passionate student of office politics at Buchanan Aircraft, a subject that definitely included Sarah's exotic, irritating mother-in-law, Tama Morris.

By this time Sarah knew sultry sullen-eyed Tama was the mistress of Buchanan's president, Adrian Van Ness. She had divorced Cliff's stepfather, the company's production chief, Buzz McCall, more or less formalizing the arrangement. Hints and prods from Susan had prompted Sarah, after weeks of hesitation, to ask Cliff about it. Was it true that Tama exercised enormous power inside Buchanan—not only from her special status but because, in Susan's words, she "knew where the bodies were buried"? Cliff had stared at her in astonishment, then burst out laughing. Flustered, Sarah had asked Cliff in her earnest English way if bodies were literally buried somewhere. "How the hell do I know?" he snarled.

When he was in the mood, Cliff could be incredibly charming—the ebullient swaggering flyboy she had loved and married in England. When he was not in the mood he was about as charming as a tarantula—a creature she had encountered in her bed on their American honeymoon in Mexico in 1945, paid for by Tama.

It was absurd but sometimes Sarah suspected her mother-in-law of putting—or at least wishing—the insect beneath her sheets. There seemed to be an irreducible wall of hostility between her and Tama. It apparently had something to do with Cliff volunteering for those extra twenty-five missions over Germany. Tama seemed to think that Sarah had put the idea in his head, when she had actually wept and begged him not to do it. When his insistence on continuing to fight what he called "our war" had been a crucial part of her decision to leave the WAAFs and marry him. She felt compelled to equal such courage, such sacrifice, with the gift of herself. Most of the time, their marriage still lived on the emotional capital of those extra twenty-five missions.

Susan began talking about Adrian Van Ness. Her mother had known him in New York. She told Sarah about Adrian's unsavory father and aloof Boston-born mother and the rumors of infidelity and criminality that had swirled around them. She added far more specific rumors about the insatiable sexual appetite of Buzz McCall, Tama's ex-husband—and his friend Frank Buchanan, the company's resident genius who had reportedly seduced Adrian's wife, Amanda.

Sarah listened to these stories with an odd mixture of disbelief and indifference. The victorious war seemed to insulate them from the failures of the older generation—and give them a sense of ownership of the future. At Cliff's suggestion, Sarah had invited Frank Buchanan to dinner a month ago. She liked him instantly; he so much resembled her father—a man without guile because his heart and soul were absorbed by creating planes. She found it hard to believe such a shy, diffident unworldly man was capable of seducing another man's wife.

Sarah had invited the Hardys to the dinner, a gesture for which Susan was enormously grateful. She was sure it had a lot to do with the Hardy Boy's rapid advancement at Buchanan. Susan disagreed with Sarah's assessment of Frank. Even in those prefeminist days, she found it hard to believe any man was without guile. That made her even more curious about Amanda Van Ness. Susan begged Sarah to quiz Cliff about her but inquiries produced nothing but grunts and snarls.

Now, her ice cream consumed, her cigarette glowing, Susan began speculating about Amanda. She was probably a nonentity. After all, she was a born Californian. They had nothing upstairs but sunshine. But Amanda was rumored to be immensely wealthy. Her brother was becoming one of the country's premier oil tycoons. Maybe Frank Buchanan had seduced her, hoping to get his hands on her money so he could take over the company and get rid of Adrian Van Ness, whom he seemed to hate.

Susan's ruminations were interrupted by a metallic *rap-rap* of the brass knocker Cliff had installed on the front door, his one contribution to beautifying their jerry-built bungalow. Sarah opened the door to confront a huge awkward man with the most Irish face she had ever seen. He introduced himself as Daniel Hanrahan, Buchanan's director of internal security. At the moment, he added, he was functioning as a chauffeur. Mrs. Van Ness was in the gray Lincoln parked at the curb. She wondered if she might pay a visit.

Bewildered and a little scared, Sarah agreed, if Mrs. Van Ness would give her five minutes to straighten up the house. She rushed to the patio to tell Susan Hardy the news. Susan flung dirty towels in the hamper, kicked toys under the couch and shoved the unwashed lunch dishes under the sink while Sarah frantically applied some makeup and put on a decent dress. As Susan tiptoed out the kitchen door, the knocker rapped again and Hanrahan ushered Amanda Van Ness into the house.

She wore her russet hair braided tightly around her long narrow face, giving her an oddly severe, almost witchy look. "I'm here for a very special reason," she said. "I want to see Tama's granddaughter."

Sarah plucked Elizabeth from her crib and carried her into the living room. "Can she sit on my lap?" Amanda said.

"Of course."

Sarah gravely introduced them and deposited Elizabeth on Amanda's lap. The little girl gazed up at Amanda's solemn face and smiled shyly. "She brings back such memories," Amanda said. "My daughter is sixteen now. Completely impossible. Adrian plans to send her to England for college. He says an American school will let her run wild."

She suddenly glared at Sarah as if she were responsible. "I hated England. I hated everything about it. Do you like California?"

Sarah managed to stammer an affirmative.

"Every woman should like California," Amanda said. "It's a sensuous, sensual climate. A world where women belong. Women don't belong in a country like England, where it's freezing and raining ten months out of the year."

Sarah murmured something defensive about enjoying summers in Sussex. Amanda glared again. "That was where Adrian used to go to meet his mistress."

She gazed at Elizabeth and her manner softened remarkably. "I'm so glad this little creature will grow up a California woman."

Sarah said something about planning to stay in California as long as Buchanan Aircraft had a job for her husband. Amanda glared again. "They'll always have a job for him. Tama and I will see to that. But that's not why I'm here. I want you to try to raise this child as a true California woman. A creature with no dependence on a man. Can you do that?"

Amazed, Sarah could only murmur she had not thought about it. "Begin thinking about it!" Amanda said. "You're a woman. Haven't you found out already how much humiliation that involves?"

She clutched Elizabeth close to her and spoke over her tousled dark head. "You think Tama isn't humiliated? Her whole life has been one long humiliation. Like mine. If it weren't for this man, I'd be a prisoner in my own house. He understands. He *knows* exactly how humiliated women are at Buchanan Aircraft."

Hanrahan turned his hat over and over in his hands and murmured something about getting back to work. Unaware of the security chief's debt of gratitude to Amanda, Sarah could only stare in astonishment, mutely asking the Irishman why he had brought this madwoman into her home. Hanrahan seemed aware of her opinion but he did not attempt to defend himself or quiet Amanda Van Ness. It never occurred to Sarah that most of what Amanda said that day might be the truth.

HOME IS THE HERO

"The best thing about the Excalibur, Captain Rickenbacker—"

"Call me Eddie, for Christ's sake."

Sweat congealed the armpits of Cliff Morris's Hathaway shirt as he tried to regain his poise before Eddie Rickenbacker's hard impatient glare. Cliff's stepfather, Buzz McCall, had the same eyes. Fighter pilot's eyes. Killer's eyes. Rickenbacker had been the top American ace in World War I, with twenty-six victories.

The year was 1948. Buchanan Aircraft's Excalibur, the plane that was supposed to create an "empire in the sky" for U.S. airlines, flew in four colors on an easel Cliff had set up in Rickenbacker's fifty-first-floor Rockefeller Center office. The whirling propellers on the four 3,500-horsepower Pratt and Whitney engines seemed ready to pull it off the page and send it roaring around the ceiling. Cliff was planning to flip through the booklet to pages displaying the luxurious interior, the sophisticated cockpit design, the huge baggage compartment.

"With a two-hundred-seat capacity, we estimate annual profits per plane of—"

"Two hundred seats!" The president of Eastern Airlines fell back in his leather cushioned swivel chair and growled with exasperation. "Buzz. The goddamn plane's too big. We're flying SkyRangers half empty. What the hell do we want with this whale?"

Buzz McCall was standing by the window, looking west across New Jersey toward California. His presence was an index of Buchanan's growing desperation as they struggled to survive in the post–World War II aviation world. Buzz had resisted coming to New York to see Rickenbacker. With some justice, he claimed he had his hands full trying to deal with the chaos on Buchanan's shrinking assembly lines.

Jim Redwood, the vice president for sales, tried to rescue the situation. He was Cliff's height, six-foot-four, with a face full of dewlaps from too much Scotch whiskey. "Eddie—our figures show a steady upturn in the market. Come 1950 there'll be an explosion. With twenty of these planes you could put National and Braniff out of business."

"If you're wrong they'll put me out of business while I'm trying to service a five-million-dollar debt. Thanks but no thanks, guys."

Buzz cursed steadily in their long ride down in the whooshing elevator. Out on the sidewalk, he jammed his finger into Cliff's chest. "The next time you get an idea like this, come to me with it, not our famous fucking marketing genius Adrian Van Ness."

Last month, *Newsweek* magazine had run a cover story on Adrian, hailing him as a model of the new postwar executive, a man who combined an uncanny instinct for the marketplace with a profound grasp of the latest technology. Ignoring the help he had gotten from Hitler and Tojo, the magazine told its readers how Adrian had brought Buchanan from bankruptcy to the biggest plane maker in the nation. Ironically, the journalists puffed him just as he was falling on his face. Betting on a steep rise in the flying public, Adrian had built the Excalibur, the biggest airliner in the world—and started selling it a month after the postwar recession sent passenger numbers plummeting.

Adrian was the toast of the aircraft business, while Buzz grappled with the thousand and one problems of Buchanan's transition from war to peacetime production. From a hundred thousand workers churning out five hundred planes a month, Buchanan had shrunk to eight thousand workers making—if they were lucky—two hundred planes a year. Adrian had put Buzz in charge of the firing—which made him the most hated man in the company.

"I'm sorry, Buzz," Jim Redwood said as they strode through the noonday crowds toward Fifth Avenue. "I thought it was worth a try. It was my idea as much as Cliff's."

"That makes you a pair of assholes," Buzz said. "Dragging me across the fucking continent to kiss Captain Eddie's ass. If my war had lasted another month I'd have passed him in the numbers game and I'd be up there running that airline and Eddie'd be a garage mechanic in Milwaukee."

"I don't know what the hell we're gonna do with this plane," Redwood said. "Rick was pretty much our last hope."

Buzz whirled on Redwood. He knew they had sold a grand total of ten Excaliburs, all to TWA because the airline's eccentric owner, millionaire Howard Hughes, liked big planes. But Buzz could never tolerate defeatism. "Listen.

We're gonna sell that plane somewhere. Maybe the army if the country wakes up to what the Russians are tryin' to pull—"

He pointed to a Daily News headline: BERLIN STILL FREE. President Truman had responded to Russian attempts to drive the Americans, British, and French out of Berlin with a massive airlift.

"If they had fifty Excaliburs redesigned for cargo, they could keep Berlin supplied till doomsday. Instead they got half-asleep pilots makin' two flights a day in C-Forty-sevens. It's just like the last war. The goddamn government makes do with yesterday's planes and the whole aircraft business stands still."

Back at the Waldorf, the desk clerk handed Cliff a telegram. He ripped it open and read: SARAH HAD A GIRL AT 6:30 A.M. TAMA. "Good Christ," he said, showing the message to Buzz. Sarah was not supposed to deliver for six weeks.

"Another girl?" Buzz said. "When you gonna stop shootin' blanks?"

"Hey. Adrian's got a girl. He's nuts about her," Jim Redwood said.

"Adrian's a fucking—aristocrat," Buzz said, avoiding Cliff's eyes.

The averted eyes, the momentary hesitation in his voice, convinced Cliff again that Buzz regretted losing Tama to Adrian. It had nothing to do with affection. He had been unfaithful to Tama with a hundred other women over the past ten years. It was the loss of face, of power, that the switch implied. The rearrangement was part of the new game the war had created. Buzz was no longer the only hero around, the tough guy who made Cliff and even Adrian twitch when he looked at them. The war, a new generation of pilots, had put things in perspective. Buzz was the ace no one remembered, the guy who came in second to Rickenbacker in France flying funny-looking planes that barely went a hundred miles an hour.

He could handle Buzz now, Cliff told himself. He had told that to Tama with not a little anger when she announced her affair with Adrian and said he had promised to protect Cliff from Buzz. A man with forty-nine missions over Germany did not need protection.

Except when he fell on his face. When an idea went sour, the way things had just gone with Rickenbacker. Anxiety swelled in Cliff's belly. Buzz would not let him forget that fiasco for months. Cliff silently cursed Adrian Van Ness and his oversized plane. He forced a smile and socked Buzz on the shoulder. "Hey listen, Grandpa. At least I can still get it up," he said.

In the room Cliff telephoned the plant and heard the good-bad news from Tama. "Sarah's okay. The baby only weighs four pounds. They've got her in an incubator. I've never seen anything so tiny. How did the meeting go?"

"Lousy. He practically threw us out."

"The son of a bitch. I'll tell Adrian."

For a moment Cliff felt five years old. When was Tama going to stop running his life? He slammed down the phone and called the hospital. After the usual delays, a weary Sarah came on the line. "Honey, I'm sorry I wasn't there," Cliff said. "How do you feel?"

"Tired. How did things go at the big meeting?"

"Lousy."

"Oh, Cliff, I'm so sorry."

"Don't worry about it. How's the kid? Tama says she's so small you can hardly see her."

"She'll be all right. They do wonders with preemies these days."

"What'll we name her?"

Cliff had wanted a boy so badly, they had not even discussed girls' names.

"I like Margaret."

She had named their first girl Elizabeth. "What are you trying to do, turn us into a royal family?" Cliff said.

"I just like the names. Tell me about the meeting."

"There's nothing to tell. He hated the plane. It's an oversized lemon. A grapefruit."

Anxiety crawled in Cliff's chest. How many cross-examinations from the goddamn women in his life did he have to swallow? "I think you should get out of sales. This plane is making you look like—what's the word?—a loser," Sarah said.

"Listen. You have the babies. I'll worry about my goddamn career."

He slammed down the phone and stood there cursing. Why the hell had he married the daughter of an aircraft executive?

Buzz charged in, suitcase in hand. "Come on. I got us on the noon balloon out of Newark. An Excalibur."

"I thought we were going to stay until tomorrow. I've got a date with Dick Stone, my navigator on the *Rainbow Express*."

"Call him and cancel it. Let's go. We've only got an hour. I want you and Redwood there when I talk to Van Ness. We've got to convince him this plane is hopeless and figure out another move fast."

Cliff called Dick Stone and blamed the cancellation on the unexpected birth. Dick was cheerful about it. "What's the kid's name? I want to send a present. I can get it wholesale."

"The baby-wear business is good?"

"The money is great, the business is shitty. How's the plane business?"

"The exact opposite," Cliff said.

"I may call you one of these days."

"I told you, I'll kick the door open—if it's still there to kick."

Forty-five minutes later, Cliff and Buzz and Jim Redwood stood in the art-deco departure lounge of Newark Airport. Around them were about a hundred fellow businessmen in broad-brimmed felt or Panama hats, many wearing the new nylon cord summer suits, with white shirts and dark ties. Among the men were a dozen or so women wearing hats of assorted spiral shapes, blouses with large balloon sleeves and skirts that covered their knees, the "new look" of the previous year. Cliff preferred the tight skirts of the war years.

"I got a weird letter in the mail yesterday," Buzz said, trying to pass the time. "Written in words clipped from a newspaper. It said something about a dame named Califia who's gonna cut my throat. There's probably a lot of dames'd like to do that—but I can't place this one."

"Maybe it's one of Tama's movie names," Jim Redwood said. Everyone knew about Tama's vendetta against Buzz.

"Trans World Airlines Flight six-oh-seven to Los Angeles departing from Gate one-sixteen," gargled the invisible announcer.

The Excalibur sat on the runway looking twice as big as Cliff remembered it. He found himself eyeing the plane, wondering if someone had ground-tested the engines, checked the fuel lines, the electrical systems. In his seat, he listened tensely as the pilot turned over the motors, waiting for the throaty roar that announced the right fuel mixture.

Nothing to worry about, he told himself. Nothing to worry about. TWA was a first-class airline with good pilots. Down the runway they thundered, the huge engines sending vibrations of power through the fuselage that surpassed anything Cliff had ever felt aboard a B-17. He found himself bracing his legs against the footrest as if he expected a crash. *Nothing to worry about.*

Clunk the wheels retracted. The Excalibur dipped and wobbled slightly as they hit some turbulence. Pinpoints of sweat sprang out all over Cliff's body. It all came back every time he flew, the way they had become pariahs. The *Rainbow Express*'s copilot had told a friend about the double-cross they had pulled over Schweinfurt and the story spread through the 103rd Bombardment Group. Whenever the 103rd flew the Purple Heart corner, the Focke-Wulfs and Messerschmitts seemed to attack with special fury. The rest of the group started blaming their losses on the *Rainbow Express*. The thing hung over them like a gigantic hoodoo, tormenting everyone in the crew.

Inevitably, the story got to their commanding officer, Colonel Atwood, who hauled them into his office and raved about court-martials and perpetual disgrace. "We'll volunteer for another twenty-five," Dick Stone had said. Before Cliff could say or do anything, all the others volunteered. That had left Cliff no choice. He had to join them for another nine months of gambling with death over Germany.

Cliff took a deep breath. Now was the time to finish it. They had evened the score. They had flown another twenty-three missions. On the twenty-fourth, the *Rainbow Express* had taken a direct hit over Berlin. Didn't that even the score? Getting blown out of a plane clutching your parachute, somehow strapping it on as you fell toward the burning city beneath you? Yes, Cliff told himself. It evened the score.

"Jesus Christ, you're still jumpy in a plane, ain't you," Buzz said.

"I'm just jumpy for a drink," Cliff said.

Suddenly Cliff wanted to tell Buzz what had happened over Schweinfurt. Instead of the old antagonism, the submerged quarrel for Tama's love, they finally had something to share as men. Buzz had risked death in the air on the western front. Maybe he would tell him what happened over Schweinfurt was all right.

For a moment the words crowded into Cliff's throat. Across the aisle Jim

Redwood, eager for his first Scotch of the day, buzzed for the stewardess. "What'll it be, guys?" he said.

Jim would never understand what he wanted to tell Buzz. The sales chief was always introducing Cliff as his "assistant war hero," reciting his number of missions, his miraculous survival over Berlin. Cliff let the moment pass.

The Excalibur climbed to 27,000 feet and the captain told them their route to Los Angeles. The stewardesses brought them their drinks. A tall sinewy redhead who wore her blue garrison cap at a cocky angle got their attention. "There's a live one," Cliff said. Her partner, a short chipper brunette, was not bad either.

On they flew into deepening dusk. The Excalibur's fuel tanks were big enough to skip landing at Chicago, a standard requirement for other cross-country flights. The stewardesses served dinner. Cliff asked the redhead if she lived in Los Angeles.

"Mayn-hattun Beach," she said, with an accent that had to be Tennessee or Kentucky.

"We work for Buchanan Aircraft in Santa Monica."

"As a test pilot?" she asked.

"No. In sales."

"If you see someone named Billy McCall tell him Cassie Trainor says hello."

His stepbrother's name filled Cliff's throat with bile. But years of practice enabled him to conceal it. "Say hello to his father, Buzz," he said.

Cassie eyed Buzz skeptically. "You don't look like him."

"He took after his mother," Buzz said.

"Billy must be quite a pilot. He likes to test *everythin'* to the limit of its structural capacity," Cassie said.

"I know all about it. I'm the same way," Cliff said.

"It runs in the family," Buzz said.

Billy had just become a major in the newly created U.S. Air Force. Recently Buzz had brought him to California to help them test an experimental jet Frank Buchanan was developing at Muroc Air Base in the Mojave Desert.

"There's some sort of club you belong to?"

"The Honeycomb Club. Maybe you'd like to work there. The hours and the pay are a lot better than this job," Buzz said.

Cassie's penciled eyebrows rose. "So I've heard."

Cliff could almost feel the heat. Cassie had cut loose. She was on her own in California, playing the big-girl game. A lot of stewardesses went this route. There was no limit to what they would try if you got them early. Timing was important. It did not take long for a woman to get her heart broken and turn morose, sullen, bitchy.

Cliff considered himself a student of women. Even a collector, a connoisseur. Cassie's down-home drawl added a touch of fire, a suggestion of sultry southern blood. She was ready to do things Cliff could never suggest to Lady Sarah, his private name for his English wife.

"You ready to go for some of that tonight?" Buzz asked Cliff, as the stewardesses began serving after-dinner drinks.

He had been planning to get Cassie Trainor's phone number for future reference and go to the hospital to see Sarah and the baby. But Buzz's offer was not something Cliff could afford to turn down. It implied Buzz was ready to forget about dragging him to see Captain Eddie—if Cliff forgot about how crudely his old pal rejected him. It even suggested a sort of truce between them, an admission that Cliff was a man now, ready to play games with women Buzz's way. "Sure," Cliff said.

By the time they landed in Los Angeles, twelve hours and ten minutes after leaving Newark, Cliff and Buzz had dates with Cassie and the chipper brunette, whose name was Barbara. Cassie offered to find a date for Jim Redwood but he did not feel in a celebrating mood and went home.

"What the hell's the matter with Redwood?" Cliff said, as they waited in the terminal for Cassie and Barbara to change out of their uniforms. "Sometimes I think he's queer. You can't get him interested half the time."

"A dame broke his heart years ago," Buzz said. "It happened to me with Billy's mother. I swore I'd never let it happen again."

On that point, he and Buzz were in agreement. Exactly where that left Sarah was something Cliff did not think about very often. Sarah was part of the war, something he had brought home, along with the forty-nine missions and the memory of Schweinfurt.

With Buzz in charge of the party, they headed for the Trocadero, a place Cassie and Barbara considered as prehistoric as the Great Pyramid. They ate the terrible food and drank a lot of wine and ogled the aging screen stars. Buzz tried to impress Barbara by claiming he had dated some of them in his stunt-flying days. On the way out he squeezed Gloria Swanson's arm and gave her a big hello. To Cliff's surprise, she smiled and said: "Hi, Buzz."

At ninety miles an hour they hurtled up the coast highway to Buzz's house in Pacific Palisades. There they persuaded Cassie and Barbara to audition for the Honeycomb Club. Barbara had good breasts and a dark wild pussy but she was shy about taking off her clothes. Cassie had no inhibitions about that or anything else. She was an instant winner. Sex popped out of every pore of her long lithe body.

Barbara and Buzz went for a swim in the pool and Cassie continued her audition with Cliff in Buzz's king-sized bed. She was just drunk enough to let him do anything and enjoy it. It was beautiful fucking, exactly the way Cliff liked it. Almost impersonal, so you could concentrate on the performance, the electricity in every touch, every thrust. Yet not completely impersonal, not like whorehouse sex. Pleasure, not money was the payoff. Cliff was proud of his ability to please a woman.

Power was almost as important. With each stroke, each moan of desire, their failure to sell the Excalibur dwindled, the world outside the walls of the bedroom was somehow less threatening, less relentless. Clifford Morris was in absolute control here, a man defying luck, eluding memory and rules, a kind of outlaw.

Finally, there was no more juice in the joystick. They lay side by side laughing, fondling. "Am I as good as Billy?" Cliff said.

"You're better," Cassie said. "You're more fun. You didn't scare me."

"How did he scare you?"

"Never mind."

Billy knew zilch about how to acquire a woman. That was what Cliff liked to do. Not just screw them and walk away à la Buzz. He liked to come back for seconds, thirds, fourths, fifths, to arouse flutters of love, to toy with the possibility of loving them in return.

"Billy's still out at Muroc testing one of our planes. Why don't you call him right now and tell him I'm better?"

"Why not?" Cassie said.

Cliff found Billy's number in Buzz's address book. Cassie dialed him and said: "Hey, Billy. You probably don't remember me. I'm just some stewardess you fucked one night in Manhattan Beach. I'm here with Cliff Morris and I want to tell you—"

Strange things began happening in Cassie's body. She shook as if she was having convulsions.

"I want to tell you—"

The tremors became more violent. Cliff grabbed her, afraid she was going to fly off the bed.

"I want to tell you—"

Cassie flung the phone against the wall and curled into a ball. She bit the back of her hand and sobbed and sobbed. "What the hell's the matter with you?" Cliff said.

Cassie rolled over on her back and smiled at him. "Nothin'," she said. "Get me a drink and we'll go for the record."

"Some other night," Cliff said, putting his hand on her damp pussy in a comforting—and acquiring—way.

DOES OOO WUVUMS WIDDLE ME?

"Mr. Stone? Mr. Pesin wants to see you immediately."

It was around five o'clock on the day Cliff had called to cancel their dinner date. The vice president of nothing in particular at Pesin's Baby Wear was sitting in his office reading a symposium, "Religion and the Intellectuals," in the *Partisan Review*. For the past three weeks, Dick Stone had not had time to do much reading. No one at Pesin's Baby Wear had time to do anything but entertain buyers.

Twice a year they invaded New York like a horde of Visigoths, insulting, demanding, cajoling, sneering, greedy for tickets to Broadway shows, free dinners, exotic sex. Everyone on the executive level of Pesin's Baby Wear, the comptroller, the production chief, the vice presidents, the designers, were all hurled into the task of keeping these obnoxious provincials happy. As son-in-law and heir apparent to the business. Dick Stone was expected to be more jovial, more amusing, more charming than anyone else.

Pesin's Baby Wear was grossing about ten million dollars a year, reason enough, in the opinion of most people, to be very very charming. Sam Pesin had made this obvious more than once, in what he called little hints.

This afternoon, Sam was pondering the usual rush-hour traffic jamming Seventh Avenue when Dick Stone walked into the office. Sam was a short energetic man who disliked the word *energetic*. He maintained energetic people were usually dumb. *Dynamic* was the word he preferred. Last year he had put up most of the money for a testimonial dinner at which the Seventh Avenue Association had hailed him as the dynamo of the baby-wear business.

"Maybe it's time we had a talk," Sam said.

"I'm listening," Dick said.

"It's not about the grandson. I can wait another year for him. It's about the business. Your attitude toward it."

Trouble, Dick thought. He had been half-expecting it since he declined to escort a half-dozen buyers to the Copacabana last Monday. He had given them the name of the headwaiter and a guarantee they had a front table. All they had to do was sign for anything they wanted to eat, drink, or squeeze. But the headwaiter had gotten a bigger tip from someone else. Instead of topping it the schnooks had left in a huff.

"Greenberg's buyer, Shapiro. He went home without giving us a single order. He never even came back to shake hands good-bye."

"That's too bad."

"Too bad? That's two hundred thousand dollars' worth of bad. They've got stores from one end of New England to the other. The same thing happened with Levitt. He's always good for fifty thousand dollars. He's got everything in Pennsylvania south of Lancaster in his pocket. Nothing."

"Is it all my fault? Or is it possible that there's something wrong with this year's line?"

"There's nothing wrong with this year's line that some dynamic selling couldn't fix. What the hell happened to you Monday night? How come you left those people on their own at the Copa?"

"Nancy and I had tickets to *Death of a Salesman*."

"Oh, this is beautiful. You go see a show about a goddamned failure written by a smartass Communist while our clients are left standing around the Copa with their fingers up their asses. Is this what an MBA does for you?"

"I tipped the headwaiter fifty bucks. Is it my fault if he's a fink?"

"It's nobody's but your fault. But it's only a symptom of an overall thing. An overall attitude, Dick. I brought you in here when you married Nancy. I was frankly delighted to have a guy with brains, a hero who bombed the Nazis no less, on the payroll. But I expected some gratitude. Some dynamism. You don't seem to really *care*, you know what I mean? You just seem to be going through the motions."

"You're right," Dick said. "I don't care. I don't give a shit whether yellow or blue is the in color for bibs this year. Or whether dresses for one-year-olds should have lace collars. Or whether the Lone Ranger should be on our overalls. I not only don't give a shit, I don't give a fuck."

At six-one, Stone had about eight inches on Sam Pesin. He had added twenty pounds to his burly thick-necked body since the war. The dynamo of the baby-wear business did not make a sound as his berserk son-in-law strode out of the office.

Dick squeezed into the packed F train at Sixth Avenue and 42nd Street and rode under the East River. What the hell was happening to him? Was he losing his mind? Was his father finally getting to him?

His father had been disappointed by his decision to go into business. His high marks in college, his intellectual interests, had led Rabbi Saul Stone to expect his only son to choose a profession—the law or medicine or academe. Dick did not completely understand the decision himself. It had something to do with an inchoate desire to become—or remain—part of the American world in which he had participated as an airman. He liked being an American first and a Jew more or less second. His father, worried about the number of Jews marrying Christians in his congregation and elsewhere, had nodded impatiently when Dick tried to explain this to him. "Just be sure you marry a nice Jewish girl," he had said.

Was that why he had married Nancy Pesin? Dick wondered as the F train groaned and creaked through the East River tunnel at ten miles an hour. It had seemed logical in so many other ways. She was in the top third of her class at Barnard, a reader and something of a thinker. She had a good disposition and her figure was definitely A+. Inheriting Pesin's Baby Wear was a not-unpleasant prospect. It dovetailed with another inchoate desire—to acquire enough money to pursue a career as a writer and thinker in the *Partisan Review* league.

At last the F Train was through the tunnel, rocketing toward bucolic Forest Hills. Dick walked to the apartment house through the warm June dusk, wondering if Sam Pesin had called his daughter to complain about her ungrateful husband. Nancy had passed little hints of her own about Daddy's dissatisfaction.

Up to the third floor in the shiny new high-rise off Queens Boulevard. The aromas of a half dozen dinners mingled in the hall. Veal cordon bleu, his nose told him the minute he opened his door. Nancy was on the telephone in the kitchen, gassing with her best friend and fellow Barnard graduate, Helene Feldman.

"It's the most devastating experience I've ever had in the theater."

She was talking about *Death of a Salesman*.

The living room had an oriental rug on the floor, prints from the Museum of Modern Art on the wall, traditional furniture from Sloane's, except for an immense television set in a mahogany case in front of the window. A Christmas gift from Daddy. In the dining area, the table was set, with a spray of fresh tulips in a vase in the center of it. A shaker sat on the coffee table with martinis for two. What could he complain about? Dick wondered. Wasn't this the American dream come true? Wouldn't Willy Loman call him a lucky SOB?

"Oh—here's my one and only. I'll call you tomorrow, *dollink*."

Nancy hung up and emerged from the kitchen, smiling broadly. She was wearing a frilly apron over a dark red dress inset with panels of blue. The energy she put into getting good marks at Barnard now went into being the compleat housewife, with a touch of upper-middle-class chic. "Here he is, home from the garment wars to his little balaboosta," she bubbled.

She threw her arms around him, nestling her body as close as possible and kissed him on the lips. Her tongue played around his mouth. "Does ooo wuvums widdle me?" she gurgled.

From the sky above them came the distant grumble of a plane landing at La Guardia Airport. The apartment house was only a block from one of the approach patterns. "No," Dick said.

The word spoke itself. It was an eruption, an explosion of memory and impulse and desire. He was back in Sam Pesin's office telling him he did not give a fuck and simultaneously in his father's temple in Rego Park listening to him compare the metaphor of the promised land to Thomas Jefferson's pursuit of happiness. He was on the telephone hearing Cliff Morris tell him the plane business was great.

Nancy had not used baby talk when he dated her, nor when they began sleeping together, in her last term at Barnard. She had been passionate but shy in those encounters. The baby talk had started on their honeymoon. Dick soon discovered it had deep roots. Sam Pesin talked that way to his daughter whenever they met. *Does oo wuvums Daddykins?* he would gurgle. Why had it suddenly become intolerable?

Nancy stepped back. Dick could see her thinking: how could he mean that? Not love this beautiful apartment, the great dinners I cook for him every night, followed by equally scrumptious screwing? Not love the perfect deal I've handed him? All he has to do is put up with the dynamo for another ten years or so and take over and run the business his way? No?

"I've had it with your father and I've had it with you and your stupid baby talk," Dick said. "I want a divorce."

Nancy's pretty face puckered like a two-year-old. Wailing, she fled into the bathroom. Dick sat down on the couch and tried to think about what he was doing. He was frightened by his inability to understand this defiant inner self, this Samson who was ready to pull down the walls and ceiling.

He could only compare what he had just done to volunteering for another twenty-five missions to get the stench of Schweinfurt out of his soul. That too had seemed an act of insanity. It would have been easy enough to blame the whole thing on Cliff Morris and let Colonel Atwood court-martial him, as he had been longing to do since training days. Only their tail gunner, Mike Shannon, seemed to understand why Dick had volunteered. Mike had been the first member of the crew to follow his lead. Where did these explosions of anger or need or morality—Dick did not know what to call them—come from?

He had no answer to the larger question. He only knew the source of this convulsion, the root of the *no* he had just snarled in his wife's face. It was the sense of being swallowed by Jewishness again. He wanted to be part of the American world of 1948, the America that had just won the greatest war in history. Instead he was stuck in a Jewish corner of New York where he felt as separated from the rest of the country as if he had emigrated to Israel.

Dick heard Cliff Morris telling him the plane business was great and the pay was shitty. Why did that appeal to him? Was there a moral dimension in those words? Or was it simply the fact that the airplane business was in California, as far away from New York as he could get?

Or was there some unfinished business between him and Cliff, something to do with those five minutes over Schweinfurt in a plane built by Buchanan Aircraft, five minutes that distorted and confused something deep in his soul—maybe in both their souls?

With an angry shake of his large head, Dick Stone told himself to cut the bullshit. When he got going he was worse than his father the rabbi. He was a goddamn mystic.

He strode into the bedroom and began throwing clothes in a suitcase. If Cliff Morris welched on his promise, he would talk his way into Buchanan on his own. Or into Lockheed or Douglas or North American. One way or another, he was on his way to California to get into the plane business.

PEACETIME BLUES

In his split-level house in south Los Angeles, Cliff Morris was awakened by his three-year-old, Liz, giving him a big wet kiss. "You smell funny, Daddy," she said.

"I feel funny too," Cliff said. "They call it a hangover."

He gulped aspirins and drove to the hospital, surprising Sarah. "I haven't even combed my hair," she said.

Cliff was tempted to tell her that would not make much difference. Sarah had gained about thirty pounds with this latest baby. The trim brunette who filled out her WAAF uniform in all the right places at Thorpe Abbots Air Base had almost vanished in rolls of fat. She swore she was going to lose weight—a song Cliff had heard before. Sarah could not resist six ounces of heavy cream on her breakfast cereal and a half pound of butter on every slice of bread.

Fat or thin, Sarah still wanted to know everything that was happening at Buchanan Aircraft. What were they going to do if the Excalibur did not sell?

Was there a market for it abroad? Could they reduce it in size? Cliff's replies were curt. He did not know the answers. He was in an impromptu training program, supposedly learning the aircraft business, while the company tried to cope with its postwar poverty. Her executive-level questions only reminded him of his insignificance.

He took a look at the tiny creature sleeping on her stomach in the incubator and drove to the Buchanan plant in Santa Monica. He remembered the way the windowless sandstone buildings always took him by surprise in his boyhood. They suddenly appeared in the middle of a neat neighborhood of one-family stucco houses, as if they had been built there by mistake. The plant now sprawled over a dozen blocks, most of it a series of hangars only one story taller than the houses around it. In the center was a hexagonal six-story tower built during the war years, with a top-floor dining room enclosed in glass. The whole place was separated from the neighborhood by a high chain-link fence.

The retired LA cop at the desk in the bare main lobby gave him a cheery hello and signed him in. Cliff clipped a badge to the handkerchief pocket of his suit coat and strode down the dim central corridor. On the left behind a blue-painted brick wall was the factory. On the right was a maze of narrow corridors leading to offices.

In the engineering and design departments rows of men bent over desks and drawing boards. They all wore identical white shirts and solid-color ties. Artificial ceilings had been inserted to lower the hangar height of the building. Overhead fluorescent lights cast a cold silver glow on the desks and their occupants. The men were mostly silent, concentrating fiercely on their tasks. Cliff did not envy them. In spite of their expensive engineering educations, they were as expendable as the assembly line workers. Thousands of them had already been fired in the great postwar cutback.

Cliff finally reached the tower in the center of the building where several flights of stairs led to an office that had the same low-budget look. Tama Morris was sitting behind another secondhand desk, wearing the usual tight nylon blouse. She had a weight problem too but she controlled it by fierce dieting. The scars of a recent face-lift were visible at the edges of her carefully combed dark hair. Thanks to willpower and the doctors, she looked younger than Sarah.

"Hi," Cliff said. "Anything I should know before I see the great man about our disaster in New York?"

"There's a big decision coming up on that goddamn plane Frank wants to build."

Cliff had seen a drawing of the plane; it was bizarre—all wing and no tail or fuselage. "Does he really think that thing will fly?"

"I think he's trying to wreck the company. First the Excalibur, now this monstrosity."

"The Excalibur was Adrian's idea."

"I didn't hear you say that. I hope you don't say it again."

As usual, Tama was playing Adrian's game for him, blaming his mistakes on other people.

"Incidentally," Tama said. "Do you know anything about this?"

She pulled a letter from her desk drawer. It was written with words clipped from a newspaper or a magazine. For Tama's name separate letters from headlines were used. *Beloved TAMA do not despair. You will be freed from your bondage soon. CALIFIA.*

"Did Sarah send this? Is it her idea of a joke?" Tama said.

"It's some nut. Buzz got one a couple of days ago from the same dame."

"You're sure it's not Sarah?"

The hostility between Tama and Sarah was one more irritation in his life. Women! Cliff retreated to his office where he found a stack of phone messages from local airlines in search of replacement parts for their fifteen-year-old SkyRangers. As he returned the calls, he could hear Jim Redwood in the next office, trying to sell the Excalibur to Pan American for their South American routes.

Another call—this one not so routine. Dick Stone was on the line asking Cliff to get him a job at Buchanan. Could he do it? Did he want him around? Old Shylock could be a difficult character. But he could be an ally. Sarah was always telling him to build alliances with people his own age. "I'll see what I can do, Dick. I'll call you back tomorrow."

At twelve o'clock a whistle gave a long low hoot and the assembly line went to lunch. The executives headed for their dining room on the top floor of the tower. As Cliff and Jim Redwood strolled in, a new Excalibur took off from the company field, the roar of its motors rattling the glasses in the well-stocked bar.

About a dozen men in rumpled dark business suits were standing in two clusters on the other side of the room, drinks in their hands. One group were designers, the other engineers. As usual they were not speaking to each other.

Cliff and Jim each ordered a glass of the house single-malt Scotch, Inverness. Most people thought it tasted like week-old rainwater but Buzz McCall said it was a man's drink. Adrian backed him because it was cheap—and he never drank it. Cliff and Jim headed for the engineers, who were grouped around Buzz.

"Where the hell did you go last night?" Buzz said. "When I came back from the pool Cassie was horny as hell. I had to satisfy her and Barbara."

"He's full of shit," Jim Redwood said. "He passed out in the pool and almost drowned. Barbara had to rescue him. She called me this morning and told me all about it."

Buzz threatened to slug him but Redwood just grinned. He had been an all-American tackle for UCLA in the twenties. "I thought we were going to talk to Adrian," he said.

"I talked to him by myself. I told him what I thought of wasting my time trying to sell a plane we never should have built in the first place. We ought to be concentrating on military stuff based on that jet Billy is testing at Muroc. If we get something like that into the Air Force we'll have enough money to develop two new airliners. But first we gotta get our resident genius to cooperate."

He glowered toward the bar. "Frank wants to talk to Cliff about that goddamn flying nightmare he's trying to build."

At the bar, Pat was surrounded by six of seven of his favorite designers. In contrast to the prevailing crew cuts, his reddish brown hair flowed over his ears and partway down his neck. Instead of a business suit, he wore an ancient leather flight jacket, which was cracking in a half-dozen places.

"Cliff," Frank said. "I heard about your latest frustration in New York. Since we don't have a plane to sell—and you're in a sort of training program—would you be interested in working with me as project manager of a new plane we hope to get into production? It's called the Talus."

"I might be," Cliff said warily.

"This plane could change the history of aviation. It's completely different from the planes you flew during the war. They used most of their engine power to overcome the drag of their fuselages and tails."

"Sounds like you're going to break the sound barrier and then some," Cliff said.

"There's no such a thing as a sound barrier," Frank said. "There are only underpowered, badly designed planes that can't survive the buffeting they take at very high speeds."

"That's verbiage, Buchanan, and you know it," roared Buzz McCall from his cluster of followers.

"No, it's intuition. Something an engineer doesn't believe in, until the facts hit him between the eyes."

"Intuition," Buzz growled, striding toward them, backed by his entourage. "That's a designer's name for something that can't fly until an engineer tells him how to make it work."

"You're telling me, I suppose, that the Talus won't fly?"

"Not without killing a lot of people."

"We'll see who's right in a month or two," Frank said.

"If I have anything to say about it, nobody'll see a goddamn thing!" Buzz roared. "We've got enough problems with the plane that could save our asses, if you'd only get to work on it. Billy's risking his neck every day flying it and you're ignoring him to work on your crazy castrated gooney bird."

"White Lightning is a research tool, not a production model. We're learning a lot about flying in the ionosphere."

"While we go broke on the ground," Buzz said.

"If we'd built the Talus instead of the Excalibur, we'd be ten years ahead of everyone else," Frank said.

"Bullshit," Buzz bellowed.

"Even if we fail, we'll go down gloriously, contributing to the advance of flight."

"Fuck glorious failure," Buzz said. "I'm for staying in business first, last, and forever."

229

" 'Sacrifices must be expected,' " Frank said. "Do you recognize those words, Cliff?"

Cliff shook his head.

"Otto Lilienthal said them in 1896, shortly before he died of a broken neck trying to demonstrate his erroneous principles of aerodynamics. Without his two thousand glider flights the Wright Brothers would probably still be trying to get off their sand dune at Kitty Hawk. Otto was a brave man, even if he was a German."

By this time a waitress in a tight black cocktail dress had served everyone another round of Inverness. Cliff told himself he had to learn to pace his drinks to get through these lunches. Frank was only warming up. They drank to the Talus. In spite of Buzz's refusal to toast a "dead kraut," the designers downed another round to Otto Lilienthal.

"Gentlemen. I'm sorry I'm late," Adrian Van Ness said, somewhere on the outer fringes of the crowd.

"You're always late," Frank said. "Is it a way of reminding us of your importance?"

Antagonism flickered between Frank and Adrian every time they met. By this time everyone knew why. It was the company's dirty secret, never mentioned above a whisper. Giving up Amanda Van Ness had filled Frank with bitterness. It came out in unexpected explosions of temper and in a reckless insistence on the right to experiment with radical new designs like the Talus.

Everyone sat down at a long table in front of the window overlooking the airfield. Two waitresses began serving hot dogs and baked beans. Gone were the war days when they feasted on black market lamb and steak. Everyone except Adrian Van Ness drank more Inverness. A waitress served him red wine.

More drunken arguments broke out at various points between engineers and designers. Jim Redwood said Pan American still might buy twenty Excaliburs. Everyone sneered. Jim had given them too many blue-sky promises.

"I want to take Cliff out of sales for a while to keep things organized on the Talus prototype," Frank said.

"Who said we're going to build that?" Adrian said.

"I did," Frank said.

"Do you have any idea how much we're losing on the Excalibur? Lockheed is killing us with this talk of a Super Constellation. Douglas, Boeing are both bringing out hundred-seat models."

"All the more reason to gamble on something radical," Frank said. "Something those play-it-safe boys wouldn't try in a million years."

"How much will it cost?"

"Four—five million—for the prototype. Overall development shouldn't go beyond twenty million."

"What do you think, Jim?" Adrian said, turning to their sales director.

"I vote no. It may fly but it won't sell," Redwood said, avoiding Frank's eyes. They were good friends. "It's too experimental. It looks like a fucking

230

boomerang. People are scared to death of jet engines. The goddamn things don't have propellers."

"It won't be experimental when it breaks the speed record from here to New York," Frank shouted, bringing his fist down on the table with a crash that sent Inverness cascading toward the ceiling. "I guarantee you this plane will outclimb and outfly every commercial airliner in the sky."

"We don't have five million dollars to spend on a fantasy," Adrian said.

"Borrow it!" Frank roared. "High finance is what you're good at, isn't it? Call up one of your Wall Street friends."

"I don't have any Wall Street friends anymore," Adrian snapped. "As far as they're concerned, we're back to being a cottage industry. The war's over. We've saved the world for the goddamned automobile."

For a moment Adrian's eyes met Cliff's. He seemed to be trying to ask him for something. Support? Sympathy?

"Mortgage the real estate then," Frank said. "This plane has to be built. If I can't build it here, I'll go elsewhere."

Adrian finished his wine. "We had some money in the bank until we ran into trouble with Excalibur." He drummed his fingers on the tabletop.

"The Talus will have a hundred seats in a cabin roomy enough to jitterbug in. At six hundred miles an hour," Frank said.

"Six million an hour is more like it," Buzz said. "Don't you have any idea how much fuel those jet engines use?"

"They'll solve that problem within a year—two at the most."

"That's not what I hear from Curtiss Wright. They don't see any future for jets except in pursuit planes," Buzz said.

"Then I don't see any future for Curtiss Wright," Frank said.

"All right," Adrian said. "We'll build a Talus prototype. Providing Buzz gets the Air Force into the act to put up at least half the money."

"Absolutely not," Frank said. "I don't agree to that condition. I made a promise to myself never to build another bomber. We don't need one. We've got the atomic bomb and no one else does. The B-Twenty-nine can take care of anyone who threatens us for the next twenty years."

"What if the Russians get the bomb?" Adrian said. "From what I hear in Washington, they grabbed more German scientists than we did when the Reich went kaput. They've built a pretty good imitation B-Twenty-nine—that Tupolev Tu4—the one they call the Bull."

"What about the White Lightning? A jet derived from that design could put us back in the big time," Buzz said.

"We don't need fighter planes any more than we need bombers," Frank said.

"I predict we're gonna need bombers and fighter planes—a lot of them—to deal with Joe Stalin and his pals," Buzz said.

"It's your sort of mentality that's created the cold war," Frank said.

"Listen to the guy!" Buzz exploded. "He's a fucking Communist."

"Let's be kind to our old friend," Adrian said. "His problem is political naivete."

"You can call me any name you please," Frank said. "Are we going to build the Talus?"

Adrian's eyes roved the table. Cliff thought he saw some sort of message pass between him and Buzz. "Maybe we ought to humor the crazy bastard," Buzz said.

"I want it designed for prop as well as jet engines," Adrian said. "I agree with Jim about the public's attitude toward jets."

"To the future," Frank Buchanan said, raising his glass of Inverness. His designers rose with him, each at least as drunk.

"Aren't you going to join us?" Frank called to Cliff.

"You bet," Cliff said, lurching to his feet. Only then did he discover neither Buzz nor Adrian nor Jim Redwood was with him. It was too late to sit down without looking like a fink. He found Adrian's eyes again. They were stony.

The hell with him, Cliff decided. The hell with Tama too. Who knew what could happen if Frank pulled this plane off? It was a gambler's business. He and Frank might start telling Adrian and Buzz what to do.

"I predict it will kill a lot of people," Buzz said.

"Sacrifices must be expected," Frank said.

"Remember, you'll be operating on borrowed money," Adrian said.

Cliff Morris wondered if he ought to call Dick Stone and tell him he was crazy to come anywhere near the Buchanan Aircraft Company.

MYSTERY BUSINESS

Six weeks after he walked out on Nancy Pesin, Dick Stone trudged off a Douglas DC-6 at Los Angeles airport with Irwin Shaw's *The Young Lions* under his arm. A smiling, crew-cutted Cliff Morris mashed his hand. They got into Cliff's white Buick convertible and in a few minutes were on a six-lane highway, roaring along at eighty-five miles an hour. "How do you like this?" Cliff said. "It's the Hollywood Freeway. They're going to build a whole network of these things."

"How many people do they lose on it each week?"

"A half dozen or so. Everybody drives fast—it's the western approach to things. Fast cars, fast planes, fast women."

"I'm ready for all three."

"I can't believe it. Old Shylock is busting loose."

"Yeah," Dick said. He had never liked the Shylock joke.

"What happened between you and Nancy?"

"Diarrhea of the mouth."

"Is there a dame who doesn't have that problem?"

"I'm hoping to find one."

"It may take you the rest of your life."

"I'll wait."

"I've thought about splitting a couple of times. But we've got two kids now."

"Hey, I'm not trying to start a fashion."

Cliff's reaction gave Dick an instant attack of guilt. Maybe he should have tried harder with Nancy—asked her to come to California with him. Maybe distance would have eliminated the baby talk. But Sam Pesin had too much money to eliminate the source of it.

"How's business?"

"If you didn't have an MBA, I couldn't have gotten you near the place. We've made a couple of wrong moves. It's part of the sport, you know? You bet half the company on a plane. We did it on the Excalibur, a double-decker transcontinental job. Nobody wants to go near it."

"What's wrong with your marketing people?"

"Marketing, schmarketing. In this business we operate on hunches. Rabbits' feet. Everything gets decided in Adrian Van Ness's head. Other companies aren't that different. Nothing happens at Douglas until Don Douglas makes up his mind. At North American Dutch Kindelberger came back from Washington the other day with a three-million-dollar contract on the back of an envelope. He couldn't read it until he sobered up."

"Don't you have a chain of command?" Dick asked.

"Sure," Cliff said. "Most of the time someone's trying to wrap it around some other guy's throat and pull it tight. This is a man's business, Dick. You've got to learn to talk back, fight dirty, play rough."

"Are you still in sales?"

"There's nothing to sell. I'm a project manager on a new plane. It's the damndest thing you've ever seen. All wing and no fuselage. If it flies I'm a hero. If it crashes I'm a bum."

They rocketed off the freeway down a ramp to a broad boulevard, where the traffic moved much slower. Eventually they reached Cliff's ranch house in a development that rambled up and down a half-dozen hills. It looked like a transplant from Long Island or Westchester—except for the palm trees on the streets and the mountains looming in the distance.

"Here's your home away from home," he said.

As Cliff helped carry his bags up the walk, a beaming Sarah Morris opened the door. "Dick," she said in her low liquid voice that brought back the years in England. "How good to see you."

Cliff dumped his share of the bags in the hall. "You two behave yourselves while I try to calm down a couple of designers who want to assassinate half the engineering department," he said, heading back to his car.

Sarah had gained over forty pounds and looked much too matronly to keep a lothario like Cliff Morris happy. Dick dismissed that unpleasant thought as she led him into a living room full of inexpensive furniture. "I see you're reading *The Young Lions*. What do you think of it?" she asked.

"It's ten times better than *The Naked and the Dead*. I especially liked the German side of the story."

"I agree on both counts. I hoped Mr. Mailer would teach me a bit about the American male, a mystery I need to penetrate. I'm afraid all I learned were naughty words."

"Do you still read Gerard Manley Hopkins?"

"Hopkins?" For a moment she looked blank. "Oh, that poor old Jesuit. No. How did you know I ever read him?"

"You—you mentioned him to Cliff—the night we met. The first night."

She gave him a peculiar look. Did she remember where and how she had mentioned him to Cliff?

" 'Like a daregale skylark scanted in a cage,' " he said.

Sarah's eyes came alive. " 'Man's spirit in his bonehouse, meanhouse dwells.' Yes. Yes. I remember how much I used to love that passage. I don't remember mentioning it to Cliff."

She made a wry face. "I can't imagine ever reciting poetry to Cliff. It's a sad commentary on how quickly romance vanishes, I suppose."

She served him tea and scones covered with an inch of butter and another inch of raspberry jam. The tea was deliciously strong, brewed in the pot as only the English make it.

"I don't know why we revolted because you taxed this stuff. I would have paid gladly," Dick said.

Sarah nodded, pleased. She stirred in some milk and sugar. "It must have been very painful—getting divorced."

Dick shrugged. "The worst part is wondering how you got involved in the first place. How you could have made such a dumb mistake."

There was a painful pause and Dick wondered if Sarah was applying the words to herself. He changed the subject to California. How did she like it? She struggled to be enthusiastic but ended up saying she had many acquaintances but few friends.

Her daughters awoke from their naps. Elizabeth, the three-year-old, was a little beauty. Dick felt a pang at the sight of her. If he had stayed with Nancy, would they have had a child like this?

Eventually Cliff came home and banged Dick on the back and told him Adrian Van Ness was looking forward to meeting a guy with an MBA. Buchanan was having a tough time right now like the rest of the industry but the coming decade was going to be stupendous. This hot air contradicted most of what Cliff had said in the car driving from the airport. Was he sorry he had told the truth the first time? Or was he talking for Sarah's benefit? If so, he was wasting his breath.

Gone was the adoration with which Sarah had gazed at Cliff at their wedding, just after he had volunteered for another twenty-five missions. Her tight mouth made it clear she was all too familiar with Cliff's tendency to talk big. It made Dick feel better about his decision to flee Nancy Pesin. Was seeing, knowing too much, an enemy of love?

234

Dinner was pleasant. Cliff talked sports, Sarah talked books. Dick was able to keep them both happy. He wondered what they would have said to each other if he were not at the table.

At midnight, in bed in the guest room, Dick listened to the rising wind. A Santa Ana, Cliff Morris had called it. A weird California phenomenon that swept down from the mountains and across the deserts with near hurricane force, hurling cars off highways, blowing roofs off houses. Tomorrow the weather would be hot and sticky.

Dick found himself remembering his father's distress when he appeared at his parents' house in Rego Park the night of the cosmic no. On the stairs going up to his old bedroom, his father had seized his arm. "Why such bitterness?" he cried. "It is something I've done?"

Dick almost tried to explain one last time. A new metaphor flared in his mind. The last mission over Berlin. Leaping from the doomed bomber. It was a kind of birth—like a butterfly from a burning chrysalis. But it would have been futile. He could not talk frankly to the rabbi. He had become a professional advice giver, a spokesman for Jewishness.

He looked past his father at his mother and was shaken by what he saw there. Her face was sad but her eyes said: *go.* In a flash he saw deep into his parents' marriage. She did not want him to be a secular replica of this pompous man she no longer loved. How did she know that Saul Stone, the articulate boy she had fallen in love with one teenage summer in Bradley Beach, New Jersey, would become a verbose Reform rabbi?

In another flash, Dick saw the evolution. His grandfather had abandoned his Orthodox faith for the glory, the power of modern culture, in particular the German culture into which he had been born. His son, reacting against the father as sons have a way of doing, had doubled back to Reform Judaism, trying to hold the old and the new together. His son had repudiated him—for what? Was it for another faith, Americanism? Maybe freedom was a better name.

Dick drifted down into sleep in the middle of these thoughts and dreamt he was flying through the darkness on a gigantic arrow, to which he clung with total desperation. A hand was seizing his shoulder, trying to tear him off. He fought with amazing fury to resist it. "Wha—?"

Cliff Morris was shaking him awake. "Hey, Navigator. You got a telephone call."

"Your mother gave me the number," Nancy Pesin Stone said. "I just want to tell you one last time what a rotten no good son of a bitch you are."

A fugitive from Jewish wrath and pain, Dick Stone was almost afraid to meet Adrian Van Ness the next morning. What if he turned out to be an anti-Semite? He could hear Sam Pesin chortling, his father mocking him with his compassionate smile.

To Dick's immense relief, Adrian Van Ness was exactly what he imagined a Protestant aristocrat would be like. Urbane, unhurried, he slouched in the big leather chair behind his desk, wrinkles of quizzical surprise on his forehead because Dick had recognized the paintings by Klee and Matisse on his wall. "I picked them up in Paris in the twenties. You're the first person who's even known they were serious paintings," he said.

Cliff Morris squirmed and said nothing. Dick smiled, pleased at being recognized as a fellow member of the shadowy brotherhood of the elite, those with superior taste, judgment, wisdom. He was only a novice in this undefined unrepresentative band. But he was eager to grow in wisdom and age and grace.

"We could use someone with an MBA to bring a little order out of our chaotic accounting methods," Adrian Van Ness said. "Basically we spend money on developing new planes and take in money for planes we've sold and add things up at the end of the quarter to see how we're doing. That frequently leads to rude shocks. For your first assignment, I want you to take a look at one of our biggest, riskiest projects, the X-Forty-nine, also known as the Talus."

"What is it?"

"Some people call it a flying wing. I call it a headlong catastrophe," Adrian said, his hooded eyes flickering toward Cliff.

"Why don't you stop it?"

"You'll find out the answer to that question by going to see the man who's designing the thing."

A surly Cliff called Frank Buchanan's secretary, who reported he was in the wind tunnel studying some aerodynamic problems in the Talus. "Let's go meet the rest of the big shots," Cliff said.

They found Buzz McCall on the factory floor conferring with a foreman. They had to talk above the rattle of rivet guns, the shriek of metal cutters. "You're the navigator?" Buzz yelled.

"That's right," Stone shouted.

"Now you're going to play cost cutter?" Buzz bellowed. "Come see me tomorrow in my office. We'll discuss the next layoff. Then you can go explain it to the union."

"We've got some pretty tough unions in the garment industry," Dick shouted.

Buzz looked at him if he had just confessed he was an embezzler and went back to talking to the foreman. "Don't let it bother you," Cliff said as they retreated to the office side of the building. "He treats everybody that way."

The treasurer, a big easygoing man named Thompson, welcomed Dick as an ally. "It isn't easy to track costs in this crazy business," he said. "You've got to prorate guys selling planes at the Twenty-One Club in New York and birdbrains on the assembly line connecting hydraulic controls backwards. Then there's Tama's stable. That's one we've got to cover under miscellaneous. And the Honeycomb Club. That's ten feet under miscellaneous, in never-never land."

Thompson grinned at Cliff as he said this, apparently presuming he had already explained all this to Dick. Outside the treasurer's office, Dick asked for the explanation. Cliff wryly told him how Tama's stable of willing women employees helped sell planes.

Welcome to the United States of America, Dick thought, recalling his repugnance when he escorted Pesin Baby Wear buyers to whorehouses in Harlem.

"And the Honeycomb Club?"

"We'll let you see that for yourself one of these nights when Frank's in the mood."

Cliff hoped Frank Buchanan would join them for lunch in the company dining room. But he stayed in the wind tunnel. Dick met a half-dozen lesser designers and as many engineers. He was amazed by the acrimony flickering between the two groups. He was even more amazed by the amount of Inverness Scotch everyone consumed. Dick's first taste brought tears to his eyes. He had no intention of swallowing another drop until Buzz McCall wondered if all Jews were timid drinkers. Almost strangling, Dick matched him belt for belt.

"Believe it or not, eventually you get to like the swill," Cliff said.

After lunch Dick wobbled through routine security and physical examinations. Security chief Hanrahan only seemed interested in whether he had any Communist relatives. Owlish Kirk Willoughby, the company doctor, wanted to know if he had been to the Honeycomb Club yet. When Dick said no, he asked him to send him a memo on his first impressions. He was collecting opinions.

Cliff called to report Frank Buchanan had finally emerged from the wind tunnel. Five minutes later, Dick sat in the chief designer's cluttered office listening to him sneer: "An MBA? What does that stand for? Master of bullshit? Nothing personal, but I have a rather low opinion of so-called business schools. I don't think they can teach you anything helpful about making planes. I've never gone near a university. Neither has Jack Northrop or Ed Heinemann, the best designer at Douglas. Can you explain why this uncanny gift should suddenly manifest itself in the human race?"

The man was everything Adrian Van Ness was not. Passionate, sincere, childishly enthusiastic. All traits Dick Stone, the rationalist, considered dangerous, although he had adored them in his grandfather. But it was one thing to enjoy passion and enthusiasm in a professor of literature at the City College of New York and another to approve them in a man who was supposedly in business to make money.

"Stop and think about it for a moment," Frank Buchanan continued. "Our teachers were two self-educated mechanics who ran a bicycle shop in Ohio, Orville and Wilbur Wright. Can you imagine anything more unlikely—except the story of the Savior being born in a manger?"

"I don't happen to believe in the Savior," Dick said.

"I don't either, in any literal sense," Frank Buchanan said. "But you can't be Jewish and not believe in some of his ideals. They're all in the Old Testament."

"I'm sorry," Dick said in a softer tone. "My father's a rabbi but—he didn't persuade me."

"Maybe I can, before we're through," Frank said. "I was brought up to believe all the great religions reflect the same spiritual truths. Reading poetry taught me everything in the material world is an emblem, a shadowing forth of a spiritual world. That's what makes the plane so important. In spite of the

237

way we've already abused it, I still think it can become a symbol of our ascent to a new spiritual synthesis."

Dick Stone cleared his throat. He was not here to discuss metaphysics. "That's very interesting. Mr. Van Ness wants me to review the Talus's costs and do an analysis of them. Estimate future outlays, that sort of thing."

"You can't do it. We're building a plane, Stone, not an automobile or locomotive!" Frank roared. "We don't know what she'll run into up there in the sky. You've flown. Don't you remember days when the plane got thrown all over the horizon? When she shuddered and yawed and groaned like a man on the rack?"

"As far as I was concerned, it did that every time we flew," Dick said.

"I know what you mean. I flew in World War One and I was terrified every moment. The peacetime sky isn't quite as deadly but it's full of mysteries. Forces that reveal themselves in new ways every time we challenge them in a different airplane. That's why you can't worry about costs, you can't start whining about budgets. By the way, can you fly?"

"No."

"Take my advice and learn. It will help you deal with a lot of people in this business, especially our chief of production, Buzz McCall."

Dick found himself confused by the mixture of hostile and friendly signals in this encounter. "Mr. Buchanan," he said. "I promise you that nothing in the job I'm going to do will interfere with your goals."

"You shouldn't make promises like that when you're working for Adrian Van Ness," Frank said.

His bitterness shook the reassurance Dick Stone had felt in Adrian Van Ness's office. The sky was the not only place where they were exploring mysteries. There seemed to be almost as many loose inside Buchanan Aircraft.

MOTHER KNOWS BEST

The doorbell rang just as Sarah Chapman Morris was sitting down to lunch. She was ravenous. Perhaps it had something to do with nursing. She remembered overeating when she nursed Elizabeth. On her plate was a ham and cheese sandwich—double slices of both with mayonnaise and lettuce on well-buttered white bread. For a side dish she was finishing up some macaroni left over from dinner. For dessert there was chocolate pudding she had made for the children two days ago; it should be eaten before it spoiled. She asked Maria, her Mexican maid, to answer the front door. It was probably some magazine salesman.

Into the dining room stalked her mother-in-law with a huge pink rabbit. "Oh, isn't that sweet," Sarah said, jumping up to kiss her. "Can I give you some lunch?"

"I never eat lunch," Tama said. "How's the baby?"

"Just fine," Sarah said. "Would you like to see her?"

She put the macaroni in the oven and they went upstairs. In the nursery Elizabeth was playing mother with Margaret, who now weighed ten pounds and was thriving. Liz was pretending to read a copy of *Winnie the Pooh*. Tama gave her a perfunctory kiss and picked up Margaret. "She's looking more and more like Cliff," she said.

The baby's hair was dark and she did seem to have Cliff's fine nose. But she had the Chapman family's blue eyes. Sarah decided not to point this out. Lately she had begun trying to conciliate her mother-in-law.

Tama put Margaret back in her crib. "Maybe I'll have a cup of coffee," she said. "Black."

Sarah served the coffee, rescued the macaroni and resumed her lunch. She sliced the sandwich and licked some oozing mayonnaise off her fingers. Tama sipped her coffee and said: "Do you know where Cliff spends a lot of his time these days?"

"He's been awfully busy with this experimental plane—"

"He spends it with a redhead named Cassie Trainor. He met her on the plane the night after Margaret was born."

Sarah tried to read Tama's expression. Was she mocking her? Sympathizing with her? The wide dark eyes were opaque, the heavy-boned, strong-jawed face expressionless. Sarah suddenly remembered Amanda Van Ness's visit, a year ago, when she told her all the women at Buchanan Aircraft were humiliated. Was this some sort of initiation?

"How do you know this? Did he tell you?" Sarah said, all interest in food gone.

She had wondered more than once if Cliff was faithful. They did not make love nearly as often as they had in England during the first year of their marriage. It was an impossible subject to discuss with your husband. It was also impossible to check up on a man who had a hundred excuses for his absences. She knew from her own experience that everyone in the aircraft business worked horrendous hours. She had barely seen her own father when he was involved in designing a plane.

"Of course he didn't tell me," Tama said. "I had security check him out. Dan Hanrahan and I are old friends. He runs security checks on my girls all the time."

Although she knew how Tama's girls helped sell Buchanan's planes, her casual reference to them shocked Sarah. The woman had no shame! But Sarah was much too absorbed by Tama's revelation about Cliff to give the girls more than a passing reproach. "Why are you telling me? Wouldn't it be better if I didn't know?"

"Not if he stays married to you. I can't figure out what you've got on him. It sure as hell isn't sex."

"Really! I know you've always disliked me. But I can't see why you've chosen this moment to become completely rude—"

"Whether I like you or not has nothing to do with it. You're married to my son. I happen to *love* him. Last night you entertained Dick Stone, a guy who knew you in England. What do you think went through his head when he saw you?"

Tama strode into the living room and came back with a framed picture of Sarah and Cliff on their wedding day. She pointed to the slim WAAF and said: "She's turned into a fat slob. That's what Dick Stone thought."

"This is insufferable!" Sarah cried. "I refuse to listen to another word. Please leave my house this instant."

Tama ignored her. "Stone is the sort of guy they're going to start hiring at Buchanan, if they make it into the next decade. People from your generation, who judge a man by the looks of his wife as much as by his own looks or his ability on the job. Cliff's got everything he needs to go to the top of this company. But he can't do it with a fat slob for a wife."

"My weight gain is connected to having children," Sarah said, almost strangling with indignation. "It's a natural thing. My mother gained weight the same way and never lost it."

"And I bet your father's got a couple of Cassie Trainors in his past—and maybe in his present."

"You really are insufferable!"

"Cut out the Greer Garson act and listen to me. Do you think you're the first woman who married some guy during a war and then found out he's not Mr. Perfect? I married Cliff's father in 1918 when I was sixteen years old. When he came back from France I realized I couldn't stand the sight of him. He got me pregnant before I got up the nerve to dump him and the Catholic Church."

"This is irrelevant. I still love Cliff."

"If you were telling the truth you wouldn't be standing there forty pounds overweight. I've still got that letter you wrote me when we both thought he was dead. All that baloney about always remembering his heroism. Not one word about the possibility that he was still alive somewhere in Germany. I figured it out on the spot. You were glad he was dead."

"No!" Sarah said, tears of shame mingling with the rage already blurring her eyes. The woman was an uncanny monster. How, where, did she acquire the skill to uncover that secret sin, unspoken, unconfessed, unadmitted to anyone?

"I want to love him. I try to love him," Sarah said. "But he makes it so— so difficult. Now—telling me this—you've made it impossible."

"Whether you love him or not isn't the point," Tama said in the same merciless voice. "Your responsibility is to those two kids upstairs. They're going to have enough trouble being women. You want them to have a failure for a father?"

"I try to talk to Cliff about the business. He isn't interested in my opinions."

"That's because you're about as subtle as a kick in the shins. You want to run him. Meanwhile you're turning into Margaret Rutherford in front of his eyes. You can't get a man's attention with ideas. You want to help Cliff get somewhere? Stop eating. Get down to a hundred and ten pounds and buy yourself some decent clothes. Look like a young executive's wife. Talk like one. Smile. Tell amusing stories. Charm the socks off guys like Jim Redwood and Adrian Van Ness. You can do it. They like that English accent. They think it's classy. Especially Adrian. He's nuts about everything English. He worked in London in the twenties."

"I—I don't know what to say," Sarah said. "Except to—to—express my astonishment at your utter lack of consideration for my feelings. Now—would you please leave?"

She turned her back on Tama—something she hadn't done to anyone since she was five. It was childish but the awful thing was, she felt childish. She felt reduced to the shy stammering creature she had been in grade school by this overbearing woman, so much older, yet still possessing the sheen of youth.

Tama walked past her to the table and picked up her gloves and purse. "When you calm down maybe you'll be glad I did this," she said.

Tama strolled to the mirror over the sideboard to check her makeup. "You may not think so right now but you can do it. This is America, not England, where you go on doing the same stupid things for five hundred years because that was the way your mother and father did it. In America we believe you can change your life, create yourself. You know what my mother did for a living? She washed clothes for the Anglos in San Juan Capistrano. My father weeded their gardens—when he felt like working. You want to know what it's like to be Mexican in California? Pick up some dirt and put it in your mouth."

Tama dug into her purse for her car keys. "Now my name is Morris instead of Moreno and I'm driving that car out front. I've got a five-figure salary and an unlimited expense account and one of the most powerful men in California, maybe in the country, in my life. You may not approve of my morals but it's a hell of a lot better than ironing shirts."

She pushed the dark wave on her forehead firmly into place and smiled at Sarah. *Smiled.* Sarah could not believe the woman's effrontery. Tama strode to the white Cadillac convertible at the curb. Sarah wandered dazedly around her house. On the second or third circuit, she passed her uneaten lunch. She dumped it into the garbage. She opened the door of her white American refrigerator and stared at the glowing interior. In the center sat the chocolate pudding.

She reached out a trembling finger and put a speck of it in her mouth. Tama had it all wrong. Sarah was only trying to make up for those five horrible war years when there was no sugar, no sweets, no pleasures that were not forbidden, sinful.

She had sinned for England. She had opened herself to Cliff, to the cascades of pleasure he sent surging through her body. She sinned for England and the only sweetness available in a world at war and told herself it was love.

But it was, it was, it was love. Love was offering, gift, commitment. She had lived all three, she was Elizabeth Barrett Browning plumbing heights and depths, a Bronte heroine clutched by dark desire. Now she was trying to deny it all, get back to Englishness again in suburban Los Angeles. Enjoy afternoon tea and scones and sweets and occasional sex with her preoccupied husband.

Oh God, oh God, oh God, Tama was right. She was re-creating her mother's life with a tiny change to make herself feel progressive, modern. She would be more involved in her husband's business. More participatory. She must have gotten the idea from a *Good Housekeeping* article on how to live happily ever after.

Sarah found herself in the living room staring at the portrait of the slim bride in the WAAF's uniform. *Like a daregale skylark scanted in a cage.* Was that why Dick Stone had asked her if she still read Gerard Manley Hopkins? He was seeing an English skylark in a cage of fat?

Sarah went back to the refrigerator and threw the chocolate pudding into the garbage. She poured the heavy cream she used on her fruit desserts down the sink. Out went the whipped cream, the jams. She transferred chocolate chip cookies, macaroons, and other snacks from handy jars to the back of her kitchen cabinet.

Finally there was nothing left in the cabinets but condiments and canned fruit and nothing in the refrigerator but milk and veal for dinner and salad greens and an array of baby food. She seized a jar of spinach, untwisted the cap, and spooned some of the mush into her mouth.

"Mommy," Elizabeth said, wide-eyed in the doorway. "Why are you eating that?"

"I'm playing a game with myself," Sarah said. "It's called growing up. I'm going back to being a little girl like you and then I'm going to grow up all over again. Fast."

"That sounds like fun," Elizabeth said. "Is it an English game?"

"No. It's American," Sarah said.

HONEYCOMB

Dick Stone spent the rest of his first week at Buchanan Aircraft acquiring an office in the executive tower and a blond secretary named Regina who helped him requisition some secondhand furniture and a used dictating machine. At Adrian Van Ness's suggestion he began analyzing the company's financial records. He also began educating himself in the intricacies of the aircraft business. This meant asking engineers, designers, purchasing agents, and foremen innumerable basic questions. Most people were delighted to explain their sometimes arcane specialties, especially the engineers, who felt no one appreciated them. He listened to endless horror stories of idiocies they had prevented the designers from perpetrating on various planes.

Late Friday afternoon, Cliff Morris called and told Dick to meet him in Frank Buchanan's office. The chief designer was in a more cheerful mood. "This fellow swears you're not one of Adrian Van Ness's finks," he said. "He's persuaded me to introduce you to the Honeycomb Club. Did you pick up any Greek history in your marvelous MBA course?"

"A little," Dick said.

"That's where the club's name comes from. From the same story that gave me the name for the Talus—the life of the great Athenian designer, Daedalus. Talus was his nephew. Daedelus murdered him because the boy was on his way to surpassing him. I chose the name for our new plane to remind us how often original ideas are destroyed in the name of the great god profit."

"Hey, Frank, be careful," Cliff said. "That's my god you're bad-mouthing."

Frank smiled and continued his explanation. "Daedelus and his son Icarus were our first fliers. They fled to Crete after murdering Talus. King Minos made them virtual slaves, creating buildings and machines for his nation. Daedalus decided to escape and he designed wings for himself and Icarus.

"He gave the boy the first aerial advice. Fly the middle course between the sea and the sun. But Icarus, like many a pilot since, became drunk with the exaltation of flight. He soared into the upper air, where the sun melted the wax on his wings. They fell off and he plummeted into the sea, atoning for the murder of Talus. Isn't it marvelous the way these old myths contain fundamental spiritual ideas? Contrary to appearances, you don't get away with murder or anything else in this life."

Again, Dick was struck by Frank Buchanan's resemblance to his grandfather. He had heard the same passionate rendition of *Faust*, *Till Eulenspiegel*, the *Niebelungenlied* from him. He made the stories meaningful in the same way, linking them to history and experience.

Buchanan shrugged into an old flight jacket. He summoned two designers about the same age as Dick and Cliff. Sam Hardy was short, thin and scholarly looking. Jeff Hall was angular and wry. They trooped downstairs to a battered prewar blue Ford. Sliding behind the wheel, Frank headed west through the gathering dusk to the coast road, continuing to talk about Daedelus. "Like the fliers of today, he was a worshipper of Aphrodite, the goddess of love. In Sicily he designed a temple in the shape of a golden honeycomb for her on the promontory of Eryx. You're about to visit the California version of the shrine."

Buchanan swung onto a two-lane highway that wound between steep-sided hills. "Topanga Canyon," Jeff Hall said. "The Greenwich Village of Los Angeles."

"Where I'd be living if I wasn't married to the Nightstalker," Sam Hardy said.

They turned into a narrow dirt road with thick woods on both sides and rocketed up an almost vertical hill into a parking lot. Before them in the glow of concealed searchlights sat a building with a distinct resemblance to an airplane hangar. Swinging doors spun them into a lobby that was painted gold; the walls and ceiling were scalloped like the inside of a honeycomb. A slim smiling redhead strolled toward them, wearing nothing whatsoever.

Stone stared in disbelief. Nothing! Not even a G-string.

243

"Hello, Frank," she cooed and kissed Buchanan on the cheek. "And Cliff—I hope you're not mad at me for saying no the other night."

Cliff patted her smooth tan rump. "You know how to fix that, Madeleine."

"Too late," she said, strolling away with Frank Buchanan's flight jacket. "Billy said he's going to have 'private—keep out' painted right here." She pointed cheerfully to where Cliff's hand had been a moment before.

Everyone laughed. Dick thought Cliff's jollity was forced. They sauntered into another gold-scalloped room where about two dozen mostly crew-cut men were drinking at a long bar and at scattered tables. A shapely brunette, also wearing nothing, was plinking out "The Darktown Strutters Ball" on a baby grand. Moving around the room carrying trays of drinks were a half-dozen other women, redheads, blondes, brunettes, each beautiful enough to land a long-term Hollywood contract, all of them in the same costume. Redoubling the dreamlike quality was the way none of the drinkers was paying the slightest attention to them.

"I remember the first time Buzz took me here, when I came back from Germany," Cliff said. "I thought I was dead and in some sort of flyer's heaven."

"We better explain the rules to Dick," Frank Buchanan said. "The club is dedicated to Buzz McCall's cherished belief that there are only two things worth doing, flying and fucking. The latter is not permitted on the premises. However, none of the girls works two days in a row. They're always available for late-night appointments, or matinees the following day. Presuming you strike their fancy as much as they strike yours."

"Where do they come from?" Dick asked.

"From all over the country," Cliff said. "Most of them are trying to get into the movies."

"A doctor checks them every week, so you don't have to worry about catching anything but hell from your wife if she finds out where you've been," Sam Hardy said.

"Do they get paid?" Dick asked.

"Plenty. It all comes out of the membership dues," Frank said. "The company pays the money directly to the club, just like the oil companies do for the stuffed shirts at the California Club."

"That's the most exclusive club in L.A.," Cliff explained.

"It's all a tribute to the cost-plus contract, one of the noblest inventions of the mind of man," Sam Hardy said.

"What are you drinking, boys?" asked a throaty voice. Dick Stone looked up into a pair of coned breasts, topped by luscious dark red teats. There was a woman's face above these charms, of course, with a strong-boned, western look. But in his state of shock Dick could think only of anatomy.

"We'll all have the usual, Cassie," Frank Buchanan said.

They drank Inverness at a deadly rate. Dick became more and more detached from reality. Frank Buchanan asked Cassie for a pencil and paper. He and the two young designers began sketching revised versions of the Talus. At first it resembled a boomerang, then a V-shaped projectile. Then the wing swelled and merged with a fuselage, creating a bat-like shape. The engines, eight of them, were on the back of the wing.

"The idea is to put most of the plane in the wing. Or most of the wing in the plane," Frank said. "It will take time to figure out which way to go."

A rotund totally bald man with a black cigar clenched in a corner of his mouth slapped Frank on the back. "Now what crazy goddamn thing are you cooking up?"

"A plane that flies without engines. On wish power," Frank said. He introduced Moon Davis, Buchanan's chief test pilot. With him was Harry Holland, introduced as the second best designer at Douglas, which, Frank added, smiling broadly, "wasn't saying much." Holland had lines like crevasses in his face, making his gray crew cut even more incongruous. "Seriously, Harry, why didn't you put the wings where the tail is on the DC-Six? You could have added a hundred knots to its airspeed."

"Because Don Douglas would have kicked my ass into Long Beach Harbor if I suggested it," Holland said.

"You're a slave to a tyrant, Harry. Rise up. You have nothing to lose but your paycheck."

"I didn't have the nerve to start my own company, Frank."

"I didn't have the brains to keep mine."

Hours seemed to pass. Dick kept seeing Cassie's coned breasts, forgetting who they belonged to, wanting to touch them, until Cliff whispered: "You want to play halfsies with her? There's more than enough to go around."

"Sounds good," Dick said, even though he did not really think so. He wanted to make his own selections. He eyed the other women. A brunette with soft rounded breasts reminded him of Nancy Pesin. That made him feel guilty for a moment. But too much was bombarding his senses to give guilt or any other emotion a chance.

The conversation swirled around planes of all sorts: World War I Spads, helicopters, bombers. Buchanan and Holland insulted each other's taste in fuselages, wings, tails. Buchanan drew a sketch of a Douglas airliner, making it look like a drunken bumblebee. Holland retaliated with a sketch of the Buchanan Excalibur that turned it into a flying dinosaur.

"At least we're not as bad as those myopic bastards at Boeing," Frank said, "Have they ever produced a decent-looking plane?"

Never, everyone agreed. Boeing had never produced a decent-looking plane and never would because it rained too much in Seattle. Their brains were waterlogged. Only Lockheed was admitted into the fraternity of aviation geniuses. Occasionally they produced a passable plane like the P-38. Frank even conceded Kelly Johnson, Lockheed's chief designer, knew more about tails than he did. They drank a toast to Alexander Kartveli, Republic's chief designer, for the P-47, which Frank pronounced the best fighter of the war. Dick noticed they did not drink to any engineers, salesmen, or company presidents.

Dick was close to passing out when they finally hailed Cassie to order dinner. While they read the short menu, Cliff told Cassie that Dick was famous in New

York as the man no woman could satisfy. "Now, that's a challenge," Cassie said.

Dick smiled drunkenly at her. It was all unreal. Six weeks ago he had been living a conventional life. He was a husband, supporting a wife, planning a family, moderating his desires like a good middle-class citizen and dutiful son. A single word had sent him hurtling across the continent to this lotus land where there seemed to be no limit to desire and satisfaction. It was so free it was scary.

One of Cassie's breasts was in his mouth. His tongue revolved on that dark red teat. He was free to do that some night soon. His hand roamed those firm thighs, that auburn pussy. There were no obligations, no prohibitions, no guilt. Incredible.

He ordered steak like everyone else. "Buildin' up your strength?" Cassie said.

"I'd say you're being challenged, Dick," Sam Hardy said. "With Cassie satisfaction is guaranteed."

"Unto exhaustion," Moon Davis said.

"You're just a dirty old man," Cassie said and swiveled away, her compact rump rippling.

"Now there's the kind of flutter I admire," Davis said. "Why can't you work some of that into your goddamn planes, Frank?"

"Because you'd never keep your eyes on the controls," Frank said.

They ate thick steaks washed down by more Scotch. Frank Buchanan began assaulting an idea Adrian Van Ness had launched in *Newsweek*'s profile of him, a lightweight vehicle he called the People Plane. With savage sarcasm Frank mocked the idea of a plane in every garage. "People kill themselves by the thousands driving cars. Can you imagine what they'd do flying planes? Of course, that wouldn't bother Adrian any more than it bothers those vultures in Detroit. Some people will do anything for money."

Cliff reminded Frank he used to agree with Adrian on the People Plane. "I don't agree with Adrian about anything. On principle," Frank roared.

"Douglas is fooling around with the same idea. We call it the Convertiplane," Harry Holland said. "It's half-helicopter, half-propeller driven. If you think flying a jet's dangerous you should try getting that thing back on the ground."

There was a commotion at the entrance to the dining room. A big blond man in a blue Air Force uniform was standing there, his arm around Cassie and Madeleine. "Billy!" Frank bellowed.

All around the room heads turned, expressions changed, as the other drinkers and diners and waitresses turned to gaze at the newcomer. On the women's faces was a range of emotion from patent envy to suppressed desire. On the men's faces rueful admiration was almost universal. This was obviously a celebrity. He seemed to know it too, as he strolled toward them. The grin on his face was supremely reckless, the eyes coolly defiant. He doesn't give a damn for anything or anyone, Dick Stone thought, in a burst of intuition he would confirm many times in the next twenty years. How do you get that way?

In a moment Dick was shaking hands with Major Billy McCall. Frank Buchanan flung one of his long arms around him. "You're looking at a test pilot that can fly anything we put in the air," Frank said. "The best goddamn pilot alive today."

"Hey Pops, careful," Billy said. "Lindbergh's still around."

"So's Eddie Rickenbacker, Jimmy Doolittle, and Buzz McCall," Frank roared. "The claim still stands."

He gazed at Billy with an affection that would have made Dick Stone flinch. His conscience would have immediately asked him how he could possibly deal with such unstinted love. But Billy accepted it as offhandedly as if it were a pat on the back.

"You guys thought you had it tough over Europe. This kid flew ninety-seven missions in the Pacific, bombing at fifty feet," Frank said.

"Twenty-five feet, Pops. Let's keep the record straight," Billy said.

"Yeah. We've heard all about it," Cliff Morris said. In his drunken daze, Dick Stone had trouble including him in his field of vision. On Cliff's face was not an iota of admiration. In his eyes were the polar opposite of affection. He looked at Billy with an odd mixture of loathing and—was it fear? Yes, Dick decided. His intuition, probably the only part of his alcohol-soaked brain that was operating, concluded it was definitely fear.

"What's this bullshit about Madeleine being off limits?" Cliff said.

"It's her idea, Big Shot, not mine," Billy said. "Can I help it if she only likes jet pilots?"

Billy took a swallow of Cliff's drink. "The fact is, you haven't really flown until you wrap your legs around a jet engine."

"How about around Madeleine?" Harry Holland said.

"She comes close. We put my Lustra on autopilot and tried it the other day at ten thousand feet. Sensational."

"Hey," Dick said. "Do you and Madeleine give flying lessons? That's one I'd like to take."

"In a couple of months Billy's going to become the world's fastest human," Frank said. "Our experimental jet, White Lightning's going to hit twice the speed of sound."

"Or they're going to scrape what's left of me off the desert floor with a spoon," Billy said, all traces of self-satisfaction vanishing from his face and voice. "That crate's been doing strange things in the sky. Haven't you gotten my reports?"

"I'm sorry, Billy. I've been working day and night on this new plane, the—"

"Read those goddamn things, Pops. Especially the one about tumbling from seventy to seventeen thousand feet before I figured out what to do."

"Fifty-three thousand feet!" Frank said, shaking his head. "But you pulled it out."

"Next time I may not be so lucky."

"Yes you will," Frank said. "There's absolutely nothing that can destroy your luck."

"Maybe," Billy said. "But read those goddamn reports anyway, Pops."

"I will, I will," Frank said. But when Billy joined them for several Inverness nightcaps, Frank spent most of his time talking about the Talus. Billy listened with cool indifference. At times he almost seemed bored and made little attempt to conceal it. Dick Stone was baffled by his refusal—or was it his inability?—to return Frank Buchanan's lavish affection.

Meanwhile, Sam Hardy conferred with a tall blonde named Tess about her availability. She was very cool. "Sam's problem is negative sex appeal," Cliff said.

"He's got an awful case on her," Frank said. "I'm beginning to wonder if this club is a good idea for some people."

Hardy returned to the table and ordered a double Inverness. "The bitch is treating me like my wife," he said.

At 1:45 the lights began to blink. Cliff reassured Dick that he was not passing out. It was closing time. They staggered to the door where Madeleine asked Billy to wait for her. Cliff Morris watched, glowering. Billy whispered something in Cliff's ear. Dick was standing next to them and caught the word "Cassie."

"Yeah. But ask her now, wiseguy," Cliff said.

Outside, Dick wondered who was going to drive. Frank Buchanan did not look up to it and neither did anyone else. "Pilot!" Frank roared. "We need a pilot."

Out of the darkness rushed a middle-aged Mexican. "I'm right here, Mr. Buchanan," he said.

"This club thinks of everything," Dick said.

"That's how you build planes. You try to think of everything," Frank said.

"Then you test them and find out how much they forgot," Billy said.

"I thought strafer pilots didn't worry about that sort of thing," Cliff said.

"Fuck you, Cliff. Come on out and fly it tomorrow," Billy snarled. His rage seemed out of proportion to Cliff's minor needle.

"We'll do something about it. I promise you," Frank said.

Sam Hardy slapped Billy on the back and began reciting a poem.

Wrinkle wrinkle little spar
Up above the yield so far.
Away up in the sky so high.
I sure am glad that I don't fly.

The other designer, Jeff Hall, did a little dance around Billy and added a stanza.

Sputter sputter little jet
Out of fuel would be my bet
Fuel consumption way too high.
I sure am glad that I don't fly.

"Fucking designers," Billy raged. He grabbed Hardy by the tie and began swinging him in a circle that would have sent him sailing into downtown Los Angeles. Dick Stone and Cliff Morris managed to rescue the choking victim before the crash landing took place.

"We'll fix it, Billy. I promise you," Frank said, acutely distressed.

"It's serious, Pops." He glowered at Cliff. "I bet this bastard has been throwing my stuff in the circular file, hoping I'll get splattered."

"Cliff wouldn't do a thing like that. It's my fault, Billy."

Crazy, Dick thought. Coming close to murder about a plane after spending the night talking wings and tails and rates of climb and more or less ignoring ten or fifteen beautiful naked women. Love in the aircraft business might turn out to be more complicated than it looked at first.

THE DAWN OF FLIGHT

Cliff Morris sat in his sunny dining room frowning at the front-page story in the *Los Angeles Times*.

WHITE LIGHTNING SETS

NEW ALTITUDE, SPEED RECORDS

With Air Force Major Billy McCall again at the controls, a Buchanan Aircraft experimental plane, called White Lightning by its aficionados at Muroc Air Force Base, streaked to another new speed record of 1,315 miles an hour yesterday. Launched from a B-29 high above the desert, the almost wingless rocket plane was a white blur in the cloudless blue sky as it whizzed down the prescribed course. Last week in the same plane, McCall set a new altitude record of 89,916 feet.

"I lost another four pounds last week," Sarah Morris said.

"Huh? Oh—great," Cliff said.

"I'm down to a hundred and thirteen pounds—only three pounds more than when we were married," Sarah said.

"Great. You look great," Cliff said, without raising his eyes from the paper.

Sarah did look a lot better than the fat woman he had seen in the hospital eighteen months ago, when Margaret was born. But Cliff had too much on his mind to get very excited about it. Billy McCall was setting altitude and speed records, rapidly becoming one of the most famous test pilots in the country, while he was project manager of a plane that might vanish without a trace. The Talus program was awash in problems. Frank Buchanan was threatening to quit the company. The U.S. Air Force was demanding to see a demonstration of the Talus's supposedly unique powers six months ahead of schedule.

"That's wonderful news, isn't it—about Billy McCall setting another record."

"Wonderful news for who?" he grunted.

"For Buchanan Aircraft. Isn't it?" Sarah said, blinking her blue eyes in that plaintive way that set his teeth on edge.

"Yeah," Cliff said.

"Will you be home for dinner tonight?"

"I doubt it. I may be out at Muroc for a couple of days, in fact."

There was a long pause. "Is that the truth?" Sarah said.

"Sure it's the truth. Why the hell shouldn't it be the truth?"

"Because the last time you stayed overnight at Muroc, you came home with matches from the Casino on Catalina Island in your pocket."

"I told you—we flew there to unwind—get some fresh ideas from the sea breezes. This plane is driving us all nuts."

It was not the first time Sarah had implied Cliff was unfaithful. It invariably infuriated him. He was not ready to become an old married man. But the arguments—and the unspoken threat of a divorce—made Cliff realize Sarah was important to him. Her admiration for his heroism in the air over Germany was an emotional insurance policy he did not want to lose. She was a kind of emblem of his war record, the most important achievement in his life.

He pulled her out of her chair and kissed her. "I swear to you—I've got nothing on my mind but you, the kids and this plane."

And Cassie Trainor, he silently added, thinking of that slinky slithery body in Manhattan Beach; fucking her at 3 A.M after watching her moving naked around the Honeycomb Club in that bold, languid way. Laughing. Cassie was always laughing while he did it. She made him laugh too.

Sex was so dumb sometimes. The crazy positions you tried for the hell of it. Sometimes it was better in the dark, when it was all feeling. Cassie liked it in the dark and she liked it in the shower and in the tub and on her terrace looking out at the dawning ocean pretending not to notice what he was sliding into her from behind.

Then the call to Billy. Last night she had called him while he was inside her. He stroked her while she told Billy how (*gasp*) much (*ooh*) better Cliff *wasssssss*.

Jesus. Where did all that come from? With his arm around his wife. Was it the contrast? Could he get Lady Sarah to become Cassie? Get her to stop making sex some sort of sacred performance, complete with classical music on the phonograph? It was amazing, how much she had changed when the war ended. When she wasn't kissing a lover who was liable to die the next day.

He remembered trying to get Sarah to take her clothes off and hang around naked in the beach house they had rented in Laguna in the summer of 1945. On hot days Tama had seldom worn anything in their house at Redondo Beach when he was a kid. Lady Sarah had been *horrified*. The way that snooty little English nose twitched. *Horrified*. Maybe he should have insisted on it. Torn off her clothes and screwed her on the rug.

Cliff did not like the way Sarah was looking at him. There was nothing in her eyes, not even anger. She seemed to be holding everything back. Maybe he should cut it out. Drop Cassie. But not for a while. He kissed Sarah on the cheek.

"I'll call you."

"Don't bother."

"Okay. I won't bother."

He drove swiftly down the boulevards to the Hollywood Freeway, listening to the news on the car radio. Truman was cutting the defense budget again. Douglas Aircraft had just laid off 4,000 workers, Lockheed had axed 8,000, Northrop wasn't saying how many but it sounded like it could be the whole company. Maybe Billy McCall had the right idea, staying in the Air Force.

At ninety on the freeway Cliff wondered where they would all be if it were not for Adrian's pull in the Pentagon. He had gotten them ten million dollars to turn the Talus into a bomber. Frank had called Adrian dirty names but Cliff and Buzz had convinced him that if he wanted to see his plane fly, they had to go this route. It was, of course, the way Buzz and Adrian had planned to go from the start. They knew the plane would never make it as an airliner.

An hour later, Cliff and the rest of the team were on the way to Muroc in an Enterpriser, a Buchanan two-engined plane aimed at the short-haul airline market. It was an old SkyRanger refitted with new Wright Cyclone engines. Jim Redwood had sold about eighty of them last year on the telephone. But the profit margin hardly made it worth the trouble.

Dick Stone sat beside Cliff in the front row of the Enterpriser. Dick had shared Cassie Trainor last night. Cliff liked the idea of sharing a woman. A lot of guys did it at the Honeycomb Club. Buzz said it cut down on the chances of things getting romantic—the last thing most guys wanted.

Across the aisle Buzz was trying to soothe Frank Buchanan. "If it passes all the tests, we've got ourselves a contract that could revolutionize the whole business. A billion goddamn dollars. That's what they're gonna commit to a new bomber. Later we can turn it into an airliner in about ten minutes of redesign. We could get so rich it'll be disgusting."

"It isn't ready. We're risking the lives of the test pilots. I don't like losing control of the plane this way," Frank said.

"You're not losing control of a goddamn thing. I've got these Air Force guys in my pocket."

That was not entirely true and Buzz knew it. If the generals were in Buzz's pocket they would not be flying out to Muroc for tests they knew were premature. Something was cooking in Washington that made Cliff uneasy. Buzz did not want to admit that the Air Force was full of guys who had barely heard of World War I, much less Buzz McCall.

"How was Cassie?" Cliff said.

"Okay," Dick said.

"Okay? Sounds like she wore you out, Navigator, and you don't want to admit it."

"Actually, she couldn't get enough of me. She says she's sticking to Jewish cock from now on."

"Yeah. I bet your balls are aching. That broad could use up the whole UCLA football team."

Dick smiled in that superior New York way Cliff had disliked during the war. Was he working on Cassie to give him the same treatment he was giving Billy?

"She's turning into the star of the Honeycomb Club," Buzz said, implying she was one of his girls. Cliff happened to know Cassie had turned him down twice.

In a half hour they landed at Muroc Air Force Base in the Mojave Desert. It was not a big operation. A half dozen hangars and four or five planes of various sizes sitting on the flight line, a dozen or so quonset-hut barracks and some officers' housing sprawled around a long low operations building. The natural scenery was far more spectacular. The empty desert stretched to the snowcapped Sierras without a single house or even a road in sight.

Billy McCall was waiting for them in front of the operations building in his blue Air Force uniform. "How's the fastest man alive?" Cliff said as they shook hands.

Billy acted as if that was the dumbest question of the year and led them down a couple of corridors to an office where an Air Force brigadier general named Johnson Scott was shooting the breeze with two colonels. Scott was a stocky man with a hard mouth and squinting eyes. He did not look more than thirty-five years old. "About time you guys got here," he said. "Before we go any further on this thing, let's decide whether we're operating on Air Force or civilian time."

"Air Force, General," Buzz said. "We had a little problem with our plane."

He introduced Dick and Cliff as Eighth Air Force veterans. The general grunted. A fighter pilot, he had no use for bomber jocks. But when he heard Frank Buchanan's name, his expression warmed. He began telling him how much he loved flying the long-range fighter Frank had designed toward the end of the war.

"I want to go on record with a warning that this plane isn't ready for extensive testing, General," Frank said.

"We can't wait, Mr. Buchanan. Congress is ready to vote some real money for a new strategic bomber now that the Russians have an atomic bomb. If we sit around waiting for the perfect plane the stupid bastards will forget all about the problem."

The Russians had exploded their first atomic bomb two months ago. This breakthrough had demolished most of Frank Buchanan's resistance to turning his plane into a weapon.

"I've been telling the general what a hell of a plane he's got," Billy McCall said. "I've applied to fly her in the next round of tests."

"I've been talking to your current test pilot," Scott said. "He makes this thing sound like the second coming."

"Correction," said a voice from the hall. In came Moon Davis, Buchanan's rotund chief test pilot, zipping up his flight suit. He was getting pretty old to be testing planes but Buzz would not let anyone talk about retiring him.

"I didn't say anything about the second coming," Davis protested. "I just told the general how this plane came into being. The Lord said unto Frank Buchanan, make me a vehicle swifter than the sun and lighter than the wind. And the dawn of a new age of flight began."

Buzz grinned nervously. "They say enthusiasm wins wars, General."

"So I've heard," Scott said. "But it doesn't pass appropriations. Let's get to work, gentlemen."

They climbed into a pair of jeeps and rode down the flight line to the Talus. She squatted in the glaring desert sun, simultaneously real and unreal. The tail was a minuscule fin, the fuselage was nonexistent. The plane had become a huge wing, two hundred feet from tip to tip. In the center a cabin bulged like a thyroid eye.

Cliff invited Dick Stone aboard to see the interior. Contrary to appearances, there was an amazing amount of room inside. The cabin was big enough to house a ten-man crew, with bulky radio and radar equipment, a bombsight and other war-fighting gear without the slightest crowding. Behind the compartment there was ample space for bomb racks.

"I've flown in it," Cliff said. "It's the greatest experience I've ever had in the air."

The most terrifying experience was closer to the truth. The plane had slewed and yawed all over the sky. Frank had yet to solve a lot of the stability problems.

Moon Davis came aboard with his copilot and flight engineer and Frank Buchanan. They went over the tests they planned for the flight. "Let me add something to impress Scott," Davis said. "He's out to kill this thing, Frank."

"That may be—but we aren't ready to do anything spectacular," Frank said. "I want to solve some of these problems with the engines and their position on the wing. We may have it wrong. I suspect they're underpowered. I wish I'd stuck to my hunch and insisted on using jet engines. But Adrian and everyone else screamed about costs so much—"

Cliff sensed Moon was not listening to Frank's plea for caution. They debarked and Davis warmed up the engines. The whole plane vibrated as he shoved them to full throttle. Satisfied, he taxied to the runway.

Down the long concrete ribbon Moon whizzed to lift off in one of the sharpest climbs Cliff had ever seen. The Talus made a B-17 look like an overloaded dromedary with wings.

"How do you like that, General?" Cliff said.

"Not bad," Scott said.

"It's got eight tons of iron in the bomb bays," Cliff said. "We're trying to simulate the real thing."

General Scott grunted.

At about five thousand feet, the huge aluminum creature leveled off and banked sharply to the left and right as it roared over the base. It was an eerie sensation, seeing it in the sky.

"If we flew it over L.A., they'd evacuate the city," Cliff said. "They'd be sure the Martians were coming."

"I'd be the first guy on the freeway," Dick Stone said.

Davis proceeded to put the Talus through a series of dives and climbs and banks. He cut two engines on the left wing and flew perfectly straight and level. He cut two on the right wing and duplicated the performance. "It could fly on two engines from here to New York," Cliff said.

Moon shoved the throttles to full. The Talus streaked for the distant mountains, wheeled and came back across the air base at top speed. "Four hundred miles an hour," Buzz McCall said. "With underpowered engines. The B-Thirty-six's max speed is four hundred and sixteen—with ten goddamn engines."

Convair's B-36 was the Talus's chief competitor. It was a totally unoriginal plane, an overgrown World War II bomber.

"What's the ceiling?" Scott said. "Have you solved that problem?"

"Watch."

Moon Davis was climbing now, a steady remarkably steep climb, until he was the size of a butterfly in the glaring azure sky. "Leveling off at thirty thousand feet," Davis said over the radio that stood beside the hangar door.

He banked, dove, climbed in the near stratosphere, where thin air frequently caused stability problems for standard-shaped planes. "Now, General, to show you what this plane can do, watch closely," Moon said.

Down came the Talus in a series of spirals until it was about five thousand feet above the air base. Davis leveled off and began doing stunts. Chandelles, rolls, it was dazzling—until he tried a loop. "No!" Frank Buchanan cried.

Over the vertical the huge plane came and down in a dive. Now, Cliff thought, now, pull it out. Davis tried. But the left wing crumpled under the forces he had unleashed, the motors ripped free and the Talus slid into a roaring whirling spin that sent it into the brown desert with a stupendous explosion and a fireball of flame.

"That wasn't on the checklist!" Frank cried. "Why in God's name did he think he could loop a thirty-ton plane?"

"Goddamn it," Buzz said. "Goddamn it." He said it about a hundred times as the fire trucks clanged across the dry lake bed to spray foam on the wreckage. There was no hope for Moon Davis or his crew. It would be a miracle if they could even identify the bodies.

Flying back to Santa Monica, everyone was glum. Buzz poured Inverness and they drank a toast to Moon. "He put some great planes in the air," he said.

Buzz took responsibility for the crash. "I told Moon to try it," he said. "We had to do something wild to get their attention."

"It was partly my idea," Billy McCall said. He had hitched a ride to Santa Monica with them. "I want to fly it, Pops."

He smiled mockingly at Cliff, who could hardly object to Billy as a test pilot now. Ordinarily he would have done everything short of assassination to keep him out of the project. Cliff wondered if he had just seen his career explode and burn on the desert floor. He heard himself telling Dick Stone that if the Talus succeeded he was a hero and if it failed he was a bum.

"What happens now?" Dick asked.

"We've got another prototype almost ready to roll out," Frank Buchanan said.

"You'll keep testing?"

"Of course we'll keep testing. You can't let these setbacks throw you," Frank said.

"I haven't seen a plane yet that didn't kill at least three pilots," Buzz said.

"Sacrifices must be expected?" Cliff said.

"Exactly," Frank said, pleased that he remembered the phrase.

Include me out, Cliff thought. But how? They landed at Buchanan Field in the dusk. Billy hitched a ride to the Beverly Wilshire Hotel with Buzz. No doubt he had some beautiful piece waiting for him there. Cliff got into his car and thought about driving home to tell the story of the crash to Sarah. There would be the usual dumb questions, then plaintive wifely sympathy, maybe some symphonic sex at bedtime.

Nuts. He wanted Scotch, he wanted fucking, fucking, fucking until the anger and frustration and fear drained out of him. There was only one woman who could give that to him. Cliff shoved a coin in the pay phone outside the main hangar. "Hello, Cassie?" he said.

SOARING LESSON

Sarah Morris was dressing for Buchanan's annual Christmas party, the major social event of the company year. She should be brimming with Dickensian cheer. But Christmas in California, with the temperature at seventy-five, was too bizarre to foster the traditional impulse to God bless everyone. That meant cheer depended on one's inner resources, on words like *love* and *faith*. At the moment, Sarah was very low on these emotions.

Sarah had completed Tama Morris's program to redesign her English daughter-in-law as an American wife. She had lost fifty-eight pounds and was keeping her weight at 110 with heroic dieting. But the program was a failure in the romance department. That was the main reason for Sarah's lack of Christmas cheer. A perfunctory performance in the bedroom once a week or so was still the most she could expect—and Cliff seemed to think she should be grateful for that. Several times recently she had to remind him that ten days or two weeks had passed without a touch or a kiss. Meanwhile there was a steady supply of evidence that other women were getting plenty of both.

At this point in Sarah's unChristmasy meditation, her husband emerged from the bathroom in his underwear and pulled a shirt from his dresser. He shoved his arms into it, flipped a tie under the collar and began buttoning the neck. "Christ!" he said. "There's enough starch in this collar to straighten Mulholland Drive."

"I keep telling Maria—but it doesn't do any good. Maybe she wants to make Anglos suffer."

"I thought you Brits were good at dealing with the lower orders."

"Speaking of shirts," she said. "The one you wore last night was covered with lipstick. Would you mind telling me how that happened?"

"Business," Cliff said.

"Funny business?"

"I was out with an Air Force general trying to keep him interested in the Talus."

"And you each had one of Tama's volunteers with you?"

"Mine got a little drunk. She was practically lying on top of me in the backseat. But I didn't do a goddamn thing to her. So help me. I don't fool around with the help. Tama'd give me hell, for one thing."

"But if I give you hell it doesn't matter?"

"I'm getting pretty bored with it. I've told you before—you don't have to worry about me leaving you. If I get tempted now and then, it's strictly a passing fancy. Christ, this is the twentieth century. You can't expect a man to be absolutely faithful."

Sarah almost burst into tears. She could not deal with this presumption of infidelity. For a while she had tried to compete with these invisible women. She spent hours studying herself in the mirror, trying to think of new ways to use makeup, change her hair. She prowled the department stores looking for bargains in the latest styles.

What did she get for this devotion? A demand for less starch in his shirts. Sarah stared at her husband in her dressing-table mirror. He looked ridiculous, the stiff collar making his neck bulge. How, why, had she ever fallen in love with this arrogant playboy?

Strangling in his over-starched shirt, Cliff drove them at terrifying speed down the Hollywood Freeway and out Santa Monica Boulevard to Buchanan Field, which was already crammed with parked cars. All Buchanan's employees were invited to this annual bash. The tradition apparently stretched back to 1929 or 1930 when Frank Buchanan had run the company with a lavish optimism the Great Depression had soon dimmed.

One of the biggest hangars had been cleared, except for the company's tiny experimental rocket plane, White Lightning, in which Billy McCall had recently set several more records for speed and altitude. It perched on two wheels like a defiant insect. The thin swept wings, the rapier nose, gave it a menacing look, even on the ground.

Standing nearby in his Air Force uniform was the record-breaker himself. People swarmed around him, slapping him on the back, asking him questions. Sarah had met Billy at these Christmas parties and once or twice at other Buchanan ceremonies. She knew her husband did not particularly like him. Today, that made her all the more inclined to chat with him. Billy was unquestionably one of the handsomest men she had ever seen, almost as tall as Cliff and much younger looking, even though they were roughly the same age. Sarah decided it was the blond hair, the fair skin.

"Congratulations from your sister-in-law, Sarah," she said, holding out her hand.

"I haven't forgotten you," Billy said, giving her hand a brief squeeze. "I may be dumb and a little deaf from flying Samsons too close to the water, but I'm not blind."

"Is that a compliment?"

"It's a fact," Billy said, smiling.

"I've been following your exploits."

"I don't deserve any credit for them. I just switch on the rockets in this excuse for a plane and go along for the ride."

In the distance, a band began to play. There was a wooden dance floor at the far end of the hangar. "Want to risk a fox trot?" he said.

They moved onto the uncrowded floor to the latest hit, "Mona Lisa." "That's you," Billy said, as the singer began gushing the saccharine words. "Mona Lisa."

"Why?"

"The way you smile. It's different from most women's. Sort of wary—and mysterious."

"Appearances are deceptive. I'm neither."

"It's a mystery to me how you've stayed married to Cliff."

"You don't like Cliff very much, do you?" Sarah said.

"I don't like him at all."

"I happen to love him."

"Come on. You loved a wartime hero. A pilot. Now you're stuck with a salesman on the make. You must feel like you've gotten into the wrong movie halfway through. But it's not too late. There's a real pilot waiting to fly you into the wild blue."

"Who, may I ask?"

"You're dancing with him."

"Really," Sarah said.

"Really," Billy mocked. "I can usually get into Los Angeles on a day's notice. Buchanan and a couple of other companies keep a suite reserved at the Beverly Wilshire, in case they want us test pilots for some publicity. Just call this number—"

He palmed a card from his pocket and slipped it into her hand. "I'm ready when you are."

"I admire your nerve, Major," Sarah said. "But not your morals."

"Think it over," Billy said. "At the very least, you'll get even."

It took Sarah a moment to realize Billy knew all about Cliff's romps with other women. Cliff probably bragged about them. The band switched to "That Lucky Old Sun" and Billy swung her into a smooth lindy. Whirling at the end

257

of his muscular arm, Sarah's bewilderment changed to cool decisive lust. Why not dispense once and for all with her adolescent ideas about love and partnership and see herself for what she really was—a young, attractive, neglected wife who was being propositioned by one of the two or three most famous pilots in America?

"You're a beautiful woman, Sarah," Billy said.

It had been years since she heard those words from her husband. "You're a rather handsome man, Major," she said.

A big hand seized Sarah by the shoulder and spun her out of Billy McCall's grasp. "Maybe it's time I danced with my wife," Cliff said.

He put his broad shoulders between her and Billy. "What's that wiseguy telling you about me?"

"He's predicting you'll be CEO of Buchanan in fifteen years," Sarah lied.

"Not if he can help it," Cliff said.

For the rest of the party, Sarah felt Billy's eyes on her. Every time she turned her head, so it seemed, there he was in the middle distance studying her, a small smile on his face. Even when she was talking to Adrian Van Ness, answering as well as she could his offhand but probing questions about how de Havilland Aircraft was doing.

Beside Adrian stood Amanda Van Ness, wearing a gauzy blue gown out of the 1920s or 1930s. Sarah's friend Susan Hardy had pointed her out earlier in the party as an example of a born Californian's total lack of style. "How are Tama's granddaughters?" Amanda said. "You must bring them both to visit me one of these days."

"They're—fine," Sarah said, abruptly flung back to her memories of Amanda's visit. "They're on their way to being very independent women. Already they ignore everything I tell them."

"Good," Amanda said. She whispered in Sarah's ear "Its more important for them to ignore their father. They need to consider men *superfluous*."

Adrian Van Ness goodnaturedly asked if Amanda was telling her he had a weakness for English women. Was he aware of his wife's bizarre opinions? Sarah wondered. Probably. But he ignored them. Sarah could not imagine anything disturbing Adrian's self-assurance.

For the third or fourth time her eyes found Billy McCall. He was standing alone, raising a drink to his lips. Sarah felt warmth gather in the center of her body. It was amazing how he could make something that simple an erotic gesture. She grew irked by Adrian's questions, which presumed her strong interest in English aviation. She was not English anymore. She was completing the process of growing up American. Maybe Billy McCall was her graduation present.

At home on Christmas Day, confronted by her two daughters and her husband and mother-in-law, Sarah told herself to forget Billy McCall. It was absurd. She was a mother and a kitchen helper, a slavey. The Morrises ate and drank what she and Maria had spent ten hours preparing for them as if they were California nobility.

Tama congratulated Sarah on charming Adrian Van Ness. "He talked about you for a half hour last night at my place."

Tama's reference to my place made it very clear that adultery was par for the course in Buchanan's executive suite. But Billy McCall was still out of the question, Sarah told herself, washing a sinkful of dishes later in the night.

The next morning at 10 A.M. the telephone rang. "This is your friend the pilot," Billy McCall said. "Just wanted to make sure you didn't lose that number."

She hung up. Out of the question. If Cliff made a single tender gesture, if he made love to her with even a hint of his old wartime ardor, she would forget it.

Instead, there was another late-night return to the nest reeking of a different perfume and a call around midnight on New Year's eve explaining that an office party had "gotten out of hand" and he would not be home at all because he was too drunk to drive. In the background she could hear women laughing.

On New Year's morning, the first day of 1950, the beginning of the second half of the century, Sarah fed the children and took down the Christmas tree. The rituals of motherhood and family completed, she went upstairs to the bedroom where she had slept alone on New Year's eve and dialed Billy McCall's number.

"This is Sarah," she said. "Are you still flying that route into the wild blue?"

Two days later, her husband in the Mojave Desert, her daughters asleep, her reliable Mexican maid, Maria, in charge of her house, Sarah drove up Los Angeles's main street, Wilshire Boulevard, to the hotel that shared its name, and walked to a white lobby phone.

"May I speak to Major McCall, please?"

A pause while the operator found the number and she had one last chance to flee. There was something so tawdry about coming to his room like a prostitute. Then Billy's voice was on the line. "Sarah? I'm on the other side of the lobby."

He strolled toward her in casual California clothes, the shirt open at the throat. Sarah felt another rush of warmth. The blond hair reminded her of several boys on whom she had teenage crushes; then the raw-boned western face. He was a remarkable blend of English and American good looks.

Was she feeling sexual desire for the first time? Were the feelings she had experienced with Cliff a kind of spiritual immolation? Do you have to grow up American to want a man? Sarah's heart pounded. She could not turn back now.

"I figured we'd go for a plane ride first," Billy said. "A friend of mine's got this place in the desert near Palm Springs."

They drove to Los Angeles Airport, where Billy kept a dark green single-engined plane. He told her it was a Lustra, one of Buchanan's first aircraft. He had rebuilt it himself and installed a new engine. Behind the cockpit he had created a miniature sitting room with a cushioned swivel chair, a couch and a small bar. In minutes they were soaring over the lights of Los Angeles and then

259

over the darkness of the desert toward a horizon filled with stars. "I love to fly at night," Billy said.

Some random lights appeared below them. Billy talked to someone on the radio and a half-dozen more powerful lights came on, illuminating a single runway. He landed without even the hint of a bounce and left the plane beside a small control tower. They walked to a station wagon in a nearby parking lot and drove a few miles into the desert to a house surrounded by a high adobe wall.

Billy unlocked a carved wooden gate and they entered a dark courtyard. He touched a switch just inside the gate and lights glowed around a rectangular pool with two chaises beside it and a bathhouse at the far end. The mission-style house remained in darkness a few dozen feet away.

Billy disappeared into the house and returned with a bottle of Scotch and some ice. "First we get just a little drunk," Billy said, pouring her a generous splash.

"To dull the conscience?" Sarah said.

"To forget about getting even," Billy said. "That's the wrong reason for coming here."

They sat down side by side on chaises facing the pool. Sarah sipped her Scotch. It burned deep in her throat. "Tell me what it feels like to go thirteen hundred miles an hour," she said.

"Like hitting a home run and scoring a touchdown in the same day."

She shook her head, dismissing these male metaphors. "Make me see it, feel it. The whole thing."

Billy hunched forward, balancing his glass on his knee. He picked it up and stretched out on the chaise. "You never know if the goddamn plane is going to explode. Two have, already. They didn't even find pieces of the pilots. With our model, it's twice as likely to happen because we're relying on rocket fuel. We were supposed to get jet engines but Westinghouse never came through with the power."

He took a hefty swallow of Scotch. "It's like flying down a tunnel of fire. Any second you expect to disappear. Your body feels like it's already vanished. You're scared in a new way, different from combat. You feel like you're going down God's throat and He doesn't like it. Afterward you just want to get drunk."

He smiled briefly at her. "That's the bad flight. Want to hear about the good flight?"

"Yes," Sarah said.

Billy poured himself more Scotch. "The altitude flight. That's the good flight."

He lay back on the chaise again and his voice dwindled to a murmur. "The first boost that pulls you away from the B-Twenty-nine is nothing to what you get when you ignite all four tubes at thirty thousand feet and start to climb. The altimeter goes up a thousand feet a second and suddenly you're at sixty thousand feet. You can feel the difference. She doesn't want to fly in that thin air. But she does as long as you've got that power in the tail. You keep going up, up with nothing but a little aileron throw to keep the wings steady. Then you're at seventy-six thousand and the rockets sputter off."

"It's perfectly quiet?" Sarah said.

Billy nodded. "You've left the world. There's only this blue-black sky and you and the plane. You feel her vibrations as if they're happening in your own body. At the same time you're incredibly aware of your body. As if it's part of the inside of the plane. You can feel every cell, every muscle, every ounce of fluid. They're awake, alive in a different way inside you. Everything you see is somehow more intense. Black is blacker, white is whiter. You feel like you're on the edge of the unknowable."

"You're not afraid?"

Billy's voice almost faded against the desert wind blowing at the gate, the bubbling water in the pool. "Fear seems independent, a ghost sitting on your shoulder. It doesn't belong to you anymore. You don't feel the slightest concern for the future. Everything is now. Nothing has any meaning but this experience. The stuff on the dials, the rocket pressures, the altimeter, the angle of attack light, are meaningless. You stop worrying about everything. You have this feeling that no matter what the dials say, the ship is going to keep flying."

Billy reached out and took her empty glass. "That's what I want us to have tonight. An experience like that."

For a moment Sarah was afraid. She banished it. She breathed Billy's courage, his faith in surviving the unknown. Her dominant emotion remained curiosity. Billy had not mentioned the word *love*. She wondered if this was a new kind of man she was confronting, a being indifferent to old ideas and feelings.

"First a swim," Billy said. He stood up and began undressing. Zip, flip, he was naked. His penis was a long dangling tube. "Come on," he said, lifting her to her feet. Unbutton, zip, slip, and she was naked too. Billy picked her up and walked slowly down the steps into the pool.

The water was incredibly cold. He lowered her into it and let her go, then dove deep beside her. She watched him swim underwater to the other end of the pool, each stroke a smooth flowing motion that shot him forward in the green depths. She dove and imitated him. Water flowed against her breasts, thighs. Up she came, gasping for breath. He drew her to him, his hands moving casually around her body. "Isn't this great?" he said.

He kissed her, his tongue crowding her mouth. She moved against him in the bubbling water. It *was* great or at least exotically different. What was she feeling? Sarah told herself to stop worrying about it. This was a man, a pilot, this was California, the beginning of her flight into unknowable freedom, into becoming a grown-up American woman. She was a being unto herself, Sarah, neither Chapman nor Morris. She was severing all the connections here, all thoughts and feelings for parents, husband, daughters.

They swam to the other end of the pool and Billy carried her to a chaise, where he carefully toweled her dry. "Are you using a diaphragm?" he said.

"Yes."

"Take it out. What we're going to do was designed by God. He didn't factor in diaphragms."

She went into the bathhouse and removed the diaphragm. Returning, she walked toward him with a lightness, a fearlessness, that amazed her.

Billy drew her down on the chaise and began playing with one of her nipples. Then his hand traveled down her body and grazed the hair on her mons. Again and again the tips of his fingers, then his palm, passed through the hair, producing shivers of pleasure in her belly and thighs.

"Hair is an extension of the skin," Billy whispered. "Do you like that?"

"Yes," she said.

"I think you'll like this even more."

He wet his fingers with his own saliva and began caressing her clitoris. "Just let go, stop thinking about everything," he said. "You're a woman, that's all you need to know. This is what makes you happy."

Waves of warmth began surging through Sarah's body into her throat. She began to sigh and shiver against him. "We're only at thirty thousand feet," Billy said. "We haven't even fired the rockets yet."

He began sweeping the inner wall of her vagina with his index finger, stopping at various points that seemed to treble the pleasure pounding in her body. "Oh," Sarah cried. "Do that again. Again!"

"That's the Grafenberg spot," Billy said. "He was one of the pioneer sex pilots."

Curving across her mind like a shooting star was the realization that Billy was flying her, she was his plane. But it did not matter. She was past caring, past thinking, all she wanted was more of those knowing fingers. "Don't look at me, just look at the stars," Billy said.

He took her hand and wrapped it around his penis. It was huge, pulsing. She gazed into the night sky while pleasure cascaded through her body. She was coming. It had been a year, perhaps two, since she had an orgasm with Cliff.

Billy scooped the creamy ointment from her labia and spread it across her lips. "Ambrosia," he said. "The food of the gods. You want some of mine?"

A stream of clear fluid was oozing from his penis. It was not semen. She did not know what it was. She took some on her fingers and put it in her mouth. It had no taste.

"It's coming without coming," Billy said. "It takes willpower—and practice."

His forefinger was still moving deep in her vagina, his thumb was stroking her clitoris. Now his tongue was in her mouth, then curling from her nipples down her breasts. "I think you're ready. You must have been in the mood. I've never seen anyone climb so fast," he said.

"Yes, yes, ready," Sarah gasped.

He lifted her on top of him and his penis filled her with new pleasure and something more profound, a sense of absolute surrender to every motion, every touch. Her whole body was in orgasm now. Her thighs, her breasts pulsed, a mist enveloped her eyes.

"Let go, let go of everything," Billy said and began moving inside her, each thrust sending new pleasure surging through her body and mind. There was no longer any distinction between these two realities. Sarah had receded from Chapman and dismissed Morris. She was in a world of pure feeling where only Billy McCall, the spaceship of her body beneath his hands, was real.

Billy was coming now too, she could feel the vibrations in his chest. Both his hands were on her breasts, massaging them firmly, steadily. He smiled up at her from the level chaise. "Isn't it great?" he whispered in the same low intense voice he had used describing his flight in the rocket plane.

He drew her down for a kiss that consumed her. His penis moved up her vagina as his tongue filled her mouth. In slow, careful syncopation they reversed again and again. Sarah began leaving the world. Her eyes saw nothing but the black sky and its infinity of stars. She was up there with transcendent beings, beyond fear and anxiety, soaring through the night on a fuel she had never encountered before. "Now," Billy said. "Now. Are you ready?"

"Yes, yes, yes!"

He came with a shuddering growl, clutching her breasts, holding her at arm's length, simultaneously apart and together, a new kind of human vehicle. Sarah vanished in this final eruption. There was no self at this altitude, only woman, man, primary words, primary beings. Again and again and again Billy came until the green water in the pool, the stars above it vanished in a wild wish that it would never end. She was inside something vast and smooth, a universe of black satin and simultaneously outside it, gazing down on the shining pool and their entwined bodies, glowing like stars. She was nowhere and everywhere, blinded and visionary, forever lost and eternally found to be the woman she had imagined, brave, proud, free.

When Sarah opened her eyes Billy was lying beside her, his fingertips moving slowly across the damp hair of her mons. "Now we glide down in nice, long spirals," he said. "In a half hour we'll be ready for another swim and a midnight supper."

This time the swim was more dreamlike. They emerged from the pool, put on terry cloth robes and sat down at a redwood table behind the chaises. Billy brought cold chicken and California champagne from the house. "I had a feeling you were ready for something like that," he said. "After five years of Cliff."

"Can't we leave him out of it?"

Billy shrugged. "We can try."

He raised his champagne. They touched glasses and Billy smiled. "Take a look at your eyes," he said.

She examined them in the mirror of her compact. She was appalled. The lids were a dark blue. They looked bruised. "They're engorged," Billy said. "That's what eye shadow is all about."

"How did you find out so much about women?"

"Frank Buchanan taught me most of it. He gave me books on physiology, sex techniques. It made sense. Before you fly a plane, you spend a lot of time studying the manual, finding out how she works, how far you can push the flight envelope. Why not do the same thing with a woman?"

"That's what we were doing? Pushing the envelope?" Sarah said.

"We were way up there," Billy said. "I haven't found many who can go that high. Want to do it again before we go home?"

For a moment, desire seized her, the stars beckoned. But Sarah found something in her soul resisting Billy. "Now that I'm back on earth, I think I'll stay here for a while."

"Suit yourself," Billy said.

He was stunningly, brutally indifferent. There were endless numbers of women out there waiting to be flown. Was she wrong to let him go? Desire or its echo in memory clutched at Sarah's throat. She was almost ready to change her mind.

"I've never had English pussy before. I'm gonna look for more," Billy said.

He was still smiling but he knew he was hurting her. That meant she had hurt him by saying no. She was glad she had said it. She was almost proud of her power to hurt him. She did not seem capable of arousing any other emotion in him.

Suddenly she wanted to rage at him, fling food and dishes. *I gave myself to you. I gave you everything.* She wanted to scream it in his face. She wanted to run howling into the desert to repent her surrender, to escape the temptation pulsing in Billy McCall's cock. What was happening to her?

She did none of those violent things, of course. A determination to match Billy's cool uncaring produced a frozen politeness. Sarah hated it almost as much as she feared the other impulses. What was she doing? Was she rejecting the greatest love of her life—of any woman's life? Was it waiting behind Billy's smile for the woman who risked everything to penetrate his uncaring?

No, no. It was all insane. What did those warfare words have to do with love? She still believed love was gift and gratitude, sharing and sympathy. For Billy these words did not seem to exist. It was all mockery, skill, daring. If this was the kind of love he found in the sky, she wanted none of it.

And yet, and yet—she wanted it. She wanted that ascent again, that shuddering fulfillment.

They flew back to Los Angeles in the dawn. "How do you feel?" Billy said, as the rising sun burst over the Sierras, filling the sky with vivid red.

"Good," Sarah said. It was defiant. But it was true. She felt good.

"How about a little aerial celebration?"

Billy reached over and tightened her seat belt. Without another word he leaned on the half circle of wheel in his hands and the left wing went down and they went somersaulting over it. Sarah felt all the blood in her body bulge into her face. It seemed ready to explode through her skin. Ahead of them she saw the coast of California rotating like a gigantic seesaw, sliding up and down. Then gravity slammed her against the seat and her heart was being crushed into a small rectangle and her intestines were flattened like ribbons and her thighs stripped of all sensation. Upside down now and slowly revolving with the Pacific sluicing the other way, pouring water over Alaska and the Pole.

"Like that?" Billy said.

"Yes," Sarah said, all defiance now.

They rolled in the opposite direction this time. The San Gabriel mountains crumbled into the illimitable desert and her eyes bulged with gravity. Her teeth were jammed into an eternal grimace. At any moment she thought she might bite chunks from her lungs. A whining roar from beyond the planets filled her ears.

They were level again. "What was that?" Sarah asked.

"Barrel rolls," Billy said.

It was more than a celebration. He was giving her a small sample of what he confronted when he pulled a plane out of a 10 or 11 g dive. He was letting her know his art was written with his blood and bones and flesh. He was revealing some of the things he had omitted in their ascent.

Now Billy was all business, clicking overhead switches and checking dials and talking to air traffic controllers at Los Angeles Airport, scouring the sky for other planes. They landed in the same smooth effortless way without saying another word. He walked her to the parking lot where she had left her car. She offered to drive him to the Beverly Wilshire. He said he would get a cab. They stood there in the rosy light while a DC-6 thundered down a nearby runway.

"Should I call you again sometime?" he said.

Sarah's whole body went hot and cold and hot again. "It was wonderful but—maybe not."

That was a ridiculous attempt at compromise. Say something else, something that will let him call you and somehow give you the right to refuse. But there were no second chances with Billy. "Okay," he said.

He stood there for another moment, the smile not quite as confident, his eyes almost sad. A force more powerful than will or ideas flung Sarah against him. She crushed her lips against that unyielding mouth.

Sobbing, she fumbled in her purse for her car keys. Billy found them for her. "See you around," he said.

FREEDOM FLIGHT

"Will it work in Moosejaw?"

Frank Buchanan's shout made the fluorescent lights in the plasterboard ceiling vibrate. Sam Hardy, the designer in charge of the ailerons on the Talus, trudged out of Frank's office looking as if he would be happy to impale himself on the nearest sharp object. Dick Stone did not know exactly what was wrong but he knew Frank was talking about Moosejaw, Canada, where the temperature was 40 below zero most of the winter. Ailerons had to work in that sort of weather—and in desert heat and equatorial humidity.

It was 8 P.M. and no one in the design department—at least the part of the department surrounding Frank Buchanan's office, where he kept his brightest people—showed any sign of going home. The designers called the area the Black Hole, after the infamous torture site in Calcutta. Some years later, when astronomers used the name for the mysterious time warps in space created by dead stars, the designers said both meanings were true.

Dick sat in his office just beyond this fluorescent-lit arena tapping data into a new machine he had persuaded Adrian Van Ness to buy, a Miller McCann computer. People in the design department used it too. It saved them hours of slide rule computations. That was one among several reasons why Dick had moved his office out of the executive tower to the edge of the Black Hole.

His main reason was his desire to learn as much as possible about the complications of creating a new plane. By now he knew a lot. He understood the perpetual struggle to anticipate problems like the weather in Moosejaw. He saw why there were so many designers needed to back up Frank Buchanan. He created the original concept of the plane. But every square inch of the creature had to be harmonized with the rest of it. A tail, a flap, a window, required hundreds of drawings by teams of men.

Each day Frank held design conferences with the leaders of the teams. There was a standing rule that nothing on the plane could be changed if those whose work it affected had any objections. If the man in charge of the landing-wheel system wanted to extend the struts an inch or two for what seemed to him a very good reason, everyone concerned with that area of the plane had a vote—and it was frequently negative. The resulting brawls could be spectacular.

That was only round one. When the engineering department began changing things, proclaiming this or that solution would not work, a firestorm of rage invariably swept the design department. The test pilots also had their say. Most of the time they complained about the cockpit, which was never designed to their complete satisfaction. Invariably, because Buzz McCall was a pilot, the engineering department backed them up.

Day after day, Dick was appalled to see thousands of blueprints representing ten times that many man-hours dumped in wastebaskets. Wind-tunnel tests, using scale models, often forced rude reevaluations on everyone, designers and engineers. These were the "unknowns" that only became apparent once a plane was exposed to some of the stresses it faced in the sky. When the real thing began to fly, there were likely to be more shocks—"unk-unks"—the unknown unknowns that revealed hidden flaws in the design or unidentified forces in the sky.

But no one in the Black Hole, even those who got the Moosejaw bellow several times a day, really complained. Frank Buchanan was working longer hours than men half his age. His enthusiasm for the Talus, his vision of a new kind of plane that would surpass in efficiency and safety everything now in the air, galvanized everyone.

Dick's telephone rang. "This is Kirk Willoughby," a voice said. "Remember me? The company sawbones? You haven't sent me that memo on the Honeycomb Club."

"I don't get it. Are you working for Dr. Kinsey on the side?"

"Just collecting opinions, pro and con. Believe it or not, some people think we ought to shut it down. They're afraid to say it in public because Buzz McCall will call them pansies. I'm also worried about its effect on the women. A lot of people have been getting letters from someone who calls herself Califia. She sounds a bit homicidal to me. We'd have a hell of a mess if someone got murdered and the tabloids got their hands on the story. Can't you see the headlines? Cost plus sex at Buchanan Aircraft."

Dick hung up and computed his latest cost projection on the Talus. It was so appalling, he decided not to show it to Frank Buchanan. It would only trigger another tirade on the futility of predicting costs on a radically new plane. At 10 P.M. Dick left the designers burning the midnight fluorescence in the Black Hole and drove down the boulevards to his one-bedroom apartment in Manhattan Beach.

He had moved into the Villa Hermosa, a complex of three-story buildings a few blocks from the ocean. Most of the residents were airline pilots, stewardesses, and middle-level aircraft company executives. Almost all were single. Dick was amazed by the offhand way everyone slept around. Sexual liberation pervaded all branches of the aircraft business.

As he drove through the warm California darkness, the cool sea wind caressing his face, Dick felt desire gathering in his belly, crowding his throat. Cassie Trainor would be waiting for him beside the pool tonight. For the past six months he had been sharing Cassie with Cliff Morris. That meant she agreed not to date anyone else from the Honeycomb Club.

For the first three months Dick had liked it. Cassie just seemed to want to screw. That was all Dick wanted to do too. He did not want to think about it. He wanted to enjoy this strange new world of sexual freedom on its own terms. Cassie was tireless. If he wanted to do it two, three, four, five times a night she was perfectly agreeable. She was always ready for one more. "Come on, go for the record," she would whisper mockingly. "Show up the Big Shot."

That was her nickname for Cliff. She had begun to talk about him and other members of the club. It broke Dick's concentration on pure physical pleasure and made him think about the whole arrangement. He was not interested in going for records or showing up his friends. Some members apparently thrived on this sort of stuff.

Dick changed to bathing trunks and found Cassie lounging beside the pool, the social center of the Villa Hermosa. She was listening to a TWA copilot describe his latest narrow escape trying to land in Pittsburgh or Chicago or Raleigh. "The fog was so goddamn thick the propellers sliced it like it was sausage meat. We had enough ice on the wings to throw a skating party—"

"Wait'll you see the Talus," Dick said. "No worries about ice, ever again. We've got heating coils in the wings that melt it at the flip of a switch."

"Is that supposed to excite me?" Cassie drawled. She was wearing a blue lastex two-piece bathing suit. The bottom half was cut to the minimum, making her long tawny body resemble a Modigliani painting.

"I thought heat excited you," Dick said.

"Just about anything excites Cassie," said Sue, a Pan American stewardess who was currently sleeping with the copilot. She was a honey-blond with a hefty wide-waisted torso and good breasts.

"What excites you?" Cassie said. "A full planeload of ginks lookin' up your dress?"

"No," Sue said.

"Then shut up about what excites me."

"Sorry," Sue said.

"Maybe you excite me," Cassie said. "Maybe that's where I'm goin'."

"Not tonight, I hope," Dick said.

She looked at him with surprising distaste. "No. Not tonight," she said. He realized Cassie was drunk. It was not the first time she had showed up this way. But it was the first time booze had not put her in a good humor.

"I think I'll take a swim," Dick said. He did two laps in a lazy Australian crawl. "Come on in," he called to Cassie.

She was still working on Sue. "Why the hell don't you get a job where you get paid for doin' it?" she said. "That's why you're on the goddamn plane but they don't pay you any real money for it."

"I think you ought to try diddling yourself for a change," Sue said.

With a lunge worthy of an offended tigress, Cassie raked Sue's face with her nails. The stewardess screamed and fell into the pool. Cassie dove on top of her and held her head under the water. "Hey, you're drowning her!" the bewildered copilot yelled and leaped on top of Cassie to rescue his girl. After a lot of thrashing he managed to pry her hands off Sue's throat.

"Get her out of here," Sue screamed, clutching her bleeding face.

Appalled, Dick led Cassie to his apartment. "What the hell is the matter?" he said.

"Nothin'. Nothin' for you to worry about," Cassie said. She pulled off her bottom, slipped out of her top and stood there, hands on her hips, naked. "Let's do it," she said.

"Wait a minute," Dick said. "Wait a couple of minutes. I'm not exactly in the mood after seeing you practically commit murder."

"Ain't that too damn bad. I thought you were a war hero. Forty-nine missions with the Big Shot? Why should you be bothered by a little friendly killin'? In case you're interested, this is my forty-ninth mission for the Honeycomb Club. I've been keepin' a record. Maybe you've noticed I'm kind of interested in records."

"I have noticed that," Dick said. "But something's gone wrong. You were flying high until tonight."

"How the hell would you know?"

"I guess I wouldn't. I thought you didn't want to talk about anything."

"I don't," Cassie said. "Let's fuck. I'm ready when you are."

It was the first time Dick had heard a woman say *fuck*. It only confirmed how disturbed, maybe crazy, Cassie was. "I'd like to know what's wrong first."

"Nothin'!"

"That's obviously bullshit."

Cassie walked over to the window and stared down at the pool. "It's a sort of anniversary. But I can handle it."

"What happened?"

"I met somebody three years ago today. He broke my goddamn heart. That's all. You don't care. You'd rather have it without any heart. Isn't that what all you bastards want? A nice smooth fuckin' machine?"

"I thought if you liked it and I liked it—"

"What's there to like? After the first couple of dozen times you start to feel dead down there. You start to feel death creepin' up through your whole body. Pretty soon you actually want death to show this certain bastard what he's done. You know he doesn't care but that doesn't matter. You think maybe it'll make him care—and that's all you want."

Cassie started trembling from head to foot. "Hey," Dick said. "Hey." He put his arms around her. "Hey, listen. It isn't that bad. It can't be that bad."

Cassie had crossed some sort of boundary. She had exceeded some sort of tolerance in her soul. For a moment he wondered if she was Califia, the woman who had sent threatening letters to half the executives at Buchanan. "Listen," he said. "We don't have to do it. Let's just lie down and let me hold you for a while."

He led her into the bedroom, his arm around her waist. It was strange. He did not have an erection. Until tonight, he could not look at Cassie naked without getting aroused. Touching her stirred instant desire. Was it all in his head? Dick wondered. Was the other Cassie, the fucking machine with the blank smile and mocking eyes, an ultimate expression of male freedom? While this Cassie, a woman in pain, was something else?

They lay down in the double bed, face to face, his arms around her. Gradually Cassie stopped trembling. But her tears continued for a long time, a silent bitter stream, eventually soaking the pillowcase. "Why did this guy break your heart?" he said.

"I don't know," Cassie said. "I don't think anybody ever knows till it happens, do they?"

"That's the way it works in novels," Dick said. "But in real life we usually get some warning signals and back off."

"Is that supposed to make me feel better? Tellin' me it's my fault?" Cassie said.

269

"I don't mean it that way. I'm trying to help you think about it. Look at it objectively."

"Just hold me. That helps more than anything."

They lay there, listening to laughter and shouts and splashing from the pool. Airline people lived on such crazy schedules, there were swimmers at all hours of the night. Often Dick was awakened at 3 A.M. by water polo contests between copilots and flight engineers, with stews cheering on the sidelines.

"Are all Jews this nice to women?" Cassie said.

"I don't know. I sort of doubt it," Dick said.

"You're the only one I've ever met this close. I never saw one in Noglichucky Hollow."

That was Cassie's Tennessee birthplace. She often compared it to Al Capp's Dogpatch. "Why did you leave that garden spot?" Dick asked.

"The only man I cared about got killed in the Pacific. He was a strafer pilot. You ever heard of them?"

"Sure."

"Bravest of brave. Not like you Eighth Air Force cowards bombin' from twenty thousand feet."

"We had some worries at twenty thousand feet. Focke-Wulfs and Messerschmitts," Dick said.

"That's why this other guy broke my heart. He was a strafer pilot too. I guess I thought I was sort of touching Joe. Then I found out all he wanted to do was fuck me silly. Jesus."

Dick held her a little tighter, trying to say he was sorry.

"You don't give a damn about all this. Why're you listenin'?"

"I like you."

"You mean you like to fuck me."

"I like to do that too. But I like you for other reasons."

"What are they?"

"You're honest. You say what you think."

"I don't, most of the time. Tonight it all came out."

"That's still worth a decoration. People aren't brave all the time."

"I like you too, Dick."

"Why?"

"Because you listened tonight."

Cassie began kissing him. Sad, gentle kisses at first, her tongue just touching his lips. Her hands roved his body with the same melancholy tempo. He let her make all the moves, sensing that she wanted to offer herself without immediate response from him. Soon her lips and her tongue began following her hands. She licked him like a cat, sighing, occasionally weeping.

He began to swell. Desire throbbed in his chest. But it had a different timbre. There was an ambiguity in the center of it. Part of Cassie's soul was reaching out to his soul in the California darkness. From simple screwing they had come to that perilous word, *like*. It was an unknown in the magical freedom of the

270

air fraternity. Were there unknown unknowns waiting over the horizon, hidden in words like love?

"Oh. Oh," Cassie sighed as he entered her. "Oh Dick."

It was the first time she had used that name. Until tonight she called him Stone or when she was feeling wry, Mr. Stone. He liked it. He liked the tenderness, the sadness that was intertwined with the pleasure. He liked the sense of entering a new dimension with this woman. Was it another stage of California freedom or the beginning of its loss?

"Oh now, Dick, now, come now," Cassie whispered.

It was the first time she had spoken to him about her desire. It was the first time he had thought about coming as something more than a physical release, a nice climax to the athletic performance. He came and came and Cassie melted in his arms. She cried out with a wild compound of pleasure and sadness and triumph. Had he somehow helped her to escape the hollow in which she had been trapped by war and grief? Dick did not know. He only felt a kind of awe at the unknown through which they were both moving.

For a long time Cassie lay in his arms, silent except for deep, slow sighs. Then she said: "I don't want to see the Big Shot anymore."

"So? Tell him. Isn't that the way the Honeycomb works? You're free to say no."

"He won't like it. Especially if I stay with you. He'll hold it against you."

"Maybe you ought to get the hell out of that club," Dick said.

"Why?"

"Because you're too smart. You can't not think about it."

Cassie chewed on that for a while. "Yes I can," she said.

Was he disappointed? Dick wondered. Or relieved? "Tell Cliff. I can handle him if he gets sore," Dick said.

"Good luck. Do you want to see me again, in spite of my persistence in whoriness?"

Dick sensed he was being tested. "Yes," he said. "If you feel the same way."

"Call me when you're ready," Cassie said.

The next morning, after Cassie departed for her own apartment a few blocks from the Villa Hermosa, Dick wrote a memo for Dr. Kirk Willoughby.

The first time I went to the Honeycomb Club I felt like some rich boys had invited me into their secret tree house. It was full of expensive toys you could not find anywhere else. They told me I could do anything I wanted with these toys. After all, a toy can't feel anything. The other day a surprising thing happened. One of my toys started to cry. Now I'm not so sure I want to play at the Honeycomb Club any more.

HOME TO ROOST

Sarah Morris went through the routine of mothering her two daughters, assisted by fat, earnest Maria, her Mexican maid. But Maria, the children, the house, the sunbaked streets of south Los Angeles, remained unreal. Again and again she was with Billy McCall at 81,000 feet, on the edge of the unknowable.

Perhaps the most curious thing was the disappearance of her rage against her husband. Was it some kind of ultimate sexual contentment? Or was it the satisfaction of revenge?

She did not know the answer. She only knew she alternated between being curiously happy and desperately unhappy. The happiness seemed to seize her spasmodically, when she least expected it—when she was giving the baby a bath or reading a book to her older daughter. *Happy.* A voice seemed to whisper it from a distance, almost mockingly—but not quite. Billy?

After lunch, the sleepless night caught up to her. She toppled into bed and found herself wide awake. She went over and over the scene in the airport parking lot until she convinced herself Billy was going to call her again. She told herself she did not want him to do it. The next moment, the thought of his voice on the telephone made her body dissolve. If it wasn't love, what was it? Lust? She had been taught that lust was vile, ugly, brutal. What she had felt with Billy had been none of those things.

What was it? She had to give it a name. She finally called it freedom. She had done something daring—more daring than marrying Cliff Morris in wartorn England. There was more courage in her heart than she had suspected. Why did she like that idea? Was she a test pilot by temperament? A test pilot of the spirit?

For the first time she faced the truth about the night Cliff had been reported missing over Berlin. She had wept briefly in her mother's arms. But in her heart she had been secretly relieved, she had felt an awful shameful gratitude. Tama and Billy were right. Why not admit it to herself? She had married a war, not a man, and she had been glad she did not have to spend the rest of her life with him. What kind of a woman was she?

English pussy, Billy whispered mockingly. He was hateful. But fascinating. Who knew what ideas he would bring back from 90,000, 100,000 feet?

She got up without sleeping, put on lipstick and went shopping for groceries in one of the new supermarkets. More American freedom. A thousand choices and no one telling her what to buy. What had she bought in the desert? Infidelity as a way of life? Could she become Billy McCall's mistress?

She sensed something special had happened to him too. Perhaps that was part of his anger. He hated the thought of a woman having power over him, even the power of giving him pleasure.

Pleasure. *Pleasure.* The word was inadequate. All the words in Shakespeare's language, her mother tongue, were inadequate to describe what she had found in the American desert. She was a *wanton.* She was a *bitch.* All the words she had read in books and never dreamt of possessing were suddenly part of Sarah Chapman Morris's American self.

What about love? What about that supreme value in every woman's life? Was it possible that Billy loved her? Was there a moment in a man's soul when pleasure crossed some boundary into love? She knew so little about how a man thought and felt. Cliff was still mostly a mystery to her.

Back in the house, she noticed an anxious look on Maria's face. "You hoos-ban', he call. Be late," she said.

"Don't worry about it," she said. She had not expected Cliff until tomorrow.

Maria hesitated. "He call—this morning too. I no tell you."

"That's all right," Sarah said. Sometimes Maria was too conscientious. She was so anxious to do everything right. It was almost embarrassing, the way the Americans had made the Mexicans so humble. It reminded her of stories she had heard about native servants in Kenya and India.

She ate dinner and watched television for a while. It was all so stupid—grinning game-show hosts and comedians telling fourth-rate jokes. She turned it off and read *Pride and Prejudice* for the third or fourth time. She adored Jane Austen's prose. It reflected the English world her characters inhabited, also so controlled and measured. While this American world seemed to have no visible boundaries, no signposts or rules.

At ten o'clock she turned on the television news. A handsome talking head told her about American plans to counter the threat of Russia's possession of the atomic bomb. Then came a commercial featuring dancing soup cans. Then the talking head again reporting "another tragedy in the Mojave." A Buchanan Aircraft experimental plane had crashed, killing its three-man crew. A previous model of this top-secret bomber had plunged into the desert six months ago.

A half hour later, Cliff's keys jingled in the front door. The sour look on his face was predictable. "How are you?" she said, kissing him briefly on the mouth.

"Lousy," he growled.

"I just heard the bad news—another crash."

"Yeah."

"Will they scrap the program?"

"I don't know. What've you been doing?"

"Baby tending. House running. A big market for my services."

"Is that all?"

"What else do you think I might be doing?"

"Fucking someone!"

It was the first time he had ever used that word in front of her. The first time she had ever heard it, except once, by accident during the war, when she had overheard two pilots using it.

"I really don't know what you're talking about," she said.

"I got back from the Mojave this morning. I called the house. Maria gave me some bullshit story about you staying with friends."

Maria had been trying to warn her.

"I—I had a call from an old school chum. She's in town doing a movie. We sat up so late talking I decided to stay with her rather than drive home half-asleep."

She could not believe the intensity of her deceit. She launched it without a moment's hesitation. Why didn't she just tell him she was playing the infidelity game? Remind him it was the twentieth century.

"What's her name?"

"I don't ask you these questions."

"What's her name?"

"None of your business!"

It was outrageous. She hated him. He was invading her desert idyll with his vulgar jealousy. "Let me rephrase the question. What's *his* name?"

"Billy McCall!"

She did not see the hand. It seemed to come from nowhere. He seemed to be standing too far away to hit her. But the hand came whirling to smash her in the face and send her hurtling across the living room. Her head struck the rug with a terrific thud and she lay there, unable to move, engulfed by a new emotion: shame.

She had known from the moment Billy propositioned her on the dance floor. She had known by the pool in the desert. This was the one man her husband could not tolerate as his rival. Cliff's choked raging words were superfluous. "Anybody else—I wouldn't give a fuck—anyone—anybody."

He stood over her, berserk. She wondered if she was about to die. She felt strangely indifferent to that possibility. She almost welcomed it. Would it even the score for her unholy gratitude at the news of his death over Berlin?

That had been a sin. It was a sin to secretly rejoice over the death of a man she had promised to love. She had sinned again last night with Billy.

She wanted Cliff to hit her again. She would welcome a beating that would reduce her to a pleading blob. It would clean her slate, it would leave her empty and calm in another kind of freedom, the opposite of Billy's soaring. The inward calm of the penitent prisoner in her cell.

Something completely unexpected began to happen. Her husband was kneeling beside her, saying "Oh, Oh, Sarah. Oh Jesus, Sarah." He picked her up and carried her to the couch.

Something even more amazing began to happen. Kneeling beside the couch, Cliff began blubbering. Tears and sobs. This six-foot-four hunk of masculinity was crying like a two-year-old.

The room was still spinning. A shrill telephone seemed to be ringing inside

Sarah's head. "Stop. Stop, please," she said. "You hurt me so much I just wanted to hurt you back."

He wiped his streaming eyes with his handkerchief. "My career's going down the tubes with that goddamn plane. Isn't that enough hurting? Were you going to tell me he's better than I am?"

A terrible understanding gathered force in Sarah Chapman Morris's soul. Part of it was guilt, part of it was painful wisdom. This tower of male muscle and bone, this Charles Atlas who could knock a woman twenty feet with a swing of his mighty arm, was a psychological ninety seven pound weakling. In a world without a sense of sin, it was still possible to acquire a misshapen soul.

"He isn't as good," Sarah said. "The whole thing only made me realize I love you. I was sorry I tried it."

She was saying farewell to ascent, farewell to little deaths on the edge of the unknowable. Farewell to Billy McCall, who thoroughly deserved it. She hoped it would be a long time before he found someone able to climb as fast. She was accepting a substitute for love—pity.

No. That was too brutal. She was going to create a different kind of love, a blend of sympathy and nostalgia and honor. Especially honor. That was the best part of it. She had made a pledge to this man in the country church outside Rackreath Air Base in 1943. She was honoring that pledge now—with this lie.

It was better than Billy's way, better than his uncaring freedom. Sarah had to believe that part of it. Billy did not care. If Billy cared she was forever undone. She was still enough of a romantic, enough of a Catholic, to disapprove of uncaring freedom, in spite of its enormous temptation.

Cliff was carrying her upstairs to their bedroom. It was a sad parody of Billy carrying her into the pool where she had been baptized in his new lonely faith. Her husband was pressing a cold washcloth on her face. "I didn't mean it," he said. "I was out of my mind."

It poured out, his fear and hatred of Billy, the certainty that he was going to resign from the Air Force eventually and join the company, where he would have Buzz McCall's backing—and Frank Buchanan's. Adrian Van Ness would die or retire and Billy would demolish his boyhood enemy. "All my life I've tried to be nice to the bastard. He goes right on despising me."

Sarah tried to convince her husband he was allowing himself to be haunted by a myth. "You have more brains than he has, more personality. He can only do one thing. Fly a plane."

"In the business we're in, nothing else matters."

"He could get killed next week."

"He won't. The bastard's got a charmed life."

"So do you," she said. "Forty-nine missions. Doesn't that prove something? You're lucky too."

"You're not lying? He wasn't better?"

"I'm not lying. He wasn't better," she said, the edge of mockery enabling her to tell the lie without a tremor. "I wouldn't have done it if you hadn't made me so angry about other women."

Romantic in spite of everything, she was still yearning for fidelity. "You don't know what it's like in this business—people think you're queer or hen-pecked if you walk away from it."

He was his stepfather's son. Buzz McCall had put his mark on Cliff Morris as profoundly as if he had implanted him with his genes. Why wasn't Billy marked in the same way? Where did he get that incredible desire to explore the unknowable? Why was he so endowed with freedom and its corollary, courage?

While this man, her husband, chased women into bed because he did not dare to defy the conventions of the plane business. For a moment an awful sadness sucked at Sarah's soul. She was learning too much. She wanted to drown her mind in blankness. She resisted the impulse. She was not going to despair. She had proven to herself and Tama that she had willpower. Now she would prove she had another kind of power. If Tama could change herself from a Mexican washerwoman's daughter into Adrian Van Ness's mistress, maybe Sarah could change Tama's son from a spoiled playboy to a serious husband and a successful executive.

"I want you to walk away from it for my sake," Sarah said. "I want you to promise me you'll try. If you want my love, you've got to make that promise."

There was a long silence. Was he saying farewell to someone he cared about? Someone he loved more than this demanding English bitch? "I promise," Cliff said.

She kissed him and began unbuttoning his shirt. "Do you want me?" she whispered.

"Yes," he said.

Were they crossing a boundary? Sarah wondered. One of those unmarked American zones just beyond the erogenous where love began? She could only hope so. "I want you most when you want me," she whispered. "It's like music. Two instruments playing. You meant so much to me in England. Make me feel the same way here in America."

They were both naked now. Cliff's fingers were deep in her English pussy. Sarah's breath came faster and faster. My God, maybe he *was* better than Billy! She kissed the pulsing tip of his penis, something she had never done before. Willfully, powerfully, she rolled him onto his back and mounted him, a position they seldom used—and never on her initiative.

Cliff rotated his palms on her nipples until they were as erect, as erotic as his penis. "You've been my luck from the start," he said. "No matter what I did with anyone else, she never meant anything to me. You're the only one I ever cared about."

Some antenna in her mind, perhaps stirred by a tremor in his gaze, made her suspect that was a lie. But it was a loving lie. As loving as the lie she had told him about Billy. It was enormously confusing. Love on a bed of lies.

"From the start I saw us as a team," he said, stroking her as he spoke, sending surges of pleasure through her body. Sarah summoned pity, she summoned hope. "We are, we are," she said.

From somewhere deep in her soul a caustic voice whispered. *You'll do your part. He won't even try.* Was it Billy McCall? Go to hell—or heaven—you smiling bastard, Sarah replied while her husband clutched her to his chest and came with a shuddering rush.

Power. The word whispered in Sarah's soul. She had just exercised, demonstrated, her power over this man. He had prostrated her with a swing of his mighty hand. Even that humiliation had become part of the power she had just acquired. Sarah lay in her husband's arms wondering if once a wife tasted such power, she could ever let it go.

"By the way," Cliff said. "You're not sending those letters to Tama, are you? The ones signed Califia?"

"No."

"They're driving her nuts."

Good, Sarah thought, delighted to hear her chief rival was faltering. Was she on her way to becoming an evil woman, in spite of her repentance? Life in America was incredibly complicated.

VORTEX

High above the Mojave Desert, a new version of the Talus roared through its latest tests, looking more than ever like an illustration from a science fiction novel. The entire plane was now a wing. Not a trace of a fuselage remained. Around Cliff four Air Force generals shook their heads in disbelief. "Give me three hundred copies and the Russkies won't say boo for twenty years," one said.

Three hundred copies at a million a plane was three hundred million dollars. With spare parts and the usual overrides in a cost-plus contract, they were talking about a half billion dollars. Cliff Morris, project manager of the Talus, could claim a lot of the credit for pumping that much money into Buchanan Aircraft. It was incredible the way his life had turned around in the last three months.

In Cliff's mind it was all connected to an amazing event. He had fallen in love with his wife again. The feeling seemed part of a current suddenly swirling through him and around him since their night of rage and reconciliation. Everything had been clicking, flowing, flying.

Frank Buchanan had switched to jet engines and solved most of the Talus's stability problems. The plane zoomed through one checkout after another, demonstrating speed, maneuverability, endurance—and its greatest asset, its phenomenally low drag-to-weight ratio. No other plane in existence could match it as a weight lifter.

The rest of Cliff's life seemed to reshape itself in the same magical way. A nervous Cassie Trainor told him she did not want to see him anymore. She was going to move in with Dick Stone. Two months ago he would have been furious. Now he just patted her on the behind and wished her well.

Sarah had shut off that stupid phonograph. She said she wanted to make her own music. She greeted him every night with ravenous eyes. After they made love they lay in bed, talking about the company, his ambitions, the Talus, Frank, Buzz, Adrian. He told her everything.

Sometimes she helped him see things he had missed. Mostly she told him how good he was at this project manager's job. He was good at bridging gaps between people. Maybe it was because he was big and looked like he had the answers. People trusted him. He was a war hero.

Each day he went to work without the old crawling anxiety in his belly. It was amazing. Was Sarah some sort of sorceress? At times the wartime hunch that she was his luck swelled to cosmic proportions. She was his guide, his priestess, his goddess. The boyish devotion he had once felt for his mother was transformed into something close to adoration of his wife.

There was only one thing wrong. Up there at the controls of the Talus was Billy McCall. Every time Cliff saw him, a flicker of his old fear revived. Beneath the fear was a cold unforgiving rage. It was one thing to play sex games with chippies like Cassie Trainor. Billy had seduced his wife. Yet Cliff had to pretend he knew nothing about it, he had to go on exchanging jokes and taunts with Billy in the same old way.

Billy was flying the plane that could make Cliff the crown prince of Buchanan Aircraft. Sarah told him again and again that this was cause for glee, not grief. But something dark and sullen at the bottom of Cliff's soul refused to accept it. He did not want Billy McCall to give him anything, even by accident. He did not want to owe even a shred of gratitude to the arrogant bastard.

Sarah did not understand how men hated each other. How deep it went, how impossible it was to forgive because to ask it or offer it would be a confession of weakness. He could forgive her, of course. He had forgiven her as she had forgiven him for that murderous slap.

Down, down came the Talus in a beautiful approach, not a hint of a yaw or a wobble. The tires kissed the runway as lightly as the wheels of a Piper Cub. It was hard to believe they were watching a thirty-ton plane carrying eight tons of simulated bombs. Cliff thought ruefully of how many times he had thumped the *Rainbow Express* onto the runway at Rackreath.

The generals murmured admiringly. Buzz McCall and Frank Buchanan accepted another round of congratulations. Cliff could see nothing but Billy and Sarah on a couch or bed somewhere engulfed in a green mist. The gleaming silver plane, the empty mocha desert, the distant mountains, vanished. He stood there, paralyzed until General Scott clapped him on the shoulder.

"You ready to do some selling in Washington? We'll back you with everything we've got."

"You bet," Cliff said, his tongue thick and dry in his mouth. He watched Billy taxi smoothly down the runway toward them. In a moment he was climbing out of the plane with his copilot and flight engineer. "The thing flies itself," Billy said. "You just got to tickle its clit now and then."

Inverness flowed on the old SkyRanger they flew back to Santa Monica. As far as they could see, the Talus was as good as sold. "I gottta hand it to you, wingman," Buzz McCall roared, holding out his glass to Frank Buchanan. "I thought it was a piece of fucking insanity the first time I saw it but you've made me a believer."

"I couldn't have done it without you. Without all of you," Frank said. He lurched down the aisle to pound Billy on the back. "Without this pilot at the controls."

He thumped Cliff's shoulder. "Without this *executive* pulling it all together. Adrian thought we were going to fall on our goddamn faces. Didn't know we were a family! Band of fathers—and brothers."

Frank whacked others on the back too. One of Buzz's engineers, Bruce Kelly, who ran things at the Muroc end of the line, designer Sam Hardy who had solved all sorts of problems with the Talus's ailerons. Dick Stone, who had made the cost estimates low enough to keep Adrian at bay. Frank talked exultantly of getting to work on an airliner version within six months.

"That's when we're really going to start lying about costs," he chuckled, winking at Dick.

They were so high on Inverness and anticipation they barely noticed when the plane landed at Buchanan Field. They piled out and gazed at a satisfying sight on the flight line. No less than nineteen copies of the Talus roosted there, some ready to fly, others waiting for the jet engines Frank had persuaded the Air Force to let them try.

"Let's head for the Honeycomb and pick out the best pussy on the list," Buzz said.

"Why not?" Billy said.

"Why not indeed?" Frank said.

Cliff took a deep slow breath. "Sorry," he said. "I've got to get home."

Buzz could not believe his ears. "What the fuck? Have you gone queer, Big Shot?"

"No. Married," Cliff said. "I've gone married." His face was flushing. His whole body felt like it was melting. Billy McCall was grinning at him.

"What's wrong? Afraid you're going to draw Califia?" Buzz said. Everyone had decided one of the girls at the club was Califia. Buzz liked the idea of screwing a woman who might murder you before it was over. He said it was better than stunt-flying.

Cliff struggled for breath. He could handle Buzz. If Billy said something he was going to knock him into the Pacific Ocean. "You're absolutely right," Frank said, squeezing his shoulder. "I wish I had a wife to go home to."

"I was going to let you try Madeleine tonight. That's how good I'm feeling, Big Shot," Billy said.

"She's all yours," Cliff said.

"I'm worn out. I think I'll head home too," Dick Stone said.

279

"Jesus," Buzz said. "Respectability is spreading like a fucking plague. Let's get the hell away from these pansies."

Cliff realized Frank and Dick Stone had tried to help him. It was a small comfort. He drove home in a daze. Had he really done it? Had he made a total asshole of himself for Sarah Chapman Morris's sake? Buzz would never let him forget it. Billy would be telling him all about Madeleine's cries and sighs for the next month. He must be going crazy to let a woman—a foreigner who knew absolutely nothing about Americans—mess him up this way.

He parked the car in the driveway and trudged slowly across the lawn to front door. Sarah met him just inside, her eyes shining. "I hope you've got good news," she said.

"Pretty good," he said.

"Mine is very good. I'm pregnant."

It was the current again. Carrying him in the right direction. His response came from somewhere outside his mind. "It's going to be a boy."

"I'm sure of it too."

They made the tenderest love of Cliff's life that night. Sex had never been tender for him. He never thought of women as fragile. He liked them big and muscular. Maybe it was because there was so much of Tama—and he saw it all in the Redondo Beach house. Sarah was fragile, especially that night. She was like a precious object, a vase or a statue that a harsh touch could smash.

He did not even want to do it at first. "I'm afraid I'll hurt the kid," he said.

"You won't. I want you. I want you more than ever."

He rested her on top of him again. It was beautiful and slow and almost sad. He kept thinking of what Billy was probably doing with Madeleine, what Cassie Trainor might be doing for Dick Stone. Why couldn't he have both worlds? Why was Sarah inflicting this choice on him? For a moment wisps of the green fog drifted through his mind, he saw her with Billy. But he concentrated on loving Sarah, on the current that was carrying them both toward some sort of special happiness.

Afterward they talked about the Talus, the hopes it was igniting. The day after tomorrow Billy was going to fly it to Washington. Adrian Van Ness and the top people from the project team were going to join him there and display the plane to senators and congressmen. The Air Force was going to back them with all the influence they could muster.

They could not fail. The current was irresistible now. Cliff rubbed Sarah's stomach and said: "What'll we name him?"

"It's your choice if it's a boy."

"Charles. But I'm going to call him Charlie."

Princess Elizabeth, England's future queen, had just named her first son Charles. Tears streamed down Sarah's face. "Oh Cliff, I do love you. No matter what happens in the future, let's never forget these three months."

"Don't worry about the future," Cliff said. "It's going to get better and better."

Sarah sighed. "You Americans are all such optimists."

The next day, the chill in that comment made it difficult for Cliff to share the ebullience of the Buchanan team on the flight to Washington. Over the Rockies, he noticed Adrian was not joining the celebration. He sat alone, looking out the window of the Lockheed Super Constellation.

"What's the boss worried about?" Cliff said, sitting down beside him.

"The usual thing a boss worries about. Money,"

"Won't this contract take the pressure off?"

"It would—if we get it."

"Is there any doubt? Our only competition is that ridiculous B-Thirty-six. The other day General Scott called it a B-Twenty-nine with elephantiasis."

The boss managed a smile. "Maybe I'm worried about the government's overall policy. It doesn't seem to have one. We're drifting from event to event. While the Communists take over huge chunks of the world."

"Like China."

Adrian nodded. "The Democrats will never recover from that one unless they do something dramatic with the defense budget. Stay sober when we get to Washington. Talk to people your age—majors, lieutenant colonels, congressional aides. Sometimes they know more about what's coming than the people at the top."

"Sure," Cliff said, flattered that the Adrian was confiding so much to him.

They landed at National Airport and ensconced themselves in a pair of suites at the Shoreham. The next day at Muroc Billy climbed into the jet-engine version of the Talus and streaked across the nation in four hours and twenty-five minutes. He came within twelve minutes of breaking the transcontinental speed record, which had been set by a Lockheed P80A "Shooting Star"—a fighter plane.

Billy roared over Washington and landed at Andrews Air Force Base in Maryland. The afternoon papers carried pictures and front page stories. The next day, President Truman inspected the Talus and remarked, "This looks like one hell of an airplane. We ought to have some."

Everyone at Buchanan could almost hear the rustle of money. The Air Force announced it was interested in buying four hundred copies. That would put the contract close to a billion dollars. At the Shoreham, Billy was the center of a nonstop party for senators and congressmen from the armed services committees, Air Force generals, and Pentagon officials.

Cliff remembered Adrian's orders to stay sober and listen. Standing with two Air Force lieutenant colonels, he heard one say: "this thing fits beautifully into NSC Sixty-eight."

"What's that? A new way to sink the Navy?" Cliff asked.

The Navy and the Air Force had been battling ferociously over their share of the budget in the consolidated Department of Defense. The lieutenant colonel grinned and shook his head. "Top secret for the time being. We're still putting it together. A new policy statement."

They flew back to California that night. On the plane, Cliff told Adrian about NSC-68. "Interesting," Adrian said. "NSC stands for the National Security Council. It's one of Truman's better ideas. They're supposed to advise the president on defense policy—instead of letting a lot of kitchen cabinet pals make up his mind for him, Roosevelt-style."

In California, the ebullience continued to build. Buzz McCall drew up plans for rehiring 20,000 workers. Frank Buchanan put the design department to work on converting the Talus to an airliner. Jet engines still guzzled too much fuel to make a commercial plane profitable. They would have to go back to props, which meant a lot of expensive changes. Jim Redwood talked to Cliff about joining him in an expanded sales department as second in command.

The Air Force continued to test the Talus at Muroc. Other pilots found it a difficult plane to handle. Perhaps they lacked Billy McCall's skills—or his determination to make the plane perform for Frank's sake. There was a third crash, killing another three-man crew. But three crashes were not considered excessive for a radically new plane. Frank was sure another redesign of the ailerons would solve the problem.

One hot day in June of 1950 Cliff was summoned to Adrian Van Ness's office. He charged up the stairs wondering if the good news from Washington had finally arrived. The CEO was standing at the window, looking down on Buchanan Field, where nineteen completed copies of the Talus now sat on the flight line. "I've got a little present for you," he said.

He handed Cliff a check for a thousand dollars. "A bonus for staying sober in Washington and hearing about NSC Sixty-eight. It's the most important state paper since the Monroe Doctrine. It proposes a policy to deal with the Communist threat. It's what they call a forward strategy—a network of bases around the world that'll support our allies and enable us to meet a Soviet challenge wherever and whenever it appears. Do you see why that could be very important to Buchanan Aircraft?"

Cliff nodded. "Air power. That's where we're ahead of the Russians. Most of those forward bases will be for planes. We'll need fighters to defend them, transports to supply them."

"Exactly," Van Ness said. "After I finished reading NSC Sixty-eight, I slept for eight hours. It's the first time I've done that since the war ended."

Adrian moved some papers around his desk for a few moments. "But it doesn't mean our worries are over."

He moved a few more papers. "How's the Talus doing? Buzz tells me you've still got those stability problems."

"Frank thinks he's got them licked."

"I want the reports on it. All of them. Don't say anything about this to Buchanan."

There was a hostile sound to the way he used Frank's last name. "Why not?" Cliff asked.

"Because you just got a direct order from me not to," Adrian said.

"What's going on?"

"A lot of things I can't explain to you."

"Mr. Van Ness—Adrian—" Cliff was never sure which name to use. "I think

I'm entitled to an explanation. I've put a year and a half of my life into this plane."

"If we don't get this bomber off our backs, we'll have to lay off three or four thousand people—and you'll be one of them."

"I thought it was worth a billion dollars if the Air Force buys it!" Cliff gasped, trying to comprehend what Adrian was saying.

"The powers that be in Washington, in particular the Secretary of the Air Force, don't want to buy it. They prefer Convair's B-Thirty-six. Do you know who Floyd Odlum is?"

"He's head of Convair."

"The Secretary of the Air Force vacations regularly at his house in Palm Springs. Consolidated's going to build the B-Thirty-six in Texas. The Speaker of the House of Representatives, Sam Rayburn, is from Texas. One of the slickest, crookedest operators in the U.S. Senate, Lyndon Johnson, is from Texas. They want that billion dollars to go to Texas, not to California."

"Why the hell should we let them do that, if their plane isn't as good as ours?"

Adrian Van Ness smiled briefly. The flash of bitter humor exposed Cliff to a world of power and intrigue that he barely knew existed. "I've been told by the Secretary of the Air Force, personally, if we encourage our friends among the generals and pilots to fight for our plane—and they could fight very effectively—we'll never get another contract from the Air Force or the Navy or the Marines. We'll be back to trying to sell planes to airlines that don't need them."

"So you're going to give the Secretary the stability reports and he can use them to beat the Air Force generals' brains in when they complain?"

This time Adrian Van Ness's smile was almost pleasant. "I begin to think I haven't misjudged you after all, Cliff."

"Yes you have. I don't buy it. If Frank knew about this, he could fight back. He could give them data that proves we've solved most of the problems. Or will in a couple of months."

"That won't do him or you or me any good. It will just make the blood flow on both sides. Consolidated has the votes—in the Pentagon and in Congress. What is there about growing up in California that makes people so naive?"

Cliff felt a flush of anxiety and humiliation. Adrian was talking to him as if he were a child. Cliff heard Buzz sneer *momma's boy*. "I'm trying to educate you, Cliff. You could go a long way in this company," Adrian said. "We need someone with a good personality and no moral principles worth mentioning."

Cliff tried to choke down that compliment. It was so oblique, it was not easy to get down his throat. He gulped and gulped, trying to make excuses for Adrian Van Ness. Maybe if you were born rich it was hard to treat people as equals. Maybe it had something to do with graduating from Harvard.

"It's for the good of the company," Adrian said. "It's even for Frank's good. He's got years and years of planes to design for us."

"But he loves this plane," Cliff said. "It's the most original thing he's ever created."

"Frank gives every plane that ultimate rating. He tends to think in extremes. You have to learn to use people like him. And people like Buzz, for that matter."

With an inrush of regret Cliff realized Adrian Van Ness had him figured exactly right. He would do this rotten thing. He would help Adrian sabotage the plane Frank Buchanan had worked on day and night for eighteen months. He would betray a man who had been his second father and friend.

Why? Was something missing inside him? Was this another moment of truth like the one over Schweinfurt? Cliff twisted away from answering that question. Courage had nothing to do with it. Adrian was right. It was for the good of the company. He was bending before the power of the Pentagon and Congress and making Cliff bend before his power. That was the way power worked.

For a moment Cliff thought of Sarah and the current of love that seemed to be carrying him toward some special happiness. What did that mean now? "Get moving," Adrian said. "I need those stability reports before the end of the day."

Cliff nodded obediently. He was being sucked into a vortex that swirled invisibly around Adrian Van Ness the way knots of force swarmed around a wing and fuselage in flight. He had watched them testing models of the Talus in the wind tunnel, charting these vicious unpredictable unknowns. He had learned a lot about building airplanes in the last eighteen months. Now he was learning how they were destroyed.

LAYING ON OF HANDS

Dick Stone sat before his computer putting together a cost estimate for redesigning the Talus as an airliner. Frank Buchanan burst into his office with a painting of the plane soaring over the Rockies. "We need a new name for it," he said. "Something dignified—but with commercial appeal."

"How about the Aurora," Dick said. "Didn't Moon Davis say it took him back to the dawn of flight?"

"Wonderful!" Frank said, whacking him on the back.

Frank wandered around the Black Hole, showing the painting to everyone. He returned to tell Dick the name had won unanimous approval. "Now all we've got to do is sell it to Adrian Van Ness. He thinks naming planes is his prerogative."

About a half hour later, Cliff Morris dropped into Dick's office. "How's it going?" he said.

"Great," Dick said. "I'll have an estimate for the airliner version ready by the end of the day."

Cliff closed the door. "That may be premature. We're having some problems with the bomber. It takes more than a good design to sell a plane to the government. We need some help from you."

"Who's *we*?"

"Adrian Van Ness and your old buddy."

That was supposed to impress Dick and to some extent it did. "We want you to revise your cost estimates on the Talus," Cliff said.

"Scale them down to the minimum?"

"No. Raise them to the maximum."

"What the hell's the point of that?"

"Look. Trust me. I can't explain everything right now. A maximum evaluation would be very helpful with the problem we're having."

"How about a minimum explanation, at least?"

"It's—it's got something to do with keeping Congress happy. Adrian wants a high and a low so no one will scream if we come out on the high side. Don't mention it to Frank. He won't understand the politics. It'll only upset him."

Dick put together an upscale cost estimate that brought the Talus close to two million dollars a copy. It was not hard to do, since Frank was still grappling with some unknown unknowns in the plane's controls. At lunch the next day, Adrian Van Ness smiled arcanely at him and squeezed his arm. "I appreciate that estimate," he said. "It's nice to have another realist at work around here."

Dick did not get the point but he nodded and smiled back, not inclined to dispute a compliment from this WASP, which for him at this point meant White Anglo-Saxon Paragon.

At home, he continued to enjoy Cassie Trainor. She was still working at the Honeycomb Club, playing a defiant game with him, daring him to love her in spite of her refusal to take his advice. He played the game right back, dating other women whenever he felt like it. He was not quite ready to love Cassie but he liked her more and more. She entertained him with impersonations of horny airline passengers and panting Buchanan executives. Cassie had developed a contempt for the male sex that was invigorating, as long as it did not get personal.

On weekends, they did not see as much of each other because Dick spent Saturday and Sunday in the air with Billy McCall in his dark green Lustra I. Billy had been surly at first. He made it clear that he was teaching Dick to fly strictly as a favor to Frank Buchanan. Like most pilots, he had a low opinion of navigators, except when he needed one. Frank had apparently told him it was important to keep the computer guru happy so he would send Adrian Van Ness only soothing reports.

Billy loved flying too much to remain surly in the air. From the start he taught Dick the way Frank Buchanan had taught him. Frank called it the laying on of hands. For the first several hours Dick simply kept his hands on the yoke and imitated everything Billy did, while he explained it. By now Dick had mastered taking off and landing and other elementary maneuvers, such as the turn and the climb and the dive. Today they were going to explore something more ambitious: spins.

Ten miles at sea, Billy began his lecture. "An airplane is a three-axis all-attitude vehicle," he said. "It can be flown in any attitude accidentally or on purpose. I want you to be able to fly this baby upside down, in an inverted spin if necessary. I want you to be able to handle every kind of spin in the vocabulary."

He proceeded to put the plane into an oscillatory spin, a translational spin and a flat spin, which Dick later learned was usually fatal in a single-engine plane. Each time they pulled out with Dick's sweaty hands on the yoke and numb feet on the elevators while gravity threatened to pound his chest cavity to jelly.

Returning to the Buchanan airport, Dick made a classy landing, lining up the plane in the middle of the runway in spite of a tricky crosswind. Billy pushed back his fifty missions cap and socked him on the shoulder. "You're ready to solo," he said. "Only thing left to discuss is philosophy."

"What do you mean?"

"What you believe is up there in the sky. You think there's a Big Air Traffic Controller who's gonna take care of you when you get your ass in a tight spot?"

Dick shook his head.

"You don't think there's anything up there?"

Dick nodded.

"You're wrong," Billy said, staring at the northeast runway, where a blue Cessna was taking off. "There's two ladies up there. The Lady of Luck and the Lady of Death. They go for some guys, no one knows why. Sometimes guys go for them. No one can figure that one out either. Except they're both beautiful."

The Cessna's right wing dropped alarmingly. The pilot was obviously a student. Billy paused while the instructor jerked the plane level and climbed for survival. "Sometimes you can feel the Lady of Death's hands resting on top of yours on the throttles. The Lady of Luck just watches and smiles. Pretty soon you figure out she doesn't give a damn. Only thing to do then is laugh in both their faces."

Billy smiled bleakly and socked him on the shoulder again. "Now you're ready to go. Take her down to Laguna and back," he said. "Keep an eye out for other planes. They'll be a lot of them around today."

The Lustra was a very forgiving plane. It lifted off the runway as if it were part balloon and in ten minutes Dick was at five thousand feet, about five miles off Long Beach. He looked around him and felt a loosening in the center of his chest.

Freedom! He could go north or south, climb into that azure sky or dive toward that dark blue sea. He could loop or roll if he had the nerve. The sky filled his eyes. He owned it. He owned that burning sun and that iridescent blue dome, he owned the ocean and the coast line with its thousands of little houses and tiny boats in narrow harbors. He even owned that big-bellied Southwest Air Lines DC 3 plodding toward him en route from San Diego to San Francisco or Seattle.

Dick banked and dove and climbed. He did not try any loops or snap rolls or immelmans. He was an unstable mixture of courage and caution. Having seen a few planes crash, he knew how dangerous flying was. The stunts could wait for a little more confidence.

Closer to shore, he swooped low enough to watch the surfers riding the big waves. He wondered if he might see Cassie. She often surfed at Laguna. Sure enough, there she was. He recognized the streaming auburn hair, the long lithe body swaying on the board as it slithered and bounced down the almost vertical incline while the white mountain of water crested just behind her.

That did it. Dick lowered the nose, picked up speed and hauled on the yoke to climb into the blank blue sky and go over the vertical into his first loop.

Cassie recognized the plane. She paddled out on her board and stood up to wave. Dick did three snap rolls and came out of the third one with the nose much too high. He was within a whisker of stalling into a probably fatal spin at five hundred feet.

Sweating, he roared up to a thousand feet for another loop and a few chandelles. He was on his way to becoming the hot pilot of his repressed dreams. Screw those punctilious medical bureaucrats who had turned him into a navigator because he had astigmatism in one eye! Dick Stone was flying in California.

Back at the airport, Dick's landing was not quite so classy. The crosswind was blowing harder and he almost hit the runway with his left wing. He pancaked to safety. Billy frowned but the Lustra was undamaged. He signed Dick's log book and they adjourned to a nearby bar to celebrate.

Billy drank hard as usual. He was in a lousy mood. "You know Sarah, Cliff's wife?" he asked.

"Sure."

"What do you think of her?"

"Nice woman. Smart."

"How's she put up with him? I mean—do you think she really loves him?"

"I don't know," Dick said, his loyalty to Cliff tying his tongue. "Women are funny about that sort of thing. You have some reason to doubt it?"

Billy shook his head. It was hard to tell whether he was saying yes and it did not matter, or no and he did not care. Dick wondered if there was a third possibility.

He drove home in a boozy glow, hoping Cassie would be there to help him celebrate his first solo. Not only was she there, she had a bottle of champagne in a bucket and frosted glasses in the freezer.

"How did you recognize the plane?"

"I've flown in it," she said.

"Oh."

Cassie smiled mockingly. "Jealous, Mr. Stone? I can't believe it."

"Curious."

"It didn't work out. I didn't want to fly as high as Billy likes to go."

Dick decided it was none of his business. "You'd rather hang around with a nice, unimaginative front-office man? Dull, normal sex once a week?"

"That's right," Cassie said. "I hate excitement."

He started undressing her. She was only wearing shorts and a pullover shirt. In ten seconds she was naked. Dick ran his hands down the firm breasts, the supple belly, into the warm luxurious pussy. "You're a bitch," he said. "Why the hell do I like that sort of woman?"

They spent most of Sunday in bed. Dick drove to work in a state of semi-exaltation. Was he falling in love with Cassie? She was unquestionably American. You could not get more American than Noglichucky Hollow, Sevier County, Tennessee.

He put Cassie out of his head and looked forward to telling Frank Buchanan about soloing. He was pretty sure Frank would tell Buzz McCall at lunch. He wanted to see the surly surprise on the SOB's swarthy face when he found out the navigator had turned pilot.

Dick never got a chance to say a word about soloing. When he walked into the design department, the place looked like the mental ward at the county hospital. People were tearing up blueprints and cursing and pounding their desks and glaring out the windows as if they might jump, even though they were on the first floor. "What's wrong?" he asked.

"They've canceled the Talus," Sam Hardy said. "The fucking Secretary of the Air Force awarded the contract to Convair's B-Thirty-six. It's the god-damndest decision I've ever heard. Even the Russians can build a better plane than that lumbering behemoth."

"Where's Frank?" Dick said.

"Upstairs arguing with Adrian Van Ness. Trying to keep something alive."

Dick wondered if his cost estimate had anything to do with the disaster. Had he exaggerated too much? Where was Cliff Morris?

Frank appeared in the doorway to the corridor with tears in his eyes. "It's all over," he said. "Not only have they canceled our contract. They've ordered us to destroy all nineteen of the prototypes we've built. Today. They want them chopped up by sundown. They want all the tools, jigs, designs destroyed. They want to wipe the Talus off the face of the earth. Adrian's surrendering to the slimy bastards. For the good of the company."

"Why?" Dick said, more and more appalled at what he may have helped to do. "What's their reason?"

"Stability problems. Somehow they've gotten their hands on our internal reports. Did you ever give them to anyone, Dick?"

"Never."

"No matter. It's easy enough to rifle files at three A.M. Adrian may have done it himself. He's perfectly capable of it."

Frank turned to his demoralized staff. "I'm quitting. I don't intend to spend the rest of my life designing planes for lying politicians to destroy. I advise you gentleman to imitate my example as soon as you can afford it."

"Wait a second, Frank," Dick said. "We're not going to let you do this. There's a hundred other planes waiting for you to design."

Emotion drained from Frank's face. "That's what Adrian just said."

"Dick's right, Frank," Cliff Morris said. He threaded his way through the empty desks. "Adrian's right too, even if he is an SOB."

Frank found it hard to believe Cliff was defending Adrian. "Cliff, you're hoping Sarah will have a son, aren't you?"

"Sure."

"If he does, you'll love him in a special way, won't you?"

"Sure," Cliff said, growing more and more uneasy.

"You'd be in despair if he were killed?"

"Of course, but—"

"This was my son."

"I'm quitting with you," Sam Hardy said. "We'll start another company." Dozens of similar declarations swept the Black Hole.

"Let's do some drinking on my expense account before we go," Frank said.

The designers departed for the Honeycomb Club. Dick wandered into in his office and discovered Cliff was there waiting for him. "Do I get the maximum explanation now?" he said.

"The problem didn't go away. We—we never had a chance," Cliff said.

Dick stared at his blank computer screen. Things began coalescing in his head. "Especially after you gave Adrian all the reports about the stability problems and my upscale cost estimate."

"Dick. You've got to be realistic. This is a business, not a goddamn experimental flight laboratory. Adrian's traded that plane for a promise of an order for two hundred Excaliburs, redesigned as troop and cargo transports. So Frank's heart is broken for a while. He'll get over it."

A week ago, a month ago, Dick Stone might have nodded and agreed with these words. But something remarkable had just happened to him. He had become a pilot. He had learned to fly in a plane designed by Frank Buchanan. He had been taught by a pilot who had learned from Frank by the same mystic laying on of hands.

"I'm sorry. I don't like the sound of that. I don't know exactly why."

"You better learn to like it if you want to keep working for Adrian," Cliff said. "He wants you to wipe out everything you've got on the computer about the Talus. Then we'll go to work on my files."

"No!" Dick smashed both his fists down on the desk. "I won't do it. I won't let you do it. Don't you have any appreciation for this plane? What it means—not just to Frank but to the whole history of flying?"

"I appreciate it as much as you do," Cliff said. "But I appreciate keeping the goddamn company in business too."

"I'd rather stand on Hollywood and Vine with a tin cup."

"That won't be necessary," Adrian Van Ness said.

He paused in the doorway, smiling sardonically. "Maybe Dick is right," he said to Cliff. "We'll just pretend to destroy the files. We'll tell the SOBs in Washington we've wiped them out to the last comma. What's another lie in this messy business? We've got an underground vault we built during the war in case the Japs bombed us. We'll put them there. But you both have to promise me not to tell Frank Buchanan. As far as he's concerned—the wipeout was total."

"Why?" Dick asked, not even trying to conceal his contempt.

"You can't trust an emotional basket case like Frank."

Slumped on the couch, Cliff nodded wearily. Adrian Van Ness turned to Dick. How did he know he was vowing to tell Frank Buchanan the truth? "You agree, Dick? Or would you prefer an actual wipeout?" Adrian asked.

Adrian's smile made everything perfectly clear. He was the man in charge. Dick nodded numbly. Now he knew what Frank Buchanan meant about making noble promises when you worked for Adrian Van Ness.

Was this a second laying on of hands? Not if he could help it, Dick vowed. In his head a voice whispered: *What do you think of California freedom now?*

TRIO IN BLUE

She had lost him, Sarah thought, watching her defeated husband slouch across the lawn to his white Buick convertible. The destruction of the Talus had ruined something less visible but far more important between her and Cliff. She had failed to comfort him, reach him, last night as they made love. She was four months' pregnant. But that had not made the difference. She felt a new—or old—distance between them, a strange, almost bitter withdrawal to the status of perfunctory husband again.

An hour later, helping Maria hang the wash in the backyard, Sarah was startled by a swooping plane. She looked up in time to see the green Lustra zooming straight up into the blue sky and tipping into a loop that turned into a spin that flowed into a half-dozen snap rolls.

How did Billy know? She watched him inscribe himself against the sky like the rhythmic line of a modern abstract painter. Intricately doubling back on himself, exploding into effervescent heaps of loops, he wrote coded messages in lazy barrel rolls and unbelievably intricate inverted spins. It was painting and music combined in a dance of death-defying skill. She could almost hear the orchestral crescendos as he stood the plane on its tail, its back, its wingtips. She saw him at the controls, gravity pounding at his chest and brain.

Sarah wanted to be with him. She wanted to share the danger and the exaltation. But she knew she could only do it by calling that scribbled number on the card Billy had given her five months ago. He would never call her. He would only send her this coded declaration of his mastery of the sky. A terrible sadness seeped into her soul.

●　　●　　●

Cliff Morris and Dick Stone spent the day storing the records of the Talus in the underground vault. They did not have much to say to each other. There was no trace of Frank Buchanan or his designers, which added to the sense of desolation as they collected blueprints and reports and stuffed them into boxes.

That night Cliff called Sarah and told her he would be working late. He and Dick Stone went looking for Frank Buchanan. He was not at the Honeycomb Club. In fact, no one was at the Honeycomb Club. The place looked as if it had been hit by a couple of fragmentation bombs. A tearful Madeleine, wearing slacks and a sweater, told them the designers had started a brawl with the engineers that wrecked the place.

Madeleine said Frank and Billy McCall and a half-dozen designers had left there last night so drunk they could hardly walk but they insisted on driving Frank's Ford. She hoped they were not dead at the bottom of one of Topanga's ravines.

They took Madeleine along and drove to Frank's house in Las Tunas Canyon, several miles north of Topanga. They found their heroes were not dead but were all drunker than they had been the night before, if that was possible. Cassie Trainor and a half-dozen other women from the Honeycomb Club were trying to console them.

Cliff accepted some Inverness and told them he and Dick had stored the records of the Talus against Adrian's orders. "Who knows what'll happen in the next couple of years? Adrian might change his mind. Or a new secretary of the Air Force might decide to go for it," he said.

Cliff looked steadily at Dick Stone, waiting to see if he would let him get away with the lie. He said nothing. Was he here for the same reason? To regain a few shreds of his manhood?

"Your loyalty is touching, Cliff," Frank said. "But nothing can alter the fundamental facts. Our plane is lying in pieces in some junkyard in El Segundo or Long Beach. Getting drunk is the only sensible response. Join us."

He refilled Cliff's glass to the top with Inverness. Across the room, Cassie Trainor smiled at him. She had her clothes on. But Cliff's imagination undressed her in a flash of desire. He was quite certain that if he drank this Scotch and joined the party, Cassie would soon be wearing nothing and so would he.

In another flash Cliff saw Sarah mounting him. He saw the delight in her eyes, the pleasure of being on top, in control. Was that where the current had been carrying him? She was no longer his magic princess. He was here to regain another kind of current, the sense of being a man among men, even if they were writhing in defeat. A man who fucked beautiful women for consolation. Cliff began drinking the Inverness.

Night and day blended with music and laughter and a trip to Malibu Point, not far from the mouth of Las Tunas Canyon, where Cliff and Billy demonstrated the art of riding killer waves and several designers who tried to imitate them almost drowned. Cassie was also very good on the board. "How about riding something else for old time's sake?" Cliff said.

"Sure," she said, smiling past him at Billy.

After a lot more Inverness, Cliff and Dick joined the designers in a vow never to work another day for Buchanan Aircraft Company. Cliff was pretty sure no one would remember it when they sobered up.

Much, much later, Cliff was on a bed with Cassie. She was telling him he was better than Billy while his hand roamed her auburn pussy making her laugh and sigh. They tried it in every position and she liked it more and more. He was so drunk he could keep it up forever. Finally she was on top, crying *Oh Oh Oh* with each thrust.

In a flash Cassie changed from a laughing, drunken dream girl riding up and down on Cliff's equipment to Sarah with sadness in her eyes. In another flash Sarah went from sad to witchy, to the snarling, whining, jealous wife of a year ago. Who had done it? Who had switched the reel and changed this movie from a farce to a possible tragedy? Who had changed Cliff Morris from a drunken bachelor to a louse of a husband?

Frank Buchanan was standing beside the bed, telling Cliff to go home, it was all right for a bum like him to live this way but Cliff had a wife, children. Behind Frank, Dick Stone stood in the doorway with a frown on his face. Was he sore about Cassie? Was he telling him to listen to Frank?

Frank. There was only one thing to do. He had to confess what he had done. He had to tell him. Cliff shoved Cassie aside and sat up, almost weeping. *I looted the files. I gave them to Adrian. Without telling you.* But another face in the doorway stopped him before he could speak.

"Pops is right," Billy McCall said, his arm around Madeleine. They were in bathing suits, just back from another swim at Malibu Point. "You got to man the home front, Big Shot."

"Home front?"

"While we bachelors go fight another goddamn war."

Billy flipped on the radio beside the bed. An announcer began babbling about an invasion of South Korea by North Korea with thousands of tanks and planes. American planes were trying to help the South Koreans. President Truman had announced the United States was going to support them with everything in its arsenal.

Madeleine and Cassie started to cry. "Come on," Billy said, putting his arm around both of them. "It isn't so bad. I can't wait to fly a jet in combat."

"We don't have a decent jet fighter," Frank said. "Nothing that can handle MIGs, if the Russians come into the war."

"Get to work, Pops," Billy said. "Don't let Califia jinx this one."

To everyone's astonishment, Frank started to weep. "I'll try, Billy. I'll try," he said.

Cliff drove home in a daze to find an enraged, almost hysterical wife. "Where have you been? I called your office and they said no one had seen you for two days."

"I was with Frank Buchanan. He's coming apart over the Talus cancellation. I was trying—"

He realized the impossibility of telling Sarah the truth. She would forgive nothing—neither the betrayal of Frank Buchanan nor the betrayal of her with Cassie.

"Trying what?" Sarah cried.

"Honey, listen, calm down. You're upset about this thing in Korea. Unless it turns into World War Three I'm not going to get drafted. A war's good for the plane business. We'll do okay. We'll be fine."

"I'm not upset about the war. I don't care whether you go or stay," Sarah said.

"In that case maybe I'll go," Cliff said.

"I take it back," Sarah said. She clung to him, sobbing. "Oh, Cliff, I need you. I need you so much."

It was the first time she had ever used that word, need. It made Cliff wonder what had happened to his wife during the two drunken days he had been trying to regain his manhood.

Dick Stone drove slowly home to Manhattan Beach with Cassie Trainor, listening to excited radio newsmen reporting massive tank-led assaults by the North Koreans and the continuing collapse of the South Korean army.

"Are you sore at me?"

"I didn't particularly like finding you in bed with Cliff."

"It was seeing Billy," Cassie said. "I couldn't help it." She stared out at the dark ocean for a moment. "He was the one I told you about—the strafer—on Joe's anniversary."

She was confessing a wound. But Dick was unable to muster any sympathy. The new war was hardening his emotions. He was back in the 103rd Bombardment Group accepting Colonel Atwood's announcement that everyone, even Dick Stone, was going to die.

"I'm tired of what you can't help. Maybe it's time you started blaming yourself instead of God or fate or whatever the hell you talk to in the sky over Noglichucky Hollow."

"Maybe you're right," Cassie said, gazing sadly out at the sea.

"Quit that goddamn Honeycomb Club."

"Then what?"

"I don't know. Go to college, maybe. You can go free here in California."

"What's the point? We could all get blown up tomorrow."

"So what? You go on living the best way you can. You're not doing that. You'd rather feel sorry for yourself."

"I'd rather have you feel sorry for me. But all you do is preach me self-improvement sermons," Cassie said.

"You've got a self that needs improving."

"So do you."

"I know," Dick said, thinking of his surrender to Adrian Van Ness.

The telephone was ringing as they walked into Dick's apartment. It was none other than Buchanan's president, sounding very impatient. "Where have you been?" he said. "I've been trying to get hold of you for hours. Get up here as soon as you can. This war in Korea means we have to move fast."

Dick roared up the coast highway to Buchanan Aircraft's headquarters. Adrian Van Ness was in his office with Buzz McCall. They were both looking angry. "The war means we can bid on a contract for two hundred new transports for the Air Force," Adrian said. "With the Excalibur still in limited production, we're years ahead of everyone. We can convert it overnight. I want you to go to work on the costs. Buzz will give you the data."

"Goddamn it, Adrian, there's more to this than profits," Buzz said. "Maybe we ought to get the Talus back on the burner. We owe it to Frank to at least try."

Adrian shoved papers around his desk. "I don't feel we owe Frank Buchanan anything. He's disappeared for the last three days. Half the design department has gone with him. The rest of them are sitting down there getting drunk on company time. The man is an anarchist. I should have gotten rid of him years ago."

"We're not gonna sell the Excalibur as is," Buzz said. "The Air Force wants more range and speed. We'll have to put those new turboprop engines on it. They're the best thing that's come out of the jet-engine research. We need Frank to design a wing that can handle those engines. You can't get along without him, Adrian. As usual."

For a moment Dick thought Adrian was going to snarl a curse at Buzz. But his voice remained calm. "Then get him back. He'll listen to you."

Buzz lit a cigarette. "Adrian, sometimes I don't think you belong in this business. You don't know how to gamble. When's the last time you flew a plane?"

"I don't know. Nineteen twenty-five, I think. When I left England."

"You should have kept flying. That's the only way to keep the instinct alive. Every time you step into a plane you're riskin' something. You've got to risk the fuckin' company the same way. Bet it on something new out there. It's a sporty game, Adrian. A game for real men."

Buzz blew smoke in Adrian's face. "That flying wing turned out to be a hell of a plane. You never should have let those Texas pricks destroy it. We did something rotten when we let that happen, Adrian."

Adrian's hooded eyes swung toward Dick. He seemed to be saying something to him. Something very confusing. A kind of plea or apology. The eyes returned to Buzz. "I thought you blamed it on your ex-girlfriend, Califia. The one who wants to kill us all."

"She's another reason for fighting back. I can't stand the thought of a dame jinxing us this way."

"You really think they have supernatural power?"

"I don't know whether it's supernatural. But some of them have power," Buzz said.

"I guess I should start worrying. She's writing to me too. Threatening me with all sorts of exotic punishments. Like strapping me to the propellers of an Excalibur and starting the motor."

Buzz did not even try to smile. He took Califia seriously. "Can't security find that dame?" Dick said. In a corner of his mind he was still worried she might be Cassie.

"She's smart as hell," Buzz said. "Mails the stuff from different boxes all over L.A."

"Getting back to the real world—will you talk to Frank?" Adrian said.

Buzz stubbed out his cigarette. "I'll talk to him. Not for your sake or my sake. Those kids flying World War Two crates over Korea are gonna need some new planes."

Buzz strode out, slamming the door. It echoed through the empty building as if a bomb had exploded. Adrian Van Ness gazed after him with undisguised hatred on his face. It took him a full minute to control himself. "Get to work, young fellow," he said with a forced smile. "I'm sorry to ruin your evening. Were you involved in something pleasant?"

"I would have been if you'd called ten minutes later," Dick said.

Adrian stared at the door Buzz had just slammed. "We don't have room for sentiment in this business," he said. "I can be as sporty as Buzz at betting the company. But I don't think we should do it if we have a safer choice. Don't you agree?"

This time Adrian was unquestionably reaching out to him, claiming him in some subtle and totally unexpected way. Dick let him know he was not accepting the offer. "I'll get to work," he said.

Four hours later, a weary Dick Stone knocked on Adrian Van Ness's door. Buchanan's president was walking up and down the office, listening to a multiband shortwave radio on his desk. "This is Mercury Two confirming a red alert," a deep voice said. "All leaves are canceled. Pilots will report to their duty bases." The radio added instructions for Air National Guard and Air Force reserve units.

"It's a real war all right," Adrian said. "Truman's sending in a division of infantry. We've already started bombing North Korea. What do the figures tell us?"

"Assuming Buzz's data is correct we can produce two hundred transports at five hundred thousand a copy. We can make as much money on that plane as we could make on the Talus."

Dick's cold monotone made it clear he was still on Frank Buchanan's side. "Put in an expense chit for five hundred dollars for the night's work," Adrian Van Ness said.

Dick drove back down the coast highway in the cool final hour of the night, the war news crackling out of the radio like slivers of steel. There were still a fair number of cars and strollers along the ocean in Santa Monica and Venice. In the Villa Hermosa compound in Manhattan Beach, a volleyball game was going strong in the shallow end of the pool, girls against boys. He looked at the tanned lunging bodies, the laughing faces and wondered how many of the men might soon be dying on Korean hillsides, how many of the women might be weeping in lonely apartments.

In his bedroom, he found Cassie prowling up and down like a caged panther, listening to the radio. "Our guys are gettin' creamed," she said. She was wearing his dark blue bathrobe, a wedding present from his mother.

Dick flipped off the radio. "The hell with it."

Cassie eyed him warily. "You feel like it?"

He nodded. He needed her. He needed the touch of a woman's flesh to defeat the way the new war was restoring the old one to memory. "I'm sorry about what I said in the car. I understand about Joe and Billy. I'm glad you told me."

"It's the war. I feel bad about it too," Cassie said, slipping out of the bathrobe and wrapping her long arms around him.

Suddenly Dick was kissing his ex-wife, remembering what she had meant: life, pleasure, the future, all the things he had consigned to oblivion in order to fly those forty-nine missions without coming apart. He had finally obeyed Colonel Atwood's injunction to think of himself as a dead man. But it had been a hard order.

Now he finally understood. Nancy Pesin had been the resurrection of Richard Stone. Perhaps first he had needed to be reborn as a Jew before he could resume his American journey. Perhaps he had been too cruel in achieving the second birth. But birth, life was full of pain, some of it necessary.

Oh, woman woman woman. He kissed the tears on Cassie's tan cheeks, he plunged his hands deep in her thick auburn hair. She was clinging to him, murmuring: "Dick, Dick, I think I love you. Will you let me love you? Will you try to love me? I'll quit the club. I'll think about goin' to college."

"Good, good," he said, unable to respond with love. Was he clinging to his California freedom? He was beginning to think it was an illusion.

As Dick came he saw Adrian Van Ness standing in a dark corner of his mind, smiling at them. Did those hooded eyes contain some sort of supernatural knowledge or power?

No. He was smiling because the war was going to make Buchanan Aircraft prosperous again. From even deeper darkness, a voice whispered this was wrong. It wounded the intensity of Dick's coming, his taking of Cassie Trainor in the name of many loves. The voice, perhaps also the sum of many voices, wondered if he deserved happiness as long as he worked for the Buchanan Aircraft Company.

WARRIOR

Frank Buchanan stood beside the single waterlogged bomb-pitted concrete runway that constituted Suwon Airfield, his eyes obsessively scanning the icy blue Korean sky. The runway stood in the middle of a sea of mud. Snow and mud intermingled on the hills sloping down to the field. He felt like a man simultaneously living two bad dreams.

One was his own life, full of anguished yearning for Amanda—and snarling hatred for Adrian Van Ness. Buzz McCall and this new war had lured him back to Buchanan Aircraft. But nothing could persuade Frank to talk to Adrian. That partly explained his inability to deal with the rest of this bad dream—the fear that Amanda was drifting into madness. He knew she was the source of Califia's letters. But he did not know what to do about it. The day before he left for Korea, he had telephoned her. His voice triggered an explosion of rage that left him bewildered and appalled. She seemed to hate him and Adrian with equal ferocity.

The other bad dream was the war in Korea. Unlike the global brawl with Germany and Japan, this was a war about which most of America seemed indifferent. No one gave the men who were risking their lives any glittering slogans, like making the world safe for democracy or fighting for the Four Freedoms. Few reporters got enthusiastic about a struggle that had turned into a stalemate.

Twenty-five miles away, in the front lines along the border of North Korea, a half-million American infantrymen were confronting a million Chinese. Only America's control of the air had enabled the infantry to survive the enemy's overwhelming numerical superiority. Relentless pounding by light and heavy bombers had reduced Chinese supplies to a trickle, leaving them incapable of mounting an offensive.

Most of the planes fighting this crucial part of the war were propeller-driven B-29s and B-26s from World War II. But the decisive struggle for air superiority was taking place far away, along the Yalu River border between Russia and North Korea. Billy McCall was up there now, leading eight F-86 North American Sabrejets from the 337th Squadron into unequal combat with Russian-built MIG-15s. The jet engine was on its way to transforming air warfare—and the entire world of flight.

Each day, the American pilots took off from Suwon and other fields and flew over the desolate mountains and valleys of North Korea to the Yalu. From there, they could look down on hundreds of MIG-15s, parked in gleaming rows beside 7,200-foot-long runways on their airfields across the river. But the Americans could not bomb or strafe them. That might bring on a wider war with Communist China, the politicians in Washington said. As if a million men trying to kill Americans was not a war about as wide as wars could get.

Frank returned to the 337th operations room to listen to Billy and his friends discussing the situation. First came Billy's voice: "This is Black Leader. Thirty-six lining up at Antung."

"Hell, only twenty-four takin' off at Tatungkou," drawled another voice, a Floridian who was Blue Leader, head of another squadron.

"It'll be at least three for everybody," grunted the nasal New England voice of White Leader. "I count fifty at Takushan."

Antung, Tatungkou, Takushan were three of the sacrosanct Chinese airfields. They placed the MIG-15s only minutes away from attacking the B-29s and B-26s pounding the Communist supply lines in Korea. If the MIGs got at these World War II planes, it was no contest. Their gunners could not deal with planes flying at 684 miles an hour, armed with .23- and .37-millimeter cannon. It was up to the American jet pilots to keep the MIGs out of North Korea.

Flying from bases two hundred miles away, the Americans never had more than thirty minutes of fuel on which to fight. In all of Korea, they only had fifty Sabrejets to confront an estimated five hundred Chinese MIG-15s. In almost every fight, the Americans were outnumbered four or five to one.

Minutes later, the radio erupted with battle language. "Honchos at six o'clock," Billy said. Honchos were MIG pilots who wanted to fight. Everyone was sure they were Russians. Two days ago, Billy had shot one down and proved it. When the pilot ejected, he lost his helmet and his blond hair streamed in the wind.

Then came the fragmented cries and shouts of combat.

"Break left, Black Leader. Honcho on your tail."

"Break right. I got him. I got him."

"Reverse and pick us up at three o'clock!"

Frank was in the swerving, diving, twisting Sabrejet with Billy, feeling the terrific force of 5g turns that can wipe out a man's mind like a blow on the head, swiveling his neck 360 degrees to see MIGs diving on them at seven-hundred miles an hour, cursing the Sabrejets' inability to outclimb a MIG or outturn him above 25,000 feet. Tormented by the exhaustion of taking this high-speed punishment day after day, while the Communists had enough pilots to send fresh teams into the air.

For Frank, worst of all was the knowledge that he could have given Billy a better plane if he had not thrown his heart and soul and the entire Buchanan design department into the dream of the flying wing. He denounced himself as a self-indulgent poseur. He was here to make amends, to find out from the pilots themselves what they needed to restore American superiority in the air.

Frank listened, hungry for the sound of Billy's voice, as the dogfight ended as abruptly as it began. The overall commander for the day's operations reported: "Flights reforming and returning—all MIGs' chased across the Yalu." Then Billy came on reporting a rough engine. "I think I've got part of a MIG in there," he said. "He blew up only about two hundred yards ahead of me and I flew right through the debris."

With calm efficiency, he climbed to 40,000 feet and told everyone to relax. He was only eighty miles from the base now and could glide in if the engine flamed out.

Frank hurried to the control tower to watch the squadron land. Billy's wingman, a twenty-two year old from Georgia, did an exultant victory roll before getting into the landing pattern—announcing he had gotten his fourth MIG. Billy had shot down eleven. In a few minutes Billy appeared overhead, coasting serenely, a silver sliver against the blue sky. Behind him came two other pilots making deadstick landings. In five minutes everyone was on the ground, heading for the operations room for a debriefing.

Frank limped after them on his bad leg and listened as Billy described a new MIG tactic. Usually the Communist pilots stayed high to take advantage of the MIG's superiority above 25,000 feet. The Americans had grown used to looking for contrails left by jet engines in the thin upper air. Today the Communists had positioned another squadron well below the contrail height to pounce on the Americans while they were watching the higher trails.

"From now on we've got to keep some sections low," Billy said.

"Does that mean we get one day off every fifth week instead of every fourth week?" his wingman asked.

"It means you're getting up tomorrow to run three miles instead of two."

The pilots ran every day. Like prizefighters, they had to stay in shape to handle the pounding of the g forces. Billy's wingman was notoriously reluctant to take any exercise.

The briefing over, the celebration began. They had downed four more MIGs today. Billy's victory raised his score to twelve—one of the highest of the war. They piled into jeeps and headed for the Korean capital of Seoul, twenty miles away. Frank rode beside Billy, remembering Buzz driving at the same reckless speed to the bars and brothels of Toul in World War I. Planes changed but pilots remained pilots.

Two hours later, in a smoky nightclub known as the Mocambo, Frank heard far more about the Sabrejet and air-to-air combat than he could get in an official briefing. "We need a plane that can let us hunt them instead of the other way around," Billy said.

"We can build one—but it'll be tough to fly," Frank said. "The wings will have to be even thinner than a MIG's. It'll be a flying gun platform, pure and simple, like the MIG."

"Why don't we have one right now? I thought that's what we were trying to put together in the White Lightning."

"We were—but the Air Force wasn't enthusiastic. Americans are always trying to combine everything in one plane. An interceptor close support attack heavy bomber that can fly around the world without refueling."

"Where the hell did those Russian meatheads get that beautiful MIG airframe, Pops?"

"The same place we got the design for the Sabrejet—from the Germans.

They're the ones who proved you needed a swept wing to get a plane above five hundred miles an hour."

"What about the engine?" Billy's wingman asked. "I thought we made the best engines in the world. But those MIGs can just run away from us anytime they feel like it."

"The British make the best engines," Frank said. "The MIG has a Rolls Royce Nene. The Labour government sold fifty-five of them to the Russians in 1946."

"That wasn't too smart, was it," Billy said.

"The British are in a state of mental and spiritual collapse," Frank said. "They've canceled one brilliant airplane after another since World War II ended. They didn't have a plane to put the engine into."

Korean bar girls swarmed around them. The wingman was telling one how he shot down his fourth MIG. She smiled and ordered champagne for both of them. Everyone but Billy had a girl. He glowered at the wingman, who was using both hands to demonstrate the way he dove, upped his flaps and got his MIG as it roared past him.

"I've lost two wingmen so far. I'm gonna lose him too. He doesn't take it seriously up there. Sometimes I think flying these jets should be limited to old crocks like me, Pops. The goddamn things are so fast, they respond to the slightest touch. And there's no sound. The noise is all going the other way. You start to think you're indestructible, like Superman."

"Maybe it would help to have a plane that makes the pilot concentrate on staying alive."

Billy nodded. "I like that idea. Then we got to figure out what to stay alive for. The land of the free and the home of the brave? Seems to me nobody back home gives a shit whether we're living or dying out here."

"Some of us do, Billy. More than you'd think, from the newspapers."

Billy pondered their images in the bar's cracked mirror. He and Frank both looked shattered into a hundred pieces. "How can this be happening, Pops? Explain to me why we're out here with fifty planes fighting the other guys with five hundred and fifty?"

"It's an old American tradition, to disarm after every war we fight."

Billy looked saturnine. He was no longer a boy. He was still a flier, still convinced flying was the only worthwhile thing a man could do. But fighting this war had turned him into a man who was angry at his country. That was a far more dangerous anger than the anger at God that had occasionally flared in his soul in New Guinea. Frank felt the same anger permeating his own soul, inflaming his mind, clouding his judgment.

"If I get through this thing in one piece, I'm gonna do everything I can to make damn sure this doesn't happen again," Billy said. "I'm not gonna salute and say yes, sir to the politicians. I'm gonna say fuck you, sir. I'm not the only pilot who thinks that way."

"Maybe we can team up. If we can design some guts into Adrian Van Ness."

"How are things back at the Honeycomb Club?"

"Not the same since Madeleine quit. They've got a new manager—a dyke who bullies the girls. They don't stay long enough to get to know them. Doc Willoughby's campaigning to close it. He says it's wrecking half the marriages in the company. Where did Madeleine go, anyway?"

Billy ordered another Scotch. It was rotgut stuff, made in Japan. "Good old Madeleine," he said. "She was something."

"Where did she go?"

"You really want to know?"

"Why shouldn't I?"

"Makes me look like a heel, Pops."

"Why?"

Billy called for a pen and scribbled an address. "Go ask her."

Frank hailed a pedicab and the grunting driver dragged him along the freezing avenues to a narrow alley near the city's central market. Frank knocked. The door opened and there stood Madeleine. But it was not the smiling glossy-haired glowing woman who used to greet him at the Honeycomb Club. This Madeleine wore a face dulled by alcohol and unhappiness. "Frank!" she said. "What are you doing out here?"

"Trying to help win this stupid war." He held up the scrap of paper. "Billy gave me your address."

She invited him into a tiny apartment, barely warmed by two laboring space heaters. Moisture oozed from the walls. Dirty dishes and pots filled the sink. "I followed him out here," Madeleine said. "I love him. I thought he loved me. Instead he gave me a thousand dollars and told me to go back on the next plane. I haven't done it. But the money's running out."

She started to weep. "What's wrong with him, Frank? He made me so happy. I thought I made him happy."

"You did. You did," Frank said. "But—"

What? He did not know what was wrong with Billy. Did flying at mach 2 make some men unfit for ordinary happiness? Was Billy living out his brother Craig's dictum on women: they're only good for one thing? Frank no longer believed that. But he had not been able to make happiness with a woman part of his own life. Nor had Billy's other father, Buzz McCall.

Was Billy, in that peculiar symbiosis a son can contract from a father, imitating him and Buzz in a deeper, lonelier way? Marrying himself to the Air Force and a struggle to keep it on the cutting edge of flight, while a swelling bitterness demolished his soul?

"Do you want me? Is that why you're here?" Madeleine said. "He sends people here all the time. I've thrown them all out. But I'll make an exception for you."

Frank took several hundred dollars out of his wallet and crushed it into her trembling hands. "Go home," he said. "He can't help it. Bad things are happening up there in the sky. That's where he lives these days. It isn't your fault."

301

"I love him, Frank!"

Gazing into Madeleine's once beautiful face, Frank Buchanan had a wrenching intimation that this was not the last time he would hear this cry from a woman trying to understand the mystery of Billy's flight from happiness.

BOOK SIX

SCORPION

Champagne glass in hand, Adrian Van Ness stood in the doorway of the Buchanan Aircraft chalet at the 1955 Paris Air Show watching Major Billy McCall streak overhead in the company's new supersonic jet, the Scorpion. Around Adrian stood a cluster of Air Force generals and executives from Pratt & Whitney, builders of the jet's engine. "That almost makes me wish we still had a war in Korea," one of the generals said. "I'd love to see that thing up against a MIG-Fifteen."

Adrian murmured agreement. Everyone declared the Scorpion the most audacious airplane ever built, a marvel of lightweight construction and design. It had already set six world speed and altitude records. It could outclimb, outdive, outturn every fighter plane in the world, sending designers in other companies reeling back to their drawing boards.

Frank Buchanan had created the Scorpion after spending three months in Korea with Billy McCall and other pilots. Unfortunately, the war it was designed to fight had ended. The Communists had abandoned their plan to unify Korea at the point of a gun. The cold war continued, of course.

The Scorpion had also set a record for killing pilots. Six had died in the testing process, exploring what happened to an airframe at Mach 2. Many more had died learning to fly her since she became operational. The Scorpion did not tolerate mistakes. The thin, astonishingly short swept wings had inspired some people to call it a missile with a man in it. A pilot who forgot his flaps on a final turn to land never got a chance to correct his error. An engine failure left the Scorpion with the aerodynamic characteristics of a bathtub.

Although the generals admired the plane, the Air Force was not rushing to buy large numbers of it. Their current order was a puny hundred copies. But

Adrian had an answer to that problem: he was selling it to the rest of the free world—with the help of Prince Carlo Pontecorvo.

Ponty had emerged from World War II as a hero of the underground resistance to Naziism. He had helped organize the continental struggle with British guns and money and finally led one of the most successful guerrilla groups in his native Italy. His book, *Code Name Zorro*, described dozens of narrow escapes in night drops, ambushes, and near-betrayals.

While Adrian struggled to keep Buchanan aloft in the turbulent postwar world, Ponty had been absorbed by the fight to beat back communism in Italy and France. He had been a conduit for millions of dollars funneled into the contest by the Central Intelligence Agency to support politicians with the courage to resist Moscow's collaborators. Now, with the left wing thrown on the defensive by the surging prosperity of the 1950s, he was in an ideal position to become Buchanan's roving representative.

Buchanan had brought planes to other Paris Air Shows, of course. It was the preeminent event of the aviation world. Every nation that either made planes or bought them poured into the City of Light for a wild week of partying and dickering and eyeing the competition. Le Bourget Airport became a sort of world's fair of aviation, with the latest model airframes and engines on display or roaring overhead.

Adrian returned to the air-conditioned interior of the chalet as Billy McCall began doing a series of stunts over the field that had the grandstands shouting applause. In a sitting room Ponty was watching Billy on closed-circuit television. With him was Frank Buchanan, Buzz McCall, and florid General Heinz Gumpert, second-in-command of the West German Air Force. "I wish we could get him to train our pilots to fly your plane that way—without fear," Gumpert said.

"It's the only way to fly any plane," said Buzz McCall.

"Especially this one," Ponty said.

Six months ago, Ponty had persuaded the West Germans to buy no fewer than four hundred Scorpions. Harsh necessity had required the victors of the Second World War to rearm Germany. Risk aside, it was painless. They had billions in surplus marks from their miraculous economic revival, enough to buy the west's latest weaponry.

Adrian was not especially surprised to learn the deal involved that old reliable lubricant, douceurs. Last month, Ponty had coolly informed him three million dollars should be deposited in a certain Swiss bank. He would withdraw appropriate sums to reward the German politicians and generals who had participated in the decision to buy the planes. The great-grandson of the man who bought up the entire Congress of the United States to build the first transcontinental railroad smiled his agreement. He had brought the money to Europe and dispatched Dick Stone to Zurich to deposit it yesterday.

Adrian's daughter Victoria joined them, wide-eyed at Billy's aerobatics. "He can make that plane do anything!" she cried, as Billy put the Scorpion through a climbing roll with flaps and landing gear extended, no more than a hundred feet above the runways.

"It's not supposed to be able to do *that*," Frank Buchanan groaned.

Now twenty-four, Victoria had not inherited her grandmother Clarissa's regal beauty nor her mother Amanda's winsome femininity. In low heels, she was almost as tall as Adrian. Her Englishy tweeds, a style he currently favored, made her resemblance to him almost dismaying. Adrian told himself there was something plaintive, even appealing about her homeliness. She made no attempt to disguise it with makeup or high fashion. Far more important to Adrian was her intellectual sophistication. She had spent the past four years at Somerville, one of Oxford's colleges for women. She had become a good minor poet and had an admirable grasp of English and American history and literature.

Adrian had sent her to school in England for a number of reasons. The sloppy, sulky postwar California teenager with nothing but pop music and movies in her head had driven him to outbursts of rage. But the main reason had been his deteriorating marriage—and his affair with Tama Morris. Whole weeks passed without him and Amanda discussing anything more significant than the weather. She never displayed the slightest interest in probing his vague excuses for spending two or three nights a week at Tama's Malibu cottage. With Victoria at home, this kind of routine would have been unthinkable.

Victoria was also well on her way to getting her name into Clarissa's will—something Adrian would never do as long as he stayed in the aircraft business. That was another reason Adrian had sent her to England. Victoria, of course, had no idea that she was a weapon in this lifelong power struggle.

On the TV screen the Scorpion was replaced by the plane that was creating an even bigger sensation at this year's show—the jet-powered British airliner, the Comet. It was a sleek swept-wing affair with four Rolls-Royce Avon engines. The pilot made a swooping pass over the grandstand, banked and climbed to 10,000 feet almost as fast as the Scorpion.

As if it were a cue, Clarissa entered the sitting room. She had let her hair go white, which added a grace note to her hauteur. She wore only black suits and gowns now, heightening the play of light on her proud, lined face. "That's the sort of airliner you'd have in production right now, Adrian, if you'd listened to me," she said.

"I told him exactly the same thing," Frank Buchanan said, without turning his head in Adrian's direction. In the five years since the cancellation of the Talus, they had yet to exchange a civil word. Most of the time his chief designer communicated through memos or messages carried by Cliff Morris or Dick Stone.

"Jets guzzle fuel," Adrian said. "The flying public has no confidence in them."

"I'm looking forward to flying on her," Clarissa said, as the Comet continued to perform in the sky above Le Bourget.

"I wouldn't, if I were you," Frank Buchanan said.

"Why?"

"That crash off Calcutta worried me."

"A woman my age doesn't fret about sudden death, Mr. Buchanan. In some ways it would be a blessing."

"Grandmother!" Victoria protested, tears in her eyes.

"I like your mother. She reminds me of my own. Indomitable," Ponty said.

Adrian heard the irony in Ponty's voice. He had met Ponty's mother. She was a dragon in the operatic Italian tradition, an interesting contrast to Clarissa's controlled severity. Women! Incredible how they haunted a man's life.

The sale of four hundred Scorpions to the Germans had encouraged Ponty to introduce Adrian to someone else who could help them sell planes in Europe—and possibly in America. Madame George was a thin gray-haired French woman with a severe smoker's cough and watery red eyes. Madame explained in excellent English the advantages of using one of her girls to persuade a potential customer. The fee was five thousand dollars. Adrian had recoiled—until he met several of the girls.

They were the most exquisite women he had ever seen, all perfectly groomed and dressed with Madame George's infallible good taste. They were well-read and au courant politically. Panache seemed to characterize all of them, a serene self-assurance that was never grossly sexual but was subtly, persistently erotic. Ponty had chosen his latest mistress from Madame George's collection and he advised Adrian to consider doing the same thing.

"It's not inexpensive, of course," the Prince said. "The girl must have a suitable apartment, charge accounts, an air travel card. But you could pass most of the expenses through the company, no?"

No, Adrian thought, although he assured Ponty he would consider it. He already had a mistress who was quite enough for a busy man with only a moderate sex drive to handle. But he had to admit to himself that Madame George's girls made Tama Morris look shopworn—or maybe just worn.

That night, in Tama's room at the Crillon, Adrian asked her if she thought Madame George's girls were worth the price. Tama scoffed. "We could bring six or eight of our girls over here for five thousand dollars," she said. "They could have a great time and do us a lot more good."

Adrian sighed. More and more, Tama showed her limitations, mental as well as physical. She was provincial. California did not travel to Paris. He had discovered this at the last two air shows. At home he had grown more and more weary of Tama's compulsion to play office politics. Even before he met Madame George and her girls, he had begun to think it was time to shed Tama.

"I'm going to use them for people at the top," Adrian said. "People the Prince can reach. They expect something more than a quick lay."

"You get some liquor into our girls and they'll do anything," Tama said. "They're from California. They don't have any inhibitions."

"Maybe the buyers do. They're getting more sophisticated—like the planes. That's something I've been trying to explain to Cliff."

Cliff and Jim Redwood had been trying to sell an upgraded version of the

Excalibur with very little success. "People don't want a 1940s plane in 1955," Tama snarled. She was always ferocious when Adrian criticized Cliff.

"Maybe I don't want a 1930s woman in 1955," Adrian said.

"There's plenty of other people who do," Tama shouted. "Anytime you want to take a walk, go ahead. I'm sick and tired of playing *Back Street* for you. If you had any guts you'd have divorced your creep of a wife and married me years ago."

"Thank God I'm not impulsive," Adrian said, stalking to the door.

"Adrian!"

Tama was standing at the French window overlooking the Place de la Concorde. In her lacy pink negligee she was a parody of the movie queen she had never become. She looked frightened—and old. "I didn't mean any of that, Adrian."

"I did," he said, slamming the door.

WENN DAS HERZ AUCH BRICHT

She was the most beautiful woman Dick Stone had ever seen. Tall, with chestnut hair that shimmered in a glowing aura around her high-cheeked, fragile-boned face. Her expression was mildly bemused, even disdainful, the wide oval eyes unillusioned. For the first time Dick was glad he had come to the Paris Air Show.

He worked his way through the jammed salon of the Buchanan Chalet, squeezing past U.S. Air Force generals and Royal Air Force air marshals and German Air Force colonels and their wives and/or mistresses. Occasionally, his quarry disappeared behind a pair of massive military shoulders. From the opposite side of the room, he saw Billy McCall moving in the same direction. But Billy got waylaid by one of the more routinely beautiful women who thronged the room and suddenly Dick was standing in front of her without the slightest idea what to say.

"Can I help you?" he said. "I sort of work here."

"For the Americans?"

"I am one," Dick said, mildly flattered that she did not think so at first glance.

He had spent the past six weeks in Germany working out the financial details of the sale of four hundred Scorpions to the Federal Republic's air force. It was the first time he had returned to Europe since he had bombed it in the *Rainbow Express*. A strange atavism had seized him as he walked the streets of Munich and Bonn. The land of his ancestors had spoken to him with a confusing mixture of menace and affection.

By now, Dick and the rest of the world knew about the Holocaust. He knew that one of the worst concentration camps, Buchenwald, was only a few miles

309

outside Weimar, that paradigm of kultur he had objected to bombing. He wondered what his grandfather would think of his schizoid fatherland now.

"I was told to look for General Heinz Gumpert," she said.

Dick knew the suave ex-fighter pilot well. He was the West German Air Force's vice chief of staff. They had spent many hours negotiating the complex problems of training pilots to fly the unforgiving Scorpions, teaching ground crews to maintain them, subcontracting to German companies the rights to make spare parts and some of the sophisticated electronic equipment in the plane. He had found the general agreeable but formal—and a tough negotiator. Every time a Scorpion crashed—they seemed to go down at the rate of one a week—he demanded a new concession from Buchanan Aircraft.

"The general's in the far corner, describing how he almost shot me down at least a dozen times during the war," Dick said. "Why not let me get you a drink first?"

"You were a bomber pilot?" she said, with just the slightest accent.

"A bomber navigator," Dick said, steering her to the bar.

She ordered a Vermouth Cassis and smiled a thank you as he handed it to her. Close up, she was even more beautiful. Her neck was rather long and supple, her body a landscape of subtle curves and planes. She was wearing a clinging mocha silk dress with thin straps that left her shoulders and arms bare and revealed most of her long spectacular legs. Her only jewelry was a gold-link bracelet on her right wrist.

"A very scared navigator," Dick said.

"Not nearly as scared as those you were bombing," she said.

"You were—are—German?" he said.

"I lived in Schweinfurt," she said.

"We bombed it many times," Dick said.

"Every time I prayed you would hit our house and destroy us all. But you never did."

"Why?"

There was a pause. In the depths of her wide gray eyes Dick thought he saw contempt. "Do you know Heine, the German poet?" she asked.

"My grandfather used to read him to me."

"How odd. So did my grandfather."

Suddenly she was someplace else, miles from this crowded room full of important people. The cool commanding line of her mouth broke and Dick thought she was going to weep. She sipped her drink and the mask of blasé uncaring returned. Softly, casually, she recited:

Anfangs wollt' ich fast verzagen
Und ich glaubt ich trüg es nie.

Dick knew the verse.

At first I thought I could not bear
The depths of my despair.

He also knew the lines that followed it. He spoke them as softly as she had
spoken hers.

Und ich hab' es doch getragen—
Aber fragt mich nur nicht, wie?
Yet O yet I bore it.
Never never ask me how.

"Do they also apply?" Dick asked.

"Yes," she said, smiling as if it were all a joke.

"Are you an old friend of General Gumpert?"

"I have never seen him before in my life."

She smiled serenely at his confusion. "Madame George has asked me to make
his stay in Paris more enjoyable. Most Germans—especially those who fly
planes—tend to be uncultured. They need guidance, counsel in reading French
menus, touring the Louvre—"

Her mockery was exquisite—and touching because it included herself. The
reference to Madame George explained everything to Dick, of course. In the
past week he had paid astonishing sums to Madame George for the services of
her beautiful creatures. He should have known—in fact, he must have known—
this woman was one of her stable.

The word *stable* suddenly seemed impossible or at least intolerable. "Americans need just as much cultural help, perhaps more," he said.

"Oh, no. You are the conquerors. Have you not mastered culture too?"

"Not really," Dick said, smiling. "What's your name?"

"Amalie."

The name of Heinrich Heine's first great love.

"Why do you live in Paris?"

He was fumbling for conversation, trying to prevent her departure to General
Gumpert.

"Because Madame de Stael said here a woman can live without being happy."

"Can I see you again, after you've improved the general's culture?"

"Why?"

For the first time in his life, Dick spoke to a woman without even an attempt
at calculation, saying exactly what leaped to his lips. "Because you're so beautiful."

A wisp of a smile played across her mouth. It was impossible to tell if she
was pleased or bored by the compliment. "Are you Jewish?" she said.

"What difference does that make?" he snapped.

She shrugged. "You don't look it. But then, what is a Jew supposed to look
like? I've never quite understood that question."

"You're Jewish?"

"I'm not supposed to answer that question. Or better, it should never come up."

Cliff Morris slapped Dick on the shoulder. "Hey—is this General Gumpert's dinner date you're monopolizing, Stone?"

"I'm afraid so," he said. Dick began to introduce her to Cliff and realized he did not know her last name.

"Borne," she said.

The name of one of the many German Jews Heinrich Heine both hated and admired. Dick watched Cliff lead her through the crowd to General Gumpert, whose angular face was consumed by anticipation at the sight of her.

Cliff drifted back to the bar. "Two more fucking Scorpions crashed this morning," he said. "Adrian told Madame George to send us the top of the line."

For the rest of the party, Dick could not take his eyes off Amalie Borne. Occasionally her eyes strayed around the room but she never missed a beat in her conversation with Gumpert. The general was obviously absorbing immense amounts of culture.

The party began to wind down. Dick realized he had lost all interest in finding himself a date for the night. There were plenty of available women, journalists and public relations assistants and models from a dozen nations at the air show. With a little effort, a man could line up a different adventure every night. He turned his back on Amalie Borne and retreated to the bar to order Buchanan's favorite, Inverness single malt Scotch.

Dick drank the swill and brooded about his erratic love life. He had talked Cassie Trainor into going to college and she wound up getting a full scholarship to Stanford, putting an end to their nights and weekends at the Villa Hermosa. Cassie had wept at the thought of leaving him—but she took the scholarship. Now they were occasional lovers—she had others in Palo Alto, Dick was sure. He had more than a few among the swinging singles of the Villa Hermosa.

He felt a hand brush his suit-coat pocket. When he turned, Amalie Borne was going out the door with Gumpert and Adrian Van Ness and Tama Morris. In his pocket he found a small white card with a telephone number on it.

Dick called the next morning at 10:30. A maid with a heavy French accent was barely polite. It took several minutes to persuade her to let him speak to Miss Borne. Amalie's dusky voice finally came on the line. Dick suggested lunch at Verfours, a five-star restaurant. She said it might be better if they lunched at her apartment. Natalie, her cook, was making a bouillabaisse.

The apartment was in the fashionable Faubourg St. Germain, in one of those huge buildings with immense doors reinforced by black-iron grillwork, guarded by a concierge. The elevator rose with the serene majesty of an ascending balloon. The French maid greeted him at the door with a frown. She was about forty, with the face of a gorgon on Nôtre Dame. She led him down a short hall to a sunny living room, where Amalie was seated on a dark red couch, wearing a blue peignoir. A bottle of champagne tilted in a silver ice bucket on a nearby secretary.

"I hope you don't mind," she said. "I hate to go out to lunch. Dressing to Madame's standards is too exhausting to do more than once a day."

"Of course."

"After lunch we'll roam Paris a bit, if you're in the mood. I walk a minimum of five miles every afternoon. What do you do for your aircraft company?"

"I keep track of the money."

"Ah. A man of importance."

"Not really. I have very little say on how it's spent."

"But you will, eventually?"

"Possibly."

"What is your fascination with planes? You like to live dangerously?"

Dick shrugged. "The test pilots are the ones who take the real chances."

"From what General Gumpert was saying last night, everyone who flies your planes takes chances."

"That's true of the plane he's buying. It's very fast and very dangerous."

"And you enjoy the vicarious encounter with death this plane creates?"

"Not really."

"You don't despise the Germans? You haven't deliberately sold them a plane that will kill their new pilots?"

"No."

"You're not here to find out if General Gumpert was sufficiently entertained to forget the recent crashes?"

"No!"

She smiled as if this was amusing. "Would you like to open the champagne? Or shall I call Annette?"

"Allow me."

The wire was recalcitrant. It took him five minutes to free the cork. Finally they raised their glasses and Dick said: "To Heinrich Heine."

"*Ich grolle nicht*," she said, referring to one of Heine's most famous love poems, which began: *I won't complain although my heart is breaking.*

"Tell me how and why you lived in Schweinfurt during the war."

"You know the story of Anne Frank, the girl who hid in a Dutch attic? I lived a similar existence in Schweinfurt. The Nazis took my parents away to a concentration camp in 1939 when I was eleven. My mother left me with their dearest friends, the Starkes, whose house was at the end of our street. They hid me in their attic for the entire war."

"Why did you pray every time we bombed Schweinfurt that we'd kill them—and you?"

She gave him a puzzled smile. "I don't understand?"

"You told me you did that—at the air show yesterday."

"Oh! It was so noisy. You must have misunderstood me. I prayed the very opposite. Those dear devout people saved my life. I told the whole story to General Gumpert last night. He broke down and wept. Imagine? A famous fighter pilot, with one hundred and fifty kills to his credit, weeping in this very room, after his fourth bottle of champagne, because I made him ashamed to be a German?"

She's lying, Dick thought. I'm not going crazy. That is irony you are hearing, savage irony of the sort Heinrich Heine used in his prose, when he was demolishing an enemy. "Remarkable," Dick said. "Perhaps you should write a book. It might make some people think better of the Germans."

"Perhaps I will when I'm old and feebleminded. Are you married?"

"No."

"I thought all Americans married at twenty-one and had dozens of children."

"I'm divorced."

"You must tell me what went wrong. I collect misalliances. It's helpful as well as amusing."

"My wife talked baby talk to me. I couldn't stand it."

"Why didn't you simply tell her to stop?"

"I didn't think she would—or could. She was a Jewish princess."

"You mean she was spoiled by indulgent parents."

"That's part of it."

"I had parents like that. You should have been more understanding, compassionate."

He shook his head. "She made me realize I didn't want a Jewish wife."

"Why not?"

"That's hard to explain. My grandfather went to his grave in 1939 believing German anti-Semitism was a passing thing, a minor flaw in a nation that had produced the greatest music, the greatest literature, the greatest philosophy of modern times."

"My grandfather—and my father—believed the same thing," Amalie Borne said.

"I want to prove to myself—and perhaps to others—that Jews can be Americans first—now that Germany's failed them."

"Fascinating," Amalie Borne said.

For the first time, Dick felt he had gotten her attention. It was also the first time he had ever tried to explain his feelings about Jewishness in such detail to anyone—including himself.

Amalie held out her glass for more champagne. "But ultimately perhaps as foolish as the dream of German assimilation?"

"Perhaps. But people in the plane business like to live dangerously."

The fishy, garlicky odor of bouillabaisse began to fill the apartment. Annette opened a table before the sunny windows and they sat down to steaming dishes of it, with a Puligny Montrachet which Annette opened with a flourish that made Dick ashamed of his struggle with the champagne. They discussed recent German literature, notably the Catholic novelist Heinrich Böll, whom Amalie urged Dick to read. "Among his many virtues, he never was and never will be a Nazi," she said.

The wine flowed and Dick asked her how she came to Paris. For a moment she seemed to ponder what to tell him.

"An American general brought me here—and left me when his wife arrived, after the war. For a while I almost starved. Then I met Madame George and began my ascent. I'm now as spoiled as my father ever dreamt of making me. Somewhere I like to think he's smiling."

"Considering what you went through during the war, you're entitled," Dick said.

She laughed and his body almost dissolved. It was more than her beauty, it was the mystery, the aura of hidden pain that surrounded her. Absurd romantic ideas crowded Dick's brain. He would rescue her from the degradation of one-night stands with macho slobs like Gumpert. He would take her to America, convince her it was a refuge she could trust.

Over dessert of *profiteroles au chocolat*, Amalie proclaimed their mission for the afternoon: to see Heinrich Heine's Paris. Germany's greatest romantic poet had lived in the City of Light for the last twenty-five years of his life in protest against the anti-Semitism and conservative politics that kept him in a frenzy of ambivalence about his fatherland.

They began with a stroll down the Champs Elysées, the poet's favorite boulevard, where he and his friend Balzac used to parade arm in arm. Then a taxi whirled them to the site of the glove shop in the narrow Passage Choiseul where Heine had met Mathilde, the nineteen-year-old peasant girl who would dominate—and ultimately destroy—his life. "I come here often to try to understand the way fate waylays a man," Amalie said.

"He loved her."

"He loved a great many women. Too many. Mathilde was woman's revenge. She was all body and no mind."

Another taxi took them to streets where the poet and Mathilde had lived— Rue d'Amsterdam, the Grande Rue des Batignolles, the Avenue Matignon, where he died. In each site, Amalie meditated on Heine's erratic, erotic life. Gradually Dick saw him looming over her, part guardian angel, part idol, part threat.

"He was an old-fashioned romantic," Dick said as Amalie recalled the poet's last love affair with the adventuress he called Mouche.

"What does that mean, exactly?"

"He fell in love with almost every woman he met."

"We moderns don't believe in love?"

"Not that effervescent kind. We're more inclined to make distinctions. Sex is not the same as love."

"How profound. Tell me more, Mr. Stone."

Confused by her sudden hostility, Dick blundered on. "We—we Americans anyway—believe in falling in love with one woman—and hoping the love will grow deeper and richer and more powerful as life goes on. For romantics falling was the most important part of love. I prefer the American approach."

"That's so naive," she said, looking up at the sagging shutters and crooked windows of the half-dozen nineteenth-century houses still standing on the Avenue Matignon. Once more Dick sensed he had gotten her attention.

"I don't know," he said. "At the end, didn't Heine wail, *'Worte, Worte, keine Taten!'*—words, words, no deeds. That's the verdict on romanticism in my opinion."

"You don't understand romanticism—or me!" she said, springing out of the taxi and striding down the street.

In his bad French, Dick told the driver to pursue her.

They kept pace with Amalie while he leaned out the window, reciting the rest of Heine's disillusioned cry: *"Immer Geist und keinen Braten/ keine Knödel in der Suppe."*—Always spirit and no roast, no dumplings in the soup.

"You're disgusting," she said. "Disgusting and naive."

"How about dinner at Verfours tonight?"

"I'm engaged."

"Tomorrow night?"

"Don't you have airplanes to worry about?"

"They can wait. I've fallen in love with you. But I want to get beyond Heine."

"There's nothing beyond him. There never will be!"

They continued to creep along beside the striding defiant Amalie for another block, while other taxis and cars beeped angrily behind them. Dick cheerfully recited more Heine. *"Lass mich mit gluhnden Zangen kneipen, Lass grausam schinden mein Gesicht."* Let me be pinched with red hot tongs, let my face be flayed from my skull, only do not make me wait any longer.

As they approached the Champs Elysées, Amalie's frown vanished. When he tried *"Noch einmal, eh mein Lebenslicht,"* in which the poet prayed that before his "life's light" was extinguished, he would be blessed once more by a woman's love, she capitulated and got back in the cab. They did not say a word all the way back to her apartment. As she got out she said: "What time, at Verfours?"

Verfours said a reservation was *impossible*. A face-to-face conference with the headwaiter and 150 dollars created a table. On the way back to his hotel, Dick realized he was supposed to be at a reception for Buchanan Aircraft at the West German embassy. He arrived as the party was breaking up. General Gumpert was still there, however, and was impossible to avoid.

"That was a fascinating creature you found for me last night, Dick," he said. "She spoke better German than I did, in spite of being born in Corsica."

"We thought you'd find her interesting, General," Dick said. "Will you be seeing her again?"

"We were supposed to go to Verfours tonight but she's ill."

"Too bad."

"You've heard about the new crashes? The newspapers are going to crucify us, I'm afraid."

"I believe it was one of Germany's aeronautic pioneers who said sacrifices must be expected."

316

"Does that include my career?" Gumpert said.

"I hope not, General."

Behind his soothing manner, Dick was thinking: *Fuck you, you Nazi bastard.* He was appalled. Did Amalie Borne have something to do with it? Had she reawakened a primitive Jewish identity in his soul?

Prince Carlo materialized to rescue Dick, an irony in itself. Dick instinctively disliked this urbane aristocrat. The Prince put his arm around Gumpert's shoulder. "Never be discouraged by a defeat in love, General. Tonight we'll go to a little place I have in the country, where complaisance is guaranteed. Would you care to join us, Stone?"

"No—I have a previous engagement."

That could easily get him fired from Buchanan Aircraft.

The Prince walked him to the door, sighing over the problems of the Scorpion. He was going to need more money—a great deal more—to deal with it. Adrian Van Ness had authorized another draft of three million dollars. Would Dick see that it was deposited in the Swiss account tomorrow?

Dick fled to his hotel for a hasty shower and a dash to Verfours, where Amalie awaited him at their table, chatting with the headwaiter in flawless French. They were apparently old friends. After champagne cocktails, they feasted on truffles and pheasant under glass and a raspberry tart whose crust seemed mostly air.

Amalie insisted on hearing more about Dick's love life. Mixing irony and humor, he described the liaisons, the weekend flings, the one night stands of the Manhattan Beach aeronauts. He portrayed them as delayed adolescents— and did not mention Cassie Trainor.

"Now, like Heine when he encountered Mathilde, you're weary with debauchery and long for the simple affection of an unspoiled heart?" Amalie asked.

"You could say that. But I wish you wouldn't."

"How fortunate that we met," Amalie said. "Perhaps I'm was wrong about fate being a dark presence in our lives."

After dinner they lingered over a forty-year-old brandy Amalie selected. Dick tried not to look at the bill as he handed the waiter his American Express card. It probably exceeded his salary for the month.

They rode back to the Faubourg St. Germain through the mostly deserted midnight streets. A soft rain had fallen while they dined; the macadam gleamed beneath the lampposts. At the apartment, Amalie fumbled for her key and Dick stood by the cab, wondering if he should pay the fare. "Ten francs, *s'il vous plait*," the driver rasped, perhaps trying to tell him that any Frenchman who escorted a woman this beautiful to her apartment would follow her upstairs if he had to climb the facade.

Dick paid him as the heavy door groaned open. "I have more of that brandy," Amalie said.

He kissed her as they walked into her apartment. She did not resist, but she did not respond, either. "It's all wrong," she whispered. "You must know that."

"I only know I love you."

"Shhh. Annette doesn't approve of you."

317

"Why not?"

"You're too young. You can't possibly be rich enough."

"I'm not."

"Oh. Can't you see, can't you hear?"

"I only see a beautiful woman who doesn't believe in American love."

" 'Lieb Liebchen, leg's Händchen aufs Herze mein.' Do you know that verse?"

"Yes," Dick said. It was the Heine poem that had resounded in his head over Schweinfurt, about a lover's hammering heart becoming a psychic coffin.

"That's the literal truth about me. Nicht worte, worte. The truth."

" 'Tobende eile mich treibend erfasst,' " Dick murmured, kissing her neck. A wild unrest is desolating me, another line from one of Heine's cries of romantic despair. Did he mean it? Was she using the other line to tell him of a twentieth-century despair? Dick only knew he could not retreat now. She was mystery and memory, Jewishness and the guilt of the navigator of the Rainbow Express. He pressed his lips against her pulsing throat and she seemed to crumple against him. The straight firm body dissolved into helplessness, sadness.

Undressed in the shadowy lamplight, she was a landscape, a country of love. A flat soft stomach descended to full thighs, ascended to coned breasts. She reached out to him like a plaintive child as he lay down beside her. "Kommt, kommt," she whispered. "Kommt feins liebchen heut." Come, come, come sweet love today. It was from the first verse of one of Heine's most famous song cycles.

Entering her was the most profound moment of Dick Stone's life. He felt like a conqueror of space and time, returning to the old world in his grandfather's name with a new and bolder love for it, an American love that could both master and transform its tormented history. Amalie gave herself without reservation, shuddering, sighing, almost sobbing and at the climax retreating into a dark silence, to emerge with a small final cry.

After another five minutes of silence, she whispered: "The brandy is in the armoire in the living room."

He returned with glasses and the bottle. She drank some and held out her arms to him again. "Now, now," she whispered. "Now must come worte worte. Now that you've had the meat, Heinrich."

In the same slow insistent whisper, she began telling him the story of her six years in the attic at Schweinfurt. Accepting her had been an impulsive act of charity on the part of her parents' friends, the Starkes. Soon she became a dangerous burden. Their attitude began to change. She could hear them arguing in the bedroom below her. Herr Starke wanted to turn her in, Frau Starke urged him to wait until Germany won the war.

Then Germany began to lose the war. The Starkes' son, who was the same age as Amalie, was killed on the Russian front. Mrs. Starke had a stroke during one of the air raids. Herr Starke, who was one of the managers of the ball-bearing works the Rainbow Express tried so often to destroy, began visiting Amalie in the attic with less than compassionate motives.

"He always reviled me while we did it," she whispered. *"Judenshit,"* he would say. *"Juden Juden Judenshit.* Every other obscene word in the language."

Unreality seized Dick's mind. The way Amalie was whispering the story somehow seemed more bizarre and horrifying than the story itself. Dick wanted it shouted. He wanted it broadcast over loudspeakers so that everyone in Germany, from General Gumpert to Heinrich Böll to Chancellor Konrad Adenauer could hear it. He wanted it put on every radio and television network in the United States. He wanted the entire world to confront the story of Amalie Borne.

"Now do you see how impossible it is for us?"

"I only see the impossibility of anything but marrying you, living with you for the rest of my life."

"The Prince would never permit it. He would ask for your job, your head."

"What does he have to do with it?"

"I'm his mistress. Who do you think pays for this apartment, for Annette, for the cook?"

"And he'd send you to Gumpert for—"

"He had confidence in my ability to elude Herr General."

"You're making this up."

"I wish I were. I wish I could convince you how much I'm risking at this very moment. There must be a risk for you too."

"The hell with that. I can't believe you prefer to be kept by that titled crook when you could come to America with me—"

"I don't believe in your America. What I see of your countrymen here in Europe makes me think you're no better than us. Possibly worse, because you lie to yourselves about your goodness and virtue."

"That has very little to do with whether two people love each other."

"I'm not at all sure you're right. In fact I suspect you're wrong."

Desperation clutched at Dick's throat. She was eluding him. "When can I see you again?"

"There's no point to it. Think about what I've said, what I've become—and you'll understand." She kissed him gently on the lips. "I'm sure you will. You're an intelligent man."

In the meantime, Dick realized, they—or at least she—would have this Heinesque romantic memory. He struggled into his clothes and trudged into the dawn, resolved to defeat both the Prince and the poet.

The next day, the last day of the air show, Billy McCall led a squadron of U.S. Scorpions in aerobatics that were the sensation of the week. Spain, Portugal, Italy, all expressed an interest in acquiring the plane. Adrian Van Ness was ecstatic. Everyone on the Buchanan team was pressed into charming the new customers. Dick found himself taking a Spanish general and his wife to dinner at the Ritz. As they chatted about Mexico and California, which the general had recently visited, there was a stir at the other end of the long narrow dining room. Amalie and Prince Carlo sat down at a table, along with

Adrian Van Ness and another of Madame George's girls, almost as beautiful as Amalie.

The encounter only redoubled Dick's resolve to convince Amalie of the possibility of American happiness. The following day, he telephoned her apartment. Annette answered. The moment she recognized him, she flung a stream of hostile French over the line from which he extracted the absence of Miss Borne. He rushed from the hotel to the nearest flower shop, bought two dozen roses and rode to the Faubourg St. Germain in a steady rain, almost suffocating himself and the driver with the scent in the airtight cab.

The concierge allowed him to ascend when he displayed the telephone number in Amalie's handwriting. But Annette barred the door, insisting Miss Borne was not at home. In fact, she was not in Paris.

"Where is she?" Dick practically shouted, hoping Amalie would hear him.

"Rome."

He retreated forlornly into the rain. At the Buchanan Chalet, exhibits were being dismantled, photographers, French public relations people, were waiting to be paid. Dick wrote out checks and tried to join in the exorbitant cheer that the success of the Scorpion had created. Adrian Van Ness came by, looking almost effervescent. "Did you get that money to the Prince?" he asked.

"I'll do it by the end of the day."

"Good. He's off to Rome, where I think he'll need it. You can't get anything done in Italy without spreading a lot of it around."

"So I hear."

"He took that fabulous girl with him. He and Madame George have been feuding about her. She wanted a villa in Cannes. He was resisting the cost. So Madame sent her to entertain General Gumpert. The next night, Ponty heard she was at Verfours with some American."

Adrian smiled in a strange, almost wistful way. "You get a whole new idea of worldliness when you spend some time with Europeans."

The next day as Dick was checking out of his hotel, the desk clerk handed him a letter. The handwriting was strange—almost a child's scrawl. He stuffed it into his pocket and did not read it until he was aboard the plane. On sky blue paper was one of Heinrich Heine's best known love poems. But it was not a testament of love here. Amalie Borne was asking him, one last time, to understand.

Ich grolle nicht, und wenn das Herz auch bricht,
Ewig verlor'nes Lieb! Ich grolle nicht.
Wie du auch strahlst in Diamantenpracht,
Es fällt kein Strahl in deines Herzens Nacht.
I shall not complain, although my heart
is breaking
Love forever lost! I shall not
complain.

However much you gleam in the diamond's
glow
No light can reach the darkness in your heart.

The DC-6 labored west toward America against a strong head wind. The pilot told them they would be at least a half hour late.

No, Dick thought, as the engines throbbed in his head, no. He refused to understand. He would somehow penetrate the darkness in Amalie's heart. She would be his talisman of forgiveness for the bombs, for abandoning Jewishness, an emblem of hope and triumph.

Dick did not realize he was like a pilot trying to land at a strange airport in night and fog, talking to air traffic controllers in a language they did not understand.

QUEEN OF THE NIGHT

With a hundred million dollars' worth or orders for Scorpions on the books, Adrian Van Ness should have left Paris a happy man. Instead, he was miserable. De Havilland Aircraft had picked up at least two hundred orders for Comets and the British were suddenly the world leaders of commercial aviation. Frank Buchanan blamed it on Adrian's timid refusal to build a jet-powered airliner and was whispering "I told you so" through all ranks of the company, making Adrian look like Casper Milquetoast.

Tama kept throwing contrite looks at him but he ignored her. Their affair was over as far as Adrian was concerned. He might even end her connection with Buchanan Aircraft if he could think of a good reason. Madame George's girls had made him feel sexually invulnerable.

Adrian's main concern was what to do about the next generation Buchanan airliner. The Scorpion's sales gave them the money to build one. If he hoped to keep Buchanan in the major leagues with Lockheed, Boeing, Douglas, he had to make a decision soon. To jet or not to jet, that was the question. Buzz McCall sat next to him halfway to California, arguing for a jet. He showed him a Frank Buchanan sketch of a plane twice the size of the Comet with the Pratt & Whitney engines they were using in the Scorpion in pods on the wings.

Adrian resisted the idea. Part of the reason was personal. A few rows ahead, Frank Buchanan sat talking to Dick Stone. The back of Frank's head was a kind of statement of his persistent contempt. Adrian saw Buzz as Frank's spokesman, with no opinion of his own worth discussing.

"I don't think we should rush into this," Adrian said. "I want to commission a survey of the public attitude toward jets. I'm not sure people want to fly at six hundred miles an hour."

Buzz saw the survey as another proof of Adrian's basic problem: lack of nerve. "Adrian, Americans want to go as fast as possible. Even the car business understands that. Why the hell do you think they've decorated the fuckin' fenders and hoods and grilles with all those fins and streamline effects? They want to make them look like planes."

In California, the debate continued to rage through the usual drunken lunches in the executive dining room. Frank and Buzz converted everyone, even young people like Cliff Morris and Dick Stone, whom Adrian hoped he had brought into his executive aura. One day, after a particularly vitriolic (and alcoholic) lunch, at which a jet had been favored by a five to one margin, Adrian went back to his office teetering on the brink of decision. Something deep in his mind still resisted the idea of admitting Frank Buchanan was right.

His secretary buzzed him. "Victoria is calling from London."

"Hello, darling, how are you?" Adrian said.

"Haven't you heard the news?" Victoria cried. "Grandmother's plane crashed. Everyone died. She's gone!"

Within minutes, Adrian had the British embassy in Washington on the telephone. They ruefully confirmed that a Comet 3 en route from Naples to London had crashed off the island of Elba. "No survivors?" Adrian said dazedly.

"None, I'm afraid. The ambassador, I'm sure, joins me in expressing our deepest regret."

Adrian hung up and sat motionless behind his desk for a long time. The whine of a jet engine out on the airfield meant another Scorpion was about to be flight-tested. As it rose to a shrill wail, Adrian tried to absorb the meaning of Clarissa's death. He told himself a fifty-five-year-old man did not fall apart over the death of his eighty-three-year-old mother. But for Adrian it was a primary event. He felt like someone who had spent most of his life guarding a door against a dangerous intruder. Now the door had swung open to reveal no one was there.

Or was it the other way around? Had he, all his life, been trying to burst into a guarded room and now, suddenly, the door was open and the secrets he had been determined to discover, the oracle he had been longing to interrogate, had vanished? He was free in a new mysterious way he had to explore.

Should he divorce Amanda and marry Tama? No, that had never been more than a remote possibility and now it was out of the question. He began to understand his involvement with Tama in a new way. In his imagination, he had seen himself introducing her to his mother as his wife, relishing the shock and dismay on Clarissa Ames Van Ness's face. Tama's middle-class taste, her sensuality, were polar opposites of Clarissa's standards. Of course, he had never done it because he also loved his mother.

And feared her.

And hated her.

And pitied her.

Adrian struggled to place all his emotions on the table so he would know, like the gambler who was getting ready to bet his money and his life, the status of the deck. Was he free of Clarissa's accusing voice, free of *ruined*? When it wailed in his head now would it belong to no one in particular? Could he ignore it if he chose?

The decision, the great decision to jet or not to jet, was part of this new freedom. Should he bet the net assets of the company on a plane that had just crashed?

No. In some unassailable blindly superstitious corner of his mind, Adrian felt his mother's death was a retribution—and a warning. He had spent his life rejecting most of her advice. Now she had died aboard the world's first jet airliner, the plane she had wanted him to build. It was an omen no one in the aircraft business, where fate so often seems to be sitting in on every hand, could resist.

It was also an irresistible opportunity to use his presumed grief with masterful effect. He called in Frank Buchanan and Buzz McCall and told them the news. They were appalled and sympathetic, of course. Adrian nodded and briskly turned the conversation to business. He predicted that this crash, the second Comet to go down this year, would cast a fatal shadow over the plane. One more crash and it would be out of business. "I seriously think it could finish jet-powered air travel for twenty years," he said.

Instead of an intercontinental jet plane like Boeing and Douglas were building, Adrian had a better idea. "At the last meeting of the Conquistadors, at least three airline presidents told me they needed an intermediate range plane that could take off from La Guardia and other small airports. Let's build one for them—with turboprops."

Pratt & Whitney had produced this compromise between a jet engine and a propeller. Buchanan had used it successfully on the Excalibur-derived transports they had built for the Air Force at the start of the Korean War.

"I like the idea of an intermediate plane," Frank said. "But why not make it a jet? The Comet isn't crashing because of its engines. It's the pressurized cabin. The Brits didn't take into account the effect of the extreme changes in air pressure at the altitude a jet flies. It's metal fatigue, not engine failure that's bringing them down. They're just disintegrating up there in the sky."

"You're telling me to build a plane that may kill people the way that thing just killed my mother?" Adrian shouted.

"All right," Frank said. "I'll give you your turboprop."

Buzz and Frank departed, shaking their heads. Adrian strode up and down the office in a terrific state of agitation. "The son of a bitch, the son of a bitch," he kept saying. He realized his reaction made no sense. What was happening to him? Had he lost his emotional bearings?

At home, Adrian found Amanda working in the garden. Beneath a large old-fashioned sun hat, she looked oddly youthful, as girlish as when he first met her. "My mother's dead," he said. "She died in the crash of the Comet."

"I know," Amanda said. "Tama called to tell you how sorry she was. She wants you to call her."

Amanda patted earth around a newly planted bulb. "Are you going to marry

Tama now?" she said in a dry, almost toneless voice. She had begun talking that way about a year ago. Adrian thought it was another way of telling him how much she hated him.

"Why should I do that?"

"You don't love her?"

"I don't know what you're talking about."

"Adrian—I've known for years. I was glad. For her sake. For yours. I knew you only stayed with me because of your mother."

"That's not true!" Adrian shouted. "It was for Victoria's sake. For your sake too—if you only gave me a chance to show it instead of crawling into bed with that slob Frank Buchanan."

"That was meant to be, Adrian. There was nothing either of us could do about it."

"I did something about it."

"I knew you would."

"What the hell is the matter with you? Why don't you talk to me like a human being, an adult woman, instead of in that voice of the living dead?"

"Call Tama. She needs you," Amanda said and left him there in the garden.

He called Tama. She was at her Malibu beach house. He could hear the surf crashing. She was out on the deck with the white telephone in her hand. "Adrian," she said. "I called to tell you how sorry I am about your mother. How sorry I am about everything. Will this—make a difference, Adrian? I mean—will you feel free to—"

"I've always been perfectly free to do what I pleased. What I've done—and haven't done—are for very good reasons," he said.

"Oh, God Adrian, I haven't been able to eat or sleep since that argument in Paris. I didn't mean any of those stupid things I said. I love you. Doesn't that make any difference? Can't you forgive me?"

"There's nothing to forgive. I was unpleasant too. I'm afraid our little fling has just run out of gas."

"Little fling? Adrian—it's been almost ten years. I divorced Buzz. I've told you what you mean to me. Told you and told you."

"I know. But you don't mean that to me. You never have. You were—very helpful. I needed you badly when it began."

Adrian was trying not to be cruel and failing miserably. He could not control the anger at women that lurked deep in his soul. "It might be best if you left the company, Tama. It's not a healthy situation for either of us. I'm sure you can get more money doing the same thing at Douglas or North American. Everyone says you're the best publicity woman in the business."

"Adrian!"

"I'm only being sensible, Tama. I'll arrange for severance pay tomorrow. It'll be very generous, I assure you. If you invest it well you'll never have to work again."

"Adrian!"

The telephone was a wonderful invention, Adrian thought, as he hung up.

It enabled a man to say things to a woman he could never say face to face.

Adrian showered and dressed for dinner in his usual deliberate fashion. He put on one of his new pink shirts—a daring style that some people thought might replace white as the color of choice—and one of his newest Savile Row suits. A resolve—a wish—was growing in his mind and heart. A decision to reorder his life. Victoria would be coming home in a year. Why not bring her into a house where her father loved her mother, his wife, in a new profound way?

Wife. Why did his mother's death give that word new depth and resonance? *Wife*—was Amanda the victim of his long bitter need to fend off Clarissa Van Ness? Had he kept her at the same taut arm's length in his mind and heart? Was it possible that he was now free, not to take a mistress selected by Madame George, but to love his wife?

At dinner he talked about Victoria. He praised her intelligence, her cheerful disposition, her budding gifts as a poet. He gave Amanda more than her share of the wine. Over dessert, with the housekeeper safely clanking pots in the kitchen, he took Amanda's hand and made his plea. He told her about his ruined American father, his discovery of his English father, his mother's obsessive attempts to control him. He confessed the whole truth about selling her share of Cadwallader Groves to her brother.

"This has been the most momentous day of my life. I've seen so much. Especially how I've let my quarrel with my mother hurt us. I've only known one way to deal with a woman—warily, fearfully, if you prefer the whole truth. That's why I could never find a way to explain our reconciliation in 1931—I mean really explain it. I should have insisted on the absolute truth that I've always loved you and money had nothing to do with it. But I couldn't do it. Pride—that spirit of defiance my mother stirred in me—was always in the way. Now I'm free to ask you to forgive me. Can you—will you?"

"What about Tama?"

"Forget Tama. She was never more than a consolation."

Amanda's eyes blazed with unnatural light. "That is more unforgivable than all the rest of it, Adrian. Forever unforgivable!"

"Why?" Adrian gasped. He had no idea Tama Morris meant anything to Amanda. As far as he knew, they had not met more than a dozen times.

Amanda tore her hand away and flung back her chair. Another emotion seemed to overwhelm her. She trembled violently. Tears ran down her cheeks. "Oh, Adrian," she said. "If only you'd said this years ago."

She fled to her bedroom. Adrian retreated to his study in a near frenzy. There would be no sleep tonight or any other foreseeable night. His stomach ached. He gulped antacid pills and poured himself a tumbler of port. For a long time he sat on the terrace watching the planes land at Los Angeles International Airport. He tried to think of a name for his new turboprop.

Starduster. Yes, he liked it. Lockheed named their planes after stars. This claimed the whole galaxy. He poured himself more port and decided maybe the Prince was right. One of Madame George's girls was the way to go. He could set her up in New York. It would be easy to keep it a secret from everyone, even Victoria.

But it was Amanda's love he wanted. A love he had neglected, denied, abandoned. It was the only way he could ever expiate the enormous echoing guilt that was throbbing in his belly now when he thought of how much unhappiness he had caused Clarissa Ames Van Ness.

An hour or two after midnight, the telephone rang. It was Dan Hanrahan, Buchanan's chief of security. "Adrian?" he said. "I'm at Tama Morris's house. I think you better get out here right away."

"What's wrong?"

"She's dead. Killed herself."

A full moon splashed ironic gold on the heaving Pacific as Adrian drove down the boulevards and up the coast highway, his brain clutched in an icy fist. *It's not your fault,* he repeated to himself. *It's not anyone's fault.*

Buzz McCall opened Tama's front door. The last person Adrian wanted to see. Buzz looked like a man who had just fallen out of a plane without a parachute. "I found her," he said. "I called Dan."

Buzz struggled to control himself. Adrian could not believe it. The ultimate tough guy, bawling. "She's in there." He pointed to the bathroom.

Hanrahan was taking photographs of Tama. She lay in her big oblong tub—her Roman tub, she used to call it. Her heavy-lidded eyes were open, staring sightlessly at a photograph of her and Adrian which had been taken at the rollout of a Buchanan plane. The water in the tub was dark red.

"Did she cut her wrists?" Adrian asked.

Hanrahan shook his head. "A knitting needle in the heart."

He handed Adrian a letter. "I found this on her pillow. She left one for Buzz and another one for Cliff."

Adrian opened the envelope and read the bold scrawl. *I can't prove my love in any other way I guess so here goes. I'm too old to start hopping from bed to bed the way I lived before I met you. If there's another place I hope we meet there so you can say you're sorry. Tama.*

"What did she say to Buzz?"

Hanrahan dug the letter out of his pocket. *If you weren't such a louse I'd have come home to you with my broken heart. But I knew there was no point to it. I really loved you in the old days but you ruined it. Good-bye, you bastard.*

"Cliff's still got his," Hanrahan said.

"He's here?"

"She called them both before she did it."

"What do we do?"

"Call the cops. But I think you better talk to Cliff first. He said some wild things when I first got here."

Adrian handed both letters to Hanrahan. "Burn them," he said.

He walked into the living room to find Buzz and Cliff glaring at each other. Cliff must have been walking on the beach. His shoes were soaked and sandy.

"You're a pair of bastards," Cliff shouted. "All you ever did was fuck her around."

"Shut up," Buzz snarled. "If you were a man instead of a fuckin' crybaby maybe she'd have asked you for help."

"Prick!" Cliff shouted and hit Buzz with a terrific roundhouse right that sent him hurtling across the living room through the glass doors to the deck. Cliff lunged after him. Buzz struggled to his feet just in time to get another punch in the face that sent him crashing through the deck's bamboo railing onto the beach below. Cliff jumped on top of him screaming, "Prick! Prick!"

Hanrahan started after them. Adrian seized his arm. "Let them fight it out," he said.

It was no contest. Buzz was almost sixty years old and he was only half Cliff's size. Cliff pounded him to the sand again and again in the ghostly moonlight. In Adrian's eyes each punch was a demolition of Buzz McCall, the swaggering sultan of the assembly line, the man who called him a coward, who had possibly—no, probably—killed Beryl Suydam.

Cliff finally knocked Buzz into the surf, where he seized his stepfather by the throat and began drowning him. "Now," Adrian said and Hanrahan leaped to the beach and rescued Buzz. The security chief took the battered loser home and Adrian descended the familiar ladder to the beach and put his arm around Cliff, who stood with his back to the house, watching the white combers rumble toward them in the darkness.

"I loved her," Adrian said. "We had a nasty fight in Paris. It was partly about business. I decided it wasn't working anymore and told her I wanted her to leave the company. With generous severance pay of course. I had no idea anything like this would happen. She never gave a hint, I swear it, Cliff. Not a hint. She was always so independent, proud."

"Yeah, proud," Cliff said, rubbing his eyes with a fist like a three-year-old.

"Cliff," Adrian said. "I'm going to do my best to make this up to you—and to myself. You've always had a great future with this company. But now—"

Cliff bowed his head, struggling to control his grief. The surf sent ghostly fingers up the beach toward them. "We're going to build a new commercial airliner. I'm going to make you the project manager. Then I'm going to switch you to sales when we start selling it. So you can get maximum credit for it."

"Thanks, thanks," Cliff said.

It was marvelous what you could do with power, Adrian thought. You can triumph over grief, regret, guilt—even hatred. At least, he hoped he was triumphing.

The next morning, Adrian told Amanda about Tama's death. He did not want her to read it in the newspaper first. He also wanted to find out more about her friendship, relationship, whatever it was, with Tama.

Amanda told him nothing. All she said, over and over, was: "Adrian, the time has finally come. You'll have to pay a price for this. A terrible price."

"I didn't do anything that a thousand other men haven't done! I did it for your sake! Because I love you. I've always loved you. I wanted to come back to you."

Whether it was true or not, Adrian now believed it. He was desperate for some kind of resolution, for relief from emotions that were tearing him to pieces. At the office he dictated a statement about Tama Morris's "tragic death," expounding on her years of "stellar contributions" to the company.

That night Adrian brought home a huge bouquet of roses for Amanda. She ignored them. She also continued to ignore his questions about her friendship with Tama.

"How did she die?" she asked.

Adrian told her. Amanda smiled. "A true warrior," she said.

"Warrior?" Adrian said.

Amanda refused to say another word. Adrian began to grow alarmed. But he did not know what to do. He was almost as irrational as Amanda at this point. He spent the night in his study, dictating his conception of the Starduster. It would carry 175 passengers and a crew of six at 450 miles an hour. It would have a cruising range of 2,700 miles, just short of transcontinental. He dictated letters to nineteen airline presidents, all members of the Conquistadores del Cielo, asking their opinion of the profitability of such a plane.

Adrian went to bed at 3 A.M. so exhausted he was sure sleep was only an eyeblink away. But the vision of Tama in the bathtub's crimson water loomed in the darkness. Her husky voice whispered: *Love me, really love me, Adrian.*

I'm sorry, Adrian whispered to the heedless ghost.

A sound in the darkness. Someone had stumbled into a chair a few feet from the bedroom door. Adrian reached for the gun he kept in the drawer of his night table at Dan Hanrahan's suggestion, when Califia started sending him menacing letters. Hanrahan had also taught him how to use it.

Footsteps came toward the bed. A figure was outlined against the starlit window. Adrian rolled out of bed and crouched behind the night table. "Who's that?" he said.

"It's Califia, Adrian, come to avenge her beloved Tama and all the women you've degraded in your vicious clubhouse with its golden face."

Amanda? Adrian switched on the light and almost dropped the gun. His wife was standing at the foot of the bed, naked, a long carving knife in her hand. Somehow she had cut herself across the top of her right breast, a deep slice that had already coated the breast and half her torso with oozing blood.

"What in Christ are you doing?" Adrian screamed.

"I'm going to kill you, Adrian. In Tama's name. Only then can Califia sleep content in her gold-and-ivory tomb."

She walked toward him, the knife raised. "I can use this," Adrian cried, brandishing the gun.

"Bullets can't harm Califia. She's immortal," Amanda said in the toneless voice that had been irritating Adrian for months.

She rounded the corner of the bed and lunged at him. Adrian thrust the lamp in front of him for a shield and the knife sank into the green shade. Amanda pulled it out and tried to raise it again for another thrust. With a snarl Adrian shoved the lamp in her face, knocking her onto the bed. He dove for the knife arm and they wrestled wildly across the double bed, Amanda screaming now, a shrill wail worthy of a jet engine.

In the melee Amanda received an ugly slash on the neck below her left ear but she continued to do her utmost to kill Adrian. He finally seized her wrist with both hands and smashed it against the other night table. The knife flew free but he still had a madwoman to contend with. Amanda clawed at his eyes, kicked, kneed, all the while shrilling her war cry.

Cursing, terrified, Adrian wound her into the sheet and shouted for their Mexican housekeeper. She stood in the doorway, bug-eyed at the blood-smeared bed, the wrecked lamp, the knife. "Call Dr. Kirk Willoughby," he said. He gave her the number from memory. "Tell him it's an emergency. *Emergencia!*"

She scampered away and he was left with Amanda raving. "Kill me. Kill me now!" she screamed. "I want to die like a warrior in the service of my queen. I don't want to spend another hour as a prisoner of you loathsome men."

"Shut up!" Adrian jammed his hand over her mouth and pressed the sheet into the wounds on her neck and breast, stanching the flow of blood.

Kirk Willoughby found him in this position when he arrived. Adrian told him what had happened and begged him to deal with Amanda without calling a hospital ambulance. He dreaded what people in the company and the aircraft business would say if the story got into the newspapers.

"They'll think I attacked her," he said.

"You'll both be attacked by Califia, Queen of California, the moment I free myself," Amanda screamed, resuming her wild thrashing.

Amanda kicked and spit and clawed furiously at Willoughby when he tried to approach her. "We'll be glad to submit to your royal whims, your highness, if you'll let us tend to your wounds," Willoughby said.

"Bring Sarah Morris to me. The mother of Tama's granddaughters. I have a message for her," Amanda said.

Willoughby's eyes sought Adrian's. He nodded. He was ready to do anything to satisfy this madwoman. He called Cliff Morris and told him to bring Sarah to the house. Thanks to the freeway, they arrived in fifteen minutes. Adrian explained Amanda's delusion and advised Sarah to pretend to be a subject of Queen Califia.

By that time Willoughby had given Amanda an injection of morphine and stitched her wounds. She was propped against the back of the bed, looking weirdly regal with the sheet robed around her. She seemed pleased to see Sarah, who could only stare incomprehensibly at her.

"You must explain to your daughters exactly what happened tonight," Amanda said. "I was distressed to see that my breasts had grown back and resolved to amputate one, as an example to my followers. I wanted to be sure none of us would ever be enslaved in their gold-smeared club in Topanga Canyon. The loss of blood weakened me and I was unable to kill the chief scum bearer, Amanda's husband. Will you tell them that?"

"Yes, your majesty," Sarah said.

"Assure them my followers haven't deserted me. They're out there in the night, waiting to be summoned. But I've failed them with my weakness for male vileness and luxury. I never should have signed even a temporary truce with them. I've paid a terrible price for it. I've lost my dearest truest follower, Tama. You knew her and loved her, didn't you?

"I did, your majesty," Sarah said. "She was a wonderful woman."

"I let him destroy her," Amanda said, glaring at Adrian. "I watched and let him destroy her because I thought she was happy. I didn't believe any woman could be happy with this monster but I let her try. I let her die of unhappiness. Now I want to die too."

"We'll talk about it tomorrow, your majesty," Willoughby said. He had called an ambulance from a private sanitarium in the San Fernando Valley. The attendants were at the door. Strapped to the stretcher, Amanda left them screaming: "Tell your daughters they can kill Califia a thousand times but she'll always return!"

Adrian thanked Sarah Morris and got her and Cliff out of the house as quickly as possible. He did not like the way she was looking at him. There seemed to be an unspoken accusation in her eyes. He ordered the housekeeper to clean up the bedroom and retreated to his study. Around him lay the pieces of his personal life, like the wreckage of a crashed plane.

Adrian banished the mess from his sight and whispered the name of his new airliner: "Starduster." It was going to make a billion dollars for Buchanan Aircraft. Did that justify Tama's sightless stare, Amanda's blood-soaked madness, Sarah Morris's accusing glare?

Of course not. The two things had nothing to do with each other. He was a man who made planes and had trouble with women. The two things had nothing to do with each other. Nothing! For a few desperate minutes, Adrian almost believed it.

WHAT DO WOMEN REALLY WANT?

Starduster, Starduster, Starduster. She was sick of it, Sarah Morris thought, as her husband orated another aspostrophe to the plane that was going to make their fortune. Usually she tolerated these monologues at the dinner table. Why was she irked by a Saturday morning version? What was wrong with her? Didn't she want to make a fortune?

Already, the Starduster had doubled Cliff's salary. They had moved from south Los Angeles to a stone-and-stucco house on the upper slope of the Palos Verdes peninsula, with a marvelous view of the ocean. It was a nice place to live, washed by sea breezes, largely free of the noxious gases that created smog attacks in the rest of Los Angeles.

Maybe her alienation was simply British. While the Starduster gathered momentum, her father and his colleagues at de Havilland were frantically trying to find out why the Comet had disintegrated in midair three times. They were conducting enormously expensive tests that were driving the company to the edge of bankruptcy. Her mother related the doleful story to Sarah in weekly letters. When she tried to talk to Cliff about it, he had gloated—yes, gloated— over the Comet's failure. In a flash her English self, her English pride, had been reborn inside her American persona.

"*Bzzzzzzz*." Her six-year-old son came racing into the living room flying a scale model of a B-17 in his upraised hand. He rounded the couch and a wingtip caught a lamp shade. The lamp toppled onto a vase and water and tulips spewed all over the couch. "Oh!" Sarah cried, seizing him in a near death grip.

"It's okay, it's okay," Cliff said. "He didn't mean it. Right, Charlie?"

"Right," Charlie said, twisting away from Sarah. The mockery in his green eyes, the curve of his smile, left Sarah shaking inside. Was she looking at Billy McCall's son? The rest of Charlie diminished the fear. He had jet-black hair and a physique that seemed closer to Cliff's thick-boned body than Billy's lean sinewy frame. But Billy's father, Buzz McCall, was thick-boned and dark to the point of swarthiness.

Cliff was oblivious to the resemblance. Charlie was his son, the light of his life, the reason he went to work every morning with a smile on his face. Charlie and the Starduster. They had transformed Cliff's life, rescued him from the morose, sullen husband who had emerged from the destruction of the Talus. Sarah told herself she should be grateful for that. But gratitude kept eluding her. Maybe it was because another secret separated her even more brutally from Cliff's happiness.

It lay upstairs at the bottom of her jewelry box. A letter that had arrived the day after Tama committed suicide. On the blue-bordered page were three words: *I was wrong.* Sarah knew why Tama had killed herself. Cliff had choked out the awful story the night of her death. The next day the letter arrived, addressed to Sarah.

Since that day it arrived again and again in Sarah's mind. *I was wrong* reverberated through her soul. Wrong about what? Sarah asked. The answers were endlessly puzzling and often demoralizing. Wrong about what a person can accomplish in America? Wrong about the power of love? Wrong about Cliff? Wrong about leaving her first unloved husband, Cliff's lost father, disobeying the injunction of the Catholic Church? Wrong about trusting Adrian Van Ness? Wrong about redesigning Sarah Chapman to be an executive's wife?

Some—perhaps all—of these questions caused sadness to seep through Sarah's soul. She awoke in the gray predawn light and prowled the rooms of her house. She stood in the doorway and contemplated her two daughters and her son, blissfully asleep in the peaceful year 1957 and wondered what their futures would be. It was the age of Ike, the general and president who ruled a prosperous, self-satisfied America. She read magazines that declared the family was the natural center of a woman's life, the only social entity to which she should ever belong. The editors of the *Ladies Home Journal* told her that an incredible 97 percent of American women had taken marriage vows.

Where did that leave Tama's *I was wrong?* Where did it leave Sarah? Another voice answered that question. *Humiliated*, Amanda Van Ness whispered. It was a year since she had been summoned to her audience with Queen Califia in Adrian Van Ness's blood-smeared bedroom. The episode still partook too much of a nightmare to think coherently about it. But it had engraved Amanda on Sarah's consciousness as a primary being, a symbolic woman. Again and again she found herself returning to Amanda's first visit to their tract house in south Los Angeles, when she had warned Sarah and her daughters against humiliation.

Sarah had told no one about her midnight visit to the Van Ness house. But everyone in the company soon knew about Amanda's breakdown. Susan Hardy said Buzz McCall had gotten the story from the Mexican housekeeper, whom Adrian had fired a week after the incident. Buzz claimed Adrian had known Amanda was Califia, the woman who had sent threatening letters to half the executives in the company. Buzz claimed it was a plot to close the Honeycomb Club. For Susan, the discovery of the existence of the club had been a humiliation. Sarah, more sure of her ability to match the Honeycomb's women in the bedroom, had only been dismayed. Now she wondered if she too should feel humiliated in the name of other women who felt that way.

After helping Sarah clean up the mess on the couch, Cliff headed for another weekend of work on the Starduster. Charlie and his sister Margaret went off to a play group at the country club, and Elizabeth, now a precocious fourteen, vanished in a swirl of hair spray and mascara with a troop of equally precocious girlfriends. Sarah helped Maria make the beds and then went out on the porch to read *The Lonely Crowd*, a book that argued Americans were shifting their values from inner moral codes to the opinions of those around them. Sarah suspected they had been doing that since 1776—but California was a giant laboratory that seemed to prove every word of the sociologist's argument.

Grrrr. Her concentration was broken by another plane, this one's motor not created by the voice of a six-year-old. Over the ocean, a green monoplane was tracing a Jackson Pollock line against the blue sky, rolling, diving, looping, spinning in and out of near disaster again and again, carving the air into forms that built wildly, musically on one another. There was a rhythm to it, violent, spasmodic, that found an echo in Sarah's inner ear. It resembled the new music, rock and roll, which her daughter Elizabeth found exhilarating and Cliff found infuriating. The pilot ended his performance with the most dangerous stunt in the aerobatic book, a *lomcevak*. He climbed almost vertically until he stalled and then tumbled down, tail over nose, wing over wing as if he and the machine had simultaneously gone berserk. He regained control less than fifty feet off the water and roared skyward for a farewell loop.

Sarah gripped the railing of the porch with both hands, feeling as weak, as feeble as a ninety-year-old. Billy McCall was back in Los Angeles. Whenever he arrived, he announced his presence to her this way. It had become a cruel game they played with each other. The next time she saw him at a Buchanan party or ceremony, she would smile and tell him how much she enjoyed his performance. He would nod and tell her he was working on a whole new repertoire out in the desert.

I was wrong. What was Tama telling her? Wrong to cling to Cliff and her children, in spite of the sadness that washed through her body like a tide of sludge? Wrong to trust her body to deliver happiness? Wrong to be born a woman? Maybe that was the fundamental mistake.

That night when Cliff came home Sarah kissed him and said: "I want to learn to fly."

"What?" He looked at her as if she had gone insane.

"I've always wanted to learn. Will you teach me?"

He shook his head. "I haven't flown a plane since I left the army. You know that."

"You could brush up easily enough. Then you could teach me."

He started to get angry—or ashamed. "Sarah—we've got three kids to raise. Flying is dangerous. Dangerous as hell."

"How can you say that? When you're busy trying to sell the whole world on how safe it is."

"The airlines are pretty safe. But flying around in a private plane isn't. Unless you do it all the time and keep your skills sharp. That's why I gave it up. I didn't have the time. Or the money."

He was lying. He gave it up because he was afraid of it. How did she know that? Was Billy McCall whispering it to her? "Why the hell do you want to learn?" Cliff asked, trying to control his exasperation.

"For the thrill of it! Because I've got three kids am I condemned to being a hausfrau for the rest of my life?"

"I sure as hell hope you're going to stay around and raise them. Flying isn't thrilling once you learn. Did you ever talk to an airline pilot? They're bored stiff most of the time. It's like driving a truck."

"Dick Stone seems to think it's still thrilling."

"That's because he flies up to Palo Alto to see a girl who likes doing it at ten thousand feet."

Sarah shook her head. "He loves it. You can see it on his face, in his eyes, when he talks about it."

"I don't care whether you love it or hate it. You're still not entitled to risk your neck learning how to fly—with three kids to raise."

She could not tell him she wanted to invade Billy McCall's sky, she wanted to face him as an equal. That was the only way she could respond to his challenge. The other way, the telephone call for another flight to the desert, was the really ruinous choice. That would separate her from Cliff, the children, forever. Dying in the wreckage of a plane would not do that. It would leave her enshrined in their hearts as a cynosure of courage, a martyr of the air.

I was wrong, Tama said. *Humiliated*, Amanda whispered.

Sarah glared at her husband, fighting despair. "I want to learn!" she said. "I'm going to learn! If you won't teach me I'll find someone else."

Cliff kissed her on the forehead as if she were a tired child. He put his arm around her and chucked her under the chin. "Okay," he said. "You can take your first lesson on Charlie's twenty-first birthday."

He was eluding her. The Starduster was taking him away from her in a new way. The collapse of the Talus had thrown him backward to the sullen playboy. Now he was moving ahead or beyond her, on a wave of pride, confidence, that she could not share, that she almost resented. Why couldn't she rejoice in his renewed American optimism?

I was wrong, Tama said. *Humiliated*, Amanda whispered. The words dislocated everything. "I'm going to fly someday. I really am!" she said.

A week later, on another sunny Saturday after Cliff had gone to work, a cable arrived from England. FATHER KILLED IN CRASH. FUNERAL TOMORROW. DON'T TRY TO COME. MOTHER. A transcontinental transatlantic phone call told her the rest of the story. Working overtime on the redesigned Comet, her father had spent the night before last at the factory, getting snatches of sleep on a cot in his office. Everyone else was doing the same thing, including the engineers who were installing new wing flaps. They had to disconnect the aileron controls to do this and in their exhaustion reattached them backwards.

The next morning, her father and three members of his design team went up to test the flaps. A crosswind caused the plane to yaw. The pilot tried to compensate with the aileron. The wing responded in the wrong direction. He applied more pressure and the wing struck the ground. The plane cartwheeled across the airport into a line of trees, killing everyone aboard.

I was wrong, Tama whispered. Sarah threw herself on the bed and wept for the rest of the day. She was still weeping when Cliff arrived around four o'clock. He had heard the news at Buchanan. He held her in his arms and told her how sorry he was. "You see what I mean about planes being dangerous?" he said.

She wanted to scream insults at him. He was using this tragic accident to destroy her wish, her hope, for freedom. He was frightening her into being an inferior, a passenger, for the rest of her life. *Humiliated*, Amanda whispered. Would she end up like her, locked in an asylum?

Somehow this justified more tears. She wept all night and into the next day. She realized her grief made no sense. She had never been close to her father. He was seldom home. But he had always been cheerful and affectionate with her, especially when she was little. He called her Lamby. It was a silly name from a game they used to play. She would sit in his lap and insist she was his lamby pie. He would pretend to eat her.

Cliff was right about the danger of flying. There was a very good chance that she might kill herself trying to become Billy McCall's equal. But that only seemed to justify more tears. She thought of Lamby and Billy and Tama's letter and Amanda's fate and wept and wept for a world hopelessly out of joint. Her father was dead, his jet plane in ruins, while the Starduster carried Cliff farther and farther away from her.

Frank Buchanan came to dinner and tried to console her with memories of her father from their friendship in England before the first World War. He talked about going to Ezra Pound's apartment in Kensington, where they gave an assembly of poets a lecture on aerodynamics. Her father had fallen in love with one of the poets. Frank intimated it was not a platonic attachment. That only made Sarah remember Tama's suggestion that he probably had a secret love life. She burst into tears and fled to her bedroom.

After a week of almost continuous weeping, Cliff became seriously alarmed and asked Dr. Kirk Willoughby to arrange a meeting with a psychiatrist. Dr. Eric Montague looked a lot like Willoughby. He was losing most of his hair. His skin was pink, his face round and bland. He gave Sarah pills that stopped the weeping but she remained intransigently gloomy. She declined to tell him why. She said it was none of his business.

"You have to put your life in perspective, Mrs. Morris," Dr. Montague said. He talked a lot about perspective. He seemed to think that was Sarah's problem. He assured her getting the right perspective on her life would banish her depression. He urged her to tell him all her secrets. It was the only way to achieve perspective.

I was wrong, Tama said. *Humiliated*, Amanda whispered. How could she trust any of these Americans, even ones with English names like Montague? She would tell him nothing. Especially about Billy McCall. She clutched that pain to her private heart with absolute ferocity. She would use the pills to defeat the gloom and become a dutiful mother and wife again. She would stick to her diet and remain as attractive as possible and every time she saw Billy McCall she would hope he was—what was the American phrase?—eating his heart out.

Yes. She liked that. She had eaten her own traitor heart in defiance of him. She hoped in the end Billy would be an empty man, flying planes faster and faster and faster to nowhere.

I was wrong, Tama said. *Humiliated*, Amanda whispered. From now on Sarah would be right, right, right. Nobly, sacrificially right in the name of private righteousness. No one would ever humiliate her again.

SAVING THE QUEEN

On the third floor of the Buena Vista mental hospital, Adrian Van Ness peered through the one-way mirror at his wife. Amanda strode up and down the small bare room shouting orders to an invisible army of Amazon warriors. "We must ride, my darlings. We must ride to revenge our beloved Tama!"

She was naked as usual. She refused to wear clothes. The wounds she had inflicted on herself still scarred her throat and breast. With a sigh Adrian retreated to the office of the hospital's director, a tall, owlish German named Farber. Amanda's mother had died in this asylum. Willoughby had brought her here because he hoped Farber's experience with the mother might give him some insights into Amanda's breakdown. That was now a failed hope.

"The prognosis remains the same?" Adrian said.

"I'm afraid so," Farber said.

For a year, Amanda had alternated between periods of paranoid calm and episodes of manic frenzy. They had tried the new psychotropic drugs on her but they had had almost no effect, beyond calming her. The delusion that she was Queen Califia remained intact.

"You both recommend the operation?" Adrian asked.

"I have reservations, moral and medical," Willoughby said. "For one thing, it's irreversible."

"That's part of its beauty, my dear fellow," Dr. Farber said.

"There are alternatives. Every month they announce a new drug," Willoughby said.

"But they don't affect the delusion," Farber said. "Whereas on this point the medical evidence is overwhelming in favor of our other alternative."

Willoughby said nothing about a third alternative but his eyes accused Adrian. Frank Buchanan had begged Adrian to let him take Amanda away with him and nurse her back to sanity. He vowed to devote the rest of his life to the task. Adrian demurred. He wanted Frank to devote the rest of his life to Buchanan Aircraft.

"Will I be accused of—of mutilating her?" Adrian asked.

"Of course not. It is still a medically respectable operation," Farber said in his heavy German way. "It does not threaten the life or health of the patient. The recovery rate is above ninety-five percent."

"She won't be a zombie, will she? I don't want a zombie for a wife," Adrian said.

"Not if the operation is a success," Farber said.

They were talking about a prefrontal lobotomy. It was a very simple operation from a surgical point of view. Amanda would be anesthetized and a steel needle, about the size of a ten penny nail, would be pushed through the front of her brain. The delusion that was consuming her would vanish. If it worked, she would be a docile woman for the rest of her life, capable of happiness albeit on a reduced scale.

The operation appealed to Adrian for several reasons. Victoria was coming home from England and he dreaded the idea of her seeing her mother in her violent Queen Califia state. A tranquilized Amanda, living at home with her husband and daughter, was immensely preferable to this madwoman in her cell.

The operation appealed to Adrian even more as an act of power. Amanda had escaped him by her flight to madness. He liked the idea of recapturing her, even though it meant keeping her as his wife for the rest of their lives. Adrian's profoundly conservative instincts had no quarrel with that idea. Perhaps most important, it put Amanda forever beyond Frank Buchanan's reach.

"Do it," Adrian said.

Willoughby grimaced, suggesting he still preferred Frank Buchanan's option. Adrian found ironic satisfaction in the doctor's pain. It was a preview of what Frank would feel. On the way back to the factory, Adrian tried to appease Willoughby with some news he knew the doctor would approve. "We're closing the Honeycomb Club," he said.

For several years Willoughby had been telling Adrian the club was a mistake. He had documented numerous broken marriages and an unacceptably high rate of alcoholism among its members. Amanda's homicidal diatribe had forced Adrian to accept his responsibility for it. "I expected a tantrum from Buzz McCall but he didn't say a word," Adrian said.

"He hasn't sobered up since Tama died," Willoughby said.

The next morning at Buchanan Aircraft, Adrian confronted another decision laden with future insomnia attacks: the design and production plans for the Starduster. It was a beautiful plane, of course, as beautiful as anything the company had ever built. But it was expensive. The SkyRanger, the pioneering all-metal plane that had saved the company in the 1930s, sold for fifty thousand dollars. The Starduster's price tag was 3.8 million dollars. The development costs would be a minimum of twenty million dollars—and Frank Buchanan's memorandum warned of unknowns in the turboprop engine that could significantly raise this figure.

Adrian sat there, contemplating the design. The huge Allison engines seemed to dwarf the short wing. Was this another hot plane like the Scorpion, which was still killing a pilot a week in Germany? His chief designer assured him it was the opposite—a plane that any decent pilot could fly safely. The monster propellers—fourteen feet long—would sweep a tremendous airstream under the short wings. The wing itself was a completely new airfoil, remarkably low in drag-to-weight ratio.

The net assets of Buchanan Aircraft—the value of its buildings, equipment, and property—were no more than thirty million. To build this plane, Adrian Van Ness would have to bet his company on his salesmen's ability to sell it to the world's airlines. That in turn depended on whether it could compete with the long-range jets that Boeing and Douglas were building.

As Adrian sat there contemplating the plane that could destroy him, he saw Amanda, sedated, her skull shaved, on the operating table. Dr. Farber approached, his thyroid eyes glittering above his face mask. He saw the terror in Amanda's eyes—and the rage.

Adrian shuddered and almost became ill. But he continued to watch in fascination as the steel needle was pressed against Amanda's temple, then slowly, steadily, tapped into the frontal lobe.

It was over. He had become this woman's master. His docile wife who would henceforth symbolize his mastery over all women—and most men.

That morning in the spring of 1957, Adrian Van Ness could with some justification have been called insane. His mother's death, Tama's suicide, Amanda's madness had catapulted him into a new spiritual dimension, a world of desperate, haunted need.

Suddenly he saw how he could guarantee the Starduster's success. He rushed up the two flights of stairs to the glass-walled executive dining room. Frank Buchanan and his designers were in their usual huddle around the bar, Buzz McCall and his engineers disdainfully drinking before the opposite windows. Cliff Morris, Dick Stone, and others were in smaller groups. Everyone turned to the door as Adrian entered, their eyes bright with anticipation.

Adrian walked over to Buzz McCall, the man who had told him he had no guts because he canceled the Talus. "How are things going with the SkyMaster program?" This was another generation of big transports they were building for the Air Force.

"Couldn't be better. We're two months ahead of schedule."

"Good. We're going to need half your engineers for the Starduster."

"Are you changing the design?"

Adrian shook his head. "We're going to have the most elaborate preflight testing program in the history of aviation. We're going to sell this plane on the basis of its safety! By implication, we're going to be telling people that the jets aren't as safe. The Starduster's going to be the only plane in the world that can claim it's crash proof."

"I don't think you can—or should—say that about any plane," Jim Redwood said.

"I agree," Buzz McCall said. "Until you get perfect pilots, planes are always gonna crash."

"I intend to say that about this plane—and prove it!" Adrian said.

He pointed to Buzz McCall and his engineers. "I want you to come up with tests no one's ever tried before. I want someone to attack the fuselage with an ax while it's under pressure—to prove it won't disintegrate like the Comet. I want landing gear strong enough to carry six tons more than the plane's gross weight. I want those wings twisted on racks, loaded with tons of sandbags and put into simulated four-hundred-mile-an-hour dives. I want a one-sixteenth scale model put through a hundred thousand wind tunnel tests. Forget about costs. Just concentrate on proving that this is the world's safest airplane!"

"Brilliant!" Jim Redwood boomed.

"Fantastic!" cried Bruce Simons, their raffish public relations director, who drank almost as much as Redwood.

"I like it," Cliff Morris said.

Adrian appreciated but discounted this praise. Redwood, Simons, and Cliff were all students of the power curve. For some reason he did not entirely understand, he wanted Frank Buchanan to say something even more extravagant. But his chief designer turned away without a word.

After lunch, Frank caught Adrian at his office door. "How's Amanda?" he asked.

The question unnerved Adrian more than a challenge to his plans for the

Starduster. "The same. But I have some hopes of bringing her home soon. They've developed a new therapy that seems effective."

"What is it? Another drug? I have grave reservations about them. I question whether we should let the doctors play God with other people's minds."

"It—does involve drugs," Adrian said, an evasion at best.

"My offer still stands, Adrian," Frank said. "I feel I'm as responsible as you."

"I don't think either one of us is responsible," Adrian snapped. "It's an inherited disease."

"That's a trivial explanation," Buchanan said. "I prefer a spiritual answer. She's in revolt against the real world because between us we've made it intolerable for her."

"I have no such guilty feelings," Adrian lied. "Maybe I should have spent more time with her. But I had an aircraft company to keep alive."

"Are you sure she's not worse? All last night I heard her calling my name. This morning, around six A.M. it suddenly stopped. I wondered if she'd died."

"She's quite well," Kirk Willoughby said, from the doorway to the stairs. "I saw her this morning at the sanitarium."

"I'm—glad to hear it," Frank said and retreated down the stairs.

Willoughby followed Adrian into his office. "Is she all right?" he said.

"She's out of the anesthetic and quite calm. She recognized me. She didn't react negatively when I mentioned your name. She smiled when I mentioned Victoria."

"When did they do it?"

"Very early. About six A.M."

Adrian struggled for calm. "Do you believe Buchanan's story? Do you believe in psychic communication?"

"No."

"It's done. We can both live with it, can't we?"

"We can try," Willoughby said.

Two days later, Dr. Farber was on the telephone, informing Adrian that the operation was a "complete success." Adrian soon learned that the medical world measured success in ways quite different from the aircraft business. Amanda emerged from the surgery tranquilized, her violent fantasies obliterated. In fact she was so passive she refused to get out of bed for the first several days. But firm nursing soon overcame this reluctance.

Amanda had another reaction that Farber said was not unusual in lobotomies, although it seemed bizarre to Adrian—extreme tactile sensitivity. She screamed in agony when an adhesive bandage was removed. She could not endure even the slightest squeeze of her arm, her hand. In a word, her skin was so sensitive to pain she was untouchable.

"There is one other problem," Farber continued in his bland professional way. "About thirty percent of those who have lobotomies became extraordinarily outspoken. Their inclination to physical violence vanishes, but in an interesting compensation, they develop a tendency to make cruel and tactless remarks. Amanda seems to be among this thirty percent."

Was that a mocking smile in Willoughby's eyes? For a moment Adrian was tempted to get a new medical director. "In the aircraft business, we call these unpleasant surprises unk-unks," Willoughby said.

Two weeks later, Adrian brought Amanda home from the hospital. When he arrived to pick her up, Dr. Farber revealed a final qualification of the completely successful operation. "I think she can deal with most social situations. But I must make one recommendation. I don't think she can handle sexual intercourse. Aside from the pain you might cause if you touched her too aggressively, it might arouse memories in the deepest part of her psyche. We don't really understand how the brain—the mind—works."

For a moment Adrian hoped Willoughby would challenge Farber on this prohibition. But Willoughby said nothing. Did he think Adrian Van Ness was getting exactly what he deserved? Was he sitting in judgment on him in Frank Buchanan's name? Struggling for composure, Adrian took Amanda home. Around-the-clock nurses guaranteed her safety. She was quiet and completely submissive. She spent most of her time watching television, mostly game shows and sitcoms. She had no interest in the news. When she asked why she could not remember so many things from the past, Adrian blamed a head injury in a car accident.

A month later, Adrian decided Amanda was well enough to attend Buchanan's Christmas party. Her presence was especially important this year. The pièce de résistance in the center of the hangar was a gleaming white mockup of the Starduster. Everyone tramped through it while new employees were told in heroically sentimental terms the story of how the first SkyRanger rolled out six weeks ahead of Victoria Van Ness—and flew to glory. Everyone hoped Amanda was casting an equally favorable aura on the Starduster.

Amanda wore a ruby red Balenciaga chemise selected by Adrian. Older employees swarmed around them to shake her hand. The foreman of the work gang on the original SkyRanger, now the assistant manager of their Mojave Desert plant, was among them. He had brought along a picture of the original party. There stood Amanda, eight months pregnant, blinking into the flashbulbs. She looked at it and said: "I was pretty, wasn't I, Adrian."

"Yes," Adrian said.

"But you were rather vile looking, even then."

Everyone laughed. They thought she was being funny.

By far the happiest man at the party was Frank Buchanan—for the first hour. He kissed Amanda and said the new Starduster would be finished twelve months ahead of schedule, to celebrate her recovery.

After two attempts to talk to Amanda, Frank drew Adrian aside and snarled: "What've you done to her? What've you and Willoughby done?"

"Done?" Adrian said, glancing nervously around to make sure no one was within earshot. "We've cured her. Brought her back from a raving madwoman—"

"She doesn't remember me. She doesn't remember anything. I told her I

340

was going to send her a copy of Pound's newest *Cantos*. She didn't know who he was! Ezra Pound! The greatest poet of the twentieth century! She doesn't remember Helen Hunt Jackson, Mary Austin—none of her favorite writers."

"She's had severe memory loss," Adrian said. "It's not unusual after acute psychosis."

"You're not telling me the truth, you bastard," Frank said. He had a full glass of Inverness in his hand. "I dare you to tell me. I want to know where the woman I loved has gone."

"I loved her too, a long time ago," Adrian said. "I tried to love her again but it was impossible, thanks to you. Now it's impossible for both of us. But I promise you, as a man of honor, I'll take care of her for the rest of our lives."

Frank looked over his shoulder at the mock-up of the Starduster. "After a crime like this—a crime in which I'm willing to admit I share—do you think that plane will fly? Do you think we're worthy of it? Do you think the guardians of this universe will permit it? All I see in that plane is doom, Adrian. Death and doom!"

Eight hours later, at 3:30 A.M., Adrian sat in his study, unable to sleep, haunted by Frank Buchanan's words. For the hundredth time he rejected them. Why was he listening to a maniac's ideas about spiritual rewards and punishment? Adrian closed his aching eyes and saw the Starduster soar skyward on her huge propellers. This was the plane of his manhood, his liberation from the petty power-plays of Buzz McCall and his world of military procurement, of fawning over generals and politicians. The plane that would trump the jets on which millions were being gambled at Boeing and Douglas and Convair. The plane that proclaimed his supremacy over every man and woman in his universe. He was in command of his fate at last, a true conqueror of the sky.

DYNAMIC COUPLING

On a hot August day in 1958, Cliff Morris watched the first Starduster roll out of Buchanan's main hangar in Santa Monica. A band played and thousands of the men and women who had worked on her cheered. "You're looking at a plane that will sell a thousand copies!" Adrian Van Ness roared into the microphone.

Cliff had never seen Adrian so wound up. Gone was his usual aloof air of command. He was closer to a southern stump speaker whipping the faithful into a frenzy. Over and over, he called it the safest plane in the world.

Beside him on the platform stood his wife, Amanda, in a powder blue suit. She stared into the distance, barely listening to Adrian. Their daughter Victoria, back from England with a British accent that almost matched Sarah's, wore a forced smile that suggested she would rather be someplace else. She had matured into a tall, thick-bodied young woman with Adrian's heavy face and wary eyes and her mother's auburn hair.

Adrian was telling the faithful they had orders for 150 Stardusters on the books—worth a reassuring 380 million dollars. He had wanted two hundred—the shortfall was an index of the ferocious competition they were getting from Boeing and Douglas, who had salesmen prowling the country bad-mouthing Adrian's turboprop in favor of the pure jets their companies were developing. Adrian, playing cheerleader, made the 150 orders sound like a vote of confidence.

Goodwin J. "Goodie" Knight, California's governor, said the plane made him proud of the state, the aircraft headquarters of the nation. Eddie Rickenbacker, chairman of Eastern Airlines, who had ordered fifty copies, said he could hardly wait to put it to work. C. E. Smith, the balding benevolent dictator who ran American Airlines, added a similar apostrophe.

While everyone drank champagne, Cliff took Sarah and the children through the passenger compartments to the cockpit. "Wow," Charlie said, gazing at the array of instruments. "Is this more stuff than you had on the *Rainbow Express*, Dad?"

"About six times as much," Cliff said.

"When can we fly in her?" Elizabeth asked.

"Maybe when we go skiing in Colorado next Christmas," Cliff said.

"Let's hope it's as safe as they say it is," Sarah said. "I'm glad we don't have to fly in it for a while."

Cliff almost growled with irritation. He had a very large personal stake in this plane. Adrian had not only made him the project manager, he had put him in the office next to his own, with a new title, Assistant to the President. "This is the safest plane in the entire world," Cliff said.

Cliff was not just echoing Adrian Van Ness. He had seen the incredible things they had done to guarantee the Starduster's durability. They had fired four-pound carcasses of electrocuted chickens out of a compressed air cannon at the cockpit windows at 450 miles an hour to make sure the outer glass and inner vinyl panes were tough enough. They had hurled frozen ice balls—make believe hailstones—into the engine air-intake ducts to see if they caused damage. They had loaded tons of sandbags on the wings and vibrated them in the company's wind tunnel to guarantee they were strong enough to support the big turboprop engines. The Starduster had passed every test.

"Every aircraft company wants to believe that about a new plane," Sarah said.

Cliff knew she was really talking about the de Havilland Comet. He had sensed her hostility to his recital of the Starduster's virtues from the day he went to work on it. Adrian's decision to make safety its greatest virtue had sharpened her antagonism. It was more than the Comet and her father's death struggling to redesign it. Something else had gone wrong between them.

Sarah never stopped picking at him. She said his ties were too loud and bought him a whole new set. She decided he was getting fat and put him on a protein diet. She wondered why he never read a book. She told him he was too old to be driving a convertible and nagged him into buying a sedan. Yet in the bedroom, she was a tigress. She thought he was a no-taste numbskull but she wanted him almost every night. Was it part of that word, *need*, that had erupted the night the Korean War began?

Like most husbands, Cliff had no idea what was happening in his wife's psyche. He did not know he was in a bitter inner war between Sarah's traitor heart and her marriage vows. He was never home when Billy McCall wove his coded messages in the sky. "I was talking to Frank Buchanan before the ceremony," Sarah said. "He seems awfully dubious about this plane."

Cliff ground his teeth. In private and now in public, Frank had been incredibly negative about the Starduster. He said he was proud of its design but he was sure it would never be a success. No one understood the reason for this uncharacteristic gloom. Dick Stone and others theorized it was a residue of bitterness from the destruction of the Talus.

One month later, the first ten Stardusters started flying for Eastern Airlines. Another ten would be delivered to American in the next thirty days. Braniff, Northwest, were next in line. It was time to build on this sales momentum. A week later Jim Redwood and Cliff flew to Chicago and picked up the first New York–bound flight of an American Airlines Starduster. The plane was almost full and the chief pilot could not stop praising it over the intercom. He told the passengers the Starduster was the fastest-climbing, best-handling plane he had ever flown. He invited Jim and Cliff into the cockpit and thanked Cliff for making a number of changes a committee from ALPA, (the Airline Pilots Association) had suggested. "Usually you arrogant bastards ignore ninety percent of what we say."

Back in their seats, Jim said: "You've got to hand it to Adrian. He's always thinking ahead."

"Yeah," Cliff said, with minimal enthusiasm.

Cliff had not completely forgiven Adrian for Tama's suicide. For a while he had carried her farewell note in his wallet. *I'm sorry to say good-bye this way. But I know you can take it like a man. That's all I ever wanted you to be—a man.* He had finally torn it up and told himself to stop thinking about it. Lately he tried to see the Starduster as a final gift from Tama, a flying carpet to the success she had always wanted for him.

The landing at La Guardia was pure powder puff. It was hard to believe the pilot was putting a four-engine plane on the runway. At the Waldorf, they unpacked and Redwood suggested a late supper at 21. They were halfway through their thirty-dollar steaks when one of the owners strolled over to them. Redwood had long made the restaurant his New York headquarters.

"Bad luck about your new plane, Jim."

"What plane?"

"The Starduster. One just crashed in south Jersey."

The steak congealed in Cliff's mouth. "What the hell should we do?" Red-

343

wood wondered. He was thinking of tomorrow, when they were scheduled to call on TWA to sell Stardusters.

"Let's find out if it's more than a rumor," Cliff said.

He telephoned Buchanan Aircraft and asked for Adrian. "His line's been busy for the past hour," the operator said.

"Get me Frank Buchanan."

In a moment Frank was on the line. "It was an Eastern plane. No survivors," he said. "Ten days after the plane went into service. I knew something like this was going to happen."

"Jim Redwood and I will go down there and see what we can do."

"Good idea. It will save us the price of flying someone from here."

The Starduster had crashed in farm country not far from Camden. By the time they got there the site was swarming with state troopers, local police, and officials from the Civil Aeronautics Board. The man in charge was the CAB's regional investigator, a tall, thin deadpan type named Jeremiah Coyne. He shook their hands and said: "Take a look. It ain't pretty. They never are."

In the headlights from a half dozen police cars they could see hundreds, perhaps thousands of pieces of Eastern Flight 915 scattered across a vegetable field—strips of torn aluminum and yellow insulating material and chunks of the seats and tail surfaces. Mingled with the metal and plastic were pieces of human bodies—a leg here, an arm there. In a tree near the farmer's barn dangled two headless corpses, upside down. The stench of burnt kerosene and scorched metal and seared flesh lingered in the humid air.

"This thing didn't crash," Cliff said. "It disintegrated."

"That's about right," Coyne said. "We just found the left wing and the engines in the woods, a mile and a half from here."

"Are there any witnesses?" Redwood asked.

"The farmer and his wife were awake. He says they heard a weird sound—a sort of high-pitched whine—then a terrific explosion. The next thing they knew pieces of the plane started raining out of the sky."

Jim Redwood seized Cliff's arm and led him back to their car. His face was shiny with sweat. The grisly debris of the crash had made him queasy. "This isn't our job. Let Buzz send a couple of his engineers out here to pick up the pieces. We've got important appointments tomorrow."

The next morning, Cliff watched Redwood bombard executives at TWA with statistics on the Starduster's projected performance. They listened politely, agreed that it sounded like a marvelous plane—but said they would wait to hear the results of the CAB investigation of the New Jersey crash. "Midair disintegration is not exactly the sort of thing that suggests a crash-proof plane," TWA's brusque president, Jack Frye, said.

A disheartened Jim Redwood decided to return to California. Cliff Morris called Adrian Van Ness and told him he wanted to stay with the CAB investigation. "Go ahead," Adrian said. "I'm sure it's pilot error. Maybe you can stop ALPA from blaming it on the plane. That's their favorite tactic."

There was an hysterical trill in Adrian's voice. His legendary calm had seemingly vanished for good. Cliff called Frank Buchanan and told him what the farmer had said about the high-pitched whine just before the explosion.

"A runaway propeller at supersonic speed might cause that sound," he said. "But it wouldn't tear off a wing. Those are the strongest wings I've ever put on a plane. Only God could tear those wings off!"

In a warehouse on the outskirts of Camden, the CAB investigators began trying to put the pieces of Starduster YP448, its Buchanan serial number, back together. It was a slow, disheartening job and mostly it told them what had not happened. There was no evidence of an inflight fire started by a tire blowout or a hot wheel brake. The fire definitely occurred after the wing broke off. Had the pilot attempted a violent evasive maneuver to avoid another plane? The Federal Aviation Authority reported no plane had been within ten miles of the doomed Starduster.

In desperation, Jeremiah Coyne convened a meeting of every expert he could think of, including officials from the Army's Bureau of Aircraft Accident Research and the Los Angeles FAA personnel who had given the Starduster its airworthiness certificate. For five days they hurled possible causes at each other and discarded them. "If this lasts another day," the pilot who was representing Eastern cracked, "we may decide the accident never happened."

Cliff Morris flew back to California to report the impasse to Adrian Van Ness. "Pilot error," Adrian snarled, pacing his office like a man about to face a firing squad. "That damn fool tried some stunt to show off the plane."

"The pilot had over forty thousand hours in his logbook," Cliff said. "He was fifty-six years old. He wasn't the damn fool type."

"Every pilot's a damn fool when no one's watching."

Cliff went home to confront an unhappy wife. "I missed you so much," Sarah said.

"I know. But I'm trying to solve a problem that could put us out of business."

She turned away as if she were stifling a nasty reply. *You're getting what you deserve for your hot air about safety.* Was that what she was thinking? It did not make for loving thoughts. For the first time in his life, Cliff said he was too tired for sex and went to sleep with a cold good night kiss.

The next morning at the office, Cliff toiled on an interim report on the New Jersey crash for the engineering department. His telephone rang. "Cliff," Frank Buchanan said. "Another one's gone down. An American flight. Over Iowa."

At lunch the gloom in the executive dining room was thicker than any conceivable smog attack. Adrian Van Ness sat at the head of the table like a zombie. "Are you going to keep on yelling 'pilot error' now?" Frank Buchanan asked.

"It's possible," Adrian said, clutching his wineglass. "Coincidences happen all the time. We don't even know why this one crashed yet."

"It's another wing failure. I feel it in my gut," Frank shouted. "But it's impossible. That wing was designed to handle every stress known to aeronautical science. Am I right, Buzz?"

"Yeah," Buzz said. He was drinking Invernesses by the gulp.

"How do we know that's true?" Adrian snarled. "Maybe the chief engineer was too drunk to read the report that warned us of the problem."

"If you're right, the man who sent in that report can have my fucking job, as of now!" Buzz roared, glaring at his engineers. There were no takers.

Again, Cliff volunteered to represent Buchanan at the crash site. At Los Angeles Airport, he had tickets on American's Starduster Special flight to Chicago. The man ahead of him on the line asked the clerk: "What kind of plane are you flying?"

When the clerk told him, the man said: "I'll take TWA."

In Iowa, Cliff shook hands with Jeremiah Coyne again. The CAB had ordered him to ignore his regional title and take charge of the crash site. "If you thought New Jersey was bad, get a grip on your nerves," he said.

American's Flight 444, en route from Chicago to Denver, had been flying through apparently perfect weather—blue sky, virtually no wind. About twenty-five miles south of Sauk City, two loud explosions startled farmers for miles around. Looking up, they saw a huge cloud of ugly black smoke. Out of the cloud hurtled Flight 444, minus both wings. Down came the smoking fuselage in a vertical dive to smash into a cornfield at approximately seven hundred miles an hour.

Cliff stood at the edge of the crater the Starduster had dug. It was forty feet deep and at first glance the 100-foot-long fuselage had disappeared in it. Jeremiah Coyne told Cliff that beneath the swirling smoke the long silver tube containing some seventy-three men women and children had been telescoped to less than thirty feet.

As Cliff gulped air to control his stomach, a thin sallow-faced man with bloodless lips walked up to the rim and cried: "Propeller fatigue. It causes more crashes than anything else and those CAB bastards cover it up every time." He merged a dozen reporters into an audience and made a speech about corruption in the CAB and Federal Aviation Authority. "They're tools of the aircraft companies," he yelled.

"That's the local congressman," Coyne said. "The son of a bitch will say anything for publicity. We haven't even found the goddamn propellers yet."

The similarities with the New Jersey crash were numerous and chilling. The wings had come down some two miles from the fuselages's crater. The breakup had apparently happened with no warning. There was no record of a distress signal, which every veteran pilot would send if he had an engine fire. "The biggest difference," Coyne said in his undertaker's drone, "is clear air turbulence. We've got reports from two pilots who said they ran into a lot of it just before the crash. An Air Force jock riding a B-Fifty-seven almost got his head rammed through his canopy."

In his pilot days Cliff had encountered some mild clear air turbulence. It was one of the most treacherous phenomenons of flight. Without any warning, a plane could collide with a swirl of air that knocked it up or down or sideways. It was like hitting a pothole in the sky. But the Starduster was built to fly through such obstacles with no more than an "oops" from the pilot to reassure the jangled customers.

Once more Cliff participated in the grisly ritual of collecting pieces of the smashed plane and watching the CAB's experts sifting it for clues. In a week they were at the same impasse they had reached in New Jersey. Something had torn the wings off the Starduster. But no one could explain how or why it happened.

This did not stop Jeremiah Coyne from coming up with a solution. "Ground it."

"Let's not do anything until I have a chance to talk to the man who designed this plane, Frank Buchanan," Cliff said.

Frank's name was enough to check the rush to execution. Cliff flew back to California with the news and Adrian summoned the top brass to his office. He seemed dazed, unable to comprehend what was happening. Instead of taking charge, he let Cliff make his trumpet-of-doom report.

Buzz McCall was inclined to accept the sentence. "They grounded the DC-Sixes in 1948 for six months," he said. "It didn't ruin them."

He was recalling a series of disastrous midair fires on Douglas DC-6s caused by a misplaced air scoop that sucked gas into the heating system during a fuel transfer from one wing tank to another.

"Grounding will ruin this plane and this company," Adrian said.

"There's only one alternative. Limit the airspeed," Frank Buchanan said. "Cut it to two hundred and fifty."

"That's slower than a DC-Six or a Constellation!" Adrian said.

"I know that. But it will keep the plane in the air. Meanwhile let's launch the biggest emergency research program in aircraft history to find out what's wrong," Frank said. "If we sit here and wait for the CAB to tell us, we'll deserve to be out of business."

"How much will it cost?" Adrian said.

"I have no idea. If I were you I'd go to the nearest moneylender and tell him you want a line of credit as wide as the Mississippi at its mouth and twice as long."

Adrian's face was a grimace of pain. "All right. I'll call the CAB."

On the way downstairs, Frank seized Cliff's arm. "Find out if there were any modifications made on the engines or the wings of any of the planes since they went into service."

Cliff found there had been one fairly important change made after delivery. Passengers sitting near the huge propellers had complained of vibrations. The engineers had tilted the nacelles of the engines slightly, which in turn altered the angle of the propeller blades. Presto, the vibration vanished. Buzz's boys had checked with design before doing this and Frank Buchanan's initials were at the bottom of the page beside *approved*.

When Cliff reported this to Frank Buchanan, he smiled forlornly. "That's our first clue," he said. "Now we're ready to find out why the Starduster has been crashing. We'll give it a scientific name. But the real reason will be unnameable, Cliff. It's a punishment for Adrian's evil will, his indifference to moral laws."

The ferocity of Frank's hatred for Adrian made Cliff his defender. "I've got reasons to dislike him too, Frank," he said. "But there's a whole company at stake here. Thousands of people's lives will be messed up if we go broke—including my own. Let's find that scientific explanation for their sakes."

"Are you ready to risk your life to find it, Cliff? I sense so much evil swirling around this plane—it's going to be very dangerous."

Cliff thought of Tama's farewell note. *Be a man.* Maybe that too was part of the gift she was trying to give him with the Starduster. "I'll take my chances if you will," he said.

Two months later, Cliff sat in the cockpit of a Starduster, strapped in by two sets of seat belts, as the plane headed for the Sierra Wave, a piece of sky above the Sierra Nevada Mountains famous for its turbulence. At the controls was Lieutenant Colonel Billy McCall, borrowed from the Air Force at Frank Buchanan's request. Frank sat beside him in the copilot's seat. Frank had insisted on Billy. He seemed to think he had some special power to resist the forces that were trying to destroy the Starduster.

Day after day for weeks now, they had flown Stardusters into the Sierra Wave, subjecting the planes to turbulence more violent than anything an airliner would ordinarily encounter in the sky. The company's two thousand engineers then virtually dismantled the planes to study the effect of this extraordinary stress.

In a half hour, the jagged snowcapped Sierras loomed on the horizon. By this time they had acquired personalities. They were a tribe of evil giants, spewing murderous winds. "Hang on!" Billy shouted as an updraft sent the airliner bouncing a thousand feet. A second later, a howling wind shear cut the air from beneath the wings, leaving the propellers clawing in a near vacuum. They dropped straight down like a stalled helicopter for three thousand feet.

To Cliff's amazement, they did not slide into a spin. Somehow, Billy kept the plane perfectly trimmed. "Jesus, Pops, I'm glad you thought of asking me to this party. I haven't had this kind of fun since the old White Lightning rocket plane days," Billy said.

"Get back up to twenty-five thousand feet," Frank said. "We're going to give these wings the ultimate test today."

In the passenger compartment, the seats had been replaced by sandbags weighing 97,000 pounds, the full gross load of the plane. Billy slowly climbed back to 25,000 feet, relit the cigar clenched in the corner of his mouth asked: "Now?"

"Now," Frank said.

They dove into that cauldron of violent air, down, down with the airspeed needle rising up the dial in weird counterpoint to their descent. Past 400 miles an hour, past 425, the Skyduster's top speed, toward 500 miles an hour, probably faster than any commercial airliner had ever gone before. The raw brown slopes of the Sierras hurtled toward them.

"Pull it out," Frank said.

"Hold together, you son of a bitch!" Billy howled and hauled on the yoke. The motors literally screamed in protest. The fuselage did a conga. The wings flapped as if they were made of feathers. The g forces hammered at Cliff's brain. The memory of Schweinfurt swelled in his belly. But he fought his panic with new weapons. Tama's farewell message: *Be a man.* Knowing his son Charlie would remember him dying this way. A wild resolve to prove he was just as tough as Billy McCall.

Memory, fear, love, hate coalesced in the plane's roaring struggle to survive the Sierra Wave's turbulence. The next thing Cliff knew Frank Buchanan was asking him: "What kind of stress readings did you get on the outer wing?"

They were still alive. The wings had stayed on.

"High," Cliff said, handing him the numbers he had just copied with a shaking hand from the dials of the special instruments in front of him.

"That's an understatement," Frank said, studying the figures. "That part of the wing is taking ten times more bending force than the rest of the wing. Who could believe that would happen from tilting a motor a few inches?"

Back they flew to Buchanan Field. "One more trip like that and they're going to need a spoon to get me out of this plane," Cliff said.

"Hey Big Shot, you're doing okay," Billy said. "I'm starting to believe you really flew those forty-nine missions over Krautland. I always thought Tama made it up for a press release."

"We're finding something new on every flight," Frank said. "Today could be the breakthrough. I'm betting those outboard engine nacelles will show us something."

Along with risking his life, Cliff was accumulating a graduate education in aerodynamics from Frank's inflight lectures. By now he knew there were a hundred different kinds of flutter that can attack a plane in flight. Designers had learned to check it in various ways so it did not explode into an uncontrolled spasm that ripped steel struts and aluminum skin to shreds. They were trying to find out if a new unsuspected kind of flutter had gotten loose in the Starduster's wing.

Billy roared in for his usual perfect landing at Buchanan Field. Buzz McCall and his engineers swarmed around the plane. "I thought so," Frank said, pointing to the struts holding the nacelles of the outboard engines. Two of them had bent inward from the g forces of the dive.

"The same sort of bends on the engines from the New Jersey crash," Cliff said.

"Exactly," Frank said. "In the Iowa crash, there were two struts broken. On to the wind tunnel. Cliff, ask Adrian to join our demonstration."

It was getting dark but Frank Buchanan had long since stopped paying attention to the clock. So had Adrian Van Ness. Cliff found him in his office conferring with Winthrop Standish, the company's solemn, hawk-nosed attorney. The families of the victims of the two crashes were suing the airlines and Buchanan for millions of dollars. Adrian was trying to fend off the suits, clinging to his theory of pilot error.

Adrian greeted Cliff with a bleak smile. "You're back from the Sierra Wave in one piece. That's the good news. Any bad news?"

"Frank thinks we've got it figured out. He'd like you to come down to the wind tunnel," Cliff said.

"What's going to happen down there?" Adrian asked.

"I don't know exactly."

"That's part of your job—to find out in advance, Cliff. So I can deal with it. Forethought. You can't use it without information."

"Frank isn't giving out any information."

Cliff found it difficult to sympathize with Adrian's fear that Frank would use the Starduster to diminish his power in the company. Those trips to the Sierra Wave had built something hard and cold into the center of Cliff's self. He was risking his life to save this plane. It made him impatient with Adrian's obsession with personal power.

In Buchanan's wind tunnel Adrian and Cliff found a one-sixteenth scale model of the Starduster sitting on a special mount, which could be manipulated to simulate movements in actual flight. Carefully, Frank Buchanan sawed through some of the struts and braces on the two outboard engines. They then adjourned to the control room and turned on the wind while Billy McCall "flew" the model from a panel in front of the window.

"When I drop my hand, pull up the nose and cut the airspeed," Frank said. "That's what the pilot probably did in Iowa when he hit clear air turbulence."

The wind whooshed through the big gray tunnel for another minute, the miniature Starduster bouncing in the turbulence. Frank's hand dropped, Billy jerked the model's nose up and cut the airspeed fifty knots on his toy throttle. Before their appalled eyes, the small Starduster suddenly shook like a bone in the mouth of an angry dog. Thirty seconds later—Cliff was timing it on a stopwatch at Frank's orders—both wings snapped off.

Frank switched off the wind. It died away like the moan of an angry ghost. "Whirl mode," he said.

"What is it?" Adrian said. He looked as if he were barely breathing.

"An extremely rare type of flutter. Two physicists wrote a paper on it in 1938. I'd forgotten it like everyone else until the wings started coming off."

Even Billy McCall, who thought he could handle anything he encountered in the sky, was aghast. "Why, Frank?" Buzz McCall said. "Why didn't it just damp out like it would on any piston plane?"

"Because the Starduster has turboprop engines," Frank said. "Those turbines are spinning at thirteen thousand revolutions a minute. The propellers are turning at a thousand. The whole thing is a giant gyroscope. The moment a jolt broke or bent one of those weakened struts, the engine started to wobble. That started the propeller wobbling and the whole vibration was transmitted to the wing, which was built to flutter at three vibrations a second. Whirl mode, for some reason, slows down from ten to five to three cycles per second. The moment both the wing and whirl mode got to three per second you got—"

"Dynamic coupling," said Frank's favorite designer, Sam Hardy.

350

"Exactly," Frank said. "What happens when a high musical note breaks a glass tuned to the same vibration level."

"Dynamic coupling," Buzz muttered. He shuffled out of the wind tunnel building like a man who had suddenly aged twenty years.

"It's not your fault," Frank called after him. "It's not the fault of anyone who built the plane. It's the sort of thing that can happen when you play God with other people's lives—and call a plane crash-proof."

"That's not true!" Adrian Van Ness cried, backing away from Frank as if he were some sort of supernatural being. "I've never done anything that wasn't for the good of this company. I've lived for this company! Are you going to listen to me or this madman?"

Billy McCall was smiling, enjoying Adrian's terror. Buzz McCall was gone—wiped out by believing whirl mode was a curse Tama had put on him. The rest of the executives, mostly designers, swayed in the firestorm of emotion between Adrian and Frank Buchanan. Someone had to take charge. It was like flying the *Rainbow Express* over Germany. You had to be a leader whether you liked it or not, whether you believed in what you were doing or thought it was mostly insanity.

Cliff Morris knew he looked like a leader—and he knew how to act like one. In that compressed room, with an explosion about to blow the company apart, he was the only man with some faith in the future. He still believed in the Starduster. It was Tama's gift to him. It had already given him a new sense of manhood.

"Wait a minute!" he roared. "Wait a minute! We've got a problem to solve. This isn't a courtroom. It's not the Spanish Inquisition either. Let's all go back to our offices and sit down and try to solve it! It's either that or start looking for other jobs."

"He's right," croaked a perspiring, trembling Adrian Van Ness, his eyes full of gratitude. That was the moment Cliff knew he was on his way to becoming president of Buchanan Aircraft.

GOING SUPER

Hatred—he was surrounded by hatred, Adrian Van Ness thought, staring into the darkness at 3 A.M. the next morning. The idea steadied him. Hatred was a force, a kind of airflow. He would use it to soar above the haters on wings of guile.

Insomnia added a dry, cold clarity to Adrian's mind. He had sat at the dinner table last night and confronted Amanda's mindless hostility. He remembered the moment of decision, when he had ordered the nail driven into her brain. Did this woman—or any other woman or invisible spiritual entity in the universe have the ability to harm him? No, Adrian decided. Although the world was frequently incomprehensible, he did not believe it was controlled or even occasionally manipulated by invisible powers.

Amanda was counterbalanced by his daughter Victoria. Her presence reminded him of Buchanan's first breakthrough to prosperity. If there was such a thing as luck, she was his talisman of good fortune. He told her nothing about the crisis at the company, of course. But he drew strength from her plaintive sympathy for his public woes with the Starduster.

Philosophy aside, Frank Buchanan had demonstrated Adrian's pilot error theory was nonsense. Their design was responsible for killing 120 people. They, not the airlines, could be liable for all the damages in the pending lawsuits. If this information in its present version got out, they might be headed for the nearest bankruptcy court. As a crucial first step he had to regain Frank's support for the plane.

He summoned Cliff Morris and Dick Stone to his office. "Do you agree with Frank—that I'm responsible for the Starduster's crashes?" he asked.

They both shook their heads. He discounted Cliff's sincerity, although he was grateful for his support. He had sentimental ties to Frank and was, like most salesmen, a believer in luck. Dick Stone's negative was the one Adrian valued. He was a fellow believer in the intellect's cold unillusioned view of the world.

They discussed how to persuade Frank Buchanan to fix the Starduster's fluttering wing. Cliff volunteered to talk to him. Before the end of the day he was back with good news. Frank was ready to cooperate. "He even came up with a name for the redesign program—Project Rainbow."

"How much will it cost?" Adrian said, ignoring the gibe in Project Rainbow.

"He's discussing it with Dick Stone right now. It'll be damn expensive, you can be sure of that."

The success of Project Rainbow required someone who did not get drunk at lunch and stay ossified for the rest of the day. Adrian hired an executive from North American and put him in charge of the engineering department. Buzz McCall sat in his office, a ghost of the swaggering son of a bitch who had intimidated everyone for two decades.

At Dick Stone's suggestion, Adrian decided to let Bruce Simons tell the whole truth about Project Rainbow. Bruce called in TV and newsreel cameras to film the one hundred Stardusters in service as they flew to Buchanan Field and had their motors stripped and wings rebuilt. Simultaneously, Adrian told Buchanan's lawyers to negotiate a settlement with the airlines, accepting a 50 percent liability in the damage suits. The costs were terrifying but the Scorpion was still in production and bankers were impressed by Project Rainbow's boldness.

The CAB demanded a few more trips to the Sierra Wave to convince them that whirl mode was under control in the Starduster's redesigned wings. They declared Project Rainbow a success and lifted the speed restrictions on the Stardusters already in service. There were celebrations in the engineering and design departments. But Adrian, reading the memorandums from salesmen in the field, did not join them. In spite of Bruce Simons's heroic publicity effort, the public refused to fly on the plane.

Nevertheless, Adrian pressed grimly ahead. He hired a half-dozen veteran plane salesmen to push their troubled product. He sent Cliff Morris and Bruce Simons out to support them with hoopla and advice. They soon grew weary of hearing "yes, but" from airline executives when they swore the new Starduster was worry-free and certain to regain the public's affection. The coup de grâce was American Airlines, which had an option to buy another forty copies. They canceled the order and refused to talk to anyone from Buchanan.

In desperation, Adrian himself flew to New York and joined Cliff and Jim Redwood in a final plea to American's boss, C. E. Smith. Adrian brought Dick Stone with a briefcase full of cost projections to prove how many millions the Starduster could save, compared to a jet. He even borrowed Billy McCall to give the airline brass a chance to shake the hand of a famous test pilot and hear him describe what the new Starduster could do. They arrived at American's headquarters equipped with a motion picture camera and screen, to show Smith some of Billy's adventures on the Sierra Wave.

Adrian knew they were licked when they walked into Smith's office and confronted glowering red-faced Bill Horton, the airline's resident son of a bitch. "C.E.'s had to fly to Tulsa," Horton growled. "What the hell have you got in mind? You look like you're ready to show me *Gone with the Wind*."

"We want to prove the Starduster is not gone with the wind, Bill," Adrian said.

"If you can do that, you can also sell me some beachfront property in Arizona," Horton said. "Don't embarrass yourself and me, Adrian. The plane is dead. Kaput. Let me show you something."

He pressed a button and a movie screen slid down the wall. Another button and onto the screen roared a swept-wing four-motored jet airliner with American markings. "That's the Boeing Seven-oh-seven," Horton said. "We'll have forty of them in service next fall."

Five minutes later, the Buchanan team stood on the Avenue of the Americas, beaten men. *Ruined* crooned in Adrian's head. "Gentlemen," Adrian said, "You are now privileged to experience failure. They say it can be good for the soul. So far my encounters with it have made me doubt that."

"Adrian," Cliff Morris said. "You give me some money and support and I'll sell this fucking plane overseas. I'll sell enough to break even on this thing. I swear it."

"Breaking even was not exactly what I had in mind," Adrian said.

"It's better than going broke."

This was the tougher, more determined Cliff who had emerged from the Sierra Wave and saved Adrian from humiliation at Frank Buchanan's revengeful hands. But Adrian doubted his ability to penetrate the maze of a foreign culture to sell a commercial plane overseas. Perhaps teaming him with Prince Carlo was the answer. Ponty could deal with the subtleties, Cliff could provide the hard American sell.

At the 21 Club the young men drank Inverness and Adrian drank Sherry and listened to Billy McCall talk about the problems of the Strategic Air Command, where he was flying a Convair B-58 Hustler. It was the first bomber to hit Mach 2, twice the speed of sound. Billy had nothing good to say for it. The plane had escape capsules that could chop off a man's hand if he was not careful when he ejected. At Mach 2, the skin temperatures reached 130 degrees in the nose, threatening to cook the pilot. To slow down from supersonic to subsonic speeds, the pilot had to transfer fuel to keep the aircraft in balance, a frequently fatal maneuver. In fact, the Hustler had already killed more pilots than the Scorpion.

"After all that," Billy said, "the goddamn thing is too small. It can't carry enough bombs to do anyone serious harm."

"What do they need?"

"A supersonic bomber that won't kill pilots and can deliver a real load," Billy said. "They're going to ask for bids on it in a couple of months."

"I'm not sure I can interest Frank Buchanan," Adrian said. "He's vowed never to design another bomber. Can you talk him into it?"

"Sure," Billy said.

Adrian saw anxiety in Cliff's eyes. Interesting. Cliff did not like Billy's intrusion into the company's business. Adrian filed the insight for future reference. "A supersonic bomber could become the model for the next-generation airliner," he mused. "It's only a question of time before we go super there too."

"I don't give a damn what you do in the airline game," Billy said. "I just want one thing understood. If the politicians try the sort of shit they pulled on the Talus, we fight."

"Agreed," Adrian said, mentally reserving the right to change his mind.

"Let's all shake on that," Dick Stone said.

Disconcerted, Adrian had to shake hands all around. He would have to give Dick a lecture on the need for greater detachment.

None of them realized they were entering a nightmare that would haunt them for the next twenty years. Nor did Adrian Van Ness, smiling hopefully at Billy McCall, foresee he was face to face with heartbreak.

LIMA BLUES

"Hemingway," Prince Carlo Pontecorvo said, banking the Starduster so that it was practically flying at a 180-degree angle along the flank of Machu Picchu. "I've hunted with him often. He too is haunted by his mother, who cast fundamental doubts on his manhood. It's an extremely common affliction. It requires a man to repeatedly look death in the face."

Sarah Morris was sure the belly of the plane was grazing the slope of the mountain. She got a swooping glimpse of the ruined palaces of the Inca kings. Her face and other parts of her body turned to rubber and bulged in unpredictable directions as the g forces sucked at them. Below the narrow saddleback on which the lost city stood, precipices plunged to a raging brown river. Around them loomed black snow-streaked mountains waiting to devour the bits and pieces of the Starduster.

The restored wings shuddered, the big engines whined as the palaces and the mountain itself vanished in swirling clouds. Cliff Morris, sitting in the copilot's seat, looked back at Sarah. "How do you like this?" he said.

He's afraid. Sarah read the fear on Cliff's face with a wife's practiced eyes. He's afraid but he isn't showing it. That's the way men deal with it. "I love it," she said.

The man who had forbidden her to learn to fly because it was too dangerous was now letting this corrupt aristocrat risk both their lives to sell this abominable plane. The Prince was not cleared to fly the Starduster. But the Prince thought he was cleared to fly anything, ride anything, sail anything, shoot anything, climb anything, love anything. He was the ultimate nobleman, the creature that a thousand years of Europe's civilization had strained and groaned and bled to produce. Sarah loathed him. She hated what he was doing to Cliff. She hated the male arrogance the Prince personified. The Prince and Adrian Van Ness were two of a kind.

I was wrong, Tama whispered. Wrong about trusting men like the Prince and Adrian Van Ness? Undoubtedly. With the help of Dr. Montague's pills, Sarah had achieved a bitter stability in defiance of them all—Cliff, Billy, Adrian, even her father, that missing person in her life who had done nothing to help her understand men.

"I didn't see *anything*," Amalie Borne said, filing her fingernails in the observer's seat beside Sarah. She was another example of Europe's decadence. The more time she spent with Amalie and the Prince, the better Sarah understood why England had always remained aloof from the continent, why so many Americans were isolationists.

The Prince banked in a wide circle and dove at the mountain again as if he were determined to commit suicide. He peeled away at the last second, leaving their hearts, stomachs and lungs behind. Sarah struggled to raise her eyelids, to hold up her head, heavy as a chunk of granite, against the g forces. Again she saw nothing but a blur of trees and crumbling walls. "That's much better!" Amalie said.

They flew on to Lima, the capital of Peru, where the Prince allowed Buchanan's assigned pilot to land the plane with the chief pilot of Peru's airline in the copilot's seat. Landings, unless they were in jungle clearings or on crevasse-gashed glaciers, bored him. He lectured them on the history of the place as they looked down on broad white beaches and the sprawling city in the lush splendor of the Rimac Valley, seven miles from the sea. "When the American pilgrims were sitting down to their first Thanksgiving dinner, wondering if they could survive another year of semi-starvation, Lima was a hundred years old, the capital of Spain's overseas empire."

What was he telling them? Lima was part of Europe, which entitled him to include it in his personal imperium? Something like that, Sarah was sure of it. She had become sure of a lot of things on this trip.

At Jorge Chavez International Airport they were greeted by a smiling delegation of Peruvian airline executives and their brothers or brothers-in-law in the ruling political party. They trooped through the Starduster exclaiming at its roominess, its comfort. No one said a word about its penchant for crashing. Its reputation as a jinxed plane had failed to penetrate South America.

With the help of the Prince, Cliff was rescuing his reputation as a jinxed executive. From Mexico south to Brazil and Argentina, then over the Andes to Chile and Bolivia and now Peru, he had sold an astonishing 150 Stardusters. It was exactly the sort of plane they were looking for south of the border, where there was not enough money to lengthen airport runways to handle jets.

Cliff had invited Sarah to join him in Santiago for a celebration when they sold their 150th plane. He explained that the Prince was along to impress the South Americans, all of whom doted on European nobility. But Sarah took one look at Amalie and suspected more complex, less moral motives.

That night, on the top floor of Cesar's Hotel, looking down on Lima's ghostly white Plaza de Armas, where Conquistador Francisco Pizarro once strutted, Cliff told Sarah the Prince was also along to dispense bribes to the executives who bought the planes and the politicians who supplied their state-run airlines with the money. There was not a hint of concern or contrition in his voice. He tried to make it sound clever, amusing.

"You could go to jail!" Sarah cried.

"Not a chance," Cliff assured her. "There's no law against bribing foreigners. Everybody does it. There isn't a country in the world where the guys in charge don't expect a piece of the action when they buy something as expensive as a plane."

As a convincer, he told her how they had already sold almost a thousand Scorpions to Germany, Holland, Spain, Portugal, the same way. "I still think it's wrong," Sarah said.

"We're rescuing this plane, maybe the company, from oblivion," Cliff snarled. "Adrian sent the Prince along to make sure I didn't have another flop on my record. He knows three strikes are out in any game. You want to keep shopping on Wilshire Boulevard? Be nice to the Prince. And Amalie."

"Does she sleep with them?"

"I don't ask. The Prince handles that part of it. Most of the time I don't think so."

I was wrong, Tama whispered. Was she asking Sarah to tell Cliff not to trust Adrian Van Ness? She could see how much the Prince subtracted from Cliff's accomplishment. He could see it too, she was sure of it. But he was telling himself he still deserved most of the credit for the 200 million dollars in orders they had already rolled up. He had brought her down here to sell her the lie.

They spent the weekend in the forty-room mansion of the suave chairman of the board of Peruvian Airlines, who spoke perfect English and talked nonchalantly with the Prince about Cannes, Antibes, Portofino. The house was in the center of an immense valley, fifty miles from Lima. Cliff made love to her in a bed that looked as if it belonged in the palace of Versailles. He did not even mention the Starduster. He had decided to be indifferent to her disapproval. As his big body crushed her into the mattress, Sarah thought:. *Now I know how it feels to be fucked.* Amanda Van Ness whispered: *humiliated*

Cliff did not have the slightest idea what she was thinking. Afterward he cradled her in his arms and talked about moving to a bigger house in Palos Verdes, on the bluffs. In the morning they stood at the window and gazed at the mountain-rimmed valley with its terraced miles of coffee trees. "He owns it all," Cliff said.

"Why do you have to bribe him?"

"He likes Yankee dollars."

"Did Amalie sleep with him?"

"Jesus Christ!" Cliff said. "Maybe you better go home. The kids probably miss you."

Sarah heard the rest of the sentence. *But I won't.* She was swept by confused regret. After the struggle to solve the Starduster's crashes, she had found a new Cliff Morris in her house, neither the sullen playboy nor the husband who sought her advice, but a man who had discovered something inside himself that he liked, in spite of the Starduster's commercial failure.

Sarah had liked this man too. She liked the way he played basketball with Charlie in the yard when he came home from work, the way he was noticeably kinder, more patient with the girls. She realized he had done something that helped him play a father's role, especially with Charlie.

Now he was doing something he hoped Charlie would never do, something he could not admit to him. He had wanted her to know about it—and forgive him. No, more than that, he had wanted her to collaborate with him, rejoice in his clever corruption, his friendship with the Prince and his elegant whore.

I was wrong, Tama whispered. "Maybe I should get home," Sarah said. "When's the next flight?"

"I'll find out," Cliff said.

She was saying no. She was refusing to join him. She might be doing more than that. She was feeling something that had been growing in her since his refusal to let her fly and his cunning misuse of her father's death. She was telling him she no longer cared about his planes.

Where did that leave Billy McCall and his coded messages in the sky? Receding, receding over the far horizon, dwindling to a speck of memory, regret, contempt. She was freeing herself from both these Americans, with their strange ability to turn admiration into its opposite, to turn her inside out, to crush her heart and mind with g forces and contorted appeals for love.

Sarah saw the sadness in Cliff's eyes. And the fear. He hated what she was telling him. But she also saw the cold resolve. Whatever he had learned out there on the Sierra Wave, he was no longer afraid of his fear, his self-doubt. Maybe he was not even afraid of losing her.

Suddenly Sarah wanted to find out if that was true. She wanted to show him she still cared about the memory of those three months when they had loved each other without reservations, the months that ended with her discovery that she was pregnant with Charlie. She wanted him to know she remembered that time, no matter what she felt about his planes. "I'm sorry," she whispered.

Cliff stood at the window, staring down the valley toward history-laden Lima. "I am too," he said.

MORALITY PLAYS

Upside down in his Aero Commander, Dick Stone flew cheerfully over the dark green surf-washed cliffs near Cape Mendocino, in Humboldt County. "How do you like this?" he asked.

Cassie Trainor laughed. "You're a maniac at heart!" she shouted. You could not scare Cassie.

Aerodynamically, Dick was becoming a very good pilot. Psychodynamically, he was a mess. For three years, he had flown to Palo Alto to see Cassie as she majored in American Studies at Stanford. He had watched her self-confidence grow as she discovered that coming from Noglichucky Hollow did not limit her ability to think and learn. Outwardly, Cassie turned into an all-American girl not unlike her classmates in their brass-button blazers and pleated skirts.

Dick was fascinated by the Stanford scene, shot through with California sunshine. These western Americans seemed to have discovered the secret of life without angst. They were so good-natured, so well-intentioned, so confident that a future of married love, hard work, babies, success, would create happiness. Their optimism, their laughing serenity, seemed to confirm his decision to become a complete American, to abandon the Jewish side of his hyphen. But beyond the sunshine stood Amalie Borne, whispering: *Never ask me how.*

Dick banked the Aero Commander and headed out to sea. Climbing to ten thousand feet, he turned to Cassie and said: "Time for the autopilot?"

Cassie was already taking off her clothes. There was a mattress spread out on the cabin floor. Dick set the autopilot's slave—a tiny claw that fastens onto a heading—and waited a moment to make sure the plane was obeying its robotic commands. Then he struggled out of his pants and shirt. It was not easy to undress in a plane and it was even harder to dress. But in between there was an unforgettable reward.

It was part feeling, the vibration of the metal skin, the roar of the motors and the rush of the airflow, and part idea, knowing where you were, hurtling between the sky and the earth at 150 miles an hour. It was a marvelous blend of sensation and power. Cassie called it angel love. She said it was the way angels would do it, if they had bodies.

For Dick there was an even more important idea at first. He was challenging Billy McCall for supremacy in Cassie's soul. He was daring Billy's two ladies of the sky to make a move on him. He was blending danger and love to prove how much he wanted to make Cassie free and happy.

It had worked, it had broken Billy's spell. By now it had become a ritual. But it could not free Dick Stone from Amalie Borne's spell. She was always there in the shadows, mocking his attempt to be a macho American lover.

Lately he had begun to imagine him and Cassie as two lovelorn robots in a science fiction movie, two machines who had accidentally acquired the ability to love each other. He thought of his penis as a piston operating with the same methodical frenzy displayed by the gleaming metal rods in the Aero Commander's growling engines. They were parts of the plane, extensions of technology, not two fleshy warm caring bodies and souls.

Insanity. He had only seen Amalie Borne once in the last three years, at the 1957 Paris air show. Again their eyes had met across a crowded room. But this time Dick read the enormous sadness in them. She had left for Rome the following day without speaking to him.

Why was he being haunted by a woman who disdained him? Amalie answered the question with a mocking sigh: *Never ask me how.*

Cassie was above him and Dick had both his palms pressed against the hard teats of her coned breasts, while the engines pounded between his shoulder blades. He raised his head and rotated his tongue on the teats. Cassie bit the bone and flesh on his shoulder. The blue sky stared in both windows. Off to the left and right he could see the propellers whirling. He put both hands on her firm smooth rump and moved her up and down. Her tongue slithered up his neck and into his mouth. He breathed the perfume of her auburn hair, the sweet deodorized smell of her flesh. "Dick, Dick," Cassie cried. "I wish it could last forever."

There was a romantic answer to that question. Will you marry me and make it try to last almost as long as forever? But Dick could not say the words. Did Cassie expect them, want them? Money was not a problem. He was now the assistant treasurer of Buchanan Aircraft. Cliff Morris had rescued the Starduster from red ink by selling two hundred copies in South America. Cliff thought he could do almost as well in the Middle East. The design department was in a frenzy, working on a top-secret supersonic bomber. The Lady of Luck might not give a damn but she was smiling on Buchanan Aircraft.

He came and came and came and Cassie cried out with joy and raked her nails across his chest. There was still a delicious blend of desire and animosity in their lovemaking. She was still a creature to be tamed, mastered. She still resisted surrender—which made it so much sweeter when she came.

Sighing, Cassie put on her slacks and blouse and Dick got his pants and shirt back on and they flew north along the Santa Cruz coast to the Santa Lucia mountains, with the Hearst Castle sitting in the middle of their huge rocky faces like a rich child's toy. They had flown all over California in the last three years, seeing it from the air in all its immensity and splendor. From Muir Beach, a sliver of white sand between dragon's jaws of green crouching headlands to the great Central Valley with its stupendous swaths of fruit and vegetable farms to Death Valley's narrow wasteland.

He was heading for their favorite site—the winding serenity of the Russian River as it descends between green hills to the sea at Jenner in Sonoma County. Soon they were swooping over it at 1,000 feet. "It's what heaven must look like," Cassie said.

"I thought you didn't believe in heaven anymore," Dick said.

"That changes my mind," Cassie said, gazing down at the looping ribbon of water.

For a moment Dick wondered if this was more important than the love they had just consummated on autopilot. He had shared his ownership of California from the air—the word *ownership* kept forcing itself into his mind—with this woman. Could he ever do it with anyone else? Amalie Borne? That might be a betrayal of Cassie far worse than sexual infidelity.

They landed at the small airport on the outskirts of Palo Alto and Cassie helped Dick tie down the Aero Commander. They drove to a roadside restaurant in Cassie's 1950 Ford and discussed her future. She was going to graduate in four months. What did he think she should do? Could he get her a job at Buchanan?

Again the unspoken question dangled between them. "You might be better off at Douglas or Lockheed. If you're set on the aircraft business."

"Why?"

"The Honeycomb Club. People remember you."

Instantly, he hated himself for saying it. "Is that what's wrong? Is that what's worrying you?"

"Nothing's worrying me."

"That's not true. We haven't been honest with each other—in the old way—for a long time. A couple of years. We talk about American history and literature. But never about us."

"Maybe there isn't anything to talk about," Dick said.

"Really?" Cassie said. "You mean that?"

Dick was hating himself, the conversation, more and more. How could he lose control of the situation this way? "We're not exactly romantic lovers."

"Whoever said we were?"

She had him. All the cards were in her hand. All the pain too. "Look, I don't mean any of this the way it sounds. I like you a hell of a lot. I wouldn't have spent all this time with you—"

"Maybe you're tired of starring in *Pygmalion*. Especially now the statue's startin' to talk back."

"You've been talking back since the night I met you. I like it."

"But you don't want to marry someone from the Honeycomb. It wouldn't fit the executive image. Is that it?"

"In this business? Are you kidding? It could make me the next president."

She did not like that either. Her eyes were bright with tears. A nerve pulsed in her temple. "I guess I'd just like to hear you say you love me."

There it was. The trump card of the 1950s, played between the heavy coffee cups and the thick plates of this roadside restaurant in the last year of the decade. "I do. But I'm not sure about the rest of it. Can you give me more time?"

"Sure."

He picked up her hand and was shocked to see how badly she had been chewing her nails. One or two fingers were raw, bitten to the quick. Maybe it was not as easy to become an all-American girl as some coeds made it look at Stanford.

Three days later, Adrian Van Ness called Dick into his office and told him to withdraw four million dollars from the Los Angeles branch of the Swiss bank in which they had set up a special account during the 1955 Paris Air Show. "The Prince is at the Ambassador. Take it over to him. It's for the Starduster sales in South America. Carry it on the books under extraordinary expenses."

So much for Cliff Morris's miraculous sale of two hundred planes, which he was celebrating all over Los Angeles, along with his promotion to sales vice president. Something deep in Dick's nature opposed this way of doing business. But he could not resist the way Adrian took him into the inner circle of the company's policies. It was a level of trust that no one else had achieved. It was Adrian's way of saying people like them, intelligent, sophisticated people, understood the way the world worked.

Dick could not decide what troubled him most, his own inner resistance or the way Adrian Van Ness seemed utterly unbothered by the bribery. Knowing nothing about Adrian's early commitment to Oakes Ames and his epic example of making ends justify means, Dick fell back on uneasy rationalizations. The money went to foreigners to keep Americans working. Buchanan was not breaking any laws. They were not even losing money for the stockholders—the bribes were merely added to the cost of the planes.

Dick brooded on these conundrums as he drove to the Ambassador with the four million dollars in his briefcase. At the desk in the ornate lobby, the clerk told him the Prince's line was busy. He wandered down a corridor full of shops—jeweled Swiss watches, the latest fashions in furs, dresses, shoes. A figure in the dress shop froze him to the deep-piled carpet. A tall woman with a mane of flowing chestnut hair. Amalie Borne.

Of course it made sense. The Prince was here. Why should he leave her in Europe with the meter running? Dick stepped into the shop. "It's nice to see some foreigners have a conscience," he said. "I bet before you're through with these shops, fifty percent of our lend-lease debts will be settled."

She turned, her smile arch—but pleased. "You're absolutely right," she said. "But I gather it can't be done without your assistance. Why aren't you upstairs? Your arrival has been anxiously awaited all morning."

"The line is busy."

"He's on the phone to his wife in Milan or his mother in Rome. He calls them every day."

"How admirable. It makes me feel guilty. I haven't called my mother in six months."

"Such schadenfreude. You ought to be ashamed of yourself."

"Can I buy you a cup of coffee?"

"You can do more than that. You can help me carry these dresses to our suite."

"I'm not interested in three way conversations."

"Why not? They allay suspicions."

He let the smiling saleswoman pile three large boxes on his arms and followed her to the elevator. "What sort of a tip can I expect?"

"If by tip you mean advice—I've already given you all I have."

In the suite, the Prince was just finishing his telephone call. "Ciao, Mamma," he crooned. "Ciao." He kissed the receiver and hung up.

"I encountered this old friend at the desk when I picked up our mail," Amalie said. "We met at the Paris Air Show. He took me to Verfours for dinner, saving me from starvation when you abandoned me for some disgusting Germans."

"I'm happy to see you again, Dick," the Prince said. "You have the full amount? Some of our friends in South America are growing rather urgent."

"It's right here," Dick said, handing him the briefcase.

The Prince opened it to make sure the amount was correct. The money was in five-thousand-dollar bills. "James Madison has such an engaging visage," the Prince said.

"I've already counted it," Dick said.

"We're flying to New York today," the Prince explained. "Then on to Rio. Any mistakes might be inconvenient."

"Of course."

"I'm taking an apartment in New York. At the Waldorf Towers," Amalie said.

"Oh?" Dick said. "I seem to recall you detested Americans."

"That sounds just like her," the Prince said, briskly shuffling through his mail. "She specializes in outrageous opinions."

"All of which are based on experience," Amalie said.

"If you come to New York, give us a call, Dick," the Prince said. "We won't be there often but we'd enjoy seeing you. Especially if the circumstances are as pleasant as they are today."

Dick knew he should say something equally ironic. But he looked at Amalie and said nothing. "This new supersonic plane—will it be ready soon?" the Prince asked.

"According to rumor, yes," Dick said.

"Business will be brisk. I hear the British and the French are working on one. And the Russians. If they can steal someone's plans."

"But not the Italians?"

"Lately our talent seems confined to cars."

"And women?" Amalie said.

The Prince smiled. Dick was mute. All his feelings for this woman were being aroused again, after he had struggled so long to banish them. She was boldly inviting him to visit her in New York, converting the Prince into her mouthpiece. What did it mean?

"Now you may buy me that coffee you offered when we met downstairs," she said.

"I'll call room service, darling," the Prince said.

"No. You have your usual long distance calls to make. I can't be witty while you're talking business. Didn't you notice that in South America?"

The Prince shrugged. "Pay no attention to anything she says, Dick."

In the lounge, Amalie ordered Coffee Amaretto. "He's so charming. And so disgusting," she said.

"Why don't you leave him?"

"I dislike complicated decisions."

"I still have that note you sent me."

She smiled, her eyebrows lifting. "It was a deft ending to our story, don't you think?"

"It wasn't a story."

"Dear Dick. Dick. It was."

"What do you mean?"

"I'm not Jewish. I'm Polish. I worked in Schweinfurt as a forced laborer throughout the war. I met Madame George there. She was in the same precarious situation. We agreed that if we survived, we would arrange to live splendidly after the war. She conceived the idea of telling men stories to enliven our friendships. I was practicing on you. It worked rather well, you must admit. I passed it on to Madame and another girl has used it on a Jewish banker from New York with great success."

"You're lying."

"I wish I was. I would have long since hired a writer to tell it to the world. It might make more money than that simpering little goody-goody, Anne Frank."

"I still think you're lying."

She shrugged. "Think what you please. Tell me what Adrian Van Ness is like."

"He's very shrewd—and he doesn't have a moral bone in his body."

"Does he have a mistress?"

"Not at the moment, as far as I know. His wife's had some sort of breakdown. He devotes a lot of his time to her."

"Is he generous?"

"Yes, on the whole."

"I dislike your reservations. I prefer simplicity in a man."

"Why are you so interested?"

"I'm at his disposal when I'm in New York. I suspect it may turn out to be the other way around. When he is in New York, I'll be summoned from Paris, Rome, wherever I happen to be."

"Why? Are you and the Prince separating?"

"No. He simply can't afford me any longer. His wife has been speculating on the Paris Bourse. She's mortgaged a great many of her estates and has no cash to spare. He depends almost entirely on Buchanan for his livelihood these days."

"He's selling shares in you!"

"You put it crudely—but I suppose it's true. I'm an asset. I suggest impossible dreams to men. They believe your planes fly without crashing."

"Will you be in New York soon?"

"Tomorrow. I have no intention of going to South America again. I found their food atrocious, their wine abominable, their men vile, their women pathetic. The whole continent is drenched in the despairing knowledge that they're doomed to perpetual inferiority to the Yankee colossus. I found myself believing you Americans may rule the world in spite of your naïveté."

"I'll see you in New York, next week."

"I'll make you miserable."

"I'll make you happy."

Did he really believe it? Was he ready to betray Cassie Trainor, abandon his all-American girl for this mocking elusive woman who clutched sadness to her being like a second skin? Dick was catapulted back to his first fantasies of what it would be like to bomb Germany. He had imagined himself hunched over his maps, giving the pilot headings in a calm, intense Hemingwayesque voice. Reality had been horrifically different. His heart had pounded, his voice had croaked and trembled.

Was it a warning? Perhaps. But the plane was already in the air. He was on his way to a strange country on a mission of redemption, not destruction. Wouldn't that make a difference?

In his heart Dick already knew the answer. He was rewriting the ethics of betrayal as Adrian Van Ness rewrote the ethics of selling planes. The consequences might be bitter. But he accepted the risk in the name of that elusive word, love.

BOOK SEVEN

WAR GAMES

A gasp ran through the crowd as the great white plane emerged from the main hangar of the Buchanan plant on the edge of the Mojave Desert. No one had ever seen anything like it before, except in science fiction magazine illustrations. It was two hundred feet long and weighed three hundred tons. A stiletto fuselage tapered to a flat span of triangle wing surface set above an engine intake duct the size of a hotel hallway. Head-on it resembled a winged creature out of the dawn of time, craning its beaked head toward the light. Everyone realized they were looking at the most original airplane ever designed—the BX experimental bomber, the Warrior.

"This one's gonna make history," Lieutenant Colonel Billy McCall said, throwing an arm around Frank Buchanan.

"It almost made me history," Frank Buchanan said. Only a few people inside the company knew how much inner agony this creature of the sky had cost their chief designer. He had been profoundly reluctant to build a plane that delivered nuclear weapons. No one but Billy McCall, implicitly reminding Frank of the promise he had made in New Guinea, could have persuaded him.

Thanks to Billy's early warning, Buchanan had a running start on the competition when the Air Force issued an invitation to six aircraft companies to submit designs for Weapon System 151. The requirements for the plane were mind-boggling. It had to be able to fly at mach 3, have a global range, carry 25,000 pounds of pounds—and be able to land on existing runways. Four of the six companies blanched and decided not to bid. Only Boeing and Buchanan competed and they both submitted designs that were so complicated, the Air Force suggested scrapping the project.

At that point, Frank Buchanan discovered an obscure technical paper published by the National Advisory Committee for Aeronautics that proposed an aircraft flying at supersonic speeds could belly-slide on the shock wave it was creating, like a surfer riding just ahead of a big comber. Frank asked for a forty-five-day extension of the competition and lashed himself and his equally exhausted fellow designers into an immense effort to incorporate this principle, called compression lift, into their design. Buchanan won the contract to produce two prototypes.

Adrian Van Ness took one look at the plane and uttered a prophecy of his own. "That's the supersonic airliner of 1965."

"I was hoping someone would say that," Frank murmured, looking past Adrian as if he did not exist. He was still unable to speak his name without loathing.

"You better start building a new factory," said burly square-jawed General Curtis LeMay, head of the Strategic Air Command. "I want two hundred and fifty of these by 1963."

Two hundred and fifty planes at thirty million dollars a copy was 750 million dollars. With the usual follow-ons for spare parts it was a billion-dollar contract. "Will that fly in Washington?" Adrian asked.

Since the end of the Korean War, each year had seen bruising battles between the armed forces over the shrinking Pentagon budget. So far, the Air Force had won most of the fights. General LeMay reflected this momentum in his answer. "We'll make it fly."

Cliff Morris did not have the slightest doubt that Curtis LeMay could deliver on this promise. To him and other veterans of the air war over Germany, LeMay was an almost mythical figure. He had devised the tactics that enabled them to survive and frequently flew in the lead plane to sustain their sagging morale. He had crowned his wartime achievements by creating the Strategic Air Command, whose mission was to warn the Russians against any more Korean-type adventures. Currently equipped with subsonic B-52s built by Boeing, SAC's strategy of intimidation seemed to be working. As the year 1960 began, communism was quiescent throughout the world except for some sporadic guerrilla fighting in a remote southeast Asian enclave called Vietnam.

Cliff could see why General LeMay was ecstatic over the Warrior. It could cruise at 2,200 miles an hour at 70,000 feet, giving it an 800-mph advantage over any fighter plane known to exist. It could fly 20,000 miles without refueling, eliminating the fleet of vulnerable flying tankers that the B-52s needed for global warfare. If it was not the ultimate weapon, it was as close as anyone had come to it yet.

"Now all you've got to do is pray your bloody Congress doesn't go missile crazy," said a weary English voice on Cliff's right.

Everyone looked at Derek Chapman—and at Cliff—with an uneasy mixture of dismay and dislike. Cliff found himself wishing there was some way he could make Derek disappear, instantly. He was turning into a hoodoo, an albatross, a walking, talking intimation of bad luck.

Unfortunately, Derek was his brother-in-law. Making him disappear was impossible. Short, stocky, and balding, he seemed an affable, tolerable relative when he showed up in California, wondering if he could get a job in Buchanan's design department. Frank Buchanan was delighted to hire this son of his old British friend. Derek joined the department in the final stages of the superhuman effort on the Warrior and made some valuable contributions to positioning the canards, the small tail-like wings on the nose that enabled the plane to achieve compression lift.

But Derek's conversation soon gave everyone the creeps. He brought with him from England a tale of woe that sent chills through Buchanan Aircraft. He talked endlessly, bitterly about the way England's aircraft industry had been decimated by the emergence of the missile.

Last year, Russia's German rocket scientists had beaten America's German rocket scientists in a secret race and fired a capsule called *Sputnik* into orbit around the earth. Nikita Khrushchev, Russia's new strongman, had proclaimed his missiles made American bombers obsolete and the Soviet Union was the number one global power. In the United States, this development had no immediate impact on the aircraft industry, beyond inspiring several companies to set up missile divisions. In England, where budget problems were far more severe, the minister of defense had canceled virtually every advanced aircraft in development, sending a half-dozen companies lurching toward bankruptcy.

It was unthinkable, Cliff told himself. It could never happen in America. A plane like the Warrior represented all Frank Buchanan and his cohorts had learned from the experimental rocket planes, the Talus flying wing, supersonic fighters like the Scorpion, the agonizing research into flutter to rescue the Starduster. When Buchananites looked at the BX's sweeping cursives and sharp obliques, they thought of the test pilots who had died in earlier planes, the designers and engineers who had collapsed with heart attacks or heartbreak when their ideas or their endurance failed them. They felt the pride of creating another leading edge in the history of flight.

The Air Force was equally unenthusiastic about missiles, as Cliff Morris had learned in more than one drunken evening with Billy McCall and his fellow colonels. Hot pilots all, they were horrified by the thought of turning into the silo sitters of the sixties. They had put on their uniforms to fly planes and they refused to believe that a hunk of hurtling metal with a fire in its ass and a computer for a brain could replace them. The Warrior was their answer to the missile.

These were the emotions vibrating through Buchanan Aircraft and the Air Force in the weeks after the Warrior rollout. Billy and a half-dozen other pilots began putting the plane through a series of tests that made everyone more and more euphoric. Never had they seen a prototype perform more precisely on or above its specifications. Heat problems were nonexistent, thanks to the exotic metals such as titanium Frank had used for the skin. At supersonic speeds there was not a hint of flutter or buffet.

Cliff frequently flew with Billy and enjoyed coming home to tell Sarah and the kids that he had been to Chicago or Hawaii and back that day. They got to Chicago in less than an hour, to Hawaii in less than two. Frank gave him a model of the plane for Charlie. Cliff solemnly swore him not to show it to anyone, because it was still top secret. Charlie loved it, of course.

Sarah watched, unenthused. "Why are you making him a pilot?" she said. "He may not be any good at it." Charlie did not do well in math or science in school.

Cliff curtly informed Sarah he was not necessarily making the kid a pilot, he might be making him an airline or aircraft executive. "I hope not," Sarah said.

Since their disagreement in South America, they had been observing a Korean-style armed truce. It frequently broke down, with Charlie often the battleground. Cliff's solution was brutal but effective. He stayed away from home as much as possible, using his new title of sales vice president as his excuse. He spent weeks on the road schmoozing with Air Force contacts in the Pentagon and at Wright Patterson Air Force Base and engine honchos at Pratt & Whitney and General Electric, getting a line on the latest thinking in the field.

In Washington Cliff began picking up some very bad vibes on the future of the Warrior. Back at Edwards (formerly Muroc) Air Force Base, Billy McCall bitterly confirmed the rumors. "They're talkin' about junkin' it, just like they did the flyin' wing," Billy said. "The gutless son of a bitch you've got for a boss will probably go right along with it."

"Not if I have anything to say about it," Cliff said, remembering Adrian's pledge.

Cliff reported the bad semi-news to Adrian and was encouraged by his reaction. "We've got to keep that plane alive," Adrian said. "It represents our chance to take the world commercial market away from Boeing and Douglas when we go supersonic. I'll talk to some people at the White House."

Adrian had been chairman of the California Business Executives for Eisenhower in both elections. He had some chits to play. A week later, as the big plane roared through a series of high-altitude tests, he telephoned Cliff. "Get all the pertinent data together and reduce it to one page. That's the most Ike ever reads about anything. Be at LAX tonight. We're flying to Georgia to settle the Warrior eyeball-to-eyeball."

Twenty-four hours later, Cliff sat in a pine-paneled room at the Augusta National Golf Club, listening to Air Force General Nathan Twining, chairman of the Joint Chiefs of Staff, tell President Dwight D. Eisenhower why America needed Buchanan Aircraft's Warrior bomber. Beside Twining sat General Curtis LeMay. Behind them was a row of colonels and lieutenant colonels, including Billy McCall.

Adrian Van Ness and Frank Buchanan sat beside Cliff, ready to expand the one-page memorandum on the Warrior's performance envelope, if the president requested it. Dick Stone was also on hand with a briefcase full of financial information. Ike was flanked by his Secretary of Defense, Neil McElroy, and his science adviser, Dr. George Kistiakowski.

McElroy backed Twining with a strong plea for the Warrior, even if it never dropped a single nuclear bomb. He saw enormous possibilities for it as a reconnaissance plane, a military transport—and a commercial carrier. Cliff sensed

Frank Buchanan's tension, as the president listened, deadpan. "I'm allergic to using military funds to develop a commercial plane," Ike said.

The astonishment on most faces was unforgettable. For a moment Cliff was sure Frank Buchanan was going to ask Ike where he thought Boeing got the 707 jetliner. All you had to do was glance at their military planes to see the connection. Anyone in the room could have told this man, who was supposed to have access to every piece of pertinent information on any subject under the sun, that leapfrogging from military to commercial models and back again was what the American aircraft business had done since its foundation. But the power of the presidency silenced everyone, even Frank.

"Mr. President," said Air Force Chief of Staff General Thomas White, "We need this plane because we think a flexible defense is basic to the nation's security. A bomber is under the control of a man, not a computer, like a missile. It can be recalled. It can take evasive actions, improvise avenues of attack. It can force the enemy to deploy defenses that absorb a lot of his energy and attention."

"You've got Boeing's B-Fifty-twos for that job," Eisenhower said.

"They're subsonic, Mr. President. Their highest speed is six-twenty miles an hour. This plane can go three times that speed! We've got a plane that represents the greatest breakthrough in aerodynamics, in the whole science of flight, in two decades. We can't dismiss it. We can't afford to do that. The morale of the Air Force is at stake here!"

"It's your job to worry about the morale of the Air Force," Ike growled, his ground soldier's animus showing. "Mine is to worry about the economy, the morale of the whole country. It may be a great plane but a missile can do its job as well or better. That's all there is to it."

Cliff found himself thinking about Sarah's moral outrage at bribing half of South America to sell the Starduster and half of Europe to sell the Scorpion. Didn't this justify it? There sat the president of the United States, dismissing the greatest plane ever designed by an American. Consigning it to the junkyard. Where did that leave Boy Scout ideas like patriotism, loyalty, integrity? Adrian's attitude was the only one that made sense. You had to survive in this business by making your own rules.

Dr. Kistiakowski, Eisenhower's science advisor, now waded in. He dismissed General White's argument about the virtues of a plane versus a missile. If anything, the plane was more vulnerable. The CIA had recently reported alarming improvements in Soviet radar and antiaircraft missilery. They now had weapons capable of destroying a plane at 70,000 feet, no matter how fast it was going.

Cliff turned expectantly to his hero, General LeMay and his cohorts, expecting a furious counterattack. Instead, the generals and the colonels looked dumbfounded. The CIA had not said a word to them about such developments. It was Cliff's first glimpse of the way the American defense establishment operated, not as a team but as a collection of warring tribes.

The meeting broke up with the Air Force and Buchanan Aircraft in disarray.

"Now maybe you'll understand why I chopped up the Talus," Adrian said to Frank Buchanan as they rode back to their hotel in downtown Atlanta. "You see the stupidity, the arrogance, the infighting we have to deal with? The quality of the plane is irrelevant."

"I wish I'd taken my mother's advice and stuck to painting pottery," Frank said.

As they sat in the hotel bar gloomily sipping Scotch, Billy McCall joined them with General LeMay. "What's the next step?" Frank Buchanan asked. "Do we chop it up?"

"Like hell," LeMay said. "That goddamn plane is gonna fly or I'm gonna get court-martialed. That fucking infantryman knows as much about air strategy as I do about molecular biology. He's only gonna be in office another fourteen months. There's two political parties in this country and the other one is looking for an issue to beat Ike and his boy Tricky Dick next year. This plane could be it. What we want to know is, will you guys cooperate?"

"What do you want us to do?" Adrian said.

"Spend some money," LeMay said. "We're gonna bring congressmen out to fly in that bomber by the dozen. We want you to make sure they're well entertained."

"Can you protect us if Ike starts canceling other contracts?"

"We'll try," Lemay said. "But we can't guarantee anything."

Adrian looked at Cliff and Dick Stone. Was he remembering his pledge to fight for the plane? It was hard to read his impassive face. Was he thinking of his billion-dollar Starduster dream that would have made them independent of this gut-shredding political game? Probably. "We're with you," he said. "Cliff here will be in charge of the reception committee."

Cliff sat with Frank Buchanan on the flight back to California. "I'm amazed," Frank said. "I never thought Adrian had this much guts."

"He wants that supersonic airliner," Cliff said, trying to play peacemaker.

"So do I," Frank said ruefully, as if it pained him to agree with Adrian on anything.

First on LeMay's invitation list was the Senate Majority Leader, Lyndon Johnson, who was running for president. The tall, stooped Texan came to the Mojave factory on a swing through California to try to line up money and support. He had a memo in his hand when he got off his Air Force plane. "Is this bullshit or the God's honest truth?" he said, handing it to Cliff.

The memo was a hymn to the power and beauty of the Warrior. It declared the bomber was the issue that could make Johnson president. "The truth, Senator," Cliff said, raising his right hand. "I wrote it myself."

Cliff introduced Johnson to Billy McCall and they took a walk around the Warrior, as it crouched on its eight-wheeled landing gear in the desert sunshine. "That's the damndest plane I've ever seen," Johnson said. "Looks like a bald eagle with its neck stretched."

"Wait'll you fly in it, Senator," Billy said.

"You couldn't get me into that thing for all the gold in Fort Knox," Johnson said.

"I hope you have time to watch her go up," Cliff said.

Johnson shook his head. "I'm meetin' eleven oilmen in the Bel Air Hotel in exactly one hour. But this thing—it's got my support."

"We were hoping we could entertain you in other ways, Senator," Cliff said. "Buchanan's got some of the best-looking girls in Los Angeles on the payroll."

"Don't worry about me, son. I can get my own pussy anytime, anyplace," Johnson said.

The next day, the *Los Angeles Times* carried a story announcing Senator Johnson's "all-out backing" of the Warrior. "This is the greatest plane of the century," he said. "If we can't afford to build this plane to defend ourselves, we don't deserve to remain a free people. General Eisenhower is showing his age when he dismisses it as nothing more than a manned missile. I've flown in it. I've witnessed its miraculous technology in action. I am going to urge the Congress of the United States to fund it, no matter what the president says."

Cliff came home in a celebratory mood. He suggested cocktails on the patio before dinner and told Sarah the inside story of Johnson's endorsement. "We didn't even have to pay anyone overtime to entertain him," he said.

"You're still doing that?" she said, implying that Tama's stable should have died with her. "It's sickening to think a man like him is running for president. He sounds as bad as the Prince. Is his endorsement worth anything? You can't trust him, can you?"

"I'm getting awfully tired of your sermons on morality," Cliff said. "Did it ever occur to you that you're hopelessly out of your depth?"

"Did it ever occur to you that I might like a husband with some integrity, some genuine pride in what he's doing?"

"I've got pride," Cliff roared. For months he had tried to ignore the anger he had felt about her judgment on the Starduster sales. This new disapproval seemed to justify unleashing it with compound fury. "I've got all the pride I need. I'm proud of the plane. I'm proud of the way we're selling it. You don't build planes in a fucking convent school and you don't sell them in a church."

"Shhh, the children will hear you," Sarah said.

"Let them hear me!" Cliff shouted. "I'm not ashamed of what I'm doing. You're the one who should be ashamed, trying to undermine me with them, with myself. Trying to destroy my self-confidence. You're worse than your goddamn brother. He's sitting around telling everyone we're going down the tubes the same way you stupid limeys went, chopping up planes because the Russians found out how to shoot off a goddamn rocket."

She was trembling. Her eyes were swimming with tears.

"Maybe Derek—and I—can't help trying to tell you the truth. It's a bad habit among us stupid limeys."

He saw how impossible it was going to be to talk to her about anything from now on. "I'm sorry about the limey stuff. Let's forget it."

373

The next day at lunch Adrian congratulated Cliff for the Johnson endorsement. "You can expect a visit from the mick from Massachusetts within the month," he said.

Adrian was talking about Senator John F. Kennedy, who had recently announced he was a candidate for the White House. Showing the built-in prejudices of his Boston ancestry, Adrian found it hard to believe any Irish-American could be presidential material. Within two weeks, the Kennedy office called to arrange a visit. A week later, JFK bounded off another Air Force plane and seized Cliff's hand with an almost lethal grip. "Where is this superbomber?" he asked.

Cliff introduced the senator to Billy McCall and he promptly recited three of the four records Billy had set in high-altitude flight. Billy grinned. "You must have had a hell of a briefing."

In the desert sunshine Kennedy seemed almost unnaturally youthful. Compared to him the drooping Johnson looked like an old man. As they rode down the flight line, Kennedy said: "We've got a mutual friend who says hello."

"Who?"

"Your old tail gunner, Mike Shannon. He's handling my campaign in New Jersey. Doing a great job. He told me what a hell of thing you did over there. Going for another twenty-five missions."

Cliff managed to grope his way past the memory of Schweinfurt to embellish the myth. "That's what happens when you fall in love with an English girl."

"Still married to her?"

"More or less."

Kennedy grinned. They understood each other. They were men of the world. A good feeling. Cliff's hopes soared. Shannon was a good omen all by himself.

The Warrior awed Kennedy. He walked around it twice. "It flies?" he said.

"Want to find out for yourself?"

"You bet. Should I make out a will?"

"Not to worry," Billy said. "We've got a parachute for you."

"What happens when you bail out at mach three?" Kennedy asked as they strapped in and Billy turned the engines over.

"You lose your head," Billy said. "And your legs and your arms and anything else that happens to be stickin' out."

"Let's go," Kennedy said.

It was as wild a ride as Cliff Morris had ever had in the bomber. Billy sent her right up to the red line, 2,273 mph. He took evasive action against imaginary fighters, rolling right and left, diving from 70,000 to 50,000 feet. Kennedy never showed even a quiver of nerves. "Where the hell are we now?" he said, looking down at the clouds obscuring the earth beneath them.

"Over Alaska," Billy said. "We'll be home in an hour."

On the ground, Kennedy thanked them and said: "I hear you fellows are good at other kinds of entertainment."

"We do have that reputation, Senator," Cliff said.

"What have you got that I haven't seen?" Kennedy said. "Lyndon told me you fixed him up with the greatest night of his life. But that raunchy bastard has no taste worth mentioning."

To avoid duplication, Kennedy let Cliff flip through his address book. It was full of names of movie stars that left him momentarily speechless. "Johnson's girl was one of our best," Cliff said. "But she's a little old for you. I've got another one from the top of our A list—"

"I'll be in meetings till about eleven tonight. Tell her to come by my room at the Bel Air around midnight," Kennedy said.

"She'll be there," Cliff said.

Kennedy flew on to LAX and Cliff got on the phone to Adrian. He told him how much the senator liked the plane—and what he expected for the evening. "She can't be one of the secretaries, Adrian. Have you got anything special in reserve?"

"I've got someone in New York. She can be here by eight o'clock. One of Madame George's girls."

The next morning, Cliff phoned the Bel Air from his office and got through to Kennedy. "I just wanted to make sure everything went all right on the entertainment front."

"It was special, all right. Where did you find her? I'm putting her in the front of my book," Kennedy said.

"Are you going to make a statement about the plane?"

"It's being typed."

Cliff had barely hung up when his secretary somewhat nervously informed him there was a woman who wanted to see him. She had asked to see Adrian Van Ness, who was in a meeting and had shunted her to Cliff. Ten seconds later, Cliff was face to face with the angriest, most beautiful woman he had ever seen. Amalie Borne glared at him and said: "Mr. Morris. Did you have anything to do with arranging my introduction to the famous Senator Kennedy?"

"In a way."

"I have a message I wish you would deliver to Mr. Van Ness. I am not a whore. I resent being treated like a whore. If I am ever treated this way again by you or Mr. Van Ness I will retaliate with every resource at my disposal."

"What the hell happened?"

"I have no intention of discussing it with you. Simply give him my message—and also tell him I have bought a few things at the hotel. The bills will signify in a very small way my outrage. I knew in my heart I should have nothing to do with you Americans."

Later in the day Cliff found Adrian Van Ness and passed on Amalie's message, including the warning about bills of outrage. Adrian told him not to worry about it. He showed him a copy of the *Los Angeles Examiner* with Kennedy's endorsement of the Warrior on the front page. "She got results. No need to worry about the bills if we land the contract."

Cliff could not resist finding out what sort of bills Amalie had run up. He told the story to Dick Stone over lunch and asked him to check with the accounting department. He was amazed by Dick's reaction. "You approve using a woman like that to sell this goddamn bomber?"

"Christ, you sound like Lady Sarah. I spent two months in South America with Amalie. She didn't exactly impress me as a Girl Scout."

"I met her in Paris. She's telling the truth. She's not a whore!"

"She works for Madame George, doesn't she?"

"You have the moral sensibility of a hound dog, Captain."

"If I'm reading you right, you're making a big mistake, Navigator. Stay away from that broad. She doesn't play by the usual rules."

"We're not talking baseball!"

Cliff was amazed by Dick's fury. It was out of character. "Hey, listen. Between her and Cassie Trainor, when it comes to dames, your taste doesn't exactly run to Snow White. I don't get this moral outrage act. Calm down and find out how much she charged us for being treated like a whore. Maybe that'll change your mind."

Later that afternoon, a memo arrived from the assistant treasurer.

TO: Cliff Morris
RE: Entertainment expenses for the BX Bomber.

According to bills received today from the Ambassador Hotel, the following charges were made to the account labeled Adrian Van Ness Extraordinary: one white mink coat, $50,000. One Chinchilla coat: $85,000. One bracelet inlaid with diamonds and rubies, $65,000.

Yours Truly,
Richard Stone
Ex-Moralist

WOMAN TALK

In the splendid new terminal TWA had recently built at Los Angeles International Airport, Sarah's brother Derek looked shabby and prematurely old—a veritable image of his once powerful country. Derek was going back to England after less than six months in California. His wife and daughter had already departed. He had stayed to complete some assignments at Buchanan.

"I'm thinking of writing a book," Derek said. "Aborted. About all the wonderful planes our idiotic government canceled. What do you think?"

"Do it," Sarah said.

Perhaps it would get the disappointment out of his system. He was so bitter. It was the real reason he and his wife had soured on California. They had soured on their country, their lives. He said he was going back to renew the struggle for the lost planes. But he was really fleeing the casual abundance, the assumption of unlimited success that pervaded America. He told Sarah he was afraid he would end up hating Americans and he did not want to do that. He did not think they were bad people, on the whole. Just spoiled.

His decision to go home stirred special pain in Sarah. She had encouraged Derek to come to California. She had persuaded Cliff to get him a job. She saw now it was a desperate attempt to cling to her English self, that moral idealist who had said no to Cliff in Peru. But it had not worked. Derek was so bitter, his wife was so intimidated by California's casual manners and morals, they had only made Sarah realize how American she had become.

"I've been meaning to ask you—but never quite found the courage," Sarah said. "Was Father faithful? Or did he have his girlfriends, like so many aircraft people over here?"

"I think he sowed a few wild oats. Most men do. But I doubt if he did much in his later years. He didn't have time, for one thing." Derek smiled bleakly. "Painful to say, but the damn planes get more attractive than women in the long run."

His Boeing 707 began boarding passengers. "Come see us," he said, kissing Sarah on the cheek.

She stood on the terminal's sunny upper deck watching the plane take off. What would he have said if she suddenly announced she was going with him? She was leaving them all—American husband, daughters, son. She imagined herself yielding to some drastic impulse like that more and more often lately.

She hated the way she and Cliff had drifted apart again to become polite, slightly hostile strangers. She wondered if he was faithful during his weeks on the road. She doubted it but she did not have the energy, the anger, to accuse him.

She rode an escalator to the lower floor, oblivious to the faces flowing past her. "Sarah!" called a woman's voice.

It was her old friend Susan Hardy. She lived several blocks from them on Palos Verdes. Her husband Sam was ascending on the design side at about the same pace Cliff was rising on the sales side of Buchanan. Susan had the same wicked tongue and disillusioned view of men and California. She had continued snacking in the afternoons and drinking hard in the evenings. She was now at least fifty pounds overweight.

"I've got an hour before my flight," she said, hefting a bag. "Feel like a drink?"

"I'd love some tea."

Susan gave her a wry look. Sarah could almost hear her thinking: goody-goody. They found a restaurant that served both liquor and tea. At the last minute Sarah decided she would have a Scotch and soda after all.

"Where are you going?" she said.

"New York," Susan said. "I'm going home to talk it over with my mother. I think I've had it with Mr. Five by One."

That was one of her milder epithets for her husband. For a while Sam and Susan had made a kind of revue of their alienation. But it had grown less amusing as it became clear they really did not get along and the humor was mostly serious insult.

"I'm so sorry."

"Nothing to be sorry about. Under California's wonderful new community property law, I'm going to take him for fifty percent of everything he owns. Then we'll see how much he spends on his Las Tunas Canyon cunt."

Why did you marry him in the first place? Sarah wondered. Why didn't you try to hold him? Lose weight, control your tongue? Appalling. She was applying Tama's approach to this bitter, unhappy woman. But Sam Hardy was not Cliff Morris. He was a thin, balding man with pipe-stem arms and a scrawny neck.

Was she still in love with Cliff on some fundamental physical level that transcended the hostility, the alienation that flickered between them? She remembered the night of reconciliation, his whispering *you're my luck* when he was inside her. She had loved that idea. It appealed to the mystical streak in her soul.

"He met her at the Honeycomb Club," Susan continued. "He set her up in this house that cost twice as much as ours—"

Swept by self-reproach, Sarah tried to listen. A woman was sharing her pain and she was thinking about herself. Her egotism was shameful. Sarah could only shake her head while Susan told her about Sam Hardy's obsession with this beautiful woman.

"She can barely stand the sight of him, dates other men—but takes his money."

"How awful," Sarah said.

"It's not that bad," Susan said, knocking down the last of her Scotch in a barroom swallow. "I'd rather see a woman sticking it to the bastard that way than the kind of thing that usually happens. Have you heard about Madeleine West, one of Billy McCall's ex-girls? She followed him to Korea and back to this country. He wouldn't even look at her. She became a drunk, a streetwalker. Last month she drove her car into the desert, soaked the cushions with gasoline and struck a match. Died like a test pilot."

"My God."

"Some women are vulnerable, Sarah. I'm glad I'm not one of them. I hope you aren't. I haven't heard anything about Cliff lately. Have you got him under control?"

"I hope so," she said, gulping the rest of her drink.

Susan departed for New York. Sarah drove slowly home to Palos Verdes thinking about the woman who had immolated herself in the desert. They were all loathsome! Cliff, Adrian Van Ness, even Dick Stone. But none of them could equal the loathsomness of Lieutenant Colonel William McCall.

I was wrong, Tama whispered. For the first time Sarah began to suspect she knew what it meant.

SCHEHERAZADE AT WORK

"I arrived at the great man's room at midnight, as directed. He was on the telephone. He interrupted his call long enough to tell me to take a shower and lie down on the bed in the next room. Only the supposedly enormous importance of my visit persuaded me to stay. He was still talking on the phone when I came out of the bathroom. I lay there for ten minutes, listening to him debate with someone named Bobby whether or not to support your wonderful plane.

"Finally he strolled into the room, pulled down the sheet and examined me as if I was a cadaver on a slab. Five minutes later I was back in the bathroom. I took another shower. Never in my life have I felt so unclean! When I came out, he was on the telephone again, trying to arrange a date with another woman. He blew me a kiss as I departed."

Dick Stone lay beside Amalie Borne in the rose-and-gold bedroom of her Waldorf Towers apartment, listening to her describe her visit to John F. Kennedy. They were both naked. On the television screen at the foot of the bed Walter Cronkite and other talking heads were excitedly reporting the 1960 election returns. The race between Kennedy and Richard Nixon was still too close to call.

As far as Buchanan Aircraft was concerned, it was a no-lose situation. Kennedy's support for the Warrior had forced Nixon to abandon Eisenhower's cancellation and promise to build the plane. Nixon had stumped through California the day before the election, telling everyone the Warrior would provide an unbeatable defense against Soviet Russia—and 20,000 jobs.

On a chair in the corner was another briefcase full of James Madisons for the Prince, two million dollars' worth. He was arriving tomorrow to pick it up. After several false starts, intensive lubrication had persuaded the government of Italy to buy 150 upgraded Scorpions as fighter bombers. Frank Buchanan did not approve of burdening the plane with the extra weight—it would make it even more lethal to fly—but Adrian Van Ness decided not to turn down a hundred-million-dollar contract.

Dick was no longer worrying about the ethics of overseas bribery. He was more troubled by the moral perceptions of Amalie Borne. *I'm not a whore*, she had cried—and paid herself 175,000 dollars for the humiliation John F. Kennedy had inflicted on her. Dick's normally controlled, reflective self wavered in the violent emotions this woman stirred in him. He still believed the story she had told him in Paris was true. But tonight, after dinner at the Chambord with two bottles of wine, they had made love and she told him a different story.

She was the illegitimate daughter of Rudolf Hess, the Nazi leader who had fled Germany to England early in the war, supposedly to try to arrange a truce with England in return for a promise to depose Hitler. "That's why I prayed for your bombs to destroy Schweinfurt," she whispered in the shadowy bedroom, while taxis honked on Park Avenue forty floors below them.

She described growing up in a Germany that regarded her mother as twice a pariah, as the woman who had seduced Hess from the arms of his faithful wife—and urged him to go to England to try to rescue Europe from Hitler's madness.

Bewilderment sucked at Dick's brain. He was not psychologically equipped to deal with a woman like this. Was she simply crazy? Or was she compelled to create myths because the truth was too unbearable to remember?

"Now this Irishman, this case of satyriasis, is going to be your president," Amalie said, as the television cut to Kennedy's headquarters and he expressed confidence in eventual victory. "But you don't care, do you? As long as he funds your bomber."

"I care a great deal. I'm not a slave of the business. I have other hopes and dreams for myself, the country."

"What are they? Tell me? I collect illusions."

"Let's talk about us instead."

"Another illusion. How much money do you personally expect to earn from this bomber and other planes you hope to foist on the warmongers of this world?"

"I have no idea. I'll be happy with a reasonable amount."

"There is no such thing as a reasonable amount of money." Amalie pointed to the briefcase in the corner. "Is that a reasonable amount?"

"That depends on what you want to do with it."

"Would it be reasonable for us to take that two million dollars and disappear? Go to South America or Lebanon? Would you do that for me?"

"You'd spend it in six months and I wouldn't be able to make any more. We'd starve."

"I've starved before."

"Are you serious?"

"Are you?"

She was challenging him to abandon his career, his respectability, for her. He wanted her to do the abandoning, to join him in rational affection, reasonable happiness. How could he convince her it was possible? "I'm serious about loving you in the real world."

"You don't love anyone else? Some American or Jewish girl? I hear a frantic note in your voice, as if you were using the absurdity of loving me to escape her."

"I was fond of one woman I met in California. I still am. But it doesn't compare to my feelings for you."

"Does she want to marry you?"

"She did for a while. Now she's getting more interested in literature."

That was not entirely true. Cassie was teaching freshman English at Oxnard, a small private boarding school for girls north of Los Angeles. But she was still waiting for him to make up his mind about the step beyond saying he loved her. His excuses were growing more and more fraudulent. She knew something was wrong—and he did not have the courage to tell her what it was.

"Do you really see me as a housewife pushing a vacuum? Shopping at the supermarket? Changing diapers?" Amalie said.

"There are servants who can do those things."

"You don't have the courage to say yes. You knew I'd laugh in your face."

"I have the courage to love you. You're the one who doesn't have the courage to believe it."

"Take me again. Slower this time. You're the only man in years who's aroused me."

They made love while the dark TV screen stared at them like the blind eye of fate. An eye that refused to blink shut, no matter how many buttons were pushed or pulled. The touches, the kisses, were simultaneously sad and joyous. When it ended with the same small cry, Dick felt strong enough to challenge God himself. "Now tell me the truth. Admit what you said in Paris was true."

"How many times do I have to deny it? As your reward for that half hour of happiness, I'll finally tell you the truth. I'm not German. I'm Swedish. I was recruited by Madame George on a visit to Stockholm. I speak excellent German because that's what we were all taught in school until 1944, when it dawned on everyone that Hitler was going to lose. Then we started studying English. I devoted six months to mastering Heine because Madame George insists all of us must know at least one major writer so we can discuss him intelligently. Heine was perfect for me because he was Jewish. I was able to make so many German industrialists squirm as I quoted him. It never dawned on me until I met you that he could be used in other ways."

"Why would you take up such a life? What did it offer you?"

"Money—and a chance to prove to my father what I contended throughout the war—that the Swedes were the whores of Europe."

Dick turned on the television set. Nixon had carried California, proving his switch to the Warrior was good politics even if—according to rumor—it infuriated Eisenhower. But Kennedy was carrying another crucial state, Illinois. "It's going to be President Kennedy," Dick said.

"I'll say this much for him. He has a reasonable amount of money," Amalie said.

They went to sleep and Dick dreamt he was walking beside Amalie down an arcade of shops, immensely longer than the little alley in the Ambassador Hotel in Los Angeles. It stretched over the horizon and Amalie methodically bought fur coats and diamond bracelets and pearl necklaces. She piled them all in the trunk and front seat of a gleaming red Ferrari that he was driving slowly behind her as she went from shop to shop. At the fifth or sixth stop, as Amalie piled a dozen pairs of shoes in the narrow backseat, she pointed at him and burst out laughing. Dick looked down and realized he was naked.

In the morning, he awoke exhausted—and reckless. "Are you going back to Europe with the Prince?" he asked.

"I doubt it," Amalie said. "Our partnership is becoming precarious. He leaves me in New York more and more. I see now why he agreed so cheerfully to this apartment. Italian men are incapable of speaking directly. They delight in sending messages in invisible ink."

Dick casually extracted fifty thousand dollars from the Prince's money and announced they would go shopping to celebrate their engagement. Amalie was not amused. "You're teasing me," she said.

"I'm serious," he said. "I want to see you spend a reasonable amount of money."

"I know exactly where to go."

They strolled up Park Avenue to Fifty-fourth Street and east to an auto showroom that featured Italian sports cars. A red Ferrari sat in the window, a gleaming creature so sleek, so curved, so powerful looking, it was a fusion of masculine and feminine. Dick bought it for 45,000 dollars and an hour later drove it up Park Avenue to Ninety-sixth Street. Amalie drove it back to the Waldorf Towers and parked it in the garage.

Madness. He had crossed some sort of boundary, exceeded some kind of altitude limit with this woman. He was no longer Richard Stone, the astute guardian of Buchanan's finances. He was no longer the rabbi's son, with ethical principles drilled into his bones. Maybe it had something to do with knowing too much about everything. About the plane business, about the new president of the United States, about Amalie Borne.

Two hours later the Prince arrived, looking somewhat tired. He explained that negotiating bribes with Italians was the most exhausting process in the world. There was always someone else to be paid—cousins, uncles, in-laws. But the deal was still set, if Buchanan agreed to a new wrinkle. The planes would be assembled in Italy.

Dick saw no objection but he checked with Cliff Morris to make sure. Cliff cleared it with Adrian and called back. "Nixon just conceded," he said. "Kennedy's the president. I think it's great. I trust him more than Tricky Dick."

"Yeah," Dick said with obvious unenthusiasm.

"Still brooding about Amalie? Have you seen her?"

"She's right here," Dick said.

"Ask her what she thinks of sleeping with JFK now. She may be getting invitations to the White House."

"She says JFK's got your problem. Satyriasis."

"Fuck you."

In the next room, the Prince was looking confused. He had just finished counting the money. "We seem to be a little short, Dick. With the added costs I've mentioned, my share of this arrangement will barely pay my barber."

"It must have been a mistake at the bank," Dick said. "I'll take care of it today. They have a branch in New York."

"Please enter it in the books as such," the Prince said. "I would not want to give Adrian the least impression of dishonesty."

"Don't worry. I'll take full responsibility."

"I'm to stay here in this dreadful city," Amalie said. "My lord and master thinks I will be happier here. He promises to return in a month. In the meantime I must rely on you for entertainment, Mr. Stone."

"I'll do my best," Dick said.

The Prince smiled. But his eyes betrayed a certain lack of amusement. "Madame George sends you a thousand kisses," he said to Amalie.

"Tell her I return every one," Amalie replied.

"She's her favorite," the Prince explained to Dick. "Ever since the war, no one has come close to her in Madame's affection. Others come—and often go abruptly. Madame can be severe."

"Our love is mutual—and undying," Amalie said, informing the Prince that his threat had failed.

The Prince began talking about the significance of Kennedy's victory. It would mean billions for Buchanan on the Warrior bomber, of course. But it was the Warrior's descendant, the supersonic airliner, that the Prince was urgently awaiting. In other respects, he wished Nixon had won. The Republicans guaranteed American stability. The Democrats were a party of political adventurers.

Dick barely listened to the Prince's monologue. He gazed at Amalie's beautiful face with its impenetrable glaze of smiling disillusion and told himself love was there behind the mask. Love that would somehow outshine the diamonds and restore the wonder and pity of that night in Paris. Love that would enable him to be an American and a Jew in a way that was beyond the gift of Cassie Trainor or any other all-American girl.

CAPITOL PUNISHMENT

"In the councils of government," President Dwight D. Eisenhower droned, "we must guard against the acquisition of unwarranted influence, whether sought or unsought, by the military industrial complex. The potential for the disastrous rise of misplaced power exists and will persist. We must never let the weight of this combination endanger our liberties or democratic processes."

"The son of a bitch," Adrian Van Ness said. "He'll make me a registered Democrat yet."

It was January 7, 1961. Dick Stone and Cliff Morris were in Adrian's office, along with a half-dozen other Buchanan executives, watching Dwight Eisenhower's farewell address to the nation. General Curtis LeMay had told them not to miss it. He said the word was out that Ike was going to get even with the Air Force for defying him on the Warrior bomber.

"That idea is going to haunt us," Adrian said. "Every loudmouth who wants to take a cheap shot at the aircraft business will use Ike as his authority."

Cliff was inclined to be skeptical. "Our guys are in the White House and he isn't," he said. "Isn't that what counts?"

"Let's see if they're our guys before we start celebrating," Adrian said.

Again, Cliff put Adrian's attitude down to his WASP prejudices against seeing an Irish-American win the presidency. Cliff was equally unimpressed by Dick Stone's loathing for Kennedy. So he wasn't the world's most considerate lover. Cliff suspected a lot of Dick's antipathy was ethnic rivalry. He was sore because a Jew didn't get there first.

The prospect of a billion-dollar contract for the Warrior was not the only reason Cliff liked Jack Kennedy. His election also had an unexpected warming influence on his marriage. Suddenly there was this wonderful idealist in the White House, telling everyone in Churchillian accents that it was time to do battle for freedom around the world. Suddenly the Warrior, even the Scorpion, did not seem quite so tainted by Adrian Van Ness's amoral methods.

Naturally, Cliff did not say a word to Sarah about Kennedy's sex life. He had stopped sharing almost everything like that with her. He seldom had anything to say about his work, period. She seldom asked about it. Their marriage was polite, tranquil—and empty.

Cliff did not worry about it very much. He was working too hard. There were always some congressmen or their aides in town to inspect the Warrior and enjoy the pleasures of Los Angeles, escorted by several of Buchanan's willing secretaries. Adrian supplemented midweek entertainment with weekend cruises aboard an ultramodern 150-foot yacht, the SS *Rainbow*.

On the night of JFK's inauguration, Cliff summoned Sarah and the kids around the TV screen to watch the news reports of Kennedy's speech. He had heard it in full at work—everyone was hoping he might say something about the Warrior. Cliff was genuinely moved by Kennedy's peroration, telling the world that a new generation of Americans was taking charge of the country, a generation that would pay any price, bear any burden, in the defense of freedom.

At work, everyone had cheered and slapped each other on the back, assuming that the price included a billion dollars for the Warrior. At home, hearing it again, the speech had a much more personal meaning. The hundreds of hours of boredom and fear in the *Rainbow Express* acquired purpose. Cliff Morris had helped to create this triumphant generation that was taking charge of the world. He held Sarah's hand and said: "Doesn't that make you proud of being an American?"

"Yes," Sarah said. "I think I finally feel like one."

Her expression reminded Cliff of the way she looked in England during the war—simultaneously innocent and sexy. That night, as they went to bed, he reached out to her and she responded to his kiss in the old yearning way.

"Maybe we ought to try to forget some things I've said—and you said," Sarah whispered.

"That sounds great to me," Cliff said.

For a little while they were lovers again.

In the morning at breakfast, Charlie asked Cliff if JFK was a better president than Eisenhower. "He's better than Ike and Truman and Roosevelt," Cliff said. "And maybe better than Lincoln and Washington and Jefferson too. He's going to tell the Russians where to go and he'll give us the money to build the greatest plane in the world."

"The Warrior?" Charlie said. "Any chance of a ride in that thing, Dad?"

"Maybe."

"I've made up my mind. I definitely want to be a pilot."

Cliff glanced uneasily at Sarah, fearing the abrupt end of their newfound harmony. But she only smiled and said: "You'll change your mind a lot about what you want to be before you're twenty-one."

Everything was possible in John F. Kennedy's America.

One week later, Cliff Morris sat in a plane to Washington, D.C., rereading with disbelief a story in the *Los Angeles Times*. KENNEDY ADMINISTRATION CANCELS NEW BOMBER. With sarcasm dripping from every word, Adrian Van Ness had told him to find out what happened—and see if there was any possibility of rescuing the situation. Buchanan had kept ten thousand workers on the payroll, sitting around doing almost nothing, while they waited for Kennedy to get elected and the billion for the bomber to arrive.

By four o'clock Cliff was in Curtis LeMay's office in the Pentagon listening to his bitter explanation. "It's the gang of Harvard whiz kids Kennedy's installed at the Pentagon," he said. "They put the data into a fucking computer and it came out *m-i-s-s-i-l-e*. You won't believe these double-domed characters. They wear glasses eight inches thick and they're about thirty years old. They sit there telling Curtis LeMay he doesn't know what he's talking about."

"I'm here to find out if we should lay off ten thousand workers tomorrow," Cliff said. "It's costing us about ten million bucks a month to keep them playing cards and shooting craps on the assembly line."

LeMay chomped on a cigar and growled: "You keep right on paying those guys. You can get it back from the contract. We're gonna fly that bomber. I don't give a goddamn what a bunch of fucking Ph.D's who never saw a war say. We'll go up to the hill and get it this spring. You ever met Carl Vinson?"

Cliff shook his head. He had heard of the legendary chairman of the House Armed Services Committee, who was now eighty years old. "Truman wanted to make him secretary of defense," LeMay said. "Old Carl turned him down. He said he'd rather run things from where he sat. He wants that fucking bomber. But the first thing you've got to do is build some of it in Georgia."

"Why?" Cliff said.

"Because that spells *j-o-b-s*," LeMay said.

No further explanation was necessary. It was obviously the Air Force's answer to *m-i-s-s-i-l-e-s*. "That's a big decision," Cliff said. "I'll have to talk to Adrian Van Ness."

"Talk fast. We haven't got a day to waste," LeMay said. "While you're at it, talk to him about opening a plant in Oklahoma."

"Why?"

"Because Bobby Kerr, the head of the Senate Finance Committee, is from the fucking state. If necessary we'll throw in another Air Force base to make the bastard delirious."

"Can I make the call from here?" Cliff said.

He sat down outside LeMay's office and called Adrian. He got the idea instantly. "We'll be ready and eager to open plants in Georgia and Oklahoma. The extraordinary size of the Warrior program will require that sort of decentralization. You might mention that there'll be a vast expansion in the future, when we go from the bomber to the supersonic transport."

"I'll do that. In the meantime, ship me Dick Stone and a ton of data on the plane. We'll start selling it on Capitol Hill tomorrow morning."

Dick arrived that night with the data. They headed for the White House, where their old crewmate Mike Shannon now had an office in the West Wing, in charge of Congressional liaison. The pintsized Shannon had become a scaled-down Jack Kennedy, complete with the haircut and one-button suit. Everything but a Boston accent. They adjourned to the Jockey Club, the best restaurant in Washington, and compared notes on the last fifteen years of their lives.

Shannon had married Teresa, the girl of his lovelorn *Rainbow Express* dreams and found out she was a nun. He had stashed her and four kids somewhere in Maryland. "How the hell is Lady Sarah?" Shannon asked Cliff. "You still getting it on with her?"

"About as much as you are with Sister Teresa," Cliff lied. He could never resist being one of the boys. "Stone here's the only guy who's done it right. Still a bachelor."

"That's because he's a Jewish atheist. No worries about sin," Shannon said.

"Is that right?" Cliff asked, remembering Dick's fury over Amalie Borne.

"Just guilt. Jews don't even have to commit sins to feel guilty," Dick said.

They finally got around to the bomber. Shannon explained it all very carefully to them. The president hated the idea of canceling it. He was Irish and a promise was a promise. But Robert McNamara, the secretary of defense, was not Irish in spite of his name. He had canceled the plane without clearing it with Kennedy. That had left the president in a very negative frame of mind.

"If you can get some support in Congress, you won't find anyone in the White House fighting you. Do you get the idea?" Shannon said.

"How about a little fighting in our favor?"

"I might manage some guerrilla stuff," Shannon said, with a knowing grin.

"To the *Rainbow Express*," Cliff said, raising his Scotch.

There was a split-second of hesitation before Shannon and Dick Stone raised their glasses. Cliff realized they were both remembering Schweinfurt. They were avoiding his eyes. Especially Navigator Shylock. *You son of a bitch, you wouldn't be here if it wasn't for me.* Cliff almost shouted the words in his face.

Shannon inadvertently rescued them. "Jack wonders if you've still got that dame he met in L.A. on the payroll. Amalie Borne? Can you fix him up?"

Cliff smiled wryly at Dick. "Sure. If she's willing."

"Let me know. We've got a back door to the White House Jackie hasn't found yet."

At the hotel, Cliff got on the telephone to Adrian Van Ness, even though it was 4:30 A.M. in California. Could Amalie Borne be persuaded to spend another night with JFK?

"I don't think there's a woman alive who can resist the most powerful man in the world," Adrian said. "Just in case, tell her she can buy any fur coat in the store at Bergdorf's if she keeps him contented."

Cliff called Amalie at 7:45 A.M. the next day. "I'll be delighted to see your president," Amalie cooed. "Tell him to call me about arrangements."

Adrian was right, as usual. Where did that leave Dick Stone? Cliff decided to tough it out with him. At lunch he said: "I called your dream girl in New York. She said she'd be delighted to see JFK again."

"I'm not surprised," Stone said. "She collects examples of how low people can sink. Especially Americans."

"I don't get it," Cliff said, although to some extent he understood it all too well. It was not that different from Sarah's disgust with the way they did business overseas.

"She's in despair," Dick said. "She lives in a state of despair."

"She sure as hell doesn't act that way."

"That's one of the interesting things about despair. I've been reading up on it. It's totally different from depression. It's liberating. Once you give up all hope, you're free to do anything."

"Women are nuts," Cliff said.

"Maybe we're the crazy ones. We just happen to be running the show," Dick said.

Each day before Cliff hit the congressional trail, he called Sarah in Los Angeles. Each day he heard loneliness eating away the feelings they had rediscovered the night of Kennedy's inauguration. It was very confusing and upsetting. He was here in Washington because Jack Kennedy had broken his promise to build the Warrior. Covertly, he was helping the Kennedys sabotage McNamara to build a plane that the secretary of defense, theoretically Curtis LeMay's commander, had canceled. It was double-crosses inside double-crosses, with a touch of mutiny.

Maybe Dick Stone was right. Maybe they were the crazy ones. But the plane had to fly. Everything depended on it. Every day, Adrian Van Ness was on the telephone reminding him of that fact.

Sometimes Billy McCall flew in to join Cliff and Dick Stone to see a congressman or senator who was into airplanes and wanted to talk to the famous test pilot. At the end of the day they regrouped in Cliff's room at the Shoreham Hotel and considered how to entertain themselves for the evening. Frequently Mike Shannon joined them and recruited some girls from his little black Congressional liaison book for fun and games.

In his head, Cliff resisted and regretted the idea in advance. But it was impossible to explain without getting a sneer from Billy and squawks of disbelief from Shannon and mocking smiles from Dick Stone, who seemed to take savage pleasure in watching him go along with the gang. At times Cliff almost believed

Dick knew he did not want to do it and was forcing him to play the game by Kennedy rules in revenge for Amalie.

Sometimes, in bed with one of Shannon's stable at the very moment of climax, Cliff would be seized with drunken regret. He would whisper a plea that he wished Sarah could hear: *I'm sorry*. At other times he remembered the night in Lima and exulted in the impersonality, the virtuosity of the fucking; it was a defiant throwback to his bachelor youth.

Meanwhile, Mike Shannon was assuring him that they were making excellent progress in their double-cross campaign on Capitol Hill. More and more congressman and senators were starting to wonder if McNamara knew what he was doing when he canceled the Warrior. Mike was in there pouring subtle salt on the tails of the more difficult birds. General Curtis LeMay also had a swarm of lesser generals and colonels working at it.

Then came the morning Cliff opened his copy of the *Washington Post* to find the front page black with disastrous headlines. President Kennedy had tried to overthrow Fidel Castro. The expedition was a fiasco. The attacking force was barely 2,500 men and their only air support were some World War II Douglas Invader bombers that Castro's jets shot down in about twenty seconds.

Cliff called Mike Shannon to find out what happened. His voice shook as he told the story. "Adlai Stevenson talked the president into canceling the air support for those poor bastards. The plan called for a squadron of Navy jets to go in there and blow Fidel's planes away. All he had were some T-Thirty-three jet trainers. Without them, the Invaders could've bombed the shit out of Castro's troops and turned the whole battle around."

Shannon ranted on about the influence of Stevenson and his circle of "fucking idealists" in the Kennedy administration. Cliff had more important things on his mind. "What does this do to our hearings on the Warrior?"

Shannon told him to forget about the Warrior for a year. It would take them at least that long to regain their leverage with Congress. "We're still spending ten million a month on those cardplayers and crapshooters in California," Cliff said.

"Give me a couple of days. I'll find something for you."

Shannon set up a lunch with Carl Vinson and a congressman from Iowa, whom Mike called "the Creature." He turned out to be the man who had stood beside the second Starduster's grave and blamed it all on the FAA and bad propellers. The eighty-year-old Vinson was sympathetic to Buchanan's plight in a courtly if somewhat fuzzy way. He told the Creature to get out the current list of defense projects and see if there was something in it for Buchanan.

Cliff took one look at the list and almost started to palpitate. It was a preview of what the Air Force, the Navy and the Marines were going to buy for the next five years. Skimming it, Cliff saw a hundred-million-dollar Navy request for ninety antisubmarine planes. The aircraft had to be big enough to carry a couple of tons of electronic gear, fast enough to get out to the deepest part of the ocean in a hurry, and slow enough to all but hover over the trouble spot.

"We've got a commercial plane that fits that description as if it was designed for it. The Starduster."

"One of them crashed in my district!" the Creature said. "We can't send our boys in blue out to sea in an unsafe plane."

Cliff labored to point out that the redesigned Starduster had been flying for two years without a crash. The Creature continued to agitate. Finally, Chairman Vinson said: "Down, boy. Let's have a couple of admirals decide how safe it is."

The Creature departed and Carl Vinson poured Cliff a glass of the best bourbon he had ever tasted. "Don't pay any attention to that fellow," he said. "He ain't worth a cup of warm spit. But he knows how to get elected and you've got to deal with him."

Vinson sipped his bourbon and studied Cliff with eyes that were no longer fuzzy. "Son," he said, "don't ever be ashamed to ask for money to build a good plane. This is the richest country in the world. Also the most thoughtless, wasteful, foolish. No one can imagine the United States of America losin' a war. But I can 'cause I come from a country that lost one. My Daddy fought for the Confederacy. He used to sit and talk by the hour about how sure they were that the pusillanimous Yankees could never lick 'em."

Congressman Vinson poured himself more bourbon. "You know how much this country spends on alcohol?"

Cliff shook his head.

"Ten billion a year."

"On cigarettes?"

Cliff shook his head.

"Seven billion a year."

"On hair spray and cosmetics and jewelry?"

Cliff shook his head.

"Seven billion a year."

On and on went the list of trivialities on which Americans spent billions, Vinson scribbling down the numbers and sipping his bourbon. Finally, without benefit of an adding machine, he added it up: fifty billion dollars a year.

"That's why it don't bother me much to spend a couple of hundred million on a good plane."

The next day, Cliff got an urgent call from the Creature. He said he had found new evidence that the Starduster was still unsafe. Cliff raced to the Congressional Office building in a cab, taking Dick Stone along for a backup.

In his office, the Creature announced he did not really have any hard evidence. In fact, his mind could easily be changed. "I've been hearin' rumors about a certain tall dark beauty Jack Kennedy's sneakin' into the White House. French. She does things only the French know how to do. How about fixin' me up for a night with her?"

Cliff contemplated the congressman's sallow, wide-pored cheeks with their overlay of five o'clock shadow. His chest was sunken; his wrists had odd bony knobs. He brushed at a cowlick and grinned expectantly.

"I wish I could do it," Cliff said. "But she's gone back to Europe. I think Jackie got wise to her. Jack told her to get out of the country for six months."

In the corridor, after hearing the congressman whine ominously about the Starduster for another ten minutes, Dick Stone said: "Thanks."

"Forget it," Cliff said. "We've got old Carl Vinson on our side. He tows that asshole around so he won't have to keep taking out his glasses to read the fine print on things."

Within two weeks, a team of admirals flew to Los Angeles to look at the Starduster. Within another month, Buchanan had the contract and Cliff and Dick Stone were splitting a fifty-thousand-dollar bonus. Cliff decided to fly home to celebrate. Dick preferred New York—and Amalie. He really had a bad case. Cliff gave him Buzz McCall's old lecture about not letting any woman get to you but it was a waste of breath.

Poor Buzz was not a very good example for anyone these days. He got drunk at lunch and stayed that way in his back office, where a few old loyalists visited him pretending to ask his advice, trying to make him feel like he was still in charge. Adrian kept talking about firing him but he was afraid Frank Buchanan would quit with him. Frank still blamed the Starduster crashes on Adrian. He said Buzz was an innocent victim.

Cliff boomed into Los Angeles aboard a 707 feeling ten feet tall about the bonus and the new career for the Starduster. The kids greeted him with yells of glee. Sarah's smile was more wary. What was wrong now? Out on the patio, he sipped his martini and tried to find out. "You look like you've got some news you don't want to tell me," he said.

"In a way, I have. Billy McCall is going to marry Victoria Van Ness."

For a moment the yard, the blue California sky above them seemed to contract to the cockpit of a spinning plane. How could she sit there smiling in that ridiculous way when she had just told him his career was ruined, his dream of becoming Buchanan's president was shredded, his life was a smashed burning wreck? Was she *glad*?

"Don't be afraid. We can handle it," Sarah said.

Her eyes were unnaturally bright. She looked happy in an odd wild way that Cliff had never seen before. That night in their bedroom Sarah made all the moves. She was as inventive as Cassie Trainor at the crest of her Honeycomb days. "Stay calm, keep your head. We'll destroy them. I *promise* you," she said, as he came.

They were together again. Cliff could sense a current flowing between them. But it was different from the old soaring tenderness. This current had a dark acrid quality; it cleared the passages, like Inverness Scotch. It would take Cliff a long time to figure out what it was.

SERPENTS IN THE SKY

As he came.

As she came.

And *went*. Went went went went

Out of that familiar bedroom. Away from the soothing sound of the Pacific surf.

Went went went went streaking over the mountains into the desert. Metempsychosis. The transfer of the soul. It was happening as Sarah came and went.

She was in the desert becoming another woman. Leaving behind a different woman in her husband's arms. A soulless woman. Her soul, the source, the vessel of love and hate, her soul had entered Victoria Van Ness. Everything you read and see and hear from that woman henceforth belongs to Sarah, *is* Sarah. At least, that is what Sarah henceforth wanted to believe.

With the men and their endless deceptions of themselves and each other, Sarah had merely penetrated their souls, peered dispassionately into the accumulated darkness and confusion. But with Victoria it was entrance, becoming, acquiring. There was no alternative. Otherwise, Sarah could not have tolerated the idea, much less the reality, of Billy McCall marrying Victoria Van Ness.

It began in the desert, in the doorway of a little shack, not much bigger than the Watch Office at Bedlington Royal Air Force Base where Sarah had talked to pilots in distress. Into the boxy little building she had walked to discover Billy McCall and Victoria Van Ness. Behind Sarah in the desert sun stood a covey of Congressmen and their wives, *oohing* and *aahing* at the sight of the Warrior's winged immensity.

Sarah had followed Mike Shannon into the shack, unable to resist another encounter with Billy. She was wearing a thousand-dollar violet Dior suit. Her hair had been done, her face and body oiled and massaged that morning at Monsieur Jacques, the best beauty salon on Rodeo Drive. Earlier in the morning the scale had said 110—exactly what she weighed when she broke the altitude record with Billy ten years ago. She wanted him to see all of her, she wanted him to eat another piece of his frozen heart.

Instead she found him telling Shannon he could not entertain the congressmen and their wives in the Warrior. He was taking a vacation—his first in years. He was going to Catalina Island for the weekend. Billy had turned to Victoria Van Ness and asked her if she liked Catalina.

Victoria glared at Sarah, a paradigm of defiance, of naïveté, of shame. "I love it," she said.

That was when Sarah divided. When the soulless part of her fled back to her bedroom to create inventive sex with her bewildered husband and her soul entered Victoria, became her willful, innocent, angry, driven self on the way to immolation and despair. Turning away in anguish, Sarah's eyes had found a distant Joshua tree. She had raised her metaphorical arms like that dumb plant and sworn eternal hatred and revenge.

Is all that perfectly *clear?* Now we can tell how it happened calmly, consecutively, the way stories are told.

The romance began aboard the SS *Rainbow*, the yacht Adrian had bought to entertain congressmen, Air Force generals, airline executives, and other visiting VIP's in the struggle to keep the Warrior alive. Adrian pressed Victoria Van Ness into service as a hostess. Amanda's unpredictable, mostly hostile tongue made her an impossible candidate for this crucial task. She was liable to say almost anything about Adrian, the plane, or the country. When she was aboard, Frank Buchanan became almost as unmanageable.

Victoria had come home from England a troubled young woman. She was very intelligent but her education had been almost entirely literary. Adrian had supervised it from a distance, trying to keep her mind uncontaminated by the hatred of capitalism that infected so much of British academic life. He wanted her to be a cultivated woman in the tradition of the previous century, indifferent to politics and business. It was an impossible dream and he did not come close to achieving it.

Instead, he got an amateur poet with an intense interest in business and politics, which she understood in a literary, emotional way, like most British (or American) members of the intelligentsia. Adrian, no longer a member of the intelligentsia, barely noticed this. He was far more satisfied with something else Victoria had brought home—4.5 million dollars from Clarissa's will.

Adrian was somewhat nonplussed to discover that there was a clause in the will forbidding Victoria ever to loan a cent of her inheritance to her father. Adrian explained it away (he thought) as an old, long-since-irrelevant quarrel. A father with a company grossing a half billion dollars a year hardly needed to worry about borrowing money. He did not know that while he was at work, Amanda told Victoria the clause proved his own mother did not trust Adrian. It was another proof—Amanda was always looking for proofs—of his hatefulness.

After five years in England Victoria found herself a stranger in a strange land. Los Angeles in the late fifties and early sixties changed faster in a half decade than most cities changed in a half century. Her friends were scattered; new dances, new music, new styles, pervaded the shops and nightclubs and beaches. Even more disturbing was the discovery that her father wanted her to be his companion, his social colleague, in her mother's place—as well her mother's keeper.

This was not a conscious decision on Adrian's part. Such things seldom are. He was living from week to week, month to month, like most people, hoping Amanda might somehow become the docile, polite wife he had envisioned when Dr. Farber recommended the lobotomy. Ninety percent of his time and emotions were consumed by the travails of the Warrior and other more mundane crises.

Buchanan had become a company racked by labor problems. Without Buzz McCall to keep the unions in line, there was a walkout a day on the assembly lines. The engineering department was also in chaos. Many of Buzz's best people deserted to Boeing and Douglas, who were building the commercial planes Adrian hungered to produce.

There was no hope of Buchanan penetrating the airline market now. Boeing's 707s ruled the transcontinental and transatlantic skies, with Douglas's DC8s not far behind. Buchanan was trapped inside the military industrial complex—unless the Warrior flew and catapulted them into the lead for the next-generation airliner, a supersonic jet that could cross the Atlantic in three hours and the Pacific in six. The possibility sat inside the angular, beaknosed fuselage of the Warrior. Is it so surprising that a man as driven as Adrian found it difficult to think coherently about his daughter's problems?

One of the most frequent weekend guests aboard the SS *Rainbow* was Lieutenant Colonel William McCall. Senators and congressmen and their aides liked to chat with a man who had flown planes higher and faster than anyone else—and was a Korean War ace in the bargain, with fifteen Migs on his escutcheon. Billy did not enjoy being ogled and verbally pawed this way. The more he saw of legislators swilling Buchanan's booze and gorging themselves on the gourmet meals served by the *Rainbow*'s French chef, the more disgusted he became with the government of the United States of America.

The *Rainbow* usually cruised off Baja California. Sometimes Billy would fly a Scorpion down to an airstrip the Pentagon, with the cooperation of the Mexican government, had carved out of the rugged desert on that arid peninsula and give the VIPs a demonstration of his readiness to risk death at supersonic speeds, sending the plane spinning, rolling, looping around the sky like the aerial equivalent of a dervish.

It was hardly surprising that Victoria Van Ness, a lonely young woman with a lifelong fascination for planes, would soon find Billy McCall the most attractive man she had ever seen. He seemed to be all the things her smooth, loquacious, lying father was not. Fearless, dedicated, indifferent to wealth (Frank Buchanan told her a lieutenant colonel made less money than a riveter on Buchanan's assembly line)—all the attributes an idealist could admire without reservations.

One night in the spring of 1962, the SS *Rainbow* cruised serenely through the placid waters of the Gulf of California. In the main cabin, six congressman were dining on pâté de foie gras and Alaska king crab. The one even his fellow congressmen called the Creature was drunk and pawing the hapless secretary Adrian Van Ness had assigned as his escort. On deck, Lieutenant Colonel Billy McCall picked out the constellations: the Great Bear, the Little Dipper. A full moon cast a swath of gold from the horizon to the hull of the ship.

Beside him Victoria Van Ness said: "Thinking of landing in a crater up there, Colonel?"

"Nope. Too old," Billy said. "I volunteered but they turned me down."

They were talking about the race to beat the Russians to the moon, which

President Kennedy had announced as one of the objectives of his administration. "That's hard to believe. I would think they'd want the best pilots they could find," Victoria said.

"They turned Chuck Yeager down too."

"How old are you?"

"Thirty-nine."

Victoria Van Ness sighed. "I'll be thirty this year. Now, *that's* old."

Billy laughed. "I know what you mean."

They were silent for a moment. "I guess you can't stand the congressmen either," Victoria said.

"They're pretty boring. But it's part of my job to stand them, these days."

"They disgust me. It's like watching pigs at feeding time. How much did it cost to fly them out here?"

"Oh, counting my salary and my copilot's and engineer's and the fuel— maybe fifty thousand dollars."

"The more I learn about the plane business, the less I like it."

"How about the planes? Do you like them?"

"I love planes. I love flying. The Warrior is the most awesomely beautiful aircraft I've ever seen."

"You're all right, then. If you didn't care about the planes, I'd know we were in trouble."

"Why?"

"Aren't you going to own the company someday?"

"I have no idea what arrangements Daddy—my father—has made in his will. I'm not a businesswoman. Unlike you, my future is a question mark."

"What's my unquestioned future?"

"Someday you'll be chief of staff of the Air Force."

"Not a chance. They've got kids coming out of the Air Force Academy who know twice as much as I'll ever know about engineering or aerodynamics."

"You're teasing me. Frank Buchanan says you know as much about airplane design and engines as anyone in the country."

"Seat-of-the-pants stuff. I can't talk the game. Except maybe some folk wisdom like, 'if it looks like a good plane it probably will be a good plane.' "

"Would it surprise you if I told you I love you?"

There was a very long pause. The ultimate pilot, the man who always knew exactly what to do in a flight emergency, did not know what to say, think, feel.

"I know you prefer beautiful women. Am I wasting my breath?"

"What do you mean when you say you're in love with me? What's it like?"

"I think about you day and night. I have trouble sleeping. I have a sudden impulse to smash windows. Or burst into tears. I write poetry about you."

"Let's hear some of it."

Victoria turned away from him and spoke the words to the dark Pacific's starry sky.

"There are too many horizons.
The sky keeps bending into question marks

While the clouds proceed, somnolent as cattle
Into the pastures of the night.
In the farthest stratosphere, a man conspires
Lonely as a hero in a myth.
Jung says we must go beneath the rainbow.
I say beyond it
Always always always beyond it
Where angels laugh at folly
And weep genuine tears."

"Would you repeat that?" Billy said.

Victoria recited the poem again.

"That's beautiful," he said. "That's almost as beautiful as flying. Have you flown in the Warrior?"

"No."

"We'll see if we can work it out. It's the most fantastic experience I've ever had."

"I've loved you for a long time, girlishly. You're extremely handsome and you make planes like the Scorpion do miraculous things in the air. But since I've come home, I've stopped being girlish. You're the only man in this business besides Frank Buchanan who seems to have retained a shred of integrity. You smile and talk flying with slobs like the congressmen and crooks like my father but I sense you're as lonely as I am."

"You've got that all wrong," Billy said.

Of course Victoria had most of it right but it was too painful for Billy to admit. At thirty-nine, he was heading into middle age without thinking about it, relying on the same instinctual skills that had enabled him to survive in the sky. He had no children and no special woman in his life. The result was a profound loneliness. Billy dealt with it stoically, the way a warrior deals with pain.

His lifestyle simultaneously deepened and disguised his loneliness. His good looks had weathered well. There were bleak Gary Cooperish lines in his face and skeptical wrinkles on his brow. He remained irresistible to women of all ages. His enthusiasm for flying them had not significantly diminished. A certain boredom, a first cousin of loneliness, was beginning to bother him. He told himself it was just getting to be a long time between wars.

The problem that made Billy's loneliness hard to bear was his anger. It lurked beneath the surface of his relaxed cocky manner, revealing itself in sarcasm and occasional flashes of temper. But it was always there in his personal sky like a blue storm swirling off the jet stream, invisible until it struck.

"Let's think about it," he said. "Let's fly together first and think about it."

Victoria fled to Frank Buchanan. He was the invisible third in this explosive equation. Victoria had, like most women, found his honesty, his spontaneity, his love of poetry, irresistible. She had confided her feelings about Billy to him and he had urged her to be bold, to be a modern woman and speak first.

That night, Frank too was boycotting the congressmen. He sat in his state-room sketching a design for a supersonic airliner. "It didn't work!" Victoria cried. "All he wants to do is give me a ride in the Warrior. He's treating me like a teenager!"

"That's a very significant first step. Be patient. You're just like your mother. You expect miracles on demand."

Did Frank find secret savage satisfaction in encouraging Victoria Van Ness? Unquestionably. But he was also thinking about Billy, whom he continued to love without reservations, a fathering love that grew stronger as Buzz McCall receded into negligibility in both their lives. What could be more marvelous (and more savagely satisfying) than the prospect of Billy retiring from the Air Force as a general in five or ten years and becoming president of Buchanan Aircraft with the backing of the majority stockholder, his wife?

Frank made sure that the Warrior had a busy schedule in the coming week. The big plane was being used in an Air Force–funded research program called HICAT, an acronym for High Altitude Clear Air Turbulence. Everyone from NACA, the National Advisory Committee for Aeronautics (forerunner to NASA) had become seriously concerned about the discovery of clear air turbulence in the stratosphere. If a supersonic plane was going to be developed, the location and magnitude of this menace had to be explored. It was bad enough to hit CAT at low or medium altitudes in a prop plane. Hitting it in a supersonic jet would magnify the impact a hundred times. It was the difference between a car going over a bump in a driveway and a bus hitting a boulder on a high-speed highway.

Frank had absolute confidence in the design integrity of the Warrior. So he did not have the slightest qualm about assigning Billy to investigate one of the toughest problems confronting supersonic flights over the North Pole, a phenomenon called the Polar Night Vortex, which contains winds of up to 380 miles per hour. It also tends to have sudden seasonal drops in temperature of as much as forty degrees, creating awesome windshears. Meteorologists using pictures from weather satellites and data from sounding rockets had been able to locate this jet stream in a general way. Billy was ordered to cruise close to it and see what sort of HICAT he encountered. The Warrior was loaded with gear to monitor its force and the impact on the plane's surfaces.

"I gather Victoria Van Ness has spoken to you about flying in the Warrior," Frank said. "She won't be able to do it once it goes back under Air Force control. Why don't you take her up on the next flight?"

"Won't her father have a goddamn fit?" Billy said. "This is sort of dangerous, Pops."

"Her father doesn't have to know about it." Frank paused to let Billy absorb the message he was sending. "You don't need a beautiful woman for a wife. It usually complicates things."

That afternoon, Billy invited Victoria on the flight. The next morning, she arrived at the Mojave field almost an hour early. Billy matter-of-factly found her a flight suit. "Did you tell your father where you're going?" he said.

"No. I hope you don't feel compelled to file a report."

"I never feel compelled to do anything," Billy said.

Victoria sat in the observer's jump seat behind Billy and the copilot, an easygoing Texan who was properly impressed by the boss's daughter. Into the stratosphere the big plane soared while the mach needle climbed up the dial toward 3. There were slight jolts as they went through mach 1 and 2. The loudest sound in the cockpit was duct rumble, which Billy had explained in advance. It was created by pressure fluctuations in the engines as air entered them at supersonic speed. Otherwise, the ride was unbelievably smooth and quiet. The thunder of the huge motors was flung miles behind them as they cruised on the shock waves the nose canards drove beneath the wings.

"Sixty thousand feet," the copilot said. "Getting close to the top of the ride, Billy."

"Here comes the hard part," Billy said. "Make damn sure you're belted in, Victoria."

"Don't worry about me," she said. "Look at that sun! The horizon!"

The morning sun was a burning white disc, filling the blue-black sky with incredibly intense light. The horizon ahead of them seemed infinite. Billy did not have time to admire the scenery. He was concentrating on leveling off at precisely the correct pitch attitude. A mistake would create weightlessness, a scary phenomenon he did not want Victoria to experience.

They eased into horizontal cruise at mach 3 without losing contact with gravity. Billy explained what might have happened. "That's gonna be one of the problems if they turn this big baby into an airliner. A half degree off pitch and the martinis'll be floatin' against the ceilin'."

Victoria laughed. "I love that idea."

"Come to think of it, so do I," Billy said.

They roared toward Alaska in search of the Polar Vortex. Billy talked to meteorologists in Fairbanks and Point Barrow to find out what they were learning from their weather balloons about the jet stream's current location. His copilot plotted a course to bring them parallel to it for a two-hundred-mile run.

"You can't see this thing," Billy said. "That's the spooky part of it. It's like playing games with a huge invisible serpent in the sky. Are you belted in real good, Victoria?"

"I'm practically part of the seat."

"Are you having a good time?"

"The time of my life."

"Here we go," the copilot said.

Victoria gazed out the cockpit window at a sky of perfect blue. She had never seen anything as pure, as serene, in her life. But somewhere in its light-filled heart the jet stream coiled, hurling vortices that smashed against the giant bomber with a ferocity that made her face, her neck, ache.

"Put it on autopilot?" the copilot said.

Billy shook his head. The autopilot was one way of dealing with turbulence.

It relieved the pilot of the struggle for control of the plane. But Billy did not trust a spinning gyroscope to do his thinking for him when he was on the edge of the unknown.

Suddenly they hit a windshear unlike anything Billy had ever encountered before. It made the bomber pitchdown—the nose dropped below the horizon—and simultaneously scythed away a column of air a mile wide beneath the wings. The Warrior plunged into a dive that took them over the red line on every instrument on the panel.

"We're hitting mach three five," the copilot gasped.

"Pull!" Billy shouted, hauling on the yoke with all his strength. The copilot imitated his example. It had no visible effect. They were going straight down, seventy tons of bomber headed for the frozen earth.

Some three miles down, the Warrior hit the bottom of the shear and responded to the controls. "Hang on!" Billy said. The wings rose, the fuselage groaned, the engines "unstarted" with a series of violent jolts as their internal shock waves readjusted themselves to normal flight. The g forces smashed Billy down in his seat and almost tore his brain apart. But he hung on to the yoke.

"Are we going back up there?" the shaken copilot said.

Billy looked over his shoulder at Victoria Van Ness. For the first time it occurred to him that she had not made a sound. Most other woman he knew would have been blubbering and wailing by now. Victoria was smiling. "Are you game for it?" Billy said.

Victoria nodded. They climbed back up to 70,000 feet and completed their jolting two-hundred-mile run along the edge of the vortex. Billy banked the Warrior into a 160-degree turn and headed back to the Mojave. On the ground, Victoria sat in Billy's office while he wrote a report of the flight. As he finished, in charged Mike Shannon.

"Hello, Miss Van Ness," he said. "What brings you out to the desert?" They had met on the SS *Rainbow*. Shannon was a frequent weekend guest.

"A supersonic ride in a top-secret plane," she said.

"She's some crate, isn't she?" Mike said. "Billy. I've got that load of congressmen out on the runway. Remember I called you about them? Are you ready to go up?"

"Can't do it, Mike. We'll have to reschedule it for tomorrow. Talk to Frank about it."

"What the hell's wrong?"

"I'm taking a vacation, Mike. The first one in years."

That was the moment when Sarah Chapman Morris appeared in the doorway. From Billy's point of view the timing could not have been more delicious. In the violent incandescence of the next five minutes, Sarah saw he knew exactly what she was feeling and he was still determined to win their long, mutilating struggle for spiritual supremacy. What he did not know, what he would never know, was Sarah's power to become Victoria Van Ness, to be the secret lover inside her awkward clumsy body, to live in the manic fire of her imagination until she won, won, won!

Two hours later, Billy circled over Santa Catalina Island in his green Lustra. The white twelve-story casino presided over the yachts in Avalon's picture-postcard harbor. The sand of Pebbly Beach gleamed against the blue-black Pacific. The interior valleys were lush with tropical foliage. It was a miniature continent.

"Remember the song?" Billy said. "I lost my heart in Avalon?"

"It's one of my favorites," Victoria said.

Billy flipped the Lustra into an inverted spin. The island, the sea, whirled inside Victoria's head as if it were being stirred by a giant whisk. "How did you know we were going to pull that bomber out?" he said, as they hurtled toward the water.

"I just knew," Victoria said, as calmly as if she were riding along Wilshire Boulevard in her red Triumph convertible. "I knew you'd do it."

"If that shear was another mile deep, no one could have done it."

"It wasn't," she said.

Billy pulled the Lustra out at 250 feet and asked for clearance at the island's airport, at the head of a deep canyon northwest of Avalon. The air traffic controller said there wasn't a plane within ten miles. He whipped the Lustra into a 180-degree turn and came in much too fast. He had to burn his brakes to stop before they rolled off the runway.

"That's the worst landing I've made in twenty years," Billy said. "And it's all your fault."

Victoria smiled. "Will you to teach me to fly?"

"Sure," Billy said.

Billy and Victoria spent two days on Santa Catalina Island. Travel writers call it the nearest thing to Shangri-la in California. That would make it the ultimate unreality in a world where realism has never been in large supply. Billy rented a thatched cottage on Papeete Beach, site of a dozen South Sea movies. In those days it included abandoned movie sets, such as the Continental Hotel in which Jean Harlow had played Sadie Thompson.

They made soaring love beneath the palm trees, they swam in the looming surf. Billy flew Victoria with a concentration, an intensity, he borrowed from memories of other women, from the metaphor of their flight together. She was an assignment given to him by the one man who could persuade him to do anything. In his instinctual, intuitive way he sensed the combination of hatred and love in Frank Buchanan's soul that was animating them. Billy saw it as another unknown, another serpent to challenge in the sky of the future. He had the same attitude toward the serpentine realities that awaited them on the mainland.

For Victoria those forty-eight hours of love became the fulcrum of her life. She had no idea love involved such a shocking surrender of the deepest self. Her previous encounters with poetry-quoting Oxford dons and randy fellow students became instantly insignificant. She now belonged to Billy in an absolute way that transcended—but did not abolish—her father's will to power and her mother's rage for moral purity.

How Victoria affected Billy is a question that people still debate. Unquestionably he became something different from the Billy McCall who had laid a thousand women without caring—except for a few who touched something inside him, usually, as in Sarah Chapman's case, quickly smothered by his anger.

Victoria dared Billy to become a being he had been taught to dismiss with contempt. "I want to be your wife, I want you to be my husband," Victoria said. "*Husband.* It's the most beautiful word in the English language. One of the oldest. It goes back beyond English to ancient Norse and German, *hus* meaning 'house' and *bondi* meaning 'to dwell.' I want to dwell in your house, in your heart, I want to live there forever."

"*Bondi,*" Billy said. "That's the name of a beach in Sydney. Not many husbands there. Or wives."

Husband. It was the most unnerving challenge Billy ever faced—infinitely more unsettling than exploring the stratosphere in rocket planes or supersonic bombers. Billy responded to it in the only way that interested him, in the only way he knew. He made it dangerous.

Billy had no idea just how dangerous a sky inhabited by Sarah-Victoria-Amanda would become. No one did. Not even Sarah. For the moment she swooped hungrily above Catalina, a lonely cormorant, feeding on the last shreds of her hateful heart.

BILE

Adrian Van Ness vomited his lunch and dinner into the toilet bowl. Pain throbbed in his chest. His head pounded. *Ruined* whined in his soul in a new more menacing way. Was he having a coronary? It had been a day of shocks— the worst day in his life. It made his discovery of his mother's infidelity, even the stock market crash of 1929, seem insignificant.

First had come a report from Cliff Morris on the ferocious struggle for the Warrior bomber. Congress, defying Secretary of Defense McNamara and his whiz kids, had voted a hundred million dollars to build another ten copies. It was a compromise, far short of a commitment to the billion-dollar program General Curtis LeMay had wanted. The secretary was still using the power of his office and the mathematical wizardry of his aides to try to kill the plane.

Then Morris delivered the shock. It was of earthquake proportions. McNamara, with the Kennedys' approval, was abolishing the cost-plus contract. In all future Defense Department contracts with airframe and engine companies, the contractor would have to deliver his product within the limits of his original estimate—and pay any cost overruns out of his own pocket.

This amounted to a whole new way of doing business, piling on a military aircraft design the same gut-wrenching risks that a new commercial plane required a company to swallow. For something as experimental as the Warrior bomber, it meant betting the company three or four times over if future testing revealed unforeseen problems—the unk unks almost every plane contained.

"Can't you talk to your boy wonder from Massachusetts?" Adrian shouted.

Wretchedly, Cliff Morris confessed his mounting disillusion with the Kennedys and the whole Democratic Party. "It's a can of worms and no one knows what happened to the lid. I think maybe Jack left it under Marilyn Monroe's bed. One thing's for sure, most of the time he doesn't pay attention."

"He's paying attention to Amalie Borne. She's been to the White House five times. I'm paying her bills in New York and he's getting all the action," Adrian snarled.

Cliff's only vestige of good news was a report that the Pentagon, in line with JFK's drive to beef up conventional forces, was looking for a new close support plane, something subsonic with a high-load capacity and plenty of endurance. Maybe Frank Buchanan had something in his files from the Korean War that they could wrap around a jet engine.

"What about a new transport—something really big?" Adrian said. Attack planes were small, compact, and cheap. The current one being used by the Navy was a Douglas job called Heinemann's Hot Rod, after their chief designer. It was so small pilots claimed you did not strap into it—you strapped it on.

"I'm working on it," Cliff said. "But LeMay is so in love with our goddamn bomber he doesn't want us to think about anything else. He's going down fighting on the thing and there's nothing we can do but go with him."

All this was only a prelude to the ultimate shock. Adrian had come home for dinner at 8 P.M. to find Amanda in an unusually cheerful mood. Most of the time she either ignored him or glowered sullenly and asked questions about the "accident" that made it so difficult for her to remember many things.

"For once I have some good news," she said.

"Oh?" Adrian said.

"Victoria is going to be married."

Adrian felt five, perhaps ten years older in ten seconds. Struggling for aplomb, he sat down, tossed a leg over his knee and said: "Who's the lucky fellow?" He half suspected he was hearing a fantasy from Amanda's damaged brain.

"Billy McCall. I told her I was a little disappointed that she was marrying a man whose profession was bombing people—but on the whole, considering how dim I thought her chances of marrying anyone were, I think it's good news, don't you?"

"Shut up, for God's sake," Adrian snarled and stormed upstairs in search of his daughter.

He found Victoria lying on her bed, staring dreamily at the ceiling. "Is it true?" he said.

"We love each other," she said. "We spent the weekend on Catalina together."

"It's a mistake," Adrian shouted, losing all his vaunted self-control.

"I thought you'd feel that way. That's why I didn't discuss it with you."

"The man's a mental vacuum. All he can talk about is planes."

"He talks about them wonderfully. Better than you, Daddy. Better than anyone. Haven't you watched the way those congressmen listen to him? He's authentic. Real—in a way most men can't even approach."

Adrian heard the reminder that he needed Billy if he had any hope of getting a billion dollars to build the Warrior. But he still could not control his chagrin. "It's romantic nonsense. Sleep with him for six months if you want to—you have my permission. But don't marry him."

"I told you—I *love* him."

"I heard you—and I hope you heard me. Most love is an illusion. Give it six months either to solidify—or dissipate."

"We're getting married as soon as possible."

"Why? Why such an idiotic rush?"

Victoria sat up and glared at him with Amanda's eyes, full of her old ominous intensity. "Otherwise I'll lose him. And if you keep talking this way—you'll lose him too. I'll see to it."

Adrian was meeting his willful match. Stunned but still frantic, he retreated. "How did this happen? I have a right to know."

She told him everything without reserve, including Frank Buchanan's role. Adrian saw it all in the worst possible light, of course. He was ashen, trembling, by the time she finished. "I thought you loved me," he said. "I thought you at least loved me."

He was really saying, how could you betray me to my enemies? But he had never explained how or why Frank Buchanan was his enemy. Victoria heard the words as an old-fashioned reproach for deserting him.

"I do love you!" she cried. "But you can't expect me to stay ten years old for the rest of my life. Besides—"

Victoria was about to tell him how much she loathed the way he did business. But she saw how wounded he was already and let pity deflect her anger into a more ordinary reproach. "Do you really expect me to be your creature indefinitely? To wait until you're ready to dispose of me to the man of your choice? Some superannuated character like Prince Carlo?"

"I never dreamt of such a thing."

What had he dreamt? Finally Adrian was forced to confront the halfway house in which his fears and his hopes had trapped his fatherhood. He had confessed too much to hold his daughter's admiration and not enough to win her forgiveness. Wretched, wretched, a wretched performance for a man whose gift was forethought.

Adrian flushed the vomit down the toilet and stumbled back to bed. In the doorway of her bedroom stood Amanda in a long ruby night robe, her russet hair streaming down her back. She smiled and said: "My poor husband. Can I get you anything?"

For a moment Adrian struggled with a terrifying inrush of fear. Was this woman in touch with some sort of supernatural power that enabled her to inflict pain and disappointment on him? Were all women in some profound way enemies to a man's deepest hopes? Rationality trembled in a swirl of terror. Adrian fled to his room and called Kirk Willoughby. He came to the house and found nothing physically wrong with Buchanan's anguished President.

The next day, Adrian retreated into acquiescence, even into apology with Victoria. He had no other choice. He struggled to welcome William Craig McCall as his son-in-law. He tried to impose reason—his word for control—on the situation.

"What are you going to do? Where are you going to live?" he asked his daughter, as wedding plans went forward.

"That's up to Billy," Victoria said.

"You're going to be an Air Force wife? Have you seen the houses they live in on most bases? You'd have more room in a Starduster."

"I remember Mother telling me we were never going to be rich, that I should adjust my expectations to realities. I was very proud of her for asking me to do that. It made me feel grown-up, serious."

"Are you going to have children?"

"Not right away. Billy doesn't want any—as long as he's test-flying."

"You don't fly forever, even in the Air Force. It would make much more sense if he retired and came to work here. He could do it in stages. He could be the air force manager for the Warrior program, assuming we get the contract—and then transfer to the civilian side."

"I'm not sure that's a good idea. I'd rather see him work for some other aircraft company."

"You're not being realistic. Each company has a different personality. This is the one he knows. Where he has friends—"

Victoria struggled to trust the secretive, subtle man she called Daddy and thought of as father—an infinitely more awesome word. Adrian struggled to control his anger. Neither succeeded. "I think you'll find he needs protection for a while at least," Adrian said.

"That's ridiculous!"

"Pilots are like athletes, very naive about the world outside their planes. When you spend your life in the military, that only adds to the naïveté."

In one of those bizarre but all too common repetitions, Adrian was sowing doubts about Billy deep in Victoria's psyche in much the same way his mother had undermined Amanda. Victoria felt the doubts as wounds, inflicted in revenge. Her mother, listening in the distance, let her outspokenness run rampant as soon as Adrian left for work.

"Isn't he perfectly hateful?" Amanda said. "I'm sure he was this way before my accident. I can't remember exactly why I hated him but now I'm sure I was right."

HEART OF DARKNESS

Outside the window, Saint Elmo's fire flickered along the wings of the Pan Am 707 as they approached Africa. Dick Stone found himself wishing it was a real fire, not one of nature's electrical stunts. Beside him, Amalie Borne read *Elle*, the French fashion magazine, relentlessly tearing out page after page of dresses she intended to buy in Paris.

It was insane, his doomed irresistible love for this woman. By now he had embezzled over three hundred thousand dollars from Buchanan Aircraft to buy her dresses and diamond necklaces and gold bracelets. The withdrawals were carried on the books as extraordinary overseas expenses, part of the millions handed over to the Prince and other agents. Buchanan's auditors had long since accepted these expenses as perfectly legal under American law. There was no immediate danger of being caught.

For someone with Dick Stone's conscience, punishment was almost superfluous. He was his own accuser, judge, and victim. He seldom slept more than four hours a night. He rarely looked at another woman. His airline and aircraft friends at the Villa Hermosa called him the hermit. Cassie Trainor wrote him sarcastic letters from Oxnard. Dick wrote evasive replies to Cassie and long letters to Amalie, full of bad imitations of Heine, or meditations on America and Europe, desperately trying to explain what was happening to him—while compounding the disaster.

In return, Amalie wrote him savagely detailed descriptions of her visits to the Kennedy White House, each as demeaning as her original encounter with JFK in Los Angeles. She told him, without moderating a phrase, how important this was to her career in Europe, where Kennedy, after his 1961 visit to Paris with Jackie, had become a near-mythical figure. Madame George had a waiting list of over twenty cabinet ministers, bankers, industrialists, generals, who were begging for a chance to escort her to Cannes, St. Moritz, Amalfi. But she stayed in New York, because she loved Richard Stone—and was certain her price would continue to rise.

By now Dick had learned to deconstruct the word *love*, to see how strangely Amalie dealt with its elements. Sacrifice was part of love, was it not? She sacrificed money, fame, for his sake. But the arrangement was strictly temporary. Next week or the week after, love might end as abruptly as a sleeper awoke from a dream—or a nightmare. Forever was not part of Amalie's love, except as a possibility. It was not exiled from the palace but it was not permitted in the throne room either. Forever watched wistfully from a dim alcove, awaiting a summons that might never come.

Fidelity was an exile in the strictly literal sense. But it was allowed to reenter the country under an assumed name, to travel in a dozen different disguises, all designed to wrench the heart. Fidelity sidled onstage as a thought at moments when obscene acts were being performed. It slithered past as a sigh when the bedroom plunged into lonely darkness. It pirouetted as a robed, hooded dancer while headwaiters bowed and Château Haut-Brion was poured.

Desire was never an exile but postponement was its constant fate. Love was not sovereign in Amalie's world. It was a deposed queen without offspring or supporters, a creature for whom tears were shed, fealty pledged—without the slightest hope that these rituals would achieve anything significant. The world was ruled by darker powers. These could only be propitiated by deception, endless, perpetually charming deception.

Dick had renounced, once and for all, his desire to know the truth about her past. She had forced him to capitulate, to accept her as a woman who seized the foreground of his vision and held it by her force and guile and affection and disdain and lust and beauty and intelligence and indifference and concern and laughter and tears.

A dozen, two dozen more words could be added to that sentence without exhausting the catalogue of Dick's love. The words and their multiple meanings trooped over the green horizon into Africa, as the big plane roared up the mouth of the Congo toward Brazzaville. The Prince was there, awaiting them and the money Dick had in his briefcase. Pontecorvo and Cliff Morris had sold eighty-two Stardusters in sixteen African countries.

En route to California with the orders, Cliff had eaten dinner with Dick and Amalie the night before they left New York. The former commander of the *Rainbow Express* talked about his adventures flying in Ethiopia, the Congo, and other countries with pilots who had trouble reading the English words on the dials. As usual, Cliff omitted the Prince's role in his triumphal progress.

Clearly seeing a rival on the horizon, Cliff devoted much of their dinner to sarcastic comments about Billy McCall's imminent marriage to Victoria Van Ness. He tried to make marrying the boss's daughter the equivalent of moral turpitude. Dick, his brain sodden with Amalie Borne, barely listened.

Amalie announced she was coming with Dick yesterday as he was packing his suitcase. "Why?" he said, resisting the idea of the Prince regaining her.

"There's no need to worry about sharing me with him," she said. "Didn't I tell you he's impotent? Some say the Gestapo gelded him. Others think his mother is responsible. Still others say he prefers six-year-old choirboys, like his ancestor, Pope Innocent."

As usual, Dick capitulated. He could not stop her from flying to Brazzaville with her own money. Now they were circling above the mixture of squatters' shacks and gleaming white skyscrapers that constituted this typical African capital. They drove down roads that were narrow causeways through seas of mud to the Intercontinental Hotel, where the Prince greeted them with his usual cordiality.

"Ah, Stone," he said. "Never did I dream that the Santa Claus of my life would turn out to be Jewish. I risked my life a great many times to save Jews from the Germans. Do you think you're my reward?"

"Perhaps."

"But what have I done to deserve this?" he said, seizing Amalie by the arms and spinning her around. She was looking spectacular in a gray black-belted Dior suit with a pleated skirt.

"There's nothing in heaven or on earth you could do, dear Carlo," she said. "Haven't you read your St. Augustine? We can't merit God's grace."

"I'm a Pelagian by trade," he said. "In other times I would have been burned at the stake before the age of thirty."

"Not merely for your beliefs," Amalie said, letting him kiss her on the cheek.

"And the money, Stone. This time it's been carefully counted by our Swiss literalists?"

"Yes," Stone said, never sure when the Prince—or Amalie for that matter—was taunting him.

"The commander of the Nigerian Army is in town. He would love to meet the uncrowned queen of the American White House," the Prince said.

"Tell him I'm vacationing—and Stone here is my CIA escort—with orders to kill anyone who so much as looks at me."

"That could lead to Stone's disappearance, Amalie dear. Is that what you're trying to arrange?"

"Why should I even think of such a thing?"

The Prince shrugged and opened the inevitable bottle of Moet et Chandon. "Perhaps then you plan to poison me and decamp with the money?"

Amalie laughed. "I can make twice that in the next year."

In spite of the air-conditioning, which was at Arctic level, Dick discovered he was bathed in sweat. Amalie had not come here for a vacation, he was sure of that much. The Prince was equally sure of it. He was as alert, as coiled, as a duelist with a rapier in his hand.

They drank champagne and the Prince discussed Africa. He said it was not much different from Calabria, where his family had owned vast estates until Mussolini confiscated them. He predicted a hundred years of anarchy and chaos in the wake of the departing Europeans. Planes were the only hope of binding the continent together. The totally corrupt governments would never manage to build roads or rail lines.

"And for binding the world together, how goes the supersonic transport?" Pontecorvo asked.

"Slowly. We're still fighting over the supersonic bomber," Dick said.

"The potential for commercial profits, Stone, is astounding. I don't understand this hesitation. The British and the French are discussing a consortium to build one."

"The Democrats are in power. They like to spend money on public housing, education, civil rights programs."

"But this plane will create thousands of jobs."

"I know. But the Democrats don't think that way."

"I thought steps were being taken to persuade them?"

He smiled at Amalie, his tufted eyebrows raised.

406

"You don't understand these Kennedys," Amalie said. "You're deceived by the photographs, the TV footage, where Prince Hal seems incarnate. Off-camera, they're crude, foul-mouthed gangsters."

Much later, after a dinner marked by several similar exchanges between Amalie and the Prince, Dick sat in his room staring across the tilted shacks and littered streets of Brazzaville at the jungle. He had knocked on Amalie's door an hour ago—she was in the room across the hall—and gotten no answer. That could only mean she was with the Prince—unless she was with the Nigerian general.

A knock. Amalie stood at the door in a long blue robe. She stepped into the room and opened her arms to him. The kiss came from her. She pressed her whole body against him and let her lips wander across his face, his neck. "Oh, Richard, Richard," she whispered, a name she only used when she was amorous. "Do you feel it out there—the jungle, the heart of darkness? I wanted to come to Africa and make love to you in the middle of it. I wanted to streak my face and my breasts and my thighs with Congo mud, I wanted to lure you once and for all from your middle-class fears and follies, I wanted to find a primeval wildness lurking in your bourgeois American heart."

"We'll go now. I'll rent a car. I'll shoot a rhinoceros for you. I'll wear the horn on my forehead."

He was tuned to her mockery, her fantasy, now.

"I didn't let him touch me. We talked business. Nothing but business. But from now on you'll have to be on guard."

"Why?"

"Later, I'll explain later. Coat me with jungle mud, now. Then lick it off. Taste Africa in my body. Create it inside me."

He breathed the perfume in her hair. He accepted her nakedness, so white, so sinuous, as the geography she was demanding. She was a continent not unlike Africa, capricious, incomprehensible, corrupt. But Dick had learned to think as well as feel in his explorations of the many Amalie Bornes he had encountered. When it was over, when she smiled and sighed childishly in his arms, he asked her again for an explanation.

"It's of no consequence. The Prince and I have parted. I grew weary of playing the waitress to his maitre d'. I wanted a share of his salary. He indignantly refused. So now, like you and Lockheed, we are competitors."

"What does that mean?"

"It means in some situations, you and Adrian Van Ness may have to decide who is more useful, the Prince or Amalie Borne."

"And in the meantime, we're responsible for your happiness?"

"Of course. Exactly how you arrange that part of it, I leave to your discretion."

Dick did not need a further explanation to grasp Amalie's plan. With him in charge of arrangements, she expected a cascade of cash. Why did she insist on piling burden after burden on their love? Was she still trying to make him hear the warning she had given him the day they met?

In the morning Amalie announced she wanted to see a gorilla colony about forty miles from Brazzaville. The hotel operated a van that took tourists to visit the site. There was only one other person in the van besides the hulking black driver—a short foxy-faced man in a well-pressed business suit who asked them if they would mind if he smoked. Amalie grandly gave him permission and he was soon conversing knowledgeably with them about Africa. His name was Korda and he was a sales representative for the Israeli aircraft industry. He apparently did a brisk business selling helicopters, trainers, and fighters to every country on the continent.

"Mr. Stone is with the American aircraft industry," Amalie said. "A company called Buchanan."

Korda praised the Scorpion fighter extravagantly as they got out and viewed the gorilla colony from a respectful distance. They watched the great apes swinging through the trees, while the females perched on lower branches and nursed and nuzzled their young. Occasionally one of the younger apes would beat his chest and roar defiance at the intruders. Amalie adored the show.

"Now I understand the Americans and the Russians, the French and Germans, the Arabs and the Israelis," she said.

"Unmolested, they're quite peace loving," Korda said.

"Aren't we all," Amalie said.

Korda was silent for the first few minutes of their ride back to Brazzaville. Then he stubbed out a half smoked cigarette and said: "Miss Borne tells me you might be interested in helping Israel to defend herself."

"Oh?" Dick said.

Korda leaned forward in a suavely confidential way, though there was no need to worry about being overheard. "We might find some of the research your designers and engineers invested in your supersonic bomber, the Warrior, quite useful. Compression lift could be invaluable in a new fighter-bomber we're developing."

"No doubt," Dick said.

"You might even persuade your chief designer to give us some personal help. I understand he's quite fond of you."

"I'm quite fond of him too," Dick said. "I'm even fonder of the United States of America. They have first call on Frank Buchanan's mind—and my loyalty."

"We could enable you to be extremely generous to Miss Borne—"

"You must be hard of hearing," Dick said. "Or do I have to translate the word *loyalty* into Hebrew?"

Back at the hotel, Amalie blended innocence and mockery. "I don't understand you, Stone. I thought I was giving you a chance to resolve all your conflicts. You could be a free American primate, beating your chest and cavorting with me in our various bedrooms and a loyal Jew on the side—with a reasonable amount of money in the bargain."

Was it another redefinition of love, the worst imaginable burden she could invent? Or was she testing him in some subterranean way to see if he was worthy of the truth? Dick struggled to control a vortex of emotions: rage, regret, shame. "You don't seem to understand. You don't want to understand—"

The mocking eyes never wavered. "I've always thought my problem was understanding too much."

In New York, Amalie persuaded him to stay overnight to cure his jetlag. He had never seen her so amorous. The next day, Dick flew on to Los Angeles, exhausted and appalled. *She was a whore. She loved him. She was a whore. She loved him.* The sentences rebounded crazily in his head for the entire flight. He tried to tell himself her mockery of love simultaneously affirmed it.

He had barely arrived in his office when his secretary told him Adrian Van Ness wanted to see him. He found Buchanan's president standing by the window watching an antisubmarine version of the Starduster taxiing out for takeoff. There were dark pouches under his eyes. Adrian was starting to look old.

"How was Africa?" Adrian said with forced jauntiness.

"I only saw twenty-four hours of it."

"How many of those were devoted to Amalie Borne?"

"A few," Dick said, deciding it was foolish to lie if Adrian already knew Amalie had spent the night with him. Had the Prince in his pique played tattletale?

"We've got some problems with her," Dick said.

"I'm not surprised, considering the encouragement you've been giving her. Women are unstable creatures, Dick. They're particularly prone to fantasies of power."

Adrian watched the new Starduster climb into the blue sky. "Let's talk about the money first. There seems to be three hundred thousand withdrawn from our Swiss account on your signature without any authorization from me."

"I used the money to buy presents for Amalie," Dick said.

The words dangled in midair in the quiet office for a long moment. What did he feel? Dick wondered. Fearful? Was he looking at a prison sentence for embezzlement? To his surprise—and dismay—he realized his dominant emotion was relief. He had just shed an intolerable burden.

Quizzical wrinkles sprouted on Adrian's brow. "A not entirely objectionable policy—if she can help us get Kennedy to deliver on the Warrior and the supersonic airliner. Is that all there is to it—a desire to keep our princess happy?"

"You obviously know everything. Why don't you just fire me and get it over with?" Dick said. "I'm in love with her. I probably would have stolen twice that if you hadn't caught me."

Adrian seemed to find the criminal language offensive. "The Swiss reported the first fifty thousand. I asked Hanrahan to have you watched," he said.

"I'll clean out my desk and go quietly," Dick said. "I'll sign an agreement to pay it back over the next ten years."

"Don't be ridiculous," Adrian said. "You're not the first man who lost his head over a beautiful woman. I've done it myself. The important thing is to learn a lesson from it. To learn something about yourself—and about women.

You can make the money back for us in a year by helping us get a grip on our finances. Those Kennedy bastards in Washington have abolished the cost-plus contract. We're going to have to keep track of every screw, every gallon of paint—and somehow restrain the madmen in the design department, led by their resident maniac, you know who. They think nothing of burning up a million dollars in a mock-up they chop to pieces the next day. You're going to have to do more than project earnings now. You're going to have to create a whole cost-control system."

Dick sat there, numb. "I'm not fired?"

"Dick," Adrian said in his gentlest tone. "Have you gone deaf?"

The similarity to his conversation with the Israeli made Dick shudder. "I—I can't do any of those things. I can't do anything with her on my mind. I'm starting to hate the company, the whole business, because of the way we're using her."

"I think you'll soon find it's the other way around, if the Prince is right. He called me last night from Brazzaville. He says Amalie has quite a lot of his correspondence in a safe deposit box, location unknown. It would embarrass a half-dozen governments if she sent copies to a newspaper."

"She's threatened to do this?"

"She hasn't threatened to do anything yet. She's waiting to see how well you negotiate for her."

"She told the Prince I was going to do that?"

"She saw it as another way to intimidate him."

It made sickening, demoralizing sense. There had to be a purpose beyond or behind the fantasy selves, the mockery of love in the very moment of transcendence. The luminous intelligence that transfixed him had analyzed reality and drawn its own bitter conclusions.

"Is she Jewish?"

Dick knew how absurd the question sounded. But he did not care. It suddenly became the most important fact in the world to him.

"Does it matter?" Adrian said.

In those offhand words, Dick saw the cold hard face of reality as defined by Adrian Van Ness. If he was going to accept the salvation Adrian was offering him, he would have to accept it as the only reality.

Ruefully, bitterly, Dick recounted Amalie's Schweinfurt story. Adrian shook his head in equally rueful admiration. "Women are amazing," he said. "They have the most diabolical imaginations."

He leaned back in his chair and picked up a stainless-steel model of the Scorpion on his desk. "To get practical for a moment," he said. "We have to deal very carefully with Amalie. She may still be useful to us with the Kennedys."

"She doesn't think so."

"There are many ways to be useful beyond the obvious one. We have pictures of her leaving the White House, for instance. Naturally I hope we never have to use them. It would be very dangerous for us—and for her."

A new kind of unreality clouded Dick's brain. Was he sitting here with Adrian Van Ness, talking about Amalie Borne as if she was disposable, loseable, like a copy of a plane in a war?

"For the time being, it's important not to alarm her. Go back to New York in a week or so and assure her that all is well. Spend enough money to convince her. But begin trying to find out where she's stashed the Prince's correspondence. That will no doubt take some doing, but it should be enjoyable."

Adrian was assigning Dick Stone the role he had played with Beryl Suydam. The lover who was not a lover, who was a secret enemy—and still a lover. Dick did not understand why, but he could see that Adrian was enjoying himself.

"Of course I understand it won't be entirely enjoyable," Adrian said. "It will take a lot of self-control. But I think you can do it."

Adrian held out his hand. "Do we understand each other, Dick?"

Dick accepted the hand. Adrian squeezed hard, unusual for him. "Thanks," Dick said.

"Nonsense. It's to our mutual advantage, I assure you."

Gazing into those subtle eyes, the shy yet shrewd smile, Dick heard that reassurance not once but twice and then three times. Adrian too was an expert at expanding the meaning of words. Mutual advantage encompassed much more than Dick's ability to set up a cost-control system for Buchanan Aircraft. It involved years and years of future arrangements with people like the Prince, in which Dick Stone's acquiescence, his readiness to bury unpleasant costs deep in Buchanan's records, were guaranteed. As he walked out of the office, Dick was no longer a prisoner of love. But he was a prisoner of Adrian Van Ness.

DEATH IN THE DESERT

Cliff Morris sat in the oak-paneled committee room beside Dick Stone and Mike Shannon, watching Adrian Van Ness testify before the Senate Armed Services Committee. Adrian had just finished arguing for the survival of the Warrior bomber. He had laid special stress on its future as a supersonic airliner.

"The plane," Adrian continued, "has won the enthusiastic applause of veteran pilots such as Colonel Billy McCall, one of the first men to break the sound barrier, holder of a half-dozen high-altitude records."

"Excuse me, Mr. Van Ness," said the lean hunched senator from Iowa, shoving his sallow face so close to the microphone he seemed to be swallowing it. "Isn't he your son-in-law? Isn't his correct rank lieutenant colonel?"

"Yes to both questions, Senator," Adrian said, as reporters grinned and several staffers in the seats around them tittered. "Lieutenant colonels are normally referred to in ordinary discourse as colonels—"

"But he is your son-in-law."

"Yes. But Colonel McCall is the sort of man who would only tell the exact truth about any plane he flew. His reputation as a test pilot is the point here."

"Of course, Mr. Van Ness," the senator sneered.

It was the Creature. He had run for the Senate in 1962 with John F. Kennedy's reluctant endorsement and won. His venal style—in particular his utter indifference to facts—had not changed an iota. Before the hearings began, he had given Mike Shannon a list of things he wanted in return for his support for the bomber. They included an Air Force base within shouting distance of his hometown, an invitation to be the principle speaker at the Air Force Association annual dinner, and a Buchanan factory in Iowa as big as the one they had promised Robert Kerr in Oklahoma. Shannon urged Cliff to say yes. But Cliff said the package was too much for any freshman senator to ask and with Adrian's approval had said no.

Beside Adrian Van Ness, Billy McCall sat very straight and silent in his blue Air Force uniform. In the front row of the spectators' seats, Victoria Van Ness wore a powder blue suit of almost identical color. It was one of her small ways of stating her devotion to Billy. Beside her sat her secret enemy, Sarah Morris.

They pretended to be warm friends. At Sarah's suggestion, Cliff had adopted the same policy toward Billy. It was not that difficult; since the Starduster days, he and Billy had become wary semi-friends. Behind his back, Cliff sabotaged Billy in large and small ways, according to Sarah's plan. He referred to him as "the son-in-law" in conversation with other executives. He wryly predicted Billy would never put up with marriage and hinted he already was straying from Victoria's bed. Cliff had balked in the negotiations with the Creature because he wanted the senator to come into the hearings angry at Buchanan, even if it risked the future of the Warrior.

The bomber was in trouble for far more serious reasons. Defense Secretary Robert McNamara was showing the Kennedys he had learned to play the Byzantine politics of Washington. With the help of the fighter pilots in the Air Force, who resented the influence of General LeMay and his Strategic Air Command bomber jocks, the secretary of defense was promoting another plane, called the TFX or F-111, a smaller, cheaper supersonic bomber that could double as a fighter. General Dynamics and Boeing had been invited to bid on it and their lobbyists and favorite senators and congressmen were pushing it, creating confusion in the ranks of the Warrior backers.

Lieutenant Colonel McCall took Adrian's place in the witness chair. "Why do you think a plane is superior to a missile?" the Creature asked. "Is it because you'd be flying it?"

"They wouldn't let an old man like me fly a serious mission, Senator," Billy said. "We've got young fellows with a lot more stamina and brains than I have."

"The mission this plane would execute would be very dangerous, am I correct?"

"No question."

"The Russians would do everything in their power to stop it?"

412

"Definitely."

"You seem awfully complacent about letting younger men risk their lives while you sit home giving them orders, Colonel."

"You risk your life every time you fly a plane like the Warrior," Billy snapped.

"Oh?" the Senator said. "I thought this was a breakthrough design, the plane of the twenty-first century, twenty-five years ahead of schedule. Now you're telling us it's radically unsafe?"

"No, sir," Billy said. "But it's a very hot plane. You have to know what you're doing."

"And you—or your father-in-law—nevertheless maintain that this radically unsafe vehicle can become a supersonic airliner? You're asking us to fund a plane that would risk the life of every passenger—every taxpaying passenger?"

"Sir," Billy said. "I wish you'd stop trying to put words in my mouth."

"I wish you would learn a little respect for the civilian arm of this government, Lieutenant Colonel McCall," the senator shouted." I wish the Air Force could find someone with a reasonably objective view of this plane. What can we expect to learn from a special pleader like you?"

Don't answer him, Cliff Morris thought. That was the only way to deal with the Creature. You had to let him dump garbage on your head and hope that you won the sympathy vote.

Cliff was shocked to find himself rooting for Billy. Wasn't that what any man would do, watching another man getting creamed by this piece of political slime? Yet last night he and Sarah had drunk to the possibility that Billy would fall on his face in these hearings.

Cliff watched Billy struggle to control his rage. He had flown 113 missions in two wars to defend the land of the free and the home of the brave. He had seen several hundred friends die in burning or exploding planes to make the world safe for democracy. Now the senator was telling him he did not respect or understand it.

"Senator," Billy said. "Senator—sir—the supersonic airliner would be a different plane. It would be a descendant of the Warrior, which is ready to operate as a bomber. There's a whole range of problems that need to be solved before we can create an airliner. We can learn a lot about them from producing the Warrior."

"Tell me, Lieutenant Colonel McCall, will you be promoted to full colonel if the Warrior gets funded?" the senator sneered.

"I have no idea, sir."

"That's all we need to hear from you."

"Sir—I have a prepared statement. I haven't gotten one word of—"

"Leave it on the table. It will be inserted in the record."

Cliff and Sarah rode back to the Shoreham Hotel with Billy and Victoria and Dick Stone. "That son of a bitch," Billy said. "That son of a bitch."

He did not even look at Victoria. She patted his hand and said: "Daddy thinks you handled him very well."

413

"So do I," Sarah said, with cool concealed malice. Billy glared at her and for a moment Cliff wondered if he understood the whole game.

Cliff looked out at the massive government buildings along Pennsylvania Avenue, so formidable, so majestic, until you knew what happened inside them. "We thought he was on our side," he lied. "The White House told us he'd protect us from the Republicans on the committee. But he must have made a deal with McNamara. They're going to move Wright Patterson Air Base to Iowa. Maybe throw in the Air Force Academy."

The Warrior, the first plane to cruise above mach 3, the breakthrough to hypersonic flight, was dead. Cliff told himself it would have happened even without Billy McCall's flagellation. That had simply been the coup de grâce, a gratuitous insult to an already expiring victim. The McNamara ploy of a cheaper alternative, the F111, was not the only reason. The billions Kennedy was asking for missiles and spaceships to the moon and a bigger army and navy had Congress much too edgy to think seriously about the bomber. The tide had been running against Buchanan for a good year.

At their suite, Billy poured himself a full glass of Inverness and drank it down before the rest of the party arrived. Victoria watched, not saying a word. But her eyes swam with tears. "I'll be in our room," she said.

"Don't wait up," Billy said.

"Let's go shopping," Sarah said cheerfully. "Cheer ourselves up." She and Victoria walked out arm in arm. Sarah's guile was breathtaking. Cliff could hardly believe his dreamy-eyed idealistic little WAAF had turned into this ultimate doubletalker.

The party—or the wake—was going to be an all-male show. Adrian arrived with General Curtis LeMay and the usual squadron of lesser generals. LeMay poured himself a glass of Inverness almost as deep as the one Billy had consumed. "Let's drink to a great plane, ruined by our gutless wonder in the White House."

General LeMay held forth for an hour on the frauds and follies of John F. Kennedy. The Bay of Pigs and then the Berlin Wall, which neither Truman nor Eisenhower would have tolerated for ten seconds. The Cuban missile crisis, which passed up a perfect excuse to get rid of Castro and instead left the bearded blowhard with a guarantee that we would never invade his miserable island. Now Kennedy was committing just enough men to South Vietnam to get us involved in a first-class war—but not enough to end it decisively.

Mike Shannon struggled to defend his fellow Irish-American. But even he found it rough going, after two and a half years of slashing around Washington. He talked about the enormous pressures on a president. All right, JFK was not King Arthur or Lancelot; he did not even approximate a white knight. But he was trying to do the job. He wanted the bomber. But McNamara had stolen the Defense Department from the White House. The ex-automaker and his Harvard Business School doubledomes sat across the Potomac like an arrogant baron and his retainers telling the president to get lost. It was bewildering but probably true.

Adrian Van Ness turned to Curtis LeMay. "General, after two and a half years we've got two supersonic bombers that we can't afford to fly again and pieces of another ten lying around the Mojave desert. We've got McNamara's auditors breathing down our necks every time we turn around to make sure we don't make a personal telephone call on the contract."

"I know, I know," LeMay said. "But you're still on the inside track for the SST."

"Right next to Boeing and Lockheed," Adrian said. "Do you think they're going to let us walk away with it?"

"Fuck 'em all," Billy McCall said and poured himself another glass of Inverness.

"Haven't you had enough of that?" Adrian said.

Billy looked at him for a long moment, then chug-a-lugged it and walked out.

Adrian sighed. "I'd like more than a place at the supersonic starting gate. We deserve some sort of guarantee that we'll receive special consideration. We've already spent fifteen million dollars of our own money on the Warrior. We've supplied our peerless leader with some very charming late-night entertainment. I think you ought to remind him of all that, Mike."

"If I did that, the only thing you'd ever get in the air would be a kite," Shannon said. "Who do you think you are, Brazil or some other semi-independent country? You don't know how to deal with Irish-Americans, Adrian. You never threaten them. You keep reminding them they owe you a very big favor."

They flew back to California, where Adrian laid off ten thousand workers and sold the assorted pieces of the ten follow-on Warriors for scrap. Frank Buchanan tried to be philosophic. He had become convinced since the Russians shot down Lockheed's spy plane, the U-2, at 70,000 feet with an antiaircraft missile that the Warrior was probably obsolete anyway. Those huge engine ducts would leave a signature a foot high on a radar screen.

"From now on," he said, "We have to build stealth into our planes. We have to make them invisible to radar."

Not without relish, he reminded everyone that the Talus never appeared on Air Force radar screens when it was being tested. A flying wing was the ultimate stealth bomber. But he presumed Adrian did not have the guts to revive the plane.

Frank was busy designing the ground-support plane Cliff had urged them to produce. Frank called it the Thunderer, a somewhat blasphemous reference (in his mind) to John the Baptist. "When this fellow drops his payload," he said, "whoever's on the other end will think it's the second coming."

It was unusual for Frank to sound so bloodthirsty. He was worried about the situation in Vietnam, where the Army, deprived of its airplanes since the creation of the Air Force in 1948, was trying to get back in the air with helicopters. Frank thought the helicopter was a lousy way to support troops on the ground. It was too vulnerable to antiaircraft fire and it couldn't drop bombs. He showed

Cliff the armor plate he was weaving around the stubby thick-bodied plane on his drawing board. "This thing will bring our kids back alive," he said. "And it can carry more bombs than a World War II B-Twenty-nine."

At home, Cliff discussed something even more important from his point of view: Billy McCall. His career in the Air Force was finished. If the Warrior had come through, Billy would no doubt have jumped to general in a year and been on his way to command of SAC. But now he was an aging bomberjock who had failed to deliver. Cliff was inclined to think they could stop worrying about Billy. Sarah disagreed. Every day she warned him the danger was greater than ever. Now Billy was certain to retire from the Air Force and join the company.

With the Warrior gone, Adrian became more and more obsessed with the supersonic airliner. He called it their declaration of independence. He quoted figures from Dick Stone that made everyone feel like they were on cocaine. The worldwide market for the plane was worth ten billion dollars. Unfortunately Buchanan was close to the limit of their resources. They needed a massive injection of government money.

Every time Cliff went to Washington, he called the White House to remind Mike Shannon about the Big Favor. He brought along a suitcase full of data on the wind tunnel tests of Frank Buchanan's latest design. The figures demonstrated that their SST could go as fast as the Warrior—at least 2,200 mph. This was some six hundred miles an hour faster than the plane the British and French were building. He naturally omitted some of the more unnerving problems they had not yet solved, such as duct rumble, which would terrify even the hardiest passenger.

Then there was the sonic boom, the noise a jet made when it went through the sound barrier. The Air Force was flying Scorpions over places like Oklahoma City and then sending in teams of researchers to find out how many people were bothered when God seemed to be cracking a giant whip in the sky. The answer seemed to be quite a few—especially when windows shattered and babies woke up screaming and cats and dogs went zooey.

A true patrician, Adrian dismissed these problems as trivialities—like noise complaints near airports. People would get used to booms—or they would find a way to eliminate them. Cliff was not so sure. He could see someone like the Creature using the boom to beat their brains out. Of course, even the scummiest senator could be persuaded by a determined president. But Jack Kennedy did not seem very determined.

As 1963 ran down, the promise of the Big Favor dwindled with it. From the White House came only silence. On June 4, 1963, Juan Trippe, president of Pan American, announced he was taking an option on six Concordes—the name the British and French had given their SST to conceal the immense amount of wrangling behind the scenes. The news drove Adrian Van Ness slightly crazy. He urged Cliff to read all about the Profumo scandal in England. A call girl named Christine Keeler was wrecking political careers and threatening to bring down the government. Once more Adrian talked about menacing the Kennedys with Amalie Borne. Once more Cliff talked him out of it.

At midnight on June 5, 1963, Cliff's phone rang. His daughter Elizabeth walked into the study where Cliff was plowing through more SST reports and said in a dazed voice: "It's President Kennedy." At eighteen, Liz was in search of idols and had found one.

"Hello, Cliff," said the rich Boston baritone. "You've been a very patient fellow. I think I've got some good news for you. Can you come to Colorado Springs tomorrow? I'm speaking at the Air Force Academy graduation. I think you'll be interested in part of the speech."

"I'll be there, Mr. President."

"Good. Good. How's that beautiful doll—what's her name?"

"Amalie?"

"Yeah. Can you bring her along?"

"Sure."

"I think she'll be an improvement on anything we could pick up in Colorado Springs, wouldn't you say?"

Cliff called Amalie Borne in New York. She was very difficult. She wanted a special fee beyond the money Buchanan was paying her. She demanded a private plane. Cliff conceded the fee but balked at the private plane. She finally agreed to meet Cliff in Denver the following morning at 10 A.M. From there they would fly in a Buchanan company plane to Colorado Springs. Dick Stone and his accountants could worry about how much it cost them later.

The next day, Cliff sat beside Amalie and Mike Shannon in the fifth row of the presidential party, looking out at forty thousand people packing Falcon Stadium. In the near distance loomed the snowcapped Rockies. Directly in front of them sat 493 young men, the fifth graduating class of the Air Force Academy. At the microphone, after some preliminary jokes and a somber review of the perilous world in which the graduates would serve, John F. Kennedy said: "Neither the economics nor the politics of international air competition permit us to stand still. Today the challenging new frontier in commercial aviation is supersonic flight. In my judgment the government should immediately commence a new program in partnership with private industry to develop a supersonic transport superior to that being built in any country in the world."

The majestic setting matched Cliff's soaring hopes. Ten billion dollars in sales, here we come! He was making triumphant love to Sarah. He was getting drunk with Frank Buchanan and Billy McCall, telling them, especially Billy, that he was in charge of the company's future now. He could junk Sarah's dirty campaign to ruin Billy. He did not have to be afraid of him anymore.

That was the way it went for that magical summer of 1963. Everyone and everything seemed to coalesce. Adrian Van Ness cheerfully ate his words and raised Cliff's salary. The Navy issued a request for bids on a new attack plane and were dazzled by Frank's Thunderer. Sarah grew passionate in bed with a man who was going to leave Billy McCall so far behind in the race for Buchanan's presidency the famous pilot shrank to toy soldier size.

417

Cliff did not even worry when Victoria talked Billy into quitting the Air Force to become Buchanan's chief test pilot. Adrian Van Ness said he was delighted. Billy's reputation inside the aircraft world would add momentum to their head start on the SST.

Unreeling, like a terrific technicolor movie that went on and on with resounding background music mingling with the roar of jet engines, that was the way Cliff Morris saw his life in the summer and fall of 1963. Even Amalie Borne seemed pleased by another flurry of visits to the White House. Only Dick Stone seemed unhappy about that—he was apparently still hung up on the dame.

Cliff took Dick to lunch and told him to marry Cassie Trainor. She was the answer to Amalie. It would give her exactly what she deserved—the brush-off—and straighten out Dick's muddled love life. For the first time in their lives, Dick admitted Cliff might be right.

Cliff even managed to continue to sell Stardusters overseas—a nice round eighty to Japan, Thailand, Australia, and India. Sarah gave a dinner party to celebrate and invited Billy and Victoria. Mike Shannon did his imitation of the Creature. It was the hit of the evening. By now Mike was practically working full time for Buchanan, talking up their SST as the only one that made sense.

Congress grumbled and yammered about putting up the money for the new plane but there was not much doubt that they would acquiesce, once they shook a few goodies from the White House tree. Adrian committed two million dollars to building a full size mockup, even though Frank Buchanan was still fussing with a lot of details, such as a new double delta wing that would make the plane much safer to land.

On November 22, 1963, Cliff whistled his way up the Hollywood Freeway to the Mojave to take a first look at a test model of the Thunderer. He was standing on the runway in the brilliant desert sunshine, admiring the barrel-shaped plane, when Frank Buchanan walked toward him with a peculiar look on his face.

"Someone just shot Kennedy," Frank said.

"He's dead?"

"They think so."

That was where Cliff heard it, with another set of mountains in the distance, reminding him of the golden figure facing the snowy crests of the Rockies, urging Americans to accept the challenge of another dawn of flight. It seemed simultaneously horrible—and just right—that he heard it here from Frank Buchanan.

"I've had a feeling from things Dick Stone told me that he was vulnerable to evil," Frank said. "No one can get away with treating women like disposable spare parts indefinitely. The good spirits turn their backs on that kind of a man."

Billy McCall came roaring onto the runway in his wife's red Triumph. He hurtled toward them at sixty miles an hour and skidded to a stop in front of the Thunderer. "I just heard it on the radio. Someone shot Kennedy's head off in Dallas. Isn't that the best goddamn news you've heard in a year?"

It was 11:30 A.M. and Billy was drunk. Standing in the violent desert sun, Cliff suddenly felt engulfed by an alien darkness. It did not come from California. It seemed to be spilling over those guardian mountains from the invisible heart of America. It made a mess of the triumphant technicolor movie of his life.

Cliff tried to tell himself Billy was elated because he shared Curtis LeMay's opinion of Kennedy as a fraud. But Cliff could not escape the feeling that Billy's smile also said he knew his half brother's climb to the executive stratosphere had just aborted. His career was in a vertical dive.

Frank Buchanan seemed to sense the old hatred crackling between them. He tried to defuse it. "Let's have a cup of coffee, Billy," he said. "I want you sober before you fly this plane. Join us, Cliff?"

"No thanks," Cliff said.

MINDS AND HEARTS

"What is it, Stone, what's wrong? Why did you stop loving me?" Amalie Borne said.

"I didn't stop," Dick Stone said, his leaden voice betraying the lie.

They were lying on the bed in her Waldorf Towers apartment, after making love for the last time. Dick had come to New York determined to demand a final yes or no. Before he could speak, Amalie had told him she did not want to see him again.

"What is wrong with your whole country?" she said, clicking on the TV set from the switch on the night table. "I begin to think you are more hysterical than the Italians, more corrupt than the English, more grandiose than the French, more militarist than the Germans, bigger liars than the Russians."

On the television screen a sheriff's posse and state troopers in Selma, Alabama were attacking Negro marchers with whips and clubs and tear gas. It was the spring of 1965. John F. Kennedy had been dead eighteen months. Lyndon Johnson had been elected president in his own right by the biggest majority in American history and proclaimed the Great Society—a swarm of federal programs that would give citizens of all ages and colors and creeds equal opportunity, equal housing, equal education, equal health care. He was discovering some serious unk-unks in this grand design.

"I still love you," Dick insisted. It was true. He was just redefining the word again, as they had defined and redefined it from the beginning. Love had become virtually identifiable with lust, with the compulsion to have this woman whenever he was near her. Only regret differentiated it from whorehouse fucking.

"But there's no joy in it, no daring anymore. Nothing forbidden. We're like a married couple, Stone. It's too disgusting to tolerate any longer."

She switched channels. Helicopters whirred over a green jungle to disgorge helmeted South Vietnamese troops beside a rice paddy. Johnson was determined to prove he was just as tough on communism as Jack Kennedy. He was putting more and more men and planes into this confusing war. He had another thirty thousand troops suppressing a Communist uprising in the Dominican Republic.

"Your ridiculous ideas about love were driving me crazy, Stone. You should have done what Adrian Van Ness suggested, fucked me with lies on your lips. I would have adored that, when you finally told me."

"I couldn't do it. I'm not one of Nietzsche's *Übermenschen*. Sometimes I think you really want to be fucked by a Nazi. Nothing else really excites you."

"What a fascinating idea. You're not as unoriginal as I thought, Stone."

The insults, the diatribes about America, about his personal shortcomings, had become more and more violent since Kennedy's assassination. Gone was the aura of the woman who slept with the most powerful man in the world. Adrian, sensing Amalie's isolation, or perhaps acting on revengeful advice from the Prince, had demanded she surrender all the incriminating papers she had stolen or face immediate cancellation of their agreement. A tearful Amalie had handed the documents over to Dick—after Xeroxing them and mailing them to Madame George. The Prince called a week later and told her that Madame George had turned the copies over to him. Henceforth, Amalie was simply another Buchanan employee.

"Richard, Richard," she said, rolling over on top of him. "Can't you believe me when I say that the only way I can prove my love is by saying good-bye?"

"I don't believe you. I don't accept it," he said, redefining both words. He believed she was both proving her love and punishing him for failing to protect her from Adrian. He accepted it as the price he was paying for his freedom but in a deeper part of his soul he rejected it as unbearable.

"You're as incomprehensible as the rest of your country. I wish I never left Europe. I understood Europe. Here nothing makes sense except money and a sort of blind desire. You all want to fuck but none of you care."

Dick was seized for the thousandth time with a yearning to know if she was Jewish, if the first story was the true one. But now he was afraid of the truth. He wanted to escape this woman. She was destroying him.

"Shannon says I must come to your magnificent capital tomorrow. There's a senator who yearns to meet me. I told him it was out of the question."

Mike Shannon had become Buchanan's field commander in the struggle for the supersonic airliner. He disliked Amalie. She transcended his Irish-American imagination in too many ways.

"Why can't you go?" Dick asked.

"I have nothing to wear. My clothes are falling apart from endless dry cleaning. Either you double my allowance or I'm going back to Paris. Even if I starve, at least it will be in a city I love."

"You're getting fifty thousand dollars a year for clothes now."

"Jackie Kennedy spends that in a month."

"I'll talk to Adrian. Meanwhile, go see the senator. He's very important at the moment. If he votes the right way, you too will be able to fly supersonically."

"And you'll make ten billion dollars."

She rolled off him and lay on her back, staring at the blue ceiling. "I don't need you any more, Stone. I need a man who doesn't care about me. Who doesn't care about himself. Who doesn't care about anything. A man who does reckless acts because they're always preferable to cautious ones. Because he's compelled to risk himself again and again. Is Cliff Morris such a man?"

"No," Dick said.

He put on his clothes, shoved one of her silver-backed white brushes through his hair and walked to the door. Amalie did not look at him. She continued to stare at the empty ceiling. Dick closed the door until he could no longer see her.

"Good-bye, Amalie."

"Good-bye Stone."

Six months later, Dick sat in his car beneath Chimney Rock, a great steep-sided pinnacle of weathered stone in the coastal mountains north of Los Angeles. There was not another car, another human being, in sight. He put his arms around Cassie Trainor and kissed her gently, firmly.

"How about it? Are you ready to get married?" he said.

He had flown up to the Oxnard School the week after he said good-bye to Amalie and began trying to regain his all-American girl. It had not been easy. Cassie was as beautiful as ever. Her auburn hair still seemed to emanate sunlight. She stood as straight, her figure was as slim and firm as a twenty-year-old, thanks to a fierce program of jogging, swimming, and tennis. But some of the spontaneity, the vivacity had been replaced by thoughtfulness. She was a reader and a thinker now.

Nevertheless she responded to his invitation to try to turn back the clock. She too wanted to regain some of that mocking stewardess who had cut loose in Manhattan Beach a decade ago. But it was mostly the other Cassie who emerged as the woman he was marrying. Now she talked back to him, not about whoriness and the Honeycomb Club but about his literary taste and political opinions.

Cassie persuaded him to reread Faulkner and Hemingway and admit her fellow southerner was superior. She read aloud from her favorite southern poet, the long-forgotten James Bannister Tabb, who blended some of Poe's music with a priestly tenderness. Cassie knew who she was in relation to the rest of the country: a southern woman who could live anywhere in America. Dick found himself attracted in an unexpectedly intense way.

For six months they had spent their weekends exploring what Cassie called "lost California," particularly in the mountains that look down on State 1 as it twists along the rugged coast below Oxnard. It reminded her of the empty landscape around Noglichucky Hollow in Tennessee.

They drove east along Route 58 to a hundred-year-old saloon at Pozo, with tractor seats for bar stools. Through fields of barley ablaze with fireweed, the farmer's enemy, they searched for the ruins of Adelaida, a town that no longer existed. Past stands of oaks and meadows sprinkled with wildflowers they roamed the Los Padres National Forest. Dick found Cassie's desire to share this scenery profoundly touching. It was a kind of statement of the loneliness she had felt when he had more or less abandoned her in Oxnard.

Now he was asking her the question that he had been unable to ask because Amalie Borne's shadow loomed between them. He told himself these six months had banished Amalie's presence. He was in love with this thoughtful American woman he had helped to create.

Cassie kissed him in a sad gentle way and gazed up at Chimney Rock for a moment as if she was remembering shadows in her own life. "I wish we'd done it four years ago," he said. "Why did it take us so long?"

"Emotional retardation," Stone said. "I hadn't quite finished growing from a boy to a man."

He had debated whether to tell her about Amalie Borne and decided it would be a mistake. It was more than a little ironic. He had created an educated woman but he could not bring himself to trust her to be mature about the most important relationship in her life. But Amalie had left Dick too bruised, too wounded, for irony.

The wedding was a small, almost private affair in a white-steepled Baptist church near Oxnard. Most of the guests were from Buchanan Aircraft. Cliff Morris was Dick's best man. One of Cassie's favorite students was her maid of honor. Frank Buchanan gave the bride away. Billy McCall and Victoria, Adrian Van Ness and Amanda completed the party.

Adrian's toast was both a wish and a warning: "May the bride realize she's marrying a man—and an aircraft company."

"God help her!" Amanda said.

Everyone laughed. "I'm not joking!" Amanda said.

"That's what makes it so amusing," Adrian said.

"I would love to be married to an aircraft company. I can't think of anything more exciting," Victoria Van Ness McCall said.

"When you're married to the right man, everything is exciting," Sarah Morris said.

Even though he was well lit on champagne, Dick sensed an undercurrent of malice in Sarah's remark. His years of penetrating the mockery in Amalie's conversation had sharpened his ear for nuances. Sarah's eyes had a feverish glow. She seemed much too excited for a wedding that was decidedly unromantic. Was she needling Victoria—implying that Billy was the wrong man? Or comparing him to Cliff?

Whatever was implied, Victoria ignored it. "I found that out long ago," she said.

She smiled at Billy. A word from Dick's struggle with Amalie lurched into his mind: *voracity*. There were times when he wondered if she had wanted to annihilate him with her relentless reports of her assignations. This was another kind of voracity. For a moment Dick felt sorry for Billy McCall.

The newlyweds departed for a two-week honeymoon on Maui. They rented a plane and flew to other islands. They drank rum swizzles and swam and played tennis, at which Cassie usually beat her out-of-shape husband. By night they made tender love and discussed their future. Cassie wanted to have children and then think about going back to graduate school to get a Ph.D. in American Studies. She had read the recent best-seller, *The Feminine Mystique*, but she still thought a family was more important than a career. "You can take the girl out of the South but you can't take the South out of the girl," she said.

The telephone rang. It was Adrian Van Ness. "Dick," he said. "I hate to interrupt your honeymoon. But I'm afraid you'll have to consider cutting it short. We just heard from Mike Shannon that Johnson's going into Vietnam with both feet. He's committing a hundred and twenty-five thousand men next week and he'll have four hundred thousand there by the end of the year. The Air Force and the Navy and the Marines are letting bids for a dozen different planes. We need you to help us cost out these proposals—"

"I'll call you in the morning," Dick said, slamming down the phone.

"Your leader?" Cassie said.

"If I die and go to heaven or hell, I'm sure Adrian Van Ness will have my telephone number," he said.

He was remembering the night the Korean War began. Making love to Cassie with Adrian Van Ness watching in a corner of his mind. Wondering if he could ever deserve happiness while working for Buchanan Aircraft. Amalie Borne's voice began whispering mockery in that same invisible place.

"Will you love me even if I'm unfaithful with an aircraft company?" he said, putting his arms around Cassie.

"I believe that was in the contract," she said.

She was still his all-American girl.

BOOK EIGHT

HATRED AT WORK

"We're out of it."

Cliff Morris was calling from Washington, where the Federal Aviation Authority was selecting the winner in the design competition for the supersonic airliner. With the usual help from Mike Shannon, who had numerous friends in Lyndon Johnson's White House, Cliff had gotten the bad news a month in advance of the announcement.

"Who won?" Adrian said.

"Boeing."

The one company in the business who did not need the contract. Boeing's new jumbo jet, the 747, was on its way to dominating the intercontinental commercial market. Its medium-range 727 was equally triumphant in the short and middle distances in the United States. Worse, Boeing's supersonic design was the one most people in the aircraft business had dismissed. But the Seattle plane maker had Senator Henry (Scoop) Jackson, better known as the senator from Boeing, on their side. Buchanan and Lockheed, the other two supersonic finalists, were among a half dozen California aircraft companies, all busily cutting each other's throats in Washington. They had no such blunt instrument to get the attention of the bureaucrats.

"Adrian, that thing is never going to fly," Cliff said. "Frank says their swing wing won't work. The environmentalists are already screaming it's going to pollute the upper atmosphere. The sonic boom means it can only fly over water. Guys like the Creature are going to eat Boeing for dinner, with Scoop Jackson for dessert. They'll never vote the money for it."

"I hope you're right," Adrian said, hearing the desperation in Cliff's voice. He had spent most of 1966 in Washington in this losing struggle to rescue their plane. Adrian knew how Cliff would translate the comment. If you are wrong you can say good-bye to your hopes of becoming Buchanan's president.

"We've got the Thunderer. The Navy's nuts about it and McNamara wants the Air Force to buy it. We're first in line on this new monster transport. It's a two-billion-dollar contract, Adrian. They're ready to go for a new high-performance fighter, to replace the Scorpion. We're near the head of the line for that too. The Air Force loves Frank's design."

"What else is cooking?"

"Vietnam is going from bad to worse. We'll have six hundred thousand men in there by the end of the year."

Ruined stopped howling in Adrian's head. He had chosen well when he put Cliff Morris in charge of Buchanan's sales. He had become an adept pupil of the Oakes Ames school of political management. Buchanan now operated a virtual hotel on the Chesapeake where Pentagon civilian and military brass mingled with senators and congressmen for weekends of golfing, shooting, and luxury drinking and dining while Cliff and Mike Shannon and a staff of thirty sold Buchanan planes. At crucial moments Cliff injected Amalie Borne into the game with a sense of climax that Adrian himself would find it hard to match.

But the supersonic airliner. None of the other planes Cliff was talking about meant anything to Adrian compared to the SST. He strode out of his office and took the elevator to the ground floor. Walking swiftly down the maze of corridors, greeted by startled security guards at checkpoints, he reached the hangar where Buchanan's two-million-dollar SST mockup sat, bathed in overhead fluorescent lights.

Gleaming white, three hundred feet long, it was a hollow plane, with no wiring, no hydraulics, no engines inside the huge ducts. But it had a full complement of seats, galleys, lavatories, carpets, and other accessories to give visitors the feel of a finished product. They had used the mockup for a thousand publicity pictures. Now Adrian saw it with different eyes.

It was the Warrior bomber with windows. After some early experimentation with a modified wing, Frank Buchanan had developed a strange indifference to doing more design work on it. Adrian, still in the grip of the illusion of favoritism the Kennedys had created, had not protested. After all, the plane had actually flown at mach 3, something none of their competitors could claim.

Much too late, Adrian remembered Billy McCall's candid admission to the Senate committee that the SST had a whole range of problems that the builder of a bomber did not have to worry about. Fuel economy, landing speed, the complete elimination of duct rumble, or surge, as the British called it. Frank Buchanan had dismissed Adrian's pleas to tackle these problems. He insisted they could be dealt with in the testing and production phase when they would not be spending their own money. Besides, he was too busy with the military planes Cliff had just mentioned.

Behind Frank's smiling refusal, Adrian now saw another motive: hatred. Frank did not want Buchanan Aircraft to win the competition. He did not want Adrian Van Ness to be able to go to the next meeting of the Conquistadores del Cielo and sit down with Don Douglas and Bill Allen of Boeing and Roger

Lewis of General Dynamics as the man who was making the most famous plane in the world, the man whose company's name was on everyone's lips.

Frank Buchanan did not want Adrian Van Ness to go to sleep at night thinking that all around the world, tens of thousands of people were whizzing over oceans and continents in Buchanan Aircraft's SST. With uncanny malice, Frank was depriving Adrian of his deepest wish, his hungriest hope.

Hatred. Adrian felt it beating on him, with the glaring intensity of those overhead lights. There was no place he could escape it. At home it confronted him in Amanda's malevolent eyes, in her relentlessly hostile remarks. It stared at him from his son-in-law's cold gray eyes. Even Victoria, the one person in the world from whom he expected an exemption, seemed to reflect it in her moody alienation. Was this his only reward for his years of struggle and anguish?

"Mr. Van Ness? Any news from Washington?"

It was Terry Pakenham, the foreman who had supervised the work on the mockup. A big thick-necked man with the flushed face of a drinker, he had been with Buchanan since 1946.

"We lost. Chop it up," Adrian said.

"Chop it up?" Pakenham said. "Jesus—can't we give it to a museum or something?" Pakenham had tears in his eyes. Adrian kept forgetting how the men who worked on a plane fell in love with it.

Although he felt nothing but rage, Adrian put his hand on Pakenham's arm. "I'm sorry," he said. "Boeing's won it."

"With that goddamn swing wing? Christ, who did they pay off?" Pakenham roared.

Back in his office, Adrian found the company's attorney, Winthrop Standish, and a lawyer from one of Los Angeles's major law firms waiting impatiently for him. The appointment was on his calendar. He apologized and braced himself for more bad news. Last year Lyndon Johnson had passed a civil rights act designed to banish racial discrimination from American life. Since there were virtually no blacks or Mexicans in the aircraft industry, Adrian had paid little attention to it. Almost as an afterthought, a congressman had suggested adding women to the list of those against whom it would be a crime to discriminate. There were quite a lot of women in the aircraft business—all working at lowly jobs.

Adrian squirmed in his chair. The doleful expressions on the legal faces said everything in advance. "Ed here doesn't agree with your inclination to fight these discrimination suits, Adrian," Standish said.

"Why not?" Adrian said testily. Sixteen women in the design department were suing Buchanan, claiming they had been denied meaningful promotion.

"For one thing, Frank Buchanan says he'll testify in their favor. He says he would have been happy to promote them if the company's policy permitted it."

"If a jury hears that, it'll be treble damages," Ed intoned.

"What about the sex-harassment case from Audrey Sinclair?" Adrian said. "That bitch used to work at the Honeycomb Club!"

"Frank—and Buzz McCall—both admit to having sexual relations with her," Standish said, wiping his brow. "Frank says he never approved of the Honeycomb Club."

"Never approved of it?" Adrian shouted. "He donated the land for it!"

"Adrian," Standish said. "That's irrelevant. The point is what he's saying now. What he might say to a jury. Can you imagine what the papers would do with that story? They'd dig up a half-dozen other women who worked there. We'd be smeared as the company who used government money to pay for sex orgies."

"If it makes you feel any better," Ed intoned, "All the aircraft companies are getting hit with these suits."

But how many of them have a chief designer ready to testify against them? Adrian wondered, almost strangling on his rage. The lawyers departed to negotiate away his money. Adrian stared at his reflection in the window. A rumble. The prototype of the Thunderer, their new ground support plane, was coming in for a landing, his son-in-law Billy McCall at the controls.

Crash, you son of a bitch, Adrian prayed. Crash. He wanted to take something away from Frank Buchanan. Something precious and irreplaceable.

He would do the next best thing. He would deprive Frank of someone else who had been tolerated long enough. Once more Adrian lunged out of his office to stride down corridors to the remote cubicle where Buzz McCall sat plastered for most of each day.

Voices. Billy McCall was in the office, having a drink with Buzz, talking about the air war in Vietnam. "It's the goddamndest mess I've ever seen," Billy said. "The fucking president picks out the targets. Or one of McNamara's Pentagon assholes does it for him. Then everybody says it proves air power can't do the job."

Adrian charged into the office. "Hello, Billy," he said. "Buzz. I've got some bad news. We've lost the SST contract. Under the circumstances we've got to cut costs. You're off the payroll at the end of the week."

"Adrian—Chrissake—gimme somethin' to do. Still make a contribution," Buzz mumbled.

Adrian glanced at Billy. Loathing was all he saw in his eyes. "This is a business, not a goddamn rest home," Adrian snarled.

Other words leaped to his lips. *He killed the only woman I ever loved. I've been waiting twenty-five years to do this.* But he did not speak them.

Back in his office, Adrian struggled for self-control. He could fire Frank Buchanan too. But that would be a mistake. Only time, his ally in the past, time and forethought, could bring him revenge on the scale he sought. In the meantime he had to remember who he was, he had to cope with the hatred in other ways.

His first target, now that Buzz was gone for good, was Billy McCall. He had to get that defiant bastard under control. He wanted to break him, not only because it would wound Frank Buchanan. He wanted to deliver the empty shell to Victoria so she could see for herself what a hoax she had married.

A month later, Cliff Morris came booming into Los Angeles with the proposal for the new transport. There would be a pro forma competition with Douglas and Convair but Buchanan was the guaranteed winner. It was going to be the biggest plane in the world, able to carry an entire battalion of troops into combat. The contract was now worth three billion dollars—a nice consolation for the loss of the SST and the Warrior.

There were several flies in this soothing ointment. The plane would have to be built in Louisiana to keep the new head of the House Armed Services Committee happy—and it would be a fixed-cost contract, a TPP, they were now calling it—a Total Performance Package. The potential overruns—no one had ever built a plane of this size before—were scary.

"Who do you think should be the project manager?" Adrian said.

"Billy McCall," Cliff said.

"What does he know about running something this big?" Adrian snorted.

"Not a damn thing," Cliff said. "But we've got Mike Shannon to cover our asses in Washington. He says half the senators and two-thirds of the congressmen on the armed services committees think this TPP idea is idiotic. We can get back most of an overrun on appeal."

"So?"

"So it's a good chance to see what kind of a manager Billy is. If he can't hack it now's the time to find out."

Adrian suddenly read all the meanings in Cliff's matter-of-fact voice. Here was the ally he was looking for, someone who hated Billy McCall even more than he did.

"I think you're right," Adrian said. "Now's the time."

TICKET TO PARADISE

After calling the ground controller three times on the wrong frequencies, I find the right one. Billy's eyes roll. We taxi onto the tarmac. I set the altimeter wrong. Billy is yelling at me not to use brakes and power at the same time. When I search his face, trying to understand the source of his rage, he tells me to get my eyes back on the taxiway where they belong.

At run-up I get the tower frequency wrong. Finally we are set for takeoff, with a plane just behind us, which rattles me even more than usual. The wheels lift off before I realize it and I am pulling the nose up into a stall. Billy yells at me to get into a lower nose position, to pick up speed as lift increases. Why can't I remember any of these things?

Suddenly we are airborne in a bell jar full of haze. Water droplets make the air glossy, like taffy, iridescent in places. The airport, the runway, the ground disappear. I think it's marvelous and ask Billy if he thinks so too. "When are you going to make your turn?" Billy yells.

A quick look for oncoming traffic in the haze, then I bank left, still climbing toward 2,000 feet. I shoot through the ceiling because I haven't changed the plane's attitude and reduced the power at the right time. Worse, I am supposed to be flying a rectangle around the airport and already I'm arcing far out to sea.

"Why are we out here? Where are we going?" Billy yells. "Why are we still climbing?"

"I don't know!" I scream back.

"Do something. Don't just sit there. Do something!"

I cut the throttle back and bank sharply toward the airport again. It's a terrible bank. The turn indicator ball tumbles far left. Billy points to it and yells "Jesus Christ!"

"We're supposed to be flying a base leg at right angles!" Billy shouts. "Are we too high or too low to make the runway?"

"I don't know," I say, beginning to sob.

"Do something!" Billy shouts.

I throttle back and we drop dead toward the telephone wires on the west side of the airport. Too low. I gun the throttle and now we are too high. I see the aim point but need flaps to steepen our descent.

I look at the ground, trying to estimate my airspeed. We seem to be going like mad. "How many times do I have to tell you to look at the instruments, not the ground?" Billy says.

I come in too hard and too fast and worst of all not on the center line but at an angle. "Fix it!" Billy says.

I try pedaling: right rudder, left rudder. Nothing happens.

"Don't just jiggle the rudder. Use it. Get us back on that center line with our nose straight! Now! Fast! Fast!"

The runway looms under us at ten feet. I try to level out the nose. He yanks the yoke back hard and settles us in. "Victoria," he says. "This plane is not designed to land on its nose. You were diving at five feet off the ground!"

Sarah Chapman Morris sat on the sunny deck of Victoria Van Ness McCall's futuristic house on a ridge in Topanga Canyon, reading the story of Billy McCall's attempts to teach Victoria how to fly. It was a disaster from the first lesson to the last one. Victoria had a poetic mind. Flight to her was an experience in beauty. The plane was a creature as mysterious as an animal or a bird. She simply could not grasp the hard technical details of conquering the sky. She either ignored the dials or chased them obsessively when Billy yelled at her to watch them. She made major changes in pitch at low altitudes, where life or death required delicacy. She admired clouds when she should have been looking for other planes in her approach pattern.

She had written it all down with unsparing accuracy, portraying herself as a hopeless pilot. She wanted Billy to read it and laugh and say something cheerful and kind. She was showing it to Sarah because she needed a confidante and

432

Sarah was always there, smiling sadly, eager to listen to every awful thing Billy was doing to destroy his marriage.

A doe bounded out of the trees and dashed across the clearing. A moment later she was followed by a buck. Somewhere in the nearby woods the buck caught up to his quarry. Sarah and Victoria listened to the thrashing and panting. Sarah saw the whole thing in the theater of her mind, the rutting, the submission.

Did Victoria see it too? Of course. She was Sarah. Sarah was Victoria. She got up and took one of the tranquilizers Dr. Kirk Willoughby had prescribed for her. "I hate my mind!" she said to Sarah. "Do you ever feel that way?"

"Of course. All women do," Sarah said.

Victoria told Sarah she did not know where her husband was. He might be flying over China Lake, the Navy testing center, in the Thunderer or lying on the sand at Malibu with some acid-dropping teenager. She did not know and she did not want to know.

She could call Frank Buchanan and ask him if Billy was at China Lake, turning over the Thunderer to the Navy for testing. If Frank said no, she would burst into tears. If he said yes she would burst into tears anyway.

Victoria showed Sarah a list of the things she hated Billy to do. She had written them down yesterday. She was thinking of showing it to him. She was even thinking of having it printed in headline-size type and posting it on the wall of their bedroom.

1. Fly without me.
2. Go to Malibu without me.
3. Go to Laguna Beach without me.
4. Insult Cliff Morris.
5. Criticize Sarah Morris.
6. Talk to any woman under thirty.
7. Read the newspapers aloud.
8. Look at the news on TV.
9. Say what the fuck.
10. Say why the fuck.
11. Say how the fuck.
12. Drink in front of me.
13. Drink without me.
14. Talk about World War II or Korea.
15. Talk about Vietnam.
16. Ask me if I believe in God.
17. Ask me why I don't really like to fuck.
18. Tell me I don't really like to fuck.
19. Tell me why some women are better fuckers.

Sarah Morris said it was a very good list. She told Victoria a better way to handle Billy. She had to find something to do outside the house, something that made her look independent without being independent. Because Billy would not tolerate real independence. Sarah urged Victoria to become cochairperson of one of her committees. There was scarcely a volunteer activity in Los Angeles Sarah did not either run from behind the scenes or chair or both. She was always raising money for starving Chicano artists or scholarships for ghetto blacks or a new campaign to eliminate smog. Sarah told Victoria being a committeeperson was very good preparation for becoming an executive's wife. After all, Billy was bound to become a Buchanan Aircraft executive. He might even become president.

Victoria frowned. Lately she had begun to dislike the way Sarah pronounced Billy's name. Sarah knew she disliked it but she could not stop pronouncing it that way, with a throb, a thud of hatred in it. "I heard Billy made some wonderful suggestions to improve the Thunderer," Sarah said.

Billy, Victoria thought. "Oh? Who told you that?"

"I think it was Frank Buchanan. I was talking to him at the benefit for the Downtown Arts. He's such a sweet man. He adores Billy."

Billy. Victoria thought.

"But then we all do. We're so lucky to have gotten him away from the Air Force. It's such a shame about the SST, though. Cliff is just crushed by it. He so looked forward to working with Billy on it. They would have made a perfect team."

Billy, Victoria thought.

Sarah urged Victoria to join the Committee to Rebuild Watts. A mob had burned down most of this black Los Angeles slum earlier in the year. She said Cliff was going to chair a subcommittee to get more blacks into the aircraft industry workforce. Maybe Billy could join him. That would give him and Victoria something to share, outside the house.

Billy, Victoria thought.

"Your father's going to be honorary chairman. I was talking to him the other day and he complained he never sees you. This would be a good excuse. He wishes he saw more of you—and Billy."

Billy, Victoria thought.

Sarah could see Victoria trying to understand what she disliked in the way Sarah said *Billy*. Victoria shook her head. "I don't want that sort of help. Especially not from *him*."

"That's not being realistic, Victoria," Sarah said. "He wants to help you—and Billy in every way he can."

Victoria sat there, trying to understand why she was suddenly unable to stand Sarah. Was it because of the way she said *Billy* or was it because she was English? That lovely vanilla accent carried Victoria back to Oxford, to days when she sat around talking about ways to save the world. Now all she thought about was how to save her marriage.

The telephone rang. It was Frank Buchanan. "I have some more books for your mother," he said. "Can I drop them off some time today?"

"I don't think she reads them, Frank," Victoria said.

"It doesn't matter. Just having them in the house, in her room, could make a difference. A book releases emanations. Not as much as a mind but—"

Frank's mysticism was lost on Victoria. She had her father's cold objectivity toward life on matters that did not involve Billy McCall.

"I know it sounds foolish. But it means a great deal to me. I'm very fond of your mother," Frank said.

Sarah had told Victoria that Amanda and Frank had been lovers. She had revealed almost all Buchanan's secrets, carefully portraying Adrian as a much-misunderstood man, hoping it would eventually reach his ears.

"How's Billy?" Frank asked.

"Fine. He's up at China Lake today, isn't he? Delivering the Thunderer?"

"I don't know. I'm spending my days and nights on another plane. A monster transport. I hope it won't look like a monster, of course."

"It won't, I'm sure of that," Victoria said.

"I'll drop off the books on the way home."

Sarah was in the kitchen fixing lunch. Victoria was about to help her when the phone rang again. "Is Billy there?" her father said.

Billy, Victoria thought. He pronounced it the same way. "No," she said.

"Do you know where he is?"

"I thought he was at China Lake. Delivering the Thunderer."

"He did that last week."

Victoria struggled to stifle an impulse to weep. This was the third time Adrian had called in search of Billy. Was he trying to tell her something? Or find out something?

"I just thought you and he might want to hear some good news," Adrian said. "We've gotten a three-billion-dollar contract to build the world's biggest transport for the Air Force. I'm going to make Billy the project manager. He'll be perfect for the job. He'll be able to handle the usual maddening interference from the Pentagon. Cliff Morris will keep Congress at bay. He and Billy will work together beautifully. Do you think he'll do it?"

Sarah, listening on the extension in the kitchen, heard her weeks of patient persuasion pay off. Victoria's resistance dissolved. "I hope so. It's exactly what he needs. More responsibility."

"Ah. I've finally done something right?"

"What do you mean?"

"Ever since you married, I've felt you regarded me as the scum of the earth."

"That's not true!"

"Maybe it's just neurosis at work."

"I'm grateful, Daddy. I really am."

"I'm not doing it for that reason. But it's nice to hear."

"How's mother?"

"About the same. Wondering aloud why you don't give her a grandchild."

"Maybe now we will. If Billy isn't flying any more, there goes his last excuse."

"That thought occurred to me."

"You Machievelli."

"Disraeli. I think of myself as Disraeli. His Victoria was difficult too, at times."

Victoria hung up and sat there, suffused by wistful nostalgic love. Sarah brought a tray of chicken salad and iced tea out on the deck. As Victoria started to tell her the good news, the buck and the doe emerged from the woods. He was nuzzling her. Out of the trees whizzed an arrow that struck the buck squarely in the chest. He bounded high in the air and came down on crumpling legs. The doe vanished into the woods in three huge leaps. Two men emerged from the woods with longbows and quivers of arrows on their shoulders. There were broad grins on their brutal faces.

"You sons of bitches!" Victoria screamed.

She ran into the house and seized Billy's shotgun off the wall. From a drawer she scooped a handful of shells and shoved them into the chamber. Outside the men were standing beside the deer, glaring at the house. Victoria aimed the gun in their general direction and fired. The men fled into the trees.

Victoria reloaded the gun and ran down to the buck, who lay on his side, barely breathing. One eye rolled up toward her; it seemed to ask a question she could not answer. Victoria put the muzzle of the shotgun behind his ear and pulled the trigger. She turned to a trembling Sarah and said: "Sometimes I think the world would be a better place without men, don't you?"

Sarah was enormously tempted to agree with her. But her hateful heart whispered: *it's too soon.*

HOUSE ON FIRE

"Where's Liz?" Cliff Morris asked as the family assembled in the living room to drive to Buchanan's 1967 Christmas party.

"She's not coming," Sarah said.

"Why not?"

"She says she refuses to toast the war machine."

Cliff's face darkened. Seventeen-year-old Charlie grinned in anticipation. He loved these brawls between Liz and her father. He was 100 percent on Cliff's side. Their quiet middle child, Margaret, looked stricken. She tried to stay neutral but she secretly sided with her older sister.

"Liz!" Cliff roared.

Liz slouched downstairs. She was a brunette beauty with her father's chiseled features. Her silken hair streamed to her waist. She wore blue jeans and a work shirt, the uniform of her generation. She had graduated from Stanford last year and was getting a master's in art history at UCLA. Her boyfriend, a political scientist, was the leading antiwar activist on the campus.

"Either you come to this party or you move out of this house," Cliff said.

"I'll be gone when you come back," Liz said.

"You better get ready to pay your own tuition from now on," Cliff said.

"I'll get a job. Maybe on your assembly line. What will you do when they catch me sabotaging one of your murder machines?"

"I'll personally escort you to jail!" Cliff roared.

"Commie freako," Charlie said.

"Junior fascist pig," Liz replied.

"Shut up, all of you!" Margaret wailed.

"Second the motion," Sarah said. As usual, she remained perfectly calm, in total control of her feelings. She had become the family arbiter, the semi-outsider who was able to adjudicate among these overwrought Americans. "We'll discuss this tomorrow. You can postpone your evacuation for a day, Liz."

The Christmas party was bigger, louder, more crowded than ever. It spread over three hangars, with a dance band in each one. New planes were on display, the sturdy ground-support craft, the Thunderer, already in production, a mock-up of a needle-nosed high-performance fighter, the SkyDemon, and a gigantic painting of the projected new transport, the Colossus. Buchanan was booming. The workforce was over fifty thousand. The champagne flowed. But Sarah Morris sensed an undercurrent of malaise.

For one thing, everyone, even Cliff, had to pass through a metal detector to get in. There were uniformed security guards at the doors; dozens more roamed the hangar floors. These days every company in the aircraft industry was the target of a continuous stream of bomb threats and vows to sabotage the production line. In California particularly, the rising protest against the war in Vietnam had focused on the American bombing offensive, Operation Rolling Thunder.

What multiplied the malaise was the failure of the offensive. The Communists seemed as potent as ever and they were shooting down an appalling number of American planes. For the disciples of air power this was a very disturbing development that they tried desperately to explain away. One part of Sarah's mind secretly exulted in this spectacle. Another part—her public self—deplored and regretted it and even sympathized with Cliff as he struggled to explain it to Charlie and his sisters.

Cliff went off to work the crowd in the next hangar. They always separated at big parties to achieve maximum contact. Susan Hardy cruised toward Sarah, a dark brown Scotch in her stubby hand. She was virtually spherical now, with a balloon body supporting a smaller balloon face. She never wore anything but immense flapping muumuus, which covered everything including her feet. But her eyes retained their fierce intelligence and there was nothing spherical about her tongue. She had become a virulent critic of the war.

"I saw a top-secret report on our actual plane losses over 'Nam," she said. "The numbers are unbelievable."

Susan always started her conversations in the middle these days. She was full of energy; an hour or two with her left Sarah feeling exhausted. Susan's divorce from Sam Hardy was a spectacular success. She had taken half of everything he owned—in cash. Sam had been forced to sell almost every piece of real property in his name except his car. Susan proceeded to compound the torment by getting a job in Buchanan's public relations department, which enabled her to keep tabs on her ex-husband's anemic love life and self-destructive drinking.

Lately Susan had become interested in attacking the American war machine—a target more worthy of her mammoth animosity. She had been trying to enlist Sarah in the campaign but she was much too busy fighting her private war against Billy McCall to be helpful.

"You must hear things from Cliff, Sarah. Just pass them along to me. I know what to do with them," Susan said sotto voce, while Margaret and Charlie gazed at the swirling crowd and the planes.

"I never know what's important and what isn't," Sarah lied. She was using Susan to rehearse her role as the sweet, slightly bewildered wife. She was not about to risk Cliff's career to feed Susan's insatiable appetite for revenge on the whole male sex. She only wanted revenge on one particular male.

"Sarah, you're looking so lovely," Adrian Van Ness said, as Susan Hardy ballooned conspiratorially off toward the bar. "It must have something to do with growing up in England. All that rain on your skin."

Beside Adrian stood Victoria Van Ness McCall and her husband. Billy gave Sarah his usual mocking smile. She returned it with maximum malice. *You won't be smiling at this time next year, hero,* she thought. *You'll be the laughingstock of the aircraft business.*

Sarah knew all about the plan to put Billy in charge of the giant transport and watch him fall on his face. She had given Cliff the idea one night after they had cavorted on that dark current that electrified their bedroom. *Get Adrian to give him some big job. Something he can't handle,* she had whispered.

Sarah introduced Charlie and Margaret. "We thought it was time they started enjoying the fun," she said.

"Have you finished testing the Thunderer, Colonel?" Charlie asked Billy.

"The first ones'll be over 'Nam in a couple of months."

"Could you give me a look at the cockpit?"

"Sure," Billy said.

For a moment, watching them stroll away, Sarah almost cried "Stop!" or something equally absurd. Charlie was as tall as Billy now. He was still mesmerized by planes. The physical resemblance remained oblique. No one but her would ever know the possible, even the probable secret.

"You can cross me off your benefit list," Victoria said. "We'll be leaving for Louisiana soon. Billy can hardly wait to get to work on the Colossus."

A pulse throbbed in Sarah's throat. Adrian had been almost too amenable to making Billy the project manager of the Colossus. Sarah had grown alarmed. She did not trust Adrian. Those hooded eyes were too cold. What if Billy pulled it off—built the biggest plane in the world?

Victoria talked about her determination to have a child. Billy had finally agreed to it. She hoped it would be a girl. Her father would adore a granddaughter. "Isn't it strange the way most men favor boys, but Daddy doesn't? I can't imagine how he would have treated me if I'd been a boy."

It was a kind of fugue in two themes, Daddy's fondness and Billy's readiness to have a child. The ideas, the images, wound strands of wire around Sarah's throat until she found it more and more difficult to breathe.

"Fascinating," Sarah said, watching Charlie and Billy climb up on the Thunderer's wing and lean into the cockpit. In profile the faces were virtually identical.

"I've been thinking of putting most of my money into Buchanan stock. Daddy said if I did he'd give me a seat on the board. I think he's teasing but it's a good idea, don't you think? A statement of confidence in the company's future?"

Sarah gazed into Victoria's wide heavy face and confronted Adrian's cold analytical eyes. Was it possible she knew Sarah was her secret enemy? This babble was all part of a carefully calculated plan to unnerve her? For the twentieth time Sarah discounted the idea. She possessed this woman. She *was* her. Every touch, every kiss, Victoria experienced in Billy's arms belonged to Sarah.

"How does Billy feel about that fellow who set a new speed record out at Edwards the other day?" Sarah asked.

An Air Force major had flown another experimental plane, the X-15, made by North American, at an astonishing 4,138 miles an hour.

"He hasn't said a word to me about it," Victoria said.

Frank Buchanan limped toward them, his lined face exuding Christmas cheer. He kissed Sarah and Margaret, then Victoria. "I just saw your mother," he said to Victoria. "She's improved a great deal. We had a very pleasant conversation. It's remarkable how much of her memory has returned."

"I almost wish it hadn't. She remembers every bad thing I ever did or said," Victoria replied.

"It's just her old determination to speak the truth no matter how much it upsets people," Frank said. "She told me I was getting uglier by the minute."

"We adore you anyway," Sarah said.

"That's what an old lecher likes to hear," Frank said, giving her a hug.

Charlie and Billy rejoined their circle. Frank shook hands with them. Sarah could see Charlie was practically exploding with some sort of good news. "You look like you've just seen all your Christmas presents in advance," she said.

"Colonel McCall says before he goes to Louisiana he'd like to teach me to fly," Charlie said. "If it's okay with you and Dad."

"He knows more about the inside of a cockpit than I did when I was his age," Billy said.

"Say yes, Mom. I'll handle Dad," Charlie said.

Billy's smile radiated mockery. Did he know? Sarah wondered. Was he showing her what he could do in retaliation? Take away the son she loved more than both her daughters?

Was that true? Did she love anything or anyone any more? Was it all possession, greed, desire? Sarah relived the vow she had made that day in the desert when she heard Billy inviting Victoria to Catalina. That oath of eternal hatred and revenge spoken to the sun and wind and emptiness. Was that the only thing she loved?

"How can we refuse an offer like that from the best pilot in the country?" Sarah said.

She was in perfect control of her feelings as usual. "Do you wish you'd been flying that new rocket plane out in the desert?" she asked Billy. "It wiped out your old speed record rather completely."

"Only kids go for records," Billy said. His smile was as bright—and mean-ingless—as ever. He was in perfect control of his feelings too.

"I can't wait to get up there," Charlie said.

"I think we've got a born pilot here," Frank Buchanan said.

ASSASSIN TIME

"Cassie? Listen—I'm afraid it's another late night."

"It's okay. I understand. I married an aircraft company."

The joke was starting to wear thin. Dick could hear the weariness in Cassie's voice. "It's this goddamn TPP contract—you've never seen anything like it," he said.

"I know, I know."

"Kiss Jake for me."

"The last time I did that, he said, 'Daddy? Who's he?' "

Dick slammed down the phone and cursed Adrian Van Ness, Secretary of Defense Robert McNamara, and the aircraft business, in that order. For the past six months he had barely seen his wife and son. The design and engineering departments had been working with him on the Total Performance Package for the giant transport, the C-116—known as the Colossus. It was turning into the most elaborate document ever contrived by the mind of man. Every possible contingency in the development of the plane, every imaginable expense, had to be analyzed, described, and costed in quintuplicate. As Buchanan's money man, Dick was intricately involved in this process, which Frank Buchanan repeatedly called idiotic.

No matter how hard they tried, they were never going to be able to anticipate the problems that might arise in developing a plane this big. Rolls-Royce was still trying to design an engine strong enough to lift it. The Air Force was still debating crucial factors such as the takeoff and landing speed.

Billy McCall, the plane's project manager, agreed with Frank Buchanan about the idiocy of it all. Like everyone else, Dick assumed Billy had gotten this job because he was Adrian Van Ness's son-in-law. He did not have the executive experience to handle something this complex. He was simultaneously supposed to supervise the construction of a new plant in Louisiana and keep track of the paperwork in Santa Monica. It was impossible and Billy did not even try. He let Dick handle the Santa Monica end of it.

A week later—a week in which he spent exactly eight hours at home, most of them asleep—Dick stood with his hands on his hips, watching forklifters trundle tons of paper into the yawning interior of an Excalibur-derived transport. The TPP was taking up the entire cargo space of a plane that ten short years ago was the biggest set of wings in the air.

Billy McCall frowned beside him. "Do you really expect us to pay attention to all that wastepaper, Stone?" he said.

"Somebody does. The Secretary of Defense, for openers."

"It's like marriage, Stone. You can't let the bastards grind you down."

By this time everyone in the company knew that Victoria had failed to tame Billy. The old-timers, for whom Billy was a sexual as well as an aerobatic hero, had rooted against her all the way. They called Victoria "the Queen B" (for bitch) and eagerly retold Billy's acts of defiance, such as failing to show up for Adrian's sixty-fifth birthday party. There was a drumfire of names of women Billy was supposedly fucking at ten thousand feet.

Dick had declined Billy's random invitations to join him in continuing bachelorhood. He was worried about the unhappiness in Cassie's eyes. Practically from the day they married, the whole company had gone into a wartime production mode. The workforce doubled and so did Dick's responsibilities.

"Still flying?" Billy asked.

"I don't have time."

"That's what worries me about this fucking job," Billy said.

Dick watched the Excalibur's cargo doors grind shut on the tons of Total Performance Package paper. He shared Billy's contempt for this harebrained attempt to control costs. They were fighting a war in Vietnam for which the Colossus was desperately needed. They had wasted six months writing the contract for it.

"Let's celebrate a little, Stone. You can't be an old married man all your life."

They headed for a nearby bar. Billy wanted to talk about Vietnam. He was appalled by the way the air war was being fought. Thousands of planes and pilots were being lost while the key targets in North Vietnam, the port of Haiphong, and the Red River dams, were off-limits.

"We could starve them to death in three months if we took out those two items," Billy said.

Dick was not sure he was right. He tried not to think about the war. But he knew it was sapping the morale of the company. Alcoholism and absenteeism among the workforce had soared as parents quarreled with sons and daughters. The old élan, the sense of being on the leading edge of Jack Kennedy's defense of freedom anywhere in the world, was gone. They had developed a siege mentality.

Billy began talking about how much he hated being grounded. He berated himself for giving up the chief test pilot's job to become "a fucking bean counter." Dick was surprised. He thought Billy was as ambitious as the next man. Becoming project manager for the Colossus was a very big promotion.

"Why did you take it?" Dick asked.

Billy was pretty drunk by now. He stared at his image in the mirror. He was still wearing his flight jacket and fifty missions hat, defying his elevation to the executive ranks. "Believe it or not, Stone, I did it to keep my wife happy. Does that make any sense to you?"

"Hell, yes. If you don't keep them happy they can make you damn miserable."

Billy finished his Scotch and shook his head. "It doesn't make a damn bit of sense to me."

Dick should have seen trouble plummeting out of the sky toward them like a Starduster shattered by whirl mode. But so many other things seemed on the verge of spinning out of control in the year 1967, he found it hard to focus on a single problem. It was especially hard to worry about Billy, who had repeatedly established his ability to live dangerously and somehow survive. It never occurred to him that on the ground Billy was as vulnerable as the rest of them.

Billy and Victoria departed for Louisiana. For nine months Dick did not give them or the giant plane more than a passing thought. Other planes, the endless war, the seething unrest in American cities and on college campuses, the birth of a daughter, absorbed his attention. A new chief engineer, a brilliant, cheerful Californian named Edwards, collaborated with him on a study that revealed Buchanan's assembly line workers only spent 26 percent of their time actually making planes. The rest was spent looking for tools, schmoozing with friends, and betting on horses and football pools. Edwards hired more supervisors, decentralized tool storage, and raised production rates 40 percent—with fewer workers. Adrian was enormously impressed.

Then came a summons from Buchanan's president. "We're getting very bad vibes on the Colossus program," Adrian said. "I want you to fly to Louisiana tonight and find out what's happening."

Dick flew to New Orleans and drove north a hundred miles to Knowlesville, in the heart of Louisiana redneck country. The Buchanan factory was by far the largest structure in the landscape. It loomed above the tree line ten miles away. Dick introduced himself to the plant security manager, got a badge and went for a walk along the assembly line. The fuselage of the Colossus prototype was taking shape—a whale-shaped creature as high as a four-story building. The wings were so large, they were being fabricated on another line and would be lowered through the sliding roof for final assembly.

"Hey, Clint," one welder said to the man working next to him as he adjusted his mask, "you think this big sumbitch is evuh gonna fly?"

"Hell no," Clint said.

Beyond the prototype fuselage, Dick did not like what he saw. Workers were standing around shooting the breeze. On the line where they were fabricating the tails, a half-dozen were rolling dice.

"Where's your foreman?" Dick said, as a wiry little man with a mean mouth and shifty eyes won the pile of bills in the pot.

Embarrassed shrugs all around. "Maybe upstairs lookin' for someone to play some acey-deucey," the little man drawled. Everyone laughed and threw more money into the pot.

In the plant manager's office, Dick found balding, bearded Joe Timberlake, a Buchanan old hand, who had run their Mojave plant with admirable efficiency. Joe looked harassed and wan. Everything was wrong. Louisiana's unions were corrupt on a scale unknown in California. Everyone wanted payoffs or daily walkouts and slowdowns would begin to occur. The education level of the workforce was low and they did not train well or, for that matter, particularly like factory work. The supervisors and foremen they had brought with them from California hated the place and were going home in droves. The engineers kept getting wind-tunnel data from California that required expensive design changes.

By the time Dick got to Project Manager Billy McCall's office, he was braced for bad news. He expected a gaunt grim-eyed ghost of the relaxed test pilot he had seen in California. Instead, Billy was tipped back in his chair, his feet on the desk, exchanging hangar talk about his Korean War days with the colonel who was the Air Force's plant representative.

The colonel departed and Dick asked Billy how things were going. "Couldn't be better," he said. "We're a little behind schedule but we'll catch up with some overtime next week. We'll have the monster ready to roll on graduation day."

"How's Victoria?"

"Haven't seen her in about a week. She's in New York tryin' to find out why she can't get pregnant."

"Adrian's worried about costs. We've got to stay inside that bid, you know."

"Ah, hell Dick, that contract's a lot of boilerplate. We've had generals down here and I told them we were probably over budget but they said not to sweat about it, we'd figure something out up the line. The important thing is to get the big bitch rolled out. They really need her in 'Nam."

"I hope you're right. How much are we over budget right now?"

"I haven't got any idea," Billy said.

More than a little stunned, Dick managed to mutter: "Adrian wants some facts. Can I see the books?"

"Sure. You gonna be here long?"

"It depends on how long it takes me to get the facts."

"We're not far from New Orleans. Lot of action down there. Some great light-chocolate stuff. I can fly us down there before you can say pussy galore. The old Lustra's parked out on the runway."

"Sorry. I'm married to a girl who wouldn't appreciate a husband with the clap."

"Christ," Billy said, with a disgusted chuckle. He was the only man Dick ever met who smiled when he was disappointed. "Is there a bachelor left in the goddamn company?"

"Sam Hardy. But I hear he's about to get married again."

"Buzz always said designers weren't in touch with reality. That proves it."

"Where are you cooking the books?"

Billy grinned and led him down a corridor to an office presided over by dapper, energetic Paul Casey, one of Buchanan's best accountants. He had two assistants hired locally and four or five clerical workers. The sight of Dick made all three accountants extremely nervous. Dick retired to Casey's office and told him he was here to examine the books.

Casey began talking very fast to explain why the books were not up to date. The engineers were so busy revising the plans they were always weeks behind with their cost estimates. They were hiring and firing over two hundred workers a week and it was impossible to do more than estimate the obligations to state unemployment insurance, medical plans and the like. They kept getting bills from trucking companies they never heard of—about three months late.

Around midnight, as exhaustion bleared his eyes, Dick began to get some idea of the Colossus's finances. He wiped his glasses and set them firmly on his head again, as if he needed to achieve maximum clarity. "Based on these figures," he said, "estimating all the overtime costs in the past two months, you could be two hundred million dollars over budget."

Casey sighed like a defeated philosopher.

"That's half the fucking net worth of the company!"

Casey groaned like a man undergoing surgery without an anesthetic.

"If the pattern continues, by the time we build a hundred and twenty-four of those things, we'll be two billion dollars over. Two billion!"

Casey gurgled like a drowning man.

"You could buy the whole fucking state of Louisiana for two billion dollars."

"I wish we could—and then sink it," Casey said.

"These are just estimates. I'm going to stay here until we get exact figures, if I have to start reading labels on packing cases and calling up suppliers personally."

"Billy kept telling me not worry about it," Casey moaned.

Dick called Cassie from his motel the next morning to tell her he would not be home for at least a week. She said it was perfectly all right, even though she was starting to wonder what would happen if she tried to stay married to him and divorced the aircraft company.

The joke was no longer thin. "I'm sorry Babe. I really am," Dick said.

Dick called Adrian next. When he gave him the figures there was a long silence, which Dick presumed was astonishment. "I'll call Mike Shannon in Washington and tell him to go to work on damage control," Adrian said. "If this stuff gets out, McNamara will crucify us. He's never forgiven us for the brawl over the Warrior. Can we bury the costs in our budget for the time being?"

Adrian was asking him to cook the books. Dick reluctantly agreed to do it.

444

"Eventually we've got to get the money back or find someone richer than Rockefeller to finance us for the rest of the century," he warned.

"I'm betting on Shannon to get the money. But it may take time. What's Billy got to say for himself?"

"Not a hell of a lot. He doesn't think there's anything to worry about. I suggest you give him an assistant who can get tough with the unions, the suppliers, the whole goddamn Mafioso circus that runs this state."

There was a long pause. Then Adrian said: "I'm inclined to do something much more drastic."

"Wait a minute, Adrian. You've got some responsibility for this mess. You sent Billy down here without an iota of advice, as far as I can see."

"I thought he was a mature, responsible executive," Adrian said. "Are you defending someone who's in danger of costing us two billion dollars?"

"I see no point in crucifying him. Why the hell didn't you let him go on testing planes? Flying's the only thing he likes to do."

"Dick—may I remind you that I make the decisions on who should—and should not—be crucified? That's part of my job. Maybe the most important part."

Dick found the choice of words—*remind you*—and the metaphor—singularly repugnant. He began to realize something was going on here more important— to Adrian, at least—than the two-billion-dollar overrun.

"I'm sending someone absolutely trustworthy down to help you straighten out this mess," Adrian said. "Cliff Morris will be on a plane in two hours."

Dick drove to the plant in Knowlesville, wondering if he should talk to Billy before Adrian started setting up the cross and handing out the nails. As he went past the project manager's door on the way to the accounting department, he heard Billy call: "Hey, Dick."

Billy had the usual smile on his face. Dick felt a spear of guilt. "Dick," Billy said, still smiling. "I thought we were friends."

"We are."

"Does a friend call the biggest prick in California and tell him his buddy's fucked up?" Billy said. "I just got off the phone with God, otherwise known as Daddy, and more widely as Adrian Van Ness. He dumped about a ton of shit on my head, most of which came from you."

"Billy—I was sent down here with the responsibility for finding out where we are on this job. You're putting the whole fucking company at risk, do you realize that?"

"Oh, ain't that awful. Puttin' you and Adrian and all the other fuckin' front office paper shufflers at risk. Now they're sendin' the number one asskisser in the aircraft business, Mr. Supersalesman Cliff Morris himself down here to straighten things out. You gonna stay around to help him shove the shaft up my butt?"

"I've got work to do," Dick said. "I hope you and Adrian discussed how to get these costs under control."

"As a matter of fact, I told him it was impossible, if he was gonna have this goddamn thing ready for Lyndon Johnson to inspect on October nineteenth. That's rollout day. I'll bet you a hundred dollars Big Cliff, so well-known for his courage, decides I'm right—after he fires me."

"He isn't going to fire you. Nobody can fire you."

"I can quit. That's what I'll do before I take a single order from that shitheel. Jesus Christ, Dick, couldn't you have come to me first and talked this over? Don't you know Adrian and Cliff and his English bitch of a wife have been tryin' to hang my scalp out to dry since the day I married Victoria? Where've you been?"

Score another one for Amalie Bourne, Dick thought. He had lost touch with what was happening all around him in Buchanan Aircraft. "Maybe you're right, but two billion dollars is still a hell of a lot of money."

"Shit. The missile division blew three billion on that Crusader rocket for the Navy and no one got the firing squad. That fucking thing never even flew. At least we'll have a plane—a great plane—to show for the money."

"But we'll be in hock for a hundred years to pay it off."

"Dick—you should've kept flyin'. You're only two degrees away from turning into Adrian Van Ness."

For a man who seemed indifferent to office politics, Billy had an uncanny ability to deliver a kick to the solar plexus. More kicks were coming. By the time Cliff Morris arrived in Knowlesville that night, Dick had received a call from Frank Buchanan, defending Billy and blaming most of the cost overrun on the Air Force, which kept changing its mind about the plane.

Cliff could not have looked more grim as he stalked into Dick's temporary office. But the moment he closed the door, a gloating smile appeared. "It looks like the son-in-law has finally fucked up," he said.

Again Dick had the unpleasant sense of discovering he was not on the inside of what was happening. He was a passenger, an employee, performing a function.

"What are you going to do?" he asked.

"I don't know. Maybe get the son of a bitch indicted—if you can get us the evidence. Gross malfeasance, that sort of thing."

"You're not getting any help from me."

"Dick—Adrian told me your cooperation was *guaranteed*," Cliff said.

Ignoring that ugly threat, Dick told Cliff why impaling Billy McCall would not work. Frank Buchanan was backing Billy 150 percent. He asked Cliff to imagine Frank testifying at a congressional hearing. Buchanan would never get another government contract.

"If you're trying to knock Billy out of the race for the top job, you've already done it. The board of directors will have to be told about this eventually and they'll blame him. Push him too far and we'll all be looking for new jobs—and maybe indicted in the bargain."

Cliff denied trying to knock Billy out of the race for anything. He was down here to straighten out a mess, that was all he had on his mind. But there was no more talk about indicting Billy—or firing him. After touring the plant and talking to Billy for an hour, Cliff flew black to Los Angeles. Dick spent the next ten days in Knowlesville, grappling with financial chaos. Grimly applying a cost-per-pound analysis to the plane based on the current production pace, he verified the probability of a two-billion-dollar overrun. Each night he called Cassie, who told him it was still perfectly all right. Throughout the ten days, Billy McCall never said another word to him. He stalked past Dick as if he were invisible.

Back in California, Dick went to work on revising the budget for the current fiscal year to hide the overrun. Adrian's smile was almost beatific as he surveyed the result. "A beautiful job," he murmured. "What would we do without you, Dick?"

He paused and shuffled papers on his desk, always a signal for an announcement. "The next thing I want is a report clearly stating in layman's language—in fact, in language a woman can understand—Billy's gross incompetence on this job."

"Why?"

"There's a particular woman I want to read it. Eventually, I'll want the board of directors to read it too. It's an odd combination of personal and company business. But you understand how those things happen, Dick."

So much for Dick's noble defense of his friend Billy in Knowlesville. Adrian was applying the screws in person now, while Amalie Borne stood in the distance, smiling. The report was as impersonal as a tombstone in a veteran's cemetery. It simply stated the facts, the dates, the figures, comparing what the costs had been predicted to be in the TPP contract and what they turned out to be under Billy McCall's supervision.

"Another beautiful job," Adrian said, the day after Dick handed in the report. He sat Dick next to him at lunch and began telling him his plans for the future. "We're going back into the commercial airliner market. Between the Thunderer and the Colossus, if we can recover those cost overruns, we can finance a new jet to fill a hole in the market—a medium-sized wide body that will make Boeing's humpbacked Seven-forty-sevens look like aborted whales who forgot to die. I'd like you to talk it up to Frank Buchanan."

Again, Dick sensed Adrian was reaching out to him, trying to enlist him as a loyal follower. But Dick was not ready to forgive Adrian for forcing him to betray Amalie Borne and Billy McCall. "Do we need another billion-dollar loss leader right now?" he said.

Hubris faded from Adrian's eyes. "Maybe you're right," he said. They did not exchange another word for days.

Planning for the rollout of the Colossus soon gathered manic intensity. Rumors about the cost overrun were loose in the Pentagon. A civilian employee had turned whistle-blower and was testifying in secret to the subcommittee on government operations, run by penny-pinching Senator William Proxmire with their old senatorial enemy, the Creature, as his right-hand impaler.

Mike Shannon flew in for a conference with Adrian, Cliff Morris, and Dick. "I want Amalie Borne down there for Johnson," Shannon said. "He's looking for consolation these days."

In the face of massive protests against the war in Vietnam, Lyndon Johnson had abandoned another run for the presidency. Cassie, a passionate admirer of Tennessee's James K. Polk, who won the Mexican War in spite of similar criticism, called LBJ the greatest coward in American history.

"Amalie's getting harder and harder to handle," Cliff said.

Amalie had turned into a cost overrun in her own right. She was supposed to work with Shannon in Washington or with the Prince in Europe. She frequently balked at doing either. When she showed up, she often coolly said good night to her escort at the door of her room without even making a decent excuse.

"We'll send Billy to New York to fly her down in style," Adrian said.

His cold eyes asked Dick what he was going to say about that idea. It was a perfect way to make it clear to everyone how low Billy had fallen—from project manager to company pilot. Dick said nothing. It was none of his business, he told himself for the twentieth time. He was just a spectator at this crucifixion.

Knowlesville had never seen anything like the Colossus rollout. All day, Air Force jets roared in with VIP's, climaxed by Air Force One itself, with the President. The Secret Service alone filled every local motel room and most of the high and mighty were booked into New Orleans hotels, which they undoubtedly preferred.

Cassie did not make the trip. She was still nursing their nine-month-old daughter. Frank Buchanan sat next to Dick on the plane, denouncing the way Adrian was abusing Billy, hoping to recruit Dick as an ally. Cliff Morris sat across the aisle reading a magazine, avoiding all Frank's attempts to draw him into the discussion. Next to him sat Sarah of the wide smile. When she lost the smile she looked haggard.

And you, of course, are deliriously happy? sneered a savage voice in Dick's head. It unmistakably belonged to Amalie Borne. She was among the last to arrive, sauntering from Billy's green Lustra in a green suit precisely the same color as the plane. Billy, defiantly wearing his flight jacket and fifty-missions hat, escorted her to the VIP grandstand where she was greeted by Mike Shannon and led to a seat in one of the rear rows.

Dick noticed how Lyndon Johnson followed Amalie's progress. He could almost hear Shannon—or Adrian—selling her to Johnson as Jack Kennedy's favorite. That would make her irresistible to a man who had ruined his presidency by compulsively competing with the ghost of JFK.

An Air Force band struck up "Off We Go Into the Wild Blue Yonder" and the doors of Factory One slowly opened. Out came the snout of the monster, looming over the two tractors that were towing her. A murmur ran through the crowd as the entire plane emerged. The tail was as high as an eight-story building. The four jet engines each looked big enough to swallow a Volkswagen. The whole thing was painted a deep black, which somehow added to the awesome bulk.

Adrian rose to thank everyone for coming and introduced the President of the United States. Johnson stooped over the bank of microphones and recited some of the Colossus's statistics. It could carry 750,000 pounds at close to the speed of sound. The Colossus fleet, when it was finished next year, could airlift an entire armored division any place in the world. If an enemy thought they could attack American soldiers defending freedom in distant lands, they would have to deal with this "new presence" which made us able to strike back anywhere, anytime.

"Now I know how we're going to win in Vietnam," Cliff Morris whispered in Dick's ear. "We're going to drown them in bullshit."

The President was followed by two or three Air Force generals, whose voices choked with emotion when they talked about the wonders of the plane. Finally came the chairman of the House Armed Services Committee, who congratulated the Air Force and Buchanan for building such a marvelous plane and a wonderful factory in Knowlesville, creating twenty thousand new jobs and an "economic renaissance" in Knowles County.

As Adrian stepped to the microphone to thank everyone for coming to the ceremony and urged them to go through the plane and join them on the factory floor for champagne and refreshments, a yellow Jaguar streaked around the corner of Hangar One and tore across the concrete runways to a gate at the far end of the field. Dick's eyes were not good enough to see who was driving. But Cliff Morris's twenty-twenty pilot's eyes were still in excellent shape.

"Holy Christ," Cliff gasped. "That's Billy—and Amalie Borne."

The reception was a melee in which the Secret Service struggled to keep most people at a distance from the lame duck President, who stood forlornly in a corner. An agitated Adrian Van Ness told Dick to get Johnson some champagne. As he returned with the bottle he heard Adrian trying to explain Amalie's departure.

"She must have been taken ill. That was my son-in-law driving her. Probably to a hospital. You remember him? Billy McCall? The test pilot?"

"It's all right, Adrian," Johnson said. "The way my luck's been runnin' she'd probably've given me the syph."

As Dick poured champagne for the president and a half-dozen aides, he saw Victoria McCall in the middle distance, sobbing hysterically. Sarah Morris was trying to calm her.

Much later, as their plane zoomed into the sky toward California, Victoria was still sobbing on Sarah's shoulder in a rear seat. Adrian glared across the aisle at Frank Buchanan. Dick had never seen him so angry.

"Is there anything you want to say in defense of your protégé before I fire him?" Adrian snarled.

"Not really," Frank said, with a sigh. "He's his mother's son."

A confusing mixture of sadness and happiness suffused Frank's face. He was wrestling with memories of Sammy that neither Adrian nor Dick could possibly understand.

"If I have anything to say about it, he won't be my son-in-law much longer," Adrian said.

Dick tried not to think about Billy and Amalie. He tried not to imagine what they were doing in New Orleans as he flew back to California and Cassie. He realized Billy was the man Amalie wanted, the hero who dared without caring whether he survived. She was the perfect answer to Billy's rage, a woman who did not care what he did to her.

Dick told himself he no longer cared what happened to either of them. But he could not prevent images from forming and reforming behind his eyes, an obscene kaleidoscope of lips and thighs and breasts. In spite of his desperate good intentions, Dick joined Adrian and Cliff in hoping Billy McCall would run out of luck on the ground and in the sky.

THE LADY OF DEATH

Wagner's "Ride of the Valkyries" poured from the stereo while Victoria Van Ness McCall sat on the deck of her Topanga Canyon home and made another list for Billy. Beside her sat her only friend, Sarah Chapman Morris.

Victoria had gotten out the earlier lists and had them printed up and hung them all around the house. There were lists of things she did not want Billy to do and lists of things she wanted him to do and lists of books she wanted him to read and lists of movies she wanted him to see and lists of songs she wanted him to hear, above all Wagner's *Ring* Cycle. She wanted him to understand through music, not words, how completely their souls were joined. She was Brunhilde, his Valkyrian beloved, born to be a warrior's bride.

She was now compiling a list of all the lists and their locations so Billy could consult them quickly, efficiently, when he decided to love her again. Her father called six times a day, begging her to come home, telling her he had fired Billy and she should divorce him. He had a lawyer sitting in his office with the papers drawn. All she had to do was sign them. He sent her a copy of a report full of incomprehensible numbers, proving Billy was stupid and possibly a crook.

Victoria told Sarah she was now convinced her mother was right, her father only cared about his power. He hated Billy because he had destroyed Adrian's power over her. Now he was trying to regain her without caring, without even thinking of what that would mean. She would have to leave Topanga and go back to Hancock Park. Back to childhood. She would have to abandon her lists, her hopes, her absolute faith that Billy would come back to her.

With intensity that approached delirium, Victoria told Sarah her father did not understand how a woman conquered a warrior like Billy. He refused to surrender to power, to money, to threats, to promises. Only one thing could break his will—submission. Patient, absolute, total submission. The women who were reading and praising this book, *The Feminine Mystique* were as foolish as Adrian. The feminists were really disguised men, with men's sterile imaginations. They had no ability to envision the power, the drama, the peace, of submission.

Submission annihilated hatred and fear and regret and anger. It left a woman with a feeling of ultimate power because nothing could destroy submission. Nothing Billy or any other man could possibly do—not the vilest betrayal in the history of love—could touch the pure white peace submission created in a woman's soul. Submission was not easy to achieve. But when it happened—oh, that inpouring of pure whiteness, of lightness, the burning essence of the sun and stars. She had found a name for it in Ezra Pound's Cantos: *the Immaculata*.

Only one thing worried Victoria—her dreams. Last night and for several previous nights she had dreamt she was two women. One wore the beautiful white robe of submission. The other wore a breastplate of black armor and a girdle of gleaming brass, with a cup of stainless steel over her pubic hair. She kept menacing the smiling white-robed women with a sword. But the white-robed woman only smiled and ignored the ugly steel tip the Amazon kept holding against her throat.

Her lists of lists completed, Victoria resumed work on a poem in praise of Billy McCall, the warrior pilot. In a low sibilant voice she recited it for Sarah.

Only once has a woman matched his cruel altitude
She took flight and soared beyond his stratosphere
And it changed her life forever.
She saw the world as a bright teacup
And dreaded the idea of breaking it.
So she coasted over seas and stars
Until her exhausted heart wore wings
That scorn horizons. Yet the pilot's eyes
Remained as blind as Oedipus
In his dotage. Why, why? The questions
Linger in the golden twilight
Like deer on a Chinese mountain.

Victoria shook her head and tore the poem to shreds. She told Sarah those words were too self-indulgent, egotistic. They were about her, not about Billy, the warrior who had been betrayed by his country, by his friends, by his gods. She understood so much. She understood the source of Billy's rage. America the good the true the beautiful, the country a warrior would rejoice to defend had become America the foul, the false, the farcical. That was why she was his only hope of salvation. Billy, the ultimate warrior, had to accept the supreme value of submission, which he would transmute into acceptance of history's blunders and deformities. She who could not conceive a child would give birth to the perfect warrior, shorn of his rage but not of his courage.

Crash, bam, slam. A car lunged up the almost vertical road and screamed to a stop in the yard below the deck. It was the yellow Jaguar she had bought Billy for their fifth wedding anniversary. Billy got out. Victoria's joy was beyond words. She turned up "The Ride of the Valkyries" so there was no need to speak.

He stood there, his hands on his hips for a moment, smiling at Victoria and Sarah. The smile meant nothing, Victoria had learned that by this time. "What the hell are you doing here?" Billy said to Victoria. Sarah might as well have been invisible.

"Waiting for you," Victoria said. "Sarah's keeping me company."

"You're too much," Billy said, still smiling.

Amalie Borne was wearing the green suit she had worn in Louisiana. She blended into the trees for a moment, as if she were an animal, a deer. Sarah saw Victoria was glad Billy had brought her. Victoria thought Billy wanted her to see how beautiful Amalie was, how impossible it had been for him to resist her.

"What are you going to do?" Victoria said.

"I don't know. We were gonna stay here for a while. But we can't do that now. I guess we'll go to Catalina."

SarahVictoria knew what Billy was trying to do. He was trying to erase all their memories. He was using Amalie Borne to erase her. It was ridiculously easy to stop him. She even knew the next question he was going to ask. He thought it was supremely brutal. He did not realize he was dealing with supreme submission.

"You want to come?" Billy asked.

"I'd love to come," Victoria said.

Billy shook his head, still smiling. "You *are* too much," he said.

Amalie Borne followed Billy up the steps to the deck. Victoria turned the volume knob of the record player to full. "You like Wagner?" Amalie said, above the booming "Ride of the Valkyries." The effort disfigured her perfect face.

"Yes. I've been urging him on Billy. I think he's the perfect musician for pilots!" Victoria shouted. "So much soaring. Don't you agree?"

"I hate him," Amalie cried. "He's sick, like the rest of Germany."

"I don't agree!" Victoria shouted. "I heard him for the first time at the Hollywood Bowl when I was ten. It made me sense the mountains all around us, even when you couldn't see them in the darkness. Grandeur. That's what I want Billy to feel."

"He feels it already. It's his essence," Amalie shouted. She was beginning to lose her composure.

Billy came out carrying an old battered suitcase. It had contained all his possessions when they moved in. "Still travelin' light," he said, smiling at Victoria and Sarah.

With no warning whatsoever he smashed Sarah in the face with his open hand. She flew across the deck and landed on her back in a perfect replay of her previous punishment from Cliff. Except here there was no rug. Her head struck the wooden deck with stunning force.

From a great distance Sarah heard Victoria cry: "Why did you do that?"

"She's been askin' for it for a long time," Billy said.

Victoria listened to the "Ride of the Valkyries" fade as they descended the mountain. Jammed in the Jaguar's narrow backseat, she suddenly understood why she disliked the way Sarah and her father pronounced Billy's name. She saw the entire scheme, from Billy's appointment as project manager to his brutal removal. She saw Sarah's part in it and for a moment could not believe her vileness. She had told her everything, even about the Immaculata. Somehow the purity of her hope became soiled, ruined.

"Do you know what you're doing?" Amalie said.

"Do you?" Billy said, rocketing up the narrow road toward Burbank Airport, where he parked his Lustra. It would be Victoria's first ride in the plane in two—or was it three?—years. She thought of their happy first year, when they flew all over California in it. Above all she remembered the precious day they had made love at ten thousand feet. Billy had told her she was the forty-ninth woman who had done it with him at that altitude.

Was I the best? Why had she asked that stupid question? She knew it was a mistake the moment she had said the words. Maybe that was the beginning of Billy trying to tell her the truth about himself and her refusing to listen. But she would listen now with the perfect attention, the exquisite silence of submission.

The Lustra was sitting on the flight line, gassed and gleaming. Billy said he and Amalie had been using it to fly all over California. She had seen everything now, even Baja. Only Catalina remained. Only Santa Catalina. Shangri-la. He had erased Victoria from everything else.

"You'll love it," Victoria said. "We spent our honeymoon there. We loved it, didn't we, Billy?"

"Yeah," Billy said. He was giving the Lustra a walkaround. He kicked the tires, hauled on the wing struts.

"Let's go," Amalie said. She was impatient. A hopeful sign. Billy disliked impatient women.

"You want to get there in one piece?" Billy said. "This plane's almost as old as I am."

"I don't care, really," Amalie said.

A thrill ran through Victoria's soul. She was as daring as Billy, as indifferent to death. That was undoubtedly why he chose her. But Victoria could match her with the perfect acceptance of submission.

"She's sore because your Daddy fired both of us," Billy said, as he taxied out on the runway. "Cut off our salaries. Ain't that awful?"

"I have plenty of money," Victoria said.

"She does," Billy said. "She's worth four or five million."

"Disgusting," Amalie said.

"Yeah," Billy said. "Someone with no fuckin' brains worth mentioning and no figure to match. But I guess there's gotta be some compensation for everyone. You think that way? The big Air Traffic Controller in the sky evens things out?"

"No," Amalie said.

"Me neither," Billy said.

"Frank Buchanan believes in God," Victoria said. "He told me to trust Him. He said you'd come back to me and you have."

"With me," Amalie said.

Billy rammed the throttle forward and the Lustra hurtled down the runway, its big engine thundering. Up, up, they climbed, until California lay beneath them, unfortunately obscured by a thick layer of smog.

"What a disgusting country," Amalie said, looking down at the gray mass of gases. "You can't even breathe freely. Yet you talk of defending the world against tyranny."

"Hey, I told you I didn't go for that kind of crapflak," Billy said.

"Are you responsible for his patriotism?" Amalie said.

"No," Victoria said.

"I haven't been a patriot for a long time," Billy said.

"But you won't let anyone else be unpatriotic," Amalie said.

"Shut up," Billy said. "Take off your clothes."

"Why?" Amalie said, not moving.

"We're going to fuck at ten thousand feet," Billy said.

He turned to Victoria and said: "Can you handle it?"

"Yes," Victoria said.

Billy had failed to teach her how to fly. Now he was teaching her—he was daring her to learn—something else. The robotic submission of the autopilot. Click. He shoved Victoria into the pilot's seat and she was flying the plane while he methodically stripped Amalie Borne.

Victoria did not see any of it. She refused to turn her head. She could not hear any of it either. The sighs, the growls, the groans, were swallowed by the roar of the motor. Click. She was in a state of perfect submission, like the autopilot's slave. Below them gleamed the dark blue Pacific. Up ahead loomed Catalina, with its rim of white beaches, its miniature mountains and valleys. Their continent. Shangri-la.

Suddenly the other Victoria was in the copilot's seat. The amazon. Blood streamed from her maddened eyes. Her pupils were drenched with it. The veins had burst from too much weeping. She had both hands on the yoke and she shoved it forward, tearing it out of Victoria's robotic grip. Submission, the Immaculata—what had happened to them?

The Lustra plunged down down down. Billy and Amalie were flung in a sickening tangle against the back of Victoria's seat. Somehow Billy struggled to his knees and reached over Victoria's shoulder and pulled on the yoke with all his strength.

"Let go, let go!" Billy roared. "I love you. Let go!"

But Victoria could not let go. She had become the other woman, Califia's daughter, the Lady of Death. Her hands were fastened to the yoke with an eternal persistence, an absolute, relentless refusal. All she could offer Billy was her final submission. She kissed him on the mouth as the Lustra struck the water and exploded into a thousand burning fragments.

AN EMPTY SKY

For a week after the crash, Sarah Morris lay in her bed with the electric blanket turned up full, shaking and shivering with violent chills. Death had suddenly declared her life random, superfluous, vacant.

Again and again she saw Amalie Borne walk from the green Lustra in the harsh Louisiana sunlight. A line from a poem seemed to swirl around her. *All in green went my love riding.*

Occasionally Sarah's husband stood in the doorway watching her, disgust on his handsome face. She was proving what he had suspected for a long time. She had never stopped loving Billy McCall. Sarah did not care what he saw. She could not conceal her pain, her terror.

"Adrian's resigning," Cliff said, on the seventh day. "I'm the new president."

I was wrong, Sarah thought. To whom should she send her confession? Her older American daughter, Elizabeth, stoned on LSD and other drugs most of the time in San Francisco? Her straight younger daughter Margaret, studying Chinese history at Stanford? Or her son Charlie, everyone's favorite halfback at University High?

Would any of them understand her babble? *I want to warn you against the way love can turn to hatred. The more violent the love the more violent the hatred. I did not believe anything so bizarre could happen to me until I killed him. I killed him and his innocent wife.*

"Get out of that goddamn bed," Cliff said. "We've got work to do. Whatever happened in that plane, it wasn't our fault."

Not your fault, of course not your fault, Sarah thought. You wouldn't have had the patience or the guile to weave the web of hatred around them until the moment of helplessness, of vulnerability, arrived.

I was wrong. She wanted to send it to Billy. He was the only one who would understand it.

"Did you hear me?" Cliff said, looming over her. "Get up. Let's get to work. I've got the job of a lifetime and you're acting like someone in a fucking Greek tragedy. They weren't the first people killed in a plane crash and they won't be the last."

He was using his war, his male indifference to everything but victory, success, to ignore the impossibility of the crash being an accident. His big hand seized her arm and literally dragged her out of bed.

"We're in this together, right?" he said.

Sarah nodded, fascinated by the way he used the argot of the criminal, the murderer, to confirm their partnership. It was thoroughly accurate, even if it betrayed his previous denial. It also underscored who was chiefly responsible for the crime. Sarah Chapman Morris was the real perpetrator. She had borrowed Cliff's adolescent hatred and welded it to her thwarted love to create a death mechanism.

Innocently, of course. Oh, so innocently hoping for the worst. Oh. Oh. Oh. How could she deny it? How could she ever purify her lost vicious heart?

Sarah saw the future, exactly as it unreeled for the next four years. She would become a woman named Mrs. Clifford Morris. She would write invitations, serve on committees, chair benefits, court senators and congressmen, awe hotel clerks and banquet managers, travel to England, France, Japan, China, with her husband while he bribed people to buy Buchanan's planes.

She would go to endless Los Angeles dinner parties where the women left the table after dessert and had coffee upstairs, isolated in a splendid bedroom or dressing room with demitasse cups and rock sugar ordered from London and cinnamon sticks in lieu of demitasse spoons. On the hostesses' elaborate dressing table there would be enormous bottles of Fracas and Gardenia and Tuberose. The dessert that preceded the retreat would invariably be served on Flora Danica plates and would be infallibly preceded by finger bowls on doilies. Wearing Pucci silks to the floor, she would spend these dinners trying not to suffocate while talking through spectacular table arrangements of flowers from their premier florist, David Jones.

Some larger parties would be held in tents with pink lights and chili from Chasen's. In fact, Mrs. Sarah Morris would become moderately famous for the size and style of her tent parties. Once, instead of chili from Chasen's she served burgers from Jimmy Murphy's. Between the dinner parties there would be lunches at places like the Bistro Garden and afternoons of committees, committees, committees.

I was wrong. Maybe the only person who could understand it was the late Sarah Chapman Morris. Maybe she should send the letter to herself and put it in a drawer hoping to find it by accident in five or ten years. Maybe it would have the power to free her from hatred's web.

Once or twice childhood pleas for mercy formed on her grimaced lips. *Immaculate Heart of Mary pray for us* But the words were murmured by a stranger named Sarah Chapman in furtive sleepless hours before dawn. By daylight and lamplight, the other person she had become, Mrs. Clifford Morris, wife of Buchanan Aircraft's president, was much too busy to pray.

For a week after the crash Adrian sat in his office unable to think, barely able to speak. At home Amanda wept and said unbearable things about getting what he deserved. He nodded his assent. He was numb. His only support was a voice that whispered from a vanished England: *It does a man no good to whine.*

At the end of the week, Frank Buchanan burst into the office. He had not come to work since the news of the crash. "Have you learned anything?" he asked, his voice, his hands trembling. He looked like an Old Testament prophet, with his mane of white hair, a five-day beard.

"I don't know. Have you?" Adrian asked.

"The futility, the stupidity of hatred. I was guilty of it, Adrian. But I never dreamt it would lead to anything like this."

Forethought, Adrian numbly told himself. He's here to mock forethought, to ridicule all my gods. "I wished them happiness, Adrian. I truly did," Frank said. "But my hatred of you permeated the whole thing. I'm resigning from the company. I've created enough evil for one lifetime."

For the first time Adrian was able to face the part his hatred had played in the tragedy. For a moment he almost conceded the limitations of forethought, admitted our mortal inability to control fate. He saw himself walking to Frank Buchanan and embracing the man he had hated for so long, asking his forgiveness in turn. Of course he did no such thing. The voice of the man still determined to play the great game remained in control.

"Frank," Adrian said. "The evil was created long before either of us was born. You can't resign from the company. Without you there is no company, there never would have been one. Now it's up to both of us to save it. I'm resigning as president. Cliff Morris will take over. I'm moving to Washington to make sure we don't get massacred by that two-billion-dollar cost overrun."

"Amanda will never be happy in Washington," Frank said.

"Amanda will never be happy anywhere," Adrian said.

"Be kind to her, Adrian. If I hear even a hint of evidence that you're mistreating her—"

"She's all I've got left too!" Adrian cried.

They were enemies again. But Frank Buchanan was still working for the company.

A month later, Frank sat beside Buzz McCall's bed watching him die of congestive heart failure, liver failure, emphysema and a half-dozen other complications. Frank tried to console him with the thought that Sammy was waiting for him on the other side.

"I hope not," Buzz said. "That means Tama'll be there too. Between them I'll never get any rest."

He browbeat Frank into giving him a cigarette. "Dames," he said. "We never figured them out, did we? None of us. Even Adrian."

"Especially Adrian," Frank said.

"What the fuck did Tama and Amanda have in common? That still baffles me."

"Womanhood," Frank said.

The word struck Buzz like a bullet. He closed his eyes and pulled on the cigarette. A few minutes later he slipped into delirium. He talked to Sammy, to

Tama and other women. "Bitches, fucking bitches," he muttered.

Suddenly he was conscious again. He glared at Frank. "There's only one thing I ever did to a dame I regret," he said. "I helped the goddamn Brits kill that Commie spy Adrian was fucking. I felt bad about that. She was a hell of a pilot."

A moment later he was gone. A terrific tremor of grief and rage ripped through Frank's body and mind. "Mother was right. You're evil. It's a different kind of evil from Adrian's but it's still evil!" he cried.

He was talking to Craig as much as to Buzz. To Billy and all the other pilots who had turned flight into a license to run wild on the ground. Another earthquake-sized tremor shook him. He seized Buzz's dangling hand and kissed it tenderly.

"But I loved you. I loved all of you," he whispered.

No one at Buchanan mourned Buzz. They were all too busy mourning Billy. "How could it happen?" the chief mourner, Sam Hardy, said over and over again. "Flying to fucking Catalina. How could that happen to Billy?"

Hardy was still Frank's favorite designer, already designated as his heir apparent. Typically, Frank saw only the man's unique gifts and ignored Sam's personal problems. His pursuit of one of the beauties of the Honeycomb Club had wrecked his marriage and turned him into an alcoholic. Kirk Willoughby had stabilized him with psychotherapy and Alcoholics Anonymous. Now he seemed to be coming apart again.

Hardy had fallen off the wagon and had a brawl with his second wife, which had them teetering on divorce. He spent hours talking to Frank about Billy, apparently oblivious to the pain it caused him. There was nothing Billy could not do in a plane. There was no plane—or woman—he could not master. Hardy recalled nights of stupendous drinking with Billy at the Honeycomb Club and stuporous fucking in the dawn. He even remembered a song about a test pilot's woes he had once sung to Billy outside the club at 3 A.M. When he got to the refrain: "Gee I'm glad that I don't fly," Sam wept.

In an odd way the extravagance of Hardy's grief steadied Frank. He began to suspect Sam was weeping as much for himself as for Billy. He was mourning the end of his youth, which Billy's death seemed to confirm and even symbolize. Of course youth had been gradually expiring for a long time, as it always does. But in California it was easier to deny this obvious fact. A man with money could get a tan, put on a tank top and head for the beach in his convertible with a willing twenty-five-year old beside him. Frank stopped being a patient listener when Sam Hardy tried to translate Billy's death into an obituary for the aircraft business. "Everyone knows the glory days are over. From now on this is just another big business, like making fucking automobiles," Sam moaned.

"That is absolute bullshit!" Frank roared. "As long as there's a sky up there and men want to fly faster and faster and higher and higher in it they'll be new planes to make. Stop feeling so goddamn sorry for yourself and get to work!"

Was that Buzz talking? His way of saying good-bye? Frank hoped so. Hardy stopped drinking and had a whole new design for their high-performance fighter, the SkyDemon, on Frank's desk within a week.

Dick Stone also knew the crash could not have been an accident. He responded by becoming a workaholic. He could no longer believe he deserved the happiness Cassie and his son and daughter promised him. In death Amalie Borne's shadow loomed like an impassable barrier between him and any possible promised land. Dick's already heroic hours became a grind of inhuman proportions. Secretaries quit in steady succession until he finally found a Japanese-American who viewed his midnight hours as a challenge to her national reputation for stamina.

Cassie stopped joking about being married to an aircraft company. She *was* married to one. The man she thought she was marrying had become almost transparent. She could not see any other reality in her life except Buchanan Aircraft. Inevitably, she began asking why.

Watching the marriage unravel, Sarah began to wonder if Dick was her only hope of redemption. She did not understand the word or the idea. She only knew it had something to do with forgiveness. She somehow understood she could offer it to him—and he could offer it to her. How or when or where she had no idea. For the time being the skylark was in a cage known as Mrs. Clifford Morris, an entity Dick Stone could only regard with repugnance. She could hardly blame him. She had the same reaction every time she looked in the mirror.

BOOK NINE

LIGHTS! ACTION! CAMERA!

The senator from Iowa's puffy face was a study in righteous frustration. "Do you mean to tell me that you take no responsibility for wasting two billion dollars of the taxpayers' money?" he screamed.

Cliff Morris smiled patiently at the Creature. "*Waste* is hardly an apt word, Senator. We will soon have a fleet of transports that can airlift an entire army overseas. We simply maintain that the responsibility for their unexpectedly high cost should be shared by Buchanan and the Air Force. I only wish our project manager, former Lieutenant Colonel William McCall, were still alive so he could explain to you in detail how Air Force officers assured him again and again that they would share this responsibility. Billy was my half-brother—and one of my closest friends. He told me this repeatedly."

"Who were these officers?" the Creature bellowed. "I want them in this committee room. I want them court-martialed!"

"As I explained to you, Senator, Colonel McCall died in a private plane crash—"

The Creature ranted about corporate greed and military incompetence. The chairman of the subcommittee, the senior senator from Connecticut, home of Pratt & Whitney, who made the engines for the Thunderer and a lot of other Buchanan planes, rapped him into silence and said he agreed with most of what Clifford Morris had said. The country was on its way to having an airlift capacity second to none. Cliff smiled and thanked the senator. In Cliff's head Billy McCall whispered: *nice going, you lying son of a bitch.*

A half hour later, Mike Shannon slapped Cliff on the back as they descended the Capitol steps. "He never laid a glove on you."

Washington broiled in its usual June heat and humidity. They plunged into the air-conditioned white limousine at the bottom of the steps and headed for a reception at the Norwegian embassy. Norway had just bought a half-dozen

463

antisubmarine versions of the Starduster to help guard NATO's northern flank.

Unreeling, it was another technicolor movie of Cliff Morris's life—and this time he was both the director and the star. It was 1970—the second year of his reign. From the moment he became Buchanan's president, he started playing the part.

Gone was Adrian's low-keyed patrician style. Cliff installed himself with a party at the Bel Air Hotel for five hundred people. He hired a personal public relations man and got himself and Sarah a stream of press clippings as they elbowed their way into Los Angeles's upper class. He bought a magnificent new house on a Palos Verdes promontory and another one almost as splendid in the desert outside Palm Springs. He drove around Los Angeles in a white Mercedes licensed *Buchanan 1*.

Gone too was Adrian Van Ness's hesitation about betting the company. Nothing was too splendid or too ambitious for Buchanan Aircraft. The war in Vietnam devoured planes. The assembly lines churned day and night. Cliff announced they were abandoning their tacky Depression-era hangars in Santa Monica for glossy new headquarters in El Segundo, on the edge of Los Angeles airport. He saw a seller's market with Cliff the salesman supreme. He was going to sell, sell, sell everything on Buchanan's menu around the world.

On the commercial airline side of the game, the view was very encouraging to a gambler like Cliff. The jets had created a revolution in air travel. Throughout the sixties, airline revenues climbed month by month as Boeing's 747s and 727s and Douglas's DC8s and DC9s flew crammed with passengers from nose to tail. The airlines were awash in cash and were practically begging the aircraft and engine companies to sell them new planes—especially ones that could fill a hole in the market. Cliff revived Adrian's idea for a medium-sized wide-body. Hoping to stir Frank Buchanan's enthusiasm, Cliff called it the Aurora, in memory of the airliner that was supposed to emerge from the Talus bomber.

Dick Stone, eyeing the two-billion-dollar cost overrun on the Colossus, asked why, if there was a hole in the market, they had to fall into it. But Cliff was determined to succeed where Adrian had failed. The Aurora was given top priority. Hundreds of new designers and engineers were hired to go all-out on a prototype. Millions of dollars were spent on marketing studies and sales brochures.

The days of one or two salesmen pitching a plane in the office of an airline president were over. Each airline now had a committee of engineers and sales and marketing representatives almost as unwieldy as the Pentagon's review boards. All these people had to be wined, dined, persuaded, while Dick Stone muttered about the outflow of cash.

To keep him quiet, Cliff embarked on a world tour to sell the Colossus and the Thunderer to America's allies. The Prince was summoned from his European haunts to join in the quest. The results were disquieting. Other aircraft companies had discovered the secret of Buchanan's overseas success and were imitating them. As often happens, the newcomers did it better. Lockheed, for instance, hired Prince Bernhard of the Netherlands to dispense their bribes. The going rate for persuasion soared with this influx of competition. At home it was matched by a runaway inflation in costs and wages as the country began paying for Lyndon Johnson's cowardly decision not to raise taxes to finance the war in Vietnam.

The Prince seemed to have lost much of his old enthusiasm for commercial combat. He complained endlessly about his liver. One night in Paris he got drunk and lost his savoir faire. "Why did you kill Amalie?" he asked. "Did she threaten to spill the beans, as you call it?"

Cliff spent an hour trying to convince him that the crash was an accident. He did not succeed. The Prince found it hard to believe anyone like Billy McCall ever existed. He was a purely American phenomenon.

The Colossus proved particularly hard to sell overseas because very few of America's allies felt a compelling need to project their power beyond their borders. Italy, for instance, finally agreed to buy four of the giant planes, mostly because the Prince raised Buchanan's under-the-table offer to astronomical heights. It would have been a personal insult to turn down such an inducement, one of the bribed politicians later explained. The huge craft were parked on a military airfield near Milan, waiting for another Mussolini to invade Africa, perhaps. There was no other visible use for them.

Cliff chose to ignore these and other portents. It was easy enough to argue that in the military procurement game, nothing much had changed. The infighting for a head start on new contracts for missiles and planes and radar systems was as ferocious as ever. Congress's arrogance and greed in the politics of procurement were not noticeably different. The new president, Richard Nixon, was an advocate of a strong America. The defense budget remained gigantic.

As the limousine nosed into the rush-hour traffic, Mike Shannon told Cliff that the Senate committee would undoubtedly approve the plan to pay Buchanan three-fourths of the two-billion cost overrun immediately. The remaining $500,000,000 would have to be appealed to several layers of Air Force review boards. But they would get the money eventually. "The White House is with us all the way. Adrian's doing a great job there."

Those last words abruptly cooled Cliff's satisfaction with his performance before the subcommittee. Adrian Van Ness had settled in Charlottesville, Virginia and made President Richard Nixon his target number one in Washington. He had succeeded so well, Cliff was virtually superfluous in that arena. Cliff did not like being superfluous anywhere.

The Norwegian reception was in the ballroom of the Hay-Adams Hotel, across Lafayette Park from the White House. After shaking the required hands, Cliff looked for more worthwhile targets. Standing in a corner was scowling Colonel Anthony Sirocca, one of Curtis LeMay's deputies in the struggle for the Warrior. Tony was in war plans these days, on his way to his first star.

They exchanged bone-crushing handshakes and Cliff went to work on behalf of Buchanan's close support plane, the Thunderer. McNamara had tried to persuade the Air Force to buy it but they had resisted mightily, in spite of (or because of) the enthusiasm the Navy and Marines had for its performance in Vietnam. They were still resisting the new secretary of defense. Tony listened, his Sicilian eyes glittering with hostility, while Cliff poured on the persuasion.

"I've got a kid in the Marines who may end up flying one of those things. I'm not blowing smoke when I say it's a good plane," Cliff said.

The superstitious side of Cliff's salesman's psyche seized him by the throat. Was he risking Charlie's life, using him to sell the plane? No—he believed in the Thunderer. He had been out to Vietnam. He had talked to the Marine and Navy pilots who were flying it. They called it the Iron Blimp and joked about its speed. But they all swore by its ability to put bombs on a target and take fantastic punishment from ground fire.

Two months ago, Charlie had quit UCLA in his sophomore year and enlisted as a Marine air cadet. Cliff had been moved by the decision. He knew what it meant—Charlie was choosing his father's side in the quarrel that was tearing the country apart.

Sarah, better known to Cliff by an unspoken nickname, the Smiling Zombie, had lost her English self-control and begged Cliff to stop him. But Cliff had already bragged to half the executives in the company the day he got the news. He told Sarah to stiffen her English lip and smile proudly at his side.

Mentioning Charlie softened the resistance in Tony Sirocca's dark eyes. "It may be a good plane, Cliff," he said. "But right now we're more interested in the big one. If that contract doesn't keep you happy for the next ten years, we'll start to think nothing satisfies you guys."

"What the hell are you talking about?" Cliff said.

Tony looked baffled. "The new bomber. Son of the Warrior. We need a production schedule, fast. Like the day before yesterday."

Cliff could only shake his head in bewilderment while a flush of humiliation traveled through his body. "Adrian Van Ness sold the package to Tricky Dick at a private dinner last week," Sirocca said. "Doesn't Adrian bother to tell you little details like a ten-billion-dollar deal?"

"I guess it slipped what's left of his mind," Cliff said.

"Frank Buchanan's got to redesign her for a completely new mission. Instead of flying high she's gotta go low—fifty, twenty-five feet low. With a profile that will go through the other guys' radar like the fucking invisible man."

"How many copies?" Cliff said.

"Two hundred."

"What's the big number?"

"We're figuring fifty million a plane."

That was ten billion dollars, all right. The biggest contract in Buchanan's history. It would require a virtual reorganization of the production lines. The chairman of the board had not bothered to mention a word of this to the company's president.

"Nixon wants a bomber good enough to scare the shit out of the Chinese and the Russians," Sirocca explained. "The B-Fifty-twos can't handle those SAM missiles."

"How many planes have we lost over Vietnam?"

"Six thousand," Sirocca said. "I wish I could have gotten someone to listen to Frank Buchanan when he told us to go stealth ten years ago."

"I'll talk to Frank this afternoon," Cliff said.

Pretending to be the man in charge. In charge of what? The washroom? Cliff blundered across the ballroom toward the door, avoiding eyes, faces. Who should be arriving but the Creature and an entourage of flunkies, most of them from left-wing think tanks that specialized in trashing the military-industrial complex. The Creature was their darling these days.

"You got away from us this time, Morris," the senator said. "But we put some salt on your tail. The next time you'll tell the truth."

For the Creature, this was almost friendly chitchat. Ordinarily, Cliff would have slapped him on the back and said something about being old friends. But his salesman's personality was submerged by his rage at Adrian Van Ness.

"The next time, Senator, maybe I'll give the committee a little history of how many lies I've heard you tell since we met at the crash of the Starduster in nineteen fifty-eight," he said.

"You can't threaten me!" the Creature snarled. "This only proves how much you've got to hide."

Leaving Mike Shannon at the party, Cliff taxied to Buchanan's Washington office, which now had a staff of fifty working to keep Congress and the Pentagon happy and eager to do business. It cost them fifteen million a year. Dick Stone was appalled but Cliff insisted it was money well spent.

Mike Shannon's busty red-haired secretary, Jeremy Anderson, gave Cliff a sultry look. Shannon had obviously touted him as one of the great lovers of the century. "Adrian Van Ness has been trying to get in touch with you," Jeremy said.

"I'm about to get in touch with him—in spades," Cliff growled.

"Cliff?" Adrian said. "I've been meaning to call you. I was down in Florida with the president and his friend Rebozo."

"We're going to build another bomber," Cliff said. "I just found it out by accident from an Air Force colonel. He was nice enough to wipe the egg off my face."

"Now Cliff—"

"Now Adrian, listen to me, once and for fucking all. You can be a hell of a big help to us here. But not if you start crossing all my wires without telling me."

"Cliff—I apologize."

"Okay. Let's forget it. Let's figure out how the hell we can take on a ten-billion-dollar bomber program, finish the Colossus without going broke, do another production run on the Thunderer and incidentally get the Aurora in the air."

"How does that look, by the way?"

"Not good. Lockheed is coming up fast on the rail with that goddamn L Ten-eleven. Douglas is building a DC-Ten. The airlines are trying to play us off against each other."

"Can't you work your usual magic overseas?"

"The Prince has run out of gas."

"Then it's up to you. Surely you've learned how to play the game by now. Take Dick Stone along if you still need a partner."

Cliff cursed silently. The Aurora had become his personal challenge, the plane he needed to show the company and the world that he could do it better than his predecessor. Adrian seemed to know it and take pleasure in his difficulties.

"Adrian," Cliff said, "I think we should let someone else build this bomber. It's more than we can handle."

"Cliff—may I remind you I'm still the chairman of the board? I will personally ask you to explain to the other directors why you turned down a ten-billion-dollar contract."

"Because I don't think we should spread ourselves so thin. Because I can see the same headaches we ran into on the Warrior, times ten. Who says Nixon can get this thing through Congress?"

"That's irrelevant. If you expect me to go back to the president of the United States and tell him we don't want to make a plane that I've convinced him no one else can build—you better look up the telephone number of Lockheed's personnel department."

Cliff had not felt so humiliated since Buzz McCall panicked him in Sky-Ranger II when he was seventeen. He was not Buchanan's chief executive officer. He was Adrian Van Ness's errand boy. In a corner of his mind Billy whispered: *having fun, Big Shot?*

"Okay. I'll talk to Frank about the bomber."

"Let me know if there's a problem. I have some moves I can make with him, these days. We're almost friends."

That only proves Frank Buchanan is one of the simpletons of all time, Cliff thought.

"Ten billion dollars, Cliff! I thought you'd be crawling down the wire to kiss me. I hope you'll communicate a lot more enthusiasm to the workforce when the contract comes through."

"Don't worry, I'll take care of it," Cliff snarled and slammed down the phone.

Jeremy Anderson still had the phone in her hand as Cliff burst out of the office. She had been listening on her extension. "You've got the makings of a third-rate spy!" he roared. "Get me a seat on an eight A.M. plane."

"I was just trying to see if you were still on the phone," Jeremy said, with a guilty pout. "Mike's on line five."

Jeremy's spying was a symptom of Cliff's weakness. Mike Shannon's political skills extended to playing power games inside Buchanan Aircraft. For the moment he was poised between Adrian, Cliff, and Dick Stone.

"What do you want?" Cliff snapped at Shannon.

"What the hell did you say to the Creature? He spent a half hour tearing my ass off."

Cliff's rage deepened. There was only one thing to do, swallow his humiliation and take most of the credit for reviving the Warrior. Adrian's undercover role in its sale would be known only to a handful of top executives such as Dick Stone. If Cliff handled it right, it might not even be known to them.

"Fuck him," Cliff said. "I just got the word from Tony Sirocca. We've got the contract of everyone's dreams. Ten billion bucks to build the next-generation bomber. Son of the Warrior."

"That's no reason to make an enemy out of the Creature," Shannon said.

"Don't worry about it," Cliff said. "We don't have to worry about anything from now on."

The next morning, Cliff flew to California aboard an American Airlines 707. Seated next to him was an angular, not especially pretty brunette with her hair pulled back in a severe ponytail. She was wearing gogo boots, Levi's, and a denim jacket with a *Peace Now* button on the lapel. It irritated him that someone with enough money to fly first class was wearing this revolutionary outfit.

Cliff pulled a copy of *Aviation News* from his briefcase and snapped it open. On its cover was a picture of Buchanan's new high-performance fighter, the SkyDemon.

His companion got the message. "Are you a pilot?" she said.

"I used to be. Now I make them. I made this one," he said, pointing to the picture of the SkyDemon climbing at a 90-degree angle.

Silence for a half hour. The story on the SkyDemon was positive. Bruce Simons had done a good job. When Cliff looked again, his seat companion was reading a copy of the *Hollywood Reporter*, the bible of West Coast show business. He remembered Tama reading it in the old days.

"You an actress?" he said.

She nodded. "You've probably never heard of me."

"My mother was one. You've probably never heard of her either. Everyone can't be a star."

"How did you get into the plane business?"

"Come on. Say it. How did you get to be a warmonger? That's what you're thinking."

Her smile was rueful but warm. "You don't look like a warmonger," she said.

"Fly forty-nine missions over Germany with guys throwing bullets and shells at you from all directions. It's an instant cure for warmongering. I hate it as much as you do. My son'll be a Marine flier in six months. I'd give a million bucks to make that button on your chest come true."

"Fascinating," she said. "What are you doing to make it happen?"

"Building this," he said, pointing to the SkyDemon. "And other planes that'll make us strong enough to end the war we're in—and make sure another one doesn't start."

She sighed. "You sound like my father. What about trusting people? Just saying we've had enough killing?"

"Who's your father?"

"Robert Sorrento. A character actor. He died last year."

"Character actor, hell. I remember him coming to our house at Redondo Beach to see my mother on Sunday afternoons. He was the handsomest, suavest guy I ever saw. Everyone was sure he was going to be the next Valentino. I used to wish he was my father."

"Was your father in the movies?"

"I don't know what he was in. My mother divorced him before I was born."

"I never saw much of my father either until I got old enough to loan him money."

Suddenly they were telling each other the hidden parts of their lives. He described Tama and her lovers and his stepfather Buzz. She told him about her screenwriter mother, who had lived with a dozen movie actors and executives after she ditched Robert Sorrento. Their tone was rueful, wry, nostalgic. The more they talked, the more they realized they shared a past.

Cliff revealed his long-defunct ambition to become a director. "I guess I always liked to run things," he said.

"How do you direct something as huge as an aircraft company?"

"You pick a good supporting cast—and make yourself the star."

That blew her away. She seemed ready to forgive him for his warmongering. She seemed ready to do a lot of things. Cliff could almost feel the rising warmth.

"I've never seen an aircraft factory. What's it like?" she asked.

"You'll see one today—unless you've got a movie to make."

"I should be so lucky," she said.

They drove from LAX to the new headquarters at El Segundo in Cliff's white Mercedes. He took off her *Peace Now* button and put it in his pocket as they strolled into the building.

"What's your name?" Cliff asked, as the guard opened the visitor's book.

"My real name's Angela Perry. Use that instead of my screen name."

"Don't want to be seen consorting with the enemy?"

She laughed and Cliff felt twenty years younger. He thought of Sarah the Smiling Zombie waiting for him on Palos Verdes, their occasional perfunctory sex in the big bedroom off the windswept terrace. This woman was adventure, conquest—he had no doubt whatsoever he could change her half-baked opinions about plane makers. This visit was the first step.

In a moment they were walking down the assembly line, with dozens of skeletal Thunderers hoisted on jigs. The scream of metal, the hammer of rivet guns filled the huge hangar, which was as long as two football fields. From the balcony dangled a tremendous American flag.

"The workers bought that flag themselves," Cliff said. "It's their way of saying they believe in what they're doing."

Cliff grabbed a balding pot-bellied supervisor by the arm, reading his name off his security badge. "How's things, Eddie? Any problems?"

"Not with this plane, Mr. Morris," Eddie said.

"This young lady's thinking of making a movie about the business. I'm showing it to her from the inside."

Eddie got the idea. "You couldn't get a better guide," he said. "Except maybe Billy McCall, eh, Mr. Morris? And he's not around any more."

"Yeah," Cliff said, returning Eddie's knowing smile, even if he did not have any enthusiasm for the comparison. He was a star. Performing.

Angela was awed by the immensity, the complexity of the show. Exactly what Cliff wanted to happen. They climbed up on the jigs and she sat in the cockpit of a half-finished Thunderer to look at the bewildering instrument panel.

"Imagine yourself in a nine-g pull-out in one of these," Cliff said. "You fly them in your mind all the time. That's the best part of making a plane."

They went into the next hangar, where they were making a half-dozen prototypes of the SkyDemon. They were like slim, stripped swallows compared to the pigeon-breasted Thunderers. Cliff told her how fast the Demons climbed, how incredibly maneuverable they were at fifty thousand feet. In the next hangar, a Colossus was being checked for final delivery to the Air Force. The plane's stupendous black bulk loomed above them.

"You build that too?" Angela said.

"The biggest in the world," Cliff said.

A scene in the technicolor movie of his life began scripting itself in Cliff's mind. A scene that surpassed anything Billy McCall had ever attempted with a woman at ten thousand feet. Careerwise, Cliff Morris was at thirty, maybe forty thousand feet. Eventually he would get rid of Adrian Van Ness and be up there, cruising at sixty thousand. In the meantime he would do something that would send Adrian a message—and make Cliff Morris a legend in his own right.

Back in the headquarters building, they shot up to the sixteenth floor in the noiseless elevator and strolled into Cliff's corner office. His Mexican secretary's eyes widened as she got a look at Angela.

"Mr. Morris," she said. "We didn't expect you until tomorrow."

"Emergencia," he said.

The oak-paneled office had a painting of the *Rainbow Express* fighting its way home from Germany on one wall. It was a duplicate of the one Sarah had given Cliff for the Palm Springs house when he became president. The wall opposite the door was glass, giving them a magnificent view of the airport and the city beyond it, unfortunately almost obscured by smog. They watched a Boeing 727 charge down the runway and head for the sky. Cliff put his arm around Angela's waist and gave her his supersalesman's smile.

She knew exactly what he wanted to do. She wanted to do it too. She wanted to do it here, with the *Rainbow Express* declaring Cliff's miraculous ability to challenge fate and survive. Compounding their desire was the sense of being linked in some mystic way. Destiny, a wild inevitability throbbed between them.

Cliff lifted her against him and kissed her—gently at first, then harder and harder, his hands roving her body. He picked her up and carried her across the room to his executive-sized desk. With a sweep of his arm, he knocked pens, memos, clock onto the carpeted floor. She lay on one elbow while he sat down in his swivel chair and buzzed his secretary.

"No calls, no nothing, for the next two hours. I'm not here."

Cliff began undressing her. He liked what he saw as the Levi's and the jacket and the work shirt came off. The black lace panties and bra suggested she had not let the counterculture obliterate her identity as a child of Hollywood. He flipped the underwear away and ran his hands across coned breasts, a flat muscular stomach, and a dark tangled pussy above remarkably fine legs.

"Now that's a design I like," he said as he undressed.

In a moment he was naked. She boldly took his penis in her hand and slid it into her mouth. An enormous throb of pleasure surged through Cliff's body. He sensed a wish to demonstrate she could be leader as well as led, but for Cliff that was erotic. He liked semi-defiant women. His fingers roved her pussy until they found the zone of desire and vulnerability, the symbolic opening that signified her ultimate surrender. In and out his finger moved while more jets thundered into the sky beyond the windows.

In his head Cliff heard Billy McCall whisper admiringly: *you crazy son of a bitch*. He saw the realization dawn on his secretary's face, saw her whispering the story to friends in the ladies' room and the cafeteria tomorrow, saw the whispers traveling like electricity from secretaries to bosses to the workers on the line to the security guards.

I'll be goddamned, they would think and probably say to their friends. *Billy McCall isn't dead after all. Would you ever think Big Cliff had that much balls?*

Security Chief Dan Hanrahan would come to him in a day or two and tell him Angela was tied up with every left-wing cause in Hollywood. He would solemnly inform Cliff that unless he desisted immediately he would have to tell Adrian Van Ness.

That's exactly what I want you to do, Cliff would say. *While you're at it ask him what the fuck is he going to do about it?*

Be a man, Tama had said. He was working at it. He spread Angela against the window overlooking the airport and slid the joystick into her. The glass was hot against his palms. He imagined the heat on her breasts and belly. "How do you like that?" Cliff asked.

"I like it. I love it. I love you," she said as the jets thundered skyward. She untied her ponytail and her dark hair fell over her shoulders in a silky shower.

It was a fantastic scene in the script Cliff was writing for the technicolor movie of his life. There was only one thing wrong. He had no control over how the movie was going to end.

A FRIEND IN NEED

It was close to midnight on December 23, 1972. Dick Stone sat in the White House's Oval Office beside Cliff Morris, Mike Shannon, Adrian Van Ness, President Richard Nixon, and several aides as the opening credits of *Lusty Lady* unrolled. Dick had brought the film from California. Adrian had introduced it as a "little treat" he thought the president would enjoy.

"Whoa!" the president chuckled, when he saw who Angela Perry was. "This *is* a treat."

In the past two years, Angela had made three movies that zoomed her from semi-obscurity to stardom. Cliff Morris was largely responsible. He had introduced her to a half-dozen studio executives with whom he had become chummy since his ascent to Buchanan's presidency.

"She made it years ago, before she changed her name," Adrian said. "One of our security people tracked it down."

The plot involved an anemic scoutmaster and his sexy wife, who take a troop of Boy Scouts camping. The Scouts all look like leftover members of the Waffen SS—blond muscular hunks who eye the wife lecherously from the first frame. In the third frame the scoutmaster falls off a cliff and disappears beneath a foaming waterfall. The Scouts proceed to enjoy Angela in every position and through every available orifice—leaving them all exhausted, while she pants for more.

The president thought it was wonderful. He laughed and laughed. When it finally ended—with a naked Angela inspecting the exhausted members of each gasping Scout—Nixon insisted on Adrian getting him a print for private showings to members of Congress.

The president knew nothing about Cliff's connection to Angela, of course. He had no idea Adrian was showing the film not only for his delectation but to embarrass Cliff into ending his fling with this Jane Fonda clone before she messed up his career—and Buchanan Aircraft.

Neither gratitude nor Cliff's arguments had altered Angela's politics. She had joined Hanoi Jane and other Hollywood luminaries in raising millions to defeat Nixon for reelection. To their chagrin he had won in a landslide, thanks largely to a last-minute announcement that "peace" had been signed with the North Vietnamese.

The announcement would never have been made without a massive application of American air power. For the first time, targets that Curtis LeMay and other air-war experts had wanted to bomb for seven years were taken off the prohibited list. Navy planes—Buchanan Thunderers—had mined Haiphong harbor and Boeing's B-52s had pounded Hanoi. For the heavies it had been anything but a joyride. The fifteen-year-old B-52s had taken horrendous losses from Soviet SAM missiles and the enormous concentration of radar-guided antiaircraft guns around the Communist capital. Morale among the B-52 crews had plummeted alarmingly and there was even a rumor of a mutiny. But the Communists, knowing nothing of this development, saw a future of even more devastating raids and began serious peace negotiations.

Along with a print of *Lusty Lady*, Dick had brought Buchanan's 13,000 page condensation of the thirteen-million page Total Performance Package contract bid for the new bomber, which was going to be simply called the BX to make it sound as futuristic as possible. Cliff had wanted to call it Warrior II but Adrian—and Nixon—thought that would unnecessarily arouse congressmen who had voted against the previous bomber. Besides, the BX was an essentially new plane, smaller, slimmer. It was not as fast as the Warrior because it was designed to fly at fifty feet, where mach 3 speed would be suicidal. But the plane had something the Warrior mortally lacked—stealth. Its carbon epoxy fuselage, its virtually invisible engine ducts, left no trace of its path on a radar screen.

After the movie, Adrian signaled Dick Stone to begin his presentation of the BX. Dick struggled to his feet, feeling as if his flesh were sludge and his brain were full of L.A. smog. The TPP contract had consumed him and his staff eighteen hours a day for the past four months. He had finished working on this presentation aboard his flight from LAX. Taking a deep breath to clear his head, Dick set up a rack for his charts and did the job in five smooth minutes. He stressed that the price they were bidding was fifty million dollars a plane. But Dick made it clear that the ultimate cost would be closer to a hundred million dollars. The electronic equipment—especially the ground-hugging radar—they were putting into the plane was fantastically expensive.

"It's all right to surprise Congress, but we don't want to surprise you, Mr. President," Adrian said.

Nixon nodded contentedly. "As long as you know something in advance, damage control is never a problem."

"I trust that goes for the unpleasant noises our Democratic sore losers are making over that break-in at the Watergate apartments," Adrian said.

"Of course," Nixon said. "It never should have happened in the first place. The boys got carried away by our momentum."

A final flip and Dick displayed the mock-up of the BX, flying directly into the camera, its needle nose emanating menace. "Beautiful," Nixon said. "With two hundred of those in the barn, Hanoi won't say boo for the next twenty years—and Peking will be nicer than ever."

"What's the matter with Morris?" one of Nixon's aides asked. "Doesn't he like the plane? He hasn't said a word for a half hour."

"Like it?" Cliff said. "That's the greatest plane, pound for pound, we've ever built. That anyone's ever built. You don't like something that fantastic. You love it."

"I hope Cliff and Mike'll be in the trenches when we send it up to the hill,"

Nixon said. "In spite of the landslide, we're going to need all the help we can get."

"You can depend on Cliff and Mike, Mr. President. Right?" Adrian said.

"You're damn right," Cliff said.

They trudged into the cold Washington night, Dick lugging the film and his presentation kit. "You fucking son of a bitch," Cliff said to Adrian.

"Give him the film," Adrian said. "Hanrahan spent a lot of time and money looking for it."

Dick handed Cliff the film. He flung the hexagonal can into the middle of Lafayette Park. "I wouldn't leave it there if I were you. It can't do your beloved any good," Adrian said.

"Go get it," Cliff said to Mike Shannon.

Cursing, Shannon waded through the muddy grass to retrieve the can. "I recommend a nightly viewing," Adrian said. "I'll even pay for renting a projector."

Adrian hailed a taxi and disappeared into the chilly darkness. Cliff shouted defiant curses after him.

"You're out of your goddamn mind," Dick Stone said.

"Second the motion," Mike Shannon said.

"Fuck you both," Cliff raged. He glared at Dick. "Did you know about this stunt?"

"All I did was carry the can from California," Dick said. "No one told me what was in it."

Shannon hailed a cab and they rode to the Buchanan company apartment in the Watergate complex. Even before Cliff took off his overcoat, he poured a full glass of Inverness and drank half of it in one gulp. "Fuck you and your bomber, Dick," he bellowed. "I'm staying till we get the Aurora straightened out. Then I'm through."

"What are you going to do?"

"First get a divorce from the Smiling Zombie, also known as Lady Sarah. Then become a movie producer. It'll be a snap compared to the fucking aircraft business."

"You'll be a sensation," Dick said. "You're as ruthless as Harry Cohn, as egocentric as Louis B. Mayer, as mean as Jack Warner."

"Second that motion too," Shannon said.

"I'm serious. Angela wants me to produce her next film."

"You'll be working for her. It's insanity," Dick said.

"It's love. Nobody believes it but it really is love, Dick."

There was a desperate appeal in Cliff's voice. He was asking Dick to understand—and simultaneously reminding him why he expected some sympathy from him. But the memory of his obsession with Amalie Borne was still too painful for sympathy. In his mind, Dick evaded the word *love* as if it were a SAM missile. He had not heard the word from Cassie for a long time. Only the children were holding them together. They were a pair of actors pretending affection whenever they performed in front of their special audience. There had been one too many quarrels about his heroic working hours, one too many pleas that Cliff was spending 50 percent of his time thinking about Angela and someone had to hold Buchanan Aircraft together.

"Cliff—the Aurora program is almost out of control. No one else but you can straighten it out. Lockheed and Douglas are mopping up the domestic market. If you can't make at least a hundred overseas sales, we're going to do a Convair."

Dick was talking about the record loss Convair had taken trying to break into the commercial jet market several years ago—440 million dollars. At the time it was the largest corporate loss in the history of American business.

"I've got a tour all lined up. Starting in Japan. If I don't sell fifty copies in Japan I'll buy you a fucking DC-Ten."

"Cliff—you should be on call for this BX thing," Shannon said.

"You're gonna have to fly solo, Tailgunner."

"In that case, I think I'll get a decent night's sleep."

"Kiss Jeremy for me," Cliff said.

"I will," Shannon said. "Just make goddamn sure you don't try for any on your own."

He departed with a defiant slam of the door. The telephone rang as Cliff poured himself another triple Inverness. "Answer that, will you, Dick?" Cliff said. "If it's Angela tell her I'm asleep. I can't talk to her after seeing that fucking film."

"This is Tony Sirocca," said a gravelly voice. "Is Cliff there?"

There was death in General Sirocca's voice. Dick did not understand why or how he knew it. Maybe he simply felt the Lady's icy fingers on his flesh. Maybe he deduced at IBM-compatible speed that death was the general's principal business and he did not call people late at night for any other reason.

"It's for you. The Pentagon," Dick said.

Cliff grabbed the telephone, feet spread wide in a fighting stance, ready to tell someone else off. Within ten seconds he was bending, crumpling as if Tony Sirocca had kicked him in the groin. "Oh Jesus," he gasped.

He spun on his heel and fell onto the couch, the phone still clutched to his cheek. "There's no hope?" he whispered. "He couldn't have gotten back out to sea? I mean—it's one tough plane, Tony."

Cliff was aging like someone in a science fiction film as he talked. His checks caved in, his chest collapsed, his legs curled up. "Sure, Tony, sure. I appreciate your calling," he said. "I'll call his mother. She couldn't have handled the usual routine. I'm not sure I could."

Cliff did not hang up. He did not have the strength. "Charlie's gone," he said. He slumped there, arms akimbo, one hand still clutching the white telephone. "He flew flak suppression over Hanoi for the B-Fifty-twos. A direct hit tore the wing off the plane."

"Jesus. I thought he was on his way home," Dick said.

Charlie had been aboard a carrier off Vietnam for almost a year, flying Buchanan Thunderers. "They canceled his orders—they were trying everything to protect the B-Fifty-twos," Cliff said.

Dick thought of his nine-year-old son in California, the love he felt when he watched him playing or sleeping. It was so acute, it was almost pain. He poured Cliff another full glass of Inverness. "Anesthesia," he said.

"No," Cliff said. "I've got to call Sarah."

"I'll call her."

He went into the bedroom and dialed Sarah's number in California. The phone rang and rang. Finally a sleepy voice answered. "Sarah?" Stone said. "This is Dick. Dick Stone. I'm calling for Cliff. He just got some terrible news."

"Charlie's dead," she said. "I've been expecting it."

Dick was so staggered he could only gasp: "Why?"

"The sins of the fathers," Sarah said. "And mothers."

"Sarah—I know this is a hell of a shock. But that doesn't make sense."

"Yes it does. You're the one who doesn't make sense, Dick. Trying to rationalize, organize, a business that was shot through with evil from the start."

Suddenly her empty voice was vibrating with rage. "Why are you telling me this?" she hissed. "Doesn't he have the guts to talk to me?"

"Sarah—"

"Get him on the phone. Get the chief executive murderer on the phone. I insist!"

Dick felt his flesh shriveling in the ferocity of the hatred that was coming over the line. "No, Sarah. It would be better if you talked in a few days."

"I'm on the line, Sarah," Cliff said. "Say it to me, not to Dick. I know you've been wanting to say it for a long time. Maybe it'll make you feel better."

"Don't try to soothe me with California pop psychology," Sarah raged. "This isn't an encounter group. It's a marriage. A word, a reality, you've never even tried to understand. A marriage you've betrayed and betrayed until you turned me into a betrayer in my own cowardly way and I helped you betray our son, the best, the finest, the dearest son two parents as worthless as us could ever hope to have—betrayed him to your friends the generals—"

"Betray—betray?" Cliff snarled. "You're the world-class expert in that department, sweetheart. How many goddamn years did you pretend to love me while you were secretly yearning for Billy McCall's cock? Tell me the truth for once. Did you imagine you were doing it with him every time we did it? Was there ever anyone else there behind those saintly closed eyes when you came?"

"I stopped loving him a long time ago. He was more loathsome than you—but I'll say this for him. He wasn't a hypocrite. He didn't lie to his women. He didn't play smarmy husband. If I had to choose between you and him—I'd take him for his honesty—his mad loathsome honesty."

"Why don't you get in a fucking plane and imitate him?" Cliff shouted. "You can be honest together at the bottom of the Pacific. Then I can marry a woman who loves me."

"You don't know the meaning of the word *love*. You never did. It was all slavering appetite. Beach blanket bingo. California fucking. Marriage American style."

"How about English style? Twenty years of playing let's pretend. Appetite had nothing to do with it? You didn't like what you were getting? You were just doing your duty? Is that why you crawled in bed with me in dear old England?"

"All England proved was you can take the boy out of America but you can't take America out of the boy. You're loathsome people. I can't believe you were ever English, that we share one drop of your vile blood. My deepest regret— my only regret—is that my son died in the service of your vicious amoral country."

Hatred, hatred, it was like a million cages of hissing snakes writhing across the landscape, Dick thought. Slithering, biting, thrashing across America over Vietnam, the rise and fall of Negro hopes, the virulent political divisions Nixon seemed to encourage. Women like Sarah concentrated it in their tormented hearts. Why did he find himself almost paralyzed by dread?

Dick slammed down the phone. He did not want to hear another word. He sat in the bedroom while Cliff and Sarah reviled each other for another twenty minutes. Dick stared out the window at the curving ultramodern architecture of the Watergate complex, struggling against a sense of disorientation, disintegration. Were there any certainties in this hate-racked America? Was Adrian Van Ness's smooth assurance that Richard Nixon was the president who would solve all Buchanan's problems worth anything?

As Cliff Morris whirled around the globe selling planes and pursuing Angela Perry, most of the day-to-day decision making had gravitated into Dick's hands. More than ever he felt the weight of being responsible for the survival of Buchanan and the thousands of designers, engineers, salesmen, and assembly-line workers who had put years of their lives into the company.

Thunk. Cliff had hung up. He was draining his glass of Inverness as Dick returned to the living room. "Does that happen often?" Dick said.

Cliff shook his head. "I knew it was there, waiting to come out. The way you know some things in a marriage. You know them but you don't think about them."

Dick nodded, thinking about his own tense marriage. Maybe it was time for some emergency repairs. Exactly what these should or could be, he had no idea.

Dick drank and listened to Cliff talk about Tama and Buzz and Adrian and Billy and the dirty game Cliff and Sarah had played to destroy him. Cliff did not feel guilty about it because Billy was going to destroy him if he got the big job. That was the game they were playing—kill or be killed—the game that had started when Billy had moved into Cliff's house at the age of eleven. It was all so stunningly inevitable, Dick was reduced to speechlessness again.

They went from Billy to Charlie and the mess the United States of America had made of the war in Vietnam. They did not have an answer much less an explanation. They talked as men, as friends, as survivors of an earlier war—and could only agree that America had failed to use its air power in a decisive way. Whether this was the whole truth or only part of it, whether it was even true, was beyond their competence that night. They were dealing with pain, loss, grief, not strategy.

By the time dawn began tinting the Washington sky, they had both drunk so much Inverness they no were longer making sense. Dick hoisted Cliff to his feet and towed him into the bedroom and sprawled him on the king-size bed.

"Dick," Cliff said. "Never forget this. Y'real friend."

"Just promise me one thing. You won't become a movie producer."

Cliff shook his head. "Gonna build that bomber. For Charlie. Gonna make it so fucking good no president has to send kids eyeball to eyeball with flak batteries."

For Charlie and for Billy McCall. Dick was still struggling with his own memories of the part he had played in Billy's destruction.

In the living room, Dick called Cassie in California. "I know you won't like this—but I'm not going to make it home for Christmas." He explained what had happened—why he felt Cliff needed a friend to stay with him for a few days.

"Doesn't he have a wife?" Cassie said.

"They're through. Between this and Angela—she's ditching him."

"Sarah?" Cassie said. She had been on several of Sarah's benefit committees. They had not become friends. Sarah, performing as that empty vessel, Mrs. Clifford Morris, had no friends.

Dick gave Cassie a brief summary of the dialogue between Sarah and Cliff. "I didn't think she could be that impolite," Cassie said.

Dread sucked at Dick's nerves again. He could think of nothing to say. "When can we look forward to celebrating Christmas?" Cassie asked. "Anytime before New Year's?"

"I hope so. I'll call you."

"We'll be so grateful."

Dick collapsed on the couch and slept until noon. He awoke with an even more acute sense of dread. It seemed to ooze from the walls of the Watergate complex. Wrong, wrong, whispered a warning voice in his head. Everything was going wrong. Politically, personally. He heard the bitterness in Cassie's voice and suddenly wanted to be on a plane to California as soon as possible.

Cliff was still snoring. Dick called Adrian and told him about Charlie. "Good God. How did Sarah take it?" Adrian asked.

Dick gave him a succinct summary. "This will make Cliff inseparable from that left-wing Hollywood slut," Adrian said. "She'll rush to console him. For an artist of her minor talents, real-life drama like this is irresistible. It supplies the emotion her imagination lacks."

Adrian sighed. "Are you ready to be the next president of Buchanan Aircraft, Dick?"

"I don't think this is the time or place to bring that up," Dick said.

"I suppose not," Adrian said. "But I'm not withdrawing the question."

Dick went out in search of breakfast. There was no food in the apartment. When he returned Cliff was on the phone. "Wear a fur coat. It's cold as hell," he said. "I'll be waiting at the gate."

Cliff hung up and smiled almost cheerfully at Dick. "I called Angela. She's flying in. You don't have to hang around. Don't you want to get home for Christmas?"

"I missed my plane."

"I'll get you on an Air Force plane."

A call to the Pentagon located a Colossus that was flying replacement crews to Thailand to maintain the B-52 bombing threat until the Communists signed a peace treaty. Dick sat with the young pilots and bombardiers and gunners, listening to them discuss the tactics that were being used over Vietnam. They all thought the generals were idiotic.

"It's World War II stuff," one freckled-faced redhead said to Dick, as if this was synonymous with prehistoric. "We should be coming in low, under the radar."

Dick thought of the BX, the invisible plane they should be flying—that they would be flying if the U.S. Congress was not a collection of pinheads. It had taken a full year to negotiate the TPP contract and write up its 13 million pieces of paper. Buchanan's enemies in the Senate, people like Proxmire and the Creature, were already threatening to block funding for the program. That meant its supporters and the Air Force would keep it alive by turning it into a stealth item in the budget. This accumulated stupidity and hatred left these kids flying bombers that were almost as old as they were into skies full of radar-guided missiles and antiaircraft shells.

They landed at Vandenberg Air Base in California to refuel and Dick hitched a ride to Los Angeles with a civilian employee. He did not call Cassie. He decided it would be fun to surprise her and the kids. He bailed his car out of LAX and roared up the Ventura Freeway to their house in Nichols Canyon. It was about six o'clock when he unlocked the front door. He found nine-year-old Jake (for John) and seven-year-old Catherine watching television.

"Daddy!" they yelled and danced around him.

"Where's Mommy?"

"She's visiting up street," Jake said. "At Dennisons."

The Dennisons were real estate brokers. Dick had bought the house through them. Lately they had hired a publicity man and became known as "brokers to the stars." They sold houses for fabulous prices in Malibu, Westwood.

An hour later, there was still no sign of Cassie. "Did Mom say when she'd be home?" Dick asked.

"No," Catherine said. "Sometime she stays up there a long time."

"What do you do for dinner?"

"We heat up TV trays in the microwave. Mom showed me how to turn it on," Jake said.

"I think I'll go tell Mom I'm here."

Dick walked up the steep winding road, his mind racing ahead to what he might find at Dennisons, then denying it as absurd. When he reached the sprawling two-story house, clinging, like his own, to the steep slope of the canyon, he thought it looked deserted. There was only one car in the open garage—a 1960 Dodge. Usually there were three or four, including some flashy sports cars. The Dennisons raced them as a hobby.

Dick rang the bell. Silence. He rang it again and again. Silence. He pounded on the door. Carl Dennison jerked it open. He was a big freckle-faced man with a handlebar mustache and slightly protruding teeth.

"Dick!" he said. "What can I do for you?"

"I'm looking for Cassie."

"Cassie? I haven't seen her."

He was a very inept liar.

"The kids told me she was visiting you. Where's your wife?"

"She—she's away."

"Cassie!" Dick shouted. "Guess who's home for Christmas."

Silence. Dennison stood there, anxiety exuding from every pore. "Listen," he said. "This was a onetime thing. She didn't know Doris had split. We started talking and got carried away—"

"Cassie!" Dick roared.

He shoved Dennison aside and strode into the house. The place was all but stripped of furniture. Doris had apparently split in a moving van. He found Cassie sitting on the edge of an unmade bed off the living room, pulling on a pair of blue jeans. On top she was still naked. She looked ashamed—and defiant. With great deliberation she put on an old denim shirt and buttoned it.

"Merry Christmas," Cassie said.

Dick realized she was drunk. "Let's go home," he said.

They walked stiff-legged downhill to their house. "Reminds me of my stewardess days," Cassie said. "Walking down the aisle while the plane was climbing. Gave all the ginks a good look at the equipment."

"How long has this been going on?" Dick said.

"Not long. Let's have dinner and argue later, when the kids are in bed."

They struggled through dinner with the kids doing all the talking—mostly about school. Dick gave them a laundered version of visiting the White House, which impressed Jake. They watched a dramatization of Dickens's *A Christmas Carol* until nine o'clock. Unreality clawed at Dick's brain. In Washington Cliff Morris grieved for his son, blasted out of the sky by Russian missiles over Hanoi. He sat in California watching sentiments that moved nineteenth-century Londoners to tears, trying to think of what to say to his adulterous wife.

Cassie put the kids to bed. Dick waited in the living room. She finally appeared, a half glass of bourbon in her hand. He grabbed it away from her and threw it into the fireplace. Seeing her on the booze upset him more than her infidelity.

"Why?" he said. "That's what I want to know. Do you love him?"

She shook her head.

"Then—why?"

"He talked me into it. He made me feel sorry for him. It was better than feeling nothing—the way I feel with you."

"You need help," Dick said. "I'll talk to our medical director. He'll suggest a therapist."

"Great," Cassie said. "It'll be nice to have an intelligent adult to talk to for a change."

"We can work this out. It won't be easy but I'll try to understand."

"I don't want your lousy understanding," Cassie said. "I don't want your goddamn condescending forgiveness either."

She strode defiantly to the bar and filled another glass with bourbon. "You want to know the real reason for this mess?" she said, her voice thickening with tears. "I could put up with your impossible hours. I want to see us win this damn war as much as you do. I could even put up with your stupid guilt about killin' Billy McCall. What I can't stand is knowin' you don't love me. You never have. I don't know what the hell you love besides your miserable airplane company."

Are you ready to be the next president of Buchanan Aircraft, Dick? whispered Adrian Van Ness.

Was this the price he was paying? Was that his secret motive from the start? A sly ambition, nurtured in the small hours of the morning, watching Cliff Morris flounder? No. Dick denied the accusation. He was working for those kids on their way to fly obsolete planes into a vortex of radar-guided antiaircraft fire over Hanoi. Maybe he was no longer working for the greater glory of the United States of America. He was still working for the fliers, for the brotherhood of the air against the greedy ignorant groundlings.

True enough, true enough. But that commitment did not explain why he had lost his all-American girl.

Dick saw Cliff Morris in that king-size bed in the Watergate apartment, entangled with Angela, emptying his grief, his pain, into her. Breaking through loss and bitterness to clutch at joy. *Freedom*—that was what the image said. In some incomprehensible way, the word, the image, belonged to California, even though it was being enacted in Washington. It was not just the freedom to fuck. It was an inward thing, a kind of space between a man's mind and heart where a person lived. Why had Dick Stone lost his space? What was wrong with him?

At first I thought I could not bear
The depths of my despair

Amalie. She was still there, barring his way to happiness.

ECHO CHAMBER

"That was beautiful," Susan Hardy said when Sarah Morris finished telling her husband how much she hated him. Susan helped Sarah weep for Charlie through the rest of that long night. They wept as women and drank like men. Susan let Sarah read aloud the letters Charlie had written her from Vietnam, telling her how much he loved to fly, how unafraid he was of dying. *If I have to die in order to fly I'll take it. I've been dying to fly all my life. It's logical.*

Sarah could see him laughing as he wrote it. He could make a joke out of anything, even death. Courage was as natural to him as breathing.

"Burn them," Susan said.

"Burn them?"

"They're dangerous. Your husband would try to publish them. He'd try to make Charlie a martyr of the air. He'd inspire thousands, millions, of others to think that way. We'd never eliminate the war love from their souls."

Burn them? Sarah could not strike the match. She let Susan do it. She piled the letters in the fireplace and burned them with her zippo. "Zip and they're zapped," Susan said. A bad joke.

Susan had not abandoned their friendship when Cliff became president of Buchanan. She sent Sarah notices of meetings of Women Concerned About the War and similar groups with capital letters. Sarah sent her money. After Billy and Victoria died and she became Mrs. Clifford Morris, the hollow woman, going through the motions of celebrity, Sarah sent Susan even more money.

In return Susan kept Sarah informed about the latest gossip at Buchanan, which she obtained through her "network." Sarah was confused by the term at first. She thought a network was something that broadcast television and radio shows. Susan explained this network broadcast the kind of information women needed to survive in a male-dominated world. She told her Cliff had seduced an actress named Angela-something in his office and was now seeing her almost nightly in her house above Mulholland Drive.

Of course Susan had no idea Mrs. Clifford Morris did not care whom her husband was seeing or what he was doing with her. She was actually relieved that she was not required to be Sarah, to play that part in the bedroom where she had shivered and shaken with horror and terror for the deaths her hatred, her inverted love, had caused. Sarah understood why Cliff was equally reluctant to visit her there, even if he did not understand why, even if he was simply trying to avoid the dead weight of her despair, a potentially fatal drag on his salesman's buoyancy.

If Sarah did not care, what explained that explosion of hatred? Was it simply a performance to please Susan, her only friend? Or was Mrs. Clifford Morris in touch with Sarah on some subterranean level? Perhaps that was it. Lately Mrs. Clifford Morris had been giving Susan Hardy more and more money and going to some of her capital-letter groups with her. She listened to angry women telling each other how their husbands and lovers had abused and exploited them. Many were from the aircraft business but not all. The aircraft business did not have a monopoly on macho males who only wanted one thing from a woman. At these meetings for some peculiar reason Mrs. Clifford Morris found herself able to get in touch with her previous incarnation, Sarah.

Now she sat and watched Charlie's letters burn. Having just resigned as Mrs. Clifford Morris, she had to let Sarah do her thinking. She thought it was a shame. She wept uncontrollably and remembered things that Mrs. Clifford Morris had successfully forgotten. Charlie zooming around the house with a model plane in his hand, smashing lamps and vases. Cliff beside her in the bed upstairs, sharing his fears and hopes about the Talus and other planes.

"You can't stay here any longer," Susan decreed. "You need a different site to launch your new consciousness."

Oh, good, thought the ghost of Mrs. Clifford Morris. I will be neither Mrs. nor Miss. I will be Ms. A nice foreshortening of the self—an alphabetical lobotomy.

They would move to the desert and convert Mrs. Clifford Morris's vacation house into a center for Women for Peace and Freedom. That was Susan's latest capital letter group. After thinking about it carefully, Susan decided it would be better if Ms. Sarah Morris did not divorce Clifford Morris for the time being. Divorce was an ultimate weapon, which should be used when a man was least able to cope with it. For the time being Cliff Morris was riding high on money from the war machine. Better to wait until he was dumped by his Hollywood dream girl or by Buchanan or both and then stick it to him.

A marvelous phrase that summed up msdom, Sarah thought. In the new age that would unfold in their desert encounter sessions, they would acquire the ability to stick it to all of them.

"All the murderers and their war machine," Susan said. She was one of the leaders of the antiwar movement in California. Major politicians conferred with her before making statements. She was in touch with gays and lesbians in San Francisco who were organizing their own political movement. Excitement, energy, surrounded Susan, turning her into a pillar of fire. Out of the flames would emerge a new kind of beast, a woman who could stick it to them.

Once upon a time there was a war machine you loved.

That was Miss Sarah Chapman talking, that difficult, crotchety ghost. Eventually she would dwindle into pale voiceless insignificance, along with Mrs. Clifford Morris, who was totally insignificant from the start to finish of her brief but expensive existence.

"We're going to discover a new declaration of independence, a new pursuit of happiness," Susan said as they piled clothes and shoes in the back of the car.

"A new declaration of independence," Ms. Sarah Morris said. "A new pursuit of happiness."

Miss Sarah Chapman tried to point out that her English ancestors had recoiled from these grandiose phrases. Ms. Sarah Morris merely smiled tolerantly. For the time being she was an echo chamber in which the words resounded defiantly. But that would change. Eventually they could become part of her bones and blood, her new American self.

Want to bet? whispered Miss Sarah Chapman, that persistent English ghost.

In the desert, visitors other than Susan Hardy's cohorts in Women for Peace and Freedom (WFPF) kept the ghost alive. First Sarah's daughter Elizabeth, precariously balanced between drug-free hope and drug-drenched despair. Elizabeth could not deal with a mother who hated her father, who denied her brother was a hero and burned his letters, who told her the man she loved, the doctor who had rescued her from the needles and nightmares of San Francisco's Haight-Asbury because she was so beautiful and now wanted to marry her was a male fraud and tyrant who only wanted to own a toy woman he had created. For one thing Sarah was not sure if that was true, just because Susan Hardy said it was. Even then she saw msdom was not always synonymous with wisdom.

Next came daughter Margaret on the long-distance telephone from England, where she was continuing to become the world's leading expert on China. She had been closer to Charlie than anyone else in the family and she required special comforting. You cannot be a comforter when your soul is consumed by hatred. So Ms. Sarah Morris had to call on the ghost of Miss Sarah Chapman to remember how deep, how pervasive, the love of planes and flight ran in Charlie's blood. She talked about her father and about Cliff. She urged Margaret to go out to Bedlington Royal Air Force base and imagine the *Rainbow Express* landing with one engine while Miss Sarah Chapman stood in front of the Watch Office praying her in. She had to make Margaret, who valued thought above feeling (or told herself she did), accept the awful inevitability of Charlie's death.

Finally, unexpectedly, the most important visitor: Frank Buchanan. He came with tears on his face, hobbling on a cane since arthritis had invaded his bad leg. He brought with him a letter of sympathy, signed by every single worker in Buchanan's El Segundo factory, where the Thunderer was built. Five thousand signatures, five thousand members of the fraternity of the air saying they were sorry and proud and sad for one of their own. Frank put the hundreds of sheets of soiled paper on Sarah's coffee table and she saw them being passed from jig to jig, signed while metal shrieked and rivet guns clattered and the gigantic American flag fluttered feebly on the wall.

Oblivious to her hatred, Frank talked of Billy and Cliff as boys, when he taught them to fly. He told her of his mother's faith—of a world soul that connected everyone, the living and the dead, in which evil fought an eternal war with good. How he had dreamt in his youth that his planes would be weapons of inspiration on the side of the good—but now he had begun to think of them as creatures of evil. They had destroyed too many people he loved, beginning with Amanda.

That was when Sarah learned Califia's fate—what had happened to Amanda Van Ness. Bewildered, appalled, Ms. Sarah Morris realized this lonely old man too needed to be comforted, consoled, forgiven. The ghost of Miss Sarah Chapman was still real enough to feel the ancient tug of daughterhood, the almost extinct wish her own lost father had never fulfilled. It was the first of many visits Frank would pay, in spite of Susan Hardy's growls of hostility.

But the ghost of Miss Sarah Chapman was still only a ghost. Most of the time Ms. Sarah Morris and her hatred prevailed. It was not entirely her fault. America seethed with hatred during those last years of Nixon's reign, with the lying president's face on the television screens night after night. Ms. Sarah even welcomed into their vituperative fraternity Cassie Trainor Stone, who became a contributor to WFPF and a member of their encounter sessions.

Listening to Cassie pour out her loathing for her absentee husband and the other Buchanan males she had known in her Honeycomb Club days, Ms. Sarah shuddered at the thought of earnest Dick Stone trying to survive this firestorm of female hatred. When Cassie announced she was divorcing Dick and returning to her Tennessee birthplace, the house resounded with mscheers. But Ms. Sarah Morris found herself feeling sorry for the failed husband.

It was the ghost of Miss Sarah Chapman again, trickily refusing to fade away, remembering the earnest navigator who hated to bomb civilians, who in turn remembered her as a daregale skylark scanted in a cage. Was she still one? Ms. Sarah Morris wondered. Had she only changed cages?

A week or so later, Dick Stone was on the telephone with a voice leaden enough to send whole flocks of skylarks spinning to earth in 13g dives. The Marines had awarded Charlie a Distinguished Flying Cross. They wanted to present it at a ceremony at Buchanan's headquarters. Cliff was in Morocco trying to sell Auroras to Arabs and Africans and could not make it. Would she come?

Once more evading Susan Hardy's doubts, Ms. Sarah Morris said yes. It was wonderful publicity for the company, of course. She rationalized it to herself and Susan by arguing that by helping to keep Buchanan airborne she was helping herself. She was making sure the pie would be big and juicy when she stuck it to Cliff with the Big Divorce that divided his assets in half.

It was a heartrending ceremony, which Ms. Sarah Morris survived only by letting the ghost of Miss Sarah Chapman take complete charge until it was over. The patriotic speeches, the pictures of Charlie, the whirring TV cameras and kleig lights would have been unendurable for the msshapened soul of Sarah Morris. She would have erupted into obscenities and denunciations of the war machine in the middle of it. Miss Sarah Chapman, who believed in heroes and dying for God and Country, even read one of Charlie's favorite poems, William Butler Yeats's "An Irish Airman Foresees His Death," in which a boy in another war tried to explain why "a lonely tumult of delight" lured him into the sky's murderous embrace.

Afterward, in Dick Stone's office, Ms. Sarah had dazedly returned to her body as Frank Buchanan and others told her how much they had loved the poem. Finally she was alone with Dick, who was looking almost as ravaged as she felt. Insomnia had gouged ridges in his face. He looked like he was barely holding on.

"I'm sorry about Cassie," Ms. Sarah said. "I'm afraid you didn't get much support from our little group of *ms*creants."

He smiled gamely at the joke. "Maybe I didn't deserve any," he said. "Are you going to divorce Cliff?"

"Eventually," Ms. Sarah said and teetered on the brink of revealing the whole program. Why not let Big Cliff know—Dick would of course tell him—all about their plan to stick it to him? Instead, Miss Sarah Chapman took control again. An echoing voice whispered: *like a daregale skylark scanted in a cage*. She realized this mournful man confronting her was her only hope of happiness. He understood everything about her life, even the sad secret of never loving Cliff, of the wizzo WAAF drunk on bourbon and glory who had thrown herself into the big pilot's arms.

In the same terrible moment Ms. Sarah Morris realized she could be this man's hope as well. She saw the knowledge in his haunted eyes—heard his oblique wish in the question about divorce. They valued the same things— honor and honesty and authentic feeling—things that Cliff could never care about if he lived to be a thousand. In a way they were both victims of that voracious all-American hero-pilot-salesman-playboy-pseudo-CEO. Victims of this devouring America with its manic pursuit of money and power and weaponry unto death.

But Ms. Sarah Morris's bitter lips were sealed against testaments of possible love. Dick Stone's lips, hands, heart, were equally encased in that unwritten law scorched on the male brain stem—thou shalt not seduce your best friend's wife. Trapped, sealed, condemned to pirouetting in separate space capsules through the long gray years unto eternity. So there was nothing else to do but murmur meaningless words about how grateful she was to be asked to Charlie's enshrinement and slink back to her desert abode, her Gaza where she waited, eyeless, for the chance to bring down the temple in the name of her mserable revenge.

THE MEANING OF MEANING

Cliff Morris stood at the window of his corner office in Buchanan Aircraft's El Segundo headquarters watching thousands of protestors massed on the company's airfield at twilight, each carrying a lighted candle of peace. Inside the main factory building sat a gleaming white prototype of the BX bomber.

"I still think we should call out the National Guard," Cliff said. "These assholes could attack the plane—destroy it."

"That's exactly what I'm hoping they'll do," Dick Stone said. "But we won't get that lucky."

"Is it worth it, Dick? All this strife, this hatred?" Frank Buchanan said.

"Yes," Dick said.

"Do you agree, Cliff?" Frank asked.

"Yeah," Cliff said with minimal enthusiasm.

He did not like the way Dick Stone had taken charge of this crisis. He did not like the way Dick had taken charge of almost everything in the day-to-day operations of Buchanan. But there was not much he could do about it. Adrian Van Ness had made Dick executive vice president.

"We can't back down now. Among other things, we can't afford it," Dick said.

It was the brutal truth. In Washington, for the third year in a row Adrian Van Ness had won a billion dollars from Congress to keep the BX alive. That was not enough to build more than the prototype but it had provided Buchanan with desperately needed cash. Unfortunately, Adrian had been unable to talk the Air Force into swallowing the five-hundred-million-dollar cost overrun on the Colossus. That cloud of red ink still loomed over the company. Last year their high-performance fighter, the SkyDemon, had lost the fly-off with General Dynamics F-16, leaving behind it another pool of red ink deep enough to drown them.

Meanwhile, Cliff flailed around the globe frantically searching for orders for his baby, the widebody commercial jet, the Aurora. He had been able to sell 30 to the Japanese with bribes even the Prince would have considered excessive. He was now working on the Egyptians and other national airlines in the Middle East. There the bribes were certain to be even more stupendous. Almost everywhere else, Lockheed was making him look silly with their own highly developed grease machine. So far Cliff had orders for a paltry 120 copies—leaving him and the company up to their ears in another deluge of red ink.

There were times when Cliff wondered if some kind of curse, some evil spirit, began pursuing the company the day he became CEO. Any hope of selling the Aurora domestically vanished when the Arabs created OPEC and raised oil prices into the stratosphere in 1973. The airlines' profits vanished in a swirl of hydrocarbons. Then a careless pilot flew an Aurora into a Florida swamp, killing everyone aboard and triggering a swarm of multimillion-dollar lawsuits.

Nixon, the president who had revived the BX bomber, was gone along with his landslide. Gone too was Vietnam—in Communist hands, abandoned by a Congress who had ignored President Gerald Ford's pathetic cry, "Our friends are dying!" But the BX had survived, thanks to heroic lobbying by Adrian, Mike Shannon, and Buchanan's Washington staff. They had beaten back the onslaughts of the Creature and the other critics of the Military Industrial Complex in and out of Congress.

This year, the nation's 200th anniversary, the critics had changed their tactics. One of the Creature's staffers, a Quaker named Jacob Woolman, decided the BX was the perfect issue to revive the noble emotions of the antiwar movement. He had organized a national crusade against the plane, which was cresting tonight beneath their windows.

A Buchanan helicopter rose from the roof of the main building and hovered over the crowd. From its open doors fluttered thousands of pieces of paper. The demonstrators picked them up and read them by candlelight. It was a statement signed by Cliff, welcoming them to Buchanan Field and assuring them that there were no police or National Guard troops anywhere near the premises.

We respect your right to protest. In return, we are confident you will respect our property and the millions of dollars worth of tools and equipment used to build planes that defend this country and give thousands of skilled workers jobs.

Dick Stone had written the statement. Dick had assessed the mood of the country and decided conciliation, not confrontation, was the way to go. "Instead of them making us look bad, we'll make them look bad," Dick said. Adrian Van Ness liked the idea; hardly surprising—it showed how much Dick had learned from the master of forethought.

The statement was part of the game plan. So was banning the police. Whenever pickets appeared outside their headquarters building, Dick sent them coffee and sandwiches. He had Cliff's picture taken talking to them.

"Don't pay any attention to those lying words," Jacob Woolman screamed from the platform. Behind him a rock band struck up "We Shall Overcome." Woolman, still bedecked in sixties love beads, led the crowd through the hymn. A Catholic priest who had become famous during the same tormented decade read one of his poems about a Vietnamese child killed by American bombs. Woolman gave a ranting hysterical speech in which he attacked the Military Industrial Complex of the United States and Israel. He linked the Palestinians in their refugee camps with the blacks in the ghettos and the villagers in Vietnam.

"Did you hear that, Stone? He's attacking Israel. Why don't you go down there and punch him in the mouth?" Cliff said.

"If it gets the Israeli lobby on our side, I'll hug him instead," Dick said.

Bruce Simons, their public relations director, returned from a tour of the crowd. He grabbed Cliff by the arm. "I found Sarah. She's not going to make a statement, thank God."

Cliff nodded glumly. Sarah was another reason why he was keeping a low profile tonight. She was down there with the demonstrators, using their son Charlie as her justification. Charlie—and Billy McCall. She said she was doing penance for her sins against them both—whatever that meant. Sin was not an idea Cliff understood. It smelled musty, absurd, a word from another century.

She had made no attempt to divorce him after their explosion of mutual loathing the night Charlie died. Somehow that made Cliff feel safe. She was still part of his luck, no matter how badly it seemed to be running. She was still the figure on the runway as he fought to bring the shattered *Rainbow Express* home from Schweinfurt.

Sarah spent most of her time at their Palm Springs house, which Cliff ceded as her turf. They kept in touch on family matters, especially their problems with their older daughter, Elizabeth, who spent a year in a drug rehab center and another year with her mother putting her mind back together. Sarah had done a good job with her. Elizabeth was now happily married to the doctor who had rescued her.

Dick Stone told Bruce Simons to make Woolman's attack on Israel the lead in his statement to the press. "Stress how pained we all were because the heroic Israelis fly so many of our planes," he said.

The roar of airliners landing at LAX kept drowning out the music and the speakers. In about an hour the crowd began to dissolve. By eleven o'clock the protest was over. Everyone agreed by the standards of the sixties it was a flop. Dick Stone telephoned Adrian Van Ness with the good news. He was not very responsive. His voice crackled over the speakerphone on Cliff's desk, sounding like someone from outer space.

"One more trip over Niagara Falls survived," he said, "Any good news on the Aurora?"

Cliff went into overdrive about the prospects for Mideast sales. The Egyptians, the Moroccans, the Tunisians were in love with the plane. It was a lie, of course. What they loved were the James Madisons in Cliff's briefcase.

"Let me know when love translates into cash," Adrian said. Panic roiled Cliff's flesh but he concealed it with his usual skill.

Downstairs Dick Stone thanked Dan Hanrahan and his security men for playing the game his way. Trying to minimize his surly performance during the demonstration, Cliff shifted gears. "Good flight plan, Navigator. Feel like relaxing over a drink?"

Dick shook his head. "I've got a date with a couple of union leaders at eight o'clock tomorrow morning."

Watching Dick trudge back to his office, Cliff thought he saw signs of strain. Several sources had told him Dr. Willoughby had barred booze from Dick's diet and was holding him together with a careful mix of tranquilizers and anti-depressants. It had been a year since Cassie divorced him and went back to Tennessee.

Up the freeways Cliff roared to Angela Perry's house in Holmby Hills, his home away from home in Los Angeles these days. A party was in progress as he arrived. There always seemed to be a party in progress. There were the usual nubile starlets in miniskirts and pretty boys in Gucci jeans, dancing to rock music that blasted from the most expensive stereo system in California.

Cliff found Angela in bed, watching the evening news with one of the ex-sixties activists sitting on the floor beside her. His name was Sam something but Cliff always called him Lenin Jr. He had been tear-gassed in Chicago in 1968 and had showed up at all the other right places from Woodstock to Altamont to Kent State to acquire a niche in the Movement's hall of fame. He looked like Pinocchio, except that his nose was not quite as long. He had the same cockeyed eyes and smarmy smile. He also (in Cliff's opinion) thought like someone with a brain made of wood.

Cliff kissed Angela and rubbed her swollen stomach. She was nine months pregnant. "How is he?"

"Restless," she said.

The child was her idea. She had declared she would have it during that unforgettable Christmas weekend they spent in Washington after Charlie's death. Conception had turned out to be much more difficult than either of them imagined. Angela was in her early forties and Cliff was fifty-two. They had wound up consulting fertility experts and counting sperm and ova.

She had finally conceived—and Cliff asked her to marry him. Her producer, her publicity man, her agent, were horrified. Marrying a right-wing warmonger would destroy her image. After listening to everyone, including several tirades from Cliff, Angela decided it would be better to have a love child without benefit of a marriage license. It was the in thing to do in seventies Hollywood—it would enhance her image as a free spirit.

On television a reporter was asking Jacob Woolman why he had attacked Israel in his assault on the BX. "Because Israel is part of the American war machine!" he shrilled.

Cliff grinned. Bruce Simons had done his job. The reporter was an old Buchanan friend, whom they had taken on junkets to the Paris Air Show and other plush ports of call. By the time Woolman stopped denouncing Israel, his movement would be yesterday's news.

"How could he be so stupid!" Lenin Jr. groaned.

"How come you weren't there tonight, hero?" Cliff said.

"I saw no point in playing into your Machiavellian hands," Lenin Jr. said.

Cliff had made no secret of their strategy. He enjoyed outraging Angela's friends by bragging about the way Buchanan outwitted protestors and congressmen to build warplanes.

"You *are* awful," Angela said in an unusually weary voice.

Cliff kicked Lenin Jr. in the shins. "Beat it, Vladimir," he said.

Lenin Jr. slouched out of the bedroom and Cliff lay down beside her. "You'll feel a lot better in a week," he said.

"Irv said this kid has cost us fifty million dollars." Irv was her producer.

"Sid's turned down *seven* firm offers for major films." Sid was her agent.

"Arnie says people are screaming for new stills. It's amazing how fast an image gets used up."

Arnie was her publicity man.

"You'll be back at work in a month, I'm sure of it."

"I better be."

"I've got to go to New York tomorrow."

"You promised you'd stay for the week! So you'd be here—"

"Honey, there's a guy flying in from Saudi Arabia who swears he can sell a hundred Auroras for us in the Middle East."

"For the usual five million a plane?"

Angela was fascinated by the gritty side of the plane business. She collected stories of corporate corruption to convince herself that her left-wing friends had it right, America was hopeless.

"Maybe six million," Cliff said. For a while he had bragged about the bribes he paid overseas. But Angela's reaction started to remind him of Sarah. Lately he had kept his mouth shut.

"I want you here all week. You promised me!"Angela said, combining moral disapproval and sheer willfulness.

"I'll fly out the minute I hear you've gone into labor."

"I've begun to wonder exactly where this relationship is going," Angela said, her mouth in a Bette Davis pout.

"Honey, you're feeling lousy. Let's talk about it next month. When we've got something to celebrate."

"You'll have something to celebrate. I'll have stitches. You won't be able to touch me for another two months."

"Hey, it's not that bad. Women have been doing this for a long time."

"I'm not women."

"You seem to be forgetting what this means to us."

"What does it mean? You've gone right on making your dirty deals, building your rotten planes. What kind of a future will this baby have with someone like you running the country?"

Cliff was very tired. He had flown in from London two days ago and spent most of the next two days and nights conferring with Dick Stone and Dan Hanrahan on preparations for the protest. The CEO thought he deserved a few words of sympathy, maybe even praise from someone, especially Angela. He liked the rueful way she admired his executive skills and simultaneously damned them. It corresponded to the way he often felt about himself. Instead of sympathy, he was getting left-wing drivel.

"I wish I was running the fucking country! I'm mostly trying to keep our heads above the goddamn mess people like you and Lenin Jr. have created over the last ten years."

"You bastard," she said. "You're standing there in your Hong Kong tailored suit pulling down three hundred thousand a year and he doesn't have a cent. He gave up his career, his life, to try to change this country and people like you have made him a laughingstock. I'm proud I tried to help him. I'm going to go on trying to help him. We're not going to quit because you can outwit a simpleton like Jacob Woolman."

"I'm not going to quit either. I'm not going to quit loving you."

That had always worked in the past. Angela's anger had invariably evaporated into tears. But tonight the words thudded against the wall behind her like wet wads of paper. She barely noticed them. Alarm shivered Cliff's nerves. Was another woman going to turn on him?

"I'm serious!" she said. "I'm beginning to think—"

Her face went from rage to terror in a blink. "Oh my God!" she screamed as the first labor pain struck.

"Call the doctor!" Cliff roared to the rockers in the living room. "Get my car!" he shouted to Lenin Jr.

The baby arrived three hours later. It was a boy, making Cliff wonder if his luck was turning. Within the hour he was dancing him around the room in his arms, crooning to him while Lenin Jr. watched from the doorway, his smile not quite so smarmy. Angela watched too, barely smiling.

"Isn't this worth it?" Cliff said. "Even worth putting up with me? What are we going to name him?"

"*Not* Charlie. I don't want him to know anything about him. How he died, why we—"

"I didn't expect Charlie. How about something nice and neutral like Frank?"

"After Frank Buchanan, the designer of the BX?" Lenin Jr. said. "I hope not."

Cliff stifled an impulse to kick him in the stomach. "Honey, I've got to get back to New York. Do you understand?"

Angela said she understood but she seemed to be looking at Lenin Jr. when she said it. In New York, the Saudi sheik turned out to be an Iranian with an unpronounceable name who wanted ten million up front to "reassure his contacts." Cliff told him to get lost and headed for Washington, where a lot of things were happening that dropped Angela and their nameless child to the bottom of his list of worries. The 1976 presidential campaign was gathering steam and it was time to collect endorsements from the candidates on the BX bomber. Gerald Ford was no problem. The Republicans had revived the plane and it had virtually become part of their platform.

The Democrats were another matter. Remnants of George McGovern's routed peace-now unilateral disarmers were all over the place, pretending that 1972 never happened and the war in Vietnam was Nixon's fault. The Democratic front-runner, Jimmy Carter, was an Annapolis man with no built-in fondness for the Air Force. On the contrary, he had undoubtedly heard endless diatribes at the Naval Academy about how the blue suiters had tried to take the Navy's planes away from them.

Nevertheless, after immense wheedling and all-out pressure from key members of the House and Senate Armed Services Committees, Carter endorsed the BX before he got the nomination. That temporarily stifled rumblings from the Creature, Proxmire, and their ilk who were hungry for another attack on the plane.

Cliff called Angela every night. He begged her to bring the baby to Washington. She refused. Her stitches were agony as she had predicted and the baby screamed all night, every night. After the Republican convention, there was a political hiatus and Cliff flew to California determined to settle a few things. He had decided to insist on marrying Angela to give his son a father. He was not going to put up with any more advice from Irv or Arnie or Sid or Lenin Jr. about anything.

He arrived to find the Holmby Hills house swarming with photographers. *People* magazine was doing a story on Angela's defiance of conventional morals. She was posing with the love child in her arms, looking more desirable than Cliff had ever seen her.

"What the hell are you doing here?" hissed a voice in Cliff's ear.

It was Lenin Jr. and he was not wearing his smarmy smile.

"Did I hear you right?" Cliff said.

"The last thing she wants is your over-age face in this story," he said in the same stage whisper. "Get out. Come back in two hours."

Cliff drove to the office and conferred with Frank Buchanan on some ECPs (Engineering Change Proposals) for a new run of the Colossus. Adrian had persuaded the Air Force to buy another fifty-four copies of the monster. Cliff had lunch with Dick Stone and predicted Carter would win the election and immediately order up the BX, solving all their financial problems with an influx of ten billion dollars.

"I don't like Carter's looks," Dick said. "That shit-eating smile reminds me of the Creature."

"It's as good as in the barn," Cliff insisted. "Incidentally, I'm going to marry Angela. Do you think it will upset Adrian?"

"Not any more than you would if you married Jane Fonda."

"Angela's not political in that obvious way," Cliff said.

"The hell she isn't," Dick said.

Back at the office, Cliff, never inclined to temporizing, put through a call to Adrian and asked him bluntly if he was opposed to him marrying Angela Perry. "I wouldn't dream of objecting personally. But I shudder to think of the board's reaction," Adrian said.

The board of directors was a bunch of retired aerospace executives who never had a thought Adrian did not put in their heads. Adrian was much too smooth to let Cliff go to them and decry his interference in his private life.

On Cliff's telephone, the red lights and the green lights began blinking simultaneously. His secretary was pressing all the buttons. What the hell was happening? He got rid of Adrian. A second later the door swung open and he found himself face-to-face with Angela, Irv the producer, Arnie the publicity man, Sid the agent—and Lenin Jr. "What's this?" he said.

"This," Angela said, sweeping past him, "is the conference we were supposed to have an hour ago at my place. Didn't Lee (Lenin Jr.'s real name) tell you to come back in two hours?"

"I've got other things to do," Cliff said.

"Maybe this is a better place to talk," Angela said.

Cliff knew exactly what she meant. He could not tell from their expressions whether Irv or Arnie or Sid knew. But the sneer on Lenin Jr.'s face suggested he knew what Cliff and Angela had done in this office to launch their romance.

"I flew out here to talk to you—alone," Cliff said. He asked Sid and Arnie and Irv if they would like a tour of the plant. "It might give you some ideas for special effects," he said. He suggested Lenin Jr. go with them and pretend he was visiting Disneyland.

"They're here because I asked them to be here," Angela said. She positioned herself by the window, looking spectacular in a cream-colored blouse and long blue gaucho skirt. "I agree with you that our son needs a father. I'm prepared to marry you. I think, in spite of many profound disagreements, we could be

494

reasonably happy. But I have to consider my career, my public image, the expectations I've raised among millions of movie goers."

It's a script, Cliff thought. She's reciting lines.

"This is especially true in the light of Buchanan's recent defiance of popular protests against your new nuclear bomber. You'd have to give everyone in the movie colony very convincing evidence that you've changed your mind about this and other weapon systems that strike at the hopes and yearnings of millions of Americans still living in poverty. Arnie here has prepared a statement which I'd like you to make at our wedding."

Arnie, who was about five-feet-nothing, with a completely bald head that rumor had it he shaved daily, fished a piece of paper out of his briefcase and handed it to Cliff with a somewhat nervous grin.

Irv the producer, who was about six-feet-two and vaguely resembled a whooping crane, cleared his throat and said: "There's nothing personal in this, Cliff, please understand that."

Sid the agent, who had the eyes of a starving piranha in a face that was mostly suet, reiterated this sentiment.

The statement began with Cliff's apology for having devoted twenty-five years of his life to serving the Military Industrial Complex. It confessed to the American people that Buchanan had devoured millions of dollars to build planes that the country did not need, planes that did nothing but kill people. It specifically repudiated the BX bomber as a "monstrosity" that would only increase the probability of a nuclear war. It ended with a glowing tribute to the way Angela had helped him to confess these atrocious sins and led him to the "altar of love and peace."

Cliff read the whole thing twice. "Arnie," he said, walking toward the tiny publicity man. "This is wonderful stuff. It's good enough to eat."

Arnie responded with a vaguely alarmed smile. He rubbed his shiny pink head, perhaps hoping for luck as Cliff's six-foot-four frame loomed over him.

"That's exactly what you're going to do. Eat it." Cliff grabbed Arnie by the shirt and jammed the sheet of paper into his mouth, pinched his nose and said: "Chew."

Arnie started turning blue. "You're killing him!" Angela screamed.

"Down on the floor—everyone!" Lenin Jr. yelled.

He fell to the rug and curled into a ball. Angela imitated him. Irv and Sid followed, with considerably more difficulty. Sid weighed about three hundred pounds and elongated Irv found folding up difficult.

"You are now confronted with a sit-in to protest the BX bomber!" Lenin Jr. shouted. "We have press releases prepared and our chauffeur is waiting for a prearranged signal to distribute them to TV and newspapers."

Arnie was chewing frantically but was still turning blue. Cliff let go of his nose and he spluttered pieces of the statement all over the rug. Cliff grabbed him by his collar and the seat of his pants and threw him out of the office headfirst. He did the same thing with Irv, Sid, and Lenin Jr.

Cliff slammed the door and stood with his back to it. "Get up," he said to Angela.

"Lee predicted you'd be violent," Angela said. She was starring in her own protest movie, loving every minute of it.

Cliff dragged her to her feet and pressed her against the window. "You can do this here? You can do this to me here?" he said.

"I'm trying to stop you from doing something worse to me. Something you've been trying to do since we started. Ruin my career. Reduce me to your obedient servant."

Outside an Aurora came whining down in its final glide. Angela was like that plane, an expensive fantasy that proved once more he was a man among men. But Cliff was not going to let Angela humiliate him. His luck might be running all wrong but he was still the pilot who had brought the *Rainbow Express* back from Schweinfurt. He had ridden the Starduster out to the Sierra Wave.

"Admit you still love me," Cliff said, standing over her.

"I don't. I've stopped," she said.

"Bullshit. I told you I'd never stop loving you and I never will. Can you turn your back on that? Can you trade that for the left-wing rubbish you just spouted?"

"It isn't rubbish. It gives my life meaning. You can't give it meaning!"

"I can give it the only meaning that matters!" he shouted.

Meaning. Cliff stepped back, stunned by the impact of those words on himself. They rebounded from the sun-filled glass like twenty-millimeter shells exploding against his body with the memory of so many other meanings that mattered. Suddenly he was talking to Sarah. He was remembering the year before and the year after Charlie was born. What was he doing, trying to make this woman part of that kind of meaning?

"At least—I thought I could—until you came here and ruined it," Cliff said.

Flabby fists pounded on the office door. "Angela! Are you all right?" Lenin Jr. cried.

Cliff yanked the door open and yelled "Boo!" Irv, Arnie, and Sid practically jumped out of their double knits. "She's all yours, boys," he said.

Angela stood there, trying to figure out how to rescue the scene. None of her four directors had a clue. She started to sob. That was definitely not in the script. She was admitting Cliff was right. She had ruined the reckless mixture of defiance and communion they had created in this unlikely place.

For a moment Cliff wanted to take her in his arms and tell her he was sorry too. But someone or something inside him whispered *no*. A hard, cold, bitter *no*. Without saying a word, he watched the entourage escort their meal ticket to the elevator.

Some people think it was Cliff Morris's finest hour in the plane business. Would he have done it, would he have clung to that resolute no, if he had known what a mess it was going to make of the technicolor movie of his life?

Some people—the handful who know the whole story of Cliff's life—say yes. More worldly-wise types point out that Cliff's movie was already way over budget and desperately in need of some sort of resolution—even if it turned out to be one he loathed.

AMORALITY PLAY

Beyond the porch of Adrian Van Ness's Virginia mansion, autumn colors glittered in the brilliant sunshine. In the distance, Jefferson's Monticello shimmered on its hilltop, a symbol of classic purity and purpose. Dick Stone sat beside Adrian in this quintessential American setting, discussing how to rescue the Buchanan Corporation from imminent extinction.

Cliff Morris's finest hour in the plane business was about to become everyone's worst nightmare. His beloved, Angela, and her left-wing lover, Lenin Jr., had revenged themselves by sending Buchanan's inveterate enemy in the Senate, the Creature from the cornfields of Iowa, a succinct summary of Cliff's boasts about bribing politicians around the world to sell Buchanan's planes. The Creature was trying to line up his fellow solons to hold hearings on this suddenly nefarious practice.

The Creature had friends inside Carter's White House who were backing him for reasons of their own. Washington was aswirl with rumors that the president was about to renege on his campaign promise and cancel the BX bomber. The hearings would smear Buchanan with enough mud to make a counterattack by their backers in Congress impossible.

Carter was turning into the unreliable president Dick had predicted the first time he saw him. His administration was an unstable congeries of ex–sixties activists and moderate Democrats like Carter himself, incapable of dealing with the pressure tactics of the left. The liberals were demanding a pound of flesh from the Military Industrial Complex and the BX bomber was the most tempting slice.

The Van Ness housekeeper emerged to report that Cliff was on the telephone. "Put him on," Adrian said. He gestured to Dick to pick up another extension.

" 'Lo, Adrian? Lissen. News isn't good on the Aurora. Only thing to do is end production run. Can't sell another fuckin' copy."

Dick had already told Adrian their wide-body jet was on its way to becoming the white whale of the business. "When are you going to stop drinking?" Adrian said.

"Hey—jus' had a couple for lunch."

"It sounds like a couple of dozen."

"Yeah, yeah. Lissen. I'll be in California for next few days."

"The action is in Washington, Cliff. That's why Dick Stone is here. Where the hell have you been? Mike Shannon has spent the last two days calling you all over the world."

"Adrian—man has a right to a personal life."

"Pussy," Adrian said. "That's all she is, Cliff. You can get the same thing in your own office. There's no reason to get drunk over her."

"Adrian I loved the goddamn woman. She's got my kid!"

Adrian hung up and stared coldly at Dick Stone. "We've got to do something about him—fast."

Dick Stone nodded mournfully. For a year now, Cliff Morris had spent half his time trying to revive his affair with Angela and the other half vainly trying to sell the Aurora while red ink gushed through the Buchanan Corporation.

For months Dick had been conferring with Adrian by telephone about how to service Buchanan's terrifying debts, which were now close to a billion dollars. He was growing more and more weary of shouldering the burden. The loss of the BX could easily shove them into bankruptcy. As the corporation's money man, he saw that as a personal defeat. He was not sure how well he could handle it. Without Cassie and his children, he was vulnerable to crushing bouts of depression.

Dick had come east expecting an aging Adrian Van Ness to let him suggest a drastic answer to their problems—perhaps selling the missile division or some other part of the company to raise cash. Instead, he had found Adrian full of determination to rely on the same combination of guile and grease that had kept them aloft so far. He seemed to be thriving on Washington's rampant intrigue and devious power plays. He had no intention of letting Buchanan get shoved out of any part of what he liked to call the great game.

"Are they canceling the whole BX program?" Dick said.

"That remains to be seen. We might be able to salvage something," Adrian said. "Much will depend on whether we can survive these hearings. Do you have our Geneva, Tokyo, and Casablanca files up to date?"

These were the cities through which overseas bribes were funneled. Dick nodded, not trying to conceal his distaste. "Dick, Dick," Adrian said. "The persistence of your Jewish conscience is the only thing about you that distresses me."

Adrian was shocked by the figures Dick spread before him. "My God," he said. "Cliff Morris is a bigger spender than I thought."

In Japan, Cliff had paid five million dollars a plane to sell the Aurora. Prices had been slightly lower in the Mideast and Europe but Africa and South America were worse—no less than seven million dollars per plane in some countries. It came to an appalling $190 million dollars in the last three years for the Aurora program alone. Cliff had been equally reckless in pushing the business jet that Adrian had christened the Argusair. The supersalesman turned CEO had paid roughly twenty million dollars to peddle 200 of them.

"How much are we likely to lose on the Aurora?"

"Two hundred million," Dick said.

"Mea culpa, mea culpa," Adrian said, scanning the figures.

Amanda Van Ness came out on the porch wearing a high-necked black silk dress and pearls. She looked ten, perhaps twenty years younger than Adrian. Everyone marveled at her smooth skin, her gleaming russet hair.

"The guests are arriving," Amanda said. "You aren't even dressed. How are you, Mr. Stone?"

"Fine. How are you, Mrs. Van Ness?"

"As well as can be expected in exile. What was the temperature in California when you left?"

"Eighty-one."

"Now you know why I hate my husband," Amanda said.

Not knowing what else to do, Dick pretended to be amused. Adrian's smile was strained.

"Have you seen Frank Buchanan lately?" Amanda asked.

"I speak to him on the phone every few days," Dick said.

"Give him my love," Amanda said.

Frank had retreated to a mountain overlooking the Mojave Desert in search of wisdom, leaving Sam Hardy as Buchanan's chief designer. But there was so much knowledge in Frank's ancient head, Dick was constantly begging him for advice in their continuing struggle to perfect the BX.

Adrian's smile vanished with the mention of Frank Buchanan's name. The word *love* made him twitch as if his wife had just struck him with a dart. He shook a pill from a dark brown plastic bottle and gulped it. Dick suddenly recalled Kirk Willoughby muttering about Adrian's heart.

Dick retreated upstairs, put on a fresh suit and joined Adrian as he greeted a swirl of Pentagon undersecretaries and congressmen and senators. Vietnamese servants disposed of their luggage. The VIPs had cocktails on the lawn under ancient oaks, supposedly planted in Jefferson's era. Most of the guests were moderate Democrats like Buchanan's old friend and supporter, the senior senator from Connecticut. Adrian did not waste his time or money on the Creature and his pals. The moderates fretted over the way the Russians were extending their influence in Africa and the Mideast. Adrian suggested the BX and another production run of the Colossus might give the United States the muscle to stop them.

Adrian concentrated on one of Carter's Georgians who was part of the White House inner circle. He plied him with several glasses of twenty-year-old bourbon and then asked, with an air of weary casualness: "Has the president made up his mind on the BX?"

"I'm afraid so," was the drawled reply. "He walked the floor for three nights and finally decided it was the one major weapons system we could cut without endangerin' our strategic posture."

"In a way I'm relieved," Adrian said. "No one likes to hang by the thumbs indefinitely. We've got other things on our plate we can get to now."

A gong summoned them to dinner. Adrian fell in step beside Dick. "Isn't that fellow from *Jawgia* a wonder?" he murmured. "A year ago he never thought of anything more strategic than how to write a press release. Now he's picked up the jargon that spells life and death for the country—and thinks he understands it."

Adrian produced one of his more enigmatic smiles. "I'm glad he came, for your sake. One of the purposes of this soiree is to display the pinheads with whom we're doomed to deal."

In the paneled dining room, Adrian began the meal by introducing the entire Vietnamese weekend staff to the guests. Each told what he had done in his former life. One had been a cabinet minister with an economics degree from the Sorbonne, another was a surgeon who had directed Saigon's main hospital, a third had been a professor of history.

The professor was writing a book on the war. "He thinks if we had the BX in time South Vietnam might be independent today," Adrian said.

The Carter aide squirmed. So did most of the other Democrats. At the end of the evening they conferred with the senator from Connecticut about the progress of the Creature's hearings. They learned he had persuaded Frank Church, a fellow superliberal, to investigate Buchanan with his subcommittee on multinational corporations.

"What if I gave you an unsigned memorandum, telling in considerable detail how all the other aircraft companies have been committing the same overseas sins for a long time?" Adrian asked. "You could slip it to the Creature to prove your heart is in the right place on this issue."

"What the hell would that accomplish?" the senator said. He was a little slow when it came to Machiavellian tactics.

Dick saw instantly what Adrian had in mind. The Creature would find the added targets irresistible. Spreading the blame would take a lot of the heat off Buchanan. But Dick could not figure out why Adrian regarded the hearings with such equanimity from a personal point of view. He had been involved in these overseas payments for two decades.

The rest of the weekend slid by. There was a private visit to Monticello, golf for those who played it, horseback riding for others, led by Amanda, who still rode like a teenager, bounding over ditches and fences. Adrian and Dick Stone followed at a more sedate pace. Dick was not at home on a horse and Adrian was not much better.

"Still enduring divorce?" Adrian said.

"More or less."

"You could be worse off. Try living with a woman who hates you."

"Why does she?" Dick said, surprised by Adrian's confessional impulse.

"Everyone pays a price for trying to reach beyond the rainbow," Adrian said. "Amanda's mine." He pointed toward Monticello. "Read a biography of him sometime. You'll see how many prices he paid."

They ambled on through the autumn sunshine. "Once I told Frank Buchanan it was the pots of gold I was reaching for. Now I know it's something far less tangible. I think we're all pursuing an image of ourselves, a personal apotheosis."

"What was—is—yours?" Dick asked.

"To be a man of substance." Adrian smiled wryly. "So substantial I'd be forever beyond the reach of ruin. What better place to do that than the aircraft business? It says wonders for my judgment, don't you think?"

"You could have done worse. Trying to beat the horses. Or the tables in Las Vegas."

Adrian chuckled. He was enjoying himself. Dick had seldom seen him so genial. "I haven't figured out the gold beyond your rainbow, Dick. What is it?"

"Maybe I haven't either," Dick said warily.

"You should. It's the final step to maturity."

For an uneasy moment Dick felt he had failed a question in an examination where a perfect score was expected.

As soon as their guests departed, Adrian announced they were flying to California. "We've got to put Cliff back together for those hearings," he said. "Find out where Angela is living these days."

That was no challenge for their security men. All they had to do was read the gossip columns about the spectacular new house Angela had built in the Malibu colony. Leaving Amanda in Virginia with the housekeeper, Adrian and Dick flew to LAX and drove up the coast to Malibu. Dick telephoned Angela from a nearby restaurant and asked if they could see her.

Angela met them in white slacks, blue boating jacket, a white beret. With her was Lenin Jr. in his inevitable blue jeans. "I'll get right to the point," Adrian said. "How much will it take to persuade you to kick Cliff out once and for all?"

Angela laughed. "What an outrageous idea," she said. But Dick could see it appealed to her. She gave her revolutionary friend a conspiratorial smile.

"Two million dollars," he said. "Off the books, of course."

"Done," Adrian said. "Give them a check, Dick."

Dick wrote a check on Buchanan's Swiss account and handed it to Angela. "Don't deposit it anyplace but in Switzerland," Adrian said.

They drove to Buchanan's headquarters. "Be sure to include in the explanation for that check something about services rendered," Adrian said.

This time Adrian was much too far ahead of Dick. "I don't get it," he said.

"We're buying silence," Adrian said. "They might have done us a lot of damage at the Creature's hearings. Now Cliff can go down with dignity."

Security Chief Hanrahan informed them Cliff was at the Beverly Wilshire. They drove to the grand old lady of Los Angeles hotels and found the chief executive officer in his underwear, halfway through a bottle of Inverness. A two-day stubble sprouted on his chin.

"What the hell do you want?" Cliff growled.

"Is that what I get for flying three thousand miles to see you?" Adrian said.

"For what? To fire me? Go ahead. I don't give a goddamn."

"What happened? Did Angela throw you out once and for all?"

"Yeah. Yesterday."

Adrian pretended to be amused. "She is clever."

"Clever?"

"She just accepted my offer of two million dollars to throw you out—after she'd done it."

"You're a fucking liar!" Cliff roared.

Dick showed him the carbon of the check he had just written. "I'll get it back," Cliff said, jamming his feet into his pants.

"Sit down," Adrian said, shoving Cliff backward onto the bed. "I'm seventy-eight years old. I had hoped before I died I'd see this company sound, secure, ready to fly into the next century. Instead I've got a self-pitying pussy-chasing playboy in charge and a conscience-stricken ex-student of the Torah as second in command. Do you think I might be entitled to feel just a little sorry for myself?"

"Most people—including me—will say you're getting pretty much what you deserve," Cliff said.

"I know that," Adrian said. "That's why I just spent two million dollars to prove something to you—instead of pleading for sympathy."

"What else is happening?" Cliff said. He was not stupid. He knew Adrian always had another motive.

"Carter's canceling the BX the day after tomorrow. There may be hearings. I want you sober for them. I want you to cut out the booze and Angela absolutely and totally. Will you promise me abstinence on both counts?"

Dick held up the carbon of the check again. He still did not completely understand the game Adrian was playing. But he wanted to straighten Cliff out for personal as well as corporate reasons. They were still friends.

Back in Adrian's car, Dick got another surprise. "I want you to come out to the desert with me and tell the workforce the BX is canceled."

"Isn't that Cliff's job?"

"I want them to hear it from you."

"Why?" Dick said.

"Because such matters may soon become part of your job."

What was Adrian saying? Dick Stone was the next Buchanan president? Then why sober up Cliff? Why not just fire him and let Angela and Sarah worry about the consequences?

The next day, Adrian and Dick flew to the Mojave. The sweep of the desert beyond the factory brought back a surge of memories. The White Lightning, the Talus, the Scorpion, the Warrior. Billy McCall swaggering from the cockpit, Cassie waiting in the bedroom at the Villa Hermosa. Amalie whispering her mocking conundrums. So many betrayals, so many failures, so much heartbreak.

Yet the planes flew. Was that the only thing that mattered? The Colossus filled the sky with thunder. The Aurora was a majestic flow of cursives and thrust in a thousand takeoffs. The new fighter, the SkyDemon, defied gravity, flying straight up as fast as it flew horizontally, even if the goddamn Air Force had rejected it.

Dick rode with Adrian to the fourth floor balcony of the huge plant, the length of four football fields and the width of two. A dozen fuselages of the BX rested on jigs while workers swarmed around them, riveting, wiring, welding. The usual big American flag dangled from the balcony.

"Ladies and gentlemen," Dick said over the public address system. "Could I have your attention? You know me, Dick Stone. You know how proud I am of the work you've done on this plane and other planes. But in this business we've learned a long time ago that hard work, dedication, isn't always appreciated. We just got some bad news from Washington. Tomorrow President Carter is canceling the BX. That means a lot of you may lose your jobs. I thought you ought to know that as soon as possible. But I also want you to know I'm going to do everything I can to keep this plane alive. We're going to try everything to keep you with us. That's a promise!"

The words, especially the promise, were spontaneous. Adrian Van Ness had simply ordered Dick to deliver the news of the cancelation. How he did it was up to him. The sight of that gigantic flag, the unfinished planes on the jigs, had demolished the rational side of Dick's nature—and banished the depression that wrapped his emotions in a leaden overcoat most of the time.

Dick went down on the plant floor to deal with angry questions and furious threats. Some people wanted to trash the BX skeletons on the spot. Others offered to work on half pay to finish them. Most were resigned but very bitter. They had been hired and fired and rehired by Buchanan and other companies too often.

When Dick returned to the plant manager's office where Adrian was waiting for him, he was bathed in sweat. But he had learned something about himself. "We're going to keep that goddamn plane alive, somehow," he said.

"I was hoping I'd hear that," Adrian said.

For the next six months Dick struggled to make good on that vow. He picked up subcontracting programs from Boeing and General Dynamics and Tony Sirocca scraped together thirty million dollars from the Air Force's Independent Research and Development Fund to do some work on a mach 3 stealth fighter. He grew so absorbed in the struggle, he almost forgot about the Creature and his friends in Washington.

But Adrian, deep in his end of the great game, had not forgotten this threat to their existence. One afternoon in April of 1978, he jangled Dick's nerves with an updated version of Paul Revere's cry. "To arms, to arms, the dimwits are coming."

"Dimwits?" Dick said.

"Congressmen," Adrian said. "The hearings are about to begin."

A few days later Church subcommittee staffers arrived with subpoenas for Buchanan's overseas records. Dick naturally warned Cliff. He brushed it off with a shrug. "It's not against the law. How come it's any of their business in the first place?"

"If they feel like it, they can make anything their business," Dick said. "If I were you I'd start talking to our lawyers."

The lawyers did not have much to offer. Since no one was being accused of a crime, they could not advise Cliff or Adrian to take the fifth amendment. Cliff was reassured to learn Adrian was going to be the first witness.

"I'll just follow his lead," Cliff said.

Dick flew to Washington with Cliff a month later. The hearings were held in one of the Senate's cavernous paneled chambers, with batteries of microphones on the witness table and TV cameras whirring on the sidelines. Adrian sat down in the central chair at the table opposite the senators and they went to work.

"Mr. Van Ness," Senator Church said in his best Eagle Scout manner. "Would you tell us about Buchanan's overseas payments?"

"We never made any while I was chief executive officer," Adrian said. "If we've made any in recent years, they've been without my knowledge."

"You have had no connection with the company since you retired as president?" the Creature sneered.

"Only as a stockholder—and board member."

"Aren't you chairman of the board?" Senator Church asked.

"At the moment, yes. But the title gives me no executive authority. I've been living in Virginia since I retired. Which would make it rather difficult to run a billion dollar corporation in California, even if I wanted to."

"Your innocence is much too studied for my taste, Mr. Van Ness," growled the Creature, who had, if possible, grown uglier with age.

"That is your problem, Senator, not mine," Adrian said. "I am proud to say that except for a few parking tickets, I have never been convicted—or even investigated—for any crime. My reputation—and the reputation of the Buchanan Corporation as far as I know it—is spotless."

"We have evidence to the contrary before this committee!" the Creature roared. "Millions of dollars in what you call overseas payments were nothing but bribes. Bribes to foreigners!"

"I know nothing about it," Adrian said.

There was a lot more sparring, in which Adrian steadfastly denied everything. Mockingly, he wondered if the Creature knew that it was not a crime for an American businessman to persuade foreigners to buy his products by sweetening the deal with some extra dollars. He recounted memories of his days as a merchant banker in London, when douceurs were regularly used to guarantee or enhance overseas investments. He discussed the foreign policy of the Roman empire, which for three hundred years included the fine art of buying friendship with hostile tribes on its borders.

Again and again, when it came to specific details he referred the senators to the next witness, Buchanan's current president, Clifford Morris. The hearings adjourned for lunch with the solons in an exasperated mood.

Adrian, Cliff, Dick Stone, and Mike Shannon taxied to the exclusive Cosmos Club, which Adrian had joined when he came to Washington. He had reserved a private dining room so they could confer without eavesdroppers.

The waiter had barely poured their drinks and departed when Cliff snarled: "Do you think you can get away with this act?"

"I hope so," Adrian said.

"Don't we have records of how you and the Prince operated in the fifties and sixties?"

"The IRS only requires you to keep records for three years," Adrian said. "When Dick computerized everything in nineteen seventy-six, all that material was obliterated."

"Is that true?" Cliff asked Dick.

Dick nodded. "Why wasn't I told?" Cliff roared.

"You've never had the slightest interest in anything that mundane," Dick said.

"I've still got news for you, Adrian. I'm not going to be anyone's fall guy," Cliff said. "If I go, you're going with me."

"I don't think you mean that, Cliff," Adrian said. "I think you care more about this company—even about me—than that threat implies. If you reveal we've been doing these naughty things for decades, it would destroy our image. Newspapers would print vicious cartoons of planes soaring over rainbows with bags of money in them. No bank in the world would loan us a nickel. We'd be out of business."

"Why the hell should I let you put me out of business?" Cliff raged.

"I'm not at all sure that's going to happen," Adrian said. "For one thing, I've supplied the committee with a lot of information that makes it clear we're not alone in making off-the-books overseas payments. If there's one executive who can survive this scandal, it's you. Who else can match your war record? Forty-nine missions over Germany. I'm sure our board of directors will back you without reservations."

Cliff gulped his drink, unconvinced. "It's a gamble, I admit," Adrian said. "But I don't see any other sensible way to deal with it. Do you really want to put the whole company at risk for the sake of petty revenge? Especially when your big mouth got us into this mess?"

He told Cliff where the Creature had obtained the original evidence to start the investigation. Cliff cursed and poured himself another drink.

"There's one more thing I might mention," Adrian continued. "Another more personal reason why you might want to protect me. All these years, I've protected you from a scandal that could have destroyed you any time it was leaked to the press."

"What the fuck are you talking about?" Cliff said.

"During World War II I got a call from a general I did several favors for—Newton Slade. He told me the Red Cross in Geneva had reported a complaint from the German government about a B-Seventeen with a rainbow on its nose that faked a midair surrender over Schweinfurt, then shot down the German pilots who were escorting it to a nearby airfield."

There was total silence in the dining room for a full minute. "General Slade quashed the matter as a personal favor for me," Adrian said. "He sent me the papers. I've saved them all these years. I had a feeling they might be useful someday."

Adrian smiled at Dick Stone and Mike Shannon. "A little example of fore-thought."

Loathing, that was the only emotion Dick felt for Adrian Van Ness, sitting opposite him in that elegant dining room with the memories of Schweinfurt and other raids clotting the air until it was almost impossible to breathe. Dick wanted to snarl a curse in Adrian's face, urge Cliff to tell the whole truth and damn the consequences. But everything Adrian had said about the consequences of the truth was true. They would be out of business. His vow to those workers in Palmdale would be aborted. But the worst pain would be inflicted on Sarah Chapman Morris. Why did he know that? Why did he still remember the adulation in her blue eyes that day beside the smoking ruin of the *Rainbow Express*?

Dick said nothing. He let Cliff think he agreed with Adrian Van Ness. In a certain sickening sense he did agree with him. Cliff accepted his silence as a final verdict. He poured himself a full water glass of Scotch.

"Okay," he said. "I'll play your lousy game."

The hearings resumed that afternoon with Cliff in the witness chair. The Creature began with a right cross. "Mr. Morris," he said. "According to our records, you paid two hundred and twenty million dollars in bribes to interested parties overseas in the past three years, all carried on your books as extraordinary expenses. Could you explain what that term means?"

"Senator," Cliff said. "I resent you calling those payments bribes. I see them under a variety of headings—gifts, payments for special services, agents' fees."

The senators began going through the transactions, one by one, asking Cliff wryly, when he denied the bribe, exactly what he thought the word's *special services* or *agent* meant. The Japanese example was particularly ripe. He had paid millions to a front man for the ruling party, a minor right-wing political zealot, who had a record of virulent anti-Americanism—the last man that an American company would hire as an agent.

The solons wanted to know all about the special services for which Cliff had paid millions in the Mideast. "Were they the world's most expensive hoochy-koochy dancers?" one senator asked.

Cliff was soon begging for mercy. "I'm not an authority on linguistics," he pleaded.

"But you're a walking encyclopedia on how to bribe people," the Creature chortled. "You ought to write a book on it."

The audience roared with glee. Another senator asked Cliff about the various code words used to conceal payments. The word for consultant was *haywire*. "Why did you choose that word?" the Creature asked.

"We let the computer pick it out at random," Cliff said.

"I'm glad to hear at least your computers have a conscience," another senator said. He outscored the Creature on the laugh meter with that one.

Cliff laboriously tried to explain that Buchanan only did what other plane makers, oil companies, ITT, did overseas. He blamed it all on the foreigners who expected the payments. A senator from Delaware asked him if he would condone stealing the designs of a competitor's plane because an opponent did it.

"That's against the law of the United States," Cliff said. "As I've tried to tell you, there is no law prohibiting overseas payments—"

"Do you or don't you steal competitors' designs?" the Creature howled.

"No, sir," Cliff said, as the galleries exploded with laughter again.

Cliff soon became a target of opportunity. "You've cheated people who trust you!" another senator thundered. "It reminds me of the crook who was asked why he did such a thing and he replied: who else can you cheat?"

Boffo. The audience laughed a full five minutes.

So it went for three gruesome days, while Mike Shannon and Dick Stone occasionally bowed their heads to avoid contemplating the butchery. Each night Cliff retreated to his hotel room and got drunk, rejecting their attempts to talk to him.

Frank Buchanan called Dick to offer his sympathy and support for Cliff. "Can't you stop it?" he said. "Why are you letting Adrian make him the fall guy? If it keeps up I'll fly in and volunteer to tell the whole truth."

"Tell Frank it's for the good of the company," Adrian said, when Dick reported the call.

With complete indifference to the careers they were destroying, the senators began reading into the record Cliff's correspondence with prominent politicians in Holland, Japan, Germany, Italy. Adrian decided this was going too far and told Buchanan's Washington attorneys, one of whom was a former secretary of state, to extract an intervention from the State Department that brought Cliff's ordeal to an abrupt halt. No less a personage than the incumbent secretary of state wrote a letter to the attorney general stating that any further disclosure of names would have "grave consequences for the United States."

The infuriated senators turned on the other aircraft companies. They roasted Lockheed's executives over a slow fire. The treasurer of the company could not handle it and committed suicide rather than face the tormentors. As the other companies went on the coals, an embittered Cliff Morris flew back to California. Adrian invited Dick Stone to Charlottesville for the weekend. They sat on the porch in the twilight, gazing at Monticello in the distance.

"If all goes well, in about three months we'll persuade Cliff to resign," Adrian said. "He'll go quietly, I hope—and the purification rite will be complete. We can go to the banks here and in London and get the money we need to keep us going until Ronald Reagan is elected. He's given me his solemn promise that he'll build the BX."

Loathing was all Dick felt for Adrian. He could not disguise it. He did not even try. Adrian's face became florid, his eyes bulged with the intensity of the emotion that seemed to seize him from nowhere.

"You have to see the situation historically, Dick," he said. "My great-grandfather, Oakes Ames, was denounced by Congress in 1869—denounced by the same people who took his bribes to build the Union Pacific Railroad—which had a lot to do with winning the Civil War by keeping the West in the Union. Our situation is virtually identical. The same hypocrites who took our campaign contributions and our hospitality are trying to wreck us for five minutes' worth of publicity, without so much as a passing thought for the planes we're building to defend the country."

It was the final performance of the student of history who had discovered Oakes Ames's fate on a night of anguish in London. But Dick Stone was too disgusted to understand, much less sympathize with Adrian Van Ness. Instead he heard it as one more betrayal of his shining expectations of the American world he had longed to join after World War II.

Dick realized Adrian had revealed more of himself to him than to anyone else in his life. Dick still refused to give him his approval. He did not care if it cost him the CEO's job. Adrian was unquestionably offering it to him. But Dick could not abrogate thirty years of friendship with Cliff, the memories of the *Rainbow Express*. He still sat in judgment on Adrian. He refused to forgive him for anything—selling out Frank and the Talus, destroying Billy McCall—and now, Cliff Morris.

"Cliff's not the greatest human being in the world but he deserves something better than this for a payoff. He evened things for that moment of panic over Schweinfurt with another twenty-four missions. I don't want the CEO's job on these terms, Adrian."

An almost hysterical trill crept into Adrian's voice. "Cliff'll be well paid in retirement. Isn't that better than letting him wind up in some flophouse in downtown Los Angeles?"

"What if it doesn't work?" Dick said. "What if Reagan—presuming he gets elected—double-crosses us like every other president since Kennedy?"

"He might. But it's still the best gamble in town."

They were betting the company again. Dick heard Buzz McCall telling Adrian you had to be a man to do that. He felt the lure, the excitement of risk beating in his blood. But he resisted surrendering on Adrian's terms.

"I think we've got to offer the banks, the stockholders, something more than a presidential promise, Adrian," Dick said. "We've got to offer a vision—the plane of tomorrow. We're the ones who can build it. A hypersonic plane that can fly the Pacific in a couple of hours. That's the kind of plane company I want to run. If you make me CEO, that's what you're going to get."

"Vision?" Adrian said, shaking his head in bewilderment. "We're playing for time."

Dick ignored the pleading note in Adrian's voice. "I want seed money for the hypersonic plane as soon as possible. Our best bet is England. You've still got clout there. We can promise Rolls-Royce the engine contract as a quid pro quo."

"England," Adrian muttered. "I haven't been to England for a long time."

"Why not?" Dick said in the same brutal uncaring voice.

508

"Memories," Adrian said. "Memories I've never shared with anyone."

"You'll have to face them for a week or two," Dick said, utterly indifferent to what these memories might be.

"Could you come with me?" Adrian said. "I'll need a good numbers man."

Dick Stone ignored the plea to share the English memories. He was in control now. Adrian had lost all his leverage—moral, psychological, financial. "I'll give you the numbers on paper," Dick said. "I don't intend to let Cliff run the company without me around even for five minutes."

Loathing. Dick knew Adrian saw it on his face, heard it in his voice. He would have to live with it. He was living with Amanda's hatred. Dick was surprised when a plea for sympathy shredded Adrian's vaunted self-control.

"Why do I have to do all the dirty work?" he cried.

"I seem to recall you telling me it does a man no good to whine," Dick Stone said.

FALL OF A CONQUEROR

Exhausted from a week of nonstop partying and negotiating in London, Adrian Van Ness dozed in the comfortable seat of his Argusair business jet. Instead of dreaming of executive power and glory, he was back on Shakespeare's Cliff at Dover, watching Bleriot fly the English channel. His mother and Goeffrey Tillotson were there, exclaiming in awe and admiration as the fragile plane clattered over their heads. Geoffrey Tillotson pointed at Dover Castle and began predicting that the plane would make forts and every other weapon of war obsolete.

He was interrupted in mid-sentence by a passionate kiss from Clarissa Ames Van Ness. She was announcing there was something more important than forts, armies, ships—and planes. They sank to the green grass, wrapped in each other's arms.

"Stop it!" Adrian cried. "Stop it or I'll jump!"

He teetered on the brink of the white chalk bluff. Below him tiny figures ran along the brown sand. Clarissa and Geoffrey paid no attention to him. They also ignored the stares and titters of the people around them.

"Stop *iiiiiiit!*" Adrian cried and leaped into space, arms spread wide in a pathetic imitation of flight.

"Wake *up.*"

A hand shook Adrian Van Ness's shoulder. The chairman of the board of the Buchanan Corporation confronted his preternaturally youthful wife. "You were having a bad dream," Amanda said. Her smile was pleased, even gloating.

The skin was still taut on Amanda's fine-boned high-cheeked face. Her auburn hair still retained its youthful color. No one could explain the phenomenon to Adrian. Dr. Kirk Willoughby wondered if it had something to do with reduced brain activity. "Maybe it's thinking too much that wears us out," Buchanan's medical director had said.

As usual Amanda was wearing a dress with a ruffled collar that concealed the scars she had inflicted on herself long ago. The collar combined with her heavy-lidded eyes, her sullen mouth, her slightly pointed chin, to justify the nickname Mike Shannon, the Buchanan Corporation's Washington manager, had given her: the Queen of Spades.

Adrian turned his head to escape his wife's nasty smile. Outside the small octagonal window beside his seat was a blue sky shot through with glaring light. The dulled roar of two Pratt & Whitney jet engines surrounded him. They were cruising at 547 miles an hour nine miles above the Atlantic Ocean. In front of them dozed two of the most powerful politicians in Washington. Adrian had taken them to London to support his plea for British cash to keep Buchanan airborne.

The stratosphere's blue dome arced upward in a slowly deepening hue until it became the velvety black of space. Adrian thought about the men Buchanan had sent up that arc in rocket planes and in jets, probing the boundaries of flight. In memory's glaring light, Billy McCall swaggered out to the needle-nosed rocket plane, White Lightning, his smile disguising his fear—and his rage. Billy had assumed this feat assured him mastery of the other vehicle on which he loved to soar—the American woman. But there he collided with un-knowns—and unknown unknowns—he had never encountered in the sky.

Up here in the stratosphere, the upper air that pilots call light country, Adrian found it easy to contemplate the ironies of four and a half decades in the aircraft business. Irony seemed normal in the stratosphere. Below, in the troposphere, where humans lived their daily lives, detachment was not so simple.

Unfortunately, men and women had to live in the troposphere. Outside the Argusair's tilted windows, the stratosphere's temperature was 210 degrees below zero. Winds were tearing along the jet's wings and fuselage with the force of seven hurricanes. A man or woman could survive for only a few convulsive seconds in that icy oxygenless world. Inside the Argusair, thanks to the wizardry of late-twentieth-century technology, Adrian and Amanda and the two politicians sat in seventy-two-degree comfort and safety.

For a moment this physical security was unbearable to Adrian. What if he spun the aluminum wheel that locked the Argusair's pressurized cabin door and sent Amanda and the politicians and himself spewing into the stratosphere? The pilots, sealed in their cockpit, would survive to tell the story. Would Dick Stone—and one or two others—read about it with guilty eyes?

What nonsense.

The ironist at the center of Adrian's soul regained control of his vehicle. He smiled at his antagonistic wife. "I was dreaming we were back in California," he said. "On the porch of Casa Felicidad. You were kissing me."

"Why were you saying 'stop it'?" Amanda asked.

"Frank Buchanan was there, shaking his fist at me."

"You're lying, as usual," Amanda said.

Needles of pain shot through Adrian's chest. For another moment the ironist's hands trembled on the controls. In recent years Adrian found it more and more difficult to laugh at the unrelenting hatred underlying Amanda's gibes. Last year he had developed angina pectoris, a convulsive knotting of the heart muscle, not unusual in men his age. Adrian wondered if it was a reaction to Amanda's malevolence. Kirk Willoughby, not a believer in psychosomatic illness, dismissed the idea.

Adrian gulped two pills, nitrogen and some exotic new anticoagulant his heart specialist had prescribed as an alternative to surgery. Lighting a small black Havana cigar against the doctor's orders, he checked to make sure the politicians were asleep and began dictating a letter to Dick Stone:

"I saw the Chancellor of the Exchequer and half the bankers in London over the past seven days. At first none of them was inclined to lend us a cent in the aftermath of the bribery hearings. I told them we were about to purge ourselves by offering a public sacrifice for our sins. They instantly understood the charade—which they perform regularly for the electorate—and grew attentive. The senator and the congressman virtually guaranteed some kind of government loan to prevent our demise. With the chancellor, I put on my boldest face and told him if he wanted to get aboard a hypersonic plane, His Majesty's Government had better be prepared to commit a hundred million pounds a year to engine development at their sacred entity, Rolls-Royce. Let me state here my grave doubts about this terrifyingly risky improvisation you've added to my psychodrama. Nonetheless I hope we can raise a glass a year from now and say we're still glad we make planes for a living."

"Have you ever been truly glad about anything?" Amanda said.

The question returned Adrian to the troposphere at sea level, to the real world of gains and losses, fears and compulsions, love and hate. In his weary mind Amanda again became a being with mysterious powers. Angina gouged his chest. He gulped more pills.

Did he deserve this legacy of stifled rage and morbid bitterness? For the thousandth time Adrian pondered the choices he had made and said no. He regretted many things but he refused to wear sackcloth and ashes for the past. At seventy-nine, he resolutely turned his face to the future and insisted that the past was another country, another time, another life, in which he had done nothing that his household gods disapproved.

Turbulence. Adrian buckled his seat belt. They were descending from light country through gumbo-thick clouds above Washington, D.C. He plugged the dictating machine into the radio telephone on the cabin wall and pressed a button. The letter whizzed to a satellite launched with a Buchanan rocket and down to Buchanan's private communications system. In five minutes typists at Buchanan's headquarters in El Segundo, California, would be transcribing it for Dick Stone's eyes.

The Argusair shivered and shook as she encountered the heavy lower air. In the seat in front of him, the senator from Connecticut awoke with a groan. He had gotten very drunk on their last night in London, after the final meeting with the Chancellor of the Exchequer. The exquisite Eurasian Adrian had imported from Singapore for his delectation had demanded double her usual fee.

Across the aisle from the senator, his counterpart on the House of Representatives Armed Services Committee, a lean, intense Texan who could hold his liquor and his women, laughed and said: "Don't you throw up on me, you son of a bitch."

Lately, the senator was drunk most of the time. Only two weeks ago, Adrian had visited him in his office at 9 A.M. and found him incoherent. The senator's wife had recently died and he was miserable without her. Adrian was still amazed by the unpredictable ways the goddess of fate threatened the survival of the Buchanan Corporation—and the United States of America.

Fortuna was the only deity forty years of making and selling planes had taught Adrian to worship. Fortuna and her tormented opposite, Prometheus, whose name meant forethought. From Prometheus had come the gift of fire that had enabled men and women to achieve dominion over the other creatures of the earth—and ultimately to soar above the world and look down on it with exalted or exultant or ironic eyes. In the Argusair's jet engines were raging flames, kindled, caged, controlled, and directed by man's transcendent mind.

Greek, he had become Greek, Adrian told himself, trying to twist his mind away from memories this visit to England had evoked. His British friends had dragged him to the Imperial War Museum, where they had put together a special exhibit to celebrate the fortieth anniversary of World War II. A good part of it was devoted to airpower, naturally. There was an entire room about the Nelson bomber and its accomplishments, with ample credit given to their American friends at Buchanan Aircraft. In one of the final photographs, Beryl Suydam stood beside the bomber she had flown to her doom. Her smile had turned Adrian's chest into an excruciating knot. He had gulped pills for the rest of the day.

From the Argusair's cockpit came blond, hazel-eyed Elizabeth Hardy, their copilot. "We'll be landing in about five minutes. How is everyone back here?"

"Fine," Adrian said.

Buchanan had gotten some good publicity (for a change) when they made Ms. Hardy (designer Sam Hardy's daughter) copilot of their number one business jet. But tonight, the sight of this beautiful young woman in her trim blue uniform stirred an enormous echoing regret in Adrian's soul. For a moment he felt hollow, a cave of winds through which meaningless words blew eternally.

Hardy returned to the cockpit. Adrian could hear the pilot, Jerry Quinn, talking to the air traffic controllers at National Airport, reporting altitude, airspeed, confirming their approach pattern. Visibility was low as usual in Washington, D.C. in December. The senator stirred restlessly. He was a nervous flier. Adrian remained calm. The Argusair had the best instrument landing system in the world, made by Buchanan's avionics division. It could land at midnight in a Heathrow or Gatwick fog—and find the center of the runway every time.

With no warning the plane rolled forty degrees to the left and dove straight for the ground. The senator emitted a belch of terror and the congressman, who had flown bombers over Italy during World War II, yelled "Jesus Christ! Outside the window Adrian glimpsed the silver bulk of a commercial airliner hurtling past them in the murk.

Jerry Quinn pulled the Argusair out of its dive and gasped over the intercom: "That idiot should have been a thousand feet above us."

Amanda'a smile mocked forethought; it derided his plane's infallible instrument landing system, its computers that made it almost impossible to stall, its aerodynamic grace. Again angina pierced Adrian's chest. He gulped pills and the pain subsided.

The Argusair's landing gear came down with a reassuring whir. They were in their final approach, the engines shrill as the fire scream became more audible at this lower speed. *Thud.* They were on the ground, the engines howling a final protest at their return to this alien element.

The senator and the congressman departed, thanking Adrian for their free ride across the Atlantic and the several thousand dollars' worth of hospitality the Buchanan Corporation had bestowed on them during their week in London. Adrian said he hoped to see them soon in Charlottesville.

Onto the plane bounded Mike Shannon, Buchanan's man in Washington. He kissed Amanda's hand and called her "Your Majesty"—unaware that there was a grisly irony in the title.

"Any *good* news?" Adrian said.

Shannon shook his head. "They're not going to let up on us. I think it's time to drop the guillotine on Cliff."

Shannon was in on the purification ritual. But he did not like it. He and Dick Stone did not like it—or Adrian Van Ness. They had made that very clear. Adrian was indifferent to Shannon's opinion. But Dick Stone's judgment on him was like a hair shirt. Why couldn't he see how necessity and history exculpated everything?

With a final mock obeisance to Amanda, the Irishman vanished into the dusk. In ten minutes the Argusair was over Charlottesville for another landing, this time without heroics. While Elizabeth Hardy taxied to the terminal, Jerry Quinn emerged from the cabin, apologizing again for the near-miss over Washington, vowing to file a report with the FAA. He was an angular Californian, so brimming with vitality he made Adrian flinch.

"This is one terrific plane," Quinn said. "She handles better than an F-Sixteen."

Just out of the Air Force, Jerry did not realize he was reminding his employer of a plane that was making one of Buchanan's rivals, General Dynamics, three billion dollars.

Quinn unloaded the Van Ness luggage and they found a porter who wheeled it ahead of them to Adrian's gray Bentley in the airport's long-term parking lot. The chairman of Rolls-Royce had given Adrian the car when he chose their engines for the Colossus. Adrian thought of what that monster had cost him. His ironist's hands trembled on the controls in his mind—and his physical hands clutched the icy wheel convulsively. Memory! It was pursuing him like a wolf pack tonight.

The engine purred at a flip of the ignition key. Amanda ostentatiously buckled herself into the seat beside Adrian. For several years she had been urging him to hire a chauffeur. She insisted he was getting too old to drive a high-powered car. Adrian ignored her, as usual. He did not like chauffeurs or butlers or any other kind of servant. They tended to learn too much about a man— knowledge that could turn out to be inconvenient in certain situations. A housekeeper was the only servant he permitted—and he replaced her frequently.

A mixture of sleet and snow began falling from the twilit sky. "It's below zero!" Amanda said, turning up the collar of her mink coat. Each day at breakfast she told Adrian the temperature in Los Angeles.

Amanda fretted about their latest housekeeper, Mrs. Welch, who was a tippler. Amanda was sure the refrigerator would be empty, they would have to drive back to Charlottesville for dinner. Adrian let her complain. Mrs. Welch was a dunce, but Adrian liked stupid housekeepers. They were unlikely to notice much.

Adrian swung up the drive of their estate past a line of bare ancient oaks. "Not a light," Amanda said, as they drove beneath the portico of the big red-brick mansion. "I wouldn't be surprised if she's passed out upstairs."

Adrian steered the Bentley into the garage on the left of the house and unloaded the bags. Amanda preceded him up the steps into the kitchen. "Oh, where is that switch," she said, as Adrian balanced two heavy suitcases on the top step.

Click. The fluorescent light illuminated the gleaming stainless-steel stove and oven, the walk-in refrigerator, the food processor, and other amenities Adrian had installed, mostly to mock Amanda's refusal to cook anything more complicated than an egg. He heaved a sigh and let the suitcases thud to the floor. Jet lag seemed to be draining life itself from his thick body. Seventy-nine-year-old men should not fly the Atlantic twice in a week.

"Mrs. Welch? Mrs. Welch?" Amanda called up the backstairs. Her voice echoed through the silent house. Annoying. Adrian did not like Amanda to be right about anything. She gloated over small triumphs for days.

He lugged the suitcases upstairs and dropped Amanda's unceremoniously at the door of her bedroom. There were limits to his readiness to play servant. In his bedroom, he flung his bag on a luggage rack and strode into his study. There were no lights flashing on the eight-line telephone on his desk. Good. He did not want to do any thinking without a night's sleep.

Adrian poured himself an ounce of forty-year-old port. It was like swallowing silk—or memory. English memories. For a moment he recalled the dream of watching Louis Bleriot fly the channel and the lie he had told Amanda about it. The port turned rancid on his tongue. Both scenarios were metaphors loaded with threats. He was assailed by a terrific wish to somehow outwit time and memory, to shed the burdens of the past. But the ironist at the center of his mind knew time and memory were as inescapable as the thing they eventually became, history.

Adrian looked around the study, trying to savor the mementos of a long life. There he was, accepting a medal for maximum production of B-17s from FDR. There was Ike, conferring another medal in a private ceremony for developing the first supersonic jet fighter. There was John F. Kennedy only a few weeks before Dallas, haunted Lyndon Johnson, tormented Richard Nixon, each grasping Adrian Van Ness's hand, each implicitly admitting how much they needed him and his planes.

The planes were everywhere, beautiful handmade models dangling from wires, full-color photos of fighters in 9 G dives and vertical climbs, bombers roaring over Berlin, Pyongyang, Hanoi, airliners soaring aloft from Bali, Los Angeles, London.

Beside the telephone on his desk lay a small yellow booklet, with a title in scrolled letters on its cover, *Conquistadores del Cielo*. It contained the membership list of this exclusive club. When Adrian had invented it in 1935 they had been a long way from being conquerors of the sky. He picked up the booklet and flipped through the pages, recalling names that were no longer there. He had outlasted so many of the hotheads, the macho swaggerers, the dictatorial spouters.

But the title—was it still ironic? Was the Buchanan Corporation—and Adrian Van Ness—about to become victims of the sky's eternal indifference to life and death? In a flash Adrian was back in the Argusair remembering how often planes had broken his heart, robbed him of love, left him with nothing but irony's exhausting consolation.

Conquistadores del Cielo. The title was pure mockery now. He had conquered nothing, his life had been a series of desperate maneuvers, of hairbreadth escapes and humiliating betrayals.

It does a man no good to whine, whispered that fathering voice, dim now with years and distance. He was still playing the Great Game, Adrian told himself with growing desperation. Why was that no longer a consolation?

Knock. Knock. Knock. Knuckles resounded on the door. It was an unusual rhythm, imperious, demanding. *Knock. Knock. Knock.* Adrian strode to the heavy oak door and flung it open. What he saw in the shadowy hall sent him stumbling, spinning back into the room with a cry of terror on his lips. Queen Califia was standing there, her russet hair streaming, a knife in her upraised hand!

A bolt of pain tore through Adrian's chest. The ironist's hands were ripped from the controls. The room whirled; the vehicle was in a catastrophic spin. Another slash of pain. The anticoagulants—where were they? Adrian clutched the vial in his pocket. He had taken the last one on the plane. The rest were in his suitcase.

"Help!" he cried.

His eyes were entangled with the dangling planes, he was on his back trying to focus on the study door. "Help. Please!" he cried.

Above the house a prop plane began landing at the Charlottesville airport. The motors thundered in the night sky, blending with a voice in Adrian's head roaring *ruined*. Both sounds were swallowed by a tremendous whine, as if all the model planes had somehow acquired life-sized jet engines and were diving on him.

Then silence, the sensation of sinking into a dark pool rimmed with light. Finally a woman's silken voice whispering: *it wasn't your fault, it wasn't anyone's fault.*

Amanda remained frozen in the doorway, her hand raised to deliver another angry knock on the door. She had no idea what she could do to help her husband. When she found the courage to venture into the room it was much too late.

"I wasn't going to hurt you, Adrian," Amanda said. "I only wanted to tell you I found Mrs. Welch upstairs, passed out—and there's not a scrap of food in the house."

BOOK TEN

MESSAGES

Dozing on the couch in his office after his return from his visit to the BX bomber, Dick Stone could have sworn he heard a voice whispering: *apotheosis*. He awoke with a violent start and lay there, slowly absorbing the fact, the reality, the event.

Adrian Van Ness was dead. The telephone call he and Cliff Morris had received last night in the board room was not imagination, not wish or nightmare or conjecture. The Buchanan Aircraft Corporation was swirling around him like a huge ungainly space vehicle with no one at the controls.

Apotheosis, the voice whispered again. It was time for him to find the gold beyond his rainbow, maybe to begin paying the price Adrian and others had paid to make the flight. With the help of his tireless Japanese secretary, Jill Kioso, who had apparently slept on the couch in her office, by noon Dick had called every member of the board of directors and told them Cliff Morris was going to resign and asked them to support him as the next Buchanan president. He read them portions of Adrian's last letter to bolster his case. Most of them agreed without much enthusiasm. Several said they wanted to hear from Cliff too.

Next Dick called the heads of Buchanan's divisions, aerospace, missiles, electronics, assuring them there was no cause for panic, he was in charge and was not going to let Adrian's death alter the company's course in any way. Here the reaction was much more positive. He worked more closely with these men than Cliff; they trusted him. Dick spent another hour telling the same story to chief designer Sam Hardy. Without him, there would be no hypersonic plane in Buchanan's future.

Hardy almost applauded when he heard Cliff was leaving. Sam still resented Cliff's cracks about his negative sex appeal from the Honeycomb Club days. There was no loyalty crisis in the Black Hole—although Hardy's moodiness could eventually become a problem.

519

Around five P.M. Dick's secretary laid a sheaf of incoming telephone calls on his desk. Most were from Buchanan supporters in Congress and friends in the aircraft industry. On top was a memo from Dr. Kirk Willoughby, reporting his inconclusive meeting with Frank Buchanan. That was bad news. Dick was going to need Frank's support, especially if Cliff found a backer who wanted to keep him as president. Such a man would only be interested in one thing—dismantling Buchanan for a quick profit, an idea that might also appeal to some members of the board.

"Dan Hanrahan's on the phone from Virginia," Jill Kioso said.

That was the call Dick was waiting for. "Everything's under control. I'm here in the house. I've got the contents of Adrian's safe. It's not that much— barely fills his attaché case. They're shipping the body from the hospital to a crematorium in Los Angeles. I'll bring Mrs. Van Ness back on the plane with me."

"How is she?"

"Fine. All she talks about is Frank Buchanan. I'm glad I came here for that reason alone. You can't let a reporter anywhere near her."

"We'll handle that."

"We're catching a ten A.M. plane. In case Frank's interested."

"I'll tell him if he calls. We can't call him. He's disconnected his phone."

"There's one problem I can't handle without a truck. Mrs. Van Ness showed me a secret room off Adrian's study. The bookcase revolves and you're in this little alcove. There's a trunk in there, full of gold. I guess it was Adrian's way of steadying his nerves when he bet the company on a big one."

Dick heard Adrian saying: *I wanted to be a man of substance, forever beyond the reach of ruin.* "Can anybody else find the room?"

"Not likely."

"Leave the trunk there for the time being. We'll get Shannon to move it out when things calm down."

Six hours later, Hanrahan strode into Dick's office with the attaché case in his hand. "Here's the goods. Mrs. Van Ness is at the Bel Air with my wife. They're old friends."

Dick opened the attaché case, not knowing what he would find. On top were a dozen photographs of Victoria at all ages, from babyhood to her wedding day. Why did Adrian keep them in his safe? Probably because he could not bear to look at them after her death.

Next was correspondence with various presidents, none of it especially startling. Then a folder of poems about the beauty and majesty of flight. Dick was astonished to discover Adrian's name at the bottom of each one. Adrian a poet! That cold-eyed bastard? It was astonishing.

Then came a series of letters from an Englishman named Tillotson, written in the 1930s, full of encouragement and general business advice. Each began with the words: "My dear son." There were copies of Adrian's replies, obviously typed himself, which began: "Dear Father." Mysteries within mysteries. One of these Dear Father letters was particularly revealing. It was written just after

520

Victoria was born. Adrian told Tillotson how much the child meant to him, how badly he wanted to be a "complete father" even though fate and circumstances had prevented him from knowing one in his boyhood.

Next came a sheaf of papers from a primitive forties or early fifties copier. It was mostly in German, which Dick had no trouble reading—although many of the words had faded. It was the protest the Germans had filed with the Red Cross in Geneva in 1943, accusing the *Rainbow Express* of violating the rules of war over Schweinfurt. On top of the first page was a handwritten scrawl from General Newton Slade, telling Adrian he could consider the matter closed.

Finally there was an envelope with a letter in French thanking Adrian for rescuing her from the "bureaucratic Apaches." The rest was an apostrophe to the beauty of California. Only southern France could compete with it. The letter was signed "Madame George." It was dated 1971.

Apotheosis. This time Dick could have sworn he heard Adrian whispering the word. His mouth dry, his pulse skittering, Dick called Hanrahan and asked him if he knew anything about Madame George. "She's living in San Juan Capistrano," he said. "I flew to France and brought her here in 1970. The French cops busted up her operation when she refused to pay them off at double the usual rates. Adrian brought her over to make sure she didn't decide to write her memoirs. He paid for it out of his own pocket and ordered me never to mention it to you under any circumstances."

"Why not?"

There was a long pause. "It seemed to have something to do with your Jewish conscience."

Apotheosis. This time Dick was sure he heard it.

Dick called in Bruce Simons, their director of public relations, and discussed plans for a memorial service for Adrian. He sketched a speech he wanted to make to the board and told him to get a writer working on it. He called Shannon in Washington to find out what was being said and done in the rumor capital of the world.

"It's pretty quiet," Shannon said. "Carter's looking worse and worse. The Democrats are starting to pull in their left-wing horns. I think they'll let us alone—if you can get Cliff to resign. Nothing else is gonna keep the Creature happy. What's the word on the Big Shot?"

"I don't know where he is."

"Wurra wurra," Shannon said.

Dick ate supper at his desk, talking to chief designer Sam Hardy and the project manager for a new mach 3 high-performance fighter. They showed him slides of incredible vortices on the wings at a high angle of attack and told him how much they were learning about wing loading from the pictures. The research might be very useful in designing the hypersonic airliner.

He spent the next several hours devouring reports from the missile and avionics divisions. When he looked at the clock on his desk, it was 11 P.M. The telephone rang. Cliff, ready to be reasonable? Dick grabbed the phone with hope uppermost.

"Stone here," he said.

"Guilford—Tom," said a shaky voice. "We just lost it. The big one. The BX. It went down about eighty miles from here, on a low-level practice run."

"I'll be there in an hour."

Dick summoned Sam Hardy from the Black Hole and Public Relations Director Bruce Simons from his bed. Their Hydra pilot got his instructions from the tower at Dreamland and in exactly one hour they descended from the starry sky at the crash site. The desert floor was eerily illuminated by huge searchlights the Air Force had flown in to begin the inevitable investigation. Pieces of the plane were scattered across a mile of desert. Most of them were blackened and twisted into junkyard objects. Only the needle nose, ripped off on impact, had escaped the fire and was relatively intact. It lay on its side like a decapitated head, reinforcing the desolation.

"What happened?" Dick asked, as General Anthony Sirocca shook his hand.

"All we know right now is they hit something big. It might have been a bird."

A bird big enough to disable a seventy-ton hundred-million-dollar bomber? Dick could almost hear the anti-defense lobbyists chortling.

A haggard Tom Guilford joined them along with the boyish colonel in charge of the investigation. "We've found all four motors. There's parts of a very large bird in one of them," the colonel said. "It might have been a Canada snow goose. We've got a guy who was stationed in Alaska for a while. He says he'd bet on it from the feathers and the size of the feet. Those birds weigh twenty-five or thirty pounds."

"Why wasn't that designed in?" Dick asked Sam Hardy.

"Snow geese and other birds that size fly at much higher altitudes," Hardy said. "We designed in resistance to birds of up to nine pounds."

"The fucking plane is supposed to go up to seventy thousand feet!"

"But its mission is low-altitude attack. At high altitudes, if a big bird disabled an engine, there'd be plenty of time to handle the problem."

Dick sighed. It was always the same story. Trying to anticipate chance, outwit fate, and save money. For some reason, at least once in every plane, fate—or was it Billy McCall's Lady of Luck?—wanted to let you know who was running things.

"We can't tell the real story," Bruce Simons pleaded. "They'll crucify us. A plane with a history like this being knocked down by a goddamn bird."

Dick stared stonily at Sam Hardy. He was looking more and more miserable. Leave it to Frank Buchanan to pick a bleeder for his successor. The guy was brilliant but he had Frank's soft heart.

"We'll tell the real story," Dick said. "Call it a one-in-a-million accident. Let them laugh for a day. Then design in fifty-pound birds. Fucking eagles and vultures wearing armor plate!"

"It'll add a hundred pounds to each engine," Hardy said. "We'll have to redesign the whole wing."

"So redesign it! Call up your wife and tell her she's not going to see you for the next six months."

He turned to Sirocca. "Who was flying her?"

"That kid who took you back the other night in your Rube Goldberg plane."

"I was afraid you were going to say that."

They flew back to El Segundo in a miasma of gloom. It reminded Dick of the time the Talus crashed. Were they heading for another chop session?

"Has Cliff resigned?" Bruce Simons asked.

"Not yet," Dick said.

Dick could see what Bruce was thinking. If Cliff has any brains left, he can wrap this crash around Dick Stone's neck and let him try to dance with it. After all, Dick was the guy who proclaimed from the balcony of the Mojave factory two years ago that he was not going to let the BX die. Bruce—or Dick—could see Cliff declaiming to the board that he had always been opposed to the plane, he had tried to talk Adrian out of building it, the thing had gotten them a billion dollars' worth of bad publicity. It was the reason why the senators had attacked him so viciously.

It was so simple it was almost irresistible. There was only one person who could stop Cliff: Sarah. Again, Dick felt the wrench of inevitability tearing at his fragile hopes. It was becoming more and more impossible to ask her anything else.

Back in the office, there was a memo from his tireless Japanese secretary on his desk: *Sarah Morris called. She would like to see you at 9 A.M. tomorrow morning.*

Hope or ruination? Dick wondered. There was only one thing to do: gamble everything on telling the truth.

Apotheosis, Adrian Van Ness whispered.

EXILE'S RETURN

Leaving the desert behind her in the rosy dawn, Sarah Chapman Morris drove along Interstate 10 past the stupendous rock formations of Joshua Tree National Monument. At times she had the road to herself, making her feel she was the last human being alive on the planet. She turned on the car radio and listened to a woman announcer with a honey-smooth voice.

"At the top of the hour, the top of the news. President Carter's budget for fiscal 1980 will include money for an additional six wings in the Tactical Air Force. That's good news for Southland's aerospace companies, especially General Dynamics, which produces the F-Sixteen jet fighter.

"The Buchanan Corporation announced it will hold a memorial service for

Adrian Van Ness, former chief executive officer and chairman of the board, early next week. Van Ness died in Virginia two days ago. A Buchanan spokesman said he had not been active in the firm for some years."

Sarah smiled wanly to herself, remembering how it felt to be an insider, aware of the superficiality of the news. She had spent yesterday disentangling herself from Susan Hardy. It had not been easy. Susan had accused her of desertion, abandoning all their good causes. With Cliff on the brink at Buchanan, now was the time to stick it to him.

"It's almost nineteen eighty," Sarah had said. "A new decade. Time for a change."

She angled west on state roads until she reached the San Diego Freeway and joined the river of cars roaring north toward Los Angeles. Trucks lumbered past on the right; red, blue, and yellow sedans and sports cars whizzed past on the left. After thirty-five years, she still found driving in southern California a terrifying experience.

She zoomed past L.A.'s downtown with its glossy new skyline, remembering the way it looked in 1945—less prepossessing than a medium-sized British city such as Bristol. In another twenty minutes of survival driving, she was on Santa Monica Boulevard, heading for Dick Stone's house in Nichols Canyon. He had suggested they meet there rather than at company headquarters.

Dick's hair had grown completely gray—almost white. But he still had a lot of vitality in his burly body and wide square-jawed face. His features would have driven a woman to despair but they made him look ruggedly masculine. He smiled and kissed her on the cheek.

"Thanks for coming—and a second thanks for coming early."

"Things must be frantic."

"You've heard the old saying, 'If you can keep your head while those about you—.' So far mine's on my shoulders, I think."

He led her into the kitchen and served scrambled eggs and bacon, hot from the stove. They were delicious. "Some career woman would love to marry a man who can cook like this," Sarah said.

Dick's smile was feeble. "How's Cassie and the kids?" Sarah asked.

"Tennessee agrees with Cassie. She's almost cheerful on the telephone. The kids are okay."

"Has she married again?"

Dick shook his head. "Thank God for small favors."

"What are we here to talk about?"

"Cliff. He's got to resign. If he tries to hang on, we'll go under. If he goes gracefully, we'll complete Adrian's purification rite and borrow enough money to keep us airborne until the next president, Ronald Reagan, gives us ten billion to build the BX bomber."

He smiled tentatively. "I was going to use paper plates in case you started to throw things. But I decided to take a chance on being civilized, no matter how barbarous we may sound to your peace-loving ears."

"I'm not a protester by nature," Sarah said. "Where do I come into this sordid picture?"

Dick avoided her eyes. The words came out in chunks, as if each took a special effort. "I'm hoping you can talk to Cliff—as a wife. Convince him—it's what has to be done. Those hearings—finished him—as an executive."

"That's all he ever wanted to be. You might as well say they've finished him as a human being."

Dick buttered some toast, then seemed to change his mind about eating it. He moved his plate aside. "I hope that isn't true. I like to think there's life after aerospace. I was hoping you felt the same way, after backing away from it for a few years."

"I've caught a glimpse of it. But has Cliff?"

Dick took a deep breath. "We've been friends a long time. But we've never talked on this level. Here goes. Did Cliff ever tell you about certain things that happened—one in particular—aboard the *Rainbow Express*?"

Sarah shook her head. Twenty minutes later, she was sitting at the table, the rest of her eggs and bacon cold, the fork grasped in a hand that had lost most of its feeling, attached to a body that was in a similar condition.

"That's why you volunteered for the extra twenty-five missions?" she cried.

She flung the fork across the bare dining room. A bachelor's room, with nothing on the walls, just essential furniture, a table, chairs, a sideboard. They were all bachelors at heart, essentially indifferent to women, except as commodities, as bodies to screw, as minds to manipulate.

"Why are you telling me this? Cliff said he did it for me! For England! I'm supposed to love a liar! Why did you volunteer? Why didn't you let him get court-martialed?"

"Because I felt guilty about it too. The extra missions were my idea."

It was almost a snarl. There was ferocity in his voice. She remembered he had flown those missions too. "I begin to think you're all in need of a purification rite," she said.

"Maybe. But you're not completely exempt, Sarah. Cliff's never been the same since the night he got the news about Charlie and you unloaded on him. After that he was a setup for the movie star."

"He'd been a setup for a long time before that," Sarah said, her eyes swimming with angry tears. She had been very successful at not thinking about that night for a long time.

"Not the way he was after that night. We were working on him—kidding him out of it. After that Angela wrote the script. It led straight to the hearings, in case you're interested. She and her friends supplied the information that started the senators sniffing around."

"What else should I know?"

"Cliff was going to take Adrian, the whole company down with him—until Adrian told him he knew about the *Rainbow Express*. After that, he was a willing victim."

"Some victim!"

"I know. We high-minded types want our victims refined of the dross. Ar-

525

chetypes. Most victims are like Cliff. They deserve quite a lot of what they get. But not all of it."

"Now you expect me to follow through with the charade—for the good of Adrian Van Ness's company?"

"Maybe there's a better reason. I'm convinced Cliff went through with those hearings mainly because he couldn't bear the thought of you finding out what happened over Schweinfurt. That's a clue—no more than that, I'll admit—to what he still feels about you."

"You want me to love him!"

The word shimmered and whirled between them like an explosion, showering them both with regret. Sarah was sure this man felt the same wish, the same hope—and he was thrusting it aside. For what? A corporation? A plane? He was asking her to do the impossible.

Dick fussed with his eggs. "I'm the last guy in the world with the right to use that word."

"Why, Dick?"

"Things have happened to me too."

He began talking about Amalie Borne. Dazedly, Sarah heard the anguish at the heart of the story—and what else he was telling her, perhaps inadvertently. Sarah was not the woman of his secret dreams. She was something else, not to be mocked or derided, no; perhaps even worthy of desire. But not an ultimate desire, eliciting reckless adoration, total commitment.

"Did you ever tell Cassie about Amalie?" she asked.

He shook his head.

"Sounds to me like you can't take your own advice about the truth, Navigator. Telling it—accepting it—forgiving it."

"It's myself I can't forgive!"

He almost roared the words. Again she saw his ferocity, saw how formidable he could be when necessary. Adrian had chosen well. Cliff never had this inner anger, this readiness for ruthless combat.

Dick went back to talking about the company. He made her understand their peril. Buchanan was drowning in red ink. She was their improbable savior. The irony was almost too rich. Why didn't she simply laugh in his face and tell him how glad she would be to see the BX, all the planes, spin down into that red flood?

Before she could answer that question Dick Stone was talking about another plane, more daring, more innovative than anyone had ever built. He called it the Orient Express. It would be a hypersonic transport carrying passengers across the Pacific and around the world at 3,500 miles an hour, flying at 120,000 feet. Sarah listened, mesmerized by the fire in his gray eyes.

He was one of the creatures of the sky. Billy McCall's blood brother. She was eighteen again, walking down a country lane with swaggering Cliff Morris, in love with pilots.

God, God, God, he had her, he had her believing again in the beauty, the magic, the mystery of flight.

"I've discussed it with our new chief designer, Sam Hardy. He thinks it may not be as expensive as it sounds. For some crazy reason, the problems with shock waves and vortexes are mostly just below and just beyond the sound barrier. The faster you go the cleaner the whole thing gets. Imagine giving average people a chance to see how the world looks from a hundred-and-twenty-thousand feet?"

"When will it fly?"

"I'm not sure. It'll take all the money we get for the BX and everything we can borrow."

"Betting the company again."

"That's what it takes to sell planes for a living."

"Where's Cliff?"

"I don't know. In your house in Palos Verdes, probably."

"I'm not sure I can do it."

Dick looked at his watch. He had a six-billion-dollar corporation in El Segundo waiting to devour him. "There's something else you should know. The BX prototype crashed last night. We're going to announce it this afternoon. If you get a chance, remind Cliff that the night Charlie died, we talked about building it together as a sort of memorial to him—and Billy McCall."

Somehow she managed to remain calm. The man's daring was beyond belief. "You might give this to him too. It was in Adrian's safe."

He handed her a worn brown envelope stuffed with papers. "It's the protest the Germans filed about what we did over Schweinfurt."

The thing scorched her hand. Somehow she was hoping Dick had made it up, that Cliff would deny it. Without another word Dick drew her to him for a quick, fierce kiss. "No matter what happens—thank you. Thanks—for everything."

For another moment Sarah gazed into those angry gray eyes and saw what she had seen a dozen times before—a wish that somehow fate, life, God, had arranged things differently and he was the man she was going to see in Palos Verdes. Or there was no man in Palos Verdes and he could finally say to her: *Skylark—I'm going to get you out of that cage once and for all.*

And she would reply: *I've been waiting thirty years to hear that.*

Maybe it was enough to know—without ever speaking it—how much love had been possible between them. Maybe, in a certain sense, the love already existed, even though they had barely touched each other beyond the polite kisses of hello and good-bye. At least this last kiss had gone beyond politeness.

QUESTING

The Hydra descended from the cloudless blue sky, its tilt rotors whirling. Cliff Morris climbed out and toiled up the slope to Frank Buchanan's shack. Sweat streamed down his face after ten steps. He had spent the previous thirty-six hours trying to see Angela Perry. His nemesis, Lenin Jr., had stonily insisted she could not come to the phone. Cliff had finally landed on her lawn at 4 A.M. and stalked into the house, ignoring a pistol Vladimir brandished.

The meeting had been a disaster. Angela not only denied for the tenth time Lenin Jr. had leaked anything to the Creature's committee, she announced she was going to marry the left-wing ferret and elect him governor of California. She said he would be a better father to their son, now a wispy, scared-looking three-year-old.

Cliff was devastated by the thought that the boy was going to grow up as he did, with a succession of indifferent or hostile fathers. Angela was certain to change husbands as often as she changed dress styles. He gave Lenin Jr. two years at best—the only consolation he could find in the fiasco.

That defeat made this visit to Frank Buchanan all the more important. This morning he had called a half dozen members of the board of directors to line up their support. Most of them had been wary, when they were not explicitly negative. But all of them had hesitated when Cliff told them he had Frank's backing.

Frank was on the porch, waving, a smile on his wide, weathered face. It was going to be a breeze. Frank loved him. He had always loved him. He had been a father to him and Billy McCall. Their skyfather.

Cliff had stopped in Palm Springs for a couple of Scotches at the airport bar. Just enough to project confidence in the product. The first law of successful sales. With a product like Clifford Morris, how could he fail?

"Cliff," Frank Buchanan said. "What a welcome sight for a lonely old man."

Inside the house, Frank gestured Cliff to the cracked, creased leather chair he had taken with him when he left Buchanan for the definitive last time.

"I've got some idea why you're here. I've already heard the news."

"I came here to ask your help, Frank."

"I can't imagine what I can do," Frank said.

"The board of directors will meet in a few days to discuss the future of the company. Right now it doesn't look like we'll have a future. We're up to our ears in red ink. A lot of the money has gone into funding the goddamn BX bomber. I know you designed it and maybe you don't like to hear me call it that. It's a great plane, Frank. But it's going to ruin us unless we do something drastic. I've got an idea that can save the plane—and get us out of the bomber business."

"I've wanted to do that all my life," Frank said.

Cliff leaped out of his chair, propelled by the sheer intensity of his desire. He was back thirty years, selling planes to Eddie Rickenbacker and other vanished titans of the airline business, to Arab sheiks and Bolivian tin mine tycoons. This was the climax of all the sales pitches he had ever made.

"It's time someone told the American people the defense industry isn't a free enterprise. We're a branch of the U.S. government. Let's sell the military stuff to Washington and give Congress and the Pentagon direct control of making warplanes. Let them fuck it up. They'll have no one to blame but themselves."

Frank Buchanan dolefully shook his shaggy head. "I talked about doing something like that when they were protesting the BX a few years ago. But Adrian convinced me it was wrong. The French tried it in the thirties. It was a disaster. They practically destroyed their aircraft industry. They didn't have a single decent plane to fight Hitler."

"We can do better," Cliff said. "NASA put a man on the moon."

"NASA buys everything it flies from private companies like us. What would we do with the money, presuming Congress deigns to pay us anything?"

"We'll use it to build planes that will make the country and the world a better place. Inexpensive, fuel-efficient commuter planes and cargo planes. Airliners with fly-by-wire avionics that make it practically impossible for them to crash. All the things you talked about doing but never did because you were always designing a new fighter or bomber or transport."

But they were beautiful. They were all beautiful planes.

For a moment Cliff's antennae glimpsed this response on Frank Buchanan's face. He was eluding the sales pitch, sliding away into that world of aerodynamic ambition Cliff had never reached.

Cliff redoubled his intensity, seizing Frank's arm, deepening, darkening his voice. "I can sell those planes, Frank. That's what I'm good at. With your name on the designs, we can give Boeing and Douglas a run for the money."

"Cliff," Frank said. "I'm touched—and flattered—that you think my ancient reputation could have any influence on the current boards of directors or the forty-year-old airline executives who buy planes these days."

"I'd handle all the details," Cliff said. "There wouldn't be any pressure. Not a bit of strain."

Not a bit of power, either.

Again, Cliff caught the edge of the negative response.

"What does Dick Stone think of all this?"

"I haven't discussed it with him. I suspect he mostly thinks getting rid of Adrian is a wonderful opportunity to grab my job."

"The last time I talked to Dick, he wasn't this pessimistic. He told me the boys in the Black Hole were working on a hypersonic plane. He seemed to think it was feasible."

"Maybe it was, before those Senate hearings. Now no banker in the world will loan us money. We've got to think in terms of survival, Frank. This is a public relations ploy that could save the company."

Up and down the cabin Cliff paced, distancing himself now, so Frank would have the feeling that he made the decision on his own, without being overwhelmed. He was putting every twist and turn, every shred and scrap of his experience into this pitch. It had to fly!

"There are people on the board who've been waiting for a chance to disagree with Adrian's habit of putting us in hock to the goddamn Pentagon. They didn't have the guts to do it while he was alive. They'll do it now if you back me up. It isn't too late. We can change the whole nature of this industry. You know as well as I do that it doesn't make sense anymore. If it ever did."

Cliff stopped. Frank did not seem to be listening. His eyes were not registering any of these ideas. He was somewhere else, listening, speaking to another person.

"Have you seen—or spoken to—Amanda?" he asked.

"No," Cliff said, bewildered, amazed, dismayed by the persistence of love in a man of eighty-three. Who, what would he love when he was eighty-three, if the booze let him get that far? Angela? The idea was ridiculous.

"Cliff," Frank said. "Forgive me. But I can't do it. The Buchanan Corporation is Adrian Van Ness's company. It was mine for a little while but Adrian made it his creation. I'd feel like a liar—a fraud—if I walked into the boardroom and pretended I wanted to change the way Adrian did things out of some superior wisdom. Much as I loathed some of the things he did, I have to admit that without him, Buchanan wouldn't exist today."

Life drained from Cliff's face and body. He slumped into the leather chair. Frank barely noticed his collapse. He was thinking about something more important.

"Dick Stone's instinct is sound, Cliff. Build for the future. A hypersonic plane! I'd bet the company on that anytime. Buchanan has the know-how, the guts to reach into the next century. I've got a few ideas I'll send down to the Black Hole in a week or two, free of charge."

"Where the hell are we going to get the *money*?" Cliff said.

"I don't know. We've always gotten the money somewhere, somehow. I know you don't agree with me, Cliff. But I think we're all under guidance in this thing. We never would have survived this long without some kind of higher protection."

Cliff's exasperation made it clear that he had no faith in Frank's spiritual universe. "You're telling me I should I should watch the company destruct to build the plane of Dick Stone's dreams?"

"It's the plane of all our dreams, Cliff. The next plane always becomes the plane of everyone's dreams. You've seen it happen. You know what I mean."

"I know what you mean but I'm sick of it. I'm sick of living on the goddamn edge of failure year after year."

Frank Buchanan let those words drift up to the dark ceiling. "Maybe you should resign, Cliff, if you really feel that way."

Cliff said nothing. Did Frank sense how close he was to despair? There was concern on his face, affection. "You love it, Cliff. In spite of all the disappointments, the heartbreak. You love the planes."

Cliff could not respond to this exhortation. His body seemed to be turning into some heavy mushy substance that his bones could not support. His voice sounded like a microphone in an echo chamber.

"Maybe I do. But they've cost me so goddamn much—"

"They've cost us all too much. But if you're a man you learn to take it."

A man. The words evoked so many things Cliff wanted to forget. Buzz using that word as a taunt. Tama telling him that was all she wanted him to be. A man. What did it mean? They did not think you had the stuff that goes into the word, into the gut.

"Would you say that to me—would you throw me out this way—if Billy was sitting here asking you for help?" Cliff said.

He imagined the words echoing across the desert, all the way to the house where Sarah lived with her feminist friends. She did not care either. Cliff had failed her test of manhood too.

"Yes," Frank said. "I would have said it with far less hesitation. Billy was born to fly. Much as I hate to say it, that seemed to incapacitate him for the rest of life."

"Frank—it still stinks. I don't deserve to go out this way! I've sold a hundred and fifty million dollars' worth of planes for this company! I lost—"

He could not say the name. He could not invoke Charlie for any deal, however sweet. Frank Buchanan seized his arm. Tears streamed down his lined face.

"I know what you've lost, Cliff. We've all had our losses. Even Adrian. But the planes are flying. That's the important thing."

Cliff struggled to raise his head, his heart to match that apotheosis. But he still wanted the sweet deal, more swaggering years as a man of importance in Los Angeles. If he could not have them, there was Tama's choice, the disappearance. Maybe it was the way to go. The way to tell all of them what they had done. To leave them choking with remorse and guilt. Dick Stone, Sarah, Angela. Even this man.

Cliff stared down at the desert, remembering the darkness that had spilled over the mountains with the news of Jack Kennedy's death. Maybe now it was time to swallow it, to let it swallow him the way it had swallowed Tama and so many others.

"Don't," Frank Buchanan said. "I know what you're thinking. Don't do it. For all our sakes."

That only made the choice more tempting.

IS THERE LIFE AFTER AEROSPACE?

Sarah Morris spent most of the morning driving around Los Angeles. She parked in front of their ranch house in their old development, remembering the pudgy English war bride gorging on sweets until Tama launched her redesign program. She strolled through the faded lobby of the Beverly Wilshire, where the trim American wife had met Billy McCall. She wandered past the opulent shops on Rodeo Drive where she had shopped and charged as Mrs. Clifford Morris. So many lost or discarded selves. Who was she, anyway?

She called her daughters to tell them what she might do. Elizabeth, no longer in revolt against the establishment—she now had two sons by her San Francisco doctor—encouraged her. Margaret, on her way to being one of the country's leading Chinese scholars at Stanford, was scathingly negative. She wondered how Sarah could go back to a man who was still a glorified adolescent.

That afternoon Sarah drove to Palos Verdes, full of doubt and hesitation. She tried to regain the night of mutual surrender with the big playboy who had wept and vowed never to hit her again. But she could not stop remembering the night in Lima when he had fucked her with triumphant indifference to her feelings.

The house looked deserted, even abandoned. Blinds drooped at odd angles, curtains dangled. Cliff's white Mercedes in the driveway was the only sign of life, and that might have been left behind by the fugitive she was seeking. Inside, the living room made her wince. Newspapers and magazines littered the couches. Ashtrays were full of butts. An empty Scotch bottle stood on an end table. The smell of liquor hung in the stale air.

She flung open some windows and the terrace door. The sea wind swirled through the place, blowing papers every which way. Footsteps thudded in the study. Cliff stood there in his shorts, running his hand through his uncombed hair.

"Hello," Sarah said.

He was not as gray as Dick Stone. Probably because he was getting touch-ups regularly. That was what a man did when he pursued a younger woman. But there were fault lines in his face that revealed age and loss—he was too much of a man's man to ask a plastic surgeon to remove them.

"I'm on the telephone," he said.

Sarah picked up the extension in the living room and listened to him talking to a man with a Texas drawl. He was telling Cliff he was not interested in a takeover of the Buchanan Corporation.

"It'd be like rustlin' a herd of starved longhorns, Cliff. I'd lose my shirt keepin' you alive before I could get you to market."

Cliff started telling him about a new missile the rocket division was developing. He suggested Buchanan might merge with Northrop and the raider could take over both companies. He read him a glowing report on Northrop's finances in a recent issue of *Aviation Week*.

"Sorry, Cliff boy," drawled the prospect. "I'm on the prowl for a drug company with a cure for arthritis. That sort of thing. You hear 'bout one, let me know. There'll be a finder's fee."

The line went dead. Cliff emerged from the study again, pulling on a pair of chinos. "What brings you here?" he said.

"I'd like to come home," Sarah said. "Is it possible?"

"It's still your house as much as it's mine," Cliff said. "That's the law in California."

"Am I welcome?"

"Give me one reason why you should be."

"I spent the last year in the desert looking at a Joshua tree. Eventually it started talking to me. It said go home and ask your husband to forgive you."

Cliff padded to the bar and poured himself a drink. Was he trying to blot her out in advance? Sarah looked past him at the windows opening on the Pacific and kept talking.

"In order to do that I had to ask myself if I forgave him. The answer was maybe. There was another reason. The longer I looked at that tree raising those stubby arms to the sky, the more I began to realize how much I wanted to try to love you again as my husband—someone who tried to achieve certain things in his life and succeeded sometimes—and failed sometimes. The way I tried to love you and failed and tried again and succeeded. Then failed because of so many things. Peru, the Prince, Vietnam, Charlie—Billy. Things we didn't expect. So we weren't very good at coping with them."

"Who sent you here?" Cliff said.

"Dick Stone called me. He told me about Adrian. Before he died, Adrian sent me a copy of the letter he wrote you, urging you to resign."

"That's why Dick called you! Can't you see that? He wants you to help him get rid of me. How the hell can you play Dick's game and tell me you love me?"

For a moment the whole room blurred. Sarah felt the wind blowing through her flesh into her bones, shattering them one by one. Was it finally ultimately impossible?

"I'm playing my own game," she said, her voice sounding as if she was shouting into a gale. "I'm trying to convince you there's life after aerospace. There's a life we can have together we never had except in fits and starts and failures."

"I don't want your goddamn pity!" Cliff roared. "I want a woman who loves a man, not a has-been!"

For a moment Sarah almost gave up. The wind tugged at more than her bones and flesh. It was blowing away everything, memory, hope, understanding. The word *has-been* seemed to abrogate both their lives. All Cliff could see was his corporate title. He did not exist outside it.

She tried one more time, clutching the back of a chair for stability. "I don't see a has-been. I see the man who brought the *Rainbow Express* back from Schweinfurt with more holes in it than anyone could count. I see a man who volunteered for another twenty-five missions because he was ashamed of something he'd done on that raid. A man who had the courage to do that—in spite of his fear—is a man I want to spend the rest of my life trying to love."

Cliff clutched his glass as if it were the only thing keeping him erect. "Who told you about Schweinfurt? Adrian? That son of a bitch—"

"Dick Stone told me. He said he had enough confidence in my judgment—to believe I could share it with you—in the right way. He gave me this—for you. He found it in Adrian's papers."

Cliff grabbed the envelope stuffed with the German protest. He flipped through the sheets of paper and slowly crumpled them into a moist mass in his big hands. He began breathing in deep gulps. Tears gushed from his eyes.

"I should have told you. But I never thought you'd forgive me—I never had that much confidence. I was—"

"Afraid. Not of me. But of your idea of me. Little Miss England, the hero-worshipping cockteaser. Afraid of that stupid idiotic girl who only knew what she could see and touch and kiss. You were so handsome—and I was so young. You were almost as young."

The wind was roaring through the room now, a gale, a cyclone. "Cliff—let's say good-bye to both those sad wonderful people. Good-bye forever—without regrets. With affection."

He hunched over his drink, refusing to abandon his misery. "I lied to you."

"That was part of being in love. I lied to you too. Telling you I was in love with you when I was really in love with an idea, with the drama, with the heroic anguish of watching you take off and praying you back again."

Neither of them had moved an inch. They were like a pair of talking stanchions. Sarah felt the wind shoving her toward him but she was afraid he would flee.

"You had a hero—now you've got a has-been," he said, regret, ambition still gouging him. "Do you expect me to believe you love both guys? Why don't you tell me to go down fighting? Why are we going to let that bastard Adrian Van Ness have the final say?"

"You did go down fighting. In those hearings. That's when I started to love you again. I saw you really didn't believe you'd done anything wrong. I watched the rest of those hearings and saw why you played the game that way. Everyone else was doing it. In a sense—a very special sense—you didn't do anything wrong."

She walked to the bar and put her hand on his arm. "But in another sense you did. It was wrong. All those men you bribed—in Japan—Holland—Germany—they've gone to jail. They were breaking their laws, if you weren't. We were both right—and both wrong that night in Lima. I didn't—I couldn't love you enough to explain it."

"Because of Billy?" he snarled.

The wind almost flung her across the room and out the door. She had to cling to something and it turned out to be his arm. "You could say that. It wouldn't be completely untrue. But he was only part of it. The other part was the way we'd failed—we hadn't loved each other before he arrived on the scene."

He was facing her on the bar stool, listening, seeming to agree. He abruptly turned away. "Yeah," he said, in the same bitter voice.

A wildness swelled in Sarah's throat. It reminded her of the night with Billy McCall in the desert. She had gone too far. She was not going to let this man escape her.

"You know what I see us doing?" she said.

"What?"

"Learning to fly. Buying a plane and flying it together, all over the country, the world. I'd feel so close to Charlie. Closer than we could ever get on the ground—"

A different man confronted her. Defeated and full of an emotion darker than anger. An ominous compound of bitterness and violence. "You really want to fly with me? After what happened to Billy? That wasn't an accident, you know. Somebody put that plane into that dive. I've thought about doing the same thing. I don't know when the impulse will suddenly get too strong to resist. You ready to fly with that kind of pilot?"

"Yes," Sarah said. "I'm ready to fly with that kind of pilot."

"I mean it," Cliff said. "I sat here half the day thinking about how to do it. Thinking about Tama—"

Sarah walked past him into the master bedroom. In the back of a drawer full of old lingerie, she found Tama's letter. *I was wrong.* The words glared up at her again, full of even more meanings now. She walked back to the living room and handed it to Cliff.

"Your mother sent this to me the night she died. I saved it for some reason. Maybe so I could give it to you now."

"What does it mean?" Cliff said dazedly, clutching the blue-bordered page.

"Whatever you want it to mean."

"Jesus," Cliff said. "Jesus."

He ran his fingers over the words. "Sarah," he said. "It means so many god-damn things. Wrong about marrying Buzz. Wrong about putting that son of a bitch in charge of my life. Wrong about trusting Adrian. Wrong about—"

"Yes," Sarah said, putting her hand on the paper too, letting all the wrongs she had committed and had been committed against her mingle in the words. "Maybe she's saying she was wrong about what she did that night too. It would be so wrong for you to do it now and leave me without the only man I ever tried to love."

Tears streamed down her face. Cliff's arms were around her. His lips were in her hair, on her throat. "Sarah, Sarah. It's okay. It's not going to happen now. You're right. Everything you've been saying is right. Dick Stone can have

535

the goddamn company and welcome to it. I've got you. That's enough for me."

He was still the salesman, selling himself on the idea. She knew it would not be that simple. She knew there would be times when he would see an Aurora soaring into the sky or a Colossus rumbling toward a runway and he would hunger for the glory days. But she promised the good angels who had brought her here and given her the words of consolation and hope that she would not falter, she would not fail again.

The telephone rang. They both gazed at it, recognizing it as an enemy, the world beyond these walls, intruding with a demand or a question. "Answer it, will you?" Cliff said. "If it's Dick, tell him he'll have my letter of resignation on his desk tomorrow morning."

"This is Mark Casey of the *Los Angeles Times*," said the smooth voice in Sarah's ear. "Is Cliff Morris there? We just got word of the crash of Buchanan's experimental bomber. I was hoping he might have a comment on it."

It was an ultimate test. Why not find out now? For a moment Sarah wondered if she should remind Cliff of the night he had promised to build the plane as a memorial to Charlie. She decided not to take Dick Stone's advice. She wanted this to be a test of what they had just said to each other, nothing else.

She told Cliff who it was and why he was calling. All the implications flashed across his face. Here was his chance to destroy Dick Stone, to create a vacuum that the board of directors might ask him to fill, for want of a better candidate.

"Hello, Mark," Cliff said. "It's a shame about the plane. I know. I agree. There are times when some planes seem jinxed. They break your heart along with your pocketbook. This is one of them—"

Cliff was looking at Sarah as he said the next words. But she sensed he was also seeing something or someone else she could not share.

"But these things happen in the aircraft business. One of the fathers of flight, the German, Otto Lilienthal, summed it up on his deathbed with a famous phrase—sacrifices must be expected. That's our motto—it's every planemaker's motto. We'll find out what went wrong and fix it so it won't happen again. We'll have another prototype of the BX ready to fly in a month or so."

They went out on the terrace, arm in arm. A mile or two at sea, a green plane was doing stunts. Loops, barrel rolls, immelmans. Writing his artistry on the blue dome of the sky. Sarah's heart almost stopped beating.

"That guy can fly," Cliff said.

"We'll be doing the same thing soon."

"I'm not that good," Cliff said.

"Yes you are," Sarah said, and almost believed it.

DESTINIES

Throughout the day, while the uproar over the crash of the BX swirled around him, part of Dick Stone's mind was elsewhere—with Sarah in the house at Palos Verdes, trying to imagine what was happening between her and Cliff, realizing ruefully that he could not do it. No matter how well you knew a couple, there was a zone of intimacy they alone had experienced.

At other times he traveled to San Juan de Capistrano to ask an old woman a crucial question. For some reason he postponed it, although disappearing for a couple of hours might have been the best way to handle the maddening mixture of condescension and scorn that descended on the company from the media and Washington.

The Creature and his cohorts in Congress churned out a sickening mixture of jokes and sneers about the crash of the BX. Editorial writers and TV anchors rushed to wonder if anyone in the American aircraft industry knew what they were doing, citing a dozen other failed programs.

Apotheosis, Adrian Van Ness whispered. It was perfect on-the-job training for a man who might soon become chief executive officer of an aircraft company. The media and the politicians were proving once more that Adrian was right in his cold-eyed assessment of them. Still Dick delayed his trip to San Juan de Capistrano. He found himself wondering if he really wanted to be CEO of this shot-up machine. Buchanan was an updated version of the *Rainbow Express*, staggering home on one and a half engines—with no one praying them in.

That night, pacing his lonely house in Nichols Canyon, Dick told himself if Sarah failed with Cliff, he would step aside and let the Big Shot and the wreck go down in flames together. *Apotheosis*, Adrian whispered. Somehow it had a mocking sound. As if he was telling him to stop kidding himself.

At 8 A.M. the next morning when Dick arrived bleary-eyed for work, his secretary handed him Cliff Morris's letter of resignation. With it was a note from Sarah. "It's your turn, Navigator."

It was time for his trip to San Juan de Capistrano. Following Hanrahan's directions, Dick found Madame George in a comfortable cottage a block from the semi-restored mission. She was a withered chip of a woman but her mind was clear. Of course she remembered Adrian Van Ness. And Richard Stone. And Amalie Borne.

"Dear Amalie. She was both the best and the worst of my girls," she whispered in her husky baritone.

"She told me a story—the night I met her," Dick said. "She said she was Jewish—raised in Schweinfurt." He choked out the rest of it, feeling like he was in a plane coming out of a 13 G dive that was turning his body and brain to mush.

"I know the whole story. She told it to me in 1945."

"Was it true?"

"Absolutely. I was in Schweinfurt myself for most of the war. A forced laborer imported from France. When the Reich collapsed, I met Amalie there, roaming like a wolf girl in the ruins. I went to her so-called protector and forced him to give me all the cash he had—or I would tell the Americans what he had done to her."

Madame George lit a cigarette. "I told the Americans anyway. The money got us to Paris. But Amalie. Dear Amalie—I tried so hard to help her forget the past, to live in the present, surrounded by beauty and love—"

Tears streamed down Dick's face, turning the room, the husky-voiced old woman, into a blur. "I loved her," he said.

"You were not alone," Madame George said. "Prince Carlo—so many others loved her. She could not love anyone in return. It was as if those nights in the attic, the furnaces in the crematoriums had annihilated her heart. All anyone can do—all you should do—is forgive her."

"I do. I do," Dick said, wiping his streaming eyes.

Suddenly Jewishness was no longer an unwanted burden, it was part of his history because it was part of his love and that love justified everything, the bombs on German cities and the treachery over Schweinfurt and the embezzled money and the bombers and fighters and attack planes Buchanan built to defend America. His history was part of the pain of all history, pain that only love and courage could confront.

Was this his apotheosis? To be both American and Jewish without regret or shame or hesitation? To be both so passionately they were one thing?

Dick drove back to his house in Nichols Canyon. He walked through the empty rooms thinking of Cassie and the children. A huge corporation was crouched a few miles away, waiting to leap on his back. But he felt incomprehensibly free for the first time in a decade. He was ready to fly to Tennessee and tell Cassie the truth at last. Maybe she would laugh in his face. Maybe not. Whatever happened at tomorrow's board meeting, it seemed almost unimportant now.

Twenty-four hours later, Dick stood in the darkened boardroom of the Buchanan Corporation, finishing his first speech as president. "The hypersonic transport—the Orient Express—will fly people farther and faster than they've ever flown before. It will create the kind of revolution in air travel to the Far East that the subsonic jets have created in Europe. Imagine Japan and China only two hours away!

"But this is not the final installment of my dreams for this company, gentlemen. I have one more to share with you, based on a plane we built—and mistakenly destroyed—thirty years ago."

He punched a switch on the slide projector and onto the screen glided a gigantic flying wing. "This is the transport of the future, the airlifter to end them all. It will be five hundred feet from wingtip to wingtip and it will carry as much cargo as a ten-thousand-ton freighter. We're calling it the Buchanan."

The screen went dark. The lights came up. Frank Buchanan was sitting next to Dick. "You should have given me some warning, at least," he said with a sad smile.

Dick squeezed his shoulder and turned to the board. "There's one more thing I want to say. Something that may surprise some of you and even make you reconsider the support most of you have promised me when you vote in a few minutes.

"We've done some things wrong in this company. You know what some of them are. I'm not going to list our sins. I could explain why we made some of these mistakes. The explanation would satisfy most of you. But an explanation is not an excuse—or a license to go on making the same mistakes. I want you to know I think they were wrong and we're not going to do them anymore."

Dick stepped away from the lectern. "That's it, gentlemen. Those are my dreams and my principles. If you disagree with them, now is the time to stop me."

The board endorsed Richard Schiller Stone and his program unanimously, while Frank Buchanan smiled his approval. The directors had already accepted Cliff Morris's letter of resignation and voted him the generous pension suggested by the new CEO. Dick thanked them and invited everyone outside for Adrian Van Ness's memorial service.

On the sunny terrace of the headquarters building was an urn containing Adrian's ashes. The clerical and middle-management employees formed a wide semicircle. Beyond them, several thousand members of the day shift stood in their coveralls. A clergyman recited the Twenty-third Psalm. Dick turned to Frank Buchanan and asked him if he would say a few words. It was a calculated risk. Dick had debated it with Bruce Simons and Kirk Willoughby only a few hours ago. Simons had been jittery about it. Willoughby thought Frank would not say anything too outrageous.

Frank limped to the microphone. "Adrian Van Ness's contribution to flight was a special awareness that no matter how high we soared or how fast we flew, we were still flying through history. He tried to help us cope with the tangled tormented past that creates so much of the turbulence in our lives. Sometimes he succeeded, sometimes he failed. But ultimately there was courage in his struggle—courage we designers and engineers and pilots did not always appreciate. May his courage—and all the other varieties of courage in our sky—help us to continue the struggle to solve flight's mysteries and endure its failures and heartbreaks in the years to come."

Overhead, while Frank was speaking, a prop plane began circling. Down, down it spiraled until everyone recognized it as a SkyRanger, Buchanan's first airliner. From its open door showered a rainbow of rose petals.

Dick watched Frank pick up one of the red petals and press it into Amanda

Van Ness's hand. Earlier in the day, he had witnessed their reunion in his office. Kirk Willoughby had examined Amanda and said she was capable of living happily with Frank. Dan Hanrahan had snorted and said he did not need a doctor to tell him that.

A few feet away, Sarah Morris scooped up a handful of petals and flung them back into the sky. She stood on tiptoes and kissed Cliff Morris on the cheek. Dick picked up a yellow petal and imagined pressing it into Cassie's hand. Had they crossed another boundary? Were some of them, at least, beyond the rainbow?

Apotheosis, Adrian whispered one last time. *You'll make your compromises like I did. If the Orient Express and the Flying Wing turn out to be paper airplanes you'll go to work on the next-generation bomber, fighter, helicopter, dirigible if the Air Force wants it. You'll double the plant capacity and try to do everything simultaneously if you get the orders. You'll probably kill yourself from overwork in the process.*

Maybe, Dick Stone whispered to his American father. *Maybe.*

BEYOND THE RAINBOW

The icy desert wind hissed out of the night through the open door of Frank Buchanan's cabin on the slope above Tahquitz Canyon. He sat there, ignoring the cold, pen in hand on the open page of his loose-leaf folder.

A Buchanan helicopter had flown him out to the cabin to clean it out. He was moving to a house in Topanga Canyon with Amanda. On impulse, he had told the pilot he wanted to spend one more night here. The helicopter would return in the morning.

Frank had held Amanda in his arms and the last vestige of his hatred for Adrian Van Ness had been cleansed from his soul. From Amanda had also come a suggestion that had given him new hope for Billy. Previously he had only tried to reach him. Frank had no fears for someone as innocent as Victoria. But Amanda had convinced him that he should try to reach both of them.

"Wherever he is, she's there too," she said.

Still only silence, except for the wind. "I'm waiting," Frank whispered.

From the shelf above his head, a book catapulted across the room and struck the opposite wall. It lay on the floor, its pages fluttering in the wind like the wings of a spent bird.

Frank picked it up and spread it open in the lamplight. His fingers were on the last page of Ezra Pound's Cantos. His eyes found the final lines.

Immaculata. Introibo
For those who drink of the bitterness.

The Immaculata! The light beyond the rainbow, beyond Eden, beyond the suns and stars. Billy had reached it with Victoria's help. Soon he and Amanda would be there too, embracing them.

But first there was the Orient Express. One last wing to design. Shakily, Frank's ancient fingers began sketching the ultimate plane.